Tax Statutes and Statutory Instruments
2000-2001

With Concessions and Statements of Practice

Consultant Editors
**Ian Barlow MA FCA
and David Milne QC MA FCA**

CRONER ⓒ CCH

Important disclaimer

This publication is designed to provide accurate and authoritative information in regard to the subject matter covered. Readers entering into transactions on the basis of such information should seek the services of a competent professional adviser as this publication is sold with the understanding that the publisher is not engaged in rendering legal or accounting advice or other professional services. The publisher and the editors expressly disclaim all and any liability and responsibility to any person, whether a purchaser or reader of this publication or not, in respect of anything and of the consequences of anything, done or omitted to be done by any such person in reliance, whether wholly or partially, upon the whole or any part of the contents of this publication.

The publisher advises that the Acts, regulations, extra-statutory concessions, statements of practice and other materials emanating from the Revenue departments ('official materials') in this publication are not the authorised official versions. In their preparation, however, the greatest care has been taken to ensure exact conformity with the law as enacted, and with the official materials as issued.

While copyright in all official materials resides in the Crown, copyright in tables, indexes and annotations relating to them is vested in the publisher. Crown copyright material is reproduced with the permission of the controller of HMSO.

Copyright in the treaties, conventions, regulations, directives and other materials issued by institutions of the European Communities is vested in the relevant institutions. Again, those European materials reproduced in this publication are not the authorised official versions, but the greatest care has been taken to ensure exact conformity with the original materials as promulgated.

Extracts from technical releases issued by the Institute of Chartered Accountants in England and Wales are reproduced by kind permission of the Institute.

ISBN 086325 548 5
ISSN 0264-3073

Croner.CCH Group Ltd
Telford Road, Bicester, Oxfordshire OX26 4LB
Telephone +44(0)1869 253300, Facsimile +44(0)1869 874700.

Typeset in the UK by Croner.CCH Group Ltd
Printed and bound in the UK by Clays Ltd, St Ives plc.

Foreword

A number of issues stand out in considering this year's Finance Act.
The first, and most obvious, is its length; it is the longest ever by a wide margin.
Neither the tax authorities nor tax advisers will be able to cope for ever with this
increasing volume of legislation. Many professional bodies have issued pleas for a
halt to this process, and for some fundamental thinking about the shape of our tax
system. It is time for these to be taken seriously.

The second issue, which is closely linked to the first, is the increasing complexity
of the tax system as more and more features are added to it to deal with particular
situations. To some extent complexity is the price of equity, as taxpayers' different
circumstances are recognised; it also results from efforts to use the tax system to
engineer behavioural changes (many of which may be desirable). However, there is a
point where the multiplicity of rules becomes an impediment to the efficient
functioning of business.

The third issue is tax avoidance. As so often in the past, anti-avoidance legislation
continues to feature prominently, this time in the detailed provisions of Schedules 24
to 26 on the capital gains of trusts. These are a response to sophisticated tax planning,
and few will dispute that it is appropriate for the Government to take action against
it (even if they do not agree with the detail). Many will also feel that this is an
unproductive use of the time and talents both of parliamentary draftsmen who must
produce the relevant material, and of professional advisers who must digest it. At one
time it seemed that either judicial development of the Ramsay doctrine or the
introduction of a statutory General Anti-Avoidance Rule (or so-called mini-GAARs)
would supersede the ad hoc introduction of detailed legislation to plug particular
loopholes as they emerged. Now that looks less likely, but the search for some more
rational approach to this whole question will continue.

The fourth issue is the nature and quality of the drafting of our tax legislation.
As it happens, Schedules 24 to 26, which provided us with an example of complex
anti-avoidance rules, also provide an example of outstanding clarity in the expression
of those rules. However, the same cannot be said of all parts of the Bill. The Tax Law
Rewrite project has been under way now for the last four years. It is encouraging to
see some of the expertise gained over that time being employed in the drafting of the
annual Finance Acts, but legislation in the new style remains comparatively rare. We
recognise that the speed required in the Finance Bill process imposes particular
constraints, but there is scope to employ the new drafting techniques more widely in
dealing with proposals which have been announced well in advance of the Budget. It
is sometimes objected that amending legislation cannot follow the new style until the
existing provisions which it amends have been dealt with by the Rewrite team, but in
our opinion these difficulties can be overstated. To the extent that they remain, our
response is that the drafting Rewrite team, and indeed the Office of the Parliamentary
Counsel as a whole, should be enlarged so that greater priority can be given to this
work. It is not sufficient to say that the expertise of a trained and experienced
parliamentary draftsman is a scarce resource. Indeed it is, and we recognise that the
necessary training takes time, but the answer is to start now.

The fifth issue is the question of whether the UK is offering a competitive tax
régime to international businesses. In an increasingly global economy, companies
which are disadvantaged by the tax system in one country will simply go elsewhere.
The realisation of this no doubt prompted the changes to the double tax relief
provisions in the Finance Act which were made at Report Stage. Increasingly, we

shall see our tax system influenced by the pressure of the international market, as well as by the decisions of international bodies such as the European Union and the OECD.

As ever, we are most grateful to the CCH editorial staff for their painstaking work on updating these volumes, and we are confident that practitioners will continue to find them invaluable.

Ian Barlow MA, FCA
David Milne QC, MA FCA

28 June 2000

Editorial Note

Comment on the growing length of finance bills in general, and of this year's in particular, is now so frequent as to risk becoming a cliché. Yet, most of this year's 591 pages consist in new, substantive provisions – climate change levy, tonnage tax, all-employee share option schemes, enterprise incentives, corporate venturing, and so forth; amendment of the Taxes Acts, while extensive, occupies a smaller proportion of finance bill space than in previous years.

Nevertheless, the unprecedented size of the Bill has not precluded other areas of the statute book from overflowing into the tax system. Practitioners in NICs, since last April a Revenue tax, must now look to some quite diverse sources. The new framework for NICs foreshadowed in the November 1998 pre-Budget Report, and the enabling powers under which the IR35 regulations were made for national insurance purposes, were both introduced in the Welfare Reform and Pensions Act 1999. This year, the Child Support, Pensions and Social Security Act 2000 was the medium for the extension of Class 1A contributions to most benefits in kind, and the new rules whereby an earner can agree to be liable for secondary contributions due on share options. This year's editions of the NIC statutes reflect those changes to the Social Security legislation reproduced in Volume 1B.

Other new tax provisions are enacted in the Limited Liability Partnerships Act 2000, of particular interest to partners in law and accountancy practices, and in the Financial Services and Markets Act 2000 (another statute on which the legislators have indulged their prolixity). Neither are yet in force, but given the likelihood that they soon will be, we reproduce the prospective tax changes (see ICTA 1988, s. 76A, 118ZA and following, TCGA 1992, s. 59A and 156A, IHTA 1984, s. 267A, etc.).

The new climate change levy (mostly in FA 2000, Schedule 6) is to be found at the back of the Green volume dedicated to indirect tax, where there is still space for expansion. This will doubtless be filled by other new environmental taxes in future years.

The Human Rights Act 1998 (reproduced in both Red and Green volumes) enters into force on 2 October 2000, and will bind all public authorities, defined as 'a court or tribunal, and any person certain of whose functions are functions of a public nature' (HRA 1998, section 6). This clearly includes the Revenue authorities, and it will be interesting to see how the new jurisprudence develops in the tax field. For example, what impact will it have on the exercise by the Revenue departments of their powers of investigation, or in the wake of the Grabiner report?

The Revenue continue to publish explanatory and interpretative material on their website, and in the bi-monthly Tax Bulletin. This material, though not binding, is nevertheless helpful for practitioners in advising clients on the Revenue's likely attitude to events and transactions, and this year there is a new section with a selection of Tax Bulletin articles which do not rank as official interpretations (see volume 1B). A new medium seems to have emerged for Revenue pronouncements – FAQs, or Frequently Asked Questions, posted on the IR website. Much use has been made of this mainly electronic format over the past year as the debate on IR35 has developed, and we would welcome readers' views on whether FAQs could usefully be reproduced in these volumes, in paper form.

Since October 1999 the old Family Credit and Disability Working Allowance have become part of the tax system – at least to the extent that the Revenue are responsible for them. So this year we have expanded the Tax Credits section in volume 1B by adding the crucial social security regulations, as amended to refer to Working Families' Tax Credit and Disabled Person's Tax Credit, and also the Tax Credits (Payments by Employers) Regulations 1999 (SI 1999/3219). We are very grateful to

Ferret Information Systems Ltd, specialist publishers of social security materials, for their considerable help in preparing these editions of the regulations. The Tax Credits section is set to grow in future years, with the announcements in the March Budget of an integrated child credit and an employment tax credit, scheduled for 2003, and the added possibility of a pensioners' tax credit.

Just as we were clearing these volumes, the Tax Law Rewrite Project published the final draft of the Capital Allowances Bill for a last round of consultation. This innovative measure is due to be introduced in Parliament in November 2000 and to become an act in March 2001. While this process will not make capital allowances any easier conceptually, at least the law will be more clearly expressed and better structured than before. It will be some years before all the remaining direct tax primary legislation can be consolidated in this way, but meantime we look forward to reproducing, next year, probably the first intelligible tax statute in history.

We are grateful to all those who have supplied us with helpful comments over the past year, and trust that they will see them reflected in this year's text. The editorial team is eager to receive suggestions and also constructive criticisms from users — please do not hesitate to make your contribution. We hope that these books will continue to provide a useful source for all tax specialists of our continually developing tax laws and practice.

Robin Williamson
Senior Technical Editor
Croner.CCH

Publisher's Note

Volume 1A contains the text of the *Finance Act* 2000, the *Taxes Management Act* 1970, the *Income and Corporation Taxes Act* 1988, the *Capital Allowances Act* 1990 and the *Taxation of Chargeable Gains Act* 1992. It also contains all other significant acts affecting the imposition and collection of income tax, corporation tax and capital gains tax and the granting of capital allowances. All enactments and amendments made up to and including the *Finance Act* 2000 are incorporated. Enactments are presented in chronological order.

The companion vol. 1B includes the statutory instruments, EC directives, and Inland Revenue extra-statutory concessions, statements of practice and decisions and interpretations relevant to the taxes covered in vol. 1A. A selection of important Revenue press releases is also included, as are selected extracts from ICAEW technical releases, selected releases from the Chartered Institute of Taxation, and Law Society *Gazette* extracts. The volume also includes extracts from Revenue booklet IR20, the Treasury General Consents, the Series 7 Prospectus for Certificates of Tax Deposit and other such documents, and lists of clearance procedures, current Inland Revenue pamphlets and double taxation agreements.

Volume 1B also now includes all relevant material on National Insurance contributions, the *Tax Credits Act* 1999, inheritance tax and petroleum revenue tax.

Volume 2 of this series covers value added tax, stamp duties, insurance premium tax, landfill tax and climate change levy.

The legislation in vol. 1A is reproduced so as to show those provisions which are in force in 2000–01. All relevant provisions of the *Finance Act* 2000 are included in full text. Other acts have been abridged by the omission of the full text of provisions which either amend earlier enactments (unless the amendment is prospective) or have been repealed.

Prospective changes for which no effective date in 2000–01 has been announced at the time of going to press are noted under the provisions to be amended or in the case of, for example, entirely new sections, at the place where they will appear when they enter into force, with reference made to the place where the text of the changes can be found. Prospective changes, which enter into force during 2000–01, are made to the provisions amended, substituted, etc. with a 'history' note setting out the 'former' provisions in smaller type beneath. This is the style adopted for instance, for the corporation tax self-assessment provisions, which are generally effective for accounting periods ending on or after 1 July 1999. Where prospective legislation is amended before it takes effect it is shown in amended form at the place where it is introduced, but the 'target' legislation to be amended carries only a brief description of the amendment.

Where, because of subsequent amendments, provisions do not appear as originally enacted, the former wording is only reproduced where it is either in force in 2000–01 or likely to be of practical relevance to 2000–01 liabilities. Details of such amendments and, where appropriate, former wording in smaller type appear as history notes beneath the amended provisions. In some cases whole sections are involved and these appear in smaller type in their entirety. This treatment is not adopted for provisions which were repealed and re-enacted by consolidating statutes, for which reference should be made to past editions of *Tax Statutes and Statutory Instruments*.

Derivation notes under provisions of the *Income and Corporation Taxes Act* 1988, the *Capital Allowances Act* 1990 and the *Taxation of Chargeable Gains Act* 1992 indicate the former enactments.

Extensive cross references appear throughout, at the end of each section or paragraph, both to other provisions of the Taxes Acts and to extraneous legislation. Cross references under a section, paragraph etc. are of two types. First, there are references to provisions which explicitly mention that section, paragraph, etc. Secondly, there are references to provisions explicitly mentioned *in* that section, paragraph, etc. The order of cross references is first to list those involving the act in point; then those involving the *Income and Corporation Taxes Act* 1988; then those involving other Taxes Acts in chronological order; and then those involving extraneous acts, again in chronological order. Effective, or implicit, cross references are mentioned by way of editorial note (see below).

Relevant statutory instruments, extra-statutory concessions, statements of practice, Revenue decisions and interpretations (these are all reproduced) are noted. Other related materials (Inland Revenue press releases and booklets, releases from accountancy bodies and the Law Society, etc.) which affect particular provisions are also noted even if they are not reproduced. European material related to the provision in question is also noted, and editorial notes are inserted where additional comment is appropriate.

While Parliamentary materials or their equivalent had in other jurisdictions long been used as an aid to the interpretation of legislative acts, the decision of the House of Lords in *Pepper (HMIT) v Hart and related appeals* [1992] BTC 591 that ministerial statements may be so used in limited circumstances was an innovation in the UK. The cases in which such use can be made of Parliamentary material are at present limited to circumstances where legislation is ambiguous, obscure or leads to an absurdity; the material relied upon consists of statements by a minister or other promoter of the Bill; and the statements relied upon are clear. A range of annotations covering Parliamentary material are grouped together under the generic heading of **"Hansard"**. Editorial judgment has been used in selecting some of the more significant such references, or those with the most widespread application: the coverage of Parliamentary material in the footnotes is by no means exhaustive.

As part of the Revenue's response to the government's code of practice on access to government information, the Revenue's guidance manuals have been made available to the public. The manuals provide Revenue staff with guidance on the interpretation of tax law and the operation of the tax system. References to useful material contained in the manuals appear under the heading '**Revenue manuals**'. Editorial judgment has been used in selecting the references.

The publisher advises that the acts, regulations and other official material in this publication are not the authorised official versions. However, the greatest care has been taken to ensure exact conformity with the law as enacted and with the text of extra-statutory material. Some changes in printing style have been adopted for convenience and to improve readability. For example, marginal notes appearing in the official statutes have been reproduced in bold type in the first line of the section to which they relate. Many words and phrases have also been reproduced in bold where they are defined in the legislation so that the definitions can be located more easily.

A comprehensive topic index to this volume is in vol. 1B, with a separate index of definitions in vol. 1A. An exhaustive table of destinations showing where pre-consolidation enactments can now be traced in the *Income and Corporation Taxes Act* 1988, the *Capital Allowances Act 1990* and the *Taxation of Chargeable Gains Act* 1992 can be found at p. 6,967. The table also includes destinations for PAYE and sub-contractor regulations following the 1993 consolidations in the *Income Tax (Sub-contractors in the Construction Industry) Regulations* 1993 (SI 1993/743) and the *Income Tax (Employments) Regulations* 1993 SI 1993/744.

ENDING OF VOCATIONAL TRAINING RELIEF AND OF EXTRA STATUTORY

[Inland Revenue Press Release 125/00, 25 July 2000]

CONCESSION A64

The introduction of the individual learning account (ILA) framework, whereby discounts will be available for a wide range of work-related and other developmental learning, means that, as planned, Vocational Training Relief (VTR) will end on 31 August.

Treasury regulations have been made today confirming this and an Extra Statutory Concession which gives relief in certain circumstances for employees training costs is also being withdrawn from the same date.

The decision to end VTR and this concession to coincide with the launching of the ILA framework was originally announced in the March 1999 Budget (Press Release No 3).

DETAILS

1. Vocational Training Relief (VTR) is a tax relief available to individuals who pay for certain costs of their own vocational training. In the March 1999 Budget the Chancellor announced that VTR would be fully abolished in 2000-01 when the national framework for ILAs was launched. Higher rate tax relief was withdrawn from 6 April 1999.

2. With the new discounts under ILAs becoming available from September 2000, in his pre-Budget Report of November 1999 the Chancellor indicated that VTR would end after August 2000. Relief for VTR payments will therefore not be available for any payments made after 31 August 2000, but relief at the basic rate will continue for payments made up to and including that date.

3. Extra Statutory Concession A64, which gives tax relief in very limited circumstances for expenditure on job related training courses that employees pay for themselves, is also being withdrawn for payments after 31 August 2000. The Budget 1999 Press Release announced that it would be withdrawn at he same time as VTR.

Croner.CCH Group Ltd
August 2000

ABBREVIATIONS

The following abbreviations are commonly used throughout this publication.

ACT	advance corporation tax
AEA	Administration of Estates Act 1925
AIM	Alternative Investment Market
AIS	accrued income scheme
App.	appendix
APR	annual percentage rate
APRT	advance petroleum revenue tax
art.	article(s)
BB	Customs and Excise Business Briefs
BEN	business economic note
BES	business expansion scheme
BN	Budget Notes
BSA 1986	Building Societies Act 1986
B(S)A 1985	Bankruptcy (Scotland) Act 1985
BTC	British Tax Cases, 1982–current (CCH)
CA 1985	Companies Act 1985
CAA 1968	Capital Allowances Act 1968
CAA 1990	Capital Allowances Act 1990
CCH	CCH Editions Limited (or associated CCH companies)
C & E Commrs	Commissioners of Customs and Excise
CED(GR)A 1979	Customs and Excise Duties (General Reliefs) Act 1979
CEMA 1979	Customs and Excise Management Act 1979
CFC	controlled foreign company
CGT	capital gains tax
CGTA 1979	Capital Gains Tax Act 1979
Ch.	Chapter(s) (of a statute/SI etc.)
CIC	close investment-holding company
cl.	clause(s)
col.	column(s)
Commr; Commrs	commissioner; commissioners
Conv.	convention
CPA 1947	Crown Proceedings Act 1947
CRT	composite rate tax
CT	corporation tax
CTD	certificates of tax deposits
CTT	capital transfer tax
CTTA 1984	Capital Transfer Tax Act 1984
Dir.	EC directives
DLT	development land tax
DLTA 1976	Development Land Tax Act 1976
DSS	Department of Social Security
DTI	Department of Trade and Industry
EC	European Community/Communities
edn.	edition
EEC	European Economic Community
EEIG	European Economic Interest Grouping

e.g.	(exempli gratia) for example
EIS	enterprise investment scheme
ESC	extra-statutory concession
ESOP	employee stock ownership plan
ESOT	employee share ownership trust
etc.	(et cetera) and so on
et seq.	(et sequens) and the following
EU	European Union
FA	Finance Act
FI	Films Act 1985
FII	franked investment income
F(No. 2)A	Finance (No. 2) Act
FYA	first-year allowance
Grp.	Group (VAT legislation)
HA 1988	Housing Act 1988
HM	Her Majesty
HMIT	Her Majesty's Inspector of Taxes
HMSO	Her Majesty's Stationery Office
IA	initial allowance
IA 1986	Insolvency Act 1986
ICAEW	Institute of Chartered Accountants in England and Wales
ICAS	Institute of Chartered Accountants of Scotland
ICTA 1970	Income and Corporation Taxes Act 1970
ICTA 1988	Income and Corporation Taxes Act 1988
i.e.	(id est) that is
IHT	inheritance tax
IHTA 1984	Inheritance Tax Act 1984
INA 1978	Interpretation Act 1978
IoT	Institute of Taxation
IR Commrs	Commissioners of Inland Revenue
IRDec.	Inland Revenue decision
IRInt.	Inland Revenue interpretaion
IRRA 1980	Inland Revenue Regulation Act 1980
IT	income tax
LAUTRO	Life Assurance and Unit Trust Regulatory Organisation
LFT	landfill tax
LIFFE	London International Financial Futures and Options Exchange
LPA 1925	Law of Property Act 1925
LSG	Law Society Gazette
MCT	mainstream corporation tax
MIRAS	mortgage interest relief at source
Misc.	miscellaneous items (denoted by number)
NB	(nota bene) note well
NHA 1980	National Heritage Act 1980
NI	Northern Ireland
NIC	National Insurance contributions
NR	Customs and Excise News Releases

O.	Order(s)
OJ	Official Journal of the European Communities
OJ "L" series	Official Journal of the European Communities, Legislation Series (cited by year, issue number and page, for example OJ 1989 L1/1 is the first page of the first issue of the legislation series of the Official Journal for 1989)
OPB	Occupational Pensions Board
Ors	others
OTA 1975	Oil Taxation Act 1975
OTA 1983	Oil Taxation Act 1983
p.; pp.	page; pages
p.a.	per annum (each year)
PACE 1994	Police and Criminal Evidence Act 1994
para.	paragraph(s)
PAYE	pay as you earn
PCTA 1968	Provisional Collection of Taxes Act 1968
PEP	personal equity plan
PET	potentially exempt transfer
PLDA 1808	Probate and Legacy Duties Act 1808
PN	Customs and Excise Press Notices
PPS	personal pension scheme
PR	press release(s)
PRP	profit-related pay
PRT	petroleum revenue tax
PRTA 1980	Petroleum Revenue Tax Act 1980
PSA 1993	Pension Schemes Act 1993
PSO	Pensions Schemes Office
Pt.	Part(s)
QCB	qualifying corporate bond
r.	rule(s)
RA 1898	Revenue Act 1898 and similarly coded for appropriate subsequent years
reg.	regulations
Regulations	EC Regulations
RPI	retail prices index
RSC	Rules of the Supreme Court 1965
s.	section(s)
SA 1891	Stamp Act 1891
SAYE	save as you earn
SCA 1981	Supreme Court Act 1981
Sch.	Schedule(s)
SDMA 1891	Stamp Duty Management Act 1891
SDRT	stamp duty reserve tax
SD(TP)A 1992	Stamp Duty (Temporary Provisions) Act 1992
SERPS	state earnings-related pension scheme
SFO	Superannuation Funds Office
SI	statutory instrument
SMP	statutory maternity pay
SP	Inland Revenue statement of practice
SRO	self-regulating organisation
SR & O	statutory rules and orders

SSA 1975	Social Security Act 1975
SSA 1980	Social Security Act 1980
SSA 1986	Social Security Act 1986
SSA 1989	Social Security Act 1989
SSAA 1992	Social Security Administration Act 1992
SSAP	Statement of Standard Accounting Practice
SSCBA 1992	Social Security Contributions and Benefits Act 1992
SS(CP)A 1992	Social Security (Consequential Provisions) Act 1992
SSHBA 1982	Social Security Housing Benefits Act 1982
SS(MP)A 1977	Social Security (Miscellaneous Provisions) Act 1977
SSP	statutory sick pay
SSPA 1975	Social Security Pensions Act 1975
SSPA 1994	Statutory Sick Pay Act 1994
STA 1963	Stock Transfer Act 1963
subcl.	subclause(s)
subpara.	subparagraph(s)
subs.	subsection(s)
TAURUS	Transfer and Automated Registration of Uncertified Stock
TCGA 1992	Taxation of Chargeable Gains Act 1992
TESSA	tax-exempt special savings account
TMA 1970	Taxes Management Act 1970
TR	technical release
TSBA 1985	Trustee Savings Bank Act 1985
TULR(C)A 1992	Trade Union and Labour Relations (Consolidation) Act 1992
TWDV	tax written-down value
UCITS	Undertakings for Collective Investment in Transferable Securities
UK	United Kingdom
USM	Unlisted Securities Market
VAT	value added tax
VATA 1983	Value Added Tax Act 1983
VCT	Venture Capital Trust
vol.	volume(s)
WDA	writing down allowance
WDV	written-down value
WFT	windfall tax
¶	CCH paragraph

About the Publisher

Croner.CCH is part of the Wolters Kluwer Group. Wolters Kluwer is the leading international publisher specialising in tax, business and law publishing throughout Europe, the US and the Asia Pacific region. The group produces a wide range of information services in different media for the accounting and legal professions and for business. The UK operation also acts as distributor of the publications of the overseas affiliates.

All Croner.CCH publications are designed to be practical and authoritative reference works and guides and are written by our own highly qualified and experienced editorial team and specialist outside authors.

Croner.CCH publishes information packages including electronic products, loose-leaf reporting services, newsletters and books on UK and European legal topics for distribution world-wide. The UK operation also acts as distributor of the publications of the overseas affiliates.

Croner.CCH
Telford Road
Bicester
Oxfordshire
OX6 0XD
Telephone: (01869) 253300

Croner.CCH Group Ltd,
Croner House, London Road, Kingston-upon-Thames,
Surrey, KT2 6SR. Part of the Wolters Kluwer Group
Telephone: 020 8547 3333

About the Consultant Editors

Ian Barlow joined KPMG in 1973 and promoted to partner in 1985. He is UK Head of Tax and Legal and Chairman of KPMG's European Tax and Legal practice. Ian's professional qualifications are MA Engineering Science – Cambridge University, FCA (ICAEW) and CA (Canadian). He is liaison partner for our Canadian and Channel Islands. Ian is a member of the following external committees: Tax Law Rewrite Project, Chaired by Lord Howe; IFS Tax Law Review Committee; ICAEW Tax Faculty Committee; and CBI London Regional Committee and Tax Committee.

David Milne QC read law at Jesus College, Oxford and was articled to Whinney Murray & Co, qualifying as a chartered accountant in 1969. He was called to the Bar in 1970, and since 1972 has been a member of Pump Court Tax Chambers, specialising in all forms of tax litigation and dispute resolution. He has been a QC since 1987, a Crown Court Recorder since 1994 and a General Commissioner (for Lincoln's Inn) since 1996, and is currently Chairman of the Revenue Bar Association.

Acknowledgment

CCH kindly acknowledges the endorsement of this publication by the Chartered Institute of Taxation.

THE CHARTERED INSTITUTE
═ OF ═
TAXATION

CCH kindly acknowledges the endorsement of this publication by the Tax Faculty of the Institute of Chartered Accountants in England and Wales.

Table of Contents

Table of Contents

VALUE ADDED TAX

Table of Contents

VALUE ADDED TAX

Table of Contents

VAT STATUTES

Table of Contents

> **Note**: Only those extant parts of these Acts which relate to value added tax are reproduced here.

PROVISIONAL COLLECTION OF TAXES ACT 1968

(1968 Chapter 2)

[1st February 1968]

ARRANGEMENT OF SECTIONS

1 Temporary statutory effect of House of Commons resolutions affecting income tax, purchase tax or customs or excise duties

1(1)   This section applies only to [not relevant to VAT] value added tax, [not relevant to VAT].

1(1A)   [Repealed by FA 1993, s. 205(3), s. 213 and Sch. 23, Pt. VI.]

1(2)   Subject to that, and to the provisions of subsections (4) to (8) below, where the House of Commons passes a resolution which–

(a)   provides for the renewal for a further period of any tax in force or imposed during the previous financial year (whether at the same or a different rate, and whether with or without modifications) or for the variation or abolition of any existing tax, and

(b)   contains a declaration that it is expedient in the public interest that the resolution should have statutory effect under the provisions of this Act,

the resolution shall, for the period specified in the next following subsection, have statutory effect as if contained in an Act of Parliament and, where the resolution provides for the renewal of a tax, all enactments which were in force with reference to that tax as last imposed by Act of Parliament shall during that period have full force and effect with respect to the tax as renewed by the resolution.

In this section references to the **renewal of a tax** include references to its reimposition, and references to the abolition of a tax include references to its repeal.

1(3)   The said period is–

(a)   in the case of a resolution passed in November or December in any year, one expiring with 5th May in the next calendar year;

(aa)   in the case of a resolution passed in February or March in any year, one expiring with 5th August in the same calendar year; and

(b)   in the case of any other resolution, one expiring at the end of four months after the date on which it is expressed to take effect or, if no such date is expressed, after the date on which it is passed.

1(4)   A resolution shall cease to have statutory effect under this section unless within the next thirty days on which the House of Commons sits after the day on which the resolution is passed–

(a)   a Bill renewing, varying or, as the case may be, abolishing the tax is read a second time by the House, or

(b)   a Bill is amended by the House in Committee or on Report, or by any Standing Committee of the House so as to include provision for the renewal, variation or, as the case may be, abolition of the tax.

1(5)   A resolution shall also cease to have statutory effect under this section if–

(a)   the provisions giving effect to it are rejected during the passage of the Bill containing them through the House, or

(b)   an Act comes into operation renewing, varying or, as the case may be, abolishing the tax, or

(c)   Parliament is dissolved or prorogued.

1(6)   Where, in the case of a resolution providing for the renewal or variation of a tax, the resolution ceases to have statutory effect by virtue of subsection (4) or (5) above, or the period specified in subsection (3) above terminates, before an Act comes into operation renewing or varying the tax, any money paid in pursuance of the resolution shall be repaid or made good, and any deduction made in pursuance of the resolution shall be deemed to be an unauthorised deduction.

1(7)   Where any tax as renewed or varied by a resolution is modified by the Act renewing or varying the tax, any money paid in pursuance of the resolution which would not have been payable under the new conditions affecting the tax shall be repaid or made good, and any deduction made in pursuance of the resolution shall, so far as it would not have been authorised under the new conditions affecting the tax, be deemed to be an unauthorised deduction.

1(8)   When during any session a resolution has had statutory effect under this section, statutory effect shall not be again given under this section in the same session to the same resolution or to a resolution having the same effect.

History – S. 1(1A) repealed by FA 1993, s. 205(3) and s. 213 and Sch. 23 Pt. VI, in relation to resolutions passed after 27 July 1993. Former s. 1(1A) was inserted by FA 1985, s. 97.
In s. 1(3)(a), references to "November or December" and "5th May in the next calendar year" substituted and in s. 1(4), the word "thirty" substituted by FA 1993, s. 205(5), in relation to resolutions passed after 27 July 1993.
S. 1(3)(aa) was inserted by F(No. 2)A 1997, s. 50(1), with effect in relation to resolutions passed after 31 July 1997.
In s. 1(4)(b), the words "in Committee ... of the House" inserted by FA 1968, s. 60.
Application extended to petroleum revenue tax, stamp duty reserve tax, value added tax and car tax by OTA 1975, s. 11; FA 1986, s. 86(3); FA 1972, s. 1(5) and FA 1972, s. 52(11) and Sch. 7, para. 2(4) respectively.
References to provisions of ICTA 1988 substituted by Sch. 29, para. 32 of that Act.
Cross references – FA 1997, s. 49(9): transitional provisions for set-offs etc.

2   Payments and deductions made on account, and before renewal, of any temporary tax within s. 1

2(1)   Any payment or deduction made on account of a temporary tax to which section 1 above applies and within one month after the date of its expiry shall, if the payment or deduction would have been a legal payment or deduction if the tax had not expired, be deemed to be a legal payment or deduction, subject to the condition that–

(a)   if a resolution for the renewal or reimposition of the tax is not passed by the House of Commons within that month, or such a resolution is passed within that month but ceases to have statutory effect under the said section 1, any money so paid or deducted shall be repaid or made good, and

(b)   if the tax is ultimately renewed or reimposed at a different rate, or with modifications, any amount paid or deducted which could not properly have been paid or deducted under the new conditions affecting the tax shall be repaid or made good.

2(2)   In this section **"temporary tax"** means a tax which has been imposed, or renewed or reimposed, for a limited period not exceeding eighteen months, and was in force or imposed during the previous financial year.

3   Customs and excise: provisions for securing duties under resolutions not having statutory effect

3(1)   The following provisions of this section shall have effect where the House of Commons passes a resolution providing for the imposition as from a specified date of any duty of customs or excise, not being a resolution to which statutory effect can be given under section 1 of this Act.

3(2)   If the duty so imposed is a duty of customs, the Commissioners may require any person who, on or after the specified date, imports or clears from warehouse any goods to which the resolution applies to give security that he will, if and when an Act giving effect to the resolution comes into operation, pay the duty chargeable in respect of the goods under that Act.

3(2A)   Subsection (2) above shall apply for the purposes of a duty of excise imposed as mentioned in subsection (1) above to the extent that the duty is charged on goods imported into the United Kingdom, as it applies for the purposes of a duty of customs so imposed.

3(3)   If the duty is a duty of excise, then–

(a)   where it is a duty of excise charged otherwise than on goods; or

(b)   where it is a duty of excise charged on goods, to the extent that it is charged on goods produced or manufactured in the United Kingdom, the Commissioners may make regulations for the purpose of securing the payment of such duty as may by law become chargeable in the event of an Act giving effect to the resolution coming into operation, and may by those regulations apply to the duty and to any trade or business in connection with which the duty may become chargeable and to any person carrying on, or premises used for the purpose of, that trade or business any provision of the revenue trade provisions of the customs and excise Acts.

3(4)   If any person contravenes or fails to comply with regulations made under this section, he shall be liable to a penalty of level 3 on the standard scale, and any goods in respect of which the offence was committed shall be liable to forfeiture.

3(5)   This and the next following section shall be construed as one with the Customs and Excise Management Act 1979.

History – S. 3(2A) was inserted by CEMA 1979, s. 177(1) and Sch. 4.
In s. 3(3), the words "then– . . . in the United Kingdom," and the words "the revenue trade . . . and Excise Acts" were substituted by CEMA 1979, s. 177(1) and Sch. 4.
In s. 3(4), the words "level 3 on the standard scale" were substituted by the Criminal Justice Act 1982, s. 37, 38 and 46.
In s. 3(5), the words "the Customs and Excise Management Act 1979" were substituted by CEMA 1979, s. 177(1) and Sch. 4.
Note – Level 3 on the standard scale is £1,000 operative from 1 October 1992.

4   Customs and excise: alteration of rate of drawback where rate of duty altered by resolution having statutory effect

4   Where the rate of any duty of excise is altered by any resolution of the House of Commons having statutory effect, and any Bill which has been introduced into the House to give effect to that resolution provides for an alteration of the rate of drawback to be allowed in respect of that duty, then, so long as the resolution continues to have statutory effect, drawback shall be allowed in accordance with the rate provided in the Bill, subject to any necessary adjustment in case the rate of drawback as enacted by Parliament differs from the rate provided in the Bill.

History – In s. 4, the words "duty of excise" were substituted by CEMA 1979, s. 177(1) and Sch. 4.

5   House of Commons resolution giving provisional effect to motions affecting taxation

5(1)   This section shall apply if the House of Commons resolves that provisional statutory effect shall be given to one or more motions to be moved by the Chancellor of the Exchequer, or some other Minister, and which, if agreed to by the House, would be resolutions–

(a)   to which statutory effect could be given under section 1 of this Act, or

(b)   to which section 3 of this Act could be applied,

(c)   [Repealed by FA 1993, s. 205(6)(a), s. 213 and Sch. 23, Pt. VI.]

5(2)   Subject to subsection (3) below, on the passing of the resolution under subsection (1) above, sections 1 to 3 of this Act and section 822 of the Income and Corporation Taxes Act 1988 (over-deductions from preference dividends before passing of annual Act) shall apply as if each motion to which the resolution applies had then been agreed to by a resolution of the House.

5(3)   Subsection (2) above shall cease to apply to a motion if that motion, or a motion containing the same proposals with modifications, is not agreed to by a resolution of the House (in this section referred to as **"a confirmatory resolution"**) within the next ten days on which the House sits after the resolution under subsection (1) above is passed, and, if it ceases to apply, all such adjustments, whether by way of discharge or repayment of tax, or discharge of security, or otherwise, shall be made as may be necessary to restore the position to what it would have been if subsection (2) above had never applied to that motion, and to make good any deductions which have become unauthorised deductions.

5(4)   The enactments specified in subsection (2) above shall have effect as if–

(a)   any confirmatory resolution passed within the said period of ten sitting days had been passed when the resolution under subsection (1) above was passed, and

(b)   everything done in pursuance of the said subsection (2) by reference to the motion to which the confirmatory resolution relates had been done by reference to the confirmatory resolution,

but any necessary adjustments shall be made, whether by way of discharge or repayment of tax, or modification of the terms of any security, or further assessment, or otherwise, where the proposals in the confirmatory resolution are not the same as those in the original motion to which that resolution relates.

History – S. 5(1)(c) and word "or" immediately preceding it and in s. 5(2), reference to ICTA 1988, s. 822 substituted by FA 1993, s. 205(6), s. 213 and Sch. 23, Pt. VI, in relation to resolutions passed after 27 July 1993.
References to provisions of ICTA 1988 substituted by Sch. 29, para. 32 of that Act.

6   Short title, repeals and saving as respects Northern Ireland

6(1)   This Act may be cited as the Provisional Collection of Taxes Act 1968.

6(2)   [Amending provision, not reproduced here.]

6(3)   [Repealed by Northern Ireland Constitution Act 1973, s. 41(1)(a) and Sch. 6, Pt. I.]

History – S. 6(3) was repealed by Northern Ireland Constitution Act 1973, s. 41(1)(a) and Sch. 6, Pt. I, with effect from 18 July 1973.

FINANCE ACT 1972

(1972 Chapter 41)

[*27th July 1972*]

PART VII – MISCELLANEOUS

127   Disclosure of information between Revenue departments

127(1)   No obligation as to secrecy or other restriction upon the disclosure of information imposed by statute or otherwise shall prevent either–

(a)   the Commissioners of Inland Revenue or an authorised officer of those Commissioners; or

(b)   the Commissioners of Customs and Excise or an authorised officer of those Commissioners;

from disclosing information to the other Commissioners or an authorised officer of the other Commissioners for the purpose of assisting them in the performance of their duties.

127(2)   Information obtained in pursuance of this section shall not be disclosed except–

(a)   to the Commissioners or an authorised officer of the Commissioners on whose behalf it was obtained; or

(b)   for the purpose of any proceedings connected with a matter in relation to which those Commissioners perform duties.

European material – Directive 77/799 as amended by 79/1070: disclosure of information between tax authorities of member states.

Official publications – 700/47.

Other material – Customs and Excise news release 12/88, 8 March 1988 (not reproduced): from 1 April 1988 exchange of information between the Inland Revenue and Customs to take place at local level as well as head office level, concentrating on larger cases of suspected tax evasion.

Notes – FA 1978, s. 77: disclosure of information to tax authorities in other member states.
FA 1980, s. 17: mutual recovery and disclosure of information between member states (extending FA 1978, s. 77 to VAT).
FA 1989, s. 182: disclosure of information by various officials subject to criminal sanctions.
Other provisions under which Customs and Excise may disclose personal information to other Government departments include:
- FA 1993, s. 37;
- Land Registration Act 1925, s. 129;
- Charities Act 1992, s. 52(2);
- Parliamentary Commissioner Act 1967, s. 8;
- National Audit Act 1983, s. 8;
- Data Protection Act 1984, s. 17;
- Housing Act 1985, s. 62.

Customs may also disclose personal information to the police under:
- Drug Trafficking Offences Act 1986, s. 30;
- Prevention of Terrorism (Temporary Provisions) Act 1989, s. 17 and Sch. 17.

FINANCE ACT 1977

(1977 Chapter 36)

[*29th July 1977*]

PART I – CUSTOMS AND EXCISE

11   Recovery of duty etc. due in other member States

11(1)   This section applies where, in accordance with the Directive of the Council of the European Communities dated 15th March 1976 No. 76/308/EEC, an authority in a member State makes a request for the recovery in the United Kingdom of any sum claimed by that authority in that State.

11(2)   Subject to the following provisions, where this section applies the Commissioners or the Intervention Board for Agricultural Produce may recover the sum specified in the request as if it were a debt due to the Crown.

11(3)   Proceedings for the recovery of any sum under this section shall be stayed if the defendant satisfies the court that proceedings relevant to his liability on the claim in relation to which the request has been made are pending, or are about to be instituted, before a court, tribunal or other competent body in the member State in question; but any such stay may be removed if the proceedings in the member State are not prosecuted or instituted with reasonable expedition.

11(4)   It shall be a defence to proceedings under this section for the defendant to show that a final decision on the claim has been given in his favour by a court, tribunal or other competent body in the member State in question; and if he shows that such a decision has been given in respect of part of the claim it shall be a defence to the proceedings in so far as they relate to that part.

11(5)   For the purposes of subsection (3) above proceedings shall be regarded as pending so long as an appeal may be brought against any decision in the proceedings; and for the purposes of subsection (4) above a final decision is one against which no appeal lies or against which an appeal lies within a period which has expired without an appeal having been brought.

11(6)   In proceedings under this section any averment in the pleadings that a request has been made as mentioned in subsection (1) above for the recovery of the sum which is the subject of the proceedings shall be conclusive evidence of that fact; and except as provided in subsection (4) above no question shall be raised in any such proceedings as to the defendant's liability on the claim in relation to which the request has been made.

11(7)   In relation to proceedings under this section in Scotland–

(a)   the reference in subsection (3) above–

      (i) to **proceedings being stayed** shall be construed as a reference to their being sisted;
      (ii) to **a stay being removed** shall be construed as a reference to a sist being recalled; and
(b)   the references in subsections (3), (4) and (6) above to **a defendant** shall be construed as references to a defender.

11(8)   This section shall not have effect in relation to a request for the recovery of any sum which became due before 15th March 1976.

Note – FA 1980, s. 17: mutual recovery and disclosure of information between member states.

FINANCE ACT 1978

(1978 Chapter 42)

[31st July 1978]

PART V – MISCELLANEOUS AND SUPPLEMENTARY

77   Disclosure of information to tax authorities in other member States

77(1) No obligation as to secrecy imposed by statute or otherwise shall preclude the Commissioners of Inland Revenue or an authorised officer of those Commissioners from disclosing to the competent authorities of another member State any information required to be so disclosed by virtue of the Directive of the Council of the European Communities dated 19th December 1977 No. 77/799/EEC.

77(2) Neither the Commissioners nor an authorised officer shall disclose any information in pursuance of the said Directive unless satisfied that the competent authorities of the other State are bound by, or have undertaken to observe, rules of confidentiality with respect to the information which are not less strict than those applying to it in the United Kingdom.

77(3) Nothing in this section shall permit the Commissioners of Inland Revenue or an authorised officer of those Commissioners to authorise the use of information disclosed by virtue of the said Directive other than for the purposes of taxation or to facilitate legal proceedings for failure to observe the tax laws of the receiving State.

Cross reference – FA 1980, s. 17: mutual recovery and disclosure of information between member states (extending FA 1978, s. 77 to VAT).

Official publications – 700/47.

Notes – FA 1972, s. 127: disclosure of information between Revenue departments.
FA 1989, s. 182: disclosure of information by various officials subject to criminal sanctions.
See note to FA 1972, s. 127 for details of other provisions under which Customs and Excise may disclose personal information to other government departments.

CUSTOMS AND EXCISE MANAGEMENT ACT 1979

(1979 Chapter 2)

[22nd February 1979]

ARRANGEMENT OF SECTIONS

PART I – PRELIMINARY

1   Interpretation

1(1)   In this Act, unless the context otherwise requires–

"**aerodrome**" means any area of land or water designed, equipped, set apart or commonly used for affording facilities for the landing and departure of aircraft;

"**approved wharf**" has the meaning given by section 20A below;

"**armed forces**" means the Royal Navy, the Royal Marines, the regular army and the regular air force, and any reserve or auxiliary force of any of those services which has been called out on permanent service, or called into actual service, or embodied;

"**assigned matter**" means any matter in relation to which the Commissioners are for the time being required in pursuance of any enactment to perform any duties;

"**boarding station**" means a boarding station for the time being appointed under section 19 below;

"**boundary**" means the land boundary of Northern Ireland;

"**British ship**" means a British ship within the meaning of the Merchant Shipping Act 1894, so, however, as not to include a ship registered in any country other than the United Kingdom, the Channel Islands, the Isle of Man or a colony within the meaning of the British Nationality Act 1948;

"**claimant**", in relation to proceedings for the condemnation of any thing as being forfeited, means a person claiming that the thing is not liable to forfeiture;

"**coasting ship**" has the meaning given by section 69 below;

"**commander**", in relation to an aircraft, includes any person having or taking the charge or command of the aircraft;

"**the Commissioners**" means the Commissioners of Customs and Excise;

"**Community transit goods**"–

(a)   in relation to imported goods, means–

(i) goods which have been imported under the internal or external Community transit procedure for transit through the United Kingdom with a view to exportation where the importation was and the transit and exportation are to be part of one Community transit operation; or

(ii) goods which have, at the port or airport at which they were imported, been placed under the internal or external Community transit procedure for transit through the United Kingdom with a view to exportation where the transit and exportation are to be part of one Community transit operation which commenced at that port or airport;

(b) in relation to goods for exportation, means–

(i) goods which have been imported as mentioned in paragraph (a)(i) of this definition and are to be exported as part of the Community transit operation in the course of which they were imported; or

(ii) goods which have, under the internal or external Community transit procedure, transited the United Kingdom from the port or airport at which they were imported and are to be exported as part of the Community transit operation which commenced at that port or airport;

and for the purposes of para. (a)(i) above the Isle of Man shall be treated as if it were part of the United Kingdom;

"container" includes any bundle or package and any box, cask or other receptacle whatsoever;

"the customs and excise Acts" means the Customs and Excise Acts 1979 and any other enactment for the time being in force relating to customs or excise;

"the Customs and Excise Acts 1979" means–

this Act,

the Customs and Excise Duties (General Reliefs) Act 1979,

the Alcoholic Liquor Duties Act 1979,

the Hydrocarbon Oil Duties Act 1979, and

the Tobacco Products Duty Act 1979;

"customs warehouse" means a place of security approved by the Commissioners under subsection (2) (whether or not it is also approved under subsection (1)) of section 92 below;

"customs and excise airport" has the meaning given by section 21(7) below;

"customs and excise station" has the meaning given by section 26 below;

"designation order" has the meaning given by section 100A(5);

"drawback goods" means goods in the case of which a claim for drawback has been or is to be made;

"dutiable goods", except in the expression "dutiable or restricted goods", means goods of a class or description subject to any duty of customs or excise, whether or not those goods are in fact chargeable with that duty, and whether or not that duty has been paid thereon;

"dutiable or restricted goods" has the meaning given by section 52 below;

"examination station" has the meaning given by section 22A below;

"excise duty point" has the meaning given by section 1 of the Finance (No. 2) Act 1992;

"excise licence trade" means, subject to subsection (5) below, a trade or business for the carrying on of which an excise licence is required;

"excise warehouse" means a place of security approved by the Commissioners under subsection (1) (whether or not it is also approved under subsection (2)) of section 92 below, and, except in that section, also includes a distiller's warehouse;

"exporter", in relation to goods for exportation or for use as stores, includes the shipper of the goods and any person performing in relation to an aircraft functions corresponding with those of a shipper;

"free zone" has the meaning given by section 100A(2);

"free zone goods" are goods which are within a free zone;

"goods" includes stores and baggage;

"holiday", in relation to any part of the United Kingdom, means any day that is a bank holiday in that part of the United Kingdom under the Banking and Financial Dealings Act 1971, Christmas Day, Good Friday and the day appointed for the purposes of customs and excise for the celebration of Her Majesty's birthday;

"hovercraft" means a hovercraft within the meaning of the Hovercraft Act 1968;

"importer", in relation to any goods at any time between their importation and the time when they are delivered out of charge, includes any owner or other person for the time being possessed of or beneficially interested in the goods and, in relation to goods imported by means of a pipe-line, includes the owner of the pipe-line;

"justice" and **"justice of the peace"** in Scotland includes a sheriff and in Northern Ireland, in relation to any powers and duties which can under any enactment for the time being in force be exercised and performed only by a resident magistrate, means a resident magistrate;

"land" and **"landing"**, in relation to aircraft, include alighting on water;

"law officer of the Crown" means the Attorney General or in Scotland the Lord Advocate or in Northern Ireland the Attorney General for Northern Ireland;

"licence year", in relation to an excise licence issuable annually, means the period of 12 months ending on the date on which that licence expires in any year;

"master", in relation to a ship, includes any person having or taking the charge or command of the ship;

"night" means the period between 11 pm and 5 am;

"occupier", in relation to any bonded premises, includes any person who has given security to the Crown in respect of those premises;

"officer" means, subject to section 8(2) below, a person commissioned by the Commissioners;

"owner", in relation to an aircraft, includes the operator of the aircraft;

"owner", in relation to a pipe-line, means (except in the case of a pipe-line vested in the Crown which in pursuance of arrangements in that behalf is operated by another) the person in whom the line is vested and, in the said excepted case, means the person operating the line;

"perfect entry" means an entry made in accordance with regulation 5 of the Customs Controls on Importation of Goods Regulations 1991 or warehousing regulations, as the case may require;

"pipe-line" has the meaning given by section 65 of the Pipe-lines Act 1962 (that Act being taken, for the purposes of this definition, to extend to Northern Ireland);

"port" means a port appointed by the Commissioners under section 19 below;

"prescribed area" means such an area in Northern Ireland adjoining the boundary as the Commissioners may by regulations prescribe;

"prescribed sum", in relation to the penalty provided for an offence, has the meaning given by section 171(2) below;

"prohibited or restricted goods" means goods of a class or description of which the importation, exportation or carriage coastwise is for the time being prohibited or restricted under or by virtue of any enactment;

"proper", in relation to the person by, with or to whom, or the place at which, anything is to be done, means the person or place appointed or authorised in that behalf by the Commissioners;

"proprietor", in relation to any goods, includes any owner, importer, exporter, shipping or other person for the time being possessed of or beneficially interested in those goods;

"Queen's warehouse" means any place provided by the Crown or appointed by the Commissioners for the deposit of goods for security thereof and of the duties chargeable thereon;

"registered excise dealer and shipper" means a revenue trader approved and registered by the Commissioners under section 100G below;

"registered excise dealers and shippers regulations" means regulations under section 100G below;

"the revenue trade provisions of the customs and excise Acts" means–

(a)   the provisions of the customs and excise Acts relating to the protection, security, collection or management of the revenues derived from the duties of excise on goods produced or manufactured in the United Kingdom;

(b)   *the provisions of the customs* and excise Acts relating to any activity or facility for the carrying on or provision of which an excise licence is required;

(c)   the provisions of the Betting and Gaming Duties Act 1981 (so far as not included in paragraph (b) above);

(d)   the provisions of Chapter II of Part I of the Finance Act 1993;

(e)   the provisions of sections 10 to 15 of, and Schedule 1 to, the Finance Act 1997;

"revenue trader" means–

(a)   any person carrying on a trade or business subject to any of the revenue trade provisions of the customs and excise Acts or which consists of or includes–

    (i)   the buying, selling, importation, exportation, dealing in or handling of any goods of a class or description which is subject to a duty of excise (whether or not duty is chargeable on the goods);

    (ia)   the buying, selling, importation, exportation, dealing in or handling of tickets or chances on the taking of which lottery duty is or will be chargeable;

    (ib)   being (within the meaning of sections 10 to 15 of the Finance Act 1997) the provider of any premises for gaming;

    (ic)   the organisation, management or promotion of any gaming (within the meaning of the Gaming Act 1968 or the Betting, Gaming, Lotteries and Amusements (Northern Ireland) Order 1985); or

    (ii)   the financing or facilitation of any such transactions or activities as are mentioned in sub-paragraph (i), (ia), (ib) or (ic) above

    whether or not that trade or business is an excise licence trade;

(b)   any person who is a wholesaler or an occupier of an excise warehouse (so far as not included in paragraph (a) above),

and includes a registered club;

"ship" and **"vessel"** include any boat or other vessel whatsoever (and, to the extent provided in section 2 below, any hovercraft);

"shipment" includes loading into an aircraft, and **"shipped"** and cognate expressions shall be construed accordingly;

"stores" means, subject to subsection (4) below, goods for use in a ship or aircraft and includes fuel and spare parts and other articles of equipment, whether or not for immediate fitting;

"tons register" means the tons of a ship's net tonnage as ascertained and registered according to the tonnage regulations of the Merchant Shipping Act 1894 or, in the case of a ship which is not registered under that Act, ascertained in like manner as if it were to be so registered;

"transit goods", except in the expression **"Community transit goods"**, means imported goods entered on importation for transit or transhipment;

"transit or transhipment", in relation to the entry of goods, means transit through the United Kingdom or transhipment with a view to the re-exportation of the goods in question or transhipment of those goods for use as stores;

"transit shed" has the meaning given by section 25A below;

"United Kingdom waters" means any waters (including inland waters) within the seaward limits of the territorial sea of the United Kingdom;

"vehicle" includes a railway vehicle;

"victualling warehouse" means a place of security approved by the Commissioners under subsection (2) (whether or not it is also a place approved under subsection (1)) of section 92 below;

"warehouse", except in the expressions **"Queen's warehouse"** and **"distiller's warehouse"**, means a place of security approved by the Commissioners under subsection (1) or (2) or subsections (1) and (2) of section 92 below and, except in that section, also includes a distiller's warehouse; and **"warehouse"** and cognate expressions shall, subject to subsection (4) of that section and any regulations made by virtue of section 93(2)(da)(i) or (ee) or (4) below, be construed accordingly;

"warehousing regulations" means regulations under section 93 below.

1(2)   This Act and the other Acts included in the Customs and Excise Acts 1979 shall be construed as one Act but where a provision of this Act refers to this Act that reference is not to be construed as including a reference to any of the others.

1(3)   Any expression used in this Act or in any instrument made under this Act to which a meaning is given by any other Act included in the Customs and Excise Acts 1979 has, except where the context otherwise requires, the same meaning in this Act or any such instrument as in that Act; and for ease of reference the Table below indicates the expressions used in this Act to which a meaning is given by any other such Act–

Alcoholic Liquor Duties Act 1979

"beer"

"brewer" and "brewer for sale"
"cider"
"compounder"
"distiller"
"distiller's warehouse"
"dutiable alcoholic liquor"
"licensed", in relation to producers of wine or made-wine
"made-wine"
"producer of made-wine"
"producer of wine"
"proof"
"rectifier"
"registered club"
"spirits"
"wine"

Hydrocarbon Oil Duties Act 1979

"rebate"
"refinery"

Tobacco Products Duty Act 1979

"tobacco products"

1(4)   Subject to section 12 of the Customs and Excise Duties (General Reliefs) Act 1979 (by which goods for use in naval ships or establishments may be required to be treated as exported), any goods for use in a ship or aircraft as merchandise for sale by retail to persons carried therein shall be treated for the purposes of the customs and excise Acts as stores, and any reference in those Acts to the consumption of stores shall, in relation to goods so treated, be construed as referring to the sale thereof as aforesaid.

1(5)   A person who deals in or sells tobacco products in the course of a trade or business carried on by him shall be deemed for the purposes of this Act to be carrying on an excise licence trade (and to be a revenue trader) notwithstanding that no excise licence is required for carrying on that trade or business.

1(6)   In computing for the purposes of this Act any period expressed therein as **a period of clear days** no account shall be taken of the day of the event from which the period is computed or of any Sunday or holiday.

1(7)   The provisions of this Act in so far as they relate to customs duties apply, notwithstanding that any duties are imposed for the benefit of the Communities, as if the revenue from duties so imposed remained part of the revenues of the Crown.

Prospective repeal – In s. 1(1), definition of "perfect entry" is to be repealed from a date to be appointed by Customs and Excise Commissioners (FA 1981, s. 139 and Sch. 19, Pt. I).

Prospective insertion – In s. 1(1), definition of "representative" is to be inserted by FA 1997, s. 50(2) and Sch. 6, para. 2(4), with effect from a day to be appointed. The definition reads as follows:

""**representative**", in relation to any person from whom the Commissioners assess an amount as being excise duty due, means his personal representative, trustee in bankruptcy or interim or permanent trustee, any receiver or liquidator appointed in relation to him or any of his property or any other person acting in a representative capacity in relation to him;".

History – In s. 1(1):

*   The definition of "approved route" was omitted by SI 1992/3095, reg. 3(1), 10(2) and Sch. 2, operative from 1 January 1993. The definition read as follows:
    ""**approved route**" has the meaning given by section 26 below;".
*   In the definition of "approved wharf", the words "section 20A" were substituted for the words "section 20" by SI 1991/2724, reg. 6(2)(a), operative from 1 January 1992.
*   In the definition of "Community transit goods", the words "and for the purposes of para. (a)(i)" to "United Kingdom" were inserted by Isle of Man Act 1979, s. 13 and Sch. 1, with effect from 1 April 1980.
*   In the definition of "the Customs and Excise Acts 1979", the words "the Matches and Mechanical Lighters Duties Act 1979" which appeared after the words "Oil Duties Act 1979" were repealed by F(No. 2)A 1992, s. 82 and Sch. 18, Pt. II, with effect from 1 January 1993.
*   The definition of "customs warehouse" was omitted by SI 1991/2725, reg. 3(2)(a), with effect from 1 January 1992, but not in relation to the application of the Act by virtue of former VATA 1983, s. 24(1). The definition read as follows:
    ""**customs warehouse**" means a place of security approved by the Commissioners under subsection (2) below (whether or not it is also approved under subsection (1)) of section 92 below;".
*   The definitions of "designation order", "free zone", "free zone goods" and "free zone regulations" were inserted by FA 1984, s. 8 and Sch. 4, Pt. II, para. 1.
*   In the definition of "examination station", the words "section 22A" were substituted for the words "section 22" by SI 1991/2724, reg. 6(2)(b), operative from 1 January 1992.
*   The definition of "excise duty point" was inserted by F(No. 2)A 1992, s. 1 and Sch. 1, para. 1, operative from 1 January 1993 (SI 1992/3261 (C 102)).
*   The definition of "free zone goods" was substituted by VATA 1994, s. 100(1) and Sch. 14, para. 6, with effect from 1 September 1994. The former definition, which was inserted by FA 1984, s. 8 and Sch. 4, Pt. II, para. 1, read as follows:

""**free zone goods**" has the meaning given by section 100B(2);".
- In the former definition of "free zone goods", "100C(4)(d)" was substituted for "100B(2)" by SI 1991/2727, reg. 4(a), operative from 1 January 1992.
- The "free zone regulations" definition was omitted by SI 1991/2727, reg. 4(b), operative from 1 January 1992. The former definition, which was inserted by FA 1984, s. 8 and Sch. 4, Pt. II, para. 1 read as follows:
""**free zone regulations**" has the meaning given by section 100B(1);".
The definition of "nautical mile" was repealed by the Territorial Sea Act 1987, s. 3(4) and Sch. 2, operative from 1 October 1987 (SI 1987/1270).
- In the definition of "occupier", the words "includes any" were substituted for the words "means the" by F(No. 2)A 1992, s. 3 and Sch. 2, para. 1, operative from 9 December 1992 (SI 1992/3104 (C 96)).
- In the definition of "perfect entry", the words "regulation 5 . . . Regulations 1991" were substituted for the words "section 37 below" by SI 1992/3095, reg. 10(1) and Sch. 1, para. 2, operative from 1 January 1993.
- The definitions of "registered excise dealer and shipper" and "registered excise dealers and shippers regulations" were inserted by FA 1991, s. 11(1).
- In the definition of "the revenue trade provisions of the customs and excise Acts", the word "and" which appeared at the end of para. (c) was repealed by FA 1997, s. 113 and Sch. 18, Pt. II, with effect in relation to any gaming on or after 1 October 1997.
- In the definition of "the revenue trade provisions of the customs and excise Acts", para. (d) was inserted by FA 1993, s. 30(2) and the word "and" which appeared at the end of para. (b) was repealed by FA 1993, s. 213 and Sch. 23, Pt. I(7) in connection with the imposition of lottery duty, operative from 1 December 1993 (SI 1993/2842 (C 60)). In the definition the words "Betting and Gaming Duties Act 1981" were substituted by Sch. 5, para. 5(a) to that Act.
- In the definition of "the revenue trade provisions of the customs and excise Acts", para. (e) was inserted by FA 1997, s. 13 and Sch. 2, para. 2(2), with effect from 19 March 1997.
- In the definition of "revenue trader", the word "or" which appeared at the end of para. (a)(ia) was repealed by FA 1997, s. 113 and Sch. 18, Pt. II, with effect in relation to any gaming on or after 1 October 1997.
- In the definition of "revenue trader", para. (a)(ia), and the words in para. (ii) following "activities", were inserted by FA 1993, s. 30(3), and the word "or" which appeared at the end of para. (a)(i) was repealed by FA 1993, s. 213 and Sch. 23, Pt. I(7) in connection with the imposition of lottery duty, operative from 1 December 1993 (SI 1993/2842 (C 60)), and the words "or which consists of . . . transactions or activities" were inserted by FA 1991, s. 11(2).
- In the definition of "revenue trader", sub-para. (ib) and (ic) were inserted by FA 1997, s. 13 and Sch. 2, para. 2(3), with effect from 19 March 1997.
- In the definition of "revenue trader", in para. (a)(ii) the words ", (ia), (ib) or (ic)" were substituted for the words "or (ia)" by FA 1997, s. 13 and Sch. 2, para. 2(4), with effect from 19 March 1997.
- In the definition of "revenue trader", para. (b) and the word "and" immediately preceding it were inserted by FA 1981, s. 11(1) and Sch. 8, para. 1(1).
- In the definition of "transit or transhipment", the words "or transhipment of those goods for use as stores" were inserted by F(No. 2)A 1987, s. 103(3).
- In the definition of "transit shed", the words "section 25A" were substituted for the words "section 25" by SI 1991/2724, reg. 6(2)(c), operative from 1 January 1992.
- The definition of "United Kingdom waters" was inserted by Territorial Sea Act 1987, s. 3(1) and Sch. 1, para. 4(1), operative from 1 October 1987 (SI 1987/1270) and the former definition of "nautical mile" was repealed from the same date by s. 3(4) and Sch. 2 of that Act.
- The definition of "victualling warehouse" was inserted by SI 1991/2725, reg. 3(2)(b), operative from 1 January 1992, but not in relation to the application of the Act by virtue of former VATA 1983, s. 24(1).
- In the definition of "warehoused" and cognate expressions, the words "any regulations . . . or (4) below" were inserted by F(No. 2)A 1992, s. 3 and Sch. 2, para. 1, operative from 9 December 1992 (SI 1992/3104 (C 96)).

Cross references – Police and Criminal Evidence Act 1984, s. 114(1): application of that Act to Customs and Excise.

2   Application to hovercraft

2(1) This Part, Parts III to VII and Parts X to XII of this Act shall apply as if references to ships or vessels included references to hovercraft, and the said Parts III to VII shall apply in relation to an approved wharf or transit shed which is not in a port as if it were in a port.

2(2) All other provisions of the customs and excise Acts shall apply as if references (however expressed) to goods or passengers carried in or moved by ships or vessels included references to goods or passengers carried in or moved by hovercraft.

2(3) In all the provisions of the customs and excise Acts **"landed"**, **"loaded"**, **"master"**, **"shipped"**, **"shipped as stores"**, **"transhipment"**, **"voyage"**, **"waterborne"** and cognate expressions shall be construed in accordance with subsections (1) and (2) above.

2(4) References in the customs and excise Acts to **goods imported or exported by land, or conveyed into or out of Northern Ireland by land** , include references to goods imported, exported or conveyed across any part of the boundary of Northern Ireland; and it is hereby declared that in those Acts references to vehicles include references to hovercraft proceeding over land or water or partly over land and partly over water.

2(5) Any power of making regulations or other instruments relating to the importation or exportation of goods conferred by the customs and excise Acts may be exercised so as to make provision for the importation or exportation of goods by hovercraft which is different from the provision made for the importation or exportation of goods by other means.

3   Application to pipe-lines

3(1) In the customs and excise Acts **"shipping"** and **"loading"** and cognate expressions, where used in relation to importation or exportation, include, in relation to importation or exportation by means of a pipe-line, the conveyance of goods by means of the pipe-line and the charging and discharging of goods into and from the pipe-line, but subject to any necessary modifications.

3(2) In the customs and excise Acts **"importer"**, in relation to goods imported by means of a pipe-line, includes the owner of the pipe-line.

3(3) Any power of making regulations or other instruments relating to the importation or exportation of goods conferred by the customs and excise Acts may be exercised so as to make provision for the importation or exportation of goods by means of a pipe-line which is different from the provision made for the importation or exportation of goods by other means.

4   Application to certain Crown aircraft

4(1) The provisions of the Customs and Excise Acts 1979 relating to aircraft shall apply in relation to any aircraft belonging to or employed in the service of Her Majesty other than a military aircraft.

4(2) In this section **"military aircraft"** includes naval and air force aircraft and any aircraft commanded by a person in naval, military or air force service detailed for the purpose of such command.

5   Time of importation, exportation, etc.

5(1) The provisions of this section shall have effect for the purposes of the customs and excise Acts.

5(2) Subject to subsections (3) and (6) below, the time of importation of any goods shall be deemed to be–

(a) where the goods are brought by sea, the time when the ship carrying them comes within the limits of a port;

(b) where the goods are brought by air, the time when the aircraft carrying them lands in the United Kingdom or the time when the goods are unloaded in the United Kingdom, whichever is the earlier;

(c) where the goods are brought by land, the time when the goods are brought across the boundary into Northern Ireland.

5(3) In the case of goods brought by sea of which entry is not required under regulation 5 of the Customs Controls on Importation of Goods Regulations 1991, the time of importation shall be deemed to be the time when the ship carrying them came within the limits of the port at which the goods are discharged.

5(4) Subject to subsections (5) and (7) below, the time of exportation of any goods from the United Kingdom shall be deemed to be–

(a) where the goods are exported by sea or air, the time when the goods are shipped for exportation;

(b) where the goods are exported by land, the time when they are cleared by the proper officer at the last customs and excise station on their way to the boundary.

5(5) In the case of goods of a class or description with respect to the exportation of which any prohibition or restriction is for the time being in force under or by virtue of any enactment which are exported by sea or air, the time of exportation shall be deemed to be the time when the exporting ship or aircraft departs from the last port or customs and excise airport at which it is cleared before departing for a destination outside the United Kingdom.

5(6) Goods imported by means of a pipe-line shall be treated as imported at the time when they are brought within the limits of a port or brought across the boundary into Northern Ireland.

5(7) Goods exported by means of a pipe-line shall be treated as exported at the time when they *are charged into that pipe-line for exportation.*

5(8) A ship shall be deemed to have arrived at or departed from a port at the time when the ship comes within or, as the case may be, leaves the limits of that port.

History – In s. 5(3), the words "regulation 5 ... 1991" were substituted for the words "section 37 below" by SI 1992/3095, reg. 10(1) and Sch. 1, para. 3, operative from 1 January 1993.

PART II – ADMINISTRATION

APPOINTMENT AND DUTIES OF COMMISSIONERS, OFFICERS, ETC.

6   Appointment and general duties of Commissioners, etc.

6(1) Her Majesty may from time to time, under the Great Seal of the United Kingdom, appoint persons to be Commissioners of Customs and Excise, and any person so appointed shall hold office during Her Majesty's pleasure and may be paid such remuneration and allowances as the Treasury may determine.

6(2) In addition to the duties conferred on them by or under any other enactment, the Commissioners shall, subject to the general control of the Treasury, be charged with the duty of collecting and accounting for, and otherwise managing, the revenues of customs and excise.

6(3) The Commissioners may commission such officers and appoint or authorise such other persons to discharge any duties in relation to any assigned matter on such terms and conditions, and may pay to them such remuneration and allowances, as the Commissioners may with the sanction of the Treasury determine.

6(4) The Commissioners may at their pleasure suspend, reduce, discharge or restore any officer or person so commissioned, appointed or authorised.

6(5) The days on which and the hours between which offices of customs and excise are to be open or officers are to be available for the performance of particular duties shall be such as the Commissioners may direct.

History – In s. 6(1) and (3), references to Treasury were substituted by SI 1981/1670.

Cross references – Criminal Justice (International Co-operation) Act 1990 (Exercise of Powers) Order 1991 (SI 1991/1297): obtaining evidence relevant to overseas investigations.
SI 1997/1431, reg. 2(1): officer commissioned for distress and other purposes.

OFFENCES IN CONNECTION WITH COMMISSIONERS, OFFICERS, ETC.

15   Bribery and collusion

15(1) If any Commissioner or officer or any person appointed or authorised by the Commissioners to discharge any duty relating to an assigned matter–

(a) directly or indirectly asks for or takes in connection with any of his duties any payment or other reward whatsoever, whether pecuniary or other, or any promise or security for any such payment or reward, not being a payment or reward which he is lawfully entitled to claim or receive; or

(b) enters into or acquiesces in any agreement to do, abstain from doing, permit, conceal or connive at any act or thing whereby Her Majesty is or may be defrauded or which is otherwise unlawful, being an act or thing relating to an assigned matter,

he shall be guilty of an offence under this section.

15(2) If any person–

(a) directly or indirectly offers or gives to any Commissioner or officer or to any person appointed or authorised by the Commissioners as aforesaid any payment or other reward whatsoever, whether pecuniary or other, or any promise or security for any such payment or reward; or

(b) proposes or enters into any agreement with any Commissioner, officer or person appointed or authorised as aforesaid,

in order to induce him to do, abstain from doing, permit, conceal or connive at any act or thing whereby Her Majesty is or may be defrauded or which is otherwise unlawful, being an act or thing relating to an assigned matter, or otherwise to take any course contrary to his duty, he shall be guilty of an offence under this section.

15(3) Any person committing an offence under this section shall be liable on summary conviction to a penalty of level 5 on the standard scale and may be arrested.

History – In s. 15(3), the words "level 5 on the standard scale" were substituted by Criminal Justice Act 1982, s. 37, 38 and 46, operative from 28 October 1982, and the word "arrested" was substituted by Police and Criminal Evidence Act 1984, s. 114(1), operative from 1 January 1986 (SI 1985/1934 (C 48)).

Note – Standard scale, level 5: £5,000 operative from 1 October 1992 (Criminal Justice Act 1982, s. 74, 75 as amended by Criminal Justice Act 1991, s. 17).

16   Obstruction of officers, etc.

16(1) Any person who–

(a)　obstructs, hinders, molests or assaults any person duly engaged in the performance of any duty or the exercise of any power imposed or conferred on him by or under any enactment relating to an assigned matter, or any person acting in his aid; or

(b)　does anything which impedes or is calculated to impede the carrying out of any search for any thing liable to forfeiture under any such enactment or the detention, seizure or removal of any such thing; or

(c)　rescues, damages or destroys any thing so liable to forfeiture or does anything calculated to prevent the procuring or giving of evidence as to whether or not any thing is so liable to forfeiture; or

(d)　prevents the arrest of any person by a person duly engaged or acting as aforesaid or rescues any person so arrested,

or who attempts to do any of the aforementioned things, shall be guilty of an offence under this section.

16(2)　A person guilty of an offence under this section shall be liable–

(a)　on summary conviction, to a penalty of the prescribed sum, or to imprisonment for a term not exceeding 3 months, or to both; or

(b)　on conviction on indictment, to a penalty of any amount, or to imprisonment for a term not exceeding 2 years, or to both.

16(3)　Any person committing an offence under this section and any person aiding or abetting the commission of such an offence may be arrested.

History – In s. 16(1)(d), (3), references to "arrest" and "arrested" were substituted by Police and Criminal Evidence Act 1984, s. 114(1), operative from 1 January 1986 (SI 1985/1934 (C 48)).

COMMISSIONERS' RECEIPTS AND EXPENSES

17　Disposal of duties, etc.

17(1)　Save for such sums as may be required for any disbursements permitted by section 10 of the Exchequer and Audit Departments Act 1866, all money and securities for money collected or received in Great Britain for or on account of customs or excise shall be paid or remitted to and accounted for by the Bank of England in such manner as the Commissioners may with the approval of the Treasury direct, and shall be placed to the account in the books of the Bank entitled "the General Account of the Commissioners of Customs and Excise".

17(2)　The Bank shall deliver to the Commissioners each day a statement in writing of the money or securities for money, if any, received on that day from or on account of the Commissioners, and every statement so delivered shall be deemed to be a sufficient acknowledgement by the Bank of the receipt of the money and securities specified therein.

17(3)　Any money and securities for money standing to the credit of the General Account shall be dealt with as provided in section 10 of the Exchequer and Audit Departments Act 1866 subject, however, to section 2 of the Isle of Man Act 1979 (payments of Isle of Man share of common duties).

17(4)　All money and securities for money collected or received in Northern Ireland for or on account of–

(a)　duties of customs or excise on goods imported into or manufactured or produced in Northern Ireland; or

(b)　any duties of excise specified in any order of the Treasury for the time being in force under section 37(3) of the Northern Ireland Constitution Act 1973,

shall be dealt with as provided in section 10 of the Exchequer and Audit Departments Act 1866.

17(5)　Notwithstanding anything in section 10 of the Exchequer and Audit Departments Act 1866 or in subsection (1) above as to the disbursements which may be made out of money collected or received for or on account of customs or excise–

(a)　[Repealed by FA 1989, s. 17 and Sch. 17, Pt. I.]

(b)　no repayment of sums overpaid in error shall be made unless the claim thereto is made and evidence in support thereof is submitted to the Commissioners within 6 years of the date of the overpayment and the claim is established to the satisfaction of the Commissioners.

Paragraph (b) above does not apply to a claim for a repayment under section 137A below.

17(6)　Any reference in this section to **money and securities for money collected or received for or on account of customs or excise** or of any duties thereof includes a reference to any sums received under or by virtue of any enactment relating to customs or excise or to those duties by way of pecuniary penalties or the pecuniary proceeds of any forfeiture, costs, or otherwise howsoever.

History – In s. 17(3), the reference to Isle of Man Act 1979, s. 2 was substituted by Isle of Man Act 1979, Sch. 1, para. 3, with effect from 1 April 1980.
S. 17(5)(a) was repealed by FA 1989, s. 17 and Sch. 17, Pt. I, with effect from 1 April 1980.
– In s. 17(5), words after para. (b) were inserted by FA 1995, s. 20(2), in relation to payments made on or after 1 December 1995 (SI 1995/2892).

Cross references – Copyright, Designs and Patents Act 1988, s. 112(5) (power of Commissioners of Customs and Excise to make regulations as to giving of notice by owner of copyright for preventing importation of infringing copies): s. 17 applies to fees paid in pursuance of regulations made under that section.
FA 1994, Sch. 7, para. 32(a): all money and securities for money collected or received for or on account of insurance premium tax if collected or received in Great Britain to be placed to the general account kept under s. 17.

PART III – CUSTOMS AND EXCISE CONTROL AREAS

19 Appointment of ports, etc.

19(1) The Commissioners may by order made by statutory instrument appoint and name as a port for the purposes of customs and excise any area in the United Kingdom specified in the order.

19(2) The appointment of any port for those purposes made before 1st August 1952 may be revoked, and the name or limits of any such port may be altered, by an order under subsection (1) above as if the appointment had been made by an order under that subsection.

19(3) The Commissioners may in any port from time to time appoint boarding stations for the purpose of the boarding of or disembarkation from ships by officers.

21 Control of movement of aircraft, etc. into and out of the United Kingdom

21(1) Save as permitted by the Commissioners, the commander of an aircraft entering the United Kingdom from a place outside the United Kingdom shall not cause or permit the aircraft to land–

(a) for the first time after its arrival in the United Kingdom; or

(b) at any time while it is carrying passengers or goods brought in that aircraft from a place outside the United Kingdom and not yet cleared,

at any place other than a customs and excise airport.

21(1A) Subsection (1) above shall not apply by virtue only of the fact that the aircraft is carrying goods brought in it from a place outside the customs territory of the Community.

21(2) Save as permitted by the Commissioners, no person importing from a place within the customs territory of the Community or concerned in so importing any goods in any aircraft shall bring the goods into the United Kingdom at any place other than a customs and excise airport.

21(3) Save as permitted by the Commissioners–

(a) no person shall depart on a flight to a place or area outside the United Kingdom from any place in the United Kingdom other than a customs and excise airport; and

(b) the commander of any aircraft engaged in a flight from a customs and excise airport to a place or area outside the United Kingdom shall not cause or permit it to land at any place in the United Kingdom other than a customs and excise airport specified in the application for clearance for that flight.

21(4) Subsections (1) to (3) above shall not apply in relation to any aircraft flying from or to any place or area outside the United Kingdom to or from any place in the United Kingdom which is required by or under any enactment relating to air navigation, or is compelled by accident, stress of weather or other unavoidable cause, to land at a place other than a customs and excise airport; but subject to subsection (5) below,–

(a) the commander of any such aircraft–

(i) shall immediately report the landing to an officer or constable and shall on demand produce to him the journey log book belonging to the aircraft,

(ii) shall not without the consent of an officer permit any goods carried in the aircraft to be unloaded from, or any of the crew or passengers to depart from the vicinity of, the aircraft, and

(iii) shall comply with any directions given by an officer with respect to any such goods; and

(b)   no passenger or member of the crew shall without the consent of an officer or constable leave the immediate vicinity of any such aircraft.

21(4A)   Subsection (4)(a)(ii) and (iii) above shall not apply in relation to goods brought in the aircraft from a place outside the customs territory of the Community.

21(5)   Nothing in subsection (4) above shall prohibit–

(a)   the departure of passengers or crew from the vicinity of an aircraft; or

(b)   the removal of goods from an aircraft,

where that departure or removal is necessary for reasons of health, safety or the preservation of life or property.

21(6)   Any person contravening or failing to comply with any provision of this section shall be liable on summary conviction to a penalty of £200, or to imprisonment for a term not exceeding 3 months, or to both.

21(7)   In this Act **"customs and excise airport"** means an aerodrome for the time being designated as a place for the landing or departure of aircraft for the purposes of the customs and excise Acts by an order made by the Secretary of State with the concurrence of the Commissioners which is in force under an Order in Council made in pursuance of section 60 of the Civil Aviation Act 1982.

21(8)   References in this section to a **place or area outside the United Kingdom** do not include references to a place or area in the Isle of Man and in subsection (3)(b) above the reference to a place in the United Kingdom includes a reference to a place in the Isle of Man.

History – S. 21(1A) was inserted by SI 1991/2724, reg. 6(4)(a), operative from 1 January 1992.
In s. 21(2), the words "from a place within the customs territory of the Community" and "so" were inserted by SI 1991/2727, reg. 6(4)(b), operative from 1 January 1992.
S. 21(4A) was inserted by SI 1991/2724, reg. 6(5), operative from 1 January 1992.
In s. 21(7), the reference to Civil Aviation Act 1982, s. 60 was substituted by Sch. 15, para. 23 of that Act.
S. 21(8) was inserted by Isle of Man Act 1979, Sch. 1, para. 4, with effect from 1 April 1980.

Cross reference – F(No. 2)A 1992, s. 4(3)(a): enforcement powers under s. 21 not exercisable in relation to any person or thing entering or leaving the UK so as to prevent, restrict or delay the movement of that person or thing between different member states.

30   Control of movement of uncleared goods within or between port or airport and other places

30(1)   The Commissioners may from time to time give general or special directions as to the manner in which, and the conditions under which, goods to which this section applies, or any class or description of such goods, may be moved within the limits of any port or customs and excise airport or between any port or customs and excise airport and any other place.

30(2)   This section applies to goods chargeable with any duty which has not been paid, to drawback goods, and to any other goods which have not been cleared out of charge.

30(3)   Any directions under subsection (1) above may require that any goods to which this section applies shall be moved only–

(a)   by persons licensed by the Commissioners for that purpose;

(b)   in such ships, aircraft or vehicles or by such other means as may be approved by the Commissioners for that purpose;

and any such licence or approval may be granted for such period and subject to such conditions and restrictions as the Commissioners think fit and may be revoked at any time by the Commissioners.

30(4)   Any person contravening or failing to comply with any direction given or condition or restriction imposed, or the terms of any licence granted, by the Commissioners under this section shall be liable on summary conviction to a penalty of level 2 on the standard scale.

History – In s. 30(4), the words "level 2 on the standard scale" were substituted by Criminal Justice Act 1982, s. 37, 46 and 54.

Cross reference – Channel Tunnel (Customs and Excise) Order 1990 (SI 1990/2167), Schedule, para. 3: Customs approved area is within a port.

Note – Standard scale level 2 in Criminal Justice Act 1982, s. 37 was increased to £500, operative from 1 October 1992.

31   Control of movement of goods to and from inland clearance depot, etc.

31(1)   The Commissioners may by regulations impose conditions and restrictions as respects–

(a)   the movement of imported goods between the place of importation and a place approved by the Commissioners for the clearance out of charge of such goods, a free zone – or the place of exportation of such goods; and (aa)   the movement of goods between–

      (i)   a free zone and a place approved by the Commissioners for the clearance out of charge of such goods,

      (ii)   such a place and a free zone, and

      (iii)   a free zone and another free zone;

(b)   the movement of goods intended for export between a place approved by the Commissioners for the examination of such goods, or a place designated by the proper officer under section 53(4) or 58(3) below, and the place of exportation.

31(2)   Regulations under subsection (1) above may in particular–

(a)   require the goods to be moved within such period and by such route as may be specified by or under the regulations;

(b)   require the goods to be carried in a vehicle or container complying with such requirements and secured in such manner as may be so specified;

(c)   prohibit, except in such circumstances as may be so specified, any unloading or loading of the vehicle or container or any interference with its security.

31(2A)   Any documents required to be made or produced as a result of regulations made under subsection (1) above shall be made or produced in such form and manner and contain such particulars as the Commissioners may direct; but the Commissioners may relax any requirement imposed under the regulations that any specific document be made or produced and if they do so may impose substituted requirements.

31(3)   If any person contravenes or fails to comply with any regulation under subsection (1) above or any requirement imposed by or under any such regulation or a direction made under subsection (2A) above or any requirement imposed under that subsection, that person and the person then in charge of the goods shall each be liable on summary conviction to a penalty of level 4 on the standard scale and any goods in respect of which the offence was committed shall be liable to forfeiture.

History – In s. 31(1), the words in para. (a) ", a free zone", and para. (aa), were inserted by FA 1984, s. 8 and Sch. 4, Pt. II, para. 2(b); and the words in para. (a) "or the place of exportation of such goods" and in para. (b) ", or a place . . . 58(3) below," were inserted by FA 1981, s. 10(2) and Sch. 7, Pt. II, para. 1(2), except in relation to goods, exported before 1 October 1981. S. 31(2A), and in s. 31(3) the words "or a direction . . . under that subsection" were inserted by FA 1981, s. 10(2) and Sch. 7, Pt. II, para. 1(3), (4), except in relation to goods exported before 1 October 1981.
In s. 31(3), the reference to level 4 on the standard scale was substituted by Criminal Justice Act 1982, s. 37, 46 and 54.

Statutory instrument – Control of Movement of Goods Regulations 1984 (SI 1984/1176).

Note – Standard scale in relation to s. 31(3): level 4 in Criminal Justice Act 1982, s. 37 increased to £2,500, operative from 1 October 1992.

PART IV – CONTROL OF IMPORTATION

INWARD ENTRY AND CLEARANCE

37A   Initial and supplementary entries

37A(1)   The Commissioners may–

(a)   give such directions as they think fit for enabling an entry under regulation 5 of the Customs Controls on Importation of Goods Regulations 1991 to consist of an initial entry and a supplementary entry where the importer is authorised for the purposes of this section in accordance with the directions; and

(b)   include in the directions such supplementary provision in connection with entries consisting of initial and supplementary entries as they think fit.

37A(1A)   Without prejudice to section 37 above, a direction under that section may–

(a)   provide that where the importer is not authorised for the purposes of this section but a person who is so authorised is appointed as his agent for the purpose of entering the goods, the entry may consist of an initial entry made by the person so appointed and a supplementary entry so made; and

(b)   make such supplementary provision in connection with entries consisting of initial and supplementary entries made as mentioned in paragraph (a) above as the Commissioners think fit.

37A(2)   Where–

(a)   an initial entry made under subsection (1) above has been accepted and the importer has given security by deposit of money or otherwise to the satisfaction of the Commissioners for payment of the unpaid duty, or

(b)   an initial entry made under subsection (1A) above has been accepted and the person making the entry on the importer's behalf has given such security as is mentioned in paragraph (a) above,

the goods may be delivered without payment of any duty chargeable in respect of the goods, but any such duty shall be paid within such time as the Commissioners may direct.

37A(3)   An importer who makes an initial entry under subsection (1) above shall complete the entry by delivering the supplementary entry within such time as the Commissioners may direct.

37A(3A)   A person who makes an initial entry under subsection (1A) above on behalf of an importer shall complete the entry by delivering the supplementary entry within such time as the Commissioners may direct.

37A(4)   For the purposes of the customs and excise Acts an entry of goods shall be taken to have been **delivered** when an initial entry of the goods has been delivered, and **accepted** when an initial entry has been accepted.

History – S. 37A(1) was substituted by SI 1992/3095, reg. 10(1) and Sch. 1, para. 5, operative from 1 January 1993.
In s. 37A(1)(b), the word "may", which appeared at the beginning, was omitted by FA 1990, s. 7 and Sch. 3, para. 2(2), s. 132 and Sch. 19, Pt. I, in relation to goods imported on or after 26 July 1990.
S. 37A(1A) was inserted by FA 1990, s. 7 and Sch. 3, para. 2(3), in relation to goods imported on or after 26 July 1990.
In s. 37A(2), the words from the beginning to " . . . the goods may" were substituted for the following words:
"Where an initial entry of goods has been accepted the goods may, on the importer giving security by deposit of money or otherwise to the satisfaction of the Commissioners for payment of the unpaid duty,"
by FA 1990, s. 7 and Sch. 3, para. 2(4), in relation to goods imported on or after 26 July 1990.
In s. 37A(3), the words "under subsection (1) above", and s. 37A(3A) were inserted by FA 1990, s. 7 and Sch. 3, para. 2(5), (6), in relation to goods imported on or after 26 July 1990.
S. 37A was inserted by FA 1984, s. 9 and Sch. 5, para. 2, with effect from 26 July 1984.

37B   Postponed entry

37B(1)   The Commissioners may, if they think fit, direct that where–

(a)   such goods as may be specified in the direction are imported by an importer authorised for the purposes of this subsection;

(b)   the importer has delivered a document relating to the goods to the proper officer, in such form and manner, containing such particulars and accompanied by such documents as the Commissioners may direct; and

(c)   the document has been accepted by the proper officer,

the goods may be delivered before an entry of them has been delivered or any duty chargeable in respect of them has been paid.

37B(1A)   The Commissioners may, if they think fit, direct that where–

(a)   such goods as may be specified in the direction are imported by an importer who is not authorised for the purposes of this subsection;

(b)   a person who is authorised for the purposes of this subsection is appointed as his agent for the purpose of entering the goods;

(c)   the person so appointed has delivered a document relating to the goods to the proper officer, in such form and manner, containing such particulars and accompanied by such documents as the Commissioners may direct; and

(d)   the document has been accepted by the proper officer,

the goods may be delivered before an entry of them has been delivered or any duty chargeable in respect of them has been paid.

37B(2)   The Commissioners may, if they think fit, direct that where–

(a)   such goods as may be specified in the direction are imported by an importer authorised for the purposes of this subsection;

(b)   the goods have been removed from the place of importation to a place approved by the Commissioners for the clearance out of charge of such goods; and

(c)   the conditions mentioned in subsection (3) below have been satisfied,

the goods may be delivered before an entry of them has been delivered or any duty chargeable in respect of them has been paid.

37B(3)   The conditions are that–

(a)   on the arrival of the goods at the approved place the importer delivers to the proper officer a notice of the arrival of the goods in such form and containing such particulars as may be required by the directions;

(b)   within such time as may be so required the importer enters such particulars of the goods and such other information as may be so required in a record maintained by him at such place as the proper officer may require; and

(c)   the goods are kept secure in the approved place for such period as may be required by the directions.

37B(3A)   The Commissioners may, if they think fit, direct that where–

(a)   such goods as may be specified in the direction are imported by an importer who is not authorised for the purposes of this subsection;

(b)   a person who is authorised for the purposes of this subsection is appointed as his agent for the purpose of entering the goods;

(c)   the goods have been removed from the place of importation to a place approved by the Commissioners for the clearance out of charge of such goods; and

(d)   the conditions mentioned in subsection (3B) below have been satisfied,

the goods may be delivered before an entry of them has been delivered or any duty chargeable in respect of them has been paid.

37B(3B)   The conditions are that–

(a)   on the arrival of the goods at the approved place the person appointed as the agent of the importer for the purpose of entering the goods delivers to the proper officer a notice of the arrival of the goods in such form and containing such particulars as may be required by the directions;

(b)   within such time as may be so required the person appointed as the agent of the importer for the purpose of entering the goods enters such particulars of the goods and such other information as may be so required in a record maintained by him at such place as the proper officer may require; and

(c)   the goods are kept secure in the approved place for such period as may be required by the directions.

37B(4)   The Commissioners may direct that the condition mentioned in subsection (3)(a) or (3B)(a) above shall not apply in relation to any goods specified in the direction and such a direction may substitute another condition.

37B(5)   No goods shall be delivered under subsection (1) or (2) above unless the importer gives security by deposit of money or otherwise to the satisfaction of the Commissioners for the payment of any duty chargeable in respect of the goods which is unpaid.

37B(5A)   No goods shall be delivered under subsection (1A) or (3A) above unless the person appointed as the agent of the importer for the purpose of entering the goods gives security by deposit of money or otherwise to the satisfaction of the Commissioners for the payment of any duty chargeable in respect of the goods which is unpaid.

37B(6)   Where goods of which no entry has been made have been delivered under subsection (1) or (2) above the importer shall deliver an entry of the goods under regulation 5 of the Customs Controls on Importation of Goods Regulations 1991 within such time as the Commissioners may direct.

37B(6A)   Where goods of which no entry has been made have been delivered under subsection (1A) or (3A) above, the person appointed as the agent of the importer for the purpose of entering the goods shall deliver an entry of the goods under section 37(1) above within such time as the Commissioners may direct.

37B(7)   For the purposes of section 43(2)(a) below such an entry shall be taken to have been accepted–

(a)   in the case of goods delivered by virtue of a direction under subsection (1) or (1A) above, on the date on which the document mentioned in that subsection was accepted;

(b)   in the case of goods delivered by virtue of a direction under subsection (2) above, on the date on which particulars of the goods were entered as mentioned in subsection (3)(b) above; and

(c)   in the case of goods delivered by virtue of a direction under subsection (3A) above, on the date on which particulars of the goods were entered as mentioned in subsection (3B)(b) above.

History – S. 37B(1A), (3A), (3B) and in s. 37B(4) the words "or (3B)(a)" were inserted by FA 1990, s. 7 and Sch. 3, para. 3(2)–(4), in relation to goods imported on or after 26 July 1990.
In s. 37B(5), the words "subsection (1) or (2) above" were substituted for the words "this section" by FA 1990, s. 7 and Sch. 3, para. 3(5), in relation to goods imported on or after 26 July 1990.
S. 37B(5A) was inserted by FA 1990, s. 7 and Sch. 3, para. 3(6), in relation to goods imported on or after 26 July 1990.
In s. 37B(6), the words "subsection (1) or (2) above" were substituted for the words "this section" by FA 1990, s. 7 and Sch. 3, para. 3(6), in relation to goods imported on or after 26 July 1990.
In s. 37B(6), the words "regulation 5 of the Customs Controls on Importation of Goods Regulations 1991" were substituted for the words "section 37(1) above" by SI 1992/3095, reg. 10(1) and Sch. 1, para. 6, operative from 1 January 1993.
S. 37B(6A), in s. 37B(7)(a) the words "or (1A)", the word "and" after s. 37B(7)(b), and s. 37B(7)(c) were inserted by FA 1990, s. 7 and Sch. 3, para. 3(8), (9), in relation to goods imported on or after 26 July 1990.
S. 37B was inserted by FA 1984, s. 9 and Sch. 5, para. 2, with effect from 26 July 1984.

37C   Provisions supplementary to s. 37A and 37B

37C(1)   The Commissioners may, if they think fit–

(a)   authorise any person for the purposes of section 37A, or 37B(1), (1A), (2) or (3A) above; and

(b)   suspend or cancel the authorisation of any person where it appears to them that he has failed to comply with any requirement imposed on him by or under this Part of this Act or that there is other reasonable cause for suspension or cancellation.

37C(2)   The Commissioners may give directions–

(a)   imposing such requirements as they think fit on any person authorised under this section; or
(b)   varying any such requirements previously imposed.

37C(3)   If any person without reasonable excuse contravenes any requirement imposed by or under section 37A, 37B or this section he shall be liable on summary conviction to a penalty of level 4 on the standard scale.

History – In s. 37C(1)(a), the word "person" was substituted for the word "importer" and the words ", (1A), (2) or (3A)" were substituted for the words "or (2)", by FA 1990, s. 7 and Sch. 3, para. 4, in relation to goods imported on or after 26 July 1990. In s. 37C(1)(b) and (2)(a) the word "person" was substituted for the word "importer" by FA 1990, s. 7 and Sch. 3, para. 4, in relation to goods imported on or after 26 July 1990.
S. 37C was inserted by FA 1984, s. 9 and Sch. 5, para. 2, with effect from 26 July 1984.

Note – Standard scale in relation to s. 37C: level 4 in Criminal Justice Act 1982, s. 37 increased to £2,500, operative from 1 October 1992.

38B   Correction and cancellation of entry

38B(1)   Where goods have been entered for home use or for free circulation the importer may correct any of the particulars contained in an entry of the goods after it has been accepted if–

(a)   the goods have not been cleared from customs and excise charge;
(b)   he has not been notified by an officer that the goods are to be examined; and
(c)   the entry has not been found by an officer to be incorrect.

38B(2)   The proper officer may permit or require any correction allowed by subsection (1) above to be made by the delivery of a substituted entry.

38B(3)   An entry of goods may at the request of the importer be cancelled at any time before the goods are cleared from customs and excise charge if the importer proves to the satisfaction of the Commissioners that the entry was delivered by mistake or that the goods cannot be cleared for free circulation.

History – S. 38B was inserted by FA 1981, s. 10(1) and Sch. 6, para. 4, operative from 1 April 1982 (SI 1982/205).

41   Failure to comply with provisions as to entry

41   Without prejudice to any liability under any other provision of the Customs and Excise Acts 1979, any person making entry of goods on their importation who fails to comply with any of the requirements of this Part of this Act in connection with that entry shall be liable on summary conviction to a penalty of level 2 on the standard scale, and the goods in question shall be liable to forfeiture but this section shall not apply to–

(a)   any failure which has been or may be remedied by virtue of section 38B(1); or
(b)   any failure in respect of an entry which by virtue of section 38B(3) has been or may be cancelled at his request.

History – The words from "but this section" to the end were inserted by FA 1981, s. 10(1) and Sch. 6, para. 6, operative from 1 April 1982 (SI 1982/205); and the words "level 2 on the standard scale" were substituted by Criminal Justice Act 1982, s. 31 and 46.

Cross reference – Channel Tunnel (Customs and Excise) Order 1990 (SI 1990/2167), Schedule, para. 6: vehicle arriving through the tunnel treated as a ship arriving at a port.

Note – Level 2 on the standard scale is £500, operative from 1 October 1992.

42   Power to regulate unloading, removal, etc. of imported goods

42(1)   The Commissioners may make regulations–

(a)   prescribing the procedure to be followed by a ship arriving at a port, an aircraft arriving at a customs and excise airport, or a person conveying goods into Northern Ireland by land;

(b)   regulating the unloading, landing, movement and removal of goods on their importation;

and different regulations may be made with respect to importation by sea, air or land respectively.

42(2)   If any person contravenes or fails to comply with any regulation made under this section or with any direction given by the Commissioners or the proper officer in pursuance of any such regulation, he shall be liable on summary conviction to a penalty of level 3 on the standard scale and any goods in respect of which the offence was committed shall be liable to forfeiture.

42(3)   Subsection (1)(b) above shall not apply in relation to goods imported on or after 1st January 1992 from a place outside the customs territory of the Community or to any goods which are moving under the procedure specified in Article 3.3 of Council Regulation (EEC) No. 2726/90 (transit procedures).

History – In s. 42(2), the words "level 3 on the standard scale" were substituted by Criminal Justice Act 1982, s. 37, 38 and 46. S. 42(3) was inserted by SI 1991/2724, reg. 6(9), operative from 1 January 1992.
In s. 42(3), words following "Community" were added by SI 1992/3095, reg. 3(2), operative from 1 January 1993.

Cross reference – Channel Tunnel (Customs and Excise) Order 1990 (SI 1990/2167), Schedule, para. 6: vehicle arriving through the tunnel treated as a ship arriving at a port.

Statutory instrument – Customs and Excise (Single Market etc.) Regulations 1992 (SI 1992/3095).

European material – Regulation 2726/90 of 17 September 1990 on Community transit, OJ 1990 L262/1.

Note – Level 3 on the standard scale is £1,000, operative from 1 October 1992.

PROVISIONS AS TO DUTY ON IMPORTED GOODS

43   Duty on imported goods

43(1)   Save as permitted by or under the customs and excise Acts or section 2(2) of the European Communities Act 1972 or any Community regulation or other instrument having the force of law, no imported goods shall be delivered or removed on importation until the importer has paid to the proper officer any duty chargeable thereon, and that duty shall, in the case of goods of which entry is made, be paid on making the entry.

43(2)   Subject to subsections (2A), (2B), (2C) and (2D) below, the duties of customs or excise and the rates thereof chargeable on imported goods–

(a)   if entry is made thereof, except where the entry is for warehousing, or if they are declared under section 78 below, shall be those in force with respect to such goods at the time when the entry is accepted or the declaration is made;

(b)   if entry or, in the case of goods entered by bill of sight, perfect entry is made thereof for warehousing, shall be ascertained in accordance with warehousing regulations;

(c)   if no entry is made thereof and the goods are not declared under section 78 below shall be–

    (i)   as respects Community customs duties, those in force with respect to such goods at the time of their entry into the customs territory of the Community; and

    (ii)   as respects other duties, those in force with respect to such goods at the time of their importation.

43(2A)   Where the Commissioners require a duty of customs to be paid because of a failure to comply with a condition or other obligation imposed under section 47 or 48 below (not being a condition or obligation required to be complied with before the goods were allowed to be removed or delivered) the duty shall be charged as if entry of the goods had been accepted at the time when the non-compliance occurred.

43(2B)   Where any duties of customs are chargeable in respect of waste or debris resulting from the destruction of imported goods in free circulation, those duties and their rates shall be those in force at the time when the goods were destroyed.

43(2C)   As respects goods which have been unlawfully removed from customs charge, subsection (2)(c) above shall have effect with respect to any duties of customs as if they had entered the customs territory of the Community, or, as the case may be, had been imported at the time of their removal.

43(2D)   Nothing in the provisions of subsections (1) and (2) above or of subsection (6) below or in any exception to any of those provisions made by or under any of sections 44 to 48 below shall have effect for the purposes of any duty of excise chargeable on any goods for which–

(a)　the excise duty point is fixed by regulations under section 1 of the Finance (No. 2) Act 1992; and

(b)　the applicable rate of duty is determined in accordance with subsection (2) of that section.

43(3)　Any goods brought or coming into the United Kingdom by sea otherwise than as cargo, stores or baggage carried in a ship shall be chargeable with the like duty, if any, as would be applicable to those goods if they had been imported as merchandise; and if any question arises as to the origin of the goods they shall, unless that question is determined under section 120 below, section 14 of the Customs and Excise Duties (General Reliefs) Act 1979 (produce of the sea or continental shelf) or under a Community regulation or other instrument having the force of law, be deemed to be the produce of such country as the Commissioners may on investigation determine.

43(4)　Where, in accordance with approval given by the Commissioners, entry of goods is made by any method involving the use of a computer, subsection (2) above shall have effect as if the reference in paragraph (a) to the time of the delivery of the entry were a reference to the time when particulars contained in the entry are accepted by the computer.

43(5)　Subject to sections 10 and 11 of the Customs and Excise Duties (General Reliefs) Act 1979 (reliefs for re-imported goods) and save as provided by or under any such enactments or instruments as are mentioned in subsection (1) above, any goods which are re-imported into the United Kingdom after exportation from the United Kingdom or the Isle of Man, whether they were manufactured or produced in or outside the United Kingdom and whether or not any duty was paid thereon at a previous importation, shall be treated for the purpose of charging duty–

(a)　as if they were being imported for the first time; and

(b)　in the case of goods manufactured or produced in the United Kingdom, as if they had not been so manufactured or produced.

43(6)　Where entry of goods is made otherwise than for warehousing and there is a reduction in the rate of duty of customs or excise chargeable on the goods between–

(a)　the time mentioned in subsection (2)(a) above; and

(b)　the time when the goods are cleared from customs and excise charge,

the rate of the duty chargeable on the goods shall, if the importer so requests, be that in force at the time mentioned in paragraph (b) above unless clearance of the goods has been delayed by reason of any act or omission for which the importer is responsible.

43(7)　Notwithstanding section 6(5) of the European Communities Act 1972 **"duty of customs"** in subsection (6) above does not include any agricultural levy.

43(8)　Where samples are taken of goods under section 38A above and the quantity of the goods covered by the entry which is subsequently delivered does not include the samples the duties of customs and the rates of those duties chargeable on the samples shall be those in force at the time when the application under subsection (1) of that section was made and shall be determined by reference to the particulars contained in the application.

43(9)　Where a substituted entry is delivered under section 38(2) or 38B(2) above the entry referred to in subsection (2)(a) above is the original entry.

Prospective repeal – FA 1981, s. 139 and Sch. 19, Pt. I repeals the words in s. 43(2)(b) "or, in the case of goods entered by bill of sight, perfect entry", and s. 43(4), with effect from a date to be appointed by Customs and Excise Commissioners.

History – In s. 43(2), the words "(2C) and (2D)" were substituted for the words "and (2C)" by F(No. 2)A 1992, s. 1 and Sch. 1, para. 2(a), operative from 1 January 1993 (SI 1992/3261 (C 102)). In s. 43(2), the reference to subsections (2A), (2B) and (2C) was inserted, and para. (c) was substituted, by SI 1982/1324, reg. 2, operative from 15 October 1982. S. 43(2)(a) was substituted by FA 1981, s. 10(1) and Sch. 6, para. 7(2), operative from 1 April 1982 (SI 1982/205).
S. 43(2A)–(2C) was inserted by SI 1982/1324, reg. 2, operative from 15 October 1982.
S. 43(2D) was inserted by F(No. 2)A 1992, s. 1 and Sch. 1, para. 2(b), operative from 1 January 1993 (SI 1992/3261 (C 102)). In s. 43(5), the words "after exportation from the United Kingdom or the Isle of Man" were substituted by Isle of Man Act 1979, Sch. 1, para. 8, with effect from 1 April 1980.
S. 43(6)–(9) were inserted by FA 1981, s. 10(1) and Sch. 6, para. 7, with effect from 1 April 1982.

Cross references – Postal Packets (Customs and Excise) Regulations 1986 (SI 1986/260): application of s. 43 to postal packets. VAT Regulations 1995 (SI 1995/2518), reg. 118(c): s. 43(5) does not apply in relation to any tax chargeable on the importation of goods from places outside the member states other than duties of customs and excise or Community customs duties.

44　Exclusion of s. 43(1) for importers etc. keeping standing deposits

44　Where the Commissioners so direct, section 43(1) above shall not apply if and so long as the importer or his agent pays to, and keeps deposited with, the Commissioners a sum by way of standing deposit sufficient in their opinion to cover any duty which may become payable in respect of goods entered by that importer or agent, and if the importer or agent complies with such other conditions as the Commissioners may impose.

45   Deferred payment of customs duty

45(1) The Commissioners may by regulations provide for the payment of customs duty to be deferred in such cases as may be specified by the regulations and subject to such conditions as may be imposed by or under the regulations; and duty of which payment is deferred under the regulations shall be treated, for such purposes as may be specified thereby, as if it had been paid.

45(2) Regulations under this section may make different provision for goods of different descriptions or for goods of the same description in different circumstances.

46   Goods to be warehoused without payment of duty

46 Any goods which are on their importation permitted to be entered for warehousing shall be allowed, subject to such conditions or restrictions as may be imposed by or under warehousing regulations, to be warehoused without payment of duty.

47   Relief from payment of duty of goods entered for transit or transhipment

47 Where any goods are entered for transit or transhipment, the Commissioners may allow the goods to be removed for that purpose, subject to such conditions and restrictions as they see fit, without payment of duty.

48   Relief from payment of duty of goods temporarily imported

48 In such cases as the Commissioners may by regulations prescribe, where the Commissioners are satisfied that goods are imported only temporarily with a view to subsequent re-exportation, they may permit the goods to be delivered on importation, subject to such conditions as they see fit to impose, without payment of duty.

FORFEITURE, OFFENCES, ETC. IN CONNECTION WITH IMPORTATION

49   Forfeiture of goods improperly imported

49(1) Where–

(a) except as provided by or under the Customs and Excise Acts 1979, any imported goods, being goods chargeable on their importation with customs or excise duty, are, without payment of that duty–

    (i) unshipped in any port,

    (ii) unloaded from any aircraft in the United Kingdom,

    (iii) unloaded from any vehicle in, or otherwise brought across the boundary into, Northern Ireland, or

    (iv) removed from their place of importation or from any approved wharf, examination station or transit shed; or

(b) any goods are imported, landed or unloaded contrary to any prohibition or restriction for the time being in force with respect thereto under or by virtue of any enactment; or

(c) any goods, being goods chargeable with any duty or goods the importation of which is for the time being prohibited or restricted by or under any enactment, are found, whether before or after the unloading thereof, to have been concealed in any manner on board any ship or aircraft or, while in Northern Ireland, in any vehicle; or

(d) any goods are imported concealed in a container holding goods of a different description; or

(e) any imported goods are found, whether before or after delivery, not to correspond with the entry made thereof; or

(f) any imported goods are concealed or packed in any manner appearing to be intended to deceive an officer,

those goods shall, subject to subsection (2) below, be liable to forfeiture.

49(2) Where any goods, the importation of which is for the time being prohibited or restricted by or under any enactment, are on their importation either–

(a) reported as intended for exportation in the same ship, aircraft or vehicle; or

(b) entered for transit or transhipment; or

(c) entered to be warehoused for exportation or for use as stores,

the Commissioners may, if they see fit, permit the goods to be dealt with accordingly.

Cross references – Postal Packets (Customs and Excise) Regulations 1986 (SI 1986/260).

Channel Tunnel (Customs and Excise) Order 1990 (SI 1990/2167), Schedule, para. 7: goods unloaded etc. from a vehicle brought through the tunnel treated as unloaded etc. from an aircraft.

50 Penalty for improper importation of goods

50(1) Subsection (2) below applies to goods of the following descriptions, that is to say–

(a) goods chargeable with a duty which has not been paid; and

(b) goods the importation, landing or unloading of which is for the time being prohibited or restricted by or under any enactment.

50(2) If any person with intent to defraud Her Majesty of any such duty or to evade any such prohibition or restriction as is mentioned in subsection (1) above–

(a) unships or lands in any port or unloads from any aircraft in the United Kingdom or from any vehicle in Northern Ireland any goods to which this subsection applies, or assists or is otherwise concerned in such unshipping, landing or unloading; or

(b) removes from their place of importation or from any approved wharf, examination station, transit shed or customs and excise station any goods to which this subsection applies or assists or is otherwise concerned in such removal,

he shall be guilty of an offence under this subsection and may be arrested.

50(3) If any person imports or is concerned in importing any goods contrary to any prohibition or restriction for the time being in force under or by virtue of any enactment with respect to those goods, whether or not the goods are unloaded, and does so with intent to evade the prohibition or restriction, he shall be guilty of an offence under this subsection and may be arrested.

50(4) Subject to subsection (5), (5A) or (5B) below, a person guilty of an offence under subsection (2) or (3) above shall be liable–

(a) on summary conviction, to a penalty of the prescribed sum or of three times the value of the goods, whichever is the greater, or to imprisonment for a term not exceeding 6 months, or to both; or

(b) on conviction on indictment, to a penalty of any amount, or to imprisonment for a term not exceeding 7 years, or to both.

50(5) In the case of an offence under subsection (2) or (3) above in connection with a prohibition or restriction on importation having effect by virtue of section 3 of the Misuse of Drugs Act 1971, subsection (4) above shall have effect subject to the modifications specified in Schedule 1 to this Act.

50(5A) In the case of an offence under subsection (2) or (3) above in connection with the prohibition contained in section 20 of the Forgery and Counterfeiting Act 1981, subsection (4)(b) above shall have effect as if for the words "2 years" there were substituted the words "10 years".

50(5B) In the case of an offence under subsection (2) or (3) above in connection with the prohibition contained in regulation 2 of the Import of Seal Skins Regulations 1996, subsection (4) above shall have effect as if–

(a) for paragraph (a) there were substituted the following–

"(a)   on summary conviction, to a fine not exceeding the statutory maximum or to imprisonment for a term not exceeding three months, or both"; and

(b) in paragraph (b) for the words "7 years" there were substituted the words "2 years".

50(6) If any person–

(a) imports or causes to be imported any goods concealed in a container holding goods of a different description; or

(b) directly or indirectly imports or causes to be imported or entered any goods found, whether before or after delivery, not to correspond with the entry made thereof,

he shall be liable on summary conviction to a penalty of three times the value of the goods or level 3 on the standard scale, whichever is the greater.

50(7) In any case where a person would, apart from this subsection, be guilty of–

(a) an offence under this section in connection with the importation of goods contrary to a prohibition or restriction; and

(b) a corresponding offence under the enactment or other instrument imposing the prohibition or restriction, being an offence for which a fine or other penalty is expressly provided by that enactment or other instrument,

he shall not be guilty of the offence mentioned in paragraph (a) of this subsection.

History – In s. 50(2), (3), the word "arrested" was substituted by Police and Criminal Evidence Act 1984, s. 114(1), operative from 1 January 1986 (SI 1985/1934 (C 48)).
The words in s. 50(4) "or (5A)", and s. 50(5A), were inserted by Forgery and Counterfeiting Act 1981, s. 23(1), with effect from 28 October 1981.
In s. 50(4), the words "(5), (5A) or (5B)" were substituted by SI 1996/2686, reg. 4(1), operative from 15 November 1996.
In s. 50(4)(b), "7 years" was substituted by FA 1988, s. 12(1)(a), in relation to offences committed after 29 July 1988.
S. 50(5B) was inserted by SI 1996/2686, reg. 4(1), operative from 15 November 1996.
In s. 50(6), the words "level 3 on the standard scale" were substituted by virtue of Criminal Justice Act 1982, s. 37, 38 and 46.

Cross references – Channel Tunnel (Customs and Excise) Order 1990 (SI 1990/2167), Schedule, para. 8: vehicle unloader etc. treated as unshipper in a port and remover etc. from customs approved area treated as from an approved wharf.

Notes – Level 3 on the standard scale is £1,000, operative from 1 October 1992.

PART VII – CUSTOMS AND EXCISE CONTROL: SUPPLEMENTARY PROVISIONS

ADDITIONAL PROVISIONS AS TO INFORMATION

77   Information in relation to goods imported or exported

77(1)   An officer may require any person–

(a)   concerned with the shipment for carriage coastwise of goods of which for that purpose an entry is required by regulation 5 of the Customs Controls on Importation of Goods Regulations 1991 or on entry or specification is required by or under this Act; or

(b)   concerned in the carriage, unloading landing or loading of goods which are being or have been imported or exported,

to furnish in such form as the officer may require any information relating to the goods and to produce and allow the officer to inspect and take extracts from or make copies of any invoice, bill of lading or other book or document whatsoever relating to the goods.

77(2)   If any person without reasonable cause fails to comply with a requirement imposed on him under subsection (1) above he shall be liable on summary conviction to a penalty of level 3 on the standard scale.

77(3)   Where any prohibition or restriction to which this subsection applies, that is to say, any prohibition or restriction under or by virtue of any enactment with respect to–

(a)   the exportation of goods to any particular destination; or

(b)   the exportation of goods of any particular class or description to any particular destination,

is for the time being in force, then, if any person about to ship for exportation or to export any goods or, as the case may be, any goods of that class or description, in the course of making entry thereof before shipment or exportation makes a declaration as to the ultimate destination thereof, and the Commissioners have reason to suspect that the declaration is untrue in any material particular, the goods may be detained until the Commissioners are satisfied as to the truth of the declaration, and if they are not so satisfied the goods shall be liable to forfeiture.

77(4)   Any person concerned in the exportation of any goods which are subject to any prohibition or restriction to which subsection (3) above applies shall, if so required by the Commissioners, satisfy the Commissioners that those goods have not reached any destination other than that mentioned in the entry delivered in respect of the goods.

77(5)   If any person required under subsection (4) above to satisfy the Commissioners as mentioned in that subsection fails to do so, then, unless he proves–

(a)   that he did not consent to or connive at the goods reaching any destination other than that mentioned in the entry delivered in respect of the goods; and

(b)   that he took all reasonable steps to secure that the ultimate destination of the goods was not other than that so mentioned,

he shall be liable on summary conviction to a penalty of three times the value of the goods or level 3 on the standard scale, whichever is the greater.

History – In s. 77(1)(a), the words "for that purpose ... under this Act" were substituted for the words "an entry or specification is required for that purpose by or under this Act" by SI 1992/3095, reg. 10(1) and Sch. 1, para. 7, operative from 1 January 1993. In s. 77, certain words before the word "shipment" were omitted by FA 1987, s. 10 and Sch. 16, Pt. III.
In s. 77(2), (5), the words "level 3 on the standard scale" were substituted by Criminal Justice Act 1982, s. 37, 38 and 46.

Cross reference – Postal Packets (Customs and Excise) Regulations 1986 (SI 1986/260).

Note – Level 3 on the standard scale is £1,000, operative from 1 October 1992.

77A   Information powers

77A(1)   Every person who is concerned (in whatever capacity) in the importation or exportation of goods for which for that purpose an entry is required by regulation 5 of the Customs Controls on Importation of Goods Regulations 1991 or an entry or specification is required by or under this Act shall–

(a)   furnish to the Commissioners, within such time and in such form as they may reasonably require, such information relating to the goods or to the importation or exportation as the Commissioners may reasonably specify; and

(b)   if so required by an officer, produce or cause to be produced for inspection by the officer–

(i)   at the principal place of business of the person upon whom the demand is made or at such other place as the officer may reasonably require, and

(ii)   at such time as the officer may reasonably require,

any documents relating to the goods or to the importation or exportation.

77A(2)   Where, by virtue of subsection (1) above, an officer has power to require the production of any documents from any such person as is referred to in that subsection, he shall have the like power to require production of the documents concerned from any other person who appears to the officer to be in possession of them; but where any such other person claims a lien on any document produced by him, the production shall be without prejudice to the lien.

77A(3)   An officer may take copies of, or make extracts from, any document produced under subsection (1) or subsection (2) above.

77A(4)   If it appears to him to be necessary to do so, an officer may, at a reasonable time and for a reasonable period, remove any document produced under subsection (1) or subsection (2) above and shall, on request, provide a receipt for any document so removed; and where a lien is claimed on a document produced under subsection (2) above, the removal of the document under this subsection shall not be regarded as breaking the lien.

77A(5)   Where a document removed by an officer under subsection (4) above is reasonably required for the proper conduct of a business, the officer shall, as soon as practicable, provide a copy of the document, free of charge, to the person by whom it was produced or caused to be produced.

77A(6)   Where any documents removed under the powers conferred by this section are lost or damaged, the Commissioners shall be liable to compensate their owner for any expenses reasonably incurred by him in replacing or repairing the documents.

77A(7)   If any person fails to comply with a requirement under this section, he shall be liable on summary conviction to a penalty of level 3 on the standard scale.

History – In s. 77A(1), the words "for that purpose ... this Act" were substituted for the words "an entry or specification is required for that purpose by or under this Act" by SI 1992/3095, reg. 10(1) and Sch. 1, para. 7, operative from 1 January 1993. S. 77A was inserted by FA 1987, s. 10.

Cross reference – FA 1994, s. 20(5)(b): any power under s. 77A ceases to be exercisable in relation to a person to the extent that goods are customs goods.

78   Customs and Excise control of persons entering or leaving the United Kingdom

78(1)   Any person entering the United Kingdom shall, at such place and in such manner as the Commissioners may direct, declare any thing contained in his baggage or carried with him which–

(a)   he has obtained outside the United Kingdom; or

(b)   being dutiable goods or chargeable goods, he has obtained in the United Kingdom without payment of duty or tax,

and in respect of which he is not entitled to exemption from duty and tax by virtue of any order under section 13 of the Customs and Excise Duties (General Reliefs) Act 1979 (personal reliefs).

In this subsection **"chargeable goods"** means goods on the importation of which value added tax is chargeable or goods obtained in the United Kingdom before 1st April 1973 which are chargeable goods within the meaning of the Purchase Tax Act 1963; and **"tax"** means value added tax or purchase tax.

78(1A)   Subsection (1) above does not apply to a person entering the United Kingdom from the Isle of Man as respects anything obtained by him in the Island unless it is chargeable there with duty or value added tax and he has obtained it without payment of the duty or tax.

78(1B) Subsection (1) above does not apply to a person entering the United Kingdom from another member State, except–

(a) where he arrives at a customs and excise airport in an aircraft in which he began his journey in a place outside the member States; or

(b) as respects such of his baggage as–

    (i) is carried in the hold of the aircraft in which he arrives at a customs and excise airport, and

    (ii) notwithstanding that it was transferred on one or more occasions from aircraft to aircraft at an airport in a member State, began its journey by air from a place outside the member States.

78(2) Any person entering or leaving the United Kingdom shall answer such questions as the proper officer may put to him with respect to his baggage and any thing contained therein or carried with him, and shall, if required by the proper officer, produce that baggage and any such thing for examination at such place as the Commissioners may direct.

78(2A) Subject to subsection (1A) above, where the journey of a person arriving by air in the United Kingdom is continued or resumed by air to a destination in the United Kingdom which is not the place where he is regarded for the purposes of this section as entering the United Kingdom, subsections (1) and (2) above shall apply in relation to that person on his arrival at that destination as they apply in relation to a person entering the United Kingdom.

78(3) Any person failing to declare any thing or to produce any baggage or thing as required by this section shall be liable on summary conviction to a penalty of three times the value of the thing not declared or of the baggage or thing not produced, as the case may be, or level 3 on the standard scale, whichever is the greater.

78(4) Any thing chargeable with any duty or tax which is found concealed, or is not declared, and any thing which is being taken into or out of the United Kingdom contrary to any prohibition or restriction for the time being in force with respect thereto under or by virtue of any enactment, shall be liable to forfeiture.

History – S. 78(1A) was inserted by Isle of Man Act 1979, s. 13 and Sch. 1.
S. 78(1B) was inserted by SI 1992/3095, reg. 3(10), operative from 1 January 1993.
S. 78(2A) was inserted by F(No. 2)A 1992, s. 5, with effect from 1 January 1993.
In s. 78(3), the words "level 3 on the standard scale" were substituted by Criminal Justice Act 1982, s. 37, 38 and 46.

Cross references – F(No. 2)A 1992, s. 4(3)(g): enforcement powers under s. 78 not exercisable in relation to any person or thing entering or leaving the UK so as to prevent, restrict or delay the movement of that person or thing between different member states.
Customs and Excise Duties (Personal Reliefs for Goods Permanently Imported) Order 1992 (SI 1992/3193), art. 8(2): goods to be declared for relief.

Note – Standard scale, level 3: £1,000, operative from 1 October 1992 (Criminal Justice Act 1982, s. 74 and 75 as amended by Criminal Justice Act 1991, s. 17).

79 Power to require evidence in support of information

79(1) The Commissioners may, if they consider it necessary, require evidence to be produced to their satisfaction in support of any information required by or under Parts III to VII of this Act to be provided in respect of goods imported or exported.

79(2) Without prejudice to subsection (1) above, where any question as to the duties chargeable on any imported goods, or the operation of any prohibition or restriction on importation, depends on any question as to the place from which the goods were consigned, or any question where they or other goods are to be treated as grown, manufactured or produced, or any question as to payments made or relief from duty allowed in any country or territory, then–

(a) the Commissioners may require the importer of the goods to furnish to them, in such form as they may prescribe, proof of–

    (i) any statement made to them as to any fact necessary to determine that question, or

    (ii) the accuracy of any certificate or other document furnished in connection with the importation of the goods and relating to the matter in issue,

and if such proof is not furnished to their satisfaction, the question may be determined without regard to that statement or to that certificate or document; and

(b) if in any proceedings relating to the goods or to the duty chargeable thereon the accuracy of any such certificate or document comes in question, it shall be for the person relying on it to furnish proof of its accuracy.

PART VIIIA – FREE ZONES

100A   Designation of free zones

100A(1)   The Treasury may by order designate any area in the United Kingdom as a special area for customs purposes.

100A(2)   An area so designated shall be known as a **"free zone"**.

100A(3)   An order under subsection (1) above–

(a)   shall have effect for such period as shall be specified in the order;

(b)   may be made so as to take effect, in relation to the area or any part of the area designated by a previous order under this section, on the expiry of the period specified in the previous order;

(c)   shall appoint one or more persons as the responsible authority or authorities for the free zone;

(d)   may impose on any responsible authority such conditions or restrictions as may be specified; and

(e)   may be revoked if the Commissioners are satisfied that there has been a failure to comply with any condition or restriction.

100A(4)   The Treasury may by order–

(a)   from time to time vary–

       (i) the conditions or restrictions imposed by a designation order; or

       (ii) with the agreement of the responsible authority, the area designated; or

(b)   appoint one or more persons as the responsible authority or authorities for a free zone either in addition to or in substitution for any person appointed as such by a designation order.

100A(5)   In this Act **"designation order"** means an order made under subsection (1) above.

100A(6)   Any order under this section shall be made by statutory instrument.

History – S. 100A was inserted by FA 1984, s. 8 and Sch. 4, Pt. I, with effect from 26 July 1984.

Statutory instruments – Free Zone (Birmingham Airport) Designation Order 1991 (SI 1991/1737) (SI 1994/2509: substitution of responsible authority).
Free Zone (Liverpool) Designation Order 1991 (SI 1991/1738).
Free Zone (Prestwick Airport) Designation Order 1991 (SI 1991/1739 as varied by SI 1994/143).
Free Zone (Southampton) Designation Order 1991 (SI 1991/1740 as varied by SI 1994/1410 and SI 1996/2615).
Free Zone (Port of Tilbury) Designation Order 1992 (SI 1992/1282 as varied by SI 1994/2216).
Free Zone (Humberside) Designation Order 1994 (SI 1994/144 as varied by SI 1995/1067).
Free Zone (Port of Sheerness) Designation Order 1994 (SI 1994/2898).

100B   Free zone regulations

100B   [Repealed by VATA 1994, s. 100(2) and Sch. 15, with effect from 1 September 1994.]

100C   Free zone goods: customs duties, etc.

100C   [Repealed by VATA 1994, s. 100(2) and Sch. 15, with effect from 1 September 1994.]

100F   Powers of search

100F(1)   Any person entering or leaving a free zone shall answer such questions as any officer may put to him with respect to any goods and shall, if required by the officer, produce those goods for examination at such place as the Commissioners may direct.

100F(2)   At a time while a vehicle is entering or leaving a free zone, any officer may board the vehicle and search any part of it.

100F(3)   Any officer may at any time enter upon and inspect a free zone and all buildings and goods within the zone.

History – S. 100F was inserted by FA 1984, s. 8 and Sch. 4, Pt. I, with effect from 26 July 1984.

Statutory instrument – Free Zone Regulations (SI 1984/1177).

PART X – DUTIES AND DRAWBACKS – GENERAL PROVISIONS

GENERAL PROVISIONS RELATING TO IMPORTED GOODS

125 Valuation of goods for purpose of ad valorem duties

125(1) For the purposes of any duty for the time being chargeable on any imported goods by reference to their value (whether a Community customs duty or not), the value of the goods shall, subject to subsection (2) below, be taken according to the rules applicable in the case of Community customs duties, and duty shall be paid on that value.

125(2) In relation to an importation in the course of trade within the Communities the value of any imported goods for the purposes mentioned in subsection (1) above shall be determined on the basis of a delivery to the buyer at the port or place of importation into the United Kingdom.

125(3) The Commissioners may make regulations for the purpose of giving effect to the foregoing provisions of this section, and in particular for requiring any importer or other person concerned with the importation of goods–

(a)   to furnish to the Commissioners in such form as they may require, such information as is in their opinion necessary for a proper valuation of the goods; and

(b)   to produce any books of account or other documents of whatever nature relating to the purchase, importation or sale of the goods by that person.

125(4) If any person contravenes or fails to comply with any regulation made under subsection (3) above he shall be liable on summary conviction to a penalty of level 3 on the standard scale.

History – In s. 125(4), the words "level 3 on the standard scale" were substituted by Criminal Justice Act 1982, s. 36, 46 and 54.

Cross reference – VAT Regulations 1995 (SI 1995/2518), reg. 118(c)(ii): s. 125(1), (2) do not apply in relation to any VAT chargeable on the importation of goods from places outside the member states other than duties of customs and excise, or Community customs duties.

Statutory instrument – Free Zone Regulations 1984 (SI 1984/1177).

Note – Level 3 on the standard scale is £1,000, operative from 1 October 1992.

127 Determination of disputes as to duties on imported goods

127 [Repealed by FA 1994, s. 18(3) and Sch. 26, Pt. III and SI 1994/2679, art. 3, with effect from 1 January 1995.]

Cross references – VAT Regulations 1995 (SI 1995/2518), reg. 118(c)(iv): s. 127(1)(b) does not apply in relation to any VAT chargeable on the importation of goods from places outside the member states other than duties of customs and excise, or Community customs duties.

PART XI – ARREST OF PERSONS, FORFEITURE AND LEGAL PROCEEDINGS

History – In the heading, the word "Arrest" was substituted for the former word "detention" by Police and Criminal Evidence Act 1984, s. 114(1), operative from 1 January 1986 (SI 1985/1934 (C 48)).

FORFEITURE

139 Provisions as to detention, seizure and condemnation of goods, etc.

139(1) Any thing liable to forfeiture under the customs and excise Acts may be seized or detained by any officer or constable or any member of Her Majesty's armed forces or coastguard.

139(2) Where any thing is seized or detained as liable to forfeiture under the customs and excise Acts by a person other than an officer, that person shall, subject to subsection (3) below, either–

(a)   deliver that thing to the nearest convenient office of customs and excise; or

(b)   if such delivery is not practicable, give to the Commissioners at the nearest convenient office of customs and excise notice in writing of the seizure or detention with full particulars of the thing seized or detained.

139(3) Where the person seizing or detaining any thing as liable to forfeiture under the customs and excise Acts is a constable and that thing is or may be required for use in connection with any proceedings to be brought otherwise than under those Acts it may, subject to subsection (4) below, be retained in the custody of the police until either those proceedings are completed or it is decided that no such proceedings shall be brought.

139(4) The following provisions apply in relation to things retained in the custody of the police by virtue of subsection (3) above, that is to say–

(a) notice in writing of the seizure or detention and of the intention to retain the thing in question in the custody of the police, together with full particulars as to that thing, shall be given to the Commissioners at the nearest convenient office of customs and excise;

(b) any officer shall be permitted to examine that thing and take account thereof at any time while it remains in the custody of the police;

(c) nothing in the Police (Property) Act 1897 shall apply in relation to that thing.

139(5) Subject to subsections (3) and (4) above and to Schedule 3 to this Act, any thing seized or detained under the customs and excise Acts shall, pending the determination as to its forfeiture or disposal, be dealt with, and, if condemned or deemed to have been condemned or forfeited, shall be disposed of in such manner as the Commissioners may direct.

139(6) Schedule 3 to this Act shall have effect for the purpose of forfeitures, and of proceedings for the condemnation of any thing as being forfeited, under the customs and excise Acts.

139(7) If any person, not being an officer, by whom any thing is seized or detained or who has custody thereof after its seizure or detention, fails to comply with any requirement of this section or with any direction of the Commissioners given thereunder, he shall be liable on summary conviction to a penalty of level 2 on the standard scale.

139(8) Subsections (2) to (7) above shall apply in relation to any dutiable goods seized or detained by any person other than an officer notwithstanding that they were not so seized as liable to forfeiture under the customs and excise Acts.

Prospective insertion – In s. 139(4)(c), the words "section 31 of the Police (Northern Ireland) Act 1998" are to be substituted for the words "the Police (Property) Act 1897" by Police (Northern Ireland) Act 1998, s. 74 and Sch. 4, para. 14, with effect from a date to be appointed.

History – In s. 139(7), the words "level 2 on the standard scale" were substituted by Criminal Justice Act 1982, s. 46.

Notes – Standard scale, level 2: £500 operative from 1 October 1992 (Criminal Justice Act 1982, s. 74 and 75 as amended by Criminal Justice Act 1991, s. 17).

GENERAL PROVISIONS AS TO LEGAL PROCEEDINGS

Cross references – VATA 1994, s. 72(12): s. 145–155 apply to VAT.
CEMA 1979 – offences in connection with tax etc. in the EC.
Criminal Justice Act 1993, s. 71(7): s. 145–152 and 154 apply as if Criminal Justice Act 1993, s. 71 was contained in FA 1994, Sch. 7, para. 11: s. 145–155 apply in relation to offences under Sch. 7, para. 9 and penalties imposed under para. 10 as they apply in relation to offences and penalties under the customs and excise Acts.

145   Institution of proceedings

145(1) Subject to the following provisions of this section, no proceedings for an offence under the customs and excise Acts or for condemnation under Schedule 3 to this Act shall be instituted except by order of the Commissioners.

145(2) Subject to the following provisions of this section, any proceedings under the customs and excise Acts instituted in a magistrates' court, and any such proceedings instituted in a court of summary jurisdiction in Northern Ireland, shall be commenced in the name of an officer.

145(3) Subsections (1) and (2) above shall not apply to proceedings on indictment in Scotland.

145(4) In the case of the death, removal, discharge or absence of the officer in whose name any proceedings were commenced under subsection (2) above, those proceedings may be continued by any officer authorised in that behalf by the Commissioners.

145(5) Nothing in the foregoing provisions of this section shall prevent the institution of proceedings for an offence under the customs and excise Acts by order and in the name of a law officer of the Crown in any case in which he thinks it proper that proceedings should be so instituted.

145(6) Notwithstanding anything in the foregoing provisions of this section, where any person has been arrested for any offence for which he is liable to be arrested under the customs and excise Acts, any court before which he is brought may proceed to deal with the case although the proceedings have not been instituted by order of the Commissioners or have not been commenced in the name of an officer.

History – In s. 145(6), the references to "arrested" were substituted by Police and Criminal Evidence Act 1984, s. 114(1), operative from 1 January 1986 (SI 1985/1934 (C 48)).

146   Service of process

146(1)   Any summons or other process issued anywhere in the United Kingdom for the purpose of any proceedings under the customs and excise Acts may be served on the person to whom it is addressed in any part of the United Kingdom without any further endorsement, and shall be deemed to have been duly served–

(a)   if delivered to him personally; or

(b)   if left at his last known place of abode or business or, in the case of a body corporate, at their registered or principal office; or

(c)   if left on board any vessel or aircraft to which he may belong or have lately belonged.

146(2)   Any summons, notice, order or other document issued for the purposes of any proceedings under the customs and excise Acts, or of any appeal from the decision of the court in any such proceedings, may be served by an officer.

In this subsection **"appeal"** includes an appeal by way of case stated.

146(3)   This section shall not apply in relation to proceedings instituted in the High Court or Court of Session.

Cross reference – Channel Tunnel (Customs and Excise) Order 1990 (SI 1990/2167), Schedule, para. 22: reference to aircraft in s. 141(1)(c) includes a vehicle which has arrived from or is departing to France through the tunnel.

146A   Time limits for proceedings

146A(1)   Except as otherwise provided in the customs and excise Acts, and notwithstanding anything in any other enactment, the following provisions shall apply in relation to proceedings for an offence under those Acts.

146A(2)   Proceedings for an indictable offence shall not be commenced after the end of the period of 20 years beginning with the day on which the offence was committed.

146A(3)   Proceedings for a summary offence shall not be commenced after the end of the period of 3 years beginning with that day but, subject to that, may be commenced at any time within 6 months from the date on which sufficient evidence to warrant the proceedings came to the knowledge of the prosecuting authority.

146A(4)   For the purposes of subsection (3) above, a certificate of the prosecuting authority as to the date on which such evidence as is there mentioned came to that authority's knowledge shall be conclusive evidence of that fact.

146A(5)   In the application of this section to Scotland–

(a)   in subsection (2), **"proceedings for an indictable offence"** means proceedings on indictment;

(b)   in subsection (3), **"proceedings for a summary offence"** means summary proceedings.

146A(6)   In the application of this section to Northern Ireland–

(a)   **"indictable offence"** means an offence which, if committed by an adult, is punishable on conviction on indictment (whether only on conviction on indictment, or either on conviction on indictment or on summary conviction);

(b)   **"summary offence"** means an offence which, if committed by an adult, is punishable only on summary conviction.

146A(7)   In this section, **"prosecuting authority"** means the Commissioners and includes, in Scotland, the procurator fiscal.

History – S. 146A was inserted by FA 1989, s. 16, with effect in relation to offences committed on or after 27 July 1989.

147   Proceedings for offences

147(1)   [Repealed by FA 1989, s. 16(2), 187 and Sch. 17, Pt. I.]

147(2)   Where, in England or Wales, a magistrates' court has begun to inquire into an information charging a person with an offence under the customs and excise Acts as examining justices the court shall not proceed under section 25(3) of the Magistrates' Courts Act 1980 to try the information summarily without the consent of–

(a)   the Attorney General, in a case where the proceedings were instituted by his order and in his name; or

(b)   the Commissioners, in any other case.

147(3)   In the case of proceedings in England or Wales, without prejudice to any right to require the statement of a case for the opinion of the High Court, the prosecutor may appeal to the Crown

Court against any decision of a magistrates' court in proceedings for an offence under the customs and excise Acts.

147(4) In the case of proceedings in Northern Ireland, without prejudice to any right to require the statement of a case for the opinion of the High Court, the prosecutor may appeal to the county court against any decision of a court of summary jurisdiction in proceedings for an offence under the customs and excise Acts.

147(5) [Repealed by the Criminal Justice Act 1982, s. 78 and Sch. 16.]

History – S. 147(1) was repealed by FA 1989, s. 16(2), 187 and Sch. 17, Pt. I, with effect in relation to offences committed on or after 27 July 1989.
In s. 147(2), the reference to the Magistrates' Courts Act 1980 was substituted by s. 154 and Sch. 7, para. 176 of that Act.
S. 147(5) was repealed by the Criminal Justice Act 1982, s. 78 and Sch. 16, with effect from 28 October 1982.

148   Place of trial for offences

148(1) Proceedings for an offence under the customs and excise Acts may be commenced–

(a)   in any court having jurisdiction in the place where the person charged with the offence resides or is found; or

(b)   if any thing was detained or seized in connection with the offence, in any court having jurisdiction in the place where that thing was so detained or seized or was found or condemned as forfeited; or

(c)   in any court having jurisdiction anywhere in that part of the United Kingdom, namely–

      (i) England and Wales,
      (ii) Scotland, or
      (iii) Northern Ireland,

in which the place where the offence was committed is situated.

148(2) Where any such offence was committed at some place outside the area of any commission of the peace, the place of the commission of the offence shall, for the purpose of the jurisdiction of any court, be deemed to be any place in the United Kingdom where the offender is found or to which he is first brought after the commission of the offence.

148(3) The jurisdiction under subsection (2) above shall be in addition to and not in derogation of any jurisdiction or power of any court under any other enactment.

149   Non-payment of penalties, etc.: maximum terms of imprisonment

149(1) Where, in any proceedings for an offence under the customs and excise Acts, a magistrates' court in England or Wales or a court of summary jurisdiction in Scotland, in addition to ordering the person convicted to pay a penalty for the offence–

(a)   orders him to be imprisoned for a term in respect of the same offence; and

(b)   further (whether at the same time or subsequently) orders him to be imprisoned for a term in respect of non-payment of that penalty or default of a sufficient distress to satisfy the amount of that penalty,

the aggregate of the terms for which he is so ordered to be imprisoned shall not exceed 15 months.

149(2) [Repealed by Criminal Justice (Scotland) Act 1980, s. 83(3) and Sch. 8.]

149(3) Where, under any enactment for the time being in force in Northern Ireland, a court of summary jurisdiction has power to order a person to be imprisoned in respect of the non-payment of a penalty, or of the default of a sufficient distress to satisfy the amount of that penalty, for a term in addition and succession to a term of imprisonment imposed for the same offence as the penalty, then in relation to a sentence for an offence under the customs and excise Acts the aggregate of those terms of imprisonment may, notwithstanding anything in any such enactment, be any period not exceeding 15 months.

History – S. 149(2) was repealed by Criminal Justice (Scotland) Act 1980, s. 83(3) and Sch. 8, with effect from 13 November 1980.

150   Incidental provisions as to legal proceedings

150(1) Where liability for any offence under the customs and excise Acts is incurred by two or more persons jointly, those persons shall each be liable for the full amount of any pecuniary penalty and may be proceeded against jointly or severally as the Commissioners may see fit.

150(2) In any proceedings for an offence under the customs and excise Acts instituted in England, Wales or Northern Ireland, any court by whom the matter is considered may mitigate any pecuniary penalty as they see fit.

150(3) In any proceedings for an offence or for the condemnation of any thing as being forfeited under the customs and excise Acts, the fact that security has been given by bond or otherwise for the payment of any duty or for compliance with any condition in respect of the non-payment of which or non-compliance with which the proceedings are instituted shall not be a defence.

151 Application of penalties

151 The balance of any sum paid or recovered on account of any penalty imposed under the customs and excise Acts, after paying any such compensation or costs as are mentioned in section 139 of the Magistrates' Courts Act 1980 to persons other than the Commissioners shall, notwithstanding any local or other special right or privilege of whatever origin, be accounted for and paid to the Commissioners or as they direct.

History – In s. 151, the reference to the Magistrates' Courts Act 1980 was substituted by Sch. 7 to that Act.

152 Powers of Commissioners to mitigate penalties, etc.

152 The Commissioners may, as they see fit–

(a) stay, sist or compound any proceedings for an offence or for the condemnation of any thing as being forfeited under the customs and excise Acts; or

(b) restore, subject to such conditions (if any) as they think proper, any thing forfeited or seized under those Acts; or

(c) after judgment, mitigate or remit any pecuniary penalty imposed under those Acts; or

(d) order any person who has been imprisoned to be discharged before the expiration of his term of imprisonment, being a person imprisoned for any offence under those Acts or in respect of the non-payment of a penalty or other sum adjudged to be paid or awarded in relation to such an offence or in respect of the default of a sufficient distress to satisfy such a sum;

but paragraph (a) above shall not apply to proceedings on indictment in Scotland.

Cross references – VAT Regulations 1995 (SI 1995/2518), reg. 58(1)(c)(ii) and 64(1)(a): compounding can stop admission to cash accounting scheme.
VAT Regulations 1995 (SI 1995/2518), reg. 204(b) and 206(1)(b): admission to scheme and cancellation of certificate of flat-rate farmer.

Other material – HC Paper (1987–88) 452–i (not reproduced): the House of Commons Public Accounts Committee's Minutes of Evidence, 25 April 1988 contain a summary of Customs and Excise policy on compounding of offence proceedings under s. 152.

153 Proof of certain documents

153(1) Any document purporting to be signed either by one or more of the Commissioners, or by their order, or by any other person with their authority, shall, until the contrary is proved, be deemed to have been so signed and to be made and issued by the Commissioners, and may be proved by the production of a copy thereof purporting to be so signed.

153(2) Without prejudice to subsection (1) above, the Documentary Evidence Act 1868 shall apply in relation to–

(a) any document issued by the Commissioners;

(b) any document issued before 1st April 1909, by the Commissioners of Customs or the Commissioners of Customs and the Commissioners of Inland Revenue jointly;

(c) any document issued before that date in relation to the revenue of excise by the Commissioners of Inland Revenue,

as it applies in relation to the documents mentioned in that Act.

153(3) That Act shall, as applied by subsection (2) above, have effect as if the persons mentioned in paragraphs (a) to (c) of that subsection were included in the first column of the Schedule to that Act, and any of the Commissioners or any secretary or assistant secretary to the Commissioners were specified in the second column of that Schedule in connection with those persons.

153(4) A photograph of any document delivered to the Commissioners for any customs or excise purpose and certified by them to be such a photograph shall be admissible in any proceedings, whether civil or criminal, to the same extent as the document itself.

History – S. 153(4) was inserted by FA 1981, s. 11(1) and Sch. 8, para. 9, with effect from 27 July 1981.

154 Proof of certain other matters

154(1) An averment in any process in proceedings under the customs and excise Acts–

(a)   that those proceedings were instituted by the order of the Commissioners; or

(b)   that any person is or was a Commissioner, officer or constable, or a member of Her Majesty's armed forces or coastguard; or

(c)   that any person is or was appointed or authorised by the Commissioners to discharge, or was engaged by the orders or with the concurrence of the Commissioners in the discharge of, any duty; or

(d)   that the Commissioners have or have not been satisfied as to any matter as to which they are required by any provision of those Acts to be satisfied; or

(e)   that any ship is a British ship; or

(f)   that any goods thrown overboard, staved or destroyed were so dealt with in order to prevent or avoid the seizure of those goods,

shall, until the contrary is proved, be sufficient evidence of the matter in question.

154(2)   Where in any proceedings relating to customs or excise any question arises as to the place from which any goods have been brought or as to whether or not–

(a)   any duty has been paid or secured in respect of any goods; or

(b)   any goods or other things whatsoever are of the description or nature alleged in the information, writ or other process; or

(c)   any goods have been lawfully imported or lawfully unloaded from any ship or aircraft; or

(d)   any goods have been lawfully loaded into any ship or aircraft or lawfully exported or were lawfully waterborne; or

(e)   any goods were lawfully brought to any place for the purpose of being loaded into any ship or aircraft or exported; or

(f)   any goods are or were subject to any prohibition of or restriction on their importation or exportation,

then, where those proceedings are brought by or against the Commissioners, a law officer of the Crown or an officer, or against any other person in respect of anything purporting to have been done in pursuance of any power or duty conferred or imposed on him by or under the customs and excise Acts, the burden of proof shall lie upon the other party to the proceedings.

Cross references – VATA 1994, s. 72(12): application to VAT.
Channel Tunnel (Customs and Excise) Order 1990 (SI 1990/2167), Schedule, para. 23: application of s. 154(2) to goods on a vehicle using the Channel Tunnel.

155   Persons who may conduct proceedings

155(1)   Any officer or any other person authorised in that behalf by the Commissioners may, although he is not a barrister, advocate or solicitor, conduct any proceedings before any magistrates' court in England or Wales or court of summary jurisdiction in Scotland or Northern Ireland or before any examining justices, being proceedings under any enactment relating to an assigned matter or proceedings arising out of the same circumstances as any proceedings commenced under any such enactment, whether or not the last mentioned proceedings are persisted in.

155(2)   Any person who has been admitted as a solicitor and is employed by the Commissioners may act as a solicitor in any proceedings in England, Wales or Northern Ireland relating to any assigned matter notwithstanding that he does not hold a current practising certificate.

PART XII – GENERAL AND MISCELLANEOUS

GENERAL POWERS, ETC.

157   Bonds and security

157(1)   Without prejudice to any express requirement as to security contained in the customs and excise Acts, the Commissioners may, if they see fit, require any person to give security by bond or otherwise for the observance of any condition in connection with customs or excise.

157(2)   Any bond taken for the purposes of any assigned matter–

(a)   shall be taken on behalf of Her Majesty; and

(b)   shall be valid notwithstanding that it is entered into by a person under full age; and

(c)   may be cancelled at any time by or by order of the Commissioners.

159   Power to examine and take account of goods

159(1)   Without prejudice to any other power conferred by the Customs and Excise Acts 1979, an officer may examine and take account of any goods–

(a)   which are imported; or

(b)   which are in a warehouse or Queen's warehouse; or

(bb)   which are in a free zone; or

(c)   which have been loaded into any ship or aircraft at any place in the United Kingdom or the Isle of Man; or

(d)   which are entered for exportation or for use as stores; or

(e)   which are brought to any place in the United Kingdom for exportation or for shipment for exportation or as stores; or

(f)   in the case of which any claim for drawback, allowance, rebate, remission or repayment of duty is made;

and may for that purpose require any container to be opened or unpacked.

159(2)   Any examination of goods by an officer under the Customs and Excise Acts 1979 shall be made at such place as the Commissioners appoint for the purpose.

159(3)   In the case of such goods as the Commissioners may direct, and subject to such conditions as they see fit to impose, an officer may permit goods to be skipped on the quay or bulked, sorted, lotted, packed or repacked before account is taken thereof.

159(4)   Any opening, unpacking, weighing, measuring, repacking, bulking, sorting, lotting, marking, numbering, loading, unloading, carrying or landing of goods or their containers for the purposes of, or incidental to, the examination by an officer, removal or warehousing thereof shall be done, and any facilities or assistance required for any such examination shall be provided, by or at the expense of the proprietor of the goods.

159(5)   If any imported goods which an officer has power under the Customs and Excise Acts 1979 to examine are without the authority of the proper officer removed from customs and excise charge before they have been examined, those goods shall be liable to forfeiture.

159(6)   If any goods falling within subsection (5) above are removed by a person with intent to defraud Her Majesty of any duty chargeable thereon or to evade any prohibition or restriction for the time being in force with respect thereto under or by virtue of any enactment, that person shall be guilty of an offence under this subsection and may be arrested.

159(7)   A person guilty of an offence under subsection (6) above shall be liable–

(a)   on summary conviction, to a penalty of the prescribed sum or of three times the value of the goods, whichever is the greater, or to imprisonment for a term not exceeding 6 months, or to both; or

(b)   on conviction on indictment, to a penalty of any amount, or to imprisonment for a term not exceeding 7 years, or to both.

159(8)   Without prejudice to the foregoing provisions of this section, where by this section or by or under any other provision of the Customs and Excise Acts 1979 an account is authorised or required to be taken of any goods for any purpose by an officer, the Commissioners may, with the consent of the proprietor of the goods, accept as the account of those goods for that purpose an account taken by such other person as may be approved in that behalf by both the Commissioners and the proprietor of the goods.

History – S. 159(1)(bb) was inserted by FA 1984, s. 8 and Sch. 4, Pt. II, para. 5.
In s. 159(1)(c), the reference to the Isle of Man was inserted by Isle of Man Act 1979, Sch. 1, para. 22.
In s. 159(6), the word "arrested" was substituted by Police and Criminal Evidence Act 1984, s. 114(1), operative from 1 January 1986 (SI 1985/1934).
In s. 159(7)(b), "7 years" was substituted by FA 1988, s. 12(1)(a), in relation to offences committed after 29 July 1988.

Cross reference – Channel Tunnel (Customs and Excise) Order 1990 (SI 1990/2167), Schedule, para. 24: in s. 159(1)(c), goods loaded into a ship to include goods loaded etc. on to a vehicle departing for or arriving from France through the tunnel.

164   Power to search persons

164(1)   Where there are reasonable grounds to suspect that any person to whom this section applies (referred to in this section as **"the suspect"**) is carrying any article–

(a)   which is chargeable with any duty which has not been paid or secured; or

(b)   with respect to the importation or exportation of which any prohibition or restriction is for the time being in force under or by virtue of any enactment, an officer may exercise the powers conferred by subsection (2) below and, if the suspect is not under arrest, may detain him for so long as may be necessary for the exercise of those powers and (where applicable) the exercise of the rights conferred by subsection (3) below.

164(2)   The officer may require the suspect–

(a)   to permit such a search of any article which he has with him; and

(b)   subject to subsection (3) below, to submit to such searches of his person, whether rub-down, strip or intimate,

as the officer may consider necessary or expedient; but no such requirement may be imposed under paragraph (b) above without the officer informing the suspect of the effect of subsection (3) below.

164(3)   If the suspect is required to submit to a search of his person, he may require to be taken–

(a)   except in the case of a rub-down search, before a justice of the peace or a superior of the officer concerned; and

(b)   in the excepted case, before such a superior;

and the justice or superior shall consider the grounds for suspicion and direct accordingly whether the suspect is to submit to the search.

164(3A)   A rub-down or strip search shall not be carried out except by a person of the same sex as the suspect; and an intimate search shall not be carried out except by a suitably qualified person.

164(4)   This section applies to the following persons, namely–

(a)   any person who is on board or has landed from any ship or aircraft;

(b)   any person entering or about to leave the United Kingdom;

(c)   any person within the dock area of a port;

(d)   any person at a customs and excise airport;

(e)   any person in, entering or leaving any approved wharf or transit shed which is not in a port;

(ee)   any person in, entering or leaving a free zone;

(f)   in Northern Ireland, any person travelling from or to any place which is on or beyond the boundary.

164(5)   In this section–

    "intimate search" means any search which involves a physical examination (that is, an examination which is more than simply a visual examination) of a person's body orifices;

    "rub-down search" means any search which is neither an intimate search nor a strip search;

    "strip search" means any search which is not an intimate search but which involves the removal of an article of clothing which–

    (a)   is being worn (wholly or partly) on the trunk; and

    (b)   is being so worn either next to the skin or next to an article of underwear;

    "suitably qualified person" means a registered medical practitioner or a registered nurse.

164(6)   Notwithstanding anything in subsection (4) of section 48 of the Criminal Justice (Scotland) Act 1987 (detention and questioning by customs officers), detention of the suspect under subsection (1) above shall not prevent his subsequent detention under subsection (1) of that section.

History – In s. 164(1), the words "(referred to in this section as "the suspect")", and "an officer may . . . subsection (3) below" were substituted by FA 1988, s. 10(1).
S. 164(2)–(3A) were substituted by FA 1988, s. 10(2) for former s. 164(2) and (3).
S. 164(4)(ee) was inserted by FA 1984, s. 8 and Sch. 4, Pt. II, para. 6.
S. 164(5), (6) were inserted by FA 1988, s. 10(3).

Cross reference – Channel Tunnel (Customs and Excise) Order 1990 (SI 1990/2167), Schedule, para. 25: search of persons applies to persons in, entering or leaving a customs approved area.

165   Power to pay rewards

165   Subject to any directions of the Treasury as to amount, the Commissioners may at their discretion pay rewards in respect of any service which appears to them to merit reward rendered to them by any person in relation to any assigned matter.

166   Agents

166(1)   If any person requests an officer or a person appointed by the Commissioners to transact any business relating to an assigned matter with him on behalf of another person, the officer or person so appointed may refuse to transact that business with him unless written authority from that other person is produced in such form as the Commissioners may direct.

166(2)   Subject to subsection (1) above, anything required by the Customs and Excise Acts 1979 to be done by the importer or exporter of any goods may, except where the Commissioners otherwise require, be done on his behalf by an agent.

GENERAL OFFENCES

167   Untrue declarations, etc.

167(1)   If any person either knowingly or recklessly–

(a)   makes or signs, or causes to be made or signed, or delivers or causes to be delivered to the Commissioners or an officer, any declaration, notice, certificate or other document whatsoever; or

(b)   makes any statement in answer to any question put to him by an officer which he is required by or under any enactment to answer,

being a document or statement produced or made for any purpose of any assigned matter, which is untrue in any material particular, he shall be guilty of an offence under this subsection and may be arrested; and any goods in relation to which the document or statement was made shall be liable to forfeiture.

167(2)   Without prejudice to subsection (4) below, a person who commits an offence under subsection (1) above shall be liable–

(a)   on summary conviction, to a penalty of the prescribed sum, or to imprisonment for a term not exceeding 6 months, or to both; or

(b)   on conviction on indictment, to penalty of any amount, or to imprisonment for a term not exceeding 2 years, or to both.

167(3)   If any person–

(a)   makes or signs, or causes to be made or signed, or delivers or causes to be delivered to the Commissioners or an officer, any declaration, notice, certificate or other document whatsoever; or

(b)   makes any statement in answer to any question put to him by an officer which he is required by or under any enactment to answer,

being a document or statement produced or made for any purpose of any assigned matter, which is untrue in any material particular, then, without prejudice to subsection (4) below, he shall be liable on summary conviction to a penalty of level 4 on the standard scale.

167(4)   Where by reason of any such document or statement as is mentioned in subsection (1) or (3) above the full amount of any duty payable is not paid or any overpayment is made in respect of any drawback, allowance, rebate or repayment of duty, the amount of the duty unpaid or of the overpayment shall be recoverable as a debt due to the Crown or may be summarily recovered as a civil debt.

167(5)   [Not reproduced; relates to excise duty.]

History – In s. 167(1), the word "arrested" was substituted by Police and Criminal Evidence Act 1984, s. 114(1), operative from 1 January 1986 (SI 1985/1934 (C 48)).
In s. 167(3), the words "level 4 on the standard scale" were substituted by Criminal Justice Act 1982, s. 37, 38 and 47.

Cross references – FA 1985, s. 10(5), (6): "document" in CEMA 1979, s. 167 has the same meaning as in Civil Evidence Act 1968, Pt. I.
Statistics of Trade (Customs and Excise) Regulations 1992 (SI 1992/2790): maximum term of imprisonment is three months where a person is summarily convicted of an offence contrary to s. 167(1) in connection with the operation of the Intrastat system.

Note – Standard scale, level 4: £2,500, operative from 1 October 1992 (Criminal Justice Act 1982, s. 74 and 75 as amended by Criminal Justice Act 1991, s. 17).

168   Counterfeiting documents, etc.

168(1)   If any person–

(a)   counterfeits or falsifies any document which is required by or under any enactment relating to an assigned matter or which is used in the transaction of any business relating to an assigned matter; or

(b)   knowingly accepts, receives or uses any such document so counterfeited or falsified; or

(c)   alters any such document after it is officially issued; or

(d)   counterfeits any seal, signature, initials or other mark of, or used by, any officer for the verification of such a document or for the security of goods or for any other purpose relating to an assigned matter,

he shall be guilty of an offence under this section and may be arrested.

168(2)   A person guilty of an offence under this section shall be liable–

(a)   on summary conviction, to a penalty of the prescribed sum, or to imprisonment for a term not exceeding 6 months, or to both; or

(b)   on conviction on indictment, to a penalty of any amount, or to imprisonment for a term not exceeding 2 years, or to both.

History – In s. 168(1), the word "arrested" was substituted by Police and Criminal Evidence Act 1984, s. 114, operative from 1 January 1984 (SI 1985/1934 (C 48)).

Cross references – FA 1985, s. 10(5), (6): "document" in CEMA 1979, s. 168 has the same meaning as in the Civil Evidence Act 1968, Pt. I.

Statistics of Trade (Customs and Excise) Regulations 1992 (SI 1992/2790): maximum term of imprisonment is three months where a person is summarily convicted of an offence contrary to s. 168(1) in connection with the operation of the Intrastat system.

171   General provisions as to offences and penalties

171(1)   Where–

(a)   by any provision of any enactment relating to an assigned matter a punishment is prescribed for any offence thereunder or for any contravention of or failure to comply with any regulation, direction, condition or requirement made, given or imposed thereunder; and

(b)   any person is convicted in the same proceedings of more than one such offence, contravention or failure,

that person shall be liable to that punishment for each such offence, contravention or failure of which he is so convicted.

171(2)   In this Act the **"prescribed sum"**, in relation to the penalty provided for an offence, means–

(a)   if the offence was committed in England or Wales, the prescribed sum within the meaning of section 32 of the Magistrates' Courts Act 1980 (£1,000 or other sum substituted by order under section 143(1) of that Act);

(b)   if the offence was committed in Scotland, the prescribed sum within the meaning of subsection (8) of section 225 of the Criminal Procedure (Scotland) Act 1995 (£5,000 or other sum substituted by order under subsection (4) of that section);

(c)   if the offence was committed in Northern Ireland, the prescribed sum within the meaning of Article 4 of the Fines and Penalties (Northern Ireland) Order 1984 (£2,000 or other sum substituted by order under Article 17 of that Order).

171(2A)   [Repealed by Statute Law (Repeals) Act 1993, s. 1(1) and Sch. 1, Pt. XIV, Grp. 2.]

171(3)   Where a penalty for an offence under any enactment relating to an assigned matter is required to be fixed by reference to the value of any goods, that value shall be taken as the price which those goods might reasonably be expected to have fetched, after payment of any duty or tax chargeable thereon, if they had been sold in the open market at or about the date of the commission of the offence for which the penalty is imposed.

171(4)   Where an offence under any enactment relating to an assigned matter which has been committed by a body corporate is proved to have been committed with the consent or connivance of, or to be attributable to any neglect on the part of, any director, manager, secretary or other similar officer of the body corporate or any person purporting to act in any such capacity, he as well as the body corporate shall be guilty of that offence and shall be liable to be proceeded against and punished accordingly.

In this subsection **"director"**, in relation to any body corporate established by or under any enactment for the purpose of carrying on under national ownership any industry or part of an industry or undertaking, being a body corporate whose affairs are managed by the members thereof, means a member of that body corporate.

171(5)   Where in any proceedings for an offence under the customs and excise Acts any question arises as to the duty or the rate thereof chargeable on any imported goods, and it is not possible to ascertain the relevant time specified in section 43 above or the relevant excise duty point, that duty or rate shall be determined as if the goods had been imported without entry at the time when the proceedings were commenced or, as the case may be, as if the time when the proceedings were commenced was the relevant excise duty point.

History – In s. 171(2), the words in para. (a) "or Wales", and para. (c), were inserted by SI 1984/703, operative from *19 July 1984; and the reference in s. 171(2)(a)* to Magistrates' Courts Act 1980 was substituted by Sch. 7, para. 178 of that Act. In s. 171(2)(c), "£2,000" was substituted by SI 1984/253, operative from 1 September 1984.

In s. 171(2)(b), the words "subsection (8) of section 225 of the Criminal Procedure (Scotland) Act 1995" to the end of para. (b) were substituted by Criminal Procedure (Consequential Provisions) (Scotland) Act 1995, Sch. 4, para. 18(5), with effect from 1 April 1996.

S. 171(2A) was repealed by Statute Law (Repeals) Act 1993, s. 1(1) and Sch. 1, Pt. XIV, Grp. 2, with effect from 5 November 1993. Former s. 171(2A) read as follows:

"**171(2A)**   In this Act **"the standard scale"** has the meaning assigned to it by section 75 of the Criminal Justice Act 1982."

In s. 171(5), the words "or the relevant excise duty point" and the words "or, as the case may be . . . excise duty point." were inserted by F(No. 2)A 1992, s. 3 and Sch. 2, para. 9, operative from 9 December 1992 (SI 1992/3104 (C 96)).

SCHEDULES

SCHEDULE 3 – PROVISIONS RELATING TO FORFEITURE

Sections 139, 143 and 145

NOTICE OF SEIZURE

1(1) The Commissioners shall, except as provided in sub-paragraph (2) below, give notice of the seizure of any thing as liable to forfeiture and of the grounds therefor to any person who to their knowledge was at the time of the seizure the owner or one of the owners thereof.

1(2) Notice need not be given under this paragraph if the seizure was made in the presence of–

(a)   the person whose offence or suspected offence occasioned the seizure; or

(b)   the owner or any of the owners of the thing seized or any servant or agent of his; or

(c)   in the case of any thing seized in any ship or aircraft, the master or commander.

Cross reference – Postal Packets (Customs and Excise) Regulations 1986 (SI 1986/260), reg. 5(k): modification of para. 1 in the case of a thing brought by post into the UK.

2   Notice under paragraph 1 above shall be given in writing and shall be deemed to have been duly served on the person concerned–

(a)   if delivered to him personally; or

(b)   if addressed to him and left or forwarded by post to him at his usual or last known place of abode or business or, in the case of a body corporate, at their registered or principal office; or

(c)   where he has no address within the United Kingdom, or the Isle of Man or his address is unknown, by publication of notice of the seizure in the London, Edinburgh or Belfast Gazette.

History – In para. 2(c), the reference to the Isle of Man was inserted by Isle of Man Act 1979, Sch. 1.

NOTICE OF CLAIM

3   Any person claiming that any thing seized as liable to forfeiture is not so liable shall, within one month of the date of the notice of seizure or, where no such notice has been served on him, within one month of the date of the seizure, give notice of his claim in writing to the Commissioners at any office of customs and excise.

4(1)   Any notice under paragraph 3 above shall specify the name and address of the claimant and, in the case of a claimant who is outside the United Kingdom and the Isle of Man, shall specify the name and address of a solicitor in the United Kingdom who is authorised to accept service of process and to act on behalf of the claimant.

4(2)   Service of process upon a solicitor so specified shall be deemed to be proper service upon the claimant.

History – In para. 4(1), the reference to the Isle of Man was inserted by Isle of Man Act 1979, Sch. 1.

CONDEMNATION

5   If on the expiration of the relevant period under paragraph 3 above for the giving of notice of claim in respect of any thing no such notice has been given to the Commissioners, or if, in the case of any such notice given, any requirement of paragraph 4 above is not complied with, the thing in question shall be deemed to have been duly condemned as forfeited.

6   Where notice of claim in respect of any thing is duly given in accordance with paragraphs 3 and 4 above, the Commissioners shall take proceedings for the condemnation of that thing by the court, and if the court finds that the thing was at the time of seizure liable to forfeiture the court shall condemn it as forfeited.

7   Where any thing is in accordance with either of paragraphs 5 or 6 above condemned or deemed to have been condemned as forfeited, then, without prejudice to any delivery up or sale of the thing by the Commissioners under paragraph 16 below, the forfeiture shall have effect as from the date when the liability to forfeiture arose.

PROCEEDINGS FOR CONDEMNATION BY COURT

8 Proceedings for condemnation shall be civil proceedings and may be instituted–

(a)   in England or Wales either in the High Court or in a magistrates' court;

(b)   in Scotland either in the Court of Session or in the sheriff court;

(c)   in Northern Ireland either in the High Court or in a court of summary jurisdiction.

9 Proceedings for the condemnation of any thing instituted in a magistrates' court in England or Wales, in the sheriff court in Scotland or in a court of summary jurisdiction in Northern Ireland may be so instituted–

(a)   in any such court having jurisdiction in the place where any offence in connection with that thing was committed or where any proceedings for such an offence are instituted; or

(b)   in any such court having jurisdiction in the place where the claimant resides or, if the claimant has specified a solicitor under paragraph 4 above, in the place where that solicitor has his office; or

(c)   in any such court having jurisdiction in the place where that thing was found, detained or seized or to which it is first brought after being found, detained or seized.

10(1) In any proceedings for condemnation instituted in England, Wales or Northern Ireland, the claimant or his solicitor shall make oath that the thing seized was, or was to the best of his knowledge and belief, the property of the claimant at the time of the seizure.

10(2) In any such proceedings instituted in the High Court, the claimant shall give such security for the costs of the proceedings as may be determined by the Court.

10(3) If any requirement of this paragraph is not complied with, the court shall give judgment for the Commissioners.

Cross reference – Postal Packets (Customs and Excise) Regulations 1986 (SI 1986/260), reg. 5(k): para. 10(1) disapplied in the case of a thing brought by post into the UK.

11(1) In the case of any proceedings for condemnation instituted in a magistrates' court in England or Wales, without prejudice to any right to require the statement of a case for the opinion of the High Court, either party may appeal against the decision of that court to the Crown Court.

11(2) In the case of any proceedings for condemnation instituted in a court of summary jurisdiction in Northern Ireland, without prejudice to any right to require the statement of a case for the opinion of the High Court, either party may appeal against the decision of that court to the county court.

12 Where an appeal, including an appeal by way of case stated, has been made against the decision of the court in any proceedings for the condemnation of anything, that thing shall, pending the final determination of the matter, be left with the Commissioners or at any convenient office of customs and excise.

PROVISIONS AS TO PROOF

13 In any proceedings arising out of seizure of any thing, the fact, form and manner of the seizure shall be taken to have been as set forth in the process without any further evidence thereof, unless the contrary is proved.

14 In any proceedings, the condemnation by a court of any thing as forfeited may be proved by the production either of the order or certificate of condemnation or of a certified copy thereof purporting to be signed by an officer of the court by which the order or certificate was made or granted.

SPECIAL PROVISIONS AS TO CERTAIN CLAIMANTS

15 For the purposes of any claim to, or proceedings for the condemnation of, any thing, where that thing is at the time of seizure the property of a body of a body corporate, of two or more partners or of any number of persons exceeding five, the oath required by paragraph 10 above to be taken and any other thing required by this Schedule or by any rules of the court to be done by, or by any person authorised by, the claimant or owner may be taken or done by, or by any other person authorised by, the following persons repectively, that is to say–

(a)   where the owner is a body corporate, the secretary or some duly authorised officer of that body;

(b)   where the owners are in partnership, any one of those owners;

(c)   where the owners are any number of persons exceeding five not being in partnership, any two of those persons on behalf of themselves and their co-owners.

POWER TO DEAL WITH SEIZURES BEFORE CONDEMNATION, ETC.

16 Where any thing has been seized as liable to forfeiture the Commissioners may at any time if they see fit and notwithstanding that the thing has not yet been condemned, or is not yet deemed to have been condemned, as forfeited–

(a)   deliver it up to any claimant upon his paying to the Commissioners such sum as they think proper, being a sum not exceeding that which in their opinion represents the value of the thing, including any duty or tax chargeable thereon which has not been paid;

(b)   if the thing seized is a living creature or is in the opinion of the Commissioners of a perishable nature, sell or destroy it.

17(1)   If, where any thing is delivered up, sold or destroyed under paragraph 16 above, it is held in proceedings taken under this Schedule that the thing was not liable to forfeiture at the time of its seizure, the Commissioners shall, subject to any deduction allowed under sub-paragraph (2) below, on demand by the claimant tender to him–

(a)   an amount equal to any sum paid by him under sub-paragraph (a) of that paragraph; or

(b)   where they have sold the thing, an amount equal to the proceeds of sale; or

(c)   where they have destroyed the thing, an amount equal to the market value of the thing at the time of its seizure.

17(2)   Where the amount to be tendered under sub-paragraph (1)(a), (b) or (c) above includes any sum on account of any duty or tax chargeable on the thing which had not been paid before its seizure the Commissioners may deduct so much of that amount as represents that duty or tax.

17(3)   If the claimant accepts any amount tendered to him under sub-paragraph (1) above, he shall not be entitled to maintain any action on account of the seizure, detention, sale or destruction of the thing.

17(4)   For the purposes of sub-paragraph (1)(c) above, the market value of any thing at the time of its seizure shall be taken to be such amount as the Commissioners and the claimant may agree or, in default of agreement, as may be determined by a referee appointed by the Lord Chancellor (not being an official of any government department or an office-holder in, or a member of the staff of, the Scottish Administration), whose decision shall be final and conclusive; and the procedure on any reference to a referee shall be such as may be determined by the referee.

History – In para. 17(4), the words "or an office-holder in, or a member of the staff of, the Scottish Administration" were inserted by Scotland Act 1998 (Consequential Modifications) (No. 2) Order 1999 (SI 1999/1820), art. 4 and Sch. 2, para. 59, operative from 1 July 1999.

FINANCE ACT 1980

(1980 Chapter 48)

[*1st August 1980*]

17   Mutual recovery and disclosure of information between member States

17(1)   In section 11(1) of the Finance Act 1977 (recovery of duty etc. due in other member States) the reference to the Directive there mentioned shall include a reference to that Directive as extended to value added tax by the Directive of the Council of the European Communities dated 6th December 1979 No. 79/1071/EEC and to excise duties by the Directive of the Council of the European Communities dated 14th December 1992 No. 92/108/EEC.

17(2)   In section 77 of the Finance Act 1978 (disclosure of information to tax authorities in other member States)–

(a)   references to the Directive mentioned in subsection (1) shall include references to that Directive as extended to value added tax by the Directive of the Council of the European Communities dated 6th December 1979 No. 79/1070/EEC and to excise duties by the Directive of the Council of the European Communities dated 25th February 1992 No. 92/12/EEC; and

(b)   references to the **Commissioners of Inland Revenue** and an **authorised officer** of those Commissioners shall include references to the Commissioners of Customs and Excise and an authorised officer of those Commissioners.

17(2A) The references in subsections (1) and (2) above to **excise duties** are references to any duty on mineral oils, on alcohol and alcoholic beverages or on manufactured tobacco.

17(3) Subsection (1) above shall have effect as respects any request made on or after 1st January 1981 for the recovery of a sum becoming due after the passing of this Act; and subsection (2) above shall come into force on 1st January 1981.

History – In s. 17(1), the words "and to excise" to the end were inserted by FA 1993, s. 22(1), with effect as respects a request for the recovery of a sum becoming due on or after 27 July 1993.
In s. 17(2)(a), the words "and to excise . . . 92/12/EEC" and s. 17(2A) were inserted by FA 1993, s. 22(2)–(3), with effect from 27 July 1993.

European material – Directive 79/1070 (OJ 1979 L331/8).
Directive 79/1071 (OJ 1979 L331/10).
Directive 92/12 (OJ 1992 L76/1).
Directive 92/108 (OJ 1992 L390/124).

Official publications – 700/47.

COMPANIES ACT 1985

(1985 Chapter 6)

[11th March 1985]

ARRANGEMENT OF SECTIONS

PART XXVI – Interpretation

PART XXVI – Interpretation

736   "Subsidiary", "holding company" and "wholly-owned subsidiary"

736(1) A company is a **"subsidiary"** of another company, its **"holding company"**, if that other company–

(a)   holds a majority of the voting rights in it, or

(b)   is a member of it and has the right to appoint or remove a majority of its board of directors, or

(c)   is a member of it and controls alone, pursuant to an agreement with other shareholders or members, a majority of the voting rights in it,

or if it is a subsidiary of a company which is itself a subsidiary of that other company.

736(2) A company is a **"wholly-owned subsidiary"** of another company if it has no members except that other and that other's wholly-owned subsidiaries or persons acting on behalf of that other or its wholly-owned subsidiaries.

736(3) In this section **"company"** includes any body corporate.

History – See history note after s. 736A.

Cross references – S. 43A: control of a body corporate by a body corporate in relation to VAT groups.

736A   *Provisions supplementing s. 736*

736A(1) The provisions of this section explain expressions used in section 736 and otherwise supplement that section.

736A(2) In section 736(1)(a) and (c) the references to the voting rights in a company are to the rights conferred on shareholders in respect of their shares or, in the case of a company not having a share capital, on members, to vote at general meetings of the company on all, or substantially all, matters.

736A(3) In section 736(1)(b) the reference to the right to appoint or remove a majority of the board of directors is to the right to appoint or remove directors holding a majority of the voting rights at meetings of the board on all, or substantially all, matters; and for the purposes of that provision–

(a)   a company shall be treated as having the right to appoint to a directorship if–

      (i) a person's appointment to it follows necessarily from his appointment as director of the company, or

      (ii) the directorship is held by the company itself; and

(b)   a right to appoint or remove which is exercisable only with the consent or concurrence of another person shall be left out of account unless no other person has a right to appoint or, as the case may be, remove in relation to that directorship.

736A(4) Rights which are exercisable only in certain circumstances shall be taken into account only–

(a)   when the circumstances have arisen, and for so long as they continue to obtain, or

(b)   when the circumstances are within the control of the person having the rights;

and rights which are normally exercisable but are temporarily incapable of exercise shall continue to be taken into account.

736A(5) Rights held by a person in a fiduciary capacity shall be treated as not held by him.

736A(6) Rights held by a person as nominee for another shall be treated as held by the other; and rights shall be regarded as held as nominee for another if they are exercisable only on his instructions or with his consent or concurrence.

736A(7) Rights attached to shares held by way of security shall be treated as held by the person providing the security–

(a)   where apart from the right to exercise them for the purpose of preserving the value of the security, or of realising it, the rights are exercisable only in accordance with his instructions;

(b)   where the shares are held in connection with the granting of loans as part of normal business activities and apart from the right to exercise them for the purpose of preserving the value of the security, or of realising it, the rights are exercisable only in his interests.

736A(8) Rights shall be treated as held by a company if they are held by any of its subsidiaries; and nothing in subsection (6) or (7) shall be construed as requiring rights held by a company to be treated as held by any of its subsidiaries.

736A(9) For the purposes of subsection (7) rights shall be treated as being exercisable in accordance with the instructions or in the interests of a company if they are exercisable in accordance with the instructions of or, as the case may be, in the interests of–

(a)   any subsidiary or holding company of that company, or

(b)   any subsidiary of a holding company of that company.

736A(10) The voting rights in a company shall be reduced by any rights held by the company itself.

736A(11) References in any provision of subsections (5) to (10) to rights held by a person include rights falling to be treated as held by him by virtue of any other provision of those subsections but not rights which by virtue of any such provision are to be treated as not held by him.

736A(12) In this section **"company"** includes any body corporate.

History – S. 736, 736A substituted for the former s. 736 by CA 1989, s. 144(1) as from 1 November 1990 subject to transitional provisions (see SI 1990/1392 (C 41), art. 2(d) and also art. 6); the former s. 736 read as follows:
"**736** "Holding company", "subsidiary" and "wholly-owned subsidiary"
736(1) For the purposes of this Act, a company is deemed to be a subsidiary of another if (but only if) –
  (a)   that other either –
      (i) is a member of it and controls the composition of its board of directors, or
      (ii) holds more than half in nominal value of its equity share capital, or
      (iii) the first-mentioned company is a subsidiary of any company which is that other's subsidiary.
The above is subject to subsection (4) below in this section.
736(2) For purposes of subsection (1), the composition of a company's board of directors is deemed to be controlled by another company if (but only if) that other company by the exercise of some power exercisable by it without the consent or concurrence of any other person can appoint or remove the holders of all or a majority of the directorships.
736(3) For purposes of this last provision, the other company is deemed to have power to appoint to a directorship with respect to which any of the following conditions is satisfied –
  (a)   that a person cannot be appointed to it without the exercise in his favour by the other company of such a power as is mentioned above, or

(b)   that a person's appointment to the directorship follows necessarily from his appointment as director of the other company, or
(c)   that the directorship is held by the other company itself or by a subsidiary of it.
736(4) In determining whether one company is a subsidiary of another –
(a)   any shares held or power exercisable by the other in a fiduciary capacity are to be treated as not held or exercisable by it,
(b)   subject to the two following paragraphs, any shares held or power exercisable–
   (i)   by any person as nominee for the other (except where the other is concerned only in a fiduciary capacity), or
   (ii)   by, or by a nominee for, a subsidiary of the other (not being a subsidiary which is concerned only in a fiduciary capacity),
are to be treated as held or exercisable by the other,
(c)   any shares held or power exercisable by any person by virtue of the provisions of any debentures of the first-mentioned company or of a trust deed for securing any issue of such debentures are to be disregarded,
(d)   any shares held or power exercisable by, or by a nominee for, the other or its subsidiary (not being held or exercisable as mentioned in paragraph (c)) are to be treated as not held or exercisable by the other if the ordinary business of the other or its subsidiary (as the case may be) includes the lending of money and the shares are held or the power is exercisable as above mentioned by way of security only for the purposes of a transaction entered into in the ordinary course of that business.
736(5) For purposes of this Act–
(a)   a company is deemed to be another's holding company if (but only if) the other is its subsidiary, and
(b)   a body corporate is deemed the wholly-owned subsidiary of another if it has no members except that other and that other's wholly-owned subsidiaries and its or their nominees.
736(6) In this section **"company"** includes any body corporate."

736B   Power to amend s. 736 and 736A

736B(1)   The Secretary of State may by regulations amend sections 736 and 736A so as to alter the meaning of the expressions "holding company", "subsidiary" or "wholly-owned subsidiary".

736B(2)   The regulations may make different provision for different cases or classes of case and may contain such incidental and supplementary provisions as the Secretary of State thinks fit.

736B(3)   Regulations under this section shall be made by statutory instrument which shall be subject to annulment in pursuance of a resolution of either House of Parliament.

736B(4)   Any amendment made by regulations under this section does not apply for the purposes of enactments outside the Companies Acts unless the regulations so provide.

736B(5)   So much of section 23(3) of the Interpretation Act 1978 as applies section 17(2)(a) of that Act (effect of repeal and re-enactment) to deeds, instruments and documents other than enactments shall not apply in relation to any repeal and re-enactment effected by regulations made under this section.

History – S. 736B inserted by CA 1989, s. 144(3) as from 1 November 1990 subject to transitional provisions (see SI 1990/1392 (C 41), art. 2(d) and also art. 6).

745   Northern Ireland

745(1)   Except where otherwise expressly provided, nothing in this Act (except provisions relating expressly to companies registered or incorporated in Northern Ireland or outside Great Britain) applies to or in relation to companies so registered or incorporated.

745(2)   Subject to any such provision, and to any express provision as to extent, this Act does not extend to Northern Ireland.

746   Commencement

746   This Act comes into force on 1st July 1985.

History – In s. 746, the words "Except as provided by section 243(6)," formerly appearing at the beginning were repealed by CA 1989, s. 212 and Sch. 24 as from 1 April 1990 subject to any relevant transitional or saving provisions (see SI 1990/355 (C 13), art. 5(1)(b), (2)).

747   Citation

747   This Act may be cited as the Companies Act 1985.

FINANCE ACT 1985

(1985 Chapter 54)

[25th July 1985]

PART I – CUSTOMS AND EXCISE, VALUE ADDED TAX AND CAR TAX

Chapter I – Customs and Excise

OTHER PROVISIONS

10   Computer records etc.

10(1)   Any provision made by or under any enactment which requires a person, in connection with any assigned matter,–

(a)   to produce, furnish or deliver any document, or cause any document to be produced, furnished or delivered, or

(b)   to permit the Commissioners of Customs and Excise (in this section referred to as **"the Commissioners"**) or a person authorised by them–

    (i) to inspect any document, or

    (ii) to make or take extracts from or copies of or remove any document,

shall have effect as if any reference in that provision to a document were a reference to anything in which information of any description is recorded and any reference to a copy of a document were a reference to anything onto which information recorded in the document has been copied, by whatever means and whether directly or indirectly.

10(2)   In connection with any assigned matter, a person authorised by the Commissioners to exercise the powers conferred by this subsection–

(a)   shall be entitled at any reasonable time to have access to, and inspect and check the operation of, any computer and any associated apparatus or material which is or has been in use in connection with any document to which this subsection applies; and

(b)   may require–

    (i) the person by whom or on whose behalf the computer is or has been so used, or

    (ii) any person having charge of, or otherwise concerned with the operation of, the computer, apparatus or material,

to afford him such reasonable assistance as he may require for the purposes of paragraph (a) above.

10(3)   Subsection (2) above applies to any document, within the meaning given by subsection (1) above, which, in connection with any assigned matter, a person is or may be required by or under any enactment–

(a)   to produce, furnish or deliver, or cause to be produced, furnished or delivered; or

(b)   to permit the Commissioners or a person authorised by them to inspect, make or take extracts from or copies of or remove.

10(4)   Any person who–

(a)   obstructs a person authorised under subsection (2) above in the exercise of his powers under paragraph (a) of that subsection, or

(b)   without reasonable excuse fails to comply within a reasonable time with a requirement under paragraph (b) of that subsection,

shall be liable on summary conviction to a penalty of level 4 on the standard scale.

10(5)   In each of the enactments mentioned in subsection (6) below (which create offences in relation, among other matters, to false documents) **"documents"** shall have the meaning given by subsection (1) above.

10(6)   The enactments referred to in subsection (5) above are–

(a)   paragraph 4(1) of Schedule 1 to the Miscellaneous Transferred Excise Duties Act (Northern Ireland) 1972 (false statements and documents in connection with pool betting duty);

(b)   paragraph 8(1) of Schedule 2 to that Act (false statements and documents in connection with general betting duty);

(c)   section 167 of the Customs and Excise Management Act 1979 (untrue declarations etc.);

(d)   section 168 of that Act (counterfeit documents etc.);

(e)   section 15 of the Customs and Excise Duties (General Reliefs) Act 1979 (false statements and documents in connection with reliefs);

(f)   paragraph 13(3) of Schedule 1 to the Betting and Gaming Duties Act 1981 (false statements and documents in connection with betting duty);

(g)   paragraph 7(3) of Schedule 2 to that Act (false statements and documents in connection with gaming licence duty);

(h)   paragraph 8(2) of Schedule 1 to the Car Tax Act 1983 (false documents etc.).

10(7)   [Repealed by Civil Evidence Act 1995, s. 15 and Sch. 1, para. 11 and Sch. 2.]

10(8)   In this section **"assigned matter"** means any matter which is an assigned matter for the purposes of the Customs and Excise Management Act 1979.

History – In s. 10(1), the words "were a reference to anything" to the end were substituted by Civil Evidence Act 1995, s. 15 and Sch. 1, para. 11(2), operative from 31 January 1997 (SI 1996/3217).
In s. 10(3), the words ", within the meaning given by subsection (1) above," were substituted by Civil Evidence Act 1995, s. 15 and Sch. 1, para. 11(3), operative from 31 January 1997 (SI 1996/3217).
In s. 10(4), words at the end were repealed by Statute Law (Repeals) Act 1993, s. 1(1) and Sch. 1, Pt. XIV, Grp. 2, with effect from 5 November 1993.
In s. 10(5), the words "the meaning given by subsection (1) above" were substituted by Civil Evidence Act 1995, s. 15 and Sch. 1, para. 11(4), operative from 31 January 1997 (SI 1996/3217).
S. 10(7) was repealed by Civil Evidence Act 1995, s. 15 and Sch. 1, para. 11(5) and Sch. 2, operative from 31 January 1997 (SI 1996/3217).

INSOLVENCY ACT 1986

(1986 Chapter 45)

[25th July 1986]

ARRANGEMENT OF SECTIONS

PART IV – WINDING UP OF COMPANIES REGISTERED UNDER THE COMPANIES ACT

CHAPTER VIII – PROVISIONS OF GENERAL APPLICATION IN WINDING UP

PREFERENTIAL DEBTS

PART IX – BANKRUPTCY

CHAPTER IV – ADMINISTRATION BY TRUSTEE

PART XII – PREFERENTIAL DEBTS IN COMPANY AND INDIVIDUAL INSOLVENCY

PART XIX – FINAL PROVISIONS

SCHEDULES

PART IV – WINDING UP OF COMPANIES REGISTERED UNDER THE COMPANIES ACT

Chapter VIII – Provisions of General Application in Winding Up

PREFERENTIAL DEBTS

175   Preferential debts (general provision)

175(1)   In a winding up the company's preferential debts (within the meaning given by section 386 in Part XII) shall be paid in priority to all other debts.

175(2)   Preferential debts–

(a)   rank equally among themselves after the expenses of the winding up and shall be paid in full, unless the assets are insufficient to meet them, in which case they abate in equal proportions; and

(b)   so far as the assets of the company available for payment of general creditors are insufficient to meet them, have priority over the claims of holders of debentures secured by, or holders of, any floating charge created by the company, and shall be paid accordingly out of any property comprised in or subject to that charge.

PART IX – BANKRUPTCY

Chapter IV – Administration by trustee

328   Priority of debts

328(1)   In the distribution of the bankrupt's estate, his preferential debts (within the meaning given by section 386 in Part XII) shall be paid in priority to other debts.

328(2)   Preferential debts rank equally between themselves after the expenses of the bankruptcy and shall be paid in full unless the bankrupt's estate is insufficient for meeting them, in which case they abate in equal proportions between themselves.

328(3)   Debts which are neither preferential debts nor debts to which the next section applies also rank equally between themselves and, after the preferential debts, shall be paid in full unless the bankrupt's estate is insufficient for meeting them, in which case they abate in equal proportions between themselves.

328(4)   Any surplus remaining after the payment of the debts that are preferential or rank equally under subsection (3) shall be applied in paying interest on those debts in respect of the periods during which they have been outstanding since the commencement of the bankruptcy; and interest on preferential debts ranks equally with interest on debts other than preferential debts.

328(5)   The rate of interest payable under subsection (4) in respect of any debt is whichever is the greater of the following–

(a)   the rate specified in section 17 of the Judgments Act 1838 at the commencement of the bankruptcy, and

(b)   the rate applicable to that debt apart from the bankruptcy.

328(6)   This section and the next are without prejudice to any provision of this Act or any other Act under which the payment of any debt or the making of any other payment is, in the event of bankruptcy, to have a particular priority or to be postponed.

PART XII – PREFERENTIAL DEBTS IN COMPANY AND INDIVIDUAL INSOLVENCY

Note – Re application of Pt. XII to insolvent partnerships, see the Insolvent Partnerships Order 1994 (SI 1994/2421), especially reg. 10, 11, Sch. 7.

386   Categories of preferential debts

386(1)   A reference in this Act to the preferential debts of a company or an individual is to the debts listed in Schedule 6 to this Act [not relevant to VAT]; VAT, [not relevant to VAT] and references to preferential creditors are to be read accordingly.

386(2)   In that Schedule **"the debtor"** means the company or the individual concerned.

386(3)   Schedule 6 is to be read with Schedule 4 to the Pension Schemes Act 1993 (occupational pension scheme contributions).

History – In s. 386(3), the words "Schedule 4 to the Pension Schemes Act 1993" substituted for the former words "Schedule 3 to the Social Security Pensions Act 1975" by Pension Schemes Act 1993, s. 190 and Sch. 8, para. 18, operative from 7 February 1994 (SI 1994/86 (C 3), art. 2).

387   "The relevant date"

387(1)   This section explains references in Schedule 6 to the relevant date (being the date which determines the existence and amount of a preferential debt).

387(2)   For the purposes of section 4 in Part I (meetings to consider company voluntary arrangement), the relevant date in relation to a company which is not being wound up is–

(a)   where an administration order is in force in relation to the company, the date of the making of that order, and

(b)   where no such order has been made, the date of the approval of the voluntary arrangement.

387(3)   In relation to a company which is being wound up, the following applies–

(a)   if the winding up is by the court, and the winding-up order was made immediately upon the discharge of an administration order, the relevant date is the date of the making of the administration order;

(b)   if the case does not fall within paragraph (a) and the company–

     (i) is being wound up by the court, and

     (ii) had not commenced to be wound up voluntarily before the date of the making of the winding-up order,

the relevant date is the date of the appointment (or first appointment) of a provisional liquidator or, if no such appointment has been made, the date of the winding-up order;

(c)   if the case does not fall within either paragraph (a) or (b), the relevant date is the date of the passing of the resolution for the winding up of the company.

387(4)   In relation to a company in receivership (where section 40 or, as the case may be, section 59 applies), the relevant date is–

(a)   in England and Wales, the date of the appointment of the receiver by debenture-holders, and

(b)   in Scotland, the date of the appointment of the receiver under section 53(6) or (as the case may be) 54(5).

387(5)   For the purposes of section 258 in Part VIII (individual voluntary arrangements), the relevant date is, in relation to a debtor who is not an undischarged bankrupt, the date of the interim order made under section 252 with respect to his proposal.

387(6)   In relation to a bankrupt, the following applies–

(a)   where at the time the bankruptcy order was made there was an interim receiver appointed under section 286, the relevant date is the date on which the interim receiver was first appointed after the presentation of the bankruptcy petition;

(b)   otherwise, the relevant date is the date of the making of the bankruptcy order.

PART XIX – FINAL PROVISIONS

438   Repeals

438   The enactments specified in the second column of Schedule 12 to this Act are repealed to the extent specified in the third column of that Schedule.

439 Amendment of enactments

439(1) The Companies Act is amended as shown in Parts I and II of Schedule 13 to this Act, being amendments consequential on this Act and the Company Directors Disqualification Act 1986.

439(2) The enactments specified in the first column of Schedule 14 to this Act (being enactments which refer, or otherwise relate, to those which are repealed and replaced by this Act or the Company Directors Disqualification Act 1986) are amended as shown in the second column of that Schedule.

439(3) The Lord Chancellor may by order make such consequential modifications of any provision contained in any subordinate legislation made before the appointed day and such transitional provisions in connection with those modifications as appear to him necessary or expedient in respect of–

(a)   any reference in that subordinate legislation to the Bankruptcy Act 1914;

(b)   any reference in that subordinate legislation to any enactment repealed by Part III or IV of Schedule 10 to the Insolvency Act 1985; or

(c)   any reference in that subordinate legislation to any matter provided for under the Act of 1914 or under any enactment so repealed.

439(4) An order under this section shall be made by statutory instrument subject to annulment in pursuance of a resolution of either House of Parliament.

Note – See the Insolvency (Amendment of Subordinate Legislation) Order 1986 (SI 1986/2001) (and also the Insolvency (Land Registration Rules) Order 1986 (SI 1986/2245)).

440 Extent (Scotland)

440(1) [Not relevant to VAT.]

440(2) The following provisions of this Act do not extend to Scotland–

(a)   [Not relevant to VAT;]

(b)   the second Group of Parts;

(c), (d) [Not relevant to VAT.]

441 Extent (Northern Ireland)

441(1) [Not relevant to VAT.]

441(2) Subject as above, and to any provision expressly relating to companies incorporated elsewhere than in Great Britain, nothing in this Act extends to Northern Ireland or applies to or in relation to companies registered or incorporated in Northern Ireland.

443 Commencement

443 This Act comes into force on the day appointed under section 236(2) of the Insolvency Act 1985 for the coming into force of Part III of that Act (individual insolvency and bankruptcy), immediately after that part of that Act comes into force for England and Wales.

Note – The relevant date is 29 December 1986 (SI 1986/1924 (C 71)).

SCHEDULES

SCHEDULE 6 – THE CATEGORIES OF PREFERENTIAL DEBTS

Section 386

CATEGORY 1: DEBTS DUE TO INLAND REVENUE

1,2 [Not relevant to VAT.]

CATEGORY 2: DEBTS DUE TO CUSTOMS AND EXCISE

3 Any value added tax which is referable to the period of 6 months next before the relevant date (which period is referred to below as **"the 6-month period"**).

For the purposes of this paragraph–

(a)   where the whole of the prescribed accounting period to which any value added tax is attributable falls within the 6-month period, the whole amount of that tax is referable to that period; and

(b)   in any other case the amount of any value added tax which is referable to the 6-month period is the proportion of the tax which is equal to such proportion (if any) of the accounting reference period in question as falls within the 6-month period;

and in sub-paragraph (a) **"prescribed"** means prescribed by regulations under the Value Added Tax Act 1994.

History – In para. 3, "1994" was substituted for "1983" by VATA 1994, s. 100(1), 101(1) and Sch. 14, para. 8, with effect from 1 September 1994 subject to savings provisions in Sch. 13.

INCOME AND CORPORATION TAXES ACT 1988

(1988 Chapter 1)

[*9th February 1988*]

PART XI – CLOSE COMPANIES

Chapter I – Interpretive Provisions

416   Meaning of "associated company" and "control"

416(1)   For the purposes of this Part, a company is to be treated as another's **"associated company"** at a given time if, at that time or at any other time within one year previously, one of the two has control of the other, or both are under the control of the same person or persons.

416(2)   For the purposes of this Part, a person shall be taken to have control of a company if he exercises, or is able to exercise or is entitled to acquire, direct or indirect control over the company's affairs, and in particular, but without prejudice to the generality of the preceding words, if he possesses or is entitled to acquire–

(a)   the greater part of the share capital or issued share capital of the company or of the voting power in the company; or

(b)   such part of the issued share capital of the company as would, if the whole of the income of the company were in fact distributed among the participators (without regard to any rights which he or any other person has as a loan creditor), entitle him to receive the greater part of the amount so distributed; or

(c)   such rights as would, in the event of the winding-up of the company or in any other circumstances, entitle him to receive the greater part of the assets of the company which would then be available for distribution among the participators.

416(3)   Where two or more persons together satisfy any of the conditions of subsection (2) above, they shall be taken to have control of the company.

416(4)   For the purposes of subsection (2) above a person shall be treated as entitled to acquire anything which he is entitled to acquire at a future date, or will at a future date be entitled to acquire.

416(5)   For the purposes of subsections (2) and (3) above, there shall be attributed to any person any rights or powers of a nominee for him, that is to say, any rights or powers which another person possesses on his behalf or may be required to exercise on his direction or behalf.

416(6)   For the purposes of subsections (2) and (3) above, there may also be attributed to any person all the rights and powers of any company of which he has, or he and associates of his have, control or any two or more such companies, or of any associate of his or of any two or more associates of his, including those attributed to a company or associate under subsection (5) above, but not those attributed to an associate under this subsection; and such attributions shall be made under this subsection as will result in the company being treated as under the control of five or fewer participators if it can be so treated.

History – In s. 416(1), the former words which occurred between "this Part," and "a company" were repealed by FA 1989, s. 187 and Sch. 17, Pt. V, in relation to accounting periods beginning after 31 March 1989.

Derivations – S. 416(1) (as originally enacted): ICTA 1970, s. 302(1), as amended by FA 1972, Sch. 24, para. 21 and Sch. 28, Pt. VI.
S. 416(2)–(4): ICTA 1970, s. 302(2)–(4), as substituted by FA 1972, s. 94(2) and Sch. 17, para. 5.
S. 416(5), (6): ICTA 1970, s. 302(5), (6).

Cross references – S. 155(1): meaning of control for capital gains tax purposes taken as that in this section.
Sch. 28B, para. 13(3): for the purposes of venture capital trust provisions, a person has control of a company if he would be so taken for the purposes of Pt. XI by virtue of s. 412(2)–(6).
S. 801A: restriction of relief for underlying tax.
Sch. 5AA: application of definition of "associated company" for purposes of taxing guaranteed returns on futures and options.
FA 1986, s. 90(5): application of definition of "control" to Inland bearer instruments.
TCGA 1992, s. 96(10) and Sch. 5, para. 2, 8, 9: meaning of control for purposes of the attribution of gains of non-resident or dual resident settlements to beneficiaries by reference to payments by and to certain companies.
TCGA 1992, s. 179(9A): meaning of "control" for purposes of de-grouping charges.
TCGA 1992, s. 191(7): director who controls a chargeable non-resident company or a company controlling that company can be charged with unpaid tax on chargeable gains.

Extra-statutory concessions – C8: a recognised money-broker not to be treated as participator of company carrying on business as stock jobber solely by reason of short-term loans/advances arising in ordinary course of respective trades.
C9: circumstances in which the Board will not, by concession, treat companies as associated where not under common control except by reference to certain factors (e.g. fixed rate preference shares, loan creditors, holdings by trustee companies, etc.); in determining whether two companies are controlled by the same persons, a relative of a participator, in connection with the term "associate", will normally include only spouse and/or minor children.
C28: limited circumstances in which, under loan relationship provisions, lending and borrowing companies may be treated as not connected for purposes of claiming relief for bad or doubtful debt, or a loss arising from such a debt, subject to election by company for concession to apply to all loan relationships within its scope.

Revenue interpretations – IRInt. 167: Revenue view on interaction between FA 1996, s. 87(8) ("connected persons" for purposes of loan relationship rules) and s. 416.

PART XV – SETTLEMENTS

Chapter IA – Liability of Settlor

SUPPLEMENTARY PROVISIONS

660G   Meaning of "settlement" and related expressions

660G(1)   In this Chapter–

> **"settlement"** includes any disposition, trust, covenant, agreement, arrangement or transfer of assets, and
>
> **"settlor"**, in relation to a settlement, means any person by whom the settlement was made.

660G(2)   A person shall be deemed for the purposes of this Chapter to have made a settlement if he has made or entered into the settlement directly or indirectly, and, in particular, but without prejudice to the generality of the preceding words, if he has provided or undertaken to provide funds directly or indirectly for the purpose of the settlement, or has made with any other person a reciprocal arrangement for that other person to make or enter into the settlement.

660G(3)   References in this Chapter to **income arising under a settlement** include, subject to subsection (4) below, any income chargeable to income tax by deduction or otherwise, and any income which would have been so chargeable if it had been received in the United Kingdom by a person domiciled, resident and ordinarily resident in the United Kingdom.

660G(4)   Where the settlor is not domiciled, or not resident, or not ordinarily resident, in the United Kingdom in a year of assessment, references in this Chapter to income arising under a settlement do not include income arising under the settlement in that year in respect of which the settlor, if he were actually entitled thereto, would not be chargeable to income tax by deduction or otherwise by reason of his not being so domiciled, resident or ordinarily resident.

But where such income is remitted to the United Kingdom in circumstances such that, if the settlor were actually entitled to that income when remitted, he would be chargeable to income tax by reason of his residence in the United Kingdom, it shall be treated for the purposes of this Chapter as arising under the settlement in the year in which it is remitted.

History – S. 660G inserted by FA 1995, s. 74 and Sch. 17, para. 1 with effect for 1995–96 and subsequent years of assessment in relation to every settlement, whenever and whenever it was made or entered into.

Revenue Manuals – Trust Manual TM4710: before 1995–96 only parental settlements on children included "transfer of assets" and extension in 1995 of "transfer of assets" to definition of all settlements was not intended to bring non-parental settlements within the scope of Pt. XV if they would not have been so prior to 1995–96.

PART XIX – SUPPLEMENTAL

MISCELLANEOUS

827   VAT penalties etc.

827(1)   Where, under Part IV of the Value Added Tax Act 1994 (value added tax), a person is liable to make a payment by way of–

(a)   penalty under any of sections 60 to 70; or

(b)   interest under section 74; or

(c)   surcharge under section 59;

the payment shall not be allowed as a deduction in computing any income, profits or losses for any tax purposes.

827(1A)   Where a person is liable to make a payment by way of a penalty under any of sections 8 to 11 of the Finance Act 1994 (penalties relating to excise), that payment shall not be allowed as a deduction in computing any income, profits or losses for any tax purposes.

827(1B)   Where a person is liable to make a payment by way of–

(a)   penalty under any of paragraphs 12 to 19 of Schedule 7 to the Finance Act 1994 (insurance premium tax), or

(b)   interest under paragraph 21 of that Schedule,

the payment shall not be allowed as a deduction in computing any income, profits or losses for any tax purposes.

827(1C)   [Not relevant to VAT.]

827(2)   A sum paid to any person by way of supplement under section 79 of that Act (VAT repayment supplements) shall be disregarded for all purposes of corporation tax and income tax.

History – In s. 827(1), the words "Part IV of the Value Added Tax Act 1994" were substituted for the words "Chapter II of Part I of the Finance Act 1985", in s. 827(1)(a) the words "60 to 70" were substituted for the words "13 to 17A", in s. 827(1)(b) "74" was substituted for "18" and in s. 827(1)(c) "59" was substituted for "19" by VATA 1994, s. 100(1) and Sch. 14, para. 10(2), with effect from 1 September 1994.
In s. 827(1)(a), "17A" was substituted for "17" by F(No. 2)A 1992, s. 14 and Sch. 3, para. 95, operative from 1 January 1993 (SI 1992/3261 (C 102)).
S. 827(1A) was inserted by FA 1994, s. 18(7), with effect in relation to any chargeable period ending after the coming into force of the provision which provides for the imposition of the penalty in question.
S. 827(1B) was inserted by FA 1994, s. 64 and Sch. 7, para. 31, consequential upon the introduction of insurance premium tax by FA 1994, Pt. III, with effect from 1 October 1994.
In s. 827(2), the words "79 of that Act" were substituted for the words "20 of the Finance Act 1985" by VATA 1994, s. 100(1) and Sch. 14, para. 10(2), with effect from 1 September 1994.

INTERPRETATION

839   Connected persons

839(1)   For the purposes of, and subject to, the provisions of the Tax Acts which apply this section, any question whether a person is connected with another shall be determined in accordance with the following provisions of this section (any provision that one person is connected with another being taken to mean that they are connected with one another).

839(2)   A person is connected with an individual if that person is the individual's wife or husband, or is a relative, or the wife or husband of a relative, of the individual or of the individual's wife or husband.

839(3)   A person, in his capacity as trustee of a settlement, is connected with–

(a)   any individual who in relation to the settlement is a settlor,

(b)   any person who is connected with such an individual, and

(c)   any body corporate which is connected with that settlement.

In this subsection **"settlement"** and **"settlor"** have the same meaning as in Chapter IA of Part XV (see section 660G(1) and (2)).

839(3A)   For the purpose of subsection (3) above a body corporate is connected with a settlement if–

(a)   it is a close company (or only not a close company because it is not resident in the United Kingdom) and the participators include the trustees of the settlement; or

(b)   it is controlled (within the meaning of section 840) by a company falling within paragraph (a) above.

839(4) Except in relation to acquisitions or disposals of partnership assets pursuant to bona fide commercial arrangements, a person is connected with any person with whom he is in partnership, and with the wife or husband or relative of any individual with whom he is in partnership.

839(5) A company is connected with another company–

(a)   if the same person has control of both, or a person has control of one and persons connected with him, or he and persons connected with him, have control of the other; or

(b)   if a group of two or more persons has control of each company, and the groups either consist of the same persons or could be regarded as consisting of the same persons by treating (in one or more cases) a member of either group as replaced by a person with whom he is connected.

839(6) A company is connected with another person if that person has control of it or if that person and persons connected with him together have control of it.

839(7) Any two or more persons acting together to secure or exercise control of a company shall be treated in relation to that company as connected with one another and with any person acting on the directions of any of them to secure or exercise control of the company.

839(8) In this section–

> **"company"** includes any body corporate or unincorporated association, but does not include a partnership, and this section shall apply in relation to any unit trust scheme as if the scheme were a company and as if the rights of the unit holders were shares in the company;
> **"control"** shall be construed in accordance with section 416; and
> **"relative"** means brother, sister, ancestor or lineal descendant.

In relation to any period during which section 470(2) has effect the reference above to a unit trust scheme shall be construed as a reference to a unit trust scheme within the meaning of the Prevention of Fraud (Investments) Act 1958 or the Prevention of Fraud (Investments) Act (Northern Ireland) 1940.

History – S. 839(3) substituted for previous version, and s. 839(3A) added, by FA 1995, s. 74 and Sch. 17, para. 20 for 1995–96 and subsequent years of assessment.
S. 839(8) repealed in part (words at end of subsection relating to former meaning of unit trust scheme) by FA 1987, Sch. 16, Pt. VI, with effect from 29 April 1988 by virtue of SI 1988/745.

Derivations – (as originally enacted) – ICTA 1970, s. 533.

Cross references – S. 591D(8): s. 839 applies for the purposes of s. 591D, relating to the cessation of approval of certain retirement benefits schemes.
S. 660G: "settlement" includes any disposition, trust, covenant, agreement, arrangement or transfer of assets and "settlor" means any person by whom the settlement was made.
Sch. 7, para. 4: application of s. 839 in determining employment with a person who is connected with employer.
Sch. 28B, para. 13(2): s. 839 applied for purposes of determining qualifying holdings in relation to venture capital trusts.
FA 1997, Sch. 12, para. 25(2): s. 839 applied for the purposes of determining connected persons in relation to leasing arrangements.
SI 1997/1154, reg. 5(3)(e), 7(4)(c), 15: modification of s. 839(8) in its application to open-ended investment companies, holdings in, and assets of, such companies, and transactions involving such companies.

Revenue interpretations – IRInt. 153: consortium claims to group relief following the decision in the case of Steele v EVC International NV.

Revenue Manuals – IR, Schedule E Manual, vol. II, SE 3523: Revenue guidance on exemption from charge on beneficial loans in respect of loans made for a fixed period at a fixed rate of interest.

Notes – TCGA 1992, s. 286: corresponding provision for capital gains tax.

FINANCE ACT 1988

(1988 Chapter 39)

[*29th July 1988*]

PART I – CUSTOMS AND EXCISE

MANAGEMENT

8   Disclosure of information as to imports

8(1)   The Commissioners may, for the purpose of supplementing the information as to imported goods which may be made available to persons other than the Commissioners, disclose information to which this section applies to such persons as they think fit.

8(2)   Such information may be so disclosed on such terms and conditions (including terms and conditions as to the payment of fees or charges to the Commissioners and the making of the information available to other persons) as the Commissioners think fit.

8(3)   This section applies to information consisting of the names and addresses of persons declared as consignees in entries of imported goods, arranged by reference to such classifications of imported goods as the Commissioners think fit.

8(4)   This section shall be construed as if it were contained in the Customs and Excise Management Act 1979.

10   Power to search persons

10(1)   [Amends CEMA 1979, s. 164(1).]

10(2)   [Substitutes CEMA 1979, s. 164(2), (3) and (3A) for former s. 164(2) and (3).]

10(3)   [Inserts CEMA 1979, s. 164(5).]

11   Time limits for arrest and proceedings

11(1)   [Not reproduced.]

11(2)   [Had substituted CEMA 1979, s. 147(1); repealed by FA 1989, s. 187 and Sch. 17, Pt. I, with effect in relation to offences committed on or after 27 July 1989.]

11(3)   This section has effect in relation to offences committed after the passing of this Act.

12   Punishment of offences

12(1)   [Amends provisions as below.]

(a)   [Amends CEMA 1979, s. 50(4)(b), 53(9)(b), 63(6)(b), 68(3)(b), 100(4)(b), 159(7)(b) and 170(3)(b).]

(b)–(d)   [Not reproduced.]

12(2)–(5)   [Not reproduced.]

12(6)   This section has effect in relation to offences committed after the passing of this Act.

FINANCE ACT 1989

(1989 Chapter 26)

[*27th July 1989*]

PART I – CUSTOMS AND EXCISE

Chapter I – Customs and Excise

GENERAL

16   Time limits for proceedings

16(1)   [Inserts CEMA 1979, s. 146A.]

16(2)   [Repeals CEMA 1979, s. 147(1).]

16(3)   [Amends Vehicles (Excise) Act 1971, s. 28(5).]

16(4)   This section shall have effect in relation to offences committed on or after the day on which this Act is passed.

17   Disbursements in Port of London

17   [Repeals CEMA 1979, s. 17(5)(a).]

PART III – MISCELLANEOUS AND GENERAL

MISCELLANEOUS

182   Disclosure of information

Prospective insertion – S. 182(4)(a)(iii) and 182(4)(a)(iv) are to be inserted by the Government of Wales Act 1998, s. 125 and Sch. 12, para. 31(2), with effect from a date to be appointed. New s. 182(4)(a)(iii) and 182(4)(a)(iv) read as follows:
of the Auditor General for Wales and any member of his staff, or
of the Welsh Administration Ombudsman and any member of his staff,"
In s. 182(4)(a)(i) the word "or" is to be repealed by the Government of Wales Act 1998, s. 152 and Sch. 18, Pt. I, with effect from a date to be appointed.
In s. 182(6), the words ", the Parliamentary Commissioner, the Auditor General for Wales or the Welsh Administration Ombudsman" are to be substituted for the words "or the Parliamentary Commissioner," by the Government of Wales Act 1998, s. 125 and Sch. 12, para. 31(3), with effect from a date to be appointed.

182(1)   A person who discloses any information which he holds or has held in the exercise of tax functions is guilty of an offence if it is information about any matter relevant, for the purposes of those functions, to tax or duty in the case of any identifiable person.

182(2)   In this section **"tax functions"** means functions relating to tax or duty–

(a)   of the Commissioners, the Board and their officers,

(b)   of any person carrying out the administrative work of any tribunal mentioned in subsection (3) below, and

(c)   of any other person providing, or employed in the provision of, services to any person mentioned in paragraph (a) or (b) above.

182(3)   The **tribunals** referred to in subsection (2)(b) above are–

(a)   [Not relevant to VAT.],

(b)   any value added tax tribunal,

(c)   [Not relevant to VAT.], and

(d)   [Not relevant to VAT.].

182(4)   A person who discloses any information which–

(a)   he holds or has held in the exercise of functions–

    (i) of the Comptroller and Auditor General and any member of the staff of the National Audit Office, or

    (ii) of the Parliamentary Commissioner for Administration and his officers,

(b)   is, or is derived from, information which was held by any person in the exercise of tax functions, and

(c)   is information about any matter relevant, for the purposes of tax functions, to tax or duty in the case of any identifiable person,

is guilty of an offence.

182(5)   Subsections (1) and (4) above do not apply to any disclosure of information–

(a)   with lawful authority,

(b)   with the consent of any person in whose case the information is about a matter relevant to tax or duty, or

(c)   which has been lawfully made available to the public before the disclosure is made.

182(6)   For the purposes of this section a disclosure of any information is made with lawful authority if, and only if, it is made–

(a)   by a Crown servant in accordance with his official duty,

(b)   by any other person for the purposes of the function in the exercise of which he holds the information and without contravening any restriction duly imposed by the person responsible,

(c)   to, or in accordance with an authorisation duly given by, the person responsible,

(d)   in pursuance of any enactment or of any order of a court, or

(e)   in connection with the institution of or otherwise for the purposes of any proceedings relating to any matter within the general responsibility of the Commissioners or, as the case requires, the Board,

and in this subsection **"the person responsible"** means the Commissioners, the Board, the Comptroller or the Parliamentary Commissioner, as the case requires.

182(7)   It is a defence for a person charged with an offence under this section to prove that at the time of the alleged offence–

(a)   he believed that he had lawful authority to make the disclosure in question and had no reasonable cause to believe otherwise, or

(b)   he believed that the information in question had been lawfully made available to the public before the disclosure was made and had no reasonable cause to believe otherwise.

182(8)   A person guilty of an offence under this section is liable–

(a)   on conviction on indictment, to imprisonment for a term not exceeding two years or a fine or both, and

(b)   on summary conviction, to imprisonment for a term not exceeding six months or a fine not exceeding the statutory maximum or both.

182(9)   No prosecution for an offence under this section shall be instituted in England and Wales or in Northern Ireland except–

(a)   by the Commissioners or the Board, as the case requires, or

(b)   by or with the consent of the Director of Public Prosecutions or, in Northern Ireland, the Director of Public Prosecutions for Northern Ireland.

182(10)   In this section–

     "the Board" means the Commissioners of Inland Revenue,

     "the Commissioners" means the Commissioners of Customs and Excise,

     "Crown servant" has the same meaning as in the Official Secrets Act 1989, and

     "tax or duty" means any tax or duty within the general responsibility of the Commissioners or the Board.

182(11)   In this section–

(a)   references to the **Comptroller and Auditor General** include the Comptroller and Auditor General for Northern Ireland,

(b)   references to the **National Audit Office** include the Northern Ireland Audit Office, and

(c)   references to the **Parliamentary Commissioner for Administration** include the Health Service Commissioner for England, the Health Service Commissioner for Wales, the Health Service Commissioner for Scotland, the Assembly Ombudsman for Northern Ireland and the Northern Ireland Commissioner for Complaints.

182(12)   This section shall come into force on the repeal of section 2 of the Official Secrets Act 1911.

History – In s. 182(11)(c), the words "Assembly Ombudsman for Northern Ireland" were substituted by SI 1996/1298 (NI), art. 21(1) and Sch. 5.

Cross references – FA 1972, s. 127; FA 1978, s. 77; FA 1980, s. 17; FA 1989, s. 182 – other provisions relating to disclosure of information.

Statutory instruments – S. 182 entered into force on 1 March 1990 by virtue of SI 1990/200.
European material – Directive 77/799: disclosure to tax authorities in other member states.
Official publications – 700/47.

FINANCE ACT 1990

(1990 Chapter 29)

[*26th July 1990*]

PART I – CUSTOMS AND EXCISE AND VALUE ADDED TAX

Chapter I – Customs and Excise

OTHER PROVISIONS

7   Entry of goods on importation

7   Schedule 3 to this Act (which amends the provisions of the Customs and Excise Management Act 1979 about initial and supplementary entries and postponed entry) shall have effect in relation to goods imported on or after the day on which this Act is passed.

SCHEDULES

SCHEDULE 3 – ENTRY OF GOODS ON IMPORTATION

Section 7

1   The Customs and Excise Management Act 1979 shall be amended as follows.

2(1)   Section 37A (initial and supplementary entries) shall be amended as follows.

2(2)   [Amends CEMA 1979, s. 37A(1)(b).]

2(3)   [Inserts CEMA 1979, s. 37A(1A).]

2(4)   [Amends CEMA 1979, s. 37A(2).]

2(5)   [Amends CEMA 1979, s. 37A(3).]

2(6)   [Inserts CEMA 1979, s. 37A(3A).]

3(1)   Section 37B (postponed entry) shall be amended as follows.

3(2)   [Inserts CEMA 1979, s. 37B(1A).]

3(3)   [Inserts CEMA 1979, s. 37B(3A) and (3B).]

3(4)   [Amends CEMA 1979, s. 37B(4).]

3(5)   [Amends CEMA 1979, s. 37B(5).]

3(6)   [Inserts CEMA 1979, s. 37B(5A).]

3(7)   [Amends CEMA 1979, s. 37B(6).]

3(8)   [Inserts CEMA 1979, s. 37B(6A).]

3(9)   [Amends CEMA 1979, s. 37B(7).]

4(1)   Section 37C (provisions supplementary to sections 37A and 37B) shall be amended as follows.

4(2)   [Amends CEMA 1979, s. 37C(1)(a).]

4(3)   [Amends CEMA 1979, s. 37C(1)(b).]

4(4)   [Amends CEMA 1979, s. 37C(2)(a).]

FINANCE ACT 1993

(1993 Chapter 34)

[*27th July 1993*]

PART I – CUSTOMS AND EXCISE AND VALUE ADDED TAX

Chapter I – General

MISCELLANEOUS

22   Mutual recovery and disclosure of information

22(1)   [Amends FA 1980, s. 17(1).]

22(2)   [Amends FA 1980, s. 17(2)(a).]

22(3)   [Inserts FA 1980, s. 17(2A).]

22(4)   Subsection (1) above shall have effect as respects a request for the recovery of a sum only if it is a sum becoming due on or after the day on which this Act is passed.

European material – Directive 79/1070: OJ 1979 L331/8.
Directive 92/12: OJ 1992 L76/1.
Directive 92/108: OJ 1992 L390/124.

Note – FA 1993 passed on 27 July 1993.

23   VAT and customs duty on vehicles subject to VED

23(1)   Where an application is made for a licence under the Vehicles (Excise) Act 1971 for a vehicle which–

(a)   appears to the Secretary of State to have been removed into the United Kingdom from a place outside the United Kingdom; and

(b)   is not already registered under that Act,

he may refuse to issue the licence unless subsection (2) below applies to the vehicle.

23(2)   This subsection applies to a vehicle if the Secretary of State is satisfied in relation to the removal of that vehicle into the United Kingdom–

(a)   that any value added tax charged on the acquisition of that vehicle from another member State, or on any supply involving its removal into the United Kingdom, has been or will be paid or remitted;

(b)   that any value added tax or customs duty charged on the importation of the vehicle from a place outside the member States has been or will be paid or remitted; or

(c)   that no such tax or duty has been charged on the acquisition or importation of the vehicle or on any supply involving its removal into the United Kingdom.

23(3)   This section shall have effect in relation to any application made on or after the day on which this Act is passed.

VALUE ADDED TAX ACT 1994

(1994 Chapter 23)

[*5th July 1994*]

ARRANGEMENT OF SECTIONS

PART I – THE CHARGE TO TAX

PART II – RELIEFS, EXEMPTIONS AND REPAYMENTS
RELIEFS ETC. GENERALLY AVAILABLE

IMPORTS, OVERSEAS BUSINESSES ETC.

PART III – APPLICATION OF ACT IN PARTICULAR CASES

PART IV – ADMINISTRATION, COLLECTION AND ENFORCEMENT
GENERAL ADMINISTRATIVE PROVISIONS

DEFAULT SURCHARGES AND OTHER PENALTIES AND CRIMINAL OFFENCES

SCHEDULES

PART I – THE CHARGE TO TAX

IMPOSITION AND RATE OF VAT

1   Value added tax

1(1)   Value added tax shall be charged, in accordance with the provisions of this Act–

(a)   on the supply of goods or services in the United Kingdom (including anything treated as such a supply),

(b)   on the acquisition in the United Kingdom from other member States of any goods, and

(c)   on the importation of goods from places outside the member States,

and references in this Act to **VAT** are references to value added tax.

1(2)   VAT on any supply of goods or services is a liability of the person making the supply and (subject to provisions about accounting and payment) becomes due at the time of supply.

1(3)   VAT on any acquisition of goods from another member State is a liability of the person who acquires the goods and (subject to provisions about accounting and payment) becomes due at the time of acquisition.

1(4)   VAT on the importation of goods from places outside the member States shall be charged and payable as if it were a duty of customs.

Derivations – S. 1(1): VATA 1983, s. 1, as amended by F(No. 2)A 1992, s. 14 and Sch. 3, para. 2.
S. 1(2): VATA 1983, s. 2(3).
S. 1(3): VATA 1983, s. 2A(4), as inserted by F(No. 2)A 1992, s. 14 and Sch. 3, para. 3.
S. 1(4): VATA 1983, s. 2B(1), as inserted by F(No. 2)A 1992, s. 14 and Sch. 3, para. 3.

Official publications – Customs Internal Guidance Manuals, vol. V1.1 and V1.2: the user's guide and VAT law.

2   Rate of VAT

2(1)   Subject to the following provisions of this section, VAT shall be charged at the rate of 17.5 per cent and shall be charged–

(a)   on the supply of goods or services, by reference to the value of the supply as determined under this Act; and

(b)   on the acquisition of goods from another member State, by reference to the value of the acquisition as determined under this Act; and

(c)   on the importation of goods from a place outside the member States, by reference to the value of the goods as determined under this Act.

2(1A)   VAT charged on–

(a)   any supply for the time being falling within paragraph 1 of Schedule A1; or

(b)   any equivalent acquisition or importation,

shall be charged at the rate of 5 per cent.

2(1B)   The reference in subsection (1A) above to an **equivalent acquisition or importation** , in relation to any supply for the time being falling within paragraph 1 of Schedule A1, is a reference (as the case may be) to–

(a)   any acquisition from another member State of goods the supply of which would be such a supply; or

(b)   any importation from a place outside the member States of any such goods.

2(1C)   The Treasury may by order vary Schedule A1 by adding to or deleting from it any description of supply for the time being specified in it or by varying any other provision for the time being contained in it.

2(2)   The Treasury may by order increase or decrease the rate of VAT for the time being in force by such percentage thereof not exceeding 25 per cent as may be specified in the order, but any such order shall cease to be in force at the expiration of a period of one year from the date on which it takes effect, unless continued in force by a further order under this subsection.

2(3)   In relation to an order made under subsection (2) above to continue, vary or replace a previous order, the reference in that subsection to the rate for the time being in force is a reference to the rate which would be in force if no order under that subsection had been made.

History – In s. 2(1), the words "and paragraph 7 of Schedule 13" which appeared after the words "provisions of this section" were omitted by FA 1995, s. 21(2), with effect in relation to any supply made on or after 1 April 1995 and any acquisition or importation taking place on or after that date.
In s. 2(1A), the words "5 per cent" were substituted for the words "8 per cent" by F(No. 2)A 1997, s. 6(1), with effect in relation to any supply made on or after 1 September 1997 and any acquisition or importation taking place on or after that date.
S. 2(1A)–(1C) were inserted by FA 1995, s. 21(2), with effect in relation to any supply made on or after 1 April 1995 and any acquisition or importation taking place on or after that date.

Derivations – (as originally enacted) VATA 1983, s. 9, as amended by FA 1991, s. 13 and F(No. 2)A 1992, s. 14 and Sch. 3, para. 11.

Statutory instruments – VAT (Reduced Rate) Order 1998 (SI 1998/1375).
S. 88: change in rate of VAT.
VAT Regulations 1995 (SI 1995/2518), reg. 15: change in the rate.

Other material – HM Customs and Excise Business Brief 9/94, 30 March 1994: how retailers account for VAT at the eight per cent fuel rate.

3   Taxable persons and registration

3(1)   A person is a **taxable person** for the purposes of this Act while he is, or is required to be, registered under this Act.

3(2)   Schedules 1 to 3A shall have effect with respect to registration.

3(3)   Persons registered under any of those Schedules shall be registered in a single register kept by the Commissioners for the purposes of this Act; and, accordingly, references in this Act to being registered under this Act are references to being registered under any of those Schedules.

3(4)   The Commissioners may by regulations make provision as to the inclusion and correction of information in that register with respect to the Schedule under which any person is registered.

History – In s. 3(2), the words "Schedules 1 to 3A" were substituted for the words "Schedules 1 to 3" by FA 2000, s. 136(1), with effect in relation to supplies made on or after 21 March 2000.

Derivations – VATA 1983, s. 2C, as inserted by F(No. 2)A 1992, s. 14 and Sch. 3, para. 3.

Cross references – S. 96(2): "being registered" construed.

Statutory instruments – VAT Regulations 1995 (SI 1995/2518, as amended by SI 2000/794).

Official publications – Customs Internal Guidance Manual, vol. V1.5: taxable person.

SUPPLY OF GOODS OR SERVICES IN THE UNITED KINGDOM

4   Scope of VAT on taxable supplies

4(1)   VAT shall be charged on any supply of goods or services made in the United Kingdom, where it is a taxable supply made by a taxable person in the course or furtherance of any business carried on by him.

4(2) A **taxable supply** is a supply of goods or services made in the United Kingdom other than an exempt supply.

Derivations – VATA 1983, s. 2(1), (2).

Cross references – S. 31(1): "exempt supply" defined.
S. 96(1): "taxable supply" defined.
CAA 1990, s. 159A: capital allowances and additional VAT liabilities and rebates.

Official publications – Customs Internal Guidance Manual, vol. V1.6: business.
Customs Internal Guidance Manual, vol. V1.7: VAT liability.

5   Meaning of supply: alteration by Treasury order

5(1) Schedule 4 shall apply for determining what is, or is to be treated as, a supply of goods or a supply of services.

5(2) Subject to any provision made by that Schedule and to Treasury orders under subsection (3) to (6) below–

(a)   "**supply**" in this Act includes all forms of supply, but not anything done otherwise than for a consideration;

(b)   anything which is not a supply of goods but is done for a consideration (including, if so done, the granting, assignment or surrender of any right) is a **supply of services**.

5(3) The Treasury may by order provide with respect to any description of transaction–

(a)   that it is to be treated as a supply of goods and not as a supply of services; or

(b)   that it is to be treated as a supply of services and not as a supply of goods; or

(c)   that it is to be treated as neither a supply of goods nor a supply of services;

and without prejudice to the foregoing, such an order may provide that paragraph 5(4) of Schedule 4 is not to apply, in relation to goods of any prescribed description used or made available for use in prescribed circumstances, so as to make that a supply of services under that paragraph and may provide that paragraph 6 of that Schedule shall not apply, in such circumstances as may be described in the order, so as to make a removal of assets a supply of goods under that paragraph.

5(4) Without prejudice to subsection (3) above, the Treasury may by order make provision for securing, with respect to services of any description specified in the order, that where–

(a)   a person carrying on a business does anything which is not a supply of services but would, if done for a consideration, be a supply of services of a description specified in the order; and

(b)   such other conditions as may be specified in the order are satisfied,

such services are treated for the purposes of this Act as being supplied by him in the course or furtherance of that business.

5(5) The Treasury may by order make provision for securing, subject to any exceptions provided for by or under the order, that where in such circumstances as may be specified in the order goods of a description so specified are taken possession of or produced by a person in the course or furtherance of a business carried on by him and–

(a)   are neither supplied to another person nor incorporated in other goods produced in the course or furtherance of that business; but

(b)   are used by him for the purpose of a business carried on by him,

the goods are treated for the purposes of this Act as being both supplied to him for the purpose of that business and supplied by him in the course or furtherance of it.

5(6) The Treasury may by order make provision for securing, with respect to services of any description specified in the order, that where–

(a)   a person, in the course or furtherance of a business carried on by him, does anything for the purpose of that business which is not a supply of services but would, if done for a consideration, be a supply of services of a description specified in the order; and

(b)   such other conditions as may be specified in the order are satisfied,

such services are treated for the purposes of this Act as being both supplied to him for the purpose of that business and supplied by him in the course or furtherance of it.

5(7) For the purposes of this section, where goods are manufactured or produced from any other goods, those other goods shall be treated as incorporated in the first-mentioned goods.

5(8) An order under subsection (4) or (6) above may provide for the method by which the value of any supply of services which is treated as taking place by virtue of the order is to be calculated.

Derivations – VATA 1983, s. 3, as amended by F(No. 2)A 1992, s. 14 and Sch. 3, para. 4.

Cross references – S. 43(2): groups of companies.
S. 43(2D)(b): group supplies using an overseas member.

S. 44(1)(c): supplies to groups.
Sch. 6, para. 6(1)(a), 7(a): value of supply where s. 5(5) applies.
Sch. 9, Grp. 14, Note (12)(c): supplies where input tax cannot be recovered.
Sch. 9A, para. 1(6): anti-avoidance and VAT groups where determining whether there is a credit for input tax.
VAT (Cars) Order 1992 (SI 1992/3122), art. 5, 8(2)(c), 8(5)(a)(iii) and 8(5)(c)(iii): relief for second-hand motor cars.
Customs and Excise (Personal Reliefs for Special Visitors) Order 1992 (SI 1992/3156), art. 2: "supply".
VAT (Input Tax) Order 1992 SI 1992/3222), art. 4(3): disallowance of input tax.
VAT (Special Provisions) Order 1995 ((SI 1995/1268), art. 5: non-supply where a going concern.
VAT (Special Provisions) Order 1995 (SI 1995/1268), art. 12(5)(a)(v) and 12(5)(c)(iii): relief for certain goods (works of art, antiques, collectors' items and second-hand goods).
VAT Regulations 1995 (SI 1995/2518), reg. 78(a): calculations of consideration under trading stamp scheme.
VAT Regulations 1995 (SI 1995/2518), reg. 81(2): time of supply of goods for private use and free supplies of services.
VAT (Fiscal Warehousing) (Treatment of Transactions) Order 1996 (SI 1996/1255): meaning of "supply".

Statutory instruments – VAT (Treatment of Transactions) Order 1986 (SI 1986/896).
VAT (Tour Operators) Order 1987 (SI 1987/1806).
VAT (Self-supply of Construction Services) Order 1989 (SI 1989/472).
VAT (Water) Order 1989 (SI 1989/1114): whether a supply of goods or services.
VAT (Treatment of Transactions) Order 1992 (SI 1992/1282).
VAT (Removal of Goods) Order 1992 (SI 1992/3111).
VAT (Cars) Order 1992 (SI 1992/3122, as amended by SI 1995/1269, SI 1995/1667, SI 1999/2832).
VAT (Supply of Temporarily Imported Goods) Order 1992 (SI 1992/3130).
VAT (Supply of Services) Order 1993 (SI 1993/1507, as amended by SI 1995/1668, SI 1998/762).
VAT (Treatment of Transactions) Order 1995 (SI 1995/958, as amended by SI 1999/3119).
VAT (Special Provisions) Order 1995 (SI 1995/1268, as amended by SI 1995/1385, SI 1999/3120).
VAT (Treatment of Transactions) (Trading Stamps) Order 1995 (SI 1995/3042).
VAT (Fiscal Warehousing) (Treatment of Transactions) Order 1996 (SI 1996/1255).

Official publications – 706/1: "Self-supply of stationery".
Customs Internal Guidance Manual, vol. V1-3: supply and consideration.

Notes – VAT Regulations 1995 (SI 1995/2518), reg. 20: non-application of certain invoicing requirements if supply is not made for consideration.

6 Time of supply

6(1) The provisions of this section shall apply, subject to sections 18, 18B and 18C, for determining the time when a supply of goods or services is to be treated as taking place for the purposes of the charge to VAT.

6(2) Subject to subsections (4) to (14) below, a supply of goods shall be treated as taking place–

(a)   if the goods are to be removed, at the time of the removal;

(b)   if the goods are not to be removed, at the time when they are made available to the person to whom they are supplied;

(c)   if the goods (being sent or taken on approval or sale or return or similar terms) are removed before it is known whether a supply will take place, at the time when it becomes certain that the supply has taken place or, if sooner, 12 months after the removal.

6(3) Subject to subsections (4) to (14) below, a supply of services shall be treated as taking place at the time when the services are performed.

6(4) If, before the time applicable under subsection (2) or (3) above, the person making the supply issues a VAT invoice in respect of it or if, before the time applicable under subsection (2)(a) or (b) or (3) above, he receives a payment in respect of it, the supply shall, to the extent covered by the invoice or payment, be treated as taking place at the time the invoice is issued or the payment is received.

6(5) If, within 14 days after the time applicable under subsection (2) or (3) above, the person making the supply issues a VAT invoice in respect of it, then, unless he has notified the Commissioners in writing that he elects not to avail himself of this subsection, the supply shall (to the extent that it is not treated as taking place at the time mentioned in subsection (4) above) be treated as taking place at the time the invoice is issued.

6(6) The Commissioners may, at the request of a taxable person, direct that subsection (5) above shall apply in relation to supplies made by him (or such supplies made by him as may be specified in the direction) as if for the period of 14 days there were substituted such longer period as may be specified in the direction.

6(7) Where any supply of goods involves both–

(a)   the removal of the goods from the United Kingdom; and

(b)   their acquisition in another member State by a person who is liable for VAT on the acquisition in accordance with provisions of the law of that member State corresponding, in relation to that member State, to the provisions of section 10,

subsections (2), (4) to (6) and (10) to (12) of this section shall not apply and the supply shall be treated for the purposes of this Act as taking place on whichever is the earlier of the days specified in subsection (8) below.

6(8)   The days mentioned in subsection (7) above are–

(a)   the 15th day of the month following that in which the removal in question takes place; and

(b)   the day of the issue, in respect of the supply, of a VAT invoice or of an invoice of such other description as the Commissioners may by regulations prescribe.

6(9)   Where a taxable person provides a document to himself which–

(a)   purports to be a VAT invoice in respect of a supply of goods or services to him by another taxable person; and

(b)   is in accordance with regulations under paragraph 2 of Schedule 11 treated as the VAT invoice required by the regulations to be provided by the supplier,

subsections (5) and (6) above shall have effect in relation to that supply as if–

     (i)   the provision of the document to himself by the first-mentioned taxable person were the issue by the supplier of a VAT invoice in respect of the supply; and

     (ii)   any notice of election given or request made by the first-mentioned taxable person for the purposes of those provisions had been given or made by the supplier.

6(10)   The Commissioners may, at the request of a taxable person, by direction alter the time at which supplies made by him (or such supplies made by him as may be specified in the direction) are to be treated as taking place, either–

(a)   by directing those supplies to be treated as taking place–

     (i)   at times or on dates determined by or by reference to the occurrence of some event described in the direction; or

     (ii)   at times or on dates determined by or by reference to the time when some event so described would in the ordinary course of events occur,

the resulting times or dates being in every case earlier than would otherwise apply; or

(b)   by directing that, notwithstanding subsections (5) and (6) above, those supplies shall (to the extent that they are not treated as taking place at the time mentioned in subsection (4) above) be treated as taking place–

     (i)   at the beginning of the relevant working period (as defined in his case in and for the purposes of the direction); or

     (ii)   at the end of the relevant working period (as so defined).

6(11)   Where goods are treated as supplied by an order under section 5(5), the supply is treated as taking place when they are appropriated to the use mentioned in that section.

6(12)   Where there is a supply of goods by virtue only of paragraph 5(1) of Schedule 4, the supply is treated as taking place when the goods are transferred or disposed of as mentioned in that paragraph.

6(13)   Where there is a supply of services by virtue only of paragraph 5(4) of Schedule 4, the supply is treated as taking place when the goods are appropriated to the use mentioned in that paragraph.

6(14)   The Commissioners may by regulations make provision with respect to the time at which (notwithstanding subsections (2) to (8) and (11) to (13) above or section 55(4)) a supply is to be treated as taking place in cases where–

(a)   it is a supply of goods or services for a consideration the whole or part of which is determined or payable periodically, or from time to time, or at the end of any period, or

(b)   it is a supply of goods for a consideration the whole or part of which is determined at the time when the goods are appropriated for any purpose, or

(c)   there is a supply to which section 55 applies, or

(d)   there is a supply of services by virtue of paragraph 5(4) of Schedule 4 or an order under section 5(4);

and for any such case as is mentioned in this subsection the regulations may provide for goods or services to be treated as separately and successively supplied at prescribed times or intervals.

6(14A)   In relation to any services of a description specified in an order under section 7(11), this section and any regulations under this section or section 8(4) shall have effect subject to section 97A.

6(15)   In this Act **"VAT invoice"** means such an invoice as is required under paragraph 2(1) of Schedule 11, or would be so required if the person to whom the supply is made were a person to whom such an invoice should be issued.

History – In s. 6(1), the words "sections 18, 18B and 18C" were substituted by FA 1996, s. 6 and Sch. 3, para. 1, with effect from 1 June 1996 and apply to any acquisition of goods from another member State and any supply taking place on or after that day.
S. 6(14A) was inserted by FA 1998, s. 22(2), with effect from 17 March 1998.

Derivations – S. 6(1)–(3): VATA 1983, s. 4.
S. 6(4)–(6): VATA 1983, s. 5(1)–(3).
S. 6(7), (8): VATA 1983, s. 5(3A), (3B), as inserted by F(No. 2)A 1992, s. 14 and Sch. 3, para. 6(1).
S. 6(9)–(13): VATA 1983, s. 5(4)–(8).
S. 6(14): VATA 1983, s. 5(9), as amended by FA 1993, s. 45(2) and Sch. 23, Pt. II(3).
S. 6(15): VATA 1983, s. 5(10), as amended by F(No. 2)A 1992, s. 14 and Sch. 3, para. 6(3).

Cross references – S. 17(5)(b): free zone goods.
S. 36(8): s. 6 applies for determining the time when a supply is to be treated as taking place for the purpose of construing that section (post-April 1989 system of bad debt relief).
S. 55(4): gold supplies – non-application of s. 6.
S. 88: supplies spanning change of rate.
S. 96(1): "VAT invoice" defined.
Sch. 11, para. 2(9), 3(3): regulations to cover time when invoice treated as issued.
VAT Regulations 1995 (SI 1995/2518), reg. 13(5): time limit for providing VAT invoice.
VAT Regulations 1995 (SI 1995/2518), reg. 14(3): consignment or delivery note not treated as a VAT invoice if it is so endorsed.
VAT Regulations 1995 (SI 1995/2518), reg. 18 and 19: invoicing requirements.
VAT Regulations 1995 (SI 1995/2518), reg. 84: land compulsorily purchased or total consideration for land not determinable at the time of the grant or assignment.
VAT Regulations 1995 (SI 1995/2518), reg. 86(1): supplies of water, gas or any form of power etc.
VAT Regulations 1995 (SI 1995/2518), reg. 86(5): time of supply of water, gas or any form of power, etc.
VAT Regulations 1995 (SI 1995/2518), reg. 88: supplier's goods in possession of buyer.
VAT Regulations 1995 (SI 1995/2518), reg. 89: retention payments.
VAT Regulations 1995 (SI 1995/2518), reg. 95: supplies spanning change of rate, etc.

Statutory instruments – VAT Regulations 1995 (SI 1995/2518, as amended by SI 1997/1525, SI 1997/2887, SI 1999/599).

Extra-statutory concessions – 3.6 (Notice 48 (1999 edn)): tax point and coin-operated machines.

Official publications – 700/44: "Barristers and advocates: tax point on ceasing practice".
701/48: time of supply and corporate purchasing cards.
Customs Internal Guidance Manual, vol. V1.11: time of supply.

Notes – S. 29: VAT due by recipient, not by supplier.
S. 56(6): fuel for private use: the time of supply is the time at which the fuel is put into the tank.
VAT (Tour Operators) Order 1987 (SI 1987/1806), art. 4: time of supply.
VAT Regulations 1995 (SI 1995/2518), Pt. XI: time of supply.
VAT Regulations 1995 (SI 1995/2518), reg. 13(3): self-billing and VAT invoice.

7   Place of supply

7(1)   This section shall apply (subject to sections 14, 18 and 18B) for determining, for the purposes of this Act, whether goods or services are supplied in the United Kingdom.

7(2)   Subject to the following provisions of this section, if the supply of any goods does not involve their removal from or to the United Kingdom they shall be treated as supplied in the United Kingdom if they are in the United Kingdom and otherwise shall be treated as supplied outside the United Kingdom.

7(3)   Goods shall be treated–

(a)   as supplied in the United Kingdom where their supply involves their installation or assembly at a place in the United Kingdom to which they are removed; and

(b)   as supplied outside the United Kingdom where their supply involves their installation or assembly at a place outside the United Kingdom to which they are removed.

7(4)   Goods whose place of supply is not determined under any of the preceding provisions of this section shall be treated as supplied in the United Kingdom where–

(a)   the supply involves the removal of the goods to the United Kingdom by or under the directions of the person who supplies them;

(b)   the supply is a transaction in pursuance of which the goods are acquired in the United Kingdom from another member State by a person who is not a taxable person;

(c)   the supplier–

        (i)   is liable to be registered under Schedule 2; or

        (ii)   would be so liable if he were not already registered under this Act or liable to be registered under Schedule 1; and

(d)   the supply is neither a supply of goods consisting in a new means of transport nor anything which is treated as a supply for the purposes of this Act by virtue only of paragraph 5(1) or 6 of Schedule 4.

7(5)   Goods whose place of supply is not determined under any of the preceding provisions of this section and which do not consist in a new means of transport shall be treated as supplied outside the United Kingdom where–

(a)   the supply involves the removal of the goods, by or under the directions of the person who supplies them, to another member State;

(b)   the person who makes the supply is taxable in another member State; and

(c)   provisions of the law of that member State corresponding, in relation to that member State, to the provisions made by subsection (4) above make that person liable to VAT on the supply;

but this subsection shall not apply in relation to any supply in a case where the liability mentioned in paragraph (c) above depends on the exercise by any person of an option in the United Kingdom corresponding to such an option as is mentioned in paragraph 1(2) of Schedule 2 unless that person has given, and has not withdrawn, a notification to the Commissioners that he wishes his supplies to be treated as taking place outside the United Kingdom where they are supplies in relation to which the other requirements of this subsection are satisfied.

7(6)   Goods whose place of supply is not determined under any of the preceding provisions of this section shall be treated as supplied in the United Kingdom where–

(a)   their supply involves their being imported from a place outside the member States; and

(b)   the person who supplies them is the person by whom, or under whose directions, they are so imported.

7(7)   Goods whose place of supply is not determined under any of the preceding provisions of this section but whose supply involves their removal to or from the United Kingdom shall be treated–

(a)   as supplied in the United Kingdom where their supply involves their removal from the United Kingdom without also involving their previous removal to the United Kingdom; and

(b)   as supplied outside the United Kingdom in any other case.

7(8)   For the purposes of the preceding provisions of this section, where goods, in the course of their removal from a place in the United Kingdom to another place in the United Kingdom, leave and re-enter the United Kingdom the removal shall not be treated as a removal from or to the United Kingdom.

7(9)   The Commissioners may by regulations provide that a notification for the purposes of subsection (5) above is not to be given or withdrawn except in such circumstances, and in such form and manner, as may be prescribed.

7(10)   A supply of services shall be treated as made–

(a)   in the United Kingdom if the supplier belongs in the United Kingdom; and

(b)   in another country (and not in the United Kingdom) if the supplier belongs in that other country.

7(11)   The Treasury may by order provide, in relation to goods or services generally or to particular goods or services specified in the order, for varying the rules for determining where a supply of goods or services is made.

History – In s. 7(1), the words "sections 14, 18 and 18B" were substituted by FA 1996, s. 26 and Sch. 3, para. 2, with effect from 1 June 1996 and apply to any acquisition of goods from another member State and any supply taking place on or after that day.

Derivations – S. 7(1), (2): VATA 1983, s. 6(1), (2), as amended by FA 1987, s. 12(2), F(No. 2)A 1992, s. 14 and Sch. 3, para. 7(1), (2) and FA 1993, s. 44(3).
S. 7(3)–(7): VATA 1983, s. 6(2A), (2B), (2C), (2D), (3) and F(No. 2)A 1992, s. 14 and Sch. 3, para. 7(3).
S. 7(8): VATA 1983, s. 6(4), as amended by F(No. 2)A 1992, s. 14 and Sch. 3, para. 7(4).
S. 7(9): VATA 1983, s. 6(4A), as inserted by F(No. 2)A 1992, s. 14 and Sch. 3, para. 7(5).
S. 7(10): VATA 1983, s. 6(5).
S. 7(11): VATA 1983, s. 6(6), as amended by F(No. 2)A 1992, s. 14 and Sch. 3, para. 7(6).

Cross references – S. 67(6)(a): VAT chargeable under s. 7(4) is relevant VAT.
VAT (Isle of Man) Order 1982 (SI 1980/1067), art. 1(4)(a): place of supply.
VAT (Tour Operators) Order 1987 (SI 1987/1806), art. 5(1): modification of place of supply provision.
VAT (Removal of Goods) Order 1992 (SI 1992/3111), art. 4: application of Sch. 4, para. 6.
VAT Regulations 1995 (SI 1995/2518), reg. 135: supplies of goods subject to excise duty to persons who are not taxable in another member state.

Statutory instruments – VAT (Place of Supply of Services) Order 1992 (SI 1992/3121, as amended by SI 1995/3038, SI 1996/2992, SI 1997/1524, SI 1998/763).
VAT (Place of Supply of Goods) Order 1992 (SI 1992/3283).
VAT Regulations 1995 (SI 1995/2518).

Official publications – 741.
Customs Internal Guidance Manual, vol. V1.4: place of supply.

Notes – VAT (Isle of Man) Order 1982 (SI 1982/1067), art. 2: Isle of Man treated as part of the UK.

8   Reverse charge on supplies received from abroad

8(1)   Subject to subsection (3) below, where relevant services are–

(a)   supplied by a person who belongs in a country other than the United Kingdom, and

(b)   received by a person (**"the recipient"**) who belongs in the United Kingdom for the purposes of any business carried on by him,

then all the same consequences shall follow under this Act (and particularly so much as charges VAT on a supply and entitles a taxable person to credit for input tax) as if the recipient had himself supplied the services in the United Kingdom in the course or furtherance of his business, and that supply were a taxable supply.

8(2)   In this section **"relevant services"** means services of any of the descriptions specified in Schedule 5, not being services within any of the descriptions specified in Schedule 9.

8(3)   Supplies which are treated as made by the recipient under subsection (1) above are not to be taken into account as supplies made by him when determining any allowance of input tax in his case under section 26(1).

8(4)   In applying subsection (1) above, the supply of services treated as made by the recipient shall be assumed to have been made at a time to be determined in accordance with regulations prescribing rules for attributing a time of supply in cases within that subsection.

8(5)   The Treasury may by order add to, or vary, Schedule 5.

8(6)   The power of the Treasury by order to add to or vary Schedule 5 shall include power, where any services whose place of supply is determined by an order under section 7(11) are added to that Schedule, to provide that subsection (1) above shall have effect in relation to those services as if a person belongs in the United Kingdom for the purposes of paragraph (b) of that subsection if, and only if, he is a taxable person.

8(7)   The power of the Treasury by order to add to or vary Schedule 5 shall include power to make such incidental, supplemental, consequential and transitional provision in connection with any addition to or variation of that Schedule as they think fit.

8(8)   Without prejudice to the generality of subsection (7) above, the provision that may be made under that subsection includes–

(a)   provision making such modifications of section 43(2A) to (2E) as the Treasury may think fit in connection with any addition to or variation of that Schedule; and

(b)   provision modifying the effect of any regulations under subsection (4) above in relation to any services added to the Schedule.

History – S. 8(7) was inserted by FA 1997, s. 42, with effect from 19 March 1997.
S. 8(8) was inserted by FA 1997, s. 42, with effect from 19 March 1997.

Derivations – S. 8(1)–(5): VATA 1983, s. 7(1)–(5), as amended by FA 1987, s. 19(2) and Sch. 2, para. 1.
S. 8(6): VATA 1983, s. 7(6), as inserted by F(No. 2)A 1992, s. 14 and Sch. 3, para. 8.

Cross references – S. 43(2C)(c): group supplies using an overseas member.
S. 96(8): determination of country where supplier or recipient belongs should take account of s. 8(6).
Sch. 6, para. 8: value of supply under s. 8.
VAT (Place of Supply of Services) Order 1992 (SI 1992/3121), art. 16: services supplied where received.
VAT Regulations 1995 (SI 1995/2518), reg. 29(2): claims for input tax supported by invoice from supplier.
VAT Regulations 1995 (SI 1995/2518), reg. 82: services from outside the UK.
VAT Regulations 1995 (SI 1995/2518), reg. 175(b)(ii): persons to whom regulations apply.
VAT (Reverse Charge) (Anti-avoidance) Order 1997 (SI 1997/2513), art. 4(1): telecommunication services supplied on or after 1 July 1997.

Statutory instruments – VAT Regulations 1995 (SI 1995/2518).
VAT (Reverse Charge) (Anti-avoidance) Order 1997 (SI 1997/1523).
VAT (Place of Supply of Services) (Amendment) Order 1998 (SI 1998/763).

9   Place where supplier or recipient of services belongs

9(1)   Subsection (2) below shall apply for determining, in relation to any supply of services, whether the supplier belongs in one country or another and subsections (3) and (4) below shall apply (subject to any provision made under section 8(6)) for determining, in relation to any supply of services, whether the recipient belongs in one country or another.

9(2)   The supplier of services shall be treated as **belonging** in a country if–

(a)   he has there a business establishment or some other fixed establishment and no such establishment elsewhere; or

(b)   he has no such establishment (there or elsewhere) but his usual place of residence is there; or

(c)   he has such establishments both in that country and elsewhere and the establishment of his which is most directly concerned with the supply is there.

9(3)   If the supply of services is made to an individual and received by him otherwise than for the purposes of any business carried on by him, he shall be treated as belonging in whatever country he has his usual place of residence.

9(4) Where subsection (3) above does not apply, the person to whom the supply is made shall be treated as belonging in a country if–

(a) either of the conditions mentioned in paragraphs (a) and (b) of subsection (2) above is satisfied; or

(b) he has such establishments as are mentioned in subsection (2) above both in that country and elsewhere and the establishment of his at which, or for the purposes of which, the services are most directly used or to be used is in that country.

9(5) For the purposes of this section (but not for any other purposes)–

(a) a person carrying on a business through a branch or agency in any country shall be treated as having a business establishment there; and

(b) **"usual place of residence"**, in relation to a body corporate, means the place where it is legally constituted.

Derivations – S. 9(1): VATA 1983, s. 8(1), as amended by F(No. 2)A 1992, s. 14 and Sch. 3, para. 9.
S. 9(2)–(5): VATA 1983, s. 8(2)–(5).

Cross references – S. 96(8): determination of country where supplier or recipient belongs in accordance with s. 9.
VAT (Tour Operators) Order 1987 (SI 1987/1806), art. 5(1): modification of place of supply provision.

ACQUISITION OF GOODS FROM MEMBER STATES

10   Scope of VAT on acquisitions from member States

10(1) VAT shall be charged on any acquisition from another member State of any goods where–

(a) the acquisition is a taxable acquisition and takes place in the United Kingdom;

(b) the acquisition is otherwise than in pursuance of a taxable supply; and

(c) the person who makes the acquisition is a taxable person or the goods are subject to a duty of excise or consist in a new means of transport.

10(2) An acquisition of goods from another member State is a **taxable acquisition** if–

(a) it falls within subsection (3) below or the goods consist in a new means of transport; and

(b) it is not an exempt acquisition.

10(3) An acquisition of goods from another member State falls within this subsection if–

(a) the goods are acquired in the course or furtherance of–

    (i) any business carried on by any person; or

    (ii) any activities carried on otherwise than by way of business by any body corporate or by any club, association, organisation or other unincorporated body;

(b) it is the person who carries on that business or, as the case may be, those activities who acquires the goods; and

(c) the supplier–

    (i) is taxable in another member State at the time of the transaction in pursuance of which the goods are acquired; and

    (ii) in participating in that transaction, acts in the course or furtherance of a business carried on by him.

Derivations – VATA 1983, s. 2A(1)–(3), as inserted by F(No. 2)A 1992, s. 14 and Sch. 3, para. 3.

Cross references – S. 96(1): "taxable acquisition" defined.
Customs and Excise (Personal Reliefs for Special Visitors) Order 1992 (SI 1992/3156), art. 2: "acquisition".

11   Meaning of acquisition of goods from another member State

11(1) Subject to the following provisions of this section, references in this Act to the **acquisition of goods from another member State** shall be construed as references to any acquisition of goods in pursuance of a transaction in relation to which the following conditions are satisfied, that is to say–

(a) the transaction is a supply of goods (including anything treated for the purposes of this Act as a supply of goods); and

(b) the transaction involves the removal of the goods from another member State;

and references in this Act, in relation to such an acquisition, to the supplier shall be construed accordingly.

11(2) It shall be immaterial for the purposes of subsection (1) above whether the removal of the goods from the other member State is by or under the directions of the supplier or by or under the directions of the person who acquires them or any other person.

11(3) Where the person with the property in any goods does not change in consequence of anything which is treated for the purposes of this Act as a supply of goods, that supply shall be treated for the purposes of this Act as a transaction in pursuance of which there is an acquisition of goods by the person making it.

11(4) The Treasury may by order provide with respect to any description of transaction that the acquisition of goods in pursuance of a transaction of that description is not to be treated for the purposes of this Act as the acquisition of goods from another member State.

Derivations – VATA 1983, s. 8A, as inserted by F(No. 2)A 1992, s. 14 and Sch. 3, para. 10.

Cross reference – VAT (Cars) Order 1992 (SI 1992/3122, as amended by SI 1995/1269), art. 4(2): non-supplies.

Statutory instruments – VAT (Treatment of Transactions) (No. 2) Order 1992 (SI 1992/3132): taking possession of gold by the Central Bank is not an acquisition of goods from another member state.
VAT (Special Provisions) Order 1995 (SI 1995/1268).

Official publications – 725: "The single market".
Customs Internal Guidance Manual, vol. V1.16: single market.

12 Time of acquisition

12(1) Subject to sections 18 and 18B and any regulations under subsection (3) below, where goods are acquired from another member State, the acquisition shall be treated for the purposes of this Act as taking place on whichever is the earlier of–

(a) the 15th day of the month following that in which the event occurs which, in relation to that acquisition, is the first relevant event for the purposes of taxing the acquisition; and

(b) the day of the issue, in respect of the transaction in pursuance of which the goods are acquired, of an invoice of such a description as the Commissioners may by regulations prescribe.

12(2) For the purposes of this Act the event which, in relation to any acquisition of goods from another member State, is the **first relevant event** for the purposes of taxing the acquisition is the first removal of the goods which is involved in the transaction in pursuance of which they are acquired.

12(3) The Commissioners may by regulations make provision with respect to the time at which an acquisition is to be treated as taking place in prescribed cases where the whole or part of any consideration comprised in the transaction in pursuance of which the goods are acquired is determined or payable periodically, or from time to time, or at the end of a period; and any such regulations may provide, in relation to any case to which they apply, for goods to be treated as separately and successively acquired at prescribed times or intervals.

History – In s. 12(1), the words "sections 18 and 18B" were substituted by FA 1996, s. 26 and Sch. 3, para. 3, with effect from 1 June 1996 and apply to any acquisition of goods from another member State and any supply taking place on or after that day.

Derivations – VATA 1983, s. 8B, as inserted by F(No. 2)A 1992, s. 14 and Sch. 3, para. 10.

Cross references – Sch. 7, para. 5: "relevant time" defined.
Sch. 11, para. 2(9), 3(3): regulations to cover time when invoice treated as issued.
VAT Regulations 1995 (SI 1995/2518), reg. 83: form of invoice where acquisition takes place at time specified in s. 12(1)(b).

Statutory instruments – VAT Regulations 1995 (SI 1995/2518).

Notes – S. 96(1): "another member state".

13 Place of acquisition

13(1) This section shall apply (subject to sections 18 and 18B) for determining for the purposes of this Act whether goods acquired from another member State are acquired in the United Kingdom.

13(2) The goods shall be treated as acquired in the United Kingdom if they are acquired in pursuance of a transaction which involves their removal to the United Kingdom and does not involve their removal from the United Kingdom, and (subject to the following provisions of this section) shall otherwise be treated as acquired outside the United Kingdom.

13(3) Subject to subsection (4) below, the goods shall be treated as acquired in the United Kingdom if they are acquired by a person who, for the purposes of their acquisition, makes use of a number assigned to him for the purposes of VAT in the United Kingdom.

13(4) Subsection (3) above shall not require any goods to be treated as acquired in the United Kingdom where it is established, in accordance with regulations made by the Commissioners for the purposes of this section that VAT–

(a) has been paid in another member State on the acquisition of those goods; and

(b) fell to be paid by virtue of provisions of the law of that member State corresponding, in relation to that member State, to the provision made by subsection (2) above.

13(5) The Commissioners may by regulations make provision for the purposes of this section–

(a) for the circumstances in which a person is to be treated as having been assigned a number for the purposes of VAT in the United Kingdom;

(b) for the circumstances in which a person is to be treated as having made use of such a number for the purposes of the acquisition of any goods; and

(c) for the refund, in prescribed circumstances, of VAT paid in the United Kingdom on acquisitions of goods in relation to which the conditions specified in subsection (4)(a) and (b) above are satisfied.

History – In s. 13(1), the words "sections 18 and 18B" were substituted by FA 1996, s. 26 and Sch. 3, para.4, with effect from 1 June 1996 and apply to any acquisition of goods from another member State and any supply taking place on or after that day.

Derivations – VATA 1983, s. 8C, as inserted by F(No. 2)A 1992, s. 14 and Sch. 3, para. 10, and as amended (subs. (1)) by FA 1993, s. 44(3)(b).

Cross references – S. 60: VAT evasion includes refunds under s. 13(5).
S. 72: VAT evasion includes refunds under s. 13(5).
S. 83(d): appeals.

14   Acquisitions from persons belonging in other member States

14(1) Subject to subsection (3) below, where–

(a) a person (**"the original supplier"**) makes a supply of goods to a person who belongs in another member State (**"the intermediate supplier"**);

(b) that supply involves the removal of the goods from another member State and their removal to the United Kingdom but does not involve the removal of the goods from the United Kingdom;

(c) both that supply and the removal of the goods to the United Kingdom are for the purposes of the making of a supply by the intermediate supplier to another person (**"the customer"**) who is registered under this Act;

(d) neither of those supplies involves the removal of the goods from a member State in which the intermediate supplier is taxable at the time of the removal without also involving the previous removal of the goods to that member State; and

(e) there would be a taxable acquisition by the customer if the supply to him involved the removal of goods from another member State to the United Kingdom,

the supply by the original supplier to the intermediate supplier shall be disregarded for the purposes of this Act and the supply by the intermediate supplier to the customer shall be treated for the purposes of this Act, other than Schedule 3, as if it did involve the removal of the goods from another member State to the United Kingdom.

14(2) Subject to subsection (3) below, where–

(a) a person belonging in another member State makes such a supply of goods to a person who is registered under this Act as involves their installation or assembly at a place in the United Kingdom to which they are removed; and

(b) there would be a taxable acquisition by the registered person if that supply were treated as not being a taxable supply but as involving the removal of the goods from another member State to the United Kingdom,

that supply shall be so treated except for the purposes of Schedule 3.

14(3) Neither subsection (1) nor subsection (2) above shall apply in relation to any supply unless the intermediate supplier or, as the case may be, the person making the supply complies with such requirements as to the furnishing (whether before or after the supply is made) of invoices and other documents, and of information, to–

(a) the Commissioners, and

(b) the person supplied,

as the Commissioners may by regulations prescribe; and regulations under this subsection may provide for the times at which, and the form and manner in which, any document or information is to be furnished and for the particulars which it is to contain.

14(4) Where this section has the effect of treating a taxable acquisition as having been made, section 12(1) shall apply in relation to that acquisition with the omission of the words from "whichever" to "acquisition; and" at the end of paragraph (a).

14(5) For the purposes of this section a person **belongs in another member State** if–

(a) he does not have any business establishment or other fixed establishment in the United Kingdom and does not have his usual place of residence in the United Kingdom;

(b) he is neither registered under this Act nor required to be so registered;

(c)   he does not have a VAT representative and is not for the time being required to appoint one; and

(d)   he is taxable in another member State;

but, in determining for the purposes of paragraph (b) above whether a person is required to be registered under this Act, there shall be disregarded any supplies which, if he did belong in another member State and complied with the requirements prescribed under subsection (3) above, would fall to be disregarded by virtue of this section.

14(6)   Without prejudice to section 13(4), where–

(a)   any goods are acquired from another member State in a case which corresponds, in relation to another member State, to the case specified in relation to the United Kingdom in subsection (1) above; and

(b)   the person who acquires the goods is registered under this Act and would be the intermediate supplier in relation to that corresponding case,

the supply to him of those goods and the supply by him of those goods to the person who would be the customer in that corresponding case shall both be disregarded for the purposes of this Act, other than the purposes of the information provisions referred to in section 92(7).

14(7)   References in this section to a **person being taxable in another member State** shall not include references to a person who is so taxable by virtue only of provisions of the law of another member State corresponding to the provisions of this Act by virtue of which a person who is not registered under this Act is a taxable person if he is required to be so registered.

14(8)   This section does not apply in relation to any supply of goods by an intermediate supplier to whom the goods were supplied before 1st August 1993.

Derivations – VATA 1983, s. 8D, as inserted by FA 1993, s. 44.

Cross references – S. 7(1): place of supply.
Sch. 13, para. 6: application of VATA 1983, s. 32B due to s. 14(8).
VAT Regulations 1995 (SI 1995/2518), reg. 11 and 12: notification of intended supply by intermediate supplier and person belonging in another member state.
VAT Regulations 1995 (SI 1995/2518), reg. 17–19: invoicing requirements.
VAT Regulations 1995 (SI 1995/2518), reg. 175: repayments to Community traders.

Statutory instrument – VAT Regulations 1995 (SI 1995/2518).

IMPORTATION OF GOODS FROM OUTSIDE THE MEMBER STATES

15   General provisions relating to imported goods

15(1)   For the purposes of this Act goods are **imported from a place outside the member States** where–

(a)   having been removed from a place outside the member States, they enter the territory of the Community;

(b)   they enter that territory by being removed to the United Kingdom or are removed to the United Kingdom after entering that territory; and

(c)   the circumstances are such that it is on their removal to the United Kingdom or subsequently while they are in the United Kingdom that any Community customs debt in respect of duty on their entry into the territory of the Community would be incurred.

15(2)   Accordingly–

(a)   goods shall not be treated for the purposes of this Act as imported at any time before a Community customs debt in respect of duty on their entry into the territory of the Community would be incurred, and

(b)   the person who is to be treated for the purposes of this Act as importing any goods from a place outside the member States is the person who would be liable to discharge any such Community customs debt.

15(3)   Subsections (1) and (2) above shall not apply, except in so far as the context otherwise requires or provision to the contrary is contained in regulations under section 16(1), for construing any references to importation or to an importer in any enactment or subordinate legislation applied for the purposes of this Act by section 16(1).

Derivations – VATA 1983, s. 2B(2)–(4), as inserted by F(No. 2)A 1992, s. 14 and Sch. 3, para. 3.

16   Application of customs enactments

16(1)   Subject to such exceptions and adaptations as the Commissioners may by regulations prescribe and except where the contrary intention appears–

(a) the provision made by or under the Customs and Excise Acts 1979 and the other enactments and subordinate legislation for the time being having effect generally in relation to duties of customs and excise charged on the importation of goods into the United Kingdom; and

(b) the Community legislation for the time being having effect in relation to Community customs duties charged on goods entering the territory of the Community,

shall apply (so far as relevant) in relation to any VAT chargeable on the importation of goods from places outside the member States as they apply in relation to any such duty of customs or excise or, as the case may be, Community customs duties.

16(2) Regulations under section 16 of the Post Office Act 1953 (which provides for the application of customs enactments to postal packets) may make special provision in relation to VAT.

Derivations – S. 16(1): VATA 1983, s. 24(1), as substituted by F(No. 2)A 1992, s. 14 and Sch. 3, para. 25.
S. 16(2): VATA 1983, s. 24(4).
Cross references – S. 84(9): appeals.
S. 93(2): territories included in reference to other member states.
VAT Regulations 1995 (SI 1995/2518), reg. 118–120: provisions excepted from scope of s. 16(1).
VAT Regulations 1995 (SI 1995/2518), reg. 121: adaptation of CEMA 1979, s. 125(3).
VAT Regulations 1995 (SI 1995/2518), reg. 142: application of customs and excise legislation.
Statutory instruments – Free Zone Regulations 1984 (SI 1984/1177).
VAT Regulations 1995 (SI 1995/2518), Pt. XVI: importation and removal from warehouse.
VAT (Amendment) (No. 2) Regulations 2000 (SI 2000/634).
Notes – Postal Packets (Customs and Excise) Regulations 1986 (SI 1986/260).

17 Free zone regulations

17(1) This section applies in relation to VAT chargeable on the importation of goods from places outside the member States; and in this section **"free zone"** has the meaning given by section 100A(2) of the Management Act.

17(2) Subject to any contrary provision made by any directly applicable Community provision, goods which are chargeable with VAT may be moved into a free zone and may remain as free zone goods without payment of VAT.

17(3) The Commissioners may by regulations (**"free zone regulations"**) make provision with respect to the movement of goods into, and the removal of goods from, any free zone and the keeping, securing and treatment of goods which are within a free zone, and subject to any provision of the regulations, **"free zone goods"** means goods which are within a free zone.

17(4) Without prejudice to the generality of subsection (3), free zone regulations may make provision–

(a) for enabling the Commissioners to allow goods to be removed from a free zone without payment of VAT in such circumstances and subject to such conditions as they may determine;

(b) for determining where any VAT becomes payable in respect of goods which cease to be free zone goods–

(i) the rates of any VAT applicable; and

(ii) the time at which those goods cease to be free zone goods;

(c) for determining for the purpose of enabling VAT to be charged in respect of free zone goods in a case where a person wishes to pay that VAT notwithstanding that the goods will continue to be free zone goods, the rate of VAT to be applied; and

(d) permitting free zone goods to be destroyed without payment of VAT in such circumstances and subject to such conditions as the Commissioners may determine.

17(5) The Commissioners, with respect to free zone goods or the movement of goods into any free zone, may by regulations make provision–

(a) for relief from the whole or part of any VAT chargeable on the importation of goods into the United Kingdom in such circumstances as they may determine;

(b) in place of, or in addition to, any provision made by section 6 or any other enactment, for determining the time when a supply of goods which are or have been free zone goods is to be treated as taking place for the purposes of the charge to VAT; and

(c) as to the treatment, for the purposes of VAT, of goods which are manufactured or produced within a free zone from other goods or which have other goods incorporated in them while they are free zone goods.

Derivations – S. 17(2): CEMA 1979, s. 100C(1), as inserted by FA 1984, s. 8 and Sch. 4, Pt. I, and as amended by SI 1991/2727.
S. 17(3): CEMA 1979, s. 100B, as inserted by FA 1984, s. 8 and Sch. 4, Pt. I, and as amended by SI 1991/2727.

S. 17(4): CEMA 1979, s. 100C(3), (4), as inserted by FA 1984, s. 8 and Sch. 4, Pt. I, and as amended by SI 1991/2727.

Statutory instrument – Free Zone Regulations 1984 (SI 1984/1177).

Official publications – Customs Internal Guidance Manual, vol. V1.19: warehousing and free zones for imports.

GOODS SUBJECT TO A WAREHOUSING REGIME

18 Place and time of acquisition or supply

18(1) Where–

(a) any goods have been removed from a place outside the member States and have entered the territory of the Community;

(b) the material time for any acquisition of those goods from another member State or for any supply of those goods is while they are subject to a warehousing regime and before the duty point; and

(c) those goods are not mixed with any dutiable goods which were produced or manufactured in the United Kingdom or acquired from another member State,

then the acquisition or supply mentioned in paragraph (b) above shall be treated for the purposes of this Act as taking place outside the United Kingdom.

18(2) Subsection (3) below applies where–

(a) any dutiable goods are acquired from another member State; or

(b) any person makes a supply of–

(i) any dutiable goods which were produced or manufactured in the United Kingdom or acquired from another member State; or

(ii) any goods comprising a mixture of goods falling within sub-paragraph (i) above and other goods.

18(3) Where this subsection applies and the material time for the acquisition or supply mentioned in subsection (2) above is while the goods in question are subject to a warehousing regime and before the duty point, that acquisition or supply shall be treated for the purposes of this Act as taking place outside the United Kingdom if the material time for any subsequent supply of those goods is also while the goods are subject to the warehousing regime and before the duty point.

18(4) Where the material time for any acquisition or supply of any goods in relation to which subsection (3) above applies is while the goods are subject to a warehousing regime and before the duty point but the acquisition or supply nevertheless falls, for the purposes of this Act, to be treated as taking place in the United Kingdom–

(a) that acquisition or supply shall be treated for the purposes of this Act as taking place at the earlier of the following times, that is to say, the time when the goods are removed from the warehousing regime and the duty point; and

(b) in the case of a supply, any VAT payable on the supply shall be paid (subject to any regulations under subsection (5) below)–

(i) at the time when the supply is treated as taking place under paragraph (a) above; and

(ii) by the person by whom the goods are so removed or, as the case may be, together with the duty or agricultural levy, by the person who is required to pay the duty or levy.

18(5) The Commissioners may by regulations make provision for enabling a taxable person to pay the VAT he is required to pay by virtue of paragraph (b) of subsection (4) above at a time later than that provided for by that paragraph.

18(5A) Regulations under subsection (5) above may in particular make provision for either or both of the following–

(a) for the taxable person to pay the VAT together with the VAT chargeable on other supplies by him of goods and services;

(b) for the taxable person to pay the VAT together with any duty of excise deferment of which has been granted to him under section 127A of the Customs and Excise Management Act 1979;

and they may make different provision for different descriptions of taxable person and for different descriptions of goods.

18(6) In this section–

"dutiable goods" means any goods which are subject–

(a) to a duty of excise; or

(b)   in accordance with any provision for the time being having effect for transitional purposes in connection with the accession of any State to the European Communities, to any Community customs duty or agricultural levy of the Economic Community;

"the duty point", in relation to any goods, means–

(a)   in the case of goods which are subject to a duty of excise, the time when the requirement to pay the duty on those goods takes effect; and

(b)   in the case of goods which are not so subject, the time when any Community customs debt in respect of duty on the entry of the goods into the territory of the Community would be incurred or, as the case may be, the corresponding time in relation to any such duty or levy as is mentioned in paragraph (b) of the definition of dutiable goods;

"material time"–

(a)   in relation to any acquisition or supply the time of which is determined in accordance with regulations under section 6(14) or 12(3), means such time as may be prescribed for the purpose of this section by those regulations;

(b)   in relation to any other acquisition, means the time of the event which, in relation to the acquisition, is the first relevant event for the purposes of taxing it; and

(c)   in relation to any other supply, means the time when the supply would be treated as taking place in accordance with subsection (2) of section 6 if paragraph (c) of that subsection were omitted;

"warehouse" means any warehouse where goods may be stored in any member State without payment of any one or more of the following, that is to say–

(a)   Community customs duty;

(b)   any agricultural levy of the Economic Community;

(c)   VAT on the importation of the goods into any member State;

(d)   any duty of excise or any duty which is equivalent in another member State to a duty of excise.

18(7)   References in this section to **goods being subject to a warehousing regime** is a reference to goods being kept in a warehouse or being transported between warehouses (whether in the same or different member States) without the payment in a member State of any duty, levy or VAT; and references to the removal of goods from a warehousing regime shall be construed accordingly.

History – S. 18(5) and (5A) were substituted for former s. 18(5) by FA 1995, s. 29, with effect from 1 May 1995.

Derivations – (as originally enacted) – VATA 1983, s. 35, as substituted by F(No. 2)A 1992, s. 14 and Sch. 3, para. 35.

Cross references – S. 6(1): time of supply.
S. 7(1): place of supply.
S. 12(1): time of acquisition.
S. 13(1): place of acquisition.
Sch. 6, para. 3: valuation.
Sch. 7, para. 2(2): valuation.
Sch. 11, para. 2(8): accounting for VAT.
VAT (Isle of Man) Order 1982 (SI 1982/1067), art. 8: taxable person includes a person who is a taxable person under the Manx Act.
VAT Regulations 1995 (SI 1995/2518), reg. 43(2): goods removed from warehousing regime.
VAT Regulations 1995 (SI 1995/2518), reg. 97(2): valuation of acquisitions.
ICTA 1988, s. 203F(6): PAYE payment in the form of a readily convertible asset.

Statutory instruments – VAT Regulations 1995 (SI 1995/2518), Pt. XVI: importation and removal from warehouse.

Official publications – Customs Internal Guidance Manual, vol. V1.19: warehousing and free zones for imports.

18A   Fiscal warehousing

18A(1)   The Commissioners may, if it appears to them proper, upon application approve any registered person as a fiscal warehousekeeper; and such approval shall be subject to such conditions as they shall impose.

18A(2)   Subject to those conditions and to regulations made under section 18F such a person shall be entitled to keep a fiscal warehouse.

18A(3)   **"Fiscal warehouse"** means such place in the United Kingdom in the occupation or under the control of the fiscal warehousekeeper, not being retail premises, as he shall notify to the Commissioners in writing; and such a place shall become a fiscal warehouse on receipt by the Commissioners of that notification or on the date stated in it as the date from which it is to have effect, whichever is the later, and, subject to subsection (6) below, shall remain a fiscal warehouse so long as it is in the occupation or under the control of the fiscal warehousekeeper or until he shall notify the Commissioners in writing that it is to cease to be a fiscal warehouse.

18A(4)   The Commissioners may in considering an application by a person to be a fiscal warehousekeeper take into account any matter which they consider relevant, and may without prejudice to the generality of that provision take into account all or any one or more of the following–

(a)   his record of compliance and ability to comply with the requirements of this Act and regulations made hereunder;

(b)   his record of compliance and ability to comply with the requirements of the customs and excise Acts (as defined in the Management Act) and regulations made thereunder;

(c)   his record of compliance and ability to comply with Community customs provisions;

(d)   his record of compliance and ability to comply with the requirements of other member States relating to VAT and duties equivalent to duties of excise;

(e)   if the applicant is a company the records of compliance and ability to comply with the matters set out at (a) to (d) above of its directors, persons connected with its directors, its managing officers, any shadow directors or any of those persons, and, if it is a close company, the records of compliance and ability to comply with the matters set out at (a) to (d) above of the beneficial owners of the shares of the company or any of them; and

(f)   if the applicant is an individual the records of compliance and ability to comply with the matters set out at (a) to (d) above of any company of which he is or has been a director, managing officer or shadow director or, in the case of a close company, a shareholder or the beneficial owner of shares,

and for the purposes of paragraphs (e) and (f) **"connected"** shall have the meaning given by section 24(7), **"managing officer"** the meaning given by section 61(6), **"shadow director"** the meaning given by section 741(2) of the Companies Act 1985 and **"close company"** the meaning given by the Taxes Act.

18A(5)   Subject to subsection (6) below, a person approved under subsection (1) shall remain a fiscal warehousekeeper until he ceases to be a registered person or until he shall notify the Commissioners in writing that he is to cease to be a fiscal warehousekeeper.

18A(6)   The Commissioners may if they consider it appropriate from time to time–

(a)   impose conditions on a fiscal warehousekeeper in addition to those conditions, if any, which they imposed under subsection (1), and vary or revoke any conditions previously imposed;

(b)   withdraw approval of any person as a fiscal warehousekeeper, and

(c)   withdraw fiscal warehouse status from any premises.

18A(7)   Any application by or on behalf of a person to be a fiscal warehousekeeper shall be in writing in such form as the Commissioners may direct and shall be accompanied by such information as they shall require.

18A(8)   Any approval by the Commissioners under subsection (1) above, and any withdrawal of approval or other act by them under subsection (6) above, shall be notified by them to the fiscal warehousekeeper in writing and shall take effect on such notification being made or on any later date specified for the purpose in the notification.

18A(9)   Without prejudice to the provisions of section 43 concerning liability for VAT, in subsections (1) and (2) above **"registered person"** includes any body corporate which under that section is for the time being treated as a member of a group.

History – S. 18A was inserted by FA 1996, s. 26 and Sch. 3, para. 5, with effect from 1 June 1996 and applies to any acquisition of goods from another member State and any supply taking place on or after that day.

Cross references – S. 69(1)(g): breach of regulations.
S. 83(da): appeals against Commissioners' decision.
ICTA 1988, s. 203F(6): PAYE payment in the form of a readily convertible asset.

18B   Fiscally warehoused goods: relief

18B(1)   Subsections (3) and (4) below apply where–

(a)   there is an acquisition of goods from another member State;

(b)   those goods are eligible goods;

(c)   either–

     (i)   the acquisition takes place while the goods are subject to a fiscal warehousing regime; or

     (ii)   after the acquisition but before the supply, if any, of those goods which next occurs, the acquirer causes the goods to be placed in a fiscal warehousing regime; and

(d)   the acquirer, not later than the time of the acquisition, prepares and keeps a certificate that the goods are subject to a fiscal warehousing regime, or (as the case may be) that he will cause paragraph (c)(ii) above to be satisfied; and the certificate shall be in such form and be kept for such period as the Commissioners may by regulations specify.

18B(2)   Subsections (3) and (4) below also apply where–

(a)   there is a supply of goods;

(b)   those goods are eligible goods;

(c)   either–

> (i)   that supply takes place while the goods are subject to a fiscal warehousing regime; or
>
> (ii) after that supply but before the supply, if any, of those goods which next occurs, the person to whom the former supply is made causes the goods to be placed in a fiscal warehousing regime;

(d)   in a case falling within paragraph (c)(ii) above, the person to whom the supply is made gives the supplier, not later than the time of the supply, a certificate in such form as the Commissioners may by regulations specify that he will cause paragraph (c)(ii) to be satisfied; and

(e)   the supply is not a retail transaction.

18B(3)   The acquisition or supply in question shall be treated for the purposes of this Act as taking place outside the United Kingdom if any subsequent supply of those goods is while they are subject to the fiscal warehousing regime.

18B(4)   Where subsection (3) does not apply and the acquisition or supply in question falls, for the purposes of this Act, to be treated as taking place in the United Kingdom, that acquisition or supply shall be treated for the purposes of this Act as taking place when the goods are removed from the fiscal warehousing regime.

18B(5)   Where–

(a)   subsection (4) above applies to an acquisition or a supply,

(b)   the acquisition or supply is taxable and not zero-rated, and

(c)   the acquirer or supplier is not a taxable person but would be were it not for paragraph 1(9) of Schedule 1, paragraph 1(7) of Schedule 2 and paragraph 1(6) of Schedule 3, or any of those provisions,

VAT shall be chargeable on that acquisition or supply notwithstanding that the acquirer or the supplier is not a taxable person.

18B(6)   In this section **"eligible goods"** means goods–

(a)   of a description falling within Schedule 5A;

(b)   upon which any import duties, as defined in article 4(10) of the Community Customs Code of 12th October 1992 (Council Regulation (EEC) No. 2913/92), either have been paid or have been deferred under article 224 of that Code or regulations made under section 45 of the Management Act;

(c)   (in the case of goods imported from a place outside the member States) upon which any VAT chargeable under section 1(1)(c) has been either paid or deferred in accordance with Community customs provisions, and

(d)   (in the case of goods subject to a duty of excise) upon which that duty has been either paid or deferred under section 127A of the Management Act.

18B(7)   For the purposes of this section, apart from subsection (4), an acquisition or supply shall be treated as taking place at the **material time** for the acquisition or supply.

18B(8)   The Treasury may by order vary Schedule 5A by adding to or deleting from it any goods or varying any description of any goods.

History – S. 18B was inserted by FA 1996, s. 26 and Sch. 3, para. 5, with effect from 1 June 1996 and applies to any acquisition of goods from another member State and any supply taking place on or after that day.

Cross references – S. 62(1)(a)(ii) and 62(1A): penalty for incorrect certificate.
Sch. 3, para. 1(6): valuation and disregarding last acquisition or supply of goods before removal from fiscal warehousing.
VAT (Fiscal Warehousing) (Treatment of Transactions) Order 1996 (SI 1996/1255): meaning of "eligible goods".
ICTA 1988, s. 203F(6): PAYE payment in the form of a readily convertible asset.

Statutory instruments – VAT Regulations 1995 (SI 1995/2518, as amended by SI 1996/1250).

18C   Warehouses and fiscal warehouses: services

18C(1)   Where–

(a)   a taxable person makes a supply of specified services;

(b)   those services are wholly performed on or in relation to goods while those goods are subject to a warehousing or fiscal warehousing regime;

(c)   (except where the services are the supply by an occupier of a warehouse or a fiscal warehousekeeper of warehousing or fiscally warehousing the goods) the person to whom the supply is made gives the supplier a certificate, in such a form as the Commissioners may by regulations specify, that the services are so performed;

(d)   the supply of services would (apart from this section) be taxable and not zero-rated; and

(e)   the supplier issues to the person to whom the supply is made an invoice of such a description as the Commissioners may by regulations prescribe,

his supply shall be zero-rated.

18C(2)   If a supply of services is zero-rated under subsection (1) above ("**the zero-rated supply of services**") then, unless there is a supply of the goods in question the material time for which is–

(a)   while the goods are subject to a warehousing or fiscal warehousing regime, and

(b)   after the material time for the zero-rated supply of services,

subsection (3) below shall apply.

18C(3)   Where this subsection applies–

(a)   a supply of services identical to the zero-rated supply of services shall be treated for the purposes of this Act as being, at the time the goods are removed from the warehousing or fiscal warehousing regime or (if earlier) at the duty point, both made (for the purposes of his business) to the person to whom the zero-rated supply of services was actually made and made by him in the course or furtherance of his business,

(b)   that supply shall have the same value as the zero-rated supply of services,

(c)   that supply shall be a taxable (and not a zero-rated) supply, and

(d)   VAT shall be charged on that supply even if the person treated as making it is not a taxable person.

18C(4)   In this section "**specified services**" means–

(a)   services of an occupier of a warehouse or a fiscal warehousekeeper of keeping the goods in question in a warehousing or fiscal warehousing regime;

(b)   in relation to goods subject to a warehousing regime, services of carrying out on the goods operations which are permitted to be carried out under Community customs provisions or warehousing regulations as the case may be; and

(c)   in relation to goods subject to a fiscal warehousing regime, services of carrying out on the goods any physical operations (other than any prohibited by regulations made under section 18F), for example, and without prejudice to the generality of the foregoing words, preservation and repacking operations.

History – S. 18C was inserted by FA 1996, s. 26 and Sch. 3, para. 5, with effect from 1 June 1996 and applies to any acquisition of goods from another member State and any supply taking place on or after that day.

Cross references – S. 62(1)(a)(ii): penalty for incorrect certificate.
VAT Regulations 1995 (SI 1995/2518), reg. 13(1): obligation to provide a VAT invoice.
ICTA 1988, s. 203F(6): PAYE payment in the form of a readily convertible asset.

Statutory instruments – VAT Regulations 1995 (SI 1995/2518, as amended by SI 1996/1250).

18D   Removal from warehousing: accountability

18D(1)   This section applies to any supply to which section 18B(4) or section 18C(3) applies (supply treated as taking place on removal or duty point) and any acquisition to which section 18B(5) applies (acquisition treated as taking place on removal where acquirer not a taxable person).

18D(2)   Any VAT payable on the supply or acquisition shall (subject to any regulations under subsection (3) below) be paid–

(a)   at the time when the supply or acquisition is treated as taking place under the section in question; and

(b)   by the person by whom the goods are removed or, as the case may be, together with the excise duty, by the person who is required to pay that duty.

18D(3)   The Commissioners may by regulations make provision for enabling a taxable person to pay the VAT he is required to pay by virtue of subsection (2) above at a time later than that provided by that subsection; and they may make different provisions for different descriptions of taxable persons and for different descriptions of goods and services.

History – S. 18D was inserted by FA 1996, s. 26 and Sch. 3, para. 5, with effect from 1 June 1996 and applies to any acquisition of goods from another member State and any supply taking place on or after that day.

Cross references – ICTA 1988, s. 203F(6): PAYE payment in the form of a readily convertible asset.

Statutory instruments – VAT Regulations 1995 (SI 1995/2518, as amended by SI 1996/1250).

18E   Deficiency in fiscally warehoused goods

18E(1)   This section applies where goods have been subject to a fiscal warehousing regime and, before being lawfully removed from the fiscal warehouse, they are found to be missing or deficient.

18E(2)   In any case where this section applies, unless it is shown to the satisfaction of the Commissioners that the absence of or deficiency in the goods can be accounted for by natural waste or other legitimate cause, the Commissioners may require the fiscal warehousekeeper to pay immediately in respect of the missing goods or of the whole or any part of the deficiency, as they see fit, the VAT that would have been chargeable.

18E(3)   In subsection (2) **"VAT that would have been chargeable"** means VAT that would have been chargeable on a supply of the missing goods, or the amount of goods by which the goods are deficient, taking place at the time immediately before the absence arose or the deficiency occurred, if the value of that supply were the open market value; but where that time cannot be ascertained to the Commissioners' satisfaction, that VAT shall be the greater of the amounts of VAT which would have been chargeable on a supply of those goods–

(a)   if the value of that supply were the highest open market value during the period (the relevant period) commencing when the goods were placed in the fiscal warehousing regime and ending when the absence or deficiency came to the notice of the Commissioners, or

(b)   if the rate of VAT chargeable on that supply were the highest rate chargeable on a supply of such goods during the relevant period and the value of that supply were the highest open market value while that rate prevailed.

18E(4)   This section has effect without prejudice to any penalty incurred under any other provision of this Act or regulations made under it.

History – S. 18E was inserted by FA 1996, s. 26 and Sch. 3, para. 5, with effect from 1 June 1996 and applies to any acquisition of goods from another member State and any supply taking place on or after that day.

Cross references – ICTA 1988, s. 203F(6): PAYE payment in the form of a readily convertible asset.

18F   Sections 18A to 18E: supplementary

18F(1)   In sections 18A to 18E and this section–

"**duty point**" has the meaning given by section 18(6);

"**eligible goods**" has the meaning given by section 18B(6);

"**fiscal warehouse**" means a place notified to the Commissioners under section 18A(3) and from which such status has not been withdrawn;

"**fiscal warehousekeeper**" means a person approved under section 18A(1);

"**material time**"–

(a)   in relation to any acquisition or supply the time of which is determined in accordance with regulations under section 6(14) or 12(3), means such time as may be prescribed for the purpose of this section by those regulations;

(b)   in relation to any other acquisition, means the time when the goods reach the destination to which they are despatched from the member State in question;

(c)   in relation to any other supply of goods, means the time when the supply would be treated as taking place in accordance with subsection (2) of section 6 if paragraph (c) of that subsection were omitted; and

(d)   in relation to any other supply of services, means the time when the services are performed;

"**warehouse**", except in the expression "fiscal warehouse", has the meaning given by section 18(6);

"**warehousing regulations**" has the same meaning as in the Management Act.

18F(2)   Any reference in sections 18A to 18E or this section to **goods being subject to a fiscal warehousing regime** is, subject to any regulations made under subsection (8)(e) below, a reference to eligible goods being kept in a fiscal warehouse or being transferred between fiscal warehouses in accordance with such regulations; and any reference to the removal of goods from a fiscal warehousing regime shall be construed accordingly.

18F(3)   Subject to subsection (2) above, any reference in sections 18C and 18D to **goods being subject to a warehousing regime** or to the **removal of goods from a warehousing regime** shall have the same meaning as in section 18(7).

18F(4)   Where as a result of an operation on eligible goods subject to a fiscal warehousing regime they change their nature but the resulting goods are also eligible goods, the provisions of sections 18B to 18E and this section shall apply as if the resulting goods were the original goods.

18F(5) Where as a result of an operation on eligible goods subject to a fiscal warehousing regime they cease to be eligible goods, on their ceasing to be so sections 18B to 18E shall apply as if they had at that time been removed from the fiscal warehousing regime; and for that purpose the proprietor of the goods shall be treated as if he were the person removing them.

18F(6) Where–

(a)   any person ceases to be a fiscal warehousekeeper; or

(b)   any premises cease to have fiscal warehouse status,

sections 18B to 18E and this section shall apply as if the goods of which he is the fiscal warehousekeeper, or the goods in the fiscal warehouse, as the case may be, had at that time been removed from the fiscal warehousing regime; and for that purpose the proprietor of the goods shall be treated as if he were the person removing them.

18F(7) The Commissioners may make regulations governing the deposit, keeping, securing and treatment of goods in a fiscal warehouse, and the removal of goods from a fiscal warehouse.

18F(8) Regulations may, without prejudice to the generality of subsection (7) above, include provisions–

(a)   in relation to –

      (i)   goods which are, have been or are to be subject to a fiscal warehousing regime,

      (ii)   other goods which are, have been or are to be kept in fiscal warehouses,

      (iii)   fiscal warehouse premises, and

      (iv)   fiscal warehousekeepers and their businesses,

      as to the keeping, preservation and production of records and the furnishing of returns and information by fiscal warehousekeepers and any other persons;

(b)   requiring goods deposited in a fiscal warehouse to be produced to or made available for inspection by an authorised person on request by him;

(c)   prohibiting the carrying out on fiscally warehoused goods of such operations as they may prescribe;

(d)   regulating the transfer of goods from one fiscal warehouse to another;

(e)   concerning goods which, though kept in a fiscal warehouse, are not eligible goods or are not intended by a relevant person to be goods in respect of which reliefs are to be enjoyed under sections 18A to 18E and this section;

(f)   prohibiting the fiscal warehousekeeper from allowing goods to be removed from the fiscal warehousing regime without payment of any VAT payable under section 18D on or by reference to that removal and, if in breach of that prohibition he allows goods to be so removed, making him liable for the VAT jointly and severally with the remover,

and may contain such incidental or supplementary provisions as the Commissioners think necessary or expedient.

18F(9) Regulations may make different provision for different cases, including different provision for different fiscal warehousekeepers or descriptions of fiscal warehousekeeper, for fiscal warehouses of different descriptions or for goods of different classes or descriptions or of the same class or description in different circumstances.

History – S. 18F was inserted by FA 1996, s. 26 and Sch. 3, para. 5, with effect from 1 June 1996 and applies to any acquisition of goods from another member State and any supply taking place on or after that day.

Cross references – VAT (Fiscal Warehousing) (Treatment of Transactions) Order 1996 (SI 1996/1255): meaning of "material time".

ICTA 1988, s. 203F(6): PAYE payment in the form of a readily convertible asset.

Statutory instruments – VAT Regulations 1995 (SI 1995/2518, as amended by SI 1996/1250).

DETERMINATION OF VALUE

19   Value of supply of goods or services

19(1) For the purposes of this Act the value of any supply of goods or services shall, except as otherwise provided by or under this Act, be determined in accordance with this section and Schedule 6, and for those purposes subsections (2) to (4) below have effect subject to that Schedule.

19(2) If the supply is for a consideration in money its value shall be taken to be such amount as, with the addition of the VAT chargeable, is equal to the consideration.

19(3) If the supply is for a consideration not consisting or not wholly consisting of money, its value shall be taken to be such amount in money as, with the addition of the VAT chargeable, is equivalent to the consideration.

19(4) Where a supply of any goods or services is not the only matter to which a consideration in money relates, the supply shall be deemed to be for such part of the consideration as is properly attributable to it.

19(5) For the purposes of this Act the **open market value** of a supply of goods or services shall be taken to be the amount that would fall to be taken as its value under subsection (2) above if the supply were for such consideration in money as would be payable by a person standing in no such relationship with any person as would affect that consideration.

Derivations – VATA 1983, s. 10, as amended by F(No. 2)A 1992, s. 14 and Sch. 3, para. 12.

Cross references – S. 52: trading stamp schemes.
VAT (Tour Operators) Order 1987 (SI 1987/1806), art. 9(2) and 14(2): value of supply.
VAT Regulations 1995 (SI 1995/2518), reg. 77: modification of s. 19(5) if a supply of goods in exchange for trading stamps under a trading stamp scheme.
VAT Regulations 1995 (SI 1995/2518), reg. 172B(1): writing off debts where claimant is a tour operator.

Extra-statutory concessions – 3.7 (Notice 48 (1999 edn)): minor items supplied in linked-supplies schemes.

Official publications – Customs Internal Guidance Manuals, vol. V1.12 and V1.17: VAT valuation and business promotion schemes.

Other material – Customs and Excise Business Brief 8/92, 15 June 1992 (not reproduced): VAT charges on staff discounts – from 15 May 1992 VAT payable only on price paid (which includes consideration from a third party).

Notes – Price Marking Order 1991 (SI 1991/1382), art. 9: indication of price exclusive of VAT.

20　Valuation of acquisitions from other member States

20(1) Subject to section 18C, for the purposes of this Act the value of any acquisition of goods from another member State shall be taken to be the value of the transaction in pursuance of which they are acquired.

20(2) Where goods are acquired from another member State otherwise than in pursuance of a taxable supply, the value of the transaction in pursuance of which they are acquired shall be determined for the purposes of subsection (1) above in accordance with this section and Schedule 7, and for those purposes–

(a)　　subsections (3) to (5) below have effect subject to that Schedule; and

(b)　　section 19 and Schedule 6 shall not apply in relation to the transaction.

20(3) If the transaction is for a consideration in money, its value shall be taken to be such amount as is equal to the consideration.

20(4) If the transaction is for a consideration not consisting or not wholly consisting of money, its value shall be taken to be such amount in money as is equivalent to the consideration.

20(5) Where a transaction in pursuance of which goods are acquired from another member State is not the only matter to which a consideration in money relates, the transaction shall be deemed to be for such part of the consideration as is properly attributable to it.

History – In s. 21(1), at the beginning the words "Subject to section 18C," were inserted by FA 1996, s. 26 and Sch. 3, para. 6, with effect from 1 June 1996 and apply to any acquisition of goods from another member state and any supply taking place on or after that day.

Derivations – VATA 1983, s. 10A, as inserted by F(No. 2)A 1992, s. 14 and Sch. 3, para. 13.

Cross references – S. 52: trading stamp schemes.
Sch. 7, para. 1(4): valuation.

Notes – Regulation 2454/93, Pt. I, Title V: customs value.

21　Value of imported goods

21(1) For the purposes of this Act, the value of goods imported from a place outside the member States shall (subject to subsections (2) to (4) below) be determined according to the rules applicable in the case of Community customs duties, whether or not the goods in question are subject to any such duties.

21(2) For the purposes of this Act the value of any goods imported from a place outside the member States shall be taken to include the following so far as they are not already included in that value in accordance with the rules mentioned in subsection (1) above, that is to say–

(a)　　all taxes, duties and other charges levied either outside or, by reason of importation, within the United Kingdom (except VAT);

(b)　　all incidental expenses, such as commission, packing, transport and insurance costs, up to the goods' first destination in the United Kingdom; and

(c)　　if at the time of the importation of the goods from a place outside the member States a further destination for the goods is known, and that destination is within the United Kingdom or another member State, all such incidental expenses in so far as they result from the transport of the goods to that other destination;

and in this subsection **"the goods' first destination"** means the place mentioned on the consignment note or any other document by means of which the goods are imported into the United Kingdom, or in the absence of such documentation it means the place of the first transfer of cargo in the United Kingdom.

21(3) Subject to subsection (2) above, where–

(a)   goods are imported from a place outside the member States for a consideration which is or includes a price in money payable as on the transfer of property;

(b)   the terms on which those goods are so imported allow a discount for prompt payment of that price;

(c)   those terms do not include provision for payment of that price by instalments; and

(d)   payment of that price is made in accordance with those terms so that the discount falls to be allowed,

the value of the goods shall be taken for the purposes of this Act to be reduced by the amount of the discount.

21(4) Subject to subsection (6D) below, for the purposes of this Act, the value of any goods falling within subsection (5) below which are imported from a place outside the member States shall be taken to be an amount equal to 28.58 per cent of the amount which, apart from this subsection, would be their value for those purposes.

21(5) The goods that fall within this subsection are–

(a)   any work of art;

(b)   any antique, not falling within paragraph (a) above or (c) below, that is more than one hundred years old;

(c)   any collection or collector's piece that is of zoological, botanical, mineralogical, anatomical, historical, archaeological, palaeontological, ethnographic, numismatic or philatelic interest.

21(6) In this section **"work of art"** means, subject to subsections (6A) and (6B) below–

(a)   any mounted or unmounted painting, drawing, collage, decorative plaque or similar picture that was executed by hand;

(b)   any original engraving, lithograph or other print which–

      (i) was produced from one or more plates executed by hand by an individual who executed them without using any mechanical or photomechanical process; and

      (ii) either is the only one produced from the plate or plates or is comprised in a limited edition;

(c)   any original sculpture or statuary, in any material;

(d)   any sculpture cast which–

      (i) was produced by or under the supervision of the individual who made the mould or became entitled to it by succession on the death of that individual; and

      (ii) either is the only cast produced from the mould or is comprised in a limited edition;

(e)   any tapestry or hanging which–

      (i) was made by hand from an original design; and

      (ii) either is the only one made from the design or is comprised in a limited edition;

(f)   any ceramic executed by an individual and signed by him;

(g)   any enamel on copper which–

      (i) was executed by hand;

      (ii) is signed either by the person who executed it or by someone on behalf of the studio where it was executed;

      (iii) either is the only one made from the design in question or is comprised in a limited edition; and

      (iv) is not comprised in an article of jewellery or an article of a kind produced by goldsmiths or silversmiths;

(h)   any mounted or unmounted photograph which–

      (i) was printed by or under the supervision of the photographer;

      (ii) is signed by him; and

      (iii) either is the only print made from the exposure in question or is comprised in a limited edition;

21(6A) The following do not fall within subsection (5) above by virtue of subsection (6)(a) above, that is to say–

(a)   any technical drawing, map or plan;

(b)   any picture comprised in a manufactured article that has been hand-decorated; or

(c)   anything in the nature of scenery, including a backcloth.

21(6B)   An item comprised in a limited edition shall be taken to be so comprised for the purposes of subsection (6)(d) to (h) above only if–

(a)   in the case of sculpture casts–

        (i) the edition is limited so that the number produced from the same mould does not exceed eight; or

        (ii) the edition comprises a limited edition of nine or more casts made before 1st January 1989 which the Commissioners have directed should be treated, in the exceptional circumstances of the case, as a limited edition for the purposes of subsection (6)(d) above;

(b)   in the case of tapestries and hangings, the edition is limited so that the number produced from the same design does not exceed eight;

(c)   in the case of enamels on copper–

        (i) the edition is limited so that the number produced from the same design does not exceed eight; and

        (ii) each of the enamels in the edition is numbered and is signed as mentioned in subsection (6)(g)(ii) above;

(d)   in the case of photographs–

        (i) the edition is limited so that the number produced from the same exposure does not exceed thirty; and

        (ii) each of the prints in the edition is numbered and is signed as mentioned in subsection (6)(h)(ii) above.

21(6C)   For the purposes of this section a collector's piece is of **philatelic interest** if–

(a)   it is a postage or revenue stamp, a postmark, a first-day cover or an item of pre-stamped stationary; and

(b)   it is franked or (if unfranked) it is not legal tender and is not intended for use as such.

21(6D)   Subsection (4) above does not apply in the case of any goods imported from outside the member States if–

(a)   the whole of the VAT chargeable on their importation falls to be relieved by virtue of an order under section 37(1); or

(b)   they were exported from the United Kingdom during the period of twelve months ending with the date of their importation.

21(7)   An order under section 2(2) may contain provision making such alteration of the percentage for the time being specified in subsection (4) above as the Treasury consider appropriate in consequence of any increase or decrease by that order of the rate of VAT.

History – In s. 21(1), the words "to (4)" were substituted for the words "and (3)" by FA 1995, s. 22(1), in relation to goods imported at any time on or after 1 May 1995.

S. 21(2)(b) and (c) were substituted for former s. 21(2)(b) by FA 1996, s. 27(3), in relation to goods imported on or after 1 January 1996. Former s. 21(2)(b) reads as follows:

"(b)   all costs by way of commission, packing, transport and insurance up to the port or place of importation."

S. 21(4)–(7) were inserted by FA 1995, s. 22(1), in relation to goods imported at any time on or after 1 May 1995.

In s. 21(4), the words "Subject to subsection (6D) below," were inserted by FA 1999, s. 12(1)(a), with effect in relation to goods imported at any time on or after 27 July 1999.

In s. 21(4), the words "28.58 per cent" were substituted for the words "14.29 per cent" by FA 1999, s. 12(1)(b), with effect in relation to goods imported at any time on or after 27 July 1999.

S. 21(5) – (6D) were substituted for the former s. 21(5) and (6) by FA 1999, s. 12(2), with effect in relation to goods imported at any time on or after 27 July 1999. Former s. 21(5) and (6) read as follows:

"(5)   The goods which fall within this subsection are–

  (a)   any work of art which was obtained by any person before 1st April 1973 otherwise than by his producing it himself or by succession on the death of the person who produced it;

  (b)   any work of art which was–

  (i)   exported from the United Kingdom before 1st April 1973,

  (ii)   exported from the United Kingdom on or after that date and before 1st January 1993 by a person who, had he supplied it in the United Kingdom at the date when it was exported, would not have had to account for VAT on the full value of the supply, or

  (iii)   exported from the United Kingdom on or after 1st January 1993 by such a person to a place which, at the time, was *outside the member States, being, in each case,* a work of art which has not been imported between the time when it was exported and the importation in question;

  (c)   any antique more than one hundred years old, being neither a work of art nor pearls or loose gem stones; and

  (d)   collectors' pieces of zoological, botanical, mineralogical, anatomical, historical, archaeological, paleontological or ethnographic interest.

(6)   In this section **"work of art"** means goods falling within any of the following descriptions, that is to say–

  (a)   paintings, drawings and pastels executed by hand but not comprised in manufactured articles that have been hand-painted or hand-decorated;

(b)   original engravings, lithographs and other prints;
(c)   original sculptures and statuary, in any material."

Derivations – S. 21(1), (2): VATA 1983, s. 11(1), (2), as amended by F(No. 2)A 1992, s. 14 and Sch. 3, para. 14.
S. 21(3): VATA 1983, s. 11(2A), as inserted by F(No. 2)A 1992, s. 14 and Sch. 3, para. 14.

Cross references – VAT (Input Tax) Order (SI 1992/3222), art. 2: definition of collectors' items.
VAT (Input Tax) Order (SI 1992/3222), art. 2: definition of work of art.
VAT (Special Provisions) Order (SI 1995/1268), art. 2: definition of collectors' items.
VAT (Special Provisions) Order (SI 1995/1268), art. 2: definition of work of art.
VAT Regulations 1995 (SI 1995/2518), reg. 121: adaptation of CEMA 1979, s. 125(3).

Other material – Customs and Excise News Release 20/95, 3 April 1995; concessionary delay of introduction of FA 1995 changes until 1 June 1995.

22   Value of certain goods

22   [S. 22 was omitted and repealed by FA 1996, s. 28(1) and 205 and Sch. 41, Pt. IV(2), in relation to supplies made on or after 1 January 1996.]

Derivations – VATA 1983, s. 12.

23   Gaming machines

23(1)   Where a person plays a game of chance by means of a gaming machine, then for the purposes of VAT (but without prejudice to subsection (2) below) the amount paid by him to play shall be treated as the consideration for a supply of services to him.

23(2)   The value to be taken as the value of supplies made in the circumstances mentioned in subsection (1) above in any period shall be determined as if the consideration for the supplies were reduced by an amount equal to the amount (if any) received in that period by persons (other than the person making the supply and persons acting on his behalf) playing successfully.

23(3)   The insertion of a token into a machine shall be treated for the purposes of subsection (1) above as the payment of an amount equal to that for which the token can be obtained; and the receipt of a token by a person playing successfully shall be treated for the purposes of subsection (2) above–

(a)   if the token is of a kind used to play the machine, as the receipt of an amount equal to that for which such a token can be obtained;

(b)   if the token is not of such a kind but can be exchanged for money, as the receipt of an amount equal to that for which it can be exchanged.

23(4)   In this section–

"game of chance" has the same meaning as in the Gaming Act 1968; and
"gaming machine" means a machine in respect of which the following conditions are satisfied, namely–

(a)   it is constructed or adapted for playing a game of chance by means of it; and

(b)   a player pays to play the machine (except where he has an opportunity to play payment-free as the result of having previously played successfully), either by inserting a coin or token into the machine or in some other way; and

(c)   the element of chance in the game is provided by means of the machine.

Derivations – VATA 1983, s. 13.

Cross reference – Sch. 11, para. 9: power to require opening of gaming machines.

PAYMENT OF VAT BY TAXABLE PERSONS

24   Input tax and output tax

24(1)   Subject to the following provisions of this section, **"input tax"**, in relation to a taxable person, means the following tax, that is to say–

(a)   VAT on the supply to him of any goods or services;

(b)   VAT on the acquisition by him from another member State of any goods; and

(c)   VAT paid or payable by him on the importation of any goods from a place outside the member States,

being (in each case) goods or services used or to be used for the purpose of any business carried on or to be carried on by him.

24(2)   Subject to the following provisions of this section, **"output tax"**, in relation to a taxable person, means VAT on supplies which he makes or on the acquisition by him from another member State of goods (including VAT which is also to be counted as input tax by virtue of subsection (1)(b) above).

24(3) For the purposes of subsections (1) and (2) above, where goods or services are supplied to a company, goods are acquired by a company from another member State or goods are imported by a company from a place outside the member States and the goods or services which are so supplied, acquired or imported are used or to be used in connection with the provision of accommodation by the company, they shall not be treated as used or to be used for the purposes of any business carried on by the company to the extent that the accommodation is used or to be used for domestic purposes by–

(a)   a director of the company, or

(b)   a person connected with a director of the company.

24(4) The Treasury may by order provide with respect to any description of goods or services that, where goods or services of that description are supplied to a person who is not a taxable person, they shall, in such circumstances as may be specified in the order, be treated for the purposes of subsections (1) and (2) above as supplied to such other person as may be determined in accordance with the order.

24(5) Where goods or services supplied to a taxable person, goods acquired by a taxable person from another member State or goods imported by a taxable person from a place outside the member States are used or to be used partly for the purposes of a business carried on or to be carried on by him and partly for other purposes, VAT on supplies, acquisitions and importations shall be apportioned so that only so much as is referable to his business purposes is counted as his input tax.

24(6) Regulations may provide–

(a)   for VAT on the supply of goods or services to a taxable person, VAT on the acquisition of goods by a taxable person from other member States and VAT paid or payable by a taxable person on the importation of goods from places outside the member States to be treated as his input tax only if and to the extent that the charge to VAT is evidenced and quantified by reference to such documents as may be specified in the regulations or the Commissioners may direct either generally or in particular cases or classes of cases;

(b)   for a taxable person to count as his input tax, in such circumstances, to such extent and subject to such conditions as may be prescribed, VAT on the supply to him of goods or services or on the acquisition of goods by him from another member State or paid by him on the importation of goods from places outside the member States notwithstanding that he was not a taxable person at the time of the supply, acquisition or payment;

(c)   for a taxable person that is a body corporate to count as its input tax, in such circumstances, to such extent and subject to such conditions as may be prescribed, VAT on the supply, acquisition or importation of goods before the company's incorporation for appropriation to the company or its business or on the supply of services before that time for its benefit or in connection with its incorporation;

(d)   in the case of a person who has been, but is no longer, a taxable person, for him to be paid by the Commissioners the amount of any VAT on a supply of services made to him for the purposes of the business carried on by him when he was a taxable person.

24(7) For the purposes of this section **"director"** means–

(a)   in relation to a company whose affairs are managed by a board of directors or similar body, a member of that board or similar body;

(b)   in relation to a company whose affairs are managed by a single director or similar person, that director or person;

(c)   in relation to a company whose affairs are managed by the members themselves, a member of the company,

and a person is **connected** with a director if that person is the director's wife or husband, or is a relative, or the wife or husband of a relative, of the director or of the director's wife or husband.

Derivations – S. 24(1), (2): VATA 1983, s. 14(3), as amended by F(No. 2)A 1992, s. 14 and Sch. 3, para. 15(2).
S. 24(3): VATA 1983, s. 14(3A), as inserted by FA 1990, s. 12(2) and amended by F(No. 2)A 1992, s. 14 and Sch. 3, para. 15(3).
S. 24(4): VATA 1983, s. 14(3B), as inserted by FA 1991, s. 14.
S. 24(5): VATA 1983, s. 14(4), as amended by F(No. 2)A 1992, s. 14 and Sch. 3, para. 15(4).
S. 24(6): VATA 1983, s. 14(9), as amended by F(No. 2)A 1992, s. 14 and Sch. 3, para. 15(5).
S. 24(7): VATA 1983, s. 14(11), as inserted by FA 1990, s. 12(3).

Cross references – S. 18A(4): fiscal warehousing and meaning of "connected".
S. 56(5): no apportionment of VAT by reference to fuel for private use.
S. 96(1): "input tax" and "output tax" defined.
CAA 1990, s. 159A(7): additional liabilities and rebates.
VAT (Isle of Man) Order 1982 (SI 1982/1067), art. 7: references to VAT include references to VAT chargeable under Pt. I of the Manx Act.

VAT (Tour Operators) Order 1987 (SI 1987/1806), art. 12: disallowance of input tax on goods or services acquired by tour operator for re-supply.
VAT (Input Tax) (Person Supplied) Order 1991 (SI 1991/2306), art. 3: road fuel bought by employees treated as supplied to employer.
VAT (Cars) Order 1992 (SI 1992/3122), art. 5(2)(c): self-supplies.
VAT (Input Tax) Order 1992 (SI 1992/3222), art. 7: input tax on certain motor cars excluded from credit.
VAT (Supply of Services) Order 1993 (SI 1993/1507), art. 6: non-application of that order in respect of any services unless input tax credited.
VAT Regulations 1995 (SI 1995/2518), Pt. XIV: input tax and partial exemption.
Landfill Tax Regulations 1996 (SI 1996/1527), reg. 37(2): contents of a landfill invoice.

Statutory instruments – VAT Regulations 1995 (SI 1995/2518, as amended by SI 1997/1086).

Official publications – 700/64: motor expenses.
700/65: business entertainment.
Customs Internal Guidance Manual, vol. V1.13: input tax.
Customs Internal Guidance Manual, vol. V1.15: partial exemption.

Other material – Customs and Excise News Release 3/94, 29 November 1994: relaxation of conditions for input tax recovery on cars.

Notes – S. 60(2)(b): penalty for VAT evasion.
S. 63 and 64: misdeclaration penalties.
S. 79(1)(a): repayment supplement.
S. 83(c): appeal with respect to the amount of any input tax which may be credited.
VAT Regulations 1995 (SI 1995/2518), reg. 65(2): input tax credit.

25   Payment by reference to accounting periods and credit for input tax against output tax

25(1)   A taxable person shall–

(a)   in respect of supplies made by him, and

(b)   in respect of the acquisition by him from other member States of any goods,

account for and pay VAT by reference to such periods (in this Act referred to as **"prescribed accounting periods"**) at such time and in such manner as may be determined by or under regulations and regulations may make different provision for different circumstances.

25(2)   Subject to the provisions of this section, he is entitled at the end of each prescribed accounting period to credit for so much of his input tax as is allowable under section 26, and then to deduct that amount from any output tax that is due from him.

25(3)   If either no output tax is due at the end of the period, or the amount of the credit exceeds that of the output tax then, subject to subsections (4) and (5) below, the amount of the credit or, as the case may be, the amount of the excess shall be paid to the taxable person by the Commissioners; and an amount which is due under this subsection is referred to in this Act as a **"VAT credit"**.

25(4)   The whole or any part of the credit may, subject to and in accordance with regulations, be held over to be credited in and for a subsequent period; and the regulations may allow for it to be so held over either on the taxable person's own application or in accordance with general or special directions given by the Commissioners from time to time.

25(5)   Where at the end of any period a VAT credit is due to a taxable person who has failed to submit returns for any earlier period as required by this Act, the Commissioners may withhold payment of the credit until he has complied with that requirement.

25(6)   A deduction under subsection (2) above and payment of a VAT credit shall not be made or paid except on a claim made in such manner and at such time as may be determined by or under regulations; and, in the case of a person who has made no taxable supplies in the period concerned or any previous period, payment of a VAT credit shall be made subject to such conditions (if any) as the Commissioners think fit to impose, including conditions as to repayment in specified circumstances.

25(7)   The Treasury may by order provide, in relation to such supplies, acquisitions and importations as the order may specify, that VAT charged on them is to be excluded from any credit under this section; and–

(a)   any such provision may be framed by reference to the description of goods or services supplied or goods acquired or imported, the person by whom they are supplied, acquired or imported or to whom they are supplied, the purposes for which they are supplied, acquired or imported, or any circumstances whatsoever; and

(b)   such an order may contain provision for consequential relief from output tax.

Derivations – S. 25(1), (2): VATA 1983, s. 14(1), (2), as amended by F(No. 2)A 1992, s. 14 and Sch. 3, para. 15(1).
S. 25(3)–(6): VATA 1983, s. 14(5)–(8).
S. 25(7): VATA 1983, s. 14(10), as amended by F(No. 2)A 1992, s. 14 and Sch. 3, para. 15(6).

Cross references – S. 32(5): relief for supply of certain second-hand goods.

S. 33(6): VAT excluded from credit under s. 25(7).
S. 34: capital goods.
S. 53: tour operators.
S. 54: farmers etc.
S. 69(5): breaches of regulatory regulations.
S. 78(1)(b): interest in certain cases of official error.
S. 79(5)(a): repayment supplement.
S. 81: interest by way of credit.
S. 96(1): "prescribed accounting period" and "VAT credit" defined.
Sch. 4, para. 5: supply of goods or services.
Sch. 6, para. 1: supply at market value.
Sch. 7, para. 1(1)(d): acquisitions from other member states.
FA 1997, s. 47(8): entitlement to a repayment under VATA 1994, s. 80.
FA 1997, s. 49(6): transitional provision for set-offs, etc.
VAT (Tour Operators) Order 1987 (SI 1987/1806), art. 12: disallowance of input tax on goods or services acquired by tour operator for re-supply.
VAT (Cars) Order 1992 (SI 1992/3122): art. 4(1) and 5: treatment of transaction as non-supply or self-supply.
VAT (Special Provisions) Order 1995 (SI 1995/2518), art. 11(2): self-supply.
VAT (Supply of Services) Order 1993 (SI 1993/1507), art. 6: non-application of that order in respect of any services unless input tax credited.
VAT Regulations 1995 (SI 1995/2518), reg. 6(3): transfer of a going concern.
VAT Regulations 1995 (SI 1995/2518), reg. 20: inapplicable invoicing requirements.
VAT Regulations 1995 (SI 1995/2518), reg. 29: claims for input tax made on return and necessary documentary evidence.
VAT Regulations 1995 (SI 1995/2518), reg. 34: correction of returns.
VAT Regulations 1995 (SI 1995/2518), reg. 49: prescribed accounting period and annual accounting.
VAT Regulations 1995 (SI 1995/2518), reg. 101(3)(c): exclusion from partial exemption calculation of supply of goods where VAT is not charged by an order made under s. 14(10).
VAT Regulations 1995 (SI 1995/2518), reg. 177(1): non-repayable VAT to Community traders.
VAT Regulations 1995 (SI 1995/2518), reg. 190(1): non-repayable VAT to third country traders.
VAT Regulations 1995 (SI 1995/2518), reg. 198: computation of repayment supplement.
VAT Regulations 1995 (SI 1995/2518), reg. 209(1): reclaim of farmers' flat-rate addition.
Statutory instruments – VAT (Input Tax) Order 1992 (SI 1992/3222 as amended by SI 1995/281, SI 1995/1267, SI 1995/1666, SI 1998/2767, SI 1999/2930, SI 1999/3118).
VAT Regulations 1995 (SI 1995/2518, as amended by SI 1996/542, SI 1996/1198, SI 1997/1086, SI 1997/1614, SI 2000/258, SI 2000/794).
Extra-statutory concessions – 3.13 (Notice 48 (1999 edn)): repayment of import VAT to shipping agents/freight forwarders.
Other material – Customs and Excise Press Notice 761, 20 September 1982: input tax recovery where goods received from fraudulent supplier.
Customs and Excise Press Notice 1148, 28 October 1986 (not reproduced): where input tax is apportioned between business and non-business activities (s. 14(4)) and the income-based method of apportionment is used the figure of total income should generally include any grants and donations.
Form VAT 426 Insolvent traders: claim for input tax after deregistration.
Form VAT 427(A) Claim for input tax on goods and services supplied before cancellation of registration.
Form VAT 427(B) Claim for relief from VAT on certain services supplied after cancellation of registration.
Form VAT 427(C) Claim for relief from VAT on bad debts identified after cancellation of registration.
Form VAT 435 (1993) VAT refunds for entitled EC residents, and crews of ships and aircraft, exporting goods from the EC.
Notes – VAT Regulations 1995 (SI 1995/2518), reg. 6: obligation to furnish a return or account for VAT where registration number is transferred.

26   Input tax allowable under section 25

26(1)   The amount of input tax for which a taxable person is entitled to credit at the end of any period shall be so much of the input tax for the period (that is input tax on supplies, acquisitions and importations in the period) as is allowable by or under regulations as being attributable to supplies within subsection (2) below.

26(2)   The supplies within this subsection are the following supplies made or to be made by the taxable person in the course or furtherance of his business–

(a)   taxable supplies;

(b)   supplies outside the United Kingdom which would be taxable supplies if made in the United Kingdom;

(c)   such other supplies outside the United Kingdom and such exempt supplies as the Treasury may by order specify for the purposes of this subsection.

26(3)   The Commissioners shall make regulations for securing a fair and reasonable attribution of input tax to supplies within subsection (2) above, and any such regulations may provide for–

(a)   determining a proportion by reference to which input tax for any prescribed accounting period is to be provisionally attributed to those supplies;

(b)   adjusting, in accordance with a proportion determined in like manner for any longer period comprising two or more prescribed accounting periods or parts thereof, the provisional attribution for any of those periods;

(c)   the making of payments in respect of input tax, by the Commissioners to a taxable person (or a person who has been a taxable person) or by a taxable person (or a person who has been a taxable person) to the Commissioners, in cases where events prove inaccurate an estimate on the basis of which an attribution was made; and

(d) preventing input tax on a supply which, under or by virtue of any provision of this Act, a person makes to himself from being allowable as attributable to that supply.

26(4) Regulations under subsection (3) above may make different provision for different circumstances and, in particular (but without prejudice to the generality of that subsection) for different descriptions of goods or services; and may contain such incidental and supplementary provisions as appear to the Commissioners necessary or expedient.

Derivations – S. 26(1)–(3): VATA 1983, s. 15(1)–(3), as substituted by FA 1987, s. 12(1), and as amended by FA 1989, s. 26, and by F(No. 2)A 1992, s. 14 and Sch. 3, para. 16.
S. 26(4): VATA 1983, s. 15(4).

Cross references – S. 8(3): ignore self-supplies for s. 26(1) purposes of VAT recovery.
S. 33: refunds.
S. 43(2C)(a): group supplies using an overseas member.
S. 44: supplies to groups.
S. 54: farmers etc.
S. 83(e), 84(4): appeals to tribunals.
Sch. 1, para. 10(2)(b): voluntary registration.
Sch. 4, para. 5: supply of goods or services.
Sch. 6, para. 1: supply at market value.
Sch. 7, para. 1(1)(d): acquisitions from other member states.
Sch. 9, Grp. 14, Note (4): supplies where input tax cannot be recovered.
Sch. 10, para. 2(3AAA)(a)(ii) and 3A(7): election to waive exemption and anti-avoidance.
Sch. 10, para. 3A: grants of land to connected persons who are not fully taxable.
FA 1999, s. 13(1): supplies of gold.
VAT (Tour Operators) Order 1987 (SI 1987/1806), art. 12: disallowance of input tax on goods or services acquired by tour operator for re-supply.
VAT (Cars) Order 1992 (SI 1992/3122), art. 5(2): self-supplies.
VAT (Supply of Services) Order 1993 (SI 1993/1507), art. 6: non-application unless input tax credited under s. 25 or 26.
VAT (Special Provisions) Order 1995 (SI 1995/1268), art. 11(2): self-supply.
VAT Regulations 1995 (SI 1995/2518), reg. 32(4): tax allowable portion in VAT account.
VAT Regulations 1995 (SI 1995/2518), reg. 99(1): partial exemption and supplies specified in an order under s. 26(2)(c).
VAT Regulations 1995 (SI 1995/2518), reg. 103(1): attribution of input tax to supplies specified in an order under s. 26(2)(c).
VAT Regulations 1995 (SI 1995/2518), reg. 105(5): treatment of input tax attributable to exempt supplies as being attributable to taxable supplies.
VAT Regulations 1995 (SI 1995/2518), reg. 209(1): reclaim of farmers' flat-rate addition.
VAT (Input Tax) (Specified Supplies) Order 1999 (SI 1999/3121) s. 26(2)(c): supplies.

Statutory instruments – VAT Regulations 1995 (SI 1995/2518, as amended by SI 1995/3147, SI 1996/1250, SI 1997/1086, SI 1997/1614, SI 1999/599, SI 1999/3114, SI 2000/258, SI 2000/794).
VAT (Input Tax) (Specified Supplies) Order 1999 (SI 1999/3121).

Official publications – 700/56: Insolvency.

27 Goods imported for private purposes

27(1) Where goods are imported by a taxable person from a place outside the member States and–

(a) at the time of importation they belong wholly or partly to another person; and
(b) the purposes for which they are to be used include private purposes either of himself or of the other,

VAT paid or payable by the taxable person on the importation of the goods shall not be regarded as input tax to be deducted or credited under section 25; but he may make a separate claim to the Commissioners for it to be repaid.

27(2) The Commissioners shall allow the claim if they are satisfied that to disallow it would result, in effect, in a double charge to VAT; and where they allow it they shall do so only to the extent necessary to avoid the double charge.

27(3) In considering a claim under this section, the Commissioners shall have regard to the circumstances of the importation and, so far as appearing to them to be relevant, things done with, or occurring in relation to, the goods at any subsequent time.

27(4) Any amount allowed by the Commissioners on the claim shall be paid by them to the taxable person.

27(5) The reference above to a person's **private purposes** is to purposes which are not those of any business carried on by him.

Derivations – VATA 1983, s. 26, as amended by F(No. 2)A 1992, s. 14 and Sch. 3, para. 27.

Cross references – S. 83(f): appeals.
VAT (Isle of Man) Order 1982 (SI 1982/1067), art. 7: references to VAT include references to VAT chargeable under Pt. I of the Manx Act.
VAT (Isle of Man) Order 1982 (SI 1982/1067), art. 8: taxable person includes a person who is a taxable person under the Manx Act.

28 Payments on account of VAT

28(1) The Treasury may make an order under this section if they consider it desirable to do so in the interests of the national economy.

28(2) An order under this section may provide that a taxable person of a description specified in the order shall be under a duty–

(a)   to pay, on account of any VAT he may become liable to pay in respect of a prescribed accounting period, amounts determined in accordance with the order, and

(b)   to do so at such times as are so determined.

28(2AA) An order under this section may provide for the matters with respect to which an appeal under section 83 lies to a tribunal to include such decisions of the Commissioners under that or any other order under this section as may be specified in the order.

28(2A) The Commissioners may give directions, to persons who are or may become liable by virtue of any order under this section to make payments on account of VAT, about the manner in which they are to make such payments; and where such a direction has been given to any person and has not subsequently been withdrawn, any duty of that person by virtue of such an order to make such a payment shall have effect as if it included a requirement for the payment to be made in the manner directed.

28(3) Where an order is made under this section, the Commissioners may make regulations containing such supplementary, incidental or consequential provisions as appear to the Commissioners to be necessary or expedient.

28(4) A provision of an order or regulations under this section may be made in such way as the Treasury or, as the case may be, the Commissioners think fit (whether by amending provisions of or made under the enactments relating to VAT or otherwise).

28(5) An order or regulations under this section may make different provision for different circumstances.

History – S. 28(2AA) was inserted by FA 1997, s. 43, with effect from 19 March 1997.
S. 28(2A) was inserted by FA 1996, s. 34, with effect from 29 April 1996.
Derivations – VATA 1983, s. 38C, as inserted by FA 1992, s. 6.
Statutory instruments – VAT (Payments on Account) Order 1993 (SI 1993/2001, as amended by SI 1995/291, SI 1996/1196, SI 1997/2542).
VAT Regulations 1995 (SI 1995/2518, as amended by SI 1996/1198).
Official publications – 700/60: payments on account.

29   Invoices provided by recipients of goods or services

29   Where–

(a)   a taxable person (**"the recipient"**) provides a document to himself which purports to be an invoice in respect of a taxable supply of goods or services to him by another taxable person; and

(b)   that document understates the VAT chargeable on the supply,

the Commissioners may, by notice served on the recipient and on the supplier, elect that the amount of VAT understated by the document shall be regarded for all purposes as VAT due from the recipient and not from the supplier.

Derivations – FA 1988, s. 22.

PART II – RELIEFS, EXEMPTIONS AND REPAYMENTS

RELIEFS ETC. GENERALLY AVAILABLE

30   Zero-rating

30(1) Where a taxable person supplies goods or services and the supply is zero-rated, then, whether or not VAT would be chargeable on the supply apart from this section–

(a)   no VAT shall be charged on the supply; but

(b)   it shall in all other respects be treated as a taxable supply;

and accordingly the rate at which VAT is treated as charged on the supply shall be nil.

30(2) A supply of goods or services is zero-rated by virtue of this subsection if the goods or services are of a description for the time being specified in Schedule 8 or the supply is of a description for the time being so specified.

30(2A) A supply by a person of services which consist of applying a treatment or process to another person's goods is zero-rated by virtue of this subsection if by doing so he produces goods, and either–

(a)   those goods are of a description for the time being specified in Schedule 8; or

(b)   a supply by him of those goods to the person to whom he supplies the services would be of a description so specified.

30(3) Where goods of a description for the time being specified in that Schedule, or of a description forming part of a description of supply for the time being so specified, are acquired in the United Kingdom from another member State or imported from a place outside the member States, no VAT shall be chargeable on their acquisition or importation, except as otherwise provided in that Schedule.

30(4) The Treasury may by order vary Schedule 8 by adding to or deleting from it any description or by varying any description for the time being specified in it.

30(5) The export of any goods by a charity to a place outside the member States shall for the purposes of this Act be treated as a supply made by the charity–

(a)   in the United Kingdom, and

(b)   in the course or furtherance of a business carried on by the charity.

30(6) A supply of goods is zero-rated by virtue of this subsection if the Commissioners are satisfied that the person supplying the goods–

(a)   has exported them to a place outside the member States; or

(b)   has shipped them for use as stores on a voyage or flight to an eventual destination outside the United Kingdom, or as merchandise for sale by retail to persons carried on such a voyage or flight in a ship or aircraft,

and in either case if such other conditions, if any, as may be specified in regulations or the Commissioners may impose are fulfilled.

30(7) Subsection (6)(b) above shall not apply in the case of goods shipped for use as stores on a voyage or flight to be made by the person to whom the goods were supplied and to be made for a purpose which is private.

30(8) Regulations may provide for the zero-rating of supplies of goods, or of such goods as may be specified in the regulations, in cases where–

(a)   the Commissioners are satisfied that the goods have been or are to be exported to a place outside the member States or that the supply in question involves both–

      (i) the removal of the goods from the United Kingdom; and

      (ii) their acquisition in another member State by a person who is liable for VAT on the acquisition in accordance with provisions of the law of that member State corresponding, in relation to that member State, to the provisions of section 10; and

(b)   such other conditions, if any, as may be specified in the regulations or the Commissioners may impose are fulfilled.

30(8A) Regulations may provide for the zero-rating of supplies of goods, or of such goods as may be specified in regulations, in cases where–

(a)   the Commissioners are satisfied that the supply in question involves both–

      (i) the removal of the goods from a fiscal warehousing regime within the meaning of section 18F(2); and

      (ii) their being placed in a warehousing regime in another member State, or in such member State or States as may be prescribed, where that regime is established by provisions of the law of that member State corresponding, in relation to that member State, to the provisions of sections 18A and 18B; and

(b)   such other conditions, if any, as may be specified in the regulations or the Commissioners may impose are fulfilled.

30(9) Regulations may provide for the zero-rating of a supply of services which is made where goods are let on hire and the Commissioners are satisfied that the goods have been or are to be removed from the United Kingdom during the period of the letting, and such other conditions, if any, as may be specified in the regulations or the Commissioners may impose are fulfilled.

30(10) Where the supply of any goods has been zero-rated by virtue of subsection (6) above or in pursuance of regulations made under subsection (8), (8A) or (9) above and–

(a)   the goods are found in the United Kingdom after the date on which they were alleged to have
        been or were to be exported or shipped or otherwise removed from the United Kingdom; or

(b)   any condition specified in the relevant regulations under subsection (6), (8), (8A) or (9)
        above or imposed by the Commissioners is not complied with,

and the presence of the goods in the United Kingdom after that date or the non-observance of the
condition has not been authorised for the purposes of this subsection by the Commissioners, the
goods shall be liable to forfeiture under the Management Act and the VAT that would have been
chargeable on the supply but for the zero-rating shall become payable forthwith by the person to
whom the goods were supplied or by any person in whose possession the goods are found in the
United Kingdom; but the Commissioners may, if they think fit, waive payment of the whole or part
of that VAT.

History – S. 30(2A) was inserted by FA 1996, s. 29(2), with effect for supplies made on or after 1 January 1996.
S. 30(5) was substituted by FA 1995, s. 28(1), in relation to transactions occurring on or after 1 May 1995.
S. 30(8A) was added by FA 1996, s. 26 and Sch. 3, para. 7, with effect from 1 June 1996 and applies to any acquisition of goods
from another member State and any supply taking place on or after that day.
In s. 30(10), both the words "subsection (8), (8A) or (9)" were substituted and the words "subsection (6), (8), (8A) or (9)" were
substituted by FA 1996, s. 26 and Sch. 3, para. 7, with effect from 1 June 1996 and apply to any acquisition of goods from
another member State and any supply taking place on or after that day.

Derivations – S. 30(1), (2): VATA 1983, s. 16(1), (2).
S. 30(3): VATA 1983, s. 16(3), as amended by F(No. 2)A 1992, s. 14 and Sch. 3, para. 17(1).
S. 30(4): VATA 1983, s. 16(4).
S. 30(5): VATA 1983, s. 16(5).
S. 30(6): VATA 1983, s. 16(6), as amended by FA 1986, s. 12(1), and F(No. 2)A 1992, s. 14 and Sch. 3, para. 17(2).
S. 30(7): VATA 1983, s. 16(6A), as inserted by FA 1990, s. 13.
S. 30(8), (9): VATA 1983, s. 16(7), (8), as amended by F(No. 2)A 1992, s. 14 and Sch. 3, para. 17(3).
S. 30(10): VATA 1983, s. 16(9), as amended by FA 1986, s. 12(2).

Cross references – S. 84(9)(a): appeals.
S. 88(7): supplies spanning change of rate.
Sch. 8, Grp. 5, Note (13): s. 30(3) does not apply to goods forming part of a description of supply in that group (construction of
dwellings etc.).
VAT (Removal of Goods) Order 1992 (SI 1992/3111), art. 4(c): non-application of Sch. 4, para. 6.
VAT (Input Tax) Order 1992 (SI 1992/3222), art. 7(2): disallowance of input tax.
VAT Regulations 1995 (SI 1995/2518), reg. 123 and 124: temporary importations zero-rated, re-importation of certain goods by
non-taxable persons and re-importation of motor cars and works of art.
VAT Regulations 1995 (SI 1995/2518), reg. 138(2): territories to be treated as excluded from or included in the territory of the
Community and of the member states.

Statutory instruments – VAT (Tour Operators) Order 1987 (SI 1987/1806).
VAT (Transport) Order 1994 (SI 1994/3014).
VAT (Construction of Buildings) Order 1995 (SI 1995/280).
VAT (Protected Buildings) Order 1995 (SI 1995/283).
VAT (Supply of Pharmaceutical Goods) Order 1995 (SI 1995/652).
VAT (Transport) Order 1995 (SI 1995/653).
VAT Regulations 1995 (SI 1995/2518, as amended by SI 1995/3147, SI 1996/210, SI 1999/438, SI 2000/258).
VAT (Ships and Aircraft) Order 1995 (SI 1995/3039).
VAT (Tax Free Shops) Order 1995 (SI 1995/3041).
VAT (Anti-avoidance (Heating)) Order 1996 (SI 1996/1661).
VAT (Registered Social Landlords) (No. 1) Order 1997 (SI 1997/50).
VAT (Drugs, Medicines and Aids for the Handicapped) Order 1997 (SI 1997/2744).
VAT (Abolition of Zero-Rating for Tax-Free Shops) Order 1999 (SI 1999/1642).
VAT (Drugs, Medicines, Aids for the Handicapped and Charities Etc) Order 2000 (SI 2000/503).
VAT (Charities and Aids for the Handicapped) Order 2000 (SI 2000/805).
VAT (Protective Helmets) Order 2000 (SI 2000/1517).

Extra-statutory concessions – 3.14 (Notice 48 (1999 edn)): zero-rating of free-zone goods.
3.17 (Notice 48 (1999 edn)): zero-rating of supplies of training for foreign governments.
4.1 (Notice 48 (1999 edn)): zero-rating of sailaway boats.
4.2 (Notice 48 (1999 edn)): zero-rating of certain goods supplied to diplomatic missions, international organisations, NATO
Forces etc. in other EC countries.
5.1 (Notice 48 (1999 edn)): zero-rating by duty-free shops.
5.2 (Notice 48 (1999 edn)): zero-rating of marine fuel as stores for vessels.

Official publications – 703: Exports and removals of goods from the UK.
704: Retail exports.
705: Personal exports of new motor vehicles to destinations outside the EC from 1 January 1993.
705A: VAT: supplies of vehicles under the personal export scheme for removal from the European Community.
725: The single market.
728: Motor vehicles, boats, aircraft: intra-EC movements by persons not registrable for VAT.
703/1: Supply of freight containers for export or removal from the United Kingdom.
703/2: Sailaway boats supplied for export outside the European Community.
703/3: Sailaway boat scheme.
704/1: VAT refunds for travellers departing from the European Community.
704/2: Traveller's guide to the retail export scheme.
704/3: Guide to tax-free shopping – the VAT refund scheme.
Customs Internal Guidance Manual, vol. V1.16: single market.
Customs Internal Guidance Manual, vol. V1.20: general export.

Hansard – HC debates, 23 June 1992: statement made by the Paymaster General on zero-rating and the single market:
"Provided that the supplier has acted in good faith and with due prudence and provided that he holds documentary evidence that
the goods have left the UK, he will not be liable to account for VAT on the transaction if the VAT number subsequently proves
to be false. I hope that this explanation will reassure those who have been worried about this matter."

Other material – Form VAT 403 Tax-free sales of new motor vehicles for use before export.

Form VAT 407 (1993) VAT refunds for overseas visitors to the UK exporting goods from the EC.
Form VAT 410 Personal export of a new motor vehicle.
Form VAT 411 New means of transport for removal from the UK to another member state of the EC.
Form VAT 418 Personal export of a new motor vehicle – payment of VAT.
Form VAT 436 (1993) VAT-free purchase of a sailaway boat for export outside the EC.

Notes – S. 50: zero-rating of certain commodities.
S. 48(1): "ship" defined.
VAT Regulations 1995 (SI 1995/2518), reg. 136 and 137: territories to be treated as excluded from or included in the territory of the community and of the member states.

31   Exempt supplies and acquisitions

31(1)   A supply of goods or services is an exempt supply if it is of a description for the time being specified in Schedule 9 and an acquisition of goods from another member State is an exempt acquisition if the goods are acquired in pursuance of an exempt supply.

31(2)   The Treasury may by order vary that Schedule by adding to or deleting from it any description of supply or by varying any description of supply for the time being specified in it, and the Schedule may be varied so as to describe a supply of goods by reference to the use which has been made of them or to other matters unrelated to the characteristics of the goods themselves.

Derivations – VATA 1983, s. 17, as amended by F(No. 2)A 1992, s. 14 and Sch. 3, para. 18.

Cross references – FA 1999, s. 13(2): supplies of gold.

Statutory instruments – VAT (Education) (No. 2) Order 1994 (SI 1994/2969).
VAT (Land) Order 1995 (SI 1995/282).
VAT (Cultural Services) Order 1996 (SI 1996/1256).
VAT (Pharmaceutical Chemists) Order 1996 (SI 1996/2949).
VAT (Finance) Order 1997 (SI 1997/510).
VAT (Sport, Sports Competitions and Physical Education) Order 1998 (SI 1998/764).
VAT (Osteopaths) Order 1998 (SI 1998/1294).
VAT (Finance) Order 1999 (SI 1999/594).
VAT (Chiropractors) Order 1999 (SI 1999/1575).
VAT (Sport, Sports Competitions and Physical Education) Order 1999 (SI 1999/1994).
VAT (Supplies of Goods where Input Tax cannot be recovered) Order 1999 (SI 1999/2833).
VAT (Subscriptions to Trade Unions, Professional and Other Public Interest Bodies) Order 1999 (SI 1999/2834).
VAT (Investment Gold) Order 1999 (SI 1999/3116).
VAT (Fund-Raising Events by Charities and Other Qualifying Bodies) Order 2000 (SI 2000/802).

Notes – S. 88: supplies spanning change of rate, etc.

32   Relief on supply of certain second-hand goods

32   [Repealed by FA 1995, s. 24(2) and 162 and Sch. 29, Pt. VI(3), operative from 1 June 1995 (SI 1995/1374 (C 28)).]

History – Former s. 32 is reproduced below:
"**32(1)**   The Treasury may by order make provision for securing a reduction of the VAT chargeable on the supply of goods of such descriptions as may be specified in the order in cases where no VAT was chargeable on a previous supply of the goods and such other conditions are satisfied as may be specified in the order or as may be imposed by the Commissioners in pursuance of the order.
32(2)   The amount of the reduction that may be secured by an order under this section shall not exceed the amount of VAT that would have been chargeable on the previous supply had VAT been chargeable on it at the same rate as that at which the VAT to be reduced would be chargeable but for the reduction.
32(3)   An order under this section making provision for reducing the VAT chargeable on the supply of goods of any description may include provision–
  (a)   for giving relief from the VAT chargeable on the acquisition of goods of that description from another member State or the importation of goods of that description from a place outside the member States; and
  (b)   for securing the like reduction where no VAT was chargeable on the acquisition of goods of that description from another member State or the importation of goods of that description from a place outside the member States as where no VAT was chargeable on a previous supply of the goods.
32(4)   An order under this section may extend to cases where the previous supply or the acquisition or importation took place before VAT was chargeable on any supply, acquisition or importation.
32(5)   The preceding provisions of this section shall, with the necessary modifications, apply in relation to cases where consequential relief from VAT was given on a previous supply by an order under section 25(7) but the relief did not extend to the whole amount of the VAT.
32(6)   An order under this section may make different provision for goods of different descriptions and for different circumstances.
32(7)   In this section references to **a supply on which no VAT was chargeable** include references to a transaction treated by virtue of an order under section 5(3) as neither a supply of goods nor a supply of services."

Derivations – VATA 1983, s. 18, as amended by F(No. 2)A 1992, s. 14 and Sch. 3, para. 19.

Cross references – VAT (Isle of Man) Order 1982 (SI 1982/1067), art. 7: references to VAT include references to VAT chargeable under Pt. I of the Manx Act.
VAT (Input Tax) Order 1992 (SI 1992/3222), art. 4(3): disallowance of input tax.
VAT Regulations 1995 (SI 1995/2518), reg. 20: non-application of certain invoicing requirements.

Statutory instruments – VAT (Cars) Order 1992 (SI 1992/3122).

Official publications – 718.

33   Refunds of VAT in certain cases

33(1)   Subject to the following provisions of this section, where–

(a)   VAT is chargeable on the supply of goods or services to a body to which this section applies, on the acquisition of any goods by such a body from another member State or on the importation of any goods by such a body from a place outside the member States, and

(b)   the supply, acquisition or importation is not for the purpose of any business carried on by the body,

the Commissioners shall, on a claim made by the body at such time and in such form and manner as the Commissioners may determine, refund to it the amount of the VAT so chargeable.

33(2)   Where goods or services so supplied to or acquired or imported by the body cannot be conveniently distinguished from goods or services supplied to or acquired or imported by it for the purpose of a business carried on by it, the amount to be refunded under this section shall be such amount as remains after deducting from the whole of the VAT chargeable on any supply to or acquisition or importation by the body such proportion thereof as appears to the Commissioners to be attributable to the carrying on of the business; but where–

(a)   the VAT so attributable is or includes VAT attributable, in accordance with regulations under section 26, to exempt supplies by the body, and

(b)   the VAT attributable to the exempt supplies is in the opinion of the Commissioners an insignificant proportion of the VAT so chargeable,

they may include it in the VAT refunded under this section.

33(3)   The bodies to which this section applies are–

(a)   a local authority;

(b)   a river purification board established under section 135 of the Local Government (Scotland) Act 1973, and a water development board within the meaning of section 109 of the Water (Scotland) Act 1980;

(c)   an internal drainage board;

(d)   a passenger transport authority or executive within the meaning of Part II of the Transport Act 1968;

(e)   a port health authority within the meaning of the Public Health (Control of Disease) Act 1984, and a port local authority and joint port local authority constituted under Part X of the Public Health (Scotland) Act 1897;

(f)   a police authority and the Receiver for the Metropolitan Police District;

(g)   a development corporation within the meaning of the New Towns Act 1981 or the New Towns (Scotland) Act 1968, a new town commission within the meaning of the New Towns Act (Northern Ireland) 1965 and the Commission for the New Towns;

(h)   a general lighthouse authority within the meaning of Part VIII of the Merchant Shipping Act 1995;

(i)   the British Broadcasting Corporation;

(j)   a nominated news provider, as defined by section 31(3) of the Broadcasting Act 1990; and

(k)   any body specified for the purposes of this section by an order made by the Treasury.

33(4)   No VAT shall be refunded under this section to a general lighthouse authority which in the opinion of the Commissioners is attributable to activities other than those concerned with the provision, maintenance or management of lights or other navigational aids.

33(5)   No VAT shall be refunded under this section to a nominated news provider which in the opinion of the Commissioners is attributable to activities other than the provision of news programmes for broadcasting by holders of regional Channel 3 licences (within the meaning of Part I of the Broadcasting Act 1990).

33(6)   References in this section to **VAT chargeable** do not include any VAT which, by virtue of any order under section 25(7), is excluded from credit under that section.

Prospective repeal – In s. 33(3)(f) at the end, the words "and the Receiver for the Metropolitan Police District" are to be repealed by Greater London Authority Act 1999, s. 423 and Sch. 27, para. 68 and Sch. 34, Pt. VII, with effect from a day to be appointed.

History – In s. 33(3)(h), the words "Part VIII of the Merchant Shipping Act 1995" were substituted by Merchant Shipping Act 1995, s. 314(2) and Sch. 13, para. 95, with effect from 1 January 1996.

Derivations – S. 33(1), (2): VATA 1983, s. 20(1), (2), as amended by F(No. 2)A 1992, s. 14 and Sch. 3, para. 21.
S. 33(3): VATA 1983, s. 20(3) and para. (j), as substituted by the Broadcasting Act 1990, s. 203(1) and Sch. 20, para. 37.
S. 33(4): VATA 1983, s. 20(4).
S. 33(5): VATA 1983, s. 20(4A), as inserted by the Broadcasting Act 1990, s. 203(1) and Sch. 20, para. 37.
S. 33(6): VATA 1983, s. 20(5).

Cross references – S. 63(9): misdeclaration penalty.
S. 79: repayment supplement.
S. 90(3): input tax repaid due to a restoration of a lower rate.
Sch. 9, Grp. 14, Note (9): supplies where input tax cannot be recovered.

Sch. 10, para. 3A: election to tax and use of land for ineligible purposes.
VAT (Isle of Man) Order 1982 (SI 1982/1067), art. 7: references to VAT include references to VAT chargeable under Pt. I of the Manx Act.

Official publications – 749.

Other material – Form VAT 126.

Notes – The following bodies have been specified by a Treasury Order:

• Anglian Water Authority	SI 1973/2121
• Authorities established under Local Government Act 1985, s. 10	SI 1986/532
• Broads Authority	SI 1999/2076
• Charter Trustees constituted by Local Government Act 1972, s. 246(4) or (5)	SI 1986/336
• Charter Trustees established by an order made under Local Government Act 1972, s. 17	SI 1997/2558
• Commission for Local Administration in England	SI 1976/2028
• Commission for Local Administration in Wales	SI 1976/2028
• Commission for Local Authority Accounts in Scotland	SI 1976/2028
• Commission for Local Administration in Scotland	SI 1976/2028
• Environment Agency	SI 1995/1978
• Fire authority constituted by a combination scheme made under Fire Services Act 1947, s. 6	SI 1995/2999
• Greater London Authority	SI 2000/1046
• Inner London Education Authority	SI 1985/1101
• Inner London Interim Education Authority	SI 1985/1101
• London Fire and Civil Defence Authority	SI 1985/1101
• London Fire and Emergency Planning Authority	SI 2000/1517
• London Residuary Body	SI 1985/1101
• Magistrates' courts committee established under Justices of the Peace Act 1979, s. 19	SI 1986/336
• Metropolitan county Fire and Civil Defence Authority	SI 1985/1101
• Metropolitan county Passenger Transport Authority	SI 1985/1101
• Metropolitan county Police Authority	SI 1985/1101
• Metropolitan county Residuary Body	SI 1985/1101
• National Park authority within the meaning of Environment Act 1995, s. 63	SI 1995/2999
• National Rivers Authority	SI 1989/1217
• North West Water Authority	SI 1973/2121
• Northumbria Interim Police Authority	SI 1985/1101
• Northumbrian Water Authority	SI 1973/2121
• Probation committee constituted by Powers of Criminal Courts Act 1973, s. 47(1) and Sch. 3, para. 2	SI 1986/336
• Severn-Trent Water Authority	SI 1973/2121
• South West Water Authority	SI 1973/2121
• Southern Water Authority	SI 1973/2121
• Thames Water Authority	SI 1973/2121
• Waste regulation and disposal bodies established under Local Government Act 1985, s. 10	
• Welsh National Water Authority	SI 1973/2121
• Wessex Water Authority	SI 1973/2121
• Yorkshire Water Authority	SI 1973/2121

34   Capital goods

34(1) The Treasury may by order make provision for the giving of relief, in such cases, to such extent and subject to such exceptions as may be specified in the order, from VAT paid on the supply, acquisition or importation for the purpose of a business carried on by any person of machinery or plant or any specified description of machinery or plant in cases where that VAT or part of that VAT cannot be credited under section 25 and such other conditions are satisfied as may be specified in the order.

34(2) Without prejudice to the generality of subsection (1) above, an order under this section may provide for relief to be given by deduction or refunding of VAT and for aggregating or excluding the aggregation of value where goods of the same description are supplied, acquired or imported together.

Derivations – VATA 1983, s. 36, as amended by F(No. 2)A 1992, s. 14 and Sch. 3, para. 36.

35   Refund of VAT to persons constructing certain buildings

35(1) Where–

(a)   a person carries out works to which this section applies,

(b)   his carrying out of the works is lawful and otherwise than in the course or furtherance of any business, and

(c)   VAT is chargeable on the supply, acquisition or importation of any goods used by him for the purposes of the works,

the Commissioners shall, on a claim made in that behalf, refund to that person the amount of VAT so chargeable.

35(1A) The works to which this section applies are–

(a)   the construction of a building designed as a dwelling or number of dwellings;

(b)   the construction of a building for use solely for a relevant residential purpose or relevant charitable purpose; and

(c) a residential conversion.

35(1B) For the purposes of this section goods shall be treated **as used for the purposes** of works to which this section applies by the person carrying out the works in so far only as they are building materials which, in the course of the works, are incorporated in the building in question or its site.

35(1C) Where–

(a) a person (**"the relevant person"**) carries out a residential conversion by arranging for any of the work of the conversion to be done by another (**"a contractor"**),

(b) the relevant person's carrying out of the conversion is lawful and otherwise than in the course or furtherance of any business,

(c) the contractor is not acting as an architect, surveyor or consultant or in a supervisory capacity, and

(d) VAT is chargeable on services consisting in the work done by the contractor,

the Commissioners shall, on a claim made in that behalf, refund to the relevant person the amount of VAT so chargeable.

35(1D) For the purposes of this section works constitute a **residential conversion** to the extent that they consist in the conversion of a non-residential building, or a non-residential part of a building, into–

(a) a building designed as a dwelling or a number of dwellings;

(b) a building intended for use solely for a relevant residential purpose; or

(c) anything which would fall within paragraph (a) or (b) above if different parts of a building were treated as separate buildings.

35(2) The Commissioners shall not be required to entertain a claim for a refund of VAT under this section unless the claim–

(a) is made within such time and in such form and manner, and

(b) contains such information, and

(c) is accompanied by such documents, whether by way of evidence or otherwise, as the Commissioners may by regulations prescribe or, in the case of documents,

as the Commissioners may determine in accordance with the regulations.

35(3) This section shall have effect–

(a) as if the reference in subsection (1) above to the **VAT chargeable on the supply of any goods** included a reference to VAT chargeable on the supply in accordance with the law of another member State; and

(b) in relation to VAT chargeable in accordance with the law of another member State, as if references to **refunding VAT to any person** were references to paying that person an amount equal to the VAT chargeable in accordance with the law of that member State;

and the provisions of this Act and of any other enactment or subordinate legislation (whenever passed or made) so far as they relate to a refund under this section shall be construed accordingly.

35(4) The notes to Group 5 of Schedule 8 shall apply for construing this section as they apply for construing that Group.

35(5) The power of the Treasury by order under section 30 to vary Schedule 8 shall include–

(a) power to apply any variation made by the order for the purposes of this section; and

(b) power to make such consequential modifications of this section as they may think fit.

History – S. 35(1)–(1D) were substituted for former s. 35(1) by FA 1996, s. 30(1), in relation to any case in which a claim for repayment under s. 35 is made on or after 29 April 1996.
In former s. 35(1), the word "building" was substituted in each place where it occurred by FA 1995, s. 33(2), with effect as if s. 35(1) had been originally enacted with this substitution.
In s. 35(2), the words "or, in the case of documents, as the Commissioners may determine in accordance with the regulations" were inserted by FA 1996, s. 30(2), in relation to any case in which a claim for repayment under s. 35 is made on or after 29 April 1996.
S. 35(4) and (5) were inserted by FA 1996, s. 30(3), in relation to any case in which a claim for repayment under s. 35 is made on or after 29 April 1996.

Derivations – S. 35(1) and (2) (as originally enacted): VATA 1983, s. 21(1) and (2), as substituted by FA 1989, s. 18 and Sch. 3, para. 5, and as amended by F(No. 2)A 1992, s. 14 and Sch. 3, para. 23(1).
S. 35(3) (as originally enacted): VATA 1983, s. 21(2A), as inserted by F(No. 2)A 1992, s. 14 and Sch. 3, para. 23(2).

Cross references – S. 60(2)(c): penalties.
S. 72(2): evasion of VAT.
S. 83(g): appeals.
S. 90(3): input tax repaid following a restoration of a lower rate.
VAT (Isle of Man) Order 1982 (SI 1982/1067), art. 7: references to VAT include references to VAT chargeable under Pt. I of the Manx Act.
VAT (Isle of Man) Order 1982 (SI 1982/1067), art. 9: s. 35 does not apply to the construction of dwellings within the Isle of Man.

VAT Regulations 1995 (SI 1995/2518), reg. 200 and 201.

Statutory instruments – VAT Regulations 1995 (SI 1995/2518).

Extra-statutory concessions – Customs and Excise News Release 15/96, 13 March 1996 (not reproduced): commissioners may refund VAT where a charity is in business and converts a certain type of property to a dwelling, if for example it is stopped by legal constraints from selling the converted property.

Official publications – 719: VAT refunds for "do-it-yourself" builders and converters.

Other material – Form SHP2: questionnaire – self-build/self-help.
Form VAT 431.

36   Bad debts

36(1)   Subsection (2) below applies where–

(a)   a person has supplied goods or services and has accounted for and paid VAT on the supply,

(b)   the whole or any part of the consideration for the supply has been written off in his accounts as a bad debt, and

(c)   a period of 6 months (beginning with the date of the supply) has elapsed.

36(2)   Subject to the following provisions of this section and to regulations under it the person shall be entitled, on making a claim to the Commissioners, to a refund of the amount of VAT chargeable by reference to the outstanding amount.

36(3)   In subsection (2) above **"the outstanding amount"** means–

(a)   if at the time of the claim no part of the consideration written off in the claimant's accounts as a bad debt has been received, an amount equal to the amount of the consideration so written off;

(b)   if at that time any part of the consideration so written off has been received, an amount by which that part is exceeded by the amount of the consideration written off;

and in this subsection **"received"** means received either by the claimant or by a person to whom has been assigned a right to receive the whole or any part of the consideration written off.

36(3A)   For the purposes of this section, where the whole or any part of the consideration for the supply does not consist of money, the amount in money that shall be taken to represent any non-monetary part of the consideration shall be so much of the amount made up of–

(a)   the value of the supply, and

(b)   the VAT charged on the supply,

as is attributable to the non-monetary consideration in question.

36(4)   A person shall not be entitled to a refund under subsection (2) above unless–

(a)   the value of the supply is equal to or less than its open market value.

(b)   [Repealed by FA 1997, s. 39(1) and 113 and Sch. 18, Pt. IV(3).]

36(4A)   Where–

(a)   a person is entitled under subsection (2) above to be refunded an amount of VAT, and

(b)   that VAT has at any time been included in the input tax of another person,

that other person shall be taken, as from the time when the claim for the refund is made, not to have been entitled to any credit for input tax in respect of the VAT that has to be refunded on that claim.

36(5)   Regulations under this section may–

(a)   require a claim to be made at such time and in such form and manner as may be specified by or under the regulations;

(b)   require a claim to be evidenced and quantified by reference to such records and other documents as may be so specified;

(c)   require the claimant to keep, for such period and in such form and manner as may be so specified, those records and documents and a record of such information relating to the claim and to anything subsequently received by way of consideration as may be so specified;

(d)   require the repayment of a refund allowed under this section where any requirement of the regulations is not complied with;

(e)   require the repayment of the whole or, as the case may be, an appropriate part of a refund allowed under this section where any part (or further part) of the consideration written off in the claimant's accounts as a bad debt is subsequently received either by the claimant or, except in such circumstances as may be prescribed, by a person to whom has been assigned a right to receive the whole or any part of that consideration;

(ea)   make provision, where there is a repayment by virtue of paragraph (e) above, for restoring the whole or any part of an entitlement to credit for input tax;

(f)   include such supplementary, incidental, consequential or transitional provisions as appear to the Commissioners to be necessary or expedient for the purposes of this section;

(g)   make different provision for different circumstances.

36(6)   The provisions which may be included in regulations by virtue of subsection (5)(f) above may include rules for ascertaining–

(a)   whether, when and to what extent consideration is to be taken to have been written off in accounts as a bad debt;

(b)   whether anything received is to be taken as received by way of consideration for a particular supply;

(c)   whether, and to what extent, anything received is to be taken as received by way of consideration written off in accounts as a bad debt.

36(7)   The provisions which may be included in regulations by virtue of subsection (5)(f) above may include rules dealing with particular cases, such as those involving receipt of part of the consideration or mutual debts; and in particular such rules may vary the way in which the following amounts are to be calculated–

(a)   the outstanding amount mentioned in subsection (2) above, and

(b)   the amount of any repayment where a refund has been allowed under this section.

36(8)   Section 6 shall apply for determining the time when a supply is to be treated as taking place for the purposes of construing this section.

History – In s. 36(1)(a), the words "for a consideration in money" were omitted and repealed by FA 1998, s. 23(1) and 165(1) and Sch. 27, Pt II, with effect in relation to claims made on or after 31 July 1998.
S. 36(3) was substituted by FA 1999, s. 15(1), with effect for the purposes of the making of any refund or repayment after 9 March 1999, but do not have effect in relation to anything received on or before that day. Former s. 36(3) reads as follows:
"**36(3)**   In subsection (2) above **"the outstanding amount"** means–
(a)   if at the time of the claim the person has received no part of the consideration written off in his accounts as a bad debt, an amount equal to the amount of the consideration so written off;
(b)   if at that time he has received any part of the consideration so written off, an amount by which that part is exceeded by the amount of the consideration so written off."
In s. 36(3)(a), the word "part" was substituted by FA 1998, s. 23(2)(a), with effect in relation to claims made on or after 31 July 1998.
In s. 36(3)(b), the words "any part" and "that part" were substituted by FA 1998, s. 23(2)(b), with effect in relation to claims made on or after 31 July 1998.
S. 36(3A) was inserted by FA 1998, s. 23(3), with effect in relation to claims made on or after 31 July 1998.
In s. 36(4)(a), the word "and" at the end was repealed by FA 1997, s. 113 and Sch. 18, Pt. IV(3), with effect in relation to supplies made on or after 19 March 1997.
S. 36(4)(b) was repealed by FA 1997, s. 39(1) and 113 and Sch. 18, Pt. IV(3), with effect in relation to supplies made on or after 19 March 1997. Former s. 36(4)(b) reads as follows:
"(b)   in the case of a supply of goods, the property in the goods has passed to the person to whom they were supplied or to a person deriving title from, through or under that person."
S. 36(4A) was inserted by FA 1997, s. 39(2), with effect in relation to any entitlement under s. 36 to a refund of VAT charged on a supply made after 26 November 1996.
In s. 36(5)(c), the words "anything subsequently received" were substituted by FA 1998, s. 23(4)(a), with effect in relation to claims made on or after 31 July 1998.
In s. 36(5)(e), the words "where any part (or further part) of the consideration written off in the claimant's accounts as a bad debt is subsequently received either by the claimant or, except in such circumstances as may be prescribed, by a person to whom has been assigned a right to receive the whole or any part of that consideration" were substituted for the words "where the claimant subsequently receives any part (or further part) of the consideration written off in his accounts as a bad debt" by FA 1999, s. 15(2), with effect for the purposes of the making of any refund or repayment after 9 March 1999, but do not have effect in relation to anything received on or before that day.
In s. 36(5)(e), the words "part or (further part)" were substituted by FA 1998, s. 23(4)(b), with effect in relation to claims made on or after 31 July 1998.
S. 36(5)(ea) was inserted by FA 1997, s. 39(4), with effect from 19 March 1997.
In s. 36(6)(b), the words "anything received" were substituted by FA 1998, s. 23(5), with effect in relation to claims made on or after 31 July 1998.
In s. 36(6)(c), the words "anything received" were substituted by FA 1998, s. 23(5), with effect in relation to claims made on or after 31 July 1998.
In s. 36(7), the words "receipt of part of the consideration" were substituted by FA 1998, s. 23(6), with effect in relation to claims made on or after 31 July 1998.
Derivations – FA 1990, s. 11, as amended by FA 1991, s. 15 and FA 1993, s. 48.
Cross references – S. 60(2)(c): penalties.
S. 72(2): evasion of VAT.
S. 83(h): appeals.
Sch. 13, para. 9: transitional provisions and savings.
FA 1999, s. 15(4): until such day as the Commissioners may specify in regulations made under s. 36, SI 1995/2518, Pt. XIX, except reg. 171, read as if a reference to a payment being received by the claimant were a reference to a payment being received either by the claimant or by a person to whom a right to receive it has been assigned.
VAT (Isle of Man) Order 1982 (SI 1982/1067), art. 7: references to VAT include references to VAT chargeable under Pt. I of *the Manx Act.*
VAT Regulations 1995 (SI 1995/2518), reg. 165: claim for refund (as amended by SI 1999/3029).
Statutory instruments – VAT Regulations 1995 (SI 1995/2518, as amended by SI 1996/2960, as amended by SI 1997/1086).
Extra-statutory concessions – Customs allow relief for certain bad debts in relation to barter transactions arising before the amendments made by FA 1998 (Business Brief 21/97, 3 October 1997).
Official publications – 700/18.
Customs Internal Guidance Manual, vol. V1-22: bad debt relief.

IMPORTS, OVERSEAS BUSINESSES ETC.

37 Relief from VAT on importation of goods

37(1) The Treasury may by order make provision for giving relief from the whole or part of the VAT chargeable on the importation of goods from places outside the member States, subject to such conditions (including conditions prohibiting or restricting the disposal of or dealing with the goods) as may be imposed by or under the order, if and so far as the relief appears to the Treasury to be necessary or expedient, having regard to any international agreement or arrangements.

37(2) In any case where–

(a)   it is proposed that goods which have been imported from a place outside the member States by any person (**"the original importer"**) with the benefit of relief under subsection (1) above shall be transferred to another person (**"the transferee"**), and

(b)   on an application made by the transferee, the Commissioners direct that this subsection shall apply,

this Act shall have effect as if, on the date of the transfer of the goods (and in place of the transfer), the goods were exported by the original importer and imported by the transferee and, accordingly, where appropriate, provision made under subsection (1) above shall have effect in relation to the VAT chargeable on the importation of the goods by the transferee.

37(3) The Commissioners may by regulations make provision for remitting or repaying, if they think fit, the whole or part of the VAT chargeable on the importation of any goods from places outside the member States which are shown to their satisfaction to have been previously exported from the United Kingdom or removed from any member State.

37(4) The Commissioners may by regulations make provision for remitting or repaying the whole or part of the VAT chargeable on the importation of any goods from places outside the member States if they are satisfied that the goods have been or are to be re-exported or otherwise removed from the United Kingdom and they think fit to do so in all the circumstances and having regard–

(a)   to the VAT chargeable on the supply of like goods in the United Kingdom;

(b)   to any VAT which may have become chargeable in another member State in respect of the goods.

Derivations – S. 37(1): VATA 1983, s. 19(1), as amended by F(No. 2)A 1992, s. 14 and Sch. 3, para. 20(1).
S. 37(2): VATA 1983, s. 19(1A), as inserted by FA 1986, s. 13, and as amended by F(No. 2)A 1992, s. 14 and Sch. 3, para. 20(2).
S. 37(3), (4): VATA 1983, s. 19(2), (3), as amended by F(No. 2)A 1992, s. 14 and Sch. 3, para. 20(3), (4).

Cross references – FA 1999, s. 13(3): supplies of gold.
VAT (Input Tax) Order 1992 (SI 1992/3222), art. 4(3): disallowance of input tax.

Statutory instruments – VAT (Imported Goods) Relief Order 1984 (SI 1984/746, as amended by SI 1995/3222).
VAT (Small Non-Commercial Consignments) Relief Order 1986 (SI 1986/939).
VAT (Imported Gold) Relief Order 1992 (SI 1992/3124).
VAT (Special Provisions) (Amendment) Order 1995 (SI 1995/957).
VAT Regulations 1995 (SI 1995/2518).
VAT (Importation of Investment Gold) Relief Order 1999 (SI 1999/3115).

Official publications – 702, 702/4, 702/6, 702/7, 702/9.

Other material – Form C79: Customs and Excise monthly VAT certificate.
Form C88: export and import declaration.
Forms C1200–1207: duty deferment.
Form VAT 905 Claim for relief from VAT on imports of second-hand works of art, etc.
Form VAT 977 Temporary import of goods for repair, renovation, modification or treatment.

38 Importation of goods by taxable persons

38 The Commissioners may by regulations make provision for enabling goods imported from a place outside the member States by a taxable person in the course or furtherance of any business carried on by him to be delivered or removed, subject to such conditions or restrictions as the Commissioners may impose for the protection of the revenue, without payment of the VAT chargeable on the importation, and for that VAT to be accounted for together with the VAT chargeable on the supply of goods or services by him or on the acquisition of goods by him from other member States.

Derivations – VATA 1983, s. 25, as amended by F(No. 2)A 1992, s. 14 and Sch. 3, para. 26.

Cross reference – VAT (Isle of Man) Order 1982 (SI 1982/1067), art. 8: taxable person includes a person who is a taxable person under the Manx Act.

Statutory instrument – VAT Regulations 1995 (SI 1995/2518).

Other material – Customs and Excise Business Brief 22/93, 14 July 1993 (not reproduced): simplification for intra-EC processing of goods.

Note – S. 30(3): zero-rating.

39   Repayment of VAT to those in business overseas

39(1)   The Commissioners may, by means of a scheme embodied in regulations, provide for the repayment, to persons to whom this section applies, of VAT on supplies to them in the United Kingdom or on the importation of goods by them from places outside the member States which would be input tax of theirs if they were taxable persons in the United Kingdom.

39(2)   This section–

(a)   applies to persons carrying on business in another member State, and

(b)   shall apply also to persons carrying on business in other countries, if, pursuant to any Community Directive, rules are adopted by the Council of the Communities about refunds of VAT to persons established elsewhere than in the member States,

but does not apply to persons carrying on business in the United Kingdom.

39(3)   Repayment shall be made in such cases only, and subject to such conditions, as the scheme may prescribe (being conditions specified in the regulations or imposed by the Commissioners either generally or in particular cases); and the scheme may provide–

(a)   for claims and repayments to be made only through agents in the United Kingdom;

(b)   either generally or for specified purposes–

     (i)   for the agents to be treated under this Act as if they were taxable persons; and

     (ii)   for treating claims as if they were returns under this Act and repayments as if they were repayments of input tax; and

(c)   for generally regulating the methods by which the amount of any repayment is to be determined and the repayment is to be made.

Derivations – VATA 1983, s. 23, as amended by FA 1987, s. 19(2) and Sch. 2, para. 2, and by F(No. 2)A 1992, s. 14 and Sch. 3, para. 24.

Cross references – S. 54(5): farmers etc.
S. 60(2)(d): penalties.
S. 72(2)(d): offences.
Sch. 4, para. 5(5): disposals of assets for which a VAT repayment is claimed.
Sch. 9, Grp. 14, Notes (8) and (9): supplies where input tax cannot be recovered.
Sch. 9A, para. 6(2)(c): anti-avoidance and VAT groups.
VAT (Isle of Man) Order 1982 (SI 1982/1067), art. 7: references to VAT include references to VAT chargeable under Pt. I of the Manx Act.

Statutory instruments – VAT Regulations 1995 (SI 1995/2518).

European material – Directive 79/1072, eighth VAT directive.
Directive 86/560, thirteenth VAT directive.

Official publications – 723.

Other material – Forms VAT 65 and 65A.

40   Refunds in relation to new means of transport supplied to other member States

40(1)   Subject to subsection (2) below, where a person who is not a taxable person makes such a supply of goods consisting in a new means of transport as involves the removal of the goods to another member State, the Commissioners shall, on a claim made in that behalf, refund to that person, as the case may be–

(a)   the amount of any VAT on the supply of that means of transport to that person, or

(b)   the amount of any VAT paid by that person on the acquisition of that means of transport from another member State or on its importation from a place outside the member States.

40(2)   The amount of VAT refunded under this section shall not exceed the amount that would have been payable on the supply involving the removal if it had been a taxable supply by a taxable person and had not been zero-rated.

40(3)   The Commissioners shall not be entitled to entertain a claim for refund of VAT under this section unless the claim–

(a)   is made within such time and in such form and manner;

(b)   contains such information; and

(c)   is accompanied by such documents, whether by way of evidence or otherwise,

as the Commissioners may by regulations prescribe.

Derivations – VATA 1983, s. 20A, as inserted by F(No. 2)A 1992, s. 14 and Sch. 3, para. 22.

Cross references – S. 60(2)(c): penalties.
S. 72(2): evasion of VAT.
S. 83(j): appeals.
S. 90(3): input tax repaid following a restoration of a lower rate.
VAT Regulations 1995 (SI 1995/2518), reg. 146: claim for a VAT refund on new means of transport.

Statutory instrument – VAT Regulations 1995 (SI 1995/2518).

PART III – APPLICATION OF ACT IN PARTICULAR CASES

41 Application to the Crown

41(1)   This Act shall apply in relation to taxable supplies by the Crown as it applies in relation to taxable supplies by taxable persons.

41(2)   Where the supply by a Government department of any goods or services does not amount to the carrying on of a business but it appears to the Treasury that similar goods or services are or might be supplied by taxable persons in the course or furtherance of any business, then, if and to the extent that the Treasury so direct, the supply of those goods or services by that department shall be treated for the purposes of this Act as a supply in the course or furtherance of any business carried on by it.

41(3)   Where VAT is chargeable on the supply of goods or services to a Government department, on the acquisition of any goods by a Government department from another member State or on the importation of any goods by a Government department from a place outside the member States and the supply, acquisition or importation is not for the purpose–

(a)   of any business carried on by the department, or

(b)   of a supply by the department which, by virtue of a direction under subsection (2) above, is treated as a supply in the course or furtherance of a business,

then, if and to the extent that the Treasury so direct and subject to subsection (4) below, the Commissioners shall, on a claim made by the department at such time and in such form and manner as the Commissioners may determine, refund to it the amount of the VAT so chargeable.

41(4)   The Commissioners may make the refunding of any amount due under subsection (3) above conditional upon compliance by the claimant with requirements with respect to the keeping, preservation and production of records relating to the supply, acquisition or importation in question.

41(5)   For the purposes of this section goods or services obtained by one Government department from another Government department shall be treated, if and to the extent that the Treasury so direct, as supplied by that other department and similarly as regards goods or services obtained by or from the Crown Estate Commissioners.

41(6)   In this section **"Government department"** includes the Scottish Administration, the National Assembly for Wales, a Northern Ireland department, a Northern Ireland health and social services body, any body of persons exercising functions on behalf of a Minister of the Crown, including a health service body as defined in section 60(7) of the National Health Service and Community Care Act 1990, and any part of a Government department (as defined in the foregoing) designated for the purposes of this subsection by a direction of the Treasury.

41(7)   For the purposes of subsection (6) above, a National Health Service trust established under Part I of the National Health Service and Community Care Act 1990 or the National Health Service (Scotland) Act 1978 and a Primary Care Trust shall be regarded as a body of persons exercising functions on behalf of a Minister of the Crown.

41(8)   In subsection (6) **"a Northern Ireland health and social services body"** means–

(a)   a health and social services body as defined in Article 7(6) of the Health and Personal Social Services (Northern Ireland) Order 1991; and

(b)   a Health and Social Services trust established under that Order.

History – In s. 41(6), the words "the Scottish Administration" were inserted by the Scotand Act 1998, s. 125 and Sch. 8, para. 30, with effect from 6 May 1999 (SI 1998/3178).
In s. 41(6), the words ", the National Assembly for Wales," were inserted by the Government of Wales Act 1998, s. 125 and Sch. 12, para. 35, with effect from 1 April 1999 (SI 1999/782).
In s. 41(7), the words "and a Primary Care Trust" were inserted by the Health Act 1999, s. 65 and Sch. 4, para. 86, with effect from 1 April 2000 (SI 1999/2342).

Derivations – S. 41(1), (2): VATA 1983, s. 27(1), (2).
S. 41(3), (4): VATA 1983, s. 27(2A), (2B), as inserted by FA 1984, s. 11, and as amended by F(No. 2)A 1992, s. 14 and Sch. 3, para. 28.
S. 41(5): VATA 1983, s. 27(3).
S. 41(6): VATA 1983, s. 27(4), as amended by the National Health Service and Community Care Act 1990, s. 60 and Sch. 8, para. 9, and SI 1991/195, art. 5.
S. 41(7): VATA 1983, s. 27(5), as inserted by the National Health Service and Community Care Act 1990, s. 61(4).
S. 41(8): VATA 1983, s. 27(6), as inserted by SI 1991/195, art. 5.

Sch. 10, para. 3A: election to tax and a Government department.
Sch. 9, Grp. 10, Note (3)(b): a s. 41(6) government department is not a "non-profit making body" for the purposes of exemption for sport, sports competitions and physical education.
Sch. 9, Grp. 13, Note (1)(b): meaning of "public body".

Cross references – Sch. 9, Grp. 14, Note (9): supplies where input tax cannot be recovered.
FA 1999, s. 21(3): VAT accounting by government departments.

Official publications – Customs Internal Guidance Manual, vol. V1-14: government and public bodies.

Notes – Treasury's directions (and amendments to directions) are published in the London Gazette.

42 Local authorities

42 A local authority which makes taxable supplies is liable to be registered under this Act, whatever the value of the supplies; and accordingly Schedule 1 shall apply, in a case where the value of the taxable supplies made by a local authority in any period of one year does not exceed the sum for the time being specified in paragraph 1(1)(a) of that Schedule, as if that value exceeded that sum.

Derivations – VATA 1983, s. 28(1), as amended by FA 1990, s. 10(8).

Official publications – 749: "Local authorities and similar bodies".

43 Groups of companies

43(1) Where under sections 43A to 43C any bodies corporate are treated as members of a group, any business carried on by a member of the group shall be treated as carried on by the representative member, and–

(a) any supply of goods or services by a member of the group to another member of the group shall be disregarded; and

(b) any supply which is a supply to which paragraph (a) above does not apply and is a supply of goods or services by or to a member of the group shall be treated as a supply by or to the representative member; and

(c) any VAT paid or payable by a member of the group on the acquisition of goods from another member State or on the importation of goods from a place outside the member States shall be treated as paid or payable by the representative member and the goods shall be treated–

    (i) in the case of goods acquired from another member State, for the purposes of section 73(7); and

    (ii) in the case of goods imported from a place outside the member States, for those purposes and the purposes of section 38,

as acquired or, as the case may be, imported by the representative member;

and all members of the group shall be liable jointly and severally for any VAT due from the representative member.

43(1A) [Repealed by FA 1996, s. 31(5) and 205 and Sch. 41, Pt. IV(5).]

43(1AA) Where–

(a) it is material, for the purposes of any provision made by or under this Act (**"the relevant provision"**), whether the person by or to whom a supply is made, or the person by whom goods are acquired or imported, is a person of a particular description,

(b) paragraph (b) or (c) of subsection (1) above applies to any supply, acquisition or importation, and

(c) there is a difference that would be material for the purposes of the relevant provision between–

    (i) the description applicable to the representative member, and

    (ii) the description applicable to the body which (apart from this section) would be regarded for the purposes of this Act as making the supply, acquisition or importation or, as the case may be, as being the person to whom the supply is made,

the relevant provision shall have effect in relation to that supply, acquisition or importation as if the only description applicable to the representative member were the description in fact applicable to that body.

43(1AB) Subsection (1AA) above does not apply to the extent that what is material for the purposes of the relevant provision is whether a person is a taxable person.

43(2) An order under section 5(5) or (6) may make provision for securing that any goods or services which, if all the members of the group were one person, would fall to be treated under that section as supplied to and by that person, are treated as supplied to and by the representative member and may provide for that purpose that the representative member is to be treated as a person of such description as may be determined under the order.

43(2A) A supply made by a member of a group (**"the supplier"**) to another member of the group (**"the UK member"**) shall not be disregarded under subsection (1)(a) above if–

(a)   it would (if there were no group) be a supply of services falling within Schedule 5 to a person belonging in the United Kingdom;

(b)   those services are not within any of the descriptions specified in Schedule 9;

(c)   the supplier has been supplied (whether or not by a person belonging in the United Kingdom) with any services falling within paragraphs 1 to 8 of Schedule 5 which do not fall within any of the descriptions specified in Schedule 9;

(d)   the supplier belonged outside the United Kingdom when it was supplied with the services mentioned in paragraph (c) above; and

(e)   the services so mentioned have been used by the supplier for making the supply to the UK member.

43(2B) Subject to subsection (2C) below, where a supply is excluded by virtue of subsection (2A) above from the supplies that are disregarded in pursuance of subsection (1)(a) above, all the same consequences shall follow under this Act as if that supply–

(a)   were a taxable supply in the United Kingdom by the representative member to itself, and

(b)   without prejudice to that, were made by the representative member in the course or furtherance of its business.

43(2C) Except in so far as the Commissioners may by regulations otherwise provide, a supply which is deemed by virtue of subsection (2B) above to be a supply by the representative member to itself–

(a)   shall not be taken into account as a supply made by the representative member when determining any allowance of input tax under section 26(1) in the case of the representative member;

(b)   shall be deemed for the purposes of paragraph 1 of Schedule 6 to be a supply in the case of which the person making the supply and the person supplied are connected within the meaning of section 839 of the Taxes Act (connected persons); and

(c)   subject to paragraph (b) above, shall be taken to be a supply the value and time of which are determined as if it were a supply of services which is treated by virtue of section 8 as made by the person by whom the services are received.

43(2D) For the purposes of subsection (2A) above where–

(a)   there has been a supply of the assets of a business of a person (**"the transferor"**) to a person to whom the whole or any part of that business was transferred as a going concern (**"the transferee"**),

(b)   that supply is either–

       (i) a supply falling to be treated, in accordance with an order under section 5(3), as being neither a supply of goods nor a supply of services, or

       (ii) a supply that would have fallen to be so treated if it had taken place in the United Kingdom,

    and

(c)   the transferor was supplied with services falling within paragraphs 1 to 8 of Schedule 5 at a time before the transfer when the transferor belonged outside the United Kingdom,

those services, so far as they are used by the transferee for making any supply falling within that Schedule, shall be deemed to have been supplied to the transferee at a time when the transferee belonged outside the United Kingdom.

43(2E) Where, in the case of a supply of assets falling within paragraphs (a) and (b) of subsection (2D) above–

(a)   the transferor himself acquired any of the assets in question by way of a previous supply of assets falling within those paragraphs, and

(b)   there are services falling within paragraphs 1 to 8 of Schedule 5 which, if used by the transferor for making supplies falling within that Schedule, would be deemed by virtue of that subsection to have been supplied to the transferor at a time when he belonged outside the United Kingdom,

that subsection shall have effect, notwithstanding that the services have not been so used by the transferor, as if the transferor were a person to whom those services were supplied and as if he were a person belonging outside the United Kingdom at the time of their deemed supply to him; and this subsection shall apply accordingly through any number of successive supplies of assets falling within paragraphs (a) and (b) of that subsection.

43(3)   [Repealed by FA 1999, s. 16 and Sch. 2, para. 1(3) and s. 139(1) and Sch. 20, Pt. II(1), with effect in accordance with the transitional provisions in FA 1999, Sch. 2, para. 6.]

43(4)   [Repealed by FA 1999, s. 16 and Sch. 2, para. 1(3) and s. 139(1) and Sch. 20, Pt. II(1), with effect in accordance with the transitional provisions in FA 1999, Sch. 2, para. 6.]

43(5)   [Repealed by FA 1999, s. 16 and Sch. 2, para. 1(3) and s. 139(1) and Sch. 20, Pt. II(1), with effect in accordance with the transitional provisions in FA 1999, Sch. 2, para. 6.]

43(5A)   [Repealed by FA 1999, s. 16 and Sch. 2, para. 1(3) and s. 139(1) and Sch. 20, Pt. II(1), with effect in accordance with the transitional provisions in FA 1999, Sch. 2, para. 6.]

43(6)   [Repealed by FA 1999, s. 16 and Sch. 2, para. 1(3) and s. 139(1) and Sch. 20, Pt. II(1), with effect in accordance with the transitional provisions in FA 1999, Sch. 2, para. 6.]

43(7)   [Repealed by FA 1999, s. 16 and Sch. 2, para. 1(3) and s. 139(1) and Sch. 20, Pt. II(1), with effect in accordance with the transitional provisions in FA 1999, Sch. 2, para. 6.]

43(8)   [Repealed by FA 1999, s. 16 and Sch. 2, para. 1(3) and s. 139(1) and Sch. 20, Pt. II(1), with effect in accordance with the transitional provisions in FA 1999, Sch. 2, para. 6.]

43(9)   Schedule 9A (which makes provision for ensuring that this section is not used for tax avoidance) shall have effect.

History – In s. 43(1), the words "sections 43A to 43C" were substituted for the words "the following provisions of this section" by FA 1999, s. 16 and Sch. 2, para. (1(2), with effect in accordance with the transitional provisions in FA 1999, Sch. 2, para. 6. In s. 43(1)(b), the words "supply which is a . . . and is a supply" were substituted by FA 1995, s. 25(2), with effect in relation to any supply made on or after 1st March 1995, and any supply made before that date in the case of which both the body making the supply and the body supplied continued to be members of the group in question until at least that date.
S. 43(1A) was repealed by FA 1996, s. 31(5) and 205 and Sch. 41, Pt. IV(5), in relation to supplies made on or after 29 April 1996.
Former s. 43(1A) was inserted by FA 1995, s. 25(2), with effect in relation to any supply made on or after 1 March 1995, and any supply made before that date in the case of which both the body making the supply and the body supplied continued to be members of the group in question until at least that date.
S. 43(1AA) was inserted by FA 1997, s. 40(1), with effect in relation to any supply made after 26 November 1996 and in relation to any acquisition or importation taking place after that date.
S. 43(1AB) was inserted by FA 1997, s. 40(1), with effect in relation to any supply made after 26 November 1996 and in relation to any acquisition or importation taking place after that date.
In s. 43(2), the words "and may provide . . . under the order" were inserted by FA 1997, s. 40(2), with effect from 19 March 1997.
S. 43(2A) was inserted by FA 1997, s. 41(1), with effect in relation to supplies made on or after 26 November 1996.
In s. 43(2A)(c), the words "any services falling within paragraphs 1 to 8 of Schedule 5 which do not fall within any of the descriptions specified in Schedule 9" were substituted for the words "services falling within any of paragraphs 1 to 8 of Schedule 5" by FA 1997, s. 41(4), in relation to supplies made after 19 March 1997.
S. 43(2B) was inserted by FA 1997, s. 41(1), with effect in relation to supplies made on or after 26 November 1996.
S. 43(2C) was inserted by FA 1997, s. 41(1), with effect in relation to supplies made on or after 26 November 1996.
In s. 43(2C), at the beginning, the words "Except in so far as the Commissioners may by regulations otherwise provide," were inserted by FA 1997, s. 41(5), in relation to supplies made after 19 March 1997.
S. 43(2D) was inserted by FA 1997, s. 41(1), with effect in relation to supplies made on or after 26 November 1996.
S. 43(2E) was inserted by FA 1997, s. 41(1), with effect in relation to supplies made on or after 26 November 1996.
S. 43(3) was repealed by FA 1999, s. 16 and Sch. 2, para. 1(3) and s. 139(1) and Sch. 20, Pt. II(1), with effect in accordance with the transitional provisions in FA 1999, Sch. 2, para. 6. Former s. 43(3) reads as follows:
"**43(3)**   Two or more bodies corporate are eligible to be treated as members of a group if each is resident or has an established place of business in the United Kingdom and–
   (a)   one of them controls each of the others; or
   (b)   one person (whether a body corporate or an individual) controls all of them; or
   (c)   two or more individuals carrying on a business in partnership control all of them."
S. 43(4) was repealed by FA 1999, s. 16 and Sch. 2, para. 1(3) and s. 139(1) and Sch. 20, Pt. II(1), with effect in accordance with the transitional provisions in FA 1999, Sch. 2, para. 6. Former s. 43(4) reads as follows:
"**43(4)**   Where an application to that effect is made to the Commissioners with respect to two or more bodies corporate eligible to be treated as members of a group, then, from the beginning of a prescribed accounting period they shall be so treated, and one of them shall be the representative member, unless the Commissioners refuse the application; but they shall not refuse it unless it appears to them necessary to do so for the protection of the revenue."
S. 43(5) was repealed by FA 1999, s. 16 and Sch. 2, para. 1(3) and s. 139(1) and Sch. 20, Pt. II(1), with effect in accordance with the transitional provisions in FA 1999, Sch. 2, para. 6. Former s. 43(5) reads as follows:
"**43(5)**   Where any bodies corporate are treated as members of a group and an application to that effect is made to the Commissioners, then, from the beginning of a prescribed accounting period–
   (a)   a further body eligible to be so treated shall be included among the bodies so treated; or
   (b)   a body corporate shall be excluded from the bodies so treated; or
   (c)   another member of the group shall be substituted as the representative member; or
   (d)   the bodies corporate shall no longer be treated as members of a group,
unless the Commissioners refuse the application under subsection (5A) below."
In former s. 43(5), words after para. (d) were substituted by FA 1995, s. 25(3), with effect in relation to applications made on or after 1 May 1995.
S. 43(5A) was repealed by FA 1999, s. 16 and Sch. 2, para. 1(3) and s. 139(1) and Sch. 20, Pt. II(1), with effect in accordance with the transitional provisions in FA 1999, Sch. 2, para. 6. Former s. 43(5A) reads as follows:
"**43(5A)**   If it appears to the Commissioners necessary to do so for the protection of the revenue, they may–
   (a)   refuse any application made to the effect mentioned in paragraph (a) or (c) of subsection (5) above; or

(b)   refuse any application made to the effect mentioned in paragraph (b) or (d) of that subsection in a case that does not appear to them to fall within subsection (6) below."

Former s. 43(5A) was inserted by FA 1995, s. 25(4), with effect in relation to applications made on or after 1 May 1995.

S. 43(6) was repealed by FA 1999, s. 16 and Sch. 2, para. 1(3) and s. 139(1) and Sch. 20, Pt. II(1), with effect in accordance with the transitional provisions in FA 1999, Sch. 2, para. 6. Former s. 43(6) reads as follows:

"**43(6)**   Where a body corporate is treated as a member of a group as being controlled by any person and it appears to the Commissioners that it has ceased to be so controlled, they shall, by notice given to that person, terminate that treatment from such date as may be specified in the notice."

S. 43(7) was repealed by FA 1999, s. 16 and Sch. 2, para. 1(3) and s. 139(1) and Sch. 20, Pt. II(1), with effect in accordance with the transitional provisions in FA 1999, Sch. 2, para. 6. Former s. 43(7) reads as follows:

"**43(7)**   An application under this section with respect to any bodies corporate must be made by one of those bodies or by the person controlling them and must be made not less than 90 days before the date from which it is to take effect, or at such later time as the Commissioners may allow."

S. 43(8) was repealed by FA 1999, s. 16 and Sch. 2, para. 1(3) and s. 139(1) and Sch. 20, Pt. II(1), with effect in accordance with the transitional provisions in FA 1999, Sch. 2, para. 6. Former s. 43(8) reads as follows:

"**43(8)**   For the purposes of this section a body corporate shall be taken to **control** another body corporate if it is empowered by statute to control that body's activities or if it is that body's holding company within the meaning of section 736 of the Companies Act 1985; and an individual or individuals shall be taken to **control** a body corporate if he or they, were he or they a company, would be that body's holding company within the meaning of that Act."

S. 43(9) was inserted by FA 1996, s. 31(1) with effect from 29 April 1996.

Derivations – S. 43(1): VATA 1983, s. 29(1), as amended by F(No. 2)A 1992, s. 14 and Sch. 3, para. 29.
S. 43(2): VATA 1983, s. 29(2).
S. 43(3): VATA 1983, s. 29(3), (3A), as respectively substituted and inserted by FA 1991, s. 16.
S. 43(4)–(8): VATA 1983, s. 29(4)–(8), as amended (s. 29(8)) by the Companies Consolidation (Consequential Provisions) Act 1985, Sch. 2, and by CA 1989, s. 144(4) and Sch. 18, para. 27.

Cross references – S. 8(8): power of the Treasury to modify s. 43(2A)–(2E).
S. 18A(9): fiscal warehousing and "registered person".
S. 56: fuel for private use.
S. 67(2)(b): unauthorised issue of invoices.
S. 83(k): appeals against refusal of an application.
Sch. 9, Grp. 10, Notes (15): sport, sports competitions and physical education in relation to disregarded supplies under s. 43(1)(a).
Sch. 9, Grp. 14, Note (14): supplies where input tax cannot be recovered.
Sch. 9A, para. 7(1): anti-avoidance and groups.
Sch. 10, para. 3(7): buildings and land.
FA 1997, s. 43(4): modified application of s. 43(2A) (see history note above).
FA 1997, s. 43(5): modified application of s. 43(2C) (see history note above).
FA 1999, Sch. 2, para. 2, 6: transitional provisions for revised group provisions.
VAT (Isle of Man) Order 1982 (SI 1982/1067), art. 10: determination of which member of a group is to be the representative member.
VAT (Isle of Man) Order 1982 (SI 1982/1067), art. 11(6): notification by representative member if a member has an establishment in the Isle of Man.
VAT (Tour Operators) Order (SI 1987/1806), art. 13: disqualification from membership of VAT group.
VAT (Self-supply of Construction Services) Order 1989 (SI 1989/472), art. 3(3): construction work by one group member for another member.
VAT (Cars) Order 1992 (SI 1992/3122), art. 7: self-supplies.
VAT (Payments on Account) Order 1993 (SI 1993/2001), art. 17: group members treated as one person for the purposes of payments on account.
VAT (Special Provisions) Order 1995 (SI 1995/1268), art. 11(4): self-supply.
VAT Regulations 1995 (SI 1995/2518), reg. 41(2): accounting etc. by reference to the duty point and period in which VAT is chargeable.
VAT Regulations 1995 (SI 1995/2518), reg. 52(1): annual accounting unavailable to group members.
VAT Regulations 1995 (SI 1995/2518), reg. 114(5A)(a): capital goods scheme and group members.
VAT Regulations 1995 (SI 1995/2518), reg. 115(6): adjustments to the deduction of input tax on capital items.
VAT (Reverse Charge) (Anti-avoidance) Order 1997 (SI 1997/2513), art. 4(1): telecommunication services supplied on or after 1 July 1997.

Statutory instruments – VAT (Cars) Order 1992 (SI 1992/3122, as amended by SI 1995/1269, SI 1995/1667).
VAT (Special Provisions) Order 1995 (SI 1995/1268).

Extra-statutory concessions – 3.2 (Notice 48 (1999 edn)): group supplies using an overseas member – anticipation of legislative changes.
3.3 (Notice 48 (1999 edn)): group supplies using an overseas member – transitional relief.

Official publications – 700/2 and 700/3.

Other material – Forms VAT 36 and VAT 50–58.
Customs and Excise Press Notice 843, 23 June 1983 (not reproduced): property transactions within VAT groups.

43A   Groups: eligibility

43A(1)   Two or more bodies corporate are eligible to be treated as members of a group if each is established or has a fixed establishment in the United Kingdom and–

(a)   one of them controls each of the others,

(b)   one person (whether a body corporate or an individual) controls all of them, or

(c)   two or more individuals carrying on a business in partnership control all of them.

43A(2)   For the purposes of this section a body corporate shall be taken to **control** another body corporate if it is empowered by statute to control that body's activities or if it is that body's holding company within the meaning of section 736 of the Companies Act 1985.

43A(3)   For the purposes of this section an individual or individuals shall be taken to **control** a body corporate if he or they, were he or they a company, would be that body's holding company within the meaning of that section.

History – S. 43A was inserted by FA 1999, s. 16 and Sch. 2, para. 2, with effect in accordance with the transitional provisions in FA 1999, Sch. 2, para. 6.

Cross references – Sch. 9A, para. 7(1): anti-avoidance and groups.
FA 1999, Sch. 2, para. 2, 6: transitional provisions for revised group provisions.

43B   Groups: applications

43B(1)   This section applies where an application is made to the Commissioners for two or more bodies corporate, which are eligible under section 43A(1), to be treated as members of a group.

43B(2)   This section also applies where two or more bodies corporate are treated as members of a group and an application is made to the Commissioners–

(a)   for another body corporate, which is eligible under section 43A(1) to be treated as a member of the group,

(b)   for a body corporate to cease to be treated as a member of the group,

(c)   for a member to be substituted as the group's representative member, or

(d)   for the bodies corporate no longer to be treated as members of a group.

43B(3)   An application with respect to any bodies corporate–

(a)   must be made by one of them or by the person controlling them, and

(b)   in the case of an application for the bodies to be treated as a group, must appoint one of them as the representative member.

43B(4)   Where this section applies in relation to an application it shall, subject to subsection (6) below, be taken to be granted with effect from–

(a)   the day on which the application is received by the Commissioners, or

(b)   such earlier or later time as the Commissioners may allow.

43B(5)   The Commissioners may refuse an application, within the period of 90 days starting with the day on which it was received by them, if it appears to them–

(a)   in the case of an application such as is mentioned in subsection (1) above, that the bodies corporate are not eligible under section 43A(1) to be treated as members of a group,

(b)   in the case of an application such as is mentioned in subsection (2)(a) above, that the body corporate is not eligible under section 43A(1) to be treated as a member of the group, or

(c)   in any case, that refusal of the application is necessary for the protection of the revenue.

43B(6)   If the Commissioners refuse an application it shall be taken never to have been granted.

History – S. 43B was inserted by FA 1999, s. 16 and Sch. 2, para. 2, with effect in accordance with the transitional provisions in FA 1999, Sch. 2, para. 6.

Cross references – S. 83(k): appeals against the refusal of an application.
S. 84(4A): restricted power of tribunal to allow an appeal.
Sch. 9A, para. 3(8): form of direction in relation to anti-avoidance and groups.
Sch. 9A, para. 7(1): anti-avoidance and groups.
FA 1999, Sch. 2, para. 2, 6: transitional provisions for revised group provisions.

43C   Groups: termination of membership

43C(1)   The Commissioners may, by notice given to a body corporate, terminate its treatment as a member of a group from a date–

(a)   which is specified in the notice, and

(b)   which is, or falls after, the date on which the notice is given.

43C(2)   The Commissioners may give a notice under subsection (1) above only if it appears to them to be necessary for the protection of the revenue.

43C(3)   Where–

(a)   a body is treated as a member of a group, and

(b)   it appears to the Commissioners that the body is not, or is no longer, eligible under section 43A(1) to be treated as a member of the group,

the Commissioners shall, by notice given to the body, terminate its treatment as a member of the group from a date specified in the notice.

43C(4)   The date specified in a notice under subsection (3) above may be earlier than the date on which the notice is given but shall not be earlier than–

(a)   the first date on which, in the opinion of the Commissioners, the body was not eligible to be treated as a member of the group, or

(b)   the date on which, in the opinion of the Commissioners, the body ceased to be eligible to be treated as a member of the group.

History – S. 43C was inserted by FA 1999, s. 16 and Sch. 2, para. 2, with effect in accordance with the transitional provisions in FA 1999, Sch. 2, para. 6.

Cross references – S. 83(ka): appeals against the giving of a notice under s. 43C(1) or (3).
S. 84(4B): effect of notice pending determination of an appeal.
S. 84(4C) and 84(4D): restricted power of tribunal to allow an appeal.
Sch. 9A, para. 2(2): relevant event where Customs terminate group membership.
Sch. 9A, para. 7(1): anti-avoidance and groups.
FA 1999, Sch. 2, para. 2, 6: transitional provisions for revised group provisions.

44   Supplies to groups

44(1)   Subject to subsections (2) to (4) below, subsection (5) below applies where–

(a)   a business, or part of a business, carried on by a taxable person is transferred as a going concern to a body corporate treated as a member of a group under section 43;

(b)   on the transfer of the business or part, chargeable assets of the business are transferred to the body corporate; and

(c)   the transfer of the assets is treated by virtue of section 5(3)(c) as neither a supply of goods nor a supply of services.

44(2)   Subsection (5) below shall not apply if the representative member of the group is entitled to credit for the whole of the input tax on supplies to it and acquisitions and importations by it–

(a)   during the prescribed accounting period in which the assets are transferred, and

(b)   during any longer period to which regulations under section 26(3)(b) relate and in which the assets are transferred.

44(3)   Subsection (5) below shall not apply if the Commissioners are satisfied that the assets were assets of the taxable person transferring them more than 3 years before the day on which they are transferred.

44(4)   Subsection (5) below shall not apply to the extent that the chargeable assets consist of capital items in respect of which regulations made under section 26(3) and (4), and in force when the assets are transferred, provide for adjustment to the deduction of input tax.

44(5)   The chargeable assets shall be treated for the purposes of this Act as being, on the day on which they are transferred, both supplied to the representative member of the group for the purpose of its business and supplied by that member in the course or furtherance of its business.

44(6)   A supply treated under subsection (5) above as made by a representative member shall not be taken into account as a supply made by him when determining the allowance of input tax in his case under section 26.

44(7)   The value of a supply treated under subsection (5) above as made to or by a representative member shall be taken to be the open market value of the chargeable assets.

44(8)   For the purposes of this section, the **open market value** of any chargeable assets shall be taken to be the price that would be paid on a sale (on which no VAT is payable) between a buyer and a seller who are not in such a relationship as to affect the price.

44(9)   The Commissioners may reduce the VAT chargeable by virtue of subsection (5) above in a case where they are satisfied that the person by whom the chargeable assets are transferred has not received credit for the full amount of input tax arising on the supply to or acquisition or importation by him of the chargeable assets.

44(10)   For the purposes of this section, assets are **chargeable assets** if their supply in the United Kingdom by a taxable person in the course or furtherance of his business would be a taxable supply (and not a zero-rated supply).

Derivations – S. 44(1)–(3): VATA 1983, s. 29A(1)–(3), as inserted by FA 1987, s. 15, and as amended by FA 1990, s. 14(2) and F(No. 2)A 1992, s. 14 and Sch. 3, para. 30(1), (2).
S. 44(4): VATA 1983, s. 29A(3A), as inserted by FA 1990, s. 14(3).
S. 44(5)–(10): VATA 1983, s. 29A(4)–(9), as amended (s. 29A(8)) by F(No. 2)A 1992, s. 14 and Sch. 3, para. 30(3).

45   Partnerships

45(1)   The registration under this Act of persons–

(a)   carrying on a business in partnership, or

(b)   carrying on in partnership any other activities in the course or furtherance of which they acquire goods from other member States,

may be in the name of the firm; and no account shall be taken, in determining for any purpose of this Act whether goods or services are supplied to or by such persons or are acquired by such persons from another member State, of any change in the partnership.

45(2) Without prejudice to section 36 of the Partnership Act 1890 (rights of persons dealing with firm against apparent members of firm), until the date on which a change in the partnership is notified to the Commissioners a person who has ceased to be a member of a partnership shall be regarded as continuing to be a partner for the purposes of this Act and, in particular, for the purpose of any liability for VAT on the supply of goods or services by the partnership or on the acquisition of goods by the partnership from another member State.

45(3) Where a person ceases to be a member of a partnership during a prescribed accounting period (or is treated as so doing by virtue of subsection (2) above) any notice, whether of assessment or otherwise, which is served on the partnership and relates to, or to any matter arising in, that period or any earlier period during the whole or part of which he was a member of the partnership shall be treated as served also on him.

45(4) Without prejudice to section 16 of the Partnership Act 1890 (notice to acting partner to be notice to the firm) any notice, whether of assessment or otherwise, which is addressed to a partnership by the name in which it is registered by virtue of subsection (1) above and is served in accordance with this Act shall be treated for the purposes of this Act as served on the partnership and, accordingly, where subsection (3) above applies, as served also on the former partner.

45(5) Subsections (1) and (3) above shall not affect the extent to which, under section 9 of the Partnership Act 1890, a partner is liable for VAT owed by the firm; but where a person is a partner in a firm during part only of a prescribed accounting period, his liability for VAT on the supply by the firm of goods or services during that accounting period or on the acquisition during that period by the firm of any goods from another member State shall be such proportion of the firm's liability as may be just.

Derivations – VATA 1983, s. 30, as amended by F(No. 2)A 1992, s. 14 and Sch. 3, para. 31.

Note – VAT Regulations 1995 (SI 1995/2518), reg. 7: notice by partnerships.

46   Business carried on in divisions or by unincorporated bodies, personal representatives etc.

46(1) The registration under this Act of a body corporate carrying on a business in several divisions may, if the body corporate so requests and the Commissioners see fit, be in the names of those divisions.

46(2) The Commissioners may by regulations make provision for determining by what persons anything required by or under this Act to be done by a person carrying on a business is to be done where a business is carried on in partnership or by a club, association or organisation the affairs of which are managed by its members or a committee or committees of its members.

46(3) The registration under this Act of any such club, association or organisation may be in the name of the club, association or organisation; and in determining whether goods or services are supplied to or by such a club, association or organisation or whether goods are acquired by such a club, association or organisation from another member State, no account shall be taken of any change in its members.

46(4) The Commissioners may by regulations make provision for persons who carry on a business of a taxable person who has died or become bankrupt or has had his estate sequestrated or has become incapacitated to be treated for a limited time as taxable persons, and for securing continuity in the application of this Act in cases where persons are so treated.

46(5) In relation to a company which is a taxable person, the reference in subsection (4) above to the taxable person having become **bankrupt** or having had his estate **sequestrated** or having become **incapacitated** shall be construed as a reference to its being in liquidation or receivership or to an administration order being in force in relation to it.

46(6) References in this section to a **business** include references to any other activities in the course or furtherance of which any body corporate or any club, association, organisation or other unincorporated body acquires goods from another member State.

Derivations – S. 46(1)–(4): VATA 1983, s. 31(1)–(4), as amended (s. 31(3)) by F(No. 2)A 1992, s. 14 and Sch. 3, para. 32(1). S. 46(5): VATA 1983, s. 31(5), as inserted by FA 1985, s. 31. S. 46(6): VATA 1983, s. 31(6), as inserted by F(No. 2)A 1992, s. 14 and Sch. 3, para. 32(2).

Cross references – S. 67(2)(c): unauthorised issue of invoices. VAT (Payments on Account) Order 1993 (SI 1993/2001), art. 16(1): duty to make payment on account. VAT Regulations 1995 (SI 1995/2518), reg. 52(1): annual accounting unavailable if a division.

Statutory instruments – VAT Regulations 1995 (SI 1995/2518, as amended by SI 1996/1250).

Notes – VAT Regulations 1995 (SI 1995/2518), reg. 8: club, association or organisation and joint and several responsibility.

47   Agents etc.

47(1)   Where–

(a)   goods are acquired from another member State by a person who is not a taxable person and a taxable person acts in relation to the acquisition, and then supplies the goods as agent for the person by whom they are so acquired; or

(b)   goods are imported from a place outside the member States by a taxable person who supplies them as agent for a person who is not a taxable person,

then, if the taxable person acts in relation to the supply in his own name, the goods shall be treated for the purposes of this Act as acquired and supplied or, as the case may be, imported and supplied by the taxable person as principal.

47(2)   For the purposes of subsection (1) above a person who is not resident in the United Kingdom and whose place or principal place of business is outside the United Kingdom may be treated as not being a **taxable person** if as a result he will not be required to be registered under this Act.

47(2A)   Where, in the case of any supply of goods to which subsection (1) above does not apply, goods are supplied through an agent who acts in his own name, the supply shall be treated both as a supply to the agent and as a supply by the agent.

47(3)   Where services are supplied through an agent who acts in his own name the Commissioners may, if they think fit, treat the supply both as a supply to the agent and as a supply by the agent.

History – In s. 47(1), the words "then, if the taxable person ... the goods shall" were substituted for the words "the goods may" by FA 1995, s. 23(1), in relation to goods acquired or imported on or after 1 May 1995.
S. 47(2A) was inserted by FA 1995, s. 23(2), in relation to any supply taking place on or after 1 May 1995.
In s. 47(3), the words "goods or" which appeared after the word "Where" were omitted and repealed by FA 1995, s. 23(3) and 162 and Sch. 29, Pt. VI(2), in relation to any supply taking place on or after 1 May 1995.

Derivations – S. 47(1) (as originally enacted): VATA 1983, s. 32(2), as substituted by F(No. 2)A 1992, s. 14 and Sch. 3, para. 33.
S. 47(2) and (3) (as originally enacted): VATA 1983, s. 32(3), (4).

Official publications – 700 (2000 edn), para. 10.1.

Other material – Customs and Excise Business Brief 20/93, 30 June 1993 (not reproduced): s. 32(4) can apply to the treatment of repossessed property sales.
Customs and Excise News Release 20/95, 3 April 1995: concessionary delay in the introduction of certain FA 1995 changes until 1 June 1995.

48   VAT representatives

48(1)   Where any person–

(a)   is a taxable person for the purposes of this Act or, without being a taxable person, is a person who makes taxable supplies or who acquires goods in the United Kingdom from one or more other member States;

(b)   does not have any business establishment or other fixed establishment in the United Kingdom; and

(c)   in the case of an individual, does not have his usual place of residence in the United Kingdom,

the Commissioners may direct that person to appoint another person (in this Act referred to as a **"VAT representative"**) to act on his behalf in relation to VAT.

48(2)   With the agreement of the Commissioners, any person who has not been required to appoint a VAT representative under subsection (1) above may do so if he is a person in relation to whom the conditions specified in paragraph (a) to (c) of that subsection are satisfied.

48(3)   Where any person is appointed by virtue of this section to be the VAT representative of another **("his principal")**, then, subject to subsections (4) to (6) below, the VAT representative–

(a)   shall be entitled to act on his principal's behalf for any of the purposes of this Act, of any other enactment (whenever passed) relating to VAT or of any subordinate legislation made under this Act or any such enactment;

(b)   shall, subject to such provisions as may be made by the Commissioners by regulations, secure (where appropriate by acting on his principal's behalf) his principal's compliance with and discharge of the obligations and liabilities to which his principal is subject by virtue of this Act, any such other enactment or any such subordinate legislation; and

(c)   shall be personally liable in respect of–

     (i)   any failure to secure his principal's compliance with or discharge of any such obligation or liability; and

     (ii)   anything done for purposes connected with acting on his principal's behalf, as if the obligations and liabilities imposed on his principal were imposed jointly and severally on the VAT representative and his principal.

48(4) A VAT representative shall not be liable by virtue of subsection (3) above himself to be registered under this Act, but regulations made by the Commissioners may–

(a) require the registration of the names of VAT representatives against the names of their principals in any register kept for the purposes of this Act; and

(b) make it the duty of a VAT representative, for the purposes of registration, to notify the Commissioners, within such period as may be prescribed, that his appointment has taken effect or has ceased to have effect.

48(5) A VAT representative shall not by virtue of subsection (3) above be guilty of any offence except in so far as–

(a) the VAT representative has consented to, or connived in, the commission of the offence by his principal;

(b) the commission of the offence by his principal is attributable to any neglect on the part of the VAT representative; or

(c) the offence consists in a contravention by the VAT representative of an obligation which, by virtue of that subsection, is imposed both on the VAT representative and on his principal.

48(6) The Commissioners may by regulations make provision as to the manner and circumstances in which a person is to be appointed, or is to be treated as having ceased to be, another's VAT representative; and regulations under this subsection may include such provision as the Commissioners think fit for the purposes of subsection (4) above with respect to the making or deletion of entries in any register.

48(7) Where a person fails to appoint a VAT representative in accordance with any direction under subsection (1) above, the Commissioners may require him to provide such security, or further security, as they may think appropriate for the payment of any VAT which is or may become due from him.

48(7A) A sum required by way of security under subsection (7) above shall be deemed for the purposes of–

(a) section 51 of the Finance Act 1997 (enforcement by distress) and any regulations under that section, and

(b) section 52 of that Act (enforcement by diligence),

to be recoverable as if it were VAT due from the person who is required to provide it.

48(8) For the purposes of this Act a person shall not be treated as having been directed to appoint a VAT representative, or as having been required to provide security under subsection (7) above, unless the Commissioners have either–

(a) served notice of the direction or requirement on him; or

(b) taken all such other steps as appear to them to be reasonable for bringing the direction or requirement to his attention.

History – S. 48(7A) was inserted by FA 1997, s. 53(6), with effect from 1 July 1997 (SI 1997/1432 (C 54)).

Derivations – VATA 1983, s. 32A, as inserted by F(No. 2)A 1992, s. 14 and Sch. 3, para. 34.

Cross reference – S. 69(1)(b): breaches of regulatory provisions.
S. 83(1): appeals.
S. 96: "VAT representative" defined.
Sch. 11, para. 4, 5: administration powers.
VAT Regulations 1995 (SI 1995/2518), reg. 10: VAT representatives – notification to the commissioners, etc.

Statutory instrument – VAT Regulations 1995 (SI 1995/2518).

Other material – Form VAT 1TR.

49   Transfers of going concerns

49(1) Where a business carried on by a taxable person is transferred to another person as a going concern, then–

(a) for the purpose of determining whether the transferee is liable to be registered under this Act he shall be treated as having carried on the business before as well as after the transfer and supplies by the transferor shall be treated accordingly; and

(b) any records relating to the business which, under paragraph 6 of Schedule 11, are required to be preserved for any period after the transfer shall be preserved by the transferee instead of by the transferor, unless the Commissioners, at the request of the transferor, otherwise direct.

49(2) Without prejudice to subsection (1) above, the Commissioners may by regulations make provision for securing continuity in the application of this Act in cases where a business carried on by a taxable person is transferred to another person as a going concern and the transferee is registered under this Act in substitution for the transferor.

49(3)   Regulations under subsection (2) above may, in particular, provide–

(a)   for liabilities and duties under this Act (excluding sections 59 to 70) of the transferor to become, to such extent as may be provided by the regulations, liabilities and duties of the transferee; and

(b)   for any right of either of them to repayment or credit in respect of VAT to be satisfied by making a repayment or allowing a credit to the other;

but no such provision as is mentioned in paragraph (a) or (b) of this subsection shall have effect in relation to any transferor and transferee unless an application in that behalf has been made by them under the regulations.

Derivations – VATA 1983, s. 33.

Statutory instrument – VAT Regulations 1995 (SI 1995/2518, as amended by SI 1997/1086).

Official publications – 700/9.
Customs Internal Guidance Manual, vol. V1.10: transfer of a going concern.

Notes – Sch. 1, para. 2(2): registration and transfer of a going concern.
VAT (Special Provisions) Order 1995 (SI 1995/1268), art. 5(1): transfer of a "going concern" treated as a non-supply.
VAT Regulations 1995 (SI 1995/2518), reg. 6: registration and notification and transfer of a going concern.
VAT Regulations 1995 (SI 1995/2518), reg. 114(6) and (7): capital goods scheme and transfer of a going concern.

50   Terminal markets

50(1)   The Treasury may by order make provision for modifying the provisions of this Act in their application to dealings on terminal markets and such persons ordinarily engaged in such dealings as may be specified in the order, subject to such conditions as may be so specified.

50(2)   Without prejudice to the generality of subsection (1) above, an order under this section may include provision–

(a)   for zero-rating the supply of any goods or services or for treating the supply of any goods or services as exempt;

(b)   for the registration under this Act of any body of persons representing persons ordinarily engaged in dealing on a terminal market and for disregarding such dealings by persons so represented in determining liability to be registered under this Act, and for disregarding such dealings between persons so represented for all the purposes of this Act;

(c)   for refunding, to such persons as may be specified by or under the order, input tax attributable to such dealings on a terminal market as may be so specified,

and may contain such incidental and supplementary provisions as appear to the Treasury to be necessary or expedient.

50(3)   An order under this section may make different provision with respect to different terminal markets and with respect to different commodities.

Derivations – VATA 1983, s. 34.

Statutory instruments – VAT (Terminal Markets) Order 1973 (SI 1973/173, as amended by SI 1997/1836, SI 1999/3117): zero-rating.

Official publications – 701/9.

50A   Margin schemes

50A(1)   The Treasury may by order provide, in relation to any such description of supplies to which this section applies as may be specified in the order, for a taxable person to be entitled to opt that, where he makes supplies of that description, VAT is to be charged by reference to the profit margin on the supplies, instead of by reference to their value.

50A(2)   This section applies to the following supplies, that is to say–

(a)   supplies of works of art, antiques or collectors' items;

(b)   supplies of motor vehicles;

(c)   supplies of second-hand goods; and

(d)   any supply of goods through a person who acts as an agent, but in his own name, in relation to the supply.

50A(3)   An option for the purposes of an order under this section shall be exercisable, and may be withdrawn, in such manner as may be required by such an order.

50A(4)   Subject to subsection (7) below, the **profit margin on a supply** to which this section applies shall be taken, for the purposes of an order under this section, to be equal to the amount (if any) by which the price at which the person making the supply obtained the goods in question is exceeded by the price at which he supplies them.

50A(5) For the purposes of this section the price at which a person has obtained any goods and the price at which he supplies them shall each be calculated in accordance with the provisions contained in an order under this section; and such an order may, in particular, make provision stipulating the extent to which any VAT charged on a supply, acquisition or importation of any goods is to be treated as included in the price at which those goods have been obtained or are supplied.

50A(6) An order under this section may provide that the consideration for any services supplied in connection with a supply of goods by a person who acts as an agent, but in his own name, in relation to the supply of the goods is to be treated for the purposes of any such order as an amount to be taken into account in computing the profit margin on the supply of the goods, instead of being separately chargeable to VAT as comprised in the value of the services supplied.

50A(7) An order under this section may provide for the total profit margin on all the goods of a particular description supplied by a person in any prescribed accounting period to be calculated by–

(a)   aggregating all the prices at which that person obtained goods of that description in that period together with any amount carried forward to that period in pursuance of paragraph (d) below;

(b)   aggregating all the prices at which he supplies goods of that description in that period;

(c)   treating the total profit margin on goods supplied in that period as being equal to the amount (if any) by which, for that period, the aggregate calculated in pursuance of paragraph (a) above is exceeded by the aggregate calculated in pursuance of paragraph (b) above; and

(d)   treating any amount by which, for that period, the aggregate calculated in pursuance of paragraph (b) above is exceeded by the aggregate calculated in pursuance of paragraph (a) above as an amount to be carried forward to the following prescribed accounting period so as to be included, for the period to which it is carried forward, in any aggregate falling to be calculated in pursuance of paragraph (a) above.

50A(8) An order under this section may–

(a)   make different provision for different cases; and

(b)   make provisions of the order subject to such general or special directions as may, in accordance with the order, be given by the Commissioners with respect to any matter to which the order relates.

History – S. 50A was inserted by FA 1995, s. 24(1), with effect from 1 May 1995.

Cross references – VAT (Special Provisions) Order 1995 (SI 1995/1268, as amended by SI 1997/1616, art. 7 and 8): treatment of transaction where goods removed to UK.
VAT Regulations 1995 (SI 1995/2518), reg. 134: supplies to persons taxable in another member state.
VAT Regulations 1995 (SI 1995/2518), reg. 135: supplies of goods subject to excise duty to persons who are not taxable in another member state.
VAT Regulations 1995 (SI 1995/2518), reg. 172A(1): writing off debts where claimant has opted.

Statutory instruments – VAT (Cars) Order 1992 (SI 1992/1269, as amended by SI 1995/1269, SI 1995/1667, SI 1997/1615, SI 1998/759, SI 1999/2832).
VAT (Special Provisions) Order 1995 (SI 1995/1268, as amended by SI 1998/760, SI 1999/2831, SI 1999/3120).
VAT (Input Tax) (Amendment) (No. 2) Order 1999 (SI 1995/1268).

Extra-statutory concessions – 3.8 (Notice 48 (1999 edn)): use of margin scheme for vehicle sales when incomplete records have been kept.

Official publications – 718.

Notes – VAT (Input Tax) Order 1992 (SI 1992/3222), art. 4: disallowance of input tax.

51   Buildings and land

51(1) Schedule 10 shall have effect with respect to buildings and land.

51(2) The Treasury may by order amend Schedule 10.

Derivations – VATA 1983, s. 35A, as inserted by FA 1989, s. 18 and Sch. 3, para. 6.
Statutory instruments – VAT (Buildings and Land) Order 1994 (SI 1994/3013).
VAT (Buildings and Land) Order 1995 (SI 1995/279).
VAT (Registered Social Landlords) (No. 2) Order 1997 (SI 1997/51).
VAT (Buildings and Land) Order 1999 (SI 1999/593).

51A   *Co-owners etc. of buildings and land*

Prospective insertion – S. 51A is to be inserted by FA 1995, s. 26(1), with effect from a day to be appointed by statutory instrument.

51A(1) This section applies to a supply consisting in the grant, assignment or surrender of any interest in or right over land in a case where there is more than one person by whom the grant, assignment or surrender is made or treated as made; and for this purpose–

(a)   a licence to occupy land, and

(b)   in relation to land in Scotland, a personal right to call for or be granted any interest or right in or over land,

shall be taken to be a right over land.

51A(2)   The persons who make or are treated as making a supply to which this section applies ("**the grantors**") shall be treated, in relation to that supply and in relation to any other such supply with respect to which the grantors are the same, as a single person ("**the property-owner**") who is distinct from each of the grantors individually.

51A(3)   Registration under this Act of the property-owner shall be in the name of the grantors acting together as a property-owner.

51A(4)   The grantors shall be jointly and severally liable in respect of the obligations falling by virtue of this section on the property-owner.

51A(5)   Any notice, whether of assessment or otherwise, which is addressed to the property-owner by the name in which the property-owner is registered and is served on any of the grantors in accordance with this Act shall be treated for the purposes of this Act as served on the property-owner.

51A(6)   Where there is any change in some, but not all, of the persons who are for the time being to be treated as the grantors in relation to any supply to which this section applies–

(a)   that change shall be disregarded for the purposes of this section in relation to any prescribed accounting period beginning before the change is notified in the prescribed manner to the Commissioners; and

(b)   any notice (whether of assessment or otherwise) which is served, at any time after such a notification, on the property-owner for the time being shall, so far as it relates to, or to any matter arising in, such a period, be treated for the purposes of this Act as served on whoever was the property-owner in that period.

52   Trading stamp schemes

52   The Commissioners may by regulations modify sections 19 and 20 and Schedules 6 and 7 for the purpose of providing (in place of the provision for the time being contained in those sections and Schedules) for the manner of determining for the purposes of this Act the value of–

(a)   a supply of goods, or

(b)   a transaction in pursuance of which goods are acquired from another member State,

in a case where the goods are supplied or acquired under a trading stamp scheme (within the meaning of the Trading Stamps Act 1964 or the Trading Stamps Act (Northern Ireland) 1965) or under any scheme of an equivalent description which is in operation in another member State.

Derivations – VATA 1983, s. 37, as substituted by F(No. 2)A 1992, s. 14 and Sch. 3, para. 37.

Statutory instrument – VAT Regulations 1995 (SI 1995/2518, as amended by SI 1995/3043).

53   Tour operators

53(1)   The Treasury may by order modify the application of this Act in relation to supplies of goods or services by tour operators or in relation to such of those supplies as may be determined by or under the order.

53(2)   Without prejudice to the generality of subsection (1) above, an order under this section may make provision–

(a)   for two or more supplies of goods or services by a tour operator to be treated as a single supply of services;

(b)   for the value of that supply to be ascertained, in such manner as may be determined by or under the order, by reference to the difference between sums paid or payable to and sums paid or payable by the tour operator;

(c)   for account to be taken, in determining the VAT chargeable on that supply, of the different rates of VAT that would have been applicable apart from this section;

(d)   excluding any body corporate from the application of section 43;

(e)   as to the time when a supply is to be treated as taking place.

53(3)   In this section "**tour operator**" includes a travel agent acting as principal and any other person providing for the benefit of travellers services of any kind commonly provided by tour operators or travel agents.

53(4) Section 97(3) shall not apply to an order under this section, notwithstanding that it makes provision for excluding any VAT from credit under section 25.

Derivations – VATA 1983, s. 37A, as inserted by FA 1987, s. 16.

Cross references – VAT Regulations 1995 (SI 1995/2518), reg. 172B(1): writing off debts where claimant is a tour operator.

Statutory instruments – VAT (Tour Operators) Order 1987 (SI 1987/1806, as amended by SI 1995/1495).

Official publications – 709/5.

54   Farmers etc.

54(1) The Commissioners may, in accordance with such provision as may be contained in regulations made by them, certify for the purposes of this section any person who satisfies them–

(a)   that he is carrying on a business involving one or more designated activities;

(b)   that he is of such a description and has complied with such requirements as may be prescribed; and

(c)   where an earlier certification of that person has been cancelled, that more than the prescribed period has elapsed since the cancellation or that such other conditions as may be prescribed are satisfied.

54(2) Where a person is for the time being certified under this section, then (whether or not that person is a taxable person) so much of any supply by him of any goods or services as, in accordance with provision contained in regulations, is allocated to the relevant part of his business shall be disregarded for the purpose of determining whether he is, has become or has ceased to be liable or entitled to be registered under Schedule 1.

54(3) The Commissioners may by regulations provide for an amount included in the consideration for any taxable supply which is made–

(a)   in the course or furtherance of the relevant part of his business by a person who is for the time being certified under this section;

(b)   at a time when that person is not a taxable person; and

(c)   to a taxable person,

to be treated, for the purpose of determining the entitlement of the person supplied to credit under sections 25 and 26, as VAT on a supply to that person.

54(4) The amount which, for the purposes of any provision made under subsection (3) above, may be included in the consideration for any supply shall be an amount equal to such percentage as the Treasury may by order specify of the sum which, with the addition of that amount, is equal to the consideration for the supply.

54(5) The Commissioners' power by regulations under section 39 to provide for the repayment to persons to whom that section applies of VAT which would be input tax of theirs if they were taxable persons in the United Kingdom includes power to provide for the payment to persons to whom that section applies of sums equal to the amounts which, if they were taxable persons in the United Kingdom, would be input tax of theirs by virtue of regulations under this section; and references in that section, or in any other enactment, to a repayment of VAT shall be construed accordingly.

54(6) Regulations under this section may provide–

(a)   for the form and manner in which an application for certification under this section, or for the cancellation of any such certification, is to be made;

(b)   for the cases and manner in which the Commissioners may cancel a person's certification;

(c)   for entitlement to a credit such as is mentioned in subsection (3) above to depend on the issue of an invoice containing such particulars as may be prescribed, or as may be notified by the Commissioners in accordance with provision contained in regulations; and

(d)   for the imposition on certified persons of obligations with respect to the keeping, preservation and production of such records as may be prescribed and of obligations to comply with such requirements with respect to any of those matters as may be so notified;

and regulations made by virtue of paragraph (b) above may confer on the Commissioners power, if they think fit, to refuse to cancel a person's certification, and to refuse to give effect to any entitlement of that person to be registered, until the end of such period after the grant of certification as may be prescribed.

54(7) In this section references, in relation to any person, to the **relevant part of his business** are references–

(a)   where the whole of his business relates to the carrying on of one or more designated activities, to that business; and

(b)   in any other case, to so much of his business as does so relate.

54(8)   In this section **"designated activities"** means such activities, being activities carried on by a person who, by virtue of carrying them on, falls to be treated as a farmer for the purposes of Article 25 of the directive of the Council of the European Communities dated 17th May 1977 No. 77/388/EEC (common flat-rate scheme for farmers), as the Treasury may by order designate.

Derivations – VATA 1983, s. 37B, as inserted by F(No. 2)A 1992, s. 16.

Cross references – S. 67(7)(a): unauthorised issue of invoices.
S. 83(m): appeals.
Sch. 4, para. 8(3): where a person ceases to be a taxable person in consequence of having been certified under s. 54, the deemed supply on deregistration does not apply.
VAT Regulations 1995 (SI 1995/2518), reg. 209(1): claims by taxable persons for farmers' flat-rate amounts to be treated as credits for input tax.

Statutory instruments – VAT (Flat-rate Scheme for Farmers) (Designated Activities) Order 1992 (SI 1992/3220).
VAT (Flat-rate Scheme for Farmers) (Percentage Addition) Order 1992 (SI 1992/3221).
VAT Regulations 1995 (SI 1995/2518).

Official publications – 700/46: "Agricultural flat-rate scheme".

Other material – Form VAT 98.

55   Customers to account for tax on supplies of gold etc.

55(1)   Where any person makes a supply of gold to another person and that supply is a taxable supply but not a zero rated supply, the supply shall be treated for purposes of Schedule 1–

(a)   as a taxable supply of that other person (as well as a taxable supply of the person who makes it); and

(b)   in so far as that other person is supplied in connection with the carrying on by him of any business, as a supply made by him in the course or furtherance of that business;

but nothing in paragraph (b) above shall require any supply to be disregarded for the purposes of that Schedule on the grounds that it is a supply of capital assets of that other person's business.

55(2)   Where a taxable person makes a supply of gold to a person who–

(a)   is himself a taxable person at the time when the supply is made; and

(b)   is supplied in connection with the carrying on by him of any business,

it shall be for the person supplied, on the supplier's behalf, to account for and pay tax on the supply, and not for the supplier.

55(3)   So much of this Act and of any other enactment or any subordinate legislation as has effect for the purposes of, or in connection with, the enforcement of any obligation to account for and pay VAT shall apply for the purposes of this section in relation to any person who is required under subsection (2) above to account for and pay any VAT as if that VAT were VAT on a supply made by him.

55(4)   Section 6(4) to (10) shall not apply for determining when any supply of gold is to be treated as taking place.

55(5)   References in this section to **a supply of gold** are references to–

(a)   any supply of goods consisting in fine gold, in gold grain of any purity or in gold coins of any purity;

(b)   any supply of goods containing gold where the consideration for the supply (apart from any VAT) is, or is equivalent to, an amount which does not exceed, or exceeds by no more than a negligible amount, the open market value of the gold contained in the goods; or

(c)   any supply of services consisting in the application to another person's goods of a treatment or process which produces goods a supply of which would fall within paragraph (a) above.

55(6)   The Treasury may by order provide for this section to apply, as it applies to the supplies specified in subsection (5) above, to such other supplies of–

(a)   goods consisting in or containing any precious or semi-precious metal or stones; or

(b)   services relating to, or to anything containing, any precious or semi-precious metal or stones,

as may be specified or described in the order.

History – In s. 55(5)(a), at the end, the word "or" was omitted and repealed by FA 1996, s. 29(3) and 205 and Sch. 41, Pt. IV(2), with effect for supplies made on or after 1 January 1996. S. 55(5)(a), was substituted by FA 1996, s. 32(1), in relation to any supply after 28 November 1995.
In s. 55(5)(b), at the end, the word "; or" was inserted by FA 1996, s. 29(3), with effect for supplies made on or after 1 January 1996.
S. 55(5)(c) was inserted by FA 1996, s. 29(3), with effect for supplies made on or after 1 January 1996.

Derivations – VATA 1983, s. 37C, as inserted by FA 1993, s. 45.

Cross references – S. 6(14): time of supply.
VAT (Terminal Markets) Order 1973 (SI 1973/173), art. 5 and 7: terminal markets.
VAT (Importation of Investment Gold) Relief) Order 1999 (SI 1999/3115), art. 4: customers to account for VAT on supplies of investment gold.
Statutory instruments – VAT (Terminal Markets) Order 1973 (SI 1973/173, as amended by SI 1999/3117): zero-rating.
VAT (Investment Gold) Order 1999 (SI 1999/3116).

56   Fuel for private use

56(1)   The provisions of this section apply where, in any prescribed accounting period, fuel which is or has previously been supplied to or imported or manufactured by a taxable person in the course of his business–

(a)   is provided or to be provided by the taxable person to an individual for private use in his own vehicle or a vehicle allocated to him and is so provided by reason of that individual's employment; or

(b)   where the taxable person is an individual, is appropriated or to be appropriated by him for private use in his own vehicle; or

(c)   where the taxable person is a partnership, is provided or to be provided to any of the individual partners for private use in his own vehicle.

56(2)   For the purposes of this section fuel shall not be regarded as provided to any person for his **private use** if it is supplied at a price which–

(a)   in the case of fuel supplied to or imported by the taxable person, is not less than the price at which it was so supplied or imported; and

(b)   in the case of fuel manufactured by the taxable person, is not less than the aggregate of the cost of the raw material and of manufacturing together with any excise duty thereon.

56(3)   For the purposes of this section and section 57–

(a)   **"fuel for private use"** means fuel which, having been supplied to or imported or manufactured by a taxable person in the course of his business, is or is to be provided or appropriated for private use as mentioned in subsection (1) above;

(b)   any reference to **fuel supplied to a taxable person** shall include a reference to fuel acquired by a taxable person from another member State and any reference to fuel imported by a taxable person shall be confined to a reference to fuel imported by that person from a place outside the member States;

(c)   any reference to an **individual's own vehicle** shall be construed as including any vehicle of which for the time being he has the use, other than a vehicle allocated to him;

(d)   subject to subsection (9) below, a vehicle shall at any time be taken to be **allocated to an individual** if at that time it is made available (without any transfer of the property in it) either to the individual himself or to any other person, and is so made available by reason of the individual's employment and for private use; and

(e)   fuel provided by an employer to an employee and fuel provided to any person for private use in a vehicle which, by virtue of paragraph (d) above, is for the time being taken to be allocated to the employee shall be taken to be **provided to the employee by reason of his employment** .

56(4)   Where under section 43 any bodies corporate are treated as members of a group, any provision of fuel by a member of the group to an individual shall be treated for the purposes of this section as provision by the representative member.

56(5)   In relation to the taxable person, tax on the supply, acquisition or importation of fuel for private use shall be treated for the purposes of this Act as input tax, notwithstanding that the fuel is not used or to be used for the purposes of a business carried on by the taxable person (and, accordingly, no apportionment of VAT shall fall to be made under section 24(5) by reference to fuel for private use).

56(6)   At the time at which fuel for private use is put into the fuel tank of an individual's own vehicle or of a vehicle allocated to him, the fuel shall be treated for the purposes of this Act as supplied to him by the taxable person in the course or furtherance of his business for a consideration determined in accordance with subsection (7) below (and, accordingly, where the fuel is appropriated by the taxable person to his own private use, he shall be treated as supplying it to himself in his private capacity).

56(7)   In any prescribed accounting period of the taxable person in which, by virtue of subsection (6) above, he is treated as supplying fuel for private use to an individual, the consideration for all the supplies made to that individual in that period in respect of any one vehicle shall be that which, by virtue of section 57, is appropriate to a vehicle of that description, and that consideration shall be taken to be inclusive of VAT.

56(8) In any case where–

(a)   in any prescribed accounting period, fuel for private use is, by virtue of subsection (6) above, treated as supplied to an individual in respect of one vehicle for a part of the period and in respect of another vehicle for another part of the period; and

(b)   at the end of that period one of those vehicles neither belongs to him nor is allocated to him,

subsection (7) above shall have effect as if the supplies made to the individual during those parts of the period were in respect of only one vehicle.

56(9) In any prescribed accounting period a vehicle shall not be regarded as **allocated to an individual by reason of his employment** if–

(a)   in that period it was made available to, and actually used by, more than one of the employees of one or more employers and, in the case of each of them, it was made available to him by reason of his employment but was not in that period ordinarily used by any one of them to the exclusion of the others; and

(b)   in the case of each of the employees, any private use of the vehicle made by him in that period was merely incidental to his other use of it in that period; and

(c)   it was in that period not normally kept overnight on or in the vicinity of any residential premises where any of the employees was residing, except while being kept overnight on premises occupied by the person making the vehicle available to them.

56(10) In this section and section 57–

"**employment**" includes any office; and related expressions shall be construed accordingly; "**vehicle**" means a mechanically propelled road vehicle other than–

(a)   a motor cycle as defined in section 185(1) of the Road Traffic Act 1988 or, for Northern Ireland, in Article 37(1)(f) of the Road Traffic (Northern Ireland) Order 1981, or

(b)   an invalid carriage as defined in that section or, for Northern Ireland, in Article 37(1)(g) of that Order.

Derivations – S. 56(1), (2): FA 1986, s. 9(1), (2).
S. 56(3)(a): FA 1986, s. 9(3)(a).
S. 56(3)(b): FA 1986, s. 9(3)(aa), as inserted by F(No. 2)A 1992, s. 14 and Sch. 3, para. 94.
S. 56(3)(c)–(e): FA 1986, s. 9(3)(b)–(d).
S. 56(4): FA 1986, s. 9(4).
S. 56(5): FA 1986, s. 9(5), as amended by F(No. 2)A 1992, s. 14 and Sch. 3, para. 94.
S. 56(6)–(10): FA 1986, s. 9(6)–(10), as amended by the Road Traffic (Consequential Provisions) Act 1988, s. 4 and Sch. 3, para. 32.

Extra-statutory concessions – 3.1 (Notice 48 (1999 edn)): scale charge avoided if no input tax recovered on any road fuel.

Other material – Customs and Excise News Release 24/87, 25 March 1987 (not reproduced): VAT scale charges apply only to cars and not to other motor vehicles according to the terms of the derogation made under Directive 77/388 of 17 May 1977, art. 27 (the sixth VAT directive).

57   Determination of consideration for fuel supplied for private use

57(1) This section has effect to determine the consideration referred to in section 56(7) in respect of any one vehicle; and in this section–

"**the prescribed accounting period**" means that in respect of supplies in which the consideration is to be determined; and

"**the individual**" means the individual to whom those supplies are treated as made.

57(1A) Where the prescribed accounting period is a period of 12 months, the consideration appropriate to any vehicle is that specified in relation to a vehicle of the appropriate description in the second column of Table A below.

57(2) Where the prescribed accounting period is a period of 3 months, the consideration appropriate to any vehicle is that specified in relation to a vehicle of the appropriate description in the third column of Table A below.

57(3) Where the prescribed accounting period is a period of one month, the consideration appropriate to any vehicle is that specified in relation to a vehicle of the appropriate description in the fourth column of Table A below.

TABLE A

Description of vehicle (Type of engine and cylinder capacity in cubic centimetres)	12 month period	3 month period	1 month period
	£	£	£
Diesel engine			
2000 or less	930	232	77
More than 2000	1180	295	98
Any other type of engine			
1400 or less	1025	256	85
More than 1400 but not more than 2000	1300	325	108
More than 2000	1915	478	159

57(4)   The Treasury may by order taking effect from the beginning of any prescribed accounting period beginning after the order is made substitute a different Table for Table A for the time being set out above.

57(5)   Where, by virtue of section 56(8), subsection (7) of that section has effect as if, in the prescribed accounting period, supplies of fuel for private use made in respect of 2 or more vehicles were made in respect of only one vehicle, the consideration appropriate shall be determined as follows–

(a)   if each of the 2 or more vehicles falls within the same description of vehicle specified in Table A above, that Table shall apply as if only one of the vehicles were to be considered throughout the whole period, and

(b)   if one of those vehicles falls within a description of vehicle specified in that Table which is different from the other or others, the consideration shall be the aggregate of the relevant fractions of the consideration appropriate for each description of vehicle under that Table.

57(6)   For the purposes of subsection (5)(b) above, **the relevant fraction** in relation to any vehicle is that which the part of the prescribed accounting period in which fuel for private use was supplied in respect of that vehicle bears to the whole of that period.

57(7)   In the case of a vehicle having an internal combustion engine with one or more reciprocating pistons, its cubic capacity for the purposes of Table A above is the capacity of its engine as calculated for the purposes of the Vehicle Excise and Registration Act 1994.

57(8)   In the case of a vehicle not falling within subsection (7) above, its cubic capacity shall be such as may be determined for the purposes of Table A above by order by the Treasury.

History – S. 57(1A) was inserted by FA 1995, s. 30(2), in relation to prescribed accounting periods beginning on or after 6 April 1995.
In s. 57(2), the word "third" was substituted by FA 1995, s. 30(3), in relation to prescribed accounting periods beginning on or after 6 April 1995.
In s. 57(3), Table A was substituted by SI 2000/811, art. 2, operative from the beginning of the first prescribed accounting period which begins after 5 April 2000. The former Table A read as follows:

TABLE A

Description of vehicle (Type of engine and cylinder capacity in cubic centimetres)	12 month period	3 month period	1 month period
	£	£	£
Diesel engine			
2000 or less	785	196	65
More than 2000	995	248	82
Any other type of engine			
1400 or less	850	212	70
More than 1400 but not more than 2000	1075	268	89
More than 2000	1585	396	132

In s. 57(3), Table A was substituted by SI 1998/788, art. 2, operative from the beginning of the first prescribed accounting period which begins after 5 April 1998.
In s. 57(3), the word "fourth" was substituted by FA 1995, s. 30(4), in relation to prescribed accounting periods beginning on or after 6 April 1995.
In s. 57(3), Table A was substituted by SI 1995/3040, art. 2, operative from the beginning of the first prescribed accounting period which begins after 5 April 1996.
In s. 57(3), Table A was substituted by FA 1995, s. 30(5), in relation to prescribed accounting periods which begin after 5 April 1995 but before 6 April 1996.

Derivations – S. 57(1): FA 1986, s. 9 and Sch. 6, para. 1.
S. 57(2) and (3) (both as originally enacted): FA 1986, s. 9 and Sch. 6, para. 2; Table A substituted by SI 1993/765 and amended by SI 1993/2952.
S. 57(4): FA 1986, s. 9 and Sch. 6, para. 4, as amended by FA 1993, s. 43(3).
S. 57(5): FA 1986, s. 9 and Sch. 6, para. 5(1), as amended by FA 1993, s. 43(2)(a), (b).
S. 57(6): FA 1986, s. 9 and Sch. 6, para. 5(2).
S. 57(7): FA 1986, s. 9 and Sch. 6, para. 6(1), as amended by FA 1993, s. 43(2)(c).
S. 57(8): FA 1986, s. 9 and Sch. 6, para. 6(2), as amended by FA 1993, s. 43(2)(d).
Statutory instruments – VAT (Increase of Consideration for Fuel) Order 1995 (SI 1995/3040).
VAT (Increase of Consideration for Fuel) Order 1996 (SI 1996/2948).
VAT (Increase of Consideration for Fuel) Order 1998 (SI 1998/788).
VAT (Increase of Consideration for Fuel) Order 2000 (SI 2000/811).

PART IV – ADMINISTRATION, COLLECTION AND ENFORCEMENT

Extra-statutory concessions – Default surcharge, civil penalties and default interest are not applied to post-insolvency VAT returns (Notice 700/56/99, para. 5.5).
Official publications – Customs Internal Guidance Manual, vol. V1.27: civil penalties.

GENERAL ADMINISTRATIVE PROVISIONS

58   General provisions relating to the administration and collection of VAT

58   Schedule 11 shall have effect, subject to section 92(6), with respect to the administration, collection and enforcement of VAT.

Derivations – VATA 1983, s. 38, as amended by F(No. 2)A 1992, s. 14 and Sch. 3, para. 38.
Statutory instruments – VAT Regulations 1995 (SI 1995/2518, as amended by SI 1996/1250, SI 1997/1614, SI 1997/2437, SI 2000/258).

DEFAULT SURCHARGES AND OTHER PENALTIES AND CRIMINAL OFFENCES

59   The default surcharge

59(1)   Subject to subsection (1A) below if, by the last day on which a taxable person is required in accordance with regulations under this Act to furnish a return for a prescribed accounting period–

(a)   the Commissioners have not received that return, or

(b)   the Commissioners have received that return but have not received the amount of VAT shown on the return as payable by him in respect of that period,

then that person shall be regarded for the purposes of this section as being in **default** in respect of that period.

59(1A)   A person shall not be regarded for the purposes of this section as being in default in respect of any prescribed accounting period if that period is one in respect of which he is required by virtue of any order under section 28 to make any payment on account of VAT.

59(2)   Subject to subsection (9) and (10) below, subsection (4) below applies in any case where–

(a)   a taxable person is in default in respect of a prescribed accounting period; and

(b)   the Commissioners serve notice on the taxable person (a **"surcharge liability notice"**) specifying as a **surcharge period** for the purposes of this section a period ending on the first anniversary of the last day of the period referred to in paragraph (a) above and beginning, subject to subsection (3) below, on the date of the notice.

59(3)   If a surcharge liability notice is served by reason of a default in respect of a prescribed accounting period and that period ends at or before the expiry of an existing surcharge period already notified to the taxable person concerned, the surcharge period specified in that notice shall be expressed as a continuation of the existing surcharge period and, accordingly, for the purposes of this section, that existing period and its extension shall be regarded as a single surcharge period.

59(4)   Subject to subsections (7) to (10) below, if a taxable person on whom a surcharge liability notice has been served–

(a)   is in default in respect of a prescribed accounting period ending within the surcharge period specified in (or extended by) that notice, and

(b) has outstanding VAT for that prescribed accounting period,

he shall be liable to a surcharge equal to whichever is the greater of the following, namely, the specified percentage of his outstanding VAT for that prescribed accounting period and £30.

59(5) Subject to subsections (7) to (10) below, the **specified percentage** referred to in subsection (4) above shall be determined in relation to a prescribed accounting period by reference to the number of such periods in respect of which the taxable person is in default during the surcharge period and for which he has outstanding VAT, so that–

(a) in relation to the first such prescribed accounting period, the specified percentage is 2 per cent;

(b) in relation to the second such period, the specified percentage is 5 per cent;

(c) in relation to the third such period, the specified percentage is 10 per cent; and

(d) in relation to each such period after the third, the specified percentage is 15 per cent.

59(6) For the purposes of subsection (4) and (5) above a person has **outstanding VAT** for a prescribed accounting period if some or all of the VAT for which he is liable in respect of that period has not been paid by the last day on which he is required (as mentioned in subsection (1) above) to make a return for that period; and the reference in subsection (4) above to a person's outstanding VAT for a prescribed accounting period is to so much of the VAT for which he is so liable as has not been paid by that day.

59(7) If a person who, apart from this subsection, would be liable to a surcharge under subsection (4) above satisfies the Commissioners or, on appeal, a tribunal that, in the case of a default which is material to the surcharge–

(a) the return or, as the case may be, the VAT shown on the return was despatched at such a time and in such a manner that it was reasonable to expect that it would be received by the Commissioners within the appropriate time limit, or

(b) there is a reasonable excuse for the return or VAT not having been so despatched,

he shall not be liable to the surcharge and for the purposes of the preceding provisions of this section he shall be treated as not having been in default in respect of the prescribed accounting period in question (and, accordingly, any surcharge liability notice the service of which depended upon that default shall be deemed not to have been served).

59(8) For the purposes of subsection (7) above, a default is **material to a surcharge if**–

(a) it is the default which, by virtue of subsection (4) above, gives rise to the surcharge; or

(b) it is a default which was taken into account in the service of the surcharge liability notice upon which the surcharge depends and the person concerned has not previously been liable to a surcharge in respect of a prescribed accounting period ending within the surcharge period specified in or extended by that notice.

59(9) In any case where–

(a) the conduct by virtue of which a person is in default in respect of a prescribed accounting period is also conduct falling within section 69(1), and

(b) by reason of that conduct, the person concerned is assessed to a penalty under that section,

the default shall be left out of account for the purposes of subsections (2) to (5) above.

59(10) If the Commissioners, after consultation with the Treasury, so direct, a default in respect of a prescribed accounting period specified in the direction shall be left out of account for the purposes of subsections (2) to (5) above.

59(11) For the purposes of this section references to a thing's being done by any day include references to its being done on that day.

History – In s. 59(1), the words "Subject to subsection (1A) below" were inserted by FA 1996, s. 35(3) in relation to any prescribed accounting period ending on or after 1 June 1996 but a liability to make a payment on account of VAT shall be disregarded for the purposes of the amendments made by this section if the payment is one becoming due before that date.
S. 59(1A) was inserted by FA 1996, s. 35(3) in relation to any prescribed accounting period ending on or after 1 June 1996 but a liability to make a payment on account of VAT shall be disregarded for the purposes of the amendments made by this section if the payment is one becoming due before that date .
S. 59(11) was inserted by FA 1996, s. 35(4) in relation to any prescribed accounting period ending on or after 1 June 1996 but a liability to make a payment on account of VAT shall be disregarded for the purposes of the amendments made by this section if the payment is one becoming due before that date.

Derivations – S. 59(1): FA 1985, s. 19(1).
S. 59(2): FA 1985, s. 19(2)(a), (c), as amended by FA 1993, s. 49 and Sch. 2, para. 5(1).
S. 59(3): FA 1985, s. 19(3), as amended by FA 1993, s. 49 and Sch. 2, para. 5(2).
S. 59(4): FA 1985, s. 19(4), as substituted by FA 1993, s. 49 and Sch. 2, para. 6(1).
S. 59(5): FA 1985, s. 19(5), as amended by FA 1993, s. 49 and Sch. 2, para. 6(2), 7.
S. 59(6): FA 1985, s. 19(5A), as inserted by FA 1993, s. 49 and Sch. 2, para. 6(3).
S. 59(7)–(10): FA 1985, s. 19(6)–(9).

Cross references – S. 69(4)(a) and (9)(b): breaches of regulatory provisions.
S. 76(1): assessment.
S. 83(n): appeal against a default surcharge.
ICTA 1988, s. 827(1): surcharge is not a deduction in computing any income, profits or losses for any tax purpose.
VAT Tribunals Rules 1986 (SI 1986/590), r. 2: "reasonable excuse appeal" defined.
VAT Regulations 1995 (SI 1995/2518), reg. 64(1): surcharge can stop use of cash accounting scheme.
Official publications – 700/50: default surcharge.
700/56/99, para. 5.5: generally no default surcharge applies to post-insolvency returns.
Notes – S. 71: "reasonable excuse" defined.
A late return and/or payment could cause Customs:
- to make a control visit and require the immediate production of documents and within a reasonable time the furnishing of information (Sch. 11, para. 7);
- to require a person for the protection of the revenue to give security as a condition of making future supplies (Sch. 11, para. 4(2));
- to issue an estimated assessment in the absence of a return (s. 73(1));
- to extend the 30-day period during which Customs must make certain repayments if no repayment supplement is to arise (s. 79(3));
- to require monthly returns (VAT Regulations 1995 (SI 1995/2518), reg. 25(1)(a));
- to refuse consent to a tribunal hearing an appeal until all returns arrive (s. 84(2); VAT Tribunals Rules 1986 (SI 1986/590), r. 33(1)(a)) except under the r. 11(4), hardship get-out);
- to refuse to make a repayment which is due (s. 25(5));
- to terminate use of the cash accounting scheme (VAT Regulations 1995 (SI 1995/2518), reg. 58 and 64; and
- to refuse authorisation to use the annual accounting scheme or to terminate any authorisation (VAT Regulations 1995 (SI 1995/2518), reg. 51 and 55)).

59A   Default surcharge: payments on account

59A(1)   For the purposes of this section a taxable person shall be regarded as in **default** in respect of any prescribed accounting period if the period is one in respect of which he is required, by virtue of an order under section 28, to make any payment on account of VAT and either–

(a)   a payment which he is so required to make in respect of that period has not been received in full by the Commissioners by the day on which it became due; or

(b)   he would, but for section 59(1A), be in default in respect of that period for the purposes of section 59.

59A(2)   Subject to subsections (10) and (11) below, subsection (4) below applies in any case where–

(a)   a taxable person is in default in respect of a prescribed accounting period; and

(b)   the Commissioners serve notice on the taxable person (a **"surcharge liability notice"**) specifying as a surcharge period for the purposes of this section a period which–

     (i) begins, subject to subsection (3) below, on the date of the notice; and

     (ii) ends on the first anniversary of the last day of the period referred to in paragraph (a) above.

59A(3)   If–

(a)   a surcharge liability notice is served by reason of a default in respect of a prescribed accounting period, and

(b)   that period ends at or before the expiry of an existing surcharge period already notified to the taxable person concerned,

the surcharge period specified in that notice shall be expressed as a continuation of the existing surcharge period; and, accordingly, the existing period and its extension shall be regarded as a single surcharge period.

59A(4)   Subject to subsections (7) to (11) below, if–

(a)   a taxable person on whom a surcharge liability notice has been served is in default in respect of a prescribed accounting period,

(b)   that prescribed accounting period is one ending within the surcharge period specified in (or extended by) that notice, and

(c)   the aggregate value of his defaults in respect of that prescribed accounting period is more than nil,

that person shall be liable to a surcharge equal to whichever is the greater of £30 and the specified percentage of the aggregate value of his defaults in respect of that prescribed accounting period.

59A(5)   Subject to subsections (7) to (11) below, the **specified percentage** referred to in subsection (4) above shall be determined in relation to a prescribed accounting period by reference to the number of such periods during the surcharge period which are periods in respect of which the taxable person is in default and in respect of which the value of his defaults is more than nil, so that–

(a)   in relation to the first such prescribed accounting period, the specified percentage is 2 per cent;

(b)   in relation to the second such period, the specified percentage is 5 per cent;

(c)   in relation to the third such period, the specified percentage is 10 per cent; and

(d)   in relation to each such period after the third, the specified percentage is 15 per cent.

59A(6)   For the purposes of this section the **aggregate value of a person's defaults** in respect of a prescribed accounting period shall be calculated as follows–

(a)   where the whole or any part of a payment in respect of that period on account of VAT was not received by the Commissioners by the day on which it became due, an amount equal to that payment or, as the case may be, to that part of it shall be taken to be the value of the default relating to that payment;

(b)   if there is more than one default with a value given by paragraph (a) above, those values shall be aggregated;

(c)   the total given by paragraph (b) above, or (where there is only one default) the value of the default under paragraph (a) above, shall be taken to be the value for that period of that person's defaults on payments on account;

(d)   the value of any default by that person which is a default falling within subsection (1)(b) above shall be taken to be equal to the amount of any outstanding VAT less the amount of unpaid payments on account; and

(e)   the aggregate value of a person's defaults in respect of that period shall be taken to be the aggregate of–

     (i) the value for that period of that person's defaults (if any) on payments on account; and

     (ii) the value of any default of his in respect of that period that falls within subsection (1)(b) above.

59A(7)   In the application of subsection (6) above for the calculation of the aggregate value of a person's defaults in respect of a prescribed accounting period–

(a)   the amount of outstanding VAT referred to in paragraph (d) of that subsection is the amount (if any) which would be the amount of that person's outstanding VAT for that period for the purposes of section 59(4); and

(b)   the amount of unpaid payments on account referred to in that paragraph is the amount (if any) equal to so much of any payments on account of VAT (being payments in respect of that period) as has not been received by the Commissioners by the last day on which that person is required (as mentioned in section 59(1)) to make a return for that period.

59A(8)   If a person who, apart from this subsection, would be liable to a surcharge under subsection (4) above satisfies the Commissioners or, on appeal, a tribunal–

(a)   in the case of a default that is material for the purposes of the surcharge and falls within subsection (1)(a) above–

     (i) that the payment on account of VAT was despatched at such a time and in such a manner that it was reasonable to expect that it would be received by the Commissioners by the day on which it became due, or

     (ii) that there is a reasonable excuse for the payment not having been so despatched, or

(b)   in the case of a default that is material for the purposes of the surcharge and falls within subsection (1)(b) above, that the condition specified in section 59(7)(a) or (b) is satisfied as respects the default,

he shall not be liable to the surcharge and for the purposes of the preceding provisions of this section he shall be treated as not having been in default in respect of the prescribed accounting period in question (and, accordingly, any surcharge liability notice the service of which depended upon that default shall be deemed not to have been served).

59A(9)   For the purposes of subsection (8) above, a default is **material** to a surcharge if–

(a)   it is the default which, by virtue of subsection (4) above, gives rise to the surcharge; or

(b)   it is a default which was taken into account in the service of the surcharge liability notice upon which the surcharge depends and the person concerned has not previously been liable to a surcharge in respect of a prescribed accounting period ending within the surcharge period specified in or extended by that notice.

59A(10)   In any case where–

(a)   the conduct by virtue of which a person is in default in respect of a prescribed accounting period is also conduct falling within section 69(1), and

(b)   by reason of that conduct, the person concerned is assessed to a penalty under section 69,

the default shall be left out of account for the purposes of subsections (2) to (5) above.

59A(11)   If the Commissioners, after consultation with the Treasury, so direct, a default in respect of a prescribed accounting period specified in the direction shall be left out of account for the purposes of subsections (2) to (5) above.

59A(12)   For the purposes of this section the Commissioners shall be taken not to receive a payment by the day on which it becomes due unless it is made in such a manner as secures (in a case where the payment is made otherwise than in cash) that, by the last day for the payment of that amount, all the transactions can be completed that need to be completed before the whole amount of the payment becomes available to the Commissioners.

59A(13)   In determining for the purposes of this section whether any person would, but for section 59(1A), be in default in respect of any period for the purposes of section 59, subsection (12) above shall be deemed to apply for the purposes of section 59 as it applies for the purposes of this section.

59A(14)   For the purposes of this section references to a **thing's being done** by any day include references to its being done on that day.

History – S. 59A was inserted by FA 1996, s. 35(2), in relation to any prescribed accounting period ending on or after 1 June 1996, but a liability to make a payment on account of VAT shall be disregarded for the purposes of the amendments made by this section if the payment is one becoming due before that date.

59B   Relationship between sections 59 and 59A

59B(1)   This section applies in each of the following cases, namely–

(a)   where a section 28 accounting period ends within a surcharge period begun or extended by the service on a taxable person (whether before or after the coming into force of section 59A) of a surcharge liability notice under section 59; and

(b)   where a prescribed accounting period which is not a section 28 accounting period ends within a surcharge period begun or extended by the service on a taxable person of a surcharge liability notice under section 59A.

59B(2)   In a case falling within subsection (1)(a) above section 59A shall have effect as if–

(a)   subject to paragraph (b) below, the section 28 accounting period were deemed to be a period ending within a surcharge period begun or, as the case may be, extended by a notice served under section 59A; but

(b)   any question–

      (i) whether a surcharge period was begun or extended by the notice, or

     (ii) whether the taxable person was in default in respect of any prescribed accounting period which was not a section 28 accounting period but ended within the surcharge period begun or extended by that notice,

were to be determined as it would be determined for the purposes of section 59.

59B(3)   In a case falling within subsection (1)(b) above section 59 shall have effect as if–

(a)   subject to paragraph (b) below, the prescribed accounting period that is not a section 28 accounting period were deemed to be a period ending within a surcharge period begun or, as the case may be, extended by a notice served under section 59;

(b)   any question–

      (i) whether a surcharge period was begun or extended by the notice, or

     (ii) whether the taxable person was in default in respect of any prescribed accounting period which was a section 28 accounting period but ended within the surcharge period begun or extended by that notice,

were to be determined as it would be determined for the purposes of section 59A; and

(c)   that person were to be treated as having had outstanding VAT for a section 28 accounting period in any case where the aggregate value of his defaults in respect of that period was, for the purposes of section 59A, more than nil.

59B(4)   In this section **"a section 28 accounting period"**, in relation to a taxable person, means any prescribed accounting period ending on or after the day on which the Finance Act 1996 was passed in respect of which that person is liable by virtue of an order under section 28 to make any payment on account of VAT.

History – S. 59B was inserted by FA 1996, s. 35(5).

60   VAT evasion: conduct involving dishonesty

60(1)   In any case where–

(a)   for the purpose of evading VAT, a person does any act or omits to take any action, and

(b)   his conduct involves dishonesty (whether or not it is such as to give rise to criminal liability),

he shall be liable, subject to subsection (6) below, to a penalty equal to the amount of VAT evaded or, as the case may be, sought to be evaded, by his conduct.

60(2)   The reference in subsection (1)(a) above to **evading VAT** includes a reference to obtaining any of the following sums–

(a)   a refund under any regulations made by virtue of section 13(5);

(b)   a VAT credit;

(c)   a refund under section 35, 36 or 40 of this Act or section 22 of the 1983 Act; and

(d)   a repayment under section 39,

in circumstances where the person concerned is not entitled to that sum.

60(3)   The reference in subsection (1) above to the **amount of the VAT evaded or sought to be evaded by** a person's conduct shall be construed–

(a)   in relation to VAT itself or a VAT credit as a reference to the aggregate of the amount (if any) falsely claimed by way of credit for input tax and the amount (if any) by which output tax was falsely understated; and

(b)   in relation to the sums referred to in subsection (2)(a), (c) and (e) above, as a reference to the amount falsely claimed by way of refund or repayment.

60(4)   Statements made or documents produced by or on behalf of a person shall not be inadmissible in any such proceedings as are mentioned in subsection (5) below by reason only that it has been drawn to his attention–

(a)   that, in relation to VAT, the Commissioners may assess an amount due by way of a civil penalty instead of instituting criminal proceedings and, though no undertaking can be given as to whether the Commissioners will make such an assessment in the case of any person, it is their practice to be influenced by the fact that a person has made a full confession of any dishonest conduct to which he has been a party and has given full facilities for investigation, and

(b)   that the Commissioners or, on appeal, a tribunal have power under section 70 to reduce a penalty under this section,

and that he was or may have been induced thereby to make the statements or produce the documents.

60(5)   The proceedings mentioned in subsection (4) above are–

(a)   any criminal proceedings against the person concerned in respect of any offence in connection with or in relation to VAT, and

(b)   any proceedings against him for the recovery of any sum due from him in connection with or in relation to VAT.

60(6)   Where, by reason of conduct falling within subsection (1) above, a person is convicted of an offence (whether under this Act or otherwise), that conduct shall not also give rise to liability to a penalty under this section.

60(7)   On an appeal against an assessment to a penalty under this section, the burden of proof as to the matters specified in subsection (1)(a) and (b) above shall lie upon the Commissioners.

Derivations – S. 60(1): FA 1985, s. 13(1), as amended by FA 1993, s. 49 and Sch. 2, para. 3(2)(a).
S. 60(2)(a): FA 1985, s. 13(2)(ba), as inserted by F(No. 2)A 1992, s. 14 and Sch. 3, para. 77(1)(b).
S. 60(2)(b): FA 1985, s. 13(2)(a).
S. 60(2)(c): FA 1985, s. 13(2)(b), (d), as amended by F(No. 2)A 1992, s. 14 and Sch. 3, para. 77(1)(a), and as inserted by FA 1990, s. 11.
S. 60(2)(d): FA 1985, s. 13(2)(c).
S. 60(3): FA 1985, s. 13(3).
S. 60(4)–(6): FA 1985, s. 13(5)–(7).
S. 60(7): FA 1985, s. 27(1).
Cross references – S. 77(4): assessments.
ICTA 1988, s. 827(1): penalty is not a deduction in computing any income, profits or losses for any tax purpose.
VAT Tribunals Rules 1986 (SI 1986/590), r. 2: "evasion penalty appeal" defined.
VAT Regulations 1995 (SI 1995/2518), reg. 58(1) and 64(1): an assessment under s. 60 can stop use of cash accounting.
VAT Regulations 1995 (SI 1995/2518), reg. 204(b) and 206(1): an assessment under s. 60 can stop use of flat-rate scheme for farmers.
Official publications – 730.

61   VAT evasion: liability of directors etc.

61(1)   Where it appears to the Commissioners–

(a)   that a body corporate is liable to a penalty under section 60, and

(b)   that the conduct giving rise to that penalty is, in whole or in part, attributable to the dishonesty of a person who is, or at the material time was, a director or managing officer of the body corporate (a **"named officer"**),

the Commissioners may serve a notice under this section on the body corporate and on the named officer.

61(2)   A notice under this section shall state–

(a)   the amount of the penalty referred to in subsection (1)(a) above (**"the basic penalty"**), and

(b)   that the Commissioners propose, in accordance with this section, to recover from the named officer such portion (which may be the whole) of the basic penalty as is specified in the notice.

61(3)   Where a notice is served under this section, the portion of the basic penalty specified in the notice shall be recoverable from the named officer as if he were personally liable under section 60 to a penalty which corresponds to that portion; and the amount of that penalty may be assessed and notified to him accordingly under section 76.

61(4)   Where a notice is served under this section–

(a)   the amount which, under section 76, may be assessed as the amount due by way of penalty from the body corporate shall be only so much (if any) of the basic penalty as is not assessed on and notified to a named officer by virtue of subsection (3) above; and

(b)   the body corporate shall be treated as discharged from liability for so much of the basic penalty as is so assessed and notified.

61(5)   No appeal shall lie against a notice under this section as such but–

(a)   where a body corporate is assessed as mentioned in subsection (4)(a) above, the body corporate may appeal against the Commissioners' decision as to its liability to a penalty and against the amount of the basic penalty as if it were specified in the assessment; and

(b)   where an assessment is made on a named officer by virtue of subsection (3) above, the named officer may appeal against the Commissioners' decision that the conduct of the body corporate referred to in subsection (1)(b) above is, in whole or part, attributable to his dishonesty and against their decision as to the portion of the penalty which the Commissioners propose to recover from him.

61(6)   In this section a **"managing officer"**, in relation to a body corporate, means any manager, secretary or other similar officer of the body corporate or any person purporting to act in any such capacity or as a director; and where the affairs of a body corporate are managed by its members, this section shall apply in relation to the conduct of a member in connection with his functions of management as if he were a director of the body corporate.

Derivations – S. 61(1)–(5): FA 1986, s. 14(1)–(5).
S. 61(6): FA 1986, s. 14(8).
Cross references – S. 18A(4): fiscal warehousing and meaning of "managing officer".
S. 83(o): appeals.
S. 84(6): "penalty" defined.
Sch. 12, para. 9(j): tribunal procedures.
ICTA 1988, s. 827(1): penalty is not a deduction in computing any income, profits or losses for any tax purpose.
VAT Tribunals Rules 1986 (SI 1986/590), r. 2: "evasion penalty appeal" defined.
VAT Tribunals Rules 1986 (SI 1986/590), r. 19(3A): appeals brought by different persons which relate to the penalty.
Note – CEMA 1979, s. 171(4): director's liability.

62   Incorrect certificates as to zero-rating etc.

62(1)   *Subject to subsections (3) and (4) below, where*–

(a)   a person to whom one or more supplies are, or are to be, made–

      (i) gives to the supplier a certificate that the supply or supplies fall, or will fall, wholly or partly within paragraph 1 of Schedule A1, Group 5 or 6 of Schedule 8 or Group 1 of Schedule 9, or

      (ii) gives to the supplier a certificate for the purposes of section 18B(2)(d) or 18C(1)(c), and

(b)   the certificate is incorrect,

the person giving the certificate shall be liable to a penalty.

62(1A)   Subject to subsections (3) and (4) below, where–

(a)   a person who makes, or is to make, an acquisition of goods from another member State prepares a certificate for the purposes of section 18B(1)(d), and

(b)   the certificate is incorrect,

the person preparing the certificate shall be liable to a penalty.

62(2)   The amount of the penalty shall be equal to–

(a)   in a case where the penalty is imposed by virtue of subsection (1) above, the difference between–

> (i)   the amount of the VAT which would have been chargeable on the supply or supplies if the certificate had been correct; and
>
> (ii)   the amount of VAT actually chargeable;

(b)   in a case where it is imposed by virtue of subsection (1A) above, the amount of VAT actually chargeable on the acquisition.

62(3)   The giving or preparing of a certificate shall not give rise to a penalty under this section if the person who gave or prepared it satisfies the Commissioners or, on appeal, a tribunal that there is a reasonable excuse for his having given or prepared it.

62(4)   Where by reason of giving or preparing a certificate a person is convicted of an offence (whether under this Act or otherwise), the giving or preparing of the certificate shall not also give rise to a penalty under this section.

History – S. 62(1), 62(1A) and 62(2) were substituted for the former s. 62(1) and (2) by FA 1999, s. 17(1), with effect in relation to certificates given or, as the case may be, prepared on or after 27 July 1999. Former s. 62(1) and (2) read as follows:
"**62(1)**   Subject to subsection (3) and (4) below, where–
    (a)   a person by whom one or more acquisitions or to whom one or more supplies are, or are to be, made–
         (i)   gives to the supplier a certificate that the supply or supplies fall, or will fall, wholly or partly within Group 5 or 6 of Schedule 8 or Group 1 of Schedule 9;
         (ii)   gave to the supplier a certificate that the supplies fell within Group 7 of Schedule 5 to the 1983 Act for the purposes of paragraph 13(4)(f) of Schedule 3 to the Finance Act 1989;
         (iii)   prepares a certificate in accordance with section 18B(1)(d) or gives a supplier a certificate in accordance with section 18B(2)(d); or
         (iv)   gives the supplier a certificate in accordance with section 18C(1)(c); and
    (b)   the certificate is incorrect,
the person giving or preparing or who gave the certificate shall be liable to a penalty.
62(2)   The amount of the penalty shall be equal to the difference between the amount of the VAT which would have been chargeable on the supply or supplies if the certificate had been correct and the amount of VAT actually so chargeable."
In s. 62(1)(a), the words "by whom one or more acquisitions or" were inserted by FA 1996, s. 26 and Sch. 3, para. 8(2), with effect from 1 June 1996 and apply to any acquisition of goods from another member State and any supply taking place on or after that day.
In s. 62(1)(a)(i), the word "or" at the end was repealed by FA 1996, s. 26 and Sch. 3, para. 8(2) and s. 205 and Sch. 41, Pt. IV(1), with effect from 1 June 1996 and applies to any acquisition with goods from another member State and any supply taking place on or after that day.
In s. 62(1)(a)(ii), the word "and" at the end was repealed by FA 1996, s. 26 and Sch. 3, para. 8(2) and s. 205 and Sch. 41, Pt. IV(1), with effect from 1 June 1996 and applies to any acquisition of goods from another member State and any supply taking place on or after that day.
S. 62(1)(a)(iii) and (iv) were inserted by FA 1996, s. 26 and Sch. 3, para. 8(2), with effect from 1 June 1996 and applies to any acquisition of goods from another member State and any supply taking place on or after that day.
In s. 62(1), in the passage following para. (b), the words "or preparing" were inserted by FA 1996, s. 26 and Sch. 3, para. 8(3), with effect from 1 June 1996 and apply to any acquisition of goods from another member State and any supply taking place on or after that day.
In s. 62(3), the words "or preparing" were inserted by FA 1996, s. 26 and Sch. 3, para. 8(3), with effect from 1 June 1996 and apply to any acquisition of goods from another member State and any supply taking place on or after that day. In s. 62(3), the words "or prepared" were inserted both after the word "gave" and the word "given" by FA 1996, s. 26 and Sch. 3, para. 8(4), with effect from 1 June 1996 and apply to any acquisition of goods from another member State and any supply taking place on or after that day.
In s. 62(4), the words "or preparing" were inserted in two places by FA 1996, s. 26 and Sch. 3, para. 8(3), with effect from 1 June 1996 and apply to any acquisition of goods from another member State and any supply taking place on or after that day.

Derivations – FA 1985, s. 13A, as inserted by FA 1989, s. 23.

Cross references – ICTA 1988, s. 827(1): penalty is not a deduction in computing any income, profits or losses for any tax purpose.
VAT Tribunals Rules 1986 (SI 1986/590), r. 2: "reasonable excuse appeal" defined.

Official publications – 708.

63   Penalty for misdeclaration or neglect resulting in VAT loss for one accounting period equalling or exceeding certain amounts

63(1)   In any case where, for a prescribed accounting period–

(a)   a return is made which understates a person's liability to VAT or overstates his entitlement to a VAT credit, or

(b)   an assessment is made which understates a person's liability to VAT and, at the end of the period of 30 days beginning on the date of the assessment, he has not taken all such steps as are reasonable to draw the understatement to the attention of the Commissioners, and the circumstances are as set out in subsection (2) below, the person concerned shall be liable, subject to subsection (10) and (11) below, to a penalty equal to 15 per cent of the VAT which would have been lost if the inaccuracy had not been discovered.

63(2)   The circumstances referred to in subsection (1) above are that the VAT for the period concerned which would have been lost if the inaccuracy had not been discovered equals or exceeds whichever is the lesser of £1,000,000 and 30 per cent of the relevant amount for that period.

63(3)   Any reference in this section to the VAT for a prescribed accounting period which would have been lost if an inaccuracy had not been discovered is a reference to the amount of the understatement of liability or, as the case may be, overstatement of entitlement referred to, in relation to that period, in subsection (1) above.

63(4)   In this section **"the relevant amount"**, in relation to a prescribed accounting period, means–

(a)   for the purposes of a case falling within subsection (1)(a) above, the gross amount of VAT for that period; and

(b)   for the purposes of a case falling within subsection (1)(b) above, the true amount of VAT for that period.

63(5)   In this section **"the gross amount of tax"**, in relation to a prescribed accounting period, means the aggregate of the following amounts, that is to say–

(a)   the amount of credit for input tax which (subject to subsection (8) below) should have been stated on the return for that period, and

(b)   the amount of output tax which (subject to that subsection) should have been so stated.

63(6)   In relation to any return which, in accordance with prescribed requirements, includes a single amount as the aggregate for the prescribed accounting period to which the return relates of–

(a)   the amount representing credit for input tax, and

(b)   any other amounts representing refunds or repayments of VAT to which there is an entitlement,

references in this section to **the amount of credit for input tax** shall have effect (so far as they would not so have effect by virtue of subsection (9) below) as references to the amount of that aggregate.

63(7)   In this section **"the true amount of VAT"**, in relation to a prescribed accounting period, means the amount of VAT which was due from the person concerned for that period or, as the case may be, the amount of the VAT credit (if any) to which he was entitled for that period.

63(8)   Where–

(a)   a return for any prescribed accounting period overstates or understates to any extent a person's liability to VAT or his entitlement to a VAT credit, and

(b)   that return is corrected, in such circumstances and in accordance with such conditions as may be prescribed, by a return for a later such period which understates or overstates, to the corresponding extent, that liability or entitlement,

it shall be assumed for the purposes of this section that the statements made by each of those returns (so far as they are not inaccurate in any other respect) are correct statements for the accounting period to which it relates.

63(9)   This section shall have effect in relation to a body which is registered and to which section 33 applies as if–

(a)   any reference to **a VAT credit** included a reference to a refund under that section, and

(b)   any reference to **credit for input tax** included a reference to VAT chargeable on supplies, acquisitions or importations which were not for the purposes of any business carried on by the body.

63(10)   Conduct falling within subsection (1) above shall not give rise to liability to a penalty under this section if–

(a)   the person concerned satisfies the Commissioners or, on appeal, a tribunal that there is a reasonable excuse for the conduct, or

(b)   at a time when he had no reason to believe that enquiries were being made by the Commissioners into his affairs, so far as they relate to VAT, the person concerned furnished to the Commissioners full information with respect to the inaccuracy concerned.

63(11)   Where, by reason of conduct falling within subsection (1) above–

(a)   a person is convicted of an offence (whether under this Act or otherwise), or

(b)   a person is assessed to a penalty under section 60,

that conduct shall not also give rise to liability to a penalty under this section.

Derivations – S. 63(1): FA 1985, s. 14(1), as amended by FA 1992, s. 7(1).
S. 63(2): FA 1985, s. 14(2), as substituted by FA 1988, s. 16(2), and as amended by FA 1993, s. 49 and Sch. 2, para. 1.
S. 63(3): FA 1985, s. 14(4), as amended by FA 1988, s. 16(3) and FA 1994, s. 45(2).
S. 63(4)–(6): FA 1985, s. 14(4A), (4B), (4C), as inserted by FA 1993, s. 49 and Sch. 2, para. 1(2).
S. 63(7): FA 1985, s. 14(5), as amended by FA 1988, s. 16(4).
S. 63(8), (9): FA 1985, s. 14(5A), (5B), as inserted by FA 1988, s. 16(5), and as amended by F(No. 2)A 1992, s. 14 and Sch. 3, para. 78, FA 1993, s. 49 and Sch. 2, para. 1(3) and by FA 1994, s. 45(3).
S. 63(10), (11): FA 1985, s. 14(6), (7), as amended by FA 1988, s. 148 and Sch. 14, Pt. III.

Cross references – S. 83(n): an appeal against a penalty under s. 63.
ICTA 1988, s. 827(1): penalty is not a deduction in computing any income, profits or losses for any tax purpose.
VAT Tribunals Rules 1986 (SI 1986/590), r. 2: "reasonable excuse appeal" defined.

Official publications – 700/42: misdeclaration penalty.
700/45: how to correct errors and make adjustments or claims.
700/56/99, para. 5.5: generally no penalty applies to post-insolvency returns.

Hansard – HC Debates, 23 June 1992: statement made by the Paymaster General on serious misdeclaration penalty and the single market:
"Customs must reserve the right to assess and collect tax that is properly due. However, in considering whether to impose any serious misdeclaration penalty, Customs will take a sympathetic view of genuine errors made as a result of misunderstanding the new provisions for the first year of their operation. There have been similar arrangements in the past and it is right to make some now."
HC Debates, 16 May 1989, col. 70 (not reproduced): statement by the Economic Secretary to the Treasury that Customs will take a lenient view (for penalty purposes) of genuine misunderstandings under and unfamiliarity with the FA 1989 regime for buildings and land during the first 12 to 18 months. However, Customs reserve the right to collect properly due VAT and default interest.

Other material – Customs and Excise News Release 26/91, 19 March 1991: penalty relaxation.
Customs and Excise News Release 14/92, 10 March 1992: Customs will not normally impose the penalty unless the net tax underdeclared or overclaimed exceeds £2,000 in a prescribed accounting period.

Notes – s. 71: "reasonable excuse" defined.

64   Repeated misdeclarations

64(1)   In any case where–

(a)   for a prescribed accounting period (including one beginning before the commencement of this section), a return has been made which understates a person's liability to VAT or overstates his entitlement to a VAT credit; and

(b)   the VAT for that period which would have been lost if the inaccuracy had not been discovered equals or exceeds whichever is the lesser of £500,000 and 10 per cent of the gross amount of tax for that period,

the inaccuracy shall be regarded, subject to subsection (5) and (6) below, as **material** for the purposes of this section.

64(2)   Subsection (3) below applies in any case where–

(a)   there is a material inaccuracy in respect of any prescribed accounting period;

(b)   the Commissioners serve notice on the person concerned (a **"penalty liability notice"**) specifying a penalty period for the purposes of this section;

(c)   that notice is served before the end of 5 consecutive prescribed accounting periods beginning with the period in respect of which there was the material inaccuracy; and

(d)   the period specified in the penalty liability notice as the penalty period is the period of 8 consecutive prescribed accounting periods beginning with that in which the date of the notice falls.

64(3)   If, where a penalty liability notice has been served on any person, there is a material inaccuracy in respect of any of the prescribed accounting periods falling within the penalty period specified in the notice, that person shall be liable, except in relation to the first of those periods in respect of which there is a material inaccuracy, to a penalty equal to 15 per cent of the VAT for the prescribed accounting period in question which would have been lost if the inaccuracy had not been discovered.

64(4)   Subsections (3), (5), (8) and (9) of section 63 shall apply for the purposes of this section as they apply for the purposes of that section.

64(5)   An inaccuracy shall not be regarded as **material** for the purposes of this section if–

(a)   the person concerned satisfies the Commissioners or, on appeal, a tribunal that there is a reasonable excuse for the inaccuracy; or

(b)   at a time when he had no reason to believe that enquiries were being made by the Commissioners into his affairs, so far as they relate to VAT, the person concerned furnished to the Commissioners full information with respect to the inaccuracy.

64(6)   Subject to subsection (6A) below, where by reason of conduct falling within subsection (1) above–

(a)   a person is convicted of an offence (whether under this Act or otherwise), or

(b)   a person is assessed to a penalty under section 60 or 63,

the inaccuracy concerned shall not be regarded as material for the purposes of this section.

64(6A)   Subsection (6) above shall not prevent an inaccuracy by reason of which a person has been assessed to a penalty under section 63–

(a)   from being regarded as a material inaccuracy in respect of which the Commissioners may serve a penalty liability notice under subsection (2) above; or

(b)   from being regarded for the purposes of subsection (3) above as a material inaccuracy by reference to which any prescribed accounting period falling within the penalty period is to be treated as the first prescribed accounting period so falling in respect of which there is a material inaccuracy.

64(7)   Where subsection (5) or (6) above requires any inaccuracy to be regarded as not material for the purposes of the serving of a penalty liability notice, any such notice served in respect of that inaccuracy shall be deemed not to have been served.

History – S. 64(6), (6A) and (7) were substituted for former s. 64(6) and (7) by FA 1996, s. 36(1), in relation to inaccuracies contained in returns made on or after 29 April 1996. Former s. 64(6) and (7) read as follows:
"**64(6)**   Where by reason of conduct falling within subsection (1) above–
(a)   a person is convicted of an offence (whether under this Act or otherwise); or
(b)   a person is assessed to a penalty under section 60 or 63,
the inaccuracy concerned shall not be regarded as **material** for the purposes of this section except, in the case of an inaccuracy by reason of which a person is assessed to a penalty under section 63, for the purposes of subsection (2)(a) above.
64(7)   In any case where subsection (5) or (6) above applies, any penalty liability notice the service of which depended upon the inaccuracy concerned shall be deemed not to have been served."

Derivations – S. 64: FA 1985, s. 14A, as inserted by FA 1988, s. 17.
S. 64(1): FA 1985, s. 14A(1), as amended by FA 1993, s. 49 and Sch. 2, para. 2(1).
S. 64(2), (3): FA 1985, s. 14A(2), (3), as substituted by FA 1993, s. 49 and Sch. 2, para. 2(2).
S. 64(4): FA 1985, s. 14A(4), as amended by FA 1993, s. 49 and Sch. 2, para. 2(3).
S. 64(5): FA 1985, s. 14A(5).
S. 64(6): FA 1985, s. 14A(6), as amended by FA 1993, s. 49 and Sch. 2, para. 2(4).
S. 64(7): FA 1985, s. 14A(7).

Cross references – ICTA 1988, s. 827(1): penalty is not a deduction in computing any income, profits or losses for any tax purpose.
VAT Tribunals Rules 1986 (SI 1986/590), r. 2: "reasonable excuse appeal" defined.

Official publications – 700/42.
700/56/99, para. 5.5: generally no penalty applies to post-insolvency returns.

65   Inaccuracies in EC sales statements

65(1)   Where–

(a)   an EC sales statement containing a material inaccuracy has been submitted by any person to the Commissioners;

(b)   the Commissioners have, within 6 months of discovering the inaccuracy, issued that person with a written warning identifying that statement and stating that future inaccuracies might result in the service of a notice for the purposes of this section;

(c)   another EC sales statement containing a material inaccuracy (**"the second inaccurate statement"**) has been submitted by that person to the Commissioners;

(d)   the submission date for the second inaccurate statement fell within the period of 2 years beginning with the day after the warning was issued;

(e)   the Commissioners have, within 6 months of discovering the inaccuracy in the second inaccurate statement, served that person with a notice identifying that statement and stating that future inaccuracies will attract a penalty under this section;

(f)   yet another EC sales statement containing a material inaccuracy is submitted by that person to the Commissioners; and

(g)   the submission date for the statement falling within paragraph (f) above is not more than 2 years after the service of the notice or the date on which any previous statement attracting a penalty was submitted by that person to the Commissioners,

that person shall be liable to a penalty of £100 in respect of the statement so falling.

65(2)   Subject to subsection (3) and (4) below, an EC sales statement shall be regarded for the purposes of this section as containing a material inaccuracy if, having regard to the matters required to be included in the statement, the inclusion or omission of any information from the statement is misleading in any material respect.

65(3) An inaccuracy contained in an EC sales statement shall not be regarded as **material** for the purposes of this section if–

(a) the person who submitted the statement satisfies the Commissioners or, on appeal, a tribunal that there is a reasonable excuse for the inaccuracy; or

(b) at a time when he had no reason to believe that enquiries were being made by the Commissioners into his affairs, that person furnished the Commissioners with full information with respect to the inaccuracy.

65(4) Where, by reason of the submission of a statement containing a material inaccuracy by any person, that person is convicted of an offence (whether under this Act or otherwise), the inaccuracy to which the conviction relates shall be regarded for the purposes of this section as not being material.

65(5) Where the only statement identified in a warning or notice served for the purposes of subsection (1)(b) or (e) above is one which (whether by virtue of either or both of subsection (3) and (4) above or otherwise) is regarded as containing no material inaccuracies, that warning or notice shall be deemed not to have been issued or served for those purposes.

65(6) In this section–

"**EC sales statement**" means any statement which is required to be submitted to the Commissioners in accordance with regulations under paragraph 2(3) of Schedule 11; and

"**submission date**", in relation to such a statement, means whichever is the earlier of the last day for the submission of the statement to the Commissioners in accordance with those regulations and the day on which it was in fact submitted to the Commissioners.

Derivations – FA 1985, s. 14B, as inserted by F(No. 2)A 1992, s. 14 and Sch. 3, para. 79.

Cross references – S. 77(2)(a): assessments.
ICTA 1988, s. 827(1): penalty is not a deduction in computing any income, profits or losses for any tax purpose.
VAT Tribunals Rules 1986 (SI 1986/590), r. 2: "reasonable excuse appeal" defined.

66   Failure to submit EC sales statement

66(1) If, by the last day on which a person is required in accordance with regulations under this Act to submit an EC sales statement for any prescribed period to the Commissioners, the Commissioners have not received that statement, that person shall be regarded for the purposes of this section as being in default in relation to that statement until it is submitted.

66(2) Where any person is in default in respect of any EC sales statement the Commissioners may serve notice on him stating–

(a) that he is in default in relation to the statement specified in the notice;

(b) that (subject to the liability mentioned in paragraph (d) below) no action will be taken if he remedies the default before the end of the period of 14 days beginning with the day after the service of the notice;

(c) that if the default is not so remedied, that person will become liable in respect of his default to penalties calculated on a daily basis from the end of that period in accordance with the following provisions of this section; and

(d) that that person will become liable, without any further notices being served under this section, to penalties under this section if he commits any more defaults before a period of 12 months has elapsed without his being in default.

66(3) Where a person has been served with a notice under subsection (2) above, he shall become liable under this section–

(a) if the statement to which the notice relates is not submitted before the end of the period of 14 days beginning with the day after the service of the notice, to a penalty in respect of that statement; and

(b) whether or not that statement is so submitted, to a penalty in respect of any EC sales statement the last day for the submission of which is after the service and before the expiry of the notice and in relation to which he is in default.

66(4) For the purposes of this section a notice served on any person under subsection (2) above shall continue in force–

(a) except in a case falling within paragraph (b) below, until the end of the period of 12 months beginning with the day after the service of the notice; and

(b) where at any time in that period of 12 months that person is in default in relation to any EC sales statement other than one in relation to which he was in default when the notice was served, until a period of 12 months has elapsed without that person becoming liable to a penalty under this section in respect of any EC sales statement.

66(5)   The amount of any penalty to which a person who has been served with a notice under subsection (2) above is liable under this section shall be whichever is the greater of £50 and–

(a)   in the case of a liability in respect of the statement to which the notice relates, a penalty of £5 for every day for which the default continues after the end of the period of 14 days mentioned in subsection (3)(a) above, up to a maximum of 100 days; and

(b)   in the case of a liability in respect of any other statement, a penalty of the relevant amount for every day for which the default continues, up to a maximum of 100 days.

66(6)   In subsection (5)(b) above **"the relevant amount"**, in relation to a person served with a notice under subsection (2) above, means–

(a)   £5, where (that person not having been liable to a penalty under this section in respect of the statement to which the notice relates) the statement in question is the first statement in respect of which that person has become liable to a penalty while the notice has been in force;

(b)   £10 where the statement in question is the second statement in respect of which he has become so liable while the notice has been in force (counting the statement to which the notice relates where he has become liable in respect of that statement); and

(c)   £15 in any other case.

66(7)   If a person who, apart from this subsection, would be liable to a penalty under this section satisfies the Commissioners or, on appeal a tribunal, that–

(a)   an EC sales statement has been submitted at such a time and in such a manner that it was reasonable to expect that it would be received by the Commissioners within the appropriate time limit; or

(b)   there is a reasonable excuse for such a statement not having been dispatched,

he shall be treated for the purposes of this section and section 59 to 65 and 67 to 71, 73, 75 and 76 as not having been in default in relation to that statement and, accordingly, he shall not be liable to any penalty under this section in respect of that statement and any notice served under subsection (2) above exclusively in relation to the failure to submit that statement shall have no effect for the purposes of this section.

66(8)   If it appears to the Treasury that there has been a change in the value of money since 1st January 1993 or, as the case may be, the last occasion when the sums specified in subsection (5) and (6) above were varied, they may by order substitute for the sums for the time being specified in those subsection such other sums as appear to them to be justified by the change; but an order under this section shall not apply to any default in relation to a statement the last day for the submission of which was before the order comes into force.

66(9)   In this section **"EC sales statement"** means any statement which is required to be submitted to the Commissioners in accordance with regulations under paragraph 2(3) of Schedule 11.

Derivations – FA 1985, s. 17A(1)–(8), (10), as inserted by F(No. 2)A 1992, s. 14 and Sch. 3, para. 82.

Cross references – S. 77(2)(a): assessments.
ICTA 1988, s. 827(1): penalty is not a deduction in computing any income, profits or losses for any tax purpose.
VAT Tribunals Rules 1986 (SI 1986/590), r. 2: "reasonable excuse appeal" defined.

Official publications – 700/56/99, para. 5.5: generally no penalty applies to post-insolvency returns.

67   Failure to notify and unauthorised issue of invoices

Notes – In relation to a person who became liable to be registered under Sch. 1, para. 1(2) (transfer of a going concern) before 1 January 1996 but who had not notified the Commissioners of the liability before that date, s. 67(3)(a) has effect as if the words "1st January 1996" were substituted for the words "the date with effect from which he is, in accordance with that paragraph, required to be registered" by virtue of FA 1996, s. 37(3).

67(1)   In any case where–

(a)   a person fails to comply with any of paragraphs 5, 6, 7 and 14(2) and (3) of Schedule 1 with paragraph 3 of Schedule 2, with paragraph 3 or 8(2) of Schedule 3 or paragraph 3, 4 or 7(2) or (3) of Schedule 3A, or

(b)   a person fails to comply with a requirement of regulations under paragraph 2(4) of Schedule 11, or

(c)   an unauthorised person issues one or more invoices showing an amount as being VAT or as including an amount attributable to VAT, he shall be liable, subject to subsection (8) and (9) below, to a penalty equal to the specified percentage of the relevant VAT or, if it is greater or the circumstances are such that there is no relevant VAT, to a penalty of £50.

67(2) In subsection (1)(c) above, **"an unauthorised person"** means anyone other than–

(a)   a person registered under this Act; or

(b)   a body corporate treated for the purposes of section 43 as a member of a group; or

(c)   a person treated as a taxable person under regulations made under section 46(4); or

(d)   a person authorised to issue an invoice under regulations made under paragraph 2(12) of Schedule 11; or

(e)   a person acting on behalf of the Crown.

67(3) In subsection (1) above **"relevant VAT"** means (subject to subsections (5) and (6) below)–

(a)   in relation to a person's failure to comply with paragraph 5, 6 or 7 of Schedule 1, paragraph 3 of Schedule 2, paragraph 3 of Schedule 3 or paragraph 3 or 4 of Schedule 3A, the VAT (if any) for which he is liable for the period beginning on the date with effect from which he is, in accordance with that paragraph, required to be registered and ending on the date on which the Commissioners received notification of, or otherwise became fully aware of, his liability to be registered; and

(b)   in relation to a person's failure to comply with sub-paragraph (2) or (3) of paragraph 14 of Schedule 1, with sub-paragraph (2) of paragraph 8 of Schedule 3 or with sub-paragraph (2) or (3) of paragraph 7 of Schedule 3A, the VAT (if any) for which, but for any exemption from registration, he would be liable for the period beginning on the date of the change or alteration referred to in that sub-paragraph and ending on the date on which the Commissioners received notification of, or otherwise became fully aware of, that change or alteration; and

(c)   in relation to a person's failure to comply with a requirement of regulations under paragraph 2(4) of Schedule 11, the VAT on the acquisition to which the failure relates; and

(d)   in relation to the issue of one or more invoices as are referred to in subsection (1)(c) above, the amount which is, or the aggregate of the amounts which are–

      (i) shown on the invoice or invoices as VAT, or

      (ii) to be taken as representing VAT.

67(4) For the purposes of subsection (1) above the **specified percentage** is–

(a)   5 per cent where the relevant VAT is given by subsection (3)(a) or (b) above and the period referred to in that paragraph does not exceed 9 months or where the relevant VAT is given by subsection (3)(c) above and the failure in question did not continue for more than 3 months;

(b)   10 per cent where that VAT is given by subsection (3)(a) or (b) above and the period so referred to exceeds 9 months but does not exceed 18 months or where that VAT is given by subsection (3)(c) and the failure in question continued for more than 3 months but did not continue for more than 6 months; and

(c)   15 per cent in any other case.

67(5) Where–

(a)   the amount of VAT which (apart from this subsection) would be treated for the purposes of subsection (1) above as the relevant VAT in relation to a failure mentioned in subsection (3)(a) above includes VAT on an acquisition of goods from another member State; and

(b)   the Commissioners are satisfied that VAT has been paid under the law of another member State on the supply in pursuance of which those goods were acquired,

then, in the determination of the amount of the **relevant VAT** in relation to that failure, an allowance shall be made for the VAT paid under the law of that member State; and the amount of the allowance shall not exceed the amount of VAT due on the acquisition but shall otherwise be equal to the amount of VAT which the Commissioners are satisfied has been paid on that supply under the law of that member State.

67(6) Where–

(a)   the amount of VAT which (apart from this subsection) would be treated for the purposes of subsection (1) above as the relevant VAT in relation to a failure mentioned in subsection (3)(a) above includes VAT chargeable by virtue of section 7(4) on any supply; and

(b)   the Commissioners are satisfied that VAT has been paid under the law of another member State on that supply,

then, in the determination of the amount of the **relevant VAT** in relation to that failure, an allowance shall be made for the VAT paid under the law of the other member State; and the amount of the allowance shall not exceed the amount of VAT chargeable by virtue of section 7(4) on that supply but shall otherwise be equal to the amount of VAT which the Commissioners are satisfied has been paid on that supply under the law of that other member State.

67(7)   This section shall have effect in relation to any invoice which–

(a)   for the purposes of any provision made under section 54(3) shows an amount as included in the consideration for any supply, and

(b)   either–

    (i)   fails to comply with the requirements of any regulations under that section; or

    (ii) is issued by a person who is not for the time being authorised to do so for the purposes of that section,

as if the person issuing the invoice were an unauthorised person and that amount were shown on the invoice as an amount attributable to VAT.

67(8)   Conduct falling within subsection (1) above shall not give rise to liability to a penalty under this section if the person concerned satisfies the Commissioners or, on appeal, a tribunal that there is a reasonable excuse for his conduct.

67(9)   Where, by reason of conduct falling within subsection (1) above–

(a)   a person is convicted of an offence (whether under this Act or otherwise), or

(b)   a person is assessed to a penalty under section 60,

that conduct shall not also give rise to liability to a penalty under this section.

67(10)   If it appears to the Treasury that there has been a change in the value of money since 25th July 1985 or, as the case may be, the last occasion when the power conferred by this subsection was exercised, they may by order substitute for the sum for the time being specified in subsection (1) above such other sum as appears to them to be justified by the change.

67(11)   An order under subsection (10) above shall not apply in relation to a failure to comply which ended on or before the date on which the order comes into force.

History – In s. 67(1)(a), the words ", 7" were inserted by FA 1996, s. 37(1)(a), in relation to any person who becomes liable to be registered under Sch. 1, para. 1(2) (transfer of a going concern) on or after 1 January 1996 and any person who became liable to be registered under Sch. 1, para. 1(2) before 1 January 1996 but who had not notified the Commissioners of the liability before that date.
In s. 67(1)(a), the words, "with paragraph 3 or 8(2) of Schedule 3 or paragraph 3, 4 or 7(2) or (3) of Schedule 3A" were substituted for the words "or with paragraph 3 or 8(2) of Schedule 3" by FA 2000, s. 136(2)(a), with effect in relation to supplies made on or after 21 March 2000.
In s. 67(3)(a), the words, "6 or 7" were substituted for the words "or 6" by FA 1996, s. 37(1)(b), in relation to any person who becomes liable to be registered under Sch. 1, para. 1(2) (transfer of a going concern) on or after 1 January 1996 and any person who became liable to be registered under Sch. 1, para. 1(2) before 1 January 1996 but who had not notified the Commissioners of the liability before that date. However, in relation to a person who became liable to be registered under Sch. 1, para. 1(2) before 1 January 1996 but who had not notified the Commissioners of the liability before that date, s. 67(3)(a) has effect as if the words "1st January 1996" were substituted for the words "the date with effect from which he is, in accordance with that paragraph, required to be registered" by virtue of FA 1996, s. 37(3).
In s. 67(3)(a), the words ", paragraph 3 of Schedule 3 or paragraph 3 or 4 of Schedule 3A" were substituted for the words "or paragraph 3 of Schedule 3" by FA 2000, s. 136(2)(b), with effect in relation to supplies made on or after 21 March 2000.
In s. 67(3)(b), the words, "with sub-paragraph (2) of paragraph 8 of Schedule 3 or with sub-paragraph (2) or (3) of paragraph 7 of Schedule 3A" were substituted for the words "or with sub-paragraph (2) of paragraph 8 of Schedule 3" by FA 2000, s. 136(2)(c), with effect in relation to supplies made on or after 21 March 2000.
In s. 67(4)(a), the words "5 per cent" were substituted for the words "10 per cent" by FA 1995, s. 32(1)(a), where a penalty is assessed on or after 1 January 1995 except in the case of a supplementary assessment if the original assessment was made before 1 January 1995.
In s. 67(4)(b), the words "10 per cent" were substituted for the words "20 per cent" by FA 1995, s. 32(1)(b), where a penalty is assessed on or after 1 January 1995 except in the case of a supplementary assessment if the original assessment was made before 1 January 1995.
In s. 67(4)(c), the words "15 per cent" were substituted for the words "30 per cent" by FA 1995, s. 32(1)(c), where a penalty is assessed on or after 1 January 1995 except in the case of a supplementary assessment if the original assessment was made before 1 January 1995.

Derivations – S. 67(1): FA 1985, s. 15(1)(a), (aa), (b), as amended by FA 1988, s. 18(1) and F(No. 2)A 1992, s. 14 and Sch. 3, para. 80(1).
S. 67(2): FA 1985, s. 15(2).
S. 67(3): FA 1985, s. 15(3), as amended by FA 1988, s. 18(2) and F(No. 2)A 1992, s. 14 and Sch. 3, para. 80(2).
S. 67(4): FA 1985, s. 15(3A), as inserted by FA 1988, s. 18(3), and as amended by F(No. 2)A 1992, s. 14 and Sch. 3, para. 80(3).
S. 67(5), (6): FA 1985, s. 15(3B), (3C), as inserted by F(No. 2)A 1992, s. 14 and Sch. 3, para. 80(4).
S. 67(7): FA 1985, s. 15(3D), as inserted by FA 1992, s. 16(5).
S. 67(8)–(11): FA 1985, s. 15(4)–(7).

Cross references – S. 74(4): unauthorised person.
S. 77(4)(b): assessments.
S. 83(n): appeals.

ICTA 1988, s. 827(1): penalty is not a deduction in computing any income, profits or losses for any tax purpose.
FA 1995, s. 32(2): amendments made to s. 67 by FA 1995 apply to corresponding provision in FA 1985, s. 15(3A).
VAT Tribunals Rules 1986 (SI 1986/590), r. 2: "reasonable excuse appeal" defined.
Official publications – 700/41.
Notes – S. 71: "reasonable excuse" defined.

68   Breaches of walking possession agreements

68(1)   This section applies where–

(a)   in accordance with regulations under section 51 of the Finance Act 1997 (enforcement by distress), a distress is authorised to be levied on the goods and chattels of a person (a **"person in default"**) who has refused or neglected to pay any VAT due or any amount recoverable as if it were VAT due, and

(b)   the person levying the distress and the person in default have entered into a walking possession agreement, as defined in subsection (2) below.

68(2)   In this section a **"walking possession agreement"** means an agreement under which, in consideration of the property distrained upon being allowed to remain in the custody of the person in default and of the delaying of its sale, the person in default–

(a)   acknowledges that the property specified in the agreement is under distraint and held in walking possession; and

(b)   undertakes that, except with the consent of the Commissioners and subject to such conditions as they may impose, he will not remove or allow the removal of any of the specified property from the premises named in the agreement.

68(3)   Subject to subsection (4) below, if the person in default is in breach of the undertaking contained in a walking possession agreement, he shall be liable to a penalty equal to half of the VAT or other amount referred to in subsection (l)(a) above.

68(4)   The person in default shall not be liable to a penalty under subsection (3) above if he satisfies the Commissioners or, on appeal, a tribunal that there is a reasonable excuse for the breach in question.

68(5)   This section does not extend to Scotland.

History – In s. 68(1)(a), the words "section 51 of the Finance Act 1997 (enforcement by distress)" were substituted for the words "paragraph 5(4) of Schedule 11" by FA 1997, s. 53(7), with effect from 1 July 1997 (SI 1997/1432 (C 54)).
Derivations – FA 1985, s. 16.
Cross references – S. 83(n): an appeal against a penalty under s. 68.
ICTA 1988, s. 827(1): penalty is not a deduction in computing any income, profits or losses for any tax purpose.
VAT Tribunals Rules 1986 (SI 1986/590), r. 2: "reasonable excuse appeal" defined.
Notes – S. 71: "reasonable excuse" defined.

69   Breaches of regulatory provisions

69(1)   If any person fails to comply with a regulatory requirement, that is to say, a requirement imposed under–

(a)   paragraph 11 or 12 of Schedule 1, paragraph 5 of Schedule 2, paragraph 5 of Schedule 3 or paragraph 5 of Schedule 3A; or

(b)   any regulations made under section 48 requiring a VAT representative, for the purposes of registration, to notify the Commissioners that his appointment has taken effect or has ceased to have effect; or

(c)   paragraph 6(1) or 7 of Schedule 11; or

(d)   any regulations or rules made under this Act, other than rules made under paragraph 9 of Schedule 12; or

(e)   any order made by the Treasury under this Act; or

(f)   any regulations made under the European Communities Act 1972 and relating to VAT; or

(g)   section 18A in the form of a condition imposed by the Commissioners under subsection (1) or (6) of that section,

he shall be liable, subject to subsection (8) and (9) below and section 76(6), to a penalty equal to the prescribed rate multiplied by the number of days on which the failure continues (up to a maximum of 100) or, if it is greater, to a penalty of £50.

69(2)   If any person fails to comply with a requirement to preserve records imposed under paragraph 6(3) of Schedule 11, he shall be liable, subject to the following provisions of this section, to a penalty of £500.

69(3)   Subject to subsection (4) below, in relation to a failure to comply with any regulatory requirement, the prescribed rate shall be determined by reference to the number of occasions in the period of 2 years preceding the beginning of the failure in question on which the person concerned has previously failed to comply with that requirement and, subject to the following provisions of this section, the prescribed rate shall be–

(a)   if there has been no such previous occasion in that period, £5;

(b)   if there has been only one such occasion in that period, £10; and

(c)   in any other case, £15.

69(4)   For the purposes of subsection (3) above–

(a)   a failure to comply with any regulatory requirement shall be disregarded if, as a result of the failure, the person concerned became liable for a surcharge under section 59 or 59A;

(b)   a continuing failure to comply with any such requirement shall be regarded as one occasion of failure occurring on the date on which the failure began;

(c)   if the same omission gives rise to a failure to comply with more than one such requirement, it shall nevertheless be regarded as the occasion of only one failure; and

(d)   in relation to a failure to comply with a requirement imposed by regulations as to the furnishing of a return or as to the payment of VAT, a previous failure to comply with such a requirement as to either of those matters shall be regarded as a previous failure to comply with the requirement in question.

69(5)   Where the failure referred to in subsection (1) above consists–

(a)   in not paying the VAT due in respect of any period within the time required by regulations under section 25(1), or

(b)   in not furnishing a return in respect of any period within the time required by regulations under paragraph 2(1) of Schedule 11,

the prescribed rate shall be whichever is the greater of that which is appropriate under subsection (3)(a) to (c) above and an amount equal to one-sixth, one-third or one-half of 1 per cent of the VAT due in respect of that period, the appropriate fraction being determined according to whether subsection (3)(a), (b) or (c) above is applicable.

69(6)   For the purposes of subsection (5) above, the **VAT due**–

(a)   if the person concerned has furnished a return, shall be taken to be the VAT shown in the return as that for which he is accountable in respect of the period in question, and

(b)   in any other case, shall be taken to be such VAT as has been assessed for that period and notified to him under section 73(1).

69(7)   If it appears to the Treasury that there has been a change in the value of money since 25th July 1985 or, as the case may be, the last occasion when the power conferred by this subsection was exercised, they may by order substitute for the sums for the time being specified in subsection (2) and (3)(a) to (c) above such other sums as appear to them to be justified by the change; but an order under this subsection shall not apply to a failure which began before the date on which the order comes into force.

69(8)   A failure by any person to comply with any regulatory requirement or the requirement referred to in subsection (2) above shall not give rise to liability to a penalty under this section if the person concerned satisfies the Commissioners or, on appeal, a tribunal that there is a reasonable excuse for the failure; and a failure in respect of which the Commissioners or tribunal have been so satisfied shall be disregarded for the purposes of subsection (3) above.

69(9)   Where, by reason of conduct falling within subsection (1) or (2) above–

(a)   a person is convicted of an offence (whether under this Act or otherwise), or

(b)   a person is assessed to a surcharge under section 59 or 59A, or

(c)   *a person is assessed to a penalty under section 60 or 63,*

that conduct shall not also give rise to liability to a penalty under this section.

69(10)   This section applies in relation to failures occurring before as well as after the commencement of this Act, and for that purpose any reference to any provision of this Act includes a reference to the corresponding provision of the enactments repealed by this Act.

History – In s. 69(1)(a), the words, "paragraph 5 of Schedule 3 or paragraph 5 of Schedule 3A" were substituted for the words "or paragraph 5 of Schedule 3" by FA 2000, s. 136(3), with effect in relation to supplies made on or after 21 March 2000. S. 69(1)(g) and the word "; or" immediately after para. (f) were inserted by FA 1996, s. 26 and Sch. 3, para. 9, with effect from 1 June 1996 and apply to any acquisition of goods from another member State and any supply taking place on or after that day. In s. 69(4)(a), the words "or 59A" were inserted by FA 1996, s. 35(6), in relation to any prescribed accounting period ending on or after 1 June 1996, but a liability to make a payment on account of VAT shall be disregarded for the purposes of the amendments made by FA 1996, s. 35 if the payment is one becoming due before that date.

In s. 69(9)(b), the words "or 59A" were inserted by FA 1996, s. 35(6), in relation to any prescribed accounting period ending on or after 1 June 1996, but a liability to make a payment on account of VAT shall be disregarded for the purposes of the amendments made by FA 1996, s. 35 if the payment is one becoming due before that date.

Derivations – S. 69(1): FA 1985, s. 17(1), as amended by FA 1988, s. 19(1)(b).
S. 69(1)(a): FA 1985, s. 17(1)(a), as amended by FA 1988, s. 19(1)(a) and F(No. 2)A 1992, s. 14 and Sch. 3, para. 81(a).
S. 69(1)(b): FA 1985, s. 17(1)(aa), as inserted by F(No. 2)A 1992, s. 14 and Sch. 3, para. 81(b).
S. 69(1)(c)–(f): FA 1985, s. 17(1)(b)–(e), as inserted (s. 1(d), (e)) by FA 1986, s. 15(1).
S. 69(2): FA 1985, s. 17(2).
S. 69(3): FA 1985, s. 17(3), as amended by FA 1988, s. 19(2).
S. 69(4): FA 1985, s. 17(4)(a), (c)–(e).
S. 69(5)–(9): FA 1985, s. 17(5)–(7), (9), (10).

Cross references – S. 59(9): default surcharge.
S. 69A(1): non-application of s. 69.
S. 83(n): appeals.
ICTA 1988, s. 827(1): penalty is not a deduction in computing any income, profits or losses for any tax purpose.
VAT Tribunals Rules 1986 (SI 1986/590), r. 2: "reasonable excuse appeal" defined.

Notes – S. 71: "reasonable excuse" defined.

BREACH OF RECORD-KEEPING REQUIREMENTS ETC. IN RELATION TO TRANSACTIONS IN GOLD

69A   Breach of record-keeping requirements etc. in relation to transactions in gold

69A(1)   This section applies where a person fails to comply with a requirement of regulations under section 13(5)(a) or (b) of the Finance Act 1999 (gold: duties to keep records or provide information).

Where this section applies, the provisions of section 69 do not apply.

69A(2)   A person who fails to comply with any such requirement is liable to a penalty not exceeding 17.5% of the value of the transactions to which the failure relates.

69A(3)   For the purposes of assessing the amount of any such penalty, the value of the transactions to which the failure relates shall be determined by the Commissioners to the best of their judgement and notified by them to the person liable.

69A(4)   No assessment of a penalty under this section shall be made more than 2 years after evidence of facts sufficient in the opinion of the Commissioners to justify the making of the assessment comes to their knowledge.

69A(5)   The reference in subsection (4) above to **facts sufficient to justify the making of the assessment** is to facts sufficient–

(a)   to indicate that there had been a failure to comply with any such requirement as is referred to in subsection (1) above, and

(b)   to determine the value of the transactions to which the failure relates.

69A(6)   A failure by any person to comply with any such requirement as is mentioned in subsection (1) above shall not give rise to a liability to a penalty under this section if the person concerned satisfies the Commissioners or, on appeal, a tribunal, that there is a reasonable excuse for the failure.

69A(7)   Where by reason of conduct falling within subsection (1) above a person–

(a)   is assessed to a penalty under section 60, or
(b)   is convicted of an offence (whether under this Act or otherwise),

that conduct shall not also give rise to a penalty under this section.

History – S. 69A was inserted by FA 2000, s. 137(2), with effect from 28 July 2000.

70   Mitigation of penalties under sections 60, 63, 64 and 67

70(1)   Where a person is liable to a penalty under section 60, 63, 64, 67 or 69A , the Commissioners or, on appeal, a tribunal may reduce the penalty to such amount (including nil) as they think proper.

70(2)   In the case of a penalty reduced by the Commissioners under subsection (1) above, a tribunal, on an appeal relating to the penalty, may cancel the whole or any part of the reduction made by the Commissioners.

70(3)   None of the matters specified in subsection (4) below shall be matters which the Commissioners or any tribunal shall be entitled to take into account in exercising their powers under this section.

70(4)   Those matters are–

(a)   the insufficiency of the funds available to any person for paying any VAT due or for paying the amount of the penalty;

(b)   the fact that there has, in the case in question or in that case taken with any other cases, been no or no significant loss of VAT;

(c)   the fact that the person liable to the penalty or a person acting on his behalf has acted in good faith.

History – In s. 70(1), the words ", 67 or 69A" were substituted for the words "or 67" by FA 2000, s. 137(3), with effect from 28 July 2000.

Derivations – FA 1985, s. 15A, as inserted by FA 1993, s. 49 and Sch. 2, para. 3(1).

Cross references – S. 84(6): appeals.

VAT Tribunals Rules 1986 (SI 1986/590), r. 2: "mitigation appeal" defined.

71   Construction of sections 59 to 70

71(1)   For the purpose of any provision of sections 59 to 70 which refers to a **reasonable excuse** for any conduct–

(a)   an insufficiency of funds to pay any VAT due is not a reasonable excuse; and

(b)   where reliance is placed on any other person to perform any task, neither the fact of that reliance nor any dilatoriness or inaccuracy on the part of the person relied upon is a reasonable excuse.

71(2)   In relation to a prescribed accounting period, any reference in sections 59 to 69 to **credit for input tax** includes a reference to any sum which, in a return for that period, is claimed as a deduction from VAT due.

Derivations – FA 1985, s. 33(2), (3).

72   Offences

72(1)   If any person is knowingly concerned in, or in the taking of steps with a view to, the fraudulent evasion of VAT by him or any other person, he shall be liable–

(a)   on summary conviction, to a penalty of the statutory maximum or of three times the amount of the VAT, whichever is the greater, or to imprisonment for a term not exceeding 6 months or to both; or

(b)   on conviction on indictment, to a penalty of any amount or to imprisonment for a term not exceeding 7 years or to both.

72(2)   Any reference in subsection (1) above or subsection (8) below to the **evasion of VAT** includes a reference to the obtaining of–

(a)   the payment of a VAT credit; or

(b)   a refund under section 35, 36 or 40 of this Act or section 22 of the 1983 Act; or

(c)   a refund under any regulations made by virtue of section 13(5); or

(d)   a repayment under section 39;

and any reference in those subsections to the **amount of the VAT** shall be construed–

    (i)   in relation to VAT itself or a VAT credit, as a reference to the aggregate of the amount (if any) falsely claimed by way of credit for input tax and the amount (if any) by which output tax was falsely understated, and

    (ii) in relation to a refund or repayment falling within paragraph (b), (c) or (d) above, as a reference to the amount falsely claimed by way of refund or repayment.

72(3)   If any person–

(a)   with intent to deceive produces, furnishes or sends for the purposes of this Act or otherwise makes use for those purposes of any document which is false in a material particular; or

(b)   in furnishing any information for the purposes of this Act makes any statement which he knows to be false in a material particular or recklessly makes a statement which is false in a material particular,

he shall be liable–

    (i)   on summary conviction, to a penalty of the statutory maximum or, where subsection (4) or (5) below applies, to the alternative penalty specified in that subsection if it is greater, or to imprisonment for a term not exceeding 6 months or to both; or

    (ii) on conviction on indictment, to a penalty of any amount or to imprisonment for a term not exceeding 7 years or to both.

72(4)   In any case where–

(a)   the document referred to in subsection (3)(a) above is a return required under this Act, or

(b)   the information referred to in subsection (3)(b) above is contained in or otherwise relevant to such a return,

the **alternative penalty** referred to in subsection (3)(i) above is a penalty equal to three times the aggregate of the amount (if any) falsely claimed by way of credit for input tax and the amount (if any) by which output tax was falsely understated.

72(5)   In any case where–

(a)   the document referred to in subsection (3)(a) above is a claim for a refund under section 35, 36 or 40 of this Act or section 22 of the 1983 Act, for a refund under any regulations made by virtue of section 13(5) or for a repayment under section 39, or

(b)   the information referred to in subsection (3)(b) above is contained in or otherwise relevant to such a claim,

the **alternative penalty** referred to in subsection (3)(i) above is a penalty equal to 3 times the amount falsely claimed.

72(6)   The reference in subsection (3)(a) above to **furnishing, sending or otherwise making use of a document which is false in a material particular, with intent to deceive**, includes a reference to furnishing, sending or otherwise making use of such a document, with intent to secure that a machine will respond to the document as if it were a true document.

72(7)   Any reference in subsection (3)(a) or (6) above to **producing, furnishing or sending a document** includes a reference to causing a document to be produced, furnished or sent.

72(8)   Where a person's conduct during any specified period must have involved the commission by him of one or more offences under the preceding provisions of this section, then, whether or not the particulars of that offence or those offences are known, he shall, by virtue of this subsection, be guilty of an offence and liable–

(a)   on summary conviction, to a penalty of the statutory maximum or, if greater, 3 times the amount of any VAT that was or was intended to be evaded by his conduct, or to imprisonment for a term not exceeding 6 months or to both, or

(b)   on conviction on indictment to a penalty of any amount or to imprisonment for a term not exceeding 7 years or to both.

72(9)   Where an authorised person has reasonable grounds for suspecting that an offence has been committed under the preceding provisions of this section, he may arrest anyone whom he has reasonable grounds for suspecting to be guilty of the offence.

72(10)   If any person acquires possession of or deals with any goods, or accepts the supply of any services, having reason to believe that VAT on the supply of the goods or services, on the acquisition of the goods from another member State or on the importation of the goods from a place outside the member States has been or will be evaded, he shall be liable on summary conviction to a penalty of level 5 on the standard scale or three times the amount of the VAT, whichever is the greater.

72(11)   If any person supplies goods or services in contravention of paragraph 4(2) of Schedule 11, he shall be liable on summary conviction to a penalty of level 5 on the standard scale.

72(12)   Subject to subsection (13) below, sections 145 to 155 of the Management Act (proceedings for offences, mitigation of penalties and certain other matters) shall apply in relation to offences under this Act (which include any act or omission in respect of which a penalty is imposed) and penalties imposed under this Act as they apply in relation to offences and penalties under the customs and excise Acts as defined in that Act; and accordingly in section 154(2) as it applies by virtue of this subsection the reference to **duty** shall be construed as a reference to VAT.

72(13)   In subsection (12) above the references to **penalties** do not include references to penalties under sections 60 to 70.

Derivations – S. 72(1): VATA 1983, s. 39(1), as amended by FA 1985, s. 12(2).
S. 72(2): VATA 1983, s. 39(1A), as inserted by FA 1985, s. 12(3) and para. (ba), as inserted by F(No. 2)A 1992, s. 14 and Sch. 3, para. 39(1)(b), as amended by FA 1990, s. 11(11)(a) and F(No. 2)A 1992, s. 14 and Sch. 3, para. 39(1)(a).
S. 72(3): VATA 1983, s. 39(2), as amended by FA 1985, s. 12(2), (4).
S. 72(4)–(7): VATA 1983, s. 39(2A), (2B), (2C), (2D), as inserted by FA 1985, s. 12(5), and as amended (s. 39(2B)) by F(No. 2)A 1992, s. 14 and Sch. 3, para. 38(2).
S. 72(8): VATA 1983, s. 39(3), as amended by FA 1985, s. 12(2).
S. 72(9): VATA 1983, s. 39(3A), as inserted by FA 1985, s. 12(6).
S. 72(10): VATA 1983, s. 39(4), as amended by F(No. 2)A 1992, s. 14 and Sch. 3, para. 39(3).
S. 72(11): VATA 1983, s. 39(5).
S. 72(12): VATA 1983, s. 39(9).
S. 72(13): FA 1985, s. 33(5)(a), as amended by F(No. 2)A 1992, s. 14 and Sch. 3, para. 86.

Cross reference – Sch. 11, para. 10(4): definition of "a fraud offence".

Official publications – 12: Compounding, seizure and restoration.

Other material – ICAEW Technical Release TAX 27/95 (not reproduced): professional conduct in relation to taxation.

Notes – S. 96(1): definition of "invoice".

Level 5 on the standard scale is £5,000 with effect from 1 October 1992 (Criminal Justice Act 1982, s. 37).

ASSESSMENTS OF VAT AND OTHER PAYMENTS DUE

73   Failure to make returns etc.

73(1)   Where a person has failed to make any returns required under this Act (or under any provision repealed by this Act) or to keep any documents and afford the facilities necessary to verify such returns or where it appears to the Commissioners that such returns are incomplete or incorrect, they may assess the amount of VAT due from him to the best of their judgment and notify it to him.

73(2)   In any case where, for any prescribed accounting period, there has been paid or credited to any person–

(a)   as being a repayment or refund of VAT, or

(b)   as being due to him as a VAT credit,

an amount which ought not to have been so paid or credited, or which would not have been so paid or credited had the facts been known or been as they later turn out to be, the Commissioners may assess that amount as being VAT due from him for that period and notify it to him accordingly.

73(3)   An amount–

(a)   which has been paid to any person as being due to him as a VAT credit, and

(b)   which, by reason of the cancellation of that person's registration under paragraph 13(2) to (6) of Schedule 1, paragraph 6(2) of Schedule 2, paragraph 6(2) or (3) of Schedule 3 or paragraph 6(1) or (2) of Schedule 3A ought not to have been so paid,

may be assessed under subsection (2) above notwithstanding that cancellation.

73(4)   Where a person is assessed under subsection (1) and (2) above in respect of the same prescribed accounting period the assessments may be combined and notified to him as one assessment.

73(5)   Where the person failing to make a return, or making a return which appears to the Commissioners to be incomplete or incorrect, was required to make the return as a personal representative, trustee in bankruptcy, interim or permanent trustee, receiver, liquidator or person otherwise acting in a representative capacity in relation to another person, subsection (1) above shall apply as if the reference to VAT due from him included a reference to VAT due from that other person.

73(6)   An assessment under subsection (1), (2) or (3) above of an amount of VAT due for any prescribed accounting period must be made within the time limits provided for in section 77 and shall not be made after the later of the following–

(a)   2 years after the end of the prescribed accounting period; or

(b)   one year after evidence of facts, sufficient in the opinion of the Commissioners to justify the making of the assessment, comes to their knowledge,

but (subject to that section) where further such evidence comes to the Commissioners' knowledge after the making of an assessment under subsection (1), (2) or (3) above, another assessment may be made under that subsection, in addition to any earlier assessment.

73(7)   Where a taxable person–

(a)   has in the course or furtherance of a business carried on by him, been supplied with any goods, acquired any goods from another member State or otherwise obtained possession or control of any goods, or

(b)   has, in the course or furtherance of such a business, imported any goods from a place outside the member States,

the Commissioners may require him from time to time to account for the goods; and if he fails to prove that the goods have been or are available to be supplied by him or have been exported or otherwise removed from the United Kingdom without being exported or so removed by way of supply or have been lost or destroyed, they may assess to the best of their judgment and notify to him the amount of VAT that would have been chargeable in respect of the supply of the goods if they had been supplied by him.

73(7A) Where a fiscal warehousekeeper has failed to pay VAT required by the Commissioners under section 18E(2), the Commissioners may assess to the best of their judgment the amount of that VAT due from him and notify it to him.

73(7B) Where it appears to the Commissioners that goods have been removed from a warehouse or fiscal warehouse without payment of the VAT payable under section 18(4) or section 18D on that removal, they may assess to the best of their judgment the amount of VAT due from the person removing the goods or other person liable and notify it to him.

73(8) In any case where–

(a) as a result of a person's failure to make a return for a prescribed accounting period, the Commissioners have made an assessment under subsection (1) above for that period,

(b) the VAT assessed has been paid but no proper return has been made for the period to which the assessment related, and

(c) as a result of a failure to make a return for a later prescribed accounting period, being a failure by a person referred to in paragraph (a) above or a person acting in a representative capacity in relation to him, as mentioned in subsection (5) above, the Commissioners find it necessary to make another assessment under subsection (1) above,

then, if the Commissioners think fit, having regard to the failure referred to in paragraph (a) above, they may specify in the assessment referred to in paragraph (c) above an amount of VAT greater than that which they would otherwise have considered to be appropriate.

73(9) Where an amount has been assessed and notified to any person under subsection (1), (2), (3), (7), (7A) or (7B) above it shall, subject to the provisions of this Act as to appeals, be deemed to be an amount of VAT due from him and may be recovered accordingly, unless, or except to the extent that, the assessment has subsequently been withdrawn or reduced.

73(10) For the purposes of this section notification to a personal representative, trustee in bankruptcy, interim or permanent trustee, receiver, liquidator or person otherwise acting as aforesaid shall be treated as notification to the person in relation to whom he so acts.

History – In s. 73(3)(b), the words ", paragraph 6(2) or (3) of Schedule 3 or paragraph 6(1) or (2) of Schedule 3A" were substituted for the words "or paragraph 6(2) or (3) of Schedule 3" by FA 2000, s. 136(4), with effect in relation to supplies made on or after 21 March 2000.
S. 73(7A) and (7B) were inserted by FA 1996, s. 26 and Sch. 3, para. 10, with effect from 1 June 1996 and apply to any acquisition of goods from another member State and any supply taking place on or after that day.
In s. 73(9), the words ", (7), (7A) or (7B)" were substituted by FA 1996, s. 26 and Sch. 3, para. 11, with effect from 1 June 1996 and apply to any acquisition of goods from another member State and any supply taking place on or after that day.
Derivations – S. 73(1): VATA 1983, s. 38 and Sch. 7, para. 4(1).
S. 73(2), (3): VATA 1983, s. 38 and Sch. 7, para. 4(2), (2A), as substituted by FA 1988, s. 15(2), and as amended by FA 1990, s. 15(1) and F(No. 2)A 1992, s. 14 and Sch. 3, para. 66(1).
S. 73(4), (5): VATA 1983, s. 38 and Sch. 7, para. 4(3), (4), as construed (s. 4(4)) by the Bankruptcy (Scotland) Act 1985, s. 75(11).
S. 73(6): VATA 1983, s. 38 and Sch. 7, para. 4(5), as amended by FA 1988, s. 15(3) and F(No. 2)A 1992, s. 14 and Sch. 3, para. 66(2).
S. 73(7): VATA 1983, s. 38 and Sch. 7, para. 4(6), as amended by FA 1985, s. 23 and Sch. 7, para. 1(2) and F(No. 2)A 1992, s. 14 and Sch. 3, para. 66(3).
S. 73(8): VATA 1983, s. 38 and Sch. 7, para. 4(6A), as inserted by FA 1985, s. 23 and Sch. 7, para. 1(3).
S. 73(9): VATA 1983, s. 38 and Sch. 7, para. 4(9), as amended by FA 1988, s. 15(4).
S. 73(10): VATA 1983, s. 38 and Sch. 7, para. 4(10), as construed by the Bankruptcy (Scotland) Act 1985, s. 75(11).
Cross references – S. 43(1)(c)(i): groups.
S. 69(6)(b): a penalty can be assessed for not accounting for VAT assessed under s. 73(1).
S. 74(1) and (5): interest.
S. 76(5) and 77(1): other assessment time limits.
S. 77(6): supplementary assessments.
S. 83(p): appeals.
S. 92(7): definition of "relevant information powers".
Sch. 13, para. 20: assessments of amounts paid or credited before 1 September 1994.
VAT Regulations 1995 (SI 1995/2518), reg. 54(1)(h): expulsion from annual accounting scheme if unpaid assessment.
VAT Regulations 1995 (SI 1995/2518), reg. 181: claim treated as a return.
VAT Regulations 1995 (SI 1995/2518), reg. 194(1): distraint on goods and chattels.
VAT Regulations 1995 (SI 1995/2518), reg. 212: claim treated as a return.
Distress for Customs and Excise Duties and Other Indirect Taxes Regulations (SI 1997/1431), reg. 5(2): restrictions on levying distress.
Notes – S. 25(1): definition of "prescribed accounting period".
VAT Regulations 1995 (SI 1995/2518), reg. 6(3)(a): obligation to furnish a return or account for VAT where registration number is transferred.

74   Interest on VAT recovered or recoverable by assessment

74(1) Subject to section 76(8), where an assessment is made under any provision of section 73 and, in the case of an assessment under section 73(1) at least one of the following conditions is fulfilled, namely–

(a) the assessment relates to a prescribed accounting period in respect of which either–

       (i)   a return has previously been made, or

       (ii)   an earlier assessment has already been notified to the person concerned,

(b)   the assessment relates to a prescribed accounting period which exceeds 3 months and begins on the date with effect from which the person concerned was, or was required to be, registered,

(c)   the assessment relates to a prescribed accounting period at the beginning of which the person concerned was, but should no longer have been, exempted from registration under paragraph 14(1) of Schedule 1 or, under paragraph 8 of Schedule 3 or under paragraph 7 of Schedule 3A,

the whole of the amount assessed shall, subject to subsection (3) below, carry interest at the rate applicable under section 197 of the Finance Act 1996 from the reckonable date until payment.

74(2)   In any case where–

(a)   the circumstances are such that an assessment falling within subsection (1) above could have been made, but

(b)   before such an assessment was made the VAT due or other amount concerned was paid (so that no such assessment was necessary),

the whole of the amount paid shall, subject to subsection (3) below, carry interest at the rate applicable under section 197 of the Finance Act 1996 from the reckonable date until the date on which it was paid.

74(3)   Where (apart from this subsection)–

(a)   the period before the assessment in question for which any amount would carry interest under subsection (1) above; or

(b)   the period for which any amount would carry interest under subsection (2) above,

would exceed 3 years, the part of that period for which that amount shall carry interest under that subsection shall be confined to the last 3 years of that period.

74(4)   Where an unauthorised person, as defined in section 67(2), issues an invoice showing an amount as being VAT or as including an amount attributable to VAT, the amount which is shown as VAT or, as the case may be, is to be taken as representing VAT shall carry interest at the rate applicable under section 197 of the Finance Act 1996 from the date of the invoice until payment.

74(5)   The references in subsection (1) and (2) above to the **reckonable date** shall be construed as follows–

(a)   where the amount assessed or paid is such an amount as is referred to in section 73(2)(a) or (b), the reckonable date is the seventh day after the day on which a written instruction was issued by the Commissioners directing the making of the payment of the amount which ought not to have been repaid or paid to the person concerned; and

(b)   in all other cases the reckonable date is the latest date on which (in accordance with regulations under this Act) a return is required to be made for the prescribed accounting period to which the amount assessed or paid relates; and

(c)   in the case of an amount assessed under section 73(7) the sum assessed shall be taken for the purposes of paragraph (b) above to relate to the period for which the assessment was made;

and interest under this section shall run from the reckonable date even if that date is a non-business day, within the meaning of section 92 of the Bills of Exchange Act 1882.

74(6)   [Repealed by FA 1996, s. 205 and Sch. 41, Pt. VIII(1).]

74(7)   Interest under this section shall be paid without any deduction of income tax.

History – In s. 74(1)(c), the words ", under paragraph 8 of Schedule 3 or under paragraph 7 of Schedule 3A" were substituted for the words "under paragraph 8 of Schedule 3" by FA 2000, s. 136(5), with effect in relation to supplies made on or after 21 March 2000.

In s. 74(1), the words "the rate applicable under section 197 of the Finance Act 1996" substituted for the words "the prescribed rate" by FA 1996, s. 197(6)(d)(i), for periods beginning on or after 1 April 1997 and will have effect in relation to interest running from before that day, as well as from that day or from after that day.

In s. 74(2), the words "the rate applicable under section 197 of the Finance Act 1996" substituted for the words "the prescribed rate" by FA 1996, s. 197(6)(d)(i), for periods beginning on or after 1 April 1997 and will have effect in relation to interest running from before that day, as well as from that day or from after that day.

In s. 74(4), the words "the rate applicable under section 197 of the Finance Act 1996" substituted for the words "the prescribed rate" by FA 1996, s. 197(6)(d)(i), for periods beginning on or after 1 April 1997 and will have effect in relation to interest running from before that day, as well as from that day or from after that day.

S. 74(6) repealed by FA 1996, s. 205 and Sch. 41, Pt. VIII(1), for periods beginning on or after 1 April 1997 and shall have effect in relation to interest running from before that day, as well as from that day or from after that day. Former s. 74(6) reads as follows:

"**74(6)**   In this section **"the prescribed rate"** means such rate as may be prescribed by order made by the Treasury; and such an order–

(a)   may prescribe different rates for different purposes; and

(b) shall apply to interest for periods beginning on or after the date when the order is expressed to come into force, whether or not interest runs from before that date."

Derivations – S. 74(1): FA 1985, s. 18(1), as amended by FA 1988, s. 14(8)(b), FA 1990, s. 16(2), F(No. 2)A 1992, s. 14 and Sch. 3, para. 83 and FA 1993, s. 49 and Sch. 2, para. 4(1).
S. 74(2): FA 1985, s. 18(3), as amended by FA 1988, s. 18(4)(b), FA 1990, s. 16(3) and FA 1993, s. 49 and Sch. 2, para. 4(1).
S. 74(3): FA 1985, s. 18(3A), as inserted by FA 1993, s. 49 and Sch. 2, para. 4(2).
S. 74(4)–(7): FA 1985, s. 18(6)–(8)(a), (b), (9), as amended (s. 18(7)) by FA 1990, s. 16(5).

Cross references – Sch. 9A, para. 6(9) and 6(10): assessments concerning anti-avoidance and VAT groups.
ICTA 1988, s. 827(1): interest is not a deduction in computing any income, profits or losses for any tax purpose.

Statutory instruments – The rate of interest has been set as follows:

Period of application	%
From 6/2/00	8.5
6/3/99–5/2/00	7.5
6/1/99–5/3/99	8.5
6/7/98–5/1/99	9.5
6/2/96–5/7/98	6.25
6/3/95–5/2/96	7
6/10/94–5/3/95	6.25
6/1/94–5/10/94	5.5
6/3/93–5/1/94	6.25
6/12/92–5/3/93	7
6/11/92–5/12/92	7.75
6/10/91–5/11/92	9.25
6/7/91–5/10/91	10
6/5/91–5/7/91	10.75
6/3/91–5/5/91	11.5
6/11/90–5/3/91	12.25
1/4/90–5/11/90	13

For interest accruing on or after 6 July 1998, the interest rate changes on the sixth day of any month, in accordance with the formulae specified in SI 1998/1461, when the rounded average of the base lending rates of six clearing banks at the close of business 12 working days prior to that day, the "reference rate" (RR) changes from the rounded average of those rates at the close of business on the corresponding day in the previous month.

Official publications – 700/43.
700/56/99, para. 5.5: generally no default interest applies to post-insolvency returns.

75   Assessments in cases of acquisitions of certain goods by non-taxable persons

75(1)   Where a person who has, at a time when he was not a taxable person, acquired in the United Kingdom from another member State any goods subject to a duty of excise or consisting in a new means of transport and–

(a)   notification of that acquisition has not been given to the Commissioners by the person who is required to give one by regulations under paragraph 2(4) of Schedule 11 (whether before or after the commencement of this Act);

(b)   the Commissioners are not satisfied that the particulars relating to the acquisition in any notification given to them are accurate and complete; or

(c)   there has been a failure to supply the Commissioners with the information necessary to verify the particulars contained in any such notification,

they may assess the amount of VAT due on the acquisition to the best of their judgment and notify their assessment to that person.

75(2)   An assessment under this section must be made within the time limits provided for in section 77 and shall not be made after whichever is the later of the following–

(a)   2 years after the time when a notification of the acquisition of the goods in question is given to the Commissioners by the person who is required to give one by regulations under paragraph 2(4) of Schedule 11;

(b)   one year after evidence of the facts, sufficient in the opinion of the Commissioners to justify the making of the assessment, comes to their knowledge,

but (subject to section 77) where further such evidence comes to the Commissioners' knowledge after the making of an assessment under this section, another assessment may be made under this section, in addition to any earlier assessment.

75(3)   Where an amount has been assessed and notified to any person under this section, it shall, subject to the provisions of this Act as to appeals, be deemed to be an amount of VAT due from him and may be recovered accordingly, unless, or except to the extent that, the assessment has subsequently been withdrawn or reduced.

75(4)   For the purposes of this section, notification to a personal representative, trustee in bankruptcy, interim or permanent trustee, receiver, liquidator or person otherwise acting in a representative capacity in relation to the person who made the acquisition in question shall be treated as notification to the person in relation to whom he so acts.

Derivations – VATA 1983, s. 38 and Sch. 7, para. 4A, as inserted by F(No. 2)A 1992, s. 14 and Sch. 3, para. 67 and as construed by the Bankruptcy (Scotland) Act 1985, s. 75(11).

Cross reference – S. 83(p): appeals.

76   Assessment of amounts due by way of penalty, interest or surcharge

76(1)   Where any person is liable–

(a)   to a surcharge under section 59 or 59A, or

(b)   to a penalty under any of sections 60 to 69A, or

(c)   for interest under section 74,

the Commissioners may, subject to subsection (2) below, assess the amount due by way of penalty, interest or surcharge, as the case may be, and notify it to him accordingly; and the fact that any conduct giving rise to a penalty under any of sections 60 to 69A may have ceased before an assessment is made under this section shall not affect the power of the Commissioners to make such an assessment.

76(2)   Where a person is liable to a penalty under section 69 for any failure to comply with such a requirement as is referred to in subsection (1)(c) to (f) of that section, no assessment shall be made under this section of the amount due from him by way of such penalty unless, within the period of 2 years preceding the assessment, the Commissioners have issued him with a written warning of the consequences of a continuing failure to comply with that requirement.

76(3)   In the case of the penalties, interest and surcharge referred to in the following paragraphs, the assessment under this section shall be of an amount due in respect of the prescribed accounting period which in the paragraph concerned is referred to as **"the relevant period"**–

(a)   in the case of a surcharge under section 59 or 59A, the relevant period is the prescribed accounting period in respect of which the taxable person is in default and in respect of which the surcharge arises;

(b)   in the case of a penalty under section 60 relating to the evasion of VAT, the relevant period is the prescribed accounting period for which the VAT evaded was due;

(c)   in the case of a penalty under section 60 relating to the obtaining of the payment of a VAT credit, the relevant period is the prescribed accounting period in respect of which the payment was obtained;

(d)   in the case of a penalty under section 63, the relevant period is the prescribed accounting period for which liability to VAT was understated or, as the case may be, for which entitlement to a VAT credit was overstated; and

(e)   in the case of interest under section 74, the relevant period is the prescribed accounting period in respect of which the VAT (or amount assessed as VAT) was due.

76(4)   In any case where the amount of any penalty, interest or surcharge falls to be calculated by reference to VAT which was not paid at the time it should have been and that VAT (or the supply which gives rise to it) cannot be readily attributed to any one or more prescribed accounting periods, it shall be treated for the purposes of this Act as VAT due for such period or periods as the Commissioners may determine to the best of their judgment and notify to the person liable for the VAT and penalty, interest or surcharge.

76(5)   Where a person is assessed under this section to an amount due by way of any penalty, interest or surcharge falling within subsection (3) above and is also assessed under section 73(1), (2), (7), (7A) or (7B) for the prescribed accounting period which is the relevant period under subsection (3) above, the assessments may be combined and notified to him as one assessment, but the amount of the penalty, interest or surcharge shall be separately identified in the notice.

76(6)   An assessment to a penalty under section 67 by virtue of subsection (1)(b) of that section may be combined with an assessment under section 75 and the 2 assessments notified together but the amount of the penalty shall be separately identified in the notice.

76(7)   In the case of an amount due by way of penalty under section 66 or 69 or interest under section 74–

(a)   a notice of assessment under this section shall specify a date, being not later than the date of the notice, to which the aggregate amount of the penalty which is assessed or, as the case may be, the amount of interest is calculated; and

(b)   if the penalty or interest continues to accrue after that date, a further assessment or assessments may be made under this section in respect of amounts which so accrue.

76(8)   If, within such period as may be notified by the Commissioners to the person liable to a penalty under section 66 or 69 or for interest under section 74—

(a)   a failure or default falling within section 66(1) or 69(1) is remedied, or

(b)   the VAT or other amount referred to in section 74(1) is paid,

it shall be treated for the purposes of section 66 or 69 or, as the case may be, section 74 as paid or remedied on the date specified as mentioned in subsection (7)(a) above.

76(9)   If an amount is assessed and notified to any person under this section, then unless, or except to the extent that, the assessment is withdrawn or reduced, that amount shall be recoverable as if it were VAT due from him.

76(10)   For the purposes of this section, notification to a personal representative, trustee in bankruptcy, interim or permanent trustee, receiver, liquidator or person otherwise acting in a representative capacity in relation to another shall be treated as notification to the person in relation to whom he so acts.

History – In s. 76(1), the words "or 59A" were inserted by FA 1996, s. 35(7), in relation to any prescribed accounting period ending on or after 1 June 1996, but a liability to make a payment on account of VAT shall be disregarded for the purposes of the amendments made by FA 1996, s. 35 if the payment is one becoming due before that date.
In s. 76(1), in both places, the words "to 69A" were substituted for the words "to 69" by FA 2000, s. 137(4), with effect from 28 July 2000.
In s. 76(3)(a), the words "or 59A" were inserted by FA 1996, s. 35(7), in relation to any prescribed accounting period ending on or after 1 June 1996, but a liability to make a payment on account of VAT shall be disregarded for the purposes of the amendments made by FA 1996, s. 35 if the payment is one becoming due before that date.
In s. 76(5), the words ", (7), (7A) or (7B)" were substituted by FA 1996, s. 26 and Sch. 3, para. 11, with effect from 1 June 1996 and apply to any acquisition of goods from another member State and any supply taking place on or after that day.
In s. 76(10), the word "another" was substituted by FA 1997, s. 45(6), and this substitution is deemed always to have had effect.
Derivations – S. 76(1) (as originally enacted): FA 1985, s. 21(1), as amended by FA 1988, s. 19(3) and F(No. 2)A 1992, s. 14 and Sch. 3, para. 84(1).
S. 76(2): FA 1985, s. 21(1A), as inserted by FA 1988, s. 19(3).
S. 76(3)–(5) (as originally enacted): FA 1985, s. 21(2)–(4).
S. 76(6): FA 1985, s. 21(4A), as inserted by F(No. 2)A 1992, s. 14 and Sch. 3, para. 84(2).
S. 76(7)–(10) (as originally enacted): FA 1985, s. 21(5)–(8), as amended (s. 21(5), (6)) by F(No. 2)A 1992, s. 14 and Sch. 3, para. 84(3), (4) and as construed by the Bankruptcy (Scotland) Act 1985, s. 75(11).
Cross references – S. 61(4): assessments of penalties on directors.
S. 69(1): breaches of regulatory provisions.
S. 83(q): appeals.
Sch. 9A, para. 6(10): assessments concerning anti-avoidance and VAT groups.
VAT Regulations 1995 (SI 1995/2518), reg. 54(1)(h): expulsion from annual accounting scheme if unpaid assessment.
VAT Regulations 1995 (SI 1995/2518), reg. 58(1): unpaid assessment under s. 76 can stop use of cash accounting.
Notes – S. 81: set off of credits.
Sch. 11, para. 5: recovery of VAT.

77   Assessments: time limits and supplementary assessments

77(1)   Subject to the following provisions of this section, an assessment under section 73, 75 or 76, shall not be made—

(a)   more than 3 years after the end of the prescribed accounting period or importation or acquisition concerned, or

(b)   in the case of an assessment under section 76 of an amount due by way of a penalty which is not among those referred to in subsection (3) of that section, 3 years after the event giving rise to the penalty.

77(2)   Subject to subsection (5) below, an assessment under section 76 of an amount due by way of any penalty, interest or surcharge referred to in subsection (3) of that section may be made at any time before the expiry of the period of 2 years beginning with the time when the amount of VAT due for the prescribed accounting period concerned has been finally determined.

77(2A)   Subject to subsection (5) below, an assessment under section 76 of a penalty under section 65 or 66 may be made at any time before the expiry of the period of 2 years beginning with the time when facts sufficient in the opinion of the Commissioners to indicate, as the case may be—

(a)   that the statement in question contained a material inaccuracy, or

(b)   that there had been a default within the meaning of section 66(1),

came to the Commissioners' knowledge.

77(3)   In relation to an assessment under section 76, any reference in subsection (1) or (2) above to the **prescribed accounting period concerned** is a reference to that period which, in the case of the penalty, interest or surcharge concerned, is the relevant period referred to in subsection (3) of that section.

77(4)   Subject to subsection (5) below, if VAT has been lost–

(a)   as a result of conduct falling within section 60(1) or for which a person has been convicted of fraud, or

(b)   in circumstances giving rise to liability to a penalty under section 67,

an assessment may be made as if, in subsection (1) above, each reference to 3 years were a reference to 20 years.

77(5)   Where, after a person's death, the Commissioners propose to assess a sum as due by reason of some conduct (howsoever described) of the deceased, including a sum due by way of penalty, interest or surcharge–

(a)   the assessment shall not be made more than 3 years after the death; and

(b)   if the circumstances are as set out in subsection (4) above, the modification of subsection (1) above contained in that subsection shall not apply but any assessment which (from the point of view of time limits) could have been made immediately after the death may be made at any time within 3 years after it.

77(6)   If, otherwise than in circumstances falling within section 73(6)(b) or 75(2)(b), it appears to the Commissioners that the amount which ought to have been assessed in an assessment under that section or under section 76 exceeds the amount which was so assessed, then–

(a)   under the like provision as that assessment was made, and

(b)   on or before the last day on which that assessment could have been made,

the Commissioners may make a supplementary assessment of the amount of the excess and shall notify the person concerned accordingly.

History – In s. 77(1)(a) and (b). the words "3 years" wherever they occur were substituted for the words "6 years" by FA 1997, s. 47(10), with effect in relation to any assessment made on or after 18 July 1996.
S. 77(2) and 77(2A) were substituted for the former s. 77(2) by FA 1999, s. 18(1), with effect in relation to any amount by way of penalty, interest or surcharge which becomes due on or after 27 July 1999. Former s. 77(2) reads as follows:
"**77(2)**   Subject to subsection (5) below, an assessment under section 76 of an amount due by way of any penalty, interest or surcharge referred to in subsection (3) of that section may be made at any time before the expiry of the period of 2 years beginning–
   (a)   in the case of a penalty under section 65 or 66, with the time when facts sufficient in the opinion of the Commissioners to indicate, as the case may be–
      (i)   that the statement in question contained a material inaccuracy; or
      (ii)   that there had been a default within the meaning of section 66(1),
      came to the Commissioners' knowledge; and
   (b)   in any other case, with the time when the amount of VAT due for the prescribed accounting period concerned has been finally determined."
In s. 77(4). the words "3 years" were substituted for the words "6 years" by FA 1997, s. 47(10), with effect in relation to any assessment made on or after 18 July 1996.
Derivations – FA 1985, s. 22(1)–(5), (7), as amended (s. 22(1), (2), (7)) by F(No. 2)A 1992, s. 14 and Sch. 3, para. 85.
Cross references – S. 83(r): appeals.
Sch. 9A, para. 6(9) and 6(10): assessments concerning anti-avoidance and VAT groups.
Notes – Limitation Act 1980, s. 37(3)(a): the normal statute of limitations does not apply to any proceedings by the Crown for the recovery of any tax or interest on any tax.

INTEREST, REPAYMENT SUPPLEMENTS ETC. PAYABLE BY COMMISSIONERS

78   Interest in certain cases of official error

Notes – S. 78 has effect in relation to any claim made on or after 18 July 1996 and is deemed always to have had effect in relation to such a claim with the substitution of s. 78(11) as made below.
S. 78 has effect and is deemed always to have had effect with the substitution of s. 78(12)(a) as made below.

78(1)   Where, due to an error on the part of the Commissioners, a person has–

(a)   accounted to them for an amount by way of output tax which was not output tax due from him and which they are in consequence liable to repay to him, or

(b)   failed to claim credit under section 25 for an amount for which he was entitled so to claim credit and which they are in consequence liable to pay to him, or

(c)   (otherwise than in a case falling within paragraph (a) or (b) above) paid to them by way of VAT an amount that was not VAT due and which they are in consequence liable to repay to him, or

(d)   suffered delay in receiving payment of an amount due to him from them in connection with VAT,

then, if and to the extent that they would not be liable to do so apart from this section, they shall pay interest to him on that amount for the applicable period, but subject to the following provisions of this section.

78(1A)   In subsection (1) above–

(a)   references to an **amount which the Commissioners are liable** in consequence of any matter to pay or repay to any person are references, where a claim for the payment or repayment has to be made, to only so much of that amount as is the subject of a claim that the Commissioners are required to satisfy or have satisfied; and

(b)   the amounts referred to in paragraph (d) do not include any amount payable under this section.

78(2)   Nothing in subsection (1) above requires the Commissioners to pay interest–

(a)   on any amount which falls to be increased by a supplement under section 79; or

(b)   where an amount is increased under that section, on so much of the increased amount as represents the supplement.

78(3)   Interest under this section shall be payable at the rate applicable under section 197 of the Finance Act 1996.

78(4)   The **"applicable period"** in a case falling within subsection (1)(a) or (b) above is the period–

(a)   beginning with the appropriate commencement date, and

(b)   ending with the date on which the Commissioners authorise payment of the amount on which the interest is payable.

78(5)   In subsection (4) above, the **"appropriate commencement date"**–

(a)   in a case where an amount would have been due from the person by way of VAT in connection with the relevant return, had his input tax and output tax been as stated in that return, means the date on which the Commissioners received payment of that amount; and

(b)   in a case where no such payment would have been due from him in connection with that return, means the date on which the Commissioners would, apart from the error, have authorised payment of the amount on which the interest is payable;

and in this subsection **"the relevant return"** means the return in which the person accounted for, or (as the case may be) ought to have claimed credit for, the amount on which the interest is payable.

78(6)   The **"applicable period"** in a case falling within subsection (1)(c) above is the period–

(a)   beginning with the date on which the payment is received by the Commissioners, and

(b)   ending with the date on which they authorise payment of the amount on which the interest is payable.

78(7)   The **"applicable period"** in a case falling within subsection (1)(d) above is the period–

(a)   beginning with the date on which, apart from the error, the Commissioners might reasonably have been expected to authorise payment of the amount on which the interest is payable, and

(b)   ending with the date on which they in fact authorise payment of that amount.

78(8)   In determining in accordance with subsection (4), (6) or (7) above the applicable period for the purposes of subsection (1) above, there shall be left out of account any period by which the Commissioners' authorisation of the payment of interest is delayed by the conduct of the person who claims the interest.

78(8A)   The reference in subsection (8) above to a **period by which the Commissioners' authorisation of the payment of interest is delayed** by the conduct of the person who claims it includes, in particular, any period which is referable to–

(a)   any unreasonable delay in the making of the claim for interest or in the making of any claim for the payment or repayment of the amount on which interest is claimed;

(b)   any failure by that person or a person acting on his behalf or under his influence to provide the Commissioners–

    (i) at or before the time of the making of a claim, or

    (ii) subsequently in response to a request for information by the Commissioners,

with all the information required by them to enable the existence and amount of the claimant's entitlement to a payment or repayment, and to interest on that payment or repayment, to be determined; and

(c)   the making, as part of or in association with either–

    (i) the claim for interest, or

    (ii) any claim for the payment or repayment of the amount on which interest is claimed,

of a claim to anything to which the claimant was not entitled.

78(9) In determining for the purposes of subsection (8A) above whether any period of delay is referable to a **failure by any person to provide information** in response to a request by the Commissioners, there shall be taken to be so referable, except so far as may be prescribed, any period which–

(a) begins with the date on which the Commissioners require that person to provide information which they reasonably consider relevant to the matter to be determined; and

(b) ends with the earliest date on which it would be reasonable for the Commissioners to conclude–

    (i) that they have received a complete answer to their request for information;

    (ii) that they have received all that they need in answer to that request; or

    (iii) that it is unnecessary for them to be provided with any information in answer to that request.

78(10) The Commissioners shall only be liable to pay interest under this section on a claim made in writing for that purpose.

78(11) A claim under this section shall not be made more than three years after the end of the applicable period to which it relates.

78(12) In this section–

(a) references to the **authorisation by the Commissioners of the payment of any amount** include references to the discharge by way of set-off (whether under section 81(3) or otherwise) of the Commissioners' liability to pay that amount; and

(b) any reference to **a return** is a reference to a return required to be made in accordance with paragraph 2 of Schedule 11.

History – S. 78(1A) was inserted by FA 1997, s. 44(1) and this insertion is deemed always to have had effect.
In s. 78(3), the words "the rate applicable under section 197 of the Finance Act 1996" substituted for the words:
"such rates as may from time to time be prescribed by order made by the Treasury; and any such order–
(a) may prescribe different rates for different purposes; and
(b) shall apply to interest for periods beginning on or after the date on which the order is expressed to come into force, whether or not interest runs from before that date;
and the first such order may prescribe, for cases where interest runs from before the date on which that order is expressed to come into force, rates for periods ending before that date."
by FA 1996, s. 197(6)(d)(ii), for periods beginning on or after 1 April 1997 and will have effect in relation to interest running from before that day, as well as from that day or from after that day.
S. 78(8), (8A) and (9) were substituted for former s. 78(8) and (9) by FA 1997, s. 44(4), with effect for the purposes of determining whether any period beginning on or after 19 March 1997 is left out of account.
S. 78(11) was substituted by FA 1997, s. 44(2) and s. 78 has effect in relation to any claim made on or after 18 July 1996 and is deemed always to have had effect in relation to such a claim with the substitution of s. 78(11).
S. 78(12)(a) was substituted by FA 1997, s. 44(3) and s. 78 has effect and is deemed always to have had effect with the substitution of s. 78(1)(a).

Derivations – S. 78 (as originally enacted): VATA 1983, s. 38A, as inserted by FA 1991, s. 17.
S. 78(1)–(8) (as originally enacted): VATA 1983, s. 38A(1)–(8).
S. 78(9) (as originally enacted): VATA 1983, s. 38A(8A), as inserted by F(No. 2)A 1992, s. 15(2).
S. 78(10)–(12) (as originally enacted): VATA 1983, s. 38A(9)–(11).

Cross references – S. 83(s): appeals.
FA 1997, s. 44(6): amendments corresponding to those made by FA 1997, s. 44(1) and (3) are deemed to have had effect, for the purposes of the cases to which the enactments applied, in relation to the enactments directly or indirectly re-enacted in s. 78.

Statutory instruments – The rate of interest has been set as follows:

Period of application	%
From 6/2/00	5
6/3/99–5/2/00	4
6/1/99–5/3/99	5
1/4/97–5/1/99	6
6/2/93–31/3/97	8
16/10/91–5/2/93	10.25
1/4/91–15/10/91	12
1/11/89–31/3/91	14.25
1/11/89–31/10/89	13
1/11/88–31/12/88	12.25
1/8/88–31/10/88	11
1/5/88–31/7/88	9.5
1/12/87–30/4/88	11
1/11/87–30/11/87	11.25
1/4/87–31/10/87	11.75
1/1/87–31/3/87	12.25
1/8/86–31/12/86	11.5
1/4/84–31/7/86	12
1/4/83–31/3/84	12.5
1/7/82–31/3/83	13
1/3/82–30/6/82	14
1/12/81–28/2/82	15
1/1/81–30/11/81	12.5

Period of application	%
1/1/80–31/12/80	15
1/3/79–31/12/79	12.5
1/2/77–28/2/79	10
1/3/74–31/1/77	9
1/4/73–28/2/74	8

For interest accruing on or after 6 July 1998, the interest rate changes on the sixth day of any month, in accordance with the formulae specified in SI 1998/1461, when the rounded average of the base lending rates of six clearing banks at the close of business 12 working days prior to that day, the "reference rate" (RR) changes from the rounded average of those rates at the close of business on the corresponding day in the previous month.

Revenue interpretations – IRInt. 109: VAT repayments and interest received by sports clubs.

Notes – Interest paid under s. 78 can be assessed to income tax or corporation tax.

78A   Assessment for interest overpayments

78A(1) Where–

(a) any amount has been paid to any person by way of interest under section 78, but

(b) that person was not entitled to that amount under that section,

the Commissioners may, to the best of their judgement, assess the amount so paid to which that person was not entitled and notify it to him.

78A(2) An assessment made under subsection (1) above shall not be made more than two years after the time when evidence of facts sufficient in the opinion of the Commissioners to justify the making of the assessment comes to the knowledge of the Commissioners.

78A(3) Where an amount has been assessed and notified to any person under subsection (1) above, that amount shall be deemed (subject to the provisions of this Act as to appeals) to be an amount of VAT due from him and may be recovered accordingly.

78A(4) Subsection (3) above does not have effect if or to the extent that the assessment in question has been withdrawn or reduced.

78A(5) An assessment under subsection (1) above shall be a recovery assessment for the purposes of section 84(3A).

78A(6) Sections 74 and 77(6) apply in relation to assessments under subsection (1) above as they apply in relation to assessments under section 73 but as if the reference in subsection (1) of section 74 to the **reckonable date** were a reference to the date on which the assessment is notified.

78A(7) Where by virtue of subsection (6) above any person is liable to interest under section 74–

(a) section 76 shall have effect in relation to that liability with the omission of subsections (2) to (6); and

(b) section 77, except subsection (6), shall not apply to an assessment of the amount due by way of interest;

and (without prejudice to the power to make assessments for interest for later periods) the interest to which any assessment made under section 76 by virtue of paragraph (a) above may relate shall be confined to interest for a period of no more than two years ending with the time when the assessment to interest is made.

78A(8) For the purposes of this section notification to a personal representative, trustee in bankruptcy, interim or permanent trustee, receiver, liquidator or person otherwise acting in a representative capacity in relation to another shall be treated as notification to the person in relation to whom he so acts.

History – S. 78A was inserted by FA 1997, s. 45(1), with effect from 4 December 1996 in relation to amounts paid by way of interest at any time on or after 18 July 1996.

Cross references – S. 83(sa): appeals.
FA 1997, s. 49(4): transitional provisions for set-offs.

79   Repayment supplement in respect of certain delayed payments or refunds

79(1) In any case where–

(a) a person is entitled to a VAT credit, or

(b) a body which is registered and to which section 33 applies is entitled to a refund under that section,

and the conditions mentioned in subsection (2) below are satisfied, the amount which, apart from this section, would be due by way of that payment or refund shall be increased by the addition of a supplement equal to 5 per cent of that amount or £50, whichever is the greater.

79(2) The said conditions are–

(a)   that the requisite return or claim is received by the Commissioners not later than the last day on which it is required to be furnished or made, and

(b)   that a written instruction directing the making of the payment or refund is not issued by the Commissioners within the relevant period, and

(c)   that the amount shown on that return or claim as due by way of payment or refund does not exceed the payment or refund which was in fact due by more than 5 per cent of that payment or refund or £250, whichever is the greater.

79(2A)   The **relevant period** in relation to a return or claim is the period of 30 days beginning with the later of–

(a)   the day after the last day of the prescribed accounting period to which the return or claim relates, and

(b)   the date of the receipt by the Commissioners of the return or claim.

79(3)   Regulations may provide that, in computing the period of 30 days referred to in subsection (2A) above, there shall be left out of account periods determined in accordance with the regulations and referable to–

(a)   the raising and answering of any reasonable inquiry relating to the requisite return or claim,

(b)   the correction by the Commissioners of any errors or omissions in that return or claim, and

(c)   in the case of a payment, the following matters, namely–

> (i) any such continuing failure to submit returns as is referred to in section 25(5), and
>
> (ii) compliance with any such condition as is referred to in paragraph 4(1) of Schedule 11.

79(4)   In determining for the purposes of regulations under subsection (3) above whether any period is referable to the raising and answering of such an inquiry as is mentioned in that subsection, there shall be taken to be so referable any period which–

(a)   begins with the date on which the Commissioners first consider it necessary to make such an inquiry, and

(b)   ends with the date on which the Commissioners–

> (i) satisfy themselves that they have received a complete answer to the inquiry, or
>
> (ii) determine not to make the inquiry or, if they have made it, not to pursue it further,

but excluding so much of that period as may be prescribed; and it is immaterial whether any inquiry is in fact made or whether it is or might have been made of the person or body making the requisite return or claim or of an authorised person or of some other person.

79(5)   Except for the purpose of determining the amount of the supplement–

(a)   a supplement paid to any person under subsection (1)(a) above shall be treated as an amount due to him by way of credit under section 25(3), and

(b)   a supplement paid to any body under subsection (1)(b) above shall be treated as an amount due to it by way of refund under section 33.

79(6)   In this section **"requisite return or claim"** means–

(a)   in relation to a payment, the return for the prescribed accounting period concerned which is required to be furnished in accordance with regulations under this Act, and

(b)   in relation to a refund, the claim for that refund which is required to be made in accordance with the Commissioners' determination under section 33.

79(7)   If the Treasury by order so direct, any period specified in the order shall be disregarded for the purpose of calculating the period of 30 days referred to in subsection (2A) above.

History – In s. 79(2)(b), the words "the relevant period" were substituted for the words "the period of 30 days beginning on the date of the receipt by the Commissioners of that return or claim" by FA 1999, s. 19(2), with effect in relation to returns and claims received by the Commissioners on or after 9 March 1999.
S. 79(2A) was inserted by FA 1999, s. 19(3), with effect in relation to returns and claims received by the Commissioners on or after 9 March 1999.
In s. 79(3), the words "subsection (2A)" were substituted for the words "subsection (2)(b)" by FA 1999, s. 19(4), with effect in relation to returns and claims received by the Commissioners on or after 9 March 1999.
In s. 79(7), the words "subsection (2A)" were substituted for the words "subsection (2)(b)" by FA 1999, s. 19(4), with effect in relation to returns and claims received by the Commissioners on or after 9 March 1999.

Derivations – S. 79(1)–(3): FA 1985, s. 20(1)–(3), as substituted by FA 1988, s. 20 and as amended by FA 1994, s. 46(2).
S. 79(4): FA 1985, s. 20(3A), as inserted by F(No. 2)A 1992, s. 15(1).
S. 79(5)–(7): FA 1985, s. 20(4), (5), (7), as substituted by FA 1988, s. 20.

Cross references – ICTA 1988, s. 827(2): a repayment supplement is disregarded for purposes of corporation tax and income tax.
VAT Regulations 1995 (SI 1995/2518), reg. 198: computation of period for repayment supplement.

Statutory instruments – VAT Regulations 1995 (SI 1995/2518).

Official publications – 700/58.

Revenue interpretations – IRInt. 122: period of account in which VAT refunds to opticians should be recognised when computing results for direct tax purposes.

80   Recovery of overpaid VAT

80(1)   Where a person has (whether before or after the commencement of this Act) paid an amount to the Commissioners by way of VAT which was not VAT due to them, they shall be liable to repay the amount to him.

80(2)   The Commissioners shall only be liable to repay an amount under this section on a claim being made for the purpose.

80(3)   It shall be a defence, in relation to a claim under this section, that repayment of an amount would unjustly enrich the claimant.

80(3A)   Subsection (3B) below applies for the purposes of subsection (3) above where–

(a)   there is an amount paid by way of VAT which (apart from subsection (3) above) would fall to be repaid under this section to any person (**"the taxpayer"**) and

(b)   the whole or part of the cost of the payment of that amount to the Commissioners has, for practical purposes, been borne by a person other than the taxpayer.

80(3B)   Where, in a case to which this subsection applies, loss or damage has been or may be incurred by the taxpayer as a result of mistaken assumptions made in his case about the operation of any VAT provisions, that loss or damage shall be disregarded, except to the extent of the quantified amount, in the making of any determination–

(a)   of whether or to what extent the repayment of an amount to the taxpayer would enrich him; or

(b)   of whether or to what extent any enrichment of the taxpayer would be unjust.

80(3C)   In subsection (3B) above –

"the quantified amount" means the amount (if any) which is shown by the taxpayer to constitute the amount that would appropriately compensate him for loss or damage shown by him to have resulted, for any business carried on by him, from the making of the mistaken assumptions;

"VAT provisions" means the provisions of–

(a)   any enactment, subordinate legislation or Community legislation (whether or not still in force) which relates to VAT or to any matter connected with VAT; or

(b)   any notice published by the Commissioners under or for the purposes of any such enactment or subordinate legislation.

80(4)   The Commissioners shall not be liable, on a claim made under this section, to repay any amount paid to them more than three years before the making of the claim.

80(4A)   Where–

(a)   any amount has been paid, at any time on or after 18th July 1996, to any person by way of a repayment under this section, and

(b)   the amount paid exceeded the Commissioners' repayment liability to that person at that time,

the Commissioners may, to the best of their judgement, assess the excess paid to that person and notify it to him.

80(4B)   For the purposes of subsection (4A) above the Commissioners' repayment liability to a person at any time is–

(a)   in a case where any provision affecting the amount which they were liable to repay to that person at that time is subsequently deemed to have been in force at that time, the amount which the Commissioners are to be treated, in accordance with that provision, as having been liable at that time to repay to that person; and

(b)   in any other case, the amount which they were liable at that time to repay to that person.

80(4C)   Subsections (2) to (8) of section 78A apply in the case of an assessment under subsection (4A) above as they apply in the case of an assessment under section 78A(1).

80(5)   [S. 80(4) substituted for former s. 80(4), (5) by FA 1997, s. 47(1): see history note below.]

80(6)   A claim under this section shall be made in such form and manner and shall be supported by such documentary evidence as the Commissioners prescribe by regulations; and regulations under this subsection may make different provision for different cases.

80(7)   Except as provided by this section, the Commissioners shall not be liable to repay an amount paid to them by way of VAT by virtue of the fact that it was not VAT due to them.

History – S. 80(3A) was inserted by FA 1997, s. 46(1), with effect for the purposes of making any repayment on or after 19 March 1997, even if the claim for that repayment was made before that day.
S. 80(3B) was inserted by FA 1997, s. 46(1), with effect for the purposes of making any repayment on or after 19 March 1997, even if the claim for that repayment was made before that day.
S. 80(3C) was inserted by FA 1997, s. 46(1), with effect for the purposes of making any repayment on or after 19 March 1997, even if the claim for that repayment was made before that day.
S. 80(4) was substituted for former s. 80(4), (5) by FA 1997, s. 47(1), subject to FA 1997, s. 47(3) and (4) with effect from 18 July 1996 as a provision applying, for the purposes of the making of any repayment on or after that date, to all claims under VATA 1994, s. 80, including claims made before that date and claims relating to payments made before that date. Former s. 80(4) and 80(5) read as follows:
"80(4) No amount may be claimed under this section after the expiry of 6 years from the date on which it was paid, except where subsection (5) below applies.
80(5) Where an amount has been paid to the Commissioners by reason of a mistake, a claim for the repayment of the amount under this section may be made at any time before the expiry of 6 years from the date on which the claimant discovered the mistake or could with reasonable diligence have discovered it."
S. 80(4A) was inserted by FA 1997, s. 47(6), with effect from 4 December 1996.
S. 80(4B) was inserted by FA 1997, s. 47(6), with effect from 4 December 1996.
S. 80(4C) was inserted by FA 1997, s. 47(6), with effect from 4 December 1996.

Derivations – S. 80: FA 1989, s. 24(1)–(7) and SI 1989/2271.

Cross references – S. 83(t): appeals.
FA 1997, s. 47(2), (3), (4), (8) and (12): time limits for repayments and entitlement to a repayment under VATA 1994, s. 80.
VAT Regulations 1995 (SI 1995/2518), reg. 37: claim under s. 80 to be made in writing to the commissioners; form of claim.
VAT Regulations 1995 (SI 1995/2518), reg. 43A: reimbursement arrangements for a claim under s. 80.
VAT Regulations 1995 (SI 1995/2518), reg. 43B: reimbursement arrangements for a claim under s. 80.

Statutory instruments – VAT Regulations 1995 (SI 1995/2518).

Other material – Form VAT 652.
Customs' note (not reproduced) on consultation exercise associated with the former VAT (Accounting and Records) Regulations 1989 (SI 1989/2248): Customs regard "unjust enrichment" (see s. 80(3)) as equivalent to "windfall profit" for the supplier, e.g. where the supplier has wrongly charged VAT to customers, discovers the error but is unable or unwilling to credit the customers with the amount wrongly charged.
HM Customs and Excise Business Brief 13/94, 16 June 1994: VAT refunds on surrendered road fund licences.

80A   Arrangements for reimbursing customers

80A(1) The Commissioners may by regulations make provision for reimbursement arrangements made by any person to be disregarded for the purposes of section 80(3) except where the arrangements–

(a)   contain such provision as may be required by the regulations; and

(b)   are supported by such undertakings to comply with the provisions of the arrangements as may be required by the regulations to be given to the Commissioners.

80A(2) In this section **"reimbursement arrangements"** means any arrangements for the purposes of a claim under section 80 which–

(a)   are made by any person for the purpose of securing that he is not unjustly enriched by the repayment of any amount in pursuance of the claim; and

(b)   provide for the reimbursement of persons who have for practical purposes borne the whole or any part of the cost of the original payment of that amount to the Commissioners.

80A(3) Without prejudice to the generality of subsection (1) above, the provision that may be required by regulations under this section to be contained in reimbursement arrangements includes–

(a)   provision requiring a reimbursement for which the arrangements provide to be made within such period after the repayment to which it relates as may be specified in the regulations;

(b)   provision for the repayment of amounts to the Commissioners where those amounts are not reimbursed in accordance with the arrangements;

(c)   provision requiring interest paid by the Commissioners on any amount repaid by them to be treated in the same way as that amount for the purposes of any requirement under the arrangements to make reimbursement or to repay the Commissioners;

(d)   provision requiring such records relating to the carrying out of the arrangements as may be described in the regulations to be kept and produced to the Commissioners, or to an officer of theirs.

80A(4) Regulations under this section may impose obligations on such persons as may be specified in the regulations–

(a)   to make the repayments to the Commissioners that they are required to make in pursuance of any provisions contained in any reimbursement arrangements by virtue of subsection (3)(b) or (c) above;

(b)   to comply with any requirements contained in any such arrangements by virtue of subsection (3)(d) above.

80A(5) Regulations under this section may make provision for the form and manner in which, and the times at which, undertakings are to be given to the Commissioners in accordance with the regulations; and any such provision may allow for those matters to be determined by the Commissioners in accordance with the regulations.

80A(6) Regulations under this section may–

(a) contain any such incidental, supplementary, consequential or transitional provision as appears to the Commissioners to be necessary or expedient; and

(b) make different provision for different circumstances.

80A(7) Regulations under this section may have effect (irrespective of when the claim for repayment was made) for the purposes of the making of any repayment by the Commissioners after the time when the regulations are made; and, accordingly, such regulations may apply to arrangements made before that time.

History – S. 80A was inserted by FA 1997, s. 46(2), with effect from 19 March 1997.

Statutory instruments – VAT (Amendment) Regulations 1998 (SI 1998/59), as amended by SI 1999/438.

80B Assessments of amounts due under section 80A arrangements

80B(1) Where any person is liable to pay any amount to the Commissioners in pursuance of an obligation imposed by virtue of section 80A(4)(a), the Commissioners may, to the best of their judgement, assess the amount due from that person and notify it to him.

80B(2) Subsections (2) to (8) of section 78A apply in the case of an assessment under subsection (1) above as they apply in the case of an assessment under section 78A(1).

History – S. 80A was inserted by FA 1997, s. 46(2), with effect from 19 March 1997.

Cross references – S. 83(ta): appeals against an assessment under s. 80B(1).

81 Interest given by way of credit and set-off of credits

81(1) Any interest payable by the Commissioners (whether under an enactment or instrument or otherwise) to a person on a sum due to him under or by virtue of any provision of this Act shall be treated as an amount due by way of credit under section 25(3).

81(2) Subsection (1) above shall be disregarded for the purpose of determining a person's entitlement to interest or the amount of interest to which he is entitled.

81(3) Subject to subsection (1) above, in any case where–

(a) an amount is due from the Commissioners to any person under any provision of this Act, and

(b) that person is liable to pay a sum by way of VAT, penalty, interest or surcharge,

the amount referred to in paragraph (a) above shall be set against the sum referred to in paragraph (b) above and, accordingly, to the extent of the set-off, the obligations of the Commissioners and the person concerned shall be discharged.

81(3A) Where–

(a) the Commissioners are liable to pay or repay any amount to any person under this Act,

(b) that amount falls to be paid or repaid in consequence of a mistake previously made about whether or to what extent amounts were payable under this Act to or by that person, and

(c) by reason of that mistake a liability of that person to pay a sum by way of VAT, penalty, interest or surcharge was not assessed, was not enforced or was not satisfied,

any limitation on the time within which the Commissioners are entitled to take steps for recovering that sum shall be disregarded in determining whether that sum is required by subsection (3) above to be set against the amount mentioned in paragraph (a) above.

81(4) [Substituted by FA 1995, s. 27(2).]

81(4A) Subsection (3) above shall not require any such amount as is mentioned in paragraph (a) of that subsection (**"the credit"**) to be set against any such sum as is mentioned in paragraph (b) of that subsection (**"the debit"**) in any case where–

(a) an insolvency procedure has been applied to the person entitled to the credit;

(b) the credit became due after that procedure was so applied; and

(c) the liability to pay the debit either arose before that procedure was so applied or (having arisen afterwards) relates to, or to matters occurring in the course of, the carrying on of any business at times before the procedure was so applied.

81(4B) Subject to subsection (4C) below, the following are the times when an **insolvency procedure** is to be taken, for the purposes of this section, to be applied to any person, that is to say–

(a)   when a bankruptcy order, winding-up order, administration order or an award of sequestration is made in relation to that person;

(b)   when that person is put into administrative receivership;

(c)   when that person, being a corporation, passes a resolution for voluntary winding up;

(d)   when any voluntary arrangement approved in accordance with Part I or VIII of the Insolvency Act 1986, or Part II or Chapter II of Part VIII of the Insolvency (Northern Ireland) Order 1989 comes into force in relation to that person;

(e)   when a deed of arrangement registered in accordance with the Deeds of Arrangement Act 1914 or Chapter I of Part VIII of that Order of 1989 takes effect in relation to that person;

(f)   when that person's estate becomes vested in any other person as that person's trustee under a trust deed.

81(4C) In this section references, in relation to any person, to the **application of an insolvency procedure** to that person shall not include–

(a)   the making of a bankruptcy order, winding-up order, administration order or an award of sequestration at a time when any such arrangement or deed as is mentioned in subsection (4B)(d) to (f) above is in force in relation to that person;

(b)   the making of a winding-up order at any of the following times, that is to say–

    (i) immediately upon the discharge of an administration order made in relation to that person;

    (ii) when that person is being wound up voluntarily;

    (iii) when that person is in administrative receivership;

    or

(c)   the making of an administration order in relation to that person at any time when that person is in administrative receivership.

81(4D) For the purposes of this section a person shall be regarded as **being in administrative receivership** throughout any continuous period for which (disregarding any temporary vacancy in the office of receiver) there is an administrative receiver of that person, and the reference in subsection (4B) above to a person being put into administrative receivership shall be construed accordingly.

81(5) In this section–

(a)   **"administration order"** means an administration order under Part II of the Insolvency Act 1986 or an administration order within the meaning of Article 5(1) of the Insolvency (Northern Ireland) Order 1989;

(b)   **"administrative receiver"** means an administrative receiver within the meaning of section 251 of that Act of 1986 or Article 5(1) of that Order of 1989; and

(c)   **"trust deed"** has the same meaning as in the Bankruptcy (Scotland) Act 1985.

History – S. 81(3A) was inserted by FA 1997, s. 48(1), with effect from 18 July 1996 as a provision applying for determining the amount of any payment or repayment by the Commissioners on or after that date, including a payment or repayment in respect of a liability arising before that date.
S. 81(4A)–(4D) were substituted for former s. 81(4) by FA 1995, s. 27(2), in relation to amounts becoming due from the Commissioners of Customs and Excise at times on or after 1 May 1995.
In s. 81(5), the words "this section" were substituted by FA 1995, s. 27(3), in relation to amounts becoming due from the Commissioners of Customs and Excise at times on or after 1 May 1995.

Derivations – S. 81(1), (2): VATA 1983, s. 38B, as inserted by FA 1991, s. 17.
S. 81(3)–(5) (as originally enacted): FA 1988, s. 21, as amended by FA 1994, s. 47(1).

Cross references – S. 78(12)(a): payments and overpayments in relation to set-offs.
Sch. 13, para. 21: s. 81(4) and (5) omitted in relation to amounts due before 10 May 1994.
FA 1997, s. 49(1)(d) and (2) and (6): transitional provisions for set-offs.
VAT Regulations 1995 (SI 1995/2518), reg. 46 and 48: calculation of payment on account.

PART V – APPEALS

82   Appeal tribunals

82(1) Any reference in this Act to **a tribunal** is a reference to a tribunal constituted in accordance with Schedule 12, and that Schedule shall have effect generally with respect to appointments to and the procedure and administration of the tribunals.

82(2) The tribunals shall continue to have jurisdiction in relation to matters relating to VAT conferred upon them by this Part of this Act and jurisdiction in relation to matters relating to customs and excise conferred by Chapter II of Part I of the Finance Act 1994.

82(3) Officers and staff may be appointed under section 27 of the Courts Act 1971 (court staff) for carrying out the administrative work of the tribunals in England and Wales.

82(4) The Secretary of State may make available such officers and staff as he may consider necessary for carrying out the administrative work of the tribunals in Scotland.

Derivations – S. 82(1): VATA 1983, s. 40(1) and Sch. 8, para. 1 and FA 1985, s. 30(1) and Sch. 8.
S. 82(2): VATA 1983, s. 40 and FA 1994, s. 7(1).
S. 82(3), (4): FA 1985, s. 30 and Sch. 8, para. 6.

Cross references – S. 96: definition of "tribunal".

Notes – Human Rights Act 1998, s. 6(3): acts of public authorities, including a court or tribunal.
Human Rights Act 1998, Sch. 1, Pt. I, art. 6: right to a fair trial.

83   Appeals

83 Subject to section 84, an appeal shall lie to a tribunal with respect to any of the following matters–

(a)   the registration or cancellation of registration of any person under this Act;

(b)   the VAT chargeable on the supply of any goods or services, on the acquisition of goods from another member State or, subject to section 84(9), on the importation of goods from a place outside the member States;

(c)   the amount of any input tax which may be credited to a person;

(d)   any claim for a refund under any regulations made by virtue of section 13(5);

(da)   a decision of the Commissioners under section 18A–

    (i) as to whether or not a person is to be approved as a fiscal warehousekeeper or the conditions from time to time subject to which he is so approved;

    (ii) for the withdrawal of any such approval; or

    (iii) for the withdrawal of fiscal warehouse status from any premises;

(e)   the proportion of input tax allowable under section 26;

(f)   a claim by a taxable person under section 27;

(fa)   a decision contained in a notification under paragraph (4) of article 12A of the Value Added Tax (Payments on Account) Order 1993 that an election under paragraph (1) of that article shall cease to have effect.

(g)   the amount of any refunds under section 35;

(h)   a claim for a refund under section 36 or section 22 of the 1983 Act;

(j)   the amount of any refunds under section 40;

(k)   the refusal of an application such as is mentioned in section 43B(1) or (2);

(ka)   the giving of a notice under section 43C(1) or (3);

(l)   the requirement of any security under section 48(7) or paragraph 4(2) of Schedule 11;

(m)   any refusal or cancellation of certification under section 54 or any refusal to cancel such certification;

(n)   any liability to a penalty or surcharge by virtue of any of sections 59 to 69A;

(o)   a decision of the Commissioners under section 61 (in accordance with section 61(5));

(p)   an assessment–

    (i) under section 73(1) or (2) in respect of a period for which the appellant has made a return under this Act; or

    (ii) under subsections (7), (7A) or (7B) of that section; or

    (iii) under section 75;

    or the amount of such an assessment;

(q)   the amount of any penalty, interest or surcharge specified in an assessment under section 76;

(r)   the making of an assessment on the basis set out in section 77(4);

(s)   any liability of the Commissioners to pay interest under section 78 or the amount of interest so payable;

(sa)   an assessment under section 78A(1) or the amount of such an assessment;

(t)   a claim for the repayment of an amount under section 80, an assessment under subsection (4A) of that section or the amount of such an assessment;

(ta)   an assessment under section 80B(1) or the amount of such an assessment;

(u)   any direction or supplementary direction made under paragraph 2 of Schedule 1;

(v)   any direction under paragraph 1 or 2 of Schedule 6 or under paragraph 2 of Schedule 4 to the 1983 Act;

(w)   any direction under paragraph 1 of Schedule 7;

(wa)   any direction or assessment under Schedule 9A;

(x)   any refusal to permit the value of supplies to be determined by a method described in a notice published under paragraph 2(6) of Schedule 11;

(y)   any refusal of authorisation or termination of authorisation in connection with the scheme made under paragraph 2(7) of Schedule 11;

(z)   any requirements imposed by the Commissioners in a particular case under paragraph 3(2)(b) of Schedule 11.

History – S. 83(da) was added by FA 1996, s. 26 and Sch. 3, para. 12, with effect from 1 June 1996 and applies to any acquisition of goods from another member State and any supply taking place on or after that day.
S. 83(fa) was inserted by SI 1997/2542, art. 2, with effect from 1 December 1997.
S. 83(k) and (ka) were substituted for former s. 83(k) by FA 1999, s. 16 and Sch. 2, para. 3, with effect in accordance with the transitional provisions in FA 1999, Sch. 2, para. 6. Former s. 83(k) reads as follows:
    "(k)   any refusal of an application under section 43;"
In s. 83(n), the words "59 to 69A" were substituted for the words "59 to 69" by FA 2000, s. 137(5), with effect from 28 July 2000.
In s. 83(p)(ii), the words "subsections (7), (7A) or (7B)" were substituted by FA 1996, s. 26 and Sch. 3, para. 12, with effect from 1 June 1996 and apply to any acquisition of goods from another member State and any supply taking place on or after that day.
S. 83(sa) was inserted by FA 1997, s. 45(2), with effect from 4 December 1996 in relation to assessments made on or after that date.
In s. 83(t), the words ", an assessment under subsection (4A) of that section or the amount of such an assessment" were inserted by FA 1997, s. 47(7), with effect from 4 December 1996.
S. 83(ta) was inserted by FA 1997, s. 46(3), with effect from 19 March 1997.
S. 83(wa) was inserted by FA 1996, s. 31(3), with effect from 29 April 1996.

Derivations – S. 83(a): VATA 1983, s. 40(1)(a).
S. 83(b): VATA 1983, s. 40(1)(b), as amended by F(No. 2)A 1992, s. 14 and Sch. 3, para. 40(a).
S. 83(c): VATA 1983, s. 40(1)(c).
S. 83(d): VATA 1983, s. 40(1)(fa), as inserted by F(No. 2)A 1992, s. 14 and Sch. 3, para. 40(c).
S. 83(e): VATA 1983, s. 40(1)(d), as substituted by FA 1987, s. 19(2) and Sch. 2, para. 4.
S. 83(f): VATA 1983, s. 40(1)(g).
S. 83(g): VATA 1983, s. 40(1)(e).
S. 83(h): VATA 1983, s. 40(1)(f), as amended by FA 1990, s. 11(11)(b).
S. 83(j): VATA 1983, s. 40(1)(da), as inserted by F(No. 2)A 1992, s. 14 and Sch. 3, para. 40(b).
S. 83(k): VATA 1983, s. 40(1)(h).
S. 83(l): VATA 1983, s. 40(1)(n), as amended by F(No. 2)A 1992, s. 14 and Sch. 3, para. 40(f).
S. 83(m): VATA 1983, s. 40(1)(hza), as inserted by F(No. 2)A 1992, s. 16(2).
S. 83(n): VATA 1983, s. 40(1)(o), as inserted by FA 1985, s. 24(1) and as amended by F(No. 2)A 1992, s. 14 and Sch. 3, para. 40(g).
S. 83(o): FA 1986, s. 14(6).
S. 83(p): VATA 1983, s. 40(1)(m), as amended by F(No. 2)A 1992, s. 14 and Sch. 3, para. 40(e).
S. 83(q), (r): VATA 1983, s. 40(1)(p), (q), as inserted by FA 1985, s. 24(1).
S. 83(s): VATA 1983, s. 40(1)(ha), as inserted by FA 1991, s. 17(2).
S. 83(t): VATA 1983, s. 40(1)(s), as inserted by FA 1989, s. 24(9).
S. 83(u): VATA 1983, s. 40(1)(hh), as inserted by FA 1986, s. 10(2).
S. 83(v): VATA 1983, s. 40(1)(j).
S. 83(w): VATA 1983, s. 40(1)(ja), as inserted by F(No. 2)A 1992, s. 14 and Sch. 3, para. 40(d).
S. 83(x): VATA 1983, s. 40(1)(k).
S. 83(y): VATA 1983, s. 40(1)(r), as inserted by SI 1987/1427, reg. 11.
S. 83(z): VATA 1983, s. 40(1)(l).

Cross references – S. 28(2AA): appeals and payments on account.
FA 1997, s. 49(5): matters specified in s. 83 include an assessment under FA 1997, s. 49 and the amount of such an assessment.
FA 1999, Sch. 2, para. 2, 6: transitional provisions for revised group provisions.
VAT (Isle of Man) Order 1982 (SI 1982/1067), art. 8: taxable person includes a person who is a taxable person under the Manx Act.
VAT Regulations 1995 (SI 1995/2518), reg. 182: repayments claimed treated as the amount of any input tax which may be credited.
VAT Regulations 1995 (SI 1995/2518), reg. 195: repayment claimed treated as the amount of any input tax which may be credited.
Civil Procedure Rules 1998 (SI 1998/3132), Sch. 1, O. 45, r. 14(1) and (3): enforcement of decisions of tribunals.

Extra-statutory concessions – 3.4 and 3.5 (Notice 48 (1999 edn)): undercharge not pursued by Customs if a genuine misunderstanding or written ruling.

Official publications – 700/50   Default surcharge appeals.
700/51   VAT enquiries guide.
700/55   VAT input tax appeals: luxuries, amusements and entertainment.
930   What if I don't pay?
1000   Complaints and putting things right: our code of practice.
VAT – appeals and applications to the tribunals – explanatory leaflet.
AO2   How to complain about HM Customs and Excise, published by the Adjudicator's Office.
Customs Internal Guidance Manual, vol. V1.29: tribunal appeals.

Other material – Forms Trib. 1–37.

Notes – Parliamentary Commissioner Act 1967: investigation by the Ombudsman.
Tribunals and Inquiries Act 1992.
Rules of the Supreme Court (Revision) 1965 (SI 1965/1776), Sch. 1, O. 45, r. 14(1): enforcement of decisions of tribunals.
VAT Tribunals Rules 1986 (SI 1986/590).
Treaty establishing the European Community, art. 177: reference to the Court of Justice of the European Communities.
In the Queen's printer's version, no text has been allocated to the letter "i".

84   Further provisions relating to appeals

84(1)   References in this section to an **appeal** are references to an appeal under section 83.

84(2) An appeal shall not be entertained unless the appellant has made all the returns which he was required to make under paragraph 2(1) of Schedule 11 and has paid the amounts shown in those returns as payable by him.

84(3) Where the appeal is against a decision with respect to any of the matters mentioned in section 83(b), (n), (p) or (q) it shall not be entertained unless–

(a) the amount which the Commissioners have determined to be payable as VAT has been paid or deposited with them; or

(b) on being satisfied that the appellant would otherwise suffer hardship the Commissioners agree or the tribunal decides that it should be entertained notwithstanding that that amount has not been so paid or deposited.

84(3A) An appeal against an assessment which is a recovery assessment for the purposes of this subsection, or against the amount of such an assessment, shall not be entertained unless–

(a) the amount notified by the assessment has been paid or deposited with the Commissioners; or

(b) on being satisfied that the appellant would otherwise suffer hardship, the Commissioners agree, or the tribunal decides, that the appeal should be entertained notwithstanding that that amount has not been so paid or deposited.

84(4) Subject to subsection (11) below, where–

(a) there is an appeal against a decision of the Commissioners with respect to, or to so much of any assessment as concerns, the amount of input tax that may be credited to any person or the proportion of input tax allowable under section 26, and

(b) that appeal relates, in whole or in part, to any determination by the Commissioners–

    (i) as to the purposes for which any goods or services were or were to be used by any person, or

    (ii) as to whether or to what extent the matters to which any input tax was attributable were or included matters other than the making of supplies within section 26(2), and

(c) VAT for which, in pursuance of that determination, there is no entitlement to a credit is VAT on the supply, acquisition or importation of something in the nature of a luxury, amusement or entertainment,

the tribunal shall not allow the appeal or, as the case may be, so much of it as relates to that determination unless it considers that the determination is one which it was unreasonable to make or which it would have been unreasonable to make if information brought to the attention of the tribunal that could not have been brought to the attention of the Commissioners had been available to be taken into account when the determination was made.

84(4A) Where an appeal is brought against the refusal of an application such as is mentioned in section 43B(1) or (2) on the grounds stated in section 43B(5)(c)–

(a) the tribunal shall not allow the appeal unless it considers that the Commissioners could not reasonably have been satisfied that there were grounds for refusing the application,

(b) the refusal shall have effect pending the determination of the appeal, and

(c) if the appeal is allowed, the refusal shall be deemed not to have occurred.

84(4B) Where an appeal is brought against the giving of a notice under section 43C(1) or (3)–

(a) the notice shall have effect pending the determination of the appeal, and

(b) if the appeal is allowed, the notice shall be deemed never to have had effect.

84(4C) Where an appeal is brought against the giving of a notice under section 43C(1), the tribunal shall not allow the appeal unless it considers that the Commissioners could not reasonably have been satisfied that there were grounds for giving the notice.

84(4D) Where–

(a) an appeal is brought against the giving of a notice under section 43C(3), and

(b) the grounds of appeal relate wholly or partly to the date specified in the notice,

the tribunal shall not allow the appeal in respect of the date unless it considers that the Commissioners could not reasonably have been satisfied that it was appropriate.

84(5) Where, on an appeal against a decision with respect to any of the matters mentioned in section 83(p)–

(a) it is found that the amount specified in the assessment is less than it ought to have been, and

(b) the tribunal gives a direction specifying the correct amount, the assessment shall have effect as an assessment of the amount specified in the direction, and that amount shall be deemed to have been notified to the appellant.

84(6) Without prejudice to section 70, nothing in section 83(q) shall be taken to confer on a tribunal any power to vary an amount assessed by way of penalty, interest or surcharge except in so far as it is necessary to reduce it to the amount which is appropriate under sections 59 to 70; and in this subsection **"penalty"** includes an amount assessed by virtue of section 61(3) or (4)(a).

84(7) Where there is an appeal against a decision to make such a direction as is mentioned in section 83(u), the tribunal shall not allow the appeal unless it considers that the Commissioners could not reasonably have been satisfied that there were grounds for making the direction.

84(7A) Where there is an appeal against a decision to make such a direction as is mentioned in section 83(wa), the cases in which the tribunal shall allow the appeal shall include (in addition to the case where the conditions for the making of the direction were not fulfilled) the case where the tribunal are satisfied, in relation to the relevant event by reference to which the direction was given, that–

(a)   the change in the treatment of the body corporate, or

(b)   the transaction in question,

had as its main purpose or, as the case may be, as each of its main purposes a genuine commercial purpose unconnected with the fulfilment of the condition specified in paragraph 1(3) of Schedule 9A.

84(8) Where on an appeal it is found–

(a)   that the whole or part of any amount paid or deposited in pursuance of subsection (3) above is not due; or

(b)   that the whole or part of any VAT credit due to the appellant has not been paid,

so much of that amount as is found not to be due or not to have been paid shall be repaid (or, as the case may be, paid) with interest at such rate as the tribunal may determine; and where the appeal has been entertained notwithstanding that an amount determined by the Commissioners to be payable as VAT has not been paid or deposited and it is found on the appeal that that amount is due, the tribunal may, if it thinks fit, direct that that amount shall be paid with interest at such rate as may be specified in the direction.

84(9) No appeal shall lie under this section with respect to the subject-matter of any decision which by virtue of section 16 is a decision to which section 14 of the Finance Act 1994 (decisions subject to review) applies unless the decision–

(a)   relates exclusively to one or both of the following matters, namely whether or not section 30(3) applies in relation to the importation of the goods in question and (if it does not) the rate of tax charged on those goods; and

(b)   is not one in respect of which notice has been given to the Commissioners under section 14 of that Act requiring them to review it.

84(10) Where an appeal is against a decision of the Commissioners which depended upon a prior decision taken by them in relation to the appellant, the fact that the prior decision is not within section 83 shall not prevent the tribunal from allowing the appeal on the ground that it would have allowed an appeal against the prior decision.

84(11) Subsection (4) above shall not apply in relation to any appeal relating to the input tax that may be credited to any person at the end of a prescribed accounting period beginning before 27th July 1993.

History – In s. 84(2), the words ", except in the case of an appeal against a decision with respect to the matter mentioned in section 83(1)," which appeared after the words "Schedule 11 and" were omitted and repealed by FA 1995, s. 31(1) and 162 and Sch. 29, Pt. VI(4), in relation to appeals brought after 1 May 1995.

S. 84(3A) was inserted by FA 1997, s. 45(3), with effect from 4 December 1996 in relation to assessments made on or after that date.

S. 84(4A) was inserted by FA 1999, s. 16 and Sch. 2, para. 4, with effect in accordance with the transitional provisions in FA 1999, Sch. 2, para. 6.

S. 84(4B) was inserted by FA 1999, s. 16 and Sch. 2, para. 4, with effect in accordance with the transitional provisions in FA 1999, Sch. 2, para. 6.

S. 84(4C) was inserted by FA 1999, s. 16 and Sch. 2, para. 4, with effect in accordance with the transitional provisions in FA 1999, Sch. 2, para. 6.

S. 84(4D) was inserted by FA 1999, s. 16 and Sch. 2, para. 4, with effect in accordance with the transitional provisions in FA 1999, Sch. 2, para. 6.

In s. 84(7), the words "that there were grounds for making the direction"were substituted for the words "as to the matters in sub-paragraph (2)(a) to (d) of paragraph 2 of Schedule 1 or, as the case may be, as to the matters in sub-paragraph (4) of that paragraph" by FA 1997, s. 31(3), with effect in relation to the making of directions on or after 19 March 1997.

S. 84(7A) was inserted by FA 1996, s. 31(4) with effect from 29 April 1996.

Derivations – S. 84(2) (as originally enacted): VATA 1983, s. 40(2), as amended by FA 1985, s. 24(3).

S. 84(3): VATA 1983, s. 40(3), as amended by FA 1985, s. 24(4).
S. 84(4): VATA 1983, s. 40(3ZA), as inserted by FA 1993, s. 46(1).
S. 84(5): VATA 1983, s. 40(3B), as inserted (as (3A)) by FA 1985, s. 24(5), as amended by FA 1986, s. 10(3).
S. 84(6): VATA 1983, s. 40(1A), as inserted by FA 1985, s. 24(2) and as amended by FA 1993, s. 49 and Sch. 2, para. 3(2)(c).
S. 84(7) (as originally enacted): VATA 1983, s. 40(3A), as inserted by FA 1986, s. 10(3).
S. 84(8)–(10): VATA 1983, s. 40(4)–(6), as amended by FA 1994, s. 18(3).
S. 84(11): FA 1993, s. 46(2).
Cross references – S. 78A(5): an assessment for overpayment of interest is a recovery assessment for the purpose of s. 84(3A), Sch. 13, para. 22(2): s. 84(5) substituted before appointed day.
FA 1999, Sch. 2, para. 2, 6: transitional provisions for revised group provisions.
VAT Tribunals Rules 1986 (SI 1986/590), r. 16(2): direction under s. 84(8) for payment of a sum with interest.

85   Settling appeals by agreement

85(1)   Subject to the provisions of this section, where a person gives notice of appeal under section 83 and, before the appeal is determined by a tribunal, the Commissioners and the appellant come to an agreement (whether in writing or otherwise) under the terms of which the decision under appeal is to be treated–

(a)   as upheld without variation, or

(b)   as varied in a particular manner, or

(c)   as discharged or cancelled,

the like consequences shall ensue for all purposes as would have ensued if, at the time when the agreement was come to, a tribunal had determined the appeal in accordance with the terms of the agreement (including any terms as to costs).

85(2)   Subsection (1) above shall not apply where, within 30 days from the date when the agreement was come to, the appellant gives notice in writing to the Commissioners that he desires to repudiate or resile for the agreement.

85(3)   Where an agreement is not in writing–

(a)   the preceding provisions of this section shall not apply unless the fact that an agreement was come to, and the terms agreed, are confirmed by notice in writing given by the Commissioners to the appellant or by the appellant to the Commissioners, and

(b)   references in those provisions to the **time when the agreement was come to** shall be construed as references to the time of the giving of that notice of confirmation.

85(4)   Where–

(a)   a person who has given a notice of appeal notifies the Commissioners, whether orally or in writing, that he desires not to proceed with the appeal; and

(b)   30 days have elapsed since the giving of the notification without the Commissioners giving to the appellant notice in writing indicating that they are unwilling that the appeal should be treated as withdrawn,

the preceding provisions of this section shall have effect as if, at the date of the appellant's notification, the appellant and the Commissioners had come to an agreement, orally or in writing, as the case may be, that the decision under appeal should be upheld without variation.

85(5)   References in this section to an **agreement being come to** with an appellant and the **giving of notice or notification** to or by an appellant include references to an agreement being come to with, and the giving of notice or notification to or by, a person acting on behalf of the appellant in relation to the appeal.

Derivations – FA 1985, s. 25.

Note – In the Queen's printer's version, in s. 85(2) after the word "resile", the word "for" appears to have been substituted in error for the word "from".

86   Appeals to Court of Appeal

86(1)   The Lord Chancellor may by order provide that–

(a)   in such classes of appeal as may be prescribed by the order, and

(b)   subject to the consent of the parties and to such other conditions as may be so prescribed,

an appeal from a tribunal shall lie to the Court of Appeal.

86(2)   An order under this section may provide that section 11 of the Tribunals and Inquiries Act 1992 (which provides for appeals to the High Court from a tribunal) shall have effect, in relation to any appeal to which the order applies, with such modifications as may be specified in the order.

86(3)   This section does not extend to Scotland.

Derivations – FA 1985, s. 26(1), (2)(a), (3), as amended by Tribunals and Inquiries Act 1992, s. 18(1) and Sch. 3, para. 17.
Cross references – Civil Procedure Rules 1998 (SI 1998/3132), Sch. 1, O. 22(1): appeals from tribunals to Court of Appeal.
Statutory instruments – VAT Tribunals Appeals Order 1986 (SI 1986/2288): appeals from tribunals to Court of Appeal.

VAT Tribunals Appeals (Northern Ireland) Order 1994 (SI 1994/1978): appeals from tribunal in Northern Ireland to Court of Appeal.

87 Enforcement of registered or recorded tribunal decisions etc.

87(1) If the decision of a tribunal in England and Wales on an appeal under section 83 is registered by the Commissioners in accordance with rules of court, payment of–

(a) any amount which, as a result of the decision, is, or is recoverable as, VAT due from any person, and

(b) any costs awarded to the Commissioners by the decision,

may be enforced by the High Court as if that amount or, as the case may be, the amount of those costs were an amount due to the Commissioners in pursuance of a judgment or order of the High Court.

87(2) If the decision of a tribunal in Scotland on an appeal under section 83–

(a) confirms or varies an amount which is, or is recoverable as, VAT due from any person, or

(b) awards costs to the Commissioners,

the decision may be recorded for execution in the Books of Council and Session and shall be enforceable accordingly.

87(3) Subsection (4) below shall apply in relation to the decision of a tribunal in Northern Ireland on an appeal under section 83 where–

(a) any amount is, or is recoverable as, VAT due from any person, as a result of the decision, whether with or without an award of costs to the Commissioners; or

(b) any costs are awarded to the Commissioners by the decision.

87(4) Where this subsection applies–

(a) payment of the amount mentioned in paragraph (a) of subsection (3) above or, as the case may be, the amount of the costs mentioned in paragraph (b) of that subsection may be enforced by the Enforcement of Judgments Office; and

(b) a sum equal to any such amount shall be deemed to be payable under a money judgment within the meaning of Article 2(2) of the Judgments Enforcement (Northern Ireland) Order 1981, and the provisions of that Order shall apply accordingly.

87(5) Any reference in this section to a **decision of a tribunal** includes a reference to an order (however described) made by a tribunal for giving effect to a decision.

Derivations – FA 1985, s. 29.

Cross references – Civil Procedure Rules 1998 (SI 1998/3132), Sch. 1, O. 45, r. 14(1) and (3): enforcement of decisions of tribunals.

PART VI – SUPPLEMENTARY PROVISIONS

CHANGE IN RATE OF VAT ETC. AND DISCLOSURE OF INFORMATION

88 Supplies spanning change of rate etc.

88(1) This section applies where there is a change in the rate of VAT in force under section 2 or in the descriptions of exempt or zero-rated supplies or exempt or zero-rated acquisitions.

88(2) Where–

(a) a supply affected by the change would, apart from section 6(4), (5), (6) or (10), be treated under section 6(2) or (3) as made wholly or partly at a time when it would not have been affected by the change; or

(b) a supply not so affected would apart from section 6(4), (5), (6) or (10) be treated under section 6(2) or (3) as made wholly or partly at a time when it would have been so affected,

the rate at which VAT is chargeable on the supply, or any question whether it is zero-rated or exempt, shall if the person making it so elects be determined without regard to section 6(4), (5), (6) or (10).

88(3) Any power to make regulations under this Act with respect to the time when a supply is to be treated as taking place shall include power to provide for this section to apply as if the references in subsection (2) above to section 6(4), (5), (6) or (10) included references to specified provisions of the regulations.

88(4) Where–

(a)   any acquisition of goods from another member State which is affected by the change would not have been affected (in whole or in part) if it had been treated as taking place at the time of the event which, in relation to that acquisition, is the first relevant event for the purposes of taxing the acquisition; or

(b)   any acquisition of goods from another member State which is not so affected would have been affected (in whole or in part) if it had been treated as taking place at the time of that event,

the rate at which VAT is chargeable on the acquisition, or any question whether it is zero-rated or exempt, shall, if the person making the acquisition so elects, be determined as at the time of that event.

88(5)   Regulations under paragraph 2 of Schedule 11 may make provision for the replacement or correction of any VAT invoice which–

(a)   relates to a supply in respect of which an election is made under this section, but

(b)   was issued before the election was made.

88(6)   No election may be made under this section in respect of a supply to which section 6(9) or paragraph 7 of Schedule 4 applies.

88(7)   References in this section to an **acquisition being zero-rated** are references to an acquisition of goods from another member State being one in relation to which section 30(3) provides for no VAT to be chargeable.

Derivations – S. 88(1): VATA 1983, s. 41(1), as amended by F(No. 2)A 1992, s. 14 and Sch. 3, para. 41(1).
S. 88(2), (3): VATA 1983, s. 41(2), (3).
S. 88(4): VATA 1983, s. 41(3A), as inserted by F(No. 2)A 1992, s. 14 and Sch. 3, para. 41(2).
S. 88(5), (6): VATA 1983, s. 41(4), (5).
S. 88(7): VATA 1983, s. 41(6), as inserted by F(No. 2)A 1992, s. 14 and Sch. 3, para. 41(3).

Cross references – VAT Regulations 1995 (SI 1995/2518), reg. 15: change of rate and credit notes.
VAT Regulations 1995 (SI 1995/2518), reg. 95: supplies spanning change of rate, etc.

Statutory instrument – VAT Regulations 1995 (SI 1995/2518).

89   Adjustments of contracts on changes in VAT

89(1)   Where, after the making of a contract for the supply of goods or services and before the goods or services are supplied, there is a change in the VAT charged on the supply, then, unless the contract otherwise provided, there shall be added to or deducted from the consideration for the supply an amount equal to the change.

89(2)   Subsection (1) above shall apply in relation to a tenancy or lease as it applies in relation to a contract except that a term of a tenancy or lease shall not be taken to provide that the rule contained in that subsection is not to apply in the case of the tenancy or lease if the term does not [refer] specifically to VAT or this section.

89(3)   References in this section to a **change in the VAT charged on a supply** include references to a change to or from no VAT being charged on the supply (including a change attributable to the making of an election under paragraph 2 of Schedule 10).

Derivations – S. 89(1): VATA 1983, s. 42(1).
S. 89(2): VATA 1983, s. 42(1A), as inserted by FA 1989, s. 18 and Sch. 3, para. 7(a).
S. 89(3): VATA 1983, s. 42(2), as amended by FA 1989, s. 18 and Sch. 3, para. 7(b).

Notes – In the Queen's printer's version, in s. 89(2) after "term does not", the word "refer" appears to have been omitted in error, but is in the above version in square brackets.

90   Failure of resolution under Provisional Collection of Taxes Act 1968

90(1)   Where–

(a)   by virtue of a resolution having effect under the Provisional Collection of Taxes Act 1968 VAT has been paid at a rate specified in the resolution on the supply of any goods or services by reference to a value determined under section 19(2) or on the acquisition of goods from another member State by reference to a value determined under section 20(3), and

(b)   by virtue of section 1(6) or (7) or 5(3) of that Act any of that VAT is repayable in consequence of the restoration in relation to that supply or acquisition of a lower rate,

the amount repayable shall be the difference between the VAT paid by reference to that value at the rate specified in the resolution and the VAT that would have been payable by reference to that value at the lower rate.

90(2)   Where–

(a)   by virtue of such a resolution VAT is chargeable at a rate specified in the resolution on the supply of any goods or services by reference to a value determined under section 19(2) or on the acquisition of goods from another member State by reference to a value determined under section 20(3), but

(b)   before the VAT is paid it ceases to be chargeable at that rate in consequence of the restoration in relation to that supply or acquisition of a lower rate,

the VAT chargeable at the lower rate shall be charged by reference to the same value as that by reference to which VAT would have been chargeable at the rate specified in the resolution.

90(3)   The VAT that may be credited as input tax under section 25 or refunded under section 33, 35 or 40 does not include VAT that has been repaid by virtue of any of the provisions mentioned in subsection (1)(b) above or that would be repayable by virtue of any of those provisions if it had been paid.

Derivations – VATA 1983, s. 43, as amended by F(No. 2)A 1992, s. 14 and Sch. 3, para. 42.

91   Disclosure of information for statistical purposes

91(1)   For the purpose of the compilation or maintenance by the Department of Trade and Industry or the Office for National Statistics of a central register of businesses, or for the purpose of any statistical survey conducted or to be conducted by that Department or Office, the Commissioners or an authorised officer of the Commissioners may disclose to an authorised officer of that Department or Office particulars of the following descriptions obtained or recorded by them in pursuance of this Act–

(a)   numbers allocated by the Commissioners on the registration of persons under this Act and reference numbers for members of a group;

(b)   names, trading styles and addresses of persons so registered or of members of groups and status and trade classifications of businesses; and

(c)   actual or estimated value of supplies.

91(2)   Subject to subsection (3) below, no information obtained by virtue of this section by an officer of the Department of Trade and Industry or the Office for National Statistics may be disclosed except to an officer of a Government department (including a Northern Ireland department) for the purpose for which the information was obtained, or for a like purpose.

91(3)   Subsection (2) above does not prevent the disclosure–

(a)   of any information in the form of a summary so framed as not to enable particulars to be identified as particulars relating to a particular person or to the business carried on by a particular person; or

(b)   with the consent of any person, of any information enabling particulars to be identified as particulars relating only to him or to a business carried on by him.

91(4)   If any person who has obtained any information by virtue of this section discloses it in contravention of this section he shall be liable–

(a)   on summary conviction to a fine not exceeding the statutory maximum; and

(b)   on conviction on indictment to imprisonment for a term not exceeding 2 years or to a fine of any amount or to both.

91(5)   In this section, references to the **Department of Trade and Industry** or the **Office for National Statistics** include references to any Northern Ireland department carrying out similar functions.

History – In s. 91(1), (2) and (5), the reference to the Office for National Statistics was substituted by SI 1996/273, Sch. 2, para. 27, operative from 1 April 1996.

Derivations – VATA 1983, s. 44, as amended (s. 44(1), (2), (5)) by SI 1989/992.

Notes – FA 1972, s. 127: disclosure of information between Revenue departments. See notes to FA 1972, s. 127 for details of other provisions under which Customs and Excise may disclose personal information to other government departments and the police.
FA 1978, s. 77; FA 1980, s. 17: disclosure to tax authorities in other member states.
FA 1989, s. 182: disclosure by tax officials.
SSAA 1992, s. 123: disclosure by DSS.
Charities Act 1992, s. 52: information disclosure to and by the charity commissioners.

INTERPRETATIVE PROVISIONS

92   Taxation under the laws of other member States etc.

92(1)   Subject to the following provisions of this section, references in this Act, in relation to another member State, to **the law of that member State** shall be construed as confined to so much of the law of that member State as for the time being has effect for the purposes of any Community instrument relating to VAT.

92(2)   Subject to the following provisions of this section–

(a)   references in this Act to **a person being taxable in another member State** are references to that person being taxable under so much of the law of that member State as makes provision for purposes corresponding, in relation to that member State, to the purposes of so much of this Act as makes provision as to whether a person is a taxable person; and

(b)   references in this Act to **goods being acquired by a person in another member State** are references to goods being treated as so acquired in accordance with provisions of the law of that member State corresponding, in relation to that member State, to so much of this Act as makes provision for treating goods as acquired in the United Kingdom from another member State.

92(3)   Without prejudice to subsection (5) below, the Commissioners may by regulations make provision for the manner in which any of the following are to be or may be proved for any of the purposes of this Act, that is to say–

(a)   the effect of any provisions of the law of any other member State;

(b)   that provisions of any such law correspond or have a purpose corresponding, in relation to any member State, to or to the purpose of any provision of this Act.

92(4)   The Commissioners may by regulations provide–

(a)   for a person to be treated for prescribed purposes of this Act as taxable in another member State only where he has given such notification, and furnished such other information, to the Commissioners as may be prescribed;

(b)   for the form and manner in which any notification or information is to be given or furnished under the regulations and the particulars which it is to contain;

(c)   for the proportion of any consideration for any transaction which is to be taken for the purposes of this Act as representing a liability, under the law of another member State, for VAT to be conclusively determined by reference to such invoices or in such other manner as may be prescribed.

92(5)   In any proceedings (whether civil or criminal), a certificate of the Commissioners–

(a)   that a person was or was not, at any date, taxable in another member State; or

(b)   that any VAT payable under the law of another member State has or has not been paid,

shall be sufficient evidence of that fact until the contrary is proved, and any document purporting to be a certificate under this subsection shall be deemed to be such a certificate until the contrary is proved.

92(6)   Without prejudice to the generality of any of the powers of the Commissioners under the relevant information provisions, those powers shall, for the purpose of facilitating compliance with any Community obligations, be exercisable with respect to matters that are relevant to a charge to VAT under the law of another member State, as they are exercisable with respect to matters that are relevant for any of the purposes of this Act.

92(7)   The reference in subsection (6) above to the **relevant information provisions** is a reference to the provisions of section 73(7) and Schedule 11 relating to–

(a)   the keeping of accounts;

(b)   the making of returns and the submission of other documents to the Commissioners;

(c)   the production, use and contents of invoices;

(d)   the keeping and preservation of records; and

(e)   the furnishing of information and the production of documents.

Derivations – VATA 1983, s. 46A, as amended by F(No. 2)A 1992, s. 14 and Sch. 3, para. 44.

Statutory instrument – VAT Regulations 1995 (SI 1995/2518).

93   Territories included in references to other member States etc.

93(1)   The Commissioners may by regulations provide for the territory of the Community, or for the member States, to be treated for any of the purposes of this Act as including or excluding such territories as may be prescribed.

93(2)   Without prejudice to the generality of the powers conferred by subsection (1) and section 16, the Commissioners may, for any of the purposes of this Act, by regulations provide for prescribed provisions of any customs and excise legislation to apply in relation to cases where any territory is treated under subsection (1) above as excluded from the territory of the Community, with such exceptions and adaptations as may be prescribed.

93(3)   In subsection (2) above the reference to **customs and excise legislation** is a reference to any enactment or subordinate or Community legislation (whenever passed, made or adopted) which has effect in relation to, or to any assigned matter connected with, the importation or exportation of goods.

93(4)   In subsection (3) above **"assigned matter"** has the same meaning as in the Management Act.

Derivations – VATA 1983, s. 46B, as inserted by F(No. 2)A 1992, s. 14 and Sch. 3, para. 44.
Statutory instrument – VAT Regulations 1995 (SI 1995/2518).

94   Meaning of "business" etc.

94(1)   In this Act **"business"** includes any trade, profession or vocation.

94(2)   Without prejudice to the generality of anything else in this Act, the following are deemed to be the carrying on of a business–

(a)   the provision by a club, association or organisation (for a subscription or other consideration) of the facilities or advantages available to its members; and

(b)   the admission, for a consideration, of persons to any premises.

94(3)   [Repealed by FA 1999, s. 20(1) and 139(1) and Sch. 20, Pt. II(2).]

94(4)   Where a person, in the course or furtherance of a trade, profession or vocation, accepts any office, services supplied by him as the holder of that office are treated as supplied in the course or furtherance of the trade, profession or vocation.

94(5)   Anything done in connection with the termination or intended termination of a business is treated as being done in the course or furtherance of that business.

94(6)   The disposition of a business as a going concern, or of its assets or liabilities (whether or not in connection with its reorganisation or winding up), is a supply made in the course or furtherance of the business.

History – S. 94(3) was repealed by FA 1999, s. 20(1) and 139(1) and Sch. 20, Pt. II(2), with effect from 1 December 1999 (SI 1999/2769 (C. 68)). Former s. 94(3) reads as follows:
"**94(3)**   Where a body has objects which are in the public domain and are of a political, religious, philanthropic, philosophical or patriotic nature, it is not to be treated as carrying on a business only because its members subscribe to it, if a subscription obtains no facility or advantage for the subscriber other than the right to participate in its management or receive reports on its activities."

Derivations – VATA 1983, s. 47.

Cross references – Sch. 9, Grp. 12: a s. 94(3) non-profit making body is a "qualifying body" for the purpose of the exemption for fund-raising events.

Official publications – 700/34: staff.

Notes – VAT (Special Provisions) Order 1995 (SI 1995/1268), art. 5: "going concern" transfers.

95   Meaning of "new means of transport"

95(1)   In this Act **"means of transport"** in the expression **"new means of transport"** means, subject to subsection (2) below, any of the following, that is to say–

(a)   any ship exceeding 7.5 metres in length;

(b)   any aircraft the take-off weight of which exceeds 1550 kilograms;

(c)   any motorized land vehicle which–

    (i) has an engine with a displacement or cylinder capacity exceeding 48 cubic centimetres; or

    (ii) is constructed or adapted to be electrically propelled using more than 7.2 kilowatts.

95(2)   A ship, aircraft or motorized land vehicle does not fall within subsection (1) above unless it is intended for the transport of persons or goods.

95(3)   For the purposes of this Act a means of transport shall be treated as **new** , in relation to any supply or any acquisition from another member State, at any time unless at that time–

(a)   the period that has elapsed since its first entry into service is–

    (i) in the case of a ship or aircraft, a period of more than 3 months; and

    (ii) in the case of a land vehicle, a period of more than 6 months; and

(b)   it has, since its first entry into service, travelled under its own power–

    (i) in the case of a ship, for more than 100 hours;

    (ii) in the case of an aircraft, for more than 40 hours; and

(iii) in the case of a land vehicle, for more than 6000 kilometres.

95(4) The Treasury may by order vary this section–

(a) by adding or deleting any ship, aircraft or vehicle of a description specified in the order to or from those which are for the time being specified in subsection (1) above; and

(b) by altering, omitting or adding to the provisions of subsection (3) above for determining whether a means of transport is new.

95(5) The Commissioners may by regulations make provision specifying the circumstances in which a means of transport is to be treated for the purposes of this section as having first entered into service.

History – In s. 95(3), the words from the beginning to the end of para. (a) were substituted for the following words:
"For the purposes of this Act a means of transport shall be treated as **new** at any time unless at that time–
(a) a period of more than 3 months has elapsed since its first entry into service; and"
by SI 1994/3128, art. 2(2), operative in relation to means of transport whose first entry into service is on or after 1 January 1995.
In s. 95(3)(b)(iii), the words "6000 kilometres" were substituted for the words "3000 kilometres" by SI 1994/3128, art. 2(3), operative in relation to means of transport whose first entry into service is on or after 1 January 1995.
Derivations – S. 95(1): VATA 1983, s. 47A(1), as inserted by F(No. 2)A 1992, s. 14 and Sch. 3, para. 45 and as amended by SI 1992/3127, art. 2.
S. 95(2): VATA 1983, s. 47A(1A), as inserted by SI 1992/3127.
S. 95(3)–(5) (as originally enacted): VATA 1983, s. 47A(2)–(4), as inserted by F(No. 2)A 1992, s. 14 and Sch. 3, para. 45.
Cross references – VAT Regulations 1995 (SI 1995/2518), reg. 14(2)(e): contents of invoice provided to a person in another member state.
VAT Regulations 1995 (SI 1995/2518), reg. 29(2): claims for input tax on an acquisition from another member state of a new means of transport.
VAT Regulations 1995 (SI 1995/2518), reg. 147(1): first entry into service of a means of transport.
Statutory instruments – VAT (Means of Transport) Order 1994 (SI 1994/3128).
VAT Regulations 1995 (SI 1995/2518).
Note – VAT Regulations 1995 (SI 1995/2518), reg. 155: supplies of new means of transport to persons departing to another member state.

96   Other interpretative provisions

96(1) In this Act–

"**the 1983 Act**" means the Value Added Tax Act 1983;

"**another member State**" means, subject to section 93(1), any member State other than the United Kingdom, and "**other member States**" shall be construed accordingly;

"**assignment**", in relation to Scotland, means assignation;

"**authorised person**" means any person acting under the authority of the Commissioners;

"**the Commissioners**" means the Commissioners of Customs and Excise;

"**copy**", in relation to a document, means anything onto which information recorded in the document has been copied, by whatever means and whether directly or indirectly;

"**document**" means anything in which information of any description is recorded;

"**fee simple**"–

(a) in relation to Scotland, means the estate or interest of the proprietor of the dominium utile or, in the case of land not held on feudal tenure, the estate or interest of the owner;

(b) in relation to Northern Ireland, includes the estate of a person who holds land under a fee farm grant;

"**invoice**" includes any document similar to an invoice;

"**input tax**" has the meaning given by section 24;

"**interim trustee**" has the same meaning as in the Bankruptcy (Scotland) Act 1985;

"**local authority**" has the meaning given by subsection (4) below;

"**major interest**", in relation to land, means the fee simple or a tenancy for a term certain exceeding 21 years, and in relation to Scotland means–

(a) the estate or interest of the proprietor of the dominium utile; or

(b) in the case of land not held on feudal tenure, the estate or interest of the owner, or the lessee's interest under a lease for a period of not less than 20 years;

"**the Management Act**" means the Customs and Excise Management Act 1979;

"**money**" includes currencies other than sterling;

"**output tax**" has the meaning given by section 24;

"**permanent trustee**" has the same meaning as in the Bankruptcy (Scotland) Act 1985;

"**prescribed**" means prescribed by regulations;

"**prescribed accounting period**" has the meaning given by section 25(1);

"**quarter**" means a period of 3 months ending at the end of March, June, September or December;

"**regulations**" means regulations made by the Commissioners under this Act;

"**ship**" includes hovercraft;

"**subordinate legislation**" has the same meaning as in the Interpretation Act 1978;

"**tax**" means VAT;

"**taxable acquisition**" has the meaning given by section 10(2);

"**taxable person**" means a person who is a taxable person under section 3;

"**taxable supply**" has the meaning given by section 4(2);

"**the Taxes Act**" means the Income and Corporation Taxes Act 1988;

"**tribunal**" has the meaning given by section 82;

"**VAT**" means value added tax charged in accordance with this Act or, where the context requires, with the law of another member State;

"**VAT credit**" has the meaning given by section 25(3);

"**VAT invoice**" has the meaning given by section 6(15);

"**VAT representative**" has the meaning given by section 48;

and any reference to a particular section, Part or Schedule is a reference to that section or Part of, or Schedule to, this Act.

96(2) Any reference in this Act to being **registered** shall be construed in accordance with section 3(3).

96(3) Subject to section 93–

(a) the question whether or not goods have entered the territory of the Community;

(b) the time when any Community customs debt in respect of duty on the entry of any goods into the territory of the Community would be incurred; and

(c) the person by whom any such debt would fall to be discharged,

shall for the purposes of this Act be determined (whether or not the goods in question are themselves subject to any such duties) according to the Community legislation applicable to goods which are in fact subject to such duties.

96(4) In this Act "**local authority**" means the council of a county, district, London borough, parish or group of parishes (or, in Wales, community or group of communities), the Common Council of the City of London, the Council of the Isles of Scilly, and any joint committee or joint board established by two or more of the foregoing and, in relation to Scotland, a regional, islands or district council within the meaning of the Local Government (Scotland) Act 1973, any combination and any joint committee or joint board established by two or more of the foregoing and any joint board to which section 226 of that Act applies.

96(5) Any reference in this Act to the **amount of any duty of excise on any goods** shall be taken to be a reference to the amount of duty charged on those goods with any addition or deduction falling to be made under section 1 of the Excise Duties (Surcharges or Rebates) Act 1979.

96(6) [Repealed by the Civil Evidence Act 1995, s. 15(2) and Sch. 2.]

96(7) [Repealed by the Civil Evidence Act 1995, s. 15(2) and Sch. 2.]

96(8) The question whether, in relation to any supply of services, the supplier or the recipient of the supply **belongs** in one country or another shall be determined (subject to any provision made under section 8(6)) in accordance with section 9.

96(9) Schedules 8 and 9 shall be interpreted in accordance with the notes contained in those Schedules; and accordingly the powers conferred by this Act to vary those Schedules include a power to add to, delete or vary those notes.

96(10) The descriptions of Groups in those Schedules are for ease of reference only and shall not affect the interpretation of the descriptions of items in those Groups.

96(10A) Where–

(a) the grant of any interest, right, licence or facilities gives rise for the purposes of this Act to supplies made at different times after the making of the grant, and

(b) a question whether any of those supplies is zero-rated or exempt falls to be determined according to whether or not the grant is a grant of a description specified in Schedule 8 or 9 or paragraph 2(2) or (3) of Schedule 10,

that question shall be determined according to whether the description is applicable as at the time of supply, rather than by reference to the time of the grant.

96(11) References in this Act to the **United Kingdom** include the territorial sea of the United Kingdom.

History – In s. 96(1), the definitions of "copy" and "document" inserted by the Civil Evidence Act 1995, s. 15(1) and Sch. 1, para. 20 with effect from 31 January 1997, the appointed day by virtue of SI 1996/3217 (C. 101).
In s. 96(1), in the definition of "major interest" in para. (b) which relates to Scotland, the words "of not less than 20 years" were substituted for the words "exceeding 21 years" by FA 1998, s. 24, with effect from 31 July 1998.
S. 96(6) and (7) were repealed by the Civil Evidence Act 1995, s. 15(2) and Sch. 2, with effect from 31 January 1997, the appointed day by virtue of SI 1996/3217 (C. 101).
S. 96(10A) was inserted by FA 1997, s. 35(1). Amendments corresponding to this insertion are deemed to have had effect, for the purposes of the cases to which it applies, in relation to the Value Added Tax Act 1983; and any provisions about the coming into force of any amendment of that Act shall be deemed to have had effect accordingly. Nothing in FA 1997, s. 35(1) is taken to affect the operation, in relation to times before its repeal took effect, of VATA 1994, Sch. 10, para. 4 or of any enactment re-enacted in that paragraph.

Derivations – (as originally enacted) S. 96(1): VATA 1983, s. 48(1), as amended by FA 1987, s. 13 and FA 1989, s. 18 and Sch. 3, para. 9 and F(No. 2)A 1992, s. 14 and Sch. 3, para. 46(1).
S. 96(2): VATA 1983, s. 48(9), as inserted by F(No. 2)A 1992, s. 14 and Sch. 3, para. 46(4).
S. 96(3): VATA 1983, s. 48(1A), as inserted by F(No. 2)A 1992, s. 14 and Sch. 3, para. 46(2).
S. 96(4): VATA 1983, s. 20(6).
S. 96(5): VATA 1983, s. 48(1B), as inserted by F(No. 2)A 1992, s. 14 and Sch. 3, para. 46(2).
S. 96(6), (7): VATA 1983, s. 48(4).
S. 96(8)–(11): VATA 1983, s. 48(5)–(8), as amended by F(No. 2)A 1992, s. 14 and Sch. 3, para. 46.

Cross references – VAT (Imported Goods) Relief Order 1984 (SI 1984/746), art. 2(3): definition of "document" not applied. Territorial Sea Act 1987, Pt. 3: "territorial sea" extended to 12 nautical miles, with effect from 1 October 1987 (SI 1987/1270). The limits of the territorial sea in the Straits of Dover and near the Isle of Man are determined by Territorial Sea (Limits) Order 1987 (SI 1987/1269).

Statutory instruments – VAT (Tour Operators) Order 1987 (SI 1987/1806).
VAT (Education) (No. 2) Order 1994 (SI 1994/2969).
VAT (Transport) Order 1994 (SI 1994/3014).
VAT (Construction of Buildings) Order 1995 (SI 1995/280).
VAT (Protected Buildings) Order 1995 (SI 1995/283).
VAT (Supply of Pharmaceutical Goods) Order 1995 (SI 1995/652).
VAT (Tax Free Shops) Order 1995 (SI 1995/3041).
VAT (Cultural Services) Order 1996 (SI 1996/1256).
VAT (Pharmaceutical Chemists) Order 1996 (SI 1996/2949).
VAT (Finance) Order 1997 (SI 1997/510).
VAT (Drugs, Medicines and Aids for the Handicapped) Order 1997 (SI 1997/2744).
VAT (Finance) Order 1999 (SI 1999/594).
VAT (Abolition of Zero-Rating for Tax-Free Shops) Order 1999 (SI 1999/1642).
VAT (Sport, Sports Competitions and Physical Education) Order 1999 (SI 1999/1994).
VAT (Supplies of Goods where Input Tax cannot be recovered) Order 1999 (SI 1999/2833).
VAT (Subscriptions to Trade Unions, Professional and Other Public Interest Bodies) Order 1999 (SI 1999/2834).
VAT (Investment Gold) Order 1999 (SI 1999/3116).
VAT (Drugs, Medicines, Aids for the Handicapped and Charities Etc) Order 2000 (SI 2000/503).
VAT (Fund-Raising Events by Charities and Other Qualifying Bodies) Order 2000 (SI 2000/802).
VAT (Charities and Aids for the Handicapped) Order 2000 (SI 2000/805).
VAT (Protective Helmets) Order 2000 (SI 2000/1517).

SUPPLEMENTARY PROVISIONS

97   Orders, rules and regulations

97(1)   Any order made by the Treasury or the Lord Chancellor under this Act and any regulations or rules under this Act shall be made by statutory instrument.

97(2)   A statutory instrument containing an order under section 86 or rules under paragraph 9 of Schedule 12 shall be subject to annulment in pursuance of a resolution of either House of Parliament.

97(3)   An order to which this subsection applies shall be laid before the House of Commons; and unless it is approved by that House before the expiration of a period of 28 days beginning with the date on which it was made, it shall cease to have effect on the expiration of that period, but without prejudice to anything previously done thereunder or to the making of a new order.

In reckoning any such period no account shall be taken of any time during which Parliament is dissolved or prorogued or during which the House of Commons is adjourned for more than 4 days.

97(4)   Subject to section 53(4), subsection (3) above applies to–

(aa)   an order under section 2(1C);

(a)   an order under section 5(4) or 28;

(ab)   an order under paragraph 5(7) of Schedule 4 substituting a lesser sum for the sum for the time being specified in paragraph 5(2)(a) of that Schedule;

(b)   [S. 97(4)(b) was repealed by FA 1996, s. 205 and Sch. 41, Pt. IV(2).]

(c)   an order under this Act making provision–

       (i)   for increasing the rate of VAT in force at the time of the making of the order;

       (ii)   for excluding any VAT from credit under section 25;

       (iii)   for varying Schedule 8 or 9 so as to abolish the zero-rating of a supply or to abolish the exemption of a supply without zero-rating it;

(d)   an order under section 51, except one making only such amendments as are necessary or expedient in consequence of provisions of an order under this Act which–

    (i)   vary Schedule 8 or 9; but

    (ii)   are not within paragraph (c) above;

(e)   an order under section 54(4) or (8).

97(5)   A statutory instrument made under any provision of this Act except–

(a)   an order made under section 79, or

(b)   an instrument as respects which any other Parliamentary procedure is expressly provided, or

(c)   an instrument containing an order appointing a day for the purposes of any provision of this Act, being a day as from which the provision will have effect, with or without amendments, or will cease to have effect,

shall be subject to annulment in pursuance of a resolution of the House of Commons.

History – S. 97(4)(aa) was inserted by FA 1995, s. 21(4), with effect in relation to any supply made on or after 1 April 1995 and any acquisition or importation taking place on or after that date.
S. 97(4)(ab) was inserted by FA 1996, s. 33(3) with effect from 29 April 1996.
S. 97(4)(b) was repealed by FA 1996, s. 205 and Sch. 41, Pt. IV(2). Former s. 97(4)(b) read as follows:
  "(b)   an order as a result of which goods of any description become goods to which section 22(3) applies;"

Derivations – S. 97(1): VATA 1983, s. 45(1).
S. 97(2): FA 1985, s. 26(2)(b), 27(3)(c).
S. 97(3): VATA 1983, s. 45(3).
S. 97(4): VATA 1983, s. 45(4), as amended by FA 1987, s. 16(2) and FA 1992, s. 6(2) and para. (d), as inserted by FA 1989, s. 18 and Sch. 3, para. 8 and para. (e), as inserted by F(No. 2)A 1992, s. 16(3).
S. 97(5): VATA 1983, s. 45(2) and FA 1985, s. 15(8), 17(8), 17A(9), 18(8)(c).

Cross references – FA 1999, s. 13(6): supplies of gold.
VAT (Isle of Man) Order 1982 (SI 1982/1067), art. 7: references to VAT include references to VAT chargeable under Pt. I of the Manx Act.

Statutory instruments – VAT Regulations 1995 (SI 1995/2518).

Notes – S. 2(2): increasing the rate of VAT.
S. 25(4): excluding tax from credit under s. 24.
S. 30(4) and s. 31(2): abolishing the zero-rating or exemption of a supply.

97A   Place of supply orders: transitional provision

97A(1)   This section shall have effect for the purpose of giving effect to any order made on or after 17th March 1998 under section 7(11), if–

(a)   the order provides for services of a description specified in the order to be treated as supplied in the United Kingdom;

(b)   the services would not have fallen to be so treated apart from the order;

(c)   the services are not services that would have fallen to be so treated under any provision re-enacted in the order; and

(d)   the order is expressed to come into force in relation to services supplied on or after a date specified in the order (**"the commencement date"**).

97A(2)   Invoices and other documents provided to any person before the commencement date shall be disregarded in determining the time of the supply of any services which, if their time of supply were on or after the commencement date, would be treated by virtue of the order as supplied in the United Kingdom.

97A(3)   If there is a payment in respect of any services of the specified description that was received by the supplier before the commencement date, so much (if any) of that payment as relates to times on or after that date shall be treated as if it were a payment received on the commencement date.

97A(4)   If there is a payment in respect of services of the specified description that is or has been received by the supplier on or after the commencement date, so much (if any) of that payment as relates to times before that date shall be treated as if it were a payment received before that date.

97A(5)   Subject to subsection (6) below, a payment in respect of any services shall be taken for the purposes of this section to relate to the time of the performance of those services.

97A(6)   Where a payment is received in respect of any services the performance of which takes place over a period a part of which falls before the commencement date and a part of which does not–

(a)   an apportionment shall be made, on a just and reasonable basis, of the extent to which the payment is attributable to so much of the performance of those services as took place before that date;

(b)   the payment shall, to that extent, be taken for the purposes of this section to relate to a time before that date; and

(c)   the remainder, if any, of the payment shall be taken for those purposes to relate to times on or after that date.

History – S. 97A was inserted by FA 1998, s. 22(1), with effect from 17 March 1998.

Cross references – VATA 1994, s. 6(14A): time of supply.

98   Service of notices

98   Any notice, notification, requirement or demand to be served on, given to or made of any person for the purposes of this Act may be served, given or made by sending it by post in a letter addressed to that person or his VAT representative at the last or usual residence or place of business of that person or representative.

Derivations – VATA 1983, s. 46, as amended by F(No. 2)A 1992, s. 14 and Sch. 3, para. 43.

Cross reference – Interpretation Act 1978, s. 7: "service by post".

99   Refund of VAT to Government of Northern Ireland

99   The Commissioners shall refund to the Government of Northern Ireland the amount of the VAT charged on the supply of goods or services to that Government, on the acquisition of any goods by that Government from another member State or on the importation of any goods by that Government from a place outside the member States, after deducting therefrom so much of that amount as may be agreed between them and the Department of Finance and Personnel for Northern Ireland as attributable to supplies, acquisitions and importations for the purpose of a business carried on by the Government of Northern Ireland.

Derivations – VATA 1983, s. 49, as amended by F(No. 2)A 1992, s. 14 and Sch. 3, para. 47.

Cross reference – VAT (Isle of Man) Order 1982 (SI 1982/1067), art. 7: references to VAT include references to VAT chargeable under Pt. I of the Manx Act.

100   Savings and transitional provisions, consequential amendments and repeals

100(1)   Schedule 13 (savings and transitional provisions) and Schedule 14 (consequential amendments) shall have effect.

100(2)   The enactments and Orders specified in Schedule 15 are hereby repealed to the extent mentioned in the third column of that Schedule.

100(3)   This section is without prejudice to the operation of sections 15 to 17 of the Interpretation Act 1978 (which relate to the effect of repeals).

101   Commencement and extent

101(1)   This Act shall come into force on 1st September 1994 and Part I shall have effect in relation to the charge to VAT on supplies, acquisitions and importations in prescribed accounting periods ending on or after that date.

101(2)   Without prejudice to section 16 of the Interpretation Act 1978 (continuation of proceedings under repealed enactments) except in so far as it enables proceedings to be continued under repealed enactments, section 78 shall have effect on the commencement of this Act to the exclusion of section 39 of the 1983 Act.

101(3)   This Act extends to Northern Ireland.

101(4)   Paragraph 23 of Schedule 13 and paragraph 7 of Schedule 14 shall extend to the Isle of Man but no other provision of this Act shall extend there.

102   Short title

102   This Act may be cited as the Value Added Tax Act 1994.

SCHEDULES

SCHEDULE A1 – CHARGE AT REDUCED RATE

History – Sch. A1 was inserted by FA 1995, s. 21(3), in relation to any supply made on or after 1 April 1995 and any acquisition or importation taking place on or after that date.

THE SUPPLIES

1(1) Subject to the following provisions of this Schedule, the supplies falling within this paragraph are–

(a)　supplies for qualifying use of–
　　(i) coal, coke or other solid substances held out for sale solely as fuel;
　　(ii) coal gas, water gas, producer gases or similar gases;
　　(iii) petroleum gases, or other gaseous hydrocarbons, whether in a gaseous or liquid state;
　　(iv) fuel oil, gas oil or kerosene; or
　　(v) electricity, heat or air-conditioning.

(aa)　supplies of services of installing List A energy-saving materials in residential accommodation or in a building intended for use solely for a relevant charitable purpose;

(ab)　supplies of List A energy-saving materials by a person who installs those materials in residential accommodation or a building intended for use solely for a relevant charitable purpose;

(b)　supplies to a qualifying person of any services of installing List B energy-saving materials in the qualifying person's sole or main residence;

(c)　supplies of List B energy-saving materials made to a qualifying person by a person who installs those materials in the qualifying person's sole or main residence;

(d)　supplies to a qualifying person of services of connecting, or reconnecting, a mains gas supply to the qualifying person's sole or main residence;

(e)　supplies of goods made to a qualifying person by a person connecting, or reconnecting, a mains gas supply to the qualifying person's sole or main residence, being goods whose installation is necessary for the connection, or reconnection, of the mains gas supply;

(f)　supplies to a qualifying person of services of installing, maintaining or repairing a central heating system in the qualifying person's sole or main residence;

(g)　supplies of goods made to a qualifying person by a person installing, maintaining or repairing a central heating system in the qualifying person's sole or main residence, being goods whose installation is necessary for the installation, maintenance or repair of the central heating system;

(h)　supplies consisting in the leasing of goods that form the whole or part of a central heating system installed in the sole or main residence of a qualifying person;

(i)　supplies of goods that form the whole or part of a central heating system installed in a qualifying person's sole or main residence and that, immediately before being supplied, were goods leased under arrangements such that the consideration for the supplies consisting in the leasing of the goods was, in whole or in part, funded by a grant made under a relevant scheme;

(j)　supplies to a qualifying person of services of installing qualifying security goods in the qualifying person's sole or main residence; and

(k)　supplies of qualifying security goods made to a qualifying person by a person who installs those goods in the qualifying person's sole or main residence.

1(1B) Where a grant is made under a relevant scheme in order to fund a supply of a description falling within any of paragraphs (b) to (k) of sub-paragraph (1) above ("**the relevant supply**") and also to fund a supply to which none of those paragraphs applies ("**the non-relevant supply**") then the proportion of the grant that is to be attributed, for the purposes of sub-paragraph (1A) above, to the relevant supply shall be the same proportion as the consideration reasonably attributable to that supply bears to the consideration for that supply and for the non-relevant supply.

1(2) In this paragraph **"qualifying use"** means–

(a)　domestic use; or

(b)　use by a charity otherwise than in the course or furtherance of a business.

1(3) Where there is a supply of goods partly for qualifying use and partly not–

(a)   if at least 60 per cent of the goods are supplied for qualifying use, the whole supply shall be treated as a supply for qualifying use; and

(b)   in any other case, an apportionment shall be made to determine the extent to which the supply is a supply for qualifying use.

History – Para. 1(1) was substituted by SI 1998/1375, art. 3, operative from 1 July 1998; the former para. 1(1) read as follows:
"**1(1)** The supplies falling within this paragraph are supplies for qualifying use of–
(a)   coal, coke or other solid substances held out for sale solely as fuel;
(b)   coal gas, water gas, producer gases or similar gases;
(c)   petroleum gases, or other gaseous hydrocarbons, whether in a gaseous or liquid state;
(d)   fuel oil, gas oil or kerosene; or
(e)   electricity, heat or air-conditioning."
Para. 1(1)(aa) was inserted by FA 2000, s. 135 and Sch. 35 , para. 2(2), operative in relation to supplies made on or after 1 April 2000.
Para. 1(1)(ab) was inserted by FA 2000, s. 135 and Sch. 35 , para. 2(2) , operative in relation to supplies made on or after 1 April 2000.
In para. 1(1)(b), the words "List B" were inserted by FA 2000, s. 135 and Sch. 35, para. 2(3), operative in relation to supplies made on or after 1 April 2000.
In para. 1(1)(b), the word "and" at the end was repealed by FA 2000, s. 156 and Sch. 40, Pt. IV, operative in relation to supplies made on or after 1 April 2000.
In para. 1(1)(c), the words "List B" were inserted by FA 2000, s. 135 and Sch. 35, para. 2(3), operative in relation to supplies made on or after 1 April 2000.
Para. 1(1)(d)–(k) were inserted by FA 2000, s. 135 and Sch. 35 , para. 2(4), operative in relation to supplies made on or after 1 April 2000.
Para. 1(1A) was substituted by FA 2000, s. 135 and Sch. 35 , para. 3, operative in relation to supplies made on or after 1 April 2000. Former para. 1(1A) reads as follows:
"(1A)   A supply to which sub-paragraph (1)(b) or (c) above applies is a supply falling within this paragraph only to the extent that the consideration for it is or is to be funded by a grant made under a relevant scheme."
Former para. 1(1A) was inserted by SI 1998/1375, art. 3, operative from 1 July 1998.
Para. 1(1B) was inserted by SI 1998/1375, art. 3, operative from 1 July 1998.
In para. 1(1B), the words "any of paragraphs (b) to (k) of sub-paragraph (1)" were substituted for the words "sub-paragraph (1)(b) or (c)" and the words "none of those paragraphs" were substituted for the words "neither of those sub-paragraphs" by FA 2000, s. 135 and Sch. 35, para. 4, operative in relation to supplies made on or after 1 April 2000.

Cross references – S. 62(1)(a): penalty for incorrect certificate.

INTERPRETATION

2   For the purposes of this Schedule the following supplies are always for **domestic use** –

(a)   a supply of not more than one tonne of coal or coke held out for sale as domestic fuel;

(b)   a supply of wood, peat or charcoal not intended for sale by the recipient;

(c)   a supply to a person at any premises of piped gas (that is, gas within paragraph 1(1)(a)(ii) above, or petroleum gas in a gaseous state, provided through pipes) where the gas (together with any other piped gas provided to him at the premises by the same supplier) was not provided at a rate exceeding 150 therms a month or, if the supplier charges for the gas by reference to the number of kilowatt hours supplied, 4397 kilowatt hours a month;

(d)   a supply of petroleum gas in a liquid state where the gas is supplied in cylinders the net weight of each of which is less than 50 kilogrammes and either the number of cylinders supplied is 20 or fewer or the gas is not intended for sale by the recipient;

(e)   a supply of petroleum gas in a liquid state, otherwise than in cylinders, to a person at any premises at which he is not able to store more than two tonnes of such gas;

(f)   a supply of not more than 2,300 litres of fuel oil, gas oil or kerosene;

(g)   a supply of electricity to a person at any premises where the electricity (together with any other electricity provided to him at the premises by the same supplier) was not provided at a rate exceeding 1000 kilowatt hours a month.

History – In para. 2(c), the words "paragraph 1(1)(a)(ii)" were substituted for the words "paragraph 1(1)(b)" by SI 1998/1375, art. 4, operative from 1 July 1998.

3(1)   For the purposes of this Schedule supplies not within paragraph 2 above are for **domestic use** if and only if the goods supplied are for use in–

(a)   a building, or part of a building, which consists of a dwelling or number of dwellings;

(b)   a building, or part of a building, used for a relevant residential purpose;

(c)   self-catering holiday accommodation;

(d)   a caravan; or

(e)   a houseboat.

3(2)   *For the purposes of this Schedule* **use for a relevant residential purpose** *means use as–*

(a)   a home or other institution providing residential accommodation for children;

(b)   a home or other institution providing residential accommodation with personal care for persons in need of personal care by reason of old age, disablement, past or present dependence on alcohol or drugs or past or present mental disorder;

(c)   a hospice;

(d)   residential accommodation for students or school pupils;

(e)   residential accommodation for members of any of the armed forces;

(f)   a monastery, nunnery or similar establishment; or

(g)   an institution which is the sole or main residence of at least 90 per cent of its residents,

except use as a hospital, a prison or similar institution or an hotel or inn or similar establishment.

3(3) For the purposes of this Schedule **self-catering holiday accommodation** includes any accommodation advertised or held out as such.

3(4) In this Schedule **"houseboat"** means a boat or other floating decked structure designed or adapted for use solely as a place of permanent habitation and not having means of, or capable of being readily adapted for, self-propulsion.

4(1) Paragraph 1(1)(a)(i) above shall be deemed to include combustible materials put up for sale for kindling fires but shall not include matches.

4(2) Paragraph 1(1)(a)(ii) and (iii) above shall not include any road fuel gas (within the meaning of the Hydrocarbon Oil Duties Act 1979) on which a duty of excise has been charged or is chargeable.

4(3) Paragraph 1(1)(a)(iv) above shall not include hydrocarbon oil on which a duty of excise has been or is to be charged without relief from, or rebate of, such duty by virtue of the provisions of the Hydrocarbon Oil Duties Act 1979.

4(4) In this Schedule **"fuel oil"** means heavy oil which contains in solution an amount of asphaltenes of not less than 0.5 per cent or which contains less than 0.5 per cent but not less than 0.1 per cent of asphaltenes and has a closed flash point not exceeding 150 degrees C.

4(5) In this Schedule **"gas oil"** means heavy oil of which not more than 50 per cent by volume distils at a temperature not exceeding 240 degrees C and of which more than 50 per cent by volume distils at a temperature not exceeding 340 degrees C.

4(6) In this Schedule **"kerosene"** means heavy oil of which more than 50 per cent by volume distils at a temperature not exceeding 240 degrees C.

4(7) In this Schedule **"heavy oil"** shall have the same meaning as in the Hydrocarbon Oil Duties Act 1979.

History – The word "(i)" in sub-paragraph (1) was inserted after the words "Paragraph (1)(a)"; in sub-paragraph (2) for "Paragraph 1(1)(b) and (c)" was substituted by "Paragraph 1(1)(a)(ii) and (iii)"; and in sub-paragraph (3) for "Paragraph 1(1)(d)" was substituted "Paragraph 1(1)(a)(iv)" by SI 1998/1375, art. 5, operative from 1 July 1998.

Extra-statutory concessions – 3.16 (Notice 48 (1999 edn)): connection to gas or electricity mains supply.
5.2 (Notice 48 (1999 edn)): certain supplies of marine and aviation fuel may be zero-rated.

Official publications – 701/19.

Hansard – 1 December 1993: statement on behalf of the Chancellor of the Exchequer that VAT on domestic fuel bills will apply to the standing charge.
24 January 1994: statement on behalf of the Chancellor of the Exchequer on circumstances when VAT will be added to service charges in respect of the supply of energy:
"Certain services associated with the supply of energy, for example maintenance of appliances and pipes on the consumer's side of the meter, are already subject to the standard rate of VAT. Other services which are currently seen as an integral part of the supply of energy, such as meter rental and disconnection and reconnection services, will continue to follow the liability of the fuel and for domestic consumers will therefore be subject to 8 per cent VAT from 1 April 1994 ... First-time connection to the gas and electricity mains will, however, continue to be relieved for VAT."

Other material – HM Customs and Excise Business Brief 9/94, 30 March 1994: how retailers account for the former eight per cent fuel rate.

5(1) For the purposes of this paragraph–

(a)   **"the Contributions and Benefits Act"** means the Social Security Contributions and Benefits Act 1992; and

(b)   **"the Northern Ireland Act"** means the Social Security Contributions and Benefits (Northern Ireland) Act 1992.

5(2) For the purposes of paragraph 1(1) above a person to whom a supply is made is **"a qualifying person"** if at the time of the supply he–

(a)   is aged 60 or over; or

(b)   is in receipt of one or more of the benefits mentioned in sub-paragraph (3) below.

5(3) The benefits referred to in sub-paragraph (2) above are as follows–

(a)   council tax benefit under Part VII of the Contributions and Benefits Act;

(b)   disability living allowance under Part III of the Contributions and Benefits Act or Part III of the Northern Ireland Act;

(c)   disabled person's tax credit under Part VII of the Contributions and Benefits Act or Part VII of the Northern Ireland Act.

(d)   working families' tax credit under Part VII of the Contributions and Benefits Act or Part VII of the Northern Ireland Act.

(e)   housing benefit under Part VII of the Contributions and Benefits Act or Part VII of the Northern Ireland Act;

(f)   an income-based jobseeker's allowance within the meaning of section 1(4) of the Jobseekers Act 1995 or Article 3(4) of the Jobseekers (Northern Ireland) Order 1995;

(g)   income support under Part VII of the Contributions and Benefits Act or Part VII of the Northern Ireland Act;

(h)   disablement pension under Part V of the Contributions and Benefits Act or Part V of the Northern Ireland Act, which is payable at the increased rate provided for under section 104 (constant attendance allowance) of the Act concerned; and

(i)   war disablement pension under the Naval, Military and Air Forces Etc. (Disablement and Death) Service Pensions Order 1983, which is payable at the increased rate provided for under article 14 (constant attendance allowance) or article 26A (mobility supplement) of that Order.

5(3A)   For the purposes of paragraph 1(1)(aa) and (ab) above **"residential accommodation"** means–

(a)   a building, or part of a building, that consists of a dwelling or a number of dwellings;

(b)   a building, or part of a building, used for a relevant residential purpose;

(c)   a caravan used as a place of permanent habitation; or

(d)   a houseboat.

5(3B)   For the purposes of paragraph 1(1)(aa) and (ab) above **"use for a relevant charitable purpose"** means use by a charity in either or both of the following ways, namely–

(a)   otherwise than in the course or furtherance of a business;

(b)   as a village hall or similarly in providing social or recreational facilities for a local community.

5(4)   For the purposes of paragraph 1(1)(aa) and (ab) above **"List A energy-saving materials"** means any of the following–

(a)   insulation for walls, floors, ceilings, roofs or lofts or for water tanks, pipes or other plumbing fittings;

(b)   draught stripping for windows and doors;

(c)   central heating system controls (including thermostatic radiator valves);

(d)   hot water system controls;

(e)   solar panels;

(f)   wind turbines;

(g)   water turbines.

5(4A)   For the purposes of paragraph 1(1)(b) and (c) above **"List B energy-saving materials"** means any of the following–

(a)   gas-fired room heaters that are fitted with thermostatic controls;

(b)   electric storage heaters;

(c)   closed solid fuel fire cassettes;

(d)   electric dual immersion water heaters with foam-insulated hot water tanks;

(e)   gas-fired boilers;

(f)   oil-fired boilers;

(g)   radiators.

5(4B)   For the purposes of paragraph 1(1)(j) and (k) above, **"qualifying security goods"** means any of the following–

(a)   locks or bolts for windows;

(b)   locks, bolts or security chains for doors;

(c)   spy holes;

(d)   smoke alarms.

5(5)   *For the purposes of paragraph 1 above a scheme is a* **"relevant scheme"** *if it is one which*–

(a)   has as one of its objectives the funding of the installation of energy-saving materials in the homes of any persons who are qualifying persons, and

(b)   disburses, whether directly or indirectly, its grants in whole or in part out of funds made available to it in order to achieve that objective–

      (i) by the Secretary of State,

(ii) by the European Community,

(iii) under an arrangement approved by the Director General of Electricity Supply, the Director General of Electricity Supply for Northern Ireland or the Director General of Gas Supply, or

(iv) by a local authority.

History – Para. 5 was inserted by SI 1998/1375, art. 6, operative from 1 July 1998.
In para. 5(3)(c), the words "disabled person's tax credit" were substituted for the words "disability working allowance" by FA 2000, s. 135 and Sch. 35, para. 5, in relation to supplies made after 1 April 2000.
In para. 5(3)(d), the words "working families' tax credit" were substituted for the words "family credit" by FA 2000, s. 135 and Sch. 35, para. 6, in relation to supplies made on or after 1 April 2000.
Para. 5(3A) was inserted by FA 2000, s. 135 and Sch. 35, para. 7, in relation to supplies made on or after 1 April 2000.
Para. 5(3B) was inserted by FA 2000, s. 135 and Sch. 35, para. 7, in relation to supplies made on or after 1 April 2000.
In para. 5(4), at the beginning, the words "For the purposes of paragraph 1(1)(aa) and (ab) above **"List A energy-saving materials"** means" were substituted for the words "For the purposes of paragraph 1(1)(b) and (c) above **"energy-saving materials"**means" by FA 2000, s. 135 and Sch. 35, para. 8(2), in relation to supplies made on or after 1 April 2000.
In para. 5(4)(c), the words "(including thermostatic radiator valves)" were inserted by FA 2000, s. 135 and Sch. 35, para. 8(3), in relation to supplies made on or after 1 April 2000.
Para. 5(4)(e) was inserted by FA 2000, s. 131 and Sch. 35, para. 8(4), in relation to supplies made on or after 1 April 2000.
Para. 5(4)(f) and (g) were inserted by FA 2000, s. 135 and Sch. 35, para. 8(5), in relation to supplies made on or after xx July 2000.
Para. 5(4A) was inserted by FA 2000, s. 135 and Sch. 35, para. 9, in relation to supplies made on or after 1 April 2000.
Para. 5(4B) was inserted by FA 2000, s. 135 and Sch. 35, para. 9, in relation to supplies made on or after 1 April 2000.
In para. 5(5), the words "paragraph 1" were substituted for the words "paragraph 1(1A) and (1B)" by FA 2000, s. 131 and Sch. 35, para. 10, in relation to supplies made on or after 1 April 2000.

Extra-statutory concessions – 3.16 (Notice 48 (1999 edn)): connection to gas or electricity mains supply.
5.2 (Notice 48 (1999 edn)): certain supplies of marine and aviation fuel may be zero-rated.

Official publications – 701/19.

Hansard – 1 December 1993: statement on behalf of the Chancellor of the Exchequer that VAT on domestic fuel bills will apply to the standing charge.
24 January 1994: statement on behalf of the Chancellor of the Exchequer on circumstances when VAT will be added to service charges in respect of the supply of energy:
"Certain services associated with the supply of energy, for example maintenance of appliances and pipes on the consumer's side of the meter, are already subject to the standard rate of VAT. Other services which are currently seen as an integral part of the supply of energy, such as meter rental and disconnection and reconnection services, will continue to follow the liability of the fuel and for domestic consumers will therefore be subject to 8 per cent VAT from 1 April 1994 ... First-time connection to the gas and electricity mains will, however, continue to be relieved for VAT."

Other material – HM Customs and Excise Business Brief 9/94, 30 March 1994: how retailers account for the former eight per cent fuel rate.

SCHEDULE 1 – REGISTRATION IN RESPECT OF TAXABLE SUPPLIES

Section 3(2)

LIABILITY TO BE REGISTERED

1(1) Subject to sub-paragraphs (3) to (7) below, a person who makes taxable supplies but is not registered under this Act becomes liable to be registered under this Schedule–

(a) at the end of any month, if the value of his taxable supplies in the period of one year then ending has exceeded £52,000; or 54k

(b) at any time, if there are reasonable grounds for believing that the value of his taxable supplies in the period of 30 days then beginning will exceed £52,000. 54k

1(2) Where a business carried on by a taxable person is transferred to another person as a going concern and the transferee is not registered under this Act at the time of the transfer, then, subject to sub-paragraph (3) to (7) below, the transferee becomes liable to be registered under this Schedule at that time if–

(a) the value of his taxable supplies in the period of one year ending at the time of the transfer has exceeded £52,000; or

(b) there are reasonable grounds for believing that the value of his taxable supplies in the period of 30 days beginning at the time of the transfer will exceed £52,000.

1(3) A person does not become liable to be registered by virtue of sub-paragraph (1)(a) or (2)(a) above if the Commissioners are satisfied that the value of his taxable supplies in the period of one year beginning at the time at which, apart from this sub-paragraph, he would become liable to be registered will not exceed £50,000.

1(4) In determining the value of a person's supplies for the purposes of sub-paragraph (1)(a) or (2)(a) above, supplies made at a time when he was previously registered under this Act shall be disregarded if–

(a)   his registration was cancelled otherwise than under paragraph 13(3) below, paragraph 6(2) of Schedule 2, paragraph 6(3) of Schedule 3 or paragraph 6(2) of Schedule 3A, and

(b)   the Commissioners are satisfied that before his registration was cancelled he had given them all the information they needed in order to determine whether to cancel the registration.

1(5)   A person shall be treated as having become liable to be registered under this Schedule at any time when he would have become so liable under the preceding provisions of this paragraph but for any registration which is subsequently cancelled under paragraph 13(3) below, paragraph 6(2) of Schedule 2, paragraph 6(3) of Schedule 3 or paragraph 6(2) of Schedule 3A.

1(6)   A person shall not cease to be liable to be registered under this Schedule except in accordance with paragraph 2(5), 3 or 4 below.

1(7)   In determining the value of a person's supplies for the purposes of sub-paragraph (1) or (2) above, supplies of goods or services that are capital assets of the business in the course or furtherance of which they are supplied and any taxable supplies which would not be taxable supplies apart from section 7(4) shall be disregarded.

1(8)   Where, apart from this sub-paragraph, an interest in, right over or licence to occupy any land would under sub-paragraph (7) above be disregarded for the purposes of sub-paragraph (1) or (2) above, it shall not be if it is supplied on a taxable supply which is not zero-rated.

1(9)   In determining the value of a person's supplies for the purposes of sub-paragraph (1) or (2) above, supplies to which section 18B(4) (last acquisition or supply of goods before removal from fiscal warehousing) applies and supplies treated as made by him under section 18C(3) (self-supply of services on removal of goods from warehousing) shall be disregarded.

History – Turnover thresholds were varied by statutory instrument under para. 15 as follows:

SI	Period of application	Past turnover £	Future turnover £
2000/804	From 1/4/2000	52,000	50,000
1999/595	1/4/99–31/3/2000	51,000	49,000
1998/761	1/4/98–31/3/99	50,000	48,000
1997/1628	1/12/97–31/3/98	49,000	47,000
1996/2950	27/11/96–30/11/97	48,000	46,000
1995/3037	29/11/95–26/11/96	47,000	45,000
1994/2905	30/11/94–28/11/95	46,000	44,000
1993/2953	1/12/93–29/11/94	45,000	43,000

In para. 1(4)(a), the words ", paragraph 6(3) of Schedule 3 or paragraph 6(2) of Schedule 3A" were substituted for the words "or paragraph 6(3) of Schedule 3" by FA 2000, s. 136(6), with effect in relation to supplies made on or after 21 March 2000.
In para. 1(5), the words ", paragraph 6(3) of Schedule 3 or paragraph 6(2) of Schedule 3A" were substituted for the words "or paragraph 6(3) of Schedule 3" by FA 2000, s. 136(6), with effect in relation to supplies made on or after 21 March 2000.
Para. 1(9) was added by FA 1996, s. 26 and Sch. 3, para. 13, with effect from 1 June 1996 and applies to any acquisition of goods from another member State and any supply taking place on or after that day.
Derivations – Para. 1(1): VATA 1983, s. 2C(2) and Sch. 1, para. 1(1), as substituted by FA 1990, s. 10(2), as amended by F(No. 2)A 1992, s. 14 and Sch. 3, para. 48(1), SI 1993/766 and SI 1993/2953.
Para. 1(2): VATA 1983, s. 2C(2) and Sch. 1, para. 1(2), as substituted by FA 1990, s. 10(2), as amended by F(No. 2)A 1992, s. 14 and Sch. 3, para. 48(2), SI 1993/766 and SI 1993/2953.
Para. 1(3): VATA 1983, s. 2C(2) and Sch. 1, para. 1(3), as substituted by FA 1990, s. 10(2), as amended by SI 1993/766 and SI 1993/2953.
Para. 1(4): VATA 1983, s. 2C(2) and Sch. 1, para. 1(4), as substituted by FA 1987, s. 14(2), as amended by FA 1990, s. 10(3), F(No. 2)A 1992, s. 14 and Sch. 3, para. 48(3).
Para. 1(5), (6): VATA 1983, Sch. 1, para. 1(4A), (4B), as inserted by F(No. 2)A 1992, s. 14 and Sch. 3, para. 48(4).
Para. 1(7): VATA 1983, s. 2C(2) and Sch. 1, para. 1(5), as substituted by FA 1987, s. 14(2), as amended by FA 1988, s. 14(2) and FA 1990, s. 10(4) and F(No. 2)A 1992, s. 14 and Sch. 3, para. 48(5).
Para. 1(8): VATA 1983, s. 2C(2) and Sch. 1, para. 1(6), as inserted by FA 1989, s. 18 and Sch. 3, para. 10(a), as amended by FA 1990, s. 10(5).
Cross references – S. 55: customers accounting for VAT on supplies of gold, etc.
S. 67 and 69: penalties.
VAT (Isle of Man) Order 1982 (SI 1982/1067), art. 11(1): person registered under the Manx Act.
VAT (Special Provisions) Order 1995 (SI 1995/1268), art. 11(2)(b): value self-supply disregarded.
VAT Regulations 1995 (SI 1995/2518), Pt. II: registration and notification.
VAT Regulations 1995 (SI 1995/2518), reg. 21: "relevant figure" defined.
VAT Regulations 1995 (SI 1995/2518), reg. 25(1): first return period.
VAT Regulations 1995 (SI 1995/2518), reg. 185: repayments to third country traders.
VAT Regulations 1995 (SI 1995/2518), reg. 203 and 208: relevant part of business disregarded and cancellation of certificate.
Official publications – 700/1: should I be registered for VAT.
 700/2: VAT group treatment.
700/67: VAT registration scheme for racehorse owners.
Customs Internal Guidance Manual, vol. V1.28: registration and de-registration.
Other material – Customs and Excise Press Notice 762, 20 September 1982: separation of business activities.
Customs and Excise News Release 65/90, 25 September 1990: evidence to register property owners and developers as intending traders.
Memorandum of understanding of 16 March 1993 between Customs and Excise and the thoroughbred horseracing and breeding industry (not reproduced): registration of racehorse owners.
Customs and Excise News Release 44/93, 19 March 1993: registration of general practitioners and general dental practitioners.
Notes – S. 4(2): definition of "taxable supply".

S. 42: registration of local authorities.
S. 49(1): transfer of going concern.
S. 83(a): appeals concerning registration.

1A(1)   Paragraph 2 below is for the purpose of preventing the maintenance or creation of any artificial separation of business activities carried on by two or more persons from resulting in an avoidance of VAT.

1A(2)   In determining for the purposes of sub-paragraph (1) above whether any separation of business activities is artificial, regard shall be had to the extent to which the different persons carrying on those activities are closely bound to one another by financial, economic and organisational links.

History – Para. 1A was inserted by FA 1997, s. 31(1), with effect in relation to the making of directions on or after 19 March 1997.

Official publications – 700/61: artificial separation of business activities.

2(1)   Without prejudice to paragraph 1 above, if the Commissioners make a direction under this paragraph, the persons named in the direction shall be treated as a single taxable person carrying on the activities of a business described in the direction and that taxable person shall be liable to be registered under this Schedule with effect from the date of the direction or, if the direction so provides, from such later date as may be specified therein.

2(2)   The Commissioners shall not make a direction under this paragraph naming any person unless they are satisfied–

(a)   that he is making or has made taxable supplies; and

(b)   that the activities in the course of which he makes or made those taxable supplies form only part of certain activities, the other activities being carried on concurrently or previously (or both) by one or more other persons; and

(c)   that, if all the taxable supplies of the business described in the direction were taken into account, a person carrying on that business would at the time of the direction be liable to be registered by virtue of paragraph 1 above;

(d)   [Para. 2(2)(d) was omitted and repealed by FA 1997, s. 31(2)(c) and 113 and Sch. 18, Pt. IV(1).]

2(3)   A direction made under this paragraph shall be served on each of the persons named in it.

2(4)   Where, after a direction has been given under this paragraph specifying a description of business, it appears to the Commissioners that a person who was not named in that direction is making taxable supplies in the course of activities which should be regarded as part of the activities of that business, the Commissioners may make and serve on him a supplementary direction referring to the earlier direction and the description of business specified in it and adding that person's name to those of the persons named in the earlier direction with effect from–

(a)   the date on which he began to make those taxable supplies, or

(b)   if it was later, the date with effect from which the single taxable person referred to in the earlier direction became liable to be registered under this Schedule.

2(5)   If, immediately before a direction (including a supplementary direction) is made under this paragraph, any person named in the direction is registered in respect of the taxable supplies made by him as mentioned in sub-paragraph (2) or (4) above, he shall cease to be liable to be so registered with effect from whichever is the later of–

(a)   the date with effect from which the single taxable person concerned became liable to be registered; and

(b)   the date of the direction.

2(6)   In relation to a business specified in a direction under this paragraph, the persons named in the direction, together with any person named in a supplementary direction relating to that business (being the persons who together are to be treated as the taxable person), are in sub-paragraph (7) and (8) below referred to as **"the constituent members"**.

2(7)   Where a direction is made under this paragraph then, for the purposes of this Act–

(a)   the taxable person carrying on the business specified in the direction shall be registrable in such name as the persons named in the direction may jointly nominate by notice in writing given to the Commissioners not later than 14 days after the date of the direction or, in default of such a nomination, in such name as may be specified in the direction;

(b)   any supply of goods or services by or to one of the constituent members in the course of the activities of the taxable person shall be treated as a supply by or to that person;

(c) any acquisition of goods from another member State by one of the constituent members in the course of the activities of the taxable person shall be treated as an acquisition by that person;

(d) each of the constituent members shall be jointly and severally liable for any VAT due from the taxable person;

(e) without prejudice to paragraph (d) above, any failure by the taxable person to comply with any requirement imposed by or under this Act shall be treated as a failure by each of the constituent members severally; and

(f) subject to paragraph (a) to (e) above, the constituent members shall be treated as a partnership carrying on the business of the taxable person and any question as to the scope of the activities of that business at any time shall be determined accordingly.

2(8) If it appears to the Commissioners that any person who is one of the constituent members should no longer be regarded as such for the purposes of paragraph (d) and (e) of sub-paragraph (7) above and they give notice to that effect, he shall not have any liability by virtue of those paragraphs for anything done after the date specified in that notice and, accordingly, on that date he shall be treated as having ceased to be a member of the partnership referred to in paragraph (f) of that sub-paragraph.

History – In para. 2(2)(b), the words "which should properly be regarded as those of the business described in the direction" which appeared after the words "of certain activities" were omitted and repealed by FA 1997, s. 31(2)(a) and 113 and Sch. 18, Pt. IV(1), with effect in relation to the making of directions on or after 19 March 1997.
In para. 2(2)(c), the words "the business described in the direction" were substituted for the words "that business" by FA 1997, s. 31(2)(b), with effect in relation to the making of directions on or after 19 March 1997.
In para. 2(2)(c), the word "and" which appeared at the end was repealed by FA 1997, s. 113 and Sch. 18, Pt. IV(1), with effect in relation to the making of directions on or after 19 March 1997.
Para. 2(2)(d) was omitted and repealed by FA 1997, s. 31(2)(c) and 113 and Sch. 18, Pt. IV(1), with effect in relation to the making of directions on or after 19 March 1997. Former para. 2(2)(d) reads as follows: that the main reason or one of the main reasons for the person concerned carrying on the activities first referred to in paragraph (b) above in the way he does is the avoidance of a liability to be registered (whether that liability would be his, another person's or that of 2 or more persons jointly)."
In para. 2(4), the word "properly" which appeared after the words "activities which should" was omitted and repealed by FA 1997, s. 31(2) and 113 and Sch. 18, Pt. IV(1), with effect in relation to the making of directions on or after 19 March 1997.
Derivations – Para. 2(1): VATA 1983, s. 2C(2) and Sch. 1, para. 1A(1), as inserted by FA 1986, s. 10(1) and as amended by F(No. 2)A 1992, s. 14 and Sch. 3, para. 49(1).
Para. 2(2), (3) (as originally enacted): VATA 1983, s. 2C(2) and Sch. 1, para. 1A(2), (3), as inserted by FA 1986, s. 10(1).
Para. 2(3): VATA 1983, s. 2C(2) and Sch. 1, para. 1A(3), as inserted by FA 1986, s. 10(1).
Para. 2(4)(as originally enacted): VATA 1983, s. 2C(2) and Sch. 1, para. 1A(4), as inserted by FA 1986, s. 10(1), as amended by F(No. 2)A 1992, s. 14 and Sch. 3, para. 49(1).
Para. 2(5), (6): VATA 1983, s. 2C(2) and Sch. 1, para. 1A(5), (6), as inserted by FA 1986, s. 10(1).
Para. 2(7): VATA 1983, s. 2C(2) and Sch. 1, para. 1A(7), as inserted by FA 1986, s. 10(1), as amended by F(No. 2)A 1992, s. 14 and Sch. 3, para. 49(2).
Para. 2(8): VATA 1983, s. 2C(2) and Sch. 1, para. 1A(8), as inserted by FA 1986, s. 10(1).
Cross references – S. 83(u): appeals.

3 A person who has become liable to be registered under this Schedule shall cease to be so liable at any time if the Commissioners are satisfied in relation to that time that he–

(a) has ceased to make taxable supplies; or

(b) is not at that time a person in relation to whom any of the conditions specified in paragraph 1(1)(a) and (b) and (2)(a) and (b) above is satisfied.

Derivations – VATA 1983, s. 2C(2) and Sch. 1, para. 1B, as inserted by F(No. 2)A 1992, s. 14 and Sch. 3, para. 50.
Cross reference – VAT Regulations 1995 (SI 1995/2518), reg. 205: effective date of certificate for flat-rate farmer.

4(1) Subject to sub-paragraph (2) below, a person who has become liable to be registered under this Schedule shall cease to be so liable at any time after being registered if the Commissioners are satisfied that the value of his taxable supplies in the period of one year then beginning will not exceed £50,000.

4(2) A person shall not cease to be liable to be registered under this Schedule by virtue of sub-paragraph (1) above if the Commissioners are satisfied that the reason the value of his taxable supplies will not exceed £50,000 is that in the period in question he will cease making taxable supplies, or will suspend making them for a period of 30 days or more.

4(3) In determining the value of a person's supplies for the purposes of sub-paragraph (1) above, supplies of goods or services that are capital assets of the business in the course or furtherance of which they are supplied and any taxable supplies which would not be taxable supplies apart from section 7(4) shall be disregarded.

4(4) Where, apart from this sub-paragraph, an interest in, right over or licence to occupy any land would under sub-paragraph (3) above be disregarded for the purposes of sub-paragraph (1) above, it shall not be if it is supplied on a taxable supply which is not zero-rated.

History – Turnover thresholds were varied by statutory instrument under para. 15 as follows:

SI	Period of application	£
2000/804	From 1/4/2000	50,000
1999/595	1/4/99–31/3/2000	49,000
1998/761	1/4/98–31/3/99	48,000
1997/1628	1/12/97–31/3/98	47,000
1996/2950	27/11/96–30/11/97	46,000
1995/3037	29/11/95–26/11/96	45,000
1994/2905	30/11/94–28/11/95	44,000
1993/2953	1/12/93–29/11/94	43,000

Derivations – Para. 4(1), (2) (as originally enacted): VATA 1983, s. 2C(2) and Sch. 1, para. 2(1), (2), as substituted by FA 1987, s. 14(3), as amended by F(No. 2)A 1992, s. 14 and Sch. 3, para. 51(1), (2), SI 1993/766 and SI 1993/2953.
Para. 4(3): VATA 1983, s. 2C(2) and Sch. 1, para. 2(3), as substituted by FA 1987, s. 14(3), as amended by FA 1988, s. 14(2).
Para. 4(4): VATA 1983, s. 2C(2) and Sch. 1, para. 2(4), as inserted by FA 1989, s. 18 and Sch. 3, para. 10(b).
Official publications – 700/11; 700/44 and 700/56.
Notes – S. 4(2): definition of "taxable supplies".
S. 45(2): retiring partner's notice.
S. 69: penalty for breaching regulation.
S. 83(a): appeals concerning deregistration.
VAT Regulations 1995 (SI 1995/2518), Pt. II: notification to commissioners.
VAT Regulations 1995 (SI 1995/2518), reg. 23: final statement on deregistration.

NOTIFICATION OF LIABILITY AND REGISTRATION

5(1) A person who becomes liable to be registered by virtue of paragraph 1(1)(a) above shall notify the Commissioners of the liability within 30 days of the end of the relevant month.

5(2) The Commissioners shall register any such person (whether or not he so notifies them) with effect from the end of the month following the relevant month or from such earlier date as may be agreed between them and him.

5(3) In this paragraph **"the relevant month"**, in relation to a person who becomes liable to be registered by virtue of paragraph 1(1)(a) above, means the month at the end of which he becomes liable to be so registered.

Derivations – VATA 1983, s. 2C(2) and Sch. 1, para. 3, as substituted by FA 1990, s. 10(6), as amended by F(No. 2)A 1992, s. 14 and Sch. 3, para. 52.
Cross references – VAT (Terminal Markets) Order 1973 (SI 1973/173), art. 6: terminal markets and non-application of para. 5.
VAT (Isle of Man) Order 1982 (SI 1982/1067), art. 11: person registered under the Manx Act.
Other material – Taxline 1993/71 (not reproduced): Customs may treat sympathetically late registration applications by artists who had not registered previously on the ground that they were employees working under a contract of employment, but after deliberation they are treated as self-employed.

6(1) A person who becomes liable to be registered by virtue of paragraph 1(1)(b) above shall notify the Commissioners of the liability before the end of the period by reference to which the liability arises.

6(2) The Commissioners shall register any such person (whether or not he so notifies them) with effect from the beginning of the period by reference to which the liability arises.

Derivations – VATA 1983, s. 2C(2) and Sch. 1, para. 4, as substituted by FA 1990, s. 10(6).
Cross references – VAT (Terminal Markets) Order 1973 (SI 1973/173), art. 6: terminal markets and non-application of para. 6.
VAT (Isle of Man) Order 1982 (SI 1982/1067), art. 11: person registered under the Manx Act.

7(1) A person who becomes liable to be registered by virtue of paragraph 1(2) above shall notify the Commissioners of the liability within 30 days of the time when the business is transferred.

7(2) The Commissioners shall register any such person (whether or not he so notifies them) with effect from the time when the business is transferred.

Derivations – VATA 1983, s. 2C(2) and Sch. 1, para. 4A, as inserted by FA 1990, s. 10(6).
Cross references – VAT (Terminal Markets) Order 1973 (SI 1973/173), art. 6: terminal markets and non-application of para. 7.
VAT (Isle of Man) Order 1982 (SI 1982/1067), art. 11: person registered under the Manx Act.

8 Where a person becomes liable to be registered by virtue of paragraph 1(1)(a) above and by virtue of paragraph 1(1)(b) or 1(2) above at the same time, the Commissioners shall register him in accordance with paragraph 6(2) or 7(2) above, as the case may be, rather than paragraph 5(2) above.

Derivations – VATA 1983, s. 2C(2) and Sch. 1, para. 4B, as inserted by FA 1990, s. 10(6).
Cross references – VAT (Terminal Markets) Order 1973 (SI 1973/173), art. 6: terminal markets and non-application of para. 8.
VAT (Isle of Man) Order 1982 (SI 1982/1067), art. 11: person registered under the Manx Act.
VAT Regulations 1995 (SI 1995/2518), reg. 5: notification to commissioners.
VAT Regulations 1995 (SI 1995/2518), reg. 99(1): effective date of registration and accounting periods for partial exemption.
Statutory instruments – VAT (Special Provisions) Order 1995 (SI 1995/1268), art. 5: going concern.

ENTITLEMENT TO BE REGISTERED

9 Where a person who is not liable to be registered under this Act and is not already so registered satisfies the Commissioners that he–

(a) makes taxable supplies; or

(b) is carrying on a business and intends to make such supplies in the course or furtherance of that business,

they shall, if he so requests, register him with effect from the day on which the request is made or from such earlier date as may be agreed between them and him.

Derivations – VATA 1983, s. 2C(2) and Sch. 1, para. 5, as substituted by FA 1988, s. 14(4), as amended by F(No. 2)A 1992, s. 14 and Sch. 3, para. 53.

Cross references – Sch. 3, para. 4(4): registration in respect of acquisitions from other member states.
VAT Regulations 1995 (SI 1995/2518), reg. 6: transfer of VAT registration number.

Other material – Customs and Excise News Release 65/90, 25 September 1990: evidence required from intending traders (property owners and developers).

10(1) Where a person who is not liable to be registered under this Act and is not already so registered satisfies the Commissioners that he–

(a) makes supplies within sub-paragraph (2) below; or

(b) is carrying on a business and intends to make such supplies in the course or furtherance of that business,

and (in either case) is within sub-paragraph (3) below, they shall, if he so requests, register him with effect from the day on which the request is made or from such earlier date as may be agreed between them and him.

10(2) A supply is within this sub-paragraph if–

(a) it is made outside the United Kingdom but would be a taxable supply if made in the United Kingdom; or

(b) it is specified for the purposes of subsection (2) of section 26 in an order made under paragraph (c) of that subsection.

10(3) A person is within this sub-paragraph if–

(a) he has a business establishment in the United Kingdom or his usual place of residence is in the United Kingdom; and

(b) he does not make and does not intend to make taxable supplies.

10(4) For the purposes of this paragraph–

(a) a person carrying on a business through a branch or agency in the United Kingdom shall be treated as having a **business establishment** in the United Kingdom, and

(b) **"usual place of residence"**, in relation to a body corporate, means the place where it is legally constituted.

History – Para. 10(2) was substituted by FA 1997, s. 32, with effect from 19 March 1997.

Derivations – VATA 1983, s. 2C(2) and Sch. 1, para. 5A, as inserted by FA 1988, s. 14(4), as amended by F(No. 2)A 1992, s. 14 and Sch. 3, para. 53, repealed in part by F(No. 2)A 1992, s. 82 and Sch. 18, Pt. V.

Cross references – Sch. 3, para. 4(4): registration in respect of acquisitions from other member states.
VAT Regulations 1995 (SI 1995/2518), reg. 5: registration and notification.
VAT Regulations 1995 (SI 1995/2518), reg. 25(4): final return by person who deregisters.

NOTIFICATION OF END OF LIABILITY OR ENTITLEMENT ETC.

11 A person registered under paragraph 5, 6 or 9 above who ceases to make or have the intention of making taxable supplies shall notify the Commissioners of that fact within 30 days of the day on which he does so unless he would, when he so ceases, be otherwise liable or entitled to be registered under this Act if his registration and any enactment preventing a person from being liable to be registered under different provisions at the same time were disregarded.

Derivations – VATA 1983, s. 2C(2) and Sch. 1, para. 7, as substituted by FA 1988, s. 14(5), and as amended by F(No. 2)A 1992, s. 14 and Sch. 3, para. 54.

Cross references – VAT Regulations 1995 (SI 1995/2518), reg. 5 and 6: notification to commissioners of variation of the register, etc. and transfer of VAT registration number.

12 A person registered under paragraph 10 above who–

(a) ceases to make or have the intention of making supplies within sub-paragraph (2) of that paragraph; or

(b) makes or forms the intention of making taxable supplies,

shall notify the Commissioners of that fact within 30 days of the day on which he does so unless, in the case of a person ceasing as mentioned in sub-paragraph (a) above, he would, when he so ceases, be otherwise liable or entitled to be registered under this Act if his registration and any enactment preventing a person from being liable to be registered under different provisions at the same time were disregarded.

Derivations – VATA 1983, s. 2C(2) and Sch. 1, para. 7/
2)A 1992, s. 14 and Sch. 3, para. 55.
Cross reference – VAT Regulations 1995 (SI 1995/2518)

CANCELLATIΟ

13(1) Subject to sub-paragraph (4) below
that he is not liable to be registered under
registration with effect from the day on wh
agreed between them and him.

13(2) Subject to sub-paragraph (5) belov
person has ceased to be registrable, they
which he so ceased or from such later

13(3) Where the Commissioners are s
registered he was not registrable, they

13(4) The Commissioners shall not u
with effect from any time unless they
subject to a requirement to be registered und...

13(5) The Commissioners shall not under sub-paragraph (2) a...
with effect from any time unless they are satisfied that it is not a time when th...
subject to a requirement, or entitled, to be registered under this Act.

13(6) In determining for the purposes of sub-paragraph (4) or (5) above whether a person would be subject to a requirement, or entitled, to be registered at any time, so much of any provision of this Act as prevents a person from becoming liable or entitled to be registered when he is already registered or when he is so liable under any other provision shall be disregarded.

13(7) In this paragraph, any reference to a **registered person** is a reference to a person who is registered under this Schedule.

Derivations – Para. 13(1): VATA 1983, s. 2C(2) and Sch. 1, para. 8A(1), as substituted by FA 1988, s. 14(6), and as amended by F(No. 2)A 1992, s. 14 and Sch. 3, para. 56.
Para. 13(2): VATA 1983, s. 2C(2) and Sch. 1, para. 9(1), as substituted by FA 1988, s. 14(6), as amended by F(No. 2)A 1992, s. 14 and Sch. 3, para. 57.
Para. 13(3): VATA 1983, s. 2C(2) and Sch. 1, para. 10, as substituted by FA 1988, s. 14(6).
Para. 13(4): VATA 1983, s. 2C(2) and Sch. 1, para. 8A(1A), as inserted by F(No. 2)A 1992, s. 14 and Sch. 3, para. 56, 57.
Para. 13(5): VATA 1983, s. 2C(2) and Sch. 1, para. 8A(1B), 9(1B), as inserted by F(No. 2)A 1992, s. 14 and Sch. 3, para. 56, 57.
Para. 13(6): VATA 1983, s. 2C(2) and Sch. 1, para. 8(1B), 9(1B), as inserted by F(No. 2)A 1992, s. 14 and Sch. 3, para. 56(2) and 57(2).
Para. 13(7): VATA 1983, Sch. 1, para. 8A(2), 9(2).
Cross reference – VAT Regulations 1995 (SI 1995/2518), reg. 5(2): notification not needed to commissioners of variation of the register, etc.
Official publications – Customs Internal Guidance Manual, vol. V1.28: registration and de-registration.

EXEMPTION FROM REGISTRATION

14(1) Notwithstanding the preceding provisions of this Schedule, where a person who makes or intends to make taxable supplies satisfies the Commissioners that any such supply is zero-rated or would be zero-rated if he were a taxable person, they may, if he so requests and they think fit, exempt him from registration under this Schedule until it appears to them that the request should no longer be acted upon or is withdrawn.

14(2) Where there is a material change in the nature of the supplies made by a person exempted under this paragraph from registration under this Schedule, he shall notify the Commissioners of the change–

(a) within 30 days of the date on which it occurred; or
(b) if no particular day is identifiable as the day on which it occurred, within 30 days of the end of the quarter in which it occurred.

14(3) Where there is a material alteration in any quarter in the proportion of taxable supplies of such a person that are zero-rated, he shall notify the Commissioners of the alteration within 30 days of the end of the quarter.

Derivations – VATA 1983, s. 2C(2) and Sch. 1, para. 11, as substituted by FA 1988, s. 14(7), as amended by F(No. 2)A 1992, s. 14 and Sch. 3, para. 58.

POWER TO VARY SPECIFIED SUMS BY ORDER

15 The Treasury may by order substitute for any of the sums for the time being specified in this Schedule such greater sums as they think fit.

, para. 12, as substituted by FA 1988, s. 14(7).
egistration Limits) Order 1994 (SI 1994/2905).
er 1995 (SI 1995/3037).
der 1996 (SI 1996/2950).
Order 1997 (SI 1997/1628).
Order 1998 (SI 1998/761).
ts) Order 1999 (SI 1999/595).
mits) Order 2000 (SI 2000/804).

SUPPLEMENTARY

a supply of goods or services shall be determined for the purposes of this
basis that no VAT is chargeable on the supply.
TA 1983, s. 2C(2) and Sch. 1, para. 13, as substituted by FA 1987, s. 14(10).

otification required under this Schedule shall be made in such form and shall contain
iculars as the Commissioners may by regulations prescribe.
ons – VATA 1983, s. 2C(2) and Sch. 1, para. 14.

tory instrument – VAT Regulations 1995 (SI 1995/2518).

In this Schedule **"registrable"** means liable or entitled to be registered under this Schedule.

Derivations – VATA 1983, s. 2C(2) and Sch. 1, para. 9(2), as substituted by FA 1988, s. 14(6), and as amended by F(No. 2)A 1992, s. 14 and Sch. 3, para. 57.

19 References in this Schedule to **supplies** are references to supplies made in the course or furtherance of a business.

Derivations – VATA 1983, s. 2C(2) and Sch. 1, para. 15, as amended by F(No. 2)A 1992, s. 82 and Sch. 18, Pt. V.

Cross references – S. 42: local authorities.
S. 54(2): farmers etc.
S. 55(1): supplies of gold.
S. 67 and s. 69(1)(a): penalties.
S. 83(a): appeals.
VAT (Special Provisions) Order 1995 (SI 1995/1268), art. 11(2): no self-supplies if not registrable.
VAT Regulations 1995 (SI 1995/2518), Pt. II: registration details.
VAT Regulations 1995 (SI 1995/2518), reg. 206: cancellation of certificate of flat-rate farmer.

Forms – VAT 1–22, 62, 63 and 68.

Official publications – 700/1, 700/2.

Notes – S. 49(1)(a): "going concern" transfers.
S. 96(1): definition of "taxable supplies".

SCHEDULE 2 – REGISTRATION IN RESPECT OF SUPPLIES FROM OTHER MEMBER STATES

Section 3(2)

LIABILITY TO BE REGISTERED

1(1) A person who–

(a)   is not registered under this Act; and

(b)   is not liable to be registered under Schedule 1,

becomes liable to be registered under this Schedule on any day if, in the period beginning with 1st January of the year in which that day falls, that person has made relevant supplies whose value exceeds £70,000.

1(2) A person who is not registered or liable to be registered as mentioned in sub-paragraph (1)(a) and (b) above becomes liable to be registered under this Schedule where–

(a)   that person has exercised any option, in accordance with the law of any other member State where he is taxable, for treating relevant supplies made by him as taking place outside that member State;

(b)   the supplies to which the option relates involve the removal of goods from that member State and, apart from the exercise of the option, would be treated, in accordance with the law of that member State, as taking place in that member State; and

(c)   that person makes a relevant supply at a time when the option is in force in relation to him.

1(3) A person who is not registered or liable to be registered as mentioned in sub-paragraph (1)(a) and (b) above becomes liable to be registered under this Schedule if he makes a supply in relation to which the following conditions are satisfied, that is to say–

(a)   it is a supply of goods subject to a duty of excise;

(b) it involves the removal of the goods to the United Kingdom by or under the directions of the person making the supply;

(c) it is a transaction in pursuance of which the goods are acquired in the United Kingdom from another member State by a person who is not a taxable person;

(d) it is made on or after 1st January 1993 and in the course or furtherance of a business carried on by the supplier; and

(e) it is not anything which is treated as a supply for the purposes of this Act by virtue only of paragraph 5(1) or 6 of Schedule 4.

1(4) A person shall be treated as having become liable to be registered under this Schedule at any time when he would have become so liable under the preceding provisions of this paragraph but for any registration which is subsequently cancelled under paragraph 6(2) below, paragraph 13(3) of Schedule 1, paragraph 6(3) of Schedule 3 or paragraph 6(2) of Schedule 3A.

1(5) A person shall not cease to be liable to be registered under this Schedule except in accordance with paragraph 2 below.

1(6) In determining for the purposes of this paragraph the value of any relevant supplies, so much of the consideration for any supply as represents any liability of the supplier, under the law of another member State, for VAT on that supply shall be disregarded.

1(7) For the purposes of sub-paragraphs (1) and (2) above supplies to which section 18B(4) (last acquisition or supply of goods before removal from fiscal warehousing) applies shall be disregarded.

History – In para. 1(4), the words ", paragraph 6(3) of Schedule 3 or paragraph 6(2) of Schedule 3A" were substituted for the words "or paragraph 6(3) of Schedule 3" by FA 2000, s. 136(6), with effect in relation to supplies made on or after 21 March 2000.
Para. 1(7) was added by FA 1996, s. 26 and Sch. 3, para. 14, with effect from 1 June 1996 and applies to any acquisition of goods from another member State and any supply taking place on or after that day.
Derivations – VATA 1983, s. 2C(2) and Sch. 1A, para. 1, as inserted by F(No. 2)A 1992, s. 14 and Sch. 3, para. 59.
Cross references – S. 18B(5): relief for fiscally warehoused goods if disregard last acquisition or supply of goods before removal from warehousing.
VAT Regulations 1995 (SI 1995/2518), reg. 25(1): first return period.
VAT Regulations 1995 (SI 1995/2518), reg. 98(1): notification to the commissioners of removal of goods to another member state.

2(1) Subject to sub-paragraph (2) below, a person who has become liable to be registered under this Schedule shall cease to be so liable if at any time—

(a) the relevant supplies made by him in the year ending with 31st December last before that time did not have a value exceeding £70,000 and did not include any supply in relation to which the conditions mentioned in paragraph 1(3) above were satisfied; and

(b) the Commissioners are satisfied that the value of his relevant supplies in the year immediately following that year will not exceed £70,000 and that those supplies will not include a supply in relation to which those conditions are satisfied.

2(2) A person shall not cease to be liable to be registered under this Schedule at any time when such an option as is mentioned in paragraph 1(2) above is in force in relation to him.
Derivations – VATA 1983, s. 2C(2) and Sch. 1A, para. 2, as inserted by F(No. 2)A 1992, s. 14 and Sch. 3, para. 59.

NOTIFICATION OF LIABILITY AND REGISTRATION

3(1) A person who becomes liable to be registered under this Schedule shall notify the Commissioners of the liability within the period of 30 days after the day on which the liability arises.

3(2) The Commissioners shall register any such person (whether or not he so notifies them) with effect from the day on which the liability arose or from such earlier time as may be agreed between them and him.
Derivations – VATA 1983, s. 2C(2) and Sch. 1A, para. 3, as inserted by F(No. 2)A 1992, s. 14 and Sch. 3, para. 59.
Cross references – S. 67: penalties.
VAT Regulations 1995 (SI 1995/2518), reg. 5: registration and notification.
Other material – Form VAT 1A.

REQUEST TO BE REGISTERED

4(1) Where a person who is not liable to be registered under this Act and is not already so registered–

(a) satisfies the Commissioners that he intends–

   (i) to exercise an option such as is mentioned in paragraph 1(2) above and, from a specified date, to make relevant supplies to which that option will relate;

(ii) from a specified date to make relevant supplies to which any such option that he has exercised will relate; or

(iii) from a specified date to make supplies in relation to which the conditions mentioned in paragraph 1(3) above will be satisfied; and

(b) requests to be registered under this Schedule,

the Commissioners may, subject to such conditions as they think fit to impose, register him with effect from such date as may be agreed between them and him.

4(2) Conditions imposed under sub-paragraph (1) above–

(a) may be so imposed wholly or partly by reference to, or without reference to, any conditions prescribed for the purposes of this paragraph; and

(b) may, whenever imposed, be subsequently varied by the Commissioners.

4(3) Where a person who is entitled to be registered under paragraph 9 or 10 of Schedule 1 requests registration under this paragraph, he shall be registered under that Schedule, and not under this Schedule.

Derivations – VATA 1983, s. 2C(2) and Sch. 1A, para. 4, as inserted by F(No. 2)A 1992, s. 14 and Sch. 3, para. 59.

NOTIFICATION OF MATTERS AFFECTING CONTINUANCE OF REGISTRATION

5(1) Any person registered under this Schedule who ceases to be registrable under this Act shall notify the Commissioners of that fact within 30 days of the day on which he does so.

5(2) A person registered under paragraph 4 above by reference to any intention of his to exercise any option or to make supplies of any description shall notify the Commissioners within 30 days of exercising that option or, as the case may be, of the first occasion after his registration when he makes such a supply, that he has exercised the option or made such a supply.

5(3) A person who has exercised such an option as is mentioned in paragraph 1(2) above which, as a consequence of its revocation or otherwise, ceases to have effect in relation to any relevant supplies by him shall notify the Commissioners, within 30 days of the option's ceasing so to have effect, that it has done so.

5(4) For the purposes of this paragraph, a person **ceases to be registrable under this Act** where–

(a) he ceases to be a person who would be liable or entitled to be registered under this Act if his registration and any enactment preventing a person from being liable to be registered under different provisions at the same time were disregarded; or

(b) in the case of a person who (having been registered under paragraph 4 above) has not been such a person during the period of his registration, he ceases to have any such intention as is mentioned in sub-paragraph (1)(a) of that paragraph.

Derivations – VATA 1983, s. 2C(2) and Sch. 1A, para. 5, as inserted by F(No. 2)A 1992, s. 14 and Sch. 3, para. 59.

Cross references – S. 69(1)(a): penalties.
VAT Regulations 1995 (SI 1995/2518), reg. 5(2) and (3): notification to commissioners of variation of the register, etc.

CANCELLATION OF REGISTRATION

6(1) Subject to paragraph 7 below, where a person registered under this Schedule satisfies the Commissioners that he is not liable to be so registered, they shall, if he so requests, cancel his registration with effect from the day on which the request is made or from such later date as may be agreed between them and him.

6(2) Where the Commissioners are satisfied that, on the day on which a person was registered under this Schedule, he–

(a) was not liable to be registered under this Schedule; and

(b) in the case of a person registered under paragraph 4 above, did not have the intention by reference to which he was registered,

they may cancel his registration with effect from that day.

6(3) Subject to paragraph 7 below, where the Commissioners are satisfied that a person who has been registered under paragraph 4 above and is not for the time being liable to be registered under this Schedule–

(a) has not, by the date specified in his request to be registered, begun to make relevant supplies, exercised the option in question or, as the case may be, begun to make supplies in relation to which the conditions mentioned in paragraph 1(3) above are satisfied; or

(b) has contravened any condition of his registration,

they may cancel his registration with effect from the date so specified or, as the case may be, the date of the contravention or from such later date as may be agreed between them and him.

Derivations – VATA 1983, s. 2C(2) and Sch. 1A, para. 6, as inserted by F(No. 2)A 1992, s. 14 and Sch. 3, para. 59.

CONDITIONS OF CANCELLATION

7(1) The Commissioners shall not, under paragraph 6(1) above, cancel a person's registration with effect from any time unless they are satisfied that it is not a time when that person would be subject to a requirement to be registered under this Act.

7(2) The Commissioners shall not, under paragraph 6(3) above, cancel a person's registration with effect from any time unless they are satisfied that it is not a time when that person would be subject to a requirement, or entitled, to be registered under this Act.

7(3) The registration of a person who has exercised such an option as is mentioned in paragraph 1(2) above shall not be cancelled with effect from any time before 1st January which is, or next follows, the second anniversary of the date on which his registration took effect.

7(4) In determining for the purposes of this paragraph whether a person would be subject to a requirement, or entitled, to be registered at any time, so much of any provision of this Act as prevents a person from becoming liable or entitled to be registered when he is already registered or when he is so liable under any other provision shall be disregarded.

Derivations – VATA 1983, s. 2C(2) and Sch. 1A, para. 7, as inserted by F(No. 2)A 1992, s. 14 and Sch. 3, para. 59.

POWER TO VARY SPECIFIED SUMS BY ORDER

8 The Treasury may by order substitute for any of the sums for the time being specified in this Schedule such greater sums as they think fit.

Derivations – VATA 1983, s. 2C(2) and Sch. 1A, para. 8, as inserted by F(No. 2)A 1992, s. 14 and Sch. 3, para. 59.

SUPPLEMENTARY

9 Any notification required under this Schedule shall be made in such form and shall contain such particulars as the Commissioners may by regulations prescribe.

Derivations – VATA 1983, s. 2C(2) and Sch. 1A, para. 9, as inserted by F(No. 2)A 1992, s. 14 and Sch. 3, para. 59.

Statutory instruments – VAT Regulations 1995 (SI 1995/2518, as amended by SI 2000/794).

10 For the purposes of this Schedule a supply of goods is a **relevant supply** where–

(a)   the supply involves the removal of the goods to the United Kingdom by or under the directions of the person making the supply;

(b)   the supply does not involve the installation or assembly of the goods at a place in the United Kingdom;

(c)   the supply is a transaction in pursuance of which goods are acquired in the United Kingdom from another member State by a person who is not a taxable person;

(d)   the supply is made on or after 1st January 1993 and in the course or furtherance of a business carried on by the supplier; and

(e)   the supply is neither an exempt supply nor a supply of goods which are subject to a duty of excise or consist in a new means of transport and is not anything which is treated as a supply for the purposes of this Act by virtue only of paragraph 5(1) or 6 of Schedule 4.

Derivations – VATA 1983, s. 2C(2) and Sch. 1A, para. 10, as inserted by F(No. 2)A 1992, s. 14 and Sch. 3, para. 59.

Cross references – S. 7: place of supply.
S. 67 and s. 69(1)(a): penalties.
Official publications – 700/1A.

SCHEDULE 3 – REGISTRATION IN RESPECT OF ACQUISITIONS FROM OTHER MEMBER STATES

Section 3(2)

LIABILITY TO BE REGISTERED

1(1) A person who–

(a)   is not registered under this Act; and

(b)   is not liable to be registered under Schedule 1 or 2, becomes liable to be registered under this Schedule at the end of any month if, in the period beginning with 1st January of the year in which that month falls, that person has made relevant acquisitions whose value exceeds £52,000. 54K

1(2) A person who is not registered or liable to be registered as mentioned in sub-paragraph (1)(a) and (b) above becomes liable to be registered under this Schedule at any time if there are reasonable grounds for believing that the value of his relevant acquisitions in the period of 30 days then beginning will exceed £52,000.

1(3) A person shall be treated as having become liable to be registered under this Schedule at any time when he would have become so liable under the preceding provisions of this paragraph but for any registration which is subsequently cancelled under paragraph 6(3) below, paragraph 13(3) of Schedule 1, paragraph 6(2) of Schedule 2 or paragraph 6(2) of Schedule 3A.

1(4) A person shall not cease to be liable to be registered under this Schedule except in accordance with paragraph 2 below.

1(5) In determining the value of any person's relevant acquisitions for the purposes of this paragraph, so much of the consideration for any acquisition as represents any liability of the supplier, under the law of another member State, for VAT on the transaction in pursuance of which the acquisition is made, shall be disregarded.

1(6) In determining the value of a person's acquisitions for the purposes of sub-paragraph (1) or (2) above, acquisitions to which section 18B(4) (last acquisition or supply of goods before removal from fiscal warehousing) applies shall be disregarded.

History – Turnover threshold varied by statutory instrument under para. 9 as follows:

SI	Period of application	£
2000/804	From 1/4/2000	52,000
1999/595	1/4/99–31/3/2000	51,000
1998/761	1/4/98–31/3/99	50,000
1997/1628	1/1/98–31/3/98	49,000
1996/2950	1/1/97–31/12/97	48,000
1995/3037	1/1/96–31/12/96	47,000
1994/2905	1/1/95–31/12/95	46,000
1993/2953	1/1/94–31/12/94	45,000

In para. 1(3), the words ", paragraph 6(2) of Schedule 2 or paragraph 6(2) of Schedule 3A" were substituted for the words "or paragraph 6(2) of Schedule 2" by FA 2000, s. 136(7), with effect in relation to supplies made on or after 21 March 2000.
Para. 1(6) was added by FA 1996, s. 26 and Sch. 3, para. 15, with effect from 1 June 1996 and applies to any acquisition of goods from another member State and any supply taking place on or after that day.

Derivations – VATA 1983, s. 2C(2) and Sch. 1B, para. 1, as inserted by F(No. 2)A 1992, s. 14 and Sch. 3, para. 59, and as amended by SI 1993/766 and SI 1993/2953.

Cross references – S. 14: acquisitions from persons belonging in other member states.
S. 18B(5): relief for fiscally warehoused goods if disregard last acquisition or supply of goods before removal from fiscal warehousing.
VAT Regulations 1995 (SI 1995/2518), reg. 25(1): first return period.
VAT Regulations 1995 (SI 1995/2518), reg. 206 and 208: flat-rate farmers.

2(1) Subject to sub-paragraph (2) below, a person who has become liable to be registered under this Schedule shall cease to be so liable if at any time–

(a)   his relevant acquisitions in the year ending with 31st December last before that time did not have a value exceeding £52,000; and

(b)   the Commissioners are satisfied that the value of his relevant acquisitions in the year immediately following that year will not exceed £52,000.

2(2) A person shall not cease to be liable to be registered under this Schedule at any time if there are reasonable grounds for believing that the value of that person's relevant acquisitions in the period of 30 days then beginning will exceed £52,000.

History – Turnover threshold varied by statutory instrument under para. 9 as follows:

SI	Period of application	£
2000/804	From 1/4/2000	52,000
1999/595	1/4/99–31/3/2000	51,000
1998/761	1/4/98–31/3/99	50,000
1997/1628	1/1/98–31/3/98	49,000
1996/2950	1/1/97–31/12/97	48,000
1995/3037	1/1/96–31/12/96	47,000
1994/2905	1/1/95–31/12/95	46,000
1993/2953	1/1/94–31/12/94	45,000

Derivations – VATA 1983, s. 2C(2) and Sch. 1B, para. 2, as inserted by F(No. 2)A 1992, s. 14 and Sch. 3, para. 59, and as amended by SI 1993/766 and SI 1993/2953.

Cross references – VAT Regulations 1995 (SI 1995/2518), reg. 205: effective date of certificate for flat-rate farmer.

NOTIFICATION OF LIABILITY AND REGISTRATION

3(1) A person who becomes liable to be registered under this Schedule shall notify the Commissioners of the liability–

(a)   in the case of a liability under sub-paragraph (1) of paragraph 1 above, within 30 days of the end of the month when he becomes so liable; and

(b)   in the case of a liability under sub-paragraph (2) of that paragraph, before the end of the period by reference to which the liability arises.

3(2) The Commissioners shall register any such person (whether or not he so notifies them) with effect from the relevant time or from such earlier time as may be agreed between them and him.

3(3) In this paragraph **"the relevant time"**–

(a)   in a case falling within sub-paragraph (1)(a) above, means the end of the month following the month at the end of which the liability arose; and

(b)   in a case falling within sub-paragraph (1)(b), means the beginning of the period by reference to which the liability arose.

Derivations – VATA 1983, s. 2C(2) and Sch. 1B, para. 3, as inserted by F(No. 2)A 1992, s. 14 and Sch. 3, para. 59.
Cross references – S. 67: penalty for failure to notify.
VAT (Terminal Markets) Order 1973 (SI 1973/173), art. 6 : terminal markets and non-application of para. 3.
VAT Regulations 1995 (SI 1995/2518), reg. 5: registration and notification.
Other material – Form VAT 1B.

ENTITLEMENT TO BE REGISTERED ETC

4(1) Where a person who is not liable to be registered under this Act and is not already so registered satisfies the Commissioners that he makes relevant acquisitions, they shall, if he so requests, register him with effect from the day on which the request is made or from such earlier date as may be agreed between them and him.

4(2) Where a person who is not liable to be registered under this Act and is not already so registered–

(a)   satisfies the Commissioners that he intends to make relevant acquisitions from a specified date; and

(b)   requests to be registered under this Schedule,

the Commissioners may, subject to such conditions as they think fit to impose, register him with effect from such date as may be agreed between them and him.

4(3) Conditions imposed under sub-paragraph (2) above–

(a)   may be so imposed wholly or partly by reference to, or without reference to, any conditions prescribed for the purposes of this paragraph, and

(b)   may, whenever imposed, be subsequently varied by the Commissioners.

4(4) Where a person who is entitled to be registered under paragraph 9 or 10 of Schedule 1 requests registration under this paragraph, he shall be registered under that Schedule, and not under this Schedule.

Derivations – VATA 1983, s. 2C(2) and Sch. 1B, para. 4, as inserted by F(No. 2)A 1992, s. 14 and Sch. 3, para. 59.

NOTIFICATION OF MATTERS AFFECTING CONTINUANCE OF REGISTRATION

5(1) Any person registered under this Schedule who ceases to be registrable under this Act shall notify the Commissioners of that fact within 30 days of the day on which he does so.

5(2) A person registered under paragraph 4(2) above shall notify the Commissioners, within 30 days of the first occasion after his registration when he makes a relevant acquisition, that he has done so.

5(3) For the purposes of this paragraph a person **ceases to be registrable under this Act** where–

(a)   he ceases to be a person who would be liable or entitled to be registered under this Act if his registration and any enactment preventing a person from being liable to be registered under different provisions at the same time were disregarded; or

(b)   in the case of a person who (having been registered under paragraph 4(2) above) has not been such a person during the period of his registration, he ceases to have any intention of making relevant acquisitions.

Derivations – VATA 1983, s. 2C(2) and Sch. 1B, para. 5, as inserted by F(No. 2)A 1992, s. 14 and Sch. 3, para. 59.
Cross references – S. 69(1)(a): penalty for breach of regulations.
VAT Regulations 1995 (SI 1995/2518), reg. 5: notification to commissioners of variation of the register, etc.

CANCELLATION OF REGISTRATION

6(1) Subject to paragraph 7 below, where a person registered under this Schedule satisfies the Commissioners that he is not liable to be so registered, they shall, if he so requests, cancel his registration with effect from the day on which the request is made or from such later date as may be agreed between them and him.

6(2) Subject to paragraph 7 below, where the Commissioners are satisfied that a person registered under this Schedule has ceased since his registration to be registrable under this Schedule, they may cancel his registration with effect from the day on which he so ceased or from such later date as may be agreed between them and him.

6(3) Where the Commissioners are satisfied that, on the day on which a person was registered under this Schedule, he–

(a)   was not registrable under this Schedule; and

(b)   in the case of a person registered under paragraph 4(2) above, did not have the intention by reference to which he was registered,

they may cancel his registration with effect from that day.

6(4) Subject to paragraph 7 below, where the Commissioners are satisfied that a person who has been registered under paragraph 4(2) above and is not for the time being liable to be registered under this Schedule–

(a)   has not begun, by the date specified in his request to be registered, to make relevant acquisitions; or

(b)   has contravened any condition of his registration,

they may cancel his registration with effect from the date so specified or, as the case may be, the date of the contravention or from such later date as may be agreed between them and him.

6(5) For the purposes of this paragraph a person is **registrable under this Schedule** at any time when he is liable to be registered under this Schedule or is a person who makes relevant acquisitions.

Derivations – VATA 1983, s. 2C(2) and Sch. 1B, para. 6, as inserted by F(No. 2)A 1992, s. 14 and Sch. 3, para. 59.

Cross reference – VAT Regulations 1995 (SI 1995/2518), reg. 5: notification to commissioners of variation of the register, etc.

CONDITIONS OF CANCELLATION

7(1) The Commissioners shall not, under paragraph 6(1) above, cancel a person's registration with effect from any time unless they are satisfied that it is not a time when that person would be subject to a requirement to be registered under this Act.

7(2) The Commissioners shall not, under paragraph 6(2) or (4) above, cancel a person's registration with effect from any time unless they are satisfied that it is not a time when that person would be subject to a requirement, or entitled, to be registered under this Act.

7(3) Subject to sub-paragraph (4) below, the registration of a person who–

(a)   is registered under paragraph 4 above; or

(b)   would not, if he were not registered, be liable or entitled to be registered under any provision of this Act except paragraph 4 above,

shall not be cancelled with effect from any time before the 1st January which is, or next follows, the second anniversary of the date on which his registration took effect.

7(4) Sub-paragraph (3) above does not apply to cancellation under paragraph 6(3) or (4) above.

7(5) In determining for the purposes of this paragraph whether a person would be subject to a requirement, or entitled, to be registered at any time, so much of any provision of this Act as prevents a person from becoming liable or entitled to be registered when he is already registered or when he is so liable under any other provision shall be disregarded.

Derivations – VATA 1983, s. 2C(2) and Sch. 1B, para. 7, as inserted by F(No. 2)A 1992, s. 14 and Sch. 3, para. 59.

EXEMPTION FROM REGISTRATION

8(1) *Notwithstanding the preceding provisions of this Schedule, where a person who makes or intends to make relevant acquisitions satisfies the Commissioners that any such acquisition would be an acquisition in pursuance of a transaction which would be zero-rated if it were a taxable supply by a taxable person, they may, if he so requests and they think fit, exempt him from registration under this Schedule until it appears to them that the request should no longer be acted upon or is withdrawn.*

8(2)　Where a person who is exempted under this paragraph from registration under this Schedule makes any relevant acquisition in pursuance of any transaction which would, if it were a taxable supply by a taxable person, be chargeable to VAT otherwise than as a zero-rated supply, he shall notify the Commissioners of the change within 30 days of the date on which he made the acquisition.

Derivations – VATA 1983, s. 2C(2) and Sch. 1B, para. 8, as inserted by F(No. 2)A 1992, s. 14 and Sch. 3, para. 59.

Cross reference – S. 67: penalty for late notification.

POWER TO VARY SPECIFIED SUMS BY ORDER

9　The Treasury may by order substitute for any of the sums for the time being specified in this Schedule such greater sums as they think fit.

Derivations – VATA 1983, s. 2C(2) and Sch. 1B, para. 9, as inserted by F(No. 2)A 1992, s. 14 and Sch. 3, para. 59.

Statutory instruments – VAT (Increase of Registration Limits) Order 1994 (SI 1994/2905).
VAT (Increase of Registration Limits) Order 1995 (SI 1995/3037).
VAT (Increase of Registration Limits) Order 1996 (SI 1996/2950).
VAT (Increase of Registration Limits) Order 1997 (SI 1997/1628).
VAT (Increase of Registration Limits) Order 1998 (SI 1998/761).
VAT (Increase of Registration Limits) Order 1999 (SI 1999/595).
VAT (Increase of Registration Limits) Order 2000 (SI 2000/804).

SUPPLEMENTARY

10　Any notification required under this Schedule shall be made in such form and shall contain such particulars as the Commissioners may by regulations prescribe.

Derivations – VATA 1983, s. 2C(2) and Sch. 1B, para. 10, as inserted by F(No. 2)A 1992, s. 14 and Sch. 3, para. 59.

Statutory instruments – VAT Regulations 1995 (SI 1995/2518, as amended by SI 2000/794).

11　For the purposes of this Schedule an acquisition of goods from another member State is a **relevant acquisition** where–

(a)　it is a taxable acquisition of goods other than goods which are subject to a duty of excise or consist in a new means of transport;

(b)　it is an acquisition otherwise than in pursuance of a taxable supply and is treated, for the purposes of this Act, as taking place in the United Kingdom; and

(c)　the event which, in relation to that acquisition, is the first relevant event for the purposes of taxing that acquisition occurs on or after 1st January 1993.

Derivations – VATA 1983, s. 2C(2) and Sch. 1B, para. 11, as inserted by F(No. 2)A 1992, s. 14 and Sch. 3, para. 59.

Official publications – 700/1B.

SCHEDULE 3A – REGISTRATION IN RESPECT OF DISPOSALS OF ASSETS FOR WHICH A VAT REPAYMENT IS CLAIMED

Section 3(2)

History – Sch. 3A was inserted by FA 2000, s. 132(8) and Sch. 36, with effect in relation to relevant supplies made on or after 21 March 2000

LIABILITY TO BE REGISTERED

1(1)　A person who is not registered under this Act, and is not liable to be registered under Schedule 1, 2 or 3, becomes liable to be registered under this Schedule at any time–

(a)　if he makes relevant supplies; or

(b)　if there are reasonable grounds for believing that he will make such supplies in the period of 30 days then beginning.

1(2)　A person shall be treated as having become liable to be registered under this Schedule at any time when he would have become so liable under sub-paragraph (1) above but for any registration which is subsequently cancelled under paragraph 6(2) below, paragraph 13(3) of Schedule 1, paragraph 6(2) of Schedule 2 or paragraph 6(3) of Schedule 3.

1(3)　A person shall not cease to be liable to be registered under this Schedule except in accordance with paragraph 2 below.

2　A person who has become liable to be registered under this Schedule shall cease to be so liable at any time if the Commissioners are satisfied that he has ceased to make relevant supplies.

NOTIFICATION OF LIABILITY AND REGISTRATION

3(1) A person who becomes liable to be registered by virtue of paragraph 1(1)(a) above shall notify the Commissioners of the liability before the end of the period of 30 days beginning with the day on which the liability arises.

3(2) The Commissioners shall register any such person (whether or not he so notifies them) with effect from the beginning of the day on which the liability arises.
Cross references – VAT Regulations 1995 (SI 1995/2518), reg. 5: notification of liability and registration.

4(1) A person who becomes liable to be registered by virtue of paragraph 1(1)(b) above shall notify the Commissioners of the liability before the end of the period by reference to which the liability arises.

4(2) The Commissioners shall register any such person (whether or not he so notifies them) with effect from the beginning of the period by reference to which the liability arises.
Cross references – VAT Regulations 1995 (SI 1995/2518), reg. 5: notification of liability and registration.

NOTIFICATION OF END OF LIABILITY

5(1) Subject to sub-paragraph (2) below, a person registered under paragraph 3 or 4 above who ceases to make or have the intention of making relevant supplies shall notify the Commissioners of that fact within 30 days of the day on which he does so.

5(2) Sub-paragraph (1) above does not apply if the person would, when he so ceases, be otherwise liable or entitled to be registered under this Act if his registration and any enactment preventing a person from being liable to be registered under different provisions at the same time were disregarded.
Cross references – VAT Regulations 1995 (SI 1995/2518), reg. 5: notification of liability and registration.

CANCELLATION OF REGISTRATION

6(1) Subject to sub-paragraph (3) below, where the Commissioners are satisfied that a registered person has ceased to be liable to be registered under this Schedule, they may cancel his registration with effect from the day on which he so ceased or from such later date as may be agreed between them and him.

6(2) Where the Commissioners are satisfied that on the day on which a registered person was registered he was not registrable, they may cancel his registration with effect from that day.

6(3) The Commissioners shall not under sub-paragraph (1) above cancel a person's registration with effect from any time unless they are satisfied that it is not a time when that person would be subject to a requirement, or entitled, to be registered under this Act.

6(4) In determining for the purposes of sub-paragraph (3) above whether a person would be subject to a requirement, or entitled, to be registered at any time, so much of any provision of this Act as prevents a person from becoming liable or entitled to be registered when he is already registered or when he is so liable under any other provision shall be disregarded.

EXEMPTION FROM REGISTRATION

7(1) Notwithstanding the preceding provisions of this Schedule, where a person who makes or intends to make relevant supplies satisfies the Commissioners that any such supply is zero-rated or would be zero-rated if he were a taxable person, they may, if he so requests and they think fit, exempt him from registration under this Schedule.

7(2) Where there is a material change in the nature of the supplies made by a person exempted under this paragraph from registration under this Schedule, he shall notify the Commissioners of the change–

(a)   within 30 days of the date on which the change occurred; or

(b)   if no particular date is identifiable as the day on which it occurred, within 30 days of the end of the quarter in which it occurred.

7(3) Where there is a material alteration in any quarter in the proportion of relevant supplies of such a person that are zero-rated, he shall notify the Commissioners of the alteration within 30 days of the end of the quarter.

7(4) If it appears to the Commissioners that a request under sub-paragraph (1) above should no longer have been acted upon on or after any day, or has been withdrawn on any day, they shall register the person who made the request with effect from that day.

SUPPLEMENTARY

8   Any notification required under this Schedule shall be made in such form and shall contain such particulars as the Commissioners may by regulations prescribe.

Statutory instruments – VAT (Amendment) (No. 3) Regulations 2000 (SI 2000/794).

9(1)   For the purposes of this Schedule a supply of goods is a **relevant supply** where–

(a)   the supply is a taxable supply;

(b)   the goods are assets of the business in the course or furtherance of which they are supplied; and

(c)   the person by whom they are supplied, or a predecessor of his, has received or claimed, or is intending to claim, a repayment of VAT on the supply to him, or the importation by him, of the goods or of anything comprised in them.

9(2)   In relation to any goods, a person is the **predecessor** of another for the purposes of this paragraph if–

(a)   that other person is a person to whom he has transferred assets of his business by a transfer of that business, or part of it, as a going concern;

(b)   those assets consisted of or included those goods; and

(c)   the transfer of the assets is one falling by virtue of an order under section 5(3) (or under an enactment re-enacted in section 5(3)) to be treated as neither a supply of goods nor a supply of services;

and the reference in this paragraph to a person's **predecessor** includes references to the predecessors of his predecessor through any number of transfers.

9(3)   The reference in this paragraph to a **repayment of VAT** is a reference to such a repayment under a scheme embodied in regulations made under section 39.

SCHEDULE 4 – MATTERS TO BE TREATED AS SUPPLY OF GOODS OR SERVICES

Section 5

1(1)   Any transfer of the whole property in goods is a supply of goods; but, subject to sub-paragraph (2) below, the transfer–

(a)   of any undivided share of the property, or

(b)   of the possession of goods,

is a supply of services.

1(2)   If the possession of goods is transferred–

(a)   under an agreement for the sale of the goods, or

(b)   under agreements which expressly contemplate that the property also will pass at some time in the future (determined by, or ascertainable from, the agreements but in any case not later than when the goods are fully paid for),

it is then in either case a supply of the goods.

Derivations – VATA 1983, s. 3 and Sch. 2, para. 1.

Cross references – Sch. 8, Grp. 5, Note (11), Grp. 6, Note (8): supply of services described in para. 1(1) not included in item 2 of those groups (zero-rating: construction of dwellings etc.; alteration of protected buildings).

2   [Repealed by FA 1996, s. 29(4) and s. 205 and Sch. 41, Pt. IV(2) in relation to supplies made on or after 1 January 1996]

3   The supply of any form of power, heat, refrigeration or ventilation is a supply of goods.

Derivations – VATA 1983, s. 3 and Sch. 2, para. 3.

Note – VAT (Water) Order 1989 (SI 1989/1114), art. 2: a water supply is a supply of goods.

4   The grant, assignment or surrender of a major interest in land is a supply of goods.

Derivations – VATA 1983, s. 3 and Sch. 2, para. 4, as amended by FA 1989, s. 18 and Sch. 3, para. 11(a).

Cross reference – VAT Regulations 1995 (SI 1995/2518), reg. 85(1): leases treated as a supply of goods and consideration is payable periodically.

Note – S. 96(1): "major interest" defined.

5(1)   Subject to sub-paragraph (2) below, where goods forming part of the assets of a business are transferred or disposed of by or under the directions of the person carrying on the business so as no longer to form part of those assets, whether or not for a consideration, that is a supply by him of goods.

5(2) Sub-paragraph (1) above does not apply where the transfer or disposal is–

(a) a gift of goods made in the course or furtherance of the business (otherwise than as one forming part of a series or succession of gifts made to the same person from time to time) where the cost to the donor of acquiring or, as the case may be, producing the goods was not more than £~~15~~; 50

(b) subject to sub-paragraph (3) below, a gift to any person of a sample of any goods.

5(2A) For the purposes of determining the cost to the donor of acquiring or producing goods of which he has made a gift, where–

(a) the acquisition by the donor of the goods, or anything comprised in the goods, was by means of a transfer of a business, or a part of a business, as a going concern,

(b) the assets transferred by that transfer included those goods or that thing, and

(c) the transfer of those assets is one falling by virtue of an order under section 5(3)(or under an enactment re-enacted in section 5(3)) to be treated as neither a supply of goods nor a supply of services,

the donor and his predecessor or, as the case may be, all of his predecessors shall be treated as if they were the same person.

5(3) Where–

(a) a person is given a number of samples by the same person (whether all on one occasion or on different occasions), and

(b) those samples are identical or do not differ in any material respect from each other,

sub-paragraph (1) above shall apply to all except one of those samples or, as the case may be, to all except the first to be given.

5(4) Where by or under the directions of a person carrying on a business goods held or used for the purposes of the business are put to any private use or are used, or made available to any person for use, for any purpose other than a purpose of the business, whether or not for a consideration, that is a supply of services.

5(5) Neither sub-paragraph (1) nor sub-paragraph (4) above shall require anything which a person carrying on a business does otherwise than for a consideration in relation to any goods to be treated as a supply except in a case where that person or any of his predecessors is a person who (disregarding this paragraph) has or will become entitled

(a) under sections 25 and 26, to credit for the whole or any part of the VAT on the supply, acquisition or importation of those goods or of anything comprised in them; or

(b) under a scheme embodied in regulations made under section 39, to a repayment of VAT on the supply or importation of those goods or of anything comprised in them..

5(5A) In relation to any goods or anything comprised in any goods, a person is the **predecessor** of another for the purposes of this paragraph if–

(a) that other person is a person to whom he has transferred assets of his business by a transfer of that business, or a part of it, as a going concern;

(b) those assets consisted of or included those goods or that thing; and

(c) the transfer of the assets is one falling by virtue of an order under section 5(3) (or under an enactment re-enacted in section 5(3)) to be treated as neither a supply of goods nor a supply of services;

and references in this paragraph to a person's predecessors include references to the predecessors of his predecessors through any number of transfers.

5(6) Anything which is a supply of goods or services by virtue of sub-paragraph (1) or (4) above is to be treated as made in the course or furtherance of the business (if it would not otherwise be so treated); and in the case of a business carried on by an individual–

(a) sub-paragraph (1) above applies to any transfer or disposition of goods in favour of himself personally; and

(b) sub-paragraph (4) above applies to goods used, or made available for use, by himself personally.

5(7) The Treasury may by order substitute for the sum for the time being specified in sub-paragraph (2)(a) above such sum, not being less than £10, as they think fit.

History – In para. 5(2)(a), the words "of acquiring or, as the case may be, producing the goods was" were substituted by FA 1998, s. 21(2), with effect where the time when the goods are transferred or disposed of or, as the case may be, put to use, used or made available for use is on or after 17 March 1998.
In para. 5(2)(a), the amount "£15" was substituted by FA 1996, s. 33(1), in relation to gifts made after 28 November 1995.

Para. 5(2A) was inserted by FA 1998, s. 21(3), with effect where the time when the goods are transferred or disposed of or, as the case may be, put to use, used or made available for use is on or after 17 March 1998.
In para. 5(5), the words "sub-paragraph (4) above" were substituted by FA 1995, s. 33(3)(a), with effect as if para. 5(5) had been originally enacted with this substitution.
In para. 5(5), the words "or any of his predecessors is a person who (disregarding this paragraph) has or will become" were substituted by FA 1998, s. 21(4), with effect where the time when the goods are transferred or disposed of or, as the case may be, put to use, used or made available for use is on or after 17 March 1998.
Para. 5(5)(a) and (b) were substituted for the words "under sections 25 and 26 to credit for the whole or any part of the VAT on the supply, acquisition or importation of those goods or of anything comprised in them" by FA 2000, s. 136(9), with effect in relation to supplies made on or after 21 March 2000.
Para. 5(5A) was inserted by FA 1998, s. 21(5), with effect where the time when the goods are transferred or disposed of or, as the case may be, put to use, used or made available for use is on or after 17 March 1998.
In para. 5(6)(b), the words "sub-paragraph (4) above" were substituted by FA 1995, s. 33(3)(a), with effect as if para. 5(6)(b) had been originally enacted with this substitution.
Para. 5(7) was inserted by FA 1996, s. 33(2) with effect from 29 April 1996

Derivations – Para. 5(1): VATA 1983, s. 3 and Sch. 2, para. 5(1), as amended by FA 1989, s. 18 and Sch. 3, para. 11(b).
Para. 5(2): VATA 1983, Sch. 2, para. 5(2), as amended by FA 1993, s. 47(2).
Para. 5(3): VATA 1983, s. 3 and Sch. 2, para. 5(2A), as inserted by FA 1993, s. 47(3).
Para. 5(4): VATA 1983, s. 3 and Sch. 2, para. 5(3).
Para. 5(5): VATA 1983, s. 3 and Sch. 2, para. 5(3A), as inserted by FA 1993, s. 47(4).
Para. 5(6): VATA 1983, s. 3 and Sch. 2, para. 5(4).

Cross references – S. 6: time of supply.
S. 97(4)(ab): approval of an order by the House of Commons.
Sch. 2: registration in respect of supplies from other member states.
Sch. 6, para. 6(1)(b), 7, 8(b): valuation rules.
Sch. 7, para. 3(1): valuation of acquisitions from other member states.
Sch. 8, Grp. 5, Note (11), Grp. 6, Note (8): supply of services described in para. 5(3) not included in item 2 of those groups (zero-rating: construction of dwellings, etc.; alteration of protected buildings).
Sch. 9, Grp. 10, Note (7): sport, sports competitions and physical education.
VAT Regulations 1995 (SI 1995/2518), reg. 81: time of supply and goods for private use and free supplies of services.

Official publications – 700/35: business gifts and samples.

Other material – Customs and Excise Press Notice 889, 1 March 1984: procedure for use of "tax certificate" on a gift of goods costing more than £10.

6(1)   Where, in a case not falling within paragraph 5(1) above, goods forming part of the assets of any business–

(a)   are removed from any member State by or under the directions of the person carrying on the business; and

(b)   are so removed in the course or furtherance of that business for the purpose of being taken to a place in a member State other than that from which they are removed,

then, whether or not the removal is or is connected with a transaction for a consideration, that is a supply of goods by that person.

6(2)   Sub-paragraph (1) above does not apply–

(a)   to the removal of goods from any member State in the course of their removal from one part of that member State to another part of the same member State; or

(b)   to goods which have been removed from a place outside the member States for entry into the territory of the Community and are removed from a member State before the time when any Community customs debt in respect of any Community customs duty on their entry into that territory would be incurred.

Derivations – VATA 1983, s. 3 and Sch. 2, para. 5A, as inserted by F(No. 2)A 1992, s. 14 and Sch. 3, para. 60(1).

Cross references – Sch. 2: registration in respect of supplies from other member states.
Sch. 6, para. 6(1)(b): valuation rules.
Sch. 7, para. 3(1): valuation of acquisitions from other member states.
VAT (Removal of Goods) Order 1992 (SI 1992/3111), art. 4 and 5: application of para. 6.

7   Where in the case of a business carried on by a taxable person goods forming part of the assets of the business are, under any power exercisable by another person, sold by the other in or towards satisfaction of a debt owed by the taxable person, they shall be deemed to be supplied by the taxable person in the course or furtherance of his business.

Derivations – VATA 1983, s. 3 and Sch. 2, para. 6.

Cross references – S. 88(6): supplies spanning change of rate.
VAT Regulations 1995 (SI 1995/2518), reg. 13(2): VAT invoice provided by auctioneer, etc.
VAT Regulations 1995 (SI 1995/2518), reg. 27: returns by auctioneer, etc.

Other material – Form VAT 833.

8(1)   Where a person ceases to be a taxable person, any goods then forming part of the assets of a business carried on by him shall be deemed to be supplied by him in the course or furtherance of his business immediately before he ceases to be a taxable person, unless–

(a)   the business is transferred as a going concern to another taxable person; or

(b)   the business is carried on by another person who, under regulations made under section 46(4), is treated as a taxable person; or

(c)   the VAT on the deemed supply would not be more than £1,000.

8(2) This paragraph does not apply to any goods in the case of which the taxable person can show to the satisfaction of the Commissioners–

(a) that no credit for input tax has been allowed to him in respect of the supply of the goods, their acquisition from another member State or their importation from a place outside the member States;

(b) that the goods did not become his as part of the assets of a business which was transferred to him as a going concern by another taxable person; and

(c) that he has not obtained relief in respect of the goods under section 4 of the Finance Act 1973.

8(3) This paragraph does not apply where a person ceases to be a taxable person in consequence of having been certified under section 54.

8(4) The Treasury may by order increase or further increase the sum specified in sub-paragraph (1)(c) above.

History – In para. 8(1)(c), the words "£1,000" were substituted for the words "£250" by SI 2000/266, art. 2, operative in relation to a person who ceases to be a taxable person on or after 1 April 2000.

Derivations – Para. 8(1): VATA 1983, s. 3 and Sch. 2, para. 7(1).
Para. 8(2): VATA 1983, s. 3 and Sch. 2, para. 7(2), as amended by F(No. 2)A 1992, s. 14 and Sch. 3, para. 60(2)(a) and (b).
Para. 8(3): VATA 1983, s. 3 and Sch. 2, para. 7(2A), as inserted by F(No. 2)A 1992, s. 16(4).
Para. 8(4): VATA 1983, s. 3 and Sch. 2, para. 7(3).

Cross references – VAT (Isle of Man) Order 1982 (SI 1982/1067), art. 11(8): persons registered under the Manx Act.
VAT Regulations 1995 (SI 1995/2518), reg. 115(3)(b): capital goods scheme.
VAT Regulations 1995 (SI 1995/2518), reg. 208: further certification.

Statutory instruments – VAT (Deemed Supply of Goods) Order 2000 (SI 2000/266).

9(1) Subject to sub-paragraphs (2) and (3) below, paragraphs 5 to 8 above have effect in relation to land forming part of the assets of, or held or used for the purposes of, a business as if it were goods forming part of the assets of, or held or used for the purposes of, a business.

9(2) In the application of those paragraphs by virtue of sub-paragraph (1) above, references to transfer, disposition or sale shall have effect as references to the grant or assignment of any interest in, right over or licence to occupy the land concerned.

9(3) Except in relation to–

(a) the grant or assignment of a major interest; or

(b) a grant or assignment otherwise than for a consideration,

in the application of paragraph 5(1) above by virtue of sub-paragraph (1) above the reference to a **supply of goods** shall have effect as a reference to a supply of services.

Derivations – VATA 1983, s. 3 and Sch. 2, para. 8, as inserted by FA 1989, s. 18 and Sch. 3, para. 11(c).

Cross references – Sch. 9, Grp. 10, Note (7): sport, sports competitions and physical education.

SCHEDULE 5 – SERVICES SUPPLIED WHERE RECEIVED

Section 8

Cross references – S. 8(7): power of the Treasury to amend Sch. 5.
S. 43(2A)(c), (2D) and (2E): group supplies using an overseas member and services falling within Sch. 5, para. 1–8.

1 Transfers and assignments of copyright, patents, licences, trademarks and similar rights.
Derivations – VATA 1983, s. 7 and Sch. 3, para. 1.

2 Advertising services.
Derivations – VATA 1983, s. 7 and Sch. 3, para. 2.

3 Services of consultants, engineers, consultancy bureaux, lawyers, accountants and other similar services; data processing and provision of information (but excluding from this head any services relating to land).
Derivations – VATA 1983, s. 7 and Sch. 3, para. 3.

4 Acceptance of any obligation to refrain from pursuing or exercising, in whole or part, any *business activity or any such rights* as are referred to in paragraph 1 above.
Derivations – VATA 1983, s. 7 and Sch. 3, para. 4.

5 Banking, financial and insurance services (including reinsurance, but not including the provision of safe deposit facilities).
Derivations – VATA 1983, s. 7 and Sch. 3, para. 5.

6 The supply of staff.

Derivations – VATA 1983, s. 7 and Sch. 3, para. 6.

7   The letting on hire of goods other than means of transport.

Derivations – VATA 1983, s. 7 and Sch. 3, para. 6A, as added by SI 1985/799.

7A   Telecommunications services, that is to say services relating to the transmission, emission or reception of signals, writing, images and sounds or information of any nature by wire, radio, optical or other electromagnetic systems, including the transfer or assignment of the right to use capacity for such transmission, emission or reception.

History – Para. 7A was inserted by SI 1997/1523, art. 3(2), with effect in relation to any services performed on or after 1 July 1997.

Cross references – VAT Regulations 1995 (SI 1995/2518), reg. 90(5): relevant telecommunications services.
VAT (Reverse Charge) (Anti-avoidance) Order 1997 (SI 1997/1523), art. 2: "relevant telecommunications services".

8   The services rendered by one person to another in procuring for the other any of the services mentioned in paragraphs 1 to 7A above.

History – In para. 8, the words "paragraphs 1 to 7A" were substituted for the words "paragraphs 1 to 7" by SI 1997/1523, art. 3(3), with effect in relation to any services performed on or after 1 July 1997.

Derivations – (as originally enacted) VATA 1983, s. 7 and Sch. 3, para. 7, as amended by SI 1985/799.

9   Any services not of a description specified in paragraphs 1 to 7 and 8 above when supplied to a recipient who is registered under this Act.

History – In para. 9, the words "paragraphs 1 to 7 and 8" were substituted for the words "paragraphs 1 to 8" by SI 1997/1523, art. 3(4), with effect in relation to any services performed on or after 1 July 1997.

Derivations – (as originally enacted) VATA 1983, s. 7 and Sch. 3, para. 8, as added by SI 1992/3128, art. 2 and as substituted by SI 1993/2328 art. 3.

10   Section 8(1) shall have effect in relation to any service–

(a)   which are of a description specified in paragraph 9 above; and

(b)   whose place of supply is determined by an order under section 7(11) to be in the United Kingdom,

as if the recipient belonged in the United Kingdom for the purposes of section 8(1)(b).

Derivations – SI 1993/2328, art. 4.

Cross references – S. 8: reverse charge on supplies received from abroad.
S. 43(2A)(a): group supplies using an overseas member.
VAT (Place of Supply of Services) Order 1992 (SI 1992/3121), art. 16: services supplied where received.

Notes – In the Queen's printer's version, in Sch. 5, para. 10 the word "service" would appear to have been used in error instead of the word "services".

SCHEDULE 5A – GOODS ELIGIBLE TO BE FISCALLY WAREHOUSED

Section 18B

History – Sch. 5A was inserted by FA 1996, s. 26 and Sch. 3, para. 18, with effect from 1 June 1996 and applies to any acquisition of goods from another member State and any supply taking place on or after that day.

Description of goods	*Combined nomenclature code of the European Communities*
Tin	8001
Copper	7402
	7403
	7405
	7408
Zinc	7901
Nickel	7502
Aluminium	7601
Lead	7801
Indium	ex 811291
	ex 811299

Description of goods	Combined nomenclature code of the European Communities
Cereals	1001 to 1005
	1006: unprocessed rice only
	1007 to 1008
Oil seeds and oleaginous fruit	1201 to 1207
Coconuts, Brazil nuts and cashew nuts	0801
Other nuts	0502
Olives	071120
Grains and seeds (including soya beans)	1201 to 1207
Coffee, not roasted	0901 11 00
	0901 12 00
Tea	0902
Cocoa beans, whole or broken, raw or roasted	1801
Raw sugar	1701 11
	1701 12
Rubber, in primary forms or in plates, sheets or strip	4001
	4002
Wool	5101
Chemicals in bulk	Chapters 28 and 29
Mineral oils (including propane and butane; also including crude petroleum oils)	2709
	2710
	2711 12
	2711 13
Silver	7106
Platinum (palladium, rhodium)	7110 11 00
	7110 21 00
	7110 31 00
Potatoes	0701
Vegetable oils and fats and their fractions, whether or not refined, but not chemically modified	1507 to 1515

SCHEDULE 6 – VALUATION: SPECIAL CASES

Section 19

1(1) Where–

(a) the value of a supply made by a taxable person for a consideration in money is (apart from this paragraph) less than its open market value, and

(b) the person making the supply and the person to whom it is made are connected, and

(c) if the supply is a taxable supply, the person to whom the supply is made is not entitled under sections 25 and 26 to credit for all the VAT on the supply,

the Commissioners may direct that the value of the supply shall be taken to be its open market value.

1(2) A direction under this paragraph shall be given by notice in writing to the person making the supply, but no direction maybe given more than 3 years after the time of the supply.

1(3) A direction given to a person under this paragraph in respect of a supply made by him may include a direction that the value of any supply–

(a) which is made by him after the giving of the notice, or after such later date as may be specified in the notice, and

(b) as to which the conditions in paragraphs (a) to (c) of sub-paragraph (1) above are satisfied,

shall be taken to be its open market value.

1(4) For the purposes of this paragraph any question whether a person is **connected** with another shall be determined in accordance with section 839 of the Taxes Act.

1(5) This paragraph does not apply to a supply to which paragraph 10 below applies.

Derivations – VATA 1983, s. 10(6), 11(4) and Sch. 4, para. 1, as amended by FA 1987, s. 17(1).

Cross references – S. 43(2C)(b): group supplies using an overseas member.
S. 83(v): appeals.
Sch. 9A, para. 1(9): anti-avoidance and VAT groups where there is a direction.
Notes – S. 19(5): "open market value" defined.
ICTA 1988, s. 839 is reproduced in *Tax Statutes and Statutory Instruments*, vol. 1A.

2   Where–

(a)   the whole or part of a business carried on by a taxable person consists in supplying to a number of persons goods to be sold, whether by them or others, by retail, and

(b)   those persons are not taxable persons,

the Commissioners may by notice in writing to the taxable person direct that the value of any such supply by him after the giving of the notice or after such later date as may be specified in the notice shall be taken to be its open market value on a sale by retail.

Derivations – VATA 1983, s. 10(6), 11(4) and Sch. 4, para. 3.

Cross reference – S. 83(v): appeals.

3(1)   Where–

(a)   any goods whose supply involves their removal to the United Kingdom–
   (i)   are charged in connection with their removal to the United Kingdom with a duty of excise; or
   (ii)   on that removal are subject, in accordance with any provision for the time being having effect for transitional purposes in connection with the accession of any State to the European Communities, to any Community customs duty or agricultural levy of the Economic Community; or

(b)   the time of supply of any dutiable goods, or of any goods which comprise a mixture of dutiable goods and other goods, is determined under section 18(4) to be the duty point,

then the value of the supply shall be taken for the purposes of this Act to be the sum of its value apart from this paragraph and the amount, so far as not already included in that value, of the duty or, as the case may be, agricultural levy which has been or is to be paid in respect of the goods.

3(2)   In this paragraph **"dutiable goods"** and **"duty point"** have the same meanings as in section 18.

Derivations – VATA 1983, s. 10(6), 11(4) and Sch. 4, para. 3A, as inserted by F(No. 2)A 1992, s. 14 and Sch. 3, para. 61(2), as amended by FA 1993, s. 50(2), 213 and Sch. 23.

4(1)   Where goods or services are supplied for a consideration in money and on terms allowing a discount for prompt payment, the consideration shall be taken for the purposes of section 19 as reduced by the discount, whether or not payment is made in accordance with those terms.

4(2)   This paragraph does not apply where the terms include any provision for payment by instalments.

Derivations – VATA 1983, s. 10(6), 11(4) and Sch. 4, para. 4.

5   Where a right to receive goods or services for an amount stated on any token, stamp or voucher is granted for a consideration, the consideration shall be disregarded for the purposes of this Act except to the extent (if any) that it exceeds that amount.

Derivations – VATA 1983, s. 10(6), 11(4) and Sch. 4, para. 6.

6(1)   Where there is a supply of goods by virtue of–

(a)   a Treasury order under section 5(5); or

(b)   paragraph 5(1) or 6 of Schedule 4 but otherwise than for a consideration; or

(c)   paragraph 8 of that Schedule,

then, except where paragraph 10 below applies, the value of the supply shall be determined as follows.

6(2)   The value of the supply shall be taken to be–

(a)   such consideration in money as would be payable by the person making the supply if he were, at the time of the supply, to purchase goods identical in every respect (including age and condition) to the goods concerned; or

(b)   where the value cannot be ascertained in accordance with paragraph (a) above, such consideration in money as would be payable by that person if he were, at that time, to purchase goods similar to, and of the same age and condition as, the goods concerned; or

(c)   where the value can be ascertained in accordance with neither paragraph (a) nor paragraph (b) above, the cost of producing the goods concerned if they were produced at that time.

6(3) For the purposes of sub-paragraph (2) above the amount of consideration in money that would be payable by any person if he were to purchase any goods shall be taken to be the amount that would be so payable after the deduction of any amount included in the purchase price in respect of VAT on the supply of the goods to that person.

Derivations – VATA 1983, s. 10(6), 11(4) and Sch. 4, para. 7, as amended by F(No. 2)A 1992, s. 14 and Sch. 3, para. 61(3).

7 Where there is a supply of services by virtue of–

(a)   a Treasury order under section 5(4); or

(b)   paragraph 5(4) of Schedule 4 (but otherwise than for a consideration),

the value of the supply shall be taken to be the full cost to the taxable person of providing the services except where paragraph 10 below applies.

History – In para. 7(b), the words "paragraph 5(4)" were substituted by FA 1995, s. 33(3)(b), with effect as if para. 7(b) had been originally enacted with this substitution.

Derivations – (as originally enacted) – VATA 1983, s. 10(6), 11(4) and Sch. 4, para. 8.

8 Where any supply of services is treated by virtue of section 8 as made by the person by whom they are received, the value of the supply shall be taken–

(a)   in a case where the consideration for which the services were in fact supplied to him was a consideration in money, to be such amount as is equal to that consideration; and

(b)   in a case where that consideration did not consist or not wholly consist of money, to be such amount in money as is equivalent to that consideration.

Derivations – VATA 1983, s. 10(6), 11(4) and Sch. 4, para. 8A, as inserted by F(No. 2)A 1992, s. 14 and Sch. 3, para. 61(4).

Cross references – VAT (Reverse Charge) (Anti-avoidance) Order 1997 (SI 1997/2513), art. 7 and 8: value of relevant telecommunications services.

9(1) This paragraph applies where a supply of services consists in the provision of accommodation falling within paragraph (d) of Item 1 of Group 1 in Schedule 9 and–

(a)   that provision is made to an individual for a period exceeding 4 weeks; and

(b)   throughout that period the accommodation is provided for the use of the individual either alone or together with one or more other persons who occupy the accommodation with him otherwise than at their own expense (whether incurred directly or indirectly).

9(2) Where this paragraph applies–

(a)   the value of so much of the supply as is in excess of 4 weeks shall be taken to be reduced to such part thereof as is attributable to facilities other than the right to occupy the accommodation; and

(b)   that part shall be taken to be not less than 20 per cent.

Derivations – VATA 1983, s. 10(6), 11(4) and Sch. 4, para. 9, as amended by FA 1986, s. 11 and FA 1989, s. 18 and Sch. 3, para. 4(2).

Official publications – 709/3.

10(1) This paragraph applies to a supply of goods or services, whether or not for a consideration, which is made by an employer and consists of–

(a)   the provision in the course of catering of food or beverages to his employees, or

(b)   the provision of accommodation for his employees in a hotel, inn, boarding house or similar establishment.

10(2) The value of a supply to which this paragraph applies shall be taken to be nil unless the supply is for a consideration consisting wholly or partly of money, and in that case its value shall be determined without regard to any consideration other than money.

Derivations – VATA 1983, s. 10(6), 11(4) and Sch. 4, para. 10.

Cross reference – VAT (Supply of Services) Order 1993 (SI 1993/1507), art. 6: disapplication where services of a description within para. 10(1).

11(1) Subject to the following provisions of this paragraph, where–

(a)   there is a supply of goods or services; and

(b)   any sum relevant for determining the value of the supply is expressed in a currency other than sterling,

then, for the purpose of valuing the supply, that sum is to be converted into sterling at the market rate which, on the relevant day, would apply in the United Kingdom to a purchase with sterling by the person to whom they are supplied of that sum in the currency in question.

11(2) Where the Commissioners have published a notice which, for the purposes of this paragraph, specifies–

(a)   rates of exchange; or

(b)   methods of determining rates of exchange,

a rate specified in or determined in accordance with the notice, as for the time being in force, shall apply (instead of the rate for which sub-paragraph (1) above provides) in the case of any supply by a person who opts, in such manner as may be allowed by the Commissioners, for the use of that rate in relation to that supply.

11(3)   An option for the purposes of sub-paragraph (2) above for the use of a particular rate or method of determining a rate–

(a)   shall not be exercised by any person except in relation to all such supplies by him as are of a particular description or after a particular date; and

(b)   shall not be withdrawn or varied except with the consent of the Commissioners and in such manner as they may require.

11(4)   In specifying a method of determining a rate of exchange a notice published by the Commissioners under sub-paragraph (2) above may allow a person to apply to the Commissioners for the use, for the purpose of valuing some or all of his supplies, of a rate of exchange which is different from any which would otherwise apply.

11(5)   On an application made in accordance with provision contained in a notice under sub-paragraph (4) above, the Commissioners may authorise the use with respect to the applicant of such a rate of exchange, in such circumstances, in relation to such supplies and subject to such conditions as they think fit.

11(6)   A notice published by the Commissioners for the purposes of this paragraph may be withdrawn or varied by a subsequent notice published by the Commissioners.

11(7)   The time by reference to which the appropriate rate of exchange is to be determined for the purpose of valuing any supply is the time when the supply takes place; and, accordingly, the day on which it takes place is the relevant day for the purposes of sub-paragraph (1) above.

Derivations – VATA 1983, s. 10(6), 11(4) and Sch. 4, para. 11, as substituted by F(No. 2)A 1992, s. 14 and Sch. 3, para. 61(5).

12   Regulations may require that in prescribed circumstances there is to be taken into account, as constituting part of the consideration for the purposes of section 19(2) (where it would not otherwise be so taken into account), money paid in respect of the supply by persons other than those to whom the supply is made.

Derivations – VATA 1983, s. 10(6), 11(4) and Sch. 4, para. 12.

13   A direction under paragraph 1 or 2 above may be varied or withdrawn by the Commissioners by a further direction given by notice in writing.

Derivations – VATA 1983, s. 10(6), 11(4) and Sch. 4, para. 13.

SCHEDULE 7 – VALUATION OF ACQUISITIONS FROM OTHER MEMBER STATES: SPECIAL CASES

Section 20

1(1)   Where, in the case of the acquisition of any goods from another member State–

(a)   the relevant transaction is for a consideration in money;

(b)   the value of the relevant transaction is (apart from this paragraph) less than the transaction's open market value;

(c)   the supplier and the person who acquires the goods are connected; and

(d)   that person is not entitled under sections 25 and 26 to credit for all the VAT on the acquisition,

the Commissioners may direct that the value of the relevant transaction shall be taken to be its open market value.

1(2)   A direction under this paragraph shall be given by notice in writing to the person by whom the acquisition in question is made; but no direction may be given more than 3 years after the relevant time.

1(3)   A direction given to a person under this paragraph in respect of a transaction may include a direction that the value of any transaction–

(a)   in pursuance of which goods are acquired by him from another member State after the giving of the notice, or after such later date as may be specified in the notice; and

(b)   as to which the conditions in paragraphs (a) to (d) of sub-paragraph (1) above are satisfied,

shall be taken to be its open market value.

1(4) For the purposes of this paragraph the **open market value** of a transaction in pursuance of which goods are acquired from another member State shall be taken to be the amount which would fall to be taken as its value under section 20(3) if it were for such consideration in money as would be payable by a person standing in no such relationship with any person as would affect that consideration.

1(5) For the purposes of this paragraph any question whether a person is **connected** with another shall be determined in accordance with section 839 of the Taxes Act.

1(6) A direction under this paragraph may be varied or withdrawn by the Commissioners by a further direction given by notice in writing.

Derivations – VATA 1983, s. 10A and Sch. 4A, para. 1, as inserted by F(No. 2)A 1992, s. 14 and Sch. 3, para. 62.

Cross reference – S. 83(w): appeals.

Note – ICTA 1988, s. 839 of the Taxes Act is reproduced in *Tax Statutes and Statutory Instruments*, vol. 1A.

2(1) Where, in such cases as the Commissioners may by regulations prescribe, goods acquired in the United Kingdom from another member State–

(a) are charged in connection with their removal to the United Kingdom with a duty of excise; or

(b) on that removal are subject, in accordance with any provision for the time being having effect for transitional purposes in connection with the accession of any State to the European Communities, to any Community customs duty or agricultural levy of the Economic Community,

then the value of the relevant transaction shall be taken for the purposes of this Act to be the sum of its value apart from this paragraph and the amount, so far as not already included in that value, of the duty or, as the case may be, agricultural levy which has been or is to be paid in respect of those goods.

2(2) Sub-paragraph (1) above shall not require the inclusion of any amount of duty or agricultural levy in the value of a transaction in pursuance of which there is an acquisition of goods which, under subsection (4) of section 18, is treated as taking place before the time which is the duty point within the meaning of that section.

Derivations – VATA 1983, s. 10A and Sch. 4A, para. 2, as inserted by F(No. 2)A 1992, s. 14 and Sch. 3, para. 62.

Cross reference – VAT Regulations 1995 (SI 1995/2518), reg. 97(1): value of acquisitions.

Statutory instrument – VAT Regulations 1995 (SI 1995/2518).

3(1) Where goods are acquired from another member State in pursuance of anything which is treated as a supply for the purposes of this Act by virtue of paragraph 5(1) or 6 of Schedule 4, the value of the relevant transaction shall be determined, in a case where there is no consideration, as follows.

3(2) The value of the transaction shall be taken to be–

(a) such consideration in money as would be payable by the supplier if he were, at the time of the acquisition, to purchase goods identical in every respect (including age and condition) to the goods concerned; or

(b) where the value cannot be ascertained in accordance with paragraph (a) above, such consideration in money as would be payable by the supplier if he were, at that time, to purchase goods similar to, and of the same age and condition as, the goods concerned; or

(c) where the value can be ascertained in accordance with neither paragraph (a) nor paragraph (b) above, the cost of producing the goods concerned if they were produced at that time.

3(3) For the purposes of sub-paragraph (2) above the amount of consideration in money that would be payable by any person if he were to purchase any goods shall be taken to be the amount that would be so payable after the deduction of any amount included in the purchase price in respect of VAT on the supply of the goods to that person.

Derivations – VATA 1983, s. 10A and Sch. 4A, para. 3, as inserted by F(No. 2)A 1992, s. 14 and Sch. 3, para. 62.

4(1) Subject to the following provisions of this paragraph, where–

(a) goods are acquired from another member State; and

(b) any sum relevant for determining the value of the relevant transaction is expressed in a currency other than sterling,

then, for the purpose of valuing the relevant transaction, that sum is to be converted into sterling at the market rate which, on the relevant day, would apply in the United Kingdom to a purchase with sterling by the person making the acquisition of that sum in the currency in question.

4(2) Where the Commissioners have published a notice which, for the purposes of this paragraph, specifies–

(a) rates of exchange; or

(b) methods of determining rates of exchange,

a rate specified in or determined in accordance with the notice, as for the time being in force, shall apply (instead of the rate for which sub-paragraph (1) above provides) in the case of any transaction in pursuance of which goods are acquired by a person who opts, in such manner as may be allowed by the Commissioners, for the use of that rate in relation to that transaction.

4(3) An option for the purposes of sub-paragraph (2) above for the use of a particular rate or method of determining a rate–

(a) shall not be exercised by any person except in relation to all such transactions in pursuance of which goods are acquired by him from another member State as are of a particular description or after a particular date; and

(b) shall not be withdrawn or varied except with the consent of the Commissioners and in such manner as they may require.

4(4) In specifying a method of determining a rate of exchange a notice published by the Commissioners under sub-paragraph (2) above may allow a person to apply to the Commissioners for the use, for the purpose of valuing some or all of the transactions in pursuance of which goods are acquired by him from another member State, of a rate of exchange which is different from any which would otherwise apply.

4(5) On an application made in accordance with provision contained in a notice under sub-paragraph (4) above, the Commissioners may authorise the use with respect to the applicant of such a rate of exchange, in such circumstances, in relation to such transactions and subject to such conditions as they think fit.

4(6) A notice published by the Commissioners for the purposes of this paragraph may be withdrawn or varied by a subsequent notice published by the Commissioners.

4(7) Where goods are acquired from another member State, the appropriate rate of exchange is to be determined for the purpose of valuing the relevant transaction by reference to the relevant time; and, accordingly, the day on which that time falls is the **relevant day** for the purposes of sub-paragraph (1) above.

Derivations – VATA 1983, s. 10A and Sch. 4A, para. 4, as inserted by F(No. 2)A 1992, s. 14 and Sch. 3, para. 62.

Official publications – 700, para. 3.1(f) (2000 edn) and 725: values expressed in a foreign currency.

5 In this Schedule–

"relevant transaction", in relation to any acquisition of goods from another member State, means the transaction in pursuance of which the goods are acquired;

"the relevant time", in relation to any such acquisition, means–

(a) if the person by whom the goods are acquired is not a taxable person and the time of acquisition does not fall to be determined in accordance with regulations made under section 12(3), the time of the event which, in relation to that acquisition, is the first relevant event for the purposes of taxing the acquisition; and

(b) in any other case, the time of acquisition.

Derivations – VATA 1983, s. 10A and Sch. 4A, para. 5, as inserted by F(No. 2)A 1992, s. 14 and Sch. 3, para. 62.

Cross reference – VAT Regulations 1995 (SI 1995/2518), reg. 96: acquisitions from another member state.

SCHEDULE 8 – ZERO-RATING

Section 30

Cross references – S. 30(2A): zero-rating of services which consist of applying a treatment or process to another person's goods.
S. 96(10A)(b): interpretation and references to grants.
Sch. 8 is interpreted in accordance with the notes contained in that schedule (s. 96(9)). The descriptions of the groups in that schedule are for ease of reference only and do not affect the interpretation (s. 96(10)).

Extra-statutory concessions – 3.11 (Notice 48 (1999 edn)): incorrect customer declaration for zero-rating under Grp. 2, 5, 6, 14 or 16.

Notes – VAT Regulations 1995 (SI 1995/2518), reg. 20: non-application of certain invoicing requirements where supply is zero-rated other than a supply for the purposes of acquisition.

Part I – Index to Zero-Rated Supplies of Goods and Services

History – Grp. 14 was repealed by SI 1999/1642, art. 2(a), with effect in relation to supplies made on or after 1 July 1999.

Part II – The Groups

GROUP 1 – FOOD

The supply of anything comprised in the general items set out below, except–

(a) a supply in the course of catering; and

(b) a supply of anything comprised in any of the excepted items set out below, unless it is also comprised in any of the items overriding the exceptions set out below which relates to that excepted item.

General items

Item No.

1. Food of a kind used for human consumption.
2. Animal feeding stuffs.
3. Seeds or other means of propagation of plants comprised in item 1 or 2.
4. Live animals of a kind generally used as, or yielding or producing, food for human consumption.

Excepted items

Item No.

1. Ice cream, ice lollies, frozen yogurt, water ices and similar frozen products, and prepared mixes and powders for making such products.
2. Confectionery, not including cakes or biscuits other than biscuits wholly or partly covered with chocolate or some product similar in taste and appearance.
3. Beverages chargeable with any duty of excise specifically charged on spirits, beer, wine or made-wine and preparations thereof.
4. Other beverages (including fruit juices and bottled waters) and syrups, concentrates, essences, powders, crystals or other products for the preparation of beverages.
5. Any of the following when packaged for human consumption without further preparation, *namely, potato crisps, potato sticks, potato puffs*, and similar products made from the potato, or from potato flour, or from potato starch, and savoury food products obtained by the swelling of cereals or cereal products; and salted or roasted nuts other than nuts in shell.
6. Pet foods, canned, packaged or prepared; packaged foods (not being pet foods) for birds other than poultry or game; and biscuits and meal for cats and dogs.

7. Goods described in items 1, 2 and 3 of the general items which are canned, bottled, packaged or prepared for use–
  (a) in the domestic brewing of any beer;
  (b) in the domestic making of any cider or perry;
  (c) in the domestic production of any wine or made-wine.

Items overriding the exceptions
Item No.
1. Yoghurt unsuitable for immediate consumption when frozen.
2. Drained cherries.
3. Candied peels.
4. Tea, maté, herbal teas and similar products, and preparations and extracts thereof.
5. Cocoa, coffee and chicory and other roasted coffee substitutes, and preparations and extracts thereof.
6. Milk and preparations and extracts thereof.
7. Preparations and extracts of meat, yeast or egg.

Notes:
(1) **"Food"** includes drink.
(2) **"Animal"** includes bird, fish, crustacean and mollusc.
(3) A supply of anything in the course of **catering** includes–
  (a) any supply of it for consumption on the premises on which it is supplied; and
  (b) any supply of hot food for consumption off those premises;

and for the purposes of paragraph (b) above **"hot food"** means food which, or any part of which–
>   (i) has been heated for the purposes of enabling it to be consumed at a temperature above the ambient air temperature; and
>   (ii) is at the time of the supply above that temperature.

(4) Item 1 of the items overriding the exceptions relates to item 1 of the excepted items.
(5) Items 2 and 3 of the items overriding the exceptions relate to item 2 of the excepted items; and for the purposes of item 2 of the excepted items **"confectionery"** includes chocolates, sweets and biscuits; drained, glacé or crystallised fruits; and any item of sweetened prepared food which is normally eaten with the fingers.
(6) Items 4 to 7 of the items overriding the exceptions relate to item 4 of the excepted items.
(7) Any supply described in this Group shall include a supply of services described in paragraph 1(1) of Schedule 4.

History – In Note (6), the words "Items 4 to 7" were substituted for the words "Items 4 to 6" by FA 1999, s. 14 and this substitution is deemed always to have had effect.

Derivations – VATA 1983, s. 16 and Sch. 5, Grp. 1, as amended by FA 1984, s. 10 and Sch. 6, para. 1, SI 1988/507, SI 1986/530, SI 1992/628 and SI 1993/2498.

Cross references – VAT Regulations 1995 (SI 1995/2518), reg. 73(1): apportionment where retail scheme user's supplies include supplies both of food under Grp. 1 and in the course of catering.
VAT Regulations 1995 (SI 1995/2518), reg. 86(1): time of supply of water comprised in any of the excepted items.

Official publications – 701/14, 701/15, 701/37, 701/38, 701/40, 709/1 and 709/2.

Other material – Customs and Excise Press Notice 805, 21 February 1983: treatment of fruit and nut mixtures.
Customs and Excise Business Brief 3, 6 June 1991 (not reproduced): hotels should not zero-rate packed lunches supplied to guests. Customs consider this amounts to standard-rated catering.
Customs and Excise Business Brief 15/92, 5 October 1992 (not reproduced): zero-rating for fresh fish used as bait.
Customs and Excise Business Brief 5/93, 3 February 1993 (not reproduced): zero-rating for total parenteral nutrition.
Customs and Excise Business Brief 8/94, 28 March 1994 (not reproduced): zero-rating for glucose, dextrose and horlicks tablets.
Customs and Excise Business Brief 6/95, 28 March 1995 (not reproduced): zero-rating for live ostriches and fertilised ostrich eggs.

GROUP 2 – SEWERAGE SERVICES AND WATER

Item No.
1. Services of–
  (a) reception, disposal or treatment of foul water or sewage in bulk, and
  (b) emptying of cesspools, septic tanks or similar receptacles which are used otherwise than in connection with the carrying on in the course of a business of a relevant industrial activity.
2. The supply, for use otherwise than in connection with the carrying on in the course of a business of a relevant industrial activity, of water other than–
  (a) distilled water, deionised water and water of similar purity,
  (b) water comprised in any of the excepted items set out in Group 1, and
  (c) water which has been heated so that it is supplied at a temperature higher than that at which it was before it was heated.

Note:

"Relevant industrial activity" means any activity described in any of Divisions 1 to 5 of the 1980 edition of the publication prepared by the Central Statistical Office and known as the Standard Industrial Classification.

History – Grp. 2, item 2(c) and the word "and" immediately before were inserted and the word "and" at the end of Grp. 2, item 2(a) was omitted by SI 1996/1661, art. 2, operative in relation to any supply made on or after 27 June 1996 and any acquisition or importation taking place on or after that date.

Derivations – VATA 1983, s. 16 and Sch. 5, Grp. 2, as amended by FA 1989, s. 19.

Official publications – 701/16.

GROUP 3 – BOOKS, ETC.

Item No.
1. Books, booklets, brochures, pamphlets and leaflets.
2. Newspapers, journals and periodicals.
3. Children's picture books and painting books.
4. Music (printed, duplicated or manuscript).
5. Maps, charts and topographical plans.
6. Covers, cases and other articles supplied with items 1 to 5 and not separately accounted for.

Note:

Items 1 to 6–
  (a) do not include plans or drawings for industrial, architectural, engineering, commercial or similar purposes; but
  (b) include the supply of the services described in paragraph 1(1) of Schedule 4 in respect of goods comprised in the items.

Derivations – VATA 1983, s. 16 and Sch. 5, Grp. 3.

Extra-statutory concessions – 3.15 (Notice 48 (1999 edn)): printed matter published in instalments.

Official publications – 701/10.

GROUP 4 – TALKING BOOKS FOR THE BLIND AND HANDICAPPED AND WIRELESS SETS FOR THE BLIND

Item No.
1. The supply to the Royal National Institute for the Blind, the National Listening Library or other similar charities of–
  (a) magnetic tape specially adapted for the recording and reproduction of speech for the blind or severely handicapped;
  (b) apparatus designed or specially adapted for the making on a magnetic tape, by way of the transfer of recorded speech from another magnetic tape, of a recording described in paragraph (f) below;
  (c) apparatus designed or specially adapted for transfer to magnetic tapes of a recording made by apparatus described in paragraph (b) above;
  (d) apparatus for re-winding magnetic tape described in paragraph (f) below;
  (e) apparatus designed or specially adapted for the reproduction from recorded magnetic tape of speech for the blind or severely handicapped which is not available for use otherwise than by the blind or severely handicapped;
  (f) magnetic tape upon which has been recorded speech for the blind or severely handicapped, such recording being suitable for reproduction only in the apparatus mentioned in paragraph (e) above;
  (g) apparatus solely for the making on a magnetic tape of a sound recording which is for use by the blind or severely handicapped;
  (h) parts and accessories (other than a magnetic tape for use with apparatus described in paragraph (g) above) for goods comprised in paragraphs (a) to (g) above;
  (i) the supply of a service of repair or maintenance of any goods comprised in paragraphs (a) to (h) above.
2. The supply to a charity of–
  (a) wireless receiving sets; or
  (b) apparatus solely for the making and reproduction of a sound recording on a magnetic tape permanently contained in a cassette,

being goods solely for gratuitous loan to the blind.

Note:

The supply mentioned in items 1 and 2 includes the letting on hire of goods comprised
Derivations – VATA 1983, s. 16 and Sch. 5, Grp. 4, as amended by SI 1986/530 and SI 1992/628.

GROUP 5 – CONSTRUCTION OF BUILDINGS, ETC.

Item No.
1.   The first grant by a person–
  (a) constructing a building–
      (i) designed as a dwelling or number of dwellings; or
      (ii) intended for use solely for a relevant residential or a relevant charitable purpose; or
  (b) converting a non-residential building or a non-residential part of a building into a building
      designed as a dwelling or number of dwellings or a building intended for use solely for a
      relevant residential purpose,
of a major interest in, or in any part of, the building, dwelling or its site.
2.   The supply in the course of the construction of–
  (a) a building designed as a dwelling or number of dwellings or intended for use solely for a
      relevant residential purpose or a relevant charitable purpose; or
  (b) any civil engineering work necessary for the development of a permanent park for residential
      caravans,
of any services related to the construction other than the services of an architect, surveyor or any
person acting as a consultant or in a supervisory capacity.
3.   The supply to a relevant housing association in the course of conversion of a non-
     residential building or a non-residential part of a building into–
  (a) a building or part of a building designed as a dwelling or number of dwellings; or
  (b) a building or part of a building intended for use solely for a relevant residential purpose,
of any services related to the conversion other than the services of an architect, surveyor or any
person acting as a consultant or in a supervisory capacity.
4.   The supply of building materials to a person to whom the supplier is supplying services
     within item 2 or 3 of this Group which include the incorporation of the materials into the
     building (or its site) in question.

Notes:
(1) **"Grant"** includes an assignment or surrender.
(2) A building is **designed as a dwelling** or a number of dwellings where in relation to each
dwelling the following conditions are satisfied–
  (a) the dwelling consists of self-contained living accommodation;
  (b) there is no provision for direct internal access from the dwelling to any other dwelling or part
      of a dwelling;
  (c) the separate use, or disposal of the dwelling is not prohibited by the terms of any covenant,
      statutory planning consent or similar provision; and
  (d) statutory planning consent has been granted in respect of that dwelling and its construction
      or conversion has been carried out in accordance with that consent.
(3) The **construction of, or conversion of a non-residential building** to, a building designed
as a dwelling or a number of dwellings includes the construction of, or conversion of a non-
residential building to, a garage provided that–
  (a) the dwelling and the garage are constructed or converted at the same time; and
  (b) the garage is intended to be occupied with the dwelling or one of the dwellings.
(4) **Use for a relevant residential purpose** means use as–
  (a) a home or other institution providing residential accommodation for children;
  (b) a home or other institution providing residential accommodation with personal care for
      persons in need of personal care by reason of old age, disablement, past or present
      dependence on alcohol or drugs or past or present mental disorder;
  (c) a hospice;
  (d) residential accommodation for students or school pupils;
  (e) residential accommodation for members of any of the armed forces;
  (f) a monastery, nunnery or similar establishment; or
  (g) an institution which is the sole or main residence of at least 90 per cent of its residents,
except use as a hospital, prison or similar institution or an hotel, inn or similar establishment.
(5) Where a number of buildings are–

(a) constructed at the same time and on the same site; and

(b) are intended to be used together as a unit solely for a relevant residential purpose;

then each of those buildings, to the extent that they would not be so regarded but for this Note, are to be treated as **intended for use solely for a relevant residential purpose** .

(6) **Use for a relevant charitable purpose** means use by a charity in either or both the following ways, namely–

(a) otherwise than in the course or furtherance of a business;

(b) as a village hall or similarly in providing social or recreational facilities for a local community.

(7) Subject to Note (9) below **"non-residential"** in relation to a building or part of a building, means–

(a) neither designed nor adapted for use as a dwelling or number of dwellings nor for a relevant residential purpose, or

(b) if so designed or adapted, was constructed before, and has not been used as a dwelling or number of dwellings or for a relevant residential purpose since, 1st April 1973.

(8) References to **a non-residential building** or **a non-residential part of a building** do not include a reference to a garage occupied together with a dwelling.

(9) The conversion, other than to a building designed for a relevant residential purpose, of a non-residential part of a building which already contains a residential part is not included within items 1(b) or 3 unless the result of that conversion is to create an additional dwelling or dwellings.

(10) Where–

(a) part of a building that is constructed is designed as a dwelling or number of dwellings or is intended for use solely for a relevant residential purpose or relevant charitable purpose (and part is not); or

(b) part of a building that is converted is designed as a dwelling or number of dwellings or is used solely for a relevant residential purpose (and part is not)–

then in the case of–

(i) a grant or other supply relating only to the part so designed or intended for that use (or its site) shall be treated as relating to a building so designed or intended for such use;

(ii) a grant or other supply relating only to the part neither so designed nor intended for such use (or its site) shall not be so treated; and

(iii) any other grant or other supply relating to, or to any part of, the building (or its site), an apportionment shall be made to determine the extent to which it is to be so treated.

(11) Where, a service falling within the description in items 2 or 3 is supplied in part in relation to the construction or conversion of a building and in part for other purposes, an apportionment may be made to determine the extent to which the supply is to be treated as falling within item 2 or item 3.

(12) Where all or part of a building is intended for use solely for a relevant residential purpose or a relevant charitable purpose–

(a) a supply relating to the building (or any part of it) shall not be taken for the purposes of items 2 and 4 as relating to a building intended for such use unless it is made to a person who intends to use the building (or part) for such a purpose; and

(b) a grant or other supply relating to the building (or any part of it) shall not be taken as relating to a building intended for such use unless before it is made the person to whom it is made has given to the person making it a certificate in such form as may be specified in a notice published by the Commissioners stating that the grant or other supply (or a specified part of it) so relates.

(13) The grant of an interest in, or in any part of–

(a) a building designed as a dwelling or number of dwellings; or

(b) the site of such a building;

is not within item 1 if–

(i) the interest granted is such that the grantee is not entitled to reside in the building or part, throughout the year; or

(ii) residence there throughout the year, or the use of the building or part as the grantee's principal private residence, is prevented by the terms of a covenant, statutory planning consent or similar permission.

(14) Where the major interest referred to in item 1 is a tenancy or lease–

(a) if a premium is payable, the grant falls within that item only to the extent that it is made for consideration in the form of the premium; and

(b) if a premium is not payable, the grant falls within that item only to the extent that it is made for consideration in the form of the first payment of rent due under the tenancy or lease.

(15) The reference in item 2(b) of this Group to the **construction of a civil engineering work** does not include a reference to the conversion, reconstruction, alteration or enlargement of work.

(16) For the purpose of this Group, **the construction of a building** does not include–

(a) the conversion, reconstruction or alteration of an existing building; or

(b) any enlargement of, or extension to, an existing building except to the extent the enlargement or extension creates an additional dwelling or dwellings; or

(c) subject to Note (17) below, the construction of an annexe to an existing building.

(17) Note (16)(c) above shall not apply where an annexe is intended for use solely for a relevant charitable purpose and–

(a) is capable of functioning independently from the existing building; and

(b) the only access or where there is more than one means of access, the main access to:

    (i) the annexe is not via the existing building; and

    (ii) the existing building is not via the annexe.

(18) A building only **ceases to be an existing building** when:

(a) demolished completely to ground level; or

(b) the part remaining above ground level consists of no more than a single facade or where a corner site, a double facade, the retention of which is a condition or requirement of statutory planning consent or similar permission.

(19) A caravan is not a **residential caravan** if residence in it throughout the year is prevented by the terms of a covenant, statutory planning consent or similar permission.

(20) Item 2 and Item 3 do not include the supply of services described in paragraph 1(1) or 5(4) of Schedule 4.

(21) In item 3 **"relevant housing association"** means–

(a) a registered social landlord within the meaning of Part I of the Housing Act 1996,

(b) a registered housing association within the meaning of the Housing Associations Act 1985 (Scottish registered housing associations), or

(c) a registered housing association within the meaning of Part II of the Housing (Northern Ireland) Order 1992 (Northern Irish registered housing associations).

(22) **"Building materials"**, in relation to any description of building, means goods of a description ordinarily incorporated by builders in a building of that description, (or its site), but does not include–

(a) finished or prefabricated furniture, other than furniture designed to be fitted in kitchens;

(b) materials for the construction of fitted furniture, other than kitchen furniture;

(c) electrical or gas appliances, unless the appliance is an appliance which is–

    (i) designed to heat space or water (or both) or to provide ventilation, air cooling, air purification, or dust extraction; or

    (ii) intended for use in a building designed as a number of dwellings and is a door-entry system, a waste disposal unit or a machine for compacting waste; or

    (iii) a burglar alarm, a fire alarm, or fire safety equipment or designed solely for the purpose of enabling aid to be summoned in an emergency; or

    (iv) a lift or hoist;

(d) carpets or carpeting material.

(23) For the purposes of Note (22) above the **incorporation of goods in a building** includes their installation as fittings.

(24) Section 30(3) does not apply to goods forming part of a description of supply in this Group.

History – In Grp. 5, item 3 the words "relevant housing association" were substituted by SI 1997/50, art. 2(a), operative from 1 March 1997.
Grp. 5, Note (21) was substituted by SI 1997/50, art. 2(b), operative from 1 March 1997.
Grp. 5 was substituted by SI 1995/280, art. 2, operative from 1 March 1995. Former Grp. 5 read as follows:
"Item No.
1.   The grant by a person constructing a building–
        (a)   designed as a dwelling or number of dwellings; or
        (b)   intended for use solely for a relevant residential purpose or a relevant charitable purpose,
of a major interest in, or in any part of, the building or its site.
2.   The supply in the course of the construction of–
        (a)   a building designed as a dwelling or number of dwellings or intended for use solely for a relevant residential purpose or a relevant charitable purpose; or

(b)   any civil engineering work necessary for the development of a permanent park for residential caravans,

of any services other than the services of an architect, surveyor or any person acting as consultant or in a supervisory capacity.

3.   The supply to a person of–

(a)   materials; or

(b)   builders' hardware, sanitary ware or other articles of a kind ordinarily installed by builders as fixtures,

by a supplier who also makes to the same person supplies within item 2 of this Group or Group 6 below of services which include the use of the materials or the installation of the articles.

Notes:

(1)   **"Grant"** includes assignment.

(2)   **"Dwelling"** includes a garage constructed at the same time as a dwelling for occupation together with it.

(3)   Use for a **relevant residential purpose** means use as–

(a)   a home or other institution providing residential accommodation for children;

(b)   a home or other institution providing residential accommodation with personal care for persons in need of personal care by reason of old age, disablement, past or present dependence on alcohol or drugs or past or present mental disorder;

(c)   a hospice;

(d)   residential accommodation for students or school pupils;

(e)   residential accommodation for members of any of the armed forces;

(f)   a monastery, nunnery or similar establishment; or

(g)   an institution which is the sole or main residence of at least 90 per cent of its residents,

except use as a hospital, a prison or similar institution or an hotel, inn or similar establishment.

(4)   Use for a **relevant charitable purpose** means use by a charity in either or both of the following ways, namely–

(a)   otherwise than in the course or furtherance of a business;

(b)   as a village hall or similarly in providing social or recreational facilities for a local community.

(5)   Where part of a building is designed as a dwelling or number of dwellings or intended for use solely for a relevant residential purpose or a relevant charitable purpose (and part is not)–

(a)   a grant or other supply relating only to the part so designed or intended for such use (or its site) shall be treated as relating to a building so designed or intended for such use;

(b)   a grant or other supply relating only to the part neither so designed nor intended for such use (or its site) shall not be so treated; and

(c)   in the case of any other grant or other supply relating to, or to any part of, the building (or its site), an apportionment shall be made to determine the extent to which it is to be so treated.

(6)   Where all or part of a building is intended for use solely for a relevant residential purpose or a relevant charitable purpose–

(a)   a supply relating to the building (or any part of it) shall not be taken for the purposes of item 2 or 3 as relating to a building intended for such use unless it is made to a person who intends to use the building (or part) for such a purpose, and

(b)   a grant or other supply relating to the building (or any part of it) shall not be taken as relating to a building intended for such use unless before it is made the person to whom it is made has given to the person making it a certificate in such form as may be specified in a notice published by the Commissioners stating that the grant or other supply (or a specified part of it) so relates.

(7)   The grant of an interest in, or in any part of–

(a)   a building designed as a dwelling or number of dwellings, or

(b)   the site of such a building,

is not within item 1 if–

(i)   the interest granted is such that the grantee is not entitled to reside in the building, or part, throughout the year; or

(ii)   residence there throughout the year, or the use of the building or part as the grantee's principal private residence, is prevented by the terms of a covenant, statutory planning consent or similar permission.

(8)   Where the major interest referred to in item 1 is a tenancy or lease–

(a)   if a premium is payable, the grant falls within that item only to the extent that it is made for consideration in the form of the premium; and

(b)   if a premium is not payable, the grant falls within that item only to the extent that it is made for consideration in the form of the first payment of rent due under the tenancy or lease.

(9)   The reference in item 2 to the **construction of a building or work** does not include a reference to–

(a)   the conversion, reconstruction, alteration or enlargement of an existing building or work; or

(b)   any extension or annexation to an existing building which provides for internal access to the existing building or of which the separate use, letting or disposal is prevented by the terms of any covenant, statutory planning consent or similar permission;

and the reference in item 1 to a **person constructing a building** shall be construed accordingly.

(10) A caravan is not a **residential caravan** if residence in it throughout the year is prevented by the terms of a covenant, statutory planning consent or similar permission.

(11) Item 2 does not include the supply of services described in paragraph 1(1) or 5(3) of Schedule 4.

(12) The goods referred to in item 3 do not include–

(a)   finished or prefabricated furniture, other than furniture designed to be fitted in kitchens;

(b)   materials for the construction of fitted furniture, other than kitchen furniture;

(c)   domestic electrical or gas appliances, other than those designed to provide space heating or water heating or both; or

(d)   carpets or carpeting material.

(13) Section 30(3) does not apply to goods forming part of a description of supply in this Group."

Cross references – S. 35: refund of tax to a person constructing a building lawfully and otherwise than in the course or furtherance of any business.

S. 35(4): notes to Grp. 5 apply for construing s. 35.

S. 62: penalty for giving incorrect certificate that a supply or supplies fall within Grp. 5.

Sch. 9, Grp. 1, Note (3): Notes (2)–(6) above apply also to that group (exemptions: land).

Sch. 10, para. 1: zero-rated supply followed by change of use within ten years of completion of building.

Sch. 10, para. 2(2B)(b): buildings intended to be used as dwellings and zero-rating under item 1(b).

Sch. 10, para. 8: notes to Grp. 8 apply with modifications in relation to Sch. 10.

VAT Regulations 1995 (SI 1995/2518), reg. 101(3)(b)(i): exclusion of item 1 supplies from partial exemption calculation.

VAT Regulations 1995 (SI 1995/2518), reg. 116(3): disregarding certain zero-rated supplies for capital goods scheme.

Official publications – 708, 742 and 742/3.

Customs Internal Guidance Manual, vol. V1.8: land and property.

Customs Internal Guidance Manual, vol. V1.18A: construction.

Other material – Customs and Excise Business Brief 15/92, 5 October 1992 (not reproduced): VAT relief extended to extractor fans and hard wired smoke detectors installed in new housing where installation required by building regulations.

Customs and Excise News Release 44/91, 26 April 1991: meaning of "person constructing".

Customs and Excise News Release 72/90, 29 October 1990 (not reproduced): fitted wardrobes.

Customs and Excise Press Notice 841, 17 June 1983 (not reproduced): fixed electric storage radiators may be zero-rated as articles of a kind ordinarily installed by builders as fixtures (item 3(b)); "fixed" means permanently wired to a fixed spur mains outlet and securely attached to the building.
Customs and Excise Press Notice 1108, 2 May 1986 (not reproduced): generally, telecommunications equipment does not fall within item 3(b); exceptions for fixed network termination points and necessary fixed cabling for distributing system throughout a new building before its first time occupation.
Notes – S. 96(1): "major interest" defined.

GROUP 6 – PROTECTED BUILDINGS

Item No.
1.   The first grant by a person substantially reconstructing a protected building, of a major interest in, or in any part of, the building or its site.
2.   The supply, in the course of an approved alteration of a protected building, of any services other than the services of an architect, surveyor or any person acting as consultant or in a supervisory capacity.
3.   The supply of building materials to a person to whom the supplier is supplying services within item 2 of this Group which include the incorporation of the materials into the building (or its site) in question.

Notes:
(1) **"Protected building"** means a building which is designed to remain as or become a dwelling or number of dwellings (as defined in Note (2) below) or is intended for use solely for a relevant residential purpose or a relevant charitable purpose after the reconstruction or alteration and which, in either case, is–
   (a)   a listed building, within the meaning of–
        (i)   the Planning (Listed Buildings and Conservation Areas) Act 1990; or
        (ii)   the Planning (Listed Buildings and Conservation Areas) (Scotland) Act 1997; or
        (iii)   the Planning (Northern Ireland) Order 1991; or
   (b)   a scheduled monument, within the meaning of–
        (i)   the Ancient Monuments and Archaeological Areas Act 1979; or
        (ii)   the Historic Monuments and Archaeological Objects (Northern Ireland) Order 1995.
(2) A building is designed to remain as or become a **dwelling** or number of dwellings where in relation to each dwelling the following conditions are satisfied–
   (a)   the dwelling consists of self-contained living accommodation;
   (b)   there is no provision for direct internal access from the dwelling to any other dwelling or part of a dwelling;
   (c)   the separate use, or disposal of the dwelling is not prohibited by the terms of any covenant, statutory planning consent or similar provision,

and includes a garage (occupied together with a dwelling) either constructed at the same time as the building or where the building has been substantially reconstructed at the same time as that reconstruction.
(3) Notes (1), (4), (6), (12) to (14) and (22) to (24) of Group 5 apply in relation to this Group as they apply in relation to that Group but subject to any appropriate modifications.
(4) For the purposes of item 1, a protected building shall not be regarded as **substantially reconstructed** unless the reconstruction is such that at least one of the following conditions is fulfilled when the reconstruction is completed–
   (a)   that, of the works carried out to effect the reconstruction, at least three-fifths, measured by reference to cost, are of such a nature that the supply of services (other than excluded services), materials and other items to carry out the works, would, if supplied by a taxable person, be within either item 2 or item 3 of this Group; and
   (b)   that the reconstructed building incorporates no more of the original building (that is to say, the building as it was before the reconstruction began) than the external walls, together with other external features of architectural or historic interest;

and in paragraph (a) above **"excluded services"** means the services of an architect, surveyor or other person acting as consultant or in a supervisory capacity.
(5) Where part of a protected building that is substantially reconstructed that is designed to remain as or become a dwelling or a number of dwellings or is intended for use solely for a relevant residential or relevant charitable purpose (and part is not)–
   (a)   a grant or other supply relating only to the part so designed or intended for such use (or its site) shall be treated as relating to a building so designed or intended for such use;
   (b)   a grant or other supply relating only to the part neither so designed nor intended for such use (or its site) shall not be so treated; and

   (c)   in the case of any other grant or other supply relating to, or to any part of, the building (or its site), an apportionment shall be made to determine the extent to which it is to be so treated.

(6) **"Approved alteration"** means–

   (a)   in the case of a protected building which is an ecclesiastical building to which section 60 of the Planning (Listed Buildings and Conservation Areas) Act 1990 applies, any works of alteration; and

   (b)   in the case of a protected building which is a scheduled monument within the meaning of the Historic Monuments Act (Northern Ireland) 1971 and in respect of which a protection order, within the meaning of that Act, is in force, works of alteration for which consent has been given under section 10 of that Act; and

   (c)   in any other case, works of alteration which may not, or but for the existence of a Crown interest or Duchy interest could not, be carried out unless authorised under, or under any provision of–

      (i)   Part I of the Planning (Listed Buildings and Conservation Areas) Act 1990,

     (ii)   Part I of the Planning (Listed Buildings and Conservation Areas) (Scotland) Act 1997,

    (iii)   Part V of the Planning (Northern Ireland) Order 1991,

    (iv)   Part I of the Ancient Monuments and Archaeological Areas Act 1979,

and for which, except in the case of a Crown interest or Duchy interest, consent has been obtained under any provision of that Part,

but does not include any works of repair or maintenance, or any incidental alteration to the fabric of a building which results from the carrying out of repairs, or maintenance work.

(7) For the purposes of paragraph (a) of Note (6), a building used or available for use by a minister of religion wholly or mainly as a residence from which to perform the duties of his office shall be treated as not being an **ecclesiastical building**.

(8) For the purposes of paragraph (c) of Note (6) **"Crown interest"** and **"Duchy interest"** have the same meaning as in section 50 of the Ancient Monuments and Archaeological Areas Act 1979.

(9) Where a service is supplied in part in relation to an approved alteration of a building, and in part for other purposes, an apportionment may be made to determine the extent to which the supply is to be treated as falling within item 2.

(10) For the purposes of item 2 the construction of a building separate from, but in the curtilage of, a protected building does not constitute an **alteration** of the protected building.

(11) Item 2 does not include the supply of services described in paragraph 1(1) or 5(4) of Schedule 4.

History – In Note (1)(a)(ii), the words "the Planning (Listed Buildings and Conservation Areas) (Scotland) Act 1997" were substituted for the words "the Town and Country Planning (Scotland) Act 1972" by Planning (Consequential Provisions) (Scotland) Act 1997, s. 4 and Sch. 2, para. 57(a), with effect from 27 May 1997.

In Note (1)(b)(ii), the words "the Historic Monuments and Archaeological Objects (Northern Ireland) Order 1995" were substituted by SI 1995/1625 (NI 9), Sch. 3, para. 4, operative from 29 August 1995.

In former Note (4), certain amendments were apparently made by SI 1995/1625 (NI 9), Sch. 3, para. 4 and Sch. 4, operative from 29 August 1995, to the text of Note (4) prior to its substitution with effect from 1 March 1995. Note (4) is generally now Note (6). In practice, the substituted Note (6) above should be considered with such amendments in mind. The amendments are:

   (1)   Note (6)((b) is repealed;

   (2)   the word "or" is added at the end of Note (6)(c)(iv); and

   (3)   Note (6)(c)(v) is inserted as reads "(v) Part II of the Historic Monuments and Archaeological Objects (Northern Ireland) Order 1995,".

In Note (6)(c)(ii), the words "Part I of the Planning (Listed Buildings and Conservation Areas) (Scotland) Act 1997" were substituted for the words "Part IV of the Town and Country Planning (Scotland) (Consequential Provisions) (Scotland) Act 1997, s. 4 and Sch. 2, para. 57(b), with effect from 27 May 1997. In the Queen's Printer's version of Planning (Consequential Provisions) (Scotland) Act 1997, para. 57(b) refers to substituting words in Note (4)(c)(ii) which apparently should refer to Note (6)(c)(ii).

Grp. 6 was substituted by SI 1995/283, art. 2, operative from 1 March 1995. Former Grp. 6 read as follows:

"Item No.

  1.   The grant, by a person substantially reconstructing a protected building, of a major interest in, or in any part of, the building or its site.

  2.   The supply, in the course of an approved alteration of a protected building, of any services other than the services of an architect, surveyor or any person acting as consultant or in a supervisory capacity.

Notes:

(1) **"Protected building"** means a building which is designed to remain as or become a dwelling or number of dwellings or is intended for use solely for a relevant residential purpose or a relevant charitable purpose after the reconstruction or alteration and which, in either case, is–

   (a)   a listed building, within the meaning of–

      (i)   the Planning (Listed Buildings and Conservation Areas) Act 1990; or

     (ii)   the Town and Country Planning (Scotland) Act 1972" or

    (iii)   the Planning (Northern Ireland) Order 1991; or

   (b)   a scheduled monument, within the meaning of–

      (i)   the Ancient Monuments and Archaeological Areas Act 1979, or

     (ii)   the Historic Monuments Act (Northern Ireland) 1971.

(2) Notes (1) to (8) to Group 5 above apply in relation to this Group as they apply in relation to that Group.

(3) For the purposes of item 1, a protected building shall not be regarded as **substantially reconstructed** unless the reconstruction is such that at least one of the following conditions is fulfilled when the reconstruction is completed–

(a) that, of the works carried out to effect the reconstruction, at least three-fifths, measured by reference to cost, are of such a nature that the supply of services (other than excluded services), materials and other items to carry out the works, would, if supplied by a taxable person, be within either item 2 of this Group or item 3 of Group 5, as it applies to a supply by a person supplying services within item 2 of this Group; and

(b) that the reconstructed building incorporates no more of the original building (that is to say, the building as it was before the reconstruction began) than the external walls, together with other external features of architectural or historic interest;

and in paragraph (a) above **"excluded services"** means the services of an architect, surveyor or other person acting as consultant or in a supervisory capacity.

(4) **"Approved alteration"** means–

(a) in the case of a protected building which is an ecclesiastical building which is for the time being used for ecclesiastical purposes or would be so used but for the works in question, any works of alteration; and

(b) in the case of a protected building which is a scheduled monument within the meaning of the Historic Monuments Act (Northern Ireland) 1971 and in respect of which a protection order, within the meaning of that Act, is in force, works of alteration for which consent has been given under section 10 of that Act; and

(c) in any other case, works of alteration which may not, or but for the existence of a Crown interest or Duchy interest could not, be carried out unless authorised under, or under any provision of–

    (i) Part I of the Planning (Listed Buildings and Conservation Areas) Act 1990,

    (ii) Part IV of the Town and Country Planning (Scotland) Act 1972,

    (iii) Part V of the Planning (Northern Ireland) Order 1991, or

    (iv) Part I of the Ancient Monuments and Archaeological Areas Act 1979,

and for which, except in the case of a Crown interest or Duchy interest, consent has been obtained under any provision of that Part;

and in paragraph (c) above **"Crown interest"** and **"Duchy interest"** have the same meaning as in section 50 of the said Act of 1979.

(5) For the purposes of paragraph (a) of Note (4), a building used or available for use by a minister of religion wholly or mainly as a residence from which to perform the duties of his office shall be treated as not being an **ecclesiastical building**.

(6) In item 2 **"alteration"** does not include repair or maintenance; and where any work consists partly of an approved alteration and partly of other work, an apportionment shall be made to determine the supply which falls within item 2.

(7) For the purposes of item 2 the construction of a building separate from, but in the curtilage of, a protected building does not constitute an **alteration** of the protected building.

(8) Item 2 does not include the supply of services described in paragraph 1(1) or 5(3) of Schedule 4."

Cross references – S. 62: penalty for giving incorrect certificate that a supply or supplies fall within Grp. 6.
Sch. 13, para. 10: supplies during construction of buildings and works.
VAT Regulations 1995 (SI 1995/2518), reg. 101(3)(b)(i): exclusion of item 1 supplies from partial exemption calculation.
VAT Regulations 1995 (SI 1995/2518), reg. 116(3): disregarding certain zero-rated supplies for capital goods scheme.

Official publications – 708, 742 and 742/3.

Notes – Planning (Northern Ireland) Order 1991 (SI 1991/1220 (NI 11)), art. 42: "listed building" defined.

GROUP 7 – INTERNATIONAL SERVICES

Item No.

1. The supply of services of work carried out on goods which, for that purpose, have been obtained or acquired in, or imported into, any of the member States and which are intended to be, and in fact are, subsequently exported to a place outside the member States–

   (a) by or on behalf of the supplier; or

   (b) where the recipient of the services belongs in a place outside the member States, by or on behalf of the recipient.

2. The supply of services consisting of the making of arrangements for–

   (a) the export of any goods to a place outside the member States;

   (b) a supply of services of the description specified in item 1 of this Group; or

   (c) any supply of services which is made outside the member States.

Note:

This Group does not include any services of a description specified in Group 2 or Group 5 of Schedule 9.

Derivations – VATA 1983, s. 16 and Sch. 5, Grp. 9, as substituted by SI 1992/3223, art. 2.

Official publications – 741.

Other material – Customs and Excise Press Notice 1121, 26 June 1986 (not reproduced): trading of sterling commercial paper may fall under item 6 if the recipient belongs in a country (not the Isle of Man) which is not an EC member state.
Customs and Excise Business Brief 26/93, 31 August 1993 (not reproduced): services valuing goods or working on goods performed in the UK for customers outside the UK is zero-rated by extra-statutory concession from 1 September 1993. Thus the overseas customers no longer need to claim refund of UK VAT. The concession also extends to "domestic" freight transport where the domestic leg of the journey is directly linked to an intra-Community movement of goods.
Customs and Excise Business Brief 32/93, 14 October 1993 (not reproduced): training services, other than exempt training, supplied in the UK to overseas governments for the purpose of their sovereign activities zero-rated by extra-statutory concession from 1 October 1993.

Notes – S. 9: "belongs" defined.

GROUP 8 – TRANSPORT

Item No.
1. The supply, repair or maintenance of a qualifying ship or the modification or conversion of any such ship provided that when so modified or converted it will remain a qualifying ship.
2. The supply, repair or maintenance of a qualifying aircraft or the modification or conversion of any such aircraft provided that when so modified or converted it will remain a qualifying aircraft.
2A. The supply of parts and equipment, of a kind ordinarily installed or incorporated in, and to be installed, or incorporated in,–
   (a) the propulsion, navigation or communication systems; or
   (b) the general structure,
of a qualifying ship or, as the case may be, aircraft.
2B. The supply of life jackets, life rafts, smoke hoods and similar safety equipment for use in a qualifying ship or, as the case may be, aircraft.
3.
   (a) The supply to and repair or maintenance for a charity providing rescue or assistance at sea of–
      (i) any lifeboat;
      (ii) carriage equipment designed solely for the launching and recovery of lifeboats;
      (iii) tractors for the sole use of the launching and recovery of lifeboats;
      (iv) winches and hauling equipment for the sole use of the recovery of lifeboats.
   (b) The construction, modification, repair or maintenance for a charity providing rescue or assistance at sea of slipways used solely for the launching and recovery of lifeboats.
   (c) The supply of spare parts or accessories to a charity providing rescue or assistance at sea for use in or with goods comprised in paragraph (a) above or slipways comprised in paragraph (b) above.
4. Transport of passengers–
   (a) in any vehicle, ship or aircraft designed or adapted to carry not less than 12 passengers;
   (b) by the Post Office;
   (c) on any scheduled flight; or
   (d) from a place within to a place outside the United Kingdom or vice versa, to the extent that those services are supplied in the United Kingdom.
5. The transport of goods from a place within to a place outside the member States or vice versa, to the extent that those services are supplied within the United Kingdom.
6. Any services provided for–
   (a) the handling of ships or aircraft in a port, customs and excise airport or outside the United Kingdom; or
   (b) the handling or storage, in a port or customs and excise airport or on land adjacent to a port, of goods carried in a ship or aircraft.
6A. Air navigation services.
7. Pilotage services.
8. Salvage or towage services.
9. Any services supplied for or in connection with the surveying of any ship or aircraft or the classification of any ship or aircraft for the purposes of any register.
10. The making of arrangements for–
   (a) the supply of, or of space in, any ship or aircraft;
   (b) the supply of any service included in items 1 and 2, 3 to 9 and 11; or
   (c) the supply of any goods of a description falling within items 2A or 2B.
11. The supply–
   (a) of services consisting of
      (i) the handling or storage of goods at, or their transport to or from, a place at which they are to be exported to or have been imported from a place outside the member States; or
      (ii) the handling or storage of such goods in connection with such transport; or
   (b) to a person who receives the supply for the purpose of a business carried on by him and who belongs outside the United Kingdom, of services of a description specified in paragraph (a) of item 6, item 6A, item 9 or paragraph (a) of item 10 of this Group.

12.   The supply of a designated travel service to be enjoyed outside the European Community, to the extent to which the supply is so enjoyed.

13.   Intra-Community transport services supplied in connection with the transport of goods to or from the Azores or Madeira or between those places, to the extent that the services are treated as supplied in the United Kingdom.

Notes:

(A1) In this Group–

   (a)   a **"qualifying ship"** is any ship of a gross tonnage of not less than 15 tons which is neither designed nor adapted for use for recreation or pleasure; and

   (b)   a **"qualifying aircraft"** is any aircraft of a weight of not less than 8,000 kilogrammes which is neither designed nor adapted for use for recreation or pleasure.

(1) In items 1 and 2 the supply of a qualifying ship or, as the case may be, aircraft includes the supply of services under a charter of that ship or aircraft except where the services supplied under such a charter consist wholly of any one or more of the following–

   (a)   transport of passengers;

   (b)   accommodation;

   (c)   entertainment;

   (d)   education;

being services wholly performed in the United Kingdom.

(2) Items 1, 2, 2A, 2B and 3 include the letting on hire of the goods specified in the items.

(2A) Items 2A and 2B do not include the supply of parts and equipment to a Government department unless–

   (a)   they are installed or incorporated in the course of a supply which is treated as being made in the course or furtherance of a business carried on by the department; or

   (b)   the parts and equipment are to be installed or incorporated in ships or aircraft used for the purpose of providing rescue or assistance at sea.

(3) Item 3 shall not apply unless, before the supply is made, the recipient of the supply gives to the person making the supply a certificate stating–

   (a)   the name and address of the recipient;

   (b)   that the supply is of a description specified in item 3 of this Group.

(4) **"Lifeboat"** means any vessel used or to be used solely for rescue or assistance at sea.

(4A) Item 4 does not include the transport of passengers–

   (a)   in any vehicle to, from or within–

       (i)   a place of entertainment, recreation or amusement; or

       (ii)   a place of cultural, scientific, historical or similar interest,

       by the person, or a person connected with him, who supplies a right of admission to, or a right to use facilities at, such a place;

   (b)   in any motor vehicle between a car park (or land adjacent thereto) and an airport passenger terminal (or land adjacent thereto) by the person, or a person connected with him, who supplies facilities for the parking of vehicles in that car park; or

   (c)   in an aircraft where the flight is advertised or held out to be for the purpose of–

       (i)   providing entertainment, recreation or amusement; or

       (ii)   the experience of flying, or the experience of flying in that particular aircraft,

       and not primarily for the purpose of transporting passengers from one place to another.

(4B) For the purposes of Note (4A) any question whether a person is **connected** with another shall be determined in accordance with section 839 of the Taxes Act.

(4C) In Note (4A)(b) **"motor vehicle"** means a mechanically propelled vehicle intended or adapted for use on the roads.

(5) Item 6 does not include the letting on hire of goods.

(6) **"Port"** and **"customs and excise airport"** have the same meanings as in the Management Act.

(6A) **"Air navigation services"** has the same meaning as in the Civil Aviation Act 1982.

(7) Except for the purposes of item 11, paragraph (a) of item 6, item 6A, item 9 and paragraph (a) of item 10 only include supplies of services where the ships or aircraft referred to in those paragraphs are qualifying ships or, as the case may be, aircraft.

(8) **"Designated travel service"** has the same meaning as in the Value Added Tax (Tour Operators) Order 1987.

(9) **"Intra-Community transport services"** means–

(a)   the Intra-Community transport of goods within the meaning of the Value Added Tax (Place of Supply of Services) Order 1992;

(b)   ancillary transport services within the meaning of the Value Added Tax (Place of Supply of Services) Order 1992 which are provided in connection with the Intra-Community transport of goods; or

(c)   the making of arrangements for the supply by or to another person of a supply within (a) or (b) above or any other activity which is intended to facilitate the making of such a supply,

and, for the purpose of this Note only, the Azores and Madeira shall each be treated as a separate member State.

History – Item 1 was substituted by SI 1995/3039, art. 2(a), operative from 1 January 1996. Former item 1 read as follows:
"1.   The supply, repair or maintenance of any ship which is neither–
    (a)   a ship of a gross tonnage of less than 15 tons; nor
    (b)   a ship designed or adapted for use for recreation or pleasure."
Item 2 was substituted by SI 1995/3039, art. 2(b), operative from 1 January 1996. Former item 2 read as follows:
"2.   The supply, repair or maintenance of any aircraft which is neither
    (a)   an aircraft of a weight of less than 8,000 kilogrammes; nor
    (b)   an aircraft designed or adapted for use for recreation or pleasure."
Item 2A was inserted by SI 1995/3039, art. 2(c), operative from 1 January 1996.
Item 2B was inserted by SI 1995/3039, art. 2(c), operative from 1 January 1996.
Item 6A was inserted by SI 1995/653, art. 3, operative from 1 April 1995.
In item 10(a), the word "or" at the end was deleted by SI 1995/3039, art. 2(d)(i), operative from 1 January 1996.
In item 10(b), the words "items 1 and 2, 3 to 9 and 11; or" were substituted for the words "items 1 to 9 and 11" by SI 1995/3039, art. 2(d)(ii), operative from 1 January 1996.
Item 10(c) was inserted by SI 1995/3039, art. 2(d)(iii), operative from 1 January 1996.
In item 11(b), the words "item 6A," were inserted by SI 1995/653, art. 4, operative from 1 April 1995.
Note (A1) was inserted by SI 1995/3039, art. 2(e), operative from 1 January 1996.
In Note (1), the word "qualifying" was inserted by SI 1995/3039, art. 2(f), operative from 1 January 1996.
In Note (2), the words ", 2A, 2B" were inserted by SI 1995/3039, art. 2(g), operative from 1 January 1996.
Note (2A) was inserted by SI 1995/3039, art. 2(h), operative from 1 January 1996.
Note (4A) was inserted by SI 1994/3014, art. 3, operative from 1 April 1995.
Note (4B) was inserted by SI 1994/3014, art. 3, operative from 1 April 1995.
Note (4C) was inserted by SI 1994/3014, art. 3, operative from 1 April 1995.
Note (6A) was inserted by SI 1995/653, art. 5, operative from 1 April 1995.
In Note (7), the words "only include supplies . . . may be, aircraft." at the end were substituted for the words "do not include the supply of any services where the ships or aircraft referred to in those paragraphs are of the descriptions specified in paragraphs (a) and (b) of item 1 or in paragraphs (a) and (b) of item 2" by SI 1995/3039, art. 2(i), operative from 1 January 1996.
In Note (7), the words "item 6A," were inserted by SI 1995/653, art. 6, operative from 1 April 1995.

Derivations – Grp. 8, items 1 and 2: VATA 1983, s. 16 and Sch. 5, Grp. 10, items 1 and 2.
Grp. 8, item 3: VATA 1983, s. 16 and Sch. 5, Grp. 10, item 3, as amended by SI 1984/631, SI 1990/752, art. 3(a) and (b) and SI 1992/628, art. 3.
Grp. 8, item 4: VATA 1983, s. 16 and Sch. 5, Grp. 10, item 4, as amended by SI 1990/752, art. 4.
Grp. 8, item 5: VATA 1983, s. 16 and Sch. 5, Grp. 10, item 5, as substituted by SI 1992/3223, art. 3(a).
Grp. 8, item 6: VATA 1983, s. 16 and Sch. 5, Grp. 10, item 6, as amended by SI 1990/752, art. 6.
Grp. 8, items 7 and 8: VATA 1983, s. 16 and Sch. 5, Grp. 10, items 7 and 8.
Grp. 8, item 9: VATA 1983, s. 16 and Sch. 5, Grp. 10, item 9, as amended by SI 1990/752, art. 7.
Grp. 8, item 10: VATA 1983, s. 16 and Sch. 5, Grp. 10, item 10, as amended by SI 1992/3223, art. 3(b).
Grp. 8, item 11 (as originally enacted): VATA 1983, s. 16 and Sch. 5, Grp. 10, item 12, as substituted by SI 1992/3223, art. 3(d).
Grp. 8, item 12: VATA 1983, s. 16 and Sch. 5, Grp. 10, item 13, as inserted by SI 1987/1806, art. 11(1).
Grp. 8, item 13: VATA 1983, s. 16 and Sch. 5, Grp. 10, item 14, as added by SI 1992/3126, art. 2(a).
Note (1): VATA 1983, s. 16 and Sch. 5, Grp. 10, Note (1), as substituted by SI 1990/752, art. 9.
Note (2): VATA 1983, s. 16 and Sch. 5, Grp. 10, Note (2), as amended by SI 1984/631.
Note (3): VATA 1983, s. 16 and Sch. 5, Grp. 10, Note (2A), as inserted by SI 1990/752, art. 10.
Note (4): VATA 1983, s. 16 and Sch. 5, Grp. 10, Note (3), as substituted by SI 1990/752, art. 11.
Notes (5)–(7) (as originally enacted): VATA 1983, s. 16 and Sch. 5, Grp. 10, Notes (4)–(6).
Note (8): VATA 1983, s. 16 and Sch. 5, Grp. 10, Note (7), as inserted by SI 1987/1806, art. 11(2).
Note (9): VATA 1983, s. 16 and Sch. 5, Grp. 10, Note (8), as added by SI 1992/3126, art. 2(b).

Extra-statutory concessions – 3.12 (Notice 48 (1999 edn)): buses with special features for carrying disabled persons.

Official publications – 744A: passenger transport.
744B: freight transport.
744C: ships aircraft and associated services.
744D: international services – zero-rating.

Notes – S. 96(1): "ship" defined.

GROUP 9 – CARAVANS AND HOUSEBOATS

Item No.

1.   Caravans exceeding the limits of size for the time being permitted for the use on roads of a trailer drawn by a motor vehicle having an unladen weight of less than 2,030 kilogrammes.

2.   Houseboats being boats or other floating decked structures designed or adapted for use solely as places of permanent habitation and not having means of, or capable of being readily adapted for, self-propulsion.

3.   The supply of such services as are described in paragraph 1(1) or 5(3) of Schedule 4 in respect of a caravan comprised in item 1 or a houseboat comprised in item 2.

Note:

This Group does not include–
  (a) removable contents other than goods of a kind mentioned in item 3 of Group 5; or
  (b) the supply of accommodation in a caravan or houseboat.
Derivations – VATA 1983, s. 16 and Sch. 5, Grp. 11, as amended by FA 1989, s. 18 and Sch. 3, para. 3.
Official publications – 701/20.

GROUP 10 – GOLD

Item No.
1.   The supply, by a Central Bank to another Central Bank or a member of the London Gold Market, of gold held in the United Kingdom.
2.   The supply, by a member of the London Gold Market to a Central Bank, of gold held in the United Kingdom.

Notes:
(1) **"Gold"** includes gold coins.
(2) Section 30(3) does not apply to goods forming part of a description of supply in this Group.
(3) Items 1 and 2 include–
  (a) the granting of a right to acquire a quantity of gold; and
  (b) any supply described in those items which by virtue of paragraph 1 of Schedule 4 is a supply of services.
Derivations – VATA 1983, s. 16 and Sch. 5, Grp. 12.
Official publications – 701/21.

GROUP 11 – BANK NOTES

Item No.
1.   The issue by a bank of a note payable to bearer on demand.
Derivations – VATA 1983, s. 16 and Sch. 5, Grp. 13.

GROUP 12 – DRUGS, MEDICINES, AIDS FOR THE HANDICAPPED, ETC.

Item No.
1.   The supply of any qualifying goods dispensed to an individual for his personal use where the dispensing is by a person registered in the register of pharmaceutical chemists kept under the Pharmacy Act 1954 or the Pharmacy (Northern Ireland) Order 1976, on the prescription of a person registered in the register of medical practitioners, the register of medical practitioners with limited registration or the dentists' register.
1A. The supply of any qualifying goods in accordance with a requirement or authorisation under–
  (a) regulation 20 of the National Health Service (Pharmaceutical Services) Regulations 1992;
  (b) regulation 34 of the National Health Service (General Medical Services) (Scotland) Regulations 1995; or
  (c) regulation 12 of the Pharmaceutical Services Regulations (Northern Ireland) 1997,
by a person registered in the register of medical practitioners or the register of medical practitioners with limited registration.
2.   The supply to a handicapped person for domestic or his personal use, or to a charity for making available to handicapped persons by sale or otherwise, for domestic or their personal use, of–
  (a) medical or surgical appliances designed solely for the relief of a severe abnormality or severe injury;
  (b) *electrically or mechanically* adjustable beds designed for invalids;
  (c) commode chairs, commode stools, devices incorporating a bidet jet and warm air drier and frames or other devices for sitting over or rising from a sanitary appliance;
  (d) chair lifts or stair lifts designed for use in connection with invalid wheelchairs;
  (e) hoists and lifters designed for use by invalids;
  (f) motor vehicles designed or substantially and permanently adapted for the carriage of a person in a wheelchair or on a stretcher and of no more than 5 other persons;
  (g) equipment and appliances not included in paragraph (a) to (f) above designed solely for use by a handicapped person;
  (h) parts and accessories designed solely for use in or with goods described in paragraph (a) to (g) above;

(i)   boats designed or substantially and permanently adapted for use by handicapped persons.

3.   The supply to a handicapped person of services of adapting goods to suit his condition.

4.   The supply to a charity of services of adapting goods to suit the condition of a handicapped person to whom the goods are to be made available, by sale or otherwise, by the charity.

5.   The supply to a handicapped person or to a charity of a service of repair or maintenance of any goods specified in item 2, 6, 18 or 19 and supplied as described in that item.

6.   The supply of goods in connection with a supply described in item 3, 4 or 5.

7.   The supply to a handicapped person or to a charity of services necessarily performed in the installation of equipment or appliances (including parts and accessories therefor) specified in item 2 and supplied as described in that item.

8.   The supply to a handicapped person of a service of constructing ramps or widening doorways or passages for the purpose of facilitating his entry to or movement within his private residence.

9.   The supply to a charity of a service described in item 8 for the purpose of facilitating a handicapped person's entry to or movement within any building.

10.   The supply to a handicapped person of a service of providing, extending or adapting a bathroom, washroom or lavatory in his private residence where such provision, extension or adaptation is necessary by reason of his condition.

11.   The supply to a charity of a service of providing, extending or adapting a bathroom, washroom or lavatory for use by handicapped persons–

  (a) in residential accommodation, or

  (b) in a day-centre where at least 20 per cent of the individuals using the centre are handicapped persons,

where such provision, extension or adaptation is necessary by reason of the condition of the handicapped persons.

12.   The supply to a charity of a service of providing, extending or adapting a washroom or lavatory for use by handicapped persons in a building, or any part of a building, used principally by a charity for charitable purposes where such provision, extension or adaptation is necessary to facilitate the use of the washroom or lavatory by handicapped persons.

13.   The supply of goods in connection with a supply described in items 8, 9, 10 or 11.

14.   The letting on hire of a motor vehicle for a period of not less than 3 years to a handicapped person in receipt of a disability living allowance by virtue of entitlement to the mobility component or of mobility supplement where the lessor's business consists predominantly of the provision of motor vehicles to such persons.

15.   The sale of a motor vehicle which had been let on hire in the circumstances described in item 14, where such sale constitutes the first supply of the vehicle after the end of the period of such letting.

16.   The supply to a handicapped person of services necessarily performed in the installation of a lift for the purpose of facilitating his movement between floors within his private residence.

17.   The supply to a charity providing a permanent or temporary residence or day-centre for handicapped persons of services necessarily performed in the installation of a lift for the purpose of facilitating the movement of handicapped persons between floors within that building.

18.   The supply of goods in connection with a supply described in item 16 or 17.

19.   The supply to a handicapped person for domestic or his personal use, or to a charity for making available to handicapped persons by sale or otherwise for domestic or their personal use, of an alarm system designed to be capable of operation by a handicapped person, and to enable him to alert directly a specified person or a control centre.

20.   The supply of services necessarily performed by a control centre in receiving and responding to calls from an alarm system specified in item 19.

Notes:

(1) Section 30(3) does not apply to goods forming part of a description of supply in item 1 or item 1A, nor to other goods forming part of a description of supply in this Group, except where those other goods are acquired from another member State or imported from a place outside the member States by a handicapped person for domestic or his personal use, or by a charity for

making available to handicapped persons, by sale or otherwise, for domestic or their personal use.

(2) For the purposes of item 1 a person who is not registered in the visiting EEC practitioners list in the register of medical practitioners at the time he performs services in an urgent case as mentioned in subsection (3) of section 18 of the Medical Act 1983 is to be treated as being **registered** in that list where he is entitled to be registered in accordance with that section.

(2A) In items 1 and 1A, **"qualifying goods"** means any goods designed or adapted for use in connection with any medical or surgical treatment except–
  (a) hearing aids;
  (b) dentures; and
  (c) spectacles and contact lenses.

(3) **"Handicapped"** means chronically sick or disabled.

(4) Item 2 shall not include hearing aids (except hearing aids designed for the auditory training of deaf children), dentures, spectacles and contact lenses but shall be deemed to include–
  (a) clothing, footwear and wigs;
  (b) invalid wheelchairs, and invalid carriages; and
  (c) renal haemodialysis units, oxygen concentrators, artificial respirators and other similar apparatus.

(5) The supplies described in items 1, 1A and 2 include supplies of services of letting on hire of the goods respectively comprised in those items.

(5A) In item 1 the reference to **personal use** does not include any use which is, or involves, a use by or in relation to an individual while that individual, for the purposes of being provided (whether or not by the person making the supply) with medical or surgical treatment, or with any form of care–
  (a) is an in-patient or resident in a relevant institution which is a hospital or nursing home; or
  (b) is attending at the premises of a relevant institution which is a hospital or nursing home.

(5B) Subject to Notes (5C) and (5D), in item 2 the reference to **domestic or personal use** does not include any use which is, or involves, a use by or in relation to a handicapped person while that person, for the purposes of being provided (whether or not by the person making the supply) with medical or surgical treatment, or with any form of care–
  (a) is an in-patient or resident in a relevant institution; or
  (b) is attending at the premises of a relevant institution.

(5C) Note (5B) does not apply for the purpose of determining whether any of the following supplies falls within item 2, that is to say–
  (a) a supply to a charity;
  (b) a supply by a person mentioned in any of paragraphs (a) to (g) of Note (5H) of an invalid wheelchair or invalid carriage;
  (c) a supply by a person so mentioned of any parts or accessories designed solely for use in or with an invalid wheelchair or invalid carriage.

(5D) Note (5B) applies for the purpose of determining whether a supply of goods by a person not mentioned in any of paragraphs (a) to (g) of Note (5H) falls within item 2 only if those goods are–
  (a) goods falling within paragraph (a) of that item;
  (b) incontinence products and wound dressings; or
  (c) parts and accessories designed solely for use in or with goods falling within paragraph (a) of this Note.

(5E) Subject to Note (5F), item 2 does not include–
  (a) a supply made in accordance with any agreement, arrangement or understanding (whether or not legally enforceable) to which any of the persons mentioned in paragraphs (a) to (g) of Note (5H) is or has been a party otherwise than as the supplier; or
  (b) any supply the whole or any part of the consideration for which is provided (whether directly or indirectly) by a person so mentioned.

(5F) A supply to a handicapped person of an invalid wheelchair or invalid carriage is excluded from item 2 by Note (5E) only if–
  (a) that Note applies in relation to that supply by reference to a person falling within paragraph (g) of Note (5H); or
  (b) the whole of the consideration for the supply is provided (whether directly or indirectly) by a person falling within any of paragraphs (a) to (f) of Note (5H).

(5G) In Notes (4), (5C) and (5F), the references to an **invalid wheelchair** and to an **invalid carriage** do not include references to any mechanically propelled vehicle which is intended or adapted for use on roads.

(5H) The **persons** referred to in Notes (5C) to (5F) are–
  (a) a Health Authority or Special Health Authority in England and Wales;
  (b) a Health Board or Special Health Board in Scotland;
  (c) a Health and Social Services Board in Northern Ireland;
  (d) the Common Services Agency for the Scottish Health Service, the Northern Ireland Central Services Agency for Health and Social Services and the Isle of Man Health Services Board;
  (e) a National Health Service trust established under Part I of the National Health Service and Community Care Act 1990 or the National Health Service (Scotland) Act 1978;
  (ea) a Primary Care Trust established under section 16A of the National Health Service Act 1977;
  (f) a Health and Social Services trust established under Article 10 of the Health and Personal Social Services (Northern Ireland) Order 1991; or
  (g) any person not falling within any of paragraphs (a) to (f) above who is engaged in the carrying on of any activity in respect of which a relevant institution is required to be approved, licensed or registered or as the case may be, would be so required if not exempt.

(5I) In Notes (5A), (5B) and (5H), **"relevant institution"** means any institution (whether a hospital, nursing home or other institution) which provides care or medical or surgical treatment and is either–
  (a) approved, licensed or registered in accordance with the provisions of any enactment or Northern Ireland legislation; or
  (b) exempted by or under the provisions of any enactment or Northern Ireland legislation from any requirement to be approved, licensed or registered,

and in this Note the references to the **provisions of any enactment** or **Northern Ireland legislation** include references only to provisions which, so far as relating to England, Wales, Scotland or Northern Ireland, have the same effect in every locality within that part of the United Kingdom.

(5J) For the purposes of item 11 **"residential accommodation"** means–
  (a) a residential home, or
  (b) self-contained living accommodation,

provided as a residence (whether on a permanent or temporary basis or both) for handicapped persons, but does not include an inn, hotel, boarding house or similar establishment or accommodation in any such type of establishment.

(5K) In this Group **"washroom"** means a room that contains a lavatory or washbasin (or both) but does not contain a bath or a shower or cooking, sleeping or laundry facilities.

(6) Item 14 applies only–
  (a) where the vehicle is unused at the commencement of the period of letting; and
  (b) where the consideration for the letting consists wholly or partly of sums paid to the lessor by the Department of Social Security or the Ministry of Defence on behalf of the lessee in respect of the mobility component of the disability living allowance or mobility supplement to which he is entitled.

(7) In item 14–
  (a) **"disability living allowance"** is a disability living allowance within the meaning of section 71 of the Social Security Contributions and Benefits Act 1992, or section 71 of the Social Security Contributions and Benefits (Northern Ireland) Act 1992; and
  (b) **"mobility supplement"** is a mobility supplement within the meaning of Article 26A of the Naval, Military and Air Forces etc. (Disablement and Death Service Pensions Order 1983, Article 25A of the Personal Injuries (Civilians) Scheme 1983, Article 3 of the Motor Vehicles (Exemption from Vehicles Excise Duty) Order 1985 or Article 3 of the Motor Vehicles (Exemption from Vehicles Excise Duty) (Northern Ireland) Order 1985.

(8) Where in item 3 or 4 the goods are adapted in accordance with that item prior to their *supply to the handicapped person* or the charity, an apportionment shall be made to determine the supply of services which falls within item 3 or 4.

(9) In item 19 or 20, a **specified person or control centre** is a person or centre who or which–
  (a) is appointed to receive directly calls activated by an alarm system described in that item, and
  (b) retains information about the handicapped person to assist him in the event of illness, injury or similar emergency.

History – In item 1, the words "supply of any qualifying goods dispensed to an individual for his personal use where the dispensing is" were substituted by SI 1997/2744, art. 3, operative in relation to supplies made on or after 1 January 1998 and any acquisition or importation taking place on or after that date.
In item 1A, the word "qualifying" was inserted by SI 1997/2744, art. 4, operative in relation to supplies made on or after 1 January 1998 and any acquisition or importation taking place on or after that date.
In item 1A, the words "regulation 12 of the Pharmaceutical Services Regulations (Northern Ireland) 1997" were substituted by SI 1997/2744, art. 4, operative in relation to supplies made on or after 1 January 1998 and any acquisition or importation taking place on or after that date.
Item 1A was inserted by SI 1995/652, art. 3, operative from 1 April 1995.
Item 11 was substituted by SI 2000/805, art. 3, operative in relation to supplies made on or after 1 April 2000. Former item 11 reads as follows:
"11.   The supply to a charity of a service of providing, extending or adapting a bathroom, washroom or lavatory for use by handicapped persons in a residential home where such provision, extension or adaptation is necessary by reason of the condition of the handicapped persons."
In Note (1), the words "or item 1A" were added by SI 1995/652, art. 4, operative from 1 April 1995.
Note (2A) was inserted by SI 1997/2744, art. 5, operative in relation to supplies made on or after 1 January 1998 and any acquisition or importation taking place on or after that date.
In Note (4)(b), the words "other than mechanically propelled vehicles intended or adapted for use on roads" were deleted by SI 1997/2744, art. 6, operative in relation to supplies made on or after 1 January 1998 and any acquisition or importation taking place on or after that date.
Note (5A) was inserted by SI 1997/2744, art. 7, operative in relation to supplies made on or after 1 January 1998 and any acquisition or importation taking place on or after that date.
Note (5B) was inserted by SI 1997/2744, art. 7, operative in relation to supplies made on or after 1 January 1998 and any acquisition or importation taking place on or after that date.
Note (5C) was inserted by SI 1997/2744, art. 7, operative in relation to supplies made on or after 1 January 1998 and any acquisition or importation taking place on or after that date.
Note (5D) was inserted by SI 1997/2744, art. 7, operative in relation to supplies made on or after 1 January 1998 and any acquisition or importation taking place on or after that date.
Note (5E) was inserted by SI 1997/2744, art. 7, operative in relation to supplies made on or after 1 January 1998 and any acquisition or importation taking place on or after that date.
Note (5F) was inserted by SI 1997/2744, art. 7, operative in relation to supplies made on or after 1 January 1998 and any acquisition or importation taking place on or after that date.
Note (5G) was inserted by SI 1997/2744, art. 7, operative in relation to supplies made on or after 1 January 1998 and any acquisition or importation taking place on or after that date.
Note (5H) was inserted by SI 1997/2744, art. 7, operative in relation to supplies made on or after 1 January 1998 and any acquisition or importation taking place on or after that date.
Note (5H)(ea) was inserted by SI 2000/503, art. 3, operative in relation to supplies made on or after 1 April 2000.
Note (5I) was inserted by SI 1997/2744, art. 7, operative in relation to supplies made on or after 1 January 1998 and any acquisition or importation taking place on or after that date.
In Note (5), ", 1A" was added by SI 1995/652, art. 5, operative from 1 April 1995.
Note (5J) was inserted by SI 2000/805, art. 4, operative in relation to supplies made on or after 1 April 2000.
Note (5K) was inserted by SI 2000/805, art. 4, operative in relation to supplies made on or after 1 April 2000.

Derivations – Grp. 12, item 1: VATA 1983, s. 16 and Sch. 5, Grp. 14, item 1.
Grp. 12, item 2: VATA 1983, s. 16 and Sch. 5, Grp. 14, item 2, as amended by SI 1984/489, art. 4 and SI 1992/628, art. 4(a).
Grp. 12, item 3: VATA 1983, s. 16 and Sch. 5, Grp. 14, item 3.
Grp. 12, item 4: VATA 1983, s. 16 and Sch. 5, Grp. 14, item 4, as amended by SI 1984/489, art. 5.
Grp. 12, item 5: VATA 1983, s. 16 and Sch. 5, Grp. 14, item 5, as substituted by SI 1986/530, art. 3(a).
Grp. 12, items 6–9: VATA 1983, s. 16 and Sch. 5, Grp. 14, items 6–9.
Grp. 12, item 10: VATA 1983, s. 16 and Sch. 5, Grp. 14, item 10, as substituted by SI 1986/530, art. 3(b).
Grp. 12, item 11: VATA 1983, s. 16 and Sch. 5, Grp. 14, item 10A, as inserted by SI 1987/437.
Grp. 12, item 12: VATA 1983, s. 16 and Sch. 5, Grp. 14, item 10B, as added by SI 1992/628, art. 4(b).
Grp. 12, item 13: VATA 1983, s. 16 and Sch. 5, Grp. 14, item 11, as substituted by SI 1987/437.
Grp. 12, item 14: VATA 1983, s. 16 and Sch. 5, Grp. 14, item 12, as inserted by SI 1984/959, as amended by Disability Living Allowance and Disability Working Allowance Act 1991, s. 4 and Sch. 2, para. 13 and SI 1991/2874, art. 3(a).
Grp. 12, item 15: VATA 1983, s. 16 and Sch. 5, Grp. 14, item 12A, as inserted by SI 1992/3065, art. 2.
Grp. 12, items 16–20: VATA 1983, s. 16 and Sch. 5, Grp. 14, items 13–17, as inserted by SI 1986/530, art. 3(c).
Grp. 12, Note (1) (as originally enacted): VATA 1983, s. 16 and Sch. 5, Grp. 14, Note (1), as amended by F(No. 2)A 1992, s. 14 and Sch. 3, para. 63(1).
Grp. 12, Notes (2)–(5) (as originally enacted): VATA 1983, s. 16 and Sch. 5, Grp. 14, Notes (2)–(5).
Grp. 12, Note (6): VATA 1983, s. 16 and Sch. 5, Grp. 14, Note (6), as amended by SI 1985/919 and SI 1988/1843, art. 5(4), Sch. 3, para. 4(b).
Grp. 12, Note (7): VATA 1983, s. 16 and Sch. 5, Grp. 14, Note (7), as amended by Disability Living Allowance and Disability Working Allowance Act 1991, s. 4 and Sch. 2, para. 13(2) and Sch. 4, Social Security (Consequential Provisions) Act 1992, s. 4 and Sch. 2, para. 65, Social Security (Consequential Provisions) (Northern Ireland) Act 1992, s. 4 and Sch. 2, para. 28, SI 1985/919 and SI 1991/2874, art. 3(b).
Grp. 12, Notes (8), (9): VATA 1983, s. 16 and Sch. 5, Grp. 14, Notes (8), (9), as inserted by SI 1986/530.

Cross references – VAT (Input Tax) Order 1992 (SI 1992/3222), art. 7(2): disallowance of input tax and letting of cars. VAT Regulations 1995 (SI 1995/2518), reg. 74(1): adjustment by retail scheme user in manner prescribed by a notice published by the commissioners.

Other material – HM Customs and Excise News Release 13/95, 16 March 1995: drugs dispensed by doctors zero-rated.

GROUP 13 – IMPORTS, EXPORTS ETC.

Item No.
1.   The supply before the delivery of an entry (within the meaning of regulation 5 of the Customs Controls on Importation of Goods Regulations 1991)) under an agreement requiring the purchaser to make such entry of goods imported from a place outside the member States.
2.   The supply to or by an overseas authority, overseas body or overseas trader, charged with the management of any defence project which is the subject of an international collaboration arrangement or under direct contract with any government or government-

sponsored international body participating in a defence project under such an arrangement, of goods or services in the course of giving effect to that arrangement.

3. The supply to an overseas authority, overseas body or overseas trader of jigs, patterns, templates, dies, punches and similar machine tools used in the United Kingdom solely for the manufacture of goods for export to places outside the member States.

Notes:

(1) An **"international collaboration arrangement"** means any arrangement which–

 (a) is made between the United Kingdom Government and the government of one or more other countries, or any government-sponsored international body for collaboration in a joint project of research, development or production; and

 (b) includes provision for participating governments to relieve the cost of the project from taxation.

(2) **"Overseas authority"** means any country other than the United Kingdom or any part of or place in such a country or the government of any such country, part or place.

(3) **"Overseas body"** means a body established outside the United Kingdom.

(4) **"Overseas trader"** means a person who carries on a business and has his principal place of business outside the United Kingdom.

(5) Item 3 does not apply where the overseas authority, overseas body or overseas trader is a taxable person, another member State, any part of or place in another member State, the government of any such member State, part or place, a body established in another member State or a person who carries on business, or has a place of business, in another member State.

Derivations – VATA 1983, s. 16 and Sch. 5, Grp. 15, items 1, 3, 4, Notes (2)–(6), as amended by F(No. 2)A 1992, s. 14 and Sch. 3, para. 63(2) and (3) and s. 82 and Sch. 18, Pt. V and SI 1992/3095, reg. 10(1) and Sch. 1, para. 8.

Cross references – VAT (Isle of Man) Order 1982 (SI 1982/1067), art. 8: taxable person includes a person who is a taxable person under the Manx Act.

Official publications – 703: Exports and removals of goods from the UK.
704: Retail exports.
705: Personal exports of new motor vehicles to destinations outside the EC from 1 January 1993.
705A: VAT: supplies of vehicles under the personal export scheme for removal from the European Community.
725: The single market.
728: Motor vehicles, boats, aircraft: intra-EC movements by persons not registrable for VAT.
703/1: Supply of freight containers for export or removal from the United Kingdom.
703/2: Sailaway boats supplied for export outside the European Community.
703/3: Sailaway boat scheme.
704/1: VAT refunds for travellers departing from the European Community.
704/2: Traveller's guide to the retail export scheme.
704/3: Guide to tax-free shopping – the VAT refund scheme.
Customs Internal Guidance Manual, vol. V1.16: single market.
Customs Internal Guidance Manual, vol. V1.18: import reliefs.
Customs Internal Guidance Manual, vol. V1.20: general export.
Customs Internal Guidance Manual, vol. V1.21: personal reliefs – exports.

GROUP 14 – TAX-FREE SHOPS

Item No.

1-2. [Repealed by SI 1999/1642, art. 2(b), with effect in relation to supplies made on or after 1 July 1999.]

History – The wording of former Grp. 14 is as follows:

GROUP 14 – TAX-FREE SHOPS

Item No.

1. The supply, by a person in the course of carrying on business in a tax-free shop, to a traveller making a relevant journey, of goods which are of either of the following descriptions–

 (a) goods not included in the first column of the following Table which do not exceed a value of £75 in aggregate and which are to be carried in the traveller's personal luggage; or

 (b) goods included in the first column of the following Table which do not exceed the quantities set out in the second column of that Table and which are to be carried in the traveller's personal luggage.

Goods	Quantity
Alcoholic beverages:	
(a) with an alcoholic strength of more than 22% by volume	1 litre
or	
with an alcoholic strength of not more than 22% by volume, fortified wines and sparkling wines (including made-wines)	2 litres
(b) still wines (including made-wines)	2 litres
Perfume and Toilet Water	
Perfume	60 ml
Toilet Water	250 ml

Goods	Quantity
Tobacco products:	
Cigarettes	200
or	
Cigarillos	100
or	
Cigars	50
or	
Smoking tobacco	250 grammes

2.   The supply, of any goods within Item 1(a) or (b) above, to a traveller on board an aircraft or ship making a relevant journey by a person who supplies the traveller's air or sea transport or any other person authorised by that person.

Notes:

(1) For the purpose of determining the aggregate value of any goods referred to in Item 1(a) only the whole of the value of any item, or group of items which are normally sold as a set or collection, may be included in the aggregate value of £75.

(2) **"Tax free shop"** means any shop which is situated within an airport, port or Channel Tunnel terminal and which is approved by the Commissioners for the supply of goods for the purposes of this Group, and in this note **"Channel Tunnel terminal"** means the area situated in the vicinity of Cheriton, Folkestone referred to in section 1(7)(b) of the Channel Tunnel Act 1987.

(3) **"Relevant journey"** means a journey by air or sea from the United Kingdom to a place in another member State where the traveller is to disembark and includes, for the purposes of Item 1, a journey by a Channel Tunnel shuttle train.

(4) **"Traveller"** means any passenger travelling under a transport document for air or sea travel stating that the immediate destination is a place in another member State (including such a transport document stating that the final destination is a place outside the member States) or for shuttle train travel.

(5) Items 1 and 2 do not apply where the supply is to a traveller under 17 years of age of goods falling within Item 1(b), other than perfumes and toilet waters.

(6) In these Notes **"shuttle train"** has the meaning given by section 1(9) of the Channel Tunnel Act 1987."

In former item 1(a), the amount "£75" was substituted for "£71" by SI 1995/3041, art. 2(a), operative from 1 January 1996.
In former Note (1), the amount "£75" was substituted for "£71" by SI 1995/3041, art. 2(b), operative from 1 January 1996.

Derivations – VATA 1983, s. 16 and Sch. 5, Grp. 15A, as inserted by SI 1992/3131, art. 2, as amended by SI 1994/686, art. 2.

GROUP 15 – CHARITIES ETC.

Item No.

1.   The sale, or letting on hire, by a charity of any goods donated to it for–
    (a) sale,
    (b) letting,
    (c) sale or letting,
    (d) sale or export,
    (e) letting or export, or
    (f) sale, letting or export.

1A.   The sale, or letting on hire, by a taxable person of any goods donated to him for–
    (a) sale,
    (b) letting,
    (c) sale or letting,
    (d) sale or export,
    (e) letting or export, or
    (f) sale, letting or export,
if he is a profits-to-charity person in respect of the goods.

2.   The donation of any goods for any one or more of the following purposes–
    (a) sale by a charity or a taxable person who is a profits-to-charity person in respect of the goods;
    (b) export by a charity or such a taxable person;
    (c) letting by a charity or such a taxable person.

3.   The export of any goods by a charity to a place outside the member States.

4.   The supply of any relevant goods for donation to a nominated eligible body where the goods are purchased with funds provided by a charity or from voluntary contributions.

5.   The supply of any relevant goods to an eligible body which pays for them with funds provided by a charity or from voluntary contributions or to an eligible body which is a charitable institution providing care or medical or surgical treatment for handicapped persons.

6.   Repair and maintenance of relevant goods owned by an eligible body.

7.   The supply of goods in connection with the supply described in item 6.

8.   The supply to a charity of a right to promulgate an advertisement by means of a medium of communication with the public.

8A.   A supply to a charity that consists in the promulgation of an advertisement by means of such a medium.

8B.   The supply to a charity of services of design or production of an advertisement that is, or was intended to be, promulgated by means of such a medium.

8C.   The supply to a charity of goods closely related to a supply within item 8B.

9.   The supply to a charity, providing care or medical or surgical treatment for human beings or animals, or engaging in medical or veterinary research, of a medicinal product where the supply is solely for use by the charity in such care, treatment or research.

10.   The supply to a charity of a substance directly used for synthesis or testing in the course of medical or veterinary research.

Notes:

(1) Item 1 or 1A does not apply unless the sale or letting–
- (a)   takes place as a result of the goods having been made available–
    - (i)   to two or more specified persons, or
    - (ii) to the general public,for purchase or hire (whether so made available in a shop or elsewhere), and
- (b)   does not take place as a result of any arrangements (whether legally binding or not) relating to the goods and entered into, before the goods were made so available, by–
    - (i)   each of the parties to the sale or letting, or
    - (ii) the donor of the goods and either or both of those parties.

(1A) For the purposes of items 1, 1A and 2, goods are **donated for letting** only if they are donated for–
- (a)   letting, and
- (b)   re-letting after the end of any first or subsequent letting, and
- (c)   all or any of–
    - (i)   sale,
    - (ii) export, or
    - (iii) disposal as waste,if not, or when no longer, used for letting.

(1B) Items 1 and 1A do not include (and shall be treated as having not included) any sale, or letting on hire, of particular donated goods if the goods, at any time after they are donated but before they are sold, exported or disposed of as waste, are whilst unlet used for any purpose other than, or in addition to, that of being available for purchase, hire or export.

(1C) In Note (1) **"specified person"** means a person who–
- (a)   is handicapped, or
- (b)   is entitled to any one or more of the specified benefits, or
- (c)   is both handicapped and so entitled.

(1D) For the purposes of Note (1C) the **specified benefits** are–
- (a)   income support under Part VII of the Social Security Contributions and Benefits Act 1992 or Part VII of the Social Security Contributions and Benefits (Northern Ireland) Act 1992;
- (b)   housing benefit under Part VII of the Social Security Contributions and Benefits Act 1992 or Part VII of the Social Security Contributions and Benefits (Northern Ireland) Act 1992;
- (c)   council tax benefit under Part VII of the Social Security Contributions and Benefits Act 1992;
- (d)   an income-based jobseeker's allowance within the meaning of section 1(4) of the Jobseekers Act 1995 or article 3(4) of the Jobseekers (Northern Ireland) Order 1995;
- (e)   working families' tax credit under Part VII of the Social Security Contributions and Benefits Act 1992 or Part VII of the Social Security Contributions and Benefits (Northern Ireland) Act 1992; and
- (f)   disabled person's tax credit under Part VII of the Social Security Contributions and Benefits Act 1992 or Part VII of the Social Security Contributions and Benefits (Northern Ireland) Act 1992.

(1E) For the purposes of items 1A and 2 a taxable person is a **"profits-to-charity"** person in respect of any goods if–
- (a)   he has agreed in writing (whether or not contained in a deed) to transfer to a charity his profits from supplies and lettings of the goods, or
- (b)   *his profits from supplies and lettings of the goods are otherwise payable to a charity.*

(1F) In items 1, 1A and 2, and any Notes relating to any of those items, **"goods"** means goods (and, in particular, does not include anything that is not goods even though provision made by or under an enactment provides for a supply of that thing to be, or be treated as, a supply of goods).

(2) **"Animals"** includes any species of the animal kingdom.

(3) **"Relevant goods"** means–
  (a) medical, scientific, computer, video, sterilising, laboratory or refrigeration equipment for use in medical or veterinary research, training, diagnosis or treatment;
  (b) ambulances;
  (c) parts or accessories for use in or with goods described in paragraph (a) or (b) above;
  (d) goods of a kind described in item 2 of Group 12 of this Schedule;
  (e) motor vehicles (other than vehicles with more than 50 seats) designed or substantially and permanently adapted for the safe carriage of a handicapped person in a wheelchair provided that–
      (i) in the case of vehicles with more than 16 but fewer than 27 seats, the number of persons for which such provision shall exist shall be at least 2;
      (ii) in the case of vehicles with more than 26 but fewer than 37 seats, the number of persons for which such provision shall exist shall be at least 3;
      (iii) in the case of vehicles with more than 36 but fewer than 47 seats, the number of persons for which such provision shall exist shall be at least 4;
      (iv) in the case of vehicles with more than 46 seats, the number of persons for which such provision shall exist shall be at least 5;
      (v) there is either a fitted electrically or hydraulically operated lift or, in the case of vehicles with fewer than 17 seats, a fitted ramp to provide access for a passenger in a wheelchair;
  (f) motor vehicles (with more than 6 but fewer than 51 seats) for use by an eligible body providing care for blind, deaf, mentally handicapped or terminally sick persons mainly to transport such persons;
  (g) telecommunication, aural, visual, light enhancing or heat detecting equipment (not being equipment ordinarily supplied for private or recreational use) solely for use for the purpose of rescue or first aid services undertaken by a charitable institution providing such services.
(4) **"Eligible body"** means–
  (a) a Health Authority or Special Health Authority in England and Wales;
  (b) a Health board in Scotland;
  (c) a Health and Social Services board in Northern Ireland;
  (d) a hospital whose activities are not carried on for profit;
  (e) a research institution whose activities are not carried on for profit;
  (f) a charitable institution providing care or medical or surgical treatment for handicapped persons;
  (g) the Common Services Agency for the Scottish Health Service, the Northern Ireland Central Services Agency for Health and Social Services or the Isle of Man Health Services board;
  (h) a charitable institution providing rescue or first-aid services;
  (i) a National Health Service trust established under Part I of the National Health Service and Community Care Act 1990 or the National Health Service (Scotland) Act 1978;
  (j) a Primary Care Trust established under section 16A of the National Health Service Act 1977.
(4A) Subject to Note (5B), a charitable institution shall not be regarded as **providing care or medical or surgical treatment** for handicapped persons unless–
  (a) it provides care or medical or surgical treatment in a relevant establishment; and
  (b) the majority of the persons who receive care or medical or surgical treatment in that establishment are handicapped persons.
(4B) **"Relevant establishment"** means–
  (a) a day-centre, other than a day-centre which exists primarily as a place for activities that are social or recreational or both; or
  (b) an institution which is–
      (i) approved, licensed or registered in accordance with the provisions of any enactment or Northern Ireland legislation; or
      (ii) exempted by or under the provisions of any enactment or Northern Ireland legislation from any requirement to be approved, licensed or registered;
and in paragraph (b) above the references to **the provisions of any enactment or Northern Ireland legislation** are references only to provisions which, so far as relating to England, Wales, Scotland or Northern Ireland, have the same effect in every locality within that part of the United Kingdom.
(5) **"Handicapped"** means chronically sick or disabled.

(5A) Subject to Note (5B), items 4 to 7 do not apply where the eligible body falls within Note (4)(f) unless the relevant goods are or are to be used in a relevant establishment in which that body provides care or medical or surgical treatment to persons the majority of whom are handicapped.

(5B) Nothing in Note (4A) or (5A) shall prevent a supply from falling within items 4 to 7 where–

  (a)   the eligible body provides medical care to handicapped persons in their own homes;

  (b)   the relevant goods fall within Note (3)(a) or are parts or accessories for use in or with goods described in Note (3)(a); and

  (c)   those goods are or are to be used in or in connection with the provision of that care.

(6) Item 4 does not apply where the donee of the goods is not a charity and has contributed in whole or in part to the funds for the purchase of the goods.

(7) Item 5 does not apply where the body to whom the goods are supplied is not a charity and has contributed in whole or in part to the funds for the purchase of the goods.

(8) Items 6 and 7 do not apply unless–

  (a)   the supply is paid for with funds which have been provided by a charity or from voluntary contributions, and

  (b)   in a case where the owner of the goods repaired or maintained is not a charity, it has not contributed in whole or in part to those funds.

(9) Items 4 and 5 include the letting on hire of relevant goods; accordingly in items 4, 5 and 6 and the notes relating thereto, references to the **purchase or ownership of goods** shall be deemed to include references respectively to their hiring and possession.

(10) Item 5 includes computer services by way of the provision of computer software solely for use in medical research, diagnosis or treatment.

(10A) Neither of items 8 and 8A includes a supply where any of the members of the public (whether individuals or other persons) who are reached through the medium are selected by or on behalf of the charity.

For this purpose **"selected"** includes selected by address (whether postal address or telephone number, e-mail address or other address for electronic communications purposes) or at random.

(10B) None of items 8 to 8C includes a supply used to create, or contribute to, a website that is the charity's own.

For this purpose a website is a charity's own even though hosted by another person.

(10C) Neither of items 8B and 8C includes a supply to a charity that is used directly by the charity to design or produce an advertisement.

(11) In item 9–

  (a)   a **"medicinal product"** means any substance or article (not being an instrument, apparatus or appliance) which is for use wholly or mainly in either or both of the following ways–

      (i)   by being administered to one or more human beings or animals for a medicinal purpose;

      (ii)   as an ingredient in the preparation of a substance or article which is to be administered to one or more human beings or animals for a medicinal purpose;

  (b)   a **"medicinal purpose"** has the meaning assigned to it by section 130(2) of the Medicines Act 1968.

  (c)   **"administer"** has the meaning assigned to it by section 130(9) of the Medicines Act 1968;

(12) In items 9 and 10 **"substance"** and **"ingredient"** have the meanings assigned to them by section 132 of the Medicines Act 1968.

History – Items 1, 1A and 2 were substituted for former items 1 and 2 by SI 2000/805, art. 6, operative in relation to supplies made on or after 1 April 2000. Former item 1 reads as follows:

"1.   The supply by a charity of any goods which have been donated for sale or the supply of such goods by a taxable person who has covenanted by deed to give all the profits of that supply to a charity.

2.   The donation of any goods for sale or export by a charity described in item 1 or by a taxable person described in that item."

Items 8, 8A, 8B and 8C were substituted for former item 8 by SI 2000/805, art. 7, operative in relation to supplies made on or after 1 April 2000. Former item 8 reads as follows:

"8.   The supply to a charity, for the purpose of raising money for, or making known the objects or reasons for the objects of, the charity, of–

    (a)   the broadcast on television or radio or screening in a cinema of an advertisement; or

    (b)   the publication of an advertisement in any newspaper, journal, poster, programme, annual, leaflet, brochure, pamphlet, periodical or similar publication; or

    (c)   any goods or services in connection with the preparation of an advertisement within (b) above."

Notes (1) and (1A)–(1F) were substituted for former Note (1) by SI 2000/805, art. 8, operative in relation to supplies made on or after 1 April 2000. Former Note (1) reads as follows:

"(1)   Item 1 shall apply only if–

  (a)   the supply is a sale of goods donated to that charity or taxable person;

(b)   the sale takes place as a result of the goods having been made available to the general public for purchase (whether in a shop or elsewhere); and

(c)   the sale does not take place as a result of any arrangements (whether legally binding or not) which related to the goods and were entered into by each of the parties to the sale before the goods were made available to the general public."

Former Note (1) was substituted by FA 1997, s. 33(1), with effect in relation to supplies made on or after 26 November 1996.

In Note (4)(a), the words "Health Authority or Special Health Authority" were substituted for the words "Regional, District or Special Health Authority" by the Health Authorities Act 1995, Sch. 1, para. 127, with effect from 28 June 1995.

Note (4)(j) was added by SI 2000/503, art. 4, operative in relation to supplies made on or after 1 April 2000.

Note (4A) was inserted by FA 1997, s. 34(1), with effect in relation to supplies made on or after 26 November 1996.

Note (4B) was inserted by FA 1997, s. 34(1), with effect in relation to supplies made on or after 26 November 1996.

Note (5A) was inserted by FA 1997, s. 34(2), with effect in relation to supplies made on or after 26 November 1996.

Note (5B) was inserted by FA 1997, s. 34(2), with effect in relation to supplies made on or after 26 November 1996.

Note (10A) was inserted by SI 2000/805, art. 9, operative in relation to supplies made on or after 1 April 2000.

Note (10B) was inserted by SI 2000/805, art. 9, operative in relation to supplies made on or after 1 April 2000.

Note (10C) was inserted by SI 2000/805, art. 9, operative in relation to supplies made on or after 1 April 2000.

Derivations – Grp. 15, item 1: VATA 1983, s. 16 and Sch. 5, Grp. 16, item 1, as substituted by SI 1991/737, art. 3.

Grp. 15, item 2: VATA 1983, s. 16 and Sch. 5, Grp. 16, item 2, as amended by SI 1987/437 and SI 1990/750, art. 4.

Grp. 15, item 3: VATA 1983, s. 16 and Sch. 5, Grp. 16, item 3, as amended by F(No. 2)A 1992, s. 14 and Sch. 3, para. 63(4).

Grp. 15, items 4–7: VATA 1983, s. 16 and Sch. 5, Grp. 16, items 4–7.

Grp. 15, item 8: VATA 1983, s. 16 and Sch. 5, Grp. 16, item 8, as substituted by SI 1991/737, art. 4.

Grp. 15, item 9: VATA 1983, s. 16 and Sch. 5, Grp. 16, item 9, as inserted by SI 1986/530, art. 4(a), as amended by SI 1991/737, art. 5.

Grp. 15, item 10: VATA 1983, s. 16 and Sch. 5, Grp. 16, item 10, as inserted by SI 1987/437, as amended by SI 1991/737, art. 6.

Note (1): VATA 1983, s. 16 and Sch. 5, Grp. 16, Note (1), as substituted by SI 1990/750, art. 6.

Note (2): VATA 1983, s. 16 and Sch. 5, Grp. 16, Note (3).

Note (3): VATA 1983, s. 16 and Sch. 5, Grp. 16, Note (4), as amended by SI 1984/766, SI 1986/530, SI 1987/437, art. 3(3) and (4), SI 1989/470, SI 1990/750, art. 7 and 8 and SI 1991/737, art. 8.

Note (4) (as originally enacted): VATA 1983, s. 16 and Sch. 5, Grp. 16, Note (5), as amended by SI 1983/1717 and SI 1990/2129.

Notes (5)–(8): VATA 1983, s. 16 and Sch. 5, Grp. 16, Notes (6)–(9).

Notes (9), (10): VATA 1983, s. 16 and Sch. 5, Grp. 16, Notes (10), (11), as inserted by SI 1983/1717.

Note (11): VATA 1983, s. 16 and Sch. 5, Grp. 16, Note (12), as inserted by SI 1986/530, as amended by SI 1987/437.

Note (12): VATA 1983, s. 16 and Sch. 5, Grp. 16, Note (13), as inserted by SI 1987/437.

Extra-statutory concessions – 4.1 (Notice 48 (1999 edn)): zero-rating of sailaway boats.

5.1 (Notice 48 (1999 edn)): zero-rating by duty-free shops.

Official publications – 701/1, 701/6 and 701/7.

Customs Internal Guidance Manual, vol. V1.9: charities.

Other material – Customs and Excise Business Brief 1/95, 11 January 1995 (not reproduced): job recruitment advertisements placed by charities are, subject to conditions, eligible for zero-rating under Grp. 15, item 8.

Customs and Excise Business Brief 12/92, 29 July 1992 (not reproduced): buildings and land are not, in Customs' view, covered by the provisions of Grp. 15, item 1.

Customs and Excise Press Notice 991, 19 March 1985 (not reproduced): "computer equipment" in Note (3)(a) includes any computer, its peripherals and parts and accessories, including discs and tapes specially designed for use with the computer but not general purpose tapes or cassettes, or items such as paper, ink and cleaning fluids.

Notes – In the Queen's printer's version, Note (11)(c) ends with a semi colon when a full stop is appropriate.

GROUP 16 – CLOTHING AND FOOTWEAR

Item No.

1.   Articles designed as clothing or footwear for young children and not suitable for older persons.

2.   The supply to a person for use otherwise than by employees of his of protective boots and helmets for industrial use.

3.   Protective helmets for wear by a person driving or riding a motor bicycle.

Notes:

(1) **"Clothing"** includes hats and other headgear.

(2) Item 1 does not include articles of clothing made wholly or partly of fur skin, except–

(a) headgear;

(b) gloves;

(c) buttons, belts and buckles;

(d) any garment merely trimmed with fur skin unless the trimming has an area greater than one-*fifth of the area of the outside* material or, in the case of a new garment, represents a cost to the manufacturer greater than the cost to him of the other components.

(3) **"Fur skin"** means any skin with fur, hair or wool attached except–

(a) rabbit skin;

(b) woolled sheep or lamb skin; and

(c) the skin, if neither tanned nor dressed, of bovine cattle (including buffalo), equine animals, goats or kids (other than Yemen, Mongolian and Tibetan goats or kids), swine (including peccary), chamois, gazelles, deer or dogs.

(4) Item 2 applies only where the goods to which it refers are–

(a) goods which–

(i) are manufactured to standards approved by the British Standards Institution; and

        (ii) bear a marking indicating compliance with the specification relating to such goods; or

  (b) goods which–

        (i) are manufactured to standards which satisfy requirements imposed (whether under the law of the United Kingdom or the law of any other member State) for giving effect to the directive of the Council of the European Communities dated 21st December 1989 No. 89/686/EEC; and

        (ii) bear any mark of conformity provided for by virtue of that directive in relation to those goods.

(4A) Item 3 does not apply to a helmet unless it is of a type that on 30th June 2000 is prescribed by regulations made on or before 6th June 2000 under section 17 of the Road Traffic Act 1988 (types of helmet recommended as affording protection to persons on or in motor cycles from injury in the event of accident).

(5) Items 1, 2 and 3 include the supply of the services described in paragraph 1(1) and 5(4) of Schedule 4 in respect of goods comprised in the items, but, in the case of goods comprised in item 2, only if the goods are for use otherwise than by employees of the person to whom the services are supplied.

History – In Note (4), the words "Item 2 applies only where the goods to which it refers are–" at the beginning were substituted for the words "Items 2 and 3 apply only where the goods to which they refer are–" by SI 2000/1517, art. 3, operative in relation to supplies made on or after 30 June 2000.
Note (4A) was inserted by SI 2000/1517, art. 4, operative in relation to supplies made on or after 30 June 2000.
In Note (5), the words "5(4)" were substituted for the words "5(3)" by SI 2000/1517, art. 5, operative in relation to supplies made on or after 30 June 2000.

Derivations – VATA 1983, s. 16 and Sch. 5, Grp. 17, as amended by FA 1989, s. 22 and SI 1993/767.

Official publications – 714, 714A and 701/23.

SCHEDULE 9 – EXEMPTIONS

Sections 8 and 31

Cross references – Sch. 9 is interpreted in accordance with the notes contained in that schedule (s. 96(9)). The descriptions of the groups in that schedule are for ease of reference only and do not affect the interpretation (s. 96(10)).
S. 43(2A)(b): group supplies using an overseas member.
S. 96(10A)(b): interpretation and references to grants.

Part I – Index to Exempt Supplies of Goods and Services

History – The reference to Grp. 13 was added by SI 1999/2834, art. 3(b), operative from 1 December 1999.
The reference to Grp. 15 was added by SI 1999/3116, art. 2(2), operative from 1 January 2000.
The reference to Grp. 14 was added by SI 1999/2833, art. 2(2), operative from 1 March 2000.
The reference to Grp. 9 was amended by SI 1999/2834, art. 3(a), operative from 1 December 1999.

Part II – The Groups

GROUP 1 – LAND

Item No.

1. The grant of any interest in or right over land or of any licence to occupy land, or, in relation to land in Scotland, any personal right to call for or be granted any such interest or right, other than–

   (a) the grant of the fee simple in–
- (i) a building which has not been completed and which is neither designed as a dwelling or number of dwellings nor intended for use solely for a relevant residential purpose or a relevant charitable purpose;
- (ii) a new building which is neither designed as a dwelling or number of dwellings nor intended for use solely for a relevant residential purpose or a relevant charitable purpose after the grant;
- (iii) a civil engineering work which has not been completed;
- (iv) a new civil engineering work;

   (b) a supply made pursuant to a developmental tenancy, developmental lease or developmental licence;

   (c) the grant of any interest, right or licence consisting of a right to take game or fish unless at the time of the grant the grantor grants to the grantee the fee simple of the land over which the right to take game or fish is exercisable;

   (d) the provision in an hotel, inn, boarding house or similar establishment of sleeping accommodation or of accommodation in rooms which are provided in conjunction with sleeping accommodation or for the purpose of a supply of catering;

   (e) the grant of any interest in, right over or licence to occupy holiday accommodation;

   (f) the provision of seasonal pitches for caravans, and the grant of facilities at caravan parks to persons for whom such pitches are provided;

   (g) the provision of pitches for tents or of camping facilities;

   (h) the grant of facilities for parking a vehicle;

   (j) the grant of any right to fell and remove standing timber;

   (k) the grant of facilities for housing, or storage of, an aircraft or for mooring, or storage of, a ship, boat or other vessel;

   (l) the grant of any right to occupy a box, seat or other accommodation at a sports ground, theatre, concert hall or other place of entertainment;

   (m) the grant of facilities for playing any sport or participating in any physical recreation; and

   (n) the grant of any right, including–
- (i) an equitable right,
- (ii) a right under an option or right of pre-emption, or
- (iii) in relation to land in Scotland, a personal right,

to call for or be granted an interest or right which would fall within any of paragraph (a) or (c) to (m) above.

Notes:

(1) **"Grant"** includes an assignment or surrender and the supply made by the person to whom an interest is surrendered when there is a reverse surrender.

(1A) A **"reverse surrender"** is one in which the person to whom the interest is surrendered is paid by the person by whom the interest is being surrendered to accept the surrender.

(2) A building shall be taken to be **completed** when an architect issues a certificate of practical completion in relation to it or it is first fully occupied, whichever happens first; and a civil engineering work shall be taken to be **completed** when an engineer issues a certificate of completion in relation to it or it is first fully used, whichever happens first.

(3) Notes (2) to (10) and (12) to Group 5 of Schedule 8 apply in relation to this Group as they apply in relation to that Group.

(4) A building or civil engineering work is **new** if it was completed less than three years before the grant.

(5) Subject to Note (6), the grant of the fee simple in a building or work completed before 1st April 1989 is not excluded from this Group by paragraph (a)(ii) or (iv).

(6) Note (5) does not apply where the grant is the first grant of the fee simple made on or after 1st April 1989 and the building was not fully occupied, or the work not fully used, before that date.

(7) A tenancy of, lease of or licence to occupy a building or work is treated as becoming a **developmental tenancy**, **developmental lease** or **developmental licence** (as the case may be) when a tenancy of, lease of or licence to occupy a building or work, whose construction, reconstruction, enlargement or extension commenced on or after 1st January 1992, is treated as being supplied to and by the developer under paragraph 6(1) of Schedule 10 (except where that paragraph applies by virtue of paragraph 5(1)(b) of that Schedule).

(8) Where a grant of an interest in, right over or licence to occupy land includes a valuable right to take game or fish, an apportionment shall be made to determine the supply falling outside this Group by virtue of paragraph (c).

(9) **"Similar establishment"** includes premises in which there is provided furnished sleeping accommodation, whether with or without the provision of board or facilities for the preparation of food, which are used by or held out as being suitable for use by visitors or travellers.

(10) **"Houseboat"** includes a houseboat within the meaning of Group 9 of Schedule 8.

(11) Paragraph (e) includes–
  (a) any grant excluded from item 1 of Group 5 of Schedule 8 by Note (13) in that Group;
  (b) any supply made pursuant to a tenancy, lease or licence under which the grantee is or has been permitted to erect and occupy holiday accommodation.

(12) Paragraph (e) does not include a grant in respect of a building or part which is not a new building of–
  (a) the fee simple, or
  (b) a tenancy, lease or licence to the extent that the grant is made for a consideration in the form of a premium.

(13) **"Holiday accommodation"** includes any accommodation in a building, hut (including a beach hut or chalet), caravan, houseboat or tent which is advertised or held out as holiday accommodation or as suitable for holiday or leisure use, but excludes any accommodation within paragraph (d).

(14) A **seasonal pitch** is a pitch–
  (a) which is provided for a period of less than a year, or
  (b) which is provided for a year or a period longer than a year but which the person to whom it is provided is prevented by the terms of any covenant, statutory planning consent or similar permission from occupying by living in a caravan at all times throughout the period for which the pitch is provided.

(15) **"Mooring"** includes anchoring or berthing.

(16) Paragraph (m) shall not apply where the grant of the facilities is for–
  (a) a continuous period of use exceeding 24 hours; or
  (b) a series of 10 or more periods, whether or not exceeding 24 hours in total, where the following conditions are satisfied–
      (i) each period is in respect of the same activity carried on at the same place;
      (ii) the interval between each period is not less than one day and not more than 14 days;
      (iii) consideration is payable by reference to the whole series and is evidenced by written agreement;
      (iv) the grantee has exclusive use of the facilities; and
      (v) the grantee is a school, a club, an association or an organisation representing affiliated clubs or constituent associations.

History – Note (1) was substituted by SI 1995/282, art. 3, operative from 1 March 1995. Former Note (1) read as follows: "(1) **"Grant"** includes an assignment, other than an assignment of an interest made to the person to whom a surrender of the interest could be made."
Note (1A) was inserted by SI 1995/282, art. 4, operative from 1 March 1995.
In Note (3), the words "Notes (2) to (10) and (12)" were substituted for the words "Notes (2) to (6)" by SI 1995/282, art. 5, operative from 1 March 1995.
In Note (7), the words "(except where that . . . 5(1)(b) of that Schedule)" were inserted by SI 1995/282, art. 6, operative from 1 March 1995.
In Note (11)(a), the words "Note (13)" were substituted for the words "Note (7)" by SI 1995/282, art. 7, operative from 1 March 1995.

Derivations – Sch. 9, Grp. 1, item 1: VATA 1983, s. 8, 17 and Sch. 6, Grp. 1, item 1, para. (a), as substituted by FA 1989, s. 18 and Sch. 3, para. 4(1), as amended by SI 1991/2569, art. 2(a).
Sch. 9, Grp. 1, item 1, para. (a): VATA 1983, s. 8, 17 and Sch. 6, Grp. 1, item 1, para. (a), as substituted by FA 1989, s. 18 and Sch. 3, para. 4(1).
Sch. 9, Grp. 1, item 1, para. (b): VATA 1983, s. 8, 17 and Sch. 6, Grp. 1, item 1, para. (aa), as inserted by SI 1991/2569, art. 2(b).
Sch. 9, Grp. 1, item 1, para. (c): VATA 1983, s. 8, 17 and Sch. 6, Grp. 1, item 1, para. (b), as substituted by FA 1989, s. 18 and Sch. 3, para. 4(1), as amended by SI 1991/2569, art. 2(c).
Sch. 9, Grp. 1, item 1, para. (d): VATA 1983, s. 8, 17 and Sch. 6, Grp. 1, item 1, para. (c), as substituted by FA 1989, s. 18 and Sch. 3, para. 4(1).
Sch. 9, Grp. 1, item 1, para. (e): VATA 1983, s. 8, 17 and Sch. 6, Grp. 1, item 1, para. (d), as substituted by SI 1990/2553, art. 3(a).

Sch. 9, Grp. 1, item 1, para. (f)–(m): VATA 1983, s. 8, 17 and Sch. 6, Grp. 1, item 1, para. (g)–(k), as substituted by FA 1989, s. 18 and Sch. 3, para. 4(1).

Sch. 9, Grp. 1, item 1, para. (n): VATA 1983, s. 8, 17 and Sch. 6, Grp. 1, item 1, para. (l), as inserted by SI 1991/2569, art. 2(d).

Sch. 9, Grp. 1, Notes (1)–(6) (as originally enacted): VATA 1983, s. 8, 17 and Sch. 6, Grp. 1, Notes (1)–(6), as substituted by FA 1989, s. 18 and Sch. 3, para. 4(1).

Sch. 9, Grp. 1, Note (7) (as originally enacted): VATA 1983, s. 8, 17 and Sch. 6, Grp. 1, Note (6A), as inserted by SI 1991/2569, art. 2(e).

Sch. 9, Grp. 1, Notes (8)–(10): VATA 1983, s. 8, 17 and Sch. 6, Grp. 1, Notes (7)–(9), as substituted by FA 1989, s. 18 and Sch. 3, para. 4(1).

Sch. 9, Grp. 1, Note (11) (as originally enacted): VATA 1983, s. 8, 17 and Sch. 6, Grp. 1, Note (10), as substituted by SI 1990/2553, art. 3.

Sch. 9, Grp. 1, Notes (12), (13): VATA 1983, s. 8, 17 and Sch. 6, Grp. 1, Notes (10A), (10B), as inserted by SI 1990/2553, art. 3.

Sch. 9, Grp. 1, Notes (14)–(16): VATA 1983, s. 8, 17 and Sch. 6, Grp. 1, Note (11)–(13), as substituted by FA 1989, s. 18 and Sch. 3, para. 4(1).

Cross references – S. 62: penalty for giving incorrect certificate that a supply or supplies fall within Sch. 9, Grp. 1.
Sch. 6, para. 9: value of supplies.
Sch. 9, Grp. 14, item 1(c) and Note (16): supplies where input tax cannot be recovered.
Sch. 10, para. 2: election to waive exemption.
Sch. 10, para. 2(2A)(b): buildings intended to be used as dwellings.
Sch. 10, para. 9: notes to Grp. 1 apply with modifications in relation to Sch. 10.
VAT (Special Provisions) Order 1995 (SI 1995/1268), art. 5: going concern and non-supply where exemption waived.
VAT Regulations 1995 (SI 1995/2518), reg. 101(3)(b)(iii)–(v): exclusion from partial exemption calculation of supplies within item 1 or para. (a) of item 1 or grants where exemption waived.

Extra-statutory concessions – 3.18 (Notice 48 (1999 edn)): exempts various mandatory service charges paid by the occupants of residential property, including charges for the upkeep of common areas of the estate or flats, the provision of a caretaker or warden and the general maintenance of the exterior of the dwelling.

Official publications – 708, 742, 701/24, 742/1, 742/2 and 742/3.
Customs Internal Guidance Manual, vol. V1.8: land and property.
Customs Internal Guidance Manual, vol. V1.18A: construction.

Hansard – HC Written Answer, 17 December 1991, col. 119: statement by the Financial Secretary to the Treasury that rent-free periods are outside the scope of VAT unless services are performed in return by the tenant for the landlord.

Other material – Customs and Excise Press Notice 233, 21 March 1973: treatment of rents and service charges.
Customs and Excise Press Notice 306, 2 April 1974: service charges paid by tenants.
Customs and Excise News Release 72/88, 20 September 1988 (not reproduced): letting, for 24 hours or less, of sporting stadia (outdoors or indoors) complete with spectating and other facilities, is taxable at the standard rate (see item 1, exception (m) and Note (16)).
Customs and Excise Business Brief 35/93, 20 December 1993 (not reproduced): surrenders of property leases are exempt from VAT. Tenants who surrendered leases after 31 March 1989 and charged VAT may seek repayment of this VAT from Customs if no unjust enrichment under s. 80(3).
HM Customs and Excise Business Brief 16/94, 25 July 1994: hairdressers' chair rents and licence to occupy land.

GROUP 2 – INSURANCE

Item No.

1. The provision of insurance or reinsurance by a person who provides it in the course of–
    (a) any insurance business which he is authorised under section 3 or 4 of the Insurance Companies Act 1982 to carry on, or
    (b) any business in respect of which he is exempted under section 2 of that Act from the requirement to be so authorised.

2. The provision by an insurer or reinsurer who belongs outside the United Kingdom of–
    (a) insurance against any of the risks or other things described in Schedules 1 and 2 to the Insurance Companies Act 1982, or
    (b) reinsurance relating to any of those risks or other things.

3. The provision of insurance or reinsurance by the Export Credits Guarantee Department.

4. The provision by an insurance broker or insurance agent of any of the services of an insurance intermediary in a case in which those services–
    (a) are related (whether or not a contract of insurance or reinsurance is finally concluded) to any such provision of insurance or reinsurance as falls, or would fall, within item 1, 2 or 3; and
    (b) are provided by that broker or agent in the course of his acting in an intermediary capacity.

Notes:

(1) For the purposes of item 4 services are **services of an insurance intermediary** if they fall within any of the following paragraphs–
    (a) the bringing together, with a view to the insurance or reinsurance of risks, of–
        (i) persons who are or may be seeking insurance or reinsurance, and
        (ii) persons who provide insurance or reinsurance;
    (b) the carrying out of work preparatory to the conclusion of contracts of insurance or reinsurance;
    (c) the provision of assistance in the administration and performance of such contracts, including the handling of claims;
    (d) the collection of premiums.

(2) For the purposes of item 4 an insurance broker or insurance agent is acting **"in an intermediary capacity"** wherever he is acting as an intermediary, or one of the intermediaries, between–

    (a) a person who provides any insurance or reinsurance the provision of which falls within item 1, 2 or 3, and

    (b) a person who is or may be seeking insurance or reinsurance or is an insured person.

(3) Where–

    (a) a person (**"the supplier"**) makes a supply of goods or services to another (**"the customer"**),

    (b) the supply of the goods or services is a taxable supply and is not a zero-rated supply,

    (c) a transaction under which insurance is to be or may be arranged for the customer is entered into in connection with the supply of the goods or services,

    (d) a supply of services which are related (whether or not a contract of insurance is finally concluded) to the provision of insurance in pursuance of that transaction is made by–

        (i) the person by whom the supply of the goods or services is made, or

        (ii) a person who is connected with that person and, in connection with the provision of that insurance, deals directly with the customer,

        and

    (e) the related services do not consist in the handling of claims under the contract for that insurance,

those related services do not fall within item 4 unless the relevant requirements are fulfilled.

(4) For the purposes of Note (3) the **relevant requirements** are–

    (a) that a document containing the statements specified in Note (5) is prepared;

    (b) that the matters that must be stated in the document have been disclosed to the customer at or before the time when the transaction mentioned in Note (3)(c) is entered into; and

    (c) that there is compliance with all such requirements (if any) as to–

        (i) the preparation and form of the document,

        (ii) the manner of disclosing to the customer the matters that must be stated in the document, and

        (iii) the delivery of a copy of the document to the customer,

as may be set out in a notice that has been published by the Commissioners and has not been withdrawn.

(5) The statements referred to in Note (4) are–

    (a) a statement setting out the amount of the premium under any contract of insurance that is to be or may be entered into in pursuance of the transaction in question; and

    (b) a statement setting out every amount that the customer is, is to be or has been required to pay, otherwise than by way of such a premium, in connection with that transaction or anything that is to be, may be or has been done in pursuance of that transaction.

(6) For the purposes of Note (3) any question whether a person is **connected** with another shall be determined in accordance with section 839 of the Taxes Act.

(7) Item 4 does not include–

    (a) the supply of any market research, product design, advertising, promotional or similar services; or

    (b) the collection, collation and provision of information for use in connection with market research, product design, advertising, promotional or similar activities.

(8) Item 4 does not include the supply of any valuation or inspection services.

(9) Item 4 does not include the supply of any services by loss adjusters, average adjusters, motor assessors, surveyors or other experts except where–

    (a) the services consist in the handling of a claim under a contract of insurance or reinsurance;

    (b) the person handling the claim is authorised when doing so to act on behalf of the insurer or reinsurer; and

    (c) that person's authority so to act includes written authority to determine whether to accept or reject the claim and, where accepting it in whole or in part, to settle the amount to be paid on the claim.

(10) Item 4 does not include the supply of any services which–

    (a) are supplied in pursuance of a contract of insurance or reinsurance or of any arrangements made in connection with such a contract; and

    (b) are so supplied either–

        (i) instead of the payment of the whole or any part of any indemnity for which the contract provides, or

    (ii) for the purpose, in any other manner, of satisfying any claim under that contract, whether in whole or in part.

History – Grp. 2 was substituted by FA 1997, s. 38(1), with effect in relation to supplies made on or after 19 March 1997. Former Grp. 2 reads as follows:

"INSURANCE

Item No.

1.   The provision of insurance and reinsurance by–

  (a)   a person permitted in accordance with section 2 of the Insurance Companies Act 1982 to carry on insurance business; or

  (b)   an insurer who belongs outside the United Kingdom against any risks or other things described in Schedules 1 and 2 to the Insurance Companies Act 1982.

2.   The provision of insurance and reinsurance by the Export Credits Guarantee Department.

3.   The making of arrangements for the provision of any insurance or reinsurance in items 1 and 2.

4.   The handling of insurance claims by insurance brokers, insurance agents and persons permitted to carry on insurance business as described in item 1.

Notes:

Item 4 does not include supplies by loss adjusters, average adjusters, motor assessors, surveyors and other experts, and legal services, in connection with the assessment of any claim."

Derivations – (as originally enacted) VATA 1983, s. 8, 17 and Sch. 6, Grp. 2, as amended by SI 1990/2037.

Cross references – VAT Regulations 1995 (SI 1995/2518), reg. 105(1): treatment of input tax attributable to exempt supplies as being attributable to taxable supplies.
VAT (Input Tax) (Specified Supplies) Order 1999 (SI 1999/3121): input tax claim and supplies made outside the UK.

Official publications – 701/36.
Customs Internal Guidance Manual, vol. V2.1: insurance premium tax.

GROUP 3 – POSTAL SERVICES

Item No.

1.   The conveyance of postal packets by the Post Office.

2.   The supply by the Post Office of any services in connection with the conveyance of postal packets.

Notes:

(1) **"Postal packet"** has the same meaning as in the Post Office Act 1953, except that it does not include a telegram.

(2) Item 2 does not include the letting on hire of goods.

Derivations – VATA 1983, s. 8, 17 and Sch. 6, Grp. 3.

GROUP 4 – BETTING, GAMING AND LOTTERIES

Item No.

1.   The provision of any facilities for the placing of bets or the playing of any games of chance.

2.   The granting of a right to take part in a lottery.

Notes:

(1) Item 1 does not include–

  (a)   admission to any premises; or

  (b)   the granting of a right to take part in a game in respect of which a charge may be made by virtue of regulations under section 14 of the Gaming Act 1968 or regulations under Article 76 of the Betting, Gaming, Lotteries and Amusements (Northern Ireland) Order 1985; or

  (c)   the provision by a club of such facilities to its members as are available to them on payment of their subscription but without further charge; or

  (d)   the provision of a gaming machine.

(2) **"Game of chance"** has the same meaning as in the Gaming Act 1968 or in the Betting, Gaming, Lotteries and Amusements (Northern Ireland) Order 1985.

(3) **"Gaming machine"** means a machine in respect of which the following conditions are satisfied, namely–

  (a)   it is constructed or adapted for playing a game of chance by means of it; and

  (b)   a player pays to play the machine (except where he has an opportunity to play payment free as the result of having previously played successfully) either by inserting a coin or token into the machine or in some other way; and

  (c)   the element of chance in the game is provided by means of the machine.

Derivations – VATA 1983, s. 8, 17 and Sch. 6, Grp. 4, items 1, 2, Notes (1), (2), (4), as amended by SI 1987/517.

Official publications – 701/26–28.

GROUP 5 – FINANCE

Item No.

1. The issue, transfer or receipt of, or any dealing with, money, any security for money or any note or order for the payment of money.

2. The making of any advance or the granting of any credit.

3. The provision of the facility of instalment credit finance in a hire-purchase, conditional sale or credit sale agreement for which facility a separate charge is made and disclosed to the recipient of the supply of goods.

4. The provision of administrative arrangements and documentation and the transfer of title to the goods in connection with the supply described in item 3 if the total consideration therefor is specified in the agreement and does not exceed £10.

5. The provision of intermediary services in relation to any transaction comprised in item 1, 2, 3, 4 or 6 (whether or not any such transaction is finally concluded) by a person acting in an intermediary capacity.

5A. The underwriting of an issue within item 1 or any transaction within item 6.

6. The issue, transfer or receipt of, or any dealing with, any security or secondary security being–

   (a) shares, stocks, bonds, notes (other than promissory notes), debentures, debenture stock or shares in an oil royalty; or

   (b) any document relating to money, in any currency, which has been deposited with the issuer or some other person, being a document which recognises an obligation to pay a stated amount to bearer or to order, with or without interest, and being a document by the delivery of which, with or without endorsement, the right to receive that stated amount, with or without interest, is transferable; or

   (c) any bill, note or other obligation of the Treasury or of a government in any part of the world, being a document by the delivery of which, with or without endorsement, title is transferable, and not being an obligation which is or has been legal tender in any part of the world; or

   (d) any letter of allotment or rights, any warrant conferring an option to acquire a security included in this item, any renounceable or scrip certificates, rights coupons, coupons representing dividends or interest on such a security, bond mandates or other documents conferring or containing evidence of title to or rights in respect of such a security; or

   (e) units or other documents conferring rights under any trust established for the purpose, or having the effect of providing, for persons having funds available for investment, facilities for the participation by them as beneficiaries under the trust, in any profits or income arising from the acquisition, holding, management or disposal of any property whatsoever.

7. [Omitted by SI 1999/594, art. 4, operative in respect of supplies made on or after 10 March 1999.]

8. The operation of any current, deposit or savings account.

9. The management of an authorised unit trust scheme or of a trust based scheme by the operator of the scheme.

10. The services of the authorised corporate director of an open-ended investment company so far as they consist in managing the company's scheme property.

Notes:

(1) Item 1 does not include anything included in item 6.

(1A) Item 1 does not include a supply of services which is preparatory to the carrying out of a transaction falling within that item.

(2) This Group does not include the supply of a coin or a banknote as a collectors' piece or as an investment article.

(2A) This Group does not include a supply of services comprising the management of credit, other than such a supply made by the person granting the credit.

(2B) For the purposes of this Group a person makes **"a supply of services comprising the management of credit"** if he performs any one or more of the following in relation to a credit, a credit card, a chargecard or a similar payment card, operation–

   (a) credit checking;

   (b) valuation;

   (c) authorisation services;

   (d) taking decisions relating to a grant or an application for a grant of credit;

(e) creating and maintaining records relating to a grant or an application for a grant of credit on behalf of the credit provider; and

(f) monitoring a creditor's payment record or dealing with overdue payments.

(3) Item 2 includes the supply of credit by a person, in connection with a supply of goods or services by him, for which a separate charge is made and disclosed to the recipient of the supply of goods or services.

(4) This Group includes any supply by a person carrying on a credit card, charge card or similar payment card operation made in connection with that operation to a person who accepts the card used in the operation when presented to him in payment for goods or services.

(5) For the purposes of item 5 **"intermediary services"** consist of bringing together, with a view to the provision of financial services–

(a) persons who are or may be seeking to receive financial services, and

(b) persons who provide financial services,

together with (in the case of financial services falling within item 1, 2, 3 or 4) the performance of work preparatory to the conclusion of contracts for the provision of those financial services, but do not include the supply of any market research, product design, advertising, promotional or similar services or the collection, collation and provision of information in connection with such activities.

(5A) For the purposes of item 5 a person is **"acting in an intermediary capacity"** wherever he is acting as an intermediary, or one of the intermediaries, between–

(a) a person who provides financial services, and

(b) a person who is or may be seeking to receive financial services,

unless the financial service in question is the grant of credit and he is also making supplies of services comprising the management of credit to the grantor, or prospective grantor, of the credit.

(5B) For the purposes of Notes (5) and (5A) **"financial services"** means the carrying out of any transaction falling within item 1, 2, 3, 4 or 6.

(6) In item 9–

(a) **"authorised unit trust scheme"** and **"operator"** have the same meanings as in section 207(1) of the Financial Services Act 1986;

(b) **"trust based scheme"** has the same meaning as in regulation 2(1)(b) of the Financial Services Act 1986 (Single Property Schemes) (Exemption) Regulations 1989.

(7) For the purposes of item 10, a person is an **authorised corporate director** of an open-ended investment company if for the time being that person–

(a) is a director of the company, and

(b) has responsibility for the management of, and is managing, the company's scheme property.

(8) For the purposes of item 10 and Note (7), an open-ended investment company's **scheme property** is the property subject to the collective investment scheme constituted by that company.

(9) In Note (7), **"director"**, in relation to an open-ended investment company, includes a person occupying in relation to it the position of director (by whatever name called).

(10) For the purposes of this Group, **"collective investment scheme"** and **"open-ended investment company"** have the meanings given by section 75 of the Financial Services Act 1986.

History – Item 5, along with item 5A, was substituted for former item 5 by SI 1999/594, art. 3, operative in relation to supplies made on or after 10 March 1999. Former item 5 read as follows:

"5   The making of arrangements for any transaction comprised in item 1, 2, 3 or 4 or the underwriting of an issue within item 1."

Item 5A, along with item 5, was substituted for former item 5 by SI 1999/594, art. 3, operative in relation to supplies made on or after 10 March 1999.

Item 7 was omitted by SI 1999/594, art. 4, operative in relation to supplies made on or after 10 March 1999. Former item 7 read as follows:

"7   The making arrangements for, or the underwriting of, any transaction within item 6."

Item 10 was added by SI 1997/510, art. 2(a), operative in relation to any supply made on or after 24 March 1997.

Note (1A) was inserted by SI 1999/594, art. 5, operative in relation to supplies made on or after 10 March 1999.

Note (2A) was inserted by SI 1999/594, art. 5, operative in relation to supplies made on or after 10 March 1999.

Note (2B) was inserted by SI 1999/594, art. 5, operative in relation to supplies made on or after 10 March 1999.

Note (5), along with Notes (5A) and (5B), was substituted for former Note (5) by SI 1999/594, art. 7, operative in relation to supplies made on or after 10 March 1999. Former Note (5) read as follows:

"(5)   Item 7 includes the introduction to a person effecting transactions in securities or secondary securities within item 6 of a person seeking to acquire or dispose of such securities."

Note (5A), along with Notes (5) and (5B), was substituted for former Note (5) by SI 1999/594, art. 7, operative in relation to supplies made on or after 10 March 1999.

Note (5B), along with Notes (5) and (5A), was substituted for former Note (5) by SI 1999/594, art. 7, operative in relation to supplies made on or after 10 March 1999.

Note (7) was added by SI 1997/510, art. 2(b), operative in relation to any supply made on or after 24 March 1997.

Note (8) was added by SI 1997/510, art. 2(b), operative in relation to any supply made on or after 24 March 1997.

Note (9) was added by SI 1997/510, art. 2(b), operative in relation to any supply made on or after 24 March 1997.

Note (10) was added by SI 1997/510, art. 2(b), operative from 24 March 1997.

Derivations – Sch. 9, Grp. 5, items 1–4: VATA 1983, s. 8, 17 and Sch. 6, Grp. 5, items 1–4.
Sch. 9, Grp. 5, item 5: VATA 1983, s. 8, 17 and Sch. 6, Grp. 5, item 5, as amended by FA 1987, s. 18(1)(a).
Sch. 9, Grp. 5, item 6: VATA 1983, s. 8, 17 and Sch. 6, Grp. 5, item 6, as substituted by SI 1987/860.
Sch. 9, Grp. 5, item 7: VATA 1983, s. 8, 17 and Sch. 6, Grp. 5, item 6A, as substituted by SI 1989/2272, art. 2(2).
Sch. 9, Grp. 5, item 8: VATA 1983, s. 8, 17 and Sch. 6, Grp. 5, item 7.
Sch. 9, Grp. 5, item 9: VATA 1983, s. 8, 17 and Sch. 6, Grp. 5, item 8, as inserted by SI 1989/2272, art. 2(3).
Sch. 9, Grp. 5, Notes (1)–(3): VATA 1983, s. 8, 17 and Sch. 6, Grp. 5, Notes (1)–(3).
Sch. 9, Grp. 5, Note (4): VATA 1983, s. 8, 17 and Sch. 6, Grp. 5, Note (4), as inserted by SI 1985/432.
Sch. 9, Grp. 5, Notes (5), (6): VATA 1983, s. 8, 17 and Sch. 6, Grp. 5, Notes (5), (6), as inserted by SI 1985/2272, art. 2(4).
Cross references – VAT Regulations 1995 (SI 1995/2518), reg. 101(3)(b)(v): exclusion of Grp. 5 supplies from partial exemption calculation.
VAT Regulations 1995 (SI 1995/2518), reg. 103(2): attribution of input tax where supply within item 1 or 6.
VAT (Input Tax) (Specified Supplies) Order 1999 (SI 1999/3121), art. 3: input tax claim and supplies made outside the UK.
Official publications – 701/29 Finance.
701/43 Financial futures and options.
701/44 Securities.
Other material – Customs and Excise Press Notice 1121, 26 June 1986 (not reproduced): trading of sterling commercial paper falls under item 1.
Notes – S. 96(1): "money" defined.

GROUP 6 – EDUCATION

Item No.
1.   The provision by an eligible body of–
  (a) education;
  (b) research, where supplied to an eligible body; or
  (c) vocational training.
2.   The supply of private tuition, in a subject ordinarily taught in a school or university, by an individual teacher acting independently of an employer.
3.   The provision of examination services–
  (a) by or to an eligible body; or
  (b) to a person receiving education or vocational training which is–
      (i) exempt by virtue of items 1, 2 or 5; or
      (ii) provided otherwise than in the course or furtherance of a business.
4.   The supply of any goods or services (other than examination services) which are closely related to a supply of a description falling within item 1 (the principal supply) by or to the eligible body making the principal supply provided–
  (a) the goods or services are for the direct use of the pupil, student or trainee (as the case may be) receiving the principal supply; and
  (b) where the supply is to the eligible body making the principal supply, it is made by another eligible body.
5.   The provision of vocational training, and the supply of any goods or services essential thereto by the person providing the vocational training, to the extent that the consideration payable is ultimately a charge to funds provided pursuant to arrangements made under section 2 of the Employment and Training Act 1973, section 1A of the Employment and Training Act (Northern Ireland) 1950 or section 2 of the Enterprise and New Towns (Scotland) Act 1990.
6.   The provision of facilities by–
  (a) a youth club or an association of youth clubs to its members; or
  (b) an association of youth clubs to members of a youth club which is a member of that association.

Notes:
(1) For the purposes of this Group an **"eligible body"** is–
  (a) a school within the meaning of the Education Act 1996, the Education (Scotland) Act 1980, the Education and Libraries (Northern Ireland) Order 1986 or the Education Reform (Northern Ireland) Order 1989, which is–
      (i) provisionally or finally registered or deemed to be registered as a school within the meaning of the aforesaid legislation in a register of independent schools; or
      (ii) a school in respect of which of which grants are made by the Secretary of State to the proprietor or managers; or
      (iii) a community, foundation or voluntary school within the meaning of the School Standards and Framework Act 1998, a special school within the meaning of section 337 of the Education Act 1996 or a maintained school within the meaning of the Education and Libraries (Northern Ireland) Order 1986; or

    (iv) a public school within the meaning of section 135(1) of the Education (Scotland) Act 1980; or

    (v) [Omitted by the School Standards and Framework Act 1998, s. 140(1) and Sch. 30, para. 51(b) and s. 140(3) and Sch. 31.]

    (vi) a self-governing school within the meaning of section 1(3) of the Self-Governing Schools (Scotland) Act 1989; or

    (vii) [Omitted by the School Standards and Framework Act 1998, s. 140(1) and Sch. 30, para. 51(b) and s. 140(3) and Sch. 31.]

    (viii) a grant-maintained integrated school within the meaning of Article 65 of the Education Reform (Northern Ireland) Order 1989;

(b) a United Kingdom university, and any college, institution, school or hall of such a university;

(c) an institution–

    (i) falling within section 91(3)(a) or (b) or section 91(5)(b) or (c) of the Further and Higher Education Act 1992; or

    (ii) which is a designated institution as defined in section 44(2) of the Further and Higher Education (Scotland) Act 1992; or

    (iii) managed by a board of management as defined in section 36(1) of the Further and Higher Education (Scotland) Act 1992; or

    (iv) to which grants are paid by the Department of Education for Northern Ireland under Article 66(2) of the Education and Libraries (Northern Ireland) Order 1986;

(d) a public body of a description in Note (5) to Group 7 below;

(e) a body which–

    (i) is precluded from distributing and does not distribute any profit it makes; and

    (ii) applies any profits made from supplies of a description within this Group to the continuance or improvement of such supplies;

(f) a body not falling within paragraphs (a) to (e) above which provides the teaching of English as a foreign language.

(2) A supply by a body, which is an eligible body only by virtue of falling within Note (1)(f), shall not fall within this Group in so far as it consists of the provision of anything other than the teaching of English as a foreign language.

(3) **"Vocational training"** means–

    training, re-training or the provision of work experience for–

(a) any trade, profession or employment; or

(b) any voluntary work connected with–

    (i) education, health, safety, or welfare; or

    (ii) the carrying out of activities of a charitable nature.

(4) **"Examination services"** include the setting and marking of examinations, the setting of educational or training standards, the making of assessments and other services provided with a view to ensuring educational and training standards are maintained.

(5) For the purposes of item 5 a supply of any goods or services shall not be taken to be **essential to the provision of vocational training** unless the goods or services in question are provided directly to the trainee.

(6) For the purposes of item 6 a club is a **"youth club"** if–

(a) it is established to promote the social, physical, educational or spiritual development of its members;

(b) its members are mainly under 21 years of age; and

(c) it satisfies the requirements of Note (l)(f)(i) and (ii).

History – In Note (1)(a), the reference to the Education Act 1996 was substituted by Education Act 1996, s. 582(1) and Sch. 37, para. 125(a), with effect from 1 November 1996.

In Note (1)(a)(iii), the words at the beginning were substituted by Education Act 1996, s. 582(1) and Sch. 37, para. 125(b), with effect from 1 November 1996.

In Note (1)(a)(iii), the following words at the beginning "a community, foundation or ... Education Act 1996" were substituted for the words "a county school, voluntary school or maintained special school (other than one established in a hospital) within the meaning of the Education Act 1996" by the School Standards and Framework Act 1998, s. 140(1) and Sch. 30, para. 51(a), with effect from 1 April 1999 (SI 1998/2212).

Note (1)(a)(v) was omitted by the School Standards and Framework Act 1998, s. 140(1) and Sch. 30, para. 51(b) and s. 140(3) and Sch. 31, with effect from 1 April 1999 (SI 1998/2212). Former Note (1)(a)(v) reads as follow:

"a grant-maintained school within the meaning of the Education Act 1996; or"

In former Note (1)(a)(v), the reference to the Education Act 1996 was substituted by Education Act 1996, s. 582(1) and Sch. 37, para. 125(c), with effect from 1 November 1996.

Note (1)(a)(vii) was omitted by the School Standards and Framework Act 1998, s. 140(1) and Sch. 30, para. 51(b) and s. 140(3) and Sch. 31, with effect from 1 April 1999 (SI 1998/2212). Former Note (1)(a)(vii) reads as follow:

"a grant-maintained special school within the meaning of the Education Act 1996; or"

In former Note (1)(a)(vii), the reference to the Education Act 1996 was substituted by Education Act 1996, s. 582(1) and Sch. 37, para. 125(d), with effect from 1 November 1996.

Note (1)(e) was substituted by SI 1994/2969, art. 3, operative from 1 January 1995. Former Note (1)(e) read as follows:
"(e) a body recognised under the British Council Recognition Scheme for the teaching of English as a foreign language;".

Note (1)(f) was substituted by SI 1994/2969, art. 4, operative from 1 January 1995. Former Note (1)(f) read as follows:
"(f) a body not falling within paragraph (a) to (e) above which–
   (i)   is precluded from distributing and does not distribute any profit it makes; and
   (ii) applies any profits made from supplies of a description within this Group to the continuance or improvement of such supplies."

In Note (2), the words "(1)(f)" were substituted for the words "(1)(e)" by SI 1994/2969, art. 5, operative from 1 January 1995.

Note (3) was substituted by SI 1994/2969, art. 6, operative from 1 January 1995. Former Note (3) read as follows:
"(3) **"Vocational training"** means training or re-training for–
  (a) any trade, profession or employment; or
  (b) any voluntary work connected with–
     (i) education, health, safety, or welfare; or
     (ii) the carrying out of activities of a charitable nature;
and for the purposes of item 5, includes the provision of work experience."

Derivations – (as originally enacted) – VATA 1983, s. 8 and 17 and Sch. 6, Grp. 6, as substituted by SI 1994/1188.

Cross references – VAT (Tour Operators) Order 1987 (SI 1987/1806), art. 10(2): no charge on Grp. 6 supplies acquired by tour operator in order to supply them as a designated travel service.

Official publications – 701/30.

GROUP 7 – HEALTH AND WELFARE

Item No.

1.   The supply of services by a person registered or enrolled in any of the following–
  (a) the register of medical practitioners or the register of medical practitioners with limited registration;
  (b) either of the registers of ophthalmic opticians or the register of dispensing opticians kept under the Opticians Act 1989 or either of the lists kept under section 9 of that Act of bodies corporate carrying on business as ophthalmic opticians or as dispensing opticians;
  (c) any register kept under the Professions Supplementary to Medicine Act 1960;
  (ca) the register of osteopaths maintained in accordance with the provisions of Osteopaths Act 1993;
  (cb) the register of chiropractors maintained in accordance with the provisions of the Chiropractors Act 1994;
  (d) the register of qualified nurses, midwives and health visitors kept under section 7 of the Nurses, Midwives and Health Visitors Act 1997;
  (e) the register of dispensers of hearing aids or the register of persons employing such dispensers maintained under section 2 of the Hearing Aid Council Act 1968.

2.   The supply of any services or dental prostheses by–
  (a) a person registered in the dentists' register;
  (b) a person enrolled in any roll of dental auxiliaries having effect under section 45 of the Dentists Act 1984; or
  (c) a dental technician.

3.   The supply of any services by a person registered in the register of pharmaceutical chemists kept under the Pharmacy Act 1954 or the Pharmacy (Northern Ireland) Order 1976.

4.   The provision of care or medical or surgical treatment and, in connection with it, the supply of any goods, in any hospital or other institution approved, licensed, registered or exempted from registration by any Minister or other authority pursuant to a provision of a public general Act of Parliament or of the Northern Ireland Parliament or of a public general Measure of the Northern Ireland Assembly or Order in Council under Schedule 1 to the Northern Ireland Act 1974, not being a provision which is capable of being brought into effect at different times in relation to different local authority areas.

5.   The provision of a deputy for a person registered in the register of medical practitioners or the register of medical practitioners with limited registration.

6.   Human blood.

7.   Products for therapeutic purposes, derived from human blood.

8.   Human (including foetal) organs or tissue for diagnostic or therapeutic purposes or medical research.

9.   The supply, otherwise than for profit, by a charity or public body of welfare services and of goods supplied in connection therewith.

10.   The supply, otherwise than for profit, of goods and services incidental to the provision of spiritual welfare by a religious community to a resident member of that community in return for a subscription or other consideration paid as a condition of membership.

11.   The supply of transport services for sick or injured persons in vehicles specially designed for that purpose.

Notes:

(1) Item 1 does not include the letting on hire of goods except where the letting is in connection with a supply of other services comprised in the item.

(2) Paragraphs (a) to (d) of item 1 and paragraph (a) and (b) of item 2 include supplies of services made by a person who is not registered or enrolled in any of the registers or rolls specified in those paragraphs where the services are wholly performed or directly supervised by a person who is so registered or enrolled.

(2A) Item 3 includes supplies of services made by a person who is not registered in either of the registers specified in that item where the services are wholly performed by a person who is so registered.

(3) Item 3 does not include the letting on hire of goods.

(4) For the purposes of this Group a person who is not registered in the visiting EEC practitioners list in the register of medical practitioners at the time he performs services in an urgent case as mentioned in subsection (3) of section 18 of the Medical Act 1983 is to be treated as being registered in that list where he is entitled to be **registered** in accordance with that section.

(5) In item 9 **"public body"** means–
  (a)   a government department within the meaning of section 41(6);
  (b)   a local authority;
  (c)   a body which acts under any enactment or instrument for public purposes and not for its own profit and which performs functions similar to those of a government department or local authority.

(6) In item 9 **"welfare services"** means services which are directly connected with–
  (a)   the provision of care, treatment or instruction designed to promote the physical or mental welfare of elderly, sick, distressed or disabled persons;
  (b)   the protection of children and young persons; or
  (c)   the provision of spiritual welfare by a religious institution as part of a course of instruction or a retreat, not being a course or a retreat designed primarily to provide recreation or a holiday.

(7) Item 9 does not include the supply of accommodation or catering except where it is ancillary to the provision of care, treatment or instruction.

History – Item 1(ca) was inserted by SI 1998/1294, art. 2, operative in relation to supplies made on or after 12 June 1998. However, by concession exemption applies from 9 May 1998 (Customs and Excise Business Brief 13/98, 9 June 1998). Item 1(cb) was inserted by SI 1999/1575, art. 2, operative in relation to supplies made on or after 29 June 1999. In item 1(d), the reference to the Nurses, Midwives and Health Visitors Act was substituted by the Nurses, Midwives and Health Visitors Act 1997, s. 23(1) and Sch. 4, para. 6, with effect from 19 June 1997. Note (2A) was inserted by SI 1996/2949, art. 2, operative in relation to supplies made on or after 1 January 1997.

Derivations – Sch. 9, Grp. 7, item 1: VATA 1983, s. 8, 17 and Sch. 6, Grp. 7, item 1, as substituted by FA 1988, s. 13(2), as amended by Opticians Act 1989, s. 37(3).
Sch. 9, Grp. 7, item 2: VATA 1983, s. 8, 17 and Sch. 6, Grp. 7, item 2, as substituted by FA 1988, s. 13(2).
Sch. 9, Grp. 7, items 3–8: VATA 1983, s. 8, 17 and Sch. 6, Grp. 7, items 3–8.
Sch. 9, Grp. 7, items 9–10: VATA 1983, s. 8, 17 and Sch. 6, Grp. 7, items 9–10, as inserted by SI 1985/1900.
Sch. 9, Grp. 7, item 11: VATA 1983, s. 8, 17 and Sch. 6, Grp. 7, item 11, as inserted by SI 1989/2272, art. 3.
Sch. 9, Grp. 7, Note (1): VATA 1983, s. 8, 17 and Sch. 6, Grp. 7, Note (1).
Sch. 9, Grp. 7, Note (2): VATA 1983, s. 8, 17 and Sch. 6, Grp. 7, Note (2), as amended by FA 1988, s. 13(3).
Sch. 9, Grp. 7, Notes (3), (4): VATA 1983, s. 8, 17 and Sch. 6, Grp. 7, Notes (3), (4).
Sch. 9, Grp. 7, Notes (5)–(7): VATA 1983, s. 8, 17 and Sch. 6, Grp. 7, Notes (5)–(7), as inserted by SI 1985/1900.

Extra-statutory concessions – Item 1(ca) was inserted in relation to supplies made on or after 12 June 1998, but by concession exemption applies from 9 May 1998 (Customs and Excise Business Brief 13/98, 9 June 1998).

Official publications – 701/31.

Other material – Customs and Excise News Release 30/89, 30 March 1989: Customs' view of "otherwise than for profit" (see items 9 and 10).
Customs and Excise News Release 32/89, 5 April 1989: provision of (accommodation and) catering in a hospital to a parent of a child patient is a supply of care to the patient and therefore exempt under item 4.
IR Int 129: timing of VAT refunds to opticians.

GROUP 8 – BURIAL AND CREMATION

Item No.
1.   The disposal of the remains of the dead.
2.   The making of arrangements for or in connection with the disposal of the remains of the dead.

Derivations – VATA 1983, s. 8, 17 and Sch. 6, Grp. 8.
Official publications – 701/32.

GROUP 9 – SUBSCRIPTIONS TO TRADE UNIONS, PROFESSIONAL AND OTHER PUBLIC INTEREST BODIES

Item No.

1.   The supply to its members of such services and, in connection with those services, of such goods as are both referable only to its aims and available without payment other than a membership subscription by any of the following non-profit-making organisations–

    (a) a trade union or other organisation of persons having as its main object the negotiation on behalf of its members of the terms and conditions of their employment;

    (b) a professional association, membership of which is wholly or mainly restricted to individuals who have or are seeking a qualification appropriate to the practice of the profession concerned;

    (c) an association, the primary purpose of which is the advancement of a particular branch of knowledge, or the fostering of professional expertise, connected with the past or present professions or employments of its members;

    (d) an association, the primary purpose of which is to make representations to the government on legislation and other public matters which affect the business or professional interests of its members;

    (e) a body which has objects which are in the public domain and are of a political, religious, patriotic, philosophical, philanthropic or civic nature.

Notes:

(1) Item 1 does not include any right of admission to any premises, event or performance, to which non-members are admitted for a consideration.

(2) **"Trade union"** has the meaning assigned to it by section 1 of the Trade Union and Labour Relations (Consolidation) Act 1992.

(3) Item 1 shall include organisations and associations the membership of which consists wholly or mainly of constituent or affiliated associations which as individual associations would be comprised in the item; and **"member"** shall be construed as including such an association and **"membership subscription"** shall include an affiliation fee or similar levy.

(4) Paragraph (c) does not apply unless the association restricts its membership wholly or mainly to individuals whose present or previous professions or employments are directly connected with the purposes of the association.

(5) Paragraph (d) does not apply unless the association restricts its membership wholly or mainly to individuals or corporate bodies whose business or professional interests are directly connected with the purposes of the association.

History – In the description of Grp. 9, the words "Subscriptions to trade unions, professional and other public interest bodies" were substituted for the words "Trade unions and professional bodies" by SI 1999/2834, art. 4(a), operative from 1 December 1999.
Item 1(e) was added by SI 1999/2834, art. 4(b), operative from 1 December 1999.

Derivations – VATA 1983, s. 8, 17 and Sch. 6, Grp. 9, as amended by Trade Union and Labour Relations (Consolidation) Act 1992, s. 300(2) and Sch. 2, para. 32.

Cross references – Sch. 9, Grp. 12: an item 1 non-profit making body is a "qualifying body" for the purposes of the exemption for fund-raising events.

Official publications – 701/33.

GROUP 10 – SPORT, SPORTS COMPETITIONS AND PHYSICAL EDUCATION

Item No.

1.   The grant of a right to enter a competition in sport or physical recreation where the consideration for the grant consists in money which is to be allocated wholly towards the provision of a prize or prizes awarded in that competition.

2.   The grant, by an eligible body established for the purposes of sport or physical recreation, of a right to enter a competition in such an activity.

3.   The supply by an eligible body to an individual, except, where the body operates a membership scheme, an individual who is not a member, of services closely linked with and essential to sport or physical education in which the individual is taking part.

Notes:

(1) Item 3 does not include the supply of any services by an eligible body of residential accommodation, catering or transport.

(2) An individual shall only be considered to be a **member** of an eligible body for the purpose of Item 3 where he is granted Membership for a period of three months or more.

(2A) Subject to Notes (2C) and (3), in this Group **"eligible body"** means a non-profit making body which–

(a) is precluded from distributing any profit it makes, or is allowed to distribute any such profit by means only of distributions to a non-profit making body;

(b) applies in accordance with Note (2B) any profits it makes from supplies of a description within Item 2 or 3; and

(c) is not subject to commercial influence.

(2B) For the purposes of Note (2A)(b) the **application of profits** made by any body from supplies of a description within Item 2 or 3 is in accordance with this Note only if those profits are applied for one or more of the following purposes, namely–

(a) the continuance or improvement of any facilities made available in or in connection with the making of the supplies of those descriptions made by that body;

(b) the purposes of a non-profit making body.

(2C) In determining whether the requirements of Note (2A) for being an **eligible body** are satisfied in the case of any body, there shall be disregarded any distribution of amounts representing unapplied or undistributed profits that falls to be made to the body's members on its winding-up or dissolution.

(3) In Item 3 an **"eligible body"** does not include–

(a) a local authority;

(b) a government department within the meaning of section 41(6); or

(c) a non-departmental public body which is listed in the 1993 edition of the publication prepared by the Office of Public Service and Science and known as Public Bodies.

(4) For the purposes of this Group a body shall be taken, in relation to a sports supply, to be subject to **commercial influence** if, and only if, there is a time in the relevant period when–

(a) a relevant supply was made to that body by a person associated with it at that time;

(b) an emolument was paid by that body to such a person;

(c) an agreement existed for either or both of the following to take place after the end of that period, namely–

    (i) the making of a relevant supply to that body by such a person; or

    (ii) the payment by that body to such a person of any emoluments.

(5) In this Group **"the relevant period"**, in relation to a sports supply, means–

(a) where that supply is one made before 1st January 2003, the period beginning with 14th January 1999 and ending with the making of that sports supply; and

(b) where that supply is one made on or after 1st January 2003, the period of three years ending with the making of that sports supply.

(6) Subject to Note (7), in this Group **"relevant supply"**, in relation to any body, means a supply falling within any of the following paragraphs–

(a) the grant of any interest in or right over land which at any time in the relevant period was or was expected to become sports land;

(b) the grant of any licence to occupy any land which at any such time was or was expected to become sports land;

(c) the grant, in the case of land in Scotland, of any personal right to call for or be granted any such interest or right as is mentioned in paragraph (a) above;

(d) a supply arising from a grant falling within paragraph (a), (b) or (c) above, other than a grant made before 1st April 1996;

(e) the supply of any services consisting in the management or administration of any facilities provided by that body;

(f) the supply of any goods or services for a consideration in excess of what would have been agreed between parties entering into a commercial transaction at arm's length.

(7) A supply which has been, or is to be or may be, made by any person shall not be taken, in relation to a sports supply made by any body, to be a **relevant supply** for the purposes of this Group if–

(a) the principal purpose of that body is confined, at the time when the sports supply is made, to the provision for employees of that person of facilities for use for or in connection with sport or physical recreation, or both;

(b) the supply in question is one made by a charity or local authority or one which (if it is made) will be made by a person who is a charity or local authority at the time when the sports supply is made;

(c) the supply in question is a grant falling within Note (6)(a) to (c) which has been made, or (if it is made) will be made, for a nominal consideration;

(d) the supply in question is one arising from such a grant as is mentioned in paragraph (c) above and is not itself a supply the consideration for which was, or will or may be, more than a nominal consideration; or

(e) the supply in question–

    (i) is a grant falling within Note (6)(a) to (c) which is made for no consideration; but

    (ii) falls to be treated as a supply of goods or services, or (if it is made) will fall to be so treated, by reason only of the application, in accordance with paragraph 9 of Schedule 4, of paragraph 5 of that Schedule.

(8) Subject to Note (10), a person shall be taken, for the purposes of this Group, to have been **associated** with a body at any of the following times, that is to say–

(a) the time when a supply was made to that body by that person;

(b) the time when an emolument was paid by that body to that person; or

(c) the time when an agreement was in existence for the making of a relevant supply or the payment of emoluments,

if, at that time, or at another time (whether before or after that time) in the relevant period, that person was an officer or shadow officer of that body or an intermediary for supplies to that body.

(9) Subject to Note (10), a person shall also be taken, for the purposes of this Group, to have been **associated** with a body at a time mentioned in paragraph (a), (b) or (c) of Note (8) if, at that time, he was connected with another person who in accordance with that Note–

(a) is to be taken to have been so associated at that time; or

(b) would be taken to have been so associated were that time the time of a supply by the other person to that body.

(10) Subject to Note (11), a person shall not be taken for the purposes of this Group to have been **associated** with a body at a time mentioned in paragraph (a), (b) or (c) of Note (8) if the only times in the relevant period when that person or the person connected with him was an officer or shadow officer of the body are times before 1st January 2000.

(11) Note (10) does not apply where (but for that Note) the body would be treated as subject to commercial influence at any time in the relevant period by virtue of–

(a) the existence of any agreement entered into on or after 14th January 1999 and before 1st January 2000; or

(b) anything done in pursuance of any such agreement.

(12) For the purposes of this Group a person shall be taken, in relation to a sports supply, to have been at all times in the relevant period an **intermediary** for supplies to the body making that supply if–

(a) at any time in that period either a supply was made to him by another person or an agreement for the making of a supply to him by another was in existence; and

(b) the circumstances were such that, if–

    (i) that body had been the person to whom the supply was made or (in the case of an agreement) the person to whom it was to be or might be made; and

    (ii) Note (7) above were to be disregarded to the extent (if at all) that it would prevent the supply from being a relevant supply, the body would have fallen to be regarded in relation to the sports supply as subject to commercial influence.

(13) In determining for the purposes of Note (12) or this Note whether there are such circumstances as are mentioned in paragraph (b) of that Note in the case of any supply, that Note and this Note shall be applied first for determining whether the person by whom the supply was made, or was to be or might be made, was himself an intermediary for supplies to the body in question, and so on through any number of other supplies or agreements.

(14) In determining for the purposes of this Group whether a supply made by any person was made by an **intermediary** for supplies to a body, it shall be immaterial that the supply by that person was made before the making of the supply or agreement by reference to which that person falls to be regarded as such an intermediary.

(15) Without prejudice to the generality of subsection (1AA) of section 43, for the purpose of determining–

(a) whether a relevant supply has at any time been made to any person;

(b) whether there has at any time been an agreement for the making of a relevant supply to any person; and

(c) whether a person falls to be treated as an intermediary for the supplies to any body by reference to supplies that have been, were to be or might have been made to him, references in the preceding Notes to a **supply** shall be deemed to include references to a supply falling for other purposes to be disregarded in accordance with section 43(1)(a).

(16) In this Group–

"**agreement**" includes any arrangement or understanding (whether or not legally enforceable);

"**emolument**" means any emolument (within the meaning of the Income Tax Acts) the amount of which falls or may fall, in accordance with the agreement under which it is payable, to be determined or varied wholly or partly by reference–

(i) to the profits from some or all of the activities of the body paying the emolument; or

(ii) to the level of that body's gross income from some or all of its activities;

"**employees**", in relation to a person, includes retired employees of that person;

"**grant**" includes an assignment or surrender;

"**officer**", in relation to a body, includes–

(i) a director of a body corporate; and

(ii) any committee member or trustee concerned in the general control and management of the administration of the body;

"**shadow officer**", in relation to a body, means a person in accordance with whose directions or instructions the members or officers of the body are accustomed to act;

"**sports land**", in relation to any body, means any land used or held for use for or in connection with the provision by that body of facilities for use for or in connection with sport or physical recreation, or both;

"**sports supply**" means a supply which, if made by an eligible body, would fall within Item 2 or 3.

(17) For the purposes of this Group any question whether a person is **connected** with another shall be determined in accordance with section 839 of the Taxes Act (connected persons).

History – In item 2, the words "an eligible body" were substituted for the words "a non-profit making body" by SI 1999/1994, art. 3, with effect in relation to supplies made on or after 1 January 2000.
In item 3, the words "an eligible body" were substituted for the words "a non-profit making body" by SI 1999/1994, art. 3, with effect in relation to supplies made on or after 1 January 2000.
In Note (1), the words "an eligible body" were substituted for the words "a non-profit making body" by SI 1999/1994, art. 3, with effect in relation to supplies made on or after 1 January 2000.
In Note (2), the words "an eligible body" were substituted for the words "a non-profit making body" by SI 1999/1994, art. 3, with effect in relation to supplies made on or after 1 January 2000.
Note (2A) was inserted by SI 1999/1994, art. 4, with effect in relation to supplies made on or after 1 January 2000.
Note (2B) was inserted by SI 1999/1994, art. 4, with effect in relation to supplies made on or after 1 January 2000.
Note (2C) was inserted by SI 1999/1994, art. 4, with effect in relation to supplies made on or after 1 January 2000.
In Note (3), the words "an eligible body" were substituted for the words "a non-profit making body" by SI 1999/1994, art. 3, with effect in relation to supplies made on or after 1 January 2000.
Notes (4)–(17) were inserted by SI 1999/1994, art. 5, with effect in relation to supplies made on or after 1 January 2000.

Derivations – Sch. 9, Grp. 10, items 1, 2: VATA 1983, s. 8, 17 and Sch. 6, Grp. 10, items 1, 2.
Sch. 9, Grp. 10, item 3: VATA 1983, s. 8, 17 and Sch. 6, Grp. 10, item 3, as inserted by SI 1994/687, art. 2(b).
Sch. 9, Grp. 10, Notes (1)–(3): VATA 1983, s. 8, 17 and Sch. 6, Grp. 10, Notes (1)–(3), as substituted by SI 1994/687, art. 2(c).

Official publications – 701/34 and 701/45.

Other material – Customs and Excise News Release 13/94, 10 March 1994 (not reproduced): transitional relief and claims for refunds since 1 January 1990.

Notes – Grp. 10 was amended by SI 1998/764, but the amendments were not approved as required by VATA 1994, s. 97(3) and so the amendments ceased to have effect after 24 April 1998.
In the HMSO version of SI 1999/1994, art. 5, which inserts Note (7) from 1 January 2000, the last words read "of paragraph 5 of that Schedule", although the last words of Note (7) should probably read "or paragraph 5 of that Schedule".

GROUP 11 – WORKS OF ART ETC.

Item No.

1. The disposal of an object with respect to which estate duty is not chargeable by virtue of section 30(3) of the Finance Act 1953, section 34(1) of the Finance Act 1956 or the proviso to section 40(2) of the Finance Act 1930.

2. The disposal of an object with respect to which inheritance tax is not chargeable by virtue of paragraph 1(3)(a) or (4), paragraph 3(4)(a), or the words following paragraph 3(4), of Schedule 5 to the Inheritance Tax Act 1984.

3. The disposal of property with respect to which inheritance tax is not chargeable by virtue of section 32(4) or 32A(5) or (7) of the Inheritance Tax Act 1984.

4. The disposal of an asset in a case in which any gain accruing on that disposal is not a chargeable gain by virtue of section 258(2) of the Taxation of Chargeable Gains Act 1992.

Derivations – Sch. 9, Grp. 11: VATA 1983, s. 8, 17 and Sch. 6, Grp. 11, as amended by IHTA 1984, s. 276 and Sch. 8, para. 24, FA 1985, s. 94 and Sch. 26, para. 14, FA 1986, s. 100 and TCGA 1992, s. 290 and Sch. 10, para. 6.

Official publications – 701/12.

Notes – On and after 25 July 1986 the Capital Transfer Tax Act 1984 may be cited as the Inheritance Tax Act 1984 (FA 1986, s. 100(1)(a)), and, except in relation to liabilities arising before 25 July 1986, references to capital transfer tax have effect as references to inheritance tax (FA 1986, s. 100(1)(b)).

GROUP 12 – FUND-RAISING EVENTS BY CHARITIES AND OTHER QUALIFYING BODIES

Item No.

1.   The supply of goods and services by a charity in connection with an event–
   (a) that is organised for charitable purposes by a charity or jointly by more than one charity,
   (b) whose primary purpose is the raising of money, and
   (c) that is promoted as being primarily for the raising of money.
2.   The supply of goods and services by a qualifying body in connection with an event–
   (a) that is organised exclusively for the body's own benefit,
   (b) whose primary purpose is the raising of money, and
   (c) that is promoted as being primarily for the raising of money.
3.   The supply of goods and services by a charity or a qualifying body in connection with an event–
   (a) that is organised jointly by a charity, or two or more charities, and the qualifying body,
   (b) that is so organised exclusively for charitable purposes or exclusively for the body's own benefit or exclusively for a combination of those purposes and that benefit,
   (c) whose primary purpose is the raising of money, and
   (d) that is promoted as being primarily for the raising of money.

Notes:

(1) For the purposes of this Group **"event"** includes an event accessed (wholly or partly) by means of electronic communications.

For this purpose **"electronic communications"** includes any communications by means of a telecommunications system (within the meaning of the Telecommunications Act 1984).

(2) For the purposes of this Group **"charity"** includes a body corporate that is wholly owned by a charity if–
   (a) the body has agreed in writing (whether or not contained in a deed) to transfer its profits (from whatever source) to a charity, or
   (b) the body's profits (from whatever source) are otherwise payable to a charity.

(3) For the purposes of this Group **"qualifying body"** means–
   (a) any non-profit making organisation mentioned in item 1 of Group 9;
   (b) any body that is an eligible body for the purposes of Group 10 and whose principal purpose is the provision of facilities for persons to take part in sport or physical education; or
   (c) any body that is an eligible body for the purposes of item 2 of Group 13.

(4) Where in a financial year of a charity or qualifying body there are held at the same location more than 15 events involving the charity or body that are of the same kind, items 1 to 3 do not apply (or shall be treated as having not applied) to a supply in connection with any event involving the charity or body that is of that kind and is held in that financial year at that location.

(5) In determining whether the limit of 15 events mentioned in Note (4) has been exceeded in the case of events of any one kind held at the same location, disregard any event of that kind held at that location in a week during which the aggregate gross takings from events involving the charity or body that are of that kind and are held in that location do not exceed £1,000.

(6) In the case of a financial year that is longer or shorter than a year, Notes (4) and (5) have effect as if for "15" there were substituted the whole number nearest to the number obtained by–
   (a) first multiplying the number of days in the financial year by 15, and
   (b) then dividing the result by 365.

(7) For the purposes of Notes (4) and (5)–
   (a) an event **involves a charity** if the event is organised by the charity or a connected charity;
   (b) an event **involves a qualifying body** if the event is organised by the body.

In this Note **"organised"** means organised alone or jointly in any combination, and **"organising"** in Note (8) shall be construed accordingly.

(8) Items 1 to 3 do not include any supply in connection with an event if–
   (a) accommodation in connection with the event is provided to a person by means of a supply, or in pursuance of arrangements, made by–
      (i) the charity or any of the charities, or the qualifying body, organising the event, or

(ii) a charity connected with any charity organising the event, and

(b) the provision of the accommodation is not incidental to the event.

(9) For the purposes of Note (8) the provision of accommodation is **incidental to the event** only if accommodation provided to the person by such means, or in pursuance of such arrangements, as are mentioned in paragraph (a) of that Note–

(a) does not exceed two nights in total (whether or not consecutive), and

(b) is not to any extent provided by means of a supply to which an order under section 53 applies.

(10) For the purposes of Notes (7)(a) and (8), two charities are **connected** if–

(a) one is a charity for the purposes of this Group only by virtue of Note (2) and the other is the charity that owns it, or

(b) each is a charity for the purposes of this Group only by virtue of Note (2) and the two of them are owned by the same charity.

(11) Items 1 to 3 do not include any supply the exemption of which would be likely to create distortions of competition such as to place a commercial enterprise carried on by a taxable person at a disadvantage.

History – Grp. 12 was substituted by SI 2000/802, art. 3, operative from 1 April 2000 but the variations made by SI 2000/802 have effect only in the case of supplies made on or after 1 April 2000. However, in determining for the purposes of Note (4) as inserted whether the number of events in a series exceeds any particular number, an event is not to be disregarded solely because it was held before 1 April 2000. Former Grp. 12 reads as follows:

GROUP 12 – FUND-RAISING EVENTS BY CHARITIES AND OTHER QUALIFYING BODIES

Item No.

1. The supply of goods and services by a charity in connection with a fund-raising event organised for charitable purposes by a charity or jointly by more than one charity.

2. The supply of goods and services by a qualifying body in connection with a fund-raising event organised exclusively for its own benefit.

Notes:

(1) For the purposes of items 1 and 2 **"fund-raising event"** means a fete, ball, bazaar, gala show, performance or similar event, which is separate from and not forming any part of a series or regular run of like or similar events.

(2) For the purposes of item 1 **"charity"** includes a body corporate which is wholly owned by a charity and whose profits (from whatever source) are payable to a charity by virtue of a deed of covenant or trust or otherwise.

(3) For the purposes of item 2 **"qualifying body"** means–

(a) [Omitted by SI 1999/2834, art. 5.]

(b) any non-profit making organisation mentioned in item 1 of Group 9;

(c) any non-profit making body whose principal purpose is the provision of facilities for persons to take part in sport or physical education; or

(d) any body which is an eligible body for the purposes of item 2 of Group 13."

Former Note (3)(a) was omitted by SI 1999/2834, art. 5, operative from 1 December 1999. Former Note (3)(a) reads as follows:
"(a) any non-profit making body whose objects are of any description mentioned in section 94(3);"
Note (3) was substituted by SI 1996/1256, art. 2(a), operative from 1 June 1996. Former Note (3) reads as follows:
"For the purposes of item 2 **"qualifying body"** means any non-profit-making body which is–
(a) mentioned in either section 94(3) or Item 1 in Group 9; or
(b) established for the principal purpose of providing facilities for participating in sport or physical education."

Derivations – Sch. 9, Grp. 12, items 1, 2: VATA 1983, s. 8, 17 and Sch. 6, Grp. 12, items 1, 2, as inserted by SI 1989/470.
Sch. 9, Grp. 12, Note (1): VATA 1983, s. 8, 17 and Sch. 6, Grp. 12, Note (1), as inserted by SI 1989/470.
Sch. 9, Grp. 12, Note (2): VATA 1983, s. 8, 17 and Sch. 6, Grp. 12, Note (1A), as inserted by SI 1991/737, art. 9.
Sch. 9, Grp. 12, Note (3): VATA 1983, s. 8, 17 and Sch. 6, Grp. 12, Note (2), as substituted by SI 1994/687, art. 3.

Official publications – 701/1.

GROUP 13 – CULTURAL SERVICES ETC.

Item No.

1. The supply by a public body of a right of admission to–

(a) a museum, gallery, art exhibition or zoo; or

(b) a theatrical, musical or choreographic performance of a cultural nature.

2. The supply by an eligible body of a right of admission to–

(a) a museum, gallery, art exhibition or zoo; or

(b) a theatrical, musical or choreographic performance of a cultural nature.

Notes:

(1) For the purposes of this Group **"public body"** means–

(a) a local authority;

(b) a government department within the meaning of section 41(6); or

(c) a non-departmental public body which is listed in the 1995 edition of the publication prepared by the Office of Public Service and known as "Public Bodies".

(2) For the purposes of item 2 **"eligible body"** means any body (other than a public body) which–

(a) is precluded from distributing, and does not distribute, any profit it makes;

(b) applies any profits made from supplies of a description falling within item 2 to the continuance or improvement of the facilities made available by means of the supplies; and

(c) is managed and administered on a voluntary basis by persons who have no direct or indirect financial interest in its activities.

(3) Item 1 does not include any supply the exemption of which would be likely to create distortions of competition such as to place a commercial enterprise carried on by a taxable person at a disadvantage.

(4) Item 1(b) includes the supply of a right of admission to a performance only if the performance is provided exclusively by one or more public bodies, one or more eligible bodies or any combination of public bodies and eligible bodies.

History – Grp. 13 was added by SI 1996/1256, art. 2(b), operative from 1 June 1996.

Cross references – VATA 1994, Sch. 9, Grp. 12, Note (3) : "eligible body".

Official publications – 701/47.

GROUP 14 – SUPPLIES OF GOODS WHERE INPUT TAX CANNOT BE RECOVERED

Item No.

1. A supply of goods in relation to which each of the following conditions is satisfied, that is to say–

(a) there is input tax of the person making the supply (**"the relevant supplier"**), or of any predecessor of his, that has arisen or will arise on the supply to, or acquisition or importation by, the relevant supplier or any such predecessor of goods used for the supply made by the relevant supplier;

(b) the only such input tax is non-deductible input tax; and

(c) the supply made by the relevant supplier is not a supply which would be exempt under Item 1 of Group 1 of Schedule 9 but for an election under paragraph 2 of Schedule 10.

Notes:

(1) Subject to Note (2) below, in relation to any supply of goods by the relevant supplier, the **goods used** for that supply are–

(a) the goods supplied; and

(b) any goods used in the process of producing the supplied goods so as to be comprised in them.

(2) In relation to a supply by any person consisting in or arising from the grant of a major interest in land (**"the relevant supply"**)–

(a) any supply consisting in or arising from a previous grant of a major interest in the land is a supply of goods used for the relevant supply; and

(b) subject to paragraph (a) above, the goods used for the relevant supply are any goods used in the construction of a building or civil engineering work so as to become part of the land.

(3) Subject to Notes (7) to (10) below, **non-deductible input tax** is input tax to which Note (4) or (5) below applies.

(4) This Note applies to input tax which (disregarding this Group and regulation 106 of the Value Added Tax Regulations 1995 (de minimis rule)) is not, and will not become, attributable to supplies to which section 26(2) applies.

(5) This Note applies to input tax if–

(a) disregarding this Group and the provisions mentioned in Note (6) below, the relevant supplier or a predecessor of his has or will become entitled to credit for the whole or a part of the amount of that input tax; and

(b) the effect (disregarding this Group) of one or more of those provisions is that neither the relevant supplier nor any predecessor of his has or will become entitled to credit for any part of that amount.

(6) The provisions mentioned in Note (5) above are–

(a) Article 5 of the Value Added Tax (Input Tax) Order 1992 (no credit for input tax on goods or services used for business entertainment);

(b) Article 6 of that Order (no credit for input tax on non-building materials incorporated in building or site);

(c) Article 7 of that Order (no credit for input tax on motor cars);

(d) any provision directly or indirectly re-enacted (with or without modification) in a provision mentioned in paragraphs (a) to (c) above.

(7) For the purposes of this Group the **input tax of a person** shall be deemed to include any VAT which–

(a) has arisen or will arise on a supply to, or acquisition or importation by, that person; and

(b) would fall to be treated as input tax of that person but for its arising when that person is not a taxable person.

(8) Subject to Note (9) below, the input tax that is taken to be **non-deductible input tax** shall include any VAT which–

(a) is deemed to be input tax of any person by virtue of Note (7) above; and

(b) would be input tax to which Note (4) or (5) above would apply if it were input tax of that person and, in the case of a person to whom section 39 applies, if his business were carried on in the United Kingdom.

(9) **Non-deductible input tax** does not include any VAT that has arisen or will arise on a supply to, or acquisition or importation by, any person of any goods used for a supply of goods ("**the relevant supply**") if–

(a) that VAT; or

(b) any other VAT arising on the supply to, or acquisition or importation by, that person or any predecessor of his of any goods used for the relevant supply,

has been or will be refunded under section 33, 39 or 41.

(10) Input tax arising on a supply, acquisition or importation of goods shall be disregarded for the purposes of determining whether the conditions in Item No 1(a) and (b) are satisfied if, at a time after that supply, acquisition or importation but before the supply by the relevant supplier, a supply of the goods or of anything in which they are comprised is treated under or by virtue of any provision of this Act as having been made by the relevant supplier or any predecessor of his to himself.

(11) In relation to any goods or anything comprised in any goods, a person is a predecessor of another ("**the putative successor**") only if Note (12) or (13) below applies to him in relation to those goods or that thing; and references in this Group to a person's predecessors include references to the predecessors of his predecessors through any number of transfers and events such as are mentioned in Notes (12) and (13).

(12) This Note applies to a person in relation to any goods or thing if–

(a) the putative successor is a person to whom he has transferred assets of his business by a transfer of that business, or a part of it, as a going concern;

(b) those assets consisted of or included those goods or that thing; and

(c) the transfer of the assets is one falling by virtue of an order under section 5(3) (or under an enactment re-enacted in section 5(3)) to be treated as neither a supply of goods nor a supply of services.

(13) This Note applies to a body corporate in relation to any goods or thing if–

(a) those goods or that thing formed part of the assets of the business of that body at a time when it became a member of a group of which the putative successor was at that time the representative member;

(b) those goods or that thing formed part of the assets of the business of that body corporate, or of any other body corporate which was a member of the same group as that body, at a time when that body was succeeded as the representative member of the group by the putative successor; or

(c) those goods or that thing formed part of the assets of the putative successor at a time when it ceased to be a member of a group of which the body corporate in question was at the time the representative member.

(14) References in Note (13) above to a body corporate's being or becoming or ceasing to be a **member of a group** or the **representative member** of a group are references to its falling to be so treated for the purposes of section 43.

(15) In Notes (11) to (13) above the references to **anything comprised in other goods** shall be taken, in relation to any supply consisting in or arising from the grant of a major interest in land, to include anything the supply, acquisition or importation of which is, by virtue of Note (2) above, taken to be a supply, acquisition or importation of goods used for making the supply so consisting or arising.

(16) Notes (1) and (1A) to Group 1 shall apply for the purposes of this Group as they apply for the purposes of that Group.

History – Grp. 14 was added by SI 1999/2833, art. 2(3), operative from 1 March 2000.

GROUP 15 – INVESTMENT GOLD

Item No.

1. The supply of investment gold.

2. The grant, assignment or surrender of any right, interest, or claim in, over or to investment gold if the right, interest or claim is or confers a right to the transfer of the possession of investment gold.

3. The supply, by a person acting as agent for a disclosed principal, of services consisting of–

 (a) the effecting of a supply falling within item 1 or 2 that is made by or to his principal, or

 (b) attempting to effect a supply falling within item 1 or 2 that is intended to be made by or to his principal but is not in fact made.

Notes:

(1) For the purposes of this Group **"investment gold"** means–

 (a) gold of a purity not less than 995 thousandths that is in the form of a bar, or a wafer, of a weight accepted by the bullion markets;

 (b) a gold coin minted after 1800 that–

   (i) is of a purity of not less than 900 thousandths,

   (ii) is, or has been, legal tender in its country of origin, and

   (iii) is of a description of coin that is normally sold at a price that does not exceed 180% of the open market value of the gold contained in the coin; or

 (c) a gold coin of a description specified in a notice that has been published by the Commissioners for the purposes of this Group and has not been withdrawn.

(2) A notice under Note (1)(c) may provide that a description specified in the notice has effect only for the purposes of supplies made at times falling within a period specified in the notice.

(3) Item 2 does not include–

 (a) the grant of an option, or

 (b) the assignment or surrender of a right under an option at a time before the option is exercised.

(4) This Group does not include a supply–

 (a) between members of the London Bullion Market Association, or

 (b) by a member of that Association to a taxable person who is not a member or by such a person to a member.

History – Grp. 15 was added by SI 1999/3116, art. 2(3), operative from 1 January 2000.

Cross references – VAT (Terminal Markets) Order 1973 (SI 1973/173), art. 2(5), 4 and 5: terminal markets.
VAT (Input Tax) Order 19992 (SI 1992/3222), art. 2: definition of collectors' items.
VAT (Special Provisions) Order (SI 1995/1268), art. 2: definition of collectors' items.
VAT Regulations 19995 (SI 1995/2518), reg. 24, 31A, 31C and 103A: record keeping.
VAT (Input tax) (Specified Supplies) Order 1999 (SI 1999/3121), art. 4: input tax and s. 26.

Statutory instruments – VAT (Investment Gold) Order 1999 (SI 1999/3116), art. 3 and 4.

Official publications – 701/21 and 701/21A.

SCHEDULE 9A – ANTI-AVOIDANCE PROVISIONS: GROUPS

[Section 43]

History – Sch. 9A was inserted by FA 1996, s. 31(2) and Sch. 4, with effect from 29 April 1996.
Cross references – FA 1999, Sch. 2, para. 6: transitional provisions for revised group provisions.

POWER TO GIVE DIRECTIONS

1(1) Subject to paragraph 2 below, the Commissioners may give a direction under this Schedule if in any case–

(a) a relevant event has occurred;

(b) the condition specified in sub-paragraph (3) below is fulfilled;

(c) that condition would not be fulfilled apart from the occurrence of that event; and

(d) in the case of an event falling within sub-paragraph (2)(b) below, the transaction in question is not a supply which is the only supply by reference to which the case falls within paragraphs (a) to (c) above.

1(2) For the purposes of this Schedule, a relevant event occurs when a body corporate–

(a) begins to be, or ceases to be, treated as a member of a group; or

(b)   enters into any transaction.

1(3)   The condition mentioned in sub-paragraph (1) above is that–

(a)   there has been, or will or may be, a taxable supply on which VAT has been, or will or may be, charged otherwise than by reference to the supply's full value;

(b)   there is at least a part of the supply which is not or, as the case may be, would not be zero-rated; and

(c)   the charging of VAT on the supply otherwise than by reference to its full value gives rise or, as the case may be, would give rise to a tax advantage.

1(4)   For the purposes of this paragraph the charging of VAT on a supply ("the undercharged supply") otherwise than by reference to its full value shall be taken to give rise to a tax advantage if, and only if, a person has become entitled–

(a)   to credit for input tax allowable as attributable to that supply or any part of it, or

(b)   in accordance with regulations under section 39, to any repayment in respect of that supply or any part of it.

1(5)   The cases where a person shall be taken for the purposes of sub-paragraph (4) above to have become entitled to a credit for input tax allowable as attributable to the undercharged supply, or to a part of it, shall include any case where–

(a)   a person has become entitled to a credit for any input tax on the supply to him, or the acquisition or importation by him, of any goods or services; and

(b)   whatever the supplies to which the credit was treated as attributable when the entitlement to it arose, those goods or services are used by him in making the undercharged supply, or a part of it.

1(6)   For the purposes of sub-paragraphs (4) and (5) above where–

(a)   there is a supply of any of the assets of a business of a person ("the transferor") to a person to whom the whole or any part of that business is transferred as a going concern ("the transferee"), and

(b)   that supply is treated, in accordance with an order under section 5(3), as being neither a supply of goods nor a supply of services,

the question, so far as it falls to be determined by reference to those assets, whether a credit for input tax to which any person has become entitled is one allowable as attributable to the whole or any part of a supply shall be determined as if the transferor and the transferee were the same person.

1(7)   Where, in a case to which sub-paragraph (6) above applies, the transferor himself acquired any of the assets in question by way of a supply falling within paragraphs (a) and (b) of that sub-paragraph, that sub-paragraph shall have the effect, as respects the assets so acquired, of requiring the person from whom those assets were acquired to be treated for the purposes of sub-paragraphs (4) and (5) above as the same person as the transferor and the transferee, and so on in the case of any number of successive supplies falling within those paragraphs.

1(8)   For the purposes of this paragraph any question–

(a)   whether any credit for input tax to which a person has become entitled was, or is to be taken to have been, a credit allowable as attributable to the whole or any part of a supply, or

(b)   whether any repayment is a repayment in respect of the whole or any part of a supply,

shall be determined, in relation to a supply of a right to goods or services or to a supply of goods or services by virtue of such a right, as if the supply of the right and supplies made by virtue of the right were a single supply of which the supply of the right and each of those supplies constituted different parts.

1(9)   References in this paragraph to the full value of a supply are references to the amount which (having regard to any direction under paragraph 1 of Schedule 6) would be the full value of that supply for the purposes of the charge to VAT if that supply were not a supply falling to be disregarded, to any extent, in pursuance of section 43(1)(a).

1(10)   References in this paragraph to the supply of a right to goods or services include references to the supply of any right, option or priority with respect to the supply of goods or services, and to the supply of an interest deriving from any right to goods or services.

Cross references – S. 83(wa): appeal against direction.
S. 84(7A): appeals against direction if there is a genuine commercial purpose.

RESTRICTIONS ON GIVING DIRECTIONS

2(1) The Commissioners shall not give a direction under this Schedule by reference to a relevant event if they are satisfied that–

(a)   the change in the treatment of the body corporate, or

(b)   the transaction in question,

had as its main purpose or, as the case may be, as each of its main purposes a genuine commercial purpose unconnected with the fulfilment of the condition specified in paragraph 1(3) above.

2(2) This paragraph shall not apply where the relevant event is the termination of a body corporate's treatment as a member of a group by a notice under section 43C(1) or (3).

History – The original para. 2 became para. 2(1) following the insertion of para. 2(2) by FA 1999, s. 16 and Sch. 2, para. 5(2), with effect in accordance with the transitional provisions in FA 1999, Sch. 2, para. 6.
Para. 2(2) was inserted by FA 1999, s. 16 and Sch. 2, para. 5(2), with effect in accordance with the transitional provisions in FA 1999, Sch. 2, para. 6.

FORM OF DIRECTIONS UNDER SCHEDULE

3(1) The directions that may be given by the Commissioners under this Schedule are either–

(a)   a direction relating to any supply of goods or services that has been made, in whole or in part, by one body corporate to another; or

(b)   a direction relating to a particular body corporate.

3(2) A direction under this Schedule relating to a supply shall require it to be assumed (where it would not otherwise be the case) that, to the extent described in the direction, the supply was not a supply falling to be disregarded in pursuance of section 43(1)(a).

3(3) A direction under this Schedule relating to a body corporate shall require it to be assumed (where it would not otherwise be the case) that, for such period (comprising times before the giving of the direction or times afterwards or both) as may be described in the direction, the body corporate–

(a)   did not fall to be treated, or is not to be treated, as a member of a group, or of a particular group so described; or

(b)   fell to be treated, or is to be treated, as a member of any group so described of which, for that period, it was or is eligible to be a member.

3(4) Where a direction under this Schedule requires any assumptions to be made, then–

(a)   so far as the assumptions relate to times on or after the day on which the direction is given, this Act shall have effect in relation to such times in accordance with those assumptions; and

(b)   paragraph 6 below shall apply for giving effect to those assumptions in so far as they relate to earlier times.

3(5) A direction falling within sub-paragraph (3)(b) above may identify in relation to any times or period the body corporate which is to be assumed to have been, or to be, the representative member of the group at those times or for that period.

3(6) A direction under this Schedule may vary the effect of a previous direction under this Schedule.

3(7) The Commissioners may at any time, by notice in writing to the person to whom it was given, withdraw a direction under this Schedule.

3(8) The refusal or non-refusal by the Commissioners of an application such as is mentioned in section 43B shall not prejudice the power of the Commissioners to give a direction under this Schedule requiring any case to be assumed to be what it would have been had the application not been refused or, as the case may be, had it been refused.

History – In para. 3(8), the words "such as is mentioned in section 43B" were substituted for the words "under section 43" by FA 1999, s. 16 and Sch. 2, para. 5(3), with effect in accordance with the transitional provisions in FA 1999, Sch. 2, para. 6.

TIME LIMIT ON DIRECTIONS

4(1) A direction under this Schedule shall not be given more than six years after whichever is the later of–

(a)   the occurrence of the relevant event by reference to which it is given; and

(b)   the time when the relevant entitlement arose.

4(2) A direction under this Schedule shall not be given by reference to a relevant event occurring on or before 28th November 1995.

4(3) Subject to sub-paragraphs (1) and (2) above, a direction under this Schedule–

(a)   may be given by reference to a relevant event occurring before the coming into force of this Schedule; and

(b)   may require assumptions to be made in relation to times (including times before 29th November 1995) falling before the occurrence of the relevant event by reference to which the direction is given, or before the relevant entitlement arose.

4(4)   For the purposes of this paragraph the reference, in relation to the giving of a direction, to the relevant entitlement is a reference to the entitlement by reference to which the requirements of paragraph 1(4) above are taken to be satisfied for the purposes of that direction.

MANNER OF GIVING DIRECTIONS

5(1)   A direction under this Schedule relating to a supply may be given to–

(a)   the person who made the supply to which the direction relates; or

(b)   any body corporate which, at the time when the direction is given, is the representative member of a group of which that person was treated as being a member at the time of the supply.

5(2)   A direction under this Schedule relating to a body corporate ("the relevant body") may be given to that body or to any body corporate which at the time when the direction is given is, or in pursuance of the direction is to be treated as, the representative member of a group of which the relevant body–

(a)   is treated as being a member;

(b)   was treated as being a member at a time to which the direction relates; or

(c)   is to be treated as being, or having been, a member at any such time.

5(3)   A direction given to any person under this Schedule shall be given to him by notice in writing.

5(4)   A direction under this Schedule must specify the relevant event by reference to which it is given.

ASSESSMENT IN CONSEQUENCE OF A DIRECTION

6(1)   Subject to sub-paragraph (3) below, where–

(a)   a direction is given under this Schedule, and

(b)   there is an amount of VAT ("the unpaid tax") for which a relevant person would have been liable before the giving of the direction if the facts had accorded with the assumptions specified in the direction,

the Commissioners may, to the best of their judgment, assess the amount of unpaid tax as tax due from the person to whom the direction was given or another relevant person and notify their assessment to that person.

6(2)   In sub-paragraph (1) above the reference to an amount of VAT for which a person would, on particular assumptions, have been liable before the giving of a direction under this Schedule is a reference to the aggregate of the following–

(a)   any amount of output tax which, on those assumptions but not otherwise, would have been due from a relevant person at the end of a prescribed accounting period ending before the giving of the direction;

(b)   the amount of any credit for input tax to which a relevant person is treated as having been entitled at the end of such an accounting period but to which he would not have been entitled on those assumptions; and

(c)   the amount of any repayment of tax made to a relevant person in accordance with regulations *under section 39 but to which he would not* have been entitled on those assumptions.

6(3)   Where any assessment falls to be made under this paragraph in a case in which the Commissioners are satisfied that the actual revenue loss is less than the unpaid tax, the total amount to be assessed under this paragraph shall not exceed what appears to them, to the best of their judgement, to be the amount of that loss.

6(4)   For the purposes of the making of an assessment under this paragraph in relation to any direction, the actual revenue loss shall be taken to be equal to the amount of the unpaid tax less the amount given by aggregating the amounts of every entitlement–

(a)   to credit for input tax, or

(b)   to a repayment in accordance with regulations under section 39, which (whether as an entitlement of the person in relation to whom the assessment is made or as an entitlement of any other person) would have arisen on the assumptions contained in the direction, but not otherwise.

6(5) An assessment under this paragraph relating to a direction may be notified to the person to whom that direction is given by being incorporated in the same notice as that direction.

6(6) An assessment under this paragraph shall not be made–

(a) more than one year after the day on which the direction to which it relates was given, or

(b) in the case of any direction that has been withdrawn.

6(7) Where an amount has been assessed on any person under this paragraph and notified to him–

(a) that amount shall be deemed (subject to the provisions of this Act as to appeals) to be an amount of VAT due from him;

(b) that amount may be recovered accordingly, either from that person or, in the case of a body corporate that is for the time being treated as a member of a group, from the representative member of that group; and

(c) to the extent that more than one person is liable by virtue of any assessment under this paragraph in respect of the same amount of unpaid tax, those persons shall be treated as jointly and severally liable for that amount.

6(8) Sub-paragraph (7) above does not have effect if or to the extent that the assessment in question has been withdrawn or reduced.

6(9) Sections 74 and 77(6) apply in relation to assessments under this paragraph as they apply in relation to assessments under section 73 but as if the reference in subsection (1) of section 74 to the reckonable date were a reference to the date on which the assessment is notified.

6(10) Where by virtue of sub-paragraph (9) above any person is liable to interest under section 74–

(a) section 76 shall have effect in relation to that liability with the omission of subsections (2) to (6); and

(b) section 77, except subsection (6), shall not apply to an assessment of the amount due by way of interest;

and (without prejudice to the power to make assessments for interest for later periods) the interest to which any assessment made under section 76 by virtue of paragraph (a) above may relate shall be confined to interest for a period of no more than two years ending with the time when the assessment to interest is made.

6(11) In this paragraph **"a relevant person"**, in relation to a direction, means–

(a) the person to whom the direction is given;

(b) the body corporate which was the representative member of any group of which that person was treated as being, or in pursuance of the direction is to be treated as having been, a member at a time to which the assumption specified in the direction relates; or

(c) any body corporate which, in pursuance of the direction, is to be treated as having been the representative member of such a group.

Cross references – S. 83(wa): appeals against assessments.

INTERPRETATION OF SCHEDULE ETC.

7(1) References in this Schedule to being **treated as a member of a group** and to being **eligible to be treated as a member of a group** shall be construed in accordance with sections 43 to 43C.

7(2) For the purposes of this Schedule the giving of any notice or notification to any receiver, liquidator or person otherwise acting in a representative capacity in relation to another shall be treated as the giving of a notice or, as the case may be, notification to the person in relation to whom he so acts.

History – In para. 7(1), the words "sections 43 to 43C" were substituted for the words "section 43" by FA 1999, s. 16 and Sch. 2, para. 5(4), with effect in accordance with the transitional provisions in FA 1999, Sch. 2, para. 6.

SCHEDULE 10 – BUILDINGS AND LAND

Section 51

RESIDENTIAL AND CHARITABLE BUILDINGS: CHANGE OF USE ETC.

1(1) In this paragraph **"relevant zero-rated supply"** means a grant or other supply taking place on or after 1st April 1989 which–

(a) relates to a building intended for use solely for a relevant residential purpose or a relevant charitable purpose or part of such a building; and

(b) is zero-rated, in whole or in part, by virtue of Group 5 of Schedule 8.

1(2) Sub-paragraph (3) below applies where–

(a) one or more relevant zero-rated supplies relating to a building (or part of a building) have been made to any person,

(b) within the period of 10 years beginning with the day on which the building is completed, the person grants an interest in, right over or licence to occupy the building or any part of it (or the building or any part of it including, consisting of or forming part of the part to which the relevant zero-rated supply or supplies related), and

(c) after the grant the whole or any part of the building, or of the part to which the grant relates, (or the whole of the building or of the part to which the grant relates, or any part of it including, consisting of or forming part of the part to which the relevant zero-rated supply or supplies related) is not intended for use solely for a relevant residential purpose or a relevant charitable purpose.

1(3) Where this sub-paragraph applies, to the extent that the grant relates to so much of the building as–

(a) by reason of its intended use gave rise to the relevant zero-rated supply or supplies; and

(b) is not intended for use solely for a relevant residential purpose or a relevant charitable purpose after the grant,

it shall be taken to be a taxable supply in the course or furtherance of a business which is not zero-rated by virtue of Group 5 of Schedule 8 (if it would not otherwise be such a supply).

1(4) Sub-paragraph (5) below applies where–

(a) one or more relevant zero-rated supplies relating to a building (or part of a building) have been made to any person; and

(b) within the period of 10 years beginning with the day on which the building is completed, the person uses the building or any part of it (or the building or any part of it including, consisting of or forming part of the part to which the relevant zero-rated supply or supplies related) for a purpose which is neither a relevant residential purpose nor a relevant charitable purpose.

1(5) Where this sub-paragraph applies, his interest in, right over or licence to occupy so much of the building as–

(a) by reason of its intended use gave rise to the relevant zero-rated supply or supplies, and

(b) is used otherwise than for a relevant residential purpose or a relevant charitable purpose,

shall be treated for the purposes of this Act as supplied to him for the purpose of a business carried on by him and supplied by him in the course or furtherance of the business when he first uses it for a purpose which is neither a relevant residential purpose nor a relevant charitable purpose.

1(6) Where sub-paragraph (5) applies–

(a) the supply shall be taken to be a taxable supply which is not zero-rated by virtue of Group 5 of Schedule 8 (if it would not otherwise be such a supply); and

(b) the value of the supply shall be such that the amount of VAT chargeable on it is equal to the amount of the VAT which would have been chargeable on the relevant zero-rated supply (or, where there was more than one such supply, the aggregate amount which would have been chargeable on them) had so much of the building as is mentioned in sub-paragraph (5) above not been intended for use solely for a relevant residential purpose or a relevant charitable purpose.

Derivations – VATA 1983, s. 35A and Sch. 6A, as inserted by FA 1989, s. 18 and Sch. 3, para. 6.

Cross references – VAT Regulations 1995 (SI 1995/2518), reg. 113 and 114: capital goods scheme and land or buildings supplied for not less than £250,000.
VAT Regulations 1995 (SI 1995/2518), reg. 115(5): adjustments to the deduction of input tax on capital items.

ELECTION TO WAIVE EXEMPTION

2(1) Subject to sub-paragraph (2), (3) and (3A) and paragraph 3 below, where an election under this paragraph has effect in relation to any land, if and to the extent that any grant made in relation to it at a time when the election has effect by the person who made the election, or where that person is a body corporate by that person or a relevant associate, would (apart from this sub-paragraph) fall within Group 1 of Schedule 9, the grant shall not fall within that Group.

2(2) Sub-paragraph (1) above shall not apply in relation to a grant if the grant is made in relation to–

(a) a building or part of a building intended for use as a dwelling or number of dwellings or solely for a relevant residential purpose; or

(b) a building or part of a building intended for use solely for a relevant charitable purpose, other than as an office;

(c) a pitch for a residential caravan;

(d) facilities for the mooring of a residential houseboat.

2(2A) Subject to the following provisions of this paragraph, where–

(a) an election has been made for the purposes of this paragraph in relation to any land, and

(b) a supply is made that would fall, but for sub-paragraph (2)(a) above, to be treated as excluded by virtue of that election from Group 1 of Schedule 9,

then, notwithstanding sub-paragraph (2)(a) above, that supply shall be treated as so excluded if the conditions in sub-paragraph (2B) below are satisfied.

2(2B) The conditions mentioned in sub-paragraph (2A) above are–

(a) that an agreement in writing made, at or before the time of the grant, between–
(i) the person making the grant, and
(ii) the person to whom it is made,
declares that the election is to apply in relation to the grant; and

(b) that the person to whom the supply is made intends, at the time when it is made, to use the land for the purpose only of making a supply which is zero-rated by virtue of paragraph (b) of item 1 of Group 5 of Schedule 8.

2(3) Sub-paragraph (1) above shall not apply in relation to a grant if–

(a) the grant is made to a relevant housing association and the association has given to the grantor a certificate stating that the land is to be used (after any necessary demolition work) for the construction of a building or buildings intended for use as a dwelling or number of dwellings or solely for a relevant residential purpose; or

(b) the grant is made to an individual and the land is to be used for the construction, otherwise than in the course or furtherance of a business carried on by him, of a building intended for use by him as a dwelling.

2(3AA) Where an election has been made under this paragraph in relation to any land, a supply shall not be taken by virtue of that election to be a taxable supply if–

(a) the grant giving rise to the supply was made by a person (**"the grantor"**) who was a developer of the land; and

(b) at the time of the grant or at the time it was treated as made by virtue of sub-paragraph (3AAA) below, it was the intention or expectation of–
(i) the grantor, or
(ii) a person responsible for financing the grantor's development of the land for exempt use,

that the land would become exempt land (whether immediately or eventually and whether or not by virtue of the grant) or, as the case may be, would continue, for a period at least, to be such land.

2(3AAA) For the purposes of sub-paragraph (3AA) above a grant (**the original grant**) in relation to land made on or after 19th March 1997 and before 10th March 1999 shall be treated as being made on 10th March 1999 if at the time of the original grant–

(a) the grantor or a person responsible for financing the grantor's development of the land for *exempt use, intended or expected* that the land or a building or part of a building on, or to be constructed on, that land would become an asset falling in relation to–
(i) the grantor, or
(ii) any person to whom that land, building or part of a building was to be transferred either in the course of a supply or in the course of a transfer of a business or part of a business as a going concern, to be treated as a capital item for the purposes of any regulations

made under section 26(3) and (4) providing for adjustments relating to the deduction of input tax to be made as respects that item, and

(b)   the land or a building or part of a building on, or to be constructed on, that land had not become such an asset.

2(3AB)   [Repealed by FA 1997, s. 37(1) and 113 and Sch. 18, Pt. IV(2).]

2(4)   Subject to the following provisions of this paragraph, no input tax on any supply or importation which, apart from this sub-paragraph, would be allowable by virtue of the operation of this paragraph shall be allowed if the supply or importation took place before the first day for which the election in question has effect.

2(5)   Subject to sub-paragraph (6) below, sub-paragraph (4) above shall not apply where the person by whom the election was made–

(a)   has not, before the first day for which the election has effect, made in relation to the land in relation to which the election has effect any grant falling within Group 1 of Schedule 9; or

(b)   has before that day made in relation to that land a grant or grants so falling but the grant, or all the grants–

(i)   were made in the period beginning with 1st April 1989 and ending with 31st July 1989; and

(ii) would have been taxable supplies but for the amendments made by Schedule 3 to the Finance Act 1989.

2(6)   Sub-paragraph (5) above does not make allowable any input tax on supplies or importations taking place before 1st August 1989 unless–

(a)   it is attributable by or under regulations to grants made by the person on or after 1st April 1989 which would have been taxable supplies but for the amendments made by Schedule 3 to the Finance Act 1989, and

(b)   the election has effect from 1st August 1989.

2(7)   Sub-paragraph (4) above shall not apply in relation to input tax on grants or other supplies which are made in the period beginning with 1st April 1989 and ending with 31st July 1989 if–

(a)   they would have been zero-rated by virtue of item 1 or 2 of Group 5 of Schedule 8 or exempt by virtue of item 1 of Group 1 of Schedule 9 but for the amendments made by Schedule 3 to the Finance Act 1989; and

(b)   the election has effect from 1st August 1989.

2(8)   Sub-paragraph (4) above shall not apply in relation to any election having effect from any day on or after 1st January 1992, except in respect of the input tax on a supply or importation which took place before 1st August 1989.

2(9)   Where a person has made an exempt grant in relation to any land and has made an election in relation to that land which has effect from any day before 1st January 1992, he may apply to the Commissioners for sub-paragraph (4) above to be disapplied in respect of any input tax on a supply or importation which took place on or after 1st August 1989, but the Commissioners shall only permit the disapplication of that sub-paragraph if they are satisfied, having regard to all the circumstances of the case, and in particular to–

(a)   the total value of–

(i)   exempt grants made;

(ii) taxable grants made or expected to be made, in relation to the land; and

(b)   the total amount of input tax in relation to the land which had been incurred before the day from which the election had effect,

that a fair and reasonable attribution of the input tax mentioned in paragraph (b) above will be secured.

History – In para. 2(1), the words "(2), (3) and (3A)" were substituted by SI 1994/3013, art. 2(a)(i), operative from 30 November 1994.
Para. 2(2)(c) and (d) were inserted by SI 1995/279, art. 3(a), operative from 1 March 1995.
Para. 2(2A) was inserted by FA 1997, s. 36(1), with effect in relation to supplies made on or after 19 March 1997.
Para. 2(2B) was inserted by FA 1997, s. 36(1), with effect in relation to supplies made on or after 19 March 1997.
In para. 2(3)(a), the words "relevant housing association" were substituted by SI 1997/51, art. 2(a), operative from 1 March 1997.
In para. 2(3AA)(b), the words "or at the time it was treated as made by virtue of sub-paragraph (3AAA) below," were inserted by SI 1999/593, art. 3, operative from 10 March 1999 in respect of supplies, other than a supply arising from a relevant pre-commencement grant within the meaning of FA 1997, s. 37, made on or after that date.
Para. 2(3AA) was inserted by FA 1997, s. 37(2), in relation to any supply made on or after 19 March 1997, other than a supply arising from a relevant pre-commencement grant as defined in FA 1997, s. 37(5) and (6).
Para. 2(3AAA) was inserted by SI 1999/593, art. 4, operative from 10 March 1999 in respect of supplies, other than a supply arising from a relevant pre-commencement grant within the meaning of FA 1997, s. 37, made on or after that date

Para. 2(3AB) was repealed by FA 1997, s. 37(1) and 113 and Sch. 18, Pt. IV(2), in relation to any supply made after 26 November 1996. Para. 2(3AB) had been inserted by SI 1994/3013, art. 2(a)(ii), operative from 30 November 1994.
In para. 2(7), the word "if" was inserted after the words "31st July 1989" by SI 1995/279, art. 3(b), operative from 1 March 1995.

Derivations – Sch. 10, para. 2(1)–(7) (as originally enacted): VATA 1983, s. 35A and Sch. 6A, para. 2(1)–(7), as inserted by FA 1989, s. 18 and Sch. 3, para. 6.
Sch. 10, para. 2(8), (9): VATA 1983, s. 35A and Sch. 6A, para. 2(8), (9), as inserted by SI 1991/2569, art. 3.

Cross references – S. 89(3): adjustments of contracts on changes in VAT.
S. 96(10A)(b): interpretation and references to grants.
VAT (Special Provisions) Order 1995 (SI 1995/1268), art. 5: going concern and non-supply where exemption waived.
Sch. 9, Grp. 14, item 1(c): supplies where input tax cannot be recovered.
VAT Regulations 1995 (SI 1995/2518), reg. 101(3): attribution of input tax to taxable supplies.

Other material – Law Society's Gazette, 14 October 1992 (not reproduced): in Customs' view, an award of Mesne profits is not consideration for a supply.

3(1) An election under paragraph 2 above shall have effect–

(a) subject to the following provisions of this paragraph, from the beginning of the day on which the election is made or of any later day specified in the election; or

(b) where the election was made before 1st November 1989, from the beginning of 1st August 1989 or of any later day so specified.

3(2) An election under paragraph 2 above shall have effect in relation to any land specified, or of a description specified, in the election.

3(3) Where such an election is made in relation to, or to part of, a building (or planned building), it shall have effect in relation to the whole of the building and all the land within its curtilage and for the purposes of this sub-paragraph buildings linked internally or by a covered walkway, and complexes consisting of a number of units grouped around a fully enclosed concourse, shall be taken to be a single building (if they otherwise would not be).

3(4) Subject to sub-paragraph (5) below, an election under paragraph 2 above shall be irrevocable.

3(5) Where–

(a) the time that has elapsed since the day on which an election had effect is–
   (i) less than 3 months; or
   (ii) more than 20 years;

(b) in a case to which paragraph (a)(i) above applies–
   (i) no tax has become chargeable and no credit for input tax has been claimed by virtue of the election; and
   (ii) no grant in relation to the land which is the subject of the election has been made which, by virtue of being a supply of the assets of a business to a person to whom the business (or part of it) is being transferred as a going concern, has been treated as neither a supply of goods nor a supply of services; and

(c) the person making the election obtains the written consent of the Commissioners;

the election shall be revoked, in a case to which paragraph (a)(i) above applies, from the date on which it was made, and in a case to which paragraph (a)(ii) above applies, from the date on which the written consent of the Commissioners is given or such later date as they may specify in their written consent.

3(5A) Where–

(a) an election under paragraph 2 above is made in relation to any land, and

(b) apart from this sub-paragraph, a grant in relation to that land would be taken to have been made (whether in whole or in part) before the time when the election takes effect,

that paragraph shall have effect, in relation to any supplies to which the grant gives rise which are treated for the purposes of this Act as taking place after that time, as if the grant had been made after that time.

3(5B) Accordingly, the references in paragraph 2(9) above and sub-paragraph (9) below to **grants being exempt or taxable** shall be construed as references to supplies to which a grant gives rise being exempt or, as the case may be, taxable.

3(6) An election under paragraph 2 above shall have effect after 1 March 1995 only if–

(a) in the case of an election made before that date–
   (i) it also had effect before that date; or
   (ii) written notification of the election is given to the Commissioners not later than the end of the period of 30 days beginning with the day on which the election was made, or not later than the end of such longer period beginning with that day as the Commissioners

may in any particular case allow, together with such information as the Commissioners may require;

(b)   in the case of an election made on or after that date–

   (i) written notification of the election is given to the Commissioners not later than the end of the period of 30 days beginning with the day on which the election is made, or not later than the end of such longer period beginning with that day as the Commissioners may in any particular case allow, together with such information as the Commissioners may require; and

   (ii) in a case in which sub-paragraph (9) below requires the prior written permission of the Commissioners to be obtained, that permission has been given.

3(7)   In paragraph 2 above and this paragraph **"relevant associate"**, in relation to a body corporate by which an election under paragraph 2 above has been made in relation to any building or land, means a body corporate which under section 43–

(a)   was treated as a member of the same group as the body corporate by which the election was made at the time when the election first had effect;

(b)   has been so treated at any later time when the body corporate by which the election was made had an interest in, right over or licence to occupy the building or land (or any part of it); or

(c)   has been treated as a member of the same group as a body corporate within paragraph (a) or (b) above or this paragraph at a time when that body corporate had an interest in, right over or licence to occupy the building or land (or any part of it).

3(7A)   In paragraph 2 above–

(a)   **"houseboat"** means a houseboat within the meaning of Group 9 of Schedule 8; and

(b)   a houseboat is not a **residential houseboat** if residence in it throughout the year is prevented by the terms of a covenant, statutory planning consent or similar permission.

3(8)   In paragraph 2 above **"relevant housing association"** means–

(a)   a registered social landlord within the meaning of Part I of the Housing Act 1996,

(b)   a registered housing association within the meaning of the Housing Associations Act 1985 (Scottish registered housing associations), or

(c)   a registered housing association within the meaning of Part II of the Housing (Northern Ireland) Order 1992 (Northern Irish registered housing associations).

3(8A)   [Repealed by FA 1997, s. 37(1) and 113 and Sch. 18, Pt. IV(2).]

3(9)   Where a person who wishes to make an election in relation to any land (the relevant land) to have effect on or after 1st January 1992, has made, makes or intends to make, an exempt grant in relation to the relevant land at any time between 1st August 1989 and before the beginning of the day from which he wishes an election in relation to the relevant land to have effect, he shall not make an election in relation to the relevant land unless the conditions for automatic permission specified in a notice published by the Commissioners are met or he obtains the prior written permission of the Commissioners, who shall only give such permission if they are satisfied having regard to all the circumstances of the case and in particular to–

(a)   the total value of exempt grants in relation to the relevant land made or to be made before the day from which the person wishes his election to have effect;

(b)   the expected total value of grants relating to the relevant land that would be taxable if the election were to have effect; and

(c)   the total amount of input tax which has been incurred on or after 1st August 1989 or is likely to be incurred in relation to the relevant land,

that there would be secured a fair and reasonable attribution of the input tax mentioned in paragraph (c) above to grants in relation to the relevant land which, if the election were to have effect, would be taxable.

History – In para. 3(3), the words "complexes consisting of . . . fully enclosed concourse" were substituted by SI 1995/279, art. 4(a), operative from 1 March 1995.
Para. 3(4) was substituted by SI 1995/279, art. 4(b), operative from 1 March 1995.
Para. 3(5) was substituted by SI 1995/279, art. 4(b), operative from 1 March 1995.
Para. 3(5A) and (5B) were inserted by FA 1997, s. 35(2). These insertions are deemed always to have had effect. Amendments corresponding to these insertions are deemed to have had effect, for the purposes of the cases to which it applies, in relation to the Value Added Tax Act 1983; and any provisions about the coming into force of any amendment of that Act shall be deemed to have had effect accordingly. Nothing in FA 1997, s. 35(2) is taken to affect the operation, in relation to times before its repeal took effect, of paragraph 4 of Schedule 10 to the Value Added Tax Act 1994 or of any enactment re-enacted in that paragraph.
Para. 3(6) was substituted by SI 1995/279, art. 4(b), operative from 1 March 1995.
Para. 3(7A) was inserted by SI 1995/279, art. 4(c), operative from 1 March 1995.
Para. 3(8) was substituted by SI 1997/51, art. 2(b), operative from 1 March 1997.

Para. 3(8A) was repealed by FA 1997, s. 37(1) and 113 and Sch. 18, Pt. IV(2), in relation to any supply made after 26 November 1996. Para. 3(8A) had been inserted by SI 1994/3013, art. 2(b), operative from 30 November 1994.
In para. 3(9), the words "the conditions for automatic ... Commissioners are met or" were inserted by SI 1995/279, art. 4(d), operative from 1 March 1995.

Derivations – Sch. 10, para. 3(1)–(6) (as originally enacted): VATA 1983, s. 35A and Sch. 6A, para. 3(1)–(6), as inserted by FA 1989, s. 18 and Sch. 3, para. 6, as amended by SI 1991/2569, art. 4(a) and (b).
Sch. 10, para. 3(7), (8): VATA 1983, s. 35A and Sch. 6A, para. 3(8), (9), as inserted by FA 1989, s. 18 and Sch. 3, para. 6.
Sch. 10, para. 3(9) (as originally enacted): VATA 1983, s. 35A and Sch. 6A, para. 3(10), as inserted by SI 1991/2569, art. 4(d).
Cross references – VAT (Special Provisions) Order 1995 (SI 1995/1268), art. 5: going concern and non-supply where exemption waived.
Other material – Law Society's Gazette, 14 October 1992 (not reproduced): in Customs' view, an award of mesne profits is not consideration for a supply.

3A(1) This paragraph shall have effect for the construction of paragraph 2(3AA) and (3AAA) above.

3A(2) For the purposes of paragraph 2(3AA) and (3AAA) above, a **grant made by any person in relation to any land** is a grant made by a developer of that land if–

(a) the land or building or part of a building on that land is an asset falling in relation to that person to be treated as a capital item for the purposes of any regulations under section 26(3) and (4) providing for adjustments relating to the deduction of input tax; or

(b) that person or a person financing his development of the land for exempt use intended or expected that the land or a building or part of a building on, or to be constructed on, that land would become an asset falling in relation to–

    (i) the grantor, or

    (ii) any person to whom it was to be transferred either in the course of a supply or in the course of a transfer of a business or part of a business as a going concern, to be treated as a capital item for the purposes of the regulations referred to in sub-paragraph (a) above, unless the grant was made at a time falling after the expiry of the period over which such regulations require or allow adjustments relating to the deduction of input tax to be made as respects that item.

3A(3) In paragraph 2(3AA) and (3AAA) above and this paragraph the references to a person's being **responsible for financing** the grantor's development of the land for exempt use are references to his being a person who, with the intention or in the expectation that the land will become, or continue (for a period at least) to be, exempt land–

(a) has provided finance for the grantor's development of the land; or

(b) has entered into any agreement, arrangement or understanding (whether or not legally enforceable) to provide finance for the grantor's development of the land.

3A(4) In sub-paragraph (3)(a) and (b) above the references to **providing finance** for the grantor's development of the land are references to doing any one or more of the following, that is to say–

(a) directly or indirectly providing funds for meeting the whole or any part of the cost of the grantor's development of the land;

(b) directly or indirectly procuring the provision of such funds by another;

(c) directly or indirectly providing funds for discharging, in whole or in part, any liability that has been or may be incurred by any person for or in connection with the raising of funds to meet the cost of the grantor's development of the land;

(d) directly or indirectly procuring that any such liability is or will be discharged, in whole or in part, by another.

3A(5) The references in sub-paragraph (4) above to the **provision of funds** for a purpose referred to in that sub-paragraph include references to–

(a) the making of a loan of funds that are or are to be used for that purpose;

(b) the provision of any guarantee or other security in relation to such a loan;

(c) the provision of any of the consideration for the issue of any shares or other securities issued wholly or partly for raising such funds; or

(d) any other transfer of assets or value as a consequence of which any of such funds are made available for that purpose.

3A(6) In sub-paragraph (4) above the references to the **grantor's development of the land** are references to the acquisition by the grantor of the asset which–

(a) consists in the land or a building or part of a building on the land, and

(b) in relation to the grantor falls or, as the case may be, is intended or expected to fall to be treated for the purposes mentioned in sub-paragraph (2)(a) or (b) above as a capital item;

and for the purposes of this sub-paragraph the **acquisition of an asset** shall be taken to include its construction or reconstruction and the carrying out in relation to that asset of any other works by reference to which it falls or, as the case may be, is intended or expected to fall, to be treated for the purposes mentioned in sub-paragraph (2)(a) or (b) above as a capital item.

3A(7) For the purposes of paragraph 2(3AA) and (3AAA) above and this paragraph land is **exempt land** if, at a time falling before the expiry of the period provided in regulations made under section 26(3) and (4) for the making of adjustments relating to the deduction of input tax as respects that land–

(a)   the grantor,

(b)   a person responsible for financing the grantor's development of the land for exempt use, or

(c)   a person connected with the grantor or with a person responsible for financing the grantor's development of the land for exempt use,

is in occupation of the land without being in occupation of it wholly or mainly for eligible purposes.

3A(8) For the purposes of this paragraph, but subject to sub-paragraphs (10) and (12) below, a person's occupation at any time of any land is not capable of being occupation for **eligible purposes** unless he is a taxable person at that time.

3A(9) Subject to sub-paragraphs (10) to (12) below, a taxable person in occupation of any land shall be taken for the purposes of this paragraph to be in occupation of that land for **eligible purposes** to the extent only that his occupation of that land is for the purpose of making supplies which–

(a)   are or are to be made in the course or furtherance of a business carried on by him; and

(b)   are supplies of such a description that any input tax of his which was wholly attributable to those supplies would be input tax for which he would be entitled to a credit.

3A(10) For the purposes of this paragraph–

(a)   occupation of land by a body to which section 33 applies is occupation of the land for **eligible purposes** to the extent that the body occupies the land for purposes other than those of a business carried on by that body; and

(b)   any occupation of land by a Government department (within the meaning of section 41) is occupation of the land for **eligible purposes**.

3A(11) For the purposes of this paragraph, where land of which any person is in occupation–

(a)   is being held by that person in order to be put to use by him for particular purposes, and

(b)   is not land of which he is in occupation for any other purpose,

that person shall be deemed, for so long as the conditions in paragraphs (a) and (b) above are satisfied, to be in occupation of that land for the purposes for which he proposes to use it.

3A(12) Sub-paragraphs (8) to (11) above shall have effect where land is in the occupation of a person who–

(a)   is not a taxable person, but

(b)   is a person whose supplies are treated for the purposes of this Act as supplies made by another person who is a taxable person,

as if the person in occupation of the land and that other person were a single taxable person.

3A(13) For the purposes of this paragraph a person shall be taken to be in **occupation** of any land whether he occupies it alone or together with one or more other persons and whether he occupies all of that land or only part of it.

3A(14) Any question for the purposes of this paragraph whether one person is **connected** with another shall be determined in accordance with section 839 of the Taxes Act.

History – In para. 3A(1), the words "and (3AAA)" were inserted by SI 1999/593, art. 5(a), operative from 10 March 1999 in respect of supplies, other than a supply arising from a relevant pre-commencement grant within the meaning of FA 1997, s. 37, made on or after that date.

Para. 3A(2) was substituted by SI 1999/593, art. 5(b), operative from 10 March 1999 in respect of supplies, other than a supply arising from a relevant pre-commencement grant within the meaning of FA 1997, s. 37, made on or after that date. Former para. 3A(2) reads as follows:

"(2)   For the purposes of paragraph 2(3AA) above a grant made by any person in relation to any land is a **grant made by a developer** of that land if–

(a)   the land, or a building or part of a building on that land, is an asset falling in relation to that person to be treated as a capital item for the purposes of any regulations under section 26(3) and (4) providing for adjustments relating to the deduction of input tax; and

(b)   the grant was made at a time falling within the period over which such regulations allow adjustments relating to the deduction of input tax to be made as respects that item."

In para. 3A(3) , the words "and (3AAA)" were inserted by SI 1999/593, art. 5(c), operative from 10 March 1999 in respect of supplies, other than a supply arising from a relevant pre-commencement grant within the meaning of FA 1997, s. 37, made on or after that date.

Para. 3A(6) was substituted by SI 1999/593, art. 5(d), operative from 10 March 1999 in respect of supplies, other than a supply arising from a relevant pre-commencement grant within the meaning of FA 1997, s. 37, made on or after that date. Former para. 3A(6) reads as follows:

"(6) In sub-paragraph (4) above the references to the **grantor's development** of the land are references to the acquisition by the grantor of the asset which–

(a)   consists in the land or a building or part of a building on the land, and

(b)   in relation to the grantor falls to be treated for the purposes mentioned in sub-paragraph (2)(a) above as a capital item; and for the purposes of this sub-paragraph the acquisition of an asset shall be taken to include its construction or reconstruction and the carrying out in relation to that asset of any other works by reference to which it falls to be treated for the purposes mentioned in sub-paragraph (2)(a) above as a capital item."

In para. 3A(7), the words "and (3AAA)" were inserted by SI 1999/593, art. 5(e)(i), operative from 10 March 1999 in respect of supplies, other than a supply arising from a relevant pre-commencement grant within the meaning of FA 1997, s. 37, made on or after that date.

In para. 3A(7), the words "at a time falling within the period mentioned in sub-paragraph (2)(b) above" were substituted for the words "at a time falling within the period mentioned in sub-paragraph (2)(b) above" by SI 1999/593, art. 5(e)(ii), operative from 10 March 1999 in respect of supplies, other than a supply arising from a relevant pre-commencement grant within the meaning of FA 1997, s. 37, made on or after that date.

Para. 3A inserted by FA 1997, s. 37(3) with effect in relation to any supply made on or after 19 March 1997, other than a supply arising from a relevant pre-commencement grant, as determined in accordance with FA 1997, s. 37(5) and (6).

4   [Deleted by SI 1995/279, art. 5.]

History – Para. 4 was deleted by SI 1995/279, art. 5, operative from 1 March 1995.

Cross references – FA 1997, s. 35(4): nothing in the amendments made by that section affect the operation, in relation to times before its repeal took effect, of paragraph 4 of Schedule 10 to the Value Added Tax Act 1994 or of any enactment re-enacted in that paragraph.

Official publications – 742, 742/1, 742/2 and 742/3.

Other material – Law Society's Gazette, 14 October 1992 (not reproduced): in Customs' view, an award of mesne profits is not consideration for a supply.

DEVELOPERS OF CERTAIN NON-RESIDENTIAL BUILDINGS ETC.

5(1)   Paragraph 6 below shall apply–

(a)   on the first occasion during the period beginning with the day when the construction of a building or work within sub-paragraph (2) below is first planned and ending 10 years after the completion of the building or work on which a person who is a developer in relation to the building or work–

     (i)   grants an interest in, right over or licence to occupy the building or work (or any part of it) which is an exempt supply; or

    (ii)   is in occupation of the building, or uses the work (or any part of it) when not a fully taxable person (or, if a person treated under section 43 as a member of a group when the representative member is not a fully taxable person); or

(b)   if construction commenced before 1st March 1995 and the period referred to in paragraph (a) above has not then expired, on 1st March 1997;

whichever is the earlier.

5(2)   Subject to sub-paragraph (3) and (3A) below, the buildings and works within this sub-paragraph are–

(a)   any building neither designed as a dwelling or number of dwellings nor intended for use solely for a relevant residential purpose or a relevant charitable purpose; and

(b)   any civil engineering work, other than a work necessary for the development of a permanent park for residential caravans.

5(3)   A building or work is not within sub-paragraph (2) above if–

(a)   construction of it was commenced before 1st August 1989 or after 28th February 1995; or

(b)   a grant of the fee simple in it which falls within paragraph (a)(ii) or (iv) of item 1 of Group 1 of Schedule 9 has been made before the occasion concerned.

5(3A)   A building or work which would, apart from this sub-paragraph, fall within sub-paragraph (2) above is not within that sub-paragraph if–

(a)   construction of it was commenced before 1st March 1995 but had not been completed by that date; and

(b)   the developer–

     (i)   makes no claim after that date to credit for input tax, entitlement to which is dependent upon his being treated in due course as having made a supply by virtue of paragraph 6 below; and

    (ii)   has made no such claim prior to that date; or

      (iii) accounts to the Commissioners for a sum equal to any such credit that has previously been claimed.

5(4) For the purposes of this paragraph a taxable person is, in relation to any building or work, a **fully taxable person** throughout a prescribed accounting period if–

(a)   at the end of that period he is entitled to credit for input tax on all supplies to, and acquisitions and importations by, him in the period (apart from any on which input tax is excluded from credit by virtue of section 25(7); or

(b)   the building or work is not used by him at any time during the period in, or in connection with, making any exempt supplies of goods or services.

5(5) Subject to sub-paragraph (6) below, in this paragraph and paragraph 6 below **"developer"**, in relation to a building or work, means any person who–

(a)   constructs it;

(b)   order it to be constructed; or

(c)   finances its construction,

with a view to granting an interest in, right over or licence to occupy it (or any part of it) or to occupying or using it (or any part of it) for his own purposes.

5(6) Where–

(a)   a body corporate treated under section 43 as a member of a group is a developer in relation to a building or work;

(b)   it grants an interest in, right over or licence to occupy the building or work (or any part of it) to another body corporate which is treated under that section as a member of the group,

then, for the purposes of this paragraph and paragraph 6 below, as from the time of the grant any body corporate such as is mentioned in sub-paragraph (7) below shall be treated as also being a **developer** in relation to the building or work.

5(7) The bodies corporate referred to in sub-paragraph (6) above are any which under section 43–

(a)   was treated as a member of the same group as the body corporate making the grant at the time of the grant; or

(b)   has been so treated at any later time when the body corporate by which the grant was made had an interest in, right over or licence to occupy the building or work (or any part of it); or

(c)   has been treated as a member of the same group as a body corporate within paragraph (a) or (b) above or this paragraph at a time when that body corporate had an interest in, right over or licence to occupy the building or work (or any part of it).

5(8) Subject to sub-paragraph (10) below, sub-paragraphs (1), (2) and (3A) to (7) above shall apply in relation to any of the following reconstructions, enlargements or extensions–

(a)   a reconstruction, enlargement or extension of an existing building which is commenced on or after 1st January 1992 and before 1st March 1995 and–

    (i)   which is carried out wholly or partly on land (hereafter referred to as new building land) adjoining the curtilage of the existing building, or

    (ii) as a result of which the gross external floor area of the reconstructed, enlarged or extended building (excluding any floor area on new building land) exceeds the gross external floor area of the existing building by not less than 20 per cent of the gross external floor area of the existing building;

(b)   a reconstruction of an existing building which is commenced on or after 1st January 1992 and before 1st March 1995 and in the course of which at least 80 per cent of the area of the floor structures of the existing building are removed;

(c)   a reconstruction, enlargement or extension of a civil engineering work which is commenced on or after 1st January 1992 and before 1st March 1995 and which is carried out wholly or partly on land (hereafter referred to as new land) adjoining the land on or in which the existing work is situated,

as if references to the building or work were references to the reconstructed, enlarged or extended building or work and as if references to construction were references to reconstruction, enlargement or extension.

5(9) For the purposes of sub-paragraph (8)(a) above, **extensions to an existing building** shall include the provision of any annex having internal access to the existing building.

5(10) Sub-paragraphs (1) and (2) and sub-paragraphs (3A) to (7) above shall not apply to a reconstruction, enlargement or extension–

(a)   falling within sub-paragraph (8)(a)(i) or (ii) or (c) above where the developer has held an interest in at least 75 per cent of all of the land on which the reconstructed, enlarged or extended building or work stands, or is constructed, throughout the period of 10 years ending with the last day of the prescribed accounting period during which the reconstructed, enlarged or extended building or work becomes substantially ready for occupation or use; or

(b)   to the extent that it falls within sub-paragraph (8)(a)(ii) above or falling within sub-paragraph (8)(b) above, where the interest in, right over or licence to occupy the building concerned (or any part of it) has already been treated as supplied to and by the developer under paragraph 6(1) below.

History – Para. 5(1) was substituted by SI 1995/279, art. 6(a), operative from 1 March 1995. Former para. 5(1) read as follows:
"**5(1)**   Paragraph 6 below shall apply on the first occasion during the period beginning with the day when the construction of a building or work within sub-paragraph (2) below is first planned and ending 10 years after the completion of the building or work on which a person who is a developer in relation to the building or work–
  (a)   grants an interest in, right over or licence to occupy the building or work (or any part of it) which is an exempt supply; or
  (b)   is in occupation of the building, or uses the work (or any part of it) when not a fully taxable person (or, if a person treated under section 43 as a member of a group when the representative member is not a fully taxable person)."
In para. 5(2), the words "and (3A)" were inserted by SI 1995/279, art. 6(b), operative from 1 March 1995.
In para. 5(3)(a), the words "or after 28th February 1995" were inserted by SI 1995/279, art. 6(c), operative from 1 March 1995.
Para. 5(3A) was inserted by SI 1995/279, art. 6(d), operative from 1 March 1995.
In para. 5(4)(a), the words "acquisitions and" were inserted by SI 1995/279, art. 6(e), operative from 1 March 1995.
In para. 5(8), the words "sub-paragraphs (1), (2) and (3A) to (7)" were substituted for the words "sub-paragraphs (1), (2) and (4) to (7)" and in para. 5(8)(a), (b) and (c) the words "and before 1st March 1995" were inserted by SI 1995/279, art. 6(f)(i) and (ii), operative from 1 March 1995.
In para. 5(10), the words "sub-paragraphs (3A) to (7)" were substituted for the words "sub-paragraphs (4) to (7)" by SI 1995/279, art. 6(g), operative from 1 March 1995.

Derivations – Para. 5(1)–(7) (as originally enacted): VATA 1983, s. 35A and Sch. 6A, para. 5, as inserted by FA 1989, s. 18 and Sch. 3, para. 6.
Para. 5(8)–(10) (as originally enacted): VATA 1983, s. 35A and Sch. 6A, para. 5(8)–(10), as inserted by SI 1991/2569, art. 5.
Extra-statutory concessions – 3.10 (Notice 48 (1999 edn)): when developer's self-supply on 1 March 1997 need not be treated as made.

6(1)   Where this paragraph applies the interest in, right over or licence to occupy the buildings or work (or any part of it) held by the developer shall be treated for the purposes of this Act as supplied to the developer for the purpose of a business carried on by him and supplied by him in the course or furtherance of the business on the last day of the prescribed accounting period during which it applies, or, if later, of the prescribed accounting period during which the building or work becomes substantially ready for occupation or use.

6(2)   The supply treated as made by sub-paragraph (1) above shall be taken to be a taxable supply and the value of the supply shall be the aggregate of–

(a)   the value of grants relating to the land on which the building or work is constructed made or to be made to the developer, but excluding, in a case where construction of the building or work in question commenced before 1st January 1992, the value of any grants to be made for consideration in the form of rent the amount of which cannot be ascertained by the developer when the supply is treated as made, and in any other case excluding the value of any–

  (i)   grants made before the relevant day to the extent that consideration for such grants was in the form of rent, and to the extent that such rent was properly attributable to a building which has been demolished,

  (ii)   grants made before the relevant day in respect of a building which has been reconstructed, enlarged or extended so that the reconstruction, enlargement or extension falls within paragraph 5(8)(a)(ii) above, and does not fall also within paragraph 5(8)(b) above, to the extent that consideration for such grants was in the form of rent, and to the extent that such rent was properly attributable to the building as it existed before the commencement of the reconstruction, enlargement or extension,

  (iii)   grants made before the relevant day in respect of a building which has been so reconstructed that the reconstruction falls within paragraph 5(8)(b) above, to the extent that consideration for such grants was in the form of rent, and to the extent that such rent was properly attributable to the building before the reconstruction commenced,

  (iv)   grants falling within paragraph (b) of item 1 of Group 1 of Schedule 9, and

(b)   the value of all the taxable supplies of goods and services, other than any that are zero-rated, made or to be made for or in connection with the construction of the building or work.

6(3)   Where the rate of VAT (the lower rate) chargeable on a supply (the construction supply) falling within sub-paragraph (2)(b) above, the value of which is included in the value of a supply (the self-supply) treated as made by sub-paragraph (1) above, is lower than the rate of VAT (the current rate) chargeable on that self-supply, then VAT on the self-supply shall be charged–

(a) on so much of its value as is comprised of the relevant part of the value of the construction supply, at the lower rate; and

(b) on the remainder of its value at the current rate.

6(4) For the purposes of sub-paragraph (3)(a) above, the **relevant part of the value of the construction supply** means–

(a) where the construction supply is a supply of goods, the value of such of those goods as have actually been delivered by the supplier;

(b) where the construction supply is a supply of services, the value of such of those services as have actually been performed by the supplier,

on or before the last day upon which the lower rate is in force.

6(5) Where the value of a supply which, apart from this sub-paragraph, would be treated as made by sub-paragraph (1) above would be less than £100,000, no supply shall be treated as made by that sub-paragraph.

6(6) For the purposes of sub-paragraph (2)(a)(i) above, the **relevant day** is the day on which the demolition of the building in question commenced and, for the purposes of sub-paragraph (2)(a)(ii) and (iii) above, the relevant day is the day on which the reconstruction, enlargement or extension in question commenced.

6(7) In the application of sub-paragraphs (1) to (6) above to a reconstruction, enlargement or extension to which sub-paragraphs (1) and (2) and sub-paragraphs (3A) to (7) of paragraph 5 above apply by virtue of paragraph 5(8) above–

(a) references to the **building or work** shall be construed as references to the reconstructed enlarged or extended building or work, and references to **construction** shall be construed as references to reconstruction, enlargement or extension;

(b) the reference in paragraph (a) of sub-paragraph (2) to the **value of grants relating to the land on which the building or work is constructed** shall be construed as a reference–

  (i) in relation to a reconstruction, enlargement or extension of an existing building to the extent that it falls within paragraph 5(8)(a)(i) above and does not fall also within paragraph 5(8)(b) above, to the value of grants relating to the new building land;

  (ii) in relation to a reconstruction, enlargement or extension of an existing building, to the extent that it falls within paragraph 5(8)(a)(ii) above and does not fall also within paragraph 5(8)(b) above, to the value of grants relating to the land on which the existing building stands multiplied by the appropriate fraction;

  (iii) in relation to a reconstruction, enlargement or extension to a work falling within paragraph 5(8)(c) above, to the value of grants relating to the new land.

6(8) For the purposes of sub-paragraph (7)(b)(ii) above the **appropriate fraction** shall be calculated by dividing the additional gross external floor area resulting from the reconstruction, enlargement or extension (excluding any floor area on new building land) by the gross external floor area of the reconstructed, enlarged or extended building (excluding any floor area on new building land).

6(9) Where this paragraph applies by virtue of paragraph 5(1)(b) above it shall have effect as if–

(a) in sub-paragraph (1)–

  (i) the words "(or any part of it)" were omitted; and

  (ii) for the words "the last day" to "ready for occupation or use" there were substituted "1 March 1997";

(b) in sub-paragraph (2)(a) the words "or to be made" and the words "to be made" were omitted;

(c) in sub-paragraph (2)(b) the words "or to be made" were omitted; and

(d) sub-paragraph (5) were omitted.

History – In para. 6(7), the words "sub-paragraphs (3A) to (7)" were substituted for the words "sub-paragraphs (4) to (7)" by SI 1995/279, art. 7(a), operative from 1 March 1995.
Para. 6(9) was added by SI 1995/279, art. 7(b), operative from 1 March 1995.

Derivations – Para. 6(1): VATA 1983, s. 35A and Sch. 6A, para. 6(1), as inserted by FA 1989, s. 18 and Sch. 3, para. 6.
Para. 6(2): VATA 1983, s. 35A and Sch. 6A, para. 6(2), as inserted by FA 1989, s. 18 and Sch. 3, para. 6 and as amended by SI 1991/2569, art. 6(a).
Para. 6(3), (4): VATA 1983, s. 35A and Sch. 6A, para. 6(2A), (2B), as inserted by SI 1991/2569, art. 6(b).
Para. 6(5): VATA 1983, s. 35A and Sch. 6A, para. 6(3), as inserted by FA 1989, s. 18 and Sch. 3, para. 6.
Para. 6(6)–(8) (as originally enacted): VATA 1983, s. 35A and Sch. 6A, para. 6(4)–(6), as inserted by SI 1991/2569, art. 6(c).

Cross references – VAT Regulations 1995 (SI 1995/2518), reg. 113: capital goods scheme and land or buildings supplied for not less than £250,000.
VAT Regulations 1995 (SI 1995/2518), reg. 115(5): adjustments to the deduction of input tax on capital items.

7(1) Where a developer is a tenant, lessee or licensee and becomes liable to a charge to VAT under paragraph 6(1) above (except where that paragraph applies by virtue of paragraph 5(1)(b)) in respect of his tenancy, lease or licence he shall notify forthwith in writing his landlord, lessor or licensor (as the case may be)–

(a)   of the date from which the tenancy, lease or licence becomes a developmental tenancy, developmental lease or developmental licence for the purposes of paragraph (b) of item 1 of Group 1 of Schedule 9;

(b)   in a case falling within paragraph 5(8)(a)(ii) above, of the appropriate fraction determined in accordance with paragraph 6(8) above.

7(2) Where the appropriate fraction has been notified in accordance with sub-paragraph (1)(b) above, any supply made pursuant to the tenancy, lease or licence in question shall be treated as made pursuant to a developmental tenancy, developmental lease or developmental licence (a developmental supply) as if, and only to the extent that, the consideration for the developmental supply is for an amount equal to the whole of the consideration for the supply made pursuant to the tenancy, lease or licence, multiplied by the appropriate fraction.

History – In para. 7(1), the words "(except where that ... of paragraph 5(1)(b))" were inserted by SI 1995/279, art. 8, operative from 1 March 1995.

Derivations – (as originally enacted) – VATA 1983, s. 35A and Sch. 6A, para. 6A, as inserted by SI 1991/2569, art. 7.

Cross reference – VAT Regulations 1995 (SI 1995/2518), Pt. XV: capital goods adjustment scheme.

GENERAL

8 Where the benefit of the consideration for the grant of an interest in, right over or licence to occupy land accrues to a person but that person is not the person making the grant–

(a)   the person to whom the benefit accrues shall for the purposes of this Act be treated as the person making the grant; and

(b)   to the extent that any input tax of the person actually making the grant is attributable to the grant it shall be treated as input tax of the person to whom the benefit accrues.

Prospective amendments – Para. 8 is to become para. 8(1) and para. 8(2) and (3) are to be inserted by FA 1995, s. 26(2), with effect from a day to be appointed. The prospective para. 8(2) and (3) read as follows:

"**8(2)** Where the consideration for the grant of an interest in, right over or licence to occupy land is such that its provision is enforceable primarily–
   (a)   by the person who, as owner of an interest or right in or over that land, actually made the grant, or
   (b)   by another person in his capacity as the owner for the time being of that interest or right or of any other interest or right in or over that land,
that person, and not any person (other than that person) to whom a benefit accrues by virtue of his being a beneficiary under a trust relating to the land, or the proceeds of sale of any land, shall be taken for the purposes of this paragraph to be the person to whom the benefit of the consideration accrues.

8(3) Sub-paragraph (2) above shall not apply to the extent that the Commissioners, on an application made in the prescribed manner jointly by–
   (a)   the person who (apart from this sub-paragraph) would be taken under that sub-paragraph to be the person to whom the benefit of the consideration accrues, and
   (b)   all the persons for the time being in existence who, as beneficiaries under such a trust as is mentioned in that sub-paragraph, are persons who have or may become entitled to or to a share of the consideration, or for whose benefit any of it is to be or may be applied,
may direct that the benefit of the consideration is to be treated for the purposes of this paragraph as a benefit accruing to the persons falling within paragraph (b) above, and not (unless he also falls within paragraph (b) above) to the person falling within paragraph (a) above."

Derivations – (as originally enacted) – VATA 1983, s. 35A and Sch. 6A, para. 7, as inserted by FA 1989, s. 18 and Sch. 3, para. 6.

9 Notes (1) to (6), (10), (12) and (19) to Group 5 of Schedule 8 and Notes (1), (1A), (2) and (15) to Group 1 of Schedule 9 apply in relation to this Schedule as they apply in relation to their respective Groups but subject to any appropriate modifications.

History – In para. 9, the words "Notes (1) to (6), (10), (12) and (19)" were substituted for the words "Notes (1) to (6), and Note (10)" and "Notes (1), (1A), (2) and (15)" were substituted for the words "Notes (1) and (2)" by SI 1995/279, art. 9(a) and (b), operative from 1 March 1995.

Derivations – (as originally enacted) – VATA 1983, s. 35A and Sch. 6A, para. 8, as inserted by FA 1989, s. 18 and Sch. 3, para. 6 and as amended by SI 1991/2569, art. 8.

SCHEDULE 11 – ADMINISTRATION, COLLECTION AND ENFORCEMENT

Section 58

GENERAL

1(1) VAT shall be under the care and management of the Commissioners.

1(2) All money and securities for money collected or received for or on account of VAT shall–

(a) if collected or received in Great Britain, be placed to the general account of the Commissioners kept at the bank of England under section 17 of the Management Act;

(b) if collected or received in Northern Ireland, be paid into the Consolidated Fund of the United Kingdom in such manner as the Treasury may direct.

Derivations – VATA 1983, s. 38 and Sch. 7, para. 1.
Official publications – 48: extra-statutory concessions.
920: the single currency.
700/57: administrative agreements entered into with trade bodies.
Other material – HM Customs and Excise Business Brief 14/94, 6 July 1994: how Customs and Excise publicises VAT law interpretation.
Notes – S. 83(b): appeals.
S. 96(1): "money" defined.

ACCOUNTING FOR VAT, VAT INVOICES AND PAYMENT OF VAT

2(1) Regulations under this paragraph may require the keeping of accounts and the making of returns in such form and manner as may be specified in the regulations and may require taxable persons supplying goods or services in such cases, or to persons of such descriptions, as may be so specified to provide the persons supplied with invoices (to be known as **"VAT invoices"**) containing statements of such particulars as may be so specified of the supply, and of the persons by and to whom the goods or services are supplied and containing such an indication as may be required by the regulations of whether VAT is chargeable on the supply under this Act or the law of another member State and such particulars of any VAT which is so chargeable as may be so specified.

2(2) The regulations may, where they require a VAT invoice to be provided in connection with any description of supply, require it to be provided within a prescribed time after the supply is treated as taking place, or at such time before the supply is treated as taking place as may be required by the regulations, and allow for an invoice to be issued later than required by the regulations where it is issued in accordance with general or special directions given by the Commissioners.

2(2A) Regulations under this paragraph may confer power on the Commissioners to allow the requirements of any regulations as to the statements and other matters to be contained in a VAT invoice to be relaxed or dispensed with.

2(3) Regulations under this paragraph may require the submission to the Commissioners by taxable persons, at such times and intervals, in such cases and in such form and manner as may be–

(a) specified in the regulations; or

(b) determined by the Commissioners in accordance with powers conferred by the regulations,

of statements containing such particulars of transactions in which the taxable persons are concerned and which involve the movement of goods between member States, and of the persons concerned in those transactions, as may be prescribed.

2(4) Regulations under this paragraph may make provision in relation to cases where–

(a) any goods which are subject to a duty of excise or consist in a new means of transport are acquired in the United Kingdom from another member State by any person;

(b) the acquisition of the goods is a taxable acquisition and is not in pursuance of a taxable supply; and

(c) that person is not a taxable person at the time of the acquisition,

for requiring the person who acquires the goods to give to the Commissioners such notification of the acquisition, and for requiring any VAT on the acquisition to be paid, at such time and in such form or manner as may be specified in the regulations.

2(5) Regulations under this paragraph may provide for a notification required by virtue of sub-paragraph (4) above–

(a)   to contain such particulars relating to the notified acquisition and any VAT chargeable thereon as may be specified in the regulations; and

(b)   to be given, in prescribed cases, by the personal representative, trustee in bankruptcy, interim or permanent trustee, receiver, liquidator or person otherwise acting in a representative capacity in relation to the person who makes that acquisition.

2(6)   Regulations under this paragraph may make special provision for such taxable supplies by retailers of any goods or of any description of goods or of services or any description of services as may be determined by or under the regulations and, in particular–

(a)   for permitting the value which is to be taken as the value of the supplies in any prescribed accounting period or part thereof to be determined, subject to any limitations or restrictions, by such method or one of such methods as may have been described in any notice published by the Commissioners in pursuance of the regulations and not withdrawn by a further notice or as may be agreed with the Commissioners; and

(b)   for determining the proportion of the value of the supplies which is to be attributed to any description of supplies; and

(c)   for adjusting that value and proportion for periods comprising two or more prescribed accounting periods or parts thereof.

2(7)   Regulations under this paragraph may make provision whereby, in such cases and subject to such conditions as may be determined by or under the regulations, VAT in respect of a supply may be accounted for and paid by reference to the time when consideration for the supply is received; and any such regulations may make such modifications of the provisions of this Act (including in particular, but without prejudice to the generality of the power, the provisions as to the time when, and the circumstances in which, credit for input tax is to be allowed) as appear to the Commissioners necessary or expedient.

2(8)   Regulations under this paragraph may make provision whereby, in such cases and subject to such conditions as may be determined by or under the regulations–

(a)   VAT in respect of any supply by a taxable person of dutiable goods, or

(b)   VAT in respect of an acquisition by any person from another member State of dutiable goods,

may be accounted for and paid, and any question as to the inclusion of any duty or agricultural levy in the value of the supply or acquisition determined, by reference to the duty point or by reference to such later time as the Commissioners may allow.

In this sub-paragraph **"dutiable goods"** and **"duty point"** have the same meanings as in section 18.

2(9)   Regulations under this paragraph may provide for the time when any invoice described in regulations made for the purposes of section 6(8)(b) or 12(1)(b) is to be treated as having been issued and provide for VAT accounted for and paid by reference to the date of issue of such an invoice to be confined to VAT on so much of the value of the supply or acquisition as is shown on the invoice.

2(10)   Regulations under this paragraph may make provision–

(a)   for treating VAT chargeable in one prescribed accounting period as chargeable in another such period; and

(b)   with respect to the making of entries in accounts for the purpose of making adjustments, whether for the correction of errors or otherwise; and

(c)   for the making of financial adjustments in connection with the making of entries in accounts for the purpose mentioned in paragraph (b) above; and

(d)   for a person, for purposes connected with the making of any such entry or financial adjustment, to be required to provide to any prescribed person, or to retain, a document in the prescribed form containing prescribed particulars of the matters to which the entry or adjustment relates; and

(e)   for enabling the Commissioners, in such cases as they may think fit, to dispense with or relax a requirement imposed by regulations made by virtue of paragraph (d) above.

2(11)   Regulations under this paragraph may make different provision for different circumstances and may provide for different dates as the commencement of prescribed accounting periods applicable to different persons.

2(12)   The provisions made by regulations under this paragraph for cases where goods are treated as supplied by a taxable person by virtue of paragraph 7 of Schedule 4 may require VAT chargeable on the supply to be accounted for and paid, and particulars thereof to be provided, by such other person and in such manner as may be specified by the regulations.

2(13) Where, at the end of a prescribed accounting period, the amount of VAT due from any person or the amount of any VAT credit would be less than £1, that amount shall be treated as nil.

History – Para. 2(2A) was inserted by FA 1996, s. 38(2), with effect from 29 April 1996.
In para. 2(10)(c), at the end the word "and" was inserted by FA 1996, s. 38(3), with effect from 29 April 1996.
Para. 2(10)(d) was inserted by FA 1996, s. 38(3), with effect from 29 April 1996.
Para. 2(10)(e) was inserted by FA 1996, s. 38(3), with effect from 29 April 1996.

Derivations – Para. 2(1), (2): VATA 1983, s. 38 and Sch. 7, para. 2(1), (2), as amended by F(No. 2)A 1992, s. 14 and Sch. 3, para. 64.
Para. 2(3)–(5): VATA 1983, s. 38 and Sch. 7, para. 2(2A)–(2C), as inserted by F(No. 2)A 1992, s. 14 and Sch. 3, para. 64.
Para. 2(6): VATA 1983, s. 38 and Sch. 7, para. 2(3).
Para. 2(7): VATA 1983, s. 38 and Sch. 7, para. 2(3A), as inserted by FA 1987, s. 11(2).
Para. 2(8), (9): VATA 1983, s. 38 and Sch. 7, para. 2(3B), (3C), as inserted by F(No. 2)A 1992, s. 14 and Sch. 3, para. 64, and as amended by FA 1993, s. 50(4), s. 213 and Sch. 23, Pt. II(5).
Para. 2(10): VATA 1983, s. 38 and Sch. 7, para. 2(4), as amended by FA 1989, s. 25(2).
Para. 2(11)–(13): VATA 1983, s. 38 and Sch. 7, para. 2(5)–(7).

Cross references – S. 6(9)(b): time of supply.
S. 65(6): "EC sales statement" defined.
S. 67: failure to notify and unauthorised issue of invoices.
S. 69(5)(b): penalties.
S. 75: assessments in cases of acquisitions of certain goods by non-taxable persons.
S. 78: interest in certain cases of official error.
S. 83(x) and (y): appeals.
S. 84(2): further provisions relating to appeals.
S. 88(5): change in VAT law.
FA 1997, s. 47(8): entitlement to a repayment under VATA 1994, s. 80.
FA 1997, s. 49(6): transitional provision for set-offs, etc.
VAT (Isle of Man) Order 1982 (SI 1982/1067), art. 8: taxable person includes a person who is a taxable person under the Manx Act.
VAT Regulations 1995 (SI 1995/2518), reg. 58(1): unpaid assessment under Sch. 11 can stop use of cash accounting.
VAT Regulations 1995 (SI 1995/2518), reg. 68(c): determination of value of taxable supplies.
VAT Regulations 1995 (SI 1995/2518), reg. 194: claim treated as a return.

Statutory instruments – VAT Regulations 1995 (SI 1995/2518, as amended by SI 1995/3147, SI 1996/210, SI 1996/542, SI 1996/1250, SI 1997/1086, SI 1997/1614, SI 1997/2437, SI 2000/258).

Official publications – 727 (retail schemes), 700/12 (VAT returns), 731 (cash accounting), and 732 (annual accounting).

Other material – Forms VAT 100, VAT 193 and VAT 597.

Notes – S. 19: valuation.
S. 59: penalties.

PRODUCTION OF VAT INVOICES BY COMPUTER

3(1) For the purposes of any provision contained in or having effect under this Act which relates to VAT invoices a person shall be treated as issuing, or as providing another person with, a VAT invoice if the requisite particulars are recorded in a computer and transmitted by electronic means and without the delivery of any document.

3(2) No provision relating to VAT invoices shall be treated as complied with by the production by means of a computer of any material other than a document in writing, by delivering any such material so produced or by making any such transmission as is mentioned in sub-paragraph (1) above unless the person producing or delivering the material or making the transmission and, in the case of delivered material or a transmission, the person receiving it–

(a)   has given the Commissioners at least one month's notice in writing that he proposes to produce or deliver such material or make such transmissions or, as the case may be, receive such material or transmissions; and

(b)   complies with such requirements as may be specified in regulations or as the Commissioners may from time to time impose in his case.

3(3) Without prejudice to the generality of the powers conferred by virtue of sub-paragraph (9) of paragraph 2 above, regulations made by virtue of that sub-paragraph may provide for the preceding provisions of this paragraph to apply, subject to such exceptions and adaptations as may be prescribed, in relation to any invoice which is described in regulations made for the purposes of section 6(8)(b) or 12(1)(b), as they apply in relation to VAT invoices.

Derivations – Para. 3(1), (2): VATA 1983, s. 38 and Sch. 7, para. 3(1), (2).
Para. 3(3): VATA 1983, s. 38 and Sch. 7, para. (2A), as inserted by F(No. 2)A 1992, s. 14 and Sch. 3, para. 65.

Cross references – S. 83(z): appeals.
S. 96(6): "computer" and "document" defined.

Note – S. 96(1): "invoice" defined.

POWER TO REQUIRE SECURITY AND PRODUCTION OF EVIDENCE

4(1) The Commissioners may, as a condition of allowing or repaying any input tax to any person, require the production of such documents relating to VAT as may have been supplied to him and may, if they think it necessary for the protection of the revenue, require, as a condition of making any VAT credit, the giving of such security for the amount of the payment as appears to them appropriate.

4(2) Without prejudice to their power under section 48(7), where it appears to the Commissioners requisite to do so for the protection of the revenue they may require a taxable person, as a condition of his supplying goods or services under a taxable supply, to give security, or further security, of such amount and in such manner as they may determine, for the payment of any VAT which is or may become due from him.

Derivations – VATA 1983, s. 38 and Sch. 7, para. 5, as amended by F(No. 2)A 1992, s. 14 and Sch. 3, para. 68.

Cross references – S. 72(11): penalties.
S. 79(3): repayment supplement.
S. 83(l): appeals.
VAT (Isle of Man) Order 1982 (SI 1982/1067), art. 7: references to VAT include references to VAT chargeable under Pt. I of the Manx Act.
VAT Regulations 1995 (SI 1995/2518), reg. 198: computation of supplement.

Official publications – 700/52: Notice of requirement to give security to Customs and Excise.

Notes – S. 24(1): "input tax" defined.
S. 96(1): "taxable supply" defined.

RECOVERY OF VAT, ETC.

5(1) VAT due from any person shall be recoverable as a debt due to the Crown.

5(2) Where an invoice shows a supply of goods or services as taking place with VAT chargeable on it, there shall be recoverable from the person who issued the invoice an amount equal to that which is shown on the invoice as VAT or, if VAT is not separately shown, to so much of the total amount shown as payable as is to be taken as representing VAT on the supply.

5(3) Sub-paragraph (2) above applies whether or not–

(a)   the invoice is a VAT invoice issued in pursuance of paragraph 2(1) above; or

(b)   the supply shown on the invoice actually takes or has taken place, or the amount shown as VAT, or any amount of VAT, is or was chargeable on the supply; or

(c)   the person issuing the invoice is a taxable person;

and any sum recoverable from a person under the sub-paragraph shall, if it is in any case VAT be recoverable as such and shall otherwise be recoverable as a debt due to the Crown.

5(4)–(10)   [Repealed by FA 1997, s. 113 and Sch. 18, Pt. V.]

History – Para. 5(4)–(10) repealed by FA 1997, s. 113 and Sch. 18, Pt. V, with effect from 1 July 1997 (SI 1997/1433 (C 55)). Former para. 5(4)–(10) reads as follows:
"**5(4)** The Commissioners may by regulations make provision in respect of England and Wales and Northern Ireland for authorising distress to be levied on the goods and chattels of any person refusing or neglecting to pay any VAT due from him or any amount recoverable as if it were VAT due from him and for the disposal of any goods or chattels on which distress is levied in pursuance of the regulations and for the imposition and recovery of costs, charges, expenses and fees in connection with anything done under the regulations.
5(5) In respect of Scotland, where any VAT or any sum recoverable as if it were VAT is due and has not been paid, the sheriff, on an application by the Commissioners accompanied by a certificate by the Commissioners–
(a)   stating that none of the persons specified in the application has paid VAT or other sum due from him;
(b)   stating that payment of the amount due from each such person has been demanded from him; and
(c)   specifying the amount due from and unpaid by each such person,
shall grant a summary warrant in a form prescribed by Act of Sederunt authorising the recovery, by any of the diligences mentioned in sub-paragraph (6) below, of the amount remaining due and unpaid.
5(6) The diligences referred to in sub-paragraph (5) above are–
(a)   a poinding and sale in accordance with Schedule 5 to the Debtors (Scotland) Act 1987;
(b)   an earnings arrestment;
(c)   an arrestment and action of furthcoming or sale.
5(7) Subject to sub-paragraph (8) below and without prejudice to paragraphs 25 to 34 of Schedule 5 to the Debtors (Scotland) Act 1987 (expenses of poinding and sale), the sheriff officer's fees, together with the outlays necessarily incurred by him, in connection with the execution of a summary warrant shall be chargeable against the debtor.
5(8) No fee shall be chargeable by the sheriff officer against the debtor for collecting, and accounting to the Commissioners for, sums paid to him by the debtor in respect of the amount owing.
5(9) The Commissioners may by regulations make provision for anything which the Commissioners may do under sub-paragraph (5) to (8) above to be done by an officer of the Commissioners holding such rank as the regulations may specify.
5(10) The preceding provisions of this paragraph shall have effect as if any sum required by way of security under section 48(7) were recoverable as if it were VAT due from the person who is required to provide it."

Derivations – VATA 1983, s. 38 and Sch. 7, para. 6, as amended by FA 1984, s. 16 and Debtors (Scotland) Act 1987, s. 74(1) and Sch. 4, para. 4 and F(No. 2)A 1992, s. 14 and Sch. 3, para. 69.

Cross references – S. 68: penalty for breach of a walking possession agreement.
Limitation Act 1980, s. 37(3)(a): the normal statute of limitations does not apply to any proceedings by the Crown for the recovery of any tax or interest on any tax.
VAT (Isle of Man) Order 1982 (SI 1982/1067), art. 7: references to VAT include references to VAT chargeable under Pt. I of the Manx Act.

Statutory instruments – VAT Regulations 1995 (SI 1995/2518, as amended by SI 1996/2098).
Extra-statutory concessions – 3.9 (Notice 48 (1999 edn)): reclaim as input tax certain charges by non-registered persons.
Official publications – 700, para. 9 (2000 edn); 700/56 and 930.
Notes – S. 76(9): assessment of penalty, interest or surcharge recoverable as if it were tax due.
Sch. 12, para. 10(4): recovery of penalty awarded by tribunal.

DUTY TO KEEP RECORDS

6(1) Every taxable person shall keep such records as the Commissioners may by regulations require, and every person who, at a time when he is not a taxable person, acquires in the United Kingdom from another member State any goods which are subject to a duty of excise or consist in a new means of transport shall keep such records with respect to the acquisition (if it is a taxable acquisition and is not in pursuance of a taxable supply) as the Commissioners may so require.

6(2) Regulations under sub-paragraph (1) above may make different provision for different cases and may be framed by reference to such records as may be specified in any notice published by the Commissioners in pursuance of the regulations and not withdrawn by a further notice.

6(3) The Commissioners may require any records kept in pursuance of this paragraph to be preserved for such period not exceeding 6 years as they may require.

6(4) The duty under this paragraph to preserve records may be discharged by the preservation of the information contained therein by such means as the Commissioners may approve; and where that information is so preserved a copy of any document forming part of the records shall, subject to the following provisions of this paragraph, be admissible in evidence in any proceedings, whether civil or criminal, to the same extent as the records themselves.

6(5) The Commissioners may, as a condition of approving under sub-paragraph (4) above any means of preserving information contained in any records, impose such reasonable requirements as appear to them necessary for securing that the information will be as readily available to them as if the records themselves had been preserved.

6(6) A statement contained in a document produced by a computer shall not by virtue of sub-paragraph (4) above be admissible in evidence–

(a) [Repealed by Civil Evidence Act 1995, s. 15(2) and Sch. 2;]

(b) in criminal proceedings in England and Wales except in accordance with sections 69 and 70 of the Police and Criminal Evidence Act 1984 and Part II of the Criminal Justice Act 1988;

(c) in civil proceedings in Northern Ireland, except in accordance with sections 2 and 3 of the Civil Evidence Act (Northern Ireland) 1971; and

(d) in criminal proceedings in Northern Ireland, except in accordance with Article 68 of the Police and Criminal Evidence (Northern Ireland) Order 1989 and Part II of the Criminal Justice (Evidence, Etc.) (Northern Ireland) Order 1988.

This sub-paragraph does not apply in relation to Scotland.

History – Para. 6(6)(a) was repealed by Civil Evidence Act 1995, s. 15(2) and Sch. 2, with effect from 31 January 1997, by virtue of SI 1996/3217 (C. 101).
Derivations – Para. 6(1): VATA 1983, s. 38 and Sch. 7, para. 7(1), as amended by FA 1989, s. 25(3) and F(No. 2)A 1992, s. 14 and Sch. 3, para. 70.
Para. 6(2): VATA 1983, s. 38 and Sch. 7, para. 7(1A), as inserted by FA 1989, s. 25(1) and (4).
Para. 6(3): VATA 1983, s. 38 and Sch. 7, para. 7(2), as amended by FA 1985, s. 23 and Sch. 7, para. 2.
Para. 6(4), (5): VATA 1983, s. 38 and Sch. 7, para. 7(3), (4).
Para. 6(6) (as originally enacted): VATA 1983, s. 38 and Sch. 7, para. 7(5), as amended by PACEA 1984, Sch. 6, para. 41 and FA 1994, s. 256(3)(a) and (b).
Cross references – S. 69: penalty for failure to keep and preserve records.
FA 1999, s. 13(6): supplies of gold.
Statutory instruments – VAT Regulations 1995 (SI 1995/2518, as amended by SI 1996/1250).
Official publications – 700 (2000 edn), para. 8 (records which the commissioners generally require to be kept).
700/21: keeping records and accounts.
700/56: short period for retention of records in the case of certain insolvencies.
Notes – Insolvency Regulations 1994 (SI 1994/2507), reg. 16 and 30: period for retention of records in the case of liquidators and trustees in bankruptcy.

FURNISHING OF INFORMATION AND PRODUCTION OF DOCUMENTS

7(1) The Commissioners may by regulations make provision for requiring taxable persons to notify to the Commissioners such particulars of changes in circumstances relating to those persons or any business carried on by them as appear to the Commissioners required for the purpose of keeping the register kept under this Act up to date.

7(2) Every person who is concerned (in whatever capacity) in the supply of goods or services in the course or furtherance of a business or to whom such a supply is made, every person who is concerned (in whatever capacity) in the acquisition of goods from another member State and every person who is concerned (in whatever capacity) in the importation of goods from a place outside the member States in the course or furtherance of a business shall–

(a)   furnish to the Commissioners, within such time and in such form as they may reasonably require, such information relating to the goods or services or to the supply, acquisition or importation as the Commissioners may reasonably specify; and

(b)   upon demand made by an authorised person, produce or cause to be produced for inspection by that person–

    (i)   at the principal place of business of the person upon whom the demand is made or at such other place as the authorised person may reasonably require, and

    (ii)   at such time as the authorised person may reasonably require,

any documents relating to the goods or services or to the supply, acquisition or importation.

7(3)   Where, by virtue of sub-paragraph (2) above, an authorised person has power to require the production of any documents from any such person as is referred to in that sub-paragraph, he shall have the like power to require production of the documents concerned from any other person who appears to the authorised person to be in possession of them; but where any such other person claims a lien on any document produced by him, the production shall be without prejudice to the lien.

7(4)   For the purposes of this paragraph, the **documents** relating to the supply of goods or services, to the acquisition of goods from another member State or to the importation of goods from a place outside the member States shall be taken to include any profit and loss account and balance sheet relating to the business in the course of which the goods or services are supplied or the goods are imported or (in the case of an acquisition from another member State) relating to any business or other activities of the person by whom the goods are acquired.

7(5)   An authorised person may take copies of, or make extracts from, any document produced under sub-paragraph (2) or (3) above.

7(6)   If it appears to him to be necessary to do so, an authorised person may, at a reasonable time and for a reasonable period, remove any document produced under sub-paragraph (2) or (3) above and shall, on request, provide a receipt for any document so removed; and where a lien is claimed on a document produced under sub-paragraph (3) above the removal of the document under this sub-paragraph shall not be regarded as breaking the lien.

7(7)   Where a document removed by an authorised person under sub-paragraph (6) above is reasonably required for the proper conduct of a business he shall, as soon as practicable, provide a copy of the document, free of charge, to the person by whom it was produced or caused to be produced.

7(8)   Where any documents removed under the powers conferred by this paragraph are lost or damaged the Commissioners shall be liable to compensate their owner for any expenses reasonably incurred by him in replacing or repairing the documents.

7(9)   For the purposes of this paragraph a person to whom has been assigned a right to receive the whole or any part of the consideration for a supply of goods or services shall be treated as a **person concerned in the supply**.

History – Para. 7(9) was added by FA 1999, s. 15(3), with effect for the purposes of the making of any refund or repayment after 9 March 1999, but do not have effect in relation to anything received on or before that day.

Derivations – Para. 7(1): VATA 1983, s. 38 and Sch. 7, para. 8(1).
Para. 7(2): VATA 1983, s. 38 and Sch. 7, para. 8(2), as amended by FA 1985, s. 23 and Sch. 7, para. 3(1) and F(No. 2)A 1992, s. 14 and Sch. 3, para. 71.
Para. 7(3): VATA 1983, s. 38 and Sch. 7, para. 8(3), as substituted by FA 1985, s. 23 and Sch. 7, para. 3(1).
Para. 7(4): VATA 1983, s. 38 and Sch. 7, para. 8(4), as amended by FA 1985, s. 23 and Sch. 7, para. 3(2).
Para. 7(5)–(7): VATA 1983, s. 38 and Sch. 7, para. 8(4A)–(4C), as inserted by FA 1985, s. 23 and Sch. 7, para. 3(3).
Para. 7(8): VATA 1983, s. 38 and Sch. 7, para. 8(5).

Official publications – 989: Visits by Customs and Excise officers.
700/47: Confidentiality in VAT matters (tax advisers) – statement of practice.
Customs Internal Guidance Manual, vol. V1.24: trader's records and officers' powers.

POWER TO TAKE SAMPLES

8(1)   An authorised person, if it appears to him necessary for the protection of the revenue against mistake or fraud, may at any time take, from the goods in the possession of any person who supplies goods or acquires goods from another member State, or in the possession of a fiscal warehousekeeper, such samples as the authorised person may require with a view to determining how the goods or the materials of which they are made ought to be or to have been treated for the purposes of VAT.

8(2) Any sample taken under this paragraph shall be disposed of and accounted for in such manner as the Commissioners may direct.

8(3) Where a sample is taken under this paragraph from the goods in any person's possession and is not returned to him within a reasonable time and in good condition the Commissioners shall pay him by way of compensation a sum equal to the cost of the sample to him or such larger sum as they may determine.

History – In para. 8(1), the words ", or in the possession of a fiscal warehousekeeper," were inserted by FA 1996, s. 26 and Sch. 3, para. 16, with effect from 1 June 1996 and apply to any acquisition of goods from another member State and any supply taking place on or after that day.

Derivations – VATA 1983, s. 38 and Sch. 7, para. 9, as amended by F(No. 2)A 1992, s. 14 and Sch. 3, para. 72.

Cross references – VAT (Isle of Man) Order 1982 (SI 1982/1067), art. 7: references to VAT include references to VAT chargeable under Pt. I of the Manx Act.

POWER TO REQUIRE OPENING OF GAMING MACHINES

9 An authorised person may at any reasonable time require a person making such a supply as is referred to in section 23(1) or any person acting on his behalf–

(a)   to open any gaming machine, within the meaning of that section; and

(b)   to carry out any other operation which may be necessary to enable the authorised person to ascertain the amount which, in accordance with subsection (2) of that section, is to be taken as the value of supplies made in the circumstances mentioned in subsection (1) of that section in any period.

Derivations – VATA 1983, s. 38 and Sch. 7, para. 9A, as inserted by FA 1985, s. 23 and Sch. 7, para. 4.

Note – S. 96(1): "authorised person" defined.

ENTRY AND SEARCH OF PREMISES AND PERSONS

10(1) For the purpose of exercising any powers under this Act an authorised person may at any reasonable time enter premises used in connection with the carrying on of a business.

10(2) Where an authorised person has reasonable cause to believe that any premises are used in connection with the supply of goods under taxable supplies or with the acquisition of goods under taxable acquisitions from other member States and that goods to be so supplied or acquired are on those premises, or that any premises are used as a fiscal warehouse, he may at any reasonable time enter and inspect those premises and inspect any goods found on them.

10(3) If a justice of the peace or in Scotland a justice (within the meaning of section 308 of the Criminal Procedure (Scotland) Act 1995) is satisfied on information on oath that there is reasonable ground for suspecting that a fraud offence which appears to be of a serious nature is being, has been or is about to be committed on any premises or that evidence of the commission of such an offence is to be found there, he may issue a warrant in writing authorising, subject to sub-paragraphs (5) and (6) below, any authorised person to enter those premises, if necessary by force, at any time within one month from the time of the issue of the warrant and search them; and any person who enters the premises under the authority of the warrant may–

(a)   take with him such other persons as appear to him to be necessary;

(b)   seize and remove any documents or other things whatsoever found on the premises which he has reasonable cause to believe may be required as evidence for the purposes of proceedings in respect of a fraud offence which appears to him to be of a serious nature; and

(c)   search or cause to be searched any person found on the premises whom he has reasonable cause to believe to be in possession of any such documents or other things;

but no woman or girl shall be searched except by a woman.

10(4) In sub-paragraph (3) above **"a fraud offence"** means an offence under any provision of section 72(1) to (8).

10(5) The powers conferred by a warrant under this paragraph shall not be exercisable–

(a)   by more than such number of authorised persons as may be specified in the warrant; nor

(b)   outside such times of day as may be so specified; nor

(c)   if the warrant so provides, otherwise than in the presence of a constable in uniform.

10(6) An authorised person seeking to exercise the powers conferred by a warrant under this paragraph or, if there is more than one such authorised person, that one of them who is in charge of the search shall provide a copy of the warrant endorsed with his name as follows–

(a)   if the occupier of the premises concerned is present at the time the search is to begin, the copy shall be supplied to the occupier;

(b) if at that time the occupier is not present but a person who appears to the authorised person to be in charge of the premises is present, the copy shall be supplied to that person; and

(c) if neither paragraph (a) nor paragraph (b) above applies, the copy shall be left in a prominent place on the premises.

History – In para. 10(2), the words ", or that any premises are used as a fiscal warehouse," were inserted by FA 1996, s. 26 and Sch. 3, para. 17, with effect from 1 June 1996 and apply to any acquisition of goods from another member State and any supply taking place on or after that day.
In para. 10(3), the reference to the Criminal Procedure (Scotland) Act 1975 was substituted by Criminal Procedure (Consequential Provisions) (Scotland) Act 1995, Sch. 4, para. 91, with effect from 1 April 1996.

Derivations – VATA 1983, s. 38 and Sch. 7, para. 10, as amended by Police and Criminal Evidence Act 1984, Sch. 6, para. 41, FA 1985, s. 23 and Sch. 7, para. 5 and F(No. 2)A 1992, s. 14 and Sch. 3, para. 73.

Cross references – FA 1999, s. 13(5)(c): supplies of gold.
VAT Regulations 1995 (SI 1995/2518), reg. 31C: records of investment gold.

Notes – S. 4(2): "taxable supply" defined.
S. 96(1): "authorised person" defined.

ORDER FOR ACCESS TO RECORDED INFORMATION ETC.

11(1) Where, on an application by an authorised person, a justice of the peace or, in Scotland, a justice (within the meaning of section 308 of the Criminal Procedure (Scotland) Act 1995) is satisfied that there are reasonable grounds for believing–

(a) that an offence in connection with VAT is being, has been or is about to be committed, and

(b) that any recorded information (including any document of any nature whatsoever) which may be required as evidence for the purpose of any proceedings in respect of such an offence is in the possession of any person,

he may make an order under this paragraph.

11(2) An order under this paragraph is an order that the person who appears to the justice to be in possession of the recorded information to which the application relates shall–

(a) give an authorised person access to it, and

(b) permit an authorised person to remove and take away any of it which he reasonably considers necessary,

not later than the end of the period of 7 days beginning on the date of the order or the end of such longer period as the order may specify.

11(3) The reference in sub-paragraph (2)(a) above to giving an authorised person **access to the recorded information** to which the application relates includes a reference to permitting the authorised person to take copies of it or to make extracts from it.

11(4) Where the recorded information consists of information contained in a computer, an order under this paragraph shall have effect as an order to produce the information in a form in which it is visible and legible and, if the authorised person wishes to remove it, in a form in which it can be removed.

11(5) This paragraph is without prejudice to paragraphs 7 and 10 above.

History – In para. 11(1), the reference to the Criminal Procedure (Scotland) Act 1975 was substituted by Criminal Procedure (Consequential Provisions) (Scotland) Act 1995, Sch. 4, para. 91, with effect from 1 April 1996.

Derivations – VATA 1983, s. 38 and Sch. 7, para. 10A, as inserted by FA 1985, s. 23 and Sch. 7, para. 6.

PROCEDURE WHERE DOCUMENTS ETC. ARE REMOVED

12(1) An authorised person who removes anything in the exercise of a power conferred by or under paragraph 10 or 11 above shall, if so requested by a person showing himself–

(a) to be the occupier of premises from which it was removed, or

(b) to have had custody or control of it immediately before the removal,

provide that person with a record of what he removed.

12(2) The authorised person shall provide the record within a reasonable time from the making of the request for it.

12(3) Subject to sub-paragraph (7) below, if a request for permission to be granted access to anything which–

(a) has been removed by an authorised person, and

(b) is retained by the Commissioners for the purposes of investigating an offence,

is made to the officer in overall charge of the investigation by a person who had custody or control of the thing immediately before it was so removed or by someone acting on behalf of such a person, the officer shall allow the person who made the request access to it under the supervision of an authorised person.

12(4) Subject to sub-paragraph (7) below, if a request for a photograph or copy of any such thing is made to the officer in overall charge of the investigation by a person who had custody or control of the thing immediately before it was so removed, or by someone acting on behalf of such a person, the officer shall–

(a)   allow the person who made the request access to it under the supervision of an authorised person for the purpose of photographing it or copying it, or

(b)   photograph or copy it, or cause it to be photographed or copied.

12(5) Where anything is photographed or copied under sub-paragraph (4)(b) above the photograph or copy shall be supplied to the person who made the request.

12(6) The photograph or copy shall be supplied within a reasonable time from the making of the request.

12(7) There is no duty under this paragraph to grant access to, or to supply a photograph or copy of, anything if the officer in overall charge of the investigation for the purposes of which it was removed has reasonable grounds for believing that to do so would prejudice–

(a)   that investigation;

(b)   the investigation of an offence other than the offence for the purposes of the investigation of which the thing was removed; or

(c)   any criminal proceedings which may be brought as a result of–

(i)   the investigation of which he is in charge, or

(ii)   any such investigation as is mentioned in paragraph (b) above.

12(8) Any reference in this paragraph to the **officer in overall charge of the investigation** is a reference to the person whose name and address are endorsed on the warrant or order concerned as being the officer so in charge.

Derivations – VATA 1983, s. 38 and Sch. 7, para. 10B, as inserted by FA 1985, s. 23 and Sch. 7, para. 6.

13(1) Where, on an application made as mentioned in sub-paragraph (2) below, the appropriate judicial authority is satisfied that a person has failed to comply with a requirement imposed by paragraph 12 above, the authority may order that person to comply with the requirement within such time and in such manner as may be specified in the order.

13(2) An application under sub-paragraph (1) above shall be made–

(a)   in the case of a failure to comply with any of the requirements imposed by paragraph 12(1) and (2) above, by the occupier of the premises from which the thing in question was removed or by the person who had custody or control of it immediately before it was so removed, and

(b)   in any other case, by the person who had such custody or control.

13(3) In this paragraph **"the appropriate judicial authority"** means–

(a)   in England and Wales, a magistrates' court;

(b)   in Scotland, the sheriff; and

(c)   in Northern Ireland, a court of summary jurisdiction.

13(4) In England and Wales and Northern Ireland, an application for an order under this paragraph shall be made by way of complaint; and sections 21 and 42(2) of the Interpretation Act (Northern Ireland) 1954 shall apply as if any reference in those provisions to any enactment included a reference to this paragraph.

Derivations – VATA 1983, s. 38 and Sch. 7, para. 10C, as inserted by FA 1985, s. 23 and Sch. 7, para. 6.

EVIDENCE BY CERTIFICATE, ETC.

14(1) A certificate of the Commissioners–

(a)   that a person was or was not, at any date, registered under this Act; or

(b)   that any return required by or under this Act has not been made or had not been made at any date; or

(c)   that any statement or notification required to be submitted or given to the Commissioners in accordance with any regulations under paragraph 2(3) or (4) above has not been submitted or given or had not been submitted or given at any date; or

(d)   that any VAT shown as due in any return or assessment made in pursuance of this Act has not been paid;

shall be sufficient evidence of that fact until the contrary is proved.

14(2) A photograph of any document furnished to the Commissioners for the purposes of this Act and certified by them to be such a photograph shall be admissible in any proceedings, whether civil or criminal, to the same extent as the document itself.

14(3) Any document purporting to be a certificate under sub-paragraph (1) or (2) above shall be deemed to be such a certificate until the contrary is proved.

Derivations – VATA 1983, s. 38 and Sch. 7, para. 11, as amended by F(No. 2)A 1992, s. 14 and Sch. 3, para. 74.

Cross reference – VAT Regulations 1995 (SI 1995/2518), reg. 199: computation of supplement.

Other material – Forms VAT 886 and 887.

SCHEDULE 12 – CONSTITUTION AND PROCEDURE OF TRIBUNALS

Section 61

Notes – In the Queen's printer's version, it is stated that Sch. 12 is introduced by s. 61 when it is actually introduced by s. 82.

ESTABLISHMENT OF TRIBUNALS

1(1) There shall continue to be tribunals for England and Wales, Scotland and Northern Ireland respectively known as **VAT tribunals**.

1(2) If section 7(1) and (2) of the Finance Act 1994 have come into force before this Schedule comes into force then for any reference in this Schedule to VAT tribunals there shall, as from the commencement of this Schedule, be substituted a reference to VAT and duties tribunals.

1(3) If sub-paragraph (2) above does not apply, then, as from a day to be appointed by order made by the Commissioners by statutory instrument for the purposes of this paragraph, for any reference in this Schedule to VAT tribunals there shall be substituted a reference to VAT and duties tribunals.

1(4) Any reference in any enactment or any subordinate legislation to a **value added tax tribunal** (or to a **VAT tribunal**) shall be construed in accordance with paragraphs (1) to (3) above, and cognate expressions shall be construed similarly.

Derivations – VATA 1983, s. 40 and Sch. 8, para. 1 and FA 1994, s. 7.

Notes – FA 1994, s. 7 (with the exception of s. 7(1)(b)) came into force on 1 July 1994 (SI 1994/1690 (C 31)). FA 1994, s. 7(1)(b) came into force on 31 August 1994 (SI 1994/2143 (C 43)).

THE PRESIDENT

2(1) There shall continue to be a President of VAT tribunals, who shall perform the functions conferred on him by the following provisions of this Schedule in relation to VAT tribunals in any part of the United Kingdom.

2(2) The President shall be appointed by the Lord Chancellor after consultation with the Lord Advocate and shall be–

(a) a person who has a 10 year general qualification, within the meaning of section 71 of the Courts and Legal Services Act 1990;

(b) an advocate or solicitor in Scotland of at least 10 years' standing; or

(c) a member of the Bar of Northern Ireland or solicitor of the Supreme Court of Northern Ireland of at least 10 years' standing.

2(3) Subject to paragraph 3 below, the appointment of the President shall be for such term and subject to such conditions as may be determined by the Lord Chancellor, after consultation with the Lord Advocate, and a person who ceases to hold the office of President shall be eligible for re-appointment thereto.

Derivations – VATA 1983, s. 40 and Sch. 8, para. 2, as amended by FA 1985, s. 30 and Sch. 8, para. 2 and Courts and Legal Services Act 1990, s. 71(2) and Sch. 10, para. 52.

3(1) [Ceased to have effect.]

3(2) If the Lord Chancellor, after consultation with the Lord Advocate, considers it desirable in the public interest to do so he may authorise the President to continue in office after the end of the completed year of service mentioned in sub-paragraph (1)(a) above.

3(3) The President–

(a) may resign his office at any time; and

(b) shall vacate his office on the day on which he attains the age of 70;

but sub-paragraph (b) above is subject to section 26(4) to (6) of the 1993 Act (power to authorise continuance in office up to the age of 75).

This sub-paragraph shall come into force on the day appointed under section 31 of the 1993 Act for the coming into force of section 26 of that Act.

3(4) The Lord Chancellor may, if he thinks fit and after consultation with the Lord Advocate, remove the President from office on the ground of incapacity or misbehaviour.

3(5) The functions of the President may, if he is for any reason unable to act or his office is vacant, be discharged by a person nominated for the purpose by the Lord Chancellor after consultation with the Lord Advocate.

3(6) There shall be paid to the President such salary or fees and there may be paid to or in respect of a former President such pension, allowance or gratuity as the Lord Chancellor may with the approval of the Treasury determine.

3(7) Sub-paragraph (6) above, so far as relating to pensions allowances and gratuities, shall not have effect in relation to a person to whom Part I of the 1993 Act applies, except to the extent provided under or by that Act.

3(8) If a person ceases to be President of VAT tribunals and it appears to the Lord Chancellor that there are special circumstances which make it right that he should receive compensation, there may be paid to that person a sum of such amount as the Lord Chancellor may with the approval of the Treasury determine.

History – Para. 3(1) ceased to have effect from 31 March 1995 when the Judicial Pensions and Retirements Act 1993, s. 26 came into force (SI 1995/631 (C 15)). The former para. 3(1) read as follows:
"**3(1)** The President may resign his office at any time and shall vacate his office–
(a)   at the end of the completed year of service in which he attains the age of 72, or
(b)   if sub-paragraph (2) below applies, on the date on which he attains the age of 75.
This sub-paragraph shall cease to have effect on the day appointed under section 31 of the Judicial Pensions and Retirement Act 1993 ("**the 1993 Act**") for the coming into force of section 26 of that Act."

Derivations – Para. 3(1): VATA 1983, s. 40 and Sch. 8, para. 3(1), as substituted by Judicial Pensions and Retirement Act 1993, s. 26 and Sch. 6, para. 35(1).
Para. 3(2)–(4): VATA 1983, s. 40 and Sch. 8, para. 3(2)–(4), as amended by FA 1985, s. 30 and Sch. 8, para. 3.
Para. 3(5): VATA 1983, s. 40 and Sch. 8, para. 3(4A), as inserted by Judicial Pensions and Retirement Act 1993, s. 31 and Sch. 8, para. 16(1).
Para. 3(6): VATA 1983, s. 40 and Sch. 8, para. 3(5), as amended by FA 1985, s. 30 and Sch. 8, para. 3.

Cross references – Sch. 13, para. 5: appointment of President and chairman.
Judicial Pensions and Retirement Act 1993, s. 26: came into force on 31 March 1995 (SI 1995/631 (C 15)).

SITTINGS OF TRIBUNALS

4 Such number of VAT tribunals shall be established as the Lord Chancellor or, in relation to Scotland, the Secretary of State may from time to time determine, and they shall sit at such times and at such places as the Lord Chancellor or, as the case may be, the Secretary of State may from time to time determine.

Derivations – VATA 1983, s. 40 and Sch. 8, para. 4, as amended by FA 1985, s. 30 and Sch. 8, para. 4.

COMPOSITION OF TRIBUNALS

5(1) A VAT tribunal shall consist of a chairman sitting either with two other members or with one other member or alone.

5(2) If the tribunal does not consist of the chairman sitting alone, its decisions may be taken by a majority of votes and the chairman, if sitting with one other member, shall have a casting vote.

Derivations – VATA 1983, s. 40 and Sch. 8, para. 6.

MEMBERSHIP OF TRIBUNALS

6 For each sitting of a VAT tribunal the chairman shall be either the President or if so authorised by the President, a member of the appropriate panel of chairmen constituted in accordance with paragraph 7 below; and any other member of the tribunal shall be a person selected from the appropriate panel of other members so constituted, the selection being made either by the President or by a member of the panel of Chairmen, authorised by the President to make it.

Derivations – VATA 1983, s. 40 and Sch. 8, para. 6.

7(1) There shall be a panel of chairmen and a panel of other members of VAT tribunals for England and Wales, Scotland and Northern Ireland respectively.

7(2) One member of each panel of chairmen shall be known as Vice-President of VAT tribunals.

7(3) Appointments to a panel of chairmen shall be made by the appropriate authority, that is to say–

(a)   for England and Wales, the Lord Chancellor;

(b)   for Scotland, the Lord President of the Court of Session; and

(c)   for Northern Ireland, the Lord Chief Justice of Northern Ireland;

and appointments to a panel of other members shall be made by the Treasury.

7(4)   No person may be appointed to a panel of chairmen of tribunals for England and Wales or Northern Ireland unless he is–

(a)   a person who has a 7 year general qualification, within the meaning of section 71 of the Courts and Legal Services Act 1990; or

(b)   a member of the Bar of Northern Ireland or solicitor of the Supreme Court of Northern Ireland of at least 7 years' standing,

and no person may be appointed to a panel of chairmen of tribunals for Scotland unless he is an advocate or solicitor of not less than 7 years' standing.

7(5)   Subject to the following provisions of this paragraph, the appointment of a chairman of VAT tribunals shall be for such term and subject to such conditions as may be determined by the appropriate authority, and a person who ceases to hold the office of chairman shall be eligible for re-appointment thereto.

7(6)   A chairman of VAT tribunals–

(a)   may resign his office at any time; and

(b)   shall vacate his office on the day on which he attains the age of 70 years;

but paragraph (b) above is subject to section 26(4) to (6) of the Judicial Pensions and Retirement Act 1993 (power to authorise continuance in office up to the age of 75).

7(7)   The appropriate authority may, if he thinks fit, remove a chairman of VAT tribunals from office on the ground of incapacity or misbehaviour.

7(8)   There shall be paid to a chairman of VAT tribunals such salary or fees, and to other members such fees, as the Lord Chancellor may with the approval of the Treasury determine; and there may be paid to or in respect of a former chairman of VAT tribunals such pension, allowance or gratuity as the Lord Chancellor may with the approval of the Treasury determine.

7(9)   Sub-paragraph (8) above, so far as relating to pensions allowances and gratuities, shall not have effect in relation to a person to whom Part I of the Judicial Pensions and Retirement Act 1993 applies, except to the extent provided under or by that Act.

7(10) If a person ceases to be a chairman of VAT tribunals and it appears to the Lord Chancellor that there are special circumstances which make it right that he should receive compensation, there may be paid to that person a sum of such amount as the Lord Chancellor may with the approval of the Treasury determine.

Derivations – Para. 7(1)–(2): VATA 1983, s. 40 and Sch. 8, para. 7(1)–(2).
Para. 7(3): VATA 1983, s. 40 and Sch. 8, para. 7(3), as amended by FA 1985, s. 30 and Sch. 8, para. 5(1).
Para. 7(4): VATA 1983, s. 40 and Sch. 8, para. 7(3A), as inserted by FA 1985, s. 30 and Sch. 8, para. 5, and as amended by Courts and Legal Services Act 1990, s. 71(2) and Sch. 10, para. 52(2).
Para. 7(5): VATA 1983, s. 40 and Sch. 8, para. 7(3B), as inserted by FA 1985, s. 30 and Sch. 8, para. 5.
Para. 7(6): VATA 1983, s. 40 and Sch. 8, para. 7(3C), as inserted by Judicial Pensions and Retirement Act 1993, s. 26 and Sch. 6, para. 35(2).
Para. 7(7): VATA 1983, s. 40 and Sch. 8, para. 7(3E), as inserted by FA 1985, s. 30 and Sch. 8, para. 5.
Para. 7(8): VATA 1983, s. 40 and Sch. 8, para. 7(4), as amended by FA 1985, s. 30 and Sch. 8, para. 5(3).
Para. 7(9): VATA 1983, s. 40 and Sch. 8, para. 7(4A), as inserted by Judicial Pensions and Retirement Act 1993, s. 31 and Sch. 8, para. 16(2).
Para. 7(10): VATA 1983, s. 40 and Sch. 8, para. 7(5), as amended by FA 1985, s. 30 and Sch. 8, para. 5.
Cross reference – Judicial Pensions and Retirement Act 1993, s. 26: came into force on 31 March 1995 (SI 1995/631 (C 15)).

EXEMPTION FROM JURY SERVICE

8   No member of a VAT tribunal shall be compelled to serve on any jury in Scotland or Northern Ireland.

Derivations – VATA 1983, s. 40 and Sch. 8, para. 8.

RULES OF PROCEDURE

9   The Lord Chancellor after consultation with the Lord Advocate may make rules with respect to the procedure to be followed on appeals to and in other proceedings before VAT tribunals and such rules may include provisions–

(a)   for limiting the time within which appeals may be brought;

(b)   for enabling hearings to be held in private in such circumstances as may be determined by or under the rules;

(c)   for parties to proceedings to be represented by such persons as may be determined by or under the rules;

(d)   for requiring persons to attend to give evidence;

(e)   for discovery and for requiring persons to produce documents;

(f)   for the payment of expenses and allowances to persons attending as witnesses or producing documents;

(g)   for the award and recovery of costs;

(h)   for authorising the administration of oaths to witnesses; and

(j)   with respect to the joinder of appeals brought by different persons where a notice is served under section 61 and the appeals relate to, or to different portions of, the basic penalty referred to in the notice.

Derivations – Sch. 12, para. 9: VATA 1983, s. 40 and Sch. 8, para. 9 and FA 1985, s. 27(3).
Para. 9(a)–(d): VATA 1983, s. 40 and Sch. 8, para. 9(a)–(d).
Para. 9(e): VATA 1983, s. 40 and Sch. 8, para. 9(dd), as inserted by FA 1985, s. 27(2).
Para. 9(f)–(h): VATA 1983, s. 40 and Sch. 8, para. 9(e)–(g), as amended by FA 1985, s. 27(2).
Para. 9(j): FA 1986, s. 14(7).

Cross references – S. 69: breaches of regulatory provisions.
Landfill Tax Regulations 1996 (SI 1996/1527), reg. 48(2): distress and landfill tax.
Distress for Customs and Excise Duties and Other Indirect Taxes Regulations (SI 1997/1431), reg. 5(1)(b): restrictions on levying distress.
Distress for Customs and Excise Duties and Other Indirect Taxes Regulations (SI 1997/1431), reg. 5(2): restrictions on levying distress.

Statutory instruments – VAT Tribunals Rules 1986 (SI 1986/590) (as amended by SI 1997/255, SI 1994/2617, SI 1991/186 and SI 1986/2290).

Notes – In the Queen's printer's version, at Sch. 12, para. 9, no text has been allocated to the letter "(i)".

10(1)   A person who fails to comply with a direction or summons issued by a VAT tribunal under rules made under paragraph 9 above shall be liable to a penalty not exceeding £1,000.

10(2)   A penalty for which a person is liable by virtue of sub-paragraph (1) above may be awarded summarily by a tribunal notwithstanding that no proceedings for its recovery have been commenced.

10(3)   An appeal shall lie to the High Court or, in Scotland, the Court of Session as the Court of Exchequer in Scotland, from the award of a penalty under this paragraph, and on such an appeal the court may either confirm or reverse the decision of the tribunal or reduce or increase the sum awarded.

10(4)   A penalty awarded by virtue of this paragraph shall be recoverable as if it were VAT due from the person liable for the penalty.

Derivations – VATA 1983, s. 40 and Sch. 8, para. 10.

Note – Tribunals and Inquiries Act 1992, s. 8: procedural rules for tribunals; s. 11: appeals from tribunals.

SCHEDULE 13 – TRANSITIONAL PROVISIONS AND SAVINGS

Section 100

GENERAL PROVISIONS

1(1)   The continuity of the law relating to VAT shall not be affected by the substitution of this Act for the enactments repealed by this Act and earlier enactments repealed by and corresponding to any of those enactments (**"the repealed enactments"**).

1(2)   Any reference, whether express or implied, in any enactment, instrument or document (including this Act or any Act amended by this Act) to, or to **things done or falling to be done under or for the purposes of, any provision of this Act** shall, if and so far as the nature of the reference permits, be construed as including, in relation to the times, years or periods, circumstances or purposes in relation to which the corresponding provision in the repealed enactments has or had effect, a reference to, or as the case may be, to things done or falling to be done under or for the purposes of, that corresponding provision.

1(3)   Any reference, whether express or implied, in any enactment, instrument or document (including the repealed enactments and enactments, instruments and documents passed or made or otherwise coming into existence after the commencement of this Act) to, or to **things done or falling to be done under or for the purposes of, any of the repealed enactments** shall, if and so far as the nature of the reference permits, be construed as including, in relation to the times, years or periods, circumstances or purposes in relation to which the corresponding provision of this Act has effect, a reference to, or as the case may be to things done or falling to be done under or for the purposes of, that corresponding provision.

1(4) Without prejudice to paragraph (1) to (3) above, in any case where as respects the charge to VAT on any supply, acquisition or importation made at a time before 1st September 1994 but falling in a prescribed accounting period to which Part I applies

(a)   an enactment applicable to that charge to VAT is not re-enacted in this Act or is re-enacted with amendments which came into force after that time, or

(b)   a repealed enactment corresponding to an enactment in this Act did not apply to that charge to VAT,

any question arising under Part I and relating to that charge to VAT shall continue to be determined in accordance with the law in force at that time.

Cross references – FA 1997, s. 47(12): amendment to VATA 1994, s. 80(4) also applies to FA 1989, s. 24.

VALIDITY OF SUBORDINATE LEGISLATION

2   So far as this Act re-enacts any provision contained in a statutory instrument made in exercise of powers conferred by any Act, it shall be without prejudice to the validity of that provision, and any question as to its validity shall be determined as if the re-enacted provision were contained in a statutory instrument made under those powers.

PROVISIONS RELATED TO THE INTRODUCTION OF VAT

3   Where a vehicle in respect of which purchase tax was remitted under section 23 of the Purchase Tax Act 1963 (vehicles for use outside the United Kingdom) is brought back to the United Kingdom the vehicle shall not, when brought back, be treated as imported for the purpose of VAT chargeable on the importation of goods.

SUPPLY IN ACCORDANCE WITH PRE-21.4.75 ARRANGEMENTS

4   Where there were in force immediately before 21st April 1975 arrangements between the Commissioners and any taxable person for supplies made by him (or such supplies made by him as were specified in the arrangements) to be treated as taking place at times or on dates which, had section 6(10) been in force when the arrangements were made, could have been provided for by a direction under that section, he shall be treated for the purposes of that section as having requested the Commissioners to give a direction thereunder to the like effect, and the Commissioners may give a direction (or a general direction applying to cases of any class or description specified in the direction) accordingly.

PRESIDENT, CHAIRMEN ETC. OF TRIBUNALS

5(1)   Any appointment to a panel of chairmen of the tribunals current at the commencement of this Act and made by the Treasury before the passing of the 1983 Act shall not be affected by the repeal by this Act of paragraph 8 of Schedule 10 to that Act.

5(2)   The terms of appointment of any person who was appointed to the office of President of the tribunal or chairman or other member of the tribunals before 1st April 1986 and holds that office on the coming into force of this Act shall continue to have effect notwithstanding the re-enactment, as Schedule 12 to this Act, of Schedule 8 to the 1983 Act as amended by Schedule 8 to the Finance Act 1985.

OVERSEAS SUPPLIERS ACCOUNTING THROUGH THEIR CUSTOMERS

6   Notwithstanding the repeal by this Act of section 32B of the 1983 Act, that section shall continue to apply in relation to any supply in relation to which section 14 does not apply by virtue of section 14(8), and for the purposes to this paragraph section 32B shall have effect as if it were included in Part III of this Act, any reference in section 32B to any enactment repealed by this Act being read as a reference to the corresponding provision of this Act.

SUPPLIES OF FUEL AND POWER FOR DOMESTIC OR CHARITY USE

7   [Omitted and repealed by FA 1995, s. 21(5) and 162 and Sch. 29, Pt. VI(1), with effect in relation to any supply made on or after 1st April 1995 and any acquisition or importation taking place on or after that date.]

ZERO-RATED SUPPLIES OF GOODS AND SERVICES

8(1) A supply of services made after the commencement of this Act in pursuance of a legally binding obligation incurred before 21st June 1988 shall if–

(a) the supply fell within item 2 of Group 8A of Schedule 5 to the 1983 Act immediately before 1st April 1989, and

(b) it was by virtue of paragraph 13(1) of Schedule 3 to the Finance Act 1989 a zero-rated supply,

be a zero-rated supply for the purposes of this Act.

8(2) Where a grant, assignment or other supply is zero-rated by virtue of this paragraph, it is not a relevant zero-rated supply for the purposes of paragraph 1 of Schedule 10.

Derivations – FA 1989, s. 18 and Sch. 3, para. 13(1).

Cross reference – VAT Regulations 1995 (SI 1995/2518), reg. 116(3): adjustments to the deduction of input tax on capital items.

BAD DEBT RELIEF

9(1) [Repealed by FA 1997, s. 113 and Sch. 18, Pt. IV(3). Former para. 1(2) had kept in force claims for refunds relating to supplies made before 27 July 1990 under former VATA 1983, s. 22.]

9(2) Claims for refunds of VAT shall not be made in accordance with section 36 of this Act in relation to–

(a) any supply made before 1st April 1989; or

(b) any supply as respects which a claim is or has been made under section 22 of the 1983 Act.

History – Para. 9(1) was repealed by FA 1997, s. 113 and Sch. 18, Pt. IV(3), with effect from 19 March 1997.
Para. 9(2) was substituted by FA 1995, s. 33(4), with effect as if para. 9(2) had been originally enacted with this substitution.
Derivations – (as originally enacted) – VATA 1983, s. 22.

Official publications – 700/18.

Notes – S. 60(2)(c): penalties.
VAT Regulations 1995 (SI 1995/2518), Pt. XVIII: bad debt relief under old scheme.

SUPPLIES DURING CONSTRUCTION OF BUILDINGS AND WORKS

10(1) Nothing in paragraphs 5 and 6 of Schedule 10 shall apply–

(a) in relation to a person who has constructed a building if he incurred before 21st June 1988 a legally binding obligation to make a grant or assignment of a major interest in, or in any part of, the building or its site;

(b) in relation to a building or work if there was incurred before that date a legally binding obligation to make in relation to the building or work a supply within item 2 of Group 8 of Schedule 5 to the 1983 Act;

(c) in relation to a person who has constructed a building if–

  (i) he incurred before that date a legally binding obligation to construct the building or any development of which it forms part, and

  (ii) planning permission for the construction of the building was granted before that date, and

  (iii) he has made a grant or assignment of a major interest in, or in any part of, the building or its site before 21st June 1993.

10(2) Sub-paragraph (1) above shall not apply in any case where the Commissioners required proof of any of the matters specified in paragraph (a), (b) or (c)(i) above to be given to their satisfaction by the production of documents made before 21st June 1988 and that requirement was not complied with.

Derivations – FA 1989, s. 18 and Sch. 3, para. 13(6), (7).

OFFENCES AND PENALTIES

11 Where an offence for the continuation of which a penalty was provided has been committed under an enactment repealed by this Act, proceedings may be taken under this Act in respect of the continuance of the offence after the commencement of this Act in the same manner as if the offence had been committed under the corresponding provision of this Act.

Derivations – Transitional provision.

12 Part IV of this Act, except section 72, shall not apply in relation to any act done or omitted to be done before 25th July 1985, and the following provision of this Schedule shall have effect accordingly.

Derivations – FA 1985, s. 12(1).

13(1) Section 72 shall have effect in relation to any offence committed or alleged to have been committed at any time (**"the relevant time"**) before the commencement of this Act subject to the following provisions of this paragraph.

13(2) Where the relevant time falls between 25th July 1983 and 26th July 1985 (the dates of passing of the 1983 and 1985 Finance Acts respectively), section 72 shall apply–

(a)   with the substitution in subsection (1)(b), (3)(ii) and (8)(b) of "2 years" for "7 years";

(b)   with the omission of subsections (2) and (4) to (7).

Derivations – FA 1985, s. 12(1).

14(1) The provisions of this paragraph have effect in relation to section 59.

14(2) Section 59 shall apply in any case where a person is in default in respect of a prescribed accounting period which has ended before the commencement of this Act, but shall have effect in any case where the last day referred to in subsection (1) of that section falls before 1st October 1993 subject to the following modifications–

(a)   for the words "a prescribed accounting period" in subsection (2)(a) there shall be substituted "any two prescribed accounting periods";

(b)   with the addition of the following paragraph in subsection (2)–

"(aa)   the last day of the later one of those periods falls on or before the first anniversary of the last day of the earlier one; and";

(c)   for the words "period referred to in paragraph (a)" in subsection (2)(b) there shall be substituted "later period referred to in paragraph (aa)"; and

(d)   for the words "a default in respect of a prescribed accounting period and that period" in subsection (3) there shall be substituted "defaults in respect of two prescribed accounting periods and the second of those periods".

14(3) Section 59 shall have effect, in any case where a person has been served with a surcharge liability notice and that person is in default in respect of a prescribed accounting period because of a failure of the Commissioners to receive a return or an amount of VAT on or before a day falling before 30th September 1993 with the omission of–

(a)   subsection (4)(b);

(b)   the words in subsection (5) "and for which he has outstanding VAT"; and

(c)   subsection (6).

Derivations – FA 1993, s. 49 and Sch. 2, para. 5(3), 6(4).

15(1) Section 63 does not apply in relation to returns and assessments made for prescribed accounting periods beginning before 1st April 1990 but subject to that shall have effect in relation to the cases referred to in the following sub-paragraphs subject to the modifications there specified.

15(2) Subsection (1) shall have effect in a case falling within paragraph (b) of that subsection where the assessment was made on or before 10th March 1992 with the substitution of "20 per cent." for "15 per cent.".

15(3) In relation to any prescribed accounting period beginning before 1st December 1993 section 63 shall have effect with the substitution–

(a)   for the words in subsection (2) following "exceeds" of "either 30 per cent of the true amount of the VAT for that period or whichever is the greater of £10,000 and 5 per cent of the true amount of VAT for that period." and with the omission of subsections (4) to (6); and

(b)   for the words in subsection (8) from "subsections" to "statements" of "subsection (7) that the statement by each of those returns is a correct statement".

15(4) In relation to any prescribed accounting period beginning before 1st June 1994 section 63 shall have effect with the substitution for subsection (3) of the following subsection–

"**63(3)** Any reference in this section to the VAT for a prescribed accounting period which would have been lost if an inaccuracy had not been discovered is a reference to the aggregate of–

(a)   the amount (if any) by which credit for input tax for that period was overstated; and

(b)   the amount (if any) by which output tax for that period was understated;

but if for any period there is an understatement of credit for input tax or an overstatement of output tax, allowance shall be made for that error in determining the VAT for that period which would have been so lost."and in subsection (8) for "this section" there shall be substituted "subsection (5) and (7) above".

Derivations – Para. 15(1), (2): FA 1992, s. 7(3)–(5).
Para. 15(3): FA 1993, s. 49 and Sch. 2, para. 1(4).

Para. 15(4): FA 1994, s. 45(4).

16(1) In relation to any prescribed accounting period beginning before 1st December 1993 section 64 shall have effect subject to the following modifications–

(a) in subsection (1)(b) for the words from "whichever" to "period" there shall be substituted "whichever is the greater of £100 and 1 per cent of the true amount of VAT for that period";

(b) for subsection (2) and (3) there shall be substituted–

> "**64(2)** Subsection (3) below applies in any case where–
> (a) there is a material inaccuracy in respect of any two prescribed accounting periods, and
> (b) the last day of the later one of those periods falls on or before the second anniversary of the last day of the earlier one, and
> (c) after 29th July 1988 the Commissioners serve notice on the person concerned ("**a penalty liability notice**") specifying as a penalty period for the purposes of this section a period beginning on the date of the notice and ending on the second anniversary of that date.
>
> **64(3)** If there is a material inaccuracy in respect of a prescribed accounting period ending within the penalty period specified in a penalty liability notice served on the person concerned that person shall be liable to a penalty equal to 15 per cent of the VAT for that period which would have been lost if the inaccuracy had not been discovered."

(c) in subsection (4) for "(5)" there shall be substituted "(7)"; and

(d) in subsection (6) the words from "except" to the end shall be omitted.

16(2) A penalty liability notice shall not be served under section 64 by reference to any material inaccuracy in respect of a prescribed accounting period beginning before 1st December 1993, and the penalty period specified in any penalty liability notice served before that day shall be deemed to end with the day before that day.

Derivations – FA 1993, s. 49 and Sch. 2, para. 2(5), (6).

17 Section 70 shall not apply in relation to any penalty to which a person has been assessed before 27th July 1993 and in the case of any penalty in relation to which that section does not apply by virtue of this paragraph, section 60 shall have effect subject to the following modifications–

(a) in subsection (1) for "subsection (6)" there shall be substituted "subsection (3A) and (6)";

(b) after subsection (3) there shall be inserted–

> "**60(3A)** If a person liable to a penalty under this section has co-operated with the Commissioners in the investigation of his true liability to tax or, as the case may be, of his true entitlement to any payment, refund or repayment, the Commissioners or, on appeal, a tribunal may reduce the penalty to an amount which is not less than half what it would have been apart from this subsection; and in determining the extent of any reduction under this subsection, the Commissioners or tribunal shall have regard to the extent of the co-operation which the person concerned has given to the Commissioners in their investigation.";

(c) in subsection (4)(b) for the words from "under" to "this section" there shall be substituted "to reduce a penalty under this section, as provided in subsection (4) above, and, in determining the extent of such a reduction in the case of any person, the Commissioners or tribunal will have regard to the extent of the co-operation which he has given to the Commissioners in their investigation";

17 and in section 61(6) for "70" there shall be substituted "60(3A)".

Derivations – FA 1993, s. 49 and Sch. 2, para. 3(3).

18 Section 74 shall not apply in relation to prescribed accounting periods beginning before 1st April 1990 and subsection (3) of that section shall not apply in relation to interest on amounts assessed or, as the case may be, paid before 1st October 1993.

Derivations – FA 1985, s. 18(10) and FA 1993, s. 49 and Sch. 2, para. 4(3).

IMPORTATION OF GOODS

19 Nothing in this Act shall prejudice the effect of the Finance (No. 2) Act 1992 (Commencement No. 4 and Transitional Provisions) Order 1992 and accordingly–

(a) where Article 4 of that Order applies immediately before the commencement of this Act in relation to any importation of goods, that Article and the legislation repealed by this Act shall continue to apply in relation to that importation as if this Act had not been enacted, and

(b) where Article 5 of that Order applies in relation to any goods, this Act shall apply in relation to those goods in accordance with that Article and Article 6 of that Order.

ASSESSMENTS

20 An assessment may be made under section 73 in relation to amounts paid or credited before the commencement of this Act but—

(a)   in relation to an amount paid or credited before 30th July 1990 section 73(2) shall have effect with the omission of the words from "or which" to "out to be", and

(b)   in relation to amounts repaid or paid to any person before the passing of the Finance Act 1982 section 73 shall have effect with the omission of subsection (2).

Derivations – FA 1990, s. 15(2) and FA 1982, s. 17(4).

SET-OFF OF CREDITS

21 Section 81 shall have effect in relation to amounts becoming due before 10th May 1994 with the omission of subsections (4) and (5).

Derivations – FA 1994, s. 47(2).

VAT TRIBUNALS

22(1) Without prejudice to paragraph 1 above, section 83 applies to things done or omitted to be done before the coming into force of this Act and accordingly references in Part V to any provision of this Act includes a reference to the corresponding provision of the enactments repealed by this Act or by any enactment repealed by such an enactment.

22(2) Section 84 shall have effect before such day as may be appointed for the purposes of section 18(3) of the Finance Act 1994 with the substitution for subsection (5) of the following subsection—

> "**84(5)** No appeal shall lie with respect to any matter that has been or could have been referred to arbitration under section 127 of the Management Act as applied by section 16."

Derivations – FA 1994, s. 19(1).

ISLE OF MAN

23 Nothing in paragraph 7 of Schedule 14 shall affect the validity of any Order made under section 6 of the Isle of Man Act 1979 and, without prejudice to section 17 of the Interpretation Act 1978, for any reference in any such Order to any enactment repealed by this Act there shall be substituted a reference to the corresponding provision of this Act.

Derivations – VATA 1983, s. 50 and Sch. 10, para. 18.

SCHEDULE 14 – CONSEQUENTIAL AMENDMENTS

[Section 100(1)]

DIPLOMATIC PRIVILEGES ACT 1964 c. 81

1 In section 2(5A) of the Diplomatic Privileges Act 1964 for "2A or 2B of the Value Added Tax Act 1983" there shall be substituted "10 or 15 of the Value Added Tax Act 1994".

COMMONWEALTH SECRETARIAT ACT 1966 c. 10

2 In paragraph 10(1A) of the Commonwealth Secretariat Act 1966 for "2A or 2B of the Value Added Tax Act 1983" there shall be substituted "10 or 15 of the Value Added Tax Act 1994".

CONSULAR RELATIONS ACT 1968 c. 18

3 In section 1(8A) of the Consular Relations Act 1968 for "2A or 2B of the Value Added Tax Act 1983" there shall be substituted "10 or 15 of the Value Added Tax Act 1994".

INTERNATIONAL ORGANISATIONS ACT 1968 c. 48

4 In paragraph 19(c) of Schedule 1 to the International Organisations Act 1968 for "2A or 2B of the Value Added Tax Act 1983" there shall be substituted "10 or 15 of the Value Added Tax Act 1994".

DIPLOMATIC AND OTHER PRIVILEGES ACT 1971 c. 64

5 In section 1(5) of the Diplomatic and other Privileges Act 1971 for "2A or 2B of the Value Added Tax Act 1983" there shall be substituted "10 or 15 of the Value Added Tax Act 1994".

CUSTOMS AND EXCISE MANAGEMENT ACT 1979 c. 2

6   In section 1(1) of the Customs and Excise Management Act 1979 for the definition of "free zone goods" there shall be substituted–

""**free zone goods**" are goods which are within a free zone;".

ISLE OF MAN ACT 1979 c. 58

7(1)   In section 1(1)(d) of the Isle of Man Act for "13 of the Value Added Tax Act 1983" there shall be substituted "23 of the Value Added Tax Act 1994".

7(2)   In section 6 of that Act–

(a)   for "1983" in each place where it occurs there shall be substituted "1994";

(b)   in subsection (2)(f) for "29" there shall be substituted "43";

(c)   in subsection (4)(a) for "16(9)" there shall be substituted "30(10)";

(d)   in subsection (4)(b) for "Schedule 7" there shall be substituted "Schedule 11"; and

(e)   in subsection (4)(c) for "39(3)" there shall be substituted "72(8)".

7(3)   In section 14(4)(b) for "section 33(2A) of the Finance Act 1972" there shall be substituted "paragraph 5(3) of Schedule 11 to the VAT Act 1994".

INSOLVENCY ACT 1986 c. 45

8   In Schedule 6 to the Insolvency Act 1986 in paragraph 3 for "1983" there shall be substituted "1994".

BANKRUPTCY (SCOTLAND) ACT 1985 c. 66

9   In paragraph 8(2) of Schedule 3 to the Bankruptcy (Scotland) Act 1985 for "Value Added Tax Act 1983" there shall be substituted "Value Added Tax Act 1994".

INCOME AND CORPORATION TAXES ACT 1988 c. 1

10(1)   The Income and Corporation Taxes Act 1988 shall be subject to the following amendments.

10(2)   In section 827 for–

(a)   "Chapter II of Part I of the Finance Act 1985" there shall be substituted "Part IV of the Value Added Tax Act 1994";

(b)   "13–17A" there shall be substituted "60–70";

(c)   "18" and "19" there shall be substituted respectively "74" and "59";

(d)   "20 of the Finance Act 1985" there shall be substituted "79 of that Act".

CAPITAL ALLOWANCES ACT 1990 c. 1

11   In section 159A of the Capital Allowances Act 1990–

(a)   in subsection (6) for "1983" and "2(2)" there shall be substituted "1994" and "4(2)"; and

(b)   in subsection (7) for "14" and "1983" there shall be substituted "24" and "1994".

TRIBUNALS AND INQUIRIES ACT 1992 c. 53

12   In Parts I and II of Schedule 1 to the Tribunals and Inquiries Act 1992 for "8 to the Value Added Tax Act 1983" there shall be substituted "12 to the Value Added Tax Act 1994".

FINANCE ACT 1994 c. 9

13   In section 7 of the Finance Act 1994–

(a)   in subsection (4) for "25 and 29 of the Finance Act 1985" and "40 of the Value Added Tax Act 1983" there shall be substituted, respectively, "85 and 87 of the Value Added Tax Act 1994" and "83 of that Act"; and

(b)   in subsection (5) for "8 to the Value Added Tax Act 1983" there shall be substituted "12 to the Value Added Tax Act 1994".

History – Para. 13(a) was substituted by FA 1995, s. 33(5), with effect as if para. 13(a) had been originally enacted with this substitution.

VEHICLE EXCISE AND REGISTRATION ACT 1994 c. 22

14   In paragraph 23 of Schedule 2 to the Vehicle Excise and Registration Act 1994–

(a)   for "2C of the Value Added Tax Act 1983" there shall be substituted "3 of the Value Added Tax Act 1994";

(b)   for "(7) of section 16" there shall be substituted "(8) of section 30"; and
(c)   for "subsection (9)" there shall be substituted "subsection (10)".

SCHEDULE 15 – REPEALS

[Section 100(2)]

ACTS OF PARLIAMENT

Chapter	Short title	Extent of repeal
1979 c. 2.	Customs and Excise Management Act 1979	Sections 100B and 100C.
1983 c. 55.	Value Added Tax Act 1983	The whole Act.
1984 c. 24.	Dentists Act 1984	In Schedule 5, paragraph 16.
1984 c. 43.	Finance Act 1984	Sections 10 to 13. Schedule 6.
1984 c. 51.	Inheritance Tax Act 1984	In Schedule 8, paragraph 24.
1984 c. 60.	Police and Criminal Evidence Act 1984	In Schedule 6, paragraph 41.
1985 c. 54.	Finance Act 1985	Sections 11 to 33. Schedules 6, 7 and 8.
		In Schedule 26, paragraph 14.
1986 c. 41.	Finance Act 1986	Sections 9 to 15. Schedule 6.
1987 c. 16.	Finance Act 1987	Sections 11 to 19. Schedule 2.
1987 c. 18.	Debtors (Scotland) Act 1987	In Schedule 4, paragraph 4.
1988 c. 39.	Finance Act 1988	Sections 13 to 22.
1988 c. 54.	Road Traffic (Consequential Provisions) Act 1988	In Schedule 3, paragraph 32.
1989 c. 26.	Finance Act 1989	Sections 18 to 26. Schedule 3.
1989 c. 40.	Companies Act 1989	In Schedule 18, paragraph 27.
1989 c. 44.	Opticians Act 1989	Section 37(3).
1990 c. 11.	Planning (Consequential Provisions) Act 1990	In Schedule 2, paragraph 61.
1990 c. 19.	National Health Service and Community Care Act 1990	Section 61(4). In Schedule 8, paragraph 9.
1990 c. 29.	Finance Act 1990	Sections 10 to 16.
1990 c. 41.	Courts and Legal Services Act 1990	In Schedule 10, paragraph 52.
1990 c. 42.	Broadcasting Act 1990	In Schedule 20, paragraph 37.
1991 c. 21.	Disability Living Allowance and Disability Working Allowance Act 1991	In Schedule 2, paragraph 13.
1991 c. 31.	Finance Act 1991	Sections 13 to 18.
1992 c. 12.	Taxation of Chargeable Gains Act 1992	In Schedule 10, paragraph 6.
1992 c. 20.	Finance Act 1992	Sections 6 and 7.
1992 c. 48.	Finance (No. 2) Act 1992	Sections 14(1) and (3) to (6). Sections 15 to 17. Schedule 3, Parts I and II.
1992 c. 52.	Trade Union and Labour Relations (Consolidation) Act 1992	In Schedule 2, paragraph 32.
1992 c. 53.	Tribunals and Inquiries Act 1992	In Schedule 3, paragraph 17.
1993 c. 8.	Judicial Pensions and Retirement Act 1993	In Schedule 6, paragraph 35. In Schedule 8, paragraph 16.
1993 c. 34.	Finance Act 1993	Sections 42 to 50. Schedule 2.
1994 c. 9	Finance Act 1994	Section 7(1) and (2). In section 18(3) the words from "and for" to the end. Sections 45 and 47.
1994 c. 22	Vehicle Excise and Registration Act 1994	In Schedule 3, paragraph 21.

STATUTORY INSTRUMENTS

Number	Short title	Extent of repeal
SI 1980/440	Value Added Tax (Fuel and Power) Order 1980	The whole Order
SI 1983/1717	Value Added Tax (Charities Etc.) Order 1983	The whole Order
SI 1984/489	Value Added Tax (Handicapped Persons) Order 1984	The whole Order
SI 1984/631	Value Added Tax (Lifeboats) Order 1984	The whole Order
SI 1984/766	Value Added Tax (Charities Etc.) Order 1984	The whole Order
SI 1984/767	Value Added Tax (Marine etc. Insurance) Order 1984	The whole Order
SI 1984/959	Value Added Tax (Handicapped Persons) (No. 2) Order 1984	The whole Order
SI 1984/1784	Value Added Tax (Optical Appliances) Order 1984	The whole Order
SI 1985/18	Value Added Tax (Protected Buildings) Order 1985	The whole Order
SI 1985/431	Value Added Tax (Charities Etc.) Order 1985	The whole Order
SI 1985/432	Value Added Tax (Finance) Order 1985	The whole Order
SI 1985/799	Value Added Tax (Hiring of Goods) Order 1985	The whole Order
SI 1985/919	Value Added Tax (Handicapped Persons) Order 1985	Article 3.
SI 1985/1900	Value Added Tax (Welfare) Order 1985	The whole Order
SI 1986/530	Value Added Tax (Handicapped Persons and Charities) Order 1986	The whole Order
SI 1987/437	Value Added Tax (Charities) Order 1987	The whole Order
SI 1987/517	Value Added Tax (Betting, Gaming and Lotteries) Order 1987	The whole Order
SI 1987/518	Value Added Tax (International Services) Order 1987	The whole Order
SI 1987/1072	Value Added Tax (Construction of Buildings) (No. 2) Order 1987	Article 2
SI 1987/860	Value Added Tax (Finance) Order 1987	The whole Order
SI 1987/1259	Value Added Tax (Education) Order 1987	The whole Order
SI 1987/1806	Value Added Tax (Tour Operators) Order 1987	Article 11
SI 1988/507	Value Added Tax (Confectionery) Order 1988	The whole Order
SI 1988/1282	Value Added Tax (Training) Order 1988	The whole Order
SI 1989/267	Value Added Tax (Education) Order 1989	The whole Order
SI 1989/470	Value Added Tax (Fund-Raising Events and Charities) Order 1989	The whole Order
SI 1989/2272	Value Added Tax (Finance, Health and Welfare) Order 1989	The whole Order
SI 1990/682	Value Added Tax (Increase of Registration Limits) Order 1990	The whole Order
SI 1990/750	Value Added Tax (Charities) Order 1990	The whole Order
SI 1990/752	Value Added Tax (Transport) Order 1990	The whole Order
SI 1990/2037	Value Added Tax (Insurance) Order 1990	The whole Order
SI 1990/2129	Value Added Tax (Charities) (No. 2) Order 1990	The whole Order
SI 1990/2553	Value Added Tax (Construction of Dwellings and Land) Order 1990	The whole Order
SI 1991/737	Value Added Tax (Charities) Order 1991	The whole Order
SI 1991/738	Value Added Tax (Increase of Registration Limits) Order 1991	The whole Order
SI 1991/2534	Value Added Tax (Piped Gas) (Metrication) Order 1991	The whole Order
SI 1991/2569	Value Added Tax (Buildings and Land) Order 1991	The whole Order
SI 1992/628	Value Added Tax (Charities and Aids for Handicapped Persons) Order 1992	The whole Order
SI 1992/629	Value Added Tax (Increase of Registration Limits) Order 1992	The whole Order
SI 1992/733	Value Added Tax (Increase for Consideration for Fuel) Order 1992	The whole Order
SI 1992/3065	Value Added Tax (Motor Vehicles for the Handicapped) Order 1992	The whole Order
SI 1992/3126	Value Added Tax (Transport) Order 1992	The whole Order
SI 1992/3127	Value Added Tax (Means of Transport) Order 1992	The whole Order

Number	Short title	Extent of repeal
SI 1992/3131	Value Added Tax (Tax Free Shops) Order 1992	The whole Order
SI 1992/3223	Value Added Tax (International Services and Transport) Order 1992	The whole Order
SI 1993/765	Value Added Tax (Increase for Consideration for Fuel) Order 1993	The whole Order
SI 1993/766	Value Added Tax (Increase of Registration Limits) Order 1993	The whole Order
SI 1993/767	Value Added Tax (Protective Boots and Helmets) Order 1993	The whole Order
SI 1993/1124	Value Added Tax (Education) (No. 2) Order 1993	The whole Order
SI 1993/2214	Finance Act 1993 (Appointed Day) Order 1993	The whole Order
SI 1993/2328	Value Added Tax (Reverse Charge) Order 1993	The whole Order
SI 1993/2498	Value Added Tax (Beverages) Order 1993	The whole Order
SI 1993/2498	Value Added Tax (Beverages) Order 1983	The whole Order
SI 1993/2952	Value Added Tax (Increase of Consideration for Fuel) (No. 2) Order 1993	The whole Order
SI 1993/2953	Value Added Tax (Increase of Registration Limits) (No. 2) Order 1993	The whole Order
SI 1994/686	Value Added Tax (Tax Free Shops) Order 1994	The whole Order
SI 1994/687	Value Added Tax (Sport, Physical Education and Fund-Raising Events) Order 1994	The whole Order
SI 1994/1188	Value Added Tax (Education) Order 1994	The whole Order

Notes – In the Queen's Printer's version of the Act, the entry for SI 1993/2498 Value Added Tax (Beverages) Order 1993 appears to be duplicated, although in the second instance the year appears incorrectly as 1983.

FINANCE ACT 1995

(1995 Chapter 4)

[1st May 1995]

ARRANGEMENT OF SECTIONS

PART II – VALUE ADDED TAX AND INSURANCE PREMIUM TAX

VALUE ADDED TAX

PART VI – MISCELLANEOUS AND GENERAL

GENERAL

SCHEDULES

29.   REPEALS
         Part VI – Value Added Tax

PART II – VALUE ADDED TAX AND INSURANCE PREMIUM TAX

VALUE ADDED TAX

21   Fuel and power for domestic or charity use

21(1)   The Value Added Tax Act 1994 shall be amended as follows.

21(2)   [Amends VATA 1994, s. 2(1) and inserts VATA 1994, s. 2(1A)–2(1C).]

21(3)   [Inserts VATA 1994, Sch. A1.]

21(4)   [Inserts VATA 1994, s. 97(4)(aa).]

21(5)   [Omits VATA 1994, Sch. 13, para. 7.]

21(6)   This section shall apply in relation to any supply made on or after 1st April 1995 and any acquisition or importation taking place on or after that date.

22   Imported works of art, antiques, etc.

22(1)   [Amends VATA 1994, s. 21(1) and inserts VATA 1994, s. 21(4)–(7).]

22(2)   This section shall have effect in relation to goods imported at any time on or after the day on which this Act is passed.

23   Agents acting in their own names

23(1)   [Amends VATA 1994, s. 47(1).]

23(2)   [Inserts VATA 1994, s. 47(2A).]

23(3)   [Amends VATA 1994, s. 47(3).]

23(4)   This section shall have effect–

(a)   so far as it amends section 47(1) of that Act, in relation to goods acquired or imported on or after the day on which this Act is passed; and

(b)   for other purposes, in relation to any supply taking place on or after that day.

24   Margin schemes

24(1)   [Inserts VATA 1994, s. 50A.]

24(2)   Section 32 of that Act (relief on supply of certain second-hand goods) shall cease to have effect on such day as the Commissioners of Customs and Excise may by order made by statutory instrument appoint.

Statutory instrument – The appointed day is 1 June 1995 (SI 1995/1374 (C 28)).

25   Groups of companies

25(1)   Section 43 of the Value Added Tax Act 1994 (groups of companies) shall be amended as follows.

25(2)   [Amends VATA 1994, s. 43(1)(b). Until its repeal by FA 1996, s. 205 and Sch. 41, Pt. IV(5), FA 1995, s. 25(2) had inserted former VATA 1994, s. 43(1A).]

25(3)   [Repealed by FA 1999, s. 139(1) and Sch. 20, Pt. II(1). FA 1995, s. 25(3) had amended former VATA 1994, s. 43(5).]

25(4)   [Repealed by FA 1999, s. 139(1)) and Sch. 20, Pt. II(1). FA 1995, s. 25(4) had inserted former VATA 1994, s. 43(5A).]

25(5)   Subsection (2) above has effect in relation to–

(a)   any supply made on or after 1st March 1995, and

(b)   any supply made before that date in the case of which both the body making the supply and the body supplied continued to be members of the group in question until at least that date,

and subsections (3) and (4) above have effect in relation to applications made on or after the day on which this Act is passed.

History – S. 25(3) was repealed by FA 1999, s. 139(1) and Sch. 20, Pt. II(1), with effect in accordance with the transitional provisions in FA 1999, Sch. 2, para. 6.
S. 25(4) was repealed by FA 1999, s. 139(1) and Sch. 20, Pt. II(1), with effect in accordance with the transitional provisions in FA 1999, Sch. 2, para. 6.

26 Co-owners etc. of buildings and land

26(1) After section 51 of the Value Added Tax Act 1994 there shall be inserted the following section–

"Co-owners etc. of buildings and land

51A(1) This section applies to a supply consisting in the grant, assignment or surrender of any interest in or right over land in a case where there is more than one person by whom the grant, assignment or surrender is made or treated as made; and for this purpose–

(a) a licence to occupy land, and

(b) in relation to land in Scotland, a personal right to call for or be granted any interest or right in or over land,

shall be taken to be a right over land.

51A(2) The persons who make or are treated as making a supply to which this section applies ("**the grantors**") shall be treated, in relation to that supply and in relation to any other such supply with respect to which the grantors are the same, as a single person ("**the property-owner**") who is distinct from each of the grantors individually.

51A(3) Registration under this Act of the property-owner shall be in the name of the grantors acting together as a property-owner.

51A(4) The grantors shall be jointly and severally liable in respect of the obligations falling by virtue of this section on the property-owner.

51A(5) Any notice, whether of assessment or otherwise, which is addressed to the property-owner by the name in which the property-owner is registered and is served on any of the grantors in accordance with this Act shall be treated for the purposes of this Act as served on the property-owner.

51A(6) Where there is any change in some, but not all, of the persons who are for the time being to be treated as the grantors in relation to any supply to which this section applies–

(a) that change shall be disregarded for the purposes of this section in relation to any prescribed accounting period beginning before the change is notified in the prescribed manner to the Commissioners; and

(b) any notice (whether of assessment or otherwise) which is served, at any time after such a notification, on the property-owner for the time being shall, so far as it relates to, or to any matter arising in, such a period, be treated for the purposes of this Act as served on whoever was the property-owner in that period."

26(2) Paragraph 8 of Schedule 10 to that Act (persons to whom the benefit of consideration for the grant of an interest accrues to be treated as person making the grant) shall become sub-paragraph (1) of that paragraph, and after that sub-paragraph there shall be inserted the following sub-paragraphs–

"**8(2)** Where the consideration for the grant of an interest in, right over or licence to occupy land is such that its provision is enforceable primarily–

(a) by the person who, as owner of an interest or right in or over that land, actually made the grant, or

(b) by another person in his capacity as the owner for the time being of that interest or right or of any other interest or right in or over that land,

that person, and not any person (other than that person) to whom a benefit accrues by virtue of his being a beneficiary under a trust relating to the land, or the proceeds of sale of any land, shall be taken for the purposes of this paragraph to be the person to whom the benefit of the consideration accrues.

8(3) Sub-paragraph (2) above shall not apply to the extent that the Commissioners, on an application made in the prescribed manner jointly by–

(a) the person who (apart from this sub-paragraph) would be taken under that sub-paragraph to be the person to whom the benefit of the consideration accrues, and

(b) all the persons for the time being in existence who, as beneficiaries under such a trust as is mentioned in that sub-paragraph, are persons who have or may become entitled

to or to a share of the consideration, or for whose benefit any of it is to be or may be
applied,

may direct that the benefit of the consideration is to be treated for the purposes of this
paragraph as a benefit accruing to the persons falling within paragraph (b) above, and not
(unless he also falls within paragraph (b) above) to the person falling within paragraph (a)
above."

26(3)   This section shall come into force on such day as the Commissioners of Customs and
Excise may by order made by statutory instrument appoint, and different days may be appointed
under this subsection for different purposes.

27   Set-off of credits

27(1)   Section 81 of the Value Added Tax Act 1994 (which includes provision as to the setting off
of credits) shall be amended as follows.

27(2)   [Substitutes VATA 1994, s. 81(4A)–(4D) for VATA 1994, s. 81(4).]

27(3)   [Amends VATA 1994, s. 81(5).]

27(4)   This section shall have effect in relation to amounts becoming due from the Commissioners
of Customs and Excise at times on or after the day on which this Act is passed.

28   Transactions treated as supplies for purposes of zero-rating etc.

28(1)   [Substitutes VATA 1994, s. 30(5).]

28(2)   This section shall have effect in relation to transactions occurring on or after the day on
which this Act is passed.

29   Goods removed from warehousing regime

29   [Substitutes VATA 1994, s. 18(5) and (5A) for VATA 1994, s. 18(5).]

30   Fuel supplied for private use

30(1)   Section 57 of the Value Added Tax Act 1994 (determination of consideration for fuel
supplied for private use) shall be amended as follows.

30(2)   [Inserts VATA 1994, s. 57(1A).]

30(3)   [Amends VATA 1994, s. 57(2).]

30(4)   [Amends VATA 1994, s. 57(3).]

30(5)   [Substitutes VATA 1994, s. 57(3), Table A.]

30(6)   This section shall apply in relation to prescribed accounting periods beginning on or after
6th April 1995.

30(7)   Nothing in this section shall be taken to prejudice any practice by which the consideration
appropriate to a vehicle is arrived at where a prescribed accounting period beginning before
6th April 1995 is a period of 12 months.

31   Appeals: payment of amounts shown in returns

31(1)   [Amends VATA 1994, s. 84(2).]

31(2)   This section shall apply in relation to appeals brought after the day on which this Act is
passed.

32   Penalties for failure to notify etc.

32(1)   [Amends VATA 1994, s. 67(4).]

32(2)   Section 15(3A) of the Finance Act 1985 (provision which is repealed by the 1994 Act and
which corresponds to section 67(4)) shall have effect subject to the amendments made by
subsection (1) above.

32(3)   Subject to subsection (4) below, subsections (1) and (2) above shall apply where a penalty
is assessed on or after 1st January 1995.

32(4)   Subsections (1) and (2) above shall not apply in the case of a supplementary assessment if
the original assessment was made before 1st January 1995.

33   Correction of consolidation errors

33(1)   The Value Added Tax Act 1994 shall have effect, and be deemed always to have had effect, as if it had been enacted as follows.

33(2)   [S. 33(2) was repealed by FA 1996, s. 205 and Sch. 41, Pt. IV(4), in relation to any case in which a claim for repayment under VATA 1994, s. 35 is made on or after 29 April 1996. S. 33(2) had amended VATA 1994, s. 35(1).]

33(3)   [Amends VATA 1994, Sch. 4, para. 5(5) and (6)(b) and Sch. 6, para. 7(b).]

33(4)   [Substitutes VATA 1994, Sch. 13, para. 9(2).]

33(5)   [Substitutes VATA 1994, Sch. 14, para. 13(a).]

PART VI – MISCELLANEOUS AND GENERAL

GENERAL

162   Repeals

162   The provisions specified in Schedule 29 to this Act (which include provisions which are already spent) are hereby repealed to the extent specified in the third column of that Schedule, but subject to any provision of that Schedule.

SCHEDULES

SCHEDULE 29 – REPEALS

Section 162

Part VI – Value Added Tax

(1)   FUEL AND POWER

Chapter	Short title	Extent of repeal
1994 c. 23.	The Value Added Tax Act 1994.	In Schedule 13, paragraph 7.

This repeal has effect in accordance with section 21 of this Act.

(2)   AGENTS

Chapter	Short title	Extent of repeal
1994 c. 23.	The Value Added Tax Act 1994.	In section 47(3), the words "goods or".

This repeal has effect in accordance with section 23(4)(b) of this Act.

(3)   MARGIN SCHEMES

Chapter	Short title	Extent of repeal
1994 c. 23.	The Value Added Tax Act 1994.	Section 32.

This repeal comes into force on the day appointed by an order under section 24(2) of this Act.

(4) APPEALS

Chapter	Short title	Extent of repeal
1994 c. 23.	The Value Added Tax Act 1994.	In section 84(2) the words ", except in the case of an appeal against a decision with respect to the matter mentioned in section 83(1),".

This repeal has effect in accordance with section 31 of this Act.

FINANCE ACT 1996

(1996 Chapter 8)

[*29th April 1996*]

ARRANGEMENT OF SECTIONS

PART II –

PART VII – MISCELLANEOUS AND SUPPLEMENTAL

SCHEDULES

PART II – VALUE ADDED TAX

EC SECOND VAT SIMPLIFICATION DIRECTIVE

25   EC Second VAT Simplification Directive

25   Sections 26 to 29 of and Schedule 3 to this Act are for the purpose of giving effect to requirements of the directive of the Council of the European Communities dated 17th May 1977 No. 77/388/EEC and the amendments of that directive by the directive of that Council dated 10th April 1995 No. 95/7/EC (amendments with a view to introducing new simplification measures with regard to value added tax).

26   Fiscal and other warehousing

26(1)   The provisions of Schedule 3 to this Act shall have effect.

26(2)   Subject to subsection (3) below, this section and Schedule 3 to this Act shall come into force on such day as the Commissioners of Customs and Excise may by order made by statutory instrument appoint, and shall apply to any acquisition of goods from another member State and any supply taking place on or after that day.

26(3)   In so far as the provisions inserted by Schedule 3 to this Act confer power to make regulations they shall come into force on the day this Act is passed.

Statutory instrument – Finance Act 1996, section 26, (Appointed Day) Order 1996 (SI 1996/1249 (C 21)): to the extent that they are not in force by virtue of s. 26(3), the day appointed as the day on which s. 26 and Sch. 3 come into force is 1 June 1996.

27   Value of imported goods

27(1)   Section 21 of the Value Added Tax Act 1994 (value of imported goods) shall be amended as follows.

27(2)   [Amends VATA 1994, s. 21(2)(a).]

27(3)   [Substitutes VATA 1994, s. 21(2)(b).]

27(4)   This section shall have effect in relation to goods imported on or after 1st January 1996.

28   Adaptation of aircraft and hovercraft

28(1)   [Omits VATA 1994, s. 22.]

28(2)   This section shall apply to supplies made on or after 1st January 1996.

29   Work on materials

29(1)   The Value Added Tax Act 1994 shall be amended as follows.

29(2)   [Inserts VATA 1994, s. 30(2A).]

29(3)   [Amends VATA 1994, s. 55(5).]

29(4)   [Omits VATA 1994, Sch. 4, para. 2.]

29(5)   This section shall apply to supplies made on or after 1st January 1996.

OTHER PROVISIONS RELATING TO CHARGES TO VAT

30   Refunds in connection with construction and conversion

30(1)   [Amends VATA 1994, s. 35.]

30(2)   [Amends VATA 1994, s. 35(2).]

30(3)   [Inserts VATA 1994, s. 35(4) and (5).]

30(4)   This section applies in relation to any case in which a claim for repayment under section 35 of the Value Added Tax Act 1994 is made at any time on or after the day on which this Act is passed.

31   *Groups: anti-avoidance*

31(1)   [Inserts VATA 1994, s. 43(9).]

31(2)   [Inserts VATA 1994, Sch. 9A.]

31(3)   [Inserts VATA 1994, s. 83(wa).]

31(4)   [Inserts VATA 1994, s. 84(7A).]

31(5)   Subsection (1A) of section 43 of that Act shall not have effect in relation to supplies on or after the day on which this Act is passed.

32   Supplies of gold etc.

32(1)   [Substititutes VATA 1994, s. 55(5)(a).]

32(2)   This section applies in relation to any supply after 28th November 1995.

33   Small gifts

33(1)   [Amends VATA 1994, Sch. 4, para. 5(2)(a).]

33(2)   [Inserts VATA 1994, Sch. 4, para. 5(7).]

33(3)   [Inserts VATA 1994, s. 97(4)(ab).]

33(4)   Subsection (1) above shall apply where a gift is made after 28th November 1995.

PAYMENT AND ENFORCEMENT

34   Method of making payments on account

34   [Inserts VATA 1994, s. 28(2A).]

35   Default surcharges

35(1)   The Value Added Tax Act 1994 shall be amended as follows.

35(2)   [Inserts VATA 1994, s. 59A.]

35(3)   [Amends VATA 1994, s. 59(1) and inserts s. 59(1A).]

35(4)   [Inserts VATA 1994, s. 59(11).]

35(5)   [Inserts VATA 1994, s. 59B.]

35(6)   [Amends VATA 1994, s. 69(4)(a) and (9)(b).]

35(7)   [Amends VATA 1994, s. 76(1) and (3)(a).]

35(8)   This section applies in relation to any prescribed accounting period ending on or after 1st June 1996, but a liability to make a payment on account of VAT shall be disregarded for the purposes of the amendments made by this section if the payment is one becoming due before that date.

36   Repeated misdeclaration penalty

36(1)   [Substitutes VATA 1994, s. 64(6), (6A) and (7) for former s. 64(6) and (7).]

36(2)   This section has effect in relation to inaccuracies contained in returns made on or after the day on which this Act is passed.

37   Penalties for failure to notify

37(1)   [Amends VATA 1994, s. 67(1)(a) and (3)(a).]

37(2)   Subject to subsection (3) below, subsection (1) above shall apply in relation to–

(a)   any person becoming liable to be registered by virtue of sub-paragraph (2) of paragraph 1 of Schedule 1 to the Value Added Tax Act 1994 on or after 1st January 1996; and

(b)   any person who became liable to be registered by virtue of that sub-paragraph before that date but who had not notified the Commissioners of the liability before that date.

37(3)   In relation to a person falling within subsection (2)(b) above, section 67 of the Value Added Tax Act 1994 shall have effect as if in subsection (3)(a) for the words "the date with effect from which he is, in accordance with that paragraph, required to be registered" there were substituted "1st January 1996".

38   VAT invoices and accounting

38(1)   Paragraph 2 of Schedule 11 to the Value Added Tax Act 1994 (regulations about accounting for VAT, VAT invoices etc.) shall be amended as follows.

38(2)   [Inserts VATA 1994, Sch. 11, para. 2(2A).]

38(3)   [Amends VATA 1994, Sch. 11, para. 2(10).]

PART VII – MISCELLANEOUS AND SUPPLEMENTAL

MISCELLANEOUS: INDIRECT TAXATION

197　Setting of rates of interest

197(1)　The rate of interest applicable for the purposes of an enactment to which this section applies shall be the rate which for the purposes of that enactment is provided for by regulations made by the Treasury under this section.

197(2)　This section applies to–

(a)　[Not reproduced; relates to air passenger duty];

(b)　[Not reproduced; relates to insurance premium tax];

(c)　sections 74 and 78 of the Value Added Tax Act 1994 (interest on VAT recovered or recoverable by assessment and interest payable in cases of official error);

(d)　[Not reproduced; relates to landfill tax];

(e)　[Not reproduced; relates to excise duties, insurance premium tax and landfill tax];

(f)　[Not reproduced; relates to customs duty].

197(3)　Regulations under this section may–

(a)　make different provision for different enactments or for different purposes of the same enactment,

(b)　either themselves specify a rate of interest for the purposes of an enactment or make provision for any such rate to be determined, and to change from time to time, by reference to such rate or the average of such rates as may be referred to in the regulations,

(c)　provide for rates to be reduced below, or increased above, what they otherwise would be by specified amounts or by reference to specified formulae,

(d)　provide for rates arrived at by reference to averages or formulae to be rounded up or down,

(e)　provide for circumstances in which changes of rates of interest are or are not to take place, and

(f)　provide that changes of rates are to have effect for periods beginning on or after a day determined in accordance with the regulations in relation to interest running from before that day, as well as in relation to interest running from, or from after, that day.

197(4)　The power to make regulations under this section shall be exercisable by statutory instrument subject to annulment in pursuance of a resolution of the House of Commons.

197(5)　Where–

(a)　regulations under this section provide, without specifying the rate determined in accordance with the regulations, for a new method of determining the rate applicable for the purposes of any enactment, or

(b)　the rate which, in accordance with regulations under this section, is the rate applicable for the purposes of any enactment changes otherwise than by virtue of the making of regulations specifying a new rate,

the Commissioners of Customs and Excise shall make an order specifying the new rate and the day from which, in accordance with the regulations, it has effect.

197(6)

(a)　[Not reproduced: relates to air passenger duty.]

(b)　[Not reproduced: relates to insurance premium tax.]

(c)　[Not reproduced: relates to insurance premium tax.]

(d)　. . .

　　　(i)　[Amends VATA 1994, s. 74(1), (2) and (4).]

　　　(ii)　[Amends VATA 1994, s. 78(3).]

197(7)　Subsections (1) and (6) above shall have effect for periods beginning on or after such day as the Treasury may by order made by statutory instrument appoint and shall have effect in relation to interest running from before that day, as well as in relation to interest running from, or from after, that day; and different days may be appointed under this subsection for different purposes.

History – In s. 197(2)(c), the word "and" which appeared at the end was repealed by FA 1997, s. 113 and Sch. 18, Pt. V(1), with effect from 19 March 1997.

Cross references – FA 1997, Sch. 5, para. 17(1): recovery of excess payments by the Commissioners and interest on amounts assessed.

Statutory instruments – SI 1997/1015: sets 1 April 1997 as the appointed day for the purposes of s. 197(7).

SI 1997/1016: sets the rate of interest from 1 April 1997 at 6.25 per cent and 6 per cent per annum for the purposes of VATA 1994, s. 74 and 78 respectively, until revoked from 6 July 1996 by SI 1998/1461, reg. 3.
SI 1998/1461: sets interest rate from 6 July 1998 for the purposes of VATA 1994, s. 74 and 78 at 9.5 and 6 per cent per annum respectively.
SI 2000/631: amended Air Passenger Duty and Other Indirect Taxes (Interest Rate) Regulations 1998 (SI 1998/1461).

205   Repeals

205(1)   The enactments mentioned in Schedule 41 to this Act (which include spent provisions) are hereby repealed to the extent specified in the third column of that Schedule.

205(2)   The repeals specified in that Schedule have effect subject to the commencement provisions and savings contained in, or referred to, in the notes set out in that Schedule.

SCHEDULES

SCHEDULE 3 – VALUE ADDED TAX: FISCAL AND OTHER WAREHOUSING

Section 26

1   [Amends VATA 1994, s. 6(1).]

2   [Amends VATA 1994, s. 7(1).]

3   [Amends VATA 1994, s. 12(1).]

4   [Amends VATA 1994, s. 13(1).]

5   [Inserts VATA 1994, s. 18A–18F.]

6   [Amends VATA 1994, s. 20(1).]

7   [Inserts VATA 1994, s. 30(8A) and amends s. 30(10).]

8(1)   Section 62 of the Value Added Tax Act 1994 shall be amended as follows.

8(2)   [Amends VATA 1994, s. 62(1).]

8(3)   [Amends VATA 1994, s. 62(1), (3) and (4).]

8(4)   [Amends VATA 1994, s. 62(3).]

9   [Adds VATA 1994, s. 69(1)(g).]

10   [Adds VATA 1994, s. 73(7A) and (7B).]

11   [Amends VATA 1994, s. 73(9) and 76(5).]

12   [Adds VATA 1994, s. 83(da) and amends s. 83(p)(ii).]

13   [Adds VATA 1994, Sch. 1, para. 1(9).]

14   [Adds VATA 1994, Sch. 2, para. 1(7).]

15   [Adds VATA 1994, Sch. 3, para. 1(6).]

16   [Amends VATA 1994, Sch. 11, para. 8(1).]

17   [Amends VATA 1994, Sch. 11, para. 10(2).]

18   [Adds VATA 1994, Sch. 5A.]

SCHEDULE 4 – VALUE ADDED TAX: ANTI-AVOIDANCE PROVISIONS

Section 31

[Inserts VATA 1994, Sch. 9A.]

SCHEDULE 41 – REPEALS

Section 205

Part IV – VALUE ADDED TAX

(1) FISCAL WAREHOUSING

Chapter	Short title	Extent of repeal
1994 c. 23.	The Value Added Tax Act 1994.	In section 62(1)(a), the words ''or'' at the end of sub-paragraph (i) and ''and'' at the end of sub-paragraph (ii).

This repeal has effect in accordance with section 22(2) of this Act.

Part VIII – MISCELLANEOUS

(1) RATES OF INTEREST

Chapter	Short title	Extent of repeal
1994 c. 9.	The Finance Act 1994.	In Schedule 6, paragraph 11.
		In Schedule 7, paragraph 21(5).
1994 c. 23.	The Value Added Tax Act 1994.	Section 74(6).

Subsection (7) of section 197 of this Act applies in relation to these repeals as it applies in relation to subsection (6) of that section.

FINANCE ACT 1997

(1997 Chapter 16)

[*19th March 1997*]

ARRANGEMENT OF SECTIONS

PART III – VALUE ADDED TAX

PART III – VALUE ADDED TAX

REGISTRATION

31 Aggregation of businesses

31(1)   [Inserts VATA 1994, Sch. 1, para. 1A(1) and 1A(2).]

31(2)   [Amends VATA 1994, Sch. 1, para. 2(2).]

31(3)   [Amends VATA 1994, s. 84(7).]

31(4)   This section has effect in relation to the making of directions on or after the day on which this Act is passed.

32 Voluntary registration

32   [Substitutes VATA 1994, Sch. 1, para. 10(2).]

ZERO-RATING

33   Sale of goods donated to charity

33(1)   [Substitutes VATA 1994, Sch. 8, Grp. 15, Note (1).]

33(2)   This section has effect in relation to supplies made on or after 26th November 1996.

34   Charitable institutions providing care etc.

34(1)   [Inserts VATA 1994, Sch. 8, Grp. 15, Notes (4A) and (4B).]

34(2)   [Inserts VATA 1994, Sch. 8, Grp. 15, Notes (5A) and (5B).]

34(3)   This section has effect in relation to supplies made on or after 26th November 1996.

BUILDINGS AND LAND

35   References to grants

35(1)   [Inserts VATA 1994, s. 96(10A).]

35(2)   [Inserts VATA 1994, Sch. 10, para. 3(5A) and 3(5B).]

35(3)   Amendments corresponding to those made by subsections (1) and (2) above shall be deemed to have had effect, for the purposes of the cases to which it applied, in relation to the Value Added Tax Act 1983; and any provisions about the coming into force of any amendment of that Act shall be deemed to have had effect accordingly.

35(4)   Nothing in this section shall be taken to affect the operation, in relation to times before its repeal took effect, of paragraph 4 of Schedule 10 to the Value Added Tax Act 1994 or of any enactment re-enacted in that paragraph.

36   Buildings intended to be used as dwellings

36(1)   [Inserts VATA 1994, Sch. 10, para. 2(2A) and 2(2B).]

36(2)   This section has effect in relation to supplies made on or after the day on which this Act is passed.

37   Supplies to non-taxable persons etc.

37(1)   Paragraphs 2(3A) and 3(8A) of Schedule 10 to the Value Added Tax Act 1994 (which relate to grants of land made to connected persons where they are not fully taxable) shall not have effect in relation to any supply made after 26th November 1996.

37(2)   [Inserts VATA 1994, Sch. 10, para. 2(3AA).]

37(3)   [Inserts VATA 1994, Sch. 10, para. 3A.]

37(4)   Subsections (2) and (3) above have effect in relation to any supply made on or after the day on which this Act is passed, other than a supply arising from a relevant pre-commencement grant.

37(5)   Subject to subsection (6) below, a grant is a **relevant pre-commencement grant** for the purposes of this section if it is either–

(a)   a grant made before 26th November 1996; or

(b)   a grant made on or after that date and before 30th November 1999 in pursuance of an agreement in writing entered into before 26th November 1996.

37(6)   For the purposes of this section a grant is not a **relevant pre-commencement** grant by virtue of paragraph (b) of subsection (5) above unless the terms on which the grant has been made are terms which, as terms for which provision was made by the agreement mentioned in that paragraph, were fixed before 26th November 1996.

Cross references – VATA 1994, Sch. 10, para. 2 and 3A: anti-avoidance and electing to waive exemption.

EXEMPT INSURANCE SUPPLIES

38   Exempt insurance supplies

38(1)   [Substitutes VATA 1994, Sch. 9, Grp. 2.]

38(2)   This section has effect in relation to supplies made on or after the day on which this Act is passed.

BAD DEBT RELIEF

39   Bad debt relief

39(1)   In section 36 of the Value Added Tax Act 1994, paragraph (b) of subsection (4) (condition of bad debt relief that property in goods supplied has passed) shall not apply in the case of any claim made under that section in relation to a supply of goods made after the day on which this Act is passed.

39(2)   [Inserts VATA 1994, s. 36(4A).]

39(3)   Subsection (2) above has effect in relation to any entitlement under section 36 of that Act of 1994 to a refund of VAT charged on a supply made after 26th November 1996.

39(4)   [Inserts VATA 1994, s. 36(5)(ea).]

39(5)   No claim for a refund may be made in accordance with section 22 of the Value Added Tax Act 1983 (old scheme for bad debt relief) at any time after the day on which this Act is passed.

GROUPS OF COMPANIES

40   Groups containing bodies of different descriptions

40(1)   [Inserts VATA 1994, s. 43(1AA) and 43(1AB).]

40(2)   [Amends VATA 1994, s. 43(2).]

40(3)   Subsection (1) above has effect in relation to any supply made after 26th November 1996 and in relation to any acquisition or importation taking place after that date.

41   Group supplies using an overseas member

41(1)   [Inserts VATA 1994, s. 43(2A) –43(2E).]

41(2)   Subject to subsection (3) below, subsection (1) above has effect in relation to supplies made on or after 26th November 1996.

41(3)   Section 43 of the Value Added Tax Act 1994 shall have effect in relation to supplies made after the day on which this Act is passed with the provisions inserted by subsection (1) above modified in accordance with subsections (4) and (5) below.

41(4)   [Amends VATA 1994, s. 43(2A).]

41(5)   [Amends VATA 1994, s. 43(2C).]

INCIDENTAL AND SUPPLEMENTAL PROVISIONS ETC.

42   Services subject to the reverse charge

42   [Inserts VATA 1994, s. 8(7) and 8(8).]

43   Payments on account: appeals

43   [Inserts VATA 1994, s. 28(2AA).]

PART IV – PAYMENTS AND OVERPAYMENTS IN RESPECT OF INDIRECT TAXES

VALUE ADDED TAX

44   Liability of Commissioners to interest

44(1)   [*Inserts* VATA 1994, s. 78(1A).]

44(2)   [Substitutes VATA 1994, s. 78(11).]

44(3)   [Substitutes VATA 1994, s. 78(12)(a).]

44(4)   [Substitutes VATA 1994, s. 78(8), 78(8A) and 78(9) for former s. 78(8) and 78(9).]

44(5)   Subsection (4) above shall have effect for the purposes of determining whether any period beginning on or after the day on which this Act is passed is left out of account.

44(6)   Amendments corresponding to those made by subsections (1) and (3) above shall be deemed to have had effect, for the purposes of the cases to which the enactments applied, in relation to the enactments directly or indirectly re-enacted in section 78 of the Value Added Tax Act 1994.

45   Assessment for overpayments of interest

45(1)   [Inserts VATA 1994, s. 78A.]

45(2)   [Inserts VATA 1994, s. 83(sa).]

45(3)   [Inserts VATA 1994, s. 84(3A).]

45(4)   Subsection (1) above shall be deemed to have come into force on 4th December 1996 in relation to amounts paid by way of interest at any time on or after 18th July 1996.

45(5)   Subsections (2) and (3) above shall be deemed to have come into force on 4th December 1996 in relation to assessments made on or after that date.

45(6)   [Amends VATA 1994, s. 76(10).]

46   Repayments of overpayments: unjust enrichment

46(1)   [Inserts VATA 1994, s. 80(3A) –80(3C).]

46(2)   [Inserts VATA 1994, s. 80A and 80B.]

46(3)   [Inserts VATA 1994, s. 83(ta).]

46(4)   Subsection (1) above has effect for the purposes of making any repayment on or after the day on which this Act is passed, even if the claim for that repayment was made before that day.

47   Repayments and assessments: time limits

47(1)   [Substitutes VATA 1994, s. 80(4) for former s. 80(4) and 80(5).]

47(2)   Subject to subsections (3) and (4) below, subsection (1) above shall be deemed to have come into force on 18th July 1996 as a provision applying, for the purposes of the making of any repayment on or after that date, to all claims under section 80 of the Value Added Tax Act 1994, including claims made before that date and claims relating to payments made before that date.

47(3)   Subsection (4) below applies as respects the making of any repayment on or after 18th July 1996 on a claim under section 80 of the Value Added Tax Act 1994 if–

(a)   legal proceedings for questioning any decision (**"the disputed decision"**) of the Commissioners, or of an officer of the Commissioners, were brought by any person at any time before that date,

(b)   a determination has been or is made in those proceedings that the disputed decision was wrong or should be set aside,

(c)   the claim is one made by that person at a time after the proceedings were brought (whether before or after the making of the determination), and

(d)   the claim relates to–

> (i)   an amount paid by that person to the Commissioners on the basis of the disputed decision, or

> (ii)   an amount paid by that person to the Commissioners before the relevant date (including an amount paid before the making of the disputed decision) on grounds which, in all material respects, correspond to those on which that decision was made.

47(4)   Where this subsection applies in the case of any claim–

(a)   subsection (4) of section 80 of the Value Added Tax Act 1994 (as inserted by this section) shall not apply, and shall be taken never to have applied, in relation to so much of that claim as relates to an amount falling within subsection (3)(d)(i) or (ii) above, but

(b)   the Commissioners shall not be liable on that claim, and shall be taken never to have been liable on that claim, to repay any amount so falling which was paid to them more than three years before the proceedings mentioned in subsection (3)(a) above were brought.

47(5)   In subsection (3)(d) above–

(a)   the reference to the **relevant date** is a reference to whichever is the earlier of 18th July 1996 and the date of the making of the determination in question; and

(b)   the reference to an amount paid on the **basis of a decision**, or on any grounds, includes an amount so paid on terms (however expressed) which questioned the correctness of the decision or, as the case may be, of those grounds.

47(6)   [Inserts VATA 1994, s. 80(4A)–80(4C).]

47(7)   [Amends VATA 1994, s. 83(t).]

47(8)   Nothing contained in–

(a)   any regulations under section 25(1) of, or paragraph 2 of Schedule 11 to, that Act relating to the correction of errors or the making of adjustments, or

(b)   any requirement imposed under any such regulations,

shall be taken, in relation to any time on or after 18th July 1996, to have conferred an entitlement on any person to receive, by way of repayment, any amount to which he would not have had any entitlement on a claim under section 80 of that Act.

47(9)   Subsections (6) to (8) above shall be deemed to have come into force on 4th December 1996.

47(10)   [Amends VATA 1994, s. 77(1) and (4).]

47(11)   In this section–

    "the Commissioners" means the Commissioners of Customs and Excise; and

    "legal proceedings" means any proceedings before a court or tribunal.

47(12)   Without prejudice to the generality of paragraph 1(2) of Schedule 13 to the Value Added Tax Act 1994 (transitional provisions), the references in this section, and in subsection (4) of section 80 of that Act (as inserted by this section), to a claim under that section include references to a claim first made under section 24 of the Finance Act 1989 (which was re-enacted in section 80).

48   Set-off of credits and debits

48(1)   [Inserts VATA 1994, s. 81(3A).]

48(2)   Subsection (1) above shall be deemed to have come into force on 18th July 1996 as a provision applying for determining the amount of any payment or repayment by the Commissioners on or after that date, including a payment or repayment in respect of a liability arising before that date.

49   Transitional provision for set-offs etc.

49(1)   Where–

(a)   at any time before 4th December 1996, any person (**"the taxpayer"**) became liable to pay any sum (**"the relevant sum"**) to the Commissioners by way of VAT, penalty, interest or surcharge,

(b)   at any time on or after 18th July 1996 and before 4th December 1996 an amount was set against the whole or any part of the relevant sum,

(c)   the amount set against that sum was an amount which is treated under section 47 above as not having been due from the Commissioners at the time when it was set against that sum, and

(d)   as a consequence, the taxpayer's liability to pay the whole or a part of the relevant sum falls to be treated as not having been discharged in accordance with section 81(3) of the 1994 Act,

the Commissioners may, to the best of their judgement, assess the amount of the continuing liability of the taxpayer and notify it to him.

49(2)   In subsection (1) above the reference to the **continuing liability** of the taxpayer is a reference to so much of the liability to pay the relevant sum as–

(a)   would have been discharged if the amount mentioned in subsection (1)(b) above had been required to be set against the relevant sum in accordance with section 81(3) of the 1994 Act, but

(b)   falls, by virtue of section 47 above, to be treated as not having been discharged in accordance with section 81(3) of that Act.

49(3)   *The taxpayer's only liabilities under the 1994 Act in respect of his failure, on or after the* time mentioned in subsection (1)(b) above, to pay an amount assessable under this section shall be–

(a)   his liability to be assessed for that amount under this section; and

(b)   liabilities arising under the following provisions of this section.

49(4)   Subsections (2) to (8) of section 78A of the 1994 Act apply in the case of an assessment under subsection (1) above as they apply in the case of an assessment under section 78A(1) of that Act.

49(5)   The 1994 Act shall have effect as if the matters specified in section 83 of that Act (matters subject to appeal) included an assessment under this section and the amount of such an assessment.

49(6)   Nothing contained in–

(a)   any regulations under section 25(1) of, or paragraph 2 of Schedule 11 to, the 1994 Act relating to the correction of errors or the making of adjustments, or

(b)   any requirement imposed under any such regulations,

shall be taken, in relation to any time on or after 18th July 1996, to have conferred on any person any entitlement, otherwise than in accordance with section 81(3) of that Act, to set any amount, as an amount due from the Commissioners, against any sum which that person was liable to pay to the Commissioners by way of VAT, penalty, interest or surcharge.

49(7)   In this section–

    "the 1994 Act" means the Value Added Tax Act 1994; and

    "the Commissioners" means the Commissioners of Customs and Excise.

49(8)   This section shall be deemed to have come into force on 4th December 1996.

49(9)   Where at any time on or after 4th December 1996 and before the day on which this Act is passed any assessment corresponding to an assessment under this section was made under a resolution of the House of Commons having effect in accordance with the provisions of the Provisional Collection of Taxes Act 1968, this section has effect, on and after the day on which this Act is passed, as if that assessment were an assessment under this section and as if any appeal brought under that resolution had been brought under this section.

ENFORCEMENT OF PAYMENT

51   Enforcement by distress

51(1)   The Commissioners may by regulations make provision–

(a)   for authorising distress to be levied on the goods and chattels of any person refusing or neglecting to pay–

    (i) any amount of relevant tax due from him, or

    (ii) any amount recoverable as if it were relevant tax due from him;

(b)   for the disposal of any goods or chattels on which distress is levied in pursuance of the regulations; and

(c)   for the imposition and recovery of costs, charges, expenses and fees in connection with anything done under the regulations.

51(2)   The provision that may be contained in regulations under this section shall include, in particular–

(a)   provision for the levying of distress, by any person authorised to do so under the regulations, on goods or chattels located at any place whatever (including on a public highway); and

(b)   provision authorising distress to be levied at any such time of the day or night, and on any such day of the week, as may be specified or described in the regulations.

51(3)   Regulations under this section may–

(a)   make different provision for different cases, and

(b)   contain any such incidental, supplemental, consequential or transitional provision as the Commissioners think fit;

and the transitional provision that may be contained in regulations under this section shall include transitional provision in connection with the coming into force of the repeal by this Act of any other power by regulations to make provision for or in connection with the levying of distress.

51(4)   The power to make regulations under this section shall be exercisable by statutory instrument subject to annulment in pursuance of a resolution of the House of Commons.

51(5)   The following are **relevant taxes** for the purposes of this section, that is to say–

(a)   [not relevant to VAT];

(b)   value added tax;

(c)   [not relevant to VAT];

(d)   [not relevant to VAT];

(e)   [not relevant to VAT].

51(6)   In this section **"the Commissioners"** means the Commissioners of Customs and Excise.

51(7)   Regulations made under this section shall not have effect in Scotland.

Statutory instruments – Distress for Customs and Excise Duties and Other Indirect Taxes Regulations 1997 (SI 1997/1431).

52　Enforcement by diligence

52(1)　Where any amount of relevant tax or any amount recoverable as if it were relevant tax is due and has not been paid, the sheriff, on an application by the Commissioners accompanied by a certificate by them–

(a)　stating that none of the persons specified in the application has paid the amount due from him;

(b)　stating that payment of the amount due from each such person has been demanded from him; and

(c)　specifying the amount due from and unpaid by each such person,

shall grant a summary warrant in a form prescribed by Act of Sederunt authorising the recovery, by any of the diligences mentioned in subsection (2) below, of the amount remaining due and unpaid.

52(2)　The **diligences** referred to in subsection (1) above are–

(a)　a poinding and sale in accordance with Schedule 5 to the Debtors (Scotland) Act 1987;

(b)　an earnings arrestment;

(c)　an arrestment and action of furthcoming or sale.

52(3)　Subject to subsection (4) below and without prejudice to paragraphs 25 to 34 of Schedule 5 to the Debtors (Scotland) Act 1987 (expenses of poinding and sale) the sheriff officer's fees, together with the outlays necessarily incurred by him, in connection with the execution of a summary warrant shall be chargeable against the debtor.

52(4)　No fees shall be chargeable by the sheriff officer against the debtor for collecting, and accounting to the Commissioners for, sums paid to him by the debtor in respect of the amount owing.

52(5)　The following are **relevant taxes** for the purposes of this section, that is to say–

(a)　[not relevant to VAT];

(b)　value added tax;

(c)　[not relevant to VAT];

(d)　[not relevant to VAT];

(e)　[not relevant to VAT].

52(6)　In this section **"the Commissioners"** means the Commissioners of Customs and Excise.

52(7)　This section shall come into force on such day as the Commissioners of Customs and Excise may by order made by statutory instrument appoint, and different days may be appointed under this subsection for different purposes.

52(8)　This section extends only to Scotland.

Statutory instruments – Finance Act 1997, sections 52 and 53, (Appointed Day) Order 1997 (SI 1997/1432) (C 54): the appointed day is 1 July 1997.

53　Amendments consequential on sections 51 and 52

53(1)　[Inserts CEMA 1979, s. 117(4A).]

53(2)　[Not relevant to VAT.]

53(3)　[Not relevant to VAT.]

53(4)　[Not relevant to VAT.]

53(5)　[Not relevant to VAT.]

53(6)　[Inserts VATA 1994, s. 48(7A).]

53(7)　[Amends VATA 1994, s. 68(1)(a).]

53(8)　[Not relevant to VAT.]

53(9)　This section shall come into force on such day as the Commissioners of Customs and Excise may by order made by statutory instrument appoint, and different days may be appointed under this subsection for different purposes.

Statutory instruments – Finance Act 1997, sections 52 and 53, (Appointed Day) Order 1997 (SI 1997/1432) (C 54): the appointed day is 1 July 1997.

PART VIII – MISCELLANEOUS AND SUPPLEMENTAL

OBTAINING INFORMATION

110   Obtaining information from social security authorities

110(1)   This section applies to–

(a)   any information held by the Secretary of State or the Department of Health and Social Services for Northern Ireland for the purposes of any of his or its functions relating to social security; and

(b)   any information held by a person in connection with the provision by him to the Secretary of State or that Department of any services which that person is providing for purposes connected with any of those functions.

110(2)   Subject to the following provisions of this section, the person holding any information to which this section applies shall be entitled to supply it to–

(a)   the Commissioners of Customs and Excise or any person by whom services are being provided to those Commissioners for purposes connected with any of their functions; or

(b)   the Commissioners of Inland Revenue or any person by whom services are being provided to those Commissioners for purposes connected with any of their functions.

110(3)   Information shall not be supplied to any person under this section except for one or more of the following uses–

(a)   use in the prevention, detection, investigation or prosecution of criminal offences which it is a function of the Commissioners of Customs and Excise, or of the Commissioners of Inland Revenue, to prevent, detect, investigate or prosecute;

(b)   use in the prevention, detection or investigation of conduct in respect of which penalties which are not criminal penalties are provided for by or under any enactment;

(c)   use in connection with the assessment or determination of penalties which are not criminal penalties;

(d)   use in checking the accuracy of information relating to, or provided for purposes connected with, any matter under the care and management of the Commissioners of Customs and Excise or the Commissioners of Inland Revenue;

(e)   use (where appropriate) for amending or supplementing any such information; and

(f)   use in connection with any legal or other proceedings relating to anything mentioned in paragraphs (a) to (e) above.

110(4)   An enactment authorising the disclosure of information by a person mentioned in subsection (2)(a) or (b) above shall not authorise the disclosure by such a person of information supplied to him under this section except to the extent that the disclosure is also authorised by a general or specific permission granted by the Secretary of State or by the Department of Health and Social Services for Northern Ireland.

110(5)   In this section references to **functions relating to social security** include references to–

(a)   functions in relation to social security contributions, social security benefits (whether contributory or not) or national insurance numbers; and

(b)   functions under the Jobseekers Act 1995 or the Jobseekers (Northern Ireland) Order 1995.

110(6)   In this section **"conduct"** includes acts, omissions and statements.

110(7)   This section shall come into force on such day as the Treasury may by order made by statutory instrument appoint, and different days may be appointed under this subsection for different purposes.

REPORT TO PARLIAMENT

111   Report on VAT on energy saving materials

111   Within twelve months of this Act receiving Royal Assent the Treasury shall report to Parliament on the consequences to the Exchequer of reducing VAT on energy saving materials.

112   Interpretation

112   In this Act **"the Taxes Act 1988"** means the Income and Corporation Taxes Act 1988.

113   Repeals

113(1)   The enactments mentioned in Schedule 18 to this Act (which include spent provisions) are hereby repealed to the extent specified in the third column of that Schedule.

113(2)   The repeals specified in that Schedule have effect subject to the commencement provisions and savings contained or referred to in the notes set out in that Schedule.

114   Short title

114   This Act may be cited as the Finance Act 1997.

SCHEDULES

SCHEDULE 2 – GAMING DUTY: CONSEQUENTIAL AND INCIDENTAL AMENDMENTS

Section 13

Part I – Amendments of the Customs and Excise Management Act 1979

INTRODUCTORY

1   The Customs and Excise Management Act 1979 shall be amended in accordance with the provisions of this Part of this Schedule.

MEANING OF "REVENUE TRADE PROVISIONS" AND "REVENUE TRADER"

2(1)   This paragraph amends section 1(1) (interpretation).

2(2)   [Amends CEMA 1979, s. 1(1).]

2(3)   [Amends CEMA 1979, s. 1(1).]

2(4)   [Amends CEMA 1979, s. 1(1).]

3-7   [Not relevant to VAT.]

SCHEDULE 18 – REPEALS

Section 110

Part IV – VALUE ADDED TAX

(1) AGGREGATION OF BUSINESSES

Chapter	Short title	Extent of repeal
1994 c. 23.	The Value Added Tax Act 1994.	In Schedule 1, in paragraph 2– (a) in sub-paragraph (2)(b), the words from "which should properly" to "described in the direction"; (b) paragraph (d) of sub-paragraph (2) and the word "and" immediately preceding it; and (c) in sub-paragraph (4), the word "properly".

These repeals have effect in relation to the making of directions on or after the day on which this Act is passed.

(2) THE OPTIONS TO TAX BUILDINGS AND LAND

Chapter	Short title	Extent of repeal
1994 c. 23.	The Value Added Tax Act 1994.	In Schedule 10, paragraphs 2(3A) and 3(8A).

These repeals have effect in accordance with section 37(1) of this Act.

(3) BAD DEBT RELIEF

Chapter	Short title	Extent of repeal
1994 c. 23.	The Value Added Tax Act 1994.	In section 36(4), paragraph (b) and the word "and" immediately preceding it. In Schedule 13, paragraph 9(1).

These repeals have effect in accordance with section 39 of this Act.

Part V – INDIRECT TAXES

(1) INTEREST PAYMENTS

Chapter	Short title	Extent of repeal
1996 c. 8.	The Finance Act 1996.	In section 197(2), the word "and" at the end of paragraph (c).

(2) DISTRESS AND DILIGENCE

Chapter	Short title	Extent of repeal
1994 c. 23.	The Value Added Tax Act 1994.	In Schedule 11, paragraph 5(4) to (10).

These repeals come into force on such day as the Commissioners of Customs and Excise may by order made by statutory instrument appoint, and different days may be appointed for different purposes.

Statutory instruments – Finance Act 1997 (Repeal of Distress and Diligence enactments) (Appointed Day) Order 1997 (SI 1997/1433) (C 55): the appointed day for Pt. V(2) is 1 July 1997.

FINANCE (NO. 2) ACT 1997

(1997 Chapter 58)

[*31st July 1997*]

PART II – VALUE ADDED TAX AND EXCISE DUTIES

VALUE ADDED TAX

6   Fuel and power for domestic or charity use

6(1) [Amends VATA 1994, s. 2(1A).]

6(2) This section applies in relation to any supply made on or after 1st September 1997 and any acquisition or importation taking place on or after that date.

PART IV – MISCELLANEOUS AND SUPPLEMENTAL

PROVISIONAL COLLECTION OF TAXES

50   Statutory effect of resolutions etc.

50(1) [Inserts PCTA 1968, s. 1(3)(aa).]

50(2) [Not relevant to VAT.]

50(3) Subsection (1) above applies in relation to resolutions passed after the day on which this Act is passed.

FINANCE ACT 1998

1998 Chapter 36

[*31st July 1998*]

ARRANGEMENT OF SECTIONS

PART II – VALUE ADDED TAX

PART VI – MISCELLANEOUS AND SUPPLEMENTAL

SUPPLEMENTAL

SCHEDULES

PART II – VALUE ADDED TAX

21   Deemed supplies

21(1)   Paragraph 5 of Schedule 4 to the Value Added Tax Act 1994 (disposal of business assets) shall be amended as follows.

21(2)   [Amends VATA 1994, Sch. 4, para. 5(2)(a).]

21(3)   [Inserts VATA 1994, Sch. 4, para. 5(2A).]

21(4)   [Amends VATA 1994, Sch. 4, para. 5(5).]

21(5)   [Inserts VATA 1994, Sch. 4, para. 5(5A).]

21(6)   The preceding provisions of this section apply to any case where the time when the goods are transferred or disposed of or, as the case may be, put to use, used or made available for use is on or after 17th March 1998.

22   Changes of place of supply: transitional

22(1)   [Inserts VATA 1994, s. 97A.]

22(2)   [Inserts VATA 1994, s. 6(14A).]

22(3)   This section shall be deemed to have come into force on 17th March 1998.

23   Bad debt relief

23(1)   [Amends VATA 1994, s. 36(1)(a).]

23(2)   [Amends VATA 1994, s. 36(3)(a) and 36(3)(b).]

23(3)   [Inserts VATA 1994, s. 36(3A).]

23(4)   [Amends VATA 1994, s. 36(5)(c) and 36(5)(e).]

23(5)   [Amends VATA 1994, s. 36(6)(b) and 36(6)(c).]

23(6)   [Amends VATA 1994, s. 36(7).]

23(7)   Subsections (1) to (3) above have effect in relation to claims made on or after the day on which this Act is passed.

24   Long leases in Scotland

24   [Amends para. (b) of definition of "major interest" in VATA 1994, s. 96(1).]

PART VI – MISCELLANEOUS AND SUPPLEMENTAL

SUPPLEMENTAL

164   Interpretation

164   In this Act "the Taxes Act 1988" means the Income and Corporation Taxes Act 1988.

165   Repeals

165(1)   The enactments mentioned in Schedule 27 to this Act (which include spent provisions) are hereby repealed to the extent specified in the third column of that Schedule.

165(2)   The repeals specified in that Schedule have effect subject to the commencement provisions and savings contained or referred to in the notes set out in that Schedule.

166   Short title

166   This Act may be cited as the Finance Act 1998.

SCHEDULES

SCHEDULE 27 – REPEALS

Part II – VALUE ADDED TAX

Chapter	Short title	Extent of repeal
1994 c. 23.	The Value Added Tax Act 1994.	In section 36(1)(a) the words "for a consideration in money".

This repeal has effect in accordance with section 23(7) of this Act.

HUMAN RIGHTS ACT 1998

(1998 Chapter 42)

[*9th November 1998*]

ARRANGEMENT OF SECTIONS

INTRODUCTION

1   The Convention Rights

1(1)   In this Act **"the Convention rights"** means the rights and fundamental freedoms set out in–

(a)   Articles 2 to 12 and 14 of the Convention,

(b)   Articles 1 to 3 of the First Protocol, and

(c)   Articles 1 and 2 of the Sixth Protocol,as read with Articles 16 to 18 of the Convention.

1(2)   Those Articles are to have effect for the purposes of this Act subject to any designated derogation or reservation (as to which see sections 14 and 15).

1(3)   The Articles are set out in Schedule 1.

1(4)   The Secretary of State may by order make such amendments to this Act as he considers appropriate to reflect the effect, in relation to the United Kingdom, of a protocol.

1(5)   In subsection (4) **"protocol"** means a protocol to the Convention–

(a)   which the United Kingdom has ratified; or

(b)   which the United Kingdom has signed with a view to ratification.

1(6)   No amendment may be made by an order under subsection (4) so as to come into force before the protocol concerned is in force in relation to the United Kingdom.

2   Interpretation of Convention rights

2(1)   A court or tribunal determining a question which has arisen in connection with a Convention right must take into account any–

(a)   judgment, decision, declaration or advisory opinion of the European Court of Human Rights,

(b)   opinion of the Commission given in a report adopted under Article 31 of the Convention,

(c)   decision of the Commission in connection with Article 26 or 27(2) of the Convention, or

(d)   decision of the Committee of Ministers taken under Article 46 of the Convention,

whenever made or given, so far as, in the opinion of the court or tribunal, it is relevant to the proceedings in which that question has arisen.

2(2)   Evidence of any judgement, decision, declaration or opinion of which account may have to be taken under this section is to be given in proceedings before any court or tribunal in such manner as may be provided by rules.

2(3)   In this section **"rules"** means rules of court or, in the case of proceedings before a tribunal, rules made for the purposes of this section–

(a)   by the Lord Chancellor or the Secretary of State, in relation to any proceedings outside Scotland;

(b)   by the Secretary of State, in relation to proceedings in Scotland; or

(c)   by a Northern Ireland department, in relation to proceedings before a tribunal in Northern Ireland–

        (i)   which deals with transferred matters; and

        (ii) for which no rules made under paragraph (a) are in force.

L

3 Interpretation of legislation

3(1) So far as it is possible to do so, primary le~~...~~
and given effect in a way which is compatible wi~~...~~

3(2) This section–

(a) applies to primary legislation and subordinate legi~~...~~

(b) does not affect the validity, continuing operation ~~...~~
primary legislation; and

(c) does not affect the validity, continuing operation or e~~...~~
subordinate legislation if (disregarding any possibility of ~~...~~
prevents removal of the incompatibility.

4 Declaration of incompatibility

4(1) Subsection (2) applies in any proceedings in which a court determines ~~...~~
primary legislation is compatible with a Convention right.

4(2) If the court is satisfied that the provision is incompatible with a Conventi~~...~~
make a declaration of that incompatibility.

4(3) Subsection (4) applies in any proceedings in which a court determines whether a
of subordinate legislation, made in the exercise of a power conferred by primary legisl~~...~~
compatible with a Convention right.

4(4) If the court is satisfied–

(a) that the provision is incompatible with a Convention right, and

(b) that (disregarding any possibility of revocation) the primary legislation concerned prevents
removal of the incompatibility,

it may make a declaration of that incompatibility.

4(5) In this section **"court"** means–

(a) the House of Lords;

(b) the Judicial Committee of the Privy Council;

(c) the Courts-Martial Appeal Court;

(d) in Scotland, the High Court of Justiciary sitting otherwise than as a trial court or the Court of
Session;

(e) in England and Wales or Northern Ireland, the High Court or the Court of Appeal.

4(6) A declaration under this section ("a declaration of incompatibility")–

(a) does not affect the validity, continuing operation or enforcement of the provision in respect
of which it is given; and

(b) is not binding on the parties to the proceedings in which it is made.

5 Right of Crown to intervene

5(1) Where a court is considering whether to make a declaration of incompatibility, the Crown is
entitled to notice in accordance with rules of court.

5(2) In any case to which subsection (1) applies–

(a) a Minister of the Crown (or a person nominated by him),

(b) a member of the Scottish Executive,

(c) a Northern Ireland Minister,

(d) a Northern Ireland department,

is entitled, on giving notice in accordance with rules of court, to be joined as a party to the
proceedings.

5(3) Notice under subsection (2) may be given at any time during the proceedings.

5(4) A person who has been made a party to criminal proceedings (other than in Scotland) as the
result of a notice under subsection (2) may, with leave, appeal to the House of Lords against any
declaration of incompatibility made in the proceedings.

5(5) In subsection (4)–

"criminal proceedings" includes all proceedings before the Courts-Martial Appeal Court;
and

...ng the declaration of incompatibility or by the

"leave" means leave granted by the House of Lords.

AUTHORITIES

...es

...thority to act in a way which is incompatible with a Convention

not apply to an act if—

6 Acts of ...ne or more provisions of primary legislation, the authority could not have

6(1) It j...tly; or

righ... of one or more provisions of, or made under, primary legislation which cannot be given effect in a way which is compatible with the Convention rights, the authority ... acting so as to give effect to or enforce those provisions.

In this section **"public authority"** includes—

(a) a court or tribunal, and

(b) any person certain of whose functions are functions of a public nature, but does not include either House of Parliament or a person exercising functions in connection with proceedings in Parliament.

6(4) In subsection (3) **"Parliament"** does not include the House of Lords in its judicial capacity.

6(5) In relation to a particular act, a person is not a public authority by virtue only of subsection (3)(b) if the nature of the act is private.

6(6) **"An act"** includes a failure to act but does not include a failure to—

(a) introduce in, or lay before, Parliament a proposal for legislation; or

(b) make any primary legislation or remedial order.

7 Proceedings

7(1) A person who claims that a public authority has acted (or proposes to act) in a way which is made unlawful by section 6(1) may—

(a) bring proceedings against the authority under this Act in the appropriate court or tribunal, or

(b) rely on the Convention right or rights concerned in any legal proceedings,

but only if he is (or would be) a victim of the unlawful act.

7(2) In subsection (1)(a) **"appropriate court or tribunal"** means such court or tribunal as may be determined in accordance with rules; and proceedings against an authority include a counterclaim or similar proceeding.

7(3) If the proceedings are brought on an application for judicial review, the applicant is to be taken to have a sufficient interest in relation to the unlawful act only if he is, or would be, a victim of that act.

7(4) If the proceedings are made by way of a petition for judicial review in Scotland, the applicant shall be taken to have title and interest to sue in relation to the unlawful act only if he is, or would be, a victim of that act.

7(5) Proceedings under subsection (1)(a) must be brought before the end of—

(a) the period of one year beginning with the date on which the act complained of took place; or

(b) such longer period as the court or tribunal considers equitable having regard to all the circumstances,

but that is subject to any rule imposing a stricter time limit in relation to the procedure in question.

7(6) In subsection (l)(b) **"legal proceedings"** includes—

(a) proceedings brought by or at the instigation of a public authority; and

(b) an appeal against the decision of a court or tribunal.

7(7) For the purposes of this section, a person is a victim of an unlawful act only if he would be a victim for the purposes of Article 34 of the Convention if proceedings were brought in the European Court of Human Rights in respect of that act.

7(8) Nothing in this Act creates a criminal offence.

7(9) In this section **"rules"** means—

(a)   in relation to proceedings before a court or tribunal outside Scotland, rules made by the Lord Chancellor or the Secretary of State for the purposes of this section or rules of court,

(b)   in relation to proceedings before a court or tribunal in Scotland, rules made by the Secretary of State for those purposes,

(c)   in relation to proceedings before a tribunal in Northern Ireland–
      (i)   which deals with transferred matters; and
      (ii) for which no rules made under paragraph (a) are in force,

      rules made by a Northern Ireland department for those purposes,

and includes provision made by order under section I of the Courts and Legal Services Act 1990.

7(10)   In making rules, regard must be had for section 9.

7(11)   The Minister who has power to make rules in relation to a particular tribunal may, to the extent he considers it necessary to ensure that the tribunal can provide an appropriate remedy in relation to an act (or proposed act) of a public authority which is (or would be) unlawful as a result of section 6(l), by order add to–

(a)   the relief or remedies which the tribunal may grant; or

(b)   the grounds on which it may grant any of them.

7(12)   An order made under subsection (11) may contain such incidental, supplemental, consequential or transitional provision as the Minister making it considers appropriate.

7(13)   **"The Minister"** includes the Northern Ireland department concerned.

8   Judicial remedies

8(1)   In relation to any act (or proposed act) of a public authority which the court finds is (or would be) unlawful, it may grant such relief or remedy, or make such order, within its powers as it considers just and appropriate.

8(2)   But damages may be awarded only by a court which has power to award damages, or to order the payment of compensation, in civil proceedings.

8(3)   No award of damages is to be made unless, taking account of all the circumstances of the case, including–

(a)   any other relief or remedy granted, or order made, in relation to the act in question (by that or any other court), and

(b)   the consequences of any decision (of that or any other court) in respect of that act,

the court is satisfied that the award is necessary to afford just satisfaction to the person in whose favour it is made.

8(4)   In determining–

(a)   whether to award damages, or

(b)   the amount of an award,

the court must take into account the principles applied by the European Court of Human Rights in relation to the award of compensation under Article 41 of the Convention.

8(5)   A public authority against which damages are awarded is to be treated–

(a)   in Scotland, for the purposes of section 3 of the Law Reform (Miscellaneous Provisions) (Scotland) Act 1940 as if the award were made in an action of damages in which the authority has been found liable in respect of loss or damage to the person to whom the award is made;

(b)   for the purposes of the Civil Liability (Contribution) Act 1978 as liable in respect of damage suffered by the person to whom the award is made.

8(6)   In this section–
      "court" includes a tribunal;
      "damages" means damages for an unlawful act of a public authority; and
      "unlawful" means unlawful under section 6(l).

9   Judicial acts

9(1)   Proceedings under section 7(l)(a) in respect of a judicial act may be brought only–

(a)   by exercising a right of appeal;

(b)   on an application (in Scotland a petition) for judicial review; or

(c)   in such other forum as may be prescribed by rules.

9(2) That does not affect any rule of law which prevents a court from being the subject of judicial review.

9(3) In proceedings under this Act in respect of a judicial act done in good faith, damages may not be awarded otherwise than to compensate a person to the extent required by Article 5(5) of the Convention.

9(4) An award of damages permitted by subsection (3) is to be made against the Crown; but no award may be made unless the appropriate person, if not a party to the proceedings, is joined.

9(5) In this section–

> **"appropriate person"** means the Minister responsible for the court concerned, or a person or government department nominated by him;
> **"court"** includes a tribunal;
> **"judge"** includes a member of a tribunal, a justice of the peace and a clerk or other officer entitled to exercise the jurisdiction of a court;
> **"judicial act"** means a judicial act of a court and includes an act done on the instructions, or on behalf, of a judge; and
> **"rules"** has the same meaning as in section 7(9).

REMEDIAL ACTION

10   Power to take remedial action

10(1) This section applies if–

(a) a provision of legislation has been declared under section 4 to be incompatible with a Convention right and, if an appeal lies–

> (i) all persons who may appeal have stated in writing that they do not intend to do so;
> (ii) the time for bringing an appeal has expired and no appeal has been brought within that time; or
> (iii) an appeal brought within that time has been determined or abandoned; or

(b) it appears to a Minister of the Crown or Her Majesty in Council that, having regard to a finding of the European Court of Human Rights made after the coming into force of this section in proceedings against the United Kingdom, a provision of legislation is incompatible with an obligation of the United Kingdom arising from the Convention.

10(2) If a Minister of the Crown considers that there are compelling reasons for proceeding under this section, he may by order make such amendments to the legislation as he considers necessary to remove the incompatibility.

10(3) If, in the case of subordinate legislation, a Minister of the Crown considers–

(a) that it is necessary to amend the primary legislation under which the subordinate legislation in question was made, in order to enable the incompatibility to be removed, and

(b) that there are compelling reasons for proceeding under this section,

he may by order make such amendments to the primary legislation as he considers necessary.

10(4) This section also applies where the provision in question is in subordinate legislation and has been quashed, or declared invalid, by reason of incompatibility with a Convention right and the Minister proposes to proceed under paragraph 2(b) of Schedule 2.

10(5) If the legislation is an Order in Council, the power conferred by subsection (2) or (3) is exercisable by Her Majesty in Council.

10(6) In this section **"legislation"** does not include a Measure of the Church Assembly or of the General Synod of the Church of England.

10(7) Schedule 2 makes further provision about remedial orders.

OTHER RIGHTS AND PROCEEDINGS

11   Safeguard for existing human rights

11 A person's reliance on a Convention right does not restrict–

(a) any other right or freedom conferred on him by or under any law having effect in any part of the United Kingdom; or

(b) his right to make any claim or bring any proceedings which he could make or bring apart from sections 7 to 9.

12   Freedom of expression

12(1)   This section applies if a court is considering whether to grant any relief which, if granted, might affect the exercise of the Convention right to freedom of expression.

12(2)   If the person against whom the application for relief is made (**"the respondent"**) is neither present nor represented, no such relief is to be granted unless the court is satisfied–

(a)   that the applicant has taken all practicable steps to notify the respondent; or
(b)   that there are compelling reasons why the respondent should not be notified.

12(3)   No such relief is to be granted so as to restrain publication before trial unless the court is satisfied that the applicant is likely to establish that publication should not be allowed.

12(4)   The court must have particular regard to the importance of the Convention right to freedom of expression and, where the proceedings relate to material which the respondent claims, or which appears to the court, to be journalistic, literary or artistic material (or to conduct connected with such material), to–

(a)   the extent to which–

    (i) the material has, or is about to, become available to the public; or
    (ii) it is, or would be, in the public interest for the material to be published;
(b)   any relevant privacy code.

12(5)   In this section–

"court" includes a tribunal; and
"relief" includes any remedy or order (other than in criminal proceedings).

13   Freedom of thought, conscience and religion

13(1)   If a court's determination of any question arising under this Act might affect the exercise by a religious organisation (itself or its members collectively) of the Convention right to freedom of thought, conscience and religion, it must have particular regard to the importance of that right.

13(2)   In this section **"court"** includes a tribunal.

DEROGATIONS AND RESERVATIONS

14   Derogations

14(1)   In this act **"designated derogation"** means–

(a)   the United Kingdom's derogation from Article 5(3) of the Convention; and
(b)   any derogation by the United Kingdom from an Article of the Convention, or of any protocol to the Convention, which is designated for the purposes of this Act in an order made by the Secretary of State.

14(2)   The derogation referred to in subsection (1)(a) is set out in Part I of Schedule 3.

14(3)   If a designated derogation is amended or replaced it ceases to be a designated derogation.

14(4)   But subsection (3) does not prevent the Secretary of State from exercising his power under subsection (1)(b) to make a fresh designation order in respect of the Article concerned.

14(5)   The Secretary of State must by order make such amendments to Schedule 3 as he considers appropriate to reflect–

(a)   any designation order; or
(b)   the effect of subsection (3).

14(6)   A designation order may be made in anticipation of the making by the United Kingdom of a proposed derogation.

15   Reservations

15(1)   In this Act **"designated reservation"** means–

(a)   the United Kingdom's reservation to Article 2 of the First Protocol to the Convention; and
(b)   any other reservation by the United Kingdom to an Article of the Convention, or of any protocol to the Convention, which is designated for the purposes of this Act in an order made by the Secretary of State.

15(2)   The text of the reservation referred to in subsection (1)(a) is set out in Part II of Schedule 3.

15(3)   If a designated reservation is withdrawn wholly or in part it ceases to be a designated reservation.

15(4) But subsection (3) does not prevent the Secretary of State from exercising his power under subsection (1)(b) to make a fresh designation order in respect of the Article concerned.

15(5) The Secretary of State must by order make such amendments to this Act as he considers appropriate to reflect–

(a)   any designation order; or
(b)   the effect of subsection (3).

16   Period for which designated derogations have effect

16(1) If it has not already been withdrawn by the United Kingdom, a designated derogation ceases to have effect for the purposes of this Act–

(a)   in the case of the derogation referred to in section 14(1)(a), at the end of the period of five years beginning with the date on which section 1(2) came into force;
(b)   in the case of any other derogation, at the end of the period of five years beginning with the date on which the order designating it was made.

16(2) At any time before the period–

(a)   fixed by subsection (1)(a) or (b), or
(b)   extended by an order under this subsection,

comes to an end, the Secretary of State may by order extend it by a further period of five years.

16(3) An order under section 14(1)(b) ceases to have effect at the end of the period for consideration, unless a resolution has been passed by each House approving the order.

16(4) Subsection (3) does not affect–

(a)   anything done in reliance on the order; or
(b)   the power to make a fresh order under section 14(1)(b).

16(5) In subsection (3) **"period for consideration"** means the period of forty days beginning with the day on which the order was made.

16(6) In calculating the period for consideration, no account is to be taken of any time during which–

(a)   Parliament is dissolved or prorogued; or
(b)   both Houses are adjourned for more than four days.

16(7) If a designated derogation is withdrawn by the United Kingdom, the Secretary of State must by order make such amendments to this Act as he considers are required to reflect that withdrawal.

17   Periodic review of designated reservations

17(1) The appropriate Minister must review the designated reservation referred to in section 15(1)(a)–

(a)   before the end of the period of five years beginning with the date on which section 1(2) came into force; and
(b)   if that designation is still in force, before the end of the period of five years beginning with the date on which the last report relating to it was laid under subsection (3).

17(2) The appropriate Minister must review each of the other designated reservations (if any)–

(a)   before the end of the period of five years beginning with the date on which the order designating the reservation first came into force; and
(b)   if the designation is still in force, before the end of the period of five years beginning with the date on which the last report relating to it was laid under subsection (3).

17(3) The Minister conducting a review under this section must prepare a report on the result of the review and lay a copy of it before each House of Parliament.

JUDGES OF THE EUROPEAN COURT OF HUMAN RIGHTS

18   Appointment to European Court of Human Rights

18(1) In this section **"judicial office"** means the office of–

(a)   Lord Justice of Appeal, Justice of the High Court or Circuit judge, in England and Wales;
(b)   judge of the Court of Session or sheriff, in Scotland;
(c)   Lord Justice of Appeal, judge of the High Court or county court judge, in Northern Ireland.

18(2) The holder of a judicial office may become a judge of the European Court of Human Rights ("the Court") without being required to relinquish his office.

18(3) But he is not required to perform the duties of his judicial office while he is a judge of the Court.

18(4) In respect of any period during which he is a judge of the Court–

(a)   a Lord Justice of Appeal or Justice of the High Court is not to count as a judge of the relevant court for the purposes of section 2(1)or 4(1) of the Supreme Court Act 1981 (maximum number of judges) nor as a judge of the Supreme Court for the purposes of section 12(1) to (6) of that Act (salaries etc.);

(b)   a judge of the Court of Session is not to count as a judge of that court for the purposes of section 1(l) of the Court of Session Act 1988 (maximum number of judges) or of section 9(1)(c) of the Administration of Justice Act 1973 ("the 1973 Act") (salaries etc.);

(c)   a Lord Justice of Appeal or judge of the High Court in Northern Ireland is not to count as a judge of the relevant court for the purposes of section 2(1) or 3(1) of the Judicature (Northern Ireland) Act 1978 (maximum number of judges) nor as a judge of the Supreme Court of Northern Ireland for the purposes of section 9(1)(d) of the 1973 Act (salaries etc.);

(d)   a Circuit judge is not to count as such for the purposes of section 18 of the Courts Act 1971 (salaries etc.);

(e)   a sheriff is not to count as such for the purposes of section 14 of the Sheriff Courts (Scotland) Act 1907 (salaries etc.);

(f)   a county court judge of Northern Ireland is not to count as such for the purposes of section 106 of the County Courts Act (Northern Ireland) 1959 (salaries etc.).

18(5) If a sheriff principal is appointed a judge of the Court, section 11(1) of the Sheriff Courts (Scotland) Act 1971 (temporary appointment of sheriff principal) applies, while he holds that appointment, as if his office is vacant.

18(6) Schedule 4 makes provision about judicial pensions in relation to the holder of a judicial office who serves as a judge of the Court.

18(7) The Lord Chancellor or the Secretary of State may by order make such transitional provision (including, in particular, provision for a temporary increase in the maximum number of judges) as he considers appropriate in relation to any holder of a judicial office who has completed his service as a judge of the Court.

PARLIAMENTARY PROCEDURE

19   Statements of compatibility

19(1) A Minister of the Crown in charge of a Bill in either House of Parliament must, before Second Reading of the Bill–

(a)   make a statement to the effect that in his view the provisions of the Bill are compatible with the Convention rights ("a statement of compatibility"); or

(b)   make a statement to the effect that although he is unable to make a statement of compatibility the government nevertheless wishes the House to proceed with the Bill.

19(2) The statement must be in writing and be published in such manner as the Minister making it considers appropriate.

SUPPLEMENTAL

20   Orders etc. under this Act

20(1) Any power of a Minister of the Crown to make an order under this Act is exercisable by statutory instrument.

20(2) The power of the Lord Chancellor or the Secretary of State to make rules (other than rules of court) under section 2(3) or 7(9) is exercisable by statutory instrument.

20(3) Any statutory instrument made under section 14, 15 or 16(7) must be laid before Parliament.

20(4) No order may be made by the Lord Chancellor or the Secretary of State under section 1(4), 7(11) or 16(2) unless a draft of the order has been laid before, and approved by, each House of Parliament.

20(5)   Any statutory instrument made under section 18(7) or Schedule 4, or to which subsection (2) applies, shall be subject to annulment in pursuance of a resolution of either House of Parliament.

20(6)   The power of a Northern Ireland department to make–

(a)   rules under section 2(3)(c) or 7(9)(c), or

(b)   an order under section 7(11),

is exercisable by statutory rule for the purposes of the Statutory Rules (Northern Ireland) Order 1979.

20(7)   Any rules made under section 2(3)(c) or 7(9)(c) shall be subject to negative resolution; and section 41(6) of the Interpretation Act (Northern Ireland) 1954 (meaning of "subject to negative resolution") shall apply as if the power to make the rules were conferred by an Act of the Northern Ireland Assembly.

20(8)   No order may be made by a Northern Ireland department under section 7(11) unless a draft of the order has been laid before, and approved by, the Northern Ireland Assembly.

21   Interpretation, etc.

21(1)   In this Act–

"**amend**" includes repeal and apply (with or without modifications);

"**the appropriate Minister**" means the Minister of the Crown having charge of the appropriate authorised government department (within the meaning of the Crown Proceedings Act 1947);

"**the Commission**" means the European Commission of Human Rights;

"**the Convention**" means the Convention for the Protection of Human Rights and Fundamental Freedoms, agreed by the Council of Europe at Rome on 4th November 1950 as it has effect for the time being in relation to the United Kingdom;

"**declaration of incompatibility**" means a declaration under section 4;

"**Minister of the Crown**" has the same meaning as in the Ministers of the Crown Act 1975;

"**Northern Ireland Minister**" includes the First Minister and the deputy First Minister in Northern Ireland;

"**primary legislation**" means any–

(a)   public general Act;

(b)   local and personal Act;

(c)   private Act;

(d)   Measure of the Church Assembly;

(e)   Measure of the General Synod of the Church of England;

(f)   Order in Council–

  (i)   made in exercise of Her Majesty's Royal Prerogative;

  (ii)   made under section 38(1)(a) of the Northern Ireland Constitution Act 1973 or the corresponding provision of the Northern Ireland Act 1998; or

  (iii)   amending an Act of a kind mentioned in paragraph (a), (b) or (c);

    and includes an order or other instrument made under primary legislation (otherwise than by the National Assembly for Wales, a member of the Scottish Executive, a Northern Ireland Minister or a Northern Ireland department) to the extent to which it operates to bring one or more provisions of that legislation into force or amends any primary legislation;

"**the First Protocol**" means the protocol to the Convention agreed at Paris on 20th March 1952;

"**the Sixth Protocol**" means the protocol to the Convention agreed at Strasbourg on 28th April 1983;

"**the Eleventh Protocol**" means the protocol to the Convention (restructuring the control machinery established by the Convention) agreed at Strasbourg on 11th May 1994;

"**remedial order**" means an order under section 10;

"*subordinate legislation*" means any–

(a)   Order in Council other than one–

  (i)   made in exercise of Her Majesty's Royal Prerogative;

  (ii)   made under section 38(1)(a) of the Northern Ireland Constitution Act 1973 or the corresponding provision of the Northern Ireland Act 1998; or

  (iii)   amending an Act of a kind mentioned in the definition of primary legislation;

(b)   Act of the Scottish Parliament;

(c)   Act of the Parliament of Northern Ireland;

(d)   Measure of the Assembly established under section 1 of the Northern Ireland Assembly Act 1973;

(e)   Act of the Northern Ireland Assembly;

(f)   order, rules, regulations, scheme, warrant, byelaw or other instrument made under primary legislation (except to the extent to which it operates to bring one or more provisions of that legislation into force or amends any primary legislation);

(g)   order, rules, regulations, scheme, warrant, byelaw or other instrument made under legislation mentioned in paragraph (b), (c), (d) or (e) or made under an Order in Council applying only to Northern Ireland;

(h)   order, rules, regulations, scheme, warrant, byelaw or other instrument made by a member of the Scottish Executive, a Northern Ireland Minister or a Northern Ireland department in exercise of prerogative or other executive functions of Her Majesty which are exercisable by such a person on behalf of Her Majesty;

"transferred matters" has the same meaning as in the Northern Ireland Act 1998; and

"tribunal" means any tribunal in which legal proceedings may be brought.

21(2) The references in paragraphs (b) and (c) of section 2(1) to Articles are to Articles of the Convention as they had effect immediately before the coming into force of the Eleventh Protocol.

21(3) The reference in paragraph (d) of section 2(1) to Article 46 includes a reference to Articles 32 and 54 of the Convention as they had effect immediately before the coming into force of the Eleventh Protocol.

21(4) The references in section 2(1) to a report or decision of the Commission or a decision of the Committee of Ministers include references to a report or decision made as provided by paragraphs 3, 4 and 6 of Article 5 of the Eleventh Protocol (transitional provisions).

21(5) Any liability under the Army Act 1955, the Air Force Act 1955 or the Naval Discipline Act 1957 to suffer death for an offence is replaced by a liability to imprisonment for life or any less punishment authorised by those Acts; and those Acts shall accordingly have effect with the necessary modifications.

22 Short title, commencement, application and extent

22(1) This Act may be cited as the Human Rights Act 1998.

22(2) Sections 18, 20 and 21(5) and this section come into force on the passing of this Act.

22(3) The other provisions of this Act come into force on such day as the Secretary of State may by order appoint; and different days may be appointed for different purposes.

22(4) Paragraph (b) of subsection (1) of section 7 applies to proceedings brought by or at the instigation of a public authority whenever the act in question took place; but otherwise that subsection does not apply to an act taking place before the coming into force of that section.

22(5) This Act binds the Crown.

22(6) This Act extends to Northern Ireland.

22(7) Section 21(5), so far as it relates to any provision contained in the Army Act 1955, the Air Force Act 1955 or the Naval Discipline Act 1957, extends to any place to which that provision extends.

SCHEDULES

SCHEDULE 1 – THE ARTICLES

Section 1(3)

Part I – The Convention

RIGHTS AND FREEDOMS

ARTICLE 2

RIGHT TO LIFE

1 Everyone's right to life shall be protected by law. No one shall be deprived of his life intentionally save in the execution of a sentence of a court following his conviction of a crime for which this penalty is provided by law.

2 Deprivation of life shall not be regarded as inflicted in contravention of this Article when it results from the use of force which is no more than absolutely necessary:

(a)   in defence of any person from unlawful violence;

(b)   in order to effect a lawful arrest or to prevent the escape of a person lawfully detained;

(c)   in action lawfully taken for the purpose of quelling a riot or insurrection.

ARTICLE 3

PROHIBITION OF TORTURE

No one shall be subjected to torture or to inhuman or degrading treatment or punishment.

ARTICLE 4

PROHIBITION OF SLAVERY AND FORCED LABOUR

1 No one shall be held in slavery or servitude.

2 No one shall be required to perform forced or compulsory labour.

3 For the purpose of this Article the term **"forced or compulsory labour"** shall not include:

(a)   any work required to be done in the ordinary course of detention imposed according to the provisions of Article 5 of this Convention or during conditional release from such detention;

(b)   any service of a military character or, in case of conscientious objectors in countries where they are recognised, service exacted instead of compulsory military service;

(c)   any service exacted in case of an emergency or calamity threatening the life or well-being of the community;

(d)   any work or service which forms part of normal civic obligations.

ARTICLE 5

RIGHT TO LIBERTY AND SECURITY

1 Everyone has the right to liberty and security of person. No one shall be deprived of his liberty save in the following cases and in accordance with a procedure prescribed by law:

(a)   the lawful detention of a person after conviction by a competent court;

(b)   the lawful arrest or detention of a person for non-compliance with the lawful order of a court or in order to secure the fulfilment of any obligation prescribed by law;

(c)   the lawful arrest or detention of a person effected for the purpose of bringing him before the competent legal authority on reasonable suspicion of having committed an offence or when it is reasonably considered necessary to prevent his committing an offence or fleeing after having done so;

(d)   the detention of a minor by lawful order for the purpose of educational supervision or his lawful detention for the purpose of bringing him before the competent legal authority;

(e)   the lawful detention of persons for the prevention of the spreading of infectious diseases, of persons of unsound mind, alcoholics or drug addicts or vagrants;

(f)   the lawful arrest or detention of a person to prevent his effecting an unauthorised entry into the country or of a person against whom action is being taken with a view to deportation or extradition.

2   Everyone who is arrested shall be informed promptly, in a language which he understands, of the reasons for his arrest and of any charge against him.

3   Everyone arrested or detained in accordance with the provisions of paragraph 1(c) of this Article shall be brought promptly before a judge or other officer authorised by law to exercise judicial power and shall be entitled to trial within a reasonable time or to release pending trial. Release may be conditioned by guarantees to appear for trial.

4   Everyone who is deprived of his liberty by arrest or detention shall be entitled to take proceedings by which the lawfulness of his detention shall be decided speedily by a court and his release ordered if the detention is not lawful.

5   Everyone who has been the victim of arrest or detention in contravention of the provisions of this Article shall have an enforceable right to compensation.

ARTICLE 6

RIGHT TO A FAIR TRIAL

1   In the determination of his civil rights and obligations or of any criminal charge against him, everyone is entitled to a fair and public hearing within a reasonable time by an independent and impartial tribunal established by law. Judgement shall be pronounced publicly but the press and public may be excluded from all or part of the trial in the interest of morals, public order or national security in a democratic society, where the interests of juveniles or the protection of the private life of the parties so require, or to the extent strictly necessary in the opinion of the court in special circumstances where publicity would prejudice the interests of justice.

2   Everyone charged with a criminal offence shall be presumed innocent until proved guilty according to law.

3   Everyone charged with a criminal offence has the following minimum rights:

(a)   to be informed promptly, in a language which he understands and in detail, of the nature and cause of the accusation against him;

(b)   to have adequate time and facilities for the preparation of his defence;

(c)   to defend himself in person or through legal assistance of his own choosing or, if he has not sufficient means to pay for legal assistance, to be given it free when the interests of justice so require;

(d)   to examine or have examined witnesses against him and to obtain the attendance and examination of witnesses on his behalf under the same conditions as witnesses against him;

(e)   to have the free assistance of an interpreter if he cannot understand or speak the language used in court.

ARTICLE 7

NO PUNISHMENT WITHOUT LAW

1   No one shall be held guilty of any criminal offence on account of any act or omission which did not constitute a criminal offence under national or international law at the time when it was committed. Nor shall a heavier penalty be imposed than the one that was applicable at the time the criminal offence was committed.

2   This Article shall not prejudice the trial and punishment of any person for any act or omission which, at the time when it was committed, was criminal according to the general principles of law recognised by civilised nations.

ARTICLE 8

RIGHT TO RESPECT FOR PRIVATE AND FAMILY LIFE

1   Everyone has the right to respect for his private and family life, his home and his correspondence.

2   There shall be no interference by a public authority with the exercise of this right except such as is in accordance with the law and is necessary in a democratic society in the interests of national security, public safety or the economic well-being of the country, for the prevention of disorder or crime, for the protection of health or morals, or for the protection of the rights and freedoms of others.

ARTICLE 9

FREEDOM OF THOUGHT, CONSCIENCE AND RELIGION

1 Everyone has the right to freedom of thought, conscience and religion; this right includes freedom to change his religion or belief and freedom, either alone or in community with others and in public or private, to manifest his religion or belief, in worship, teaching, practice and observance.

2 Freedom to manifest one's religion or beliefs shall be subject only to such limitations as are prescribed by law and are necessary in a democratic society in the interests of public safety, for the protection of public order, health or morals, or for the protection of the rights and freedoms of others.

ARTICLE 10

FREEDOM OF EXPRESSION

1 Everyone has the right to freedom of expression. This right shall include freedom to hold opinions and to receive and impart information and ideas without interference by public authority and regardless of frontiers. This Article shall not prevent States from requiring the licensing of broadcasting, television or cinema enterprises.

2 The exercise of these freedoms, since it carries with it duties and responsibilities, may be subject to such formalities, conditions, restrictions or penalties as are prescribed by law and are necessary in a democratic society, in the interests of national security, territorial integrity or public safety, for the prevention of disorder or crime, for the protection of health or morals, for the protection of the reputation or rights of others, for preventing the disclosure of information received in confidence, or for maintaining the authority and impartiality of the judiciary.

ARTICLE 11

FREEDOM OF ASSEMBLY AND ASSOCIATION

1 Everyone has the right to freedom of peaceful assembly and to freedom of association with others, including the right to form and to join trade unions for the protection of his interests.

2 No restrictions shall be placed on the exercise of these rights other than such as are prescribed by law and are necessary in a democratic society in the interests of national security or public safety, for the prevention of disorder or crime, for the protection of health or morals or for the protection of the rights and freedoms of others. This Article shall not prevent the imposition of lawful restrictions on the exercise of these rights by members of the armed forces, of the police or of the administration of the State.

ARTICLE 12

RIGHT TO MARRY

Men and women of marriageable age have the right to marry and to found a family, according to the national laws governing the exercise of this right.

ARTICLE 14

PROHIBITION OF DISCRIMINATION

The enjoyment of the rights and freedoms set forth in this Convention shall be secured without discrimination on any ground such as sex, race, colour, language, religion, political or other opinion, national or social origin, association with a national minority, property, birth or other status.

ARTICLE 16

RESTRICTIONS ON POLITICAL ACTIVITY OF ALIENS

Nothing in Articles 10, 11 and 14 shall be regarded as preventing the High Contracting Parties from imposing restrictions on the political activity of aliens.

ARTICLE 17

PROHIBITION OF ABUSE OF RIGHTS

Nothing in this Convention may be interpreted as implying for any State, group or person any right to engage in any activity or perform any act aimed at the destruction of any of the rights and freedoms set forth herein or at their limitation to a greater extent than is provided for in the Convention.

ARTICLE 18

LIMITATION ON USE OF RESTRICTIONS RIGHTS

The restrictions permitted under this Convention to the said rights and freedoms shall not be applied for any purpose other than those for which they have been prescribed.

Part II – THE FIRST PROTOCOL

ARTICLE 1

PROTECTION OF PROPERTY

Every natural or legal person is entitled to the peaceful enjoyment of his possessions. No one shall be deprived of his possessions except in the public interest and subject to the conditions provided for by law and by the general principles of international law.

The preceding provisions shall not, however, in any way impair the right of a State to enforce such laws as it deems necessary to control the use of property in accordance with the general interest or to secure the payment of taxes or other contributions or penalties.

ARTICLE 2

RIGHT TO EDUCATION

No person shall be denied the right to education. In the exercise of any functions which it assumes in relation to education and to teaching, the State shall respect the right of parents to ensure such education and teaching in conformity with their own religious and philosophical convictions.

ARTICLE 3

RIGHT TO FREE ELECTIONS

The High Contracting Parties undertake to hold free elections at reasonable intervals by secret ballot, under conditions which will ensure the free expression of the opinion of the people in the choice of the legislature.

Part III – THE SIXTH PROTOCOL

ARTICLE 1

ABOLITION OF THE DEATH PENALTY

The death penalty shall be abolished. No one shall be condemned to such penalty or executed.

ARTICLE 2

DEATH PENALTY IN TIME OF WAR

A State may make provision in its law for the death penalty in respect of acts committed in time of war or of imminent threat of war; such penalty shall be applied only in the instances laid down in the law and in accordance with its provisions. The State shall communicate to the Secretary General of the Council of Europe the relevant provisions of that law.

SCHEDULE 2 – REMEDIAL ORDERS

Section 10

ORDERS

1(1) A remedial order may–

(a) contain such incidental, supplemental, consequential or transitional provision as the person making it considers appropriate;

(b) be made so as to have effect from a date earlier than that on which it is made;

(c) make provision for the delegation of specific functions;

(d) make different provision for different cases.

1(2) The power conferred by sub-paragraph (1)(a) includes–

(a) power to amend primary legislation (including primary legislation other than that which contains the incompatible provision); and

(b) power to amend or revoke subordinate legislation (including subordinate legislation other than that which contains the incompatible provision).

1(3) A remedial order may be made so as to have the same extent as the legislation which it affects.

1(4) No person is to be guilty of an offence solely as a result of the retrospective effect of a remedial order.

PROCEDURE

2 No remedial order may be made unless–

(a) a draft of the order has been approved by a resolution of each House of Parliament made after the end of the period of 60 days beginning with the day on which the draft was laid; or

(b) it is declared in the order that it appears to the person making it that, because of the urgency of the matter, it is necessary to make the order without a draft being so approved.

ORDERS LAID IN DRAFT

3(1) No draft may be laid under paragraph 2(a) unless–

(a) the person proposing to make the order has laid before Parliament a document which contains a draft of the proposed order and the required information; and

(b) the period of 60 days, beginning with the day on which the document required by this sub-paragraph was laid, has ended.

3(2) If representations have been made during that period, the draft laid under paragraph 2(a) must be accompanied by a statement containing–

(a) a summary of the representations; and

(b) if, as a result of the representations, the proposed order has been changed, details of the changes.

URGENT CASES

4(1) If a remedial order ("the original order") is made without being approved in draft, the person making it must lay it before Parliament, accompanied by the required information, after it is made.

4(2) If representations have been made during the period of 60 days beginning with the day on which the original order was made, the person making it must (after the end of that period) lay before Parliament a statement containing–

(a) a summary of the representations; and

(b) if, as a result of the representations, he considers it appropriate to make changes to the original order, details of the changes.

4(3) If sub-paragraph (2)(b) applies, the person making the statement must–

(a) *make a further remedial order replacing the original order*; and

(b) lay the replacement order before Parliament.

4(4) If, at the end of the period of 120 days beginning with the day on which the original order was made, a resolution has not been passed by each House approving the original or replacement order, the order ceases to have effect (but without that affecting anything previously done under either order or the power to make a fresh remedial order).

DEFINITIONS

5   In this Schedule–

"Representations" means representations about a remedial order (or proposed remedial order) made to the person making (or proposing to make) it and includes any relevant Parliamentary report or resolution; and

"Required information" means–

(a)   an explanation of the incompatibility which the order (or proposed order) seeks to remove, including particulars of the relevant declaration, finding or order; and

(b)   a statement of the reasons for proceeding under section 10 and for making an order in those terms.

CALCULATING PERIODS

6   In calculating any period for the purposes of this Schedule, no account is to be taken of any time during which–

(a)   Parliament is dissolved or prorogued; or

(b)   both Houses are adjourned for more than four days.

SCHEDULE 3 – DEROGATION AND RESERVATION

Sections 14 and 15

Part I – DEROGATION

THE 1988 NOTIFICATION

The United Kingdom Permanent Representative to the Council of Europe presents his compliments to the Secretary General of the Council, and has the honour to convey the following information in order to ensure compliance with the obligations of Her Majesty's Government in the United Kingdom under Article 15(3) of the Convention for the Protection of Human Rights and Fundamental Freedoms signed at Rome on 4 November 1950.

There have been in the United Kingdom in recent years campaigns of organised terrorism connected with the affairs of Northern Ireland which have manifested themselves in activities which have included repeated murder, attempted murder, maiming, intimidation and violent civil disturbance and in bombing and fire raising which have resulted in death, injury and widespread destruction of property. As a result, a public emergency within the meaning of Article 15(1) of the Convention exists in the United Kingdom.

The Government found it necessary in 1974 to introduce and since then, in cases concerning persons reasonably suspected of involvement in terrorism connected with the affairs of Northern Ireland, or of certain offences under the legislation, who have been detained for 48 hours, to exercise powers enabling further detention without charge, for periods of up to five days, on the authority of the Secretary of State. These powers are at present to be found in Section 12 of the Prevention of Terrorism (Temporary Provisions) Act 1984, Article 9 of the Prevention of Terrorism (Supplemental Temporary Provisions) Order 1984 and Article 10 of the Prevention of Terrorism (Supplemental Temporary Provisions) (Northern Ireland) Order 1984.

Section 12 of the Prevention of Terrorism (Temporary Provisions) Act 1984 provides for a person whom a constable has arrested on reasonable grounds of suspecting him to be guilty of an offence under Section 1, 9 or 10 of the Act, or to be or to have been involved in terrorism connected with the affairs of Northern Ireland, to be detained in right of the arrest for up to 48 hours and thereafter, where the Secretary of State extends the detention period, for up to a further five days. Section 12 substantially re-enacted Section 12 of the Prevention of Terrorism (Temporary Provisions) Act 1976 which, in turn, substantially re-enacted Section 7 of the Prevention of Terrorism (Temporary Provisions) Act 1974.

Article 10 of the Prevention of Terrorism (Supplemental Temporary Provisions) (Northern Ireland) Order 1984 (SI 1984/417) and Article 9 of the Prevention of Terrorism (Supplemental Temporary Provisions) Order 1984 (SI 1984/418) were both made under Sections 13 and 14 of and Schedule 3 to the 1984 Act and substantially re-enacted powers of detention in Orders made under the 1974 and 1976 Acts. A person who is being examined under Article 4 of either Order on his arrival in, or on seeking to leave, Northern Ireland or Great Britain for the purpose of determining whether he is or has been involved in terrorism connected with the affairs of Northern Ireland, or whether there are grounds for suspecting that he has committed an offence under Section 9 of the 1984 Act, may be detained under Article 9 or 10, as appropriate, pending the conclusion of his examination. The period of this examination may exceed 12 hours if an examining officer has reasonable grounds for suspecting him to be or to have been involved in acts of terrorism connected with the affairs of Northern Ireland.

Where such a person is detained under the said Article 9 or 10 he may be detained for up to 48 hours on the authority of an examining officer and thereafter, where the Secretary of State extends the detention period, for up to a further five days.

In its judgment of 29 November 1988 in the Case of *Brogan and Others,* the European Court of Human Rights held that there had been a violation of Article 5(3) in respect of each of the applicants, all of whom had been detained under Section 12 of the 1984 Act. The Court held that even the shortest of the four periods of detention concerned, namely four days and six hours, fell outside the constraints as to time permitted by the first part of Article 5(3). In addition, the Court held that there had been a violation of Article 5(5) in the case of each applicant.

Following this judgment, the Secretary of State for the Home Department informed Parliament on 6 December 1988 that, against the background of the terrorist campaign, and the over-riding need to bring terrorists to justice, the Government did not believe that the maximum period of detention should be reduced. He informed Parliament that the Government were examining the matter with a view to responding to the judgment. On 22 December 1988, the Secretary of State further informed Parliament that it remained the Government's wish, if it could be achieved, to find a judicial process under which extended detention might be reviewed and where appropriate authorised by a judge or other judicial officer. But a further period of reflection and consultation was necessary before the Government could bring forward a firm and final view.

Since the judgment of 29 November 1988 as well as previously, the Government have found it necessary to continue to exercise, in relation to terrorism connected with the affairs of Northern Ireland, the powers described above enabling further detention without charge for periods of up to 5 days, on the authority of the Secretary of State, to the extent strictly required by the exigencies of the situation to enable necessary enquiries and investigations properly to be completed in order to decide whether criminal proceedings should be instituted. To the extent that the exercise of these powers may be inconsistent with the obligations imposed by the Convention the Government has availed itself of the right of derogation conferred by Article 15(1) of the Convention and will continue to do so until further notice.

Dated 23 December 1988.

THE 1989 NOTIFICATION

The United Kingdom Permanent Representative to the Council of Europe presents his compliments to the Secretary General of the Council, and has the honour to convey the following information.

In his communication to the Secretary General of 23 December 1988, reference was made to the introduction and exercise of certain powers under Section 12 of the Prevention of Terrorism (Temporary Provisions) Act 1984, Article 9 of the Prevention of Terrorism (Supplemental Temporary Provisions) Order 1984 and Article 10 of the Prevention of Terrorism (Supplemental Temporary Provisions) (Northern Ireland) Order 1984.

These provisions have been replaced by section 14 of and paragraph 6 of Schedule 5 to the Prevention of Terrorism (Temporary Provisions) Act 1989, which make comparable provision. They came into force on 22 March 1989. A copy of these provisions is enclosed.

The United Kingdom Permanent Representative avails himself of this opportunity to renew to the Secretary General the assurance of his highest consideration.

23 March 1989

Part II – RESERVATION

At the time of signing the present (First) Protocol, I declare that, in view of certain provisions of the Education Acts in the United Kingdom, the principle affirmed in the second sentence of Article 2 is accepted by the United Kingdom only so far as it is compatible with the provision of efficient instruction and training, and the avoidance of unreasonable public expenditure.

Dated 20 March 1952. Made by the United Kingdom Permanent Representative to the Council of Europe.

SCHEDULE 4 – JUDICIAL PENSIONS

Section 18(6)

DUTY TO MAKE ORDERS ABOUT PENSIONS

1(1) The appropriate Minister must by order make provision with respect to pensions payable to or in respect of any holder of a judicial office who serves as an ECHR judge.

1(2) A pensions order must include such provision as the Minister making it considers is necessary to secure that–

(a)   an ECHR judge who was, immediately before his appointment as an ECHR judge, a member of a judicial pension scheme is entitled to remain as a member of that scheme;

(b)   the terms on which he remains a member of the scheme are those which would have been applicable had he not been appointed as an ECHR judge; and

(c)   entitlement to benefits payable in accordance with the scheme continues to be determined as if, while serving as an ECHR judge, his salary was that which would (but for section 18(4)) have been payable to him in respect of his continuing service as the holder of his judicial office.

CONTRIBUTIONS

2 A pensions order may, in particular, make provision–

(a)   for any contributions which are payable by a person who remains a member of a scheme as a result of the order, and which would otherwise be payable by deduction from his salary, to be made otherwise than by deduction from his salary as an ECHR judge; and

(b)   for such contributions to be collected in such manner as may be determined by the administrators of the scheme.

AMENDMENTS OF OTHER ENACTMENTS

3 A pensions order may amend any provision of or made under, a pensions Act in such manner and to such extent as the Minister making the order considers necessary or expedient to ensure the proper administration of any scheme to which it relates.

DEFINITIONS

4 In this Schedule–

"appropriate Minister" means–

(a)   in relation to any judicial office whose jurisdiction is exercisable exclusively in relation to Scotland, the Secretary of State; and

(b)   otherwise, the Lord Chancellor;

"ECHR judge" means the holder of a judicial office who is serving as a judge of the Court;

"judicial pension scheme" means a scheme established by and in accordance with a pensions Act;

"pensions Act" means–

(a)   the County Courts Act (Northern Ireland) 1959;

(b)   the Sheriff's Pensions (Scotland) Act 1961;

(c)   the Judicial Pensions Act 1981; or

(d)   the Judicial Pensions and Retirement Act 1993; and

"pensions order" means an order made under paragraph 1.

FINANCE ACT 1999

(1999 chapter 16)

[*27 July 1999*]

ARRANGEMENT OF SECTIONS

PART II – VALUE ADDED TAX

12   Works of art, antiques, etc.

12(1) [AmendsVATA 1994, s. 21(4).]

12(2) [SubstitutesVATA 1994, s. 21(5)–(6D)for former s. 21(5)and(6).]

12(3) This section has effect in relation to goods imported at any time on or after the day on which this Act is passed.

13   Gold

13(1) Notwithstanding the words preceding paragraph (a) in section 26(3) of the Value Added Tax Act 1994 (input tax allowable against output tax), regulations which–

(a)   are made under section 26(3), and

(b)   have effect in respect of exempt supplies which relate to gold,

may provide that input tax is allowable, as being attributable to the supplies, only in relation to specified matters.

13(2) An order under section 31(2) of that Act (exempt supplies and acquisitions) which provides for certain supplies which relate to gold to be exempt supplies may–

(a) provide that a supply which would be an exempt supply by virtue of the order shall, if the supplier so chooses, be a taxable supply;

(b) make provision by reference to notices to be published by the Commissioners.

13(3) An order under section 37(1) of that Act (relief on importation of goods) which gives relief from VAT on certain importations of gold may make provision by reference to notices to be published by the Commissioners.

13(4) Provision made by virtue of subsection (2) or (3) above may be expressed–

(a) to apply only in specified circumstances;

(b) to apply subject to compliance with specified conditions (which may include conditions relating to general or specific approval of the Commissioners).

13(5) Regulations may–

(a) require specified persons to keep specified records in relation to specified transactions concerning gold;

(b) require specified persons to give specified information to the Commissioners about specified transactions concerning gold;

(c) provide for paragraph 10(2) of Schedule 11 to that Act (entry and inspection of premises) to apply in relation to specified transactions concerning gold as it applies in relation to the supply of goods under taxable supplies.

13(6) The provisions of that Act (including, in particular, section 97 and paragraph 6(2) to (6) of Schedule 11) shall apply in relation to regulations under subsection (5) above as they apply in relation to regulations under paragraph 6(1) of Schedule 11 to that Act.

13(7) In this section **"the Commissioners"** means the Commissioners of Customs and Excise.

Cross references – VATA 1994, s. 69A: penalty for failure to comply with record-keeping requirements.

Statutory instruments – VAT (Amendment) (No. 4) Regulations 1999 (SI 1994/3114).
VAT (Importation of Investment Gold) Relief Order 1999 (SI 1994/3115).
VAT (Investment Gold) Order 1999 (SI 1999/3116).

14 Preparations etc. of meat, yeast or egg

14 [Amends VATA 1994, Sch. 8, Grp. 1, Note (6).]

15 Assignment of debts

15(1) [Substitutes VATA 1994, s. 36(3).]

15(2) [Amends VATA 1994, s. 36(5)(e).]

15(3) [Adds VATA 1994, Sch. 11, para. 7(9).]

15(4) [S. 15(4) ceased to have effect by SI 1999/3029, reg. 5.]

15(5) Subsections (1) and (4) above have effect for the purposes of the making of any refund or repayment after 9th March 1999, but do not have effect in relation to anything received on or before that day.

History – S. 15(4) ceased to have effect by SI 1999/3029, reg. 5, operative from 1 December 1999. Former s. 15(4) reads as follows:
"**15(4)** Until such day as the Commissioners may specify in regulations made under section 36 of that Act, Part XIX of the Value Added Tax Regulations 1995 (bad debt relief), except regulation 171, shall be read as if a reference to a payment being received by the claimant were a reference to a payment being received either by the claimant or by a person to whom a right to receive it has been assigned."

16 Groups of companies

16 Schedule 2 to this Act (which makes changes to provisions about the treatment of bodies corporate as members of a group) shall have effect.

17 Penalties for incorrect certificates

17(1) [Substitutes VATA 1994, s. 62(1),(1A)and(2)for former s. 62(1)and(2).]

17(2) Subsection (1) above has effect in relation to certificates given or, as the case may be, prepared on or after the day on which this Act is passed.

18 EC sales statements: time limits for assessments to penalties

18(1) [Substitutes VATA 1994, s. 77(2)and(2A)for formers. 77(2).]

18(2) Subsection (1) above has effect in relation to any amount by way of penalty, interest or surcharge which becomes due on or after the day on which this Act is passed.

19   Period before repayment supplement payable

19(1)   Section 79 of the Value Added Tax Act 1994 (repayment supplement) shall be amended as follows.

19(2)   [AmendsVATA 1994, s. 79(2)(b).]

19(3)   [InsertsVATA 1994, s. 79(2A).]

19(4)   [AmendsVATA 1994, s. 79(3) and (7).]

19(5)   This section has effect in relation to returns and claims received by the Commissioners on or after 9th March 1999.

20   Meaning of "business"

20(1)   [RepealsVATA 1994, s. 94(3).]

20(2)   This section shall come into force in accordance with such provision as the Commissioners of Customs and Excise may make by order made by statutory instrument.

Statutory instruments – FA 1999, section 20, (Appointed Day) Order 1999 (SI 1999/2769 (C. 68)): brought s. 20 into force from 1 December 1999.

21   Accounting for VAT by Government departments

21(1)   Where–

(a)   a Government department makes supplies of goods or services that are taxable supplies for the purposes of the Value Added Tax Act 1994, and

(b)   its receipts include amounts paid to it in respect of the making of those supplies,

the receipts of the department to be paid into the Consolidated Fund shall be confined to the amounts remaining after deducting, from the amounts otherwise falling to be paid into that Fund, all such amounts in respect of the department's liabilities to pay value added tax to the Commissioners of Customs and Excise as the department may be authorised to deduct in accordance with arrangements made by the Treasury.

21(2)   Arrangements made by the Treasury for the purposes of this section shall apply only to such Government departments and in such cases, and shall have effect subject to such conditions and to the compliance by the department with such accounting and other requirements, as may be provided for in the arrangements.

21(3)   In this section **"Government department"** includes any person or body of persons carrying out functions on behalf of the Crown or of any Minister of the Crown and any part of a Government department (as so defined) which is designated for the purposes of section 41 of the Value Added Tax Act 1994.

21(4)   This section has effect in relation to the financial year beginning with 1st April 1999 and subsequent financial years and shall be deemed to have had effect in relation to earlier financial years.

21(5)   For the purposes of applying this section in relation to the financial year beginning with 1st April 1999 or in relation to any earlier financial year, any arrangements applying to a Government department which–

(a)   were made or approved before the passing of this Act, and

(b)   allowed that department to deduct amounts in respect of value added tax liabilities before making payments into the Consolidated Fund,

shall be deemed to have been made by the Treasury for the purposes of this section.

PART VIII – MISCELLANEOUS AND SUPPLEMENTAL

GENERAL ADMINISTRATION OF TAX

131   Economic and monetary union: taxes and duties

131   The Commissioners of Inland Revenue and the Commissioners of Customs and Excise may incur expenditure in order to secure that, if the United Kingdom were to move to the third stage of economic and monetary union, they would be able to exercise their functions relating to taxes and duties (including agricultural levies of the European Community).

132 Power to provide for use of electronic communications

132(1) Regulations may be made, in accordance with this section, for facilitating the use of electronic communications for–

(a) the delivery of information the delivery of which is authorised or required by or under any legislation relating to a taxation matter;

(b) the making of payments under any such legislation.

132(2) The power to make regulations under this section is conferred–

(a) on the Commissioners of Inland Revenue in relation to matters which are under their care and management; and

(b) on the Commissioners of Customs and Excise in relation to matters which are under their care and management.

132(3) For the purposes of this section provision for facilitating the use of electronic communications includes any of the following–

(a) provision authorising persons to use electronic communications for the delivery of information to tax authorities, or for the making of payments to tax authorities;

(b) provision requiring electronic communications to be used for the making to tax authorities of payments due from persons using such communications for the delivery of information to those authorities;

(c) provision authorising tax authorities to use electronic communications for the delivery of information to other persons or for the making of any payments;

(d) provision as to the electronic form to be taken by any information that is delivered to any tax authorities using electronic communications;

(e) provision requiring persons to prepare and keep records of information delivered to tax authorities by means of electronic communications, and of payments made to any such authorities by any such means;

(f) provision for the production of the contents of records kept in accordance with any regulations under this section;

(g) provision imposing conditions that must be complied with in connection with any use of electronic communications for the delivery of information or the making of any payment;

(h) provision, in relation to cases where use is made of electronic communications, for treating information as not having been delivered, or a payment as not having been made, unless conditions imposed by any such regulations are satisfied;

(i) provision, in relation to such cases, for determining the time when information is delivered or a payment is made;

(j) provision, in relation to such cases, for determining the person by whom information is to be taken to have been delivered or by whom a payment is to be taken to have been made;

(k) provision, in relation to cases where information is delivered by means of electronic communications, for authenticating whatever is delivered.

132(4) The power to make provision under this section for facilitating the use of electronic communications shall also include power to make such provision as the persons exercising the power think fit (including provision for the application of conclusive or other presumptions) as to the manner of proving for any purpose–

(a) whether any use of electronic communications is to be taken as having resulted in the delivery of information or the making of a payment;

(b) the time of delivery of any information for the delivery of which electronic communications have been used;

(c) the time of the making of any payment for the making of which electronic communications have been used;

(d) the person by whom information delivered by means of electronic communications was delivered;

(e) the contents of anything so delivered;

(f) the contents of any records;

(g) any other matter for which provision may be made by regulations under this section.

132(5) Regulations under this section may–

(a) allow any authorisation or requirement for which such regulations may provide to be given or imposed by means of a specific or general direction given by the Commissioners of Inland Revenue or the Commissioners of Customs and Excise;

(b)   provide that the conditions of any such authorisation or requirement are to be taken to be satisfied only where such tax authorities as may be determined under the regulations are satisfied as to specified matters;

(c)   allow a person to refuse to accept delivery of information in an electronic form or by means of electronic communications except in such circumstances as may be specified in or determined under the regulations;

(d)   allow or require use to be made of intermediaries in connection with–

(i)   the delivery of information, or the making of payments, by means of electronic communications; or

(ii)   the authentication or security of anything transmitted by any such means.

132(6)   Power to make provision by regulations under this section shall include power–

(a)   to provide for a contravention of, or any failure to comply with, a specified provision of any such regulations to attract a penalty of a specified amount not exceeding £1,000;

(b)   to provide that specified enactments relating to penalties imposed for the purposes of any taxation matter (including enactments relating to assessments, review and appeal) are to apply, with or without modifications, in relation to penalties under such regulations;

(c)   to make different provision for different cases;

(d)   to make such incidental, supplemental, consequential and transitional provision in connection with any provision contained in any such regulations as the persons exercising the power think fit.

132(7)   The power to make regulations under this section shall be exercisable by statutory instrument subject to annulment in pursuance of a resolution of the House of Commons.

132(8)   References in this section to the delivery of information include references to any of the following (however referred to)–

(a)   the production or furnishing to a person of any information, account, record or document;

(b)   the giving, making, issue or surrender to, or service on, any person of any notice, notification, statement, declaration, certificate or direction;

(c)   the imposition on any person of any requirement or the issue to any person of any request;

(d)   the making of any return, claim, election or application;

(e)   the amendment or withdrawal of anything mentioned in paragraphs (a) to (d) above.

132(9)   References in this section to a taxation matter are references to any of the matters which are under the care and management of the Commissioners of Inland Revenue or of the Commissioners of Customs and Excise.

132(10)   In this section–

"**electronic communications**" includes any communications by means of a telecommunication system (within the meaning of the Telecommunications Act 1984);

"**legislation**" means any enactment, Community legislation or subordinate legislation;

"**payment**" includes a repayment;

"**records**" includes records in electronic form;

"**subordinate legislation**" has the same meaning as in the Interpretation Act 1978;

"**tax authorities**" means–

(a)   the Commissioners of Inland Revenue or the Commissioners of Customs and Excise,

(b)   any officer of either body of Commissioners; or

(c)   any other person who for the purposes of electronic communications is acting under the authority of either body of Commissioners.

Statutory instruments – VAT Regulations 1995 (SI 1995/2518, as amended by SI 2000/258).

133   Use of electronic communications under other provisions

133(1)   Without prejudice to section 132 above, where any power to make subordinate legislation for or in connection with the delivery of information or the making of payments is conferred in relation to any taxation matter on–

(a)   the Commissioners of Inland Revenue,

(b)   the Commissioners of Customs and Excise, or

(c)   the Treasury,

that power shall be taken (to the extent that it would not otherwise be so taken) to include power to make any such provision in relation to the delivery of that information or the making of those payments as could be made by any person by regulations in exercise of a power conferred by that section.

133(2) Provision made in exercise of the powers conferred by section 132 above or subsection (1) above shall have effect notwithstanding so much of any enactment or subordinate legislation as (apart from the provision so made) would require–

(a) any information to be delivered, or

(b) any amount to be paid,

in a form or manner that would preclude the use of electronic communications for its delivery or payment, or the use in connection with its delivery or payment of an intermediary.

133(3) Schedule 3A to the Taxes Management Act 1970 (electronic lodgment of tax returns etc.) shall cease to have effect.

133(4) Subsection (3) above shall come into force on such day as the Treasury may by order made by statutory instrument appoint; and different days may be appointed under this subsection for different purposes.

133(5) Expressions used in this section and section 132 above have the same meanings in this section as in that section.

Statutory instruments – VAT Regulations 1995 (SI 1995/2518, as amended by SI 2000/258).

SUPPLEMENTAL

138 Interpretation

138 In this Act **"the Taxes Act 1988"** means the Income and Corporation Taxes Act 1988.

139 Repeals

139(1) The enactments mentioned in Schedule 20 to this Act (which include provisions that are spent or of no practical utility) are hereby repealed to the extent specified in the third column of that Schedule.

139(2) The repeals specified in that Schedule have effect subject to the commencement provisions and savings contained or referred to in the notes set out in that Schedule.

140 Short title

140 This Act may be cited as the Finance Act 1999.

SCHEDULES

SCHEDULE 2 – VAT: GROUPS OF COMPANIES

Section 16

Part 1 – VALUE ADDED TAX

AMENDMENT OF VALUE ADDED TAX ACT 1994

1(1) Section 43 of the Value Added Tax Act 1994 (groups of companies) shall be amended as follows.

1(2) [Amends VATA 1994, s. 43(1).]

1(3) [Repeals VATA 1994, s. 43(3)–(8).]

2 [Inserts VATA 1994, s. 43A–43C.]

3 [Substitutes VATA 1994, s. 83(k) and (ka) for former s. 83(k).]

4 [Inserts VATA 1994, s. 84(4A)–(4D).]

5(1) Schedule 9A to the Value Added Tax Act 1994 (groups: anti-avoidance) shall be amended as follows.

5(2) [Inserts VATA 1994, Sch. 9A, para. 2(2)and consequently existing para. 2 becomes para. 2(1).]

5(3) [Amends VATA 1994, Sch. 9A, para. 3(8).]

5(4)   [Amends VATA 1994, Sch. 9A, para. 7(1).]

TRANSITIONAL PROVISIONS

6(1)   In this paragraph–

"**the old law**" means sections 43, 83 and 84 of, and Schedule 9A to, the Value Added Tax Act 1994 as they have effect without the amendments in paragraphs 1 to 5 of this Schedule, and

"**the new law**" means sections 43 to 43C, 83 and 84 of, and Schedule 9A to, that Act as they have effect by virtue of paragraphs 1 to 5 of this Schedule.

6(2)   Where, immediately before this Schedule comes into force, two or more bodies corporate are treated as members of a group by virtue of the old law–

(a)   they shall continue to be treated as members of a group, and

(b)   in their treatment as members of a group after this Schedule comes into force, they shall be treated as if any application under the old law by virtue of which they are treated as members of a group had been an equivalent application under the new law.

6(3)   Where an application under section 43 of the Value Added Tax Act 1994 is received by the Commissioners, and has neither taken effect nor been refused before the day on which this Act is passed, the old law shall apply to determine whether the application is to take effect; but where it is determined under this sub-paragraph that an application is to take effect–

(a)   it shall be treated as if it were an equivalent application under the new law, and

(b)   it shall be taken to have been granted under the new law at the time when it would have taken effect in accordance with the old law.

6(4)   In a case to which sub-paragraph (2) or (3) above applies, the power under section 43C(3) shall not be used to terminate the treatment of a body corporate as a member of a group–

(a)   on the ground that the body corporate is not established, and does not have a fixed establishment, in the United Kingdom, and

(b)   from a date before 1st January 2000.

6(5)   Where an application which purports to be an application under the old law is received by the Commissioners after the day on which this Act is passed–

(a)   it shall be treated as if it were an application under the new law, and

(b)   section 43B of the new law shall apply notwithstanding any provision in the application for a date from which it is to take effect.

SCHEDULE 20 – REPEALS

Section 139

Part II – VALUE ADDED TAX

(1) GROUPS OF COMPANIES

Chapter	Short title	Extent of repeal
1994 c. 23.	The Value Added Tax Act 1994.	Section 43(3) to (8).
1995 c. 4.	The Finance Act 1995.	Section 25(3) and (4).

These repeals have effect subject to paragraph 6 of Schedule 2 to this Act.

(2) MEANING OF "BUSINESS"

Chapter	Short title	Extent of repeal
1994 c. 23.	The Value Added Tax Act 1994.	Section 94(3).

Subsection (2) of section 20 of this Act shall apply in relation to this repeal as it applies in relation to that section.

FINANCE ACT 2000

(2000 Chapter 17)

[*28 July 2000*]

ARRANGEMENT OF SECTIONS

PART V – OTHER TAXES

VALUE ADDED TAX

135   Supplies to which reduced rate applies

135(1)   Schedule 35 to this Act (which amends Schedule A1 to the Value Added Tax Act 1994 for the purpose of extending the range of supplies to which the reduced rate of value added tax applies) has effect.

135(2)   The amendments made by that Schedule have effect in relation to supplies made on or after 1st April 2000.

135(3)   Subsection (2) does not apply to the amendment made by paragraph 8(5) of that Schedule.

That amendment has effect in relation to supplies made after the day on which this Act is passed.

136   Disposals of assets for which a VAT repayment is claimed

136(1)   In section 3(2) of the Value Added Tax Act 1994 (taxable persons and registration), for "Schedules 1 to 3" there shall be substituted "Schedules 1 to 3A".

136(2)   In section 67 of that Act (failure to notify)–

(a)   in subsection (1)(a), for "or with paragraph 3 or 8(2) of Schedule 3" there shall be substituted ", with paragraph 3 or 8(2) of Schedule 3 or paragraph 3, 4 or 7(2) or (3) of Schedule 3A";

(b)   in subsection (3)(a), for "or paragraph 3 of Schedule 3" there shall be substituted ", paragraph 3 of Schedule 3 or paragraph 3 or 4 of Schedule 3A"; and

(c)   in subsection (3)(b), for "or with sub-paragraph (2) of paragraph 8 of Schedule 3" there shall be substituted ", with sub-paragraph (2) of paragraph 8 of Schedule 3 or with sub-paragraph (2) or (3) of paragraph 7 of Schedule 3A".

136(3)   In section 69(1)(a) of that Act (breaches of regulatory provisions), for "or paragraph 5 of Schedule 3" there shall be substituted ", paragraph 5 of Schedule 3 or paragraph 5 of Schedule 3A".

136(4)   In section 73(3)(b) of that Act (failure to make returns etc.), for "or paragraph 6(2) or (3) of Schedule 3" there shall be substituted ", paragraph 6(2) or (3) of Schedule 3 or paragraph 6(1) or (2) of Schedule 3A".

136(5)   In section 74(1)(c) of that Act (interest on VAT recovered or recoverable by assessment), for "under paragraph 8 of Schedule 3" there shall be substituted ", under paragraph 8 of Schedule 3 or under paragraph 7 of Schedule 3A".

136(6)   In the following provisions of that Act–

(a)   paragraph 1(4)(a) and (5) of Schedule 1 (registration in respect of taxable supplies); and

(b)   paragraph 1(4) of Schedule 2 (registration in respect of supplies from other member States),

for "or paragraph 6(3) of Schedule 3" there shall be substituted ", paragraph 6(3) of Schedule 3 or paragraph 6(2) of Schedule 3A".

136(7)   In paragraph 1(3) of Schedule 3 to that Act (registration in respect of acquisitions from other member States), for "or paragraph 6(2) of Schedule 2" there shall be substituted ", paragraph 6(2) of Schedule 2 or paragraph 6(2) of Schedule 3A".

136(8)   After Schedule 3 to that Act there shall be inserted the Schedule 3A set out in Schedule 36 to this Act.

136(9)   In paragraph 5(5) of Schedule 4 to that Act (matters to be treated as a supply of goods or services), for the words from "under sections 25 and 26" to the end there shall be substituted–

"(a)   under sections 25 and 26, to credit for the whole or any part of the VAT on the supply, acquisition or importation of those goods or of anything comprised in them; or

(b)   under a scheme embodied in regulations made under section 39, to a repayment of VAT on the supply or importation of those goods or of anything comprised in them.".

136(10)   Subsections (1) to (7) and (9) above have effect in relation to supplies made on or after 21st March 2000; and subsection (8) above and Schedule 36 to this Act have effect in relation to relevant supplies (within the meaning of Schedule 3A to that Act) made on or after that date.

137   Gold: penalty for failure to comply with record-keeping requirements etc.

137(1)   Part IV of the Value Added Tax Act 1994 (administration, collection and enforcement) is amended as follows.

137(2)   After section 69 (breaches of regulatory provisions) insert–

"Breach of record-keeping requirements etc. in relation to transactions in gold

69A(1)   This section applies where a person fails to comply with a requirement of regulations under section 13(5)(a) or (b) of the Finance Act 1999 (gold: duties to keep records or provide information).

Where this section applies, the provisions of section 69 do not apply.

69A(2)   A person who fails to comply with any such requirement is liable to a penalty not exceeding 17.5% of the value of the transactions to which the failure relates.

69A(3)   For the purposes of assessing the amount of any such penalty, the value of the transactions to which the failure relates shall be determined by the Commissioners to the best of their judgement and notified by them to the person liable.

69A(4)   No assessment of a penalty under this section shall be made more than 2 years after evidence of facts sufficient in the opinion of the Commissioners to justify the making of the assessment comes to their knowledge.

69A(5)   The reference in subsection (4) above to facts sufficient to justify the making of the assessment is to facts sufficient–

(a)   to indicate that there had been a failure to comply with any such requirement as is referred to in subsection (1) above, and

(b)   to determine the value of the transactions to which the failure relates.

69A(6) A failure by any person to comply with any such requirement as is mentioned in subsection (1) above shall not give rise to a liability to a penalty under this section if the person concerned satisfies the Commissioners or, on appeal, a tribunal, that there is a reasonable excuse for the failure.

69A(7) Where by reason of conduct falling within subsection (1) above a person–
(a) is assessed to a penalty under section 60, or
(b) is convicted of an offence (whether under this Act or otherwise),

that conduct shall not also give rise to a penalty under this section.".

137(3) In section 70(1) of that Act (mitigation of penalties), for "or 67" substitute ", 67 or 69A".

137(4) In section 76(1) of that Act (assessment of amount due by way of penalty etc.), for "to 69" (in both places) substitute "to 69A".

137(5) In section 83 of that Act (appeals), in paragraph (n) for "59 to 69" substitute "59 to 69A".

PART VI – MISCELLANEOUS AND SUPPLEMENTARY PROVISIONS

INCENTIVES FOR ELECTRONIC COMMUNICATIONS

143   Power to provide incentives to use electronic communications

143(1) Regulations may be made in accordance with Schedule 38 to this Act for providing incentives to use electronic communications.

143(2) Anything received by way of incentive under any such regulations shall not be regarded as income for any purposes of the Tax Acts.

SUPPLEMENTARY PROVISIONS

156   Repeals

156(1) The enactments mentioned in Schedule 40 to this Act (which include provisions that are spent or of no practical utility) are repealed to the extent specified in the third column of that schedule.

156(2) The repeals specified in that Schedule have effect subject to the commencement provisions and savings contained or referred to in the notes set out in that Schedule.

157   Short title

157 This Act may be sited as the Finance Act 2000.

SCHEDULES

SCHEDULE 35 – VALUE ADDED TAX: CHARGE AT REDUCED RATE

Section 131

1 Schedule A1 to the Value Added Tax Act 1994 (charge at reduced rate) has effect with the *following amendments.*

2(1) Paragraph 1(1) (supplies benefitting from the reduced rate) is amended as follows.

2(2) After paragraph (a) insert–
"(aa) supplies of services of installing List A energy-saving materials in residential accommodation or in a building intended for use solely for a relevant charitable purpose;
(ab) supplies of List A energy-saving materials by a person who installs those materials in residential accommodation or a building intended for use solely for a relevant charitable purpose;".

2(3) In each of paragraphs (b) and (c), before "energy-saving materials" insert "List B".

2(4) After paragraph (c) insert–

"(d) supplies to a qualifying person of services of connecting, or reconnecting, a mains gas supply to the qualifying person's sole or main residence;

(e) supplies of goods made to a qualifying person by a person connecting, or reconnecting, a mains gas supply to the qualifying person's sole or main residence, being goods whose installation is necessary for the connection, or reconnection, of the mains gas supply;

(f) supplies to a qualifying person of services of installing, maintaining or repairing a central heating system in the qualifying person's sole or main residence;

(g) supplies of goods made to a qualifying person by a person installing, maintaining or repairing a central heating system in the qualifying person's sole or main residence, being goods whose installation is necessary for the installation, maintenance or repair of the central heating system;

(h) supplies consisting in the leasing of goods that form the whole or part of a central heating system installed in the sole or main residence of a qualifying person;

(i) supplies of goods that form the whole or part of a central heating system installed in a qualifying person's sole or main residence and that, immediately before being supplied, were goods leased under arrangements such that the consideration for the supplies consisting in the leasing of the goods was, in whole or in part, funded by a grant made under a relevant scheme;

(j) supplies to a qualifying person of services of installing qualifying security goods in the qualifying person's sole or main residence; and

(k) supplies of qualifying security goods made to a qualifying person by a person who installs those goods in the qualifying person's sole or main residence."

3 For paragraph 1(1A) (supplies benefit from reduced rate only if funded by grants) substitute–

"**1(1A)** A supply to which any of paragraphs (b) to (k) of sub-paragraph (1) above applies is a supply falling within this paragraph only to the extent that the consideration for it–

(a) is, or is to be, funded by a grant made under a relevant scheme; or

(b) in the case of a supply to which paragraph (i) of that sub-paragraph applies–

(i) is, or is to be, funded by such a grant, or

(ii) is a payment becoming due only by reason of the termination (whether by the passage of time or otherwise) of the leasing of the goods in question."

4 In paragraph 1(1B) (interpretation of sub-paragraph (1A)), for "sub-paragraph (1)(b) or (c)" substitute "any of paragraphs (b) to (k) of sub-paragraph (1)" and for "neither of those sub-paragraphs" substitute "none of those paragraphs".

5 In paragraph 5(3)(c), for "disability working allowance" substitute "disabled person's tax credit".

6 In paragraph 5(3)(d), for "family credit" substitute "working families' tax credit".

7 In paragraph 5 (interpretation), after sub-paragraph (3) insert–

"**5(3A)** For the purposes of paragraph 1(1)(aa) and (ab) above "residential accommodation" means–

(a) a building, or part of a building, that consists of a dwelling or a number of dwellings;

(b) a building, or part of a building, used for a relevant residential purpose;

(c) a caravan used as a place of permanent habitation; or

(d) a houseboat.

5(3B) For the purposes of paragraph 1(1)(aa) and (ab) above "use for a relevant charitable purpose" means use by a charity in either or both of the following ways, namely–

(a) otherwise than in the course or furtherance of a business;

(b) as a village hall or similarly in providing social or recreational facilities for a local community."

8(1) Paragraph 5(4) (meaning of "energy-saving materials") is amended as follows.

8(2) For "For the purposes of paragraph 1(1)(b) and (c) above "energy-saving materials" means" substitute "For the purposes of paragraph 1(1)(aa) and (ab) above "List A energy-saving materials" means".

8(3) In paragraph (c), after "central heating system controls" insert "(including thermostatic radiator valves)".

8(4) After paragraph (d) insert–

"(e)   solar panels."

8(5)   After paragraph (e) (which is inserted by sub-paragraph (4) above) insert–

"(f)   wind turbines;
(g)   water turbines."

9   In paragraph 5, after sub-paragraph (4) insert–

"5(4A)   For the purposes of paragraph 1(1)(b) and (c) above "List B energy-saving materials" means any of the following–

(a)   gas-fired room heaters that are fitted with thermostatic controls;
(b)   electric storage heaters;
(c)   closed solid fuel fire cassettes;
(d)   electric dual immersion water heaters with foam-insulated hot water tanks;
(e)   gas-fired boilers;
(f)   oil-fired boilers;
(g)   radiators.

5(4B)   For the purposes of paragraph 1(1)(j) and (k) above, "qualifying security goods" means any of the following–

(a)   locks or bolts for windows;
(b)   locks, bolts or security chains for doors;
(c)   spy holes;
(d)   smoke alarms."

10   In paragraph 5(5) (meaning of "relevant scheme"), for "paragraph 1(1A) and (1B)" substitute "paragraph 1".

SCHEDULE 36 – NEW SCHEDULE 3A TO THE VALUE ADDED TAX ACT 1994

Section 132(8)

The Schedule inserted after Schedule 3 to the Value Added Tax Act 1994 is as follows:

"SCHEDULE 3A – REGISTRATION IN RESPECT OF DISPOSALS OF ASSETS FOR WHICH A VAT REPAYMENT IS CLAIMED

LIABILITY TO BE REGISTERED

1(1)   A person who is not registered under this Act, and is not liable to be registered under Schedule 1, 2 or 3, becomes liable to be registered under this Schedule at any time–

(a)   if he makes relevant supplies; or
(b)   if there are reasonable grounds for believing that he will make such supplies in the period of 30 days then beginning.

1(2)   A person shall be treated as having become liable to be registered under this Schedule at any time when he would have become so liable under sub-paragraph (1) above but for any registration which is subsequently cancelled under paragraph 6(2) below, paragraph 13(3) of Schedule 1, paragraph 6(2) of Schedule 2 or paragraph 6(3) of Schedule 3.

1(3)   A person shall not cease to be liable to be registered under this Schedule except in accordance with paragraph 2 below.

2   A person who has become liable to be registered under this Schedule shall cease to be so liable at any time if the Commissioners are satisfied that he has ceased to make relevant supplies.

NOTIFICATION OF LIABILITY AND REGISTRATION

3(1)   A person who becomes liable to be registered by virtue of paragraph 1(1)(a) above shall notify the Commissioners of the liability before the end of the period of 30 days beginning with the day on which the liability arises.

3(2)   The Commissioners shall register any such person (whether or not he so notifies them) with effect from the beginning of the day on which the liability arises.

4(1)   A person who becomes liable to be registered by virtue of paragraph 1(1)(b) above shall notify the Commissioners of the liability before the end of the period by reference to which the liability arises.

4(2)   The Commissioners shall register any such person (whether or not he so notifies them) with effect from the beginning of the period by reference to which the liability arises.

NOTIFICATION OF END OF LIABILITY

5(1)   Subject to sub-paragraph (2) below, a person registered under paragraph 3 or 4 above who ceases to make or have the intention of making relevant supplies shall notify the Commissioners of that fact within 30 days of the day on which he does so.

5(2)   Sub-paragraph (1) above does not apply if the person would, when he so ceases, be otherwise liable or entitled to be registered under this Act if his registration and any enactment preventing a person from being liable to be registered under different provisions at the same time were disregarded.

CANCELLATION OF REGISTRATION

6(1)   Subject to sub-paragraph (3) below, where the Commissioners are satisfied that a registered person has ceased to be liable to be registered under this Schedule, they may cancel his registration with effect from the day on which he so ceased or from such later date as may be agreed between them and him.

6(2)   Where the Commissioners are satisfied that on the day on which a registered person was registered he was not registrable, they may cancel his registration with effect from that day.

6(3)   The Commissioners shall not under sub-paragraph (1) above cancel a person's registration with effect from any time unless they are satisfied that it is not a time when that person would be subject to a requirement, or entitled, to be registered under this Act.

6(4)   In determining for the purposes of sub-paragraph (3) above whether a person would be subject to a requirement, or entitled, to be registered at any time, so much of any provision of this Act as prevents a person from becoming liable or entitled to be registered when he is already registered or when he is so liable under any other provision shall be disregarded.

EXEMPTION FROM REGISTRATION

7(1)   Notwithstanding the preceding provisions of this Schedule, where a person who makes or intends to make relevant supplies satisfies the Commissioners that any such supply is zero-rated or would be zero-rated if he were a taxable person, they may, if he so requests and they think fit, exempt him from registration under this Schedule.

7(2)   Where there is a material change in the nature of the supplies made by a person exempted under this paragraph from registration under this Schedule, he shall notify the Commissioners of the change–
(a)   within 30 days of the date on which the change occurred; or
(b)   if no particular date is identifiable as the day on which it occurred, within 30 days of the end of the quarter in which it occurred.

7(3)   Where there is a material alteration in any quarter in the proportion of relevant supplies of such a person that are zero-rated, he shall notify the Commissioners of the alteration within 30 days of the end of the quarter.

7(4)   If it appears to the Commissioners that a request under sub-paragraph (1) above should no longer have been acted upon on or after any day, or has been withdrawn on any day, they shall register the person who made the request with effect from that day.

SUPPLEMENTARY

8   Any notification required under this Schedule shall be made in such form and shall contain such particulars as the Commissioners may by regulations prescribe.

9(1)   For the purposes of this Schedule a supply of goods is a relevant supply where–
(a)   the supply is a taxable supply;

(b) the goods are assets of the business in the course or furtherance of which they are supplied; and

(c) the person by whom they are supplied, or a predecessor of his, has received or claimed, or is intending to claim, a repayment of VAT on the supply to him, or the importation by him, of the goods or of anything comprised in them.

9(2) In relation to any goods, a person is the predecessor of another for the purposes of this paragraph if–

(a) that other person is a person to whom he has transferred assets of his business by a transfer of that business, or part of it, as a going concern;

(b) those assets consisted of or included those goods; and

(c) the transfer of the assets is one falling by virtue of an order under section 5(3) (or under an enactment re-enacted in section 5(3)) to be treated as neither a supply of goods nor a supply of services;

and the reference in this paragraph to a person's predecessor includes references to the predecessors of his predecessor through any number of transfers.

9(3) The reference in this paragraph to a repayment of VAT is a reference to such a repayment under a scheme embodied in regulations made under section 39.".

SCHEDULE 37 – LANDFILL TAX: NEW PART VIII OF SCHEDULE 5 TO THE FINANCE ACT 1996

Section 138

"Part VIII – Secondary Liability: Controllers of Landfill Sites

MEANING OF CONTROLLER

48(1) For the purposes of this Part of this Schedule a person is the controller of the whole, or a part, of a landfill site at a given time if he determines, or is entitled to determine, what disposals of material, if any, may be made–

(a) at every part of the site at that time, or

(b) at that part of the site at that time,

as the case may be.

48(2) But a person who, because he is an employee or agent of another, determines or is entitled to determine what disposals may be made at a landfill site or any part of a landfill site is not the controller of that site or, as the case may be, that part of that site.

48(3) Where a person is the controller of the whole or a part of a landfill site, that site or, as the case may be, that part of the site is referred to in this Part of this Schedule as being under his control.

48(4) Any reference in this Part of this Schedule to a controller (without more) is a reference to a controller of the whole or a part of a landfill site.

SECONDARY LIABILITY

49(1) Where–

(a) a taxable disposal is made at a landfill site,

(b) at the time when that disposal is made a person is the operator of the landfill site by virtue of section 67(a), (c) or (e) of this Act, and

(c) at that time a person other than the operator mentioned in paragraph (b) above is the controller of the whole or a part of the landfill site,

the controller shall be liable to pay to the Commissioners an amount of the landfill tax chargeable on the disposal.

49(2) The amount which the controller is liable to pay shall be determined in accordance with the following provisions of this paragraph.

49(3) In a case where the whole of the landfill site is under the control of the controller, he shall be liable to pay the whole of the landfill tax chargeable.

49(4) In a case where a part of the landfill site is under the control of the controller, he shall be liable to pay an amount of the landfill tax calculated in accordance with sub-paragraphs (5) and (6) below.

49(5) The amount of landfill tax which the controller is liable to pay is the amount which would have been chargeable had a separate taxable disposal consisting of the amount of material referred to in sub-paragraph (6) below been made at the time of the disposal mentioned in sub-paragraph (1)(a) above.

49(6) That amount of material is the amount by weight of the material comprised in the disposal mentioned in sub-paragraph (1)(a) above which was disposed of on the part of the landfill site under the control of the controller.

49(7) If the amount mentioned in sub-paragraph (6) above is nil, the controller shall have no liability under sub-paragraph (1) above in relation to landfill tax chargeable on the disposal.

49(8) For the purposes of sub-paragraph (1)(b) and (c) above–
(a)   section 61 of this Act, and
(b)   any regulations made under section 62 of this Act,
shall not apply for determining the time when the disposal in question is made.

OPERATOR ENTITLED TO CREDIT

50(1) This paragraph applies where–
(a)   the operator of a landfill site is liable to pay landfill tax on a taxable disposal by reference to a particular accounting period,
(b)   a controller of the whole or a part of that site is (apart from this paragraph) liable under paragraph 49 above to pay an amount of that tax, and
(c)   for the accounting period in question the operator is entitled to credit under regulations made under section 51 of this Act.

50(2) The amount of the tax which the controller is (apart from this sub-paragraph) liable to pay shall be reduced by the amount calculated in accordance with the following formula–

$$\frac{A \times C}{G}$$

where–
        A is the amount of tax mentioned in sub-paragraph (1)(b) above;
        C is the amount of credit mentioned in sub-paragraph (1)(c) above; and
        G is the operator's gross tax liability for the accounting period in question.

50(3) For the purposes of sub-paragraph (2) above, the operator's gross tax liability for the accounting period in question is the gross amount of landfill tax–
(a)   which is chargeable on disposals made at all landfill sites of which he is the operator, and
(b)   for which he is required to account by reference to that accounting period.

50(4) In sub-paragraph (3) above, **the gross amount of landfill tax** means the amount of tax before any credit or any other adjustment is taken into account in the period in question.

50(5) If the amount calculated in accordance with the formula in sub-paragraph (2) above is greater than the amount of tax mentioned in sub-paragraph (1)(b) above, the amount of the tax which the controller is liable to pay shall be reduced to nil.

PAYMENT OF SECONDARY LIABILITY

51(1) This paragraph applies where a controller is liable under paragraph 49 above (after taking account of any reduction under paragraph 50 above) to pay an amount of landfill tax ("the relevant amount").

51(2) The controller is required to pay the relevant amount to the Commissioners only if–
(a)   a notice containing the required information is served on him, or
(b)   other reasonable steps are taken with a view to bringing the required information to his attention,
before the end of the period of two years beginning with the day immediately following the relevant accounting day.

51(3) The relevant accounting day is the last day of the accounting period by reference to which the landfill site operator liable to pay the landfill tax in question is required to account for that tax.

51(4) If the controller is required to pay the relevant amount by virtue of this paragraph, the amount shall be paid before the end of the period of thirty days beginning with the day immediately following the notification day.

51(5) The notification day is—
(a)   in a case where notice is served on a controller as mentioned in sub-paragraph (2)(a) above, the day on which the notice is served, or
(b)   in a case where other reasonable steps are taken as mentioned in sub-paragraph (2)(b) above, the day on which the last of those steps is taken.

51(6) For the purposes of sub-paragraph (2) above the required information is the relevant amount and, if that amount is one reduced in accordance with paragraph 50 above, also—
(a)   the amount of the controller's liability under paragraph 49 above apart from the reduction,
(b)   the amount of credit to which the operator is entitled, and
(c)   the operator's gross tax liability.

ASSESSMENTS

52(1) Where an amount of landfill tax is—
(a)   assessed under section 50 of this Act, and
(b)   notified to a licensed operator,
the Commissioners may also determine that a controller of the whole or a part of any landfill site operated by the licensed operator shall be liable to pay so much of the amount assessed as they consider just and equitable.

52(2) A controller is required to pay an amount determined under sub-paragraph (1) above only if—
(a)   a notice stating the amount is served on him, or
(b)   other reasonable steps are taken with a view to bringing the amount of the liability to his attention,
before the expiry of the period of two years beginning with the day immediately following the assessment day.

52(3) The assessment day is the day on which the assessment in question is notified to the licensed operator.

52(4) If a controller is required to pay an amount by virtue of this paragraph, it shall be paid before the end of the period of thirty days beginning with the day immediately following the notification day.

52(5) The notification day is—
(a)   in a case where notice is served on a controller as mentioned in sub-paragraph (2)(a) above, the day on which the notice is served, or
(b)   in a case where other reasonable steps are taken as mentioned in sub-paragraph (2)(b) above, the day on which the last of those steps is taken.

52(6) For the purposes of this paragraph a licensed operator is a person who is the operator of a landfill site by virtue of section 67(a), (c) or (e) of this Act.

ASSESSMENT WITHDRAWN OR REDUCED

53(1) Where—
(a)   a controller is liable to pay an amount determined under paragraph 52 above, and
(b)   the assessment notified to the licensed operator is withdrawn or reduced,
the Commissioners may determine that the controller's liability is to be cancelled or to be reduced to such an amount as they consider just and equitable.

53(2) Sub-paragraphs (3) to (5) below apply where the Commissioners make a determination under sub-paragraph (1) above that the controller's liability is to be reduced (but not cancelled).

53(3) In such a case they shall—
(a)   serve the controller with notice stating the amount of the reduced liability, or

(b)   take other reasonable steps with a view to bringing the reduced amount to the controller's attention.

53(4)   If the controller has already been served with notice of the amount determined under paragraph 52 above, or if other steps have already been taken to bring that amount to his attention–

(a)   the Commissioners shall serve the notice mentioned in sub-paragraph (3)(a) above, or take the steps mentioned in sub-paragraph (3)(b) above, before the end of the period of thirty days beginning with the day immediately following that on which they make the determination under sub-paragraph (1) above, and

(b)   the reduced amount shall be payable, or treated as having been payable, on or before the day on which the amount referred to in sub-paragraph (1)(a) above would have been payable apart from this paragraph.

53(5)   In a case where the controller has not been served with notice of the amount determined under paragraph 52 above, or no other steps have been taken to bring that amount to his attention, he shall be liable to pay the reduced amount only if–

(a)   the notice mentioned in sub-paragraph (3)(a) above is served, or

(b)   the other steps mentioned in sub-paragraph (3)(b) above are taken,

before the expiry of the period of two years beginning with the day immediately following that on which the Commissioners make the determination under sub-paragraph (1) above.

53(6)   Sub-paragraph (7) below applies where–

(a)   the Commissioners make a determination under sub-paragraph (1) above that the controller's liability is to be cancelled, and

(b)   the controller has already been served with notice of the amount determined under paragraph 52 above, or other steps have already been taken to bring that amount to his attention.

53(7)   In such a case the Commissioners shall–

(a)   serve the controller with notice stating that the liability has been cancelled, or

(b)   take other reasonable steps with a view to bringing the cancellation to the controller's attention,

before the end of the period of thirty days beginning with the day immediately following that on which they make the determination that the liability is to be cancelled.

ADJUSTMENTS

54(1)   This paragraph applies in any case where the liability of a licensed operator to pay landfill tax is adjusted otherwise than by–

(a)   his being entitled to credit under regulations made under section 51 of this Act,

(b)   his being notified of an amount assessed under section 50 of this Act, or

(c)   the withdrawal or reduction of an assessment under section 50 of this Act which was notified to him.

54(2)   In such a case the Commissioners may determine that a controller of the whole or any part of a landfill site operated by the licensed operator–

(a)   shall be liable to pay to the Commissioners such an amount as they consider just and equitable, or

(b)   shall be entitled to an allowance of such an amount as they consider just and equitable.

54(3)   A controller is required to pay an amount determined under sub-paragraph (2)(a) above only if–

(a)   a notice stating the amount is served on him, or

(b)   other reasonable steps are taken with a view to bringing the amount of the liability to his attention,

before the end of the period of two years beginning with the day immediately following the relevant accounting day.

54(4)   The relevant accounting day is the last day of the accounting period of the operator within which the adjustment in question was taken into account.

54(5)   If a controller is required to pay an amount by virtue of sub-paragraph (3) above, it shall be paid before the end of the period of thirty days beginning with the day immediately following the notification day.

54(6)   The notification day is–

(a)   in a case where notice is served on a controller as mentioned in sub-paragraph (3)(a)
       above, the day on which the notice is served, or

(b)   in a case where other reasonable steps are taken as mentioned in sub-paragraph (3)(b)
       above, the day on which the last of those steps is taken.

54(7)   The Commissioners may determine in what manner a controller is to benefit from an
allowance determined under sub-paragraph (2)(b) above.

54(8)   For the purposes of this paragraph a licensed operator is a person who is the operator
of a landfill site by virtue of section 67(a), (c) or (e) of this Act.

AMOUNTS PAYABLE TO BE TREATED AS TAX

55   An amount which a controller is required to pay under paragraph 52, 53 or 54(2)(a)
above or under paragraph 58 below shall be deemed to be an amount of tax due from him
and shall be recoverable accordingly.

CONTROLLER NOT CARRYING OUT TAXABLE ACTIVITY

56   A controller is not to be treated for the purposes of this Act as carrying out a taxable
activity by reason only of any liability under this Part of this Schedule.

JOINT AND SEVERAL LIABILITY

57(1)   In any case where the condition in sub-paragraph (4), (5) or (6) below is satisfied,
the controller and the operator shall be jointly and severally liable for the principal liability.

57(2)   But the amount which may be recovered from the controller in consequence of such
liability shall not exceed the amount of the secondary liability.

57(3)   For the purposes of this paragraph–
(a)   the principal liability is the amount referred to in sub-paragraph (4)(a), (5)(a) or (6)(a)
       below, as the case may be, and
(b)   the secondary liability is the amount referred to in sub-paragraph (4)(b), (5)(b) or
       (6)(b) below, as the case may be.

57(4)   The condition in this sub-paragraph is satisfied if–
(a)   the operator of a landfill site is liable under section 41 of this Act for landfill tax, and
(b)   a controller is liable under paragraph 49 above, after taking account of any reduction
       under paragraph 50 above, to pay an amount of that tax.

57(5)   The condition in this sub-paragraph is satisfied if–
(a)   the operator of a landfill site is notified of the amount of an assessment made under
       section 50 of this Act, and
(b)   in consequence of a determination made under paragraph 52 above by the
       Commissioners in connection with the assessment, a controller is liable to pay an
       amount (after taking account of any reduction under paragraph 53 above).

57(6)   The condition in this sub-paragraph is satisfied if–
(a)   the liability of the operator of a landfill site to pay landfill tax is adjusted in such a
       way that paragraph 54 above applies, and
(b)   in consequence of a determination made under paragraph 54(2)(a) above by the
       Commissioners in connection with the adjustment, a controller is liable to pay an
       amount.

INTEREST PAYABLE BY A CONTROLLER

58(1)   This paragraph applies where–
(a)   the operator of a landfill site and the controller of the whole or a part of that site are
       by virtue of paragraph 57 above jointly and severally liable for an amount, and
(b)   that amount carries interest by virtue of any provision of this Schedule.

58(2)   The controller and the operator shall be jointly and severally liable to pay the
interest.

58(3)   But the amount which may be recovered from the controller in consequence of such
liability shall not exceed the amount calculated in accordance with the following formula–

$$\frac{(I - [A + B]) \times S}{P}$$

where–
      I is the total amount of interest in question;
      A is the amount of interest carried for the period which–
      (a)   begins with the first day of the period for which interest is carried, and
      (b)   ends with the day on which the controller becomes liable to pay the secondary
           liability;
      B is the amount of interest carried for any day falling after that on which the
      secondary liability is met in full;
      S is the amount of the secondary liability;
      P is the amount of the principal liability.
    In this paragraph secondary liability and principal liability have the same meaning as in
paragraph 57 above.

58(4)   The controller is liable for an amount of interest only if–
(a)   a notice stating the amount is served on him, or
(b)   other reasonable steps are taken with a view to bringing the amount of the liability to
      his attention,
before the end of the period of two years beginning with the day immediately following the
final day.

58(5)   The final day is the last day of the period for which the interest in question is carried.

58(6)   If the controller is required to pay an amount in accordance with this paragraph, it
shall be paid before the end of the period of thirty days beginning with the day immediately
following the notification day.

58(7)   The notification day is–
(a)   in a case where notice is served on a controller as mentioned in sub-paragraph (4)(a)
      above, the day on which the notice is served, or
(b)   in a case where other reasonable steps are taken as mentioned in sub-paragraph (4)(b)
      above, the day on which the last of those steps is taken.

58(8)   Where by virtue of sub-paragraph (2) above a controller is liable to pay interest
which arises under paragraph 27 above, paragraph 28 above shall apply in relation to that
interest as it applies to interest which a person is liable under paragraph 27 above to pay.

REVIEWS

59   Section 54 of this Act shall apply to a decision of the Commissioners under this Part of
this Schedule–
(a)   that a person is a controller,
(b)   that a person is liable under this Part of this Schedule to pay any amount (including a
      penalty under paragraph 60 below),
(c)   that a person is not entitled under this Part of this Schedule to an allowance, or
(d)   as to the amount of any liability or any allowance under this Part of this Schedule,
as it applies to the other decisions of the Commissioners specified in subsection (1) of that
section.

NOTICE THAT PERSON IS, OR IS NO LONGER, A CONTROLLER

60(1)   This paragraph applies where–
(a)   on the date when this paragraph comes into force, a person is a controller of the whole
      or a part of a landfill site, or
(b)   after that date, a person becomes or ceases to be a controller of the whole or a part of a
      landfill site.

60(2)   The controller, and the operator of the landfill site in question, shall be under a duty
to secure that notice which complies with the requirements of sub-paragraph (3) below
appropriate to the case in question is given to the Commissioners.

60(3)   *The requirements of this sub-paragraph are that the notice–*
(a)   states that a person is, has become or has ceased to be a controller,
(b)   identifies that person and the site under his control or formerly under his control,
(c)   states the date when he became or ceased to be the controller, and
(d)   is given within the period of thirty days beginning with the day immediately
      following–

     (i) the day when this paragraph comes into force, in a case falling within sub-paragraph (1)(a) above, or

     (ii) the day when the person in question becomes or ceases to be the controller, in a case falling within sub-paragraph (1)(b) above.

60(4) If a person fails to comply with sub-paragraph (2) above, he is liable to a penalty of £250.

60(5) Paragraph 25 above applies to a penalty under sub-paragraph (4) above as it applies to a penalty under Part V of this Schedule.

EXTENSION OF TIME LIMITS WHERE NOTICE NOT SERVED

61(1) This paragraph applies where–

(a) a person is liable under paragraph 49 above to pay an amount of landfill tax or liable under paragraph 58 above to pay interest, or

(b) the Commissioners are entitled under paragraph 52, 53 or 54 above to determine an amount which a person is liable to pay.

61(2) The reference to two years in paragraph 51(2), 52(2), 53(5), 54(3) or 58(4) above (as the case may be) shall be treated as a reference to twenty years if the requirement of paragraph 60(2) above to give notice to the Commissioners in relation to the person mentioned in sub-paragraph (1) above being or becoming a controller has not been complied with."

SCHEDULE 38 – REGULATIONS FOR PROVIDING INCENTIVES FOR ELECTRONIC COMMUNICATIONS

Section 139(1)

INTRODUCTION

1(1) Regulations may be made in accordance with this Schedule for providing incentives to use electronic communications–

(a) for the purposes mentioned in section 132(1) of the Finance Act 1999 (power to provide for use of electronic communications for delivery of information and making of payments), or

(b) for any other communications with the tax authorities or in connection with taxation matters.

1(2) The power to make regulations under this Schedule is conferred–

(a) on the Commissioners of Inland Revenue in relation to matters which are under their care and management, and

(b) on the Commissioners of Customs and Excise in relation to matters which are under their care and management.

KINDS OF INCENTIVE

2(1) The incentives shall be of such description as may be provided for in the regulations.

2(2) They may, in particular, take the form of–

(a) discounts;

(b) the allowing of additional time to comply with any obligations under tax legislation (including obligations relating to the payment of tax or other amounts); or

(c) the facility to deliver information or make payments at more convenient intervals.

CONDITIONS OF ENTITLEMENT

3(1) The regulations may make provision as to the conditions of entitlement to an incentive.

3(2) They may, in particular, make entitlement conditional–

(a) on the use of electronic communications for all communications or payments (or all communications and payments of a specified description) with, to or from the tax authority concerned, and

(b) on the use of specified means of electronic communication or payment acceptable to the tax authority concerned.

3(3) The regulations may make provision for an appeal against a decision that the conditions of entitlement are not met.

WITHDRAWAL OF ENTITLEMENT

4(1) The regulations may make provision for the withdrawal of an incentive in specified circumstances.

4(2) If they do, they may make provision–

(a) for giving notice of the withdrawal,
(b) for an appeal, and
(c) for the recovery of an amount not exceeding the value of the incentive.

4(3) The regulations may provide that specified enactments relating to assessments, appeals and recovery of tax are to apply, with such adaptations as may be specified, in relation to the withdrawal of an incentive.

POWER TO AUTHORISE PROVISION BY DIRECTIONS

5 The regulations may authorise the making of any such provision as is mentioned in paragraph 3 or 4 by means of a specific or general direction given by the Commissioners of Inland Revenue or the Commissioners of Customs and Excise.

POWER TO PROVIDE FOR PENALTIES

6(1) The regulations may provide for contravention of, or failure to comply with, a specified provision of any such regulations to attract a penalty of a specified amount not exceeding £1,000.

6(2) If they do, they may provide that specified enactments relating to penalties imposed in relation to any taxation matter (including enactments relating to assessments, review and appeals) are to apply, with or without modifications, in relation to penalties under the regulations.

GENERAL SUPPLEMENTARY PROVISIONS

7(1) Power to make provision by regulations under this Schedule includes power–

(a) to make different provision for different cases; and
(b) to make such incidental, supplemental, consequential and transitional provision in connection with any provision contained in any such regulations as the persons exercising the power think fit.

7(2) The power to make regulations under this Schedule is exercisable by statutory instrument subject to annulment in pursuance of a resolution of the House of Commons.

INTERPRETATION

8(1) In this Schedule–

"**discount**" includes payment;
"**electronic communications**" includes any communications by means of a telecommunication system (within the meaning of the Telecommunications Act 1984);
"**legislation**" means any enactment, Community legislation or subordinate legislation;
"**payment**" includes a repayment;
"**subordinate legislation**" has the same meaning as in the Interpretation Act 1978;
"**taxation matter**" means any of the matters under the care and management of the Commissioners of Inland Revenue or the Commissioners of Customs and Excise;
"**tax authorities**" means–
(a) the Commissioners of Inland Revenue or the Commissioners of Customs and Excise,
(b) any officer of either body of Commissioners; or
(c) any other person who for the purposes of electronic communications is acting under the authority of either body of Commissioners;
"**tax legislation**" means legislation relating to any taxation matter.

8(2) References in this Schedule to the delivery of information have the same meaning as in section 132 of the Finance Act 1999.

SCHEDULE 39 – NEW SCHEDULE 1AA TO THE TAXES MANAGEMENT ACT 1970

Section 144(2)

The Schedule inserted after Schedule 1 to the Taxes Management Act 1970 is as follows:

"SCHEDULE 1AA – ORDERS FOR PRODUCTION OF DOCUMENTS

INTRODUCTION

1   The provisions of Schedule supplement section 20BA.

AUTHORISED OFFICER OF THE BOARD

2(1)   In section 20BA(1) an **"authorised officer of the Board"** means an officer of the Board authorised by the Board for the purposes of that section.

2(2)   The Board may make provision by regulations as to–
(a)   the procedures for approving in any particular case the decision to apply for an order under that section, and
(b)   the descriptions of officer by whom such approval may be given.

NOTICE OF APPLICATION FOR ORDER

3(1)   A person is entitled–
(a)   to notice of the intention to apply for an order against him under section 20BA, and
(b)   to appear and be heard at the hearing of the application,
unless the appropriate judicial authority is satisfied that this would seriously prejudice the investigation of the offence.

3(2)   The Board may make provision by regulations as to the notice to be given, the contents of the notice and the manner of giving it.

OBLIGATIONS OF PERSON GIVEN NOTICE OF APPLICATION

4(1)   A person who has been given notice of intention to apply for an order under section 20BA(4) shall not–
(a)   conceal, destroy, alter or dispose of any document to which the application relates, or
(b)   disclose to any other person information or any other matter likely to prejudice the investigation of the offence to which the application relates.
      This is subject to the following qualifications.

4(2)   Sub-paragraph (1)(a) does not prevent anything being done–
(a)   with the leave of the appropriate judicial authority,
(b)   with the written permission of an officer of the Board,
(c)   after the application has been dismissed or abandoned, or
(d)   after any order made on the application has been complied with.

4(3)   Sub-paragraph (1)(b) does not prevent a professional legal adviser from disclosing any information or other matter–
(a)   to, or to a representative of, a client of his in connection with the giving by the adviser of legal advice to the client; or
(b)   to any person–
         (i)   in contemplation of, or in connection with, legal proceedings; and
         (ii)   for the purpose of those proceedings.
      This sub-paragraph does not apply in relation to any information or other matter which is disclosed with a view to furthering a criminal purpose.

4(4)   A person who fails to comply with the obligation in sub-paragraph (1)(a) or (b) above may be dealt with as if he had failed to comply with an order under section 20BA.

EXCEPTION OF ITEMS SUBJECT TO LEGAL PRIVILEGE

5(1)   Section 20BA does not apply to items subject to legal privilege.

5(2)   For this purpose **"items subject to legal privilege"** means–

(a)   communications between a professional legal adviser and his client or any person representing his client made in connection with the giving of legal advice to the client;

(b)   communications between a professional legal adviser and his client or any person representing his client or between such an adviser or his client or any such representative and any other person made in connection with or in contemplation of legal proceedings and for the purposes of such proceedings; and

(c)   items enclosed with or referred to in such communications and made–

       (i)   in connection with the giving of legal advice; or

       (ii)   in connection with or in contemplation of legal proceedings and for the purposes of such proceedings,

when they are in the possession of a person who is entitled to possession of them.

5(3)   Items held with the intention of furthering a criminal purpose are not subject to legal privilege.

RESOLUTION OF DISPUTES AS TO LEGAL PRIVILEGE

6(1)   The Board may make provision by regulations for the resolution of disputes as to whether a document, or part of a document, is an item subject to legal privilege.

6(2)   The regulations may, in particular, make provision as to–

(a)   the custody of the document whilst its status is being decided;

(b)   the appointment of an independent, legally qualified person to decide the matter;

(c)   the procedures to be followed; and

(d)   who is to meet the costs of the proceedings.

COMPLYING WITH AN ORDER

7(1)   The Board may make provision by regulations as to how a person is to comply with an order under section 20BA.

7(2)   The regulations may, in particular, make provision as to–

(a)   the officer of the Board to whom the documents are to be produced,

(b)   the address to which the documents are to be taken or sent, and

(c)   the circumstances in which sending the documents by post complies with the order.

7(3)   Where an order under section 20BA applies to a document in electronic or magnetic form, the order shall be taken to require the person to deliver the information recorded in the document in a form in which it is visible and legible.

PROCEDURE WHERE DOCUMENTS ARE DELIVERED

8(1)   The provisions of section 20CC(3) to (9) apply in relation to a document delivered to an officer of the Board in accordance with an order under section 20BA as they apply to a thing removed by an officer of the Board as mentioned in subsection (1) of section 20CC.

8(2)   In section 20CC(9) as applied by sub-paragraph (1) above the reference to the warrant concerned shall be read as a reference to the order concerned.

SANCTION FOR FAILURE TO COMPLY WITH ORDER

9(1)   If a person fails to comply with an order made under section 20BA, he may be dealt with as if he had committed a contempt of the court.

9(2)   For this purpose **"the court"** means–

(a)   in relation to an order made by a Circuit judge, the Crown Court;

(b)   in relation to an order made by a sheriff, a sheriff court;

(c)   in relation to an order made by a county court judge, a county court in Northern Ireland.

NOTICE OF ORDER ETC.

10   The Board may make provision by regulations as to the circumstances in which notice of an order under section 20BA, or of an application for such an order, is to be treated as having been given.

GENERAL PROVISIONS ABOUT REGULATIONS

11 Regulations under this Schedule–

(a) may contain such incidental, supplementary and transitional provision as appears to the Board to be appropriate, and

(b) shall be made by statutory instrument which shall be subject to annulment in pursuance of a resolution of either House of Parliament.".

SCHEDULE 40 – REPEALS

Part IV – Value Added Tax

Chapter	Short title	Extent of repeal
1994 c. 23.	The Value Added Tax Act 1994.	In Schedule A1, in paragraph 1(1), the word "and" at the end of paragraph (b).

VAT STATUTORY INSTRUMENTS

Table of Contents

> **Note**: Not all current statutory instruments are reproduced in full text in this division. If a current statutory instrument merely amends an existing Act or statutory instrument, then the existing Act or statutory instrument itself is amended and a history note is added thereto. The amending statutory instrument is not reproduced in this division, but it is listed below together with a note indicating its effect. Similarly, if a statutory instrument merely brings a current provision into operation, i.e. it is a commencement order or an appointed day order, then it is also listed below together with an appropriate note. If a statutory instrument only partly relates to VAT, only that part is reproduced.

continued over

continued over

continued over

continued over

continued over

continued over

continued over

continued over

VALUE ADDED TAX (TERMINAL MARKETS) ORDER 1973

(SI 1973/173, as amended by SI 1975/385, SI 1980/304, SI 1981/338, SI 1981/955, SI 1984/202, SI 1985/1046, SI 1987/806, SI 1997/1836, SI 1999/3117)

Made 6 February 1973 by the Treasury under sec. 26 of the Finance Act 1972 [VATA 1994, s. 50].
Operative from 1 April 1973.

1 This Order may be cited as the Value Added Tax (Terminal Markets) Order 1973 and shall come into operation on 1st April 1973.

2(1) The Interpretation Act 1889 [Interpretation Act 1978] shall apply for the interpretation of this Order as it applies for the interpretation of an Act of Parliament.

2(2) This Order applies to the following terminal markets–

>the London Metal Exchange,
>
>the London Rubber Market,
>
>the London Cocoa Terminal Market,
>
>the London Coffee Terminal Market,
>
>the London Sugar Terminal Market,
>
>the London Vegetable Oil Terminal Market,
>
>the London Wool Terminal Market,
>
>the London Bullion Market,
>
>the London Meat Futures Market,
>
>the London Grain Futures Market,
>
>the London Soya Bean Meal Futures Market,
>
>the Liverpool Barley Futures Market,
>
>the International Petroleum Exchange of London,
>
>the London Potato Futures Market,
>
>the London Platinum and Palladium Market, and
>
>the London Securities and Derivatives Exchange Limited (OMLX).

2(3) References in this Order to a **member of a market** include any person ordinarily engaged in dealings on the market.

2(4) Notwithstanding paragraph 3 above, for the purposes of this Order a person is to be regarded as **being a member of the London Bullion Market** only if that person is a member of the London Bullion Market Association.

2(5) In this Order–

>**"investment gold"** has the same meaning as that expression has for the purposes of Group 15 of Schedule 9 to the Value Added Tax Act 1994;
>
>**"the Act"** means the Value Added Tax Act 1994.

History – In art. 2(2), the words "the London Bullion Market" were substituted for the words "the London Gold Market" by SI 1999/3117, art. 3, operative in relation to supplies made on or after 1 January 2000.
In art. 2(2), the words "the London Silver Market", which appeared after the words "the London Bullion Market", were deleted by SI 1999/3117, art. 3, operative in relation to supplies made on or after 1 January 2000.
In art. 2(2), the words "the London Platinum and Palladium Market" were inserted by SI 1987/806 operative from 1 June 1987.
In art. 2(2), the words "the London Gold Futures Market" were deleted by SI 1985/1046, operative from 1 August 1985. This SI also revoked, from 1 August 1985, SI 1981/995 which had extended zero-rating to supplies in the course of dealings on the London Gold Futures Market. The London Gold Futures Market closed on 26 June 1985.
Art. 2(2) variously amended by SI 1975/385, SI 1980/304, SI 1981/338, SI 1981/955 and SI 1984/202.
Art. 2(2) amended by SI 1997/1836 from 1 September 1997 by the insertion of "the London Securities and Derivatives Exchange Limited (OMLX)".
Art. 2(4) was inserted by SI 1999/3117, art. 4, operative in relation to supplies made on or after 1 January 2000.
Art. 2(5) was inserted by SI 1999/3117, art. 5, operative in relation to supplies made on or after 1 January 2000.

3(1) The following supplies of goods or services in the course of dealings on a terminal market to which this Order applies are hereby zero-rated, subject to the conditions specified in this Article–

(a)   the sale by or to a member of the market of any goods, other than investment gold, ordinarily dealt with on the market,

(b)   the grant by or to a member of the market of a right to acquire such goods,

(c) where a sale of goods or the grant of a right zero-rated under sub-paragraph (a) or (b) above is made, or where a supply of a description falling within article 4 or 5 below is made, in dealings between members of the market acting as agents, the supply by those members to their principals of their services in so acting.

3(2) The zero-rating of a sale by virtue of paragraph (1)(a) above is subject to the condition that the sale is either–

(a) a sale which, as a result of other dealings on the market, does not lead to a delivery of the goods by the seller to the buyer, or

(b) a sale by and to a member of the market which–

    (i) if the market is the London Metal Exchange, is a sale between members entitled to deal in the ring,

    (ii) if the market is the London Cocoa Terminal Market, the London Coffee Terminal Market, the London Meat Futures Market, the International Petroleum Exchange of London, the London Potato Futures Market, the London Soya Bean Meal Futures Market, the London Sugar Terminal Market, the London Vegetable Oil Terminal Market or the London Wool Terminal Market, is a sale registered with the International Commodities Clearing House Limited,

    (iii) if the market is the London Grain Futures Market, is a sale registered in the Clearing House of the Grain and Feed Trade Association Limited, and

    (iv) if the market is the Liverpool Barley Futures Market, is a sale registered at the Clearing House of the Liverpool Corn Trade Association Limited.

3(3) The zero-rating of the grant of a right by virtue of paragraph (1)(b) above is subject to the condition that either–

(a) the right is exercisable at a date later than that on which it is granted, or

(b) any sale resulting from the exercise of the right would be a sale with respect to which the condition specified in paragraph (2) above is satisfied.

History – In art. 3(1)(a), the words ", other than investment gold," were inserted by SI 1999/3117, art. 6, operative in relation to supplies made on or after 1 January 2000.
In art. 3(1)(c), the words ", or where a supply of a description falling within article 4 or 5 below is made," were inserted by SI 1999/3117, art. 7, operative in relation to supplies made on or after 1 January 2000.
Art. 3(2)(b)(ii) variously amended by SI 1975/385, SI 1981/338 and SI 1984/202.

4 Supplies between taxable persons which but for Note 4(a) to Group 15 of Schedule 9 to the Act (exemption for investment gold) would have fallen within that Group are hereby zero-rated.

History – Art. 4 was inserted by SI 1999/3117, art. 8, operative from 1 January 2000.

Cross references – VAT Regulations 1995 (SI 1995/2518), reg. 33A: records in relation to investment gold.

Official publications – 701/21 and 701/21A.

5 Subject to articles 6 and 7 below, section 55(1) to (4) of the Act (customers to account for tax on supplies of gold) shall apply to any supply between taxable persons which but for Note 4(b) to Group 15 of Schedule 9 to the Act would have fallen within that Group.

History – Art. 5 was inserted by SI 1999/3117, art. 8, operative from 1 January 2000.

6 Subject to article 7 below, where a taxable person who is not a member of the London Bullion Market Association makes or receives a supply falling within the description in article 5 is liable to be registered under Schedule 1 or under Schedule 3 to the Act solely by virtue of that supply or acquisition, paragraphs 5 to 8 of Schedule 1 or paragraph 3 of Schedule 3 to the Act (notification of liability and registration) shall not apply.

History – Art. 6 was inserted by SI 1999/3117, art. 8, operative from 1 January 2000.

Cross references – VAT Regulations 1995 (SI 19995/2518), reg. 33B: records in relation to investment gold.

7 Notwithstanding section 55(2) of the Act, where articles 5 and 6 above apply, it shall be for the London Bullion Market Association member, on the non-member's behalf, to keep a record of the supplies and to pay to the Commissioners of Customs and Excise the net amount of VAT, and not for the person who is not a member.

History – Art. 7 was inserted by SI 1999/3117, art. 8, operative from 1 January 2000.

Official publications – 701/9.

VALUE ADDED TAX (REFUND OF TAX) (NO. 2) ORDER 1973

(SI 1973/2121)

Made on 14 December 1973 by the Treasury under s. 15(3) of the Finance Act 1972 [VATA 1994, s. 33(3)]. Operative from 10 January 1974.

1   This Order may be cited as The Value Added Tax (Refund of Tax) (No. 2) Order 1973 and shall come into operation on 10th January 1974.

2   The Interpretation Act 1889 [Interpretation Act 1978] shall apply for the interpretation of this Order as it applies for the interpretation of an Act of Parliament.

3   The following bodies are hereby specified for the purposes of section 15 of the Finance Act 1972 [VATA 1994, s. 33]:

   Welsh National Water Development Authority
   North West Water Authority
   Northumbrian Water Authority
   Yorkshire Water Authority
   Anglian Water Authority
   Thames Water Authority
   Southern Water Authority
   Wessex Water Authority
   South West Water Authority
   Severn-Trent Water Authority

CUSTOMS DUTIES (DEFERRED PAYMENT) REGULATIONS 1976

(SI 1976/1223, as amended by SI 1978/1725)

Made on 2 August 1976 by the Commissioners of Customs and Excise under s. 16(2) of the Finance (No. 2) Act 1975 and s. 15 of the Finance Act 1976.

CITATION AND COMMENCEMENT

1   These Regulations may be cited as the Customs Duties (Deferred Payment) Regulations 1976 and shall come into operation on 1st September 1976.

INTERPRETATION

2(1)   In these Regulations–

   "approved" means approved by the Commissioners to apply for deferment of payment of duty on behalf of himself or another and **"approve"** and **"approval"** shall be construed accordingly;

   "deferment" means deferment of payment of customs duty granted under these Regulations and **"deferred"** shall be construed accordingly;

   "payment day" means the 15th day of the month next following that in which the amount of duty deferred is entered into the Commissioners' accounts, or in the case of import entries scheduled periodically, the 15th day of the period following that in which deferment is granted (save that where that day in either case falls on a non-working day it shall be the next working day thereafter);

   "period" means a period commencing on the 16th day of any month and ending on the 15th day of the month next following.

2(2)   The Interpretation Act 1889 [Interpretation Act 1978] shall apply for the interpretation of these Regulations as it applies for the interpretation of an Act of Parliament.

2(3) Where any document used or required for the purpose of deferment refers to a provision of the Customs Duties (Deferred Payment) Regulations 1972 such reference shall, unless the contrary intention appears, be construed as referring to the corresponding provision of these Regulations.

2(4) Any approval granted by a Collector under the Customs Duties (Deferred Payments) Regulations 1972 and in force immediately before the commencement of these Regulations shall have effect as if granted under these Regulations.

History – Various amendments made to reg. 2(1) by SI 1978/1725.

APPLICATION

3 These Regulations apply in the case of customs duty payable, apart from these Regulations, on the making of entry of goods chargeable therewith.

History – Reg. 3 amended by SI 1978/1725.

APPROVAL

4(1) A person who wishes to be approved for the purposes of these Regulations shall apply to the Commissioners in such form and manner as they shall determine, furnish security for payment on payment day of the amount of customs duty in respect of which he seeks deferment, and make arrangements with the Commissioners for the payment of that duty on payment day.

4(2) If satisfied with the security and arrangements as aforesaid, the Commissioners shall in writing approve the applicant with respect to an amount of customs duty not exceeding that for which he has furnished security;

Provided that such approval may be limited to the deferment of customs duty payable, apart from these Regulations, on the making of entry within any named Collection.

4(3) The Commissioners may, for reasonable cause, at any time vary or revoke any approval granted under this Regulation.

4(4) A person to whom approval has been granted under this Regulation shall forthwith notify the Commissioners of any change in the particulars furnished, the security given, or the arrangements for payment provided for in paragraph (1) above.

History – Reg. 4(1) amended by SI 1978/1725.

GRANT OF DEFERMENT

5 Subject to Regulations 3, 4, 6 and 7, the Commissioners shall, upon application by an approved person in such form and manner as they shall determine, grant deferment of customs duty until payment day.

History – Reg. 5 amended by SI 1978/1725.

PAYMENT

6 On each payment day an approved person shall pay to the Commissioners in accordance with the arrangements referred to in Regulation 4(1) the total amount of customs duty of which he has been granted deferment until that payment day.

7 If at any time after entry has been made the Commissioners are satisfied that–

(a) the full amount of customs duty payable has not been shown on the entry or periodic schedule then, save as the Commissioners otherwise allow, the balance shall forthwith be paid by the person making entry of the goods and no deferment in respect thereof shall be permitted;

(b) customs duty in excess of the amount payable has been shown on the entry or periodic schedule, the Commissioners shall repay the excess, but the total amount shown shall nevertheless be paid on payment day.

History – Reg. 7 amended by SI 1978/1725.

8 Without prejudice to Regulation 6, for the purposes of–

(a) sections 34(1) and 260(1) of the Customs and Excise Act 1952 and the Warehousing Regulations 1975; and

(b) any relief by way of repayment or suspension of customs duty, or agricultural levy falling to be treated as such, under–

    (i) the Inward Processing Relief Regulations 1977,

    (ii) the Customs Duties and Agricultural Levies (Goods for Free Circulation) Regulations 1977,

    (iii) Regulation 4 of the Import Duties (Outward Processing Relief) Regulations 1976, and

(iv) Article 4 of the Agricultural Levies (Outward Processing Relief) Order 1976

duty shall be deemed to have been paid at the time when deferment thereof was granted.
History – Reg. 8 substituted by SI 1978/1725.

WAREHOUSING

9 [Repealed by SI 1978/1725, reg. 10, operative from 1 January 1979. It had amended the Warehousing Regulations 1975, reg. 8(5).]

VALUE ADDED TAX (REFUND OF TAX) ORDER 1976

(SI 1976/2028)

Made on 29 November 1976 by the Treasury under s. 15(3) of the Finance Act 1972 [VATA 1994, s. 33(3)]. Operative from 1 April 1977.

1 This Order may be cited as The Value Added Tax (Refund of Tax) Order 1976 and shall come into operation on 1st April 1977.

2 The Interpretation Act 1889 [Interpretation Act 1978] shall apply for the interpretation of this Order as it applies for the interpretation of an Act of Parliament.

3 The following bodies are hereby specified for the purposes of section 15 of the Finance Act 1972 [VATA 1994, s. 33]:–

the Commission for Local Administration in England

the Commission for Local Administration in Wales

the Commissioner for Local Administration in Scotland

the Commission for Local Authority Accounts in Scotland.

VALUE ADDED TAX (ISLE OF MAN) ORDER 1982

(SI 1982/1067)

Made on 30 July 1982 by Her Majesty under s. 6 of the Isle of Man Act 1979. Operative from 1 October 1982.

1(1) This Order may be cited as the Value Added Tax (Isle of Man) Order 1982 and shall come into operation on 1st October 1982.

1(2) In this Order:–

"the United Kingdom Act" means the Finance Act 1972 [VATA 1994];

"the Manx Act" means the Value Added Tax and Other Taxes Act 1973; and

"the Finance Board" means the Finance Board of the Isle of Man,

and any other word or expression used in this Order to which meaning is given in or under Part I of the United Kingdom Act shall have, except where the context otherwise requires, the same meaning in this Order as in or under that Part of that Act.

1(3) For the purposes of this Order, the Interpretation Act 1978 shall apply to the Manx Act and to any instrument of a legislative character made thereunder as if the Manx Act were an Act of Parliament.

1(4) For the purposes of this Order:–

(a) a supply shall be treated as made in the United Kingdom if it would be so treated under section 8 or 8A of the United Kingdom Act [VATA 1994, s. 7] if Article 2 below were disregarded; and

(b) a supply shall be treated as made in the Isle of Man if it would be so treated under one or other of those sections if they were amended by substituting for the words "United Kingdom" wherever they occur the words "Isle of Man".

2 Subject to the provisions of this Order Part I of the United Kingdom Act shall have effect as if the Isle of Man were part of the United Kingdom.

3(1) Notwithstanding Article 2 above, the removal of goods to the United Kingdom from the Isle of Man shall be treated for the purposes of Part I of the United Kingdom Act as the importation of those goods into the United Kingdom if they are goods which have previously been imported into or supplied in the United Kingdom or the Isle of Man and either:–

(a)   value added tax was chargeable on that previous importation or supply under Part I of the Manx Act but was not accounted for or paid at the rate which would have applied under Part I of the United Kingdom Act if the importation had been made into, or the supply had been made in, the United Kingdom; or

(b)   that previous importation or supply was wholly or partly relieved from tax chargeable under Part I of the United Kingdom Act or value added tax chargeable under Part I of the Manx Act subject to a condition and that condition has not been complied with.

3(2)   The amount of tax chargeable under Part I of the United Kingdom Act on the removal into the United Kingdom from the Isle of Man of such goods as are mentioned in paragraph (1) above shall be reduced by an amount equal to any value added tax chargeable under Part I of the Manx Act which has been accounted for or paid on any earlier importation of those goods into, or supply of those goods in, the United Kingdom or the Isle of Man.

4   Tax shall not be charged under the United Kingdom Act:–

(a)   on the importation of goods into the Isle of Man except where the importation is by a taxable person otherwise than in the course or furtherance of a business carried on by him; or

(b)   on the importation of goods into the United Kingdom by a person who is a taxable person for the purposes of the Manx Act where the importation is in the course or furtherance of a business carried on by him.

5   Any requirement imposed by or under the Manx Act shall be treated as a requirement imposed by or under the United Kingdom Act.

6   Any permission, direction, notice, determination or other thing given, made or done under the Manx Act by the Finance Board shall be treated as given, made or done by the Commissioners under the United Kingdom Act.

7   Sections 3(3)(a), (4), (8) and (9), 5, 14(3), 15, 15A, 17(1), 32(1), 33, 36(1), 43(4)(b) and 51 of the United Kingdom Act [VATA 1994, 16(1), 24, 32, 33, 35, 39, 97(4)(b) and 99 and Sch. 11, para. 4, 5 and 8], section 16 of the Finance Act 1977 [VATA 1994, s. 27] and section 12(1) of the Finance Act 1978 [VATA 1994, s. 36] shall have effect as if the references to tax in those sections included references to value added tax chargeable under Part I of the Manx Act.

8   A person who is a taxable person for the purposes of the Manx Act shall be treated as a taxable person for the purposes of sections 18, 27(3), 30(2), 34(1) and 40(1)(k) of, and Note (6) to Item 4 of Group 15 of Schedule 4 to, the United Kingdom Act [VATA 1994, s. 38, 18(3) and 83(f) and Sch. 8, Grp. 13, item 3 and Note (5) and Sch. 11, para. 2(2) and 6] and of section 16 of the Finance Act 1977 [VATA 1994, s. 27].

9   Section 15A of the United Kingdom Act [VATA 1994, s. 35] shall not apply to the construction of dwellings within the Isle of Man.

10(1)   This Article shall have effect for enabling the Commissioners to determine for the purposes of section 21 of the United Kingdom Act [VATA 1994, s. 43] which member of a group is to be the representative member in cases where supplies are made both in the United Kingdom and in the Isle of Man.

10(2)   Where bodies corporate, which are treated as members of a group under the said section 21 have establishments both in the United Kingdom and in the Isle of Man, or do not have an establishment in either country, the Commissioners may at any time determine that another member of the group shall be substituted as the representative member from such date as they may determine.

11(1)   This Article shall have effect, where a person would, apart from this Article, be liable to be registered both under Part I of the United Kingdom Act and under Part I of the Manx Act, for determining, or enabling the Commissioners to determine whether that person is to be registered under the United Kingdom Act or the Manx Act and for transferring a person registered under one Act to the register kept under the other.

11(2)   A person, who by virtue of paragraph 1(a) or (b) of Schedule 1 to the United Kingdom Act [VATA 1994, Sch. 1, para. 1] is liable to be registered shall, if he has an establishment both in the United Kingdom and in the Isle of Man or does not have an establishment in either country, be registered either under Part I of the United Kingdom Act or under Part I of the Manx Act, as the Commissioners shall determine, but unless or until the Commissioners determine that such a person shall be registered under Part I of the Manx Act, he shall be required to be registered under Part I of the United Kingdom Act.

11(3) Paragraphs 3, 5 and 6 of Schedule 1 to the United Kingdom Act [VATA 1994, Sch. 1, para. 5–8] shall not apply to a person registered or required to be registered under Part I of the Manx Act.

11(4) The Commissioners may determine that any person to whom paragraph 3, 5 or 6 of Schedule 1 to the United Kingdom Act [VATA 1994, Sch. 1, para. 5–8] applies shall be registered under Part I of the Manx Act.

11(5) Where a person, who is or was required to notify the Commissioners under paragraph 3, 5 or 6 of Schedule 1 to the United Kingdom Act [VATA 1994, Sch. 1, para. 5–8], has an establishment in the Isle of Man, he may notify the Isle of Man Finance Board and such notification shall be deemed for the purposes of that paragraph to be notification to the Commissioners.

11(6) Any person, registered under Part I of the United Kingdom Act on or after 1st April 1980, who–

(a)   has no establishment in the Isle of Man, or

(b)   is the representative member of a group of bodies corporate, within the meaning of section 21 of the United Kingdom Act [VATA 1994, s. 43] , no member of which has an establishment in the Isle of Man,

shall notify the Commissioners if, at any later time, he or any member of the group has such an establishment and such notification shall be treated for the purposes of Schedule 1 to the United Kingdom Act [VATA 1994, Sch. 1] and any regulations made thereunder as an event which could necessitate the cancellation of that person's, or that group of bodies corporate's, registration.

11(7) Where a person, who is registered under Part I of the United Kingdom Act, has establishments both in the United Kingdom and in the Isle of Man, or does not have an establishment in either country, the Commissioners may, at any time, determine that he shall be registered under Part I of the Manx Act.

11(8) Where the Commissioners determine that a person, who is registered under Part I of the United Kingdom Act, shall be registered under Part I of the Manx Act, he shall cease to be, or required to be, registered under Part I of the United Kingdom Act from such date as they may determine, but, for the purposes of paragraph 7 of Schedule 2 to the United Kingdom Act [VATA 1994, Sch. 4, para. 8], he shall not cease to be a taxable person.

11(9) Where a person, who is registered under Part I of the Manx Act, has establishments both in the United Kingdom and in the Isle of Man or does not have an establishment in either country, the Commissioners may, at any time, determine that he shall be registered under Part I of the United Kingdom Act and, if they so determine, they shall register him with effect from such date as they may determine.

11(10) Where a person who was registered under Part I of the Manx Act is, pursuant to a determination of the Commissioners to that effect, registered under Part I of the United Kingdom Act, any amount of value added tax required to be paid under Part I of the Manx Act shall be deemed to have been an amount of tax due under Part I of the United Kingdom Act.

11(11) Section 18(1) of the Finance (No. 2) Act 1975 [VATA 1994, s. 22] shall not apply where the person to whom the supply is made is registered under Part I of the Manx Act.

12(1) For the purposes of Articles 10 and 11 above a person shall be deemed to have an establishment in a country if–

(a)   there is a place in that country from which he carries on a business; or

(b)   he carries on business through a branch or agent in that country.

12(2) For the purposes of paragraph (1) above an agent is a person who has the authority or capacity to create legal relations between his principal and a third party.

13 In section 3(8)(bb) of the United Kingdom Act the words "under either of those Parts" are hereby repealed.

14 This Order revokes:–

(a)   the Value Added Tax (Isle of Man) Order 1980, except so much of it as relates to the Rules, Regulations and Orders specified in Schedule 2 to that Order; and

(b)   so much of the Value Added Tax (Isle of Man) (No. 2) Order 1980 as relates to the amendment of the Finance Act 1972, and accordingly the Finance Acts amended by those Orders shall have effect as if the Orders had not been made.

VALUE ADDED TAX (ISLE OF MAN) (NO. 2) ORDER 1982

(SI 1982/1068)

Made on 30 July 1982 by Her Majesty under s. 6 of the Isle of Man Act 1979. Operative from 1 October 1982.

1(1) This Order may be cited as the Value Added Tax (Isle of Man) (No. 2) Order 1982 and shall come into operation on 1st October 1982.

1(2) In this Order–

"the United Kingdom Act" means the Finance Act 1972 [VATA 1994] and **"the Manx Act"** means the Value Added Tax and Other Taxes Act 1973,

and any other word or expression used in this Order to which meaning is given in or under Part I of the United Kingdom Act shall have, except where the context otherwise requires, the same meaning in this Order as in or under that Part of that Act.

1(3) For the purposes of this Order, the Interpretation Act 1978 shall apply to the Manx Act and to any instrument of a legislative character made thereunder as if the Manx Act were an Act of Parliament.

2 In statutory instruments made under Part I of the United Kingdom Act references to the United Kingdom shall be construed as including references to the Isle of Man.

3 In the statutory instruments referred to in column 1 of the Schedule to this Order, the word or expression appearing in column 2 thereof shall, to the extent prescribed therein, be construed as including references to their equivalents specified in column 3, whether or not the same word or expression is used in their equivalents in the Manx Act or regulations made thereunder.

4 Regulation 51(4) of the Value Added Tax (General) Regulations 1980 shall not apply to a person determined by the Commissioners under paragraph (7) or (8) of Article 11 of the Value Added Tax (Isle of Man) Order 1982 to be required to be registered under Part I of the Manx Act.

5 Article 2(a) of the Tribunals and Inquiries (Value Added Tax Tribunals) Order 1972 and Rule 30(2) of the Value Added Tax Tribunals Rules 1972 [Value Added Tax Tribunals Rules 1986, r. 29(2)] shall have effect as if the words "England and Wales" included the Isle of Man.

6 This Order revokes:–

(a)   so much of the Value Added Tax (Isle of Man) Order 1980 as relates to the Rules, Regulations and Orders specified in Schedule 2 to that Order;

(b)   so much of the Value Added Tax (Isle of Man) (No. 2) Order 1980 as relates to the Order specified in the Schedule to that Order; and

(c)   the Value Added Tax (Isle of Man) (No. 3) Order 1980,

and accordingly the instruments amended by those Orders shall have effect as if the Orders had not been made.

SCHEDULE

Article 3

Column 1	Column 2	Column 3
STATUTORY INSTRUMENT	WORDS	MANX EQUIVALENT
The Value Added Tax (Treatment of Transactions) (No. 1) Order 1973		
In Article 3(a)	"taxable person"	a person defined as such in section 2(2) of the Manx Act
The Value Added Tax (Do-it-yourself Builders) (Relief) Regulations 1975		
In Regulation 1(2)	"value added tax"	value added tax chargeable under Part I of the Manx Act
The Value Added Tax (Bad Debt Relief) Regulations 1978		
In Regulation 4(b)(i)	"invoice"	a document defined as such in section 30(2) of the Manx Act
	"Regulations"	the corresponding provisions made under the Manx Act
The Value Added Tax (Cars) Order 1980		
In Article 4(1)	"Tax"	value added tax chargeable under Part I of the Manx Act
	"taxable person", where secondly occurring	a person defined as such in section 2(2) of the Manx Act
In Article 5(2)(b)	"tax"	value added tax chargeable under Part I of the Manx Act
In Article 6(1)(b)	"tax", where secondly occurring	
In Article 6(1)(c)	"tax", where first occurring	value added tax chargeable under Part I of the Manx Act
In Article 6(2)(c)	"tax", wherever occurring	
The Value Added Tax (General) Regulations 1980		
In Regulation 8(1)	"taxable person", where secondly occurring	a person defined as such in section 2(2) of the Manx Act
In Regulation 8(3)	"taxable person", where secondly occurring	a person defined as such in section 2(2) of the Manx Act
	"regulation"	the corresponding provision made under the Manx Act
In Regulation 10(1)	"taxable person", where secondly occurring	a person defined as such in section 2(2) of the Manx Act

Column 1	Column 2	Column 3
STATUTORY INSTRUMENT	WORDS	MANX EQUIVALENT
In Regulations 14 and 15	"the Act"	the corresponding provision of the Manx Act
	"invoice"	a document defined as such in section 30(2) of the Manx Act
In Regulations 16(1)(b) and 17	"invoice"	a document defined as such in section 30(2) of the Manx Act
In Regulation 18(1)	"invoice"	a document defined as such in section 30(2) of the Manx Act
In Regulation 18(2)	"invoice", wherever occurring	a document defined as such in section 30(2) of the Manx Act
In Regulation 18(2)(b)	"tax"	value added tax chargeable under Part I of the Manx Act
In Regulation 18(2)(c)	"tax", where first occurring	
In Regulations 19, 20, 21 and 22	"invoice"	a document defined as such in section 30(2) of the Manx Act
In Regulation 29(1)	"tax", where secondly occurring	value added tax chargeable under Part I of the Manx Act
In Regulation 29(2)	"tax", where first occurring	
In Regulation 29(4)	"tax"	
In Regulation 30(5)	"registered person"	a person defined as such in regulations made under the Manx Act
In Regulation 33	"taxable person", wherever occurring	a person defined as such in section 2(2) of the Manx Act
	"tax"	value added tax chargeable under Part I of the Manx Act
In Regulation 33(a)	"the Act"	the corresponding provisions of the Manx Act
In Regulation 33(b)	"registration number", wherever occurring	a number defined as such in regulations made under the Manx Act
In Regulation 33(a) and 33(b)	"Commissioners"	the Isle of Man Finance Board
In Regulation 34	"tax"	value added tax chargeable under Part I of the Manx Act
	"taxable person"	a person defined as such in section 2(2) of the Manx Act
	"registration number"	a number defined as such in regulations made under the Manx Act
In Regulation 39(a)	"taxable person"	a person defined as such in section 2(2) of the Manx Act
In Regulation 39(c)(i)	"tax", where secondly occurring	value added tax chargeable under Part I of the Manx Act
In Regulation 39(d)	"tax", where first occurring	
	"the Act"	the Manx Act

Column 1	Column 2	Column 3
STATUTORY INSTRUMENT	WORDS	MANX EQUIVALENT
In Regulation 40(1)(a)	"tax", where secondly occurring	value added tax chargeable under Part I of the Manx Act
In Regulation 42	"port", "airport" or "depot", wherever occurring	a place in the Isle of Man corresponding to such a port, airport or depot
In Regulation 55(1)	"proper officer", wherever occurring	a person defined as such in regulations made under the Manx Act
	"tax", where secondly occurring	value added tax chargeable under Part I of the Manx Act
In Regulation 55(1)(a)	"registered person"	a person defined as such in regulations made under the Manx Act
	"regulation 8"	the corresponding provision made under the Manx Act
In Regulation 55(1)(c) and 55(1)(d)	"tax", wherever occurring	value added tax chargeable under Part I of the Manx Act
In Regulation 58(1)	"tax", wherever occurring	value added tax chargeable under Part I of the Manx Act
	"the Act", where first occurring	the Manx Act
	"the Act", where secondly occurring	the corresponding provision of the Manx Act
In Regulation 59(a)	"tax", wherever occurring	value added tax chargeable under Part I of the Manx Act
	"Act"	the Manx Act
In Regulation 59(c), 59(e), 59(f) and 59(g)	"tax", wherever occurring	value added tax chargeable under Part I of the Manx Act
The Value Added Tax (Repayment to Community Traders) Regulations 1980		
In Regulation 3	"tax", where firstly and secondly occurring	value added tax chargeable under Part I of the Manx Act
In Regulation 4(b)(ii)	"tax"	
	"section 8B of the Act"	section 8B of the Manx Act
In Regulation 6(1)	"tax", wherever occurring	value added tax chargeable under Part I of the Manx Act
In Regulation 7(1)	"tax", where firstly and secondly occurring	value added tax chargeable under Part I of the Manx Act
In Regulation 7(1)(b)(ii)	"section 3 of the Act"	section 3 of the Manx Act
In Regulations 8 and 12	"tax", wherever occurring	value added tax chargeable under Part 1 of the Manx Act

VALUE ADDED TAX (IMPORTED GOODS) RELIEF ORDER 1984

(SI 1984/746, as amended by SI 1987/155 and 2108, SI 1988/1193, 2212,
SI 1992/3120, SI 1995/3222)

*Operative from 1 July 1984. Made by the Treasury in pursuance of the Value Added Tax Act 1983,
s. 19(1), 45(1), (2) [VATA 1994, s. 37(1), 97(1) and (5)].*

CITATION AND COMMENCEMENT

1   This Order may be cited as the Value Added Tax (Imported Goods) Relief Order 1984 and shall come into operation on 1st July 1984.

INTERPRETATION

2(1)   In this Order–

"**abroad**" means a place outside the member States;

"**alcoholic beverages**" means beverages falling within headings 22.03 to 22.08;

"**approved**" means approved by the Secretary of State;

"**exported**" means exported to a place outside the member States and "**exportation**" shall be construed accordingly;

"**sent**" means sent from a place outside the member States;

"**third country**" means a place outside the member States;

"**tobacco products**" has the same meaning as in section 1 of the Tobacco Products Duty Act 1979.

2(2)   In this Order, references to a heading or subheading are references to a heading or subheading of the Combined Nomenclature of the European Economic Community.

2(3)   Section 48(4) of the Value Added Tax Act 1983 [VATA 1994, s. 96(6), (7)] (definition of "document" etc.) shall not apply for the purposes of this Order.

2(4)   Except where it appears in Article 3(2) "**import**" means import from a place outside the member States and "**importation**" and "**imported**" shall be construed accordingly;

2(5)   Except where it appears in Note (3) to Group 7 of Schedule 2, for "**United Kingdom**" there shall be substituted "**member States**".

History – In art. 2(1), the definition of "abroad" substituted by SI 1992/3120, art. 3(a), operative from 1 January 1993. The former definition read as follows:
""**abroad**" means in a country outside the United Kingdom;"
Art. 2(1) amended by SI 1988/1193 which in the definition of "alcoholic beverages" for the heading "22.09" there was substituted the heading "22.08", operative from 1 August 1988.
In art. 2(1), definitions of "exported", "sent" and "third country" inserted by SI 1992/3120, art. 3(b), operative from 1 January 1993.
Art. 2(2) amended by SI 1987/2108 on 1 January 1988. The former art. 2(2) read as follows:
"**2(2)**   In this Order, references to a heading or subheading are references to a heading or subheading of the common customs tariff of the European Economic Community."
Art. 2(4) and (5) inserted by SI 1992/3120, art. 3(c), operative from 1 January 1993.

APPLICATION

3(1)   This Order shall apply without prejudice to relief from tax on the importation of goods afforded under or by virtue of any other enactment.

3(2)   Nothing in this Order shall be construed as authorising a person to import anything from a place outside or within the member States in contravention of any prohibition or restriction for the time being in force with respect thereto under or by virtue of any enactment.

History – Art. 3(2) substituted by SI 1992/3120, art. 4, operative from 1 January 1993. Former art. 3(2) read as follows:
"**3(2)**   Nothing in this Order shall be construed as authorising a person to import any thing in contravention of any prohibition or restriction for the time being in force with respect thereto under or by virtue of any enactment."

RELIEF FOR UNITED NATIONS GOODS

4   No tax shall be payable on the importation, for whatever purpose, of goods produced by the United Nations or by a United Nations organisation, being goods–

(a)   of a description specified in Part I of Schedule 1 to this Order, or

(b)   classified under any heading or subheading specified in column 1 of Part II of Schedule 1 to this Order and within the limits of relief specified in column 2 thereof in relation to such heading or subheading.

RELIEF FOR GOODS OF OTHER DESCRIPTIONS

5(1) Subject to the provisions of this Order, no tax shall be payable on the importation of goods of a description specified in any item in Schedule 2 to this Order.

5(2) Schedule 2 shall be interpreted in accordance with the notes therein contained, except that the descriptions of Groups in that Schedule are for ease of reference only and shall not affect the interpretation of the descriptions of items in those Groups.

CONDITION AS TO USE OR PURPOSE OF GOODS IN SCHEDULE 2

6(1) Where relief has been afforded in respect of any goods by virtue of an item comprised in Schedule 2 which describes the goods by reference to a use or purpose, it shall be a condition of the relief that the goods are put to such use or the purpose fulfilled in the United Kingdom.

6(2) Without prejudice to paragraph (1) above, where relief has been afforded by virtue of item 5, 6 or 7 of Group 3 of Schedule 2 in respect of goods for demonstration or use, it shall be a condition of the relief that, in the course of, or as a result of, such demonstration or use, the goods are consumed or destroyed or rendered incapable of being used again for the same purpose.

6(3) Without prejudice to paragraph (1) above, where relief has been afforded by virtue of item 1 of Group 4 of Schedule 2 in respect of goods for examination, analysis or testing, the relief shall be subject to the following conditions:–

(a) the examination, analysis or testing shall be completed within such time as the Commissioners may require; and

(b) any goods not completely used up or destroyed in the course of, or as a result of, such examination, analysis or testing, and any products resulting therefrom, shall forthwith be destroyed or rendered commercially worthless, or exported.

RESTRICTION ON DISPOSAL OF GOODS IN SCHEDULE 2, GROUP 6

7(1) Without prejudice to article 6(1) above and subject to paragraph (2) below, where relief is afforded in respect of any goods by virtue of Group 6 of Schedule 2, it shall be a condition of the relief that the goods are not lent, hired-out or transferred, except in accordance with the provisions of that Group relating to those goods.

7(2) Paragraph (1) above shall not apply and relief shall continue to be afforded where goods are lent, hired-out or transferred to an organisation which would be entitled to relief by virtue of Group 6 of Schedule 2, if importing the goods on that date, on condition that–

(a) prior notification in writing is received by the Commissioners; and

(b) the goods are used solely in accordance with the provisions of Group 6 relating thereto.

SUPPLEMENTARY PROVISIONS AS TO GOODS IN SCHEDULE 2, GROUP 6

8 Where any goods in respect of which relief has been afforded by virtue of Group 6 of Schedule 2–

(a) are to be lent, hired-out, transferred or used except in accordance with the provisions of this Order relating to those goods; or

(b) remain in the possession of an organisation which has ceased to fulfil any condition subject to which it is approved,

and written notification thereof is given to the Commissioners, the tax payable on the goods shall be determined as if the goods had been imported on the date when the tax becomes due, provided that where the amount of the tax first relieved is less, such lesser amount shall become payable.

REVOCATION

9 The Value Added Tax (Imported Goods) Relief (No. 1) Order 1973 and the Value Added Tax (Health) Order 1983 are hereby revoked.

SCHEDULE 1 – RELIEF FOR GOODS PRODUCED BY THE UNITED NATIONS OR A UNITED NATIONS ORGANISATION

Article 4

Part I

1 Holograms for laser projection.

2 Multi-media kits.

3 Materials for programmed instruction, including materials in kit form, with the corresponding printed materials.

Part II

Column 1 Heading or subheading	Column 2 Limits of Relief
370400 10	Limited to films of an educational, scientific or cultural character.
37 05	Limited to films of an educational, scientific or cultural character.
370690 51	Limited to newsreels (with or without soundtrack) depicting events of current news value at the time of importation and, in the case of each importer, not exceeding two copies of each subject for copying.
370610 99 370690 91 370690 99	Limited to— (i) archival film material (with or without soundtrack) intended for use in connection with newsreel films; (ii) recreational film particularly suited for children and young people; and (iii) other films of an educational, scientific or cultural character.
49 11	Limited to— (i) microcards or other information storage media required in computerised information and documentation services of an educational, scientific or cultural character; and (ii) wall charts designed solely for demonstration and education.
85 24	Limited to those of an educational, scientific or cultural character.
90 23	Limited to— (i) patterns, models and wall charts of an educational, scientific or cultural character, designed solely for demonstration and education; and (ii) mock-ups or visualisations of abstract concepts such as molecular structures or mathematical formulae.

History – Sch. 1, Pt. II substituted by SI 1987/2108, operative from 1 January 1988. The former Sch. 1, Pt. II read as follows:

"Column 1 Heading or subheading	Column 2 Limits of Relief		
37.04 A.II	Limited to those of an educational, scientific or cultural character.	49.11B	Limited to–
			(i) microcards or other information storage media required in computerised information and documentation services of an educational, scientific or cultural character;
37.05	Limited to those of an educational, scientific or cultural character.		
37.07B.II.(a)	Limited to those depicting events of current news value at the time of importation and, in the case of each importer, not exceeding two copies of each subject for copying.		(ii) wall charts designed solely for demonstration and education.
(b)	Limited to–	90.21	Limited to–
	(i) archival film material (with or without soundtrack) intended for use in connection with newsreel films;		(i) patterns, models and wall charts of an educational, scientific or cultural character, designed solely for demonstration and education; and
	(ii) recreational films particularly suited for children and young people;		(ii) mock-ups or visualisations of abstract concepts such as molecular structures or mathematical formulae.
	(iii) other films of an educational, scientific or cultural character.		
		92.12B	Limited to those of an educational, scientific or cultural character."

SCHEDULE 2 – RELIEF FOR GOODS OF OTHER DESCRIPTIONS

Article 5

GROUP 1 – CAPITAL GOODS AND EQUIPMENT ON TRANSFER OF ACTIVITIES

Item No.

1. Capital goods and equipment imported by a person for the purposes of a business he has ceased to carry on abroad and which he has notified the Commissioners is to be carried on by him in the United Kingdom and concerned exclusively with making taxable supplies.

2. [Revoked by SI 1992/3120, art. 5(a).]

Notes:

(1) **"Capital goods and equipment"** includes livestock other than livestock in the possession of dealers, but does not include–

(a) food of a kind used for human consumption or animal feeding stuffs;

(b) fuel;

(c) stocks of raw materials and finished or semi-finished products; or

(d) any motor vehicle in respect of which deduction of input tax is disallowed by article 4 of the Value Added Tax (Cars) Order 1980.

(2) For the purposes of item 1, a person is not to be treated as intending to carry on a business in the United Kingdom if such business is to be merged with, or absorbed by, another business already carried on there.

(3) Item 1 applies only where the goods–

(a) have been used in the course of the business for at least twelve months before it ceased to be carried on abroad;

(b) are imported within twelve months of the date on which such business ceased to be carried on abroad, or within such longer period as the Commissioners allow; and

(c) are appropriate both to the nature and size of the business to be carried on in the United Kingdom.

(4) [Revoked by SI 1992/3120, art. 5(a).]

History – Item 2 and Note (4) were revoked by SI 1992/3120, art. 5(a), operative from 1 January 1993. Former item 2 and Note (4) read as follows:

"2. Capital goods and equipment belonging to, and imported for the purposes of, a charitable or philanthropic organisation which has notified the Commissioners of the transfer of its principal place of business from another member State to the United Kingdom."

"(4) Item 2 does not apply to any goods supplied exempt from tax to the charitable or philanthropic organisation in question for the purpose of being exported in the course of its humanitarian, charitable or teaching activities."

GROUP 2 – AGRICULTURE AND ANIMALS

3   [Revoked by SI 1992/3120, art. 5(a), operative from 1 January 1993.]

History – Former Grp. 2 read as follows:
"Item No.

1. Products obtained by a relevant person from any agricultural activity carried on by him on relevant land, imported by or on behalf of such person.

2. Seeds, fertilizers and products for the treatment of soil and crops, imported by or on behalf of a relevant person in quantities not exceeding those necessary for his use in the course of any agricultural activity carried on by him on relevant land.

3. Products obtained by a person established in the United Kingdom from fishing or fish-farming in rivers and lakes adjoining the boundary, imported by or on behalf of such person.

4. Thoroughbred horses, not more than six months old, born of a mare covered in the United Kingdom which was exported temporarily by the breeder in order to give birth.

Notes:

(1)   In item 1, **"relevant person"** means a person established in the United Kingdom for the purpose of any agricultural activity which is principally carried on by him on land in the United Kingdom adjoining the boundary.

(2)   **"Agricultural activity"** includes stock-farming, bee-keeping, horticulture and forestry.

(3)   In item 1, **"relevant land"** means land in the Irish Republic adjoining the boundary.

(4)   Item 1 applies to stock-farming products only where such products are obtained from an animal which has been reared or supplied in, or imported into, the United Kingdom and in respect of which any tax chargeable has been paid and not repaid.

(5)   In item 2, **"relevant person"** means a person established in the Irish Republic for the purpose of any agricultural activity which is principally carried on by him on land in the Irish Republic adjoining the boundary.

(6)   In item 2, **"relevant land"** means land in the United Kingdom adjoining the boundary.

(7)   **"Boundary"** means the land boundary of Northern Ireland.

(8)   Items 1 and 3 do not apply to products which have undergone any treatment other than that which normally follows the activity as a result of which they were obtained."

GROUP 3 – PROMOTION OF TRADE

Item No.

1.   Articles of no intrinsic commercial value sent free of charge by suppliers of goods and services for the sole purpose of advertising.

2.   Samples of negligible value of a kind and in quantities capable of being used solely for soliciting orders for goods of the same kind.

3.   Printed advertising matter, including catalogues, price lists, directions for use or brochures, which relates to goods for sale or hire by a person established outside the United Kingdom, or to transport, commercial insurance or banking services offered by a person established in a third country, and which clearly displays the name of the person by whom such goods or services are offered.

4.   Goods to be distributed free of charge at an event, as small representative samples, for use or consumption by the public.

5.   Goods imported solely for the purpose of being demonstrated at an event.

6.   Goods imported solely for the purpose of being used in the demonstration of any machine or apparatus displayed at an event.

7.   Paints, varnishes, wallpaper and other materials of low value to be used in the building, fitting-out and decoration of a temporary stand at an event.

8.   Catalogues, prospectuses, price lists, advertising posters, calenders (whether or not illustrated), unframed photographs and other printed matter or articles advertising goods displayed at an event, supplied without charge for the purpose of distribution free of charge to the public at such event.

Notes:

(1) Where the Commissioners so require, item 2 applies only to goods which are rendered permanently unusable, except as samples, by being torn, perforated, clearly and indelibly marked, or by any other process.

(2) Save in the case of imported printed matter intended for distribution free of charge and relating to either goods for sale or hire, item 3 does not apply to–

(a)   any consignment containing two or more copies of different documents;

(b)   any consignment containing two or more copies of the same document, unless the total gross weight of such consignment does not exceed one kilogram; or

(c)   any goods which are the subject of grouped consignments from the same consignor to the same consignee.

(3) *"Event" means any of the following–*

(a)   any trade, industrial, agricultural or craft exhibition, fair or similar show or display, not being an exhibition, fair, show or display organised for private purposes in a shop or on business premises with a view to the sale of the goods displayed;

(b)   any exhibition or meeting which is primarily organised–

    (i)   for a charitable purpose, or

    (ii) to promote any branch of learning, art, craft, sport or scientific, technical, educational, cultural or trade union activity, or tourism, or

    (iii) to promote friendship between peoples, or

    (iv) to promote religious knowledge or worship;

(c)   any meeting of representatives of any international organisation or international group of organisations; and

(d)   any representative meeting or ceremony of an official or commemorative character.

(4) In item 4, **"representative samples"** means goods which are–

(a)   imported free of charge or obtained at such event from goods imported in bulk;

(b)   identifiable as advertising samples of low value;

(c)   not easily marketable and, where appropriate, packaged in quantities which are less than the lowest quantity of the same goods as marketed; and

(d)   intended to be consumed at such event, where the goods comprise foodstuffs or beverages not packaged as described in paragraph (c) above.

(5) Items 4, 5 and 6 do not apply to fuels, alcoholic beverages or tobacco products.

(6) Items 4 to 8 apply only where the aggregate value and quantity thereof is appropriate to the nature of the event, the number of visitors and the extent of the exhibitor's participation in it.

History – In item 3, the words "or to services offered by a person established in another member State" which appeared after the words "United Kingdom" deleted by SI 1992/3120, art. 5(b), operative from 1 January 1993.
Item 3 was substituted on 1 January 1989 by SI 1988/2212, art. 4(a). The former item 3 read as follows:
"3. Printed advertising matter, including catalogues, price lists, directions for use or brochures, which relate to goods for sale or hire, or to transport, commercial insurance or banking services, and which clearly display the name of a person established abroad by whom such goods or services are offered."
In Note (2), the words "or to services offered by a person established in a member State other than the United Kingdom" which appeared after the words "or hire" deleted by SI 1992/3120, art. 5(d), operative from 1 January 1993.
Note (2) was amended on 1 January 1989 by SI 1988/2212, art. 4(b). The former Note (2) read as follows:
"(2) Item 3 does not apply in the case of–
(a) any consignment containing two or more copies of different documents;
(b) any consignment containing two or more copies of the same document, unless the total gross weight of such consignment does not exceed one kilogram; or
(c) any goods which are the subject of grouped consignments from the same consignor to the same consignee."

GROUP 4 – GOODS FOR TESTING, ETC.

Item No.

1.   Goods imported for the purpose of examination, analysis or testing to determine their composition, quality or other technical characteristics, to provide information or for industrial or commercial research.

Item 1 does not apply to goods exceeding the quantities necessary for such purposes or where the examination, analysis or testing, itself constitutes a sales promotion.

GROUP 5 – HEALTH

Item No.

1.   Animals specially prepared for laboratory use and sent free of charge to a relevant establishment.

2.   [Revoked by SI 1992/3120, art. 5(a), operative from 1 January 1993.]

3.   Biological or chemical substances sent to a relevant establishment from a place outside the member States.

4.   Human blood.

5.   Products for therapeutic purposes, derived from human blood.

6.   Human (including foetal) organs or tissue for diagnostic or therapeutic purposes or medical research.

7.   Reagents for use in blood type grouping, or for the detection of blood grouping incompatibilities, by approved institutions or laboratories, exclusively for non-commercial medical or scientific purposes.

8.   Reagents for use in the determination of human tissue types by approved institutions or laboratories, exclusively for non-commercial medical or scientific purposes.

9.   Pharmaceutical products imported by or on behalf of persons or animals for their use while visiting the United Kingdom to participate in an international sporting event.

10.   Samples of reference substances approved by the World Health Organisation for the quality control of materials used in the manufacture of medicinal products.

Notes:

(1) In items 1 and 3, **"relevant establishment"** means–

(a)   a public establishment, or a department of such establishment, principally engaged in education or scientific research; or

(b)   a private establishment so engaged, which is approved.

(2) Item 3 applies only where the goods fulfil the conditions laid down under or by virtue of Article 60 of Council Regulation (EEC) No. 918/83.

(3) Items 4, 5, 6, 7 and 8 include special packaging essential for transport of the goods and any solvents or accessories necessary for their use.

(4) In items 7 and 8, **"reagents"** means all reagents, whether of human, animal, plant, or other, origin.

(5) Item 10 applies only to samples addressed to consignees authorised to receive them free of tax.

History – Former item 2 read as follows:
"2. Biological or chemical substances sent free of charge from another member State to a relevant establishment."
In item 3, the words "a place outside the member States" substituted for the words "outside the Community" by SI 1992/3120, art. 5(c), operative from 1 January 1993.
Item 10 was inserted on 1 January 1989 by SI 1988/2212, art. 5(a).
In Note (1), the figure ", 2" which appeared after the words "In items 1" deleted by SI 1992/3120, art. 5(e), operative from 1 January 1993.
Note (2) was amended on 1 January 1989 by SI 1988/2212, art. 5(b) which substituted "Article 60" for "Article 60(1)(b)".
Note (5) was inserted on 1 January 1989 by SI 1988/2212, art. 5(c).

GROUP 6 – CHARITIES, ETC.

Item No.

1.   Basic necessities obtained without charge for distribution free of charge to the needy by a relevant organisation.

2.   Goods donated by a person established abroad to a relevant organisation for use to raise funds at occasional charity events for the benefit of the needy.

3.   Equipment and office materials donated by a person established abroad to a relevant organisation for meeting its operating needs or carrying out its charitable aims.

4.   Goods imported by a relevant organisation for distribution or loan, free of charge, to victims of a disaster affecting the territory of one or more member States.

5.   Goods imported by a relevant organisation for meeting its operating needs in the relief of a disaster affecting the territory of one or more member States.

6.   Articles donated to and imported by a relevant organisation for supply to blind or other physically or mentally handicapped persons and which are specially designed for the education, employment or social advancement of such persons.

7.   Spare parts, components or accessories for any article of a kind mentioned in item 6, including tools for its maintenance, checking, calibration or repair.

Notes:

(1) In items 1 to 5, **"relevant organisation"** means a State organisation or other approved charitable or philanthropic organisation.

(2) In item 1, **"basic necessities"** means food, medicines, clothing, blankets, orthopaedic equipment and crutches, required to meet a person's immediate needs.

(3) Items 1, 2 and 3 do not include alcoholic beverages, tobacco products, coffee, tea or motor vehicles other than ambulances.

(4) Items 2, 3 and 6 do not apply where there is any commercial intent on the part of the donor.

(5) Items 4 and 5 apply only where the Commission of the European Communities has made a Decision authorising importation of the goods.

(6) In item 6, **"relevant organisation"** means an approved organisation principally engaged in the education of, or the provision of assistance to, blind or other physically or mentally handicapped persons.

(7) In item 6, **"supply"** means any loan, hiring-out or transfer, for consideration or free of charge, other than on a profit-making basis.

(8) Item 7 applies only where the goods are imported with an article of a kind mentioned in item 6 to which they relate, or, if imported subsequently, are identifiable as being intended for that article, where relief from tax on that article has been afforded by virtue of item 6, or would have been so afforded if such article were imported with the goods which relate to it.

GROUP 7 – PRINTED MATTER, ETC.

Item No.

1.   Documents sent free of charge to public services in the United Kingdom.

2.   Foreign government publications and publications of official international bodies intended for free distribution.

3. Ballot papers for elections organised by bodies abroad.
4. Specimen signatures and printed circulars concerning signatures, forming part of exchanges of information between bankers or public services.
5. Official printed matter sent to a Central Bank in the United Kingdom.
6. Documents sent by companies incorporated abroad to bearers of, or subscribers to, securities issued by such companies.
7. Files, archives and other documents for use at international meetings, conferences or congresses and reports of such gatherings.
8. Plans, technical drawings, traced designs and other documents sent by any person for the purpose of participating in a competition in the United Kingdom or to obtain or fulfil an order executed abroad.
9. Documents to be used in examinations held in the United Kingdom on behalf of institutions established abroad.
10. Printed forms to be used as official documents in the international movement of vehicles or goods pursuant to international conventions.
11. Printed forms, labels, tickets and similar documents set to travel agents in the United Kingdom by transport and tourist undertakings abroad.
12. Used commercial documents.
13. Official printed forms from national or international authorities.
14. Printed matter conforming to international standards, for distribution by an association in the United Kingdom and sent by a corresponding association abroad.
15. Documents sent for the purpose of free distribution to encourage persons to visit foreign countries, in particular to attend cultural, tourist, sporting, religious, trade or professional meetings or events.
16. Foreign hotel lists and yearbooks published by or on behalf of official tourist agencies and timetables for foreign transport services, for free distribution.
17. Yearbooks, lists of telephone and telex numbers, hotel lists, catalogues for fairs, specimens of craft goods of negligible value and literature on museums, universities, spas or other similar establishments, supplied as reference material to accredited representatives or correspondents appointed by official national tourist agencies and not intended for distribution.
18. Official publications issued under the authority of the country of exportation, international institutions, regional or local authorities and bodies governed by public law established in the country of exportation.
19. Printed matter distributed by foreign political organisations on the occasion of elections to the European Parliament or national elections in the country in which the printed matter originates.

Notes:

(1) Items 15 and 16 do not apply where the goods contain more than 25 per cent of private commercial advertising.

(2) Items 18 and 19 apply only to publications or printed matter on which value added tax or any other tax has been paid in the third country from which they have been exported and which have not benefited, by virtue of their exportation, from any relief from payment thereof.

(3) In item 19, **"foreign political organisations"** means those which are officially recognised as such in the United Kingdom.

(4) In item 11 **"travel agent"** includes airlines, national railway undertakings, ferry operators and similar organisations.

(5) In items 2, 15, 16 and 19 **"foreign"** means from a country other than the United kingdom.

History – Items 18 and 19 inserted, operative from 1 January 1989 by SI 1988/2212, art. 6(a).
Note (2) substituted by SI 1992/3120, art. 5(f), operative from 1 January 1993. Former Note (2) read as follows:
"(2) Items 18 and 19 apply only to publications or printed matter on which value added tax or any other tax has been paid in the country of exportation and which have not benefited, by virtue of their exportation, from any relief from payment thereof."
Notes (1)–(3) substituted, operative from 1 January 1989 by SI 1988/2212, art. 6(b) for the former Note which read as follows:
"*Note:* Items 15 and 16 do not apply where the goods contain more than 25 per cent of private commercial advertising."
Notes (4) and (5) inserted by SI 1992/3120, art. 5(g) and (h), operative from 1 Janaury 1993.

GROUP 8 – ARTICLES SENT FOR MISCELLANEOUS PURPOSES

Item No.

1. Material relating to trademarks, patterns or designs and supporting documents and applications for patents, imported for the purpose of being submitted to bodies competent to deal with protection of copyright or industrial or commercial patent rights.

2.   Objects imported for the purpose of being submitted as evidence, or for the like purpose, to a court or other official body in the United Kingdom.

3.   Photographs, slides and stereotype mats for photographs, whether or not captioned, sent to press agencies and publishers of newspapers or magazines.

4.   Recorded media, including punched cards, sound recordings and microfilm, sent free of charge for the transmission of information.

5.   Any honorary decoration conferred by a government or Head of State abroad on a person resident in the United Kingdom and imported on his behalf.

6.   Any cup, medal or similar article of an essentially symbolic nature, intended as a tribute to activities in the arts, sciences, sport, or the public service, or in recognition of merit at a particular event, which is either–

(a)   donated by an authority or person established abroad for the purpose of being presented in the United Kingdom, or

(b)   awarded abroad to a person resident in the United Kingdom and imported on his behalf.

7.   Goods (other than alcoholic beverages or tobacco products) sent on an occasional basis as gifts in token of friendship or goodwill between bodies, public authorities or groups carrying on an activity in the public interest.

8.   Any consignment of goods (other than alcoholic beverages, tobacco products, perfumes or toilet waters) not exceeding £18 in value.

9.   Awards, trophies and souvenirs of a symbolic nature and of limited value intended for distribution free of charge at business conferences or similar international events to persons normally resident in a country other than the United Kingdom.

Items 5, 6, 7 and 9 do not apply to any importation of a commercial character.

History – In item 8, the amount "£18" was substituted for "£15" by SI 1995/3222, art. 2, operative from 1 January 1996. Item 8 amended by SI 1990/2548, art. 2, operative from 1 January 1991 by the substitution of "£15" for "£7".
Item 8 amended on 1 January 1989 by SI 1988/2212, art. 7(a). Former item 8 read as follows:
"8. Any consignment of goods (other than alcoholic beverages, tobacco products, perfumes or toilet waters) not exceeding £7 in value, sent by post."
Item 8 amended on 9 March 1987 by SI 1987/155 by the substitution of "£7" for "£6".
Item 9 was inserted on 1 January 1989 by SI 1988/2212, art. 7(b).
The Note was substituted on 1 January 1989 by SI 1988/2212, art. 7(c). The former Note read as follows:
"*Note:* Items 5, 6 and 7 do not apply to any importation–
(a) of a commercial character; or
(b) in respect of which relief from tax has been afforded by virtue of Part XII of the Customs and Excise Duties (Personal Reliefs for Goods Permanently Imported) Order 1983."

GROUP 9 – WORKS OF ART AND COLLECTORS' PIECES

Item No.

1.   Works of art and collectors' pieces imported by approved museums, galleries or other institutions for a purpose other than sale.

Item 1 applies only where the goods are–

(a)   of an educational, scientific or cultural character; and

(b)   imported free of charge or, if for a consideration, are not supplied to the importer in the course or furtherance of any business.

GROUP 10 – TRANSPORT

Item No.

1.   Fuel contained in the standard tanks of a vehicle or of a special container, for use exclusively by such vehicle or such special container.

2.   Fuel, not exceeding 10 litres for each vehicle, contained in portable tanks carried by a vehicle, for use exclusively by such vehicle.

3.   Lubricants contained in a vehicle, for use exclusively by such vehicle.

4.   Litter, fodder and feedingstuffs contained in any means of transport carrying animals, for the use of such animals during their journey.

5.   Disposable packings for the stowage and protection of goods during their transportation to the United Kingdom.

Notes:

(1) **"Standard tanks"** means any of the following–

(a)   tanks permanently fitted to a vehicle and which are fitted to all vehicles of that type by the manufacturer, to supply directly fuel for the purpose of propulsion and, where appropriate, for the operation, during transport, of refrigeration systems and other systems;

(b)   gas tanks fitted to vehicles designed for the direct use of gas as a fuel;

(c)   tanks fitted to ancillary systems with which a vehicle is equipped; and

(d)   tanks permanently fitted to a special container and which are fitted to all special containers of that type by the manufacturer, to supply directly fuel for the operation, during transport, of refrigeration systems and other systems with which special containers are equipped.

(2) **"Vehicle"** means any motor road vehicle.

(3) **"Special container"** means any container fitted with specially designed apparatus for refrigeration systems, oxygenation systems, thermal insulation systems and other systems.

(4) Item 2 does not apply in the case of any special purpose vehicle or a vehicle which, by its type of construction and equipment, is designed for and capable of transporting goods or more than nine persons, including the driver.

(5) Item 3 applies only to lubricants necessary for the normal operation of the vehicle during its journey.

(6) Item 5 applies only where the cost of the packings is included in the consideration for the goods transported.

History – Grp. 10 was substituted on 1 January 1989 by SI 1988/2212, art. 8. Former Grp. 10 read as follows:
"Item No.
1. Fuel and lubricants contained in a vehicle imported into the United Kingdom, for use exclusively by such vehicle.
2. Fuel, not exceeding 10 litres for each vehicle, contained in portable tanks carried by a vehicle imported into the United Kingdom, for use exclusively by such vehicle.
3. Litter, fodder and feedingstuffs contained in a vehicle carrying animals, for the use of such animals during their journey to the United Kingdom.
4. Disposable packings for the stowage and protection of goods during their transportation to the United Kingdom.
Notes:
(1) **"Vehicle"** means any motor road vehicle.
(2) Item 1 applies only to–
(a) fuel contained in the standard tanks permanently fitted to the vehicle and which are fitted to all vehicles of that type by the manufacturer, to supply fuel directly for propulsion or refrigeration; and
(b) lubricants necessary for the normal operation of the vehicle during its journey.
(3) Item 2 does not apply in the case of a vehicle which, by its type of construction and equipment, is designed for and capable of transporting more than nine persons, including the driver, or goods, or any special purpose vehicle.
(4) Item 4 applies only where the cost of the packings is included in the consideration for the goods transported."

GROUP 11 – WAR GRAVES, FUNERALS, ETC.

Item No.

1.   Goods imported by an approved organisation for use in the construction, upkeep or ornamentation of cemeteries, tombs and memorials in the United Kingdom which commemorate war victims of other countries.

2.   Coffins containing human remains.

3.   Urns containing human ashes.

4.   Flowers, wreaths and other ornamental objects accompanying goods described in items 2 or 3.

5.   Flowers, wreaths and other ornamental objects, imported without any commercial intent by a person resident abroad, for use at a funeral or to decorate a grave.

CONTROL OF MOVEMENT OF GOODS REGULATIONS 1984

(SI 1984/1176)

Made on 1 August 1984, by the Commissioners of Customs and Excise under the Customs and Excise Management Act 1979, s. 31. Operative from 1 August 1984.

CITATION AND COMMENCEMENT

1   These Regulations may be cited as the Control of Movement of Goods Regulations 1984 and shall come into operation on 1st August 1984.

REVOCATION

2   The Control of Movement of Goods Regulations 1981 are hereby revoked.

INTERPRETATION

3   In these Regulations–

     "the Act" means the Customs and Excise Management Act 1979;

     "approved place"–

(a)   in relation to imported goods means a place approved by the Commissioners under section 20 or 25 of the Act for the clearance out of charge of such goods, and

(b)   in relation to goods intended for export means a place appointed under section 159 of the Act for the examination of goods which is approved by the Commissioners under section 31 of the Act for the examination of such goods before their movement to a place of exportation;

"the loader" shall have the same meaning as in section 57 of the Act; that is to say the owner of the ship or aircraft in which the goods are to be exported or a person appointed by him;

"place of importation" and **"place of exportation"** shall, where appropriate, include a free zone;

"removal" means a movement of goods which is authorised under these Regulations and **"remove"** and **"removed"** shall be construed accordingly;

"removal document" means a document to be obtained from or approved by the Commissioners made in such form and containing such particulars as the Commissioners may direct under section 31(2A) of the Act and for the purpose of regulation 15 shall include a copy of the application referred to in regulations 5, 6 and 7 stamped by the proper officer.

4(1)   These Regulations shall not apply where any goods are moved under the internal or external Community transit procedure.

4(2)   The application of regulations 11 and 13 of these Regulations to goods carried under the provisions of an international convention having effect in the United Kingdom shall be without prejudice to any such provisions.

RESTRICTIONS ON THE MOVEMENT OF GOODS

5   Subject to regulation 10, no imported goods not yet cleared from customs and excise charge shall be moved between their place of importation and either an approved place or a free zone and, in the case of transit goods, between their place of importation and a place of exportation unless the movement is authorised by the proper officer upon application made to him.

6   Subject to regulation 10, no goods shall be moved between–

(a)   a free zone and a place approved for the clearance out of charge of such goods,

(b)   such a place and a free zone, and

(c)   a free zone and another free zone,

unless the movement is authorised by the proper officer upon application made to him.

7   Subject to regulations 9 and 10, no goods intended for export and made available at an approved place or a place designated by the proper officer under sections 53(4) or 58(3) of the Act for the purposes of examination shall be moved between any such place and a place of exportation unless the movement is authorised by the proper officer upon application made to him.

8   Save as the Commissioners may otherwise allow, the applications referred to in regulations 5, 6 and 7 above shall be made in writing on a document obtained from or approved by the Commissioners for that purpose and shall be made–

(a)   in the case of imported goods, by the importer or the person in charge of the goods,

(b)   in the case of goods intended for export, by the exporter or the person in charge of the goods, and

(c)   in any other case, by the proprietor of the goods or the person in charge of the goods.

LOCAL EXPORT CONTROL

9(1)   Where a notice under section 58A(3)(a)(i) of the Act is delivered by the exporter such notice shall replace the application required under regulation 7.

9(2)   Where the notice is for a single movement of goods, if the authority of the proper officer, *required under regulation 7, is neither given nor refused* by the date and time for the movement specified in that notice, it shall be deemed to be given on the date and immediately before the time so specified.

9(3)   Where the notice is for more than one movement of goods, if the authority of the proper officer, required under regulation 7, is neither given nor refused, it shall be deemed to be given immediately before each movement commences.

STANDING PERMISSION TO REMOVE

10   Where the Commissioners so permit, during a period specified by them, goods may be moved as contemplated in regulations 5, 6 and 7 without an application to the proper officer; and, unless the proper officer previously gives or refuses his authority, it shall be deemed to be given immediately before the movement commences.

REQUIREMENT FOR REMOVAL DOCUMENT

11   Before any removal commences the person by whom, or on whose behalf, the goods are being moved shall be in possession of a removal document.

SPECIFICATION OF VEHICLES ETC.

12(1)   The Commissioners may, in respect of any class or description of goods, require that vehicles or containers in which goods of a particular class or description are removed shall be of a type specified by them for the removal of such goods.

12(2)   Save as provided by paragraph (3) below, no person shall remove any goods in respect of which a requirement under paragraph (1) above has been imposed unless the vehicle or container in which they are carried conforms to such requirement.

12(3)   The proper officer, upon application made to him by the person in charge of goods to be removed, may for the purposes of the removal in question relax any requirement imposed under paragraph (1) above.

SPECIFICATION OF ROUTES

13   Vehicles and containers proceeding under a removal shall be moved by such routes as the Commissioners may specify.

SECURITY OF GOODS, VEHICLES AND CONTAINERS

14(1)   Before any goods are removed they or the vehicle or container carrying them shall be secured or identified by any such seals, locks or marks as the Commissioners may specify.

14(2)   Where in the United Kingdom, seals, locks or marks are affixed for any customs or excise purpose in order to secure or identify the goods to be removed or the vehicles or containers carrying the goods, they shall be so affixed by the proper officer or by such other person as the Commissioners may authorise.

15(1)   Save in the circumstances hereunder mentioned, no person shall at any time during a removal–

(a)   wilfully break, open or remove any seal, lock or mark affixed for any customs or excise purpose on any goods or to a vehicle or container; or

(b)   load or unload or assist in the loading or unloading of a vehicle or container.

15(2)   The circumstances referred to in paragraph (1) above are–

(a)   where authorisation has been given by the proper officer; or

(b)   in accordance with any general or special permission given by the Commissioners; or

(c)   in an emergency in order to safeguard the goods or to protect life or property.

COMPLETION OF REMOVALS, TIME LIMITS AND ACCIDENTS

16(1)   Save as the Commissioners otherwise allow, the person in charge of goods proceeding under a removal shall complete the removal by producing the goods, together with the vehicle or container in which they are carried if such vehicle or container has been secured or identified, and delivering a removal document to the proper officer at the approved place or, in the case of goods intended for export, at the place of exportation.

16(2)   The Commissioners may allow the removal of goods intended for export to be completed by the person in charge of the goods placing them, together with any container in which they are carried if such container has been secured or identified, under the control of the loader and delivering the removal document to him.

17   The person in charge of goods proceedings under a removal shall complete the removal within such period as the Commissioners may specify.

18   Where as a result of an accident or other occurrence arising during a removal a vehicle or container is delayed or diverted from a specified route the person in charge of the goods shall as soon as practicable give sufficient notification of the accident or occurrence as required by the Commissioners to the local office of customs and excise.

FREE ZONE REGULATIONS 1984

(SI 1984/1177, as amended by SI 1988/710)

Made on 1 August 1984, by the Commissioners of Customs and Excise under the Value Added Tax Act 1983, s. 24 [VATA 1994, s. 16] and under the Customs and Excise Management Act 1979, s. 100B(1), 100C(3), (4), 100D(1), (2) and 125(3). Operative from 6 August 1984.

Notes – CEMA 1979, s. 100B and 100C were repealed by VATA 1994, s. 100(2) and Sch. 15, with effect from 1 September 1994.
CEMA 1979, s. 100D was repealed by SI 1991/2727, except as provided by reg. 3(2) of those regulations, operative from 1 January 1992. From the date the administration of free zones is governed by EC Council Regulation 2504/88 and Commission Regulation 2562/90.

ARRANGEMENT OF REGULATIONS

REGULATION

REGULATION
27.   RELIEF FROM IMPORT TAX FOLLOWING SUPPLY TO NON-REGISTERED
         PERSON

PART I – PRELIMINARY

CITATION AND COMMENCEMENT

1   These Regulations may be cited as the Free Zone Regulations 1984 and shall come into operation on 6th August 1984.

INTERPRETATION

2 In these Regulations–

"chargeable operation" means any operation carried out on Community goods which are free zone goods where, because of Commission Regulation (EEC) 1371/81 and the nature of the operation, agricultural levy becomes chargeable or a negative monetary compensatory amount payable;

"Community goods" means goods which fulfil the conditions of Article 9(2) of the EEC Treaty, and goods covered by the Treaty establishing the European Coal and Steel Community which are in free circulation in the Community in accordance with that Treaty;

"tax" means value added tax;

"transfer to another customs procedure providing for suspension of, or relief from, customs duty or agricultural levy" in regulation 11 (requirement for entry) shall not be taken to include the removal of free zone goods from one free zone to another or from a free zone to a place for the clearance out of charge of imported goods.

PART II – SECURITY OF FREE ZONES

SECURITY AND RECOVERY OF EXPENDITURE BY COMMISSIONERS

3   The Commissioners may by direction impose obligations on the responsible authority for a free zone to ensure the security of that free zone; and where the responsible authority fails to comply with such direction and the Commissioners thereby incur any expenditure, such expenditure shall be recoverable on demand by the Commissioners as a civil debt from that responsible authority.

RESIDENCE IN FREE ZONES NOT PERMITTED

4   The responsible authority shall not permit any person to take up residence within a free zone.

PART III – GOODS CHARGEABLE WITH EXCISE DUTY

EXCISE GOODS WHICH MAY BECOME FREE ZONE GOODS WITHOUT PAYMENT OF EXCISE DUTY

5   Goods chargeable with excise duty may be moved into a free zone in accordance with these Regulations without payment of that duty and remain as free zone goods; provided that they are goods which, by or under the customs and excise Acts, the Commissioners may allow to be removed or delivered without payment of excise duty and which have been allowed to be so removed or delivered.

PART IV – MOVEMENT OF GOODS INTO FREE ZONE

GOODS TO BECOME FREE ZONE GOODS

6(1)   Goods moved into a free zone shall not be free zone goods unless, within such time as the Commissioners may direct, such particulars as the Commissioners may direct have been entered in a record to be kept by the occupier of the premises at which the goods are received or, if the Commissioners so direct, by the responsible authority.

6(2)   [Revoked by SI 1988/710, reg. 3(b).]

History – In reg. 6(1), the words "such time as the Commissioners may direct" were substituted for "the relevant period" by SI 1988/710, reg. 3(a), operative from 10 May 1988.
The revocation of reg. 6(2) operates from 10 May 1988. Former reg. 6(2) read as follows:
"**6(2)**   In this regulation **"relevant period"**, in respect of imported goods, shall have the same meaning as in section 40(4) of the Customs and Excise Management Act 1979 and in respect of any other goods shall mean a period not exceeding 14 days from the time the goods are moved into the free zone."

ACKNOWLEDGMENT OF COMMUNITY STATUS OF FREE ZONE GOODS

7(1)   Where the proprietor of free zone goods wishes to obtain an acknowledgment that the goods are Community goods he shall deliver to the proper officer, within the relevant period, a document in such form and containing such particulars as the Commissioners may direct together with such supporting evidence as will enable the officer to establish to his satisfaction that they are Community goods, and, if so satisfied, the proper officer shall provide a written acknowledgment of such Community status.

7(2)   The written acknowledgment referred to in paragraph (1) above shall consist of a copy of the document containing particulars of the goods, endorsed by the proper officer.

7(3)   In this regulation **"relevant period"** shall mean a period not exceeding 7 days from the time the goods become free zone goods or from the time an entry for free circulation under regulation 17(2) is accepted.

GOODS FROM ANOTHER CUSTOMS PROCEDURE

8   Goods moved into a free zone which are subject to another customs procedure shall not be free zone goods until the proprietor of the goods has presented them to the proper officer and that procedure has been discharged.

PART V – OPERATIONS

OPERATIONS ON FREE ZONE GOODS

9(1)   Operations on free zone goods shall only be permitted in accordance with this regulation and subject to any prohibition or restriction imposed by or under any enactment for the time being in force.

9(2)   Any operation is prohibited in which goods that are not free zone goods are mixed with or incorporated into free zone goods.

9(3)   The Commissioners shall allow, subject to such conditions as they may impose, operations to be carried out on free zone goods as follows–

(a)   where only Community goods are involved, any operation;

(b)   where any other goods are involved–

     (i)   the usual forms of handling listed in Article 1.1 of Council Directive 71/235/EEC,

     (ii)   processing under customs control for free circulation in accordance with Council Regulation (EEC) 2763/83, or

     (iii)   any operation carried out in accordance with the Inward Processing Relief Regulations 1977.

9(4)   A person intending to carry out any operation shall–

(a)   before commencing an operation referred to in paragraph (3)(a) above, inform the proper officer of his intention and, in addition, where the operation is a chargeable operation enter such particulars as the Commissioners may require in a record to be kept by him,

(b)   before commencing an operation referred to in paragraph (3)(b)(i) above, notify the proper officer of his intention, and

(c)   before commencing any other operation, make a declaration by entering such particulars as the Commissioners may require in a record to be kept by him.

9(5)   A person intending to carry out an operation referred to in paragraph (3)(b)(i) above may, at the time he notifies the proper officer of his intention to carry out the operation, apply for a written acknowledgment that the operation is to commence and the application shall be in such form as the Commissioners may direct and contain such particulars as the Commissioners may require to enable them to apply regulation 25(4).

9(6)   The written acknowledgment referred to in paragraph (5) above, shall consist of a copy of the application endorsed by the proper officer.

9(7)   Save as provided by this regulation, free zone goods shall not be used or consumed in a free zone unless they are entered in accordance with regulation 17(1).

9(8)   Notwithstanding paragraph (3) above, free zone goods chargeable with excise duty which have been removed or delivered without payment of that duty by or under the customs and excise Acts before becoming free zone goods may only be used or consumed in the free zone without payment of that duty where such use or consumption does not affect the relief from excise duty under the requirements of those Acts applicable to the relief; and paragraph and excise Acts before becoming free zone goods may only be used or consumed in the free zone without payment of that duty where such use or consumption does not affect the relief from excise duty under the requirements of those Acts applicable to the relief; and paragraph (7) above shall only apply to such goods if they are also chargeable with a duty of customs or agricultural levy which has not been paid.

9(9)   Where an operation is carried out on free zone goods otherwise than in accordance with this regulation, they shall cease to be free zone goods, and shall be liable to forfeiture.

PART VI – ENTRY, REMOVAL AND PAYMENT OF DUTY ETC.

PROCEDURE FOR ENTERING FREE ZONE GOODS

10(1)   Free zone goods, required by these Regulations to be entered, shall be entered by the proprietor of the goods delivering to the proper officer an entry thereof in such form and manner, containing such particulars and accompanied by such documents as the commissioners may direct.

10(2)   Acceptance of an entry by the proper officer shall be signified in such manner as the Commissioners may direct.

10(3)   Where free zone goods are required to be entered under regulation 17, the Commissioners may direct that if the proprietor of the goods–

(a)   enters such particulars as the Commissioners may direct in a record to be kept by him, and

(b)   furnishes a schedule to the proper officer at such place and at such intervals as the Commissioners may direct containing such particulars extracted from the record and accompanied by such documents as the Commissioners may direct,

an entry of the goods shall be taken to have been delivered and accepted when the particulars are entered in the record.

ENTRY REQUIRED BEFORE REMOVAL FOR HOME USE ETC.

11   Subject to regulation 12, before any free zone goods are removed from a free zone for–

(a)   home use, or

(b)   transfer to another customs procedure providing for suspension of, or relief from, customs duty or agricultural levy,

the goods shall be entered for such purpose.

Extra-statutory concessions – 3.14 (Notice 48 (1999 edn)): free zone goods may be zero-rated if supplier and customer agree that customer will clear the goods for removal to home use.

REMOVAL WITHOUT ENTRY

12(1)   Upon application by the proprietor of free zone goods, the Commissioners may allow the goods to be removed from the free zone for the purposes set out in regulation 11 without the goods being entered, if such particulars as the Commissioners may direct are entered in a record to be kept by the proprietor of the goods.

12(2)   Where goods are allowed to be removed from the free zone in accordance with paragraph (1) above, the proprietor of the goods shall comply with such conditions as the Commissioners may impose.

GOODS TO BE REMOVED AFTER ENTRY ETC.

13   Subject to regulations 15 and 16, free zone goods which have been entered under regulation 11 or in respect of which the particulars required under regulation 12 have been entered in the record, shall be removed, forthwith, from the free zone.

REMOVAL OF GOODS FOR EXPORT ETC.

14 Part V of the Customs and Excise Management Act 1979 (procedures for the export of goods) and any prohibition or restriction on the export of goods or their shipment as stores, imposed by or under any enactment for the time being in force, shall apply to goods removed from a free zone for export or shipment as stores.

RESTRICTION ON REMOVAL OF GOODS

15 No goods shall be removed from a free zone except with the authority of and in accordance with any requirement made by the proper officer.

PAYMENT OF DUTY BEFORE REMOVAL OF GOODS

16 Save as the Commissioners may otherwise allow and subject to such conditions as they may impose, no goods shall be removed from a free zone until any customs duty and agricultural levy chargeable thereon has been paid; and where the goods have been entered under regulation 11(a), such duty and levy shall be paid at the time the entry is delivered.

ENTRY OF GOODS WHICH ARE TO REMAIN IN FREE ZONE

17(1) Free zone goods to be used or consumed in a free zone, as provided in regulation 9(7), shall be entered for home use.

17(2) Where the proprietor of free zone goods wishes to pay any customs duty or agricultural levy chargeable on the goods and for the goods to remain as free zone goods, the goods shall be entered for free circulation.

PAYMENT OF DUTY ETC. ON GOODS TO REMAIN IN FREE ZONE AFTER ENTRY

18(1) Where goods are entered under regulation 17, any customs duty and agricultural levy chargeable thereon shall be paid at the time the entry is delivered.

18(2) As an exception to paragraph (1) above, where the goods are entered for free circulation, tax on importation shall not be paid at the time customs duty is paid.

AGRICULTURAL LEVY CHARGEABLE BECAUSE OF CHARGEABLE OPERATION

19 Where agricultural levy becomes chargeable or a negative monetary compensatory amount payable, because of a chargeable operation, a schedule in such form and containing such particulars of the goods and the operation as the Commissioners may direct shall be furnished by the proprietor of the goods to the proper officer at such place and at such intervals as the Commissioners may direct, and any agricultural levy so chargeable shall be paid at the time the schedule is furnished.

CUSTOMS DUTY ETC. DEEMED TO HAVE BEEN PAID

20 For the purposes of these Regulations, customs duty and agricultural levy shall be deemed to have been paid if payment thereof has been deferred under the Customs Duties (Deferred Payment) Regulations 1976, secured to the satisfaction of the Commissioners or otherwise accounted for.

DESTRUCTION OF FREE ZONE GOODS

21 Subject to such conditions as the Commissioners may impose, free zone goods may be destroyed and no customs duty or agricultural levy shall be payable on them:

Provided that where any scrap or waste resulting from their destruction is entered for removal for home use, duty and levy shall be chargeable thereon in accordance with regulation 25.

PART VII – CONTROLS

PRODUCTION OF GOODS

22 Goods in a free zone shall be produced to the proper officer for examination on request.

SEGREGATION ETC. OF GOODS

23 The proper officer may require any goods in a free zone to be segregated and marked or otherwise identified.

KEEPING OF RECORDS AND PROVISION OF INFORMATION

24(1) In addition to any requirement in that regard imposed by or under these Regulations, the Value Added Tax Act 1983 [VATA 1994] or the Inward Processing Relief Regulations 1977, the occupier of any premises upon which free zone goods are kept or, where the Commissioners so direct, the responsible authority on his behalf, shall keep such records relating to the goods as the Commissioners may direct.

24(2) Any records required to be kept under these Regulations shall be kept in the free zone or such other place as the Commissioners may allow and be kept in such form and be preserved for such time, not exceeding three years from the date the goods are removed from the free zone, as the Commissioners may direct.

24(3) The person keeping the record shall–

(a) furnish to the Commissioners, within such time and in such form as they may require, such information relating to the goods as the Commissioners may direct, and

(b) upon demand made by the proper officer produce to him any records and any document relating to the goods for inspection by the proper officer and permit him to take copies of or to make extracts from them or remove them at a reasonable time and for a reasonable purpose:

Provided that if the information that would otherwise be contained in any record or document is not made or preserved in a form which is easily readable or which is not readable without the aid of equipment, the person keeping the record or document, shall, at the request of the proper officer produce the information contained in the record or document in the form of a transcript or other permanent legible reproduction.

PART VIII – CUSTOMS DUTY ETC. CHARGEABLE ON FREE ZONE GOODS

CUSTOMS DUTY CHARGEABLE ON FREE ZONE GOODS

25(1) Except as provided in paragraph (5) of this regulation (compensating products from inward processing), the customs duty and agricultural levy and the rate thereof chargeable, or the negative monetary compensatory amount and the rate thereof payable, on free zone goods–

(a) removed from a free zone for home use, or

(b) remaining in a free zone after being entered for home use or free circulation;

shall be those in force for goods of that class or description at the time of acceptance of the entry or, where the goods are allowed to be removed without entry, those in force at the time the particulars required under regulation 12 are entered in the record.

25(2) The agricultural levy and the rate thereof chargeable or the negative monetary compensatory amount and the rate thereof payable on free zone goods because of a chargeable operation thereon shall be those in force for goods of that class or description at the time the operation commenced.

25(3) Except as provided in paragraph (4) below, the value for customs purposes of free zone goods of any class or description shall be that ascertained or accepted by the Commissioners at the time of the acceptance of the entry for home use or free circulation.

25(4) Where goods which are removed from a free zone have undergone any of the usual forms of handling referred to in regulation 9(3)(b)(i), provided that the proprietor of the goods–

(a) if the goods are entered, produces with the entry, or

(b) in any other case, produces to the proper officer at such time as the Commissioners may direct,

the written acknowledgment referred to in regulation 9(5), the quantity of goods, their class or description and value shall, at his option, be those accepted or ascertained at the date of the acknowledgment.

25(5) Notwithstanding any other provision of this regulation, where any goods imported into the United Kingdom are granted an authorisation, or have been granted in another Member State an authorisation, for inward processing relief and the Commissioners have allowed compensating products, derived from such goods which have become free zone goods, to be entered for home use or free circulation, the customs duty and agricultural levy chargeable shall be either–

(a)   the amount calculated in accordance with the Inward Processing Relief Regulations 1977, or

(b)   at the option of the proprietor of the goods and provided that the Commissioners are satisfied that the amount is at least equal to the amount ascertainable under sub-paragraph (a) above, the amount calculated in accordance with paragraph (1) above.

25(6)   In this regulation, **"compensating products"** shall have the same meaning as in the Inward Processing Relief Regulations 1977.

PART IX – VALUE ADDED TAX

TAX CHARGE ON REMOVAL FROM FREE ZONE OF MANUFACTURED GOODS

26   [Revoked by SI 1988/710, reg. 4, operative from 10 May 1988.]

History – Reg. 26 formerly read as follows:
"**26**   Goods manufactured or produced within a free zone from free zone goods shall, for the purposes of the charge to tax, be treated as free zone goods upon which no customs duty has been paid, whether or not the goods are chargeable with customs duty and whether or not such duty has been paid."

RELIEF FROM IMPORT TAX FOLLOWING SUPPLY TO NON-REGISTERED PERSON

27   Where free zone goods have been supplied whilst in the free zone to a person who is neither registered nor liable to be registered for tax and he enters the goods for home use, the amount of tax payable shall be reduced by the amount of tax paid on the supply.

VALUE ADDED TAX (REFUND OF TAX) ORDER 1985

(SI 1985/1101)

Made on 17 July 1985 by the Treasury under s. 20(3) of the Value Added Tax Act 1983 [VATA 1994, s. 33(3)]. Operative from 1 August 1985.

1   This Order may be cited as the Value Added Tax (Refund of Tax) Order 1985 and shall come into operation on 1st August 1985.

2   The following bodies established under the Local Government Act 1985 are hereby specified for the purposes of section 20 of the Value Added Tax Act 1983 [VATA 1994, s. 33(3)]:

> The Inner London Education Authority
> The Inner London Interim Education Authority
> The Northumbria Interim Police Authority
> The London Fire and Civil Defence Authority
> The London Residuary Body
> A metropolitan county Police Authority
> A metropolitan county Fire and Civil Defence Authority
> A metropolitan county Passenger Transport Authority
> A metropolitan county Residuary Body.

COMPANIES (DEPARTMENT OF TRADE AND INDUSTRY) FEES ORDER 1985

(SI 1985/1784 (L 15))

Made on 18 November 1985 by the Lord Chancellor and the Treasury under s. 663(4) of the Companies Act 1985 and s. 2 of the Public Offices Fees Act 1879. Operative from 1 December 1985.

3(1)   All fees shall be taken in cash.

3(2)   When a fee is paid to an officer of a court the person paying the fee shall inform the officer that the fee relates to a proceeding for or in the winding-up of a company.

4 Where Value Added Tax is chargeable in respect of the provision of any service for which a fee is prescribed in the Schedule, there shall be payable in addition to that fee the amount of the Value Added Tax.

Notes – Companies Act 1985, s. 663(4) is reproduced below:

"**663(4)** There shall be paid in respect of proceedings under this Act in relation to the winding up of companies in England and Wales such fees as the Lord Chancellor may, with the sanction of the Treasury, direct; and the Treasury may direct by whom and in what manner the fees are to be collected and accounted for."

POSTAL PACKETS (CUSTOMS AND EXCISE) REGULATIONS 1986

(SI 1986/260, as amended by SI 1986/1019)

Made on 14 February 1986 by the Treasury under s. 16(2) of the Post Office Act 1953. Operative from 1 March 1986.

1 These Regulations may be cited as the Postal Packets (Customs and Excise) Regulations 1986 and shall come into force on 1 March 1986.

2(1) In these Regulations–

"**Act of 1979**" means the Customs and Excise Management Act 1979;

"**Commissioners**" means Commissioners of Customs and Excise;

"**the customs and excise Acts**" has the meaning given by section 1(1) of the Act of 1979;

"**datapost packet**" means a postal packet containing goods which is posted in the United Kingdom as a datapost packet for transmission to a place outside the United Kingdom either in accordance with the terms of a contract entered into between the Post Office and the sender of the packet, or in accordance with the provisions of Schemes made under section 28 of the Post Office Act 1969; or which is received at a post office in the United Kingdom from a place outside the United Kingdom for transmission and delivery in the United Kingdom as if it were a datapost packet;

"**dutiable goods**" has the meaning given by section 1(1) of the Act of 1979 but includes goods chargeable with value added tax and goods subject to any other charge on importation;

"**duty**" and "**duty of customs or excise**" include value added tax and any other charge on imported goods;

"**exporter**" and "**importer**" have the meanings assigned to them by section 1(1) of the Act of 1979;

"**inland post**" means the post for transmission of those postal packets to which the Post Office Inland Post Scheme 1979 applies;

"**letter packet**" means a packet transmitted at the letter rate of postage and containing goods;

"**prescribed**" means prescribed by the provisions of the Universal Postal Convention and Detailed Regulations made thereunder which are for the time being in force;

"**proper**" in relation to an officer means appointed or authorised by the Commissioners or the Post Office to perform any duty in relation to a postal packet.

2(2) In these Regulations (except in relation to the inland post) the expressions "**printed packet**" and "**small packet**" have the same meanings as in the Post Office Overseas Letter Post Scheme 1982 and "**parcel**" has the same meaning as in the Post Office Overseas Parcel Post Scheme 1982.

2(3) In these Regulations, in relation to the inland post, the expression "**parcel**" has the same meaning as in the Post Office Inland Post Scheme 1979, and references to printed packets, small packets and datapost packets shall, in relation to the inland post, be deemed to be omitted.

3 The Postal Packets (Customs and Excise) Regulations 1975 are hereby revoked.

4 Section 16 of the Post Office Act 1953 shall apply to all postal packets, other than postcards, which are posted in the United Kingdom for transmission to any place outside it or which are brought by post into the United Kingdom.

5   In their application to goods contained in such postal packets, the following provisions of the Act of 1979 shall be subject to the following modifications and exceptions–

(a)   In the application of section 5, subsection (3) shall be omitted and subsection (4) shall apply with the modification that the time of exportation of goods shall be the time when they are posted (or redirected) in the United Kingdom for transmission to a place outside it.

(b)   Section 37 shall apply only in any case, or class of cases, in which the Commissioners require an entry to be made in accordance with that section, and paragraph (b) of subsection (5) thereof shall apply with the modification that any direction made by the Commissioners as to goods not permitted to be entered for warehousing may be restricted to goods of any description specified in the direction which are brought by post into the United Kingdom.

(c)   Section 40 shall apply only where the Commissioners have required entry to be made, and, where they have so required, shall apply only to the extent, and with the modification, set out in Regulation 14 of these Regulations.

(d)   In the application of section 43, subsection (1) shall not apply, and paragraph (c) of subsection (2) shall apply with the substitution for sub-paragraphs (i) and (ii) of the words "those in force at the time when, the packet containing the goods having been presented to the proper officer of customs and excise, the amount of duty appearing to be due is assessed by him".

(e)   In the application of section 49, subsection (1)(a) shall be omitted.

(f)   For references in–

     (i)   section 53 to "exported", "shipped for exportation", and "exported or shipped for exportation";

     (ii)   section 56 to "shipped or exported by land", "exported", and "shipped";

     (iii)   section 58 to "shipped for exportation", and "shipped";

     (iv)   section 58A to "shipped for exportation or exported by land", and "shipped",

there shall be substituted references to "posted in the United Kingdom for transmission to any place outside it".

(g)   Section 58B shall apply only in any cases, or class of cases, in which the Commissioners require a specification to be delivered.

(h)   Section 77(1) shall apply to goods brought by post into the United Kingdom or posted in the United Kingdom for transmission to any place outside it, if an entry or specification is required of such goods when they are imported or exported otherwise than by post.

(ij)   Section 99 shall apply to any goods deposited in a Queen's Warehouse under Regulation 14 of these Regulations as it applies to goods so deposited under or by virtue of any provision of the Act of 1979.

(k)   Paragraph 1 of Schedule 3 shall, in the case of a thing brought by post into the United Kingdom, apply with the substitution, for the words "to any person who to their knowledge was at the time of seizure the owner or one of the owners thereof", of the following–

"to any person:

     (a)   who to their knowledge was at the time of the seizure the owner or one of the owners of the postal packet containing the thing; or

     (b)   who appears to them to be the sender of the postal packet containing the thing; or

     (c)   to whom the postal packet containing the thing was addressed"

and paragraph 10(1) shall not apply.

History – Reg. 5(d) substituted on 1 July 1986 by SI 1986/1019. Former reg. 5(d) read as follows:
     "(d)   In the application of section 43, subsection (1) shall not apply, and paragraph (c) of subsection (2) shall apply with the substitution of subparagraphs (i) and (ii) for the words "at the time when, the packet containing the goods having been presented to the proper officer of customs and excise, the amount of duty appearing to be due is assessed by him"."

5A   In its application to goods contained in postal packets brought into the United Kingdom, regulation 5 of the Customs Controls on Importation of Goods Regulations 1991 shall apply only in any case, or class of cases, in which the Commissioners require an entry to be made in accordance with that regulation.

History – Reg. 5A was inserted by SI 1992/3224, reg. 3(b), operative from 1 January 1993.

6   Dutiable goods shall not be brought by post into the United Kingdom from a place situated outside the United Kingdom and the Isle of Man for delivery in the United Kingdom or the Isle of Man except–

(a)   in a parcel, a letter packet, a small packet or a datapost packet; or

(b)   in a printed packet, provided that the goods are of such a description as to be transmissible in such a packet under paragraph 22 of the Post Office Overseas Letter Post Scheme 1982.

7(1)   This Regulation relates to–

(a)   parcels brought by post into the United Kingdom;

(b)   packets brought by post into the United Kingdom, being printed packets containing or consisting of dutiable goods, small packets, letter packets or datapost packets.

7(2)   Every parcel referred to in paragraph (1)(a) of this Regulation shall have affixed to it, or be accompanied by, a customs declaration fully and correctly stating the nature, quantity and value of the goods which it contains or of which it consists, and such other particulars as the Commissioners or the Post Office may require:

Provided that the Commissioners may, at the request of the Post Office, relax the requirements of this paragraph by allowing the bringing in by post into the United Kingdom of any number of parcels accompanied by a single customs declaration containing the particulars prescribed above if the parcels are brought in together, sent by or on behalf of the same person and addressed to a single addressee.

7(3)   Every packet referred to in paragraph (1)(b) of this Regulation, of which packet the value exceeds £270, shall have attached to it a full and correct customs declaration of the kind described in paragraph (2) of this Regulation and, in addition, shall bear on the outside the top portion of a green label in the prescribed form:

Provided that any packet referred to in this paragraph, being a registered letter packet containing any article of value, may have the customs declaration referred to in this paragraph enclosed in it.

7(4)   Every packet referred to in paragraph (1)(b) of this Regulation, of which packet the value does not exceed £270, shall either–

(a)   bear on the outside a green label in the prescribed form, in which the declaration as to the description, net weight and value of the contents shall be fully and correctly completed; or

(b)   bear on the outside the top portion of a green label in the prescribed form and, in addition, have attached to it a full and correct customs declaration of the kind prescribed in paragraph (2) of this Regulation:

Provided that any packet referred to in this paragraph, being a registered letter packet containing any article of value, may have the customs declaration referred to in sub-paragraph (b) of this paragraph enclosed in it.

8(1)   This Regulation relates to–

(a)   parcels posted in the United Kingdom for transmission to any place outside it;

(b)   packets posted in the United Kingdom for transmission to any place outside it, being printed packets containing or consisting of goods which are dutiable in the country of destination, small packets, letter packets or datapost packets.

8(2)   Every parcel referred to in paragraph (1)(a) of this Regulation shall have affixed to it, or be accompanied by, a customs declaration fully and correctly stating the nature, quantity and value of the goods which it contains or of which it consists, and such other particulars as the Commissioners or the Post Office may require:

Provided that the Commissioners may, at the request of the Post Office, relax the requirements of this paragraph by allowing the exportation by post of any number of parcels accompanied by a single customs declaration containing the particulars prescribed above if the parcels are posted simultaneously at the same post office by or on behalf of the same person and are addressed to a single addressee.

8(3)   Every packet referred to in paragraph (1)(b) of this Regulation, of which packet the value exceeds £270, shall bear on the outside the top portion of a green label in the prescribed form and, in addition, shall have attached to it, or, if the postal administration of the country of destination so requires, enclosed in it, a full and correct customs declaration of the kind described in paragraph (2) of this Regulation:

Provided that any packet referred to in this paragraph, being a registered letter packet containing any article of value, may have the customs declaration referred to in this paragraph enclosed in it if the sender so prefers.

8(4) Every packet referred to in paragraph (1)(b) of this Regulation, of which packet the value does not exceed £270, shall either–

(a)   bear on the outside a green label in the prescribed form, in which the declaration as to the description, net weight and value of the contents shall be fully and correctly completed; or, if the sender so prefers,

(b)   bear on the outside the top portion of a green label in the prescribed form and, in addition, have attached to it or, if the postal administration of the country of destination so requires, enclosed in it, a full and correct customs declaration of the kind described in paragraph (2) of this Regulation:

Provided that any packet referred to in this paragraph, being a registered letter packet containing any article of value, may have the customs declaration referred to in sub-paragraph (b) of this paragraph enclosed in it if the sender so prefers.

9(1) Without prejudice to the application of Regulations 7(1)(b), (3) and (4), and 8(1)(b), (3) and (4) of these Regulations to any printed packet contained in it, every mail bag containing printed packets containing or consisting of goods which are dutiable in the country of destination, brought by post into the United Kingdom or posted in the United Kingdom for transmission to any place outside it under the provisions of paragraph 30 of the Post Office Overseas Letter Post Scheme 1982 shall have affixed to the bag label a green label in the prescribed form.

9(2) Regulations 7 and 8 of these regulations and paragraph (1) of this Regulation shall not apply to a postal packet or mail bag which–

(a)   contains only Community goods, and

        (i)   having been posted elsewhere in the territory of the Community, is brought by post to the United Kingdom for delivery there, or which

        (ii)   is posted in the United Kingdom for delivery in the territory of the Community, or

(b)   is posted in a place situated outside the United Kingdom for delivery in another place so situated.

History – Reg. 9(2) was substituted by SI 1992/3224, reg. 3(c), operative from 1 January 1993.

10 Without prejudice to the provisions of Regulations 7, 8 and 9 of these Regulations, every postal packet containing goods to be exported by post without payment of any duty of customs or excise to which they are subject, or on drawback or repayment of such duty, shall on its removal to the post office–

(a)   be accompanied by such shipping bill, declaration or other document containing such particulars as the Commissioners may require; and

(b)   have affixed to its outer cover in the form and manner so required a label having printed thereon the words "Exported by Post under Customs and Excise Control", or be distinguished in such other manner as may be so required.

11 The proper officer of the Post Office is hereby authorised to perform in relation to any postal packet or the goods which it contains such of the duties required by virtue of the customs and excise Acts to be performed by the importer or exporter of goods as the Commissioners may require.

12 In such cases or classes of case as the Commissioners may so require, the proper officer of the Post Office shall produce to the proper officer of customs and excise postal packets arriving in the United Kingdom or about to be despatched from the United Kingdom and, if the proper officer of customs and excise so requires, shall open for customs examination any packets so produced.

13 The proper officer of the Post Office accepting any outgoing packet in respect of which the requirements of paragraph (b) of Regulation 10 of these Regulations have been duly complied with shall endorse a certificate of the posting of the packet on the appropriate document and shall give it to the sender.

14(1) If goods are brought by post into the United Kingdom, and an officer of customs and excise sends to the addressee of the packet in which they are contained, or to any other person who is for the time being the importer of the goods, a notice requiring entry to be made of them or requiring a full and accurate account of them to be delivered to the proper officer of customs and excise but entry is not made or such account is not delivered with 28 days of the date of such notice or within such longer period as the Commissioners may allow, then unless the Commissioners have required the packet to be delivered to them under Regulation 17 of these Regulations the Post Office shall–

(a)   return the goods to the sender of the packet in which they were contained, or otherwise export them from the United Kingdom in accordance with any request or indication appearing on the packet; or

(b)   deliver the goods to the proper officer of customs and excise; or

(c)   with the permission of the Commissioners, and under the supervision of the proper officer of customs and excise, destroy them.

14(2)   Where goods have been delivered to him in accordance with paragraph 1(b) of this Regulation, the proper officer of customs and excise may cause the goods to be deposited in a Queen's Warehouse and section 40(3) of the Act of 1979 shall apply to the goods as it applies to goods so deposited under the said Section 40.

15(1)   On delivering a postal packet the proper officer of the Post Office may demand payment of any duty or other sum due to the Commissioners in respect of it, and any sum so received shall be paid over to the Commissioners by the Post Office.

15(2)   If payment is not made of any duty so demanded, then, subject to paragraph (3) of this Regulation, the Post Office may, with the agreement of the Commissioners, dispose of the goods contained in the packet as it sees fit.

15(3)   If any amount demanded in accordance with paragraph (1) of this Regulation, but not paid, is an amount other than duty, the Post Office shall deliver the packet to the proper officer of Customs and Excise.

16   If dutiable goods are brought by post into the United Kingdom in any postal packet contrary to Regulation 6 of these Regulations, or if any postal packet or mail bag to which Regulations 7, 8 and 9 of these Regulations or any of them apply does not contain, does not have affixed or attached to it, or is not accompanied by, the declaration, or does not bear the green label, required by those Regulations or any of them, or if the contents of any postal packet do not agree with the green label or customs declaration affixed or attached to the packet, or by which it is accompanied, or if the other requirements of these Regulations or any of them are not complied with in every material respect, then in every such case the postal packet or mail bag and all its contents shall be liable to forfeiture.

17   If the Commissioners require any postal packet to be delivered to them on the ground that any goods contained in it are liable to forfeiture under the customs and excise Acts (including these Regulations) the proper officer of the Post Office shall deliver the packet to the proper officer of Customs and Excise.

18   Nothing in these Regulations shall authorise the sending or bringing of any article out of or into the United Kingdom by post contrary to any provisions of the Post Office Overseas Parcel Post Scheme 1982, the Post Office Overseas Letter Post Scheme 1982 or the Post Office Inland Post Scheme 1979 which are applicable thereto.

Cross references – Customs and Excise Duties (Personal Reliefs for Goods Permanently Imported) Order 1992 (SI 1992/3193), art. 8(2): goods to be declared for relief.

ADMINISTRATIVE RECEIVERS (VALUE ADDED TAX CERTIFICATES) (SCOTLAND) RULES 1986

(SI 1986/304 (S 23))

Made on 20 February 1986 by the Secretary of State under s. 106 and para. 23(d) of Sch. 5 to the Insolvency Act 1985. Operative from 1 April 1986.

1(1)   These Rules may be cited as the Administrative Receivers (Value Added Tax Certificates) (Scotland) Rules 1986 and shall come into operation on 1st April 1986.

1(2)   In these Rules references to "the 1983 Act" are to the Value Added Tax Act 1983 [VATA 1994], and the expression **"administrative receiver"** has the same meaning as in Part II of the Insolvency Act 1985.

Notes – Insolvency Act 1985, Pt. II was repealed by Insolvency Act 1986, s. 438 and Sch. 12. Insolvency Act 1986, s. 51 and 251 now defines "administrative receiver" in Scotland.

APPLICATION OF THESE RULES

2   These Rules apply to a company for the purposes of section 22 of the 1983 Act [VATA 1994, Sch. 13, para. 9] where a person is appointed to act as its administrative receiver under section 467 of the Companies Act 1985 (power to appoint receivers under the law of Scotland).

ISSUE OF CERTIFICATE OF INSOLVENCY

3   In accordance with this Rule, it is the duty of the administrative receiver to issue a certificate in the terms of paragraph (b) of section 22(3) of the 1983 Act (which specifies the circumstances in which a company is deemed insolvent for the purposes of the section) forthwith upon his forming the opinion described in that paragraph.

FORM OF CERTIFICATE

4(1)   There shall be specified in the certificate–

(a)   the name of the company and its registered number;

(b)   the full name of the administrative receiver and the date of his appointment as such; and

(c)   the date on which the certificate is issued.

4(2)   The certificate shall be intituled "CERTIFICATE OF INSOLVENCY FOR THE PURPOSES OF SECTION 22(3)(b) OF THE VALUE ADDED TAX ACT 1983".

NOTIFICATION TO CREDITORS

5(1)   Notice of the issue of the certificate shall be given by the administrative receiver, within 3 months of his appointment or within 2 months of issuing the certificate whichever is the later, to all of the company's unsecured creditors of whose address he is then aware and who have, to his knowledge, made supplies to the company, with a charge to value added tax, at any time before his appointment.

5(2)   Thereafter, he shall give the notice to any such creditor of whose address and supplies to the company he becomes aware.

5(3)   He is not under obligation to provide any creditor with a copy of the certificate.

PRESERVATION OF CERTIFICATE WITH COMPANY'S RECORDS

6   The certificate shall be retained with the company's accounting records, and section 222 of the Companies Act 1985 (where and for how long records are to be kept) applies to the certificate as it applies to those records.

VALUE ADDED TAX (REFUND OF TAX) ORDER 1986

(SI 1986/336)

Made on 25 February 1986 by the Treasury under s. 20(3) of the Value Added Tax Act 1983 [VATA 1994, s. 33(3)]. Operative from 1 April 1986.

1   This Order may be cited as the Value Added Tax (Refund of Tax) Order 1986 and shall come into operation on 1st April 1986.

2   The following bodies are hereby specified for the purposes of section 20 of the Value Added Tax Act 1983 [VATA 1994, s. 33]:

A *probation committee* constituted by section 47(a) of, and paragraph 2 of Schedule 3 to, the Powers of Criminal Courts Act 1973

A magistrates' courts committee established under section 19 of the Justices of the Peace Act 1979

The charter trustees constituted by section 246(4) or (5) of the Local Government Act 1972

ADMINISTRATIVE RECEIVERS (VALUE ADDED TAX CERTIFICATES) RULES 1986

(SI 1986/385)

Made on 27 February 1986 by the Lord Chancellor under s. 106 of the Insolvency Act 1985. Operative from 1 April 1986.

CITATION AND COMMENCEMENT

1(1) These Rules may be cited as the Administrative Receivers (Value Added Tax Certificates) Rules 1986 and shall come into force on 1st April 1986.

1(2) In these Rules references to "the 1983 Act" are to the Value Added Tax Act 1983.

APPLICATION OF THESE RULES

2 These Rules apply to a company for the purposes of section 22 of the 1983 Act where a person is appointed to act as its administrative receiver except where such a person is appointed under section 467 of the Companies Act 1985 (power to appoint receivers under the law of Scotland).

ISSUE OF CERTIFICATE OF INSOLVENCY

3 In accordance with this Rule, it is the duty of the administrative receiver to issue a certificate in the terms of paragraph (b) of section 22(3) of the 1983 Act (which specifies the circumstances in which a company is deemed insolvent for the purposes of the section) forthwith upon his forming the opinion described in that paragraph.

FORM OF CERTIFICATE

4(1) There shall in the certificate be specified:

(a) the name of the company and its registered number;

(b) the full name of the administrative receiver and the date of his appointment as such; and

(c) the date on which the certificate is issued.

4(2) The certificate shall be intituled "CERTIFICATE OF INSOLVENCY FOR THE PURPOSES OF SECTION 22(3)(b) OF THE VALUE ADDED TAX ACT 1983".

NOTIFICATION TO CREDITORS

5(1) Notice of the issue of the certificate shall be given by the administrative receiver within 3 months of his appointment or within 2 months of issuing the certificate, whichever is the later, to all of the company's unsecured creditors of whose address he is then aware and who have, to his knowledge, made supplies to the company, with a charge to value added tax, at any time before his appointment.

5(2) Thereafter, he shall give the notice to any such creditor of whose address and supplies to the company he becomes aware.

5(3) He is not under obligation to provide any creditor with a copy of the certificate.

PRESERVATION OF CERTIFICATE WITH COMPANY'S RECORDS

6 The certificate shall be retained with the company's accounting records, and section 222 of the Companies Act 1985 (where and for how long records are to be kept) applies to the certificate as it applies to those records.

VALUE ADDED TAX (REFUND OF TAX) (NO. 2) ORDER 1986

(SI 1986/532)

Made on 18 March 1986 by the Treasury under s. 20(3) of the Value Added Tax Act 1983 [VATA 1994, s. 33(3)]. Operative from 1 April 1986.

CITATION AND COMMENCEMENT

1 This Order may be cited as the Value Added Tax (Refund of Tax) (No. 2) Order 1986 and shall come into operation on 1st April 1986.

2 The following bodies are hereby specified for the purposes of section 20 of the Value Added Tax Act 1983 [VATA 1994, s. 33]:

Authorities established under section 10 of the Local Government Act 1985.

VALUE ADDED TAX TRIBUNALS RULES 1986

(SI 1986/590, as amended by SI 1997/255, SI 1994/2617, SI 1991/186, SI 1986/2290)

Made on 26 March 1986 by the Commissioners of Customs and Excise under Sch. 8, para. 9 of the Value Added Tax Act 1983 [VATA 1994, Sch. 12, para. 9] and under s. 10 of the Tribunals and Inquiries Act 1971 [Tribunals and Inquiries Act 1992, s. 13]. Operative from 1 May 1986.

History – In the Arrangement of Rules, in the entries relating to r. 7 and 8 the words "an evasion" were substituted by SI 1997/255, r. 3(a), operative from 1 March 1997.
In the Arrangement of Rules, the entry relating to r. 8A was inserted by SI 1997/255, r. 3(b), operative from 1 March 1997.

ARRANGEMENT OF RULES

CITATION, COMMENCEMENT, REVOCATION AND SAVINGS

1(1)   These rules may be cited as the Value Added Tax Tribunals Rules 1986 and shall come into operation on 1st May 1986.

1(2)   The Value Added Tax Tribunals Rules 1972, the Value Added Tax Tribunals (Amendment) Rules 1974, the Value Added Tax Tribunals (Amendment) Rules 1977, and the Value Added Tax Tribunals (Amendment) (No. 2) Rules 1977 are hereby revoked.

1(3)   Anything begun under or for the purpose of any rules revoked by these rules may be continued under or, as the case may be, for the purpose of the corresponding provision of these rules.

1(4)   Where any document in any appeal to, or other proceedings before, a tribunal refers to a provision of any rules revoked by these rules, such reference shall, unless a contrary intention appears, be construed as referring to the corresponding provision of these rules.

Official publications – 700/51: VAT enquiries guide.
700/54: What if I don't pay?
700/55: VAT input tax appeals: luxuries, amusements and entertainment.
1000: Complaints and putting things right: our code of practice.
VAT – appeals and applications to the tribunals – explanatory leaflet.
AO2: How to complain about HM Customs and Excise, published by the Adjudicator's Office.
Customs Internal Guidance Manual, vol. V1.29: tribunal appeals.

Other material – Forms Trib. 1–37.

INTERPRETATION

2   In these rules, unless the context otherwise requires,–

   "the Act" means the Value Added Tax Act 1994;

   "the 1985 Act" means the Finance Act 1985;

   "the 1994 Act" means the Finance Act 1994;

   "the 1996 Act" means the Finance Act 1996;

   "appellant" means a person who brings an appeal under section 83 of the Act or sections 16 or 60 of the 1994 Act or section 55 of the 1996 Act;

   "the appropriate tribunal centre" means the tribunal centre for the time being appointed by the President for the area in which is situated the address to which the disputed decision was sent by the Commissioners or the tribunal centre to which the appeal against the disputed decision may be transferred under these rules;

   "chairman" has the same meaning as in Schedule 12 to the Act, and includes the President and any Vice-President;

   "the Commissioners" means the Commissioners of Customs and Excise;

   "costs" includes fees, charges, disbursements, expenses and remuneration;

   "date of notification" in relation to any document, means the date on which a proper officer sends that document, or a copy of that document, to any person under these rules;

   "disputed decision" means the decision of the Commissioners against which an appellant or intending appellant appeals or desires to appeal to a tribunal;

   "evasion penalty appeal" means an appeal against an assessment to a penalty under section 60 or section 61 of the Act, or section 8 of or paragraph 12 of Schedule 7 to the 1994 Act or paragraph 18 or 19 of Schedule 5 to the 1996 Act which is not solely a mitigation appeal and any accompanying appeal by the appellant against an assessment for the amount of tax alleged to have been evaded by the same conduct as that in the appeal against the assessment to a penalty;

   "hardship direction" means a direction that an appeal or an intended appeal should be entertained notwithstanding that the amount which the Commissioners have determined to be payable as tax has not been paid or deposited with them;

"mitigation appeal" means an appeal which, according to the notice of appeal or other document received from the appellant at the appropriate tribunal centre, is against a decision of the Commissioners with respect to the amount of a penalty on grounds confined to those set out in section 13(4) of the 1985 Act (in respect of penalties imposed before 27th July 1993), or with respect to the amount of a penalty or (as the case may be) interest solely under section 70 of the Act, section 8(4) of or paragraph 13 of Schedule 7 to the 1994 Act or paragraph 25 or 28 of Schedule 5 to the 1996 Act;

"the President" means the President of VAT and Duties Tribunals or the person nominated by the Lord Chancellor to discharge for the time being the functions of the President;

"proper officer" means a member of the administrative staff of the VAT and duties tribunals appointed by a chairman to perform the duties of a proper officer under these rules; or other document received from the appellant at the appropriate tribunal centre, is against a decision of the Commissioners with respect to the liability to or the amount of a penalty or surcharge on grounds confined to those set out in sections 59(7), 62(3), 63(10), 64(5), 65, 66, 67(8), 68(4), or 69(8) of the Act or sections 9, 10 or 11 of or paragraphs 14 to 19 of Schedule 7 to, the Finance Act 1994;

"reasonable excuse appeal" means an appeal which, according to the notice of appeal or other document received from the appellant at the appropriate tribunal centre, is against a decision of the Commissioners with respect to any liability to or amount of any penalty or surcharge on grounds confined to those set out in sections 59(7), 62(3), 63(10), 64(5), 65(3), 66(7), 67(8), 68(4), or 69(8) of the Act or section 10(4) or 11(4) of or any of paragraphs 14(3), 15(5), 16(4), 17(3), 18(2) or 19(4) of Schedule 7 to the 1994 Act;

"the Registrar" means the Registrar of the VAT and duties tribunals or any member of the administrative staff of the VAT and duties tribunals authorised by the President to perform for the time being all or any of the duties of a Registrar under these rules;

"tax" in relation to an appeal or application, means any tax, duty, levy or security to which that appeal or application relates;

"tribunal centre" means an administrative office of the VAT and duties tribunals;

"Vice-President" means a Vice-President of the VAT and Duties Tribunals.

History – In r. 2, the words "VAT and duties tribunals" wherever they appear were substituted by SI 1994/2617, r. 4(a), operative from 1 November 1994.
In r. 2, in the definition of "the Act", "1994" was substituted for "1983" by SI 1994/2617, r. 4(b), operative from 1 November 1994.
In r. 2, the definition of "the 1985 Act" was inserted by SI 1994/2617, r. 4(c), operative from 1 November 1994.
In r. 2, the definition of "the 1994 Act" was inserted by SI 1997/255, r. 4(a), operative from 1 March 1997.
In r. 2, the definition of "the 1996 Act" was inserted by SI 1997/255, r. 4(a), operative from 1 March 1997.
In r. 2, in the definition of "appellant", the words "the 1994 Act or section 55 of the 1996 Act" were substituted by SI 1997/255, r. 4(b), operative from 1 March 1997.
In r. 2, in the definition of "appellant", the words "section 83 of the Act ... Finance Act 1994" were substituted by SI 1994/2617, r. 4(d), operative from 1 November 1994.
In r. 2, in the definition of "chairman", the number "12" was substituted by SI 1997/255, r. 4(c), operative from 1 March 1997.
In r. 2, in the definition of "date of notification", the word "a" was inserted before the word "copy" by SI 1997/255, r. 4(d), operative from 1 March 1997.
In r. 2, the definition of "date of notification" was inserted by SI 1991/186, r. 3, operative from 1 March 1991.
In r. 2, in the definition of "evasion penalty appeal", the words "the 1994 Act or paragraph 18 or 19 of Schedule 5 to the 1996 Act" were substituted by SI 1997/255, r. 4(e), operative from 1 March 1997.
In r. 2, the definition of "evasion penalty appeal" was inserted by SI 1994/2617, r. 4(e), operative from 1 November 1994.
In r. 2, the definition of "hardship direction" was inserted by SI 1991/186, r. 3, operative from 1 March 1991.
In r. 2, in the definition of "mitigation appeal", the words "on grounds confined" to the end were substituted by SI 1997/255, r. 4(f), operative from 1 March 1997.
In r. 2, in the definition of "mitigation appeal", the words "(in respect of penalties ... the Finance Act 1994" were inserted by SI 1994/2617, r. 4(f), operative from 1 November 1994.
In r. 2, in the definition of "the President", the word "Duties" was substituted for the word "duties" by SI 1997/255, r. 4(g), operative from 1 March 1997.
In r. 2, in the definition of "the President", the words "the VAT and duties Tribunals" were substituted by SI 1994/2617, r. 4(g), operative from 1 November 1994.
In r. 2, in the definition of "reasonable excuse appeal", the following words "any liability to or the amount of any", "65(3)", "66(7)", and "section 10(4) or ... the 1994 Act" were substituted by SI 1997/255, r. 4(h), operative from 1 March 1997.
In r. 2, the definition of "reasonable excuse appeal" was substituted by SI 1994/2617, r. 4(h), operative from 1 November 1994.
In r. 2, in the definition of "the Registrar", the word "President" was substituted by SI 1994/2617, r. 4(i), operative from 1 November 1994.
In r. 2, the definition of "tax" was inserted by SI 1994/2617, r. 4(j), operative from 1 November 1994.
In r. 2, the definition of "section 13 penalty appeal" was omitted by SI 1994/2617, r. 4(k), operative from 1 November 1994.
In r. 2, in the definition of "Vice-President", the words "the VAT and Duties Tribunals" were substituted by SI 1997/255, r. 4(i), operative from 1 March 1997.

METHOD OF APPEALING

3(1) An appeal to a tribunal shall be brought by a notice of appeal served at the appropriate tribunal centre.

3(2)   A notice of appeal shall be signed by or on behalf of the appellant and shall–

(a)   state the name and address of the appellant;

(aa)   state the date (if any) with effect from which the appellant was registered for tax and the nature of his business;

(b)   state the address of the office of the Commissioners from which the disputed decision was sent;

(c)   state the date of the document containing the disputed decision and the address to which it was sent;

(d)   have attached thereto a copy of the document containing the disputed decision; and

(e)   set out, or have attached thereto a document containing, the grounds of the appeal, including in a reasonable excuse appeal, particulars of the excuse relied upon.

3(3)   A notice of appeal shall have attached thereto a copy of any letter from the Commissioners extending the appellant's time to appeal against the disputed decision and of any further letter from the Commissioners notifying him of a date from which his time to appeal against the disputed decision shall run.

3(4)   Subject to any direction made under rule 13, the parties to an appeal shall be the appellant and the Commissioners.

History – R. 3(2)(aa) was inserted by SI 1994/2617, r. 5(a), operative from 1 November 1994.
In r. 3(2)(d), the words "set out, or" at the start were deleted by SI 1994/2617, r. 5(b), operative from 1 November 1994.

TIME FOR APPEALING

4(1)   Subject to paragraph (2) of this rule and any direction made under rule 19, a notice of appeal shall be served at the appropriate tribunal centre before the expiration of 30 days after the date of the document containing the disputed decision of the Commissioners.

4(2)   If, during the period of 30 days after the date of the document containing the disputed decision, the Commissioners shall have notified the appellant by letter that his time to appeal against the disputed decision is extended until the expiration of 21 days after a date set out in such letter, or to be set out in a further letter to him, a notice of appeal against that disputed decision may be served at the appropriate tribunal centre at any time before the expiration of the period of 21 days set out in such letter or further letter.

ACKNOWLEDGMENT AND NOTIFICATION OF AN APPEAL

5   A proper officer shall send–

(a)   an acknowledgment of the service of a notice of appeal at the appropriate tribunal centre to the appellant; and

(b)   a copy of the notice of appeal and of any accompanying document or documents to the Commissioners;

and the acknowledgment and such copy of the notice of appeal shall state the date of service and the date of notification of the notice of appeal.

History – R. 5 amended by SI 1991/186, r. 4 from 1 March 1991 which inserted the words "and the date of notification".

NOTICE THAT AN APPEAL DOES NOT LIE OR CANNOT BE ENTERTAINED

6(1)   Where the Commissioners contend that an appeal does not lie to, or cannot be entertained by, a tribunal they shall serve a notice to that effect at the appropriate tribunal centre containing the grounds for such contention and applying for the appeal to be struck out or dismissed, as the case may be, as soon as practicable after the receipt by them of the notice of appeal.

6(2)   Any notice served by the Commissioners under this rule shall be accompanied by a copy of the disputed decision unless a copy thereof has been served previously at the appropriate tribunal centre by either party to the appeal.

6(3)   In a reasonable excuse or a mitigation appeal the hearing of any application made by the Commissioners under the provisions of this rule may immediately precede the hearing of the substantive appeal.

6(4)   A proper officer shall send a copy of any notice or certificate served under this rule and of any document or documents accompanying the same to the appellant.

STATEMENT OF CASE, DEFENCE AND REPLY IN AN EVASION PENALTY APPEAL

7(1)   Unless a tribunal shall otherwise direct, in an evasion penalty appeal–

(a)   the Commissioners shall within 42 days of the date of notification of the notice of appeal or the withdrawal or dismissal of any application made by them under rule 6 hereof (whichever shall be the later) serve at the appropriate tribunal centre a statement of case in the appeal setting out the matters and facts on which they rely for the making of the penalty assessment and (where also disputed) the making of the assessment for the tax alleged to have been evaded by the same conduct;

(aa)   a statement of case served by the Commissioners in accordance with (a) above shall include full particulars of the alleged dishonesty and shall state the statutory provision under which the penalty or tax is assessed or the decision is made;

(b)   the appellant shall within 42 days of the date of notification of such statement of case serve at the appropriate tribunal centre a defence thereto setting out the matters and facts on which he relies for his defence; and

(c)   the Commissioners may within 21 days of the date of notification of such defence serve at the appropriate tribunal centre a reply to a defence and shall do so if it is necessary thereby to set out specifically any matter or any fact showing illegality, or

      (i)   which they allege makes the defence not maintainable; or

     (ii)   which, if not specifically set out, might take the appellant by surprise; or

    (iii)   which raises any issue of fact not arising out of the statement of case.

7(2)   At any hearing of an evasion penalty appeal the Commissioners shall not be required to prove, or to bring evidence relating to, any matter or fact which is admitted by the appellant in his defence.

7(3)   Every statement of case, defence and reply hereunder shall be divided into paragraphs numbered consecutively, each allegation being so far as convenient contained in a separate paragraph.

7(4)   Each such document shall contain in summary form a brief statement of the matters and facts on which the party relies but not the evidence by which those facts are to be proved.

7(5)   A party may raise a point of law in such documents.

History – In the heading to r. 7, the words "an evasion" were substituted by SI 1997/255, r. 5, operative from 1 March 1997. In r. 7, the words "an evasion penalty appeal" were substituted wherever they appear by SI 1994/2617, r. 6(a), operative from 1 November 1994.
R. 7(1)(aa), was inserted by SI 1994/2617, r. 6(b), operative from 1 November 1994.
In r. 7(1)(a)–(c), the word "notification" was substituted in three places by SI 1991/186, r. 5, operative from 1 March 1991.

STATEMENT OF CASE IN AN APPEAL OTHER THAN AN EVASION PENALTY APPEAL AND REASONABLE EXCUSE AND MITIGATION APPEALS

8   Unless a tribunal otherwise directs, in appeals other than reasonable excuse and mitigation appeals and evasion penalty appeals the Commissioners shall within the period of 30 days after–

(a)   the date of notification of the notice of appeal; or

(b)   the date of notification of the notice of withdrawal of any application under rule 6 in the appeal; or

(c)   the date on which a direction dismissing any application under rule 6 in the appeal is released in accordance with rule 30;

whichever shall be the latest serve at the appropriate tribunal centre a statement of case in the appeal setting out the matters and facts on which they rely to support the disputed decision and the statutory provision under which the tax or penalty is assessed or the decision is made.

History – In the heading to r. 8, the words "an evasion" were substituted by SI 1997/255, r. 5, operative from 1 March 1997.
In r. 8, the words "evasion penalty appeals" were substituted by SI 1994/2617, r. 7(a), operative from 1 November 1994.
In r. 8, the words "within the period ... be the latest" were substituted by SI 1991/186, r. 6, operative from 1 March 1991.
In r. 8 at the end, the words "and the statutory provision ... the decision is made" were inserted by SI 1994/2617, r. 7(b), operative from 1 November 1994.

FURTHER PROVISIONS ABOUT STATEMENTS OF CASE

8A   Where on an appeal against a decision with respect to an assessment or the amount of an assessment the Commissioners wish to contend that an amount specified in the assessment is less than it ought to have been, they shall so state in their statement of case in that appeal, indicating the amount of the alleged deficiency and the manner in which it has been calculated.

History – R. 8A was inserted by SI 1997/255, r. 6, operative from 1 March 1997.

FURTHER AND BETTER PARTICULARS

9 A tribunal may at any time direct a party to an appeal to serve further particulars of his case at the appropriate tribunal centre for the appeal within such period from the date of such direction (not being less than 14 days from the date thereof) as it may specify therein.

History – R. 9(1) was redesignated r. 9 by SI 1997/255, r. 7(1), operative from 1 March 1997.
R. 9(2) was omitted by SI 1997/255, r. 7(2), operative from 1 March 1997.

ACKNOWLEDGMENT OF AND NOTIFICATION OF SERVICE OF FORMAL DOCUMENTS SERVED IN AN APPEAL

10(1) Any statement of case served by the Commissioners under rule 7 or rule 8 of these rules shall be accompanied by a copy of the disputed decision unless a copy of the disputed decision has been served previously at the appropriate tribunal centre by either party to the appeal.

10(2) In a reasonable excuse or a mitigation appeal the Commissioners shall serve a copy of the disputed decision at the appropriate tribunal centre as soon as practicable after the receipt by them of the copy of the notice of appeal unless a copy of the disputed decision has been so served previously by the appellant.

10(3) A proper officer shall send–

(a) an acknowledgement of the service at the appropriate tribunal centre of any statement of case, defence, reply or particulars in any appeal to the party serving the same; and

(b) a copy of such document or particulars and any other document accompanying the same to the other party to the appeal.

METHOD OF APPLYING FOR A DIRECTION

11(1) An application to a tribunal, made otherwise than at a hearing, for

(a) the issue of a witness summons; or

(b) a direction (including a hardship direction or a direction for the setting aside of a witness summons)

shall be made by notice served at the appropriate tribunal centre.

11(2) A notice under this rule shall–

(a) state the name and address of the applicant;

(b) state the direction sought or details of the witness summons sought to be issued or set aside; and

(c) set out, or have attached thereto a document containing, the grounds of the application.

11(3) In addition to the requirement of paragraph (2) hereof, any notice of application by an intending appellant shall–

(a) state the address of the office of the Commissioners from which the disputed decision was sent;

(b) state the date of the disputed decision and the address to which it was sent;

(c) set out shortly the disputed decision or have attached thereto a copy of the document containing the same; and

(d) have attached thereto a copy of any letter from the Commissioners extending the applicant's time to appeal the disputed decision and of any letter from the Commissioners notifying him of a date from which his time of appeal against the disputed decision shall run.

11(4) A notice of application for a hardship direction shall be served at the appropriate tribunal centre within the period for the service of a notice of appeal.

11(5) Except as provided by rule 22, the parties to an application shall be the parties to the appeal or intended appeal.

11(6) Except as provided by rule 22, a proper officer shall send–

(a) an acknowledgment of the service of a notice of application at the appropriate tribunal centre to the applicant; and

(b) a copy of such notice of application and of accompanying document or documents to the other party to the application (if any);

and the acknowledgment and copy of the notice of application shall state the date of service and the date of notification of the notice of application.

11(7) Within 14 days of the date of notification of a notice of application the other party to the application (if any) shall indicate whether or not he consents thereto and, if he does not consent thereto, the reason therefor.

History – R. 11(1) amended by SI 1991/186, r. 7, operative from 1 March 1991.
R. 11(4) amended by SI 1991/186, r. 8, operative from 1 March 1991.
R. 11(6) amended by SI 1991/186, r. 9 from 1 March 1991 which inserted the words "and the date of notification".
R. 11(7) amended by SI 1991/186, r. 10 from 1 March 1991 which substituted the word "notification".

PARTNERS

12 One or more partners in a firm which is not a legal person distinct from the partners of whom it is composed may appeal against a decision of the Commissioners relating to the firm or its business, or apply to a tribunal in an appeal or intended appeal, in the name of the firm and, unless a tribunal shall otherwise direct, the proceedings shall be carried on in the name of the firm, but with the same consequences as would have ensued if the appeal or application had been brought in the names of the partners.

History – In r. 12 at the beginning, the words "One or more partners" were substituted by SI 1994/2617, r. 8, operative from 1 November 1994.

DEATH OR BANKRUPTCY OF AN APPELLANT OR APPLICANT

13(1) This rule applies where, in the course of proceedings, the liability or interest of the applicant or appellant passes to another person (**"the successor"**) by reason of death, insolvency or otherwise.

13(2) The tribunal may direct, on the application of the Commissioners or the successor, and with the written consent of the successor, that the successor shall be substituted for the applicant or appellant in the proceedings.

13(3) Where the tribunal is satisfied that there is no person interested in the application or appeal, or the successor fails to give written consent for his substitution in the proceedings within a period of two months after being requested to do so by the tribunal it may, of its own motion or on application by the Commissioners and after giving prior written notice to the successor, dismiss the application or appeal.

History – R. 13 was substituted by SI 1994/2617, r. 9, operative from 1 November 1994.

AMENDMENTS

14(1) For the purposes of determining the issues in dispute or of correcting an error or defect in an appeal or application or intended appeal, a tribunal may at any time, either of its own motion or on the application of any party to the appeal or application, or any other person interested, direct that a notice of appeal, notice of application, statement of case, defence, reply, particulars or other document in the proceedings be amended in such manner as may be specified in such direction on such terms as it may think fit.

14(2) This rule shall not apply to a decision or direction of a tribunal.

TRANSFERS BETWEEN TRIBUNAL CENTRES

15 A tribunal on the application of a party to an appeal may direct that the appeal and all proceedings in the appeal be transferred to such tribunal centre as may be specified in such direction whereupon, for the purposes of these rules, the tribunal centre specified in such direction shall become the appropriate tribunal centre for such appeal and all proceedings therein, without prejudice to the power of a tribunal to give a further direction relating thereto under this rule.

WITHDRAWAL OF AN APPEAL OR APPLICATION

16(1) An appellant or applicant may at any time withdraw his appeal or application by serving at the appropriate tribunal centre a notice of withdrawal signed by him or on his behalf, and a proper officer shall send a copy thereof to the other parties to the appeal.

16(2) The withdrawal of an appeal or application under this rule shall not prevent a party to such appeal or application from applying under rule 29 for an award or direction as to his or their costs or under section 84(8) of the Act or under section 56(3), (4) or (5) of the 1996 Act for a direction *for the payment or repayment of a* sum of money with interest or prevent a tribunal from making such an award or direction if it thinks fit so to do.

History – In r. 16(1), the words "the other parties to the appeal" were substituted by SI 1994/2617, r. 10(a), operative from 1 November 1994.
In r. 16(2), the words "section 84(8)" were substituted by SI 1994/2617, r. 10(b), operative from 1 November 1994.
In r. 16(2) the words "or under section 56(3), (4) or (5) of the 1996 Act" were inserted by SI 1997/255, r. 8, operative from 1 March 1997.

APPEAL OR APPLICATION ALLOWED BY CONSENT

17 Where the parties to an appeal or application have agreed upon the terms of any decision or direction to be given by a tribunal, a tribunal may give a decision or make a direction in accordance with those terms without a hearing.

POWER OF A TRIBUNAL TO STRIKE OUT OR DISMISS AN APPEAL

18(1) A tribunal shall–

(a) strike out an appeal where no appeal against the disputed decision lies to a tribunal; and

(b) dismiss an appeal where the appeal cannot be entertained by a tribunal.

18(2) A tribunal may dismiss an appeal for want of prosecution where the appellant or the person to whom the interest of liability of the appellant has been assigned or transmitted, or upon whom such interest or liability has devolved, has been guilty of inordinate and inexcusable delay.

18(3) Except in accordance with rule 17, no appeal shall be struck out or dismissed under this rule without a hearing.

POWER OF A TRIBUNAL TO EXTEND TIME AND TO GIVE DIRECTIONS

19(1) A tribunal may of its own motion or on the application of any party to an appeal or application extend the time within which a party to the appeal or application or any other person is required or authorised by these rules or any decision or direction of a tribunal to do anything in relation to the appeal or application (including the time for service for a notice of appeal or notice of application) upon such terms as it may think fit.

19(2) A tribunal may make a direction under paragraph (1) of this rule of its own motion without prior notice or reference to any party or other person and without a hearing.

19(3) Without prejudice to the preceding provisions of this rule a tribunal may of its own motion or on the application of a party to an appeal or application or other person interested give or make any direction as to the conduct of or as to any matter or thing in connection with the appeal or application which it may think necessary or expedient to ensure the speedy and just determination of the appeal including the joining of other persons as parties to the appeal.

19(3A) Where a notice is served under section 61 of the Act or paragraph 19 of Schedule 5 to the 1996 Act and appeals are brought by different persons which relate to, or to different portions of, the basic penalty referred to in the notice, the tribunal may, of its own motion or on the application of any party to any such appeal, give any direction it thinks fit as to the joinder of the appeals.

19(4) If any party to an appeal or application or other person fails to comply with any direction of a tribunal, a tribunal may allow or dismiss the appeal or application.

19(5) A tribunal may, of its own motion or on the application of any party to an appeal or application, waive any breach or non-observance of any provision of these rules or of any decision or direction of a tribunal upon such terms as it may think just.

History – In r. 19(3), the words "of its own motion or" were inserted by SI 1994/2617, r. 11(a), operative from 1 November 1994.
In r. 19(3), the words "including the joining ... to the appeal" were inserted by SI 1994/2617, r. 11(b), operative from 1 November 1994.
In r. 19(3A), the words "or paragraph 19 of Schedule 5 to the 1996 Act" were inserted by SI 1997/255, r. 9, operative from 1 March 1997.
R. 19(3A), was inserted by SI 1994/2617, r. 12, operative from 1 November 1994.
In r. 19(4), the word "application" was substituted by SI 1991/186, r. 11, operative from 1 March 1991.

DISCLOSURE, INSPECTION AND PRODUCTION OF DOCUMENTS

20(1) Each of the parties to an appeal other than a reasonable excuse or a mitigation appeal and each of the parties to an application for a hardship direction shall, before the expiration of the time set out in paragraph (2) of this rule, serve at the appropriate tribunal centre a list of the documents in his possession, custody or power which he proposes to produce at the hearing of the appeal or application.

20(1A) The list of documents to be served by the Commissioners in accordance with paragraph (1) shall contain a reference to the documents relied upon in reaching a decision on a review under section 15 or 59 of the 1994 Act or section 54 of the 1996 Act.

20(2) The time within which a list of documents shall be served under paragraph (1) of this rule shall be–

(a) in an evasion penalty appeal, a period of 15 days after the last day for the service by the Commissioners of any reply pursuant to rule 7(1)(c) hereof;

(b)   in any other appeal except a reasonable excuse appeal or a mitigation appeal, a period of 30 days after–

       (i)   the date of notification of the notice of appeal; or

       (ii)   the date of notification of the notice of withdrawal of any application under rule 6 in the appeal; or

       (iii)   the date on which a direction dismissing any application under rule 6 in the appeal is released in accordance with rule 30;

     whichever shall be the latest;

(c)   in an application for a hardship direction, a period of 30 days after the date of notification of the application.

20(3)   In addition, and without prejudice to the foregoing provisions of this rule, a tribunal may, where it appears necessary for disposing fairly of the proceedings, on the application of a party to an appeal direct that the other party to the appeal shall serve at the appropriate tribunal centre for the appeal within such period as it may specify a list of the documents or any class of documents which are or have been in his possession, custody or power relating to any question in issue in the appeal, and may at the same time or subsequently order him to make and serve an affidavit verifying such list.

20(4)   If a party desires to claim that any document included in a list of documents served by him in pursuance of a direction made under paragraph (3) of this rule is privileged from production in the appeal, that claim must be made in the list of documents with a sufficient statement of the grounds of privilege.

20(5)   A proper officer shall send a copy of any list of documents and affidavit served under paragraph (1) or paragraph (3) of this rule to the other party to the appeal or application and such other party shall be entitled to inspect and take copies of the documents set out in such list which are in the possession, custody or power of the party who made the list and are not privileged from production in the appeal at such time and place as he and the party who served such list of documents may agree or a tribunal may direct.

20(6)   At the hearing of an appeal or application a party shall produce any document included in a list of documents served by him in relation to such appeal or application under paragraph (1) or paragraph (3) of this rule which is in his possession, custody or power and is not privileged from production when called upon so to do by the other party to the appeal or application.

History – In r. 20(1), the words "each of the parties" in each place and "a hardship direction" were substituted by SI 1991/186, r. 12, operative from 1 March 1991.
In r. 20(1A), the words "the 1994 Act or section 54 of the 1996 Act" were substituted by SI 1997/255, r. 10, operative from 1 March 1997.
R. 20(1A), was inserted by SI 1994/2617, r. 13, operative from 1 November 1994.
In r. 20(2)(a), the words "an evasion penalty appeal" were substituted by SI 1994/2617, r. 14, operative from 1 November 1994.
R. 20(2)(b) and (c) were substituted for former r. 20(2)(b) by SI 1991/186, r. 13, operative from 1 March 1991.

WITNESS STATEMENTS

21(1)   A party to an appeal may, within the time specified in paragraph (6) of this rule, serve at the appropriate tribunal centre a statement in writing (in these rules called **"a witness statement"**) containing evidence proposed to be given by any person at the hearing of the appeal.

21(2)   A witness statement shall contain the name, address and description of the person proposing to give the evidence contained therein and shall be signed by him.

21(3)   A proper officer shall send a copy of a witness statement served at the appropriate tribunal centre to the other party to the appeal and such copy shall state the date of service and the date of notification of the witness statement and shall contain or be accompanied by a note to the effect that unless a notice of objection thereto is served in accordance with paragraph (4) of this rule, the witness statement may be read at the hearing of the appeal as evidence of the facts stated therein without the person who made the witness statement giving oral evidence thereat.

21(4)   If a party objects to a witness statement being read at the hearing of the appeal as evidence of any fact stated therein he shall serve a notice of objection to such witness statement at the appropriate tribunal centre not later than 14 days after the date of notification of such witness statement whereupon a proper officer shall send a copy of the notice of objection to the other party and the witness statement shall not be read or admitted in evidence at such hearing but the person who signed such witness statement may give evidence orally at the hearing.

21(5)   Subject to paragraph (4) of this rule, unless a tribunal shall otherwise direct, a witness statement signed by any person and duly served under this rule shall be admissible in evidence at the hearing of the appeal as evidence of any fact stated therein of which oral evidence by him at that hearing would be admissible.

21(6)   The time within which a witness statement may be served under this rule shall be–

(a)   in the case of an evasion penalty appeal, before the expiration of 21 days after the last day for the service by the Commissioners of a reply pursuant to paragraph (1)(c) of rule 7;

(b)   in the case of a mitigation appeal or a reasonable excuse appeal, before the expiration of 21 days after the date of notification of the Notice of Appeal; and

(c)   in the case of any other appeal, before the expiration of 21 days after the date of notification of the Commissioners' statement of case.

History – In r. 21(3), the words "and the date of notification of the witness statement" were inserted by SI 1991/186, r. 14(a), operative from 1 March 1991.
In r. 21(4), words after "notification of such witness statement" were omitted by SI 1997/255, r. 11, operative from 1 March 1997.
In r. 21(4) and (6)(b), the word "notification" was substituted by SI 1991/186, r. 14(b) and (c), operative from 1 March 1991.
In r. 21(6)(a), the words "an evasion penalty appeal" were substituted by SI 1994/2617, r. 15, operative from 1 November 1994.
In r. 21(6)(c), the words "notification . . . case" were substituted by SI 1991/186, r. 14(d), operative from 1 March 1991.

AFFIDAVITS AND DEPOSITIONS MADE IN OTHER LEGAL PROCEEDINGS

21A(1)   If–

(a)   an affidavit or deposition made in other legal proceedings (whether civil or criminal) is specified as such in a list of documents served under rule 20(1) by a party to an appeal or application or (in the case of an appeal or application to which rule 20(1) does not apply) in a notice served by such a party at the appropriate tribunal centre, and

(b)   it is stated in that list or notice that the party serving the list or notice proposes to give that affidavit or deposition in evidence at the hearing of the appeal or application and that the person who made that affidavit or deposition is dead, or outside the United Kingdom or unfit by reason of his bodily or mental condition to attend as a witness or (as the case may be) that despite the exercise of reasonable diligence it has not been possible to find him,

then, subject to the following paragraphs of this rule, the affidavit or deposition shall be admissible at the hearing of the appeal or application as evidence of any fact stated therein of which oral evidence by the person who made the affidavit or deposition would be admissible.

21A(2)   The time within which a notice may be served under paragraph (1) of this rule shall be before the expiration of 21 days after the date of notification of the notice of appeal or notice of application.

21A(3)   When a proper officer sends a copy of any such list or notice as is mentioned in paragraph (1) of this rule to any person pursuant to rule 20(5) or rule 11(6)(b), he shall also send to that person a copy of this rule.

21A(4)   If a party objects to an affidavit or deposition being read and admitted as evidence under paragraph (1) of this rule, he shall serve a notice of application for directions with regard to that affidavit or deposition at the appropriate tribunal centre not later than 21 days after the date of notification of the list of documents or notice (as the case may be).

21A(5)   At the hearing of an application under paragraph (4) of this rule a tribunal may give directions as to whether, and if so how and on what conditions, the affidavit or deposition may be admitted as evidence and (where applicable) as to the manner in which the affidavit or deposition is to be proved, and the affidavit or deposition shall be admissible as evidence to the extent and on the conditions (if any) specified in the direction but not further or otherwise.

21A(6)   The members of the tribunal hearing an application under paragraph (4) of this rule shall not sit on the hearing of the appeal or application to which the first-mentioned application relates.

History – R. 21A was inserted by SI 1991/186, r. 15(1), operative from 1 March 1991.

WITNESS SUMMONSES AND SUMMONSES TO THIRD PARTIES

22(1)   Where a witness is required by a party to an appeal or application to attend the hearing of an appeal or application to give oral evidence or to produce any document in his possession, custody or power necessary for the purpose of that hearing, a chairman or the Registrar shall, upon the application of such party, issue a summons requiring the attendance of such witness at such hearing or the production of the document, wherever such witness may be in the United Kingdom or the Isle of Man.

22(2)   Where a party to an appeal or application desires to inspect any document necessary for the purpose of the hearing thereof which is in the possession, custody or power of any other person in the United Kingdom or the Isle of Man (whether or not such other person is a party to that appeal or application) a chairman or the Registrar shall, upon the application of such party, issue a summons requiring either–

(a)   the attendance of such other person at such date, time and place as the chairman or the Registrar may direct and then and there to produce such document for inspection by such party or his representative and to allow such party or his representative then and there to peruse such document and to take a copy thereof; or

(b)   such other person to post the document by ordinary post to an address in the United Kingdom or Isle of Man by First Class Mail in an envelope duly prepaid and properly addressed to the party requiring to inspect the same.

22(3)   A chairman or the Registrar may issue a summons under this rule without prior notice or reference to the applicant or any other person and without a hearing and the only party to the application shall be the applicant.

22(4)   A summons issued under this rule shall be signed by a chairman or the Registrar and must be served–

(a)   where the witness or third party is an individual, by leaving a copy of the summons with him and showing him the original thereof,

(b)   where the witness or third party is a body corporate, by sending a copy of the summons by post to, or leaving it at, the registered or principal office in the United Kingdom or the Isle of Man of the body to be served,

not less than 4 days before the day on which the attendance of the witness or third party or the posting of the document is thereby required. A summons issued under this rule shall contain a statement, or be accompanied by a note, to the effect that the witness or third party may apply, by a notice served at the tribunal centre from which the summons was issued, for a direction that the summons be set aside.

22(5)   A witness summons issued under this rule for the purpose of a hearing and duly served shall have effect until the conclusion of the hearing at which the attendance of the witness is thereby required.

22(6)   No person shall be required to attend to give evidence or to produce any document at any hearing or otherwise under paragraph (2) of this rule which he could not be required to give or produce on the trial of an action in a court of law.

22(7)   No person shall be bound to attend any hearing or to produce or post any document for the purpose of a hearing or for inspection and perusal in accordance with a summons issued under this rule unless a reasonable and sufficient sum of money to defray the expenses of coming to, attending at and returning from such hearing or place of inspection and perusal was tendered to him at the time when the summons was served on him.

22(8)   A tribunal may, upon the application of any person served at the appropriate tribunal centre, set aside a summons served upon him under this rule.

22(9)   The parties to an application to set aside a summons issued under this rule shall be the applicant and the party who obtained the issue of the summons.

History – In r. 22(4), the words from the beginning to "is thereby required." were substituted by SI 1991/186, r. 16, operative from 1 March 1991.
In r. 22(4)(b), the words "in the United . . . of Man" were inserted by SI 1994/2617, r. 16, operative from 1 November 1994.

NOTICE OF HEARINGS

23(1)   A proper officer shall send a notice stating the date and time when, and the place where, an appeal will be heard to the parties to the appeal which, unless the parties otherwise agree, shall not be earlier than 14 days after the date on which the notice is sent.

23(2)   Unless a tribunal otherwise directs, an application made at a hearing shall be heard forthwith, and no notice thereof shall be sent to the parties thereto.

23(3)   Subject to paragraph (2) of this rule, a proper officer shall send a notice stating the date and time when, and the place where, an application will be heard which, unless the parties shall otherwise agree, shall be not earlier than 14 days after the date on which the notice is sent–

(a)   in the case of an application for the issue of a witness summons, to the applicant;

(b)   in the case of an application to set aside the issue of a witness summons, to the applicant and the party who obtained the issue of the witness summons;

(c)   in the case of any other application, to the parties to the application.

23(4) A proper officer shall send a notice stating the date and time when, and the place where, a hearing for the purpose of giving directions relating to an appeal will take place to the parties to the appeal which, unless the parties otherwise agree, shall be not earlier than 14 days after the date on which the notice is sent.

History – In r. 23(1), the word "the" was inserted before the word "place" by SI 1997/255, r. 12(a), operative from 1 March 1997.
R. 23(4) was inserted by SI 1997/255, r. 12(b), operative from 1 March 1997.

HEARINGS IN PUBLIC OR IN PRIVATE

24(1) The hearing of an appeal shall be in public unless a tribunal, on the application of a party thereto, directs that the hearing or any part of the hearing shall take place in private.

24(2) Unless a tribunal otherwise directs, the hearing of any application made otherwise than at or subsequent to the hearing of an appeal shall take place in private.

24(3) Any member of the Council on Tribunals or the Scottish Committee of the Council on Tribunals in his capacity as such a member may attend the hearing of any appeal or application notwithstanding that the appeal or application takes place in private.

REPRESENTATION AT A HEARING

25 At the hearing of an appeal or application–

(a)   any party to the appeal or application (other than the Commissioners) may conduct his case himself or may be represented by any person whom he may appoint for the purpose; and

(b)   the Commissioners may be represented at any hearing at which they are entitled to attend by any person whom they may appoint for the purpose.

FAILURE TO APPEAR AT A HEARING

26(1) If, when an appeal or application is called on for hearing no party thereto appears in person or by his representative, a tribunal may dismiss or strike out the appeal or application, but a tribunal may, on the application of any such party or of any person interested served at the appropriate tribunal centre within 14 days after the date when the decision or direction of the tribunal was released in accordance with rule 30, reinstate such appeal or application on such terms as it may think just.

26(2) If, when an appeal or application is called on for hearing, a party does not appear in person or by his representative, the tribunal may proceed to consider the appeal or application in the absence of that party.

26(3) Subject to paragraph (4) below, the tribunal may set aside any decision or direction given in the absence of a party on such terms as it thinks just, on the application of that party or of any other person interested served at the appropriate tribunal centre within 14 days after the date when the decision or direction of the tribunal was released.

26(4) Where a party makes an application under paragraph (3) above and does not attend the hearing of that application, he shall not be entitled to apply to have a decision or direction of the tribunal on the hearing of that application set aside.

History – In r. 26(1), the words "or direction" were inserted by SI 1991/186, r. 17, operative from 1 March 1991.
In r. 26(2), words at the end were omitted by SI 1994/2617, r. 17(a), operative from 1 November 1994.
R. 26(3) and (4) were inserted by SI 1994/2617, r. 17(b), operative from 1 November 1994.

PROCEDURE AT A HEARING

27(1) At the hearing of an appeal or application other than an evasion penalty appeal the tribunal shall allow–

(a)   the appellant or applicant or his representative to open his case;

(b)   the appellant or applicant to give evidence in support of the appeal or application and to produce documentary evidence;

(c)   the appellant or applicant or his representative to call other witnesses to give evidence in support of the appeal or application or to produce documentary evidence, and to re-examine any such witness following his cross-examination;

(d)   the other party to the appeal or application or his representative to cross-examine any witness called to give evidence in support of the appeal or application (including the appellant or applicant if he gives evidence);

(e)   the other party to the appeal or application or his representative to open his case;

(f)   the other party to the appeal or application to give evidence in opposition to the appeal or application and to produce documentary evidence;

(g)   the other party to the appeal or application or his representative to call other witnesses to give evidence in opposition to the appeal or application or to produce documentary evidence and to re-examine any such witness following his cross-examination;

(h)   the appellant or applicant or his representative to cross-examine any witness called to give evidence in opposition to the appeal or application (including the other party to the appeal or application if he gives evidence);

(i)   the other party to the appeal or application or his representative to make a second address closing his case; and

(j)   the appellant or applicant or his representative to make a final address closing his case.

27(2)   At the hearing of an evasion penalty appeal, or an appeal against a penalty imposed under section 114(2) of the Customs and Excise Management Act 1979 or section 22 or section 23 of the Hydrocarbon Oil Duties Act 1979, the tribunal shall follow the same procedure as is set out in paragraph (1) of this rule for the hearing of an appeal or application, but as if there were substituted–

(a)   "the Commissioners" for "the appellant or applicant";

(b)   "their" for "his" in sub-paragraphs (a), (c), (h) and (j);

(c)   "in opposition to" for "in support of" in sub-paragraphs (b), (c) and (d); and

(d)   "in support of" for "in opposition to" in sub-paragraphs (f), (g) and (h).

27(3)   At the hearing of an appeal or application the chairman and any other member of the tribunal may put any question to any witness called to give evidence thereat (including a party to the appeal or application if he gives evidence).

27(4)   Subject to the foregoing provisions of this rule, a tribunal may regulate its own procedure as it may think fit and in particular may determine the order in which the matters mentioned in paragraphs (1) and (2) are to take place.

27(5)   A chairman or the Registrar may postpone the hearing of any appeal or application.

27(6)   A tribunal may adjourn the hearing of any appeal or application on such terms as it may think just.

History – In r. 27(1), the words "an evasion penalty appeal" were substituted by SI 1994/2617, r. 18(a), operative from 1 November 1994.
In r. 27(1)(c), the words "or application" were inserted by SI 1994/2617, r. 18(b), operative from 1 November 1994.
R. 27(2) was substituted by SI 1994/2617, r. 19, operative from 1 November 1994.
In r. 27(4), the words "and in particular may . . . (1) and (2) are to take place" were added at the end by SI 1994/2617, r. 20, operative from 1 November 1994.

EVIDENCE AT A HEARING

28(1)   Subject to paragraph (4) and (5) of rule 21 and to rule 21A a tribunal may direct or allow evidence of any fact to be given in any manner it may think fit and shall not refuse evidence tendered to it on grounds only that such evidence would be inadmissible in a court of law.

28(2)   A tribunal may require oral evidence of a witness (including a party to an appeal or application) to be given on oath or affirmation and for that purpose a chairman and any member of the administrative staff of the tribunals on the direction of a chairman shall have power to administer oaths or take affirmations.

28(3)   At the hearing of an appeal or application the tribunal shall allow a party to produce any document set out in his list of documents served under rule 20 and unless a tribunal otherwise directs–

(a)   any document contained in such a list of documents which appears to be an original document shall be deemed to be an original document printed, written, signed or executed as it respectively appears to have been; and

(b)   any document contained in such list of documents which appears to be a copy shall be deemed to be a true copy.

History – R. 28(1) amended by SI 1991/186, r. 15(2) from 1 March 1991 which inserted the words "and to rule 21A".

AWARDS AND DIRECTIONS AS TO COSTS

29(1)   A tribunal may direct that a party or applicant shall pay to the other party to the appeal or application–

(a)   within such period as it may specify such sum as it may determine on account of the costs of such other party of and incidental to and consequent upon the appeal or application; or

(b)   the costs of such other party of and incidental to and consequent upon the appeal or application to be taxed by a Taxing Master of the Supreme Court or a district judge of the High Court of Justice in England and Wales or by the Auditor of the Court of Session in Scotland or by the Taxing Master of the Supreme Court of Northern Ireland or by the Taxing Master of the High Court of Justice of the Isle of Man on such basis as it shall specify.

29(2)   Where a tribunal gives a direction under paragraph 1(b) of this rule in proceedings in England and Wales the provisions of Order 62 of the Rules of the Supreme Court 1965 shall apply, with the necessary modifications, to the taxation of the costs as if the proceedings in the tribunal were a cause or matter in the Supreme Court of Judicature in England.

29(3)   Where a tribunal gives a direction under paragraph 1(b) of this rule in proceedings in Scotland the provisions of Chapter 42 of the Act of Sederunt (Rules of the Court of Session 1994) shall apply, with the necessary modifications, to the taxation of the costs as if those proceedings were a cause or matter in the Court of Session in Scotland.

29(4)   Where a tribunal gives a direction under paragraph 1(b) of this rule in proceedings in Northern Ireland the provisions of Order 62 of the Rules of the Supreme Court (Northern Ireland) 1980 shall apply, with the necessary modifications, to the taxation of the costs as if those proceedings were a cause or matter in the High Court of Northern Ireland.

29(5)   Any costs awarded under this rule shall be recoverable as a civil debt.

History – R. 29(1)(b) amended by SI 1991/186, r. 18 from 1 March 1991 which substituted the words "Taxing Master of the Supreme Court or a district judge of the High Court of Justice in England and Wales".
In r. 29(3), the words "Chapter 42 of the Act . . . of Session 1994)" were substituted by SI 1994/2617, r. 21, operative from 1 November 1994.
In r. 29(4), the word "provisions" was substituted by SI 1994/2617, r. 22, operative from 1 November 1994.

Notes – Civil Procedure Rules 1998 (SI 1998/3132) replaced the Rules of the Supreme Court.

DECISIONS AND DIRECTIONS

30(1)   At the conclusion of the hearing of an appeal the chairman may give or announce the decision of the tribunal but subject to paragraph (8) of this rule the decision shall be recorded in a written document containing the findings of fact by the tribunal and its reasons for the decision which shall be signed by a chairman; provided that if a party to the appeal shall so request by notice in writing served at the appropriate tribunal centre within one year of the date on which the decision is released in accordance with this rule the outcome of the appeal and any award and direction as to costs or for the payment or repayment of any sum of money with or without interest given or made by the tribunal during or at the conclusion of the hearing of the appeal shall be recorded in a written direction which shall be signed by a chairman or the Registrar.

30(2)   At the conclusion of the hearing of an application the chairman may give or announce the decision of the tribunal but in any event the outcome of the application and any award or direction given or made by the tribunal during or at the conclusion of the hearing shall be recorded in a written direction which shall be signed by a chairman or the Registrar; provided that if a party to the application shall so request by notice in writing served at the appropriate tribunal centre within 14 days of the date on which the direction is released in accordance with this rule the decision of the tribunal on the application shall be recorded in a written document containing the findings of fact by the tribunal and its reasons for the decision which shall be signed by a chairman.

30(3)   A proper officer shall send a copy of the decision and of any direction in an appeal to each party to the appeal and a duplicate of the direction and of any decision in an application to each party to the application.

30(4)   Every decision in an appeal shall bear the date when the copies thereof are released to be sent to the parties and such copies and any direction, and all copies of any direction, recording the outcome of the appeal shall state that date.

30(5)   Every direction on an application shall bear the date when the copies thereof are released to be sent to the parties and such copies and any decision on that application given or made under the proviso to paragraph (2) of this rule and all copies thereof shall state that date.

30(6)   A chairman or the Registrar may correct any clerical mistake or other error in expressing his manifest intention in a decision or direction signed by him but if a chairman or the Registrar corrects any such document after a copy thereof has been sent to a party, a proper officer shall as soon as practicable thereafter send a copy of the corrected document, or the page or pages which have been corrected, to that party.

30(7) Where a copy of a decision or a direction dismissing an appeal or application or containing a decision or direction given or made in the absence of a party is sent to a party or other person entitled to apply under rule 26 to apply to have the appeal or application reinstated or the decision or direction set aside, the copy shall contain or be accompanied by a note to that effect.

30(8) If, at the conclusion of the hearing of a mitigation appeal or a reasonable excuse appeal the chairman gives or announces the decision of the tribunal, he may ask the parties present at the hearing whether they require the decision to be recorded in a written document in accordance with paragraph (1) of this rule, and if none of the parties present requires this the provisions of this rule shall apply as if the appeal had been an application.

History – R. 30(1) amended by SI 1991/186, r. 19 from 1 March 1991 which substituted the words "subject to paragraph (8) of this rule" and the words "date on which the decision is released in accordance with this rule".
R. 30(2) amended by SI 1991/186, r. 20 from 1 March 1991 which substituted the words "date on which the direction is released in accordance with this rule".
R. 30(7) amended by SI 1991/186, r. 21 from 1 March 1991 which inserted the words "or the decision or direction set aside".
R. 30(8) was substituted by SI 1994/2617, r. 23, operative from 1 November 1994.

APPEALS FROM TRIBUNAL

30A A party who wishes to appeal from a decision of the tribunal direct to the Court of Appeal shall apply to the tribunal in accordance with rule 11 for a certificate under Article 2(b) of the Value Added Tax Tribunals Appeals Order 1986 or Article 2(b) of the Value Added Tax Tribunals Appeals (Northern Ireland) Order 1994, as appropriate, at the conclusion of the hearing or within 21 days after the date when the decision of the tribunal was released in accordance with rule 30.

History – In r. 30A the words "or Article 2(b) of . . . 1994, as appropriate," were inserted by SI 1994/2617, r. 24, operative from 1 November 1994.
R. 30A was inserted by SI 1986/2290, operative from 12 January 1987.

SERVICE AT A TRIBUNAL CENTRE

31(1) Service of a notice of appeal, notice of application or other document shall be effected by the same being handed to a proper officer at the appropriate tribunal centre or by the same being received by post at the appropriate tribunal centre or by a facsimile of the same being received at the appropriate tribunal centre by facsimile transmission process.

31(2) Any notice of appeal, notice of application or other document (including a facsimile of a document) handed in or received at a tribunal centre other than the appropriate tribunal centre may be sent by post in a letter addressed to a proper officer at the appropriate tribunal centre, or handed back to the person from whom it was received, or sent by post in a letter addressed to the person from whom it appears to have been received or by whom it appears to have been sent.

History – R. 31(1) amended by SI 1991/186, r. 23(a) from 1 March 1991 which inserted the words "or by a facsimile of the same being received at the appropriate tribunal centre by facsimile transmission process".
R. 31(2) amended by SI 1991/186, r. 23(b) from 1 March 1991 which inserted the words "(including a facsimile of a document)".

SENDING OF DOCUMENTS TO THE PARTIES

32(1) Any document authorised or required to be sent to the Commissioners may be sent to them by post in a letter addressed to them at the address of their office from which the disputed decision appears to have been sent, or handed or sent to them by post or in such manner and at such address as the Commissioners may from time to time request by a general notice served at the appropriate tribunal centre.

32(2) Any document authorised or required to be sent to any party to an appeal or application other than the Commissioners may be sent by post in a letter addressed to him at his address stated in his notice of appeal or application, or sent by post in a letter addressed to any person named in his notice of appeal or application as having been instructed to act for him in connection therewith at the address therein stated, or sent by post in a letter addressed to such person and at such address as he may specify from time to time by notice served at the appropriate tribunal centre; provided that where partners appeal or apply to a tribunal in the name of their firm, any document sent by post in a letter addressed to the firm at the address of the firm stated in the notice of appeal or notice of application or to any person named in the notice of appeal or application as having been instructed to act for the firm at the address therein stated or to such other address as such partners may from time to time specify by notice served at the appropriate tribunal centre, shall be deemed to have been duly sent to all such partners.

32(3) Subject to the foregoing provisions of this rule any document authorised or required to be sent to any party to an appeal or application or other person may be sent by post in a letter addressed to him at his usual or last known address or addressed to him or to such other person at such address as he may from time to time specify by notice served at the appropriate tribunal centre.

32(4) Any reference in this rule to the sending of any document to any party to an appeal or application or to any other person by post shall be construed as including a reference to the transmission of a facsimile of such document by facsimile transmission process.

History – R. 32(4) was inserted by SI 1991/186, r. 24, operative from 1 March 1991.

DELEGATION OF POWERS TO THE REGISTRAR

33(1) All or any of the following powers of a tribunal or a chairman under these rules shall be exercisable by the Registrar, that is to say–

(a) power to give or make any direction by consent of the parties to the appeal or application;

(b) power to give or make any direction on the application of one party which is not opposed by the other party to the application;

(c) power to issue a witness summons;

(d) power to postpone any hearing; and

(e) power to extend the time for the service of any notice of appeal, notice of application or other document at the appropriate tribunal centre for a period not exceeding one month without prior notice or reference to any party or other person and without a hearing.

33(2) The Registrar shall have power to sign a direction recording the outcome of an appeal and any award or direction given or made by the tribunal during or at the conclusion of the hearing of an appeal as provided by rule 30(1) and to sign any document recording any direction given or made by him under this rule.

TABLE OF DESTINATIONS OF VAT TRIBUNALS RULES 1972

This table shows the destination of the provisions of the *VAT Tribunals Rules* 1972 following the consolidation and amendments made by the *VAT Tribunals Rules* 1986 on 1 May 1986.

Rule (1972 Rules)	Rule (1986 Rules)	Notes
1	1	
2	2	
3(1), (2)	3(1), (2)	
(3)	3(4)	
4	4(1), (2)	
5	5	
6(1)	8, 10(1), 11(7)	
(2)	6(1), (4)	
7(1)	20(1), (2)	
(2)	10(3)	
(3)	20(5)	
(4)	20(6)	
8(1)	21(1), (6)	
(2)–(5)	21(2)–(5)	
9(1)	22(1), (3)	
(2)	22(4)	
(3)	22(5)	
(4)	22(6)	
(5)	22(7)	
(6)	22(8)	
10	12	
11	13	
12	14	
13(1)	15	
(2)	–	
14	16(1)	
15	17	

Rule (1972 Rules)	Rule (1986 Rules)	Notes
16(1)	18(1)	
(2)	18(3)	
17(1)	19(3)	
(2)	–	
18	19(1), (2)	
19(1), (2)	11(1)	
(3)	11(2)	
(4)	–	
20(1), (2)	11(4)	
(3)	11(3)	
(4)	11(5)	
21	–	VATA 1983, Sch. 7, para. 4(7), (8) repealed, with effect from 25 July 1985.
22	11(6)	
23(1)–(3)	23(1)–(3)	
(4)	–	
24	24	
25	25	
26	26	
27(1), (2)	27(1)	
(3)	27(3)	
(4)	27(4)	
28	28	
29(1)	30(1), (2)	
(2)	30(3)	
(3)	30(6)	
(4)	30(7)	
30	29	
31(1)	27(5)	
(2)	27(6)	
(3)	9(1)	
(4)	–	
32	31	
33	32	

VALUE ADDED TAX (TREATMENT OF TRANSACTIONS) ORDER 1986

(SI 1986/896)

Made by the Treasury under the Value Added Tax Act 1983, s. 3(3)(c) [VATA 1994, s. 5(3)(c)].
Operative from 1 July 1986.

CITATION AND COMMENCEMENT

1 This Order may be cited as the Value Added Tax (Treatment of Transactions) Order 1986 and shall come into operation on 1st July 1986.

INTERPRETATION

2 In this Order–

"**articles in pawn**" means articles subject to a pledge;

"**pawnee**", "**pawnor**" and "**pledge**" have the same meaning as in section 189 of the Consumer Credit Act 1974.

TREATMENT OF TRANSACTION

3 The following description of a transaction shall be treated as neither a supply of goods nor a supply of services:

the supply by a taxable person of goods the property in which passed to him as a pawnee by virtue of section 120(1)(a) of the Consumer Credit Act 1974–

(a) where the supply is to a person who was pawnor of those goods, and

(b) where the supply is made not later than three months from the date when the taxable person acquired the property in the goods.

VALUE ADDED TAX (SMALL NON-COMMERCIAL CONSIGNMENTS) RELIEF ORDER 1986

(SI 1986/939, as amended by SI 1992/3118, SI 1991/2535, SI 1989/2273, SI 1987/154)

*Made by the Treasury under the Value Added Tax Act 1983, s. 19(1) [VATA 1994, s. 37(1)].
Operative from 1 July 1986.*

Whereas it appears to the Treasury expedient that the relief from value added tax provided by this Order should be allowed with a view to conforming with Article 2(1) of Council Directive No. 74/651/EEC (as last amended by Council Directive No. 85/349/EEC) on the tax reliefs to be allowed on the importation of certain goods when sent in small consignments from a State which is a member of the European Economic Community to another such State and with Article 5(1) of Council Directive No. 78/1035/EEC (as last amended by Council Directive No. 85/576/EEC) on the tax reliefs to be allowed on the importation of certain goods when sent in small consignments from a State which is not a member of the European Economic Community to a State which is a member thereof:

CITATION AND COMMENCEMENT

1 This Order may be cited as the Value Added Tax (Small Non-Commercial Consignments) Relief Order 1986 and shall come into operation on 1st July 1986.

REVOCATION

2 The Value Added Tax (Imported Goods) Relief Order 1980 and the Value Added Tax (Imported Goods) Relief (Amendment) Order 1985 are hereby *revoked*.

RELIEF FROM VALUE ADDED TAX

3(1) Subject to the provisions of this Order, no tax is payable on the importation from a place outside the member States of goods forming part of a small consignment of a non-commercial character.

3(2) In this Order **"small consignment"** means a consignment (not forming part of a larger consignment) containing goods with a value for customs purposes not exceeding £36.

3(3) For the purposes of this Order a consignment is of a non-commercial character only if the following requirements are met, namely–

(a) it is consigned by one private individual to another;

(b) it is not imported for any consideration in money or money's worth;

(c) it is intended solely for the personal use of the consignee or that of his family and not for any commercial purpose.

History – In art. 3(1), the words "from a place outside the member States" inserted by SI 1992/3118, art. 3, operative from 1 January 1993. In art. 3(2), "£36." substituted for the words at the end by SI 1992/3118, art. 4, operative from 1 January 1993. The words formerly at the end were:
    "(a)   £75 in the case of a consignment from a member State;
    (b)   £32 in any other case."
In art. 3(2)(a), "£75" substituted for "£71" by SI 1989/2273, operative from 1 January 1990.
In art. 3(2), "£71" and "£32" substituted for "£58" and "£27" respectively by SI 1987/154, operative from 9 March 1987.

CONDITIONS OF RELIEF

4   No relief shall be given under this order unless the consignment is of an occasional nature.

History – Art. 4 substituted by SI 1992/3118, art. 5, operative from 1 January 1993. Former art. 4 read as follows:
"**4(1)**   In the case of goods consigned from another member State, no relief shall be given under this Order unless the goods were acquired in the Economic Community subject to the taxation normally imposed in the domestic market of a member State and without relief from excise duty or turnover tax chargeable there.
4(2)   In the case of goods consigned from a country which is not a member State, no relief shall be given under this Order unless the consignment is of an occasional nature."

QUANTITATIVE RESTRICTION ON RELIEF FOR CERTAIN GOODS

5   Where a small consignment of a non-commercial character contains goods of any of the following descriptions, namely–

(a)   tobacco products (being cigarettes, cigars or smoking tobacco);

(b)   alcohol and alcoholic beverages (being spirits or wine), tafia and saké; or

(c)   perfumes or toilet waters,

in excess of the quantity shown in relation to goods of that description in the Schedule to this Order, no relief under this Order shall be given in respect of any goods of that description contained in that consignment.

RELIEF NOT APPLICABLE TO TRAVELLERS' BAGGAGE

6   This Order does not apply to goods contained in the baggage of a person entering the United Kingdom or carried with such a person.

SCHEDULE

Article 5

(1)	Tobacco products–	
	cigarettes	50
	or	
	cigarillos (cigars with a maximum weight each of 3 grammes)	25
	or	
	cigars	10
	or	
	smoking tobacco	50 grammes
(2)	Alcohol and alcoholic beverages–	
	distilled beverages and spirits of an alcoholic strength exceeding 22% by volume; undenatured ethyl alcohol of 80% by volume and over	1 litre
	or	
	distilled beverages and spirits, and aperitifs with a wine or alcohol base, tafia, saké or similar beverages of an alcoholic strength of 22% by volume or less; sparkling wines and fortified wines	1 litre
	or	
	still wines	2 litres
(3)	Perfumes	50 grammes
	or	
	toilet waters	250 millilitres

History – In Schedule, para. (3), the quantity "250 millilitres" substituted for ".25 litre or 8 ounces" by SI 1991/2535, operative from 30 November 1991.

INSOLVENCY RULES 1986
(SI 1986/1925)

Made on 10 November 1986 by the Lord Chancellor under the Insolvency Act 1986, s. 411, 412.
Operative from 29 December 1986.

PART 2 – ADMINISTRATION PROCEDURE

Note – VATA 1983, s. 22 is repealed, in relation to any supply made on or after 26 July 1990, by FA 1990, s. 11(9), 132 and Sch. 19, Pt. III. See VATA 1994, Sch. 13, para. 9.

Chapter 6 – VAT Bad Debt Relief

2.56   Issue of certificate of insolvency

2.56(1)   In accordance with this Rule, it is the duty of the administrator to issue a certificate in the terms of paragraph (b) of section 22(3) of the Value Added Tax Act 1983 (which specifies the circumstances in which a company is deemed insolvent for the purposes of that section) forthwith upon his forming the opinion described in that paragraph.

2.56(2)   There shall in the certificate be specified–

(a)   the name of the company and its registered number;

(b)   the name of the administrator and the date of his appointment;

(c)   the date on which the certificate is issued.

2.56(3)   The certificate shall be intituled "CERTIFICATE OF INSOLVENCY FOR THE PURPOSES OF SECTION 22(3)(b) OF THE VALUE ADDED TAX ACT 1983".

2.57   Notice to creditors

2.57(1)   Notice of the issue of the certificate shall be given by the administrator within 3 months of his appointment or within 2 months of issuing the certificate, whichever is the later, to all of the company's unsecured creditors of whose address he is then aware and who have, to his knowledge, made supplies to the company, with a charge to value added tax, at any time before his appointment.

2.57(2)   Thereafter, he shall give the notice to any such creditor of whose address and supplies to the company he becomes aware.

2.57(3)   He is not under obligation to provide any creditor with a copy of the certificate.

2.58   Preservation of certificate with company's records

2.58(1)   The certificate shall be retained with the company's accounting records, and section 222 of the Companies Act (where and for how long records are to be kept) shall apply to the certificate as it applies to those records.

2.58(2)   It is the duty of the administrator, on vacating office, to bring this Rule to the attention of the directors or (as the case may be) any successor of his as administrator.

PART 3 – ADMINISTRATIVE RECEIVERSHIP

Chapter 6 – VAT Bad Debt Relief

Note – VATA 1983, s. 22 is repealed, in relation to any supply made on or after 26 July 1990, by FA 1990, s. 11(9), 132 and Sch. 19, Pt. III. See VATA 1994, Sch. 13, para. 9.

3.36   Issue of certificate of insolvency

3.36(1)   In accordance with this Rule, it is the duty of the administrative receiver to issue a certificate in the terms of paragraph (b) of section 22(3) of the Value Added Tax Act 1983 (which specifies the circumstances in which a company is deemed insolvent for the purposes of that section) forthwith upon his forming the opinion described in that paragraph.

3.36(2)   There shall in the certificate be specified–

(a)   the name of the company and its registered number;

(b)   the name of the administrative receiver and the date of his appointment; and

(c)   the date on which the certificate is issued.

3.36(3) The certificate shall be intituled "CERTIFICATE OF INSOLVENCY FOR THE PURPOSES OF SECTION 22(3)(B) OF THE VALUE ADDED TAX ACT 1983".

VALUE ADDED TAX TRIBUNALS APPEALS ORDER 1986

(SI 1986/2288)

Made on 18 December 1986 by the Lord Chancellor under s. 26 of the Finance Act 1985 [VATA 1994, s. 86]. Operative on 12 January 1987.

1   This Order may be cited as the Value Added Tax Tribunals Appeals Order 1986 and shall come into operation on 12th January 1987.

2   If any party to proceedings before a value added tax tribunal is dissatisfied in point of law with a decision of the tribunal he may, notwithstanding section 13 of the Tribunals and Inquiries Act 1971 [Tribunals and Inquiries Act 1992, s. 11], appeal from the tribunal direct to the Court of Appeal if–

(a)   the parties consent;

(b)   the tribunal endorses its decision with a certificate that the decision involves a point of law relating wholly or mainly to the construction of an enactment, or of a statutory instrument, or of any of the Community Treaties or of any Community Instruments, which has been fully argued before it and fully considered by it; and

(c)   the leave of a single judge of the Court of Appeal has been obtained pursuant to section 54(6) of the Supreme Court Act 1981.

Cross references – VAT Tribunals Rules 1986 (SI 1986/590), r. 30A: appeals direct to Court of Appeal.

VALUE ADDED TAX (TOUR OPERATORS) ORDER 1987

(SI 1987/1806, as amended by SI 1990/751, SI 1992/3125, SI 1995/1495)

Made on 14 October 1987 by the Treasury under s. 3(3), 6(6), 16(4), 37A(1) and (2) and 48(6) of the Value Added Tax Act 1983 [VATA 1994, s. 5(3), 7(11), 30(4), 53(1) and (2) and 96(9)]. Operative on 1 April 1988.

CITATION AND COMMENCEMENT

1   This Order may be cited as the Value Added Tax (Tour Operators) Order 1987 and shall come into force on 1st April 1988.

SUPPLIES TO WHICH THIS ORDER APPLIES

2   This Order shall apply to any supply of goods or services by a tour operator where the supply is for the benefit of travellers.

MEANING OF "DESIGNATED TRAVEL SERVICE"

3(1)   Subject to paragraphs (2), (3) and (4) of this article, a **"designated travel service"** is a supply of goods or services–

(a)   acquired for the purposes of his business; and

(b)   supplied for the benefit of a traveller without material alteration or further processing;

by a tour operator in a member State of the European Community in which he has established his business or has a fixed establishment.

3(2)   The supply of one or more designated travel services, as part of a single transaction, shall be treated as a single supply of services.

3(3) The Commissioners of Customs and Excise may on being given notice by a tour operator that he is a person who to the order of a taxable person–

(a) acquires goods or services from another taxable person; and

(b) supplies those goods or services, without material alteration or further processing, to the taxable person who ordered the supply for use in the United Kingdom by that person for the purpose of that person's business other than by way of re-supply–

treat supplies within sub-paragraph (b) as not being designated travel services.

3(4) The supply of goods and services of such description as the Commissioners of Customs and Excise may specify shall be deemed not to be a designated travel service.

Official publication – 709/5.

TIME OF SUPPLY

4(1) Sections 4 and 5 of the Value Added Tax Act 1983 [VATA 1994, s. 6] shall not apply to any supply comprising in whole or in part a designated travel service.

4(2) Subject to paragraphs (3) and (4) of this article, all supplies comprising in whole or in part a designated travel service shall, at the election of the tour operator making the supplies, be treated as taking place either–

(a) when the traveller commences a journey or occupies any accommodation supplied, whichever is the earlier; or

(b) when any payment is received by the tour operator in respect of that supply which, when aggregated with any earlier such payment, exceeds 20% of the total consideration, to the extent covered by that and any earlier such payment, save insofar as any earlier such payment has already been treated as determining the time of part of that supply.

4(3) Save as the Commissioners of Customs and Excise may otherwise allow, all supplies comprising in whole or in part a designated travel service made by the same tour operator shall, subject to paragraph (4) of this article, be treated as taking place at the time determined under one only of the methods specified in paragraph (2) of this article.

4(4) Where–

(a) a tour operator uses the method specified in paragraph (2)(b) to determine the time of a supply; and

(b) payment is not received in respect of all or part of the supply;

notwithstanding paragraph (3), the time of any part of that supply, which has not already been determined under paragraph (2)(b), shall be determined in accordance with paragraph (2)(a).

PLACE OF SUPPLY

5(1) The application of sections 6 and 8 of the Value Added Tax Act 1983 shall [VATA 1994, s. 7 and 9] be modified in accordance with paragraph (2) below.

5(2) A designated travel service shall be treated as supplied in the member State in which the tour operator has established his business or, if the supply was made from a fixed establishment, in the member State in which the fixed establishment is situated.

History – Art. 5 substituted by SI 1992/3125, art. 2(a), operative from 1 January 1993. Former art. 5 read as follows:
"**5(1)** The application of sections 6 and 8 of the Value Added Tax Act 1983 in relation to a supply of services or of a designated travel service shall be modified in accordance with the provisions of this article.
(2) A designated travel service shall be treated as supplied in the member State of the European Community in which the tour operator has established his business or, if the supply was made from a fixed establishment, in the member State in which the fixed establishment is situated and in no other place.
(3) Any supply by a tour operator, not being a designated travel service, of transport of persons or of services ancillary to such transport, shall be treated as being made in the country in which the services are performed to the extent that they are performed in that country.
(3A) For the purposes of paragraph (3), in determining the extent to which those services are performed in that country, the following shall be treated as performed wholly in that country:
    (a) those services which are performed partly outside the territorial jurisdiction of that country, provided that the means of transport by which the services are performed does not put in at or land in another country;
    (b) those services which are performed between places in that country in the course of a journey from–
        (i) that country to another country, or
        (ii) another country to that country,
notwithstanding that the services performed between those places are performed partly outside the territorial jurisdiction of that country."
Art. 5(3) and (3A) substituted by SI 1990/751, art. 3 from 1 May 1990 for the former art. 5(3) which read as follows:
"**5(3)** Any supply by a tour operator, not being a designated travel service, of transport of persons or their effects shall be treated as being made:
    (a) in the country in which the services are performed to the extent that they are performed in that country; or
    (b) wholly in the country in which the services are performed or partly performed notwithstanding that they may be partly performed outside the territorial jurisdiction of that country, provided that they are not also partly performed in any other country."

"**(4)**   Subject to paragraph (7) any supply by a tour operator, not being a designated travel service, of cultural, artistic, sporting, entertainment, educational, scientific or related services or of the right of attendance at conferences, shall be treated as being made in the place where the services are performed."
Art. 5(4) amended by SI 1990/751, art. 3(b) from 1 May 1990 by the insertion of the words "Subject to paragraph (7)".
"**(5)**   Subject to paragraph (7) any supply by a tour operator, not being a designated travel service, of accommodation, or of facilities for camping in tents and caravans, or for parking vehicles, shall be treated as being made in the place where the accommodation or facilities are provided."
Art. 5(5) amended by SI 1990/751, art. 3(b) from 1 May 1990 by the insertion of the words "Subject to paragraph (7)".
"**(6)**   Any supply by a tour operator by way of hire of any means of transport which apart from this paragraph, would be treated as being made outside the European Community, shall be treated as being made within the United Kingdom where the means of transport is used within the United Kingdom.
(7)   Paragraphs (3) and (3A) shall apply to any supply of goods or services comprised in a pleasure cruise as they apply to the services described therein, as if the reference in those paragraphs to performed were a reference to provided, the reference to services were a reference to goods or services, the reference to the means of transport by which the services are performed were a reference to the cruise ship upon board which the goods or services are provided, and the reference to journey were a reference to cruise.
(8)   In this Order, **"pleasure cruise"** includes a cruise wholly or partly for the purposes of education or training."
Art. 5(7) and (8) inserted by SI 1990/751, art 3(c) from 1 May 1990.

6 [Revoked by SI 1992/3125, operative from 1 January 1993. Article 6 had substituted SI 1984/1685, art. 4 and 5, operative from 1 April 1988.]

VALUE OF A DESIGNATED TRAVEL SERVICE

7   Subject to articles 8 and 9 of this Order, the value of a designated travel service shall be determined by reference to the difference between sums paid or payable to and sums paid or payable by the tour operator in respect of that service, calculated in such manner as the Commissioners of Customs and Excise shall specify.

8(1)   Where–
(a)   a supply of goods or services is acquired for a consideration in money by a tour operator, for the purpose of supplying a designated travel service, and
(b)   the value of the supply is (apart from this article) greater than its open market value, and
(c)   the person making the supply and the tour operator to whom it is made are connected,
the Commissioners of Customs and Excise may direct that the value of the supply shall be deemed to be its open market value for the purpose of calculating the value of the designated travel service.

8(2)   A direction under this article shall be given by notice in writing to the tour operator acquiring the supply, but no direction may be given more than three years after the time of the supply.

8(3)   A direction given to a tour operator under this paragraph, in respect of a supply acquired by him, may include a direction that the value of any supply–
(a)   which is acquired by him after the giving of the notice, or after such later date as may be specified in the notice, and
(b)   as to which the conditions in sub-paragraph (a) to (c) of paragraph (1) above are satisfied,
shall be deemed to be its open market value for the purpose of calculating the value of the designated travel service.

8(4)   For the purposes of this article any question whether a person is **connected** with another shall be determined in accordance with section 533 of the Income and Corporation Taxes Act 1970 [ICTA 1988, s. 839].

9(1)   Where–
(a)   goods and services have been acquired prior to the commencement of this Order; and
(b)   input tax credit has been claimed in respect of those goods and services; and
(c)   the goods and services are supplied as a designated travel service or as part of a designated travel service after the commencement of this Order;
article 7 of this Order shall not apply in determining the value of that part of a designated travel service referable to goods and services on which input tax has been claimed.

9(2)   The value of that part of the designated travel service to which, by virtue of paragraph (1) of this article, article 7 of this Order does not apply shall be calculated in accordance with section 10 of the Value Added Tax Act 1983 [VATA 1994, s. 19].

TAX CHARGEABLE ON CERTAIN DESIGNATED TRAVEL SERVICES

10   [Revoked by SI 1995/1495, art. 2, operative from 1 January 1996.]
History – Former art. 10 reads as follows:
"**10(1)**   The application of the Value Added Tax Act 1983 [VATA 1994] shall, in relation to those supplies made by a tour operator, which are described in the following paragraphs, be modified in accordance with those paragraphs.
10(1A)   Where a tour operator acquires certain services, that is to say transport of passengers–

    (a)   within or outside the United Kingdom–
        (i)   in any vehicle, ship or aircraft designed or adapted to carry not less than twelve passengers, or
        (ii)   on any scheduled flight, or
    (b)   from a place within to a place outside the United Kingdom or vice versa

in order to supply them as a designated travel service or as part of such a service, the rate at which tax shall be charged shall be nil on that portion of the value of the designated travel service supplied which is attributable to those services.

10(2)   Where a tour operator acquires goods or services of a description for the time being specified in Group 6 of Schedule 6 to the Value Added Tax Act 1983 [VATA 1994, Sch. 9, Grp. 6], in order to supply them as a designated travel service, or part of such a service, no tax shall be chargeable on that portion of the value of the designated travel service supplied, which is attributable to the goods and services specified in the Schedule."

Former art. 10(1) and (1A) were substituted by SI 1990/751, art. 4(a), operative from 1 May 1990 for the former art. 10(1), which read as follows:

        "TAX CHARGEABLE ON ZERO-RATED AND EXEMPT DESIGNATED TRAVEL SERVICES

10(1)   Where a tour operator acquires goods or services of a description for the time being specified in Schedule 5 of the Value Added Tax Act 1983, in order to supply them as a designated travel service or part of such a service, the rate at which tax shall be charged shall be nil on that portion of the value of the designated travel service supplied which is attributable to the goods and services specified in the Schedule."

Former art. 10(2) amended by SI 1990/751, art. 4(b), operative from 1 May 1990 by the insertion of the words "Group 6 of".

AMENDMENT OF ZERO-RATING PROVISIONS

11(1)   [Inserted former VATA 1983, Sch. 5, Grp. 10, item 13, operative from 1 April 1988.]

11(2)   [Repealed by VATA 1994, s. 100(2) and Sch. 15, with effect from 1 September 1994. Inserted former VATA 1983, Sch. 5, Grp. 10, Note (7), operative from 1 April 1988.]

DISALLOWANCE OF INPUT TAX

12   Input tax on goods or services acquired by a tour operator for re-supply as a designated travel service shall be excluded from credit under sections 14 and 15 of the Value Added Tax Act 1983 [VATA 1994, s. 24–26].

DISQUALIFICATION FROM MEMBERSHIP OF GROUP OF COMPANIES

13   A tour operator shall not be eligible to be treated as a member of a group for the purposes of section 29 of the Value Added Tax Act 1983 [VATA 1994, s. 43] if any other member of the proposed or existing group–

(a)   has an overseas establishment;

(b)   makes supplies outside the United Kingdom which would be taxable supplies if made within the United Kingdom; and

(c)   supplies goods or services which will become, or are intended to become, a designated travel service.

OPTION NOT TO TREAT SUPPLY AS DESIGNATED TRAVEL SERVICE

14(1)   Where a tour operator supplies a designated travel service he may treat that supply as not being a designated travel service if:

(a)   there are reasonable grounds for believing that the value of all such supplies in the period of one year then beginning will not exceed one per cent of all supplies made by him during that period; and

(b)   he makes no supplies of designated travel services consisting of accommodation or transport.

14(2)   For the purposes of this article the value of any supplies shall be calculated in accordance with section 10 of the Value Added Tax Act 1983 [VATA 1994, s. 19].

EXCISE WAREHOUSING (ETC.) REGULATIONS 1988

(SI 1988/809)

Made on 29 April 1988 by the Commissioners of Customs and Excise under s. 93 of the Customs and Excise Management Act 1979 and s. 2(3A), 15 and 56(1) of the Alcoholic Liquor Duties Act 1979.

ARRANGEMENT OF REGULATIONS

REGULATION

PART I – PRELIMINARY

PART I – PRELIMINARY

CITATION AND COMMENCEMENT

1 These Regulations may be cited as the Excise Warehousing (Etc) Regulations 1988 and shall come into force on 1st June 1988, but the Commissioners may give consent and agree conditions, restrictions or requirements under regulation 5 (variation of provisions at request of occupier or proprietor) before that date.

INTERPRETATION

2 *In these Regulations, unless the context otherwise requires–*

    "duty" means excise duty;

    "occupier" means the occupier of an excise warehouse, and in the case of a distiller's warehouse means the distiller;

    "package" includes any bundle, case, carton, cask, or other container whatsoever;

"**proprietor**" means the proprietor of goods in an excise warehouse or of goods which have been in, or are to be deposited in, or are treated as being in, an excise warehouse, and "**proprietorship**" shall be construed accordingly;

"**warehoused**" means warehoused or rewarehoused in an excise warehouse, and

"**warehousing**" and "**rewarehousing**" shall be construed accordingly.

APPLICATION

3(1) Except as provided by or under the Hydrocarbon Oil Duties Act 1979, Parts I to IV of these Regulations apply to all goods chargeable with a duty of excise.

3(2) Part V of these Regulations applies for all purposes of the Alcoholic Liquor Duties Act 1979.

DESIGNATED FILE

4(1) For the purposes of these Regulations delivery to the proper officer of anything in writing–

(a) shall be effected by placing it in the relevant designated file; and

(b) the time of such delivery shall be when it is placed in that designated file,

but the proper officer may direct that delivery shall be effected in another manner.

4(2) Nothing in a designated file shall be removed without the permission of the proper officer.

4(3) Nothing in a designated file shall be altered in any way, and an amendment to anything in it shall be made by depositing a notice of amendment in the designated file.

4(4) The designated file shall be kept at such place as the Commissioners direct and, if kept at the excise warehouse, shall be provided by the occupier.

4(5) The designated file shall be a receptacle approved by the Commissioners for the secure keeping of written material, and different files may be approved for different purposes.

4(6) For the purposes of these Regulations delivery to the proper officer of anything not in writing shall be effected in such manner, and be subject to such conditions, as the Commissioners direct.

VARIATION OF PROVISIONS AT REQUEST OF OCCUPIER OR PROPRIETOR

5(1) The Commissioners may, if they see fit, consent in writing to an application by an occupier or proprietor for variation of any condition, restriction or requirement contained in or arising under regulations 11 to 24 below, and may make that consent subject to compliance with such other condition, restriction or requirement (as the case may be) as may be agreed by them and the applicant in writing.

5(2) Where under paragraph (1) above any condition or restriction is varied or another is substituted for it, then, if the varied or substituted condition or restriction is one–

(a) subject to which goods may be deposited in, secured in, kept in or removed from an excise warehouse or made available there to their owner for any prescribed purpose; or

(b) subject to which an operation may be carried out on goods in an excise warehouse,

breach of the varied or substituted condition or restriction shall give rise to forfeiture of those goods, provided that breach of the original condition or restriction would have given rise to forfeiture.

LIMITATION OF PENALTIES

6 If any person contravenes or fails to comply with any of these Regulations or with any condition imposed under these Regulations and in consequence is liable to a penalty under section 15(7) of the Alcoholic Liquor Duties Act 1979 (breach of regulations relating to a distiller's warehouse), and by reason of that contravention or failure is also liable to a penalty under section 93(6) of the Customs and Excise Management Act 1979 (breach of warehousing regulations) the amount of the penalty imposed under the said section 15(7) shall not exceed the penalty specified by the said section 93(6).

MANNER OF COMMISSIONERS' DIRECTIONS ETC.

7(1) Where, by or under these Regulations, it is provided that the Commissioners may–

(a) make a direction or requirement;

(b) give their permission or consent;

(c) grant approval; or

(d) impose a condition or restriction,

then they may do so only in writing; and they may make a direction or requirement or impose a condition or restriction by means of a public notice.

7(2) Any request for the proper officer to give his permission or grant approval under these Regulations shall, if he or the Commissioners direct, be made in writing.

7(3) Any right granted to the Commissioners or the proper officer by these Regulations to–

(a) make a direction or requirement;

(b) give permission or consent;

(c) grant approval; or

(d) impose a condition or restriction,

shall include a right to revoke, vary or replace any such direction, requirement, permission, consent, approval, condition or restriction.

FORM OF ENTRIES ETC.

8(1) Except as the Commissioners otherwise allow, and subject to paragraph (2) below, any entry, account, notice, specification, record or return required by or under these Regulations shall be in writing.

8(2) This regulation does not apply to the records referred to in regulation 22(3) and (4) below (records kept for the purposes of any relevant business or activity).

REVOCATION

9 The Excise Warehousing (Etc.) Regulations 1982 and the Excise Warehousing (Etc) (Amendment) Regulations 1986 are hereby revoked.

PART II – PROCEDURES FOR EXCISE WAREHOUSES AND WAREHOUSED GOODS

TIME OF WAREHOUSING

10 Goods brought to an excise warehouse for warehousing shall be deemed to be warehoused when they are put in the excise warehouse.

RECEIPT OF GOODS INTO WAREHOUSE

11(1) Subject to paragraph (6) below, when goods are warehoused the occupier shall immediately deliver to the proper officer an entry of the goods in such form and containing such particulars as the Commissioners direct.

11(2) When goods are warehoused the occupier shall take account of the goods and deliver a copy of that account to the proper officer by the start of business on the next day after warehousing that the warehouse is open.

11(3) The occupier shall, if there is any indication that the goods may have been subject to loss or tampering in the course of removal to the excise warehouse, immediately inform the proper officer and retain the goods intact for his examination.

11(4) Except as the proper officer may otherwise allow, the occupier shall, within 5 days of goods being warehoused, send a certificate of receipt for the goods to the person from whom they were received identifying the goods and stating the quantity which has been warehoused.

11(4A) Where goods are warehoused in circumstances where duty may be drawn back the certificate of receipt mentioned in paragraph (4) above shall–

(a) be in such form and contain such particulars as the Commissioners may require, and

(b) be endorsed on one of the copies of the warehousing advice note that accompanied the goods,

and in this paragraph **"warehousing advice note"** means a document (in such form and containing such particulars as the Commissioners may require) drawn up by the person to whom the certificate of receipt will be sent.

11(5) Except as the proper officer otherwise allows the occupier shall give only one receipt required by paragraph (4) above for each lot or parcel of goods warehoused.

11(6) In the case of spirits warehoused at the distillery where they were produced satisfaction of the requirements of regulation 21 of the Spirits Regulations 1982 shall be deemed to be compliance with the requirements of entry and account in paragraphs (1) and (2) above.

11(7) Should the occupier fail to comply with any condition or restriction imposed by or under paragraphs (1), (2), (3) or (6) above any goods in respect of which the failure occurred shall be liable to forfeiture.

History – Reg. 11(4A) was inserted by SI 1995/1046, Pt. V, reg. 15(b), operative from 1 June 1995.

SECURING, MARKING AND TAKING STOCK OF WAREHOUSED GOODS

12(1) The occupier shall take all necessary steps to ensure that no access is had to warehoused goods other than as allowed by or under these Regulations.

12(2) Goods shall be warehoused in the packages and lots in which they were first entered for warehousing.

12(3) The occupier shall–

(a) legibly and uniquely mark and keep marked warehoused goods so that at any time they can be identified in the stock records; and

(b) stow warehoused goods so that safe and easy access may be had to each package or lot.

12(4) The occupier shall, when required by the proper officer to do so, promptly produce to him any warehoused goods which have not lawfully been removed from the warehouse.

12(5) The occupier shall take stock of all goods in the warehouse–

(a) monthly in the case of bulk goods in vats or in storage tanks; and

(b) annually in the case of all other goods,

and shall take stock at such other times and to such extent as the Commissioners may for reasonable cause require.

12(6) In accordance with the Commissioners' directions the occupier shall–

(a) balance his stock accounts and reconcile the quantities of those balances with his Excise Warehouse Returns; and

(b) balance his stock accounts so that they can be compared with the result of any stock-taking.

12(7) The occupier shall notify the proper officer immediately in writing of any deficiency, surplus or other discrepancy concerning stocks or records of stocks whenever or however discovered.

12(8) Any goods–

(a) found not to be marked in accordance with paragraph (3) above; or

(b) found to be in excess of the relevant stock account and not immediately notified to the proper officer,

shall be liable to forfeiture.

PROPRIETOR'S EXAMINATION OF GOODS

13 The proprietor of warehoused goods may, provided that the occupier has first given his consent and has given at least 6 hours' notice to the proper officer–

(a) examine the goods and their packaging;

(b) take any steps necessary to prevent any loss therefrom; or

(c) display them for sale.

OPERATIONS

14(1) Except as provided by or under this regulation or by or under sections 57 and 58 of the Alcoholic Liquor Duties Act 1979 (mixing of spirits with made-wine or wine), no operation shall be carried out on warehoused goods.

14(2) The Commissioners may allow the operations described in Schedule 1 to these Regulations to be carried out on warehoused goods, and may allow other operations if they are satisfied that the control of the goods and the security and collection of the revenue will not be prejudiced.

14(3) Save as the proper officer may allow in cases of emergency for the preservation of the goods, no operation shall be commenced unless the occupier has delivered to the proper officer a notice of the proposed operation with a specification of the goods involved, and 24 hours have elapsed following the delivery of that notice.

14(4) Before commencing any operation on goods the occupier shall ensure that an account is taken of those goods and that immediately after completion of the operation an account is taken of the out-turn quantities.

14(5) The occupier shall deliver to the proper officer a notice containing such detail of the accounts required by paragraph (4) above as the proper officer requires.

14(6) The occupier shall ensure that–

(a) any operation is carried out in part of the warehouse approved by the Commissioners for that purpose, or in such other part as the proper officer allows; and

(b) such other requirements as the proper officer may impose in any particular circumstances are observed.

14(7) Any goods in respect of which this regulation is not observed shall be liable to forfeiture.

14(8) Nothing in paragraph (2) above shall permit the mixing of spirits with wine or made-wine while that operation is excluded from the provisions of section 93(2)(c) of the Customs and Excise Management Act 1979.

REMOVAL FROM WAREHOUSE – OCCUPIER'S RESPONSIBILITIES

15 The occupier shall ensure that–

(a) notice of intention to remove the goods is given to the proper officer in accordance with any directions made by the Commissioners;

(b) an entry of the goods is delivered to the proper officer in such form and containing such particulars as the Commissioners may direct;

(c) no goods are removed until any duty chargeable has been paid, secured, or otherwise accounted for;

(d) no goods are removed contrary to any condition or restriction imposed by the proper officer;

(e) an account of the goods is taken in such manner and to such extent as the proper officer requires and a copy of the account is delivered to the proper officer; and

(f) when goods are removed other than for home use, a certificate of receipt is obtained showing that all the goods arrived at the place to which they were entered on removal and, if no such receipt is obtained within 21 days of the removal, notice of that fact is given to the proper officer for the excise warehouse from which the goods were removed.

REMOVAL FROM WAREHOUSE – ENTRY

16(1) Goods may be entered for removal from warehouse for–

(a) home use, if so eligible;

(b) exportation;

(c) shipment as stores; or

(d) removal to the Isle of Man;

provided that where goods are warehoused in circumstances where duty may be drawn back they may not, under this paragraph, be entered for removal from warehouse for any purpose that may result in their being consumed in the United Kingdom or the Isle of Man.

16(2) The Commissioners may allow goods to be entered for removal from warehouse for–

(a) rewarehousing in another excise warehouse;

(b) temporary removal for such purposes and such periods as they may allow;

(c) scientific research and testing;

(d) removal to premises where goods of the same class or description may, by or under the customs and excise Acts, be kept without payment of excise duty;

(e) denaturing or destruction; or

(f) such other purpose as they permit,

and may by direction impose conditions and restrictions on the entry of goods or classes of goods for any of the above purposes.

16(3) Save as the Commissioners direct no goods may be removed from warehouse unless they have been entered in accordance with this regulation.

16(4) Goods entered for home use may be removed from warehouse only if–

(a) the duty has been paid to the Commissioners;

(b)   the removal is in accordance with provisions of, or under, the customs and excise Acts, allowing payment of the duty to be deferred; or

(c)   the removal is permitted under an arrangement approved by the Commissioners for the payment of duty on the day the goods are removed.

16(5) Goods entered for a purpose other than home use may be removed from warehouse without payment of duty only if security for that duty is given (by bond or otherwise) to the satisfaction of the Commissioners and the security is such as to remain in force until the accomplishment of the purpose for which entry is made.

History – In reg. 16(1), the words "provided that, where" to the end were inserted by SI 1995/1046, Pt. V, reg. 15(c), operative from 1 June 1995.

Cross references – VAT Regulations 1995 (SI 1995/2518), reg. 119: regulations excepted from legislation applied as mentioned in VATA 1994, s. 16(1).

REMOVAL FROM WAREHOUSE – GENERAL

17(1) Any goods removed from an excise warehouse without payment of duty as samples or for scientific research and testing and which are no longer required for the purpose for which they were removed shall be–

(a)   destroyed to the satisfaction of the proper officer;

(b)   rewarehoused in an excise warehouse; or

(c)   diverted to home use on payment of the duty chargeable thereon.

17(2) The proper officer may require any goods entered for removal from an excise warehouse for any purpose, other than home use, to be secured or identified by the use of a seal, lock or mark, and any such requirement may continue after the goods have been removed.

17(3) In such cases as the Commissioners may direct the proper officer may impose conditions and restrictions on the removal of goods from an excise warehouse in addition to those imposed elsewhere in these Regulations.

17(4) Any goods in respect of which any of the provisions of these Regulations relating to removal of goods from an excise warehouse (other than regulation 15(f)) is contravened shall be liable to forfeiture.

17(5) The Commissioners may direct that any provision of these Regulations relating to removal of goods from an excise warehouse shall not apply in the case of hydrocarbon oils.

ENTRY OF GOODS NOT IN WAREHOUSE

18 Except in such cases as the Commissioners direct, goods which are to be warehoused and goods which have been lawfully removed from an excise warehouse without payment of duty may, with the permission of the proper officer, be entered or further entered by their proprietor for any of the purposes referred to in paragraphs (1) and (2) of regulation 16 above as if they were to be removed from the excise warehouse:

Provided that where any such goods are packaged and part only is to be further entered, that part shall consist of one or more complete packages.

SAMPLES

19(1) The Commissioners may make directions–

(a)   allowing the proprietor of warehoused goods to draw samples thereof for such purposes and subject to such conditions as they specify; and

(b)   allowing the removal of samples from an excise warehouse with or without payment of duty,

and no sample shall be drawn or removed except as allowed by, and in accordance with directions *and conditions under, this* regulation.

19(2) Any samples drawn or removed in breach of this regulation shall be liable to forfeiture.

Cross references – VAT Regulations 1995 (SI 1995/2518), reg. 119: regulations excepted from legislation applied as mentioned in VATA 1994, s. 16(1).

PART III – RETURNS AND RECORDS

RETURNS

20(1) The occupier shall complete and sign an Excise Warehouse Return and shall deliver such return to the proper officer within 14 days of the end of the stock period to which it relates.

20(2)   A return shall be in such form and contain such particulars of goods received into, stored in and delivered from an excise warehouse as the Commissioners direct, and different provisions may be made for goods of different classes or descriptions.

20(3)   The Commissioners may direct that separate returns be made in respect of goods of different classes or descriptions.

20(4)   The occupier shall support each return with such schedules and further information relating to the goods as the Commissioners may require.

20(5)   "Stock period" means one calendar month or such other period, not exceeding 5 weeks, as the proper officer, at the request of the occupier, allows.

RECORDS TO BE KEPT

21(1)   The occupier shall, in relation to goods in an excise warehouse, keep the records prescribed by Schedule 2 to these Regulations.

21(2)   The proprietor of goods in an excise warehouse, or of goods which have been removed from an excise warehouse without payment of duty, or which are to be warehoused, may be required by the proper officer to keep the records prescribed by Schedule 3 to these Regulations in so far as they relate to his proprietorship of the goods.

21(3)   In addition to the other records required by this regulation the occupier shall, in relation to his occupation of the warehouse, keep such records of the receipt and use of goods received into the excise warehouse other than for warehousing therein as the proper officer requires.

21(4)   Records required by or under this regulation shall—

(a)   be entered up promptly;

(b)   identify the goods to which they relate;

(c)   in the case of an occupier be kept at the warehouse;

(d)   in the case of a proprietor be kept at his principal place of business in the United Kingdom, or at such other place as the proper officer allows; and

(e)   be kept in such form and manner and contain such information as the Commissioners direct.

PRESERVATION OF RECORDS

22(1)   The occupier shall preserve, for not less than 3 years from the lawful removal of the goods or such shorter period as the Commissioners direct, all records which he is required to keep by virtue of regulation 21(1) above, but no record shall be destroyed until the relevant stock accounts have been balanced and any discrepancy reconciled.

22(2)   The proprietor shall preserve, for not less than 3 years from when he ceased to be the proprietor of the goods, or for such shorter period as the Commissioners direct, all records which he is required to keep by virtue of regulation 21(2) above.

22(3)   Each occupier and proprietor shall preserve all records (other than those referred to in paragraphs (1) and (2) above) kept by him for the purposes of any relevant business or activity for not less than 3 years from the events recorded in them, except that such records need not be preserved if they are records which (or records of a class which) the Commissioners have directed as not needing preservation.

22(4)   The requirements to preserve records imposed by paragraph (3) above may be discharged by the preservation in a form approved by the Commissioners of the information contained in those records.

PRODUCTION OF RECORDS

23(1)   The occupier or the proprietor shall, when required by the Commissioners, produce or cause to be produced to the proper officer any records, copy records or information which he was required by these Regulations to preserve.

23(2)   Production under paragraph (1) above shall—

(a)   take place at such reasonable time as the proper officer requires; and

(b)   take place at the excise warehouse or at such other place as the proper officer may reasonably require.

23(3)   The proper officer may inspect, copy or take extracts from and may remove at a reasonable time and for a reasonable period any record produced or required to be produced to him under this regulation, and the occupier and proprietor shall permit such inspection, copying, extraction and removal.

23(4) Where the records required to be produced by this regulation are preserved in a form which is not readily legible, or which is legible only with the aid of equipment, the occupier or proprietor shall, if the proper officer so requires, produce a transcript or other permanently legible reproduction of the records and shall permit the proper officer to retain that reproduction.

INFORMATION FOR THE PROTECTION OF THE REVENUE

24(1) The occupier or the proprietor shall furnish the Commissioners with any information relating to any relevant business or activity of his which they specify as information which they think it is necessary or expedient for them to be given for the protection of the revenue.

24(2) Such information shall be furnished to the Commissioners within such time, and at such place and in such form as they may reasonably require.

FURTHER PROVISION AS TO RECORDS

25 For the purposes of regulations 21 to 24 above, in relation to a proprietor–

(a) goods which are to be warehoused shall be treated as if they were warehoused in the warehouse to which they are being removed; and

(b) goods which have been removed from warehouse without payment of duty shall be treated as if they were warehoused in the warehouse from which they have been removed.

PART IV – DUTY CHARGEABLE ON WAREHOUSED GOODS

DUTY CHARGEABLE ON GOODS REMOVED FOR HOME USE

26 The duty and the rate thereof chargeable on any warehoused goods removed from an excise warehouse for home use shall be those in force for goods of that class or description at the time of their removal.

DUTY CHARGEABLE ON GOODS DIVERTED TO HOME USE AFTER REMOVAL WITHOUT PAYMENT OF DUTY

27(1) The duty and the rate thereof chargeable on any goods removed from an excise warehouse without payment of duty and in respect of which duty is payable under regulation 17(1)(c) above shall be those in force for goods of that class or description at the time of payment of the duty.

27(2) The duty and the rate thereof chargeable on any goods which have been entered for home use under regulation 18 above shall be those in force for goods of that class or description–

(a) where removal for home use is allowed under section 119 of the Customs and Excise Management Act 1979 on the giving of security for the duty chargeable thereon, at the time of giving of the security, or

(b) in any other case, at the time of payment.

DUTY CHARGEABLE ON MISSING OR DEFICIENT GOODS

28 The duty and the rate thereof chargeable on any goods found to be missing or deficient and upon which duty is payable under section 94 of the Customs and Excise Management Act 1979, shall be those in force for goods of that class or description at the time the loss or deficiency occurred:

Provided that where that time cannot be ascertained to the proper officer's satisfaction, the rate of duty chargeable on such goods shall be the highest rate applicable thereto from the time of their deposit in the excise warehouse, or, where appropriate, from the time that the last account of them was taken, until the loss or deficiency came to the notice of the proper officer.

CALCULATION OF DUTY

29(1) Where duty is charged on any such goods as are referred to in regulation 26 above, the quantity of those goods shall be ascertained by reference to any account taken in accordance with these Regulations at the time of their removal from the excise warehouse or, if no account is taken, the quantity declared to and accepted by the proper officer as the quantity of goods being removed or, if greater, the actual quantity of goods being removed.

29(2)   Where duty is charged on any such goods as are referred to in regulations 27 or 28 above the quantity of such goods shall be ascertained by reference to the last account taken in accordance with these Regulations, or, if no account has been taken, the quantity declared to and accepted by the proper officer as the quantity of goods on which duty is to be charged, or, if greater, the actual quantity of goods.

ASCERTAINMENT OF QUANTITY BY TAKING AN ACCOUNT

30(1)   Where the quantity of warehoused goods is to be ascertained by taking an account thereof, it shall be ascertained for the purposes of these Regulations by reference to weight, measure, strength, original gravity or number as the case may require.

30(2)   Where under these Regulations an occupier is required to deliver a copy of an account of goods he shall deliver to the proper officer a notice giving such details of the account as the proper officer requires, and the taking of the account shall not be complete until that notice has been delivered.

PART V – ASCERTAINMENT OF DUTY BY REFERENCE TO LABELS ETC.

ASCERTAINMENT OF DUTY BY REFERENCE TO LABELS ETC.

31(1)   Subject to paragraph (2) of this regulation, for the purpose of charging duty on any spirits, wine or made-wine contained in any bottle or other container the strength, weight and volume of the spirits, wine or made-wine shall be ascertained conclusively by reference to any information given on the bottle or other container by means of a label, or otherwise, or by reference to any documents relating to the bottle or other container, notwithstanding any other legal provision.

31(2)   The method of ascertaining the strength, weight or volume, or any of them, referred to in paragraph (1) above shall not be used if another method would produce a result upon which a greater amount of duty would be charged than would be the case if the method in paragraph (1) above were used.

SCHEDULE 1 – OPERATIONS WHICH MAY BE PERMITTED ON WAREHOUSED GOODS

(Regulation 14(2))

1   Sorting, separating, packing or repacking and such other operations as are necessary for the preservation, sale, shipment or disposal of the goods.

2   The rectifying and compounding of spirits.

3   The rendering sparkling of wine and made-wine.

4   The mixing of a fermented liquor or a liquor derived from a fermented liquor with any other liquor or substance so as to produce made-wine.

5   The mixing of lime or lemon juice with spirits for shipment as stores or for exportation.

6   Denaturing.

7   Reducing.

8   Marrying.

9   Blending.

SCHEDULE 2 – RECORDS TO BE KEPT BY THE OCCUPIER

(Regulation 21(1))

Records of:

(a)   goods deposited in the excise warehouse, from where and from whom received, and date of warehousing;

(b)   goods removed from the excise warehouse, the purpose of the removal, date of removal and (if the purpose of the removal is other than for home use) the place to which the goods are removed;

(c)   stock of warehoused goods;

(d)   deficiencies and increases in stock;

(e)   operations performed;

(f)   deficiencies and increases in operation;

(g)   accounts taken of goods deposited in the excise warehouse, removed from the excise warehouse, put into operation, received from operation, and of stocks in the excise warehouse;

(h)   samples drawn from warehoused goods, samples removed from warehouse, and the person to whom samples are delivered;

(i)   the manner in which duty is paid or accounted for when goods chargeable with duty are removed for home use;

(j)   the manner in which security is given when goods chargeable with duty are removed for purposes other than home use, and the dates when certificates of receipt or shipment are received;

(k)   notices delivered to the proper officer and of the manner and time of delivery;

(l)   times when the excise warehouse is opened and closed;

(m)   names and titles of keyholders to the excise warehouse;

(n)   the name and address of the proprietor of each lot or parcel of goods, and of changes of proprietorship.

SCHEDULE 3 – RECORDS WHICH THE PROPRIETOR MAY BE REQUIRED TO KEEP

(Regulation 21(2))

Records of:

(a)   goods which are to be warehoused in an excise warehouse;

(b)   goods which have been warehoused in an excise warehouse;

(c)   goods which have been removed from an excise warehouse otherwise than for home use on payment of the duty chargeable, and all movements of such goods;

(d)   his stock of goods in each excise warehouse;

(e)   operations performed;

(f)   samples drawn, removed from warehouse and, where that removal is other than on payment of the duty chargeable, their use, location and disposal;

(g)   the time and manner in which the duty chargeable on goods to which regulation 21(2) relates is paid, secured or accounted for.

VALUE ADDED TAX (SELF-SUPPLY OF CONSTRUCTION SERVICES) ORDER 1989

(SI 1989/472)

Made on 14 March 1989 by the Treasury under s. 3(6) and (8) and 29(2) of the Value Added Tax Act 1983 [VATA 1994, s. 5(6) and (8) and 43(2)]. Operative 1 April 1989.

1   This Order may be cited as the Value Added Tax (Self-supply of Construction Services) Order 1989 and shall come into force on 1st April 1989.

2   In this Order **"the Act"** means the Value Added Tax Act 1983 [VATA 1994].

3(1)   Where a person, in the course or furtherance of a business carried on by him, for the purpose of that business and otherwise than for a consideration, performs any of the following services, that is to say–

(a)   the construction of a building; or

(b)   the extension or other alteration of, or the construction of an annexe to, any building such that additional floor area of not less than 10 per cent of the floor area of the original building is created; or

(c)   the construction of any civil engineering work; or

(d)   in connection with any such services as are described in sub-paragraph (a), (b) or (c) above, the carrying out of any demolition work contemporaneously with or preparatory thereto,

then, subject to each of the conditions specified in paragraph (2) below being satisfied, those services shall be treated for the purposes of the Act as both supplied to him for the purpose of that business and supplied by him in the course or furtherance of it.

3(2)   The conditions mentioned in paragraph (1) above are that–

(a)   the value of such services is not less than £100,000; and

(b)   such services would, if supplied for a consideration in the course or furtherance of a business carried on by a taxable person, be chargeable to tax at a rate other than nil.

3(3)   The preceding provisions of this article shall apply in relation to any bodies corporate which are treated for the purposes of section 29 of the Act [VATA 1994, s. 43] as members of a group as if those bodies were one person, but anything done which would fall to be treated by virtue of this Order as services supplied to and by that person shall be treated as supplied to and by the representative member.

4(1)   The value of any supply of services which is to be treated as taking place by virtue of this Order is the open market value of such services.

4(2)   Where any services of a description specified in article 3(1) above are in the process of being performed on the day this Order comes into force, the value of such services for the purposes of this Order shall be the value of such part of those services as are performed on or after that day.

VALUE ADDED TAX (WATER) ORDER 1989

(SI 1989/1114)

Made on 3 July 1989 by the Treasury under s. 3(3) of the Value Added Tax Act 1983 [VATA 1994, s. 5(3)]. Operative on 1 August 1989.

1   This Order may be cited as the Value Added Tax (Water) Order 1989 and shall come into force on 1st August 1989.

2   The supply of water insofar as it is not otherwise a supply of goods shall be treated as a supply of goods and not as a supply of services.

VALUE ADDED TAX (REFUND OF TAX) ORDER 1989

(SI 1989/1217)

Made on 14 July 1989 by the Treasury, in exercise of the powers conferred on them by s. 20(3) of the Value Added Tax Act 1983 [VATA 1994, s. 33(3)].

1   This Order may be cited as the Value Added Tax (Refund of Tax) Order 1989 and shall come into force on 1st August 1989.

2   The National Rivers Authority (a body corporate established by section 1 of the Water Act 1989) is hereby specified for the purposes of section 20 of the Value Added Tax Act 1983 [VATA 1994, s. 33].

EUROPEAN COMMUNITIES (PRIVILEGES OF THE EUROPEAN SCHOOL) ORDER 1990

(SI 1990/237)

Made on 14 February 1990; coming into force on 15 February 1990.

Whereas Her Majesty in pursuance of the Regency Acts 1937 to 1953 was pleased, by Letters Patent dated the 18th day of January 1990, to delegate to the six Counsellors of State therein named or any two or more of them full power and authority during the period of Her Majesty's absence from the United Kingdom to summon and hold on Her Majesty's behalf Her Privy Council and to signify thereat Her Majesty's approval for anything for which Her Majesty's approval in Council is required;

And whereas a draft of this Order has been laid before Parliament and has been approved by a resolution of each House of Parliament;

Now, therefore, Her Majesty Queen Elizabeth The Queen Mother and His Royal Highness The Prince Charles, Prince of Wales, being authorised thereto by the said Letters Patent, and in pursuance of the powers conferred by section 2(2) of the European Communities Act 1972, and by and with the advice of Her Majesty's Privy Council, do on Her Majesty's behalf order, and it is hereby ordered, as follows:

PART I – GENERAL

1 This Order may be cited as the European Communities (Privileges of the European School) Order 1990 and shall come into force on the day after the day on which it is made.

2(1) For the purposes of this Order, **"the School"** means the European School established at Culham; **"staff members"** means the headmaster, deputy heads, secondary school teachers, primary school teachers, kindergarten teachers and educational advisers appointed, assigned or seconded to the School in accordance with Article 12(2) and (3) of the Statute of the European School.

2(2) In this Order **"the 1961 Convention Articles"** means the Articles (being certain Articles of the Vienna Convention on Diplomatic Relations signed in 1961) which are set out in Schedule 1 to the Diplomatic Privileges Act 1964.

PART II – THE SCHOOL

3 The School shall have the legal capacities of a body corporate.

4 Within the scope of its official activities, the School shall have exemption from taxes on income and capital gains.

5 The School shall have relief, under arrangements made by the Secretary of State, by way of refund of value added tax paid on the supply of goods or services of substantial value which are necessary for the official activities of the School, such relief to be subject to compliance with such conditions as may be imposed in accordance with the arrangements; provided that no refund shall be made in respect of any claim for goods or services where the value of the goods or services does not amount in the aggregate to £100.

6 The School shall have exemption from duties (whether of customs or excise) and taxes on the importation of goods imported by or on behalf of the School and necessary for the exercise of its official activities, such exemption to be subject to compliance with such conditions as the Commissioners of Customs and Excise may prescribe for the protection of the Revenue.

PART III – STAFF MEMBERS

7 Staff members shall enjoy:

(a)   provided that they are seconded to the School by a member State other than the United Kingdom and are subject to its social security legislation, exemptions whereby for the purposes of the enactments relating to social security including enactments in force in *Northern Ireland*–

    (i)   services rendered for the School by them shall be deemed to be excepted from any class of employment in respect of which contributions or premiums under those enactments are payable, but

    (ii) no person shall be rendered liable to pay any contribution or premium which he would not be required to pay if those services were not deemed to be so excepted;

(b)   unless they are British citizens, British Dependent Territories citizens or British Overseas citizens or are permanently resident in the United Kingdom, the like exemption from duties and taxes on the importation of furniture and personal effects (including one motor car each) which–

(i) at the time when they first enter the United Kingdom to take up their post, are imported for personal use or for that of their families forming part of their households, and

(ii) were in their ownership or possession or which they were under contract to purchase immediately before they so entered the United Kingdom,

as in accordance with paragraph 1 of Article 36 of the 1961 Convention Articles is accorded to a diplomatic agent; and

(c)

(i) in the case of staff members who are seconded to the School by a member State other than the United Kingdom, exemption from income tax in respect of salaries and emoluments paid to them by the School as well as those paid to them by the member State which seconded them;

(ii) in the case of staff members who are seconded to the School by the United Kingdom, exemption from income tax in respect of salaries and emoluments paid to them by the School.

Other material – Department of Education and Science press release 86/90, 14 March 1990: applies certain tax exemptions for years prior to entry into force of this Order by extra-statutory concession.

CHANNEL TUNNEL (CUSTOMS AND EXCISE) ORDER 1990

(SI 1990/2167)

Made on 1 November 1990 by the Commissioners of Customs and Excise in exercise of the powers conferred upon them by s. 11(1)(a), (c), (d), (g) and (h), 11(2), 11(3)(a) and (d), and 13(1) and (2) of the Channel Tunnel Act 1987 and of all other powers enabling them in that behalf.

CITATION AND COMMENCEMENT

1   This Order may be cited as the Channel Tunnel (Customs and Excise) Order 1990 and shall come into force on 1st December 1990.

INTERPRETATION

2(1)   In this Order–

"**the Act of 1979**" means the Customs and Excise Management Act 1979;

"**the Act of 1987**" means the Channel Tunnel Act 1987;

"**customs approved area**" has the meaning given by article 3(1) below;

"**the tunnel**" except in the expression "**tunnel system**" means that part of the tunnel system comprising the tunnels specified in section 1(7)(a) of the Act 1987 or any of those tunnels.

2(2)   In this Order the following expressions have the meanings assigned to them by section 1 of the Act of 1979;

"**approved wharf**"

"**the boundary**"

"**commander**"

"**the Commissioners**"

"**the customs and excise Acts**"

"**customs and excise airport**"

"**goods**"

"**officer**"

"**owner**"

"**port**"

"**proper**"

"**ship**"

"**shipped**" and cognate expressions.

2(3)   [Neither relevant nor reproduced.]

2(4)   [Neither relevant nor reproduced.]

2(5)   [Neither relevant nor reproduced.]

History – In art. 2(2), the word "proper" was inserted by SI 1993/1813, art. 8, Sch. 5, para. 7 and 8(a), operative from 1 August 1993.

CHANNEL TUNNEL CUSTOMS APPROVED AREAS

3   [Neither relevant nor reproduced.]

MODIFICATION OF THE ACT OF 1979

4   The Act of 1979 shall be modified in accordance with the provisions of the Schedule to this Order.

TIME OF IMPORTATION, EXPORTATION ETC.

5   [Neither relevant nor reproduced.]

MODIFICATIONS OF THE ACT OF 1979

Article 4

PART II OF THE ACT OF 1979: ADMINISTRATION

A1   In section 17(1) (disposal of duties, etc) the references to Great Britain shall be construed as including a reference to a control zone in France.

Prospective insertion – In para. A1, the words "or Belgium" are to be inserted at the end by SI 1994/1405, art. 8 and Sch. 4, para. 7, with effect from a day to be appointed.

History – Para. A1 was inserted by SI 1993/1813, art. 8 and Sch. 5, Pt. II, para. 11, operative from 2 August 1993.

PART III OF THE ACT OF 1979: CUSTOMS AND EXCISE CONTROL AREAS

A2(1)   For the purposes of section 21 (control of movement of aircraft, etc, into and out of the United Kingdom) references to an aircraft shall be treated as including references to a through train, and in relation to such trains section 21 shall be construed in accordance with sub-paragraphs (2) to (5).

A2(2)   References to a customs and excise airport shall be construed as references to a terminal control point or a place which is a customs approved area.

A2(3)   References to a flight shall be construed as references to a journey, and the references in section 21(4) to flying shall be construed accordingly.

A2(4)   References to landing shall be construed as references to stopping for the purpose of enabling passengers or crew to board or leave the train or goods to be loaded onto or unloaded from it.

A2(5)   References to the commander of an aircraft shall be construed as references to the train manager of a train.

History – Para. A2 was inserted by SI 1993/1813, art. 8, Sch. 5, Pt. II, para. 11, operative from 2 August 1993.

1   [Neither relevant nor reproduced.]

2   [Neither relevant nor reproduced.]

3   [Neither relevant nor reproduced.]

4   [Neither relevant nor reproduced.]

PART IV OF THE ACT OF 1979: CONTROL OF IMPORTATION

5   [Neither relevant nor reproduced.]

6   In section 42(1)(a) (power to regulate the unloading, removal, etc. of imported goods) the reference to a ship arriving at a port shall be construed as including a reference to a vehicle arriving at a customs approved area through the tunnel from France.

7   In section 49(1) (forfeiture of goods improperly imported)–

    (a)   the reference in paragraph (a)(ii) to goods unloaded from any aircraft in the United Kingdom shall be construed as including a reference to goods unloaded from a through train or shuttle train which has brought them into the United Kingdom and a reference to goods otherwise brought through the tunnel into the United Kingdom; and

    (b)   the reference in paragraph (c) to goods found to have been concealed on board any aircraft shall be construed as including references to goods found concealed–

       (i)   on a through train or shuttle train has brought them into the United Kingdom,

(ii) on a through train while it constitutes a control zone in France, or

(iii) in a road vehicle in a control zone in France within the tunnel system.

Prospective insertion – In para. 7(b)(ii), the words "or Belgium" are to be inserted at the end before the word ", or" by SI 1994/1405, art. 8 and Sch. 4, with effect from a day to be appointed.

History – Para. 7 was substituted by SI 1993/1813, art. 8, Sch. 5, Pt. II, operative from 2 August 1993.

8   Section 50(2) (penalty for improper importation of goods) shall have effect as if–

(a) any person who unloads or assists or is otherwise concerned in the unloading of those goods mentioned in section 50(1) from any vehicle which has arrived from France through the tunnel, or who brings or assists or is otherwise concerned in the bringing of such goods into a control zone in France, were a person who unships such goods in a port; and

(b) any person who removes or assists or is otherwise concerned in the removal of such goods from any customs approved area were a person who removes such goods from an approved wharf.

Prospective insertion – In para. 8(a), the words "or Belgium" are to be inserted after the words "through the tunnel" by SI 1994/1405, art. 8 and Sch. 4, with effect from a day to be appointed.
In para. 8(b), the words "or Belgium" are to be inserted after the words "zone in France" by SI 1994/1405, art. 8 and Sch. 4, with effect from a day to be appointed.

History – In para. 8(a) the words "or who brings . . . zone in France" were inserted by SI 1993/1813, art. 8, Sch. 5, Pt. II, operative from 2 August 1993.

PART V OF THE ACT OF 1979: CONTROL OF EXPORTATION

9   [Neither relevant nor reproduced.]

10   [Neither relevant nor reproduced.]

11   [Neither relevant nor reproduced.]

12   [Neither relevant nor reproduced.]

13   [Neither relevant nor reproduced.]

14   [Neither relevant nor reproduced.]

15   [Neither relevant nor reproduced.]

16   [Neither relevant nor reproduced.]

PART VII OF THE ACT OF 1979: CUSTOMS AND EXCISE CONTROL: SUPPLEMENTARY PROVISIONS

17   [Neither relevant nor reproduced.]

18   [Neither relevant nor reproduced.]

19   [Neither relevant nor reproduced.]

PART X OF THE ACT OF 1979: DUTIES AND DRAWBACKS – GENERAL PROVISIONS

20   [Neither relevant nor reproduced.]

PART XI OF THE ACT OF 1979: DETENTION OF PERSONS, FORFEITURE AND LEGAL PROCEEDINGS

21   [Neither relevant nor reproduced.]

Notes – The heading immediately before para. 21 incorporates the original title of CEMA 1979, Pt. XI which, under the Police and Criminal Evidence Act 1984, s. 145(6), requires the substitution of "arrest" for "detention".

22   In section 146(1) (service of process) the reference in paragraph (c) to **an aircraft** shall be construed as including a reference to a vehicle which has arrived from or is departing to France through the tunnel, and in relation to such a vehicle the second reference to the United Kingdom shall be construed as including a reference to a control zone in France within the tunnel system.

History – In para. 22, the words "and in relation to such" to the end were inserted by SI 1993/1813, art. 8, Sch. 5, Pt. II, operative from 2 August 1993.

23   In section 154(2) (proof of certain other matters) any reference to **goods loaded or to be loaded into or unloaded from an aircraft** shall be construed respectively as including references to goods loaded or to be loaded onto or unloaded from a vehicle which is departing to or has arrived from France through the tunnel.

24　In section 159(1) (power to examine and take account of goods) the reference in paragraph (c) to **goods which have been loaded into a ship** shall be construed as including a reference to goods which have been loaded onto a vehicle for exportation through the tunnel.

25　The persons to whom section 164 (search of persons) applies shall be taken to include any person who is–

(a)　in the tunnel system in the United Kingdom;

(b)　in a through train in the United Kingdom;

(c)　in, entering or leaving a customs approved area in the United Kingdom; or

(d)　in a control zone in France.

Prospective insertion – In para. 25(d), the words "or Belgium" are to be inserted at the end by SI 1994/1405, art. 8 and Sch. 4, with effect from a day to be appointed.

History – Para. 25 was substituted by SI 1993/1813, art. 8, Sch. 5, Pt. II, operative from 2 August 1993.

PLANNING (NORTHERN IRELAND) ORDER 1991

(SI 1991/1220 (NI 11))

Made on 21 May 1991

PART V – ADDITIONAL PLANNING CONTROL

Buildings of special architectural or historic interest

LISTS OF BUILDINGS OF SPECIAL ARCHITECTURAL OR HISTORIC INTEREST

42(1)　The Department–

(a)　shall compile lists of buildings of special architectural or historic interest; and

(b)　may amend any list so compiled.

42(2)　In considering whether to include a building in a list compiled under this Article the Department may take into account not only the building itself but also–

(a)　any respect in which its exterior contributes to the architectural or historic interest of any group of buildings of which it forms part; and

(b)　the desirability of preserving, on the ground of its architectural or historic interest, any feature of the building which consists of a man-made object or structure fixed to the building or which forms a part of the land and which is comprised within the curtilage of the building.

42(3)　Before compiling or amending any list under this Article, the Department shall consult with the Historic Buildings Council and with the appropriate district council.

42(4)　As soon as may be after any list has been compiled under this Article, or any amendments of such a list have been made, the Department shall cause a copy of so much of the list, or so much of the amendments, as related to the area of a district council to be deposited with the clerk of that council.

42(5)　As soon as may be after the inclusion of any building in a list under this Article, whether on the compilation of the list or by its amendment, or as soon as may be after any such list has been amended by the exclusion of any building from it, the Department shall serve a notice in the prescribed form on every owner and occupier of the building, stating that the building has been included in, or excluded from, the list, as the case may be.

42(6)　The Department shall keep available for inspection by the public at all reasonable hours copies of lists and amendments of lists compiled or made under this Article.

42(7)　In this Order **"listed building"** means a building which is for the time being included in a list compiled under this Article; and, for the purposes of the provisions of this Order relating to listed buildings, the following shall be treated as part of the building–

(a)　any object or structure within the curtilage of the building and fixed to the building;

(b)　any object or structure within the curtilage of the building which, although not fixed to the buildings, forms part of the land and has done so since before 1st October 1973.

CRIMINAL JUSTICE (INTERNATIONAL CO-OPERATION) ACT 1990 (EXERCISE OF POWERS) ORDER 1991

(SI 1991/1297)

Made on 4 June 1991 by the Treasury, in exercise of the powers conferred on them by s. 7(7) and 8(5) of the Criminal Justice (International Co-operation) Act 1990.

1 This Order may be cited as the Criminal Justice (International Co-operation) Act 1990 (Exercise of Powers) Order 1991 and shall come into operation on 1st July 1991.

2 In this Order–

"**the Act**" means the Criminal Justice (International Co-operation) Act 1990;

"**officer**" means a person commissioned by the Commissioners of Customs and Excise under section 6(3) of the Customs and Excise Management Act 1979.

3 In England and Wales and Northern Ireland, any powers exercisable by a constable under section 7 of the Act, shall also be exercisable by an officer or by any person acting under the direction of an officer.

4 In Scotland, any powers to enter, search or seize granted under section 8(1) of the Act shall also be exercisable by an officer or by any person acting under the direction of an officer.

PRICE MARKING ORDER 1991

(SI 1991/1382)

Made on 3 June 1991, operative fom 1 September 1991

Note – Only art. 9 relates to VAT and is reproduced here.

VALUE ADDED TAX AND OTHER TAXES

9(1) This article applies to goods other than motor fuel.

9(2) In this article "**VAT**" means the value added tax chargeable on the supply of the goods or services in question and "**other tax**" means any other tax or duty to which any goods or services are subject.

9(3) Subject to the provisions of article 8 above, where a person indicates in accordance with this Order that any goods are or may be for sale by retail, the selling price or the unit price that is indicated on or in relation to those goods shall be indicated in such a manner as to be inclusive of any VAT or other tax relating to those goods.

9(4) The indication of price may be indicated exclusive of any VAT or other tax where the sale of goods on any premises or arising out of any advertisement is mainly to persons carrying on business and where, in addition to the indication of price, there is displayed either–

(a) a statement of the price inclusive of VAT and any other tax payable with equal prominence to the indication of price; or

(b) a statement of the amount of the VAT or other tax payable expressed as a sum of money with equal prominence to the indication of price; or

(c) prominent general statements that VAT or other tax is payable in addition to the prices indicated and stating the amount of the VAT or other tax expressed as a percentage.

9(5) The provisions of this Order shall be complied with notwithstanding any change in the rate or coverage of VAT or any other tax, provided that where there is any such change a retailer who adjusts his prices in consequence thereof may–

(a) by means of a general notice or notices for a period of 14 days from the date any such change takes effect, indicate that any goods subject to that change are not for sale at the price indicated and that such price will be adjusted to take account of the change if, but only if, any such notice is prominently displayed, is unambiguous and easily identifiable as referring to the goods in question and is clearly legible to prospective purchasers;

(b) continue to distribute any catalogue or sales literature printed or ordered to be printed before a change is announced if, but only if–

(i)   there is firmly attached thereto a label which prominently states that some or all of the prices printed therein are to be adjusted to reflect the change, and

(ii)   it includes sufficient information to enable prospective purchasers to establish the adjusted prices of any goods listed, or

(iii) it refers to and is accompanied by a supplement which enables them to do so.

FREE ZONE (BIRMINGHAM AIRPORT) DESIGNATION ORDER 1991

(SI 1991/1737)

Made on 24 July 1991 by the Treasury, in exercise of the powers conferred on them by s. 100A of the Customs and Excise Management Act 1979 and of all other powers enabling them in that behalf.

CITATION AND COMMENCEMENT

1   This Order may be cited as The Free Zone (Birmingham Airport) Designation Order 1991 and shall come into force on 6th August 1991.

DESIGNATION OF AREA AS FREE ZONE

2(1)   An area of 2.77 acres, in the Metropolitan Borough of Solihull in the County of West Midlands, shown enclosed by a red line on a map (in this article referred to as "**the map**"), being of a scale of 5 inches to a mile, and signed by a Collector of Customs and Excise, shall be a free zone.

2(2)   The map shall be kept by the Commissioners at their Headquarters, New King's Beam House, 22 Upper Ground, London SE1 9PJ and a copy thereof at the offices of the responsible authority.

2(3)   The map or the copy thereof may, on application, be inspected by members of the public at reasonable hours without charge.

APPOINTMENT OF RESPONSIBLE AUTHORITY

3   The responsible authority for the free zone shall be The Prudential Assurance Company Limited whose Registered Office is at 142 Holborn Bars, London EC1N 2NH.

PERIOD OF VALIDITY OF ORDER

4   This Order shall have effect for a period of 10 years from the date of coming into force.

CONDITIONS IMPOSED ON RESPONSIBLE AUTHORITY

5   The responsible authority shall–

(a)   maintain an office in the free zone or at such other place as the Commissioners may allow at which shall be kept any records, for which the responsible authority is responsible, relating to the free zone and the business carried on therein;

(b)   keep separate accounts in connection with the free zone;

(c)   provide such information in connection with the free zone and the operation thereof to any person authorised by the Treasury, as that person may reasonably require;

(d)   provide, free of expense to the Crown, such accommodation and facilities including furniture, fittings and equipment as the Commissioners may reasonably require and such accommodation and facilities shall be properly maintained, heated, lighted, ventilated and kept clean by the responsible authority;

(e)   provide, free of expense to the Crown, such area of land within the free zone as the Commissioners may reasonably require for the examination of goods and vehicles and shall provide and maintain such appliances and afford such other facilities which are reasonably necessary to enable an account to be taken of any goods or make any examination or search;

(f)   not permit a person to establish or carry on any trade or business in the free zone unless that person is authorised by the Commissioners to carry on such a trade or business in the free zone.

HEALTH AND SAFETY

7   Without prejudice to the responsibilities of persons occupying premises within the free zone, the responsible authority shall ensure that the working conditions within the free zone are safe and without risk to the health and safety of persons employed by the Commissioners and shall comply with any requirements concerning health and safety imposed by any competent authority.

Note – The above statutory instrument as published does not have an art. 6.

FREE ZONE (LIVERPOOL) DESIGNATION ORDER 1991

(SI 1991/1738)

Made on 24 July 1991 by the Treasury, in exercise of the powers conferred on them by s. 100A of the Customs and Excise Management Act 1979.

CITATION AND COMMENCEMENT

1   This Order may be cited as The Free Zone (Liverpool) Designation Order 1991 and shall come into force on 6th August 1991.

DESIGNATION OF AREA AS FREE ZONE

2(1)   An area of 787 acres, in the County of Merseyside, consisting of 121 acres in the Metropolitan Borough of Wirral together with 666 acres in the Borough of Sefton, shown enclosed by a red line on maps (in this article referred to as **"the maps"**), entitled Docks Plan Sheet No. 10 and Freeport Docks Plan Sheet No. 11 respectively, being of a scale of 25 inches to a mile, and signed by a Collector of Customs and Excise, shall be a free zone.

2(2)   The maps shall be kept by the Commissioners at their Headquarters, New King's Beam House, 22 Upper Ground, London SE1 9PJ and copies thereof at the offices of the responsible authority.

2(3)   The maps or the copies thereof may, on application, be inspected by members of the public at reasonable hours without charge.

APPOINTMENT OF RESPONSIBLE AUTHORITY

3   The responsible authority for the free zone shall be The Mersey Docks and Harbour Company whose Head Office is at Pier Head, Liverpool.

PERIOD OF VALIDITY OF ORDER

4   This Order shall have effect for a period of 10 years from the date of coming into force.

CONDITIONS IMPOSED ON RESPONSIBLE AUTHORITY

5   The responsible authority shall not permit the area designated by this Order to function as a free zone before the Commissioners are satisfied that the area is secure and have so notified the responsible authority in writing.

6   The responsible authority shall–

(a)   maintain an office in the free zone or at such other place as the Commissioners may allow at which shall be kept any records, for which the responsible authority is responsible, relating to the free zone and the business carried on therein;

(b)   keep separate accounts in connection with the free zone;

(c)   provide such information in connection with the free zone and the operation thereof to any person authorised by the Treasury, as that person may reasonably require;

(d)   provide, free of expense to the Crown, such accommodation and facilities including furniture, fittings and equipment as the Commissioners may reasonably require and such accommodation and facilities shall be properly maintained, heated, lighted, ventilated and kept clean by the responsible authority;

(e)   provide, free of expense to the Crown, such area of land within the free zone as the Commissioners may reasonably require for the examination of goods and vehicles and shall provide and maintain such appliances and afford such other facilities which are reasonably necessary to enable an account to be taken of any goods or make any examination or search;

(f)   not permit a person to establish or carry on any trade or business in the free zone unless that person is authorised by the Commissioners to carry on such a trade or business in the free zone.

HEALTH AND SAFETY

7   Without prejudice to the responsibilities of persons occupying premises within the free zone, the responsible authority shall ensure that the working conditions within the free zone are safe and without risk to the health and safety of persons employed by the Commissioners and shall comply with any requirements concerning health and safety imposed by any competent authority.

FREE ZONE (PRESTWICK AIRPORT) DESIGNATION ORDER 1991

(SI 1991/1739)

Made on 24 July 1991 by the Treasury, in exercise of the powers conferred on them by s. 100A of the Customs and Excise Management Act 1979 and of all other powers enabling them in that behalf.

CITATION AND COMMENCEMENT

1   This Order may be cited as The Free Zone (Prestwick Airport) Designation Order 1991 and shall come into force on 6th August 1991.

DESIGNATION OF AREA AS FREE ZONE

2(1)   An area of 5.799 acres, in the parish of Ayr in the County of Ayr, shown enclosed by a red line on a map (in this article referred to as **"the map"**), being of a scale of 25 inches to a mile, and signed by a Collector of Customs and Excise, shall be a free zone.

2(2)   The map shall be kept by the Commissioners at their Headquarters, New King's Beam House, 22 Upper Ground, London SE1 9PJ and a copy thereof at the offices of the responsible authority.

2(3)   The map or the copy therefore [*sic*] may, on application, be inspected by members of the public at reasonable hours without charge.

Cross references – Free Zone (Prestwick Airport) Designation (Variation) Order 1994 (SI 1994/143).

APPOINTMENT OF RESPONSIBLE AUTHORITY

3   The responsible authority for the free zone shall be Freeport Scotland Ltd whose Registered Office is at Burns House, Burns Statue Square, Ayr KA7 1UT.

PERIOD OF VALIDITY OF ORDER

4   This Order shall have effect for a period of 10 years from the date of coming into force.

CONDITIONS IMPOSED ON RESPONSIBLE AUTHORITY

5   There [*sic*] responsible authority shall not permit the area designated by this Order to function as a free zone before the Commissioners are satisfied that the area is secure and have so notified the responsible authority in writing.

6   The responsible authority shall—

(a)   *maintain an office in the free zone* or at such other place as the Commissioners may allow at which shall be kept any records, for which the responsible authority is responsible, relating to the free zone and the business carried on therein;

(b)   keep separate accounts in connection with the free zone;

(c)   provide such information in connection with the free zone and the operation thereof to any person authorised by the Treasury, as that person may reasonably require;

(d)   provide, free of expense to the Crown, such accommodation and facilities including furniture, fittings and equipment as the Commissioners may reasonably require and such accommodation and facilities shall be properly maintained, heated, lighted, ventilated and kept clean by the responsible authority;

(e)   provide, free of expense to the Crown, such area of land within the free zone as the Commissioners may reasonably require for the examination of goods and vehicles and shall provide and maintain such appliances and afford such other facilities which are reasonably necessary to enable an account to be taken of any goods or make any examination or search;

(f)   not permit a person to establish or carry on any trade or business in the free zone unless that person is authorised by the Commissioners to carry on such a trade or business in the free zone.

HEALTH AND SAFETY

7   Without prejudice to the responsibilities of persons occupying premises within the free zone, the responsible authority shall ensure that the working conditions within the free zone are safe and without risk to the health and safety of persons employed by the Commissioners and shall comply with any requirements concerning health and safety imposed by any competent authority.

FREE ZONE (SOUTHAMPTON) DESIGNATION ORDER 1991

(SI 1991/1740)

Made on 24 July 1991 by the Treasury, in exercise of the powers conferred on them by s. 100A of the Customs and Excise Management Act 1979 and of all other powers enabling them in that behalf.

CITATION AND COMMENCEMENT

1   This Order may be cited as The Free Zone (Southampton) Designation Order 1991 and shall come into force on 6th August 1991.

DESIGNATION OF AREA AS FREE ZONE

2(1)   An area of 6.8 acres, in the City of Southampton, Hampshire, shown enclosed by a red line on a map (in this article referred to as **"the map"**), being of a scale of 25 inches to a mile, and signed by a Collector of Customs and Excise, shall be a free zone.

2(2)   The map shall be kept by the Commissioners at their Headquarters, New King's Beam House, 22 Upper Ground, London SE1 9PJ and a copy thereof at the offices of the responsible authority.

2(3)   The map or the copy thereof may, on application, be inspected by members of the public at reasonable hours without charge.

Cross references – Free Zone (Southampton) Designation (Variation) Order 1994 (SI 1994/1410).

APPOINTMENT OF RESPONSIBLE AUTHORITY

3   The responsible authority for the free zone shall be Southampton Free Trade Zone Limited whose Registered Office is at 150 Holborn, London EC1N 2LR.

PERIOD OF VALIDITY OF ORDER

4   This Order shall have effect for a period of 10 years from the date of coming into force.

CONDITIONS IMPOSED ON RESPONSIBLE AUTHORITY

5   The responsible authority shall–

(a)   maintain an office in the free zone or at such other place as the Commissioners may allow at which shall be kept any records, for which the responsible authority is responsible, relating to the free zone and the business carried on therein;

(b)   keep separate accounts in connection with the free zone;

(c)   provide such information in connection with the free zone and the operation thereof to any person authorised by the Treasury, as that person may reasonably require;

(d)   provide, free of expense to the Crown, such accommodation and facilities including furniture, fittings and equipment as the Commissioners may reasonably require and such accommodation and facilities shall be properly maintained, heated, lighted, ventilated and kept clean by the responsible authority;

(e)   provide, free of expense to the Crown, such area of land within the free zone as the Commissioners may reasonably require for the examination of goods and vehicles and shall provide and maintain such appliances and afford such other facilities which are reasonably necessary to enable an account to be taken of any goods or make any examination or search;

(f)   not permit a person to establish or carry on any trade or business in the free zone unless that person is authorised by the Commissioners to carry on such a trade or business in the free zone.

HEALTH AND SAFETY

6   Without prejudice to the responsibilities of persons occupying premises within the free zone, the responsible authority shall ensure that the working conditions within the free zone are safe and without risk to the health and safety of persons employed by the Commissioners and shall comply with any requirements concerning health and safety imposed by any competent authority.

VALUE ADDED TAX (INPUT TAX) (PERSON SUPPLIED) ORDER 1991
(SI 1991/2306)

Made on 17 October 1991 by the Treasury, in exercise of the powers conferred on them by s. 14(3B) of the Value Added Tax Act 1983 [VATA 1994, s. 24(4)] and of all other powers enabling them in that behalf.

1   This Order may be cited as the Value Added Tax (Input Tax) (Person Supplied) Order 1991 and shall come into force on 1st December 1991.

2   Article 3 below shall apply where road fuel is supplied to a person who is not a taxable person and a taxable person pays to him–

(a)   the actual cost to him of the fuel; or

(b)   an amount, the whole or part of which approximates to and is paid in order to reimburse him for the cost of the fuel, determined by reference to –

  (i)   the total distances travelled by the vehicle in which the fuel is used (whether or not including distances travelled otherwise than for the purposes of the business of the taxable person), and

  (ii) the cylinder capacity of the vehicle,

whether or not the taxable person makes any payment in order to reimburse him for any other cost.

3   Where this article applies, the fuel shall be treated for the purpose of section 14(3) of the Value Added Tax Act 1983 [VATA 1994, s. 24(2)] as having been supplied to the taxable person for the purpose of a business carried on by him and for a consideration equal to the amount paid by him under article 2(a) or (b) above, as the case may be (excluding any reimbursement of any cost other than the cost of the fuel).

VALUE ADDED TAX (TREATMENT OF TRANSACTIONS) ORDER 1992
(SI 1992/630)

Made on 10 March 1992 by the Treasury, in exercise of the powers conferred on them by s. 3(3) of the Value Added Tax Act 1983 [VATA 1994, s. 5(3)] and of all other powers enabling them in that behalf.

1   This Order may be cited as the Value Added Tax (Treatment of Transactions) Order 1992 and shall come into force on 1st April 1992.

2   Where an employer gives an employee a choice between–

(a)   a particular rate of wages, salary or emoluments, or

(b)   in the alternative a lower rate of wages, salary or emoluments and, in addition, the right to the private use of a motor car provided by the employer, and the employee chooses the alternative described in paragraph (b) above, then the provision to the employee of the right to use the motor car privately shall be treated as neither a supply of goods nor a supply of services (if it otherwise would be) to the extent only that the consideration for the provision of the motor car for the employee's private use is the difference between the wages, salary or emoluments available to him under paragraphs (a) and (b) of this article.

Other material – Customs Business Brief 9/92, 19 June 1992 (not reproduced): clarification of the VAT position in cases of trading down, trading up; guidance generally on sacrificing benefits and retrospection.

FREE ZONE (PORT OF TILBURY) DESIGNATION ORDER 1992

(SI 1992/1282)

Made by the Treasury, in exercise of the powers conferred on them by s. 100A of the Customs and Excise Management Act 1979.

CITATION AND COMMENCEMENT

1   This Order may be cited as the Free Zone (Port of Tilbury) Designation Order 1992 and shall come into force on 3rd June 1992.

DESIGNATION OF AREA AS A FREE ZONE

2(1)   An area of 750 acres, in the Borough of Thurrock in the County of Essex, shown enclosed by a blue line on a map (in this article referred to as **"the map"**), being of a scale of 1:5000, and signed by a Collector of Customs and Excise, shall be a free zone.

2(2)   The map shall be kept by the Commissioners at their Headquarters, New King's Beam House, 22 Upper Ground, London SE1 9PJ and a copy thereof at the offices of the responsible authority.

2(3)   The map or the copy thereof may, on application, be inspected by members of the public at reasonable hours without charge.

Cross references – Free Zone (Port of Tilbury) Designation (Variation) Order 1992 (SI 1994/2216).

APPOINTMENT OF RESPONSIBLE AUTHORITY

3   The responsible authority for the free zone shall be Port of Tilbury London Limited whose Registered Office is at Leslie Ford House, Tilbury Dock, Essex RM18 7EH.

PERIOD OF VALIDITY OF ORDER

4   This Order shall have effect for a period of 10 years from the date of coming into force.

CONDITIONS IMPOSED ON RESPONSIBLE AUTHORITY

5   The responsible authority shall–

(a)   maintain an office in the free zone or at such other place as the Commissioners may allow at which shall be kept any records, for which the responsible authority is responsible, relating to the free zone and the business carried on therein;

(b)   keep separate accounts in connection with the free zone;

(c)   provide such information in connection with the free zone and the operation thereof to any person authorised by the Treasury, as that person may reasonably require;

(d)   provide, free of expense to the Crown, such accommodation and facilities including furniture, fittings and equipment as the Commissioners may reasonably require and such accommodation and facilities shall be properly maintained, heated, lighted, ventilated and kept clean by the responsible authority;

(e)   provide, free of expense to the Crown, such area of land with the free zone as the *Commissioners* may reasonably require for the examination of goods and vehicles and shall provide and maintain such appliances and afford such other facilities which are reasonably necessary to enable an account to be taken of any goods or make any examination or search;

(f)   not permit a person to establish or carry on any trade or business in the free zone unless that person is authorised by the Commissioners to carry on such a trade or business in the free zone.

HEALTH AND SAFETY

6 Without prejudice to the responsibilities of persons occupying premises within the free zone, the responsible authority shall ensure that the working conditions within the free zone are safe and without risk to the health and safety of persons employed by the Commissioners and shall comply with any requirements concerning health and safety imposed by any competent authority.

STATISTICS OF TRADE (CUSTOMS AND EXCISE) REGULATIONS 1992

(SI 1992/2790, as amended by SI 1996/2968, SI 1993/3015, SI 1993/541, SI 1997/2864)

Made on 6 November 1992 by the Commissioners of Customs and Excise, in exercise of the powers conferred on them by s. 2(2) of the European Communities Act 1972, being the department designated for the purpose of that subsection in relation to the receipt, regulation and control of statistics relating to the trading of goods between the United Kingdom and other Member States of the Communities and of all other powers enabling them in that behalf.

CITATION, COMMENCEMENT AND INTERPRETATION

1(1) These Regulations may be cited as the Statistics of Trade (Customs and Excise) Regulations 1992 and shall come into force on 1st December 1992.

1(2) In these Regulations–

"**the Act**" means the Customs and Excise Management Act 1979;

"**arrival stage**" has the meaning assigned to it by Article 28 of the Principal Regulation;

"**assimilation threshold**" has the meaning assigned to it by Article 28 of the Principal Regulation;

"**authorised person**" means any person acting under the authority of the Commissioners;

"**dispatch stage**" has the meaning assigned to it by Article 28 of the Principal Regulation;

"**document**" includes in addition to a document in writing–

(a) any photograph;

(b) any disc tape, sound track or other device in which sounds or other data (not being visual images) are recorded so as to be capable (with or without the aid of some other equipment) of being reproduced therefrom; and

(c) any film, negative, tape or other device in which one or more visual images are recorded so as to be capable (as aforesaid) of being reproduced therefrom;

"**film**" includes a microfilm;

"**goods**" has the meaning assigned to it by Article 2 of the Principal Regulation;

"**Intrastat system**" has the meaning assigned to it by Article 6 of the Principal Regulation;

"**Member State**" has the meaning assigned to it by Article 2 of the Principal Regulation;

"**periodic declaration**" means the declaration referred to in Article 13 of the Principal Regulation or the periodic tax declaration referred to in Article 28(4) of the Principal Regulation;

"**Principal Regulation**" means Council Regulation (EEC) No. 3330/91;

"**reference period**" means the period specified in Article 20(7) of the Principal Regulation;

"**register of intra-Community operators**" means the register compiled by the Commissioners in accordance with Article 10 of the Principal Regulation;

"**supplementary declaration**" means the periodic declaration which a person on the register of intra-Community operators is required to submit to the Commissioners apart from any periodic declaration which is also a "return" for the purposes of regulation 58 of the Value Added Tax (General) Regulations 1985;

"**threshold Regulation**" means Commission Regulation (EEC) No. 2256/92.

1(3) In these Regulations, unless defined above, words and expressions shall have the meanings assigned to them by section 1 of the Act.

History – In reg. 1(2), the definitions of "ancillary costs sample survey", "business day", "commodity code" and "supplementary units" were omitted by SI 1997/2864, reg. 3, operative from 1 January 1998.
In reg. 1(2), the former definitions of "ancillary costs sample survey", "business day", "commodity code" and "supplementary units" inserted by SI 1993/541, reg. 3, operative from 1 April 1993.

APPLICATION OF INTRASTAT SYSTEM

2(1) The Intrastat system shall be under the care and management of the Commissioners.

2(2) The Commissioners shall be the competent national department to whom periodic declarations shall be sent in accordance with Article 13 of the Principal Regulation.

Official publications – 60.
Customs Internal Guidance Manual, vol. S8.42: Intrastat.

SUPPLEMENTARY DECLARATIONS

3(1) For the purposes of the application of Article 9 of the Threshold Regulation–

(a)   the assimilation threshold at the arrival stage shall be £233,000; and

(b)   the assimilation threshold at the dispatch stage shall be £233,000.

3(2) Any supplementary declaration shall be furnished–

(a)   at such place as the Commissioners shall direct; and

(b)   subject to paragraph (3) below, no later than the tenth day following the end of the reference period to which it relates.

3(3) For the purpose of calculating the period following the end of the reference period mentioned in paragraph (2) above no account shall be taken of any day upon which the place designated by the Commissioners for receipt of supplementary declarations is not open to the public for business.

History – In reg. 3(1), the threshold of £225,000 was substituted by SI 1997/2864, reg. 4, operative from 1 January 1998. The threshold was varied by statutory instrument as follows:

SI	Period of application	£
1999/3269	From 1 January 2000	233,000
1998/2973	1 January 1999 to 31 December 1999	230,000
1997/2864	1 January 1998 to 31 December 1998	225,000
1996/2968	1 January 1997 to 31 December 1997	195,000
1994/2946	1 January 1996 to 31 December 1996	160,000
1994/2914	1 January 1995 to 31 December 1995	150,000
1993/3015	1 January 1994 to 31 December 1994	140,000
–	1 January 1993 to 31 December 1993	135,000

4(1) Subject to paragraph (4) below, unless a supplementary declaration is made in a form prescribed for the purpose in accordance with Article 12(1) of the Principal Regulation it shall be made in the form set out in the Schedule to these Regulations as is appropriate in the circumstances of the case.

4(2) Supplementary declarations may be furnished to the place specified by the Commissioners in accordance with paragraph (3) of regulation 3 above by post or in person when that place is open to the public for business.

4(3) Supplementary declarations sent by post shall not be presumed to have been furnished without proof of posting.

4(4) The Commissioners may–

(a)   on the application of a person who is mentioned in the register of intra-Community operators; or

(b)   without application in such circumstances as they may direct,

permit, subject to such conditions as they deem necessary or expedient, any person to furnish supplementary declarations by electronic means.

4(5) The Commissioners may at any time for reasonable cause revoke or vary any permission given under paragraph (4) above.

ANCILLARY COSTS SAMPLE SURVEYS

4A [Omitted by SI 1997/2864, art. 5, operative from 1 January 1998.]

History – Former reg. 4A was inserted by SI 1993/541, reg. 4, operative from 1 April 1993.

DUTY TO KEEP AND RETAIN RECORDS

5(1) Every person who is mentioned in the register of intra-Community operators, shall–

(a)   keep a copy of every periodic declaration he makes or which is made on his behalf;

(b)   keep copies of all documents which he or anyone acting on his behalf used for the purpose of compiling his periodic declarations;

(c)   produce or cause to be produced periodic declarations and documents mentioned in paragraphs (a) and (b) above when required to do so by an authorised person;

(d)   permit an authorised person exercising the powers mentioned in paragraph (c) above to make copies or extracts of those periodic declarations and documents or to remove them for a reasonable period.

5(2)   The Commissioners may require periodic declarations and documents mentioned in paragraph (1) above to be preserved for such period not exceeding six years as they may require.

5(3)   For the purpose of exercising any powers granted by this regulation an authorised person may at any reasonable time enter premises used in connection with the carrying on of a business by a person mentioned in the register of intra-Community operators or another person compiling periodic declarations on his behalf.

History – In reg. 5(1)(a), the words "and every return for the purposes of an ancillary costs sample survey" which appeared after the word "declaration" were inserted by SI 1993/541, reg. 5(1)(a), operative from 1 April 1993, but omitted by SI 1997/2864, reg. 6(1)(a), operative from 1 January 1998.
In reg. 5(1)(b), the words "the documents mentioned in paragraph (a) above" substituted for the words "his periodic declarations" by SI 1993/541, reg. 5(1)(b), operative from 1 April 1993, but this substitution was reversed by SI 1997/2864, reg. 6(1)(b), operative from 1 January 1998.
In reg. 5(1)(c), the words "any such copies as are" substituted for the words "periodic declarations and documents" by SI 1993/541, reg. 5(1)(c), operative from 1 April 1993, but this substitution was reversed by SI 1997/2864, reg. 6(1)(c), operative from 1 January 1998.
In reg. 5(1)(d), the words "further copies of, or of extracts from, those copies" substituted for the words "copies or extracts of those periodic declarations and documents" by SI 1993/541, reg. 5(1)(d), operative from 1 April 1993, but this substitution was reversed by SI 1997/2864, reg. 6(1)(d), operative from 1 January 1998.
In reg. 5(2), the words "the copies" substituted for the words "periodic declarations and documents" by SI 1993/541, reg. 5(2), operative from 1 April 1993, but this substitution was reversed by SI 1997/2864, reg. 6(2), operative from 1January 1998.

OFFENCES AND EVIDENCE

6(1)   If any person required to furnish a supplementary declaration in accordance with the Intrastat system fails to do so he shall be liable on summary conviction to a penalty not exceeding level 4 on the standard scale.

6(2)   Any failure to furnish a supplementary declaration includes a failure to furnish such supplementary declaration in the form and manner required by these Regulations, or the Principal Regulation.

6(3)   Subject to paragraph (4) below, for the purpose of the rules against charging more than one offence in the same information–

(a)   failure to furnish one or more supplementary declarations of trade in goods dispatched to other Member States for any given reference period shall constitute one offence; and

(b)   failure to furnish one or more supplementary declarations of trade in goods received from other Member States for any given reference period shall constitute one offence.

6(4)   If the failure in respect of which a person is convicted under paragraph (1) above is continued after the conviction he shall be guilty of a further offence and may on summary conviction thereof be punished accordingly.

6(5)   If, following a request made by the Commissioners in accordance with Article 9(2) of the Principal Regulation, any person is required to provide information and fails to do so in accordance with the conditions set out in the request for such information he shall be liable on summary conviction to a penalty not exceeding level 4 on the standard scale.

6(5A)   [Omitted by SI 1997/2864, art. 7(a), operative from 1 January 1998.]

6(6)   If the failure in respect of which a person is convicted under paragraph (5) above is continued after the conviction he shall be guilty of a further offence and may on summary conviction thereof be punished accordingly.

6(7)   In any proceedings for an offence mentioned in this regulation it shall be a defence for the accused to prove that he took all reasonable precautions and exercised all due diligence to avoid the commission of such an offence by himself, any person under his control or any person to whom he transferred the task of providing information in accordance with Article 9(1) of the Principal Regulation.

History – In reg. 6, para. (5A) was inserted by SI 1993/541, reg. 6, operative from 1 April 1993, but was omitted by SI 1997/2864, reg. 7(a), operative from 1 January 1998.
In para. (6) the words "or (5A)" were inserted by SI 1993/541, reg. 6, operative from 1 April 1993, but were omitted by SI 1997/2864, reg. 7(b), operative from 1 January 1998.

7(1)   In any legal proceedings, whether civil or criminal, where any question arises concerning a document furnished or created for the purposes of the Intrastat system this regulation shall apply.

7(2)   Where any document does not consist of legible visual images its content may be proved in any proceedings by production of a copy of the information in the form of legible visual images.

History – In reg. 7(2), the words "form and" which appeared after the words "images its" omitted by SI 1993/541, reg. 7, operative from 1 April 1993.

8(1)   A certificate of the Commissioners–

(a)   that a person was or was not a party responsible for providing information in accordance with the Intrastat system;

(b)   that a person was or was not mentioned in the register of intra-Community operators;

(c)   that any information required for purposes connected with the Intrastat system has not been given or had not been given at any date;

(d)   that a copy produced in accordance with paragraph (2) of regulation 7 above is, both as to form and content, identical to that received by electronic means in accordance with paragraph (4) of regulation 4 above

shall be sufficient evidence of that fact until the contrary is proved.

8(2)   A photograph of any document furnished to the Commissioners for the purposes of these Regulations and certified by them to be such a photograph shall be admissible in any proceedings, whether civil or criminal, to the same extent as the document itself.

8(3)   Any document purporting to be a certificate under paragraph (1) or (2) above shall be deemed to be such a certificate until the contrary is proved.

ACCESS TO RECORDED INFORMATION

9(1)   Where, on an application by an authorised person, a justice of the peace or, in Scotland, a justice (within the meaning of section 462 of the Criminal Procedure (Scotland) Act 1975) is satisfied that there are reasonable grounds for believing–

(a)   that an offence in connection with the Intrastat system is being, has been or is about to be committed, and

(b)   that any recorded information (including any document of any nature whatsoever) which may be required as evidence for the purpose of any proceedings in respect of such an offence is in the possession of any person,

he may make an order in accordance with this regulation.

9(2)   An order made in accordance with this regulation is an order that the person who appears to the justice to be in possession of the recorded information to which the application relates shall–

(a)   give an authorised person access to it, and

(b)   permit an authorised person to remove and take away any of it which he reasonably considers necessary,

not later than the end of the period of seven days beginning on the date of the order or the end of such longer period as the order may specify.

9(3)   The reference in sub-paragraph (2)(a) above to giving an authorised person **access to the recorded information** to which the application relates includes a reference to permitting the authorised person to take copies of it or to make extracts from it.

9(4)   Where the recorded information consists of information contained in a computer, an order made in accordance with this regulation shall have effect as an order to produce the information in a form in which it is visible and legible and, if the authorised person wishes to remove it, in a form in which it can be removed.

10(1)   An authorised person who removes anything in the exercise of a power conferred by or under regulation 9 above shall, if so requested by a person showing himself–

(a)   to be the occupier of premises from which it was removed, or

(b)   to have had custody or control of it immediately before the removal,

provide that person with a record of what he removed.

10(2)   The authorised person shall provide the record within a reasonable time from the making of the request for it.

10(3)   Subject to paragraph (7) below, if a request for permission to be granted access to anything which–

(a)   has been removed by an authorised person, and

(b)   is retained by the Commissioners for the purpose of investigating an offence,

is made to the officer in overall charge of the investigation by a person who had custody or control of the thing immediately before it was so removed or by someone acting on behalf of such a person, the officer shall allow the person who made the request access to it under the supervision of an authorised person.

10(4)   Subject to paragraph (7) below, if a request for a photograph or copy of any such thing is made to the officer in overall charge of the investigation by a person who had custody or control of the thing immediately before it was so removed, or by someone acting on behalf of such a person, the officer shall–

(a)   allow the person who made the request access to it under the supervision of an authorised person for the purpose of photographing it or copying it; or

(b)   photograph or copy it, or cause it to be photographed or copied.

10(5)   Where anything is photographed or copied under sub-paragraph (4)(b) above the photograph or copy shall be supplied to the person who made the request.

10(6)   The photograph or copy shall be supplied within a reasonable time from the making of the request.

10(7)   There is no duty under this regulation to grant access to, or to supply a photograph or copy of, anything if the officer in overall charge of the investigation for the purposes of which it was removed has reasonable grounds for believing that to do so would prejudice–

(a)   that investigation;

(b)   the investigation of an offence other than the offence for the purposes of the investigation of which the thing was removed; or

(c)   any criminal proceedings which may be brought as a result of–

(i)   the investigation of which he is in charge, or

(ii)   any such investigation as is mentioned in sub-paragraph (b) above.

10(8)   Any reference in this regulation to the **officer in overall charge** of the investigation is a reference to the person whose name and address are endorsed on the order concerned as being the officer so in charge.

11(1)   Where, on an application made as mentioned in paragraph (2) below, the appropriate judicial authority is satisfied that a person has failed to comply with a requirement imposed by regulation 10 above, the authority may order that person to comply with the requirement within such time and in such manner as may be specified in the order.

11(2)   An application under paragraph (1) above shall be made

(a)   in the case of a failure to comply with any of the requirements imposed by paragraphs (1) and (2) of regulation 10 above, by the occupier of the premises from which the thing in question was removed or by the person who had custody or control of it immediately before it was so removed, and

(b)   in any other case, by the person who has such custody or control.

11(3)   In this regulation **"the appropriate judicial authority"** means–

(a)   in England and Wales, a magistrates' court;

(b)   in Scotland, the sheriff; and

(c)   in Northern Ireland, a court of summary jurisdiction, as defined in Article 2(2)(a) of the *Magistrates' Court (Northern Ireland) Order 1981*.

11(4)   In England and Wales and Northern Ireland, an application for an order under this regulation shall be made by way of complaint; and sections 21 and 42(2) of the Interpretation Act (Northern Ireland) 1954 shall apply as if any reference in those provisions to any enactment included a reference to this regulation.

SUPPLEMENTARY

12   Where in connection with the operation of the Intrastat system a person is convicted of an offence contrary to section 167(1) or section 168(1) of the Act, section 167(2)(a) and section 168(2)(a) of the Act shall have effect as if, in each case, for the words "6 months" there were substituted the words "3 months".

13 The following provisions of the Act shall apply to these Regulations as they apply to the customs and excise Acts–

    Sections 145 to 148 (proceedings for offences, etc.);

    Sections 150 to 154 (incidental provisions as to legal proceedings, mitigation of penalties, proof and other matters).

History – Reg. 13 inserted by SI 1993/3015, reg. 4, operative from 1 January 1994.

SCHEDULE

Regulation 4

Form C 1500	Intra EC trade statistics – supplementary declaration – Intrastat – arrivals
Form C 1500 (cont.)	Continuation sheet for form C 1500
Form C 1501	Intra EC trade statistics – supplementary declaration – Intrastat – dispatches
Form C 1501 (cont.)	Continuation sheet for form C 1501

[Forms not reproduced.]

VALUE ADDED TAX (REMOVAL OF GOODS) ORDER 1992

(SI 1992/3111)

Made on 9 December 1992 by the Treasury, in exercise of the powers conferred on them by s. 3(3) of the Value Added Tax Act 1983 [VATA 1994, s. 5(3)] and of all other powers enabling them in that behalf.

1 This Order may be cited as the Value Added Tax (Removal of Goods) Order 1992 and shall come into force on 1st January 1993.

2 In this Order–

    "the Act" means the Value Added Tax Act 1983 [VATA 1994];

    "the member State of arrival" means the member State to which the goods are removed;

    "the member State of dispatch" means the member State from which the goods are removed;

    "the owner" means the person who is carrying on the business of which the goods form part of the assets;

    "registered" means either registered under the Act or registered under the provisions of the law of another member State corresponding thereto;

    "temporary importation relief" means relief, other than partial relief, from payment of any duty incurred on the entry of goods into the territory of the Community which is afforded by virtue of any of the Community Regulations specified in the Schedule to this Order.

3 For the purposes of this Order, a person is treated as being established in a member State if he has there a business establishment or some other fixed establishment or carries on a business there through a branch or agency.

4 Subject to article 5 below, paragraph 5A of Schedule 2 to the Act [VATA 1994, Sch. 4, para. 6] shall not apply to the following removals of goods from a member State to a place in any other member State–

(a)   where the supply of the goods would be treated as having been made in a member State *other than the member* State of dispatch by virtue of section 6(2A), (2B) or (2C) of the Act [VATA 1994, s. 7(3)–(5)];

(b)   where the supply of the goods would be treated as having been made in the member State of dispatch by virtue of the Value Added Tax (Place of Supply of Goods) Order 1992;

(c)   where the goods have been removed by or under the directions of the owner for the purpose of–

(i) his delivering them to a person to whom he is supplying those goods; or

(ii) his taking possession of them from a person who is supplying those goods to him,

and that supply is or will be zero-rated by virtue of section 16(6) or (7) of the Act [VATA 1994, s. 30(6) or (8)];

(d) where—

    (i) the owner is registered in the member State of dispatch and is not registered in the member State of arrival;

    (ii) the goods have been removed for the purpose of delivering them to a person other than the owner who is to produce goods by applying a treatment or process to the goods removed; and

    (iii) the owner intends that the goods produced will be returned to him by their removal to the member State of dispatch upon completion of the treatment or process;

(e) where—

    (i) the goods have been removed for the purpose of delivering them to a person other than the owner who is to value or carry out any work on the goods; and

    (ii) the supply made by the person to whom the goods have been delivered is or will be a supply of services treated as having been made in the member State of arrival;

(f) where—

    (i) the owner is established in the member State of dispatch and is not established in the member State of arrival;

    (ii) they are removed for the sole purpose of their being used by the owner in the course of a supply of services to be made by him;

    (iii) at the time of their removal there exists a legally binding obligation to make that supply of services; and

    (iv) the owner intends to remove them to the member State of dispatch upon his ceasing to use them in the course of making the supply;

(g) where—

    (i) temporary importation relief would have been afforded had the goods been imported from a place outside the member States; and

    (ii) the owner intends to export the goods to a place outside the member States or remove them to a member State other than the member State of arrival, in either case, not later than 2 years after the day upon which the goods were removed;

(h) where the goods are removed in accordance with an intention described in paragraph (d)(iii), (f)(iv) or (g)(ii) above;

(i) where goods which have been removed under the conditions described in paragraph (e) above are removed to the member State of dispatch when the valuation or work has been completed.

5 In the case of a removal falling within paragraph (d), (f) or (g) above, it shall be a condition of paragraph 5A or Schedule 2 to the Act [VATA 1994, Sch. 4, para. 6] not applying that the relevant intention of the owner is fulfilled.

Cross references – VAT Regulations 1995 (SI 1995/2518), reg. 24, 42: accounting payment and records.

COMMUNITY LEGISLATION RELATING TO TEMPORARY IMPORTATION RELIEF

Article 2

Council Regulation (EEC) No. 3599/82
Council Regulation (EEC) No. 1855/89
Council Regulation (EEC) No. 3312/89
Commission Regulation (EEC) No. 2249/91

VALUE ADDED TAX (PLACE OF SUPPLY OF SERVICES) ORDER 1992

(SI 1992/3121, as amended by SI 1995/3038, SI 1996/2992, SI 1997/1524, SI 1998/763).)

Made on 9 December 1992 by the Treasury, in exercise of the powers conferred on them by s. 6(6) of the Value Added Tax Act 1983 [VATA 1994, s. 7(11)] and of all other powers enabling them in that behalf.

PART I – PRELIMINARY

CITATION AND COMMENCEMENT

1   This Order may be cited as the Value Added Tax (Place of Supply of Services) Order 1992 and shall come into force on 1st January 1993.

INTERPRETATION

2   In this Order–

"**the Act**" means the Value Added Tax Act 1994;

"**ancillary transport services**" means loading, unloading, handling and similar activities;

"**intra-Community transport of goods**" means the transportation of goods which begins in one member State and ends in a different member State;

"**pleasure cruise**" includes a cruise wholly or partly for the purposes of education or training;

"**registration number**" means an identifying number assigned to a person by a member State for the purposes of value added tax in that member State.

History – In art. 2, the words "Value Added Tax Act 1994" were substituted for "Value Added Tax Act 1983" by SI 1995/3038, art. 3, operative from 1 January 1996.

REVOCATION

3   The Value Added Tax (Place of Supply) Order 1984 is hereby revoked.

PART II – RULES FOR DETERMINING PLACE OF SUPPLY OF SERVICES

4   The rules for determining where a supply of goods or of services is made shall be varied in accordance with the following provisions of this Order.

SERVICES RELATING TO LAND

5   Where a supply of services consists of–

(a)   the grant, assignment or surrender of–

    (i)   any interest in or right over land;

    (ii)   a personal right to call for or be granted any interest in or right over land; or

    (iii)   a licence to occupy land or any other contractual right exercisable over or in relation to land;

(b)   any works of construction, demolition, conversion, reconstruction, alteration, enlargement, repair or maintenance of a building or civil engineering work;

(c)   services such as are supplied by estate agents, auctioneers, architects, surveyors, engineers and others involved in matters relating to land,

it shall be treated as made where the land in connection with which the supply is made is situated.

TRANSPORT

6   Subject to articles 7 and 10 below, services consisting of the transportation of passengers or goods shall be treated as supplied in the country in which the transportation takes place, and only to the extent that it takes place in that country.

7　For the purposes of article 6 above, there shall be treated as taking place wholly in a country any transportation which takes place partly outside the territorial jurisdiction of that country where–

(a)　it takes place in the course of a journey between two points in that country, whether or not as part of a longer journey involving travel to or from another country; and

(b)　the means of transport used does not put in or land in another country in the course of the journey between those two points.

8　Any–

(a)　goods or services provided as part of a pleasure cruise; or

(b)　services consisting of the transportation of any luggage or motor vehicle accompanying (in either case) a passenger,

shall be treated as supplied in the same place as the transportation of the passenger is treated as supplied (whether or not they would otherwise be treated as supplied separately); and, for the purpose of this article, a pleasure cruise shall be treated as the transportation of passengers.

9　Subject to article 14 below, where a supply consists of ancillary transport services, it shall be treated as made where those services are physically performed.

10　Subject to article 14 below, where a supply of services consists of the intra-Community transport of goods, it shall be treated as made in the member State in which the transportation of the goods begins.

SERVICES OF INTERMEDIARIES

11　Subject to article 14 below, where services consist of the making of arrangements for the intra-Community transport of goods or of any other activity intended to facilitate the making of such a supply, they shall be treated as supplied in the member State where the transportation of the goods begins.

12　Subject to article 14 below where services consist of the making of arrangements for the supply by or to another person of ancillary transport services in connection with the intra-Community transport of goods or of any other activity intended to facilitate the making of such a supply, they shall be treated as supplied in the member State where the ancillary transport services are physically performed.

13　Subject to article 14 below, where services consist of the making of arrangements for a supply by or to another person or of any other activity intended to facilitate the making of such a supply, being a supply which is not of a description within articles 9 or 10 above or 16 below, those services shall be treated as supplied in the same place as the supply by or to that other person is treated as made.

USE OF CUSTOMER'S REGISTRATION NUMBER

14　Where a supply of services–

(a)　falls within articles 10 to 13 above;

(aa)　consists of the valuation of, or work carried out on, any goods which are then dispatched or transported out of the member State where those services were physically carried out; or

(b)　consists of ancillary transport services provided in connection with the intra-Community transport of goods,

and the recipient of those services makes use, for the purpose of the supply, of a registration number, then, notwithstanding any provision of this Order to the contrary, the supply shall be treated as made in the member State which issued the registration number if, and only if, the supply would otherwise be treated as taking place in a different member State.

History – In art. 14, at the end of para. (a), the word "or" was deleted by SI 1995/3038, art. 4(a), operative from 1 January 1996.
In art. 14(aa), the words "which are then dispatched or . . . physically carried out" were substituted by SI 1996/2992, art. 2(a), operative from 1 January 1997.
Art. 14, para. (aa) was inserted by SI 1995/3038, art. 4(b), operative from 1 January 1996.

SERVICES SUPPLIED WHERE PERFORMED

15　Where a supply of services consists of–

(a)　cultural, artistic, sporting, scientific, educational or entertainment services;

(b)　services relating to exhibitions, conferences or meetings;

(c)　services ancillary to, including those of organising, any supply of a description within paragraph (a) or (b) above; or

(d)   the valuation of, or work carried out on, any goods, save as provided by Article 14 above,

it shall be treated as made where the services are physically carried out.

History – In art. 15(c), the word "or" was added at the end by SI 1996/2992, art. 2(b), operative from 1 January 1997.
In art. 15(d), the words "save as provided by Article 14 above," were inserted by SI 1995/3038, art. 5, operative from 1 January 1996.

SERVICES SUPPLIED WHERE RECEIVED

16   Where a supply consists of any services of a description specified in any of paragraphs 1 to 8 of Schedule 5 to the Act and the recipient of that supply–

(a)   belongs in a country, other than the Isle of Man, which is not a member State; or

(b)   is a person who belongs in a member State, but in a country other than that in which the supplier belongs, and who–

    (i)   receives the supply for the purpose of a business carried on by him; and

    (ii)   is not treated as having himself supplied the services by virtue of section 8 of the Act,

it shall be treated as made where the recipient belongs.

History – In art. 16, the words "paragraphs 1 to 8 of Schedule 5" were substituted by SI 1995/3038, art. 6(a), operative from 1 January 1996.
Art. 16(b) was substituted by SI 1995/3038, art. 6(b), operative from 1 January 1996.

HIRE OF MEANS OF TRANSPORT

17   Where a supply of services consists of–

(a)   the letting on hire of any means of transport; or

(b)   services described in paragraph 7 or 7A of Schedule 5 to the Act,

and those services would be treated, apart from this article, as supplied in the United Kingdom, they shall not be treated as supplied in the United Kingdom to the extent that the effective use and enjoyment of the services takes place outside the member States.

History – Art. 17 was substituted by SI 1998/763, art. 3, operative in relation to any services supplied on or after 18 March 1998.
In former art. 17, the words "to the extent that" were substituted by SI 1997/1524, art. 3, operative in relation to any services performed on or after 1 July 1997.

18   Where a supply of services consists of–

(a)   the letting on hire of any means of transport; or

(b)   services described in paragraph 7 or 7A of Schedule 5 to the Act,

and those services would be treated, apart from this article, as supplied in a place outside the member States, they shall be treated as supplied in the United Kingdom to the extent that the effective use and enjoyment of the services takes place in the United Kingdom.

History – Art. 18 was substituted by SI 1998/763, art. 4, operative in relation to any services supplied on or after 18 March 1998.
In former art. 18, the words "to the extent that" were substituted by SI 1997/1524, art. 4, operative in relation to any services performed on or after 1 July 1997.

19   [Omitted by SI 1998/763, art. 5, operative in relation to any services supplied on or after 18 March 1998.]

History – Former art. 19 was inserted by SI 1997/1524, art. 5, operative in relation to any services performed on or after 1 July 1997.

20   [Omitted by SI 1998/763, art. 5, operative in relation to any services supplied on or after 18 March 1998.]

History – Former art. 20 was inserted by SI 1997/1524, art. 5, operative in relation to any services performed on or after 1 July 1997.

Cross references – VAT Regulations 1995 (SI 1995/2518), reg. 90(5): relevant telecommunications services.

21(1)   The place of supply of a right to services shall be the same as the place of supply of the services to which the right relates (whether or not the right is exercised).

21(2)   The reference to a **right to services** in para. (1) above shall include a reference to any right, option or priority with respect to the supply of services and to the supply of an interest deriving from any right to services.

History – Art. 21 was inserted by SI 1997/1524, art. 5, operative in relation to any services performed on or after 1 July 1997.

VALUE ADDED TAX (CARS) ORDER 1992

(SI 1992/3122 as amended by SI 1993/2951, SI 1995/1269, SI 1995/1667,
SI 1997/1615, SI 1998/759, SI 1999/2832)

Made on 9 December 1992 by the Treasury, in exercise of the powers conferred on them by s. 3(3), 3(5), 18(1), 18(2), 18(3), 18(4), 18(5), 18(6) and 29(2) of the Value Added Tax Act 1983 [VATA 1994, s. 5(3) and (5), 32(1)–(6) and 43(2)] and of all other powers enabling them in that behalf.

CITATION AND COMMENCEMENT

1 This Order may be cited as the Value Added Tax (Cars) Order 1992 and shall come into force on 1st January 1993.

INTERPRETATION

2 In this Order–

"**the Act**" means the Value Added Tax Act 1994;

"**the Manx Act**" means the Value Added Tax Act 1994;

"**finance agreement**" means an agreement for the sale of goods whereby the property in those goods is not to be transferred until the whole of the price has been paid and the seller retains the right to repossess the goods;

"**insurer**" means a person permitted, in accordance with section 2 of the Insurance Companies Act 1982 to effect and carry out contracts of insurance against risks of loss of or damage to goods;

"**motor car**" means any motor vehicle of a kind normally used on public roads which has three or more wheels and either–

(a)　is constructed or adapted solely or mainly for the carriage of passengers; or

(b)　has to the rear of the driver's seat roofed accommodation which is fitted with side windows or which is constructed or adapted for the fitting of side windows;

but does not include–

(i)　vehicles capable of accommodating only one person;

(ii)　vehicles which meet the requirements of Schedule 6 to the Road Vehicles (Construction and Use) Regulations 1986 and are capable of carrying twelve or more seated persons;

(iii)　vehicles of not less than three tonnes unladen weight (as defined in the Table to regulation 3(2) of the Road Vehicles (Construction and Use) Regulations 1986);

(iv)　vehicles constructed to carry a payload (the difference between a vehicle's kerb weight (as defined in the Table to regulation 3(2) of the Road Vehicles (Construction and Use) Regulations 1986) and its maximum gross weight (as defined in that Table)) of one tonne or more;

(v)　caravans, ambulances and prison vans;

(vi)　vehicles constructed for a special purpose other than the carriage of persons and having no other accommodation for carrying persons than such as is incidental to that purpose;

"**auctioneer**" means a person who sells or offers for sale goods at any public sale where persons become purchasers by competition, being the highest bidders.

History – In art. 2, in the definition of "the Act", the year "1994" was substituted for "1983" by SI 1995/1269, art. 3(a), operative from 1 June 1995.
In art. 2, the definition of "the Manx Act" was inserted by SI 1995/1269, art. 3(b), operative from 1 June 1995.
In art. 2, in the definition of "the Manx Act", the words "Value Added Tax Act 1996" were substituted by SI 1998/759, art. 3, operative from 18 March 1998.
In art. 2, the definition of "car dealer" was omitted by SI 1999/2832, art. 3(a), operative from 1 December 1999. The former definition reads as follows:
""**car dealer**" means a taxable person who carries on a business which consists of or includes the sale of motor cars;"
In art. 2, the definition of "motor car" was substituted by SI 1999/2832, art. 3(b), operative from 1 December 1999. The former definition reads as follows:
""**motor car**" means any motor vehicle of a kind normally used on public roads which has three or more wheels and either–
　　(a)　is constructed or adapted solely or mainly for the carriage of passengers; or
　　(b)　has to the rear of driver's seat roofed accommodation which is fitted with side windows or which is constructed or adapted for the fitting of side windows;
but does not include–
　　(i)　vehicles capable of accommodating only one person or suitable for carrying twelve or more persons;
　　(ii)　vehicles of not less than three tonnes unladen weight;"

(iii)   caravans, ambulances and prison vans;

(iv)   vehicles of a type approved by the Assistant Commissioner of Police of the Metropolis conforming to the conditions of fitness for the time being laid down by him for the purposes of the London Cab Order 1934; or

(v)   vehicles constructed for a special purpose other than the carriage of persons and having no other accommodation for carrying persons than such as is incidental to that purpose;"

In art. 2, the definition of "auctioneer" was inserted by SI 1995/1269, art. 3(c), operative from 1 June 1995.

Extra-statutory concessions – 3.12 (Notice 48 (1999 edn)): buses with special facilities for carrying disabled persons – capacity to carry under 12 passengers due to wheelchair facilities – input tax may be recoverable.

REVOCATIONS

3   The provisions specified in the first column of the Schedule to this Order are hereby revoked to the extent specified in the second column of that Schedule.

TREATMENT OF TRANSACTIONS

4(1)   Subject to paragraphs (1A) to (2) below, each of the following descriptions of transactions shall be treated as neither a supply of goods nor a supply of services–

(a)   the disposal of a used motor car by a person who repossessed it under the terms of a finance agreement, where the motor car is in the same condition as it was in when it was repossessed;

(b)   the disposal of a used motor car by an insurer who has taken it in the settlement of a claim under a policy of insurance, where the motor car is disposed of in the same condition as it was in when it was so taken;

(c)   the disposal of a motor car for no consideration;

(d)   services in connection with a supply of a used motor car provided by an agent acting in his own name to the purchaser of the motor car the consideration for which is taken into account by virtue of article 8(8) below in calculating the price at which the agent sold the motor car;

(e)   services in connection with the sale of a used motor car provided by an auctioneer acting in his own name to the vendor or the purchaser of the motor car the consideration for which is taken into account by virtue of article 8(9) below in calculating the price at which the auctioneer obtained (or as the case be) sold the motor car;

(f)   a relevant supply of services by a taxable person to whom a motor car has been let on hire or supplied or by whom a motor car has been acquired from another member State or imported.

4(1A)   Paragraph (1) above shall not apply in relation to a case falling within paragraph (1)(a) to (c) above unless the tax on any previous supply, acquisition or importation was wholly excluded from credit under section 25 of the Act.

4(1B)   Paragraph (1) above shall not apply in relation to a case falling within paragraph (1)(f) above unless the tax on any previous letting on hire, supply, acquisition or importation was wholly or partly excluded from credit under section 25 of the Act.

4(1C)   For the purposes of paragraph (1)(f) above a **relevant supply of services** is–

(a)   the letting on hire of a motor car to any person for no consideration or for a consideration which is less than that which would be payable in money if it were a commercial transaction conducted at arms length; or

(b)   the making available of a motor car (otherwise than by letting it on hire) to any person (including, where the taxable person is an individual, himself, and where the taxable person is a partnership, a partner) for private use, whether or not for a consideration.

4(2)   Nothing in paragraph (1)(a) or (b) above shall be construed as meaning that a transaction is not a supply for the purposes of section 11(1)(a) of the Act.

History – In art. 4(1), the words "Subject to paragraphs (1A) to (2) below," were inserted by SI 1995/1667, art. 3(a), operative from 1 August 1995.
In art. 4(1)(c), the words "where, on a previous supply of the motor car or on its acquisition from another member State or on its importation, tax charged thereon had been excluded from any credit by virtue of an order made under section 25(7) of the Act" which appeared at the end were deleted by SI 1995/1667, art. 3(b), operative from 1 August 1995.
In art. 4(1)(c) in the deleted words, the words "25(7)" were substituted for the words "14(10)" by SI 1995/1269, art. 4(a), operative from 1 June 1995.
Art. 4(1)(d) and (e) were inserted by SI 1995/1269, art. 4(c), operative from 1 June 1995.
Art. 4(1)(f), was added by SI 1995/1667, art. 3(c), operative from 1 August 1995.
Art. 4(1A)–(1C), were inserted by SI 1995/1667, art. 3(d), operative from 1 August 1995.
In art. 4(2), the words "11(1)(a)" were substituted for the words "8A(1)(a)" by SI 1995/1269, art. 4(b), operative from 1 June 1995.

4A   Paragraph 5(4) of Schedule 4 to the Act shall not apply in relation to a motor car to which article 5 below applies which is used or made available in circumstances where, but for the operation of that paragraph, it would be treated by virtue of that article as supplied to and by a taxable person.

History – In art. 4A, the words "article 5" were substituted for the words "either article 5 or article 6" by SI 1999/2832, art. 4(a), operative from 1 December 1999.
In art. 4A, the words "that article" were substituted for the words "one or other of those articles" by SI 1999/2832, art. 4(b), operative from 1 December 1999.
Art. 4A was inserted by SI 1995/1667, art. 4, operative from 1 August 1995.

SELF-SUPPLIES

5(1) This article applies to any motor car–

(a) which has been produced by a taxable person otherwise than by the conversion of a vehicle obtained by him;

(b) which has been produced by the taxable person by the conversion of another vehicle (whether a motor car or not) and in relation to which the condition in paragraph (2) below is satisfied;

(c) which was supplied to, or acquired from another member State or imported by, a taxable person and in relation to which the condition in paragraph (2) below is satisfied, or

(d) which was transferred to a taxable person as an asset of a business or part of a business in the course of the transfer of that business or part of a business as a going concern–

  (i) in circumstances where the transfer was treated as neither a supply of goods nor a supply of services by virtue of an Order made or having effect as if made under section 5(3) of the Act;

  (ii) in the hands of the transferor or any predecessor of his the motor car was one to which this article applied by virtue of subparagraph (a), (b) or (c) above; and

  (iii) the motor car has not been treated as supplied by virtue of this article to and by the transferor or any of his predecessors.

5(2) The condition referred to in paragraph (1)(b) and (c) above is that the tax on the supply to, or acquisition or importation by, the taxable person of the motor car or the vehicle from which it was converted, as the case may be, was not wholly excluded from credit under section 25 of the Act.

5(2A) For the purposes of paragraph (1)(d) above a person is a predecessor of a transferor if–

(a) he transferred the motor car as an asset of a business or part of a business which he transferred as a going concern–

  (i) to the transferor, or

  (ii) where the motor car has been the subject of more than one such transfer, to a person who made one of those transfers; and

(b) the transfer of the motor car was treated as neither a supply of goods nor a supply of services by virtue of any Order made or having effect as if made under section 5(3) of the Act.

5(3) Where a motor car to which this article applies–

(a) has not been supplied by the taxable person in the course or furtherance of a business carried on by him; and

(b) is used by him such that had it been supplied to, or imported or acquired from another member State by, him at that time his entitlement to credit under section 25 of the Act in respect of the VAT chargeable on such a supply, importation or acquisition from another member State would have been wholly excluded by virtue of article 7 of the Value Added Tax (Input Tax) Order 1992,

it shall be treated for the purposes of the Act as both supplied to him for the purposes of a business carried on by him and supplied by him for the purposes of that business.

History – In art. 5(1)(b), the word "or" at the end was omitted by SI 1999/2832, art. 5(a), operative from 1 December 1999.
In art. 5(1), the word "or" and para. (d) were substituted for the words "but does not apply to any motor car to which article 6 below applies" which appeared after para. (c) by SI 1999/2832, art. 5(b), operative from 1 December 1999.
Art. 5(2A) was inserted by SI 1999/2832, art. 6, operative from 1 December 1999.
Art. 5(3) was substituted by SI 1999/2832, art. 7, operative from 1 December 1999. Former art. 5(3) reads as follows:
"**5(3)** Where a motor car to which this article applies–
(a) has not been supplied by the taxable person in the course or furtherance of a business carried on by him; and
(b) is used by him such that it is not used exclusively for the purposes of a business carried on by him,
it shall be treated for the purposes of the Act as both supplied to him for the purposes of a business carried on by him and supplied by him for the purposes of that business."
Art. 5 was substituted by SI 1995/1667, art. 5, operative from 1 August 1995. Former art. 5 read as follows:
"**5(1)** This article applies to the following motor cars produced or obtained by a taxable person in the course or furtherance of any business carried on by him, that is to say–
(a) any motor car produced by him otherwise than by the conversion of a vehicle obtained by him;

(b)   any motor car produced by him by the conversion of another vehicle (whether a motor car or not) and in respect of which the conditions specified in paragraph (2) below are satisfied;

(c)   any motor car obtained by him and in respect of which the conditions specified in paragraph (2) below are satisfied.

5(2)   The conditions mentioned in paragraph (1) above are–

(a)   that the motor car or other vehicle was supplied to the taxable person or was acquired by him from another member State or was imported by him; and

(b)   tax was chargeable on that supply, acquisition or importation; and

(c)   the taxable person is entitled to credit for that tax under sections 25 and 26 of the Act.

5(3)   Save in the case of a motor car to which article 6 below applies, where a motor car to which this article applies–

(a)   is neither supplied by the taxable person in the course or furtherance of any business carried on by him, nor converted into another vehicle (whether a motor car or not) in the course or furtherance of that business; but

(b)   is used by him for the purpose of that business,

the motor car shall be treated for the purposes of the Act as both supplied to him for the purposes of that business and supplied by him in the course or furtherance of that business, except where the Commissioners are satisfied that the motor car is, or is to be, used solely for the purpose of research and development in his business as a producer of motor cars (other than as a producer of motor cars solely by the conversion of vehicles)."

In former art. 5(2)(c), the words "25 and 26" were substituted for the words "14 and 15" by SI 1995/1269, art. 5, operative from 1 June 1995.

6   [Omitted by SI 1999/2832, art. 8.]

History – Art. 6 was omitted by SI 1999/2832, art. 8, operative from 1 December 1999. Former art. 6 reads as follows:

"6(1)   This article applies to any motor car which has been supplied to, or acquired from another member State or imported by, a taxable person primarily for the purpose of–

(a)   being provided by him for hire with the services of a driver for the purpose of carrying passengers;

(b)   being provided by him for self-drive hire; or

(c)   being used as a vehicle in which instruction in the driving of a motor car is to be given by him.

6(1A)   Where a motor car to which this article applies–

(a)   is neither supplied nor converted into another vehicle (whether a motor car or not) by the taxable person, in either case, in the course or furtherance of any business carried on by him; and

(b)   is used by him primarily for a purpose other than one of the purposes described in paragraph (1) above, but is not used exclusively for the purposes of a business carried on by him,

it shall be treated for the purposes of the Act as both supplied to him for the purposes of that business and supplied by him in the course or furtherance of that business.

6(2)   In this article **"self-drive hire"** means hire where the hirer is the person normally expected to drive the motor car and the period of hire to each hirer, together with the period of hire of any other motor car expected to be hired to him by the taxable person–

(a)   will normally be less than 30 consecutive days; and

(b)   will normally be less than 90 days in any period of 12 months."

Former art. 6(1) and (1A) were substituted for former art. 6(1) and (1A) by SI 1995/1667, art. 6, operative from 1 August 1995. In former art. 6(1)(d), the words "under an agreement which imposes a" were substituted for the words "who is not a taxable person on" by SI 1993/2951, art. 2(a), operative from 1 January 1994.

Former art. 6(1A) was inserted by SI 1993/2951, art. 2(b), operative from 1 January 1994.

6A   [Omitted by SI 1999/2832, art. 8.]

History – Art. 6A was omitted by SI 1999/2832, art. 8, operative from 1 December 1999. Former art. 6A reads as follows:

"6A   For the purposes of articles 5 and 6 above article 7 of the Value Added Tax (Input Tax) Order 1992 shall apply for the purpose of determining whether a motor car is used exclusively for the purposes of the taxable person's business as it would apply for the purpose of determining whether he so intended to use it."

Former art. 6A was inserted by SI 1995/1667, art. 7, operative from 1 August 1995.

7   Article 5 above shall apply in relation to any bodies corporate which are treated for the purposes of section 43 of the Act as members of a group as if those bodies were one person, but any motor car which would fall to be treated as supplied to and by that person shall be treated as supplied to and by the representative member.

History – In art. 7, the words "Article 5" were substituted for the words "Articles 5 and 6" by SI 1999/2832, art. 9, operative from 1 December 1999.

In art. 7, the number "43" was substituted for the number "29" by SI 1995/1269, art. 6, operative from 1 June 1995.

RELIEF FOR SECOND-HAND MOTOR CARS

8(1)   Subject to complying with such conditions (including the keeping of such records and accounts) as the Commissioners may direct in a notice published by them for the purposes of this Order or may otherwise direct, and subject to paragraph (3) below, where a person supplies a used motor car which he took possession of in any of the circumstances set out in paragraph (2) below, he may opt to account for the VAT chargeable on the supply on the profit margin on the supply instead of by reference to its value.

8(2)   The circumstances referred to in paragraph (1) above are that the taxable person took possession of the motor car pursuant to–

(a)   a supply in respect of which no VAT was chargeable under the Act or under Part I of the Manx Act;

(b)   a supply on which VAT was chargeable on the profit margin in accordance with paragraph (1) above, or a corresponding provision made under the Manx Act or a corresponding provision of the law of another member State;

(bb)   a supply received before 1st March 2000 to which the provisions of article 7(4) of the Value Added Tax (Input Tax) Order 1992 applied;

(c)   a transaction except one relating to the transfer of the assets of a business or part of a business as a going concern which was treated by virtue of any Order made or having effect as if made under section 5(3) of the Act or under the corresponding provisions of the Manx Act as being neither a supply of goods nor a supply of services;

(d)   a transaction relating to the transfer of the assets of a business or part of a business as a going concern which was treated as neither a supply of goods nor a supply of services if the transferor took possession of the goods in any of the circumstances described in this paragraph.

8(3)   This article does not apply to—

(a)   a supply which is a letting on hire;

(b)   the supply by any person of a motor car which was produced by him, if it was neither previously supplied by him in the course or furtherance of any business carried on by him nor treated as so supplied by virtue of article 5 above;

(c)   any supply if an invoice or similar document showing an amount as being VAT or as being attributable to VAT is issued in respect of the supply;

(d)   [Deleted by SI 1995/1667, art. 8(b).]

8(4)   [Deleted by SI 1995/1667, art. 8(c).]

8(5)   Subject to paragraph (6) below, for the purposes of determining the **profit margin**—

(a)   the price at which the motor car was obtained shall be calculated as follows—

     (i)   (where the taxable person took possession of the used motor car pursuant to a supply) in the same way as the consideration for the supply would be calculated for the purposes of the Act;

     (ii)   (where the taxable person is a sole proprietor and the used motor car was supplied to him in his private capacity) in the same way as the consideration for the supply to him as a private individual would be calculated for the purposes of the Act;

     (iii)   (where the taxable person took possession of the goods pursuant to a transaction relating to the transfer of the assets of a business or part of a business as a going concern which was treated by virtue of any Order made or having effect as if made under section 5(3) of the Act, or under the corresponding provisions of the Manx Act, as neither a supply of goods nor a supply of services) as being the price at which the earliest of his predecessors obtained the goods;

(b)   the price at which the motor car is sold shall be calculated in the same way as the consideration for the supply would be calculated for the purposes of the Act;

(c)   in relation to any goods, a person is the predecessor of another for the purposes of this article if—

     (i)   that other person is a person to whom he has transferred assets of his business by a transfer of that business, or a part of it, as a going concern;

     (ii)   those assets consisted of or included those goods; and

     (iii)   the transfer of the assets is one falling by virtue of an Order made or having effect as if made under section 5(3) of the Act, or under the corresponding provisions of the Manx Act, to be treated as neither a supply of goods nor a supply of services;

and the reference in sub-paragraph (a) above to a person's predecessors includes a reference to the predecessors of his predecessors through any number of transfers.

8(6)   Subject to paragraph (7) below, where the taxable person is an agent acting in his own name the price at which the motor car was obtained shall be calculated in accordance with paragraph 5(a) above but the selling price calculated in accordance with paragraph 5(b) above shall be increased by the amount of any consideration payable to the taxable person in respect of services supplied by him to the purchaser in connection with the supply of the motor car.

8(7)   Instead of calculating the price at which the motor car was obtained or supplied in accordance with paragraph (6) above, an auctioneer acting in his own name may—

(a)   calculate the price at which the motor car was obtained by deducting from the successful bid the consideration for any services supplied by him to the vendor in connection with the sale of the motor car;

(b)   calculate the price at which the motor car was supplied by adding to the successful bid the consideration for any supply of services by him to the purchaser in connection with the sale of the motor car,

in either (or both) cases excluding the consideration for supplies of services that are not chargeable to VAT.

History – In art. 8(2)(bb), the words "received before 1st March 2000" were inserted by SI 1999/2832, art. 10, operative from 1 March 2000.
Art. 8(2)(bb) was inserted by SI 1995/1667, art. 8(a), operative from 1 August 1995.
Art. 8(2)(c) was substituted by SI 1997/1615, art. 3, with effect from 3 July 1997. Former art. 8(2)(c) reads as follows:
"(c)   a transaction which was treated by virtue of any Order made under section 5(3) of the Act or under the corresponding provisions of the Manx Act as being neither a supply of goods nor a supply of services."
Art. 8(2)(d) was inserted by SI 1997/1615, art. 4, with effect from 3 July 1997.
Art. 8(3)(d) was deleted by SI 1995/1667, art. 8(b), operative from 1 August 1995. Former art. 8(3)(d) read as follows:
"(d)   save where it has previously been treated as supplied by him by virtue of article 6 above, the supply by a taxable person of a motor car where its supply to him or its acquisition by him from another member State, or its importation by him, was primarily for any of the following purposes–
          (i)   being provided by him for hire with the services of a driver for the purpose of carrying passengers;
being provided by him for self-drive hire;
being used as a vehicle in which instruction in the driving of a motor car is to be given by him; or
the letting on hire to a person who is not a taxable person on condition that he uses the motor car primarily for one of the purposes described in paragraphs (i) to (iii)."
Art. 8(4) was deleted by SI 1995/1667, art. 8(c), operative from 1 August 1995. Former art. 8(4) read as follows:
"**8(4)**   For the purposes of paragraph (3)(d) above **"self-drive hire"** means hire where the hirer is the person normally expected to drive the motor car and the period of hire to each hirer, together with the period of hire of any of any other motor car expected to be hired to him by the taxable person–
          (a)   will normally be less than 30 consecutive days; and
          (b)   will normally be less than 90 days in any period of 12 months."
art. 8(5)(a)(iii) was inserted by SI 1998/759, art. 4(1), operative from 18 March 1998.
art. 8(5)(c) was inserted by SI 1998/759, art. 4(2), operative from 18 March 1998.
Art. 8 was substituted by SI 1995/1269, art. 7, operative from 1 June 1995. Former art. 8 read as follows:
"**8(1)**   Subject to paragraph (2) below–
(a)   on the supply by any person of a used motor car, tax shall be chargeable as if the supply were for a consideration equal to the excess of–
          (i)   the consideration for which the motor car is supplied by him, over
the consideration for which the motor car was obtained by him,
          and accordingly shall not be charged unless there is such an excess;
(b)   on the supply by a person of a used motor car which was acquired by him from another member State, or imported by him, the consideration for which the motor car was obtained by him shall be taken to be the value of its acquisition or, as the case may require, its value for the purposes of charging tax on importation, together with any tax chargeable in respect of the acquisition, or, as the case may be, the importation of the motor car;
(c)   on the supply by a person of a used car previously treated under article 5 above as supplied by him, paragraph (a) above shall apply as if for the consideration referred to in sub-paragraph (ii) there were substituted the amount by reference to which tax was chargeable on the previous supply plus the tax so chargeable.
8(2)   This article does not apply to–
(a)   a supply which is a letting on hire;
(b)   the supply by any person of a motor car which was produced by him, if it was neither previously supplied by him in the course or furtherance of any business carried on by him nor treated as so supplied by virtue of article 5 above;
(c)   any supply if an invoice or similar document showing an amount as being tax or as being attributable to tax is issued in respect of the supply;
(d)   a supply by a car dealer unless he keeps such records and accounts as the Commissioners may specify in a notice published by them for the purposes of this Order or may recognise as sufficient for those purposes;
(e)   save where it has previously been treated as supplied by him by virtue of article 6 above, the supply by a taxable person of a motor car where its supply to him, or its acquisition by him from another member State, or its importation by him, was primarily for any of the following purposes–
being provided by him for hire with the services of a driver for the purpose of carrying passengers;
being provided by him for self-drive hire;
being used as a vehicle in which instruction in the driving of a motor car is to be given by him; or
the letting on hire to a person under an agreement which imposes a condition that he uses the motor car primarily for one of the purposes described in paragraphs (i) to (iii) above.
8(3)   For the purposes of paragraph (2)(e) above **"self-drive hire"** means hire where the hirer is the person normally expected to drive the motor car and the period of hire to each hirer, together with the period of hire of any other motor car expected to be hired to him by the taxable person–
          (a)   will normally be less than 30 consecutive days; and
          (b)   will normally be less than 90 days in any period of 12 months.
8(4)   Where a car dealer has failed to keep all such records and accounts as the Commissioners have specified, and the Commissioners do not recognise other records and accounts kept as sufficient, tax shall be chargeable as provided in paragraph (5) below if the following conditions are satisfied–
(a)   such records as the Commissioners have specified are available in relation to the purchase of the motor car or in relation to the supply of the motor car by him;
(b)   the Commissioners are of the opinion that the mark-up achieved by him does not exceed 100 per cent; and
(c)   the supply is otherwise eligible for the relief afforded by this article.
8(5)   *The tax chargeable in the circumstances referred to in paragraph (4) above shall be either–*
(a)   *where only the specified records in relation to the purchase of the motor car are available, as if the supply by the car dealer were for a consideration equal to the consideration for which the motor car was purchased by him; or*
(b)   *where only the specified records in relation to the supply by him are available, as if the supply by the car dealer were for a consideration equal to half the consideration for which the motor car was supplied by him."*
In former art. 8(2)(e)(iv), the words "under an agreement which imposes a" were substituted for the words "who is not a taxable person on" by SI 1993/2951, art. 2(c), operative from 1 January 1994.

Official publications – Notice 718.

REVOCATIONS

Provision	Extent of Revocation
The Value Added Tax (Cars) Order 1980 (No. 442)	The whole Order insofar as it contains provisions which were subject to annulment in pursuance of a resolution of the House of Commons by virtue of section 43(3) of the Finance Act 1972
The Value Added Tax (Cars) (Amendment) Order 1984 (No. 33)	The whole Order
The Value Added Tax (Cars) (Amendment) Order 1989 (No. 959)	The whole Order
The Value Added Tax (Cars) (Amendment) Order 1990 (No. 315)	The whole Order
The Value Added Tax (Cars) (Amendment) Order 1992 (No. 627)	The whole Order insofar as not previously revoked.

VALUE ADDED TAX (IMPORTED GOLD) RELIEF ORDER 1992

(SI 1992/3124)

Whereas it appears necessary to the Treasury that the relief from value added tax provided by this Order should be allowed with a view to conforming with art. 14.1(j) of Council Directive 77/388 and art. 189 of the EEC Treaty:

Now therefore the Treasury, by virtue of the powers conferred on them by s. 19(1) of the Value Added Tax Act 1988 [VATA 1994, s. 37(1)] and of all other powers enabling them in that behalf, hereby make the following Order:

1 This Order may be cited as the Value Added Tax (Imported Gold) Relief Order 1992 and shall come into force on 1st January 1993.

2 The tax chargeable upon the importation of gold (including gold coins) from a place outside the Member States shall not be payable where the importation is by a Central Bank.

3 The Value Added Tax (Imported Goods) Relief Order 1977 is hereby revoked.

VALUE ADDED TAX (SUPPLY OF TEMPORARILY IMPORTED GOODS) ORDER 1992

(SI 1992/3130)

Made on 9 December 1992 by the Treasury, in exercise of the powers conferred on them by s. 3(3) of the Value Added Tax Act 1983 [VATA 1994, s. 5(3)] and of all other powers enabling them in that behalf.

1 This Order may be cited as the Value Added Tax (Supply of Temporarily Imported Goods) Order 1992 and shall come into force on 1st January 1993.

2(1) Where goods held under temporary importation arrangements are supplied, that supply shall be treated as neither a supply of goods nor a supply of services provided that—

(a)   the goods remain eligible for temporary importation arrangements; and

(b)   the supply is to a person established outside the member States.

2(2)   **"Goods held under temporary importation arrangements"** means goods placed under customs arrangements with total relief from customs duty within the meaning of Council Regulation (EEC) No. 3599/82, whether or not the goods are subject to customs duty.

VALUE ADDED TAX (TREATMENT OF TRANSACTIONS) (NO. 2) ORDER 1992

(SI 1992/3132)

Made on 9 December 1992 by the Treasury, in exercise of the powers conferred on them by s. 8A(4) of the Value Added Tax Act 1983 [VATA 1994, s. 11(4)] and of all other powers enabling them in that behalf.

1   This Order may be cited as the Value Added Tax (Treatment of Transactions) (No. 2) Order 1992, and shall come into force on 1st January 1993.

2(1)   Where gold is supplied to a Central Bank by a supplier in another member State, and the transaction involves the removal of the gold from that or some other member State to the United Kingdom, the taking possession of the gold by the Central Bank concerned is not to be treated for the purposes of the Value Added Tax Act 1983 [VATA 1994] as the acquisition of goods from another member State.

2(2)   For the purposes of this article, **gold** includes gold coins.

CUSTOMS AND EXCISE (PERSONAL RELIEFS FOR SPECIAL VISITORS) ORDER 1992

(SI 1992/3156)

Made on 10 December 1992 by the Commissioners of Customs and Excise, in exercise of the powers conferred on them by s. 13A of the Customs and Excise Duties (General Reliefs) Act 1979 and of all other powers enabling them in that behalf.

PART I – PRELIMINARY

1   This Order may be cited as the Customs and Excise (Personal Reliefs for Special Visitors) Order 1992 and shall come into force on 1st January 1993.

PART II – INTERPRETATION

2   In this Order–

"acquisition" means an acquisition of goods from another member State within the meaning of section 2A of the Value Added Tax Act 1983 [VATA 1994, s. 10], and **"acquired"** shall be construed accordingly;

"duty" means any duty of customs or duty of excise;

"importation" means an importation from a place outside the member States, and

"imported" shall be construed accordingly;

"relief" means the remission of any duty or tax which is chargeable and which a person, whether the person upon whom the relief is conferred or some other person, would be liable to pay were it not for the relief conferred;

"supply" means a supply within the meaning of section 3 of the Value Added Tax Act 1983 [VATA 1994, s. 5] and **"supplied"** shall be construed accordingly;

"tax" means value added tax;

"United Kingdom national" means a British citizen, a British Dependent Territories citizen, a British National (Overseas) or a British Overseas citizen;

"used", in relation to a person's use of consumable property, includes having the property at his disposal;

"**warehouse**" means a warehouse within the meaning of section 1(1) of the Customs and Excise Management Act 1979, and "**removal from warehouse**" shall be construed accordingly.

PART III – CONDITIONS ATTACHING TO PART VI RELIEFS

3   In this Part–

"**entitled person**" means an entitled person for the purposes of Part VI.

4   It shall be a condition of the relief conferred under article 16 below that the entitled person deliver or cause to be delivered to the supplier of the motor vehicle a certificate in the form numbered 1 in the Schedule to this Order–

(a)   containing full information in respect of the matters specified therein; and

(b)   signed–

    (i)   as to Part A, by the entitled person upon whom the relief is conferred;

    (ii)   as to Part B, by the head of the mission or other body or organisation of which the entitled person is a member;

    (iii)   as to Part C, by the Secretary of State or a person authorised to sign on his behalf; and

    (iv)   as to Part D, by the supplier,

before the supply is made.

PART IV – CONDITIONS ATTACHING TO PART VII RELIEFS

5(1)   In this Part–

"**entitled person**" means an entitled person for the purposes of Part VII.

5(2)   For the purposes of articles 6 and 7 below, any reference to a certificate shall be construed as including a reference to a copy of such a certificate.

6(1)   It shall be a condition of relief conferred under article 19 below that the entitled person deliver or cause to be delivered in accordance with paragraph (2) below five certificates in the form numbered 2 in the Schedule to this Order–

(a)   containing full information in respect of the matters specified therein; and

(b)   signed–

    (i)   as to Part A, by the entitled person upon whom the relief is conferred; and

    (ii)   as to Part B, by the officer commanding the visiting force or other body or organisation of which the entitled person is a member or by a person authorised to sign on his behalf.

6(2)   The certificates referred to in paragraph (1) above shall be delivered before the supply is made as follows:

(a)   two certificates shall be delivered to the visiting force or other body or organisation of which the entitled person is a member;

(b)   two certificates shall be delivered to the proper officer; and

(c)   one certificate shall be delivered to the supplier of the motor vehicle.

7(1)   It shall be a condition of relief conferred under article 20 below in respect of a motor vehicle that the entitled person deliver or cause to be delivered in accordance with paragraph (2) below four certificates in the form numbered 3 in the Schedule to this Order–

(a)   containing full information in respect of the matters specified therein; and

(b)   signed–

    (i)   as to Part A, by the entitled person upon whom the relief is conferred; and

    (ii)   as to Part B, by the officer commanding the visiting force or other body or organisation of which the entitled person is a member or by a person authorised to sign on his behalf.

7(2)   The certificates referred to in paragraph (1) above shall be delivered before the goods are removed by or on behalf of the entitled person as follows:

(a)   one certificate shall be delivered to the visiting force or other body or organisation of which the entitled person is a member; and

(b)   three certificates shall be delivered to the proper officer.

PART V – CONDITIONS ATTACHING TO ALL RELIEFS

8   In this Part–

"**entitled person**" means an entitled person for the purposes of either part VI or Part VII of this Order.

9   An entitled person upon whom any relief is conferred under any Part of this Order shall be bound by the conditions described in the following provisions of this Part and in Part III or IV above, as the case may be.

10(1)   It shall be a condition of the relief that the goods shall not be lent, hired-out, given as security or transferred by the entitled person or any other person without the prior authorisation in writing of the Commissioners.

10(2)   Where the Commissioners authorise such disposal as is mentioned in paragraph (1) above, they may discharge the relief and the entitled person to whom the relief was afforded shall forthwith pay the duty or tax at the rate then in force, provided that where a lower rate was in force when relief was afforded the amount payable shall be determined by reference to the lower rate.

11   It shall be a condition of the relief that the goods are used exclusively by the entitled person or members of his family forming part of his household.

12   Where relief has been afforded and subsequently the Commissioners are not satisfied that any condition attaching to such relief, whether by virtue of a provision of this Order or otherwise, has been complied with, then, unless the Commissioners sanction the non-compliance in writing, the duty or tax shall become payable forthwith and the goods shall be liable to forfeiture.

13   Where relief has been afforded, but any duty or tax subsequently becomes payable by virtue of article 12 above, the following persons shall be jointly and severally liable to pay it–

(a)   the entitled person upon whom the relief was conferred;

(b)   any person who, at or after the time of the non-compliance with the condition which has caused the duty or tax to become payable, has been in possession of the goods.

PART VI – DIPLOMATS ETC.

14   In this Part–

"**entitled person**" means:

(a)   any person enjoying any privilege or immunity by virtue [of] his being–

   (i)   a diplomatic agent for the purposes of the Diplomatic Privileges Act 1964,

   (ii)   a senior officer of the Commonwealth Secretariat for the purposes of the Commonwealth Secretariat Act 1966,

   (iii)   a consular officer for the purposes of the Consular Relations Act 1968,

   (iv)   a representative or a person recognised as holding a rank equivalent to a diplomatic agent for the purposes of the International Organisations Act 1968, or

(b)   any person enjoying, under or by virtue of section 2 of the European Communities Act 1972, any privilege or immunity similar to those enjoyed under or by virtue of the enactments referred to in paragraph (a) above by the persons therein specified,

who is neither a United Kingdom national nor a permanent resident of the United Kingdom.

15   Where any tobacco product or beverage containing alcohol is removed from warehouse in the course of its being supplied to an entitled person, payment of any duty or tax chargeable in respect of the removal from warehouse or supply shall not be required.

16(1)   Subject to the following provisions of this article, where an entitled person purchases a motor vehicle which has been manufactured in a country, other than the United Kingdom, which is–

(a)   a member State; or

(b)   a member of the European Free Trade Association,

payment of any tax chargeable in respect of the supply shall not be required.

16(2)   No relief shall be afforded under paragraph (1) above if the entitled person has previously been afforded relief in respect of any other motor vehicle, whether under paragraph (1) above or otherwise, unless he has disposed of all previous motor vehicles in respect of which relief has been so afforded and paid any duty or tax which was required to be paid under article 10(2) above.

16(3)   Where the spouse of the entitled person is present in the United Kingdom, paragraph (2) above shall apply as if the words "(or all but one)" were inserted after the words "motor vehicles".

17   Nothing in this Part of this Order shall be taken as conferring relief in respect of any duty or tax which is subject to remission or refund by or under any of the enactments referred to in article 14 above.

PART VII – VISITING FORCES AND HEADQUARTERS

18   In this Part–

"entitled person" means a person who is–

(a)   for the purposes of any provision of the Visiting Forces Act 1952, a serving member of a visiting force of a country, other than the United Kingdom, which is a party to the North Atlantic Treaty, or a person recognised by the Secretary of State as a member of a civilian component of such a force, or

(b)   a person who is a military or civilian member of a headquarters or organisation designated for the purposes of any provision of the International Headquarters and Defence Organisations Act 1964,

who is neither a United Kingdom national nor a permanent resident of the United Kingdom.

19   Subject to article 22 below, where an entitled person purchases a motor vehicle which has been manufactured in a country which is–

(a)   a member State; or

(b)   a member of the European Free Trade Association,

payment of any tax in respect of the supply shall not be required.

20   Subject to article 22 below, where an entitled person imports, acquires or removes from [a] warehouse any goods, payment of any duty or tax chargeable in respect of the importation, acquisition or removal from [a] warehouse shall not be required.

21   Subject to article 22 below, where a gift of goods, other than tobacco products or beverages containing alcohol, is made to an entitled person by dispatching them to him from a place outside the United Kingdom, payment of any duty or tax chargeable in respect of their acquisition or importation shall not be required.

22(1)   No relief shall be afforded under this Part of this Order in respect of a motor vehicle if the entitled person has previously been afforded relief under this Order in respect of any other motor vehicle, unless he has disposed of all previous motor vehicles in respect of which relief has been so afforded and paid any duty or tax which was required to be paid under article 10(2) above.

22(2)   Where the spouse of the entitled person is present in the United Kingdom, paragraph (1) above shall apply as if the words "(or all but one)" were inserted after the words "motor vehicles".

SCHEDULE

Form No. 1: C 428

Form No. 2: C & E 941 A

Form No. 3: C 941

[Forms not reproduced.]

CUSTOMS AND EXCISE DUTIES (PERSONAL RELIEFS FOR GOODS PERMANENTLY IMPORTED) ORDER 1992

(SI 1992/3193)

Made on 16 December 1992 by the Commissioners of Customs and Excise, in exercise of the powers conferred on them by s. 7 and 13 of the Customs and Excise Duties (General Reliefs) Act 1979 and of all other powers enabling them in that behalf.

PART I – PRELIMINARY

CITATION AND COMMENCEMENT

1   This Order may be cited as the Customs and Excise Duties (Personal Reliefs for Goods Permanently Imported) Order 1992 and shall come into force on 1st January 1993.

INTERPRETATION

2   In this Order–

"declared for relief" has the meaning assigned to it by article 8 below;

"household effects" means furnishings and equipment for personal household use;

"motor vehicle" shall include a trailer;

"normal residence" means a person's principal place of abode situated in the country where he is normally resident;

"normally resident" has the meaning assigned to it by article 3 below;

"occupational ties" shall not include attendance by a pupil or student at a school, college or university;

"personal ties" shall mean family or social ties to which a person devotes most of his time not devoted to occupational ties;

"property" means any personal property intended for personal use or for meeting household needs and shall include household effects, household provisions, household pets and riding animals, cycles, motor vehicles, caravans, pleasure boats and private aircraft, provided that there shall be excluded any goods which, by their nature or quantity, indicate that they are being imported for a commercial purpose;

"third country", shall have the meaning given by Article 3.1 of Council Directive 77/388/EEC;

"used", in relation to a person's use of consumable property, shall include having the property at his disposal.

RULES FOR DETERMINING WHERE A PERSON IS NORMALLY RESIDENT

3(1)   This article shall apply for the purpose of determining, in relation to this Order, where a person is normally resident.

3(2)   A person shall be treated as being normally resident in the country where he usually lives–

(a)   for a period of, or periods together amounting to, at least 185 days in a period of twelve months;

(b)   because of his occupational ties; and

(c)   because of his personal ties.

3(3)   In the case of a person with no occupational ties, paragraph (2) above shall apply with the omission of sub-paragraph (b), provided his personal ties show close links with that country.

3(4)   Where a person has his occupational ties in one country and his personal ties in another country, he shall be treated as being normally resident in the latter country provided that either–

(a)   his stay in the former country is in order to carry out a task of a definite duration, or

(b)   he returns regularly to the country where he has his personal ties.

3(5)   Notwithstanding paragraph (4) above, a United Kingdom citizen whose personal ties are in the United Kingdom but whose occupational ties are in a third country may for the purposes of relief under this Order be treated as normally resident in the country of his occupational ties, provided he has lived there for a period of, or periods together amounting to, at least 185 days in a period of twelve months.

SUPPLEMENTARY

4 For the purposes of this Order–

(a)   any reference to a person who has been normally resident in a third country and who intends to become normally resident in the United Kingdom shall be taken as a reference to a person who intends to comply with the requirements of paragraphs (2), (3) or (4) of article 3 above, as the case may be, for being treated as normally resident in the United Kingdom;

(b)   the date on which a person becomes normally resident in the United Kingdom shall be the date when having given up his normal residence in a third country he is in the United Kingdom for the purpose of fulfilling such intention as is mentioned in paragraph (a) above.

PART II – PROVISIONS COMMON TO CERTAIN RELIEFS

PROPERTY MAY BE IN SEPARATE CONSIGNMENTS

5 Except as otherwise provided by this Order, where property in respect of which relief is afforded is permitted to be imported over a period it may be imported in more than one consignment during such period.

CONDITION AS TO SECURITY FOR CERTAIN IMPORTATIONS

6 Where any goods are declared for relief under this Order–

(a)   before the date on which a person becomes normally resident in the United Kingdom, or

(b)   if he intends to become so resident on the occasion of his marriage before such marriage has taken place,

the relief shall be subject to the condition that there is furnished to the Commissioners such security as they may require.

RESTRICTION ON DISPOSAL WITHOUT AUTHORISATION

7(1) Except as provided by or under this Order, where relief is afforded under any Part of this Order, it shall be a condition of the relief that the goods are not lent, hired-out, given as security or transferred in the United Kingdom within a period of twelve months from the date on which relief was afforded, unless such disposal is authorised by the Commissioners.

7(2) Where the Commissioners authorise any such disposal as is mentioned in paragraph (1) above, they may discharge the relief and the person to whom the relief was afforded shall forthwith pay tax at the rate then in force, provided that where a lower rate was in force when relief was afforded the amount payable shall be determined by reference to the lower rate.

PART III – PROVISIONS COMMON TO ALL RELIEFS

GOODS TO BE DECLARED FOR RELIEF

8(1) A person shall not be entitled to relief from payment of duty or tax in respect of any goods under any Part of this Order unless the goods are declared for relief to the proper officer.

8(2) For the purposes of this Order, the expression **"declared for relief"** shall refer to the act by which a person applies for relief on importation of the goods or on their removal from another customs procedure and includes, as the case may be, any declaration under section 78 of the Customs and Excise Management Act 1979, or any entry under the Postal Packets (Customs and Excise) Regulations 1986, the Excise Warehousing (etc.) Regulations 1988, or regulation 5 of the Customs Controls on Importation of Goods Regulations 1991, or any entry required by Article 40 of Commission Regulation (EEC) No. 2561/90.

FULFILMENT OF INTENTION TO BE A CONDITION

9 Where relief from payment of duty or tax is afforded under any Part of this Order subject to a specified intention on the part of a person in relation to his becoming normally resident in the United Kingdom, or the use of the goods in respect of which relief is afforded, it shall be a condition of the relief that such intention be fulfilled.

ENFORCEMENT

10 Where relief from payment of duty or tax has been afforded under any Part of this Order and subsequently the Commissioners are not satisfied that any condition subject to which such relief was afforded has been complied with, then, unless the Commissioners sanction the non-compliance, the duty or tax shall become payable forthwith by the person to whom relief was afforded (except to the extent that the Commissioners may see fit to waive payment of the whole or any part thereof) and the goods shall be liable to forfeiture.

PART IV – PERSONS TRANSFERRING THEIR NORMAL RESIDENCE FROM A THIRD COUNTRY

11(1) Subject to the provisions of this Part, a person entering the United Kingdom shall not be required to pay any duty or tax chargeable in respect of property imported into the United Kingdom on condition that–

(a) he has been normally resident in a third country for a continuous period of at least twelve months;

(b) he intends to become normally resident in the United Kingdom;

(c) the property has been in his possession and used by him in the country where he has been normally resident, for a period of at least six months before its importation;

(d) the property is intended for his personal or household use in the United Kingdom; and

(e) the property is declared for relief–

    (i) not earlier than six months before the date on which he becomes normally resident in the United Kingdom, and

    (ii) not later than twelve months following that date.

11(2) A person shall not be afforded relief under this Part unless the Commissioners are satisfied that the goods have borne, in their country of origin or exportation, the customs or other duties and taxes to which goods of that class or description are normally liable and that such goods have not, by reason of their exportation, been subject to any exemption from, or refund of, such duties and taxes as aforesaid, or any turnover tax, excise duty or other consumption tax.

11(3) For the purposes of this Part, **"property"** shall not include–

(a) beverages containing alcohol;

(b) tobacco products;

(c) any motor road vehicle which by its type of construction and equipment is designed for and capable of transporting more than nine persons including the driver, or goods, or any special purpose vehicle or mobile workshop; and

(d) articles for use in the exercise of a trade or profession, other than portable instruments of the applied or liberal arts.

Extra-statutory concessions – 5.3–5.7 (Notice 48 (1999 edn)): personal reliefs for goods permanently imported from third countries.

SUPPLEMENTARY

12 Where the Commissioners are satisfied that a person has given up his normal residence in a third country but is prevented by occupational ties from becoming normally resident in the United Kingdom immediately, they may allow property to be declared for relief earlier than as prescribed in article 11(1)(e)(i) above, subject to such conditions and restrictions as they think fit.

PART V – ADDITIONAL RELIEF FOR PROPERTY IMPORTED ON MARRIAGE FROM A THIRD COUNTRY

RELIEF

13(1) Subject to the provisions of this article, in addition to the relief afforded by Part IV, a person entering the United Kingdom shall not be required to pay any duty or tax chargeable in respect of property imported into the United Kingdom on condition that–

(a)   he has been normally resident in a third country for a continuous period of at least twelve months;

(b)   he intends to become normally resident in the United Kingdom on the occasion of his marriage; and

(c)   the property is declared for relief within the period provided by article 15 below.

13(2)   In this article **"property"** shall be limited to household effects and trousseaux, other than tobacco products and beverages containing alcohol.

WEDDING GIFTS

14(1)   Subject to the provisions of this article, a person to whom article 13(1) above applies shall not be required to pay any duty or tax chargeable in respect of any wedding gift imported into the United Kingdom by him or on his behalf on condition that such wedding gift is–

(a)   given or intended to be given to him on the occasion of his marriage by a person who is normally resident in a third country;

(b)   declared for relief within the period provided by article 15 below.

14(2)   Relief shall not be afforded under this article in respect of any wedding gift the value of which exceeds £800.

14(3)   For the purpose of affording relief from any duty or tax under this article, a wedding gift shall be treated as if it were liable to Community customs duty and valued in accordance with the rules applicable to such duty.

14(4)   In this article **"wedding gift"** means any property customarily given on the occasion of a marriage, other than tobacco products or beverages containing alcohol.

TIME LIMIT FOR RELIEF

15   The property to which this Part applies shall be declared for relief–

(a)   not earlier than two months before the date fixed for the solemnisation of the marriage; and

(b)   not later than four months following the date of the marriage.

PART VI – PUPILS AND STUDENTS

RELIEF FOR SCHOLASTIC EQUIPMENT

16(1)   Without prejudice to relief afforded under any other Part of this Order and subject to the provisions of this article, a person entering the United Kingdom shall not be required to pay any duty or tax chargeable in respect of scholastic equipment imported into the United Kingdom on condition that–

(a)   he is a pupil or student normally resident in a third country who has been accepted to attend a full-time course at a school, college or university in the United Kingdom; and

(b)   such equipment belongs to him and is intended for his personal use during the period of his studies.

16(2)   For the purposes of this article, **"scholastic equipment"** shall mean household effects which represent the normal furnishings for the room of a pupil or student, clothing, uniforms, and articles or instruments normally used by pupils or students for the purpose of their studies, including calculators or typewriters.

16(3)   The provisions of article 7 above shall not apply to relief afforded under this Part.

PART VII – HONORARY DECORATIONS, AWARDS AND GOODWILL GIFTS

RELIEF FOR HONORARY DECORATIONS AND AWARDS

17   Subject to article 20 below, a person entering the United Kingdom shall not be required to pay any duty or tax chargeable on the importation into the United Kingdom of any goods on condition that–

(a)   he is normally resident in the United Kingdom; and

(b)   such goods comprise–

      (i)   any honorary decoration which has been conferred on him by a government in a third country or

      (ii) any cup, medal or similar article of an essentially symbolic nature which has been awarded to him in a third country as a tribute to his activities in the arts, sciences, sport, or the public service, or in recognition of merit at a particular event.

RELIEF FOR GIFTS RECEIVED BY OFFICIAL VISITORS IN A THIRD COUNTRY

18   Subject to article 20 below, a person entering the United Kingdom shall not be required to pay any duty or tax chargeable on the importation into the United Kingdom of any goods on condition that–

(a)   he is normally resident in the United Kingdom;

(b)   he is returning from an official visit to a third country;

(c)   the goods were given to him by the host authorities of such country on the occasion of his visit; and

(d)   the goods are not intended for a commercial purpose.

RELIEF FOR GIFTS BROUGHT BY OFFICIAL VISITORS

19   Subject to article 20 below, a person entering the United Kingdom shall not be required to pay any duty or tax chargeable on the importation into the United Kingdom of any goods on condition that–

(a)   he is normally resident in a third country;

(b)   he is paying an official visit to the United Kingdom;

(c)   the goods are in the nature of an occasional gift which he intends to offer to the host authorities during his visit; and

(d)   the goods are not intended for a commercial purpose.

SUPPLEMENTARY

20(1)   Part II shall not apply to relief afforded under this Part.

20(2)   No relief shall be afforded under this Part in respect of beverages containing alcohol, tobacco products or importations having a commercial character.

PART VIII – PERSONAL PROPERTY ACQUIRED BY INHERITANCE

RELIEF FOR LEGACIES IMPORTED FROM A THIRD COUNTRY

21(1)   Without prejudice to relief afforded under any other Part of this Order and subject to the provisions of this article, a person who has become entitled as a legatee to property situated in a third country shall not be required to pay any duty or tax chargeable on the importation thereof into the United Kingdom, on condition that–

(a)   he is either–

      (i)   normally resident in the United Kingdom or the Isle of Man; or

      (ii) a secondary resident who is not normally resident in a third country; or

      (iii) an eligible body;

(b)   he furnishes proof to the officer of his entitlement as legatee to the property; and

(c)   save as the Commissioners otherwise allow, the property is imported by or for such person not later than two years from the date on which his entitlement as legatee is finally determined.

21(2)   No relief shall be afforded under paragraph (1) above in respect of goods specified in the Schedule to this Order.

21(3)   For the purposes of this Part–

    "eligible body" means a body solely concerned with carrying on a non-profit making activity and which is incorporated in the United Kingdom or the Isle of Man;

"secondary resident" means a person who, without being normally resident in the United Kingdom or the Isle of Man has a home situated in the United Kingdom which he owns or is renting for at least twelve months.

PART IX – REVOCATION

22   The following statutory instruments are revoked–

The Customs and Excise Duties (Reliefs for Goods Permanently Imported) Order 1983;

The Customs and Excise Duties (Relief for Imported Legacies) Order 1984;

The Customs and Excise Duties (Relief for Imported Legacies) Order 1984 (Amendment) Order 1985;

The Customs and Excise Duties (Reliefs for Goods Permanently Imported) (Amendment) Order 1991.

SCHEDULE

Article 21(2)

1   Beverages containing alcohol.

2   Tobacco products.

3   Any motor road vehicle which, by its type of construction and equipment, is designed for and capable of transporting more than nine persons including the driver, or goods, or any special purpose vehicle or mobile workshop.

4   Articles, other than portable instruments of the applied or liberal arts used in the exercise of a trade or profession before his death by the person from whom the legatee has acquired them.

5   Stocks of new materials and finished or semi-finished products.

6   Livestock and stocks of agricultural products exceeding the quantities appropriate to normal family requirements.

VALUE ADDED TAX (FLAT-RATE SCHEME FOR FARMERS) (DESIGNATED ACTIVITIES) ORDER 1992

(SI 1992/3220)

Made on 16 December 1992 by the Treasury, in exercise of the powers conferred on them by s. 37B(8) of the Value Added Tax Act 1983 [VATA 1994, s. 54(8)] and of all other powers enabling them in that behalf.

1   This Order may be cited as the Value Added Tax (Flat-rate Scheme for Farmers) (Designated Activities) Order 1992, and shall come into force on 1st January 1993.

2(1)   Subject to paragraph (2) below, the activities described in any part of the Schedule to this Order are designated activities for the purposes of section 37B of the Value Added Tax Act 1983 [VATA 1994, s. 54].

2(2)   The activities described in Part VI of the Schedule are not designated activities for the purposes of section 37B of the Act [VATA 1994, s. 54], unless:

(a)   the person performing them also carries out designated activities falling within one or more of Parts I to V of the Schedule (other designated activities), and

(b)   in carrying out the activities described in Part VI–

(i)   he performs them himself, or they are performed by his employees (or both), and

(ii)   any equipment he uses in carrying them out, or hires to another, for agricultural purposes is equipment which he also uses for carrying out his other designated activities.

SCHEDULE

Article 2

PART I – CROP PRODUCTION

1   General agriculture, including viticulture.

2   Growing of fruit and of vegetables, flowers and ornamental plants, whether in the open or under glass.

3   Production of mushrooms, spices, seeds and propagating materials; nurseries.

PART II – STOCK FARMING

1   General stock farming.

2   Poultry farming.

3   Rabbit farming.

4   Beekeeping.

5   Silkworm farming.

6   Snail farming.

PART III – FORESTRY

1   Growing, felling and general husbandry of trees in a forest, wood or copse.

PART IV – FISHERIES

1   Fresh-water fishing.

2   Fish farming.

3   Breeding of mussels, oysters and other molluscs and crustaceans.

4   Frog farming.

PART V – PROCESSING

1   The processing by a person of products deriving from his activities falling within Parts I to IV above, using only such means as are normally employed in the course of such activities.

PART VI – SERVICES

1   Field work, reaping and mowing, threshing, bailing [*sic*], collecting, harvesting, sowing and planting.

2   Packing and preparing for market (including drying, cleaning, grinding, disinfecting and ensilaging) of agricultural products for market.

3   Storage of agricultural products.

4   Stock minding, rearing and fattening.

5   Hiring out of equipment for use in any of the activities described in this Schedule.

6   Technical assistance in relation to any of the activities described in this Schedule.

7   Destruction of weeds and pests, dusting and spraying of crops and land.

8   Operation of irrigation and drainage equipment.

9   Lopping, tree felling and other forestry services.

VALUE ADDED TAX (FLAT-RATE SCHEME FOR FARMERS) (PERCENTAGE ADDITION) ORDER 1992

(SI 1992/3221)

Made on 16 December 1992 by the Treasury, in exercise of the powers conferred on them by s. 37B(4) of the Value Added Tax Act 1983 [VATA 1994, s. 54(4)] and of all other powers enabling them in that behalf.

1   This Order may be cited as the Value Added Tax (Flat-rate Scheme for Farmers) (Percentage Addition) Order 1992, and shall come into force on 1st January 1993.

2   The percentage referred to in section 37B(4) of the Value Added Tax Act 1983 [VATA 1994, s. 54(5)] shall be 4 per cent.

VALUE ADDED TAX (INPUT TAX) ORDER 1992

(SI 1992/3222 as amended by SI 1993/2954, SI 1995/281, SI 1995/1267, SI 1995/1666, SI 1998/2767, SI 1999/2930, SI 1999/3118)

Made on 16 December 1992 by the Treasury, in exercise of the powers conferred on them by s. 14(10) of the Value Added Tax Act 1983 [VATA 1994, s. 25(7)] and of all other powers enabling them in that behalf.

CITATION AND COMMENCEMENT

1   This Order may be cited as the Value Added Tax (Input Tax) Order 1992, and shall come into force on 1st January 1993.

INTERPRETATION

2   In this Order–

"**the Act**" means the Value Added Tax Act 1994;

"**the Manx Act**" means the Value Added Tax and Other Taxes Act 1973;

"**antiques**" means objects other than works of art or collectors' items, which are more than 100 years old;

"**collectors' items**" means any collection or collector's piece falling within section 21(5) of the Act but excluding investment gold coins within the meaning of Note 1(b) and (c) to Group 15 of Schedule 9 to the Act;

"**building materials**" means any goods the supply of which would be zero-rated if supplied by a taxable person to a person to whom he is also making a supply of a description within either item 2 or item 3 of Group 5, or item 2 of Group 6, of Schedule 8 to the Act;

"**motor car**" means any motor vehicle of a kind normally used on public roads which has three or more wheels and either–

(a)   is constructed or adapted solely or mainly for the carriage of passengers; or

(b)   has to the rear of the driver's seat roofed accommodation which is fitted with side windows or which is constructed or adapted for the fitting of side windows;

but does not include–

(i)   vehicles capable of accommodating only one person;

(ii)   vehicles which meet the requirements of Schedule 6 to the Road Vehicles (Construction and Use) Regulations 1986 and are capable of carrying twelve or more seated persons;

(iii)   vehicles of not less than three tonnes unladen weight (as defined in the Table to regulation 3(2) of the Road Vehicles (Construction and Use) Regulations 1986);

(iv)   vehicles constructed to carry a payload (the difference between a vehicle's kerb weight (as defined in the Table to regulation 3(2) of the Road Vehicles (Construction and Use) Regulations 1986) and its maximum gross weight (as defined in that Table)) of one tonne or more;

(v)   caravans, ambulances and prison vans;

(vi)   vehicles constructed for a special purpose other than the carriage of persons and having no other accommodation for carrying persons than such as is incidental to that purpose;

"**motor dealer**" means a person whose business consists in whole or in part of obtaining supplies of, or acquiring from another member State or importing, new or second-hand motor cars for resale with a view to making an overall profit on the sale of them (whether or not a profit is made on each sale);

"**motor manufacturer**" means a person whose business consists in whole or part of producing motor cars including producing motors cars by conversion of a vehicle (whether a motor car or not);

"**Second-hand goods**" means tangible moveable property (including motor cars) that is suitable for further use as it is or after repair other than works of art, collectors' items or antiques and other than precious metals and precious stones;

"**stock in trade**" means new or second-hand motor cars (other than second-hand motor cars which are not qualifying motor cars within the meaning of article 7(2A) below) which are–

(a)   produced by a motor manufacturer or, as the case may require, supplied to or acquired from another member State or imported by a motor dealer, for the purpose of resale, and

(b)   are intended to be sold by–

(i) a motor manufacturer within 12 months of their production, or

(ii) by a motor dealer within 12 months of their supply, acquisition from another member State or importation, as the case may require,

and such motor cars shall not cease to be stock in trade where they are temporarily put to a use in the motor manufacturer's or, as the case may be, the motor dealer's business which involves making them available for private use;

"**work of art**" has the same meaning as in section 21 of the Act.

History – In art. 2, in the definition of "the Act", the year "1994" was substituted for the year "1983" by SI 1995/281, art. 3(a), operative from 1 March 1995.

In art. 2, the definition of "antiques" was inserted by SI 1995/1267, art. 3(b), operative from 1 June 1995.

In art. 2, the definition of "collectors' items" was substituted by SI 1999/3118, art. 3(a), operative from 1 January 2000. The former definition reads as follows:

"**collectors' items**" means the following goods–

postage or revenue stamps, postmarks, first-day covers, pre-stamped stationery and the like, franked, or if unfranked not being of legal tender and not being intended for use as legal tender.

collections and collectors' pieces of zoological, botanical, mineralogical, anatomical, historical, archaeological, palaeontological, ethnographic or numismatic interest;."

In art. 2, the former definition of "collectors' items" was inserted by SI 1995/1267, art. 3(b), operative from 1 June 1995.

In art. 2, the definition of "building materials" was inserted by SI 1995/281, art. 3(b), operative from 1 March 1995.

In art. 2, the definition of "caravan" was omitted by SI 1995/1267, art. 3(a), operative from 1 June 1995. The former definition reads as follows:

"**caravan**" includes a motor caravan but does not include a caravan of a description specified in item 1 of Group 9 of Schedule 8 to the Act;".

In the former definition of "caravan", the words "item 1 of . . . to the Act" were substituted for the words "item 1 of Group 11 of Schedule 5 to the Act" by SI 1995/281, art. 3(c), operative from 1 March 1995.

In art. 2, the definition of "firearms" was omitted by SI 1995/1267, art. 3(a), operative from 1 June 1995. The former definition reads as follows:

"**firearms**" means rifles, shotguns, pistols (including revolvers) and air guns but does not include a weapon specified by section 5(1) of the Firearms Act 1968;".

In art. 2, the definition of "motor car" was substituted by SI 1999/2930, art. 3(a), operative from 1 December 1999. The former definition reads as follows:

"**motor car**" means any motor vehicle of a kind normally used on public roads which has three or more wheels and either–

(a)   is constructed or adapted solely or mainly for the carriage of passengers; or

(b)   has to the rear of the driver's seat roofed accommodation which is fitted with side windows or which is constructed or adapted for the fitting of side windows;

but does not include–

(i)   vehicles capable of accommodating only one person or suitable for carrying twelve or more persons;

(ii)   vehicles of not less than three tonnes unladen weight;

(iii)   caravans, ambulances and prison vans;

(iv)   vehicles of a type approved by the Assistant Commissioner of Police of the Metropolis as conforming to the condition of fitness for the time being laid down by him for the purposes of the London Cab Order 1934; or

(v)   vehicles constructed for a special purpose other than the carriage of persons and having no other accommodation for carrying persons than such as is incidental to that purpose;."

In art. 2, the definition of "motorcycle" was omitted by SI 1995/1267, art. 3(a), operative from 1 June 1995. The former definition reads as follows:

"**motor cycle**" includes a motor bicycle, motor tricycle or motor scooter (whether or not a sidecar is attached), a bicycle or tricycle with an attachment for propelling it by mechanical means and any mechanically propelled vehicle with three wheels capable of accommodating only one person;".

In art. 2, the definition of "motor dealer" was inserted by SI 1999/2930, art. 3(b), operative from 1 December 1999.

In art. 2, the definition of "motor manufacturer" was inserted by SI 1999/2930, art. 3(b), operative from 1 December 1999.

In art. 2, the definition of "printed matter" was omitted by SI 1999/2930, art. 3(c), operative from 1 December 1999. The former definition reads as follows:

"**printed matter**" includes printed stationery but does not include anything produced by typing, duplicating or photocopying;."

In art. 2, the definition of "stock in trade" was inserted by SI 1999/2930, art. 3(d), operative from 1 December 1999.

In art. 2, the definition of "works of art", "antiques" and "collectors' pieces" was omitted by SI 1995/1267, art. 3(a), operative from 1 June 1995. The former definition reads as follows:

"**works of art**", "**antiques**" and "**collectors' pieces**" means the following goods–

(a)   paintings, drawings and pastels, executed by hand, other than hand-painted or hand-decorated manufactured articles;

(b)   original engravings, prints and lithographs;

(c)   original sculptures and statuary, in any material;

(d)   antiques, of an age exceeding one hundred years, except pearls and loose gem stones;

(e)   collections and collectors' pieces of zoological, botanical, mineralogical, anatomical, historical, archaeological, palaeontological or ethnographic interest."

In art. 2, the definition of "second-hand goods" was inserted by SI 1995/1267, art. 3(c), operative from 1 June 1995.

In art. 2, the definition of "work of art" was substituted for the definition of "works of art" by SI 1999/3118, art. 3(b), operative from 1 January 2000. The former definition reads as follows:

""**works of art**" means the following goods–

> pictures, collages and similar decorative plaques, paintings and drawings, executed entirely by hand by the artist, other than plans and drawings for architectural, engineering, industrial, commercial, topographical or similar purposes, hand-decorated manufactured articles, theatrical scenery, studio back cloths or the like of painted canvas;
>
> original engravings, prints and lithographs, being impressions produced in limited numbers directly in black and white or in colour of one or of several plates executed entirely by hand by the artist irrespective of the process or of the material employed by him, but not including any mechanical or photomechanical process original sculptures and statuary, in any material, provided that they are executed entirely by the artist; sculpture casts the production of which is limited to eight copies (or, in relation to statuary casts produced before 1st January 1989, such greater number of copies as the Commissioners of Customs and Excise may in any particular case allow) and supervised by the artist or his successors in title;
>
> tapestries and wall textiles made by hand from original designs provided by artists, provided that there are not more than eight copies of each;
>
> individual pieces of ceramics executed entirely by the artist and signed by him;
>
> enamels on copper, executed entirely by and, limited to eight numbered copies bearing the signature of the artist or the studio, excluding articles of jewellery and goldsmiths' and silversmiths' wares;
>
> photographs taken by the artist, printed by him or under his supervision, signed and numbered and limited to 30 copies, all sizes and mounts included."

In art. 2, the former definition of "works of art" was inserted by SI 1995/1267, art. 3(c), operative from 1 June 1995.

REVOCATIONS

3   The provisions specified in the first column of the Schedule to this Order are hereby revoked to the extent specified in the second column of that Schedule.

DISALLOWANCE OF INPUT TAX

4(1)   Subject to paragraph (4) below, tax charged on the–

(a)   supply;

(b)   acquisition from another member State; or

(c)   importation,

any goods such as are described in paragraph (2) below which are supplied to, or acquired from another member State or imported by, a taxable person in the circumstances described in paragraph (3) below shall be excluded from any credit under section 25 of the Act;

4(2)   The goods referred to in paragraph (1) above are–

(a)   works of art, antiques and collectors' items;

(b)   second-hand goods;

4(3)   The circumstances of the supply, acquisition from another member State or importation referred to in paragraph (1) above are–

(a)   a supply on which, by virtue of an Order made under section 50A of the Act or a corresponding provision of the Manx Act or by virtue of a corresponding provision of the law of another member State, VAT was chargeable on the profit margin;

(b)   (if the goods are a work of art, an antique or a collectors' item) the taxable person imported it himself;

(c)   (if the goods are a work of art) it was supplied to the taxable person by, or acquired from another member State by him from its creator or his successor in title;

4(4)   Paragraph (1) above shall only apply to exclude from credit, tax chargeable on a supply of goods to or an acquisition or importation of goods by a taxable person in the circumstances set out in paragraph (3)(b) and (c) above if the taxable person–

(a)   has opted to account for VAT chargeable on his supplies of such goods on the profit margin and

(b)   has not elected to account for VAT chargeable on his supply of the goods by reference to its value, in accordance with the provisions of an Order made under section 50A of the Act.

History – Art. 4(3)(aa) was omitted by SI 1999/2930, art. 4, operative from 1 March 2000. Former art. 4(3)(aa) reads as follow:
"

> (aa)   a supply which, for the purposes of the charge to VAT, was treated as if it were for a consideration calculated in accordance with article 7(4) below;".

Art. 4(3)(aa) was inserted by SI 1995/1666, art. 3, operative from 1 August 1995.
Art. 4 was substituted by SI 1995/1267, art. 4, operative from 1 June 1995. Former art. 4 reads as follows:
"**4(1)**   Tax charged on the–
> (a)   supply;
> (b)   acquisition from another member State; or
> (c)   importation,

of any goods such as are described in paragraph (2) below which are supplied, acquired or imported in any of the circumstances described in paragraph (3) below shall be excluded from any credit under section 25 of the Act.
4(2)   The goods referred to in paragraph (1) above are–
> (a)   works of art, antiques and collectors' pieces;

(b)   used motor cycles;
(c)   used caravans;
(d)   used boats and outboard motors;
(e)   used electronic organs;
(f)   used aircraft;
(g)   used firearms.

4(3)   The circumstances of the supply to, or acquisition or importation by, a taxable person of goods described in paragraph (2) above are as follows–

(a)   a supply in respect of which no tax was chargeable under the Act or under Part I of the Manx Act;
(b)   a supply on which tax chargeable under either of those Acts was chargeable by virtue of any Order made under section 32 of the Act or a corresponding provision made under the Manx Act;
(c)   a transaction which was treated by virtue of any Order made under section 5(3) of the Act or under a corresponding provision of the Manx Act as being neither a supply of goods nor a supply of services; or
(d)   (if the goods are a work of art, an antique or a collectors' piece) their acquisition from another member State or their importation and (whether by virtue of an Order made under section 37(1) of the Act or otherwise) no tax was chargeable on their acquisition or, as the case may be, their importation."

In former art. 4(1), the number "25" was substituted for "14" by SI 1995/281, art. 4(a), operative from 1 March 1995.
In former art. 4(3)(b), the number "32" was substituted for "18" by SI 1995/281, art. 4(b), operative from 1 March 1995.
In former art. 4(3)(c), "5(3)" was substituted for "3(3)" by SI 1995/281, art. 4(c), operative from 1 March 1995.
In former art. 4(3)(d), "37(1)" was substituted for "19(1)" by SI 1995/281, art. 4(c), operative from 1 March 1995.

5(1)   Tax charged on any goods or services supplied to a taxable person, or on any goods acquired by a taxable person, or on any goods imported by a taxable person, is to be excluded from any credit under section 25 of the Act, where the goods or services in question are used or to be used by the taxable person for the purposes of business entertainment.

5(2)   Where, by reason of the operation of paragraph (1) above, a taxable person has claimed no input tax on a supply of any services, tax shall be charged on a supply by him of the services in question, as if that supply were for a consideration equal to the excess of–

(a)   the consideration for which the services are supplied by him, over

(b)   the consideration for which the services were supplied to him,

and accordingly shall not be charged unless there is such an excess.

5(3)   For the purposes of this article, **"business entertainment"** means entertainment including hospitality of any kind provided by a taxable person in connection with a business carried on by him, but does not include the provision of any such entertainment for either or both–

(a)   employees of the taxable person;

(b)   if the taxable person is a body corporate, its directors or persons otherwise engaged in its management,

unless the provision of entertainment for persons such as are mentioned in sub-paragraph (a) and (b) above is incidental to its provision for others.

5(4)   [Omitted by SI 1999/2930, art. 5(b).]

History – In art. 5(1), the number "25" was substituted for "14" by SI 1995/281, art. 5, operative from 1 March 1995.
In art. 5(2), the words "a supply, acquisition or importation of any goods, or on" which appeared after the words "no input tax on" were omitted by SI 1999/2930, art. 5(a)(i), operative from 1 March 2000.
In art. 5(2), the words "on a supply by him of the goods in question not being a letting on hire or" which appeared after the words "tax shall be charged" were omitted by SI 1999/2930, art. 5(a)(i), operative from 1 March 2000.
Art. 5(2)(a) and (b) were substituted by SI 1999/2930, art. 5(a)(ii), operative from 1 March 2000. Former art. 5(2)(a) and (b) read as follows:
"
(a)   the consideration for which the goods or services are supplied by him, over
(b)   the relevant amount,".
Art. 5(4) was omitted by SI 1999/2930, art. 5(b), operative from 1 March 2000. Former art. 5(4) reads as follows:
"5(4)   For the purposes of sub-paragraph (b) of paragraph (2) above, the **"relevant amount"** is–
(a)   if the goods or services in question had been supplied to the taxable person, the consideration for the supply to him;
(b)   if the goods in question had been acquired by him from another member State, the value of their acquisition plus the tax chargeable thereon;
(c)   if the goods in question had been imported by him, the value of the goods for the purposes of charging tax on importation plus any tax chargeable on their importation."

Cross references – VATA 1994, Sch. 9, Grp. 14, Note (6)(a): supplies where input tax cannot be recovered.

Extra-statutory concessions – 3.10 (Notice 48 (1999 edn)): meals and accommodation provided by representative sporting bodies to amateurs.

6   Where a taxable person constructing, or effecting any works to a building, in either case for the purpose of making a grant of a major interest in it or any part of it or its site which is of a description in Schedule 8 to the Act, incorporates goods other than building materials in any part of the building or its site, input tax on the supply, acquisition or importation of the goods shall be excluded from credit under section 25 of the Act.

History – Art. 6 was substituted by SI 1995/281, art. 6, operative from 1 March 1995. Former art. 6 reads as follows:
"6(1)   Subject to paragraph (2) below where a taxable person constructing a building or effecting works to any building, in either case for the purpose of granting a major interest in it or in any part of it, incorporates goods in any part of the building or its site which is used for the purpose of a dwelling, input tax on the supply, or acquisition or importation of the goods shall be excluded from any credit under section 14 of the Act.

6(2)   Paragraph (1) above shall not apply to materials, builders' hardware, sanitary ware or other articles of a kind ordinarily installed by builders as fixtures except–

    (a)   finished or prefabricated furniture, other than furniture designed to be fitted in kitchens;

    (b)   materials for the construction of fitted furniture, other than kitchen furniture;

    (c)   domestic electrical or gas appliances, other than those designed to provide space heating or water heating or both;

    (d)   carpets or carpeting materials."

Cross references – VATA 1994, Sch. 9, Grp. 14, Note (6)(b): supplies where input tax cannot be recovered.

Other material – Customs and Excise Business Brief 13/93, 29 April 1993 (not reproduced): fitted and built-in wardrobes – input tax recovery by house builders.

Customs and Excise Business Brief 3/94, 15 February 1994 (not reproduced): vanity (or vanitory) units are not fitted furniture and are not subject to VAT. Input tax relating to base units incorporating a wash hand basin installed in bathrooms, cloakrooms or bedrooms of new dwellings is recoverable by the housebuilder.

7(1)   Subject to paragraph (2) to (2H) below tax charged on–

(a)   the supply (including a letting on hire) to a taxable person;

(b)   the acquisition by a taxable person from another member State; or

(c)   the importation by a taxable person,

of a motor car shall be excluded from any credit under section 25 of the Act.

7(2)   Paragraph (1) above does not apply where–

(a)   the motor car is–

      (i)   a qualifying motor car;

      (ii)   supplied (including on a letting on hire) to, or acquired from another member State or imported by, a taxable person; and

      (iii)   the relevant condition is satisfied;

(aa)   the motor car forms part of the stock in trade of a motor manufacturer or a motor dealer;

(b)   the supply is a letting on hire of a motor car which is not a qualifying motor car (other than a supply on a letting on hire of a motor car which is not a qualifying motor car by virtue only of the application of paragraph (2C) below, to a person whose supply on a letting on hire prior to 1st August 1995 resulted in the application of that paragraph);

(c)   the motor car is unused and is supplied to a taxable person whose only taxable supplies are concerned with the letting of motor cars on hire to another taxable person whose business consists predominantly of making supplies of a description falling within item 14 of Group 12 of Schedule 8 to the Act; or

(d)   the motor car is unused and is supplied on a letting on hire to a taxable person whose business consists predominantly of making supplies of a description falling within item 14 of Group 12 of Schedule 8 to the Act, by a taxable person whose only taxable supplies are concerned with the letting on hire of motor cars to such a taxable person.

7(2A)   Subject to paragraph (2B) and (2C) below, for the purposes of paragraph (2)(a) and (b) above a motor car is a **qualifying motor car** if–

(a)   it has never been supplied, acquired from another member State, or imported in circumstances in which the VAT on that supply, acquisition or importation was wholly excluded from credit as input tax by virtue of paragraph (1) above; or

(b)   a taxable person has elected for it to be treated as such.

7(2B)   A taxable person may only elect for a motor car to be treated as a qualifying motor car if it–

(a)   is first registered on or after 1st August 1995;

(b)   was supplied to, or acquired from another member State or imported by, him prior to that date in circumstances in which the VAT on that supply, acquisition or importation was wholly excluded from credit as input tax by virtue of paragraph (1) above; and

(c)   had not been supplied on a letting on hire by him prior to 1st August 1995.

7(2C)   A motor car that is supplied, acquired from another member State or imported on or after 1st August 1995 and which would, apart from this paragraph, be a qualifying motor car by virtue of sub-paragraph (a) of paragraph (2A) above shall not be such a car if it was supplied on a letting on hire prior to that date by the person to whom it is supplied or by whom it is acquired or imported (as the case may be).

7(2D)   References in this article to **registration of a motor car** mean registration in accordance with section 21 of the Vehicle Excise and Registration Act 1994.

7(2E)   For the purposes of paragraph (2)(a) above the **relevant condition** is that the letting on hire, supply, acquisition or importation (as the case may be) is to a taxable person who intends to use the motor car either–

(a)   exclusively for the purposes of a business carried on by him, but this is subject to paragraph (2G) below; or

(b)   primarily for a relevant purpose.

7(2F)   For the purposes of paragraph (2E) above a **relevant purpose**, in relation to a motor car which is let on hire or supplied to, or acquired or imported by, a taxable person (as the case may be), is any of the following purposes–

(a)   to provide it on hire with the services of a driver for the purpose of carrying passengers;

(b)   to provide it for self-drive hire; or

(c)   to use it as a vehicle in which instruction in the driving of a motor car is to be given by him.

7(2G)   A taxable person shall not be taken to intend to **use a motor car exclusively for the purposes of a business** carried on by him if he intends to–

(a)   let it on hire to any person either for no consideration or for a consideration which is less than that which would be payable in money if it were a commercial transaction conducted at arms length; or

(b)   make it available (otherwise than by letting it on hire) to any person (including, where the taxable person is an individual, himself, or where the taxable person is a partnership, a partner) for private use, whether or not for a consideration.

7(2H)   Where paragraph (1) above applies to a supply of a motor car on a letting on hire it shall apply to the tax charged on that supply as if for the word "tax" there were substituted "one half of the tax".

7(3)   In this article–

(a)   [Deleted by SI 1995/1666, art. 7.]

(b)   **"self-drive hire"** means hire where the hirer is the person normally expected to drive the motor car and the period of hire to each hirer, together with the period of hire of any other motor car expected to be hired to him by the taxable person–

  (i)   will normally be less than 30 consecutive days; and

  (ii)   will normally be less than 90 days in any period of 12 months.

7(4)   [Omitted by SI 1999/2930, art. 6(c), operative from 1 March 2000.]

7(5)   [Omitted by SI 1999/2930, art. 6(c), operative from 1 March 2000.]

History – In art. 7(1), the words "to (2H)" were inserted by SI 1995/1666, art. 4(a), operative from 1 August 1995.
In art. 7(1)(a), the words "(including a letting on hire)" were inserted by SI 1995/1666, art. 4(b), operative from 1 August 1995.
In art. 7(1), the number "25" was substituted for "14" by SI 1995/281, art. 7(a), operative from 1 March 1995.
In art. 7(2)(a)(ii), the words "supplied (including on a letting on hire) to" were substituted for the words "let on hire or supplied to" by SI 1998/2767, art. 2(a), operative on 13 November 1998 in respect of VAT charged on supplies received, or acquisitions from another member state or importations made, on or after that date.
Art. 7(2)(aa) was inserted by SI 1999/2930, art. 6(a), operative from 1 December 1999.
In art. 7(2)(b), all the words after the words"qualifying motor car" were inserted by SI 1998/2767, art. 2(b), operative on 13 November 1998 in respect of VAT charged on supplies received, or acquisitions from another member state or importations made, on or after that date.
Art. 7(2) was substituted by SI 1995/1666, art. 5, operative from 1 August 1995. Former art. 7(2) read as follows:
"**7(2)**   Paragraph (1) above does not apply where–
  (a)   the supply is a letting on hire; or
  (b)   the motor car is supplied, acquired or imported for the purpose of its conversion into a vehicle which is not a motor car; or
  (c)   the motor car is unused and is supplied to, or acquired or imported by, the taxable person for the purpose of being sold; or
  (d)   the motor car is unused and forms part of the assets of the taxable person's business and is supplied by him in the circumstances–
    (i)   described in paragraph 6 of Schedule 4 to the Act (removal of business assets to another member State), and
    (ii)   by way of a zero-rated supply by virtue of regulations made under section 30(8) of the Act; or
  (e)   the motor car is unused and is supplied to, or acquired or imported by, a taxable person whose business includes the production of motor cars (other than the production of motor cars solely by the conversion of vehicles) and the motor car is for the purpose of research and development to be carried out by him; or
  (f)   the motor car is unused and is supplied to a taxable person whose only taxable supplies are concerned with the *letting of motor cars on hire* to another taxable person whose business consists predominantly of making supplies of a description falling within item 14 of group 12 of Schedule 8 to the Act; or
  (g)   the motor car is supplied to, or acquired or imported by, a taxable person for the primary purpose of–
    (i)   being provided by him for hire with the services of a driver for the purpose of carrying passengers;
    (ii)   being provided by him for self-drive hire;
    (iii)   being used as a vehicle in which instruction in the driving of a motor car is to be given by him; or
    (iv)   the letting on hire to a person under an agreement which imposes a condition that he uses the motor car primarily for one of the purposes described in sub-paragraphs (i) to (iii) above."

In former art. 7(2)(d)(i), the words "paragraph 6 of Schedule 4 to the Act" were substituted for "paragraph 5A of Schedule 2 to the Act" by SI 1995/281, art. 7(b), operative from 1 March 1995.

In former art. 7(2)(d)(ii), "30(8)" was substituted for "16(7)" by SI 1995/281, art. 7(c), operative from 1 March 1995.

In former art. 7(2)(f), the words "item 14 of group 12 of Schedule 8" were substituted for the words "item 12 of Group 14 of Schedule 5" by SI 1995/281, art. 7(d), operative from 1 March 1995.

In former art. 7(2)(g)(iv), the words "under an agreement which imposes a" were substituted for the words "who is not a taxable person on" by SI 1993/2954, art. 2, operative from 1 January 1994.

Art. 7(2A) was inserted by SI 1995/1666, art. 6, operative from 1 August 1995.

In art. 7(2A), the words "and (b)" were inserted by SI 1999/2930, art. 6(b), operative from 1 December 1999.

Art. 7(2B)–(2H) were inserted by SI 1995/1666, art. 6, operative from 1 August 1995.

Art. 7(3)(a) was deleted by SI 1995/1666, art. 7, operative from 1 August 1995. Former art. 7(3)(a) reads as follows:

"(a) **"sold"** includes being supplied under a hire-purchase agreement;"

Art. 7(4) was omitted by SI 1999/2930, art. 6(c), operative from 1 March 2000. Former art. 7(4) reads as follows:

"**7(4)** On the supply by a taxable person of a motor car (other than one which is a qualifying motor car by virtue of paragraph (2A)(b) above) in respect of which tax has been wholly excluded from credit by virtue of paragraph (1) above, or of any other provision made or having effect as if made under section 25(7) of the Act, tax shall be chargeable as if the supply were for a consideration equal to the excess of–

    (a)   the consideration for which the motor car is supplied by him, over

    (b)   the relevant amount,

and accordingly shall not be charged unless there is such an excess."

In former art. 7(4), the words "(other than one which ... excluded from credit" were substituted for the words "in respect of which tax has been excluded from any credit" by SI 1995/1666, art. 8, operative from 1 August 1995.

In former art. 7(4), "25(7)" was substituted for "14(10)" by SI 1995/281, art. 7(e), operative from 1 March 1995.

Art. 7(5) was omitted by SI 1999/2930, art. 6(c), operative from 1 March 2000. Former art. 7(5) reads as follows:

"**7(5)** For the purposes of paragraph (4)(b) above, the **relevant amount** is–

    (a)   if the motor car had been obtained by the taxable person by way of a supply to him by another taxable person, the consideration for that supply;

    (b)   if the motor car had been treated as supplied by the taxable person to himself by virtue of an order made under section 5(5) of the Act, the value of that supply plus the tax chargeable thereon;

    (c)   if the motor car had been acquired by the taxable person from another member State, the value of that acquisition plus the tax chargeable thereon;

    (d)   if the motor car had been imported by the taxable person, the value of the motor car for the purposes of charging tax on importation together with any tax chargeable on its importation."

In former art. 7(5)(b), "5(5)" was substituted for "3(5)" by SI 1995/281, art. 7(f), operative from 1 March 1995.

Cross references – VATA 1994, Sch. 9, Grp. 14, Note (6)(c): supplies where input tax cannot be recovered.

VAT (Cars) Order 1992 (SI 1992/3122), art. 8(2)(bb): relief for second-hand motor cars.

Extra-statutory concessions – 3.12 (Notice 48 (1999 edn)): buses with special facilities for carrying disabled treated as if had at least 12 seats.

REVOCATIONS

Article 3

Provision	Extent of Revocation
The Value Added Tax (Cars) Order 1980 (No. 442)	The whole Order insofar as it contains provisions in respect of which approval by the House of Commons was required under section 43(4) of the Finance Act 1972
The Value Added Tax (Special Provisions) Order 1981 (No. 1741)	The whole Order insofar as it contains provisions in respect of which approval by the House of Commons was required under section 43(4) of the Finance Act 1972
The Value Added Tax (Special Provisions) (Amendment) (No. 2) Order 1984 (No. 736)	The whole Order
The Value Added Tax (Handicapped Persons) Order 1985 (No. 919)	Article 2
The Value Added Tax (Construction of Buildings) (No. 2) Order 1987 (No. 1072)	Article 3
The Value Added Tax (Special Provisions) (Amendment) Order 1988 (No. 1124)	The whole Order
The Value Added Tax (Cars) (Amendment) (No. 2) Order 1992 (No. 1654)	The whole Order

VALUE ADDED TAX (PLACE OF SUPPLY OF GOODS) ORDER 1992

(SI 1992/3283)

Made on 23 December 1992 by the Treasury, in exercise of the powers conferred on them by s. 6(6) of the Value Added Tax Act 1983 [VATA 1994, s. 7(11)] and of all other powers enabling them in that behalf.

1 This Order may be cited as the Value Added Tax (Place of Supply of Goods) Order 1992 and shall come into force on 1st January 1993.

2 The rules for determining where a supply of goods is made shall be varied in accordance with the following provisions of this Order.

3 In this Order–

"Community transport" means the transportation of passengers between the point of departure and the point of arrival in the course of which–

(a) there is a stop in a member State other than that in which lies the point of departure; and

(b) there is no stop in a country which is not a member State;

"homeward stage" means that part of the return trip which ends at the first stop in the country in which the return trip commenced and which involves only such other stops, if any, as are in member States where there have previously been stops (in the course of that return trip);

"pleasure cruise" includes a cruise wholly or partly for the purposes of education or training;

"point of arrival" means the last place in the member States where it is expected that passengers who have commenced their journey at a place in a member State will terminate their journey or, where there is to follow a leg which will involve a stop in a place outside the member States, the last such place before such leg is undertaken;

"point of departure" means the first place in the member States where it is expected that passengers will commence their journey or, where there has been a leg which involved a stop in a place outside the member States, the first such place after such leg has been completed;

"return trip" means any journey involving two or more countries where it is expected that the means of transport will stop in the country from which it originally departed.

4 Subject to the following provisions of this Order, where goods are supplied on board a ship, aircraft or train in the course of a Community transport, those goods shall be treated as supplied at the point of departure.

5 Subject to the following provisions of this Order, any goods supplied on board a ship or aircraft in the course of a Community transport for consumption on board shall be treated as supplied outside the member States.

6 For the purposes of this Order–

(a) part of transportation where it is expected that a different means of transport will be used shall be treated as separate transportation; and

(b) the homeward stage of a return trip shall be treated as separate transportation.

7 This Order shall not apply to any goods supplied as part of a pleasure cruise.

VALUE ADDED TAX (SUPPLY OF SERVICES) ORDER 1993

(SI 1993/1507, as amended by SI 1995/1668, SI 1998/762)

Made by the Treasury, in exercise of the powers conferred on them by s. 3(4) and (8) of the Value Added Tax Act 1983 [VATA 1994, s. 5(4) and (8)] and of all other powers enabling them in that behalf. Operative from 1 August 1993.

1 This Order may be cited as the Value Added Tax (Supply of Services) Order 1993 and shall come into force on 1st August 1993.

2 In this Order–

"the Act" means the Value Added Tax Act 1994.

History – In art. 2, the year "1994" was substituted for the year "1983" by SI 1995/1668, art. 3, operative from 1 August 1995.

3 Subject to articles 6, 6A and 7 below, where a person carrying on a business puts services which have been supplied to him to any private use or uses them, or makes them available to any person for use, for a purpose other than a purpose of the business he shall be treated for the purposes of the Act as supplying those services in the course or furtherance of the business.

History – In art. 3, the words "6, 6A and 7" were substituted for the words "6 and 7" by SI 1995/1668, art. 4, operative from 1 August 1995.

4 In the case of a business carried on by an individual, this Order shall apply to services used or made available for use, by himself personally.

5 The value of a supply which a person is treated as making by virtue of this Order shall be taken to be that part of the value of the supply of the services to him as fairly and reasonably represents the cost to him of providing the services.

6 This Order shall not apply in respect of any services–

(a) which are used, or made available for use, for a consideration;

(b) except those in respect of which the person carrying on the business has or will become entitled under sections 25 and 26 of the Act to credit for the whole or any part of the tax on their supply to him;

(c) in respect of which any part of the tax on their supply to the person carrying on the business was not counted as being input tax of his by virtue of an apportionment made under section 24(5) of the Act; or

(d) of a description within paragraph 10(1) of Schedule 6 to the Act.

History – In art. 6(b), the words "has or will become" were substituted by SI 1998/762, art. 3, operative in relation to services which are put to any private use, or used or made available to any person for use for a purpose other than a purpose of the business, on or after 18 March 1998.
In art. 6(b), the words "25 and 26" were substituted for the words "14 and 15" by SI 1995/1668, art. 5(a), operative from 1 August 1995.
In art. 6(c), the reference "24(5)" was substituted for "14(4)" by SI 1995/1668, art. 5(b), operative from 1 August 1995.
In art. 6(d), the reference "6" was substituted for "4" by SI 1995/1668, art. 5(c), operative from 1 August 1995.

6A(1) This Order shall not apply to any supply of services consisting of the letting on hire of a motor car where one half of the tax on that letting on hire was excluded from credit under section 25 of the Act by virtue of article 7 of the Value Added Tax (Input Tax) Order 1992.

6A(2) In paragraph (1) above, **"motor car"** has the same meaning as in article 2 of the Value Added Tax (Input Tax) Order 1992.

History – Art. 6A was inserted by SI 1995/1668, art. 6, operative from 1 August 1995.

7 Nothing in this Order shall be construed as making any person liable for any tax which, taken together with any tax for which he was liable as a result of a previous supply of the same services which he was treated as making by virtue of this Order, would exceed the amount of input tax for which he has or will become entitled to credit under sections 25 and 26 of the Act in respect of the services used, or made available for use, by him; and, where the tax chargeable would otherwise exceed the amount of that credit–

(a) he shall not be treated as making a supply of the services where the amount of that credit has already been equalled or exceeded; and

(b) in any other case, the value of the supply shall be reduced accordingly.

History – In art. 7, the words "has or will become entitled" were substituted by SI 1998/762, art. 4(a), operative in relation to services which are put to any private use, or used or made available to any person for use for a purpose other than a purpose of the business, on or after 18 March 1998.

In art. 7, the words "credit under sections 25 and 26 of the Act" were substituted by SI 1998/762, art. 4(b), operative in relation to services which are put to any private use, or used or made available to any person for use for a purpose other than a purpose of the business, on or after 18 March 1998.

8   Where–

(a)   there is a supply of any of the assets of a business of a person (**"the transferor"**) to a person to whom the whole or any part of that business is transferred as a going concern (**"the transferee"**), and

(b)   that supply is treated in accordance with an Order made under section 5(3) of the Act (or under an enactment re-enacted in section 5(3) of the Act) as being neither a supply of goods nor a supply of services,

the liability of the transferee to tax in accordance with articles 5, 6(b) and 7 above, shall be determined as if the transferor and the transferee were the same person.

History – Art. 8 was added by SI 1998/762, art. 5, operative in relation to services which are put to any private use, or used or made available to any person for use for a purpose other than a purpose of the business, on or after 18 March 1998.

9   Where a transferor has himself acquired any assets by way of a supply falling within paragraphs (a) and (b) of article 8 above, that article shall have the effect of requiring the person from whom those assets were acquired to be treated for the purposes of determining the liability of the transferee to tax in accordance with articles 5, 6(b) and 7 above as the same person as the transferor and the transferee, and so on in the case of any number of successive supplies falling within those paragraphs.

History – Art. 9 was added by SI 1998/762, art. 5, operative in relation to services which are put to any private use, or used or made available to any person for use for a purpose other than a purpose of the business, on or after 18 March 1998.

VALUE ADDED TAX (PAYMENTS ON ACCOUNT) ORDER 1993

(SI 1993/2001, as amended by SI 1995/291, SI 1996/1196, SI 1997/2542)

Made on 9 August 1993 by the Treasury, in exercise of the powers conferred on them by s. 38C(1), (2), (4) and (5) of the Value Added Tax Act 1983 [VATA 1994, s. 28(1), (2), (4) and (5)] and of all other powers enabling them in that behalf. Operative from 2 September 1993.

Whereas the Treasury consider it desirable to make an order under section 38C of the Value Added Tax Act 1983 [VATA 1994, s. 28] in the interests of the national economy:

Now, therefore, the Treasury, in exercise of the powers conferred on them by section 38C(1), (2), (4) and (5) of the Value Added Tax Act 1983 [VATA 1994, s. 28(1), (2), (4) and (5)] and of all other powers enabling them in that behalf, hereby make the following Order:

CITATION AND COMMENCEMENT

1   This Order may be cited as the Value Added Tax (Payments on Account) Order 1993 and shall come into force on 2nd September 1993.

INTERPRETATION

2(1)   In this Order–

"**the Act**" means the Value Added Tax Act 1994;

"**the basic period**" means, in relation to a taxable person falling within article 5 or 6 below, the period of one year in which there ended the prescribed accounting periods in respect of which his liability to pay a total amount of tax exceeding £2,000,000 caused him to become such a taxable person;

"**Controller**" means the Controller, Customs and Excise, Value Added Tax Central Unit;

"**reference period**" has the meaning ascribed to it in article 11(1) below.

2(2)   Any reference in articles 13 to 15 below to the total amount of tax by reference to which a taxable person's payments on account fall to be calculated being "**reduced accordingly**" or "**increased accordingly**" is in each case a reference to a reduction or increase of the same proportion as the difference between the total amount of tax by reference to which his payments on account are currently calculated and the total amount of tax, excluding the tax on goods imported from countries other than member States, which he was, or (as the case may be) which the Commissioners are satisfied that he will be, liable to pay in respect of the prescribed accounting periods the ends of which fall within the year referred to in the relevant provision of the article in question.

History – In art. 2(1), in the definition of "the Act", the year "1994" was substituted by SI 1996/1196, art. 3(a), operative from 1 June 1996.
In art. 2(1), the definition of "credit transfer" was omitted by SI 1996/1196, art. 3(b), operative from 1 June 1996.

REVOCATION

3(1)　Subject to paragraph (2) below, the Value Added Tax (Payments on Account) (No. 2) Order 1992 is hereby revoked.

3(2)　The duty under the Value Added Tax (Payments on Account) (No. 2) Order 1992 of any taxable person to make a payment on account in respect of a prescribed accounting period beginning before 2nd September 1993 shall not be affected by the revocation of that Order which shall continue to have effect in relation to any such payment on account.

PAYMENTS ON ACCOUNT

4(1)　A taxable person falling within article 5 or 6 below shall be under a duty to pay, on account of any tax he may become liable to pay in respect of each prescribed accounting period exceeding one month beginning on or after 1st April each year, amounts (in this Order referred to as **"payments on account"**) determined in accordance with this Order at times so determined, provided that in the case of a taxable person falling within article 6 below there shall be no duty to pay such amounts in respect of a prescribed accounting period other than one beginning after the basic period.

4(2)　Where such a taxable person has a prescribed accounting period exceeding one month which begins on or after 2nd March each year and ends on or before 30th June each year, he shall be under a like duty to make payments on account also in respect of that prescribed accounting period.

History – In art. 4(1), the words "1st April each year" were substituted by SI 1995/291, art. 3, operative from 2 March 1995 except that it does not apply where there is a duty to make a payment on account in respect of a prescribed accounting period beginning before that date.
Art. 4(2) was substituted by SI 1995/291, art. 4, operative from 2 March 1995 except that it does not apply where there is a duty to make a payment on account in respect of a prescribed accounting period beginning before that date.

Cross references – VAT Regulations 1995 (SI 1995/2518), reg. 44: payments on account.

Official publications – 700/60.

PERSONS TO WHOM THIS ORDER APPLIES

5(1)　Subject to paragraph (2) below and article 16 below, a taxable person falls within this article in any year if the total amount of tax which he was liable to pay in respect of the prescribed accounting periods the ends of which fell within the period of one year ending on the last day of his last prescribed accounting period ending before the previous 1st December exceeded £2,000,000.

5(2)　Where in any year ending 30th November a prescribed accounting period of the taxable person did not begin on the first day or did not end on the last day of a month, the period of one year shall, for the purpose of this article, be regarded as having comprised those prescribed account periods which related to the tax periods ending within the year ending 30th November of that year to which references are shown in the certificate of registration issued to him.

History – Art. 5 was substituted by SI 1995/291, art. 5, operative from 2 March 1995 except that it does not apply where there is a duty to make a payment on account in respect of a prescribed accounting period beginning before that date. Former art. 5 read as follows:
"**5(1)**　Subject to paragraph (2) below and article 16 below, a taxable person falls within this article if the total amount of tax which he was liable to pay in respect of the prescribed accounting periods the ends of which fell within the period of one year ending on the last day of his last prescribed accounting period ending before 1st June 1993 exceeded £2,000,000.
5(2)　Where in the year ending 31st May 1993 a prescribed accounting period of the taxable person did not begin on the first day or did not end on the last day of a month, the period of one year shall, for the purpose of this article, be regarded as having comprised those prescribed accounting periods which related to the tax periods ending within the year ending 31st May 1993 to which references are shown in the certificate of registration issued to him."

6(1)　Subject to paragraph (2) below and article 16 below, a taxable person who does not fall within article 5 above shall fall within this article if the total amount of tax which he was liable to pay in respect of the prescribed accounting periods the ends of which fell within any one period of one year ending on the last day of a prescribed accounting period of his ending after 30th November of the previous year exceeded £2,000,000.

6(2)　Where in the period of the year referred to in paragraph (1) above a prescribed accounting period of the taxable person did not begin on the first day or did not end on the last day of a month, that period of one year shall, for the purpose of this article, be regarded as having comprised those prescribed accounting periods which related to the tax periods ending within that period of one year to which references are shown in the certificate of registration issued to him.

History – In art. 6(1), the words "30th November of the previous year" were substituted by SI 1995/291, art. 6, operative from 2 March 1995 except that it does not apply where there is a duty to make a payment on account in respect of a prescribed accounting period beginning before that date.

CESSATION OF DUTY TO MAKE PAYMENTS ON ACCOUNT

7   If the total amount of tax which a taxable person who is under a duty to make payments on account was liable to pay in respect of the prescribed accounting periods the ends of which fell within any one period of one year ending after the end of the basic period was less than £1,600,000, then, with effect from the date of the written approval by the Commissioners of a written application by the taxable person to that effect, he shall not be under a duty to make payments on account.

TIME FOR PAYMENT

8   Subject to article 9 below, in respect of each prescribed accounting period a payment on account shall be made to the Controller not later than–

(a)   the last day of the month next following the end of the first complete month included therein, and

(b)   the last day of the month next following the end of the second complete month included therein.

History – In art. 8, the words " Subject to article 9 below," were substituted by SI 1996/1196, art. 4, operative from 1 June 1996.

9   Where a prescribed accounting period does not begin on the first day or does not end on the last day of a month–

(a)   the first payment on account shall be made not later than the last day of the month next following the end of the first complete month included therein, and

(b)   the second payment on account shall be made not later than the last day of the month next following the end of the second complete month included therein,

except that where–

(i)   a prescribed accounting period does not comprise more complete months than one, the first payment on account shall be made not later than the last day of that month and the second payment on account shall be made not later than the end of the prescribed accounting period, or

(ii)   a prescribed accounting period comprises an incomplete month followed by two complete months, the first payment on account shall be made not later than the end of the first complete month and the second payment on account shall be made not later than the end of the second complete month, or

(iii)   a prescribed accounting period comprises an incomplete month followed by two complete months and an incomplete month, the first payment on account shall be made not later than the end of the first complete month and the second payment on account shall be made not later than the end of the second complete month.

History – In art. 9 at the beginning, the words " Subject to article 10 below," were omitted by SI 1996/1196, art. 5, operative from 1 June 1996.

10   [Omitted by SI 1996/1196, art. 6, operative from 1 June 1996.]

CALCULATION OF THE PAYMENTS ON ACCOUNT

11(1)   Subject to paragraph (2) below and articles 12A, 13, 14 and 15 below, the amount of each payment on account to be made by a taxable person who falls within article 5 above shall equal one twenty-fourth of the total amount of tax, excluding the tax on goods imported from countries other than member States, which he was liable to pay in respect of the prescribed accounting periods the ends of which fell within the period (in this Order referred to as **"the reference period"**)–

(a)   1st October to 30th September in the basic period where he has a prescribed accounting period beginning in April in any year in which he is under a duty to make payments on account,

(b)   1st November to 31st October in the basic period where he has a prescribed accounting period beginning in May in any year in which he is under a duty to make payments on account, and

(c)   1st December to 30th November in the basic period where he has a prescribed accounting period beginning in June in any year in which he is under a duty to make payments on account.

11(2)   Where in the period of the year mentioned in sub-paragraph (a), (b) or (c) of paragraph (1) above a prescribed accounting period of the taxable person did not begin on the first day or did not end on the last day of a month, the reference period shall, for the purpose of paragraph (1), be regarded as having comprised those prescribed accounting periods which related to the tax periods ending within the period of the year mentioned in sub-paragraph (a), (b) or (c) of paragraph (1) as appropriate to which references are shown in the certificate of registration issued to him.

History – In art. 11(1), the number "12A" was inserted by SI 1996/1196, art. 7, operative from 1 June 1996.
In art. 11(1), the word "one twenty-fourth" was substituted by SI 1996/1196, art. 7, operative from 1 June 1996.
Art. 11(1)(a) was substituted by SI 1995/291, art. 7, operative from 2 March 1995 except that it does not apply where there is a duty to make a payment on account in respect of a prescribed accounting period beginning before that date.
Art. 11(1)(b) was substituted by SI 1995/291, art. 8, operative from 2 March 1995 except that it does not apply where there is a duty to make a payment on account in respect of a prescribed accounting period beginning before that date.
Art. 11(1)(c) was substituted by SI 1995/291, art. 9, operative from 2 March 1995 except that it does not apply where there is a duty to make a payment on account in respect of a prescribed accounting period beginning before that date.

12   Subject to articles 12A, 13, 14 and 15 below, the amount of each payment on account to be made by a taxable person who falls within article 6 above shall equal one twenty-fourth of the total amount of tax, excluding the tax on goods imported from countries other than member States, which he was liable to pay in respect of the prescribed accounting periods the ends of which fell within the basic period.

History – In art. 12, the number "12A" was inserted by SI 1996/1196, art. 8, operative from 1 June 1996.
In art. 12, the word "one twenty-fourth" was substituted by SI 1996/1196, art. 8, operative from 1 June 1996.

12A(1)   Subject to paragraph (5) below a taxable person who is under a duty to make payments on account may instead of paying the amount calculated in accordance with paragraphs 11 or 12 above elect to pay an amount equal to his liability to VAT (excluding the tax on goods imported from countries other than member States) for the preceding month.

12A(2)   A person making an election under paragraph (1) above shall notify the Commissioners in writing of–

(a)   the election and

(b)   the date (being a date not less than 30 days after the date of the notification) on which it is to take effect.

12A(3)   Subject to paragraph (4) below, an election under paragraph (1) above shall continue to have effect until a date notified by the taxable person in writing to the Commissioners, which date shall not be earlier than the first anniversary of the date on which the election took effect.

12A(4)   Where the Commissioners are satisfied that an amount paid by a person who has elected in accordance with paragraph (1) above is less than the amount required to be paid by virtue of that paragraph the Commissioners may notify the taxable person in writing that his election shall cease to have effect from a date specified in the notification.

12A(5)   A person may not make an election under paragraph (1) above within 12 months of the date on which any previous election made by him ceased to have effect by virtue of paragraph (4) above.

History – Art. 12A was inserted by SI 1996/1196, art. 10, operative from 1 June 1996.

Cross references – VATA 1994, s. 83(fa): appeal against a decision under art. 12A(4) that an election under art. 12A(1) ceases to have effect.

13   If–

(a)   the total amount of tax, excluding the tax on goods imported from countries other than member States, which the taxable person was liable to pay in respect of the prescribed accounting periods the ends of which fell within any one period of one year–

     (i)   in the case of a taxable person who falls within article 5 above, ending after the end of his reference period was less than 80 per cent of the total amount of tax relevant in his case under article 11 above, or

     (ii)   in the case of a taxable person who falls within article 6 above, ending after the end of the basic period was less than 80 per cent of the total amount of tax referred to in article 12, or

(b)   where such a period of one year has not ended, the Commissioners are satisfied that the total amount of tax, excluding the tax on goods imported from countries other than member States, which the taxable person will be liable to pay in respect of the prescribed accounting periods the ends of which fall within that year will be less than 80 per cent of the total amount of tax referred to in sub-paragraph (i) or (ii) (as the case may be) of paragraph (a) above,

then, with effect from the date of the written approval by the Commissioners of a written application by the taxable person to that effect, but subject to article 14 below, the total amount of tax by reference to which his payments on account fall to be calculated shall be reduced accordingly and the amount of each payment on account beginning with the first payment on account which falls to be made after the date of that approval shall equal one twenty-fourth of the reduced amount.

History – In art. 13, the word "one twenty-fourth" was substituted by SI 1996/1196, art. 9, operative from 1 June 1996.

14 If the total amount of tax, excluding the tax on goods imported from countries other than member States, which the taxable person was liable to pay in respect of the prescribed accounting periods the ends of which fell within any one period of one year–

(a)   in the case of a taxable person who falls within article 5 above, ending after the end of his reference period exceeded by 20 per cent or more the total amount of tax by reference to which his payments on account are currently calculated, or

(b)   in the case of a taxable person who falls within article 6 above, ending after the end of the basic period exceeded by 20 per cent or more the total amount of tax by reference to which his payments on account are currently calculated,

then, with effect from the end of the period of one year first mentioned, but subject to article 15 below, the total amount of tax by reference to which his payments on account fall to be calculated shall be increased accordingly and the amount of each payment on account beginning with the first payment on account which falls to be made after the end of that period of one year shall equal one twenty-fourth of the increased amount.

History – In art. 14, the word "one twenty-fourth" was substituted by SI 1996/1196, art. 9, operative from 1 June 1996.

15 Where the payments on account payable by a taxable person have been increased by virtue of article 14 above and–

(a)   the total amount of tax, excluding the tax on goods imported from countries other than member States, which he was liable to pay in respect of the prescribed accounting periods the ends of which fell within any one period of one year ending after such increase has taken effect was less than 80 per cent of the total amount of tax by reference to which his payments on account are currently calculated, or

(b)   where such a period of one year has not ended, the Commissioners are satisfied that the total amount of tax, excluding the tax on goods imported from countries other than member States, which he will be liable to pay in respect of the prescribed accounting periods the ends of which fall within that year will be less than 80 per cent of the total amount of tax by reference to which his payments on account are currently calculated,

then, with effect from the date of the written approval by the Commissioners of a written application by the taxable person to that effect, the total amount of tax by reference to which his payments on account fall to be calculated shall be reduced accordingly and the amount of each payment on account beginning with the first payment on account which falls to be made after the date of that approval shall equal one twenty-fourth of the reduced amount.

History – In art. 15, the word "one twenty-fourth" was substituted by SI 1996/1196, art. 9, operative from 1 June 1996.

BUSINESS CARRIED ON IN DIVISIONS

16(1) Subject to paragraph (3) below, where the registration under the Act of a body corporate is and was throughout the prescribed accounting periods mentioned in article 5(1) or 6(1) above in the names of divisions under section 31(1) of the Act [VATA 1994, s. 46(1)] and those divisions are the same divisions, that body corporate shall not be under a duty to make payments on account by virtue of falling within article 5 or 6 above but shall be under a duty to make payments on account by reference to the business of any division if the total amount of tax which it was liable to pay in respect of the prescribed accounting periods of that division the ends of which fell within the period of one year ending on the last day of–

(a)   that division's last prescribed accounting period ending before 1st December of the previous year, or

(b)   a prescribed accounting period of that division ending after 30th November of the previous year,

and which was referable to the business of that division exceeded £2,000,000.

16(2)   Where a relevant division has a prescribed accounting period exceeding one month which begins on or after 2nd March each year and ends on or before 30th June each year, the body corporate shall be under a like duty to make payments on account also in respect of that prescribed accounting period.

16(3)   Articles 5(2) and 6(2) above shall apply for the purposes of this article as if for the references therein to the taxable person there were substituted references to a relevant division.

16(4)   Where payments on account fall to be made under this article, they shall be calculated and made separately in the case of each relevant division as if it were a taxable person and shall be remitted to the Controller through that division.

16(5)   In relation to a body corporate to which this article applies, references in articles 7, 13, 14 and 15 above to–

(a)   the total amount of tax which a taxable person was or will be liable to pay shall be construed as references to the total amount of such tax referable to the business of a relevant division; and

(b)   an application by the taxable person shall be construed as references to an application by the division in respect of which the application is made.

16(6)   In this article **"relevant division"** means a division by reference to the business of which a body corporate is under a duty to make payments on account by virtue of paragraph (1) above.

History – In art. 16(1)(a), the words "1st December of the previous year" were substituted by SI 1995/291, art. 10, operative from 2 March 1995, except that it does not apply where there is a duty to make a payment on account in respect of a prescribed accounting period beginning before that date.
In art. 16(1)(b), the words "30th November of the previous year" were substituted by SI 1995/291, art. 11, operative from 2 March 1995, except that it does not apply where there is a duty to make a payment on account in respect of a prescribed accounting period beginning before that date.
Art. 16(2) was substituted by SI 1995/291, art. 12, operative from 2 March 1995, except that it does not apply where there is a duty to make a payment on account in respect of a prescribed accounting period beginning before that date.

GROUPS OF COMPANIES

17   This Order shall apply in relation to any bodies corporate which are treated as members of a group under section 43 of the Act as if those bodies were one taxable person; and where there is a duty to make a payment on account it shall be the responsibility of the representative member, except that in default of payment by the representative member it shall be the joint and several responsibility of each member of the group.

History – In art. 17, the reference to "section 43" was substituted by SI 1996/1196, art. 11, operative from 1 June 1996.

FREE ZONE (PRESTWICK AIRPORT) DESIGNATION (VARIATION) ORDER 1994

(SI 1994/143)

Made on 26 January 1994 by the Treasury, in exercise of the powers conferred on them by s. 100A(4)(a)(ii) of the Customs and Excise Management Act 1979 and of all other powers enabling them in that behalf, and with the agreement of Freeport Scotland Limited. Operative from 1 February 1994.

1   This Order may be cited as the Free Zone (Prestwick Airport) Designation (Variation) Order 1994 and shall come into force on 1st February 1994.

2   The area designated a free zone by the Free Zone (Prestwick Airport) Designation Order 1991 shall be varied so as to consist of the area of 7.0359 acres in the parish of Ayr in the County of Ayr, shown enclosed by a red line on a map (being of a scale of 1:2500), marked "Map referred to in article 2 of the Free Zone (Prestwick Airport) Designation (Variation) Order 1994", signed by a Collector of Customs and Excise and dated 7th December 1993.

3   The map referred to in article 2 above shall be kept by the Commissioners at their Headquarters, New King's Beam House, 22 Upper Ground, London SE1 9PJ (and a copy thereof at the offices of Freeport Scotland Limited) in substitution for the map referred to in article 2 of the Free Zone (Prestwick Airport) Designation Order 1991.

FREE ZONE (HUMBERSIDE) DESIGNATION ORDER 1994

(SI 1994/144)

Made on 26 January 1994 by the Treasury, in exercise of the powers conferred on them by s. 100A of the Customs and Excise Management Act 1979 and of all other powers enabling them in that behalf. Operative from 1 February 1994.

CITATION AND COMMENCEMENT

1   This Order may be cited as the Free Zone (Humberside) Designation Order 1994 and shall come into force on 1st February 1994.

DESIGNATION OF AREA AS FREE ZONE

2(1)   An area of 10.322 acres, in the parish of Soneferry in the County of Humberside, shown enclosed by a red line on a map (in this article referred to as **"the map"**), being of a scale of 1:500, and signed by a Collector of Customs and Excise, shall be a free zone.

2(2)   The map shall be kept by the Commissionrs at their Headquarters, New King's Beam House, 22 Upper Ground, London SE1 9PJ and a copy thereof at the offices of the responsible authority.

2(3)   The map or a copy thereof may, on application, be inspected by members of the public at reasonable hours without charge.

Cross references – Free Zone (Humberside) Designation (Variation) Order 1995 (SI 1995/1067).

APPOINTMENT OF RESPONSIBLE AUTHORITY

3   The responsible authority for the free zone shall be Transport Development Group Limited whose Registered Office is at Windsor House, 50 Victoria Street, London SW1H 0NR.

PERIOD OF VALIDITY OF ORDER

4   This Order shall have effect for a period of 10 years from the date of coming into force.

CONDITIONS IMPOSED ON RESPONSIBLE AUTHORITY

5   The responsible authority shall–

(a)   maintain an office in the free zone or such other place as the Commissioners may allow at which shall be kept any records, for which the responsible authority is responsible, relating to the free zone and the business carried on therein;

(b)   keep separate accounts in connection with the free zone;

(c)   provide such information in connection with the free zone and the operation thereof to any person authorised by the Treasury, as that person may reasonably require;

(d)   provide, free of expense to the Crown, such accommodation and facilities including furniture, fittings and equipment as the Commissioners may reasonably require and such accommodation and facilities shall be properly maintained, heated, lighted, ventilated and kept clean by the responsible authority;

(e)   provide, free of expense to the Crown, such area of land within the free zone as the Commissioners may reasonably require for the examination of goods and vehicles and shall provide and maintain such appliances and afford such other facilities which are reasonably necessary to enable an account to be taken of any goods or make any examination or search.

HEALTH AND SAFETY

6   Without prejudice to the responsibilities of persons occupying premises within the free zone, the responsible authority shall ensure that the working conditions within the free zone are safe and without risk to the health and safety of persons employed by the Commissioners and shall comply with any requirements concerning health and safety imposed by any competent authority.

VALUE ADDED TAX TRIBUNALS APPEALS (NORTHERN IRELAND) ORDER 1994

(SI 1994/1978)

Made on 22 July 1994 by the Lord Chancellor, in exercise of the powers conferred on him by s. 26 of the Finance Act 1985 [VATA 1994, s. 86]. Operative from 1 October 1994.

1   This Order may be cited as the Value Added Tax Tribunals Appeals (Northern Ireland) Order 1994 and shall come into force on 1st October 1994.

2   If any party to proceedings before a VAT and duties tribunal in Northern Ireland is dissatisfied in point of law with a decision of the tribunal he may, notwithstanding section 11 of the Tribunals and Inquiries Act 1992, appeal from the tribunal direct to the Court of Appeal if–

(a)   the parties consent;

(b)   the tribunal endorses its decision with a certificate that the decision involves a point of law relating wholly or mainly to the construction of an enactment, or of a statutory instrument, or of any of the Community Treaties or of any Community Instrument, which has been fully argued before it and fully considered by it; and

(c)   the leave of the Court of Appeal has been obtained.

FREE ZONE (PORT OF TILBURY) DESIGNATION (VARIATION) ORDER 1994

(SI 1994/2216)

Made on 24 August 1994 by the Treasury, in exercise of the powers conferred on them by s. 100A(4)(ii) of the Customs and Excise Management Act 1979, and of all other powers enabling them in that behalf. Operative from 25 August 1994.

1   This Order may be cited as the Free Zone (Port of Tilbury) Designation (Variation) Order 1994 and shall come into force on 25th August 1994.

2   The area designated a free zone by the Free Zone (Port of Tilbury) Designation Order 1992 shall be varied so as to consist of the area of 766.9 acres in the Borough of Thurrock in the County of Essex, shown enclosed by a red line on a map (being of a scale of 1:5000), marked "Map referred to in article 2 of the Free Zone (Port of Tilbury) Designation (Variation) Order 1994", signed by a Collector of Customs and Excise and dated 16th May 1994.

3   The map referred to in article 2 above shall be kept by the Commissioners at their Headquarters, New King's Beam House, 22 Upper Ground, London SE1 9PJ (and a copy thereof at the offices of Port of Tilbury London Limited) in substitution for the map referred to in article 2 of the Free Zone (Port of Tilbury) Designation Order 1992.

FREE ZONE (BIRMINGHAM AIRPORT) (SUBSTITUTION OF RESPONSIBLE AUTHORITY) ORDER 1994

(SI 1994/2509)

Made on 23 September 1994 by the Treasury, in exercise of the powers conferred on them by s. 100A(4)(b) of the Customs and Excise Management Act 1979 and all other powers enabling them in that behalf. Operative from 24 September 1994.

1   This Order may be cited as the Free Zone (Birmingham Airport) (Substitution of Responsible Authority) Order 1994 and shall come into force on 24th September 1994.

2   The responsible authority for the area designated a free zone by article 2(1) of the Free Zone (Birmingham Airport) Designation Order 1991 shall, in substitution for The Prudential Assurance

Company Limited who were appointed by article 3 of that Order, be Prudential Portfolio Managers Limited whose Registered Office is at 142 Holborn Bars, London EC1N 2NH.

FREE ZONE (PORT OF SHEERNESS) DESIGNATION ORDER 1994

(SI 1994/2898)

Made on 15 November 1994 by the Treasury, in exercise of the powers conferred on them by s. 100A of the Customs and Excise Management Act 1979 and all other powers enabling them in that behalf. Operative from 16 November 1994.

CITATION AND COMMENCEMENT

1   This Order may be cited as the Free Zone (Port of Sheerness) Designation Order 1994 and shall come into force on 16th November 1994.

DESIGNATION OF AREA AS A FREE ZONE

2(1)   An area of 283 acres, in the Borough of Swale in the County of Kent, shown enclosed by a red line on a map (in this article referred to as **"the map"**), being of a scale of 1:2500, signed by a Collector of Customs and Excise and dated 10th August 1994, shall be a free zone.

2(2)   The map shall be kept by the Commissioners at their Headquarters, New King's Beam House, 22 Upper Ground, London SE1 9PJ and a copy thereof at the offices of the responsible authority.

2(3)   The map or a copy thereof may, on application, be inspected by members of the public at reasonable hours without charge.

APPOINTMENT OF RESPONSIBLE AUTHORITY

3   The responsible authority for the free zone shall be Medway Ports Limited whose Registered Office is at Dockyard House, Sheerness Docks, Sheerness, Kent ME12 1RX.

PERIOD OF VALIDITY OF ORDER

4   This Order shall have effect for a period of 10 years from the date of coming into force.

CONDITIONS IMPOSED ON RESPONSIBLE AUTHORITY

5   The responsible authority shall not permit the area designated by this Order to function as a free zone before the Commissioners are satisfied that the area is secure and have so notified the responsible authority in writing.

6   The responsible authority shall–

(a)   maintain an office in the free zone or at such other place as the Commissioners may allow at which shall be kept any records, for which the responsible authority is responsible, relating to the free zone and the business carried on therein;

(b)   keep separate accounts in connection with the free zone;

(c)   provide such information in connection with the free zone and the operation thereof to any person authorised by the Treasury, as that person may reasonably require;

(d)   provide, free of expense to the Crown, such accommodation and facilities including furniture, fittings and equipment as the Commissioners may reasonably require and such accommodation and facilities shall be properly maintained, heated, lighted, ventilated and kept clean by the responsible authority;

(e)   provide, free of expense to the Crown, such area of land within the free zone as the Commissioners may reasonably require for the examination of goods and vehicles and shall provide and maintain such appliances and afford such other facilities which are reasonably necessary to enable an account to be taken of any goods or make any examination or search.

HEALTH AND SAFETY

7   Without prejudice to the responsibilities of persons occupying premises within the free zone, the responsible authority shall ensure that the working conditions within the free zone are safe and without risk to the health and safety of persons employed by the Commissioners and shall comply with any requirements concerning health and safety imposed by any competent authority.

VALUE ADDED TAX (TREATMENT OF TRANSACTIONS) ORDER 1995

(SI 1995/958 as amended by SI 1999/3119)

Made on 30 March 1995 by the Treasury, in exercise of the powers conferred on them by s. 5(3) of the Value Added Tax Act 1994 and of all other powers enabling them in that behalf. Operative from 1 May 1995.

1   This Order may be cited as the Value Added Tax (Treatment of Transactions) Order 1995 and shall come into force on the day that the Finance Bill 1995 is passed.

Notes – The Finance Bill was passed on 1 May 1995.

2   In this Order–

"work of art" has the same meaning as in section 21 of the Value Added Tax Act 1994.

History – Art. 2 was substituted by SI 1999/3119, operative from 1 January 200. Former art. 2 reads as follows:
2   In this Order–
    "works of art" means–
      (a)   paintings, drawings and pastels executed by hand but not comprised in manufactured articles that have been hand-painted or hand-decorated; collages and similar decorative plaques;
      (b)   original engravings, lithographs and other prints;
      (c)   original sculptures and statuary, in any material."

3(1)   Subject to paragraph (3) below, the transfer of ownership in–

(a)   second-hand goods imported from a place outside the member States with a view to their sale by auction;

(b)   works of art imported from a place outside the member States for the purposes of exhibition, with a view to possible sale,

at a time when the second-hand goods or works of art, as the case may be, are still subject to arrangements for temporary importation with total exemption from import duty in accordance with Articles 137 to 141 and paragraph 1 Article 144 of Council Regulation (EEC) No. 2913/92 and paragraph 1(a) or (c) (as the case may require) and paragraphs 2 and 3 of Article 682 of Commission Regulation (EEC) No. 2454/93, shall be treated as neither a supply of goods nor a supply of services.

3(2)   Subject to paragraph (3) below, the provision of any services relating to a transfer of ownership falling within paragraph (1)(a) or (b) above shall be treated as neither a supply of goods nor a supply of services.

3(3)   Paragraphs (1) and (2) above shall not apply in relation to any transfer of ownership in second-hand goods which is effected otherwise than by sale by auction.

FREE ZONE (HUMBERSIDE) DESIGNATION (VARIATION) ORDER 1995

(SI 1995/1067)

Made on 11 April 1995 by the Treasury, in exercise of the powers conferred on them by s. 100A(4)(a)(ii) of the Customs and Excise Management Act 1979 and of all other powers enabling them in that behalf, and with the agreement of Transport Development Group Limited. Operative from 12 April 1995.

1   This Order may be cited as the Free Zone (Humberside) Designation (Variation) Order 1995 and shall come into force on 12th April 1995.

2   The area designated a free zone by the Free Zone (Humberside) Designation Order 1994 shall be varied so as to consist of the area of 4.479 hectares in the parish of Stoneferry in the County of Humberside, shown enclosed by a red line on a map (being of a scale of 1:500), marked "Map referred to in article 2 of the Free Zone (Humberside) Designation (Variation) Order 1995", signed by a Collector of Customs and Excise and dated 2nd February 1995.

3 The map referred to in article 2 above shall be kept by the Commissioners at their Headquarters, New King's Beam House, 22 Upper Ground, London SE1 9PJ (and a copy thereof at the offices of Transport Development Group Limited) in substitution for the map referred to in article 2 of the Free Zone (Humberside) Designation Order 1994.

VALUE ADDED TAX (SPECIAL PROVISIONS) ORDER 1995

(SI 1995/1268, as amended by SI 1995/1385, SI 1997/1616, SI 1998/760, SI 1999/2831, SI 1999/3120.)

Made on 10 May 1995 by the Treasury, in exercise of the powers conferred on them by s. 5(3) and (5), s. 11(4), s. 43(2) and s. 50A of the Value Added Tax Act 1994 and of all other powers enabling them in that behalf. Operative from 1 June 1995.

CITATION AND COMMENCEMENT

1 This Order may be cited as the Value Added Tax (Special Provisions) Order 1995, and shall come into force on 1st June 1995.

INTERPRETATION

2 In this Order–

"**finance agreement**" means an agreement for the sale of goods whereby the property in those goods is not to be transferred until the whole of the price has been paid and the seller retains the right to repossess the goods;

"**insurer**" means a person permitted, in accordance with section 2 of the Insurance Companies Act 1982, to effect and carry out contracts of insurance against risks of loss of or damage to goods;

"**marine mortgage**" means a mortgage which is registered in accordance with the Merchant Shipping (Registration, etc.) Act 1993 and by virtue of which a boat (but not any share thereof) is made a security for a loan;

"**aircraft mortgage**" means a mortgage which is registered in accordance with the Mortgaging of Aircraft Order 1972 and by virtue of which an aircraft is made security for a loan;

"**the Act**" means the Value Added Tax Act 1994;

"**the Manx Act**" means the Value Added Tax Act 1994;

"**work of art**" has the same meaning as in section 21 of the Act;

"**antiques**" means objects other than works of art or collectors' items, which are more than 100 years old;

"**collectors' items**" means any collection or collector's piece falling within section 21(5) of the Act but excluding investment gold coins within the meaning of Note 1(b) and (c) to Group 15 of Schedule 9 to the Act;

"**motor car**" means any motor vehicle of a kind normally used on public roads which has three or more wheels and either–

(a)   is constructed or adapted solely or mainly for the carriage of passengers; or

(b)   has to the rear of the driver's seat roofed accommodation which is fitted with side windows or which is constructed or adapted for the fitting of side windows;

but does not include–

(i)   vehicles capable of accommodating only one person;

(ii)   vehicles which meet the requirements of Schedule 6 to the Road Vehicles (Construction and Use) Regulations 1986 and are capable of carrying twelve or more seated persons;

(iii)   vehicles of not less than three tonnes unladen weight (as defined in the Table to regulation 3(2) of the Road Vehicles (Construction and Use) Regulations 1986);

(iv)   vehicles constructed to carry a payload (the difference between a vehicle's kerb weight (as defined in the Table to regulation 3(2) of the Road Vehicles (Construction and Use) Regulations 1986) and its maximum gross weight (as defined in that Table)) of one tonne or more;

(v)   caravans, ambulances and prison vans;

(vi)   vehicles constructed for a special purpose other than the carriage of persons and having no other accommodation for carrying persons than such as is incidental to that purpose;

"second-hand goods" means tangible movable property that is suitable for further use as it is or after repair, other than motor cars, works of art, collectors' items or antiques and other than precious metals and precious stones;

"printed matter" includes printed stationery but does not include anything produced by typing, duplicating or photo-copying;

"auctioneer" means a person who sells or offers for sale goods at any public sale where persons become purchasers by competition, being the highest bidders.

History – In art. 2, in the definition of "the Manx Act", the words "Value Added Tax Act 1994" were substituted by SI 1998/760, art. 3, operative from 18 March 1998.
In art. 2, the definition of "work of art" was substituted for the definition of "works of art" by SI 1999/3120, art. 3(b), operative from 1 January 2000. The former definition reads as follows:
""**works of art**" means the following goods–
       pictures, collages and similar decorative plaques, paintings and drawings, executed entirely by hand by the artist, other than plans and drawings for architectural, engineering, industrial, commercial, topographical or similar purposes, hand decorated manufactured articles, theatrical scenery, studio back cloths or the like of painted canvas,
       original engravings, prints and lithographs, being impressions produced in limited numbers directly in black and white or in colour of one or of several plates executed entirely by hand by the artist irrespective of the process or of the material employed by him, but not including any mechanical or photomechanical process,
       original sculptures and statuary, in any material, provided that they are executed entirely by the artist; sculpture casts the production of which is limited to eight copies (or, in relation to statuary casts produced before 1st January 1989, such greater number of copies as the Commissioners of Customs and Excise may in any particular case allow) and supervised by the artist or his successors in title;
       tapestries and wall textiles made by hand from original designs provided by artists, provided that there are not more than eight copies of each,
       individual pieces of ceramics executed entirely by the artist and signed by him,
       enamels on copper, executed entirely by hand, limited to eight numbered copies bearing the signature of the artist or the studio, excluding articles of jewellery and goldsmiths' and silversmiths' wares,
       photographs taken by the artist, printed by him or under his supervision, signed and numbered and limited to 30 copies, all sizes and mounts included;"
In art. 2, the definition of "collectors' items" was substituted by SI 1999/3120, art. 3(a), operative from 1 January 2000. The former definition reads as follows:
""**collectors' items**" means the following goods–
       postage or revenue stamps, postmarks, first-day covers, pre-stamped stationery and the like, franked, or if unfranked not being of legal tender and not being for use as legal tender,
       collections and collectors' pieces of zoological, botanical, mineralogical, anatomical, historical, archaeological, palaeontological, ethnographic or numismatic interest;"
In art. 2, the definition of "motor car" was substituted by SI 1999/2831, art. 2, operative from 1 December 1999. The former definition reads as follows:
""**motor car**" means any motor vehicle of a kind normally used on public roads which has three or more wheels and either–
      (a)   is constructed or adapted solely or mainly for the carriage of passengers; or
      (b)   has to the rear of the driver's seat roofed accommodation which is fitted with side windows or which is constructed or adapted for the fitting of side windows;
but does not include–
      (i)   vehicles capable of accommodating only one person or suitable for carrying twelve or more persons;
      (ii)   vehicles of not less than three tonnes unladen weight;
      (iii)   caravans, ambulances and prison vans;
      (iv)   vehicles of a type approved by the Assistant Commissioner of Police of the Metropolis as conforming to the condition of fitness for the time being laid down by him for the purposes of the London Cab Order 1934;
      (v)   vehicles constructed for a special purpose other than the carriage of persons and having no other accommodation for carrying persons than such as is incidental to that purpose;"

REVOCATIONS

3(1)   The Value Added Tax (Horses and Ponies) Order 1983 is hereby revoked.

3(2)   *The Value Added Tax (Special Provisions) Order 1992 is hereby revoked.*

3(3)   The Value Added Tax (Special Provisions) (Amendment) Order 1995 is hereby revoked.

TREATMENT OF TRANSACTIONS

4(1)   Each of the following descriptions of transactions shall be treated as neither a supply of goods nor a supply of services–

(a)   the disposal of any of the goods described in paragraph (3) below by a person who repossessed them under the terms of a finance agreement;

(b)   the disposal of any of the goods described in paragraph (3) below by an insurer who has taken possession of them in settlement of a claim under a policy of insurance;

(c)   the disposal of a boat by a mortgagee after he has taken possession thereof under the terms of a marine mortgage;

(d)   the disposal of an aircraft by a mortgagee after he has taken possession thereof under the terms of an aircraft mortgage;

if, in each case, the goods so disposed of are in the same condition at the time of disposal as they were when they were repossessed or taken into possession, as the case may be, and if a supply of them in the United Kingdom by the person from whom in each case they were obtained would not have been chargeable with VAT, or would have been chargeable with VAT on less than the full value of such supply.

4(2)   Paragraph (1) of this article shall not apply to reimported goods which were previously exported from the United Kingdom or the Isle of Man free of VAT chargeable under the Act or VAT chargeable under Part I of the Manx Act by reason of the zero-rating provisions of either Act, or regulations made under either Act, or to imported goods which have not borne VAT chargeable under either of those Acts in the United Kingdom or the Isle of Man.

4(3)   The goods referred to in subparagraphs (a) and (b) of paragraph (1) above are as follows:

(a)   works of art, antiques and collectors' items;

(b)   second-hand goods.

History – In art. 4(2), the words "Act, or" were inserted after the words "zero-rating provisions of either" by SI 1995/1385, art. 2, operative from 1 June 1995.

5(1)   Subject to paragraph (2) below, there shall be treated as neither a supply of goods nor a supply of services the following supplies by a person of assets of his business–

(a)   their supply to a person to whom he transfers his business as a going concern where–

    (i)   the assets are to be used by the transferee in carrying on the same kind of business, whether or not as part of any existing business, as that carried on by the transferor, and

    (ii)   in a case where the transferor is a taxable person, the transferee is already, or immediately becomes as a result of the transfer, a taxable person or a person defined as such in section 3(1) of the Manx Act;

(b)   their supply to a person to whom he transfers part of his business as a going concern where–

    (i)   that part is capable of separate operation,

    (ii)   the assets are to be used by the transferee in carrying on the same kind of business, whether or not as part of any existing business, as that carried on by the transferor in relation to that part, and

    (iii)   in a case where the transferor is a taxable person, the transferee is already, or immediately becomes as a result of the transfer, a taxable person or a person defined as such in section 3(1) of the Manx Act.

5(2)   A supply of assets shall not be treated as neither a supply of goods nor a supply of services by virtue of paragraph (1) above to the extent that it consists of–

(a)   a grant which would, but for an election which the transferor has made, fall within item 1 of Group 1 of Schedule 9 to the Act; or

(b)   a grant of a fee simple which falls within paragraph (a) of item 1 of Group 1 of Schedule 9 to the Act,

unless the transferee has made an election in relation to the land concerned which has effect on the relevant date and has given any written notification of the election required by paragraph 3(6) of Schedule 10 to the Act, no later than the relevant date.

5(3)   In paragraph (2) of this article–

    "**election**" means an election having effect under paragraph 2 of Schedule 10 to the Act;

    "**relevant date**" means the date upon which the grant would have been treated as having been made or, if there is more than one such date, the earliest of them;

    "*transferor*" and "*transferee*" include a relevant associate of either respectively as defined in paragraph 3(7) of Schedule 10 to the Act.

5(4)   There shall be treated as neither a supply of goods nor a supply of services the assignment by an owner of goods comprised in a hire-purchase or conditional sale agreement of his rights and interest thereunder, and the goods comprised therein, to a bank or other financial institution.

History – In art. 5(1)(a)(ii), the words "section 3(1)" were substituted by SI 1998/760, art. 4, operative from 18 March 1998.

In art. 5(1)(b)(iii), the words "section 3(1)" were substituted by SI 1998/760, art. 4, operative from 18 March 1998.

Official publications – 700/9.

Customs Internal Guidance Manual, vol. V1.10: transfer of a going concern.

Other material – Customs and Excise News Release 56/93, 27 July 1993 (not reproduced): where building subject to a rent-free period sold during that period, the vendor may be regarded as carrying on a property rental business even if no income has previously been received.

6   The following description of transaction shall be treated as a supply of services and not as a supply of goods–

> the exchange of a reconditioned article for an unserviceable article of a similar kind by a person who regularly offers in the course of his business to provide a reconditioning facility by that means.

7   The following description of transaction shall not be treated as the acquisition of goods from another member State–

> the removal of goods to the United Kingdom in pursuance of a supply to a taxable person, made by a person in another member State, where VAT on that supply is to be accounted for and paid in another member State by reference to the profit margin on the supply by virtue of the law of that member State corresponding to section 50A of the Act and any Orders made thereunder.

8   The following description of transaction shall be treated as neither a supply of goods nor a supply of services–

> the removal of goods to the United Kingdom in pursuance of a supply to a person, made by a person in another member State where VAT on that supply is to be accounted for and paid in another member State by reference to the profit margin on the supply by virtue of the law of that member State corresponding to section 50A of the Act and any Orders made thereunder.

9   The following description of transaction shall be treated as neither a supply of goods nor a supply of services–

> services in connection with a supply of goods provided by an agent acting in his own name to the purchaser of the goods the consideration for which is taken into account by virtue of article 12(6) below in calculating the price at which the agent obtained the goods.

10   The following description of transaction shall be treated as neither a supply of goods nor a supply of services–

> services in connection with the sale of goods provided by an auctioneer acting in his own name to the vendor or the purchaser of the goods the consideration for which is taken into account by virtue of article 12(7) below in calculating the price at which the auctioneer obtained (or as the case may be) sold the goods.

SELF-SUPPLY

11(1)   Where a person in the course or furtherance of any business carried on by him produces printed matter and the printed matter–

(a)   is not supplied to another person or incorporated in other goods produced in the course or furtherance of that business; but

(b)   is used by him for the purpose of a business carried on by him,

then, subject to paragraph (2) below, the printed matter shall be treated for the purposes of the Act as both supplied to him for the purpose of that business and supplied by him in the course or furtherance of that business.

11(2)   Paragraph (1) of this article does not apply if–

(a)   the person is a fully taxable *person;*

(b)   the value of the supplies falling to be treated as made by and to that person would not, if those were the only supplies made or to be made by that person, make him liable to be registered for VAT pursuant to the provisions of Schedule 1 to the Act; or

(c)   the Commissioners, being satisfied that the VAT (if any) which would be attributable to the supplies after allowing for any credit under sections 25 and 26 of the Act would be negligible, have given, and have not withdrawn, a direction that the paragraph is not to apply.

11(3)   For the purposes of paragraph (2)(a) above, a person is a fully taxable person if the only input tax of his to which he is not entitled to credit at the end of any prescribed accounting period or longer period is input tax which is excluded from any credit under section 25 of the Act by virtue of any Order made under sub-section (7) of that section.

11(4)   The preceding provisions of this article shall apply in relation to any bodies corporate which are treated for the purposes of section 43 of the Act as members of a group as if those bodies were one person, but any printed matter which would fall to be treated as supplied to and by that person shall be treated as supplied to and by the representative member.

RELIEF FOR CERTAIN GOODS

12(1)   Without prejudice to article 13 below and subject to complying with such conditions as the Commissioners may direct in a notice published by them for the purposes of this Order or may otherwise direct and subject to paragraph (4) below, where a person supplies goods of a description in paragraph (2) below, of which he took possession in any of the circumstances set out in paragraph (3) below, he may opt to account for the VAT chargeable on the supply on the profit margin on the supply instead of by reference to its value.

12(2)   The supplies referred to in paragraph (l) above are supplies of–

(a)   works of art, antiques and collectors' items;

(b)   second-hand goods.

12(3)   The circumstances mentioned in paragraph (l) above are–

(a)   that the taxable person took possession of the goods pursuant to–

    (i)   a supply in respect of which no VAT was chargeable under the Act or under Part I of the Manx Act;

    (ii)   a supply on which VAT was chargeable on the profit margin in accordance with paragraph (1) above or a corresponding provision made under the Manx Act or a corresponding provision of the law of another member State;

    (iii)   a transaction except one relating to the transfer of the assets of a business or part of a business as a going concern which was treated by virtue of any Order made or having effect as if made under section 5(3) of the Act or under the corresponding provisions of the Manx Act as being neither a supply of goods nor a supply of services;

    (iv)   a transaction relating to the transfer of the assets of a business or part of a business as a going concern which was treated as neither a supply of goods nor a supply of services if the transferor took possession of the goods in any of the circumstances described in this sub-paragraph; or

    (v)   (if the goods are a work of art) a supply to the taxable person by, or an acquisition from another member State by him from its creator or his successor in title;

(b)   (if the goods are a work of art, an antique or a collectors' item) that they were imported by the taxable person himself.

12(4)   A taxable person–

(a)   may not opt under paragraph (1) above where–

    (i)   the supply is a letting on hire;

    (ii)   an invoice or similar document showing an amount as being VAT or as being attributable to VAT is issued in respect of the supply;

    (iii)   the supply is of an air gun unless the taxable person is registered for the purposes of the Firearms Act 1968; or

    (iv)   the supply is of goods which are being disposed of in the circumstances mentioned in article 4(1)(a), (b), (c) or (d) above but which is not disregarded by virtue of that article;

(b)   may only exercise the option under paragraph (1) above in relation to supplies of–

    (i)   works of art of which he took possession in the circumstances mentioned in paragraph (3)(a)(v) above, or

    (ii)   works of art, antiques or collectors' items of which he took possession in circumstances set out in paragraph (3)(b) above,

if at the same time he exercises the option in relation to the other.

12(5)   Subject to paragraph (6) below, for the purposes of determining the profit margin–

(a)   the price at which goods were obtained shall be calculated as follows–

(i) (where the taxable person took possession of the goods pursuant to a supply) in the same way as the consideration for the supply would be calculated for the purposes of the Act;

(ii) (where the taxable person is a sole proprietor and the goods were supplied to him in his private capacity) in the same way as the consideration for the supply to him as a private individual would be calculated for the purposes of the Act;

(iii) (where the goods are a work of art which was acquired from another member State by the taxable person pursuant to a supply to him by the creator of the item or his successor in title) in the same way as the value of the acquisition would be calculated for the purposes of the Act plus the VAT chargeable on the acquisition;

(iv) (where the goods are a work of art, an antique or a collectors' item which the taxable person has imported himself) in the same way as the value of the goods for the purpose of charging VAT on their importation would be calculated for the purposes of the Act plus any VAT chargeable on their importation;

(v) (where the taxable person took possession of the goods pursuant to a transaction relating to the transfer of the assets of a business or part of a business as a going concern which was treated by virtue of any Order made or having effect as if made under section 5(3) of the Act, or under the corresponding provisions of the Manx Act, as neither a supply of goods nor a supply of services) as being the price at which the earliest of his predecessors obtained the goods;

(b) the price at which goods are sold shall be calculated in the same way as the consideration for the supply would be calculated for the purposes of the Act;

(c) in relation to any goods, a person is the predecessor of another for the purposes of this article if–

(i) that other person is a person to whom he has transferred assets of his business by a transfer of that business, or a part of it, as a going concern;

(ii) those assets consisted of or included those goods; and

(iii) the transfer of the assets is one falling by virtue of an Order made or having effect as if made under section 5(3) of the Act, or under the corresponding provisions of the Manx Act, to be treated as neither a supply of goods nor a supply of services;

and the reference in sub-paragraph (a) above to a person's predecessors includes a reference to the predecessors of his predecessors through any number of transfers.

12(6) Subject to paragraph (7) below, where the taxable person is an agent acting in his own name the price at which the goods were obtained shall be calculated in accordance with paragraph (5)(a) above, but the selling price calculated in accordance with paragraph (5)(b) above shall be increased by the amount of any consideration payable to the taxable person in respect of services supplied by him to the purchaser in connection with the supply of the goods.

12(7) Instead of calculating the price at which goods were obtained or supplied in accordance with paragraph (6) above an auctioneer acting in his own name may–

(a) calculate the price at which they were obtained by deducting from the successful bid the consideration for any services supplied by him to the vendor in connection with the sale of the goods;

(b) calculate the price at which they were supplied by adding to the successful bid the consideration for any supply of services by him to the purchaser in connection with the sale of the goods,

in either (or both) cases excluding the consideration for supplies of services that are not chargeable to VAT.

12(8) Where a taxable person opts under paragraph (1) above in respect of goods of which he took possession in the circumstances set out in paragraph 3(a)(iv) and (b) above, the exercise of the option shall–

(a) be notified by him to the Commissioners in writing;

(b) have effect from the date of that notification or such later date as may be specified therein;

(c) subject to paragraph (9) below, apply to all supplies of such goods made by the taxable person in the period ending 2 years after the date on which it first had effect or the date on which written notification of its revocation is given to the Commissioners, whichever is the later.

12(9) Notwithstanding paragraph (8)(c) above a taxable person may elect to account for VAT chargeable on any particular supply of such goods by reference to the value of that supply.

History – Art. 12(3)(a) was substituted by SI 1997/1616, art. 3, operative from 3 July 1997. Former art. 12(3)(a) reads as follows:
"(a)   that the taxable person took possession of the goods pursuant to –
         (i)   a supply in respect of which no VAT was chargeable under the Act or under Part I of the Manx Act;
a supply on which VAT was chargeable on the profit margin in accordance with paragraph (1) above or a corresponding provision made under the Manx Act or a corresponding provision of the law of another member State;
a transaction which was treated by virtue of any Order made under Section 5(3) of the Act or under the corresponding provisions of the Manx Act as being neither a supply of goods nor a supply of services; or
(if the goods are a work of art) a supply to the taxable person by, or an acquisition from another member State by him from its creator or his successor in title;".
Art. 12(5)(a)(v) was inserted by SI 1998/760, art. 6(1), operative from 18 March 1998.
In art. 12(4)(b)(i), the words "(3)(a)(v)" were substituted by SI 1998/760, art. 5, operative from 18 March 1998.
Art. 12(5)(c) and the words at the end of art. 12(5) were added by SI 1998/760, art. 6(2), operative from 18 March 1998.
Official publications – 718.
Customs Internal Guidance Manual, vol. V1.23: chapter 7, margin scheme for second-hand goods.

GLOBAL ACCOUNTING

13(1) Subject to complying with such conditions as the Commissioners may direct in a notice published by them for the purposes of this Order or may otherwise direct, and subject to paragraph (2) below, a taxable person who has opted under article 12(1) above may account for VAT on the total profit margin on goods supplied by him during a prescribed accounting period, calculated in accordance with paragraph (3) below, instead of the profit margin on each supply.

13(2) Paragraph (1) above does not apply to supplies of–

(a)   motor vehicles;

(b)   aircraft;

(c)   boats and outboard motors;

(d)   caravans and motor caravans;

(e)   horses and ponies;

(f)   any other individual items whose value calculated in accordance with article 12(5)(a) above, exceeds £500.

13(3) The **total profit margin** for a prescribed accounting period shall be the amount (if any) by which the total selling price calculated in accordance with paragraph (4) below, exceeds the total purchase price calculated in accordance with paragraph (5) below.

13(4) For the purposes of paragraph (3) above the total selling price shall be calculated by aggregating for all goods sold during the period the prices (calculated in accordance with article 12(5) or (6) above as appropriate) for which they were sold.

13(5) For the purposes of paragraph (3) above the total purchase price shall be calculated by aggregating for all goods obtained during the period the prices (calculated in accordance with article 12(5) above) at which they were obtained and adding to that total the amount (if any) carried forward from the previous period in accordance with paragraph (6) below;

13(6) If in any prescribed accounting period the total purchase price calculated in accordance with paragraph (5) above exceeds the total selling price, the excess amount shall be carried forward to the following prescribed accounting period for inclusion in the calculation of the total purchase price for that period.

History – Art. 13(3) was substituted by SI 1999/3120, art. 4, operative from 1 January 2000. The former definition reads as follows:
"3   The total profit margin for a prescribed accounting period shall be the amount (if any) by which the total selling price calculated in accordance with paragraph (5) below, exceeds the total purchase price calculated in accordance with paragraph (4) below."
Official publications – 718.

VALUE ADDED TAX (REFUND OF TAX) ORDER 1995

(SI 1995/1978)

Made on 26 July 1995 by the Treasury, in exercise of the powers conferred on them by s. 33(3) of the Value Added Tax Act 1994 and of all other powers enabling them in that behalf. Operative from 18 August 1995.

1 This Order may be cited as the Value Added Tax (Refund of Tax) Order 1995 and shall come into force on 18th August 1995.

2 The Environment Agency (a body corporate established by section 1 of the Environment Act 1995) is hereby specified for the purposes of section 33 of the Value Added Tax Act 1994.

VALUE ADDED TAX REGULATIONS 1995

(SI 1995/2518, as variously amended)

Made on 27 September 1995 by the Commissioners of Customs and Excise, in exercise of the powers conferred on them by sections 3(4), 6(14), 7(9), 8(4), 12(3), 14(3), 16(1) and (2), 18(5) and (5A), 24(3), (4) and (6), 25(1), (4) and (6), 26(1), (3) and (4), 28(3), (4) and (5), 30(8), 35(2), 36(5), 37(3) and (4), 38, 39(1), 40(3), 46(2) and (4), 48(3)(b), (4) and (6), 49(2) and (3), 52, 54(1), (2), (3) and (6), 58, 79(3), 80(6), 88(3) and (5), 92(4), 93(1) and (2), 95(5) and 97(1) of, and paragraph 17 of Schedule 1, paragraph 9 of Schedule 2, paragraph 10 of Schedule 3, paragraphs 2(1) and (2) of Schedule 7, and paragraphs 2(1), (2), (3), (4), (5), (6), (7), (8), (9), (10), (11) and (12), 5(4) and (9), 6(1) and (2) and 7(1) of Schedule 11 to, the Value Added Tax Act 1994 and of all other powers enabling them in that behalf, hereby make the following Regulations coming into force 20 October 1995.

ARRANGEMENT OF REGULATIONS

REGULATION

REGULATION

SCHEDULES

SCHEDULE

1.   FORMS
1A.   THE FISCAL WAREHOUSING RECORD WHICH IS REFERRED TO IN PARAGRAPH (3) OF REGULATION 145F SHALL HAVE THE FEATURES AND COMPLY WITH THE REQUIREMENTS SET OUT BELOW
2.   REVOCATIONS

PART I – PRELIMINARY

CITATION AND COMMENCEMENT

1 These Regulations may be cited as the Value Added Tax Regulations 1995 and shall come into force on 20th October 1995.

INTERPRETATION – GENERAL

2(1) In these Regulations unless the context otherwise requires–

"**the Act**" means the Value Added Tax Act 1994 and any reference to a Schedule to the Act includes a reference to a Schedule as amended from time to time by Order of the Treasury;

"**alphabetical code**" means the alphabetical prefix as set out below which shall be used to identify the member State–

Austria–AT

Belgium–BE

Denmark–DK

Finland–FI

France–FR

Germany–DE

Greece–EL

Ireland–IE

Italy–IT

Luxembourg–LU

Netherlands–NL

Portugal–PT

Spain–ES

Sweden–SE

United Kingdom–GB;

"**Collector**" includes Deputy Collector and Assistant Collector;

"**the Community**" means the European Community;

"**continental shelf**" means a designated area within the meaning of the Continental Shelf Act 1964;

"**Controller**" means the Controller, Customs and Excise Value Added Tax Central Unit;

"**datapost packet**" means a postal packet containing goods which is posted in the United Kingdom as a datapost packet for transmission to a place outside the United Kingdom in *accordance with the terms of* a contract entered into between the Post Office and the sender of the packet; or which is received at a post office in the United Kingdom from a place outside the United Kingdom for transmission and delivery in the United Kingdom as if it were a datapost packet;

"**fiscal or other warehousing regime**" means "fiscal warehousing regime or warehousing regime";

"**prescribed accounting period**", subject to regulation 99(1), means a period such as is referred to in regulation 25;

"**proper officer**" means the person appointed or authorised by the Commissioners to act in respect of any matter in the course of his duties;

"**registered person**" means a person registered by the Commissioners under Schedule 1, 2, 3 or 3A to the Act;

"**registration number**" means the number allocated by the Commissioners to a taxable person in the certificate of registration issued to him;

"**return**" means a return which is required to be made in accordance with regulation 25;

"**specified date**" means the date specified in a person's application for registration for the purpose of VAT as that on which he expects to make his first taxable supply.

2(2) A reference in these Regulations to "this Part" is a reference to the Part of these Regulations in which that reference is made.

2(3) In these Regulations any reference to a form prescribed in Schedule 1 to these Regulations shall include a reference to a form which the Commissioners are satisfied is a form to the like effect.

History – In reg. 2(1), the definition of "fiscal or other warehousing regime" was inserted by SI 1996/1250, reg. 4, operative from 1 June 1996.
In reg. 2(1), in the definition of "registered person", the words "Schedule 1, 2, 3 or 3A" were substituted for the words "Schedule 1, 2 or 3" by SI 2000/794, reg. 3, operative from 22 March 2000.

REVOCATIONS AND SAVINGS

3(1) The Regulations described in Schedule 2 to these Regulations are hereby revoked.

3(2) Anything begun under or for the purpose of any Regulations revoked by these Regulations shall be continued under or, as the case may be, for the purpose of the corresponding provision of these Regulations.

3(3) Where any document used or required for the purpose of VAT refers to a provision of a regulation revoked by these Regulations, such reference shall, unless the context otherwise requires, be construed as a reference to the corresponding provision of these Regulations.

REQUIREMENT, DIRECTION, DEMAND OR PERMISSION

4 Any requirement, direction, demand or permission by the Commissioners, under or for the purposes of these Regulations, may be made or given by a notice in writing, or otherwise.

PART II – REGISTRATION AND PROVISIONS FOR SPECIAL CASES

Official publications – 700, para. 11.1ff. (2000 edn).
Customs Internal Guidance Manual, vol. V1.28: registration and de-registration.

REGISTRATION AND NOTIFICATION

5(1) Where any person is required under paragraph 5(1) or 6(1) of Schedule 1, paragraph 3(1) of Schedule 2, paragraph 3(1) of Schedule 3 or paragraph 3(1) or 4(1) of Schedule 3A to the Act to notify the Commissioners of his liability to be registered, the notification shall contain the particulars (including the declaration) set out in forms numbered 1, 6, 7 and 7A respectively in Schedule 1 to these Regulations and shall be made in those forms;

provided that, where the notification is made by a partnership, the notification shall also contain the particulars set out in the form numbered 2 in that Schedule.

5(2) Every registered person except one to whom paragraph 11, 12, 13(1), (2) or (3) of Schedule 1, paragraph 5 of Schedule 2, paragraph 5 of Schedule 3 or paragraph 5 of Schedule 3A of the Act applies, shall, within 30 days of any changes being made in the name, constitution or ownership of his business, or of any other event occurring which may necessitate the variation of the register or cancellation of his registration, notify the Commissioners in writing of such change or event and furnish them with full particulars thereof.

5(3) Every notification by a registered person under paragraph 11 or 12 of Schedule 1, paragraph 5 of Schedule 2, paragraph 5 of Schedule 3 or paragraph 5 of Schedule 3A to the Act shall be made in writing to the Commissioners and shall state–

(a) the date on which he ceased to make, or have the intention of making, taxable supplies; or

(b) where paragraph 12(a) of Schedule 1 to the Act applies, the date on which he ceased to make, or have the intention of making, supplies within paragraph 10(2) of that Schedule; or

(c) where paragraph 12(b) of Schedule 1 to the Act applies, the date on which he made, or formed the intention of making, taxable supplies; or

(d)   where paragraph 5(1) of Schedule 2 to the Act applies, the date on which he ceased to be registrable by virtue of paragraph 5(4) of that Schedule; or

(e)   where paragraph 5(1) of Schedule 3 to the Act applies, the date on which he ceased to be registrable by virtue of paragraph 5(3) of that Schedule; or

(f)   where paragraph 5(1) of Schedule 3A to the Act applies, the date on which he ceased to make, or have the intention of making, relevant supplies within the meaning of paragraph 9 of that Schedule.

History – Reg. 5 was substituted by SI 2000/794, reg. 4, operative from 22 March 2000. Former reg. 5 reads as follows:
"**5(1)** Where any person is required under paragraph 5(1) or 6(1) of Schedule 1, paragraph 3(1) of Schedule 2, or paragraph 3(1) of Schedule 3 to the Act to notify the Commissioners of his liability to be registered, the notification shall contain the particulars (including the declaration) set out in the forms numbered 1, 6 and 7 respectively in Schedule 1 to these Regulations and shall be made in those forms;

provided that, where the notification is made by a partnership, the notification shall also contain the particulars set out in the form numbered 2 in that Schedule.

5(2) Every registered person except one to whom paragraph 11, 12, 13(1), (2) or (3) of Schedule 1, paragraph 5 of Schedule 2, or paragraph 5 of Schedule 3 to the Act applies shall, within 30 days of any changes being made in the name, constitution or ownership of his business, or of any other event occurring which may necessitate the variation of the register or cancellation of his registration, notify the Commissioners in writing of such change or event and furnish them with full particulars thereof.

5(3) Every notification by a registered person under paragraph 11 or 12 of Schedule 1, paragraph 5 of Schedule 2, or paragraph 5 of Schedule 3 to the Act shall be made in writing to the Commissioners and shall state–
(a)   the date on which he ceased to make, or have the intention of making, taxable supplies; or
(b)   where paragraph 12(a) of Schedule 1 to the Act applies, the date on which he ceased to make, or have the intention of making, supplies within paragraph 10(2) of that Schedule; or
(c)   where paragraph 12(b) of Schedule 1 to the Act applies, the date on which he made, or formed the intention of making, taxable supplies; or
(d)   where paragraph 5(1) of Schedule 2 to the Act applies, the date on which he ceased to make, or have the intention of making, supplies; or
(e)   where paragraph 5(1) of Schedule 3 to the Act applies, the date on which he ceased to make, or have the intention of making, a relevant acquisition within paragraph 6(2) of that Schedule."

TRANSFER OF A GOING CONCERN

6(1) Where–

(a)   a business is transferred as a going concern,

(b)   the registration under Schedule 1 to the Act of the transferor has not already been cancelled,

(c)   on the transfer of the business the registration of the transferor under that Schedule is to be cancelled and either the transferee becomes liable to be registered under that Schedule or the Commissioners agree to register him under paragraph 9 of that Schedule, and

(d)   an application is made in the form numbered 3 in Schedule 1 to these Regulations by or on behalf of both the transferor and the transferee of that business,

the Commissioners may as from the date of the said transfer cancel the registration under Schedule 1 to the Act of the transferor and register the transferee under that Schedule with the registration number previously allocated to the transferor.

6(2) An application under paragraph (1) above shall constitute notification for the purposes of paragraph 11 of Schedule 1 to the Act.

6(3) Where the transferee of a business has under paragraph (1) above been registered under Schedule 1 to the Act in substitution for the transferor of that business, and with the transferor's registration number–

(a)   any liability of the transferor existing at the date of the transfer to make a return or to account for or pay VAT under regulation 25 or 41 shall become the liability of the transferee,

(b)   any right of the transferor, whether or not existing at the date of the transfer, to credit for, or to repayment of, input tax shall become the right of the transferee,

(c)   any right of either the transferor, whether or not existing at the date of the transfer, or the transferee to payment by the Commissioners under section 25(3) of the Act shall be satisfied by payment to either of them,

(d)   any right of the transferor, whether or not existing at the date of the transfer, to claim a refund under section 36 of the Act shall become the right of the transferee, and

(e)   any liability of the transferor, whether or not existing at the date of the transfer, to account for an amount under Part XIXA of these Regulations, shall become that of the transferee.

6(4) In addition to the provisions set out in paragraph (3) above, where the transferee of a business has been registered in substitution for, and with the registration number of, the transferor during a prescribed accounting period subsequent to that in which the transfer of the business took place but with effect from the date of the transfer of the business, and any–

(a)   return has been made,

(b)   VAT has been accounted for and paid, or

(c)   right to credit for input tax has been claimed,

either by or in the name of the transferee or the transferor, it shall be treated as having been done by the transferee.

History – Reg. 6(3)(d), (e) added by SI 1997/1086, reg. 3, operative from 1 May 1997.

Cross references – Reg. 25(4I): authorisation to make VAT returns electronically.

Official publications – 700/9.

NOTICE BY PARTNERSHIP

7(1)   Where any notice is required to be given for the purposes of the Act or these Regulations by a partnership, it shall be the joint and several liability of all the partners to give such notice, provided that a notice given by one partner shall be a sufficient compliance with any such requirement.

7(2)   Where, in Scotland, a body of persons carrying on a business which includes the making of taxable supplies is a partnership required to be registered, any notice shall be given and signed in the manner indicated in section 6 of the Partnership Act 1890.

REPRESENTATION OF CLUB, ASSOCIATION OR ORGANISATION

8   Anything required to be done by or under the Act, these Regulations or otherwise by or on behalf of a club, association or organisation, the affairs of which are managed by its members or a committee or committees of its members, shall be the joint and several responsibility of–

(a)   every member holding office as president, chairman, treasurer, secretary or any similar office; or in default of any thereof,

(b)   every member holding office as a member of a committee; or in default of any thereof,

(c)   every member,

provided that if it is done by any official, committee member or member referred to above, that shall be sufficient compliance with any such requirement.

DEATH, BANKRUPTCY OR INCAPACITY OF TAXABLE PERSON

9(1)   If a taxable person dies or becomes bankrupt or incapacitated, the Commissioners may, from the date on which he died or became bankrupt or incapacitated treat as a taxable person any person carrying on that business until some other person is registered in respect of the taxable supplies made or intended to be made by that taxable person in the course or furtherance of his business or the incapacity ceases, as the case may be; and the provisions of the Act and of any Regulations made thereunder shall apply to any person so treated as though he were a registered person.

9(2)   Any person carrying on such business shall, within 21 days of commencing to do so, inform the Commissioners in writing of that fact and of the date of the death, the date of the bankruptcy order, or of the nature of the incapacity and the date on which it began.

9(3)   In relation to a company which is a taxable person, the references in paragraph (1) above to the taxable person becoming **bankrupt** or **incapacitated** shall be construed as references to the company going into liquidation or receivership or to an administration order being made in relation to it.

History – In reg. 9(2), the words "the date of the bankruptcy order," were inserted by SI 1996/1250, reg. 5, operative from 1 June 1996.

VAT REPRESENTATIVES

10(1)   Where any person is appointed by virtue of section 48 of the Act to be the VAT representative of another (in this regulation referred to as **"his principal"**), the VAT representative shall notify the Commissioners of his appointment on the form numbered 8 in Schedule 1 to these Regulations within 30 days of the date on which his appointment became effective and the notification shall contain the particulars (including the declaration) set out in that form.

10(2)   The notification referred to in this regulation shall be accompanied by evidence of the VAT representative's appointment.

10(3)   Where a person is appointed by virtue of section 48 of the Act to be a VAT representative, the Commissioners shall register the name of that VAT representative against the name of his principal in the register kept for the purposes of the Act.

10(4) Every VAT representative who is registered in accordance with this regulation shall, within 30 days of any changes being made in the name, constitution or ownership of his business or of his ceasing to be a person's VAT representative, or of any other event occurring which may necessitate the variation of the register, notify the Commissioners in writing of such change, cessation or event and furnish them with full particulars thereof.

10(5) For the purposes of this regulation the date upon which the appointment of a VAT representative (**"the first VAT representative"**) shall be regarded as having ceased shall be treated as being whichever is the earliest of the following times–

(a)   when the Commissioners receive any notification in accordance with regulation 5(2), or

(b)   when the Commissioners receive a notification of appointment in accordance with paragraph (1) above of a person other than the first VAT representative, or

(c)   when the Commissioners receive a notification of cessation in accordance with regulation 5(2), or

(d)   when the Commissioners receive a notification of cessation in accordance with paragraph (4) above, or

(e)   when a VAT representative dies, becomes insolvent or becomes incapacitated,

provided that if the Commissioners have not received a notification such as is mentioned in all or any of sub-paragraphs (a), (c) or (d) above and another person has been appointed as a VAT representative by virtue of section 48 of the Act, the Commissioners may treat the date of cessation as the date of appointment of that other person.

10(6) In relation to a company which is a VAT representative, the references in paragraph (5)(e) above to the VAT representative becoming **insolvent** or **incapacitated** shall be construed as references to its going into liquidation or receivership or to an administration order being made in relation to it.

NOTIFICATION OF INTENDED SECTION 14(1) SUPPLIES BY INTERMEDIATE SUPPLIERS

11(1) An intermediate supplier who has made or intends to make a supply to which he wishes section 14(1) of the Act to apply shall notify the Commissioners and the customer in writing of his intention to do so.

11(2) A notification under this regulation shall contain the following particulars–

(a)   the name and address of the intermediate supplier,

(b)   the number including the alphabetical code, by which the intermediate supplier is identified for VAT purposes, which was used or is to be used for the purpose of the supply to him by the original supplier,

(c)   the date upon which the goods were first delivered or are intended to be first delivered, and

(d)   the name, address and registration number of the customer to whom the goods have been supplied or are to be supplied.

11(3) A notification under this regulation shall be made no later than the provision, in accordance with regulation 18, of the first invoice in relation to the supply to which it relates, and sent to–

(a)   the office designated by the Commissioners for the receipt of such notifications, and

(b)   the customer.

11(4) Notifications under this regulation shall be made separately in relation to each customer to whom it is intended to make supplies to which the intermediate supplier wishes section 14(1) of the Act to apply.

11(5) Where an intermediate supplier has complied with the requirements of this regulation in relation to the first supply to a customer to which section 14(1) of the Act applies, those requirements shall be deemed to have been satisfied in relation to all subsequent supplies to that customer while the intermediate supplier continues to belong in another member State.

NOTIFICATION OF INTENDED SECTION 14(2) SUPPLIES BY PERSONS BELONGING IN OTHER MEMBER STATES

12(1) A person belonging in another member State who has made or who intends to make a supply to which he wishes section 14(2) of the Act to apply shall notify the Commissioners and the registered person in writing of his intention to do so.

12(2) A notification under this regulation shall contain the following particulars–

(a)   the name and address of the person belonging in another member State,

(b)   the number including the alphabetical code by which the person belonging in another member State is identified for VAT purposes in the member State in which he belongs,

(c)   the date upon which the installation or assembly of the goods was commenced or is intended to commence, and

(d)   the name, address and registration number of the registered person to whom the goods have been supplied or are to be supplied.

12(3)   A notification under this regulation shall be made no later than the provision, in accordance with regulation 19, of the first invoice in relation to the supply to which it relates, and sent to–

(a)   the office designated by the Commissioners for the receipt of such notifications, and

(b)   the registered person to whom the goods are to be supplied.

12(4)   Notifications under this regulation shall be made separately in relation to each registered person to whom it is intended to make supplies to which the person belonging in another member State wishes section 14(2) of the Act to apply.

12(5)   Where a person belonging in another member State has complied with the requirements of this regulation in relation to the first supply to a registered person to which section 14(2) of the Act applies, those requirements shall be deemed to have been satisfied in relation to all subsequent supplies to that registered person while the person making the supply continues to belong in another member State.

PART III – VAT INVOICES AND OTHER INVOICING REQUIREMENTS

Official publications – 700, para. 6.1ff. (2000 edn).

OBLIGATION TO PROVIDE A VAT INVOICE

13(1)   Save as otherwise provided in these Regulations, where a registered person–

(a)   makes a taxable supply in the United Kingdom to a taxable person, or

(b)   makes a supply of goods or services other than an exempt supply to a person in another member State, or

(c)   receives a payment on account in respect of a supply he has made or intends to make from a person in another member State,

he shall provide such persons as are mentioned above with a VAT invoice (unless, in the case of that supply, he is entitled to issue and issues a VAT invoice pursuant to section 18C(1)(e) of the Act and regulation 145D(1) below in relation to the supply by him of specified services performed on or in relation to goods while those goods are subject to a fiscal or other warehousing regime).

13(2)   The particulars of the VAT chargeable on a supply of goods described in paragraph 7 of Schedule 4 to the Act shall be provided, on a sale by auction, by the auctioneer, and, where the sale is otherwise than by auction, by the person selling the goods, on a document containing the particulars prescribed in regulation 14(1); and such a document issued to the buyer shall be treated for the purposes of paragraph (1)(a) above as a VAT invoice provided by the person by whom the goods are deemed to be supplied in accordance with the said paragraph 7.

13(3)   Where a registered person provides a document to himself which purports to be a VAT invoice in respect of a supply of goods or services to him by another taxable person registered in the United Kingdom, that document may, with the approval of the Commissioners, be treated as the VAT invoice required to be provided by the supplier under paragraph (1)(a) above.

13(4)   Where the person who makes a supply to which regulation 93 relates gives an authenticated receipt containing the particulars required under regulation 14(1) to be specified in a VAT invoice in respect of that supply, that document shall be treated as the VAT invoice required to be provided under paragraph (1)(a) above on condition that no VAT invoice or similar document which was intended to be or could be construed as being a VAT invoice for the supply to which the receipt relates is issued.

13(5) The documents specified in paragraphs (1), (2), (3) and (4) above shall be provided within 30 days of the time when the supply is treated as taking place under section 6 of the Act, or within such longer period as the Commissioners may allow in general or special directions.

History – In reg. 13(1), the words after the word "invoice" to the end were inserted by SI 1996/1250, reg. 6, operative from 1 June 1996.

Cross references – Reg. 31A(2)(a): record-keeping and investment gold.

CONTENTS OF VAT INVOICE

14(1) Subject to paragraph (2) below and regulation 16 and save as the Commissioners may otherwise allow, a registered person providing a VAT invoice in accordance with regulation 13 shall state thereon the following particulars–

(a)   an identifying number,

(b)   the time of the supply,

(c)   the date of the issue of the document,

(d)   the name, address and registration number of the supplier,

(e)   the name and address of the person to whom the goods or services are supplied,

(f)   the type of supply by reference to the following categories–

       (i)   a supply by sale,

       (ii)   a supply on hire purchase or any similar transaction,

       (iii)   a supply by loan,

       (iv)   a supply by way of exchange,

       (v)   a supply on hire, lease or rental,

       (vi)   a supply of goods made from the customer's materials,

       (vii)   a supply by sale on commission,

       (viii)   a supply on sale or return or similar terms, or

       (ix)   any other type of supply which the Commissioners may at any time by notice specify,

(g)   a description sufficient to identify the goods or services supplied,

(h)   for each description, the quantity of the goods or the extent of the services, and the rate of VAT and the amount payable, excluding VAT, expressed in sterling,

(i)   the gross total amount payable, excluding VAT, expressed in sterling,

(j)   the rate of any cash discount offered,

(k)   each rate of VAT chargeable and the amount of VAT chargeable, expressed in sterling, at each such rate, and

(l)   the total amount of VAT chargeable, expressed in sterling.

14(2) Where a registered person provides to a person in another member State a VAT invoice he shall state thereon the following particulars, and save as the Commissioners may otherwise allow–

(a)   the information specified in sub-paragraphs (a) to (g) and (j) of paragraph (1) above,

(b)   the letters "GB" as a prefix to his registration number,

(c)   the registration number, if any, of the recipient of the supply of goods or services and which registration number, if any, shall contain the alphabetical code of the member State in which that recipient is registered,

(d)   the gross amount payable, excluding VAT,

(e)   where the supply is of a new means of transport (as defined in section 95 of the Act) a description sufficient to identify it as such,

(f)   for each description, the quantity of the goods or the extent of the services, and where a positive rate of VAT is chargeable, the rate of VAT and the amount payable, excluding VAT, expressed in sterling, and

(g)   where the supply of goods is a taxable supply, the information as specified in sub-paragraphs (k) and (l) of paragraph (1) above.

14(3) Where a taxable supply takes place as described in section 6(2)(c) or section 6(5) of the Act, any consignment or delivery note or similar document or any copy thereof issued by the supplier before the time of supply shall not, notwithstanding that it may contain all the particulars set out in paragraph (1) above, be treated as a VAT invoice provided it is endorsed "This is not a VAT invoice".

14(4) Where a registered person provides an invoice containing the particulars specified in paragraphs (1) and (3) above, and specifies thereon any goods or services which are the subject of an exempt or zero-rated supply, he shall distinguish on the invoice between the goods or services which are the subject of an exempt, zero-rated or other supply and state separately the gross total amount payable in respect of each supply and rate.

14(5) Where a registered person provides a VAT invoice relating in whole or in part to a supply the VAT upon which is required to be accounted for and paid by the person supplied, on the supplier's behalf, the supplier shall state that fact, and the amount of VAT so to be accounted for and paid, on the VAT invoice.

14(6) Where a registered person provides a VAT invoice relating in whole or in part to a supply of the letting on hire of a motor car other than for self-drive hire, he shall state on the invoice whether that motor car is a qualifying vehicle under article 7(2A) of the Value Added Tax (Input Tax) Order 1992.

History – In reg. 14(1), the words "and save as the Commissioners may otherwise allow," were inserted by SI 1996/1250, reg. 7(1), operative from 1 June 1996.
In reg. 14(2), the comma after the words "VAT invoice" was omitted by SI 1996/1250, reg. 7(2), operative from 1 June 1996. In reg. 14(2), the words "and save as the Commissioners may otherwise allow," were inserted by SI 1996/1250, reg. 7(2), operative from 1 June 1996.
Reg. 14(6) was inserted by SI 1995/3147, reg. 3, operative from 1 January 1996.

Cross references – Reg. 31A(2)(a): record-keeping and investment gold.

Official publications – 701/48: corporate purchasing cards.

CHANGE OF RATE, CREDIT NOTES

15 Where there is a change in the rate of VAT in force under section 2 of the Act or in the descriptions of exempt or zero-rated supplies, and a VAT invoice which relates to a supply in respect of which an election is made under section 88 of the Act was issued before the election was made, the person making the supply shall, within 14 days after any such change, provide the person to whom the supply was made with a credit note headed "Credit note – change of VAT rate" and containing the following particulars–

(a)   the identifying number and date of issue of the credit note,

(b)   the name, address and registration number of the supplier,

(c)   the name and address of the person to whom the supply is made,

(d)   the identifying number and date of issue of the VAT invoice,

(e)   a description sufficient to identify the goods or services supplied, and

(f)   the amount being credited in respect of VAT.

RETAILERS' INVOICES

16(1) Subject to paragraph (2) below, a registered person who is a retailer shall not be required to provide a VAT invoice, except that he shall provide such an invoice at the request of a customer who is a taxable person in respect of any supply to him; but, in that event, if, but only if, the consideration for the supply does not exceed £100 and the supply is other than to a person in another member State, the VAT invoice need contain only the following particulars–

(a)   the name, address and registration number of the retailer,

(b)   the time of the supply,

(c)   a description sufficient to identify the goods or services supplied,

(d)   the total amount payable including VAT, and

(e)   for each rate of VAT chargeable, the gross amount payable including VAT and the VAT rate applicable.

16(2) Where a registered person provides an invoice in accordance with this regulation, the invoice shall not contain any reference to any exempt supply.

SECTION 14(6) SUPPLIES TO PERSONS BELONGING IN OTHER MEMBER STATES

17(1) Where a registered person makes a supply such as is mentioned in section 14(6) of the Act he shall provide the person supplied with an invoice in respect of that supply.

17(2) An invoice provided under this regulation shall–

(a)   comply with the requirements of regulations 13 and 14, and

(b)   bear the legend "VAT: EC ARTICLE 28 SIMPLIFICATION INVOICE".

SECTION 14(1) SUPPLIES BY INTERMEDIATE SUPPLIERS

18(1)   On each occasion that an intermediate supplier makes or intends to make a supply to which he wishes section 14(1) of the Act to apply he shall, subject to paragraph (3) below, provide the customer with an invoice.

18(2)   An invoice provided under this regulation by an intermediate supplier shall–

(a)   comply with the provisions of the law corresponding, in relation to the member State which provided the intermediate supplier with the identification number for VAT purposes used or to be used by him for the purpose of the supply to him by the original supplier of the goods which were subsequently removed to the United Kingdom, to regulation 17,

(b)   be provided no later than 15 days after the time that the supply of the goods would, but for section 14(1) of the Act, have been treated as having taken place by or under section 6 of the Act,

(c)   cover no less than the extent of the supply which would, but for section 14(1) of the Act, have been treated as having taken place by or under section 6 of the Act at the time that such an invoice is provided, and

(d)   bear the legend "VAT: EC ARTICLE 28 SIMPLIFICATION INVOICE".

18(3)   Where an intermediate supplier makes a supply such as is mentioned in paragraph (1) above, and he has already provided the customer with an invoice that complies with the requirements of sub-paragraphs (a), (c) and (d) of paragraph (2) above, he shall not be required to provide the customer with a further invoice in relation to that supply.

18(4)   Where an intermediate supplier makes a supply such as is mentioned in paragraph (1) above and he provides the customer with an invoice such as is described in paragraphs (2) and (3) above, that invoice shall be treated as if it were an invoice for the purpose of regulation 83.

18(5)   Where an intermediate supplier makes a supply such as is mentioned in paragraph (1) above and he provides the customer with an invoice that complies only with the requirements of paragraph (2)(a) above, that invoice shall, for the purposes of this regulation only, be treated as if it were a VAT invoice.

SECTION 14(2) SUPPLIES BY PERSONS BELONGING IN OTHER MEMBER STATES

19(1)   On each occasion that a person belonging in another member State makes or intends to make a supply to which he wishes section 14(2) of the Act to apply he shall, subject to paragraph (3) below, provide the registered person with an invoice.

19(2)   An invoice provided under this regulation by a person belonging in another member State shall–

(a)   comply with the provisions of the law of the member State in which he belongs corresponding in relation to that member State to the provisions of regulation 14,

(b)   be provided no later than 15 days after the time that the supply of the goods would, but for section 14(2) of the Act, have been treated as having taken place by or under section 6 of the Act,

(c)   cover no less than the extent of the supply which would, but for section 14(2) of the Act, have been treated as having taken place by or under section 6 of the Act at the time that such an invoice is provided, and

(d)   bear the legend "SECTION 14(2) VATA INVOICE".

19(3)   Where a person belonging in another member State makes a supply such as is mentioned in paragraph (1) above, and he has already provided the registered person with an invoice that complies with the requirements of sub-paragraphs (a), (c) and (d) of paragraph (2) above, he shall not be required to provide the registered person with a further invoice in relation to that supply.

19(4)   Where a person belonging in another member State makes a supply such as is mentioned in paragraph (1) above and he provides the registered person with an invoice such as is described in paragraphs (2) and (3) above, that invoice shall be treated as if it were an invoice for the purpose of regulation 83.

19(5)   Where a person belonging in another member State makes a supply such as is mentioned in paragraph (1) above, and he provides the registered person with an invoice that complies only with the requirements of paragraph (2)(a) above, that invoice shall, for the purposes of this regulation only, be treated as if it were a VAT invoice.

GENERAL

20 Regulations 13, 14, 15, 16, 17, 18 and 19 shall not apply to the following supplies made in the United Kingdom–

(a)   any zero-rated supply other than a supply for the purposes of an acquisition in another member State,

(b)   any supply to which an order made under section 25(7) of the Act applies,

(c)   any supply on which VAT is charged although it is not made for consideration, or

(d)   any supply to which an order made under section 32 of the Act applies.

PART IV – EC SALES STATEMENTS

INTERPRETATION OF PART IV

21 In this Part–

     "form" means the form numbered 12 in Schedule 1 to these Regulations;

     "registered in another member State" means registered in accordance with the measures adopted by the competent authority in another member State for the purposes of the common system of VAT and **"registered"** shall be construed accordingly;

     "relevant figure" means the sum of the amount mentioned in paragraph 1(1)(a) of Schedule 1 to the Act and £25,500;

     "statement" means the statement which a taxable person is required to submit in accordance with this Part of these Regulations;

     "total value" means the consideration for the supply including the costs of any freight transport services and services ancillary to the transport of goods charged by the supplier of the goods to the customer.

History – In reg. 21, the definition of contract work was omitted by SI 1996/210, reg. 3, operative from 1 March 1996. In reg. 21, the definition of processing work was omitted by SI 1996/210, reg. 3, operative from 1 March 1996.

SUBMISSION OF STATEMENTS

22(1) Subject to paragraph (6) below and save as the Commissioners may otherwise allow or direct, every taxable person who in any period of a quarter has made a supply of, or has dispatched, or has transported, or has transferred, goods to a person who is or was registered in another member State shall in relation to that period submit to the Commissioners, no later than 42 days after the end of that period, a statement in the form numbered 12 in Schedule 1 to these Regulations containing full information as specified in paragraph (3) or (5) below, as the case may require and a declaration signed by him that the statement is true and complete;

provided that–

(a)   the Commissioners may allow a taxable person to submit those statements in respect of periods of one month;

(b)   where a taxable person satisfies the Commissioners either that–

         (i)   at the end of any month, the value of his taxable supplies in the period of one year then ending is less than the relevant figure, or

         (ii)   at any time, there are reasonable grounds for believing that the value of his taxable supplies in the period of one year beginning at that or any later time will not exceed the relevant figure,

     and either that–

         (iii)   at the end of any month, the value of his supplies to persons registered in other member States in the period of one year then ending is less than £11,000, or

         (iv)   at any time, there are reasonable grounds for believing that the value of his supplies to *persons registered in* other member States in the period of one year beginning at that or any later time will not exceed £11,000,

     the Commissioners may allow that person to submit a statement which relates to the period of the year mentioned in sub-paragraphs (i) to (iv) above and which contains full information as specified in paragraph (3)(a) to (d) below and a declaration signed by him that the statement is true and complete;

(c)   where the Commissioners have allowed a taxable person under regulation 25 to make returns in respect of periods longer than 3 months and that person satisfies the Commissioners either that–

      (i)   at the end of any month, the value of his taxable supplies in the period of one year then ending is less than £145,000, or

      (ii)   at any time, there are reasonable grounds for believing that the value of his taxable supplies in the period of one year beginning at that or any later time will not exceed £145,000,

    and either that–

      (iii)   at the end of any month, the value of his supplies to persons registered in other member States in the period of one year then ending is less than £11,000, or

      (iv)   at any time, there are reasonable grounds for believing that the value of his supplies to persons registered in other member States in the period of one year beginning at that or any later time will not exceed £11,000,

    the Commissioners may allow that person to submit statements in respect of periods identical to those that have been allowed for the making of his returns and each statement shall contain full information as specified in paragraphs (3) and (5) below, as the case may require, and a declaration signed by him that the statement is true and complete; and

(d)   where the Commissioners consider it necessary in a particular case, they may allow or direct a taxable person to submit statements to a specified address.

22(2)   Where the Commissioners allow a statement to be submitted as is mentioned in the proviso to paragraph (1) above, that statement shall be submitted–

(a)   where sub-paragraph (a) of the proviso applies, no later than 42 days after the end of the quarter in which the month in question occurs;

(b)   where sub-paragraph (b) of the proviso applies, no later than 42 days after the end of the period of the year to which the statement relates; and

(c)   where sub-paragraph (c) of the proviso applies, no later than 42 days after the end of the period in respect of which the Commissioners have allowed a return to be furnished.

22(3)   Save as the Commissioners may otherwise allow or direct, a taxable person shall in any statement such as is mentioned in paragraph (1) above specify–

(a)   his name, address and registration number which number shall include the prefix GB,

(b)   the date of the submission of the statement,

(c)   the date of the last day of the period to which the statement refers,

(d)   the registration number of each person acquiring or deemed to have acquired goods in the period, including the alphabetical code of the member State in which each such person is registered, and

(e)   the total value of the goods supplied in the period to each person mentioned in sub-paragraph (d) above.

22(4)   [Reg. 22(4) was omitted by SI 1996/210, reg. 6.]

22(5)   Where a taxable person makes a supply such as is mentioned in regulation 18(1), he shall specify in the statement required under paragraph (1) above the following–

(a)   the information mentioned in paragraph (3) above,

(b)   the figure "2" in the box marked "indicator" on the form numbered 12 in Schedule 1 to these Regulations, and

(c)   the total value of the goods supplied by him.

22(6)   Every taxable person who in any period of a quarter has made a supply of a new means of transport to a person for the purpose of acquisition by him in another member State shall in relation to that period submit to the Commissioners no later than 42 days after the end of that period a statement containing the particulars (including the declaration made by him) set out in the form numbered 13 in Schedule 1 to these Regulations,

provided that where the Commissioners consider it necessary in a particular case, they may allow or direct a taxable person to submit the statement to a specified address.

History – In reg. 22(1), the words "(3) or (5)" were substituted by SI 1996/210, reg. 4, operative from 1 March 1996. In reg. 22(1)(c), the words "(3) and (5)" were substituted by SI 1996/210, reg. 4, operative from 1 March 1996. Note that in the Queen's Printer's version of SI 1996/210, the substitution apparently incorrectly required the substitution of the words "(3) or (5)" for the words "(3), (4) and (5)".

In reg. 22(3)(e), words after "paragraph (d) above" were omitted by SI 1996/210, reg. 5, operative from 1 March 1996. Reg. 22(4) was omitted by SI 1996/210, reg. 6, operative from 1 March 1996.

FINAL STATEMENTS

23   Any taxable person who ceases to be registered under Schedule 1 to the Act shall, unless another person has been registered with the registration number of and in substitution for him under regulation 6(3), submit to the Commissioners a final statement on either of the forms in Schedule 1 to these Regulations numbered 12 or 13 or both, as the case may require, and unless the Commissioners in any case otherwise allow or direct, and such statement shall contain–

(a)   the information specified in paragraphs (3) and (5) of regulation 22, or the full information required by the form numbered 13 in Schedule 1 to these Regulations or both, as the case may require, and

(b)   a declaration signed by him that the statement is true and complete,

and the statement shall be submitted no later than 42 days after the date with effect from which his registration has been cancelled.

History – In reg. 23(a), the words "(3) and (5)" were substituted by SI 1996/210, reg. 7, operative from 1 March 1996.

PART V – ACCOUNTING, PAYMENT AND RECORDS

Official publications – 700, para. 8.1ff and 9.1ff (2000 edn) and Notice 700/21.

INTERPRETATION OF PART V

24   In this Part–

"increase in consideration" means an increase in the consideration due on a supply made by a taxable person which is evidenced by a credit or debit note or any other document having the same effect and **"decrease in consideration"** is to be interpreted accordingly;

"insolvent person" means–

(a)   an individual who has been adjudged bankrupt;

(b)   a company in relation to which–

     (i)   a voluntary arrangement under Part I of the Insolvency Act 1986 has been approved,

     (ii)   an administration order has been made,

     (iii)   an administrative receiver has been appointed,

     (iv)   a resolution for voluntary winding up has been passed, or

     (v)   an order for its winding-up has been made by the court at a time when it had not already gone into liquidation by passing a resolution for voluntary winding-up;

"investment gold" has the same meaning as that expression has for the purposes of Group 15 of Schedule 9 to the Act;

"negative entry" means an amount entered into the VAT account as a negative amount;

"positive entry" means an amount entered into the VAT account as a positive amount;

"VAT allowable portion" "VAT payable portion" and **"VAT account"** have the meanings given in regulation 33;

"the Removal Order" means the Value Added Tax (Removal of Goods) Order 1992;

"the owner" has the same meaning as in article 2 of the Removal Order.

History – In reg. 24, the definition of investment gold was inserted by SI 1999/3114, reg. 3, operative from 1 January 2000.
Notes – In the Queen's Printer's version of the regulations, in the definition of "VAT allowable portion", the reference to regulation 33 should be a reference to regulation 32.

MAKING OF RETURNS

25(1)   Every person who is registered or was or is required to be registered shall, in respect of every period of a quarter or in the case of a person who is registered, every period of 3 months ending on the dates notified either in the certificate of registration issued to him or otherwise, not later than the last day of the month next following the end of the period to which it relates, make to the Controller a return on the form numbered 4 in Schedule 1 to these Regulations ("Form 4") showing the amount of VAT payable by or to him and containing full information in respect of the other matters specified in the form and a declaration, signed by him, that the return is true and complete;

provided that–

(a)   the Commissioners may allow or direct a person to make returns in respect of periods of one month and to make those returns within one month of the periods to which they relate;

(b)   the first return shall be for the period which includes the effective date determined in accordance with Schedules 1, 2, 3 and 3A to the Act upon which the person was or should have been registered, and the said period shall begin on that date;

(c)   where the Commissioners consider it necessary in any particular case to vary the length of any period or the date on which any period begins or ends or by which any return shall be made, they may allow or direct any person to make returns accordingly, whether or not the period so varied has ended;

(d)   where the Commissioners consider it necessary in any particular case, they may allow or direct a person to make returns to a specified address.

25(2)   Any person to whom the Commissioners give any direction in pursuance of the proviso to paragraph (1) above shall comply therewith.

25(3)   Where for the purposes of this Part the Commissioners have made a requirement of any person pursuant to regulation 30–

(a)   the period in respect of which taxable supplies were being made by the person who died or became incapacitated shall end on the day previous to the date when death or incapacity took place; and

(b)   subject to sub-paragraph (1)(c) above, a return made on his behalf shall be made in respect of that period no later than the last day of the month next following the end of that period; and

(c)   the next period shall start on the day following the aforesaid period and it shall end, and all subsequent periods shall begin and end, on the dates previously determined under paragraph (1) above.

25(4)   Any person who–

(a)   ceases to be liable to be registered, or

(b)   ceases to be entitled to be registered under either or both of paragraphs 9 and 10 of Schedule 1 to the Act,

shall, unless another person has been registered with his registration number in substitution for him under regulation 6, make to the Controller a final return on the form numbered 5 in Schedule 1 to these Regulations ("Form 5") and any such return shall contain full information in respect of the matters specified in the form and a declaration, signed by him, that the return is true and complete and shall be made, in the case of a person who was or is registered, within one month of the effective date for cancellation of his registration, and in the case of any other person, within one month of the date upon which he ceases to be liable to be registered, and in either case shall be in respect of the final period ending on the date aforementioned and be in substitution for the return for the period in which such date occurs.

25(4A)   A person may make a return required by this regulation on an electronic version of Form 4 or Form 5 (as appropriate) using electronic communications.

25(4B)   Such a method of making a return shall be referred to in this Part as an **"electronic return system"**.

25(4C)   A person may only make a return by way of an electronic return system on condition that–

(a)   the electronic return system in question takes a form approved by the Commissioners in a *specific or general direction*; and

(b)   that person remains authorised by the Commissioners in accordance with paragraph (4G) below.

25(4D)   No return shall be treated as having been made under paragraph (4A) above unless the conditions imposed by paragraph (4C) above are satisfied.

25(4E)   An electronic return system shall incorporate an electronic validation process.

25(4F)   Subject to paragraph (4D) above–

(a)   the use of an electronic return system shall be proved to have resulted in the **making of the return** to the Controller only if this has been successfully recorded as such by the relevant electronic validation process;

(b) the **time of making the return** to the Controller using an electronic return system shall be conclusively presumed to be the time recorded as such by the relevant electronic validation process; and

(c) the person making the return to the Controller shall be presumed to be the person identified as such by any relevant feature of the electronic return system.

25(4G) The Commissioners may on application authorise a person to make returns using an electronic return system and may revoke any such authorisation.

25(4H) The Commissioners shall pay proper regard to the following factors before authorising a person or revoking an authorisation under paragraph (4G) above–

(a) the state of development of any relevant electronic return system;

(b) the protection of the revenue;

(c) the degree of compliance of the person concerned with this Part; and

(d) any other relevant factor.

25(4I) A person shall not be authorised to make returns using an electronic return system only by reason of being–

(a) registered under regulation 6 above in substitution for a person who has been so authorised (transfer of a going concern); or

(b) required by the Commissioners under regulation 30 below to comply with the requirements of this Part (person acting in a representative capacity).

25(4J) The electronic versions of Forms 4 and 5 shall not differ in any material respect from those in Schedule 1 to these Regulations but may include relevant modifications.

25(4K) Paragraphs (1) and (4) above shall have effect in relation to a return made by way of an electronic return system as if the expression ", signed by him," were omitted.

25(4L) Paragraphs (4A) to (4K) above shall not be taken as affecting any provision except in relation to the means of making a return to the Controller.

25(5) The Commissioners may allow VAT chargeable in any period to be treated as being chargeable in such later period as they may specify.

History – In reg. 25(1), the words "("Form 4")" were inserted immediately after the words "these Regulations" by SI 2000/258, reg. 3(1), operative from 1 March 2000.
In reg. 25(1)(b), the words "Schedules 1, 2, 3 and 3A" were substituted for the words "Schedules 1, 2 and 3" by SI 2000/794, reg. 5, operative from 22 March 2000.
In reg. 25(4), the words "("Form 5")" were inserted immediately after the words "these Regulations" by SI 2000/258, reg. 3(2), operative from 1 March 2000.
Reg. 25(4A) – (4L) were inserted by SI 2000/258, reg. 3(3), operative from 1 March 2000.
Official publications – 700/12.
Notes – Customs may extend the due date for furnishing a return by seven days if any payment is made by credit transfer and they give their written approval in advance (Form VAT 459).

ACCOUNTING FOR VAT ON AN ACQUISITION BY REFERENCE TO THE VALUE SHOWN ON AN INVOICE

26 Where the time of the acquisition of any goods from another member State is determined by reference to the issue of an invoice such as is described in regulation 83, VAT shall be accounted for and paid in respect of the acquisition only on so much of its value as is shown on that invoice.

SUPPLIES UNDER SCHEDULE 4, PARAGRAPH 7

27 Where goods are deemed to be supplied by a taxable person by virtue of paragraph 7 of Schedule 4 to the Act, the auctioneer on a sale by auction or, where the sale is otherwise than by auction, the person selling the goods, shall, whether or not registered under the Act, within 21 days of the sale–

(a) furnish to the Controller a statement showing–

(i) his name and address and, if registered, his registration number,

(ii) the name, address and registration number of the person whose goods were sold,

(iii) the date of the sale,

(iv) the description and quantity of goods sold at each rate of VAT, and

(v) the amount for which they were sold and the amount of VAT charged at each rate,

(b) pay the amount of VAT due, and

(c) send to the person whose goods were sold a copy of the statement referred to in sub-paragraph (a) above, and the auctioneer or person selling the goods, as the case may be, and the person whose goods were sold shall exclude the VAT chargeable on that supply of those goods from any return made under these Regulations.

Other material – Form VAT 833.

ESTIMATION OF OUTPUT TAX

28 Where the Commissioners are satisfied that a person is not able to account for the exact amount of output tax chargeable in any period, he may estimate a part of his output tax for that period, provided that any such estimated amount shall be adjusted and exactly accounted for as VAT chargeable in the next prescribed accounting period or, if the exact amount is still not known and the Commissioners are satisfied that it could not with due diligence be ascertained, in the next but one prescribed accounting period.

CLAIMS FOR INPUT TAX

29(1) Subject to paragraphs (1A) and (2) below, and save as the Commissioners may otherwise allow or direct either generally or specially, a person claiming deduction of input tax under section 25(2) of the Act shall do so on a return made by him for the prescribed accounting period in which the VAT became chargeable.

29(1A) The Commissioners shall not allow or direct a person to make any claim for deduction of input tax in terms such that the deduction would fall to be claimed more than 3 years after the date by which the return for the prescribed accounting period in which the VAT became chargeable is required to be made.

29(2) At the time of claiming deduction of input tax in accordance with paragraph (1) above, a person shall, if the claim is in respect of–

(a)   a supply from another taxable person, hold the document which is required to be provided under regulation 13;

(b)   a supply under section 8(1) of the Act, hold the relative invoice from the supplier;

(c)   an importation of goods, hold a document authenticated or issued by the proper officer, showing the claimant as importer, consignee or owner and showing the amount of VAT charged on the goods;

(d)   goods which have been removed from warehouse, hold a document authenticated or issued by the proper officer showing the claimant's particulars and the amount of VAT charged on the goods;

(e)   an acquisition by him from another member State of any goods other than a new means of transport, hold a document required by the authority in that other member State to be issued showing his registration number including the prefix "GB", the registration number of the supplier including the alphabetical code of the member State in which the supplier is registered, the consideration for the supply exclusive of VAT, the date of issue of the document and description sufficient to identify the goods supplied; or

(f)   an acquisition by him from another member State of a new means of transport, hold a document required by the authority in that other member State to be issued showing his registration number including the prefix "GB", the registration number of the supplier including the alphabetical code of the member State in which the supplier is registered, the consideration for the supply exclusive of VAT, the date of issue of the document and description sufficient to identify the acquisition as a new means of transport as specified in section 95 of the Act;

provided that where the Commissioners so direct, either generally or in relation to particular cases or classes of cases, a claimant shall hold, instead of the document or invoice (as the case may require) specified in sub-paragraph (a), (b), (c), (d), (e) or (f) above, such other documentary evidence of the charge to VAT as the Commissioners may direct.

29(3) Where the Commissioners are satisfied that a person is not able to claim the exact amount of input tax to be deducted by him in any period, he may estimate a part of his input tax for that period, provided that any such estimated amount shall be adjusted and exactly accounted for as VAT deductible in the next prescribed accounting period or, if the exact amount is still not known and the Commissioners are satisfied that it could not with due diligence be ascertained, in the next but one prescribed accounting period.

History – Reg. 29(1A), and reference to it in reg. 29(1), inserted by SI 1997/1086, reg. 4, operative from 1 May 1997.

PERSONS ACTING IN A REPRESENTATIVE CAPACITY

30   Where any person subject to any requirements under this Part dies or becomes incapacitated and control of his assets passes to another person, being a personal representative, trustee in bankruptcy, receiver, liquidator or person otherwise acting in a representative capacity, that other person shall, if the Commissioners so require and so long as he has such control, comply with these requirements, provided that any requirement to pay VAT shall only apply to that other person to the extent of the assets of the deceased or incapacitated person over which he has control; and save to the extent aforesaid this Part shall apply to such a person, so acting, in the same way as it would have applied to the deceased or incapacitated person had that person not been deceased or incapacitated.

Cross references – Reg. 25(4I): authorisation to make VAT returns electronically.

RECORDS

31(1)   Every taxable person shall, for the purpose of accounting for VAT, keep the following records–

(a)   his business and accounting records,

(b)   his VAT account,

(c)   copies of all VAT invoices issued by him,

(d)   all VAT invoices received by him,

(da)   all certificates–

     (i)   prepared by him relating to acquisitions by him of goods from other member States, or

     (ii)   given to him relating to supplies by him of goods or services,

     provided that, owing to provisions in force which concern fiscal or other warehousing regimes, those acquisitions or supplies are either zero-rated or treated for the purposes of the Act as taking place outside the United Kingdom,

(e)   documentation received by him relating to acquisitions by him of any goods from other member States,

(f)   copy documentation issued by him relating to the transfer, dispatch or transportation of goods by him to other member States,

(g)   documentation received by him relating to the transfer, dispatch or transportation of goods by him to other member States,

(h)   documentation relating to importations and exportations by him, and

(i)   all credit notes, debit notes, or other documents which evidence an increase or decrease in consideration that are received, and copies of all such documents that are issued by him.

31(2)   The Commissioners may–

(a)   in relation to a trade or business of a description specified by them, or

(b)   for the purposes of any scheme established by, or under, Regulations made under the Act,

supplement the list of records required in paragraph (1) above by a notice published by them for that purpose.

31(3)   Every person who, at a time when he is not a taxable person, acquires in the United Kingdom from another member State any goods which are subject to a duty of excise or consist of a new means of transport shall, for the purposes of accounting for VAT, keep such records with respect to the acquisition as may be specified in any notice published by the Commissioners in pursuance of this regulation.

History – In Reg. 31(1), para. (da) was inserted by SI 1996/1250, reg. 8, operative from 1 June 1996.

31A(1)   This regulation applies where a person–

(a)   makes a supply of investment gold of a description falling within item 1 of Group 15 of Schedule 9 to the Act, or

(b)   makes a supply of a description falling within item 2 of Group 15 of Schedule 9 to the Act, which subsequently results in the transfer of the possession of the investment gold.

31A(2)   Subject to paragraph (6) below (and save as the Commissioners may otherwise allow in relation to supplies where the value is less than an amount equivalent to 15,000 euro at a rate specified in any notice published by the Commissioners for the purposes of this regulation) in addition to the requirements upon every taxable person under this Part, a person making a supply of a description falling within paragraph (1) above shall–

(a)   without prejudice to regulations 13 and 14, issue an invoice in respect of the supply containing such details as may be specified in a notice published by the Commissioners for the purposes of this regulation;

(b)   keep and maintain a record of the supply containing such details as may be specified in a notice published by the Commissioners for the purposes of this regulation;

(c)   retain such documents in relation to the supply as may be specified in a notice published by the Commissioners for the purposes of this regulation;

(d)   keep and maintain a record of the recipient of the supply containing such particulars pertaining to the recipient as may be specified in a notice published by the Commissioners for the purposes of this regulation;

(e)   keep and maintain such other records and documents as may be specified in a notice published by the Commissioners for the purposes of this regulation to allow the proper identification of each recipient of the supply;

(f)   notify the Commissioners in writing that he is making such supplies within 28 days of the first supply;

(g)   furnish to the Commissioners such information in relation to his making of the supply as may be specified in a notice published by them.

31A(3)   A taxable person shall keep and maintain, together with the account he is required to keep and maintain under regulation 32 below, a record of exempt supplies of a description falling within item 1 or 2 of Group 15 of Schedule 9 to the Act, that he makes to another taxable person.

31A(4)   Where there is a sale of investment gold, which would if that person were supplying investment gold in the course or furtherance of any business, fall within item 1 or 2 of Group 15 of Schedule 9 to the Act, by a person who is not trading in investment gold, to a person who is so trading, the purchaser shall issue on behalf of the seller an invoice containing such particulars as may be set out in a notice published by the Commissioners for the purposes of this regulation and the seller shall sign such form of declaration as may be set out in a notice published by the Commissioners for the purposes of this regulation.

31A(5)   The records required to be kept and the documents required to be retained under paragraphs (1) to (4) above shall be preserved for a minimum period of 6 years.

31A(6)   Paragraphs (2) to (5) above shall not apply to any person in respect of a supply by him of a description falling within item 1 or 2 of Group 15 of Schedule 9 to the Act the value of which does not exceed £5,000, unless the total value of those supplies to any person over the last 12 months exceeds £10,000.

History – Reg. 31A was inserted by SI 1999/3114, reg. 4, operative from 1 January 2000.
Official publications – 701/21 and 701/21A.

31B   Where a person receives a supply of a description falling within article 31A(1) above that person shall retain the purchase invoice in relation to that supply for a minimum period of 6 years.
History – Reg. 31B was inserted by SI 1999/3114, reg. 4, operative from 1 January 2000.

31C   Paragraph 10(2) of Schedule 11 to the Act shall apply in relation to supplies of a description falling within items 1 and 2 of Group 15 of Schedule 9 to the Act as it applies in relation to the supply of goods under taxable supplies.
History – Reg. 31C was inserted by SI 1999/3114, reg. 4, operative from 1 January 2000.

THE VAT ACCOUNT

32(1)   Every taxable person shall keep and maintain, in accordance with this regulation, an account to be known as the **VAT account**.

32(2)   The VAT account shall be divided into separate parts relating to the prescribed accounting periods of the taxable person and each such part shall be further divided into 2 portions to be known as **"the VAT payable portion"** and **"the VAT allowable portion"**.

32(3)   The **VAT payable portion** for each prescribed accounting period shall comprise–

(a)   a total of the output tax due from the taxable person for that period,

(b)   a total of the output tax due on acquisitions from other member States by the taxable person for that period,

(c)   every correction or adjustment to the VAT payable portion which is required or allowed by regulation 34, 35 or 38, and

(d)   every adjustment to the amount of VAT payable by the taxable person for that period which is required, or allowed, by or under any Regulations made under the Act.

32(4)   The **VAT allowable portion** for each prescribed period shall comprise–

(a)   a total of the input tax allowable to the taxable person for that period by virtue of section 26 of the Act,

(b)   a total of the input tax allowable in respect of acquisitions from other member States by the taxable person for that period by virtue of section 26 of the Act,

(c)   every correction or adjustment to the VAT allowable portion which is required or allowed by regulation 34, 35 or 38, and

(d)   every adjustment to the amount of input tax allowable to the taxable person for that period which is required, or allowed, by or under any Regulations made under the Act.

THE REGISTER OF TEMPORARY MOVEMENT OF GOODS TO AND FROM OTHER MEMBER STATES

33(1)   Every taxable person shall keep and maintain, in accordance with this regulation, a register to be known as the **register of temporary movement of goods** to and from other member States.

33(2)   Where goods have been moved to or received from another member State and they are to be returned within a period of 2 years of the date of their first removal or receipt, as the case may be, the register shall contain the following information–

(a)   the date of removal of goods to another member State,

(b)   the date of receipt of the goods mentioned in sub-paragraph (a) above when they are returned from the member State mentioned in that sub-paragraph or another member State,

(c)   the date of receipt of goods from another member State,

(d)   the date of removal of the goods mentioned in sub-paragraph (c) above when they are returned to the member State mentioned in that sub-paragraph or another member State,

(e)   a description of the goods sufficient to identify them,

(f)   a description of any process, work or other operation carried out on the goods either in the United Kingdom or in another member State,

(g)   the consideration for the supply of the goods, and

(h)   the consideration for the supply of any processing, work or other operation carried out on the goods either in the United Kingdom or another member State.

33(3)   The Commissioners may in relation to a trade or business of a description specified by them supplement the list of information required in paragraph (2) above by a notice published by them for that purpose.

33A   A person making supplies of a description falling within article 4 of the Value Added Tax (Terminal Markets) Order 1973 shall not be required to keep in relation to those supplies the records specified in regulations 31 (save for paragraph (1)(a) of that regulation), 31A, 32 and 33 of these Regulations.

History – Reg. 33A was inserted by SI 1999/3114, reg. 5, operative from 1 January 2000.

33B   Where a person of a description in article 6 of the Value Added Tax (Terminal Markets) Order 1973 makes or receives supplies of a description falling within that article, the following Parts of these Regulations shall not apply in relation to those supplies, that is to say–

(a)   Part IV;

(b)   Part V.

History – Reg. 33B was inserted by SI 1999/3114, reg. 5, operative from 1 January 2000.

CORRECTION OF ERRORS

34(1)   Subject to paragraph (1A) below, this regulation applies where a taxable person has made a return, or returns, to the Controller which overstated or understated his liability to VAT or his entitlement to a payment under section 25(3) of the Act.

34(1A)   Subject to paragraph (1B) below, any overstatement or understatement in a return where–

(a)   a period of 3 years has elapsed since the end of the prescribed accounting period for which the return was made; and

(b)   the taxable person has not (in relation to that overstatement or understatement) corrected his VAT account in accordance with this regulation before the end of the prescribed accounting period during which that period of 3 years has elapsed,

shall be disregarded for the purposes of this regulation; and in paragraphs (2) to (6) of this regulation "overstatement", "understatement" and related expressions shall be construed accordingly.

34(1B)   Paragraph (1A) above does not apply where–

(a)   the overstatement or understatement is discovered in a prescribed accounting period which begins before 1st May 1997; and

(b)   the return for that prescribed accounting period has not been made, and was not required to have been made, before that date.

34(2)   In this regulation–

(a)   **"under-declarations of liability"** means the aggregate of–

(i)   the amount (if any) by which credit for input tax was overstated in any return, and

(ii)   the amount (if any) by which output tax was understated in any return;

(b)   **"over-declarations of liability"** means the aggregate of–

(i)   the amount (if any) by which credit for input tax was understated in any return, and

(ii)   the amount (if any) by which output tax was overstated in any return.

34(3)   Where, in relation to all such overstatements or understatements discovered by the taxable person during a prescribed accounting period, the difference between–

(a)   under-declarations of liability, and

(b)   over-declarations of liability,

does not exceed £2,000, the taxable person may correct his VAT account in accordance with this regulation.

34(4)   In the VAT payable portion–

(a)   where the amount of any overstatements of output tax is greater than the amount of any understatements of output tax a negative entry shall be made for the amount of the excess; or

(b)   where the amount of any understatements of output tax is greater than the amount of any overstatements of output tax a positive entry shall be made for the amount of the excess.

34(5)   In the VAT allowable portion–

(a)   where the amount of any overstatements of credit for input tax is greater than the amount of any understatements of credit for input tax a negative entry shall be made for the amount of the excess; or

(b)   where the amount of any understatements of credit for input tax is greater than the amount of any overstatements of credit for input tax a positive entry shall be made for the amount of the excess.

34(6)   Every entry required by this regulation shall–

(a)   be made in that part of the VAT account which relates to the prescribed accounting period in which the overstatements or understatements in any earlier returns were discovered,

(b)   make reference to the returns to which it applies, and

(c)   make reference to any documentation relating to the overstatements or understatements.

34(7)   Where the conditions referred to in paragraph (3) above do not apply, the VAT account may not be corrected by virtue of this regulation.

35   Where a taxable person has made an error–

(a)   in accounting for VAT, or

(b)   in any return made by him,

then, unless he corrects that error in accordance with regulation 34, he shall correct it in such manner and within such time as the Commissioners may require.

History – Reg. 34(1A), (1B), and reference to reg. 34(1A) in reg. 34(1), inserted by SI 1997/1086, reg. 5, operative from 1 May 1997.

Official publications – 700, para. 8.9 and 8.10 (2000 edn) and Notices 700/21 and 700/45.
Form – VAT 652.

NOTIFICATION OF ACQUISITION OF GOODS SUBJECT TO EXCISE DUTY BY NON-TAXABLE PERSONS AND PAYMENT OF VAT

36(1) Where–

(a) a taxable acquisition of goods subject to excise duty takes place in the United Kingdom,

(b) the acquisition is not in pursuance of a taxable supply, and

(c) the person acquiring the goods is not a taxable person at the time of the acquisition,

the person acquiring the goods shall notify the Commissioners of the acquisition at the time of the acquisition or the arrival of the goods in the United Kingdom, whichever is the later.

36(2) The notification shall be in writing in the English language and shall contain the following particulars–

(a) the name and current address of the person acquiring the goods,

(b) the time of the acquisition,

(c) the date when the goods arrived in the United Kingdom,

(d) the value of the goods including any excise duty payable, and

(e) the VAT due upon the acquisition.

36(3) The notification shall include a declaration, signed by the person who is required to make the notification, that all the information entered in it is true and complete.

36(4) Any person required to notify the Commissioners of an acquisition of goods subject to excise duty shall pay the VAT due upon the acquisition at the time of notification and, in any event, no later than the last day on which he is required by this regulation to make such notification.

36(5) Where a person required to make notification dies or becomes incapacitated and control of his assets passes to another person, being a personal representative, trustee in bankruptcy, receiver, liquidator or person otherwise acting in a representative capacity, that other person shall, so long as he has such control, be required to make the notification referred to in this regulation, provided that the requirement to pay the VAT due upon the acquisition shall apply to that other person only to the extent of the assets of the deceased or incapacitated person over which he has control and, save to the extent aforesaid, this regulation shall apply to such person so acting in the same way as it would have applied to the deceased or incapacitated person had that person not been deceased or incapacitated.

CLAIMS FOR RECOVERY OF OVERPAID VAT

37 Any claim under section 80 of the Act shall be made in writing to the Commissioners and shall, by reference to such documentary evidence as is in the possession of the claimant, state the amount of the claim and the method by which that amount was calculated.

ADJUSTMENTS IN THE COURSE OF BUSINESS

38(1) Subject to paragraph (1A) below, this regulation applies where–

(a) there is an increase in consideration for a supply, or

(b) there is a decrease in consideration for a supply,

which includes an amount of VAT and the increase or decrease occurs after the end of the prescribed accounting period in which the original supply took place.

38(1A) Subject to paragraph (1B) below, this regulation does not apply to any increase or decrease in consideration which occurs more than 3 years after the end of the prescribed accounting period in which the original supply took place.

38(1B) Paragraph (1A) above does not apply where–

(a) the increase or decrease takes place during a prescribed accounting period beginning before 1st May 1997; and

(b) the return for the prescribed accounting period in which effect is given to the increase or decrease in the business records of the taxable person has not been made, and was not required to have been made, before that date.

38(2) Where this regulation applies, the taxable person shall adjust his VAT account in accordance with the provisions of this regulation.

38(3) The maker of the supply shall–

(a) in the case of an increase in consideration, make a positive entry; or

(b) in the case of a decrease in consideration, make a negative entry, for the relevant amount of VAT in the VAT payable portion of his VAT account.

38(4) The recipient of the supply, if he is a taxable person, shall–

(a)   in the case of an increase in consideration, make a positive entry; or

(b)   in the case of a decrease in consideration, make a negative entry,

for the relevant amount of VAT in the VAT allowable portion of his VAT account.

38(5) Every entry required by this regulation shall, except where paragraph (6) below applies, be made in that part of the VAT account which relates to the prescribed accounting period in which the increase or decrease is given effect in the business accounts of the taxable person.

38(6) Any entry required by this regulation to be made in the VAT account of an insolvent person shall be made in that part of the VAT account which relates to the prescribed accounting period in which the supply was made or received.

38(7) None of the circumstances to which this regulation applies is to be regarded as giving rise to any application of regulations 34 and 35.

History – Reg. 38(1A), (1B), and reference to reg. 38(1A) in reg. 38(1), inserted by SI 1997/1086, reg. 6, operative from 1 May 1997.

CALCULATION OF RETURNS

39(1) Where a person is required by regulations made under the Act to make a return to the Controller, the amounts to be entered on that return shall be determined in accordance with this regulation.

39(2) In the box opposite the legend "VAT due in this period on sales and other outputs" shall be entered the aggregate of all the entries in the VAT payable portion of that part of the VAT account which relates to the prescribed accounting period for which the return is made, except that the total of the output tax due in that period on acquisitions from other member States shall be entered instead in the box opposite the legend "VAT due in this period on acquisitions from other EC member States".

39(3) In the box opposite the legend "VAT reclaimed in this period on purchases and other inputs" (including acquisitions from other member States) shall be entered the aggregate of all the entries in the VAT allowable portion of that part of the VAT account which relates to the prescribed accounting period for which the return is made.

39(4) Where any correction has been made and a return calculated in accordance with these Regulations then any such return shall be regarded as correcting any earlier returns to which regulations 34 and 35 apply.

VAT TO BE ACCOUNTED FOR ON RETURNS AND PAYMENT OF VAT

40(1) Any person making a return shall in respect of the period to which the return relates account in that return for–

(a)   all his output tax,

(b)   all VAT for which he is accountable by virtue of Part XVI of these Regulations,

(c)   all VAT which he is required to pay as a result of the removal of goods from a fiscal warehousing regime, and

(d)   all VAT which he is required to pay as a result of a supply of specified services (performed on or in relation to goods at a time when they are subject to a warehousing regime) being zero-rated under section 18C(1) of the Act where–

    (i)   that warehousing regime is one where goods are stored without payment of any duty of excise,

    (ii)   those goods are subject to a duty of excise,

    (iii) those goods have been the subject of an acquisition from another member State and the material time for that acquisition was while those goods were subject to that warehousing regime, and,

    (iv)   there was no supply of those goods while they were subject to that warehousing regime.

The amounts to be entered on that return shall be determined in accordance with these Regulations.

40(2) Any person required to make a return shall pay to the Controller such amount of VAT as is payable by him in respect of the period to which the return relates not later than the last day on which he is required to make that return.

40(2A)   Where a return is made in accordance with regulation 25 above using an electronic return system, the relevant payment to the Controller required by paragraph (2) above shall be made solely by means of electronic communications that are acceptable to the Commissioners for this purpose.

40(3)   The requirements of paragraphs (1) or (2) above shall not apply where the Commissioners allow or direct otherwise.

History – Reg. 40 was substituted by SI 1996/1250, reg. 9, operative from 1 June 1996.
Reg. 40(2A) was inserted by SI 2000/258, reg. 4, operative from 1 March 2000.

40A   Where the Commissioners in exercise of their power under section 28(2A) of the Act have directed the manner in which payments on account under section 28 of the Act are to be made, a person who is liable to make such payments shall also pay any amount of VAT payable in respect of a return for any prescribed accounting period in the like manner.

History – Reg. 40A was inserted by SI 1996/1198, reg. 3, operative from 1 June 1996.

ACCOUNTING ETC. BY REFERENCE TO THE DUTY POINT, AND PRESCRIBED ACCOUNTING PERIOD IN WHICH VAT ON CERTAIN SUPPLIES IS TO BE TREATED AS BEING CHARGEABLE

41(1)   Where in respect of–

(a)   any supply by a taxable person of dutiable goods, or

(b)   an acquisition by any person from another member State of dutiable goods,

the time of supply or acquisition, as the case may be, precedes the duty point in relation to those goods, the VAT in respect of that supply or acquisition shall be accounted for and paid, and any question as to the inclusion of any duty in the value of the supply or acquisition shall be determined, by reference to the duty point or by reference to such later time as the Commissioners may allow.

41(2)–(3)   [Omitted by SI 1996/1250, reg. 10.]

History – Reg. 41(2) and (3) were omitted by SI 1996/1250, reg. 10, operative from 1 June 1996, except where 28 April 1996 falls within the prescribed accounting period of a taxable person, and that prescribed accounting period ends on or after 1 June 1996, the omissions do not, in relation to that taxable person, have effect until the day after the end of that prescribed accounting period.

ACCOUNTING FOR VAT ON THE REMOVAL OF GOODS

42(1)   This regulation applies where goods have been removed from a member State to a place in any other member State, and that removal falls within any of paragraphs (d), (f) or (g) of article 4 of the Removal Order.

42(2)   Except where paragraph (3) below applies in respect of the same prescribed accounting period, the owner shall not make any entry in the VAT payable portion of that part of his VAT account which relates to the prescribed accounting period in which he would be liable to account for any VAT chargeable in respect of the removal.

42(3)   Where–

(a)   the condition described in article 5 of the Removal Order has not been complied with, and

(b)   an amount of VAT has become payable,

the owner shall make a positive entry for the relevant amount of VAT in the VAT payable portion of that part of his VAT account which relates to the prescribed accounting period in which the condition was not complied with.

GOODS REMOVED FROM WAREHOUSING REGIME

43(1)   This regulation applies to a registered person who is an approved person within the meaning of the Excise Duties (Deferred Payment) Regulations 1992 in respect of goods which are at a specified warehouse.

43(2)   Where a person to whom this regulation applies is–

(a)   the person who is liable under section 18(4)(b) of the Act to pay VAT on a supply of goods while the goods are subject to a warehousing regime, or

(b)   liable under section 18D(2) of the Act to pay VAT on a supply of services to which section 18C(3) of the Act applies (specified services performed on or in relation to goods which are subject to a warehousing regime),

he may pay that VAT at or before the relevant time determined in accordance with paragraph (3) below instead of at the time provided for by sections 18(4)(b) or 18D(2)(a) of the Act.

43(3)   For the purposes of paragraph (2) above the **relevant time** means–

(a)   in relation to hydrocarbon oils, the 15th day of the month immediately following the month in which the hydrocarbon oils were removed from the warehousing regime;

(b)   in relation to any other goods subject to a duty of excise, the day (payment day) on which the registered person is required to pay the excise duty on the goods in accordance with regulation 5 of the Excise Duties (Deferred Payment) Regulations 1992.

43(4)   Where any goods of a kind chargeable to a duty of excise qualify for any relief of that duty, that relief shall be disregarded for the purposes of determining the relevant time under paragraph (3) above.

History – Reg. 43(2) was replaced by SI 1996/1250, reg. 11, operative from 1 June 1996.

PART VA – REIMBURSEMENT ARRANGEMENTS

INTERPRETATION OF PART VA

43A   In this Part–

"**claim**" means a claim made (irrespective of when it was made) under section 80 of the Act for repayment of an amount paid to the Commissioners by way of VAT which was not VAT due to them; and "**claimed**" and "**claimant**" shall be construed accordingly;

"**reimbursement arrangements**" means any arrangements (whether made before, on or after 30th January 1998) for the purposes of a claim which–

(a)   are made by a claimant for the purpose of securing that he is not unjustly enriched by the repayment of any amount in pursuance of the claim; and

(b)   provide for the reimbursement of persons (consumers) who have, for practical purposes, borne the whole or any part of the cost of the original payment of that amount to the Commissioners;

"**relevant amount**" means that part (which may be the whole) of the amount of a claim which the claimant has reimbursed or intends to reimburse to consumers.

History – Reg. 43A was inserted by SI 1998/59, reg. 2, operative from 11 February 1998 and was originally numbered reg. 37A, but was renumbered as reg. 43A by SI 1999/438, reg. 3, operative from 1 April 1999.

REIMBURSEMENT ARRANGEMENTS – GENERAL

43B   Without prejudice to regulation 43H below, for the purposes of section 80(3) of the Act (defence by the Commissioners that repayment by them of an amount claimed would unjustly enrich the claimant) reimbursement arrangements made by a claimant shall be disregarded except where they–

(a)   include the provisions described in regulation 43C below; and

(b)   are supported by the undertakings described in regulation 43G below.

History – Reg. 43B was inserted by SI 1998/59, reg. 2, operative from 11 February 1998 and was originally numbered reg. 37B, but was renumbered as reg. 43B by SI 1999/438, reg. 3, operative from 1 April 1999. The cross references to reg. 37A to 37H were substituted accordingly by SI 1999/438, reg. 4, operative from 1 April 1999.

REIMBURSEMENT ARRANGEMENTS – PROVISIONS TO BE INCLUDED

43C   The provisions referred to in regulation 43B(a) above are that–

(a)   reimbursement for which the arrangements provide will be completed by no later than 90 days after the repayment to which it relates;

(b)   no deduction will be made from the relevant amount by way of fee or charge (howsoever expressed or effected);

(c)   reimbursement will be made only in cash or by cheque;

(d)   any part of the relevant amount that is not reimbursed by the time mentioned in paragraph (a) above will be repaid by the claimant to the Commissioners;

(e)   any interest paid by the Commissioners on any relevant amount repaid by them will also be treated by the claimant in the same way as the relevant amount falls to be treated under paragraphs (a) and (b) above; and

(f)   the records described in regulation 43E below will be kept by the claimant and produced by him to the Commissioners, or to an officer of theirs in accordance with regulation 43F below.

History – Reg. 43C was inserted by SI 1998/59, reg. 2, operative from 11 February 1998 and was originally numbered reg. 37C, but was renumbered as reg. 43C by SI 1999/438, reg. 3, operative from 1 April 1999. The cross references to reg. 37A to 37H were substituted accordingly by SI 1999/438, reg. 5, operative from 1 April 1999.

REPAYMENTS TO THE COMMISSIONERS

43D   The claimant shall, without prior demand, make any repayment to the Commissioners that he is required to make by virtue of regulation 43C(d) and (e) above within 14 days of the expiration of the period of 90 days referred to in regulation 43C(a) above.

History – Reg. 43D was inserted by SI 1998/59, reg. 2, operative from 11 February 1998 and was originally numbered reg. 37D, but was renumbered as reg. 43D by SI 1999/438, reg. 3, operative from 1 April 1999. The cross references to reg. 37A to 37H were substituted accordingly by SI 1999/438, reg. 6, operative from 1 April 1999.

RECORDS

43E   The claimant shall keep records of the following matters–

(a)   the names and addresses of those consumers whom he has reimbursed or whom he intends to reimburse;

(b)   the total amount reimbursed to each such consumer;

(c)   the amount of interest included in each total amount reimbursed to each consumer;

(d)   the date that each reimbursement is made.

History – Reg. 43E was inserted by SI 1998/59, reg. 2, operative from 11 February 1998 and was originally numbered reg. 37E, but was renumbered as reg. 43E by SI 1999/438, reg. 3, operative from 1 April 1999.

PRODUCTION OF RECORDS

43F(1)   Where a claimant is given notice in accordance with paragraph (2) below, he shall, in accordance with such notice produce to the Commissioners, or to an officer of theirs, the records that he is required to keep pursuant to regulation 43E above.

43F(2)   A notice given for the purposes of paragraph (1) above shall–

(a)   be in writing;

(b)   state the place and time at which, and the date on which the records are to be produced; and

(c)   be signed and dated by the Commissioners, or by an officer of theirs,

and may be given before or after, or both before and after the Commissioners have paid the relevant amount to the claimant.

History – Reg. 43F was inserted by SI 1998/59, reg. 2, operative from 11 February 1998 and was originally numbered reg. 37F, but was renumbered as reg. 43F by SI 1999/438, reg. 3, operative from 1 April 1999. The cross references to reg. 37A to 37H were substituted accordingly by SI 1999/438, reg. 7, operative from 1 April 1999.

UNDERTAKINGS

43G(1)   Without prejudice to regulation 43H(b) below, the undertakings referred to in regulation 43B(b) above shall be given to the Commissioners by the claimant no later than the time at which he makes the claim for which the reimbursement arrangements have been made.

43G(2)   The undertakings shall be in writing, shall be signed and dated by the claimant, and shall be to the effect that–

(a)   at the date of the undertakings he is able to identify the names and addresses of those consumers whom he has reimbursed or whom he intends to reimburse;

(b)   he will apply the whole of the relevant amount repaid to him, without any deduction by way of fee or charge or otherwise, to the reimbursement in cash or by cheque, of such consumers by no later than 90 days after his receipt of that amount (except insofar as he has already so reimbursed them);

(c)   he will apply any interest paid to him on the relevant amount repaid to him wholly to the reimbursement of such consumers by no later than 90 days after his receipt of that interest;

(d)   he will repay to the Commissioners without demand the whole or such part of the relevant amount repaid to him or of any interest paid to him as he fails to apply in accordance with the undertakings mentioned in sub-paragraphs (b) and (c) above;

(e)   he will keep the records described in regulation 43E above; and

(f)   he will comply with any notice given to him in accordance with regulation 43F above concerning the production of such records.

History – Reg. 43G was inserted by SI 1998/59, reg. 2, operative from 11 February 1998 and was originally numbered reg. 37G, but was renumbered as reg. 43G by SI 1999/438, reg. 3, operative from 1 April 1999. The cross references to reg. 37A to 37H were substituted accordingly by SI 1999/438, reg. 8, operative from 1 April 1999.

REIMBURSEMENT ARRANGEMENTS MADE BEFORE 11TH FEBRUARY 1998

43H   Reimbursement arrangements made by a claimant before 11th February 1998 shall not be disregarded for the purposes of section 80(3) of the Act if, not later than 11th March 1998–

(a)   he includes in those arrangements (if they are not already included) the provisions described in regulation 43C above; and

(b)   gives the undertakings described in regulation 43G above.

History – Reg. 43H was inserted by SI 1998/59, reg. 2, operative from 11 February 1998 and was originally numbered reg. 37H, but was renumbered as reg. 43H by SI 1999/438, reg. 3, operative from 1 April 1999. The cross references to reg. 37A to 37H were substituted accordingly by SI 1999/438, reg. 9, operative from 1 April 1999.

PART VI – PAYMENTS ON ACCOUNT

INTERPRETATION OF PART VI

44   In this Part–

"body corporate" means a body corporate which is under a duty to make payments on account by virtue of the Value Added Tax (Payments on Account) Order 1993 and

"relevant division" means a division of a body corporate by reference to the business of which that body corporate is under such a duty;

"payments on account" has the same meaning as in the Value Added Tax (Payments on Account) Order 1993.

PAYMENTS ON ACCOUNT

45   Save in a case to which regulation 48 applies, the Commissioners shall give to a taxable person who is under a duty to make payments on account notification in writing of–

(a)   the amounts that he is under a duty to pay,

(b)   how those amounts have been calculated, and

(c)   the times for payment of those amounts.

46   Save in a case to which regulation 48 applies, if in respect of a prescribed accounting period the total amount of the payment on account made by the taxable person exceeds the amount of VAT due from him in respect of that period, the amount of excess shall be paid to him by the Commissioners if and to the extent that it is not required by section 81 of the Act to be set against any sum which he is liable to pay to them.

46A(1)   A payment on account and a payment in respect of a return to which regulation 40A above applies shall not be treated as having been made by the last day on which it is required to be made unless it is made in such a manner as secures that all the transactions can be completed that need to be completed before the whole of the amount becomes available to the Commissioners.

46A(2)   For the purposes of this regulation and regulation 47 below, references to a **payment being made by any day** include references to its being made on that day.

History – Reg. 46A was inserted by SI 1996/1198, reg. 4, operative from 1 June 1996.

47   Where a taxable person fails to make a payment on account by the last day by which he is required to make it, that payment on account shall be recoverable as if it were VAT due from him.

48(1)   The Commissioners shall notify a relevant division in writing of–

(a)   the amounts of the payments on account that the body corporate is under a duty to make by reference to the business of that division,

(b)   how those amounts have been calculated, and

(c)   the times for payment of those amounts.

48(2)   If in respect of a prescribed accounting period the total amount of the payments on account made by a body corporate by reference to the business of a particular relevant division exceeds the amount of VAT due from the body corporate in respect of that period by reference to that business, the amount of the excess shall be paid to the body corporate through that division by the

Commissioners if and to the extent that it is not required by section 81 of the Act to be set against any sum which the body corporate is liable to pay to them.

48(3) Section 81 of the Act shall not require any amount which is due to be paid by the Commissioners to a body corporate under paragraph (2) above by reference to the business of a particular relevant division to be set against any sum due from the body corporate otherwise than by reference to that business or to the liabilities of the body corporate arising in connection with that division.

Official publications – 700/60: payments on account.
Customs Internal Guidance Manual, vol. V1.23, chapter 8: payments on account.

PART VII – ANNUAL ACCOUNTING

History – Pt. VII was substituted by SI 1996/542, operative from 1 April 1996 except for a taxable person who is on 31 March 1996 authorised under reg. 50 it is operative from the first day of his next current accounting year.

INTERPRETATION OF PART VII

49   In this Part–

"**authorised person**" means a person who has been authorised by the Commissioners in accordance with regulation 50(1), and

"**authorised**" and "**authorisation**" shall be construed accordingly;

"**transitional accounting period**" means the period commencing on the first day of a person's prescribed accounting period in which the Commissioners authorise him to use the scheme, and ending on the day immediately preceding the first day of that person's first current accounting year, and is a prescribed accounting period within the meaning of section 25(1) of the Act;

"**current accounting year**" means the period of 12 months commencing on a date indicated by the Commissioners in their notification of authorisation of a person, or while a person remains authorised the most recent anniversary thereof, and is a prescribed accounting period within the meaning of section 25(1) of the Act;

"**the scheme**" means the annual accounting scheme established by regulations 50 and 51;

"**credit transfer**" means the transfer of funds from one bank account to another under a mandate given by the payer to the bank making the transfer;

"**the quarterly sum**" means a sum equal to 20 per cent of the total amount of VAT which a taxable person was liable to pay to the Commissioners in the 12 months–

(a)   immediately preceding the first day of his current accounting year; or

(b)   for the purposes of regulation 51, immediately preceding the first day of his transitional accounting period;

"**the agreed quarterly sum**" means a sum agreed with the Commissioners, not being less than 20 per cent of a taxable person's estimated liability for VAT in his current accounting year;

"**the monthly sum**" means a sum equal to 10 per cent of the total amount of VAT which a taxable person was liable to pay to the Commissioners in the 12 months–

(a)   immediately preceding the first day of his current accounting year; or

(b)   for the purposes of regulation 51, immediately preceding the first day of his transitional accounting period;

"**the agreed monthly sum**" means a sum agreed with the Commissioners, not being less than 10 per cent of a taxable person's estimated liability for VAT, in his current accounting year;

"**working day**" means any day of the week other than Saturday, Sunday, a bank holiday or a *public holiday*;

"**relevant quarterly date**" means the last working day of the fourth and, where a period has such months, the seventh and the tenth months of a transitional accounting period;

"**relevant monthly date**" means the last working day of the fourth and each successive month of a transitional accounting period.

ANNUAL ACCOUNTING SCHEME

50(1)   The Commissioners may, subject to the requirements of this Part, authorise a taxable person to pay and account for VAT by reference to any transitional accounting period, and any subsequent current accounting year at such times, and for such amounts, as may be determined in accordance with the scheme.

50(2)   A taxable person authorised to pay and account for VAT in accordance with the scheme shall–

(a)   pay to the Commissioners by credit transfer–

    (i)   in cases to which paragraph (3) below applies, the quarterly sum, or as the case may be, the agreed quarterly sum, no later than the last working day of each of the fourth, seventh and tenth months of his current accounting year, save that where that sum does not exceed £400 no quarterly payment need be made; or

    (ii)   in all other cases, the monthly sum, or as the case may be, the agreed monthly sum, in nine equal monthly instalments, commencing on the last working day of the fourth month of his current accounting year; and

(b)   make by the last working day of the second month following the end of that current accounting year a return in respect of that year, together with any outstanding payment due to the Commissioners in respect of his liability for VAT for the current accounting year declared on that return.

50(3)   This paragraph applies where the value of taxable supplies made by a taxable person in the period of 12 months ending on the day before the first day of his current accounting year–

(a)   does not exceed £100,000; or

(b)   where he was paying quarterly sums under the scheme in that period, does not exceed £110,000.

51   An authorised person shall, where in any given case the transitional accounting period is–

(a)   4 months or more–

    (i)   if the value of his taxable supplies during the period of 12 months immediately preceding the first day of his transitional accounting period did not exceed £100,000, pay to the Commissioners by credit transfer on each relevant quarterly date the quarterly sum, save that where that sum does not exceed £400 no quarterly payment need be made; or

    (ii)   in all other cases, pay to the Commissioners by credit transfer on each relevant monthly date the monthly sum; and

    (iii)   make by the last working day of the second month following the end of his transitional accounting period a return in respect of that period, together with any outstanding payment due to the Commissioners in respect of his liability for VAT declared on that return; or

(b)   less than 4 months, make by the last working day of the first month following the end of his transitional accounting period a return in respect of that period, together with any outstanding payment due to the Commissioners in respect of his liability for VAT declared on that return.

ADMISSION TO THE SCHEME

52(1)   A taxable person shall be eligible to apply for authorisation under regulation 50(1) if–

(a)   he has been registered for at least 12 months at the date of his application for authorisation;

(b)   he has reasonable grounds for believing that the value of taxable supplies made or to be made by him in the period of 12 months beginning on the date of his application for authorisation will not exceed £300,000;

(c)   his registration is not in the name of a group under section 43(1) of the Act;

(d)   his registration is not in the name of a division under section 46(1) of the Act; and

(e)   he has not in the 12 months preceding the date of his application for authorisation ceased to operate the scheme.

52(2)   The Commissioners may refuse to authorise a person under regulation 50(1) where they consider it necessary to do so for the protection of the revenue.

53(1)　An authorised person shall continue to account for VAT in accordance with the scheme until he ceases to be authorised.

53(2)　An authorised person ceases to be authorised when–

(a)　at the end of any transitional accounting period or current accounting year the value of taxable supplies made by him in that period or, as the case may be, year has exceeded £375,000; or

(b)　his authorisation is terminated in accordance with regulation 54 below;

(c)　he–

    (i)　becomes insolvent and ceases to trade, other than for the purpose of disposing of stocks and assets; or

    (ii)　ceases business or ceases to be registered; or

    (iii)　dies, becomes bankrupt or incapacitated;

(d)　he ceases to operate the scheme of his own volition.

54(1)　The Commissioners may terminate an authorisation in any case where–

(a)　a false statement has been made by or on behalf of an authorised person in relation to his application for authorisation; or

(b)　an authorised person fails to make by the due date a return in accordance with regulation 50(2)(b) or regulation 51(a)(iii) or (b); or

(c)　an authorised person fails to make any payment prescribed in regulation 50 or 51; or

(d)　where they receive a notification in accordance with paragraph (2) below; or

(e)　at any time during an authorised person's transitional accounting period or current accounting year they have reason to believe, that the value of taxable supplies he will make during the period or as the case may be year, will exceed £375,000; or

(f)　it is necessary to do so for the protection of the revenue; or

(g)　an authorised person has not, in relation to a return made by him prior to authorisation, paid to the Commissioners all such sums shown as due thereon; or

(h)　an authorised person has not, in relation to any assessment made under either section 73 or section 76 of the Act, paid to the Commissioners all such sums shown as due thereon.

54(2)　Where an authorised person has reason to believe that the value of taxable supplies made by him during a transitional accounting period or current accounting year will exceed £375,000, he shall within 30 days notify the Commissioners in writing.

55(1)　The date from which an authorised person ceases to be authorised in accordance with Regulation 53(2) shall be–

(a)　where regulation 53(2)(a) applies, the day following the last day of the relevant transitional accounting period or current accounting year;

(b)　where regulation 53(2)(b) applies, the day on which the Commissioners terminate his authorisation;

(c)　where regulation 53(2)(c) applies, the day on which any one of the events mentioned in that paragraph occurs; and

(d)　where regulation 53(2)(d) applies, the date on which the Commissioners are notified in writing of the authorised persons decision to cease using the scheme.

55(2)　Where an authorised person ceases to be authorised, he or as the case may be, his representative, shall–

(a)　if his authorisation ceases before the end of his transitional accounting period or current accounting year, make a return within 2 months of the date specified in paragraph (1)(b), (1)(c) or (1)(d) above, together with any outstanding payment due to the Commissioners in respect of his liability for VAT for that part of the period or year arising before the date he ceased to be authorised; or

(b)　if his authorisation ceases at the end of his transitional accounting period or current accounting year, make a return together with any outstanding payment due to the Commissioners in respect of his liability for VAT in accordance with regulation 51 or 50 above; and in either case, from the day following the day on which he ceases to be authorised, account for and pay VAT as provided for otherwise than under this Part.

Official publications – 732.
Customs Internal Guidance Manual, vol. V1.23, chapter 1: annual accounting.

Other material – Form VAT 600: application to join the annual accounting scheme.

PART VIII – CASH ACCOUNTING

INTERPRETATION OF PART VIII

56 In this Part–

    "money" means banknotes or coins;

    "notice" means any notice published pursuant to this Part.

CASH ACCOUNTING SCHEME

57 A taxable person may, subject to this Part and to such conditions as are described in a notice published by the Commissioners, account for VAT in accordance with a scheme (hereinafter referred to in this Part as **"the scheme"**) by which the operative dates for VAT accounting purposes shall be–

(a)   for output tax, the day on which payment or other consideration is received or the date of any cheque, if later; and

(b)   for input tax, the date on which payment is made or other consideration is given, or the date of any cheque, if later.

Official publications – 731.
Customs Internal Guidance Manual, vol. V1.23, chapter 4: cash accounting.

ADMISSION TO THE SCHEME

58(1) Without prejudice to paragraph (4) below, a taxable person shall be eligible to begin to operate the scheme from the beginning of any prescribed accounting period if–

(a)   he has reasonable grounds for believing that the value of taxable supplies to be made by him in the period of one year then beginning will not exceed £350,000,

(b)   he has made all returns which he is required to make, and has–

    (i)   paid to the Commissioners all such sums shown as due on those returns and on any assessments made either under section 76 of, or Schedule 11 to, the Act, or

    (ii)   agreed an arrangement with the Commissioners for any outstanding amount of such sums as are referred to in sub-paragraph (i) above to be paid in instalments over a specific period, and

(c)   he has not in the period of one year preceding that time–

    (i)   been convicted of any offence in connection with VAT,

    (ii)   made any payment to compound proceedings in respect of VAT under section 152 of the Customs and Excise Management Act 1979,

    (iii)   been assessed to a penalty under section 60 of the Act, or

    (iv)   by virtue of regulation 64(1), ceased to be entitled to continue to operate the scheme.

58(2) The scheme shall not apply to–

(a)   lease purchase agreements;

(b)   hire purchase agreements;

(c)   *conditional sale agreements;*

(d)   credit sale agreements;

(e)   supplies where a VAT invoice is issued and full payment of the amount shown on the invoice is not due for a period in excess of 6 months from the date of the issue of the invoice; or

(f)   supplies of goods or services in respect of which a VAT invoice is issued in advance of the delivery or making available of the goods or the performance of the services as the case may be.

58(3) Sub-paragraph (2)(f) above shall not apply where goods have been delivered or made available in part or where services have been performed in part and the VAT invoice in question relates solely to that part of the goods which have been delivered or made available or that part of the services which have been performed.

58(4) A person shall not be entitled to begin to operate the scheme if the Commissioners consider it is necessary for the protection of the revenue that he shall not be so entitled.

History – Reg. 58 was substituted by SI 1997/1614, reg. 3, operative from 3 July 1997. Former reg. 58 reads as follows:
"**58(1)** A taxable person shall be eligible to begin to operate the scheme if–
(a)   at any time, he has reasonable grounds for believing that the value of taxable supplies made or to be made by him in the period of one year then beginning will not exceed £350,000,
(b)   he has made all returns which he is required to make, and has–
                    (i)   paid to the Commissioners all such sums shown as due on those returns and on any assessments made either under section 76 of, or Schedule 11 to, the Act, or
agreed an arrangement with the Commissioners for any outstanding amount of such sums as are referred to in sub-paragraph (i) above to be paid in instalments over a specified period, and
(c)   he has not in the period of one year preceding that time–
been convicted of any offence in connection with VAT,
made any payment to compound proceedings in respect of VAT under section 152 of the Customs and Excise Management Act 1979,
been assessed to a penalty under section 60 of the Act, or
by virtue of regulation 64(1), ceased to be entitled to continue to operate the scheme.
58(2) The scheme shall not apply to lease purchase agreements, hire purchase agreements, conditional sale agreements, credit sale agreements or supplies where a VAT invoice is issued and full payment of the amount shown on the invoice is not due for a period in excess of 12 months from the date of the issue of the invoice."

59 Without prejudice to the right of a person to withdraw from the scheme, the Commissioners may vary the terms of the scheme by publishing a fresh notice or publishing a notice which amends an existing notice.

History – In reg. 59, the words "or publishing a notice which amends an existing notice" were inserted by SI 1997/1614, reg. 4, operative from 3 July 1997.

60(1) Without prejudice to regulation 64 below, a person shall withdraw from the scheme immediately at the end of a prescribed accounting period of his if the value of taxable supplies made by him in the period of one year ending at the end of the prescribed accounting period in question has exceeded £437,500.

60(2) Subject to regulations 61 to 63 below a person may withdraw from the scheme at the end of any prescribed accounting period.

60(3) The requirement in paragraph (1) above shall not apply where the Commissioners allow or direct otherwise.

History – Reg. 60 was substituted by SI 1997/1614, reg. 5, operative from 3 July 1997. Former reg. 60 reads as follows:
"**60(1)** A person who becomes eligible to begin to operate the scheme may do so at the beginning of his next prescribed accounting period.
60(2) A person may, subject to regulation 64, remain in the scheme unless at the end of one of his prescribed accounting periods the value of taxable supplies made by him in a period of one year then ending has exceeded £437,500 and the value of the taxable supplies made by him in the period of one year then beginning has exceeded £350,000, in which case he shall cease to operate the scheme with effect from the end of the second mentioned period of one year.
60(3) A person may withdraw from the scheme at the end of one of his prescribed accounting periods where–
(a)   he derives no benefit from remaining in the scheme, or
(b)   he is unable, by reason of his accounting system, to comply with the requirements of the scheme"

61 A person who ceases to operate the scheme either of his own volition or because the value of taxable supplies made by him exceeds the level provided for in regulation 60(1), shall account for and pay on a return made for the prescribed accounting period in which he ceased to operate the scheme–

(a)   all VAT which he would have been required to pay to the Commissioners during the time when he operated the scheme, if he had not then been operating the scheme, less

(b)   all VAT accounted for and paid to the Commissioners in accordance with the scheme, subject to any adjustment for credit for input tax.

History – Reg. 61 was substituted by SI 1997/1614, reg. 6, operative from 3 July 1997. Former reg. 61 reads as follows:
"**61** A person who ceases to operate the scheme either of his own volition or because the value of taxable supplies made by him exceeds the level provided for in regulation 60 may continue to use the scheme for supplies made and received while he operated the scheme, but shall not otherwise account for and pay VAT under this Part."

62 Where a person operating the scheme becomes insolvent he shall within 2 months of the date of insolvency account for VAT due on all supplies made and received up to the date of insolvency which has not otherwise been accounted for, subject to any credit for input tax.

History – Reg. 62 was substituted by SI 1997/1614, reg. 7, operative from 3 July 1997. Former reg. 62 reads as follows:
"**62** Where a person operating the scheme becomes insolvent and ceases to trade, other than for the purpose of disposing of stocks and assets, he shall within 2 months account for VAT on supplies made and received in the previous 6 months which has not otherwise been accounted for, subject to any adjustment for credit for input tax."

63(1) Where a person operating the scheme ceases business or ceases to be registered he shall within 2 months or such longer period as the Commissioners may allow, make a return accounting for, and pay, VAT due on all supplies made and received up to the date of cessation which has not otherwise been accounted for, subject to any adjustment for credit for input tax.

63(2) Where a business or part of a business carried on by a person operating the scheme is transferred as a going concern and regulation 6(1) does not apply, the transferor shall within 2 months or such longer period as the Commissioners may allow, make a return accounting for, and pay, VAT due on all supplies made and received which has not otherwise been accounted for, subject to credit for input tax.

63(3) Where a business carried on by a person operating the scheme is transferred in circumstances where regulation 6(1) applies, the transferee shall continue to account for and pay VAT as if he were a person operating the scheme on supplies made and received by the transferor prior to the date of transfer.

History – Reg. 63(1) was substituted by SI 1997/1614, reg. 8(a), operative from 3 July 1997. Former reg. 63(1) reads as follows:
"**63(1)** Where a person operating the scheme ceases business or ceases to be registered, or dies or becomes bankrupt or incapacitated, he or his representative shall within 2 months or such longer period as the Commissioners may allow make a return accounting for, and pay, VAT on supplies made and received during the previous 6 months which has not otherwise been accounted for, subject to any adjustment for credit for input tax, and VAT in respect of any payment or other consideration received for earlier supplies must be accounted for and paid when received."
Reg. 63(2) was substituted by SI 1997/1614, reg. 8(b), operative from 3 July 1997. Former reg. 63(2) reads as follows:
"**(2)** Where a business or part of a business carried on by a person operating the scheme is transferred as a going concern and regulation 6(1) does not apply, the transferor shall within 2 months make a return accounting for, and pay, VAT on supplies made and received during the previous 6 months which has not otherwise been accounted for, subject to any adjustment for credit for input tax, and VAT in respect of any payment or other consideration received for earlier supplies must be accounted for and paid when received."
In reg. 63(3), the words "6(1)" were substituted for the words "6(2)" by SI 1997/1614, reg. 8(c), operative from 3 July 1997.

WITHDRAWAL FROM THE SCHEME

64(1) A person shall not be entitled to continue to operate the scheme where–

(a)   he has, while operating the scheme, been convicted of an offence in connection with VAT or has made a payment to compound such proceedings under section 152 of the Customs and Excise Management Act 1979,

(b)   he has while operating the scheme been assessed to a penalty under section 60 of the Act,

(c)   he has failed to leave the scheme as required by regulation 60(1) above, or

(d)   the Commissioners consider it necessary for the protection of the revenue that he shall not be so entitled.

64(2) A person who, by virtue of paragraph (1) above, ceases to be entitled to continue to operate the scheme shall account for and pay on a return made for the prescribed accounting period in which he ceased to be so entitled–

(a)   all VAT which he would have been required to pay to the Commissioners during the time when he operated the scheme, if he had not then been operating the scheme, less

(b)   all VAT accounted for and paid to the Commissioners in accordance with the scheme, subject to any adjustment for credit for input tax.

History – Reg. 64 was substituted by SI 1997/1614, reg. 9, operative from 3 July 1997. Former reg. 64 reads as follows:
"**64(1)** A person shall not be entitled to continue to operate the scheme where–
(a)   he has, while operating the scheme, been convicted of an offence in connection with VAT or has made a payment to compound such proceedings under section 152 of the Customs and Excise Management Act 1979,
(b)   he has while operating the scheme been assessed to a penalty under section 60, 63, 67 or 69 of the Act or to a surcharge under section 59 of the Act,
(c)   he has failed to leave the scheme as required by regulation 60(2),
(d)   he has claimed input tax as though he had not been operating the scheme, or
(e)   the Commissioners consider it is necessary for the protection of the revenue that he shall not be so entitled.
64(2) A person who, by virtue of paragraph (1) above, ceases to be entitled to continue to operate the scheme shall account for and pay on a return made for the prescribed accounting period in which he ceased to be so entitled–
(a)   all VAT which he would have been required to pay to the Commissioners during the time when he operated the scheme, if he had not then been operating the scheme, less
(b)   all VAT accounted for and paid to the Commissioners in accordance with the scheme,
subject to any adjustment for credit for input tax.
64(3) A person who ceases to operate the scheme may be required to account for and pay on a return made for the prescribed accounting period in which he ceased to operate the scheme–
(a)   all VAT which he would have been required to pay to the Commissioners during the time when he operated the scheme, if he had not then been operating the scheme, less
(b)   all VAT accounted for and paid to the Commissioners in accordance with the scheme,
subject to any adjustment for credit for input tax, notwithstanding that he has already withdrawn from the scheme of his own volition."

ACCOUNTING

65(1) Except in the circumstances set out in regulations 61 to 63, VAT shall be accounted for and paid to the Commissioners by the due date prescribed for the accounting period in which payment or other consideration for the supply is received.

65(2)   Input tax may be credited either in the prescribed accounting period in which payment or consideration for a supply is given, or in such later period as may be agreed with the Commissioners.

65(3)   A person operating the scheme shall obtain and keep for a period of 6 years, or such lesser period as the Commissioners may allow, a receipted and dated VAT invoice from any taxable person to whom he has made a payment in money in respect of a taxable supply, and in such circumstances a taxable person must on request provide such a receipted and dated VAT invoice.

65(4)   A person operating the scheme shall keep for a period of 6 years, or such lesser period as the Commissioners may allow, a copy of any receipt which he gives under paragraph (3) above.

PART IX – SUPPLIES BY RETAILERS

INTERPRETATION OF PART IX

66   In this Part–

"**notice**" means any notice or leaflet published by the Commissioners pursuant to this Part;

"**scheme**" means a method as referred to in regulation 67.

Official publications – 727 and 727/2–727/5.
Customs Internal Guidance Manual, vol. V1.23, chapter 10: retail schemes.

RETAIL SCHEMES

67(1)   The Commissioners may permit the value which is to be taken as the value, in any prescribed accounting period or part thereof, of supplies by a retailer which are taxable at other than the zero rate to be determined by a method agreed with that retailer or by any method described in a notice published by the Commissioners for that purpose; and they may publish any notice accordingly.

67(2)   The Commissioners may vary the terms of any method by–

(a)   publishing a fresh notice,

(b)   publishing a notice which amends an existing notice, or

(c)   adapting any method by agreement with any retailer.

68   The Commissioners may refuse to permit the value of taxable supplies to be determined in accordance with a scheme if it appears to them–

(a)   that the use of any particular scheme does not produce a fair and reasonable valuation during any period,

(b)   that it is necessary to do so for the protection of the revenue, or

(c)   that the retailer could reasonably be expected to account for VAT in accordance with regulations made under paragraph 2(1) of Schedule 11 to the Act.

69   No retailer may at any time use more than one scheme except as provided for in any notice or as the Commissioners may otherwise allow.

NOTIFICATION OF USE OF A SCHEME

70   [Omitted by SI 1997/2437, reg. 2, operative from 1 November 1997.]

CHANGING SCHEMES

71   Save as the Commissioners may otherwise allow, a retailer who accounts for VAT on the basis of taxable supplies valued in accordance with any scheme shall, so long as he remains a taxable person, continue to do so for a period of not less than one year from the adoption of that scheme by him, and any change by a retailer from one scheme to another shall be made at the end of any complete year reckoned from the beginning of the prescribed accounting period in which he first adopted the scheme.

CEASING TO USE A SCHEME

72(1)   A retailer shall notify the Commissioners before ceasing to account for VAT on the basis of taxable supplies valued in accordance with these regulations.

72(2)   A retailer may be required to pay VAT on such proportion as the Commissioners may consider fair and reasonable of any sums due to him at the end of the prescribed accounting period in which he last used a scheme.

SUPPLIES UNDER SCHEDULE 8, GROUP 1

73 [Omitted by SI 1997/2437, reg. 2, operative from 1 November 1997.]

SUPPLIES UNDER SCHEDULE 8, GROUP 12

74 [Omitted by SI 1997/2437, reg. 2, operative from 1 November 1997.]

CHANGE IN VAT

75 Where pursuant to any enactment there is a change in the VAT charged on any supply, including a change to or from no VAT being charged on such supply, a retailer using any scheme shall take such steps relating to that scheme as are directed in any notice applicable to him or as may be agreed between him and the Commissioners.

PART X – TRADING STAMPS

INTERPRETATION OF PART X

76 [Revoked by SI 1995/3043, reg. 2, operative from 1 June 1996.]

TRADING STAMP SCHEME

77 [Revoked by SI 1995/3043, reg. 2, operative from 1 June 1996.]
78 [Revoked by SI 1995/3043, reg. 2, operative from 1 June 1996.]
79 [Revoked by SI 1995/3043, reg. 2, operative from 1 June 1996.]
80 [Revoked by SI 1995/3043, reg. 2, operative from 1 June 1996.]

PART XI – TIME OF SUPPLY AND TIME OF ACQUISITION

Official publications – 700, para. 5.1ff. (2000 edn).

GOODS FOR PRIVATE USE AND FREE SUPPLIES OF SERVICES

81(1) Where the services referred to in paragraph 5(4) of Schedule 4 to the Act are supplied for any period, they shall be treated as being supplied on the last day of the supplier's prescribed accounting period, or of each such accounting period, in which the goods are made available or used.

81(2) Where services specified in an order made by the Treasury under section 5(4) of the Act are supplied for any period, they shall be treated as being supplied on the last day of the supplier's prescribed accounting period, or of each such accounting period, in which the services are performed.

SERVICES FROM OUTSIDE THE UNITED KINGDOM

82 Services which are treated as made by a taxable person under section 8(1) of the Act shall be treated as being supplied when the supplies are paid for or, if the consideration is not in money, on the last day of the prescribed accounting period in which the services are performed.

Cross references – VAT (Reverse Charge) (Anti-avoidance) Order 1997 (SI 1997/1523), art. 4(1): modification of reg. 82 in relation to telecommunication services supplied on or after 1 July 1997 so they are not chargeable to VAT in another member state.

TIME OF ACQUISITION

83 Where the time that goods are acquired from another member State falls to be determined in accordance with section 12(1)(b) of the Act by reference to the day of the issue, in respect of the *transaction in pursuance of which the goods are acquired*, of an invoice of such description as the Commissioners may by regulations prescribe, the invoice shall be one which is issued by the supplier under the provisions of the law of the member State where the goods were supplied, corresponding in relation to that member State, to the provisions of regulations 13 and 14.

SUPPLIES OF LAND – SPECIAL CASES

84(1) Where by or under any enactment an interest in, or right over, land is compulsorily purchased and, at the time determined in accordance with section 6(2) or (3) of the Act, the person **(the grantor)** from whom it is purchased does not know the amount of payment that he is to receive in respect of the purchase then goods or, as the case may require, services shall be treated as supplied each time the grantor receives any payment for the purchase.

84(2) Where a person (**the grantor**) grants or assigns the fee simple in any land, and at the time of the grant or assignment, the total consideration for it is not determinable, then goods shall be treated as separately and successively supplied at the following times–

(a)   the time determined in accordance with section 6(2), (4), (5), (6), (9) or (10) of the Act, as the case may require, and

(b)   the earlier of the following times–

      (i)   each time that any part of the consideration which was not determinable at the time mentioned in sub-paragraph (a) above is received by the grantor, or

      (ii)   each time that the grantor issues a VAT invoice in respect of such a part.

LEASES TREATED AS SUPPLIES OF GOODS

85(1) Subject to paragraph (2) below, where the grant of a tenancy or lease is a supply of goods by virtue of paragraph 4 of Schedule 4 to the Act, and the whole or part of the consideration for that grant is payable periodically or from time to time, goods shall be treated as separately and successively supplied at the earlier of the following times–

(a)   each time that a part of the consideration is received by the supplier, or

(b)   each time that the supplier issues a VAT invoice relating to the grant.

85(2) Where in respect of the grant of a tenancy or lease such as is mentioned in paragraph (1) above the supplier, at or about the beginning of any period not exceeding one year, issues a VAT invoice containing, in addition to the particulars specified in regulation 14, the following particulars–

(a)   the dates on which any parts of the consideration are to become due for payment in the period,

(b)   the amount payable (excluding VAT) on each such date, and

(c)   the rate of VAT in force at the time of the issue of the VAT invoice and the amount of VAT chargeable in accordance with that rate on each of such payments,

goods shall be treated as separately and successively supplied each time that a payment in respect of the tenancy or lease becomes due or is received by the supplier, whichever is the earlier.

85(3) Where, on or before any of the dates that a payment is due as stated on an invoice issued as described in paragraph (2) above, there is a change in the VAT chargeable on supplies of the description to which the invoice relates, that invoice shall cease to be treated as a VAT invoice in respect of any such supplies for which payments are due after the change (and not received before the change).

SUPPLIES OF WATER, GAS OR ANY FORM OF POWER, HEAT, REFRIGERATION OR VENTILATION

86(1) Except in relation to a supply to which subsections (7) and (8) of section 6 of the Act apply, and subject to paragraphs (2) and (3) below, a supply of–

(a)   water other than–

      (i)   distilled water, deionised water and water of similar purity, and

      (ii)   water comprised in any of the excepted items set out in Group 1 of Schedule 8 to the Act, or

(b)   coal gas, water gas, producer gases or similar gases, or

(c)   petroleum gases, or other gaseous hydrocarbons, in a gaseous state, or

(d)   any form of power, heat, refrigeration or ventilation,

shall be treated as taking place each time that a payment in respect of the supply is received by the supplier, or a VAT invoice relating to the supply is issued by the supplier, whichever is the earlier.

86(2) Subject to paragraph (3) below, where the whole or part of the consideration for a supply such as is described in paragraph (1)(a), (b) or (c) above or of power in the form of electricity is determined or payable periodically or from time to time, goods shall be treated as separately and successively supplied at the earlier of the following times–

(a)   each time that a part of the consideration is received by the supplier, or

(b)   each time that the supplier issues a VAT invoice relating to the supply.

86(3) Where separate and successive supplies as described in paragraph (2) above are made under an agreement which provides for successive payments, and the supplier at or about the beginning of any period not exceeding one year, issues a VAT invoice containing, in addition to the particulars specified in regulation 14, the following particulars–

(a)   the dates on which payments under the agreement are to become due in the period,

(b)   the amount payable (excluding VAT) on each such date, and

(c)   the rate of VAT in force at the time of issue of the VAT invoice and the amount of VAT chargeable in accordance with that rate on each of such payments,

goods shall be treated as separately and successively supplied each time that payment in respect of the supply becomes due or is received by the supplier, whichever is the earlier.

86(4)   Where, on or before any of the dates that a payment is due as stated on an invoice issued as described in paragraph (3) above, there is a change in the VAT chargeable on supplies of the description to which the invoice relates, that invoice shall cease to be treated as a VAT invoice in respect of any such supplies for which payments are due after the change (and not received before the change).

86(5)   A supply mentioned in paragraph (1)(a), (b), (c) or (d) above to which subsections (7) and (8) of section 6 of the Act apply shall be treated as taking place on the day of the issue of a VAT invoice in respect of the supply.

ACQUISITIONS OF WATER, GAS OR ANY FORM OF POWER, HEAT, REFRIGERATION OR VENTILATION

87   Where goods described in regulation 86(1)(a), (b), (c) or (d) are acquired from another member State and the whole or part of any consideration comprised in the transaction in pursuance of which the goods are acquired is payable periodically, or from time to time, goods shall be treated as separately and successively acquired on each occasion that the supplier issues, in respect of the transaction, an invoice such as is described in regulation 83.

SUPPLIER'S GOODS IN POSSESSION OF BUYER

88(1)   Except in relation to a supply mentioned in section 6(2)(c) of the Act, or to a supply to which subsections (7) and (8) of section 6 of the Act apply, where goods are supplied under an agreement whereby the supplier retains the property therein until the goods or part of them are appropriated under the agreement by the buyer and in circumstances where the whole or part of the consideration is determined at that time, a supply of any of the goods shall be treated as taking place at the earliest of the following dates–

(a)   the date of appropriation by the buyer,

(b)   the date when a VAT invoice is issued by the supplier, or

(c)   the date when a payment is received by the supplier.

88(2)   If, within 14 days after appropriation of the goods or part of them by the buyer as mentioned in paragraph (1) above, the supplier issues a VAT invoice in respect of goods appropriated, the provisions of section 6(5) of the Act shall apply to that supply.

RETENTION PAYMENTS

89   Where any contract (other than one of a description falling within regulation 93 below) for the supply of goods (other than for a supply to which subsections (7) and (8) of section 6 of the Act apply) or for the supply of services provides for the retention of any part of the consideration by a person pending full and satisfactory performance of the contract, or any part of it, by the supplier, goods or services (as the case may require) shall be treated as separately and successively supplied at the following times–

(a)   the time determined in accordance with section 6(2), (3), (4), (5), (6), (9), (10) or (13) of the Act, as the case may require, and

(b)   the earlier of the following times–

       (i)   the time that a payment in respect of any part of the consideration which has been retained, pursuant to the terms of the contract, is received by the supplier, or

       (ii)   the time that the supplier issues a VAT invoice relating to any such part.

History – In reg. 89, the words "(other than one of a description falling within regulation 93 below)" were inserted by SI 1997/2887, reg. 3, operative from 1 January 1998.

CONTINUOUS SUPPLIES OF SERVICES

90(1)   Subject to paragraph (2) below, where services, except those to which regulation 93 applies, are supplied for a period for a consideration the whole or part of which is determined or payable periodically or from time to time, they shall be treated as separately and successively supplied at the earlier of the following times–

(a)   each time that a payment in respect of the supplies is received by the supplier, or

(b)   each time that the supplier issues a VAT invoice relating to the supplies.

90(2)   Where separate and successive supplies of services as described in paragraph (1) above are made under an agreement which provides for successive payments, and the supplier at or about the beginning of any period not exceeding one year, issues a VAT invoice containing, in addition to the particulars specified in regulation 14, the following particulars–

(a)   the dates on which payments under the agreement are to become due in the period,

(b)   the amount payable (excluding VAT) on each such date, and

(c)   the rate of VAT in force at the time of issue of the VAT invoice and the amount of VAT chargeable in accordance with that rate on each of such payments,

services shall be treated as separately and successively supplied each time that a payment in respect of them becomes due or is received by the supplier, whichever is the earlier.

90(3)   Where, on or before any of the dates that a payment is due as stated on an invoice issued as described in paragraph (2) above, there is a change in the VAT chargeable on supplies of the description to which the invoice relates, that invoice shall cease to be treated as a VAT invoice in respect of any such supplies for which payments are due after the change (and not received before the change).

90(4)   This regulation shall not apply to any relevant services–

(a)   where the period to which a payment falling within paragraph (1), (2) or (3) above relates, ends before 1st July 1997; or

(b)   which are treated as supplied on 1st July 1997 by virtue of regulation 90A below.

90(5)   In this regulation and in regulations 90A and 90B below, **"relevant services"** means services within the description contained in paragraph 7A of Schedule 5 to the Act which are treated as supplied in the United Kingdom by virtue of article 18 of the Value Added Tax (Place of Supply of Services) Order 1992.

History – In reg. 90(1), the words ", except those to which regulation 93 applies," were inserted by SI 1997/2887, reg. 4, operative from 1 January 1998.
In reg. 90(5), the words "article 18" were substituted for the words "article 20" by SI 1998/765, reg. 2, operative from 18 March 1998.
Reg. 90(4) and (5) were added by SI 1997/1525, reg. 3, operative from 1 July 1997.
Official publications – 700, para. 5.2 (2000 edn).

90A   Where–

(a)   relevant services are supplied for a period for a consideration the whole or part of which is determined or payable periodically or from time to time;

(b)   the period covered by the payment referred to in sub-paragraph (c) below ends on or after 1st July 1997; and

(c)   a payment in respect of the services was made before 1st July 1997,

the services shall be treated as supplied on 1st July 1997.

History – Reg. 90A was inserted by SI 1997/1525, reg. 4, operative from 1 July 1997.

90B   Where relevant services are treated as supplied on or after 1st July 1997 by virtue of regulation 90 or 90A above, the supply shall be treated as taking place only to the extent covered by the lower of–

(a)   the payment; and

(b)   so much of the payment as is properly attributable to such part of the period covered by the payment as falls after 30th June 1997.

History – Reg. 90B was inserted by SI 1997/1525, reg. 4, operative from 1 July 1997.

ROYALTIES AND SIMILAR PAYMENTS

91   Where the whole amount of the consideration for a supply of services was not ascertainable at the time when the services were performed and subsequently the use of the benefit of those services by a person other than the supplier gives rise to any payment of consideration for that supply which is–

(a)   in whole or in part determined or payable periodically or from time to time or at the end of any period,

(b)   additional to the amount, if any, already payable for the supply, and

(c)   not a payment to which regulation 90 applies,

a further supply shall be treated as taking place each time that a payment in respect of the use of the benefit of those services is received by the supplier or a VAT invoice is issued by the supplier, whichever is the earlier.

SUPPLIES OF SERVICES BY BARRISTERS AND ADVOCATES

92   Services supplied by a barrister, or in Scotland, by an advocate, acting in that capacity, shall be treated as taking place at whichever is the earliest of the following times–

(a)   when the fee in respect of those services is received by the barrister or advocate,

(b)   when the barrister or advocate issues a VAT invoice in respect of them, or

(c)   the day when the barrister or advocate ceases to practise as such.

Official publications – 700/44.

SUPPLIES IN THE CONSTRUCTION INDUSTRY

93(1)   where services, or services together with goods, are supplied in the course of the construction, alteration, demolition, repair or maintenance of a building or any civil engineering work under a contract which provides for payment for such supplies to be made periodically or from time to time, those services or goods and services shall be treated as separately and successively supplied at the earliest of the following times–

(a)   each time that a payment is received by the supplier,

(b)   each time that the supplier issues a VAT invoice, or

(c)   where the services are services to which paragraph (2) below applies, to the extent that they have not already been treated as supplied by virtue of sub-paragraphs (a) and (b) above–

      (i)   if the services were performed on or after 9th December 1997 and before 9th June 1999, the day which falls eighteen months after the date on which those services were performed, or

     (ii)   if the services are performed on or after 9th June 1999, the day on which the services are performed.

93(2)   This paragraph applies if, at the time the services were, or as the case may require, are performed–

(a)   it was, or as the case may require, is the intention or expectation of–

      (i)   the supplier, or

     (ii)   a person responsible for financing the supplier's cost of supplying the services or services together with goods,

that relevant land would, or as the case may require, will become (whether immediately or eventually) exempt land or, as the case may be, continue (for a period at least) to be such land, or

(b)   the supplier had, or as the case may require, has received (and used in making his supply) any supply of services or of services together with goods the time of supply of which–

      (i)   was, or

     (ii)   but for the issue by the supplier of those services or services together with goods of a VAT invoice (other than one which has been paid in full), would have been,

determined by virtue of paragraph (1)(c) above.

93(3)   For the purposes of this regulation **relevant land** is land on which the building or civil engineering work to which the construction services relate is, or as the case may be, was situated.

93(4)   In this regulation references to a person's being **responsible for financing** the supplier's cost of supplying the services or goods and services are references to his being a person who, with the intention or in the expectation that relevant land will become, or continue (for a period at least) to be, exempt land–

(a)   has provided finance for the supplier's cost of supplying the services or services together with goods, or

(b)   has entered into any agreement, arrangement or understanding (whether or not legally enforceable) to provide finance for the supplier's cost of supplying the services or services together with goods.

93(5) In this regulation references to **providing finance** for the supplier's cost of supplying services or services together with goods are references to doing any one or more of the following, that is to say–

(a)   directly or indirectly providing funds for meeting the whole or any part of the supplier's cost of supplying the services or services together with goods,

(b)   directly or indirectly procuring the provision of such funds by another,

(c)   directly or indirectly providing funds for discharging, in whole or in part any liability that has been or may be incurred by any person for or in connection with the raising of funds to meet the supplier's cost of supplying the services or services together with goods,

(d)   directly or indirectly procuring that any such liability is or will be discharged, in whole or in part, by another.

93(6) The references in paragraph (5) above to the **provision of funds** for a purpose referred to in that paragraph include references to–

(a)   the making of a loan of funds that are or are to be used for that purpose,

(b)   the provision of any guarantee or other security in relation to such a loan,

(c)   the provision of any of the consideration for the issue of any shares or other securities issued wholly or partly for raising those funds, or

(d)   any other transfer of assets or value as a consequence of which any of those funds are made available for that purpose,

but do not include references to funds made available to the supplier by paying to him the whole or any part of the consideration payable for the supply of the services or services together with goods.

93(7) In this regulation references to the supplier's **cost of supplying the services or services together with goods** are to–

(a)   amounts payable by the supplier for supplies to him of services or of goods used or to be used by him in making the supply of services or of services together with goods, and

(b)   the supplier's staff and other internal costs of making the supply of services or of services together with goods.

93(8) For the purposes of this regulation relevant land is **exempt land** if–

(a)   the supplier,

(b)   a person responsible for financing the supplier's cost of supplying the services or goods and services, or

(c)   a person connected with the supplier or with a person responsible for financing the supplier's cost of supplying the services or goods and services,

(d)   is in occupation of the land without being in occupation of it wholly or mainly for eligible purposes.

93(9) For the purposes of this regulation, but subject to paragraphs (11) and (13) below, a person's occupation at any time of any land is not capable of being **occupation for eligible purposes** unless he is a taxable person at that time.

93(10) Subject to paragraphs (11) and (13) below, a taxable person in occupation of any land shall be taken for the purposes of this regulation to be in occupation of that land for eligible purposes to the extent only that his occupation of that land is for the purpose of making supplies which–

(a)   are or are to be made in the course or furtherance of a business carried on by him, and

(b)   are supplies of such a description that any input tax of his which was wholly attributable to those supplies would be input tax for which he would be entitled to credit.

93(11) For the purposes of this regulation–

(a)   occupation of land by a body to which section 33 of the Act applies is occupation of the land for eligible purposes to the extent that the body occupies the land for purposes other than those of a business carried on by that body, and

(b)   any occupation of land by a government department (within the meaning of section 41 of the Act) is occupation of the land for eligible purposes.

93(12) For the purposes of this regulation, where land of which a person is in occupation–

(a)   is being held by that person in order to be put to use by him for particular purposes, and

(b)   is not land of which he is in occupation for any other purpose,

(c)   that person shall be deemed, for so long as the conditions in sub-paragraphs (a) and (b) above are satisfied, to be in occupation of the land for the purposes for which he proposes to use it.

93(13)   Paragraphs (9) to (12) above shall have effect where land is in the occupation of a person who–

(a)   is not a taxable person, but

(b)   is a person whose supplies are treated for the purposes of the Act as supplies made by another person who is a taxable person,

(c)   as if the person in occupation of the land and that other person were a single taxable person.

93(14)   For the purposes of this regulation a person shall be taken to be in **occupation of any land** whether he occupies it alone or together with one or more other persons and whether he occupies all of that land or only part of it.

93(15)   For the purposes of this regulation, any question as to whether one person is **connected** with another shall be determined in accordance with section 839 of the Taxes Act.

History – Reg. 93 was substituted by SI 1999/1374, reg. 2, operative from 9 June 1999. Former reg. 93 reads as follows:
"93(1)   Where services, or services together with goods, are supplied in the course of the construction, alteration, demolition, repair or maintenance of a building or any civil engineering work under a contract which provides for payment for such supplies to be made periodically or from time to time, those services or goods and services shall be treated as separately and successively supplied at the earliest of the following times–
(a)   each time that a payment is received by the supplier,
(b)   each time that the supplier issues a VAT invoice, or
(c)   to the extent that they have not already been treated as supplied by virtue of sub-paragraphs (a) and (b) above and subject to paragraph (2) below, the day which falls eighteen months after the date on which those services were performed.
93(2)   Sub-paragraph (1)(c) above does not apply unless the services were performed on or after 9th December 1997."
Reg. 93 was substituted by SI 1997/2887, reg. 5, operative from 1 January 1998. Former reg. 93 reads as follows:
"93   Where services, or services together with goods, are supplied in the course of the construction, alteration, demolition, repair or maintenance of a building or of any civil engineering work under a contract which provides for payment for such supplies to be made periodically or from time to time, a supply shall be treated as taking place at the earlier of the following times–
(a)   each time that a payment is received by the supplier where the consideration for the contract is wholly in money, or
(b)   each time that the supplier issues a VAT invoice."

GENERAL

94   Subject to regulation 90B above, where under this Part of these Regulations a supply is treated as taking place each time that a payment (however expressed) is received or an invoice is issued, the supply is to be treated as taking place only to the extent covered by the payment or invoice.

History – In reg. 94, the words "Subject to regulation 90B above, where under this Part" were substituted for the words "Where under this Part" by SI 1997/1525, reg. 5, operative from 1 July 1997.

94A   In this Part a reference to **receipt of payment** (however expressed) includes a reference to receipt by a person to whom a right to receive it has been assigned.

History – Reg. 94A was inserted by SI 1999/599, reg. 3 operative in respect of payments received on or after 10 March 1999.

SUPPLIES SPANNING CHANGE OF RATE ETC.

95   Section 88 of the Act shall apply as if the references in subsection (2) of that section to section 6(4), (5), (6) and (10) of the Act included references to regulations 81, 82, 84, 85, 86(1) to (4) and 88 to 93 of these Regulations.

PART XII – VALUATION OF ACQUISITIONS

INTERPRETATION OF PART XII

96   In this Part–

    "relevant transaction", in relation to any acquisition of goods from another member State, and **"relevant time"** in relation to any such acquisition, have the meanings given in paragraph 5 of Schedule 7 to the Act.

VALUATION OF ACQUISITIONS

97(1)   Subject to paragraph (2) below, the value of the relevant transaction in relation to any goods acquired in the United Kingdom from another member State where–

(a)   the goods are charged in connection with their removal to the United Kingdom with a duty of excise; or

(b)   on that removal are subject, in accordance with any provision for the time being having effect for transitional purposes in connection with the accession of any State to the European

Communities, to any Community customs duty or agricultural levy of the Economic Community,

shall be taken, for the purposes of the Act, to be the sum of its value apart from paragraph 2 of Schedule 7 to the Act and the amount, so far as not already included in that value, of the excise duty, Community customs duty or, as the case may be, agricultural levy which has been or is to be paid in respect of those goods.

97(2) Paragraph (1) above does not apply to a transaction in pursuance of which there is an acquisition of goods which, under subsection (4) of section 18 of the Act, is treated as taking place before the duty point within the meaning of that section.

PART XIII – PLACE OF SUPPLY

DISTANCE SALES FROM THE UNITED KINGDOM

98(1) Where a person has exercised an option in the United Kingdom corresponding to an option mentioned in paragraph 1(2) of Schedule 2 to the Act, in respect of supplies involving the removal of goods to another member State, he shall notify the Commissioners in writing of the exercise of that option not less than 30 days before the date on which the first supply to which the option relates is made.

98(2) The notification referred to in paragraph (1) above shall contain the name of the member State to which the goods have been, or are to be, removed under the direction or control of the person making the supply.

98(3) Any person who has notified the Commissioners in accordance with paragraph (1) above shall within 30 days of the date of the first supply as is mentioned in that paragraph furnish to the Commissioners documentary evidence that he has notified the member State of the exercise of his option.

98(4) Where a person has notified the Commissioners in accordance with paragraph (1) above he may withdraw his notification by giving a further written notification but that further notification must specify the date upon which the first notification is to be withdrawn, which date must not be earlier than–

(a)   the 1st January which is, or next follows, the second anniversary of the date of the making of the first supply mentioned above to which the option relates, and

(b)   the day 30 days after the receipt by the Commissioners of the further notification,

and not later than 30 days before the date of the first supply which he intends to make after the withdrawal.

PART XIV – INPUT TAX AND PARTIAL EXEMPTION

INTERPRETATION OF PART XIV AND LONGER PERIODS

99(1) In this Part–

(a)   **"exempt input tax"** means–

    (i) input tax or a proportion of input tax, which is attributable to exempt supplies in accordance with the method used under regulation 101, or a method approved or directed to be used under regulation 102 as the case may be, and

    (ii) input tax, or a proportion of input tax, which is attributable to exempt supplies of a description falling within regulation 103A, but not any input tax allowable under that regulation, and

    (iii) input tax, or a proportion of input tax, which is attributable to supplies outside the United Kingdom which would be exempt if made in the United Kingdom, not being supplies specified in an order under section 26(2)(c) of the Act, according to the extent to which the goods or services on which the input tax was incurred are used or to be used in making such supplies or in accordance with a method approved or directed to be used under regulation 102, as the case may be;

(b)   **"prescribed accounting period"** means–

    (i) a prescribed accounting period such as is referred to in regulation 25, or

(ii) a special accounting period, where the first prescribed accounting period would otherwise be 6 months or longer, save that this paragraph shall not apply where the reference to the prescribed accounting period is used solely in order to identify a particular return;

(c) **"special accounting period"** means each of a succession of periods of the same length as the next prescribed accounting period which does not exceed 3 months, and–

(i) the last such period shall end on the day before the commencement of that next prescribed accounting period, and

(ii) the first such period shall commence on the effective date of registration determined in accordance with Schedule 1, 2, 3 or 3A to the Act and end on the day before the commencement of the second such period;

(d) the **"tax year"** of a taxable person means–

(i) the first period of 12 calendar months commencing on the first day of April, May or June, according to the prescribed accounting periods allocated to him, next following his effective date of registration determined in accordance with Schedule 1, 2, 3 or 3A to the Act, or

(ii) any subsequent period of 12 calendar months commencing on the day following the end of his first, or any subsequent, tax year,

save that the Commissioners may approve or direct that a tax year shall be a period of other than 12 calendar months or that it shall commence on a date other than that determined in accordance with paragraph (i) or (ii) above;

(e) the **"registration period"** of a taxable person means the period commencing on his effective date of registration determined in accordance with Schedule 1, 2, 3 or 3A to the Act and ending on the day before the commencement of his first tax year.

99(2) In this Part, any reference to **goods** or **services** shall be construed as including a reference to anything which is supplied by way of a supply of goods or a supply of services respectively.

99(3) The provisions of paragraphs (4), (5), (6) and (7) below shall be used for determining the longer period applicable to taxable persons under this Part.

99(4) A taxable person who incurs exempt input tax during any tax year shall have applied to him a longer period which shall correspond with that tax year unless he did not incur exempt input tax during his immediately preceding tax year or registration period, in which case his longer period shall–

(a) begin on the first day of the first prescribed accounting period in which he incurs exempt input tax, and

(b) end on the last day of that tax year,

except where he incurs exempt input tax only in the last prescribed accounting period of his tax year, in which case no longer period shall be applied to him in respect of that tax year.

99(5) A taxable person who incurs exempt input tax during his registration period shall have applied to him a longer period which shall begin on the first day on which he incurs exempt input tax and end on the day before the commencement of his first tax year.

99(6) In the case of a taxable person ceasing to be taxable during a longer period applicable to him, that longer period shall end on the day when he ceases to be taxable.

99(7) The Commissioners may approve in the case of a taxable person who incurs exempt input tax, or a class of such persons, that a longer period shall apply which need not correspond with a tax year.

History – Reg. 99(1)(a) was substituted by SI 1999/3114, reg. 6, operative from 1 January 2000. Former reg. 99(1)(a) reads as follows:
"(a) **"exempt input tax"** means–
　　　　　(i)　input tax, or a proportion of input tax, which is attributable to exempt supplies in accordance with the method used under regulation 101, or a method approved or directed to be used under regulation 102 as the case may be, and
input tax, or a proportion of input tax, which is attributable to supplies outside the United Kingdom which would be exempt if made in the United Kingdom, not being supplies specified in an order under section 26(2)(c) of the Act, according to the extent to which the goods or services on which the input tax was incurred are used or to be used in making such supplies or in accordance with a method approved or directed to be used under regulation 102, as the case may be;"
In reg. 99(1)(c), the words ", 2, 3 or 3A" were inserted by SI 2000/794, reg. 6, operative from 22 March 2000.
In reg. 99(1)(d), the words ", 2, 3 or 3A" were inserted by SI 2000/794, reg. 6, operative from 22 March 2000.
In reg. 99(1)(e), the words ", 2, 3 or 3A" were inserted by SI 2000/794, reg. 6, operative from 22 March 2000.

100 Nothing in this Part shall be construed as allowing a taxable person to deduct the whole or any part of VAT on the importation or acquisition by him of goods or the supply to him of goods or services where those goods or services are not used or to be used by him in making supplies in the course or furtherance of a business carried on by him.

Official publications – 706 and 706/2.
Customs Internal Guidance Manual, vol. V1.15: partial exemption.

Other material – Form VAT 427.

ATTRIBUTION OF INPUT TAX TO TAXABLE SUPPLIES

101(1)   Subject to regulation 102, the amount of input tax which a taxable person shall be entitled to deduct provisionally shall be that amount which is attributable to taxable supplies in accordance with this regulation.

101(2)   In respect of each prescribed accounting period–

(a)   goods imported or acquired by and goods or services supplied to, the taxable person in the period shall be identified,

(b)   there shall be attributed to taxable supplies the whole of the input tax on such of those goods or services as are used or to be used by him exclusively in making taxable supplies,

(c)   no part of the input tax on such of those goods or services as are used or to be used by him exclusively in making exempt supplies, or in carrying on any activity other than the making of taxable supplies, shall be attributed to taxable supplies, and

(d)   there shall be attributed to taxable supplies such proportion of the input tax on such of those goods or services as are used or to be used by him in making both taxable and exempt supplies as bears the same ratio to the total of such input tax as the value of taxable supplies made by him bears to the value of all supplies made by him in the period.

101(3)   In calculating the proportion under paragraph (2)(d) above, there shall be excluded–

(a)   any sum receivable by the taxable person in respect of any supply of capital goods used by him for the purposes of his business,

(b)   any sum receivable by the taxable person in respect of any of the following descriptions of supplies made by him, where such supplies are incidental to one or more of his business activities–

     (i)   any supply which falls within item 1 of Group 5, or item 1 of Group 6, of Schedule 8 to the Act,

     (ii)   any grant which falls within item 1 of Group 1 of Schedule 9 to the Act,

     (iii)   any grant which falls within paragraph (a) of item 1 of Group 1 of Schedule 9 to the Act,

     (iv)   any grant which would fall within item 1 of Group 1 of Schedule 9 to the Act but for an election having effect under paragraph 2 of Schedule 10 to the Act, and

     (v)   any supply which falls within Group 5 of Schedule 9 to the Act,

(c)   that part of the value of any supply of goods on which output tax is not chargeable by virtue of any order made by the Treasury under section 25(7) of the Act unless the taxable person has imported, acquired or been supplied with the goods for the purpose of selling them, and

(d)   the value of any supply which, under or by virtue of any provision of the Act, the taxable person makes to himself.

101(4)   The ratio calculated for the purpose of paragraph (2)(d) above shall be expressed as a percentage and, if that percentage is not a whole number, it shall be rounded up to the next whole number.

101(5)   [Omitted by SI 1996/1250, reg. 14(b).]

History – In reg. 101(2)(a), the words "subject to paragraph (5) below" were omitted by SI 1996/1250, reg. 14(a), operative from 1 June 1996, except where 28 April 1996 falls within the prescribed accounting period of a taxable person, and that prescribed accounting period ends on or after 1 June 1996, the omission does not, in relation to that taxable person, have effect until the day after the end of that prescribed accounting period.
Reg. 101(5) was omitted by SI 1996/1250, reg. 14(b), operative from 1 June 1996, except where 28 April 1996 falls within the prescribed accounting period of a taxable person, and that prescribed accounting period ends on or after 1 June 1996, the omission does not, in relation to that taxable person, have effect until the day after the end of that prescribed accounting period.

USE OF OTHER METHODS

102(1)   Subject to paragraph (2) below and regulation 103, the Commissioners may approve or direct the use by a taxable person of a method other than that specified in regulation 101, save that where the use of a method was allowed prior to 1st August 1989 there shall not be included in the calculation (if the method in question would otherwise allow it)–

(a)   the value of any supply which, under or by virtue of any provision of the Act, the taxable person makes to himself, and

(b)   the input tax on such a supply.

102(2)   Notwithstanding any provision of any method approved or directed to be used under this regulation which purports to have the contrary effect, in calculating the proportion of any input tax on goods or services used or to be used by the taxable person in making both taxable and exempt supplies which is to be treated as attributable to taxable supplies, the value of any supply within regulation 101(3) shall be excluded.

102(3)   A taxable person using a method as approved or directed to be used by the Commissioners under paragraph (1) above shall continue to use that method unless the Commissioners approve or direct the termination of its use.

102(4)   Any direction under paragraph (1) or (3) above shall take effect from the date upon which the Commissioners give such direction or from such later date as they may specify.

ATTRIBUTION OF INPUT TAX TO FOREIGN AND SPECIFIED SUPPLIES

103(1)   Input tax incurred by a taxable person in any prescribed accounting period on goods imported or acquired by, or goods or services supplied to, him which are used or to be used by him in whole or in part in making–

(a)   supplies outside the United Kingdom which would be taxable supplies if made in the United Kingdom, or

(b)   supplies specified in an Order under section 26(2)(c) of the Act other than supplies of a description falling within regulation 103A below,

shall be attributed to taxable supplies to the extent that the goods or services are so used or to be used expressed as a proportion of the whole use or intended use.

103(2)   Where–

(a)   input tax of the description in paragraph (1) above has been incurred on goods or services which are used or to be used in making both–

     (i)   a supply within item 1 or 6 of Group 5 of Schedule 9 to the Act, and

     (ii)   any other supply, and

(b)   the supply mentioned in sub-paragraph (a)(i) above is incidental to one or more of the taxable person's business activities,

that input tax shall be attributed to taxable supplies in accordance with paragraph (1) above notwithstanding any provision of any method that the taxable person is required or allowed to use under this Part of these Regulations which purports to have the contrary effect.

103(3)   For the purpose of attributing to taxable supplies any input tax of the description in paragraph (2) above, it shall be deemed to be the only input tax incurred by the taxable person in the prescribed accounting period concerned.

History – In reg. 103(1)(b), the words "other than supplies of a description falling within regulation 103A below," were inserted by SI 1999/3114, reg. 7, operative from 1 January 2000.

103A(1)   This regulation applies to a taxable person who makes supplies of a description falling within item 1 or 2 of Group 15 of Schedule 9 to the Act.

103A(2)   Input tax incurred by him in any prescribed accounting period in respect of supplies by him of a description falling within paragraph (1) above shall be allowable as being attributable to those supplies only to the following extent, that is to say where it is incurred–

(a)   on investment gold supplied to him which but for an election made under the Value Added Tax (Investment Gold) Order 1999, or but for Note 4(b) to Group 15 of Schedule 9 to the Act would have fallen within item 1 or 2 of that Group, or on investment gold acquired by him;

(b)   on a supply to him, an acquisition by him, or on an importation by him of gold other than investment gold which is to be transformed by him or on his behalf into investment gold;

(c)   on services supplied to him comprising a change of form, weight or purity of gold.

103A(3)   Where a taxable person produces investment gold or transforms any gold into investment gold he shall also be entitled to credit for input tax incurred by him on any goods or services supplied to him, any acquisitions of goods by him or any importations of goods by him, but only to the extent that they are linked to the production or transformation of that gold into investment gold.

103A(4) Where input tax has been incurred on goods or services which are used or to be used in making supplies of a description falling within item 1 or 2 of Group 15 of Schedule 9 to the Act and any other supply, that input tax shall be attributed to the supplies falling within item 1 or 2 to the extent that the goods or services are so used or to be used, expressed as a proportion of the whole use or intended use.

103A(5) Where input tax is attributed to supplies of a description falling within item 1 or 2 of Group 15 of Schedule 9 to the Act under paragraph (4) above, the taxable person shall be entitled to credit for only so much input tax as is reasonably allowable under paragraph (2) or (3) above.

103A(6) For the purpose of attributing input tax to supplies of a description falling within item 1 or 2 of Group 15 of Schedule 9 to the Act under paragraph (4) above, any input tax of the description in that paragraph shall be deemed to be the only input tax incurred by the taxable person in the prescribed accounting period concerned.

History – Reg. 103A was inserted by SI 1999/3114, reg. 8, operative from 1 January 2000.
Official publications – 701/21 and 701/21A.

ATTRIBUTION OF INPUT TAX ON SELF-SUPPLIES

104 Where under or by virtue of any provision of the Act a person makes a supply to himself, the input tax on that supply shall not be allowable as attributable to that supply.

TREATMENT OF INPUT TAX ATTRIBUTABLE TO EXEMPT SUPPLIES AS BEING ATTRIBUTABLE TO TAXABLE SUPPLIES

105 [Omitted by SI 1999/599, reg. 4. In relation to a taxable person whose registration period (as defined by reg. 99(1)(e)) commenced before 10 March 1999 and ends after that day, the omission has effect from the commencement of his first tax year (as defined by reg. 99(1)(d)(i)). However, in relation to a taxable person who was registered before 10 March 1999, and whose registration period (as defined by reg. 99(1)(e)) did not commence before 10 March 1999 and end after that day, the omission has effect from the first day of the first of his tax years commencing after that day.]

History – Former reg. 15 reads as follows:
"**105(1)** Subject to paragraphs (2) and (4) below, there shall be treated as attributable to taxable supplies any exempt input tax attributable to supplies of the following descriptions–
(a)   any deposit of money,
(b)   the grant of any lease or tenancy of, or any licence to occupy, any land where in any longer period–
         (i)   the input tax attributable to all such supplies by the grantor is less than £1,000, and
no exempt input tax is incurred by the grantor in respect of any exempt supply other than a supply of a description specified in this regulation,
(c)   any services comprised in item 3 of Group 2 of Schedule 9 to the Act,
(d)   services of arranging–
any mortgage, or
any hire purchase, credit sale or conditional sale transaction, and
(e)   the assignment of any debt due to the assignor in respect of a supply of goods or services made by him.
105(2) Paragraph (1) above shall not apply where the supply is made by the taxable person in the course of carrying on a business of, or a business similar to, any of the following–
(a)   a bank,
(b)   an accepting house,
(c)   an insurance company, agent or broker,
(d)   an investment trust or unit trust,
(e)   an investment company,
(f)   a Stock Exchange broker/dealer or share dealing company,
(g)   a trustee of a pension fund,
(h)   a unit trust management company,
(i)   a building society,
(j)   a discount house,
(k)   a finance house,
(l)   a friendly society,
(m)   a money lender,
(n)   a money broker,
(o)   a mortgage broker,
(p)   a pawnbroker,
(q)   a debt factor, or
(r)   a credit or charge card company.
105(3) For the purpose of paragraph (2) above, a taxable person who carries on one or more of the businesses specified in that paragraph shall not be treated as having made the supply in the course of carrying on such a business if he made the supply exclusively in the course of carrying on a business which is not so specified.
105(4)   Paragraph (1) above shall not apply where the exempt input tax of the taxable person, excluding any exempt input tax attributable to supplies of the descriptions specified in that paragraph, cannot be treated as attributable to taxable supplies under regulation 106.
105(5) In this regulation–
         "**supplies**", except in the expression "taxable supplies", shall be construed as including supplies outside the United Kingdom which would be exempt if made in the United Kingdom, other than supplies specified in an Order under section 26(2)(c) of the Act, and
         "**supply**" shall be construed accordingly."

106(1)   Where in any prescribed accounting period or in any longer period the exempt input tax of a taxable person–

(a)   does not amount to more than £625 per month on average, and

(b)   does not exceed one half of all his input tax for the period concerned,

all such input tax in that period shall be treated as attributable to taxable supplies.

106(2)   In the application of paragraph (1) above to a longer period–

(a)   any treatment of exempt input tax as attributable to taxable supplies in any prescribed accounting period shall be disregarded, and

(b)   no account shall be taken of any amount or amounts which may be deductible or payable under regulation 115.

Cross references – VATA 1994, Sch. 9, Grp. 14, Note (4): supplies where input tax cannot be recovered.

ADJUSTMENT OF ATTRIBUTION

107(1)   Where a taxable person to whom a longer period is applicable has provisionally attributed an amount of input tax to taxable supplies in accordance with a method, and where all his exempt input tax in that longer period cannot be treated as attributable to taxable supplies under 106, and save as the Commissioners may dispense with the following requirement to adjust, he shall–

(a)   determine for the longer period the amount of input tax which is attributable to taxable supplies according to the method used in the prescribed accounting periods,

(b)   ascertain whether there has been, overall, an over-deduction or an under-deduction of input tax, having regard to the above-mentioned determination and to the sum of the amounts of input tax, if any, which were deducted in the returns for the prescribed accounting periods, and

(c)   include any such amount of over-deduction or under-deduction in a return for the first prescribed accounting period next following the longer period, except where the Commissioners allow another return to be used for this purpose.

107(2)   Where a taxable person to whom a longer period is applicable has provisionally attributed an amount of input tax to taxable supplies in accordance with a method, and where all his exempt input tax in that longer period can be treated as attributable to taxable supplies under 106, he shall–

(a)   calculate the difference between the total amount of his input tax for that longer period and the sum of the amounts of input tax deducted in the returns for the prescribed accounting periods, and

(b)   include any such amount of under-deduction in a return for the first prescribed accounting period next following the longer period, except where the Commissioners allow another return to be used for this purpose.

History – In reg. 107(1), the words "105 or" were omitted by SI 1999/599, reg. 5. In relation to a taxable person whose registration period (as defined by reg. 99(1)(e)) commenced before 10 March 1999 and ends after that day, the omission has effect from the commencement of his first tax year (as defined by reg. 99(1)(d)(i)). However, in relation to a taxable person who was registered before 10 March 1999, and whose registration period (as defined by reg. 99(1)(e)) did not commence before 10 March 1999 and end after that day, the omission has effect from the first day of the first of his tax years commencing after that day.

In reg. 107(2), the words "105 or" were omitted by SI 1999/599, reg. 5, operative from the same date as that identical omission made to reg. 107(1).

108(1)   This regulation applies where a taxable person has deducted an amount of input tax which has been attributed to taxable supplies because he intended to use the goods or services in making either–

(a)   taxable supplies, or

(b)   both taxable and exempt supplies,

and during a period of 6 years commencing on the first day of the prescribed accounting period in which the attribution was determined and before that intention is fulfilled, he uses or forms an intention to use the goods or services concerned in making exempt supplies or, in the case of an attribution within sub-paragraph (a) above, in making both taxable and exempt supplies.

108(2)   Subject to regulation 110 and save as the Commissioners otherwise allow, where this regulation applies the taxable person shall on the return for the prescribed accounting period in which the use occurs or the intention is formed, as the case may be, account for an amount equal to the input tax which has ceased to be attributable to taxable supplies in accordance with the method which he was required to use when the input tax was first attributed and he shall repay the said amount to the Commissioners.

108(3) For the purposes of this regulation any question as to the nature of any supply shall be determined in accordance with the provisions of the Act and any Regulations or Orders made thereunder in force at the time when the input tax was first attributed.

109(1) This regulation applies where a taxable person has incurred an amount of input tax which has not been attributed to taxable supplies because he intended to use the goods or services in making either–

(a)   exempt supplies, or

(b)   both taxable and exempt supplies,

and during a period of 6 years commencing on the first day of the prescribed accounting period in which the attribution was determined and before that intention is fulfilled, he uses or forms an intention to use the goods or services concerned in making taxable supplies or, in the case of an attribution within sub-paragraph (a) above, in making both taxable and exempt supplies.

109(2) Subject to regulation 110 and where this regulation applies, the Commissioners shall, on receipt of an application made by the taxable person in such form and manner and containing such particulars as they may direct, pay to him an amount equal to the input tax which has become attributable to taxable supplies in accordance with the method which he was required to use when the input tax was first attributed.

109(3) For the purposes of this regulation any question as to the nature of any supply shall be determined in accordance with the provisions of the Act and any Regulations or Orders made thereunder in force at the time when the input tax was first attributed.

110(1) Subject to paragraph (2) below, in this regulation, in regulations 108 and 109 above and in Part XV of these Regulations–

(a)   **"exempt supplies"** includes supplies outside the United Kingdom which would be exempt if made in the United Kingdom, other than supplies of a description falling within subparagraph (b) below; and

(b)   **"taxable supplies"** includes supplies of a description falling within regulation 103(1) above.

110(2) Subject to paragraph (3) below, for the purposes of identifying the use, or intended use, of goods and services in regulations 108 and 109 above and in Part XV of these Regulations–

(a)   **"exempt supplies"** shall be construed as including supplies of a description falling within regulation 103A(1) above, but only to the extent that there is, or would be, no credit for input tax on goods and services under that regulation; and

(b)   **"taxable supplies"** shall be construed as including supplies of a description falling within regulation 103A(1) above, but only to the extent that there is, or would be, credit for input tax on goods and services under that regulation.

110(3) Any adjustment under regulations 108 and 109 above shall not cause any more or any less input tax to be credited, as the case may be, in respect of supplies of a description falling within regulation 103A(1) above than would be allowed or required under that regulation.

110(4) Subject to regulation 103, where–

(a)   regulation 108 or 109 applies,

(b)   the use to which the goods or services concerned are put, or to which they are intended to be put, includes the making of any supplies outside the United Kingdom, and

(c)   at the time when the taxable person was first required to attribute the input tax he was not required to use a method approved or directed under regulation 102 or that method did not provide expressly for the attribution of input tax attributable to supplies outside the United Kingdom,

the amount for which the taxable person shall be liable to account under regulation 108 or the amount which he is entitled to be paid under regulation 109, as the case may be, shall be calculated by reference to the extent to which the goods or services concerned are used or intended to be used in making taxable supplies, expressed as a proportion of the whole use or intended use.

History – Reg. 110 was substituted by SI 1999/3114, reg. 9, operative from 1 January 2000. Former reg. 110 reads as follows:
"**110(1)** *In this regulation and regulations 108 and 109*–
(a)   **"exempt supplies"** includes supplies outside the United Kingdom which would be exempt if made in the United Kingdom, other than supplies within sub-paragraph (b) below, and
(b)   **"taxable supplies"** includes the supplies referred to in regulation 103.
110(2) Subject to regulation 103, where–
(a)   regulation 108 or 109 applies,
(b)   the use to which the goods or services concerned are put or to which they are intended to be put includes the making of any supplies outside the United Kingdom, and

(c)   at the time when the taxable person was first required to attribute the input tax he was not required to use a method approved or directed under regulation 102 or that method did not provide expressly for the attribution of input tax attributable to supplies outside the United Kingdom,

the amount for which the taxable person shall be liable to account under regulation 108 or the amount which he is entitled to be paid under regulation 109, as the case may be, shall be calculated by reference to the extent to which the goods or services concerned are used or intended to be used in making taxable supplies, expressed as a proportion of the whole use or intended use."

EXCEPTIONAL CLAIMS FOR VAT RELIEF

111(1) Subject to paragraphs (2) and (4) below, on a claim made in accordance with paragraph (3) below, the Commissioners may authorise a taxable person to treat as if it were input tax–

(a)   VAT on the supply of goods or services to the taxable person before the date with effect from which he was, or was required to be, registered, or paid by him on the importation or acquisition of goods before that date, for the purpose of a business which either was carried on or was to be carried on by him at the time of such supply or payment, and

(b)   in the case of a body corporate, VAT on goods obtained for it before its incorporation, or on the supply of services before that time for its benefit or in connection with its incorporation, provided that the person to whom the supply was made or who paid VAT on the importation or acquisition–

    (i)   became a member, officer or employee of the body and was reimbursed, or has received an undertaking to be reimbursed, by the body for the whole amount of the price paid for the goods or services,

    (ii)   was not at the time of the importation, acquisition or supply a taxable person, and

    (iii)   imported, acquired or was supplied with the goods, or received the services, for the purpose of a business to be carried on by the body and has not used them for any purpose other than such a business.

111(2) No VAT may be treated as if it were input tax under paragraph (1) above–

(a)   in respect of

    (i)   goods or services which had been supplied, or

    (ii)   save as the Commissioners may otherwise allow, goods which had been consumed,

    by the relevant person before the date with effect from which the taxable person was, or was required to be, registered;

(b)   subject to paragraph (2A) below, in respect of goods which had been supplied to, or imported or acquired by, the relevant person more than 3 years before the date with effect from which the taxable person was, or was required to be, registered,

(c)   in respect of services performed upon goods to which sub-paragraph (a) or (b) above applies; or

(d)   in respect of services which had been supplied to the relevant person more than 6 months before the date with effect from which the taxable person was, or was required to be, registered.

111(2A) Paragraph (2)(b) above does not apply where–

(a)   the taxable person was registered before 1st May 1997; and

(b)   he did not make any return before that date.

111(2B) In paragraph (2) above references to the **relevant person** are references to-

(a)   the taxable person; or

(b)   in the case of paragraph (1)(b) above, the person to whom the supply had been made, or who had imported or acquired the goods, as the case may be.

111(3) Subject to paragraphs (3A) and (3B) below, a claim under paragraph (1) above shall, save as the Commissioners may otherwise allow, be made on the first return the taxable person is required to make and, as the Commissioners may require, be supported by invoices and other evidence.

111(3A) Where the taxable person was registered before 1st May 1997 and has not made any returns before that date paragraph (3) above shall have effect as if for the words "the first return the taxable person is required to make" there were substituted the words "the first return the taxable person makes".

111(3B) The Commissioners shall not allow a person to make any claim under paragraph (3) above in terms such that the VAT concerned would fall to be claimed as if it were input tax more than 3 years after the date by which the first return he is required to make is required to be made.

111(4) A taxable person making a claim under paragraph (1) above shall compile and preserve for such period as the Commissioners may require–

(a)   in respect of goods, a stock account showing separately quantities purchased, quantities used in the making of other goods, date of purchase and date and manner of subsequent disposals of both such quantities, and

(b)   in respect of services, a list showing their description, date of purchase and date of disposal, if any.

111(5) Subject to paragraph (6) below, if a person who has been, but is no longer, a taxable person makes a claim in such manner and supported by such evidence as the Commissioners may require, they may pay to him the amount of any VAT on the supply of services to him after the date with effect from which he ceased to be, or to be required to be, registered and which was attributable to any taxable supply made by him in the course or furtherance of any business carried on by him when he was, or was required to be, registered.

111(6) Subject to paragraph (7) below, no claim under paragraph (5) above may be made more than 3 years after the date on which the supply of services was made.

111(7) Paragraph (6) above does not apply where–

(a)   the person ceased to be, or ceased to be required to be, registered before 1st May 1997; and

(b)   the supply was made before that date.

History – Reg. 111(2) substituted, and reg. 111(2A), (2B) inserted by SI 1997/1086, reg. 7(a), (b), operative from 1 May 1997. Reg. 111(2) formerly read as follows:
"**111(2)**   No VAT may be treated as input tax under paragraph (1) above–
> (a)   in respect of goods or services which had been supplied, or, in respect of goods, save as the Commissioners may otherwise allow, consumed–
>> (i)   by the taxable person, or
>> (ii)   in the case of paragraph (1)(b) above, by the person who imported, acquired or was supplied with the goods or services,before the date with effect from which the taxable person was, or was required to be, registered,
> (b)   in respect of services performed upon goods to which sub-paragraph (a) above applies, or
> (c)   in respect of services which had been supplied–
>> (i)   to the taxable person, or
>> (ii)   in the case of paragraph (1)(b) above, to the person who received the services,more than 6 months before the date of the taxable person's registration."

In reg. 111(3), the words "Subject to paragraphs (3A) and (3B) below," were inserted and the words "the first return the taxable person is required to make" were substituted for the words "the first return the taxable person makes" by SI 1997/1086, reg. 7(c), (d), operative from 1 May 1997.
Reg. 111(3A), (3B) inserted by SI 1997/1086, reg. 7(e), operative from 1 May 1997.
Reg. 111(6), (7), and reference to reg. 111(6) in reg. 111(5), inserted by SI 1997/1086, reg. 7(f), (g), operative from 1 May 1997.

PART XV – ADJUSTMENTS TO THE DEDUCTION OF INPUT TAX ON CAPITAL ITEMS

INTERPRETATION OF PART XV

112(1) Any expression used in this Part to which a meaning is given in Part XIV of these Regulations shall, unless the contrary intention appears, have the same meaning in this Part as it has in that Part and in particular, exempt supplies and taxable supplies shall be accorded the same meanings as defined in regulation 110 above.

112(2) Any reference in this Part to a **capital item** shall be construed as a reference to a capital item to which this Part applies by virtue of regulation 113, being an item which a person (hereinafter referred to as **"the owner"**) uses in the course or furtherance of a business carried on by him, and for the purpose of that business, otherwise than solely for the purpose of selling the item.

History – In reg. 112(1), the words "and in particular, exempt supplies ... defined in regulation 110 above" were inserted by SI 1999/3114, reg. 10, operative from 1 January 2000.

CAPITAL ITEMS TO WHICH THIS PART APPLIES

113 The capital items to which this Part applies are items of any of the following descriptions–

(a)   a computer or an item of computer equipment of a value of not less than £50,000 supplied to, or imported or acquired by, the owner,

(b)   land, a building or part of a building or a civil engineering work or part of a civil engineering work where the value of the interest therein supplied to the owner, by way of a taxable supply which is not a zero-rated supply, is not less than £250,000 excluding so much of that value as may consist of rent (including charges reserved as rent) which is neither payable nor paid more than 12 months in advance nor invoiced for a period in excess of 12 months,

(c)   a building or part of a building where–

    (i)   the owner's interest in, right over, or licence to occupy, the building or part of the building is treated as supplied to him under paragraph 1(5) of Schedule 10 to the Act, and

    (ii)   the value of that supply, determined in accordance with paragraph 1(6)(b) of that Schedule, is not less than £250,000,

(d)   a building or part of a building where–

    (i)   the owner's interest in, right over, or licence to occupy, the building or part of the building was, on or before 1st March 1997, treated as supplied to him under paragraph 6(1) of Schedule 10 to the Act, and

    (ii)   the value of that supply, determined in accordance with paragraph 6(2) of that Schedule, was not less than £250,000,

(e)   a building other than one falling or capable of falling within paragraphs (c) or (d) above constructed by the owner and first brought into use by him on or after 1st April 1990 where the aggregate of–

    (i)   the value of taxable grants relating to the land on which the building is constructed made to the owner on or after 1st April 1990, and

    (ii)   the value of all the taxable supplies of goods and services, other than any that are zero-rated, made or to be made to him for or in connection with the construction of the building on or after 1st April 1990,

is not less than £250,000,

(f)   a building which the owner alters, or an extension or an annex which he constructs, where–

    (i)   additional floor area is created in the altered building, extension or annex, of not less than 10 per cent. of the floor area of the building before the alteration in question is carried out, or the extension or annex in question is constructed, and

    (ii)   the value of all the taxable supplies of goods and services, other than any that are zero-rated, made or to be made to the owner for or in connection with the alteration, extension or annex in question on or after 1st April 1990, is not less than £250,000,

(g)   a civil engineering work constructed by the owner and first brought into use by him on or after 3rd July 1997 where the aggregate of–

    (i)   the value of the taxable grants relating to the land on which the civil engineering work is constructed made to the owner on or after 3rd July 1997, and

    (ii)   the value of all the taxable supplies of goods and services, other than any that are zero-rated, made or to be made to him for or in connection with the construction of the civil engineering work on or after 3rd July 1997,

is not less than £250,000, and

(h)   a building which the owner refurbishes or fits out where the value of capital expenditure on the taxable supplies of services and of goods affixed to the building, other than any that are zero-rated, made or to be made to the owner for or in connection with the refurbishment or fitting out in question on or after 3rd July 1997 is not less than £250,000.

History – In reg. 113(b), the words "land, a building or part of a building or a civil engineering work or part of a civil engineering work" were substituted for the words "land or a building or part of a building" by SI 1997/1614, reg. 10(a)(i), operative from 3 July 1997.

In reg. 113(b), the words "(including charges reserved as rent) which is neither payable" to the end were added by SI 1997/1614, reg. 10(a)(ii), operative from 3 July 1997.

In reg. 113(d)(i), the words "was, on or before 1st March 1997, treated" were substituted for the words "is treated" by SI 1997/1614, reg. 10(b), operative from 3 July 1997.

In reg. 113(d)(ii), the word "was" was substituted for the word "is" by SI 1997/1614, reg. 10(c), operative from 3 July 1997.

In reg. 113(e), the word "and" at the end was omitted by SI 1997/1614, reg. 10(d), operative from 3 July 1997.

In reg. 113(f), the comma at the end was added by SI 1997/1614, reg. 10(e), operative from 3 July 1997.

Reg. 113(g) was added by SI 1997/1614, reg. 10(e), operative from 3 July 1997.

Reg. 113(h) was added by SI 1997/1614, reg. 10(e), operative from 3 July 1997.

PERIOD OF ADJUSTMENT

114(1) The proportion (if any) of the total input tax on a capital item which may be deducted under Part XIV shall be subject to adjustments in accordance with the provisions of this Part.

114(2) Adjustments shall be made over a period determined in accordance with the following paragraphs of this regulation.

114(3) The **period of adjustment** relating to a capital item of a description falling within–

(a)   regulation 113(a) shall consist of 5 successive intervals,

(b)   regulation 113(b), where the interest in the land, building or part of the building or civil engineering work or part of the civil engineering work in question has less than 10 years to run at the time it is supplied to the owner, shall consist of 5 successive intervals, and

(c)   any other description shall consist of 10 successive intervals,

determined in accordance with paragraphs (4) to (5B) and (7) below.

114(4) Subject to paragraphs (5A), (5B) and (7) below, the **first interval** applicable to a capital item shall be determined as follows–

(a)   where the owner is a registered person when he imports, acquires or is supplied with the item as a capital item, the first interval shall commence on the day of the importation, acquisition or supply and shall end on the day before the commencement of his tax year following that day;

(b)   where the owner is a registered person when he appropriates to use an item as a capital item, the first interval shall commence on the day he first so uses it and shall end on the day before the commencement of his tax year following that day;

(c)   where the capital item is of a description falling within regulation 113(c), the first interval shall commence on the day the owner's interest in, right over, or licence to occupy, the building or part of the building is treated as supplied to him under paragraph 1(5) of Schedule 10 to the Act and shall end on the day before the commencement of his tax year following that day;

(d)   where the capital item is of a description falling within regulation 113(d), the first interval shall commence on the later of the following days–

    (i) 1st April 1990,

    (ii) the day the owner first uses the building (or part of the building),

and shall end on the day before the commencement of his tax year following the day of commencement of the first interval;

(e)   where the capital item is of a description falling within regulation 113(e) (f), (g) or (h), the first interval shall commence on the day the owner first uses the building or the altered building or the extension or annex or the civil engineering work or the building which has been refurbished or fitted out in question, and shall end on the day before the commencement of his tax year following that day;

(f)   where the owner is not a registered person when he first uses an item as a capital item, and subsequently–

    (i) becomes a registered person, the first interval shall correspond with his registration period, or

    (ii) is included among bodies treated as members of a group under section 43 of the Act, the first interval shall correspond with, or be that part still remaining of, the then current tax year of that group.

114(5) Subject to paragraphs (5A) (5B) and (7) below, each subsequent interval applicable to a capital item shall correspond with a longer period applicable to the owner, or if no longer period applies to him, a tax year of his.

114(5A) On the first occasion during the period of adjustment applicable to a capital item that the owner of the item–

(a)   being a registered person subsequently becomes a member of a group under section 43 of the Act;

(b)   being a member of a group under section 43 ceases to be a member of that group (whether or not he becomes a member of another such group immediately thereafter); or

(c)   transfers the item in the course of the transfer of his business or part of his business as a going concern (the item therefore not being treated as supplied) in circumstances where the new owner is not, under regulation 6(1) above, registered with the registration number of and in substitution for the transferor,

the interval then applying shall end on the day before he becomes a member of a group or the day that he ceases to be a member of the group or transfers the business or part of the business (as the case may require) and thereafter each subsequent interval (if any) applicable to the capital item shall end on the successive anniversaries of that day.

114(5B)   Where the extent to which a capital item is used in making taxable supplies does not change between what would, but for this paragraph, have been the first interval and the first subsequent interval applicable to it and the length of the two intervals taken together does not exceed 12 months the first interval applicable to the capital item shall end on what would have been the day that the first subsequent interval expired.

114(6)   [Omitted by SI 1997/1614, reg. 11(e).]

114(7)   Where the owner of a capital item transfers it during the period of adjustment applicable to it in the course of the transfer of his business or a part of his business as a going concern (the item therefore not being treated as supplied) and the new owner is, under regulation 6(1) above, registered with the registration number of, and in substitution for the transferor, the interval applying to the capital item at the time of the transfer shall end on the last day of the longer period applying to the new owner immediately after the transfer or, if no longer period then applies to him, shall end on the last day of his tax year following the day of transfer.

History – In reg. 114(3)(b), the words "or civil engineering work or part of the civil engineering work" were inserted by SI 1997/1614, reg. 11(a)(i), operative from 3 July 1997.
In reg. 114(3), the words "paragraphs (4) to (5B) and (7)" were substituted for the words "paragraphs (4) to (7)" by SI 1997/1614, reg. 11(a)(ii), operative from 3 July 1997.
In reg. 114(4), the words "paragraphs (5A), (5B) and (7)" were substituted for the words "paragraphs (6) and (7)" by SI 1997/1614, reg. 11(b)(i), operative from 3 July 1997.
In reg. 114(4)(e), the words "(e), (f), (g) or (h)" were substituted for the words "(e) or (f)" by SI 1997/1614, reg. 11(b)(ii), operative from 3 July 1997.
In reg. 114(4)(e), the words "or the civil engineering work or the building which has been refurbished or fitted out" were inserted by SI 1997/1614, reg. 11(b)(ii), operative from 3 July 1997.
In reg. 114(5), the words "paragraphs (5A), (5B) and (7)" were substituted for the words "paragraphs (6) and (7)" by SI 1997/1614, reg. 11(c), operative from 3 July 1997.
Reg. 114(5A) was inserted by SI 1997/1614, reg. 11(d), operative from 3 July 1997.
Reg. 114(5B) was inserted by SI 1997/1614, reg. 11(d), operative from 3 July 1997.
Reg. 114(6) was omitted by SI 1997/1614, reg. 11(e), operative from 3 July 1997. Former reg. 114(6) reads as follows:
"**114(6)**   Where the owner of a capital item—
(a)   is a registered person and subsequently becomes a member of a group under section 43 of the Act during the period of adjustment applicable to the capital item, the interval then applying to it shall end on the day before the owner is first so included and each subsequent interval (if any) applicable to the capital item shall end on the last day of a longer period applicable to that group, or if no longer period applies, shall end on the last day of a tax year of that group;
(b)   ceases to be a member of such a group during the period of adjustment applicable to the capital item, the interval then applying to it shall end on the day that the owner so ceases and the next interval (if any) applicable to the capital item shall correspond with the registration period of the owner and each subsequent interval thereafter (if any) shall correspond with a longer period applying to the owner, or if no longer period applies, shall correspond with a tax year of the owner,
provided that if the owner of a capital item ceases to be a member of such a group (the first group) during the period of adjustment applicable to the capital item, and is immediately thereafter included in another such group (the second group), the interval applying to the capital item immediately before the owner ceases to be a member of the first group shall end on the day that the owner so ceases and each subsequent interval (if any) shall end on the last day of a longer period applicable to the second group, or if no longer period applies, shall end on the last day of a tax year of the second group."
Reg. 114(7) was omitted by SI 1997/1614, reg. 11(f), operative from 3 July 1997. Former reg. 114(7) reads as follows:
"**(7)**   Where the owner of a capital item transfers it during the period of adjustment applicable to it, in the course of the transfer of his business or of part of his business as a going concern, the interval then applying to the capital item shall end on the day of the transfer, and each subsequent interval (if any) applicable to the capital item shall end on the last day of a longer period applying to the new owner or, if no longer period applies, shall end on the day before the commencement of a tax year of the new owner, provided that where the new owner has, under regulation 6(1), been registered with the registration number of and in substitution for the transferor, the interval applying to the capital item at the time of the transfer shall not end on the day of the transfer (and shall accordingly end on the last day of the longer period applying to the new owner immediately after the transfer or, if no longer period then applies to him, shall end on the last day of his tax year following the day of the transfer)."

METHOD OF ADJUSTMENT

115(1)   Where in a subsequent interval applicable to a capital item, the extent to which it is used in making taxable supplies increases from the extent to which it was so used or to be used at the time that the original entitlement to deduction of the input tax was determined, the owner may deduct for that subsequent interval an amount calculated as follows—

(a)   where the capital item falls within regulation 114(3)(a) or (b)—

$$\frac{\textit{the total input tax on the capital item}}{5} \times \text{the adjustment percentage;}$$

(b)   where the capital item falls within regulation 114(3)(c)—

$$\frac{\text{the total input tax on the capital item}}{10} \times \text{the adjustment percentage.}$$

115(2) Where in a subsequent interval applicable to a capital item, the extent to which it is used in making taxable supplies decreases from the extent to which it was so used or to be used at the time that the original entitlement to deduction of the input tax was determined, the owner shall pay to the Commissioners for that subsequent interval an amount calculated in the manner described in paragraph (1) above.

115(3) Where the whole of the owner's interest in a capital item is supplied by him, or the owner is deemed or, but for the fact that the VAT on the deemed supply (whether by virtue of its value or because it is zero-rated or exempt) would have been not more than the sum specified in paragraph 8(1) of Schedule 4 to the Act, would have been deemed to supply a capital item pursuant to that paragraph during an interval other than the last interval applicable to the capital item, then if the supply (or deemed supply) of the capital item is–

(a)   a taxable supply, the owner shall be treated as using the capital item for each of the remaining complete intervals applicable to it wholly in making taxable supplies, or

(b)   an exempt supply, the owner shall be treated as not using the capital item for any of the remaining complete intervals applicable to it in making any taxable supplies,

and the owner shall, except where paragraph (3A) below applies calculate for each of the remaining complete intervals applicable to it, in accordance with paragraph (1) or (2) above, as the case may require, such amount as he may deduct or such amount as he shall be liable to pay to the Commissioners, provided that the aggregate of the amounts that he may deduct in relation to a capital item pursuant to this paragraph shall not exceed the output tax chargeable by him on the supply of that capital item.

115(3A) This paragraph applies if the total amount of input tax deducted or deductible by the owner of a capital item as a result of the initial deduction, any adjustments made under paragraph (1) or (2) above and the adjustment which would apart from this paragraph fall to be made under paragraph (3) above would exceed the output tax chargeable by him on the supply of that capital item.

115(3B) Save as the Commissioners may otherwise allow, where paragraph (3A) above applies the owner may deduct, or as the case may require, shall pay to the Commissioners such amount as results in the total amount of input tax deducted or deductible being equal to the output tax chargeable by him on the supply of the capital item.

115(4) If a capital item is–

(a)   irretrievably lost or stolen or is totally destroyed, or

(b)   is of a kind falling within regulation 114(3)(b) and the interest in question expires,

during the period of adjustment applicable to it, no further adjustment shall be made in respect of any remaining complete intervals applicable to it.

115(5) For the purposes of this regulation–

     "the original entitlement to deduction" means the entitlement to deduction determined in accordance with Part XIV of these Regulations;

     "the total input tax on the capital item" means, in relation to a capital item falling within–

     (a)   regulation 113(a) or (b), the VAT charged on the supply to, or on the importation or acquisition by, the owner of the capital item, other than VAT charged on rent (including charges reserved as rent) which is neither payable nor paid more than 12 months in advance nor invoiced for a period in excess of 12 months (if any),

     (b)   regulation 113(c) or (d), the VAT charged on the supply which the owner is treated as making to himself under paragraph 1(5) or 6(1) of Schedule 10 to the Act, as the case may require,

     (c)   regulation 113(e) (f), (g) or (h), the aggregate of the VAT charged on the supplies described in regulation 113(e) (f), (g) or (h), as the case may require, other than VAT charged on rent (if any),

and shall include, in relation to any capital item, any VAT treated as input tax under regulation 111 which relates to the capital item, other than such VAT charged on rent (if any); and for the purposes of this paragraph references to **"the owner"** shall be construed as references to the person who incurred the total input tax on the capital item;

"**the adjustment percentage**" means the difference (if any) between the extent, expressed as a percentage, to which the capital item was used or to be used for the making of taxable supplies at the time the original entitlement to deduction of the input tax was determined, and the extent to which it is so used or is treated under paragraph (3) above as being so used in the subsequent interval in question.

115(6) Subject to paragraph (8) below, a taxable person claiming any amount pursuant to paragraph (1) above, or liable to pay any amount pursuant to paragraph (2) above, shall include such amount in a return for the second prescribed accounting period next following the interval to which that amount relates, except where the Commissioners allow another return to be used for this purpose, provided that where an interval has come to an end under regulation 114(5A)–

(a)　because the owner of the capital item has ceased to be a member of a group under section 43 of the Act, any amount claimable from the Commissioners or payable to them (as the case may be) in respect of that interval shall be included in a return for that group for the second prescribed accounting period after the end of the tax year of the group in which the interval in question fell, or

(b)　because the owner has transferred part of his business as a going concern, and he remains a registered person after the transfer, any amount claimable from the Commissioners or payable to them (as the case may be) in respect of that interval shall be included in a return by him for the second prescribed accounting period after the end of his tax year in which the interval in question fell,

except where the Commissioners allow another return to be used for this purpose.

115(7) Subject to paragraph (8) below, a taxable person claiming any amount or amounts, or liable to pay any amount or amounts, pursuant to paragraph (3) above, shall include such amount or amounts in a return for the second prescribed accounting period next following the interval in which the supply (or deemed supply) in question takes place except where the Commissioners allow another return to be used for this purpose.

115(8) The Commissioners shall not allow the taxable person to use a return other than that specified in paragraph (6) above, paragraph (a) or (b) of that paragraph or paragraph (7) above (in each case, "the specified return"), as the case may be, unless it is the return for a prescribed accounting period commencing within 3 years of the end of the prescribed accounting period to which the specified return relates.

History – In reg. 115(1), the words "in the first interval applicable to it" were substituted for the words "or to be used at the time that the original entitlement to deduction of the input tax was determined" by SI 1999/599, reg. 6(a), operative in respect of subsequent adjustment intervals (within the meaning of Pt. XV) commencing on or after 10 March 1999.
In reg. 115(2), the words "in the first interval applicable to it" were substituted for the words "or to be used at the time that the original entitlement to deduction of the input tax was determined" by SI 1999/599, reg. 6(a), operative in respect of subsequent adjustment intervals (within the meaning of Pt. XV) commencing on or after 10 March 1999.
In reg. 115(3), the words "the sum specified in paragraph 8(1) of Schedule 4 to the Act" were substituted for the words "£250" by SI 2000/258, reg. 5(a), operative from 1 March 2000.
In reg. 115(3), the words "pursuant to that paragraph" were substituted for the words "pursuant to paragraph 8(1) of Schedule 4 to the Act" by SI 2000/258, reg. 5(b), operative from 1 March 2000.
In reg. 115(5), the definition "the original entitlement to deduction" was inserted by SI 1999/599, reg. 6(b)(i), operative in respect of subsequent adjustment intervals (within the meaning of Pt. XV) commencing on or after 10 March 1999.
In reg. 115(5), in the definition "the adjustment percentage", the words "was used or to be used for the making of taxable supplies at the time the original entitlement to deduction of the input tax was determined" were substituted for the words "is used (or is regarded as being used) in making taxable supplies in the first interval applicable to it" by SI 1999/599, reg. 6(b)(ii), operative in respect of subsequent adjustment intervals (within the meaning of Pt. XV) commencing on or after 10 March 1999.
Reg. 115(8), and reference to it in reg. 115(7), inserted by SI 1997/1086, reg. 8, operative from 1 May 1997.
In reg. 115(3), the words ", except where paragraph (3A) below applies" were inserted by SI 1997/1614, reg. 12(a), operative from 3 July 1997.
Reg. 115(3A) was inserted by SI 1997/1614, reg. 12(b), operative from 3 July 1997.
Reg. 115(3B) was inserted by SI 1997/1614, reg. 12(b), operative from 3 July 1997.
In reg. 115(5)(a), the words "(including charges reserved as rent) which is neither payable nor paid more than 12 months in advance nor invoiced for a period in excess of 12 months" were inserted by SI 1997/1614, reg. 12(c)(i), operative from 3 July 1997.
In reg. 115(5)(c), the words "(e), (f), (g) or (h)" were substituted for the words "(e) and (f)" in both places by SI 1997/1614, reg. 12(c)(ii), operative from 3 July 1997.
In reg. 115(6), the words "regulation 114(5A)" were inserted by SI 1997/1614, reg. 12(d)(i), operative from 3 July 1997.
In reg. 115(6)(a), the words "regulation 114(6)(b)" were omitted by SI 1997/1614, reg. 12(d)(ii), operative from 3 July 1997.
In reg. 115(6)(b), the words "regulation 114(7)" were omitted by SI 1997/1614, reg. 12(d)(iii), operative from 3 July 1997.

ASCERTAINMENT OF TAXABLE USE OF A CAPITAL ITEM

116(1) Subject to regulation 115(3) and (3B) and paragraphs (2), (A2) and (3) below, for the purposes of this Part, an attribution of the total input tax on the capital item shall be determined for each subsequent interval applicable to it in accordance with the method used under Part XIV for that interval and the proportion of the input tax thereby determined to be attributable to taxable supplies shall be treated as being the extent to which the capital item is used in making taxable supplies in that subsequent interval.

116(A2)   Subject to paragraph (2) below, the attribution of the total input tax on a capital item for subsequent intervals determined in accordance with regulation 114(5A) above shall be determined by such method as is agreed with the Commissioners.

116(2)   In any particular case the Commissioners may allow another method by which, or may direct the manner in which, the extent to which a capital item is used in making taxable supplies in any subsequent interval applicable to it is to be ascertained.

116(3)   Where the owner of a building which is a capital item of his grants or assigns a tenancy or lease in the whole or any part of that building and that grant or assignment is a zero-rated supply to the extent only as provided by–

(a)   note (14) to Group 5 of Schedule 8 to the Act, or

(b)   that note as applied to Group 6 of that Schedule by note (3) to Group 6, or

(c)   paragraph 8 of Schedule 13 to the Act,

any subsequent exempt supply of his arising directly from that grant or assignment shall be disregarded in determining the extent to which the capital item is used in making taxable supplies in any interval applicable to it.

History – In reg. 116(1), the words "and (3B)" were inserted by SI 1997/1614, reg. 13(a)(i), operative from 3 July 1997.
In reg. 116(1), the words ", (A2)" were inserted by SI 1997/1614, reg. 13(a)(ii), operative from 3 July 1997.
Reg. 116(A2) was inserted by SI 1997/1614, reg. 13(b), operative from 3 July 1997.
In reg. 116(3)(a), the number "(14)" was substituted by SI 1995/3147, reg. 5(a), operative from 1 January 1996.
In reg. 116(3)(b), the number "(3)" was substituted by SI 1995/3147, reg. 5(b), operative from 1 January 1996.

Notes – CAA 1990, s. 159A: capital allowances and additional VAT liabilities and rebates.

PART XVI – IMPORTATIONS, EXPORTATIONS AND REMOVALS

Official publications – Importation: Notices 700, 702, 702/4, 702/6 and 702/7.
Exportation: Notices 700, 703, 704, 705, 701/22, 703/1, 703/2, 703/3 and 704/1–3.
Customs Internal Guidance Manual, vol. V1.16: single market.
Customs Internal Guidance Manual, vol. V1.18: import reliefs.
Customs Internal Guidance Manual, vol. V1.19: warehousing and free zones for imports.
Customs Internal Guidance Manual, vol. V1.20: general exports.
Customs Internal Guidance Manual, vol. V1.21: personal reliefs – exports.

Other material – Importation: Form C79, VAT 905 and 977.
Exportation: Form VAT 403, 407, 410, 415, 418, 435, 436 and 444.

INTERPRETATION OF PART XVI

117(1)   In regulation 127 **"approved inland clearance depot"** means any inland premises approved by the Commissioners for the clearance of goods for customs and excise purposes.

117(2)   For the purposes of regulation 128 **"container"** means an article of transport equipment (lift-van, moveable tank or other similar structure)–

(a)   fully or partially enclosed to constitute a compartment intended for containing goods,

(b)   of a permanent character and accordingly strong enough to be suitable for repeated use,

(c)   specially designed to facilitate the carriage of goods, by one or more modes of transport, without intermediate reloading,

(d)   designed for ready handling, particularly when being transferred from one mode of transport to another,

(e)   designed to be easy to fill and to empty, and

(f)   having an internal volume of one cubic metre or more,

and the term **"container"** shall include the accessories and equipment of the container, appropriate for the type concerned, provided that such accessories and equipment are carried with the container, but shall not include vehicles, accessories or spare parts of vehicles, or packaging.

117(3)   [Omitted by SI 1999/438, reg. 10(1).]

117(4)   In regulations 130 and 131 **"goods"** does not include–

(a)   a motor vehicle, or

(b)   a boat intended to be exported under its own power.

117(5)–(6)   [Omitted by SI 1996/210, reg. 9.]

117(7) For the purposes of regulation 129 **"overseas authority"** means any country other than the United Kingdom or any part of or place in such a country or the government of any such country, part or place.

117(7A) In regulations 130(a)(i) and 131 the words **"overseas visitor"** refer to a traveller who is not established within the member States.

117(7B) For the purposes of paragraph (7A) above, a traveller is not established within the member States only if that traveller's domicile or habitual residence is situated outside the member States.

117(7C) Solely for the purposes of paragraph (7B) above, the traveller's domicile or habitual residence is the place entered as such in a valid–

(a)   identity document,

(b)   identity card, or

(c)   passport.

117(7D) A document referred to in sub-paragraph (a), (b) or (c) of paragraph (7C) above is valid for the purposes of that paragraph only if–

(a)   it is so recognised by the Commissioners; and

(b)   it is not misleading as to the traveller's true place of domicile or habitual residence.

117(8) In regulation 132 **"overseas visitor"** means a person who, during the 2 years immediately preceding the date of the application mentioned in regulation 132, has not been in the member States for more than 365 days, or who during the 6 years immediately preceding the date of the application has not been in the member States for more than 1,095 days.

117(9) In regulations 130 and 131 **"ship"** includes a hovercraft within the meaning of the Hovercraft Act 1968.

117(10) In regulations 140 and 144 **"customs territory of the Community"** has the same meaning as it has for the purposes of Council Regulation (EEC) No. 2913/92.

History – Reg. 117(3) was omitted by SI 1999/438, reg. 10(1), operative from 1 April 1999. Former reg. 117(3) reads as follows:
"**117(3)** In regulation 127 **"export house"** means any person registered in the United Kingdom who in the course of his business in the United Kingdom arranges or finances the export of goods from the United Kingdom to a place outside the member States."
Reg. 117(4) was substituted by SI 1996/210, reg. 8, operative from 1 March 1996.
Reg. 117(5) was omitted by SI 1996/210, reg. 9, operative from 1 March 1996.
Reg. 117(6) was omitted by SI 1996/210, reg. 9, operative from 1 March 1996.
Reg. 117(7A) was inserted by SI 1999/438, reg. 10(2), operative from 1 April 1999.
Reg. 117(7B) was inserted by SI 1999/438, reg. 10(2), operative from 1 April 1999.
Reg. 117(7C) was inserted by SI 1999/438, reg. 10(2), operative from 1 April 1999.
Reg. 117(7D) was inserted by SI 1999/438, reg. 10(2), operative from 1 April 1999.
In reg. 117(8), the words "regulation 132" were substituted for the words "this Part of these Regulations" by SI 1999/438, reg. 10(3)(a), operative from 1 April 1999.
In reg. 117(8), the words "the date of the supply mentioned in regulations 130 and 131 or" which appeared after the words "immediately preceding" were omitted by SI 1999/438, reg. 10(3)(b), operative from 1 April 1999.
In reg. 117(8), the words "for the purposes of regulation 132," which appeared after the words "or who" were omitted by SI 1999/438, reg. 10(3)(b), operative from 1 April 1999.

ENACTMENTS EXCEPTED

118 There shall be excepted from the enactments which are to apply as mentioned in section 16(1) of the Act–

(a)   the Alcoholic Liquor Duties Act 1979–

      (i)   section 7 (exemption from duty on spirits in articles used for medical purposes),

      (ii)   section 8 (repayment of duty on spirits for medical or scientific purposes),

      (iii)   section 9 (remission of duty on spirits for methylation),

      (iv)   *section 10 (remission of duty on spirits for use in art or manufacture),*

      (v)   section 22(4) (drawback on exportation of tinctures or spirits of wine), and

      (vi)   sections 42 and 43 (drawback on exportation and warehousing of beer),

(b)   the Hydrocarbon Oil Duties Act 1979–

      (i)   section 9 (relief for certain industrial uses),

      (ii)   section 15 (drawback of duty on exportation etc. of certain goods),

      (iii)   section 16 (drawback of duty on exportation etc. of power methylated spirits),

      (iv)   section 17 (repayment of duty on heavy oil used by horticultural producers),

      (v)   section 18 (repayment of duty on fuel for ships in home waters),

    (vi) section 19 (repayment of duty on fuel used in fishing boats etc.),

    (vii) section 20 (relief from duty on oil contaminated or accidentally mixed in warehouse), and

    (viii) section 20AA (power to allow reliefs),

(c)   the Customs and Excise Management Act 1979–

    (i) section 43(5) (provisions as to duty on re-imported goods),

    (ii) section 125(1) and (2) (valuation of goods for the purpose of ad valorem duties),

    (iii) section 126 (charge of excise duty on manufactured or composite imported articles), and

    (iv) section 127(1)(b) (determination of disputes as to duties on imported goods),

(d)   the Customs and Excise Duties (General Reliefs) Act 1979 other than sections 8 and 9(b),

(e)   the Isle of Man Act 1979, sections 8 and 9 (removal of goods from Isle of Man to United Kingdom),

(f)   the Tobacco Products Duty Act 1979, section 2(2) (remission or repayment of duty on tobacco products), and

(g)   the Finance Act 1999, sections 126 and 127 (interest on unpaid customs debts and on certain repayments relating to customs duty).

History – In reg. 118(e), the word "and" at the end was omitted by SI 2000/634, reg. 3(1), operative from 1 April 2000.
In reg. 118(f), the word "and" at the end was inserted by SI 2000/634, reg. 3(2), operative from 1 April 2000.
Reg. 118(g) was inserted by SI 2000/634, reg. 3(2), operative from 1 April 2000.

REGULATIONS EXCEPTED

119   The provision made by or under the following subordinate legislation shall be excepted from applying as mentioned in section 16(1) of the Act–

(a)   regulations 16(4) and (5) and 19(1)(b) of the Excise Warehousing (Etc) Regulations 1988 (certain removals from warehouse);

(b)   any regulations made under section 197(2)(f) of the Finance Act 1996 (rate of interest on overdue customs duty and on repayments of amounts paid by way of customs duty).

History – Reg. 119 was substituted by SI 2000/634, reg. 4, operative from 1 April 2000. Former reg. 119 reads as follows: "**119** Regulations 16(4) and (5) and 19(1)(b) of the Excise Warehousing (Etc.) Regulations 1988 shall be excepted from the subordinate legislation which is to apply as mentioned in section 16(1) of the Act."

COMMUNITY LEGISLATION EXCEPTED

120(1)   Council Regulation (EEC) No. 918/83 on conditional reliefs from duty on the final importation of goods, and any implementing Regulations made thereunder shall be excepted from the Community legislation which is to apply as mentioned in section 16(1) of the Act.

120(2)   The following Articles shall be excepted from the Community legislation which is to apply as mentioned in section 16(1) of the Act–

(a)   in Council Regulation (EEC) No. 2913/92 establishing the Community Customs Code–

    (i) Articles 126 to 128 (drawback system of inward processing relief),

    (ii) Articles 130 to 136 (processing for free circulation),

    (iii) Article 137 so far as it relates to partial relief on temporary importation, and Article 142,

    (iv) Articles 145 to 160 (outward processing),

    (v) Articles 185 to 187 (returned goods),

    (vi) Article 229(b) (interest payable on a customs debt),

    (vii) Articles 232(1)(b), (2) and (3) (interest on arrears of duty), and

    (viii) Article 241, second and third sentences only (interest on certain repayments by the authorities),

(b)   in Commission Regulation (EEC) No. 2454/93 which contains provisions implementing the Community Customs Code–

    (i) Articles 624 to 647 (drawback system of inward processing relief),

    (ii) Articles 650 to 669 (processing for free circulation),

    (iii) Article 690 (partial relief on temporary importation),

    (iv) Articles 748 to 787 (outward processing), and

(v) Articles 844 to 856 and 882 (returned goods).

120(3)   Council Regulation (EEC) No. 2658/87 on the tariff and statistical nomenclature and on the Common Customs Tariff and implementing Regulations made thereunder (end use relief), save and in so far as the said Regulations apply to goods admitted into territorial waters–

(a) in order to be incorporated into drilling or production platforms, for purposes of the construction, repair, maintenance, alteration or fitting-out of such platforms, or to link such drilling or production platforms to the mainland of the United Kingdom, or

(b) for the fuelling and provisioning of drilling or production platforms,

shall be excepted from the Community legislation which is to apply as mentioned in section 16(1) of the Act.

History – In reg. 120(2)(a)(v), the word "and" at the end was omitted by SI 2000/634, reg. 5(1), operative from 1 April 2000. Reg. 120(2)(a)(vii) and (viii) were added by SI 2000/634, reg. 5(2), operative from 1 April 2000.

ADAPTATIONS

121(1)   The provision made by the following enactments shall apply, as mentioned in section 16(1) of the Act, subject to the adaptations prescribed by this regulation.

121(2)   Section 125(3) of the Customs and Excise Management Act 1979 (valuation of goods) shall have effect as if the reference to the preceding subsections of that section included a reference to section 21 of the Act.

121(3)   Section 129 of the Finance Act 1999 (recovery of certain amounts by the Commissioners) shall be regarded as providing for the recovery of a repayment of any relevant VAT (import VAT).

History – Reg. 121 was substituted by SI 2000/634, reg. 6, operative from 1 April 2000. Former reg. 121 reads as follows: "**121** Section 125(3) of the Customs and Excise Management Act 1979 shall have effect in its application by virtue of section 16(1) of the Act as if the reference to the preceding subsections of that section included a reference to section 21 of the Act."

POSTAL IMPORTATIONS BY REGISTERED PERSONS IN THE COURSE OF BUSINESS

122   Goods imported by post from places outside the member States, other than by datapost packet, not exceeding £2,000 in value, or such greater sum as is determined for the time being by the Commissioners, by a registered person in the course of a business carried on by him may, with the authority of the proper officer, be delivered without payment of VAT if–

(a) the registered person has given such security as the Commissioners may require, and

(b) his registration number is shown on the customs declaration attached to or accompanying the package,

and save as the Commissioners may otherwise allow he shall account for VAT chargeable on the goods on their importation together with any VAT chargeable on the supply of goods or services by him or on the acquisition of goods by him from another member State in a return furnished by him in accordance with these Regulations for the prescribed accounting period during which the goods were imported.

TEMPORARY IMPORTATIONS

123(1)   Subject to such conditions as the Commissioners may impose, the VAT chargeable on the importation of goods from a place outside the member States shall not be payable where–

(a) a taxable person makes a supply of goods which is to be zero-rated in accordance with sub-paragraphs (a)(i) and (ii), and (b) of section 30(8) of the Act,

(b) the goods so imported are the subject of that supply, and

(c) the Commissioners are satisfied that–

(i) the importer intends to remove the goods to another member State, and

(ii) the importer is importing the goods in the course of a supply by him of those goods in accordance with the provisions of sub-paragraphs (a)(i) and (ii), and (b) of section 30(8) of the Act and any Regulations made thereunder.

123(2)   As a condition of granting the relief afforded by paragraph (1) above the Commissioners may require the deposit of security, the amount of which shall not exceed the amount of VAT chargeable on the importation.

123(3)   The relief afforded by paragraph (1) above shall continue to apply provided that the importer–

(a)   removes the goods to another member State within one month of the date of importation or within such longer period as the Commissioners may allow, and

(b)   supplies the goods in accordance with sub-paragraphs (a)(i) and (ii), and (b) of section 30(8) of the Act and any Regulations made thereunder.

REIMPORTATION OF CERTAIN GOODS BY NON-TAXABLE PERSONS

124   Subject to such conditions as the Commissioners may impose, the VAT chargeable on the importation of goods from a place outside the member States which have been previously exported from the member States shall not be payable if the Commissioners are satisfied that—

(a)   the importer is not a taxable person or, if he is, the goods are imported otherwise than in the course of his business,

(b)   the goods were last exported from the member States by him or on his behalf,

(c)   the goods—

    (i) were supplied, acquired in or imported into a member State before their export, and any VAT or other tax due on that supply, acquisition or importation was paid and neither has been, nor will be, refunded, or

    (ii) are imported by the person who made them,

(d)   the goods were not exported free of VAT by reason of the zero-rating provisions of subsection (6) or (8) of section 30 of the Act or Regulations made thereunder or free of purchase tax or by reason of the provisions of the law of another member State corresponding, in relation to that member State, to those provisions,

(e)   the goods have not been subject to process or repair outside the member States other than necessary running repairs which did not result in any increase in the value of the goods, and

(f)   the goods—

    (i) were at the time of exportation intended to be reimported, or

    (ii) have been returned for repair or replacement, or after rejection by a customer outside the member States, or because it was not possible to deliver them to such customer, or

    (iii) were prior to the time of exportation in private use and possession in the member States.

REIMPORTATION OF CERTAIN GOODS BY TAXABLE PERSONS

125   Subject to such conditions as the Commissioners may impose, the VAT chargeable on the importation of goods from a place outside the member States which have been previously exported from the member States shall not be payable if the Commissioners are satisfied that—

(a)   the importer is a taxable person importing the goods in the course of his business,

(b)   the goods were last exported from the member States by him or on his behalf,

(c)   the goods have not been subject to process or repair outside the member States other than necessary running repairs which did not result in any increase in the value of the goods,

(d)   the goods—

    (i) were owned by him at the time of exportation and have remained his property, or

    (ii) were owned by him at the time of exportation and have been returned after rejection by a customer outside the member States or because it was not possible to deliver them to such a customer, or

    (iii) have been returned from the continental shelf, and

(e)   if the goods were supplied in, acquired in or imported into a member State before their export, any VAT or other tax chargeable on that supply, acquisition or importation was accounted for or paid and neither has been, nor will be, refunded.

REIMPORTATION OF GOODS EXPORTED FOR TREATMENT OR PROCESS

126   Subject to such conditions as the Commissioners may impose, VAT chargeable on the importation of goods from a place outside the member States which have been temporarily exported from the member States and are reimported after having undergone repair, process or adaptation outside the member States, or after having been made up or reworked outside the member States, shall be payable as if such treatment or process had been carried out in the United Kingdom, if the Commissioners are satisfied that—

(a)   at the time of exportation the goods were intended to be reimported after completion of the treatment or process outside the member States, and

(b)   the ownership in the goods was not transferred to any other person at exportation or during the time they were abroad.

SUPPLIES TO EXPORT HOUSES

127   [Omitted by SI 1999/438, reg. 11, operative from 1 April 1999.]

History – Former reg. 127 reads as follows:
"**127**   Where goods are supplied to an export house but are not at any time delivered to the export house in the United Kingdom and–
(a)   the goods are delivered by the supplier direct to a port, customs and excise airport or approved inland clearance depot for immediate shipment or to an export packer for delivery direct to a port, customs and excise airport or approved inland clearance depot for immediate shipment to the order of the export house, and
(b)   the goods are exported to a place outside the member States,
the supply, subject to such conditions as the Commissioners may impose, shall be zero-rated."

EXPORT OF FREIGHT CONTAINERS

128   Where the Commissioners are satisfied that a container is to be exported to a place outside the member States, its supply, subject to such conditions as they may impose, shall be zero-rated.

SUPPLIES TO OVERSEAS PERSONS

129(1)   Where the Commissioners are satisfied that–

(a)   goods intended for export to a place outside the member States have been supplied, otherwise than to a taxable person, to–

    (i)   a person not resident in the United Kingdom,

    (ii)   a trader who has no business establishment in the United Kingdom from which taxable supplies are made, or

    (iii) an overseas authority, and

(b)   the goods were exported to a place outside the member States, the supply, subject to such conditions as they may impose, shall be zero-rated.

129(2)   This regulation shall not apply in the case of a supply to any person who is a member of the crew of any ship or aircraft departing from the United Kingdom or the Isle of Man.

Extra-statutory concessions – 4.1 (Notice 48 (1999 edn)): sailaway boats zero-rated.

Official publications – 703/2: sailaway boats supplied for export outside the European Community. 703/3: VAT-free purchases of sailaway boats.

SUPPLIES TO PERSONS DEPARTING FROM THE MEMBER STATES

130   Where the Commissioners are satisfied that–

(a)   goods have been supplied to, and delivered direct to, a ship or aircraft on behalf of–

    (i)   a member, being an overseas visitor, of the crew of any ship or aircraft departing from the United Kingdom or the Isle of Man to an immediate destination outside the member States, or

    (ii)   a person who has been resident in the member States for at least 365 days in the last 2 years immediately preceding the date of the supply of the said goods and who, at the time of the said supply, intends to depart from the United Kingdom or the Isle of Man for an immediate destination outside the member States and remain outside the member States for a period of at least 12 months, and

(b)   save as they may allow, the goods were produced to the proper officer on exportation, and

(c)   the goods were exported in that ship or aircraft or in such other ship or aircraft as the Commissioners may allow,

the supply, subject to such conditions as they may impose, shall be zero-rated.

History – In reg. 130(a)(ii), the words "who is not an overseas visitor," which appeared after the words "a person" were omitted by SI 1999/438, reg. 12, operative from 1 April 1999.

131(1)   Where the Commissioners are satisfied that–

(a)   goods have been supplied to a person who is an overseas visitor and who, at the time of the supply, intended to depart from the member States before the end of the third month following that in which the supply is effected and that the goods should accompany him,

(b)   save as they may allow, the goods were produced to the competent authorities for the purposes of the common system of VAT in the member State from which the goods were finally exported to a place outside the member States, and (c)　　the goods were exported to a place outside the member States,

the supply, subject to such conditions as they may impose, shall be zero-rated.

131(2)　This regulation shall not apply in the case of a supply to any person who is a member of the crew of any ship or aircraft departing from the member States.

History – In reg. 131(1)(a), the words "before the end of the third . . . supply is effected" were substituted by SI 1995/3147, reg. 6, operative from 1 January 1996.

132　The Commissioners may, on application by an overseas visitor who intends to depart from the member States within 15 months and remain outside the member States for a period of at least 6 months, permit him within 12 months of his intended departure to purchase, from a registered person, a motor vehicle without payment of VAT, for subsequent export, and its supply, subject to such conditions as they may impose, shall be zero-rated.

History – In reg. 132, the word "new" which appeared before the words "motor vehicle" was omitted by SI 2000/258, reg. 5, operative from 1 April 2000.

133　The Commissioners may, on application by any person who intends to depart from the member States within 9 months and remain outside the member States for a period of at least 6 months, permit him within 6 months of his intended departure to purchase, from a registered person, a motor vehicle without payment of VAT, for subsequent export, and its supply, subject to such conditions as they may impose, shall be zero-rated.

History – In reg. 133, the word "new" which appeared before the words "motor vehicle" was omitted by SI 2000/258, reg. 5, operative from 1 April 2000.

SUPPLIES TO PERSONS TAXABLE IN ANOTHER MEMBER STATE

134　Where the Commissioners are satisfied that–

(a)　　a supply of goods by a taxable person involves their removal from the United Kingdom,

(b)　　the supply is to a person taxable in another member State,

(c)　　the goods have been removed to another member State, and

(d)　　the goods are not goods in relation to whose supply the taxable person has opted, pursuant to section 50A of the Act, for VAT to be charged by reference to the profit margin on the supply,

the supply, subject to such conditions as they may impose, shall be zero-rated.

SUPPLIES OF GOODS SUBJECT TO EXCISE DUTY TO PERSONS WHO ARE NOT TAXABLE IN ANOTHER MEMBER STATE

135　Where the Commissioners are satisfied that–

(a)　　a supply by a taxable person of goods subject to excise duty involves their removal from the United Kingdom to another member State,

(b)　　that supply is other than to a person taxable in another member State and the place of supply is not, by virtue of section 7(5) of the Act, treated as outside the United Kingdom,

(c)　　the goods have been removed to another member State in accordance with the provisions of the Excise Goods (Holding, Movement, Warehousing and REDS) Regulations 1992, and

(d)　　the goods are not goods in relation to whose supply the taxable person has opted, pursuant to section 50A of the Act, for VAT to be charged by reference to the profit margin on the supply,

the supply, subject to such conditions as they may impose, shall be zero-rated.

TERRITORIES TO BE TREATED AS EXCLUDED FROM OR INCLUDED IN THE TERRITORY OF THE COMMUNITY AND OF THE MEMBER STATES

136　For the purposes of the Act the following territories shall be treated as excluded from the **territory of the Community**–

(a)　　the Channel Islands,

(b)　　Andorra,

(c)　　San Marino, and

(d)　　the Aland Islands.

137　For the purposes of the Act the following territories shall be treated as excluded from the **territory of the member States** and the **territory of the Community**–

(a)　　the Canary Islands (Kingdom of Spain),

(b)   the overseas departments of the French Republic (Guadeloupe, Martinique, Réunion, St. Pierre and Miquelon and French Guiana), and

(c)   Mount Athos (Hellenic Republic).

138(1)   For the purposes of the Act the **territory of the Community** shall be treated as excluding Austria, Finland and Sweden (the acceding States) in relation to goods to which this regulation applies.

138(2)   Subject to paragraph (4) below, the goods to which this regulation applies are—

(a)   goods which are the subject of a supply made in an acceding State before 1st January 1995 and which in pursuance of that supply are removed to the United Kingdom on or after 20th October 1995 being goods in the case of which provisions of the law of the acceding State in question having effect for purposes corresponding to those of subsection (6)(a) or (so far as it applies to exportations) subsection (8) of section 30 of the Act have prevented VAT from being charged on that supply, and

(b)   goods which were subject to a suspension regime before 1st January 1995, which by virtue of any Community legislation were to remain, for VAT purposes only, subject to that regime for a period beginning with that date and which cease to be subject to that regime on or after 20th October 1995.

138(3)   For the purposes of paragraph (2)(b) above, goods shall be treated as having become **subject to a suspension regime** if—

(a)   on their entry into the territory of the Community—

     (i)   they were placed under a temporary admission procedure with full exemption from import duties, in temporary storage, in a free zone, or under customs warehousing arrangements or inward processing arrangements, or

     (ii)   they were admitted into the territorial waters of the United Kingdom for the purpose of being incorporated into drilling or production platforms, for the purposes of the construction, repair, maintenance, alteration or fitting-out of such platforms, for the purpose of linking such platforms to the mainland of the United Kingdom, or for the purpose of fuelling or provisioning such platforms, or

(b)   they were placed under any customs transit procedure in pursuance of a supply made in the course of a business,

and (in the case in question) the time that any Community customs debt in relation to the goods would be incurred in the United Kingdom if the accession to the European Union of the acceding States were disregarded would fall to be determined by reference to the matters mentioned in sub-paragraph (a) or (b) above.

138(4)   This regulation does not apply to the following goods—

(a)   goods which are exported on or after 20th October 1995 to a place outside the member States,

(b)   goods which are not means of transport and are removed on or after 20th October 1995 from a temporary admission procedure such as is referred to in paragraph (3)(a)(i) above, in order to be returned to the person in an acceding State who had exported them from that State,

(c)   means of transport which are removed on or after 20th October 1995 from a temporary admission procedure such as is referred to in paragraph (3)(a)(i) above and which—

     (i)   were first brought into service before 1st January 1987, or

     (ii)   have a value not exceeding £4,000, or

     (iii)   have been charged in an acceding State with VAT which has not been remitted or refunded by reason of their exportation and to such other tax (if any) to which means of transport of that class or description are normally chargeable.

139   For the purposes of the Act the following territories shall be treated as included in the **"territory of the member States"** and the **"territory of the Community"**—

(i)   the Principality of Monaco (French Republic), and

(ii)   the Isle of Man (United Kingdom).

ENTRY AND EXIT FORMALITIES

140(1)   Where goods enter the United Kingdom from the territories prescribed in regulation 136 or 137 the formalities relating to the entry of goods into the customs territory of the Community contained in Council Regulation (EEC) No. 2913/92, Commission Regulation (EEC) No. 2454/93 and the Customs Controls on Importation of Goods Regulations 1991, shall be completed.

140(2) Where goods are exported from the United Kingdom to the territories prescribed in regulation 136 or 137 the formalities relating to the export of goods to a place outside the customs territory of the Community contained in Council Regulation (EEC) No. 2913/92 and Commission Regulation (EEC) No. 2454/93 shall be completed.

USE OF THE INTERNAL COMMUNITY TRANSIT PROCEDURE

141 Where goods enter the United Kingdom from the territories prescribed in regulation 136 or 137 and the said goods are intended for another member State, or other destination outside the United Kingdom transport of the goods to which destination involves their passage through another member State, the internal Community transit procedure described in Council Regulation (EEC) No. 2913/92 and Commission Regulation (EEC) No. 2454/93 shall apply.

CUSTOMS AND EXCISE LEGISLATION TO BE APPLIED

142 Subject to regulation 143, where goods are imported into the United Kingdom from the territories prescribed in regulation 136 or 137 customs and excise legislation shall apply (so far as relevant) in relation to any VAT chargeable upon such importation with the same exceptions and adaptations as are prescribed in regulations 118, 119, 120 and 121 in relation to the application of section 16(1) of the Act.

143 Where goods are imported into the United Kingdom from the territories prescribed in regulation 137, section 4 of the Finance (No. 2) Act 1992 (enforcement powers) shall apply in relation to any VAT chargeable upon such importation as if references in that section to **"member States"** excluded the territories prescribed in regulation 137.

144 Where goods are exported from the United Kingdom to the territories prescribed in regulation 136 or 137 the provisions relating to the export of goods to a place outside the customs territory of the Community contained in Council Regulation (EEC) No. 2913/92 and Commission Regulation (EEC) No. 2454/93 shall apply for the purpose of ensuring the correct application of the zero rate of VAT to such goods.

145(1) Subject to paragraph (2) below, where goods are exported from the United Kingdom to the territories prescribed in regulation 136 or 137 the provisions made by or under the Customs and Excise Management Act 1979 in relation to the exportation of goods to places outside the member States shall apply (so far as relevant) for the purpose of ensuring the correct application of the zero rate of VAT to such goods.

145(2) Where goods are being exported from the United Kingdom to the territories prescribed in regulation 137, section 4 of the Finance (No. 2) Act 1992 (enforcement powers) shall apply to such goods as if references in that section to **"member States"** excluded the territories prescribed in regulation 137.

PART XVI(A) – FISCAL AND OTHER WAREHOUSING REGIMES

History – Pt. XVI(A) was inserted by SI 1996/1250, reg. 13, operative from 1 June 1996.
Official publications – 702/9.

INTERPRETATION OF PART XVI(A)

145A(1) In this Part unless the context otherwise requires–

    "eligible goods" has the meaning given by section 18B(6);

    "fiscal warehouse" includes all fiscal warehouses kept by the same fiscal warehousekeeper;

    "material time" has the meaning given by section 18F(1) in the case of a fiscal warehousing regime and section 18(6) in the case of a warehousing regime;

    "regulation" or **"regulations"** refers to the relevant regulation or regulations of these Regulations; and,

    "section" or **"sections"** refers to the relevant section or sections of the Act.

145A(2) For the purposes of this Part, where a fiscal warehousekeeper keeps one or more fiscal warehouses there shall be associated with him a single fiscal warehousing regime; and **"relevant fiscal warehousekeeper"**, **"relevant fiscal warehouse"**, **"relevant fiscal warehousing regime"**,

"his fiscal warehouse", **"his fiscal warehousing regime"** and similar expressions shall be construed in this light.

FISCAL WAREHOUSING CERTIFICATES

145B(1) The certificate referred to in section 18B(1)(d) (certificate relating to acquisitions in or intended for fiscal warehousing) and the certificate referred to in section 18B(2)(d) (supplies of goods intended for fiscal warehousing) shall contain the information indicated in the form numbered 17 in Schedule 1 to these Regulations.

145B(2) A certificate prepared under section 18B(1)(d) by an acquirer who is not a taxable person shall be kept by him for a period of six years commencing on the day the certificate is prepared; and he shall produce it to a proper officer when that officer requests him to do so.

Notes – Form 17 is reproduced in Notice 702/9 (1998 edn.), appendix I.

CERTIFICATES CONNECTED WITH SERVICES IN FISCAL OR OTHER WAREHOUSING REGIMES

145C The certificate referred to in section 18C(1)(c) (certificate required for the zero-rating of certain services performed on or in relation to goods while those goods are subject to a fiscal or other warehousing regime) shall contain the information indicated in the form numbered 18 in Schedule 1 to these Regulations.

Notes – Form 18 is reproduced in Notice 702/9 (1998 edn.), appendix J.

VAT INVOICES RELATING TO SERVICES PERFORMED IN FISCAL OR OTHER WAREHOUSING REGIMES

145D(1) This regulation applies to the invoice referred to in section 18C(1)(e) (invoice required for the zero-rating of the supply of certain services performed on or in relation to goods while those goods are subject to a fiscal or other warehousing regime).

145D(2) The invoice shall be known as a VAT invoice and shall state the following particulars (unless the Commissioners allow any requirement of this paragraph to be relaxed or dispensed with)–

(a) an identifying number,

(b) the material time of the supply of the services in question,

(c) the date of the issue of the invoice,

(d) the name, an address and the registration number of the supplier,

(e) the name and an address of the person to whom the services are supplied,

(f) a description sufficient to identify the nature of the services supplied,

(g) the extent of the services and the amount payable, excluding VAT, expressed in sterling,

(h) the rate of any cash discount offered,

(i) the rate of VAT as zero per cent, and

(j) a declaration that in respect of the supply of services in question, the requirements of section 18C(1) will be or have been satisfied.

145D(3) The supplier of the services in question shall issue the invoice to the person to whom the supply is made within thirty days of the material time of that supply of services (or within such longer period as the Commissioners may allow in general or special directions).

FISCAL WAREHOUSING REGIMES

145E(1) Upon any eligible goods entering a fiscal warehouse the relevant fiscal warehousekeeper shall record their entry in his relevant fiscal warehousing record.

145E(2) Eligible goods shall only be subject to or in a fiscal warehousing regime at any time–

(a) while they are allocated to that regime in the relevant fiscal warehousing record;

(b) while they are not identified in that record as having been transferred; or,

(c) prior to their removal from that regime.

THE FISCAL WAREHOUSING RECORD AND STOCK CONTROL

145F(1) In addition to the records referred to in regulation 31, a fiscal warehousekeeper shall maintain a fiscal warehousing record for any fiscal warehouse in respect of which he is the relevant fiscal warehousekeeper.

145F(2) The fiscal warehousing record may be maintained in any manner acceptable to the Commissioners. In particular, it shall be capable of–

(a) ready use by any proper officer in the course of his duties; and

(b) reproduction into a form suitable for any proper officer to readily use at a place other than the relevant fiscal warehouse.

145F(3) Subject to paragraph (4) below, the fiscal warehousing record shall have the features and shall comply with the requirements set out in Schedule 1A to these Regulations.

145F(4) In respect of any goods the relevant fiscal warehousing record shall not be required to record events more than six years following–

(a) the transfer or removal of those goods from the relevant fiscal warehousing regime; or,

(b) the exit of those goods from the relevant fiscal warehouse (in the case of goods which were not allocated to the relevant fiscal warehousing regime).

145F(5) A fiscal warehousekeeper, upon receiving a request to do so from any proper officer, shall–

(a) produce his fiscal warehousing record to that officer and permit him to inspect or take copies of it or of any part of it (as that officer shall require); or,

(b) facilitate and permit that officer to inspect any goods which are stored or deposited in his fiscal warehouse (whether or not those goods are allocated to the relevant fiscal warehousing regime).

FISCAL WAREHOUSING TRANSFERS IN THE UNITED KINGDOM

145G(1) Subject to paragraphs (2) and (3) below, a fiscal warehousekeeper (**"the original fiscal warehousekeeper"**) may permit eligible goods which are subject to his fiscal warehousing regime (**"the original regime"**) to be transferred to another fiscal warehousing regime (**"the other regime"**) without those goods being treated as removed from the original regime.

145G(2) The original fiscal warehousekeeper shall not allow eligible goods to exit from his fiscal warehouse in pursuance of this regulation before he receives a written undertaking from the fiscal warehousekeeper in relation to that other fiscal warehousing regime (**"the other fiscal warehousekeeper"**) that, in respect of those eligible goods, the other fiscal warehousekeeper will comply with the requirements of paragraph (3) below.

145G(3) The other fiscal warehousekeeper, upon the entry of the goods to his fiscal warehouse, shall–

(a) record that entry in his fiscal warehousing record; and,

(b) allocate those goods to his fiscal warehousing regime.

Furthermore, within 30 days commencing with the day on which those goods left the original fiscal warehouse, he shall–

(c) deliver or cause to be delivered to the original fiscal warehousekeeper a certificate in a form acceptable to the Commissioners confirming that he has recorded the entry of those goods to his fiscal warehouse and allocated them to his fiscal warehousing regime; and,

(d) retain a copy of that certificate as part of his fiscal warehousing record.

REMOVAL OF GOODS FROM A FISCAL WAREHOUSING REGIME AND TRANSFERS OVERSEAS

145H(1) Without prejudice to sections 18F(5), 18F(6) and the following paragraphs of this regulation, eligible goods which are allocated to a fiscal warehousing regime shall only be removed from that regime at the time and in any of the following circumstances–

(a) when an entry in respect of those eligible goods is made in the relevant fiscal warehousing record which indicates the time and date of their removal from that regime;

(b) when the eligible goods are moved outside the fiscal warehouse in respect of which they are allocated to a fiscal warehousing regime (except in the case of movements between fiscal warehouses kept by the same fiscal warehousekeeper); or,

(c) at the time immediately preceding a retail sale of those eligible goods.

The person who shall be treated as the person who removes or causes the removal of the relevant goods from the relevant fiscal warehousing regime in any of the circumstances described above shall be, as the case requires, either the person who causes any of those circumstances to occur or, in the case of sub-paragraph (c), the person who makes the retail sale referred to there.

145H(2)   Subject to paragraph (3) below, eligible goods which are subject to a fiscal warehousing regime shall not be treated as removed from that regime but shall be treated as transferred or as being in the process of transfer, as the case requires, in any of the following circumstances–

(a)   where the goods in question are transferred or are in the process of transfer to another fiscal warehousing regime in pursuance of regulation 145G(1) above;

(b)   where the goods in question are transferred or are in the process of transfer to arrangements which correspond in effect, under the law of another member State, to section 18B(3) (fiscal warehousing) whether or not those arrangements also correspond in effect to section 18C(1) (zero-rating of certain specified services performed in a fiscal or other warehousing regime);

(c)   where the goods in question are exported or are in the process of being exported to a place outside the member States; or,

(d)   where the goods in question are moved temporarily to a place other than the relevant fiscal warehouse for repair, processing, treatment or other operations (subject to the prior agreement of and to conditions to be imposed by the Commissioners).

145H(3)   Where any relevant document referred to in paragraph (4) below is not received by the relevant fiscal warehousekeeper within the time period indicated there (commencing on the day on which the relevant eligible goods leave his fiscal warehouse), he shall–

(a)   make an entry by way of adjustment to his fiscal warehousing record to show the relevant goods as having been removed from his fiscal warehousing regime at the time and on the day when they left;

(b)   identify in his fiscal warehousing record the person on whose instructions he allowed the goods to leave his fiscal warehouse as the person removing those goods and that person's address and registration number (if any); and,

(c)   notify the person on whose instructions he allowed the goods to leave his fiscal warehouse that the relevant document has not been received by him in time.

145H(4)   The document and time period referred to in paragraph (3) above is, as the case requires, either–

(a)   the certificate referred to in regulation 145G(3)(c) confirming the completion of a transfer of eligible goods from the relevant fiscal warehousing regime to another fiscal warehousing regime (30 days);

(b)   a document evidencing the completion of the transfer of the eligible goods from the relevant fiscal warehousing regime directly to arrangements which correspond, in another member State, to fiscal warehousing (60 days); or,

(c)   a document evidencing the export of the eligible goods from the relevant fiscal warehousing regime to a place outside the member States (60 days).

145I(1)   A fiscal warehousekeeper shall not remove or allow the removal of any eligible goods from his fiscal warehousing regime at any time before–

(a)   he has inspected and placed on his fiscal warehousing record a copy of the relevant document issued by the Commissioners under regulation 145J(1) (removal document); or,

(b)   he is provided with the registration number of a person registered under the Act and a written undertaking from that person that any VAT payable by that person as the result of any removal of eligible goods from that fiscal warehousing regime will be accounted for on that person's return in accordance with regulation 40(1)(c).

145I(2)   Without prejudice to section 18E, where a fiscal warehousekeeper allows the removal of any eligible goods to take place from his fiscal warehousing regime otherwise than in accordance with this regulation, he shall be jointly and severally liable with the person who removes the goods for the payment of the VAT payable under section 18D(2) to the Commissioners.

145I(3)   Paragraphs (1) and (2) above shall not apply to a removal which is the result of an entry in the relevant fiscal warehousing record made by the relevant fiscal warehousekeeper in compliance with regulation 145H(3)(a) (non-receipt of a document following transfer or export).

PAYMENT ON REMOVAL OF GOODS FROM A FISCAL WAREHOUSING REGIME

145J(1)   The Commissioners may, in respect of a person who is seeking to remove or cause the removal of eligible goods from a fiscal warehousing regime–

(a)   accept from or on behalf of that person payment of the VAT payable (if any) as a result of that removal, and

(b)   issue to that person a document bearing a reference or identification number.

145J(2)   The Commissioners need not act in accordance with paragraph (1) above unless, as the case requires, they are satisfied as to–

(a)   the value and material time of any supply of the relevant goods in the fiscal warehousing regime which is treated as taking place in the United Kingdom under section 18B(4) and the status of the person who made that supply;

(b)   the nature and quantity of the relevant eligible goods;

(c)   the value of any relevant self-supplies of specified services treated as made under section 18C(3) in the course or furtherance of his business by the person who is to remove the relevant goods, or by the person on whose behalf the goods are to be removed, at the time they are removed from the fiscal warehousing regime; and,

(d)   the nature and material time of any relevant supplies of specified services in respect of which the self supplies referred to in sub-paragraph (c) above are treated as being identical (certain supplies of services on or in relation to goods while those goods are subject to the fiscal warehousing regime).

145J(3)   In paragraph (2)(a) above **"status"** is a reference to whether the person in question–

(a)   is or is required to be registered under the Act, or

(b)   would be required to be registered under the Act were it not for paragraph 1(9) of Schedule 1 to the Act, paragraph 1(7) of Schedule 2 to the Act, paragraph 1(6) of Schedule 3 to the Act, or any of those provisions.

PART XVII – NEW MEANS OF TRANSPORT

INTERPRETATION OF PART XVII

146   In this Part–

"claim" means a claim for a refund of VAT made pursuant to section 40 of the Act and **"claimant"** shall be construed accordingly;

"competent authority" means an authority having powers under the laws in force in any member State to register a vehicle for road use in that member State;

"first entry into service" in relation to a new means of transport means the time determined in relation to that means of transport under regulation 147;

"registration" means registration for road use in a member State corresponding in relation to that member State to registration in accordance with the Vehicles Excise and Registration Act 1994.

FIRST ENTRY INTO SERVICE OF A MEANS OF TRANSPORT

147(1)   For the purposes of section 95 of the Act a means of transport is to be treated as having **first entered into service**–

(a)   in the case of a ship or aircraft–

    (i)   when it is delivered from its manufacturer to its first purchaser or owner, or on its first being made available to its first purchaser or owner, whichever is the earlier, or

    (ii)   if its manufacturer takes it into use for demonstration purposes, on its being first taken into such use, and

(b)   in the case of a motorised land vehicle–

    (i)   on its first registration for road use by the competent authority in the member State of its manufacture or when a liability to register for road use is first incurred in the member State of its manufacture, whichever is the earlier,

    (ii)   if it is not liable to be registered for road use in the member State of its manufacture, on its removal by its first purchaser or owner, or on its first delivery or on its being made available to its first purchaser, whichever is the earliest, or

    (iii)   if its manufacturer takes it into use for demonstration purposes, on its first being taken into such use.

147(2) Where the times specified in paragraph (1) above cannot be established to the Commissioners' satisfaction, a means of transport is to be treated as having first entered into service on the issue of an invoice relating to the first supply of the means of transport.
Official publications – 725, s. 7 (1998 edn).

NOTIFICATION OF ACQUISITION OF NEW MEANS OF TRANSPORT BY NON-TAXABLE PERSONS AND PAYMENT OF VAT

148(1) Where–

(a)   a taxable acquisition of a new means of transport takes place in the United Kingdom,

(b)   the acquisition is not in pursuance of a taxable supply, and

(c)   the person acquiring the goods is not a taxable person at the time of the acquisition,

the person acquiring the goods shall notify the Commissioners of the acquisition within 7 days of the time of the acquisition or the arrival of the goods in the United Kingdom, whichever is the later.

148(2) The notification shall be in writing in the English language and shall contain the following particulars–

(a)   the name and current address of the person acquiring the new means of transport,

(b)   the time of the acquisition,

(c)   the date when the new means of transport arrived in the United Kingdom,

(d)   a full description of the new means of transport which shall include any registration mark allocated to it by any competent authority in another member State prior to its arrival in the United Kingdom and any chassis, hull or airframe identification number and engine number,

(e)   the consideration for the transaction in pursuance of which the new means of transport was acquired,

(f)   the name and address of the supplier in the member State from which the new means of transport was acquired,

(g)   the place where the new means of transport can be inspected, and

(h)   the date of notification.

148(3) The notification shall include a declaration, signed by the person who is required to make the notification or a person authorised in that behalf in writing, that all the information entered in it is true and complete.

148(4) The notification shall be made at, or sent to, any office designated by the Commissioners for the receipt of such notifications.

148(5) Any person required to notify the Commissioners of an acquisition of a new means of transport shall pay the VAT due upon the acquisition at the time of notification or within 30 days of the Commissioners issuing a written demand to him detailing the VAT due and requesting payment.

REFUNDS IN RELATION TO NEW MEANS OF TRANSPORT

149 A claimant shall make his claim in writing no earlier than one month and no later than 14 days prior to making the supply of the new means of transport by virtue of which the claim arises.

150 The claim shall be made at, or sent to, any office designated by the Commissioners for the receipt of such claims.

151 The claim shall contain the following information–

(a)   the name, current address and telephone number of the claimant,

(b)   the place where the new means of transport is kept and the times when it may be inspected,

(c)   the name and address of the person who supplied the new means of transport to the claimant,

(d)   the price paid by the claimant for the supply to him of the new means of transport excluding any VAT,

(e)   the amount of any VAT paid by the claimant on the supply to him of the new means of transport,

(f)   the amount of any VAT paid by the claimant on the acquisition of the new means of transport from another member State or on its importation from a place outside the member States,

(g)   the name and address of the proposed purchaser, the member State to which the new means of transport is to be removed, and the date of the proposed purchase,

(h)   the price to be paid by the proposed purchaser,

(i)   a full description of the new means of transport including, in the case of motorised land vehicles, its mileage since its first entry into service and, in the case of ships and aircraft, its hours of use since its first entry into service,

(j)   in the case of a ship, its length in metres,

(k)   in the case of an aircraft, its take-off weight in kilograms,

(l)   in the case of a motorised land vehicle powered by a combustion engine, its displacement or cylinder capacity in cubic centimetres, and in the case of an electrically propelled motorised land vehicle, its maximum power output in kilowatts, described to the nearest tenth of a kilowatt, and

(m)   the amount of the refund being claimed.

152   The claim shall be accompanied by the following documents–

(a)   the invoice issued by the person who supplied the new means of transport to the claimant or such other documentary evidence of purchase as is satisfactory to the Commissioners,

(b)   in respect of a new means of transport imported from a place outside the member States by the claimant, documentary evidence of its importation and of the VAT paid thereon, and

(c)   in respect of a new means of transport acquired by the claimant from another member State, documentary evidence of the VAT paid thereon.

153   The claim shall include a declaration, signed by the claimant or a person authorised by him in that behalf in writing, that all the information entered in or accompanying it is true and complete.

154   The claim shall be completed by the submission to the Commissioners of–

(a)   the sales invoice or similar document identifying the new means of transport and showing the price paid by the claimant's customer, and

(b)   documentary evidence that the new means of transport has been removed to another member State.

SUPPLIES OF NEW MEANS OF TRANSPORT TO PERSONS DEPARTING TO ANOTHER MEMBER STATE

155   The Commissioners may, on application by a person who is not taxable in another member State and who intends–

(a)   to purchase a new means of transport in the United Kingdom, and

(b)   to remove that new means of transport to another member State,

permit that person to purchase a new means of transport without payment of VAT, for subsequent removal to another member State within 2 months of the date of supply and its supply, subject to such conditions as they may impose, shall be zero-rated.

PART XVIII – BAD DEBT RELIEF (THE OLD SCHEME)

Notes – VATA 1983, s. 22 was repealed by FA 1990, s. 11(9), 132 and Sch. 19, Pt. III, in relation to supplies made after 26 July 1990. See now VAT 1994, s. 36.
No claim for a refund may be made in accordance with VATA 1983, s. 22 at any time after 19 March 1997 (FA 1997, s. 39(5)).

INTERPRETATION OF PART XVIII

156   [Omitted by SI 1997/1086, reg. 9, operative from 1 May 1997.]

THE MAKING OF A CLAIM TO THE COMMISSIONERS

157   [Omitted by SI 1997/1086, reg. 9, operative from 1 May 1997.]

EVIDENCE REQUIRED OF THE CLAIMANT IN SUPPORT OF THE CLAIM

158   [Omitted by SI 1997/1086, reg. 9, operative from 1 May 1997.]

159   [Omitted by SI 1997/1086, reg. 9, operative from 1 May 1997.]

PRESERVATION OF DOCUMENTS AND RECORDS AND DUTY TO PRODUCE

160   [Omitted by SI 1997/1086, reg. 9, operative from 1 May 1997.]

SET-OFF OF AMOUNTS BETWEEN THE CLAIMANT AND THE DEBTOR

161   [Omitted by SI 1997/1086, reg. 9, operative from 1 May 1997.]

DETERMINATION OF OUTSTANDING AMOUNT OF CONSIDERATION IN MONEY

162   [Omitted by SI 1997/1086, reg. 9, operative from 1 May 1997.]

REPAYMENT OF A REFUND

163   [Omitted by SI 1997/1086, reg. 9, operative from 1 May 1997.]

PROVING IN THE INSOLVENCY IN SCOTLAND

164   [Omitted by SI 1997/1086, reg. 9, operative from 1 May 1997.]

PART XIX – BAD DEBT RELIEF (THE NEW SCHEME)

Cross references – FA 1999, s. 15(4): until such day as the Commissioners may specify, SI 1995/2518, Pt. XIX, except reg. 171, read as if a reference to a payment being received by the claimant were a reference to a payment being received either by the claimant or by a person to whom a right to receive it has been assigned.

Official publications – 700/18.
Customs Internal Guidance Manual, vol. V1.22: bad debt relief.

INTERPRETATION OF PART XIX

165   In this Part–

"**claim**" means a claim in accordance with regulations 166 and 167 for a refund of VAT to which a person is entitled by virtue of section 36 of the Act and "**claimant**" shall be construed accordingly;

"**payment**" means any payment or part-payment which is made by any person by way of consideration for a supply regardless of whether such payment extinguishes the purchaser's debt to the claimant or not;

"**purchaser**" means a person to whom the claimant made a relevant supply;

"**refunds for bad debts account**" has the meaning given in regulation 168;

"**relevant supply**" means any taxable supply upon which a claim is based;

"**return**" means the return which the claimant is required to make in accordance with regulation 25;

"**security**" means–

(a)   in relation to England, Wales and Northern Ireland, any mortgage, charge, lien or other security, and

(b)   in relation to Scotland, any security (whether heritable or moveable), any floating charge and any right of lien or preference and right of retention (other than a right of compensation or set-off).

History – In reg. 165, in the definition of "payment", the words "to the claimant" which appeared after the words "by any person" were omitted by SI 1999/3029, reg. 3, operative from 1 December 1999.

TIME WITHIN WHICH A CLAIM MUST BE MADE

165A(1)   Subject to paragraph (3) below, a claim shall be made within the period of 3 years and 6 months following the later of–

(a)   the date on which the consideration (or part) which has been written off as a bad debt becomes due and payable to or to the order of the person who made the relevant supply; and

(b)   the date of the supply.

165A(2)   A person who is entitled to a refund by virtue of section 36 of the Act, but has not made a claim within the period specified in paragraph (1) shall be regarded for the purposes of this Part as having ceased to be entitled to a refund accordingly.

165A(3)   This regulation does not apply insofar as the date mentioned at sub-paragraph (a) or (b) of paragraph (1) above, whichever is the later, falls before 1st May 1997.

History – Reg. 165A inserted by SI 1997/1086, reg. 10, operative from 1 May 1997.

THE MAKING OF A CLAIM TO THE COMMISSIONERS

166(1) Save as the Commissioners may otherwise allow or direct, the claimant shall make a claim to the Commissioners by including the correct amount of the refund in the box opposite the legend "VAT reclaimed in this period on purchases and other inputs" on his return for the specified accounting period in which he becomes entitled to make the claim or, subject to regulation 165A, any later return.

166(2) If at a time the claimant becomes entitled to a refund he is no longer required to make returns to the Commissioners he shall make a claim to the Commissioners in such form and manner as they may direct.

History – In reg. 166(1), words from "for the specified accounting period" to the end added by SI 1997/1086, reg. 11, operative from 1 May 1997.
Form – VAT 427(C): claim under reg. 166(2).

NOTICE TO PURCHASER OF CLAIM

166A Where the purchaser is a taxable person the claimant shall not before, but within 7 days from, the day he makes a claim give to the purchaser a notice in writing containing the following information-

(a)   the date of issue of the notice;

(b)   the date of the claim;

(c)   the date and number of any VAT invoice issued in relation to each relevant supply;

(d)   the amount of the consideration for each relevant supply which the claimant has written off as a bad debt;

(e)   the amount of the claim.

History – Reg. 166A inserted by SI 1997/1086, reg. 12, operative from 1 May 1997.

EVIDENCE REQUIRED OF THE CLAIMANT IN SUPPORT OF THE CLAIM

167 Save as the Commissioners may otherwise allow, the claimant, before he makes a claim, shall hold in respect of each relevant supply-

(a)   either-

    (i)   a copy of any VAT invoice which was provided in accordance with Part III of these Regulations, or

    (ii)   where there was no obligation to provide a VAT invoice, a document which shows the time, nature and purchaser of the relevant goods and services, and the consideration therefor,

(b)   records or any other documents showing that he has accounted for and paid the VAT thereon, and

(c)   records or any other documents showing that the consideration has been written off in his accounts as a bad debt.

RECORDS REQUIRED TO BE KEPT BY THE CLAIMANT

168(1) Any person who makes a claim to the Commissioners shall keep a record of that claim.

168(2) Save as the Commissioners may otherwise allow, the record referred to in paragraph (1) above shall consist of the following information in respect of each claim made-

(a)   in respect of each relevant supply for that claim-

    (i)   the amount of VAT chargeable,

    (ii)   the prescribed accounting period in which the VAT chargeable was accounted for and paid to the Commissioners,

    (iii)   the date and number of any invoice issued in relation thereto or, where there is no such invoice, such information as is necessary to identify the time, nature and purchaser thereof, and

    (iv)   *any payment received therefor,*

(b)   the outstanding amount to which the claim relates,

(c)   the amount of the claim,

(d)   the prescribed accounting period in which the claim was made, and

(e)   a copy of the notice required to be given in accordance with regulation 166A.

168(3) Any records created in pursuance of this regulation shall be kept in a single account to be known as the **"refunds for bad debts account"**.

History – Reg. 168(2)(e) added by SI 1997/1086, reg. 13, operative from 1 May 1997.

PRESERVATION OF DOCUMENTS AND RECORDS AND DUTY TO PRODUCE

169(1) Save as the Commissioners may otherwise allow, the claimant shall preserve the documents, invoices and records which he holds in accordance with regulations 167 and 168 for a period of 4 years from the date of the making of the claim.

169(2) Upon demand made by an authorised person the claimant shall produce or cause to be produced any such documents, invoices and records for inspection by the authorised person and permit him to remove them at a reasonable time and for a reasonable period.

ATTRIBUTION OF PAYMENTS

170(1) Where–

(a) the claimant made more than one supply (whether taxable or otherwise) to the purchaser, and

(b) a payment is received in relation to those supplies,

the payment shall be attributed to each such supply in accordance with the rules set out in paragraphs (2) and (3) below.

170(2) The payment shall be attributed to the supply which is the earliest in time and, if not wholly attributed to that supply, thereafter to supplies in the order of the dates on which they were made, except that attribution under this paragraph shall not be made to any supply if the payment was allocated to that supply by the purchaser at the time of payment and the consideration for that supply was paid in full.

170(3) Where–

(a) the earliest supply and other supplies to which the whole of the payment could be attributed under this regulation occur on one day, or

(b) the supplies to which the balance of the payment could be attributed under this regulation occur on one day,

the payment shall be attributed to those supplies by multiplying, for each such supply, the payment received by a fraction of which the numerator is the outstanding consideration for that supply and the denominator is the total outstanding consideration for those supplies.

REPAYMENT OF A REFUND

171(1) Where a claimant–

(a) has received a refund upon a claim, and

(b) either–

    (i) a payment for the relevant supply is subsequently received, or

    (ii) a payment is, by virtue of regulation 170, treated as attributed to the relevant supply,

he shall repay to the Commissioners such an amount as equals the amount of the refund, or the balance thereof, multiplied by a fraction of which the numerator is the amount so received or attributed, and the denominator is the amount of the outstanding consideration.

171(2) The claimant shall repay to the Commissioners the amount referred to in paragraph (1) above by including that amount in the box opposite the legend "VAT due in this period on sales and other outputs" on his return for the prescribed accounting period in which the payment is received.

171(3) Save as the Commissioners may otherwise allow, where the claimant fails to comply with the requirements of regulation 167, 168, 169 or 170 he shall repay to the Commissioners the amount of the refund obtained by the claim to which the failure to comply relates; and he shall repay the amount by including that amount in the box opposite the legend "VAT due in this period on sales and other outputs" on his return for the prescribed accounting period which the Commissioners shall designate for that purpose.

171(4) If at the time the claimant is required to repay any amount, he is no longer required to make returns to the Commissioners, he shall repay such amount to the Commissioners at such time and in such form and manner as they may direct.

171(5) For the purposes of this regulation a reference to **payment** shall not include a reference to a payment received by a person to whom a right to receive it has been assigned.

History – Reg. 171(5) was inserted by SI 1999/3029, reg. 4, operative from 1 December 1999.

Cross references – FA 1999, s. 15(4): until such day as the Commissioners may specify, SI 1995/2518, Pt. XIX, except reg. 171, read as if a reference to a payment being received by the claimant were a reference to a payment being received either by the claimant or by a person to whom a right to receive it has been assigned.

WRITING OFF DEBTS

172(1) This regulation shall apply for the purpose of ascertaining whether, and to what extent, the consideration is to be taken to have been written off as a bad debt.

172(1A) Neither the whole nor any part of the consideration for a supply shall be taken to have been written off in accounts as a bad debt until a period of not less than six months has elapsed from the time when such whole or part first became due and payable to or to the order of the person who made the relevant supply.

172(2) Subject to paragraph (1A) the whole or any part of the consideration for a relevant supply shall be taken to have been written off as a bad debt when an entry is made in relation to that supply in the refunds for bad debt account in accordance with regulation 168.

172(3) Where the claimant owes an amount of money to the purchaser which can be set off, the consideration written off in the accounts shall be reduced by the amount so owed.

172(4) Where the claimant holds in relation to the purchaser an enforceable security, the consideration written off in the accounts of the claimant shall be reduced by the value of that security.

History – In reg. 172(1A), words "relevant supply" were substituted for the former words "supply in question" by SI 1997/1086, reg. 14(a), operative from 1 May 1997.
Reg. 172(1A) was added by SI 1996/2960, reg. 2(a), operative from 17 December 1996.
In reg. 14(2), words "relevant supply" substituted for the former word "supply" by SI 1997/1086, reg. 14(b), operative from 1 May 1997.
Reg. 172(2) was substituted by SI 1996/2960, reg. 2(b), operative from 17 December 1996.

WRITING OFF DEBTS – MARGIN SCHEMES

172A(1) This regulation applies where, by virtue of the claimant's having exercised an option under an order made under section 50A of the Act, the VAT chargeable on the relevant supply is charged by reference to the profit margin.

172A(2) Where this regulation applies the consideration for the relevant supply which is to be taken to have been written off as a bad debt shall not exceed the relevant amount.

172A(3) For the purposes of paragraph (2) above the **relevant amount** is–

(a)   where either

   (i) no payment has been received in relation to the relevant supply, or

   (ii) the total of such payments as have been received does not exceed the non-profit element,

   the profit margin; or

(b)   where the total of such payments as have been received exceeds the non-profit element, the amount (if any) by which the consideration for the relevant supply exceeds that total.

172A(4) In paragraph (3) above–

"non-profit element" means the consideration for the relevant supply less the profit margin.

History – Reg. 172A inserted by SI 1997/1086, reg. 15, operative from 1 May 1997.

WRITING OFF DEBTS – TOUR OPERATORS MARGIN SCHEME

172B(1) This regulation applies where, by virtue of an order under section 53 of the Act, the value of the relevant supply falls to be determined otherwise than in accordance with section 19 of the Act.

172B(2) Where this regulation applies the consideration for the relevant supply which is to be taken to have been written off as a bad debt shall not exceed the relevant amount.

172B(3) For the purposes of paragraph (2) above the **relevant amount** is–

(a)   where either

   (i) no payment has been received in relation to the relevant supply, or

   (ii) the total of any such payments as have been received does not exceed the non-profit element, the profit element; or

(b)   where the total of such payments as have been received exceeds the non-profit element, the amount (if any) by which the consideration for the relevant supply exceeds that total.

172B(4)   In this regulation–

     "non-profit element" means the consideration for the relevant supply less the profit element;

     "profit element" means the sum of–

     (a)   the value of the relevant supply; and

     (b)   the VAT chargeable on the relevant supply.

History – Reg. 172B inserted by SI 1997/1086, reg. 15, operative from 1 May 1997.

PART XIXA – REPAYMENT OF INPUT TAX WHERE CLAIM MADE UNDER PART XIX

INTERPRETATION OF PART XIXA

172C   Any expression used in this Part to which a meaning is given in Part XIX of these Regulations shall, unless the contrary intention appears, have the same meaning in this Part as it has in that Part.

History – Reg. 172C inserted by SI 1997/1086, reg. 16, operative from 1 May 1997.

REPAYMENT OF INPUT TAX

172D(1)   Where–

(a)   a claim has been made; and

(b)   the purchaser has claimed deduction of the whole or part of the VAT on the relevant supply as input tax (**"the deduction"**),

the purchaser shall make an entry in his VAT account in accordance with paragraphs (2) and (3) below.

172D(2)   The purchaser shall make a negative entry in the VAT allowable portion of that part of his VAT account which relates to the prescribed accounting period of his in which the claim has been made.

172D(3)   The amount of the **negative entry** referred to in paragraph (2) above shall be such amount as is found by multiplying the amount of the deduction by a fraction of which the numerator is the amount of the claim and the denominator is the total VAT chargeable on the relevant supply.

172D(4)   None of the circumstances to which this regulation applies is to be regarded as giving rise to any application of regulations 34 and 35.

History – Reg. 172D inserted by SI 1997/1086, reg. 16, operative from 1 May 1997.

RESTORATION OF AN ENTITLEMENT TO CREDIT FOR INPUT TAX

172E(1)   Where–

(a)   the purchaser has made an entry in his VAT account in accordance with regulation 172D (**"the input tax repayment"**);

(b)   he has made the return for the prescribed accounting period concerned, and has paid any VAT payable by him in respect of that period; and

(c)   the claimant has made a repayment in accordance with regulation 171 in relation to the claim concerned,

the purchaser shall make an entry in his VAT account in accordance with paragraphs (2) and (3) below.

172E(2)   The purchaser shall make a positive entry in the VAT allowable portion of that part of his VAT account which relates to the prescribed accounting period of his in which the repayment has been made.

172E(3)   The amount of the positive entry referred to in paragraph (2) above shall be such amount as is found by multiplying the amount of the input tax repayment by a fraction of which the numerator is the amount repaid by the claimant and the denominator is the total amount of the claim.

172E(4) None of the circumstances to which this regulation applies is to be regarded as giving rise to any application of regulations 34 and 35.

History – Reg. 172E inserted by SI 1997/1086, reg. 16, operative from 1 May 1997.

PART XX – REPAYMENTS TO COMMUNITY TRADERS

INTERPRETATION OF PART XX

173(1) In this Part–

"**calendar year**" means the period of 12 months beginning with the first day of January in any year;

"**claimant**" means a person making a claim under this Part or a person on whose behalf such a claim is made;

"**official authority**" means the authority in a member State designated to issue the certificate referred to in regulation 178(1)(b)(i).

173(2) For the purposes of this Part, a person is treated as being **established** in a country if–

(a) he has there an establishment from which business transactions are effected, or

(b) he has no such establishment (there or elsewhere) but his usual place of residence is there.

173(3) For the purposes of this Part–

(a) a person carrying on business through a branch or agency in any country is treated as having there an **establishment from which business transactions are effected**, and

(b) "**usual place of residence**", in relation to a body corporate, means the place where it is legally constituted.

REPAYMENT OF VAT

174 Subject to the other provisions of this Part a person to whom this Part applies shall be entitled to be repaid VAT charged on goods imported by him from a place outside the member States in respect of which no other relief is available or on supplies made to him in the United Kingdom if that VAT would be input tax of his were he a taxable person in the United Kingdom.

PERSONS TO WHOM THIS PART APPLIES

175 This Part applies to a person carrying on business in a member State other than the United Kingdom but does not apply to such a person in any period referred to in regulation 179 if during that period–

(a) he was established in the United Kingdom, or

(b) he made supplies in the United Kingdom of goods or services other than–

    (i) transport of freight outside the United Kingdom or to or from a place outside the United Kingdom or services ancillary thereto,

    (ii) services where the VAT on the supply is payable solely by the person to whom the services are supplied in accordance with the provisions of section 8 of the Act, and

    (iii) goods where the VAT on the supply is payable solely by the person to whom they are supplied as provided for in section 14 of the Act.

SUPPLIES AND IMPORTATIONS TO WHICH THIS PART APPLIES

176 This Part applies to any supply of goods or services made in the United Kingdom or to any importation of goods from a place outside the member States but does not apply to–

(a) a supply or importation of goods or a supply of services which the claimant has used or intends to use for the purpose of any supply by him in the United Kingdom, or

(b) a supply or importation of goods which the claimant has removed or intends to remove to another member State, or which he has exported or intends to export to a place outside the member States.

VAT WHICH WILL NOT BE REPAID

177(1) The following VAT shall not be repaid–

(a) VAT charged on a supply which if made to a taxable person would be excluded from any credit under section 25 of the Act,

(b)   VAT charged on a supply to a travel agent which is for the direct benefit of a traveller other than the travel agent or his employee.

177(2)   In this regulation a travel agent includes a tour operator and any person who purchases and resupplies services of a kind enjoyed by travellers.

METHOD OF CLAIMING

178(1)   A person claiming a repayment of VAT under this Part shall–

(a)   complete in the English language and send to the Commissioners either the form numbered 15 in Schedule 1 to these Regulations, or a form designed for the purpose by any official authority, containing full information in respect of all the matters specified in the said form and a declaration as therein set out, and

(b)   at the same time furnish–

      (i)   a certificate of status issued by the official authority of the member State in which the claimant is established either on the form numbered 16 in Schedule 1 to these Regulations or on the form designed by the official authority for the purpose, and

      (ii)   such documentary evidence of an entitlement to deduct VAT as may be required of a taxable person claiming a deduction of input tax in accordance with the provisions of regulation 29.

178(2)   Where the Commissioners are in possession of a certificate of status issued not more than 12 months before the date of the claim, the claimant shall not be required to furnish a further certificate.

178(3)   The Commissioners shall refuse to accept any document referred to in paragraph (1)(b)(ii) above if it bears an official stamp indicating that it had been furnished in support of an earlier claim.

Official publications – Notice 723.

TIME WITHIN WHICH A CLAIM MUST BE MADE

179(1)   A claim shall be made not later than 6 months after the end of the calendar year in which the VAT claimed was charged and shall be in respect of VAT charged on supplies or on importations from a place outside the member States made during a period of not less than 3 months and not more than one calendar year, provided that a claim may be in respect of VAT charged on supplies or on importations from a place outside the member States made during a period of less than 3 months where that period represents the final part of a calendar year.

179(2)   No claim shall be made for less than £16.

179(3)   No claim shall be made for less than £130 in respect of VAT charged on supplies or on importations from a place outside the member States made during a period of less than one calendar year except where that period represents the final part of a calendar year.

DEDUCTION OF BANK CHARGES

180   Where any repayment is to be made to a claimant in the country in which he is established, the Commissioners may reduce the amount of the repayment by the amount of any bank charges or costs incurred as a result thereof.

TREATMENT OF CLAIM AND REPAYMENT CLAIMED

181   For the purposes of section 73 of the Act any claim made under this Part shall be treated as a return required under paragraph 2 of Schedule 11 to the Act.

182   For the purpose of section 83(c) of the Act repayments claimed under this Part shall be treated as the amount of any input tax which may be credited to a person.

FALSE, ALTERED OR INCORRECT CLAIMS

183   If any claimant furnishes or sends to the Commissioners for the purposes of this Part any document which is false or which has been altered after issue to that person, the Commissioners may refuse to repay any VAT claimed by that claimant for the period of 2 years from the date when the claim, in respect of which the false or altered document was furnished or sent, was made.

184   Where any sum has been repaid to a claimant as a result of an incorrect claim, the amount of any subsequent repayment to that claimant may be reduced by the said sum.

PART XXI – REPAYMENTS TO THIRD COUNTRY TRADERS

INTERPRETATION OF PART XXI

185(1) In this Part–

"claimant" means a person making a claim under this Part or a person on whose behalf a claim is made and any agent acting on his behalf as his VAT representative;

"official authority" means any government body or agency in any country which is recognised by the Commissioners as having authority to act for the purposes of this Part;

"prescribed year" means the period of 12 months beginning on the first day of July in any year;

"VAT representative" means any person established in the United Kingdom and registered for VAT purposes in accordance with the provisions of Schedule 1 to the Act who acts as agent on behalf of a claimant;

"third country" means a country other than those comprising the member States of the European Community;

"trader" means a person carrying on a business who is established in a third country and who is not a taxable person in the United Kingdom.

185(2) For the purposes of this Part, a person is treated as being **established** in a country if–

(a) he has there a business establishment, or

(b) he has no such establishment (there or elsewhere) but his permanent address or usual place of residence is there.

185(3) For the purposes of this Part–

(a) a person carrying on business through a branch or agency in any country is treated as being **established** there, and

(b) where the person is a body corporate its **usual place of residence** shall be the place where it is legally constituted.

REPAYMENTS OF VAT

186 Subject to the other provisions of this Part a trader shall be entitled to be repaid VAT charged on goods imported by him into the United Kingdom in respect of which no other relief is available or on supplies made to him in the United Kingdom if that VAT would be input tax of his were he a taxable person in the United Kingdom.

VAT REPRESENTATIVES

187 The Commissioners may, as a condition of allowing a repayment under this Part, require a trader to appoint a VAT representative to act on his behalf.

PERSONS TO WHOM THIS PART APPLIES

188(1) Save as the Commissioners may otherwise allow, a trader to whom this Part applies who is established in a third country having a comparable system of turnover taxes will not be entitled to any refunds under this Part unless that country provides reciprocal arrangements for refunds to be made to taxable persons who are established in the United Kingdom.

188(2) This Part shall apply to any trader but not if during any period determined under regulation 192–

(a) he was established in any of the member States of the European Community, or

(b) he made supplies in the United Kingdom of goods or services other than–

    (i) transport of freight outside the United Kingdom to or from a place outside the United Kingdom or services ancillary thereto,

    (ii) services where the VAT on the supply is payable solely by the person to whom they are supplied in accordance with the provisions of section 8 of the Act, and

    (iii) goods where the VAT on the supply is payable solely by the person to whom they are supplied.

SUPPLIES AND IMPORTATIONS TO WHICH THIS PART APPLIES

189 This Part applies to any supply of goods or services made in the United Kingdom or to any importation of goods into the United Kingdom on or after 1st July 1994 but does not apply to any supply or importation which–

(a) the trader has used or intends to use for the purpose of any supply by him in the United Kingdom, or

(b) has been exported or is intended for exportation from the United Kingdom by or on behalf of the trader.

VAT WHICH WILL NOT BE REPAID

190(1) The following VAT shall not be repaid–

(a) VAT charged on a supply which if made to a taxable person would be excluded from any credit under section 25 of the Act,

(b) VAT charged on a supply to a travel agent which is for the direct benefit of a traveller other than the travel agent or his employee.

190(2) In this regulation a travel agent includes a tour operator or any person who purchases and resupplies services of a kind enjoyed by travellers.

METHOD OF CLAIMING

191(1) A person claiming a repayment of VAT under this Part shall–

(a) complete in the English language and send to the Commissioners either the form numbered 9 in Schedule 1 to these Regulations, or a like form produced by any official authority, containing full information in respect of all the matters specified in the said form and a declaration as therein set out, and

(b) at the same time furnish–

　(i) a certificate of status issued by the official authority of the third country in which the trader is established either on the form numbered 10 in Schedule 1 to these Regulations or on a like form produced by the official authority, and

　(ii) such documentary evidence of an entitlement to deduct input tax as may be required of a taxable person claiming a deduction of input tax in accordance with the provisions of regulation 29.

191(2) Where the Commissioners are in possession of a certificate of status issued not more than 12 months before the date of the claim, the claimant shall not be required to furnish a further such certificate.

191(3) The Commissioners shall refuse to accept any document referred to in paragraph (1)(b)(ii) above if it bears an official stamp indicating that it had been furnished in support of an earlier claim.

Official publications – Notice 723.

TIME WITHIN WHICH A CLAIM MUST BE MADE

192(1) A claim shall be made not later than 6 months after the end of the prescribed year in which the VAT claimed was charged and shall be in respect of VAT charged on supplies or on importations made during a period of not less than 3 months and not more than 12 months, provided that a claim may be made in respect of VAT charged on supplies or on importations made during a period of less than 3 months where that period represents the final part of the prescribed year.

192(2) No claim shall be made for less than £16.

192(3) No claim shall be made for less than £130 in respect of VAT charged on supplies or on importations made during a period of less than the prescribed year except where that period represents the final part of the prescribed year.

DEDUCTION OF BANK CHARGES

193 Where any repayment is to be made to a claimant in the country in which he is established, the Commissioners may reduce the amount of the repayment by the amount of any bank charges or costs incurred as a result thereof.

TREATMENT OF CLAIM AND REPAYMENT CLAIMED

194 For the purposes of section 73 of the Act any claim made under this Part shall be treated as a return required under paragraph 2 of Schedule 11 to the Act.

195 For the purpose of section 83(c) of the Act repayments claimed under this Part shall be treated as the amount of any input tax which may be credited to a person.

FALSE, ALTERED OR INCORRECT CLAIMS

196 If any claimant furnishes or sends to the Commissioners for the purposes of this Part any document which is false or which has been altered after issue to that person, the Commissioners may refuse to repay any VAT claimed by that claimant for the period of 2 years from the date when the claim, in respect of which the false or altered documents were furnished or sent, was made.

197 Where any sum has been repaid to a claimant as a result of an incorrect claim, the amount of any subsequent repayment to that claimant may be reduced by the said sum.

PART XXII – REPAYMENT SUPPLEMENT

COMPUTATION OF PERIOD

198 In computing the period of 30 days referred to in section 79(2)(b) of the Act, periods referable to the following matters shall be left out of account–

(a)   the raising and answering of any reasonable inquiry relating to the requisite return or claim,

(b)   the correction by the Commissioners of any errors or omissions in that requisite return or claim, and

(c)   in any case to which section 79(1)(a) of the Act applies, the following matters, namely–

    (i)   any such continuing failure to submit returns as is referred to in section 25(5) of the Act, and

    (ii)   compliance with any such condition as is referred to in paragraph 4(1) of Schedule 11 to the Act.

DURATION OF PERIOD

199 For the purpose of determining the duration of the periods referred to in regulation 198, the following rules shall apply–

(a)   in the case of the period mentioned in regulation 198(a), it shall be taken to have begun on the date when the Commissioners first raised the inquiry and it shall be taken to have ended on the date when they received a complete answer to their inquiry;

(b)   in the case of the period mentioned in regulation 198(b), it shall be taken to have begun on the date when the error or omission first came to the notice of the Commissioners and it shall be taken to have ended on the date when the error or omission was corrected by them;

(c)   in the case of the period mentioned in regulation 198(c)(i), it shall be determined in accordance with a certificate of the Commissioners under paragraph 14(1)(b) of Schedule 11 to the Act;

(d)   in the case of the period mentioned in regulation 198(c)(ii), it shall be taken to have begun on the date of the service of the written notice of the Commissioners which required the production of documents or the giving of security, and it shall be taken to have ended on the date when they received the required documents or the required security.

Official publications – 700, para. 9.8 (2000 edn).

PART XXIII – REFUNDS TO "DO-IT-YOURSELF" BUILDERS

INTERPRETATION OF PART XXIII

200 In this Part–

"claim" means a claim for refund of VAT made pursuant to section 35 of the Act, and

"claimant" shall be construed accordingly;

"relevant building" means a building in respect of which a claimant makes a claim.

METHOD AND TIME FOR MAKING CLAIM

201   A claimant shall make his claim in respect of a relevant building by–

(a)   furnishing to the Commissioners no later than 3 months after the completion of the building the form numbered 11 in Schedule 1 to these Regulations containing the full particulars required therein, and

(b)   at the same time furnishing to them–

     (i)   a certificate of completion obtained from a local authority or such other documentary evidence of completion of the building as is satisfactory to the Commissioners,

     (ii)   an invoice showing the registration number of the person supplying the goods, whether or not such an invoice is a VAT invoice, in respect of each supply of goods on which VAT has been paid which have been incorporated into the building or its site,

     (iii)   in respect of imported goods which have been incorporated into the building or its site, documentary evidence of their importation and of the VAT paid thereon,

     (iv)   documentary evidence that planning permission for the building had been granted, and

     (v)   a certificate signed by a quantity surveyor or architect that the goods shown in the claim were or, in his judgement, were likely to have been, incorporated into the building or its site.

Official publications   – Notice 719.

PART XXIV – FLAT-RATE SCHEME FOR FARMERS

Official publications   – 700/46.
Customs Internal Guidance Manual, vol. V1.23, chapter 2: agricultural flat-rate scheme.

INTERPRETATION OF PART XXIV

202   In this Part–

     "certified person" means a person certified as a flat-rate farmer for the purposes of the flat-rate scheme under regulation 203 and **"certified"** and **"certification"** shall be construed accordingly.

FLAT-RATE SCHEME

203(1)   The Commissioners shall, if the conditions mentioned in regulation 204 are satisfied, certify that a person is a flat-rate farmer for the purposes of the flat-rate scheme (hereinafter in this Part referred to as **"the scheme"**).

203(2)   Where a person is for the time being certified in accordance with this regulation, then (whether or not that person is a taxable person) any supply of goods or services made by him in the course or furtherance of the relevant part of his business shall be disregarded for the purpose of determining whether he is, has become or has ceased to be liable or entitled to be registered under Schedule 1 to the Act.

ADMISSION TO THE SCHEME

204   The conditions mentioned in regulation 203 are that–

(a)   the person satisfies the Commissioners that he is carrying on a business involving one or more designated activities,

(b)   he has not in the 3 years preceding the date of his application for certification–

     (i)   been convicted of any offence in connection with VAT,

     (ii)   made any payment to compound proceedings in respect of VAT under section 152 of the Customs and Excise Management Act 1979 as applied by section 72(12) of the Act,

     (iii)   been assessed to a penalty under section 60 of the Act,

(c)   he makes an application for certification on the form numbered 14 in Schedule 1 to these Regulations, and

(d)   he satisfies the Commissioners that he is a person in respect of whom the total of the amounts as are mentioned in regulation 209 relating to supplies made in the year following the date of his certification will not exceed by £3,000 or more the amount of input tax to which he would otherwise be entitled to credit in that year.

CERTIFICATION

205   Where the Commissioners certify that a person is a flat-rate farmer for the purposes of the scheme, the certificate issued by the Commissioners shall be effective from–

(a)   the date on which the application for certification is received by the Commissioners,

(b)   with the agreement of the Commissioners, an earlier date to that mentioned in sub-paragraph (a) above, or

(c)   if the person so requests, a later date which is no more than 30 days after the date mentioned in sub-paragraph (a) above,

provided that any certificate shall not be effective from a date before the date when the person's registration under Schedule 1 or 3 to the Act is cancelled and a certificate shall not be effective from a date earlier than 1st January 1993.

CANCELLATION OF CERTIFICATES

206(1)   The Commissioners may cancel a person's certificate in any case where–

(a)   a statement false in a material particular was made by him or on his behalf in relation to his application for certification,

(b)   he has been convicted of an offence in connection with VAT or has made a payment to compound such proceedings under section 152 of the Customs and Excise Management Act 1979 as applied by section 72(12) of the Act,

(c)   he has been assessed to a penalty under section 60 of the Act,

(d)   he ceases to be involved in designated activities,

(e)   he dies, becomes bankrupt or incapacitated,

(f)   he is liable to be registered under Schedule 1 or 3 to the Act,

(g)   he makes an application in writing for cancellation,

(h)   he makes an application in writing for registration under Schedule 1 or 3 to the Act, and such application shall be deemed to be an application for cancellation of his certificate,

(i)   they consider it is necessary to do so for the protection of the revenue, or

(j)   they are not satisfied that any of the grounds for cancellation of a certificate mentioned in sub-paragraphs (a) to (h) above do not apply.

206(2)   Where the Commissioners cancel a person's certificate in accordance with paragraph (1) above, the effective date of the cancellation shall be for each of the cases mentioned respectively in that paragraph as follows–

(a)   the date when the Commissioners discover that such a statement has been made,

(b)   the date of his conviction or the date on which a sum is paid to compound proceedings,

(c)   30 days after the date when the assessment is notified,

(d)   the date of the cessation of designated activities,

(e)   the date on which he died, became bankrupt or incapacitated,

(f)   the effective date of registration,

(g)   not less than one year after the effective date of his certificate or such earlier date as the Commissioners may agree,

(h)   not less than one year after the effective date of his certificate or such earlier date as the Commissioners may agree,

(i)   the date on which the Commissioners consider a risk to the revenue arises, or

(j)   the date mentioned in sub-paragraphs (a) to (h) above as appropriate.

DEATH, BANKRUPTCY OR INCAPACITY OF CERTIFIED PERSON

207(1)   If a certified person dies or becomes bankrupt or incapacitated, the Commissioners may, from the date on which he died or became bankrupt or incapacitated treat as a certified person any person carrying on those designated activities until some other person is certified in respect of the designated activities or the incapacity ceases, as the case may be; and the provisions of the Act and of any Regulations made thereunder shall apply to any person so treated as though he were a certified person.

207(2) Any person carrying on such designated activities shall, within 30 days of commencing to do so, inform the Commissioners in writing of that fact and of the date of the death, or of the nature of the incapacity and the date on which it began.

207(3) In relation to a company which is a certified person, the references in regulation 206(1)(e) and (2)(e) and in paragraph (1) above to the certified person becoming bankrupt or incapacitated shall be construed as references to its going into liquidation or receivership or to an administration order being made in relation to it.

FURTHER CERTIFICATION

208 Where a person who has been certified and is no longer so certified makes a further application under regulation 204, that person shall not be certified for a period of 3 years from the date of the cancellation of his previous certificate except–

(a)   the Commissioners may certify from the date of his further application a person who has not been registered under Schedule 1 or 3 to the Act at any time since the cancellation of his previous certificate; and

(b)   where the circumstances as are mentioned in paragraph 8(1)(c) of Schedule 4 to the Act apply, the Commissioners may certify the person mentioned in that paragraph on a date after the expiry of one year from the date of the cancellation of his previous certificate.

CLAIMS BY TAXABLE PERSONS FOR AMOUNTS TO BE TREATED AS CREDITS FOR INPUT TAX

209(1) The amount referred to in section 54(4) of the Act and included in the consideration for any taxable supply which is made–

(a)   in the course or furtherance of the relevant part of his business by a person who is for the time being certified under this part,

(b)   at a time when that person is not a taxable person, and

(c)   to a taxable person,

shall be treated, for the purpose of determining the entitlement of the person supplied to credit under sections 25 and 26 of the Act, as VAT on a supply to that person.

209(2) Subject to paragraph (3) below and save as the Commissioners may otherwise allow or direct generally or specially, a taxable person claiming entitlement to a credit of an amount as is mentioned in paragraph (1) above shall do so on the return made by him for the prescribed accounting period in which the invoice specified in paragraph (3) below is issued by a certified person.

209(3) A taxable person shall not be entitled to credit as is mentioned in paragraph (1) above unless there has been issued an invoice containing the following particulars–

(a)   an identifying number,

(b)   the name, address and certificate number of the certified person by whom the invoice is issued,

(c)   the name and address of the person to whom the goods or services are supplied,

(d)   the time of the supply,

(e)   a description of the goods or services supplied,

(f)   the consideration for the supply or, in the case of any increase or decrease in the consideration, the amount of that increase or decrease excluding the amount as is mentioned in paragraph (1) above, and

(g)   *the amount as is mentioned* in paragraph (1) above which amount shall be entitled **"Flat-rate Addition"** or **"FRA"**.

DUTY TO KEEP RECORDS

210(1) Every certified person shall, for the purposes of the scheme, keep and preserve the following records–

(a)   his business and accounting records, and

(b)   copies of all invoices specified in regulation 209(3) issued by him or on his behalf.

210(2) Every certified person shall comply with such requirements with respect to the keeping, preservation and production of records as the Commissioners may notify to him.

210(3)   Every certified person shall keep and preserve such records as are required by paragraph (1) above or by notification for a period of 6 years or such lesser period as the Commissioners may allow.

PRODUCTION OF RECORDS

211(1)   Every certified person shall–

(a)   upon demand made by an authorised person, produce or cause to be produced for inspection by that person–

       (i)   at the principal place of business of the person upon whom the demand is made or at such other place as the authorised person may reasonably require, and

       (ii)   at such time as the authorised person may reasonably require,

    any documents specified in regulation 210(1), and

(b)   permit an authorised person to take copies of, or make extracts from, or remove at a reasonable time and for a reasonable period, any document produced under paragraph (1)(a) above.

211(2)   Where a document removed by an authorised person under paragraph (1)(b) above is reasonably required for the proper conduct of a business, he shall, as soon as practicable, provide a copy of that document, free of charge, to the person by whom it was produced or caused to be produced.

211(3)   Where any documents removed under paragraph (1)(b) above are lost or damaged, the Commissioners shall be liable to compensate their owner for any expenses reasonably incurred by him in replacing or repairing the documents.

PART XXV – DISTRESS AND DILIGENCE

Official publications – 930 and 700/56.

A212   In this Part–

    "Job Band" followed by a number between "1" and "12" means the band for the purposes of pay and grading in which the job an officer performs is ranked in the system applicable to Customs and Excise.

History – Reg. A212 was inserted by SI 1996/2098, reg. 3, operative from 2 September 1996.

DISTRESS

212   [Repealed by SI 1997/1431, reg. 3(1) and Sch. 3, operative from 1 July 1997.]

History – Former reg. 212 reads as follows:
"**212(1)**   If upon written demand a person neglects or refuses to pay VAT which he is required to pay under the Act or any Order or any Regulations made thereunder or to pay any amount recoverable as if it were VAT, a Collector or an officer of rank not below that of Job Band 7 may distrain on the goods and chattels of that person and by warrant signed by him direct any authorised person to levy such distress, provided that where an amount of VAT is due under section 73(9) of the Act (other than an amount assessed as due under section 73(1) of the Act upon failure by a person to make a return) no distress shall be levied until 30 days after that amount became due.
212(2)   A levy shall be executed by or under the direction of, and in the presence of, the authorised person.
212(3)   A person in respect of whose goods and chattels a warrant has been signed shall be liable for all costs and charges in connection with anything done under this regulation.
212(4)   If the person aforesaid does not pay the sum due together with the costs and charges within 5 days of a levy, the distress shall be sold by the authorised person for payment of the sums due and all costs and charges; and costs and charges of taking, keeping and selling the distress shall be retained by the authorised person and any surplus remaining after the deduction of the costs and charges and of the sum due shall be restored to the owner of the goods distrained."
In former reg. 212(1), the words "Job Band 7" were substituted by SI 1996/2098, reg. 4, operative from 2 September 1996.

DILIGENCE

213   In Scotland, the following provisions shall have effect–

(a)   where the Commissioners are empowered to apply to the Sheriff for a warrant to authorise a Sheriff Officer to recover any amount of VAT or any sum recoverable as if it were VAT remaining due and unpaid, any application, and any certificate required to accompany that application, may be made on their behalf by a Collector of Customs and Excise or an officer of rank not below that of Job Band 7;

(b)   where, during the course of a poinding and sale in accordance with Schedule 5 to the Debtors (Scotland) Act 1987 the Commissioners are entitled as a creditor to do any acts, then any such acts, with the exception of the exercise of the power contained in paragraph 18(3) of that Schedule, may be done on their behalf by a Collector of Customs and Excise or an officer of rank not below that of Job Band 7.

History – In reg. 213(a) and (b), the words "Job Band 7" were substituted by SI 1996/2098, reg. 4, operative from 2 September 1996.

SCHEDULES

SCHEDULE 1 – FORMS

Form 1:	VAT 1	Application for VAT registration	Regulation 5(1)
Form 2:	VAT 2	Partnership details	Regulation 5(1)
Form 3:	VAT 68	Transfer of a going concern	Regulation 6(1)
Form 4:	VAT 100	Value added tax return	Regulation 25(1)
Form 5:	VAT 193	Final value added tax return	Regulations 23, 25(4)
Form 6:	VAT 1A	Application for VAT registration	Regulation 5(1)
Form 7:	VAT 1B	Application for VAT registration	Regulation 5(1)
Form 7A:	[VAT 1C]	[VAT registration notification]	Regulation 5(1)
Form 8:	VAT 1TR	Appointment of tax representative	Regulation 10
Form 9:	VAT 65A	Application by a business person not established in the Community for refund of value added tax	Regulation 191(1)
Form 10:	VAT 66A	Certificate of status of business person	Regulation 191(1)(b)
Form 11:	VAT 431	VAT refunds for DIY builders	Regulation 201(a)
Form 12:	VAT 101	EC sales list	Regulations 21–23
Form 13:	VAT 411	New means of transport	Regulations 22(6), 23
Form 14:	VAT 98	Flat rate scheme for agriculture; application for certification	Regulation 204(c)
Form 15:	VAT 65	Application by a business person established in the Community for refund of value added tax	Regulation 178(1)(a)
Form 16:	VAT 66	Certificate of status of taxable person	Regulation 178(1)(b)(i)
Form 17:		Certificate required to secure relief from VAT on purchased or acquired goods intended to be placed in a fiscal warehousing regime	Regulation 145B
Form 18:		Certificate required to secure zero-rating of services (other than the supply of warehousing) performed in a fiscal or other warehouse	Regulation 145C

History – Form 7A was added by SI 2000/794, reg. 7 and Sch. 1, operative from 22 March 2000.
Forms 17 and 18 were added by SI 1996/1250, reg. 15, operative from 1 June 1996.

Cross references – Reg. 25(4J): modification of Forms 4 and 5 in relation to making VAT returns electronically.

Notes – Forms not reproduced.

SCHEDULE 1A – THE FISCAL WAREHOUSING RECORD WHICH IS REFERRED TO IN PARAGRAPH (3) OF REGULATION 145F SHALL HAVE THE FEATURES AND COMPLY WITH THE REQUIREMENTS SET OUT BELOW

Regulation 145F

History – Sch. 1A was inserted by SI 1996/1250, reg. 16, operative from 1 June 1996.

1 Goods in and out of a fiscal warehouse and its regime.

(a) It shall accurately identify any eligible goods which enter or exit the fiscal warehouse, their nature and quantity, and the time and date when they so enter or exit.

(b) It shall accurately identify any goods which are not eligible goods and which enter or exit the fiscal warehouse for storage (other than goods which enter for purposes wholly incidental to such storage), their nature and quantity, and time and date when they so enter or exit.

(c) It shall accurately identify all eligible goods which are allocated to or removed from the fiscal warehousing regime associated with the relevant fiscal warehousekeeper, the time and date when the allocation or removal takes place, and the location of the eligible goods while they are allocated to the relevant regime.

(d) It shall accurately identify as **"transferred goods"** all eligible goods which are transferred directly from the fiscal warehousing regime to another fiscal warehousing regime, the time and date when the transfer starts, and the address of the fiscal warehouse to which the goods in question are transferred.

(e) It shall accurately identify as **"transferred goods"** all eligible goods which are transferred directly from the fiscal warehousing regime to corresponding arrangements in another member State under regulation 145H(2)(b), the date and time when the transfer starts, and the address of the place in the other member State to which the goods in question are transferred.

(f) It shall accurately identify as **"transferred goods (by reason of export)"** all eligible goods which are directly exported from the fiscal warehousing regime to a place outside the member States under regulation 145H(2)(c), the date and time when the movement of the goods which is directly associated with the export starts, and the address of the place outside the member States to which the goods in question are consigned.

2 Specified services performed in a fiscal warehouse

It shall accurately identify the nature of any services which are performed on or in relation to eligible goods while those goods are allocated to the relevant fiscal warehousing regime, the date when the services are performed, the particular eligible goods on or in relation to which they are performed, and the name, address and registration number (if any) of the supplier of those services.

3 Documents relating to transfers and specified services

(a) It shall include the written undertaking from the other fiscal warehousekeeper relating to a transfer made within the United Kingdom referred to in regulation 145G(2), the certificate from the other fiscal warehousekeeper confirming a transfer made within the United Kingdom referred to in regulation 145G(3)(c), and it shall relate them to the relevant transfer.

(b) It shall include the copy of the certificate relating to a transfer received by the relevant fiscal warehousekeeper from another fiscal warehousing regime within the United Kingdom referred to in regulation 145G(3)(d) and it shall relate that copy to the relevant allocation to his relevant fiscal warehousing regime.

(c) It shall include the document relating to the completion of a transfer to corresponding arrangements in another member State referred to in regulation 145H(4)(b) and it shall relate that document to the relevant transfer.

(d) It shall include the document relating to the completion of an export to a place outside the member States referred to in regulation 145H(4)(c) and it shall relate that document to the export in question.

4 Procedures where transfers are not completed

(a) It shall be adjusted to show a removal (and not a transfer) where the certificate of transfer within the United Kingdom referred to in regulation 145G(3)(c) is not received in time from the other fiscal warehousekeeper.

(b) It shall be adjusted to show a removal (and not a transfer) where the document referred to in [regulations] 145H(4)(b) or 145H(4)(c) concerning goods which have been transferred to corresponding arrangements in another member State, or which have been exported to a place outside the member States, is not received in time.

(c) It shall evidence any notification made under regulation 145H(3)(c) to the person on whose instructions the goods were allowed to leave the fiscal warehouse.

5 Removals from a fiscal warehousing regime

(a) It shall identify the name and address of any person who at any time removes or causes the removal of any goods from the fiscal warehousing regime and that person's registration number if he is registered under the Act.

(b) It shall include a copy of the removal document issued by the Commissioners under regulation 145J(1) and shall relate it to the relevant removal.

6 Miscellaneous

(a) It shall incorporate any modifications to the features or requirements set out in paragraphs 1 to 5 above which the Commissioners may require in respect of the relevant fiscal warehousekeeper.

(b) A fiscal warehousekeeper may, with the prior agreement of the Commissioners, maintain a fiscal warehousing record in which any of the features or requirements set out in paragraphs 1 to 5 above are relaxed or dispensed with.

SCHEDULE 2 – REVOCATIONS

Regulation 3(1)

Statutory instrument number	Title of regulations
SI 1972/1148	The Value Added Tax (Supplies by Retailers) Regulations 1972
SI 1973/293	The Value Added Tax (Trading Stamps) Regulations 1973
SI 1975/274	The Value Added Tax (Supplies by Retailers) (Amendment) Regulations 1975
SI 1979/224	The Value Added Tax (Supplies by Retailers) (Amendment) Regulations 1979
SI 1980/1537	The Value Added Tax (Repayment to Community Traders) Regulations 1980
SI 1985/886	The Value Added Tax (General) Regulations 1985
SI 1985/1650	The Value Added Tax (General) (Amendment) Regulations 1985
SI 1986/71	The Value Added Tax (General) (Amendment) Regulations 1986
SI 1986/305	The Value Added Tax (General) (Amendment) (No. 2) Regulations 1986
SI 1986/335	The Value Added Tax (Bad Debt Relief) Regulations 1986
SI 1987/193	The Value Added Tax (General) (Amendment) Regulations 1987
SI 1987/510	The Value Added Tax (General) (Amendment) (No. 2) Regulations 1987
SI 1987/1427	The Value Added Tax (Cash Accounting) Regulations 197
SI 1987/1712	The Value Added Tax (Supplies by Retailers) (Amendment) Regulations 1987
SI 1987/1916	The Value Added Tax (General) (Amendment) (No. 3) Regulations 1987
SI 1987/2015	The Value Added Tax (Repayments to Third Country Traders) Regulations 1987
SI 1988/886	The Value Added Tax (Annual Accounting) Regulations 1988
SI 1988/1343	The Value Added Tax (Repayment Supplement) Regulations 1988
SI 1988/2083	The Value Added Tax (General) (Amendment) Regulations 1988
SI 1988/2108	The Value Added Tax (General) (Amendment) (No. 2) Regulations 1988
SI 1988/2217	The Value Added Tax (Repayment to Community Traders) (Amendment) Regulations 1988
SI 1989/1132	The Value Added Tax (General) (Amendment) Regulations 1989
SI 1989/1302	The Value Added Tax (General) (Amendment) (No. 2) Regulations 1989
SI 1989/2248	The Value Added Tax (Accounting and Records) Regulations 1989
SI 1989/2255	The Value Added Tax (Bad Debt Relief) (Amendment) Regulations 1989
SI 1989/2256	The Value Added Tax (General) (Amendment) (No. 3) Regulations 1989
SI 1989/2259	The Value Added Tax ("Do-It-Yourself" Builders) (Refund of Tax) Regulations 1989
SI 1989/2355	The Value Added Tax (General) (Amendment) (No. 4) Regulations 1989
SI 1990/420	The Value Added Tax (Cash Accounting) (Amendment) Regulations 1990
SI 1990/1943	The Value Added Tax (Cash Accounting) (Amendment) (No. 2) Regulations 1990
SI 1991/371	The Value Added Tax (Refunds for Bad Debts) Regulations 1991
SI 1991/691	The Value Added Tax (General) (Amendment) Regulations 1991
SI 1991/1332	The Value Added Tax (General) (Amendment) (No. 2) Regulations 1991
SI 1991/1532	The Value Added Tax (Annual Accounting) (Amendment) Regulations 1991
SI 1992/644	The Value Added Tax (Cash Accounting) (Amendment) Regulations 1992
SI 1992/645	The Value Added Tax (General) (Amendment) Regulations 1992
SI 1992/1844	The Value Added Tax (Payments on Account) (No. 2) Regulations 1992
SI 1992/3096	The Value Added Tax (EC Sales Statements) Regulations 1992
SI 1992/3097	The Value Added Tax (Accounting and Records) (Amendment) Regulations 1992

Statutory instrument number	Title of regulations
SI 1992/3099	The Value Added Tax (Valuation of Acquisitions) Regulations 1992
SI 1992/3100	The Value Added Tax (Refunds in relation to New Means of Transport) Regulations 1992
SI 1992/3101	The Value Added Tax (Removal of Goods) (Accounting) Regulations 1992
SI 1992/3102	The Value Added Tax (General) (Amendment) (No. 4) Regulations 1992
SI 1992/3103	The Value Added Tax (Flat-rate Scheme for Farmers) Regulations 1992
SI 1993/119	The Value Added Tax (General) (Amendment) Regulations 1993
SI 1993/761	The Value Added Tax (Accounting and Records) (Amendment) Regulations 1993
SI 1993/762	The Value Added Tax (Cash Accounting) (Amendment) Regulations 1993
SI 1993/764	The Value Added Tax (General) (Amendment) (No. 2) Regulations 1993
SI 1993/856	The Value Added Tax (General) (Amendment) (No. 3) Regulations 1993
SI 1993/1222	The Value Added Tax (Repayment to Third Country Traders) (Amendment) Regulations 1993
SI 1993/1223	The Value Added Tax (Repayment to Community Traders) (Amendment) Regulations 1993
SI 1993/1224	The Value Added Tax (General) (Amendment) (No. 4) Regulations 1993
SI 1993/1639	The Value Added Tax (General) (Amendment) (No. 5) Regulations 1993
SI 1993/1941	The Value Added Tax (General) (Amendment) (No. 6) Regulations 1993
SI 1993/3027	The Value Added Tax (General) (Amendment) (No. 7) Regulations 1993
SI 1993/3028	The Value Added Tax (Cash Accounting) (Amendment) (No. 2) Regulations 1993
SI 1994/803	The Value Added Tax (Accounting and Records) (Amendment) Regulations 1994
SI 1994/3015	The Value Added Tax (General) (Amendment) Regulations 1994
SI 1995/152	The Value Added Tax (General) (Amendment) Regulations 1995
SI 1995/913	The Value Added Tax (General) (Amendment) (No. 2) Regulations 1995
SI 1995/1069	The Value Added Tax (General) (Amendment) (No. 3) Regulations 1995
SI 1995/1280	The Value Added Tax (General) (Amendment) (No. 4) Regulations 1995

Notes – In the Queen's Printer's version of the regulations, the entry for SI 1991/1532 should apparently be SI 1991/532.

VALUE ADDED TAX (REFUND OF TAX) (NO. 2) ORDER 1995

(SI 1995/2999)

Made on 22 November 1995 by the Treasury, in exercise of the powers conferred on them by s. 33(3) of the Value Added Tax Act 1994 and of all other powers enabling them in that behalf. Operative from 15 December 1995.

1 This Order may be cited as the Value Added Tax (Refund of Tax) (No. 2) Order 1995 and shall come into force on 15 December 1995.

2 The following bodies are hereby specified for the purposes of section 33 of the Value Added Tax Act 1994:

A National Park authority (within the meaning of section 63 of the Environment Act 1995)

A fire authority constituted by a combination scheme made under section 6 of the Fire Services Act 1947.

VALUE ADDED TAX (FISCAL WAREHOUSING) (TREATMENT OF TRANSACTIONS) ORDER 1996

(1996/1255)

Made on 8 May 1996 by the Treasury, in exercise of the power conferred on them by s. 5(3) of the Value Added Tax Act 1994 and of all other powers enabling them in that behalf. Operative from 1 June 1996.

1 This Order may be cited as the Value Added Tax (Fiscal Warehousing) (Treatment of Transactions) Order 1996 and shall come into force on 1st June 1996.

2(1) In this Order–

"**eligible goods**" has the meaning given by section 18B(6) of the Act;

"**material time**" has the meaning given by section 18F(1) of the Act;

"**supply**" means a supply for the purposes of section 5(2)(a) of the Act; and,

"**the Act**" means the Value Added Tax Act 1994.

2(2) In construing article 3(2) below any supply referred to in that article must be treated as taking place at the material time for that supply.

3(1) A transaction fulfilling the description set out in paragraph (2) below shall be treated as a supply of goods and not as a supply of services.

3(2) The description referred to in paragraph (1) above is that there is a supply (which is not a retail transaction) involving the transfer of any undivided share of property in eligible goods and either–

(a)   that supply takes place while the goods in question are subject to a fiscal warehousing regime, or

(b)   the transferee causes the goods in question to be placed in a fiscal warehousing regime after receiving that supply but before the supply, if any, which next occurs involving the transfer of any property in those goods.

FREE ZONE (SOUTHAMPTON) DESIGNATION (VARIATION OF AREA) ORDER 1996

(SI 1996/2615)

Made on 14 October 1996 by the Treasury, in exercise of the powers conferred on them by s. 100A(4)(a)(ii) of the Customs and Excise Management Act 1979 and of all other powers enabling them in that behalf, and with the agreement of Southampton Free Trade Zone Limited. Operative from 21 October 1996.

1 This Order may be cited as the Free Zone (Southampton) Designation (Variation of Area) Order 1996 and shall come into force on 21 October 1996.

2 The area designated a free zone by the Free Zone (Southampton) Designation Order 1991 and varied by the Free Zone (Southampton) Designation (Variation) Order 1994 shall be further varied by substituting the area referred to in article 2 of the Free Zone (Southampton) Designation (Variation) Order 1994 for an area consisting of 3.2436 hectares in the City of Southampton, Hampshire shown enclosed by a blue line on a map (being of a scale of 1:2500), marked "Map referred to in article 2 of the Free Zone (Southampton) Designation (Variation of Area) Order 1996" signed by a Collector of Customs and Excise and dated 19th March 1996.

3 The map referred to in article 2 above shall be kept by the Commissioners at their Headquarters, New King's Beam House, 22 Upper Ground, London SE1 9PJ (and a copy thereof at the registered office of Southampton Free Trade Zone Limited) in substitution for the map referred to in article 2 of the Free Zone (Southampton) Designation (Variation) Order 1994.

DISTRESS FOR CUSTOMS AND EXCISE DUTIES AND OTHER INDIRECT TAXES REGULATIONS 1997

(SI 1997/1431)

Made on 9 June 1997 by the Commissioners of Customs and Excise, in exercise of the powers conferred on them by s. 51(1), (2) and (3) of the Finance Act 1997 and of all other powers enabling them in that behalf. Operative from 1 July 1997.

CITATION AND COMMENCEMENT

1   These Regulations may be cited as The Distress for Customs and Excise Duties and Other Indirect Taxes Regulations 1997 and shall come into force on 1st July 1997.

INTERPRETATION

2(1)   In these Regulations–

"**authorised person**" means a person acting under the authority of the Commissioners;

"**costs**" means any costs, charges, expenses and fees;

"**officer**" means, subject to section 8(2) of the Customs and Excise Management Act 1979, a person commissioned by the Commissioners pursuant to section 6(3) of that Act;

"**person in default**" means a person who has refused or neglected to pay any relevant tax due from him;

"**relevant tax**" means any of the following–

(a)   any duty of customs or excise, other than vehicle excise duty;

(b)   value added tax;

(c)   insurance premium tax;

(d)   landfill tax;

(e)   any agricultural levy of the European Community;

"**VAT Act**" means the Value Added Tax Act 1994;

"**walking possession agreement**" means an agreement under which, in consideration of any goods and chattels distrained upon being allowed to remain in the custody of the person in default and of the delaying of their sale, that person–

(a)   acknowledges that the goods and chattels specified in the agreement are under distraint and held in walking possession; and

(b)   undertakes that, except with the consent of the Commissioners and subject to such conditions as they may impose, he will not remove or allow the removal of any of the specified goods and chattels from the place named in the agreement;

"**1994 Act**" means Part III of the Finance Act 1994;

"**1996 Act**" means Part III of the Finance Act 1996.

2(2)   Any reference in these Regulations to an amount of **relevant tax** includes a reference to any amount recoverable as if it were an amount of that relevant tax.

REVOCATIONS AND TRANSITIONAL PROVISIONS

3(1)   The Regulations specified in Schedule 3 are hereby revoked to the extent set out there.

3(2)   Where a warrant is signed before the coming into force of these Regulations, these Regulations shall apply to anything done, after these Regulations come into force, in relation to that warrant or as a consequence of distress being levied.

LEVYING DISTRESS

4(1)   Subject to regulation 5 below, if upon written demand a person neglects or refuses to pay any relevant tax due from him an officer may levy distress on the goods and chattels of that person and by warrant signed by him direct any authorised person to levy such distress.

4(2)   Where a warrant has been signed, distress shall be levied by or under the direction of, and in the presence of, the authorised person.

4(3)   Subject to regulation 6 below, distress may be levied on any goods and chattels located at any place whatever including on a public highway.

RESTRICTIONS ON LEVYING DISTRESS

5(1)   Where–

(a)   [not relevant to VAT]

(b)   [not relevant to VAT] or

(c)   [not relevant to VAT],

no distress shall be levied before expiry of the last day on which the person who is liable to pay the amount concerned is required, by rules made under paragraph 9 of Schedule 12 to the VAT Act, to serve a notice of appeal with respect to that decision.

5(2)   Where an amount of VAT is due under section 73(9) of the VAT Act no distress shall be levied before expiry of the last day on which the person who is liable to pay the amount concerned is required, by rules made under paragraph 9 of Schedule 12 to the VAT Act, to serve a notice of appeal with respect to that amount.

GOODS AND CHATTELS NOT SUBJECT TO LEVY

6   No distress shall be levied on any goods and chattels mentioned in Schedule 1 which at the time of levy are located in a place and used for a purpose mentioned in that Schedule.

TIMES FOR LEVYING DISTRESS

7(1)   Subject to paragraph (2) below, a levy of distress shall commence only during the period between eight o'clock in the morning and eight o'clock at night on any day of the week but it may be continued thereafter outside that period until the levy is completed.

7(2)   Where a person holds himself out as conducting any profession, trade or business during hours which are partly within and partly outside, or wholly outside the period mentioned in paragraph (1) above, a levy of distress may be commenced at any time during that period or during the hours of any day in which he holds himself out as conducting that profession, trade or business and it may be continued thereafter outside that period or those hours until the levy is completed.

COSTS

8(1)   A person in respect of whose goods and chattels a warrant has been signed shall be liable to pay to an officer or authorised person all costs, in connection with anything done under these Regulations described in column 1 of Schedule 2, as determined in accordance with column 2 of that Schedule.

8(2)   An authorised person may, after deducting and accounting for the amount of relevant tax to the Commissioners, retain costs from any amount received.

SALE

9   If any person upon whose goods and chattels distress has been levied does not pay the amount of relevant tax due together with costs within 5 days of a levy, an officer or authorised person may sell the distress for payment of the amount of relevant tax and costs; and the officer or authorised person, after deducting and retaining the amount of relevant tax and costs shall restore any surplus to the owner of the goods upon which distress was levied.

DISPUTES AS TO COSTS

10(1)   In the case of any dispute as to costs, the amount of those costs shall be taxed by a district judge of the county court of the district where the distress was levied, and he may make such order as he thinks fit as to the costs of the taxation.

10(2)   In the application of this regulation to Northern Ireland, in the case of any dispute as to costs, the amount of those costs shall be taxed in the same manner as costs in equity suits or proceedings in the county court in Northern Ireland.

SCHEDULES

SCHEDULE 1 – GOODS AND CHATTELS NOT SUBJECT TO LEVY

Regulation 6

1 Any of the following goods and chattels which are located in a dwelling house at which distress is being levied and are reasonably required for the domestic needs of any person residing in that dwelling house–

(a) beds and bedding;

(b) household linen;

(c) chairs and settees;

(d) tables;

(e) food;

(f) lights and light fittings;

(g) heating appliances;

(h) curtains;

(i) floor coverings;

(j) furniture, equipment and utensils used for cooking, storing or eating food;

(k) refrigerators;

(l) articles used for cleaning, mending, or pressing clothes;

(m) articles used for cleaning the home;

(n) furniture used for storing–

(i) clothing, bedding or household linen;

(ii) articles used for cleaning the home;

(iii) utensils used for cooking or eating food;

(o) articles used for safety in the home;

(p) toys for the use of any child within the household;

(q) medical aids and medical equipment.

2 Any of the following items which are located in premises used for the purposes of any profession, trade or business–

(a) fire fighting equipment for use on the premises;

(b) medical aids and medical equipment for use on the premises.

SCHEDULE 2 – SCALE OF COSTS

Regulation 8(1)

Matter (1)	Costs (2)
1 For attending to levy distress where payment is made of an amount of relevant tax due and distress is not levied:	£12.50
2 For levying distress–	
(a) where an amount of relevant tax demanded and due does not exceed £100:	£12.50
(b) where an amount of relevant tax demanded and due exceeds £100:	12½% on the first £100, 4% on the next £400, 2½% on the next £1,500, 1% on the next £8,000, ¼% on any additional sum.

Matter (1)	Costs (2)
3 For taking possession of distrained goods–	
(a) where a person remains in physical possession of goods at the place where distress was levied (the person to provide his own food and lodgings):	£4.50 per day.
(b) where possession is taken under a walking possession agreement:	£7.00
4 For appraising goods upon which distress has been levied:	Reasonable costs of appraisement.
5 For arranging removal and storage of goods upon which distress has been levied:	Reasonable costs of arrangement.
6 For removing and storing goods upon which distress has been levied:	Reasonable costs of removal and storage.
7 For advertising the sale of goods upon which distress has been levied:	Reasonable costs of advertising.
8 For selling the distress–	
(a) where a sale by auction is held at the auctioneer's premises:	15% of the sum realised.
(b) where a sale by auction is held elsewhere:	$7^1/_2$% of the sum realised and the auctioneer's reasonable costs.
(c) where a sale by other means is undertaken:	$7^1/_2$% of the sum realised and reasonable costs.

9 In addition to any amount specified in this scale in respect of the supply of goods or services on which value added tax is chargeable there may be added a sum equivalent to value added tax at the appropriate rate on that amount.

SCHEDULE 3 – REVOCATIONS

Regulation 3(1)

Statutory Instrument Number	Title of Regulation	Extent
SI 1994/1774	The Insurance Premium Tax Regulations 1994	regulation 42
SI 1995/2518	The Value Added Tax Regulations 1995	regulation 212
SI 1996/1527	The Landfill Tax Regulations 1996	regulation 48

VALUE ADDED TAX (REVERSE CHARGE) (ANTI-AVOIDANCE) ORDER 1997

(SI 1997/1523)

Made on 30 June 1997 by the Treasury, in exercise of the powers conferred on them by s. 8(5), (7) and (8) of the Value Added Tax Act 1994 and of all other powers enabling them in that behalf. Operative in accordance with art. 1.

CITATION AND COMMENCEMENT

1 This Order may be cited as the Value Added Tax (Reverse Charge) (Anti-avoidance) Order 1997 and shall apply in relation to any services performed on or after 1st July 1997.

INTERPRETATION

2 In this Order–

"**the Act**" means the Value Added Tax Act 1994;

"**the Regulations**" means the Value Added Tax Regulations 1995;

"**relevant telecommunications services**" means services within the description which by virtue of this Order is inserted as paragraph 7A of Schedule 5 to the Act;

"**relevant period**" means such part of a period over which relevant telecommunications services are performed as falls after 30th June 1997;

"**a supply of relevant telecommunications services by virtue of a right**" means a supply of relevant telecommunications services performed on or after 1st July 1997 which is made by virtue of the exercise of a right which had been granted before 1st July 1997.

INSERTION OF TELECOMMUNICATIONS SERVICES INTO SCHEDULE 5 TO THE ACT

3(1)   Schedule 5 to the Act shall be amended in accordance with the following paragraphs of this article.

3(2)   [Inserts VATA 1994, Sch. 5, para. 7A.]

3(3)   [Amends VATA 1994, Sch. 5, para. 8.]

3(4)   [Amends VATA 1994, Sch. 5, para. 9.]

MODIFICATION OF THE EFFECT OF REGULATION 82 OF THE REGULATIONS

4(1)   Where a supply of relevant telecommunications services is treated as if it were a taxable supply by virtue of section 8(1) or 43(2B) of the Act, the effect of regulation 82 of the Regulations shall be modified as follows–

(a)   it shall have no effect in relation to relevant telecommunications services which are performed or which, by virtue of article 10 below, are treated as performed before 1st July 1997;

(b)   it shall have no effect in relation to relevant telecommunications services which are wholly chargeable to VAT in another member State;

(c)   where–

    (i)   relevant telecommunications services are performed on or after 1st July 1997; and

    (ii)   a payment in respect of those services has been made before that date,

it shall have effect in relation to those services as if the payment was made on 1st July 1997.

4(2)   Where the circumstances mentioned in paragraph (3) below apply–

(a)   relevant telecommunications services which are paid for on or after 1st July 1997 shall be treated as being supplied only to the extent covered by the lower of–

    (i)   so much of the payment as exceeds the part of the payment for the supply by reference to which VAT is chargeable in another member State; and

    (ii)   so much of the payment as is properly attributable to the relevant period; and

(b)   relevant telecommunications services which are supplied for a consideration which is not in money shall be treated as being supplied only to the extent covered by the lower of–

    (i)   so much of the consideration as exceeds the part of the consideration for the supply by reference to which VAT is chargeable in another member State; and

    (ii)   so much of the consideration as is properly attributable to the relevant period.

4(3)   The circumstances referred to in paragraph (2) above and article 7 below are that–

(a)   relevant telecommunications services are performed on or after 1st July 1997; and

(b)   either–

    (i)   the services are chargeable to VAT in part in another member State; or

    (ii)   the period over which the services are performed commenced before 1st July 1997.

TREATMENT OF A RIGHT TO RELEVANT TELECOMMUNICATIONS SERVICES

5(1)   Subject to article 6 below, where the circumstances mentioned in article 8(3) below apply the time at which and extent to which a supply of relevant telecommunications services by virtue of a right is to be treated as made shall be determined as if the supply of relevant telecommunications services and the right were a single supply of which the supply of the right and each of those supplies constituted different parts.

5(2) Without prejudice to the generality of paragraph (1) above, the payment for a right to relevant telecommunications services or the consideration for that right, as the case may be, shall, for the purposes of article 4 above, be treated as if it were the payment or the consideration for the relevant telecommunications services supplied by virtue of the right.

RIGHTS NOT EXERCISED BEFORE 1ST JULY 1997

6 Where–

(a)   the circumstances mentioned in article 8(3) below apply;

(b)   a right to relevant telecommunications services is exercised on or after 1st July 1997;

(c)   the consideration for the right was in money; and

(d)   a payment in respect of the right was made before 1st July 1997,

the payment shall be deemed to have been made at the time of the exercise of the right.

VALUE OF SUPPLY OF RELEVANT TELECOMMUNICATIONS SERVICES

7 Where the circumstances mentioned in article 4(3) above apply, the effect of paragraph 8 of Schedule 6 to the Act shall be modified so that the value of the supply treated as made shall be taken–

(a)   in a case where the consideration for which the relevant telecommunications services were in fact supplied was a consideration in money, to be such amount as is equal to the lower of–

    (i)   so much of the consideration as exceeds the part of the consideration for the supply by reference to which VAT is chargeable in another member State; and

    (ii)   so much of the consideration as is properly attributable to the relevant period; and

(b)   in a case where that consideration did not consist or not wholly consist of money, to be such amount in money as is equivalent to the lower of–

    (i)   so much of the consideration as exceeds the part of the consideration for the supply by reference to which VAT is chargeable in another member State; and

    (ii)   so much of the consideration as is properly attributable to the relevant period.

VALUE OF RELEVANT TELECOMMUNICATIONS SERVICES SUPPLIED BY VIRTUE OF A RIGHT

8(1) For the purposes of paragraph 8 of Schedule 6 to the Act and article 7 above, where the circumstances mentioned in paragraph (3) below apply, the consideration for which the relevant telecommunications services were in fact supplied shall be deemed to be the higher of–

(a)   the consideration for which the services were in fact received; and

(b)   the lower of–

    (i)   the open market value of the relevant telecommunications services which were in fact supplied which shall be valued as if they had not been supplied by virtue of the right; and

    (ii)   the amount determined in accordance with paragraph (2) below.

8(2) The amount referred to in paragraph (1)(b)(ii) above is the sum of–

(a)   the consideration for which the relevant telecommunications services were in fact supplied; and

(b)   the consideration for the right to those services, reduced by the open market value of the right to the relevant telecommunications services which shall be valued as if the right was a right to those services to be supplied at the open market value for those services determined in accordance with paragraph (1)(b)(i) above.

8(3) The circumstances referred to in paragraph (1) above are that–

(a)   there is a supply of relevant telecommunications services by virtue of a right; and

(b)   the consideration for the relevant telecommunications services which were in fact supplied is less than the open market value of those services which shall be valued as if they had not been supplied by virtue of the right.

MEANING OF A RIGHT TO RELEVANT TELECOMMUNICATIONS SERVICES

9 References in this Order to a **right to relevant telecommunications services** include references to any right, option or priority with respect to a supply of relevant telecommunications services, and to any interest deriving from any right to relevant telecommunications services.

TIME WHEN RELEVANT TELECOMMUNICATIONS SERVICES ARE TREATED AS PERFORMED

10(1) For the purposes of this Order relevant telecommunications services which are supplied for a consideration the whole or part of which is determined or payable periodically or from time to time or in respect of which statements or invoices are issued periodically or from time to time, shall be treated as performed on the expiration of the period to which a payment, statement or invoice (as the case may be) relates.

10(2) Where paragraph (1) above applies the services shall be treated as performed to the extent covered by the payment, citation or invoice.

VALUE ADDED TAX (REFUND OF TAX) ORDER 1997

(SI 1997/2558)

Made on 27 October 1997 by the Treasury, in exercise of the powers conferred on them by s. 33(3) of the Value Added Tax Act 1994 and of all other powers enabling them in that behalf. Operative from 1 December 1997.

1 This Order may be cited as the Value Added Tax (Refund of Tax) Order 1997 and shall come into force on 1 December 1997.

2 The following bodies are hereby specified for the purposes of section 33 of the Value Added Tax Act 1994:

charter trustees established by an Order made under section 17 of the Local Government Act 1992 or by any other statutory instrument made under Part II of that Act.

AIR PASSENGER DUTY AND OTHER INDIRECT TAXES (INTEREST RATE) REGULATIONS 1998

(SI 1998/1461 as amended by SI 2000/631)

Made on 15 June 1998 by the Treasury, in exercise of the powers conferred on them by s. 197 of the Finance Act 1996 and of all other powers enabling them in that behalf. Operative from 6 July 1998.

CITATION AND COMMENCEMENT

1 These Regulations may be cited as the Air Passenger Duty and Other Indirect Taxes (Interest Rate) Regulations 1998 and shall come into force on 6th July 1998 in relation to interest accruing on or after that date.

INTERPRETATION

2(1) In these Regulations unless the context otherwise requires:

"**established rate**" means–

(a)   on the coming into force of these Regulations, 6 per cent per annum; and

(b)   in relation to any day after the first reference day after the coming into force of these Regulations, the reference rate found on the immediately preceding reference day;

"**operative day**" means the sixth day of each month;

"**reference day**" means the twelfth working day before the next operative day;

"**section 197**" means section 197 of the Finance Act 1996;

"**the relevant enactments**" are those referred to in regulations 4(1) and 5(1) below;

"**working day**" means any day other than a non-business day within the meaning of section 92 of the Bills of Exchange Act 1882.

2(2) In these Regulations **the reference rate** found on a reference day is the percentage per annum found by averaging the base lending rates at close of business on that day of–

(a) Bank of Scotland,

(b) Barclays Bank plc.,

(c) Lloyds Bank plc.,

(d) HSBC Bank plc.,

(e) National Westminster Bank plc., and

(f) The Royal Bank of Scotland plc.

and, if the result is not a whole number, rounding the result to the nearest such number, with any result midway between two whole numbers rounded down.

History – In reg. 2(1)(a), the words "6 per cent" were substituted for the words "7 per cent" by SI 2000/631, reg. 3(a), operative from 1 April 2000.
In reg. 2(2)(d), the words "HSBC Bank plc." were substituted for the words "Midland Bank plc." by SI 2000/631, reg. 3(b), operative from 1 April 2000.

3 [Revokes SI 1997/1016.]

APPLICABLE RATE OF INTEREST PAYABLE TO THE COMMISSIONERS OF CUSTOMS AND EXCISE IN CONNECTION WITH EXCISE DUTIES, INSURANCE PREMIUM TAX, VAT, LANDFILL TAX, AND CUSTOMS DUTY

4(1) For the purposes of–

(a) [neither relevant nor reproduced],

(b) [neither relevant nor reproduced],

(c) section 74 of the Value Added Tax Act 1994, and

(d) [neither relevant nor reproduced],

(e) [neither relevant nor reproduced], and

(f) [neither relevant nor reproduced],

the rate applicable under section 197 shall, subject to paragraph (2) below, be 8.5 per cent per annum.

4(2) Where on any reference day after the coming into force of these Regulations, the reference rate found on that day differs from the established rate, the rate applicable under section 197 of the Finance Act 1996 for the purposes of the enactments referred to in paragraph (1) above shall, from the next operative day, be the percentage per annum determined in accordance with the formula specified in paragraph (3) below.

4(3) The formula specified in this paragraph is–

$$RR + 2.5,$$

where–

RR is the reference rate referred to in paragraph (2) above.

History – Reg. 4 was substituted by SI 2000/631, reg. 4, operative from 1 April 2000. Former reg. 4 and its heading read as follows:

> "APPLICABLE RATE OF INTEREST PAYABLE TO THE COMMISSIONERS OF CUSTOMS AND EXCISE IN CONNECTION WITH AIR PASSENGER DUTY, INSURANCE PREMIUM TAX, VAT RECOVERED OR RECOVERABLE BY ASSESSMENT AND LANDFILL TAX
>
> **4(1)** For the purposes of–
> (a) [neither relevant nor reproduced],
> (b) [neither relevant nor reproduced],
> (c) section 74 of the Value Added Tax Act 1994, and
> (d) [neither relevant nor reproduced],
> the rate applicable under section 197 shall, subject to paragraph (2) below, be 9.5 per cent per annum.
> **4(2)** Where on any reference day after the coming into force of these Regulations, the reference rate found on that day differs from the established rate, the rate applicable under section 197 of the Finance Act 1996 for the purposes of the enactments referred to in paragraph (1) above shall, from the next operative day, be the percentage per annum determined in accordance with the formula specified in paragraph (3) below.
> **4(3)** The formula specified in this paragraph is–
>
> $$RR + 2.5,$$
>
> where–
> RR is the reference rate referred to in paragraph (2) above."

APPLICABLE RATE OF INTEREST PAYABLE BY THE COMMISSIONERS OF CUSTOMS AND EXCISE IN CONNECTION WITH AIR PASSENGER DUTY, INSURANCE PREMIUM TAX, VAT, LANDFILL TAX AND CUSTOMS DUTY

5(1)   For the purposes of–

(a)   [neither relevant nor reproduced],

(b)   [neither relevant nor reproduced],

(c)   section 78 of the Value Added Tax Act 1994,

(d)   [neither relevant nor reproduced],

(e)   [neither relevant nor reproduced],

(f)   [neither relevant nor reproduced],

the rate applicable under section 197 of the Finance Act 1996 shall be 5 per cent per annum.

5(2)   Where, on a reference day after the coming into force of these Regulations, the reference rate found on that date differs from the established rate, the rate applicable under section 197 for the purposes of the enactments referred to in paragraph (1) above shall, from the next operative day, be the percentage per annum determined in accordance with the formula specified in paragraph (3) below.

5(3)   The formula specified in this paragraph is–

$$RR - 1,$$

where–

RR is the reference rate referred to in paragraph (2) above.

History – Reg. 5 was substituted by SI 2000/631, reg. 5, operative from 1 April 2000. Former reg. 5 and its heading read as follows:

> "APPLICABLE RATE OF INTEREST PAYABLE BY THE COMMISSIONERS OF CUSTOMS AND EXCISE IN CONNECTION WITH AIR PASSENGER DUTY, INSURANCE PREMIUM TAX, CASES OF OFFICIAL ERROR IN RELATION TO VAT AND LANDFILL TAX
>
> **5(1)**   For the purposes of–
> (a)   [neither relevant nor reproduced],
> (b)   paragraph 22 of Schedule 7 to that Act,
> (c)   section 78 of the Value Added Tax Act 1994, and
> (d)   paragraph 29 of Schedule 5 to the Finance Act 1996,
> the rate applicable under section 197 of the Finance Act 1996 shall be 6 per cent per annum.
> **5(2)**   Where, on a reference day after the coming into force of these Regulations, the reference rate found on that date differs from the established rate, the rate applicable under section 197 for the purposes of the enactments referred to in paragraph (1) above shall, from the next operative day, be the percentage per annum determined in accordance with the formula specified in paragraph (3) below.
> **5(3)**   The formula specified in this paragraph is–
>
> $$RR - 1,$$
>
> where–
> RR is the reference rate referred to in paragraph (2) above."

EFFECT OF CHANGE IN APPLICABLE RATE

6   Where the rate applicable under section 197 for the purposes of any of the relevant enactments changes on an operative day by virtue of these Regulations, that change shall have effect for periods beginning on or after the operative day in relation to interest running from before that day as well as in relation to interest running from, or from after that day.

7   Where the rate applicable under section 197 for the purposes of any of the relevant enactments changes on an operative day by virtue of these Regulations, the rate in force immediately prior to any change shall continue to have effect for periods immediately prior to the change and so on in the case of any number of successive changes.

APPLICABLE RATE OF INTEREST PRIOR TO THE COMING INTO FORCE OF THESE REGULATIONS

8   The rate applicable under section 197 for interest running from before the date these regulations come into force in relation to periods prior to that date shall be that specified for the relevant *enactments in the following Tables*–

MINIMUM AMOUNT OF INTEREST PAYABLE IN CONNECTION WITH CUSTOMS DUTY

9   [neither relevant nor reproduced].

History – Reg. 9 was inserted by SI 2000/631, reg. 7, operative from 1 April 2000.

TABLE 1

[Neither relevant nor reproduced.]

TABLE 2

Paragraph 21 of Schedule 7 to the Finance Act 1994

Interest for any period	Rate %
from 1st October 1994 and before 6th February 1996	5.5
after 5th February 1996 and before 6th July 1998	6.25

TABLE 3

Section 74 of the Value Added Tax Act 1994

Interest for any period	Rate %
from 1st April 1990 and before 6th November 1990	13
after 5th November 1990 and before 6th March 1991	12.25
after 5th March 1991 and before 6th May 1991	11.5
after 5th May 1991 and before 6th July 1991	10.75
after 5th July 1991 and before 6th October 1991	10
after 5th October 1991 and before 6th November 1992	9.25
after 5th November 1992 and before 6th December 1992	7.75
after 5th December 1992 and before 6th March 1993	7
after 5th March 1993 and before 6th January 1994	6.25
after 5th January 1994 and before 6th October 1994	5.5
after 5th October 1994 and before 6th March 1995	6.25
after 5th March 1995 and before 6th February 1996	7
after 5th February 1996 and before 6th July 1998	6.25

TABLE 4

Paragraph 26 of Schedule 5 to the Finance Act 1996

Interest for any period	Rate %
from 1st April 1997 and before 6th July 1998	6.25

TABLE 5

[Neither relevant nor reproduced.]

TABLE 6

Paragraph 22 of Schedule 7 to the Finance Act 1994

Interest for any period	Rate %
after 1st October 1994 and before 1st April 1997	8
after 31st March 1997 and before 6th July 1998	6

TABLE 7

Section 78 of the Value Added Tax Act 1994

History – In Table 7 of reg. 8, the words "16th October 1991" were substituted for the words "16th October 1992" by SI 2000/631, reg. 6, operative from 1 April 2000.

Interest for any period	Rate %
from 1st April 1973 and before 1st March 1974	8
after 28th February 1974 and before 1st February 1977	9
after 31st January and before 1st March 1979	10
after 28th February 1979 and before 1st January 1980	12.5
after 31st December 1979 and before 1st January 1981	15
after 31st December 1980 and before 1st December 1981	12.5
after 30th November 1981 and before 1st March 1982	15
after 28th February 1982 and before 1st July 1982	14
after 30th June 1982 and before 1st April 1983	13
after 31st March 1983 and before 1st April 1984	12.5
after 31st March 1984 and before 1st August 1986	12
after 31st July 1986 and before 1st January 1987	11.5
after 31st December 1986 and before 1st April 1987	12.25
after 31st March 1987 and before 1st November 1987	11.75
after 31st October 1987 and before 1st December 1987	11.25
after 30th November 1987 and before 1st May 1988	11
after 30th April 1988 and before 1st August 1988	9.5
after 31st July 1988 and before 1st November 1988	11
after 31st October 1988 and before 1st January 1989	12.25
after 31st December 1988 and before 1st November 1989	13
after 31st October 1989 and before 1st April 1991	14.25
after 31st March 1991 and before 16th October 1991	12
after 15th October 1991 and before 6th February 1993	10.25
after 5th February 1993 and before 1st April 1997	8
after 31st March 1997 and before 6th July 1998	6

TABLE 8

Paragraph 29 of Schedule 5 to the Finance Act 1996

Interest for any period	Rate %
from 1st April 1997 and before 6th July 1998	6

CIVIL PROCEDURE RULES 1998

(SI 1998/3132, as amended by SI 1999/1008)

Made on 10 December 1998 by the Civil Procedure Rule Committee under s. 2 of the Civil Procedure Act 1997. Operative from 26 April 1999.

PART 50 – APPLICATION OF THE SCHEDULES

50(1) The Schedules to these Rules set out, with modifications, certain provisions previously contained in the Rules of the Supreme Court 1965 and the County Court Rules 1981.

50(2) These Rules apply in relation to the proceedings to which the Schedules apply subject to the provisions in the Schedules and the relevant practice directions.

50(3) A provision previously contained in the Rules of the Supreme Court 1965–

(a)   is headed "RSC";

(b)   is numbered with the Order and rule numbers it bore as part of the RSC; and

(c)   unless otherwise stated in the Schedules or the relevant practice direction, applies only to proceedings in the High Court.

50(4)   A provision previously contained in the County Court Rules 1981

(a)   is headed "CCR";

(b)   is numbered with the Order and rule numbers it bore as part of the CCR; and

(c)   unless otherwise stated in the Schedules or the relevant practice direction, applies only to proceedings in the county court.

50(5)   A reference in a Schedule to a rule by number alone is a reference to the rule so numbered in the Order in which the reference occurs.

50(6)   A reference in a Schedule to a rule by number prefixed by "CPR" is a reference to the rule with that number in these Rules.

50(7)   In the Schedules, unless otherwise stated,

"the Act" means–

(a)   in a provision headed "RSC", the Supreme Court Act 1981; and

(b)   in a provision headed "CCR", the County Courts Act 1984.

SCHEDULE 1 –

RSC ORDER 45 – ENFORCEMENT OF JUDGMENTS AND ORDERS: GENERAL

ENFORCEMENT OF DECISIONS OF VALUE ADDED TAX TRIBUNALS

14(1)   An application under section 29 of the Finance Act 1985 [VATA 1994, s. 87] for registration of a decision of a Value Added Tax Tribunal on an appeal under section 83 of the Value Added Tax Act 1994 shall be made by a request in writing to the head clerk of the Crown Office–

(a)   exhibiting the decision or a duly authenticated copy thereof;

(b)   stating, so far as is known to the witness, the name and occupation and the usual or last known address or place of business of the person against whom it is sought to enforce the decision; and

(c)   stating, to the best of the information and belief of the witness, the amount which as a result of the decision is, or is recoverable as, tax from such person at the date of the application and the amount then remaining unpaid of any costs awarded to the Commissioners of Customs and Excise by the decision.

14(2)   Notice of the registration of a decision must be served on the person against whom it is sought to enforce the decision by delivering it to him personally or by sending it to him at his usual or last known address or place of business or in such manner as the Court may direct.

14(3)   There shall be kept in the Central Office under the direction of the Senior Master a register of the decisions registered under section 29 of the Finance Act 1985 [VATA 1994, s. 87], and there shall be included in the register particulars of any execution issued on a decision so registered.

RSC ORDER 55 – APPEALS TO HIGH COURT FROM COURT, TRIBUNAL OR PERSON: GENERAL

APPLICATION

1(1)   Subject to paragraphs (2), (3) and (4), this Order shall apply to every appeal which by or under any enactment lies to the High Court from any court, tribunal or person.

1(2)   This Order shall not apply to an appeal by case stated or to any appeal to which the Arbitration Practice Direction applies.

1(3)   The following rules of this Order shall not apply to an appeal from a county court to a single judge under section 375 of the Insolvency Act 1986, but subject to the Insolvency Rules 1986, as amended, Order 59 shall, with the necessary modifications, apply to such an appeal as it applies to an appeal from a county court to the Court of Appeal.

1(4)   The following rules of this Order shall, in relation to an appeal to which this Order applies, have effect subject to any provision made in relation to that appeal by any other provision of these rules or by or under any enactment.

1(5)   In this Order references to a **"tribunal"** shall be construed as references to any tribunal constituted by or under any enactment other than any of the ordinary courts of law.

COURT TO HEAR APPEAL

2   Except where it is otherwise provided by these rules or by or under any enactment, an appeal to which this Order applies shall be assigned to the Queen's Bench Division and shall be heard and determined–

  (a) here the decision of the High Court on the appeal is final, by a Divisional Court, and

  (b) in any other case, by a single judge.

BRINGING AN APPEAL

3(1)   An appeal to which this Order applies shall be by way of rehearing and must be brought by notice of appeal.

3(2)   Every notice by which such an appeal is brought must state the grounds of the appeal and, if the appeal is against a judgment, order or other decision of a court, must state whether the appeal is against the whole or a part of that decision and, if against a part only, must specify the part.

3(3)   The bringing of such an appeal shall not operate as a stay of proceedings on the judgment, determination or other decisions against which the appeal is brought unless the Court by which the appeal is to be heard or the court, tribunal or person by which or by whom the decision was given so orders.

SERVICE OF NOTICE OF APPEAL AND ENTRY OF APPEAL

4(1)   The persons to be served with the notice of appeal are the following–

(a) if the appeal is against a judgment, order or other decision of a court, the registrar or clerk of the court and any party to the proceedings in which the decision was given who is directly affected by the appeal;

(b) if the appeal is against an order, determination, award or other decision of a tribunal, Minister of the Crown, government department or other person, the chairman of the tribunal, Minister, government department or person, as the case may be, and every party to the proceedings (other than the appellant) in which the decision appealed against was given.

4(2)   The notice must be served, and the appeal entered, within 28 days after the date of the judgment, order, determination or other decision against which the appeal is brought.

4(3)   In the case of an appeal against a judgment, order or decision of a court, the period specified in paragraph (2) shall be calculated from the date of the judgment or order or the date on which the decision was given.

4(4)   In the case of an appeal against an order, determination, award or other decision of a tribunal, Minister, government department or other person, the period specified in paragraph (2) shall be calculated from the date on which notice of the decision, or, in a case where a statement of the reasons for a decision was given later than such notice, on which such a statement was given to the appellant by the person who made the decision or by a person authorised in that behalf to do so.

History – In r. 4(1), the words "the notice of appeal" were substituted for the words "notice of the motion by which an appeal to which this Order applies is brought" by SI 1999/1008, r. 1, 34, operative from 26 April 1999.

DATE OF HEARING OF APPEAL

5   Unless the Court having jurisdiction to determine the appeal otherwise directs, an appeal to which this Order applies shall not be heard sooner than 21 days after service of notice of the motion by which the appeal is brought.

AMENDMENT OF GROUNDS OF APPEAL, ETC.

6(1)   The notice by which an appeal to which this Order applies is brought may be amended by the appellant, without permission, by supplementary notice served not less than 7 days before the day appointed for the hearing of the appeal, on each of the persons on whom the notice to be amended was served.

6(2)   Within 2 days after service of a supplementary notice under paragraph (1) the appellant must file two copies of the notice in the office in which the appeal is entered.

6(3) Except with the permission of the Court hearing any such appeal, no grounds other than those stated in the notice by which the appeal is brought or any supplementary notice under paragraph (1) may be relied upon by the appellant at the hearing; but that Court may amend the grounds so stated or make any other order, on such terms as it thinks just, to ensure the determination on the merits of the real question in controversy between the parties.

INTERLOCUTORY APPLICATIONS

6A(1) Unless the Court otherwise directs, any interlocutory application in proceedings to which this Order applies may be made to any Judge or a Master of the Queen's Bench Division or, as the case may be, any Judge or a District Judge of the Family Division, notwithstanding that the appeal is to be heard by a Divisional Court. In this paragraph **"interlocutory application"** includes an application for the extension of time for the service of the notice of appeal or the entry of the appeal or for the amendment of the notice of appeal.

6A(2) In relation to an order made by a Master or District Judge pursuant to paragraph (1), Order 58, rule 1 shall, where the appeal is to be heard by a Divisional Court, have effect as if a reference to that Court were substituted for the reference to a Judge sitting in private.

6A(3) This rule is without prejudice to any statutory provision or rule of law restricting the making of an order against the Crown.

History – Rule 6A was added by SI 1987/1423.

POWERS OF COURT HEARING APPEAL

7(1) In addition to the power conferred by rule 6(3) the Court hearing an appeal to which this Order applies shall have the powers conferred by the following provisions of this rule.

7(2) The Court shall have power to receive further evidence on questions of fact, and the evidence may be given in such manner as the Court may direct either by oral examination in Court, by witness statement or affidavit, by deposition taken before an examiner or in some other manner.

7(3) The Court shall have power to draw any inferences of fact which might have been drawn in the proceedings out of which the appeal arose.

7(4) It shall be the duty of the appellant to apply to the Judge or other person presiding at the proceedings in which the decision appealed against was given for a signed copy of any note made by him of the proceedings and to furnish that copy for the use of the Court; and in default of production of such a note, or if such note is incomplete, in addition to such note, the Court may hear and determine the appeal on any other evidence or statement of what occurred in those proceedings as appears to the Court to be sufficient. Except where the Court otherwise directs, a witness statement or affidavit or note by a person present at the proceedings shall not be used in evidence under this paragraph unless it was previously submitted to the person presiding at the proceedings for his comments.

7(5) The Court may give any judgment or decision or make any order which ought to have been given or made by the Court, tribunal or person and make such further or other order as the case may require or may remit the matter with the opinion of the Court for rehearing and determination by it or him.

7(6) The Court may, in special circumstances, order that such security shall be given for the costs of the appeal as may be just.

7(7) The Court shall not be bound to allow the appeal on the ground merely of misdirection, or of the improper admission or rejection of evidence, unless in the opinion of the Court substantial wrong or miscarriage has been thereby occasioned.

RIGHT OF MINISTER, ETC., TO APPEAR AND BE HEARD

8 Where an appeal to which this Order applies is against an order, determination or other decision of a Minister of the Crown or government department, the Minister or department, as the case may be, shall be entitled to appear and be heard in the proceedings on the appeal.

RSC ORDER 59 – APPEALS TO THE COURT OF APPEAL

APPEALS FROM VALUE ADDED TAX TRIBUNALS

22(1) An application to the Court of Appeal for permission to appeal from a value added tax tribunal direct to that Court under section 26 of the Finance Act 1985 [VATA 1994, s. 87] shall be made within 28 days from the date on which the tribunal certifies that its decision involves a point of law relating wholly or mainly to the construction of an enactment or of a statutory instrument, or of any of the Community Treaties or any Community Instrument, which has been fully argued before it and fully considered by it.

22(2) Such an application shall be made by the parties jointly by filing a copy of the decision, endorsed with the certificate of the tribunal and a statement of the grounds of the application, with the court, and shall be determined by a single judge of the Court of Appeal, who may do so without a hearing.

22(3) In the case of all applications, the Court shall notify the parties of the determination of the single judge, and

(a)   where permission to appeal to the Court of Appeal is granted, the appellant shall within 14 days after such notification serve the notice of appeal on the chairman of the tribunal as well as on the party or parties required to be served by rule 3;

(b)   where permission to appeal to the Court of Appeal is refused, the period specified in Order 55, rule 4(2) for appealing to the High Court shall be calculated from the date of notification of the refusal.

RSC ORDER 77 – PROCEEDINGS BY AND AGAINST THE CROWN

SUMMARY APPLICATIONS TO THE COURT IN CERTAIN REVENUE MATTERS

8(1) This rule applies to applications under section 14 of the Crown Proceedings Act 1947.

8(2) An application to which this rule applies shall be made by claim form.

8(3) The person from whom any account or information or payment is claimed or by whom any books are required to be produced must be made a defendant to the application.

8(4) A claim form under this rule–

(a)   must be entitled in the matter or matters out of which the need for the application arises and in the matter of the Crown Proceedings Act 1947; and

(b)   must refer to the enactment under which the account or information or payment or the production of books is claimed and, where information is claimed, must show (by appropriate questions or otherwise) what information is required.

8(5) Upon any application to which this rule applies, a witness statement or affidavit by a duly authorised officer of the Government department concerned setting out the state of facts upon which the application is based and stating that he has reason to think that those facts exist shall be evidence of those facts; and if evidence is filed disputing any of those facts, further evidence may be filed and the Court may either decide the matter upon the witness statements or affidavits (after any cross-examination that may have been ordered) or may direct that it be decided by oral evidence in Court.

8(6) An order in favour of the Crown on an application to which this rule applies shall, unless the Court otherwise determines, name a time within which each of its terms is to be complied with.

8(8) Nothing in this rule shall, in relation to any case in which the only remedy claimed by the Crown is the payment of money, be construed as requiring the Crown to proceed by way of an application to which this rule applies or as preventing the Crown from availing itself of any other procedure which is open to it under these rules.

JOINDER OF COMMISSIONERS OF INLAND REVENUE

8A Nothing in CPR rule 19.3 shall be construed as enabling the Commissioners of Inland Revenue to be added as a party to any proceedings except with their consent signified in writing or in such manner as may be authorised.

History – Rule 8A was added by SI 1971/1269.

RSC ORDER 91 – REVENUE PROCEEDINGS

APPEALS FROM VALUE ADDED TAX TRIBUNALS

6(1) A party to proceedings before a value added tax tribunal who is dissatisfied in point of law with a decision of the tribunal may appeal under section 11(1) of the Tribunals and Inquiries Act 1992 to the High Court and Order 94, rule 9 shall not apply in relation to such an appeal.

6(2) Such an appeal shall be heard and determined by a single judge of the Chancery Division.

6(3) Order 55, rule 4(2) shall apply in relation to any such appeal as if for the period of 28 days specified in that rule there were substituted a period of 56 days, except where the appeal is made following the refusal of the Value Added Tax Tribunal to grant a certificate under article 2(b) of the Value Added Tax Tribunal Appeals Order 1986.

6(3A) Where the tribunal has refused to grant a certificate under article 2(b) of the Value Added Tax Tribunal Appeals Order 1986, the 28 day period mentioned in Order 55, rule 4(2) shall be calculated from the date of the release of the decision of the tribunal containing the refusal.

6(4) This rule is without prejudice to the right of the parties to appeal direct to the Court of Appeal in accordance with Order 59, rule 22.

History – In r. 6(2), the words "by a single judge of the Queen's Bench Division or, where both parties consent," which appeared after the words "heard and determined" were omitted by SI 1999/1008, r. 1, 45, operative from 26 April 1999. R. 6(3A) was added by SI 1987/2206.

RSC ORDER 94 – APPLICATIONS AND APPEALS TO HIGH COURT UNDER VARIOUS ACTS: QUEEN'S BENCH DIVISION

TRIBUNALS AND INQUIRIES ACT 1992: APPEAL FROM TRIBUNAL

8(1) A person who was a party to proceedings before any such tribunal as is mentioned in section 1(1) of the Tribunals and Inquiries Act 1992 and is dissatisfied in point of law with the decision of the tribunal may appeal to the High Court.

8(2) Order 55, rule 4(1)(b) shall apply in relation to such an appeal as if for the reference to the chairman of a tribunal there were substituted–

(a)   in the case of a tribunal which has no chairman or member who acts as a chairman, a reference to the member or members of the tribunal, and

(b)   in the case of any such tribunal as is specified in paragraph 16 of Schedule 1 to the said Act of 1992, a reference to the secretary of the tribunal.

8(3) Where such an appeal is against the decision of –

(a)   the tribunal constituted under section 46 of the National Health Service Act 1977, or

(b)   a tribunal established under section 1 of the Industrial Tribunals Act 1996,

Order 55, rule 4 (2) shall apply in relation to the appeal as if for the period of 28 days therein specified there were substituted, in the case of the tribunal mentioned in sub-paragraph (a) a period of 14 days and, in the case of a tribunal mentioned in sub-paragraph (b) a period of 42 days.

TRIBUNALS AND INQUIRIES ACT 1992: CASE STATED BY TRIBUNAL

9(1) Any such tribunal as is mentioned in section 11(1) of the Tribunals and Inquiries Act 1992 may, of its own initiative or at the request of any party to proceedings before it, state in the course of proceedings before it in the form of a special case for the decision of the High Court any question of law arising in the proceedings.

9(2) Any party to proceedings before any such tribunal who is aggrieved by the tribunal's refusal to state such a case may apply to the High Court for an order directing the tribunal to do so.

9(3) A case stated by any such tribunal which has no chairman or member who acts as a chairman must be signed by the member or members of the tribunal.

VALUE ADDED TAX (REFUND OF TAX) ORDER 1999

(SI 1999/2076)

Made on 21 July 1999 by the Treasury under section 33(3) of the Value Added Tax Act 1994 and of all other powers enabling them in that behalf. Operative from 1 September 1999.

1 This Order may be cited as the Value Added Tax (Refund of Tax) Order 1999 and shall come into force on 1st September 1999.

2 The Broads Authority (a body corporate established by section 1 of the Norfolk and Suffolk Broads Act 1988) is hereby specified for the purposes of section 33 of the Value Added Tax Act 1994.

VALUE ADDED TAX (IMPORTATION OF INVESTMENT GOLD) RELIEF ORDER 1999

(SI 1999/3115)

Made on 19 November 1999 by the Treasury, in exercise of the powers conferred on them by s. 37(1) of the Value Added Tax Act 1994 and s. 13(3) and (4) of the Finance Act 1999 and of all other powers enabling them in that behalf. Operative from 1 January 2000.

1   This Order may be cited as the Value Added Tax (Importation of Investment Gold) Relief Order 1999 and shall come into force on 1st January 2000.

2   In this Order–

"**Investment gold**" has the same meaning as in Group 15 of Schedule 9 to the Value Added Tax Act 1994.

3   VAT shall not be chargeable on the importation of investment gold from places outside the member States.

Official publications – 701/21 and 701/21A.

VALUE ADDED TAX (INVESTMENT GOLD) ORDER 1999

(SI 1999/3116)

Made on 19 November 1999 by the Treasury, in exercise of the powers conferred on them by s. 31(2), 55(6) and 96(9) of the Value Added Tax Act 1994 and s. 13(2) and (4) of the Finance Act 1999 and of all other powers enabling them in that behalf. Operative from 1 January 2000.

CITATION AND COMMENCEMENT

1(1)   This Order may be cited as the Value Added Tax (Investment Gold) Order 1999 and shall come into force on 1st January 2000 and shall have effect in relation to supplies made on or after that date.

1(2)   In this Order–

"**the Commissioners**" means the Commissioners of Customs and Excise;

"**the Act**" means the Value Added Tax Act 1994;

"**relevant supply**" means a supply of investment gold within the meaning of item 1 or 2 of Group 15 of Schedule 9 to the Act made by a taxable person, to another taxable person and "**relevant supplies**" shall be construed accordingly.

EXEMPTION FOR INVESTMENT GOLD

2   [Amended VATA 1994, Sch. 9, Pt. I and inserted Sch. 9, Grp. 15.]

ELECTION TO WAIVE EXEMPTION

3(1)   Subject to paragraphs (2), (6), (7) and (8) below, where an election under this paragraph has effect in relation to a relevant supply by a taxable person who produces or transforms investment gold, which supply would (apart from this paragraph) fall within item 1 or 2 of Group 15 of Schedule 9 to the Act, the supply shall not fall within that Group.

3(2)   An election under paragraph (1) above (or an election having the like effect) or an election under paragraph (5) below shall apply in respect of an individual relevant supply made and shall have effect on or after the day from which the election is made.

3(3)   Subject to complying with such conditions as the Commissioners may direct in notices published by them for the purposes of this Order, the Commissioners may permit a taxable person to make elections in respect of relevant supplies by him of a description falling within paragraph (4) below having the like effect to an election under paragraph (1) above.

3(4)   The supplies referred to in paragraph (3) above are those relevant supplies where the investment gold supplied falls within the description in Note (1)(a) contained in Group 15 of Schedule 9 to the Act, made by a taxable person who in the normal course of his business makes supplies of gold for industrial purposes.

3(5) Subject to paragraphs (6) to (8) below, where a taxable person has made a relevant supply in respect of which an election under paragraph (1) above (or an election having the like effect) has been made, the supply of services by his agent directly linked to the relevant supply and which supply of services would (apart from this paragraph) fall within item 3 of Group 15 of Schedule 9 to the Act shall, if the agent so elects, not fall within that Group.

3(6) A person making a relevant supply in respect of which an election to waive exemption under this article has been made shall comply with such conditions as the Commissioners may specify in notices published by them for the purposes of this Order including conditions relating to the notification of an election.

3(7) An election made under paragraph (1) above (or an election having the like effect) and an election made under paragraph (5) above shall be irrevocable.

3(8) Where the Commissioners have permitted a person to make elections under paragraph (3) above, they may withdraw that permission where it appears to them to be necessary to do so for the protection of the revenue and accordingly the permission shall cease to have effect from such date as may be specified in a notification from the Commissioners.

Cross references – SI 1995/2518, reg. 103A: allowable input tax.

CUSTOMERS TO ACCOUNT FOR TAX ON SUPPLIES OF INVESTMENT GOLD

4 Section 55(1) to (4) of the Act shall apply to all supplies of a description which but for an election made under article 3 above would fall within item 1 or 2 of Group 15 of Schedule 9 to the Act.

Official publications – 701/21 and 701/21A.

VALUE ADDED TAX (INPUT TAX) (SPECIFIED SUPPLIES) ORDER 1999

(SI 1999/3121)

Made on 19 November 1999 by the Treasury, in exercise of the powers conferred on them by s. 26(2)(c) of the Value Added Tax Act 1994 and of all other powers enabling them in that behalf. Operative from 1 January 2000.

1 This Order may be cited as the Value Added Tax (Input Tax) (Specified Supplies) Order 1999 and shall come into force on 1st January 2000 and shall have effect in relation to supplies made on or after that date.

2 The supplies described in articles 3 and 4 below are hereby specified for the purposes of 26(2)(c) of the Value Added Tax Act 1994.

3 Services–

(a)   which are supplied to a person who belongs outside the member States;

(b)   which are directly linked to the export of goods to a place outside the member States; or

(c)   which consist of the provision of intermediary services within the meaning of item 4 of Group 2, or item 5 of Group 5, of Schedule 9 to the Value Added Tax Act 1994 in relation to any transaction specified in paragraph (a) or (b) above,

provided the supply is exempt, or would have been exempt if made in the United Kingdom, by virtue of any item of Group 2, or any of items 1 to 6 and item 8 of Group 5, of Schedule 9 to the Value Added Tax Act 1994.

Official publications – 703; 701/29; 701/36; 701/43; 701/44.

4 Supplies made either in or outside the United Kingdom which fall, or would fall, within item 1 or 2 of Group 15 of Schedule 9 to the Value Added Tax Act 1994 (investment gold).

Official publications – 701/21 and 701/21A.

5 [Revokes SI 1992/3123.]

VALUE ADDED TAX (REFUND OF TAX) ORDER 2000

(SI 2000/1046)

Made on 12 April 2000 by the Treasury, in exercise of the powers conferred on them by s. 33(3) of the Value Added Tax Act 1994 and of all other powers enabling them in that behalf. Operative from 8 May 2000.

1 This Order may be cited as the Value Added Tax (Refund of Tax) Order 2000 and shall come into force on 8 May 2000.

2 The Greater London Authority (a body established by section 1 of the Greater London Authority Act 1992) is specified for the purposes of section 33 of the Value Added Tax Act 1994.

VALUE ADDED TAX (REFUND OF TAX) (NO. 2) ORDER 2000

(SI 2000/1515)

Made on 7 June by the Treasury, in exercise of the powers conferred on them by s. 33(3) of the Value Added Tax Act 1994. Operative from 3 July 2000.

1 This Order may be cited as the Value Added Tax (Refund of Tax) (No. 2) Order 2000 and shall come into force on 3rd July 2000.

2 The London Fire and Emergency Planning Authority (the body corporate reconstituted by section 328 of, and Schedule 28 to, the Greater London Authority Act 1999) is specified for the purposes of section 33 of the Value Added Tax Act 1994.

VAT
EUROPEAN MATERIAL

Table of Contents

> **Note:** Proposals for directives are not reproduced in this volume.
> Not all directives and regulations are reproduced in full text in this division. If a directive or regulation merely amends an existing provision, then the existing provision itself is amended and a history note is added thereto. The amending directive or regulation is not reproduced in this division, but it is listed below together with a note indicating its effect. Similarly, if a directive or regulation merely brings a provision into operation, then it is also listed below together with an appropriate note. If a directive or regulation only partly relates to VAT, only that part is reproduced.

continued over

continued over

TREATY ESTABLISHING THE EUROPEAN COMMUNITY

(25 March 1957)

PART THREE – POLICY OF THE COMMUNITY

Title I – Common Rules

CHAPTER 2 – TAX PROVISIONS

ART. 90   [Internal taxation: imports]

90   No member state shall impose, directly or indirectly, on the products of other member states any internal taxation of any kind in excess of that imposed directly or indirectly on similar domestic products.

Furthermore, no member state shall impose on the products of other member states any internal taxation of such a nature as to afford indirect protection to other products.

History – Art. 90 was formerly art. 95 until it was renumbered by art. 12 of the Amsterdam Treaty (OJ 1997 C340/1), with effect from 1 May 1999.
Art. 95, third paragraph, was deleted by art. 6(I)(52) of the Amsterdam Treaty (OJ 1997 C340/1), with effect from 1 May 1999. That former third paragraph read as follows:
"Member states shall, not later than at the beginning of the second stage, repeal or amend any provisions existing when this treaty enters into force which conflict with the preceding rules."

ART. 91   [Internal taxation: exports]

91   Where products are exported to the territory of any member state, any repayment of internal taxation shall not exceed the internal taxation imposed on them whether directly or indirectly.

History – Art. 91 was formerly art. 96 until it was renumbered by art. 12 of the Amsterdam Treaty (OJ 1997 C340/1), with effect from 1 May 1999.

ART. 97   [Turnover tax: average rates]

97   [Omitted by art. 6(I)(53) of the Amsterdam Treaty (OJ 1997 C340/1), with effect from 1 May 1999.]

History – Former art. 97 read as follows:
"Member states which levy a turnover tax calculated on a cumulative multi-stage tax system may, in the case of internal taxation imposed by them on imported products or of repayments allowed by them on exported products, establish average rates for products or groups of products, provided that there is no infringement of the principles laid down in articles 95 and 96. Where the average rates established by a member state do not conform to these principles, the Commission shall address appropriate directives or decisions to the state concerned."

ART. 92   [Other charges]

92   In the case of charges other than turnover taxes, excise duties and other forms of indirect taxation, remissions and repayments in respect of exports to other member states may not be granted and countervailing charges in respect of imports from member states may not be imposed unless the measures contemplated have been previously approved for a limited period by the Council acting by a qualified majority on a proposal from the Commission.

History – Art. 92 was formerly art. 98 until it was renumbered by art. 12 of the Amsterdam Treaty (OJ 1997 C340/1), with effect from 1 May 1999.

ART. 93   [Indirect taxes harmonisation]

93   The Council shall, acting unanimously on a proposal from the Commission and after consulting the European Parliament and the Economic and Social Committee, adopt provisions for the harmonisation of legislation concerning turnover taxes, excise duties and other forms of indirect taxation to the extent that such harmonisation is necessary to ensure the establishment and the functioning of the internal market within the time-limit laid down in article 7A.

History – Art. 93 was formerly art. 99 until it was renumbered by art. 12 of the Amsterdam Treaty (OJ 1997 C340/1), with effect from 1 May 1999.
Art. 93 was replaced by art. G(D)(20) of the Treaty on European Union (the Maastricht Treaty) (OJ 1992 C191/1), with effect from 1 November 1993.

Note – The date laid down for the completion of the internal market was 31 December 1992.

CHAPTER 3 – APPROXIMATION OF LAWS

ART. 94   **[Removal of barriers to common market]**

94 The Council shall, acting unanimously on a proposal from the Commission and after consulting the European Parliament and the Economic and Social Committee, issue directives for the approximation of such laws, regulations or administrative provisions of the member states as directly affect the establishment or functioning of the common market.

History – Art. 94 was formerly art. 100 until it was renumbered by art. 12 of the Amsterdam Treaty (OJ 1997 C340/1), with effect from 1 May 1999.
Art. 94 was replaced by art. G(D)(21) of the Treaty on European Union (the Maastricht Treaty) (OJ 1992 C191/1), with effect from 1 November 1993.

DIRECTIVE 67/227

First directive on the harmonisation of legislation of member states concerning turnover taxes

(11 April 1967, OJ 1967, Eng. Spec. Ed., p. 14)

The Council of the European Economic Community,

Having regard to the Treaty establishing the European Economic Community, and in particular articles 99 and 100 thereof;

Having regard to the proposal from the Commission;

Having regard to the opinion of the European Parliament;

Having regard to the opinion of the Economic and Social Committee;

[1]   Whereas the main objective of the treaty is to establish, within the framework of an economic union, a common market within which there is healthy competition and whose characteristics are similar to those of a domestic market;

[2]   Whereas the attainment of this objective presupposes the prior application in member states of legislation concerning turnover taxes such as will not distort conditions of competition or hinder the free movement of goods and services within the common market;

[3]   Whereas the legislation at present in force does not meet these requirements; whereas it is therefore in the interest of the common market to achieve such harmonisation of legislation concerning turnover taxes as will eliminate, as far as possible, factors which may distort conditions of competition, whether at national or Community level, and make it possible subsequently to achieve the aim of abolishing the imposition of tax on importation and the remission of tax on exportation in trade between member states;

[4]   Whereas, in the light of the studies made, it has become clear that such harmonisation must result in the abolition of cumulative multi-stage taxes and in the adoption by all member states of a common system of value added tax;

[5]   Whereas a system of value added tax achieves the highest degree of simplicity and of neutrality when the tax is levied in as general a manner as possible and when its scope covers all stages of production and distribution and the provision of services; whereas it is therefore in the interest of the common market and of member states to adopt a common system which shall also apply to the retail trade;

[6]   Whereas, however, the application of that tax to retail trade might in some member states meet with practical and political difficulties; whereas, therefore, member states should be permitted, subject to prior consultation, to apply the common system only up to and including the wholesale trade stage, and to apply, as appropriate, a separate complementary tax at the retail trade stage, or at the preceding stage;

[7]   Whereas it is necessary to proceed by stages, since the harmonisation of turnover taxes will lead in member states to substantial alterations in tax structure and will have appreciable consequences in the budgetary, economic and social fields;

[8]   Whereas the replacement of the cumulative multi-stage tax systems in force in the majority of member states by the common system of value added tax is bound, even if the rates and exemptions are not harmonised at the same time, to result in neutrality in competition, in that within each country similar goods bear the same tax burden, whatever the length of the production and distribution chain, and that in international trade the amount of the tax burden borne by goods is known so that an exact equalisation of that amount may be ensured; whereas, therefore, provision

should be made, in the first stage, for adoption by all member states of the common system of value added tax, without an accompanying harmonisation of rates and exemptions;

[9]   Whereas it is not possible to foresee at present how and within what period the harmonisation of turnover taxes can achieve the aim of abolishing the imposition of tax on importation and the remission of tax on exportation in trade between member states; whereas it is therefore preferable that the second stage and the measures to be taken in respect of that stage should be determined later on the basis of proposals made by the Commission to the Council,

has adopted this directive:

ART. 1   [VAT: common system]

1   Member states shall replace their present system of turnover taxes by the common system of value added tax defined in article 2.

     In each member state the legislation to effect this replacement shall be enacted as rapidly as possible, so that it can enter into force on a date to be fixed by the member state in the light of the conjunctural situation; this date shall not be later than 1 January 1972.

     From the entry into force of such legislation, the member state shall not maintain or introduce any measure providing for flat-rate equalisation of turnover taxes on importation or exportation in trade between member states.

History – In art. 1, the date of 1 January 1972 was substituted for 1 January 1970 by Directive 69/463, art. 1 (OJ 1969(II), Eng. Spec. Ed., p. 551).

ART. 2   [Application]

2   The principle of the common system of value added tax involves the application to goods and services of a general tax on consumption exactly proportional to the price of the goods and services, whatever the number of transactions which take place in the production and distribution process before the stage at which tax is charged.

     On each transaction, value added tax, calculated on the price of the goods or services at the rate applicable to such goods or services, shall be chargeable after deduction of the amount of value added tax borne directly by the various cost components.

     The common system of value added tax shall be applied up to and including the retail trade stage.

History – The fourth paragraph of art. 2 was repealed by Directive 77/388, art. 36 (OJ 1977 L145/1).

ART. 3   [Second directive]

3   The Council shall issue, on a proposal from the Commission, a second directive concerning the structure of, and the procedure for applying, the common system of value added tax.

Note – A second directive (Directive 67/228) was adopted on 11 April 1967. It was superseded by the sixth directive (Directive 77/388); see Directive 77/388, art. 37.

ART. 4   [Harmonisation of turnover taxes: transitional period]

4   In order to enable the Council to discuss this, and if possible to take decisions before the end of the transitional period, the Commission shall submit to the Council, before the end of 1968, proposals as to how and within what period the harmonisation of turnover taxes can achieve the aim of abolishing the imposition of tax on importation and the remission of tax on exportation in trade between member states, while ensuring the neutrality of those taxes as regards the origin of the goods or services.

     In this connection, particular account shall be taken of the relationship between direct and indirect taxes, which differs in the various member states; of the effects of an alteration in tax systems on the tax and budget policy of member states; and of the influence which tax systems have on conditions of competition and on social conditions in the Community.

ART. 5   [Repealed]

5   [Repealed by art. 36 of Directive 77/388.]

ART. 6   [Addressees]

6   This directive is addressed to the member states.

DIRECTIVE 77/388

Sixth directive on the harmonisation of the laws of the member states relating to turnover taxes – common system of value added tax: uniform basis of assessment

(17 May 1977, OJ 1977 L145/1)

The Council of the European Communities,

Having regard to the Treaty establishing the European Economic Community, and in particular articles 99 and 100 thereof,

Having regard to the proposal from the Commission,

Having regard to the opinion of the European Parliament,

Having regard to the opinion of the Economic and Social Committee,

[1] Whereas all member states have adopted a system of value added tax in accordance with the first and second Council directives of 11 April 1967 on the harmonisation of the laws of the member states relating to turnover taxes;

[2] Whereas the decision of 21 April 1970 on the replacement of financial contributions from member states by the Communities' own resources provides that the budget of the Communities shall, irrespective of other revenue, be financed entirely from the Communities' own resources; whereas these resources are to include those accruing from value added tax and obtained by applying a common rate of tax on a basis of assessment determined in a uniform manner according to Community rules;

[3] Whereas further progress should be made in the effective removal of restrictions on the movement of persons, goods, services and capital and the integration of national economies;

[4] Whereas account should be taken of the objective of abolishing the imposition of tax on the importation and the remission of tax on exportation in trade between member states; whereas it should be ensured that the common system of turnover taxes is non-discriminatory as regards the origin of goods and services, so that a common market permitting fair competition and resembling a real internal market may ultimately be achieved;

[5] Whereas, to enhance the non-discriminatory nature of the tax, the term "taxable person" must be clarified to enable the member states to extend it to cover persons who occasionally carry out certain transactions;

[6] Whereas the term "taxable transaction" has led to difficulties, in particular as regards transactions treated as taxable transactions; whereas these concepts must be clarified;

[7] Whereas the determination of the place where taxable transactions are effected has been the subject of conflicts concerning jurisdiction as between member states, in particular as regards supplies of goods for assembly and the supply of services; whereas although the place where a supply of services is effected should in principle be defined as the place where the person supplying the services has his principal place of business, that place should be defined as being in the country of the person to whom the services are supplied, in particular in the case of certain services supplied between taxable persons where the cost of the services is included in the price of the goods;

[8] Whereas the concepts of chargeable event and of the charge to tax must be harmonised if the introduction and any subsequent alterations of the Community rate are to become operative at the same time in all member states;

[9] Whereas the taxable base must be harmonised so that the application of the Community rate to taxable transactions leads to comparable results in all the member states;

[10] Whereas the rates applied by member states must be such as to allow the normal deduction of the tax applied at the preceding stage;

[11] Whereas a common list of exemptions should be drawn up so that the Communities' own resources may be collected in a uniform manner in all the member states;

[12] Whereas the rules governing deductions should be harmonised to the extent that they affect the actual amounts collected; whereas the deductible proportion should be calculated in a similar manner in all the member states;

[13] Whereas it should be specified which persons are liable to pay tax, in particular as regards services supplied by a person established in another country;

[14]   Whereas the obligations of taxpayers must be harmonised as far as possible so as to ensure the necessary safeguards for the collection of taxes in a uniform manner in all the member states; whereas taxpayers should, in particular, make a periodic aggregate return of their transactions, relating to both inputs and outputs where this appears necessary for establishing and monitoring the basis of assessment of own resources;

[15]   Whereas member states should nevertheless be able to retain their special schemes for small undertakings, in accordance with common provisions, and with a view to closer harmonisation; whereas member states should remain free to apply a special scheme involving flat rate rebates of input value added tax to farmers not covered by normal schemes; whereas the basic principles of this scheme should be established and a common method adopted for calculating the value added of these farmers for the purposes of collecting own resources;

[16]   Whereas the uniform application of the provisions of this directive should be ensured; whereas to this end a Community procedure for consultation should be laid down; whereas the setting up of a Value Added Tax Committee would enable the member states and the Commission to co-operate closely;

[17]   Whereas member states should be able, within certain limits and subject to certain conditions, to take or retain special measures derogating from this directive in order to simplify the levying of tax or to avoid fraud or tax avoidance;

[18]   Whereas it might appear appropriate to authorise member states to conclude with non-member countries or international organisations agreements containing derogations from this directive;

[19]   Whereas it is vital to provide for a transitional period to allow national laws in specified fields to be gradually adapted,

has adopted this directive:

Notes – The table of contents below has been prepared by CCH and is not part of the directive.

CONTENTS

TITLE I – INTRODUCTORY PROVISIONS

ART. 1   [Adoption of provisions]

Member states shall modify their present value added tax systems in accordance with the following articles. They shall adopt the necessary laws, regulations and administrative provisions so that the systems as modified enter into force at the earliest opportunity and by 1 January 1978 at the latest.

TITLE II – SCOPE

ART. 2   [Subject to VAT]

The following shall be subject to value added tax:

1   the supply of goods or services effected for consideration within the territory of the country by a taxable person acting as such;
2   the importation of goods.

Cross references – VATA 1994, s. 4, 5: scope of VAT; meaning of supply.

TITLE III – TERRITORIAL APPLICATION

ART. 3   [Territory]

3(1)   For the purposes of this directive–
–   **"territory of a member state"** shall mean the territory of the country as defined in respect of each member state in paragraphs 2 and 3,
–   **"Community"** and **"territory of the Community"** shall mean the territory of the member states as defined in respect of each member state in paragraphs 2 and 3,
–   **"third territory"** and **"third country"** shall mean any territory other than those defined in paragraphs 2 and 3 as the territory of a member state.

3(2)   For the purposes of this directive, the **"territory of the country"** shall be the area of application of the treaty establishing the European Economic Community as defined in respect of each member state in article 227.

3(3)   The following territories of individual member states shall be excluded from the **"territory of the country"**:

–   Federal Republic of Germany:
              the Island of Heligoland,
              the territory of Büsingen,
–   Kingdom of Spain:
              Ceuta,
              Melilla,
–   Republic of Italy:
              Livigno,
              Campione d'Italia,
              the Italian waters of Lake Lugano.

The following territories of individual member states shall also be excluded from the **territory of the country**:

–   Kingdom of Spain:
              the Canary Islands,
–   French Republic:
              the overseas departments,
–   Hellenic Republic
              Αγιο Ορος.

3(4)   By way of derogation from paragraph 1, in view of the conventions and treaties which they have concluded respectively with the French Republic and the United Kingdom of Great Britain and Northern Ireland, the Principality of Monaco and the Isle of Man shall not be treated for the purposes of the application of this directive as third territories.

Member states shall take the measures necessary to ensure that transactions originating in or intended for–

– the Principality of Monaco are treated as transactions originating in or intended for the French Republic;

– the Isle of Man are treated as transactions originating in or intended for the United Kingdom of Great Britain and Northern Ireland.

3(5) If the Commission considers that the provisions laid down in paragraphs 3 and 4 are no longer justified, particularly in terms of fair competition or own resources, it shall submit appropriate proposals to the Council.

History – Art. 3 replaced by Directive 91/680, art. 1(1) (OJ 1991 L376/1).
Member states had to bring into force the measures necessary to comply with this directive no later than 1 January 1997. The former art. 3(2) had been amended by the Act of Accession of the Hellenic Republic, art. 21 and Annex I, Pt. VI, point 3 (OJ 1979 L291/17), Directive 80/368, art. 1 (OJ 1980 L90/41) and the Act of Accession of Spain and Portugal, art. 26 and Annex I, Pt. V, point 2 (OJ 1985 L302/23).
Art. 3(4) replaced by Directive 92/111, art. 1(1) (OJ 1992 L384/47). Member states had to bring into force the measures necessary to implement this directive no later than 1 January 1993.

TITLE IV – TAXABLE PERSONS

ART. 4 [Definitions; taxable persons]

4(1) "Taxable person" shall mean any person who independently carries out in any place any economic activity specified in paragraph 2, whatever the purpose or results of that activity.

4(2) The **economic activities** referred to in paragraph 1 shall comprise all activities of producers, traders and persons supplying services including mining and agricultural activities and activities of the professions. The exploitation of tangible or intangible property for the purpose of obtaining income therefrom on a continuing basis shall also be considered an economic activity.

4(3) Member states may also treat as a taxable person anyone who carries out, on an occasional basis, a transaction relating to the activities referred to in paragraph 2 and in particular one of the following:

(a) the supply before first occupation of buildings or parts of buildings and the land on which they stand; member states may determine the conditions of application of this criterion to transformations of buildings and the land on which they stand.

Member states may apply criteria other than that of first occupation, such as the period elapsing between the date of completion of the building and the date of first supply or the period elapsing between the date of first occupation and the date of subsequent supply, provided that these periods do not exceed five years and two years respectively.

"A building" shall be taken to mean any structure fixed to or in the ground;

(b) the supply of building land.

"Building land" shall mean any unimproved or improved land defined as such by the member states.

4(4) The use of the word "independently" in paragraph 1 shall exclude employed and other persons from the tax in so far as they are bound to an employer by a contract of employment or by any other legal ties creating the relationship of employer and employee as regards working conditions, remuneration and the employer's liability.

Subject to the consultations provided for in article 29, each member state may treat as a single taxable person persons established in the territory of the country who, while legally independent, are closely bound to one another by financial, economic and organisational links.

4(5) States, regional and local government authorities and other bodies governed by public law shall not be considered taxable persons in respect of the activities or transactions in which they engage as public authorities, even where they collect dues, fees, contributions or payments in connection with these activities or transactions.

However, when they engage in such activities or transactions, they shall be considered taxable persons in respect of these activities or transactions where treatment as non-taxable persons would lead to significant distortions of competition.

In any case, these bodies shall be considered taxable persons in relation to the activities listed in Annex D, provided they are not carried out on such a small scale as to be negligible.

Member states may consider activities of these bodies which are exempt under article 13 or 28 as activities which they engage in as public authorities.

Cross references – VATA 1994, s. 3, 4, 33, 41, 43, 94 and Sch. 1, para. 2: taxable person, taxable supply; refunds; state authorities; corporate groups; meaning of business; directions as to single taxable persons.

TITLE V – TAXABLE TRANSACTIONS

ART. 5　Supply of goods

5(1)　**"Supply of goods"** shall mean the transfer of the right to dispose of tangible property as owner.

5(2)　Electric current, gas, heat, refrigeration and the like shall be considered **tangible property**.

5(3)　Member states may consider the following to be **tangible property**:

(a)　certain interest in immovable property;

(b)　rights *in rem* giving the holder thereof a right of user over immovable property;

(c)　shares or interests equivalent to shares giving the holder thereof *de jure* or *de facto* rights of ownership or possession over immovable property or part thereof.

5(4)　The following shall also be considered supplies within the meaning of paragraph 1:

(a)　the transfer, by order made by or in the name of a public authority or in pursuance of the law, of the ownership of property against payment of compensation;

(b)　the actual handing over of goods, pursuant to a contract for the hire of goods for a certain period or for the sale of goods on deferred terms, which provides that in the normal course of events ownership shall pass at the latest upon payment of the final instalment;

(c)　the transfer of goods pursuant to a contract under which commission is payable on purchase or sale.

5(5)　Member states may consider the handing over of certain works of construction to be supplies within the meaning of paragraph 1.

5(6)　The application by a taxable person of goods forming part of his business assets for his private use or that of his staff, or the disposal thereof free of charge or more generally their application for purposes other than those of his business, where the value added tax on the goods in question or the component parts thereof was wholly or partly deductible, shall be treated as supplies made for consideration. However, applications for the giving of samples or the making of gifts of small value for the purposes of the taxable person's business shall not be so treated.

5(7)　Member states may treat as **supplies made for consideration**:

(a)　the application by a taxable person for the purposes of his business of goods produced, constructed, extracted, processed, purchased or imported in the course of such business, where the value added tax on such goods, had they been acquired from another taxable person, would not be wholly deductible;

(b)　the application of goods by a taxable person for the purposes of a non-taxable transaction, where the value added tax on such goods became wholly or partly deductible upon their acquisition or upon their application in accordance with subparagraph (a);

(c)　except in those cases mentioned in paragraph 8, the retention of goods by a taxable person or his successors when he ceases to carry out a taxable economic activity where the value added tax on such goods became wholly or partly deductible upon their acquisition or upon their application in accordance with subparagraph (a).

5(8)　In the event of a transfer, whether for consideration or not or as a contribution to a company, of a totality of assets or part thereof, member states may consider that no supply of goods has taken place and in that event the recipient shall be treated as the successor to the transferor. Where appropriate, member states may take the necessary measures to prevent distortion of competition in cases where the recipient is not wholly liable to tax.

History – Art. 5(5) replaced by Directive 95/7, art. 1(1) (OJ 1995 L102/18). Member states required to bring into force the measures necessary to comply with this directive on 1 January 1996. The former art. 5(5) read as follows:
"**5(5)**　Member states may consider the following to be supplies within the meaning of paragraph 1:
(a)　supplies under a contract to make up work from customer's materials, that is to say delivery by a contractor to his customer of movable property made or assembled by the contractor from materials or objects entrusted to him by the customer for this purpose, whether or not the contractor has provided any part of the materials used;
(b)　the handing over of certain works of construction."

Cross references – *VATA 1994, s. 5(5), 96(1) and Sch. 4*; VAT (Special Provisions) Order 1992 (SI 1992/3129), art. 5: self-supply; interpretation; matters to be treated as supplies of goods or services; supplies not supplies of goods or services. Council Decision 93/204, of 5 April 1993 authorises the UK to apply, until 31 December 1996, a measure derogating from art. 5(8) whereby a supply of goods is deemed to occur where assets, other than the capital goods subject to adjustment of the deductions initially made pursuant to legislation adopted by the UK on the basis of article 20 of the directive, are totally or partially transferred to a company which is a member of a group of enterprises treated as a single taxable person within the meaning of article 4(4) of the directive and which, as a member of that group, is not entitled to deduct tax in full, a provision whereby the company which is the recipient of the supply of assets referred to in the first indent becomes liable to tax.

ART. 6   Supply of services

6(1)   **"Supply of services"** shall mean any transaction which does not constitute a supply of goods within the meaning of article 5.

Such transactions may include *inter alia*:

–   assignments of intangible property whether or not it is the subject of a document establishing title,

–   obligations to refrain from an act or to tolerate an act or situation,

–   the performances of services in pursuance of an order made by or in the name of a public authority or in pursuance of the law.

6(2)   The following shall be treated as **supplies of services for consideration**:

(a)   the use of goods forming part of the assets of a business for the private use of the taxable person or of his staff or more generally for purposes other than those of his business where the value added tax on such goods is wholly or partly deductible;

(b)   supplies of services carried out free of charge by the taxable person for his own private use or that of his staff or more generally for purposes other than those of his business.

Member states may derogate from the provisions of this paragraph provided that such derogation does not lead to distortion of competition.

6(3)   In order to prevent distortion of competition and subject to the consultations provided for in article 29, member states may treat as a supply of services for consideration the supply by a taxable person of a service for the purposes of his undertaking where the value added tax on such a service, had it been supplied by another taxable person, would not be wholly deductible.

6(4)   Where a taxable person acting in his own name but on behalf of another takes part in a supply of services, he shall be considered to have received and supplied those services himself.

6(5)   Article 5(8) shall apply in like manner to the supply of services.

Cross references – VATA 1994, s. 5(2)(b), (3), (5), (6), 47(3), 96(1) and Sch. 4, para. 5: supply of services; whether supply a supply of goods or services; self-supply; further provisions concerning supply of services; treatment of non-residents; interpretation; transfer of business assets, business gifts and goods not used for business.
Council Decision 98/198, of 9 March 1998 authorises derogation from art. 6(2)(a) to permit the UK not to treat as supplies of services for consideration the private use of a business car hired or leased by a taxable person.

ART. 7   Imports

7(1)   **"Importation of goods"** shall mean:

(a)   the entry into the Community of goods which do not fulfil the conditions laid down in articles 9 and 10 of the treaty establishing the European Economic Community or, where the goods are covered by the treaty establishing the European Coal and Steel Community, are not in free circulation;

(b)   the entry into the Community of goods from a third territory, other than the goods covered by (a).

7(2)   The **place of import of goods** shall be the member state within the territory of which the goods are when they enter the Community.

7(3)   Notwithstanding paragraph 2, where goods referred to in paragraph 1(a) are, on entry into the Community, placed under one of the arrangements referred to in article 16(1)(B), (a), (b), (c) and (d) under arrangements for temporary importation with total exemption from import duty or under external transit arrangements, the place of import of such goods shall be the member state within the territory of which they cease to be covered by those arrangements.

Similarly, when goods referred to in paragraph 1(b) are placed, on entry into the Community, under one of the procedures referred to in article 33A(1)(b) or (c), the place of import shall be the member state within whose territory this procedure ceases to apply.

History – Art. 7 replaced by Directive 91/680, art. 1(2) as part of the transitional arrangements which are to apply in the first instance until 31 December 1996 (OJ 1991 L376/1). Member states had to bring into force the measures necessary to comply with this directive no later than 1 January 1993.
Art. 7(1)(b) replaced, and art. 7(3) amended, by Directive 92/111, art. 1(2) and (3) respectively (OJ 1992 L384/47). Member states had to bring into force the measures necessary to implement this directive no later than 1 January 1993.

Cross references – VATA 1994, s. 1(4), 15: charge on importation of goods.

TITLE VI – PLACE OF TAXABLE TRANSACTIONS

ART. 8   Supply of goods

8(1)   The **place of supply of goods** shall be deemed to be:

(a)   in the case of goods dispatched or transported either by the supplier or by the person to whom they are supplied or by a third person: the place where the goods are at the time when dispatch or transport to the person to whom they are supplied begins. Where the goods are installed or assembled, with or without a trial run, by or on behalf of the supplier, the place of supply shall be deemed to be the place where the goods are installed or assembled. In cases where the installation or assembly is carried out in a member state other than that of the supplier, the member state within the territory of which the installation or assembly is carried out shall take any necessary steps to avoid double taxation in that state;

(b)   in the case of goods not dispatched or transported: the place where the goods are when the supply takes place;

(c)   in the case of goods supplied on board ships, aircraft or trains during the part of a transport of passengers effected in the Community: at the point of the departure of the transport of passengers.

For the purposes of applying this provision–

–   **"part of a transport of passengers effected in the Community"** shall mean the part of the transport effected, without a stop in a third territory, between the point of departure and the point of arrival of the transport of passengers,

–   **"the point of departure of the transport of passengers"** shall mean the first point of passenger embarkation foreseen within the Community, where relevant after a leg outside the Community,

–   **"the point of arrival of the transport of passengers"** shall mean the last point of disembarkation of passengers foreseen within the Community of passengers who embarked in the Community, where relevant before a leg outside the Community.

In the case of a return trip, the return leg shall be considered to be a separate transport.

The Commission shall, by 30 June 1993 at the latest submit to the Council a report accompanied, if necessary, by appropriate proposals on the place of taxation of goods supplied for consumption and services, including restaurant services, provided for passengers on board ships, aircraft or trains.

By 31 December 1993, after consulting the European Parliament, the Council shall take a unanimous decision on the Commission proposal.

Until 31 December 1993, member states may exempt or continue to exempt goods supplied for consumption on board whose place of taxation is determined in accordance with the above provisions, with the right to deduct the value added tax paid at an earlier stage.

8(2)   By way of derogation from paragraph 1(a), where the place of departure of the consignment or transport of goods is in a third territory, the place of supply by the importer as defined in article 21(2) and the place of any subsequent supplies shall be deemed to be within the member state of import of the goods.

History – Art. 8(1)(a) amended by Directive 91/680, art. 1(1) (OJ 1991 L376/1).
Art. 8(1)(c) replaced by Directive 92/111, art. 1(4) (OJ 1992 L384/47).
Former art. 8(1)(c) added by Directive 91/680, art. 1(4) (OJ 1991 L376/1).
Art. 8(2) replaced by Directive 91/680, art. 1(5) (OJ 1991 L376/1).
Member states had to bring into force the measures necessary to comply with these directives no later than 1 January 1993.

Cross references – Art. 28B(B): derogation.
VATA 1994, s. 7: place of supply.
VAT (Place of Supply of Goods) Order 1992 (SI 1992/3283): implements art. 8(1)(c).

ART. 9   Supply of services

9(1)   The **place where a service is supplied** shall be deemed to be the place where the supplier has established his business or has a fixed establishment from which the service is supplied or, in the absence of such a place of business or fixed establishment, the place where he has his permanent address or usually resides.

9(2)   However:

(a)   the place of the supply of services connected with immovable property, including the services of estate agents and experts, and of services for preparing and coordinating construction works, such as the services of architects and of firms providing on-site supervision, shall be the place where the property is situated;

(b)   the place where transport services are supplied shall be the place where transport takes place, having regard to the distances covered;

(c)   the place of the supply of services relating to:

> –   cultural, artistic, sporting, scientific, educational, entertainment or similar activities, including the activities of the organisers of such activities, and where appropriate, the supply of ancillary services,
> –   ancillary transport activities such as loading, unloading, handling and similar activities,
> –   valuations of movable tangible property,
> –   work on movable tangible property,

shall be the place where those services are physically carried out;

(d)   [Deleted by Directive 84/386, art. 1.]

(e)   the place where the following services are supplied when performed for customers established outside the Community or for taxable persons established in the Community but not in the same country as the supplier, shall be the place where the customer has established his business or has a fixed establishment to which the service is supplied or, in the absence of such a place, the place where he has his permanent address or usually resides:

> –   transfers and assignments of copyrights, patents, licences, trade marks and similar rights,
> –   advertising services,
> –   services of consultants, engineers, consultancy bureaux, lawyers, accountants and other similar services, as well as data processing and the supplying of information,
> –   obligations to refrain from pursuing or exercising, in whole or in part, a business activity or a right referred to in this point (e),
> –   banking, financial and insurance transactions including reinsurance, with the exception of the hire of safes,
> –   the supply of staff,
> –   the services of agents who act in the name and for the account of another, when they procure for their principal the services referred to in this point (e),
> –   the hiring out of movable tangible property, with the exception of all forms of transport;
> –   Telecommunications. Telecommunications services shall be deemed to be services relating to the transmission, emission or reception of signals, writing, images and sounds or information of any nature by wire, radio, optical or other electromagnetic systems, including the related transfer or assignment of the right to use capacity for such transmission, emission or reception. Telecommunications services within the meaning of this provision shall also include provision of access to global information networks.

9(3)   In order to avoid double taxation, non-taxation or the distortion of competition the member states may, with regard to the supply of services referred to in 2(e) and the hiring out of forms of transport consider:

(a)   the place of supply of services, which under this article would be situated within the territory of the country, as being situated outside the Community where the effective use and enjoyment of the services take place outside the Community;

(b)   the place of supply of services, which under this article would be situated outside the Community, as being within the territory of the country where the effective use and enjoyment of the services take place within the territory of the country.

9(4)   In the case of telecommunications services referred to in paragraph 2(e) supplied by a taxable person established outside the Community to non-taxable persons established inside the Community, member states shall make use of paragraph 3(b).

History – In para. 2(e), the words "– the hiring out of movable . . . transport" inserted and, in para. 3, the words "and the hiring out of all forms of transport" substituted by Directive 84/386 (OJ 1984 L208/58).
In para. 2(e), the indent on telecommunications was added by Directive 99/59, art. 1, para. 1 (OJ 1999 L162/63). Member states had to adopt the laws and regulations and administrative provisions necessary to comply with these directives no later than 1 January 2000.
Para. 4 was added by Directive 99/59, art. 1, para. 2 (OJ 1999 L162/63). Member states had to adopt the laws and regulations and administrative provisions necessary to comply with these directives no later than 1 January 2000.

Cross references – Art. 28B(C)–(E): derogations in respect of intra-Community transport of goods and services rendered by intermediaries.
VATA 1994, s. 7: place of supply of services.
VATA 1994, s. 8; Sch. 5: reverse charge on services.
VAT (Place of Supply of Services) Order 1992 (SI 1992/3121): services relating to land, transport, intermediaries.

TITLE VII – CHARGEABLE EVENT AND CHARGEABILITY OF TAX

ART. 10   [Chargeability]

10(1)

(a) **"Chargeable event"** shall mean the occurrence by virtue of which the legal conditions necessary for tax to become chargeable are fulfilled.

(b) The tax becomes **"chargeable"** when the tax authority becomes entitled under the law at a given moment to claim the tax from the person liable to pay, notwithstanding that the time of payment may be deferred.

10(2)   The chargeable event shall occur and the tax shall become chargeable when the goods are delivered or the services are performed. Deliveries of goods other than those referred to in article 5(4)(b) and supplies of services which give rise to successive statements of account or payments shall be regarded as being completed at the time when the periods to which such statements of account or payments pertain expire.

However, where a payment is to be made on account before the goods are delivered or the services are performed, the tax shall become chargeable on receipt of the payment and on the amount received.

By way of derogation from the above provisions, member states may provide that the tax shall become chargeable, for certain transactions or for certain categories of taxable person, either:

–   no later than the issue of the invoice or of the document serving as invoice, or
–   no later than receipt of the price, or
–   where an invoice or document serving as invoice is not issued, or is issued late, within a specified period from the date of the chargeable event.

10(3)   The chargeable event shall occur and the tax shall become chargeable when the goods are imported. Where goods are placed under one of the arrangements referred to in article 7(3) on entry into the Community, the chargeable event shall occur and the tax shall become chargeable only when the goods cease to be covered by those arrangements.

However, where imported goods are subject to customs duties, to agricultural levies or to charges having equivalent effect established under a common policy, the chargeable event shall occur and the tax shall become chargeable when the chargeable event for those Community duties occurs and those duties become chargeable.

Where imported goods are not subject to any of those Community duties, member states shall apply the provisions in force governing customs duties as regards the occurrence of the chargeable event and the moment when the tax becomes chargeable.

History – Art. 10(3) replaced by Directive 91/680, art. 1(6) (OJ 1991 L376/1). Member states had to bring into force the measures necessary to comply with this directive no later than 1 January 1993.

Cross references – Art. 28D(4): derogation from art. 10(2) and (3).
VATA 1994, s. 1(2), 6(5), (14), 8(4): liability for tax; supply when invoice issued; related regulations; value and time of supply on supplies received from abroad.

TITLE VIII – TAXABLE AMOUNT

ART. 11   [Taxable amount]

11(A)   Within the territory of the country

11(A)(1)   The taxable amount shall be:

(a) in respect of supplies of goods and services other than those referred to in (b), (c) and (d) below, everything which constitutes the consideration which has been or is to be obtained by the supplier from the purchaser, the customer or a third party for such supplies including subsidies directly linked to the price of such supplies;

(b) in respect of supplies referred to in article 5(6) and (7), the purchase price of the goods or of similar goods or, in the absence of a purchase price, the cost price, determined at the time of supply;

(c) in respect of supplies referred to in article 6(2), the full cost to the taxable person of providing the services;

(d) in respect of supplies referred to in article 6(3), the open market value of the services supplied.

"Open market value" of services shall mean the amount which a customer at the marketing stage at which the supply takes place would have to pay to a supplier at arm's length within the territory of the country at the time of the supply under conditions of fair competition to obtain the services in question.

11(A)(2) The taxable amount shall include:

(a)   taxes, duties, levies and charges, excluding the value added tax itself;

(b)   incidental expenses such as commission, packing, transport and insurance costs charged by the supplier to the purchaser or customer. Expenses covered by a separate agreement may be considered to be incidental expenses by the member states.

11(A)(3) The taxable amount shall not include:

(a)   price reductions by way of discount for early payment;

(b)   price discounts and rebates allowed to the customer and accounted for at the time of the supply;

(c)   the amounts received by a taxable person from his purchaser or customer as repayment for expenses paid out in the name and for the account of the latter and which are entered in his books in a suspense account. The taxable person must furnish proof of the actual amount of this expenditure and may not deduct any tax which may have been charged on these transactions.

11(A)(4) By way of derogation from paragraphs 1, 2 and 3, member states which, on 1 January 1993, did not avail themselves of the option provided for in the third subparagraph of article 12(3)(a) may, where they avail themselves of the option provided for in Title B(6), provide that, for the transactions referred to in the second subparagraph of article 12(3)(c), the taxable amount shall be equal to a fraction of the amount determined in accordance with paragraphs 1, 2 and 3.

That fraction shall be determined in such a way that the value added tax thus due is, in any event, equal to at least 5 per cent of the amount determined in accordance with paragraphs 1, 2 and 3.

11(B)   Importation of goods

11(B)(1) The taxable amount shall be the value for customs purposes, determined in accordance with the Community provisions in force; this shall also apply for the import of goods referred to in article 7(1)(b).

11(B)(2) [Deleted by Council Directive 91/680, art. 1(7) (OJ 1991 L376/1).]

11(B)(3) The taxable amount shall include, in so far as they are not already included:

(a)   taxes, duties, levies and other charges due outside the importing member state and those due by reason of importation, excluding the value added tax to be levied;

(b)   incidental expenses, such as commission, packing, transport and insurance costs, incurred up to the first place of destination within the territory of the importing member state.

"First place of destination" shall mean the place mentioned on the consignment note or any other document by means of which the goods are imported into the importing member state. In the absence of such an indication, the first place of destination shall be taken to be the place of the first transfer of cargo in the importing member state.

The incidental expenses referred to above shall also be included in the taxable amount where they result from transport to another place of destination within the territory of the Community if that place is known when the chargeable event occurs.

11(B)(4) The taxable amount shall not include those factors referred to in (A)(3)(a) and (b).

11(B)(5) When goods have been temporarily exported from the Community and are re-imported after having undergone abroad repair, processing or adaptation, or after having been made up or reworked outside the Community, member states shall take steps to ensure that the treatment of the goods for value added tax purposes is the same as that which would have applied to the goods in question had the above operations been carried out within the territory of the country.

11(B)(6) By way of derogation from paragraphs 1 to 4, member states which, on 1 January 1993, did not avail themselves of the option provided for in the third subparagraph of article 12(3)(a) may provide that for imports of the works of art, collectors' items and antiques defined in article 26A(A)(a), (b) and (c), the taxable amount shall be equal to a fraction of the amount determined in accordance with paragraphs 1 to 4.

That fraction shall be determined in such a way that the value added tax thus due on the import is, in any event, equal to at least 5 per cent of the amount determined in accordance with paragraphs 1 to 4.

11(C)　Miscellaneous provisions

11(C)(1)　In the case of cancellation, refusal or total or partial non-payment, or where the price is reduced after the supply takes place, the taxable amount shall be reduced accordingly under conditions which shall be determined by the member states.

However, in the case of total or partial non-payment, member states may derogate from this rule.

11(C)(2)　Where information for determining the taxable amount on importation is expressed in a currency other than that of the member state where assessment takes place, the exchange rate shall be determined in accordance with the Community provisions governing the calculation of the value for customs purposes.

Where information for the determination of the taxable amount of a transaction other than an import transaction is expressed in a currency other than that of the member state where assessment takes place, the exchange rate applicable shall be the latest selling rate recorded, at the time the tax becomes chargeable, on the most representative exchange market or markets of the member state concerned, or a rate determined by reference to that or those markets, in accordance with the down [sic] by that member state. However, for some of those transactions or for certain categories of taxable person, member states may continue to apply the exchange rate determined in accordance with the Community provisions in force governing the calculation of the value for customs purposes.

11(C)(3)　As regards returnable packing costs, member states may:

– 　either exclude them from the taxable amount and take the necessary measures to see that this amount is adjusted if the packing is not returned,

– 　or include them in the taxable amount and take the necessary measures to see that this amount is adjusted where the packing is in fact returned.

History – Art. 11(A)(4) added by Directive 94/5, art. 1(a) (OJ 1994 L60/16). Member states had to bring into force the measures necessary to comply with this directive no later than 1 January 1995.
Art. 11(B)(1) replaced by Directive 92/111, art. 1(5) (OJ 1992 L384/47). Former art. 11(B)(1) replaced by Directive 91/680, art. 1(7) (OJ 1991 L376/1).
Art. 11(B)(2) deleted by Directive 92/111, art. 1(7) (OJ 1991 L376/1).
Art. 11(B)(3) replaced by Directive 91/680, art. 1(8) (OJ 1991 L376/1).
Art. 11(B)(3)(b), third subparagraph, replaced by Directive 95/7, art. 1(2) (OJ 1995 L102/18). That subparagraph previously read as follows:
"Equally, member states may include in the taxable amount the incidental expenses referred to above where they result from transport to another place of destination within the territory of the importing member state if that place is known when the chargeable event occurs."
Art. 11(B)(5) amended by Directive 91/680, art. 1(9) (OJ 1991 L376/1).
Art. 11(B)(6) added by Directive 94/5, art. 1(b) (OJ 1994 L60/16).
Member states had to bring into force the measures necessary to comply with Directive 92/111 no later than 1 January 1995, and with Directive 95/7 on 1 January 1996.
Art. 11(C)(2) replaced by Directive 91/680, art. 1(10) (OJ 1991 L376/1).
Member states had to bring into force the measures necessary to comply with this directive no later than 1 January 1993.

Cross references – VATA 1994, s. 19 and Sch. 6: value of supply.
VATA 1994, s. 21 and Sch. 6: value of imported goods.
VATA 1994, Sch. 6, para. 12 and s. 36: value given by persons not receiving supply; relief for bad debts.
Council Decision 89/466 of 18 July 1989 authorises derogation from art. 11(A)(1)(b), permitting UK to use open market value as the taxable amount for the supply, under art. 5(7)(a), (b) of buildings or parts of buildings before first occupation and of related land.
Council Decision 89/534 of 24 May 1989 authorises derogation from art. 11(A)(1)(a), permitting UK to prescribe, where a marketing structure based on the supply of goods through non-taxable persons results in non-taxation at the stage of final consumption, that the taxable amount for supplies to such persons is to be the open-market value of the goods as determined at that stage.

TITLE IX – RATES

ART. 12　[Rates]

12(1)　The rate applicable to taxable transactions shall be that in force at the time of the *chargeable event*. However:

(a)　in the cases provided for in the second and third sub-paragraphs of article 10(2), the rate to be used shall be that in force when the tax becomes chargeable;

(b)　in the cases provided for in the second and third sub-paragraphs of article 10(3), the rate applicable shall be that in force at the time when the tax becomes chargeable.

12(2)　In the event of changes in the rates, member states may:

—   effect adjustments in the cases provided for in paragraph 1(a) in order to take account of the rate applicable at the time when the goods or services were supplied,

—   adopt all appropriate transitional measures.

12(3)

(a)   The standard rate of VAT shall be fixed by each member state as a percentage of the taxable amount and shall be the same for the supply of goods and for the supply of services. From 1 January 1999 to 31 December 2000, this percentage may not be less than 15%.

On a proposal from the Commission and after consulting the European Parliament and the European and Social Committee, the Council shall decide unanimously on the level of the standard rate to be applied after 31 December 2000.

Member states may also apply either one or two reduced rates. These rates shall be fixed as a percentage of the taxable amount which may not be less than 5 per cent and shall apply only to supplies of the categories of goods and services specified in Annex H.

(b)   Member states may apply a reduced rate to supplies of natural gas and electricity provided that no risk of distortion of competition exists. A member state intending to apply such a rate must before doing so, inform the Commission. The Commission shall give a decision on the existence of a risk of distortion of competition. If the Commission has not taken that decision within three months of the receipt of the information a risk of distortion of competition is deemed not to exist.

(c)   Member states may provide that the reduced rate, or one of the reduced rates, which they apply in accordance with the third paragraph of (a) shall also apply to imports of works of art, collectors' items and antiques as referred to in article 26A(A)(a), (b) and (c).

Where they avail themselves of this option, member states may also apply the reduced rate to supplies of works of art, within the meaning of article 26A(A)(a):

—   effected by their creator or his successors in title,

—   effected on an occasional basis by a taxable person other than a taxable dealer, where these works of art have been imported by the taxable person himself or where they have been supplied to him by their creator or his successors in title or where they have entitled him to full deduction of value added tax.

(d)   [Deleted by Council Directive 96/42, art. 1 (OJ 1996 L170/34).]

(e)   [Deleted by Council Directive 98/80, art. 2 (OJ 1998 L281/31).]

Member states will take all necessary measures to combat fraud in this area from 1 January 1993. These measures may include the introduction of a system of accounting for VAT on supplies of gold between taxable persons in the same member state which provides for the payment of tax by the buyer on behalf of the seller and a simultaneous right for the buyer to a deduction of the same amount of tax as input tax.

12(4)   Each reduced rate shall be so fixed that the amount of value added tax resulting from the application thereof shall be such as in the normal way to permit the deduction therefrom of the whole of the value added tax deductible under the provisions of article 17.

On the basis of a report from the Commission, the Council shall, starting in 1994, review the scope of the reduced rates every two years. The Council, acting unanimously on a proposal from the Commission, may decide to alter the list of goods and services in Annex H.

12(5)   Subject to paragraph 3(c), the rate applicable on the importation of goods shall be that applied to the supply of like goods within the territory of the country.

12(6)   The Portuguese Republic may apply to transactions carried out in the autonomous regions of the Azores and Madeira and to direct imports to those regions, reduced rates in comparison to those applying on the mainland.

History – Art. 12(1)(b) replaced by Directive 92/111, art. 1(6) (OJ 1992 L384/47). Member states had to bring into force the measures necessary to implement this directive no later than 1 January 1993.
Art. 12(3) replaced by Directive 92/77, art. 1 (OJ 1992 L316/1). Member states had to bring into force the measures necessary to comply with this directive no later than 31 December 1992.
Art. 12(3)(a) replaced by Directive 99/49, art. 1 (OJ 1996 L338/89). Member states had to bring into force the measures necessary to implement this directive no later than 1 January 1999. Former art. 12(3)(a) reads as follows:

"(a)   The standard rate of VAT shall be fixed by each member state as a percentage of the taxable amount and shall be the same for the supply of goods and for the supply of services. From 1 January 1997 to 31 December 1998, this percentage may not be less than 15.

(b)   On a proposal from the Commission and after consulting the European Parliament and the European and Social Committee, the Council shall decide unanimously on the level of the standard rate to be applied after 31 December 1998.

(c)   Member states may also apply either one or two reduced rates. These rates shall be fixed as a percentage of the taxable amount which may not be less than 5 per cent and shall apply only to supplies of the categories of goods and services specified in Annex H."

Art. 12(3)(a) replaced by Directive 96/95, art. 1 (OJ 1996 L338/89). Member states had to bring into force the measures necessary to implement this directive no later than 1 January 1997.

Art. 12(3)(c) replaced by Directive 94/5, art. 2(a) (OJ 1994 L60/16). Member states had to bring into force the measures necessary to comply with this directive no later than 1 January 1995. Former art. 12(3)(c) read as follows:

The rules concerning the rates applied to works of art, antiques and collectors' items, shall be determined by the directive relating to the special arrangements applicable to second-hand goods, works of art, antiques and collectors' items. The Council shall adopt this directive before 31 December 1992."

Art. 12(3)(d) deleted by Directive 96/42, art. 1 (OJ 1996 L170/34). The deletion applies from 1 January 1995.

Art. 12(3)(e) deleted by Directive 98/80, art. 2 (OJ 1998 L281/31). Member states had to bring into force the measures necessary to comply with this directive on 1 January 2000. Former art. 12(3)(e) read as follows:

The rules concerning the regime and the rates applied to gold shall be determined by a directive relating to special arrangements applicable to gold. The Commission shall make such a proposal in time for its adoption by the Council, acting unanimously, before 31 December 1992."

Art. 12(4), first sentence was deleted and the subparagraph was added by Directive 92/77, art. 2 and 3 (OJ 1992 L316/1). Member states had to bring into force the measures necessary to comply with this directive no later than 31 December 1992.

Art. 12(5) replaced by Directive 94/5, art. 2(b) (OJ 1994 L60/16). Member states had to bring into force the measures necessary to comply with this directive no later than 1 January 1995. Former art. 12(5) read as follows:

The rate applicable on the importation of goods shall be that applied to the supply of like goods within the territory of the country."

Art. 12(6) inserted by the Act of Accession of Spain and Portugal 1985, art. 26, Annex I, Pt. V, point 2 (OJ 1985 L302/167).

Cross references – VATA 1994, s. 2: rate of tax.

Notes – The directive referred to in art. 12(3)(e) was not adopted by the Council by 31 December 1992.

TITLE X – EXEMPTIONS

ART. 13   Exemptions within the territory of the country

13(A)   Exemptions for certain activities in the public interest

13(A)(1)   Without prejudice to other Community provisions, member states shall exempt the following under conditions which they shall lay down for the purpose of ensuring the correct and straightforward application of such exemptions and of preventing any possible evasion, avoidance or abuse:

(a)   the supply by the public postal services of services other than passenger transport and telecommunications services, and the supply of goods incidental thereto;

(b)   hospital and medical care and closely related activities undertaken by bodies governed by public law or, under social conditions comparable to those applicable to bodies governed by public law, by hospitals, centres for medical treatment or diagnosis and other duly recognised establishments of a similar nature;

(c)   the provision of medical care in the exercise of the medical and paramedical professions as defined by the member state concerned;

(d)   supplies of human organs, blood and milk;

(e)   services supplied by dental technicians in their professional capacity and dental prostheses supplied by dentists and dental technicians;

(f)   services supplied by independent groups of persons whose activities are exempt from or are not subject to value added tax, for the purpose of rendering their members the services directly necessary for the exercise of their activity, where these groups merely claim from their members exact reimbursement of their share of the joint expenses, provided that such exemption is not likely to produce distortion of competition;

(g)   the supply of services and of goods closely linked to welfare and social security work, including those supplied by old people's homes, by bodies governed by public law or by other organisations recognised as charitable by the member state concerned;

(h)   the supply of services and of goods closely linked to the protection of children and young persons by bodies governed by public law or by other organisations recognised as charitable by the member state concerned;

(i)   children's or young people's education, school or university education, vocational training or retraining, including the supply of services and of goods closely related thereto, provided by bodies governed by public law having such as their aim or by other organisations defined by the member state concerned as having similar objects;

(j)   tuition given privately by teachers and covering school or university education;

(k)   *certain supplies of staff by religious or philosophical institutions for the purpose of subparagraphs (b), (g), (h) and (i) of this article and with a view to spiritual welfare;*

(l)   supply of services and goods closely linked thereto for the benefit of their members in return for a subscription fixed in accordance with their rules by non-profit-making organisations with aims of a political, trade-union, religious, patriotic, philosophical, philanthropic or civic nature, provided that this exemption is not likely to cause distortion of competition;

(m)   certain services closely linked to sport or physical education supplied by non-profit-making organisations to persons taking part in sport or physical education;

(n)   certain cultural services and goods closely linked thereto supplied by bodies governed by public law or by other cultural bodies recognised by the member state concerned;

(o)   the supply of services and goods by organisations whose activities are exempt under the provisions of subparagraphs (b), (g), (h), (i), (l), (m) and (n) above in connection with fund-raising events organised exclusively for their own benefit provided that exemption is not likely to cause distortion of competition. Member states may introduce any necessary restrictions in particular as regards the number of events or the amount of receipts which give entitlement to exemption;

(p)   the supply of transport services for sick or injured persons in vehicles specially designed for the purpose by duly authorised bodies;

(q)   activities of public radio and television bodies other than those of a commercial nature.

13(A)(2)

(a)   Member states may make the granting to bodies other than those governed by public law of each exemption provided for in (1)(b), (g), (h), (i), (l), (m) and (n) of this article subject in each individual case to one or more of the following conditions:

–   they shall not systematically aim to make a profit, but any profits nevertheless arising shall not be distributed, but shall be assigned to the continuance or improvement of the services supplied,

–   they shall be managed and administered on an essentially voluntary basis by persons who have no direct or indirect interest, either themselves or through intermediaries, in the results of the activities concerned,

–   they shall charge prices approved by the public authorities or which do not exceed such approved prices or, in respect of those services not subject to approval, prices lower than those charged for similar services by commercial enterprises subject to value added tax,

–   exemption of the services concerned shall not be likely to create distortions of competition such as to place at a disadvantage commercial enterprises liable to value added tax.

(b)   The supply of services or goods shall not be granted exemption as provided for in (1)(b), (g), (h), (i), (l), (m) and (n) above if:

–   it is not essential to the transactions exempted,

–   its basic purpose is to obtain additional income for the organisation by carrying out transactions which are in direct competition with those of commercial enterprises liable for value added tax.

13(B)   Other exemptions

13   Without prejudice to other Community provisions, member states shall exempt the following under conditions which they shall lay down for the purpose of ensuring the correct and straightforward application of the exemptions and of preventing any possible evasion, avoidance or abuse:

(a)   insurance and reinsurance transactions, including related services performed by insurance brokers and insurance agents;

(b)   the leasing or letting of immovable property excluding:

(1)   the provision of accommodation, as defined in the laws of the member states, in the hotel sector or in sectors with a similar function, including the provision of accommodation in holiday camps or on sites developed for use as camping sites;

(2)   the letting of premises and sites for parking vehicles;

(3)   lettings of permanently installed equipment and machinery;

(4)   hire of safes.

Member states may apply further exclusions to the scope of this exemption;

(c)   supplies of goods used wholly for an activity exempted under this article or under article 28(3)(b) when these goods have not given rise to the right to deduction, or of goods on the acquisition or production of which, by virtue of article 17(6), value added tax did not become deductible;

(d)   the following transactions:

(1)   the granting and the negotiation of credit and the management of credit by the person granting it;

      (2) the negotiation of or any dealings in credit guarantees or any other security for money and the management of credit guarantees by the person who is granting the credit;

      (3) transactions, including negotiation, concerning deposit and current accounts, payments, transfers, debts, cheques and other negotiable instruments, but excluding debt collection and factoring;

      (4) transactions, including negotiation, concerning currency, bank notes and coins used as legal tender, with the exception of collectors' items; "collectors' items" shall be taken to mean gold, silver or other metal coins or bank notes which are not normally used as legal tender or coins of numismatic interest;

      (5) transactions, including negotiation, excluding management and safekeeping, in shares, interests in companies or associations, debentures and other securities, excluding:
–   documents establishing title to goods,
–   the rights or securities referred to in article 5(3);

      (6) management of special investment funds as defined by member states;

(e)   the supply at face value of postage stamps valid for use for postal services within the territory of the country, fiscal stamps, and other similar stamps;

(f)   betting, lotteries and other forms of gambling, subject to conditions and limitations laid down by each member state;

(g)   the supply of buildings or parts thereof, and of the land on which they stand, other than as described in article 4(3)(a);

(h)   the supply of land which has not been built on other than building land as described in article 4(3)(b).

13(C) Options

Member states may allow taxpayers a right of option for taxation in cases of:

(a)   letting and leasing of immovable property;

(b)   the transactions covered in (B)(d), (g) and (h) above.

Member states may restrict the scope of this right of option and shall fix the details of its use.

Cross references – VATA 1994, s. 31(2), 94(3) and Sch. 9: Treasury power to designate exempt supplies; bodies not carrying on a business; exemptions.
The eighteenth Council directive (Directive 89/465) authorises member states taxing the transactions at points 4, 5, Annex E (i.e. transactions referred to in art. 13(A)(1)(m), (n)) at 1 January 1989 to extend the conditions of art. 13(A)(2)(a), final indent to activities under art. 13(1)(m), (n) carried out by bodies governed by public law.

ART. 14   Exemptions on importation

14(1) Without prejudice to other Community provisions, member states shall exempt the following under conditions which they shall lay down for the purpose of ensuring the correct and straightforward application of such exemption and of preventing any possible evasion, avoidance or abuse:

(a)   final importation of goods of which the supply by a taxable person would in all circumstances be exempted within the country;

(b)   [Deleted by Directive 91/680, art. 1(11).]

(c)   [Deleted by Directive 92/111, art. 1(8).]

(d)   final importation of goods qualifying for exemption from customs duties other than as provided for in the Common Customs Tariff. However, member states shall have the option of not granting exemption where this would be liable to have a serious effect on conditions of competition. This exemption shall also apply to the import of goods, within the meaning of article 7(1)(b), which would be capable of benefiting from the exemption set out above if they had been imported within the meaning of article 7(1)(a);

(e)   reimportation by the person who exported them of goods in the state in which they were exported, where they qualify for exemption from customs duties;

(f)   [Deleted by Directive 91/680, art. 1(11).]

(g)   importations of goods:
–   under diplomatic and consular arrangements, which qualify for exemption from customs duties,
–   by international organisations recognised as such by the public authorities of the host country, and by members of such organisations, within the limits and under the conditions laid down by the international conventions establishing the organisations or by headquarters agreements,

- into the territory of member states which are parties to the North Atlantic Treaty by the armed forces of other states which are parties to that treaty for the use of such forces or the civilian staff accompanying them or for supplying their messes or canteens where such forces take part in the common defence effort:

(h)   importation into ports by sea fishing undertakings of their catches, unprocessed or after undergoing preservation for marketing but before being supplied;

(i)   the supply of services, in connection with the importation of goods where the value of such services is included in the taxable amount in accordance with article 11(B)(3)(b);

(j)   importation of gold by central banks.

14(2)   The Commission shall submit to the Council at the earliest opportunity proposals designed to lay down Community tax rules clarifying the scope of the exemptions referred to in paragraph 1 and detailed rules for their implementation.

Until the entry into force of these rules, member states may:

- maintain their national provisions in force on matters related to the above provisions,

- adapt their national provisions to minimise distortion of competition and in particular the non-imposition or double imposition of value added tax within the Community,

- use whatever administrative procedures they consider most appropriate to achieve exemption.

Member states shall inform the Commission, which shall inform the other member states, of the measures they have adopted and are adopting pursuant to the preceding provisions.

History – Art. 14(1)(b) deleted by Directive 91/680, art. 1(11) (OJ 1991 L376/1).
Art. 14(1)(c) deleted by Directive 92/111, art. 1(8) (OJ 1992 L384/47).
Art. 14(1)(d) amended by Directive 91/680, art. 1(11) (OJ 1991 L376/1) and by Directive 92/111, art. 1(8) (OJ 1992 L384/47).
Art. 14(1)(e) amended, art. 14(1)(f) deleted and art. 14(1)(g) amended by Directive 91/680, art. 1(11) (OJ 1991 L376/1).
Member states had to bring into force the measures necessary to implement these directives no later than 1 January 1993.

Cross references – VATA 1994, s. 30, 37: zero-rating; relief for importation of goods.
VAT (Imported Goods) Relief Order 1984 (SI 1984/746).
VAT (Imported Gold) Relief Order 1992 (SI 1992/3124): implements art. 14(1)(j).
Customs and Excise (Personal Reliefs for Special Visitors) Order 1992 (SI 1992/3156): implements art. 14(1)(g).

ART. 15   Exemption of exports from the Community and like transactions and international transport

15   Without prejudice to other Community provisions member states shall exempt the following under conditions which they shall lay down for the purpose of ensuring the correct and straightforward application of such exemptions and of preventing any evasion, avoidance or abuse:

(1)   the supply of goods dispatched or transported to a destination outside the Community by or on behalf of the vendor;

(2)   the supply of goods dispatched or transported to a destination outside the Community by or on behalf of a purchaser not established within the territory of the country, with the exception of goods transported by the purchaser himself for the equipping, fuelling and provisioning of pleasure boats and private aircraft or any other means of transport for private use.

     In the case of the supply of goods to be carried in the personal luggage of travellers, this exemption shall apply on condition that:

- the traveller is not established within the Community,

- the goods are transported to a destination outside the Community before the end of the third month following that in which the supply is effected,

- the total value of the supply, including value added tax, is more than the equivalent in national currency of ECU 175, fixed in accordance with article 7(2) of Directive 69EEC; however, member states may exempt a supply with a total value of less than that amount.

     For the purposes of applying the second subparagraph:

- a traveller not established within the Community shall be taken to mean a traveller whose domicile or habitual residence is not situated within the Community. For the purposes of this provision, **"domicile or habitual residence"** shall mean the place entered as such in a passport, identity card or other identity documents which the member state within whose territory the supply takes place recognises as valid,

- proof of exportation shall be furnished by means of the invoice or other document in lieu thereof, endorsed by the customs office where the goods left the Community.

Each member state shall transmit to the Commission specimens of the stamps it uses for the endorsement referred to in the second indent of the third subparagraph. The Commission shall transmit this information to the tax authorities in the other member states.

(3)   the supply of services consisting of work on movable property acquired or imported for the purpose of undergoing such work within the territory of the Community, and dispatched or transported out of the Community by the person providing the services or by the customer if not established within the territory of the country or on behalf of either of them;

(4)   the supply of goods for the fuelling and provisioning of vessels:

      (a)   used for navigation on the high seas and carrying passengers for reward or used for the purpose of commercial, industrial or fishing activities;

      (b)   used for rescue or assistance at sea, or for inshore fishing, with the exception, for the latter, of ships provisions;

      (c)   of war, as defined in subheading 89.01 A of the Common Customs Tariff, leaving the country and bound for foreign ports or anchorages.

The Commission shall submit to the Council as soon as possible proposals to establish Community fiscal rules specifying the scope of and practical arrangements for implementing this exemption and the exemptions provided for in (5) to (9). Until these rules come into force, member states may limit the extent of the exemption provided for in this paragraph;

(5)   the supply, modification, repair, maintenance, chartering and hiring of the sea-going vessels referred to in paragraph 4(a) and (b) and the supply, hiring, repair and maintenance of equipment – including fishing equipment – incorporated or used therein;

(6)   the supply, modification, repair, maintenance, chartering and hiring of aircraft used by airlines operating for reward chiefly on international routes, and the supply, hiring, repair and maintenance of equipment incorporated or used therein;

(7)   the supply of goods for the fuelling and provisioning of aircraft referred to in paragraph 6;

(8)   the supply of services other than those referred to in paragraph 5, to meet the direct needs of the sea-going vessels referred to in that paragraph or of their cargoes;

(9)   the supply of services other than those referred to in paragraph 6, to meet the direct needs of aircraft referred to in that paragraph or of their cargoes;

(10)   supplies of goods and services:

      –   under diplomatic and consular arrangements,

      –   to another member state and intended for the forces of any member state which is a party to the North Atlantic Treaty, other than the member state of destination itself, for the use of those forces or of the civilian staff accompanying them, or for supplying their messes or canteens when such forces take part in the common defence effort,

      –   to international organisations recognised as such by the public authorities of the host country, and to members of such organisations, within the limits and under the conditions laid down by the international conventions establishing the organisations or by headquarters agreements,

      –   effected within a member state which is a party to the North Atlantic Treaty and intended either for the use of the forces of other states which are parties to that treaty or of the civilian staff accompanying them, or for supplying their messes or canteens when such forces take part in the common defence effort.

This exemption shall be subject to limitations laid down by the host member state until Community tax rules are adopted.

In cases where the goods are not dispatched or transported out of the country, and in the case of services, the benefit of the exemption may be given by means of a refund of the tax;

(11)   supplies of gold to central banks;

(12)   goods supplied to approved bodies which export them from the Community as part of their humanitarian, charitable or teaching activities outside the Community. This exemption may be implemented by means of a refund of the tax;

(13)   the supply of services, including transport and ancillary operations, but excluding the supply of services exempted in accordance with article 13, where these are directly connected with the export of goods or imports of goods covered by the provisions of article 7(3) or article 16(1), Title A;

(14)   services supplied by brokers and other intermediaries, acting in the name and for account of another person, where they form part of transactions specified in this article, or of transactions carried out outside the Community.

This exemption does not apply to travel agents who supply in the name and for account of the traveller services which are supplied in other member states.

(15)   the Portuguese Republic may treat sea and air transport between the islands making up the autonomous regions of the Azores and Madeira and between those regions and the mainland in the same way as international transport.

History – In the heading to art. 15, the words "from the Community" added by Directive 91/680, art. 1(12) (OJ 1991 L376/1). In art. 15, para. 1 and 2 amended by Directive 91/680, art. 1(13) (OJ 1991 L376/1).
Art. 15(2), second and third subparagraphs, replaced (with three subparagraphs) by Directive 95/7, art. 1(3) (OJ 1995 L102/18).
Art. 15(2), second and third subparagraphs, previously read as follows:
"The Commission shall submit to the Council as soon as possible proposals to establish Community fiscal rules specifying the scope of and practical arrangements for implementing this exemption for supplies made at the retail stage of goods to be carried in the personal luggage of travellers. Until these provisions come into force:

–   the benefit of the exemption shall be subject to the production of a copy of the invoice or other documents in lieu thereof, endorsed by the Customs office where the goods left the Community,

–   member states may set limits in relation to the application of this exemption, may exclude from the benefit of the exemption supplies to travellers whose domicile or habitual residence is situated in the Community and may extend the benefit of the exemption to their residents.

For the purposes of applying the second subparagraph **"domicile or habitual residence"** means the place entered as such in a passport, identity card or, failing those, other identity documents which the member state in whose territory the supply takes place recognises as valid;"
Art. 15, para. 2, second and following subparagraphs previously added by Directive 92/111, art. 1(9) (OJ 1992 L384/47).
Art. 15, para. 3 amended by Directive 92/111, art. 1(9) (OJ 1992 L384/47). Former para. 3 replaced by Directive 91/680, art. 1(14) (OJ 1991 L376/1).
Art. 15, para. 4, second subparagraph, replaced by Directive 92/111, art. 1(9) (OJ 1992 L384/47).
In art. 15, para. 10, second indent added by Directive 91/680, art. 1(15) (OJ 1991 L376/1).
In art. 15, para. 10, second subparagraph, the word "limitations" substituted by Directive 92/111, art. 1(9) (OJ 1992 L384/47); this subparagraph previously amended by Directive 91/680, art. 1(16) (OJ 1991 L376/1).
In art. 15, para. 10, third subparagraph replaced by Directive 92/111, art. 1(9) (OJ 1992 L384/47).
In art. 15, para. 12, the words "from the Community" were added after the words "which export them" and the words "outside the Community" replaced the word "abroad" by Directive 91/680 of 16 December 1991, art. 1(17) (OJ 1991 L376/1).
Art. 15, para. 13 replaced by Directive 92/111, art. 1(9) (OJ 1992 L384/47); former para. 13 replaced by Directive 91/680, art. 1(18) (OJ 1991 L376/1).
In art. 15, para. 14, the words "outside the Community" substituted by Directive 91/680, art. 1(19) (OJ 1991 L376/1).
Member states had to bring into force the measures necessary to comply with Directives 91/680 and 92/111 no later than 1 January 1993, and with Directive 95/7 on 1 January 1996.
Art. 15, para. 15 inserted by the Act of Accession of Spain and Portugal, art. 26, Annex I, Pt. V, point 2 (OJ 1985 L302/167).
Cross references – Art. 15 exemption really means zero-rating in the UK, because art. 17, para. 3(b) allows input tax to be deducted.
VATA 1994, s. 30(6), 37(1) and Sch. 8, Grp. 7, 8, 10: goods for use outside UK; relief on importation of goods; international services; transport; gold.
Customs and Excise (Personal Reliefs for Special Visitors) Order 1992 (SI 1992/3156): implements art. 15(10).

ART. 16   Special exemptions linked to international goods traffic

16(1)   Without prejudice to other Community tax provisions, member states may, subject to the consultations provided for in article 29, take special measures designed to exempt all or some of the following transactions, provided that they are not aimed at final use and/or consumption and that the amount of value added tax due on cessation of the arrangements on situations referred to at A to E corresponds to the amount of tax which would have been due had each of these transactions been taxed within the territory of the country:

A imports of goods which are intended to be placed under warehousing arrangements other than customs;

B supplies of goods which are intended to be:

(a)   produced to customs and, where applicable, placed in temporary storage;

(b)   placed in a free zone or in a free warehouse;

(c)   placed under customs warehousing arrangements or inward processing arrangements;

(d)   admitted into territorial waters:

–   in order to be incorporated into drilling or production platforms, for purposes of the construction, repair, maintenance, alteration or fitting-out of such platforms, or to link such drilling or production platforms to the mainland,

–   for the fuelling and provisioning of drilling or production platforms;

(e)   placed, within the territory of the country, under warehousing arrangements other than customs warehousing.

For the purposes of this article, warehouses other than customs warehouses shall be taken to be:

–   for products subject to excise duty, the places defined as tax warehouses for the purposes of article 4(b) of Directive 92/12/EEC,

–   for goods other than those subject to excise duty, the places defined as such by the member states. However, member states may not provide for warehousing arrangements other than customs warehousing where the goods in question are intended to be supplied at the retail stage.

Nevertheless, member states may provide for such arrangements for goods intended for:

-      taxable persons for the purposes of supplies effected under the conditions laid down in article 28k,
-      tax-free shops within the meaning of article 28k, for the purposes of supplies to travellers taking flights or sea crossings to third countries, where those supplies are exempt pursuant to article 15,
-      taxable persons for the purposes of supplies to travellers on board aircraft or vessels during a flight or sea crossing where the place of arrival is situated outside the Community,
-      taxable persons for the purposes of supplies effected free of tax pursuant to article 15, point 10.

The places referred to in (a), (b), (c) and (d) shall be as defined by the Community customs provisions in force;

C supplies of services relating to the supplies of goods referred to in B;

D supplies of goods and of services carried out;

(a)   in the places listed in B(a), (b), (c) and (d) and still subject to one of the situations specified therein;

(b)   in the places listed in B(e) and still subject, within the territory of the country, to the situation specified therein.

Where they exercise the option provided for in (a) for transactions effected in customs warehouses, member states shall take the measures necessary to ensure that they have defined warehousing arrangements other than customs warehousing which permit the provisions in (b) to be applied to the same transactions concerning goods listed in Annex J which are effected in such warehouses other than customs warehouses;

E supplies:

-      of goods referred to in article 7(1)(a) still subject to arrangements for temporary importation with total exemption from import duty or to external transit arrangements,
-      of goods referred to in article 7(1)(b) still subject to the internal Community transit procedure provided for in article 33a,

as well as supplies of services relating to such supplies.

By way of derogation from the first subparagraph of article 21(1)(a), the person liable to pay the tax due in accordance with the first subparagraph shall be the person who causes the goods to cease to be covered by the arrangements or situations listed in this paragraph.

When the removal of goods from the arrangements or situations referred to in this paragraph gives rise to importation within the meaning of article 7(3), the member state of import shall take the measures necessary to avoid double taxation within the country.

16(1A)   Where they exercise the option provided for in paragraph 1, member states shall take the measures necessary to ensure that intra-Community acquisitions of goods intended to be placed under one of the arrangements or in one of the situations referred to in paragraph 1(B) benefit from the same provisions as supplies of goods effected within the country under the same conditions.

16(2)   Subject to the consultation provided for in article 29, member states may opt to exempt intra-Community acquisitions of goods made by a taxable person and to exempt imports for and supplies of goods to a taxable person intending to export them outside the Community as they are or after processing, as well as supplies of services linked with his export business, up to a maximum equal to the value of his exports during the preceding 12 months.

When they take up this option the member states shall, subject to the consultation provided for in article 29, extend the benefit of this exemption to intra-Community acquisitions of goods by a taxable person, imports for and supplies of goods to a taxable person intending to supply them, as they are or after processing, under the conditions laid down in article 28C(A), as well as supplies of services relating to such supplies, up to a maximum equal to the value of his supplies of goods effected under the conditions laid down in article 28C(A) during the preceding twelve months.

Member states may set a common maximum amount for transactions which they exempt under the first and second subparagraphs.

16(3) The Commission shall submit to the Council at the earliest opportunity proposals concerning common arrangements for applying value added tax to the transactions referred to in paragraphs 1 and 2.

History – In art. 16(1), A–D were replaced and E was added by Directive 91/680, art. 1(20) (OJ 1991 L376/1).
Member states had to bring into force the measures necessary to comply with this directive no later than 1 January 1993.
Art. 16(1) replaced, and art. 16(1A) added, by Directive 77/388, art. 28C(E)(1), which was itself replaced by Directive 95/7 art. 9 (OJ 1995 L102/18). The former art. 16(1), (1A) read as follows:
"**16(1)** Without prejudice to other Community provisions, member states may, subject to the consultations provided for in article 29, take special measures designed to relieve from value added tax all or some of the following transactions, provided that they are not aimed at final use and/or consumption and that the amount of value added tax charged at entry for home use corresponds to the amount of the tax which should have been charged had each of these transactions been taxed on import or within the territory of the country:
A imports of goods which are intended to be placed under warehousing arrangements other than customs;
B supplies of goods which are intended to be
  (a)   produced to customs and where applicable, placed in temporary storage;
  (b)   placed in a free zone or in a free warehouse;
  (c)   placed under customs warehousing arrangements or inward processing arrangements;
  (d)   admitted into territorial waters;
      –   in order to be incorporated into drilling or production platforms, for purposes of the construction, repair, maintenance, alteration or fitting-out of such platforms, or to link such drilling or production platforms to the mainland,
      –   for the fuelling and provisioning of drilling or production platforms;
  (e)   placed under warehousing arrangements other than customs.
The places referred to in (a), (b), (c) and (d) shall be as defined by the Community customs provisions in force;
C supplies of services relating to the supplies of goods referred to in B;
D supplies of goods and of services carried out in the places listed in B and still subject to one of the arrangements specified therein;
E supplies:
  –   of goods referred to in article 7(1)(a) still subject to arrangements for temporary importation with total exemption from import duty or to external transit arrangements.
  –   of goods referred to in article 7(1)(b) still subject to the internal Community transit procedure provided for in article 33A.
as well as supplies of services relating to such supplies.
16(1A) When they take up the option provided for in paragraph 1, member states shall take the measures necessary in order to ensure that the intra-Community acquisitions of goods intended to be placed under one of the regimes or in one of the situations referred to in article 16(1)(B) benefit from the same provisions as supplies of goods carried out within the territory of the country under the same conditions".
Art. 16(1A) previously added by Directive 77/388, art. 28C(E)(1), which was itself added by Directive 92/111, art. 1(13) (OJ 1992 L384/47).
In art. 16(2), the words "intra-Community acquisition of goods made by a taxable person and" and "outside the Community", together with the second and third subparagraphs, added by Directive 77/388, art. 28C(E)(2), which was itself added by Directive 92/111, art. 1(13) (OJ 1992 L384/47).
Member states had to bring into force the measures necessary to comply with Directive 92/111, art. 1(13) by 1 January 1993.

Cross references – VATA 1994, s. 18A–F and Sch. 5A, as inserted by FA 1996, s. 26(1) and Sch. 3, para. 5 and 18: fiscal and other warehousing.
Free Zone Regulations 1984 (SI 1984/1177); Free Zone Designation Orders 1991 (SI 1991/1737–1740).

TITLE XI – DEDUCTIONS

ART. 17   Origin and scope of the right to deduct

17(1) The right to deduct shall arise at the time when the deductible tax becomes chargeable.

17(2) In so far as the goods and services are used for the purposes of his taxable transactions, the taxable person shall be entitled to deduct from the tax which he is liable to pay:

(a)   value added tax due or paid within the territory of the country in respect of goods or services supplied or to be supplied to him by another taxable person;

(b)   value added tax due or paid in respect of imported goods within the territory of the country;

(c)   value added tax due pursuant to article 5(7)(a), 6(3) and 28A(6);

(d)   value added tax due pursuant to article 28A(1)(a).

17(3) Member states shall also grant every taxable person the right to the deduction or refund of the value added tax referred to in paragraph 2 in so far as the goods and services are used for the purposes of:

(a)   transactions relating to the economic activities referred to in article 4(2), carried out in another country, which would be deductible if they had been performed within the territory of the country;

(b)   transactions which are exempt pursuant to article 14(1)(i), 15, 16(1)(B), (C), (D) or (E) or (2) or 28C(A) and (C);

(c)   any of the transactions exempt pursuant to article 13(B)(a) and (d)(1) to (5), when the customer is established outside the Community or when those transactions are directly linked with goods to be exported to a country outside the Community.

17(4) The refund of value added tax referred to in paragraph 3 shall be effected:

–   to taxable persons who are not established within the territory of the country but who are established in another member state in accordance with the detailed implementing rules laid down in Directive 79/1072.

–   to taxable persons who are not established within the territory of the Community, in accordance with the detailed implementing rules laid down in Directive 86/560.

For the purposes of applying the above:

(a)   the taxable persons referred to in article 1 of Directive 79/1072 shall also be considered for the purposes of applying the said directive as taxable persons who are not established in the country when, inside the territory of the country, they have only carried out supplies of goods and services to a person who has been designated as the person liable to pay the tax in accordance with article 21(1)(a);

(b)   the taxable persons referred to in article 1 of Directive 86/560 shall also be considered for the purposes of applying the said directive as taxable persons who are not established in the Community when, inside the territory of the country, they have only carried out supplies of goods and services to a person who has been designated as the person liable to pay the tax in accordance with article 21(1)(a);

(c)   Directives 79/1072 and 86/560 shall not apply to supplies of goods which are, or may be, exempted under article 28C(A) when the goods supplied are dispatched or transported by the acquirer or for his account.

17(5)   As regards goods and services to be used by a taxable person both for transactions covered by paragraphs 2 and 3, in respect of which value added tax is deductible, and for transactions in respect of which value added tax is not deductible, only such proportion of the value added tax shall be deductible as is attributable to the former transactions.

This proportion shall be determined, in accordance with article 19, for all the transactions carried out by the taxable person.

However, member states may:

(a)   authorise the taxable person to determine a proportion for each sector of his business, provided that separate accounts are kept for each sector;

(b)   compel the taxable person to determine a proportion for each sector of his business and to keep separate accounts for each sector;

(c)   authorise or compel the taxable person to make the deduction on the basis of the use of all or part of the goods and services;

(d)   authorise or compel the taxable person to make the deduction in accordance with the rule laid down in the first subparagraph, in respect of all goods and services used for all transactions referred to therein;

(e)   provide that where the value added tax which is not deductible by the taxable person is insignificant it shall be treated as nil.

17(6)   Before a period of four years at the latest has elapsed from the date of entry into force of this directive, the Council, acting unanimously on a proposal from the Commission, shall decide what expenditure shall not be eligible for a deduction of value added tax. Value added tax shall in no circumstances be deductible on expenditure which is not strictly business expenditure, such as that on luxuries, amusements or entertainment.

Until the above rules come into force, member states may retain all the exclusions provided for under their national laws when this directive comes into force.

17(7)   Subject to the consultation provided for in article 29, each member state may, for cyclical economic reasons, totally or partly exclude all or some capital goods or other goods from the system of deductions. To maintain identical conditions of competition, member states may, instead of refusing deduction, tax the goods manufactured by the taxable person himself or which he has purchased in the country or imported, in such a way that the tax does not exceed the value added tax which would have been charged on the acquisition of similar goods.

History – Art. 17(2)–(4) replaced by virtue of art. 28F of Directive 77/388, which was itself inserted by Directive 91/680, art. 1(22) (OJ 1991 L376/1), and amended by Directive 92/111, art. 1(18) (OJ 1992 L384/47). Member states had to bring into force the measures necessary to comply with these provisions no later than 1 January 1993.

Art. 17(2)(a) replaced by virtue of amendment of Directive 77/388, art. 28F(1) by Directive 95/7, art. 10 (OJ 1995 L102/18). Member states required to bring into force the measures necessary to comply with Directive 95/7 on 1 January 1996. The former art. 17(2)(a) read as follows:

"(a)   value added tax due or paid in respect of goods or services supplied or to be supplied to him by another taxable person liable for the tax within the territory of the country;"

Former art. 17(4) partially repealed by Directive 86/560, art. 7 with effect from 1 January 1988 (OJ 1986 L326/40).

Cross references – VATA 1994, s. 24, 25, 39 and Sch. 8, Grp. 7, items 6–9; Grp. 8, item 5: credit for input tax; tax repayments overseas; international services; transport outside the UK.

VAT Regulations 1995 (SI 1995/2518), reg. 185–197.
VAT (Input Tax) (Specified Supplies) Order 1992 (SI 1992/3123): supplies to persons outside the EC.
Directive 79/1072: refunds outside the country.
Council Decision 97/375 of 9 June 1997 authorises derogation from art. 17(1) to permit the UK to provide within an optional scheme that enterprises with an annual turnover not higher than £400,000 must postpone the right of deduction of tax until it has been paid to the supplier.
Council Decision 98/198 of 9 March 1998 authorises derogation from art. 17(2)and, (3) to permit the UK to restrict to 50% the right of the hirer or lessee of a car to deduct the VAT on the cost of hiring or leasing that car where it is used for private purposes.
Official publications – 723.

ART. 18   Rules governing the exercise of the right to deduct

18(1)   To exercise his right of deduction, a taxable person must:

(a)   in respect of deductions pursuant to article 17(2)(a), hold an invoice drawn up in accordance with article 22(3);

(b)   in respect of deductions pursuant to article 17(2)(b), hold an import document specifying him as consignee or importer and stating or permitting the calculation of the amount of tax due;

(c)   in respect of deductions pursuant to article 17(2)(c), comply with the formalities established by each member state;

(d)   when he is required to pay the tax as a customer or purchaser where article 21(1) applies, comply with the formalities laid down by each member state;

(e)   in respect of deductions pursuant to article 17(2)(d), set out in the declaration provided for in article 22(4) all the information needed for the amount of the tax due on his intra-Community acquisitions of goods to be calculated and hold an invoice in accordance with article 22(3).

18(2)   The taxable person shall effect the deduction by subtracting from the total amount of the value added tax for a given tax period the total amount of the tax in respect of which, during the same period, the right to deduct has arisen and can be exercised under the provisions of paragraph 1.

However, member states may require that as regards taxable persons who carry out occasional transactions as defined in article 4(3), the right to deduct shall be exercised only at the time of the supply.

18(3)   Member states shall determine the conditions and procedures whereby a taxable person may be authorised to make a deduction which he has not made in accordance with the provisions of paragraphs 1 and 2.

18(3A)   Member states may authorise a taxable person who does not hold an invoice in accordance with article 22(3) to make the deduction referred to in article 17(2)(d); they shall determine the conditions and arrangements for applying this provision.

18(4)   Where for a given tax period the amount of authorised deductions exceeds the amount of tax due, the member states may either make a refund or carry the excess forward to the following period according to conditions which they shall determine.

However, member states may refuse to refund or carry forward if the amount of the excess is insignificant.

History – Art. 18(1) replaced and art. 18(3A) inserted by virtue of art. 28F(2) and (3) of Directive 77/388 which was itself inserted by Directive 91/680, art. 1(22) (OJ 1991 L376/1).

Cross references – VATA 1994, s. 25; VAT Regulations 1995 (SI 1995/2518), reg. 29: credit for input tax; procedure for claiming input tax.

ART. 19   Calculation of the deductible proportion

19(1)   The proportion deductible under the first subparagraph of article 17(5) shall be made up of a fraction having:

–   as numerator, the total amount, exclusive of value added tax, of turnover per year attributable to transactions in respect of which value added tax is deductible under article 17(2) and (3),

–   as denominator, the total amount, exclusive of value added tax, of turnover per year attributable to transactions included in the numerator and to transactions in respect of which value added tax is not deductible. The member states may also include in the denominator the amount of subsidies, other than those specified in article 11(A)(1)(a).

The proportion shall be determined on an annual basis, fixed as a percentage and rounded up to a figure not exceeding the next unit.

19(2) By way of derogation from the provisions of paragraph 1, there shall be excluded from the calculation of the deductible proportion, amounts of turnover attributable to the supplies of capital goods used by the taxable person for the purposes of his business. Amounts of turnover attributable to transactions specified in article 13(B)(d), in so far as these are incidental transactions, and to incidental real estate and financial transactions shall also be excluded. Where member states exercise the option provided under article 20(5) not to require adjustment in respect of capital goods, they may include disposals of capital goods in the calculation of the deductible proportion.

19(3) The provisional proportion for a year shall be that calculated on the basis of the preceding year's transactions. In the absence of any such transactions to refer to, or where they were insignificant in amount, the deductible proportion shall be estimated provisionally, under supervision of the tax authorities, by the taxable person from his own forecasts. However, member states may retain their current rules.

Deductions made on the basis of such provisional proportion shall be adjusted when the final proportion is fixed during the next year.

Cross references – VATA 1994, s. 26: amount of allowable input tax.

ART. 20   Adjustments of deductions

20(1) The initial deduction shall be adjusted according to the procedures laid down by the member states, in particular:

(a)   where that deduction was higher or lower than that to which the taxable person was entitled;

(b)   where after the return is made some change occurs in the factors used to determine the amount to be deducted, in particular where purchases are cancelled or price reductions are obtained; however, adjustment shall not be made in cases of transactions remaining totally or partially unpaid and of destruction, loss or theft of property duly proved or confirmed, nor in the case of applications for the purpose of making gifts of small value and giving samples specified in article 5(6). However, member states may require adjustment in cases of transactions remaining totally or partially unpaid and of theft.

20(2) In the case of capital goods, adjustment shall be spread over five years including that in which the goods were acquired or manufactured. The annual adjustment shall be made only in respect of one-fifth of the tax imposed on the goods. The adjustment shall be made on the basis of the variations in the deduction entitlement in subsequent years in relation to that for the year in which the goods were acquired or manufactured.

By way of derogation from the preceding subparagraph, member states may base the adjustment on a period of five full years starting from the time at which the goods are first used.

In the case of immovable property acquired as capital goods, the adjustment period may be extended up to 20 years.

20(3) In the case of supply during the period of adjustment capital goods shall be regarded as if they had still been applied for business use by the taxable person until expiry of the period of adjustment. Such business activities are presumed to be fully taxed in cases where the delivery of the said goods is taxed; they are presumed to be fully exempt where the delivery is exempt. The adjustment shall be made only once for the whole period of adjustment still to be covered.

However, in the latter case, member states may waive the requirement for adjustment in so far as the purchaser is a taxable person using the capital goods in question solely for transactions in respect of which value added tax is deductible.

20(4) For the purposes of applying the provisions of paragraphs 2 and 3, member states may:

–   define the concept of capital goods,

–   indicate the amount of the tax which is to be taken into consideration for adjustment,

–   adopt any suitable measures with a view to ensuring that adjustment does not involve any unjustified advantage,

–   permit administrative simplifications.

20(5) If in any member state the practical effect of applying paragraphs 2 and 3 would be *insignificant, that member state* may subject to the consultation provided for in article 29 forgo application of these paragraphs having regard to the need to avoid distortion of competition, the overall tax effect in the member state concerned and the need for due economy of administration.

20(6) Where the taxable person transfers from being taxed in the normal way to a special scheme or *vice versa*, member states may take all necessary measures to ensure that the taxable person neither benefits nor is prejudiced unjustifiably.

History – Art. 20(2), last subparagraph, replaced by Directive 95/7, art. 1(4) (OJ 1995/L102/18). Member states required to bring into force the measures necessary to comply with this directive on 1 January 1996. The former art. 20(2), last subparagraph, read as follows:
In the case of immovable property acquired as capital goods the adjustment period may be extended up to ten years."
Cross references – VATA 1994, s. 34; CAA 1990, s. 159A; VAT Regulations 1995 (SI 1995/2518), reg. 35: capital goods; capital allowances and additional VAT liabilities and rebates; correction of errors.

TITLE XII – PERSONS LIABLE FOR PAYMENT FOR TAX

ART. 21   Persons liable to pay tax to the authorities

The following shall be liable to pay value added tax:

21(1)   under the internal system:

(a)   the taxable person carrying out the taxable supply of goods or of services, other than one of the supplies of services referred to in (b).

Where the taxable supply of goods or of services is effected by a taxable person who is not established within the territory of the country, member states may adopt arrangements whereby tax is payable by another person. Inter alios a tax representative or the person for whom the taxable supply of goods or of services is carried out may be designated as that other person.

However, the tax is payable by the person to whom the supply of goods is made when the following conditions are met:

  –   the taxable operation is a supply of goods made under the conditions laid down in paragraph 3 of Title E of article 28C,

  –   the person to whom the supply of goods is made is another taxable person or a non-taxable legal person identified for the purposes of value added tax within the territory of the country,

  –   the invoice issued by the taxable person not established within the territory of the country conforms to article 22(3).

However, member states may provide a derogation from this obligation in the case where the taxable person who is not established within the territory of the country has appointed a tax representative in that country.

Member states may provide that someone other than the taxable person shall be held jointly and severally liable for payment of the tax;

(b)   taxable persons to whom services covered by article 9(2)(e) are supplied or persons who are identified for value added tax purposes within the territory of the country to whom services covered by article 28B(C), (D), (E) and (F) are supplied, if the services are carried out by a taxable person established abroad; however, member states may require that the supplier of services shall be held jointly and severally liable for payment of the tax;

(c)   any person who mentions the value added tax on an invoice or other document serving as invoice;

(d)   any person effecting a taxable intra-Community acquisition of goods. Where an intra-Community acquisition of goods is effected by a person established abroad member states may adopt arrangements whereby tax is payable by another person. Inter alios, a tax representative may be designated as that other person. Member states may also provide that someone other than the person effecting the intra-Community acquisition of goods shall be held jointly and severally liable for payment of the tax;

21(2)   on importation: the person or persons designated or accepted as being liable by the member state into which the goods are imported.

History – Art. 21 replaced by virtue of art. 28G of Directive 77/388, which was itself inserted by Directive 91/680, art. 1(22) (OJ 1991 L376/1), and amended by Directive 92/111, art. 1(19) (OJ 1992 L384/47), as to the wording of art. 21(1)(a) and (b). Member states had to bring into force the measures necessary to implement these provisions no later than 1 January 1993, except as regards art. 21(1)(a), third subparagraph, for which the relevant date was 1 January 1994.
Art. 21(1)(b) was replaced by Directive 99/59, art. 1, para. 3 (OJ 1999 L162/63). Member states had to adopt the laws and regulations and administrative provisions necessary to comply with these directives no later than 1 January 2000. The former art. 21(1)(b) read as follows:
  "(b)   persons to whom services covered by article 9(2)(e) are supplied or persons who are identified for value added tax purposes within the territory of the country to whom services covered by article 28B, (C), (D), (E) and (F) are supplied, if the services are carried out by a taxable person established abroad; however, member states may require that the supplier of services shall be held jointly and severally liable for payment of the tax;"
Former art. 21(1)(b) was replaced by virtue of amendment of art. 28G of Directive 77/388 by Directive 95/7, art. 11 (OJ 1995 L102/18). Member states required to bring into force the measures necessary to comply with Directive 95/7 on 1 January 1996. The former art. 21(1)(b) read as follows:
  "(b)   persons to whom services covered by article 9(2)(e) are supplied, or persons, identified for VAT purposes within the territory of the country, to whom services referred to in article 28B(C), (D), or (E) are supplied, when the service is carried out by a taxable person established abroad; however, member states may require that the supplier of the service shall be held jointly and severally liable for payment of the tax;"

Cross references – VATA 1994, s. 1(2), (4), 8 and Sch. 11, para. 5: liability for tax; tax on importation; services subject to reverse charge; recovery of tax etc.
Council Decision 93/204, authorises the UK to apply, until 31 December 1996, a measure derogating from 21(1)(a) whereby a supply of goods is deemed to occur where assets, other than the capital goods subject to adjustment of the deductions initially made pursuant to legislation adopted by the United Kingdom on the basis of article 20 of the directive, are totally or partially transferred to a company which is a member of a group of enterprises treated as a single taxable person within the meaning of article 4(4) of the directive and which, as a member of that group, is not entitled to deduct tax in full, a provision whereby the company which is the recipient of the supply of assets referred to in the first indent becomes liable to tax.

TITLE XIII – OBLIGATIONS OF PERSONS LIABLE FOR PAYMENT

ART. 22 Obligations under the internal system

22(1)

(a) Every taxable person shall state when his activity as a taxable person commences, changes or ceases.

(b) Without prejudice to (a), every taxable person referred to in article 28A(1)(a), second subparagraph, shall state that he is effecting intra-Community acquisitions of goods when the conditions for application of the derogation provided for in that article are not fulfilled.

(c) Member states shall take the measures necessary to identify by means of an individual number:

– every taxable person, with the exception of those referred to in article 28A(4), who within the territory of the country effects supplies of goods or of services giving him the right of deduction, other than provisions of services for which tax is payable solely by the customer in accordance with article 21(1)(b) and other than a supply of goods or services to a person who has been designated as the person liable for tax in accordance with art. 21(1)(a), third paragraph. However, member states need not identify certain taxable persons referred to in article 4(3),

– every taxable person referred to in paragraph 1(b) and every taxable person who exercises the option provided for in the third subparagraph of article 28A(1)(a),

– every taxable person who, within the territory of the country, effects intra-Community acquisitions of goods for the purposes of his operations relating to the economic activities referred to in article 4(2) carried out abroad.

(d) Each individual identification number shall have a prefix in accordance with ISO International Standard No. 3166 – alpha 2 – by which the member state of issue may be identified.

(e) Member states shall take the measures necessary to ensure that their identification systems distinguish the taxable persons referred to in (c) and to ensure the correct application of the transitional arrangements for the taxation of intra-Community transactions as laid down in this title.

22(2)

(a) Every taxable person shall keep accounts in sufficient detail for value added tax to be applied and inspected by the tax authority.

(b) Every taxable person shall keep a register of the goods he has dispatched or transported or which have been dispatched or transported on his behalf out of the territory defined in article 3 but within the Community for the purposes of the transactions referred to in the fifth, sixth and seventh indents of article 28A(5)(b).

Every taxable person shall keep sufficiently detailed accounts to permit the identification of goods dispatched to him from another member state by or on behalf of a taxable person identified for purposes of value added tax in that other member state, in connection with which a service has been provided pursuant to the third or fourth indent of article 9(2)(c);

22(3)

(a) Every taxable person shall issue an invoice, or other document serving as invoice, in respect of goods and services which he has supplied or rendered to another taxable person or to a non-taxable legal person. Every taxable person shall also issue an invoice, or other document serving as invoice, in respect of the supplies of goods referred to in article 28B(B)(1) and in respect of goods supplied under the conditions laid down in article 28C(A). A taxable person shall keep a copy of every document issued.

Every taxable person shall likewise issue an invoice in respect of any payment to account made to him before any supplies of goods referred to in the first subparagraph and in respect of any payment to account made to him by another taxable person or by a non-taxable legal person before the provision of services is completed.

(b)   The invoice shall state clearly the price exclusive of tax and the relevant tax at each rate as well as any exemptions.

The invoice shall also indicate:

- in the case of the transactions referred to in article 28B(C), (D), (E) and (F), the number by which the taxable person is identified in the territory of the country and the number by which the customer is identified and under which the service has been rendered to him,
- in the case of the transactions referred to in article 28C(A)(a), the number by which the taxable person is identified in the territory of the country and the number by which the person acquiring the goods is identified in another member state,
- in the case of the supply of new means of transport, the particulars specified in article 28A(2),
- where the provisions of article 28C(E)(3) are applied, an explicit reference to that provision as well as the identification number for value added tax purposes under which the taxable person has carried out the intra-Community acquisition and the subsequent supply of goods and the number by which the person to whom this supply is made is identified for VAT purposes.

(c)   Member states shall lay down the criteria that shall determine whether a document may be considered an invoice.

22(4)

(a)   Every taxable person shall submit a return by a deadline to be determined by member states. That deadline may not be more than two months later than the end of each tax period. The tax period shall be fixed by each member state at one month, two months or a quarter. Member states may, however, set different periods provided that they do not exceed one year.

(b)   The return shall set out all the information needed to calculate the tax that has become chargeable and the deductions to be made including, where appropriate, and in so far as it seems necessary for the establishment of the basis of assessment, the total value of the transactions relative to such tax and deductions and the value of any exempt transactions.

(c)   The return shall also set out:

- on the one hand, the total value, less value added tax, of the supplies of goods referred to in article 28C(A) on which tax has become chargeable during the period.
  The following shall also be added: the total value, less value added tax, of the supplies of goods referred to in the second sentence of article 8(1)(a) and in article 28B(B)(1) effected within the territory of another member state for which tax has become chargeable during the return period where the place of departure of the dispatch or transport of the goods is situated in the territory of the country,
- on the other hand, the total amount, less value added tax of the intra-Community acquisitions of goods referred to in article 28A(1) and (6) effected within the territory of the country on which tax has become chargeable.
  The following shall also be added: the total value, less value added tax, of the supplies of goods referred to in the second sentence of article 8(1)(a) and in article 28B(B)(1) effected in the territory of the country on which tax has become chargeable during the return period, where the place of departure of the dispatch or transport of the goods is situated within the territory of another member state, and the total amount, less value added tax, of the supplies of goods made within the territory of the country for which the taxable person has been designated as the person liable for the tax in accordance with article 28C(E)(3) and under which the tax has become payable in the course of the period covered by the declaration.

22(5)   Every taxable person shall pay the net amount of the value added tax when submitting the regular return. Member states may, however, set a different date for the payment of that amount or may demand an interim payment.

22(6)

(a)   Member states may require a taxable person to submit a statement, including all the particulars specified in paragraph 4, concerning all transactions carried out in the preceding year. That statement shall provide all the information necessary for any adjustments.

(b)   Every taxable person identified for value added tax purposes shall also submit a recapitulative statement of the acquirers identified for value added tax purposes to whom he has supplied goods under the conditions provided for in article 28C(A)(a) and (d), and of consignees identified for value added tax purposes in the transactions referred to in the fifth subparagraph.

The recapitulative statement shall be drawn up for each calendar quarter within a period and in accordance with procedures to be determined by the member states, which shall take the measures necessary to ensure that the provisions concerning administrative co-operation in the field of indirect taxation are in any event complied with.

The recapitulative statement shall set out:
- the number by which the taxable person is identified for purposes of value added tax in the territory of the country and under which he effected supplies of goods in the conditions laid down in article 28C(A)(a),
- the number by which each person acquiring goods is identified for purposes of value added tax in another member state and under which the goods were supplied to him,
- for each person acquiring goods, the total value of the supplies of goods effected by the taxable person. Those amounts shall be declared for the calendar quarter during which the tax became chargeable.

The recapitulative statement shall set out:
- for the supplies of goods covered by article 28C(A)(d), the number by means of which the taxable person is identified for purposes of value added tax in the territory of the country, the number by which he is identified in the member state of arrival of the dispatch or transport and the total amount of the supplies, determined in accordance with article 28E(2).
- the amounts of adjustments made pursuant to article 11(C)(1). Those amounts shall be declared for the calendar quarter during which the person acquiring the goods is notified of the adjustment.

In the cases set out in the third subparagraph of article 28B(A)(2), the taxable person identified for VAT purposes within the territory of the country shall mention in a clear way on the recapitulative statement:
- the number by which he is identified for value added tax purposes within the territory of the country and under which he carried out the intra-Community acquisition and the subsequent supply of goods,
- the number by which, within the territory of the member state of arrival of the dispatch or transport of the goods, the consignee of the subsequent supply by the taxable person is identified,
- and, for each consignee, the total amount, less value added tax, of the supplies made by the taxable person within the territory of the member state of arrival of the dispatch or transport of the goods. These amounts shall be declared for the calendar quarter during which the tax became chargeable.

(c)   By way of derogation from (b), member states may:
- require recapitulative statements to be filed on a monthly basis,
- require that recapitulative statements give additional particulars.

(d)   In the case of supplies of new means of transport effected under the conditions laid down in article 28C(A)(b) by a taxable person identified for purposes of value added tax to a purchaser not identified for purposes of value added tax or by a taxable person as defined in article 28A(4), member states shall take the measures necessary to ensure that the vendor communicates all the information necessary for value added tax to be applied and inspected by the tax authority.

(e)   Member states may require taxable persons who in the territory of the country effect intra-Community acquisitions of goods as defined in article 28A(1)(a) and (6) to submit statements giving details of such acquisitions provided, however, that such statements may not be required for a period of less than one month.

Member states may also require persons who effect intra-Community acquisitions of new means of transport as defined in article 28A(1)(b) to provide, when submitting the return referred to in paragraph 4, all the information necessary for value added tax to be applied and inspected by the tax authority.

22(7)   Member states shall take the measures necessary to ensure that those persons who, in accordance with article 21(1)(a) and (b), are considered to be liable to pay the tax instead of a taxable person established abroad or who are jointly and severally liable with the above obligations relating to declaration and payment.

22(8) Member states may impose other obligations which they deem necessary for correct collection of the tax and for the prevention of evasion, subject to the requirement of equal treatment for domestic transactions and transactions carried out between member states, and provided that such obligations do not, in trade between member states, give rise to formalities connected with the crossing of frontiers.

22(9)

(a)   Member states may release from certain or all obligations:
- taxable persons carrying out only supplies of goods or of services which are exempt pursuant to articles 13 and 15,
- taxable persons eligible for the exemption from tax provided for in article 24 and for the derogation provided for in article 28A(1)(a), second subparagraph,
- taxable persons carrying out none of the transactions referred to in paragraph 4(c).

(b)   Member states may release taxable persons other than those referred to in (a) from certain of the obligations referred to in 2(a).

(c)   Member states may release taxable persons from payment of the tax due where the amount involved is insignificant.

22(10) Member states shall take measures to ensure that non-taxable legal persons who are liable for the tax payable in respect of intra-Community acquisitions of goods covered by the first subparagraph of article 28A(1)(a) comply with the above obligations relating to declaration and payment and that they are identified by an individual number as defined in paragraph 1(c), (d) and (e).

22(11) In the case of intra-Community acquisitions of products subject to excise duty referred to in article 28A(1)(c) as well as in the case of intra-Community acquisitions of new means of transport covered by article 28A(1)(b), member states shall adopt arrangements for declaration and subsequent payment.

22(12) Acting unanimously on a proposal from the Commission, the Council may authorise any member state to introduce particular measures to simplify the statement obligations laid down in paragraph 6(b). Such simplification measures, which shall not jeopardise the proper monitoring of intra-Community transactions, may take the following forms:

(a)   member states may authorise taxable persons who meet the following three conditions to file one-year recapitulative statements indicating the numbers by which the persons to whom those taxable persons have supplied goods under the conditions laid down in article 28C(A) are identified for purposes of value added tax in other member states:
- the total annual value, less value added tax, of their supplies of goods or provisions of services, as defined in articles 5, 6 and 28A(5), does not exceed by more than ECU 35,000 the amount of the annual turnover which is used as a reference for application of the exemption from tax provided for in article 24,
- the total annual value, less value added tax, of supplies of goods effected by them under the conditions laid down in article 28C(A) does not exceed the equivalent in national currency of ECU 15,000,
- supplies of goods effected by them under the conditions laid down in article 28C(A) are other than supplies of new means of transport;

(b)   member states which set at over three months the tax period for which taxable persons must submit the returns provided for in paragraph 4 may authorise such persons to submit recapitulative statements for the same period where those taxable persons meet the following three conditions:
- the overall annual value, less value added tax, of the goods and the services they supply, as defined in articles 5, 6 and 28A(5), does not exceed the equivalent in national currency of ECU 200,000,
- the total annual value, less value added tax, of supplies of goods effected by them under the conditions laid down in article 28C(A) does not exceed the equivalent in national currency of ECU 15,000,
- supplies of goods effected by them under the conditions laid down in article 28C(A) are other than supplies of new means of transport.

History – Art. 22 replaced by virtue of art. 28H of Directive 77/388, which was itself inserted by Directive 91/680, art. 1(22) (OJ 1991 L376/1), and amended by Directive 92/111, art. 1(20) (OJ 1992 L384/47) with regard to the wording of art. 22(1)(c), 22(3)(b), 22(4)(c), 22(6)(b) and 22(11). Member states had to bring into force the measures necessary to comply with these

Dir. 77/388, art anuary 1993, except in so far as they relate to obligations in respect of transactions referred to in ragraph, 28B(A)(2), third subparagraph, and 28C(E)(3), in respect of which the relevant date was

ended by virtue of amendments to art. 28H by Directive 95/7, art. 12 (OJ 1995 L102/18); the replacement 22(3)(b), second paragraph, first indent; art. 22(6)(b), first subparagraph, and third subparagraph, second *tion of* art. 22(6)(b), fifth subparagraph. Member states required to bring into force the measures necessary

ision of art. 95/7 on 1 January 1995. The former art. 22(2)(b) read as follows:

art. 2) Directive *xable person shall keep a register of the goods he has dispatched or transported or which have been dispatched or* n his behalf out of the territory defined in article 3 but *within the Community* for the purposes of the transactions in the fourth, fifth, sixth and seventh indents of article 28A(5)(b).

able person shall keep a register of materials dispatched to him from another member state by or on behalf of a taxable identified for purposes of value added tax in that other member state with a view to the supply to that taxable person of act work."

former art. 22(3)(b), second paragraph, first indent read as follows: in the case of the transactions referred to in article 28B(C), (D) and (E), the number by which the taxable person is identified in the territory of the country and the number by which the customer is identified and under which the service has been rendered to him,"

The former art. 22(6)(b), first subparagraph read as follows:
(b) Every taxable person identified for value added tax purposes shall also submit a recapitulative statement of the acquirers identified for value added tax purposes to whom he has supplied goods under the conditions provided for in article 28C(A)(a) and (d), and of consignees identified for value added tax purposes in the transactions referred to in the fifth and sixth subparagraphs."

The former art. 22(6)(b), third subparagraph, second indent read as follows:
" the number by which each person acquiring goods is identified for purposes of value added tax in another member state and under which the goods were supplied to him and, where appropriate, an indication that supplies of goods as defined in article 28A(5)(a) were effected for the person acquiring those goods."

The former art. 22(6)(b), fifth subparagraph read as follows:
Where goods are dispatched or transported by or on behalf of the taxable person out of the territory defined in article 3 but within the Community, with a view to the supply to the taxable person of contract work under the conditions set out in article 28A(5)(a), the recapitulative statement drawn up for the quarter during which the goods were thus dispatched or transported shall set out:
– the number by means of which the taxable person is identified for purposes of value added tax in the territory of the member state of departure of the dispatch or transport of the goods,
– the number by means of which the taxable person to whom the goods have been sent with a view to the supply of contract work is identified in the member state of arrival of the dispatch or transport of the goods,
– a statement that the goods have been dispatched or transported under the conditions referred to above, for the purposes of contract work physically carried out in the member state of arrival of the dispatch or transport."

Cross references – VATA 1994, s. 47 and Sch. 1, 11, para. 6; VAT Regulations 1995 (SI 1995/2518), Pt. III, V: recovery of tax from agents etc.; registration requirements; duty to keep records; invoices; time of supply.
VAT Regulations 1995 (SI 1995/2518), Pt. IV: EC sales statements.
Council Decision 93/609, of 22 November 1993 authorises the UK to introduce a particular measure in accordance with under subparagraph (a) of article 22(12), to simplify the obligations laid down in under subparagraph 6(b) of article 22 regarding recapitulative statements.
Regulation 3046/92, art. 8(2): information provided by tax authorities as referred to in Regulation 3330/91, art. 11(4).

ART. 23   Obligations in respect of imports

23   As regards imported goods, member states shall lay down the detailed rules for the making of the declarations and payments.

In particular, member states may provide that the value added tax payable on importation of goods by taxable persons or persons liable to tax or certain categories of these two need not be paid at the time of importation, on condition that the tax is mentioned as such in a return to be submitted under article 22(4).

TITLE XIV – SPECIAL SCHEMES

ART. 24   Special scheme for small undertakings

24(1)   Member states which might encounter difficulties in applying the normal tax scheme to small undertakings by reason of their activities or structure shall have the option, under such conditions and within such limits as they may set but subject to the consultation provided for in article 29, of applying simplified procedures such as flat-rate schemes for charging and collecting the tax provided they do not lead to a reduction thereof.

24(2)   Until a date to be fixed by the Council acting unanimously on a proposal from the Commission, but which shall not be later than that on which the charging of tax on imports and the remission of tax on exports in trade between the member states are abolished:

(a)   member states which have made use of the option under article 14 of the second Council directive of 11 April 1967 to introduce exemptions or graduated tax relief may retain them and the arrangements for applying them if they conform with the value added tax system. Those member states which apply an exemption from tax to taxable persons whose annual turnover is less than the equivalent in national currency of 5,000 European units of account at the conversion rate of the day on which this directive is adopted, may increase this exemption up to 5,000 European units of account.

Member states which apply graduated tax relief may neither increase the ceiling of the graduated tax reliefs nor render the conditions for the granting of it more favourable;

(b) member states which have not made use of this option may grant an exemption from tax to taxable persons whose annual turnover is at the maximum equal to the equivalent in national currency of 5,000 European units of account at the conversion rate of the day on which this directive is adopted; where appropriate, they may grant graduated tax relief to taxable persons whose annual turnover exceeds the ceiling fixed by the member states for the application of exemption;

(c) member states which apply an exemption from tax to taxable persons whose annual turnover is equal to or higher than the equivalent in national currency of 5,000 European units of account at the conversion rate of the day on which this directive is adopted, may increase it in order to maintain its value in real terms.

24(3) The concepts of exemption and graduated tax relief shall apply to the supply of goods and services by small undertakings.

Member states may exclude certain transactions from the arrangements provided for in paragraph 2. The provisions of paragraph 2 shall not, in any case, apply to the transactions referred to in article 4(3).

In all circumstances supplies of new means of transport effected under the conditions laid down in article 28C(A) as well as supplies of goods and services effected by a taxable person who is not established in the territory of the country shall be excluded from the exemption from tax under paragraph 2.

24(4) The turnover which shall serve as a reference for the purposes of applying the provisions of paragraph 2 shall consist of the amount, exclusive of value added tax, of goods and services supplied as defined in articles 5 and 6, to the extent that they are taxed, including transactions exempted with refund of tax previously paid in accordance with article 28(2), and the amount of the transactions exempted pursuant to article 15, the amount of real property transactions, the financial transactions referred to in article 13(B)(d), and insurance services, unless these transactions are ancillary transactions.

However, disposals of tangible or intangible capital assets of an undertaking shall not be taken into account for the purposes of calculating turnover.

24(5) Taxable persons exempt from tax shall not be entitled to deduct tax in accordance with the provisions of article 17, nor to show the tax on their invoices or on any other documents serving as invoices.

24(6) Taxable persons eligible for exemption from tax may opt either for the normal value added tax scheme or for the simplified procedures referred to in paragraph 1. In this case they shall be entitled to any graduated tax relief which may be laid down by national legislation.

24(7) Subject to the application of paragraph 1, taxable persons enjoying graduated relief shall be treated as taxable persons subject to the normal value added tax scheme.

24(8) At four-yearly intervals, and for the first time on 1 January 1982, and after consultation of the member states, the Commission shall report to the Council on the application of the provisions of this article. It shall as far as may be necessary, and taking into account the need to ensure the long-term convergence of national regulations, attach to this report proposals for:

(a) improvements to be made to the special scheme for small undertakings;

(b) the adaptation of national systems as regards exemptions and graduated value added tax relief;

(c) the adaptation of the limit of 5,000 European units of account mentioned in paragraph 2.

24(9) The Council will decide at the appropriate time whether the realisation of the objective referred to in article 4 of the first council directive of 11 April 1967 requires the introduction of a special scheme for small undertakings and will, if appropriate, decide on the limits and common implementing conditions of this scheme. Until the introduction of such a scheme, member states may retain their own special schemes which they will apply in accordance with the provisions of this article and of subsequent acts of the Council.

History – In art. 24(3), the final subparagraph was added by virtue of art. 28I of Directive 77/388, which was itself inserted by Directive 91/680, art. 1(22) (OJ 1991 L376/1) and replaced by Directive 92/111, art. 1(21) (OJ 1992 L384/47). Member states had to bring into force the measures necessary to implement these provisions no later than 1 January 1993.

ART. 25   Common flat-rate scheme for farmers

25(1)   Where the application to farmers of the normal value added tax scheme, or the simplified scheme provided for in article 24, would give rise to difficulties, member states may apply to farmers a flat-rate scheme tending to offset the value added tax charged on purchases of goods and services made by the flat-rate farmers pursuant to this article.

25(2)   For the purposes of this article, the following definitions shall apply:

—   **"farmer"**: a taxable person who carries on his activity in one of the undertakings defined below,

—   **"agricultural, forestry or fisheries undertakings"**: an undertaking considered to be such by each member state within the framework of the production activities listed in Annex A,

—   **"flat-rate farmer"**: a farmer subject to the flat-rate scheme provided for in paragraphs 3 et seq.,

—   **"agricultural products"**: goods produced by an agricultural, forestry or fisheries undertaking in each member state as a result of the activities listed in Annex A,

—   **"agricultural service"**: any service as set out in Annex B supplied by a farmer using his labour force and/or by means of the equipment normally available on the agricultural, forestry or fisheries undertaking operated by him,

—   **"value added tax charge on inputs"**: the amount of the total value added tax attaching to the goods and services purchased by all agricultural, forestry and fisheries undertakings of each member state subject to the flat-rate scheme where such tax would be deductible under article 17 by a farmer subject to the normal value added tax scheme,

—   **"flat-rate compensation percentages"**: the percentages fixed by member states in accordance with paragraph 3 and applied by them in the cases specified in paragraph 5 to enable flat-rate farmers to offset at a fixed rate the value added tax charge on inputs,

—   **"flat-rate compensation"**: the amount arrived at by applying the flat-rate compensation percentage provided for in paragraph 3 to the turnover of the flat-rate farmer in the cases referred to in paragraph 5.

25(3)   Member states shall fix the flat-rate compensation percentages, where necessary, and shall notify the Commission before applying them. Such percentages shall be based on macro-economic statistics for flat-rate farmers alone for the preceding three years. They may not be used to obtain for flat-rate farmers refunds greater than the value added tax charges on inputs. Member states shall have the option of reducing such percentages to a nil rate. The percentage may be rounded up or down to the nearest half point.

Member states may fix varying flat-rate compensation percentages for forestry, for the different sub-divisions of agriculture and for fisheries.

25(4)   Member states may release flat-rate farmers from the obligations imposed upon taxable persons by article 22.

When they exercise this option, member states shall take the measures necessary to ensure the correct application of the transitional arrangements for the taxation of intra-Community transactions as laid down in Title XVIa.

25(5)   The flat-rate percentages provided for in paragraph 3 shall be applied to the prices, exclusive of tax, of:

(a)   agricultural products supplied by flat-rate farmers to taxable persons other than those eligible within the territory of the country for the flat-rate scheme provided for in this article;

(b)   agricultural products supplied by flat-rate farmers, under the conditions laid down in article 28C(A), to non-taxable legal persons not eligible, in the member state of arrival of the dispatch or transport of the agricultural products thus supplied, for the derogation provided for in article 28A(1)(a), second subparagraph;

(c)   agricultural services supplied by flat-rate farmers to taxable persons other than those eligible within the territory of the country for the flat-rate scheme provided for in this article.

This compensation shall exclude any other form of deduction.

25(6)   In the case of the supplies of agricultural products and of agricultural services referred to in paragraph 5, member states shall provide for the flat-rate compensation to be paid either:

(a)   by the purchaser or customer. In that event, the taxable purchaser or customer shall be authorised as provided for in article 17 and in accordance with the procedures laid down by the member states, to deduct from the tax for which he is liable within the territory of the country the amount of the flat-rate compensation he has paid to flat-rate farmers.

Member states shall refund to the purchaser or customer the amount of the flat-rate compensation he has paid to flat-rate farmers in respect of any of the following transactions:

– supplies of agricultural products effected under the conditions laid down in article 28C(A) to taxable persons, or to non-taxable legal persons acting as such in another member state within which they are not eligible for the derogation provided for in the second subparagraph of article 28A(1)(a),

– supplies of agricultural products effected under the conditions laid down in article 15 and in article 16(1)(B), (D) and (E) to taxable purchasers established outside the Community, provided that the products are used by those purchasers for the purposes of the transactions referred to in article 17(3)(a) and (b) or for the purposes of services which are deemed to be supplied within the territory of the country and on which tax is payable solely by the customers under article 21(1)(b),

– supplies of agricultural services to taxable customers established within the Community but in other member states or to taxable customers established outside the Community, provided that the services are used by those customers for the purposes of the transactions referred to in article 17(3)(a) and (b) and for the purposes of services which are deemed to be supplied within the territory of the country and on which tax is payable solely by the customers under article 21(1)(b).

Member states shall determine the method by which the refunds are to be made; in particular, they may apply article 17(4); or

(b) by the public authorities.

25(7) Member states shall make all necessary provisions to check properly the payment of the flat-rate compensation to the flat-rate farmers.

25(8) As regards all supplies of agricultural products and agricultural services other than those covered by paragraph 5, the flat-rate compensation is deemed to be paid by the purchaser or customer.

25(9) Each member state may exclude from the flat-rate scheme certain categories of farmers and farmers for whom the application of the normal value added tax scheme, or the simplified scheme provided for in article 24(1), would not give rise to administrative difficulties.

Whenever they exercise the option provided for in this article, member states shall take all measures necessary to ensure that the same method of taxation is applied to supplies of agricultural products effected under the conditions laid down in article 28B(B)(1), whether the supply is effected by a flat-rate farmer or by a taxable person other than a flat-rate farmer.

25(10) Every flat-rate farmer may opt, subject to the rules and conditions to be laid down by each member state, for application of the normal value added tax scheme or, as the case may be, the simplified scheme provided for in article 24(1).

25(11) The Commission shall, before the end of the fifth year following the entry into force of this directive, present to the Council new proposals concerning the application of the value added tax to transactions in respect of agricultural products and services.

25(12) When they take up the option provided for in this article the member states shall fix the uniform basis of assessment of the value added tax in order to apply the scheme of own resources using the common method of calculation in Annex C.

History – In art. 25(4) and (9), final subparagraph added and art. 25(5) and (6) replaced by virtue of art. 28J of Directive 77/388 which was itself inserted by Directive 91/680, art. 1(22) (OJ 1991 L376/1).

Cross references – VATA 1994, s. 54: special treatment for persons involved in farming. VAT Regulations 1995 (SI 1995/2518), Pt. XXIV: flat-rate scheme for farmers.

ART. 26 Special scheme for travel agents

26(1) Member states shall apply value added tax to the operations of travel agents in accordance with the provisions of this article, where the travel agents deal with customers in their own name and use the supplies and services of other taxable persons in the provision of travel facilities. This article shall not apply to travel agents who are acting only as intermediaries and accounting for tax in accordance with article 11(A)(3)(c). In this article travel agents include tour operators.

26(2) All transactions performed by the travel agent in respect of a journey shall be treated as a single service supplied by the travel agent to the traveller. It shall be taxable in the member state in which the travel agent has established his business or has a fixed establishment from which the travel agent has provided the services. The taxable amount and the price exclusive of tax, within the meaning of article 22(3)(b), in respect of this service shall be the travel agent's margin, that is to say, the difference between the total amount to be paid by the traveller, exclusive of value added tax, and the actual cost to the travel agent of supplies and services provided by other taxable persons where these transactions are for the direct benefit of the traveller.

26(3) If transactions entrusted by the travel agent to other taxable persons are performed by such persons outside the Community, the travel agent's service shall be treated as an exempted intermediary activity under article 15(14). Where these transactions are performed both inside and outside the Community, only that part of the travel agent's service relating to transactions outside the Community may be exempted.

26(4) Tax charged to the travel agent by other taxable persons on the transactions described in paragraph 2 which are for the direct benefit of the traveller, shall not be eligible for deduction or refund in any member state.

Cross reference – VAT (Tour Operators) Order 1987 (SI 1987/1806).

Official publications – 709/5.

ART. 26A   Special arrangements applicable to second-hand goods, works of art, collectors' items and antiques

26A(A)   Definitions

26A For the purposes of this article, and without prejudice to other Community provisions:

(a)   **works of art** shall mean the objects referred to in (a) of Annex I.
However, member states shall have the option of not considering as "works of art" the items mentioned in the final three indents in (a) in Annex I;

(b)   **collectors' items** shall mean the objects referred to in (b) of Annex I;

(c)   **antiques** shall mean the objects referred to in (c) of Annex I;

(d)   **second-hand goods** shall mean tangible movable property that is suitable for further use as it is or after repair, other than works of art, collectors' items or antiques and other than precious metals or precious stones as defined by the member states;

(e)   **taxable dealer** shall mean a taxable person who, in the course of his economic activity, purchases or acquires for the purposes of his undertaking, or imports with a view to resale, second-hand goods and/or works of art, collectors' items or antiques, whether that taxable person is acting for himself or on behalf of another person pursuant to a contract under which commission is payable on purchase or sale;

(f)   **organiser of a sale by public auction** shall mean any taxable person who, in the course of his economic activity, offers goods for sale by public auction with a view to handing them over to the highest bidder;

(g)   **"principal of an organiser of a sale by public auction"** shall mean any person who transmits goods to an organiser of a sale by public auction under a contract under which commission is payable on a sale subject to the following provisions:

     –   the organiser of the sale by public auction offers the goods for sale in his own name but on behalf of his principal,

     –   the organiser of the sale by public auction hands over the goods, in his own name but on behalf of his principal, to the highest bidder at the public auction.

26A(B)   Special arrangements for taxable dealers

26A(B)(1) In respect of supplies of second-hand goods, works of art, collectors' items and antiques effected by taxable dealers, member states shall apply special arrangements for taxing the profit margin made by the taxable dealer, in accordance with the following provisions.

26A(B)(2) The supplies of goods referred to in paragraph 1 shall be supplies, by a taxable dealer, of second-hand goods, works of art, collectors' items or antiques supplied to him within the Community:

–   by a non-taxable person, or

–   by another taxable person, in so far as the supply of goods by that other taxable person is exempt in accordance with article 13(B)(c), or

–   by another taxable person in so far as the supply of goods by that other taxable person qualifies for the exemption provided for in article 24 and involves capital assets, or

–   by another taxable dealer, in so far as the supply of goods by that other taxable dealer was subject to value added tax in accordance with these special arrangements.

26A(B)(3) The taxable amount of the supplies of goods referred to in paragraph 2 shall be the profit margin made by the taxable dealer, less the amount of value added tax relating to the profit margin. That profit margin shall be equal to the difference between the selling price charged by the taxable dealer for the goods and the purchase price.

For the purposes of this paragraph, the following definitions shall apply:

-     **selling price** shall mean everything which constitutes the consideration, which has been, or is to be, obtained by the taxable dealer from the purchaser or a third party, including subsidies directly linked to that transaction, taxes, duties, levies and charges and incidental expenses such as commission, packaging, transport and insurance costs charged by the taxable dealer to the purchaser but excluding the amounts referred to in article 11(A)(3),
-     **purchase price** shall mean everything which constitutes the consideration defined in the first indent, obtained, or to be obtained, from the taxable dealer by his supplier.

26A(B)(4) Member states shall entitle taxable dealers to opt for application of the special arrangements to supplies of:

(a)   works of art, collectors' items or antiques which they have imported themselves;

(b)   works of art supplied to them by their creators or their successors in title;

(c)   works of art supplied to them by a taxable person other than a taxable dealer where the supply by that other taxable person was subject to the reduced rate pursuant to article 12(3)(c).

Member states shall determine the detailed rules for exercising this option which shall in any event cover a period at least equal to two calendar years.

If the option is taken up, the taxable amount shall be determined in accordance with paragraph 3. For supplies of works of art, collectors' items or antiques which the taxable dealer has imported himself, the purchase price to be taken into account in calculating the margin shall be equal to the taxable amount on importation, determined in accordance with article 11(B), plus the value added tax due or paid on importation.

26A(B)(5) Where they are effected in the conditions laid down in article 15, the supplies of second-hand goods, works of art, collectors' item[s] or antiques subject to the special arrangements for taxing the margin shall be exempt.

26A(B)(6) Taxable persons shall not be entitled to deduct from the tax for which they are liable the value added tax due or paid in respect of goods which have been, or are to be, supplied to them by a taxable dealer, in so far as the supply of those goods by the taxable dealer is subject to the special arrangements for taxing the margin.

26A(B)(7) In so far as goods are used for the purpose of supplies by him subject to the special arrangements for taxing the margin, the taxable dealer shall not be entitled to deduct from the tax for which he is liable:

(a)   the value added tax due or paid in respect of works of art, collectors' items or antiques which he has imported himself;

(b)   the value added tax due or paid in respect of works of art which have been, or are to be, supplied to him by their creators or their successors in title;

(c)   the value added tax due or paid in respect of works of art which have been, or are to be, supplied to him by a taxable person other than a taxable dealer.

26A(B)(8) Where he is led to apply both the normal arrangements for value added tax and the special arrangements for taxing the margin, the taxable dealer must follow separately in his accounts the transactions falling under each of these arrangements, according to rules laid down by the member states.

26A(B)(9) The taxable dealer may not indicate separately on the invoices which he issues, or on any other document serving as an invoice, tax relating to supplies of goods which he makes subject to the special arrangements for taxing the margin.

26A(B)(10) In order to simplify the procedure for charging the tax and subject to the consultation provided for in article 29, member states may provide that, for certain transactions or for certain categories of taxable dealers, the taxable amount of supplies of goods subject to the special arrangements for taxing the margin shall be determined for each tax period during which the taxable dealer must submit the return referred to in article 22(4).

In that event, the taxable amount for supplies of goods to which the same rate of value added tax is applied shall be the total margin made by the taxable dealer less the amount of value added tax relating to that margin.

The total margin shall be equal to the difference between:

– the total amount of supplies of goods subject to the special arrangements for taxing the margin effected by the taxable dealer during the period; that amount shall be equal to the total selling prices determined in accordance with paragraph 3, and

– the total amount of purchases of goods as referred to in paragraph 2 effected, during that period, by the taxable dealer; that amount shall be equal to the total purchase prices determined in accordance with paragraph 3.

Member states shall take the necessary measures to ensure that the taxable persons concerned do not enjoy unjustified advantages or sustain unjustified loss.

26A(B)(11) The taxable dealer may apply the normal value added tax arrangements to any supply covered by the special arrangements pursuant to paragraph 2 or 4.

Where the taxable dealer applies the normal value added tax arrangements to:

(a) the supply of a work of art, collectors' item or antique which he has imported himself, he shall be entitled to deduct from his tax liability the value added tax due or paid on the import of those goods;

(b) the supply of a work of art supplied to him by its creator or his successors in title, he shall be entitled to deduct from his tax liability the value added tax due or paid for the work of art supplied to him;

(c) the supply of a work of art supplied to him by a taxable person other than a taxable dealer, he shall be entitled to deduct from his tax liability the value added tax due or paid for the work of art supplied to him.

This right to deduct shall arise at the time when the tax due for the supply in respect of which the taxable dealer opts for application of the normal value added tax arrangements become chargeable.

26A(C) Special arrangements for sales by public auction

26A(C)(1) By way of derogation from B, member states may determine, in accordance with the following provisions, the taxable amount of supplies of second-hand goods, works of art, collectors' items or antiques effected by an organiser of sales by public auction, acting in his own name, pursuant to a contract under which commission is payable on the sale of those goods by public auction, on behalf of:

– a non-taxable person, or

– another taxable person, in so far as the supply of goods, within the meaning of article 5(4)(c), by that other taxable person is exempt in accordance with article 13(B)(c), or

– another taxable person, in so far as the supply of goods, within the meaning of article 5(4)(c), by that other taxable person qualifies for the exemption provided for in article 24 and involves capital assets, or

– a taxable dealer, in so far as the supply of goods, within the meaning of article 5(4)(c), by that other taxable dealer, is subject to tax in accordance with the special arrangements for taxing the margin provided for in B.

26A(C)(2) The taxable amount of each supply of goods referred to in paragraph 1 shall be the total amount invoiced in accordance with paragraph 4 to the purchaser by the organiser of the sale by public auction, less:

– the net amount paid or to be paid by the organiser of the sale by public auction to his principal, determined in accordance with paragraph 3, and

– the amount of the tax due by the organiser of the sale by public auction in respect of his supply.

26A(C)(3) The net amount paid or to be paid by the organiser of the sale by public auction to his principal shall be equal to the difference between:

– the price of the goods at public auction, and

– the amount of the commission obtained or to be obtained by the organiser of the sale by public auction from his principal, under the contract whereby commission is payable on the sale.

26A(C)(4) *The organiser of the sale by public auction must issue to the purchaser an invoice or a document in lieu itemising:*

– the auction price of the goods,

– taxes, dues, levies and charges,

– incidental expenses such as commission, packing, transport and insurance costs charged by the organiser to the purchaser of the goods.

That invoice must not indicate any value added tax separately.

26A(C)(5)   The organiser of the sale by public auction to whom the goods were transmitted under a contract whereby commission is payable on a public auction sale must issue a statement to his principal.

That statement must itemise the amount of the transaction, i.e. the auction price of the goods less the amount of the commission obtained or to be obtained from the principal.

A statement so drawn up shall serve as the invoice which the principal, where he is a taxable person, must issue to the organiser of the sale by public auction in accordance with article 22(3).

26A(C)(6)   Organisers of sales by public auction who supply goods under the conditions laid down in paragraph 1 must indicate in their accounts, in suspense accounts:

–   the amounts obtained or to be obtained from the purchaser of the goods,
–   the amount reimbursed or to be reimbursed to the vendor of the goods.

These amounts must be duly substantiated.

26A(C)(7)   The supply of goods to a taxable person who is an organiser of sales by public auction shall be regarded as being effected when the sale of those goods by public auction is itself effected.

26A(D)   Transitional arrangements for the taxation of trade between member states

During the period referred to in article 28L, member states shall apply the following provisions:

(a)   supplies of new means of transport, within the meaning of article 28A(2), effected within the conditions laid down in article 28C(A) shall be excluded from the special arrangements provided for in B and C;

(b)   by way of derogation from article 28A(1)(a), intra-Community acquisitions of second-hand goods, works of art, collectors' items or antiques shall not be subject to value added tax where the vendor is a taxable dealer acting as such and the goods acquired have been subject to tax in the member state of departure of the dispatch or transport, in accordance with the special arrangements for taxing the margin provided for in B, or where the vendor is an organiser of sales by public auction acting as such and the goods acquired have been subject to tax in the member state of departure of the dispatch or transport, in accordance with the special arrangements provided for in C;

(c)   articles 28B(B) and 28C(A)(a), (c) and (d) shall not apply to supplies of goods subject to value added tax in accordance with either of the special arrangements laid down in B and C.

History – Art. 26A was inserted by Directive 94/5, art. 3 (OJ 1994 L60/16). Member states had to bring into force the measures necessary to comply with this directive no later than 1 January 1995.

ART. 26B   Special scheme for investment gold

26B(A)   Definition

26B   For the purposes of this directive, and without prejudice to other Community provisions: "investment gold" shall mean:

(i)   gold, in the form of a bar or a wafer of weights accepted by the bullion markets, of a purity equal to or greater than 995 thousandths, whether or not represented by securities. Member states may exclude from the scheme small bars or wafers of a weight of 1g or less;

(ii)   gold coins which:
–   are of a purity equal to or greater than 900 thousandths,
–   are minted after 1800,
–   are or have been legal tender in the country of origin, and
–   are normally sold at a price which does not exceed the open market value of the gold contained in the coins by more than 80%. Such coins are not, for the purpose of this directive, considered to be sold for numismatic interest. Each member state shall inform the Commission before 1 July each year, starting in 1999, of the coins meeting these criteria which are traded in that member state. The Commission shall publish a comprehensive list of these coins in the "C" series of the *Official Journal of the European Communities* before 1 December each year. Coins included in the published list shall be deemed to fulfil these criteria for the whole year for which the list is published.

26B(B)   Special arrangements applicable to investment gold transactions

Member states shall exempt from value added tax the supply, intra-Community acquisition and importation of investment gold, including investment gold represented by certificates for allocated or unallocated gold or traded on gold accounts and including, in particular, gold loans and swaps, involving a right of owner ship or claim in respect of investment gold, as well as transactions concerning investment gold involving futures and forward contracts leading to a transfer of right of ownership or claim in respect of investment gold.

Member states shall also exempt services of agents who act in the name and for the account of another when they intervene in the supply of investment gold for their principal.

26B(C) Option to tax

Member states shall allow taxable persons who produce investment gold or transform any gold into investment gold as defined in A a right of option for taxation of supplies of investment gold to another taxable person which would otherwise be exempt under B.

Member states may allow taxable persons, who in their trade normally supply gold for industrial purposes, a right of option for taxation of supplies of investment gold as defined in A(i) to another taxable person, which would otherwise be exempt under B. Member states may restrict the scope of this option.

Where the supplier has exercised a right of option for taxation pursuant to the first or second paragraph, member states shall allow a right of option for taxation for the agent in respect of the services mentioned in the second paragraph of B.

Member states shall specify the details of the use of these options, and shall inform the Commission of the rules of application for the exercise of these options in that member state.

26B(D) Right of deduction

26B(D)(1) Taxable persons shall be entitled to deduct:

(a)   tax due or paid in respect of investment gold supplied to, them by a person who has exercised the right of option under C or supplied to them pursuant to the procedure laid down in G;

(b)   tax due or paid in respect of supply to them, or intra-Community acquisition or importation by them, of gold other than investment gold which is subsequently transformed by them or on their behalf into investment gold;

(c)   tax due or paid in respect of services supplied to them consisting of change of form, weight or purity of gold including investment gold,

if their subsequent supply of this gold is exempt under this article.

26B(D)(2) Taxable persons who produce investment gold or transform any gold into investment gold, shall be entitled to deduct tax due or paid by them in respect of supplies, or intra-Community acquisition or importation of goods or services linked to the production or transformation of that gold as if their subsequent supply of the gold exempted under this article were taxable.

26B(E) Special obligations for traders in investment gold

Member states shall, as a minimum, ensure that traders in investment gold keep account of all substantial transactions in investment gold and keep the documentation to allow identification of the customer in such transactions.

Traders shall keep this information for a period of at least five years.

Member states may accept equivalent obligations under measures adopted pursuant to other Community legislation, such as Council Directive 91/308 of 10 June 1991 on prevention of the use of the financial system for the purpose of money laundering, to meet the requirements of the first paragraph.

Member states may lay down stricter obligations, in particular on special record keeping or special accounting requirements.

26B(F) Reverse charge procedure

By way of derogation from article 21(1)(a), as amended by article 28G, in the case of supplies of gold material or semi-manufactured products of a purity of 325 thousandths or greater, or supplies of investment gold where an option referred to in C of this article has been exercised, member states may designate the purchaser as the person liable to pay the tax, according to the procedures and conditions which they shall lay down. When they exercise this option, member states shall take the measures necessary to ensure that the person designated as liable for the tax due fulfils the obligations to submit a statement and to pay the tax in accordance with article 22.

26B(G) Procedure for transactions on a regulated gold bullion market

26B(G)(1) A member state may, subject to consultationprovided for under article 29, disapply the exemption for investment gold provided for by this special scheme in respect of specific transactions, other than intra-Community supplies or exports, concerning investment gold taking place in that member state:

(a)   between taxable persons who are members of a bullion market regulated by the member state concerned, and

(b)   where the transaction is between a member of a bullion market regulated by the member state concerned and another taxable person who is not a member of that market.

Under these circumstances, these transactions shall be taxable and the following shall apply.

26B(G)(2)

(a)   For transactions under 1(a), for the purpose of simplification, the member state shall authorise suspension of the tax to be collected as well as dispense with the recording requirements of value added tax.

(b)   For transactions under 1(b), the reverse charge procedure under F shall be applicable. Where a non-member of the bullion market would not, other than for these transactions, be liable for registration for VAT in the relevant member state, the member shall fulfil the fiscal obligations on behalf of the non-member, according to, the provisions of that member state.

History – Art. 26B was inserted by Directive 98/80, art. 1 (OJ 1998 L281/31). Member states had to bring into force the measures necessary to comply with this directive no later than 1 January 2000.

TITLE XV – SIMPLIFICATION PROCEDURES

ART. 27   [Requests for derogation]

27(1)   The Council, acting unanimously on a proposal from the Commission, may authorise any member state to introduce special measures for derogation from the provisions of this directive, in order to simplify the procedure for charging the tax or to prevent certain types of tax evasion or avoidance. Measures intended to simplify the procedure for charging the tax, except to a negligible extent, may not affect the amount of tax due at the final consumption stage.

27(2)   A member state wishing to introduce the measures referred to in paragraph 1 shall inform the Commission of them and shall provide the Commission with all relevant information.

27(3)   The Commission shall inform the other member states of the proposed measures within one month.

27(4)   The Council's decision shall be deemed to have been adopted if, within two months of the other member states being informed as laid down in the previous paragraph, neither the Commission nor any member state has requested that the matter be raised by the Council.

27(5)   Those member states which apply on 1 January 1977 special measures of the type referred to in paragraph 1 above may retain them providing they notify the Commission of them before 1 January 1978 and providing that where such derogations are designed to simplify the procedure for charging tax they conform with the requirement laid down in paragraph 1 above.

Derogations – Derogations made by the UK under the procedure outlined in art. 27 are listed below.

(1) Derogations specified in Customs 1977 communication to EC Commission:

The Customs wrote to the EC Commission on 28 December 1977, listing in seven Annexes the UK's special measures for derogation from the provisions of the EC sixth directive under art. 27 of that directive. These derogations are part of the law applying in the UK. All the seven Annexes are reproduced below. It should be noted that the Annexes refer to the law as at 28 December 1977.

"Annex 1: Special VAT schemes for retailers

There are nine alphabetically identified schemes, and retailers may choose any scheme or combination of schemes for which their business is eligible, under the rules set out in Notice No. 727 and its Supplements enclosed herewith. The Notices are given vires under the Finance Act 1972, s. 30(3) [now VATA 1994, Sch. 11, para. 2(6)].

The purpose of the United Kingdom's special value added tax schemes for retailers is to simplify the calculation of output tax by retailers, in that they do not have to record full details and calculate tax on each transaction. It is considered that the special retail schemes do not derogate in principle from the provisions of the sixth directive, but only apply a totality of the considerations received or receivable in determining the tax due at different rates.

Some minor changes – e.g., to provide for credit calculations in accordance with art. 13B(d)(1) of the sixth directive – will be introduced on 1 January 1978, but these do not alter the basic framework of the schemes in use on 1 January 1977.

Annex 2: Trading stamps

Trading stamps are widely used in the United Kingdom as essentially a promissory discount, by which the consumer receives either the face value of the stamps in cash, or goods to a value generally well in excess of the face value, on redemption of books of stamps at some later date.

The financial advantage of redemption for goods provided by the promoter results in only a limited encashment of the stamps. To simplify retail accounting and avoid double taxation, the stamps are "de-supplied" under the vires of Finance Act 1972, s. 5(7) [now VATA 1994, s. 5(3)], at the time of issue by the promoter or retailer. Tax on the goods supplied by the promoter in exchange for the stamps is calculated and accounted for by him at the appropriate rate of tax, and on a valuation formula based on his charge to the retailer for the stamps, and the consideration for the goods priced in terms of a number of books of stamps in the promoter's catalogue.

Annex 3: Exemption from registration

Under the Finance Act 1972, Sch. 1, para. 11(a) [now VATA 1994, Sch. 1, para. 14(1)] the Commissioners of Customs and Excise have discretion to treat as exempt from registration any person who, although the value of his taxable supplies exceeds the exemption limits for registration, satisfies them that all these supplies are or would be zero-rated if he were a taxable person.

Traders seeking such exemption are generally in a fairly small way of business, e.g., small service traders in the construction and transport industries and food retailers, and prefer to bear the tax on their inputs rather than come under control as registered taxable persons and claim refunds of input tax.

Arrangements are in hand to take account of the activities of these traders in calculating the United Kingdom "own resources" contribution.

Annex 4: Valuation

In the United Kingdom certain companies, in the field of cosmetics for example, sell their products to individuals who are outside the tax net for re-sale to the consumer. The Commissioners of Customs and Excise have power under the Finance Act 1972, Sch. 3, para. 2 [now substituted by VATA 1994, Sch. 6, para. 2] to prevent avoidance of tax on the retail margin by requiring sales to these individuals to be taxed on their retail value.

[Following the ruling in Direct Cosmetics Ltd v C & E Commrs (1985) 2 BVC 200,069, the VAT valuation powers indicated in Annex 4 were restored on 12 June 1985: directions were issued by Customs, with effect from 1 July 1985.]

Annex 5: Operation of UK terminal markets

(1) There are in the United Kingdom a number of commodity markets. These are centres of much international merchanting trade. Some are solely "physical" markets dealing in consignments of goods, usually on c.i.f. [cost, insurance and freight] terms, for either immediate or forward delivery, e.g., the London Tea Market and the Liverpool Cotton Exchange. The normal value added tax rules are applied to transactions on these markets and are operated without distortion of competition. The application of normal value added tax rules to all transactions on the "futures" market, however, would have had damaging consequences. The eleven "futures" markets in the United Kingdom provide growers, merchants and manufacturers with the facility of buying and selling "futures" contracts in certain commodities to protect themselves against loss on their real trading operations through changes in price. "Futures" trading on each of the markets is generally confined to small groups of "ring-dealing" members. In most cases these members deal as principals on their own account; in other cases members may act as agents on behalf of outside clients. A "futures" contract is normally drawn up so as to require the eventual delivery of goods and a small percentage of contracts in fact run to maturity. This helps to maintain a close relationship between "futures" prices and "physical" prices. However, most dealings in "futures" are of the nature of financing or insurance and are not performed with the intention of acquiring goods.

(2) If value added tax had been applied without relief to all "futures" transactions, this would have distorted United Kingdom market prices which presently command international acceptance. This could have led to the loss of much of the international "futures" trade to countries outside the Community. Further, there is a very substantial volume of business on the "futures" markets which is often conducted in very short periods of the day and application of the full system of value added tax would have imposed considerable administrative burdens on the markets which it would not have been easy for them to sustain, and the pattern of trading could have been seriously disrupted. Additionally, it would have been difficult to institute effective verification of the complete chain of transactions of each "futures" market.

It was decided, therefore, that a scheme of relief was necessary for these markets. The scheme provides a simplified system of control and reduces the administrative burdens on the market without a substantial loss of revenue at the final consumption stage.

(3) In broad terms, the scheme provides that transactions on the eleven "futures" markets involving defined market members are traded free of value added tax and of the recording requirements of value added tax. The markets involved and the extent of zero-rating of those transactions are defined in the terms of Regulations made under the Finance Act 1972, s. 26 [now VATA 1994, s. 50]. These are the Value Added Tax (Terminal Markets) Order 1973 and the Value Added Tax (Terminal Markets) (Amendment) Order 1975. Copies of these Orders are enclosed with this note. The exception to the normal requirement of keeping value added tax records of these zero-rated transactions is made under the "care and management" provisions vested in the Commissioners of Customs and Excise. The zero-rating extends only to "futures" transactions in a commodity which involves a member of the relevant market and agency charges by market members in connection with these transactions. Brokerage charges are normally levied at certain specific rates and usually as part of the contract price. It is difficult to distinguish it as the service of an agent distinct from the market in which he operates. If a "futures" contract runs to maturity and delivery of the goods takes place where a non-market member is involved, the supply of both the goods and any agency service by a market member is not relieved by the Orders and normal value added tax rules apply. The Orders do not allow users of these commodities to acquire them free of tax in the United Kingdom, although it is important to bear in mind that many commodities may of course still be zero-rated under the Finance Act 1972, Sch. 4 [now VATA 1994, Sch. 8] and agency services by market members to overseas customers may also be zero-rated as an export of services.

Annex 6: Long stays in hotels

(1) The leasing and letting of immovable property is exempt from value added tax under art. 13B(b) of the sixth Council directive, unless it is, inter alia, accommodation as defined in the laws of member states in the hotel sector or in sectors with a similar function, which is taxable under para. 1 of that article.

(2) In the United Kingdom sales of new houses by builders and developers are zero-rated, and sales of second-hand houses and the leasing and letting of property are exempt, subject to certain exceptions. One of these exceptions relates to accommodation in hotels, inns, boarding houses and similar establishments which is taxable at the standard rate. The relevant legal provisions are contained in the Finance Act 1972, Sch. 5, Grp. 1, item 1(a) [see subsequently VATA 1994, Sch. 9, Grp. 1, item 1(a)].

(3) In order to reduce disparity of treatment between people who live residentially in hotels, etc., for long periods and those who occupy normal domestic accommodation, the 1972 Act also provides (in Sch. 3, para. 7 [now VATA 1994, Sch. 6, para. 9]) that where a stay in a hotel lasts more than four weeks, the value of the supply of accommodation and facilities, but not of meals and extras, is reduced for value added tax purposes for the period in excess of four weeks by excluding the value of the right to occupy the accommodation. The reduced value must not be less than 20% of the amount payable for the accommodation and facilities; if in particular cases the amount payable for facilities is higher than 20%, then tax is chargeable on that higher percentage.

(4) This arrangement has enabled the United Kingdom to avoid the considerable legislative complications which would have arisen if it had been necessary to define the various types of accommodation for value added tax purposes. It has also avoided the necessity to treat as partly exempt traders those hoteliers who provide both short and long-term accommodation; and at the same time, it has reduced economic distortion and incentives to tax evasion. It is considered that the amount of input tax which would have been borne by the hotelier if exemption had applied is negligible.

(5) All hoteliers using the provision are required to enter on their value added tax returns the full value of their supplies, irrespective of the status of the resident. Accordingly, the arrangements will have no effect on their own resources calculation.

(6) The arrangements have proved simple to operate for both officials and traders alike, at virtually nil cost to the Revenue. It is the view of the United Kingdom that they conform with the requirements of para. 1 of art. 27 of the directive and may therefore continue to apply after 1 January 1978.

Annex 7: Goods in warehouse – article 16

Imports

The present United Kingdom practice is to allow the importation and warehousing of dutiable goods without payment of value added tax if the importer quotes his registered tax number, or against security in those cases where it is not registered. Article 16(1A)(c) covers the practice but is subject to consultation under article 29.

The preamble to art. 16 (which is permissive) is unusual in that it allows member states to "take special measures designed to *relieve from value added tax* all or some of the ... transactions ...". Our system achieves this.

Similarly, article 16(1C), which allows relief on *supplies of goods* carried out in warehouse, covers our practice of disregarding all supplies in warehouse before duty is paid. We also allow removals from warehouse the benefit of the postponed accounting system (PAS) under the Finance Act 1972, s. 27(3) [now VATA 1994, s. 51]. By doing so we simply mirror the import conditions and this would appear unobjectionable.

Excise goods

In equity we allow excise goods the same treatment as customs goods. If excise goods are required to be warehoused for security of duty then we disregard supplies before duty payment and allow traders to operate the PAS under the [Finance Act 1972], s. 27(2) and (3).

This would seem to be adequately covered by the interplay of art. 16(1A)(e) – which implicitly refers to excise warehouses – and 16(1C), which refers to supplies within them.

Similar facilities are granted in respect of home produced excisable goods and in cases where imported goods and home produced goods are mixed in warehouses, e.g., the fortifying of wine with British spirits.

As stated above this practice is subject to consultation under art. 29 but until the consultation procedure is complete the United Kingdom will continue with the existing measures."

(2)   Council Decision 84/496 authorising a derogation, requested by the UK, with a view to avoiding certain types of fraud or tax evasion

(15 April 1984, OJ 1984 L264/27)

A Council decision, deemed to have been adopted in accordance with the procedure laid down in art. 27(4) of the sixth directive, authorised a measure derogating from the directive requested by the UK with a view to avoiding certain types of fraud or tax evasion on supplies of gold, gold coins and gold scrap between taxable persons by a special tax accounting scheme.

(3)   Council Decision 86/356 authorising the UK to apply flat-rate measures in respect of the non-deductible VAT charged on fuel expenditure in company cars

(21 July 1986, OJ 1986 L212/35)

The Council of the European Communities ... has adopted this decision:

Art. 1

The United Kingdom is hereby authorised to fix on a flat-rate basis the proportion of value added tax relating to expenditure on fuel used for private purposes in company cars.

Art. 2

For a transitional period, the proportion of the tax referred to in article 1 may be expressed in fixed amounts determined according to engine capacity or type of vehicle. These fixed amounts shall be adjusted annually in line with changes in the average cost of fuel.

Art. 3

Where article 2 is applied, the United Kingdom shall communicate to the Commission annually the following information, broken down by vehicle category:

(1)   The average cost of fuel per kilometre.

(2)   The average distance covered per vehicle each year on private journeys.

(3)   An estimate of the number of vehicles affected by this decision.

The system which has been set up will be reviewed on the basis of this information and taking account of the harmonisation of expenditure not eligible for a deduction of value added tax envisaged in article 17(6) of Directive 77/388.

Art. 4

This decision shall apply from 23 March 1986.

Art. 5

This decision is addressed to the United Kingdom.

(4)   Council decision authorising a derogation, requested by the UK, in respect of the supply of hotel services to long-stay residents

(10 December 1986, OJ 1986 L359/59)

A Council decision, deemed to have been adopted in accordance with the procedure laid down in art. 27(4) of the sixth directive, authorised a measure derogating from the directive requested by the UK with a view to simplifying the calculation of VAT in respect of long stays in hotels by assessing on a flat-rate basis the part of the service deemed to correspond to a letting of immovable property exempt under art. 13B(b)(i) of the directive. The measure, which replaces a previously notified derogation the scope of which was too broad, applies only to hotel services provided to individuals themselves occupying the accommodation in question.

(5)   Council decision authorising a derogation, requested by the UK, in respect of the use of open market value in non-arm's length transactions

(11 April 1987, OJ L132/22)

A Council decision, deemed to have been adopted in accordance with the procedure laid down in art. 27(4) of the sixth directive, authorised anti-avoidance measures derogating from the directive that were requested by the UK with a view to preventing taxable persons artificially reducing the price for supplies or imports of goods or for supplies of services to totally or partially exempt persons with whom they have family, legal or business ties as specified in the UK legislation. In these circumstances, the free market value may be taken as the consideration for the transaction, irrespective of whether that transaction is taxable, where otherwise there would be loss of tax.

See VATA 1994, Sch. 6, para. 1(1)(c).

(6)   Council Decision 89/466, authorising the UK to apply a measure derogating from art. 11A(1)(b) of the sixth directive on VAT in respect of land and buildings

(18 July 1989, OJ 1989 L226/23)

The Council of the European Communities ... has adopted this decision:

Art. 1

By way of derogation from article 11(A)(1)(b) of the sixth directive, the United Kingdom is hereby authorised to use the open market value as the taxable amount for the supply, within the meaning of article 5(7)(a) and (b) of the said directive, of buildings or parts of buildings before first occupation and of the land on which they stand.

Art. 2

This authorisation shall be granted pending the deletion of point 16 of Annex F to the sixth directive.

Art. 3

This directive is addressed to the United Kingdom.

(7)   Council Decision 89/534, authorising the UK to apply, in respect of certain supplies to unregistered resellers, a measure derogating from art. 11(A)(1)(a) of the sixth directive on VAT

(24 May 1989, OJ 1989 L280/54)

The Council of the European Communities ... has adopted this decision:

Art. 1

By way of derogation from article 11(A)(1)(a) of the sixth directive, the United Kingdom is hereby authorised to prescribe, in cases where a marketing structure based on the supply of goods through non-taxable persons results in non-taxation at the stage of final consumption, that the taxable amount for supplies to such persons is to be the open market value of the goods as determined at that stage.

Art. 2

The United Kingdom shall inform the Commission of any administrative decisions subsequently adopted in connection with the derogation.

Art. 3

The decision is addressed to the United Kingdom.

(8)   Council Decision 90/127, authorising the UK to apply a measure derogating from art. 5(8) and 21(1)(a) of the sixth directive on VAT in respect of assets transferred to a partially exempt company

(12 March 1990, OJ 1990 L73/32)

The Council of the European Communities . . . has adopted this decision:

Art. 1

By way of derogation from articles 5(8) and 21(1)(a) of the sixth directive (77/388), the United Kingdom is hereby authorised to apply until 31 December 1992:

–   a provision whereby a supply of goods is deemed to occur where assets other than the capital goods subject to adjustment of the deductions initially made pursuant to legislation adopted by the United Kingdom on the basis of article 20 of the sixth directive (77/388) are totally or partially transferred to a company which is a member of a group of enterprises treated as a single taxable person within the meaning of article 4(4) of the said directive and which, as a member of that group, is not entitled to deduct tax in full;

–   a provision whereby the company which is the recipient of the supply of assets referred to in the first indent becomes liable to tax.

Art. 2

This decision is addressed to the United Kingdom.

Council Decision 89/533 of 11 April 1989 allowing a similar derogation is superseded by Decision 90/127.

(9) Council Decision 93/204, authorising the UK to apply a measure derogating from art. 5(8) and 21(1)(a) of the sixth directive on VAT in respect of transfers of assets within a group

(5 April 1993, OJ 1993 L88/43)

The Council of the European Communities . . . has adopted this decision:

Art. 1

By way of derogation from articles 5(8) and 21(1)(a) of Directive 77/388, the United Kingdom is hereby authorised to apply until 31 December 1996:

–   a provision whereby a supply of goods is deemed to occur where assets, other than the capital goods subject to adjustment of the deductions initially made pursuant to legislation adopted by the United Kingdom on the basis of article 20 of the said directive, are totally or partially transferred to a company which is a member of a group of enterprises treated as a single taxable person within the meaning of article 4(4) of that directive and which, as a member of that group, is not entitled to deduct tax in full, a provision whereby the company which is the recipient of the supply of assets referred to in the first indent becomes liable to tax.

Art. 2

This decision is addressed to the United Kingdom.

(10) Council Decision 93/609, authorising the United Kingdom to apply a particular measure in accordance with art. 22(12)(a) of the sixth directive on the harmonisation of the laws of the member states relating to turnover taxes

(22 November 1993, OJ 1993 L292/51).

The Council of the European Union . . . has adopted this decision:

Art. 1

As provided for by article 22(12) of the Sixth Directive 77/388, the United Kingdom is hereby authorised, with effect from 1 January 1993 until 31 December 1996 or until the end of the transitional arrangements, should this be later, to introduce a particular measure in accordance with subparagraph (a) of article 22(12), to simplify the obligations laid down in paragraph 6(b) of article 22 regarding recapitulative statements.

Art. 2

This decision is addressed to the United Kingdom.

(11) Council Decision 97/375, authorising the UK to apply an optional measure derogating from art. 17 of the sixth directive on VAT [in respect of cash accounting]

(9 June 1997, OJ 1997 L158/43)

The Council of the European Union . . . has adopted this decision:

Art. 1

By way of derogation from the provisions of article 17(1) of Directive 77/388/EEC, the United Kingdom is hereby authorized, until 31 December 1999, to provide within an optional scheme that enterprises with an annual turnover not higher than £400,000 must postpone the right of deduction of tax until it has been paid to the supplier.

Art. 2

This decision is addressed to the United Kingdom

(12) Council Decision 98/23, authorising the UK to extend application of a measure derogating from art. 28E(1) of the sixth directive on VAT [in respect of intra-Community acquisitions of goods]

(19 December 1997, OJ 1998 L8/24)

The Council of the European Union . . . has adopted this decision:

Art. 1

By way of derogation from the provisions of article 28E(1) of Directive 77/388/EEC, the United Kingdom is hereby authorized, until 31 December 1999, to apply a special measure allowing the appropriate authorities to direct that the open-market value be taken as the taxable amount for intra-Community acquisitions of goods when the following two conditions are met:

–   the person who acquires the goods is not a fully taxable person and there are family, legal or business ties specified in national legislation, between the person acquiring the goods and the supplier,

–   a number of facts make it possible to conclude that these family, business of legal ties have influenced the determination of the taxable amount provided for in the said of article 28E

Art. 2

This decision is addressed to the United Kingdom

(13) Council Decision 98/198, authorising the UK to extend application of a measure derogating from art. 6 and 17 of the sixth directive on VAT [in respect of restriction of input tax deduction for hirers/lessees of cars and private use of business cars]

(9 March 1998, OJ 1998 L76/31)

The Council of the European Union . . . has adopted this decision:

Art. 1

By way of derogation from article 17(2) and (3) of Directive 77/388/EEC, the United Kingdom is hereby authorized to restrict to 50% the right of the hirer or lessee of a car to deduct the VAT on the cost of hiring or leasing that car where it is used for private purposes.

Art. 2
By way of derogation from article 6(2)(a) of Directive 77/388/EEC, the United Kingdom is hereby authorized not to treat as supplies of services for consideration the private use of a business car hired or leased by a taxable person.
Art. 3
This authorization shall expire on 31 December 1998.
Art. 4
This decision is addressed to the United Kingdom.

TITLE XVI – TRANSITIONAL PROVISIONS

ART. 28   [Expiry of earlier provisions]

28(1)   Any provisions brought into force by the member states under the provisions of the first four indents of article 17 of the second Council directive of 11 April 1967 shall cease to apply, in each member state, as from the respective dates on which the provisions referred to in the second paragraph of article 1 of this directive come into force.

28(1A)   Until a date which may not be later than 30 June 1999, the United Kingdom of Great Britain and Northern Ireland may, for imports of works of art, collectors' items or antiques which qualified for an exemption on 1 January 1993, apply article 11(B)(6) in such a way that the value added tax due on importation is, in any event, equal to 2.5 per cent of the amount determined in accordance with article 11(B)(1) to (4).

28(2)   Notwithstanding article 12(3), the following provisions shall apply during the transitional period referred to in article 28L.

(a)   Exemptions with refund of the tax paid at the preceding stage and reduced rates lower than the minimum rate laid down in article 12(3) in respect of the reduced rates, which were in force on 1 January 1991 and which are in accordance with Community law, and satisfy the conditions stated in the last indent of article 17 of the second Council Directive of 11 April 1967, may be maintained.

     Member states shall adopt the measures necessary to ensure the determination of own resources relating to these operations.

     In the event that the provisions of this paragraph create for Ireland distortions of competition in the supply of energy products for heating and lighting, Ireland may, on specific request, be authorised by the Commission to apply a reduced rate to such supplies, in accordance with article 12(3). In that case, Ireland shall submit its request to the Commission together with all necessary information. If the Commission has not taken a decision within three months of receiving the request, Ireland shall be deemed to be authorised to apply the proposed reduced rates.

(b)   Member states which, at 1 January 1991 in accordance with Community law, applied exemptions with refund of tax paid at the preceding stage, or reduced rates lower than the minimum laid down in article 12(3) in respect of the reduced rates, to goods and services other than those specified in Annex H, may apply the reduced rate or one of the two reduced rates provided for in article 12(3) to any such supplies.

(c)   Member states which under the terms of article 12(3) will be obliged to increase their standard rate as applied at 1 January 1991 by more than 2 per cent may apply a reduced rate lower than the minimum laid down in article 12(3) in respect of the reduced rate to supplies of categories of goods and services specified in Annex H. Furthermore, those member states may apply such a rate to restaurant services, children's clothing, children's footwear and housing. Member states may not introduce exemptions with refund of the tax at the preceding stage on the basis of this paragraph.

(d)   Member states which at 1 January 1991 applied a reduced rate to restaurant services, *children's clothing, children's footwear* and housing, may continue to apply such a rate to such supplies.

(e)   Member states which at 1 January 1991 applied a reduced rate to supplies of goods and services other than those specified in Annex H may apply the reduced rate or one of the two reduced rates provided for in article 12(3) to such supplies, provided that the rate is not lower than 12 per cent.

     This provision may not apply to supplies of second-hand goods, works of art, collectors' items or antiques subject to value added tax in accordance with one of the special arrangements provided for [in] article 26A(B) and (C).

(f)   The Hellenic Republic may apply VAT rates up to 30 per cent lower than the corresponding rates applied in mainland Greece in the departments of Lesbos, Chios, Samos, the

Dodecanese and the Cyclades, and on the following islands in the Aegean: Thasos, Northern Sporades, Samothrace and Skiros.

(g) On the basis of a report from the Commission, the Council shall, before 31 December 1994, re-examine the provisions of subparagraphs (a) to (f) above in relation to the proper functioning of the internal market in particular. In the event of significant distortions of competition arising, the Council, acting unanimously on a proposal from the Commission, shall adopt appropriate measures.

(h) Member states which, on 1 January 1993, were availing themselves of the option provided for in article 5(5)(a) as in force on that date, may apply to supplies under a contract to make up work the rate applicable to the goods after making up.

For the purposes of applying this provision, supplies under a contract to make up work shall be deemed to be delivery by a contractor to his customer of movable property made or assembled by the contractor from materials or objects entrusted to him by the customer for this purpose, whether or not the contractor has provided any part of the materials used.

(i) Member States may apply a reduced rate to supplies of live plants (including bulbs, roots and the like, cut flowers and ornamental foliage) and wood for use as firewood.

28(3) During the transitional period referred to in paragraph 4, member states may:

(a) continue to subject to tax the transactions exempt under article 13 or 15 set out in Annex E to this directive;

(b) continue to exempt the activities set out in Annex F under conditions existing in the member state concerned;

(c) grant to taxable persons the option for taxation of exempt transactions under the conditions set out in Annex G;

(d) continue to apply provisions derogating from the principle of immediate deduction laid down in the first paragraph of article 18(2);

(e) continue to apply measures derogating from the provisions of articles 5(4)(c), 6(4) and 11(A)(3)(c);

(f) provide that for supplies of buildings and building land purchased for the purpose of resale by a taxable person for whom tax on the purchase was not deductible, the taxable amount shall be the difference between the selling price and the purchase price;

(g) by way of derogation from articles 17(3) and 26(3), continue to exempt without repayment of input tax the services of travel agents referred to in article 26(3). This derogation shall also apply to travel agents acting in the name and on account of the traveller.

28(3A) Pending a decision by the Council, which, under article 3 of Directive 89/465, is to act on the abolition of the transitional derogations provided for in paragraph 3, Spain shall be authorised to exempt the transactions referred to in point 2 of Annex F in respect of services rendered by authors and the transactions referred to in points 23 and 25 of Annex F.

28(4) The transitional period shall last initially for five years as from 1 January 1978. At the latest six months before the end of this period, and subsequently as necessary, the Council shall review the situation with regard to the derogations set out in paragraph 3 on the basis of a report from the Commission and shall unanimously determine on a proposal from the Commission, whether any or all of these derogations shall be abolished.

28(5) At the end of the transitional period passenger transport shall be taxed in the country of departure for that part of the journey taking place within the Community according to the detailed rules of procedure to be laid down by the Council acting unanimously on a proposal from the Commission.

28(6) The Council, acting unanimously on a proposal from the Commission, may authorise any member state to apply for a maximum period of three years between 1 January 2000 and 31 December 2002 the reduced rates provided for in the third sub-paragraph of article 12(3)(a) to services listed in a maximum of two of the categories set out in Annex K. In exceptional cases a member state may be authorised to apply the reduced rate to services in three of the above mentioned categories.

The services concerned must satisfy the following requirements–

(a) they must be labour-intensive;

(b) they must be largely provided direct to final consumers;

(c) they must be mainly local and not likely to create distortions of competition;

(d) there must be a close link between the lower prices resulting from the rate reduction and the foreseeable increase in demand and employment.

The application of a reduced rate must not prejudice the smooth functioning of the internal market.

Any member state wishing to introduce the measure provided for in the first sub-paragraph shall inform the Commission before 1 November 1999 and shall provide it before that date with all relevant particulars, and in particular the following—

(a)   scope of the measure and detailed description of the services concerned;

(b)   particulars showing that the conditions laid down in the second and third sub-paragraphs have been met;

(c)   particulars showing the budgetary cost of the measure envisaged.

Those member states authorised to apply the reduced rate referred to in the first sub-paragraph shall, before 1 October 2002, draw up a detailed report containing an overall assessment of the measure's effectiveness in terms notably of job creation and efficiency.

Before 31 December 2002 the Commission shall forward a global evaluation report to the Council and Parliament accompanied, if necessary, by a proposal for appropriate measures for a final decision on the VAT rate applicable to labour-intensive services.

History – Art. 28(1A) inserted by Directive 94/5, art. 4 (OJ 1994 L60/16). Member states had to bring into force the measures necessary to comply with this directive no later than 1 January 1995.
Art. 28(2)(h) added by Directive 95/7, art. 1(5) (OJ 1995 L102/18). Member states required to bring into force the measures necessary to comply with this directive on 1 January 1996.
Art. 28(2)(i) inserted by Directive 96/42, art. 2 (OJ 1996 L170/34). The insertion applies from 1 January 1995.
Art. 28(2) replaced by Directive 92/77, art. 4 (OJ 1992 L316/1). Member states had to bring into force the measures necessary to comply with this directive no later than 31 December 1992.
Subparagraph added to art. 28(2)(e) by Directive 94/5, art. 5 (OJ 1994 L60/16). Member states had to bring into force the measures necessary to comply with this directive no later than 1 January 1995.
In art. 28(3)(e), a reference to art. 5(4)(c) deleted by Directive 94/5, art. 8 (OJ 1994 L60/16). Member states had to bring into force the measures necessary to comply with this directive no later than 1 January 1995.
Art. 28(3A) inserted by Directive 91/680, art. 1(21) (OJ 1991 L376/1). Member states had to bring into force the measures necessary to comply with this directive no later than 1 January 1993.
Art. 28(6) added by Directive 99/85, art. 1 (OJ 1999 L277/34). The directive entered into force on the day of its publication in the Official Journal of the European Communities, which was 28 October 1999.

TITLE XVIa – TRANSITIONAL ARRANGEMENTS FOR THE TAXATION OF TRADE BETWEEN MEMBER STATES

ART. 28A   **Scope**

28A(1)   The following shall also be subject to value added tax:

(a)   intra-Community acquisitions of goods for consideration within the territory of the country by a taxable person acting as such or by a non-taxable legal person where the vendor is a taxable person acting as such who is not eligible for the tax exemption provided for in article 24 and who is not covered by the arrangements laid down in the second sentence of article 8(1)(a) or in article 28B(B)(1).

By way of derogation from the first subparagraph, intra-Community acquisitions of goods made under the conditions set out in paragraph 1A by a taxable person or non-taxable legal person shall not be subject to value added tax.

–   by a taxable person who is eligible for the flat-rate scheme provided for in article 25, by a taxable person who carries out only goods or of services that are not deductible, or by a non-taxable legal person,

–   for a total amount, less value added tax due or paid in the member state from which the goods are dispatched or transported, not exceeding, during the current calendar year, a threshold which member states shall determine but which may not be less than the equivalent in national currency of ECU 10,000, and

–   provided that the total amount, less value added tax due or paid in the member state from which the goods are dispatched or transported, of intra-Community acquisitions of goods other than new means of transport and other than products subject to excise duty did not, during the previous calendar year, exceed the threshold referred to in the second indent.

Member states shall grant taxable persons and non-taxable legal persons eligible under the second subparagraph the right to opt for the general scheme laid down in the first subparagraph. Member states shall determine the detailed rules for the exercise of that option, which shall in any case apply for two calendar years;

(b)   intra-Community acquisitions of new means of transport effected for consideration within the country by taxable persons or non-taxable legal persons who qualify for the derogation provided for in the second subparagraph of (a) or by any other non-taxable person;

(c)   the intra-Community acquisition of goods which are subject to excise duties effected for consideration within the territory of the country by a taxable person or a non-taxable legal person who qualifies for the derogation referred to in the second subparagraph of point (a), and for which the excise duties become chargeable within the territory of the country pursuant to Directive 92/12.

28A(1A)   The following shall benefit from the derogation set out in the second subparagraph of paragraph 1(a):

(a)   intra-Community acquisitions of goods whose supply within the territory of the country would be exempt pursuant to article 15(4) to (10);

(b)   intra-Community acquisitions of goods other than those at (a), made:

–   by a taxable person for the purpose of his agricultural, forestry or fisheries undertaking, subject to the flat-rate scheme set out in article 25, by a taxable person who carries out only supplies of goods or services in respect of which value added tax is not deductible, or by a non-taxable legal person,

–   for a total amount not exceeding, during the current calendar year, a threshold which the member states shall determine but which may not be less than the equivalent in national currency of ECU 10,000, and

–   provided that the total amount of intra-Community acquisitions of goods did not, during the previous calendar year, exceed the threshold referred to in the second indent.

The threshold which serves as the reference for the application of the above shall consist of the total amount, exclusive of value added tax due or paid in the member state from which the goods are dispatched or transported, of intra-Community acquisitions of goods other than new means of transport and other than goods subject to excise duty.

28A(2)   For the purposes of this Title:

(a)   the following shall be considered as **"means of transport"**: vessels exceeding 7.5 metres in length, aircraft the take-off weight of which exceeds 1,550 kilograms and motorised land vehicles the capacity of which exceeds 48 cubic centimetres or the power of which exceeds 7.2 kilowatts, intended for the transport of persons or goods, except for the vessels and aircraft referred to in article 15(5) and (6);

(b)   the means of transport referred to in (a) shall not be considered to be "new" where both of the following conditions are simultaneously fulfilled:

–   they were supplied more than three months after the date of first entry into service. However, this period shall be increased to six months for the motorised land vehicles defined in (a),

–   they have travelled more than 6,000 kilometres in the case of land vehicles, sailed for more than 100 hours in the case of vessels, or flown for more than 40 hours in the case of aircraft.

Member states shall lay down the conditions under which the above facts can be regarded as established.

28A(3)   **"Intra-Community acquisition of goods"** shall mean acquisition of the right to dispose as owner of movable tangible property dispatched or transported to the person acquiring the goods by or on behalf of the vendor or the person acquiring the goods to a member state other than that from which the goods are dispatched or transported.

Where goods acquired by a non-taxable legal person are dispatched or transported from a third territory and imported by that non-taxable legal person into a member state other than the member state of arrival of the goods dispatched or transported, the goods shall be deemed to have been dispatched or transported from the member state of import. That member state shall grant the importer as defined in article 21(2) a refund of the value added tax paid in connection with the importation of the goods in so far as the importer establishes that his acquisition was subject to value added tax in the member state of arrival of the goods dispatched or transported.

28A(4)   Any person who from time to time supplies a new means of transport under the conditions laid down in article 28C(A) shall also be regarded as a taxable person.

The member state within the territory of which the supply is effected shall grant the taxable person *the right of deduction on the basis of* the following provisions:

–   the right of deduction shall arise and may be exercised only at the time of the supply,

–   the taxable person shall be authorised to deduct the value added tax included in the purchase price or paid on the importation or intra-Community acquisition of the means of transport, up to an amount not exceeding the tax for which he would be liable if the supply were not exempt.

Member states shall lay down detailed rules for the implementation of these provisions.

28A(5) The following shall be treated as supplies of goods effected for consideration:

(a)   [Deleted by Directive 95/7, art. 6.]

(b)   the transfer by a taxable person of goods from his undertaking to another member state.

The following shall be regarded as having been transferred to another member state: any tangible property dispatched or transported by or on behalf of the taxable person out of the territory defined in article 3 but within the Community for the purposes of his undertaking, other than for the purposes of one of the following transactions:

–   the supply of the goods in question by the taxable person within the territory of the member state of arrival of the dispatch or transport under the conditions laid down in the second sentence of article 8(1)(a) and in article 28B(B)(1),

–   the supply of the goods in question by the taxable person under the conditions laid down in article 8(1)(c),

–   the supply of the goods in question by the taxable person within the territory of the country under the conditions laid down in article 15 or in article 28C(A),

–   the supply of a service performed for the taxable person and involving work on the goods in question pysically carried out in the member state in which the dispatch or transport of the goods ends, provided that the goods, after being worked upon, are re-dispatched to that taxable person in the member state from which they had initally been dispatched or transported,

–   temporary use of the goods in question within the territory of the member state of arrival of the dispatch or transport of the goods for the purposes of the supply of services by the taxable person established within the territory of the member state of departure of the dispatch or transport of the goods,

–   temporary use of the goods in question, for a period not exceeding 24 months, within the territory of another member state in which the import of the same goods from a third country with a view to temporary use would be eligible for the arrangements for temporary importation with full exemption from import duties.

However, when one of the conditions to which the benefit of the above is subordinated is no longer met, the goods shall be considered as having been transferred to a destination in another member state. In this case, the transfer is carried out at the moment that the condition is no longer met.

28A(6) The intra-Community acquisition of goods for consideration shall include the use by a taxable person for the purposes of his undertaking of goods dispatched or transported by or on behalf of that taxable person from another member state within the territory of which the goods were produced, extracted, processed, purchased, acquired as defined in paragraph 1 or imported by the taxable person within the framework of his undertaking into that other member state.

The following shall also be deemed to be an intra-Community acquisition of goods effected for consideration: the appropriation of goods by the forces of a state party to the North Atlantic Treaty, for their use or for the use of the civilian staff accompanying them, which they have not acquired subject to the general rules governing taxation on the domestic market of one of the member states, when the importation of these goods could not benefit from the exemption set out in article 14(1)(g).

28A(7) Member states shall take measures to ensure that transactions which would have been classed as "supplies of goods" as defined in paragraph 5 or article 5 if they had been carried out within the territory of the country by a taxable person acting as such are classed as "intra-Community acquisitions of goods".

History – Art. 28A inserted by Directive 91/680, art. 1(22) (OJ 1991 L376/1).
Art. 28A(1)(a), second subparagraph, replaced, art. 28A(1)(c), art. 28A(1A), art. 28A(5)(b), final subparagraph, and art. 28A(6), second subparagraph, all added by Directive 92/111, art. 1(10) (OJ 1992 L384/47).
Member states had to bring into force the measures necessary to comply with these directives no later than 1 January 1993.
Art. 28A(2)(b) replaced by Directive 94/5, art. 6 (OJ 1994 L60/16). Member states had to bring into force the measures necessary to comply with this directive no later than 1 January 1995.
Former art. 28A(2)(b) read as follows:
"(b)   the means of transport referred to in (a) shall not be considered as "new" where both of the following conditions are fulfilled:
–   they were supplied more than three months after the date of first entry into service,
–   they have travelled more than 3,000 kilometres in the case of land vehicles, sailed for more than 100 hours in the case of vessels or flown for more than 40 hours in the case of aircraft.
Member states shall lay down the conditions under which the above facts can be regarded as established."
In art. 28A(5) the introductory sentence replaced by identical words; art. 28A(5)(a) and art. 28A(5)(b), second subparagraph, fourth indent deleted; and art. 28A(5)(b), second subparagraph, fifth indent replaced – all by Directive 95/7, art. 6 (OJ 1995 L102/18). Member states required to bring into force the measures necessary to comply with this directive on 1 January 1996. The former art. 28A(5)(a) read as follows:

"(a)   the delivery to another taxable person of contract work as defined in article 5(5)(a), physically carried out within a member state other than that within the territory of which the customer is identified for purposes of value added tax, where the following conditions are fulfilled:
- the materials used by the person undertaking the work have been dispatched or transported by or on behalf of the customer from the member state within the territory of which the customer is identified for purposes of value added tax,
- the work finished or assembled by the person undertaking the work is transported or dispatched to the customer in the member state in which the customer is identified for purposes of value added tax;"

The former art. 28A(5)(b), second subparagraph, fourth and fifth indents, read as follows:
"- the supply to the taxable person, under the conditions set out in (a), of contract work carried out in the member state of arrival of the dispatch or transport of the goods in question,
- the supply of a service performed for the taxable person and involving work on the goods in question physically carried out in the member state of arrival of the dispatch or transport of the goods."

Cross references – VAT Regulations 1995 (SI 1995/2518), Pt. XVII: refunds in relation to new means of transport (implementing art. 28A).
VAT Regulations 1995 (SI 1995/2518), reg. 42 and VAT (Removal of Goods) Order 1992 (SI 1992/3111): partially implementing art. 28A(5)(b).

ART. 28B   Place of transactions

28B(A)   Place of the intra-Community acquisition of goods

28B(A)(1)   The place of the intra-Community acquisition of goods shall be deemed to be the place where the goods are at the time when dispatch or transport to the person acquiring them ends.

28B(A)(2)   Without prejudice to paragraph 1, the place of the intra-Community acquisition of goods referred to in article 28A(1)(a) shall, however, be deemed to be within the territory of the member state which issued the value added tax identification number under which the person acquiring the goods made the acquisition, unless the person acquiring the goods establishes that that acquisition has been subject to tax in accordance with paragraph 1.

If, however, the acquisition is subject to tax in accordance with paragraph 1 in the member state of arrival of the dispatch or transport of the goods after having been subject to tax in accordance with the first subparagraph, the taxable amount shall be reduced accordingly in the member state which issued the value added tax identification number under which the person acquiring the goods made the acquisition.

For the purposes of applying the first subparagraph, the intra-Community acquisition of goods shall be deemed to have been subject to tax in accordance with paragraph 1 when the following conditions have been met–
- the acquirer establishes that he has effected this intra-Community acquisition for the needs of a subsequent supply effected in the member state referred to in paragraph 1 and for which the consignee has been designated as the person liable for the tax due in accordance with article 28C(E)(3),
- the obligations for declaration set out in the last subparagraph of article 22(6)(b) have been satisfied by the acquirer.

28B(B)   Place of the supply of goods

28B(B)(1)   By way of derogation from article 8(1)(a) and (2), the place of the supply of goods dispatched or transported by or on behalf of the supplier from a member state other than that of arrival of the dispatch or transport shall be deemed to be the place where the goods are when dispatch or transport to the purchaser ends, where the following conditions are fulfilled:
- the supply of goods is effected for a taxable person eligible for the derogation provided for in the second subparagraph of article 28a(1)(a), for a non-taxable legal person who is eligible for the same derogation or for any other non-taxable person,
- the supply is of goods other than new means of transport and other than goods supplied after assembly or installation, with or without a trial run, by or on behalf of the supplier.

Where the goods thus supplied are dispatched or transported from a third territory and imported by the supplier into a member state other than the member state of arrival of the goods dispatched or transported to the purchaser, they shall be regarded as having been dispatched or transported from the member state of import.

28B(B)(2)   However, where the supply is of goods other than products subject to excise duty, paragraph 1 shall not apply to supplies of goods dispatched or transported to the same member state of arrival of the dispatch or transport where:
- the total value of such supplies, less value added tax, does not in one calendar year exceed the equivalent in national currency of ECU 100,000, and

–   the total value, less value added tax, of the supplies of goods other than products subject to excise duty effected under the conditions laid down in paragraph 1 in the previous calendar year did not exceed the equivalent in national currency of ECU 100,000.

The member state within the territory of which the goods are when dispatch or transport to the purchaser ends may limit the thresholds referred to above to the equivalent in national currency of ECU 35,000 where that member state fears that the threshold of ECU 100,000 referred to above would lead to serious distortions of the conditions of competition. Member states which exercise this option shall take the measures necessary to inform the relevant public authorities in the member state of dispatch or transport of the goods.

Before 31 December 1994, the Commission shall report to the Council on the operation of the special ECU 35,000 thresholds provided for in the preceding subparagraph. In that report the Commission may inform the Council that the abolition of the special thresholds will not lead to serious distortions of the conditions of competition. Until the Council takes a unanimous decision on a Commission proposal, the preceding subparagraph shall remain in force.

28B(B)(3)   The member state within the territory of which the goods are at the time of departure of the dispatch or transport shall grant those taxable persons who effect supplies of goods eligible under paragraph 2 the right to choose that the place of such supplies shall be determined in accordance with paragraph 1.

The member states concerned shall determine the detailed rules for the exercise of that option, which shall in any case apply for two calendar years.

28B(C)   **Place of the supply of services in the intra-Community transport of goods**

28B(C)(1)   By way of derogation from article 9(2)(b), the place of the supply of services in the intra-Community transport of goods shall be determined in accordance with paragraphs 2, 3 and 4. For the purposes of this Title the following definitions shall apply:

–   **"the intra-Community transport of goods"** shall mean transport where the place of departure and the place of arrival are situated within the territories of two different member states.

The transport of goods where the place of departure and the place of arrival are situated within the territory of the country shall be treated as intra-Community transport of goods where such transport is directly linked to transport to goods where the place of departure and the place of arrival are situated within the territories of two different member states.

–   **"the place of departure"** shall mean the place where the transport of goods actually starts, leaving aside distance actually travelled to the place where the goods are,

–   **"the place of arrival"** shall mean the place where the transport of goods actually ends.

28B(C)(2)   The place of the supply of services in the intra-Community transport of goods shall be the place of departure.

28B(C)(3)   However, by way of derogation from paragraph 2, the place of the supply of services in the intra-Community transport of goods rendered to customers identified for purposes of value added tax in a member state other than that of the departure of the transport shall be deemed to be within the territory of the member state which issued the customer with the value added tax identification number under which the service was rendered to him.

28B(C)(4)   Member states need not apply the tax to that part of the transport corresponding to journeys made over waters which do not form part of the territory of the Community as defined in article 3.

28B(D)   **Place of the supply of services ancillary to the intra-Community transport of goods**

28B   By way of derogation from article 9(2)(c), the place of the supply of services involving activities ancillary to the intra-Community transport of goods, rendered to customers identified for purposes of value added tax in a member state other than that within the territory of which the services are physically performed, shall be deemed to be within the territory of the member state which issued the customer with the value added tax identification number under which the service was rendered to him.

28B(E)   **Place of the supply of services rendered by intermediaries**

28B(E)(1)   By way of derogation from article 9(1), the place of the supply of services rendered by intermediaries, acting in the name and for the account of other persons, where they form part of the supply of services in the intra-Community transport of goods, shall be the place of departure.

However, where the customer for whom the services rendered by the intermediary are performed is identified for purposes of value added tax in a member state other than that of the departure of the transport, the place of the supply of services rendered by an intermediary shall be deemed to be within the territory of the member state which issued the customer with the value added tax identification number under which the service was rendered to him.

28B(E)(2)   By way of derogation from article 9(1), the place of the supply of services rendered by intermediaries acting in the name and for the account of other persons, where they form part of the supply of services the purpose of which is activities ancillary to the intra-Community transport of goods, shall be the place where the ancillary services are physically performed.

However, where the customer of the services rendered by the intermediary is identified for purposes of value added tax in a member state other than that within the territory of which the ancillary service is physically performed, the place of supply of the services rendered by the intermediary shall be deemed to be within the territory of the member state which issued the customer with the value added tax identification number under which the service was rendered to him by the intermediary.

28B(E)(3)   By way of derogation from article 9(1), the place of the supply of services rendered by intermediaries acting in the name and for the account of other persons, when such services form part of transactions other than those referred to in paragraph 1 or 2 or in article 9(2)(e), shall be the place where those transactions are carried out.

However, where the customer is identified for purposes of value added tax in a member state other than that within the territory of which those transactions are carried out, the place of supply of the services rendered by the intermediary shall be deemed to be within the territory of the member state which issued the customer with the value added tax identification number under which the service was rendered to him by the intermediary.

28B(F)   Place of the supply of services in the case of valuations of or work on movable tangible property

By way of derogation from article 9(2)(c), the place of the supply of services involving valuations or work on movable tangible property, provided to customers identified for value added tax purposes in a member state other than the one where those services are physically carried out, shall be deemed to be in the territory of the member state which issued the customer with the value added tax identification number under which the service was carried out for him.

This derogation shall not apply where the goods are not dispatched or transported out of the member state where the services were physically carried out.

History – Art. 28B was inserted by Directive 91/680, art. 1(22) (OJ 1991 L376/1). Member states had to bring into force the measures necessary to implement this directive no later than 1 January 1993.
Art. 28B(A)(2), third subparagraph, was added by Directive 92/111, art. 1(11) (OJ 1992 L384/47). Member states had to bring into force the measures necessary to implement this provision no later than 1 January 1994.
In art. 28B(C)(1), first indent, comma at the end replaced by a full stop and the following subparagraph added by Directive 95/7, art. 7 (OJ 1995 L102/18). Member states had to bring into force the measures necessary to comply with this directive on 1 January 1996.
Art. 28B(F) was added by Directive 95/7, art. 7 (OJ 1995 L102/18). Member states had to bring into force the measures necessary to comply with this directive on 1 January 1996.

ART. 28C   Exemptions

28C(A)   Exempt supplies of goods

28C   Without prejudice to other Community provisions and subject to conditions which they shall lay down for the purpose of ensuring the correct and straightforward application of the exemptions provided for below and preventing any evasion, avoidance or abuse, member states shall exempt:

(a)   supplies of goods, as defined in article 5, dispatched or transported by or on behalf of the vendor or the person acquiring the goods out of the territory referred to in article 3 but within the Community, effected for another taxable person or a non-taxable legal person acting as such in a member state other than that of the departure of the dispatch or transport of the goods.
   This exemption shall not apply to supplies of goods by taxable persons exempt from tax pursuant to article 24 or to supplies of goods effected for taxable persons or non-taxable legal persons who qualify for the derogation in the second subparagraph of article 28A(1)(a);

(b)   supplies of new means of transport, dispatched or transported to the purchaser by or on behalf of the vendor or the purchaser out of the territory referred to in article 3 but within the Community, effected for taxable persons or non-taxable legal persons who qualify for the derogation provided for in the second subparagraph of article 28A(1)(a) or for any other non-taxable person;

(c) the supply of goods subject to excise duty dispatched or transported to the purchaser, by the vendor, by the purchaser or on his behalf, outside the territory referred to in article 3 but inside the Community, effected for taxable persons or non-taxable legal persons who qualify for the derogation set out in the second subparagraph of article 28A(1)(a), when the dispatch or transport of the goods is carried out in accordance with article 7(4) and (5), or article 16 of Directive 92/12.

This exemption shall not apply to supplies of goods subject to excise duty effected by taxable persons who benefit from the exemption from tax set out in article 24;

(d) the supply of goods, within the meaning of article 28A(5)(b), which benefit from the exemptions set out above if they have been made on behalf of another taxable person.

28C(B)   Exempt intra-Community acquisitions of goods

Without prejudice to other Community provisions and subject to conditions which they shall lay down for the purpose of ensuring the correct and straightforward application of the exemptions provided for below and preventing any evasion, avoidance or abuse, member states shall exempt:

(a) the intra-Community acquisition of goods the supply of which by taxable persons would in all circumstances be exempt within the territory of the country;

(b) the intra-Community acquisition of goods the importation of which would in all circumstances be exempt under article 14(1);

(c) the intra-Community acquisition of goods where, pursuant to article 17(3) and (4), the person acquiring the goods would in all circumstances be entitled to full reimbursement of the value added tax due under article 28A(1).

28C(C)   Exempt transport services

Member states shall exempt the supply of intra-Community transport services involved in the dispatch or transport of goods to and from the islands making up the autonomous regions of the Azores and Madeira as well as the dispatch or transport of goods between those islands.

28C(D)   Exempt importation of goods

Where goods dispatched or transported from a third territory are imported into a member state other than that of arrival of the dispatch or transport, member states shall exempt such imports where the supply of such goods by the importer as defined in article 21(2) is exempt in accordance with paragraph A.

Member states shall lay down the conditions governing this exemption with a view to ensuring its correct and straightforward application and preventing any evasion, avoidance or abuse.

28C(E)   Other exemptions

28C(E)(1)   [Replaces art. 16(1) and adds art. 16(1A).]

28C(E)(2)   [Amends art. 16(2).]

28C(E)(3)   Member states shall take specific measures to ensure that VAT is not charged on the intra-Community acquisition of goods effected, within the meaning of article 28B(A)(1), within its territory when the following conditions are met–

– the intra-Community acquisition of goods is effected by a taxable person who is not established in the territory of the country but who is identified for value added tax purposes in another member state,

– the intra-Community acquisition of goods is effected for the purpose of a subsequent supply of goods made by a taxable person in the territory of the country,

– the goods so acquired by this taxable person are directly dispatched or transported from another member state than that in which he is identified for value added tax purposes and destined for the person for whom he effects the subsequent supply,

– the person to whom the subsequent supply is made is a taxable person or a non-taxable legal person who is identified for value added tax purposes within the territory of the country,

– the person to whom the subsequent supply is made has been designated in accordance with the third subparagraph of article 21(1)(a) as the person liable for the tax due on the supplies effected by the taxable person not established within the territory of the country.

History – Art. 28C inserted by Council Directive 91/680, art. 1(22) (OJ 1991 L376/1). Member states had to bring into force the measures necessary to comply with this directive no later than 1 January 1993.
In art. 28C(A), point (a), the words "as defined in articles 5 and 28A(5)(a)" replaced by "as defined in article 5" by Directive 95/7, art. 8 (OJ 1995 L102/18). Member states required to bring into force the measures necessary to comply with this directive on 1 January 1996.

In art. 28C(A), point (c) replaced, and point (d) added by Directive 92/111, art. 1(12) (OJ 1992 L384/47). Member states had to bring into force the measures necessary to comply with this provision by 1 January 1993.
Art. 28C(E) replaced by Directive 92/111, art. 1(13) (OJ 1992 L384/47). Member states had to bring into force the measures necessary to comply with this provision by 1 January 1993, except in respect of art. 28(C)(E)(3) for which the relevant date is January 1994.
Art. 28C(E)(1) replaced by Directive 95/7, art. 9 (OJ 1995 L102/18). This amending provision had previously added art. 16(1A). Member states required to bring into force measures necessary to comply with Directive 95/7 on 1 January 1996.
Cross references – Customs and Excise (Personal Reliefs for Special Visitors) Order 1992 (SI 1992/3156): implements art. 28C(B).

ART. 28D   Chargeable event and chargeability of tax

28D(1)   The chargeable event shall occur when the intra-Community acquisition of goods is effected. The intra-Community acquisition of goods shall be regarded as being effected when the supply of similar goods is regarded as being effected within the territory of the country.

28D(2)   For the intra-Community acquisition of goods, tax shall become chargeable on the 15th day of the month following that during which the chargeable event occurs.

28D(3)   By way of derogation from paragraph 2, tax shall become chargeable on the issue of the invoice or other document serving as an invoice provided for in the first subparagraph of article 22(3)(a) where that invoice or document is issued to the person acquiring the goods before the fifteenth day of the month following that during which the taxable event occurs.

28D(4)   By way of derogation from article 10(2) and (3), tax shall become chargeable for supplies of goods effected under the conditions laid down in article 28C(A) on the 15th day of the month following that during which the chargeable event occurs.

However, tax shall become chargeable on the issue of the invoice provided for in the first subparagraph of article 22(3)(a) or other document serving as invoice where that invoice or document is issued before the fifteenth day of the month following that during which the taxable event occurs.

History – Art. 28D inserted by Directive 91/680, art. 1(22) (OJ 1991 L376/1).
Art. 28D(3) replaced by Directive 92/111, art. 1(14) (OJ 1992 L384/47).
Art. 28D(4), second subparagraph, replaced by Directive 92/111, art. 1(15) (OJ 1992 L384/47).
Member states had to bring into force the measures necessary to comply with these directives no later than 1 January 1993.

ART. 28E   Taxable amount and rate applicable

28E(1)   In the case of the intra-Community acquisition of goods, the taxable amount shall be established on the basis of the same elements as those used in accordance with article 11(A) to determine the taxable amount for supply of the same goods within the territory of the country.

In particular, in the case of the intra-Community acquisition of goods referred to in article 28A(6), the taxable amount shall be determined in accordance with article 11(A)(1) and paragraphs 2 and 3.

Member states shall take the measures necessary to ensure that the excise duty due or paid by the person effecting the intra-Community acquisition of a product subject to excise duty is included in the taxable amount in accordance with article 11(A)(2)(a). When, after the moment the intra-Community acquisition of goods was effected, the acquirer obtains the refund of excise duties paid in the member state from which the goods were dispatched or transported, the taxable amount shall be reduced accordingly in the member state where the intra-Community acquisition took place.

28E(2)   For the supply of goods referred to in article 28C(A)(d), the taxable amount shall be determined in accordance with article 11(A)(1)(b) and paragraphs 2 and 3.

28E(3)   The tax rate applicable to the intra-Community acquisition of goods shall be that in force when the tax becomes chargeable.

28E(4)   The tax rate applicable to the intra-Community acquisition of goods shall be that applied to the supply of like goods within the territory of the country.

History – Art. 28E inserted by Directive 91/680, art. 1(22) (OJ 1991 L376/1).
In art. 28E(1), first subparagraph, second sentence replaced, and second subparagraph, second sentence added by Directive 92/111, art. 1(16) (OJ 1992 L384/47).
Art. 28E(2) inserted, and art. 28E(3) and (4) renumbered by Directive 92/111, art. 1(17).
Member states had to bring into force the measures necessary to implement these directives no later than 1 January 1993.

Cross references – Council Decision 98/23 of 19 December 1997 authorises the UK to derogate from art. 28E(1), by directing that the open-market value be taken as the taxable amount for intra-Community acquisitions of goods where the person acquiring the goods is not a fully taxable person and there are family, legal or business ties between the person acquiring the goods and the supplier.

ART. 28F   Right of deduction

28F(1)   [Replaces art. 17(2)–(4).]

28F(2)   [Replaces art. 18(1).]

28F(3)   [Inserts art. 18(3A).]

History – Art. 28F inserted by Council Directive 91/680, art. 1(22) (OJ 1991 L376/1).
Art. 28F amended, as to the wording of the new art. 17(3)(b) and 17(4), by Directive 92/111, art. 1(1B) (OJ 1992 L384/47).
Member states had to bring into force the measures necessary to implement these directives no later than 1 January 1993.
Art. 28F amended, as to the wording of the new art. 17(2)(a), by Directive 95/7, art. 10 (OJ 1995 L102/18). Member states
required to bring into force the measures necessary to comply with this directive on 1 January 1996.

ART. 28G   Persons liable for payment of the tax

28G   [Replaces art. 21.]

History – Art. 28G inserted by Directive 91/680, art. 1(22) (OJ 1991 L376/1).
Art. 28G amended, by replacement of art. 21(1)(b), by Directive 95/7, art. 11 (OJ 1995 L102/18). Member states required to
bring into force the measures necessary to comply with this directive on 1 January 1996.
Art. 28G amended, by the replacement of new wording for art. 21(1)(a) and (b), by Directive 92/111, art. 1(19) (OJ 1992
L384/47).
Member states had to bring into force the measures necessary to implement these provisions no later than 1 January 1993,
except as regards art. 21(1)(a), third subparagraph, for which the relevant date was 1 January 1994.

ART. 28H   Obligations of persons liable for payment

28H   [Replaces art. 22.]

History – Art. 28H inserted by Directive 91/680, art. 1(22) (OJ 1991 L376/1).
Art. 28H amended, as to the wording of art. 22(1)(c), 22(3)(b), 22(4)(c), 22(6)(b) and 22(11), by Directive 92/111, art. 1(20)
(OJ 1992 L384/47).
Member states had to bring into force the measures necessary to comply with these provisions no later than 1 January 1993,
except in so far as they relate to obligations in respect of transactions referred to in art. 21(1)(a), third subparagraph, 28B(A)(2),
third subparagraph, and 28C(E)(3), in respect of which the relevant date was 1 January 1994. Art. 28H amended, by the
replacement of art. 22(2)(b); art. 22(3)(b), second subparagraph, first indent; art. 22(6)(b), first subparagraph, and third
subparagraph, second indent; and by the deletion of art. 22(6)(b), fifth subparagraph – all by Directive 95/7, art. 12 (OJ 1995
L102/18). Member states required to bring into force the measures necessary to comply with Directive 95/7 on 1 January 1996.

ART. 28I   Special scheme for small undertakings

28I   [Added subparagraph to art. 24(3).]

History – Art. 28I inserted by Directive 91/680, art. 1(22) (OJ 1991 L376/1), and replaced by Directive 92/111, art. 1(21)
(OJ 1992 L384/47). Member states had to bring into force the measures necessary to comply with these provisions no later than
1 January 1993.

ART. 28J   Common flat-rate scheme for farmers

28J(1)   [Adds subparagraph to art. 25(4).]

28J(2)   [Replaces art. 25(5) and (6).]

28J(3)   [Adds subparagraph to art. 25(9).]

History – Art. 28J inserted by Directive 91/680, art. 1(22) (OJ 1991 L376/1). Member states had to bring into force the
measures necessary to comply with this directive no later than 1 January 1993.

ART. 28K   Miscellaneous provisions

The following provisions shall apply until 30 June 1999:

28K(1)   Member states may exempt supplies by tax-free shops of goods to be carried away in the
personal luggage of travellers taking intra-Community flights or sea crossings to other member
states. For the purposes of this article:

(a)   **"tax-free shop"** shall mean any establishment situated within an airport or port which fulfils
the conditions laid down by the competent public authorities pursuant, in particular, to
paragraph 5;

(b)   **"traveller to another member state"** shall mean any passenger holding a transport
document for air or sea travel stating that the immediate destination is an airport or port
situated in another member state;

(c)   **"intra-Community flight or sea crossing"** shall mean any transport, by air or sea, starting
within the territory of the country as defined in article 3 where the actual place of arrival is
situated within another member state.

Supplies of goods effected by tax-free shops shall include supplies of goods effected on board
aircraft or vessels during intra-Community passenger transport.

This exemption shall also apply to supplies of goods effected by tax-free shops in either of two
Channel Tunnel terminals, for passengers holding valid tickets for the journey between those two
terminals.

28K(2)   Eligibility for the exemption provided for in paragraph 1 shall apply only to supplies of goods:

(a)   the total value of which per person per journey does not exceed ECU 90.

By way of derogation from article 28M, member states shall determine the equivalent in national currency of the above amount in accordance with article 7(2) of Directive 69/169. Where the total value of several items or of several supplies of goods per person per journey exceeds those limits, the exemption shall be granted up to those amounts, on the understanding that the value of an item may not be split;

(b)   involving quantities per person per journey not exceeding the limits laid down by the Community provisions in force for the movement of travellers between third countries and the Community.

The value of supplies of goods effected within the quantitative limits laid down in the previous subparagraph shall not be taken into account for the application of (a).

28K(3)   Member states shall grant every taxable person the right to a deduction or refund of the value added tax referred to in article 17(2) in so far as the goods and services are used for the purposes of his supplies of goods exempt under this article.

28K(4)   Member states which exercise the option provided for in article 16(2) shall also grant eligibility under that provision to imports, intra-Community acquisitions and supplies of goods to a taxable person for the purposes of his supplies of goods exempt pursuant to this article.

28K(5)   Member states shall take the measures necessary to ensure the correct and straightforward application of the exemptions provided for in this article and to prevent any evasion, avoidance or abuse.

History – Art. 28K inserted by Directive 91/680, art. 1(22) (OJ 1991 L376/1). Member states had to bring into force the measures necessary to comply with this directive no later than 1 January 1993.
In art. 28K(2)(a), words substituted by Directive 94/4, art. 2 and 4 (OJ 1994 L60/14). Member states had to bring into force the measures necessary to comply with this directive no later than 3 March 1994.

ART. 28L   Period of application

28L   The transitional arrangements provided for in this Title shall enter into force on 1 January 1993. Before 31 December 1994 the Commission shall report to the Council on the operation of the transitional arrangements and submit proposals for a definitive system.

The transitional arrangements shall be replaced by a definitive system for the taxation of trade between member states based in principle on the taxation in the member state of origin of the goods or services supplied. To that end, after having made a detailed examination of that report and considering that the conditions for transition to the definitive system have been fulfilled satisfactorily, the Council, acting unanimously on a proposal from the Commission and after consulting the European Parliament, shall decide before 31 December 1995 on the arrangements necessary for the entry into force and the operation of the definitive system.

The transitional arrangement shall enter into force for four years and shall accordingly apply until 31 December 1996. The period of application of the transitional arrangements shall be extended automatically until the date of entry into force of the definitive system and in any event until the Council has decided on the definitive system.

History – Art. 28L inserted by Directive 91/680, art. 1(22) (OJ 1991 L376/1).

ART. 28M   Rate of conversion

28M   To determine the equivalents in their national currencies of amounts expressed in ECUs in this Title member states shall use the rate of exchange applicable on 16 December 1991.

History – Title XVIa and art. 28A–M inserted by Directive 91/680, art. 1(22) (OJ 1991 L376/1). Member states had to bring into force the measures necessary to comply with this directive no later than 1 January 1993.

ART. 28N   Transitional measures

28N(1)   When goods:

–   entered the territory of the country within the meaning of article 3 before 1 January 1993, and

–   were placed, on entry into the territory of that country, under one of the regimes referred to in article 14(1)(b) or (c), or article 16(1)(A), and

–   have not left that regime before 1 January 1993, the provisions in force at the moment the goods were placed under that regime shall continue to apply for the period, as determined by those provisions, the goods remain under that regime.

28N(2)   The following shall be deemed to be an import of goods within the meaning of article 7(1):

(a)   the removal, including irregular removal, of goods from the regime referred to in article 14(1)(c) under which the goods were placed before 1 January 1993 under the conditions set out in paragraph 1;

(b)   the removal, including irregular removal, of goods from the regime referred to in article 16(1)(A) under which the goods were placed before 1 January 1993 under the conditions set out in paragraph 1;

(c)   the termination of a Community internal transit operation started before 1 January 1993 in the Community for the purpose of supply of goods for consideration made before 1 January 1993 in the Community by a taxable person acting as such;

(d)   the termination of an external transit operation started before 1 January 1993;

(e)   any irregularity or offence committed during an external transit operation started under the conditions set out in (c) or any Community external transit operation referred to in (d);

(f)   the use within the country, by a taxable or non-taxable person, of goods which have been supplied to him, before 1 January 1993, within another member state, where the following conditions are met–

    –   the supply of these goods has been exempted, or was likely to be exempted, pursuant to article 15(1) and (2),

    –   the goods were not imported within the country before 1 January 1993.

For the purpose of the application of (c), the expression **"Community internal transit operation"** shall mean the dispatch or transport of goods under the cover of the internal Community transit arrangement or under the cover of a T2 L document or the intra-Community movement carnet, or the sending of goods by post.

28N(3)   In the cases referred to in paragraph 2(a) to (e), the place of import, within the meaning of article 7(2), shall be the member state within whose territory the goods cease to be covered by the regime under which they were placed before 1 January 1993.

28N(4)   By way of derogation from article 10(3), the import of the goods within the meaning of paragraph 2 of this article shall terminate without the occurrence of a chargeable event when:

(a)   the imported goods are dispatched or transported outside the Community within the meaning of article 3; or

(b)   the imported goods, within the meaning of paragraph 2(a), are other than a means of transport and are dispatched or transported to the member state from which they were exported and to the person who exported them; or

(c)   the imported goods, within the meaning of paragraph 2(a), are means of transport which were acquired or imported before 1 January 1993, in accordance with the general conditions of taxation in force on the domestic market of a member state, within the meaning of article 3, and/or have not been subject by reason of their exportation to any exemption from or refund of value added tax.

This condition shall be deemed to be fulfilled when the date of the first use of the means of transport was before 1 January 1985 or when the amount of tax due because of the importation is insignificant.

History – Art. 28N added by Directive 92/111, art. 1(22) (OJ 1992 L384/47). Member states had to bring into force the measures necessary to implement this provision no later than 1 January 1993.

Cross reference – Finance (No. 2) Act 1992 (Commencement No. 4 and Transitional Provisions) Order 1992 (SI 1992/3261).

TITLE XVIb – TRANSITIONAL PROVISIONS APPLICABLE IN THE FIELD OF SECOND-HAND GOODS, WORKS OF ART, COLLECTORS' ITEMS AND ANTIQUES

ART. 28O   [Transitional provisions]

28O(1)   Member states which at 31 December 1992 were applying special tax arrangements other than those provided for in article 26A(B) to supplies of second-hand means of transport effected by taxable dealers [may] continue to apply those arrangements during the period referred to in article 28L in so far as they comply with, or are adjusted to comply with, the following conditions:

(a)　　the special arrangements shall apply only to supplies of the means of transport referred to in article 28A(2)(a) and regarded as second-hand goods within the meaning of article 26A(A)(d), effected by taxable dealers within the meaning of article 26A(A)(e), and subject to the special tax arrangements for taxing the margin pursuant to article 26A(B)(1) and (2). Supplies of new means of transport within the meaning of article 28A(2)(b) that are carried out under the conditions specified in article 28C(A) shall be excluded from these special arrangements;

(b)　　the tax due in respect of each supply referred to in (a) is equal to the amount of tax that would be due if that supply had been subject to the normal arrangements for value added tax, less the amount of value added tax regarded as being incorporated in the purchase price of the means of transport by the taxable dealer;

(c)　　the tax regarded as being incorporated in the purchase price of the means of transport by the taxable dealer shall be calculated according to the following method:

-　　the purchase price to be taken into account shall be the purchase price within the meaning of article 26A(B)(3),

-　　that purchase price paid by the taxable dealer shall be deemed to include the tax that would have been due if the taxable dealer's supplier had subjected the supply to the normal value added tax arrangements,

-　　the rate to be taken into account shall be the rate applicable within the meaning of article 12(1), in the member state within which the place of the supply to the taxable dealer, determined in accordance with article 8, is deemed to be situated;

(d)　　the tax due in respect of each supply as referred to in (a), determined in accordance with the provisions of (b), may not be less than the amount of tax that would be due if that supply had been subject to the special arrangements for taxing the margin in accordance with article 26A(B)(3).

For the application of the above provisions, the member states have the option of providing that if the supply had been subject to the special arrangements for taxation of the margin, that margin would not have been less than 10 per cent of the selling price, within the meaning of B(3);

(e)　　the taxable dealer shall not be entitled to indicate separately on the invoices he issues, or on any other document in lieu, tax relating to supplies which he is subjecting to the special arrangements;

(f)　　taxable persons shall not be entitled to deduct from the tax for which they are liable tax due or paid in respect of second-hand means of transport supplied to them by a taxable dealer, in so far as the supply of those goods by the taxable dealer is subject to the tax arrangements in accordance with (a);

(g)　　by way of derogation from article 28A(1)(a), intra-Community acquisitions of means of transport are not subject to value added tax where the vendor is a taxable dealer acting as such and the second-hand means of transport acquired has been subject to the tax, in the member state of departure of the dispatch or transport, in accordance with (a);

(h)　　Articles 28B and 28C(A)(a) and (d) shall not apply to supplies of second-hand means of transport subject to tax in accordance with (a).

28O(2)　By way of derogation from the first sentence of paragraph 1, the Kingdom of Denmark shall be entitled to apply the special tax arrangements laid down in paragraph 1(a) to (h) during the period referred to in article 28L.

28O(3)　Where they apply the special arrangements for sales by public auction provided for in article 26A(C), member states shall also apply these special arrangements to supplies of second-hand means of transport effected by an organiser of sales by public auction acting in his own name, pursuant to a contract under which commission is payable on the sale of those goods by public auction, on behalf of a taxable dealer, in so far as the supply of the second-hand means of transport, within the meaning of article 5(4)(c), by that other taxable dealer, is subject to tax in accordance with paragraphs 1 and 2.

28O(4)　For supplies by a taxable dealer of works of art, collectors' items or antiques that have been supplied to him under the conditions provided for in article 26A(B)(2), the Federal Republic of Germany shall be entitled, until 30 June 1999, to provide for the possibility for taxable dealers to apply either the special arrangements for taxable dealers, or the normal VAT arrangements according to the following rules:

(a)　　for the application of the special arrangements for taxable dealers to these supplies of goods, the taxable amount shall be determined in accordance with article 11(A)(1), (2) and (3);

(b)   in so far as the goods are used for the needs of his operations which are taxed in accordance with (a), the taxable dealer shall be authorised to deduct from the tax for which he is liable:

      –   the value added tax due or paid for works of art, collectors' items or antiques which are or will be supplied to him by another taxable dealer, where the supply by that other taxable dealer has been taxed in accordance with (a),

      –   the value added tax deemed to be included in the purchase price of the works of art, collectors' items or antiques which are or will be supplied to him by another taxable dealer, where the supply by that other taxable dealer has been subject to value added tax in accordance with the special arrangements for the taxation of the margin provided for in article 26A(B), in the member state within whose territory the place of that supply, determined in accordance with article 8, is deemed to be situated.

        This right to deduct shall arise at the time when the tax due for the supply taxed in accordance with (a) becomes chargeable;

(c)   for the application of the provisions laid down in the second indent of (b), the purchase price of the works of art, collectors' items or antiques the supply of which by a taxable dealer is taxed in accordance with (a) shall be determined in accordance with article 26A(B)(3) and the tax deemed to be included in this purchase price shall be calculated according to the following method:

      –   the purchase price shall be deemed to include the value added tax that would have been due if the taxable margin made by the supplier had been equal to 20 per cent of the purchase price,

      –   the rate to be taken into account shall be the rate applicable, within the meaning of article 12(1), in the member state within whose territory the place of the supply that is subject to the special arrangements for taxation of the profit margin, determined in accordance with article 8, is deemed to be situated;

(d)   where he applies the normal arrangements for value added tax to the supply of a work of art, collectors' item or antique which has been supplied to him by another taxable dealer and where the goods have been taxed in accordance with (a), the taxable dealer shall be authorised to deduct from his tax liability the value added tax referred to in (b);

(e)   the category of rates applicable to these supplies of goods shall be that which was applicable on 1 January 1993;

(f)   for the application of the fourth indent of article 26A(B)(2), the fourth indent of article 26A(C)(1) and article 26A(D)(b) and (c), the supplies of works of art, collectors' items or antiques, taxed in accordance with (a), shall be deemed by member states to be supplies subject to value added tax in accordance with the special arrangements for taxation of the profit margin provided for in article 26A(B);

(g)   where the supplies of works of art, collectors' items or antiques taxed in accordance with (a) are effected under the conditions provided for in article 28C(A), the invoice issued in accordance with article 22(3) shall contain an endorsement indicating that the special taxation arrangements for taxing the margin provided for in article 28O(4) have been applied.

History – Art. 28O inserted by Directive 94/5, art. 7 (OJ 1994 L60/16). Member states had to bring into force the measures necessary to comply with this directive no later than 1 January 1995.

TITLE XVIc – TRANSITIONAL MEASURES APPLICABLE IN THE CONTEXT OF THE ACCESSION TO THE EUROPEAN UNION OF AUSTRIA, FINLAND AND SWEDEN

ART. 28P   [Accession of member states]

28P(1)   For the purpose of applying this article:

–   **"Community"** shall mean the territory of the Community as defined in article 3 before accession,

–   **"new member states"** shall mean the territory of the member states acceding to the European Union by the Treaty signed on 24 June 1994, as defined for each of those member states in article 3 of this Directive,

–   **"enlarged Community"** shall mean the territory of the Community as defined in article 3, after accession.

28P(2)   When goods:

– entered the territory of the Community or of one of the new member states before the date of accession, and

– were placed, on entry into the territory of the Community or of one of the new member states, under a temporary admission procedure with full exemption from import duties, under one of the regimes referred to in article 16(1)(B)(a) to (d) or under a similar regime in one of the new member states, and

– have not left that regime before the date of accession,

the provisions in force at the moment the goods were placed under that regime shall continue to apply until the goods leave this regime, after the date of accession.

28P(3) When goods:

– were placed, before the date of accession, under the common transit procedure or under another customs transit procedure, and

– have not left that procedure before the date of accession,

the provisions in force at the moment the goods were placed under that procedure shall continue to apply until the goods leave this procedure, after the date of accession.

For the purposes of the first indent, **"common transit procedure"** shall mean the measures for the transport of goods in transit between the Community and the countries of the European Free Trade Association (EFTA) and between the EFTA countries themselves, as provided for in the Convention of 20 May 1987 on a common transit procedure.

28P(4) The following shall be deemed to be an importation of goods within the meaning of article 7(1) where it is shown that the goods were in free circulation in one of the new member states or in the Community:

(a) the removal, including irregular removal, of goods from a temporary admission procedure under which they were placed before the date of accession under the conditions set out in paragraph 2;

(b) the removal, including irregular removal, of goods either from one of the regimes referred to in article 16(1)(B)(a) to (d) or from a similar regime under which they were placed before the date of accession under the conditions set out in paragraph 2;

(c) the termination of one of the procedures referred to in paragraph 3 which was started before the date of accession in one of new member states for the purposes of a supply of goods for consideration effected before that date in that member state by a taxable person acting as such;

(d) any irregularity or offence committed during one of the procedures referred to in paragraph 3 under the conditions set out at (c).

28P(5) The use after the date of accession within a member state, by a taxable or non-taxable person, of goods supplied to him before the date of accession within the Community or one of the new member states shall also be deemed to be an importation of goods within the meaning of article 7(1) where the following conditions are met:

– the supply of those goods has been exempted, or was likely to be exempted, either under article 15(1) and (2) or under a similar provision in the new member states,

– the goods were not imported into one of the new member states or into the Community before the date of accession.

28P(6) In the cases referred to in paragraph 4, the place of import within the meaning of article 7(3) shall be the member state within whose territory the goods cease to be covered by the regime under which they were placed before the date of accession.

28P(7) By way of derogation from article 10(3), the importation of goods within the meaning of paragraphs 4 and 5 of this article shall terminate without the occurrence of a chargeable event when:

(a) the imported goods are dispatched or transported outside the enlarged Community; or

(b) the imported goods within the meaning of paragraph 4(a) are other than means of transport and are redispatched or transported to the member state from which they were exported and to the person who exported them; or

(c) the imported goods within the meaning of paragraph 4(a) are means of transport which were acquired or imported before the date of accession in accordance with the general conditions of taxation in force on the domestic market of one of the new member states or of one of the member states of the Community and/or have not been subject, by reason of their exportation, to any exemption from, or refund of, value added tax.

This condition shall be deemed to be fulfilled when the date of the first use of the means of transport was before 1 January 1987 or when the amount of tax due by reason of the importation is insignificant.

History – Art. 28P inserted by Directive 94/76, art. 1 (OJ 1994 L365/53). Member states had to bring into force the laws, regulations and administrative provisions necessary to comply with this directive no later than 1 January 1995.

TITLE XVII – VALUE ADDED TAX COMMITTEE

ART. 29   [Advisory Committee]

29(1)   An Advisory Committee on value added tax, hereinafter called **"the Committee"**, is hereby set up.

29(2)   The Committee shall consist of representatives of the member states and of the Commission.

The chairman of the Committee shall be a representative of the Commission.

Secretarial services for the Committee shall be provided by the Commission.

29(3)   The Committee shall adopt its own rules of procedure.

29(4)   In addition to points subject to the consultation provided for under this directive, the Committee shall examine questions raised by its chairman, on his own initiative or at the request of the representative of a member state, which concern the application of the Community provisions on value added tax.

TITLE XVIII – MISCELLANEOUS

ART. 30   International agreements

30   The Council, acting unanimously on a proposal from the Commission, may authorise any member state to conclude with a non-member country or an international organisation an agreement which may contain derogations from this directive. A state wishing to conclude such an agreement shall bring the matter to the notice of the Commission and provide all the information necessary for it to be considered. The Commission shall inform the other member states within one month.

The Council's decision shall be deemed to have been adopted if, within two months of the other member states being informed as laid down in the previous paragraph, the matter has not been raised before the Council.

ART. 31   Unit of account

31(1)   The unit of account used in this directive shall be the European unit of account (EUA) defined by Decision 75/250.

31(2)   When converting this unit of account into national currencies, member states shall have the option of rounding the amounts resulting from this conversion either upwards or downwards by up to 10 per cent.

Cross reference – Regulation 3308/80 (OJ 1980 L345/1): replacement of European unit of account by ECU.

ART. 32   Second-hand goods

32   [Deleted by Directive 94/5, art. 9 (OJ 1994 L60/16).]

History – Member states had to bring into force the measures necessary to comply with Directive 94/5 no later than 1 January 1995. Former art. 32 read as follows:
"The Council, acting unanimously on a proposal from the Commission, shall adopt before 31 December 1977 a Community taxation system to be applied to used goods, works of art, antiques and collectors' items. Until the Community system becomes applicable member states applying a special system to these items at the time this directive comes into force may retain that system."

ART. 33   [Taxes other than turnover taxes]

33(1)   Without prejudice to other Community provisions, in particular those laid down in the Community provisions in force relating to the general arrangements for the holding, movement and monitoring of products subject to excise duty, this directive shall not prevent a member state from maintaining or introducing taxes on insurance contracts, taxes on betting and gambling, excise duties stamp duties and, more generally, any taxes, duties or charges which cannot be characterised as turnover taxes, provided however that those taxes, duties or charges do not, in trade between member states, give rise to formalities connected with the crossing of frontiers.

33(2) Any reference in this directive to products subject to excise duty shall apply to the following products as defined by current Community provisions:

–   mineral oils
–   alcohol and alcoholic beverages,
–   manufactured tobacco.

History – Art. 33 replaced by Directive 91/680, art. 1(23) (OJ 1991 L376/1). Member states had to bring into force the measures necessary to comply with this directive no later than 1 January 1993.

ART. 33A   [Goods from or to excluded territories etc.]

33A(1) Goods referred to in article 7(1)(b) entering the Community from a territory which forms part of the Customs territory of the Community but which is considered as a third territory for the purposes of applying this directive shall be subject to the following provisions:

(a)   the formalities relating to the entry of such goods into the Community shall be the same as those laid down by the Community customs provisions in force for the import of goods into the customs territory of the Community;

(b)   when the place of arrival of the dispatch or transport of these goods is situated outside the member state where they enter the Community, they shall circulate in the Community under the internal Community transit procedure laid down by the Community customs provisions in force, in so far as they have been the subject of a declaration placing them under this regime when the goods entered the Community;

(c)   when at the moment of their entry into the Community the goods are found to be in one of the situations which would qualify them, if they were imported within the meaning of article 7(1)(a), to benefit from one of the arrangements referred to in article 16(1)(B)(a), (b), (c) and (d), or under a temporary arrangement in full exemption from import duties, the member states shall take measures ensuring that the goods may remain in the Community under the same conditions as those laid down for the application of such arrangements.

33A(2) Goods not referred to in article 7(1)(a) dispatched or transported from a member state to a destination in a territory that forms parts of the Customs territory of the Community but which is considered as a third territory for the purposes of applying this directive shall be subject to the following provisions:

(a)   the formalities relating to the export of those goods outside the territory of the Community shall be the same as the Community customs provisions in force in relation to export of goods outside the customs territory of the Community;

(b)   for goods which are temporarily exported outside the Community, in order to be reimported, the member states shall take the measures necessary to ensure that, on reimportation into the Community, such goods may benefit from the same provisions as if they had been temporarily exported outside the customs territory of the Community.

History – Art. 33A inserted by Directive 91/680, art. 1(24) (OJ 1991 L376/1) and replaced by Directive 92/111, art. 1(23) (OJ 1992 L384/47). Member states had to bring into force the measures necessary to implement these provisions no later than 1 January 1993.

TITLE XIX – FINAL PROVISIONS

ART. 34   [Commission report]

34 For the first time on 1 January 1982 and thereafter every two years, the Commission shall, after consulting the member states, send the Council a report on the application of the common system of value added tax in the member states. This report shall be transmitted by the Council to the European Parliament.

ART. 35   [Restrictions of derogations]

35 At the appropriate time the Council acting unanimously on a proposal from the Commission, after receiving the opinion of the European Parliament and of the Economic and Social Committee, and in accordance with the interests of the common market, shall adopt further directives on the common system of value added tax, in particular to restrict progressively or to repeal measures taken by the member states by way of derogation from the system, in order to achieve complete parallelism of the national value added tax systems and thus permit the attainment of the objective stated in article 4 of the first Council directive of 11 April 1967.

ART. 36   [Repeals]

36   The fourth paragraph of article 2 and article 5 of the first Council directive of 11 April 1967 are repealed.

ART. 37   [Expiry of earlier provisions]

37   Second Council Directive 67/228 of 11 April 1967 on value added tax shall cease to have effect in each member state as from the respective dates on which the provisions of this directive are brought into application.

ART. 38   [Addressees]

38   This directive is addressed to the member states.

ANNEX A – LIST OF AGRICULTURAL PRODUCTION ACTIVITIES

I.   CROP PRODUCTION
- (1)   General agriculture, including viticulture
- (2)   Growing of fruit (including olives) and of vegetables, flowers and ornamental plants, both in the open and under glass
- (3)   Production of mushrooms, spices, seeds and propagating materials; nurseries

II.   STOCK FARMING TOGETHER WITH CULTIVATION
- (1)   General stock farming
- (2)   Poultry farming
- (3)   Rabbit farming
- (4)   Beekeeping
- (5)   Silkworm farming
- (6)   Snail farming

III.   FORESTRY

IV.   FISHERIES
- (1)   Fresh-water fishing
- (2)   Fish farming
- (3)   Breeding of mussels, oysters and other molluscs and crustaceans
- (4)   Frog farming

V.   Where a farmer processes, using means normally employed in an agricultural, forestry or fisheries undertaking, products deriving essentially from his agricultural production, such processing shall also be regarded as agricultural production.

ANNEX B – LIST OF AGRICULTURAL SERVICES

Supplies of agricultural services which normally play a part in agricultural production shall be considered the supply of agricultural services, and include the following in particular:

- field work, reaping and mowing, threshing, baling, collecting, harvesting, sowing and planting
- packing and preparation for market, for example drying, cleaning, grinding, disinfecting and ensilage of agricultural products
- storage of agricultural products
- stock minding, rearing and fattening
- hiring out, for agricultural purposes, of equipment normally used in agricultural, forestry or fisheries undertakings
- technical assistance
- destruction of weeds and pests, dusting and spraying of crops and land
- operation of irrigation and drainage equipment
- lopping, tree felling and other forestry services.

ANNEX C – COMMON METHOD OF CALCULATION

Note – The classification used in this Annex is that used in the Economic Accounts for Agriculture of the Statistical Office of the European Communities (SOEC).

[Not directly relevant to flat-rate scheme for farmers.]

ANNEX D – LIST OF THE ACTIVITIES REFERRED TO IN THE THIRD PARAGRAPH OF ARTICLE 4(5)

(1)   Telecommunications

(2)   The supply of water, gas, electricity and steam

(3)   The transport of goods

(4)   Port and airport services

(5)   Passenger transport

(6)   Supply of new goods manufactured for sale

(7)   The transactions of agricultural intervention agencies in respect of agricultural products carried out pursuant to regulations on the common organisation of the market in these products

(8)   The running of trade fairs and exhibitions

(9)   Warehousing

(10)   The activities of commercial publicity bodies

(11)   The activities of travel agencies

(12)   The running of staff shops, cooperatives and industrial canteens and similar institutions.

(13)   Transactions other than those specified in article 13A(1)(q), of radio and television bodies.

ANNEX E – TRANSACTIONS REFERRED TO IN ARTICLE 28(3)(a)

(1)   [Abolished by Directive 89/465, with effect from 1 January 1990.]

(2)   Transactions referred to in Article 13(A)(1)(e)

(3)-(6)   [Abolished by Directive 89/465, with effect from 1 January 1990.]

(7)   Transactions referred to in article 13(A)(1)(q)

(8)-(10)   [Abolished by Directive 89/465, with effect from 1 January 1990.]

(11)   Supplies covered by article 13(B)(g) in so far as they are made by taxable persons who were entitled to deduction of input tax on the building concerned

(12)-(14)   [Abolished by Directive 89/465, with effect from 1 January 1990.]

(15)   The services of travel agents referred to in article 26, and those of travel agents acting in the name and on account of the traveller, for journeys outside the Community.

ANNEX F – TRANSACTIONS REFERRED TO IN ARTICLE 28(3)(b)

(1)   Admission to sporting events

(2)   Services supplied by authors, artists, performers, lawyers and other members of the liberal professions, other than the medical and paramedical professions, in so far as these are not services specified in Annex B to the second Council directive of 11 April 1967

(3)   [Abolished by Directive 89/465, with effect from 1 January 1990.]

(4)   [Abolished by Directive 89/465, with effect from 1 January 1991.]

(5)   Telecommunications services supplied by public postal services and supplies of goods incidental thereto

(6)   Services supplied by undertakers and cremation services, together with goods related thereto

(7)   Transactions carried out by blind persons or workshops for the blind provided these exemptions do not give rise to significant distortion of competition

(8)   The supply of goods and services to official bodies responsible for the construction, setting out and maintenance of cemeteries, graves and monuments commemorating war dead

(9)   [Abolished by Directive 89/465, with effect from 1 January 1992.]

(10)   Transactions of hospitals not covered by article 13(A)(1)(b)

(11)   [Abolished by Directive 89/465, with effect from 1 January 1993.]

(12)   The supply of water by public authorities

(13)   [Abolished by Directive 89/465, with effect from 1 January 1991.]

(14)   [Abolished by Directive 89/465, with effect from 1 January 1990.]

(15) [Abolished by Directive 89/465, with effect from 1 January 1991.]

(16) Supplies of those buildings and land described in article 4(3)

(17) Passenger transport
The transport of goods such as luggage or motor vehicles accompanying passengers and the supply of services related to the transport of passengers, shall only be exempted in so far as the transport of the passengers themselves is exempt

(18)-(22) [Abolished by Directive 89/465, with effect from 1 January 1990.]

(23) The supply, modification, repair, maintenance, chartering and hiring of aircraft, including equipment incorporated or used therein, used by state institutions

(24) [Abolished by Directive 89/465, with effect from 1 January 1991.]

(25) The supply, modification, repair, maintenance, chartering and hiring of warships

(26) [Deleted by Directive 98/80, with effect from 1 January 2000.]

(27) The services of travel agents referred to in article 26, and those of travel agents acting in the name and on account of the traveller, for journeys within the Community.

History – Annex F, point 26 deleted by Directive 98/80, art. 2 (OJ 1998 L281/31). Member states had to bring into force the measures necessary to comply with this directive on 1 January 2000. Former art. 12(3)(e) read as follows: "Transactions concerning gold other than gold for industrial use".

ANNEX G – RIGHT OF OPTION

(1) The right of option referred to in article 28(3)(c) may be granted in the following circumstances:

    (a) in the case of transactions specified in Annex E:
        member states which already exempt these supplies but also give right of option for taxation, may maintain this right of option

    (b) in the case of transactions specified in Annex F:
        member states which provisionally maintain the right to exempt such supplies may grant taxable persons the right to opt for taxation

(2) Member states already granting a right of option for taxation not covered by the provisions of paragraph 1 above may allow taxpayers exercising it to maintain it until at the latest the end of three years from the date the directive comes into force.

ANNEX H – LIST OF SUPPLIES OF GOODS AND SERVICES WHICH MAY BE SUBJECT TO REDUCED RATES OF VAT

In transposing the categories below which refer to goods into national legislation, member states may use the combined nomenclature to establish the precise coverage of the category concerned.

Category	Description
1.	Foodstuffs (including beverages but excluding alcoholic beverages) for human and animal consumption; live animals, seeds, plants and ingredients normally intended for use in preparation of foodstuffs; products normally intended to be used to supplement or substitute foodstuffs
2.	Water supplies
3.	Pharmaceutical products of a kind normally used for health care, prevention of diseases and treatment for medical and veterinary purposes, including products used for contraception and sanitary protection
4.	Medical equipment, aids and other appliances normally intended to alleviate or treat disability, for the exclusive personal use of the disabled, including the repair of such goods, and children's car seats
5.	Transport of passengers and their accompanying luggage
6.	Supply, including on loan by libraries, of books (including brochures, leaflets and similar printed matter, children's picture, drawing or colouring books, music printed or in manuscript, maps and hydrographic or similar charts), newspapers and periodicals, other than material wholly or substantially devoted to advertising matter
7.	Admissions to shows, theatres, circuses, fairs, amusement parks, concerts, museums, zoos, cinemas, exhibitions and similar cultural events and facilities
	Reception of broadcasting services
8.	Services supplied by or royalties due to writers, composers and performing artists

Category	Description
9.	Supply, construction, renovation and alteration of housing provided as part of a social policy
10.	Supplies of goods and services of a kind normally intended for use in agricultural production but excluding capital goods such as machinery or buildings
11.	Accommodation provided by hotels and similar establishments including the provision of holiday accommodation and the letting of camping sites and caravan parks
12.	Admission to sporting events
13.	Use of sporting facilities
14.	Supply of goods and services by organizations recognised as charities by member states and engaged in welfare or social security work, in so far as these supplies are not exempt under article 13
15.	Services supplied by undertakers and cremation services, together with the supply of goods related thereto
16.	Provision of medical and dental care as well as thermal treatment in so far as these services are not exempt under article 13
17.	Services supplied in connection with street cleaning, refuse collection and waste treatment, other than the supply of such services by bodies referred to in article 4(5).

History – Annex H appended by Directive 92/77, art. 5 (OJ 1992 L316/1). Member states had to bring into force the measures necessary to comply with this directive no later than 31 December 1992.

ANNEX I – WORKS OF ART, COLLECTORS' ITEMS AND ANTIQUES

For the purposes of this directive:

(a)   **"works of art"** shall mean:

–   pictures, collages and similar decorative plaques, paintings and drawings, executed entirely by hand by the artist, other than plans and drawings for architectural, engineering, industrial, commercial, topographical or similar purposes, hand-decorated manufactured articles, theatrical scenery, studio back cloths or the like of painted canvas (CN code 9701),

–   original engravings, prints and lithographs, being impressions produced in limited numbers directly in black and white or in colour of one or of several plates executed entirely by hand by the artist, irrespective of the process or of the material employed by him, but not including any mechanical or photomechanical process (CN code 9702 00 00),

–   original sculptures and statuary, in any material, provided that they are executed entirely by the artist; sculpture casts the production of which is limited to eight copies and supervised by the artist or his successors in title (CN code 9703 00 00); on an exceptional basis, in cases determined by the member states, the limit of eight copies may be exceeded for statuary casts produced before 1 January 1989,

–   tapestries (CN code 5805 00 00) and wall textiles (CN code 6304 00 00) made by hand from original designs provided by artists, provided that there are not more than eight copies of each,

–   individual pieces of ceramics executed entirely by the artist and signed by him,

–   enamels on copper, executed entirely by hand, limited to eight numbered copies bearing the signature of the artist or the studio, excluding articles of jewellery and goldsmiths' and silversmiths' wares,

–   photographs taken by the artist, printed by him or under his supervision, signed and numbered and limited to 30 copies, all sizes and mounts included;

(b)   **"collectors' items"** shall mean:

–   postage or revenue stamps, postmarks, first-day covers, pre-stamped stationery and the like, franked, or if unfranked not being of legal tender and not being intended for use as legal tender (CN code 9704 00 00),

–   collections and collectors' pieces of zoological, botanical, mineralogical, anatomical, historical, archaeological, palaetological, ethnographic or numismatic interest (CN code 9705 00 00);

(c)   **"antiques"** shall mean objects other than works of art or collectors' items, which are more than 100 years old (CN code 9706 00 00).

History – Annex I added by Directive 94/5, art. 9 (OJ 1994 L60/16). Member states had to bring into force the measures necessary to comply with this directive no later than 1 January 1995.

ANNEX J – [CN CODES OF GOODS]

Description of goods	CN code
Tin	8001
Copper	7402 7403 7405 7408
Zinc	7901
Nickel	7502
Aluminium	7601
Lead	7801
Indium	ex 8112 91 ec 8112 99
Cereals	1001 to 1005 1006: unprocessed rice only 1007 to 1008
Oil seeds and oleaginous fruit Coconuts, Brazil nuts and cashew nuts Other nuts Olives	1201 to 1207 0801 0802 0711 20
Grains and seeds (including soya beans)	1201 to 1207
Coffee, not roasted	0901 11 00 0901 12 00
Tea	0902
Cocoa beans, whole or broken, raw or roasted	1801
Raw sugar	1701 11 1701 12
Rubber, in primary forms or in plates, sheets or strip	4001 4002
Wool	5101
Chemicals in bulk	Chapters 28 and 29
Mineral oils (including propane and butane; also including crude petroleum oils)	2709 2710 2711 12 2711 13
Silver	7106
Platinum (palladium, rhodium)	7110 11 00 7110 21 00 7110 31 00
Potatoes	0701
Vegetable oils and fats and their fractions, whether or not refined, but not chemically modified	1507 to 1515

History – Annex J added by Directive 95/7, art. 13 (OJ 1995 L102/18). Member states required to bring into force the measures necessary to comply with this directive on 1 January 1996.

ANNEX K – LIST OF SUPPLIES OF SERVICES REFERRED TO IN ARTICLE 28(6)

(1)   Small services of repairing–
      –   bicycles,
      –   shoes and leather goods,
      –   clothing and household linen (including mending and alteration).
(2)   Renovation and repairing of private dwellings, excluding materials which form a significant part of the value of the supply.
(3)   Window cleaning and cleaning in private households.
(4)   Domestic care services (e.g. home help and care of the young, elderly, sick or disabled).
(5)   Hairdressing.

History – Annex K added by Directive 99/85, art. 2 (OJ 1999 L277/34). The directive entered into force on the day of its publication in the Official Journal of the European Communities, which was 28 October 1999.

DIRECTIVE 77/799

On the mutual assistance by the competent authorities of the member states in the field of direct and indirect taxation

(19 December 1977, OJ 1977 L336/15)

History – The title of this directive was replaced by Directive 92/12 of 25 February 1992, art. 30(1) (OJ 1992 L76/1) to add excise duties to its scope, with effect from 1 January 1993.

Notes – This directive was given effect in the UK by FA 1978, s. 77.
FA 1990, s. 125: extension of Revenue information powers to cover information needed solely by the tax authorities of another member state (enabling full compliance with obligations under the directive).

The Council of the European Communities,

Having regard to the treaty establishing the European Economic Community, and in particular article 100 thereof,

Having regard to the proposal from the Commission,

Having regard to the opinion of the European Parliament,

Having regard to the opinion of the Economic and Social Committee,

[1]   Whereas practices of tax evasion and tax avoidance extending across the frontiers of member states lead to budget losses and violations of the principle of fair taxation and are liable to bring about distortions of capital movements and of conditions of competition; whereas they therefore affect the operation of the common market;

[2]   Whereas, for these reasons, the Council adopted on 10 February, 1975, a resolution on the measures to be taken by the Community in order to combat international tax evasion and avoidance;

[3]   Whereas the international nature of the problem means that national measures, whose effect does not extend beyond national frontiers, are insufficient; whereas collaboration between administrations on the basis of bilateral agreements is also unable to counter new forms of tax evasion and avoidance, which are increasingly assuming a multinational character;

[4]   Whereas collaboration between tax administrations within the Community should therefore be strengthened in accordance with common principles and rules;

[5]   Whereas the member states should, on request, exchange information concerning particular cases; whereas the state so requested should make the necessary inquiries to obtain such information;

[6]   Whereas the member states should exchange, even without any request, any information which appears relevant for the correct assessment of taxes on income and on capital, in particular where there appears to be an artificial transfer of profits between enterprises in different member states or where such transactions are carried out between enterprises in two member states through a third country in order to obtain tax advantages, or where tax has been or may be evaded or avoided for any reason whatever;

[7]   Whereas it is important that officials of the tax administration of one member state be allowed to be present in the territory of another member state if both the states concerned consider it desirable;

[8] Whereas care must be taken to ensure that information provided in the course of such collaboration is not disclosed to unauthorised persons, so that the basic rights of citizens and enterprises are safeguarded; whereas it is therefore necessary that the member states receiving such information should not use it, without the authorisation of the member state supplying it, other than for the purposes of taxation or to facilitate legal proceedings for failure to observe the tax laws of the receiving state; whereas it is also necessary that the receiving states afford the information the same degree of confidentiality which it enjoyed in the state which provided it, if the latter so requires;

[9] Whereas a member state which is called upon to carry out inquiries or to provide information shall have the right to refuse to do so where its laws or administrative practices prevent its tax administration from carrying out these inquiries or from collecting or using this information for its own purposes, or where the provision of such information would be contrary to public policy or would lead to the disclosure of a commercial, industrial or professional secret or of a commercial process, or where the member state for which the information is intended is unable for practical or legal reasons to provide similar information;

[10] Whereas collaboration between the member states and the Commission is necessary for the permanent study of co-operation procedures and the pooling of experience in the fields considered, and in particular in the field of the artificial transfer of profits within groups of enterprises, with the aim of improving those procedures and of preparing appropriate Community rules,

has adopted this directive:

ART. 1   General provisions

1(1) In accordance with this Directive the competent authorities of the Member State shall exchange any information that may enable them to effect a correct assessment of taxes on income and capital and any information relating to the assessment of the following indirect taxes:

–   value added tax,
–   excise duty on mineral oils,
–   excise duty on alcohol and alcoholic beverages,
–   excise duty on manufactured tobacco.

1(2) There shall be regarded as taxes on income and on capital, irrespective of the manner in which they are levied, all taxes imposed on total income, on total capital, or on elements of income or of capital, including taxes on gains from the disposal of movable or immovable property, taxes on the amounts of wages or salaries paid by enterprises, as well as taxes on capital appreciation.

1(3) The taxes referred to in paragraph (2) are at present, in particular:

in Belgium:

     Impôt des personnes physiques/Personenbelasting
     Impôt des sociétés/Vennootschapsbelasting
     Impôt des personnes morales/Rechtspersonenbelasting
     Impôt des non-résidents/Belasting der niet-verblijfhouders

in Denmark:

     Indkomstskat til staten
     Selskabsskat
     Den kommunale indkomstskat
     Den amtskommunale indkomstskat
     Folkepensionsbidragene
     Sømandsskat
     Den særlige indkomstskat
     Kirkeskatten
     Formueskat til staten
     Bidrag til dagpengefonden

in Germany:

     Einkommensteuer
     Körperschaftsteuer
     Vermögensteuer
     Gewerbesteuer
     Grundsteuer

in Greece:

Φοροσ εισοδηματοσ φυσικων προσωπων
Φοροσ εισοδηματοσ νομικων προσωπων
Φοροσ~ ακινητου περιουσιασ

in Spain:

Impuesto sobre la Renta de las Personas Físicas
Impuesto sobre Sociedades
Impuesto Extraordinario sobre el Patrimonio de las Personas Físicas

in France:

Impôt sur le revenu
Impôt sur les sociétés
Taxe professionnelle
Taxe foncière sur les propriétés bâties
Taxe foncière sur les propriétés non bâties

in Ireland:

Income tax
Corporation tax
Capital gains tax
Wealth tax

in Italy:

Imposta sul reddito delle persone fisiche
Imposta sul reddito delle persone giuridiche
Imposta locale sui redditi

in Luxembourg:

Impôt sur le revenu des personnes physiques
Impôt sur le revenu des collectivités
Impôt commercial communal
Impôt sur la fortune
Impôt foncier

in Netherlands:

Inkomstenbelasting
Vennootschapsbelasting
Vermogensbelasting

in Austria:

Einkommensteuer
Körperschaftsteuer
Grundsteuer
Bodenwertabgabe
Abgabe von land- und forstwirtschaftlichen Betrieben

in Portugal:

Contribuição predial
Imposto sobre a indústria agrícola
Contribuição industrial
Imposto de capitais
Imposto profissional
Imposto complementar
Imposto de mais-valias
Imposto sobre o rendimento do petróleo
Os adicionais devidos sobre os impostos precedentes

in Finland:

Valtion tuloverot/de statliga inkomstskatterna
Yhteisöjen tulovero/inkomstskatten för samfund
Kunnallisvero/kommunalskatten
Kirkollisvero/kyrkoskatten
Kansaneläkevakuutusmaksu/folkpensionsförsäkringspremien
Sairausvakuutusmaksu/sjukförsäkringspremien
Korkotulon lähdevero/källskatten på ränteinkomst

Rajoitetusti verovelvollisen lähdevero/källskatten för
    begränsat skattskyldig
Valtion varallisuusvero/den statliga förmögenhetsskatten
Kiinteistövero/fastighetsskatten

in Sweden:

Den statliga inkomstskatten
Sjömansskatten
Kupongskatten
Den särskilda inkomstskatten för utomlands bosatta artister m.fl.
Den statliga fastighetsskatten
Den kommunala inkomstskatten
Förmögenhetsskatten

in United Kingdom:

Income tax
Corporation tax
Capital gains tax
Petroleum revenue tax
Development land tax

1(4) Paragraph (1) shall also apply to any identical or similar taxes imposed subsequently, whether in addition to or in place of the taxes listed in paragraph (3). The competent authorities of the member states shall inform one another and the Commission of the date of entry into force of such taxes.

1(5) The expression **"competent authority"** means:

in Belgium:

De minister van financiën or an authorised representative
Le ministre des finances or an authorised representative

in Denmark:

Skatteministeren or an authorised representative;

in Germany:

Der Bundesminister der Finanzen or an authorised representative

in Greece:

To Ο Υπουργειο Οικκονομικων or an authorised representative

in Spain:

El Ministro de Economía y Hacienda or an authorised representative

in France:

Le ministre de l'économie or an authorised representative

in Ireland:

The Revenue Commissioners or their authorised representative

in Italy:

Il Ministro per le finanze or an authorised representative

in Luxembourg

Le ministre des finance or an authorised representative

in Netherlands:

De minister van financiën or an authorised representative

in Austria:

Der Bundesminister für Finanzen or an authorised representative

in Portugal:

O Ministro das Finanças or an authorised representative

in Finland:

Valtiovarainministeriö or an authorised representative
Finansministeriet or an authorised representative

in Sweden:

Ministern med ansvar för skattefrågor or an authorised representative *in United Kingdom:*

> The Commissioners of Customs and Excise or an authorised representative for information required concerning value added tax and excise duty,
>
> The Commissioners of Inland Revenue or an authorised representative for all other information.

History – Para. 1 replaced by Directive 92/12 of 25 February 1992, art. 30(2)(a) (OJ 1992 L76/1) with effect from 1 January 1993. Para. 3 replaced by the Act of Accession of Austria, Finland and Sweden, annex I, Ch. XIII(B), point 1(a) (as adjusted by Decision 95/1 (OJ 1995 L1/1)) with effect from 1 January 1995. Para. 5 replaced by the Act of Accession of Austria, Finland and Sweden, annex I, Ch. XIII(B), point 1(b) (adjusted by Decision 95/1 (OJ 1995 L1/1)) with effect from 1 January 1995.

ART. 2   Exchange on request

2(1)   The competent authority of a member state may request the competent authority of another member state to forward the information referred to in article 1(1) in a particular case. The competent authority of the requested state need not comply with the request if it appears that the competent authority of the state making the request has not exhausted its own usual information, which it could have utilised, according to the circumstances, to obtain the information requested without running the risk of endangering the attainment of the sought-after result.

2(2)   For the purpose of forwarding the information referred to in paragraph (1), the competent authority of the requested member state shall arrange for the conduct of any inquiries necessary to obtain such information.

ART. 3   Automatic exchange of information

3   For categories of cases which they shall determine under the consultation procedure laid down in article 9, the competent authorities of the member states shall regularly exchange the information referred to in article 1(1) without prior request.

ART. 4   Spontaneous exchange of information

4(1)   The competent authority of a member state shall without prior request forward the information referred to in article 1(1), of which it has knowledge, to the competent authority of any other member state concerned, in the following circumstances:

(a)   the competent authority of the one member state has grounds for supposing that there may be a loss of tax in the other member state;

(b)   a person liable to tax obtains a reduction in or an exemption from tax in the one member state which would give rise to an increase in tax or to liability to tax in the other member state;

(c)   business dealings between a person liable to tax in a member state and a person liable to tax in another member state are conducted through one or more countries in such a way that a saving in tax may result in one or the other member state or in both;

(d)   the competent authority of a member state has grounds for supposing that a saving of tax may result from artificial transfers of profits within groups of enterprises;

(e)   information forwarded to the one member state by the competent authority of the other member state has enabled information to be obtained which may be relevant in assessing liability to tax in the latter member state.

4(2)   The competent authorities of the member states may, under the consultation procedure laid down in article 9, extend the exchange of information provided for in paragraph (1) to cases other than those specified therein.

4(3)   The competent authorities of the member states may forward to each other in any other case, without prior request, the information referred to in article 1(1) of which they have knowledge.

ART. 5   Time-limit for forwarding information

5   The competent authority of a member state which, under the preceding articles, is called upon to furnish information, shall forward it as swiftly as possible. If it encounters obstacles in furnishing the information or if it refuses to furnish the information, it shall forthwith inform the requesting authority to this effect, indicating the nature of the obstacles or the reasons for its refusal.

ART. 6   Collaboration by officials of the state concerned

6 For the purpose of applying the preceding provisions, the competent authority of the member state providing the information and the competent authority of the member state for which the information is intended may agree, under the consultation procedure laid down in article 9, to authorise the presence in the first member state of officials of the tax administration of the other member state. The details for applying this provision shall be determined under the same procedure.

ART. 7   Provisions relating to secrecy

7(1) All information made known to a member state under this directive shall be kept secret in that state in the same manner as information received under its domestic legislation.

In any case, such information:

- may be made available only to the persons directly involved in the assessment of the tax or in the administrative control of this assessment,
- may in addition be made known only in connection with judicial proceedings or administrative proceedings involving sanctions undertaken with a view to, or relating to, the making or reviewing the tax assessment and only to persons who are directly involved in such proceedings; such information may, however, be disclosed during public hearings or in judgments if the competent authority of the member state supplying the information raises no objection,
- shall in no circumstances be used other than for taxation purposes or in connection with judicial proceedings or administrative proceedings involving sanctions undertaken with a view to, or in relation to, the making or reviewing the tax assessment.

7(2) Paragraph (1) shall not oblige a member state whose legislation or administrative practice lays down, for domestic purposes, narrower limits than those contained in the provisions of that paragraph, to provide information if the state concerned does not undertake to respect those narrower limits.

7(3) Notwithstanding paragraph (1), the competent authorities of the member state providing the information may permit it to be used for other purposes in the requesting state, if, under the legislation of the informing state, the information could, in similar circumstances, be used in the informing state for similar purposes.

7(4) Where a competent authority of a member state considers that information which it has received from the competent authority of another member state is likely to be useful to the competent authority of a third member state, it may transmit it to the latter competent authority with the agreement of the competent authority which supplied the information.

ART. 8   Limits to exchange of information

8(1) This directive shall impose no obligation to have inquiries carried out or to provide information if the member state, which should furnish the information, would be prevented by its laws or administrative practices from carrying out these inquiries or from collecting or using this information for its own purposes.

8(2) The provision of information may be refused where it would lead to the disclosure of a commercial, industrial or professional secret or of a commercial process, or of information whose disclosure would be contrary to public policy.

8(3) The competent authority of a member state may refuse to provide information where the State concerned is unable, for practical or legal reasons, to provide similar information.

ART. 9   Consultations

9(1) For the purposes of the implementation of this directive, consultation shall be held, if necessary in a committee, between:

- the competent authorities of the member states concerned at the request of either, in respect of bilateral questions,
- the competent authorities of all the member states and the commission, at the request of one of those authorities or the commission, in so far as the matters involved are not solely of bilateral interest.

9(2)   The competent authorities of the member states may communicate directly with each other. The competent authorities of the member states may by mutual agreement permit authorities designated by them to communicate directly with each other in specified cases or in certain categories of cases.

9(3)   Where the competent authorities make arrangements on bilateral matters covered by this directive other than as regards individual cases, they shall as soon as possible inform the Commission thereof. The Commission shall in turn notify the competent authorities of the other member states.

ART. 10   Pooling of experience

10   The member states shall, together with the Commission, constantly monitor the co-operation procedure provided for in this directive and shall pool their experience, especially in the field of transfer pricing within groups of enterprises, with a view to improving such co-operation and, where appropriate, drawing up a body of rules in the fields concerned.

ART. 11   Applicability of wider-ranging provisions of assistance

11   The foregoing provisions shall not impede the fulfilment of any wider obligations to exchange information which might flow from other legal acts.

ART. 12   Final provisions

12(1)   Member states shall bring into force the necessary laws, regulations and administrative provisions in order to comply with this directive not later than January 1, 1979, and shall forthwith communicate them to the Commission.

12(2)   Member states shall communicate to the Commission the texts of any important provisions of national law which they subsequently adopt in the field covered by this directive.

ART. 13   [Addressees]

13   This directive is addressed to the member states.

DIRECTIVE 79/1072

Eighth directive on the harmonisation of the laws of the member states relating to turnover taxes – arrangements for the refund of value added tax to taxable persons not established in the territory of the country

(6 December 1979, OJ 1979 L331/11)

The Council of the European Communities,

Having regard to the Treaty establishing the European Economic Community,

Having regard to Sixth Council Directive 77/388 of 17 May 1977 on the harmonisation of the laws of the member states relating to turnover taxes – common system of value added tax (uniform basis of assessment) (OJ 1977 L145/1), and in particular article 17(4) thereof,

Having regard to the proposal from the Commission,

Having regard to the opinion of the European Parliament,

Having regard to the opinion of the Economic and Social Committee,

[1]   Whereas, pursuant to article 17(4) of Directive 77/388, the Council is to adopt Community rules laying down the arrangements governing refunds of value added tax, referred to in paragraph 3 of the said article, to taxable persons not established in the territory of the country;

[2]   *Whereas rules are required* to ensure that a taxable person established in the territory of one member country can claim for tax which has been invoiced to him in respect of supplies of goods or services in another member state or which has been paid in respect of imports into that other member state, thereby avoiding double taxation;

[3]   Whereas discrepancies between the arrangements currently in force in member states, which give rise in some cases to deflection of trade and distortion of competition, should be eliminated;

[4]   Whereas the introduction of Community rules in this field will mark progress towards the effective liberalisation of the movement of persons, goods and services, thereby helping to complete the process of economic integration;

[5]   Whereas such rules must not lead to the treatment of taxable persons differing according to the member state in the territory of which they are established;

[6]   Whereas certain forms of tax evasion or avoidance should be prevented;

[7]   Whereas, under article 17(4) of Directive 77/388, member states may refuse the refund or impose supplementary conditions in the case of taxable persons not established in the territory of the Community; whereas steps should, however, also be taken to ensure that such taxable persons are not eligible for refunds on more favourable terms than those provided for in respect of Community taxable persons;

[8]   Whereas, initially, only the Community arrangements contained in this directive should be adopted; whereas these arrangements provide, in particular, that decisions in respect of applications for refund should be notified within six months of the date on which such applications were lodged; whereas refunds should be made within the same period; whereas, for a period of one year from the final date laid down for the implementation of these arrangements, the Italian Republic should be authorised to notify the decisions taken by its competent services with regard to applications lodged by taxable persons not established within its territory and to make the relevant refunds within nine months, in order to enable the Italian Republic to reorganise the system at present in operation, with a view to applying the Community system;

[9]   Whereas further arrangements will have to be adopted by the Council to supplement the Community system; whereas, until the latter arrangements enter into force, member states will refund the tax on the services and the purchases of goods which are not covered by this directive, in accordance with the arrangements which they adopt pursuant to article 17(4) of Directive 77/388,

has adopted this directive:

ART. 1   [Taxable person: definition]

1   For the purposes of this directive, **"a taxable person not established in the territory of the country"** shall mean a person as referred to in article 4(1) of Directive 77/388 who, during the period referred to in the first and second sentences of the first subparagraph of article 7(1), has had in that country neither the seat of his economic activity, nor a fixed establishment from which business transactions are effected, nor, if no such seat or fixed establishment exists, his domicile or normal place of residence, and who, during the same period, has supplied no goods or services deemed to have been supplied in that country, with the exception of:

(a)   transport services and services ancillary thereto, exempted pursuant to article 14(1)(i), article 15 or article 16(1), B, C and D of Directive 77/388;

(b)   services provided in cases where tax is payable solely by the person to whom they are supplied, pursuant to article 21(1)(b) of Directive 77/388.

ART. 2   [Refunds to nationals of other member states]

2   Each member state shall refund to any taxable person who is not established in the territory of the country but who is established in another member state, subject to the conditions laid down below, any value added tax charged in respect of services or movable property supplied to him by other taxable persons in the territory of the country or charged in respect of the importation of goods into the country, in so far as such goods and services are used for the purposes of the transactions referred to in article 17(3)(a) and (b) of Directive 77/388 and of the provision of services referred to in article 1(b).

ART. 3   [Refunds: procedure]

3   To qualify for refund, any taxable person as referred to in article 2 who supplies no goods or services deemed to be supplied in the territory of the country shall:

(a)   submit to the competent authority referred to in the first paragraph of article 9 an application modelled on the specimen contained in Annex A, attaching originals of invoices or import documents. Member states shall make available to applicants an explanatory notice which shall in any event contain the minimum information set out in Annex C;

(b)   produce evidence, in the form of a certificate issued by the official authority of the state in which he is established, that he is a taxable person for the purposes of value added tax in that state. However, where the competent authority referred to in the first paragraph of article 9 already has such evidence in its possession, the taxable person shall not be bound to produce new evidence for a period of one year from the date of issue of the first certificate by the official authority of the state in which he is established. Member states shall not issue certificates to any taxable persons who benefit from tax exemption pursuant to article 24(2) of Directive 77/388;

(c)   certify by means of a written declaration that he has supplied no goods or services deemed to have been supplied in the territory of the country during the period referred to in the first and second sentences of the first subparagraph of article 7(1);

(d)   undertake to repay any sum collected in error.

ART. 4   [Refunds: eligibility]

4   To be eligible for the refund, any taxable person as referred to in article 2 who has supplied in the territory of the country no goods or services deemed to have been supplied in the country other than the services referred to in article 1(a) and (b) shall:

(a)   satisfy the requirements laid down in article 3(a), (b) and (d);

(b)   certify by means of a written declaration that, during the period referred to in the first and second sentences of the first subparagraph of article 7(1), he has supplied no goods or services deemed to have been supplied in the territory of the country other than services referred to in article 1(a) and (b).

ART. 5   [Eligible goods and services]

5   For the purposes of this directive, goods and services in respect of which tax may be refundable shall satisfy the conditions laid down in article 17 of Directive 77/388 as applicable in the member state of refund.

This directive shall not apply to supplies of goods which are, or may be, exempted under item 2 of article 15 of Directive 77/388.

ART. 6   [Information requirements]

6   Member states may not impose on the taxable persons referred to in article 2 any obligation, in addition to those referred to in articles 3 and 4, other than the obligation to provide, in specific cases, the information necessary to determine whether the application for refund is justified.

ART. 7   [Refunds procedure]

7(1)   The application for refund provided for in articles 3 and 4 shall relate to invoiced purchases of goods or services or to imports made during a period of not less than three months or not more than one calendar year. Applications may, however, relate to a period of less than three months where the period represents the remainder of a calendar year. Such applications may also relate to invoices or import documents not covered by previous applications and concerning transactions completed during the calendar year in question. Applications shall be submitted to the competent authority referred to in the first paragraph of article 9 within six months of the end of the calendar year in which the tax became chargeable.

If the application relates to a period of less than one calendar year but not less than three months, the amount for which application is made may not be less than the equivalent in national currency of 200 European units of account; if the application relates to a period of a calendar year or the remainder of a calendar year, the amount may not be less than the equivalent in national currency of 25 European units of account.

7(2)   The European unit of account used shall be that defined in the Finance Regulation of 21 December 1977 (OJ 1977 L356/1), as determined on 1 January of the year of the period referred to in the first and second sentences of the first subparagraph of paragraph 1. Member states may round up or down, by up to 10 per cent, the figures resulting from this conversion into national currency.

7(3)   The competent authority referred to in the first paragraph of article 9 shall stamp each invoice and/or import document to prevent their use for further application and shall return them within one month.

7(4)   Decisions concerning applications for refund shall be announced within six months of the date when the applications, accompanied by all the necessary documents required under this directive for examination of the application, are submitted to the competent authority referred to in paragraph 3. Refunds shall be made before the end of the abovementioned period, at the applicant's request, in either the member state of refund or the state in which he is established. In the latter case, the bank charges for the transfer shall be payable by the applicant.

The grounds for refusal of an application shall be stated. Appeals against such refusals may be made to the competent authorities in the member state concerned, subject to the same conditions as to form and time limits as those governing claims for refunds made by taxable persons established in the same state.

7(5) Where a refund has been obtained in a fraudulent or in any other irregular manner, the competent authority referred to in paragraph 3 shall proceed directly to recover the amounts wrongly paid and any penalties imposed, in accordance with the procedure applicable in the member state concerned, without prejudice to the provisions relating to mutual assistance in the recovery of value added tax.

7(6) In the case of fraudulent applications which cannot be made the subject of an administrative penalty, in accordance with national legislation, the member state concerned may refuse for a maximum period of two years from the date on which the fraudulent application was submitted any further refund to the taxable person concerned. Where an administrative penalty has been imposed but has not been paid, the member state concerned may suspend any further refund to the taxable person concerned until it has been paid.

Cross references – Regulation 3308/80 (OJ 1980 L345/1): replacement of European unit of account by ECU.

ART. 8   [Obsolete]

8 [Art. 8 ceased to have effect in each member state from 1 January 1988 by virtue of Directive 86/560, art. 7.]

ART. 9   [Submission requirements]

9 Member states shall make known, in an appropriate manner, the competent authority to which the application referred to in article 3(a) and in article 4(a) are to be submitted.

The certificates referred to in article 3(b) and in article 4(a), establishing that the person concerned is a taxable person, shall be modelled on the specimens contained in Annex B.

ART. 10   [Implementation]

10 Member states shall bring into force the provisions necessary to comply with this directive no later than 1 January 1981. This directive shall apply only to applications for refunds concerning value added tax charged on invoiced purchases of goods or services or in imports made as from that date.

Member states shall communicate to the Commission the texts of the main provisions of national law which they adopt in the field covered by this directive. The Commission shall inform the other member states thereof.

ART. 11   [Italian Republic]

11 By a way of derogation from article 7(4), the Italian Republic may, until 1 January 1982, extend the period referred to in this paragraph from six to nine months.

ART. 12   [Report of Commission]

12 Three years after the date referred to in article 10, the Commission shall, after consulting the member states, submit a report to the Council on the application of this directive, and in particular articles 3, 4 and 7 thereof.

ART. 13   [Addressees]

13 This directive is addressed to the member states.

ANNEX A – SPECIMEN

[Not reproduced.]

Note – If the applicant does not have a VAT registration number, the competent authority shall state the reason for this.

ANNEX B – SPECIMEN

CERTIFICATE OF STATUS OF TAXABLE PERSON

[Not reproduced.]

ANNEX C – MINIMUM INFORMATION TO BE GIVEN IN EXPLANATORY NOTES

A.   The application shall be drawn up on a form printed in one of the official languages of the European Communities. This form shall, however, be completed in the language of the country of refund.

B.   The application shall be completed in block capitals and be submitted, by 30 June of the year following that to which the application relates, to the competent authority of the state to which the application is made (see D below).

C.   The VAT registration number in the country of refund shall be given, if it is known to the applicant.

D.   The application shall be submitted to the relevant competent authorities, i.e. for:

–Belgium: ....
–Denmark: ....
–Germany: ....
–Greece: ....
–Spain: ....
–France: ....
–Ireland: ....
–Italy: ....
–Luxembourg: ....
–the Netherlands: ....
–Austria: ....
–Portugal: ....
–Finland: ....
–Sweden: ....
–the United Kingdom: ....

E.   The application shall refer to purchases of goods or services invoiced or to imports made during a period of not less than three months or more than one calendar year. However, it may relate to a period of less than three months where this period represents the remainder of a calendar year. Such an application may also relate to invoices or import documents not covered by previous applications and concerning transactions made during the calendar year in question.

F.   In 9(a), the applicant shall describe the nature of the activities for which he has acquired the goods or received the services referred to in the application for refund of the tax (e.g. participation in the International ... ... Fair, held in ... ... from ... ... to ... ... , stand No. ... ... , or international carriage of goods as from ... ... to ... ... on ... ...).

G.   *The application shall be accompanied by a certificate issued by the official authority of the state in which the applicant is established and which provides evidence that he is a taxable person for the purposes of value added tax in that state. However, where the competent authority referred to in D above already has such evidence in its possession, the applicant shall not be bound to produce new evidence for a period of one year from the date of issue of the first certificate.*

H.   The application shall be accompanied by the originals of the invoices or import documents showing the amount of value added tax borne by the applicant.

I.   The application may be used for more than one invoice or import document but the total amount of VAT claimed for 19 ... may not be less than:

BFr/Lfr ...

DKr ...

DM ...

Dr ...

Pts ...

FF ...

Ir£ ...

Lire ...

HFl ...

ASch ...

Esc ...

FM ...

SKr ...

£ ...

if the period to which it relates is less than one calendar year but not less than three months or less than:

BFr/LFr ...

DKr ...

DM ...

Dr ...

Pts ...

FF ...

Ir£ ...

Lire ...

HFl ...

ASch ...

Esc ...

FM ...

SKr ...

£ ...

if the period to which it relates is one calendar year or less than three months.

J.   Exempted transport services are those carried out in connection with the international carriage of goods, including – subject to certain conditions – transport associated with the transit, export or import of goods.

K.   Any refund obtained improperly may render the offender liable to the fines or penalties laid down by the law of the state which has made the refund.

L.   The authority in the country of refund reserves the right to make refunds by cheque or money order addressed to the applicant.

History – Point D substituted by the Act of Accession of Austria, Sweden and Finland, art. 29 and Annex I, Ch. XIII (OJ 1994 C241/1), as substituted by Decision 95/1, Annex, Ch. XIII (OJ 1995 L1/1), with effect from 1 January 1995.
Item I substituted by the Act of Accession of Austria, Sweden and Finland, art. 29 and Annex I, Ch. XIII (OJ 1994 C241/1), as substituted by Decision 95/1, Annex, Ch. XIII (OJ 1995 L1/1), with effect from 1 January 1995.

DIRECTIVE 86/560

Thirteenth directive on the harmonisation of the laws of the member states relating to turnover taxes – arrangements for

the refund of value added tax to taxable persons not established in the Community territory

(17 November 1986, OJ 1986 L326/40)

The Council of the European Communities,

Having regard to the Treaty establishing the European Economic Community, and in particular articles 99 and 100 thereof,

Having regard to Sixth Council Directive 77/388 of 17 May 1977 on the harmonisation of the laws of the member states relating to turnover taxes – common system of value added tax: uniform basis of assessment and in particular article 17(4) thereof,

Having regard to the proposal from the Commission,

Having regard to the opinion of the European Parliament,

Having regard to the opinion of the Economic and Social Committee,

[1]   Whereas article 8 of Directive 79/1072 on the arrangements for the refund of value added tax to taxable persons not established in the territory of the country provides that in the case of taxable persons not established in the territory of the Community, member states may refuse refunds or impose special conditions;

[2]   Whereas there is a need to ensure the harmonious development of trade relations between the Community and third countries based on the provisions of Directive 79/1072, while taking account of the varying situations encountered in third countries;

[3]   Whereas certain forms of tax evasion or avoidance should be prevented,

has adopted this directive:

ART. 1   [Definitions]

For the purposes of this directive–

1(1)   "A taxable person not established in the territory of the Community" shall mean a taxable person asreferred to in article 4(1) of Directive 77/388 who, during the period referred to in article 3(1) of this directive, has had in that territory neither his business nor a fixed establishment from which business transactions are effected, nor, if no such business or fixed establishment exists, his permanent address or usual place of residence, and who, during the same period, has supplied no goods or services deemed to have been supplied in the member state referred to in article 2, with the exception of–

(a)   transport services and services ancillary thereto, exempted pursuant to article 14(1)(i), article 15 or article 16(1)B, C and D of Directive 77/388;

(b)   services provided in cases where tax is payable solely by the person to whom they are supplied, pursuant to article 21(1)(b) of Directive 77/388;

1(2)   "Territory of the Community" shall mean the territories of the member states in which Directive 77/388 is applicable.

ART. 2   [Refunds]

2(1)   Without prejudice to articles 3 and 4, each member state shall refund to any taxable person not established in the territory of the Community, subject to the conditions set out below, any value added tax charged in respect of services rendered or moveable property supplied to him in the territory or the country by other taxable persons or charged in respect of the importation of goods into the country, in so far as such goods and services are used for the purposes of the transactions referred to in article 17(3)(a) and (b) of Directive 77/388 or of the provision of services referred to in point 1(b) of article 1 of this directive.

2(2)   Member states may make the refunds referred to in paragraph 1 conditional upon the granting by third states of comparable advantages regarding turnover taxes.

2(3)   Member states may require the appointment of a tax representative.

ART. 3   [Refund arrangements]

3(1)   The refunds referred to in article 2(1) shall be granted upon application by the taxable person. Member states shall determine the arrangements for submitting applications, including the time-limits for doing so, the period which applications should cover, the authority competent to receive them and the minimum amounts in respect of which applications may be submitted. They shall also determine the arrangements for making refunds, including the time limits for doing so. They shall impose on the applicant such obligations as are necessary to determine whether the application is justified and to prevent fraud, in particular the obligation to provide proof that he is engaged in an economic activity in accordance with article 4(1) of Directive 77/388. The applicant must certify, in a written declaration, that, during the period prescribed, he has not carried out any transaction which does not fulfil the conditions laid down in point 1 of article 1 of this directive.

3(2) Refunds may not be granted under conditions more favourable than those applied to Community taxable persons.

ART. 4 [Eligibility]

4(1) For the purposes of this directive, eligibility for refunds shall be determined in accordance with article 17 of Directive 77/388 as applied in the member state where the refund is paid.

4(2) Member states may, however, provide for the exclusion of certain expenditure or make refunds subject to additional conditions.

4(3) This directive shall not apply to supplies of goods which are or may be exempted under point 2 of article 15 of Directive 77/388.

ART. 5 [Commencement: procedure]

5(1) Member states shall bring into force the laws, regulations and administrative provisions necessary to comply with this directive by 1 January 1988 at the latest. This directive shall apply only to applications for refunds concerning value added tax charged on purchases of goods or services invoiced or on imports effected on or after that date.

5(2) Member states shall communicate to the Commission the main provisions of national law which they adopt in the field covered by this directive and shall inform the Commission of the use they make of the option afforded by article 2(2). The Commission shall inform the other member states thereof.

ART. 6 [Submission of report]

6 Within three years of the date referred to in article 5, the Commission shall, after consulting the member states, submit a report to the Council and to the European Parliament on the application of this directive, particularly as regards the application of article 2(2).

ART. 7 [Repeal]

7 As from the date on which this directive is implemented, and at all events by the date mentioned in article 5, the last sentence of article 17(4) of Directive 77/388 and article 8 of Directive 79/1072 shall cease to have effect in each member state.

ART. 8 [Addressees]

8 This directive is addressed to the member states.

DIRECTIVE 89/465

Eighteenth directive on the harmonisation of the laws of the member states relating to turnover taxes – abolition of certain derogations provided for in article 28(3) of the sixth directive, 77/388

(18 July 1989, OJ 1989 L226/21)

The Council of the European Communities,

Having regard to the Treaty establishing the European Economic Community, and in particular article 99 thereof,

Having regard to the proposal from the Commission,

Having regard to the opinion of the European Parliament,

Having regard to the opinion of the Economic and Social Committee,

[1]   Whereas article 28(3) of the Sixth Council Directive, 77/388, of 17 May 1977 on the harmonisation of the laws of the member states relating to turnover taxes – common system of value added tax: uniform basis of assessment, as last amended by the Act of Accession of Spain and Portugal, allows member states to apply measures derogating from the normal rules of the common system of value added tax during a transitional period; whereas that period was originally fixed at five years; whereas the Council undertook to act, on a proposal from the Commission, before the expiry of that period, on the abolition, where appropriate, of some or all of those derogations;

[2]   Whereas many of those derogations give rise, under the Communities' own resources system, to difficulties in calculating the compensation provided for in Council Regulation 1553/89 of 29 May 1989 on the definitive uniform arrangements for the collection of own resources accruing from value added tax; whereas, in order to ensure that that system operates more efficiently, there are grounds for abolishing those derogations;

[3]   Whereas the abolition of those derogations will also contribute to greater neutrality of the value added tax system at Community level;

[4]   Whereas some of the said derogations should be abolished respectively from 1 January 1990, 1 January 1991, 1 January 1992 and 1 January 1993;

[5]   Whereas, having regard to the provisions of the Act of Accession, the Portuguese Republic may, until 1 January 1994 at the latest, postpone the abolition of the exemption of the transactions referred to in points 3 and 9 in Annex F to Directive 77/388;

[6]   Whereas it is appropriate that, before 1 January 1991, the Council should, on the basis of a Commission report, review the situation with regard to the other derogations provided for in article 28(3) of Directive 77/388, including the one referred to in the second subparagraph of point 1 of article 1 of this directive, and that it should take a decision, on a proposal from the Commission, on the abolition of these derogations, bearing in mind any distortion of competition which has resulted from their application or which may arise in connection with the future completion of the internal market,

has adopted this directive:

ART. 1   [Amendments]

Directive 77/388 is hereby amended as follows:

1(1)   With effect from 1 January 1990 the transactions referred to in points 1, 3 to 6, 8, 9, 10, 12, 13 and 14 of Annex E shall be abolished.

Those member states which, on 1 January 1989, subjected to value added tax the transactions listed in Annex E, points 4 and 5, are authorised to apply the conditions of article 13(A)(2)(a), final indent, also to services rendered and goods delivered, as referred to in article 13(A)(1)(m) and (n), where such activities are carried out by bodies governed by public law.

1(2)   In Annex F:

(a)   The transactions referred to in points 3, 14 and 18 to 22 shall be abolished with effect from 1 January 1990;

(b)   The transactions referred to in points 4, 13, 15 and 24 shall be abolished with effect from 1 January 1991;

(c)   The transaction referred to in point 9 shall be abolished with effect from 1 January 1992;

(d)   The transaction referred to in point 11 shall be abolished with effect from 1 January 1993.

ART. 2   [Portuguese Republic]

2   The Portuguese Republic may defer until 1 January 1994 at the latest the dates referred to in article 1, point 2(a), for the deletion of point 3 from Annex F and in article 1, point 2(c), for the deletion of point 9 from Annex F.

ART. 3   [Review]

3   By 1 January 1991 the Council, on the basis of a report from the Commission, shall review the situation with regard to the other derogations laid down in article 28(3) of Directive 77/388, including that referred to in the second subparagraph of point 1 of article 1 of this directive and, acting on a Commission proposal, shall decide whether these derogations should be abolished, having regard to any distortions of competitions which have resulted from their having been applied or which might arise from measures to complete the internal market.

ART. 4 [Unwarranted advantages/disadvantages]

4   In respect of the transactions referred to in articles 1, 2 and 3, member states may take measures concerning deduction of value added tax in order totally or partially to prevent the taxable persons concerned from deriving unwarranted advantages or sustaining unwarranted disadvantages.

ART. 5 [Commencement]

5(1)   Member states shall take the necessary measures to comply with this directive not later than the dates laid down in articles 1 and 2.

5(2)   Member states shall inform the Commission of the main provisions of national law which they adopt in the field governed by this directive.

ART. 6 [Addressees]

6   This directive is addressed to the member states.

DIRECTIVE 92/111

Amending Directive 77/388 and introducing simplification measures with regard to value added tax

(14 December 1992, OJ 1992 L384/47)

The Council of the European Communities,

Having regard to the Treaty establishing the European Economic Community, and in particular article 99 thereof,

Having regard to the proposal from the Commission,

Having regard to the opinion of the European Parliament,

Having regard to the opinion of the Economic and Social Committee,

[1]   Whereas article 3 of Council Directive 91/680 of 16 December 1991 supplementing the common system of valued added tax and amending Directive 77/388 with a view to the abolition of fiscal frontiers sets 1 January 1993 as the date for the entry into force of these provisions in all the member states;

[2]   Whereas in order to facilitate the application of these provisions and to introduce the simplifications needed, it is necessary to supplement the common system of value added tax, as applicable on 1 January 1993, so as to clarify how the tax shall apply to certain operations carried out with third territories and certain operations carried out inside the Community, as well to define the transitional measures between the provisions in force on 31 December 1992 and those which will enter into force as from 1 January 1993;

[3]   Whereas in order to guarantee the neutrality of the common system of turnover tax in respect of the origin of goods, the concept of a third territory and the definition of an import must be supplemented;

[4]   Whereas certain territories forming part of the Community Customs territory are regarded as third territories for the purposes of applying the common system of value added tax; whereas value added tax is therefore applied to trade between the member states and those territories according to the same principles as apply to any operation between the Community and third countries; whereas it is necessary to ensure that such trade is subject to fiscal provisions equivalent to those which would be applied to operations carried out under the same conditions with territories which are not part of the Community customs territory; whereas as a result of these provisions the Seventeenth Council Directive 85/362 of 16 July 1985 on the harmonisation of the laws of the member states relating to turnover taxes – exemption from value added tax on the temporary importation of goods other than means of transport, becomes null and void;

[5]   Whereas it is necessary to state exactly how the exemptions relating to certain export operations or equivalent operations will be implemented; whereas it is necessary to adapt the other directives concerned accordingly;

[6]   Whereas it is necessary to clarify the definition of the place of taxation of certain operations carried out on board ships, aircraft or trains transporting passengers inside the Community;

[7]   Whereas the transitional arrangements for taxation of trade between the member states must be supplemented to take account both of the Community provisions relating to excise duties and the need to clarify and simplify the detailed rules for the application of the tax of certain operations which will be carried out between the member states as from 1 January 1993;

[8]   Whereas Council Directive 92/12 of 25 February 1992 on the general arrangements for products subject to excise duty and on the holding, movement and monitoring of such products lays down particular procedures and obligations in relation to declarations in the case of shipments of such products to another member state; whereas as a result the methods of applying tax to certain supplies and intra-Community acquisitions of products liable to excise duties can be simplified to the benefit both of the persons liable to pay tax and the competent administrations;

[9]   Whereas it is necessary to define the scope of the exemptions referred to in article 28C of Directive 77/388; whereas it is also necessary to supplement the provisions concerning the chargeability of the tax and the methods of determining the taxable amount of certain intra-Community operations;

[10]   Whereas, for taxable operations in the domestic market linked to intra-Community trade in goods which are carried out during the period laid down in article 28L of Directive 77/388 by taxable persons not established in the member state referred to in article 28B(A)(1) of the said directive, it is necessary to take simplification measures guaranteeing equivalent treatment in all the member states; whereas to achieve this, the provisions concerning the taxation system and the person liable to tax in respect of such operations must be harmonised;

[11]   Whereas in order to take account of the provisions relating to the person liable to pay tax in the domestic market and to avoid certain forms of tax evasion or avoidance, it is necessary to clarify the Community provisions concerning the repayment to taxable persons not established in the country of the value added tax referred to in article 17(3) of Directive 77/388 as amended by article 28F of the said directive;

[12]   Whereas the abolition as from 1 January 1993 of tax on imports and tax relief on exports for trade between the member states makes it necessary to have transitional measures in order to ensure the neutrality of the common system of valued added tax and to avoid situations of double-taxation or non-taxation;

[13]   Whereas it is therefore necessary to lay down special provisions for cases where a Community procedure, started before 1 January 1993 for the purposes of a supply effected before that date by a taxable person acting as such in respect of goods dispatched or transported to another member state, is not completed until after 31 December 1992;

[14]   Whereas such provisions should also apply to taxable operations carried out before 1 January 1993 to which particular exemptions were applied which as a result delayed the taxable event;

[15]   Whereas it is also necessary to lay down special measures for means of transport which, not having been acquired or imported subject to the general domestic tax conditions of a member state, have benefited by the application of national measures, from an exemption from tax because of their temporary import from another member state;

[16]   Whereas the application of these transitional measures, both in relation [to] trade between the member states and to operations with third territories, presupposes supplementing the definition of the operations to be made subject to taxation as from 1 January 1993 and the clarification for such cases of the concepts of the place of taxation, the taxable event and the chargeability of the tax;

[17]   Whereas, on account of the current economic situation, the Kingdom of Spain and the Italian Republic have requested that, as a transitional measure, provisions derogating from the principle of immediate deduction laid down in the first subparagraph of article 18(2) of Directive 77/388 be applied; whereas this request should be granted for a period of two years which may not be extended;

[18]   Whereas this directive lays down common provisions for simplifying the treatment of certain intra-Community operations; whereas, in a number of cases, it is for the member states to determine the conditions for implementing these provisions; whereas certain member states will not be able to complete the legislative procedure necessary to adapt their legislation on valued added tax within the period laid down; whereas an additional period should therefore be allowed for the

implementation of this directive; whereas a maximum period of twelve months is sufficient for this purpose;

[19]   Whereas it is accordingly necessary to amend Directive 77/388,

has adopted this directive:

ART. 1   [Amendments]

1(1)   Replaces Directive 77/388, art. 3(4).

1(2)   Replaces Directive 77/388, art. 7(1)(b).

1(3)   Amends Directive 77/388, art. 7(3).

1(4)   Replaces Directive 77/388, art. 8(1)(c).

1(5)   Replaces Directive 77/388, art. 11(B)(1).

1(6)   Replaces Directive 77/388, art. 12(1)(b).

1(7)   Replaces Directive 77/388, art. 12(3)(a).

1(8)   Amends Directive 77/388, art. 14(1).

1(9)   Amends Directive 77/388, art. 15.

1(10)   Amends Directive 77/388, art. 28A.

1(11)   Adds Directive 77/388, art. 28B(A)(2), third subparagraph.

1(12)   Amends Directive 77/388, art. 28C(A).

1(13)   Replaces Directive 77/388, art. 28C(E).

1(14)   Replaces Directive 77/388, art. 28D(3).

1(15)   Replaces Directive 77/388, art. 28D(4), second subparagraph.

1(16)   Amends Directive 77/388, art. 28E(1).

1(17)   Inserts Directive 77/388, art. 28E(2).

1(18)   Amends Directive 77/388, art. 28F.

1(19)   Amends Directive 77/388, art. 28G.

1(20)   Amends Directive 77/388, art. 28H.

1(21)   Replaces Directive 77/388, art. 28I.

1(22)   Adds Directive 77/388, art. 28N.

1(23)   Replaces Directive 77/388, art. 33A(1) and (2).

1(24)   Provides for Directive 85/362, exempting from VAT the temporary importation of goods other than means of transport (OJ 1985 L192/20) to cease to have effect on 31 December 1992.

1(25)   Repeals Directive 69/169, on exemption from turnover tax and excise duty of imports in international travel, art. 6 (OJ 1969, Eng. Spec. Ed., p. 22) as from 1 January 1993.

ART. 2   [Derogations]

2(1)   As from 1 January 1993 and for a period of two years, which may not be extended, the Kingdom of Spain and the Italian Republic shall be authorised to apply provisions derogating from the principle of immediate deduction provided for in the first subparagraph of article 18(2). These provisions may not have the effect of delaying by more than one month the time when the right to deduction, having arisen, may be exercised under article 18(1).

However, for taxable persons who file the returns provided for in article 22(4) for quarterly tax periods, the Kingdom of Spain and the Italian Republic shall be authorised to provide that the right to deduction which has come into being which could, under article 18(1), be exercised in a given quarter, may not be exercised until the following quarter. This provision shall only apply where the Kingdom of Spain or the Italian Republic authorises such taxable persons to opt for the filing of monthly returns.

2(2)   By way of derogation from the third subparagraph of article 15(10), the Portuguese Republic, the French Republic, the Kingdom of the Netherlands and the Federal Republic of Germany shall be authorised, in regard to contracts concluded after 31 December 1992, to abolish the repayment procedure, where it is prohibited by this directive by 1 October 1993 at the latest.

ART. 3   [Chain transactions]

3 The Council, acting unanimously on a Commission proposal, shall adopt before 30 June 1993, detailed rules for the taxation of chain transactions between taxable persons, so that such rules may enter into force on 1 January 1994.

ART. 4   [Implementation]

4(1) The member states shall adapt their present value added tax system to the provisions of this directive.

They shall adopt the necessary laws, regulations and administrative provisions for their adapted systems to enter into force on 1 January 1993.

Member states may, however, provide that information relating to transactions referred to in the last subparagraph of article 22(6)(b) for which the tax becomes payable during the first three calendar months of 1993 must appear at the latest on the summary statement signed for the second calendar quarter of 1993.

4(2) By way of derogation from the second subparagraph of paragraph 1, member states shall be authorised to adopt the necessary laws, regulations and administrative provisions in order to implement by 1 January 1994 at the latest the provisions laid down in the following paragraphs of article 1:

–   paragraph 11,
–   paragraph 13, in so far as it relates to article 28C(E)(3);
–   paragraph 19, in so far as it relates to the third subparagraph of article 21(1)(a),
–   paragraph 20, in so far as it relates to obligations in respect of the transactions referred to in the preceding indents.

Member states which, on 1 January 1993, apply measures equivalent to those mentioned above shall adopt the necessary measures to ensure that the principles laid down in article 22(6) and in current Community provisions on administrative cooperation in the area of indirect taxation are complied with as from 1 January 1993 without fail.

4(3) By way of derogation from the second subparagraph of paragraph 1, the Federal Republic of Germany shall be authorised to adopt the necessary laws, regulations and administrative provisions in order to implement by 1 October 1993 at the latest the provisions laid down in article 1(10) with regard to article 28A(1A)(a).

4(4) Member states shall inform the Commission of the provisions which they adopt to apply this directive.

4(5) Member states shall communicate the provisions of domestic law which they adopt in the field covered by this directive to the Commission.

4(6) When member states adopt these provisions, they shall contain a reference to this directive or shall be accompanied by such reference on the occasion of their official publication. The methods of making such a reference shall be laid down by the member states.

ART. 5   [Addressees]

5 This directive is addressed to the member states.

DIRECTIVE 94/5

Seventh directive supplementing the common system of value added tax and amending Directive 77/388 – special arrangements applicable to second-hand goods, works of art, collectors' items and antiques

(14 February 1994, OJ 1994 L60/16)

The Council of the European Union,

Having regard to the Treaty establishing the European Community, and in particular article 99 thereof,

Having regard to the proposal from the Commission,

Having regard to the opinion of the European Parliament,

Having regard to the opinion of the Economic and Social Committee,

[1]　Whereas, in accordance with article 32 of the Sixth Council Directive 77/388 of 17 May 1977 on the harmonisation of the laws of the member states relating to turnover taxes – Common system of value added tax: uniform basis of assessment, the Council is to adopt a Community taxation system to be applied to used goods, works of art, antiques and collectors' items;

[2]　Whereas the present situation, in the absence of Community legislation, continues to be marked by the application of very different systems which cause distortion of competition and deflection of trade both internally and between member states; whereas these differences also include a lack of harmonisation in the levying of the own resources of the Community; whereas consequently it is necessary to bring this situation to an end as soon as possible;

[3]　Whereas the Court of Justice has, in a number of judgments, noted the need to attain a degree of harmonisation which allows double taxation in intra-Community trade to be avoided;

[4]　Whereas it is essential to provide, in specific areas, for transitional measures enabling legislation to be gradually adapted;

[5]　Whereas, within the internal market, the satisfactory operation of the value added tax mechanisms means that Community rules with the purpose of avoiding double taxation and distortion of competition between taxable persons must be adopted;

[6]　Whereas it is accordingly necessary to amend Directive 77/388,

has adopted this directive:

ART. 1　[Amendments]

Directive 77/388 is hereby amended as follows:

1(1)　Adds art. 11(A)(4) and 11(B)(6).

1(2)　Replaces art. 12(3)(c) and (5).

1(3)　Inserts art. 26A.

1(4)　Inserts art. 28(1A).

1(5)　Adds subparagraph to art. 28(2)(e).

1(6)　Replaces art. 28A(2)(b).

1(7)　Inserts art. 28O.

1(8)　Amends art. 28(3)(e).

1(9)　Deleted art. 32.

1(10)　the annex to this directive shall be added as Annex I.

ART. 2　[Unjustified results]

2　Member states may take measures concerning the right to deduct value added tax in order to avoid the taxable dealers concerned enjoying unjustified advantages or sustaining unjustified loss.

ART. 3　[Combating fraud]

3　Acting unanimously on a proposal from the Commission, the Council may authorise any member state to introduce particular measures for the purpose of combating fraud, by providing that the tax due in application of the arrangements for taxing the profit margin provided for in article 26A(B) cannot be less than the amount of tax which would be due if the profit margin were equal to a certain percentage of the selling price. This percentage shall be fixed taking into account the normal profit margins realised by economic operators in the sector concerned.

ART. 4　[Commencement date]

4(1)　Member states shall adapt their present value added tax system to this directive.

They shall bring into force such laws, regulations and administrative provisions as are necessary for their system thus adapted to enter into force on 1 January 1995 at the latest.

4(2)　Member states shall inform the Commission of the provisions which they adopt to apply this directive.

4(3)　Member states shall communicate to the Commission the provisions of national law which they adopt in the field covered by this directive.

4(4) When member states adopt such provisions, they shall contain a reference to this directive or be accompanied by such reference on the occasion of their official publication. The methods of making such a reference shall be laid down by the member states.

ART. 5   [Addressees]

5   This directive is addressed to the member states.

ANNEX

[Not reproduced.]

REGULATION 3330/91

On the statistics relating to the trading of goods between member states

(7 November 1991)

The Council of the European Communities,

Having regard to the Treaty establishing the European Economic Community, and in particular article 100A thereof,

Having regard to the proposal from the Commission,

In co-operation with the European Parliament, Having regard to the opinion of the Economic and Social Committee,

[1]   Whereas abolishing physical barriers between member states is necessary to complete the internal market; whereas a satisfactory level of information on the trading of goods between member states should thus be ensured by means other than those involving checks, even indirect ones, at internal frontiers;

[2]   Whereas an analysis of the situation of the Community and the member states after 1992 reveals that a number of specific requirements will persist as regards information on the trading of goods between member states;

[3]   Whereas these requirements are not of a macro-economic nature, unlike those relating, for example, to national accounts or the balance of payments, and many of them cannot be met by means of highly aggregated data alone; whereas matters such as trade policy, sectoral analyses, competition rules, the management and guidance of agriculture and fisheries, regional development, energy projections and the organisation of transport must on the contrary be based on statistical documentation providing the most up-to-date, accurate and detailed view of the internal market;

[4]   Whereas it is precisely information on the trading of goods between member states which will contribute to measuring the progress of the internal market, thereby speeding up its completion and consolidating it on a sound basis; whereas this kind of information could prove to be one of the means of assessing the development of economic and social cohesion;

[5]   Whereas until the end of 1992 statistics relating to the trading of goods between member states will benefit from the formalities, documentation and controls which the customs authorities, for their own requirements or for those of other departments, prescribe for consignors and consignees of goods in circulation between member states, but which will disappear through the elimination of physical frontiers and tax barriers;

[6]   Whereas it will consequently be necessary to collect directly from the consignors and consignees the data necessary to compile statistics relating to the trading of goods between member states, using methods and techniques which will ensure that they are exhaustive, reliable and up to *date, without giving rise for the parties* concerned, in particular for small and medium-sized businesses, to a burden out of proportion to the results which users of the said statistics can reasonably expect;

[7]   Whereas the relevant legislation must henceforth apply to all statistics relating to the trading of goods between member states, including those statistics which are not to be harmonised or made compulsory by the Community before 1993;

[8]   Whereas the statistics relating to the trading of goods between member states are a function of the movements of goods involved; whereas they may include data on transport, which can be collected simultaneously with the data specific to each of these categories of statistics, thus lightening the overall statistical burden;

[9]   Whereas private individuals will derive obvious advantages from the internal market; whereas it is necessary to ensure that these advantages are not diminished in their eyes by requirements for statistical information; whereas the provision of such information would undoubtedly impose an obligation which private individuals would consider inconvenient at the very least and which would be impossible to check on without employing excessive measures; whereas it is therefore reasonable not to regard private individuals as responsible for providing such information, apart from suitable periodic surveys;

[10]   Whereas the new collection system to be introduced is to apply to all statistics relating to the trading of goods between member states; whereas it must therefore be defined first in a general context involving new concepts, particularly as regards the scope, the party responsible for providing the information and the transmission of data;

[11]   Whereas the actual concept of the system resides in the use of related administrative networks, and in particular that of the value added tax (VAT) authorities, to provide the statistical services with a minimum degree of indirect verification without thereby increasing the burden on taxpayers; whereas it is nonetheless necessary to avoid confusion arising in the minds of the parties responsible for providing information between their statistical and their tax obligations;

[12]   Whereas it is vital to use existing sources to compile basic documentation in each member state regarding consignors and consignees of goods which are covered by statistics of trade between member states, so as to identify, in preparation for 1992, the main parties concerned and to develop modern data transmission techniques with their assistance;

[13]   Whereas implementation alone will reveal loopholes or weaknesses in the new collection system whereas improvements and simplifications should be introduced within a reasonable period of time in order to prevent defects from having negative repercussions on the trading of goods between member states;

[14]   Whereas, among the statistics relating to the trading of goods between member states, statistics of trade between member states must receive priority, for obvious reasons of importance and continuity; whereas, however, substantial adjustments must be made to these statistics in order to take account of the new conditions on the internal market after 1992; whereas it will be necessary to review, inter alia, the definition of their content, the goods classification applicable to them and the list of data to be collected to compile them; whereas it is desirable to adopt forthwith the principle on which the statistical thresholds will operate in order to avoid small and medium-sized businesses incurring expenditure which is disproportionate to overheads;

[15]   Whereas the Commission should be assisted by a committee to ensure the regular co-operation of the member states, in particular to resolve the problems which are bound to arise in connection with information on the trading of goods between member states following the numerous innovations introduced by the new collection system;

[16]   Whereas relevant Community legislation should be supplemented systematically by provisions adopted either by the Council or by the Commission;

[17]   Whereas some of the provisions of this regulation must enter into force without delay so that the Community and its member states can prepare for the practical consequences which it will entail as from 1 January 1993;

[18]   Whereas one of these consequences is that Council Regulation 2954/85 of 22 October 1985 laying down certain measures for the standardisation and simplification of the statistics of trade between member states must be repealed and that Council Regulation 1736/75 of 24 June 1975 on the external trade statistics of the Community and statistics of trade between member states, as last amended by Regulation 1629/88, will no longer be applicable to statistics relating to the trading of goods between member states,

has adopted this regulation:

ART. 1   [Trade statistics]

1   The Community and its member states shall compile statistics relating to the trading of goods between member states, in accordance with the rules laid down by this regulation, during the transitional period which shall begin on 1 January 1993 and end on the date of change-over to a unified system of taxation in the member state of origin.

Chapter 1 – General provisions

ART. 2　[Definitions]

2　For the purposes of this regulation and without prejudice to any individual provisions:

(a)　**"trading of goods between member states"** means any movement of goods from one member state to another;

(b)　**"goods"** means all movable property, including electric current;

(c)　**"Community goods"** means goods:

－　entirely obtained in the customs territory of the Community, without the addition of goods from non-member countries or territories which are not part of the customs territory of the Community,

－　from countries or territories not forming part of the customs territory of the Community which have been released for free circulation in a member state,

－　obtained in the customs territory of the Community either from the goods referred to exclusively in the second indent or from the goods referred to in the first and second indents;

(d)　**"non-Community goods"** means goods other than those referred to in (c). Without prejudice to agreements concluded with non-member countries for the implementation of the Community transit arrangements, goods which, while fulfilling the conditions laid down in (c), are reintroduced into the customs territory of the Community after export therefrom are also considered as non-Community goods;

(e)　**"member state"**, when the term is used in the geographical sense, means its statistical territory;

(f)　**"statistical territory of a member state"** means the territory occupied by that member state within the statistical territory of the Community, as this latter is defined in article 3 of Regulation 1736/75;

(g)　**"goods in free movement on the internal market of the Community"** means goods authorised, pursuant to Directive 77/388, to move from one member state to another without prior formalities or formalities linked to the crossing of internal frontiers;

(h)　**"private individual"** means any natural person not liable to account for VAT in connection with a given movement of goods.

ART. 3　[Goods moving between member states]

3(1)　All goods which move from one member state to another shall be the subject of statistics relating to the trading of goods between member states.

In addition to the goods which move within the statistical territory of the Community, goods shall be considered as moving from one member state to another if, in so doing, they cross the external frontier of the Community, whether of [sic] not they subsequently enter the territory of a non-member state.

3(3)　Paragraph 1 shall apply both to non-Community and Community goods, whether or not they are the subject of a commercial transaction.

Note – There is no numbered para. 3(2).

ART. 4　[Goods subject to statistics]

4(1)　Of the goods referred to in article 3:

(a)　transit statistics shall be compiled on those which are transported, with or without transhipment, across a member state without being stored there for reasons not inherent in their transport;

(b)　storage statistics shall be compiled on those referred to in article 2(2) of Regulation 1736/75, as well as those which enter or leave storage facilities determined by the Commission in accordance with article 30 of this regulation;

(c)　statistics of trade between member states shall be compiled on those which do not meet the *conditions of (a) and (b)* or which, while meeting either of those conditions, are expressly designated by this regulation or by the Commission pursuant to article 30;

(d)　the Council, on a proposal from the Commission, shall determine the goods that are to be the subject of other statistics relating to the trading of goods between member states.

4(2)　Without prejudice to Community provisions on statistical returns in respect of carriage of goods, the data on the movement of goods subject to the statistics referred to in paragraph 1 shall be included, as necessary, in the list of data relating to each of these categories of statistics on the conditions and terms laid down by this regulation or by the Commission pursuant to article 30.

ART. 5   [Persons exempt]

5   Without prejudice to article 15, private individuals shall be exempt from the obligations implied by the preparation of the statistics referred to in article 4.

shall also apply to the party responsible for providing information who, being liable to account for VAT, qualifies, in the member state in which he is responsible for providing information, for one of the special schemes provided for by articles 24 and 25 of Directive 77/388. This provision shall be extended, mutatis mutandis, to legal persons not liable to account for VAT and to parties liable to account who carry out only transactions not entitling them to any deduction of VAT, who pursuant to Council Directive 91/680, are not required to submit a tax declaration.

History – Art. 5, second paragraph, amended by Regulation 3046/92, art. 22(1) and (2) (OJ 1992 L307/27), with effect from 30 October 1992.

Chapter 2 – Statistical collection system
INTRASTAT

ART. 6   [Establishment of Intrastat]

6   With a view to compiling the statistics relating to the trading of goods between member states, a statistical collection system shall be set up, hereinafter referred to as the **"Intrastat system"**.

Cross references – Statistics of Trade (Customs and Excise) Regulations 1992 (SI 1992/2790).

ART. 7   [Application]

7(1)   The Intrastat system shall be applied in the member states whenever they are deemed to be partner countries in the trading of goods between member states by virtue of paragraph 4.

7(2)   The Intrastat system shall be applied to the goods referred to in article 3:

(a)   which are in free movement on the internal market of the Community;

(b)   which, since they may move on the internal market of the Community only after completion of the formalities prescribed by Community legislation on the circulation of goods, are expressly designated either by this regulation or by the Commission pursuant to article 30.

7(3)   The collection of data on the goods referred to in article 3 to which the Intrastat system does not apply shall be regulated by the Commission pursuant to article 30 within the framework of the formalities referred to in paragraph 2(b).

7(4)   The Intrastat system shall apply:

(a)   to statistics of trade between member states, pursuant to article 17 to 28;

(b)   to transit and storage statistics, in accordance with provisions laid down by the Council on a proposal from the Commission pursuant to article 31.

7(5)   Saving a decision to the contrary by the Council on a proposal from the Commission, in particular pursuant to article 31, national provisions on the statistics referred to in paragraph 4 of this article, in so far as they relate to data collection, shall cease to apply after 31 December 1992.

Cross references – Regulation 3046/92, art. 3 (OJ 1992 L307/27): non-application of Intrastat to certain goods.

ART. 8   [Person obliged to supply information]

8   Without prejudice to article 5, the obligation to supply the information required by the Intrastat system shall be incumbent on any natural or legal person who is involved in the trading of goods between member states.

Among those incurring this obligation, the party responsible for providing information for each category of statistics covered by the Intrastat system shall be designated by the relevant specific provisions.

ART. 9   [Third party information provider]

9(1)   The party responsible for providing the information required by the Intrastat system may transfer the task of providing the information to a third party residing in a member state, but such transfer shall in no way reduce the responsibility of the said party.

The party responsible for providing information shall provide such third party with all the information necessary to fulfil his obligations as party responsible.

9(2)   The party responsible for providing information may be required, at the express request of the departments responsible for compiling statistics on the trading of goods between member states, to notify them that for a given reference period,

–   all the information which is to be the subject of the periodic declaration referred to in article 13(1) has been provided either by himself or by a third party,

–   he has transferred the task of providing the information required by the Intrastat system to that third party, whom he shall identify.

9(3)   Paragraph 1 shall not apply:

(a)   in cases where article 28(4) applies;

(b)   in member states where the periodic declaration referred to in article 13(1) is not distinct from the periodic declaration required for tax purposes and inasmuch as the tax rules in force relating to declaration obligations prevent the transfer referred to in the abovementioned paragraph 1.

9(4)   The implementing rules for paragraphs 1, 2 and 3 shall be laid down by the Commission in accordance with article 30.

Cross references – Regulation 3046/92, art. 5 (OJ 1992 L307/27): information to be provided by person referred to in art. 9(1).

ART. 10   [Register]

10(1)   Member states shall take the measures necessary to ensure that those of their departments which are responsible for compiling statistics relating to the trading of goods between member states have a register of intra-Community operators at their disposal by 1 January 1993.

10(2)   For the purposes of applying paragraph 1, a list shall be established of upon dispatch the consignors, upon arrival the consignees and where necessary the declarants, within the meaning of Commission Regulation 2792/86, who are involved from 1 January 1991 to 31 December 1992 in trade between member states.

10(3)   Paragraph 2 shall not apply in those member states which take the measures necessary to ensure that their tax authorities have at their disposal, by 1 January 1993 at the latest, a register:

(a)   listing the parties liable to account for VAT who, during the 12 months prior to that date, took part in the trading of goods between member states, as consignors upon dispatch and as consignees upon arrival;

(b)   intended to list legal persons not liable to account for VAT and parties liable to account who carry out only transactions not entitling them to any deduction of VAT who, from that date, carry out their acquisitions, within the meaning of Directive 91/680.

In those member states, the abovementioned tax authorities shall, in addition to the identification number referred to in paragraph 6, supply the statistical departments referred to in paragraph 1 with the information included in that register which is used to identify those intra-Community operators, under the conditions required for application of this regulation.

10(4)   The list of minimum data to be recorded in the register of intra-Community operators in addition to the identification number referred to in paragraph 6 shall be laid down by the Commission pursuant to article 30.

10(5)   From 1 January 1993, the register of intra-Community operators shall be managed and updated in the member states by the relevant departments on the basis of the declarations referred to in article 13(1) or the lists referred to in article 11(1), or other administrative sources.

Where required, the Commission shall draw up, in accordance with article 30, the other rules relating to the management and updating of the register of intra-Community operators to be applied in the member states by the relevant departments.

10(6)   Apart from exceptions which they shall justify to the parties responsible for providing statistical information, the relevant statistical departments shall use in their relations with those parties, and in particular with a view to application of article 13(1), the identification number allocated to those parties by the tax authorities responsible.

History – Art. 10(3)(b) amended by Regulation 3046/92, art. 22(1) and (2) (OJ 1992 L307/27), with effect from 30 October 1992.

Cross references – Regulation 3046/92, art. 6 (OJ 1992 L307/27): information necessary to identify an intra-Community operator.

Regulation 3046/92, art. 7 (OJ 1992 L307/27): justified exception where responsibility for the information, for given operations, lies with a constituent part of the operator, such as a branch office.

ART. 11   [List from tax authority]

11(1)   The tax authorities responsible in each member state shall, at least once every three months, furnish the departments in that member state responsible for compiling statistics relating to the trading of goods between member states with the lists of those liable to account for VAT who have declared that, during the period in question, they have made acquisitions in other member states or deliveries to other member states.

11(2)   The lists referred to in paragraph 1 shall also include:

(a)   parties liable to account for VAT who have declared that, during the period in question, they have conducted trading of goods between member states which, although not resulting from acquisitions or deliveries, must be the subject of a periodic tax declaration;

(b)   legal persons not liable to account for VAT and parties liable to account who carry out only transactions not entitling them to any deduction of VAT who have declared that, during the same period, they have conducted trading of goods between member states which must be the subject of a periodic tax declaration.

11(3)   The lists shall indicate, for each operator on them, the value of trading of goods between member states which the operator has mentioned in his periodic tax declaration in accordance with Directive 91/680.

11(4)   Under restrictive conditions, which the Commission shall determine pursuant to article 30, each member state's competent tax authorities shall in addition furnish the departments in that member state responsible for compiling statistics relating to the trading of goods between member states, on their own initiative or at the request of the latter, with any information capable of improving the quality of statistics which those liable to account for VAT normally submit to the competent tax authorities to comply with tax requirements.

The information communicated to them in accordance with the first subparagraph shall be treated by the statistical departments, vis-;aga-vis third parties, in accordance with the rules applied to it by the tax authorities.

11(5)   Whatever the administrative structure of the member state, the party responsible for providing statistical information may not be compelled to justify, other than within the limits laid down by paragraphs 1, 2 and 3 and by the provisions provided for in paragraph 4, the information he supplies in comparison with the data he communicates to the competent tax authorities.

11(6)   In their relations with persons liable to account for VAT regarding the periodic declaration which such persons must forward to it for tax purposes, the competent tax authorities shall draw attention to the obligations which they may incur as parties responsible for providing the information required by the Intrastat system.

11(7)   For the purpose of applying paragraphs 4 and 6, **"parties liable to account for VAT"** shall also mean legal persons not liable to account for VAT and parties liable to account who carry out only transactions not entitling them to any deduction of VAT who carry out acquisitions within the meaning of Directive 91/680.

11(8)   Administrative assistance between national departments of different member states responsible for compiling statistics relating to the trading of goods between member states shall, as necessary, be regulated by the Commission pursuant to article 30.

History – Art. 11(2)(b) amended by Regulation 3046/92, art. 22(2) (OJ 1992 L307/27), with effect from 30 October 1992. Art. 11(3) amended by Regulation 3046/92, art. 22(1) (OJ 1992 L307/27), with effect from 30 October 1992. Art. 11(7) amended by Regulation 3046/92, art. 22(1) and (2) (OJ 1992 L307/27), with effect from 30 October 1992.

Cross references – Regulation 3046/92, art. 8 (OJ 1992 L307/27): tax authorities to mention operators who, as a result of scission, merger or cessation of activity, will no longer appear on the lists referred to in art. 11(1).

ART. 12   [Statistical information media]

12(1)   The statistical information media required by the Intrastat system shall be set up by the Commission pursuant to article 30 in respect of each category of statistics relating to the trading of goods between member states.

12(2)   In order to take account of their particular administrative arrangements, member states may set up media other than those referred to in paragraph 1, provided that those responsible for providing information may choose which of these media they will use.

Member states exercising this option shall inform the Commission accordingly.

12(3)   Paragraphs 1 and 2 shall not apply:

(a)   in cases where article 28(4) applies:

(b)   in member states where the periodic declaration referred to in article 13(1) is not distinct
       from the periodic declaration required for tax purposes and inasmuch as the tax rules in force
       relating to declaration obligations prevent such application.

Cross reference – Commission Regulation 3590/92 on the statistical information media for statistics on trade between member
states (OJ 1992 L364/27).

ART. 13   [Statistical declaration]

13(1)   The statistical information required by the Intrastat system shall be covered in periodic
declarations to be sent by the party responsible for providing the information to the competent
national departments, under conditions which the Commission shall lay down pursuant to
article 30.

13(2)   The Commission shall determine pursuant to article 30:

–   where not laid down by this regulation, the reference period applicable to each category of
       statistics relating to the trading of goods between member states,

–   the procedures for the transmission of the information, especially with a view to making
       available to the parties responsible for providing information networks of regional data
       collection offices.

13(3)   The periodic declarations referred to in paragraph 1 or, in any case, the information which
they contain shall be retained by the member states for at least two years following the end of the
calendar year of the reference period to which those declarations relate.

History – Art. 13(1) was replaced by Regulation 1182/99, art. 1(1), with effect from 1 January 2001. Former art. 13(1) reads as
follows:
"**13(1)**   The statistical information required by the Intrastat system shall be covered in periodic declarations to be sent by the
party responsible for providing the information to the competent national departments, by deadlines and under conditions which
the Commission shall lay down pursuant to article 30."

ART. 14   [Penalty]

14   Failure by any party responsible for providing statistical information to fulfil his obligations
under this regulation shall be liable to the penalties which the member states shall lay down in
accordance with their national provisions.

ART. 15   [Survey]

15   Pursuant to article 30, periodic surveys may be organised on the trading of goods between
member states by private individuals and on movements of goods or on intra-Community operators
excluded from the returns benefitting from simplification measures under specific provisions
relating to the various statistics on the trading of goods.

ART. 16   [Commission's report]

16   The Commission shall report to the European Parliament and the Council in good time on the
operation of the Intrastat system for each category of statistics relating to the trading of goods
between member states covered by the Intrastat system, with a view to possible adaptation of the
system at the end of the transitional period referred to in article 1.

Chapter 3 – Statistics on trade between member states

ART. 17   [Goods leaving/entering]

17   Statistics on trade between member states shall cover, on the one hand, movements of goods
leaving the member state of dispatch and, on the other, movements of goods entering the member
state of arrival.

ART. 18   ["Dispatch"]

18(1)   The member state of dispatch shall be the member state in which the goods leaving it are
the subject of a dispatch.

        "**Dispatch**" shall mean the shipment of goods referred to in paragraph 2 to a destination in
        another member state.

18(2)   In a given member state the following may be the subject of a dispatch:

(a)   Community goods which, in that member state:

–	are not in direct or interrupted transit,
–	are in direct or interrupted transit, but, having entered that member state as non-Community goods, have subsequently been released for free circulation there;
(b)	non-Community goods placed, maintained or obtained in that member state under inward processing customs arrangements or under arrangements for processing under customs control.

ART. 19   ["Arrival"]

19   The member state of arrival shall be the member state in which the goods entering it:

(a)   as Community goods:
-   are not in direct or interrupted transit in that member state,
-   are in direct or interrupted transit in that member state but leave it following formalities for export from the statistical territory of the Community;

(b)   as non-Community goods referred to in article 18(2)(b), are:
- (1)   released for free circulation;
- (2)   maintained under inward processing customs arrangements or under arrangements for processing under customs control or again made subject to such arrangements.

ART. 20   [Supplementary provisions]

20   With a view to collecting the data required for the statistics of trade between member states, the provisions of Chapter II shall be supplemented as follows:

(1)   without prejudice to article 34, the Intrastat system shall apply to the goods referred to in articles 18(2)(a) and 19(a);

(2)   the partner countries in trading of goods between member states within the meaning of article 7(1) shall be the member state of dispatch and the member state of arrival;

(3)   within the Intrastat system, the member state of dispatch shall be defined as that in which the goods which are dispatched from there to another member state come under the terms of article 18(2)(a);

(4)   within the Intrastat system, the member state of arrival shall be defined as that in which the goods which enter from another member state come under the terms of article 19(a);

(5)   the party responsible for providing the information referred to in article 8 shall be the natural or legal person who:
- (a)   registered for value added tax in the member state of dispatch:
  - –   has concluded the contract, with the exception of transport contracts, giving rise to the dispatch of goods or, failing this,
  - –   dispatches or provides for the dispatch of the goods or, failing this,
  - –   is in possession of the goods which are the subject of the dispatch;
- (b)   registered for value added tax in the member state of arrival:
  - –   has concluded the contract, with the expection [sic] of transport contracts, giving rise to the delivery of goods or, failing this,
  - –   takes possession or provides for possession to be taken of the goods or, failing this,
  - –   is in possession of the goods which are the subject of the delivery;

(6)   the Commission shall adopt the provisions provided for in article 7(3) in due course;

(7)   the reference period referred to in the first indent of article 13(2) shall be:
- –   for goods to which the Intrastat system applies, the calendar month during which the value added tax becomes due on intra-Community deliveries or acquisitions of goods, the movements of which are to be recorded pursuant to this article; when the period to which the periodic fiscal declaration of a party liable to account for VAT refers does not correspond with a calendar month, quarter, half-year or year, the member states may adapt the periodicity of the obligations relating to the statistical declarations of that party to the periodicity of his obligations relating to fiscal declarations,
- –   for goods to which the Intrastat system does not apply, according to the circumstances:
  - –   the calendar month during which the goods are either placed or maintained under the inward processing customs procedure (suspension system) or the procedure of processing under customs control or placed in free circulation as a result of one of these procedures,

- the calendar month during which the goods, circulating between parts of the statistical territory of the Community, at least one of which is not part of the territory of the Community pursuant to Council Directive 77/388, have been subject to dispatch or arrival procedures.

History – Art. 20(3) and (4) amended by Regulation 3046/92, art. 22(1) (OJ 1992 L307/27), with effect from 30 October 1992. Art. 20(5)(a) and (b) amended by Regulation 3046/92, art. 22(3)(a) (OJ 1992 L307/27), with effect from 30 October 1992. Art. 20(7) replaced by Regulation 3046/92, art. 22(3)(b) (OJ 1992 L307/27), with effect from 30 October 1992.

Cross references – Regulation 3046/92, art. 4 (OJ 1992 L307/27): responsible person under art. 20(5).

ART. 21   [Data medium: designation of goods]

21   On the statistical data medium to be transmitted to the competent departments:

- without prejudice to article 34, goods shall be designated in such a way as to permit easy and precise classification in the finest relevant subdivision of the version of the combined nomenclature in force at the time;
- the eight-digit code number of the corresponding subdivision of the combined nomenclature shall also be given for each type of goods.

Cross reference – Regulation 3046/92, art. 21(3) (OJ 1992 L307/27): derogation from art. 21 for member states wishing more detailed information.

ART. 22   [Data medium: description of states]

22(1)   On the statistical data medium, the member states shall be described by the alphabetical or numerical codes which the Commission shall determine pursuant to article 30.

22(2)   Without prejudice to the provisions adopted by the Commission pursuant to article 30, the parties responsible for providing information shall comply, for the purposes of paragraph 1, with the instructions issued by the competent national departments regarding the compiling of statistics on trade between member states.

ART. 23   [Required data]

23(1)   For each type of goods, the statistical data medium to be transmitted to the competent departments must provide the following data:

(a)   in the member state of arrival, the member state of consignment of the goods, within the meaning of article 24(1);
(b)   in the member state of dispatch, the member state of destination of the goods, within the meaning of article 24(2);
(c)   the quantity of goods, in net mass and supplementary units;
(d)   the value of the goods;
(e)   the nature of the transaction.

23(2)   Member states may prescribe that the following additional data be provided on the statistical data medium:

(a)   in the member states of arrival, the country of origin; however, that information may only be prescribed within the limits of Community law;
(b)   in the member state of dispatch, the region of origin; in the member state of arrival, the region of destination.

23(3)   In the case of providers of statistical information whose annual value of arrivals or dispatches falls below the thresholds fixed by the Commission in accordance with the procedure established under article 30, it shall not be prescribed that data other than those listed in paragraphs 1 and 2 be provided for such arrivals or dispatches on the statistical data medium.

Apart from the data provided for in paragraphs 1 and 2, member states may, solely in respect of providers of statistical information with dispatches or arrivals of an annual value in excess of the above thresholds, prescribe that the following additional data be provided on the statistical data medium:

(a)   *the delivery terms;*
(b)   the presumed mode of transport;
(c)   the statistical procedure.

23(4)   In so far as not laid down in this regulation, the data referred to in paragraphs 1 and 2 and the rules governing their inclusion on the statistical data medium shall be defined by the Commission pursuant to article 30.

23(5) The Commission shall ensure publication of a list of the data required of providers of statistical information by the member states, as well as the thresholds referred to in paragraph 3, in the Official Journal of the European Communities.

History – Art. 23(1)(f) and (g) were deleted by Regulation 1182/99, art. 1(2)(a), with effect from 1 January 2001. Former art. 23(1)(f) and (g) read as follows:
"(f)   the delivery terms;
(g)   the presumed mode of transport."
Art. 23(2) was replaced by Regulation 1182/99, art. 2(b), with effect from 1 January 2001. Former art. 23(2) read as follows:
23(2)   Member states may not prescribe that data other than those listed in paragraph 1 be provided on the statistical data medium, except for the following:
(a)   in the member state of arrival, the country of origin however, this item may be required only as allowed by Community law;
(b)   in the member state of dispatch, the region of origin in the member state of arrival, the region of destination;
(c)   in the member state of dispatch, the port or airport of loading in the member state of arrival, the port or airport of unloading;
(d)   in the member state of dispatch and in the member state of arrival, the presumed port or airport of transhipment situated in another member state provided the latter prepares transit statistics;
(e)   where appropriate, statistical procedure."
Old art. 23(3) became art. 23(4) and new art. 23(3) was inserted by Regulation 1182/99, art. 1(2)(c), with effect from 1 January 2001.
Art. 23(5) was inserted by Regulation 1182/99, art. 1(2)(d), with effect from 1 January 2001.

Cross references – Regulation 3046/92, art. 12 (OJ 1992 L307/27): valuation of goods for art. 23(1)(d).
Regulation 3046/92, art. 17(3): obligations for member states exercising the option provided in art. 23(2)(b).
Regulation 3046/92, art. 18(3): obligations for member states exercising the options provided in art. 23(2)(c) and (d).
Regulation 3046/92, art. 19(2): obligations for member states exercising the options provided in art. 23(2)(e).

ART. 24   ["Member state of consignment"]

24(1) When, before reaching the member state of arrival, goods have entered one or more countries in transit and have been subject in those countries to halts or legal operations not inherent in their transport, the member state of consignment shall be taken to be the last member state where such halts or legal operations occurred. In other cases, the member state of consignment shall be the same as the member state of dispatch.

24(2) **"Member state of destination"** means the last country to which it is known, at the time of dispatch, that the goods are to be dispatched.

24(3) Notwithstanding article 23(1)(a), the party responsible for providing information in the member state of arrival may, in the following order:

–   if he does not know the member state of consignment, state the member state of dispatch;
–   if he does not know the member state of dispatch, state the member state of purchase, within the meaning of paragraph 4.

24(4) **"The member state of purchase"** means the member state of residence of the contracting partner of the natural or legal person who has concluded the contract, with the exception of transport contracts, giving rise to the delivery of goods in the member state of arrival.

ART. 25   [Trade statistics]

25(1) The Community and the member states shall compile statistics on trade between member states from the data referred to in article 23(1).

25(2) Member states which do not compile statistics on trade between member states from the data referred to in article 23(2) shall refrain from ordering the collection of such data.

25(3) The Community and the member states shall compile statistics on trade between member states, having regard to such provisions as the Commission may adopt pursuant to article 30 on general and specific exemptions and the statistical thresholds.

25(4) Any provision which has the effect of excluding goods referred to in articles 18 and 19 from the compilation of the statistics of trade between member states shall suspend the obligation to supply statistical information on the goods thus excluded.

Cross reference – Regulation 3046/92, art. 20 and Annex III (OJ 1992 L307/27): goods excluded from compilation and collection of data.

ART. 26   [Statistics to Commission]

26(1) Member states shall transmit to the Commission their monthly statistics on trade between member states. These statistics shall cover the data referred to in article 23(1).

26(2) Where necessary, the procedure for such transmission shall be laid down by the Commission pursuant to article 30.

26(3) Data declared confidential by the member states under the conditions referred to in article 32 shall be transmitted by them in accordance with Council Regulation 1588/90 of 11 June 1990 on the transmission of data subject to statistical confidentiality to the Statistical Office of the European Communities.

ART. 27 [Simplification]

27 Provisions regarding the simplification of statistical information shall be adopted by the Council on a proposal from the Commission.

ART. 28 [Thresholds]

28(1) For the purposes of this Chapter, statistical thresholds shall be defined as limits expressed in terms of value, at which level the obligations incumbent on parties responsible for providing information shall be suspended or reduced.

These thresholds shall apply without prejudice to the provisions of article 15.

28(2) The statistical thresholds shall be known as exclusion, assimilation or simplification thresholds.

28(3) Exclusion thresholds shall apply to the parties required to provide information referred to in the second subparagraph of article 5.

They shall apply in all member states and shall be determined, by each of the said member states, in accordance with national tax provisions adopted pursuant to Directive 77/388.

28(4) Assimilation thresholds shall exempt parties required to provide information from having to supply the declarations referred to in article 13(1) the periodic tax declaration which they make as parties liable to account for VAT, including parties within the meaning of article 11(7), shall be considered to be the statistical declaration.

Assimilation thresholds shall apply in all member states and shall be set, by each of the said member states, at higher levels than the exclusion thresholds.

28(5) Simplification thresholds shall exempt parties required to provide information from the full provisions of article 23; the declarations referred to in article 13(1) need only state for each type of goods, in addition to the code number referred to in the second indent of article 21, the member state of consignment or destination and the value of the goods.

Without prejudice to the first subparagraph of paragraph 9, they shall be applied at the levels determined by paragraph 8 in member states whose assimilation thresholds are lower than these levels.

In member states whose assimilation thresholds are set at levels equal to or, pursuant to the first subparagraph of paragraph 9, higher than those determined by paragraph 8, simplification thresholds shall be optional.

28(6) Assimilation and simplification thresholds shall be expressed in annual values of intra-Community trade operations.

They shall be determined by dispatch or arrival flows.

They shall apply separately to intra-Community operators at the dispatch stage and to intra-Community operators at the arrival stage. Without prejudice to paragraph 10, those member states which elect to use the option set out in the first subparagraph of paragraph 9 may, however, determine the obligations of those responsible for providing the information at both the dispatch and the arrival stages in accordance with the flow for which the annual value of their intra-Community operations is highest.

The assimilation and simplification thresholds may vary from one member state to another, by product group and by period.

28(7) With a view to the application of the assimilation and simplification thresholds by the member states, the Commission shall determine, pursuant to article 30, the quality requirements which must be met by the statistics compiled by the member states under article 25(1).

28(8) The simplification thresholds shall be set at ECU 100,000 for dispatch and ECU 100,000 for arrival.

Pursuant to article 30, the Commission may raise the simplification threshold levels, provided that the quality requirements referred to in paragraph 7 above are met.

28(9) Member states may, provided that the requirements set out in paragraph 7 are met, set their assimilation and simplification thresholds at levels higher than those in paragraph 8. They shall inform the Commission thereof.

Member states may, in order to comply with the requirements set out in paragraph 7, derogate to the extent necessary from the requirements of the second subparagraph of paragraph 5. They shall inform the Commission thereof.

The Commission may ask the member states to justify the measures which they take by providing it with all appropriate information.

28(10) If member states' application of the assimilation and simplification thresholds affects the quality of intra-Community trade statistics, bearing in mind the data supplied by the member states, or increases the burden on parties required to provide information, such that the objectives of this regulation are compromised, the Commission shall adopt, pursuant to article 30, provisions which restore the conditions needed to ensure the required quality or to ease the burden.

Cross reference – Regulation 2256/92 on statistical thresholds for the statistics on trade between member states (OJ 1992 L219/40).

Chapter 4 – Committee on statistics relating to the trading of goods between member states

ART. 29   [Committee's work]

29(1) A Committee on the statistics relating to the trading of goods between member states, hereinafter called **"the Committee"**, is hereby established. It shall be composed of representatives of the member states and chaired by a Commission representative.

29(2) The Committee shall draw up its rules of procedure.

29(3) The Committee may examine any question relating to the implementation of this regulation raised by its chairman, either on his own initiative or at the request of the representative of a member state.

ART. 30   [Implementation]

30(1) The provisions required for the implementation of this regulation shall be adopted according to the procedure laid down in paragraphs 2 and 3.

30(2) The representative of the Commission shall submit to the committee a draft of the measures to be taken. The Committee shall deliver its opinion on the draft within a time limit which the chairman may lay down according to the urgency of the matter. The opinion shall be delivered by the majority laid down in article 148(2) of the treaty in the case of decisions which the Council is required to adopt on a proposal from the Commission. The votes of the representatives of the member states within the committee shall be weighted in the manner set out in that article. The chairman shall not vote.

30(3) The Commission shall adopt measures which shall apply immediately. However, if these measures are not in accordance with the opinion of the committee, they shall be communicated by the Commission to the Council forthwith.

In that event, the Commission may defer application of the measures which it has decided for a period of not more than one month from the date of such communication.

The Council, acting by a qualified majority, may take a different decision within the time limit referred to in the second subparagraph.

Cross reference – Regulation 3046/92 (OJ 1992 L307/27): provisions implementing Regulation 3330/91.

Chapter 5 – Final provisions

ART. 31   [Non-trade statistics]

31 On a proposal from the Commission, the Council shall adopt the provisions necessary to enable the Community or its member states to compile the statistics other than statistics of trade between member states referred to in article 4.

ART. 32   [Member state declaration]

32(1) On a proposal from the Commission, the Council shall decide on the conditions under which the member states may declare data compiled in accordance with this regulation, or the regulations provided for herein, to be confidential.

32(2) Until the conditions referred to in paragraph 1 have been laid down, member states' provisions on this matter shall apply.

ART. 33   [Adaptations]

33 The Commission may, by the procedure laid down in article 30, adapt as necessary the provisions of this regulation:

–   to the consequences of amendments to Directive 77/388;
–   to specific movements of goods within the meaning of the statistical regulations of the Community.

Cross reference – Regulation 3046/92, art. 21(2) (OJ 1992 L307/27): procedures to be applied in respect of specific movements of goods in absence of provisions under art. 33.

ART. 34   [Simplification]

34(1) In respect both of goods subject to the Intrastat system and of other goods, the Commission may, for the purpose of facilitating the task of the parties responsible for providing information, establish in accordance with article 30 simplified data collection procedures and in particular create the conditions for increased use of automatic data processing and electronic data transmission.

34(2) In order to take account of their individual administrative arrangements, member states may establish simplified procedures other than those referred to in paragraph 1, provided that those responsible for providing information may choose the procedures they will use.

Member states exercising this option shall inform the Commission accordingly.

ART. 35   [Date in force]

35 This regulation shall enter into force on the third day following that of its publication in the *Official Journal of the European Communities*.

Except in so far as they require the Council or the Commission to adopt provisions implementing this regulation before that date, articles 1 to 9, 11, 13(1) and 14 to 27 shall apply as from the date of implementation of Council Regulation 2726/90 of 17 September 1990 on Community transit.

As from the date referred to in the second subparagraph, Regulation 2954/85 shall be repealed and Regulation 1736/75 shall cease to apply to the statistics relating to the trading of goods between member states to which it was applicable.

Notes – This regulation was published in the Official Journal on 16 November 1991.
Regulation 2726/90 on Community transit (OJ 1990 L262/1) applied as from 1 January 1993.

This regulation shall be binding in its entirety and directly applicable in all member states.

REGULATION 218/92

On administrative co-operation in the field of indirect taxation (VAT)

(27 January 1992, OJ 1992 L24/1)

The Council of the European Communities,

Having regard to the Treaty establishing the European Economic Community, and in particular article 99 thereof,

Having regard to the proposal from the Commission,

Having regard to the opinion of the European Parliament,

Having regard to the opinion of the Economic and Social Committee,

[1] Whereas the establishment of the internal market in accordance with article 8a of the treaty requires the creation of an area without internal frontiers in which the free movement of goods, persons, services and capital is ensured; whereas the internal market requires changes in the legislation on value added tax as provided in article 99 of the treaty;

[2] Whereas in order to avoid tax revenue losses for member states the tax harmonisation measures taken to complete the internal market and for the transitional period must include the establishment of a common system for the exchange of information on intra-Community transactions between the competent authorities of the member states;

[3] Whereas in order to permit the abolition of fiscal controls at internal frontiers in accordance with the aims set out in article 8a of the treaty the transitional value added tax system introduced by Directive 91/680, amending Directive 77/388, must be effectively established without the risk of fraud which might cause distortions of competition;

[4] Whereas this regulation provides for a common system for the exchange of information on intra-Community transactions, supplementing Directive 77/799, as last amended by Directive 79/1070, and intended to serve tax purposes;

[5] Whereas the member states should provide the Commission with any value added tax information which may be of interest at Community level;

[6] Whereas the establishment of a common system of administrative co-operation may affect individuals' legal positions, in particular because of the exchange of information concerning their tax positions;

[7] Whereas care must be taken to ensure that the provisions concerning the control of indirect taxes are in balance with administrations' needs for effective control and the administrative burdens imposed on taxable persons;

[8] Whereas the operation of such a system requires the establishment of a standing committee on administrative co-operation;

[9] Whereas the member states and the Commission must establish an effective system for the electronic storage and transmission of certain data for value added tax control purposes;

[10] Whereas care must be taken to ensure that information provided in the course of such collaboration is not disclosed to unauthorised persons, so that the basic rights of citizens and undertakings are safeguarded; whereas it is therefore necessary that an authority receiving such information should not, without the authorisation of the authority supplying it, use it for purposes other than taxation or to facilitate legal proceedings for failure to comply with the tax laws of the member states concerned; whereas the receiving authority must also accord such information the same degree of confidentiality as it enjoyed in the member state which provided it, if the latter so requires;

[11] Whereas the member states and the Commission must collaborate on the continuous analysis of co-operation procedures and the pooling of the experience gained in the fields in question, with the aims of improving those procedures and drawing up appropriate Community rules,

has adopted this regulation:

ART. 1   [Co-operation]

1 This regulation lays down the ways in which the administrative authorities in the member states responsible for the application of laws on value added tax shall co-operate with each other and with the Commission to ensure compliance with those laws.

To that end it lays down procedures for the exchange of value added tax information on intra-Community transactions by electronic means and any subsequent exchange of information between member states' competent authorities.

ART. 2   [Definitions]

2(1) For the purposes of this regulation:

–   **"competent authority"** shall mean the authority appointed to act as correspondent as defined in paragraph 2,

–   **"applicant authority"** shall mean the competent authority of a member state which makes a request for assistance,

–   **"requested authority"** shall mean the competent authority of a member state to which a request for assistance is made,

–   **"person"** shall mean:

     –   a natural person,

     –   a legal person or,

-    where the possibility is provided for under the legislation in force, an association of persons recognised as having the capacity to perform legal acts but lacking the legal status of a legal person,
-    **"to grant access"** shall mean authorising access to the relevant electronic data base and providing data by electronic means,
-    **"value added tax identification number"** shall mean the number provided for in article 22(1)(c), (d) and (e) of Directive 77/388,
-    **"intra-Community transactions"** shall mean the intra-Community supply of goods and the intra-Community supply of services as defined in this paragraph,
-    **"intra-Community supply of goods"** shall mean any supply of goods which must be declared in the recapitulative statement provided for in article 22(6)(b) of Directive 77/388,
-    **"intra-Community supply of services"** shall mean any supply of services covered by article 28B(C), (D) or (E) of Directive 77/388,
-    **"intra-Community acquisition of goods"** shall mean acquisition of the right to dispose as owner of movable tangible property as defined in article 28A(3) of Directive 77/388.

2(2)   Each member state shall notify the other member states and the Commission of the competent authorities appointed to act as correspondents for the purpose of applying this regulation. In addition, each member state shall nominate a central office with principal responsibility for liaison with other member states in the field of administrative co-operation.

2(3)   The Commission shall publish a list of competent authorities in the *Official Journal of the European Communities* and, where necessary, update it.

Note – The following list of competent authorities was published in accordance with art. 2(3), (OJ 1994 C302/5):
"In accordance with the provisions of Article 2(2) and (3) of Regulation (EEC) No 218/92, the expression "competent authority" means:
Belgium
L'Administration centrale de la TVA, de l'enregistrement et des domaines, 4ème service, 12ème direction
De Central Administratie van de BTW, registratie en domeinen, 4de dienst, 12de directie
Denmark
Skatteministeriet, Told- og Skattestyrelsen
Germany
Das Bundesministerium der Finanzen or an authorised representative
Greece
Υπουργος Οικονομικων
Γενικε Διευθυνση Φορολογιας και Δημοσιας Περιουσιας
14h Die;aayqynsh FPA kai EF
Grafe;aaiio VIES
Spain
El Ministro de Economía y Hacienda or an authorised representative
France
Le Directeur général des Impôts or an authorised representative
Ireland
The Revenue Commissioners or their authorised representative
Italy
Il ministro per le Finanze or an authorised representative
Luxembourg
L'Administration de l'Enregistrement et des Domaines
the Netherlands
Ministerie van Financiën
Directoraat-Generaal der Belastingen
Portugal
O Ministro das Finan;alcas or an authorised representative
United Kingdom
HM Customs and Excise
VAT Practice Directorate or an authorised representative."

TITLE I – EXCHANGE OF INFORMATION – GENERAL PROVISIONS

ART. 3   [General]

3(1)   The obligation to give assistance provided for in this regulation shall not cover the provision of information or documents obtained by the administrative authorities referred to in article 1 at the request of a judicial authority.

However, in cases of applications for assistance, such information and documents shall be provided whenever the judicial authority, to which reference must be made, gives its consent.

3(2)   This regulation shall not restrict the application of provisions of other agreements or instruments relating to co-operation on tax matters.

3(3)   This regulation shall not affect the application in the member states of the rules on mutual assistance in criminal matters.

TITLE II – EXCHANGE OF INFORMATION RELATING TO VALUE ADDED TAX IN CONNECTION WITH INTRA-COMMUNITY TRANSACTIONS

ART. 4   [Information exchange]

4(1)   The competent authority of each member state shall maintain an electronic data base in which it shall store and process the information that it collects in accordance with article 22(6)(b) of Directive 77/388. To allow the use of this information in the procedures provided for in this regulation the information shall be stored for at least five years after the end of the calendar year in which access to the information was to be granted. Member states shall ensure that their data bases are kept up to date, complete and accurate. Under the procedure laid down in article 10 criteria shall be defined to determine what amendments that are not significant, material or useful need not be made.

4(2)   From the data collected in accordance with paragraph 1, the competent authority of a member state shall obtain directly and without delay from each member state, or may have direct access to, the following information:

–   the value added tax identification numbers issued by the member state receiving the information, and

–   the total value of all intra-Community supplies of goods made to the persons to whom those numbers were issued by all operators identified for the purposes of value added tax in the member state providing the information; the values shall be expressed in the currency of the member state providing the information and shall relate to calendar quarters.

4(3)   From the data collected in accordance with paragraph 1 and solely in order to combat tax fraud the competent authority of a member state shall, wherever it considers it necessary for the control of intra-Community acquisitions of goods, obtain directly and without delay, or have direct access to, the following information:

–   the value added tax identification numbers of all persons who have made the supplies referred to in the second indent of paragraph 2, and

–   the total value of such supplies from each such person to each person to whom one of the value added tax identification numbers referred to in the first indent of paragraph 2 has been issued; the values shall be expressed in the currency of the member state providing the information and shall relate to calendar quarters.

4(4)   Where the competent authority of a member state is obliged to grant access to information under this article it shall, as regards the information referred to in paragraphs 2 and 3, do so within three months of the end of the calendar quarter to which the information relates. By way of derogation from this rule, where information is added to a data base in the circumstances provided for in paragraph 1, access to such additions shall be granted as quickly as possible and in any event no more than three months after the end of the quarter in which the additional information was collected; the conditions under which access to the corrected information may be granted shall be defined by means of the procedure laid down in article 10.

4(5)   Where, for purposes of the application of this article, the competent authorities of the member states keep information in electronic data bases and exchange such information by electronic means they shall take all measures necessary to ensure compliance with article 9.

ART. 5   [Further information requested]

5(1)   Where the information provided under article 4 is insufficient, the competent authority of a member state may at any time and in specific cases request further information. The requested authority shall provide the information as quickly as possible and in any event no more than three months after receipt of the request.

5(2)   In the circumstances described in paragraph 1 the requested authority shall at least provide the applicant authority with invoice numbers, dates and values in relation to individual transactions between persons in the member states concerned.

ART. 6   [Information access]

6(1)   The competent authority of each member state shall maintain an electronic data base which shall contain a register of persons to whom value added tax identification numbers have been issued in that member state.

6(2)   At any time the competent authority of a member state may obtain directly or have communicated to it from the data collected in accordance with article 4(1), confirmation of the validity of the value added tax identification number under which a person effected or received an intra-Community supply of goods or of services. On specific request the requested authority shall also communicate the date of issue and, where appropriate, the date of cessation of the validity of the value added tax identification number.

6(3)   Where it is so requested a competent authority shall also provide without delay the name and address of the person to whom a number has been issued, provided that such information is not stored by the applicant authority with a view to its possible use at some future time.

6(4)   The competent authority of each member state shall ensure that persons involved in the intra-Community supply of goods or of services are allowed to obtain confirmation of the validity of the value added tax identification number of any specified person.

6(5)   Where, for purposes of the application of this article, the competent authorities of the member states keep information in electronic data bases and exchange such information by electronic means they shall take all measures necessary to ensure compliance with article 9.

TITLE III – CONDITIONS GOVERNING THE EXCHANGE OF INFORMATION

ART. 7   [Information exchange regulations]

7(1)   A requested authority in one member state shall provide an applicant authority in another member state with the information referred to in article 5(2) provided that:

– the number and the nature of the requests for information made by the applicant authority within a specific period of time do not impose a disproportionate administrative burden on that requested authority,

– that applicant authority exhausts the usual sources of information which it can use in the circumstances to obtain the information requested, without running the risk of jeopardising the achievement of the desired end,

– that applicant authority requests assistance only if it would be able to provide similar assistance to the applicant authority of another member state.

In accordance with the procedure laid down in article 10 and taking into account experience of the new administrative cooperation system during its first year of operation, the Commission shall submit general criteria for the definition of the scope of these commitments before July 1994.

7(2)   If an applicant authority is unable to comply with the general provisions of paragraph 1 it shall notify the requested authority accordingly without delay, stating its reasons. If a requested authority considers that the general provisions of paragraph 1 are not complied with and that it is therefore not obliged to provide the information, it shall notify the applicant authority accordingly without delay, stating its reasons. The applicant authority and the requested authority shall attempt to reach agreement. If they fail to reach agreement within one month of notification either authority may request that the matter be examined under article 11.

7(3)   This article shall be without prejudice to the application of Directive 77/799 as regards the exchange of information referred to in article 5(1).

ART. 8   [Notification of person concerned]

8   In cases of exchanges of information as defined in article 5, where the national legislation in force in a member state provides for notification of the person concerned of the exchange of information, those provisions may continue to apply except where their application would prejudice the investigation of tax evasion in another member state. In the latter event, at the express request of the applicant authority, the requested authority shall refrain from such notification.

ART. 9   [Confidentiality]

9(1) Any information communicated in whatever form pursuant to this regulation shall be of a confidential nature. It shall be covered by the obligation of professional secrecy and shall enjoy the protection extended to similar information under both the national law of the member state which received it and the corresponding provisions applicable to Community authorities.

In any case, such information:

–   may be made available only to the persons directly concerned with the bases of assessment, collection or administrative control of taxes for the purpose of the assessment of taxes, or to persons employed by Community institutions whose duties require that they have access to it,

–   may in addition be used in connection with judicial or administrative proceedings that may involve sanctions, initiated as a result of infringements of tax law.

9(2) By way of derogation from paragraph 1, the competent authority of the member state providing the information shall permit its use for other purposes in the member state of the applicant authority, if, under the legislation of the member state of the requested authority, the information could be used in the member state of the requested authority for similar purposes.

9(3) Where the applicant authority considers that information which it has received from the requested authority is likely to be useful to the competent authority of a third member state, it may transmit it to the latter with the agreement of the requested authority.

TITLE IV – CONSULTATION AND CO-ORDINATION PROCEDURES

ART. 10   [Standing Committee]

10(1) The Commission shall be assisted by a Standing Committee on Administrative Co-operation in the field of Indirect Taxation, hereinafter referred to as "the Committee". It shall consist of representatives of the member states and have a representative of the Commission as chairman.

10(2) The measures required for the application of articles 4 and 7(1) shall be adopted in accordance with the procedure laid down in paragraphs 3 and 4 of this article.

10(3) The Commission representative shall submit to the Committee a draft of the measures to be adopted. The Committee shall deliver its opinion on that draft within a time-limit which the chairman may lay down according to the urgency of the matter. The Committee's opinion shall be delivered by a majority, the member states' votes being weighted in accordance with article 148(2) of the treaty. The chairman shall not vote.

10(4) The Commission shall adopt the measures contemplated where they are in accordance with the Committee's opinion.

Where those measures are not in accordance with the Committee's opinion or if the Committee does not deliver an opinion, the Commission shall without delay submit to the Council a proposal on the measures to be adopted. The Council shall act by a qualified majority.

If within three months of the proposal's being submitted to it the Council has not acted, the proposed measures shall be adopted by the Commission, unless the Council has decided against those measures by a simple majority.

ART. 11   [Evaluation of operation]

11 The member states and the Commission shall examine and evaluate the operation of the arrangements for administrative cooperation provided for in this regulation and the Commission shall pool the member states' experience, in particular that concerning new means of tax avoidance and evasion, with the aim of improving the operation of those arrangements. To that end the member states shall also communicate to the Commission any value added tax information on intra-Community transactions that may be of interest at Community level.

ART. 12   [Communication between member states]

12(1) On matters of bilateral interest, the competent authorities of the member states may communicate directly with each other. The competent authorities of the member states may by mutual agreement permit authorities designated by them to communicate directly with each other in specified cases or categories of cases.

12(2) For the purpose of applying this regulation, member states shall take all necessary steps to:

(a) ensure efficient internal co-ordination between the competent authorities referred to in article 1;

(b) establish direct co-operation between the authorities specially empowered for the purposes of such co-ordination;

(c) make suitable arrangements to ensure the smooth operation of the arrangements for the exchange of information provided for in this regulation.

12(3) The Commission shall communicate to the competent authority of each member state, as quickly as possible, any information which it receives and which it is able to supply.

TITLE V – FINAL PROVISIONS

ART. 13   [Expenses of applying this regulation]

13 Member states shall waive all claims for the reimbursement of expenses incurred in applying this regulation except, as appropriate, in respect of fees paid to experts.

ART. 14   [Reports to Parliament and the Commission]

14(1) Every two years after the date of entry into force of this regulation, the Commission shall report to the European Parliament and the Council on the conditions of application of this regulation on the basis, in particular, of the continuous monitoring procedures provided for in article 11.

14(2) Member states shall communicate to the Commission the texts of any provisions of national law which they adopt in the field governed by this regulation.

ART. 15   [Entry into force]

15 This regulation shall enter into force on the third day following its publication in the *Official Journal of the European Communities*.

No exchange of information under this regulation shall take place before 1 January 1993.

This regulation shall be binding in its entirety and directly applicable in all member states.

Note – The regulation was published in the Official Journal on 1 February 1992.

REGULATION 2256/92

On statistical thresholds for the statistics on trade between member states

(31 July 1992, OJ 1992 L219/40)

The Commission of the European Communities,

Having regard to the Treaty establishing the European Economic Community,

Having regard to Council Regulation 3330/91 of 7 November 1991 on the statistics relating to the trading of goods between member states, and in particular article 30 thereof,

[1] Whereas the burden on intra-Community operators must be lightened as much as possible, either by [exempting] them from statistical obligations or by simplifying procedures;

[2] Whereas this lightening of the burden must be limited only by the demands of statistics of a satisfactory quality, which must consequently be defined by common accord;

[3] Whereas, once this quality has been defined, all the member states must have their necessary instruments to ensure it, while taking account of their own economic and commercial structure; whereas it is for the member states themselves to strike the most appropriate balance between lightening of the statistical burden and quality on the basis of the information available to them;

[4] Whereas the information to be analysed by the member states in order to fix their thresholds differs, particularly as regards coverage, depending on whether they are to be introduced in 1993 or to be adapted as from 1994; whereas a distinction should therefore be drawn between the rules to

be followed on one single occasion, as in the first case, and those to be followed each year, as in the second case;

[5] Whereas the obligations of the persons responsible for providing information should be defined in such a way as to take maximum account of their interests, particularly if their intra-Community transactions are expanding;

[6] Whereas the measures provided for in this regulation are in accordance with the opinion of the Committee on Statistics relating to the trading of goods between member states,

has adopted this regulation:

ART. 1   [Assimilation/simplification threshold]

1 The member states shall set annually, in national currency, the assimilation and simplification thresholds referred to in article 28 of Regulation 3330/91, hereinafter **"the Basic regulation"**. They shall ensure when setting these thresholds that, first, they meet the quality requirements laid down in this regulation and, secondly, they exploit to the full the ensuing opportunities to relieve the burden on intra-Community operators.

ART. 2   [Meaning]

2 For the purposes of this regulation:

(a)   **"error"** means the discrepancy between the results obtained with and without application of the thresholds referred to in article 1; when a correction procedure is applied to the results obtained following application of the thresholds, the error is calculated in relation to the corrected results;

(b)   **"total value"** means:
   –   for the introduction of the thresholds in 1993, the value either of the outgoing goods or of the incoming goods, accounted for by intra-Community operators over a period of twelve months,
   –   for the adjustment of the thresholds from 1994, the value of either of the outgoing goods or of the incoming goods accounted for by intra-Community operators over a twelve-month period, other than those who are exempt under article 5 of the basic regulation;

(c)   **"coverage"** means in relation to a given total value, the proportionate value of the outgoing goods or of the incoming goods, accounted for by the intra-Community operators who lie above the assimilation threshold.

ART. 3   [Quality requirements]

3(1) For the introduction of the assimilation thresholds in 1993, the member states shall meet the following quality requirements:

(a)   Results by goods category
   Each member state shall ensure that the error in annual values does not exceed 5 per cent for 90 per cent of the eight-digit sub-headings of the combined nomenclature which represent 0.005 per cent or more of the total value of its outgoing or incoming goods.
   However, each member state may raise this quality requirement up to the point that the error in annual values does not exceed 5 per cent for 90 per cent of the eight-digit sub-headings of the combined nomenclature which represent 0.001 per cent or more of the total value of its outgoing or incoming goods.

(b)   Results by partner country
   Each member state shall ensure that the error in the annual values of its results by partner country, excluding countries which represent less than 3 per cent of the total value of its outgoing or incoming goods, does not exceed 1 per cent.

(c)   Time series
   Each member state shall ensure that:
      –   for 90 per cent of the eight-digit sub-headings of the combined nomenclature which represent the percentage of the total value of its outgoing or incoming goods laid down in point (a), and
      –   for 90 per cent of its results by partner country,
   The fluctuation over time of the error in annual values will not exceed the limits (L) laid down in the annex.

If in any member state applying the requirement leads to an increase in the number of parties responsible for providing information who are required to submit the periodic declaration laid down in article 13 of the basic regulation that is excessive in proportion to the number involved under the more stringent of the other two requirements, the member state concerned may take steps to reduce the imbalance accordingly. It shall inform the Commission of the action taken.

3(2) When a member state's share of the total value of outgoing or incoming goods in the Community is less than 3 per cent, that member state may depart from the quality requirements laid down in the first subparagraph of paragraph 1(a) and the first indent of the first subparagraph of paragraph 1(c). In such cases, the 90 per cent and 0.005 per cent shares shall be replaced by 70 per cent and 0.01 per cent respectively.

3(3) To meet the quality requirements set out in paragraphs 1 and 2, the member states shall base the calculation of their thresholds on the results of trade with the other member states for twelve-month periods prior to the introduction of the thresholds.

For member states unable to make this calculation because figures are incomplete, the assimilation thresholds shall be fixed at a level not lower than the lowest, nor higher than the highest, thresholds set by the other member states. However, this provision shall not be binding for member states which are exempt under paragraph 2.

3(4) If, for certain groups of goods, the application of the thresholds calculated in accordance with the provisions of this article yields results which, mutatis mutandis, fail to meet the quality requirements set out in paragraphs 1 and 2 above, and if the thresholds cannot be lowered without reducing the relief which article 1 guarantees to intra-Community operators, appropriate measures may be taken, at the initiative of the Commission or the request of a member state, in accordance with the procedure laid down in article 30 of the basic regulation.

ART. 4   [Simplification threshold]

4 For the introduction of the simplification thresholds in 1993, the member states may set these:

–   at levels above ECU 100,000 pursuant to the first subparagraph of article 28(9) of the basic regulation, provided that they ensure that at least 95 per cent of the total value of their outgoing or incoming goods is covered by periodic declarations containing all the information required under article 23 of the basic regulation,

–   where they are exempt under article 3(2), at levels below ECU 100,000 pursuant to the second subparagraph of article 28(9) of the basic regulation, to the extent necessary to ensure that at least 95 per cent of the total value of their outgoing or incoming goods is covered by periodic declarations containing all the information required under article 23 of the basic regulation.

ART. 5   [Publication]

5 The information relating to the information of the assimilation and simplification thresholds in 1993 shall be published not later than 31 August 1992.

ART. 6   [Assimilation threshold adjustment]

6(1) For the adjustment of the assimilation thresholds from 1994, the quality requirements specified in article 3 shall be regarded as met if the coverage is maintained at the level which obtained when the thresholds were introduced.

6(2) The condition laid down in paragraph 1 shall be met if member states:

(a)   calculate their thresholds for the year following the current year on the basis of the latest available results for their trade with the other member states over a twelve-month period, and

(b)   set their thresholds at a level which allows the same coverage for the period thus defined as for the period used as a basis for calculating their thresholds for the current year.

Member states shall notify the Commission if they use a different method to meet this condition.

6(3) Member states may lower their coverage provided that the quality requirements laid down in article 3 continue to be met.

6(4) Member states shall calculate adjustments to their assimilation thresholds each year. The thresholds shall be adjusted if the adjustment involves a change of at least 10 per cent in the threshold values for the current year.

ART. 7   [Simplification threshold adjustment]

7(1) For the adjustment of the simplification thresholds from 1994, the member states which set these thresholds

- at levels higher than the values laid down by article 28(8) of the basic regulation, shall ensure that the condition laid down in the first indent of article 4 of this regulation is met,
- at levels below these values, since they are exempt pursuant to article 3(2) above, shall ensure that they comply with the limit laid down in the second indent of article 4 of this regulation.

7(2) To ensure that the condition referred to in the first indent of article 4 is met or that the limit referred to in the second indent of article 4 is complied with, it shall be sufficient for member states to calculate the adjustment of the simplification thresholds using the method laid down in article 6(2) for adjusting the assimilation thresholds. Member states shall notify the Commission if they use a different method.

ART. 8   [Publication]

8 The information relating to the adjustment of assimilation and simplification thresholds from 1994 shall be published not later than 31 October of the preceding year.

ART. 9   [Exceeding threshold]

9(1) Parties responsible for providing information shall be freed from their obligations to the extent allowed by application of the assimilation and simplification thresholds set for a given year, provided they have not exceeded these thresholds during the previous year.

9(2) For each statistical threshold, the provisions adopted shall apply for the whole year.

However, if the value of the intra-Community transactions carried out by a party responsible for providing information at some time during the year exceeds the threshold applicable to him, he shall provide information on his intra-Community transactions from the month in which this threshold was exceeded in accordance with the provisions applying to the threshold which becomes applicable. If this provision involves the transmission of the periodic declarations referred to in article 13 of the basic regulation, the member states shall lay down the time limit for transmitting these declarations in accordance with their particular administrative arrangements.

ART. 10   [Information for Commission]

10 The member states shall communicate to the Commission the information regarding the thresholds they have calculated at least two weeks before publication. At the Commission's request, they shall also communicate the information required for assessing these thresholds, both for the period on which their calculation is based and for a given calendar year.

ART. 11   [Date in force]

11 This regulation shall enter into force on the seventh day following its publication in the *Official Journal of the European Communities*.

This regulation shall be binding in its entirety and directly applicable in all member states.

Note – The regulation was published in the Official Journal on 4 August 1992.

ANNEX

The limits (L) of the error fluctuation referred to in article 3(1)(c) are laid down as follows:

$\mid e_{i,t+1} - e_{i,t} \mid \leq L_{i,t+1,t}$ $e_{i,t}$ = error in % of CN subheading i or partner country i in year t

with

$e_{i,t} = [(V^d_{i,t} - V^c_{i,t}) / V^c_{i,t}] \cdot 100$ $V^c_{i,t}$ = annual value of CN subheading i or partner country i in year t without use of a threshold

$L_{i,t+1,t} = l_{i,t+1,t}$ if $l_{i,t+1,t} < 5$

$L_{i,t+1,t} = 5$ if $l_{i,t+1,t} \geq 5$ $V^d_{i,t}$ = annual value of CN subheading i or partner country i in year t using of a threshold

$l_{i,t+1,t} = 5 \cdot \sqrt{q_{i,t+1,t}} + 0,5$

$q_{i,t+1,t} = \mid (V^c_{i,t+1} / V^c_{i,t}) - 1 \mid$

$t \leq 1990$

REGULATION 2913/92

Establishing the Community Customs Code

(12 October 1992, OJ 1992 L302/1)

The Council of the European Communities,

Having regard to the Treaty establishing the European Economic Community, and in particular articles 28, 100A and 113 thereof,

Having regard to the proposal from the Commission,

In co-operation with the European Parliament,

Having regard to the opinion of the Economic and Social Committee,

[1] Whereas the Community is based upon a customs union; whereas it is advisable, in the interests both of Community traders and the customs authorities, to assemble in a code the provisions of customs legislation that are at present contained in a large number of Community regulations and directives; whereas this task is of fundamental importance from the standpoint of the internal market;

[2] Whereas such a Community Customs Code (hereinafter called "the code") must incorporate current customs legislation; whereas it is, nevertheless, advisable to amend that legislation in order to make it more consistent, to simplify it and to remedy certain omissions that still exist with a view to adopting complete Community legislation in this area;

[3] Whereas, based on the concept of an internal market, the code must contain the general rules and procedures which ensure the implementation of the tariff and other measures introduced at Community level in connection with trade in goods between the Community and third countries; whereas it must cover, among other things, the implementation of common agricultural and commercial policy measures taking into account the requirements of these common policies;

[4] Whereas it would appear advisable to specify that this code is applicable without prejudice to specific provisions laid down in other fields; whereas such specific rules may exist or be introduced in the context, inter alia, of legislation relating to agriculture, statistics, commercial policy or own resources;

[5] Whereas, in order to secure a balance between the needs of the customs authorities in regard to ensuring the correct application of customs legislation, on the one hand, and the right of traders to be treated fairly, on the other, the said authorities must be granted, inter alia, extensive powers of control and the said traders a right of appeal; whereas the implementation of a customs appeals system will require the United Kingdom to introduce new administrative procedures which cannot be effected before 1 January 1995;

[6] Whereas in view of the paramount importance of external trade for the Community, customs formalities and controls should be abolished or at least kept to a minimum;

[7] Whereas it is important to guarantee the uniform application of this code and to provide, to that end, for a Community procedure which enables the procedures for its implementation to be

adopted within a suitable time; whereas a Customs Code Committee should be set up in order to ensure close and effective co-operation between the member states and the Commission in this field;

[8] Whereas in adopting the measures required to implement this code, the utmost care must be taken to prevent any fraud or irregularity liable to affect adversely the general budget of the European Communities,

has adopted this regulation:

TITLE I – GENERAL PROVISIONS
Chapter 1 – Scope and basic definitions
ART. 1   [Fields of application]

1   Customs rules shall consist of this code and the provisions adopted at Community level or nationally to implement them. The code shall apply, without prejudice to special rules laid down in other fields

- to trade between the Community and third countries,
- to goods covered by the Treaty establishing the European Coal and Steel Community, the Treaty establishing the European Economic Community or the Treaty establishing the European Atomic Energy Community.

ART. 2   [Geographic scope]

2(1)   Save as otherwise provided, either under international conventions or customary practices of a limited geographic and economic scope or under autonomous Community measures, Community customs rules shall apply uniformly throughout the customs territory of the Community.

2(2)   Certain provisions of customs rules may also apply outside the customs territory of the Community within the framework of either rules governing specific fields or international conventions.

ART. 3   [Community customs territory]

3(1)   The customs territory of the Community shall comprise:

- the territory of the Kingdom of Belgium,
- the territory of the Kingdom of Denmark, except the Faroe Islands and Greenland,
- the territory of the Federal Republic of Germany, except the Island of Heligoland and the territory of Büsingen (treaty of 23 November 1964 between the Federal Republic of Germany and the Swiss Confederation),
- the territory of the Kingdom of Spain, except Ceuta and Melilla,
- the territory of the French Republic, except the overseas territories and Saint-Pierre and Miquelon and Mayotte,
- the territory of the Hellenic Republic,
- the territory of Ireland,
- the territory of the Italian Republic, except the municipalities of Livigno and Campione d'Italia and the national waters of Lake Lugano which are between the bank and the political frontier of the area between Ponte Tresa and Porto Ceresio,
- the territory of the Grand Duchy of Luxembourg,
- the territory of the Kingdom of the Netherlands in Europe,
- the territory of the Republic of Austria,
- the territory of the Portuguese Republic,
- the territory of the Republic of Finland,
- the territory of the Kingdom of Sweden,
- the territory of the United Kingdom of Great Britain and Northern Ireland and of the Channel Islands and the Isle of Man.

3(2)   Although situated outside the territory of the French Republic, the territory of the Principality of Monaco as defined in the Customs Convention signed in Paris on 18 May 1963 (*Official Journal of the French Republic* of 27 September 1963, p. 8679) shall, by virtue of that Convention, also be considered to be part of the customs territory of the Community.

3(3) The customs territory of the Community shall include the territorial waters, the inland maritime waters and the airspace of the member states, and the territories referred to in paragraph 2, except for the territorial waters, the inland maritime waters and the airspace of those territories which are not part of the customs territory of the Community pursuant to paragraph 1.

History – In art. 3(1), the fifth and thirteenth indents replaced by Regulation 82/97, art. 1(1) (OJ 1997 L17/1), with effect from 1 January 1997.
Art. 3(1) previously substituted by the Act of Accession of Austria, Sweden and Finland, art. 29 and Annex I, Ch. XIII (OJ 1994 C241/1), as substituted by Decision 95/1, Annex, Ch. XIII (OJ 1995 L1/1), with effect from 1 January 1995.
Art. 3(2) replaced by Regulation 82/97, art. 1(1) (OJ 1997 L17/1), with effect from 1 January 1997.

ART. 4 [Definitions]

4 For the purposes of this code, the following definitions shall apply:

(1) **"Person"** means:
  –   a natural person,
  –   a legal person,
  –   where the possibility is provided for under the rules in force, an association of persons recognised as having the capacity to perform legal acts but lacking the legal status of a legal person.

(2) **"Persons established in the Community"** means:
  –   in the case of a natural person, any person who is normally resident there,
  –   in the case of a legal person or an association of persons, any person that has in the Community its registered office, central headquarters or a permanent business establishment.

(3) **"Customs authorities"** means the authorities responsible inter alia for applying customs rules.

(4) **"Customs office"** means any office at which all or some of the formalities laid down by customs rules may be completed.

(5) **"Decision"** means any official act by the customs authorities pertaining to customs rules giving a ruling on a particular case, such act having legal effects on one or more specific or identifiable persons; this term covers, inter alia, binding information within the meaning of article 12.

(6) **"Customs status"** means the status of goods as Community or non-Community goods.

(7) **"Community goods"** means goods:
  –   wholly obtained or produced in the customs territory of the Community under the conditions referred to in article 23 and not incorporating goods imported from countries or territories not forming part of the customs territory of the Community. Goods obtained from goods placed under a suspensive arrangement shall not be deemed to have Community status in cases of special economic importance determined in accordance with the committee procedure,
  –   imported from countries or territories not forming part of the customs territory of the Community which have been released for free circulation,
  –   obtained or produced in the customs territory of the Community, either from goods referred to in the second indent alone or from goods referred to in first and second indents.

(8) **"Non-Community goods"** means goods other than those referred to in subparagraph 7. Without prejudice to articles 163 and 164, Community goods shall lose their status as such when they are actually removed from the customs territory of the Community.

(9) **"Customs debt"** means the obligation on a person to pay the amount of the import duties (customs debt on importation) or export duties (customs debt on exportation) which apply to specific goods under the Community provisions in force.

(10) **"Import duties"** means:
  –   customs duties and charges having an effect equivalent to customs duties payable on the importation of goods,
  –   import charges introduced under the common agricultural policy or under the specific arrangements applicable to certain goods resulting from the processing of agricultural products.

(11) **"Export duties"** means:
  –   customs duties and charges having an effect equivalent to customs duties payable on the exportation of goods,

      —   export charges introduced under the common agricultural policy or under the specific arrangements applicable to certain goods resulting from the processing of agricultural products.

(12)   **"Debtor"** means any person liable for payment of a customs debt.

(13)   **"Supervision by the customs authorities"** means action taken in general by those authorities with a view to ensuring that customs rules and, where appropriate, other provisions applicable to goods subject to customs supervision are observed.

(14)   **"Control by the customs authorities"** means the performance of specific acts such as examining goods, verifying the existence and authenticity of documents, examining the accounts of undertakings and other records, inspecting means of transport, inspecting luggage and other goods carried by or on persons and carrying out official inquiries and other similar acts with a view to ensuring that customs rules and, where appropriate, other provisions applicable to goods subject to customs supervision are observed.

(15)   **"Customs-approved treatment or use of goods"** means:
     (a)   the placing of goods under a customs procedure;
     (b)   their entry into a free zone or free warehouse;
     (c)   their re-exportation from the customs territory of the Community;
     (d)   their destruction;
     (e)   their abandonment to the Exchequer.

(16)   **"Customs procedure"** means:
     (a)   release for free circulation;
     (b)   transit;
     (c)   customs warehousing;
     (d)   inward processing;
     (e)   processing under customs control;
     (f)   temporary admission;
     (g)   outward processing;
     (h)   exportation.

(17)   **"Customs declaration"** means the act whereby a person indicates in the prescribed form and manner a wish to place goods under a given customs procedure.

(18)   **"Declarant"** means the person making the customs declaration in his own name or the person in whose name a customs declaration is made.

(19)   **"Presentation of goods to customs"** means the notification to the customs authorities, in the manner laid down, of the arrival of goods at the customs office or at any other place designated or approved by the customs authorities.

(20)   **"Release of goods"** means the act whereby the customs authorities make goods available for the purposes stipulated by the customs procedure under which they are placed.

(21)   **"Holder of the procedure"** means the person on whose behalf the customs declaration was made or the person to whom the rights and obligations of the abovementioned person in respect of a customs procedure have been transferred.

(22)   **"Holder of the authorisation"** means the person to whom an authorisation has been granted.

(23)   **"Provisions in force"** means Community or national provisions.

(24)   **"Committee procedure"** means the procedure provided for or referred to in article 249.

History – Art. 4(5), (7), (10) and (11) amended by Regulation 82/97, art. 1(2) (OJ 1997 L17/1), with effect from 1 January 1997.

Cross references – VATA 1994, s. 18B(6): "eligible goods" and fiscal warehouses.

Chapter 2 – Sundry general provisions relating in particular to the rights and obligations of persons with regard to customs rules

SECTION 1 – RIGHT OF REPRESENTATION

ART. 5   [Appointing a representative]

5(1)   Under the conditions set out in article 64(2) and subject to the provisions adopted within the framework of article 243(2)(b), any person may appoint a representative in his dealings with the customs authorities to perform the acts and formalities laid down by customs rules.

5(2)   Such representations may be:

—   direct, in which case the representative shall act in the name of and on behalf of another person, or

–   indirect, in which case the representative shall act in his own name but on behalf of another person.A member state may restrict the right to make customs declarations:

–   by direct representation, or

–   by indirect representation,so that the representative must be a customs agent carrying on his business in that country's territory.

5(3)   Save in the cases referred to in article 64(2)(b) and (3), a representative must be established within the Community;

5(4)   A representative must state that he is acting on behalf of the person represented, specify whether the representation is direct or indirect and be empowered to act as a representative. A person who fails to state that he is acting in the name of or on behalf of another person or who states that he is acting in the name of or on behalf of another person without being empowered to do so shall be deemed to be acting in his own name and on his own behalf.

5(5)   The customs authorities may require any person stating that he is acting in the name of or on behalf of another person to produce evidence of his powers to act as a representative.

SECTION 2 – DECISIONS RELATING TO THE APPLICATION OF CUSTOMS RULES

ART. 6   [Taking of decisions]

6(1)   Where a person requests that the customs authorities take a decision relating to the application of customs rules that person shall supply all the information and documents required by those authorities in order to take a decision.

6(2)   Such decision shall be taken and notified to the applicant at the earliest opportunity.

Where a request for a decision is made in writing, the decision shall be made within a period laid down in accordance with the existing provisions, starting on the date on which the said request is received by the customs authorities. Such a decision must be notified in writing to the applicant.

However, that period may be exceeded where the customs authorities are unable to comply with it. In that case, those authorities shall so inform the applicant before the expiry of the abovementioned period, stating the grounds which justify exceeding it and indicating the further period of time which they consider necessary in order to give a ruling on the request.

6(3)   Decisions adopted by the customs authorities in writing which either reject requests or are detrimental to the persons to whom they are addressed shall set out the grounds on which they are based. They shall refer to the right of appeal provided for in article 243.

6(4)   Provision may be made for the first sentence of paragraph 3 to apply likewise to other decisions.

ART. 7   [Enforceability of decisions]

7   Save in the cases provided for in the second subparagraph of article 244, decisions adopted shall be immediately enforceable by customs authorities.

ART. 8   [Annulment of decisions]

8(1)   A decision favourable to the person concerned shall be annulled if it was issued on the basis of incorrect or incomplete information and:

–   the applicant knew or should reasonably have known that the information was incorrect or incomplete, and

–   such decision could not have been taken on the basis of correct or complete information.

8(2)   The persons to whom the decision was addressed shall be notified of its annulment.

8(3)   Annulment shall take effect from the date on which the annulled decision was taken.

ART. 9   [Revocation or amendment of decisions]

9(1)   A decision favourable to the person concerned, shall be revoked or amended where, in cases other than those referred to in article 8, one or more of the conditions laid down for its issue were not or are no longer fulfilled.

9(2)   A decision favourable to the person concerned may be revoked where the person to whom it is addressed fails to fulfil an obligation imposed on him under that decision.

9(3)   The person to whom the decision is addressed shall be notified of its revocation or amendment.

9(4)   The revocation or amendment of the decision shall take effect from the date of notification. However, in exceptional cases where the legitimate interests of the person to whom the decision is addressed so require, the customs authorities may defer the date when revocation or amendment takes effect.

ART. 10   [National rules]

10   Articles 8 and 9 shall be without prejudice to national rules which stipulate that decisions are invalid or become null and void for reasons unconnected with customs legislation.

SECTION 3 – INFORMATION

ART. 11   [Requests for information]

11(1)   Any person may request information concerning the application of customs legislation from the customs authorities.

Such a request may be refused where it does not relate to an import or export operation actually envisaged.

11(2)   The information shall be supplied to the applicant free of charge. However, where special costs are incurred by the customs authorities, in particular as a result of analyses or expert reports on goods, or the return of the goods to the applicant, he may be charged the relevant amount.

SECTION 4 – OTHER PROVISIONS

ART. 13   [Powers of customs authorities]

13   The customs authorities may, in accordance with the conditions laid down by the provisions in force, carry out all the controls they deem necessary to ensure that customs legislation is correctly applied.

ART. 14   [Provision of information to customs authorities]

14   For the purposes of applying customs legislation, any person directly or indirectly involved in the operations concerned for the purposes of trade in goods shall provide the customs authorities with all the requisite documents and information, irrespective of the medium used, and all the requisite assistance at their request and by any time-limit prescribed.

Cross references – Regulation 1495/80 (OJ 1980 L154/14), art. 11A: interpreting provision of Regulation 1224/80 equivalent to art. 14.
Regulation 1496/80 (OJ 1980 L154/16): declaration of particulars relating to customs value and on documents to be furnished.

ART. 15   [Confidentiality]

15   All information which is by nature confidential or which is provided on a confidential basis shall be covered by the obligation of professional secrecy. It shall not be disclosed by the customs authorities without the express permission of the person or authority providing it; the communication of information shall be permitted where the customs authorities may be obliged or authorised to do so pursuant to the provisions in force, particularly in respect of data protection, or in connection with legal proceedings.

ART. 16   [Retention of documents]

16   The persons concerned shall keep the documents referred to in article 14 for the purposes of control by the customs authorities, for the period laid down in the provisions in force and for at least three calendar years, irrespective of the medium used. That period shall run from the end of the year in which:

(a)   in the case of goods released for free circulation in circumstances other than those referred to in (b) or goods declared for export, from the end of the year in which the declarations for release for free circulation or export are accepted;

(b)   in the case of goods released for free circulation at a reduced or zero rate of import duty on account of their end-use, from the end of the year in which they cease to be subject to customs supervision;

(c)   in the case of goods placed under another customs procedure, from the end of the year in which the customs procedure concerned is completed;

(d)   in the case of goods placed in a free zone or free warehouse, from the end of the year on which they leave the undertaking concerned.

Without prejudice to the provisions of article 221(3), second sentence, where a check carried out by the customs authorities in respect of a customs debt shows that the relevant entry in the accounts has to be corrected, the documents shall be kept beyond the time limit provided for in the first paragraph for a period sufficient to permit the correction to be made and checked.

ART. 17   [Periods, dates and time-limits]

17   Where a period, date or time-limit is laid down pursuant to customs legislation for the purpose of applying legislation, such period shall not be extended and such date or time-limit shall not be deferred unless specific provision is made in the legislation concerned.

ART. 18   [Value of the ECU]

18(1)   The value of the ECU in national currencies to be applied for the purposes of determining the tariff classification of goods and import duties shall be fixed once a month. The rates to be used for this conversion shall be those published in the *Official Journal of the European Communities* on the penultimate working day of the month. Those rates shall apply throughout the following month.

However, where the rate applicable at the start of the month differs by more than 5 per cent from that published on the penultimate working day before the 15th of that same month, the latter rate shall apply from the 15th until the end of the month in question.

18(2)   The value of the ECU in national currencies to be applied within the framework of customs legislation in cases other than those referred to in paragraph 1 shall be fixed once a year. The rates to be used for this conversion shall be those published in the *Official Journal if the European Communities* on the first working day of October, with effect from 1 January of the following year. If no rate is available for a particular national currency, the rate applicable to that currency shall be that obtaining on the last day for which a rate was published in the *Official Journal of the European Communities*.

18(3)   The customs authorities may round up or down the sum resulting form the conversion into their national currency of an amount expressed in ECUs for purposes other than determining the tariff classification of goods or import or export duties.

The rounded-off amount may not differ from the original amount by more than 5 per cent.

The customs authorities may retain unchanged the national-currency value of an amount expressed in ECUs if, at the time of the annual adjustment provided for in paragraph 2, the conversion of that amount, prior to the abovementioned rounding-off, results in a variation of less than 5 per cent in the national-currency value or a reduction in that value.

History – Art. 18 replaced by Regulation 82/97, art. 1(4) (OJ 1997 L17/1), with effect from 1 January 1997.

ART. 19   [Simplification of customs legislation]

19   The procedure of the Committee shall be used to determine in which cases and under which conditions the application of customs legislation may be simplified.

[Art. 20–26 are not reproduced.]

TITLE II – FACTORS ON THE BASIS OF WHICH IMPORT DUTIES OR EXPORT DUTIES AND THE OTHER MEASURES PRESCRIBED IN RESPECT OF TRADE IN GOODS ARE APPLIED

[Art. 27 is not reproduced.]

Chapter 3 – Value of goods for customs purposes

ART. 28   [Determination of value]

28   The provisions of this Chapter shall determine the customs value for the purposes of applying the Customs Tariff of the European Communities and non-tariff measures laid down by Community provisions governing specific fields relating to trade in goods.

ART. 29   [Transaction value]

29(1)   The customs value of imported goods shall be the transaction value, that is the price actually paid or payable for the goods when sold for export to the customs territory of the Community, adjusted, where necessary, in accordance with Articles 32 and 33, provided:

(a)   that there are no restrictions as to the disposal or use of the goods by the buyer, other than restrictions which:

-    are imposed or required by a law or by the public authorities in the Community,
-    limit the geographical area in which the goods may be resold, or
-    do not substantially affect the value of the goods;

(b)   that the sale or price is not subject to some condition or consideration for which a value cannot be determined with respect to the goods being valued;

(c)   that no part of the proceeds of any subsequent resale, disposal or use of the goods by the buyer will accrue directly or indirectly to the seller, unless an appropriate adjustment can be made in accordance with article 32; and

(d)   that the buyer and seller are not related, or, where the buyer and seller are related, that the transaction value is acceptable for customs purposes under paragraph 2.

29(2)

(a)   In determining whether the transaction value is acceptable for the purposes of paragraph 1, the fact that the buyer and the seller are related shall not in itself be sufficient grounds for regarding the transaction value as unacceptable. Where necessary, the circumstances surrounding the sale shall be examined and the transaction value shall be accepted provided that the relationship did not influence the price. If, in the light of information provided by the declarant or otherwise, the customs authorities have grounds for considering that the relationship influenced the price, they shall communicate their grounds to the declarant and he shall be given a reasonable opportunity to respond. If the declarant so requests, the communication of the grounds shall be in writing.

(b)   In a sale between related persons, the transaction value shall be accepted and the goods valued in accordance with paragraph 1 wherever the declarant demonstrates that such value closely approximates to one of the following occurring at or about the same time:

(i)   the transaction value in sales, between buyers and sellers who are not related in any particular case, of identical or similar goods for export to the Community;

(ii)   the customs value of identical or similar goods, as determined under article 30(2)(c);

(iii)   the customs value of identical or similar goods, as determined under article 30(2)(d).

In applying the foregoing tests, due account shall be taken of demonstrated differences in commercial levels, quantity levels, the elements enumerated in article 32 and costs incurred by the seller in sales in which he and the buyer are not related and where such costs are not incurred by the seller in sales in which he and the buyer are related.

(c)   The tests set forth in subparagraph (b) are to be used at the initiative of the declarant and only for comparison purposes. Substitute values may not be established under the said subparagraph.

29(3)

(a)   The price actually paid or payable is the total payment made or to be made by the buyer to or for the benefit of the seller for the imported goods and includes all payments made or to be made as a condition of sale of the imported goods by the buyer to the seller or by the buyer to a third party to satisfy an obligation of the seller. The payment need not necessarily take the form of a transfer of money. Payment may be made by way of letters of credit or negotiable instrument and may be made directly or indirectly.

(b)   Activities, including marketing activities, undertaken by the buyer on his own account, other than those for which an adjustment is provided in article 32, are not considered to be an indirect payment to the seller, even though they might be regarded as of benefit to the seller or have been undertaken by agreement with the seller, and their cost shall not be added to the price actually paid or payable in determining the customs value of imported goods.

ART. 30   [Determination of customs value other than by transaction value]

30(1)   Where the customs value cannot be determined under article 29, it is to be determined by proceeding sequentially through subparagraphs (a), (b), (c) and (d) of paragraph 2 to the first subparagraph under which it can be determined, subject to the proviso that the order of application of subparagraphs (c) and (d) shall be reversed if the declarant so requests; it is only when such value cannot be determined under a particular subparagraph that the provisions of the next subparagraph in a sequence established by virtue of this paragraph can be applied.

30(2) The customs value as determined under this article shall be:

(a) the transaction value of identical goods sold for export to the Community and exported at or about the same time as the goods being valued;

(b) the transaction value of similar goods sold for export to the Community and exported at or about the same time as the goods being valued;

(c) the value based on the unit price at which the imported goods for identical or similar imported goods are sold within the Community in the greatest aggregate quantity to persons not related to the sellers;

(d) the computed value, consisting of the sum of:

    – the cost or value of materials and fabrication or other processing employed in producing the imported goods,

    – an amount for profit and general expenses equal to that usually reflected in sales of goods of the same class or kind as the goods being valued which are made by producers in the country of exportation for export to the Community,

    – the cost or value of the items referred to in article 32(1)(e).

30(3) Any further conditions and rules for the application of paragraph 2 above shall be determined in accordance with the committee procedure.

ART. 31   [Determination of customs value where other methods cannot be used]

31(1) Where the customs value of imported goods cannot be determined under articles 29 or 30, it shall be determined, on the basis of data available in the Community, using reasonable means consistent with the principles and general provisions of:

    – the agreement on implementation of article VII of the General Agreement on Tariffs and Trade of 1994,

    – article VII of the General Agreement on Tariffs and Trade of 1994,

    – the provisions of this chapter.

31(2) No customs value shall be determined under paragraph 1 on the basis of:

(a) the selling price in the Community of goods produced in the Community;

(b) a system which provides for the acceptance for customs purposes of the higher of two alternative values;

(c) the price of goods on the domestic market of the country of exportation;

(d) the cost of production, other than computed values which have been determined for identical or similar goods in accordance with article 30(2)(d);

(e) prices for export to a country not forming part of the customs territory of the Community;

(f) minimum customs values; or

(g) arbitrary or fictitious values.

History – In art. 31(1), the words "of 1994" added to the first and second indents by Regulation 82/97, art. 1(6) (OJ 1997 L17/1), with effect from 1 January 1997.

ART. 32   [Additions to price]

32(1) In determining the customs value under article 29, there shall be added to the price actually paid or payable for the imported goods:

(a) the following, to the extent that they are incurred by the buyer but are not included in the price actually paid or payable for the goods:

    (i) commissions and brokerage, except buying commissions,

    (ii) the cost of containers which are treated as being one, for customs purposes, with the goods in question,

    (iii) the cost of packing, whether for labour or materials;

(b) the value, apportioned as appropriate, of the following goods and services where supplied *directly or indirectly by the buyer free of charge* or at reduced cost for use in connection with the production and sale for export of the imported goods, to the extent that such value has not been included in the price actually paid or payable:

    (i) materials, components, parts and similar items incorporated in the imported goods,

    (ii) tools, dies, moulds and similar items used in the production of the imported goods,

    (iii) materials consumed in the production of the imported goods,

    (iv) engineering, development, artwork, design work, and plans and sketches undertaken elsewhere than in the Community and necessary for the productions of the imported goods;

(c)   royalties and licence fees related to the goods being valued that the buyer must pay, either directly or indirectly, as a condition of sale of the goods being valued, to the extent that such royalties and fees are not included in the price actually paid or payable;

(d)   the value of any part of the proceeds of any subsequent resale, disposal or use of the imported goods that accrues directly or indirectly to the seller;

(e)

    (i) the cost of transport and insurance of the imported goods, and

    (ii) loading and handling charges associated with the transport of the imported goods

to the place of introduction into the customs territory of the Community.

32(2)   Additions to the price actually paid or payable shall be made under this article only on the basis of objective and quantifiable data.

32(3)   No additions shall be made to the price actually paid or payable in determining the customs value except as provided in this article.

32(4)   In this Chapter, the term **"buying commissions"** means fees paid by an importer to his agent for the service of representing him in the purchase of the goods being valued.

32(5)   Notwithstanding paragraph 1(c):

(a)   charges for the right to reproduce the imported goods in the Community shall not be added to the price actually paid or payable for the imported goods in determining the customs value; and

(b)   payments made by the buyer for the right to distribute or resell the imported goods shall not be added to the price actually paid or payable for the imported goods if such payments are not a condition of the sale for export to the Community of the goods.

ART. 33   [Charges excluded from customs value]

33   Provided that they are shown separately from the price actually paid or payable, the following shall not be included in the customs value:

(a)   charges for the transport of goods after their arrival at the place of introduction into the customs territory of the Community;

(b)   charges for construction, erection, assembly, maintenance or technical assistance, undertaken after importation of imported goods such as industrial plant, machinery or equipment;

(c)   charges for interest under a financing arrangement entered into by the buyer and relating to the purchase of imported goods, irrespective of whether the finance is provided by the seller or another person, provided that the financing arrangement has been made in writing and where required, the buyer can demonstrate that:

    —   such goods are actually sold at the price declared as the price actually paid or payable, and

    —   the claimed rate of interest does not exceed the level for such transactions prevailing in the country where, and at the time when, the finance was provided;

(d)   charges for the right to reproduce imported goods in the Community;

(e)   buying commissions;

(f)   import duties or other charges payable in the Community by reason of the importation or sale of the goods.

ART. 34   [Carrier media]

34   Specific rules may be laid down in accordance with the procedure of the committee to determine the customs value of carrier media for use in data processing equipment and bearing data or instructions.

ART. 35   [Exchange rate where value expressed in foreign currency]

35   Where factors used to determine the customs value of goods are expressed in a currency other than that of the member state where the valuation is made, the rate of exchange to be used shall be that duly published by the competent authorities of the member state concerned.

Such rate shall reflect as effectively as possible the current value of such currency in commercial transactions in terms of the currency of such member state and shall apply during such period as may be determined in accordance with the procedure of the committee.

Where such a rate does not exist, the rate of exchange to be used shall be determined in accordance with the procedure of the committee.

Cross reference – Regulation 1766/85 (OJ 1985 L168/21): rates of exchange to be used in determination of customs value.

ART. 36   [Customs value of goods assigned a different treatment or use]

36(1) The provisions of this chapter shall be without prejudice to the specific provisions regarding the determination of the value for customs purposes of goods released for free circulation after being assigned a different customs-approved treatment or use.

36(2) By way of derogation from articles 29, 30 and 31, the customs value of perishable goods usually delivered on consignment may, at the request of the declarant, be determined under simplified rules drawn up for the whole Community in accordance with the committee procedure.

[Art. 37–242 are not reproduced.]

TITLE VIII – APPEALS

ART. 243   [Right of appeal]

243(1) Any person shall have the right to appeal against decisions taken by the customs authorities which relate to the application of customs legislation, and which concern him directly and individually.

Any person who has applied to the customs authorities for a decision relating to the application of customs legislation and has not obtained a ruling on that request within the period referred to in article 6(2) shall also be entitled to exercise the right of appeal.

The appeal must be lodged in the member state where the decision has been taken or applied for.

243(2) The right of appeal may be exercised:

(a)   initially, before the customs authorities designated for that purpose by the member states;
(b)   subsequently, before an independent body, which may be a judicial authority or an equivalent specialised body, according to the provisions in force in the member states.

ART. 244   [Suspension of decision]

244 The lodging of an appeal shall not cause implementation of the disputed decision to be suspended.

The customs authorities shall, however, suspend implementation of such decision in whole or in part where they have good reason to believe that the disputed decision is inconsistent with customs legislation or that irreparable damage is to be feared for the person concerned.

Where the disputed decision has the effect of causing import duties or export duties to be charged, suspension of implementation of that decision shall be subject to the existence or lodging of a security. However, such security need not be required where such a requirement would be likely, owing to the debtor's circumstances, to cause serious economic or social difficulties.

ART. 245   [Implementation]

245 The provisions for the implementation of the appeals procedure shall be determined by the *member states*.

ART. 246   [Criminal appeals]

246 This title shall not apply to appeals lodged with a view to the annulment or revision of a decision taken by the customs authorities on the basis of criminal law.

TITLE IX – FINAL PROVISIONS

Chapter 1 – Customs Code Committee

ART. 247   [Established of committee]

247(1)   A Customs Code committee, hereinafter called **"the committee"**, composed of representatives of the member states with a representative of the Commission as chairman, is hereby established.

247(2)   The committee shall adopt its rules of procedure.

ART. 248   [Role of committee]

248   The committee may examine any question concerning customs legislation which is raised by its chairman, either on his own initiative or at the request of a member state's representative.

ART. 249   [Implementation of the code]

249(1)   The provisions required for the implementation of this code, including implementation of the regulation referred to in article 184, except for Title VIII and subject to articles 9 and 10 of Council Regulation 2658/87 and to paragraph 4, shall be adopted in accordance with the procedure laid down in paragraphs 2 and 3, in compliance with the international commitments entered into by the Community.

249(2)   The representative of the Commission shall submit to the committee a draft of the measures to be taken. The committee shall deliver its opinion on the draft within a time-limit which the chairman may lay down according to the urgency of the matter. The opinion shall be delivered by the majority laid down in article 148(2) of the treaty in the case of decisions which the Council is required to adopt on a proposal from the Commission. The votes of the representatives of the member states within the committee shall be weighted in the manner set out in that article. The chairman shall not vote.

249(3)

(a)   The Commission shall adopt the measures envisaged if they are in accordance with the opinion of the committee.

(b)   If the measures envisaged are not in accordance with the opinion of the committee, or if no opinion is delivered, the Commission shall, without delay, submit to the Council a proposal relating to the provisions to be adopted. The Council shall act by a qualified majority.

(c)   If, on the expiry of a period of three months from the date of referral to the Council, the Council has not acted, the proposed measures shall be adopted by the Commission.

249(4)   The provisions necessary for implementing articles 11, 12 and 21 shall be adopted by the procedure referred to in article 10 of Regulation 2658/87.

Cross reference – Regulation 2658/87 on the tariff and statistical nomenclature and on the Common Customs Tariff (OJ 1987 L256/1), art. 9 and 10: procedures for the adoption of certain measures.

Chapter 2 – Legal effects in a member state of measures taken, documents issued and findings made in another member state

ART. 250   [Customs procedure used in several member states]

250   Where a customs procedure is used in several member states,

–   the decisions, identification measures taken or agreed on, and the documents issued by the customs authorities of one member state shall have the same legal effects in other member states as such decisions, measures taken and documents issued by the customs authorities of each of those member states;

–   the findings made at the time controls are carried out by the customs authorities of a member state shall have the same conclusive force in the other member states as the findings made by the customs authorities of each of those member states.

Chapter 3 – Other final provisions

[Art. 251 and 252 are not reproduced.]

ART. 253   [Entry into force; application]

253 This regulation shall enter into force on the third day following that of its publication in the *Official Journal of the European Communities*.

It shall apply from 1 January 1994.

Title VIII shall not apply to the United Kingdom until 1 January 1995.

However, article 161 and, in so far as they concern re-exportation, articles 182 and 183 shall apply from 1 January 1993. In so far as the said articles make reference to provisions in this code and until such time as such provisions enter into force, the references shall be deemed to allude to the corresponding provisions in the regulations and directives listed in article 251.

Before 1 October 1993, the Council shall, on the basis of a Commission progress report on discussions regarding the consequences to be drawn from the monetary conversion rate used for the application of common agricultural policy measures, review the problem of trade in goods between the member states in the context of the internal market. This report shall be accompanied by Commission proposals if any, on which the Council shall take a decision in accordance with the provisions of the treaty.

Before 1 January 1998, the Council shall, on the basis of a Commission report, review this code with a view to making such adaptations as may appear necessary taking into account in particular the achievement of the internal market. This report shall be accompanied by proposals, if any, on which the Council shall take a decision in accordance with the provisions of the treaty.

This regulation shall be binding in its entirety and directly applicable in all member states.

Note – The regulation was published in the Official Journal on 19 October 1992.

REGULATION 3046/92

Laying down provisions implementing and amending Council Regulation 3330/91 on the statistics relating to the trading of goods between member states

(22 October 1992, OJ 1992 L307/27)

The Commission of the European Communities,

Having regard to the Treaty establishing the European Economic Community,

Having regard to Council Regulation 3330/91 of 7 November 1991 on the statistics relating to the trading of goods between member states, and in particular article 30 thereof,

[1] Whereas, with a view to establishing the statistics relating to the trading of goods between member states, the field of application of the Intrastat system should be precisely defined in relation to both the goods to be included and those to be excluded;

[2] Whereas the date from which the intra-Community operator shall in practice comply with his obligations to supply information must be determined; whereas the extent of the obligations of the third parry to whom the party responsible for providing the information may transfer that task should be defined;

[3] Whereas certain of the rules to be complied with by the departments concerned must be specified in detail in particular with a view to efficient management of the registers of intra-Community operation; whereas it is useful to specify the provisions relating to certain fiscal aspects of statistical information;

[4] Whereas there should be additions to the definition of the data to be reported and to the arrangements for reporting such data;

[5] Whereas a list should be drawn up of the goods to be excluded from the statistical returns relating to the trading of goods;

[6] Whereas account should be taken initially of existing simplified procedures and of the special requirements of certain sectors;

[7] Whereas the amendments to Council Directive 77/388 by Directive 91/680 require certain provisions of Regulation 3330/91 to be adapted, pursuant to the first indent of article 33 thereof;

[8] Whereas the measures provided for in this regulation are in accordance with the opinion of the Committee on the statistics relating to the trading of goods between member states,

has adopted this regulation:

ART. 1   [Meaning]

1   With a view to establishing the statistics relating to the trading of goods between member states, the Community and its member states shall apply Regulation 3330/91, hereinafter referred to as the **basic regulation**, in accordance with the rules laid down in this regulation.

ART. 2   [Application]

2(1)   In connection with trade between the Community as constituted on 31 December 1985 and Spain or Portugal, and between those two last-mentioned member states, the Intrastat system shall also apply to goods still liable to certain customs duties and charges having equivalent effect or which remain subject to other measures laid down by the Act of Accession.

2(2)   The Intrastat system shall apply to the products referred to in article 3(1) of Council Directive 92/12, regardless of the form and content of the document accompanying them, when they move between the territories of the member states.

ART. 3   [Non-application]

3(1)   The Intrastat system shall not apply:

(a)   to goods placed or obtained under the inward processing customs procedure (suspension system) or the procedure of processing under customs control;

(b)   to goods circulating between parts of the statistical territory of the Community, at least one of which is not part of the territory of the Community pursuant to Council Directive 77/388.

3(2)   The member states shall be responsible for collecting data on the goods referred to in paragraph 1 on the basis of the customs procedures applicable to such goods.

3(3)   If the statistical copy of the Single Administrative Document containing the data listed in article 23 of the basic regulation, with the exception of the information referred to in paragraph 2(e) of that article, is not available, the customs departments shall at least once a month send the relevant statistical departments a periodic list of those same data by type of goods, in accordance with the arrangements agreed upon by the said departments.

3(4)   Articles 2, 4, 8, 9, 12(1), (3), (4), (5), (6) and (7); 13, 14, 19, 21 and 22(3)(a) and (b), first indent, shall not apply to the goods referred to in paragraph 1.

The other provisions of this regulation shall apply to these goods without prejudice to any customs regulations which otherwise apply.

ART. 4   [Responsible person]

4(1)   Any natural or legal person carrying out an intra-Community operation for the first time, whether the goods are arriving or being dispatched, shall become responsible for providing the required information within the meaning of article 20(5) of the basic regulation.

4(2)   The party referred to in paragraph 1 shall provide the data on his intra-Community operations via the periodic declarations referred to in article 13 of the basic regulation as from the month during which the assimilation threshold is exceeded, in accordance with the provisions relating to the threshold which become applicable to him.

The member states shall determine the deadline for transmission in line with their particular administrative organisation.

4(3)   When the VAT registration number of a party responsible for providing the information is amended as a result of a change of ownership, name, address, legal status or similar change which does not affect his intra-Community operations to a significant extent, the rule defined in paragraph 1 need not be applied to the party in question at the time of the change. It shall remain subject to the statistical obligations to which it was subject before the change.

ART. 5   ["Declaring third party"]

5(1)   The third party referred to in article 9(1) of the basic regulation is hereinafter referred to as the declaring third party.

5(2)   The declaring third party shall provide the competent national departments with the following information:

(a)   in accordance with article 6(1), the information necessary:

       –   to identify himself,

- to identify each of the parties responsible for providing the information who have transferred this task to him;
(b) for each of the parties responsible for providing information, the data required by the basic regulation and in implementation thereof.

ART. 6   ["Intra-Community operator"]

6(1) The information necessary to identify an intra-Community operator within the meaning of article 10 of the basic regulation shall be the following:

- full name of the person or firm,
- full address including post code,
- under the circumstances laid down in article 10(6) of the basic regulation, the VAT registration number.

However, the statistical departments referred to in article 10(1) of the basic regulation may dispense with one or more of the abovementioned items of information or, under circumstances to be determined by them, exempt the intra-Community operators from providing them.

In the member states referred to in article 10(3) of the basic regulation, the information which serves to identify an intra-Community operator shall be supplied to the abovementioned statistical departments by the tax authorities referred to in the said article as and when it becomes available to the latter, unless there is an agreement to the contrary between the departments concerned.

6(2) The minimum of list data to be recorded in the register of intra-Community operators, within the meaning of article 10 of the basic regulation, shall contain, for each intra-Community operator, the following:

(a) the year and month of entry in the register;
(b) the information necessary to identify the operator as laid down in paragraph 1;
(c) where applicable, whether the operator is the consignor, consignee or declarant, or, as from 1 January 1993, a party responsible for providing information or a declaring third party, upon either consignment or receipt; in the member states referred to in article 10(3) of the basic regulation, the information stipulated in paragraph 1 of the present article shall show whether each operator in question is a consignor or a consignee;
(d) in the case of a consignor or consignee or, as from 1 January 1993, a party responsible for providing information, the total value of his intra-Community operations, by month and by flow, together with, as from that same date, the value referred to in article 11(3) of the basic regulation; however, this information need not be recorded:
  - prior to 1993, in those member states referred to in article 10(3) of the basic regulation,
  - if the checking of the information recorded as statistics using the information referred to in article 11(3) of the basic regulation and the functioning of the statistical thresholds referred to in article 28 of the said regulation are organised separately from the management of the register of intra-Community operators.

The competent national departments may record other data in the register in accordance with their requirements.

ART. 7   [Responsible person]

7 With a view to implementing article 10(6) of the basic regulation, the case where responsibility for the information, for given operations, lies not with the operator as a legal entity per se but with a constituent part of this entity, such as a branch office, a kind-of-activity unit or local unit, may be considered a justified exception.

ART. 8   [Scission, merger or cessation]

8(1) In the lists referred to in article 11(1) of the basic regulation, the tax authorities responsible shall mention intra-Community operators who, as a result of a scission, merger or cessation of activity during the period under review, will no longer appear on the said lists.

8(2) The provision of information of a fiscal nature referred to in article 11(4) of the basic regulation by a member state's administrative authorities responsible for the application of laws on value added tax to the departments in that member state responsible for compiling statistics relating to the trading of goods between member states is limited to information which those liable to account for VAT are required to provide in accordance with article 22 of Directive 77/388.

History – Art. 8(2) was added and consequently the previous paragraph was numbered art. 8(1) by Regulation 2535/98, art. 1 (OJ 1998 L 318/22), with effect from 17 December 1998.

ART. 9   [Data transmission]

9(1) The party responsible for providing information shall transmit the data required under the basic regulation and in implementation thereof:

(a)   in accordance with the Community provision in force;

(b)   direct to the competent national departments or via the collection offices which the member states have set up for this or for other statistical or administrative purposes;

(c)   for a given reference period, at his discretion:

     –   either by means of a single declaration, within a time limit which the competent national departments shall lay down in their instructions to the parties responsible for providing information and which shall be between the fifth and the tenth working day following the end of that period,

     –   or by means of several part-declarations; in this case, the competent national departments may require agreement to be reached with them on the frequency of transmission and deadlines, but the last part-declaration must be transmitted within the time limit laid down under the first indent above.

9(2) By way of derogation from paragraph 1, a party responsible for providing information who benefits from exemption by virtue of application of the assimilation threshold provided for in article 28(4) of the basic regulation must, when transmitting the information, conform only to the regulations of the tax authorities responsible.

9(3) Pursuant to article 34 of the basic regulation, the provisions of this article relating to the periodicity of the declaration shall not prevent the conclusion of an agreement providing for the supply of data in real time, when the data are transmitted electronically.

9(4) By way of derogation to paragraph 1 above, in those member states where the periodic statistical declaration is the same as the periodic tax declaration, the provisions relating to the transmission of the statistical declaration shall be drawn up in line with Community or national tax regulations.

ART. 10   [Territory code]

10 In the medium for the information, the member states whose statistical territory is described in the nomenclature of countries annexed to Council Regulation 1736/75 shall be designated by either alphabetical or numerical codes, as follows:

France:	FR or	001;
Belgium and Luxembourg:	BL or	002,
Netherlands:	NI or	003,
Germany:	DE or	004,
Italy:	IT or	005,
United Kingdom:	GB or	006,
Ireland:	IE or	007,
Denmark:	DK or	008,
Greece:	GR or	009,
Portugal:	PT or	010,
Spain:	ES or	011.

Cross reference – Regulation 1736/75 (OJ 1975 L183/3): external trade statistics of the Community and statistics of trade between member states.
Regulation 208/93 (OJ 1993 L25/11): country nomenclature for the external trade statistics of the Community and statistics of trade between member states – version valid on 1 January 1993.

ART. 11   [Meaning]

11(11) When the quantity of goods to be mentioned on the data medium is determined:

(a)   **"net mass"** shall mean the actual mass of the good excluding all packaging; it must be given in kilograms. However, the specification of net mass for the subheadings of the combined nomenclature set out in Annex IV shall be optional for the parties responsible for providing information.

(b)   **"supplementary units"** shall mean the units measuring quantity, other than the units measuring mass expressed in kilograms; they must be mentioned in accordance with the information set out in the current version of the combined nomenclature, opposite the sub-heading concerned, the list of which is published in Part I "Preliminary provisions" of the said nomenclature.

History – Art. 11(a) was substituted by Regulation 2385/96 (OJ L 326/10).

ART. 12   [Valuation]

12(1)   The value of the goods referred to in article 23(1)(d) of the basic regulation, shall be reported in the statistical information medium on the conditions defined in paragraphs 2 and 3.

12(2)   The value of the goods to be reported in the "invoiced amount" field in the statistical information medium shall be the taxable amount to be determined for taxation purposes in accordance with Directive 77/388. For products subject to excise duties, however, the amount of these duties should be excluded from the value of the goods.

Whenever the taxable amount does not have to be declared for taxation purposes, the value of the goods to be reported shall correspond to the invoice value, excluding VAT, or, failing this, to an amount which would have been invoiced in the event of any sale or purchase.

In the case of work under contract, the value of the goods to be reported, with a view to and following such operations, shall be the total amount to be invoiced in the event of any sale or purchase.

12(3)   The statistical value of the goods, as defined in paragraph 5, shall also be reported in the field provided to this end in the statistical information medium by providers of information whose arrivals or dispatches exceed the annual limits set by each member state.

The member states shall set separate limits for arrivals and dispatches at such values that 95 per cent of providers of information are exempted from the requirement to provide the statistical value. The member states may exempt more providers of information in so far as the statistical value collected covers at least 70 per cent of the total value of their dispatches or arrivals.

The limit of 95 per cent of providers of information exempted from providing the statistical value may be reduced to 90 per cent if the coverage rate of 70 per cent of the total value of their dispatches or arrivals is not reached.

The member states shall calculate these limits from the last available results for their trade with the other member states over a period of 12 months.

The member states shall publish the information on the introduction of these limits by 31 October 1997 at the latest.

The member states may adapt their limits every calendar year provided that the conditions set out at 2 above continue to be obtained. The member states concerned shall publicize changes to the limits by 31 October of the year preceding such changes.

12(4)   In derogation from paragraph 3, the member states may exempt providers of information from reporting the statistical value of goods.

In this case, the member states concerned shall calculate the statistical value of goods, as defined in paragraph 5, by kinds of goods.

12(5)   The statistical value shall be based on the goods reported by the providers of information pursuant to paragraph 2. It shall include only incidental expenses, such as transport and insurance costs, referring to the part of the route which:

–   for dispatches, is within the statistical territory of the member state of dispatch,
–   for arrivals, is within the statistical territory of the member state of arrival.

12(6)   The value of the goods defined in the preceding paragraphs shall be expressed in each national currency, whereupon the exchange rate to be applied shall be:

–   that applicable for determining the taxable amount for taxation purposes, when this is established,
–   otherwise, the official rate of exchange at the time of completing the declaration or that applicable to calculating the value for customs purposes, in the absence of any special provisions decided by the member states.

12(7)   In accordance with article 26 of the basic regulation, the value of the goods given in the results to be transmitted to the Commission shall be the statistical value defined in paragraph 5.

12(8)   At the Commission's request, the member states shall provide it with the information enabling it to assess the application of paragraph 3.

12(9) By 1 January 2000, the Commission shall examine the application of this Article, and paragraph 3 thereof in particular, and shall propose amendments to the rules governing the reporting of value, if necessary.

History – Art. 12 was replaced by Regulation 860/97, art. 1 (OJ 1997 L123/12), with effect from 1 January 1998. Former art. 12 reads as follows:

"**12(1)** The value of the goods, as referred to in article 23(1)(d) of the basic regulation, shall be given as follows:
- by type of goods, the statistical value,
- by statistical declaration, the amount invoiced.

12(2) The statistical value shall be fixed:
- upon dispatch, on the basis of the taxable amount to be determined the taxation purposes in accordance with Directive 77/388 for deliveries of goods specified under section A(1)(a) and, where appropriate, for the operations specified under section A(1)(b) of article 11 of the same directive, minus, however, any taxes deductible because of the dispatch; it shall, on the other hand, include transport and insurance costs relating to that part of the journey which takes place on the statistical territory of the member state of dispatch,
- upon arrival, on the basis of the taxable amount to be determined for taxation purposes, in accordance with article 28E of the directive referred to above, for acquisition of goods, minus, however, taxes due because of the release for consumption and transport and insurance costs relating to that part of the journey which takes place on the statistical territory of the member state of arrival.

The statistical value must be declared in accordance with the first subparagraph, even if the taxable amount does not have to be determined for taxation purposes.

For goods resulting from processing operations, the statistical value shall be established as if those goods had been produced entirely in the member state of processing.

12(3) The amount invoiced shall be the total amount (excluding VAT) of invoices or documents serving as invoices relating to all the goods included in a statistical declaration.

12(4) The party responsible for providing information may indicate the invoiced amount broken down by type of goods.

By way of derogation to paragraph 1, the member states may require the invoiced amount to be broken down by type of goods. In this case, they shall calculate the statistical value and exempt the party responsible for providing the statistical information from the need to mention it. However, those responsible for providing the information may be required to supply information on ancillary costs on a sample basis.

The second subparagraph shall apply either to all parties required to transmit the periodic declaration referred to in article 13(1) of the basic regulation or solely to those parties who benefit from the application of simplification thresholds.

12(5) The member states may exercise the option laid down in the second subparagraph of paragraph 4, even if their particular administrative organisation prevents them from taking the simplification measure which, by virtue of this subparagraph, must accompany the exercise of this option, namely, exemption from the requirement to mention the statistical value.

In the instructions relating to the statistical declaration to the parties responsible for providing information, the technical reasons why both the statistical value and the invoiced amount must be mentioned, by type of goods, shall be indicated in advance. The member states shall transmit a copy of these instructions to the Commission before 1 November 1992 and, thereafter, whenever they are updated.

12(6) In the case of work under contract, the amount invoiced shall be the amount entered in the accounts for the work, including any ancillary costs. It shall be mentioned only in the case of the dispatch and the arrival which follow the contract work.

12(7) "Ancillary costs" means the costs incurred in the movement of goods between the member state of dispatch and the member state of arrival, such as transport and insurance costs."

ART. 13 [Meaning]

13(1) For the purposes of this regulation:

(a) **"transaction"** shall mean any operation, whether commercial or not, which leads to a movement of goods covered by statistics on the trading of goods between member states;

(b) **"nature of the transaction"** shall mean all those characteristics which distinguish one transaction from another.

13(2) A distinction shall be made between transactions which differ in nature, in accordance with the list in Annex I.

The nature of the transaction shall be specified, on the information medium, by the code number corresponding to the appropriate category of column A in the above-mentioned list.

13(3) Within the limits of the list referred to in paragraph 2, the member states may prescribe the collection of data on the nature of the transaction up to the level which they use for the collection of data on trade third countries, regardless of whether they collect them in this connection as data on the nature of the transaction or as data on customs procedures.

ART. 14 [Meaning]

14(1) For the purposes of this regulation, **"delivery terms"** shall mean those provisions of the sales contract which lay down the obligations of the seller and the buyer respectively, in accordance with the Incoterms of the International Chamber of Commerce listed in Annex II.

14(2) Within the limits of the list referred to in paragraph 1 and without prejudice to paragraph 3:

(a) those member states which apply the second subparagraph of article 12(4) shall stipulate that data on delivery terms shall be collected on the information medium and shall give details of how they are to be mentioned;

(b) the other member states may stipulate that data on delivery terms shall be collected on the information medium up to the level at which they collect data on trade with third countries.

14(3)   The delivery terms shall be indicated, for each type of goods, by one of the abbreviations in the list referred to in paragraph 1.

ART. 15   [Meaning and code]

15(1)   "Presumed mode of transport" shall indicate, upon dispatch, the mode of transport determined by the active means of transport by which the goods are presumed to be going to leave the statistical territory of the member state of dispatch and, upon arrival, the mode of transport determined by the active means of transport by which the goods are presumed to have entered the statistical territory of the member state of arrival.

15(2)   The modes of transport to be mentioned on the information medium are as follows:

Code	Title
1	Transport by sea
2	Transport by rail
3	Transport by road
4	Transport by air
5	Consignments by post
7	Fixed transport installations
8	Transport by inland waterway
9	Own propulsion

The mode of transport shall be designated on the said medium by the corresponding code number.

ART. 16   [Meaning]

16(1)   "Country of origin" shall mean the country where the goods originate.

Goods which are entirely obtained in a country originate in that country.

An item in the production of which two or more countries are involved originates in the country where the last significant processing or working, economically justified and carried out in an enterprise equipped for this purpose and leading to the manufacture of a new product or representing an important stage of manufacture, takes place.

16(2)   The country of origin shall be designated by the code number given to it in the current version of the country nomenclature annexed to Regulation 1736/75, without prejudice to the last sentence of article 47 of the said regulation.

Cross references – Regulation 1736/75 (OJ 1975 L183/3): external trade statistics of the Community and statistics of trade between member states.
Regulation 208/93 (OJ 1993 L25/11): country nomenclature for the external trade statistics of the Community and statistics of trade between member states – version valid on 1 January 1993.

ART. 17   [Meaning]

17(1)   "Region of origin" shall mean the region of the member state of dispatch where the goods were produced or were erected, assembled, processed, repaired or maintained; failing this, the region of origin shall be replaced either by the region where the commercial process took place or by the region where the goods were dispatched.

17(2)   "Region of destination" shall mean the region of the member state of arrival where the goods are to be consumed or erected, assembled, processed, repaired or maintained; failing this, the region of destination shall be replaced either by the region where the commercial process is to take place or by the region to which the goods are to be dispatched.

17(3)   Each member state exercising the option provided for in article 23(2)(b) of the basic regulation shall draw up a list of its regions and determine the code, which shall have a maximum of two characters, by which those regions shall be indicated on the information medium.

ART. 18   [Meaning]

18(1)   "Port or airport of loading" shall mean the port or airport situated on the statistical territory of the member state of dispatch at which the goods are loaded onto the active means of transport on or in which they are presumed to be going to leave that territory.

18(2) "**Port or airport of unloading**" shall mean the port or airport situated on the statistical territory of the member state of arrival at which the goods are unloaded from the active means of transport on or in which they are presumed to have entered that territory.

18(3) Each member state exercising the option provided for in article 23(2)(c) or (d) of the basic regulation shall draw up a list of ports and airports to be mentioned on the information medium and shall fix the code by which they are to be indicated on that medium.

ART. 19 [Meaning]

19(1) "**Statistical procedure**" shall mean the category of dispatch or arrival within which a given intra-Community operation takes place and which is not adequately referred to in column A or column B of the list of transactions in Annex I.

19(2) Any member state wishing to exercise the option provided for in article 23(2)(e) of the basic regulation shall draw up a list of the statistical procedures to be mentioned on the information medium and shall fix the code by which they are to be indicated on that medium.

ART. 20 [Excluded data]

20 Data relating to the goods listed in Annex III shall be excluded from compilation and, consequently, pursuant to article 25(4) of the basic regulation, from collection.

ART. 21 [Meaning]

21(1) For the purposes of this regulation, "**specific movements of goods**" shall mean movements of goods having specific features which have some significance for the interpretation of the information and stem either from the movement as such or from the nature of the goods or from the transaction which results in the movement of the goods or from the consignor or consignee of the goods.

21(2) In the absence of provisions drawn up under article 33 of the basic regulation, the member states may apply, as regards data to specific movements of goods, the simplified procedures which were applied, under Regulation 1736/75, prior to the date referred to in the second paragraph of article 35 of the basic regulation.

21(3) Those member states wishing to have more detailed information than that resulting from the application of article 21 of the basic regulation may, by way of derogation from that article, organise the collection of that information, for one or more specific product groups, provided that the party responsible for providing the information is allowed to elect to supply it in accordance with either the combined nomenclature or the additional subdivisions.

Those member states exercising that option shall notify the Commission that they are doing so. At the same time, they shall state the reasons for their decision, supply the list of relevant combined nomenclature subheadings and describe the collection method they are using.

Cross reference – Regulation 1736/75 (OJ 1975 L183/3): external trade statistics of the Community and statistics of trade between member states.

ART. 22

22 [Art. 22 is not reproduced.]

ART. 23 [Entry into force]

23 This regulation shall enter into force on the seventh day following its publication in the Official Journal of the European Communities.

Those of its provisions which relate to the articles referred to in the second paragraph of article 35 of the basic regulation shall apply from the same date as those said articles.

This regulation shall be binding in its entirety and directly applicable in all member states.

Note – The regulation was published in the Official Journal (L307/33) on 23 October 1992.

ANNEX I – LIST OF TRANSACTIONS REFERRED TO IN ART. 13(2)

Column A	Column B
1. Transactions involving actual or intended transfer of ownership against compensation (financial or otherwise) (except the transactions listed under 2, 7, 8)[a][b][c]	1. Outright/purchase/sale[b] 2. Supply for sale on approval or after trial, for consignment or with the inter-mediation of a commission agent 3. Barter trade (compensation in kind) 4. Personal purchases by travellers 5. Financial leasing[c]
2. Return of goods after registration of the original transaction under code 1[d]; replacement of goods free of charge[d]	1. Return of goods 2. Replacement for returned goods 3. Replacement (e.g. under warranty) for goods not being returned
3. Transactions (not temporary) involving transfer of ownership but without compensation (financial or other)	1. Goods delivered under aid programmes operated or financed partly or wholly 2. Other general government-aid deliveries 3. Other aid deliveries (individuals, non-governmental organisations)
4. Operations with a view to processing under contract[e] or repair[f] (except those recorded under 7)	1. Processing under contract 2. Repair and maintenance against payment 3. Repair and maintenance free of charge
5. Operations following processing under contract[e] or repair[f] (except those recorded under 7)	1. Processing under contract 2. Repair and maintenance against payment 3. Repair and maintenance free of charge
6. Transactions not involving transfer of ownership, e.g. hire, loan, operational leasing[g] and other temporary uses[h] except processing under contract or repair (delivery or return)	1. Hire, loan, operational leasing 2. Other goods for temporary uses
7. Operations under joint defence projects or other joint intergovernmental production programs (e.g. Airbus)	
8. Supply of building material and equipment for works that are part of a general construction or engineering contract[i]	
9. Other transactions	

[a] This item covers most dispatches and arrivals, i.e. transactions in respect of which:
– ownership is transferred from resident to non-resident, and
– payment or compensation in kind is or will be made.
It should be noted that this also applies to goods sent between related enterprises or from/to central distribution depots, even if no immediate payments is made.

[b] Including spare parts and other replacements made against payment.

[c] Including financial leasing: the lease instalments are calculated in such a way as to cover all or virtually all of the value of the goods. The risks and rewards of ownership are transferred to the lessee. At the end of the contract the lessee becomes the legal owner of the goods.

[d] Return and replacement dispatches of goods originally recorded under items 3 to 9 of column A should be registered under the corresponding items.

[e] Processing operations (whether or not under customs supervision) should be recorded under items 4 and 5 of column A. Processing activities on processor's own account are not covered by this item, they should be registered under item 1 of column A.

[f] Repair entails the restoration of goods to their original function; this may involve some rebuilding or enhancements.

[g] Operational leasing: leasing contracts other than financial leasing (see note (c)).

(h)   This item covers goods that are exported/imported with the intention of subsequent re-import/re-export without any change of ownership taking place.

(i)   The transactions recorded under item 8 of column A involve goods which are not separately invoiced, but for which a single invoice is made covering the total value of the works. Where this is not the case, the transactions should be recorded under item 1.

ANNEX II – LIST OF DELIVERY TERMS REFERRED TO IN ARTICLE 14

First sub-box	Meaning	
		Place to be indicated[1]
Incoterm code	Incoterm ICC/ECE Geneva	
EXW	ex-works	location of works
FCA	franco carrier	. . . agreed place
FAS	free alongside ship	agreed port of loading
FOB	free on board	agreed port of loading
CFR	cost and freight (C & F)	agreed port of destination
CIF	cost, insurance, freight	agreed port of destination
CPT	carriage paid to	agreed place of destination
CIP	carriage and insurance paid to	agreed place of destination
DAF	delivered at frontier	agreed place of delivery at frontier
DES	delivered ex-ship	agreed port of destination
DEQ	delivered ex-quay	after customs clearance, agreed port
DDU	delivered duty unpaid	agreed place of destination in importing country
DDP	delivered duty paid	agreed place of delivery in importing country
XXX	delivery terms other than the above	precise statement of terms specified in the contract[1]

[1]   Provide details in box 6 if necessary (form Intrastat N only)

Second sub-division

1: place located in the territory of the member state concerned,
2: place located in another member state,
3: other (place located outside the Community).

Second sub-division

(1)   place located in the territory of the member state concerned,
(2)   place located in another member state,
(3)   other (place located outside the Community).

ANNEX III – LIST OF EXCEPTIONS REFERRED TO IN ARTICLE 20

Data shall not be required for the following goods:

(a)   means of payment which are legal tender, and securities;
(b)   emergency aid for disaster areas;
(c)   because of the diplomatic or similar nature of their intended use:
    1.   goods benefiting from diplomatic and consular or similar immunity;
    2.   gifts to a head of state or to members of a government or parliament;
    3.   items being circulated within the framework of administrative mutual aid;
(d)   provided that the trade is temporary, amongst other things:
    1.   goods intended for fairs and exhibitions;
    2.   theatrical scenery;
    3.   merry-go-rounds and other fairground attractions;

    4.   professional equipment within the meaning of the International Customs Convention of 8 June 1968;

    5.   cinematographic films;

    6.   apparatus and equipment for experimental purposes;

    7.   animals for show, breeding, racing, etc.;

    8.   commercial samples;

    9.   means of transport, containers and equipment connected with transport;

    10.   packaging;

    11.   goods on hire;

    12.   plant and equipment for civil engineering works;

    13.   goods destined for examination, analysis or test purposes;

(e)   provided that they are not the subject of a commercial transaction:

    1.   decorations, honorary distinctions prizes, commemorative badges and metals;

    2.   travel equipment, provisions and other items, including sports equipment, intended for personal use or consumption which accompany, precede or follow the traveller;

    3.   bridal outfits, items involved in moving house, or heirlooms;

    4.   coffins, funerary urns, ornamental funerary articles and items for the upkeep of graves and funeral monuments;

    5.   printed advertising material, instructions for use, price lists and other advertising items;

    6.   goods which have become unusable, or which cannot be used for industrial purposes;

    7.   ballast;

    8.   photographs, exposed and developed firms, drafts, drawings, copies of plans, manuscripts, files and records, official printed matter and printing proofs, as well as all information media used for an intra-Community exchange of information;

    9.   postage stamps;

    10.   pharmaceutical products used at international sport events;

(f)   products used under agreements providing for common measures for the protection of persons or of the environment;

(g)   goods which are the subject of non-commercial traffic between persons resident in the adjacent zones of the member states; products obtained by agricultural producers on properties located outside, but adjacent to, the statistical territory within which they have their principal undertaking;

(h)   goods leaving a given statistical territory to return after crossing a foreign territory, either directly, or with halts inherent in the transport.

REGULATION 3590/92

Concerning the statistical information media for statistics on trade between member states

(11 December 1992, OJ 1992 L364/32)

The Commission of the European Communities,

Having regard to the Treaty establishing the European Economic Community,

Having regard to Council Regulation 3330/91 of 7 November 1991, on the statistics relating to the trading of goods between member states (OJ 1991 L316/1), as amended by Commission Regulation 3046/92 (OJ 1992 L307/27) and in particular article 12 thereof,

[1]   Whereas, in the context of statistics on trade between member states, it is necessary to adopt standard statistical forms for regular use by the parties responsible for providing information in order to ensure that the declarations required of them adhere to a consistent format, irrespective of the member state where they are made; whereas the choice accorded to the parties responsible for providing information by article 12(2) of the above-mentioned regulation is only available if the Commission sets up the appropriate information media; whereas, moreover, certain member states would rather use Community media than produce national forms of their own;

[2]   Whereas it is important to provide the competent authorities with all the technical details required for the printing of these forms;

[3]   Whereas it is advisable in order to ensure uniform treatment of the parties responsible for providing information, to contribute towards the cost of these forms; whereas it is necessary to

estimate the amount of Community funds required for this; whereas this amount must be in line with the financial perspective set out in the interinstitutional agreement of 29 June 1988 on budgetary discipline and improvement of the budgetary procedure (OJ 1988 L185/33); whereas, in compliance with this agreement, the appropriations actually available must be determined in accordance with budgetary procedure;

[4]   Whereas it is necessary to take account of other modes of transmitting information, and, in particular, to promote the use of magnetic or electronic information media;

[5]   Whereas the measures provided for in this regulation reflect the opinion of the Committee on Statistics Relating to the Trading of Goods between Member States,

has adopted this regulation:

ART. 1   [Setting up of statistical information media]

1(1)   With a view to the drawing-up by the Community and its member states of statistics on trade between the member states, the statistical information media provided for in article 12, paragraph 1, of Council Regulation 3330/91, hereafter referred to as **"the basic regulation"**, shall be set up in accordance with the provisions of this regulation.

1(2)   In member states where no distinction is made between the periodic declaration and the periodic declaration required for tax purposes, the provisions necessary for the setting-up of information media shall, in so far as necessary, be adopted within the framework of Community or national tax regulations, and in conformity with the other implementing provisions of the basic regulation.

ART. 2   [Use of Intrastat forms]

2   Without prejudice to provisions adopted pursuant to article 34 of the basic regulation, Intrastat forms N-Dispatch, R-Dispatch and S-Dispatch and N-Arrival, R-Arrival and S-Arrival, specimens of which are annexed to this regulation, shall be used in conformity with the provisions set out below.

-    Forms N shall be used by parties responsible for providing information who are not subject to the dispensations resulting from the assimilation and simplification thresholds fixed by each member state, nor to the exemption provided for in the following indent.
-    Forms R shall be used by parties responsible for providing information whom the competent national authorities have exempted from giving a description of the goods.
-    Forms S shall be used by parties responsible for providing information who are subject to the dispensations resulting from the simplification threshold.

Cross reference – Explanatory notes to the forms, reproduced after this regulation.

ART. 3   [Details of forms]

3(1)   The forms referred to in article 2 shall consist of a single sheet, which shall be delivered to the competent national authorities.

The member states may, however, require parties responsible for providing information to retain a copy in accordance with the instructions of the competent national authorities.

3(2)   The forms shall be printed on paper which is suitable for writing and weighs no less than 70 g/m^2.

The colour of the paper used shall be white. The colour of the print shall be red. The paper and the print used must meet the technical requirements of optical character recognition (OCR) equipment.

The fields and subdivisions shall be measured horizontally in units of one-tenth of an inch and *vertically in units of one-sixth of an inch.*

The forms shall measure 210 × 297 mm, subject to maximum tolerances as to length of −5 mm and +8 mm.

3(3)   The conditions under which the forms may be produced using reproduction techniques departing from the provisions of paragraph 2, first and second subparagraphs, shall be determined by the member states, which shall inform the Commission accordingly.

ART. 4   [Supply of forms]

4   The member states shall, without charge, supply parties responsible for providing information with the forms reproduced in specimen in the annex hereto.

The Commission shall contribute annually, at the end of the reporting period, to the costs which the member states have incurred in printing these forms and distributing them via official postal channels. This contribution shall be calculated in proportion to the number of forms which the parties responsible for providing information have actually transmitted to the competent national authorities during the year in question.

ART. 5   [Use of magnetic or electronic media]

5 Parties responsible for providing information who wish to use magnetic or electronic media shall give prior notice of this intention to the national authorities responsible for compiling statistics on trade between member states. Parties responsible for providing information shall, in this event, comply with any relevant provisions adopted by the Commission and with any national instructions issued by the abovementioned authorities pursuant to the said provisions, bearing in mind the technical equipment available to them. These instructions shall include in their structuring rules the Cusdec message designed and updated by the United Nations Edifact Board – Message Design Group 3, and shall comply with the provisions relating to the Instat subset of that message, which the Commission shall publish in a user manual.

ART. 6   [Use of SAD]

6(1) In derogation from article 2, parties responsible for providing information who wish to use as an information medium the statistical forms of the Single Administrative Document as provided for in Council [Regulation] 717/91 (OJ 1991 L78/1) shall comply with the instructions issued by the competent national authorities. The latter shall send a copy of these instructions to the Commission.

6(2) Member states which set up media other than those provided for in article 2 or article 5 above, or paragraph 1 of this article, shall inform the Commission accordingly in advance. They shall send the Commission an example of such media and/or provide details as to their use.

ART. 7   [Entry into force]

7 This regulation shall enter into force on the seventh day following that of its publication in the *Official Journal of the European Communities.*

It shall apply from the date provided for in article 35, second indent, of the basic regulation.

This regulation shall be binding in its entirety and directly applicable in all member states.

Note – The regulation was published in the Official Journal on 12 December 1992.
The date provided for in Regulation 3330/91, art. 35, second indent, is 1 January 1993.

ANNEX

Form N – Dispatch
Form R – Dispatch
Form S – Dispatch
Form N – Arrival
Form R – Arrival
Form S – Arrival

[Forms not reproduced here.]

EXPLANATORY NOTES

To the Intrastat forms referred to in article 2 of Commission Regulation 3590/92

(OJ 1992 C349/1)

A – GENERAL

Purpose

The Intrastat forms (see Annex) are used by parties responsible for providing information to make statistical declarations on their intra-Community trade in goods to the competent national authorities. The contents of these declarations are used exclusively for statistical purposes.

Party responsible for providing information

Any natural or legal person registered for VAT in the member state of dispatch or arrival who

–   has concluded the contract, with the exception of transport contracts, giving rise to the dispatch or delivery of the goods, or, failing this,

–   dispatches or provides for the dispatch of the goods, or takes possession or provides for possession to be taken of the goods, or, failing this,

–   is in possession of the goods which are the subject of the dispatch or delivery,

is obliged to submit statistical declarations, within the limits laid down by Community law, on the intra-Community trade in goods involved.

In practice, parties responsible for providing information comprise persons liable to account for VAT, legal persons not liable to account for VAT and persons liable to account for VAT engaged solely in transactions not entitling them to any deduction, in so far as (for the purposes of intra-Community trade in goods) they are required, in the member state of dispatch, the member state of arrival or both, to submit tax returns pursuant to article 28 of the amended version of the sixth VAT directive.

Exemptions

Private individuals are exempt from the obligation to provide information, as are those parties responsible for providing information who are not required to make periodic tax returns. Parties responsible for providing information whose intra-Community trade in goods does not exceed the statistical assimilation thresholds laid down by the member states are also exempt from the obligation to submit statistical declarations.

Data pertaining to the goods in the list of exclusions set out in Annex III of Commission Regulation 3046/92 (see below under "legal bases") need not be declared.

Box of application

The Intrastat forms can be used for all trade in goods between member states, except in the case of:

–   intra-Community trade in non-Community goods (Single Administrative Document),

–   Community goods circulating between parts of the Community's statistical territory of which at least one lies outside the Community's territory within the meaning of the amended version of the sixth VAT directive, e.g. goods dispatched in France with the island of Jersey as their destination (Single Administrative Document),

–   direct transit or transit interrupted for reasons of transport. In the following cases of transit, however, a statistical declaration is required for the purposes of statistics on trade between member states:

(a)   Community goods which are moved in transit through a member state which they entered as non-Community goods and in which they were released by the customs authorities into free circulation. A declaration for the purposes of statistics on trade between member states must be submitted for such goods when they are (re)dispatched from this member state;

(b)   Community goods which are moved in transit through a member state which, after completion of the appropriate export formalities, they leave for a destination outside the statistical territory of the Community. A declaration for the purposes of statistics on trade between member states must be submitted for such goods when they enter this member state.

The Intrastat forms should not be used in member states where statistical declarations are made in association with the monthly VAT return.

Reference period

The reference period is the calendar month during which value added tax has become due for the intra-Community transactions to be recorded. The member states may adapt this definition of the reference month to the particular tax rules applicable.

Periodic transmission

Parties responsible for providing information may submit data for the calendar month in question either in a single declaration or in several partial declarations.

Transmission deadline

In the case of a single monthly declaration, the deadline for submitting the Intrastat forms is between the fifth and tenth working day following the end of the reference period. Where partial declarations are made, the abovementioned deadline applies to the last partial declaration for the reference period. The competent national authorities may require that the frequency and deadlines for the other partial declarations be agreed with them.

Data collection office

The Intrastat forms must be returned to the central, regional or local collection offices designated by the member states.

Legal bases

Council Regulation 3330/91 of 7 November 1991 on the statistics relating to the trading of goods between member states (OJ 1991 L316/1),

Commission Regulation 2256/92 of 31 July 1992 on the statistical thresholds for statistics on trade between member states (OJ 1992 L219/40),

Commission Regulation 3046/92 of 22 October 1992, laying down provisions implementing and amending Council Regulation 3330/91 on the statistics relating to the trading of goods between member states (OJ 1992 L307/27),

Commission Regulation 3590/92 of 11 December 1992 concerning the statistical information media for statistics on trade between member states (OJ 1992 L364/32).

B – USE AND COMPOSITION OF THE FORMS

Use of the forms

The forms come in three versions for dispatch on the one hand and three versions for arrival on the other:

– *Intrastat forms N*

These are the standard versions, to be used by parties responsible for providing information who do not qualify for a simplified procedure or other simplifications resulting from the statistical thresholds.

– *Intrastat forms R*

These forms may be used by parties responsible for providing information whom the competent national authorities have exempted from giving a description of the goods.

– *Intrastat forms S*

These forms may be used, in member states which make use of simplification thresholds, by parties responsible for providing information whose intra-Community transactions do not exceed the values laid down for these thresholds. These parties may also use forms Intrastat N or Intrastat R, in which case they must cross out the boxes which they are not required to complete.

Composition

The Intrastat forms consist of a single sheet, which of the forms: is to be returned to the collection office. The circumstances under which the forms may be reproduced by procedures other than that used to produce the original form are to be specified by the member states. The competent national authorities may require parties responsible for providing information to retain a copy of their declarations.

C – SUPPLY AND SAFEKEEPING OF THE FORMS

Supply of the Intrastat forms

The Intrastat forms will be made available free of charge to parties responsible for providing information.

Safekeeping

Where copies of declarations are to be kept, parties responsible for providing information should comply with the instructions of the competent national authorities.

D – OTHER STATISTICAL INFORMATION MEDIA

Other forms

Where the member states provide for national forms in addition to the Intrastat forms, parties responsible for providing information may choose between the Community and national forms in making their statistical declarations. They may also transmit their data using the statistical forms of the Single Administrative Document, but must comply with national instructions in this regard.

Magnetic media/remote transmission

Parties responsible for providing information who wish to use electronic means of data collection and transmission should contact the competent national authorities and comply with the relevant stipulations.

E – DATA REQUIRED

Intrastat forms N and R

Boxes to be completed *on dispatch*: 1, 2, 3*, 4 if appropriate, 5, 6 (Form N only), 7, 8a, 8b*, 9 (first subdivision) if appropriate, 9 (second subdivision)*, 10 (first subdivision), 10 (second subdivision)*, 11, 12*, 13, 15*, 16, 17, 18, 19 if no waiver granted, 20*.

Boxes to be completed *on arrival*: 1, 2, 3*, 4 if appropriate, 5, 6 (Form N only), 7, 8a, 8b*, 9 (first subdivision) if appropriate, 9 (second subdivision)*, 10 (first subdivision), 10 (second subdivision)*, 11, 12*, 13, 14*, 15*, 16, 17, 18, 19 if no waiver granted, 20*.

Intrastat forms S

Boxes to be completed *on dispatch*: 1, 2, 3*, 4 if appropriate, 5, 6, 7, 8, 9, 10 if no waiver granted, 11*.

Boxes to be completed *on arrival*: 1, 2, 3*, 4 if appropriate, 5, 6, 7, 8, 9, 10 if no waiver granted, 11*.

An asterisk (*) indicates that the box is to be completed if so required by the member state in question.

F – COMPLETION OF THE FORMS

Language

The Intrastat forms must be completed in an official Community language approved by the competent authorities in the member state for which the declaration is intended.

Means of completion

The Intrastat forms should be completed using a typewriter or other mechanical or comparable equipment.

If, for example, a typewriter or printer is used, the forms must be completed in such a way that the first letter entered appears in the small positioning box in the top left-hand corner of the forms. Where provided for by the member state in question, the forms may also be completed by hand, although care should be taken to write legibly.

Combined entries

Data relating to several intra-Community transactions may be combined in a single item, in so far as the data to be entered in the individual boxes are identical. This condition does not apply to the data for boxes 6 (in so far as the commodity code in box 13 is the same), 16, 17, 18 and 19 of form N, boxes 16, 17, 18 and 19 of form R or boxes 9 and 10 of form S.

Corrections

Corrections must be made in such a way that incorrect data are crossed out and, where appropriate, the correct data added. Where the competent national authorities use optical character readers, a new form should be used whenever corrections would otherwise impair the machine-readability of the data.

Use of more than one form

If a declaration or partial declaration requires more items than are present on an Intrastat form, additional forms should be used. In this case the individual items should be given continuous serial numbers (box 7 on Intrastat form N and R, box 6 on form S).

G – NOTES ON INDIVIDUAL BOXES

Information on the Community codes to be used can be found under section H of these explanatory notes.

G.1. Intrastat forms N and R

G.1.1. DISPATCH

Box 1 – Party responsible for providing information/number

Enter the surname and first name (or registered name) of the party responsible for providing information, together with the full address. The identification number allocated to the party responsible for providing information by the competent tax authority should also be stated, unless the competent statistical authorities require – and state their reasons for requiring – the use of a different number.

Box 2 – Period

Enter the reference period.

First subdivision

Enter the month in two digits (e.g. 01, 02, 03, . . . 10, 11, 12).

Second subdivision

Enter the last two digits of the year (e.g. 93, 94, 95, 96).

Box 3

On the last declaration form, mark this box with a cross if required to do so by national instructions.

Box 4 – Declaring third party/number

This box must be completed if the party responsible for providing information has instructed a third party to submit the statistical declaration. Enter the surname and first name (or registered name) of the declaring third party, together with the full address. The identification number allocated to the declaring third party by the competent tax authority should also be stated, unless the competent statistical authorities require – and state their reasons for requiring – the use of a different number.

Box 5

Name and address of the data-collection office designated by the competent national authorities.

Box 6 – Description of goods

Intrastat form N only: Enter the usual trade name of the goods, which must be sufficiently precise to allow them to be ascribed to the appropriate subdivision at the most detailed level of the combined nomenclature. See also the notes on boxes 9 and 10.

Box 7 – Item number

Enter the serial number. If more than one form is required for the declaration or partial declaration, the numbering must be continued unbroken on the second and subsequent forms.

Box 8a – Member state of destination

Enter the code number of the member state of destination using the appropriate Community code. *The member state of destination is the last country to which it is known, at the time of dispatch, that the goods are to be dispatched.*

Box 8b – Region of origin

This box need only be completed if so required by national instructions. Enter the code number of the region of origin using the appropriate national code.

Box 9 – Delivery terms

First subdivision

This subdivision must be completed, in compliance with national instructions, in member states which do not require a statement of the statistical value (box 19). In member states which do require such a statement, it need only be completed if so required by national instructions. The Community code must be used.

Second subdivision

This subdivision need only be completed if so required by national instructions. The Community code must be used.

Intrastat form N only: Additional information required by the member states on the place of delivery or the delivery terms but not included in the list of Incoterms should be entered in box 6.

Box 10 – Nature of the transaction

First subdivision

Enter the appropriate Community code from column A of the table entitled "Nature of the transaction".

Second subdivision

This subdivision need only be completed if so required by national instructions. Enter the Community code from column B of the table entitled "Nature of the transaction".

Intrastat form N only: Additional information required by the member states should be entered in box 6.

Box 11 – Presumed mode of transport

Enter the code number of the presumed mode of transport using the appropriate Community code. The presumed mode of transport is determined by the active means of transport with which the goods are thought to have left the statistical territory of the member state of dispatch.

Box 12 – Port or airport of loading

This box need only be completed if so required by national instructions. Enter the code number of the port or airport of loading using the appropriate national code.

Box 13 – Commodity code

Enter the eight-digit code of the appropriate subdivision in the version of the combined nomenclature in force at the time. For one or more product groups, the member states may provide for additional national subdivisions, provided the party responsible for providing information can choose to supply the information in accordance either with the combined nomenclature or with any such additional subdivisions.

Box 14 – Country of origin

This box need only be completed if so required by national instructions. However, the information requested can only be required within the limits of Community law. Enter the code number of the country of origin using the appropriate Community code.

Box 15 – Statistical procedure

This box need only be completed if so required by national instructions. Enter the code of the statistical procedure using the appropriate national code.

Box 16 – Net mass

Enter the mass of the goods, net of all packaging, for each item (box 7).

Box 17 – Supplementary units

Enter for each item (box 7) the quantity of the goods in supplementary units (m, m2, 1, units, etc.), in so far as the combined nomenclature provides for a supplementary unit of measurement for the goods in question.

Box 18 – Invoiced amount

Enter in box 18 of the first item (box 7) on the form the invoiced amount, exclusive of VAT, for all the goods declared, i.e. for all items in the statistical declaration. The remaining boxes 18 should not be filled in. If two or more forms are used for a declaration, the invoiced amount should be stated in box 18 of the first item on the first form only.

Parties responsible for providing information may, if they prefer, state the invoiced amount by item.

The member states may require the invoice amount to be stated by item under the following circumstances:

-     if they do not require a statement of the statistical value,
-     if they provide technical reasons for requiring both the statistical value and the invoiced amount to be stated by item.

The invoiced amount may or may not include additional costs such as transport and insurance, depending on circumstances.

The invoiced amount must be stated in the currency of the member state to which the statistical declaration is to be returned.

If the goods have not been invoiced, the amount stated should be that which would presumably have been agreed between a mutually independent seller and buyer under conditions of free competition.

In the case of transactions involving processing under contract, the invoiced amount is the amount relating solely to the processing, including additional costs but excluding VAT. This amount must only be stated for dispatches after processing has been completed. If, however, no statement of the statistical value is required, the invoiced amount must also be stated for dispatches *with* a view to processing.

In such cases the invoiced amount is calculated via the method used where goods have been invoiced.

Box 19 – Statistical value

Enter the statistical value of the goods for each item (box 7). If, however, the invoiced amount (box 18) must be stated by item, box 19 need only be completed if so required by national instructions.

The statistical value is established, on dispatch, on the basis of the taxable amount to be determined for tax purposes (amended version of the sixth VAT directive) minus, however, any taxes deductible because of the dispatch; it shall, on the other hand, include transport and insurance costs relating to that part of the journey which takes place on the statistical territory of the member state of dispatch.

It should be noted that, with the exception of VAT itself, taxes, duties, levies and dues, etc. are included in the taxable amount and must therefore also be included in the statistical value.

The statistical value must be declared in accordance with the rules described above, even in cases where the taxable amount does not have to be determined for tax purposes.

In the case of goods derived from processing, the statistical value is established, on dispatch, as if the goods had been wholly manufactured in the member state of processing.

Box 20 – Place/date/signature

This box need only be completed if so required by the competent national authorities. The party responsible for providing information or the declaring third party should place his signature in this box and state his name and the place and date.

G.1.2.   ARRIVAL

Box 1 – Party responsible for information/number

Enter the surname and first name (or registered name) of the party responsible for providing information, together with the full address.

The identification number allocated to the party responsible for providing information by the competent tax authority should also be stated, unless the competent statistical authorities require – and state their reasons for requiring – the use of a different number.

Box 2 – Period

Enter the reference period.

First subdivision

Enter the month in two digits (e.g. 01, 02, 03, ... 10, 11, 12).

Second subdivision

Enter the last two digits of the year (e.g. 93, 94, 95, 96).

Box 3

On the last declaration form, mark this box with a cross if required to do so by national instructions.

Box 4 – Declaring third party/number

This box must be completed if the party responsible for providing information has instructed a third party to submit the statistical declaration. Enter the surname and first name (or registered name) of the declaring third party, together with the full address. The identification number allocated to the declaring third party by the competent tax authority should also be stated, unless the competent statistical authorities require – and state their reasons for requiring – the use of a different number.

Box 5

Name and address of the data-collection office designated by the competent national authorities.

Box 6 – Description of goods

Intrastat form N only: Enter the usual trade name of the goods, which must be sufficiently precise to allow them to be ascribed to the appropriate subdivision at the most detailed level of the combined nomenclature. See also the notes on boxes 9 and 10.

Box 7 – Item number

Enter the serial number. If more than one form is required for the declaration or partial declaration, the numbering must be continued unbroken on the second and subsequent forms.

Box 8a – Member state of consignment

Enter the code number of the member state of consignment using the appropriate Community code. The member state of consignment is in fact the member state in which the goods were assigned the destination of the member state of arrival.

If the member state of consignment is not known, enter the member state of dispatch, which is that from which the goods were routed to another member state. In the case of Community goods, the member state of dispatch is usually also the member state of consignment. If the member state of dispatch is not known, enter the member state of purchase, i.e. the member state of residence of the party (the seller) with whom the trade contract (not the transport contract) leading to the delivery of the goods in the member state of arrival was concluded.

Box 8b – Region of destination

This box need only be completed if so required by national instructions. Enter the code number of the region of destination using the appropriate national code.

Box 9 – Delivery terms

First subdivision

This subdivision must be completed, in compliance with national instructions, in member states which do not require a statement of the statistical value (box 19). In member states which do require such a statement, it need only be completed if so required by national instructions. The Community code must be used.

Second subdivision

This subdivision need only be completed if so required by national instructions. The Community code must be used.

Intrastat form N only: Additional information required by the member states on the place of delivery or the delivery terms but not included in the list of Incoterms should be entered in box 6.

Box 10 – Nature of the transaction

First subdivision

Enter the appropriate Community code from column A of the table entitled "Nature of the transaction".

Second subdivision

This subdivision need only be completed if so required by national instructions. Enter the Community code from column B of the table entitled "Nature of transaction".

Intrastat form N only: Additional information required by the member states should be entered in box 6.

Box 11 – Presumed mode of transport

Enter the code number of the presumed mode of transport using the appropriate Community code. The presumed mode of transport is determined by the active means of transport with which the goods are thought to have entered the statistical territory of the member state of arrival.

Box 12 – Port or airport of unloading

This box need only be completed if so required by national instructions. Enter the code number of the port or airport of unloading using the appropriate national code.

Box 13 – Community code

Enter the eight-digit code of the appropriate subdivision in the version of the combined nomenclature in force at the time. For one or more product groups, the member states may provide for additional national subdivisions, provided the party responsible for providing information can choose to supply the information in accordance either with the combined nomenclature or with any such additional subdivisions.

Box 14 – Country of origin

This box need only be completed if so required by national instructions. However, the information requested can only be required within the limits of Community law. Enter the code number of the country of origin using the appropriate Community code.

Box 15 – Statistical procedure

This box need only be completed if so required by national instructions. Enter the code number of the statistical procedure using the appropriate national code.

Box 16 – Net mass

Enter the mass of the goods, net of all packaging, for each item (box 7).

Box 17 – Supplementary units

Enter for each item (box 7) the quantity of the goods in supplementary units (m, m², 1, units, etc.), in so far as the combined nomenclature provides for a supplementary unit of measurement for the goods in question.

Box 18 – Invoiced amount

Enter in box 18 of the first item (box 7) on the form the invoiced amount, exclusive of VAT, for all the goods declared, i.e. for all items in the statistical declaration. The remaining boxes 18 should not be filled in. If two or more forms are used for a declaration, the invoiced amount should be stated in box 18 of the first item on the first form only.

Parties responsible for providing information may, if they prefer, state the invoiced amount by item.

The member states may require the invoiced amount to be stated by item

–   if they do not require a statement of the statistical value,
–   if they provide technical reasons for requiring both the statistical value and the invoiced amount to be stated by item.

The invoiced amount may or may not include additional costs such as transport and insurance, depending on circumstances.

The invoiced amount must be stated in the currency of the member state to which the statistical declaration is to be returned.

If the goods have not been invoiced, the amount stated should be that which would presumably have been agreed between a mutually independent seller and buyer under conditions of free competition.

In the case of transactions involving processing under contract, the invoiced amount is the amount relating solely to the processing, including additional costs but excluding VAT. This amount must only be stated for arrivals *after* the processing has been completed. If, however, no statement of the statistical value is required, the invoiced amount must also be stated for arrivals *with a view* to processing. In such cases the invoiced amount is calculated via the method used where goods have not been invoiced.

Box 19 – Statistical value

Enter the statistical value of the goods for each item (box 7). If, however, the invoiced amount (box 18) must be indicated by item, box 19 need only be completed if so required by national instructions.

The statistical value is established, on arrival, on the basis of the taxable amount to be determined for tax purposes (amended version of the sixth VAT directive), minus however taxes due because of the release for home use and transport and insurance costs relating to that part of the journey which takes place in the statistical territory of the member state of arrival.

It should be noted that, with the exception of VAT itself, taxes, duties, levies and dues, etc. are included in the taxable amount and must therefore also be included in the statistical value.

The statistical value must be declared in accordance with the rules described above, even in cases where the taxable amount does not have to be determined for tax purposes.

In the case of goods derived from processing, the statistical value is established, on arrival, as if the goods had been wholly manufactured in the member state of processing.

Box 20 – Place/date/signature

This box need only be completed if so required by the competent national authorities. The party responsible for providing information or the declaring third party should place his signature in this box and state his name and the place and date.

G.2.   Intrastat Forms

G.2.1.   DISPATCH

Box 1 – Party responsible for providing information/number

Enter the surname and first name (or registered name) of the party responsible for providing information, together with the full address. The identification number allocated to the party responsible for providing information by the competent tax authority should also be stated, unless the competent statistical authorities require – and state their reasons for requiring – the use of a different number.

Box 2 – Period

Enter the reference period.

First subdivision

Enter the month in two digits (e.g. 01, 02, 03, ... 10, 11, 12).

Second subdivision

Enter the last two digits of the year (e.g. 93, 94, 95, 96).

Box 3

On the last declaration form, mark this box with a cross if required to do so by national instructions.

Box 4 – Declaring third party/number

This box must be completed if the party responsible for providing information has instructed a third party to submit the statistical declaration. Enter the surname and first name (or registered name) of the declaring third party, together with the full address. The identification number allocated to the declaring third party by the competent tax authority should also be stated, unless the competent statistical authorities require – and state their reasons for requiring – the use of a different number.

Box 5

Name and address of the data-collection office designated by the competent national authorities.

Box 6 – Item number

Enter the serial number. If more than one form is required for the declaration or partial declaration, the numbering must be continued unbroken on the second and subsequent forms.

Box 7 – Member state of destination

Enter the code number of the member state of destination using the appropriate Community code. The member state of destination is the *last* country to which it is known, at the time of dispatch, that the goods are to be dispatched.

Box 8 – Commodity code

Enter the eight-digit code of the appropriate subdivision in the version of the combined nomenclature in force at the time. For one or more product groups, the member states may provide for additional national subdivisions, provided the party responsible for providing information can choose to supply the information in accordance either with the combined nomenclature or with any such additional subdivisions.

Box 9 – Invoiced amount

Enter in box 9 of the first item (box 6) on the form the invoiced amount, exclusive of VAT, for all the goods declared, i.e. for all items in the statistical declaration. The remaining boxes 9 should not be filled in. If two or more forms are used for a declaration, the invoiced amount should be stated in box 9 on the first form only.

Parties responsible for providing information may, if they prefer, state the invoiced amount by item.

The member states may require the invoiced amount to be stated by item under the following circumstances:

–   if they do not require a statement of the statistical value,
–   if they provide technical reasons for requiring both the statistical value and the invoiced amount to be stated by item.

The invoiced amount may or may not include additional costs such as transport and insurance, depending on circumstances.

The invoiced amount must be stated in the currency of the member state to which the statistical declaration is to be returned.

If the goods have not been invoiced, the amount stated should be that which would presumably have been agreed between a mutually independent seller and buyer under conditions of free competition.

In the case of transactions involving processing under contract, the invoiced amount is the amount relating solely to the processing, including additional costs but excluding VAT. This amount must only be stated for dispatches *after* processing has been completed. If, however, no statement of the statistical value is required, the invoiced amount must also be stated for dispatches *with a view to* processing. In such cases the invoiced amount is calculated via the method used where goods have not been invoiced.

Box 10 – Statistical value

Enter the statistical value of the goods for each item (box 6). If, however, the invoiced amount (box 9) must be stated by item, box 10 need only be completed if so required by national instructions.

The statistical value is established, on dispatch, on the basis of the taxable amount to be determined for tax purposes (amended version of the sixth VAT directive) minus, however, any taxes deductible because of the dispatch; it shall, on the other hand, include transport and insurance costs relating to that part of the journey which takes place on the statistical territory of the member state of dispatch.

It should be noted that, with the exception of VAT itself, taxes, duties, levies and dues, etc. are included in the taxable amount and must therefore also be included in the statistical value.

The statistical value must be declared in accordance with the rules described above, even in cases where the taxable amount does not have to be determined for tax purposes.

In the case of goods derived from processing, the statistical value is established, on dispatch, as if the goods had been wholly manufactured in the member state of processing.

Box 11 – Place/date/signature

This box need only be completed if so required by national instructions. The party responsible for providing information or the declaring third party should place his signature in this box and state his name and the place and date.

G.2.2.   ARRIVAL

Box 1 – Party responsible for information/number

Enter the surname and first name (or registered name) of the party responsible for providing information, together with the full address. The identification number allocated to the party responsible for providing information by the competent tax authority should also be stated, unless the competent statistical authorities require – and state their reasons for requiring – the use of a different number.

Box 2 – Period

Enter the reference period.

First subdivision

Enter the month in two digits (e.g. 01, 02, 03, . . . 10, 11, 12).

Second subdivision

Enter the last two digits of the year (e.g. 93, 94, 95, 96).

Box 3

On the last declaration form, mark this box with a cross if required to do so by national instructions.

Box 4 – Declaring third party/number

This box must be completed if the party responsible for providing information has instructed a third party to submit the statistical declaration. Enter the surname and first name (or registered name) of the declaring third party, together with the full address. The identification number allocated to the declaring third party by the competent tax authority should also be stated, unless the competent statistical authorities require – and state their reasons for requiring – the use of a different number.

Box 5

Name and address of the data collection office designated by the competent national authorities.

Box 6

Enter the serial number. If more than one form item number is required for the declaration or partial declaration, the numbering must be continued unbroken on the second and subsequent forms.

Box 7 – Member state of consignment

Enter the code number of the member state of consignment using the appropriate Community code. The member state of consignment is in fact the member state in which the goods were assigned the destination of the member state of arrival. If the member state of consignment is not known, enter the member state of dispatch, which is that from which the goods were routed to another member state. In the case of Community goods, the member state of dispatch is usually also the member state of consignment. If the member state of dispatch is not known, enter the member state of purchase, i.e. the member state of residence of the party (the seller) with whom the trade contract (not the transport contract) leading to the delivery of the goods in the member state of arrival was concluded.

Box 8 – Commodity code

Enter the eight-digit code of the appropriate subdivision in the version of the combined nomenclature in force at the time. For one or more product groups, the member states may provide for additional national subdivisions, provided the party responsible for providing information can choose to supply the information in accordance either with the combined nomenclature or with any such additional subdivisions.

Box 9 – Invoiced amount

Enter in box 9 of the first item (box 6) on the form the invoiced amount, exclusive of VAT, for all the goods declared, i.e. for all items in the statistical declaration. The remaining boxes 9 should not be filled in. If two or more forms are used for a declaration, the invoiced amount should be stated in box 9 on the first form only.

Parties responsible for providing information may, if they prefer, state the invoiced amount by item.

The member states may require the invoiced amount to be stated by item under the following circumstances:

– if they do not require a statement of the statistical value,
– if they provide technical reasons for requiring both the statistical value and the invoiced amount to be stated by item.

The invoiced amount may or may not include additional costs such as transport and insurance, depending on circumstances.

The invoiced amount must be stated in the currency of the member state to which the statistical declaration is to be returned.

If the goods have not been invoiced, the amount stated should be that which would presumably have been agreed between a mutually independent seller and buyer under conditions of free competition.

In the case of transactions involving processing under contract, the invoiced amount is the amount relating solely to the processing, including additional costs but excluding VAT. This amount must only be stated for arrivals *after* processing has been completed. If, however, no statement of the statistical value is required, the invoiced amount must also be stated for arrivals *with a view* to processing. In such cases the invoiced amount is calculated via the method used where goods have not been invoiced.

Box 10 – Statistical value

Enter the statistical value of the goods for each item (box 6). If, however, the invoiced amount (box 9) must be stated by item, box 10 need only be completed if so required by national instructions.

The statistical value is established, on arrival, on the basis of the taxable amount to be determined for tax purposes (amended version of the sixth VAT directive), minus however taxes due because of the release for home use and transport and insurance costs relating to that part of the journey which takes place in the statistical territory of the member state of arrival.

It should be noted that, with the exception of VAT itself, taxes, duties, levies and dues, etc. are included in the taxable amount and must therefore also be included in the statistical value.

The statistical value must be declared in accordance with the rules described above, even in cases where the taxable amount does not have to be determined for tax purposes.

In the case of goods derived from processing, the statistical value is established, on arrival, as if the goods had been wholly manufactured in the member state of processing.

Box 11 – Place/date/signature

This box need only be completed if so required by national instructions. The party responsible for providing information or the declaring third party should place his signature in this box and state his name and the place and date.

H.   CODES TO BE USED

H.1.   INTRASTAT FORMS N AND R

Box 8a – Dispatch: Member state of destination; Arrival: Member state of consignment

France:	FR	or	001
Belgium and Luxembourg:	BL	or	002
Netherlands:	NL	or	003
Germany:	DE	or	004
Italy:	IT	or	005
United Kingdom:	GB	or	006
Ireland:	IE	or	007
Denmark:	DK	or	008
Greece:	GR	or	009
Portugal:	PT	or	010
Spain:	ES	or	011

The member states will decide whether the alphabetical or the numerical code is to be used.

Box 8b – Dispatch: Region of origin; Arrival: Region of destination

The code, which may contain a maximum of two digits, will be determined by the member states requiring the information.

Box 9 – Delivery terms

First subdivision

Incoterm code	Meaning Incoterm ICC/ECE Geneva	Place to be indicated[1]
EXW	ex-works	location of works
FCA	franco carrier	. . . agreed place
FAS	free alongside ship	agreed port of loading
FOB	free on board	agreed port of loading
CFR	cost and freight (C & F)	agreed port of destination
CIF	cost, insurance, freight	agreed port of destination
CPT	carriage paid to	agreed place of destination
CIP	carriage and insurance paid to	agreed place of destination
DAF	delivered at frontier	agreed place of delivery at frontier
DES	delivered ex-ship	agreed port of destination
DEQ	delivered ex-quay	after customs clearance, agreed port
DDU	delivered duty unpaid	agreed place of destination in importing country
DDP	delivered duty paid	agreed place of delivery in importing country
XXX	delivery terms other than the above	precise statement of terms specified in the contract[1]

[1] Provide details in box 6 if necessary (form Intrastat N only).

Second subdivision

1.   place located in the territory of the member state concerned;
2.   place located in another member state,
3.   other (place located outside the Community).

Box 10 – Nature of the transaction

Column A	Column B
1. Transactions involving actual or intended transfer of ownership against compensation (financial or otherwise) (except the transactions listed under 2, 7, 8)[a][b][c]	1. Outright/purchase/sale[b] 2. Supply for sale on approval or after trial, for consignment or with the intermediation of a commission agent 3. Barter trade (compensation in kind) 4. Personal purchases by travellers 5. Financial leasing[c]
2. Return of goods after registration of the original transaction under code 1[d]; replacement of goods free of charge[d]	1. Return of goods 2. Replacement for returned goods 3. Replacement (e.g. under warranty) for goods not being returned
3. Transactions (not temporary) involving transfer of ownership but without compensation (financial or other)	1. Goods delivered under aid programmes operated or financed partly or wholly 2. Other general government-aid deliveries 3. Other aid deliveries (individuals, non-governmental organisations)
4. Operations with a view to processing under contract[e] or repair[f] (except those recorded under 7)	1. Processing under contract 2. Repair and maintenance against payment 3. Repair and maintenance free of charge
5. Operations following processing under contract[e] or repair[f] (except those recorded under 7)	1. Processing under contract 2. Repair and maintenance against payment 3. Repair and maintenance free of charge

Column A	Column B
6. Transactions not involving transfer of ownership, e.g. hire, loan, operational leasing[g] and other temporary uses[h] except processing under contract or repair (delivery or return)	1. Hire, loan, operational leasing 2. Other goods for temporary uses
7. Operations under joint defence projects or other joint intergovernmental production programs (e.g. Airbus)	
8. Supply of building material and equipment for works that are part of a general construction or engineering contract[i]	
9. Other transactions	

[a]　This item covers most dispatches and arrivals, i.e. transactions in respect of which:
– ownership is transferred from resident to non-resident, and
– payment or compensation in kind is or will be made.
It should be noted that this also applies to goods sent between related enterprises or from/to central distribution depots, even if no immediate payments is made.

[b]　Including spare parts and other replacements made against payment.

[c]　Including financial leasing: the lease instalments are calculated in such a way as to cover all or virtually all of the value of the goods. The risks and rewards of ownership are transferred to the lessee. At the end of the contract the lessee becomes the legal owner of the goods.

[d]　Return and replacement dispatches of goods originally recorded under items 3 to 9 of column A should be registered under the corresponding items.

[e]　Processing operations (whether or not under customs supervision) should be recorded under items 4 and 5 of column A. Processing activities on processor's own account are not covered by this item, they should be registered under item 1 of column A.

[f]　Repair entails the restoration of goods to their original function; this may involve some rebuilding or enhancements.

[g]　Operational leasing: leasing contracts other than financial leasing (see note (c)).

[h]　This item covers goods that are exported/imported with the intention of subsequent re-import/re-export without any change of ownership taking place.

[i]　The transactions recorded under item 8 of column A involve goods which are not separately invoiced, but for which a single invoice is made covering the total value of the works. Where this is not the case, the transactions should be recorded under item 1.

Box 11 – Mode of transport

Code	Title
1	Transport by sea
2	Transport by rail
3	Transport by road
4	Transport by air
5	Consignments by post
7	Fixed transport installations
8	Transport by inland waterway
9	Own propulsion

Box 12 – Dispatch: Port or airport of loading; Arrival: Port or airport of unloading

The code is to be determined by the member states requiring this information.

Box 13 – Commodity code

Commodity code as contained in the current version of the combined nomenclature.

Box 14 – Arrival: Country of origin

Community code as contained in the current version of the country nomenclature for the external trade statistics of the Community and trade between member states.

Box 15 – Statistical procedure

The code is to be determined by the member states requiring this information.

H.2.　INTRASTAT FORM S

Box 7 – Dispatch: Member state of destination; Arrival: Member state of consignment

France:	FR	or	001
Belgium and Luxembourg:	BL	or	002
Netherlands:	NL	or	003
Germany:	DE	or	004
Italy:	IT	or	005
United Kingdom:	GB	or	006
Ireland:	IE	or	007
Denmark:	DK	or	008
Greece:	GR	or	009
Portugal:	PT	or	010
Spain:	ES	or	011

The member states will determine whether the alphabetical or the numerical code is to be used.

Box 8 – Commodity code

Commodity code as contained in the current version of the combined nomenclature.

ANNEX

Form N – Dispatch
Form R – Dispatch
Form S – Dispatch
Form N – Arrival
Form R – Arrival
Form S – Arrival

[Forms not reproduced here.]

REGULATION 2454/93

Laying down provisions for the implementation of Regulation 2913/92 establishing the Community Customs Code

(2 July 1993, OJ 1993 L253/1)

CONTENTS

CHAPTER

PART I: GENERAL IMPLEMENTING PROVISIONS

Title V – Customs Value

ANNEXES

ANNEX

PART I: GENERAL IMPLEMENTING PROVISIONS
Title V – Customs Value
CHAPTER 1 – GENERAL PROVISIONS

ART. 141   [Application]

141   In applying the provisions of Articles 28 to 36 of the Code and those of this title, member states shall comply with the provisions set out in Annex 23.

The provisions as set out in the first column of Annex 23 shall be applied in the light of the interpretative note appearing in the second column.

If it is necessary to make reference to generally accepted accounting principles in determining the customs value, the provisions of Annex 24 shall apply.

Note – The "Code" is Regulation 2913/92 (OJ 1992 L302/1).

ART. 142   [Meaning]

142(1)   For the purposes of this title:

(a)   **"the Agreement"** means the Agreement on implementation of Article VII of the General Agreement on Tariffs and Trade concluded in the framework of the multilateral trade negotiations of 1973 to 1979 and referred to in the first indent of article 31(1) of the Code;

(b)   **"produced goods"** includes goods grown, manufactured and mined;

(c)   **"identical goods"** means goods produced in the same country which are the same in all respects, including physical characteristics, quality and reputation. Minor differences in appearance shall not preclude goods otherwise conforming to the definition from being regarded as identical;

(d)   **"similar goods"** means goods produced in the same country which, although not alike in all respects, have like characteristics and like component materials which enable them to perform the same functions and to be commercially interchangeable; the quality of the goods, their reputation and the existence of a trademark are among the factors to be considered in determining whether goods are similar;

(e)   **"goods of the same class or kind"** means goods which fall within a group or range of goods produced by a particular industry or industry sector, and includes identical or similar goods.

142(2)   **"Identical goods"** and **"similar goods"**, as the case may be, do not include goods which incorporate or reflect engineering, development, artwork, design work, and plans and sketches for which no adjustment has been made under article 32(1)(b)(iv) of the Code because such elements were undertaken in the Community.

ART. 143   ["Related"]

143(1)   For the purposes of articles 29(l)(d) and 30(2)(c) of the Code, persons shall be deemed to be **"related"** only if:

(a)   they are officers or directors of one another's businesses;

(b)   they are legally recognised partners in business;

(c)   they are employer and employee;

(d)   any person directly or indirectly owns, controls or holds 5 per cent or more of the outstanding voting stock or shares of both of them;

(e)   one of them directly or indirectly controls the other;

(f)   both of them are directly or indirectly controlled by a third person;

(g)   together they directly or indirectly control a third person; or

(h)   they are members of the same family. Persons shall be deemed to be members of the same family only if they stand in any of the following relationships to one another:
  – husband and wife,
  – *parent and child,*
  – brother and sister (whether by whole or half blood),
  – grandparent and grandchild,
  – uncle or aunt and nephew or niece,
  – parent-in-law and son-in-law or daughter-in-law,
  – brother-in-law and sister-in-law.

143(2) For the purposes of this title, persons who are associated in business with one another in that one is the sole agent, sole distributor or sole concessionaire, however described, of the other shall be deemed to be **"related"** only if they fall within the criteria of paragraph 1.

ART. 144   [Settlement price]

144(1) For the purposes of determining customs value under article 29 of the Code of goods in regard to which the price has not actually been paid at the material time for valuation for customs purposes, the price payable for settlement at the said time shall as a general rule be taken as the basis for customs value.

144(2) The Commission and the member states shall consult within the Committee concerning the application of paragraph 1.

ART. 145   [Part of a larger quantity]

145 Where goods declared for free circulation are part of a larger quantity of the same goods purchased in one transaction, the price actually paid or payable for the purposes of article 29(1) of the Code shall be that price represented by the proportion of the total price which the quantity so declared bears to the total quantity purchased.

Apportioning the price actually paid or payable shall also apply in the case of the loss of part of a consignment or when the goods being valued have been damaged before entry into free circulation.

ART. 146   [Internal tax]

146 Where the price actually paid or payable for the purposes of article 29(1) of the Code includes an amount in respect of any internal tax applicable within the country of origin or export in respect of the goods in question, the said amount shall not be incorporated in the customs value provided that it can be demonstrated to the satisfaction of the customs authorities concerned that the goods in question have been or will be relieved therefrom for the benefit of the buyer.

ART. 147   [Free circulation]

147(1) For the purposes of article 29 of the Code, the fact that the goods which are the subject of a sale are declared for free circulation shall be regarded as adequate indication that they were sold for export to the customs territory of the Community. In the case of successive sales before valuation, only the last sale, which led to the introduction of the goods into the customs territory of the Community, or a sale taking place in the customs territory of the Community before entry for free circulation of the goods shall constitute such indication.

Where a price is declared which relates to a sale taking place before the last sale on the basis of which the goods were introduced into the customs territory of the Community, it must be demonstrated to the satisfaction of the customs authorities that this sale of goods took place for export to the customs territory in question.

The provisions of articles 178 to 181A shall apply.

147(2) Where goods are used in a third country between the time of sale and the time of entry into free circulation the customs value need not be the transaction value.

147(3) The buyer need satisfy no condition other than that of being a party to the contract of sale.

History – In art. 147(1) the words from "In the case of succesive sales . . ." substituted by Regulation 1762/95, art. 2(a) with effect from 28 July 1995. The former wording was:
"This indication shall also apply in the case of successive sales before valuation; in such case each price resulting from these sales may, subject to the provisions of articles 178 to 181, be taken as a basis for valuation."
In art. 147(2) the word "However, . . .", which previously appeared at the beginning of that paragraph, deleted by Regulation 1762/95, art. 2(b), with effect from 28 July 1995.

ART. 148   [Price subject to condition etc.]

148 Where, in applying article 29(1)(b) of the Code, it is established that the sale or price of imported goods is subject to a condition or consideration the value of which can be determined with respect to the goods being valued, such value shall be regarded as an indirect payment by the buyer to the seller and part of the price actually paid or payable provided that the condition or consideration does not relate to either:

(a) an activity to which article 29(3)(b) of the Code applies; or

(b)   a factor in respect of which an addition is to be made to the price actually paid or payable under the provisions of article 32 of the Code.

ART. 149   [Meaning]

149(1)   For the purposes of article 29(3)(b) of the Code, the term **"marketing activities"** means all activities relating to advertising and promoting the sale of the goods in question and all activities relating to warranties or guarantees in respect of them.

149(2)   Such activities undertaken by the buyer shall be regarded as having been undertaken on his own account even if they are performed in pursuance of an obligation on the buyer following an agreement with the seller.

ART. 150   [Identical goods]

150(1)   In applying article 30(2)(a) of the Code (the transaction value of identical goods), the customs value shall be determined by reference to the transaction value of identical goods in a sale at the same commercial level and in substantially the same quantity as the goods being valued. Where no such sale is found, the transaction value of identical goods sold at a different commercial level and/or in different quantities, adjusted to take account of differences attributable to commercial level and/or to quantity, shall be used, provided that such adjustments can be made on the basis of demonstrated evidence which clearly establishes the reasonableness and accuracy of the adjustment, whether the adjustment leads to an increase or a decrease in the value.

150(2)   Where the costs and charges referred to in article 32(1)(e) of the Code are included in the transaction value, an adjustment shall be made to take account of significant differences in such costs and charges between the imported goods and the identical goods in question arising from differences in distances and modes of transport.

150(3)   If, in applying this article, more than one transaction value of identical goods is found, the lowest such value shall be used to determine the customs value of the imported goods.

150(4)   In applying this article, a transaction value for goods produced by a different person shall be taken into account only when no transaction value can be found under paragraph 1 for identical goods produced by the same person as the goods being valued.

150(5)   For the purposes of this article, the **"transaction value of identical imported goods"** means a customs value previously determined under article 29 of the Code, adjusted as provided for in paragraphs 1 and 2 of this article.

History – In art. 150(5), reference to para. 1(b) amended to a reference to para. 1 by corrigenda (OJ 1994 L268/32).

ART. 151   [Similar goods]

151(1)   In applying article 30(2)(b) of the Code (the transaction value of similar goods), the customs value shall be determined by reference to the transaction value of similar goods in a sale at the same commercial level and in substantially the same quantity as the goods being valued. Where no such sale is found, the transaction value of similar goods sold at a different commercial level and/or in different quantities, adjusted to take account of differences attributable to commercial level and/or to quantity, shall be used, provided that such adjustments can be made on the basis of demonstrated evidence which clearly establishes the reasonableness and accuracy of the adjustment, whether the adjustment leads to an increase or a decrease in the value.

151(2)   Where the costs and charges referred to in article 32(1)(e) of the Code are included in the transaction value, an adjustment shall be made to take account of significant differences in such costs and charges between the imported goods and the similar goods in question arising from differences in distances and modes of transport.

151(3)   If, in applying this article, more than one transaction value of similar goods is found, the lowest such value shall be used to determine the customs value for the imported goods.

151(4)   In applying this article, a transaction value for goods produced by a different person shall be taken into account only when no transaction value can be found under paragraph 1 for similar goods produced by the same person as the goods being valued.

151(5)   For the purposes of this article, the transaction value of similar imported goods means a customs value previously determined under article 29 of the Code, adjusted as provided for in paragraphs 1 and 2 of this article.

History – In art. 151(5), reference to para. 1(b) amended to a reference to para. 1 by corrigenda (OJ 1994 L268/32).

ART. 152   [Sold in condition as imported]

152(1)

(a)   If the imported goods or identical or similar imported goods are sold in the Community in the condition as imported, the customs value of imported goods, determined in accordance with article 30(2)(c) of the Code, shall be based on the unit price at which the imported goods or identical or similar imported goods are so sold in the greatest aggregate quantity, at or about the time of the importation of the goods being valued, to persons who are not related to the persons from whom they buy such goods, subject to deductions for the following:

     (i)   either the commissions usually paid or agreed to be paid or the additions usually made for profit and general expenses (including the direct and indirect costs of marketing the goods in question) in connection with sales in the Community of imported goods of the same class or kind;

     (ii)   the usual costs of transport and insurance and associated costs incurred within the Community;

     (iii)   the import duties and other charges payable in the Community by reason of the importation or sale of the goods.

(b)   If neither the imported goods nor identical nor similar imported goods are sold at or about the time of importation of the goods being valued, the customs value of imported goods determined under this article shall, subject otherwise to the provisions of paragraph 1(a), be based on the unit price at which the imported goods or identical or similar imported goods are sold in the Community in the condition as imported at the earliest date after the importation of the goods being valued but before the expiration of 90 days after such importation.

152(2)   If neither the imported goods nor identical nor similar imported goods are sold in the Community in the condition as imported, then, if the importer so requests, the customs value shall be based on the unit price at which the imported goods, after further processing, are sold in the greatest aggregate quantity to persons in the Community who are not related to the persons from whom they buy such goods, due allowance being made for the value added by such processing and the deductions provided for in paragraph 1(a).

152(3)   For the purposes of this article, the unit price at which imported goods are sold in the greatest aggregate quantity is the price at which the greatest number of units is sold in sales to persons who are not related to the persons from whom they buy such goods at the first commercial level after importation at which such sales take place.

152(4)   Any sale in the Community to a person who supplies directly or indirectly free of charge or at reduced cost for use in connection with the production and sale for export of the imported goods any of the elements specified in article 32(1)(b) of the Code should not be taken into account in establishing the unit price for the purposes of this article.

152(5)   For the purposes of paragraph 1(b), the **"earliest date"** shall be the date by which sales of the imported goods or of identical or similar imported goods are made in sufficient quantity to establish the unit price.

ART. 153   [Computed value]

153(1)   In applying article 30(2)(d) of the Code (computed value), the customs authorities may not require or compel any person not resident in the Community to produce for examination, or to allow access to, any account or other record for the purposes of determining this value. However, information supplied by the producer of the goods for purposes of determining the customs value under this article may be verified in a non-Community country by the customs authorities of a member state with the agreement of the producer and provided that such authorities give sufficient advance notice to the authorities of the country in question and the latter do not object to the investigation.

153(2)   The cost or value of materials and fabrication referred to in the first indent of article 30(2)(d) of the Code shall include the cost of elements specified in article 32(1)(a)(ii) and (iii) of the Code.

It shall also include the value, duly apportioned, of any product or service specified in article 32(1)(b) of the Code which has been supplied directly or indirectly by the buyer for use in connection with the production of the imported goods. The value of the elements specified in article 32(1)(b)(iv) of the Code which are undertaken in the Community shall be included only to the extent that such elements are charged to the producer.

153(3)   Where information other than that supplied by or on behalf of the producer is used for the purposes of determining a computed value, the customs authorities shall inform the declarant, if the latter so requests, of the source of such information, the data used and the calculations based on such data, subject to article 15 of the Code.

153(5)   The **"general expenses"** referred to in the second indent of article 30(2)(d) of the Code, cover the direct and indirect costs of producing and selling the goods for export which are not included under the first indent of article 30(2)(d) of the Code.

Note – No para. 4 appears in the version of Regulation 2454/93 as published in the Official Journal.

ART. 154   [Containers]

154   Where containers referred to in article 32(1)(a)(ii) of the Code are to be the subject of repeated importations, their cost shall, at the request of the declarant, be apportioned, as appropriate, in accordance with generally accepted accounting principles.

ART. 155   [Research etc. costs]

155   For the purposes of article 32(1)(b)(iv) of the Code, the cost of research and preliminary design sketches is not to be included in the customs value.

ART. 156   [Method other than transaction value]

156   Article 33(c) of the Code shall apply mutatis mutandis where the customs value is determined by applying a method other than the transaction value.

ART. 156a   [Authorisation of derogations]

156a(1)   The customs authorities may, at the request of the person concerned, authorise:

–   by derogation from article 32(2) of the Code, certain elements which are to be added to the price actually paid or payable, although not quantifiable at the time of incurrence of the customs debt,

–   by derogation from article 33 of the Code, certain charges which are not to be included in the customs value, in cases where the amounts relating to such elements are not shown separately at the time of incurrence of the customs debt,

to be determined on the basis of appropriate and specific criteria.

In such cases, the declared customs value is not to be considered as provisional within the meaning of the second indent of article 254.

156a(2)   The authorisation shall be granted under the following conditions:

(a)   the carrying out of the procedures provided for by article 259 would, in the circumstances, represent disproportionate administrative costs;

(b)   recourse to an application of articles 30 and 31 of the Code appears to be inappropriate in the particular circumstances;

(c)   there are valid reasons for considering that the amount of import duties to be charged in the period covered by the authorisation will not be lower than that which would be levied in the absence of an authorisation;

(d)   competitive conditions amongst operators are not distorted.

History – Art. 156a inserted by Regulation 1679/96, art. 1(1) (OJ 1996 L218/1), with effect from 4 September 1996.

CHAPTER 2 – PROVISIONS CONCERNING ROYALTIES AND LICENCE FEES

ART. 157   [Meaning]

157(1)   For the purposes of article 32(l)(c) of the Code, **"royalties"** and **"licence fees"** shall be taken to mean in particular payment for the use of rights relating:

–   to the manufacture of imported goods (in particular, patents, designs, models and manufacturing know-how), or

–   to the sale for exportation of imported goods (in particular, trade marks, registered designs), or

–   to the use or resale of imported goods (in particular, copyright, manufacturing processes inseparably embodied in the imported goods).

157(2) Without prejudice to article 32(5) of the Code, when the customs value of imported goods is determined under the provisions of article 29 of the Code, a royalty or licence fee shall be added to the price actually paid or payable only when this payment:

–   is related to the goods being valued, and
–   constitutes a condition of sale of those goods.

ART. 158   [Ingredient/component]

158(1) When the imported goods are only an ingredient or component of goods manufactured in the Community, an adjustment to the price actually paid or payable for the imported goods shall only be made when the royalty or licence fee relates to those goods.

158(2) Where goods are imported in an unassembled state or only have to undergo minor processing before resale, such as diluting or packing, this shall not prevent a royalty or licence fee from being considered related to the imported goods.

158(3) If royalties or licence fees relate partly to the imported goods and partly to other ingredients or component parts added to the goods after their importation, or to post-importation activities or services, an appropriate apportionment shall be made only on the basis of objective and quantifiable data, in accordance with the interpretative note to article 32(2) of the Code in Annex 23.

ART. 159   [Trade mark]

159 A royalty or licence fee in respect of the right to use a trade mark is only to be added to the price actually paid or payable for the imported goods where:

–   the royalty or licence fee refers to goods which are resold in the same state or which are subject only to minor processing after importation,
–   the goods are marketed under the trade mark, affixed before or after importation, for which the royalty or licence fee is paid, and
–   the buyer is not free to obtain such goods from other suppliers unrelated to the seller.

ART. 160   [Royalty etc. to third party]

160 When the buyer pays royalties or licence fees to a third party, the conditions provided for in article 157(2) shall not be considered as met unless the seller or a person related to him requires the buyer to make that payment.

ART. 161   [Royalty based on price]

161 Where the method of calculation of the amount of a royalty or licence fee derives from the price of the imported goods, it may be assumed in the absence of evidence to the contrary that the payment of that royalty or licence fee is related to the goods to be valued.

However, where the amount of a royalty or licence fee is calculated regardless of the price of the imported goods, the payment of that royalty or licence fee may nevertheless be related to the goods to be valued.

ART. 162   [Recipient's residence]

162 In applying article 32(1)(c) of the Code, the country of residence of the recipient of the payment of the royalty or licence fee shall not be a material consideration.

CHAPTER 3 – PROVISIONS CONCERNING THE PLACE OF INTRODUCTION INTO THE COMMUNITY

ART. 163   [Meaning]

163(1) For the purposes of article 32(1)(e) and article 33(a) of the Code, the **place of introduction** into the customs territory of the Community shall be:

(a)   for goods carried by sea, the port of unloading, or the port of transhipment, subject to transhipment being certified by the customs authorities of that port;

(b)   for goods carried by sea and then, without transhipment, by inland waterway, the first port where unloading can take place either at the mouth of the river or canal or further inland, subject to proof being furnished to the customs office that the freight to the port of unloading is higher than that to the first port;

(c)   for goods carried by rail, inland waterway, or road, the place where the first customs office is situated;

(d)   for goods carried by other means, the place where the land frontier of the customs territory of the Community is crossed.

163(2)   The customs value of goods introduced into the customs territory of the Community and then carried to a destination in another part of that territory through the territories of Belarus, Bulgaria, the Czech Republic, Estonia, Hungary, Latvia, Lithuania, Poland, Russia, Romania, the Slovak Republic, Switzerland, or former Yugoslavia in its borders of 1 January 1991 shall be determined by reference to the first place of introduction into the customs territory of the Community, provided that goods are carried direct through the territories of those countries by a usual route across such territory to the place of destination.

163(3)   The customs value of goods introduced into the customs territory of the Community and then carried by sea to a destination in another part of that territory shall be determined by reference to the first place of introduction into the customs territory of the Community, provided the goods are carried direct by a usual route to the place of destination.

163(4)   Paragraphs 2 and 3 of this article shall also apply where the goods have been unloaded, transhipped or temporarily immobilised in the territories of Belarus, Bulgaria, the Czech Republic, Estonia, Hungary, Latvia, Lithuania, Poland, Russia, Romania, the Slovak Republic, Switzerland, or former Yugoslavia in its borders of 1 January 1991 for reasons related solely to their transport.

163(5)   For goods introduced into the customs territory of the Community and carried directly from one of the French overseas departments to another part of the customs territory of the Community or vice versa, the place of introduction to be taken into consideration shall be the place referred to in paragraphs 1 and 2 situated in that part of the customs territory of the Community from which the goods came, if they were unloaded or transhipped there and this was certified by the customs authorities.

163(6)   When the conditions specified at paragraphs 2, 3 and 5 are not fulfilled, the place of introduction to be taken into consideration shall be the place specified in paragraph 1 situated in that part of the customs territory of the Community to which the goods are consigned.

History – Art. 163(2), (4) substituted by the Act of Accession of Austria, Sweden and Finland, art. 29 and Annex I, Ch. XIII (OJ 1994 C241/1), as substituted by Decision 95/1, Annex, Ch. XIII (OJ 1995 L1/1), with effect from 1 January 1995.

CHAPTER 4 – PROVISIONS CONCERNING TRANSPORT COSTS

ART. 164   [Application]

164   In applying article 32(1)(e) and 33(a) of the Code:

(a)   where goods are carried by the same mode of transport to a point beyond the place of introduction into the customs territory of the Community, transport costs shall be assessed in proportion to the distance covered outside and inside the customs territory of the Community, unless evidence is produced to the customs authorities to show the costs that would have been incurred under a general compulsory schedule of freight rates for the carriage of the goods to the place of introduction into the customs territory of the Community;

(b)   where goods are invoiced at a uniform free domicile price which corresponds to the price at the place of introduction, transport costs within the Community shall not be deducted from that price. However, such deduction shall be allowed if evidence is produced to the customs authorities that the free-frontier price would be lower than the uniform free domicile price;

(c)   where transport is free or provided by the buyer, transport costs to the place of introduction, calculated in accordance with the schedule of freight rates normally applied for the same modes of transport, shall be included in the customs value.

ART. 165   [Postal charges]

165(1)   All postal charges levied up to the place of destination in respect of goods sent by post shall be included in the customs value of these goods, with the exception of any supplementary postal charge levied in the country of importation.

165(2)   No adjustment to the declared value shall, however, be made in respect of such charges in determining the value of consignments of a non-commercial nature.

165(3)   Paragraphs 1 and 2 are not applicable to goods carried by the express postal services known as EMS-Datapost (in Denmark, EMS-Jetpost, in Germany, EMS-Kurierpostsendungen, in Italy, CAI-Post).

ART. 166   [Air transport]

166   The air transport costs to be included in the customs value of goods shall be determined by applying the rules and percentages shown in Annex 25.

CHAPTER 5 – VALUATION OF CERTAIN CARRIER MEDIA FOR USE IN ADP EQUIPMENT

ART. 167   [Data or other instructions]

167(1)   Notwithstanding articles 29 to 33 of the Code, in determining the customs value of imported carrier media bearing data or instructions for use in data processing equipment, only the cost or value of the carrier medium itself shall be taken into account. The customs value of imported carrier media bearing data or instructions shall not, therefore, include the cost or value of the data or instructions, provided that such cost or value is distinguished from the cost or value of the carrier medium in question.

167(2)   For the purposes of this article:

(a)   the expression **"carrier medium"** shall not be taken to include integrated circuits, semiconductors and similar devices or articles incorporating such circuits or devices;

(b)   the expression **"data or instructions"** shall not be taken to include sound, cinematographic or video recordings.

CHAPTER 6 – PROVISIONS CONCERNING RATES OF EXCHANGE

ART. 168   [Meaning]

168   For the purposes of articles 169 to 171 of this chapter:

(a)   **"rate recorded"** shall mean:
-    the latest selling rate of exchange recorded for commercial transactions on the most representative exchange market or markets of the member state concerned, or
-    some other description of a rate of exchange so recorded and designated by the member state as the **"rate recorded"** provided that it reflects as effectively as possible the current value of the currency in question in commercial transactions;

(b)   **"published"** shall mean made generally known in a manner designated by the member state concerned;

(c)   **"currency"** shall mean any monetary unit used as a means of settlement between monetary authorities or on the international market.

ART. 169   [Exchange rate]

169(1)   Where factors used to determine the customs value of goods are expressed at the time when that value is determined in a currency other than that of the member state where the valuation is made, the rate of exchange to be used to determine that value in terms of the currency of the member state concerned shall be the rate recorded on the second-last Wednesday of a month and published on that or the following day.

169(2)   The rate recorded on the second-last Wednesday of a month shall be used during the following calendar month unless it is superseded by a rate established under article 171.

169(3)   Where a rate of exchange is not recorded on the second-last Wednesday indicated in paragraph 1, or, if recorded, is not published on that or the following day, the last rate recorded for the currency in question published within the preceding 14 days shall be deemed to be the rate recorded on that Wednesday.

ART. 170   [Designation of rate]

170   Where a rate of exchange cannot be established under the provisions of article 169, the rate of exchange to be used for the application of article 35 of the Code shall be designated by the member state concerned and shall reflect as effectively as possible the current value of the currency in question in commercial transactions in terms of the currency of that member state.

ART. 171   [Changing rate]

171(1)   Where a rate of exchange recorded on the last Wednesday of a month and published on that or the following day differs, by 5 per cent or more from the rate established in accordance with article 169 for entry into use the following month, it shall replace the latter rate from the first Wednesday of that month as the rate to be applied for the application of article 35 of the Code.

171(2)   Where in the course of a period of application as referred to in the preceding provisions, a rate of exchange recorded on a Wednesday and published on that or the following day differs by 5 per cent or more from the rate being used in accordance with this Chapter, it shall replace the latter rate and enter into use on the Wednesday following as the rate to be used for the application of article 35 of the Code. The replacement rate shall remain in use for the remainder of the current month, provided that this rate is not superseded due to operation of the provisions of the first sentence of this paragraph.

171(3)   Where, in a member state, a rate of exchange is not recorded on a Wednesday or, if recorded, is not published on that or the following day, the rate recorded shall, for the application in that member state of paragraphs 1 and 2, be the rate most recently recorded and published prior to that Wednesday.

ART. 172   [Periodic declaration]

172   When the customs authorities of a member state authorise a declarant to furnish or supply at a later date certain details concerning the declaration for free circulation of the goods in the form of a periodic declaration, this authorisation may, at the declarant's request, provide that a single rate be used for conversion into that member state's currency of elements forming part of the customs value as expressed in a particular currency. In this case, the rate to be used shall be the rate, established in accordance with this Chapter, which is applicable on the first day of the period covered by the declaration in question.

CHAPTER 7 – SIMPLIFIED PROCEDURES FOR CERTAIN PERISHABLE GOODS

ART. 173   [Unit value]

173(1)   For the purpose of determining the customs value of products referred to in Annex 26, the Commission shall establish for each classification heading a unit value per 100 kg net expressed in the currencies of the member states.

The unit values shall apply for periods of 14 days, each period beginning on a Friday.

173(2)   Unit values shall be established on the basis of the following elements, which are to be supplied to the Commission by member states, in relation to each classification heading:

(a)   the average free-at-frontier unit price, not cleared through customs, expressed in the currency of the member state in question per 100 kg net and calculated on the basis of prices for undamaged goods in the marketing centres referred to in Annex 27 during the reference period referred to in article 174(1);

(b)   the quantities entered into free circulation over the period of a calendar year with payment of import duties.

173(3)   The average free-at-frontier unit price, not cleared through customs, shall be calculated on the basis of the gross proceeds of sales made between importers and wholesalers. However, in the case of the London, Milan and Rungis marketing centres the gross proceeds shall be those recorded at the commercial level at which those goods are most commonly sold at those centres.

There shall be deducted from the figures so arrived at:

–   a marketing margin of 15 per cent for the marketing centres of London, Milan and Rungis and of 8 per cent for the other marketing centres,

–   costs of transport and insurance within the customs territory,

–   a standard amount of ECU 5 representing all the other costs which are not to be included in the customs value.
    This amount shall be converted into the currencies of the member states on the basis of the latest rates in force established in accordance with Article 18 of the Code,

–   import duties and other charges which are not to be included in the customs value.

173(4)   The member states may fix standard amounts for deduction in respect of transport and insurance costs in accordance with paragraph 3. Such standard amounts and the methods for calculating them shall be made known to the Commission immediately.

ART. 174   [Reference period]

174(1) The reference period for calculating the average unit prices referred to in article 173(2)(a) shall be the period of 14 days ending on the Thursday preceding the week during which new unit values are to be established.

174(2) Average unit prices shall be notified by member states not later than 12 noon on the Monday of the week during which unit values are established pursuant to article 173. If that day is a non-working day, notification shall be made on the working day immediately preceding that day.

174(3) The quantities entered into free circulation during a calendar year for each classification heading shall be notified to the Commission by all member states before 15 June in the following year.

ART. 175   [Tuesday]

175(1) The unit values referred to in article 173(1) shall be established by the Commission on alternate Tuesdays on the basis of the weighted average of the average unit prices referred to in article 173(2)(a) in relation to the quantities referred to in article 173(2)(b).

175(2) For the purpose of determining the weighted average, each average unit price as referred to in article 173(2)(a) shall be converted into ECU on the basis of the last conversion rates determined by the Commission and published in the Official Journal of the European Communities prior to the week during which the unit values are to be established. The same conversion rates shall be applied in converting the unit values so obtained back into the currencies of the member states.

175(3) The last published unit values shall remain applicable until new values are published. However, in the case of major fluctuations in price in one or more member states, as a result, for example, of an interruption in the continuity of imports of a particular product, new unit values may be determined on the basis of actual prices at the time of fixing those values.

ART. 176   [Damaged consignments]

176(1) Consignments which at the material time for valuation for customs purposes contain not less than 5 per cent of produce unfit in its unaltered state for human consumption or the value of which has depreciated by not less than 20 per cent in relation to average market prices for sound produce, shall be treated as damaged.

176(2) Consignments which are damaged may be valued:

–   either, after sorting, by application of unit values to the sound portion, the damaged portion being destroyed under customs supervision, or

–   by application of unit values established for the sound produce after deduction from the weight of the consignment of a percentage equal to the percentage assessed as damaged by a sworn expert and accepted by the customs authorities, or

–   by application of unit values established for the sound produce reduced by the percentage assessed as damaged by a sworn expert and accepted by the customs authorities.

ART. 177   [Simplified procedure system]

177(1) In declaring or causing to be declared the customs value of one or more products which he imports by reference to the unit values established in accordance with this Chapter, the person concerned joins the simplified procedure system for the current calendar year in respect of the product or products in question.

177(2) If subsequently the person concerned requires the use of a method other than the simplified procedures for the customs valuation of one or more of the products he imports, the customs authorities of the member state concerned shall be entitled to notify him that he will not be allowed to benefit from the simplified procedures for the remainder of the current calendar year in regard to the product or products concerned; this exclusion can be extended for the following calendar year. Such notified exclusion shall be communicated without delay to the Commission, which shall in turn immediately inform the customs authorities of the other member states.

CHAPTER 8 – DECLARATIONS OF PARTICULARS AND DOCUMENTS TO BE FURNISHED

ART. 178   [Form DV 1]

178(1)   Where it is necessary to establish a customs value for the purposes of articles 28 to 36 of the Code, a declaration of particulars relating to customs value (value declaration) shall accompany the customs entry made in respect of the imported goods. The value declaration shall be drawn up on a form D.V. 1 corresponding to the specimen in Annex 28, supplemented where appropriate by one or more forms D.V. 1 bis corresponding to the specimen in Annex 29.

178(2)   It shall be a particular requirement that the value declaration prescribed in paragraph 1 shall be made only by a person who has his residence or place of business in the customs territory of the Community and is in possession of the relevant facts.

178(3)   The customs authorities may waive the requirement of a declaration on the form referred to in paragraph 1 where the customs value of the goods in question cannot be determined under the provisions of article 29 of the Code. In such cases the person referred to in paragraph 2 shall furnish or cause to be furnished to the customs authorities such other information as may be requested for the purposes of determining the customs value under another article of the said Code; and such other information shall be supplied in such form and manner as may be prescribed by the customs authorities.

178(4)   The lodging with a customs office of a declaration required by paragraph 1 shall, without prejudice to the possible application of penal provisions, be equivalent to the engagement of responsibility by the person referred to in paragraph 2 in respect of:

–   the accuracy and completeness of the particulars given in the declaration,
–   the authenticity of the documents produced in support of these particulars, and
–   the supply of any additional information or document necessary to establish the customs value of the goods.

178(5)   This article shall not apply in respect of goods for which the customs value is determined under the simplified procedure system established in accordance with the provisions of articles 173 to 177.

ART. 179   [Waived art. 178(1)]

179(1)   Except where it is essential for the correct application of import duties, the customs authorities shall waive the requirement of all or part of the declaration provided for in article 178(1):

(a)   where the customs value of the imported goods in a consignment does not exceed ECU 5,000, provided that they do not constitute split or multiple consignments from the same consignor to the same consignee; or
(b)   where the importations involved are of a non-commercial nature; or
(c)   where the submission of the particulars in question is not necessary for the application of the Customs Tariff of the European Communities or where the customs duties provided for in the Tariff are not chargeable pursuant to specific customs provisions.

179(2)   The amount in ECU referred to in paragraph 1(a) shall be converted in accordance with article 18 of the Code. The customs authorities may round-off upwards or downwards the sum arrived at after conversion.

The customs authorities may maintain unamended the exchange value in national currency of the amount determined in ECU if, at the time of the annual adjustment provided for in article 18 of the Code, the conversion of this amount, before the rounding-off provided for in this paragraph, leads to an alteration of less than 5 per cent in the exchange value expressed in national currency or to a reduction thereof.

179(3)   In the case of continuing traffic in goods supplied by the same seller to the same buyer under the same commercial conditions, the customs authorities may waive the requirement that all particulars under article 178(1) be furnished in support of each customs declaration, but shall require them whenever the circumstances change and at least once every three years.

179(4)   A waiver granted under this article may be withdrawn and the submission of a D.V. 1 may be required where it is found that a condition necessary to qualify for that waiver was not or is no longer met.

ART. 180   [Computerised system]

180   Where computerised systems are used, or where the goods concerned are the subject of a general, periodic or recapitulative declaration, the customs authorities may authorise variations in the form of presentation of data required for the determination of customs value.

ART. 181   [Invoices]

181(1)   The person referred to in article 178(2) shall furnish the customs authorities with a copy of the invoice on the basis of which the value of the imported goods is declared. Where the customs value is declared in writing this copy shall be retained by the customs authorities.

181(2)   In the case of written declarations of the customs value, when the invoice for the imported goods is made out to a person established in a member state other than that in which the customs value is declared, the declarant shall furnish the customs authorities with two copies of the invoice. One of these copies shall be retained by the customs authorities; the other, bearing the stamp of the office in question and the serial number of the declaration at the said customs office shall be returned to the declarant for forwarding to the person to whom the invoice is made out.

181(3)   The customs authorities may extend the provisions of paragraph 2 to cases where the person to whom the invoice is made out is established in the member state in which the customs value is declared.

ART. 181A   [Value of imported goods]

181A(1)   The customs authorities need not determine the customs valuation of imported goods on the basis of the transaction value method if, in accordance with the procedure set out in paragraph 2, they are not satisfied, on the basis of reasonable doubts, that the declared value represents the total amount paid or payable as referred to in article 29 of the Code.

181A(2)   Where the customs authorities have the doubts described in paragraph 1 they may ask for additional information in accordance with article 178(4). If those doubts continue, the customs authorities must, before reaching a final decision, notify the person concerned, in writing if requested, of the grounds for those doubts and provide him with a reasonable opportunity to respond. A final decision and the grounds therefor shall be communicated in writing to the person concerned.

History – Art. 181A was inserted by Regulation 3245/94 (OJ L 346/94).

ANNEX 23 – INTERPRETATIVE NOTES ON CUSTOMS VALUE

First column	Second column
Reference to provisions of the Customs Code	Notes
Article 29(1)	The price actually paid or payable refers to the price for the imported goods. Thus the flow of dividends or other payments from the buyer to the seller that do not relate to the imported goods are not part of the customs value.
Article 29(1)(a), third indent	An example of such restriction would be the case where a seller requires a buyer of automobiles not to sell or exhibit them prior to a fixed date which represents the beginning of a model year.
Article 29(1)(b)	Some examples of this include: (a) the seller establishes the price of the imported goods on condition that the buyer will also buy other goods in specified quantities; (b) the price of the import goods is dependent upon the price or prices at which the buyer of the imported goods sells other goods to the seller of the imported goods;

First column	Second column
Reference to provisions of the Customs Code	Notes
	(c) the price is established on the basis of a form of payment extraneous to the imported goods, such as where the imported goods are semi-finished goods which have been provided by the seller on condition that he will receive a specified quantity of the finished goods. However, conditions or considerations relating to the production or marketing of the imported goods shall not result in rejection of the transaction value. For example, the fact that the buyer furnishes the seller with engineering and plans undertaken in the country of importation shall not result in rejection of the transaction value for the purposes of article 29(1).
Article 29(2)	1. Paragraphs 2(a) and (b) provide different means of establishing the acceptability of a transaction value. 2. Paragraph 2(a) provides that where the buyer and the seller are related, the circumstances surrounding the sale shall be examined and the transaction value shall be accepted as the customs value provided that the relationship did not influence the price. It is not intended that there should be an examination of the circumstances in all cases where the buyer and the seller are related. Such examination will only be required where there are doubts about the acceptability of the price. Where the customs authorities have no doubts about the acceptability of the price, it should be accepted without requesting further information from the declarant. For example, the customs authorities may have previously examined the relationship, or it may already have detailed information concerning the buyer and the seller, and may already be satisfied from such examination or information that the relationship did not influence the price. 3. Where the customs authorities are unable to accept the transaction value without further inquiry, they should give the declarant an opportunity to supply such further detailed information as may be necessary to enable it to examine the circumstances surrounding the sale, in this context, the customs authorities should be prepared to examine relevant aspects of the transaction, including the way in which the buyer and seller organise their commercial relations and the way in which the price in question was arrived at, in order to determine whether the relationship influenced the price. Where it can be shown that the buyer and seller, although related under the provisions of article 143 of this Regulation, buy from and sell to each other as if they were not related, this would demonstrate that the price had not been influenced by the relationship. As an example of this, if the price had been settled in a manner consistent with the normal pricing practices of the industry in question or with the way the seller settles prices for sales to buyers who are not related to him, this would demonstrate that the price had not been influenced by the relationship. As a further example, where it is shown that the price is adequate to ensure recovery of all costs plus a profit which is representative of the firm's overall profit realised over a representative period of time (e.g. on an annual basis) in sales of goods of the same class or kind, this would demonstrate that the price had not been influenced.

First column	Second column
Reference to provisions of the Customs Code	Notes
	4. Paragraph 2(b) provides an opportunity for the declarant to demonstrate that the transaction value closely approximates to a "test" value previously accepted by the customs authorities and is therefore acceptable under the provisions of article 29. Where a test under paragraph 2(b) is met, it is not necessary to examine the question of influence under paragraph 2(a). If the customs authorities already have sufficient information to be satisfied, without further detailed inquiries, that one of the tests provided in paragraph 2(b) has been met, there is no reason for them to require the declarant to demonstrate that the test can be met.
Article 29(2)(b)	A number of factors must be taken into consideration in determining whether one value **"closely approximates"** to another value. These factors include the nature of the imported goods, the nature of the industry itself, the season in which the goods are imported, and, whether the difference in values is commercially significant. Since these factors may vary from case to case, it would be impossible to apply a uniform standard such as a fixed percentage, in each case. For example, a small difference in value in a case involving one type of goods could be unacceptable while a large difference in a case involving another type of goods might be acceptable in determining whether the transaction value closely approximates to the "test" values set forth in article 29(2)(b).
Article 29(3)(a)	An example of an indirect payment would be the settlement by the buyer, whether in whole or in part, of a debt owed by the seller.
Article 30(2)(a) Article 30(2)(b)	1. In applying these provisions, the customs authorities shall, where possible, use a sale of identical or similar goods, as appropriate, at the same commercial level and in substantially the same quantity as the goods being valued. Where no such sale is found, a sale of identical or similar goods, as appropriate, that takes place under any one of the following three conditions may by used: (a) a sale at the same commercial level but in a different quantity; (b) a sale at a different commercial level but in substantially the same quantity; or (c) a sale at a different commercial level and in a different quantity. 2. Having found a sale under any one of these three conditions adjustments will then be made, as the case may be, for: (a) quantity factors only; (b) commerical level factors only; or (c) both commercial level and quantity factors. 3. [Deleted by corrigenda (OJ 1994 L268/32)]

First column	Second column
Reference to provisions of the Customs Code	Notes

	4. A condition for adjustment because of different commercial levels or different quantities is that such adjustment, whether it leads to an increase or a decrease in the value, be made only on the basis of demonstrated evidence that clearly establishes the reasonableness and accuracy of the adjustment, e.g. valid price lists containing prices referring to different levels or different quantities. As an example of this, if the imported goods being valued consist of a shipment of 10 units and the only identical or similar imported goods, as appropriate, for which a transaction value exists involved a sale of 500 units, and it is recognised that the seller grants quantity discounts, the required adjustment may be accomplished by resorting to the seller's price list and using that price applicable to a sale of 10 units. This does not require that a sale had to have been made in quantities of 10 as long as the price list has been established as being bona fide through sales at other quantities. In the absence of such an objective measure, however, the determination of a customs value under the provisions of article 30(2)(a) and (b) is not appropriate.
Article 30(2)(d)	1. As a general rule, customs value is determined under these provisions on the basis of information readily available in the Community. In order to determine a computed value, however, it may be necessary to examine the cost of producing the goods being valued and other information which has to be obtained from outside the Community. Furthermore, in most cases the producer of the goods will be outside the jurisdiction of the authorities of the member states. The use of the computed value method will generally be limited to those cases where the buyer and seller are related, and the producer is prepared to supply to the authorities of the country of importation the necessary costings and to provide facilities for any subsequent verification which may be necessary.
	2. The **"cost or value"** referred to in article 30(2)(d), first indent, is to be determined on the basis of information relating to the production of the goods being valued supplied by or on behalf of the producer. It is to be based upon the commercial accounts of the producer, provided that such accounts are consistent with the generally accepted accounting principles applied in the country where the goods are produced.

First column	Second column
Reference to provisions of the Customs Code	Notes

	3. The **"amount for profit and general expenses"** referred to in article 30(2)(d), second indent, is to be determined on the basis of information supplied by or on behalf of the producer unless his figures are inconsistent with those usually reflected in sales of goods of the same class or kind as the goods being valued which are made by producers in the country of exportation for export to the country of importation.
	4. No cost or value of the elements referred to in this article shall be counted twice in determining the computed value.
	5. It should be noted in this context that the **"amount for profit and general expenses"** has to be taken as a whole. It follows that if, in any particular case, the producer's profit figure is low and his general expenses are high, his profit and general expenses taken together may nevertheless be consistent with that usually reflected in sales of goods of the same class or kind. Such a situation might occur, for example, if a product were being launched in the Community and the producer accepted a nil or low profit to offset high general expenses associated with the launch. Where the producer can demonstrate that he is taking a low profit on his sales of the imported goods because of particular commercial circumstances, his actual profit figures should be taken into account provided that he has valid commercial reasons to justify them and his pricing policy reflects usual pricing policies in the branch of industry concerned. Such a situation might occur, for example, where producers have been forced to lower prices temporarily because of an unforeseeable drop in demand, or where they sell goods to complement a range of goods being produced in the country of importation and accept a low profit to maintain competitivity. Where the producer's own figures for profit and general expenses are not consistent with those usually reflected in sales of goods of the same class or kind as the goods being valued which are made by producers in the country of exportation for export to the country of importation, the amount for profit and general expenses may be based upon relevant information other than that supplied by or on behalf of the producer of the goods.
	6. Whether certain goods are **"of the same class or kind"** as other goods must be determined on a case-by-case basis with reference to the circumstances involved. In determining the usual profits and general expenses under the provisions of article 30(2)(d), sales for export to the country of importation of the narrowest group or range of goods, which includes the goods being valued, for which the necessary information can be provided, should be examined. For the purposes of article 30(2)(d), **"goods of the same class or kind"** must be from the same country as the goods being valued.
Article 31(1)	1. Customs values determined under the provisions of article 31(1) should, to the greatest extent possible, be based on previously determined customs values.
	2. The methods of valuation to be employed under article 31(1) should be those laid down in articles 29 and 30(2), but a reasonable flexibility in the application of such methods would be in conformity with the aims and provisions of article 31(1).

First column	Second column
Reference to provisions of the Customs Code	Notes

	3. Some examples of reasonable flexibility are as follows:
	(a) *identical goods* – the requirement that the identical goods should be exported at or about same time as the goods being valued could be flexibly interpreted; identical imported goods produced in a country other than the country of exportation of the goods being valued could be the basis for customs valuation; customs values of identical imported goods already determined under the provisions of article 30(2)(c) and (d) could be used;
	(b) *similar goods* – the requirement that the similar goods should be exported at or about the same time as the goods being valued could be flexibly interpreted; similar imported goods produced in a country other than the country of exportation of the goods being valued could be the basis for customs valuation; customs values of similar imported goods already determined under the provisions of article 30(2)(c) and (d) could be used;
	(c) *deductive method* – the requirement that the goods shall have been sold in the "condition as imported" in article 152(1)(a) of this Regulation could be flexibly interpreted; the "90 days" requirement could be administered flexibly.
Article 32(1)(b)(ii)	1. There are two factors involved in the apportionment of the elements specified in article 32(1)(b)(ii) to the imported goods – the value of the element itself and the way in which that value is to be apportioned to the imported goods. The apportionment of these elements should be made in reasonable manner appropriate to the circumstances and in accordance with generally accepted accounting principles.
	2. Concerning the value of the element, if the buyer acquires the element from a seller not related to him at a given cost, the value of the element is that cost. If the element was produced by the buyer or by a person related to him, its value would be the cost of producing it. If the element had been previously used by the buyer, regardless of whether it had been acquired or produced by him, the original cost of acquisition or production would have to be adjusted downwards to reflect its use in order to arrive at the value of the element.
	3. Once a value has been determined for the element, it is necessary to apportion that value to the imported goods. Various possibilities exist. For example, the value might be apportioned to the first shipment, if the buyer wishes to pay duty on the entire value at one time. As another example, he may request that the value be apportioned over the number of units produced up to the time of the first shipment. As a further example, he may request that the value be apportioned over the entire anticipated production where contracts or firm commitments exist for that production. The method of apportionment used will depend upon the documentation provided by the buyer.

First column	Second column
Reference to provisions of the Customs Code	Notes
	4. As an illustration of the above, a buyer provides the producer with a mould to be used in the production of the imported goods and contracts with him to buy 10,000 units. By the time of arrival of the first shipment of 1,000 units, the producer has already produced 4,000 units. The buyer may request the customs authorities to apportion the value of the mould over 1,000, 4,000 or 10,000 units.
Article 32(1)(b)(iv)	1. Additions for the elements specified in article 32(1)(b)(iv) should be based on objective and quantifiable data. In order to minimise the burden for both the declarant and customs authorities in determining the values to be added, data readily available in the buyer's commercial record system should be used insofar as possible.
	2. For those elements supplied by the buyer which were purchased or leased by the buyer, the addition would be the cost of the purchase or the lease. No addition shall be made for those elements available in the public domain, other than the cost of obtaining copies of them.
	3. The ease with which it may be possible to calculate the values to be added will depend on a particular firm's structure and management practice, as well as its accounting methods.
	4. For example, it is possible that a firm which imports a variety of products from several countries maintains the records of its design centre outside the country of importation in such a way as to show accurately the costs attributable to a given product. In such cases, a direct adjustment may appropriately be made under the provisions of article 32.
	5. In another case, a firm may carry the cost of the design centre outside the country of importation as a general overhead expense without allocation to specific products. In this instance, an appropriate adjustment could be made under the provisions of article 32 with respect to the imported goods by apportioning total design centre costs over total production benefiting from the design centre and adding such apportioned cost on a unit basis to imports.
	6. Variations in the above circumstances will, of course, require different factors to be considered in determining the proper method of allocation.
	7. In cases where the production of the element in question involves a number of countries and over a period of time, the adjustment should be limited to the value actually added to that element outside the Community.
Article 32(1)(c)	The royalties and licence fees referred to in article 32(1)(c) may include, among other things, payments in respect to patents, trademarks and copyrights.

First column	Second column
Reference to provisions of the Customs Code	Notes
Article 32(2)	Where objective and quantifiable data do not exist with regard to the additions required to be made under the provisions of article 32, the transaction value cannot be determined under the provisions of article 29. As an illustration of this, a royalty is paid on the basis of the price in a sale in the importing country of a litre of a particular product that was imported by the kilogram and made up into a solution after importation. If the royalty is based partially on the imported goods and partially on other factors which have nothing to do with the imported goods (such as when the imported goods are mixed with domestic ingredients and are no longer separately identifiable, or when the royalty cannot be distinguished from special financial arrangements between the buyer and the seller), it would be inappropriate to attempt to make an addition for the royalty. However, if the amount of this royalty is based only on the imported goods and can be readily quantified, an addition to the price actually paid or payable can be made.

First column	Second column
Reference to provisions of the Customs Code Implementing Provisions	Notes
Article 143(1)(e)	1. One person shall be deemed to control another when the former is legally or operationally in a position to exercise restraint or direction over the latter.
Article 150(1) Article 151(1)	1. The expression "and/or" allows the flexibility to use the sales and make the necessary adjustments in any one of the three conditions described in paragraph 1 of the interpretative notes to articles 30(2)(a) and (b).
Article 152(1)(a)(i)	1. The words **"profit and general expenses"** should be taken as a whole. The figure for the purposes of this deduction should be determined on the basis of information supplied by the declarant unless his figures are inconsistent with those obtaining in sales in the country of importation of imported goods of the same class or kind. Where the declarant's figures are inconsistent with such figures, the amount for profit and general expenses may be based upon relevant information other than that supplied by the declarant.
	2. In determining either the commissions or the usual profits and general expenses under this provision, the question whether certain goods are of the same class or kind as other goods must be determined on a case-by-case basis by reference to the circumstances involved. Sales in the country of importation of the narrowest group or range of imported goods of the same class or kind, which includes the goods being valued, for which the necessary information can be provided, should be examined. For the purposes of this provision, **"goods of the same class or kind"** includes goods imported from the same country as the goods being valued as well as goods imported from other countries.

First column	Second column
Reference to provisions of the Customs Code Implementing Provisions	Notes

Article 152(2)	1. Where this method of valuation is used, deductions made for the value added by further processing shall be based on objective and quantifiable data relating to the cost of such work. Accepted industry formulas, recipes, methods of construction, and other industry practices would form the basis of the calculations. 2. This method of valuation would normally not be applicable when, as a result of the further processing, the imported goods lose their identity. However, there can be instances where, although the identity of the imported goods is lost, the value added by the processing can be determined accurately without unreasonable difficulty. On the other hand, there can also be instances where the imported goods maintain their identity but form such a minor element in the goods sold in the country of importation that the use of this valuation method would be unjustified. In view of the above, each situation of this type must be considered on a case-by-case basis.
Article 152(3)	1. As an example of this, goods are sold from a price list which grants favourable unit prices for purchases made in larger quantities.

Sale quantity	Unit price	Number of sales	Total quantity sold at each price
1 to 10 units	100	10 sales of 5 units Five sales of 3 units	65
11 to 25 units	95	Five sales of 11 units	55
Over 25 units	90	One sale of 30 units One sale of 50 units	80

The greatest number of units sold at a price is 80; therefore, the unit price in the greatest aggregate quantity is 90.

2. As another example of this, two sales occur. In the first sale 500 units are sold at a price of 95 currency units each. In the second sale 400 units are sold at a price of 90 currency units each. In this example, the greatest number of units sold at a particular price is 500; therefore, the unit price in the greatest aggregate quantity is 95.

3. A third example would be the following situation where various quantities are sold at various prices

(a) Sales

Sale quantity	Unit price
40 units	100
30 units	90
15 units	100
50 units	95
25 units	105
35 units	90
5 units	100

First column	Second column
Reference to provisions of the Customs Code Implementing Provisions	Notes

	(b) Total

Total quantity sold	Unit price
65	90
50	95
60	100
25	105

In this example, the greatest number of units sold at a particular price is 65; therefore, the unit price in the greatest aggregate quantity is 90.

History – Note 3 at art. 30(2)(a) and 30(2)(b), deleted by corrigenda (OJ 1994 L268/32), is reproduced below for information: "The expression "and/or allows the flexibility to use the sales and make the necessary adjustments in any one of the three conditions described above."
The row between art. 32(2) and art. 143(1)(e) inserted by corrigenda (OJ 1994 L268/32).
The row between art. 143(1)(e) and art. 152(1)(a)(i) inserted by corrigenda (OJ 1994 L268/32).

ANNEX 24 – APPLICATION OF GENERALLY ACCEPTED ACCOUNTING PRINCIPLES FOR THE DETERMINATION OF CUSTOMS VALUE

1   **"Generally accepted accounting principles"** refers to the recognised consensus or substantial authoritative support within a country at a particular time as to which economic resources and obligations should be recorded as assets and liabilities, which changes in assets and liabilities should be recorded, how the assets and liabilities and changes in them should be measured, what information should be disclosed and how it should be disclosed, and which financial statements should be prepared. These standards may be broad guidelines of general application as well as detailed practices and procedures.

2   For the purposes of the application of the customs valuation provisions, the customs administration concerned shall utilise information prepared in a manner consistent with generally accepted accounting principles in the country which is appropriate for the article in question. For example, the determination of usual profit and general expenses under the provisions of article 152(1)(a)(i) of this Regulation would be carried out utilising information prepared in a manner consistent with generally accepted accounting principles of the country of importation. On the other hand, the determination of usual profit and general expenses under the provisions of article 30(2)(d) of the Code would be carried out utilising information prepared in a manner consistent with generally accepted accounting principles of the country of production. As a further example, the determination of an element provided for in article 32(1)(b)(ii) of the Code undertaken in the country of importation would be carried out utilising information in a manner consistent with the generally accepted accounting principles of that country.

ANNEX 25 – AIR TRANSPORT COSTS TO BE INCLUDED IN THE CUSTOMS VALUE

Introduction

1   The following table shows:

(a)   third countries listed by continent (column 1);

(b)   airports of departure in third countries (column 2);

(c)   airports of arrival in the Community with the percentages which represent the part of the air transport costs to be included in the customs value (column 3 and following columns).

2   When the goods are shipped to or from airports not included in the following table, other than the airports referred to in paragraph 3, the percentage given for the airport nearest to that of departure or arrival shall be taken.

3   As regards the French overseas departments of Guadeloupe, Guyana, Martinique and Réunion, of which territories the airports are not included in the table, the following rules shall apply:

(a)   for goods shipped direct to those departments from third countries, the whole of the air transport cost is to be included in the customs value;

(b)   for goods shipped to the European part of the Community from third countries and transhipped or unloaded in one of those departments, the air transport costs which would have been incurred for carrying the goods only as far as the place of transhipment or unloading are to be included in the customs value;

(c)   for goods shipped to those departments from third countries and transhipped or unloaded in an airport in the European part of the Community, the air transport costs to be included in the customs value are those which result from the application of the percentages given in the following table to the costs which would have been incurred for carrying the goods from the airport of departure to the airport of transhipment or unloading.

The transhipment or unloading shall be certified by an appropriate endorsement by the customs authorities on the air waybill or other air transport document, with the official stamp of the office concerned; failing this certification the provisions of the last subparagraph of article 163(6) of this Regulation shall apply.

[Table not reproduced here].

VAT EXTRA-STATUTORY MATERIAL

Table of Contents

continued over

Page

C.   Business briefs

D.   Statements of practice

OFFICIAL PUBLICATIONS

CUSTOMS AND EXCISE PUBLICATIONS HAVING LEGAL FORCE

Notice	Part having the force of law and its purpose	Enabling powers
Notice 700: *The VAT Guide*	Paragraph 3.1(f) – values expressed in foreign currency	VATA 1994 Sch. 6, para. 11
Notice 701/48: *Corporate purchasing cards*	Paragraph 4 – Line Item Detail (LID) invoices	VATA 1994 Sch. 11, para. 2
	Paragraph 5 – the Summary VAT invoice	VAT Regs. 1995 regs. 13 and 14
Notice 703: *Exports and removals of goods from the United Kingdom*	Principally paragraphs 2.2 and 8.4 but specific conditions relating to the zero-rating of particular types of supplies of goods for export outside the EC, or removal to another EC Member State, are contained throughout the Notice	VATA 1994 sections 30(6) and 30(10) VAT Regs. 1995 regs. 127, 129 and 134
Notice 703/1: *Supply of freight containers for export or removal from the United Kingdom*	Paragraphs 4 and 5 contain the conditions which must be met in full in order to zero-rate supplies (by way of sale) of freight containers for export outside the EC or for removal to another EC Member State	VATA 1994 sections 30(6) and 30(8) VAT Regs. 1995 regs. 128, 134
Notice 703/2: *Sailaway boats supplied for export outside the European Community*	Principally Part 2 which sets out the conditions to be complied with, but other paragraphs outline additional conditions which must be met	VATA 1994 section 30(8) VAT Regs. 1995 reg. 129
Notice 704: *Retail exports*	Principally paragraph 1.1 but the notice expands on the conditions for the retailer to supply goods that can be zero-rated to entitled customers	VATA 1994 section 30(8) VAT Regs. 1995 regs. 130 and 131
Notice 704/1: *VAT refunds for travellers departing from the European Community*	Principally paragraph 1.2 but the notice expands on the conditions for travellers departing from the European Community and how they may be able to get a refund on some goods bought by using the Retail Export Scheme	VATA 1994 section 30(8) VAT Regs. 1995 regs. 130 and 131
Notice 705: *VAT: Personal exports of new motor vehicles to destinations outside the European Community from 1 January 1993*	Principally the conditions set out on page 2 Other conditions and procedures to be followed by the purchaser are set out elsewhere in the Notice	VATA 1994 section 30(8) VAT Regs. 1995 regs. 132 and 133

Notice	Part having the force of law and its purpose	Enabling powers
Notice 705A: *VAT: Supplies of vehicles under the Personal Export Scheme for removal from the European Community*	Principally the conditions set out in Appendix B Other conditions and procedures to be followed by the supplier are set out elsewhere in the Notice	VATA 1994 section 30(8) VAT Regs. 1995 regs. 132 and 133
Notice 708: *Buildings and construction*	Annex A – Certificate for developers and building contractors in respect of relevant residential and relevant charitable buildings	VATA 1994 Sch. 8, Group 5 Note (12)(b)
Notice 709/2: *Catering and take-away food*	Paragraph 11 – How retailers who are unable to use one of the published retail schemes should estimate zero-rated supplies of food	VATA 1994 Sch. 11, para. 2(6) VAT Regs. 1995 regs. 66–75
Notice 709/5: *Tour operators' margin scheme*	App A–E. The notice provides that certain goods and services which would otherwise be covered by the Margin Scheme are excluded, and specifies the method of calculation for the Margin Scheme	VATA 1994, section 53 VAT (Tour Operators) Order 1987 SI No. 1806 articles 3 and 7 as amended by the Value Added Tax (Tour Operators) Orders of 1990, 1992 and 1995
Notice 718: *Margin Schemes for second-hand goods, works of art, antiques and collectors' items*	Section II: Records and Accounts Section III: Global Accounting Section IV: Auctions Section VII: Second-Hand Vehicles Section VIII: Horses and Ponies Updates 1, 2 and 3	VATA 1994 section 50A. VAT (Cars) Order 1992 (SI 3122) as amended VAT (Special Provisions) Order 1995 (SI 1268) as amended VAT (Input Tax) Order 1992 (SI 3222) as amended
Notice 725: *VAT: The Single Market*	(1) Paragraph 2.2(a) – Supplies to VAT registered customers in another EC Member State (2) Paragraph 5.5 – Values expressed in a foreign currency	VATA 1994 section 30(8) VATA 1994 Sch. 7, para. 4

Notice	Part having the force of law and its purpose	Enabling powers
Notice 727: *VAT: Retail schemes*	Paragraph 3: Who can use a retail scheme? Paragraph 5: Bespoke schemes Paragraph 6: How to choose a retail scheme Paragraph 7: The Point of Sale scheme Paragraph 8: The Apportionment Schemes Paragraph 9: The Direct Calculation schemes Paragraph 10: Using a mixture of schemes Paragraph 11: Changes of schemes Paragraph 12: Ceasing to use the schemes Appendices A–F	VATA 1994 Sch. 11, para. 2(6) VAT Regs. 1995 Part IX (regulations 66–75)
Notice 727/3: *Retail schemes: How to work the Point of Scale scheme*	Section 3: Special transactions Appendix B: Daily Gross Takings (DGT) checklist Appendix C: Business Promotion schemes	VATA 1994 Sch. 11, para. 2(6) VAT Regs. 1995 Part IX (SI 1995/2518) (regulations 66–75)
Notice 727/4: *Retail schemes. How to work the Apportionment Schemes*	Section 3: Special transactions Appendix B: Daily Gross Takings (DGT) checklist Appendix C: Business Promotion schemes	VATA 1994 Sch 11, para. 2(6) VAT Regs. 1995 Part IX (SI 1995/2518) (regulations 66–75)
Notice 727/5: *Retail schemes. How to work the Direct Calculation schemes*	Section 3: Special transactions Appendix B: Daily Gross Takings (DGT) checklist Appendix C: Business Promotion schemes	VATA 1994 Sch. 11, para. 2(6) VAT Regs. 1995 Part IX (SI 1995/2518) (regulations 66–75)
Notice 728: *Motor vehicles, boats, aircraft: intra-EC movements by private persons*	Principally paragraphs 5 – the conditions of the Scheme – and 13 – rate of exchange used to calculate the value of a NMT Other conditions and procedures to be complied with are set out elsewhere in the Notice	VATA 1994 section 30(8) VAT Regs. 1995 reg. 155 VATA 1994 Sch. 7, para. 4(2)
Notice 731: *Cash accounting*	Whole of the notice. The notice details the conditions for and rules of the cash accounting scheme which may benefit small businesses	VATA 1994 section 25 and Sch 11, para. 2(7) VAT Regs. 1995 regs. 56–65 as amended by VAT (Amendment) (No. 3) Regulations 1997
Notice 742: *Land and property*	Paragraph 8.6 – Automatic permission to opt to tax allowed subject to certain conditions	VATA 1994 Sch. 10, para. 3(9)

CUSTOMS AND EXCISE PUBLICATIONS NOT HAVING LEGAL FORCE

Publication

12	Compounding, seizure and restoration
48	Extra-statutory concessions
60	The Intrastat general guide
400	HM Customs and Excise charter standards
700	The VAT guide
702	Imports
703	Exports and removals of goods from the UK
704	Retail exports
705	Personal exports of new motor vehicles to destinations outside the EC from 1 January 1993
705A	VAT: supplies of vehicles under the personal export scheme for removal from the European Community
706	Partial exemption
708	Buildings and construction
714	Young children's clothing and footwear
714A	Young children's clothing and footwear: schedule of maximum sizes for zero-rating
718	Margin scheme for second-hand goods, works of art, antiques and collector's items
719	VAT refunds for "do-it-yourself" builders and converters
723	Refunds of VAT in the European Community and the other countries
725	The single market
727	Retail schemes
728	Motor vehicles, boats, aircraft: intra-EC movements by private persons
730	Civil evasion penalty investigations: statement of practice
732	Annual accounting
741	Place of supply of services
742	Land and property
744A	Passenger transport
744B	Freight transport
744C	Ships, aircraft and associated services
744D	International services: zero-rating
747	VAT notices having the force of law
749	Local authorities and similar bodies
989	Visits by Customs and Excise officers
990	Excise and customs appeals
999	Catalogue of publications
1000	Complaints and putting things right: our code of practice
700/1	Should I be registered for VAT?
700/1A	Should I be registered for VAT? – Distance selling
700/1B	Should I be registered for VAT? – Acquisitions
700/2	VAT group treatment
700/3	Registration for VAT: corporate bodies organised in divisions
700/4	Registration for VAT: non-established taxable persons
700/5	Hire-purchase and conditional sale: repossessions and transfers of agreements
700/7	Business promotion schemes
700/9	Transfer of a business as a going concern
700/11	Cancelling your registration
700/12	Filling in your VAT return
700/14	*Video cassette films: rental* and part-exchange
700/15	The ins and outs of VAT
700/17	Funded pension schemes
700/18	Relief from VAT on bad debts
700/21	Keeping records and accounts
700/22	Admissions

Publication

700/24	Postage and delivery charges
700/25	Taxis and hire-cars
700/28	Estate agents
700/31	Pawnbrokers: disposals of pledged goods
700/34	Staff
700/35	Business gifts and samples
700/41	Late registration penalty
700/42	Misdeclaration penalty
700/43	Default interest
700/44	Barristers and advocates: tax point on ceasing to practise
700/45	How to correct errors you find on your VAT returns
700/46	Agricultural flat-rate scheme
700/47	Confidentiality in VAT matters (tax advisers) – statement of practice
700/50	Default surcharge
700/51	VAT enquiries guide
700/52	Notice of requirement to give security to Customs and Excise
700/54	What if I don't pay?
700/55	VAT input tax appeals: luxuries, amusements and entertainment
700/56	Insolvency
700/57	VAT: administrative agreements entered into with trade bodies
700/58	Treatment of VAT repayment claims and VAT repayment supplement
700/59	VAT refunds on surrendered road fund licences
700/60	Payments on account
700/61	Artificial separation of business activities: statement of practice
700/64	Motoring expenses
700/65	Business entertainment
700/67	The VAT registration scheme for racehorse owners
701/1	Charities
701/5	Clubs and associations
701/6	Charity funded equipment for medical, veterinary etc. uses (and supplement)
701/7	VAT reliefs for people with disabilities
701/8	Postage stamps and philatelic supplies
701/9	Terminal markets – Dealings with commodities
701/10	Printed and similar matter
701/12	Sales of antiques, works of art etc. from stately homes
701/13	Gaming and amusement machines
701/14	Food
701/15	Food for animals
701/16	Sewerage services and water
701/19	Fuel and power
701/20	Caravans and houseboats
701/21	Gold
701/22	Tools for the manufacture of goods for export
701/23	Protective boots and helmets
701/24	Parking facilities
701/26	Betting and gaming
701/27	Bingo
701/28	Lotteries
701/29	Finance
701/30	Education
701/31	Health
701/32	Burial, cremation and the commemoration of the dead
701/33	Trade unions, professional bodies and learned societies
701/34	Competitions in sport and physical recreation
701/35	Youth clubs
701/36	Insurance

Publication

701/37	Live animals
701/38	Seeds and plants
701/39	VAT liability law
701/40	Abattoirs
701/41	Sponsorship
701/43	Financial futures and options
701/44	Securities
701/45	Sport and physical education
701/46	School photographs
701/47	Culture
701/48	Corporate purchasing cards
702/4	Importing computer software
702/6	Import VAT certificates
702/7	Import VAT relief for goods supplied onward to another country in the European Community
702/9	Warehouses and free zones
703/1	Supply of freight containers for export or removal from the United Kingdom
703/2	Sailaway boats supplied for export outside the European Community
703/3	VAT-free purchases of sailaway boats
704/1	VAT refunds for travellers departing from the European Community
704/2	Traveller's guide to the retail export scheme
704/3	Guide to tax-free shopping – the VAT refund scheme
706/1	Self-supply of stationery
706/2	Capital goods scheme: input tax on computers, land and buildings acquired for use in your business
708/5	Registered social landlords (Housing Associations etc.)
709/1	Industrial, staff and public sector catering
709/2	Catering and take-away food
709/3	Hotels and holiday accommodation
709/5	Tour operator's margin scheme
710/1	Theatrical agents and Nett Acts
710/2	Agencies providing nurses and nursing auxiliaries
727/2	Bespoke Retail Schemes
727/3	Retail schemes: How to work the point of sale scheme
727/4	Retail schemes: How to work the apportionment schemes
727/5	Retail schemes: How to work the direct calculation schemes
742C	Land and property: law
742/1	Letting of facilities for sport and physical recreation
742/2	Sporting rights
742/3	Scottish land law terms

Tribunal publication

Appeals and applications to the tribunals

Adjudicator's office

AO2   How to complain about Customs and Excise

Note – The publications are reproduced in the *British Value Added Tax Reporter*.

EXTRA-STATUTORY CONCESSIONS

This section contains the text of Notice 48, "Extra-statutory concessions" (1999). Only the material relating to VAT is reproduced here.

Notice 48 – Extra-statutory concessions (1999) [VAT material only]

CONTENTS

Paragraph
5 – Non-commercial transactions
5.1   VAT: VAT on goods supplied at duty-free and tax-free shops
5.2   VAT: Marine fuel
5.3   VAT and excise duties: Personal reliefs for goods permanently imported from third
         countries
5.4   VAT and excise duties: Personal reliefs for goods permanently imported from third
         countries
5.5   VAT and excise duties: Personal reliefs for goods permanently imported from third
         countries
5.6   VAT and excise duties: Personal reliefs for goods permanently imported from third
         countries
5.7   VAT and excise duties: Personal reliefs for goods permanently imported from third
         countries

2.   International Field

2.1.   VAT, excise and customs duties: Goods and services

Duty and VAT are remitted or refunded in accordance with agreements with the authorities concerned on:

(a)   goods and services imported by or supplied to visiting forces and their instrumentalities, for the official use of the force, or their instrumentalities
(b)   goods and services imported by or supplied to NATO military headquarters, organisations or agencies, for their official use
(c)   United States and Canadian Government expenditure on mutual defence or mutual aid contracts, and
(d)   temporary importations of equipment required by contractors for fulfilling NATO infrastructure contracts or in connection with the provision and maintenance of US forces defence facilities in the United Kingdom.

2.2.   VAT, excise and customs duties: UK-manufactured alcoholic liquor and tobacco products purchased by diplomats

Duty and VAT are remitted on alcoholic liquor and tobacco products of UK manufacture imported by, or supplied to, diplomatic representatives of foreign states in the United Kingdom who are entitled to similar privileges in respect of imported products of foreign manufacture under the Diplomatic Privileges Act 1964.

2.3.   VAT and excise duties: United States Air Force

Relief from VAT and/or excise duty is allowed, in accordance with conditions agreed with the United States Air Force, on:

(a)   charges for admission to air shows and open days, and
(b)   goods sold by US forces organisations during air shows and open days to persons not entitled to receive/consume them unless customs charges have been paid.

2.4.   VAT and customs duty: Gifts

Duty and VAT are remitted on gifts (whether imported or purchased in the United Kingdom) from United States forces to charitable organisations.

2.5.   VAT: American war graves

In order to place inland purchases on the same footing as imported goods, VAT is remitted on the supply of goods and services to the American Battle Monuments Commission for the maintenance of the American Military Cemetery and Memorial at Maddingley, Cambridge and Brookwood, Surrey.

2.6.   VAT and customs duty: Certain aircraft ground and security equipment

The Convention on International Civil Aviation (Chicago Convention) allows relief from duty and VAT for certain ground and security equipment imported into the territory of one Contracting State by an airline of another Contracting State operating an international service. The United Kingdom is a signatory to the Chicago Convention.

Additionally, the United Kingdom has concluded a number of Air Service Agreements which allow, on a reciprocal basis, the various reliefs detailed in the Convention, including the one mentioned above.

We have become aware that end-use relief may be being claimed erroneously in these cases. Aircraft ground and security equipment does not qualify for end-use relief. We are in the process of drawing up a new procedure to enable the relief to be correctly claimed.

In the interim period an extra-statutory concession has been agreed to allow relief for ground and security equipment to be claimed. The following list details those goods which qualify for relief and who is eligible to claim it.

Qualifying goods: The following ground and security equipment for aircraft:

(a)   Repair, maintenance and servicing equipment:
    ● all repair and maintenance material for airframes, engines and instruments
    ● specialised aircraft repair kits
    ● starter batteries and carts
    ● maintenance platforms and steps
    ● test equipment for aircraft, aircraft engines, and instruments
    ● aircraft engine heaters and coolers, and
    ● ground radio equipment.

(b)   Passenger-handling equipment:
    ● passenger − loading steps
    ● specialised passenger-weighing devices, and
    ● specialised catering equipment.

(c)   Cargo-loading equipment:
    ● vehicles for moving or loading of baggage, cargo, equipment or supplies
    ● specialised cargo-loading devices, and
    ● specialised cargo-weighing devices.

(d)   Component parts for incorporation into ground equipment including the items listed above.

(e)   Security equipment:
    ● weapon-detecting devices
    ● explosives-detecting devices, and
    ● intrusion detecting devices.

(f)   Component parts for incorporation into security equipment.

Claims for relief of duty and VAT under this concession should be addressed to the Customs Entry Processing Unit where the goods will be cleared with a copy of this advice.

3.   Concessions designed to remove inequities or anomalies in administration

3.1.   VAT: VAT on purchase of road fuel

The Value Added Tax Act 1994 section 56 (formerly Finance Act 1986 section 9) requires payment of a scale charge when road fuel purchased by a business is used for private journeys. However, where a registered person claims no input tax on purchases of road fuel, whether for business or private journeys, the VAT scale charge will not apply.

3.2.   VAT: Group supplies using an overseas member: anticipation of legislative changes

General

With effect from 26 November 1996, a resolution under the Provisional Collection of Taxes Act has created a new tax charge for the representative member of a VAT group, where supplies of a type set out in Schedule 5 to the VAT Act 1994 are purchased by an overseas group member and used for making Schedule 5 supplies to a UK group member. This new tax charge was made permanent when the Finance Act 1997 was passed on 19 March 1997. The new tax charge is given effect by section 41 of the Finance Act, which inserts the new rules into section 43 of the VAT Act 1994 at paragraphs (2A) to (2E).

Committee Stage amendments to what became section 41 reduced the impact of the new tax charge in certain specified circumstances with effect from 19 March 1997, the date when the Finance Act 1997 was passed. The impact will be further reduced when Regulations are made under section 41. This concession will allow groups to account for VAT with effect from 26 November 1996 as though the amendments and Regulations had been in force from that date. The concession falls into two parts.

First part of concession

First, a tax charge under section 41 is triggered where an overseas member of a VAT group has been supplied with services falling within any of paragraphs 1 to 8 of Schedule 5 to the VAT Act 1994 (services to be treated as supplied where received). By concession, no tax charge will be triggered by any such services which are exempt from VAT because they fall within one of the descriptions in Schedule 9 of the Act. This concession applies to supplies made between 26 November 1996 and 19 March 1997. After that date the concession is not needed, because it has been given legal effect by the passing of the Finance Act.

Second part of concession

Second, the amount of the tax charge under section 41 is calculated with reference to the value of the supply by the overseas member to the UK member. By concession, the value for calculating the tax charge may be reduced to the value of the Schedule 5 services purchased by the overseas group member, provided that the group is in a position to provide evidence in the UK of the value of those services, and that those services have not been undervalued. This concession will be given legal effect when Regulations are made under section 41.

3.3. VAT: Group supplies using an overseas member: transitional relief

General

With effect from 26 November 1996, a resolution under the Provisional Collection of Taxes Act has created a new tax charge for the representative member of a VAT group, where supplies of a type set out in Schedule 5 to the VAT Act 1994 are purchased by an overseas group member and used for making Schedule 5 supplies to a UK group member. This new tax charge was made permanent when the Finance Act 1997 was passed on 19 March 1997. The new tax charge is given effect by section 41 of the Finance Act, which inserts the new rules into section 43 of the VAT Act 1994 at paragraphs (2A) to (2E).

The time of the supply which is taxed under section 41 is the time when the supply is paid for or, if the consideration is not in money, on the last day of the prescribed accounting period in which the services are performed. Under this concession, taxpayers may treat the introduction of the new charge under section 41 as though it were a change in the rate of VAT, and covered by section 88 of the VAT Act 1994.

This means that, where the UK group member has on, or after 26 November 1996, paid for services affected by section 41, but performance of those services took place to any extent before that date, the group may account for tax only on that proportion of the services which were performed on or after 26 November 1996. Further details are contained in Notice 700, Appendix C, paragraphs 7 to 9.

Telecommunications services

Telecommunications services are not currently affected by section 41 because they do not fall within Schedule 5 of the VAT Act 1994. However, it is possible that relevant telecommunications services will be so included shortly. When that happens, appropriate rules will be introduced to determine whether and when VAT should be accounted for on these telecommunications services provided by suppliers outside the UK, but received by customers within the UK. Accordingly, this concession does not apply to telecommunications services.

3.4. VAT: Misunderstanding by a VAT trader

VAT undercharged by a registered trader on account of a bona fide misunderstanding may be remitted provided all the following conditions are fulfilled:

(a)   there is no reason to believe that the tax has been knowingly evaded

(b)   there is no evidence of negligence

(c)   the misunderstanding does not concern an aspect of the tax clearly covered in general guidance published by Customs and Excise or in specific instructions to the trader concerned, and

(d)   the tax due was not charged, could not now reasonably be expected to be charged to customers, and will not be charged.

Where, at the time the misunderstanding comes to light, there are unfulfilled firm orders from customers, for which the price quoted has been based mistakenly on the assumption that no VAT, or less VAT than properly due, would be chargeable, VAT undercharged may be remitted in respect of such orders provided conditions (a)-(d) above are met.

3.5.   VAT: Misdirection

If a Customs and Excise officer, with the full facts before him, has given a clear and unequivocal ruling on VAT in writing or, knowing the full facts, has misled a registered person to his detriment, any assessment of VAT due will be based on the correct ruling from the date the error was brought to the registered person's attention.

3.6.   VAT: Coin-operated machines

The tax point for supplies made from coin-operated machines is the date the machine is used. As an accounting convenience, however, operators may delay accounting for VAT until the takings are removed from a machine.

For all other purposes the normal tax point rules apply. Therefore in the event of a theft of takings from a machine, VAT must still be accounted for in full on any supplies that have been made from the machine.

3.7.   VAT: VAT on minor promotional items supplied in linked supplies schemes

These are schemes in which a minor article is linked, although not necessarily physically linked, with a main article (of either goods or services) and sold with it at a single price. The price paid should normally be apportioned to reflect any difference where the items are liable to VAT at different rates.

However, if the minor article:

(a)   is not charged to the customer at a separate price
(b)   costs the supplier no more than 20% of the total cost of the combined supply (excluding VAT), and
(c)   costs the supplier no more than:
- £1(excluding VAT) if included with goods intended for retail sale, or
- £5 (excluding VAT) otherwise,

the supplier may account for VAT on the minor article at the same rate as the main article – ie no apportionment is necessary.

3.8.   VAT: Use of margin scheme for vehicle sales when incomplete records have been kept

A dealer in second-hand vehicles who supplies a vehicle in circumstances in which, but for his failure to keep the necessary records relating to either the purchase or to the sale of the vehicle (but not to both), he would be entitled to account for the VAT chargeable on the supply on the profit margin on the supply rather than its value may, provided he satisfies the Commissioners that the mark-up achieved on the supply does not exceed 100%, treat the profit margin on the supply as being equal to:

(a)   where he has kept the necessary purchase records, the purchase price, and
(b)   where he has kept the necessary sales records, half of the selling price,

and accordingly account for the VAT chargeable on the supply on that profit margin.

3.9.   VAT: Recoveries under the VAT Act 1994 Schedule 11 paragraph 5

Where an amount is shown or represented as VAT on an invoice issued by a person who is neither registered nor required to be registered for VAT at the time when the invoice is issued, the provisions of Schedule 11 paragraph 5 of the VAT Act 1994 (formerly Schedule 7 paragraph 6 of the VAT Act 1983) enable the Commissioners to require that person to pay an equivalent amount to them. The Act does not provide any relief in respect of related VAT incurred by such a person. On the grounds of equity, a person making such a payment may be permitted to deduct from it the amount of VAT incurred on supplies to him of goods and services that were directly attributable to any invoiced supply in respect of which such payment is required.

Where such a person has made a supply to a taxable person and, on the invoice, showed or represented an amount as VAT, the recipient of the supply has no legal entitlement to treat that amount as his input tax. If it is clear that the taxable person who received the supply has treated such an amount as input tax in good faith, action to recover the amount so deducted may be remitted on grounds of equity.

3.10.   VAT: VAT on necessary meals and accommodation provided by recognised representative sporting bodies to amateur sports persons chosen to represent that body in a competition

The Value Added Tax (Input Tax) Order 1992 (SI 1992 No 3222) (formerly the Value Added Tax (Special Provisions) Order 1981 (SI 1981 No 1741) as amended by the VAT (Special Provisions) (Amendment) Order 1988 (SI 1988 No 1124)) prevents input tax deduction where goods or services have been provided for the purposes of business entertainment except where this entertainment is of an employee. The effect of this provision is to produce different treatment as between, for example, professional football teams and amateur football teams. This is because the professional players are employees of their clubs and input tax is deductible, while the amateur players are, by definition, not employees and input tax is blocked. This distinction between amateur and professional sportsmen has led to inequity in the VAT treatment of certain amateur representative bodies who are registered for VAT and account for output tax on "gate money" in the same way as professional clubs, but cannot recover VAT on some of their genuine business expenses.

With the overwhelming number of clubs this has provided no problem as members' subscriptions are regarded as being payment, in part, for any accommodation or meals that they may receive when playing for that club. However, problems have been encountered with certain bodies who choose, from affiliated clubs, individual amateur sports persons to represent their country or county. These persons so selected are not full subscribing members of the representational body, paying a very small nominal subscription, or no subscription at all and, therefore, the provision in Notice 700/65, paragraph 11 – entertainment of members of clubs, associations, etc. – cannot apply. To remove this inequity of treatment as between professional and amateur bodies, it has been agreed that input tax necessarily incurred on the provision of accommodation and meals for team members selected by such representative bodies may be deductible as input tax. This concession not only applies to selected players but also to the committee members of the body who are to be treated as "persons engaged in the management of a company and deemed to be employees of that company". The concession does not cover alcoholic drinks and tobacco (including cigarettes and cigars) provided for consumption by players and committee members.

3.11. VAT: Incorrect customer declaration

Where a customer provides an incorrect declaration claiming eligibility for zero-rating under Groups 2, 4, 5, 6, 8, 12 or 15 of the zero rate Schedule of the VAT Act 1994, or eligibility for a reduced rate under Schedule A1 for the qualifying use of fuel and power, and where a supplier, despite having taken all reasonable steps to check the validity of the declaration, nonetheless fails to identify the inaccuracy and in good faith makes the supplies concerned at the zero rate, or a reduced rate, Customs and Excise will not seek to recover the tax due from the supplier.

3.12. VAT: Buses with special facilities for carrying disabled persons

A vehicle constructed or adapted to have a carrying capacity of less than 12 passengers would not normally qualify for input tax deduction and subsequent fares charged to passengers would be standard-rated. But where a vehicle which would otherwise have 12 or more seats, has a carrying capacity of less than 12 passengers solely because it is equipped with facilities for persons in wheelchairs, it can be treated, for VAT purposes, as if it had at least 12 seats.

3.13. VAT: Repayment of import VAT to shipping agents and freight forwarders

Import VAT may be paid directly to shipping agents and freight forwarders where importers go into liquidation, or where an administrator or administrative receiver has been appointed who certifies that, in his or her opinion, ordinary unsecured creditors would receive nothing in a liquidation, leaving the agents unable to recover VAT paid on their behalf. The importers must have gone into a formal state of insolvency or receivership within 6 months of the date of lodgement of the Customs entry, and the goods must have remained under the agents' control throughout their stay in the UK and have been re-exported unused from the European Community.

3.14. VAT: Zero-rating of certain supplies of free zone goods

From 1 August 1991 the supply of goods subject to import VAT which are free zone goods in the UK may be zero-rated on condition that there is an agreement between the supplier and the customer that the customer will clear the goods for removal from the zone and will take responsibility for payment of the import VAT.

3.15. VAT: Printed matter published in instalments

Books are zero-rated for VAT under item 1 of Group 3 of Schedule 8 to the VAT Act 1994 (formerly item 1 of Group 3 of Schedule 5 to the VAT Act 1983). However, there is a specialist area of the market known as continuity publishing or part-works where the product is supplied in parts over varying periods but builds up into a greater whole, ie a loose-leaf book. Unless such items, when viewed independently, are books etc. at the time of supply, they are not entitled to zero-rating under the present law.

From 1 February 1993 by way of concession, if, at the time of supply, an article is or was not by itself regarded as a book, including a loose-leaf book, qualifying for zero-rating under item 1 of Group 3 of Schedule 8 to the VAT Act 1994, but is or was a part of a larger finite work which itself would fall under item 1 of Group 3 of Schedule 8 as a book, then the individual component parts may also be zero-rated where they are or were being supplied either direct by the publisher or through a distribution chain to the final consumer. From 26 October 1993 by way of further concession in relation to card-based boxed continuity series publications, such publications, even though not bound or held together other than in or by their container, and having all the other characteristics of a book, will for VAT purposes be treated as a book.

3.16. VAT: Connection to the gas or electricity mains supply

Connection to the gas or electricity mains supply, which would have been a zero-rated supply before 1 April 1994 by virtue of Group 7 of Schedule 5 to the Value Added Tax Act 1983, may continue to be treated as a zero-rated supply provided that:

(a)   it is the first connection to the gas or electricity mains supply (as the case may be) of:

      (i)   a building, or part of a building, which consists of a dwelling or number of dwellings

     (ii)   a building, or part of a building, used solely for a relevant residential purpose (within the meaning of Note 4 to Group 7)

    (iii)   a building, or part of a building, used by a charity otherwise than in the course or furtherance of a business

    (iv)   a residential caravan (that is to say a caravan on a site in respect of which there is no covenant, statutory planning consent or similar permission precluding occupation throughout the year), or

     (v)   a houseboat (within the meaning of Note 6 to Group 7), and

    (vi)   the person receiving the supply does not do so for the purpose of any business carried on by him.

3.17. VAT: Zero-rating of supplies of training for foreign governments

From 1 October 1993 the services of training (not being services comprised in any Group of Schedule 9 to the VAT Act 1994, formerly Schedule 6 to the VAT Act 1983), supplied to a foreign government in furtherance of its sovereign activities (and not its business activities), is liable to VAT at the zero rate provided the supplier retains a statement in writing from that government (or its accredited representative), that the trainees are employed in furtherance of its sovereign activities.

3.18. VAT: Exemption for all domestic service charges

The concession exempts from 1 April 1994 all mandatory service charges or similar charges paid by the occupants of residential property towards the upkeep of the dwellings or block of flats in which they reside and towards the provision of a warden, caretakers, and people performing a similar function for those occupants. The concession does not exempt service charges paid in respect of holiday accommodation as defined in paragraph 1(e) of and Notes 11-13 to Group 1, Schedule 9, VAT Act 1994 (formerly paragraph 1(d) of and Notes (10) (10A) and (10B) to Group 1, Schedule 6, VAT Act 1983).

3.19. VAT: Developer's self-supply on 1 March 1997

1. The developer's self-supply on 1 March 1997 under paragraph 5(1)(b) of Schedule 10 to the Value Added Tax Act 1994 need not be treated as made where:

(a)   construction of a building or civil engineering work is still in progress on 1 March 1997 and the value of the developer's potential self-supply including those construction costs in paragraph 6(2)(b) of Schedule 10 to the Value Added Tax Act 1994 incurred both before and on or after 28 February 1997, would be less than £100,000, or

(b)   a building or civil engineering work was completed before 1 March 1995 and either:

      (i)   the building is fully occupied or the civil engineering work is used by a "developer" who is a taxable person for non-business purposes, rather than in connection with making any exempt supplies of goods or services, and consequently the "developer" under paragraph 5(5) of Schedule 10 to the Value Added Tax Act 1994 would have been a taxable person under paragraph 5(4)(b) of that Schedule, or

    (ii)   the building has been fully occupied or the civil engineering work has been fully used before 1 March 1997, or

    (iii) the building or civil engineering work is the subject of an election to waive exemption, and input tax has been provisionally recovered in the anticipation of granting a taxable interest in it.

2.   Examples of buildings or civil engineering works which might be within paragraph 1(b)(i) above are non-business NHS hospitals, government offices, and buildings and civil engineering works occupied or used by a local authority or similar body pursuant to its statutory non-business activities.

3.   If a "developer":

(a)   has completed the construction of a building or civil engineering work before 1 March 1995, and

(b)   considers that the building or work would not have been subject to the developer's self-supply had the provisions in paragraph 5(1)(a) of Schedule 10 to the Value Added Tax Act 1994 continued after 28 February 1997, but the situation is not described in paragraphs 1(a) to 1(b) above,

then that person may make an individual request in writing to the Commissioners of Customs and Excise not to be treated as making a developer's self-supply on 1 March 1997.

Any reference in this concession to a building or civil engineering work includes a building or work which has been or is being reconstructed, enlarged or extended.

3.20.   VAT: Supplies of "relevant goods" to charities

1.   Where "relevant goods" of a kind described in Note (3) to Group 15 of the Value Added Tax Act 1994 are supplied to a charity:

(a)   whose sole purpose and function is to provide a range of care services to meet the personal needs of handicapped people (of which transport might form a part), or

(b)   which provides transport services predominantly to handicapped people,

then by concession, the supply of those goods will be zero-rated, as will the repair and maintenance of those goods and the supply of any further goods in connection with that repair and maintenance.

2.   **"Handicapped"** means chronically sick or disabled.

3.   In order to be eligible for this concession, a charity must demonstrate that it meets the requirements of sub-paragraphs (a) or (b) above by way of:

(a)   its charitable aims and objectives its publicity and advertising material

(b)   any documents which it has issued for the purpose of obtaining funding from a third party such as a local authority

(c)   its day-to-day operations, and

(d)   any other evidence that may be relevant.

3.21.   VAT: Disapplication of Repayment of Input Tax (Value Added Tax Act 1994 section 36(4)A and the VAT Regulations 1995 SI 2518 (as amended by the VAT (Amendment) Regulations 1997 SI 1086)

1.   Subject to paragraphs 3 and 4 below, section 36(4A) of the VAT Act 1994 will not apply to any person where:

(a)   an insolvency procedure has commenced in relation to that person under section 81(4B), (4C) and (5) of the VAT Act 1994;

(b)   the claimant's notification of his claim for bad debt relief in accordance with regulation 166A of the Value Added Tax Regulations 1995 (SI 1995 No 2518), is received after the insolvency procedure has commenced, and

(c)   each relevant supply upon which the claim for bad debt relief is based, was made prior to the commencement of the insolvency procedure.

2.   Paragraph 1 above applies whether or not the business of the person who is the subject of the insolvency procedure continues to be carried on.

3.   Paragraph 1 above does not apply unless the Commissioners have received notification on Form VAT 769 "Notification of Insolvency details", or such other notification as the Commissioners may require, in respect of the insolvency procedure referred to in that paragraph.

4.   Paragraph 1 above does not apply in circumstances where its application would give rise to tax avoidance.

The insolvency procedures to which the extra-statutory concession applies

The insolvency procedures included in section 81 of the Value Added Tax Act 1994 for the purposes of this concession are:

- Bankruptcy.
- Compulsory liquidation (winding up).
- Creditors' voluntary liquidation (voluntary winding up).
- Members' voluntary liquidation (voluntary winding up).
- Administrative Receivership.
- Administrative Order.
- Individual Voluntary Arrangement.
- Company Voluntary Arrangement.
- Scottish Trust Deed.
- Deed of Arrangement.

After further consultations with representatives of insolvency practitioners and colleagues within Customs who deal with insolvency policy, it has been agreed that the application of this concession should be extended to a number of other types of insolvencies that are not included in the strict interpretation of section 81 of the Value Added Tax Act 1994. Accordingly this concession will apply to the following types of insolvency that are not included in section 81.

- Partnership Voluntary Arrangement. (Insolvent Partnerships Order 1994). (Insolvent Partnerships Order (Northern Ireland) 1995).
- Partnership Liquidation. (Insolvent Partnerships Order 1994). (Insolvent Partnerships Order (Northern Ireland) 1995).
- Partnership Administration Order. (Insolvent Partnerships Order 1994). (Insolvent Partnerships Order (Northern Ireland) 1995).
- Sequestration. (Bankruptcy (Scotland) Act 1985). (Bankruptcy (Scotland) Act 1993).
- County Court Administration Order. (County Court Act 1984).Scheme of Arrangement. (Companies Act 1985).
- Deceased Persons Administration Order. (Administration of Insolvent Estates of Deceased Persons Order 1986). (Administration of Insolvent Estates of Deceased Persons Order (Northern Ireland) 1991).

Application of extra-statutory concession

The effective date for the application of the concession will be the date of the Customs claim in the insolvency. This will be the relevant date of the insolvency and the insolvency meeting date (if applicable).

In Administration Order cases the effective date will be the date of the Administration Order.

Where there is a subsequent insolvency the concession will also apply to that subsequent insolvency.

If an insolvency arrangement fails the insolvency is annulled and the requirement to account for clawback will be reinstated.

The concession will only apply to a provisional liquidation if it is followed by a permanent liquidation. In these circumstances the clawback concession will take effect from the date of the provisional liquidation.

3.22. VAT: Sales of poor quality donated goods

By concession, the supply by a charity of any goods which have been donated for sale or the supply of such goods by a taxable person who is convenanted by deed to give all the profits of that supply to a charity, shall be treated as zero-rated, provided that:

(a)   the supply is a sale of goods donated to that charity or taxable person, but

(b)   the goods, although of a kind which the charity or taxable person makes available to the general public for purchase (whether in a shop or elsewhere) are by reason of their poor quality not fit to be so made available.

3.23. VAT: Supplies by Financial Services Authority to self-regulating organisations

The payment of any amount at any time by the Investment Management Regulatory Organisation (IMRO), the Personal Investment Authority (PIA) or the Securities and Futures Authority (SFA) to the Financial Services Authority (FSA) for the supply of services by the FSA in the carrying out the regulatory functions of IMRO, PIA or SFA (as the case may be) between 1 April 1998 and

31 March 2000 shall not be treated as consideration for any supply in the course or furtherance of any business carried on by FSA.

3.24. VAT: Supplies by Financial Services Authority to self-regulating organisations

This concession extends the existing concession (see 3.23 above) in order to ensure that payments from the Registrar of Friendly Societies (RFS) and the Insurance Directorate of HM Treasury (ID) for performance by Financial Services Authority (FSA) of regulatory functions of RFS and ID shall not be treated as any supply in the course or furtherance of any business carried on by the FSA.

3.25. VAT: Charities who provide care in an institution and also supply goods to disabled persons resident in their own and other institutions

1. This concession applies in relation to a supply of goods which, apart from Note (5B) to Group 12 of Schedule 8 to the Value Added Tax 1994, would fall within paragraph (g) of item 2 of that Group, where:

(a) the goods are goods other than spectacles or contact lenses, and are designed solely for use by a visually handicapped person

(b) the goods are supplied by a charity at or below cost

(c) the recipient of the supply is a resident or is attending the premises of a relevant institution as defined in Note (5I) to the said Group 12, and

(d) the charity is not actively engaged in supplying goods within paragraph (a) above solely to handicapped persons who are resident in or attending the premises of a relevant institution as defined by Note (5I) to the said Group 12 operated, managed or controlled by the charity.

2. Where this concession applies, the supply of the goods may be treated as if it were a zero-rated supply.

3. The Commissioners may withdraw or restrict the application of this concession if they have reasonable cause to believe that it is being abused.

3.26. VAT: Resuscitation training models supplied to charities and other eligible bodies for use in first aid training

1. The concession shall operate to include in Note (3) to Group 15 of Schedule 8 to the Value Added Tax Act 1994, the following:

(i) human resuscitation training models acquired for use in first aid training in either or both cardiopulmonary resuscitation and defibrillation techniques, and

(ii) parts and accessories for use in or with the goods described in paragraph (i) above, where the parts and accessories are for use in the training of either or both cardiopulmonary resuscitation and defibrillation techniques.

2. In this concession resuscitation training model means a model which includes a head and torso designed for use in the training of cardiopulmonary resuscitation or defibrillation techniques.

3. In this concession cardiopulmonary resuscitation means a combination of expired air ventilation and chest compression.

4. The Commissioners may withdraw or restrict the application of this concession if they have reasonable cause to believe that it is being abused.

3.27. VAT: Works of art, antiques and collectors' items

The Value Added Tax (Treatment of Transactions) Order 1995 (SI 1995/958) relieves from VAT certain transactions by treating them as neither a supply of goods nor a supply of services. This Order may also be applied, in the same way that it applies to works of art, to the following goods:

(a) all works of art falling within paragraph (a) of Annex I to Council Directive 77/388/EEC (inserted by Council Directive 94/5/EC) which do not already fall within the said order

(b) collectors' items falling within paragraph (b) of the said Annex I, and

(c) antiques falling within paragraph (c) of the said Annex I.

3.28. VAT: Use of the Auctioneers' Scheme for sales of goods at auction on behalf of non-taxable persons

From 1 January 1999, an auctioneer selling, on behalf of a third party vendor who is a non-taxable person, goods which have been grown, made or produced (including bloodstock or livestock reared from birth) by that person, may enter the goods into the auctioneers' scheme provided he holds a certificate from the vendor which includes:

(a) vendor's full name and address

(b)   description of goods and date of sale
(c)   declaration that the vendor is not registered nor required to be registered for VAT
(d)   signature of vendor and date, and
(e)   signature of auctioneer and date,

and all other conditions of the scheme are met. The completed certificate must be retained with the relevant records for VAT purposes.

An example of an acceptable certificate is set out below:

AUCTIONEERS' SCHEME FOR SECOND-HAND GOODS, WORKS OF ART, ANTIQUES AND COLLECTORS' ITEMS

Extra-statutory concession number xx

Vendor's Certificate for goods grown, made or produced and sold at auction on behalf of non-taxable persons

I (full name)

of (address)

declare that I am not registered or required to be registered for VAT and that the goods detailed below are to be sold at auction on my behalf by (auctioneer's name)

Description of goods

Date of sale (to be completed by auctioneer)

Signature of vendor

Signature of auctioneer

Date

---

4.   Facilitation of exports

4.1.   VAT: Sailaway boats

Under regulation 129 of the Value Added Tax Regulations 1995, the supply of a sailaway boat to an overseas resident outside the VAT territory of the Member States may be zero-rated provided the boat is exported to a place outside the Member States within 6 months of the date of delivery, and the supplier obtains satisfactory proof of its eventual export.

As a concession and to prevent loss of UK trade, the supply of a boat to a UK resident may also be zero-rated provided:

(a)   the supplier has evidence that the UK resident intends to keep the boat outside the VAT territory of the Member States for a continuous period of at least 12 months, and

(b)   the boat is exported, within 2 months of the date of delivery, to a place outside the VAT territory of the Member States, and

(c)   the boat is not used for any commercial purposes between the time of supply and exportation, and

(d)   the supplier obtains and holds satisfactory evidence of export of the boat directly to a place outside the VAT territory of the Member States on copy 3 of the Form C88 (Single Administrative Document).

The above conditions apply to boats supplied both to UK residents who intend to keep them abroad and to UK residents intending to emigrate.

4.2.   VAT: Supplies to diplomatic missions, international organisations, NATO forces etc. in other EC countries

A VAT registered trader can zero-rate supplies of goods, (other than new means of transport), or services made to entitled persons and bodies resident or situated in other EC countries provided:

●   the goods or services are for either the official use of the entitled bodies or for the personal use of entitled members etc. thereof, and

●   the supplier obtains from the customer an application for exemption from VAT under Article 15.10 of the Sixth VAT Directive (or, if not available, a written order/certificate confirming eligibility under that Article), and

●   in the case of goods, they are removed to another EC country, and

●   the supplier obtains and keeps proof of removal of the goods to another EC country within three months of the time of supply. This should be the commercial proof of export or removal normally acceptable for VAT zero-rating purposes.

5.   Non-commercial transactions

5.1.   VAT: VAT on goods supplied at duty-free and tax-free shops

The supplier of goods which are liable to VAT and which are supplied to intending passengers at duty-free and tax-free shops approved by the Commissioners may, for those goods which are exported directly to a place outside the VAT territory of the Member States, be regarded as the exporter and zero-rate the supply.

5.2.   VAT: Marine fuel

Commercial vessels engaged on voyages within UK territorial waters (or within the limits of a port), may receive certain types of marine fuel VAT free providing the conditions set out in paragraph 7.5 of Notice 703 VAT: Exports and removals of goods from the United Kingdom are met.

This relief extends only to those supplies of fuel which were zero-rated prior to 1 July 1990 under the Value Added Tax Act 1983 Schedule 5 Group 7 item 4. It does not apply to petrol, DERV or lubricating oil.

5.3.   VAT and excise duties: Personal reliefs for goods permanently imported from third countries

Where property (including motor vehicles) which has been purchased in accordance with the terms of Article 15/10 of Directive 77/388/EEC and which otherwise qualifies for relief from payment of customs charges under Article 11 of the Customs and Excise Duties (Personal Reliefs for Goods Permanently Imported) Order 1992, relief is not to be refused solely by reason of Article 11.2 of that Order.

5.4.   **VAT and excise duties: Personal reliefs for goods permanently imported from third countries**

Where property (including motor vehicles) which has been purchased by members of UK forces (or by the civilian staff accompanying them) in countries outside the area of the European Community and which otherwise qualifies for relief from payment of customs charges under Article 11 of the Customs and Excise Duties (Personal Reliefs for Goods Permanently Imported) Order 1992, relief is not to be refused solely by reason of Article 11.2 of that Order.

5.5.   **VAT and excise duties: Personal reliefs for goods permanently imported from third countries**

Where property (including motor vehicles) which has been purchased under a UK export scheme by members of the UK diplomatic service, by members of UK forces or by the civilian staff accompanying them or by members of international organisations and which otherwise qualifies for relief from payment of customs charges under Article 11 of the Customs and Excise Duties (Personal Reliefs for Goods Permanently Imported) Order 1992, relief is not to be refused solely by reason of Article 11.2 of that Order.

5.6.   **VAT and excise duties: Personal reliefs for goods permanently imported from third countries**

Where personal belongings otherwise qualify for relief under Article 11 of the Customs and Excise Duties (Personal Reliefs for Goods Permanently Imported) Order 1992 save only that the property has not been possessed and used for the specified period, then just as relief can be granted from customs duties as "special cases justified by the circumstances" under Article 3 of Council Regulation 918/83, similar consideration shall apply in respect of VAT and excise duties and relief may be granted accordingly.

5.7.   **VAT and excise duties: Personal reliefs for goods permanently imported from third countries**

Where personal belongings otherwise qualify for relief under Article 11 of the Customs and Excise Duties (Personal Reliefs for Goods Permanently Imported) Order 1992 save only that the property is declared for relief outside the specific periods, then just as relief can be granted from customs duties as special cases under Article 6, or under Article 9 of Council Regulation 918/83, similar consideration shall apply in respect of VAT and excise duties and relief may be granted accordingly.

OTHER MATERIAL

A. PRESS NOTICES

VAT: HIRE PURCHASE ETC. – GOODS RETURNED OR REPOSSESSED [HM Customs and Excise Press Notice 754, 30 July 1982]

Customs and Excise have issued guidance to the Consumer Credit Trade Association and the Finance Houses Association on the procedure to be followed when suppliers under hire purchase and conditional sale agreements wish to reduce the tax value of a supply after the goods are returned or repossessed before all the instalments are paid.

In these circumstances the supplier may adjust the tax value of the supply and issue a credit note to the customer. Only full credit notes are acceptable – no adjustment may be made for credit notes which are issued "for VAT only".

The value on the credit note must exclude:

(a) any instalments which have been paid or damages received; and

(b) any unpaid instalments for which the supplier is pressing a claim. (If the goods are resold and the creditor decides to press a claim for the unpaid instalments not covered by the sale, he may issue a credit note for the proceeds of the sale.)

When, under the terms of the original agreement, the customer is obliged to pay at least 50 per cent of the purchase price the credit must not exceed this amount.

Similar arrangements will also apply to supplies under Romalpa type reservation of title contracts.

Further details should be obtained from local VAT offices.

VAT: VEHICLE HIRE [HM Customs and Excise Press Notice 758, 23 August 1982]

Customs and Excise announce that with effect from 1 October 1982 vehicle hirers will be required to charge VAT at the standard rate in respect of the total charge payable by the customer for the hire of the vehicle.

This will include any portion of the hire charge which may be attributable to charges for insurers.

The British Vehicle Rental and Leasing Association and the Motor Agents' Association have been consulted about the new arrangements.

Notes – This press notice followed a tribunal decision that vehicle hirers making a charge for insurance were supplying an insured vehicle, the consideration for which was the total charge payable by the customer.

VAT: GOODS OBTAINED BY FRAUD [HM Customs and Excise Press Notice 761, 20 September 1982]

VAT registered traders who have been defrauded of goods may, in certain circumstances, be able to recover VAT which they have accounted for as output tax and submitted to Customs and Excise in respect of the transaction.

If the trader reports the fraud to the police and, as a result, a conviction is obtained, he should apply in writing to his local VAT office for authority to adjust his VAT account. The application should be supported by evidence of his complaint to the police and of the conviction for the offence.

A verifiable description of the goods in question will also be required.

VAT: SEPARATION OF BUSINESS ACTIVITIES FOR VAT PURPOSES [HM Customs and Excise Press Notice 762, 20 September 1982]

Customs and Excise announce the following criteria which they would expect to be met before accepting that a previously single business had been divided into independent parts for VAT registration purposes.

(a) appropriate premises and equipment for the business should be owned or rented by the person carrying on the business;

(b) day to day records which specifically identify the business should be maintained and, where appropriate, annual accounts prepared;

(c) purchase and sale invoices should be in the name of the person making supplies in the course of carrying on the business. (Where constituents of a supply normally regarded as a single compound supply, e.g. "bed and breakfast", are claimed to be made by different persons directly to the customer, not only must each part be invoiced separately but the arrangements for the supply must also be seen to be directly between the person claiming to make the supply and the customer);

(d) the person carrying on the business should be legally responsible for all trading activities, i.e. payments for supplies should be the sole responsibility of the person carrying on the business and proceeds of sales should also be at the sole disposal of that person;

(e) any bank account for the business should be in the name of the person carrying on the business, who should also be the sole drawer to the account;

(f) wages and National Health contributions in respect of staff employed in the business should be paid by the person carrying on the business; and

(g) for income tax purposes the business should be assessed as a separate business.

This notice relates only to VAT considerations. Persons contemplating dividing their business should take into account all the other implications of this course of action, seeking professional advice as appropriate.

Failure to implement all of the points listed might affect the person's liability for VAT.

VAT: SALES OF GOODWILL [HM Customs and Excise Press Notice 790, 10 December 1982]

From 1 January 1983 Customs and Excise will treat all sales of the goodwill of a business as taxable supplies except where they are specifically relieved by law.

Unidentifiable goodwill, valued as the residual difference between the business as a whole and the sum of its identifiable assets, is currently treated as outside the scope of VAT.

Normally goodwill is sold as part of the assets of a business transferred as a going concern. Such sales will be relieved from tax if the transfer meets the provisions of the [VAT (Special Provisions) Order 1995 (SI 1995/1268), art. 5(1)].

Notes – A note to this press notice referred to the fact that sales of goodwill which can be specifically identified as an asset of the business have always been treated as taxable supplies of services (e.g. use of a trade mark or trading name, lists of customers).

VAT: REPOSSESSED GOODS [HM Customs and Excise Press Notice 931, 3 August 1984]

HM Customs and Excise announce that from 1 September 1984, a supplier who takes back goods sold under a hire purchase or conditional sale agreement from a customer who is a VAT registered trader before all the instalments have been paid, will not be allowed to reduce the value of the original sale for VAT purposes.

VAT: LEGAL SERVICES IN INSURANCE CLAIMS [HM Customs and Excise Press Notice 960, 31 December 1984]

The Commissioners of Customs and Excise have agreed with the British Insurance Association and other insurance bodies that policy-holders who are registered for VAT can count as input tax VAT incurred on legal services supplied to them in connection with an insurance claim relating to their business.

From 1 January 1985 this will apply whether the solicitor is instructed by the policy-holder or by the insurer on his behalf and whether or not in practice the proceedings are controlled by the insurer. It has also been agreed that, normally, such legal services are supplied to the policy-holder not the insurer even where the insurer exercises his right of subrogation to pursue or defend a claim in the name of the policy-holder.

The Commissioners have also agreed with the insurance bodies that Directions issued to insurance companies to ensure that input tax is not recovered on repairs and replacements are no longer necessary. The Directions, which were issued under Regulation 24(2) of the VAT (General) Regulations [1980], are to be treated as withdrawn with effect from 1 January 1985. Guidance on the VAT treatment of solicitors' and other costs in insurance claims [can be found in Leaflet 701/36].

VAT: LIABILITY GOVERNED BY STATUS OF RECIPIENT [HM Customs and Excise Press Notice 1032, 10 September 1985]

As a general principle, the determination of liability of VAT is the responsibility of the taxpayer. In certain special cases the VAT liability of supplies of goods or services depends on the status of the customer receiving them. This can present problems for the supplier where the customer, innocently or otherwise, wrongly represents his status. Where this happens the Commissioners of

Customs and Excise will not hold the supplier responsible for failing to charge the correct amount of tax, provided they are satisfied that the supplier:

(a)   acted in good faith; and

(b)   made normal and prudent checks and enquiries about the status of the customer and of any documentation of certification provided by him.

Notes – This concession only applies where the customer provides misleading information on his status rather than that of the supply.

VAT TRIBUNALS: COSTS OF UNSUCCESSFUL APPLICANTS [HM Customs and Excise Press Notice 1132, 5 August 1986]

Customs and Excise are to continue their present practice of only seeking costs in limited circumstances when there are unsuccessful appeals by taxpayers to the independent Value Added Tax Tribunals. This restatement covers both appeals against tax and those against penalties imposed under the provisions of FA 1985 [VATA 1994, s. 59–69] (for example, late notification and default surcharge).

Announcing this in answer to a Parliamentary Question in the House of Commons the Minister of State, Treasury, the Hon. Peter Brooke MP said:

> "The practice of Customs and Excise in seeking costs in unsuccessful appeals heard by the VAT Tribunals was set out by [Mr. Robert Sheldon], the Right Honourable member for Ashton-under-Lyne, when he was Financial Secretary to the Treasury, on 13 November 1978. There has been no change in policy since then, but with the new enforcement powers and rights of appeal, particularly on the grounds of reasonable excuse, enacted in the Finance Act 1985 [VATA 1994, s. 71(1)], it may be helpful to restate it. As a general rule, Customs and Excise do not seek costs against unsuccessful appellants. They do, however, ask for costs in certain narrowly defined cases so as to provide protection for public funds and the general body of taxpayers. They will therefore seek to continue to ask for costs at those exceptional Tribunal hearings of substantial and complex cases where large sums are involved and which are comparable with High Court cases, unless the appeal involves an important general point of law requiring clarification. They will also continue to consider seeking costs where the appellant has misused the Tribunal procedure – for example in frivolous or vexatious cases, or where the appellant has failed to appear or to be represented at a mutually arranged hearing without sufficient explanation, or where the appellant has first produced at a hearing relevant evidence which ought properly to have been disclosed at an earlier stage and which could have saved public funds had it been produced timeously.
>
> The new penalty provisions and right of appeal to the Value Added Tax Tribunals has made no change to this policy. Customs and Excise, with the agreement of the council on Tribunals, consider that appeals against penalties imposed under FA 1985, s. 13 [VATA 1994, s. 60] on the grounds that a person has evaded VAT and his conduct has involved dishonesty, fall to be considered as being comparable with High Court cases. Where such appeals are unsuccessful, Customs and Excise will normally seek an award of costs.
>
> In all cases the question whether or not costs should be awarded will, of course, remain entirely within the discretion of the Tribunal concerned and the amount of any such award will be fixed either by that Tribunal, or by the High Court as provided by Tribunal procedure rules.
>
> Customs and Excise, in consultation with the Council on Tribunals, will continue to keep their policy under careful scrutiny."

VAT: MEALS AND ACCOMMODATION PROVIDED BY EMPLOYERS TO THEIR EMPLOYEES [HM Customs and Excise Press Notice 1137, 20 August 1986]

In a decision released on 16 June [1986] (Robert Wright Goodfellow and Margaret Jane Goodfellow: (MAN/85/20) [No. 2107; (1986) 2 BVC 208,100]) the London VAT Tribunal held that the appellants were not accountable for VAT when they provided meals or accommodation to their employees.

The appellants generally paid their employees in accordance with the Wages Order for the time being in force for the industry under the Wages Councils Act 1979. This involved establishing the basic minimum wage applicable to the employee under the Order and then making the appropriate reduction set out in the Order, depending on the catering and accommodation provided. Customs and Excise contended that the reduction in the wage amounted to a monetary consideration for the provision of the catering and accommodation, and was therefore liable to VAT. The Tribunal held however that these calculations were no more than steps in arriving at the amount of the weekly wage to be paid: and that there was no agreement between the appellants and their employees that meals or accommodation would be provided in consideration for the reduction in their weekly remuneration. Because there was no monetary consideration, it followed that under the provisions of VATA 1983, Sch. 4, para. 10 [VATA 1994, Sch. 6, para. 10] the appellants were not liable to VAT on the amount by which the wages were reduced.

Customs and Excise have accepted the decision in the particular circumstances to which it relates. They remain of the view however that VAT registered employers must account for VAT when they provide meals or accommodation to employees for monetary consideration, for example by an agreed deduction from their wages or by means of periodical payments.

Tax incurred on purchases for the provision of meals or accommodation to employees can be deducted as input tax subject to the normal rules.

Notes – See VATA 1994, s. 24(3) for restrictions on the recovery of input tax related to directors' etc. accommodation.

B. NEWS RELEASES

VAT: SETTLEMENT OF DISPUTES [HM Customs and Excise News Release 82/87, 19 November 1987]

The Commissioners of Customs and Excise have reviewed their policy on the VAT treatment of payments made under out-of-court settlements of disputes, after proceedings have been commenced by service of originating process (or appointment of an arbitrator).

They now take the view that, where such payments are in essence compensatory and do not relate directly to supplies of goods or services, they are outside the scope of VAT. This will be so even if the settlement is expressed in terms that the payment is consideration for the plaintiff's agreement to abandon his rights to bring legal proceedings. But payments will remain taxable if, and to the extent, that they are the consideration for specific taxable supplies by the plaintiff, e.g. where the dispute concerns payment for an earlier supply, or where the plaintiff grants future rights to exploit copyright material under the settlement.

These changes of policy may be applied from 19 November 1987.

The Commissioners of Customs and Excise had previously taken the view that all payments under out-of-court settlements were generally taxable. The revised VAT liability brings the VAT treatment of out-of-court settlements into line with the VAT treatment of payments under Court orders.

VAT REGISTRATION: INTENDING TRADERS: PROPERTY OWNERS AND DEVELOPERS – OBJECTIVE EVIDENCE REQUIREMENTS [HM Customs and Excise News Release 65/90, 25 September 1990]

Following representations from the Accountancy profession and the trade, Customs and Excise have reviewed their objective evidence requirements in respect of property owners and developers who apply for VAT registration on the basis that they intend to make taxable supplies by way of business at a future date.

The evidential requirements will be relaxed with a view to reducing the burdens on business:

–   applicants will now only be required to state the nature of their intended supplies in order that local VAT office staff can confirm the liability of such supplies; in appropriate cases this may involve notification of their election to waive exemption for the relevant building or planned building;

–   applicants will also be asked to confirm that they have commenced preparatory activities and the amounts of VAT that they have incurred to date; and

–   the minimum evidence of preparatory activity that will be accepted is that an applicant has commissioned a feasibility study for which a consideration has, or will be, charged.

Further information regarding other types of acceptable evidence of preparatory activity is available from local VAT offices.

Prior to the review applicants had to produce copy documentation to show that they held title to the respective land or buildings, that full or outline planning permission had also been obtained, and firm arrangements had been made for the disposal of the property.

Note

Under paragraph 5(b) of Schedule 1 to the Value Added Tax Act 1983 [VATA 1994, Sch. 1, para. 9(b)] a person who is not liable to be registered but who can satisfy Customs and Excise that he is carrying on a business and intends to make taxable supplies in the course or furtherance of that business is entitled to be registered on an "intending trader basis."

Prior to the changes in property liability introduced in the Finance Act 1989, many supplies in the field of property ownership and development could only be exempt. In order to satisfy Customs that taxable supplies were likely to be made, an applicant had to provide objective evidence to show that title was held to the respective land or buildings, that full or outline planning permission had been obtained, and firm arrangements had been made as regards the disposal of property.

Customs have decided to relax the above criteria following representations. The minimum evidence of preparatory activity that will be accepted is that an applicant has commissioned a feasibility study for which a consideration has, or will be, charged. Other types of acceptable evidence of preparatory activity are:

–   that the applicant holds title to land or buildings, or is currently negotiating to purchase, or holds an option to purchase;
–   the applicant holds full or outline planning permission or is to apply for permission in the near future;
–   the applicant has commissioned architect's services with a view to applying for planning permission or is to apply for permission, or legal or other professional services in connection with the intended sale or letting of the property;
–   in respect of intended zero-rated sale or long lease of old people's homes, hospices and non-business charity buildings the applicant has obtained from his customers the certification required for zero-rating; and
–   in respect of the intended zero-rated sale or long lease of substantially reconstructed protected buildings, the applicant has the listed building consent for conversion to residential use and, if necessary, the relevant certification from his customers.

Local VAT offices will now accept written statements from either the applicant or his professional adviser confirming that the above types of evidence are held. They will no longer have to produce copies of planning permission and legal documentation.

More information about the election to waive exemption in respect of property transactions is in Notice [742].

VAT RELAXATIONS IN SERIOUS MISDECLARATION PENALTY [HM Customs and Excise News Release 26/91, 19 March 1991]

. . . From 20 March 1991:

–   there will be a "period of grace" during which serious misdeclaration penalty will not normally be imposed on misdeclarations made on VAT returns. This "period of grace" will extend from the end of a prescribed accounting period to the due date for furnishing the VAT return for the following accounting period;
–   serious misdeclaration penalty will not normally be imposed when a VAT return for a registered trader is misdeclared but this has been corrected by a compensating misdeclaration in respect of the same transactions for the following accounting period with no overall loss of VAT.

SERIOUS MISDECLARATION PENALTY AND DEFAULT SURCHARGE [HM Customs and Excise News Release 14/92, 10 March 1992]

. . . from 11 March, when liability to a penalty is established, Customs will not normally impose one unless the net tax underdeclared or overclaimed exceeds £2,000 in a prescribed accounting period.

VAT REGISTRATION SCHEME FOR RACEHORSE OWNERS [HM Customs and Excise News Release 10/97, 10 March 1997]

Following the review by HM Customs and Excise of the VAT Registration Scheme for Racehorse Owners, Philip Oppenheim, Exchequer Secretary, has announced that it will continue, but with some changes.

The main changes are:

–   future VAT registrations will be restricted to owners who have actually obtained sponsorship and

–   sole proprietors can apply "The Scheme" arrangements in future only to those racehorses in which they own at least a 50 per cent share.

The effective date of these changes will be the subject of discussions with the British Horseracing Board (BHB) and will be confirmed later.

The terms of a new Memorandum of Understanding will also be discussed with the BHB and issued in due course.

Customs intend to review The Scheme again in 2001/2.

Notes

The VAT Registration Scheme for Racehorse Owners was announced by the Chancellor in his Budget statement of 16 March 1993.

The Scheme provides that owners who register racehorses under the Jockey Club's Rules of Racing, and also make a declaration that they will seek income by way of sponsorship and appearance money, are accepted as intending to carry on a business for VAT purposes and may register for VAT. Once registered, owners recover VAT incurred on the purchase and upkeep of racehorses and other general overhead expenses and account for tax on sponsorship, appearance money, prize money and sales of horses.

Details of The Scheme were agreed by Customs and the racing organisation in a Memorandum of Understanding of 16 March 1993. The agreement contained a provision that Customs would review The Scheme in June 1996 and issued a Consultation Document on 3 June 1996 (News Release 39/96 refers).

VAT AVOIDANCE SCHEME ON COMPANY CARS BLOCKED [HM Customs and Excise News Release 28/98, 12 November 1998]

New VAT rules take effect from midnight to prevent businesses that lease their cars avoiding the 50 per cent restriction on VAT recovery.

The change, following today's judgement of the Court of Appeal in C & E Commissioners v. BRS, ensures that the 50 per cent restriction on input tax recovery will apply as Parliament intended to all leased business cars also used for private motoring.

Financial Secretary to the Treasury, Dawn Primarolo MP said:

> "We are acting quickly to tackle this blatant avoidance scheme marketed by some of the leading accountants. Taxes must be fair. Artificial schemes undermine fairness in the system, making the burden fall disproportionately on businesses who do not want to pay for "creative" tax advice. Business needs to understand that we will not hesitate to bring forward counter measures as and when required."

Notes

(i)   Private motoring in leased business cars is taxed by the simplified procedure of restricting recovery of input tax by business. This is often called "input tax blocking". The relevant legislation is the VAT (Input Tax) Order 1992 S. I. 1992/3222.

(ii)   Prior to 1 August 1995 an input tax block attached to the purchase of cars by leasing companies for onward leasing. In turn their customers were able to deduct all the VAT incurred on leasing charges, subject to the normal operation of the partial exemption rules. On 1 August 1995, in response to trade representations, new rules were introduced to allow leasing companies to deduct the VAT incurred on purchase. In turn a 50 per cent block was imposed on the car leasing charges paid by their customers.

(iii)   Two leading accountancy firms marketed a scheme which circumvents the input tax blocking through the use of artificial pre-leasing arrangements involving an associated "leasing company". Customs have contested this scheme in the VAT Tribunal and the Courts. They won in the High Court but have lost the argument in the Court of Appeal.

(iv)   *Amendments are made in the* Value Added Tax (Input Tax) Amendment Order 1998 SI No. 2767 laid today, which subject to Parliamentary Approval will take effect at midnight tonight.

(v)   The avoidance is being countered by making the leases to the associated "leasing company" subject to the 50 per cent block. This measure is not retrospective, as it affects future supplies of leasing.

(vi)   The measure protects £20 million revenue.

GET AN EXTRA WEEK TO PAY YOUR VAT [HM Customs and Excise News Release 21/2000, 23 May 2000]

Businesses paying their VAT electronically from 31 May can improve their cash flow because they will have an extra week to submit and pay their VAT returns.

Announcing the new electronic payment concession Paymaster General Dawn Primarolo said:

> "Electronic payment means businesses improve their cash flow because they can time payment precisely, thus aiding their financial planning. There is greater certainty that payments are made on time, reducing possible liability to penalties, and credit transfer is a more secure method of payment.

> This is part of the wider Government drive to develop electronic services, for both businesses and the public. Customs are also trialing the introduction of electronic filing of VAT returns in order that all businesses can do this from early in 2001. Businesses can already retrieve a wide amount of VAT guidance from the website 24 hours a day. We are delivering a tax system to meet the current and future needs of business."

Notes

1.   For VAT returns with a due date on or after 31 May 2000 use of electronic means of payment will be made simpler. Qualifying businesses will automatically receive the seven calendar day extension for the submission and payment of VAT returns, on a return-by-return basis. Businesses will no longer have to request this concession and, as the extension will be applied automatically, they will not be advised whether or not they have been given it.

2.   The small number of businesses in the Payment on Account and Annual Accounting schemes cannot use this concession. Virtually all businesses in the Payment on Account scheme pay VAT electronically, and those in the Annual Accounting Scheme already get extra time to pay their VAT.

3.   The automatic application of the concession on a return-by-return basis gives businesses the freedom to change payment methods without having to notify Customs. However if a business changes back to paying by cheque it will not have the extra week to make that payment.

3.   If the VAT return and electronic payment are not received on or before the seventh calendar day following the normal due date, businesses may be liable to default surcharge, the penalty regime for late payment.

4.   Any VAT liabilities can be paid by an electronic method; however, the 7 extra calendar days apply only to VAT return payments and not to other VAT payments such as assessments or underdeclarations.

Businesses can obtain further details on this concession from their local VAT Office listed under Customs and Excise in the telephone book and from Customs' Internet site – www.hmce.gov.uk.

C. BUSINESS BRIEFS

HOW CUSTOMS AND EXCISE PUBLICISES VAT LAW INTERPRETATION CHANGES [HM Customs and Excise Business Brief 14/94, 6 July 1994]

We sometimes change our view of what the VAT law means because of decisions made by the VAT Tribunal, the courts, or as a result of internal reviews.

This statement explains how we will publicise such changes. It indicates how businesses and their advisors can keep abreast of the changes.

Your position

VAT is a self assessed tax, but we will ensure that you are kept informed of changes in the law and its interpretation. You should take steps to keep yourself up to date with these and how they affect your business.

Our position

We apply what we consider to be the correct interpretation of the law relating to VAT. However we can be challenged at the VAT Tribunal and in the courts. In addition we may reconsider our interpretation and change it.

We will take all reasonable action to publicise a change before it is implemented. Our Charter commitment to provide clear, accurate and timely information about VAT reinforces this intention.

Timing of changes

Where, for whatever reason, interpretation of the law is changed, we are obliged to apply this change as quickly as possible. Delay will clearly be unfair if a change is beneficial to taxpayers.

If a change is to the advantage of the Exchequer it cannot be delayed unduly as we must collect the tax properly due. However, whenever possible we will give you time to prepare for it.

Publicity for changes

Our action will include consultation with relevant trade bodies and representative organisations. We will issue a News Release or Business Brief setting out details of the change and the justification for it. These go to a wide variety of media outlets and are available through a subscription service operated for us by the Central Office of Information.

We will also make an announcement in "VAT Notes", a broadsheet publication sent quarterly to all registered persons with their returns. Where appropriate this will include a cross reference to any other relevant publications. You are asked to read "VAT Notes" carefully and to implement any changes which affect your business.

At the earliest opportunity we will update our publications covering the subject affected by the change. These will not show dates earlier than that of the month in which they are published.

Overpayments resulting from a change

If despite taking all reasonable steps to keep yourself informed, you were not aware of a change in interpretation of the law at the time it was made, and you overcharge VAT as a result, we will normally agree to you applying the change retrospectively. You will be entitled to adjust the VAT due, subject to the provisions concerning unjust enrichment (Section 24, 1989 Finance Act [VATA 1994, s. 80]) which precludes anyone securing a repayment of VAT overpaid which benefits them rather than the person to whom they have charged the VAT.

If it is established that the overpayment occurred because of a failure on our part to publicise the change adequately we will pay you interest on the amount involved.

Underpayments resulting from a change

If you do not implement a change at the correct time you could be liable for the VAT underpaid as a result.

However, if despite you taking all reasonable steps to keep informed about changes, a change is introduced of which you could not have been aware, we will require you to pay any extra VAT only from the date when it was reasonable for you to have known about it. This would normally be not later than the date of receipt by you of "VAT Notes" referring to the change. In these special circumstances any tax underpaid would qualify to be remitted on grounds of misunderstanding.

For further information traders should contact their local VAT Office.

VAT AND HAIRDRESSERS [HM Customs and Excise Business Brief 16/94, 25 July 1994]

In its decision in the case brought by Group Montage (MAN/91/572) [No. 12,014] the VAT Tribunal found that certain agreements between the owners of a salon and the stylists constituted a licence to occupy land and were therefore exempt supplies.

Customs had given a ruling that the agreements between the two parties did not amount to a licence to occupy because no exclusive use of a particular area of the salon was granted, and that the substance and reality of the agreement was that the stylists were given the standard rated general use of the salon as a whole. The tribunal overturned that ruling and found that non-exclusivity does not mitigate against there being an exempt licence to occupy land.

This decision runs contrary to Customs' view that an exempt licence to occupy land must grant the licensee exclusive use of a clearly defined area and Customs have decided to appeal the Group Montage decision to the High Court.

There have been a number of contradictory rulings on the liability of "hairdressers chairs". For example in the case of William Walker trading as Ziska (EDN 92/334) [No. 11,825] the Tribunal Chairman accepted Customs' view that even although exclusive use may have been granted at two chairs, in substance and reality the supply was for the general right to use the facilities of the salon as a whole.

Customs recognise that this is a very difficult area, and it is not possible to provide traders with absolute certainty. Local VAT offices have been advised to judge each case individually on the basis of the substance and reality of each agreement. For further information traders should contact their local VAT office listed under Customs and Excise in the phone book.

VAT CHANGES FOR BUSINESS CARS [HM Customs and Excise Business Brief 10/95, 23 May 1995]

The Chancellor announced in last year's budget changes to the VAT treatment of business cars. These changes will, subject to Parliamentary approval, come into effect on 1 August 1995.

Draft legislation was exposed to businesses for comments and we would like to thank all those who contributed. A number of clarifying amendments to the draft legislation will be made in the light of comments received.

This edition of the Business Brief describes the way Customs intends the proposed changes to apply in practice. A VAT Information Sheet will be issued in due course.

Cars obtained for a wholly business purpose

Businesses will be able to recover the VAT in full, subject to the normal rules, on cars they buy, import or lease on or after 1 August for demonstrably wholly business purposes.

Full recovery will not apply to ordinary business cars but only to those which are not available for private motoring. In order to meet this test businesses will have to be able to demonstrate that by the very nature of its use a car is not available for the private use of a sole proprietor, partner, director, employee or other connected person.

This is a very restrictive test and the main beneficiaries of the change are expected to be leasing companies because there is no private use of the cars purchased by them, although there may be private use in the hands of their customers.

Cars that may also qualify under this test are genuine pool cars, demonstrators, and service rental ("courtesy") cars. The test is that they are not available for private use, are not allocated to a single individual and are never kept overnight at home. For this purpose a motor trade garage with attached domestic accommodation is treated as business premises.

The current relief for research and development cars used by car manufacturers will remain and is extended to research and development cars used by other companies engaged in car research and development, e.g. component manufacturers.

A business must not treat a car as being used for a wholly business purpose simply because it charges its employees for private use. In such circumstances full input tax recovery will apply only if the business operates on the same basis as a commercial leasing or hire company.

The test is that the provision of the car to the employee must be an arm's length transaction. In other words the terms and conditions of the rental and the value of the charges made must be equivalent to those that would apply if the employee was to lease or hire the car on the open market. This test will not be met where a business simply makes a charge to its employees for private motoring based upon the proportion of private use.

Cars bought or imported for the purpose of resale will meet the "wholly business purpose" test only if the business does not make the cars available for private use between the time they are purchased or imported and the time they are sold. This includes cars that are bought for the purpose of sale and lease-back.

Taxis, self-drive hire and driving school cars

Businesses are currently entitled to recover input tax on cars bought or leased primarily for the purpose of taxi hire, self-drive hire or driving school tuition. This entitlement will not change. The changes however affect the way business customers of self-drive hire companies treat the VAT incurred on their daily rentals, which is dealt with in the following section.

Business cars made available for private use

Input tax recovery will remain restricted in full on business cars bought or imported that are to be made available for private use.

Where leased business cars are to be made available for private use, businesses will only be able to recover 50 per cent of the VAT on the rental charges. The restriction will apply only to those cars on which the leasing company recovered VAT when they bought them. These will normally be cars registered on or after 1 August 1995, i.e. cars with an "N" registration prefix onwards.

We are aware that some tax practitioners are advising clients to enter into leasing contracts prior to 1 August in respect of cars that will not be supplied to the leasing company until after that date. We understand the intention is to create a situation in which both the lessor and the lessee would be entitled to full input tax recovery. Any such scheme will not work because the final version of the draft legislation will ensure that the lessor will not be entitled to input tax recovery in such circumstances.

The charges to which the 50 per cent restriction on input tax recovery will apply are all those payable under the terms of the leasing agreement for the rental of the car, including excess mileage charges.

Under contract leasing arrangements the lessor may also contract to provide the lessee with a variety of services in addition to the basic rental, typically including maintenance and roadside assistance. Where those services are supplied separately from the supply of leasing, VAT incurred on them will not be subject to the 50 per cent restriction and may be recovered in full. Customs and the leasing trade organisations will issue agreed guidelines as to what will be acceptable as evidence that leasing and maintenance are supplied separately. Where maintenance is supplied separately, excess mileage charges can be apportioned between the leasing and maintenance elements.

Under some forms of finance leasing the lessee's payments cover the full cost of the cars plus interest. When the car is sold at the end of the lease the proceeds are normally used by the lessor to rebate the monthly rental payments made by the lessee (rebates of rental). If, at the end of the full term of the lease, the lessor issues a VAT credit note for a rebate of rental to a lessee who incurred a 50 per cent input tax restriction on the rental charges on that car, the lessee may offset 50 per cent of the VAT credit against input tax previously restricted.

Customs and the leasing trade organisations are discussing the treatment of termination payments and rebates of rental where the lease is terminated early. Further guidance will be issued in due course.

The 50 per cent restriction on input tax recovery will apply to self-drive hire (daily rentals) as well as leasing. Customs will however accept that where a business hires a car for not more than five days to use for business journeys, that the car is used for a wholly business purpose and the 50 per cent restriction will not apply. Customs will monitor this concession to ensure that it is applied only to genuine short term hire arrangements.

Where a business hires a car for business use for more than five days, the 50 per cent restriction will apply unless the business can demonstrate that the car was used wholly for business journeys. Where this is claimed to be the case, appropriate records would have to be kept by the business.

Taxpayers who have mixed business and non business activities, e.g. charities, must apportion VAT on car leasing charges between business and non-business use and apply the 50 per cent input tax restriction to the VAT proportion that relates to business activities. The 50 per cent input tax restriction must be applied before any partial exemption calculation is carried out.

Charges to employees for use of a car

The input tax recovery restrictions are a proxy for more directly taxing the private use of business cars. In order to avoid instances of double taxation certain charges to employees for use of a car will not be subject to tax, with effect from 1 August. Technically these charges will be treated as neither a supply of goods or services, they will be "de-supplied".

At present any reduction of salary constituting a "salary sacrifice" is not taxable. As outlined in Business Brief 9/92, issued 19 June 1992, such sacrifices are deemed not to constitute a consideration for a supply. However actual charges to employees for use of a car, including deductions from salary, have been taxable. From 1 August a business will not have to charge VAT on any charge it makes to employees for the private use of an input tax restricted business car, including those cars first leased by the employer before 1 August where the input tax restriction was incurred by the leasing company.

The charges de-supplied will be those that represent a consideration for the provision of a car to the employee. For simplification these will include single charges, e.g. those based on the AA rate, that are based on the capital cost of the car, even if there is an element of running costs, but the provision of fuel will remain taxable. The de-supplied charges include "top up" charges, whereby an employee pays an amount for use of a better car than that to which he is strictly entitled. Any charge to cover running costs only, e.g. maintenance, will remain taxable.

The provision of fuel to employees will remain taxable under the arrangements described in Appendix C of Notice 700: The VAT Guide. If a business provides fuel at or above cost for private motoring those charges are taxable. Where a business provides fuel free or below cost, it is required to account for tax by means of the fuel scale charge.

Changes in the use of wholly business cars

As previously outlined, businesses will be able to recover input tax in full on a car which they genuinely intend to use for wholly business purposes. If a business subsequently changes its intention and makes a car available for private use, it will be deemed to make a self-supply of the car and must pay VAT on its full current value at the time of the change of use. No further output tax will be due on any real or notional charge for the private use of the car.

Sales of second hand cars

Where businesses have been able to recover all the VAT charged to them on a car they have bought, they will have to charge VAT when they sell that car. In this section a qualifying car means a car on which the seller recovered the VAT charged when he bought, acquired or imported the car. Qualifying cars will be mainly, but not exclusively, cars registered on or after 1 August 1995. A qualifying user means a buyer who will be using the car for a purpose which entitles him to recover the VAT charged by the seller.

A business selling a qualifying car must charge VAT on the full value of the sale. The seller must issue a full tax invoice to a buyer who is a qualifying user, but need not issue a tax invoice to a buyer who is not a qualifying user.

From 1 August second hand car dealers will normally be qualifying users and will not be able to use the second hand scheme for qualifying cars. Hence the current concession which allows self-hire drive firms, taxi companies and driving schools not to issue a tax invoice to dealers will lapse.

A business that sells a car which was subject to the full input tax restriction will, as now, only have to account for tax on any profit margin. A second hand car dealer, or any other business, will be able to use the second hand schemes for non-qualifying cars that it buys and resells.

At present certain disposals of cars repossessed by finance companies and cars taken by insurance companies in settlement of a claim under a policy are not taxable. From 1 August the finance or insurance company must charge VAT on the full value of the disposal, if input tax has previously been recovered on the car being sold.

VAT group registrations

A VAT group registration is treated as a single taxable person. When a group member obtains cars from outside the group to supply to other group members the intra-group transactions are irrelevant to the issue of input tax recovery.

The group company will be able to recover the VAT incurred only if the cars are to be used by the group as a whole for wholly business purposes. This will not be the case if any group member is to make the cars available for the private use of employees.

Government departments, local authorities, police authorities and health authorities

The changes will apply to local authorities and other bodies such as police authorities falling within section 33 of the 1994 VAT Act, in the same way as they apply to business. They will be able to recover tax in full on any car that is to be used wholly for the authority's non-business and/or business activity. The treatment of leasing charges, charges to employees and sales of used cars described in the above sections will apply equally to these bodies.

The Treasury Direction dated 2 March 1995 made under Section 41(3) of the 1994 VAT Act allows Government Departments and Health Authorities to recover VAT on the "hire of vehicles, including repair and maintenance" for their non-business activities. This right will not be affected by the 50 per cent input tax restriction on car leasing charges. Consequently section 41 bodies will continue to recover input tax in full on leasing charges. They must also charge VAT on employee contributions towards the use of a car on which the leasing company recovered input tax.

For further information traders and their advisers should contact their local VAT office listed under Customs and Excise in the telephone book.

VAT ON BUSINESS CARS [HM Customs and Excise Business Brief 15/95, 31 July 1995]

In this Business Brief we outline further developments to the VAT treatment of business cars which will take effect from 1 August 1995. This follows on from Business Brief 10/95 where we outlined the major VAT changes that will affect such cars.

Legislation

The European Council adopted a decision on June 29 to allow the UK to derogate from articles 6 and 17 of the Sixth VAT Directive.

Three Treasury Orders were made on 29 June and laid before Parliament on 30 June. Two of the orders required approval by a resolution of the House of Commons which was provided on 17 July. The orders will all come into force on 1 August 1995.

The orders are the VAT (Input Tax) (Amendment) (No. 3) Order 1995, SI 1995 No. 1666; the VAT (Cars) (Amendment) (No. 2) Order, SI 1995 No. 1667; and the VAT (Supply of Services) (Amendment) Order 1995, SI 1995 No. 1668.

Cut-over arrangements

In Business Brief 10/95 we explained that businesses will be able to recover VAT incurred on cars obtained on or after August for "wholly business purposes."

The change is linked to the N registration prefix for cars. However some N registration cars will be the subject of prior invoicing or prepayment. The proposed legislation therefore contains a cut-over provision that will allow a business to elect to treat as a qualifying car, a car it obtains before 1 August 1995 for wholly business purposes, but which is not first registered until on or after that date. A business cannot do this if it makes a letting or hire of the car before 1 August 1995.

A business may make the election described above on a car by car basis, or it may make a single election for all cars falling within the scope of the election provision. A bulk election will need to identify by registration number each car covered by the election.

If a business elects to adopt a car as a qualifying car as described above, it will become entitled to recover input tax incurred on the supply or importation of that car before 1 August 1995. The right to deduct tax incurred before 1 August will arise in the first VAT return period commencing on or after 1 August and not at the time the tax was incurred. The amount claimed must be clearly identified in the VAT account for that period beginning on or after 1 August.

If a car is adopted as a qualifying car it will be treated as such for all transactions on or after 1 August 1995. If it is let on hire to a business that intends to use it for business and private purposes, the 50 per cent input tax restriction will apply to VAT on the leasing charge as described in Business Brief 10/95. VAT must be charged on the full value of the car on its sale or disposal.

Invoicing arrangements

Customs has agreed with a main leasing trade organisation a recommended form of invoice for leasing companies to adopt for lettings to business customers on or after 1 August. The recommended format will clearly identify whether or not the car is a qualifying car. If the car is a qualifying car the invoice will also clearly identify the amount of tax which is potentially subject to the 50 per cent input tax restriction on leasing charges. Leasing companies should take care not to indicate the actual amount of tax the customer can recover as this will depend upon the customer's specific circumstances.

We intend to introduce VAT Regulations requiring businesses leasing cars to VAT registered businesses to specify whether or not the car is "a qualifying car under article 7(2) of the VAT (Input Tax) Order 1992 (as amended)".

Businesses are reminded that if an invoice for leasing charges is issued before 1 August the car concerned cannot be treated as a qualifying car.

Changes in "wholly business purposes"

We wish to make clear that in order to claim input tax relief on a car on the basis that the car is to be used for wholly business purposes, the business must, at the time the tax is incurred, genuinely have no intention to make that car available for private use.

Customs will look closely at all claims where there has been a purported change of intention following input tax recovery. Taxpayers are reminded that incorrect claims to relief will result in assessment with consequential interest and penalties, where appropriate.

Excess mileage charges

Where a leasing company makes rental of a car consisting of separate supplies of leasing and maintenance, Customs has agreed that any excess mileage charge may be split between the leasing and maintenance elements. One simple way of doing this would be to split the excess mileage charge on exactly the same basis as the overall rental charge.

Leasing companies may adopt another form of split, but if they do so they will be required to demonstrate from their records that the proportion attributed to maintenance is a fair and reasonable allocation of the costs incurred. Excess mileage charges must not be attributed solely to maintenance.

Traders and their advisers should contact their local VAT business advice centre listed under Customs and Excise in the telephone book.

LIABILITY OF "REVERSE SURRENDER OF LEASE" [HM Customs and Excise Business Brief 18/95, 6 September 1995]

Business Briefs 16/94 and 17/94 stated that a "reverse surrender" was standard-rated; that is, the supply made by a landlord who agreed in return for payment to accept the surrender of a lease by his tenant. HM Customs and Excise now accept that the supply was exempt, subject to an election to waive exemption made by the landlord.

A Tribunal found in the case of Central Capital Corporation Ltd (MAN/94/2393) that a landlord made a supply when he agreed in return for payment to accept the surrender of his tenant's lease, and that the supply was exempt by virtue of Article 13B(b) of the Sixth VAT Directive (EEC/77/388). Customs accept the analysis of the Tribunal, which took into account the previous decision in the case of Marbourne Ltd (LON/93/590A) that a tenant had made a supply to his landlord when he paid the landlord to accept a surrender of the lease. Customs had appealed the latter case to the High Court on the grounds that it must be the person receiving payment, the landlord, who made the supply. However, Customs consider that the correct principle has now been established, and are not pursuing the case of Marbourne because the company has ceased trading and would not have been represented before the High Court.

Landlords who charged VAT to their tenants on the assumption that the supplies they made to the tenants were compulsorily standard-rated may now claim repayment of the VAT from Customs and Excise. Landlords who had elected to waive exemption are not affected. Repayment will be conditional on there being no unjust enrichment of the claimant. This means that generally landlords will have to repay the tax to their tenants or former tenants. This may be by means of a credit note where appropriate. Claimants will have to make adjustments in their VAT accounts for input tax incurred on goods or services which had been reclaimed as attributable to the supply. Where repayment is made, tenants in turn must adjust their own input tax in respect of any initial deduction they made. A valid credit note issued by the landlord will provide evidence. If a credit note is not appropriate, for example because the tenant is not registered for VAT, landlords will be expected to make the repayment by other means.

Any landlords who wish to claim repayment without passing it on to their tenants must first explain in writing why they do not think they would be unjustly enriched.

Requests for payment of statutory interest should be made in writing to local offices in the usual way. Following the decision of the Tribunal in the case of North East Media (MAN/94/448) interest will only be paid on the net amount of any overpayment, that is the amount by which the sum paid as output tax exceeded the sum claimed as input tax.

CLAIMS FOR REPAYMENT OF OVERPAID VAT BY OPTICIANS [HM Customs and Excise Business Brief 19/95, 13 September 1995]

This Business Brief outlines the procedures for opticians to claim overpaid VAT following the recent High Court judgements in the Leightons and Eye Tech cases.

It gives guidance on acceptable methods to apportion values between taxable and exempt supplies and for restricting any associated input tax under the partial exemption rules. A detailed technical information sheet will be issued to all opticians by their professional associations. This Business Brief supplements information given in Business Briefs 31A/93 and 8/95.

Submission of claims

In Business Brief 8/95 we invited opticians to submit claims for repayment of overpaid VAT and statutory interest dating back to 1 September 1988.

Some opticians have been able to formulate and submit claims for overpaid VAT based upon existing commercial records and have had these claims accepted and paid by Customs. These traders will already have ensured that their claims were the most accurate possible and will not need to avail themselves of the methods described in this Business Brief.

There are a number of opticians who have submitted provisional claims, or who have submitted claims based upon purely arbitrary percentages of taxable and exempt sales. These may have been paid in full or in part, in some instances "without prejudice", or in some cases have had repayment partly withheld by Customs, pending the outcome of central negotiations between Customs and opticians' representatives, because the opticians have not been in a position to submit more accurate claims. These opticians should now resubmit their claims following the guidelines contained in this Business Brief and the more detailed technical information sheet.

There are many opticians who have found preparing claims difficult because the limitations of their records mean they cannot provide accurate details of the separate values of the standard rated and exempt elements of their supplies. A principle purpose of the central negotiations was to agree and publicise a number of acceptable methods which these opticians could use in formulating their claims.

Any opticians who have not yet submitted their claims because they have been awaiting the outcome of the central negotiations should now do so.

The negotiations were carried out with representatives from the Association of Optometrists, the Association of British Dispensing Opticians and the Federation of Ophthalmic and Dispensing Opticians.

Different methods of apportionment

There cannot be a standard apportionment between the standard-rated and exempt elements of spectacles that can be applied by all opticians, because no one simple method of apportionment will satisfy everybody and at the same time give a fair result.

Some independent VAT advisors and some local VAT offices have suggested that such a universal apportionment can be applied. This is not so. Each VAT registered optician should submit a claim that produces a fair result by using their existing commercial records. If these are inadequate for formulating a fair claim they should follow the guidelines outlined below and in the technical information sheet issued by their professional representatives. The results will differ from the nation-wide average to a lesser or greater degree depending upon the individual circumstances of the business and its pricing structure and policy.

After considering a number of proposals put to the Department by the profession Customs accepts there are two main methods opticians can use to make claims for overpaid VAT repayments. These are cost plus and full cost apportionment.

A number of other possible methods have also been considered but these can only apply to a very limited number of opticians.

The cost plus method

Customs consider this method only appropriate for businesses whose annual tax exclusive value of sales (outputs) since 1988 has not exceeded £500,000.

Under this method you must demonstrate the mark up actually achieved on all standard rated sales other than spectacles e.g. contact lens solutions, sunglasses, spectacle cases and other accessories. The achieved mark up for these other standard rated supplies should be applied to the cost of spectacles (frames and lenses). This figure should then be subtracted from the final selling price of the spectacles to arrive at the cost of the exempt professional service. Output tax actually due should be calculated on the marked up cost established using this method.

The full cost apportionment method

This is a more detailed method and is the one which might be applied by those VAT registered businesses whose annual tax exclusive value of sales (outputs) since 1988 has exceeded £500,000.

Under this method opticians should first identify, using standard accounting practice, the direct costs to their business of both the taxable goods and the exempt service they provide. Having established these costs an apportionment calculation should be applied to income received from the sale of spectacles.

A variation to the full cost apportionment method could be based upon time spent. This would only be an appropriate method where all dispensing time is accurately recorded and might be used as the basis for costing the exempt service involved in dispensing a pair of spectacles.

Other methods

Fixed Mark up is a method which can only be applied by those smaller businesses whose annual tax exclusive value of sales (outputs) since 1988 has not exceeded £125,000. A fixed mark up on standard rated purchases of frames and lenses of 40% should be calculated and the VAT fraction (currently 7/47) applied to this marked up value by any small business wishing to use this simple method.

Any variations to the methods described above or any alternative method will need to be agreed with your local VAT office.

For the past

In many cases it will be impossible for opticians to recalculate their proper output tax liability on a period by period basis going back to 1988. Subject to no significant alterations in trading patterns or volume of business during this period, figures for periods in the preceding 12 months can be used as being sufficiently representative to enable a claim to be made dating as far back as 1 September 1988, or such later date from which a claim is to be made.

If this is not a realistic option because the required data for the preceding 12 months is unavailable, or you are able to demonstrate that the cost of doing so would be excessive, then the next full prescribed accounting period (if you are on quarterly returns) or the next three full prescribed accounting periods (if you are on monthly returns) may be used. However if you wish to adopt this option to determine the amount of your claim you will need to readdress the claim at the end of another three months using figures for the full six month period. This is because three months might not be truly representative of a claim covering seven years.

If this revised calculation shows a material change in the amount originally claimed (£500 or more for a trader using the "cost plus" or "fixed mark up" methodologies or £1000 or 1%, whichever is the less, for a trader using any other method) an adjusted claim should be submitted, irrespective of whether this figure is higher or lower than that contained in the original claim, using the normal voluntary disclosure procedure.

For the future

Accounting systems which will enable more precise apportionments to be applied will now need to be introduced by many opticians.

Any proposed future apportionment methods will need to be approved by your local VAT office.

Some opticians will already have started introducing records sufficient to demonstrate separately each element of the mixed supply of spectacles. Where this has not yet happened and a further period of grace is required to enable the introduction of approved apportionment methods, the method adopted for the purposes of making a claim for tax overpaid in the past may continue. It will be subject to review by the local VAT office on the first routine visit after any claim for the past has been settled.

Partial exemption implications

Since opticians are now making a higher level of exempt supplies they will need to contact their local VAT office to determine the most appropriate partial exemption calculations that will need to be made. This will be necessary to determine whether or not the business can be treated as fully taxable in accordance with the "de-minimis" limits.

For further information traders and their advisers should contact their local VAT Business Advice Centre or VAT Enquiry Office listed under Customs and Excise in the telephone book.

BUSINESS ENTERTAINMENT [HM Customs and Excise Business Brief 21/95, 8 October 1995]

This Business Brief updates Customs' policy on the reclaiming of VAT incurred on staff parties and in response to recent articles it confirms the Department's policy on the entertainment of overseas customers.

In Business Brief 30/93 we outlined how the VAT Tribunal decision in KPMG, Peat Marwick McLintock (MAN 91/120) had allowed full input tax deduction on staff party expenses where both employees and guests were present, and that this decision was under appeal.

We have decided not to proceed with this appeal for technical reasons outlined below, but it continues to be our interpretation of the law that entertaining of guests at staff parties constitutes "business entertainment."

The KPMG appeal

At the Tribunal hearing both parties argued the case, on the basis of previous decisions, that where tax is incurred on an indivisible supply of goods and services to be used to a measurable degree for business entertainment the law does not provide for input tax to be apportioned between business entertainment and other business use. The Court of Appeal judgement in Thorn EMI plc has subsequently determined that the law does provide the taxpayer with such a right of apportionment.

Customs' legal advice is that it would be difficult to proceed with an appeal on the basis of an apportionment that was accepted wrongly, by both parties to the original case, as being impermissible. We have therefore withdrawn our appeal. But we have not changed our view that the entertainment of any persons other than directors and staff is business entertainment.

Customs policy on staff entertainment

Customs' interpretation of the law for input tax recovery on staff parties following the Court of Appeal judgement can be summarised as follows.

The part of the VAT incurred that relates to the entertainment of staff is input tax that can be recovered to the extent that the expenditure relates to a business purpose. This is described in paragraph 40 of Notice 700: The VAT Guide – supplement.

The part of the VAT incurred for the entertainment of other persons, including partners and guests of staff, falls within the business entertainment provisions and is non-deductible.

Entertainment of overseas customers

Before 1 August 1988 businesses were able to deduct input tax incurred on the entertainment of overseas customers. Recent articles in the accountancy press have suggested that in removing this entitlement the UK may have exceeded the derogation in article 17.6 of the Sixth Directive permitting member states to retain those input tax exclusions in force under national rules on 1 January 1978.

Article 17.6 also contains a provision that expressly excludes input tax deduction on expenditure on luxuries, amusement or entertainment. The Court of Appeal judgement in Thorn EMI plc confirmed Customs interpretation that this exclusion is binding on Member States with effect from the entry into force of the directive on 1 January 1978. The overseas customer provision did not conform with the exclusion required by the directive and was revoked.

For further information traders and their advisers should contact their local VAT Enquiry Office listed under Customs and Excise in the telephone book.

VAT AND HAIRDRESSERS [HM Customs and Excise Business Brief 13/96, 1 July 1996]

The VAT and Duties Tribunal has now ruled in favour of Customs and Excise in the case of Simon Harris Hair Design Ltd (LON/94/[346]). This decision clarifies both the VAT position of hairdressers and the advice given in Business Brief 16/94 issued on 25 July 1994.

The Tribunal Chairman found that although the agreement between the owner of the salon and the stylist had two separate charges, it nevertheless amounted to a single supply taxable at the standard rate. The company had maintained that one of the charges was an exempt license to occupy land, which would have reduced their VAT liability.

Even though each stylist had an allocated space within the salon, a license to occupy that space could not be dissociated from the right to use other facilities of the salon such as junior staff, basins and dryers.

As a result of this ruling local VAT officers have been advised to assess for VAT in cases where it is clear that stylists working in open plan salons are using the facilities of the premises as a whole.

For further information traders and their advisers should contact their local VAT Business Advice Centre listed under Customs and Excise in the telephone book.

RECOVERY OF TAX INCURRED ON REPAIRS, MAINTENANCE, RENOVATION ETC TO FARMHOUSES [HM Customs and Excise Business Brief 18/96, 27 August 1996]

Following a number of VAT Tribunal decisions HM Customs and Excise have reviewed their approach to input tax claims made by sole proprietors and partnerships in relation to farmhouses. The following sets out guidelines which have been agreed with the National Farmers Union.

However, it must be pointed out that this does not give an automatic entitlement to recover an amount of tax. Businesses should continue to consider their own particular circumstances, and use the guidelines below to assess the proportion of tax that is claimable.

The guidelines

In the case of a normal working farm where the VAT registered person is actively engaged in running it, 70 per cent of tax incurred on repairs, maintenance and renovations, may be recovered as input tax. This position is in line with that adopted by VAT Tribunals who have found that in those given circumstances the dominant purpose was to allow the farming business to be carried on, and allowed 70 per cent of the tax to be claimed.

However, where the building work is more associated with an alteration, e.g. building an extension, the amount that may be recovered will depend on the purpose for the construction. If the circumstances are such that the dominant purpose is a business one then 70 per cent can be claimed. But if the dominant purpose is a personal one we would expect the claim to be 40 per cent or less, and in some cases, depending on the facts, none of the VAT incurred would be recoverable.

Where farming is not a full-time business and occupation for the VAT registered person, i.e. income is received from either full-time employment or other sources, the amount of tax that may be claimed will be considerably less. With these kind of cases VAT Tribunals have accepted somewhere between 10 per cent and 30 per cent of tax incurred is claimable on the grounds that the dominant purpose is a personal one. Businesses should therefore assess their particular circumstances, and make claims within those parameters.

Retrospective claims

Customs policy reflects the High Court judgement in the case of The Victoria & Albert Museum. The Museum wished to revisit past input tax claims on the grounds that it could have used a different and more favourable method to calculate its input tax. The Court held there had been no error of law or fact, and consequently the Museum were not permitted to revisit those earlier tax periods. The three year capping set out in News Release 42/96 also has to be considered.

(a)   where a trader has claimed input tax of less than 70 per cent without reference to Customs.

In this situation a retrospective claim is not allowable. The trader has assessed the input tax recovery position, and made a claim. There has been no error in law or fact to be corrected.

(b)   where a trader has claimed input tax based on an officer's decision, or has been assessed.

In this instance a retrospective claim may be made but any claim will be subject to the three year capping. Where the business self-assessed its input tax at less than 70 per cent, a refund claim will be allowed to the extent of the percentage self-assessed.

Limited companies

Where the occupant of the farmhouse is a director of the company, or a person connected with the director of the company, different legislation applies. This means that only tax on supplies that are used for other than domestic purposes is claimable as input tax. If a room is used partly for business and partly for domestic purposes, VAT will only be recoverable to the extent of the business use and suitable records will need to be kept to justify the proportion of tax being claimed.

VAT PLACE OF SUPPLY RULES CHANGE FOR INTERNET SERVICES [HM Customs and Excise Business Brief 22/97, 10 October 1997]

On 1 July 1997 the VAT place of supply rules for supplies of telecommunications services, including internet services, changed. The Department has already provided extensive guidance to businesses on how to apply the changes through VAT Information Sheet 2/97 (VAT Telecommunications Services: Place of Supply) and Business Brief 10/97.

However the application of the changes to internet packages comprising a variety of related elements is less straightforward. Customs has now examined several examples of such supplies and this brief provides guidance on the appropriate VAT treatment.

This brief does not cover supplies of basic access to the Internet, even where related software, some information and customer support facilities are included. The treatment of these is addressed in paragraphs 2.3 and 2.5 of the Information Sheet. There is no change to the treatment for supplies of services which are simply delivered via the Internet. The VAT treatment of those supplies is determined by the actual nature of the services rather than their means of delivery.

Packages Comprising a Variety of Internet Related Elements

Typically these supplies present the user on log-in with a specially developed and regulated environment rather than just delivering the user directly into the Internet or World Wide Web. Subscribers are granted access to a variety of services under the terms of their membership. Emphasis is generally given to "content" prepared by the provider rather than the "communications" facilities available to subscribers in the form of basic access, e-mail, on-line (live time) correspondence.

These packages may include some or all of the following components, and may also include other similar services not mentioned.

–   Access to the Internet and World Wide Web (WWW)
–   one or more e-mail addresses;
–   access to chatline facilities;
–   web space to create own web-site (home page)
–   access to specially prepared information pages (e.g. news, weather, stock market, travel)
–   access to on-line shopping (malls, travel etc.)
–   home banking facilities;
–   games fora.

Single or Multiple Supply?

Where such Internet packages are provided for a single inclusive price there is a single supply which falls within paragraphs 1–8 of Schedule 5 to the VAT Act 1994 (as amended).

Where particular services are made available separately, each one will normally be a separate supply with its own VAT treatment.

Nature of Supply

A supply which contains a variety of elements is capable of falling within more than one paragraph of Schedule 5. For example, with effect from 1 July, basic Internet access, e-mail addresses and chatline facilities fall within paragraph 7A of that Schedule as telecommunications services. Similarly, specially composed pages of information covering topics such as weather forecasts, share prices and news services, etc. fall within paragraph 3 as the provision of information.

Since the supply gives each customer access to whichever elements of the service are required, it is not possible to determine accurately whether telecommunications services predominate. Thus the new use and enjoyment provisions for telecommunications services outlined in Information Sheet 2/97 do not apply.

What Internet Service Providers (ISPs) Should Do

ISPs who supply these packages and who are established in the UK should charge VAT on all sales to UK customers.

They should also charge UK VAT on sales to customers in other Member States who do not receive the supply for business purposes.

For business customers in other member States ISPs should satisfy themselves that the supply is made for business purposes and retain evidence to support this decision.

ISPs making this kind of supply, who are not established in the UK are not required to charge UK VAT on their sales to UK customers. Usually they will charge their own local tax on such supplies.

What VAT Registered Customers in the UK Should Do

Where a UK established business receives a package of the services described in this Business Brief from an ISP who is not established in the UK, those services are liable to VAT under the reverse charge provisions in Section 8 of the VAT Act 1994, subject to the normal rules. Business customers should declare the reverse charge on their VAT returns in the usual way.

STAFF AND BUSINESS ENTERTAINMENT – RECOVERY OF INPUT TAX [HM Customs and Excise Business Brief 25/97, 10 November 1997]

Two recent court cases have clarified the law on the recovery of input tax on staff entertainment. This Business Brief sets out Customs' revised position on the recovery of input tax on staff entertainment and clarifies the current position on the deduction of input tax on staff party expenses where both employees and guests are present.

Staff Entertainment

Customs policy on staff entertainment is described in paragraph 4 of Notice 700/65 "Business Entertainment". It is also mentioned in VAT Leaflet 700/55 "VAT input tax appeals: luxuries amusements and entertainment". Our basic rule of thumb is to treat only 50% of VAT incurred on providing entertainment to staff as input tax in order to reflect the personal benefit derived.

A recent VAT Tribunal decision, Ernst & Young (LON/96/1377), found that where Ernst & Young provided entertainment to its employees it did so for wholly business purposes and all of the VAT incurred was input tax and recoverable.

But the Tribunal also found that where Ernst & Young provided entertainment solely for the benefit of its partners such expenditure was not made for business purposes and the VAT incurred was not input tax.

Customs has accepted the decision and revised its policy on staff entertainment expenditure accordingly. The decision does not affect the treatment of entertainment provided to guests of employees which is described below.

Customs now accepts that where a business provides entertainment to its employees in order to maintain and improve staff relations it does so for wholly business purposes and any VAT incurred is input tax and recoverable, subject to the normal rules. However where the expenditure has no discernible business purpose, and no connection with the business activities, any VAT incurred is not input tax.

Notice 700/65 and VAT Leaflet 700/55 will be amended in due course.

Entertainment Where Employees and Guests are Present

A recent VAT Tribunal decision, KPMG (MAN/96/553) upheld Customs' view that input tax incurred on entertaining guests at a staff party is non-deductible under the Business Entertainment provisions. Accordingly input tax incurred on functions where both employees and guests are present should be apportioned so that only the VAT attributable to the entertainment of the employees is recovered.

Effect on taxpayers

Those businesses who have apportioned tax incurred on staff entertainment, and can show such expenditure was to benefit their staff, may make claims for the amount of VAT they have attributed to a non-business purpose. Claims should be made as detailed in VAT Leaflet 700/45/93, "How to correct errors you find on your VAT returns". Such claims will be subject to the three year cap provisions. Claims in respect of entertainment provided to persons other than employees will not be allowable.

The Future

Notwithstanding the above, Customs' position is that staff entertainment inherently involves private consumption, which, since VAT is a tax on private consumption, in principle ought to be taxed. We also consider that the general scheme of the Sixth Directive, and Article 17(6) in particular, clearly envisages that all forms of entertainment should be taxed. This area of the Directive is to be reviewed shortly as part of the Common VAT System programme and we will take this issue forward in the context of that review.

LICENSE TO OCCUPY LAND DECISION [HM Customs and Excise Business Brief 25/97, 10 November 1997]

A recent VAT and Duties Tribunal hearing has concluded that the test of exclusivity is the wrong test to apply in determining whether for VAT purposes there is a license to occupy land. Customs and Excise disagree and consider that for there to be a licence to occupy land there must be exclusive occupation.

In this case Abbotsley Golf & Squash Club Ltd (AGSC) granted Abbotsley Country Club Ltd (ACC) a non-exclusive licence over a golf course for a payment of £280,000. (VAT Tribunal Ref. LON/96/148.)

The issue was whether in doing so AGSC had granted a licence to occupy land which falls within VAT Act 1994, Schedule 9, Group 1, item 1, or merely made the golf course available to ACC with no actual occupational rights.

The Commissioners argued that the grant was not a licence to occupy land because ACC's members have no preferential rights of admission to the golf course, sharing it with other players who are not members of ACC .

The Tribunal disagreed. It ruled that the licence granted to ACC was wholly distinct from the rights ACC gives to its members to play golf on the course. The Tribunal added that a non-exclusive licence can still be a licence to occupy land because exclusivity is not a necessary requirement for a supply to be the grant of a licence to occupy land.

The Commissioners have taken further legal advice on the matter and, given the facts that ACC was granted by AGSC a licence over the entire golf course for which it paid a substantial premium, they accept the Tribunal's finding that in substance and reality ACC was granted a licence to occupy land. In the Commissioners' opinion this is because de facto ACC had an exclusive licence over a substantial area of land.

The Commissioners disagree, however, with some of the Tribunal's reasoning. First, the Tribunal Chairman stated that the test of exclusivity in determining whether there exists a licence to occupy land is the wrong test to apply. The Commissioners disagree, and consider it is a correct test to use in order to determine whether the substance of the supply is the occupation of land as opposed to something that merely makes use of land.

Second, the Tribunal held that in granting a licence over the golf course, AGSC was not granting ACC facilities for playing sport as defined in VAT Act 1994, Schedule 9, Group 1, item 1(m) and Note 16, because those facilities were created after the grant of the licence.

The Commissioners also disagree with this approach. Schedule 9, Group 1, item 1, exempts the grant of any interest in, or right over, or of any licence to occupy land. It then excludes from that certain specified interests, rights and licences. The facility referred to in item 1 (m) must in itself be an interest in, or right over, or licence to occupy land. In the Commissioners' opinion, a licence to occupy a golf course in itself amounts to the grant of facilities for playing sport.

However the Commissioners now accept that ACC was granted a licence to occupy land. Also the letting of a sports facility to a club for a period exceeding 24 hours is exempt from VAT under Note 16 referred to above.

Therefore the Commissioners have concluded it is inappropriate to appeal the Tribunal's decision purely on account of the reasoning adopted. Different reasoning would produce the same conclusion that ACC was granted a licence to occupy land.

The Commissioners wish to make it clear that they still consider the test of exclusivity to be a correct one when determining whether a licence to occupy land exists. This was confirmed in the VAT tribunal appeal of Paul James Lamb trading as Footloose (dated 13/8/97 ref.: M/96/1232) – this appeal was dismissed on the grounds that there was no exclusivity. The Commissioners also consider a golf course to be a sports facility.

The Commissioners propose, however, to re-open their earlier review on whether the law itself should include a definition of what is a licence to occupy land. Further details of this review will be released shortly in a future business brief.

VAT: LICENCE TO OCCUPY LAND [HM Customs and Excise Business Brief 22/98, 3 November 1998]

Introduction

Business Brief 25/97 announced that HM Customs and Excise planned to review the definition of the term "licence to occupy land". This Business Brief informs taxpayers of the scope of the review, invites interested parties to comment and states Customs' policy during the review period.

Background

Customs' interpretation of the law has been that for there to be a "licence to occupy land" under Schedule 9, Group 1 of the VAT Act 1994, the licensee must be granted exclusive occupation of a defined piece of land under terms that fall short of a formal tenancy. Following the tribunal decision in Abbotsley Golf and Squash Club (1997), which held that exclusivity was not necessarily required to create a "licence to occupy land", Customs have been advised that although exclusivity can be an appropriate test in many cases it is not so in every situation.

Businesses need certainty and Customs recognise that the current doubts about when there is "a licence to occupy land" benefits neither taxpayers nor its own officers. While the review is in progress, businesses may use the criteria set out in this Business Brief to determine whether a supply amounts to a "licence to occupy land" as opposed to some lesser right to come onto land.

The Review

As part of the deregulation initiative and consultation exercises on VAT and immovable property in 1993 and 1995, Customs carried out a review of the possibility of defining the term "licence to occupy land" in VAT legislation. There was differing opinion as to whether such a definition would be helpful, and Customs concluded that reliance upon case law would be sufficient. However, following the Abbotsley decision, Customs are considering ways of providing a clear and workable definition of a "licence to occupy land".

Customs would therefore welcome comments on the following questions:

–   Should a "licence to occupy land" be defined in VAT legislation, and if so how?
–   What practical tests can be applied to identify a "licence to occupy land"?
–   Is the concept of "licence to occupy land" necessary or is there an alternative?
–   What are the circumstances in which non-exclusive occupation of land can be regarded as the leasing or letting of immovable property and thus falling within the scope of the exemption in Article 13B(b) of the Sixth VAT Directive?

Please send comments on any or all of these questions by 31 January 1999 to: Ian Moules, HM Customs & Excise, VAT Policy Directorate - Land and Property Branch, 4th Floor West, New King's Beam House, 22 Upper Ground, London, SE1 9PJ. Telephone 0171 865 5478/5477.

Contributors to the previous reviews need not respond unless they wish to add to their previous submission. If you wish to receive a copy of Customs findings once the review is over please also write to the above address.

Customs' Interim Policy

Customs do not wish to prejudice the outcome of the review, but clearly while it is being conducted businesses need to know where they stand.

While the review is in progress, businesses should use the following criteria set out below to determine whether a supply amounts to a "licence to occupy land" as opposed to a lesser right to come onto land:

1.   Customs will normally continue to accept that a "licence to occupy land" exists where there is:

–   a licence in relation to a clearly defined area or piece of land, which in substance and reality permits the licensee an exclusive right of occupation during the times prescribed in the licence (this is explained in greater detail below).

2.   In addition the Tribunal in Abbotsley found a non-exclusive licence amounted to a "licence to occupy land" because as a matter of fact:

"the licence provides . . . for the physical presence of the [licensee] on the land, the physical enjoyment of the land by the [licensee, and] the exploitation of that land by the [licensee] for the purposes of the licence."

Customs accept that there can be a "licence to occupy land" where the land in question is not occupied exclusively by the licensee, provided that:

–   the licence is in relation to a clearly defined area or piece of land;
–   the licence in substance and reality allows the licensee to physically occupy the land; and
–   the rights granted are in relation to the occupation of the land thereby providing for the licensee's physical enjoyment or exploitation of the land.

What is meant by "exclusive"

For VAT purposes it is possible to have exclusive occupation of land even though the licensor can at any time come onto the land, and even though the period granted under the licence is not continuous (for example, every Tuesday and Thursday afternoon). Thus it is possible for there to be exclusive occupation if during the period of the licence the licensee alone is able to occupy the land at the times and for the purpose indicated in the licence agreement.

Examples of when there is likely to be a "licence to occupy land"

- granting a person a pitch in a market or at a car boot sale;
- hiring a hall to a person, for example for a conference or a reception;
- granting a concession to operate a shop within a shop where the concessionaire is granted an area from which to sell their goods or services;
- the provision of a stand or similar space to a person at an exhibition;
- the provision to the owner of coin operated machines of sites on which to locate his machines.

Examples of when there is unlikely to be a "licence to occupy land"

- ambulatory concessions e.g. ice-cream vans on the beach;
- hairdresser's chairs in open-plan salons;
- allowing the general public admission to premises or events.

Election to waive exemption ("option to tax")

If you have opted to tax land or a building, then the grant of a licence to occupy all or part of it will be standard rated unless that option to tax has no effect (for example, because the grant is to a charity that intends to occupy the property for non-business purposes).

Treatment of Enquiries

During the review period, requests for rulings regarding whether there is a non-exclusive "licence to occupy land" should be sent to your local VAT office. Such requests should set out the full facts of the case, indicate the guidance sought together with the reason why the taxpayer needs Customs' guidance.

VAT GROUPS AND TRANSFERS OF GOING CONCERNS (TOGCS) [HM Customs and Excise Business Brief 26/98, 18 December 1998]

This business brief clarifies Customs' policy on whether there can be a transfer of a property rental business as a going concern where the landlord and the tenant or the purchaser and the tenant are members of the same VAT group.

Background

In Kingfisher Plc 1993 the High Court found that members of a VAT group are to be considered a single taxable person for VAT purposes. The status of individual members of VAT groups has also been recently considered by the House of Lords in Thorn Materials Supply Ltd 1998 which came to the same conclusion. A question raised by those decisions is whether there can be a TOGC when the sole business activity constitutes supplies from one group member to another. With property rental between group members, if the rental supply is disregarded under Section 43(1)(a) VAT Act 1994, it is simply as though the taxable person (the group) is occupying the property itself.

Therefore, where a group member landlord sells a property which is tenanted by another group member, it is doubtful that a business exists which is making relevant supplies capable of transfer as a going concern. Conversely, where a landlord sells a property which is tenanted by a company that is a member of the new landlord's VAT group, the business ceases after the transfer because the tenant and the new landlord effectively become one taxable person.

Customs policy is as follows.

The following situations will not be considered to be TOGCS:

1. Where the purchaser of the property rental business is a member of the same VAT group as the existing tenant.

2. Where a member of a VAT group sells a property, which is being rented to another member of the group, to a third party.

The following situation will be considered to be a TOGC:

3. Where the tenant who is a member of the landlord's VAT group is only one of a number of tenants. The presence of a tenant or tenants outside the group means that the whole transaction can still be treated as a TOGC.

Implementation date

This policy will take effect from 1 January 1999. Transactions prior to this date will not be affected. If transfers of the type described at 1. and 2. take place after 1 January 1999 they can still be treated as TOGCs if a deposit or other part-payment of the purchase price is received by the seller before that date. An amendment will be made to Public Notice 700/9.

THE SINGLE CURRENCY (THE EURO) [HM Customs and Excise Business Brief 1/99, 13 January 1999]

From 1 January 1999 eleven European countries adopted a single currency (the euro). Although the UK is not one of the countries joining in the first wave, the introduction of the euro is likely to affect a wide range of UK businesses. This Business Brief explains the impact upon HM Customs and Excise's requirements. There are two main issues, paying taxes and duties in euro and accounting and invoicing in euro.

1. Paying taxes and duties in euro

UK businesses can now pay Customs and Excise taxes and duties (including arrears) in most cashless forms of the euro. Notes and coins will not be introduced until 2002. However, all declarations must continue to be made in sterling, including VAT returns and Intrastat declarations.

Exchange Rate Fluctuations

When paying in euro, the exchange rate will fluctuate between the time payment is initiated or sent to Customs and Excise and the time it is cleared. Businesses will be credited with the sterling value received by Customs and Excise. The repayment of overpayments to businesses and the payment of underpayments to Customs & Excise will be dealt with using existing debt management practices.

The shorter the delay between the time payment is made and the time it is cleared may help to minimise this fluctuation. Payments will be processed most quickly through the use of CHAPS euro (Clearing House Automated Payment System) - an electronic same day funds transfer system.

BACS direct debit

Most methods of payment can be used to pay in euro. One of the main exceptions is BACS direct debit. Although BACS direct credit is available, banks are not making BACS euro direct debit available at this time. The main impact of this is that importers who wish to use the duty deferment facility, of which one of the requirements is that direct debit be used, must continue to pay in sterling.

Conversion Costs

The costs incurred by Customs and Excise in converting euro tax and duty payments into sterling will not be passed on to businesses and will be borne by the Department.

Repayments

All repayments will continue to be made by Customs and Excise in sterling - the currency of the UK.

2. Euro accounting and invoicing in the UK

Invoicing

Customs and Excise have simplified the current requirements for tax invoices issued in currencies other than sterling, in order to facilitate the euro.

If businesses issue tax invoices in euro the invoice must also show the sterling equivalent of the total net value of goods and services at each rate of VAT and the amount of VAT, if any, at each rate. These rules are set out in HM Customs and Excise's Public Notice 700 paragraphs 6.3 and 3.1(f) but it is not now necessary to make line by line conversions.

The sterling VAT amount on tax invoices is to be used by both the supplier and the customer for VAT accounting purposes i.e. suppliers must declare the sterling VAT amounts on their sales invoices as output tax and their customers must use the same amounts for input tax purposes. These are necessary requirements in order to preserve the integrity of the tax.

VAT and Duty accounts

VAT and duty accounts must continue to be maintained in sterling.

Exchange Rates

There are 3 alternative methods that can be used to convert an amount from euro into sterling on invoices (Public notice 700, paragraph 3.1 (f)):

- the UK market selling rate at the time of the supply - rates published in national newspapers are acceptable as evidence of the rates at the relevant time;
- the period rate of exchange published by Customs and Excise for customs purposes; or - you may apply in writing to the VAT Business Advice Centre for your area for the use of a rate or method of determining a rate which you use for commercial purposes but which is not covered by the two alternatives above.

Declarations

All declarations must continue to be made in sterling, including VAT returns and Intrastat declarations. The one exception is Box 22 on the Single Administrative Document which is used for imports and exports, where euro values can be used.

Customs and Excise publications

HM Customs and Excise have published a series of information sheets in a question and answer format called "Single Currency Matters" to keep businesses informed and to give details of how businesses can pay in euro. Issues 1, 2 and 3 are now available from local Customs and Excise Business Advice Centres.

VAT: SITES FOR COIN-OPERATED MACHINES [HM Customs and Excise Business Brief 1/99, 13 January 1999]

This Business Brief gives Customs' position in light of the High Court Decision in the case of Sinclair Collis Limited. The High Court reversed the Tribunal decision. This judgement also reverses the earlier decision of "Wolverhampton and Dudley Breweries Limited". Both cases concern the siting of coin-operated amusement machines in public houses, where the supply of the machine was made by its owner. The High Court addressed the question of what was the nature of the supply by the owner of the premises, and the judgement upheld Customs' published interpretation of the law (see VAT Notice 701/13/95: Gaming and amusement machines).

Customs interpretation of the law

Where the owner of premises (such as a publican) allows the owner of a machine to site it on his premises for payment and under a written or oral agreement, this gives rise to a supply for VAT purposes. The supply is of the space on which the machine is sited. Where both parties can exercise some degree of control over the machine, or have a say in its siting, this generally results in a supply of a licence to occupy land, made by the owner of the premises to the owner of the machine.

Past confusion

In the past, there has been confusion over the VAT treatment of these supplies leading to VAT being wrongly charged by the owners of the premises and wrongly recovered by the owners' of the machines. Customs will not require businesses to take any action where, due to a genuine misunderstanding, the owners of the premises have in the past taxed supplies of sites for coin operated machines, provided that the tax wrongly charged has been accounted as output tax. Where this has happened and the owner of the machine has included the amount wrongly charged as input tax, Customs will also leave this undisturbed, provided that there is documented evidence that 17.5 per cent was added to the site rental payments and there was no other error in calculating this input tax claim.

What this means for businesses

Businesses are now expected to implement the decision of the High Court.

If you are the owner of premises

If you are the owner of premises on which a coin-operated machine is situated and you have accounted for VAT on the site rental payments received, you need not adjust this unless you wish to do so. However, if you do submit a claim for a refund, Customs will consider whether you would be unjustly enriched by such a refund. We would expect that those who included VAT in the cost of their services and passed that tax on will return the benefit of any refund to those individuals who actually bore the cost of that VAT.

From now on, you should not tax the site rental income unless you have elected to waive exemption ("opted to tax") in respect of the property in question. If you have indeed opted to tax, the site rental payments should have been taxed from the effective date of your option to tax.

If you are the owner of a machine

If you are the owner of a coin-operated machine sited on another person's premises and have in the past expressly, but wrongly, been charged VAT on the payments you have made under the site rental agreement, you can either:

(i)   do nothing, so any amounts you recovered as input tax will not be adjusted by Customs, provided that these amounts are correctly recorded in your accounts and you have documentary evidence to support the claims you have made; or

(ii)   ask the owner of the premises to refund the VAT wrongly charged. On receipt of such a refund you must remember to note your accounting records accordingly. Any refund will be limited to three years, in accordance with the three year cap provisions, which restrict the recovery of overpaid VAT.

If the owner of the premises has not charged VAT (i.e. 17.5% was not added to the site rental payments) there will have been no VAT for you to recover as input tax and you should not have done so.

VAT: PARTIAL EXEMPTION – VALUES TO BE EXCLUDED FROM THE STANDARD METHOD CALCULATION [HM Customs and Excise Business Brief 8/99, 31 March 1999]

This Business Brief is about the decision of the Court of Appeal of 17 March 1999 in the Liverpool School of Performing Arts case. In Business Brief 8/98 Customs stated their intention to appeal following the High Court decision of 30 January 1998. The case determined whether the values of supplies made outside the UK, which would be taxable supplies if made in the UK, could be included in the partial exemption standard method calculation. This is one of the methods used to establish the recoverable proportion of residual input tax. The Court of Appeal, in overturning the High Court's decision, supported Customs' view that such supplies are not to be included in that calculation. The deduction of input tax relating to these supplies is provided for separately and is determined on the basis of use.

Impact on Businesses

The Court of Appeal's decision will not, of course, affect those businesses which have continued to apply Customs' policy pending the outcome of this appeal. But it will affect those businesses which have applied the High Court's decision. Business Brief 8/98 stated that if the Courts were to find for Customs then those businesses which have applied the High Court's decision will be required to repay any overclaimed tax plus interest on amounts over £2,000. This is now the case. However, penalties will not be applied for the periods when the High Court's decision had effect (i.e. from the date of the High Court's decision until the date of the Court of Appeal decision).

VAT: THE THREE YEAR CAP AND PARTIAL EXEMPTION [HM Customs and Excise Business Brief 8/99, 31 March 1999]

This Business Brief clarifies Customs' policy about how the three year cap affects businesses' partial exemption position, illustrated by a number of examples.

Background

The purpose of the three year cap is to provide certainty and stability for both the Exchequer and the tax payer. The provisions are not intended to have any impact on the normal system of deduction and adjustments to deduction as set out in the VAT Regulations.

Any trader or business currently operating the partial exemption rules correctly will not be affected by the three cap. This also applies to businesses which discover a mistake and make the necessary correction within the three year time limit. In other words, the three year cap only affects businesses who do not claim the input tax to which they were entitled or claim input tax to which they were not entitled, and fail to correct this within 3 years.

In addition, if a business fails to make an initial deduction of input tax (or gets the initial deduction wrong) and the error falls in a period which is more than three years old, the error cannot be corrected in the partial exemption annual adjustment even if the adjustment itself is not capped. However, even though the unclaimed amount of input tax cannot be reclaimed because it is capped, the annual adjustment itself should be based on the true amounts of input and output tax.

Examples

The effects of the three year cap are illustrated in the following examples:

(i)   A partly exempt business (makes both exempt and taxable supplies) fails to use a partial exemption method and does not claim any input tax for a number of years. After an audit, the business submits a refund claim, in which the first quarter of the third tax year is "capped" (i.e. more than three years old) but the annual adjustment period itself is not "capped" (it falls within the three year period). Can the input tax in that period be recovered in the annual adjustment?

No–The trader, by failing to recover input tax in the relevant period, has failed to exercise the right to deduct. The trader is not able to claim this "capped" amount in the annual adjustment.

(ii)   A partly exempt business calculates deductible input tax in accordance with his partial exemption method. In the first two quarters he fails the de-minimis limits and so correctly restricts his exempt input tax. In the second two quarters he is able to benefit from the de-minimis limits and so correctly recovers all his input tax in those quarters. At the end of the year he is able to benefit from the de-minimis rules for the year as a whole but does not apply them. If he discovers this mistake within three years from the last day of the annual adjustment quarter is he able to correct it?

Yes–The partly exempt trader has correctly applied the de-minimis rules to each quarter. Since it is at the time of the annual adjustment that the de-minimis rules are applied to all the input tax incurred in the previous four quarters, it is at that time that any exempt input tax previously restricted may be recovered.

However, where a trader was entitled to apply the de-minimis rules to a particular period but did not do so, and that period was "capped", any affected input tax falling in that period may not be recovered in the final de-minimis calculation at the time of the annual adjustment (which itself is not "capped"). This is because the trader failed to exercise the right to deduct within the three year period.

(iii)   A business with an agreed partial exemption method mistakenly treats taxable input tax as exempt. Can this input tax be recovered at the time of the annual adjustment if the input tax is proper to a period which is "capped" (but the annual adjustment is not "capped")?

No–We would not allow the trader to recover the exempt input tax at the time of the annual adjustment. The trader has mistakenly treated taxable input tax as exempt, and so he has failed to recover it.

Similarly, if the trader had incorrectly claimed exempt input tax and the input tax was proper to a period which was "capped", we would be unable to recover it under the assessment provisions in that period or the period of the annual adjustment (even if it was not "capped").

Customs are aware that, because of the complexity of the three year cap, we have agreed some claims and settled them as if the annual adjustment can be used to override the cap, effectively giving some claimants a repayment to which they were not entitled. We do not propose to revisit any of these claims, but all future claims will be treated on a proper basis.

VAT: TOUR OPERATORS' MARGIN SCHEME (TOMS) – European Court of Justice (ECJ) decision [HM Customs and Excise Business Brief 10/99, 22 April 1999]

This business brief explains Customs' position in light of the ECJ decision in Madgett & Baldwin t/a Howden Court Hotel. The hotel, in Torquay, supplies inclusive packages to tourists from the north of England. The packages comprise coach transport between the hotel and customers' home towns, a stay at the hotel for several days and coach excursions. The coach transport is bought-in by the hotel.

Definition of tour operator

The first issue before the ECJ was to determine whether the hotel's activities were those of a tour operator and therefore subject to VAT under the TOMS. The Court supported Customs' policy that the TOMS applies in principle to anyone who buys in and resells services for the direct benefit of a traveller, but added two new criteria to Customs' definition. The first was that the travel services must be bought in and resold "habitually". The second was that bought-in travel services which take up a small proportion of the package price are "ancillary" in relation to the main supply and would not justify a supplier being regarded as a tour operator. The Court's example of "ancillary" was a taxi ride between a hotel and a local railway station.

Apportionment of packages which include in-house supplies

The second issue before the ECJ related to the method of determining the value of the in-house element of the packages. In Madgett & Baldwin's case, the VAT on the margin of the bought-in element was the same whichever method was used. The Court held that, bearing this in mind, the operator was entitled to use a method based on the market value of the in-house supplies when the cost-based calculation required complex sub-apportionment exercises, and when it was possible to identify the in-house element of the package by a market value-based method.

The way forward

Customs see the decision as being primarily about simplification, rather than the amount of VAT paid by tour operators, and consider that the cost-based apportionment set out in Notice 709/5 Tour operators' margin scheme remains a valid method of valuing in-house supplies. Customs intend to use the decision to simplify the TOMS and reduce the number of traders affected by it and will be consulting with the industry and other interested parties. A technical discussion document will be issued in May, exploring practical issues such as the interpretation and application of the terms "habitually", "ancillary" and "market value". Customs envisage this period of consultation running through to the autumn, with appropriate changes to the TOMS being made in due course.

The timing of these changes (and so any revision of Notice 709/5) is uncertain at this stage, but they are unlikely to be implemented before April 2000. In the meantime, traders should continue to use the TOMS as set out in Notice 709/5. Subject to capping, any changes which are beneficial to traders may be applied retrospectively. To protect themselves against the effects of capping, traders who consider that they have "overpaid" VAT may lodge a claim with their VAT Business Advice Centre before changes are implemented.

VAT: PASSENGER TRANSPORT SERVICES WHICH INCLUDE CATERING [HM Customs and Excise Business Brief 10/99, 22 April 1999]

This Business Brief explains Customs' position following the Sea Containers case, which considered the VAT position of passenger transport supplied with catering on a railway train. There were a number of different types of supply all of which included in-house catering which was promoted as high quality in advertising material.

The supplies included:

- charter of the whole train plus crew, with separately negotiated catering;
- charter of the whole train plus crew, with catering included in a single price;
- round trips sold to individual passengers which included high quality catering, such as five course meals and champagne lunches; and
- a stopping trip sold to individual passengers who could alight before the return journey, again including catering.

The issue for the Tribunal was whether there were single supplies of zero-rated passenger transport, or separate supplies of transport and standard-rated catering. The Tribunal found that in each case there were separate supplies.

Customs consider that this decision, in conjunction with the remarks of the European Court of Justice on single and multiple supplies in another recent case (Card Protection Plan) confirms their current policy. Where an element of catering is included with scheduled passenger transport for no extra charge (such as a meal included in the price of an airline ticket) there is a single supply of passenger transport. Where catering, or other elements such as discos, receptions etc. are included as a feature of leisure travel, there are separate supplies, and the catering and other extras are taxable at the standard rate.

As mentioned in Business Brief 5/99, Customs consider that the decision in the recent case of Pennine Boat Trips is confined to that case. Refund claims based on Pennine will not be repaid, and the decision will not be applied more generally. The treatment of cruises remains as set out in paragraph 3.13 of Notice 744A, Passenger Transport, and agreements with trade associations representing operators of boat trips on canals and rivers remain in place.

VAT: MOBILE PHONES PROVIDED TO EMPLOYEES [HM Customs and Excise Business Brief 14/99, 2 July 1999]

This Business Brief explains Customs and Excise revised policy on the VAT treatment of mobile phones provided by businesses to employees.

Background

In the 1999 Budget the Chancellor announced his intention to abolish the Inland Revenue scale charge which taxed the benefit in kind of mobile phones provided to employees. This has prompted a number of organisations to ask for similar proposals for VAT purposes. EC law would not permit the UK to stop charging VAT on the private use of business assets such as mobile phones. However Customs has reviewed its policy to ensure businesses can continue to account for VAT in a simple and flexible way.

VAT on the cost of providing and connecting a mobile phone

Where a business provides its employees with mobile phones for business use then, regardless of whether it allows private use, it can treat as input tax all the VAT it incurs on purchasing a phone and on standing charges for keeping it connected to the network providing the charges do not contain any element for calls.

VAT on mobile phone call charges

If a business does not allow its employees to make private calls, all of the VAT incurred on the call charges is input tax. Customs will accept this is the case where a business has imposed clear rules prohibiting private use and enforces them. However we realise that in practice businesses with such a policy often tolerate a small amount of private calls. We are prepared to treat such minimal use as being insignificant for VAT purposes and it will not prevent a business treating all the tax it incurs on calls as input tax.

If a business charges its employees for any private calls they make, then it may treat the VAT incurred on the calls as input tax, but must account for output tax on the amounts it charges.

If a business allows its employees to make private calls without charge, then it must apportion the VAT incurred on the call charges. It is not appropriate for businesses to adopt an alternative treatment of accounting for output tax on the private use.

Businesses can choose any apportionment method that suits their individual circumstances providing the method chosen produces a fair and reasonable result. For example businesses could analyse a sample of bills taken over a reasonable period of time and use the same ratio for future VAT recovery on mobile phone bills.

Where the phone package allows the business to make a certain quantity of calls for a fixed monthly payment and there is no separate standing charge, then it must apportion the VAT on the total charge for the package. Similarly, where the contract is for the purchase of the phone and the advance purchase of a set amount of call time for a single charge, the apportionment will also apply to the whole charge.

Further advice

You can obtain further advice from your local VAT Business Advice Centre. You will find the number under Customs and Excise in the phone book.

VAT GROUPS – PROTECTION OF THE REVENUE [HM Customs and Excise Business Brief 15/99, 12 July 1999]

In the 1999 Budget, changes to the VAT grouping rules were announced. This included a new revenue protection power. This Business Brief sets out our approach to this new power, and to our use of existing revenue protection powers contained in the grouping legislation.

Background

The VAT grouping facility was introduced with the tax in 1973 and has always contained powers to refuse certain applications for grouping, for the protection of the revenue. Over the years those powers have been amended so that, prior to the 1999 Budget, we were able to refuse applications for:

-     a new VAT group to be formed;
-     a company to be added to an existing VAT group;
-     a company to be removed from an existing VAT group;
-     the representative member of a VAT group to be changed; and
-     a VAT group to be disbanded.

1999 Budget changes

There were two changes in this area announced in the Budget. They will come into force on Royal Assent. These are that:

— grouping applications will be given immediate provisional effect from the date that we receive them. We will then have 90 days from the receipt of an application to decide whether to refuse the application for the protection of the revenue; and

— we will be able to remove a company from an existing VAT group for the protection of the revenue. This power is not subject to any 90 day limit.

How will we operate the 90 day rule?

If you have properly completed your application forms, we will aim to respond to you within 15 working days of their receipt with either:

— a new VAT registration number for the group; or

— notification that your application to amend the composition of your group has been processed.

We will also aim to inform you within 15 working days of receipt if further enquiries are to be made. Our letter will include confirmation of the date of receipt of the application.

If we consider that further enquiries do need to be made into your application we shall endeavour to complete those enquiries as soon as possible after receiving your application. We will notify you of the outcome of our enquiries as soon as they are completed. If we have not written to you to let you know the outcome by the end of the 90 day period, we will not be able to refuse the application.

If we do refuse an application it will effectively be set aside and it will be deemed never to have been allowed or effected. This may mean that:

— you will have to notify a liability to register for VAT in accordance with the normal rules; or

— we will reinstate the VAT registration number that you held when you made the application for grouping with effect from the date on which it was cancelled for you to join the group; and

— the representative member of the VAT group will have to submit a voluntary disclosure to reverse the VAT accounting done while the change had provisional effect.

It is therefore in your interest to provide information quickly in respect of your provisional grouping, if asked to do so. If you think, after reading this *Business Brief*, that your application is one which we may refuse, you must draw our attention to the relevant facts and issues at the time of your application.

What will happen when a company is to be removed from a group?

When a revenue concern is identified relating to an existing group member, we will write advising you that enquiries are being made and that the company may be removed from the group for the protection of the revenue. It is in your interests to provide information quickly when asked to do so. Any failure to provide information may mean that factors are not taken into account which may affect the outcome of our considerations. We will notify you of the outcome of our enquiries as soon as they are completed.

When a decision is made to remove a company from a group we will give written notice specifying the date from which the company is to be removed. This date cannot be before the date when the notice is given. We will normally provide sufficient notice to allow you time to reorganise your affairs but in some circumstances we may need to take prompt action.

The meaning of "for the protection of the revenue"

Even though some of the revenue protection powers for groups are new, the concept of refusing group applications for the protection of the revenue is not. Until the Budget changes are enacted, the relevant legislation is set out in section 43(4) & (5A) of the *Value Added Tax Act* 1994. The meaning of "protection of the revenue" in this context was recently discussed in the VAT & Duties Tribunal in the case of *National Westminster Bank PLC v The Commissioners of Customs & Excise* (LON/97/124).

Paragraph 72 of the decision says that:

"the protection in question under section 43(5A) may be against any loss of revenue which is not de minimis whether or not it follows from the normal operation of grouping. It certainly covers an artificial avoidance scheme but it also covers a straight forward case which would not be characterised as avoidance or abusive".

In future, we will not normally use our revenue protection powers when we consider that the revenue loss follows from the normal operation of grouping. By this, we mean the "revenue loss" which occurs because VAT is eliminated on the value added by a group member, when a supply takes place between two group members. This includes the loss arising from supplies between group members being disregarded, where the recipient of the supply would not normally be able to deduct that VAT because it makes exempt supplies. We would normally consider such revenue loss, the same as if the VAT group members were all one company, to be a natural result of grouping.

Where we consider that there seems likely to be a revenue loss that goes beyond the accepted result of grouping, we will feel entitled to use our revenue protection powers. When deciding in any particular case whether to refuse a VAT group application, or to expel a company from a VAT group, we will bear in mind the decision in *National Westminster Bank*. Paragraph 74 of that decision says:

> "the phrase "necessary for the protection of the revenue" must be considered as a totality and involves a balancing exercise in which the Commissioners must weigh the effect on the Appellant of refusal of grouping against the loss of revenue likely to result from grouping".

Weighing the likely revenue loss against the administrative cost of using our powers.

When considering whether or not to use our revenue protection powers, we will aim to follow this approach. If we have concerns that the revenue loss does go beyond the accepted consequence of VAT grouping, we will ask for relevant information about the administrative savings that grouping brings in the particular circumstances, and an estimate of the revenue impact of grouping. We will normally ask you to comment on the impact on your business of any refusal or removal on our part. For example, you may incur extra costs in having to submit an extra VAT return, or in having to account for VAT on supplies between group members. The extent of these costs will depend on how your accounting systems are set up.

We will weigh any likely abnormal revenue loss against the administrative cost to you of our refusal or removal. When that revenue cost significantly outweighs the administrative cost we will consider invoking our powers.

Decisions and appeals

We will make a judgement based on the information that you provide, and any other information that we have. If you fail to provide the information that we ask for, we will endeavour to come to a balanced decision based on the information that we already have to hand. But if you consistently fail to provide information or records which we might reasonably request in the course of our enquiries, that may be treated as sufficient grounds for exercising our revenue protection powers.

Any decision on whether to exercise our revenue protection powers will take into account the scheme of VAT as a whole. Our internal guidance will make it clear to local VAT assurance officers in what circumstances they must have headquarters' agreement before using the revenue protection powers.

If we invoke our revenue protection powers, we will write to you explaining why. If you disagree with our view, you can appeal to the VAT & Duties Tribunal who can rule on whether our decision was reasonable in the circumstances.

If you have any questions, please contact your local VAT Business Advice centre listed under Customs and Excise in your local telephone directory.

VAT: OPTION TO TAX – PROPERTY [HM Customs and Excise Business Brief 17/99, 5 August 1999]

Introduction

This *Business Brief* concerns the decision by the VAT and Duties Tribunal in the case of *Blythe Limited Partnership* ("Blythe"). Customs did not appeal the decision. This *Business Brief* provides some practical steps businesses can take to ensure there are no misunderstandings over which properties they have opted to tax ("opted"). The option to tax allows businesses who sell, or grant either leases of or licences to occupy land to tax supplies that would otherwise be exempt, and thereby recover the input tax incurred in making those supplies.

Background

Unless it is necessary to obtain Customs' written permission (para 8.6 of Notice 742 *Land and property* explains the circumstances when this would be required) to opt to tax ("to opt"), an option to tax ("an option") comprises two actions. Firstly, the business decides to opt a building or piece of land and secondly it notifies this decision to Customs. For the option to take legal effect and allow the business to charge VAT on any future rents and sales notification must be within 30 days of opting to tax ("opting").

The issue in the *Blythe* case was how many properties the limited partnership had opted and whether they were bound by the written notification from their solicitors to Customs. The solicitors had sent in a written notification of an option made by their client and attached a list of 16 properties. Blythe subsequently sold one of these properties without charging VAT. They argued that of the 16 properties they had in fact only opted 4, and the property sold was not one of these. On the basis of documentary evidence made available at the hearing, the Tribunal found that Blythe had indeed only opted 4 buildings. Consequently, Blythe was not bound by the incorrect notification with regard the other 12 properties.

How to notify an option to tax

Customs' aim has always been to make the process of notifying an option as simple and straightforward as possible. Consequently, unless a letter notifying an option is clearly wrong or it is evident that prior written permission to opt is necessary, Customs have accepted such letters at face value. Customs will continue to do so because to check the accuracy of each and every written notification would create unnecessary delay.

However, the decision in *Blythe* has shown what problems can arise if a responsible person within the business making the option does not sign the letter of notification, and if unchecked lists are attached to that letter. Where this is not already done, Customs recommend that the letter notifying an option and any accompanying list or schedule of properties, is signed as appropriate by a director, two or more partners (or trustees), an authorised administrator, or by a sole proprietor.

If a business authorises a third party to notify an option on their behalf Customs require confirmation that this person is an authorised signatory. Customs would also like to be notified if the business ever withdraws the authority from this person.

Recording the decision to opt to tax

Since the decision to opt is in law different from the act of notifying it, Customs recommend that businesses keep a written record of its decision to opt at the time it is made. How this is done is best left to the individual business concerned, for example the decision might have been made during a meeting and recorded in the minutes of that meeting. It should, however, state which property is the subject of the option and the date on which the business decided to opt. This will be helpful to both businesses and Customs if, as in the case of *Blythe*, a business claims the letter notifying the option contains an error. If there is no such written record Customs will have no choice but to treat the written notification as the proof of what properties or land the business decided to opt.

Reminder

An option applies to entire buildings and therefore extends to the entire interest held or to be acquired at a future date in that property. It will cover the sale as well as its leasing or letting unless it does not apply because of the use to which the property will be put (i.e. the property is intended for use as a dwelling).

As stated above there are certain circumstances when businesses will need to seek Customs' written permission before they can opt. Where this is the case, the business will not be able to charge VAT nor reclaim any input tax incurred making those supplies until it has received Customs' permission even if it has sent Customs a letter notifying its decision to opt.

Further advice

Further information can be obtained from your local Business Advice Centre. The address and telephone number can be found in the telephone directory listed under Customs and Excise.

VAT: LICENCES TO OCCUPY LAND [HM Customs and Excise Business Brief 21/99, 7 September 1999]

This Business Brief announces that Customs have now published their report on "licences to occupy land" following their review. It also provides a summary of Customs' revised interpretation.

Background

In *Business Brief* 22/98, Customs announced they were reviewing what constituted a "licence to occupy land" and invited businesses to respond to four questions. Customs promised to publish a report once they had completed the review. Customs published the report on 21 July 1999 and sent copies to all those who contributed to the review and those who requested a copy.

The scope of the report

Some contributors expressed the view that rather than looking at "licences to occupy land" in isolation, Customs should consider again the wording used in the Land Exemption. However, the main purpose of *Business Brief* 22/98 was to find a swift and workable solution to the immediate problem of what is a "licence to occupy land", and how this could be achieved. Customs believe while a more extensive analysis of the words used in the Land Exemption may be a useful longer term objective, it is not a realistic objective in the short time. Customs therefore limited the scope of the report to the issue of "licences to occupy land".

Customs' findings

Customs studied the various decisions by the Tribunals and Higher Courts on what constitutes a "licence to occupy land" to see whether the Courts had adopted any common criteria or tests. Unfortunately research revealed that most cases were decided on their individual facts, with little read across from one to the other. Customs concluded that in the absence of any consistent themes case law was of little assistance to this particular project.

Two other possibilities were considered. Either to publish what Customs believe to be the characteristics of a "licence to occupy land", with more detailed examples; or to consider how the term "licence to occupy land" might be defined in the law. Customs have decided against the latter because the responses to the *Business Brief* have demonstrated the extreme difficulty in achieving such a legal definition. Since the license in question is one which permits the occupation of land, Customs believe the concept of occupation can be adequately explained in guidance. Therefore Customs have decided to publish clearer guidance on when, in their opinion, a supply of land for occupation does and does not exist. Customs hope this will be helpful for businesses, clarify some areas of doubt or confusion and end some disputes.

One further issue that arose was the distinction between a lease and a licence. While this may be a relevant issue elsewhere, Customs consider it of comparatively little importance in the context of VAT. Since the licence which is exempt from VAT is a "licence to occupy land", it does not matter whether it is characterised as a lease or a licence. Both are exempt and both are equally subject to an election to waive exemption where the law permits. Lesser licences to use facilities situated on land are not within the Exemption and they are unlikely to be characterised as leases.

Customs' revised interpretation

The following is a list of characteristics that Customs believe should be present if a supply of land for occupation is to qualify for exemption.

The characteristics are:

1.   the licence is granted in return for a consideration paid by the licensee;
2.   the licence to occupy must be of a specified piece of land, even if the licence allows the licensor to change the exact area occupied, i.e. to move licensee from the third to fourth floor;
3.   the licence is for the occupation of the land by the licensee;
4.   *another person's right to enter the* specified land does not impinge upon the occupational rights of the licensee; and either
5.   the licence allows the licensee to physically enjoy the land for the purposes of the grant, for example to hold a party in a hall or graze sheep on a field; or
6.   the licence allows the licensee to economically exploit the land for the purposes of its business, for example run a nightclub or museum.

Public guidance

The Croners VAT Encyclopaedia is currently being updated. Customs will also issue an update to Public Notice 742 "*Land and property*". Both will contain the above characteristics plus two lists; the first containing examples of when Customs believe there is a "licence to occupy land", and the second a list of examples when Customs believe there is not such a licence.

In the meantime if you have not already requested a copy of the report but would like one you can either write to or fax:

John Munford, HM Customs and Excise, VAT Policy Directorate, Commercial Division, New King's Beam House, 22 Upper Ground, London, SE1 9PJ. Tel 0171 865 5747 or fax 0171 865 4824.

You can obtain further advice from your local VAT Business Advice Centre. You will find the number under Customs and Excise in the phone book.

D. STATEMENTS OF PRACTICE

VAT AVOIDANCE – GROUPS OF COMPANIES [HM Customs and Excise Statement of Practice, June 1996]

STATEMENT OF PRACTICE ON THE NEW SCHEDULE 9A OF THE VALUE ADDED TAX ACT 1994

1. Introduction

1.1   The following sets out how Customs and Excise will seek to apply the new anti-avoidance provisions for VAT groups introduced in the Finance Act 1996. This Statement has been produced jointly by the Chartered Institute of Taxation and Customs and Excise, who have incorporated comments from other professional bodies. Its purpose is solely to clarify Customs' policy in this area; it does not qualify the relevant legislation, nor does it affect a taxpayer's rights of appeal to an independent VAT tribunal.

2. Why is this legislation required?

2.1   The new provisions are designed for use only against certain categories of avoidance scheme which rely on the existence of the group registration provision contained in section 43 of the Value Added Tax Act 1994. Subsection 43(1)(a) of the Act provides that any supply of goods or services between members of the same VAT group shall be disregarded, but the schemes in question seek to exploit the "disregard" provision for the sole purpose of reducing the VAT on supplies of goods and services purchased by the group from external sources.

2.2   In addition to providing an administrative convenience to the taxpayer, a tax benefit inevitably results through the normal operation of the disregard provision, which prevents supplies between members of the group registration from being taxed or treated as exempt supplies. The tax benefit which results naturally from group registration is not necessarily VAT avoidance and Customs accept some loss of tax from the facilitation measure. The following is an example of VAT group arrangements that fall outside the scope of these anti-avoidance provisions.

Example of acceptable VAT savings from operation of grouping rules

A company carries on a variety of activities in separate divisions. These divisions "supply" goods and services to each other but, as they are all part of the one body corporate, no supply is made for VAT purposes and no output tax occurs. Input tax recovery is determined according to the taxable status of the company as a whole.

If the same business were to be carried on by a number of separately registered companies, all members of the same group of companies, then these supplies would be supplies for VAT purposes. Should any member of the group be VAT exempt, or otherwise be unable to recover its VAT in full, a VAT cost will have arisen which would not have arisen had the business been run in a single company but in separate divisions.

If all the companies are put into a single VAT group registration then the VAT position of the group is the same as a single company with divisions. No charge to output tax would arise on supplies between members of the group, but equally, no input tax could be claimed in connection with those internal supplies: recovery of such tax would be subject to the tax status and activities of the group as a whole.

2.3   Customs will, however, seek to use the new provisions where avoidance of VAT over and above such savings arise out of the facilitation measures. Examples of instances where they would seek to take action are given below.

Entry schemes

A typical entry scheme would involve the supplier acquiring goods and services, and recovering the associated VAT before moving the assets into the user's business (either by transferring the assets to another company in the user's VAT group or by joining the group itself). A common feature of such schemes is that periodic payments due from the user under the contract are staged so as to ensure that the greater part falls due when supplier and user are within the same VAT group.

Exit schemes

Under a typical exit scheme, a company wishing to use goods and services subject to VAT which it cannot recover (the "user") acts in concert with a central purchasing company (the "supplier") within its existing VAT group. The user enters into a contract with the supplier and makes a substantial pre-payment. The supplier then leaves the group, purchases the relevant goods or services and supplies them to the user. The supplier takes full recovery of VAT on the goods and services, but accounts for VAT only on the balance of the purchase price. The user is therefore able to reduce the amount of irrecoverable VAT it would otherwise have suffered on goods and services purchased for its business. **NB Customs are currently appealing a tribunal decision in connection with one such scheme.**

2.4   These examples are illustrative only and Customs will seek to apply the provisions to any similar scheme or its variation. Features common to such avoidance schemes are that input tax deduction is taken against standard-rated supplies, but output tax does not fall on the full value of those supplies because they are treated to some extent as being made between members of the same VAT group and so are disregarded for VAT. The simplest means of bringing the disregard into play is by moving a company in to or out of a VAT group at a critical moment. But a similar result could be secured by entering into some other transaction, such as the transfer of assets or the assignment of an agreement to or from a group member (see also paragraph 3.5 below covering the definition of transaction in the context of a relevant event).

3.   Scope of the new provisions

3.1   Section 31 of, and Schedule 4, to the Finance Act 1996 insert a new Schedule 9A into the VAT Act 1994. Essentially, this increases the powers available to Customs in connection with the registration of VAT groups under section 43 of the VAT Act 1994.

3.2   The new powers enable the Commissioners of Customs and Excise to direct that [VATA 1994, Sch. 9A, para. 3]:

- separately registered companies eligible to be treated as members of a VAT group may be compelled to group from a specified date; or
- a company within a group may be compelled to leave a group from a specified date; and
- a supply within a group initially treated as a disregarded supply may subsequently be subjected to tax.

3.3   To neutralise fully the tax advantage gained by an avoidance scheme, a direction may require assumptions to be made in connection with matters arising prior to its issue. Special provisions [VATA 1994, Sch. 9A, para. 6(1)] enable an assessment to be issued to recover tax which would have been due had those assumptions reflected the actual position.

Conditions for the issue of a direction under the new Schedule 9A

3.4   A direction may only be issued where all of the following conditions are present:

- **A relevant event** (defined at paragraph 3.5. below) has occurred which meets conditions which but for the occurrence of that event would not be fulfilled;
- *The conditions qualifying the relevant event are:*
  - that there has been, or will or may be, a standard-rated (or partly standard-rated) supply on which the output tax due falls to be charged otherwise than by reference to its **full value**; and
  - the charging of VAT at less than full value gives rise or would give rise to **a tax advantage**.

3.5   *Relevant event*: A relevant event is defined [VATA 1994, Sch. 9A, para. 1(2)] as occurring when a company joins or leaves a VAT group registration, or when it enters into any transaction. The word "transaction" is capable of being given a very wide meaning when considered in isolation, but the key to understanding how Customs will interpret this in the context of the provisions is that a relevant event occurs when a taxpayer *enters into* a transaction. Generally Customs will take this to mean when the taxpayer enters into a contract or other disposition, such as a gift.

Example:

Take a lease of a building. Each payment of rent could be regarded as a transaction in itself. However, the mere payment of rent would not be regarded as covered by the term "enters into any transaction" as used in the legislation.

Customs will regard the entering into of the lease by the landlord or tenant as a relevant event which would (if the other conditions are met), potentially bring a company within the scope of the provisions. Other examples falling within the scope of the provisions are an agreement for a lease, an assignment, variation or surrender. The performance of obligations under the lease, (e.g. the carrying out of repairs or the payment of rent), would not normally be caught unless, exceptionally, such obligation constituted the entering into of a separate contract.

3.6   *Full value condition*: in the context of these measures [VATA 1994, Sch. 9A, para. 1(9)], a supply at less than full value (the undercharged supply) means only those supplies which to any extent have been, or will be, disregarded under section 43 of the Value Added Tax Act 1994 because they arise between VAT group members. Supplies which, although not disregarded under section 43, are less than full value for other reasons are not covered. Customs could not, for instance, compulsorily group the parties to a lease and lease-back agreement under arrangements that had nothing to do with the operation of an intra-group disregard. This is not to say that other measures would not apply.

3.7   *Tax advantage*: A tax advantage is defined [VATA 1994, Sch. 9A, para. 1(4)] as arising in circumstances where an input tax credit or payment under section 39 of the VAT Act 1994 is taken on goods and services used to make the undercharged supply. It is not essential that the right to a tax credit or payment should be that of the supplier of the undercharged supply. The legislation specifically provides that the condition is also fulfilled where the supplier acquires the goods and/or services tax free under the provisions relating to the transfer of a business as a going concern, and the transferor or some previous owner of the business had been entitled to an input tax credit [VATA 1994, Sch. 9A, para. 1(6)]. The following example based on an entry scheme illustrates why this is necessary.

A partly exempt group of companies (the PX group) wishes to reduce the VAT on computer equipment It therefore arranges for the equipment to be provided by an associated company, Newco 1, which operates a leasing business.

Newco 1 purchases the necessary equipment and deducts input tax under its own VAT registration against its intended supplies of leasing services to the PX group.

Before entering into a lease agreement Newco 1 transfers its business, including the assets for use by PX group, as a going concern to another associated company, Newco. 2. The transfer is not subject to VAT.

Newco 2 enters into a leasing agreement with PX group and after an appropriate period joins the group to ensure that the major part of the lease rentals fall to be disregarded. Overall, the arrangements deliver the tax advantage which Schedule 9A is intended to counter even though Newco 2 has not itself had any entitlement to an input tax credit.

In providing that in such cases the transferor and the transferee shall be treated as the same person the legislation ensures that such arrangements are not excluded from the scope of these anti-avoidance measures.

3.8   Other provisions [VATA 1994, Sch. 9A, para. 1(8), 1(10)] deem that, for the purpose of determining whether the input tax credit is used to make an undercharged supply, separate rights to goods or services (including options or priorities in connection with goods or services), and the goods and services themselves shall be treated as a single supply. The intention is to ensure that variations of avoidance schemes such as that in the following example are covered.

Example (Variation on basic exit scheme)

PX Group comprising companies A and B wishes to mitigate VAT on purchase of computer equipment

A pays B 90% of cost for an option to purchase the equipment at a nominal value and the supply falls to be disregarded.

B leaves the group and registers in its own right.

A exercises its option and B supplies the goods to A after purchasing the goods and deducting input tax thereon. The argument could run that the input tax deduction was attributable only to the supply of the goods and not to the option. Without the special provision, therefore, there would not be an undercharged supply enabling a direction to be issued.

By providing that the supply of the option and the supply of the goods are to be treated as a single supply, the legislation ensures that such schemes are brought within the scope of Schedule 9A.

3.9 *Summary of conditions*: Taken together, the conditions require that the relevant event must generate a situation where standard-rated supplies, which have given rise to an input tax credit by any person, are not taxed on their full value, so leading to a tax advantage because input tax deduction is disproportionately greater than the corresponding output tax – essentially the tax advantage of an avoidance scheme such as those described earlier must be present.

Partially completed schemes

3.10 Where Customs have evidence that a scheme has been implemented (there has been a relevant event) then they can make a direction in anticipation of the conditions for the scheme being met. Clear examples of such evidence would be a lease which, because of an entry scheme, becomes an intra-group lease (even though further rental payments have yet to be made since the relevant event) and an uncompleted purchase contract. A direction cannot be issued in anticipation of the relevant event itself.

Commercial transactions

3.11 Even where a tax advantage arises, schedule 9a will not apply where the relevant event was carried through for a commercial purpose or purposes unconnected with the avoidance of VAT [VATA 1994, Sch. 9A, para. 2]. This recognises the fact that in the vast majority of cases businesses are moved into and out of vat groups for reasons which have no avoidance motivation whatsoever (e.g. a relevant event might be motivated solely for administration reasons following a change of ownership of a business). The example given at Annex 1 illustrates arrangements which customs would accept as being motivated by a genuine commercial purpose.

3.12 However, it is important to realise that where, in addition to an acceptable commercial purpose, Customs also identify other main purposes indicating VAT avoidance, they will seek to use their powers to nullify the VAT advantage derived. Examples of mixed motive transactions are given at Annexes 2 and 3, along with an indication of how Customs would view the transactions in question. While the examples are rather complex, they are intended to illustrate the basic point that no direction will be issued where Customs are satisfied that it is not one of the main purposes of the arrangement to gain a VAT advantage by having a supply disregarded in a VAT group while obtaining input tax recovery in respect of it.

3.13 In deciding issues concerning commercial purpose, Customs would be prepared to consider the term in its broadest sense where the context of any particular case allowed. The taxable trading arm of a charity, for example, would not be denied a claim to commercial purpose merely because it is part of a non-profit making body.

Time limit on directions

3.14 A direction cannot be given more than six years after the **relevant event**, or six years after the entitlement to input tax which gave rise to the **tax advantage**, whichever is the later [VATA 1994, Sch. 9A, para. 4(1)].

3.15 A direction cannot be given unless the relevant event occurs on or after 29 November 1995 [VATA 1994, Sch. 9A, para. 4(2)].

3.16 However, where a direction is appropriate, it can rely on assumptions about transactions made before that date without any limit [VATA 1994, Sch. 9A, para. 4(3)] (but see paragraph 3.18 below).

Right of appeal

3.17 Taxpayers have full rights of appeal to the VAT tribunal [VATA 1994, s. 83, 84 as amended by FA 1996, s. 31] against the issue by Customs of any direction or assessments issued under these provisions. The tribunal is entitled to consider all relevant facts and decide whether or not the conditions had been fulfilled. in addition the tribunal will be able to decide whether there had been a genuine commercial purpose.

Powers of direction – how far back will Customs go?

3.18 Customs will not seek application of any direction from a date earlier than that required to nullify the tax advantage derived from the relevant event. Usually this will be the first day of the prescribed accounting period in which the scheme commences or the relevant event occurs (whichever is the earlier). In calculating an assessment for unpaid tax according to assumptions applying to periods prior to issue of the direction, only those supplies relevant to delivery of the tax advantage will be taken into account. The assessment amount itself will be capped so that it does not exceed what, in the judgement of Customs is the actual revenue loss arising [VATA 1994, Sch. 9A, para. 6(3), 6(4)]. This means that input tax that would have been deductible on the basis of the assumptions in the direction can be taken into account in appropriate cases. All other supplies made by the parties involved will be unaffected so there will be no need for any retrospective VAT accounting adjustment in their regard. In short, the intention is that the provisions will be applied so as not to make the actions of Customs disproportionate to the mischief involved.

3.19 Nevertheless, Customs will apply these provisions vigorously where an attempt to avoid VAT is made (see also paragraph 6.3 on responsibility for authorising directions).

Is a grouping or degrouping direction irrevocable?

3.20 Once the particular tax advantage of the scheme targeted has been corrected satisfactorily, Customs will consider any subsequent application to join or leave a group subject to their normal powers of discretion in such matters.

4. Records

4.1 It is not intended that these provisions should increase the record keeping requirements of taxpayers to enable either Customs to assess under, or taxpayers to comply with, these provisions. If neither the company degrouped nor the remainder of the group have accurate records to determine the value and nature of transactions between them then an assessment will be made on the best judgement of Customs from all available records, either obtained from or made available to Customs, by the taxpayer.

4.2 Where a direction covers times after its issue the consequences of the direction will materially affect the treatment of any supplies from the date specified in the direction and such supplies will be subject to the normal accounting requirements for VAT. So, for example, a de-grouping direction could result in a separate registration being set up for the company concerned and it will have to make returns and pay tax accordingly.

5. Calculation of charge to VAT

Disregarded supplies

5.1 Where a direction is made to treat a supply as not being disregarded between group members then tax will become payable according to its value (adjusted as appropriate to take account of any direction issued under paragraph 1 of Schedule 6 of the VAT Act 1994 if the supply is less than market value). A credit will be allowed for that part of the tax which would have been deductible according to the partial exemption method of the VAT group registration.

Degrouping

5.2 Where the direction degroups a company from a group registration then (to the extent that the direction has force for tax periods after it is issued see paragraph 4.2 above) all supplies made by that company to all other members of the group, and all supplies made by other members of the group to that company will, from the date specified in the direction, be treated as taxable supplies. Action in relation to assumptions for events prior to issue of the direction will be covered by the new powers of assessment and only those transactions relevant to the tax advantage will be affected (see paragraph 3.18 [sic]).

Mandatory grouping

5.3   Normally, the purpose of a direction to group companies together will be for Customs to recoup any excess claim to input tax. In such cases, the amount of tax to be charged will be the amount of input tax recovered less the amount which would otherwise have been recoverable in accordance with the partial exemption method of the appropriate VAT group registration. A credit will also be allowed in connection with any output tax charged between the parties which would not have been due according to the assumptions specified in the direction.

Transitional provisions

5.4   The new provisions overlap with existing VAT group anti-avoidance provisions contained in section 43(1A) of the VAT Act 1994 in that they are available for use in cases where the relevant event occurs on or after 29 November 1995. But section 43(1A) remains in force for cases prior to its repeal on 29 April 1996 (Royal Assent for the Finance Bill 1996). Customs will not use the powers under Schedule 9A if an assessment under section 43(1A) could be raised to correct the mischief from an avoidance scheme.

Interaction with Capital Goods Scheme (CGS)

5.5   It is possible that assets to which the CGS applies will become the subject of a direction. indeed, the transfer of such goods to or from a VAT group registration could qualify as a relevant event meeting the necessary conditions for triggering the new provisions. in deciding whether there is a tax advantage justifying issue of a direction Customs will take into account the impact of the CGS.

Interaction with section 44 of the VATA 1994

5.6   The fact that the transfer of a business results in a charge to tax under the provisions of section 44 of VAT Act 1994 (these are to remain in force) will not preclude Customs from exercising the new powers. However, in such cases where a direction is considered necessary, credit will be allowed in calculating an assessment for unpaid tax against a charge under section 44 which would not have been due according to the assumptions specified in the direction.

6.   If Customs suspect VAT avoidance

6.1   If Customs believe a VAT avoidance scheme has been implemented then, save where fraud is also suspected, a Customs officer will discuss his concerns with the taxpayer and invite an explanation as to whether or not, for example, a particular transaction falls outside the powers under the commercial purpose test.

6.2   If Customs are subsequently satisfied that a direction and assessment should be made, then their intentions will be set out in a pre-direction letter against which the taxpayer can ask for an internal review. In taking a decision in any one case, Customs will consider all relevant circumstances including the appropriate form of direction and its future effects. Where more than one remedy is available, Customs will be prepared to adopt the taxpayer's preferred option providing this does not impose an increased administrative burden (and, obviously, the loss from the avoidance scheme is still neutralised).

Who will be responsible for authorising the issue of directions?

6.3   Implementation of the new provisions is to be closely monitored and for the next two years, at least, it has been agreed that no direction or assessment will be issued under these provisions without the authorisation of Customs & Excise Head Office, at the address given below:

       HM Customs and Excise
       VAT Policy Directorate
       VAT Collection Division (Registration Branch)
       Fourth Floor South West
       Queens Dock
       Liverpool
       L74 4AB.

ANNEX 1

The following illustrates the type of case where, should a tax advantage arise from the stated transactions alone, Customs would accept a genuine commercial reason as prevailing:

There is a movement of a company or a business to a group registration directly following the purchase of the entire issued share capital of a company or the assets of a business as a going concern where:

- the sale is for full consideration
- the buyer has no interest in the business of the seller and the seller has no interest in the business of the buyer, either before or after the transaction apart from the sale, and

the sale is not associated with any other operation, transaction or arrangement whereby the business (or the part of the business) of the company or any part of the issued share capital of the capital which is sold, or any interest in that business or company, may revert to the seller or to any person who has an interest in the business of the seller.

ANNEX 2

Example of arrangement where customs would use their powers under Schedule 9A

1   Background

A partly exempt group of companies (the PX group) wishes to buy a large number of new personal computers for £1 million plus any VAT.

2   Commercial Considerations

In structuring this purchase the PX group considers four main factors:

- *how to finance the purchase*. The group wishes to fund about half of the purchase price from its own resources, paying the balance over a four year period
- *the accounting treatment of the purchase*. The group does not wish to increase the gearing in its group balance sheet.
- *the direct tax treatment of the purchase*. The group is not expecting to make a profit this year for corporation tax purposes, although it expects to return to profitability in the relatively near future.
- *the VAT cost of the purchase*. The group wishes to minimise the incidence of irrecoverable VAT suffered.

3   Structure Chosen

The above factors having been considered, the following steps take place:

- the PX group sets up a new company (Newco) and registers it as part of its VAT group
- having taken advice on their precise terms, the PX group executes:
  - (a)   a leasing agreement between Newco and the other PX group companies, this agreement requiring an immediate 50% deposit in respect of each computer to be leased (total £500,000); and
  - (b)   an agreement to sell Newco to an unrelated Finance House (F Ltd) for a nominal sum
- the deposit is paid and Newco is sold to F Ltd
- Newco leaves the PX VAT group
- Newco buys the computers for £1 million plus VAT, recovering the VAT in full
- Newco begins to make leasing charges to the PX group. These will eventually amount to £800,000 plus VAT over the four year period.

4   Summary of Effects of Structure

The PX group has taken legal advice to the effect that:

- its arrangements do not involve it in significantly greater commercial risk than a straightforward leasing agreement
- because of the precise terms of the agreement, the computers will not be included in the group balance sheet
- the precise terms of the agreement will allow Newco to claim capital allowances on the purchase of the computers at a time when the consequent direct tax losses can be surrendered to other members of the F Ltd loss relief group, this benefit having been factored into the leasing charge
- the arrangements have the effect of
- spreading the irrecoverable VAT suffered on the purchase over a four year period; and
- reducing the absolute amount of irrecoverable VAT by 20%
- however, the PX group is advised that these VAT efficiencies will be reversed if Customs and Excise issue a direction and assessment under Schedule 9A of the VAT Act 1994.

5 Customs and Excise View of Structure

Customs and Excise would consider that an arrangement such as that described above has a number of main purposes. Customs would further consider that one of these main purposes (namely the desire to generate a VAT saving by having Newco obtain full input tax recovery against outputs some of which are disregarded under s.43(1)(a)) is not a genuine commercial purpose within the meaning of Schedule 9A, para 2. Following the procedure outlined in part 5 of this statement of practice, therefore, Customs would issue a direction in these circumstances (most probably to the effect that the 50% deposit should not have been disregarded under s.43(1)(a)). An assessment would follow the direction.

ANNEX 3

Example of arrangement where customs would not use their powers under Schedule 9A

1 Background

A partly exempt group of companies (the PX group) wishes to sell one of its bead office buildings, which is surplus to requirements following a downsizing exercise. All of the PX group companies are included in a single VAT group. The property is owned by P Ltd, the group property company, and used by M Ltd, the group management services company. M Ltd pays (and has historically paid) annual rentals in advance on 1 January under a formal 15 year lease. The PX group has elected to waive exemption in respect of all of its properties, although this currently has no effect in respect of the rentals paid by M Ltd, these being disregarded under s.43(1)(a).

It is now May 1996, and the PX group wishes to dispose of the property on or around December 1997, when M Ltd's lease (coincidentally) runs out. it will be difficult to relocate M Ltd's staff before that date. However, the directors have already found a willing buyer for the property. The buyer is unrelated to the PX group.

2 Commercial Considerations

In structuring this purchase the PX group considers four main factors:

- *cash flow*. The group would like to make the disposal as soon as possible, using the proceeds to pay off expensive debt.
- *accounting*. The group would like the profit on disposal of the building to be included in this year's results if possible.
- *direct tax*. The gain on disposal of the building can be sheltered if the disposal takes place this year.
- *VAT*. As a matter of policy the group manages the irrecoverable VAT on all of its overheads.

3 Structure Chosen

The directors manage to agree with the purchaser the following arrangements:

- P Ltd will sell the freehold of the property to the purchaser on 1 July 1996
- however, the freehold will be subject to M Ltd's lease, which will have 18 months to run by then
- the purchaser will opt to tax the property prior to sale so that the transaction can be treated as the transfer of a business as a going concern for VAT purposes
- in order to avoid the situation where the purchaser charges M Ltd VAT on the final year's rent, M Ltd pays the final year's rent to P Ltd before the sale takes place, an adjustment being made to the sale price to reflect this

4 Summary of Effects of Structure

The structure meets all of the group's commercial objectives. However, the group's advisers are concerned that the advance payment of rent by M Ltd might lead to Customs issuing a direction and assessment under Schedule 9A.

5 Customs and Excise Approach to the Arrangements

Customs and Excise would not issue a direction based on the above facts. Even though the final year's rent is advanced in order to avoid the incidence of irrecoverable VAT, it is not considered that this would have been a main purpose of the sale of the property.

CAPITAL GOODS SCHEME [HM Customs and Excise Statement of Practice, December 1997]

STATEMENT OF PRACTICE ON A BUDGET CHANGE TO THE CAPITAL GOODS SCHEME

1. Introduction

1.1 Changes to the Capital Goods Scheme announced at the time of the July 1997 budget included a test to be applied on the disposal of a capital item by the owner during the adjustment period. The test compares the total amount of input tax deducted or deductible on a capital item with the amount of output tax due on the disposal of that item. For the purposes of this Statement of Practice and the examples annexed, this test will be known as "the disposal test".

1.2 The policy objective underlying the disposal test is to ensure that partly exempt businesses such as banks, building societies, insurance companies, educational establishments, sports clubs, providers of private health-care and the like, do not obtain an unjustified tax advantage by being able to recover the input tax they incur on land or property which is to be used for exempt purposes.

1.3 The change was announced as part of a package of anti-avoidance measures in the 1997 Budget. It was introduced by The Value Added Tax (Amendment) (No. 3) Regulations 1997 (Statutory Instrument 1997 No. 1614) and came into force with effect from 3 July 1997.

1.4 It is not intended that the disposal test should be applied to bona fide commercial transactions. The legislation gives Customs the power to exclude individual transactions and this power will be used either generally or specifically in cases that do not appear to Customs to involve unjustified tax advantage. So, for example, given the policy objective, the disposal test will not be applied to sales of computer equipment.

1.5 The purpose of this Statement of Practice is to clarify Customs policy in this area. It does not qualify the relevant legislation, nor does it affect a taxpayer's right of appeal to an independent VAT tribunal.

2. Background

2.1 Generally, businesses making taxable supplies can recover VAT on goods and services they buy in for their business (input tax). Businesses making exempt supplies cannot normally recover their input tax. Businesses which make both taxable and exempt supplies can recover input tax to the extent that the goods and services on which it is incurred are used to make taxable supplies.

2.2 The Capital Goods Scheme recognises that certain major capital assets (capital items) are not consumed immediately but are used by businesses over a number of years. It is designed to be fair to both businesses and the Exchequer. The scheme applies to:

–   certain land and buildings where the VAT bearing costs of purchase or development (acquisition) amount to £250,000 or more, with an adjustment period of 10 intervals;

–   items of computer equipment of a value of £50,000 or more, with an adjustment period of 5 intervals.

2.3 An interval normally equates with the partial exemption tax year. In the first interval the owner deducts input tax incurred on a capital item to the extent that the item is used or to be used in making taxable supplies. He must then review his use of the item over the relevant adjustment period. In each subsequent interval, if the extent of taxable use differs from that which governed the initial recovery of input tax, the owner must make an adjustment. The adjustment is calculated by comparing the percentage of taxable use in the subsequent interval with the initial recovery percentage.

2.4 For example, input tax is deducted in full when a property is acquired, because it is being used exclusively in making taxable supplies. In a subsequent interval the use to which it is put changes from fully taxable to fully exempt. The owner must pay back 1/10th of the input tax originally claimed. If the owner continues to use the property for exempt purposes, similar adjustments will have to be made (and amounts paid back) at the end of each interval for the remainder of the adjustment period.

2.5 The legal basis of the scheme is Part XV of the Value Added Tax Regulations 1995 (regulations 112 to 116). Further information about the scheme can be found in VAT Leaflet 706/2/90 – Capital Goods Scheme: input tax on computers, land and buildings for use in your business.

3. Disposal of a capital item

3.1 The period of adjustment is brought to an end by the outright disposal of the capital item during the adjustment period. In effect, on termination the item is treated as if it were used for the remainder of the adjustment period in making the supply which gives rise to the termination. So, where the capital item is sold and the sale is a taxable supply, the item is treated as being used in all remaining complete intervals for the making of taxable supplies. The owner must make a final adjustment in respect of all remaining intervals to reflect this.

3.2 Prior to 3 July 1997 businesses could acquire a new commercial building as a capital item and recover all of the input tax by putting the item to taxable use in the first interval. At the beginning of interval 2, the owner could make a very substantial exempt supply (say a 999 year lease – which is not an outright disposal because the freehold interest remains) and then immediately sell the freehold of the building – that sale being a compulsory taxable supply. Because there was an exempt lease, the value of the freehold sale was very low and there was output tax only on that very low value. The taxable sale of the capital item ensured the recovery of a high proportion of the input tax incurred while very little output tax was paid. The building then ceased to be a capital item. This results in an unjustified tax advantage and is the sort of arrangement that the new rule is designed to counter.

4. The introduction of a test on disposal

4.1 With effect from 3 July 1997 where the owner of a capital item disposes of it and the total input tax deducted is greater than the output tax due on the supply of the item, the owner is required to make an adjustment so that the input tax recoverable does not exceed the output tax chargeable on the supply of the item. The input tax recoverable is the aggregate of:

- the initial deduction of input tax incurred on the purchase or development of the item,
- any adjustments made previously in respect of the item under the scheme, and
- any adjustment that would otherwise be required due to the disposal of the item.

5. Application of the provision

5.1 In principle the disposal test is wide ranging and impacts on many disposals of capital items. In practice it will only be applied where the owner of a capital item would otherwise gain an unjustified tax advantage, and then the tax charge will be limited to an adjustment amount that would ensure no unjustified tax advantage arises. The legislation includes a "save as the Commissioners otherwise allow" provision to enable Customs to exclude individual transactions. This power will be used to exclude the application of the disposal test in cases that do not appear to Customs to involve unjustified tax advantage. It will not be applied:

- to sales of computer equipment;
- where an owner disposes of an item at a loss due to market conditions (such as a general downturn in property prices);
- where the value of the item has depreciated;
- where the value of the item is reduced for other legitimate reasons (such as accepting a lower price to effect a quick sale);
- where the amount of output tax on disposal is less than the total input tax claimed only due to a reduction in the VAT rate;
- where the item is used only for taxable (including zero rated) purposes throughout the adjustment period (which includes the final disposal).

5.2 Where there is no unjustified tax advantage a business should not apply the disposal test and in such circumstances it is not necessary to apply to Customs for a specific ruling. A business need only apply the disposal test where it has entered into arrangements for tax mitigation affecting the particular capital item or its disposal. In cases of doubt or difficulty businesses should contact the local VAT office. Examples of where the disposal test should and should not be applied are set out in the annex.

5.3 Where there is an unjustified tax advantage businesses will need to work out the amount of tax to be adjusted. To do this, they will need to calculate the net tax advantage and then work out how much of the net tax advantage is unjustified. The net tax advantage is the overall benefit derived from the avoidance device. Normally the benefit is that the owner is able to secure the amount of input tax that would still be subject to adjustment under the scheme, were it not for the sale of the capital item. In order to achieve this benefit a taxable supply is made. The net tax advantage would therefore be the amount of input tax secured by the sale less any output tax due on the sale. Some form of apportionment needs to be applied to work out how much of the net tax advantage is unjustified. Normally this could be achieved by using the ratio that the value of the final taxable sale bears to the value of both the exempt supply and the final taxable sale (see example 4 in the annex).

5.4 If Customs consider that the disposal of a capital item has resulted in an unjustified tax advantage to the owner the provision will be vigorously enforced. Implementation of the provision is to be closely monitored. For the next two years, where the provision is enforced and a business requests a review of that decision, any review will be carried out by the Partial Exemption Branch, Commercial Division, VAT Policy Directorate.

5.5 This Statement of Practice may be changed or disapplied if used for the purposes of avoidance of tax.

ANNEX 1 – EXAMPLES

Example 1

A business acquires the freehold of a newly constructed commercial property for £2 million plus VAT on 1 June 1995. The business immediately occupies the building for its own business purposes. The business is partly exempt with a recovery rate of 50% and is therefore only able to deduct half of the input tax incurred under the normal partial exemption rules.

The business continues to use the building for taxable and exempt purposes for the remainder of the tax year ending on 30 April 1996 (the end of the first interval) and for the following tax year (the second interval) there is a small Capital Goods Scheme adjustment made in respect of the second interval because the overall recovery rate increases.

During the third interval, on 1 August 1997, the business disposes of the property by way of a taxable supply (sold within 3 years of completion of the construction of the building) for £2 million plus VAT. As a consequence the business is required to carry out a final adjustment and is able to deduct 7/10ths of the input tax previously restricted. The disposal test does not affect the recovery of the 7/10ths because the output tax on disposal is greater than the input tax claimed in the adjustment period.

Example 2

A business completes the construction of a £20 million office block, the whole cost of which had borne VAT, on 1 June 1995 and immediately occupies the building for its own business purposes. The business is partly exempt with a recovery rate of 50% and is therefore only able to deduct half of the input tax incurred.

The business continues to use the building for taxable and exempt purposes for the remainder of the tax year ending on 30 April 1996 (the end of the first interval) and for the following tax year (the second interval). There is a small Capital Goods Scheme adjustment made in respect of the second interval because the overall recovery rate increased.

During the third interval, on 1 August 1997, following a downturn in property prices, the business disposes of the property by way of a taxable supply (sold within 3 years of completion of construction of the building) for its open market value of £16 million plus VAT. As a consequence the business is required to carry out a final adjustment and is able to deduct 7/10ths of the input tax previously restricted. Since the output tax on disposal is less than the input tax claimed in the adjustment period, the disposal test applies. However, the owner is not required to pay any amount back to Customs because the building was sold at an open market price and not to obtain an unjustified tax advantage.

Example 3

A business acquires the 20 year leasehold interest in an office block for a premium of £10 million plus VAT (the previous owner having opted to tax) on 1 June 1995. The business immediately occupies the building for its own business purposes. The business is partly exempt with a recovery rate of 65% and is therefore only able to deduct that proportion of the input tax incurred.

The business continues to use the building for taxable and exempt purposes for the remainder of the tax year ending on 31 March 1996 (the end of the first interval) and for the following six tax years (the second to the seventh intervals). There are some small Capital Goods Scheme adjustments made in respect of the later intervals because the overall recovery rate increases or decreases as the case may be.

During the eighth interval, on 1 August 2003, following an expansion in their business, the business relocates to new premises and sells the remaining 12 years leasehold interest in the existing office block to a third party as an exempt supply (not having opted) at an open market price. As a consequence the business is required to carry out a final adjustment in respect of the ninth and tenth intervals and pay back 2/10ths of the input tax previously recovered in the first interval. In addition, since the output tax on disposal is less than the input tax claimed in the adjustment period, the disposal test applies. However, the owner is not required to pay any amount back to Customs because the building was sold at an open market price and there was no attempt to obtain an unjustified tax advantage. The Capital Goods Scheme adjustments have adequately reflected the exempt use to which the property will be put for the remaining two complete intervals.

Example 4

On 1 June 1997 a developer completes a £25 million commercial development, the whole cost of which had borne VAT (£4,375,000). The developer opts to tax the building and leases it out on a 2 year lease to a third party tenant at a market rent plus VAT. The developer is therefore able to deduct all the input tax incurred on the development under the normal partial exemption rules.

The business continues to let the building on a taxable lease for the remainder of the tax year ending on 31 March 1998 (the end of the first interval) and for the following tax year (the second interval). A Capital Goods Scheme adjustment is therefore not required for the second interval.

On 1 June 1999 (part way through the third interval) the developer grants a 99 year lease at a premium of £24m and a peppercorn rent to its wholly owned subsidiary. The subsidiary is wholly exempt.

Section 37 FA 97 (paragraph 2(3AA) Schedule 10 VATA 94) operates so as to disapply the developer's option to tax so that the premium is not subject to VAT. At the end of the third interval there is therefore an adjustment in respect of 1/10th (£437,500) of the initial input tax incurred and a proportion of 1/10th (because there was some taxable use in the first part of the third interval) is paid back to Customs (assuming a recovery rate of 50%–£218,750).

On 1 May 2000 the developer sells the freehold, subject to the 99 year lease for £250,000 plus VAT, to the wholly owned subsidiary (a compulsory taxable supply). The sale effectively ends the fourth interval. Since the building is used for exempt purposes up to the sale there is an adjustment in respect of 1/10th of the initial input tax incurred. It is a full 1/10th that is restricted because the item is only used for exempt purposes up to the disposal of the item.

As a consequence of the low value taxable disposal, since there is no change in the extent of taxable use the business is not required to carry out a final adjustment. But since the output tax on disposal is less than the input tax claimed in the adjustment period, the disposal test applies. In this instance there is an unjustified tax advantage because the high value exempt grant in the third interval enables a low value taxable sale of the freehold. At the same time the taxable sale enables full recovery of input tax in respect of the remaining six intervals (the fifth to the tenth) while only 1/10th of the input tax is restricted (in the fourth interval) to reflect the exempt grant:

Interval	Input tax claim	Output tax declared	Difference
1	4,375,000		4,375,000
2			4,375,000
3	(218,750)		4,156,250
4	(437,500)	(43,750)	3,762,500
5–10			3,762,500

In principle £3,762,500 would be due. But the net tax advantage is that the owner is able to secure the amount of input tax that would still be subject to adjustment under the scheme (intervals 5 – 10), were it not for the sale of the capital item and in order to achieve this benefit a taxable supply is made.

The amount of input tax involved is 6/10ths of £4,375,000 – £2,625,000. The amount of output tax involved is £43,750. The net tax advantage is therefore £2,581,250.

Some form of fair and reasonable apportionment needs to be applied to work out how much of the net tax advantage is unjustified. This could be achieved by using the ratio that the value of the final taxable sale bears to the value of both the exempt supply and the final taxable sale:

$$\frac{250,000}{24,250,000} \text{ or } \frac{1}{97} \times £2,581,250 = \begin{array}{l} £26,611 \text{ taxable use} \\ £2,554,639 \text{ exempt use} \end{array}$$

Thus, in practice the disposal test would be applied, but the amount due to Customs would be the value of the unjustified tax advantage £2,554,639.

TABLE OF DESTINATIONS AND DERIVATIONS

TABLE OF DESTINATIONS
AND DERIVATIONS

TABLE OF DESTINATIONS –
CEMA 1979, VATA 1983, FA 1984–FA 1994

The consolidated table below, prepared by CCH Editorial staff, relates the provisions of the former legislation (in the left-hand column) to the corresponding provisions of the *Value Added Tax Act* 1994 (VATA 1994) (in the right-hand column).

Note: The left-hand column sets out the provisions in the form they took immediately before consolidation. Provisions which repealed, or partially repealed, earlier legislation are not included. Otherwise all relevant substantive and amending provisions are included. For additional information, former substantive provisions repealed prior to the consolidation are included in the left-hand column, with an indication that they were '(Previously repealed)'. Spent provisions are treated similarly, with '(Spent)' appearing by way of a description.

Provisions which are still in force after consolidation are indicated as '(Not repealed)'.

Former Provision		Destination
	Customs and Excise Management Act 1979	
s. 100B	Free zone regulations	VATA 1994, s. 17(3)
s. 100C(1)	Free zone goods: customs duties, etc.	VATA 1994, s. 17(2)
s. 100C(2), (3)	(Previously repealed)	
s. 100C(4)(a)–(c)		VATA 1994, s. 17(5)
s. 100C(4)(d)		VATA 1994, s. 17(3)
s. 100C(5)	(Unnecessary)	
	Value Added Tax Act 1983	
s. 1	Value added tax	VATA 1994, s. 1(1)
s. 2(1), (2)	Scope of tax	VATA 1994, s. 4
s. 2(3)		VATA 1994, s. 1(2)
s. 2(4), (5)	(Previously repealed)	
s. 2A(1)–(3)	Scope of tax on acquisitions	VATA 1994, s. 10
s. 2A(4)		VATA 1994, s. 1(3)
s. 2B(1)	Scope of tax on imports	VATA 1994, s. 1(4)
s. 2B(2)–(4)		VATA 1994, s. 15
s. 2C	Taxable persons	VATA 1994, s. 3
s. 3	Meaning of "supply": alteration by Treasury order	VATA 1994, s. 5
s. 4	Time of supply	VATA 1994, s. 6(1)–(3)
s. 5(1)–(3)	Further provisions relating to time of supply	VATA 1994, s. 6(4)–(6)
s. 5(3A), (3B)		VATA 1994, s. 6(7), (8)
s. 5(4)–(10)		VATA 1994, s. 6(9)–(15)
s. 6(1), (2)	Place of supply	VATA 1994, s. 7(1), (2)
s. 6(2A)–(3)		VATA 1994, s. 7(3)–(7)
s. 6(4)		VATA 1994, s. 7(8)
s. 6(4A)		VATA 1994, s. 7(9)
s. 6(5)		VATA 1994, s. 7(10)
s. 6(6)		VATA 1994, s. 7(11)
s. 7(1)–(5)	Reverse charge on supplies received from abroad	VATA 1994, s. 8(1)–(5)
s. 7(6)		VATA 1994, s. 8(6)
s. 8	Place where supplier or recipient of services belongs	VATA 1994, s. 9
s. 8A	Meaning of acquisition of goods from another member state	VATA 1994, s. 11
s. 8B	Time of acquisition	VATA 1994, s. 12
s. 8C	Place of acquisition	VATA 1994, s. 13
s. 8D	Acquisitions from persons belonging in other member states	VATA 1994, s. 14(1)–(7)
s. 9	Rate of tax	VATA 1994, s. 2
s. 10(1)–(5)	Value of supply of goods or services	VATA 1994, s. 19
s. 10(6)	(Previously repealed)	
s. 10A	Valuation of acquisitions from other member states	VATA 1994, s. 20
s. 11(1), (2)	Value of imported goods	VATA 1994, s. 21(1), (2)
s. 11(2A)		VATA 1994, s. 21(3)

Former Provision		Destination
Value Added Tax Act 1983		
s. 11(3), (4)	(Previously repealed)	
s. 12	Value of certain goods	VATA 1994, s. 22
s. 13	Gaming machines	VATA 1994, s. 23
s. 14(1), (2)	Credit for input tax against output tax	VATA 1994, s. 25(1), (2)
s. 14(3)		VATA 1994, s. 24(1), (2)
s. 14(3A)		VATA 1994, s. 24(3)
s. 14(3B)		VATA 1994, s. 24(4)
s. 14(4)		VATA 1994, s. 24(5)
s. 14(5)–(8)		VATA 1994, s. 25(3)–(6)
s. 14(9)		VATA 1994, s. 24(6)
s. 14(10)		VATA 1994, s. 25(7)
s. 14(11)		VATA 1994, s. 24(7)
s. 15(1)	Input tax allowable under section 14	VATA 1994, s. 26(1)
s. 15(2)(a), (b)		VATA 1994, s. 26(2)(a), (b)
s. 15(2)(ba)		VATA 1994, s. 26(2)(c)
s. 15(2)(c)	(Previously repealed)	
s. 15(3)		VATA 1994, s. 26(3)
s. 15(4)		VATA 1994, s. 26(4)
s. 16(1)–(3)	Zero-rating	VATA 1994, s. 30(1)–(3)
s. 16(4), (5)		VATA 1994, s. 30(4), (5)
s. 16(6)		VATA 1994, s. 30(6)
s. 16(6A)		VATA 1994, s. 30(7)
s. 16(7), (8)		VATA 1994, s. 30(8), (9)
s. 16(9)		VATA 1994, s. 30(10)
s. 17	Exemptions	VATA 1994, s. 31
s. 18	Relief on supply of certain second-hand goods	VATA 1994, s. 32
s. 19(1)	Relief from tax on importation of goods	VATA 1994, s. 37(1)
s. 19(1A)		VATA 1994, s. 37(2)
s. 19(2), (3)		VATA 1994, s. 37(3), (4)
s. 20(1), (2)	Refund of tax in certain cases	VATA 1994, s. 33(1), (2)
s. 20(3)		VATA 1994, s. 33(3)
s. 20(4)		VATA 1994, s. 33(4)
s. 20(4A)		VATA 1994, s. 33(5)
s. 20(5)		VATA 1994, s. 33(6)
s. 20(6)		VATA 1994, s. 96(1), (4)
s. 20A	Refunds in relation to new means of transport supplied to member States	VATA 1994, s. 40
s. 21(1), (2)	Refund of tax to persons constructing certain buildings	VATA 1994, s. 35(1), (2)
s. 21(2A)		VATA 1994, s. 35(3)
s. 22	(Spent)	
s. 23	Repayment of tax to those in business overseas	VATA 1994, s. 39
s. 24(1)	Application of customs enactments	VATA 1994, s. 16(1)
s. 24(2), (3)	(Previously repealed)	
s. 24(4)		VATA 1994, s. 16(2)
s. 25	Importation of goods by taxable persons	VATA 1994, s. 38
s. 26	Goods imported for private purposes	VATA 1994, s. 27
s. 27(1), (2)	Application to Crown	VATA 1994, s. 41(1), (2)
s. 27(2A), (2B)		VATA 1994, s. 41(3), (4)
s. 27(3)		VATA 1994, s. 41(5)
s. 27(4)		VATA 1994, s. 41(6)
s. 27(5)		VATA 1994, s. 41(7)
s. 27(6)		VATA 1994, s. 41(8)
s. 28(1)	Local authorities	VATA 1994, s. 42
s. 28(2)		VATA 1994, s. 96(1), (4)
s. 29(1)	Groups of companies	VATA 1994, s. 43(1)
s. 29(2)		VATA 1994, s. 43(2)
s. 29(3)		VATA 1994, s. 43(3)

Former Provision   **Destination**

Value Added Tax Act 1983

Former Provision	Description	Destination
s. 29(3A)		VATA 1994, s. 43(3)
s. 29(4)–(8)		VATA 1994, s. 43(4)–(8)
s. 29A(1)–(3)	Supplies to groups	VATA 1994, s. 44(1)–(3)
s. 29A(3A)		VATA 1994, s. 44(4)
s. 29A(4)–(9)		VATA 1994, s. 44(5)–(10)
s. 30	Partnerships	VATA 1994, s. 45
s. 31	Business carried on in divisions or by unincorporated bodies, personal representatives, etc.	VATA 1994, s. 46
s. 32(1)	(Previously repealed)	
s. 32(2)	Agents, etc.	VATA 1994, s. 47(1)
s. 32(3), (4)		VATA 1994, s. 47(2), (3)
s. 32A	Tax representatives	VATA 1994, s. 48
s. 32B	(Previously repealed)	
s. 33(1)	Transfers of going concerns	VATA 1994, s. 49(1)
s. 33(1A)	(Previously repealed)	
s. 33(2)		VATA 1994, s. 49(2)
s. 33(3)		VATA 1994, s. 49(3)
s. 34	Terminal markets	VATA 1994, s. 50
s. 35	Goods subject to warehousing regime	VATA 1994, s. 18
s. 35A	Buildings and land	VATA 1994, s. 51
s. 36(1), (2)	Capital goods	VATA 1994, s. 34
s. 36(3)	(Previously repealed)	
s. 37	Trading stamp schemes	VATA 1994, s. 52
s. 37A	Tour operators	VATA 1994, s. 53
s. 37B	Special treatment for persons involved in farming etc.	VATA 1994, s. 54
s. 37C	Customers to account for tax on supplies of gold etc.	VATA 1994, s. 55
s. 38	Administration, collection and enforcement	VATA 1994, s. 58
s. 38A(1)–(8)	Interest in certain cases of official error	VATA 1994, s. 78(1)–(8)
s. 38A(8A)		VATA 1994, s. 78(9)
s. 38A(9)–(11)		VATA 1994, s. 78(10)–(12)
s, 38A(12)	(Spent)	
s. 38B	Interest: general treatment	VATA 1994, s. 81(1), (2)
s. 38C	Payments on account	VATA 1994, s. 28
s. 39(1)	Offences and penalties	VATA 1994, s. 72(1)
s. 39(1A)		VATA 1994, s. 72(2)
s. 39(2)		VATA 1994, s. 72(3)
s. 39(2A)–(2D)		VATA 1994, s. 72(4)–(7)
s. 39(3)		VATA 1994, s. 72(8)
s. 39(3A)		VATA 1994, s. 72(9)
s. 39(4)		VATA 1994, s. 72(10)
s. 39(5)		VATA 1994, s. 72(11)
s. 39(6)–(8)	(Previously repealed)	
s. 39(9)		VATA 1994, s. 72(12)
s. 40(1)	Appeals	VATA 1994, s. 82(1), s. 83
s. 40(1)(a)		VATA 1994, s. 83(a)
s. 40(1)(b)		VATA 1994, s. 83(b)
s. 40(1)(c)		VATA 1994, s. 83(c)
s. 40(1)(d)		VATA 1994, s. 83(e)
s. 40(1)(da)		VATA 1994, s. 83(j)
s. 40(1)(e)		VATA 1994, s. 83(g)
s. 40(1)(f)		VATA 1994, s. 83(h)
s. 40(1)(fa)		VATA 1994, s. 83(d)
s. 40(1)(g)		VATA 1994, s. 83(f)
s. 40(1)(h)		VATA 1994, s. 83(k)
s. 40(1)(hza)		VATA 1994, s. 83(m)
s. 40(1)(ha)		VATA 1994, s. 83(s)
s. 40(1)(hh)		VATA 1994, s. 83(u)
s. 40(1)(i)	(Previously repealed)	

Former Provision		Destination
Finance Act 1985		
s. 30(2)	(Spent)	
s. 30(3)		VATA 1994, Sch. 13, para. 5(2)
s. 31	Insolvency	VATA 1994, s. 46(5)
s. 32	(Previously repealed)	
s. 33(1)	(Unnecessary)	
s. 33(2), (3)		VATA 1994, s. 71(1), (2)
s. 33(4)	(Previously repealed)	
s. 33(5)		VATA 1994, s. 72(13)
Sch. 6	Section 39 of the Principal Act as amended, Excluding Subsection (8)	VATA 1994, s. 72
Sch. 7, para. 1(1)	(Previously repealed)	
Sch. 7, para. 1(2)–(6)	(Amending provisions)	VATA 1994, Sch. 11
Sch. 8, para. 1	(Unnecessary)	
Sch. 8, para. 2–5	(Amending provisions)	VATA 1994, Sch. 12
Sch. 8, para. 6(1), (2)		VATA 1994, s. 82(3), (4)
Sch. 26, para. 14	(Amending provisions)	VATA 1994, Sch. 9, Grp. 11, item 3

Finance Act 1986

Former Provision		Destination
s. 9	Fuel for private use	VATA 1994, s. 56
s. 10(1)		VATA 1994, Sch. 1, para. 2
s. 10(2)		VATA 1994, s. 83(u)
s. 10(3)		VATA 1994, s. 84(7), (5)
s. 11(1)	(Amending provision)	VATA 1994, Sch. 6, para. 9
s. 11(2)	(Unnecessary)	
s. 12(1)	(Amending provision)	VATA 1994, s. 30(6)
s. 12(2)	(Amending provision)	VATA 1994, s. 30(10)
s. 13		VATA 1994, s. 37(2)
s. 14(1)–(5)	Penalty for tax evasion: liability of directors etc.	VATA 1994, s. 61(1)–(5)
s. 14(6)		VATA 1994, s. 83(o)
s. 14(7)		VATA 1994, Sch. 12, para. 9(j)
s. 14(8)		VATA 1994, s. 61(6)
s. 14(9)	(Spent)	
s. 15(1)		VATA 1994, s. 69(1)
s. 15(2)	(Spent)	
Sch. 6, para. 1	Consideration for fuel supplied for private use	VATA 1994, s. 57(1)
Sch. 6, para. 2(1)		VATA 1994, s. 57(2)
Sch. 6, para. 2(2)		VATA 1994, s. 57(3)
Sch. 6, para. 3	(Previously repealed)	
Sch. 6, para. 4		VATA 1994, s. 57(4)
Sch. 6, para. 5		VATA 1994, s. 57(5), (6)
Sch. 6, para. 6(1)		VATA 1994, s. 57(7)
Sch. 6, para. 6(2)		VATA 1994, s. 57(8)

Finance Act 1987

Former Provision		Destination
s. 11(1)	(Amending provision)	VATA 1994, s. 25(1)
s. 11(2)		VATA 1994, Sch. 11, para. 2(7)
s. 12(1)		VATA 1994, s. 26
s. 12(2)	(Amending provision)	VATA 1994, s. 7(1)
s. 12(3)	(Previously repealed)	
s. 12(4)	(Unnecessary)	
s. 13	(Previously repealed)	
s. 14(1)	(Unnecessary)	
s. 14(2)		VATA 1994, Sch. 1, para. 1
s. 14(3)		VATA 1994, Sch. 1, para. 4

Former Provision		Destination
Finance Act 1987		
s. 14(4)–(8)	(Previously repealed)	
s. 14(9)		VATA 1994, Sch. 1, para. 14
s. 14(10)		VATA 1994, Sch. 1, para. 16
s. 15(1)		VATA 1994, s. 44
s. 15(2)	(Spent)	
s. 16(1)		VATA 1994, s. 53
s. 16(2)	(Amending provision)	VATA 1994, s. 97(4)
s. 17(1)		VATA 1994, Sch. 6, para. 1
s. 17(2)	(Spent)	
s. 18(1)		VATA 1994, Sch. 9, Grp. 5, items 5, 6A
s. 18(2)	(Spent)	
s. 19(1)	(Unnecessary)	
s. 19(2)	(Spent)	
Sch. 2, para. 1	(Amending provision)	VATA 1994, s. 8
Sch. 2, para. 2	(Amending provision)	VATA 1994, s. 39(1)
Sch. 2, para. 3	(Previously repealed)	
Sch. 2, para. 4		VATA 1994, s. 83(e)

Finance Act 1988

Former Provision		Destination
s. 13(1)	(Amending provision)	VATA 1994, Sch. 9, Grp. 7
s. 13(2)		VATA 1994, Sch. 9, Grp. 7, items 1,2
s. 13(3)	(Amending provision)	VATA 1994, Sch. 9, Grp. 7, Note (2)
s. 13(4)	(Unnecessary)	
s. 14(1)	(Amending provision)	VATA 1994, Sch. 1
s. 14(2)	(Amending provision)	VATA 1994, Sch. 1, para. 1(7), para. 4(3)
s. 14(3)	(Amending provision)	VATA 1994, Sch. 1, para. 6(3)
s. 14(4)		VATA 1994, Sch. 1, para. 9, 10
s. 14(5)		VATA 1994, Sch. 1, para. 11, 12
s. 14(6)		VATA 1994, Sch. 1, para. 13(1)–(7), para. 18
s. 14(7)		VATA 1994, Sch. 1, para. 14, 15
s. 14(8)(a)	(Previously repealed)	
s. 14(8)(b)	(Amending provision)	VATA 1994, s. 74(1)(c)
s. 15(1)	(Amending provision)	VATA 1994, s. 73
s. 15(2)		VATA 1994, s. 73(2),(3)
s. 15(3)	(Amending provision)	VATA 1994, s. 73(6)
s. 15(4)	(Amending provision)	VATA 1994, s. 73(9)
s. 16(1)	(Amending provision)	VATA 1994, s. 63
s. 16(2)		VATA 1994, s. 63(2)
s. 16(3)	(Amending provision)	VATA 1994, s. 63(3)
s. 16(4)	(Amending provision)	VATA 1994, s. 63(7)
s. 16(5)		VATA 1994, s. 63(8),(9)
s. 17		VATA 1994, s. 64
s. 18(1)	(Amending provision)	VATA 1994, s. 67(1)
s. 18(2)	(Amending provision)	VATA 1994, s. 67(3)
s. 18(3)		VATA 1994, s. 67(4)
s. 18(4)		VATA 1994, s. 74(2)
s. 18(5)	(Spent)	
s. 18(6)	(Spent)	
s. 19(1)	(Amending provision)	VATA 1994, s. 69(1)
s. 19(2)	(Amending provision)	VATA 1994, s. 69(3)
s. 19(3)	(Amending provision)	VATA 1994, s. 76(1), (2)
s. 19(4)	(Spent)	
s. 19(5)	(Spent)	
s. 20		VATA 1994, s. 79
s. 21	Set-off of credits	VATA 1994, s. 81(3)–(5)
s. 22	Invoices provided by recipients of goods or services	VATA 1994, s. 29

Finance Act 1989

Former Provision		Destination
s. 18	(Unnecessary)	

Former Provision		Destination

s. 14		VATA 1994, s. 24(4)
s. 15(1)	(Amending provision)	VATA 1994, s. 36
s. 15(2)	(Spent)	
s. 16(1)	(Unnecessary)	
s. 16(2)	(Amending provision)	VATA 1994, s. 43(3)
s. 16(3)		VATA 1994, s. 43(3)
s. 17(1)		VATA 1994, s. 78, 81
s. 17(2)		VATA 1994, s. 83(s)
s. 18(1)		VATA 1994, s. 63(1)
s. 18(2), (3)	(Spent)	

Finance Act 1992

s. 6	(Amending provision)	VATA 1994, s. 28, 97(4)
s. 7	(Amending provision)	VATA 1994, s. 63(1), 59(5)

Finance (No. 2) Act 1992

s. 14(1), (3)–(6)	(Spent)	
s. 15(1)		VATA 1994, s. 79(4)
s. 15(2)		VATA 1994, s. 78(9)
s. 15(3), (4)	(Unnecessary)	
s. 16(1)		VATA 1994, s. 54
s. 16(2)		VATA 1994, s. 83(m)
s. 16(3)		VATA 1994, s. 97(4)
s. 16(4)		VATA 1994, Sch. 4, para. 8(3)
s. 16(5)		VATA 1994, 67(7)
s. 16(6)	(Spent)	
s. 17	(Amending provision)	VATA 1994, Sch. 13, para. 7
Sch. 3, para. 1	(Unnecessary)	
Sch. 3, para. 2	(Amending provision)	VATA 1994, s. 1
Sch. 3, para. 3		VATA 1994, s. 1(3) and (4), 3, 10, 15
Sch. 3, para. 4	(Amending provision)	VATA 1994, s. 5(3) and (5)
Sch. 3, para. 5	(Amending provision)	VATA 1994, s. 6(1)
Sch. 3, para. 6	(Amending provision)	VATA 1994, s. 6
Sch. 3, para. 7	(Amending provision)	VATA 1994, s. 7
Sch. 3, para. 8		VATA 1994, s. 8(6)
Sch. 3, para. 9	(Amending provision)	VATA 1994, s. 9
Sch. 3, para. 10		VATA 1994, s. 11, 12, 13
Sch. 3, para. 11	(Amending provision)	VATA 1994, s. 2
Sch. 3, para. 12	(Amending provision)	VATA 1994, s. 19
Sch. 3, para. 13		VATA 1994, s. 20
Sch. 3, para. 14	(Amending provision)	VATA 1994, s. 21
Sch. 3, para. 15	(Amending provision)	VATA 1994, 24(1)–(3), (5) and (6), s. 25(1) and (7)
Sch. 3, para. 16	(Amending provision)	VATA 1994, s. 26
Sch. 3, para. 17	(Amending provision)	VATA 1994, s. 30
Sch. 3, para. 18	(Amending provision)	VATA 1994, s. 31(1)
Sch. 3, para. 19	(Amending provision)	VATA 1994, s. 32
Sch. 3, para. 20	(Amending provision)	VATA 1994, s. 37
Sch. 3, para. 21	(Amending provision)	VATA 1994, s. 33
Sch. 3, para. 22		VATA 1994, s. 40
Sch. 3, para. 23	(Amending provision)	VATA 1994, s. 35
Sch. 3, para. 24	(Amending provision)	VATA 1994, s. 39
Sch. 3, para. 25		VATA 1994, s. 16(1)
Sch. 3, para. 26	(Amending provision)	VATA 1994, s. 38
Sch. 3, para. 27	(Amending provision)	VATA 1994, s. 27(1)
Sch. 3, para. 28	(Amending provision)	VATA 1994, s. 41
Sch. 3, para. 29	(Amending provision)	VATA 1994, s. 43(1)

Former Provision		Destination
Finance (No. 2) Act 1992		
Sch. 3, para. 30	(Amending provision)	VATA 1994, s. 44
Sch. 3, para. 31	(Amending provision)	VATA 1994, s. 45
Sch. 3, para. 32	(Amending provision)	VATA 1994, s. 46
Sch. 3, para. 33		VATA 1994, s. 47(1)
Sch. 3, para. 34		VATA 1994, s. 48
Sch. 3, para. 35		VATA 1994, s. 18
Sch. 3, para. 36	(Amending provision)	VATA 1994, s. 34
Sch. 3, para. 37		VATA 1994, s. 52
Sch. 3, para. 38	(Amending provision)	VATA 1994, s. 58
Sch. 3, para. 39	(Amending provision)	VATA 1994, s. 72
Sch. 3, para. 40	(Amending provision)	VATA 1994, s. 82(1), s. 83
Sch. 3, para. 41	(Amending provision)	VATA 1994, s. 88
Sch. 3, para. 42	(Amending provision)	VATA 1994, s. 90
Sch. 3, para. 43	(Amending provision)	VATA 1994, s. 98
Sch. 3, para. 44		VATA 1994, s. 92, 93
Sch. 3, para. 45		VATA 1994, s. 95
Sch. 3, para. 46	(Amending provision)	VATA 1994, s. 96
Sch. 3, para. 47	(Amending provision)	VATA 1994, s. 99
Sch. 3, para. 48	(Amending provision)	VATA 1994, Sch. 1, para. 1
Sch. 3, para. 49	(Amending provision)	VATA 1994, Sch. 1, para. 2
Sch. 3, para. 50		VATA 1994, Sch. 1, para. 3
Sch. 3, para. 51	(Amending provision)	VATA 1994, Sch. 1, para. 4
Sch. 3, para. 52	(Amending provision)	VATA 1994, Sch. 1, para. 5(3)
Sch. 3, para. 53	(Amending provision)	VATA 1994, Sch. 1, para. 9, 10(1)
Sch. 3, para. 54	(Amending provision)	VATA 1994, Sch. 1, para. 11
Sch. 3, para. 55	(Amending provision)	VATA 1994, Sch. 1, para. 12
Sch. 3, para. 56	(Amending provision)	VATA 1994, Sch. 1, para. 13
Sch. 3, para. 57	(Amending provision)	VATA 1994, Sch. 1, para. 13 and 18
Sch. 3, para. 58	(Amending provision)	VATA 1994, Sch. 1, para. 14
Sch. 3, para. 59		VATA 1994, Sch. 2, 3
Sch. 3, para. 60	(Amending provision)	VATA 1994, Sch. 4
Sch. 3, para. 61	(Amending provision)	VATA 1994, Sch. 6
Sch. 3, para. 62		VATA 1994, Sch. 7
Sch. 3, para. 63	(Amending provision)	VATA 1994, Sch. 8, Grp. 12, 13 and 15
Sch. 3, para. 64	(Amending provision)	VATA 1994, Sch. 11
Sch. 3, para. 65		VATA 1994, Sch. 11, para. 3(3)
Sch. 3, para. 66	(Amending provision)	VATA 1994, s. 73
Sch. 3, para. 67		VATA 1994, s. 75
Sch. 3, para. 68	(Amending provision)	VATA 1994, Sch. 11, para. 4(2)
Sch. 3, para. 69		VATA 1994, Sch. 11, para. 5(10)
Sch. 3, para. 70	(Amending provision)	VATA 1994, Sch. 11, para. 6(1)
Sch. 3, para. 71	(Amending provision)	VATA 1994, Sch. 11
Sch. 3, para. 72	(Amending provision)	VATA 1994, Sch. 11, para. 8(1)
Sch. 3, para. 73	(Amending provision)	VATA 1994, Sch. 11, para. 10(2)
Sch. 3, para. 74		VATA 1994, Sch. 11, para. 14(1)(c)
Sch. 3, para. 75	(Unnecessary)	
Sch. 3, para. 76	(Unnecessary)	
Sch. 3, para. 77	(Amending provision)	VATA 1994, s. 60(2) and (3)
Sch. 3, para. 78	(Amending provision)	VATA 1994, s. 63(9)(b)
Sch. 3, para. 79		VATA 1994, s. 65
Sch. 3, para. 80	(Amending provision)	VATA 1994, s. 67
Sch. 3, para. 81	(Amending provision)	VATA 1994, s. 69
Sch. 3, para. 82		VATA 1994, s. 66 and 97
Sch. 3, para. 83	(Amending provision)	VATA 1994, s. 74(1)(c)
Sch. 3, para. 84	(Amending provision)	VATA 1994, s. 76
Sch. 3, para. 85	(Amending provision)	VATA 1994, s. 77
Sch. 3, para. 86	(Amending provision)	VATA 1994, s. 72(13)(a)
Sch. 3, para. 87–93	(Unnecessary)	
Sch. 3, para. 94		VATA 1994, s. 56
Sch. 3, para. 95	(Unnecessary)	

Former Provision   **Destination**

Finance (No. 2) Act 1992

Finance Act 1993

s. 42	Fuel and power for domestic or charity use	VATA 1994, Sch. 13, para. 7
s. 43	(Amending provision)	VATA 1994, s. 57
s. 44(1)	....	VATA 1994, s. 14
s. 44(2)	(Unnecessary)	
s. 44(3)	(Amending provision)	VATA 1994, s. 7(1), 13
s. 44(4)	....	VATA 1994, s. 14(8)
s. 45(1)	....	VATA 1994, s. 55
s. 45(2)	(Amending provision)	VATA 1994, s. 6(14)
s. 45(3)	(Spent)	
s. 46(1)	....	VATA 1994, s. 84(4)
s. 46(2)	(Spent)	
s. 47(1)	(Unnecessary)	
s. 47(2)	....	VATA 1994, Sch. 4, para. 5(2)
s. 47(3)	....	VATA 1994, Sch. 4, para. 5(3)
s. 47(4)	....	VATA 1994, Sch. 4, para. 5(5)
s. 48(1)	(Amending provision)	VATA 1994, s. 36
s. 48(2)	(Spent)	
s. 49	(Spent)	
s. 50(1)	(Unnecessary)	
s. 50(2)	(Amending provision)	VATA 1994, Sch. 6, para. 3
s. 50(3)	(Amending provision)	VATA 1994, Sch. 7
s. 50(4)	(Amending provision)	VATA 1994, Sch. 11, para. 2(8)
Sch. 2, para. 1(1)	(Amending provision)	VATA 1994, s. 63(2)
Sch. 2, para. 1(2)	....	VATA 1994, s. 63(4)–(6)
Sch. 2, para. 1(3)	(Amending provision)	VATA 1994, s. 63(8)
Sch. 2, para. 1(4)	(Spent)	
Sch. 2, para. 2(1)	(Amending provision)	VATA 1994, s. 64(1)
Sch. 2, para. 2(2)	....	VATA 1994, s. 64(2), (3)
Sch. 2, para. 2(3)	(Amending provision)	VATA 1994, s. 64(4)
Sch. 2, para. 2(4)	(Amending provision)	VATA 1994, s. 64(6)
Sch. 2, para. 2(5), (6)	(Spent)	
Sch. 2, para. 3(1)	....	VATA 1994, s. 70
Sch. 2, para. 3(2)	(Amending provision)	VATA 1994, s. 60(1), (4), 84(6)
Sch. 2, para. 3(3)	(Spent)	
Sch. 2, para. 4(1)	(Amending provision)	VATA 1994, s. 74(1), (2)
Sch. 2, para. 4(2)	....	VATA 1994, s. 74(3)
Sch. 2, para. 4(3)	(Spent)	
Sch. 2, para. 5(1)	(Amending provision)	VATA 1994, s. 59(2)
Sch. 2, para. 5(2)	(Amending provision)	VATA 1994, s. 59(3)
Sch. 2, para. 5(3)	(Spent)	
Sch. 2, para. 6(1)	....	VATA 1994, s. 59(4)
Sch. 2, para. 6(2)	(Amending provision)	VATA 1994, s. 59(5)
Sch. 2, para. 6(3)	....	VATA 1994, s. 59(6)
Sch. 2, para. 6(4)	(Spent)	
Sch. 2, para. 7(1)	(Amending provision)	VATA 1994, s. 59(5)
Sch. 2, para. 7(2)	(Spent)	
Sch. 2, para. 7(3)	....	VATA 1994, s. 59(5)
Sch. 2, para. 7(4)	(Spent)	
Sch. 2, para. 8	(Unnecessary)	

Value Added Tax (Reverse Charge) Order 1993 (SI 1993/2328)

art. 4	....	VATA 1994, Sch. 5, para. 10

Finance Act 1994

s. 7(1), (2)	VAT and duties tribunals	VATA 1994, s. 82(2), Sch. 12, para. 1
s. 7(3)–(4)	(Unnecessary)	
s. 7(5)	(Not a VAT provision)	

TABLE OF DERIVATIONS
VALUE ADDED TAX ACT 1994

The consolidated table below, prepared by CCH Editorial staff, relates the provisions of the *Value Added Tax Act* 1994 (VATA 1994) (in the left-hand column) to the provisions of the *Customs and Excise Management Act* 1979 (CEMA 1979), the *Value Added Tax Act* 1983 (VATA 1983) and other ancillary Acts and statutory instruments (in the right-hand column).

Section	Derivation
1(1)	VATA 1983, s. 1, as amended by F(No. 2)A 1992, s. 14 and Sch. 3, para. 2.
1(2)	VATA 1983, s. 2(3).
1(3)	VATA 1983, s. 2A(4), as inserted by F(No. 2)A 1992, s. 14 and Sch. 3, para. 3.
1(4)	VATA 1983, s. 2B(1), as inserted by F(No. 2)A 1992, s. 14 and Sch. 3, para. 3.
2	VATA 1983, s. 9, as amended by FA 1991, s. 13 and F(No. 2)A 1992, s. 14 and Sch. 3, para. 11.
3	VATA 1983, s. 2C, as inserted by F(No. 2)A 1992, s. 14 and Sch. 3, para. 3.
4	VATA 1983, s. 2(1), (2).
5	VATA 1983, s. 3, as amended by F(No. 2)A 1992, s. 14 and Sch. 3, para. 4.
6(1)–(3)	VATA 1983, s. 4.
6(4)–(6)	VATA 1983, s. 5(1)–(3).
6(7), (8)	VATA 1983, s. 5(3A), (3B), as inserted by F(No. 2)A 1992, s. 14 and Sch. 3, para. 6(1).
6(9)–(13)	VATA 1983, s. 5(4)–(8).
6(14)	VATA 1983, s. 5(9), as amended by FA 1993, s. 45(2) and Sch. 23, Pt. II(3).
6(15)	VATA 1983, s. 5(10), as amended by F(No. 2)A 1992, s. 14 and Sch. 3, para. 6(3).
7(1), (2)	VATA 1983, s. 6(1), (2), as amended by FA 1987, s. 12(2), F(No. 2)A 1992, s. 14 and Sch. 3, para. 7(1), (2) and FA 1993, s. 44(3).
7(3)–(7)	VATA 1983, s. 6(2A), (2B), (2C), (2D), (3) and F(No. 2)A 1992, s. 14 and Sch. 3, para. 7(3).
7(8)	VATA 1983, s. 6(4) and F(No. 2)A 1992, s. 14 and Sch. 3, para. 7(4).
7(9)	VATA 1983, s. 6(4A) and F(No. 2)A 1992, s. 14 and Sch. 3, para. 7(5).
7(10)	VATA 1983, s. 6(5).
7(11)	VATA 1983, s. 6(6) and F(No. 2)A 1992, s. 14 and Sch. 3, para. 7(6).
8(1)–(5)	VATA 1983, s. 7(1)–(5), as inserted by FA 1987, s. 19(2) and Sch. 2, para. 1.
8(6)	VATA 1983, s. 7(6), as inserted by F(No. 2)A 1992, s. 14, Sch. 3, para. 8.
9(1)	VATA 1983, s. 8(1), as amended by F(No. 2)A 1992, s. 14 and Sch. 3, para. 9.
9(2)–(5)	VATA 1983, s. 8 (2)–(5).
10	VATA 1983, s. 2A(1)–(3), as inserted by F(No. 2)A 1992, s. 14 and Sch. 3, para. 3.
11	VATA 1983, s. 8A, as inserted by F(No. 2)A 1992, s. 14 and Sch. 3, para. 10.
12	VATA 1983, s. 8B, as inserted by F(No. 2)A 1992, s. 14 and Sch. 3, para. 10.
13	VATA 1983, s. 8C, as inserted by F(No. 2)A 1992, s. 14 and Sch. 3, para. 10 and as amended by FA 1993, s. 44(3)(b).
14	VATA 1983, s. 8D, as inserted by FA 1993, s. 44.
15	VATA 1983, s. 2B(2)–(4), as inserted by F(No. 2)A 1992, s. 14 and Sch. 3, para. 3.
16(1)	VATA 1983, s. 24(1), as substituted by F(No. 2)A 1992, s. 14 and Sch. 3, para. 25.
16(2)	VATA 1983, s. 24(4).
17(1)	(None).
17(2)	CEMA 1979, s. 100C(1), as inserted by FA 1984, s. 8 and Sch. 4, Pt. I, and as amended by SI 1991/2727.
17(3)	CEMA 1979, s. 100B, as inserted by FA 1984, s. 8 and Sch. 4, Pt. I, and as amended by SI 1991/2727.
17(4)	CEMA 1979, s. 100C(3), (4), as inserted by FA 1984, s. 8 and Sch. 4, Pt. I, and as amended by SI 1991/2727.
18	VATA 1983, s. 35, as substituted by F(No. 2)A 1992, s. 14 and Sch. 3, para. 35.
19	VATA 1983, s. 10, as amended by F(No. 2)A 1992, s. 14 and Sch. 3, para. 12.
20	VATA 1983, s. 10A, as inserted by F(No. 2)A 1992, s. 14 and Sch. 3, para. 13.
21(1), (2)	VATA 1983, s. 11(1), (2), as amended by F(No. 2)A 1992, s. 14 and Sch. 3, para. 14.
21(3)	VATA 1983, s. 11(2A), as inserted by F(No. 2)A 1992, s. 14 and Sch. 3, para. 14.

Section	Derivation
41(5)	VATA 1983, s. 27(3).
41(6)	VATA 1983, s. 27(4), as amended by the National Health Service and Community Care Act 1990, s. 60 and Sch. 8, para. 9 and SI 1991/195, art. 5.
41(7)	VATA 1983, s. 27(5), as inserted by the National Health Service and Community Care Act 1990, s. 61(4).
41(8)	VATA 1983, s. 27(6), as inserted by SI 1991/195, art. 5.
42	VATA 1983, s. 28(1), as amended by FA 1990, s. 10(8).
43(1)	VATA 1983, s. 29(1), as amended by F(No. 2)A 1992, s. 14 and Sch. 3, para. 29.
43(2)	VATA 1983, s. 29(2).
43(3)	VATA 1983, s. 29(3), (3A), as respectively subsituted and inserted by FA 1991, s. 16.
43(4)–(8)	VATA 1983, s. 29(4)–(8), as amended (s. 29(8)) by the Companies Consolidation (Consequential Provisions) Act 1985, Sch. 2, and by CA 1989, s. 144(4) and Sch. 18, para. 27.
44(1)–(3)	VATA 1983, s. 29A, as inserted by FA 1987, s. 15, and as amended by FA 1990, s. 14(2) and F(No. 2)A 1992, s. 14 and Sch. 3, para. 30(1), (2).
44(4)	VATA 1983, s. 29A(3A), as inserted by FA 1990, s. 14(3).
44(5)–(10)	VATA 1983, s. 29A(4)–(9), as amended (s. 29A(8)) by F(No. 2)A 1992, s. 14 and Sch. 3, para. 30(3).
45	VATA 1983, s. 30, as amended by F(No. 2)A 1992, s. 14 and Sch. 3, para. 31.
46(1)–(4)	VATA 1983, s. 31(1)–(4), as amended (s. 31(3)) by F(No. 2)A 1992, s. 14 and Sch. 3, para. 32(1).
46(5)	VATA 1983, s. 31(5), as inserted by FA 1985, s. 31.
46(6)	VATA 1983, s. 31(6), as inserted by F(No. 2)A 1992, s. 14 and Sch. 3, para. 32(2).
47(1)	VATA 1983, s. 32(2), as substituted by F(No. 2)A 1992, s. 14 and Sch. 3, para. 33.
47(2), (3)	VATA 1983, s. 32(3), (4).
48	VATA 1983, s. 32A, as inserted by F(No. 2)A 1992, s. 14 and Sch. 3, para. 34.
49	VATA 1983, s. 33.
50	VATA 1983, s. 34.
51	VATA 1983, s. 35A, as inserted by FA 1989, s. 18 and Sch. 3, para. 6.
52	VATA 1983, s. 37, as substituted by F(No. 2)A 1992, s. 14 and Sch. 3, para. 37.
53	VATA 1983, s. 37A, as inserted by FA 1987, s. 16.
54	VATA 1983, s. 37B, as inserted by F(No. 2)A 1992, s. 16.
55	VATA 1983, s. 37C, as inserted by FA 1993, s. 45.
56(1), (2)	FA 1986, s. 9(1), (2).
56(3)(a)	FA 1986, s. 9(3)(a).
56(3)(b)	FA 1986, s. 9(3)(aa), as inserted by F(No. 2)A 1992, s. 14 and Sch. 3, para. 94.
56(3)(c)–(e)	FA 1986, s. 9(3)(b)–(d).
56(4)	FA 1986, s. 9(4).
56(5)	FA 1986, s. 9(5), as amended by F(No. 2)A 1992, s. 14 and Sch. 3, para. 94.
56(6)–(10)	FA 1986, s. 9(6)–(10), as amended by the Road Traffic (Consequential Provisions) Act 1988, s. 4 and Sch. 3, para. 32.
57(1)	FA 1986, s. 9 and Sch. 6, para. 1.
57(2), (3)	FA 1986, s. 9 and Sch. 6, para. 2; Table A substituted by SI 1993/765 and amended by SI 1993/2952.
57(4)	FA 1986, s. 9 and Sch. 6, para. 4, as amended by FA 1993, s. 43(3).
57(5)	FA 1986, s. 9 and Sch. 6, para. 5(1), as amended by FA 1993, s. 43(2)(a), (b).
57(6)	FA 1986, s. 9 and Sch. 6, para. 5(2).
57(7)	FA 1986, s. 9 and Sch. 6, para. 6(1), as amended by FA 1993, s. 43(2)(c).
57(8)	FA 1986, s. 9 and Sch. 6, para. 6(2), as amended by FA 1993, s. 43(2)(d).
58	VATA 1983, s. 38, as amended by F(No. 2)A 1992, s. 14 and Sch. 3, para. 38.
59(1)	FA 1985, s. 19(1).
59(2)	FA 1985, s. 19(2)(a), (c), as amended by FA 1993, s. 49 and Sch. 2, para. 5(1).
59(3)	FA 1985, s. 19(3), as amended by FA 1993, s. 49 and Sch. 2, para. 5(2).
59(4)	FA 1985, s. 19(4), as substituted by FA 1993, s. 49 and Sch. 2, para. 6(1).
59(5)	FA 1985, s. 19(5), as amended by FA 1993, s. 49 and Sch. 2, para. 6(2), 7.
59(6)	FA 1985, s. 19(5A), as inserted by FA 1993, s. 49 and Sch. 2, para. 6(3).
59(7)–(10)	FA 1985, s. 19(6)–(9).
60(1)	FA 1985, s. 13(1), as amended by FA 1993, s. 49 and Sch. 2, para. 3(2)(a).

Section	Derivation
60(2)(a)	FA 1985, s. 13(2)(ba), as inserted by F(No. 2)A 1992, s. 14 and Sch. 3, para. 77(1)(b).
60(2)(b)	FA 1985, s. 13(2)(a).
60(2)(c)	FA 1985, s. 13(2)(b), (d), as amended by F(No. 2)A 1992, s. 14 and Sch. 3, para. 77(1)(a), and as inserted by FA 1990, s. 11.
60(2)(d)	FA 1985, s. 13(2)(c).
60(3)	FA 1985, s. 13(3).
60(4)–(6)	FA 1985, s. 13(5)–(7).
60(7)	FA 1985, s. 27(1).
61(1)–(5)	FA 1986, s. 14(1)–(5).
61(6)	FA 1986, s. 14(8).
62	FA 1985, s. 13A, as inserted by FA 1989, s. 23.
63(1)	FA 1985, s. 14(1), as amended by FA 1992, s. 7(1).
63(2)	FA 1985, s. 14(2), as substituted by FA 1988, s. 16(2), and as amended by FA 1993, s. 49 and Sch. 2, para. 1.
63(3)	FA 1985, 14(4), as substituted by FA 1988, s. 16(3) and FA 1994, s. 45(2).
63(4)–(6)	FA 1985, s. 14(4A), (4B), (4C), as inserted by FA 1993, s. 49 and Sch. 2, para. 1(2).
63(7)	FA 1985, s. 14(5), as amended by FA 1988, s. 16(4).
63(8), (9)	FA 1985, s. 14(5A), (5B), as inserted by FA 1988, s. 16(5), and as amended by F(No. 2)A 1992, s. 14 and Sch. 3, para. 78, by FA 1993, s. 49 and Sch. 2, para. 1(3) and by FA 1994, s. 45(3).
63(10), (11)	FA 1985, s. 14(6), (7), as amended by FA 1988, s. 148 and Sch. 14, Pt. III.
64	FA 1985, s. 14A, as inserted by FA 1988, s. 17.
64(1)	FA 1985, s. 14A(1), as amended by FA 1993, s. 49 and Sch. 2, para. 2(1).
64(2), (3)	FA 1985, s. 14A(2), (3), as substituted by FA 1993, s. 49 and Sch. 2, para. 2(2).
64(4)	FA 1985, s. 14A(4), as amended by FA 1993, s. 49 and Sch. 2, para. 2(3).
64(5)	FA 1985, s. 14A(5).
64(6)	FA 1985, s. 14A(6), as amended by FA 1993, s. 49 and Sch. 2, para. 2(4).
64(7)	FA 1985, s. 14A(7).
65	FA 1985, s. 14B, as inserted by F(No. 2)A 1992, s. 14 and Sch. 3, para. 79.
66	FA 1985, s. 17A(1)–(8), (10), as inserted by F(No. 2)A 1992, s. 14 and Sch. 3, para. 82.
67(1)	FA 1985, s. 15(1)(a), (aa), (b), as amended by FA 1988, s. 18(1) and F(No. 2)A 1992, s. 14 and Sch. 3, para. 80(1).
67(2)	FA 1985, s. 15(2).
67(3)	FA 1985, s. 15(3), as amended by FA 1988, s. 18(2) and F(No. 2)A 1992, s. 14 and Sch. 3, para. 80(2).
67(4)	FA 1985, s. 15(3A), as inserted by FA 1988, s. 18(3), and as amended by F(No. 2)A 1992, s. 14 and Sch. 3, para. 80(3).
67(5), (6)	FA 1985, s. 15(3B), (3C), as inserted by F(No. 2)A 1992, s. 14 and Sch. 3, para. 80(4).
67(7)	FA 1985, s. 15(3D), as inserted by FA 1992, s. 16(5).
67(8)–(11)	FA 1985, s. 15(4)–(7).
68	FA 1985, s. 16.
69(1)	FA 1985, s. 17(1), as amended by FA 1988, s. 19(1)(b).
69(1)(a)	FA 1985, s. 17(1)(a), as amended by FA 1988, s. 19(1)(a) and F(No. 2)A 1992, s. 14 and Sch. 3, para. 81(a).
69(1)(b)	FA 1985, s. 17(1)(aa), as inserted by F(No. 2)A 1992, s. 14 and Sch. 3, para. 81(b).
69(1)(c)–(f)	FA 1985, s. 17(1)(b)–(e), as inserted by FA 1986, s. 15(1).
69(2)	FA 1985, s. 17(2).
69(3)	FA 1985, s. 17(3), as amended by FA 1988, s. 19(2).
69(4)	FA 1985, s. 17(4)(a), (c)–(e).
69(5)–(9)	FA 1985, s. 17(5)–(7), (9), (10).
69(10)	(Transitional provision).
70	FA 1985, s. 15A, as inserted by FA 1993, s. 49 and Sch. 2, para. 3(1).
71	FA 1985, s. 33(2), (3).
72(1)	VATA 1983, s. 39(1), as amended by FA 1985, s. 12(2).

Section	Derivation
72(2)	VATA 1983, s. 39(1A), as inserted by FA 1985, s. 12(3) and para. (ba), as inserted by F(No. 2)A 1992, s. 14 and Sch. 3, para. 39(1)(b), as amended by FA 1990, s. 11(11)(a) and F(No. 2)A 1992, s. 14 and Sch. 3, para. 39(1)(a).
72(3)	VATA 1983, s. 39(2), as amended by FA 1985, s. 12(2), (4).
72(4)–(7)	VATA 1983, s. 39(2A), (2B), (2C), (2D), as inserted by FA 1985, s. 12(5), and as amended (s. 39(2B)) by F(No. 2)A 1992, s. 14 and Sch. 3, para. 38(2).
72(8)	VATA 1983, s. 39(3), as amended by FA 1985, s. 12(2).
72(9)	VATA 1983, s. 39(3A), as inserted by FA 1985, s. 12(6).
72(10)	VATA 1983, s. 39(4), as amended by F(No. 2)A 1992, s. 14 and Sch. 3, para. 39(3).
72(11)	VATA 1983, s. 39(5).
72(12)	VATA 1983, s. 39(9).
72(13)	FA 1985, s. 33(5)(a), as amended by F(No. 2)A 1992, s. 14 and Sch. 3, para. 86.
73(1)	VATA 1983, s. 38 and Sch. 7, para. 4(1).
73(2), (3)	VATA 1983, s. 38 and Sch. 7, para. 4(2), (2A), as substituted by FA 1988, s. 15(2), and as amended by FA 1990, s. 15(1) and F(No. 2)A 1992, s. 14 and Sch. 3, para. 66(1).
73(4), (5)	VATA 1983, s. 38 and Sch. 7, para. 4(3), (4), as construed (s. 4(4)) by the Bankruptcy (Scotland) Act 1985, s. 75(11).
73(6)	VATA 1983, s. 38 and Sch. 7, para. 4(5), as amended by FA 1988, s. 15(3) and F(No. 2)A 1992, s. 14 and Sch. 3, para. 66(2).
73(7)	VATA 1983, s. 38 and Sch. 7, para. 4(6), as amended by FA 1985, s. 23 and Sch. 7, para. 1(2) and F(No. 2)A 1992, s. 14 and Sch. 3, para. 66(3).
73(8)	VATA 1983, s. 38 and Sch. 7, para. 4(6A), as inserted by FA 1985, s. 23 and Sch. 7, para. 1(3).
73(9)	VATA 1983, s. 38 and Sch. 7, para. 4(9), as amended by FA 1988, s. 15(4).
73(10)	VATA 1983, s. 38 and Sch. 7, para. 4(10), as construed by the Bankruptcy (Scotland) Act 1985, s. 75(11).
74(1)	FA 1985, s. 18(1), as amended by FA 1988, s. 14(8)(b), by FA 1990, s. 16(2), by F(No. 2)A 1992, s. 14 and Sch. 3, para. 83 and by FA 1993, s. 49 and Sch. 2, para. 4(1).
74(2)	FA 1985, s. 18(3), as amended by FA 1988, s. 18(4)(b), by FA 1990, s. 16(3) and by FA 1993, s. 49 and Sch. 2, para. 4(1).
74(3)	FA 1985, s. 18(3A), as inserted by FA 1993, s. 49 and Sch. 2, para. 4(2).
74(4)–(7)	FA 1985, s. 18(6)–(8)(a), (b), (9), as amended (s. 18(7)) by FA 1990, s. 16(5).
75	VATA 1983, s. 38 and Sch. 7, para. 4A, as inserted by F(No. 2)A 1992, s. 14 and Sch. 3, para. 67 and as construed by the Bankruptcy (Scotland) Act 1985, s. 75(11).
76(1)	FA 1985, s. 21(1), as amended by FA 1988, s. 19(3) and F(No. 2)A 1992, s. 14 and Sch. 3, para. 84(1).
76(2)	FA 1985, s. 21(1A), as inserted by FA 1988, s. 19(3).
76(3)–(5)	FA 1985, s. 21(2)–(4).
76(6)	FA 1985, s. 21(4A), as inserted by F(No. 2)A 1992, s. 14 and Sch. 3, para. 84(2).
76(7)–(10)	FA 1985, s. 21(5)–(8), as amended (s. 21(5), (6)) by F(No. 2)A 1992, s. 14 and Sch. 3, para. 84(3), (4) and, as construed by the Bankruptcy (Scotland) Act 1985, s. 75(11).
77	FA 1985, s. 22(1)–(5), (7), as amended (s. 22(1), (2), (7)) by F(No. 2)A 1992, s. 14 and Sch. 3, para. 85.
78(1)–(8)	VATA 1983, s. 38A(1)–(8), as inserted by FA 1991, s. 17.
78(9)	VATA 1983, s. 38A(8A), as inserted by F(No. 2)A 1992, s. 15(2).
78(10)–(12)	VATA 1983, s. 38A(9)–(11).
79(1)–(3)	FA 1985, s. 20(1)–(3), as substituted by FA 1988, s. 20 and as amended by FA 1994, s. 46(2).
79(4)	FA 1985, s. 20(3A), as inserted by F(No. 2)A 1992, s. 15(1).
79(5)–(7)	FA 1985, s. 20(4), (5), (7), as substituted by FA 1988, s. 20.
80	FA 1989, s. 24(1)–(7) and SI 1989/2271.
81(1), (2)	VATA 1983, s. 38B, as inserted by FA 1991, s. 17.
81(3)–(5)	FA 1988, s. 21, as amended by FA 1994, s. 47(1).
82(1)	VATA 1983, s. 40(1), Sch. 8, para. 1 and FA 1985, s. 30(1).

Section	Derivation
82(2)	VATA 1983, s. 40 and FA 1994, s. 7(1).
82(3), (4)	FA 1985, s. 30 and Sch. 8, para. 6.
83(a)	VATA 1983, s. 40(1)(a).
83(b)	VATA 1983, s. 40(1)(b), as amended by F(No. 2)A 1992, s. 14 and Sch. 3, para. 40(a).
83(c)	VATA 1983, s. 40(1)(c).
83(d)	VATA 1983, s. 40(1)(fa), as inserted by F(No. 2)A 1992, s. 14 and Sch. 3, para. 40(c).
83(e)	VATA 1983, s. 40(1)(d), as substituted by FA 1987, s. 19(2) and Sch. 2, para. 4.
83(f)	VATA 1983, s. 40(1)(g).
83(g)	VATA 1983, s. 40(1)(e).
83(h)	VATA 1983, s. 40(1)(f), as amended by FA 1990, s. 11(11)(b).
83(j)	VATA 1983, s. 40(1)(da), as inserted by F(No. 2)A 1992, s. 14 and Sch. 3, para. 40(b).
83(k)	VATA 1983, s. 40(1)(h).
83(l)	VATA 1983, s. 40(1)(n), as amended by F(No. 2)A 1992, s. 14 and Sch. 3, para. 40(f).
83(m)	VATA 1983, s. 40(1)(hza), as inserted by F(No. 2)A 1992, s. 16(2).
83(n)	VATA 1983, s. 40(1)(o), as inserted by FA 1985, s. 24(1) and as amended by F(No. 2)A 1992, s. 14 and Sch. 3, para. 40(g).
83(o)	FA 1986, s. 14(6).
83(p)	VATA 1983, s. 40(1)(m), as amended by F(No. 2)A 1992, s. 14 and Sch. 3, para. 40(e).
83(q), (r)	VATA 1983, s. 40(1)(p), (q), as inserted by FA 1985, s. 24(1).
83(s)	VATA 1983, s. 40(1)(ha), as inserted by FA 1991, s. 17(1).
83(t)	VATA 1983, s. 40(1)(s), as inserted by FA 1989, s. 24(9).
83(u)	VATA 1983, s. 40(1)(hh), as inserted by FA 1986 s. 10(2).
83(v)	VATA 1983, s. 40(1)(j).
83(w)	VATA 1983, s. 40(1)(ja), as inserted by F(No. 2)A 1992, s. 14 and Sch. 3, para. 40(d).
83(x)	VATA 1983, s. 40(1)(k).
83(y)	VATA 1983, s. 40(1)(r), as inserted by SI 1987/1427, reg. 11.
83(z)	VATA 1983, s. 40(1)(l).
84(1)	(Unnecessary).
84(2)	VATA 1983, s. 40(2), as amended by FA 1985, s. 24(3).
84(3)	VATA 1983, s. 40(3), as amended by FA 1985, s. 24(4).
84(4)	VATA 1983, s. 40(3ZA), as inserted by FA 1993, s. 46(1).
84(5)	VATA 1983, s. 40(3B), as inserted (as (3A)) by FA 1985, s. 24(5), as amended by FA 1986, s. 10(3).
84(6)	VATA 1983, s. 40(1A), as inserted by FA 1985, s. 24(2) and as amended by FA 1993, s. 49 and Sch. 2, para. 3(2)(c).
84(7)	VATA 1983, s. 40(3A), as inserted by FA 1986, s. 10(3).
84(8)–(10)	VATA 1983, s. 40(4)–(6), as amended by FA 1994, s. 18(3).
84(11)	FA 1993, s. 46(2).
85	FA 1985, s. 25.
86	FA 1985, s. 26(1), (2)(a), (3), as amended by the Tribunals and Inquiries Act 1992, s. 18(1) and Sch. 3, para. 17.
87	FA 1985, s. 29.
88(1)	VATA 1983, s. 41(1), as amended by F(No. 2)A 1992, s. 14 and Sch. 3, para. 41(1).
88(2), (3)	VATA 1983, s. 41(2), (3).
88(4)	VATA 1983, s. 41(3A), as inserted by F(No. 2)A 1992, s. 14 and Sch. 3, para. 41(2).
88(5), (6)	VATA 1983, s. 41(4), (5).
88(7)	VATA 1983, s. 41(6), as inserted by F(No. 2)A 1992, s. 14 and Sch. 3, para. 41(3).
89(1)	VATA 1983, s. 42(1).
89(2)	VATA 1983, s. 42(1A), as inserted by FA 1989, s. 18 and Sch. 3, para. 7(1).
89(3)	VATA 1983, s. 42(2), as amended by FA 1989, s. 18 and Sch. 3, para. 7(2).

Section	Derivation
90	VATA 1983, s. 43, as amended by F(No. 2)A 1992, s. 14 and Sch. 3, para. 42.
91	VATA 1983, s. 44, as amended (s. 44(1), (2), (5)) by SI 1989/992.
92	VATA 1983, s. 46A, as amended by F(No. 2)A 1992, s. 14 and Sch. 3, para. 44.
93	VATA 1983, s. 46B, as inserted by F(No. 2)A 1992, s. 14 and Sch. 3, para. 44.
94	VATA 1983, s. 47.
95(1)	VATA 1983, s. 47A(1), as inserted by F(No. 2)A 1992, s. 14 and Sch. 3, para. 45 and as amended by SI 1992/3127, art. 2.
95(2)	VATA 1983, s. 47A(1A), as inserted by SI 1992/3127.
95(3)–(5)	VATA 1983, s. 47A(2)–(4), as inserted by F(No. 2)A 1992, s. 14 and Sch. 3, para. 45.
96(1)	VATA 1983, s. 48(1), as amended by FA 1987, s. 13 and FA 1989, s. 18 and Sch. 3, para. 9 and F(No. 2)A 1992, s. 14 and Sch. 3, para. 46(1).
96(2)	VATA 1983, s. 48(9), as inserted by F(No. 2)A 1992, s. 14 and Sch. 3, para. 46(4).
96(3)	VATA 1983, s. 48(1A), as inserted by F(No. 2)A 1992, s. 14 and Sch. 3, para. 46(2).
96(4)	VATA 1983, s. 20(6).
96(5)	VATA 1983, s. 48(1B), as inserted by F(No. 2)A 1992, s. 14 and Sch. 3, para. 46(2).
96(6), (7)	VATA 1983, s. 48(4).
96(8)–(11)	VATA 1983, s. 48(5)–(8), as amended by F(No. 2)A 1992, s. 14 and Sch. 3, para. 46.
97(1)	VATA 1983, s. 45(1).
97(2)	FA 1985, s. 26(2)(b), 27(3)(c).
97(3)	VATA 1983, s. 45(3).
97(4)	VATA 1983, s. 45(4), as amended by FA 1987, s. 16(2) and FA 1992, s. 6(2) and para. (d), as inserted by FA 1989, s. 18 and Sch. 3, para. 8 and para. (e), as inserted by F(No. 2)A 1992, s. 16(3).
97(5)	VATA 1983, s. 45(2) and FA 1985, s. 15(8), 17(8), 17A(9), 18(8)(c).
98	VATA 1983, s. 46, as amended by F(No. 2)A 1992, s. 14 and Sch. 3, para. 43.
99	VATA 1983, s. 49, as amended by F(No. 2)A 1992, s. 14 and Sch. 3, para. 47.

Schedule 1

Para. 1(1)	VATA 1983, s. 2C(2) and Sch. 1, para. 1(1), as substituted by FA 1990, s. 10(2), as amended by F(No. 2)A 1992, s. 14 and Sch. 3, para. 48(1), SI 1993/766 and SI 1993/2953.
Para. 1(2)	VATA 1983, s. 2C(2) and Sch. 1, para. 1(2), as substituted by FA 1990, s. 10(2), as amended by F(No. 2)A 1992, s. 14 and Sch. 3, para. 48(2), SI 1993/766 and SI 1993/2953.
Para. 1(3)	VATA 1983, s. 2C(2) and Sch. 1, para. 1(3), as substituted by FA 1990, s. 10(2), as amended by SI 1993/766 and SI 1993/2953.
Para. 1(4)	VATA 1983, s. 2C(2) and Sch. 1, para. 1(4), as substituted by FA 1987, s. 14(2), as amended by FA 1990, s. 10(3), F(No. 2)A 1992, s. 14 and Sch. 3, para. 48(3).
Para. 1(5), (6)	VATA 1983, Sch.1, para. 1(4A), (4B), as inserted by F(No. 2)A 1992, s. 14 and Sch. 3, para. 48(4).
Para. 1(7)	VATA 1983, s. 2C(2) and Sch. 1, para. 1(5), as substituted by FA 1987, s. 14(2), as amended by FA 1988, s. 14(2) and FA 1990, s. 10(4) and F(No. 2)A 1992, s. 14 and Sch. 3, para. 48(5).
Para. 1(8)	VATA 1983, s. 2C(2) and Sch. 1, para. 1(6), as inserted by FA 1989, s. 18 and Sch. 3, para. 10(a), as amended by FA 1990, s. 10(5).
Para. 2(1)	VATA 1983, s. 2C(2) and Sch. 1, para. 1A(1), as inserted by FA 1986, s. 10(1) and as amended by F(No. 2)A 1992, s. 14 and Sch. 3, para. 49(1).
Para. 2(2), (3)	VATA 1983, s. 2C(2) and Sch. 1, para. 1A(2), (3), as inserted by FA 1986, s. 10(1).
Para. 2(4)	VATA 1983, s. 2C(2) and Sch. 1, para. 1A(4), as inserted by FA 1986, s. 10(1), as amended by F(No. 2)A 1992, s. 14 and Sch. 3, para. 49(1).
Para. 2(5), (6)	VATA 1983, s. 2C(2) and Sch. 1, para. 1A(5), (6), as inserted by FA 1986, s. 10(1).

Schedule 2	Derivation
Para. 7	VATA 1983, s. 2C(2) and Sch. 1A, para. 7, as inserted by F(No. 2)A 1992, s. 14 and Sch. 3, para. 59.
Para. 8	VATA 1983, s. 2C(2) and Sch. 1A, para. 8, as inserted by F(No. 2)A 1992, s. 14 and Sch. 3, para. 59.
Para. 9	VATA 1983, s. 2C(2) and Sch. 1A, para. 9, as inserted by F(No. 2)A 1992, s. 14 and Sch. 3, para. 59.
Para. 10	VATA 1983, s. 2C(2) and Sch. 1A, para. 10, as inserted by F(No. 2)A 1992, s. 14 and Sch. 3, para. 59.

Schedule 3	
Para. 1	VATA 1983, s. 2C(2) and Sch. 1B, para. 1, as inserted by F(No. 2)A 1992, s. 14 and Sch. 3, para. 59, and as amended by SI 1993/766 and SI 1993/2953.
Para. 2	VATA 1983, s. 2C(2) and Sch. 1B, para. 2, as inserted by F(No. 2)A 1992, s. 14 and Sch. 3, para. 59, and as amended by SI 1993/766 and SI 1993/2953.
Para. 3	VATA 1983, s. 2C(2) and Sch. 1B, para. 3, as inserted by F(No. 2)A 1992, s. 14 and Sch. 3, para. 59.
Para. 4	VATA 1983, s. 2C(2) and Sch. 1B, para. 4, as inserted by F(No. 2)A 1992, s. 14 and Sch. 3, para. 59.
Para. 5	VATA 1983, s. 2C(2) and Sch. 1B, para. 5, as inserted by F(No. 2)A 1992, s. 14 and Sch. 3, para. 59.
Para. 6	VATA 1983, s. 2C(2) and Sch. 1B, para. 6, as inserted by F(No. 2)A 1992, s. 14 and Sch. 3, para. 59.
Para. 7	VATA 1983, s. 2C(2) and Sch. 1B, para. 7, as inserted by F(No. 2)A 1992, s. 14 and Sch. 3, para. 59.
Para. 8	VATA 1983, s. 2C(2) and Sch. 1B, para. 8, as inserted by F(No. 2)A 1992, s. 14 and Sch. 3, para. 59.
Para. 9	VATA 1983, s. 2C(2) and Sch. 1B, para. 9, as inserted by F(No. 2)A 1992, s. 14 and Sch. 3, para. 59.
Para. 10	VATA 1983, s. 2C(2) and Sch. 1B, para. 10, as inserted by F(No. 2)A 1992, s. 14 and Sch. 3, para. 59.
Para. 11	VATA 1983, s. 2C(2) and Sch. 1B, para. 11, as inserted by F(No. 2)A 1992, s. 14 and Sch. 3, para. 59.

Schedule 4	
Para. 1	VATA 1983, s. 3 and Sch. 2, para. 1.
Para. 2	VATA 1983, s. 3 and Sch. 2, para. 2.
Para. 3	VATA 1983, s. 3 and Sch. 2, para. 3.
Para. 4	VATA 1983, s. 3 and Sch. 2, para. 4, as amended by FA 1989, s. 18 and Sch. 3, para. 11(a).
Para. 5(1)	VATA 1983, s. 3 and Sch. 2, para. 5(1), as amended by FA 1989, s. 18 and Sch. 3, para. 11(b).
Para. 5(2)	VATA 1983, Sch. 2, para. 5(2), as amended by FA 1993, s. 47(2).
Para. 5(3)	VATA 1983, s. 3 and Sch. 2, para. 5(2A), as inserted by FA 1993, s. 47(3).
Para. 5(4)	VATA 1983, s. 3 and Sch. 2, para. 5(3).
Para. 5(5)	VATA 1983, s. 3 and Sch. 2, para. 5(3A), as inserted by FA 1993, s. 47(4).
Para. 5(6)	VATA 1983, s. 3 and Sch. 2, para. 5(4).
Para. 6	VATA 1983, s. 3 and Sch. 2, para. 5A, as inserted by F(No. 2)A 1992, s. 14 and Sch. 3, para. 60(1).
Para. 7	VATA 1983, s. 3 and Sch. 2, para. 6.
Para. 8(1)	VATA 1983, s. 3 and Sch. 2, para. 7(1).
Para. 8(2)	VATA 1983, s. 3 and Sch. 2, para. 7(2), as amended by F(No. 2)A 1992, s. 14 and Sch. 3, para. 60(2)(a) and (b).
Para. 8(3)	VATA 1983, s. 3 and Sch. 2, para. 7(2A), as inserted by F(No. 2)A 1992, s. 16(4).
Para. 8(4)	VATA 1983, s. 3 and Sch. 2, para. 7(3).
Para. 9	VATA 1983, s. 3 and Sch. 2, para. 8, as inserted by FA 1989, s. 18 and Sch. 3, para. 11(c).

Schedule 5	
Para. 1	VATA 1983, s. 7 and Sch. 3, para. 1.
Para. 2	VATA 1983, s. 7 and Sch. 3, para. 2.
Para. 3	VATA 1983, s. 7 and Sch. 3, para. 3.

Schedule 5	Derivation
Para. 4	VATA 1983, s. 7 and Sch. 3, para. 4.
Para. 5	VATA 1983, s. 7 and Sch. 3, para. 5.
Para. 6	VATA 1983, s. 7 and Sch. 3, para. 6.
Para. 7	VATA 1983, s. 7 and Sch. 3, para. 6A, as added by SI 1985/799.
Para. 8	VATA 1983, s. 7 and Sch. 3, para. 7, as amended by SI 1985/799.
Para. 9	VATA 1983, s. 7 and Sch. 3, para. 8, as added by SI 1992/3128, art. 2 and as substituted by SI 1993/2328, art. 3.
Para. 10	SI 1993/2328, art. 4.

Schedule 6

Para. 1	VATA 1983, s. 10(6), 11(4) and Sch. 4, para. 1, as amended by FA 1987, s. 17(1).
Para. 2	VATA 1983, s. 10(6), 11(4) and Sch. 4, para. 3.
Para. 3	VATA 1983, s. 10(6), 11(4) and Sch. 4, para. 3A, as inserted by F(No. 2)A 1992, s. 14 and Sch. 3, para. 61(2), as amended by FA 1993, s. 50(2), 213 and Sch. 23.
Para. 4	VATA 1983, s. 10(6), 11(4) and Sch. 4, para. 4
Para. 5	VATA 1983, s. 10(6), 11(4) and Sch. 4, para. 6.
Para. 6	VATA 1983, s. 10(6), 11(4) and Sch. 4, para. 7, as amended by F(No. 2)A 1992, s. 14 and Sch. 3, para. 61(3).
Para. 7	VATA 1983, s. 10(6), 11(4) and Sch. 4, para. 8.
Para. 8	VATA 1983, s. 10(6), 11(4) and Sch. 4, para. 8A, as inserted by F(No. 2)A 1992, s. 14 and Sch. 3, para. 61(4).
Para. 9	VATA 1983, s. 10(6), 11(4) and Sch. 4, para. 9, as amended by FA 1986, s. 11 and FA 1989, s. 18 and Sch. 3, para. 4(2).
Para. 10	VATA 1983, s. 10(6), 11(4) and Sch. 4, para. 10.
Para. 11	VATA 1983, s. 10(6), 11(4) and Sch. 4, para. 11, as substituted by F(No. 2)A 1992, s. 14 and Sch. 3, para. 61(5).
Para. 12	VATA 1983, s. 10(6), 11(4) and Sch. 4, para. 12.
Para. 13	VATA 1983, s. 10(6), 11(4) and Sch. 4, para. 13.

Schedule 7

Para. 1	VATA 1983, s.10A and Sch. 4A, para. 1, as inserted by F(No. 2)A 1992, s. 14 and Sch. 3, para. 62.
Para. 2	VATA 1983, s. 10A and Sch. 4A, para. 2, as inserted by F(No. 2)A 1992, s. 14 and Sch. 3, para. 62.
Para. 3	VATA 1983, s. 10A and Sch. 4A, para. 3, as inserted by F(No. 2)A 1992, s. 14 and Sch. 3, para. 62.
Para. 4	VATA 1983, s. 10A and Sch. 4A, para. 4, as inserted by F(No. 2)A 1992, s. 14 and Sch. 3, para. 62.
Para. 5	VATA 1983, s. 10A and Sch. 4A, para. 5, as inserted by F(No. 2)A 1992, s. 14 and Sch. 3, para. 62.

Schedule 8

Grp. 1	VATA 1983, s. 16 and Sch. 5, Grp. 1, as amended by FA 1984, s. 10 and Sch. 6, para. 1, SI 1988/507, SI 1986/530, SI 1992/628 and SI 1993/2498.
Grp. 2	VATA 1983, s. 16 and Sch. 5, Grp. 2, as amended by FA 1989, s. 19.
Grp. 3	VATA 1983, s. 16 and Sch. 5, Grp. 3.
Grp. 4	VATA 1983, s. 16 and Sch. 5, Grp. 4, as amended by SI 1986/530 and SI 1992/628.
Grp. 5	VATA 1983, s. 16 and Sch. 5, Grp. 8, as substituted by FA 1989, s. 18 and Sch. 3, para. 1, and as amended by SI 1990/2553, art. 2.
Grp. 6, item 1	VATA 1983, s. 16 and Sch. 5, Grp. 8A, item 1, as inserted by FA 1984, s. 10 and Sch. 6, para. 8, as amended by FA 1989, s. 18 and Sch. 3, para. 2(2).
Grp. 6, item 2	VATA 1983, s. 16 and Sch. 5, Grp. 8A, item 2, as inserted by FA 1984, s. 10 and Sch. 6, para. 8.
Grp. 6, Note (1) ...	VATA 1983, s. 16 and Sch. 5, Grp. 8A, Note (1), as inserted by FA 1984, s. 10 and Sch. 6, para. 8, as amended by FA 1989, s. 18 and Sch. 3, para. 2(3) and the Planning (Consequential Provisions) Act 1990, s. 4 and Sch. 2, para. 61.
Grp. 6, Note (2) ...	VATA 1983, s. 16 and Sch. 5, Grp. 8A, Note (1A), as inserted by FA 1989, s. 18 and Sch. 3, para. 2(4).

Schedule 8	Derivation
Grp. 6, Note (3) ...	VATA 1983, s. 16 and Sch. 5, Grp. 8A, Note (2), as inserted by FA 1984, s. 10 and Sch. 6, para. 8, as amended by SI 1985/18.
Grp. 6, Note (4) ...	VATA 1983, s. 16 and Sch. 5, Grp. 8A, Note (3), as inserted by FA 1984, s. 10 and Sch. 6, para. 8, as amended by the Planning (Consequential Provisions) Act 1990, s. 4 and Sch. 2, para. 61 and the Planning (Northern Ireland) Order 1991.
Grp. 6, Note (5) ...	VATA 1983, s. 16 and Sch. 5, Grp. 8A, Note (4), as inserted by FA 1984, s. 10 and Sch. 6, para. 8.
Grp. 6, Note (6) ...	VATA 1983, s. 16 and Sch. 5, Grp. 8A, Note (6), as inserted by FA 1984, s. 10 and Sch. 6, para. 8.
Grp. 6, Note (7) ...	VATA 1983, s. 16 and Sch. 5, Grp. 8A, Note (6A), as inserted by FA 1989, s. 18 and Sch. 3, para. 2(6).
Grp. 6, Note (8) ...	VATA 1983, s. 16 and Sch. 5, Grp. 8A, Note (7), as substituted by FA 1989, s. 18 and Sch. 3, para. 2(7).
Grp. 7	VATA 1983, s. 16 and Sch. 5, Grp. 9, as substituted by SI 1992/3223, art. 2.
Grp. 8, items 1, 2	VATA 1983, s. 16 and Sch. 5, Grp. 10, items 1, 2.
Grp. 8, item 3	VATA 1983, s. 16 and Sch. 5, Grp. 10, item 3, as amended by SI 1984/631, SI 1990/752, art. 3(a) and (b) and SI 1992/628, art. 3.
Grp. 8, item 4	VATA 1983, s. 16 and Sch. 5, Grp. 10, item 4, as amended by SI 1990/752, art. 4.
Grp. 8, item 5	VATA 1983, s. 16 and Sch. 5, Grp. 10, item 5, as substituted by SI 1992/3223, art. 3(a).
Grp. 8, item 6	VATA 1983, s. 16 and Sch. 5, Grp. 10, item 6, as amended by SI 1990/752, art. 6.
Grp. 8, items 7, 8	VATA 1983, s. 16 and Sch. 5, Grp. 10, items 7, 8.
Grp. 8, item 9	VATA 1983, s. 16 and Sch. 5, Grp. 10, item 9, as amended by SI 1990/752, art. 7.
Grp. 8, item 10	VATA 1983, s. 16 and Sch. 5, Grp. 10, item 10, as amended by SI 1992/3223, art. 3(b).
Grp. 8, item 11	VATA 1983, s. 16 and Sch. 5, Grp. 10, item 12, as substituted by SI 1992/3223, art. 3(d).
Grp. 8, item 12	VATA 1983, s. 16 and Sch. 5, Grp. 10, item 13, as inserted by SI 1987/1806, art. 11(1).
Grp. 8, item 13	VATA 1983, s. 16 and Sch. 5, Grp. 10, item 14, as added by SI 1992/3126, art. 2(a).
Grp. 8, Note (1) ...	VATA 1983, s. 16 and Sch. 5, Grp. 10, Note (1), as substituted by SI 1990/752, art. 9.
Grp. 8, Note (2) ...	VATA 1983, s. 16 and Sch. 5, Grp. 10, Note (2), as amended by SI 1984/631.
Grp. 8, Note (3) ...	VATA 1983, s. 16 and Sch. 5, Grp. 10, Note (2A), as inserted by SI 1990/752, art. 10.
Grp. 8, Note (4) ...	VATA 1983, s. 16 and Sch. 5, Grp. 10, Note (3), as substituted by SI 1990/752, art. 11.
Grp. 8, Notes (5)– (7)	VATA 1983, s. 16 and Sch. 5, Grp. 10, Notes (4)–(6).
Grp. 8, Note (8) ...	VATA 1983, s. 16 and Sch. 5, Grp. 10, Note (7), as inserted by SI 1987/1806, art. 11(2).
Grp. 8, Note (9) ...	VATA 1983, s. 16 and Sch. 5, Grp. 10, Note (8), as added by SI 1992/3126, art. 2(b).
Grp. 9	VATA 1983, s. 16 and Sch. 5, Grp. 11, as amended by FA 1989, s. 18 and Sch. 3, para. 3.
Grp. 10	VATA 1983, s. 16 and Sch. 5, Grp. 12.
Grp. 11	VATA 1983, s. 16 and Sch. 5, Grp. 13.
Grp. 12, item 1	VATA 1983, s. 16 and Sch. 5, Grp. 14, item 1.
Grp. 12, item 2	VATA 1983, s. 16 and Sch. 5, Grp. 14, item 2, as amended by SI 1984/489, art. 4 and SI 1992/628, art. 4(a).
Grp. 12, item 3	VATA 1983, s. 16 and Sch. 5, Grp. 14, item 3.
Grp. 12, item 4	VATA 1983, s. 16 and Sch. 5, Grp. 14, item 4, as amended by SI 1984/489, art. 5.
Grp. 12, item 5	VATA 1983, s. 16 and Sch. 5, Grp. 14, item 5, as substituted by SI 1986/530, art. 3(a).
Grp. 12, items 6–9	VATA 1983, s. 16 and Sch. 5, Grp. 14, items 6–9.

Schedule 8	Derivation
Grp. 15, Note (4)	VATA 1983, s. 16 and Sch. 5, Grp. 16, Note (5), as amended by SI 1983/1717 and SI 1990/2129.
Grp. 15, Notes (5)– (8)	VATA 1983, s. 16 and Sch. 5, Grp. 16, Notes (6)–(9).
Grp. 15, Notes (9), (10)	VATA 1983, s. 16 and Sch. 5, Grp. 16, Notes (10), (11), as inserted by SI 1983/1717.
Grp. 15, Note (11)	VATA 1983, s. 16 and Sch. 5, Grp. 16, Note (12), as inserted by SI 1986/530, as amended by SI 1987/437.
Grp. 15, Note (12)	VATA 1983, s. 16 and Sch. 5, Grp. 16, Note (13), as inserted by SI 1987/437.
Grp. 16	VATA 1983, s. 16 and Sch. 5, Grp. 17, as amended by FA 1989, s. 22 and SI 1993/767.
Schedule 9	
Grp. 1, item 1	VATA 1983, s. 8, 17 and Sch. 6, Grp. 1, item 1, para. (a), as substituted by FA 1989, s. 18 and Sch. 3, para. 4(1), as amended by SI 1991/2569, art. 2(a).
Grp. 1, item 1, para. (a)	VATA 1983, s. 8, 17 and Sch. 6, Grp. 1, item 1, para. (a), as substituted by FA 1989, s. 18 and Sch. 3, para. 4(1).
Grp. 1, item 1, para. (b)	VATA 1983, s. 8, 17 and Sch. 6, Grp. 1, item 1, para. (aa), as inserted by SI 1991/2569, art. 2(b).
Grp. 1, item 1, para. (c)	VATA 1983, s. 8, 17 and Sch. 6, Grp. 1, item 1, para. (b), as substituted by FA 1989, s. 18 and Sch. 3, para. 4(1), as amended by SI 1991/2569, art. 2(c).
Grp. 1, item 1, para. (d)	VATA 1983, s. 8, 17 and Sch. 6, Grp. 1, item 1, para. (c), as substituted by FA 1989, s. 18 and Sch. 3, para. 4(1).
Grp. 1, item 1, para. (e)	VATA 1983, s. 8, 17 and Sch. 6, Grp. 1, item 1, para. (d), as substituted by SI 1990/2553, art. 3(a).
Grp. 1, item 1, para. (f)–(m)	VATA 1983, s. 8, 17 and Sch. 6, Grp. 1, item 1, para. (g)–(k), as substituted by FA 1989, s. 18 and Sch. 3, para. 4(1).
Grp. 1, item 1, para. (n)	VATA 1983, s. 8, 17 and Sch. 6, Grp. 1, item 1, para. (l), as inserted by SI 1991/2569, art. 2(d).
Grp. 1, Notes (1)– (6)	VATA 1983, s. 8, 17 and Sch. 6, Grp. 1, Notes (1)–(6), as substituted by FA 1989, s. 18 and Sch. 3, para. 4(1).
Grp. 1, Note (7) ...	VATA 1983, s. 8, 17 and Sch. 6, Grp. 1, Note (6A), as inserted by SI 1991/2569, art. 2(e).
Grp. 1, Notes (8)– (10)	VATA 1983, s. 8, 17 and Sch. 6, Grp. 1, Notes (7)–(9), as substituted by FA 1989, s. 18 and Sch. 3, para. 4(1).
Grp. 1, Note (11)	VATA 1983, s. 8, 17 and Sch. 6, Grp. 1, Note (10), as substituted by SI 1990/2553, art. 3.
Grp. 1, Notes (12), (13)	VATA 1983, s. 8, 17 and Sch. 6, Grp. 1, Notes (10A), (10B), as inserted by SI 1990/2553, art. 3.
Grp. 1, Notes (14)– (16)	VATA 1983, s. 8, 17 and Sch. 6, Grp. 1, Note (11)–(13), as substituted by FA 1989, s. 18 and Sch. 3, para. 4(1).
Grp. 2	VATA 1983, s. 8, 17 and Sch. 6, Grp. 2, as amended by SI 1990/2037.
Grp. 3	VATA 1983, s. 8, 17 and Sch. 6, Grp. 3.
Grp. 4	VATA 1983, s. 8, 17 and Sch. 6, Grp. 4, items 1, 2, Notes (1), (2), (4), as amended by SI 1987/517.

Schedule 9	Derivation

Grp. 5, items 1–4
.... VATA 1983, s. 8, 17 and Sch. 6, Grp. 5, items 1–4.

Grp. 5, item 5 ..... VATA 1983, s. 8, 17 and Sch. 6, Grp. 5, item 5, as amended by FA 1987, s. 18(1)(a).

Grp. 5, item 6 ..... VATA 1983, s. 8, 17 and Sch. 6, Grp. 5, item 6, as substituted by SI 1987/860.

Grp. 5, item 7 ..... VATA 1983, s. 8, 17 and Sch. 6, Grp. 5, item 6A, as substituted by SI 1989/2272, art. 2(2).

Grp. 5, item 8 ..... VATA 1983, s. 8, 17 and Sch. 6, Grp. 5, item 7.

Grp. 5, item 9 ..... VATA 1983, s. 8, 17 and Sch. 6, Grp. 5, item 8, as inserted by SI 1989/2272, art. 2(3).

Grp. 5, Notes (1)–
(3) .... VATA 1983, s. 8, 17 and Sch. 6, Grp. 5, Notes (1)–(3).

Grp. 5, Note (4) ... VATA 1983, s. 8, 17 and Sch. 6, Grp. 5, Note (4), as inserted by SI 1985/432.

Grp. 5, Notes (5),
(6) .... VATA 1983, s. 8, 17 and Sch. 6, Grp. 5, Notes (5), (6), as inserted by SI 1985/2272, art. 2(4).

Grp. 6 .... VATA 1983, s. 8, 17 and Sch. 6, Grp. 6, as substituted by SI 1994/1188.

Grp. 7, item 1 ..... VATA 1983, s. 8, 17 and Sch. 6, Grp. 7, item 1, as substituted by FA 1988, s. 13(2), as amended by Opticians Act 1989, s. 37(3).

Grp. 7, item 2 ..... VATA 1983, s. 8, 17 and Sch. 6, Grp. 7, item 2, as substituted by FA 1988, s. 13(2).

Grp. 7, items 3–8
.... VATA 1983, s. 8, 17 and Sch. 6, Grp. 7, items 3–8.

Grp. 7, items 9–10
.... VATA 1983, s. 8, 17 and Sch. 6, Grp. 7, items 9–10, as inserted by SI 1985/1900.

Grp. 7, item 11 .... VATA 1983, s. 8, 17 and Sch. 6, Grp. 7, item 11, as inserted by SI 1989/2272, art. 3.

Grp. 7, Note (1) ... VATA 1983, s. 8, 17 and Sch. 6, Grp. 7, Note (1).

Grp. 7, Note (2) ... VATA 1983, s. 8, 17 and Sch. 6, Grp. 7, Note (2), as amended by FA 1988, s. 13(3).

Grp. 7, Notes (3),
(4) .... VATA 1983, s. 8, 17 and Sch. 6, Grp. 7, Notes (3), (4).

Grp. 7, Notes (5)–
(7) .... VATA 1983, s. 8, 17 and Sch. 6, Grp. 7, Notes (5)–(7), as inserted by SI 1985/1900.

Grp. 8 .... VATA 1983, s. 8, 17 and Sch. 6, Grp. 8.

Grp. 9 .... VATA 1983, s. 8, 17 and Sch. 6, Grp. 9, as amended by Trade Union and Labour Relations (Consolidation) Act 1992, s. 300(2) and Sch. 2, para. 32.

Grp. 10, items 1, 2
.... VATA 1983, s. 8, 17 and Sch. 6, Grp. 10, items 1, 2.

Grp. 10, item 3 .... VATA 1983, s. 8, 17 and Sch. 6, Grp. 10, item 3, as inserted by SI 1994/687, art. 2(b).

Grp. 10, Notes (1)–
(3) .... VATA 1983, s. 8, 17 and Sch. 6, Grp. 10, Notes (1)–(3), as substituted by SI 1994/687, art. 2(c).

Grp. 11 .... VATA 1983, s. 8, 17 and Sch. 6, Grp. 11, as amended by IHTA 1984, s. 276 and Sch. 8, para. 24, FA 1985, Sch. 26, para. 14, FA 1986, s. 100 and TCGA 1992, s. 290 and Sch. 10, para. 6.

Grp. 12, items 1, 2
.... VATA 1983, s. 8, 17 and Sch. 6, Grp. 12, items 1, 2, as inserted by SI 1989/470.

Grp. 12, Note (1)
.... VATA 1983, s. 8, 17 and Sch. 6, Grp. 12, Note (1), as inserted by SI 1989/470.

Grp. 12, Note (2)
.... VATA 1983, s. 8, 17 and Sch. 6, Grp. 12, Note (1A), as inserted by SI 1991/737, art. 9.

Grp. 12, Note (3)
.... VATA 1983, s. 8, 17 and Sch. 6, Grp. 12, Note (2), as substituted by SI 1994/687, art. 3.

Schedule 10

Para. 1 .... VATA 1983, s. 35A and Sch. 6A, as inserted by FA 1989, s. 18 and Sch. 3, para. 6.

Para. 2(1)–(7) ...... VATA 1983, s. 35A and Sch. 6A, para. 2(1)–(7), as inserted by FA 1989, s. 18 and Sch. 3, para. 6.

Para. 2(8), (9) ...... VATA 1983, s. 35A and Sch. 6A, para. 2(8), (9), as inserted by SI 1991/2569, art. 3.

Para. 3(1)–(6) ...... VATA 1983, s. 35A and Sch. 6A, para. 3(1)–(6), as inserted by FA 1989, s. 18 and Sch. 3, para. 6, as amended by SI 1991/2569, art. 4(a) and (b).

Para. 3(7), (8) ...... VATA 1983, s. 35A and Sch. 6A, para. 3(8), (9), as inserted by FA 1989, s. 18 and Sch. 3, para. 6.

Para. 3(9) .... VATA 1983, s. 35A and Sch. 6A, para. 3(10), as inserted by SI 1991/2569, art. 4(d).

Para. 4 .... VATA 1983, s. 35A and Sch. 6A, para. 4, as inserted by SI 1991/2569.

Para. 5(1)–(7) ...... VATA 1983, s. 35A and Sch. 6A, para. 5, as inserted by FA 1989, s. 18 and Sch. 3, para. 6.

Para. 5(8)–(10) ..... VATA 1983, s. 35A and Sch. 6A, para. 5(8)–(10), as inserted by SI 1991/2569, art. 5.

Para. 6(1) .... VATA 1983, s. 35A and Sch. 6A, para. 6(1), as inserted by FA 1989, s. 18 and Sch. 3, para. 6.

Para. 6(2) .... VATA 1983, s. 35A and Sch. 6A, para. 6(2), as inserted by FA 1989, s. 18 and Sch. 3, para. 6 and as amended by SI 1991/2569, art. 6(a).

Para. 6(3), (4) ...... VATA 1983, s. 35A and Sch. 6A, para. 6(2A), (2B), as inserted by SI 1991/2569, art. 6(b).

Para. 6(5) .... VATA 1983, s. 35A and Sch. 6A, para. 6(3), as inserted by FA 1989, s. 18 and Sch. 3, para. 6.

Para. 6(6)–(8) ...... VATA 1983, s. 35A and Sch. 6A, para. 6(4)–(6), as inserted by SI 1991/2569, art. 6(c).

Para. 7 .... VATA 1983, s. 35A and Sch. 6A, para. 6A, as inserted by SI 1991/2569, art. 7.

Para. 8 .... VATA 1983, s. 35A and Sch. 6A, para. 7, as inserted by FA 1989, s. 18 and Sch. 3, para. 6.

Para. 9 .... VATA 1983, s. 35A and Sch. 6A, para. 8, as inserted by FA 1989, s. 18 and Sch. 3, para. 6 and as amended by SI 1991/2569.

Schedule 11

Para. 1 .... VATA 1983, s. 38 and Sch. 7, para. 1.

Para. 2(1), (2) ...... VATA 1983, s. 38 and Sch. 7, para. 2(1), (2), as amended by F(No. 2)A 1992, s. 14 and Sch. 3, para. 64.

Para. 2(3) .... VATA 1983, s. 38 and Sch. 7, para. 2(2A), as inserted by F(No. 2)A 1992, s. 14 and Sch. 3, para. 64.

Para. 2(4) .... VATA 1983, s. 38 and Sch. 7, para. 2(2B), as inserted by F(No. 2)A 1992, s. 14 and Sch. 3, para. 64.

Para. 2(5) .... VATA 1983, s. 38 and Sch. 7, para. 2(2C), as inserted by F(No. 2)A 1992, s. 14 and Sch. 3, para. 64.

Para. 2(6) .... VATA 1983, s. 38 and Sch. 7, para. 2(3).

Para. 2(7) .... VATA 1983, s. 38 and Sch. 7, para. 2(3A), as inserted by FA 1987, s. 11(2).

Para. 2(8), (9) ...... VATA 1983, s. 38 and Sch. 7, para. 2(3B), (3C), as inserted by F(No. 2)A 1992, s. 14 and Sch. 3, para. 64, and as amended by FA 1993, s. 50(4), s. 213 and Sch. 23, Pt. II(5).

Para. 2(10) .... VATA 1983, s. 38 and Sch. 7, para. 2(4), as amended by FA 1989, s. 25(2).

Para. 2(11) .... VATA 1983, s. 38 and Sch. 7, para. 2(5), as amended by FA 1989, s. 25(2).

Para. 2(12) .... VATA 1983, s. 38 and Sch. 7, para. 2(6), as amended by FA 1989, s. 25(2).

Para. 2(13) .... VATA 1983, s. 38 and Sch. 7, para. 2(7), as amended by FA 1989, s. 25(2).

Para. 3(1) .... VATA 1983, s. 38 and Sch. 7, para. 3(1).

Para. 3(2) .... VATA 1983, s. 38 and Sch. 7, para. 3(2).

Para. 3(3) .... VATA 1983, s. 38 and Sch. 7, para. (2A), as amended by F(No. 2)A 1992, s. 14 and Sch. 3, para. 65.

Para. 4 .... VATA 1983, s. 38 and Sch. 7, para. 5, as amended by F(No. 2)A 1992, s. 14 and Sch. 3, para. 68.

Para. 5 .... VATA 1983, s. 38 and Sch. 7, para. 6, as amended by FA 1984, s. 16, Debtors (Scotland) Act 1987, s. 74(1) and Sch. 4, para. 4 and F(No. 2)A 1992, s. 14 and Sch. 3, para. 69.

Schedule 12	Derivation
Para. 7(7)	VATA 1983, s. 40 and Sch. 8, para. 7(3E), as inserted by FA 1985, s. 30 and Sch. 8, para. 5.
Para. 7(8)	VATA 1983, s. 40 and Sch. 8, para. 7(4), as amended by FA 1985, s. 30 and Sch. 8, para. 5(3).
Para. 7(9)	VATA 1983, s. 40 and Sch. 8, para. 7(4A), as inserted by Judicial Pensions and Retirement Act 1993, s. 31 and Sch. 8, para. 16(2).
Para. 7(10)	VATA 1983, s. 40 and Sch. 8, para. 7(5), as amended by FA 1985, s. 30 and Sch. 8, para. 5.
Para. 8	VATA 1983, s. 40 and Sch. 8, para. 8.
Para. 9	VATA 1983, s. 40 and Sch. 8, para. 9 and FA 1985, s. 27(3).
Para. 9(a)–(d)	VATA 1983, s. 40 and Sch. 8, para. 9(a)–(d).
Para. 9(e)	VATA 1983, s. 40 and Sch. 8, para. 9(dd), as inserted by FA 1985, s. 27(2).
Para. 9(f)–(h)	VATA 1983, s. 40 and Sch. 8, para. 9(e)–(g), as amended by FA 1985, s. 27(2).
Para. 9(j)	FA 1986, s. 14(7).
Para. 10	VATA 1983, s. 40 and Sch. 8, para. 10.

Schedule 13	
Para. 1–6	(Transitional provisions and savings).
Para. 7(1), (2)	FA 1993, s. 42(2), (3).
Para. 7(3)	VATA 1983, Sch. 5, Grp. 7, as substituted by FA 1989, s. 21 and amended by SI 1991/2534, art. 2(2), F(No. 2)A 1992, s. 17(1), 82 and Sch. 18, Pt. V(2).
Para. 8	FA 1989, s. 18 and Sch. 3, para. 13(1).
Para. 9	VATA 1983, s. 22.
Para. 10	FA 1989, s. 18 and Sch. 3, para. 13(6), (7).
Para. 11	(Transitional provision).
Para. 12, 13	FA 1985, s. 12(1).
Para. 14	FA 1993, s. 49 and Sch. 2, para. 5(3), 6(4).
Para. 15(1), (2)	FA 1992, s. 7(3)–(5).
Para. 15(3)	FA 1993, s. 49 and Sch. 2, para. 1(4).
Para. 15(4)	FA 1994, s. 45(4).
Para. 16	FA 1993, s. 49 and Sch. 2, para. 2(5), (6).
Para. 17	FA 1993, s. 49 and Sch. 2, para. 3(3).
Para. 18	FA 1985, s. 18(10), FA 1993, s. 49 and Sch. 2, para. 4(3).
Para. 19	(Transitional provision).
Para. 20	FA 1990, s. 15(2) and FA 1982, s. 17(4).
Para. 21	FA 1994, s. 47(2).
Para. 22(1)	(Transitional provision).
Para. 22(2)	FA 1994, s. 19(1).
Para. 23	VATA 1983, s. 50 and Sch. 10, para. 18.

TABLE OF DERIVATIONS
VALUE ADDED TAX REGULATIONS 1995 (SI 1995/2518)

The consolidated table below, prepared by CCH Editorial staff, relates the provisions of the *Value Added Tax Regulations* 1995 (SI 1995/2518) to the provisions of the *Value Added Tax (General) Regulations* 1985 (SI 1985/886) and other ancillary statutory instruments (in the right-hand column).

Regulation	Derivation
reg. 1	SI 1985/886, reg. 1
reg. 2(1)	SI 1985/886, reg. 2(1), as amended by SI 1992/3102, reg. 3, SI 1993/1941, reg. 3 and SI 1995/152, reg. 3
reg. 2(2)	None
reg. 2(3)	SI 1985/886, reg. 2(2)
reg. 3	SI 1985/886, reg. 3
reg. 4	SI 1985/886, reg. 67
reg. 5	SI 1985/886, reg. 4(1)–(3), as substituted by SI 1992/3102, reg. 4(a)
reg. 6(1), (2)	SI 1985/886, reg. 4(4), (5), as substituted by SI 1992/3102, reg. 4(a)
reg. 6(3)	SI 1985/886, reg. 4(7), as amended by SI 1992/3102, reg. 4(b)
reg. 6(4)	SI 1985/886, reg. 4(8)
reg. 7	SI 1985/886, reg. 9
reg. 8	SI 1985/886, reg. 10
reg. 9(1), (2)	SI 1985/886, reg. 11(1), (2)
reg. 9(3)	SI 1985/886, reg. 11(3), as inserted by SI 1985/1650, reg. 7
reg. 10	SI 1985/886, reg. 10A, as inserted by SI 1992/3102, reg. 6
reg. 11	SI 1985/886, reg. 10B, as substituted by SI 1993/1941, reg. 4
reg. 12	SI 1985/886, reg. 10C, as inserted by SI 1993/1941, reg. 5
reg. 13	SI 1985/886, reg. 12, as substituted by SI 1992/3120, reg. 8
reg. 14(1)–(4)	SI 1985/886, reg. 13(1)–(4), as substituted by SI 1992/3102, reg. 9
reg. 14(5)	SI 1985/886, reg. 13(5), as inserted by SI 1993/856, reg. 3
reg. 15	SI 1985/886, reg. 14
reg. 16(1)	SI 1985/886, reg. 15(1), as substituted by SI 1992/3102, reg. 10
reg. 16(2)	SI 1985/886, reg. 15(2)
reg. 17	SI 1985/886, reg. 15A, as inserted by SI 1993/1941, reg. 8
reg. 18	SI 1985/886, reg. 15B, as inserted by SI 1993/1941, reg. 8
reg. 19	SI 1985/886, reg. 15C, as inserted by SI 1993/1941, reg. 8
reg. 20	SI 1985/886, reg. 16, as substituted by SI 1992/3102, reg. 11 and amended by SI 1993/1941, reg. 9
reg. 21	SI 1992/3096, reg. 1(2)
reg. 22(1)–(4)	SI 1992/3096, reg. 2(1)–(4)
reg. 22(5)	(None)
reg. 22(6)	SI 1985/886, reg. 2(5)
reg. 23	SI 1992/3096, reg. 3
reg. 24	SI 1989/2248, reg. 1(2) and SI 1992/3101, reg. 2
reg. 25(1), (2)	SI 1985/886, reg. 58(1), (2)
reg. 25(3)	SI 1985/886, reg. 58(3), as substituted by SI 1987/1916, reg. 9(a)
reg. 25(4)	SI 1985/886, reg. 58(4), as amended by SI 1986/71, and SI 1988/2108, reg. 7
reg. 25(5)	SI 1985/886, reg. 58(5)
reg. 26	SI 1985/886, reg. 58(A), as inserted by SI 1992/3102, reg. 45
reg. 27	SI 1985/886, reg. 59
reg. 28	SI 1985/886, reg. 61
reg. 29(1)	SI 1985/886, reg. 62(1), as substituted by SI 1987/1916, reg. 10
reg. 29(2)	SI 1985/886, reg. 62(1A), as substituted by SI 1992/3102, reg. 47
reg. 29(3)	SI 1985/886, reg. 62(2)
reg. 30	SI 1985/886, reg. 63
reg. 31(1), (2)	SI 1989/2248, reg. 2(1), (2), as amended by SI 1992/3097, reg. 3
reg. 31(3)	SI 1989/2248, reg. 2A, as inserted by SI 1992/3097, reg. 4
reg. 32(1), (2)	SI 1989/2248, reg. 4(1), (2)
reg. 32(3), (4)	SI 1989/2248, reg. 4(3), 4(4), as amended by SI 1992/3097, reg. 6

Regulation	Derivation
reg. 33	SI 1989/2248, reg. 4(A), as inserted by SI 1992/3097, reg. 7
reg. 34(1), (2)	SI 1989/2248, reg. 5(1), (2)
reg. 34(3)	SI 1989/2248, reg. 5(3), as amended by SI 1994/803, reg. 2 and SI 1993/761
reg. 34(4)–(7)	SI 1989/2248, reg. 5(4)–(7)
reg. 35	SI 1985/886, reg. 64
reg. 36	SI 1985/886, reg. 64C, as inserted by SI 1992/3102, reg. 48
reg. 37	SI 1989/2248, reg. 6
reg. 38	SI 1989/2248, reg. 7
reg. 39(1)	SI 1989/2248, reg. 8(1)
reg. 39(2)	SI 1989/2248, reg. 8(2), as amended by SI 1992/3097, reg. 8
reg. 39(3), (4)	SI 1989/2248, reg. 8(3), (4)
reg. 40	SI 1985/886, reg. 60
reg. 41(1)	SI 1985/886, reg. 60A, as inserted by SI 1992/3102, reg. 46
reg. 41(2), (3)	SI 1985/886, reg. 58ZA, as inserted by SI 1995/1069, reg. 4
reg. 42	SI 1992/3101, reg. 3
reg. 43	(None)
reg. 44	SI 1992/1844, reg. 2, 7(1)
reg. 45	SI 1992/1844, reg. 4
reg. 46	SI 1992/1844, reg. 5
reg. 47	SI 1992/1844, reg. 6
reg. 48	SI 1992/1844, reg. 7(2)–(4)
reg. 49	SI 1988/886, reg. 2
reg. 50	SI 1988/886, reg. 3, as amended by SI 1991/532, reg. 3
reg. 51(1)	SI 1988/886, reg. 4(1), as amended by SI 1991/532, reg. 4(a), 5
reg. 51(2)	SI 1988/886, reg. 4(2)
reg. 52(1)	SI 1988/886, reg. 5(1)
reg. 52(2)	SI 1988/886, reg. 5(2), as amended by SI 1991/532, reg. 4(b), 6(a), (b)
reg. 53	SI 1988/886, reg. 6
reg. 54	SI 1988/886, reg. 7
reg. 55(1)	SI 1988/886, reg. 8(1), as amended by SI 1991/532, reg. 7
reg. 55(2)	SI 1988/886, reg. 8(2)
reg. 56	SI 1987/1427, reg. 2, as amended by SI 1993/762, reg. 3
reg. 57	SI 1987/1427, reg. 3, as amended by SI 1993/762, reg. 4
reg. 58(1), opening words	SI 1987/1427, reg. 4(1), as amended by SI 1993/762, reg. 5(a)
reg. 58(1)(a)	SI 1987/1427, reg. 4(1)(a), as substituted by SI 1993/762, reg. 5(b)
reg. 58(1)(b)	SI 1987/1427, reg. 4(1)(b), as substituted by SI 1990/420, reg. 3 and SI 1993/3028, reg. 3(a)
reg. 58(1)(c)	SI 1987/1427, reg. 4(1)(c), as amended by SI 1993/762, reg. 5(c), 5(d) and SI 1993/3028, reg. 3(b)
reg. 58(2)	SI 1987/1427, reg. 4(3)
reg. 59	SI 1987/1427, reg. 5
reg. 60(1)	SI 1987/1427, reg. 6(1), as substituted by SI 1993/762, reg. 6(a)
reg. 60(2)	SI 1987/1427, reg. 6(2), as substituted by SI 1993/3028, reg. 4
reg. 60(3)	SI 1987/1427, reg. 6(3)
reg. 61	SI 1987/1427, reg. 7, as amended by SI 1993/762, reg. 7
reg. 62	SI 1987/1427, reg. 8, as amended by SI 1993/3028, reg. 5 and SI 1993/762, reg. 8
reg. 63(1), (2)	SI 1987/1427, reg. 9(1), (2), as amended by SI 1993/762, reg. 8 and SI 1993/3028, reg. 5
reg. 63(3)	SI 1987/1427, reg. 9(3), as amended by SI 1993/762, reg. 8
reg. 64	SI 1987/1427, reg. 10(1), as amended by SI 1993/762, reg. 9(a)–(c), (e) and 9(l)
reg. 64(2)	SI 1987/1427, reg. 10(2), as amended by SI 1993/762, reg. 9(f)
reg. 64(3)	SI 1987/1427, reg. 10(3), as amended by SI 1993/762, reg. 9(g)
reg. 65(1), (2)	SI 1987/1427, reg. 12(1), (2)
reg. 65(3), (4)	SI 1987/1427, reg. 12(3), (4), as amended by SI 1992/762, reg. 10
reg. 66	SI 1972/1148, reg. 1(2), as amended by SI 1979/224
reg. 67(1)	SI 1972/1148, reg. 2(1)
reg. 67(2)	SI 1972/1148, reg. 2(2), as substituted by SI 1979/224
reg. 68	SI 1972/1148, reg. 3, as substituted by SI 1987/1712

Regulation	Derivation
reg. 69	SI 1972/1148, reg. 4
reg. 70	SI 1972/1148, reg. 5
reg. 71	SI 1972/1148, reg. 6
reg. 72	SI 1972/1148, reg. 7
reg. 73	SI 1972/1148, reg. 10
reg. 74	SI 1972/1148, reg. 8, as substituted by SI 1975/274
reg. 75	SI 1972/1148, reg. 9, as substituted by SI 1975/274
reg. 76	SI 1973/293, reg. 2(1)
reg. 77	SI 1973/293, reg. 3
reg. 78	SI 1973/293, reg. 4, as amended by FA 1977, s. 14 and Sch. 6, para. 28
reg. 79	SI 1973/293, reg. 5
reg. 80	SI 1973/293, reg. 6
reg. 81	SI 1985/886, reg. 17
reg. 82	SI 1985/886, reg. 18
reg. 83	SI 1985/886, reg. 18A, as inserted by SI 1992/3102, reg. 12
reg. 84	SI 1985/886, reg. 18B, as inserted by SI 1992/3102, reg. 12
reg. 85	SI 1985/886, reg. 19, as substituted by SI 1989/1132, reg. 2
reg. 86(1)	SI 1985/886, reg. 20(1), as substituted by SI 1989/1132, reg. 3 and amended by SI 1992/3102, reg. 13(a)
reg. 86(2)–(4)	SI 1985/886, reg. 20(2)–(4), as substituted by SI 1989/1132, reg. 3
reg. 86(5)	SI 1985/886, reg. 20(5), as added by SI 1992/3102, reg. 13(b)
reg. 87	SI 1985/886, reg. 20A, as inserted by SI 1992/3102, reg. 14
reg. 88	SI 1985/886, reg. 21, as amended by SI 1992/3102, reg. 15(a), (b)
reg. 89	SI 1985/886, reg. 22, as substituted by SI 1992/3102, reg. 16
reg. 90	SI 1985/886, reg. 23, as substituted by SI 1989/1132, reg. 5
reg. 91	SI 1985/886, reg. 24
reg. 92	SI 1985/886, reg. 25
reg. 93	SI 1985/886, reg. 26
reg. 94	SI 1985/886, reg. 27, as substituted by SI 1992/3102, reg. 17
reg. 95	SI 1985/886, reg. 28, as amended by SI 1993/3102, reg. 18
reg. 96	SI 1992/3099, reg. 2(3)
reg. 97	SI 1992/3099, reg. 2(1), (2)
reg. 98	SI 1985/886, reg. 9A, as substituted by SI 1993/1224
reg. 99(1)	SI 1985/886, reg. 29(1), as substituted by SI 1992/3102, reg. 19 and amended by SI 1993/1639, reg. 3
reg. 99(2)	SI 1985/886, reg. 29(1A), as substituted by SI 1992/3102, reg. 19
reg. 99(3)–(7)	SI 1985/886, reg. 29(2)–(6), as substituted in error by SI 1992/3102, reg. 19 and reinstated by SI 1993/119
reg. 100	SI 1985/886, reg. 29A, as inserted by SI 1993/1639, reg. 4
reg. 101(1)	SI 1985/886, reg. 30(1)
reg. 101(2)	SI 1985/886, reg. 30(2), as amended by SI 1992/3102, reg. 20(a) and SI 1995/1069, reg. 3(a)
reg. 101(3)	SI 1985/886, reg. 30(3), as amended by SI 1992/3102, reg. 20(b) and 20(c)
reg. 101(4)	SI 1985/886, reg. 30(4)
reg. 101(5)	SI 1985/886, reg. 30(2A), as inserted by SI 1995/1069, reg. 3(b)
reg. 102(1)	SI 1985/886, reg. 31(1), as amended by SI 1994/3015, reg. 3(a)
reg. 102(2)	SI 1985/886, reg. 31(1A), as inserted by SI 1994/3015, reg. 3(b)
reg. 102(3), (4)	SI 1985/886, reg. 31(2), (3)
reg. 103	SI 1985/886, reg. 32, as substituted by SI 1994/3015, reg. 4
reg. 104	SI 1985/886, reg. 32A
reg. 105(1)–(4)	SI 1985/886, reg. 33(1)–(4)
reg. 105(5)	SI 1985/886, reg. 33(5), as inserted by SI 1993/1639, reg. 6
reg. 106(1)	SI 1985/886, reg. 33A(1), as amended by SI 1994/3015, reg. 5
reg. 106(2)	SI 1985/886, reg. 33A(2)
reg. 107	SI 1985/886, reg. 34
reg. 108(1)	SI 1985/886, reg. 35(1)
reg. 108(2)	SI 1985/886, reg. 35(2), as amended by SI 1993/1639, reg. 7
reg. 108(3)	SI 1985/886, reg. 35(3)
reg. 109(1)	SI 1985/886, reg. 36(1)

Regulation	Derivation
reg. 109(2)	SI 1985/886, reg. 36(2), as amended by SI 1993/1639, reg. 7
reg. 109(3)	SI 1985/886, reg. 36(3)
reg. 110(1)	SI 1985/886, reg. 36A(1), as inserted by SI 1993/1639, reg. 8
reg. 110(2)	SI 1985/886, reg. 36A(2), as inserted by SI 1993/1639, reg. 8 and amended by SI 1994/3015, reg. 6
reg. 111(1)	SI 1985/886, reg. 37(1), as amended by SI 1992/3102, reg. 22
reg. 111(2)	SI 1985/886, reg. 37(2), as amended by SI 1992/3102, reg. 22
reg. 111(3)–(5)	SI 1985/886, reg. 37(3)–(5)
reg. 112(1)	SI 1985/886, reg. 37A(1), as inserted by SI 1989/2355, reg. 4 and amended by SI 1992/645, reg. 4
reg. 112(2)	SI 1985/886, reg. 37A(2), as inserted by SI 1989/2355, reg. 4
reg. 113	SI 1989/886, reg. 37B, as inserted by SI 1989/2355, reg. 4 and amended by SI 1992/3102, reg. 23
reg. 114(1)–(3)	SI 1985/886, reg. 37C(1)–(3), as inserted by SI 1989/2355, reg. 4
reg. 114(4)	SI 1985/886, reg. 37C(4), as inserted by SI 1989/2355, reg. 4 and amended by SI 1992/3102, reg. 24
reg. 114(5)–(7)	SI 1985/886, reg. 37C(5)–(7), as inserted by SI 1989/2355, reg. 4
reg. 115	SI 1985/886, reg. 37D, as inserted by SI 1989/2355, reg. 4
reg. 116(1)	SI 1985/886, reg. 37E(1), as substituted by SI 1992/645, reg. 5
reg. 116(2), (3)	SI 1985/886, reg. 37E(2), (3)
reg. 117(1)	SI 1985/886, reg. 38(1)
reg. 117(2)	SI 1985/886, reg. 38(3)
reg. 117(3)	SI 1985/886, reg. 38(5), as amended by SI 1992/3102, reg. 25
reg. 117(4)	SI 1985/886, reg. 38(6), as amended by SI 1992/3102, reg. 25
reg. 117(5)	SI 1985/886, reg. 38(8), as amended by SI 1995/913, reg. 3
reg. 117(6)	SI 1985/886, reg. 38(9)
reg. 117(7)	SI 1985/886, reg. 38(10)
reg. 117(8)	SI 1985/886, reg. 38(11), as amended by SI 1992/3102, reg. 25
reg. 117(9)	SI 1985/886, reg. 38(12), as amended by SI 1992/3102, reg. 25
reg. 117(10)	SI 1985/886, reg. 38(14), as substituted by SI 1995/152, reg. 4
reg. 118	SI 1985/886, reg. 39, as amended by SI 1992/3102, reg. 26
reg. 119	SI 1985/886, reg. 39B, as inserted by SI 1992/3102, reg. 27
reg. 120(1)	SI 1985/886, reg. 40(1), as substituted by SI 1992/3102, reg. 28 and as amended by SI 1993/3027, reg. 3(a)
reg. 120(2)	SI 1985/886, reg. 40(2), as substituted by SI 1992/3102, reg. 28 and SI 1993/3027, reg. 3(b)
reg. 120(3)	SI 1985/886, reg. 40(3), as substituted by SI 1992/3102, reg. 28
reg. 121	SI 1985/886, reg. 39A, as inserted by SI 1992/3102, reg. 27
reg. 122	SI 1985/886, reg. 41, as amended by SI 1992/3102, reg. 29
reg. 123	SI 1985/886, reg. 42, as substituted by SI 1992/3102, reg. 30
reg. 124	SI 1985/886, reg. 45, as substituted by SI 1992/3102, reg. 32
reg. 125	SI 1985/886, reg. 46, as substituted by SI 1992/3102, reg. 33
reg. 126	SI 1985/886, reg. 48, as amended by SI 1992/3102, reg. 35
reg. 127	SI 1985/886, reg. 49, as amended by SI 1992/3102, reg. 36
reg. 128	SI 1985/886, reg. 50, as amended by SI 1992/3102, reg. 37
reg. 129(1)	SI 1985/886, reg. 51(1), as amended by SI 1992/3102, reg. 38
reg. 129(2)	SI 1985/886, reg. 51(2)
reg. 130	SI 1985/886, reg. 52, as substituted by SI 1992/3102, reg. 39
reg. 131	SI 1985/886, reg. 54, as amended by SI 1992/3102, reg. 41
reg. 132	SI 1985/886, reg. 56, as amended by SI 1992/3102, reg. 43
reg. 133	SI 1985/886, reg. 57, as amended by SI 1992/3102, reg. 43
reg. 134	SI 1985/886, reg. 57A, as inserted by SI 1992/3102, reg. 44 and amended by SI 1995/1280, reg. 3(a), (b)
reg. 135	SI 1985/886, reg. 57B, as inserted by SI 1992/3102, reg. 44 and amended by SI 1995/1280, reg. 4(b)
reg. 136	SI 1985/886, reg. 57D(1), as inserted by SI 1992/3102, reg. 44 and amended by SI 1995/152, reg. 5
reg. 137	SI 1985/886, reg. 57D(2), as inserted by SI 1992/3102, reg. 44
reg. 138	SI 1985/886, reg. 57DA, as inserted by SI 1995/152, reg. 6

Regulation	Derivation
reg. 139	SI 1985/886, reg. 57E, as inserted by SI 1992/3102, reg. 44
reg. 140(1)	SI 1985/886, reg. 57F(1), as inserted by SI 1992/3102, reg. 44 and amended by SI 1993/3027, reg. 4(a)
reg. 140(2)	SI 1985/886, reg. 57A(2), as inserted by SI 1992/3102, reg. 44 and amended by SI 1993/3027, reg. 4(b)
reg. 141	SI 1985/886, reg. 57G, as inserted by SI 1992/3102, reg. 44 and amended by SI 1993/3027, reg. 5
reg. 142	SI 1985/886, reg. 57H, as inserted by SI 1992/3102, reg. 44
reg. 143	SI 1985/886, reg. 57I, as inserted by SI 1992/3102, reg. 44
reg. 144	SI 1985/886, reg. 57J, as inserted by SI 1992/3102, reg. 44 and amended by SI 1993/3027, reg. 6
reg. 145(1)	SI 1985/886, reg. 57K, as inserted by SI 1992/3102, reg. 44
reg. 145(2)	SI 1985/886, reg. 57L, as inserted by SI 1992/3102, reg. 44
reg. 146	SI 1992/3100, reg. 1(2) and SI 1985/886, reg. 64B(3), as inserted by SI 1992/3102, reg. 48
reg. 147	SI 1985/886, reg. 64B(1), (2), as inserted by SI 1992/3102, reg. 48
reg. 148	SI 1985/886, reg. 64(A)(1)–(5), as inserted by SI 1992/3102, reg. 48
reg. 149	SI 1992/3100, reg. 2
reg. 150	SI 1992/3100, reg. 3
reg. 151	SI 1992/3100, reg. 4
reg. 152	SI 1992/3100, reg. 5
reg. 153	SI 1992/3100, reg. 6
reg. 154	SI 1992/3100, reg. 7
reg. 155	SI 1985/886, reg. 57C, as inserted by SI 1992/3102, reg. 44
reg. 156	SI 1986/335, reg. 2
reg. 157(1)	SI 1986/335, reg. 4(1), as amended by SI 1989/2255
reg. 157(2)	SI 1986/335, reg. 4(2)
reg. 158	SI 1986/335, reg. 5
reg. 159	SI 1986/335, reg. 6
reg. 160	SI 1986/335, reg. 7
reg. 161	SI 1986/335, reg. 8
reg. 162	SI 1986/335, reg. 9
reg. 163(1), (2)	SI 1986/335, reg. 10(1), (2), as amended by SI 1989/2255
reg. 163(3)	SI 1986/335, reg. 10(3)
reg. 164	SI 1986/335, reg. 11
reg. 165	SI 1991/371, reg. 2
reg. 166	SI 1991/371, reg. 3
reg. 167	SI 1991/371, reg. 4
reg. 168	SI 1991/371, reg. 5
reg. 169	SI 1991/371, reg. 6
reg. 170	SI 1991/371, reg. 7
reg. 171	SI 1991/371, reg. 8
reg. 172	SI 1991/371, reg. 9
reg. 173	SI 1980/1537, reg. 2
reg. 174	SI 1980/1537, reg. 3, as substituted by SI 1988/2217 and amended by SI 1992/3098, reg. 3
reg. 175	SI 1980/1537, reg. 4, as amended by SI 1993/1223, reg. 2
reg. 176	SI 1980/1537, reg. 5, as substituted by SI 1988/2217 and amended by *SI 1992/3098*, reg. 5
reg. 177	SI 1980/1537, reg. 6
reg. 178(1)	SI 1980/1537, reg. 7(1), as amended by SI 1988/2217
reg. 178(2), (3)	SI 1980/1537, reg. 7(2), (3)
reg. 179(1)	SI 1980/1537, reg. 8(1), as substituted by SI 1989/2217 and amended by SI 1992/3098, reg. 6
reg. 179(2)	SI 1980/1537, reg. 8(2)
reg. 179(3)	SI 1980/1537, reg. 8(3), as amended by SI 1989/2217 and SI 1992/3098, reg. 6
reg. 180	SI 1980/1537, reg. 9
reg. 181	SI 1980/1537, reg. 10
reg. 182	SI 1980/1537, reg. 11

Regulation	Derivation
reg. 183	SI 1980/1537, reg. 12
reg. 184	SI 1980/1537, reg. 13
reg. 185	SI 1987/2015, reg. 2
reg. 186	SI 1987/2015, reg. 3
reg. 187	SI 1987/2015, reg. 4
reg. 188(1)	SI 1987/2015, reg. 5(1)
reg. 188(2)	SI 1987/2015, reg. 5(2), as amended by SI 1993/1222, reg. 3
reg. 189	SI 1987/2015, reg. 6
reg. 190	SI 1987/2015, reg. 7
reg. 191	SI 1987/2015, reg. 8
reg. 192	SI 1987/2015, reg. 9
reg. 193	(None)
reg. 194	SI 1987/2015, reg. 10
reg. 195	SI 1987/2015, reg. 11
reg. 196	(None)
reg. 197	(None)
reg. 198	SI 1988/1343, reg. 4
reg. 199	SI 1988/1343, reg. 5
reg. 200	SI 1989/2259, reg. 2
reg. 201	SI 1989/2259, reg. 3
reg. 202	SI 1992/3103, reg. 1(2)
reg. 203	SI 1992/3103, reg. 2
reg. 204	SI 1992/3103, reg. 3
reg. 205	SI 1992/3103, reg. 4
reg. 206	SI 1992/3103, reg. 5
reg. 207	SI 1992/3103, reg. 6
reg. 208	SI 1992/3103, reg. 7
reg. 209	SI 1992/3103, reg. 8
reg. 210	SI 1992/3103, reg. 9
reg. 211	SI 1992/3103, reg. 10
reg. 212	SI 1985/886, reg. 65, as substituted by SI 1993/3027, reg. 7
reg. 213	SI 1985/886, reg. 66, as substituted by SI 1988/2083 and amended by SI 1993/3027, reg. 8

INDEX TO VALUE ADDED TAX

For a list of abbreviations used in this Index see p. xii.

Provision

.. form of .... SI 1986/304 r. 4;
SI 1986/385 r. 4
.. notification of creditors .... SI 1986/304 r. 5;
SI 1986/385 r. 5
.. preservation .... SI 1986/304 r. 6;
SI 1986/385 r. 6
. meaning .... SI 1986/304 r. 1(2)

Administrators – see Bad debt relief;
Personal representatives

Admission charges
. cultural activities, exemption ... VATA94 Sch. 9,
Grp. 13

Adult education courses – see
Education, research and
vocational training

Advertisements
. charities ... VATA94 Sch. 8, Grp. 15, item 8–8C,
Note (10A), (10B)

Advertising material
. relief, importation .. SI 1984/746 art. 5, 6, Sch. 2,
Grp. 3

Advertising services
. place of supply .... Dir. 77/388 art. 9(2)(e)
.. reverse charge .... VATA94 s. 8
.. services supplied where received VATA94
Sch. 5, para. 2;
SI 1992/3121 art. 16

Advocates
. tax point .... SI 1995/2518 reg. 92

Affidavits
. made in other legal proceedings,
used as evidence at tribunal
hearing ....SI 1986/590 r. 21A

Agents
. acting for commissioners ....CEMA79 s. 166
. acting in own name .... VATA94 s. 47
.. margin scheme – see Margin
schemes
.. used motor cars, supply of .... SI 1992/3122
art. 4(1)(d)
. general provisions .... VATA94 s. 47
. services .... Dir. 77/388 art. 6(4)
.. exemption, investment gold ... VATA94 Sch. 9,
Grp. 15, item 3;
Dir. 77/388 art. 26B(B)
.. insurance intermediary .... VATA94 Sch. 9,
Grp. 2, item 4, Note (1), (2), (7)–(10)
.. place of supply .... Dir. 77/388 art. 9(2)(e)
.. reverse charge ....VATA94 s. 8
.. services supplied where received VATA94
Sch. 5, para. 8;
SI 1992/3121 art. 16
. travel – see Tour operators; Tour
operators' margin scheme

Aggregation of businesses – see
Splitting business activities

Agricultural levy
. free zone goods ......SI 1984/1177 reg. 16–21, 25

Agriculture – see also Farmers
. flat-rate scheme for farmers – see
Farmers

Provision

. production activities, list ... Dir. 77/388 Annex A
. rate of VAT ....Dir. 77/388 art. 12(3)(d)
. services, list .... Dir. 77/388 Annex B

Air-conditioning – see Fuel and
power

Air cooling/purification appliances
. new buildings .... VATA94 Sch. 8, Grp. 5,
Note (22), (23)
. protected buildings ..... VATA94 Sch. 8, Grp. 6,
Note (3)

Aircraft – see also Transport
. aircraft mortgage, meaning .. SI 1995/1268 art. 2
. brokers and intermediaries
services ....Dir. 77/388 art. 15(14)
. chartering .... Dir. 77/388 art. 15(6)
.. supply of services ..... VATA94 Sch. 8, Grp. 8,
Note (1)
. commercial flights, goods used as
stores .... CEMA79 s. 1(4);
Dir. 77/388 art. 15(4)
. control of movement in and out
of UK ....CEMA79 s. 21
. Crown .... CEMA79 s. 4(2)
. disposal by mortgagee .... SI 1995/1268 art. 4
. fuel ....Dir. 77/388 art. 15(7)
. global accounting, exclusion .... SI 1995/1268
art. 13(2)
. goods shipped as stores .... CEMA79 s. 1(4)
.. zero-rating .... VATA94 s. 30(6), (7);
Dir. 77/388 art. 15(4)
. ground and security equipment .... ESC 2.6
. housing or storage, grant of
facilities ....VATA94 Sch. 9, Grp. 1, item 1(k)
. land/landing, meaning .... CEMA79 s. 1(1)
. margin scheme – see Margin
schemes
. military ....CEMA79 s. 4(2)
. new means of transport – see
New means of transport
. place of supply of goods, member
state in which transportation
commenced .... SI 1992/3283
. provisions ....Dir. 77/388 art. 15(7)
. qualifying
.. letting on hire .... VATA94 Sch. 8, Grp. 8,
Note (2)
.. meaning .... VATA94 Sch. 8, Grp. 8,
Note (A1)(b)
.. modification or conversion .... VATA94 Sch. 8,
Grp. 8, item 2, 10(b)
.. supply of life jackets, life rafts,
smoke hoods or similar safety
equipment .. VATA94 Sch. 8, Grp. 8, item 2B,
10(c)
.. supply of parts or equipment VATA94
Sch. 8, Grp. 8, item 2A, 10(c)
.. supply of parts or equipment to
government department ..... VATA94 Sch. 8,
Grp. 8, Note (2A)
.. supply, repair or maintenance VATA94
Sch. 8, Grp. 8, item 2, 10(b)
. related services ....Dir. 77/388 art. 15(9)

Aircraft – continued   **Provision**
. stores for use on .... CEMA79 s. 1(4);
      VATA94 s. 30(6);
      Dir. 77/388 art. 15(4)
. supplies to persons departing
    from member states .... SI 1995/2518
      reg. 130–133
. supply, modification, repair,
    maintenance, chartering and
    hiring .... Dir. 77/388 art. 15(6)
. tax-free shops – see Tax-free
    shops
. transport costs included in
    customs valuation of goods ..... Reg. 2454/93
      art. 166, Annex 25

Air guns – see Firearms

Air navigation services
. meaning ..... VATA94 Sch. 8, Grp. 8, Note (6A)
. zero-rating ..... VATA94 Sch. 8, Grp. 8, item 6A

Airports
. free zones
. . Birmingham .... SI 1991/1737;
      SI 1994/2509
. . Prestwick .... SI 1991/1739;
      SI 1994/143
. tax-free shops – see Tax-free
    shops

Alarm systems – see Distress alarms

Alcoholic beverages
. beer, meaning .... CEMA79 s. 1(3)
. cider, meaning .... CEMA79 s. 1(3)
. imported ....SI 1995/2518 reg. 118
. meaning ....SI 1984/746 art. 2(1)
. removed from warehouse, relief
    for special visitors .... SI 1992/3156 art. 15
. small consignments .... SI 1986/939
. spirits, meaning .... CEMA79 s. 1(3)
. warehoused .... SI 1988/809
. . removal, relief for special
    visitors .... SI 1992/3156 art. 15
. wine, meaning .... CEMA79 s. 1(3)
. zero-rating .... VATA94 Sch. 8, Grp. 1
. . tax-free shops ....VATA94 Sch. 8, Grp. 14

Alterations to buildings
. existing buildings .... VATA94 Sch. 8, Grp. 5,
      Note (16)(a)
. handicapped person's private
    residence/residential home ...VATA94 Sch. 8,
      Grp. 12, item 9–13
. protected buildings, zero-rating VATA94
      Sch. 8, Grp. 6

Ambulance services
. exemption ......VATA94 Sch. 9, Grp. 7, item 11;
      Dir. 77/388 art. 13(A)(1)(p)

American war graves .... ESC 2.5

Ancient monuments – see Protected
    buildings

Anglian Water Authority
. refund of VAT .... SI 1973/2121

Animals
. charities engaged in treatment/
    research
. . medicinal products .... VATA94 Sch. 8,
      Grp. 15, item 9

             Provision
. . substances directly used for
    synthesis or testing .... VATA94 Sch. 8,
      Grp. 15, item 10
. feeding stuffs, zero-rating .... VATA94 Sch. 8,
      Grp. 1
. human consumption, zero-rating VATA94
      Sch. 8, Grp. 1
. imported for laboratory use,
    relief ...... SI 1984/746 art. 5, 6, Sch. 2, Grp. 5
. meaning ....VATA94 Sch. 8, Grp. 1, Note (2),
      Grp. 15, Note (2), Grp. 16, Note (3)

Annual accounting scheme
. admission .... SI 1995/2518 reg. 52–55
. agreed monthly sum, meaning ..... SI 1995/2518
      reg. 49
. agreed quarterly sum, meaning ..... SI 1995/2518
      reg. 49
. authorisation ....SI 1995/2518 reg. 50(1)
. . application, eligibility ...SI 1995/2518 reg. 52(1)
. . cessation .... SI 1995/2518 reg. 53, 55
. . insolvency/bankruptcy/
    incapacity or death .... SI 1995/2518 reg. 53
. . refusal, protection of the
    revenue .... SI 1995/2518 reg. 52(2)
. . termination .... SI 1995/2518 reg. 54
. authorised person, meaning .... SI 1995/2518
      reg. 49
. credit transfer .... SI 1995/2518 reg. 50(2)(a)
. . meaning .... SI 1995/2518 reg. 49
. current accounting year, meaning .. SI 1995/2518
      reg. 49
. monthly sum, meaning ...... SI 1995/2518 reg. 49
. quarterly sum, meaning ..... SI 1995/2518 reg. 49
. relevant monthly date, meaning .... SI 1995/2518
      reg. 49
. relevant quarterly date, meaning ... SI 1995/2518
      reg. 49
. returns ....SI 1995/2518 reg. 50(2)(b)
. scheme, meaning ....SI 1995/2518 reg. 49
. transitional accounting period ..... SI 1995/2518
      reg. 51
. . meaning .... SI 1995/2518 reg. 49
. value of taxable supplies .... SI 1995/2518
      reg. 50(3)
. working day, meaning ...... SI 1995/2518 reg. 49

Anti-avoidance – see Avoidance of
    VAT

Antiques
. acquisitions ....Dir. 77/388 art. 26A(D)(b)
. disposal by finance house or
    insurer .... SI 1995/1268 art. 4
. imported
. . reduced rate of VAT ... Dir. 77/388 art. 12(3)(c)
. . value .... VATA94 s. 21
. input tax disallowed .... SI 1992/3222 art. 4
. margin scheme – see Margin
    schemes
. meaning .... SI 1992/3222 art. 2;
      SI 1995/1268 art. 2;
      Dir. 77/388 art. 26A(A)(c), Annex I(c)
. transactions treated as neither a
    supply of goods or services ....SI 1995/958;
      ESC 3.27

Consideration – continued   **Provision**

. supplies of services for
     consideration, meaning .. Dir. 77/388 art. 6(2)
. supply, adjustments to VAT
     account .... SI 1995/2518 reg. 38
. supply of goods/services .... VATA94 s. 19
. value
.. provisions for employees ...... VATA94 Sch. 6,
                             para. 10(1)
.. tokens/stamps/vouchers .... VATA94 Sch. 6,
                                para. 5

Constituent members

. persons treated as one direction –
     see Splitting business activities

Construction – see Civil engineering
     work; Construction services;
     Land and buildings

Construction services – see also
     Building work

. approved alteration of protected
     buildings ...... VATA94 Sch. 8, Grp. 6, item 2
.. apportionment .... VATA94 Sch. 8, Grp. 6,
                              Note (9)
.. excluded services ...... VATA94 Sch. 8, Grp. 6,
                             Note (11)
. construction of dwellings or
     residential/charitable buildings VATA94
                    Sch. 8, Grp. 5, item 2
.. apportionment .... VATA94 Sch. 8, Grp. 5,
                             Note (11)
. exclusions .... VATA94 Sch. 8, Grp. 5, Note (20)
. housing associations, conversion
     of non-residential buildings   VATA94 Sch. 8,
                    Grp. 5, item 3
.. apportionment .... VATA94 Sch. 8, Grp. 5,
                             Note (11)
. invoices .... SI 1995/2518 reg. 13(4)
. self-supply .... SI 1989/472
. tax point .... SI 1995/2518 reg. 93
. zero-rating
.. builder's certificate .... VATA94 Sch. 8, Grp. 5,
                             Note (12)(b)
.. construction of dwellings or
     residential/charitable buildings VATA94
                    Sch. 8, Grp. 5, item 2
.. excluded supply .... VATA94 Sch. 8, Grp. 5,
                             Note (12)
.. garages constructed at same
     time as dwelling ..... VATA94 Sch. 8, Grp. 5,
                             Note (3)
.. housing associations, conversion
     of non-residential buildings   VATA94 Sch. 8,
                    Grp. 5, item 3
.. protected buildings, approved
     alteration ...... VATA94 Sch. 8, Grp. 6, item 2

Consultants and consultancy
     bureaux

. place of supply of services .... Dir. 77/388
                               art. 9(2)(e)
.. reverse charge .... VATA94 s. 8
.. services supplied where received VATA94
                    Sch. 5, para. 3;
                    SI 1992/3121 art. 16

     Provision

Containers

. meaning .... CEMA79 s. 1(1)
. repeated importations, customs
     value .... Reg. 2454/93 art. 154

Continuous supplies of services

. tax point .... SI 1995/2518 reg. 90
.. telecommunications services ...... SI 1995/2518
                           reg. 90A, 90B

Contracts

. adjustment of, on changes in
     VAT .... VATA94 s. 89

Control of exportation

. postal packets .... SI 1986/260 reg. 5(f)–(h)

Control of importation

. duty on imports .... CEMA79 s. 43
.. deferred payments .... CEMA79 s. 45
.. deposits paid .... CEMA79 s. 44
.. goods to be warehoused without
     payment .... CEMA79 s. 46
. entry
.. commissioners' power to
     regulate unloading and
     removal of goods .... CEMA79 s. 42
.. correction and cancellation ... CEMA79 s. 38B
.. failure to comply with
     provisions .... CEMA79 s. 41
.. formalities .... SI 1995/2518 reg. 140
.. initial and supplementary .... CEMA79 s. 37A,
                          37C; FA90 s. 7
.. postponed .... CEMA79 s. 37B, 37C
. forfeiture of goods
.. goods improperly imported ..... CEMA79 s. 49
.. persons entering or leaving the
     UK .... CEMA79 s. 78(4)
. goods improperly imported .... CEMA79 s. 50
. forfeiture .... CEMA79 s. 49
. initial and supplementary entries
.. authorisation of importer ..CEMA79 s. 37C(1)
.. authorised agents .... CEMA79 s. 37A(1A)
.. entry of goods on importation
     direction .... CEMA79 s. 37A(1)
.. payment of duty .... CEMA79 s. 37A(2)
.. penalty .... CEMA79 s. 37C(3)
.. requirements for importer ..CEMA79 s. 37C(2)
.. time entry delivered .... CEMA79 s. 37A(4)
. offences, goods improperly
     imported .... CEMA79 s. 50
. persons entering or leaving the
     UK
.. air journeys continued ...... CEMA79 s. 78(2A)
.. answering questions etc.,
     requirement .... CEMA79 s. 78(3)
.. entry from another member
     state .... CEMA79 s. 78(1B)
.. forfeiture of goods .... CEMA79 s. 78(4)
.. goods requiring declaration ..CEMA79 s. 78(1)
.. Isle of Man .... CEMA79 s. 78(2)
.. penalty .... CEMA79 s. 78(3)
. postal packets ...... SI 1986/260 reg. 5(b), (c), (h)
. postponed entry .... CEMA79 s. 37B
.. authorisation of importer ..CEMA79 s. 37C(1)
.. authorised agents .. CEMA79 s. 37B(1A), (3A)

Fiscal warehousing – continued   **Provision**
.. operation on .... VATA94 s. 18F(4), (5)
. fiscal or other warehousing
    regime, meaning .... SI 1995/2518 reg. 2(1)
. fiscal warehousekeeper
.. application .... VATA94 s. 18A
.. approval .... VATA94 s. 18A
.. breach of conditions, penalty ... VATA94 s. 62
.. cessation .... VATA94 s. 18F(6)
.. conditions, imposition ......VATA94 s. 18A(1),
                                 (6)(a)
.. meaning ....VATA94 s. 18F(1)
.. withdrawal of approval .. VATA94 s. 18A(6)(b)
. fiscal warehouse, meaning ...VATA94 s. 18A(3),
                                   18F(1);
                    SI 1995/2518 reg. 145A(1)
. general provisions .... VATA94 s. 18A
. goods being subject to a fiscal
    warehousing regime,
    meaning .... VATA94 s. 18F(2)
. goods being subject to a
    warehousing regime,
    meaning .... VATA94 s. 18F(3)
. his fiscal warehouse, meaning ...... SI 1995/2518
                                 reg. 145A(2)
. his fiscal warehousing regime,
    meaning .... SI 1995/2518 reg. 145A(2)
. last acquisition/supply of goods
    before removal disregarded for
    registration purposes .... VATA94 Sch. 1,
    para. 1(9), Sch. 2, para. 1(7), Sch. 3, para. 1(6)
. material time, meaning .... VATA94 s. 18F(1);
                      SI 1995/2518 reg. 145A(1);
                            SI 1996/1255 art. 2(1)
. missing goods .... VATA94 s. 18E
.. failure to pay VAT, best of
    judgment assessment ...... VATA94 s. 73(7A)
. premises having fiscal warehouse
    status
.. cessation .... VATA94 s. 18A(5), 18F(6)
.. withdrawal .... VATA94 s. 18A(6)(c)
. record .... SI 1995/2518 reg. 145F
.. features/requirements .....SI 1995/2518 Sch. 1A
. regulations .... VATA94 s. 18F(7)–(9)
.. meaning .... SI 1995/2518 reg. 145A(1)
. relevant fiscal warehousekeeper,
    meaning .... SI 1995/2518 reg. 145A(2)
. relevant fiscal warehouse,
    meaning .... SI 1995/2518 reg. 145A(2)
. relevant fiscal warehousing
    regime, meaning ... SI 1995/2518 reg. 145A(2)
. relief ....VATA94 s. 18B
. removal of goods .. SI 1995/2518 reg. 145H, 145I
.. accountability .... VATA94 s. 18D
.. failure to pay VAT, best of
    judgment assessment ....VATA94 s. 73(7B)
.. payment of VAT ...... SI 1995/2518 reg. 40, 43,
                                    145J
.. removal of goods from a
    warehousing regime,
    meaning .... VATA94 s. 18F(3)
.. returns and payment of VAT ..... SI 1995/2518
                                  reg. 40
.. zero-rating ....VATA94 s. 30(8A), (10)

                                        Provision
. samples, power to take ....VATA94 Sch. 11,
                                   para. 8
. section, meaning ...... SI 1995/2518 reg. 145A(1)
. services ....VATA94 s. 18C
.. certificates .... VATA94 s. 18C(1)(c);
                            SI 1995/2518 reg. 145C
.. invoices .... VATA94 s. 18C(1)(e);
                    SI 1995/2518 reg. 13(1), 145D
.. returns and payment of VAT ..... SI 1995/2518
                                  reg. 40
. stock control ....SI 1995/2518 reg. 145F
. supply, meaning .... SI 1996/1255 art. 2(1)
. transactions treated as supply of
    goods and not supply of
    services .... SI 1996/1255
. transfers in the UK ...... SI 1995/2518 reg. 145G
. transfers overseas .. SI 1995/2518 reg. 145H, 145I
. warehouse, meaning ....VATA94 s. 18F(1)
. warehousing regulations,
    meaning .... VATA94 s. 18F(1)

Fisheries – see **Farmers**

Fishing boats – see **Boats; Ships**

Fishing undertakings
. importation of fish caught at sea,
    exemption ....Dir. 77/388 art. 14(1)(h)

Fitted furniture – see **Furniture**

Flat-rate scheme for farmers – see
    Farmers

Food – see also **Catering**
. meaning .... VATA94 Sch. 8, Grp. 1, Note (1)
. zero-rating .... VATA94 Sch. 8, Grp. 1

Footwear
. zero-rating
.. children's ..... VATA94 Sch. 8, Grp. 16, item 1
.. protective ..... VATA94 Sch. 8, Grp. 16, item 2

Foreign currency
. exchange rates – see **Exchange**
    rates
. value of supply expressed in .... VATA94 Sch. 6,
                                    para. 11;
                     Dir. 77/388 art. 11(C)(2)
.. acquisition of goods ...VATA94 Sch. 7, para. 4

Foreign VAT
. refund – see **Refund of VAT**

Forestry – see **Farmers**

Forfeiture
. compensation ....CEMA79 Sch. 3, para. 17(1)
. condemnation .... CEMA79 Sch. 3, para. 5
.. claimants ....CEMA79 Sch. 3, para. 15
.. proceedings for .... CEMA79 Sch. 3, para. 8–12
. goods
.. detention, seizure,
    condemnation ....CEMA79 s. 139
.. examination, officers'
    powers .... CEMA79 s. 159(5)
.. improperly imported ....CEMA79 s. 49
. persons entering or leaving the
    UK ....CEMA79 s. 78(4)
.. zero-rated but not
    exported .... VATA94 s. 30(10)

Insurance companies – continued   **Provision**
. . works of art, antiques,
    collectors' items and
    second-hand goods .... SI 1995/1268 art. 4
. insurer, meaning .... SI 1995/1268 art. 2
. insurers, meaning .... SI 1992/3122 art. 2

Intending trader registration
. entitlement .... VATA94 Sch. 1, para. 9, 10
. . end of, notification .. VATA94 Sch. 1, para. 11,
    12
. property owners and developers .... NR 65/90

Interest – see also **Default interest**
. given by way of credit and set off
    of credits .... VATA94 s. 81
. overpayment of VAT due to
    official error .... VATA94 s. 78
. appeals .... VATA94 s. 83(s), (sa)
. . assessment for interest
    overpayments .... VATA94 s. 78A
. . rate .... SI 1998/1461
. . setting rates .... FA96 s. 197
. repayment of VAT, tribunal's
    direction .... VATA94 s. 84(8)
. VAT recovered/recoverable by
    assessment .... VATA94 s. 74
. . setting rates .... FA96 s. 197

Intermediaries – see also **Agents**
. place of supply of services .... SI 1992/3121
    art. 11–13;
    Dir. 77/388 art. 28B(E)
. . customers registration number,
    use .... SI 1992/3121 art. 14
. services relating to exports and
    international transport .... Dir. 77/388
    art. 15(14)

Intermediate suppliers
. invoices .... SI 1995/2518 reg. 18
. notification of intended supplies ... SI 1995/2518
    reg. 11

International agreements
. member states wishing to
    conclude .... Dir. 77/388 art. 30

International co-operation
. investigations, commissioners'
    powers .... SI 1991/1297

International goods traffic
. exemption .... Dir. 77/388 art. 16

International organisations
. agreements, member states
    wishing to conclude .... Dir. 77/388 art. 30
. exemption/relief .... SI 1992/3156
. . exports .... Dir. 77/388 art. 15(10)
. . imports .... Dir. 77/388 art. 14(1)(g)
. personal reliefs for goods
    permanently imported from
    third countries .... ESC 5.5
. supplies to those other member
    states, zero-rating .... ESC 4.2

**International Petroleum Exchange
    of London**
. zero-rating .... SI 1973/173 art. 2, 3

International services   **Provision**
. zero-rating .... VATA94 Sch. 8, Grp. 7
. . training to overseas
    governments .... ESC 3.17

International transport – see
    Transport

Internet
. services, place of supply rules
    change .... BB 22/97
. submission of returns .... SI 1995/2518
    reg. 25(4A)–(4L)
. . incentives to use .... FA2000 s. 143, Sch. 38

Interpretation of statutes .... BB 14/94

Intrastat system
. adaptations .... Reg. 3330/91 art. 33
. additional data required .... Reg. 3330/91
    art. 23(2), (3)
. ancillary costs sample surveys
. . business day, meaning ... SI 1992/2790 reg. 1(2)
. . meaning .... SI 1992/2790 reg. 1(2)
. . supplementary units, meaning .... SI 1992/2790
    reg. 1(2)
. application .... Reg. 3046/92 art. 2; Reg. 3330/91
    art. 7
. arrival, meaning .... Reg. 3330/91 art. 19
. basic regulation, meaning .... Reg. 3046/92 art. 1
. cessations .... Reg. 3046/92 art. 8
. Commission's report .... Reg. 3330/91 art. 16
. committee .... Reg. 3330/91 art. 29, 30
. Community goods, meaning .... Reg. 3330/91
    art. 2(c)
. country of origin, meaning .... Reg. 3046/92
    art. 16
. data medium
. . description of states .... Reg. 3330/91 art. 22
. . designation of goods .... Reg. 3330/91 art. 21
. data required .... Reg. 3330/91 art. 23
. . list, publication .... Reg. 3330/91 art. 23(5)
. data transmission .... Reg. 3046/92 art. 9
. declaring third party .... Reg. 3046/92 art. 5
. delivery terms
. . list .... Reg. 3046/92 Annex II
. . meaning .... Reg. 3046/92 art. 14
. dispatch, meaning .... Reg. 3330/91 art. 18
. enforcement .... Reg. 3330/91 art. 35
. establishment .... Reg. 3330/91 art. 6
. excluded data .... Reg. 3046/92 art. 20
. . list .... Reg. 3046/92 Annex III
. forms
. . details .... Reg. 3590/92 art. 3
. . supply .... Reg. 3590/92 art. 4
. . use of .... Reg. 3590/92 art. 2
. goods in free movement on the
    internal market of the
    Community, meaning .. Reg. 3330/91 art. 2(g)
. goods leaving/entering ...... Reg. 3330/91 art. 17
. goods, meaning .... Reg. 3330/91 art. 2(b)
. goods moving between member
    states .... Reg. 3330/91 art. 3
. goods subject to statistics .... Reg. 3330/91 art. 4
. implementation .... Reg. 3330/91 art. 30
. intra-Community operator .. Reg. 3046/92 art. 6

	Provision
Non-taxable persons – continued	
.. assessment, time-limit and	
supplementary assessments	VATA94 s. 77
.. penalty	VATA94 s. 67
. acquisitions, notification	VATA94 Sch. 11,
	para. 2(4), (5);
	SI 1995/2518 reg. 36
. deemed taxable, Treasury	
orders	VATA94 s. 24(4)
. new means of transport – see	
New means of transport	
. re-importation of goods	SI 1995/2518 reg. 124

Northern Ireland
. computer records
.. admissibility as evidence in
    proceedings ...... VATA94 Sch. 11, para. 6(6)
.. production of .... FA85 s. 10(7)
. condemnation .... CEMA79 Sch. 3, para. 8
. enforcement of registered or
    recorded tribunal decisions
    etc. .... VATA94 s. 87(3)
. fee simple, meaning .... VATA94 s. 96(1)
. health board/agency, supplies of
    invalid wheelchairs and
    carriages and parts and
    accessories .... VATA94 Sch. 8, Grp. 12,
    Note (5C), (5F), (5H)
. legal proceedings .... CEMA79 s. 147(4)
.. non-payment of penalties,
    maximum terms of
    imprisonment .... CEMA79 s. 149(3)
. listed buildings .... SI 1991/1220 art. 42
. money and securities for money
    on account of duties .... CEMA79 s. 17(4)
. penalties
.. mitigation .... CEMA79 s. 150(2)
.. non-payment, maximum terms
    of imprisonment .... CEMA79 s. 149(3)
. recovery of VAT ... VATA94 Sch. 11, para. 5(4)
. refund of VAT to government ... VATA94 s. 99

**Northumbria Interim Police
    Authority**
. refund of VAT .... SI 1985/1101

Northumbrian Water Authority
. refund of VAT .... SI 1973/2121

North West Water Authority
. refund of VAT .... SI 1973/2121

Notes
. securities, exemption .... VATA94 Sch. 9,
    Grp. 5, item 6, 7, Note (5)

Notice
. evasion of VAT, liability of
    directors etc. .... VATA94 s. 61
. partnerships
.. former partner, to .... VATA94 s. 45(3)
.. service on partnership's
    registered name .... VATA94 s. 45(4)
. service of .... VATA94 s. 98
. tribunals .... SI 1986/590 r. 3
.. application for directions ...... SI 1986/590 r. 11
.. commissioners' contention
    appeal does not lie .... SI 1986/590 r. 6

	Provision
.. date of hearing	SI 1986/590 r. 23
.. notice of appeal – see Notice of	
appeal	

Notice of appeal
. acknowledgment .... SI 1986/590 r. 5
. form .... SI 1986/590 r. 3
. notification of commissioners ... SI 1986/590 r. 5
. service .... SI 1986/590 r. 4, 31

Nurses
. exemption ..... VATA94 Sch. 9, Grp. 7, item 1(d)

**Nursing homes – see also Health
    and welfare; Residential
    accommodation/buildings**
. care or medical/surgical treatment
.. supply of aids to handicapped
    persons .... VATA94 Sch. 8, Grp. 12,
    Note (5D), (5E)
.. supply of medical and surgical
    appliances to handicapped
    persons VATA94 Sch. 8, Grp. 12, Note (5B),
    (5C)
.. supply of qualifying goods
    dispensed to individual for
    personal use .... VATA94 Sch. 8, Grp. 12,
    Note (5A)
. relevant institution, meaning ... VATA94 Sch. 8,
    Grp. 12, Note (5I)

Nuts
. salted/roasted, zero-rating ...... VATA94 Sch. 8,
    Grp. 1

O

Offences and penalties
. acquisitions, failure to notify ..... VATA94 s. 67
. amount fixed at open market
    value .... CEMA79 s. 171(3)
. application of penalty
    payments .... CEMA79 s. 151
. bribery and collusion .... CEMA79 s. 15
. commissioners' powers to
    mitigate penalties .... CEMA79 s. 152
. control of movement of
    goods ... CEMA79 s. 21(6), 30(4), 31(3), 42(2)
. counterfeiting documents .... CEMA79 s. 168
. Customs and Excise legislation,
    application of .... VATA94 s. 72(12)
. default surcharge .... VATA94 s. 59, 59B
.. payments on account ..... VATA94 s. 59A, 59B
. disclosure of information .... FA89 s. 182;
    VATA94 s. 91(4)
. documents
.. failure to preserve .... VATA94 s. 69(2)
.. false .... CEMA79 s. 168; VATA94 s. 72
. EC sales statements
.. failure to submit .... VATA94 s. 66
.. inaccuracies .... VATA94 s. 65
. evasion of VAT – see Evasion of
    VAT
. exported goods, failure to
    provide documents .... CEMA79 s. 77
. false declarations .... CEMA79 s. 167
. fraudulent evasion of VAT .... VATA94 s. 72

Provision

Royalties
. tax point .... SI 1995/2518 reg. 91
. valuation of goods for customs
     purposes
.. amount of royalty based on
     price .... Reg. 2454/93 art. 161
.. meaning .... Reg. 2454/93 art. 157
.. recipient's residence .... Reg. 2454/93 art. 162
.. trade mark .... Reg. 2454/93 art. 159

S

Safes and safe deposit facilities
. excluded from exemption .... Dir. 77/388
                                            art. 13(B)(b)(4)
. place of supply .... Dir. 77/388 art. 9(2)(e)

Safety equipment
. qualifying ships or aircraft ..... VATA94 Sch. 8,
                                      Grp. 8, item 2B, 10(c)
.. letting on hire .... VATA94 Sch. 8, Grp. 8,
                                      Note (2)

Sailaway boat scheme
. zero-rating .... ESC 4.1

Salary sacrifice
. private use of company car .... SI 1992/630

Salvage services
. zero-rating .... VATA94 Sch. 8, Grp. 8, item 8

Samples
. accounting for ...... VATA94 Sch. 11, para. 8(2)
. compensation for non-return .. VATA94 Sch. 11,
                                            para. 8(3)
. gifts of .... VATA94 Sch. 4, para. 5(2)(b), (3);
                                            Dir. 77/388 art. 5(6)
. power to take, authorised person VATA94
                                            Sch. 11, para. 8(1)
. reference substances, importation ... SI 1984/746
                                            Sch. 2, Grp. 5
. warehoused goods .... SI 1988/809 reg. 19

Sanitary appliances
. handicapped persons .... VATA94 Sch. 8,
                              Grp. 12, item 2(c), Note (5D), (5E)

Savoury snacks
. zero-rating .... VATA94 Sch. 8, Grp. 1

Scholastic equipment
. meaning .... SI 1992/3193 art. 16(2)
. permanently imported, personal
     reliefs .... SI 1992/3193 art. 16

Schoolchildren – see Students

**Schools – see Education, research
     and vocational training**

Scientific services
. place of supply .... Dir. 77/388 art. 9(2)(c)
.. services supplied where
     performed .... SI 1992/3121 art. 15(a), (c)

Scope of VAT
. acquisition of goods .... VATA94 s. 10
. imports .... Dir. 77/388 art. 2(2)
. taxable supplies .... VATA94 s. 4;
                                            Dir. 77/388 art. 2(1)

Provision

Scotland
. access to recorded information,
     Intrastat system offences .... SI 1992/2790
                                            reg. 9–11
. administrative receivers .... SI 1986/304
. assignment, meaning .... VATA94 s. 96(1)
. commissioners' regulations for
     the recovery of VAT .... VATA94 Sch. 11,
                                            para. 5(5), (6), (9)
. computer records, production of .. FA85 s. 10(7)
. condemnation .... CEMA79 Sch. 3, para. 8
. diligence .... VATA94 Sch. 11, para. 5(5)–(9);
                                            SI 1995/2518 reg. 213
. enforcement of registered or
     recorded tribunal decisions
     etc. .... VATA94 s. 87(2)
. fraud, issue of warrant .... VATA94 Sch. 11,
                                            para. 10(3)
. health boards/agencies, supplies
     of invalid wheelchairs and
     carriages and parts and
     accessories .... VATA94 Sch. 8, Grp. 12,
                                            Note (5C), (5F), (5H)
. imported goods, determination of
     disputes as to duty payable ... CEMA79 s. 127
. land
.. fee simple, meaning .... VATA94 s. 96(1)
.. major interest, meaning ...... VATA94 s. 96(1)
. land and buildings, personal right VATA94
                                            Sch. 9, Grp. 1, item 1
.. co-ownership .... VATA94 s. 51A
. legal proceedings ..... CEMA79 s. 145(3), 147(5)
.. institution by
     commissioners .... CEMA79 s. 145(3)
.. non-payment of penalties,
     maximum terms of
     imprisonment .... CEMA79 s. 149(1)
. partnerships, registration   SI 1995/2518 reg. 7(2)
. penalties
.. mitigation .... CEMA79 s. 150(2)
.. non-payment, maximum terms
     of imprisonment .... CEMA79 s. 149(1)
. recorded information, order for
     access to .... VATA94 Sch. 11, para. 11
.. Intrastat system offences .... SI 1992/2790
                                            reg. 9–11
. recovery of VAT .... VATA94 Sch. 11,
                                            para. 5(5)–(9);
                                            SI 1995/2518 reg. 213
. refund of VAT, specified bodies ... SI 1976/2028

Sea fishing
. importation of catches .. Dir. 77/388 art. 14(1)(h)

~~Sea-going vessels – see Boats; Ships~~

**Search and entry – see Entry and
     search of premises/persons**

**Sea rescue equipment – see
     Lifeboats**

Seasonal pitches
. caravans .... VATA94 Sch. 9, Grp. 1, item 1(f)
. meaning ...... VATA94 Sch. 9, Grp. 1, Note (14)

**Second-hand goods – see also
     Moveable tangible property**
. acquisitions .... Dir. 77/388 art. 26A(D)(b)

Provision

Waste disposal units/compactors
. building designed as number of
    dwellings .... VATA94 Sch. 8, Grp. 5,
        Note (22), (23), Grp. 6, Note (3)

Water
. tax point .... SI 1995/2518 reg. 86, 87
. treated as supply of goods .... SI 1989/1114
. zero-rating .... VATA94 Sch. 8, Grp. 2

Water authorities
. refund of VAT .... VATA94 s. 33

Water heating appliances
. new buildings .... VATA94 Sch. 8, Grp. 5,
        Note (22), (23)
. protected buildings ..... VATA94 Sch. 8, Grp. 6,
        Note (3)

Wedding gifts
. meaning .... SI 1992/3193 art. 14(4)
. relief for property imported on
    marriage from a third country .. SI 1992/3193
        art. 14
.. time-limit .... SI 1992/3193 art. 15

Welfare services – see Health and
    welfare

Welsh National Water Development
    Authority
. refund of VAT .... SI 1973/2121

Wessex Water Authority
. refund of VAT .... SI 1973/2121

Wheelchairs and carriages
. handicapped persons .. VATA94 Sch. 8, Grp. 12,
        Note (5C), (5F), (5G), (5H)
.. adapted motor vehicles .... VATA94 Sch. 8,
        Grp. 12, item 2(f)

Winding up
. fees .... SI 1985/1784
. preferential debts – see
    Preferential debts
. taxable person .... VATA94 s. 46(5)

Wine – see Alcoholic beverages

Wireless sets – see Radio

Witnesses
. statements at tribunals .... SI 1986/590 r. 21
. summonses .... SI 1986/590 r. 22

Wood – see Fuel and power

Works of art
. acquisitions .... Dir. 77/388 art. 26A(D)(b)
. disposal by finance house or
    insurer .... SI 1995/1268 art. 4
. exemption .... VATA94 Sch. 9, Grp. 11
. imported
.. reduced rate of VAT ... Dir. 77/388 art. 12(3)(c)
.. value .... VATA94 s. 21
. input tax disallowed .... SI 1992/3222 art. 4
. margin scheme – see Margin
    schemes
. meaning .... VATA94 s. 21(6)–(6B);
        SI 1992/3222 art. 2;
        SI 1995/958 art. 2;
        SI 1995/1268 art. 2;
    Dir. 77/388 art. 26A(A)(a), Annex I(a)

Provision

. transactions treated as neither a
    supply of goods or services .... SI 1995/958;
        ESC 3.27

Y

Yorkshire Water Authority
. refund of VAT .... SI 1973/2121

Youth clubs
. exemption .... VATA94 Sch. 9, Grp. 6, item 6
. meaning .... VATA94 Sch. 9, Grp. 6, Note (6)

Z

Zero-rating
. alcoholic beverages ...... VATA94 Sch. 8, Grp. 1
. animal feeding stuffs .... VATA94 Sch. 8, Grp. 1
. animals for human consumption VATA94
        Sch. 8, Grp. 1
. bank notes .... VATA94 Sch. 8, Grp. 11
. biscuits .... VATA94 Sch. 8, Grp. 1
. books .... VATA94 Sch. 8, Grp. 3
. boots, protective .... VATA94 Sch. 8, Grp. 16
. caravans .... VATA94 Sch. 8, Grp. 9
. change in description of
    supplies .... VATA94 s. 88
. charities
.. advertisements .... VATA94 Sch. 8,
        Grp. 15, item 8–8C, Note (10A), (10B)
.. aids for handicapped persons –
    see Handicapped persons
.. buildings, change of use ...... VATA94 Sch. 10,
        para. 1
.. construction of buildings ...... VATA94 Sch. 8,
        Grp. 5
.. donations, sale, letting or export VATA94
    Sch. 8, Grp. 15, item 1, 1A, 2, Note (1)–(1F)
.. eligible body, meaning .... VATA94 Sch. 8,
        Grp. 15, Note (4)
.. export of goods .... VATA94 s. 30(5), Sch. 8,
        Grp. 15, item 3
.. medical care/surgical treatment,
    medicinal products for .... VATA94 Sch. 8,
        Grp. 15, item 9
.. medical/veterinary research,
    medicinal products for .... VATA94 Sch. 8,
        Grp. 15, item 9
.. provision of care or medical/
    surgical treatment for
    handicapped persons, supply
    of relevant goods .... VATA94 Sch. 8,
        Grp. 15, item 5
.. relevant goods, meaning .... VATA94 Sch. 8,
        Grp. 15, Note (3)
.. relevant goods supplied to
    eligible body .... VATA94 Sch. 8,
        Grp. 15, item 4–7
.. repair/maintenance of relevant
    goods ...... VATA94 Sch. 8, Grp. 15, item 6, 7
. children's picture and painting
    books .... VATA94 Sch. 8, Grp. 3
. clothing, children's ..... VATA94 Sch. 8, Grp. 16
. coffee .... VATA94 Sch. 8, Grp. 1
. confectionery .... VATA94 Sch. 8, Grp. 1

VALUE ADDED TAX
LIST OF DEFINITIONS AND MEANINGS

For a list of abbreviations used in this list see p. xii.

For a list of abbreviations used in this list see p. xii.

For a list of abbreviations used in this list see p. xii.

For a list of abbreviations used in this list see p. xii.

For a list of abbreviations used in this list see p. xii.

For a list of abbreviations used in this list see p. xii.

For a list of abbreviations used in this list see p. xii.

For a list of abbreviations used in this list see p. xii.

For a list of abbreviations used in this list see p. xii.

For a list of abbreviations used in this list see p. xii.

For a list of abbreviations used in this list see p. xii.

btl2 98   vat   def Mp   13100—vatdef

For a list of abbreviations used in this list see p. xii.

STAMP DUTIES

(INCLUDING STAMP DUTY RESERVE TAX)

Table of Contents

STAMP DUTIES STATUTES

Table of Contents

continued over

STAMP DUTIES MANAGEMENT ACT 1891

(1891 Chapter 38)

[*21st July 1891*]

ARRANGEMENT OF SECTIONS

APPLICATION OF ACT

1   Act to apply to all stamp duties

1   All duties for the time being chargeable by law as stamp duties shall be under the care and management of the Commissioners, and this Act shall apply to all such duties and to all fees which are for the time being directed to be collected or received by means of stamps.

MODE OF RECOVERING MONEY RECEIVED FOR DUTY

2 Moneys received for duty and not appropriated to be recoverable in High Court

2(1) Every person who, having received any sum of money as or for any duty, or any fee collected by means of a stamp, does not apply the money to the due payment of the duty or fee, and improperly withholds or detains the same, shall be accountable for the amount of the duty or fee, and the same shall be a debt from him to Her Majesty, and recoverable as such accordingly.

2(2) [Repealed by FA 1999, s. 115 and Sch. 18, para. 6(1), s. 139 and Sch. 20, Pt. V(4).]

2(3) [Repealed by FA 1999, s. 115 and Sch. 18, para. 6(1), s. 139 and Sch. 20, Pt. V(4).]

History – S. 2 amended by Crown Proceedings Act 1947, s. 14(1)(b).
S. 2(2), (3) repealed by FA 1999, 115 and Sch. 18, para. 6(1), 139 and Sch. 20, Pt. V(4), the repeal coming into force on 1 October 1999.

SALE OF STAMPS

3 Power to grant licences to deal in stamps

3 [Repealed by FA 1999, s. 115 and Sch. 18, para. 6(1), s. 139 and Sch. 20, Pt. V(4) on 1 October 1999.]

4 Penalty for unauthorised dealing in stamps, etc.

4 [Repealed by FA 1999, s. 115 and Sch. 18, para. 6(1), s. 139 and Sch. 20, Pt. V(4) on 1 October 1999.]

5 Provisions as to determination of a licence

5 [Repealed by FA 1999, s. 115 and Sch. 18, para. 6(1), s. 139 and Sch. 20, Pt. V(4) on 1 October 1999.]

6 Penalty for hawking stamps

6 [Repealed by FA 1999, s. 115 and Sch. 18, para. 6(1), s. 139 and Sch. 20, Pt. V(4) on 1 October 1999.]

8 Discount

8 [Repealed by FA 1999, s. 115 and Sch. 18, para. 6(1), s. 139 and Sch. 20, Pt. V(4) on 1 October 1999.]

ALLOWANCE FOR SPOILED STAMPS

9 Procedure for obtaining allowance

9 Subject to such regulations as the Commissioners may think proper to make, and to the production of such evidence by statutory declaration or otherwise as the Commissioners may require, allowance is to be made by the Commissioners for stamps spoiled in the cases hereinafter mentioned; (that is to say,):

(1) The stamp on any material inadvertently and undesignedly spoiled, obliterated, or by any means rendered unfit for the purpose intended, before the material bears the signature of any person or any instrument written thereon is executed by any party:

(2) [Repealed by FA 1999, s. 115 and Sch. 18, para. 6(1), s. 139 and Sch. 20, Pt. V(4).]

(3) [Repealed by FA 1999, s. 115 and Sch. 18, para. 6(1), s. 139 and Sch. 20, Pt. V(4).]

(4) The stamp on any bill of exchange signed by or on behalf of the drawer which has not been accepted or made use of in any manner whatever or delivered out of his hands for any purpose other than by way of tender for acceptance:

(5) The stamp on any promissory note signed by or on behalf of the maker which has not been made use of in any manner whatever or delivered out of his hands:

(6) The stamp on any bill of exchange or promissory note which from any omission or error has *been spoiled or rendered useless*, although the same, being a bill of exchange, may have been accepted or indorsed, or, being a promissory note, may have been delivered to the payee, provided that another completed and duly stamped bill of exchange or promissory note is produced identical in every particular, except in the correction of the error or omission, with the spoiled bill or note:

(7) The stamp used for any of the following instruments; that is to say,

(a)   An instrument executed by any party thereto, but afterwards found to be absolutely void from the beginning:

(b)   An instrument executed by any party thereto, but afterwards found unfit, by reason of any error or mistake therein, for the purpose originally intended:

(c)   An instrument executed by any party thereto which has not been made use of for any purpose whatever, and which by reason of the inability or refusal of some necessary party to sign the same or to complete the transaction according to the instrument, is incomplete and insufficient for the purpose for which it was intended:

(d)   An instrument executed by any party thereto, which by reason of the refusal of any person to act under the same, or for want of enrolment or registration within the time required by law, fails of the intended purpose or becomes void:

(e)   An instrument executed by any party thereto which becomes useless in consequence of the transaction intended to be thereby effected being effected by some other instrument duly stamped:

Provided as follows:–

(a)   That the application for relief is made within two years after the stamp has been spoiled or become useless or in the case of an executed instrument after the date of the instrument, or, if it is not dated, within two years after the execution thereof by the person by whom it was first or alone executed or within such further time as the Commissioners may prescribe in the case of any instrument sent abroad for execution or when from unavoidable circumstances any instrument for which another has been substituted cannot be produced within the said period;

(b)   That in the case of an executed instrument no legal proceeding has been commenced in which the instrument could or would have been given or offered in evidence, and that the instrument is given up to be cancelled;

(c)   [Repealed by Statute Law (Repeals) Act 1993, s. 1(1) and Sch. 1.]

History – S. 9(2) (3) repealed by FA 1999, s. 115 and Sch. 18, para. 6(1), s. 139 and Sch. 20, Pt. V(4), the repeal coming into force on 1 October 1999.
In s. 9(7)(e), the words "which is inadvertently and undesignedly spoiled, and in lieu whereof another instrument made between the same parties and for the same purpose is executed and duly stamped, or" after "thereto" omitted by FA 1996, s. 199 and Sch. 39, para. 10(1), (2) and s. 205 and Sch. 41, Pt. VIII(4), with effect from 29 April 1996, but not in relation to an instrument which has been accidentally spoiled if an application for an allowance under s. 9 was made before that date.
Reference to "two years" in proviso (a) to s. 9(7) substituted by RA 1898, s. 13. In proviso (c) application restricted to use as playing cards by Pharmacy and Medicines Act 1941.
In s. 9(7), proviso (c) repealed by Statute Law (Repeals) Act 1993, s. 1(1) and Sch. 1, Pt. IX, Grp. 1, with effect from 5 November 1993.

Cross references – FA 1970, s. 33(6): reference to stamp extended to other indications of the amount of stamp duty on composition agreements with stock exchanges etc.

Notes – See note to s. 12A.

10   Allowance for misused stamps

10   When any person has inadvertently used for an instrument liable to duty a stamp of greater value than was necessary, or has inadvertently used a stamp for an instrument not liable to any duty, the Commissioners may, on application made within two years after the date of the instrument, or, if it is not dated, within two years after the execution thereof by the person by whom it was first or alone executed, and upon the instrument, if liable to duty, being stamped with the proper duty, cancel and allow as spoiled the stamp so misused.

History – S. 10 amended by Revenue Act 1898, s. 13, substituting reference to "two years" in both places.

Cross references – FA 1970, s. 33(6): reference to stamp extended to other indications of the amount of stamp duty on composition agreements with stock exchanges etc.

11   Allowance how to be made

11   In any case in which allowance is made for spoiled or misused stamps the Commissioners may give in lieu thereof other stamps of the same denomination and value, or if required, and they think proper, stamps of any other denomination to the same amount in value, or in their discretion, the same value in money.

History – In s. 11, the words ", deducting therefrom the discount allowed on the purchase of stamps of the like description", which appeared at the end of the section, were repealed by FA 1999, s. 115 and Sch. 18, para. 6(1), s. 139 and Sch. 20, Pt. V(4), the repeal coming into force on 1 October 1999.

Cross references – FA 1999, s. 110(4): interest on repayment of duty overpaid etc. also to apply to a money payment under s. 11 in relation to instruments executed on or after 1 October 1999.

Notes – See note to s. 12A.

12   Stamps not wanted may be repurchased by the Commissioners

12   [Repealed by FA 1999, s. 115 and Sch. 18, para. 6(1), s. 139 and Sch. 20, Pt. V(4) on 1 October 1999.]

ALLOWANCE FOR LOST OR SPOILED INSTRUMENTS

12A   Lost or spoiled instruments

12A(1)   This section applies where the Commissioners are satisfied that:

(a)   an instrument which was executed and duly stamped (**"the original instrument"**) has been accidentally lost or spoiled; and

(b)   in place of the original instrument, another instrument made between the same persons and for the same purpose (**"the replacement instrument"**) has been executed; and

(c)   an application for relief under this section is made to the Commissioners; and either

(d)   where the original instrument has been lost, the applicant undertakes to deliver it up to the Commissioners to be cancelled if it is subsequently found; or

(e)   where the original instrument has been spoiled:

     (i)   the application is made within two years after the date of the original instrument, or if it is not dated, within two years after the time when it was executed, or within such further time as the Commissioners may allow; and

     (ii)   no legal proceeding has been commenced in which the original instrument has been or could or would have been given or offered in evidence; and

     (iii)   the original instrument is delivered up to the Commissioners to be cancelled.

12A(2)   Where this section applies:

(a)   the replacement instrument shall not be chargeable with any duty, but shall be stamped with the duty with which it would otherwise have been chargeable in accordance with the law in force at the time when it was executed, and shall be deemed for all purposes to be duly stamped; and

(b)   if any duty, interest, or penalty was paid in respect of the replacement instrument before the application was made, the Commissioners shall pay to such person as they consider appropriate an amount equal to the duty, interest, or penalty so paid.

12A(3)   For the purposes of this section the Commissioners may require the applicant to produce such evidence by statutory declaration or otherwise as they think fit.

History – S. 12A inserted by FA 1996, s. 199 and Sch. 39, para. 10(1), (3), with effect from 29 April 1996, but not in relation to an instrument which has been accidentally spoiled if an application for an allowance under s. 9 was made before that date. In s. 12A(2)(b), the words "or penalty" substituted for the words "fine or penalty" where they appeared (twice), by FA 1999, s. 114 and Sch. 17, para. 2(2), in relation to penalties in respect of things done or omitted on or after 1 October 1999.

Cross references – FA 1999, s. 110(5): interest on repayment of duty overpaid etc. – a payment under s. 12A(2)(b) is treated as a repayment of the duty or penalty by reference to which it is made, in relation to instruments executed on or after 1 October 1999.

Notes – S. 12A, and the amendment to s. 9(7)(e), put on a statutory footing former ESC G1 and G2.

OFFENCES RELATING TO STAMPS

13   Offences in relation to dies and stamps

13(1)   A person commits an offence who does, or causes or procures to be done, or knowingly aids, abets, or assists in doing, any of the acts following; that is to say,

(1), (2) [Repealed by Forgery Act 1913, s. 20.]

(3)   Fraudulently prints or makes an impression upon any material from a genuine die;

(4)   Fraudulently cuts, tears, or in any way removes from any material any stamp, with intent that any use should be made of such stamp or of any part thereof;

(5)   Fraudulently mutilates any stamp, with intent that any use should be made of any part of such stamp;

(6)   Fraudulently fixes or places upon any material or upon any stamp, any stamp or part of a stamp which, whether fraudulently or not, has been cut, torn, or in any way removed from *any other material, or out of or from* any other stamp;

(7)   Fraudulently erases or otherwise either really or apparently removes from any stamped material any name, sum, date, or other matter or thing whatsoever thereon written, with the intent that any use should be made of the stamp upon such material;

(8)   Knowingly sells or exposes for sale or utters or uses any stamp which has been fraudulently printed or impressed from a genuine die;

(9)   Knowingly, and without lawful excuse (the proof whereof shall lie on the person accused) has in his possession any stamp which has been fraudulently printed or impressed from a genuine die, or any stamp or part of a stamp which has been fraudulently cut, torn, or otherwise removed from any material, or any stamp which has been fraudulently mutilated, or any stamped material out of which any name, sum, date, or other matter or thing has been fraudulently erased or otherwise either really or apparently removed.

13(2)   A person guilty of an offence under this section is liable–

(a)   on summary conviction, to imprisonment for a term not exceeding six months or a fine not exceeding the statutory maximum, or both;

(b)   on conviction on indictment, to imprisonment for a term not exceeding ten years or a fine, or both.

History – In the sidenote to s. 13, the words "Offences in relation to dies and stamps" substituted for the words "Certain offences in relation to dies and stamps provided by Commissioners to be felonies" by FA 1999, s. 115 and Sch. 18, para. 5(2) in relation to things done or omitted on or after 1 October 1999.
S. 13(1) was made out of the existing s. 13 and the following alterations made to the wording of the new subsection (1):
–   the words "A person commits an offence who" substituted for the words "Every person who"; and
–   the words "shall be guilty of felony, and shall on conviction be liable to be kept in penal servitude for any term not exceeding fourteen years, or to be imprisoned for any term not exceeding two years." (which appeared at the end of the then s. 13 after item (9)) were omitted and repealed,
by FA 1999, s. 115 and Sch. 18, para. 5(3)Sch. 18, para. 5(4), s. 139 and Sch. 20, Pt. V(3) (the repeal) with effect in relation to things done or omitted on or after 1 October 1999.
S. 13(2) was inserted by FA 1999, s. 115 and Sch. 18, para. 5(5) with effect in relation to things done or omitted on or after 1 October 1999.
The Forgery Act 1913 repealed the previous s. 13(1), (2) and amended former s. 13(8), (9).
Notes – Criminal Justice Act 1948, s. 1(1); Criminal Procedure (Scotland) Act 1975, s. 221(1): reference to "penal servitude" is to be construed as a reference to "imprisonment".
Criminal Law Act 1967, s. 1: the felony/misdemeanour distinction removed.
Magistrates' Courts Act 1980, Sch. 1, para. 12: any offence is triable either summarily or upon indictment.

16   Proceedings for detection of forged dies, etc.

16   On information given before a justice upon oath that there is just cause to suspect any person of being guilty of any of the offences aforesaid, such justice may, by a warrant under his hand, cause every house, room, shop, building, or place belonging to or occupied by the suspected person, or where he is suspected of being or having been in any way engaged or concerned in the commission of any such offence, or of secreting any machinery, implements, or utensils applicable to the commission of any such offence, to be searched, and if upon such search any of the said several matters and things are found, the same may be seized and carried away, and shall afterwards be delivered over to the Commissioners.

History – S. 16 amended by Revenue Act 1898, s. 12 to include paper used for excise licences, and by Post Office Act 1969, s. 118(2).

17   Proceedings for detection of stamps stolen or obtained fraudulently

17   [Repealed by FA 1999, s. 115 and Sch. 18, para. 6(1), s. 139 and Sch. 20, Pt. V(4) on 1 October 1999.]

18   Licensed person in possession of forged stamps to be presumed guilty until contrary is proved

18   [Repealed by FA 1999, s. 115 and Sch. 18, para. 6(1), s. 139 and Sch. 20, Pt. V(4) on 1 October 1999.]

19   Mode of proceeding when stamps are seized

19   [Repealed by FA 1999, s. 115 and Sch. 18, para. 6(1), s. 139 and Sch. 20, Pt. V(4) on 1 October 1999.]

20   As to defacement of adhesive stamps

20   [Repealed by FA 1999, s. 115 and Sch. 18, para. 6(1), s. 139 and Sch. 20, Pt. V(4) on 1 October 1999.]

21   Penalty for frauds in relation to duties

21   Any person who practises or is concerned in any fraudulent act, contrivance, or device, not specially provided for by law, with intent to defraud Her Majesty of any duty shall incur a penalty not exceeding £3,000.

History – In s. 21 the words "a penalty not exceeding £3,000" substituted for the words "a fine of fifty pounds" by FA 1999, s. 114 and Sch. 17, para. 2(2) in relation to penalties in respect of things done or omitted on or after 1 October 1999.

MISCELLANEOUS

22   As to discontinuance of dies

22   Whenever the Commissioners determine to discontinue the use of any die, and provide a new die to be used in lieu thereof, and give public notice thereof in the London, Edinburgh and Belfast Gazettes, then from and after any day to be stated in the notice (such day not being within one month after the same is so published) the new die shall be the only lawful die for denoting the duty chargeable in any case in which the discontinued die would have been used; and every instrument first executed by any person, or bearing date after the day so stated, and stamped with the discontinued die, shall be deemed to be not duly stamped:

Provided as follows:

(a)   If any instrument stamped as last aforesaid, and first executed after the day so stated at any place out of the United Kingdom, is brought to the Commissioners within fourteen days after it has been received in the United Kingdom, then upon proof of the facts to the satisfaction of the Commissioners the stamp thereon shall be cancelled, and the instrument shall be stamped with the same amount of duty by means of the lawful die, without the payment of any penalty:

(b)   All persons having in their possession any material stamped with the discontinued die, and which by reason of the providing of such new die has been rendered useless, may at any time within six months after the day stated in the notice send the same to the chief office or one of the head offices, and the Commissioners may thereupon cause the stamp on such material to be cancelled, and the same material, or, if the Commissioners think fit, any other material, to be stamped with the new die, in lieu of and to an equal amount with the stamp so cancelled.

History – In s. 22, the words "London, Edinburgh and Belfast Gazettes" were substituted by FA 1998, s. 150(3), with effect from 31st July 1998.

Cross references – Revenue Act 1898, s. 10: s. 22 provisos also apply where a notice is published under that section.

23   Application of Act to excise labels

23   The provisions of this Act in reference to offences relating to stamps shall apply to any label now or hereafter provided by the Commissioners for denoting any duty of excise other than a duty of excise chargeable on goods imported into the United Kingdom and any label so provided shall be deemed to be included in the term "stamp" as defined by this Act.

History – S. 23 amended by CEMA 1979, Sch. 4, para. 12.

24   Declaration, how to be made

24   Any statutory declaration to be made in pursuance of or for the purposes of this or any other Act for the time being in force relating to duties may be made before any of the Commissioners, or any officer or person authorised by them in that behalf, or before any commissioner for oaths or any justice or notary public in any part of the United Kingdom, or at any place out of the United Kingdom, before any person duly authorised to administer oaths there.

History – S. 24 amended by Solicitors' Act 1974, s. 81(1).

Cross references – Revenue Act 1898, s. 7(6): s. 24 to include affidavits and oaths.

25   Mode of granting licences

25   [Repealed by FA 1999, s. 115 and Sch. 18, para. 6(1), s. 139 and Sch. 20, Pt. V(4) on 1 October 1999.]

26   Recovery of fines

26   [Repealed by FA 1999, s. 139 and Sch. 20, Part. V(3) on 1 October 1999.]

27   Definitions

27   In this Act, unless the context otherwise requires,–

The expression **"Commissioners"** means Commissioners of Inland Revenue:

The expression **"officer"** means officer of Inland Revenue:

The expression **"chief office"** means chief office of Inland Revenue:

The expression **"head offices"** means the head offices of Inland Revenue in Edinburgh and Belfast:

The expression **"duty"** means any stamp duty for the time being chargeable by law:

The expression **"material"** includes every sort of material upon which words or figures can be expressed:

The expression **"instrument"** includes every written document:

The expression **"die"** includes any plate, type, tool, or implement whatever used under the direction of the Commissioners for expressing or denoting any duty, or rate of duty, or the fact that any duty or rate of duty or penalty has been paid, or that an instrument is duly stamped, or is not chargeable with any duty or for denoting any fee, and also any part of any such plate, type, tool, or implement:

The expressions **"forge"** and **"forged"** include counterfeit and counterfeited:

The expression **"stamp"** means as well a stamp impressed by means of a die as an adhesive stamp for denoting any duty or fee:

The expression **"stamped"** is applicable as well to instruments and material impressed with stamps by means of a die as to instruments and material having adhesive stamps affixed thereto:

The expressions **"executed"** and **"execution"** have the same meaning as in the Stamp Act 1891:

The expression **"justice"** means justice of the peace.

History – Definitions of "die" and "stamp" extended by Post Office Act 1969, s. 118(2).
In s. 27, in the definition of "executed" and "execution", the words following "execution" substituted by FA 1994, s. 239(2), in relation to any instrument except one which, on or before 7 December 1993, has been executed for the purposes of SA 1891.

REPEAL, COMMENCEMENT, SHORT TITLE

30   Short title

30   This Act may be cited as the Stamp Duties Management Act 1891.

STAMP ACT 1891

(1891 Chapter 39)

[21st July 1891]

ARRANGEMENT OF SECTIONS

PART I – REGULATIONS APPLICABLE TO INSTRUMENTS GENERALLY

SCHEDULES
FIRST SCHEDULE – STAMP DUTIES ON INSTRUMENTS

Notes – FA 1999, Pt. VI, so far as it relates to stamp duty (s. 109–122) are to be construed as one with the Stamp Act 1891. These provisions apply to various events or actions occurring on or after 1 October 1999 – see specific sections for details of commencement.

PART I – REGULATIONS APPLICABLE TO INSTRUMENTS GENERALLY

CHARGE OF DUTY UPON INSTRUMENTS

1   Charges of duties in schedule

1   [Repealed by FA 1999, s. 139 and Sch. 20, Pt. V(2) in relation to instruments executed, or bearer instruments issued, on or after 1 October 1999 but as regards unit trust schemes subject to FA 1999, Sch. 20, Pt. V(2), para. 2. The repeal took effect from 6 February 2000 as regards unit trust schemes, by virtue of FA 1999, s. 122(4) and FA 1999, Sch. 19.]

2   All duties to be paid according to regulations of Act

2   All stamp duties for the time being chargeable by law upon any instruments are to be paid and denoted according to the regulations in this Act contained, and except where express provision is made to the contrary are to be denoted by impressed stamps only.

Cross references – Law of Property Act 1925, s. 42(2): a stipulation that a purchaser of a legal estate in land shall pay or contribute towards the costs of or incidental to the preparation of stamping is void.

3   How instruments are to be written and stamped

3(1)   Every instrument written upon stamped material is to be written in such manner, and every instrument partly or wholly written before being stamped is to be so stamped, that the stamp may appear on the face of the instrument, and cannot be used for or applied to any other instrument written upon the same piece of material.

3(2)   If more than one instrument be written upon the same piece of material, every one of the instruments is to be separately and distinctly stamped with the duty with which it is chargeable.

Cross references – FA 1988, s. 143(7), (9): disapplication to bearer instruments issued after 8 December 1987 representing "paired shares".

4   Instruments to be separately charged with duty in certain cases

4   Except where express provision to the contrary is made by this or any other Act,–

(a)   An instrument containing or relating to several distinct matters is to be separately and distinctly charged, as if it were a separate instrument, with duty in respect of each of the matters;

(b)   An instrument made for any consideration in respect whereof it is chargeable with ad valorem duty, and also for any further or other valuable consideration or considerations, is to be separately and distinctly charged, as if it were a separate instrument, with duty in respect of each of the considerations.

Cross references – FA 1989, s. 173(2): subject to s. 4, an instrument which would be chargeable with stamp duty under para. (3) of the heading "Bond, Covenant, or Instrument of any kind whatsoever" in Sch. 1, but for FA 1989, s. 173(1) (abolition of duty under that paragraph), not to be chargeable with stamp duty under any other provision of the Stamp Act 1891.

Note – Revenue Act 1909, s. 8: extension to further considerations in a lease consisting of a covenant.

5   Facts and circumstances affecting duty to be set forth in instruments

5   All the facts and circumstances affecting the liability of any instrument to duty, or the amount of the duty with which any instrument is chargeable, are to be fully and truly set forth in the instrument; and every person who, with intent to defraud Her Majesty,

(a)   executes any instruments in which all the said facts and circumstances are not fully and truly set forth; or

(b)   being employed or concerned in or about the preparation of any instrument, neglects or omits fully and truly to set forth therein all the said facts and circumstances;

shall incur a penalty not exceeding £3,000.

History – In s. 5 the words "a penalty not exceeding £3,000" substituted for the words "a fine of ten pounds" by FA 1999, 114 and Sch. 17, para. 3(2), in relation to penalties in respect of things done or omitted on or after 1 October 1999.

Notes – S. 121: in relation to fines in respect of things done or omitted before 1 October 1999, **"fines"** are penalties recoverable by High Court proceedings.

6   Mode of calculating ad valorem duty in certain cases

6(1)   Where an instrument is chargeable with ad valorem duty in respect of–

(a)   any money in any foreign or colonial currency, or

(b)   any stock or marketable security,

the duty shall be calculated on the value, on the day of the date of the instrument, of the money in British currency according to the current rate of exchange, or of the stock or security according to the average price thereof.

6(2)   Where an instrument contains a statement of current rate of exchange, or average price, as the case may require, and is stamped in accordance with that statement, it is, so far as regards the subject matter of the statement, to be deemed duly stamped, unless or until it is shown that the statement is untrue, and that the instrument is in fact insufficiently stamped.

Notes – S. 6 was disapplied for foreign and colonial currency for which a rate of exchange was specified in the Schedule to FA 1899 (s. 12 of that Act) but reapplied for instruments executed after 31 July 1985 on repeal of the said s. 12 (FA 1985, s. 88).

USE OF ADHESIVE STAMPS

9   Penalty for frauds in relation to adhesive stamps

9(1)   If any person–

(a)   Fraudulently removes or causes to be removed from any instrument any adhesive stamp, or affixes to any other instrument or uses for any postal purpose any adhesive stamp which has been so removed, with intent that the stamp may be used again; or

(b)   Sells or offers for sale, or utters, any adhesive stamp which has been so removed, or utters any instrument, having thereon any adhesive stamp which has to his knowledge been so removed as aforesaid;

he is liable to a penalty not exceeding £3,000.

9(2)   [Repealed by Revenue Act 1898.]

History – S. 9 amended by Revenue Act 1898, s. 7, and by Post Office Act 1969, s. 117(1).

In s. 9(1) the words "he is liable to a penalty not exceeding £3,000", at the end, substituted for the words "he shall, in addition to any other fine or penalty to which he may be liable, incur a fine of fifty pounds" by FA 1999, 114 and Sch. 17, para. 3(3), in relation to penalties in respect of things done or omitted on or after 1 October 1999.

Cross references – Revenue Act 1898, s. 7(5): fines incurred under s. 9 are recoverable summarily, with same right of appeal as for fines under excise Acts.

National Debt Act 1972, s. 10(1): power to apply s. 9 conferred, subject to modifications.

SSCBA 1992, Sch. 1, para. 8(3): power to apply s. 9 to National Insurance etc. conferred, subject to modifications.

Notes – S. 121: for fines in respect of things done or omitted before 1 October 1999, **"fines"** are penalties recoverable by High Court proceedings.

[DENOTING STAMPS]

Notes – Heading amended by CCH to reflect single extant section thereunder.

11   Denoting stamps

11   Where the duty with which an instrument is chargeable depends in any manner upon the duty paid upon another instrument, the payment of the last-mentioned duty shall, upon application to the Commissioners and production of both the instruments, be denoted upon the first-mentioned instrument in such manner as the Commissioners think fit.

Cross reference – FA 1984, s. 111: for the purpose of determining whether duly stamped, duty chargeable on certain conveyances, transfers, leases or tacks which are subject to agreement for a lease or tack is treated as dependent on the duty paid on the agreement.

ADJUDICATION STAMPS

12   Adjudication by Commissioners

12(1)   Subject to such regulations as the Commissioners may think fit to make, the Commissioners may be required by any person to adjudicate with reference to any executed instrument upon the questions–

(a)   whether it is chargeable with duty;

(b)   with what amount of duty it is chargeable;

(c)   whether any penalty is payable under section 15B (penalty on late stamping);

(d)   what penalty is in their opinion correct and appropriate.

12(2)   The Commissioners may require to be furnished with an abstract of the instrument and with such evidence as they may require as to the facts and circumstances relevant to those questions.

12(3)   The Commissioners shall give notice of their decision upon those questions to the person by whom the adjudication was required.

12(4)   If the Commissioners decide that the instrument is not chargeable with any duty, it may be stamped with a particular stamp denoting that it has been the subject of adjudication and is not chargeable with any duty.

12(5)   If the Commissioners decide that the instrument is chargeable with duty and assess the amount of duty chargeable, the instrument when stamped in accordance with their decision may be stamped with a particular stamp denoting that it has been the subject of adjudication and is duly stamped.

12(6)   Every instrument stamped in accordance with subsection (4) or (5) shall be admissible in evidence and available for all purposes notwithstanding any objection relating to duty.

History – S. 12 (together with s. 12A below) substituted for the former s. 12 by FA 1999, s. 109(3) and Sch. 12, para. 1. The substituted wording applies to instruments executed on or after 1 October 1999, but FA 1999, s. 109 and Sch. 12 do not apply to certain transfers or other instruments relating to units under a unit trust scheme (FA 1999, s. 122(1) and (2)).

Cross references – FA 1931, s. 28(4): notwithstanding s. 12, instrument transferring land not duly stamped unless produced to commissioners.

FA 1965, s. 90(3): instrument conveying or transferring property in contemplation of sale not duly stamped unless adjudicated under s. 12.

FA 1994, s. 244(5): certain instruments required by 244 to be produced to the Commissioners of Inland Revenue in relation to transfers of land in Northern Ireland are only duly stamped for the purposes of s. 14 if stamped with a stamp denoting that the instrument has been so produced. This applies from a day to be appointed.

FA 1995, s. 151(5): instruments mentioned in s. 151(1) not duly stamped unless duly stamped under law which would apply but for s. 151(1) or adjudicated under s. 12.

FA 2000, s. 130: no stamp duty chargeable on certain transfers to registered social landlords providing the instrument has been stamped with the duty to which it would have been liable or it has been stamped denoting that it is not chargeable with any duty in accordance with s. 12.

FA 2000, s. Sch. 32, para. 4 (stamp duty on seven year leases: transitional provisions): an instrument which ceases to be duly stamped under the provisions of Sch. 32, even if stamped in accordance with s. 12(5), is not admissible in evidence under s. 12(6) .

FA 2000, s. Sch. 32, para. 7 (stamp duty on seven year leases: transitional provisions): application of s. 12 as regards any additional duty under Sch. 32.

Electricity Act 1989, Sch. 11, para. 11(3)(b): no instrument certified as made in pursuance of a transfer scheme on privatisation to be taken to be duly stamped unless stamped in accordance with s. 12.

Education Act 1993, s. 299(5): no instrument under certain provisions of that Act to be treated as duly stamped unless stamped in accordance with s. 12.

Railways Act 1993, Sch. 9, para. 2(5): no instrument or agreement under certain provisions of that Act to be treated as duly stamped unless stamped in accordance with s. 12.

Education Act 1997, s. 53(2): no instrument under certain provisions of that Act to be treated as duly stamped unless stamped in accordance with s. 12.

Regional Development Agencies Act 1998, s. 39(2): an instrument or agreement which is certified by a Minister of the Crown as being made in pursuance of a transfer scheme under certain provisions of that Act must be stamped not chargeable with duty in accordance with s. 12.

Access to Justice Act 1999, Sch. 14, para. 34(2): no stamp duty chargeable on any scheme under para. 33 of the schedule (or on any instrument or agreement which is certified to the Commissioners of Inland Revenue by the Lord Chancellor as made in pursuance of such a scheme), providing the scheme (or instrument or agreement which is certified) has been stamped with the duty to which it would have been liable or it has been stamped denoting that it is not chargeable with any duty in accordance with s. 12.

Greater London Authority Act 1999, s. 417: no stamp duty chargeable on a transfer instrument (or an instrument or agreement which is certified to the Commissioners of Inland Revenue by a Minister of the Crown as made in pursuance of a transfer instrument or which is so certified as giving effect to a preparatory reorganisation) under an order or a scheme involving London Regional Transport under the provisions of the GLAA 1999, providing the instrument, etc. has been stamped with the duty to which it would have been liable or it has been stamped denoting that it is not chargeable with any duty in accordance with s. 12.

SI 1987/516: deeds of gift and other documents vesting title by way of gift (including deeds of arrangement) executed after 30 April 1987 no longer have to be submitted for a formal adjudication stamp (see FA 1985, s. 82 and 84).

SI 1997/1156, reg. 7(3): an instrument not chargeable with any duty under reg. 7 (instrument transferring property subject to authorised unit trust to an open-ended investment company) must be stamped not chargeable with any duty in accordance with s. 12.

Notes – Companies Act 1985, s. 88: Registrar of Companies may insist that duty payable on particulars of a contract constituting title to allotment of shares delivered for registration be adjudicated.

12A   Adjudication: supplementary provisions

12A(1) An instrument which has been the subject of adjudication by the Commissioners under section 12 shall not, if it is unstamped or insufficiently stamped, be stamped otherwise than in accordance with the Commissioners' decision on the adjudication.

12A(2) If without reasonable excuse any such instrument is not duly stamped within 30 days after the date on which the Commissioners gave notice of their decision, or such longer period as the Commissioners may allow, the person by whom the adjudication was required is liable to a penalty not exceeding £300.

12A(3) A statutory declaration made for the purposes of section 12 shall not be used against the person making it in any proceedings whatever, except in an inquiry as to the duty with which the instrument to which it relates is chargeable or as to the penalty payable on stamping that instrument.

12A(4) Every person by whom any such declaration is made shall, on payment of the duty chargeable upon the instrument to which it relates, and any interest or penalty payable on stamping, be relieved from any penalty to which he may be liable by reason of the omission to state truly in the instrument any fact or circumstance required by this Act to be so stated.

History – S. 12A (together with s. 12 above) substituted for the former s. 12 by FA 1999, 109(3) and Sch. 12, para. 1. The new section applies to instruments executed on or after 1 October 1999, but FA 1999, s. 109 and Sch. 12 do not apply to certain transfers or other instruments relating to units under a unit trust scheme (FA 1999, s. 122(1) and (2)).

Cross references – FA 2000, s. Sch. 32, para. 5 (stamp duty on seven year leases: transitional provisions): s. 12A(1) does not prevent an instrument being stamped with additional duty under Sch. 32.
FA 2000, Sch. 32, para. 7 (stamp duty on seven year leases: transitional provisions): application of s. 12A as regards any additional duty under Sch. 32.

13   Appeal against Commissioners' decision on adjudication

13(1) A person who is dissatisfied with a decision of the Commissioners on an adjudication under section 12 may appeal against it.

13(2) The appeal must be brought within 30 days of notice of the decision on the adjudication being given under section 12(3).

13(3) An appeal may only be brought on payment of–

(a) duty and any penalty in conformity with the Commissioners' decision, and

(b) any interest that in conformity with that decision would be payable on stamping the instrument on the day on which the appeal is brought.

13(4) An appeal which relates only to the penalty payable on late stamping may be brought to the Special Commissioners in accordance with section 13A below.

13(5) Any other appeal may be brought in accordance with section 13B below to the High Court of the part of the United Kingdom in which the case has arisen.

History – S. 13 (together with s. 13A and s. 13B below) substituted for the former s. 13 by FA 1999, 109(3) and Sch. 12, para. 2, but FA 1999, s. 109 does not apply to certain transfers or other instruments relating to units under a unit trust scheme (FA 1999, s. 122(1) and (2)). The substituted wording applies to instruments executed on or after 1 October 1999.

Cross references – FA 1965, s. 91 (repealed in relation to instruments executed on or after 1 October 1999): power of court to order repayment with interest in cases within former s. 13(4).
FA 2000, Sch. 32, para. 7 (stamp duty on seven year leases: transitional provisions): application of s. 13 as regards any additional duty under Sch. 32.

Notes – SI 1994/1811: Special Commissioners (Jurisdiction and Procedure) Regulations 1994.
SI 1998/3132, Sch. 1, RSC, O. 5: appeals to High Court from a general or special commissioner.

13A   Appeal to the Special Commissioners

13A(1) The following provisions apply in relation to an appeal under section 13(4).

13A(2) Notice of appeal must be given in writing to the Commissioners, specifying the grounds of appeal.

13A(3) On the hearing of the appeal the Special Commissioners may allow the appellant to put forward a ground not specified in the notice of appeal, and take it into consideration, if satisfied that the omission was not wilful or unreasonable.

13A(4) The powers conferred by sections 46A(1)(c) and (2) to (4) and sections 56B to 56D of the Taxes Management Act 1970 (power of Lord Chancellor to make regulations as to jurisdiction, practice and procedure in relation to appeals) are exercisable in relation to appeals to which this section applies.

13A(5) On the appeal the Special Commissioners may–

(a) if it appears to them that no penalty should be paid, set the decision aside;

(b)   if the amount determined appears to them to be appropriate, confirm the decision;

(c)   if the amount determined appears to them to be excessive, reduce it to such other amount (including nil) as they consider appropriate;

(d)   if the amount determined appears to them to be insufficient, increase it to such amount as they consider appropriate.

13A(6)   Section 56A of the Taxes Management Act 1970 (general right of appeal on point of law) applies in relation to a decision of the Special Commissioners under this section.

13A(7)   Without prejudice to that right of appeal, an appeal lies against the amount of a penalty determined by the Special Commissioners under this section, at the instance of the person liable to the penalty, to the High Court.

13A(8)   On an appeal under subsection (7) the court has the same powers as are conferred on the Special Commissioners by subsection (5) above.

History – S. 13A (together with s. 13 above and s. 13B below) substituted for the former s. 13 by FA 1999, 109(3) and Sch. 12, para. 2. The new section applies to instruments executed on or after 1 October 1999, but FA 1999 s. 109 and Sch. 12 do not apply to certain transfers or other instruments relating to units under a unit trust scheme (FA 1999, s. 122(1) and (2)).

Cross references – FA 2000, Sch. 32, para. 7 (stamp duty on seven year leases: transitional provisions): application of s. 13A as regards any additional duty under Sch. 32.

SI 1994/1811: Special Commissioners (Jurisdiction and Procedure) Regulations 1994.

13B   Appeal to the High Court

13B(1)   The following provisions apply in relation to an appeal under section 13(5).

13B(2)   The appellant may for the purposes of the appeal require the Commissioners to state and sign a case setting out the questions upon which they were required to adjudicate and their decision upon them.

13B(3)   The Commissioners shall thereupon state and sign a case and deliver the same to the person by whom it is required, and the case may, within 30 days thereafter, be set down by him for hearing.

13B(4)   On the appeal the court shall determine the questions submitted and may give such directions as it thinks fit with respect to the repayment of any duty or penalty paid in conformity with the Commissioners' decision.

History – S. 13B (together with s. 13 and s. 13A above) substituted for the former s. 13 by FA 1999, 109(3) and Sch. 12, para. 2. The new section applies to instruments executed on or after 1 October 1999, but FA 1999 s. 109 and Sch. 12 do not apply to certain transfers or other instruments relating to units under a unit trust scheme (FA 1999, s. 122(1) and (2)).

Cross references – FA 2000, Sch. 32, para. 7 (stamp duty on seven year leases: transitional provisions): application of s. 13B as regards any additional duty under Sch. 32.

SI 1994/1811: Special Commissioners (Jurisdiction and Procedure) Regulations 1994.

PRODUCTION OF INSTRUMENTS IN EVIDENCE

14   Terms upon which instruments not duly stamped may be received in evidence

14(1)   Upon the production of an instrument chargeable with any duty as evidence in any court of civil judicature in any part of the United Kingdom, or before any arbitrator or referee, notice shall be taken by the judge, arbitrator, or referee of any omission or insufficiency of the stamp thereon, and the instrument may, on payment to the officer of the court whose duty it is to read the instrument, or to the arbitrator or referee, of the amount of the unpaid duty, and any interest or penalty payable on stamping the same, and of a further sum of one pound, be received in evidence, saving all just exceptions on other grounds.

14(2)   The officer, or arbitrator, or referee receiving the duty and any interest or penalty shall give a receipt for the same, and make an entry in a book kept for that purpose of the payment and of the amount thereof, and shall communicate to the Commissioners the name or title of the proceeding in which, and of the party from whom, he received the duty and any interest or penalty, and the date and description of the instrument, and shall pay over to such person as the Commissioners may appoint the money received by him for the duty and any interest or penalty.

14(3)   On production to the Commissioners of any instrument in respect of which any duty, interest or penalty has been paid, together with the receipt, the payment of the duty, interest and penalty shall be denoted on the instrument.

14(4)   Save as aforesaid, an instrument executed in any part of the United Kingdom, or relating, wheresoever executed, to any property situate, or to any matter or thing done or to be done, in any part of the United Kingdom, shall not, except in criminal proceedings, be given in evidence, or be available for any purpose whatever, unless it is duly stamped in accordance with the law in force at the time when it was executed.

History – In s. 14:

- in subs. (1), the words:
  - "the instrument may" substituted for the words "if the instrument is one which may legally be stamped after the execution thereof, it may", and
  - "any interest or penalty" substituted for the words "the penalty";
- in subs. (2), the words "the duty and any interest or penalty" substituted for the words "the duty and penalty" where they appeared (three times);
- in subs. (3), the words:
  - "any duty, interest or penalty" substituted for the words "any duty or penalty", and
  - "the duty, interest and penalty" substituted for the words "the duty and penalty"; and
- in subs. (4) the word "executed" substituted for the words "first executed" where they appeared at the end of the subsection

all by FA 1999, s. 109(3) and Sch. 12, para. 3. The substitutions apply to instruments executed on or after 1 October 1999, but FA 1999 s. 109 and Sch. 12 do not apply to certain transfers or other instruments relating to units under a unit trust scheme (FA 1999, s. 122(1) and (2)).

Cross references – FA 1993, s. 204(3): regulations may be made as to the method of denoting stamp duty.
FA 1994, s. 244(5): certain instruments required by s. 244 to be produced to the Commissioners of Inland Revenue in relation to transfers of land in Northern Ireland are only duly stamped for the purposes of s. 14 if stamped with a stamp denoting that the instrument has been so produced. This applies from a day to be appointed.
FA 2000, Sch. 32, para. 4 (stamp duty on seven year leases: transitional provisions): an instrument which ceases to be duly stamped under the provisions of Sch. 32, cannot be received in evidence in accordance with s. 14(1) unless the additional duty (and any interest or penalty) is paid in accordance with subs. (1).
FA 2000, Sch. 32, para. 6 (stamp duty on seven year leases: transitional provisions): as regards any instrument subject to additional duty under Sch. 32, s. 14(4) is to apply as if reference to the law in force at the time when it was executed is a reference to the law in force on the commencement date for the purposes of Sch. 32 (28 March 2000).

Other material – Law Society's Gazette, 18 July 1990: administrative modification to adjudication procedures.

Notes – FA 1931, s. 28(4): certain instruments transferring land not duly stamped unless stamped as having been produced to the commissioners.

STAMPING OF INSTRUMENTS AFTER EXECUTION

15　Stamping after execution

15(1)　An unstamped or insufficiently stamped instrument may be stamped after being executed on payment of the unpaid duty and any interest or penalty payable.

15(2)　Any interest or penalty payable on stamping shall be denoted on the instrument by a particular stamp.

History – S. 15 (together with s. 15A and s. 15B below) substituted for the former s. 15 by FA 1999, s. 109(1). The substituted wording applies to instruments executed on or after 1 October 1999, but FA 1999, s.109(1) does not apply to certain transfers or other instruments relating to units under a unit trust scheme (FA 1999, s. 122(1) and (2)).

Cross references – FA 1994, s. 240: time for presenting agreement for a lease for stamping.
FA 1994, s. 240A(2): a lease gives effect to an agreement for a lease if it is granted subsequent to the agreement and conforms with the agreement or relates to substantially the same property and term as the agreement.
FA 1998, s. 150(2): relief from double stamp duties, etc.
FA 2000, Sch. 32, para. 7 (stamp duty on seven year leases: transitional provisions): application of s. 15 as regards any additional duty under Sch. 32.

Other material – Stamp Office leaflet SO1099 – Stamp duty interest and penalties (not reproduced): Stamp Office policy on mitigation of interest and penalties.

15A　Late stamping: interest

15A(1)　Interest is payable on the stamping of an instrument which–

(a)　is chargeable with ad valorem duty, and

(b)　is not duly stamped within 30 days after the day on which the instrument was executed (whether in the United Kingdom or elsewhere).

15A(2)　Interest is payable on the amount of the unpaid duty from the end of the period of 30 days mentioned in subsection (1)(b) until the duty is paid.

If an amount is lodged with the Commissioners in respect of the duty, the amount on which interest is payable is reduced by that amount.

15A(3)　Interest shall be calculated at the rate applicable under FA 1989, section 178 of the Finance Act 1989 (power of Treasury to prescribe rates of interest).

15A(4)　The amount of interest shall be rounded down (if necessary) to the nearest multiple of £5.

No interest is payable if that amount is less than £25.

15A(5)　Interest under this section shall be paid without any deduction of income tax and shall not be taken into account in computing income or profits for any tax purposes.

History – S. 15A (together with s. 15 above and s. 15B below) substituted for the former s. 15 by FA 1999, s. 109(1). The new section applies to instruments executed on or after 1 October 1999, but FA 1999 s. 109 does not apply to certain transfers or other instruments relating to units under a unit trust scheme (FA 1999, s. 122(1) and (2)).

Cross references – FA 1994, s. 240(2): application of s. 15A to presentation of an agreement for a lease for stamping in determining when instrument executed for purposes of interest on unpaid duty.

FA 1994, s. 240A(2): a lease gives effect to an agreement for a lease if it is granted subsequent to the agreement and conforms with the agreement or relates to substantially the same property and term as the agreement.

FA 1999, Sch. 15, para. 24: bearer instruments – interest on unpaid duty payable at the rate prescribed under FA 1989, s. 178 for the purposes of s. 15A.

FA 2000, Sch. 32, para. 7 (stamp duty on seven year leases: transitional provisions): application of s. 15A as regards any additional duty under Sch. 32.

SI 1989/1297, reg. 3(1)(d) inserted by SI 1999/2538, reg. 3(b): applicable rate of interest under FA 1989, s.178(1) as it applies to s.15A.

Other material – Stamp Office leaflet SO1099 – Stamp duty interest and penalties (not reproduced): Stamp Office policy on mitigation of interest and penalties.

15B   Late stamping: penalties

15B(1)   A penalty is payable on the stamping of an instrument which is not presented for stamping within 30 days after–

(a)   if the instrument is executed in the United Kingdom, the day on which it is so executed;

(b)   if the instrument is executed outside the United Kingdom, the day on which it is first received in the United Kingdom.

15B(2)   If the instrument is presented for stamping within one year after the end of the 30-day period mentioned in subsection (1), the maximum penalty is £300 or the amount of the unpaid duty, whichever is less.

15B(3)   If the instrument is not presented for stamping until after the end of the one-year period mentioned in subsection (2), the maximum penalty is £300 or the amount of the unpaid duty, whichever is greater.

15B(4)   The Commissioners may, if they think fit, mitigate or remit any penalty payable on stamping.

15B(5)   No penalty is payable if there is a reasonable excuse for the delay in presenting the instrument for stamping.

History – S. 15B (together with s. 15 and s. 15A above) substituted for the former s. 15 by FA 1999, s. 109(1). The new section applies to instruments executed on or after 1 October 1999, but FA 1999 s. 109 does not apply to certain transfers or other instruments relating to units under a unit trust scheme (FA 1999, s. 122(1) and (2)).

Cross references – FA 1994, s. 240(3): application of S. 15B to presentation of an agreement for a lease for stamping in determining when instrument executed for purposes of penalties.

FA 1994, s. 240A(2): a lease gives effect to an agreement for a lease if it is granted subsequent to the agreement and conforms with the agreement or relates to substantially the same property and term as the agreement.

FA 1999, Sch. 17, para. 9(1): provisions of FA 1999, Sch. 17, Pt. II (determination of penalty and appeals) do not apply to penalties on late stamping under s. 15B.

FA 2000, Sch. 32, para. 7 (stamp duty on seven year leases: transitional provisions): application of s. 15B as regards any additional duty under Sch. 32.

Other material – Stamp Office leaflet SO1099 – Stamp duty interest and penalties (not reproduced): Stamp Office policy on mitigation of interest and penalties.

ENTRIES UPON ROLLS, BOOKS, ETC.

16   Rolls, books, etc., to be open to inspection

16   Every public officer having in his custody any rolls, books, records, papers, documents, or proceedings, the inspection whereof may tend to secure any duty, or to prove or lead to the discovery of any fraud or omission in relation to any duty, shall at all reasonable times permit any person thereto authorised by the Commissioners to inspect the rolls, books, records, papers, documents, and proceedings, and to take such notes and extracts as he may deem necessary, without fee or reward, and in case of refusal shall for every offence incur a penalty not exceeding £300.

History – In s. 16 the words "a penalty not exceeding £300" substituted for the words "a fine of ten pounds" by FA 1999, s. 114 and Sch. 17, para. 3(4), in relation to penalties in respect of things done or omitted on or after 1 October 1999.

Cross references – IHTA 1984, s. 259: application to inheritance tax as in relation to stamp duties.

Note – For IHTA 1984, s. 259, see the inheritance tax division.

17   Penalty for enrolling, etc., instrument not duly stamped

17   If any person whose office it is to enrol, register, or enter in or upon any rolls, books, or records any instrument chargeable with duty, enrols, registers, or enters any such instrument not being duly stamped, he shall incur a penalty not exceeding £300.

History – In s. 17 the words "a penalty not exceeding £300" substituted for the words "a fine of ten pounds" by FA 1999, s. 114 and Sch. 17, para. 3(5), in relation to penalties in respect of things done or omitted on or after 1 October 1999.

PART II – REGULATIONS APPLICABLE TO PARTICULAR INSTRUMENTS

INSTRUMENTS OF APPRENTICESHIP

25   Meaning of instrument of apprenticeship

25   Every writing relating to the service or tuition of any apprentice, clerk, or servant placed with any master to learn any profession, trade, or employment (except articles of clerkship to a solicitor or law agent or writer to the signet) is to be deemed an instrument of apprenticeship.

BILLS OF SALE

41   Bills of sale

41   A bill of sale is not to be registered under any Act for the time being in force relating to the registration of bills of sale unless the original, duly stamped, is produced to the proper officer.

CHARTER-PARTIES

49   Provisions as to duty on charter-party

49(1)   For the purposes of this Act the expression **"charter-party"** includes any agreement or contract for the charter of any ship or vessel or any memorandum, letter, or other writing between the captain, master, or owner or any ship or vessel, and any other person for or relating to the freight or conveyance of any money, goods, or effects on board of the ship or vessel.

49(2)   [Repealed by Finance Act 1949, s. 52(10) and Sch. 11, Pt. V.]

History – S. 49(2) repealed by FA 1949, s. 52(10) and Sch. 11, Pt. V.

CONVEYANCES ON SALE

54   Meaning of "conveyance on sale"

54   [Repealed by FA 1999, s. 139 and Sch. 20, Pt. V(2) in relation to instruments executed, or bearer instruments issued, on or after 1 October 1999, but as regards unit trust schemes subject to. FA 1999, Sch. 20, Pt. V(2), para. 2. The repeal took effect from 6 February 2000 as regards unit trust schemes, by virtue of FA 1999, s. 122(4) and FA 1999, Sch. 19.]

55   How ad valorem duty to be calculated in respect of stock and securities

55(1)   Where the consideration, or any part of the consideration, for a conveyance on sale consists of any stock or marketable security, the conveyance is to be charged with ad valorem duty in respect of the value of the stock or security.

55(1A)   For the purposes of subsection (1), it is immaterial–

(a)   whether, at the time of the execution of the conveyance on sale, the stock or marketable security is or has been issued or is to be issued; and

(b)   in a case where the stock or marketable security is to be issued, when it is to be, or is, issued and whether the issue is certain or contingent.

55(2)   Where the consideration, or any part of the consideration, for a conveyance on sale consists of any security not being a marketable security, the conveyance is to be charged with ad valorem duty in respect of the amount due on the day of the date thereof for principal and interest upon the security.

History – S. 55(1A) inserted by s. 126 (2) which has effect in relation to instruments executed after 28 July 2000.

56   How consideration consisting of periodical payments to be charged

56(1)   Where the consideration, or any part of the consideration, for a conveyance on sale consists of money payable periodically for a definite period not exceeding twenty years, so that the total amount to be paid can be previously ascertained, the conveyance is to be charged in respect of that consideration with ad valorem duty on such total amount.

56(2)   Where the consideration, or any part of the consideration, for a conveyance on sale consists of money payable periodically for a definite period exceeding twenty years or in perpetuity, or for any indefinite period not terminable with life, the conveyance is to be charged in respect of that consideration with ad valorem duty on the total amount which will or may, according to the terms of sale, be payable during the period of twenty years next after the day of the date of the instrument.

56(3) Where the consideration, or any part of the consideration, for a conveyance on sale consists of money payable periodically during any life or lives, the conveyance is to be charged in respect of that consideration with ad valorem duty on the amount which will or may, according to the terms of sale, be payable during the period of twelve years next after the day of the date of the instrument.

56(4) [Repealed by FA 1971, s. 69 and Sch. 14, Pt. VI.]

History – S. 56(4) repealed by FA 1971, s. 69 and Sch. 14, Pt. VI, with effect from 1 August 1971.

Statements of practice – SP 11/91: where VAT on rent treated otherwise than as rent under the lease, duty charged on VAT element as consideration payable periodically.

57   How conveyance in consideration of a debt, etc., to be charged

57 Where any property is conveyed to any person in consideration, wholly or in part, of any debt due to him, or subject either certainly or contingently to the payment or transfer of any money or stock, whether being or constituting a charge or incumbrance upon the property or not, the debt, money, or stock is to be deemed the whole or part, as the case may be, of the consideration in respect whereof the conveyance is chargeable with ad valorem duty.

Cross references – FA 1898, s. 6: application to foreclosure decrees.
FA 1981, s. 107(1): disapplication to conveyance or transfer on sale of a dwelling-house at a discount by specified bodies.
F(No. 2)A 1983, s. 15(1): disapplication to certain conveyances by constituency associations of political parties.
SI 1987/516: certain voluntary dispositions exempt duty if not for consideration within s. 57.

Statements of practice – SP 6/90: a covenant by the transferee to pay the debt is valuable consideration, may be implied in some circumstances but does not affect any statutory exemption; procedure explained.

58   Direction as to duty in certain cases

58(1) Where property contracted to be sold for one consideration for the whole is conveyed to the purchaser in separate parts or parcels by different instruments, the consideration is to be apportioned in such manner as the parties think fit, so that a distinct consideration for each separate part or parcel is set forth in the conveyance relating thereto, and such conveyance is to be charged with ad valorem duty in respect of such distinct consideration.

58(2) Where property contracted to be purchased for one consideration for the whole by two or more persons jointly, or by any person for himself and others, or wholly for others, is conveyed in parts or parcels by separate instruments to the persons by or for whom the same was purchased for distinct parts of the consideration, the conveyance of each separate part or parcel is to be charged with ad valorem duty in respect of the distinct part of the consideration therein specified.

58(3) Where there are several instruments of conveyance for completing the purchaser's title to property sold, the principal instrument of conveyance only is to be charged with ad valorem duty, and the other instruments are to be respectively charged with such other duty as they may be liable to, but the last-mentioned duty shall not exceed the ad valorem duty payable in respect of the principal instrument.

58(4) Where a person having contracted for the purchase of any property, but not having obtained a conveyance thereof, contracts to sell the same to any other person, and the property is in consequence conveyed immediately to the sub-purchaser then, except where–

(a) the chargeable consideration moving from the sub-purchaser is less than the value of the property immediately before the contract of sale to him, and

(b) the conveyance is not one to which section 107 of the Finance Act 1981 (sales of houses at discount by local authorities etc.) applies,

the conveyance is to be charged with ad valorem duty in respect of the consideration moving from the sub-purchaser.

58(5) Where a person having contracted for the purchase of any property but not having obtained a conveyance contracts to sell the whole, or any part or parts thereof, to any other person or persons, and the property is in consequence conveyed by the original seller to different persons in parts or parcels then, except where the aggregate of the chargeable consideration for the sale of all such parts or parcels is less than the value of the whole of the property immediately before the contract for their sale or, as the case may be, the first contract for the sale of any of them, the conveyance of each part or parcel is to be charged with ad valorem duty in respect only of the consideration moving from the sub-purchaser thereof, without regard to the amount or value of the original consideration.

58(6)   Where a sub-purchaser takes an actual conveyance of the interest of the person immediately selling to him, which is chargeable with ad valorem duty in respect of the consideration moving from him, and is duly stamped accordingly, any conveyance to be afterwards made to him of the same property by the original seller shall be chargeable only with such other duty as it may be liable to, but the last-mentioned duty shall not exceed the ad valorem duty.

58(7)   Any reference in subsection (4) or subsection (5) of this section to chargeable consideration is a reference to consideration which falls to be brought into account in determining the duty (if any) chargeable on the conveyance to the sub-purchaser or, as the case may be, on the conveyance of each of the parts or parcels in question; and in any case where it is necessary for the purposes of either of those sub-sections to determine the value at any time of any property, that value shall be taken to be the price which the property might reasonably be expected to fetch on a sale at that time in the open market.

History – S. 58(4), (5) amended and (7) inserted by FA 1984, s. 112(1)–(3) to provide exceptions from calculation of duty by reference to the consideration moving from a sub-purchaser, effective when the contract for the sub-sale, or as the case may be, the first contract for sub-sale of a part or parcel is entered into after 19 March 1984.
S. 58(7) amended by FA 1985, s. 82(2) to substitute reference to open market value rather than a cross reference to repealed provisions, effective from 26 March 1985.
Cross references – FA 1991, s. 112: modifications of s. 58(1), (2), where part of the property referred to in those subsections consists of "exempt property" within FA 1991, s. 110, with effect from the "abolition day" referred to in that section.
FA 2000, Sch. 34, para. 3: modifications of s. 58(1), (2), where part of the property referred to in those subsections consists of "intellectual property" within FA 2000, s. 129, with application to instruments executed on or after 28 March 2000.

59   Certain contracts to be chargeable as conveyances on sale

59   [Repealed by FA 1999, s. 139 and Sch. 20, Pt. V(2) in relation to instruments executed, or bearer instruments issued, on or after 1 October 1999 but as regards unit trust schemes subject to FA 1999, Sch. 20, Pt. V(2), para. 2. The repeal took effect from 6 February 2000 as regards unit trust schemes, by virtue of FA 1999, s. 122(4) and FA 1999, Sch. 19.]

60   As to sale of an annuity or right not before in existence

60   Where upon the sale of any annuity or other right not before in existence such annuity or other right is not created by actual grant or conveyance, but is only secured by bond, warrant of attorney, covenant, contract, or otherwise, the bond or other instrument, or some one of such instruments, if there be more than one, is to be charged with the same duty as an actual grant or conveyance, and is for the purposes of this Act to be deemed an instrument of conveyance on sale.

61   Principal instrument, how to be ascertained

61(1)   In the cases hereinafter specified the principal instrument is to be ascertained in the following manner:

    (a), (b) [Repealed by FA 1949, s. 52 and Sch. 11, Pt. V.]
       (c) Where in Scotland there is a disposition or assignation executed by the seller, and any other instrument is executed for completing the title, the disposition or assignation is to be deemed the principal instrument.

61(2)   In any other case the parties may determine for themselves which of several instruments is to be deemed the principal instrument, and may pay the ad valorem duty thereon accordingly.

History – S. 61(1)(a), (b) repealed by FA 1949, s. 52 and Sch. 11, Pt. V.

CONVEYANCES ON ANY OCCASION EXCEPT OR MORTGAGE

62   What is to be deemed a conveyance on any occasion, not being a sale or mortgage

62   [Repealed by FA 1999, s. 139 and Sch. 20, Pt. V(2) in relation to instruments executed, or bearer instruments issued, on or after 1 October 1999 but as regards unit trust schemes subject to FA 1999, Sch. 20, Pt. V(2), para. 2. The repeal took effect from 6 February 2000 as regards unit trust schemes, by virtue of FA 1999, s. 122(4) and FA 1999, Sch. 19.]

DUPLICATES AND COUNTERPARTS

72   Provision as to duplicates and counterparts

72   [Repealed by FA 1999, s. 139 and Sch. 20, Pt. V(2) in relation to instruments executed, or bearer instruments issued, on or after 1 October 1999 but as regards unit trust schemes subject to FA 1999, Sch. 20, Pt. V(2), para. 2. The repeal took effect from 6 February 2000 as regards unit trust schemes, by virtue of FA 1999, s. 122(4) and FA 1999, Sch. 19.]

EXCHANGE AND PARTITION OR DIVISION

73   As to exchange, etc.

73   [Repealed by FA 1999, s. 139 and Sch. 20, Pt. V(2) in relation to instruments executed, or bearer instruments issued, on or after 1 October 1999 but as regards unit trust schemes subject to FA 1999, Sch. 20, Pt. V(2), para. 2. The repeal took effect from 6 February 2000 as regards unit trust schemes, by virtue of FA 1999, s. 122(4) and FA 1999, Sch. 19.]

LEASES

75   Agreements to be charged as leases

75   [Repealed by FA 1999, s. 139 and Sch. 20, Pt. V(2)]

History – Repealed by FA 1999, s. 139 and Sch. 20, Pt. V(2) in relation to instruments executed, or bearer instruments issued, on or after 1 October 1999 but as regards unit trust schemes subject to FA 1999, Sch. 20, Pt. V(2), para. 2.

Notes – Section heading amended by Croner.CCH to reflect revised contents of section, originally "Agreements for not more than thirty-five years to be charged to leases".

77   Directions as to duty in certain cases

77(1)   A lease, or agreement for a lease, or with respect to any letting, is not to be charged with any duty in respect of any penal rent, or increased rent in the nature of a penal rent, thereby reserved or agreed to be reserved or made payable, or by reason of being made in consideration of the surrender or abandonment of any existing lease, tack, or agreement of or relating to the same subject matter.

77(2)   A lease made for any consideration in respect whereof it is chargeable with ad valorem duty, and in further consideration either of a covenant by the lessee to make, or of his having previously made, any substantial improvement of or addition to the property demised to him, or of any covenant relating to the matter of the lease, is not to be charged with any duty in respect of such further consideration.

77(3-4)   [Repealed by FA 1963, s. 73 and Sch. 14, Pt. IV.]

77(5)   [Repealed by FA 1999, s. 139 and Sch. 20, Pt. V(2).]

History – In s.77(1), the word "lease" substituted for the words "lease or tack" by FA 1999, s. 112(4) and Sch. 14, para. 2 in relation to instruments executed on or after 1 October 1999.
S. 77(3), (4) repealed by FA 1963, s. 73 and Sch. 14, Pt. IV, with effect from 1 August 1963.
S. 77(5) repealed by FA 1999, s. 139 and Sch. 20, Pt. V(2), the repeal having effect in relation to instruments executed, or bearer instruments issued, on or after 1 October 1999 but as regards unit trust schemes subject to FA 1999, Sch. 20, Pt. V(2), para. 2. The repeal took effect from 6 February 2000 as regards unit trust schemes, by virtue of FA 1999, s. 122(4) and FA 1999, Sch. 19.

Cross references – RA 1909, s. 8: exclusion as respects further consideration in a lease consisting of certain covenants.

Statements of practice – SP 11/91: further stamp duty may be payable on deed of variation etc. varying terms of lease so as to provide for payment of VAT by way of additional rent.

MARKETABLE SECURITIES AND FOREIGN AND COLONIAL SHARE CERTIFICATES

83   Penalty on issuing, etc. foreign, etc. security not duly stamped

83   Every person who in the United Kingdom assigns, transfers, negotiates, any foreign security or Commonwealth government security not being duly stamped, shall incur a penalty not exceeding £300.

Prospective repeals – S. 83 repealed by FA 1990, s. 109(1), and Sch. 19, Pt. VI, for instruments executed and transfers or negotiations of bearer stock on or after a day to be appointed. (See note below.)

History – S. 83 amended by FA 1963, s. 62(4) and FA 1973, Sch. 22, Pt. V.
In s. 83 the words "a penalty not exceeding £300" substituted for the words "a fine of twenty pounds" by FA 1999, s. 114 and Sch. 17, para. 3(6), in relation to penalties in respect of things done or omitted on or after 1 October 1999.

Notes – S. 121: in relation to fines in respect of things done or omitted before 1 October 1999, **"fines"** are penalties recoverable by High Court proceedings.
The Treasury order appointing the "abolition day" for the purposes of FA 1990, s. 107–110 was to have broadly coincided with the start of paperless trading under the Stock Exchange's planned TAURUS system (IR press release, 20 March 1990). However, on 11 March 1993 it was announced that TAURUS had been abandoned (London Stock Exchange News Release 6/93).

STOCK CERTIFICATES TO BEARER

109   Penalty for issuing stock certificate unstamped

109(1)   Where the holder of a stock certificate to bearer has been entered on the register of the local authority as the owner of the share of stock described in the certificate, the certificate shall be forthwith cancelled so as to be incapable of being re-issued to any person.

109(2)   [Repealed by FA 1963, s. 73 and Sch. 14, Pt. IV.]

Prospective repeals – S. 109(1) repealed by FA 1990, s. 109(2)(a), 132 and Sch. 19, Pt. VI, where the stock certificate or other instrument is entered on or after a day to be appointed. (See note below).

History – S. 109(2) repealed by FA 1963, s. 73 and Sch. 14, Pt. IV, with effect from 1 August 1963.

Cross references – FA 1899, s. 5: extension to a company or body of persons and to instruments chargeable as stock certificates to bearer.

FA 1946, s. 56(2): extension in relation to units under a unit trust scheme to a register kept under the scheme.

Notes – The Treasury order appointing the "abolition day" for the purposes of FA 1990, s. 107–110 was to have broadly coincided with the start of paperless trading under the Stock Exchange's planned TAURUS system (IR press release, 20 March 1990). However, on 11 March 1993 it was announced that TAURUS had been abandoned (London Stock Exchange News Release 6/93).

WARRANTS FOR GOODS

111   Provisions as to warrants for goods

111(1)   For the purposes of this Act the expression **"warrant for goods"** means any document or writing, being evidence of the title of any person therein named, or his assigns, or the holder thereof, to the property in any goods, wares, or merchandise lying in any warehouse or dock, or upon any wharf, and signed or certified by or on behalf of the person having the custody of the goods, wares, or merchandise.

111(2), (3)   [Repealed by FA 1949, s. 52 and Sch. 11, Pt. V.]

History – S. 111(2), (3) repealed by FA 1949, s. 52 and Sch. 11, Pt. V.

PART III – SUPPLEMENTAL

MISCELLANEOUS

117   Conditions and agreements as to stamp duty void

117   Every condition of sale framed with the view of precluding objection or requisition upon the ground of absence or insufficiency of stamp upon any instrument executed after the sixteenth day of May one thousand eight hundred and eighty-eight, and every contract, arrangement, or undertaking for assuming the liability on account of absence or insufficiency of stamp upon any such instrument or indemnifying against such liability, absence, or insufficiency, shall be void.

119   Instruments relating to Crown property

119   Except where express provision to the contrary is made by this or any other Act, an instrument relating to property belonging to the Crown, or being the private property of the sovereign, is to be charged with the same duty as an instrument of the same kind relating to property belonging to a subject.

120   As to instruments charged with duty of £1.75

120   Any instrument which by any Act passed before the first day of January one thousand eight hundred and seventy-one and not relating to stamp duties, is specifically charged with the duty of £1.75, shall be chargeable only with the duty of 50p in lieu of the said duty of £1.75.

121   Recovery of penalties

121   [Repealed by FA 1999, s. 139 and Sch. 20, Pt. V(3) in relation to things done or omitted on or after 1 October 1999.]

122   Definitions

122(1)   In this Act, unless the context otherwise requires,–

The expression **"Commissioners"** means Commissioners of Inland Revenue:

The expression **"material"** includes every sort of material upon which words or figures can be expressed:

The expression **"instrument"** includes every written document:

The expression **"stamp"** means as well a stamp impressed by means of a die as an adhesive stamp:

The expression **"stamped"**, with reference to instruments and material, applies as well to instruments and material impressed with stamps by means of a die as to instruments and material having adhesive stamps affixed thereto:

The expressions **"executed"** and **"execution"**, with reference to instruments not under seal, mean signed and signature (but subject to subsection (1A) of this section):

The expression **"money"** includes all sums expressed in British or in any foreign or colonial currency:

The expression **"stock"** includes any share in any stocks or funds transferable at the Bank of England or at the Bank of Ireland, any strip (within the meaning of section 47 of the Finance Act 1942) of any such stocks or funds, and any share in the stocks or funds of any foreign or colonial state or government, or in the capital stock or funded debt of any county council, corporation, company, or society in the United Kingdom, or of any foreign or colonial corporation, company, or society:

The expression **"marketable security"** means a security of such a description as to be capable of being sold in any stock market in the United Kingdom:

The expression **"steward"** of a manor includes deputy steward.

122(1A)   For the purposes of this Act a deed (or, in Scotland, a deed for which delivery is required) shall be treated as executed when it is delivered or, if it is delivered subject to conditions, when the conditions are fulfilled.

122(2)   In the application of this Act to Scotland expressions referring to the High Court shall be construed as referring to the Court of Session sitting as the Court of Exchequer.

History – In s. 122(1), in the definition of "executed" and "execution", the words "(but subject to subsection (1A) of this section)" added by FA 1994, s. 239(1)(b), in relation to any instrument except one which, on or before 7 December 1993, has been executed for the purposes of SA 1891.
In s. 122(1), in the definition of "stock", the words "and India promissory notes", after "Ireland", repealed by Statute Law (Repeals) Act 1993, s. 1(1) and Sch. 1, Pt. IX, Grp. 1, with effect from 5 November 1993.
In s. 122(1), in the definition of "stock", the words "any strip . . . such stock or funds," inserted by FA 1996, s. 202 and Sch. 40, para. 1, with effect from 29 April 1996.
S. 122(1A) inserted by FA 1994, s. 239(1)(a), in relation to any instrument except one which, on or before 7 December 1993, has been executed for the purposes of SA 1891.

Cross references – FA 1942, s. 47: Treasury regulations with respect to the transfer and registration of Government stock.
FA 1986, s. 81(2): notwithstanding s. 122 the stamp denoting that instrument effecting transaction by a market maker is exempt may be of such kind as the commissioners may prescribe.

REPEAL; COMMENCEMENT; SHORT TITLE

124   Commencement

124   This Act shall come into operation on the first day of January one thousand eight hundred and ninety-two.

125   Short title

125   This Act may be cited as the Stamp Act 1891.

SCHEDULES

SCHEDULE – FIRST SCHEDULE – STAMP DUTIES ON INSTRUMENTS

History – First Schedule repealed by FA 1999, s. 139 and Sch. 20, Pt. V(2), the repeal having effect in relation to instruments executed, or bearer instruments issued, on or after 1 October 1999 (but as regards unit trust schemes, subject to FA 1999, Sch. 20, Pt. V(2), para. 2). The repeal took effect from 6 February 2000 as regards unit trust schemes, by virtue of FA 1999, s. 122(4) and FA 1999, Sch. 19.

Note – Following the repeal of the First Schedule (see note above), the following legislation should be referred to in its place in order to establish the amount of duty chargeable:

- on instruments (other than bearer instruments) executed on or after 1 October 1999 – FA 1999, Sch. 13 (brought into effect by FA 1999, 112(3)). References (express or implied) in any enactment, instrument or other document to any of the headings in Sch. 1 (other than the heading "bearer instrument") shall be construed, so far as is required for continuing its effect on or after 1 October 1999, as being or including a reference to the corresponding provision of FA 1999, Sch. 13 (FA 1999, Sch. 14, para. 1(1)); and
- on bearer instruments issued on or after 1 October 1999 – FA 1999, Sch. 15 (brought into effect by FA 1999, 113(1)). References (express or implied) in any enactment, instrument or other document to the heading "Bearer Instrument" in

Sch. 1 shall be construed, so far as is required for continuing its effect, as being or including a reference to FA 1999, Sch. 15 (FA 1999, Sch. 16, para. 1(1)).

FINANCE ACT 1895

(1895 Chapter 16)

[*30th May 1895*]

PART II – STAMPS

12   Collection of stamp duty in cases of property vested by Act or purchased under statutory power

12   Where after the passing of this Act, by virtue of any Act, whether passed before or after this Act, either –

(a)   any property is vested by way of sale in any person; or

(b)   any person is authorised to purchase property;

such person shall within three months after the passing of the Act, or the date of vesting, whichever is later, or after the completion of the purchase, as the case may be, produce to the Commissioners of Inland Revenue a copy of the Act printed by the Queen's printer of Acts of Parliament or some instrument relating to the vesting in the first case, and an instrument of conveyance of the property in the other case, duly stamped with the ad valorem duty payable upon a conveyance on sale of the property; and in default of such production, the duty with interest thereon at the rate of five per cent per annum from the passing of the Act, date of vesting, or completion of the purchase, as the case may be, shall be a debt to Her Majesty from such person.

History – S. 12 modified by FA 1946, s. 52(a) (transfer of assets upon nationalisation); FA 1952, s. 74 (transfer of assets to joint boards or joint committees of local authorities); FA 1966, s. 45(5) (transfer of property to harbour boards under harbour reorganisation schemes).

Cross references – FA 1949, s. 36, as prospectively amended by FA 1991, s. 114: exclusion of exempt property, within FA 1991, s. 110, from conveyance etc. to be produced in respect of property acquired under or in pursuance of Acts passed on or after abolition day as defined in FA 1991, s. 110.
FA 2000, Sch. 34, para. 5: exclusion of exempt intellectual property from requirements of s. 12 for an instrument of conveyance in accordance with which, by virtue of any Act, property is vested, or a person is authorised to purchase property. If the property consists wholly of intellectual property no instrument of conveyance need be produced.
The operation of s. 12 has been excluded by a number of provisions:
Land Commission Act 1967, s. 25(5) (where an instrument is exempt under that section).
Transport Act 1968, s. 160 (as amended).
Atomic Energy Authority Act 1971, s. 22(1) (property vested in the Authority is not regarded as so vested by way of sale).
Atomic Energy Authority (Weapons Group) Act 1973, s. 7 (property vested in Secretary of State for Defence not treated as vested by way of sale).
National Health Service Reorganisation Act 1973, s. 49 (transfer of property upon reorganisation).
Employment and Training Act 1973, s. 1(6) (establishment of Manpower Services Commission (now the Training Commission)).
Biological Standards Act 1975, s. 3(4).
Agriculture (Miscellaneous Provisions) Act 1976, s. 1(7) (dissolution of Sugar Board).
Race Relations Act 1976, Sch. 2, para. 10(2) (transfers of property from Race Relations Board to Commission for Racial Equality).
Aircraft and Shipbuilding Industries Act 1977, Sch. 3, para. 8 (vesting of property in acquired company); Sch. 4, para. 7 (vesting of property in public ownership).
National Health Service Act 1977, s. 96 (health authorities holding property on trust).
New Towns Act 1981, s. 71(1) (transfers of property to water authorities or district councils in accordance with the Act).
Police and Criminal Evidence Act 1984, Sch. 4, para. 15(2) (transfer of property from Police Complaints Board to Police Complaints Authority).
Railways Act 1993, Sch. 9, para. 2(6): no requirement to comply with s. 12 in relation to any instrument which is not chargeable to stamp duty under that Act.
Broadcasting Act 1996, s. 135 and Sch. 7, para. 25: no requirement to comply with s. 12 in relation to any instrument which is not chargeable to stamp duty under that provision.
Regional Development Agencies Act 1998, s. 39(3): no requirement to comply with s. 12 in relation to any instrument which is not chargeable to stamp duty under that Act.
Access to Justice Act 1999, Sch. 14, para. 34(1): no requirement to comply with s. 12 in relation to any instrument which is not chargeable to stamp duty under that Act.
Greater London Authority Act 1999, s. 417: no requirement to comply with s. 12 in relation to any instrument which is not chargeable to stamp duty under that Act.

FINANCE ACT 1898

(1898 Chapter 10)

[1st July 1898]

PART II – STAMPS

6   Removal of doubt as to 54 & 55 Vict. c. 39, ss. 54, 57, so far as regards foreclosure decrees

6   For the removal of doubts with reference to the effect of section fifty-four and fifty-seven of the Stamp Act 1891, it is hereby declared that the definition of **"conveyance on sale"** in the said section fifty-four includes a decree or order for, or having the effect of an order for, foreclosure.

Provided that –

(a)   the ad valorem stamp duty upon any such decree or order shall not exceed the duty on a sum equal to the value of the property to which the decree or order relates, and where the decree or order states that value that statement shall be conclusive for the purpose of determining the amount of the duty; and

(b)   where ad valorem stamp duty is paid upon such decree or order, any conveyance following upon such decree or order shall be exempt from the ad valorem stamp duty.

Cross references – SA 1891, s. 57: certain debts, money or stock deemed to be part of the consideration chargeable with ad valorem duty on conveyance of property.
FA 1999, Sch. 13, para. 1: definition of conveyance on sale (which replaces that in SA 1891, s. 54, s. 54 being repealed, although the wording of s. 6 is unchanged).

REVENUE ACT 1898

(1898 Chapter 46)

[12th August 1898]

PART II – STAMPS

7   Amendments of 54 & 55 Vict. c. 39

7(1)   [Repealed by F(1909–1910)A 1910.]

7(2)   Any document referring to any Act or enactment repealed by the Stamp Act 1891, shall unless the context otherwise requires be construed to refer to that Act or the corresponding enactment in that Act.

7(3)   [Repealed by Statute Law Revision Act 1908.]

7(4)   The expression **"instrument"** in section nine of the Stamp Act 1891, includes any postal packet within the meaning of the Post Office (Protection) Act 1884, and sub-section two of the said section is hereby repealed.

7(5)   [Repealed by FA 1999, s. 139 and Sch. 20, Pt. V(3).]

7(6)   Section twenty-four of the Stamp Duties Management Act 1891, is hereby declared to apply to affidavits and oaths as well as to statutory declarations.

History – S. 7(1) repealed by F(1909–1910)A 1910, Sch. 6.
S. 7(3) repealed by Statute Law Revision Act 1908.
S. 7(5) repealed by FA 1999, s. 139 and Sch. 20, Pt. V(3) with effect in relation to things done or omitted on or after 1 October 1999.

Cross references – SA 1891, s. 9: penalties for fraud in relation to adhesive stamps.
SDMA 1891, s. 24: the manner in which statutory declarations are to be made.

10   Amendment of 54 & 55 Vict. c. 38, s. 22

10(1)   Whenever the Commissioners of Inland Revenue give public notice in the London, Edinburgh, and Belfast Gazettes that the use of any die, as defined by the Stamp Duties

Management Act 1891, has been discontinued, then, whether a new die has been provided or not, from and after any day to be stated in the notice (that day not being within one month after the notice is so published), that die shall not be a lawful die for denoting the payment of duty, and every instrument first executed by any person, or bearing date, after the day so stated in the notice, and stamped with duty denoted by the discontinued die, shall be deemed to be not duly stamped.

10(2) The provisos to section twenty-two of the Stamp Duties Management Act 1891, shall apply, subject to the necessary modifications, where a notice is published under this section in the same manner as they apply where a notice is published under that section.

10(3) [Repealed by Post Office Act 1969, Sch. 11, Pt. II.]

History – Reference to the Dublin Gazette excluded by SR & O 1921/1804, art. 7(a).
S. 10(3) repealed by Post Office Act 1969, Sch. 11, Pt. II.

Cross references – SDMA 1891, s. 22 (proviso): permitted stamping of material with a new die where stamped in certain circumstances with a discontinued die.

12   Extension of certain sections of 54 & 55 Vict. c. 38, to paper used for excise licences

12 Sections fourteen, fifteen, and sixteen of the Stamp Duties Management Act 1891 (which relate to frauds in connection with the manufacture of paper), shall extend to paper used for excise licences, in like manner as if it were paper provided by the Commissioners of Inland Revenue for receiving the impression of a die.

FINANCE ACT 1899

(1899 Chapter 9)

[20th June 1899]

PART II – STAMPS

5   Extension of stamp duty on stock certificates to bearer

Notes – Section heading amended by CCH to reflect extant provisions.

5(1) [Repealed by FA 1963, s. 73 and Sch. 14, Pt. IV.]

5(2) Section one hundred and nine of the Stamp Act 1891 (which relates to the penalty for issuing stock certificates unstamped), shall apply to any instrument chargeable with stamp duty as a stock certificate to bearer in the same manner as it applies to the stock certificates to bearer named in that section, and as if "company or body of persons" were mentioned in sub-section one of that section as well as "local authority".

Prospective repeals – S. 5(2) repealed by FA 1990, s. 109(2)(b), 132 and Sch. 19, Pt. VI where the stock certificate or other instrument is entered on or after a day to be appointed. (See note below).

History – S. 5(1) and certain words in s. 5(2) repealed by FA 1963, s. 73 and Sch. 14, Pt. IV.

Notes – The Treasury order appointing the "abolition day" for the purposes of FA 1990, s. 107–110 was to have broadly coincided with the start of paperless trading under the Stock Exchange's planned TAURUS system (IR press release, 20 March 1990). However, on 11 March 1993 it was announced that TAURUS had been abandoned (London Stock Exchange News Release 6/93).

14   Construction of Part of Act

14 This Part of this Act shall be construed together with the Stamp Act 1891.

FINANCE ACT 1900

(1900 Chapter 7)

[9th April 1900]

PART II – STAMPS

10   Conveyances on sale

10   A conveyance on sale made for any consideration in respect whereof it is chargeable with ad valorem duty, and in further consideration of a covenant by the purchaser to make, or of his having previously made, any substantial improvement of or addition to the property conveyed to him, or of any covenant relating to the subject matter of the conveyance, is not chargeable, and shall be deemed not to have been chargeable, with any duty in respect of such further consideration.

FINANCE ACT 1902

(1902 Chapter 7)

[22nd July 1902]

PART II – STAMPS

9   Amendment of 54 & 55 Vict. c. 39, s. 62

9   [Repealed by FA 1999, s. 139 and Sch. 20, Pt. V(2) in relation to instruments executed, or bearer instruments issued, on or after 1 October 1999 but as regards unit trust schemes subject to FA 1999, Sch. 20, Pt. V(2), para. 2. The repeal took effect from 6 February 2000 as regards unit trust schemes, by virtue of FA 1999, s. 122(4) and FA 1999, Sch. 19.]

REVENUE ACT 1903

(1903 Chapter 46)

[14th August 1903]

PART II – STAMPS

7   Reduction of stamp duty in the case of substituted securities

7   [Repealed by FA 1999, s. 139 and Sch. 20, Pt. V(2) in relation to instruments executed, or bearer instruments issued, on or after 1 October 1999 but as regards unit trust schemes subject to FA 1999, Sch. 20, Pt. V(2), para. 2. The repeal took effect from 6 February 2000 as regards unit trust schemes, by virtue of FA 1999, s. 122(4) and FA 1999, Sch. 19.]

FINANCE ACT 1907

(1907 Chapter 13)

[*9th August 1907*]

PART II – STAMPS

7   Stamping of hire-purchase agreement

7   Any agreement for or relating to the supply of goods on hire, whereby the goods in consideration of periodical payments will or may become the property of the person to whom they are supplied, shall not be charged with any stamp duty.

History – S. 7 amended by FA 1985, s. 85(2), extending exemption to such agreements under seal (or, in Scotland, with a clause of registration), effective for instruments executed after 25 March 1985 or executed after 18 March 1985 but not stamped before 26 March 1985.

Note – S. 30(2): Pt. II to be construed together with SA 1891.

REVENUE ACT 1909

(1909 Chapter 43)

[*3rd December 1909*]

PART II – STAMPS

8   Amendment of section 77 of the Stamp Act 1891

8   The provisions of subsection (2) of section seventy-seven of the Stamp Act 1891 (which exempt a lease from stamp duty in respect of certain further considerations) shall not apply as respects any further consideration in the lease consisting of a covenant which if it were contained in a separate deed would be chargeable with ad valorem stamp duty, and accordingly the lease shall in any such case be charged with duty in respect of any such further consideration under section four of the said Act.

Notes – S. 12(1): Pt. II to be construed together with SA 1891.

LAW OF PROPERTY ACT 1925

(1925 Chapter 20)

[*9th April 1925*]

42   Provisions as to contracts

42(1)   [Not reproduced.]

42(2)   A stipulation that a purchaser of a legal estate in land shall pay or contribute towards the costs of or incidental to –

(a)   obtaining a vesting order, or the appointment of trustees of a settlement, or the appointment of trustees of a conveyance on trust for sale; or

(b)   the preparation stamping or execution of a conveyance on trust for sale, or of a vesting instrument for bringing into force the provisions of the Settled Land Act, 1925;

shall be void.

42(3)–(8)   [Not reproduced.]

42(9)   This section only applies in favour of a purchaser for money or money's worth.

FINANCE ACT 1930

(1930 Chapter 28)

[1st August 1930]

PART IV – STAMPS

42   Relief from transfer stamp duty in case of transfer of property as between associated companies

42(1)   Stamp duty under Part I of Schedule 13 to the Finance Act 1999 (conveyance or transfer on sale), shall not be chargeable on an instrument to which this section applies:

Provided that no such instrument shall be deemed to be duly stamped unless either it is stamped with the duty to which it would but for this section be liable, or it has in accordance with the provisions of section twelve of the said Act been stamped with a particular stamp denoting either that it is not chargeable with any duty or that it is duly stamped.

42(2)   This section applies to any instrument as respects which it is shown to the satisfaction of the Commissioners that –

(a)   the effect of the instrument is to convey or transfer a beneficial interest in property from one body corporate ("the transferor") to another ("the transferee"), and

(b)   the bodies in question are associated at the time the instrument is executed,

unless at the time the instrument is executed arrangements are in existence by virtue of which at that or some later time any person has or could obtain, or any persons together have or could obtain, control of the transferee but not of the transferor.

42(2A)   For the purposes of this section bodies corporate are associated at a particular time if at that time one is the parent of the other or another body corporate is the parent of each.

42(2B)   For the purposes of this section one body corporate is the parent of another at a particular time if at that time the first body–

(a)   is beneficial owner of not less than 75 per cent of the ordinary share capital of the second body;

(b)   is beneficially entitled to not less than 75 per cent of any profits available for distribution to equity holders of the second body; and

(c)   would be beneficially entitled to not less than 75 per cent of any assets of the second body available for distribution to its equity holders on a winding-up.

42(3)   The **ownership** referred to in paragraph (a) of subsection (2B) above is ownership either directly or through another body corporate or other bodies corporate, or partly directly and partly through another body corporate or other bodies corporate, and Part I of Schedule 4 to the Finance Act 1938 (determination of amount of capital held through other bodies corporate) shall apply for the purposes of that paragraph.

42(4)   In this section **"ordinary share capital"**, in relation to a body corporate, means all the issued share capital (by whatever name called) of the body corporate, other than capital the holders of which have a right to a dividend at a fixed rate but have no other right to share in the profits of the body corporate.

42(5)   Schedule 18 to the Income and Corporation Taxes Act 1988 shall apply for the purposes of paragraphs (b) and (c) of subsection (2B) as it applies for the purposes of paragraphs (a) and (b) of section 413(7) of that Act; but this is subject to subsection (6).

42(6)   In determining for the purposes of this section whether a body corporate is the parent of the transferor, paragraphs 5 (3) and 5B to 5E of Schedule 18 to the Income and Corporation Taxes Act 1988 shall not apply for the purposes of paragraph (b) or (c) of subsection (2B).

42(7)   In this section, **"control"** shall be construed in accordance with section 840 of the Income and Corporation Taxes Act 1988.

History – In s. 42(1), the words "Part I of Schedule 13 to the Finance Act 1999 (conveyance or transfer on sale)" substituted for the words "the heading "Conveyance or Transfer on Sale" in the First Schedule to the Stamp Act 1891" by 112(4) and Sch. 14, para. 3 in relation to instruments executed on or after 1 October 1999.
In s. 42(2), in paragraph (a) the words "("tranferor") to another ("tranferee")" substituted for the words "to another" by FA 2000, s. 123 (2) which has effect in relation to instruments executed after 28 July 2000.

In s. 42(2), after paragraph (b) the words "unless at the time ...... but not of the transferor" inserted by FA 2000, s. 123 (3) which has effect in relation to instruments executed after 28 July 2000.

In s. 42(2), words from "that –" to the end of para. (b) substituted by FA 1995, s. 149(1), (2), in relation to instruments executed on or after 1 May 1995.

S. 42(2) substituted by FA 1967, s. 27(2).

S. 42(2A), (2B) inserted by FA 1995, s. 149(1), (3), in relation to instruments executed on or after 1 May 1995.

In s. 42(2B), para. (a) created using the existing wording and para. (b), (c) added by FA 2000, s. 123(4) in relation to instruments executed after 28 July 2000.

In s. 42(3), the words "paragraph (a) of" inserted and the words "that paragraph" substituted for the words "this section", by FA 2000, s. 123(5) in relation to instruments executed after 28 July 2000.

In s. 42(3), reference to subsection (2B) substituted for former reference to subsection (2), and words at the end, which read "with the substitution of references to issued share capital for references to ordinary share capital." omitted and repealed by FA 1995, s. 149(1), (4), s. 162 and Sch. 29, Pt. X, in relation to instruments executed on or after 1 May 1995.

S. 42(3) substituted by FA 1967, s. 27(2).

S. 42(4) inserted by FA 1995, s. 149(1), (5) in relation to instruments executed on or after 1 May 1995.

S. 42(5) - (7) added by FA 2000, s. 123(6) in relation to instruments executed after 28 July 2000.

Cross references – FA 1967, s. 27(3): disapplication of s. 42 unless shown to the satisfaction of the commissioners that not connected with certain arrangements.

SI 1997/1156, reg. 11: disapplication of s. 42 as regards any beneficial interest in property conveyed to or from an open-ended investment company.

Statements of practice – SP 3/98: Stamp Office approach to application of anti-avoidance rules preventing exploitation of group relief.

Notes – FA 1938, Sch. 4, Pt. I read as follows:

"SCHEDULE 4 – PROVISIONS FOR DETERMINING AMOUNT OF CAPITAL HELD THROUGH OTHER BODIES CORPORATE

4(1) Where, in the case of a number of bodies corporate, the first directly owns ordinary share capital of the second and the second directly owns ordinary share capital of the third, then, for the purposes of this Schedule, the first shall be deemed to own ordinary share capital of the third through the second, and, if the third directly owns ordinary share capital of a fourth, the first shall be deemed to own ordinary share capital of the fourth through the second and third, and the second shall be deemed to own ordinary share capital of the fourth through the third, and so on.

4(2) In this Part of this Schedule–

(a)   any number of bodies corporate of which the first directly owns ordinary share capital of the next and the next directly owns ordinary share capital of the next but one and so on, and, if they are more than three, any three or more of them, are referred to as "a series";

(b)   in any series–

    (i)   that body corporate which owns ordinary share capital of another through the remainder is referred to as "the first owner";

    (ii)   that other body corporate the ordinary share capital of which is so owned is referred to as "the last owned body corporate";

    (iii)   the remainder, if one only, is referred to as an "intermediary" and, if more than one, referred to as "a chain of intermediaries";

(c)   a body corporate in a series which directly owns ordinary share capital of another body corporate in the series is referred to as an "owner";

(d)   any two bodies corporate in a series of which one owns ordinary share capital of the other directly, and not through one or more of the other bodies corporate in the series, are referred to as being directly related to one another.

4(3) Where every owner in a series owns the whole of the ordinary share capital of the body corporate to which it is directly related, the first owner shall be deemed to own through the intermediary or chain of intermediaries the whole of the ordinary share capital of the last owned body corporate.

4(4) Where one of the owners in a series owns a fraction of the ordinary share capital of the body corporate to which it is directly related, and every other owner in the series owns the whole of the ordinary share capital of the body corporate to which it is directly related, the first owner shall be deemed to own that fraction of the ordinary share capital of the last owned body corporate through the intermediary or chain of intermediaries.

4(5) Where–

(a)   each of two or more of the owners in a series owns a fraction, and every other owner in the series owns the whole, of the ordinary share capital of the body corporate to which it is directly related; or

(b)   every owner in a series owns a fraction of the ordinary share capital of the body corporate to which it is directly related;

4(5) the first owner shall be deemed to own through the intermediary or chain of intermediaries such fraction of the ordinary share capital of the last owned body corporate as results from the multiplication of those fractions.

4(6) Where the first owner in any series owns a fraction of the ordinary share capital of the last owned body corporate in that series through the intermediary or chain of intermediaries in that series, and also owns another fraction or other fractions of the ordinary share capital of the last owned body corporate, either–

(a)   directly; or

(b)   through an intermediary or intermediaries which is not a member or are not members of that series; or

(c)   through a chain or chains of intermediaries of which one or some or all are not members of that series; or

(d)   in a case where the series consists of more than three bodies corporate, through an intermediary or intermediaries which is a member or are members of the series, or through a chain or chains of intermediaries consisting of some but not all of the bodies corporate of which the chain of intermediaries in the series consists;

4(6) then, for the purpose of ascertaining the amount of the ordinary share capital of the last owned body corporate owned by the first owner, all those fractions shall be aggregated and the first owner shall be deemed to own the sum of those fractions."

S. 53(4): Pt. IV to be construed as one with SA 1891.

ICTA 1988, section 840 and Schedule 18: see *Tax Statutes and Statutory Instruments*, Vol. 1A.

FINANCE ACT 1931

(1931 Chapter 28)

[*31st July 1931*]

PART III – LAND VALUE TAX

28 Production to Commissioners of instruments transferring land

28(1) On the occasion of –

(a) any transfer on sale of the fee simple of land;

(b) the grant of any lease of land for a term of seven or more years;

(c) any transfer on sale of any such lease;

it shall be the duty of the transferee, lessee, or proposed lessee to produce to the Commissioners the instrument by means of which the transfer is effected, or the lease granted or agreed to be granted, as the case may be, and to comply with the requirements of the Second Schedule to this Act, and if he fails so to produce any such instrument within thirty days after the execution thereof or, in the case of an instrument first executed at any place out of Great Britain after the instrument is first received in Great Britain, or fails to comply with the requirements of the said Schedule, he shall be liable on summary conviction to a fine not exceeding level 3 on the standard scale.

28(2) Where in accordance with the provisions of the last foregoing subsection any agreement for any lease of land for a term of seven or more years has been produced to the Commissioners, and the requirements of the said Second Schedule with respect thereto are complied with, it shall not be necessary under this section to produce to the Commissioners the instrument granting the lease in pursuance of the agreement or to comply with the requirements of the said Schedule with respect thereto, unless that instrument is inconsistent with the agreement, but the Commissioners shall, if any such instrument is produced to them and application is made for that purpose, denote on the instrument that the instrument has been so produced.

28(3) This section shall not apply with respect to any instrument which relates solely to incorporeal hereditaments or to a grave or right of burial.

28(4) Notwithstanding anything in section twelve of the Stamp Act 1891, no instrument required by this section to be produced to the Commissioners shall be deemed, for the purposes of section fourteen of that Act, to be duly stamped unless it is stamped with a stamp denoting that the instrument has been so produced.

28(5) This section shall come into operation on the first day of September, nineteen hundred and thirty-one.

28(6) [Repealed by Statute Law (Repeals) Act 1998, s. 1(1) and Sch. 1, Pt. IV.]

History – The former reference in s. 28(1) to "a fine not exceeding four hundred pounds" has effect as a reference to a fine not exceeding "level 3 on the standard scale" (Criminal Justice Act 1982, s. 38, 46, 54).
S. 28(1) and (3) amended by Land Commission Act 1967, Sch. 14.
S. 28(6) repealed by Statute Law (Repeals) Act 1998, s. 1(1) and Sch. 1, Pt. IV with effect from 19 November 1998. The wording of subs. (6) as it applied before repeal was as follows:
"**(6)** In Schedule 2 to this Act **"local authority"**, in relation to England and Wales, has the same meaning as in the Town and Country Planning Act 1971, and, in relation to Scotland, has the same meaning as in the Town and Country Planning (Scotland) Act 1997."
Reference in s. 28(6) to the Town and Country Planning (Scotland) Act 1997 substituted by Planning (Consequential Provisions) (Scotland) Act, s. 4 and Sch. 2, para. 1(1). S. 28(6) inserted by Land Commission Act 1967, Sch. 14.

Cross references – SA 1891, s. 12: assessment of duty by commissioners.
FA 1985, s. 89(1): disapplication of s. 28 to instruments prescribed by regulations (see notes to that section for such regulations).
FA 1999, Sch. 18, para. 4: where referring to the duration of a lease, the expression "term" in relation to Scotland means "period".

Notes – For offences committed after 30 September 1992, "level 3 on the standard scale" is £1,000 (Criminal Justice Act 1982, s. 37(2); Criminal Justice Act 1991, s. 17(1), 101(1), Sch. 12, para. 6; SI 1992/333).

34 Provisions as to expenses

34 Any expenses incurred by the Commissioners for the purposes of this Part of this Act shall be paid out of moneys provided by Parliament.

History – S. 34 amended by FA 1934, Sch. 4.

SCHEDULES

SCHEDULE 2 – REQUIREMENTS IN CONNECTION WITH PRODUCTION OF INSTRUMENTS OF TRANSFER

Section 28

1 Any person required by section 28 of this Act to produce any instrument to the Commissioners shall furnish to the Commissioners with the instrument a document (signed by the transferee or lessee or by some person on his behalf and showing his address) giving particulars–

1(a) of the description of the instrument;

1(b) of the date of the instrument;

1(c) of the names and addresses of the transferor and transferee or lessor and lessee;

1(d) of the situation of the land to which the transaction relates, including any dimensions stated in the instrument and, if necessary for the identification of the land, a description of the boundaries of the land, or a plan;

1(e) of the estate or interest transferred, including, where the transaction is the assignment or grant of a lease or the transfer of a fee simple subject to a lease, the term of the lease, the date of the commencement of the term and the rent reserved;

1(f) of the consideration, if any, other than the rent shown under sub-paragraph (e), showing separately any capital payment, any debt released, any debt covenanted to be paid or to which the transaction is made subject, any periodical payment (including any charge) covenanted to be paid, any terms surrendered, any land exchanged and any other thing representing money or money's worth comprised in the consideration for the transaction;

1(g) of any minerals, mineral rights, sporting rights, timber or easements reserved, and of any restrictions, covenants or conditions affecting the value of the estate or interest transferred or granted; and

1(h) of the information given to the transferee or lessee by any relevant authority when requested, in connection with the transaction, to state what entries (if any) relating to the land to which the transaction relates were shown in any relevant register.

2 In paragraph 1(h)–

2(a) in relation to land in England or Wales–

"**relevant authority**" means a local planning authority within the meaning of the Town and Country Planning Act 1990 and
"**relevant register**" means a register kept by the authority under section 69(1) of that Act;

2(b) in relation to land in Scotland–

"**relevant authority**" means a local authority within the meaning of the Town and Country Planning (Scotland) Act 1997 and
"**relevant register**" means a register kept by the authority under section 36(1) of that Act.

History – Sch. 2 substituted for the Second Schedule by virtue of Statute Law (Repeals) Act 1998, s. 1(2) and Sch. 2, para. 10 with effect from 19 November 1998. (Sch. 2 was previously substituted by virtue of Land Commission Act 1967, Sch. 15, and amended by Planning (Consequential Provisions) Act 1990, s. 4 and Sch. 2, para. 1(2) and Planning (Consequential Provisions) (Scotland) Act 1997, s. 4 and Sch. 2, para. 1(2).)

Cross reference – FA 1999, Sch. 18, para. 4: where referring to the duration of a lease, the expression "term" in relation to Scotland means "period".

FINANCE ACT 1933

(1933 Chapter 19)

[*28th June 1933*]

PART V – MISCELLANEOUS AND GENERAL

42   Effect of non-compliance with stamp laws in case of certain bills of exchange

42   Notwithstanding any enactment to the contrary, a bill of exchange which is presented for acceptance, or accepted, or payable, outside the United Kingdom shall not be invalid by reason only that it is not stamped in accordance with the law for the time being in force relating to stamp duties, and any such bill of exchange which is unstamped or not properly stamped may be received in evidence on payment of the proper duty and penalties as provided by section fourteen of the Stamp Act 1891.

History – In s. 42, the words "and subsection (1) of section fifteen" which appeared after the words "section fourteen" repealed by FA 1999, s. 139 and Sch. 20, Pt. V(1), the repeal having effect in relation to instruments executed on or after 1 October 1999 but as regards unit trust schemes subject to FA 1999, Sch. 20, Pt. V(1), para. 2.

FINANCE ACT 1942

(5 & 6 Geo. 6, Chapter 21)

[*24 June 1942*]

PART V – MISCELLANEOUS AND GENERAL

47   Transfer and registration of Government Stock

47(1)   The Treasury may by regulations provide–

(a)   for the transfer in law by instrument in writing or otherwise of stock and registered bonds of the descriptions specified in Part I of the Eleventh Schedule to this Act;

(b)   for the keeping by the Banks of England and Ireland of registers of the holders of such stock and bonds and as to the matters to be entered in the registers, and for enabling the registers to be closed in such circumstances as may be prescribed by the regulations;

(bb)   for the redemption of such stock and bonds;

(bc)   for the exchange of any such stock and bonds (whenever issued) for strips thereof;

(bd)   for exchanges by which such strips (whether deriving from the same security or from different securities) are consolidated into a single security of a description so specified;

(c)   as to the issue, except in such cases as appear to the Treasury to be appropriate, of documents of title relating to such stock and bonds and as to evidence of title thereto;

(d)   as to the transfer of such stock or bonds from England to Ireland and from Ireland to England;

(e)   for any incidental, supplementary or transitional matters relating to such stock and bonds, and to transactions connected therewith, for which it appears to the Treasury to be necessary or expedient to provide.

47(1ZA)   Regulations under subsection (1) of this section may make provision with respect to the purchase and sale of such stock and bonds by any person, or any description of person, through the Bank of England and, in relation to purchase or sale under the regulations, may–

(a)   make provision with respect to the commission and fees payable, and

(b)   make provision limiting the amount which any person, or any description of person, may purchase or sell on any day.

47(1A)   Regulations under subsection (1) of this section may make provision authorising the Bank of England, in such circumstances and subject to such conditions as may be prescribed in the regulations, to transfer stock and bonds standing in their books in the name of a deceased person into the name of another person without requiring the production of probate, confirmation or letters of administration.

47(1B) In this section **"strip"**, in relation to any stock or bond, means a security issued under the National Loans Act 1968 which–

(a)   is issued for the purpose of representing the right to, or of securing–

        (i) a payment corresponding to a payment of interest or principal remaining to be made under the stock or bond, or

        (ii) two or more payments each corresponding to a different payment remaining to be so made;

(b)   is issued in conjunction with the issue of one or more other securities which, together with that security, represent the right to , or secure, payments corresponding to every payment remaining to be made under the stock or bond; and

(c)   is not itself a security that represents the right to, or secures, payments corresponding to a part of every payment so remaining.

47(1C) For the purposes of subsection (1B) of this section, where the balance has been struck for a dividend on any stock or bond, any payment to be made in respect of that dividend shall, at times falling after that balance has been struck, be treated as not being a payment remaining to be made under the stock or bond.

47(1D) Without prejudice to the generality of the powers conferred by the preceding provisions of this section (but subject to subsection (1E) of this section), regulations made by virtue of paragraph (bc) or (bd) of subsection (1) of this section may–

(a)   provide, for the purpose of authorising the making of exchanges, for any stock or bonds to be treated as issued on such terms as may be specified in the regulations;

(b)   contain such provision as the Treasury think fit about the circumstances in which and the conditions subject to which exchanges may be effected; and

(c)   contain any such provision as could be contained in rules made under section 14(3) of the National Loans Act 1968 (Treasury rules as to exchange of securities).

47(1E) Regulations made by virtue of subsection (1)(bc) or (bd) of this section shall not make provision for the exchange of any stock or bonds, or of any strips, in any cases other than those where the exchange is at the request of the holder or in accordance with an order made by a court.

47(1F) Regulations under this section may make different provision for different cases and contain such exceptions and exclusions as the Treasury think fit; and the powers of the Treasury to make regulations under this section are without prejudice to any of their powers under the National Loans Act 1968.

47(2) As from the date on which the first regulations made under this section come into operation, all such stock and bonds as aforesaid shall be transferable in law in manner provided by regulations so made, and in no other manner, and accordingly the enactments and Order in Council set out in Part II of the Eleventh Schedule to this Act shall be amended to the extent specified in the third column of that Part, and the enactments and Order in Council set out in Part III of the said Schedule shall be repealed to the extent specified in the third column of that Part.

47(3) When the Treasury propose to make any regulations under this section, they shall lay a draft thereof before Parliament, and if either House of Parliament within the period of forty days beginning with the day on which the draft of the regulations is laid before it resolves that the regulations shall not be made, no further proceedings shall be taken thereon, but without prejudice to the laying of new draft regulations before Parliament.

In reckoning any such period of forty days as aforesaid no account shall be taken of any time during which Parliament is dissolved or prorogued or during which both Houses are adjourned for more than four days.

47(4) Nothing in this section shall affect–

(a)   any stock in respect of which a stock certificate issued under Part V of the National Debt Act 1870, is for the time being outstanding, or any other bearer security;

(b)   [repealed by FA 1964, s. 24 and Sch. 8, para. 2, s. 26(7) and Sch. 9.]

(c)   the National Savings Stock Register or any stock or securities for the time being registered therein.

History – In s. 47(1)(a), words "or otherwise" inserted by Stock Transfer Act 1982, s. 3 and Sch. 2, para. 2.
S. 47(1)(bb) inserted by FA 1989, s. 183(1).
S. 47(1)(bc),(bd) inserted by FA 1996, s. 202(1).

In s. 47(1)(c), words "except in such cases as appear to the Treasury to be appropriate" inserted by Stock Transfer Act 1982, s. 3 and Sch. 2, para. 2.
S. 47(1ZA) inserted by Bank of England Act 1998, s. 34, with effect from 1 June 1998 (SI 1998/1120).
S. 47(1A) inserted by FA 1989, s. 183(1).
S. 47(1B)–(1F) inserted by FA 96, s. 202(2).
S. 47(4)(b)repealed by FA 1964, s. 24 and Sch. 8, para. 2, s. 26(7) and Sch. 9, and words in s. 47(4)(c) repealed by National Debt Act 1958, s. 17(1) and Schedule. Words in s. 47(4)(c) "the National Savings Stock Register"substituted by Post Office Act 1969, s. 108(1)(d).

FINANCE ACT 1944

(1944 Chapter 23)

[13th July 1944]

PART VII – MISCELLANEOUS

45   Exemption of certain assignments by seamen from stamp duty

45   Stamp duty shall not be charged, and shall be deemed never to have been chargeable, on any assignment rendered valid by Regulation forty-seven D of the Defence (General) Regulations, 1939 (which relates to assignments of wages in payment of contributions to certain bodies representing the interests of or providing benefits for seamen).

46   Extension of Barracks Act 1890, s. 11

46   Section eleven of the Barracks Act 1890 (which exempts from stamp duty contracts, conveyances and other documents made with a view to carrying into effect the purposes of that Act) shall have effect as if in the preamble to that Act (which defines the purposes of that Act) the reference to military forces included a reference to naval forces.

FINANCE ACT 1946

(1946 Chapter 64)

[1st August 1946]

ARRANGEMENT OF SECTIONS

PART VII – STAMP DUTY

PART VII – STAMP DUTY

Note – S. 67(7): Pt. VII to be construed as one with SA 1891.

52   Exemption from stamp duty of documents connected with nationalisation schemes

52   Where, by any Act passed after the beginning of the present Session which embodies any scheme for the carrying on of any industry or part of an industry, or of any undertaking, under national ownership or control, provision is made for the transfer of any property, as part of the initial putting into force of the scheme, to the Crown or to a body corporate constituted for the purposes of that scheme or any previous scheme for such national ownership or control as aforesaid–

(a) in considering whether any and if so what duty is payable under section twelve of the Finance Act 1895 (which requires Acts to be stamped as conveyances on sale in certain cases) the consideration for the transfer shall be left out of account;

(b) [Repealed by FA 1973, s. 59 and Sch. 22, Pt. V.]

(c) stamp duty shall not be payable on any conveyance, agreement or assignment made or instrument executed solely for the purpose of giving effect to the transfer.

History – S. 52(b) repealed by FA 1973, s. 59 and Sch. 22, Pt. V.

Notes – Electricity Act 1947, s.11: special provisions dealing with transfers between Electricity Boards.

54 Units under unit trust schemes to be treated as stock

54(1)–(4) [Repealed by FA 1999, s. 139 and Sch. 20, Pt. V(5).]

54(5) [Repealed by FA 1976, s. 132 and Sch. 15, Pt. VI.]

54(6) [Repealed by FA 1987, s. 72 and Sch. 16, Pt. VIII.]

History – S. 54 (in effect, S. 54(1)–(4) because of previous repeals, see history notes below) repealed by FA 1999, s. 139 and Sch. 20, Pt. V(5), the repeal having effect in relation to instruments executed on or after 6 February 2000.
S. 54(5) repealed by FA 1976, s. 132 and Sch. 15, Pt. VI.
S. 54(6) repealed by FA 1987, s. 72 and Sch. 16, Pt. VIII with effect from 29 April 1988 (by virtue of SI 1988/780).

56 Supplemental provisions

56 [Repealed by FA 1999, 139 and Sch. 20, Pt. V(5) in relation to instruments executed on or after 6 February 2000.]

57 Interpretation of Part VII

57 [Repealed by FA 1999, s. 139 and Sch. 20, Pt. V(5).]

History – S. 57 repealed by FA 1999, s. 139 and Sch. 20, Pt. V(5), the repeal having effect in relation to instruments executed on or after 6 February 2000, although the repeal of s. 57(1A) and (1B) have effect subject to FA 1999, Sch. 19, para. 17(4) (saving for existing regulations). For this continued application and the enduring use of meanings in this section (see note below) after repeal, the relevant former wording only of s. 57 is reproduced below:

"**57(1)** In this Part of this Act, except in so far as the context otherwise requires, the following expressions have the meanings hereby respectively assigned to them, that is to say–

"**unit trust scheme**" has the same meaning as in the Financial Services Act 1986 (but subject to subsection (1A) of this section);

"**unit**" means, in relation to a unit trust scheme, a right or interest (whether described as a unit, as a sub-unit, or otherwise) of a beneficiary under the trust instrument;[other definitions not reproduced]

57(1A) The Treasury may by regulations provide that any scheme of a description specified in the regulations shall be treated as not being a unit trust scheme for the purposes of this Part of this Act.

57(1B) Regulations under this section–

(a) may contain such supplementary and transitional provisions as appear to the Treasury to be necessary or expedient, and

(b) shall be made by statutory instrument, which shall be subject to annulment in pursuance of a resolution of the House of Commons.

[sub. (2)–(4) not reproduced]"

Cross references – FA 1999, s. 122(3): "unit" and "unit trust scheme" have the same meaning as in Part VII of the Finance Act 1946 (or equivalent legislation for Northern Ireland).
SI 1997/1156, reg. 3: S. 57(1A), (1B) have effect in relation to open-ended investment companies as they have effect in relation to unit trust schemes.

Statutory instruments – SI 1988/268: limited partnership schemes and approved profit sharing schemes excluded from being "unit trust schemes".
SI 1992/197: common investment fund established under the Administration of Justice Act 1982, s. 42(1) is excepted from the definition of "unit trust scheme" from 1 March 1992.
SI 1996/1584: unit trust schemes which are pension funds pooling schemes excluded from being "unit trust schemes".

FINANCE ACT 1947

(1947 Chapter 35)

[*31st July 1947*]

PART VI – STAMP DUTIES

57 Exemption of transfers of stock guaranteed by Treasury

57(1) Where the payment of principal and interest on any stock to which this section applies is guaranteed by the Treasury, transfers of the stock shall be exempt from all stamp duties.

57(2) This section applies to any stock to which it may be applied by direction of the Treasury, being stock issued by a body corporate constituted for the purposes of any scheme for the carrying on of any industry or part of an industry, or of any undertaking, under national ownership or control which may be embodied in any Act passed after the beginning of the present Session.

Prospective repeals – S. 57 repealed by FA 1990, s. 132 and Sch. 19, Pt. VI in accordance with s. 107–111 of that Act.

History – Entries in s. 57(2) repealed by Air Corporations Act 1949, s. 41 and Sch. 3.
In s. 57(2), the words from "all stock" to "and to" and "other" repealed by Electricity Act 1989, s. 112(4) and Sch. 18, with effect from 31 March 1990 (SI 1990/117).

Notes – S. 74(7): Pt. VI to be construed as one with SA 1891.
The Treasury order appointing the "abolition day" for the purposes of FA 1990, s. 107–110 was to have broadly coincided with the start of paperless trading under the Stock Exchange's planned TAURUS system (IR press release, 20 March 1990). However, on 11 March 1993 it was announced that TAURUS had been abandoned (London Stock Exchange News Release 6/93).

FINANCE ACT 1948

(1948 Chapter 49)

[*30th July 1948*]

PART VII – STAMPS

74   Exemption from stamp duty in connection with certain nationalisation schemes

74   If, by any scheme under Part IV of the Transport Act 1947, or by or under any Act passed after the beginning of the present Session which embodies any scheme for the carrying on of any industry or part of an industry, or of any undertaking, under national ownership or control, provision is made for the transfer of the undertaking of any body corporate, and for the application to any shares, stock, debentures, debenture stock or other securities of that body corporate of provisions appearing to the Treasury to correspond to the provisions of Part II of the Fifth Schedule to the Transport Act 1947, the Treasury may direct, as respects all or any of the shares, stock, debentures, debenture stock or other securities, that, as from the date of the transfer of the undertaking, transfers thereof shall be exempt from all stamp duties.

Prospective repeals – S. 74 repealed by FA 1990, s. 132 and Sch. 19, Pt. VI, in accordance with s. 107–111 of that Act. (See note below).

Cross reference – Aircraft and Shipbuilding Act 1977, Sch. 5, para. 8: extension of s. 74.

Notes – S. 82(6): Pt. VII to be construed as one with SA 1891.
The Treasury order appointing the "abolition day" for the purposes of FA 1990, s. 107–110 was to have broadly coincided with the start of paperless trading under the Stock Exchange's planned TAURUS system (IR press release, 20 March 1990). However, on 11 March 1993 it was announced that TAURUS had been abandoned (London Stock Exchange News Release 6/93).

FINANCE ACT 1949

(1949 Chapter 47)

[*30 July 1949*]

PART IV – STAMP DUTIES

36   Amendments as to conveyances on sale

36(1)–(3)   [Repealed by FA 1956.]

36(4)   Section twelve of the Finance Act 1895 (which relates to duty on property vested by Act or purchased under statutory powers), shall not require any person who is authorised after the coming into force of this section to purchase any property as mentioned in the said section twelve to include in the instrument of conveyance required by that section to be produced to the Commissioners any goods, wares or merchandise forming part of the property nor, if the property consists wholly of goods, wares or merchandise, to produce any instrument of conveyance thereof to the Commissioners.

Prospective amendments – S. 36(4) amended by FA 1991, s. 114(2), and s. 36(5) added by s. 114(3), in respect of instruments executed on or after a day to be appointed.

History – S. 36(1)–(3) repealed by FA 1956, s. 44(9) and Sch. 5.

Notes – S. 52(5): Pt. IV to be construed as one with SA 1891.

FINANCE ACT 1951

(1951 Chapter 43)

[*1st August 1951*]

PART V – MISCELLANEOUS

42   Exemption from stamp duties of transfers of International Bank stock

42(1)   Transfers of any stock of the International Bank for Reconstruction and Development shall be exempt from all stamp duties.

42(2)   This section shall have effect as from the twenty-sixth day of April, nineteen hundred and fifty-one.

Prospective repeals – S. 42 repealed by FA 1990, s. 132 and Sch. 19, Pt. VI, from a day to appointed in accordance with s. 107–111 of that Act. (See note below).

Notes – The Treasury order appointing the "abolition day" for the purposes of FA 1990, s. 107–110 was to have broadly coincided with the start of paperless trading under the Stock Exchange's planned TAURUS system (IR press release, 20 March 1990). However, on 11 March 1993 it was announced that TAURUS had been abandoned (London Stock Exchange News Release 6/93).

FINANCE ACT 1952

(1952 Chapter 33)

[*9th July 1952*]

PART VI – MISCELLANEOUS AND GENERAL

74   Stamp duties (exemption for certain transfers to joint boards or joint committees of local authorities)

74(1)   Where provision is made either –

(a)   [Repealed by Water Act 1989, s. 190 and Sch. 25, para. 18 and Sch. 27, Pt. I.]

(b)   by an order under the Public Health Act 1936, or the Local Government (Scotland) Act 1947, for the transfer of any property to a joint board constituted under section six of the said Act of 1936 or to a joint board or joint committee constituted under section one hundred and nineteen or one hundred and twenty of the said Act of 1947, as the case may be, from another local authority;

then, in considering whether any and if so what duty is payable under section twelve of the Finance Act 1895 (which relates to the stamp duty payable in connection with certain statutory conveyances), the consideration for the transfer shall be left out of account.

74(2)   [Repealed by Water Act 1989, s. 190 and Sch. 25, para. 18 and Sch. 27, Pt. I.]

74(3)   No stamp duty shall be payable on any conveyance, agreement or assignment made, or instrument executed, solely for the purpose of giving effect to a transfer of property to a joint board or joint committee constituted under section one hundred and nineteen or one hundred and twenty of the Local Government (Scotland) Act 1947, from another local authority.

74(4) In this section **"local authority"** has the meaning assigned to it by section 519 of the Income and Corporation Taxes Act 1988.

74(5) This section shall be construed as one with the Stamp Act 1891.

History – S. 74(1)(a), (2) repealed by Water Act 1989, s. 190, Sch. 25, para. 18 and Sch. 27, Pt. I, with effect from 1 September 1989 (SI 1989/1530).
S. 74(1), (3), (4) amended by FA 1974, Sch. 12. Reference to provision of ICTA 1988 substituted by Sch. 29, para. 32 of that Act.

Notes – ICTA 1988, s. 519(4): (meaning of "local authority") repealed by FA 1990, s. 127 and Sch. 18, para. 5, s. 132 and Sch. 19, Pt. IV, with deemed effect from 1 April 1990.

FINANCE ACT 1953

(1953 Chapter 34)

[*31st July 1953*]

PART IV – MISCELLANEOUS AND GENERAL

31 Stamp duties

31(1) There shall be exempt from all stamp duties instruments of the following descriptions, being instruments made or executed for the purposes of any savings committee, savings group or other similar body affiliated to the National Savings Committee or the Scottish Savings Committee, that is to say,–

(a) [Repealed by FA 1970, s. 36(8) and Sch. 8, Pt. V.]

(b) any agreement whereby a person so acting makes himself responsible for money, stamps or other things supplied for the purposes of the body he acts for.

31(2) [Repealed by FA 1963, s. 73 and Sch. 14, Pt. IV.]

31(3) This section shall be construed as one with the Stamp Act 1891.

History – S. 31(1)(a) repealed by FA 1970, s. 36(8) and Sch. 8, Pt. V.
S. 31(1)(b) amended by FA 1970 and FA 1971.
S. 31(2) repealed by FA 1963, s. 73 and Sch. 14, Pt. IV.

FINANCE ACT 1958

(1958 Chapter 56)

[*1st August 1958*]

PART VI – STAMP DUTIES

Note – S. 40(2)(f): Pt. VI to be construed as one with SA 1891.

34 Conveyances on sale, etc.

34(1)–(3) [Repealed by FA 1963.]

34(4) [*Repealed by FA 1999, s. 139 and Sch. 20, Pt. V(2).*]

34(5)–(10) [Repealed by FA 1963 and FA 1970.]

History – S. 34(1)-(3), (5)-(7), (10) repealed by FA 1963, s. 73 and Sch. 14, Pt. IV.
S. 34(4) repealed by FA 1999, s. 139 and Sch. 20, Pt. V(2), the repeal having effect in relation to instruments executed, or bearer instruments issued, on or after 1 October 1999 but as regards unit trust schemes subject to FA 1999, Sch. 20, Pt. V(2), para. 2. The repeal took effect from 6 February 2000 as regards unit trust schemes, by virtue of FA 1999, s. 122(4) and FA 1999, Sch. 19.
S. 34(8) repealed by FA 1970, s. 36(8) and Sch. 8, Pt. V.

35 Miscellaneous amendments

35(1)–(3) [Repealed by FA 1971, s. 69 and Sch. 14, Pt. VI.]

35(4) [(a), (c) repealed by Water Act 1989; (b) repealed by FA 1974, s. 57 and Sch. 14, Pt. VI.]

35(5) No stamp duty shall be chargeable under or by reference to the heading "Conveyance or Transfer on sale" in the First Schedule to the Stamp Act 1891, on any agreement made under section fourteen of the New Towns Act 1946, by a development corporation under that Act for the transfer of the whole or part of the water undertaking or sewerage undertaking of that corporation, or on any conveyance, agreement or assignment made, or instrument executed, solely for the purpose of giving effect to such a transfer.

35(6) This section shall have effect as from the beginning of August, nineteen hundred and fifty-eight.

History – S. 35(1)–(3) repealed by FA 1971, s. 69 and Sch. 14, Pt. VI.
S. 35(4)(b) repealed by FA 1974, s. 57 and Sch. 14, Pt. VI.
S. 35(4)(a), (c), (5) repealed by Water Act 1989, s. 190, Sch. 25, para. 25 and Sch. 27, Pt. I, with effect from 1 September 1989 (SI 1989/1530).

FINANCE ACT 1959

(1959 Chapter 58)

[29th July 1959]

PART IV – STAMP DUTIES

30   Stamp duty on policies of insurance

30(1)–(3) [Repealed by FA 1970, s. 36(8) and Sch. 8, Pt. IV.]

30(4) [Repealed by Statute Law (Repeals) Act 1976, FA 1970, s. 36(8) and Sch. 8, Pt. IV and FA 1989, s. 187 and Sch. 17, Pt. IX.]

30(5) [Repealed by Statute Law (Repeals) Act 1976.]

30(6) Notwithstanding the repeal of section ninety-three of the Stamp Act 1891, a contract for such insurance as is mentioned in section five hundred and six of the Merchant Shipping Act 1894 shall continue to be admissible in evidence although not embodied in a marine policy as required by section twenty-two of the Marine Insurance Act 1906.

30(7) This section shall apply in relation to instruments made or executed after the beginning of August, nineteen hundred and fifty-nine.

History – S. 30(1)–(3) repealed by FA 1970, s. 36(8) and Sch. 8, Pt. IV.
S. 30(4) repealed by Statute Law (Repeals) Act 1976, Sch. 1, Pt. XVIII, FA 1970, s. 36(8) and Sch. 8, Pt. IV and FA 1989, s. 187 and Sch. 17, Pt. IX.
S. 30(5) repealed by Statute Law (Repeals) Act 1976, Sch. I, Pt. XVIII.

Notes – S. 37(2)(d): Pt. IV to be construed as one with SA 1891.

STOCK TRANSFER ACT 1963

(1963 Chapter 18)

[10th July 1963]

ARRANGEMENT OF SECTIONS

1   Simplified transfer of securities

1(1) Registered securities to which this section applies may be transferred by means of an instrument under hand in the form set out in Schedule 1 to this Act (in this Act referred to as a stock transfer), executed by the transferor only and specifying (in addition to the particulars of the consideration, of the description and number or amount of the securities, and of the person by whom the transfer is made) the full name and address of the transferee.

1(2)   The execution of a stock transfer need not be attested; and where such a transfer has been executed for the purpose of a stock exchange transaction, the particulars of the consideration and of the transferee may either be inserted in that transfer or, as the case may require, supplied by means of separate instruments in the form set out in Schedule 2 to this Act (in this Act referred to as brokers transfers), identifying the stock transfer and specifying the securities to which each such instrument relates and the consideration paid for those securities.

1(3)   Nothing in this section shall be construed as affecting the validity of any instrument which would be effective to transfer securities apart from this section; and any instrument purporting to be made in any form which was common or usual before the commencement of this Act, or in any other form authorised or required for that purpose apart from this section, shall be sufficient, whether or not it is completed in accordance with the form, if it complies with the requirements as to execution and contents which apply to a stock transfer.

1(4)   This section applies to fully paid up registered securities of any description, being–

(a)   securities issued by any company within the meaning of the Companies Act 1985 except a company limited by guarantee or an unlimited company;

(b)   securities issued by any body (other than a company within the meaning of the said Act) incorporated in Great Britain by or under any enactment or by Royal Charter except a building society within the meaning of the Building Societies Act 1986 or a society registered under the Industrial and Provident Societies Act 1965;

(c)   securities issued by the Government of the United Kingdom, except stock or bonds in the National Savings Stock Register, and except national savings certificates;

(d)   securities issued by any local authority;

(e)   units of an authorised unit trust scheme or a recognised scheme within the meaning of the Financial Services Act 1986.

History – Reference to Companies Act 1985 substituted by Companies Consolidation (Consequential Provisions) Act 1985, Sch. 2.
S. 1 (4)(b) amended by Building Societies Act 1986, s. 120(1) and Sch. 18, Pt. I, effective from 1 January 1987 (SI 1986/1560), excepting securities issued by a building society.
S. 1 (4)(c) amended by FA 1964, Sch. 10 and Post Office Act 1969, s. 108(1)(f).
Reference to matters within the meaning of Financial Services Act 1986 substituted by s. 212(2) and Sch. 16, para. 4(a) of that Act.

2   Supplementary provisions as to simplified transfer

2(1)   Section 1 of this Act shall have effect in relation to the transfer of any securities to which that section applies notwithstanding anything to the contrary in any enactment or instrument relating to the transfer of those securities; but nothing in that section affects–

(a)   any right to refuse to register a person as the holder of any securities on any ground other than the form in which those securities purport to be transferred to him: or

(b)   any enactment or rule of law regulating the execution of documents by companies or other bodies corporate, or any articles of association or other instrument regulating the execution of documents by any particular company or body corporate.

2(2)   Subject to the provisions of this section, any enactment or instrument relating to the transfer of securities to which section 1 of this Act applies shall, with any necessary modifications, apply in relation to an instrument of transfer authorised by that section as it applies in relation to an instrument of transfer to which it applies apart from this subsection; and without prejudice to the generality of the foregoing provision, the reference in section 184 of the Companies Act 1985 (certification of transfers) to any instrument of transfer shall be construed as including a reference to a brokers transfer.

2(3)   In relation to the transfer of securities by means of a stock transfer and a brokers transfer–

(a)   any reference in any enactment or instrument (including in particular section 183(1) and (2) of the Companies Act 1985) to the delivery or lodging of an instrument (or proper instrument) of transfer shall be construed as a reference to the delivery or lodging of the stock transfer and the brokers transfer.

(b)   any such reference to the date on which an instrument of transfer is delivered or lodged shall be construed as a reference to the date by which the later of those transfers to be delivered or lodged has been delivered or lodged; and

(c)   subject to the foregoing provisions of this subsection, the brokers transfer (and not the stock transfer) shall be deemed to be the conveyance or transfer for the purposes of the enactments related to stamp duty.

2(4)   Without prejudice to subsection (1) of this section, section 1 of this Act shall have effect, in its application to Scotland, notwithstanding anything to the contrary in any enactment relating to the execution of instruments or the validity of instruments delivered with particulars left blank; but so much of subsection (2) of that section as provides that the execution of a stock transfer need not be attested shall not apply to a transfer executed in accordance with section 18 of the Conveyancing (Scotland) Act 1924 on behalf of a person who is blind or unable to write.

Prospective repeals – S. 2(3)(c) and preceding word "and" repealed by FA 1990, s. 132 and Sch. 19, Pt. VI, from a date to be appointed in accordance with s. 107–111 of that Act. (See note below).

History – Reference to provisions of the Companies Act 1985 substituted by Companies Consolidation (Consequential Provisions) Act 1985, s. 30 and Sch. 2.
In s. 2(3)(a) reference to FA 1946, s. 56(4) (in parentheses) repealed by FA 1999, s. 139 and Sch. 20, Pt. V(5), the repeal having effect in relation to instruments executed on or after 6 February 2000.

Notes – The Treasury order appointing the "abolition day" for the purposes of FA 1990, s. 107–110 was to have broadly coincided with the start of paperless trading under the Stock Exchange's planned TAURUS system (IR press release, 20 March 1990). However, on 11 March 1993 it was announced that TAURUS had been abandoned (London Stock Exchange News Release 6/93).

3   Additional provisions as to transfer forms

3(1)   References in this Act to the forms set out in Schedule 1 and Schedule 2 include references to forms substantially corresponding to those forms respectively.

3(2)   The Treasury may by order amend the said Schedules either by altering the forms set out therein or by substituting different forms for those forms or by the addition of forms for use as alternatives to those forms; and references in this Act to the forms set out in those Schedules (including references in this section) shall be construed accordingly.

3(3)   Any order under subsection (2) of this section which substitutes a different form for a form set out in Schedule 1 to this Act may direct that subsection (3) of section 1 of this Act shall apply, with any necessary modifications, in relation to the form for which that form is substituted as it applies to any form which was common or usual before the commencement of this Act.

3(4)   Any order of the Treasury under this section shall be made by statutory instrument, and may be varied or revoked by a subsequent order; and any statutory instrument made by virtue of this section shall be subject to annulment in pursuance of a resolution of either House of Parliament.

3(5)   An order under subsection (2) of this section may–

(a)   provide for forms on which some of the particulars mentioned in subsection (1) of section 1 of this Act are not required to be specified;

(b)   provide for that section to have effect, in relation to such forms as are mentioned in the preceding paragraph or other forms specified in the order, subject to such amendments as are so specified (which may include an amendment of the reference in subsection (1) of that section to an instrument under hand);

(c)   provide for all or any of the provisions of the order to have effect in such cases only as are specified in the order.

History – S. 3(5) inserted by Stock Exchange (Completion of Bargains) Act 1976, s. 6(1), 7(4).

4   Interpretation

4(1)   In this Act the following expressions have the meanings hereby respectively assigned to them, that is to say–

"**local authority**" means, in relation to England and Wales, any authority being, within the meaning of the Local Loans Act 1875, an authority having power to levy a rate and, in relation to Scotland, a county council, a town council and any statutory authority, commissioners or trustees to whom section 270 of the Local Government (Scotland) Act 1947 applies;

"**registered securities**" means transferable securities the holders of which are entered in a register (whether maintained in Great Britain or not);

"**securities**" means shares, stock, debentures, debenture stock, loan stock, bonds, units of a collective investment scheme within the meaning of the Financial Services Act 1986, and other securities of any description;

"**stock exchange transaction**" means a sale and purchase of securities in which each of the parties is a member of a stock exchange acting in the ordinary course of his business as such or is acting through the agency of such a member;

"**stock exchange**" means the Stock Exchange, London, and any other stock exchange (whether in Great Britain or not) which is declared by order of the Treasury to be a recognised stock exchange for the purposes of this Act.

4(2) Any order of the Treasury under this section shall be made by statutory instrument, and may be varied or revoked by a subsequent order.

History – Definition of "securities" amended by the Financial Services Act 1986, s. 212(2) and Sch. 16, para. 4(b), substituting reference to collective investment scheme within the meaning of that Act.

Statutory instruments – SI 1973/536: the Stock Exchange (amalgamation of the former Stock Exchange, London with other members of the former Federation of Stock Exchanges in Great Britain and Ireland) is a recognised stock exchange.

FINANCE ACT 1963

(1963 Chapter 25)

[*31st July 1963*]

ARRANGEMENT OF SECTIONS

PART IV – STAMP DUTIES

REDUCTION OF DUTIES

PART IV – STAMP DUTIES

Note – S. 73(4): Pt. IV to be construed as one with SA 1891.

REDUCTION OF DUTIES

55   Reduced duty on conveyance or transfer on sale

55 [Repealed by FA 1999, s. 139 and Sch. 20, Pt. V(2).]

History – The repeal took effect in relation to instruments executed on or after 1 October 1999, but as regards unit trust schemes, the repeal was subject to FA 1999, Sch. 20, Pt. V(2), para. 2. For unit trust schemes, the repeal took effect from 6 February 2000, by virtue of FA 1999, s. 122(4) and FA 1999, Sch. 19.

Cross references – FA 1999, s. 112(3) and Sch. 13, Pt. I: rates of duty in relation to instruments executed on or after 1 October 1999. The percentage rates specified in Sch. 13 correspond to the rates of duty generally in force at 27 July 1999 (FA 1999, s. 112(5)).

56   Reduced duty on leases

56 [Repealed by FA 1999, s. 139 and Sch. 20, Part. V(2)]

History – The repeal under FA 1999, s. 139 and Sch. 20, Part. V(2) is in relation to instruments executed on or after 1 October 1999 but as regards unit trust schemes the repeal is subject to FA 1999, Sch. 20, Pt. V(2), para. 2. The repeal took effect from 6 February 2000 as regards unit trust schemes, by virtue of FA 1999, s. 122(4) and FA 1999, Sch. 19.

Cross references – FA 1999, 112(3) and Sch. 13, Pt. II: rates of duty on leases in relation to instruments executed on or after 1 October 1999.

57   Miscellaneous reductions

57 [Repealed by FA 1999, s. 139 and Sch. 20, Pt. V(2)]

History – Repealed by FA 1999, s. 139 and Sch. 20, Pt. V(2) in relation to instruments executed on or after 1 October 1999 but as regards unit trust schemes the repeal is subject to FA 1999, Sch. 20, Pt. V(2), para. 2. The repeal took effect from 6 February 2000 as regards unit trust schemes, by virtue of FA 1999, s. 122(4) and FA 1999, Sch. 19.

Cross references – FA 1999, 112(3) and Sch. 13: rates of duty in relation to instruments executed on or after 1 October 1999.

BEARER INSTRUMENTS

59   Stamp duty on bearer instruments

59   [Repealed by FA 1999, s. 139 and Sch. 20, Pt. V(2)]

History – Repealed by FA 1999, s. 139 and Sch. 20, Pt. V(2) in relation to bearer instruments issued on or after 1 October 1999 but as regards unit trust schemes the repeal is subject to FA 1999, Sch. 20, Pt. V(2), para. 2. The repeal took effect from 6 February 2000 as regards unit trust schemes, by virtue of FA 1999, s. 122(4) and FA 1999, Sch. 19.

Cross references – FA 1999, s. 113(1) and Sch. 15: charge on bearer instruments issued on or after 1 October 1999. The percentage rates specified in Sch. 15 correspond to the rates of duty generally in force at 27 July 1999 (FA 1999, s. 113(2)).

60   Payment of duty

60   [Repealed by FA 1999, s. 139 and Sch. 20, Pt. V(2) in relation to bearer instruments issued on or after 1 October 1999 but as regards unit trust schemes the repeal is subject to FA 1999, Sch. 20, Pt. V(2), para. 2. The repeal took effect from 6 February 2000 as regards unit trust schemes, by virtue of FA 1999, s. 122(4) and FA 1999, Sch. 19.]

Cross reference – FA 1999, s. 113(1) and Sch. 15: charge on bearer instruments issued on or after 1 October 1999.

61   Ascertainment of market value

61   [Repealed by FA 1999, s. 139 and Sch. 20, Pt. V(2) in relation to bearer instruments issued on or after 1 October 1999 but as regards unit trust schemes the repeal is subject to FA 1999, Sch. 20, Pt. V(2), para. 2. The repeal took effect from 6 February 2000 as regards unit trust schemes, by virtue of FA 1999, s. 122(4) and FA 1999, Sch. 19.]

Cross references – FA 1999, s. 113(1) and Sch. 15: charge on bearer instruments issued on or after 1 October 1999.

MISCELLANEOUS

62   Commonwealth stock

62   [Repealed by FA 1999, s. 139 and Sch. 20, Pt. V(2) in relation to instruments executed, or bearer instruments issued, on or after 1 October 1999 but as regards unit trust schemes subject to FA 1999, Sch. 20, Pt. V(2), para. 2. The repeal took effect from 6 February 2000 as regards unit trust schemes, by virtue of FA 1999, s. 122(4) and FA 1999, Sch. 19.]

63   Securities for annual and other payments

63   [Repealed by FA 1999, s. 139 and Sch. 20, Pt. V(2) in relation to instruments executed, or bearer instruments issued, on or after 1 October 1999 but as regards unit trust schemes subject to FA 1999, Sch. 20, Pt. V(2), para. 2. The repeal took effect from 6 February 2000 as regards unit trust schemes, by virtue of FA 1999, s. 122(4) and FA 1999, Sch. 19.]

65   Miscellaneous exemptions

65(1)   [Repealed by FA 1999, s. 139 and Sch. 20, Pt. V(2).]

65(2)   [Repealed by FA 1999, s. 139 and Sch. 20, Pt. V(5).]

65(3)   No stamp duty shall be chargeable in respect of any form of application for legal aid under the Legal Aid Act 1974 or the Legal Aid (Scotland) Act 1967 or in respect of any form relating to the offer and acceptance of a certificate pursuant to an application for legal aid under those Acts.

History – S. 65(1) repealed by FA 1999, s. 139 and Sch. 20, Pt. V(2), the repeal having effect in relation to instruments executed, or bearer instruments issued, on or after 1 October 1999 but as regards unit trust schemes subject to FA 1999, Sch. 20, Pt. V(2), para. 2. The repeal took effect from 6 February 2000 as regards unit trust schemes, by virtue of FA 1999, s. 122(4) and FA 1999, Sch. 19.

S. 65(2) repealed by FA 1999, s. 139 and Sch. 20, Pt. V(5), the repeal having effect in relation to instruments executed, or bearer instruments issued, on or after 6 February 2000.

In s. 65(3), references to 1974 and 1967 Acts substituted by virtue of Interpretation Act 1978, s. 17(2)(a).

67   Prohibition of circulation of blank transfers

67(1)   *Where a transfer in blank relating to registered stock of any description has been delivered,* pursuant to a sale of that stock, to or to the order of the purchaser or any person acting on his behalf, any person who in Great Britain parts with possession of that transfer, or who removes it or causes or permits it to be removed from Great Britain, before it has been duly completed shall be liable to a penalty not exceeding the aggregate of £300 and an amount equal to twice the stamp duty chargeable in respect of that transfer.

67(2) For the purposes of this section **"transfer in blank"** means a transfer in which the name of the transferee has not been inserted, and a transfer shall be treated as duly completed if, and only if, the name of the transferee is inserted therein, being the name of –

(a)   the purchaser of the stock under the sale;

(b)   a person entitled to a charge upon the stock for money lent to that purchaser;

(c)   a nominee holding as a bare trustee for that purchaser or for any such person as is mentioned in paragraph (b) above; or

(d)   a person acting as the agent of that purchaser for the purposes of the sale.

67(3) [Repealed by FA 1985, s. 98 and Sch. 27.]

67(4) In this section–

(a)   **"stock"** includes securities;

(b)   references to stock include any interest in, or in any fraction of, stock or in any dividends or other rights arising out of stock and any right to an allotment of or to subscribe for stock; and

(c)   **"transfer"** includes any instrument used for transferring stock.

67(4A) Nothing in this section applies to–

(a)   an instrument which is chargeable with duty at the rate specified in paragraph 5 of Schedule 15 to the Finance Act 1999 (certain bearer instruments issued by or on behalf of non-UK companies) and is duly stamped, or

(b)   renounceable letters of allotment, letters of rights or other similar instruments where the rights under the letter or other instrument are renounceable not later than six months after its issue.

67(5) References in this section to the purchaser of any stock include references to any person to whom the rights of the purchaser are transmitted by operation of law; and in relation to a transfer chargeable with duty in accordance with section 58(4) or (5) of the Stamp Act 1891 (transfers to sub-purchasers) references in this section to the purchaser and a sale shall be construed as references to the sub-purchaser and a sub-sale.

67(6) This section shall come into force on such date as the Treasury may by order made by statutory instrument direct.

Prospective repeals – S. 67 repealed by FA 1990, s. 109(3), 132 and Sch. 19, Pt. VI, where the sale is made on or after a day to be appointed.

History – In s. 67(1) the word "penalty" substituted for the word "fine" and "£300" substituted for "£50" by FA 1999, s. 114 and Sch. 17, para. 6, in relation to penalties in respect of things done or omitted on or after 1 October 1999.
S. 67(3) repealed by FA 1985, s. 98 and Sch. 27, as a consequence of the repeal of provisions dealing with gifts inter vivos, effective for instruments executed after 25 March 1985 or executed after 18 March 1985 and stamped after 25 March 1985.
s. 67(4) and (4A) substituted for the original subs. (4) by FA 1999, s. 113(3) and Sch. 16, para. 2, in relation to bearer instruments issued on or after 1 October 1999.
S. 67(5) amended (to omit reference to donee) by FA 1985, s. 98 and Sch. 27, as a consequence of the repeal of provisions dealing with gifts inter vivos, effective for instruments executed after 25 March 1985 or executed after 18 March 1985 and stamped after 25 March 1985.

FINANCE ACT 1964

(1964 Chapter 49)

[16th July 1964]

PART III – MISCELLANEOUS

23   Exemption of service contracts from stamp duty

23(1) No stamp duty shall be chargeable on, or on any memorandum of, a contract of service in any office or employment or a contract varying or terminating such a contract.

23(2) This section shall have effect as from 6th July 1964, and if before the passing of this Act any duty has been paid which by virtue of this section is not chargeable, the Commissioners shall, on application made to them within two years after the date of the payment, cancel the relevant stamps and repay the duty.

23(3) This section shall be construed as one with the Stamp Act 1891.

FINANCE ACT 1965

(1965 Chapter 25)

[*5th August 1965*]

PART V – MISCELLANEOUS AND GENERAL

90   Stamp duty: conveyances and transfers

90(1)   Subject to the provisions of this section, any instrument whereby property is conveyed or transferred to any person in contemplation of a sale of that property shall be treated for the purposes of the Stamp Act 1891 as a conveyance or transfer on sale of that property for a consideration equal to the value of that property.

90(2)   If on a claim made to the Commissioners not later than two years after the making or execution of an instrument chargeable with duty in accordance with subsection (1) of this section, it is shown to their satisfaction –

(a)   that the sale in contemplation of which the instrument was made or executed has not taken place and the property has been re-conveyed or re-transferred to the person from whom it was conveyed or transferred or to a person to whom his rights have been transmitted on death or bankruptcy; or

(b)   that the sale has taken place for a consideration which is less than the value in respect of which duty was paid on the instrument by virtue of this section,

the Commissioners shall repay the duty paid by virtue of this section, in a case falling under paragraph (a) of this subsection, so far as it exceeds the stamp duty which would have been payable apart from this section and, in a case falling under paragraph (b) of this subsection, so far as it exceeds the stamp duty which would have been payable if the instrument had been stamped in accordance with subsection (1) of this section in respect of a value equal to the consideration in question.

90(3)   No instrument chargeable with duty in accordance with subsection (1) of this section shall be deemed to be duly stamped unless the Commissioners have been required to express their opinion thereon under section 12 of the said Act of 1891 and have expressed their opinion thereon in accordance with that section.

90(4)   The foregoing provisions of this section shall apply whether or not an instrument conveys or transfers other property in addition to the property in contemplation of the sale of which it is made or executed, but those provisions shall not affect the stamp duty chargeable on the instrument in respect of that other property.

90(5)   For the purposes of subsection (1) of this section, the value of property conveyed or transferred by an instrument chargeable with duty in accordance with that subsection shall be determined without regard to –

(a)   any power (whether or not contained in the instrument) on the exercise of which the property, or any part of or any interest in, the property, may be re-vested in the person from whom it was conveyed or transferred or in any person on his behalf;

(b)   any annuity reserved out of the property or any part of it, or any life or other interest so reserved, being an interest which is subject to forfeiture;

but if on a claim made to the Commissioners not later than two years after the making or execution of the instrument it is shown to their satisfaction that any such power as is mentioned in paragraph (a) of this subsection has been exercised in relation to the property and the property or any property representing it has been re-conveyed or re-transferred in the whole or in part in consequence of that exercise the Commissioners shall repay the stamp duty paid by virtue of this subsection, in a case where the whole of such property has been so re-conveyed or re-transferred, so far as it exceeds the stamp duty which would have been payable apart from this subsection and, in any other case, so far as it exceeds the stamp duty which would have been payable if the instrument had operated to convey or transfer only such property as is not so re-conveyed or re-transferred.

90(6)   This section shall be construed as one with the said Act of 1891.

90(7)   This section shall come into force on 1st August 1965.

History – Consequent to the repeal of provisions dealing with gifts inter vivos, s. 90(2) and (5) amended by FA 1985, s. 29 and Sch. 27 to omit the exception for certain such gifts and the valuation of gifts, effective for instruments executed after 25 March 1985 or executed after 18 March 1985 and stamped after 25 March 1988.

Cross references – SA 1891, s. 12: assessment of duty by commissioners.

91   Interest where stamp duty repaid under judgment

91   [Repealed by FA 1999, 139 and Sch. 20, Pt. V(1) in relation to instruments executed on or after 1 October 1999 but as regards unit trust schemes subject to FA 1999, Sch. 20, Pt. V(1), para. 2. The repeal took effect from 6 February 2000 as regards unit trust schemes, by virtue of FA 1999, s. 122(4) and FA 1999, Sch. 19.]

FINANCE ACT 1966

(1966 Chapter 18)

[3rd August 1966]

PART VII – MISCELLANEOUS

45   Harbour reorganisation schemes: corporation tax and stamp duty

45(1)–(4)   [Repealed by ICTA 1970, s. 538(1) and Sch. 16.]

45(5)   Where a certified harbour reorganisation scheme contains provision for the transfer of an undertaking, or of any other description of property, to a harbour authority, then, in considering whether any and if so what duty is payable under section 12 of the Finance Act 1895 (which relates to the stamp duty payable in connection with certain statutory conveyances), the consideration for the transfer shall be left out of account; and no stamp duty shall be payable on any contract or agreement for any such transfer if the contract or agreement is conditional on the making and certification of a harbour reorganisation scheme.

45(6)   In this section –

     "harbour authority" has the same meaning as in the Harbours Act 1964;

     "harbour reorganisation scheme" means any statutory provision providing for the management by a harbour authority of any harbour or group of harbours in the United Kingdom, and **"certified"**, in relation to any harbour reorganisation scheme, means certified by a Minister of the Crown or Government department as so providing with a view to securing, in the public interest, the efficient and economical development of the harbour or harbours in question.

45(7)   [Repealed by ICTA 1970, s. 538(1) and Sch. 16.]

History – S. 45(1)–(4) repealed, and s. 45(6) amended by ICTA 1970, s. 538(1) and Sch. 16.

Notes – S. 53(2): s. 45 to be construed as one with SA 1891.

FINANCE ACT 1967

(1967 Chapter 54)

[21st July 1967]

PART V – STAMP DUTIES

Notes – S. 45(3)(g): Pt. V to be construed as one with SA 1891.

27   Conveyances and transfers on sale: reduction of duty, and amendment of provisions for exemption

27(1)   [Repealed by FA 1972, s. 134 and Sch. 28, Pt. XI.]

27(2)   [Substitutes FA 1930, s. 42(2), (3).]

27(3)   The said section 42 shall not apply to any instrument executed on or after the said 1st August unless it is also shown to the satisfaction of the Commissioners that the instrument was not executed in pursuance of or in connection with an arrangement whereunder –

(a)   the consideration, or any part of the consideration, for the conveyance or transfer was to be provided or received, directly or indirectly, by a person other than a body corporate which at the time of the execution of the instrument was associated within the meaning of the said section 42 with either the transferor or the transferee (meaning, respectively, the body from whom and the body to whom the beneficial interest was conveyed or transferred), or

(b)   the said interest was previously conveyed or transferred, directly or indirectly, by such a person, or

(c)   the transferor and the transferee were to cease to be associated within the meaning of the said section 42 by reason of the transferor or a third body corporate ceasing to be the transferee's parent (within the meaning of the said section 42);

and, without prejudice to the generality of paragraph (a) above, an arrangement shall be treated as within that paragraph if it is one whereunder the transferor or the transferee, or a body corporate associated with either as there mentioned, was to be enabled to provide any of the consideration, or was to part with any of it, by or in consequence of the carrying out of a transaction or transactions involving, or any of them involving, a payment or other disposition by a person other than a body corporate so associated.

This subsection shall, as respects instruments executed on or after the said 1st August, have effect in substitution for section 50 of the Finance Act 1938.

History – S. 27(1) repealed by FA 1972, s. 134 and Sch. 28, Pt. XI.
In s. 27(3)(c), words from "the transferor" to "the said section 42" substituted by FA 1995, s. 149(1), (6), in relation to instruments executed on or after 1 May 1995.

Statements of practice – SP 3/98: Stamp Office approach to application of anti-avoidance rules preventing exploitation of group relief.

Notes – "The said section 42" means FA 1930, s. 42 and "the said 1st August" means 1 August 1967.

30   Exemption for bearer instruments relating to stock in foreign currencies

30   [Repealed by FA 1999, s. 139 and Sch. 20, Pt. V(2) in relation to bearer instruments issued on or after 1 October 1999 but as regards unit trust schemes subject to FA 1999, Sch. 20, Pt. V(2), para. 2.]

FINANCE ACT 1970

(1970 Chapter 24)

[29th May 1970]

PART III – MISCELLANEOUS

STAMP DUTIES

32   Abolition of certain stamp duties, and amendments as to rates and other matters

32   [Repealed by FA 1999, s. 139 and Sch. 20, Pt. V(2) in relation to instruments executed, or bearer instruments issued, on or after 1 October 1999 but as regards unit trust schemes subject to FA 1999, Sch. 20, Pt. V(2), para. 2. The repeal took effect from 6 February 2000 as regards unit trust schemes, by virtue of FA 1999, s. 122(4) and FA 1999, Sch. 19.]

33   Composition by stock exchanges in respect of transfer duty

33(1)   The Commissioners may enter into an agreement with, or with persons acting on behalf of, any recognised stock exchange for the composition, in accordance with the provisions of this section, of the stamp duty chargeable under or by reference to Part I or paragraph 16 of Part III of Schedule 13 to the Finance Act 1999 (conveyance or transfer on sale or otherwise) on such instruments as may be specified in the agreement.

In this subsection **"recognised stock exchange"** means the Stock Exchange, London, and any other stock exchange declared by an order in force under section 4 of the Stock Transfer Act 1963 to be a recognised stock exchange for the purposes of that Act.

33(2) An agreement under this section shall provide–

(a) for every instrument to which the agreement relates to bear on its face an indication of the amount of stamp duty chargeable thereon,

(b) for the issue in respect of every such instrument, by or on behalf of the stock exchange, of a certificate (which may relate to more than one such instrument) to the effect that stamp duty to the amount so indicated has been, or will be, accounted for to the Commissioners,

(c) for the delivery to the Commissioners, by or on behalf of the stock exchange, of periodical accounts in respect of instruments to which the agreement relates, giving such particulars with respect thereto as may be specified in the agreement, and

(d) for the payment to the Commissioners, by or on behalf of the stock exchange and on the delivery of any such account, of the aggregate amount of the stamp duty chargeable as mentioned in subsection (1) above on instruments to which the agreement relates during the period to which the account relates;

and any such agreement may contain such other terms and conditions as the Commissioners think proper.

33(3) [Repealed by FA 1976, s. 132(5) and Sch. 15.]

33(4) An instrument to which an agreement under this section relates and in respect of which a certificate to the effect mentioned in subsection (2)(b) above has been issued by or on behalf of the stock exchange in question shall be treated for the purposes of the Stamp Act 1891 as stamped with the amount of duty indicated on the face of the instrument.

33(5) A stock exchange or person making default in delivering any account required by an agreement under this section, or in paying any amount in accordance with such an agreement, shall be liable to a fine not exceeding £50 for any day during which the default continues; and, in addition, every amount payable under such an agreement shall bear interest at the rate of 5 per cent per annum, recoverable by Her Majesty, from the due date for delivery of the account by reference to which it is payable until the actual date of payment.

33(6) Except in so far as the context otherwise requires, any reference to a stamp in section 9 or 10 of the Stamp Duties Management Act 1891 (allowances for spoiled stamps) shall include a reference to any indication of an amount of stamp duty on the face of any instrument to which an agreement under this section relates.

Prospective amendments – S. 33 repealed by FA 1990, s. 109(6)(c), 132 and Sch. 19, Pt. VI, as provided by Treasury order. S. 33(1) amended by FA 1986, s. 83(1), from such day as the commissioners may appoint, as follows:
- the words "any recognised stock exchange" will be replaced by the words "any recognised investment exchange or recognised clearing house";
- the words from "In this subsection" to the end will be replaced by the words:
  "In this subsection "recognised investment exchange" and "recognised clearing house" have the same meaning as in the Financial Services Act 1986".
S. 33(2), (4), (5) amended by FA 1986, s. 83(2), from such day as the commissioner may appoint, so that the words "stock exchange" will be replaced by the words "recognised investment exchange or recognised clearing house".

History – S. 33(1) amended by FA 1976, s. 127(4), 132(5) and Sch. 15, Pt. VI. The amending provision subsequently repealed by FA 1999, 139 and Sch. 20, Pt. V(2) (following further amendment to subs. (1) – see history note below) the repeal having effect in relation to instruments executed, or bearer instruments issued, on or after 1 October 1999 but as regards unit trust schemes subject to. FA 1999, Sch. 20, Pt. V(2), para. 2.
In s. 33(1), the words "Part I or paragraph 16 of Part III of Schedule 13 to the Finance Act 1999" "(conveyance or transfer on sale or otherwise)" substituted for the words "the heading "Conveyance or Transfer on Sale" or "Conveyance or Transfer of any kind not hereinbefore described" in Schedule 1 to the Stamp Act 1891" (which had themselves been amended by FA 1976, see history note above) by FA 1999, 112(4) and Sch. 14, para. 5, in relation to instruments executed on or after 1 October 1999. (3) repealed by FA 1976, 132(5) and Sch. 15, Pt. VI.

Cross references – SDMA 1891, s. 9: procedure for obtaining allowance.
SDMA 1891, s. 10: allowance for misused stamps.
FA 1986, s. 84(2), (3): exemptions from duty from day(s) to be appointed by commissioners in respect of certain instruments effecting a transfer of stock where composition agreements under s. 33 made with investment exchange or clearing house are in force at time of transfer.

Notes – Order in force under Stock Transfer Act 1963, s. 4 declares The Stock Exchange (amalgamation of the former Stock Exchange, London, with other members of the former Federation of Stock Exchanges in Great Britain and Ireland) to be a recognised stock exchange; see also FA 1973, s. 54(1)(a) whereby references to the Stock Exchange, London shall be construed as references to The Stock Exchange.
S. 36(5): s. 33 to be construed as one with SA 1891.

SCHEDULES

SCHEDULE 7 – STAMP DUTIES

Section 32

History – Sch. 7 repealed by FA 1999, 139 and Sch. 20, Pt. V(2), the repeal having effect in relation to instruments executed, or bearer instruments issued, on or after 1 October 1999 but as regards unit trust schemes subject to FA 1999, Sch. 20, Pt. V(2). The repeal took effect from 6 February 2000 as regards unit trust schemes, by virtue of FA 1999, s. 122(4) and FA 1999, Sch. 19.

Part II – General Amendments

1 [Repealed by FA 1999, s. 139 and Sch. 20, Pt. V(2) in relation to instruments executed, or bearer instruments issued, on or after 1 October 1999 but as regards unit trust schemes subject to FA 1999, Sch. 20, Pt. V(2), para. 2. The repeal took effect from 6 February 2000 as regards unit trust schemes, by virtue of FA 1999, s. 122(4) and FA 1999, Sch. 19.]

BEARER INSTRUMENTS

6 [Repealed by FA 1999, s. 139 and Sch. 20, Pt. V(2) in relation to instruments executed, or bearer instruments issued, on or after 1 October 1999 but as regards unit trust schemes subject to FA 1999, Sch. 20, Pt. V(2), para. 2. The repeal took effect from 6 February 2000 as regards unit trust schemes, by virtue of FA 1999, s. 122(4) and FA 1999, Sch. 19.]

MORTGAGES ETC.

16 [Repealed by FA 1999, s. 139 and Sch. 20, Pt. V(2) in relation to instruments executed, or bearer instruments issued, on or after 1 October 1999 but as regards unit trust schemes subject to FA 1999, Sch. 20, Pt. V(2), para. 2. The repeal took effect from 6 February 2000 as regards unit trust schemes, by virtue of FA 1999, s. 122(4) and FA 1999, Sch. 19.]

FINANCE ACT 1971

(1971 Chapter 68)

[5th August 1971]

PART V – MISCELLANEOUS

64   Stamp duty – abolition of duty on bonds, mortgages etc.

64 [Repealed by FA 1999, s. 139 and Sch. 20, Pt. V(2)]

History – Repealed by FA 1999, s. 139 and Sch. 20, Pt. V(2) in relation to instruments executed, or bearer instruments issued, on or after 1 October 1999 but as regards unit trust schemes subject to FA 1999, Sch. 20, Pt. V(2), para. 2. The repeal took effect from 6 February 2000 as regards unit trust schemes, by virtue of FA 1999, s. 122(4) and FA 1999, Sch. 19. Despite its repeal, the abolition of duty on instruments affected by this section continues to apply. See cross reference note below.

Cross references – FA 1999, Sch. 13, para. 25(a): stamp duty not chargeable under FA 1999, Sch. 13 (charge other than on bearer instruments) on any description of instrument in respect of which duty was abolished by s. 64. See text of repealed section below.

FA 1999, Sch. 15, para. 15: stamp duty not chargeable under FA 1999, Sch. 15 (bearer instruments) on any description of instrument in respect of which duty was abolished by s. 64. See text of repealed section below.

The former wording of the section as it continues to apply after repeal (see notes above) is as follows:

"**64(1)** The following stamp duties are hereby abolished–
  (a)   except as respects any instrument increasing the rent reserved by another instrument, the duties chargeable by virtue of paragraph (1) and paragraph (2) (securities for annuities other than superannuation annuities and for certain other periodic sums) of the heading in Schedule 1 to the Stamp Act 1891 "Bond, Covenant, or Instrument of any kind whatsoever",
  (b)   the duties chargeable by virtue of the heading in that Schedule "Bond of any kind whatsoever not specifically charged with any duty", and
  (c)   the duties chargeable by virtue of the heading in that Schedule beginning "Mortgage, Bond, Debenture, Covenant".
64(2) Subject to section 4 of the said Act of 1891 (separate charges on instruments containing or relating to several distinct matters), any instrument which, but for subsection (1) above, would be chargeable with duty under a heading mentioned in that subsection shall not be chargeable with duty under any other heading in the said Schedule 1.
64(3) For the avoidance of doubt it is hereby declared that paragraph (c) of subsection (1) above does not affect the amount of any duty chargeable under the said Schedule 1 by reference to the heading mentioned in that paragraph.
64(4) This section has effect as from 1st August 1971."

FINANCE ACT 1973

(1973 Chapter 51)

[*25th July 1973*]

PART V – STAMP DUTY

50 Temporary statutory effect of House of Commons resolution affecting stamp duties

50(1) Where the House of Commons passes a resolution which –

(a) provides for the variation or abolition of an existing stamp duty; and

(b) is expressed to have effect for a period stated in the resolution in accordance with the following provisions of this section; and

(c) contains a declaration that it is expedient in the public interest that the resolution should have statutory effect under the provisions of this section;

then, subject to subsection (3) of this section, the resolution shall for the period so stated have statutory effect as if contained in an Act of Parliament.

50(2) The period to be stated in a resolution is a period expressed as beginning on a date so stated and ending on, or thirty-one days or such less number of days as may be so stated after, the earliest of the dates mentioned in this subsection; and those dates are –

(a) the thirtieth day on which, after the day the resolution is passed, the House of Commons sits without a Bill containing provisions to the same effect as the resolution being read a second time and without a Bill being amended (whether by the House or a Committee of the House or a Standing Committee) so as to include such provisions;

(b) the rejection of such provisions during the passage through the House of a Bill containing them;

(c) the dissolution or prorogation of Parliament; and

(d) the expiration of the period of six months beginning with the day on which the resolution takes effect.

50(3) A resolution shall cease to have statutory effect under this section if an Act comes into operation varying or abolishing the duty.

50(4) The ending of the period for which a resolution has statutory effect under the provisions of this section shall not affect the validity of anything done during that period.

History – S. 50(1)(a) amended by FA 1975, s. 59 and Sch. 13, Pt. I.
In s. 50(2)(a), the word "thirtieth" substituted for the words "twenty-fifth", and in s. 50(2)(d), the word "six" substituted for the word "five", by FA 1993, s. 207(1), in relation to resolutions passed after 27 July 1993.

PART VI – MISCELLANEOUS AND GENERAL

54 Amendments consequential on establishment of The Stock Exchange

54(1) In the enactments relating to stamp duty–

(a) references to the Stock Exchange, London or the London Stock Exchange, a stock exchange in the United Kingdom or a recognised stock exchange in the United Kingdom shall be construed as references to The Stock Exchange;

(b) references to quotation on a stock exchange in the United Kingdom or a recognised stock exchange in the United Kingdom shall be construed as references to listing in the Official List of The Stock Exchange; and

(c) references to a member of a stock exchange in the United Kingdom shall be construed as references to a member of the Stock Exchange;

and those enactments shall have effect subject to the amendments specified in Schedule 21 to this Act.

54(2) This section shall be deemed to have come into operation on 25th March 1973 but shall not affect the operation of any enactment in relation to anything done before that day.

History – In s. 54(1), words repealed by ICTA 1988, s. 844 and Sch. 31, with effect from 6 April 1988.

FINANCE ACT 1974

(1974 Chapter 30)

[31st July 1974]

PART IV – MISCELLANEOUS AND GENERAL

49   Increase of certain stamp duties

49   [Repealed by FA 1999, s. 139 and Sch. 20, Pt. V(2) in relation to instruments executed, or bearer instruments issued, on or after 1 October 1999 but as regards unit trust schemes subject to FA 1999, Sch. 20, Pt. V(2), para. 2. The repeal took effect from 6 February 2000 as regards unit trust schemes, by virtue of FA 1999, s. 122(4) and FA 1999, Sch. 19.]

57   Citation, interpretation, construction and repeals

57(1)   This Act may be cited as the Finance Act 1974.

57(3)   In this Act –

(a)   [Not relevant here.]
(b)   [Not relevant here.]
(c)   [Not relevant here.]
(d)   [Repealed by FA 1999, s. 139 and Sch. 20, Pt. V(2).]

57(4)   Except so far as the context otherwise requires, any reference in this Act to any enactment shall be construed as a reference to that enactment as amended, and as including a reference to that enactment as applied, by or under any other enactment, including this Act.

57(5)   If the Northern Ireland Assembly passes provisions amending or replacing any enactment of the Parliament of Northern Ireland, or any Order in Council made under section 1(3) of the Northern Ireland (Temporary Provisions) Act 1972, referred to in this Act, the reference shall be construed as a reference to the enactment or order as so amended or, as the case may be, as a reference to those provisions.

History – S. 57(3)(d) repealed by FA 1999, s. 139 and Sch. 20, Pt. V(2), the repeal having effect in relation to instruments executed, or bearer instruments issued, on or after 1 October 1999 but as regards unit trust schemes subject to FA 1999, Sch. 20, Pt. V(2), para. 2. The repeal took effect from 6 February 2000 as regards unit trust schemes, by virtue of FA 1999, s. 122(4) and FA 1999, Sch. 19.

SCHEDULES

SCHEDULE 11 – INCREASE OF CERTAIN STAMP DUTIES

Section 49

Part I – Provisions Having Effect in Great Britain

1   [Repealed by FA 1999, s. 139 and Sch. 20, Pt. V(2) in relation to instruments executed, or bearer instruments issued, on or after 1 October 1999 but as regards unit trust schemes subject to FA 1999, Sch. 20, Pt. V(2), para. 2. The repeal took effect from 6 February 2000 as regards unit trust schemes, by virtue of FA 1999, s. 122(4) and FA 1999, Sch. 19.]

FINANCE ACT 1976

(1976 Chapter 40)

[*29th July 1976*]

PART V – MISCELLANEOUS AND SUPPLEMENTARY

127   Stamp duty: stock exchange transfers

127(1)   Stamp duty shall not be chargeable on any transfer to a stock exchange nominee.

127(2), (3)   [Repealed by FA 1986, s. 114 and Sch. 23, Pt. IX(4); s. 127(2) also omitted by virtue of FA 1986, s. 85(4).]

127(4)   [Amends FA 1970, s. 33(1).]

127(5)   This section shall be construed as one with the Stamp Act 1891 and in this section –

     "stock exchange nominee" means any person designated for the purposes of this section as a nominee of The Stock Exchange by an order made by the Secretary of State;

127(6)   The power to make an order under subsection (5) above shall be exercisable by statutory instrument and includes power to vary or revoke a previous order.

127(7)   Section 33 of the Finance Act 1970 shall extend to Northern Ireland; and in the application of that section to Northern Ireland for any reference to the Stock Transfer Act 1963 there shall be substituted a reference to the Stock Transfer Act (Northern Ireland) 1963.

Prospective repeals – S. 127(1), (4)–(7) repealed by FA 1990, s. 109(6)(d), 132 and Sch. 19, Pt. VI, from a date to be appointed as provided by Treasury Order.

History – S. 127(1) amended by FA 1986, s. 84(1), by omitting the words "which is executed for the purposes of a stock exchange transaction", effective for transfers after 26 October 1986 (but these words were not repealed until 20 March 1989, by FA 1986, s. 114 and Sch. 23, Pt. IX (4) and SI 1989/291).
S. 127(2), (3) repealed by FA 1986, s. 114 and Sch. 23, Pt. IX(4) in accordance with SI 1989/291, effective from 20 March 1989; s. 127(2) also omitted by virtue of FA 1986, s. 85(4) for any transfer giving effect to a transaction carried out on or after 27 October 1986.
The definitions of "jobber" and "stock exchange transaction" in s. 127(5) and the words "and this section" which appeared after the words "of that section" in s. 127(7) were also repealed by FA 1986, s. 114 and Sch. 23, Pt. IX(4) in accordance with SI 1989/291, effective from 20 March 1989.

Cross references – FA 1986, s. 97(2): no charge to stamp duty reserve tax by reference to clearance services if transfer exempt by virtue of s. 127(1).
FA 1989, s. 175: Treasury may, by regulations, exempt a transaction involving a stock exchange nominee from charge under "Conveyance or Transfer on Sale" if also charged to stamp duty reserve tax.
FA 1989, s. 176: Treasury may, by regulations, exempt from charge or apply a reduced rate to a transaction involving a stock exchange nominee in relation to stamp duty reserve tax.

Extra-statutory concessions – G7: transfers of stock into SEPON.

FINANCE ACT 1980

(1980 Chapter 48)

[*1st August 1980*]

PART V – STAMP DUTY

97   Shared ownership transactions

97(1)   A lease to which this section applies shall, instead of being chargeable with stamp duty under Part II of Schedule 13 to the Finance Act 1999 (lease), be chargeable with stamp duty under Part I of that Schedule (conveyance or transfer on sale) as if it were a conveyance for a consideration equal to the value or sum stated in the lease in accordance with subsection (2)(d) below; and where stamp duty has been paid on a lease in accordance with this section stamp duty shall not be chargeable under that Act on any instrument executed in pursuance of the lease whereby the reversion is transferred to the lessee.

97(2)   This section applies to any lease granted by a body mentioned in subsection (3) below, being a lease which –

(a)   is of a dwelling for the exclusive use of the lessee or, if there are joint lessees, of those lessees;

(b)   is granted partly in consideration of a premium calculated by reference to –

     (i) the market value of the dwelling, or

     (ii) a sum calculated by reference to that value, and partly in consideration of rent;

(c)   provides for the lessee to acquire the reversion; and

(d)   contains a statement of the market value referred to in paragraph (b)(i) above or, as the case may be, the sum referred to in paragraph (b)(ii) above and a statement to the effect that the parties intend duty to be charged in accordance with this section by reference to that value or as the case may be, to that sum.

97(3)   The bodies referred to in subsection (2) above are –

(a)   a local housing authority within the meaning of the Housing Act 1985;

(b)   a housing association within the meaning of the Housing Associations Act 1985 or Part VII of the Housing (Northern Ireland) Order 1981;

(c)   a development corporation established by an order made, or having effect as if made, under the New Towns Act 1965;

(cc)   a housing action trust established under Part III of the Housing Act 1988;

(d)   the Commission for the New Towns;

(e)   the Development Board for Rural Wales;

(f)   the Northern Ireland Housing Executive;

(g)   the Council of the Isles of Scilly.

97(4)   For the purposes of subsection (1) above an instrument transferring a reversion shall not be regarded as executed in pursuance of a lease in respect of which duty has been paid in accordance with this section unless it contains a statement to the effect that it has been so executed.

Prospective repeal – S. 97(3)(e) repealed by the Government of Wales Act 1998, s. 152 and Sch. 18, Pt. IV with effect from a date to be appointed.

History – S. 97(1), (2) amended by FA 1981, s. 108(2)–(4) and (7), effective for instruments executed after 22 March 1981. In s. 97(1):
- the words "Part II of Schedule 13 to the Finance Act 1999 (lease)" substituted for the words "the heading "Lease or Tack" in Schedule 1 to the Stamp Act 1891"; and
- the words "Part I of that Schedule (conveyance or transfer on sale)" substituted for the words "the heading "Conveyance or Transfer on Sale" in that Schedule"by FA 1999, 112(4) and Sch. 14, para. 6, the substitutions having effect in relation to instruments executed on or after 1 October 1999.

S. 97(3)(a) and (b) substituted by Housing (Consequential Provisions) Act 1985, Sch. 2, para. 43, effective from 1 April 1986 (after extension to Northern Ireland by FA 1981, s. 108); requirement for registration in (b) omitted by FA 1987, s. 54(1), (4), for leases granted after 31 July 1987.

S. 97(3)(cc) inserted by FA 1988, s. 142(1).

Cross references – FA 1981, s. 108: power to modify charge by reference to premium obtainable with "minimum rent" imposed.

FA 1987, s. 54(2): application to a lease granted by a private sector landlord to a person with a "preserved right to buy".

98   Maintenance funds for historic buildings

98(1)   No stamp duty shall be chargeable on any instrument whereby property ceases to be comprised in a settlement if as a result of the property or part of it becoming comprised in another settlement (otherwise than by virtue of the instrument itself) there is by virtue of paragraph 9(1) or 17(1) of Schedule 4 to the Capital Transfer Tax Act 1984 there is no charge to capital transfer tax in respect of the property ceasing to be comprised in the settlement or a reduced charge to that tax by virtue of paragraph 9(4) or 17(4) of that Schedule; but where only part of the property becomes comprised in the other settlement this subsection shall not affect the stamp duty chargeable on the instrument by reference to the other part.

98(2)   An instrument in respect of which stamp duty is not chargeable by virtue only of this section or in respect of which the duty chargeable is reduced by virtue of this section shall not be treated as duly stamped unless it is stamped in accordance with section 12 of the Stamp Act 1891 with a stamp denoting that it is not chargeable with any duty or that it is duly stamped.

History – Reference to provisions of CTTA 1984 substituted by s. 276 and Sch. 8, para. 19 of that Act.

Notes – FA 1986, s. 100(1): reference to capital transfer tax to have effect as reference to inheritance tax and CTTA 1984 cited as IHTA 1984.

101   Unit trusts

101   [Repealed by FA 1999, s. 139 and Sch. 20, Pt. V(5) in relation to instruments executed on or after 6 February 2000.]

102   Conveyance in consideration of debt

102(1)   Where –

(a)   any property is conveyed to any person wholly or in part in consideration of a debt due to him; and

(b)   apart from this section the consideration in respect of which the conveyance would be chargeable with ad valorem duty by virtue of section 57 of the Stamp Act 1891 (which deems the debt to be the consideration) would exceed the value of the property conveyed,

that consideration shall be treated as reduced to that value.

102(2)   Where subsection (1) above applies in relation to any conveyance, it shall not be treated as duly stamped unless it is stamped in accordance with section 12 of the said Act of 1891 with a stamp denoting that it is not chargeable with any duty or that it is duly stamped.

FINANCE ACT 1981

(1981 Chapter 35)

[*27th July 1981*]

ARRANGEMENT OF SECTIONS

PART VI – STAMP DUTY

PART VI – STAMP DUTY

107   Sale of houses at discount by local authorities etc.

107(1)   Where a conveyance or transfer to which this section applies is subject contingently to the payment of any money (whether by virtue of that conveyance or transfer or otherwise), then, notwithstanding section 57 of the Stamp Act 1891, that money shall not be deemed to be part of the consideration in respect of which the conveyance or transfer is chargeable with ad valorem duty.

107(2)   [Repealed by FA 1985, s. 98 and Sch. 27, Pt. IX(1).]

107(3)   This section applies to any conveyance or transfer on sale of a dwelling-house (including the grant of a lease) at a discount by –

(a)   any Minister of the Crown or Northern Ireland department;

(b)   a local housing authority within the meaning of the Housing Act 1985, a county council, a district council within the meaning of the Local Government Act (Northern Ireland) 1972 or in Scotland a regional, district or islands council, the common good of such a council or any trust under its control;

(c)   the Housing Corporation;

(ca)   Housing for Wales;

(d)   the Scottish Special Housing Association;

(e)   the Northern Ireland Housing Executive;

(ea)   a registered social landlord within the meaning of Part I of the Housing Act 1996;

(f)   a housing association registered – (i) in Scotland, under theHousing Associations Act 1985, or (ii) in Northern Ireland, under Part II of the Housing (Northern Ireland) Order 1992;

(ff)   a housing action trust established under Part III of the Housing Act 1988;

(g)   a development corporation established by an order made or having effect as if made under the New Towns Act 1965 or the New Towns (Scotland) Act 1968 or an urban development corporation established by an order made under section 135 of the Local Government, Planning and Land Act 1980;

(h)   the Commission for the New Towns or a new town commission established under section 7 of the New Towns Act (Northern Ireland) 1965;

(i)   the Development Board for Rural Wales;

(j)   the Council of the Isles of Scilly;

(k)   a police authority within the meaning of section 101(1) of the Police Act 1996 or section 2(1) or 19(9)(b) of the Police (Scotland) Act 1967, or the Police Authority for Northern Ireland;

(ka)   the Service Authority for the National Crime Squad or the Service Authority for the National Crime Intelligence Service;

(l)   an Education and Libraries Board established under the Education and Libraries (Northern Ireland) Order 1972;

(m)   any person mentioned in paragraph (e), (i), (j) or (l) of section 1(10) of the Tenants' Rights, Etc. (Scotland) Act 1980;

(n)   the United Kingdom Atomic Energy Authority;

(o)   such other body as the Treasury may, by order made by statutory instrument, prescribe for the purposes of this section.

107(3A)   This section also applies to any conveyance or transfer on sale of a dwelling house where the conveyance or transfer is made pursuant to a sub-sale made at a discount by a body falling within subsection (3)(ea) or (f) above.

107(3B)   This section also applies to a conveyance or transfer on sale (including the grant of a lease) by a person against whom the right to buy under Part V of the Housing Act 1985 is exercisable by virtue of section 171A of that Act (preservation of right to buy on disposal to private sector landlord) to a person who is the qualifying person for the purposes of the preserved right to buy and in relation to whom that dwelling-house is the qualifying dwelling-house.

107(3C)   A grant under section 20 or 21 of the Housing Act 1996 (purchase grants in respect of disposals at a discount by registered social landlords) shall not be treated as part of the consideration for a conveyance or transfer to which this section applies made by a body falling within subsection (3)(ea) above.

107(4)   This section applies to instruments executed on or after 23rd March 1981 and shall be deemed to have come into force on that date.

Prospective repeal – S. 107(3)(ca), (3)(i) repealed by the Government of Wales Act 1998, s. 152 and Sch. 18, Pt. IV with effect from a date to be appointed.

History – S. 107(2) repealed by FA 1985, s. 98 and Sch. 27, Pt. IX(1).
Reference in s. 107(3)(b) and (f) to local authority within the meaning of the Housing Act 1985 and the Housing Associations Act 1985 substituted by Housing (Consequential Provisions) Act 1985, Sch. 2, para. 48, effective from 1 April 1986. S. 107(3)(ea) inserted by Housing Act 1996, s. 55 and Sch. 3, para. 1, with effect from 1 October 1996 (SI 1996/2402, art. 3). In s. 107(3)(f), the words from "registered" to the end substituted by Housing Act 1996, s. 55 and Sch. 3, para. 1(3), with effect from 1 October 1996 (SI 1996/2402, art. 3).
S. 107(3)(ff) inserted by FA 1988, s. 142(2). In s. 107(3)(k) reference to Police Act 1996, s. 101(1) substituted by Sch. 7, para. 33 of that Act, with effect from 22 August 1996. S. 107(3)(ka) inserted by Police Act 1997, s. 134(1) and Sch. 9, para. 42, with effect from 1 April 1998 (SI 1998/354).
S. 107(3)(n) inserted by FA 1984, s. 110(2).
S. 107(3)(o) inserted by FA 1984, s. 110(5).
S. 107(3)(ca) inserted by Housing Act 1988, s. 140 and Sch. 17, Pt. II, para. 105, with effect from 1 December 1988 (SI 1988/2056), Housing for Wales being a body established by that Act. In s. 107(3A), references to subsection (3)(ea), (f) substituted by Housing Act 1996, s. 55 and Sch. 3, para. 1, with effect from 1 October 1996 (SI 1996/2402, art. 3).
S. 107(3A) inserted by FA 1984, s. 110(3).
S. 107(3B) inserted by Housing and Planning Act 1986, Sch. 5, para. 18, with effect from 17 August 1992 (SI 1992/1753).
S. 107(3C) inserted by Housing Act 1996, s. 55 and Sch. 3, para. 1, with effect from 1 April 1997 (SI 1997/618).

Cross references – SA 1891, s. 57: how conveyance in consideration of a debt etc. to be charged. For transitional provisions and savings, see SI 1996/2402.

108   Shared ownership transactions

108(1)   Section 97 of the Finance Act 1980 (shared ownership transactions) shall have effect with the amendments specified in subsections (2) to (4) below.

108(2)–(4)   [Amends FA 1980, s. 97.]

108(5)   Where a lease is granted by a body mentioned in subsection (3) of the said section 97 which –

(a)   is of a dwelling for the exclusive use of the lessee or, if there are joint lessees, of those lessees;

(b)   provides that the lessee may on payment of a sum require the terms of the lease to be altered so that the rent payable under it is reduced;

(c)   is granted partly in consideration of rent and partly in consideration of a premium calculated by reference to –

    (i) the premium obtainable on the open market for the grant of a lease containing the same terms as the lease but with the substitution for the rent payable under the lease of the minimum rent, or

    (ii) a sum calculated by a reference to that premium; and

(d)   contains a statement of the minimum rent and the premium referred to in paragraph (c)(i) above or, as the case may be, the sum referred to in paragraph (c)(ii) above and a statement to the effect that the parties intend duty to be charged in accordance with this section by reference to that rent and that premium or, as the case may be, that sum,

the lease shall be chargeable to stamp duty as if the premium paid by the lessee were equal to the premium or, as the case may be, the sum, stated in the lease in accordance with paragraph (d) above and the rent payable were as so stated.

108(6)   In subsection (5) above **"minimum rent"** in relation to any lease means the lowest rent which could become payable under the lease if it were altered as mentioned in paragraph (b) of that subsection at the date when the lease is granted.

108(7)   This section applies to instruments executed on or after 23rd March 1981 and shall be deemed to have come into force on that date.

Cross references – FA 1987, s. 54(2): application ofs. 108(5), (6) to a lease granted by a private sector landlord to a person with a "preserved right to buy".

110   Pooled pension funds

110   [Repealed by FA 1999, s. 139 and Sch. 20, Pt. V(5) in relation to instruments executed on or after 6 February 2000.]

FINANCE ACT 1982

(1982 Chapter 39)

[*30th July 1982*]

PART V – STAMP DUTY

129   Exemption from duty on grants, transfers to charities, etc.

129(1)   Where any conveyance, transfer or lease is made or agreed to be made to a body of persons established for charitable purposes only or to the trustees of a trust so established or to the Trustees of the National Heritage Memorial Fund or to the National Endowment for Science, Technology and the Arts, no stamp duty shall be chargeable under Part I or II, or paragraph 1 of Part III, of Schedule 13 to the Finance Act 1999 on the instrument by which the conveyance, transfer or lease, or the agreement for it, is effected.

129(2)   An instrument in respect of which stamp duty is not chargeable by virtue only of subsection (1) above shall not be treated as duly stamped unless it is stamped in accordance with section 12 of the Stamp Act 1891 with a stamp denoting that it is not chargeable with any duty.

129(3)   This section applies to instruments executed on or after 22nd March 1982 and shall be deemed to have come into force on that date.

History – In s. 129(1) the words "under Part I or II, or paragraph 1 of Part III, of Schedule 13 to the Finance Act 1999" substituted by FA 1999, s. 112(4) and Sch. 14, para. 7, the substitution having effect in relation to instruments executed on or after 1 October 1999.
In s. 129(1) the words "or to the National Endowment for Science, Technology and the Arts" inserted by the National Lottery Act 1998, s. 24(4).

Cross references – Education Act 1993, s. 299(5): no instrument under certain provisions of that Act to be treated as duly stamped unless stamped in accordance with SA 1891, s. 12.
Education Act 1997, s. 53(2): no instrument under certain provisions of that Act to be treated as duly stamped unless stamped in accordance with SA 1891, s. 12.

Statement of practice – SP 6/90: exemption not affected by duty under SA 1891, s. 57 (property subject to debt).

Notes – For purposes of exemption under s. 129, Historic Buildings and Monuments Commission for England is treated as established for charitable purposes only (FA 1983, s. 46(3)(c)).

FINANCE (NO. 2) ACT 1983

(1983 Chapter 49)

[*26th July 1983*]

PART I – INCOME TAX, CORPORATION TAX AND CAPITAL GAINS TAX

7 Relief for local constituency associations of political parties on reorganisation of constituencies

7(1) In this section **"relevant date"** means the date of coming into operation of an Order in Council under section 3 of the House of Commons (Redistribution of Seats) Act 1949 (orders specifying new parliamentary constituencies) and, in relation to any relevant date,–

(a) **"former parliamentary constituency"** means an area which, for the purposes of parliamentary elections, was a constituency immediately before that date but is no longer such a constituency after that date; and

(b) **"new parliamentary constituency"** means an area which, for the purposes of parliamentary elections, is a constituency immediately after that date but was not such a constituency before that date.

7(2) In this section **"local constituency association"** means an unincorporated association (whether described as an association, a branch or otherwise) whose primary purpose is to further the aims of a political party in an area which at any time is or was the same or substantially the same as the area of a parliamentary constituency or two or more parliamentary constituencies and, in relation to any relevant date,–

(a) **"existing association"** means a local constituency association whose area was the same, or substantially the same, as the area of a former parliamentary constituency or two or more such constituencies; and

(b) **"new association"** means a local constituency association whose area is the same, or substantially the same, as the area of a new parliamentary constituency or two or more such constituencies.

7(3) For the purposes of this section, a **new association** is a successor to an existing association if any part of the existing association's area is comprised in the new association's area.

7(4) In any case where, before, on or after a relevant date,–

(a) an existing association disposes of land to a new association which is a successor to the existing association, or

(b) an existing association disposes of land to a body (whether corporate or unincorporated) which is an organ of the political party concerned and, as soon as practicable thereafter, that body disposes of the land to a new association which is a successor to the existing association,

the parties to the disposal or, where paragraph (b) above applies, to each of the disposals, shall be treated for the purposes of corporation tax in respect of chargeable gains or, as the case may require, capital gains tax as if the land disposed of were acquired from the existing association or the body making the disposal for a consideration of such an amount as would secure that on the disposal neither a gain nor a loss accrued to that association or body.

7(5)–(7) [Not reproduced here.]

7(8) In this section **"political party"** means a political party which qualifies for exemption under *section 24 of the Capital Transfer Tax Act 1984* (gifts to political parties).

7(9) This section applies in any case where the relevant date falls after 1st January 1983 and the disposal referred to in subsection (4) or subsection (6) above is on or after 6th April 1983.

History – Reference to CTTA 1984 substituted by s. 276 and Sch. 8, para. 23 of that Act, effective from 1 January 1985.

Notes – FA 1986, s. 100: citation of CTTA 1984 as IHTA 1984, effective from 25 July 1986.

PART III – MISCELLANEOUS AND SUPPLEMENTAL

15   Relief from stamp duty for local constituency associations of political parties on reorganisation of constituencies

15(1)   In a case falling within paragraph (a) or paragraph (b) of subsection (4) of section 7 above, section 57 of the Stamp Act 1891 shall not apply in relation to a conveyance or transfer by which the disposal or, in the case of paragraph (b), either of the disposals referred to in that paragraph is effected.

15(2)   [Repealed by FA 1985, s. 98 and Sch. 27, Pt. IX(1).]

History – Consequent to the repeal of provisions dealing with gifts inter vivos, s. 15(1) amended by FA 1985, s. 82(4), effective from 26 March 1985, to omit reference to exemption from that special charge and s. 15(2) repealed by FA 1985, s. 98 and Sch. 27, Pt. IX(1).

FINANCE ACT 1984

(1974 Chapter 30)

[26th July 1984]

PART IV – STAMP DUTY

111   Agreements for leases

111(1)   [Repealed by FA 1999, s. 139 and Sch. 20, Pt. V(2).]

111(2)   In any case where–

(a)   an interest in land is conveyed or transferred subject to an agreement for a lease for a term exceeding 35 years, or

(b)   a lease is granted subject to an agreement for a lease for a term exceeding 35 years,

then, whether or not the conveyance, transfer or lease is expressed to be so subject, it shall not be taken to be duly stamped unless there is denoted upon the conveyance, transfer or lease the duty paid on the agreement; and section 11 of the Stamp Act 1891 shall have effect for this purpose as if the duty chargeable on the conveyance, transfer or lease depended on the duty paid on the agreement.

111(3)   For the purposes of subsection (2) above, an interest conveyed or transferred or, as the case may be, a lease granted is not to be regarded as subject to an agreement for a lease if that agreement is directly enforceable against another interest in the land in relation to which the interest conveyed or transferred or, as the case may be, the lease granted is a superior interest.

111(4)   [Repealed by FA 1999, s. 139 and Sch. 20, Pt. V(1).]

111(5)   This section applies to any agreement for a lease entered into on or after 20th March 1984 and shall be deemed to have come into force on that date.

History – S. 111(1) (which amends SA 1891, s. 75) repealed by FA 1999, s. 139 and Sch. 20, Pt. V(2), the repeal having effect in relation to instruments executed, or bearer instruments issued, on or after 1 October 1999 but as regards unit trust schemes subject to FA 1999, Sch. 20, Pt. V(2).
In FA 1984, s. 111(2)(six times), (3)(three times) and (5), the word "lease" substituted for the words "lease or tack" by FA 1999, s. 112(4) and Sch. 14, para. 2 in relation to instruments executed on or after 1 October 1999.
S. 111(4) (which amends SA 1891, s. 15(2)) repealed by FA 1999, s. 139 and Sch. 20, Pt. V(1), the repeal having effect in relation to instruments executed on or after 1 October 1999 but as regards unit trust schemes subject to FA 1999, Sch. 20, Pt. V(1).

Cross references – SA 1891, s. 11: denoting stamps.
FA 1999, Sch. 18, para. 4: where referring to the duration of a lease, the expression "term" in relation to Scotland means "period".

PART VI – MISCELLANEOUS AND SUPPLEMENTARY

126   Tax exemptions in relation to designated international organisations

126(1)   Where–

(a)   the United Kingdom or any of the Communities is a member of an international organisation; and

(b)   the agreement under which it became a member provides for exemption from tax, in relation to the organisation, of the kind for which provision is made by this section;

the Treasury may, by order made by statutory instrument, designate that organisation for the purposes of this section.

126(2)   Where an organisation has been so designated, the provisions mentioned in subsection (3) below shall, with the exception of any which may be excluded by the designation order, apply in relation to that organisation.

126(3)   The provisions are–

(a)   [Repealed by ICTA 1988, s. 844and Sch. 29, para. 32.]

(b)   [Relevant only to the inheritance, capital transfer, and capital gains taxes.]

(c)   no stamp duty shall be chargeable under Schedule 15 to the Finance Act 1999 (bearer instruments) on the issue of any instrument by the organisation or on the transfer of the stock constituted by, or transferable by means of, any instrument issued by the organisation,

(d)   no stamp duty reserve tax shall be chargeable under section 93 (depositary receipts) or 96 (clearance services) of the Finance Act 1986 in respect of the issue of securities by the organisation.

126(4)   The Treasury may, by order made by statutory instrument, designate any of the Communities or the European Investment Bank for the purposes of this section, and references in subsections (2) and (3) above to an organisation designated for the purposes of this section include references to a body so designated by virtue of this subsection.

126(5)   Subsection (3) above, as it applies by virtue of subsection (4) above, shall be read as if the words "under Schedule 15 to the Finance Act 1999 (bearer instruments)" were omitted.

Prospective repeals – S. 126(3)(c), (5) repealed by FA 1990, s. 132 and Sch. 19, Pt. VI, for issues or transfers on or after a day to be appointed.

History – S. 126(3)(a) repealed by ICTA 1988, s. 844 and Sch. 29, para. 32.
In S. 126(3)(c), the words "Schedule 15 to the Finance Act 1999 (bearer instruments)" substituted for the words "the heading "Bearer Instrument" in Schedule 1 to the Stamp Act 1891" by FA 1999, s. 113(3) and Sch. 16, para. 4, the substitution applying in relation to bearer instruments issued on or after 1 October 1999.
S. 126(3)(d) inserted by FA 1990, s. 114 in relation to the issue of securities by an organisation or body designated under s. 126(1) or (4) on or after 26 July 1990 where the organisation or body is so designated before that date, and in relation to the issue of securities by the organisation or body after its designation where it is so designated on or after that date.
S. 126(4) and (5) inserted by FA 1985, s. 96(1).
In s. 126(5), the words "Schedule 15 to the Finance Act 1999 (bearer instruments)" substituted for the words "the heading "Bearer Instrument" in Schedule 1 to the Stamp Act 1891" by FA 1999, s. 113(3) and Sch. 16, para. 4, the substitution applying in relation to bearer instruments issued on or after 1 October 1999.

Cross references – FA 1985, s. 96(2): order under s. 126(4) may revoke or vary the exclusion from exemption of the European Economic Community given by European Communities (Loan Stock) (Stamp Duties) Order 1972 (see Statutory instruments, below).

Statutory instruments – The Treasury has designated the following bodies for the purposes of s. 126: The Asian Development Bank (SI 1984/1215); The African Development Bank (SI 1984/1634); The European Economic Community, The European Coal and Steel Community, The European Atomic Energy Community and The European Investment Bank (SI 1985/1172, also revoking the European Communities (Loan Stock) (Stamp Duties) Order 1972); The European Bank for Reconstruction and Development (SI 1991/1202).

Notes – FA 1986, s. 78(4), (9); 79(3), (12): exemption for instruments transferring loan capital raised or issued by designated organisations.

COMPANIES ACT 1985

(1985 Chapter 6)

[11th March 1985]

PART IV – ALLOTMENT OF SHARES AND DEBENTURES

GENERAL PROVISIONS AS TO ALLOTMENT

88   Return as to allotments, etc.

88(1)   This section applies to a company limited by shares and to a company limited by guarantee and having a share capital.

88(2)   When such a company makes an allotment of its shares, the company shall within one month thereafter deliver to the registrar of companies for registration–

(a)   a return of the allotments (in the prescribed form) stating the number and nominal amount of the shares comprised in the allotment, the names and addresses of the allottees, and the amount (if any) paid or due and payable on each share, whether on account of the nominal value of the share or by way of premium; and

(b)   in the case of shares allotted as fully or partly paid up otherwise than in cash–

     (i)   a contract in writing constituting the title of the allottee to the allotment together with any contract of sale, or for services or other consideration in respect of which that allotment was made (such contracts being duly stamped), and

     (ii)   a return stating the number and nominal amount of shares so allotted, the extent to which they are to be treated as paid up, and the consideration for which they have been allotted.

88(3)   Where such a contract as above mentioned is not reduced to writing, the company shall within one month after the allotment deliver to the registrar of companies for registration the prescribed particulars of the contract stamped with the same stamp duty as would have been payable if the contract had been reduced to writing.

88(4)   Those particulars are deemed an instrument within the meaning of the Stamp Act 1891; and the registrar may, as a condition of filing the particulars, require that the duty payable on them be adjudicated under section 12 of that Act.

88(5)   If default is made in complying with this section, every officer of the company who is in default is liable to a fine and, for continued contravention, to a daily default fine, but subject as follows.

88(6)   In the case of default in delivering to the registrar within one month after the allotment any document required by this section to be delivered, the company, or any officer liable for the default, may apply to the court for relief; and the court, if satisfied that the omission to deliver the document was accidental or due to inadvertence, or that it is just and equitable to grant relief, may make an order extending the time for the delivery of the document for such period as the court thinks proper.

SCHEDULES

SCHEDULE 14 – OVERSEAS BRANCH REGISTERS

Section 362

Part II – General Provisions With Respect to Overseas Branch Registers

8 An instrument of transfer of a share registered in an overseas branch register (other than such a register kept in Northern Ireland) is deemed a transfer of property situated outside the United Kingdom and, unless executed in a part of the United Kingdom, is exempt from stamp duty chargeable in Great Britain.

Prospective repeals – The words from "and unless" to the end repealed by FA 1990, s. 132 and Sch. 19, Pt. VI from a date to be appointed in accordance with s. 107–111 of that Act.

Notes – The Treasury order appointing the "abolition day" for the purposes of FA 1990, s. 107–110 was to have broadly coincided with the start of paperless trading under the Stock Exchange's planned TAURUS system (IR press release, 20 March 1990). However, on 11 March 1993 it was announced that TAURUS had been abandoned (London Stock Exchange News Release 6/93).

FINANCE ACT 1985

(1985 Chapter 54)

[*25th July 1985*]

ARRANGEMENT OF SECTIONS

PART III – STAMP DUTY

PART V – MISCELLANEOUS AND SUPPLEMENTARY

PART III – STAMP DUTY

Notes – S. 98(4): Pt. III to be construed as one with SA 1891.

81   Renounceable letters of allotment etc.

81(1) Subsection (2) below applies where there is an arrangement whereby–

(a)   rights under an instrument are renounced in favour of a person (A),

(b)   the rights are rights to shares in a company (company B), and

(c)   A, or a person connected with A, or A and such a person together, has or have control of company B or will have such control in consequence of the arrangement.

81(2) The instrument shall not be exempt by virtue of paragraph 24(d) of Part IV of Schedule 13 to the Finance Act 1999 (renounceable letters of allotment, etc.) from stamp duty under or by reference to Part I of that Schedule (conveyance or transfer on sale).

81(3) References in this section to shares in company B include references to its loan capital to which section 79(4) of the Finance Act 1986 does not apply by virtue of section 79(5) or (6) (convertible loan capital and excessive return capital).

81(4) In this section **"shares"** includes stock.

81(5) For the purposes of this section a person has control of company B if he has power to control company B's affairs by virtue of holding shares in, or possessing voting power in relation to, company B or any other body corporate.

81(6) For the purposes of this section one person is connected with another if he would be so connected for the purposes of the Taxation of Chargeable Gains Act 1992.

81(7) This section applies to instruments if rights are renounced under them on or after 1st August 1985, except where the arrangement concerned includes an offer for the rights and on or before 27th June 1985 the offer became unconditional as to acceptances.

Prospective repeals – S. 81 repealed by FA 1990, s. 132 and Sch. 19, Pt. V, from a date to be appointed, in accordance with s. 107–111 of that Act. (See note below).

History – S. 81(2) substituted by FA 1999, s.112(4) and Sch. 14, para. 8, the substitution having effect in relation to instruments executed on or after 1 October 1999.
In s. 81(3) the words "section 79(4) of the Finance Act 1986 does not apply by virtue of section 79(5) or (6)" substituted for the words "section 126(1) of the Finance Act 1976 does not apply by virtue of section 126(2) or (3)" by FA 1999, s.112(4) and Sch. 14, para. 8, the substitution having effect in relation to instruments executed on or after 1 October 1999.
Reference to TCGA 1992 in s. 81(6) substituted by TCGA 1992, s. 290 and Sch. 10, para. 9.

Notes – The Treasury order appointing the "abolition day" for the purposes of FA 1990, s. 107–110 was to have broadly coincided with the start of paperless trading under the Stock Exchange's planned TAURUS system (IR press release, 20 March 1990). However, on 11 March 1993 it was announced that TAURUS had been abandoned (London Stock Exchange News Release 6/93).

82   Gifts inter vivos

82(1) [Repeals F(1909–10)A 1910, s. 74.]

82(2) [Amends SA 1891, s. 58(7).]

82(3) [Amends FA 1965, s. 90(5).]

82(4) [Amends F(No. 2)A 1983, s. 15(1).]

82(5) An instrument–

(a)   in respect of which stamp duty would be chargeable by virtue of section 74 of the 1910 Actapart from this section, and

(b)   on which stamp duty is not chargeable under Part I of Schedule 13 to the Finance Act 1999 (conveyance or transfer on sale),

shall not be deemed to be duly stamped unless it has, in accordance with section 12 of the 1891 Act, been stamped with a particular stamp denoting that it is duly stamped or that it is not chargeable with any duty.

82(6) This section applies to–

(a)   instruments executed on or after 26th March 1985, and

(b)   instruments executed on or after 19th March 1985 which are stamped on or after 26th March 1985.

82(7) For the purposes of section 14(4) of the Stamp Act 1891 (instruments not to be given in evidence etc. unless stamped in accordance with the law in force at the time of first execution), the law in force at the time of execution of an instrument falling within subsection (6)(b) above shall be deemed to be that as varied in accordance with this section.

82(8) The preceding provisions of this section shall be deemed to have come into operation on 26th March 1985.

82(9) Subsection (5) above does not apply to an instrument which is required by regulations under section 87(1) or (2) below to be certified.

History – In s. 82(5), the words "Part I of Schedule 13 to the Finance Act 1999 (conveyance or transfer on sale)" substituted for the words "the heading "Conveyance or Transfer on Sale" in Schedule 1 to the Stamp Act 1891" by FA 1999, s.112(4) and Sch. 14, para. 9, the substitution having effect in relation to instruments executed on or after 1 October 1999.

Cross references – SI 1987/516, reg. 5 and Schedule: disapplication of s. 82(5) to instruments certified in accordance with those regulations.

83   Transfers in connection with divorce etc.

83(1) Stamp duty under Part I of Schedule 13 to the Finance Act 1999 (conveyance or transfer on sale) shall not be chargeable on an instrument by which property is conveyed or transferred from one party to a marriage to the other if the instrument–

(a)   is executed in pursuance of an order of a court made on granting in respect of the parties a decree of divorce, nullity of marriage or judicial separation, or

(b)   is executed in pursuance of an order of a court which is made in connection with the dissolution or annulment of the marriage or the parties' judicial separation and which is made at any time after the granting of such a decree, or

(c)   is executed at any time in pursuance of an agreement of the parties made in contemplation of or otherwise in connection with the dissolution or annulment of the marriage or their judicial separation.

83(2)   An instrument in respect of which stamp duty is not chargeable under the heading mentioned in subsection (1) above by virtue only of that subsection shall be chargeable under this subsection with stamp duty of £5.

83(3)   This section applies to instruments executed on or after 26th March 1985 and shall be deemed to have come into operation on that date.

Prospective insertion – New paragraph to be inserted after s. 83(1)(b) by Family Law Act 1996, s. 66(1) and Sch. 8, para. 33, with effect from a date to be appointed, as follows: "(bb) is executed in pursuance of an order of a court which is made at any time under section 22A, 23A or 24A of the Matrimonial Causes Act 1973, or". S. 83(1)(c) to be amended by Family Law Act 1996, s. 66(1) and Sch. 8, para. 33, with effect from a date to be appointed, by replacing the words "or their judicial separation" with ", their judicial separation or the making of a separation order in respect of them".

History – In s. 83(1), the words "Part I of Schedule 13 to the Finance Act 1999 (conveyance or transfer on sale)" substituted for the words "the heading "Conveyance or Transfer on Sale" in Schedule 1 to the Stamp Act 1891" and, in subs. (2), "£5" substituted for "50p", by FA 1999, s. 112(4) and Sch. 14, para. 10, the substitutions having effect in relation to instruments executed on or after 1 October 1999.

Cross references – SI 1987/516, reg. 2 and Schedule: exemption for certain instruments executed after 30 April 1987.

Statements of practice – SP 6/90: exemption not affected by covenants etc. within SA 1891, s. 57 (property subject to debt).

84   Death: varying dispositions, and appropriations

84(1)   Where, within the period of two years after a person's death, any of the dispositions (whether effected by will, under the law relating to intestacy or otherwise) of the property of which he was competent to dispose are varied by an instrument executed by the persons or any of the persons who benefit or would benefit under the dispositions, stamp duty under Part I of Schedule 13 to the Finance Act 1999 (conveyance or transfer on sale) shall not be chargeable on the instrument.

84(2)   Subsection (1) above does not apply where the variation is made for any consideration in money or money's worth other than consideration consisting of the making of a variation in respect of another of the dispositions.

84(3)   Subsection (1) above applies whether or not the administration of the estate is complete or the property has been distributed in accordance with the original dispositions.

84(4)   Where property is appropriated by a personal representative in or towards satisfaction of a general legacy of money, stamp duty under the heading mentioned in subsection (1) above shall not be chargeable on an instrument giving effect to the appropriation.

84(5)   Where on an intestacy property is appropriated by a personal representative in or towards satisfaction of any interest of a surviving husband or wife in the intestate's estate, stamp duty under the heading mentioned in subsection (1) above shall not be chargeable on an instrument giving effect to the appropriation.

84(6)   The reference in subsection (5) above to an interest in the intestate's estate–

(a)   includes a reference to the capital value of a life interest which the surviving husband or wife has under the Intestates' Estate Act 1952 elected to have redeemed, and

(b)   in Scotland, includes a reference to prior rights (within the meaning of the Succession (Scotland) Act 1964) but, without prejudice to subsection (7) below, not to such rights as are mentioned in that subsection.

84(7)   Where in Scotland, on an intestacy or otherwise, property is appropriated by a personal representative in or towards satisfaction of the right of a husband to *jus relicti,* of a wife to *jus relictae* or of issue to *legitim,* stamp duty under the heading mentioned in subsection (1) above shall not be chargeable on an instrument giving effect to the appropriation.

84(8)   An instrument in respect of which stamp duty is not chargeable under the heading mentioned in subsection (1) above by virtue only of subsection (1), (4), (5) or (7) above shall be chargeable under this subsection with stamp duty of £5.

84(9)   But an instrument which is chargeable under subsection (8) above shall not be treated as duly stamped unless it has, in accordance with section 12 of the Stamp Act 1891, been stamped with a particular stamp denoting that it is duly stamped.

84(10) Subject to subsection (11) below, this section applies to instruments executed on or after 26th March 1985 and shall be deemed to have come into operation on that date.

84(11) Subsections (5) to (7) above and, so far as it relates to subsection (5) or (7), subsection (8) above apply to instruments executed on or after 1st August 1985.

History – In s. 84(1), the words "Part I of Schedule 13 to the Finance Act 1999 (conveyance or transfer on sale)" substituted for the words "the heading "Conveyance or Transfer on Sale" in Schedule 1 to the Stamp Act 1891" and, in subs. (8), "£5" substituted for "50p", by FA 1999, 112(4) and Sch. 14, para. 11, the substitutions having effect in relation to instruments executed on or after 1 October 1999.

Cross references – SI 1987/516, reg. 2 and Schedule: exemption from fixed duty for certain instruments executed after 30 April 1987.
SI 1987/516, reg. 5 and Schedule: disapplication of s. 84(9) to instruments certified in accordance with those regulations.

87   Certificates

87(1) The Commissioners may make regulations providing that an instrument which is of a kind specified in them–

(a)   shall be certified to be an instrument of that kind, and

(b)   shall not be treated as duly stamped if it is not so certified.

87(2) The Treasury may make regulations providing that an instrument which is of a kind specified in them, and which would apart from this subsection be chargeable with stamp duty of a fixed amount under any provision so specified, shall not be charged with such duty under that provision if it is certified to be an instrument of that kind.

87(3) Certification under this section shall be by such method as the regulations may specify, and in particular they may provide for a certificate to be borne by or attached to or otherwise associated with an instrument in such manner as they may specify.

87(4) A certificate under this section shall be in such form and signed by such person as the regulations may specify.

87(5) Regulations under this section may contain such incidental or consequential provisions as the Commissioners or Treasury (as the case may be) think fit.

87(6) Regulations under this section may make different provision for different cases or descriptions of case.

87(7) The power to make regulations under this section shall be exercisable by statutory instrument subject to annulment in pursuance of a resolution of the House of Commons.

Statutory instruments – SI 1987/516 (as amended by SI 1999/2539): kind of instruments eligible for certification under s. 87(2).

88   Exchange rates

88 [Repeals FA 1899, s. 12 and revives the effect of SA 1891, s. 6.]

89   Exemption from section 28 of Finance Act 1931

89(1) Section 28 of the Finance Act 1931 (production to Commissioners of instruments transferring land and furnishing of particulars) shall not apply in relation to any instrument (an **"exempt instrument"**) which falls within any class prescribed for the purposes of this section by regulations made by the Commissioners.

89(2) Regulations under this section may–

(a)   provide that the particulars mentioned in Schedule 2 to the 1931 Act shall be furnished to the Commissioners, in accordance with the requirements of the regulations, in respect of exempt instruments or such descriptions of exempt instruments as may be prescribed by the *regulations*;

(b)   make different provision in relation to different cases or kinds of case and in respect of different parts of Great Britain.

89(3) Any person who fails to comply with any requirement imposed by regulations made under this section shall be liable on summary conviction to a fine not exceeding level 3 on the standard scale (as defined in section 75 of the Criminal Justice Act 1982).

89(4) The power to make regulations under this section shall be exercisable by statutory instrument; and a statutory instrument containing regulations under this section shall be subject to annulment in pursuance of a resolution of the House of Commons.

89(5) [Repeals FA 1931, s. 35(x).]

89(6) Regulations made under section 35(x)shall have effect after the commencement of this section as if they were made under this section and as if they imposed on the Keeper of the Registers of Scotland the duty mentioned in section 35(x).

Statutory instruments – SI 1985/1688: class of instrument prescribed for the purposes of s. 89(1).

PART V – MISCELLANEOUS AND SUPPLEMENTARY

96   European Communities and Investment Bank: exemptions

96(1)   [Amends FA 1984, s. 126.]

96(2)   An order made by virtue of subsection (4) of section 126 of the Finance Act 1984 may revoke or vary the European Communities (Loan Stock) (Stamp Duties) Order 1972 (which provides for exemption from stamp duty in respect of issues and transfers of loan stock of the bodies referred to in that subsection, other than the Economic Community).

Notes – For revocation of the above order, see FA 1984, s. 126.

FINANCE ACT 1986

(1986 Chapter 41)

[*25th July 1986*]

ARRANGEMENT OF SECTIONS

PART III – STAMP DUTY

SECURITIES

PART IV – STAMP DUTY RESERVE TAX
INTRODUCTION

THE PRINCIPAL CHARGE

OTHER CHARGES

GENERAL

PART III – STAMP DUTY

Notes – S. 114(4): Pt. III to be construed as one with SA 1891.

SECURITIES

64   Stock or marketable securities: reduction of rate

64   [Repealed by FA 1999, s. 139 and Sch. 20, Pt. V(2) in relation to instruments executed, or bearer instruments issued, on or after 1 October 1999.]

65   Bearers: consequential provisions etc.

65   [Repealed by FA 1999, s. 139 and Sch. 20, Pt. V(2) in relation to instruments executed, or bearer instruments issued, on or after 1 October 1999.]

66   Company's purchase of own shares

66(1)   This section applies where a company purchases its own shares under section 162 of the Companies Act 1985 or Article 47 of the Companies (Northern Ireland) Order 1982.

66(2)   The return which relates to the shares purchased and is delivered to the registrar of companies under section 169 of that Act or, as the case may be, Article 53 of that Order shall be charged with stamp duty, and treated for all purposes of the Stamp Act 1891, as if it were an instrument transferring the shares on sale to the company in pursuance of the contract (or contracts) of purchase concerned.

66(3) Subject to subsection (4) below, this section applies to any return under section 169 of the Companies Act 1985, or Article 53 of the Companies (Northern Ireland) Order 1982, which is delivered to the registrar of companies on or after the day of The Stock Exchange reforms.

66(4) This section does not apply to any return to the extent that shares to which it relates were purchased under a contract entered into before the day of The Stock Exchange reforms.

66(5) In this section **"the day of The Stock Exchange reforms"** means the day on which the rule of The Stock Exchange that prohibits a person from carrying on business as both a broker and a jobber is abolished.

Prospective repeals – S. 66 repealed by FA 1990, s. 132 and Sch. 19, Pt. VI, from a date to be appointed in accordance with s. 107–111 of that Act. (See note below).

Notes – The Companies (Northern Ireland) Order 1982 is SI 1982/1534 (NI 17).
The day of The Stock Exchange reforms was 27 October 1986.
The Treasury order appointing the "abolition day" for the purposes of FA 1990, s. 107–110 was to have broadly coincided with the start of paperless trading under the Stock Exchange's planned TAURUS system (IR press release, 20 March 1990). However, on 11 March 1993 it was announced that TAURUS had been abandoned (London Stock Exchange News Release 6/93).

DEPOSITARY RECEIPTS

67 Depositary receipts

67(1) Subject to subsection (9) below, subsection (2) or (3) below (as the case may be) applies where an instrument transfers relevant securities of a company incorporated in the United Kingdom to a person who at the time of the transfer falls within subsection (6), (7) or (8) below.

67(2) If stamp duty is chargeable on the instrument under Part I of Schedule 13 to the Finance Act 1999 (conveyance or transfer on sale), the rate at which that duty is chargeable is 1.5% of the amount or value of the consideration for the sale to which the instrument gives effect.

67(3) If stamp duty is chargeable on the instrument under paragraph 16 of Schedule 13 to the Finance Act 1999 (conveyance or transfer otherwise than on sale), then, subject to subsection (5), the rate at which that duty is chargeable is 1.5% of the value of the securities at the date the instrument is executed.

67(4) [Repealed by FA 1997, s. 99(1), 113 and Sch. 18, Pt. VII]

67(5) In a case where–

(a) securities are issued, or securities sold are transferred, and (in either case) they are to be paid for in instalments,

(b) the person to whom they are issued or transferred holds them and transfers them to another person when the last instalment is paid,

(c) the transfer to the other person is effected by an instrument in the case of which subsection (3) above applies,

(d) before the execution of the instrument mentioned in paragraph (c) above an instrument is received by a person falling (at the time of the receipt) within sub-section (6), (7) or (8) below,

(e) the instrument so received evidences all the rights which (by virtue of the terms under which the securities are issued or sold as mentioned in paragraph (a) above) subsist in respect of them at the time of the receipt, and

(f) the instrument mentioned in paragraph (c) above contains a statement that paragraphs (a), (b) and (e) above are fulfilled,

subsection (3) above shall have effect as if the reference to the value there mentioned were to an amount (if any) equal to the total of the instalments payable, less those paid before the transfer to the other person is effected.

67(6) A person falls within this subsection if his business is exclusively that of holding relevant securities–

(a) as nominee or agent for a person whose business is or includes issuing depositary receipts for relevant securities, and

(b) for the purposes of such part of the business mentioned in paragraph (a) above as consists of issuing such depositary receipts (in a case where the business does not consist exclusively of that).

67(7) A person falls within this subsection if–

(a) he is specified for the purposes of this subsection by the Treasury by order made by statutory instrument, and

(b)   his business is or includes issuing depositary receipts for relevant securities.

67(8)   A person falls within this subsection if–

(a)   he is specified for the purposes of this subsection by the Treasury by order made by statutory instrument,

(b)   he does not fall within subsection (6) above but his business includes holding relevant securities as nominee or agent for a person who falls within subsection (7)(b) above at the time of the transfer, and

(c)   he holds relevant securities as nominee or agent for such a person, for the purposes of such part of that person's business as consists of issuing depositary receipts for relevant securities (in a case where that business does not consist exclusively of that).

67(9)   Where an instrument transfers relevant securities of a company incorporated in the United Kingdom–

(a)   to a company which at the time of the transfer falls within subsection (6) above and is resident in the United Kingdom, and

(b)   from a company which at that time falls within that subsection and is so resident,

subsections (2) to (5) above shall not apply and the stamp duty chargeable on the instrument is £5.

67(10)   This section applies to any instrument executed on or after the day on which the rule of The Stock Exchange that prohibits a person from carrying on business as both a broker and a jobber is abolished.

Prospective repeals – S. 67 repealed by FA 1990, s. 132 and Sch. 19, Pt. VI, for instruments executed on or after a day to be appointed. See also FA 1990, s. 108(8) for abolition of stamp duty charge on instruments executed on or after that day which fall within s. 67(1) or (9) (or which do not fall within s. 67(1) or (9) and are not executed in pursuance of a contract).

History – S. 67(2), (3), substituted by FA 1999, s. 112(4) and Sch. 14, para. 12(2), the substitution having effect in relation to instruments executed on or after 1 October 1999.
Former s. 67(3) previously amended by FA 1997, s. 99(2)(a) and s. 67(4) repealed by FA 1997, s. 99(1), 113 and Sch. 18, Pt. VII, with effect for instruments executed on or after the day which is the commencement day for the purposes of FA 1997, s. 97, except an instrument which transfers relevant securities which were acquired by the transferor before that date. The appointed day for the purposes of FA 1997, s. 97(5) and (6) was 20 October 1997, the commencement day by virtue of SI 1997/2428 (C. 95).
In s. 67(9), the words "and is resident in the United Kingdom" and "and is so resident" shall cease to have effect by virtue of FA 2000, s. 134 (3) as follows: in the application of FA 2000, s. 134 (3) for the purposes of stamp duty, where instruments are executed after 28 July 2000, and in the application of FA 2000, s. 134 (3)for the purposes of stamp duty reserve tax, where the securities are transferred after 28 July 2000.
In s. 67(9), the words "stamp duty chargeable on the instrument is £5" substituted for the words "maximum stamp duty chargeable on the instrument shall be 50p" by FA 1999, s. 112(4) and Sch. 14, para. 12(3), the substitution having effect in relation to instruments executed on or after 1 October 1999.

Cross references – FA 1988, s. 143(6): certain foreign companies treated as incorporated in the UK in relation to instruments transferring "paired shares" executed after 28 July 1988.

Notes – The rule of The Stock Exchange which prohibited a person from carrying on business as both a broker and a jobber was abolished on 27 October 1986.

68   Depositary receipts: notification

68(1)   A person whose business is or includes issuing depositary receipts for relevant securities of a company incorporated in the United Kingdom shall notify the Commissioners of that fact before the end of the period of one month beginning with the date on which he first issues such depositary receipts.

68(2)   A person whose business includes (but does not exclusively consist of) holding relevant securities (being securities of a company incorporated in the United Kingdom)–

(a)   as nominee or agent for a person whose business is or includes issuing depositary receipts for relevant securities, and

(b)   for the purposes of such part of the business mentioned in paragraph (a) above as consists of issuing such depositary receipts (in a case where the business does not consists exclusively of that), shall notify the Commissioners of that fact before the end of the period of one month beginning with the date on which he first holds such relevant securities as such a nominee or agent and for such purposes.

68(3)   A company which is incorporated in the United Kingdom and becomes aware that any shares in the company are held by a person such as is mentioned in subsection (1) or (2) above shall notify the Commissioners of that fact before the end of the period of one month beginning with the date on which the company first becomes aware of that fact.

68(4)   A person who fails to comply with subsection (1) or (2) above shall be liable to a penalty not exceeding £1,000.

68(5) A company which fails to comply with subsection (3) above shall be liable to a penalty not exceeding £100.

68(6) [Repealed by FA 1999, s. 139 and Sch. 20, Pt. V(3).]

Prospective repeals – S. 68 repealed by FA 1990, s. 132 and Sch. 19, Pt. VI, where a person first issues or holds the securities or first becomes aware (as appropriate) on or after a day to be appointed. See also FA 1990, s. 109(4) for withdrawal of notification requirement under s. 68(1) or (2) where receipts first issued on or after that day.

History – In s. 68(4), (5) the word "penalty" substituted for the word "fine" by FA 1999, s. 114 and Sch. 17, para. 8, the substitution having effect in relation to penalties in respect of things done or omitted on or after 1 October 1999. S. 68(6) repealed by FA 1999, s. 139 and Sch. 20, Pt. V(3), the repeal having effect in relation to penalties in respect of things done or omitted on or after 1 October 1999.

Cross references – FA 1988, s. 143(6): certain foreign companies treated as incorporated in the UK in relation to instruments transferring "paired shares" executed after 28 July 1988.

69   Depository receipts: supplementary

69(1) For the purposes of sections 67 and 68 above a **depository receipt for relevant securities** is an instrument acknowledging–

(a)   that a person holds relevant securities or evidence of the right to receive them, and

(b)   that another person is entitled to rights, whether expressed as units or otherwise, in or in relation to relevant securities of the same kind, including the right to receive such securities (or evidence of the right to receive them) from the person mentioned in paragraph (a) above, except that for those purposes a depository receipt for relevant securities does not include an instrument acknowledging rights in or in relation to securities if they are issued or sold under terms providing for payment in instalments and for the issue of the instrument as evidence that an instalment has been paid.

69(2) The Treasury may by regulations provide that for subsection (1) above (as it has effect for the time being) there shall be substituted a subsection containing a different definition of a depository receipt for the purposes of sections 67 and 68 above.

69(3) References in this section and sections 67 and 68 above to **relevant securities**, or to relevant securities of a company, are to shares in or stock or marketable securities of any company (which, unless otherwise stated, need not be incorporated in the United Kingdom).

69(4) For the purposes of section 67(3) above the value of securities at the date the instrument is executed shall be taken to be the price they might reasonably be expected to fetch on a sale at that time in the open market.

69(5) [Repealed by FA 1999, s. 139 and Sch. 20, Pt. V(1).]

69(6)–(8) [Repealed by FA 1997, s. 99(2)(b), 113 and Sch. 18, Pt. VII.]

69(9) The power to make regulations or an order under this section shall be exercisable by statutory instrument subject to annulment in pursuance of a resolution of the House of Commons.

Prospective repeals – S. 69 repealed by FA 1990, s. 132 and Sch. 19, Pt. VI, in relation to s. 67, 68 as specified for those sections (see prospective repeal notes thereto).

History – S. 69(5) repealed by FA 1999, s. 139 and Sch. 20, Pt. V(1), the repeal having effect in relation to instruments executed on or after 1 October 1999, but as regards unit trust schemes subject to FA 1999, Sch. 20, Pt. V(1), para. 2. The repeal took effect from 6 February 2000 as regards unit trust schemes, by virtue of FA 1999, s. 122(4) and FA 1999, Sch. 19. S. 69(6)–(8) repealed by FA 1997, s. 99(2)(b), 113 and Sch. 18, Pt. VII, with effect for instruments executed on or after the day which is the commencement day for the purposes of FA 1997, s. 97, except an instrument which transfers relevant securities which were acquired by the transferor before that date. The appointed day for the purposes of FA 1997, s. 97(5) and (6) was 20 October 1997, the commencement day by virtue of SI 1997/2428 (C. 95).

CLEARANCE SERVICES

70   Clearance services

70(1) Subject to subsection (9) and section 97A below, subsection (2) or (3) below (as the case may be) applies where an instrument transfers relevant securities of a company incorporated in the United Kingdom to a person who at the time of the transfer falls within subsection (6), (7) or (8) below.

70(2) If stamp duty is chargeable on the instrument under Part I of Schedule 13 to the Finance Act 1999 (conveyance or transfer on sale), the rate at which that duty is chargeable is 1.5% of the amount or value of the consideration for the sale to which the instrument gives effect.

70(3) If stamp duty is chargeable on the instrument under paragraph 16 of Schedule 13 to the Finance Act 1999 (conveyance or transfer otherwise than on sale), then, subject to subsection (5), the rate at which that duty is chargeable is 1.5% of the value of the securities at the date the instrument is executed.

70(4) [Repealed by FA 1997, s. 99(3), 113 and Sch. 18, Pt VII.]

70(5) In a case where–

(a)   securities are issued, or securities sold are transferred, and (in either case) they are to be paid for in instalments,

(b)   the person to whom they are issued or transferred holds them and transfers them to another person when the last instalment is paid,

(c)   the transfer to the other person is effected by an instrument in the case of which subsection (3) above applies,

(d)   before the execution of the instrument mentioned in paragraph (c) above an instrument is received by a person falling (at the time of the receipt) within subsection (6), (7) or (8) below,

(e)   the instrument so received evidences all the rights which (by virtue of the terms under which the securities are issued or sold as mentioned in paragraph (a) above) subsist in respect of them at the time of the receipt, and

(f)   the instrument mentioned in paragraph (c) above contains a statement that paragraphs (a), (b) and (e) above are fulfilled,

subsection (3) above shall have effect as if the reference to the value there mentioned were to an amount (if any) equal to the total of the instalments payable, less those paid before the transfer to the other person is effected.

70(6) A person falls within this subsection if his business is exclusively that of holding shares, stock or other marketable securities–

(a)   as nominee or agent for a person whose business is or includes the provision of clearance services for the purchase and sale of shares, stock or other marketable securities, and

(b)   for the purposes of such part of the business mentioned in paragraph (a) above as consists of the provision of such clearance services (in a case where the business does not consist exclusively of that).

70(7) A person falls within this subsection if–

(a)   he is specified for the purposes of this subsection by the Treasury by order made by statutory instrument, and

(b)   his business is or includes the provision of clearance services for the purchase and sale of relevant securities.

70(8) A person falls within this subsection if–

(a)   he is specified for the purposes of this subsection by the Treasury by order made by statutory instrument,

(b)   he does not fall within subsection (6) above but his business includes holding relevant securities as nominee or agent for a person who falls within subsection (7)(b) above at the time of the transfer, and

(c)   he holds relevant securities as nominee or agent for such a person for the purposes of such part of that person's business as consists of the provision of clearance services for the purchase and sale of relevant securities (in a case where that business does not consist exclusively of that).

70(9) Where an instrument transfers relevant securities of a company incorporated in the United Kingdom–

(a)   to a company which at the time of the transfer falls within subsection (6) above and is resident in the United Kingdom, and

(b)   from a company which at that time falls within that subsection and is so resident,

subsections (2) to (5) above shall not apply and the stamp duty chargeable on the instrument is £5.

70(10) This section applies to any instrument executed on or after the day on which the rule of The Stock Exchange that prohibits a person from carrying on business as both a broker and a jobber is abolished.

Prospective repeals – S. 70 repealed by FA 1990, s. 132 and Sch. 19, Pt. VI, for instruments executed on or after a day to be appointed. See also FA 1990, s. 108(8) for abolition of stamp duty charge on instruments executed on or after that day which fall within s. 70(1) or (9) (or which do not fall within s. 70(1) or (9) and are not executed in pursuance of a contract).

History – S. 70(1) amended by FA 1996, s. 196(1), inserting the reference to s. 97A with effect from 1 July 1996.
S. 70(2), (3) substituted by FA 1999, s. 112(4) and Sch. 14, para. 13(2), the substitution having effect in relation to instruments executed on or after 1 October 1999 but FA 1999, s. 112 and Sch. 14 do not apply to certain transfers or other instruments relating to units under a unit trust scheme (FA 1999, s. 122(1) and (2)). The repeal took effect with regards to certain transfers or other instruments relating to units under a unit trust scheme on their execution on or after 6 February 2000 (FA 1999, s. 122(4) and FA 1999, Sch. 19).
Former s. 70(3) amended by FA 1997, s. 99(4)(a) and s. 70(4) repealed by FA 1997, s. 99(3), 113 and Sch. 18, Pt VII, with effect for instruments executed on or after the day which is the commencement day for the purposes of FA 1997, s. 97, except

an instrument which transfers relevant securities which were acquired by the transferor before that date. The appointed day for the purposes of FA 1997, s. 97(5) and (6) was 20 October 1997, the commencement day by virtue of SI 1997/2428 (C. 95). S. 70(6) amended by FA 1987, s. 52, substituting reference to shares, stock or other marketable securities for reference to relevant securities, effective for instruments executed after 31 July 1987.

In s. 70(9), the words "and is resident in the United Kingdom" and "and is so resident" shall cease to have effect by virtue of FA 2000, s. 134 (3) as follows: in the application of FA 2000, s. 134 (3) for the purposes of stamp duty, where instruments are executed after 28 July 2000, and in the application of FA 2000, s. 134 (3)for the purposes of stamp duty reserve tax, where the securities are transferred after 28 July 2000.

In s. 70(9), the words "stamp duty chargeable on the instrument is £5" substituted for the words "maximum stamp duty chargeable on the instrument shall be 50p" by FA 1999, s. 112(4) and Sch. 14, para. 13(3), the substitution having effect in relation to instruments executed on or after 1 October 1999 but FA 1999, s. 112 and Sch. 14 do not apply to certain transfers or other instruments relating to units under a unit trust scheme (FA 1999, s. 122(1) and (2)).

Cross references – FA 1988, s. 143(6): certain foreign companies treated as incorporated in the UK in relation to instruments transferring "paired shares" executed after 28 July 1988.

Notes – The rule of The Stock Exchange which prohibited a person from carrying on business as both a broker and a jobber was abolished on 27 October 1986.

71   Clearance services: notification

71(1)   A person whose business is or includes the provision of clearance services for the purchase and sale of relevant securities of a company incorporated in the United Kingdom shall notify the Commissioners of that fact before the end of the period of one month beginning with the date on which he first provides such clearance services.

71(2)   A person whose business includes (but does not exclusively consist of) holding relevant securities (being securities of a company incorporated in the United Kingdom)–

(a)   as nominee or agent for a person whose business is or includes the provision of clearance services for the purchase and sale of relevant securities, and

(b)   for the purposes of such part of the business mentioned in paragraph (a) above as consists of the provision of such clearance services (in a case where the business does not consist exclusively of that),

shall notify the Commissioners of that fact before the end of the period of one month beginning with the date on which he first holds such relevant securities as such a nominee or agent and for such purposes.

71(3)   A company which is incorporated in the United Kingdom and becomes aware that any shares in the company are held by a person such as is mentioned in subsection (1) or (2) above shall notify the Commissioners of that fact before the end of the period of one month beginning with the date on which the company first becomes aware of that fact.

71(4)   A person who fails to comply with subsection (1) or (2) above shall be liable to a penalty not exceeding £1,000.

71(5)   A company which fails to comply with subsection (3) above shall be liable to a penalty not exceeding £100.

71(6)   [Repealed by FA 1999, s. 139 and Sch. 20, Pt. V(3).]

Prospective repeals – S. 71 repealed by FA 1990, s. 132 and Sch. 19, Pt. VI, where a person first provides the services, holds the securities or becomes aware (as appropriate) on or after a day to be appointed. See also FA 1990, s. 109(4) for withdrawal of notification requirement under s. 71(1) or (2) where receipts first issued on or after that day.

History – In s. 71(4), (5) the word "penalty" substituted for the word "fine" by FA 1999, s. 114 and Sch. 17, para. 8, in relation to penalties in respect of things done or omitted on or after 1 October 1999.
S. 71(6) repealed by FA 1999, s. 139 and Sch. 20, Pt. V(3), the repeal having effect in relation to things done or omitted on or after 1 October 1999.

Cross references – FA 1988, s. 143(6): certain foreign companies treated as incorporated in the UK in relation to instruments transferring "paired shares" executed after 28 July 1988.

72   Clearance services: supplementary

72(1)   References in sections 70 and 71 above to **relevant securities**, or to relevant securities of a company, are to shares in or stock or marketable securities of any company (which, unless otherwise stated, need not be incorporated in the United Kingdom).

72(2)   For the purposes of section 70(3) above the value of securities at the date the instrument is executed shall be taken to be the price they might reasonably be expected to fetch on a sale at that time in the open market.

72(3)   [Repealed by FA 1999, s. 139 and Sch. 20, Pt. V(1).]

72(4)   [Repealed by FA 1997, s. 99(4)(b), 113 and Sch. 18, Pt. VII.]

Prospective repeals – S. 72 repealed by FA 1990, s. 132 and Sch. 19, Pt. VI, in relation to s. 70, 71 as specified for those sections (see prospective repeal notes thereto).

History – S. 72(3) repealed by FA 1999, s. 139 and Sch. 20, Pt. V(1), the repeal having effect in relation to instruments executed on or after 1 October 1999, but as regards unit trust schemes subject to FA 1999, Sch. 20, Pt. V(1), para. 2. The repeal took effect from 6 February 2000 as regards unit trust schemes, by virtue of FA 1999, s. 122(4) and FA 1999, Sch. 19.

S. 72(4) repealed by FA 1997, s. 99(4)(b), 113 and Sch. 18, Pt VII with effect for instruments executed on or after the day which is the commencement day for the purposes of FA 1997, s. 97, except an instrument which transfers relevant securities which were acquired by the transferor before that date. The appointed day for the purposes of FA 1997, s. 97(5) and (6) was 20 October 1997, the commencement day by virtue of SI 1997/2428 (C. 95).

72A Transfers between depositary receipt systems and clearance systems

72A(1) Where an instrument transfers relevant securities of a company incorporated in the United Kingdom between a depositary receipt system and a clearance system–

(a) the provisions of section 67(2) to (5) or, as the case may be, section 70(2) to (5) above shall not apply, and

(b) the stamp duty chargeable on the instrument is £5.

72A(2) A transfer between a depositary receipt system and a clearance system means a transfer–

(a) from (or to) a company that at the time of the transfer falls within section 67(6) above, and

(b) to (or from) a company that at that time falls within section 70(6) above.

72A(3) This section does not apply to a transfer from a clearance system (that is, from such a company as is mentioned in subsection (2)(b) above) if at the time of the transfer an election is in force under section 97A below in relation to the clearance services for the purposes of which the securities are held immediately before the transfer.

History – S. 72A inserted by FA 2000, s. 134 (1) which has effect in relation to instruments executed after 28 July 2000.

RECONSTRUCTIONS AND ACQUISITIONS

75 Acquisitions: reliefs

75(1) This section applies where a company (the acquiring company) acquires the whole or part of an undertaking of another company (the target company) in pursuance of a scheme for the reconstruction of the target company.

75(2) If the first and second conditions (as defined below) are fulfilled, stamp duty under Part I of Schedule 13 to the Finance Act 1999 (conveyance or transfer on sale) shall not be chargeable on an instrument executed for the purposes of or in connection with the transfer of the undertaking or part.

75(3) An instrument on which stamp duty is not chargeable by virtue only of subsection (2) above shall not be taken to be duly stamped unless it is stamped with the duty to which it would be liable but for that subsection or it has, in accordance with section 12 of the Stamp Act 1891, been stamped with a particular stamp denoting that it is not chargeable with any duty.

75(4) The first condition is that the registered office of the acquiring company is in the United Kingdom and that the consideration for the acquisition–

(a) consists of or includes the issue of non-redeemable shares in the acquiring company to all the shareholders of the target company;

(b) includes nothing else (if anything) but the assumption or discharge by the acquiring company of liabilities of the target company.

In paragraph (a) above, **"non-redeemable shares"** means shares which are not redeemable shares.

75(5) The second condition is that–

(a) the acquisition is effected for bona fide commercial reasons and does not form part of a scheme or arrangement of which the main purpose, or one of the main purposes, is avoidance of liability to stamp duty, income tax, corporation tax or capital gains tax,

(b) after the acquisition has been made, each shareholder of each of the companies is a shareholder of the other, and

(c) after the acquisition has been made, the proportion of shares of one of the companies held by any shareholder is the same as the proportion of shares of the other company held by that shareholder.

75(6) This section applies to any instrument which is executed after 24th March 1986 unless it is executed in pursuance of an unconditional contract made on or before 18th March 1986.

75(7) This section shall be deemed to have come into force on 25th March 1986.

History – In s. 75(2), the words "Part I of Schedule 13 to the Finance Act 1999 (conveyance or transfer on sale)" substituted for the words "the heading "Conveyance or Transfer on Sale" in Schedule 1 to the Stamp Act 1891" by FA 1999, s. 112(4) and Sch. 14, para. 14, the substitution having effect in relation to instruments executed on or after 1 October 1999.
In s. 75(4), the words "non-redeemable" in para. (a) inserted by FA 2000, s. 127 (2) and the definition of "non-redeemable shares" after para. (b) added by s. 127 (3) respectively, with effect in relation to instruments executed after 28 July 2000.

Cross references – FA 1995, s. 152(3)(d): powers of Treasury to make regulations providing for s. 75–77 to have effect or not to have effect in relation to open-ended companies, etc.
SI 1997/1156, reg. 7,reg. 9 : exemption from stamp duty charge for conversion of an authorised unit trust to an open-ended investment company or for amalgamation of an authorised unit trust with an open-ended investment company.
SI 1997/1156, reg. 12: disapplication of s. 75 as regards open-ended investment companies.
SI 1999/1467, reg. 3: amendment of SI 1997/1156, reg. 9 to remove time limit of 1 July 1999 for amalgamations to be exempt from stamp duty (see note above).
Other material – ICAEW Technical Release TR 631: relief not available where reconstruction of close company involves one group of shareholders taking over one part of undertaking while another group takes the remainder.

76   Acquisitions: further provisions about reliefs

76(1)   This section applies where a company (the acquiring company) acquires the whole or part of an undertaking of another company (the target company).

76(2)   If the condition mentioned in subsection (3) below is fulfilled, and stamp duty under Part I of Schedule 13 to the Finance Act 1999 (conveyance or transfer on sale) is chargeable on an instrument executed for the purposes of or in connection with–

(a)   the transfer of the undertaking or part, or

(b)   the assignment to the acquiring company by a creditor of the target company of any relevant debts (secured or unsecured) owed by the target company,

the rate at which the duty is charged under that heading shall not exceed that mentioned in subsection (4) below.

76(3)   The condition is that the registered office of the acquiring company is in the United Kingdom and that the consideration for the acquisition–

(a)   consists of or includes the issue of non-redeemable shares (within the meaning of section 75(4)(a) above) in the acquiring company to the target company or to all or any of its shareholders;

(b)   includes nothing else (if anything) but cash not exceeding 10 per cent of the nominal value of those shares, or the assumption or discharge by the acquiring company of liabilities of the target company, or both.

76(4)   The rate is 0.5% of the amount or value of the consideration for the sale to which the instrument gives effect.

76(5)   An instrument on which, by virtue only of subsection (2) above, the rate at which stamp duty is charged is not to exceed that mentioned in subsection (4) above shall not be taken to be duly stamped unless it is stamped with the duty to which it would be liable but for subsection (2) above or it has, in accordance with section 12 of the Stamp Act 1891, been stamped with a particular stamp denoting that it is duly stamped.

76(6)   In subsection (2)(b) above **"relevant debts"** means–

(a)   any debt in the case of which the assignor is a bank or trade creditor, and

(b)   any other debt incurred not less than two years before the date on which the instrument is executed.

76(7)   This section applies to any instrument executed on or after the day on which the rule of The Stock Exchange that prohibits a person from carrying on business as both a broker and a jobber is abolished.

History – In s. 76(2), the words "Part I of Schedule 13 to the Finance Act 1999 (conveyance or transfer on sale)" substituted for the words "the heading "Conveyance or Transfer on Sale" in Schedule 1 to the Stamp Act 1891" and, in subs. (4), the words "0.5%" substituted for the words "the rate of 50p for every £100 or part of £100", by FA 1999, s. 112(4) and Sch. 14, para. 15, the substitutions having effect in relation to instruments executed on or after 1 October 1999.
In s. 76(3)(a), the words "non-redeemable shares (within the meaning of section 75(4)(a) above)" substituted for the word "shares" by FA 2000, s. 127 (4), with effect in relation to instruments executed after 28 July 2000.
Cross references – FA 1995, s. 152(3)(d): powers of Treasury to make regulations providing for s. 75–77 to have effect or not to have effect in relation to open-ended companies. etc.
SI 1997/1156, reg. 7,reg. 9 : exemption from stamp duty charge for conversion of an authorised unit trust to an open-ended investment company or for amalgamation of an authorised unit trust with an open-ended investment company.
SI 1997/1156, reg. 12: disapplication of s. 76 as regards open-ended investment companies.
SI 1999/1467, reg. 3: amendment of SI 1997/1156, reg. 9 to remove time limit of 1 July 1999 for amalgamations to be exempt from stamp duty (see note above).
Notes – The rule of The Stock Exchange which prohibited a person from carrying on business as both a broker and a jobber was abolished on 27 October 1986.

77   Acquisition of target company's share capital

77(1)   Stamp duty under Part I of Schedule 13 to the Finance Act 1999 (conveyance or transfer on sale) shall not be chargeable on an instrument transferring shares in one company (the target company) to another company (the acquiring company) if the conditions mentioned in subsection (3) below are fulfilled.

77(2) An instrument on which stamp duty is not chargeable by virtue only of subsection (1) above shall not be taken to be duly stamped unless it is stamped with the duty to which it would be liable but for that subsection or it has, in accordance with section 12 of the Stamp Act 1891, been stamped with a particular stamp denoting that it is not chargeable with any duty.

77(3) The conditions are that–

(a)   the registered office of the acquiring company is in the United Kingdom,

(b)   the transfer forms part of an arrangement by which the acquiring company acquires the whole of the issued share capital of the target company,

(c)   the acquisition is effected for bona fide commercial reasons and does not form part of a scheme or arrangement of which the main purpose, or one of the main purposes, is avoidance of liability to stamp duty, stamp duty reserve tax, income tax, corporation tax or capital gains tax,

(d)   the consideration for the acquisition consists only of the issue of shares in the acquiring company to the shareholders of the target company,

(e)   after the acquisition has been made, each person who immediately before it was made was a shareholder of the target company is a shareholder of the acquiring company,

(f)   after the acquisition has been made, the shares in the acquiring company are of the same classes as were the shares in the target company immediately before the acquisition was made,

(g)   after the acquisition has been made, the number of shares of any particular class in the acquiring company bears to all the shares in that company the same proportion as the number of shares of that class in the target company bore to all the shares in that company immediately before the acquisition was made, and

(h)   after the acquisition has been made, the proportion of shares of any particular class in the acquiring company held by any particular shareholder is the same as the proportion of shares of that class in the target company held by him immediately before the acquisition was made.

77(4) In this section references to **shares** and to **share capital** include references to stock.

77(5) This section applies to any instrument executed on or after 1st August 1986.

Prospective repeals – S. 77 repealed by FA 1990, s. 132 and Sch. 19, Pt. VI, for instruments executed on or after a day to be appointed.

History – In s. 77(1), the words "Part I of Schedule 13 to the Finance Act 1999 (conveyance or transfer on sale)" substituted for the words "the heading "Conveyance or Transfer on Sale" in Schedule 1 to the Stamp Act 1891" by FA 1999, s. 112(4) and Sch. 14, para. 16, the substitution having effect in relation to instruments executed on or after 1 October 1999.

Cross references – FA 1995, s. 152(3)(d): powers of Treasury to make regulations providing for s. 75–77 to have effect or not to have effect in relation to open-ended companies. etc.

SI 1997/1156, reg. 7, reg. 9 : exemption from stamp duty charge for conversion of an authorised unit trust to an open-ended investment company or for amalgamation of an authorised unit trust with an open-ended investment company.

SI 1997/1156, reg. 12: disapplication of s. 77 as regards open-ended investment companies.

SI 1999/1467, reg. 3: amendment of SI 1997/1156, reg. 9 to remove time limit of 1 July 1999 for amalgamations to be exempt from stamp duty (see note above).

LOAN CAPITAL, LETTERS OF ALLOTMENT, ETC.

79   Loan capital: new provisions

79(1) [Repealed by FA 1999, s. 139 and Sch. 20, Pt. V(2).]

79(2) Stamp duty under Schedule 15 to the Finance Act 1999 (bearer instruments) shall not be chargeable on the issue of an instrument which relates to loan capital or on the transfer of the loan capital constituted by, or transferable by means of, such an instrument.

79(3) Stamp duty shall not be chargeable on an instrument which transfers loan capital issued or raised by–

(a)   the financial support fund of the Organisation for Economic Co-operation and Development,

(b)   the Inter-American Development Bank, or

(c)   an organisation which was a designated international organisation at the time of the transfer (whether or not it was such an organisation at the time the loan capital was issued or raised).

79(4) Subject to subsections (5) and (6) below, stamp duty shall not be chargeable on an instrument which transfers any other loan capital.

79(5) Subsection (4) above does not apply to an instrument transferring loan capital which, at the time the instrument is executed, carries a right (exercisable then or later) of conversion into shares or other securities, or to the acquisition of shares or other securities, including loan capital of the same description.

79(6) Subject to subsection (7) below, subsection (4) above does not apply to an instrument transferring loan capital which, at the time the instrument is executed or any earlier time, carries or has carried–

(a)   a right to interest the amount of which exceeds a reasonable commercial return on the nominal amount of the capital,

(b)   a right to interest the amount of which falls or has fallen to be determined to any extent by reference to the results of, or of any part of, a business or to the value of any property, or

(c)   a right on repayment to an amount which exceeds the nominal amount of the capital and is not reasonably comparable with what is generally repayable (in respect of a similar nominal amount of capital) under the terms of issue of loan capital listed in the Official List of The Stock Exchange.

79(7) Subsection (4) above shall not be prevented from applying to an instrument by virtue of subsection (6)(a) or (c) above by reason only that the loan capital concerned carries a right to interest, or (as the case may be) to an amount payable on repayment, determined to any extent by reference to an index showing changes in the general level of prices payable in the United Kingdom over a period substantially corresponding to the period between the issue or raising of the loan capital and its repayment.

79(7A) Subsection (4) above shall not be prevented from applying to an instrument by virtue of subsection (6)(b) above by reason only that the loan capital concerned carries a right to interest which–

(a)   reduces in the event of the results of a business or part of a business improving, or the value of any property increasing, or

(b)   increases in the event of the results of a business or part of a business deteriorating, or the value of any property diminishing.

79(8) Where stamp duty is chargeable under Part I of Schedule 13 of the Finance Act 1999 (conveyance or transfer on sale) on an instrument which transfers loan capital, the rate at which duty is charged under that Part shall be 0.5% of the amount or value of the consideration for the sale to which the instrument gives effect.

79(9)–(11) [Repealed by FA 1999, s. 139 and Sch. 20, Pt. V(2).]

79(12) Subsections (7), (9) of section 78 above shall apply as if references to that section included references to this.

Prospective repeals – S. 79(2)–(8) and the words "(7), (9)" in s. 79(12) repealed by FA 1990, s. 132 and Sch. 19, Pt. VI, from a date to be appointed in accordance with s. 107–111 of that Act. (See note below.)

History – S. 79(1) (which repeals FA 1963, s. 62(2), (6), FA 1967, s. 29, and FA 1976, s. 126 and equivalent Northern Ireland provisions) repealed by FA 1999, s. 139 and Sch. 20, Pt. V(2), the repeal having effect in relation to instruments executed, or bearer instruments issued, on or after 1 October 1999, but as regards unit trust schemes subject to. FA 1999, Sch. 20, Pt. V(2), para. 2. The repeal took effect from 6 February 2000 as regards unit trust schemes, by virtue of FA 1999, s. 122(4) and FA 1999, Sch. 19.

In s. 79(2), the words "Schedule 15 to the Finance Act 1999 (bearer instruments)" substituted for the words "the heading "Bearer Instrument" in Schedule 1 to the Stamp Act 1891" by FA 1999, s. 113(3) and Sch. 16, para. 5, the substitution having effect in relation to bearer instruments issued on or after 1 October 1999.

S. 79(7A) inserted by FA 2000, s. 133(1) having effect:

- for the purposes of stamp duty where the instrument is executed on or after 21 March 2000 (FA 2000, s. 133(2)); and
- for the purposes of stamp duty reserve tax (FA 2000, s. 133(3)) in relation to a charge to tax under one of the following provisions of FA 1986–

     (a)   s. 87 where –
         (i)   the agreement to transfer is conditional and the condition is satisfied on or after 21 March 2000, or
         (ii)   the agreement is not conditional and is made on or after that date;
     (b)   s. 93(1) where securities are transferred, issued or appropriated on or after 21 March 2000 (whenever the arrangement was made);
     (c)   s. 96(1) where securities are transferred or issued on or after 21 March 2000 (whenever the arrangement was made);
     (d)   s. 93(10) where securities are issued or transferred on sale, under terms there mentioned, on or after 21 March 2000; and
     (e)   s. 96(8), where securities are issued or transferred on sale, under terms there mentioned, on or after 21 March 2000.

S. 79(8) substituted by FA 1999, s. 112(4) and Sch. 14, para. 17, the substitution having effect in relation to instruments executed on or after 1 October 1999.

S. 79(9)–(11) repealed by FA 1999, s. 139 and Sch. 20, Pt. V(2), the repeal having effect in relation to instruments executed, or bearer instruments issued, on or after 1 October 1999, but as regards unit trust schemes subject to FA 1999, Sch. 20, Pt. V(2), para. 2. The repeal took effect from 6 February 2000 as regards unit trust schemes, by virtue of FA 1999, s. 122(4) and FA 1999, Sch. 19.

In s. 79(12), the words "(10) and (14)" repealed by FA 1999, s. 139 and Sch. 20, Pt. V(2), the repeal having effect in relation to instruments executed, or bearer instruments issued, on or after 1 October 1999, but as regards unit trust schemes subject to FA 1999, Sch. 20, Pt. V(2), para. 2. This was a direct consequence of the repeal of s. 78(10)–(14) by the same legislation at the same time. The repeal took effect from 6 February 2000 as regards unit trust schemes, by virtue of FA 1999, s. 122(4) and FA 1999, Sch. 19. (S. 78 is not reproduced separately in this volume as it only applied for a temporary period: see note below.)

Statements of practice – SP 3/84: S. 79(2) does not exclude from the exemption loan capital which carries an unexpired right of conversion into an acquisition of loan capital which itself comes within the terms of the exemption.

Notes – FA 1986, s. 78, referred to in s. 79(12), had effect only during the period beginning on 25 March 1986 and ending on 6 July 1986. Only the interpretative provisions of that section referred to in s. 79(12) and which continue to be relevant are therefore reproduced below for information.

"**78(7)**   In this section "**loan capital**" means–

  (a)   any debenture stock, corporation stock or funded debt, by whatever name known, issued by a body corporate or other body of persons (which here includes a local authority and any body whether formed or established in the United Kingdom or elsewhere);

  (b)   any capital raised by such a body if the capital is borrowed or has the character of borrowed money, and whether it is in the form of stock or any other form;

  (c)   stock or marketable securities issued by the government of any country or territory outside the United Kingdom.
     . . .

78(9)   In this section "**designated international organisation**" means an international organisation designated for the purposes of section 126 of the Finance Act 1984 by an order made under subsection (1) of that section."

The Treasury order appointing the "abolition day" for the purposes of FA 1990, s. 107–110 was to have broadly coincided with the start of paperless trading under the Stock Exchange's planned TAURUS system (IR press release, 20 March 1990). However, on 11 March 1993 it was announced that TAURUS had been abandoned (London Stock Exchange News Release 6/93).

80   Bearer letters of allotment etc.

80   [Repealed by FA 1999, s. 139 and Sch. 20, Pt. V(2) in relation to bearer instruments issued on or after 1 October 1999 but as regards unit trust schemes subject to FA 1999, Sch. 20, Pt. V(2), para. 2. The repeal took effect from 6 February 2000 as regards unit trust schemes, by virtue of FA 1999, s. 122(4) and FA 1999, Sch. 19.]

CHANGES IN FINANCIAL INSTITUTIONS

80A   Sales to intermediaries

80A(1)   Stamp duty shall not be chargeable on an instrument transferring stock of a particular kind on sale to a person or his nominee if–

(a)   the person is a member of an EEA exchange, or a recognised foreign exchange, on which stock of that kind is regularly traded;

(b)   the person is an intermediary and is recognised as an intermediary by the exchange in accordance with arrangements approved by the Commissioners; and

(c)   the sale is effected on the exchange.

80A(2)   Stamp duty shall not be chargeable on an instrument transferring stock of a particular kind on sale to a person or his nominee if–

(a)   the person is a member of an EEA exchange or a recognised foreign options exchange;

(b)   options to buy or sell stock of that kind are regularly traded on that exchange and are listed by or quoted on that exchange;

(c)   the person is an options intermediary and is recognised as an options intermediary by that exchange in accordance with arrangements approved by the Commissioners; and

(d)   the sale is effected on an EEA exchange, or a recognised foreign exchange, on which stock of that kind is regularly traded or subsection (3) below applies.

80A(3)   This subsection applies if–

(a)   the sale is effected on an EEA exchange, or a recognised foreign options exchange, pursuant to the exercise of a relevant option; and

(b)   options to buy or sell stock of the kind concerned are regularly traded on that exchange and are listed by or quoted on that exchange.

80A(4)   For the purposes of this section–

(a)   an intermediary is a person who carries on a bona fide business of dealing in stock and does not carry on an excluded business; and

(b)   an options intermediary is a person who carries on a bona fide business of dealing in quoted or listed options to buy or sell stock and does not carry on an excluded business.

80A(5)   The excluded businesses are the following–

(a)   any business which consists wholly or mainly in the making or managing of investments;

(b)   any business which consists wholly or mainly in, or is carried on wholly or mainly for the purpose of, providing services to persons who are connected with the person carrying on the business;

(c)   any business which consists in insurance business;

(d)   any business which consists in managing or acting as trustee in relation to a pension scheme or which is carried on by the manager or trustee of such a scheme in connection with or for the purposes of the scheme;

(e)   any business which consists in operating or acting as trustee in relation to a collective investment scheme or is carried on by the operator or trustee of such a scheme in connection with or for the purposes of the scheme.

80A(6)   A sale is effected on an exchange for the purposes of subsection (1) or (2) above if (and only if)–

(a)   it is subject to the rules of the exchange; and

(b)   it is reported to the exchange in accordance with the rules of the exchange.

80A(7)   An instrument on which stamp duty is not chargeable by virtue only of this section shall not be deemed to be duly stamped unless it has been stamped with a stamp denoting that it is not chargeable with any duty; and notwithstanding anything in section 122(1) of the Stamp Act 1891, the stamp may be a stamp of such kind as the Commissioners may prescribe.

Prospective repeal – S. 80A repealed by FA 1997, s. 113 and Sch. 18, Pt. VII, with effect, in accordance with FA 1990, s. 108, where the instrument is executed in pursuance of a contract made on or after the abolition day (see note).

History – S. 80A inserted by FA 1997, s. 97(1) with effect for instruments executed on or after 20 October 1997, the commencement day for the purposes of FA 1997, s. 97(4) and (6) by virtue of SI 1997/2428 (C. 95).

Notes – The Treasury order appointing the "abolition day" for the purposes of FA 1990, s. 107–110 was to have broadly coincided with the start of paperless trading under The Stock Exchange's planned TAURUS system (IR press release, 20 March 1990). However, on 11 March 1993 it was announced that TAURUS had been abandoned (London Stock Exchange News Release 6/93).

80B   Intermediaries: supplementary

80B(1)   For the purposes of section 80A above the question whether a person is connected with another shall be determined in accordance with the provisions of section 839 of the Income and Corporation Taxes Act 1988.

80B(2)   In section 80A above and this section–

"**collective investment scheme**" has the meaning given in section 75 of the Financial Services Act 1986;

"**EEA exchange**" means a market which appears on the list drawn up by an EEA State pursuant to Article 16 of European Communities Council Directive No. 93/22/EEC on investment services in the securities field;

"**EEA State**" means a State which is a contracting party to the agreement on the European Economic Area signed at Oporto on the 2nd May 1992 as adjusted by the Protocol signed at Brussels on the 17th March 1993;

"**insurance business**" means long term business or general business as defined in section 1 of the Insurance Companies Act 1982;

"**quoted or listed options**" means options which are quoted on or listed by an EEA exchange or a recognised foreign options exchange;

"**stock**" includes any marketable security;

"**trustee**" and "**the operator**" shall, in relation to a collective investment scheme, be construed in accordance with section 75(8) of the Financial Services Act 1986.

80B(3)   In section 80A above "**recognised foreign exchange**" means a market which–

(a)   is not in an EEA State; and

(b)   is specified in regulations made by the Treasury under this subsection.

80B(4)   In section 80A above and this section "**recognised foreign options exchange**" means a market which–

(a)   is not in an EEA State; and

(b)   is specified in regulations made by the Treasury under this subsection.

80B(5)   In section 80A above "**the exercise of a relevant option**" means–

(a)   the exercise by the options intermediary concerned of an option to buy stock; or

(b)   the exercise of an option binding the options intermediary concerned to buy stock.

80B(6)   The Treasury may by regulations provide that section 80A above shall not have effect in relation to instruments executed in pursuance of kinds of agreement specified in the regulations.

80B(7)   *The Treasury may by regulations* provide that if–

(a)   an instrument falls within subsection (1) or (2) of section 80A above, and

(b)   stamp duty would be chargeable on the instrument apart from that section,

stamp duty shall be chargeable on the instrument at a rate, specified in the regulations, which shall not exceed 0.1% of the consideration for the sale.

80B(8) The Treasury may by regulations change the meaning of **"intermediary"** or **"options intermediary"** for the purposes of section 80A above by amending subsection (4) or (5) of that section (as it has effect for the time being).

80B(9) The power to make regulations under subsections (3) to (8) above shall be exercisable by statutory instrument subject to annulment in pursuance of a resolution of the House of Commons.

Prospective repeal – S. 80B repealed by FA 1997, s. 113 and Sch. 18, Pt. VII, with effect, in accordance with FA 1990, s. 108, where the instrument is executed in pursuance of a contract made on or after the abolition day (see note).

History – S. 80B inserted by FA 1997, s. 97(1) with effect for instruments executed on or after 20 October 1997, the commencement day for the purposes of FA 1997, s. 97(4) and (6) by virtue of SI 1997/2428 (C. 95).
In s. 80B(7), "0.1%" substituted for the words "10p for every £100 or part of £100" by FA 1999, s. 112(4) and Sch. 14, para. 18, the substitution having effect in relation to instruments executed on or after 1 October 1999.

Notes – The Treasury order appointing the "abolition day" for the purposes of FA 1990, s. 107–110 was to have broadly coincided with the start of paperless trading under The Stock Exchange's planned TAURUS system (IR press release, 20 March 1990). However, on 11 March 1993 it was announced that TAURUS had been abandoned (London Stock Exchange News Release 6/93).

80C Repurchases and stock lending

80C(1) This section applies where a person (A) has entered into an arrangement with another person (B) under which–

(a) B is to transfer stock of a particular kind to A or his nominee, and
(b) stock of the same kind and amount is to be transferred by A or his nominee to B or his nominee,

and the conditions set out in subsection (3) below are fulfilled.

80C(2) Stamp duty shall not be chargeable on an instrument transferring stock to B or his nominee or A or his nominee in accordance with the arrangement.

80C(3) The conditions are–

(a) that the arrangement is effected on an EEA exchange or a recognised foreign exchange; and
(b) that stock of the kind concerned is regularly traded on that exchange.

80C(4) An arrangement does not fall within subsection (1) above if–

(a) the arrangement is not such as would be entered into by persons dealing with each other at arm's length; or
(b) under the arrangement any of the benefits or risks arising from fluctuations, before the transfer to B or his nominee takes place, in the market value of the stock accrues to, or falls on, A.

80C(5) An instrument on which stamp duty is not chargeable by virtue only of subsection (2) above shall not be deemed to be duly stamped unless it has been stamped with a stamp denoting that it is not chargeable with any duty; and notwithstanding anything in section 122(1) of the Stamp Act 1891, the stamp may be a stamp of such kind as the Commissioners may prescribe.

80C(6) An arrangement is effected on an exchange for the purposes of subsection (3) above if (and only if)–

(a) it is subject to the rules of the exchange; and
(b) it is reported to the exchange in accordance with the rules of the exchange.

80C(7) In this section–

"**EEA exchange**" has the meaning given in section 80B(2) above; and
"**recognised foreign exchange**" has the meaning given in section 80B(3) above.

80C(8) The Treasury may by regulations provide that if stamp duty would be chargeable on an instrument but for subsection (2) above, stamp duty shall be chargeable on the instrument at a rate, specified in the regulations, which shall not exceed 0.1% of the consideration for the transfer.

80C(9) The Treasury may by regulations amend this section (as it has effect for the time being) in order–

(a) to change the conditions for exemption from duty under this section; or
(b) to provide that this section does not apply in relation to kinds of arrangement specified in the regulations.

80C(10) The power to make regulations under subsection (8) or (9) above shall be exercisable by statutory instrument subject to annulment in pursuance of a resolution of the House of Commons.

Prospective repeal – S. 80C repealed by FA 1997, s. 113 and Sch. 18, Pt. VII, with effect, in accordance with FA 1990, s. 108, where the instrument is executed in pursuance of a contract made on or after the abolition day (see note below).

History – S. 80C inserted by FA 1997, s. 98(1), with effect in relation to instruments executed on or after 20 October 1997, the commencement day for the purposes of FA 1997, s. 98(3), (4) by virtue of SI 1997/2428 (C. 35).

In s. 80C(8), "0.1%" substituted for the words "10p for every £100 or part of £100" by FA 1999, s. 112(4) and Sch. 14, para. 19, the substitution having effect in relation to instruments executed on or after 1 October 1999.

Cross references – European Single Currency (Taxes) Regulations 1998 (SI 1998/3177), reg. 25: modification to cater for adoption of the euro in connection with the replacement of stock in a euroconvention.
European Single Currency (Taxes) Regulations 1998 (SI 1998/3177), reg. 27: modification to cater for adoption of the euro in connection with the payment or benefit received by transferee of stock on euroconversion.
European Single Currency (Taxes) Regulations 1998 (SI 1998/3177), reg. 29: modification to cater for adoption of the euro in connection with the renominalisation resulting in new minimum denomination in which stock can be held or traded.

Other material – IR/Customs press release, 29 July 1998: proposed tax treatment of redenominations of debt securities into euros for repo/stock lending and related purposes; cases where continuity of asset treatment will apply; and treatment of representative payments on "cashing out".

Notes – The Treasury order appointing the "abolition day" for the purposes of FA 1990, s. 107–110 was to have broadly coincided with the start of paperless trading under The Stock Exchange's planned TAURUS system (IR press release, 20 March 1990). However, on 11 March 1993 it was announced that TAURUS had been abandoned (London Stock Exchange News Release 6/93).

81   Sales to market makers

81   [Repealed by FA 1997, s. 97(2), 113 and Sch. 18, Pt VII.]

82   Borrowing of stock by market makers

82   [Repealed by FA 1997, s. 98(2), 113 and Sch. 18, Pt. VII.]

83   Composition agreements

83(1)   In section 33(1) of the Finance Act 1970 (composition by stock exchanges in respect of transfer duty)–

(a)   for the words "any recognised stock exchange" there shall be substituted "any recognised investment exchange or recognised clearing house", and

(b)   the following shall be substituted for the words from "In this subsection" to the end– "In this subsection "recognised investment exchange" and "recognised clearing house"" have the same meanings as in the Financial Services Act 1986.'"

83(2)   The words "recognised investment exchange or recognised clearing house" shall be substituted for the words "stock exchange" in section 33(2)(b), (c) and (d), (4) and (5) of the Finance Act 1970.

83(3)   This section shall come into force on such day as the Commissioners may appoint by order made by statutory instrument.

Prospective repeals – S. 83 repealed by FA 1990, s. 132 and Sch. 19, Pt. VI, from a date to be appointed in accordance with s. 107–111 of that Act.

Notes – The Treasury order appointing the "abolition day" for the purposes of FA 1990, s. 107–110 was to have broadly coincided with the start of paperless trading under the Stock Exchange's planned TAURUS system (IR press release, 20 March 1990). However, on 11 March 1993 it was announced that TAURUS had been abandoned (London Stock Exchange News Release 6/93).

84   Miscellaneous exemptions

84(1)   [Amends FA 1976, s. 127(1).]

84(2)   Stamp duty shall not be chargeable on an instrument effecting a transfer of stock if–

(a)   the transferee is a recognised investment exchange or a nominee of a recognised investment exchange, and

(b)   an agreement which relates to the stamp duty which would (apart from this subsection) be chargeable on the instrument, and was made between the Commissioners and the investment exchange under section 33 of the Finance Act 1970, is in force at the time of the transfer.

84(3)   Stamp duty shall not be chargeable on an instrument effecting a transfer of stock if–

(a)   the transferee is a recognised clearing house or a nominee of a recognised clearing house, and

(b)   an agreement which relates to the stamp duty which would (apart from this subsection) be chargeable on the instrument, and was made between the Commissioners and the clearing house under section 33 of the Finance Act 1970, is in force at the time of the transfer.

84(4)   Subsection (1) above applies to any transfer giving effect to a transaction carried out on or after the day of The Stock Exchange reforms.

84(5)   Subsection (2) above applies to any instrument giving effect to a transaction carried out on or after such day as the Commissioners may appoint by order made by statutory instrument.

84(6)   Subsection (3) above applies to any instrument giving effect to a transaction carried out on or after such day as the Commissioners may appoint by order made by statutory instrument.

Prospective repeals – S. 84 repealed by FA 1990, s. 132 and Sch. 19, Pt. VI, from a date to be appointed in accordance with s. 107–111 of that Act. (See note below).

Notes – The day of The Stock Exchange reforms was 27 October 1986.
The Treasury order appointing the "abolition day" for the purposes of FA 1990,s. 107–110 was to have broadly coincided with the start of paperless trading under the Stock Exchange's planned TAURUS system (IR press release, 20 March 1990). However, on 11 March 1993 it was announced that TAURUS had been abandoned (London Stock Exchange News Release 6/93).

85   Supplementary

85(1)   [Spent.]

85(2)   Section 34 of the Finance Act 1961 and section 4 of the Finance Act (Northern Ireland) 1961 (borrowing of stock by jobbers) shall not apply where stock is transferred in discharge of an undertaking given on or after the day of The Stock Exchange reforms.

85(3)   Section 42(1) of the Finance Act 1920 shall not apply to any transfer giving effect to a transaction carried out on or after such day as is specified for this purpose in regulations made under section 81(5) above; and different days may be so specified for different purposes.

85(4)   Section 127(2) of the Finance Act 1976 (transfer otherwise than on sale from stock exchange nominee to jobber) shall not apply to any transfer giving effect to a transaction carried out on or after the day of The Stock Exchange reforms.

85(5)   In sections 81, 82 and 84 above and this section–

(a)   **"the day of The Stock Exchange reforms"** means the day on which the rule of The Stock Exchange that prohibits a person from carrying on business as both a broker and a jobber is abolished,

(b)   references to a recognised investment exchange are to a recognised investment exchange within the meaning of the Financial Services Act 1986,

(c)   references to a recognised clearing house are to a recognised clearing house within the meaning of the Financial Services Act 1986, and

(d)   **"stock"** includes marketable security.

Prospective repeals – S. 85 repealed by FA 1990, s. 109(6)(e), 132 and Sch. 19, Pt. VI, from a date to be appointed in accordance with s. 107–111 of that Act. (See note below).

Notes – The day of The Stock Exchange reforms was 27 October 1986.
The Treasury order appointing the "abolition day" for the purposes of FA 1990, s. 107–110 was to have broadly coincided with the start of paperless trading under the Stock Exchange's planned TAURUS system (IR press release, 20 March 1990). However, on 11 March 1993 it was announced that TAURUS had been abandoned (London Stock Exchange News Release 6/93).

PART IV – STAMP DUTY RESERVE TAX

Prospective repeals – Pt. IV repealed by FA 1990, s. 132 and Sch. 19, Pt. VII, from a date to be appointed in accordance with s.110 of that Act. (See note below).

Cross references – FA 1995, s. 152(2)(b), (3)(c): powers of Treasury to make regulations applying and adapting Pt. IV in relation to open-ended investment companies etc.
Stamp Duty and Stamp Duty Reserve Tax (Open-ended Investment Companies) Regulations 1997, SI 1997/1156.
Stamp Duty and Stamp Duty Reserve Tax (Open-ended Investment Companies) (Amendment) Regulations SI 1999/1467.
FA 1999, s. 119: powers of Treasury to make regulations exempting UK depositary interests in foreign securities from charge to stamp duty reserve tax by excluding them from definition of "chargeable securities" in Pt. IV.
Stamp Duty Reserve Tax (UK Depositary Interests in Foreign Securities) Regulations 1999, SI 1999/2383.

Notes – The Treasury order appointing the "abolition day" for the purposes of FA 1990, s. 107–110 was to have broadly coincided with the start of paperless trading under the Stock Exchange's planned TAURUS system (IR press release, 20 March 1990). However, on 11 March 1993 it was announced that TAURUS had been abandoned (London Stock Exchange News Release 6/93).
Although imposed on transfers of chargeable securities, and so not technically a stamp duty, the stamp duty reserve tax provisions are included here for ease of reference.
FA 1999, s. 123(1)(b): FA 1999, Pt. VI (various changes to stamp duty and stamp duty reserve tax, largely effective from 1 October 1999), so far as it relates to stamp duty reserve tax, to be construed as one with Pt. IV.

INTRODUCTION

86   The tax: introduction

86(1)   A tax, to be known as stamp duty reserve tax, shall be charged in accordance with this Part of this Act.

86(2)   The tax shall be under the care and management of the Board.

86(3)   Section 1 of the Provisional Collection of Taxes Act 1968 shall apply to the tax; and accordingly in subsection (1) of that section after the words "petroleum revenue tax" there shall be inserted the words "stamp duty reserve tax".

86(4) Stamp duty reserve tax shall be chargeable in accordance with the provisions of this Part of this Act–

(a)   whether the agreement, transfer, issue or appropriation in question is made or effected in the United Kingdom or elsewhere, and

(b)   whether or not any party is resident or situate in any part of the United Kingdom.

Prospective repeals – S. 86 repealed by FA 1990, s. 132 and Sch. 19, Pt. VII, from a date to be appointed in relation to s. 87, 93 and 96 as provided for those sections by FA 1990, s. 110. (See note below).

History – S. 86(4) inserted by FA 1996, s. 187(1) and having effect:
- in relation to an agreement, if:
  - the agreement is conditional and the condition is satisfied on or after 1 July 1996; or
  - the agreement is not conditional and is made on or after that date; and
- in relation to a transfer, issue or appropriation made or effected on or after that date.

Cross references – FA 1995, s. 152(2)(b), (3)(c): powers of Treasury to make regulations applying and adapting Pt. IV in relation to open-ended investment companies etc.
Stamp Duty and Stamp Duty Reserve Tax (Open-ended Investment Companies) Regulations 1997, SI 1997/1156.
Stamp Duty and Stamp Duty Reserve Tax (Open-ended Investment Companies) (Amendment) Regulations SI 1999/1467, reg. 3.
FA 1999, s. 119: powers of Treasury to make regulations exempting UK depositary interests in foreign securities from charge to stamp duty reserve tax by excluding them from definition of "chargeable securities" in Pt. IV.

Other material – Inland Revenue press release, 28 November 1995: background to the 1996 amendments.

Notes – The Treasury order appointing the "abolition day" for the purposes of FA 1990, s. 107–110 was to have broadly coincided with the start of paperless trading under the Stock Exchange's planned TAURUS system (IR press release, 20 March 1990). However, on 11 March 1993 it was announced that TAURUS had been abandoned (London Stock Exchange News Release 6/93).

THE PRINCIPAL CHARGE

87   The principal charge

87(1) This section applies where a person (A) agrees with another person (B) to transfer chargeable securities (whether or not to B) for consideration in money or money's worth.

87(2) There shall be a charge to stamp duty reserve tax under this section on the relevant day.

87(3) In subsection (2) above **"the relevant day"** means–

(a)   in a case where the agreement is conditional, the day on which the condition is satisfied, and

(b)   in any other case, the day on which the agreement is made.

87(4), (5) [Repealed by FA 1996, s. 192(1), 205 and Sch. 41, Pt. VII.]

87(6) Tax under this section shall be charged at the rate of 0.5 per cent. of the amount or value of the consideration mentioned in subsection (1) above.

87(7) For the purposes of subsection (6) above the value of any consideration not consisting of money shall be taken to be the price it might reasonably be expected to fetch on a sale in the open market at the time the agreement mentioned in subsection (1) above is made.

87(7A)   Where–

(a)   there would be no charge to tax under this section, or

(b)   there would, under section 92 below, be a repayment or cancellation of tax,

in relation to some of the chargeable securities to which the agreement between A and B relates if separate agreements had been made between them for the transfer of those securities and for the transfer of the remainder, this section and sections 88(5) and 92 below shall have effect as if such separate agreements had been made.

87(7B) [Repealed by FA 1997, s. 106(3), 113 and Sch. 18, Pt. VII.]

87(8) [Repealed by FA 1996, s. 192(1), 205 and Sch. 41, Pt. VII.]

87(9) This section applies where the agreement to transfer is made on or after the day on which the rule of The Stock Exchange that prohibits a person from carrying on business as both a broker and a jobber is abolished.

87(10) This section has effect subject to sections 88 to 90 below.

Prospective repeals – S. 87 repealed by FA 1990, s. 132 and Sch. 19, Pt. VII, for agreements made or conditions satisfied (as appropriate) in accordance with FA 1990, s. 110(2) on or after a day to be appointed. (See note below).

History – S. 87(2) amended by FA 1996, s. 188(1), 205 and Sch. 41, Pt. VII and having effect in relation to an agreement to transfer securities if:
- the agreement is conditional and the condition is satisfied on or after 1 July 1996; or
- the agreement is not conditional and is made on or after that date.
S. 87(4), (5) and (8) omitted by FA 1996, s. 192(1), 205 and Sch. 41, Pt. VII, with effect in relation to an agreement to transfer securities if:
- the agreement is conditional and the condition is satisfied on or after 1 July 1996; or
- the agreement is not conditional and is made on or after that date.
S. 87(6) amended by FA 1996, s. 194(1), substituting "0.5 per cent." for "50p for every £100 or part of £100", with effect where:

- the agreement is conditional and the condition is satisfied on or after 1 July 1996; or
- the agreement is not conditional and is made on or after that date.

S. 87(7A) wording substituted, and s. 87(7B) repealed by FA 1997, s. 106(2), (3) in relation to an agreement to transfer securities if the agreement is conditional and the condition is satisfied on or after 4 January 1997, or if the agreement is not conditional and is made on or after that date (FA 1997, s. 106(9)).
S. 87(7A), (7B) inserted by FA 1987, Sch. 7, para. 2, with retrospective effect.

Cross references – FA 1989, s. 176: Treasury may, by regulations, exempt from charge or apply reduced rate to certain transactions involving a stock exchange nominee.
FA 1997, s. 100 and 101: circumstances relating to mergers of authorised unit trusts and trust property held on other trusts where s. 87 shall not apply.
FA 1999, s. 122(4): a charge under s. 87 in respect of an agreement which is **not** excepted by s. 90(1) is not affected by the provisions of FA 1999, Sch. 19 (charge to stamp duty reserve tax on surrender of units in unit trusts).
SI 1997/1156, reg. 8, 10: disapplication of s. 87 as regards an agreement to transfer securities to an open-ended investment company on the occasion of the conversion of an authorised unit trust to, or the amalgamation of an authorised unit trust with, that open-ended investment company.
SI 1999/1467, reg. 3: amendment of SI 1997/1156, reg. 10 to remove time limit of 1 July 1999 for disapplication of s. 87 as regards an agreement to transfer securities to an open-ended investment company on the occasion of the amalgamation of an authorised unit trust with that open-ended investment company (see note above).
SI 1986/1711 (as amended by SI 1988/835): management provisions including reg. 3, 4 (accountability) and reg. 7 (relief from accountability).

Other material – Inland Revenue press release, 28 November 1995: background to the 1996 amendments.

Notes – The rule of The Stock Exchange which prohibited a person from carrying on business as both a broker and a jobber was abolished on 27 October 1986.
FA 1991, s. 117: investment exchanges and clearing house – stamp duty reserve tax.
SI 1992/570: prescribes the circumstances in which agreements to transfer securities to members of LIFFE (London International Financial Futures and Options Exchange) will be exempt from stamp duty reserve tax.
The Treasury order appointing the "abolition day" for the purposes of FA 1990, s. 107–110 was to have broadly coincided with the start of paperless trading under the Stock Exchange's planned TAURUS system (IR press release, 20 March 1990). However, on 11 March 1993 it was announced that TAURUS had been abandoned (London Stock Exchange News Release 6/93).

88   Special cases
History – Heading substituted by FA 1997, s. 106(7).

88(1)   An instrument on which stamp duty is not chargeable by virtue of–

(aa)   paragraph 24(d) of Schedule 13 to the Finance Act 1999 (renounceable letters of allotment etc.),

(a)   section 127(1) of the Finance Act 1976 (transfer to stock exchange nominee), or

(b)   section 84(2) or (3) above, or

(c)   Part I of Schedule 19 to the Finance Act 1999 (transfers etc. of units in unit trusts),

shall be disregarded in construing section 92(1A) and (1B) below.

88(1A)   An instrument on which stamp duty is not chargeable by virtue of section 186 of the Finance Act 1996 (transfers of securities to members of electronic transfer systems etc.) shall be disregarded in construing section 92(1A) and (1B) below unless–

(a)   the transfer is made by a stock exchange nominee; and

(b)   the maximum stamp duty chargeable on the instrument, apart from section 186 of the Finance Act 1996, would be £5;

and in this subsection **"stock exchange nominee"** means a person designated for the purposes of section 127 of the Finance Act 1976 as a nominee of The Stock Exchange by an order made by the Secretary of State under subsection (5) of that section.

88(1B)   An instrument on which stamp duty is not chargeable by virtue of section 42 of the Finance Act 1930 or section 11 of the Finance Act (Northern Ireland) 1954 (transfer between associated bodies corporate) shall be disregarded in construing section 92(1A) and (1B) below in any case where–

(a)   the property mentioned in section 42(2)(a) of the Finance Act 1930 or, as the case may be, section 11(2)(a) of the Finance Act (Northern Ireland) 1954 consists of or includes chargeable securities of any particular kind acquired in the period of two years ending with the day on which the instrument was executed; and

(b)   the body corporate from which the conveyance or transfer there mentioned is effected acquired any of those chargeable securities–

   (i)   in a transaction which was given effect by an instrument of transfer on which stamp duty was not chargeable by virtue of section 80A above;

   (ii)   in pursuance of an agreement to transfer securities as regards which section 87 above did not apply by virtue of section 88A above;

   (iia)   in pursuance of an agreement to transfer securities which was made for the purpose of performing the obligation to transfer chargeable securities described in section 89AA(1)(a) below and as regards which section 87 above did not apply by virtue of section 89AA(2) below; or

  (iii) in circumstances with regard to which the charge to stamp duty or stamp duty reserve tax was treated as not arising by virtue of regulations under section 116 or 117 of the Finance Act 1991.

88(1C)   Where–

(a) there is an arrangement falling within subsection (1) of section 80C above (stamp duty relief for transfers in accordance with certain arrangements for B to transfer stock to A or his nominee and for A or his nominee to transfer stock of the same kind and amount back to B or his nominee), and

(b) under the arrangement stock is transferred to A or his nominee by an instrument on which stamp duty is not chargeable by virtue only of section 80C(2) above, but

(c) it becomes apparent that stock of the same kind or amount will not be transferred to B or his nominee by A or his nominee in accordance with the arrangement,

the instrument shall be disregarded in construing section 92(1A) and (1B) below.

88(1D)   Where–

(a) an instrument transferring stock in accordance with an arrangement is stamped under section 80C(5) above, but

(b) the instrument should not have been so stamped because the arrangement fell within section 80C(4)(a) or (b) above, and

(c) apart from section 80C above stamp duty would have been chargeable on the instrument,

the instrument shall be deemed to be duly stamped under section 80C(5) above, but shall be disregarded in construing section 92(1A) and (1B) below.

88(2), (3)   [Repealed by FA 1996, s. 188(3), 205 and Sch. 41, Pt. VII.]

88(4)   If chargeable securities cannot (apart from this subsection) be identified for the purposes of subsection (1B) above, securities shall be taken as follows, that is to say, securities of the same kind acquired later in the period of two years there mentioned (and not taken for the purposes of that subsection in relation to an earlier instrument) shall be taken before securities acquired earlier in that period.

88(5)   If, in the case of an agreement (or of two or more agreements between the same parties) to transfer chargeable securities–

(a) the conditions in section 92(1A) and (1B) below are not satisfied by virtue only of the application of subsection (1B) above in relation to the instrument (or any one or more of the two or more instruments) in question, but

(b) not all of the chargeable securities falling to be regarded for the purposes of that subsection as transferred by the instrument (or by the two or more instruments between them) were acquired as mentioned in paragraphs (a) and (b) of that subsection,

stamp duty reserve tax shall be repaid or cancelled under section 92 below in accordance with subsection (5A) below.

88(5A)   Any repayment or cancellation of tax falling to be made by virtue of subsection (5) above shall be determined as if (without prejudice to section 87(7A) above) there had, instead of the agreement (or the two or more agreements) in question been–

(a) a separate agreement (or two or more separate agreements) relating to such of the securities as were acquired as mentioned in paragraphs (a) and (b) of subsection (1B) above, and

(b) a single separate agreement relating to such of the securities as do not fall within those paragraphs,

and as if the instrument in question (or the two or more instruments in question between them) had related only to such of the securities as do not fall within those paragraphs.

88(6)   Where a person enters into an agreement for securities to be transferred to him or his nominee, the securities shall be treated for the purposes of subsections (1B)(a) and (4) above as acquired by that person at the time when he enters into the agreement, unless the agreement is *conditional, in which case they shall be* taken to be acquired by him when the condition is satisfied.

Prospective repeals – S. 88 repealed by FA 1990, s. 132 and Sch. 19, Pt. VII, from a date to be appointed in relation to s. 87 as specified for that section by FA 1990, s. 110(2). (See note below).

History – In s. 88(1), para. (aa) substituted for former para. (aa) and (ab) by FA 1999, s. 112(4) and Sch. 14, para. 20(2), the substitution having effect in relation to instruments executed on or after 1 October 1999.
Former s. 88(1), para. (aa) and (ab) (see history note above) inserted, and the words "92(1A) and (1B) below" substituted, by FA 1996, s. 188(2) and 192(2) respectively, with effect in relation to an agreement to transfer securities if the agreement is

conditional and the condition is satisfied on or after 1 July 1996, or the agreement is not conditional and is made on or after that date.

S. 88(1), para. (c) and the word ", or" immediately before it inserted by FA 1999, s. 122(4) and Sch. 19, para. 10(2), with effect from 6 February 2000.

In s. 88(1A)(b), "£5" substituted for 50p by FA 1999, s. 112(4) and Sch. 14, para. 20(3), the substitution having effect in relation to instruments executed on or after 1 October 1999.

S. 88(1A) originally inserted by FA 1996, s. 189, with effect in relation to an agreement to transfer securities if an instrument is executed on or after 1 July 1996 in pursuance of the agreement. The words "92(1A) and (1B) below" were substituted by FA 1996, s. 192(2) in relation to an agreement to transfer securities if the agreement is conditional and the condition is satisfied on or after 1 July 1996, or the agreement is not conditional and is made on or after that date.

In s. 88(1B)(a), words "or includes" inserted, in s. 88(1B)(b) words "any of those chargeable securities" substituted and word "or" at end repealed, and s. 88(1B)(b)(iia) inserted, by FA 1997, s. 106(5), 113 and Sch. 18, Pt. VII with effect where the instrument on which stamp duty is not chargeable by virtue of FA 1930, s. 42 or FA (NI) 1954, s. 11 is executed on or after 4 January 1997 in pursuance of an agreement to transfer securities made on or after that date (FA 1997, s. 106(10)).

S. 88(1B)(b)(i) amended by FA 1997, s. 97(3), with effect in relation to an agreement to transfer chargeable securities if the securities were acquired in a transaction which was given effect to by an instrument of transfer executed on or after 20 October 1997, the commencement day for the purposes of FA 1997, s. 97(5) and (6) by virtue of SI 1997/2428 (C. 95).

S. 88(1B)(b)(ii) amended by FA 1997, s. 102(3), by substituting "88A" with effect in relation to property consisting of chargeable securities if the securities were acquired in pursuance of an agreement to which s. 88A, 88B apply.

S. 88(1B)(b)(iia) substituted by FA 1997, s. 103(3) in relation to property consisting of chargeable securities if the securities were acquired in pursuance of an agreement to transfer securities where, in the case of an agreement which is not conditional, the agreement is made on or after 20 October 1997, or where, in the case of a conditional agreement, the condition is satisfied on or after 20 October 1997, the commencement day for the purposes of FA 1997, s. 103(8) by virtue of SI 1997/2428 (C. 95).

S. 88(1B) originally inserted by FA 1996, s. 190(1), with effect where the instrument on which stamp duty is not chargeable by virtue of FA 1930, s. 42 or FA (NI) 1954 is executed on or after 4 January 1996 in pursuance of an agreement to transfer securities on or after that date. The words "92(1A) and (1B) below" were substituted by FA 1996, s. 192(2), with effect in relation to an agreement to transfer securities if the agreement is conditional and the condition is satisfied on or after 1 July 1996, or the agreement is not conditional and is made on or after that date.

S. 88(1C) and (1D) inserted by FA 1997, s. 103(4), with effect in relation to instruments executed on or after 20 October 1997, the commencement day for the purposes of FA 1997, s. 103(7) and (8) by virtue of SI 1997/2428 (C. 95).

S. 88(2), (3) omitted by FA 1996, s. 188(3), 205 and Sch. 41, Pt. VII, with effect in relation to an agreement to transfer securities if the agreement is conditional and the condition is satisfied on or after 1 July 1996, or the agreement is not conditional and is made on or after that date.

S. 88(4) and (5) substituted, and s. 88(5A) inserted by FA 1997, s. 106(6), with effect where the instrument on which stamp duty is not chargeable by virtue of FA 1930, s. 42 or FA (NI) 1954, s. 11 is executed on or after 4 January 1997 in pursuance of an agreement to transfer securities made on or after that date (FA 1997, s. 106(10)).

S. 88(4)–(6) originally inserted by FA 1996, s. 190(2), with effect where the instrument on which stamp duty is not chargeable by virtue of FA 1930, s. 42 or s. 11 of FA (NI) 1954 is executed on or after 4 January 1996 in pursuance of an agreement to transfer securities on or after that date.

Other material – Inland Revenue press release, 28 November 1995: background to the 1996 amendments.

Notes – The Treasury order appointing the "abolition day" for the purposes of FA 1990, s. 107–110 was to have broadly coincided with the start of paperless trading under the Stock Exchange's planned TAURUS system (IR press release, 20 March 1990). However, on 11 March 1993 it was announced that TAURUS had been abandoned (London Stock Exchange News Release 6/93).

88A   Section 87: exceptions for intermediaries

88A(1)   Section 87 above shall not apply as regards an agreement to transfer securities of a particular kind to B or his nominee if–

(a)   B is a member of an EEA exchange, or a recognised foreign exchange, on which securities of that kind are regularly traded;

(b)   B is an intermediary and is recognised as an intermediary by the exchange in accordance with arrangements approved by the Board; and

(c)   the agreement is effected on the exchange.

88A(2)   Section 87 above shall not apply as regards an agreement to transfer securities of a particular kind to B or his nominee if–

(a)   B is a member of an EEA exchange or a recognised foreign options exchange;

(b)   options to buy or sell securities of that kind are regularly traded on that exchange and are listed by or quoted on that exchange;

(c)   B is an options intermediary and is recognised as an options intermediary by that exchange in accordance with arrangements approved by the Board; and

(d)   the agreement is effected on an EEA exchange, or a recognised foreign exchange, on which securities of that kind are regularly traded or subsection (3) below applies.

88A(3)   This subsection applies if–

(a)   the agreement is effected on an EEA exchange, or a recognised foreign options exchange, pursuant to the exercise of a relevant option; and

(b)   options to buy or sell securities of the kind concerned are regularly traded on that exchange and are listed by or quoted on that exchange.

88A(4)   For the purposes of this section–

(a)   an intermediary is a person who carries on a bona fide business of dealing in chargeable securities and does not carry on an excluded business; and

(b)   an options intermediary is a person who carries on a bona fide business of dealing in quoted or listed options to buy or sell chargeable securities and does not carry on an excluded business.

88A(5)   The excluded businesses are the following–

(a)   any business which consists wholly or mainly in the making or managing of investments;

(b)   any business which consists wholly or mainly in, or is carried on wholly or mainly for the purpose of, providing services to persons who are connected with the person carrying on the business;

(c)   any business which consists in insurance business;

(d)   any business which consists in managing or acting as trustee in relation to a pension scheme or which is carried on by the manager or trustee of such a scheme in connection with or for the purposes of the scheme;

(e)   any business which consists in operating or acting as trustee in relation to a collective investment scheme or is carried on by the operator or trustee of such a scheme in connection with or for the purposes of the scheme.

88A(6)   An agreement is effected on an exchange for the purposes of subsection (1) or (2) above if (and only if)–

(a)   it is subject to the rules of the exchange; and

(b)   it is reported to the exchange in accordance with the rules of the exchange.

Prospective repeal – S. 88A repealed by FA 1997, s. 113 and Sch. 18, Pt. VII, with effect in accordance with FA 1990, s. 110 (see note).

History – S. 88A inserted by FA 1997, s. 102(1) in relation to an agreement to transfer securities where, in the case of an agreement which is not conditional, the agreement is made on or after 20 October 1997, or where, in the case of a conditional agreement, the condition is satisfied on or after 20 October 1997, the commencement day appointed for the purposes of FA 1997, s. 102(6) by virtue of SI 1997/2428 (C. 35).

Notes – The Treasury order appointing the "abolition day" for the purposes of FA 1990, s. 107–110 was to have broadly coincided with the start of paperless trading under The Stock Exchange's planned TAURUS system (IR press release, 20 March 1990). However, on 11 March 1993 it was announced that TAURUS had been abandoned (London Stock Exchange News Release 6/93).

88B   Intermediaries: supplementary

88B(1)   For the purposes of section 88A above the question whether a person is connected with another shall be determined in accordance with the provisions of section 839 of the Income and Corporation Taxes Act 1988.

88B(2)   In section 88A above and this section–

"**collective investment scheme**" has the meaning given in section 75 of the Financial Services Act 1986;

"**EEA exchange**" means a market which appears on the list drawn up by an EEA State pursuant to Article 16 of European Communities Council Directive No. 93/22/EEC on investment services in the securities field;

"**EEA State**" means a State which is a contracting party to the agreement on the European Economic Area signed at Oporto on the 2nd May 1992 as adjusted by the Protocol signed at Brussels on the 17th March 1993;

"**insurance business**" means long term business or general business as defined in section 1 of the Insurance Companies Act 1982;

"**quoted or listed options**" means options which are quoted on or listed by an EEA exchange or a recognised foreign options exchange;

"**recognised foreign exchange**" and "**recognised foreign options exchange**" have the meanings given, respectively, by subsections (3) and (4) of section 80B above;

"**trustee**" and "**the operator**" shall, in relation to a collective investment scheme, be construed in accordance with section 75(8) of the Financial Services Act 1986.

88B(3)   In section 88A above "**the exercise of a relevant option**" means–

(a)   the exercise by B of an option to buy securities; or

(b)   the exercise of an option binding B to buy securities.

88B(4)   The Treasury may by regulations provide that section 88A above shall not have effect in relation to kinds of agreement specified in the regulations.

88B(5)   The Treasury may by regulations provide that if–

(a)   an agreement falls within subsection (1) or (2) of section 88A above, and

(b)   section 87 above would, apart from section 88A, apply to the agreement, section 87 shall apply to the agreement but with the substitution of a rate of tax not exceeding 0.1 per cent for the rate specified in subsection (6) of that section.

88B(6) The Treasury may by regulations change the meaning of **"intermediary"** or **"options intermediary"** for the purposes of section 88A above by amending subsection (4) or (5) of that section (as it has effect for the time being).

88B(7) The power to make regulations under subsections (4) to (6) above shall be exercisable by statutory instrument subject to annulment in pursuance of a resolution of the House of Commons.

Prospective repeal – S. 88B repealed by FA 1997, s. 113 and Sch. 18, Pt. VII, with effect in accordance with FA 1990, s. 110 (see note).

History – S. 88B inserted by FA 1997, s. 102(1) in relation to an agreement to transfer securities where, in the case of an agreement which is not conditional, the agreement is made on or after 20 October 1997, or where, in the case of a conditional agreement, the condition is satisfied on or after 20 October 1997, the commencement day appointed for the purposes of FA 1997, s. 102(6) by virtue of SI 1997/2428 (C. 35).

Notes – The Treasury order appointing the "abolition day" for the purposes of FA 1990, s. 107–110 was to have broadly coincided with the start of paperless trading under The Stock Exchange's planned TAURUS system (IR press release, 20 March 1990). However, on 11 March 1993 it was announced that TAURUS had been abandoned (London Stock Exchange News Release 6/93).

89   Section 87: exceptions for market makers etc.

89   [Repealed by FA 1997, s. 102(2), 113 and Sch. 18, Pt. VII.]

89A   Section 87: exceptions for public issue

89A(1) Section 87 above shall not apply as regards an agreement to transfer securities other than units under a unit trust scheme to B or B's nominee if–

(a)   the agreement is part of an arrangement, entered into by B in the ordinary course of B's business as an issuing house, under which B (as principal) is to offer the securities for sale to the public,

(b)   the agreement is conditional upon the admission of the securities to the Official List of The Stock Exchange,

(c)   the consideration under the agreement for each security is the same as the price at which B is to offer the security for sale, and

(d)   B sells the securities in accordance with the arrangements referred to in paragraph (a) above.

89A(2) Section 87 above shall not apply as regards an agreement if the securities to which the agreement relates are newly subscribed securities other than units under a unit trust scheme and–

(a)   the agreement is made in pursuance of an offer to the public made by A (as principal) under an arrangement entered into in the ordinary course of A's business as an issuing house,

(b)   a right of allotment in respect of, or to subscribe for, the securities has been acquired by A under an agreement which is part of the arrangement,

(c)   both those agreements are conditional upon the admission of the securities to the Official List of The Stock Exchange, and

(d)   the consideration for each security is the same under both agreements;

and for the purposes of this subsection, **"newly subscribed securities"** are securities which, in pursuance of the arrangement referred to in paragraph (a) above, are issued wholly for new consideration.

89A(3) Section 87 above shall not apply as regards an agreement if the securities to which the agreement relates are registered securities other than units under a unit trust scheme and–

(a)   the agreement is made in pursuance of an offer to the public made by A,

(b)   the agreement is conditional upon the admission of the securities to the Official List of The Stock Exchange, and

(c)   under the agreement A issues to B or his nominee a renouncable letter of acceptance, or similar instrument, in respect of the securities.

89A(4) The Treasury may by regulations amend paragraph (b) of subsection (1) above, paragraph (c) of subsection (2) above, and paragraph (b) of subsection (3) above (as they have effect for the time being); and the power to make regulations under this section shall be exercisable by statutory instrument subject to annulment in pursuance of a resolution of the House of Commons.

Prospective repeals – S. 89A repealed by FA 1990, s. 132 and Sch. 19, Pt. VII, from a date to be appointed in relation to s. 87 as specified for that section by FA 1990, s. 110(2). (See note below).

History – S. 89A inserted by F(No. 2)A 1987, s. 100(1), for agreements to transfer securities made after 7 May 1987.

Notes – For reference to a person, B, see s. 87(1).

The Treasury order appointing the "abolition day" for the purposes of FA 1990, s. 107–110 was to have broadly coincided with the start of paperless trading under the Stock Exchange's planned TAURUS system (IR press release, 20 March 1990). However, on 11 March 1993 it was announced that TAURUS had been abandoned (London Stock Exchange News Release 6/93).

89AA   Section 87: exception for repurchases and stock lending

89AA(1)   This section applies where a person (P) has entered into an arrangement with another person (Q) under which–

(a)   Q is to transfer chargeable securities of a particular kind to P or his nominee, and

(b)   chargeable securities of the same kind and amount are to be transferred by P or his nominee to Q or his nominee,

and the conditions set out in subsection (3) below are fulfilled.

89AA(2)   Section 87 above shall not apply as regards an agreement to transfer chargeable securities to P or his nominee or Q or his nominee in accordance with the arrangement.

89AA(3)   The conditions are–

(a)   that the agreement is effected on an EEA exchange or a recognised foreign exchange;

(b)   that securities of the kind concerned are regularly traded on that exchange; and

(c)   that chargeable securities are transferred to P or his nominee and Q or his nominee in pursuance of the arrangement.

89AA(4)   An arrangement does not fall within subsection (1) above if–

(a)   the arrangement is not such as would be entered into by persons dealing with each other at arm's length; or

(b)   under the arrangement any of the benefits or risks arising from fluctuations, before the transfer to Q or his nominee takes place, in the market value of the chargeable securities accrues to, or falls on, P.

89AA(5)   An agreement is effected on an exchange for the purposes of subsection (3) above if (and only if)–

(a)   it is subject to the rules of the exchange; and

(b)   it is reported to the exchange in accordance with the rules of the exchange.

89AA(6)   In this section–

     "EEA exchange" has the meaning given in section 88B(2) above;

     "recognised foreign exchange" has the meaning given in section 80B(3) above.

89AA(7)   The Treasury may by regulations provide that if section 87 would apply as regards an agreement but for subsection (2) above, section 87 shall apply as regards the agreement but with the substitution of a rate of tax not exceeding 0.1 per cent for the rate specified in subsection (6) of that section.

89AA(8)   The Treasury may by regulations amend this section (as it has effect for the time being) in order–

(a)   to change the conditions for exemption from tax under this section; or

(b)   to provide that this section does not apply in relation to kinds of arrangement specified in the regulations.

89AA(9)   The power to make regulations under subsection (7) or (8) above shall be exercisable by statutory instrument subject to annulment in pursuance of a resolution of the House of Commons.

Prospective repeal – S. 89AA repealed by FA 1997, s. 113 and Sch. 18, Pt. VII, with effect in accordance with FA 1990, s. 110 (see note).

History – S. 89AA inserted by FA 1997, s. 103(1) in relation to an agreement to transfer securities where, in the case of an agreement which is not conditional, the agreement is made on or after 20 October 1997, or where, in the case of a conditional agreement, the condition is satisfied on or after 20 October 1997 (s. 101(5)), the day appointed for the purposes of FA 1997, s. 103(8) by virtue of SI 1997/2428 (C. 35).

Cross references – European Single Currency (Taxes) Regulations 1998 (SI 1998/3177), reg. 26: modification to cater for adoption of the euro in connection with the replacement of chargeable securities in a euroconversion.
European Single Currency (Taxes) Regulations 1998 (SI 1998/3177), reg. 28: modification to cater for adoption of the euro in connection with the payment or benefit received by a transferee of chargeable securities on a euroconversion.
European Single Currency (Taxes) Regulations 1998 (SI 1998/3177), reg. 30: modification to cater for adoption of the euro in connection with the renominalisation resulting in new minimum denomination in which chargeable securities can be held or traded.

Other material – IR/Customs press release, 29 July 1998: proposed tax treatment of redenominations of debt securities into euros for repo/stock lending and related purposes; cases where continuity of asset treatment will apply; and treatment of representative payments on "cashing out".

Notes – The Treasury order appointing the "abolition day" for the purposes of FA 1990, s. 107–110 was to have broadly coincided with the start of paperless trading under The Stock Exchange's planned TAURUS system (IR press release, 20 March 1990). However, on 11 March 1993 it was announced that TAURUS had been abandoned (London Stock Exchange News Release 6/93).

89B Section 87: exceptions for stock lending and collateral security arrangements

89B [Repealed by FA 1997, s. 103(2), 113 and Sch. 18, Pt. VII.]

90 Section 87: other exceptions

90(1) Section 87 above shall not apply as regards an agreement to transfer a unit under a unit trust scheme to or from the managers under the scheme.

90(1A) Section 87 above shall not apply as regards an agreement to transfer a unit under a unit trust scheme if an instrument executed at the same time as the agreement and giving effect to the agreement would be exempt from stamp duty (if stamp duty were otherwise chargeable) by virtue of—

(a) section 42 of the Finance Act 1930 or section 11 of the Finance Act (Northern Ireland) 1954 (transfers between associated companies), or

(b) regulations under section 87(2) of the Finance Act 1985 (power to exempt instruments from stamp duty of fixed amount).

90(1B) Section 87 above shall not apply as regards an agreement to transfer trust property to the unit holder on the surrender to the managers of a unit under a unit trust scheme.

The reference here to the surrender of a unit has the same meaning as in Part II of Schedule 19 to the Finance Act 1999.

90(2) [Repealed by FA 1999, s. 139 and Sch. 20, Pt. V(5).]

90(3) Section 87 above shall not apply as regards an agreement to transfer securities constituted by or transferable by means of—

(a) a non-UK bearer instrument;

(b) [Repealed by FA 1997, s. 105(1), 113 and Sch. 18, Pt. VII.]

90(3A) Section 87 above shall not apply as regards an agreement to transfer chargeable securities constituted by or transferable by means of a UK bearer instrument unless subsection (3B), (3C) or (3E) below applies to the instrument.

90(3B) This subsection applies to any instrument which falls within the exemption conferred by paragraph 16 of Schedule 15 to the Finance Act 1999 (renounceable letters of allotment etc.) (renounceable letter of allotment etc. where rights are renounceable not later than six months after issue) [see history notes re words in second set of parentheses].

90(3C) This subsection applies to an instrument if—

(a) the instrument was issued by a body corporate incorporated in the United Kingdom;

(b) stamp duty under Schedule 15 to the Finance Act 1999 was not chargeable on the issue of the instrument by virtue only of the exemption conferred by paragraph 17 of that Schedule (non-sterling bearer instruments); and

(c) the instrument is not exempt.

90(3D) An instrument is exempt for the purposes of subsection (3C) above if—

(a) the chargeable securities in question are, or a depositary receipt for them is, listed on a recognised stock exchange; and

(b) the agreement to transfer those securities is not made in contemplation of, or as part of an arrangement for, a takeover of the body corporate which issued the instrument.

90(3E) This subsection applies to an instrument if—

(a) the instrument was issued by a body corporate incorporated in the United Kingdom;

(b) stamp duty under Schedule 15 to the Finance Act 1999 was not chargeable on the issue of the instrument—

   (i) by virtue only of the exemption conferred by section 79(2) above (bearer instruments relating to loan capital), or

   (ii) by virtue only of that provision and paragraph 17 of that Schedule (non-sterling bearer instruments);

(c) by virtue of section 79(5) (convertible loan capital) or 79(6) (loan capital carrying special rights) above, stamp duty would be chargeable on an instrument transferring the loan capital to which the instrument relates; and

(d) the instrument is not exempt.

90(3F) An instrument is exempt for the purposes of subsection (3E) above if—

(a)   the chargeable securities in question are, or a depositary receipt for them is, listed on a recognised stock exchange;

(b)   the agreement to transfer those securities is not made in contemplation of, or as part of an arrangement for, a takeover of the body corporate which issued the instrument; and

(c)   those securities do not carry any right of the kind described in section 79(5) above (right of conversion into, or acquisition of, shares or other securities) by the exercise of which chargeable securities which are not listed on a recognised stock exchange may be obtained.

90(4)   Section 87 above shall not apply as regards an agreement which forms part of an arrangement falling within section 93(1) or 96(1) below.

90(5)   Section 87 above shall not apply as regards an agreement to transfer securities which the Board are satisfied are held, when the agreement is made, for the purposes of a business within subsection (6) below.

90(6)   A business is within this subsection if, or so far as, it consists of that of holding shares, stock or other marketable securities–

(a)   as nominee or agent for a person whose business is or includes the provision of clearance services for the purchase and sale of shares, stock or other marketable securities, and

(b)   for the purpose of such part of the business mentioned in paragraph (a) above as consists of the provision of such clearance services (in a case where the business does not consist exclusively of that);

and in this subsection, **"marketable securities"** shall be construed in accordance with section 122(1) of the Stamp Act 1891.

90(7)   Section 87 above shall not apply as regards an agreement to transfer securities to–

(a)   a body of persons established for charitable purposes only, or

(b)   the trustees of a trust so established, or

(c)   the Trustees of the National Heritage Memorial Fund, or

(d)   the Historic Buildings and Monuments Commission for England, or

(e)   the National Endowment for Science, Technology and the Arts.

90(8)   For the purposes of subsections (3D) and (3F) above–

(a)   references to a **depositary receipt for chargeable securities** shall be construed in accordance with section 94(1) below;

(b)   **"recognised stock exchange"** has [the] same meaning as it has in the Tax Acts by virtue of section 841 of the Income and Corporation Taxes Act 1988;'

(c)   there is a takeover of a body corporate if a person, on his own or together with connected persons, loses or acquires control of it.

90(9)   For the purposes of subsection (8) above–

(a)   any question whether a person is connected with another shall be determined in accordance with section 286 of the Taxation of Chargeable Gains Act 1992;

(b)   **"control"** shall be construed in accordance with section 416 of the Income and Corporation Taxes Act 1988.

Prospective repeals – S. 90 repealed by FA 1990, s. 132 and Sch. 19, Pt. VII, from a date to be appointed in relation to s. 87 as specified for that section by FA 1990, s. 110(2). (See note below).

History – In s. 90(1) the words "to or from the managers" substituted for the words "to the managers" by FA 1999, s. 122(4) and Sch. 19, para. 11(2), where the relevant day for the purposes of s. 87 falls on or after 6 February 2000.
S. 90(1A) was inserted by FA 1999, s. 122(4) and Sch. 19, para. 11(3), where the relevant day for the purposes of s. 87 falls on or after 6 February 2000.
S. 90(1B) was inserted by FA 1999, s. 122(4) and Sch. 19, para. 11(4), where the surrender (within the meaning of FA 1999, Sch. 19, Pt. II) occurs on or after 6 February 2000.
S. 90(2) repealed by FA 1999, s. 139 and Sch. 20, Pt. V(5), the repeal having effect in relation to instruments executed on or after 6 February 2000.
In s. 90(3), para. (a) substituted for the previous version by FA 1999, s. 113(3) and Sch. 16, para. 6(2), the substitution applying in relation to bearer instruments issued on or after 1 October 1999.
S. 90(3)(b) repealed by FA 1997, s. 105(1), 113 and Sch. 18, Pt. VII, and s. 90(3A)–(3F) inserted by FA 1997, s. 105(2) in relation to an agreement if the inland bearer instrument in question was issued on or after 26 November 1996 and, in the case of an agreement which is not conditional, the agreement is made on or after that date or, in the case of a conditional agreement, the condition is satisfied on or after that date (s. 105(4)).
In s. 90(3A) the words "a UK bearer instrument" substituted for the words "an inland bearer instrument within the meaning of the heading "Bearer Instrument" in Schedule 1 to the Stamp Act 1891" by FA 1999, s. 113(3) and Sch. 16, para. 6(3), the substitution applying in relation to bearer instruments issued on or after 1 October 1999.
In s. 90(3B) the words "the exemption conferred by paragraph 16 of Schedule 15 to the Finance Act 1999 (renounceable letters of allotment etc.)" substituted for the words "exemption 3 in the heading "Bearer Instrument" in Schedule 1 to the Stamp Act 1891" by FA 1999, s. 113(3) and Sch. 16, para. 6(4), the substitution applying in relation to bearer instruments issued on or after 1 October 1999. (The substitution may be incomplete in that the words which appear in the second set of parentheses have been retained although they were part of the original wording.)
In s. 90(3C), para. (b) substituted by FA 1999, s. 113(3) and Sch. 16, para. 6(5), the substitution applying in relation to bearer instruments issued on or after 1 October 1999.

In s. 90(3E), para. (b) substituted by FA 1999, s. 113(3) and Sch. 16, para. 6(6), the substitution applying in relation to bearer instruments issued on or after 1 October 1999.
In s. 90(3F)(c) the words "chargeable securities which are not listed" substituted for the words "securities which are not listed" by FA 1999, s. 120(2), the substitution applying to instruments issued on or after 9 March 1999.
In s. 90(5), the words "for the purposes of a business" substituted for the words "by a person" and, in (6), the words "A business is within this subsection if, or so far as, it consists of" substituted for the words "A person is within this subsection if his business is exclusively" by FA 1999, s. 120(3), the substitutions applying to agreements to transfer securities made on or after 9 March 1999.
S. 90(5), (6) substituted and s. 90(7) inserted by FA 1987, s. 56 and Sch. 7, para. 5, 6 with retrospective effect.
S. 90(7)(e) inserted by the National Lottery Act 1998, s. 24(5).
S. 90(8),(9) inserted by FA 1997, s. 105(3) in relation to an agreement if the inland bearer instrument in question was issued on or after 26 November 1996 and, in the case of an agreement which is not conditional, the agreement is made on or after that date or, in the case of a conditional agreement, the condition is satisfied on or after that date (s. 105(4)).
Notes – The Treasury order appointing the "abolition day" for the purposes of FA 1990, s. 107–110 was to have broadly coincided with the start of paperless trading under the Stock Exchange's planned TAURUS system (IR press release, 20 March 1990). However, on 11 March 1993 it was announced that TAURUS had been abandoned (London Stock Exchange News Release 6/93).

91   Liability to tax

91(1)   Where tax is charged under section 87 above as regards an agreement, B shall be liable for the tax.

91(2)   [Repealed by F(No. 2)A 1987, s. 100(2) and Sch. 9, Pt. IV.]

Prospective repeals – S. 91 repealed by FA 1990, s. 132 and Sch. 19, Pt. VII, in relation to s. 87 as specified for that section by FA 1990, s. 110(2). (See note below).

History – S. 91(2) repealed by F(No. 2)A 1987, s. 100(2) and Sch. 9, Pt. IV.

Cross references – SI 1986/1711, reg. 7: relief from accountability for charge under s. 87 does not extend to person liable under s. 91.

Notes – For reference to a person, B, see s. 87(1).
The Treasury order appointing the "abolition day" for the purposes of FA 1990, s. 107–110 was to have broadly coincided with the start of paperless trading under the Stock Exchange's planned TAURUS system (IR press release, 20 March 1990). However, on 11 March 1993 it was announced that TAURUS had been abandoned (London Stock Exchange News Release 6/93).

92   Repayment or cancellation of tax

92(1)   If, as regards an agreement to transfer securities to B or his nominee, tax is charged under section 87 above and it is proved to the Board's satisfaction that at a time on or after the relevant day (as defined in section 87(3)) but before the expiry of the period of six years (beginning with that day) the conditions mentioned in subsections (1A) and (1B) below have been fulfilled, subsections (2) to (4A) of this section shall apply.

92(1A)   The first condition is that an instrument is (or instruments are) executed in pursuance of the agreement and the instrument transfers (or the instruments between them transfer) to B or, as the case may be, to his nominee all the chargeable securities to which the agreement relates.

92(1B)   The second condition is that the instrument (or each instrument) transferring the chargeable securities to which the agreement relates is duly stamped in accordance with the enactments relating to stamp duty if it is an instrument which, under those enactments, is chargeable with stamp duty or otherwise required to be stamped.

92(2)   If any of the tax charged has been paid, and a claim for repayment is made within the period of six years mentioned in subsection (1) above, the tax paid shall be repaid; and where the tax paid is not less than £25 it shall be repaid with interest on it at the rate applicable under section 178 of the Finance Act 1989 from the date on which the payment was made until the order for repayment is issued.

92(3)   To the extent that the tax charged has not been paid, the charge shall be cancelled by virtue of this subsection.

92(4)   [Repealed by FA 1989, s. 187 and Sch. 17, Pt. X.]

92(4A)   Interest paid under subsection (2) above shall not constitute income for any tax purposes.

92(5)   [Repealed by FA 1989, s. 187 and Sch. 17, Pt. X.]

92(6)   In this section **"the enactments relating to stamp duty"** means the Stamp Act 1891 and any enactment which amends or is required to be construed together with that Act.

92(7)   This section shall have effect in relation to a person to whom the chargeable securities are transferred by way of security for a loan to B as it has effect in relation to a nominee of B.

Prospective repeals – S. 92 repealed by FA 1990, s. 132 and Sch. 19, Pt. VII from a date to be appointed, in relation to s. 87 as specified for that section by FA 1990, s. 110(2). (See note below).

History – S. 92(1) amended by FA 1996, s. 188(4) and 192(3), and s. 92(1A), (1B) inserted by FA 1996, s. 192(4), with effect in relation to an agreement to transfer securities if:
- the agreement is conditional and the condition is satisfied on or after 1st July 1996; or
- the agreement is not conditional and is made on or after that date.

S. 92(2) amended by FA 1989, s. 179(1)(f) substituting "rate applicable under section 178 of the Finance Act 1989" for "appropriate rate", effective in relation to any period for which FA 1989, s. 178(1) has effect (periods beginning on or after 18 August 1989: SI 1989/1298).
Date from which interest runs substituted by FA 1989, s. 180(5) and deemed always to have had effect.
S. 92(4A) inserted by FA 1987, s. 56 and Sch. 7, para. 7, with retrospective effect.
The repeals of s. 92(4), (5) have effect for periods beginning on or after 18 August 1989 (SI 1989/1298).
S. 92(6) inserted by FA 1996, s. 192(5), with effect in relation to an agreement to transfer securities if:
- the agreement is conditional and the condition is satisfied on or after 1st July 1996; or
- the agreement is not conditional and is made on or after that date.
S. 92(7) inserted by FA 1997, s. 106(8) in relation to an agreement to transfer securities if the agreement is conditional and the condition is satisfied on or after 4 January 1997, or if the agreement is not conditional and is made on or after that date (FA 1997, s. 106(9)).
Cross references – SI 1989/1297, reg. 3AB(1)(d) inserted by SI 1999/2538, reg. 5(b): applicable rate of interest for the purposes of s. 92.
SI 1989/1297, reg. 3AB(1)(e): applicable rate of interest under s. 110.
Other material – Inland Revenue press release, 28 November 1995: background to the 1996 amendments.
Taxline 1997/6 (note reproduced): Stamp Duty office confirmation that no additional liability to SDRT arises where there are linking agreements.
Notes – For reference to a person, B, see s. 87(1).
SI 1989/1297, reg. 3AA: formula for determining annual rate of interest (6.25 per cent from 6 February 1996).
The Treasury order appointing the "abolition day" for the purposes of FA 1990, s. 107–110 was to have broadly coincided with the start of paperless trading under the Stock Exchange's planned TAURUS system (IR press release, 20 March 1990). However, on 11 March 1993 it was announced that TAURUS had been abandoned (London Stock Exchange News Release 6/93).

OTHER CHARGES

93   Depositary receipts

93(1)   Subject to subsection (7) below and section 95 below, there shall be a charge to stamp duty reserve tax under this section where in pursuance of an arrangement–

(a)   a person falling within subsection (2) below has issued or is to issue a depositary receipt for chargeable securities, and

(b)   chargeable securities of the same kind and amount are transferred or issued to the person mentioned in paragraph (a) above or a person falling within subsection (3) below, or are appropriated by the person mentioned in paragraph (a) above or a person falling within subsection (3) below towards the eventual satisfaction of the entitlement of the receipt's holder to receive chargeable securities.

93(2)   A person falls within this subsection if his business is or includes issuing depositary receipts for chargeable securities.

93(3)   A person falls within this subsection if his business is or includes holding chargeable securities as nominee or agent for the person who has issued or is to issue the depositary receipt.

93(4)   Subject to subsections (6) and (7) below, tax under this section shall be charged at the rate of 1.5 per cent. of the following–

(a)   in a case where the securities are issued, their price when issued;

(b)   in a case where the securities are transferred for consideration in money or money's worth, the amount or value of the consideration;

(c)   in any other case, the value of the securities.

93(5)   [Repealed by FA 1997, s. 104(1), 113 and Sch. 18, Pt. VII]

93(6)   In a case where–

(a)   securities are issued, or securities sold are transferred, and (in either case) they are to be paid for in instalments,

(b)   the person to whom they are issued or transferred holds them and transfers them to another person when the last instalment is paid,

(c)   subsection (4)(c) above applies in the case of the transfer to the other person,

(d)   before the making of the transfer to the other person an instrument is received by a person falling within subsection (2) or (3) above,

(e)   the instrument so received evidences all the rights which (by virtue of the terms under which the securities are issued or sold as mentioned in paragraph (a) above) subsist in respect of them at the time of the receipt, and

(f)   the transfer to the other person is effected by an instrument containing a statement that paragraphs (a), (b) and (e) above are fulfilled,

subsection (4)(c) above shall have effect as if the reference to the value there mentioned were to an amount (if any) equal to the total of the instalments payable, less those paid before the transfer to the other person is effected.

93(7) Where tax is (or would apart from this subsection be) charged under this section in respect of a transfer of securities, and ad valorem stamp duty is chargeable on any instrument effecting the transfer, then–

(a) if the amount of the duty is less than the amount of tax found by virtue of subsections (4) and (6) above, the tax charged under this section shall be the amount so found less the amount of the duty;

(b) in any other case, there shall be no charge to tax under this section in respect of the transfer.

93(8) Where tax is charged under the preceding provisions of this section, the person liable for the tax shall (subject to subsection (9) below) be the person who has issued or is to issue the depositary receipt.

93(9) Where tax is charged under the preceding provisions of this section in a case where securities are transferred, and at the time of the transfer the person who has issued or is to issue the depositary receipt is not resident in the United Kingdom and has no branch or agency in the United Kingdom, the person liable for the tax shall be the person to whom the securities are transferred.

93(10) Where chargeable securities are issued or transferred on sale under terms providing for payment in instalments and for an issue of other chargeable securities, and (apart from this subsection) tax would be charged under this section in respect of that issue, tax shall not be so charged but–

(a) if any of the instalments becomes payable by a person falling within subsection (2) or (3) above, there shall be a charge to stamp duty reserve tax under this section when the instalment becomes payable;

(b) the charge shall be at the rate of 1.5 per cent. of the amount of the instalment payable;

(c) the person liable to pay the instalment shall be liable for the tax.

93(11) Subject to subsection (12) below, this section applies where securities are transferred, issued or appropriated after 18th March 1986 (whenever the arrangement was made).

93(12) This section does not apply, in the case of securities which are transferred, if the Board are satisfied that they were acquired or appropriated by the transferor on or before 18th March 1986 for or towards the eventual satisfaction of the entitlement of a person to receive securities of the same kind under a depositary receipt (whether issued on or before that date or to be issued after that date).

Prospective repeal – S. 93 repealed by FA 1990, s. 132 and Sch. 19, Pt. VII, for securities transferred, issued or appropriated in accordance with FA 1990, s. 110(3), (5), (7) on or after a day to be appointed. (See note below).

History – S. 93(1)(b) amended by FA 1996, s. 193(2), inserting "the person . . . above or" and substituting "the person . . . below" for "such a person", with effect in relation to the charge under:
- s. 93(1), where securities are transferred, issued or appropriated on or after 1 July 1996 (whenever the arrangement was made);
- s. 93(10), as respects instalments payable on or after 1 July 1996.

S. 93(4) amended by FA 1997, s. 104(2)(a) with effect where securities are transferred on or after the day which is the commencement day for the purposes of FA 1997, s. 102, unless the securities were acquired by the transferor before that day (s. 104(5)). The appointed day for the purposes of FA 1997, s. 102(5) and (6) was 20 October 1997, the commencement day by virtue of SI 1997/2428 (C. 95). The amendment removed a reference to s. 93(5) following its repeal with effect from the same date (see history note below).

S. 93(4) amended by FA 1996, s. 194(2)(a), substituting "1.5 per cent." for "£1.50 for every £100 or part of £100", with effect (in relation to the charge under s. 93(1)) where securities are transferred, issued or appropriated on or after 1 July 1996 (whenever the arrangement was made).

S. 93(5) repealed by FA 1997, s. 104(1), 113 and Sch. 18, Pt. VII, with effect where securities are transferred on or after the day which is the commencement day for the purposes of FA 1997, s. 102, unless the securities were acquired by the transferor before that day (s. 104(5)). The appointed day for the purposes of FA 1997, s. 102(5) and (6) was 20 October 1997, the commencement day by virtue of SI 1997/2428 (C. 95).

S. 93(5) previously amended by FA 1996, s. 194(2)(b) with effect (in relation to the charge under s. 93(1)) where securities are transferred, issued or appropriated on or after 1 July 1996 (whenever the arrangement was made).

S. 93(6) amended by FA 1996, s. 193(3), inserting "(2) or", with effect in relation to the charge under:
- s. 93(1), where securities are transferred, issued or appropriated on or after 1 July 1996 (whenever the arrangement was made);
- s. 93(10), as respects instalments payable on or after 1 July 1996.

S. 93(7)(a) amended by FA 1997, s. 104(2)(b) with effect where securities are transferred on or after the day which is the commencement day for the purposes of FA 1997, s. 102, unless the securities were acquired by the transferor before that day (s. 104(5)). The appointed day for the purposes of FA 1997, s. 102(5) and (6) was 20 October 1997, the commencement day by virtue of SI 1997/2428 (C. 95). The amendment removed a reference to s. 93(5) following its repeal with effect from the same date (see history note above).

S. 93(10)(b) amended by FA 1996, s. 194(2)(c), substituting "1.5 per cent. of the amount" for "£1.50 for every £100 or part of £100", with effect (in relation to the charge under s. 93(10)) as respects instalments payable on or after 1 July 1996.

Cross references – FA 1984, s. 126(3)(d): no stamp duty reserve tax chargeable under s. 93 in respect of the issue of securities by certain designated international organisations.

S. 95(2): no stamp duty reserve tax chargeable under s. 93 in respect of the transfer, issue or appropriation of a UK bearer instrument except in certain circumstances.

s. 79(7A): exemption from duty for certain instruments relating to loan capital carrying a right to interest which reduces if the business results improve (or value of any property increases), or which increases if the business results deteriorate (or value of any property diminishes)(so called "ratchet loans").

Other material – Inland Revenue press release, 28 November 1995: background to the 1996 amendments.

Notes – FA 1989, s. 176: Treasury may, by regulations, exempt from charge or apply reduced rate to certain transactions involving a stock exchange nominee.
SI 1986/1711: management provisions.
The day of The Stock Exchange reforms was 27 October 1986.
The Treasury order appointing the "abolition day" for the purposes of FA 1990, s. 107–110 was to have broadly coincided with the start of paperless trading under the Stock Exchange's planned TAURUS system (IR press release, 20 March 1990). However, on 11 March 1993 it was announced that TAURUS had been abandoned (London Stock Exchange News Release 6/93).

94　Depositary receipts: supplementary

94(1)　For the purposes of section 93 above a **depositary receipt for chargeable securities** is an instrument acknowledging–

(a)　that a person holds chargeable securities or evidence of the right to receive them, and

(b)　that another person is entitled to rights, whether expressed as units or otherwise, in or in relation to chargeable securities of the same kind, including the right to receive such securities (or evidence of the right to receive them) from the person mentioned in paragraph (a) above,

except that for those purposes a depositary receipt for chargeable securities does not include an instrument acknowledging rights in or in relation to securities if they are issued or sold under terms providing for payment in instalments and for the issue of the instrument as evidence that an instalment has been paid.

94(2)　The Treasury may by regulations provide that for subsection (1) above (as it has effect for the time being) there shall be substituted a subsection containing a different definition of a depositary receipt for the purposes of section 93 above.

94(3)　For the purposes of section 93(4)(b) above the value of any consideration not consisting of money shall be taken to be the price it might reasonably be expected to fetch on a sale in the open market at the time the securities are transferred.

94(4)　For the purposes of section 93(4)(c) above the value of the securities shall be taken to be the price they might reasonably be expected to fetch on a sale in the open market at the time they are transferred or appropriated (as the case may be).

94(5)–(7)　[Repealed by FA 1997, s. 104(2)(c), s. 113 and Sch. 18, Pt. VII.]

94(8)　[Repealed by FA 1996, s. 194(3), 205 and Sch. 41, Pt. VII.]

94(9)　The power to make regulations or an order under this section shall be exercisable by statutory instrument subject to annulment in pursuance of a resolution of the House of Commons.

Prospective repeal – S. 94 repealed by FA 1990, s. 132 and Sch. 19, Pt. VII, from a date to be appointed in relation to s. 93 as specified for that section by FA 1990, s. 110(3), (5), (7). (See note below).

History – S. 94(5)–(7) repealed by FA 1997, s. 104(2)(c), s. 113 and Sch. 18, Pt. VII, with effect where securities are transferred on or after the day which is the commencement day for the purposes of FA 1997, s. 102, unless the securities were acquired by the transferor before that day (s. 104(5)). The appointed day for the purposes of FA 1997, s. 102(5) and (6) was 20 October 1997, the commencement day by virtue of SI 1997/2428 (C. 95).
In s. 94(5)(a), reference to provisions of the Taxes Act 1988 substituted by FA 1988, s. 146 and Sch. 13, para. 23, 25, effective in relation to 1988–89 and later tax years or companies' accounting periods ending after 5 April 1988.
S. 94(8) repealed by FA 1996, s. 194(3), 205 and Sch. 41, Pt. VII, with effect where securities are transferred, issued or appropriated on or after 1 July 1996.

Other material – Inland Revenue press release, 28 November 1995: background to the 1996 amendments.

Notes – For ICTA 1988, see *Tax Statutes and Statutory Instruments*, vol. 1A.
The Treasury order appointing the "abolition day" for the purposes of FA 1990, s. 107–110 was to have broadly coincided with the start of paperless trading under the Stock Exchange's planned TAURUS system (IR press release, 20 March 1990). However, on 11 March 1993 it was announced that TAURUS had been abandoned (London Stock Exchange News Release 6/93).

95　Depositary receipts: exceptions

95(1)　Where securities are transferred–

(a)　to a company which at the time of the transfer falls within subsection (6) of section 67 above and is resident in the United Kingdom, and

(b)　from a company which at that time falls within that subsection and is so resident,

there shall be no charge to tax under section 93 above in respect of the transfer.

95(2)　There shall be no charge to tax under section 93 above in respect of a transfer, issue or appropriation of a UK bearer instrument, except in the case of–

(a)　an instrument within the exemption conferred by paragraph 16 of Schedule 15 to the Finance Act 1999 (renounceable letters of allotment etc. where rights are renounceable not later than six months after issue), or

(b)   an instrument within the exemption conferred by paragraph 17 of that Schedule (non-sterling instruments) which–

    (i) does not raise new capital, and

    (ii) is not issued in exchange for an instrument raising new capital.

95(2A) For the purpose of subsection (2)(b)–

(a)   an instrument is regarded as raising new capital only if the condition in subsection (2B) is met, and

(b)   an instrument is regarded as issued in exchange for an instrument raising new capital only if the conditions in subsection (2C) are met.

95(2B) The condition mentioned in subsection (2A)(a) is that the instrument–

(a)   is issued in conjunction with–

    (i) the issue of relevant securities for which only cash is subscribed, or

    (ii) the granting of rights to subscribe for relevant securities which are granted for a cash consideration only and exercisable only by means of a cash subscription; or

(b)   is issued to give effect to the exercise of such rights as are mentioned in paragraph (a)(ii).

95(2C) The conditions mentioned in subsection (2A)(b) are that–

(a)   the instrument is issued in conjunction with the issue of relevant securities by a company in exchange for relevant securities issued by another company, and

(b)   immediately before the exchange an instrument relating to those other securities–

    (i) was regarded for the purposes of subsection (2)(b) as raising new capital or as issued in exchange for an instrument raising new capital, or

    (ii) would have been so regarded if the amendments made to this section by section 117 of the Finance Act 1999 had been in force at the time of its issue,

and accordingly was or would have been within the exception conferred by subsection (2).

95(2D) For the purposes of subsections (2B) and (2C)

"relevant securities" means chargeable securities which are either–

    (a)   shares the holders of which have a right to a dividend at a fixed rate but have no other right to share in the profits of the company, or

    (b)   loan capital within the meaning of section 78 above,

and which, in either case, do not carry any rights (of conversion or otherwise) by the exercise of which chargeable securities other than relevant securities may be obtained.

95(3) There shall be no charge to tax under section 93 above in respect of an issue by a company (**company X**) of securities in exchange for shares in another company (**company Y**) where company X–

(a)   has control of company Y, or

(b)   will have such control in consequence of the exchange or of an offer as a result of which the exchange is made

and the shares in company Y are held under a depositary receipt scheme.

95(4) For the purposes of subsection (3) above company X has **control** of company Y if company X has power to control company Y's affairs by virtue of holding shares in, or possessing voting power in relation to, company Y or any other body corporate.

95(5) For the purposes of subsection (3) above, the cases where shares are held under a depositary receipt scheme are those cases where, in pursuance of an arrangement,–

(a)   a depositary receipt for chargeable securities has been, or is to be, issued by a person falling within section 93(2) above in respect of the shares in question or shares of the same kind and *amount; and*

(b)   the shares in question are held by that person, or by a person whose business is or includes holding chargeable securities as nominee or agent for that person, towards the eventual satisfaction of the entitlement of the receipt's holder to receive chargeable securities.

95(6) Where an arrangement is entered into under which–

(a)   a company issues securities to persons in respect of their holdings of securities issued by another company, and

(b)   the securities issued by the other company are cancelled,

the issue shall be treated for the purposes of this section as an issue of securities in exchange for securities issued by the other company.

95(7) In this section **"depositary receipt for chargeable securities"** has the same meaning as in section 93 above (see section 94 above).

Prospective repeals – S. 95 repealed by FA 1990, s. 132 and Sch. 19, Pt. VII, from a date to be appointed in relation to s. 93 as specified for that section by FA 1990, s. 110(3), (5), (7).

History – In s. 95(1), the words "and is resident in the United Kingdom" and "and is so resident" shall cease to have effect by virtue of FA 2000, s. 134 (3) as follows: in the application of FA 2000, s. 134 (3) for the purposes of stamp duty, where instruments are executed after 28 July 2000, and in the application of FA 2000, s. 134 (3) for the purposes of stamp duty reserve tax, where the securities are transferred after 28 July 2000.

S. 95 (particularly subs. (2)) was amended by FA 1999 in three separate stages. Each stage applies for a specific period with an ultimate exclusion for instruments giving effect to an agreement for a company merger or takeover entered into in writing by the companies involved before 30 January 1999. The text reproduced above applies in relation to bearer instruments issued on or after 1 October 1999, subject to that exclusion. For the history of the different versions which apply at various dates, see the notes below.

S. 95(2) substituted for the version applying to bearer instruments issued on or after 9 March 1999 (see history note below) by FA 1999, s. 113(3) and Sch. 16, para. 7(1), the substitution applying in relation to bearer instruments issued on or after 1 October 1999 except that no charge to tax by virtue of subs. (2)(b) will arise in the case of an instrument which gives effect to an agreement for a company merger or takeover entered into in writing by the companies involved before 30 January 1999 (FA 1999, Sch. 16, para. 7(2)).

S. 95(2), para. (b) was substituted for the version applying to bearer instruments issued on or after 30 January 1999 (see history note below) by FA 1999, s. 117(1), the substitution applying in relation to any instrument issued on or after 9 March 1999, except one giving effect to an agreement for a company merger or takeover entered into in writing by the companies involved before 30 January 1999.

S. 95(2) was substituted by FA 1999, s. 116(1), the substitution applying to any instrument issued on or after 30 January 1999, except one giving effect to an agreement for a company merger or takeover entered into in writing by the companies involved before that date. This applied to instruments issued after that date (but before 9 March 1999, see history notes above).

S. 95(2A)–(2D) were inserted by FA 1999, s. 117(2) in relation to any instrument issued on or after 9 March 1999, except one giving effect to an agreement for a company merger or takeover entered into in writing by the companies involved before 30 January 1999.

In s. 95(3), the words after para. (b) were inserted by FA 1998, s. 151(1), where the issue by company X referred to in FA 1986, s. 95(3) (or (6)) or 97(4) (or (7)) is an issue on or after 1 May 1998.

S. 95(5) was added by FA 1998, s. 151(2), where the issue by company X referred to in FA 1986, s. 95(3) (or (6)) or 97(4) (or (7)) is an issue on or after 1 May 1998.

S. 95(6) was substituted by FA 1999, s. 117(3) in relation to any instrument issued on or after 9 March 1999, except one giving effect to an agreement for a company merger or takeover entered into in writing by the companies involved before 30 January 1999.

Former s. 95(6) was added by FA 1998, s. 151(2), where the issue by company X referred to in FA 1986, s. 95(3) (or (6)) or 97(4) (or (7)) is an issue on or after 1 May 1998.

S. 95(7) was added by FA 1998, s. 151(2), where the issue by company X referred to in FA 1986, s. 95(3) (or (6)) or 97(4) (or (7)) is an issue on or after 1 May 1998.

Notes – The Treasury order appointing the "abolition day" for the purposes of FA 1990,s. 107–110 was to have broadly coincided with the start of paperless trading under the Stock Exchange's planned TAURUS system (IR press release, 20 March 1990). However, on 11 March 1993 it was announced that TAURUS had been abandoned (London Stock Exchange News Release 6/93).

95A   Depositary receipts: exception for replacement securities

95A(1) There shall be no charge to tax under section 93 above in respect of the transfer, issue or appropriation of chargeable securities ("the new securities") issued by a company in place of existing securities of the same company ("the old securities") if the following conditions are met.

95A(2) The first condition is that the old securities are held under a depositary receipt scheme.

95A(3) The second condition is that–

(a) there was a charge to tax under section 93 above in respect of the transfer, issue or appropriation–

    (i) of the old securities, or

    (ii) of earlier securities in relation to which on a previous application of this section those securities were the new securities,

    or there would have been such a charge if that section had been in force; or

(b) there would have been such a charge but for section 95(2) or (3) above.

95A(4) The third condition is that there is an arrangement under which–

(a) the new securities are transferred, issued or appropriated as mentioned in section 93(1)(b), and

(b) the old securities are cancelled.

95A(5) For the purposes of subsection (2) above the cases in which securities are held under a depositary receipt scheme are those specified (in relation to shares) in section 95(5) above.

95A(6) The exception provided by this section applies only to the extent that the value of the new securities immediately after their issue does not exceed the value of the old securities immediately before the issue of the new securities.

History – S. 95A inserted by s. 118(1) in relation to securities issued on or after 1 May 1998.

96   Clearance services

96(1)   Subject to subsection (5) below and sections 97 and 97A below, there shall be a charge to stamp duty reserve tax under this section where–

(a)   a person (A) whose business is or includes the provision of clearance services for the purchase and sale of chargeable securities has entered into an arrangement to provide such clearance services for another person, and

(b)   in pursuance of the arrangement, chargeable securities are transferred or issued to A or to a person whose business is or includes holding chargeable securities as nominee for A.

96(2)   Subject to subsections (4) and (5) below, tax under this section shall be charged at the rate of 1.5 per cent. of the following–

(a)   in a case where the securities are issued, their price when issued;

(b)   in a case where the securities are transferred for consideration in money or money's worth, the amount or value of the consideration;

(c)   in any other case, the value of the securities.

96(3)   [Repealed by FA 1997, s. 104(3), 113 and Sch. 18, Pt. VII.]

96(4)   In a case where–

(a)   securities are issued, or securities sold are transferred, and (in either case) they are to be paid for in instalments,

(b)   the person to whom they are issued or transferred holds them and transfers them to another person when the last instalment is paid,

(c)   subsection (2)(c) above applies in the case of the transfer to the other person,

(d)   before the making of the transfer to the other person an instrument is received by A or a person whose business is or includes holding chargeable securities as nominee for A,

(e)   the instrument so received evidences all the rights which (by virtue of the terms under which the securities are issued or sold as mentioned in paragraph (a) above) subsist in respect of them at the time of the receipt, and

(f)   the transfer to the other person is effected by an instrument containing a statement that paragraphs (a), (b) and (e) above are fulfilled,

subsection 2(c) above shall have effect as if the reference to the value there mentioned were to an amount (if any) equal to the total of the instalments payable, less those paid before the transfer to the other person is effected.

96(5)   Where tax is (or would apart from this subsection be) charged under this section in respect of a transfer of securities and ad valorem stamp duty is chargeable on any instrument effecting the transfer, then–

(a)   if the amount of the duty is less than the amount of tax found by virtue of subsections (2) and (4) above, the tax charged under this section shall be the amount so found less the amount of the duty;

(b)   in any other case, there shall be no charge to tax under this section in respect of the transfer.

96(6)   Where tax is charged under the preceding provisions of this section, the person liable for the tax shall (subject to subsection (7) below) be A.

96(7)   Where tax is charged under the preceding provisions of this section in a case where securities are transferred to a person other than A, and at the time of transfer A is not resident in the United Kingdom and had no branch or agency in the United Kingdom, the person liable for the tax shall be the person to whom the securities are transferred.

96(8)   Where chargeable securities are issued or transferred on sale under terms providing for payment in instalments and for an issue of other chargeable securities, and (apart from this subsection) tax would be charged under this section in respect of that issue, tax shall not be so charged but–

(a)   if any of the instalments becomes payable by A or by a person whose business is or includes holding chargeable securities as nominee for A, there shall be a charge to stamp duty reserve tax under this section when the instalment becomes payable;

(b)   the charge shall be at the rate of 1.5 per cent. of the amount of the instalment payable;

(c)   the person liable to pay the instalment shall be liable for the tax.

96(9)   For the purposes of subsection (2)(b) above the value of any consideration not consisting of money shall be taken to be the price it might reasonably be expected to fetch on a sale in the open market at the time the securities are transferred.

96(10) For the purposes of subsection (2)(c) above the value of securities shall be taken to be the price they might reasonably be expected to fetch on a sale in the open market at the time they are transferred.

96(11) [Repealed by FA 1997, s. 104(4)(c), 113 and Sch. 18, Pt. VII.]

96(12) [Repealed by FA 1996, s. 194(5), 205 and Sch. 41, Pt. VII.]

96(13) Subject to subsection (14) below, this section applies where securities are transferred or issued after 18th March 1986 (whenever the arrangement was made).

96(14) This section does not apply, in the case of securities which are transferred, if the Board are satisfied–

(a)   that on or before 18th March 1986 the transferor (or, where the transferor transfers as agent, the principal) agreed to sell securities of the same kind and amount to the person (other than A) referred to in subsection (1)(a) above, and

(b)   that the transfer is effected in pursuance of that agreement.

Prospective repeal – S. 96 repealed by FA 1990, s. 132 and Sch. 19, Pt. VII, for securities issued or transferred in accordance with FA 1990, s. 110(4), (6), (8) on or after a day to be appointed. (See note below).

History – S. 96(1) amended by FA 1996, s. 196(2), inserting the reference to s. 97A from 1 July 1996.
S. 96(2) amended by FA 1997, s. 104(4)(a), with effect where securities are transferred on or after the day which is the commencement day for the purposes of FA 1997, s. 102 unless the securities were acquired by the transferor before that day (s. 104(5)). The appointed day for the purposes of FA 1997, s. 102(5) and (6) was 20 October 1997, the commencement day by virtue of SI 1997/2428 (C. 95). The effect of the amendment was to remove a reference to s. 96(3) following the repeal of that subsection with effect from the same date (see history note below).
In s. 96(2), "1.5 per cent." substituted for "£1.50 for every £100 or part of £100" by FA 1996, s. 194(4)(a) , with effect (in relation to the charge under s. 96(1)) where securities are transferred or issued on or after 1 July 1996 (whenever the arrangement was made) or (in relation to the charge under, and amendment of, s. 96(8)) as respects instalments payable on or after 1 July 1996.
S. 96(3) repealed by FA 1997, s. 104(3), 113 and Sch. 18, Pt. VII with effect where securities are transferred on or after the day which is the commencement day for the purposes of FA 1997, s. 102 unless the securities were acquired by the transferor before that day (s. 104(5)). The appointed day for the purposes of FA 1997, s. 102(5) and (6) was 20 October 1997, the commencement day by virtue of SI 1997/2428 (C. 95).
S. 96(3) previously amended by FA 1996, s. 194(4)(b), with effect (in relation to the charge under s. 96(1)) where securities are transferred or issued on or after 1 July 1996 (whenever the arrangement was made) or (in relation to the charge under, and amendment of, s. 96(8)) as respects instalments payable on or after 1 July 1996.
S. 96(5)(a) amended by FA 1997, s. 104(4)(b), with effect where securities are transferred on or after the day which is the commencement day for the purposes of FA 1997, s. 102 unless the securities were acquired by the transferor before that day (s. 104(5)). The appointed day for the purposes of FA 1997, s. 102(5) and (6) was 20 October 1997, the commencement day by virtue of SI 1997/2428 (C. 95). The effect of the amendment was to remove a reference to s. 96(3) following the repeal of that subsection with effect from the same date (see history note below).
In s. 96(8)(b), "1.5 per cent. of the amount" substituted for "£1.50 for every £100 or part of £100" by FA 1996, s. 194(4)(c), with effect (in relation to the charge under s. 96(1)) where securities are transferred or issued on or after 1 July 1996 (whenever the arrangement was made) or (in relation to the charge under, and amendment of, s. 96(8)) as respects instalments payable on or after 1 July 1996.
S. 96(11) repealed by FA 1997, s. 104(4)(c), 113 and Sch. 18, Pt. VII with effect where securities are transferred on or after the day which is the commencement day for the purposes of FA 1997, s. 102 unless the securities were acquired by the transferor before that day (s. 104(5)). The appointed day for the purposes of FA 1997, s. 102(5) and (6) was 20 October 1997, the commencement day by virtue of SI 1997/2428 (C. 95).
S. 96(12) repealed by FA 1996, s. 194(5), 205 and Sch. 41, Pt. VII, with effect (in relation to the charge under s. 96(1)) where securities are transferred or issued on or after 1 July 1996 (whenever the arrangement was made) or (in relation to the charge under, and amendment of, s. 96(8)) as respects instalments payable on or after 1 July 1996.

Cross references – FA 1984, s. 126(3)(d): no stamp duty reserve tax chargeable under s. 96 in respect of the issue of securities by certain designated international organisations.
FA 1986, s. 79(7A): exemption from duty for certain instruments relating to loan capital carrying a right to interest which reduces if the business results improve (or value of any property increases), or which increases if the business results deteriorate (or value of any property diminishes) (so called "ratchet loans").
FA 1986, S. 97(3): no stamp duty reserve tax chargeable under s. 96 in respect of the transfer, issue of a UK bearer instrument except in certain specified circumstances.

Other material – Inland Revenue press release, 28 November 1995: background to the 1996 amendments.

Notes – FA 1989, s. 176: Treasury may, by regulations, exempt from charge or apply reduced rate to certain transactions involving a stock exchange nominee.
SI 1986/1711: management provisions.
The Treasury order appointing the "abolition day" for the purposes of FA 1990, s. 107–110 was to have broadly coincided with the start of paperless trading under the Stock Exchange's planned TAURUS system (IR press release, 20 March 1990). However, on 11 March 1993 it was announced that TAURUS had been abandoned (London Stock Exchange News Release 6/93).

97   Clearance services: exceptions

97(1) Where securities are transferred–

(a)   to a company which at the time of the transfer falls within subsection (6) of section 70 above and is resident in the United Kingdom, and

(b)   from a company which at that time falls within that subsection and is so resident,

there shall be no charge to tax under section 96 above in respect of the transfer.

97(2) [Repealed by FA 1996, s. 196(4), 205 and Sch. 41, Pt. VII.]

97(3) There shall be no charge to tax under section 96 above in respect of a transfer or issue of a UK bearer instrument, except in the case of–

(a)   an instrument within the exemption conferred by paragraph 16 of Schedule 15 to the Finance Act 1999 (renounceable letters of allotment etc. where rights are renounceable not later than six months after issue), or

(b)   an instrument within the exemption conferred by paragraph 17 of that Schedule (non-sterling instruments) which–

        (i) does not raise new capital, and
        (ii) is not issued in exchange for an instrument raising new capital.

97(3A) For the purpose of subsection (3)(b)–

(a)   an instrument is regarded as raising new capital only if the condition in subsection (3B) is met, and

(b)   an instrument is regarded as issued in exchange for an instrument raising new capital only if the conditions in subsection (3C) are met.

97(3B) The condition mentioned in subsection (3A)(a) is that the instrument–

(a)   is issued in conjunction with–

        (i) the issue of relevant securities for which only cash is subscribed, or
        (ii) the granting of rights to subscribe for relevant securities which are granted for a cash consideration only and exercisable only by means of a cash subscription; or

(b)   is issued to give effect to the exercise of such rights as are mentioned in paragraph (a)(ii).

97(3C) The conditions mentioned in subsection (3A)(b) are that–

(a)   the instrument is issued in conjunction with the issue of relevant securities by a company in exchange for relevant securities issued by another company, and

(b)   immediately before the exchange an instrument to those other securities–

        (i) was regarded for the purposes of subsection (3)(b) as raising new capital or as issued in exchange for an instrument raising new capital, or
        (ii) would have been so regarded if the amendments made to this section by section 117 of the Finance Act 1999 had been in force at the time of its issue,

and accordingly was or would have been within the exception conferred by subsection (3).

97(3D) For the purposes of subsections (3B) and (3C) **"relevant securities"** means chargeable securities which are either–

(a)   shares the holders of which have a right to a dividend at a fixed rate but have no other right to share in the profits of the company, or

(b)   loan capital within the meaning of section 78 above, and which in either case, do not carry any rights (of conversion or otherwise) by the exercise of which chargeable securities other than relevant securities may be obtained.

97(4) There shall be no charge to tax under section 96 above in respect of an issue by a company (company X) of securities in exchange for shares in another company (company Y) where company X–

(a)   has control of company Y, or

(b)   will have such control in consequence of the exchange or of an offer as a result of which the exchange is made

and the shares in company Y are held under a clearance services scheme.

97(5) For the purposes of subsection (4) above company X has control of company Y if company X has power to **control** company Y's affairs by virtue of holding shares in, or possessing voting power in relation to, company Y or any other body corporate.

97(6) For the purposes of subsection (4) above, the cases where shares are held under a clearance services scheme are those cases where–

(a)   an arrangement falling within paragraph (a) of subsection (1) of section 96 above has been entered into; and

(b)   in pursuance of that arrangement, the shares are held by the person referred to in that paragraph as A or by a person whose business is or includes holding chargeable securities as nominee for that person.

97(7) Where an arrangement is entered into under which–

(a)   a company issues securities to persons in respect of their holdings of securities issued by another company, and

(b)   the securities issued by the other company are cancelled,

the issue shall be treated for the purposes of this section as an issue of securities in exchange for securities issued by the other company.

Prospective repeals – S. 97 repealed by FA 1990, s. 132 and Sch. 19, Pt. VII, from a date to be appointed in relation to s. 96 as specified for that section by FA 1990, s. 110(4), (6), (8). (See note below).

History – In s. 97(1), the words "and is resident in the United Kingdom" and "and is so resident" shall cease to have effect by virtue of FA 2000, s. 134 (3) as follows: in the application of FA 2000, s. 134 (3) for the purposes of stamp duty, where instruments are executed after 28 July 2000, and in the application of FA 2000, s. 134 (3) for the purposes of stamp duty reserve tax, where the securities are transferred after 28 July 2000.

S. 97 (particularly subs. (3)) was amended by FA 1999 in three separate stages. Each stage applies for a specific period with an ultimate exclusion for instruments giving effect to an agreement for a company merger or takeover entered into in writing by the companies involved before 30 January 1999. The text reproduced above applies in relation to bearer instruments issued on or after 1 October 1999, subject to that exclusion. For the history of the different versions which apply at various dates, see the notes below.

S. 97(2) repealed by FA 1996, s. 196(4), 205 and Sch. 41, Pt. VII in relation to transfers effected on or after 1 July 1996.

S. 97(3) substituted for the version applying to bearer instruments issued on or after 9 March 1999 (see history note below) by FA 1999, s. 113(3) and Sch. 16, para. 8(1), the substitution applying in relation to bearer instruments issued on or after 1 October 1999 except that no charge to tax by virtue of subs. (3)(b) will arise in the case of an instrument which gives effect to an agreement for a company merger or takeover entered into in writing by the companies involved before 30 January 1999 (FA 1999, Sch. 16, para. 8(2)).

S. 97(3), para. (b) was substituted for the version applying to bearer instruments issued on or after 30 January 1999 (see history note below) by FA 1999, s. 117(4), the substitution applying in relation to any instrument issued on or after 9 March 1999, except one giving effect to an agreement for a company merger or takeover entered into in writing by the companies involved before 30 January 1999.

S. 97(3) was substituted by FA 1999, s. 116(2), the substitution applying to any instrument issued on or after 30 January 1999, except one giving effect to an agreement for a company merger or takeover entered into in writing by the companies involved before that date. This applied to instruments issued after that date (but before 9 March 1999, see history notes above).

S. 97(3A)–(3D) were inserted by FA 1999, s. 117(5) in relation to any instrument issued on or after 9 March 1999, except one giving effect to an agreement for a company merger or takeover entered into in writing by the companies involved before 30 January 1999.

In s. 97(4), the words after para. (b) were inserted by FA 1998, s. 151(3), where the issue by company X referred to in FA 1986, s. 95(3) (or (6)) or 97(4) (or (7)) is an issue on or after 1 May 1998.

S. 97(6) was added by FA 1998, s. 151(4), where the issue by company X referred to in FA 1986, s. 95(3) (or (6)) or 97(4) (or (7)) is an issue on or after 1 May 1998.

S. 97(7) was substituted by s. 117(6) in relation to any instrument issued on or after 9 March 1999, except one giving effect to an agreement for a company merger or takeover entered into in writing by the companies involved before 30 January 1999. Former s. 97(7) was added by FA 1998, s. 151(4), where the issue by company X referred to in FA 1986, s. 95(3) (or (6)) or 97(4) (or (7)) is an issue on or after 1 May 1998.

Notes – The Treasury order appointing the "abolition day" for the purposes of FA 1990, s. 107–110 was to have broadly coincided with the start of paperless trading under the Stock Exchange's planned TAURUS system (IR press release, 20 March 1990). However, on 11 March 1993 it was announced that TAURUS had been abandoned (London Stock Exchange News Release 6/93).

97AA   Clearance services: further exception

97AA(1)   There shall be no charge to tax under section 96 above in respect of the transfer or issue of chargeable securities ("the new securities") issued by a company in place of existing securities of the same company ("the old securities") if the following conditions are met.

97AA(2)   The first condition is that the old securities are held under a clearance services scheme.

97AA(3)   The second condition is that–

(a)   there was a charge to tax under section 96 above in respect of the transfer or issue–

  (i) of the old securities, or

  (ii) of earlier securities in relation to which on a previous application of this section those securities were the new securities,

  or there would have been such a charge if that section had been in force; or

(b)   there would have been such a charge but for section 97(3) or (4) above.

97AA(4)   The third condition is that there is an arrangement under which–

(a)   the new securities are transferred or issued as mentioned in section 96(1)(b), and

(b)   the old securities are cancelled.

97AA(5)   For the purposes of subsection (2) above the cases in which securities are held under a clearance services scheme are those specified (in relation to shares) in section 97(6) above.

97AA(6)   The exception provided by this section applies only to the extent that the value of the new securities immediately after their issue does not exceed the value of the old securities immediately before the issue of the new securities.

History – S. 97AA inserted by FA 1999, s. 118(3) in relation to securities issued on or after 1 May 1998.

97A   Clearance services: election for alternative system of charge

97A(1)   A person whose business is or includes the provision of clearance services for the purchase and sale of chargeable securities or relevant securities (an **"operator"**) may, with the approval of the Board, elect that stamp duty and stamp duty reserve tax shall be chargeable in accordance with this section in connection with those clearance services.

97A(2)   An election under subsection (1) above–

(a)   shall come into force on such date as may be notified to the operator by the Board in giving their approval; and

(b)   shall continue in force unless and until it is terminated in accordance with the following provisions of this section.

97A(3)   If and so long as an election under subsection (1) above is in force, stamp duty or stamp duty reserve tax (as the case may require) shall, in connection with the clearance services to which the election relates, be chargeable in relation to–

(a)   a transfer or issue falling within section 70(1) or 96(1) above,

(b)   an agreement falling within section 90(4) above by virtue of section 96(1) above, or

(c)   an agreement falling within section 90(5) above,

as it would be chargeable apart from sections 70, 90(4) and (5) and 96 above.

97A(4)   Where stamp duty or stamp duty reserve tax is chargeable by virtue of subsection (3) above in relation to a transfer, issue or agreement, sections 70, 90(4) and (5) and 96 above shall not have effect in relation to that transfer, issue or agreement.

97A(5)   Nothing in subsection (3) or (4) above affects the application of section 70 or 96 above in relation to a transfer falling within section 70(1) or 96(1) above by the operator or his nominee to, or to a nominee of, another operator in relation to whom no election under subsection (1) above is for the time being in force.

97A(6)   The Board may require the operator, as a condition of the approval of his election under subsection (1) above, to make and maintain such arrangements as they may consider satisfactory–

(a)   for the collection of stamp duty reserve tax chargeable in accordance with this section, and

(b)   for complying, or securing compliance, with the provisions of this Part and of regulations under section 98 below, so far as relating to such tax.

97A(7)   Where the operator is not resident in the United Kingdom and has no branch or agency in the United Kingdom, the Board may require him, as a condition of the approval of his election under subsection (1) above, to appoint and, so long as the election remains in force, maintain a tax representative.

97A(8)   A person shall not be an operator's tax representative under this section unless that person–

(a)   has a business establishment in the United Kingdom, and

(b)   is approved by the Board.

97A(9)   A person who is at any time an operator's tax representative under this section–

(a)   shall be entitled to act on the operator's behalf for the purposes of stamp duty and stamp duty reserve tax in connection with the clearance services to which the operator's election under subsection (1) above relates,

(b)   shall secure (where appropriate by acting on the operator's behalf) the operator's compliance with and discharge of the obligations and liabilities to which the operator is subject, in connection with the clearance services to which the operator's election under subsection (1) above relates, by virtue of legislation relating to stamp duty or stamp duty reserve tax (including obligations and liabilities arising before he became the operator's tax representative), and

(c)   shall be personally liable in respect of any failure to secure the operator's compliance with or discharge of any such obligation or liability, and in respect of anything done for purposes connected with acting on the operator's behalf,

as if the obligations and liabilities imposed on the operator were imposed jointly and severally on the tax representative and the operator.

97A(10)   An election under subsection (1) above may be terminated–

(a)   by not less than thirty days' notice given by the operator to the Board or by the Board to the operator; or

(b)   if there is or has been a breach of a condition of the approval of the election imposed by virtue of subsection (6) or (7) above, by a notice–

    (i) given by the Board to the operator,

    (ii) taking effect on the giving of the notice or at such later time as may be specified in the notice, and

    (iii) stating that it is given by reason of the breach of condition.

97A(11)   Where an election under subsection (1) above is terminated, section 96 above shall have effect as if chargeable securities of the same amounts and kinds as are, immediately before the termination, held by the operator or his nominee in connection with the provision of the clearance services, had, immediately after the termination, been transferred to the operator or, as the case may be, to the nominee by a transfer falling within subsection (1) of that section.

97A(12)   In this section **"relevant securities"** has the same meaning as in section 70 above.

97A(13)   Nothing in section 70(9) or 97(1) above has effect to prevent a charge to stamp duty or stamp duty reserve tax arising–

(a)   on a transfer to which subsection (5) above applies, or

(b)   on a deemed transfer under subsection (11) above.

History – S. 97A inserted by FA 1996, s. 196(3), with effect from 1 July 1996.
S. 97A(13) inserted by FA 2000, s. 134(4) which has effect as follows: as FA 2000, s. 134(4) applies for the purposes of stamp duty, where instruments are executed after 28 July 2000, and as FA 2000, s. 134(4) applies for the purposes of stamp duty reserve tax, where the securities are transferred after 28 July 2000.

Other material – Inland Revenue press release, 28 November 1995: background to the 1996 amendments.

97B   Transfer between depositary receipt system and clearance system

97B(1)   There shall be no charge to tax under section 93 or 96 above where securities are transferred between a depositary receipt system and a clearance system.

97B(2)   A transfer between a depositary receipt system and a clearance system means a transfer–

(a)   from (or to) a company which at the time of the transfer falls within section 67(6) above, and

(b)   to (or from) a company which at that time falls within section 70(6) above.

97B(3)   This section does not apply to a transfer from a clearance system (that is, from such a company as is mentioned in subsection (2)(b) above) if at the time of the transfer an election is in force under section 97A above in relation to the clearance services for the purposes of which the securities are held immediately before the transfer.

History – S. 97B inserted by FA 2000, s. 134 (2) which has effect where the securities are transferred after 28 July 2000.

GENERAL

98   Administration etc.

98(1)   The Treasury may make regulations–

(a)   providing that provisions of the Taxes Management Act 1970 specified in the regulations shall apply in relation to stamp duty reserve tax as they apply in relation to a tax within the meaning of that Act, with such modifications (specified in the regulations) as they think fit;

(b)   making with regard to stamp duty reserve tax such further provision as they think fit in relation to administration, assessment, collection and recovery.

98(1A)   The power conferred on the Treasury by subsection (1) above includes power to make provision conferring or imposing on the Board functions which involve the exercise of a discretion.

98(2)   The power to make regulations under subsection (1) above shall be exercisable by statutory instrument subject to annulment in pursuance of a resolution of the House of Commons.

Prospective repeals – S. 98 repealed by FA 1990, s. 132 and Sch. 19, Pt. VII, from a date to be appointed in accordance with s. 110 of that Act. (See note below).

History – S. 98(1A) inserted by FA 1996, s. 195, with effect from 29 April 1996.

Cross references – FA 1989, s. 177: regulations under s. 98(1) may include provision as to manner or form of notice or information.
FA 1999, s. 121: power to make regulations under s. 98(1) includes power to make provision:

- applying the provisions of the Taxes Management Act 1970 relating to penalties and the payment of interest on overdue tax, and
- requiring information to be provided, or books, documents or other records to be made available for inspection, and imposing a penalty for failure to do so; and
- shall be deemed always to have included, power to make provision requiring specified descriptions of persons to account for and pay tax, and any interest on it, on behalf of the person liable to pay it.

Statutory instruments – SI 1986/1711 (as amended by SI 1988/835, SI 1989/1301, SI 1993/3110, SI 1997/2430, SI 1999/2383 and SI 1999/2536): regulations made under s. 98. Further amended by SI 1994/1813, made under TMA 1970, s. 46A, 56B.

Other material – Inland Revenue press release, 28 November 1995: background to the 1996 amendments.

Notes – The Treasury order appointing the "abolition day" for the purposes of FA 1990, s. 107–110 was to have broadly coincided with the start of paperless trading under the Stock Exchange's planned TAURUS system (IR press release, 20 March 1990). However, on 11 March 1993 it was announced that TAURUS had been abandoned (London Stock Exchange News Release 6/93).

99   Interpretation

99(1)   This section applies for the purposes of this Part of this Act.

99(1A)   **"Bearer Instrument"** has the same meaning as in Schedule 15 to the Finance Act 1999. An instrument is a **"UK bearer instrument"** or **"non-UK bearer instrument"** according to whether it is issued by or on behalf of a UK company or a non-UK company within the meaning of that Schedule.

99(2)   **"The Board"** means the Commissioners of Inland Revenue.

99(3)   Subject to the following provisions of this section,

     "chargeable securities" means–

       (a)   stocks, shares or loan capital;

       (b)   interests in, or in dividends or other rights arising out of, stocks, shares or loan capital;

       (c)   rights to allotments of or to subscribe for, or options to acquire, stocks, shares or loan capital; and

       (d)   units under a unit trust scheme.

99(4)   **"Chargeable securities"** does not include securities falling within paragraph (a), (b) or (c) of subsection (3) above which are issued or raised by a body corporate not incorporated in the United Kingdom unless–

(a)   they are registered in a register kept in the United Kingdom by or on behalf of the body corporate by which they are issued or raised, or

(b)   in the case of shares, they are paired with shares issued by a body corporate incorporated in the United Kingdom, or

(c)   in the case of securities falling within paragraph (b) or (c) of subsection (3) above, paragraph (a) or (b) above applies to the stocks, shares or loan capital to which they relate.

99(5)   **"Chargeable securities"** does not include–

(a)   securities falling within paragraph (a), (b) or (c) of subsection (3) above the transfer of which is exempt from all stamp duties, or

(b)   securities falling within paragraph (b) or (c) of subsection (3) above which relate to stocks, shares or loan capital the transfer of which is exempt from all stamp duties.

99(5A)   "Chargeable securities" does not include a unit under a unit trust scheme if–

(a)   all the trustees under the scheme are resident outside the United Kingdom and the unit is not registered in a register kept in the United Kingdom by or on behalf of the trustees under the scheme; or

(b)   under the terms of the scheme the trust property can only be invested in exempt investments.

99(5B)   For the purposes of subsection (5A)(b)–

(a)   an investment other than an interest under a collective investment scheme is an exempt investment if, and only if–

       (i)   it is not an investment on the transfer of which ad valorem stamp duty would be chargeable, and

       (ii)   it is not a chargeable security;

(b)   an interest under a collective investment scheme is an exempt investment if, and only if, the scheme is an authorised unit trust scheme or an open-ended investment company and under the terms of the scheme the property subject to the scheme–

       (i)   cannot be invested in such a way that income can arise to the trustees or the company that will be chargeable to tax in their hands otherwise than under Case III of Schedule D, and

       (ii)   can only be invested in exempt investments;

(c)   a derivative is an exempt investment if, and only if, it relates wholly to one or more exempt investments; and

(d)   funds held for the purposes of the day to day management of the unit trust scheme are not regarded as investments.

     In this subsection "authorised unit trust scheme", "collective investment scheme" and "open-ended investment company" have the same meaning as in the Financial Services Act 1986.

99(6) "**Chargeable securities**" does not include interests in depositary receipts for stocks or shares.

99(6A) For the purposes of subsection (4) above, shares issued by a body corporate which is not incorporated in the United Kingdom ("**the foreign company**") are **paired** with shares issued by a body corporate which is so incorporated ("**the UK company**") where–

(a) the articles of association of the UK company and the equivalent instruments governing the foreign company each provide that no share in the company to which they relate may be transferred otherwise than as part of a unit comprising one share in that company and one share in the other, and

(b) such units have been offered for sale to the public in the United Kingdom and, at the same time, other such units have been offered for sale to the public at a broadly equivalent price in the country in which the foreign company is incorporated.

99(6B) For the purposes of subsection (4) above, shares issued by a body corporate which is not incorporated in the United Kingdom ("**the foreign company**") are **paired** with shares issued by a body corporate which is so incorporated ("**the UK company**") where–

(a) the articles of association of the UK company and the equivalent instruments governing the foreign company each provide that no share in the company to which they relate may be transferred otherwise than as part of a unit comprising one share in that company and one share in the other, and

(b) the shares issued by the foreign company, and the shares issued by the UK company, are issued to give effect to an allotment of the shares (as part of such units) as fully or partly paid bonus shares.

99(7) A **depositary receipt for stocks or shares** is an instrument acknowledging–

(a) that a person holds stocks or shares or evidence of the right to receive them, and

(b) that another person is entitled to rights, whether expressed as units or otherwise, in or in relation to stocks or shares of the same kind, including the right to receive such stocks or shares (or evidence of the right to receive them) from the person mentioned in paragraph (a) above,

except that a depositary receipt for stocks or shares does not include an instrument acknowledging rights in or in relation to stocks or shares if they are issued or sold under terms providing for payment in instalments and for the issue of the instrument as evidence that an instalment has been paid.

99(8) The Treasury may by regulations provide that for subsection (7) above (as it has effect for the time being) there shall be substituted a subsection containing a different definition of a depositary receipt; and the power to make regulations under this subsection shall be exerciseable by statutory instrument subject to annulment in pursuance of a resolution of the House of Commons.

99(9) "**Unit trust scheme**" and related expressions have the meanings given by Part IV of Schedule 19 to the Finance Act 1999.

99(10) In interpreting "**chargeable securities**" in sections 93, 94, 95, 95A, 96, 97, 97AA and 97A above–

(a) paragraph (a) of subsection (4) above and the reference to that paragraph in paragraph (c) of that subsection shall be ignored, and

(b) the effect of paragraph 8 of Schedule 14 to the Companies Act 1985 (share registered overseas) and of section 118 of the Companies Act (Northern Ireland) 1960 and paragraph 7 of Schedule 14 of the Companies (Northern Ireland) Order 1986 (equivalent provision for Northern Ireland) shall be ignored for the purposes of subsection (5) above.

99(11) In interpreting "**chargeable securities**" in section 93 or 96 above in a case where–

(a) newly subscribed shares, or

(b) securities falling within paragraph (b) or (c) of subsection (3) above which relate to newly subscribed shares,

are issued in pursuance of an arrangement such as is mentioned in that section (or an arrangement which would be such an arrangement if the securities issued were chargeable securities), paragraph (b) of subsection (4) above and the reference to that paragraph in paragraph (c) of that subsection shall be ignored.

99(12) In subsection (11) above, "**newly subscribed shares**" means shares issued wholly for new consideration in pursuance of an offer for sale to the public.

99(13) Where the calculation of any tax in accordance with the provisions of this Part results in an amount which is not a multiple of one penny, the amount so calculated shall be rounded to the nearest penny, taking any $\frac{1}{2}$ as nearest to the next whole penny above.

Prospective repeals – S. 99 repealed by FA 1990, s. 132 and Sch. 19, Pt. VII, from a date to be appointed in accordance with s. 110 of that Act. (See note below).

History – S. 99(1A) inserted by FA 1999, s. 113(3) and Sch. 16, para. 9 in relation to bearer instruments issued on or after 1 October 1999.
S. 99(3)–(6) substituted, and (6A), (11) and (12) inserted, by FA 1988, s. 144(2)–(6), effective for an agreement to transfer chargeable securities made after 8 December 1987 and for a transfer, issue or appropriation of such securities, or an issue of securities such as are mentioned in s. 99(11), after that date in pursuance of an arrangement such as is mentioned in that subsection; reference to s. 99(6A) consequently inserted in s. 99(9) and corresponding amendments made to s. 99(10)(a).
In s. 99(5) the words "falling within paragraph (a), (b) or (c) of subsection (3) above" inserted by FA 1999, s. 122(4) and Sch. 19, para. 12(2) with effect from 6 February 2000.
S. 99(5A) and (5B) inserted by FA 1999, s. 122(4) and Sch. 19, para. 12(3) with effect from 6 February 2000.
In s. 99(6A)(b) the word "other" was substituted by FA 1990, s. 113(1), (2), for the former words "an equal number of", effective where the offers referred to in s. 99(6A) are made on or after 26 July 1990, and before the offers are made, units comprising shares in the two companies concerned were offered (whether before, on or after 26 July 1990) in circumstances where s. 99(6A) applied without amendment.
S. 99(6B) and the reference to it in s. 99(9) inserted by FA 1990, s. 113(1), (3), (4), where the shares referred to in s. 99(6B) are issued on or after 26 July 1990, and before they are issued, units comprising shares in the two companies concerned were offered (whether before, on or after 26 July 1990) in circumstances where s. 99(6A) applied without the amendment made by FA 1990, s. 113(2) (see above).
S. 99(9) substituted by FA 1999, s. 122(4) and Sch. 19, para. 12(4) with effect from 6 February 2000.
In s. 99(10), reference to s. 95A and 97AA added by FA 1999, s. 118(2) and 118(4) respectively, in relation to securities issued on or after 1 May 1998.
In s. 99(10), reference to s. 95 and 97 inserted by FA 1998, s. 151(5)(a) and (b) respectively, where the issue by company X referred to in FA 1986, s. 95(3) (or (6)) or 97(4) (or (7)) is an issue on or after 1 May 1998.
In s. 99(10), reference to s. 97A added by FA 1996, s. 196(5), with effect from 1 July 1996.
S. 99(13) inserted by FA 1996, s. 194(6), with effect from 29 April 1996.

Cross references – FA 2000, s. 122(6) (marketable securities exchanged for exempt property): definition of "qualifying property" to exclude certain items that are not chargeable securities within the meaning of Pt. IV of this act.
Broadcasting Act 1996, s. 135 and Sch. 7, para. 26: no stamp duty reserve tax on agreement to transfer chargeable securities from BBC to a wholly-owned subsidiary of the BBC where agreement is part of restructuring scheme.
SI 1997/1156, reg. 4B: modification of s. 99 in relation to open-ended investment companies.

Other material – Inland Revenue press release, 28 November 1995: background to the 1996 amendments.

Notes – SI 1992/197: common investment fund established under the Administration of Justice Act 1982, s. 42(1) is excepted from the definition of "unit trust scheme" from 1 March 1992.
SI 1992/570: "equity securities" includes shares paired with shares of a UK-incorporated company within the meaning of s. 99(6A).
The Treasury order appointing the "abolition day" for the purposes of FA 1990, s. 107–110 was to have broadly coincided with the start of paperless trading under the Stock Exchange's planned TAURUS system (IR press release, 20 March 1990). However, on 11 March 1993 it was announced that TAURUS had been abandoned (London Stock Exchange News Release 6/93).

INSOLVENCY ACT 1986

(1986 Chapter 45)

[29th December 1986]

PART IV – WINDING UP OF COMPANIES REGISTERED UNDER THE COMPANIES ACTS

Chapter VIII – Provisions of General Application in Winding Up

MISCELLANEOUS MATTERS

190   Documents exempt from stamp duty

190(1) In the case of a winding up by the court, or of a creditors' voluntary winding up, the following has effect as regards exemption from duties chargeable under the enactments relating to stamp duties.

190(2) If the company is registered in England and Wales, the following documents are exempt from stamp duty–

(a)   every assurance relating solely to freehold or leasehold property, or to any estate, right or interest in, any real or personal property, which forms part of the company's assets and which, after the execution of the assurance, either at law or in equity, is or remains part of those assets, and

(b)   every writ, order, certificate, or other instrument or writing relating solely to the property of any company which is being wound up as mentioned in subsection (1), or to any proceeding under such a winding up. **"Assurance"** here includes deed, conveyance, assignment and surrender.

190(3)   If the company is registered in Scotland, the following documents are exempt from stamp duty–

(a)   every conveyance relating solely to property, which forms part of the company's assets and which, after the execution of the conveyance, is or remains the company's property for the benefit of its creditors,

(b)   any articles of roup or sale, submission and every other instrument and writing whatsoever relating solely to the company's property, and

(c)   every deed or writing forming part of the proceedings in the winding up. **"Conveyance"** here includes assignation, instrument, discharge, writing and deed.

PART X – INDIVIDUAL INSOLVENCY: GENERAL PROVISIONS

378   Exemption from stamp duty

378   Stamp duty shall not be charged on–

(a)   any document, being a deed, conveyance, assignment, surrender, admission or other assurance relating solely to property which is comprised in a bankrupt's estate and which, after the execution of that document, is or remains at law or in equity the property of the bankrupt or of the trustee of that estate,

(b)   any writ, order, certificate or other instrument relating solely to the property of a bankrupt or to any bankruptcy proceedings.

FINANCE ACT 1987

(1987 Chapter 16)

[15th May 1987]

ARRANGEMENT OF SECTIONS

PART III – STAMP DUTY AND STAMP DUTY RESERVE TAX

STAMP DUTY

STAMP DUTY RESERVE TAX

PART VI – MISCELLANEOUS AND SUPPLEMENTARY

SCHEDULES
7.   STAMP DUTY RESERVE TAX

PART III – STAMP DUTY AND STAMP DUTY RESERVE TAX

Notes – S. 72(4): Pt. III (except s. 56 and Sch. 7) to be construed as one with SA 1891.

STAMP DUTY

48   Unit trusts
48   [Amends FA 1947, s. 57(1) and inserts s. 57(1A), (1B).]

50   Warrants to purchase Government Stock etc.

50(1)   Where an interest in, a right to an allotment of or to subscribe for, or an option to acquire or to dispose of, exempt securities is transferred to or vested in any person by any instrument, no stamp duty shall be chargeable on the instrument by virtue of Part I, or paragraph 16, of Schedule 13 to the Finance Act 1999 (conveyance or transfer on sale or otherwise).

50(2)   No stamp duty under Schedule 15 to the Finance Act 1999 (bearer instruments) shall be chargeable–

(a)   on the issue of an instrument which relates to such an interest, right or option as is mentioned in subsection (1) above, or

(b)   on the transfer of the interest, right or option constituted by, or transferable by means of, such an instrument.

50(3)   For the purposes of this section, **"exempt securities"** means–

(a)   securities the transfer of which is exempt from all stamp duties,

(b)   securities constituted by or transferable by means of an instrument the issue of which is exempt from stamp duty under paragraph 1 of Schedule 15 to the Finance Act 1999 (issue of bearer instrument) by virtue of paragraph 17 of that Schedule (certain non-sterling instruments), or

(c)   securities the transfer of which is exempt from stamp duty under that Schedule by virtue of paragraph 17 of that Schedule or section 79(2) of the Finance Act 1986;

and **"securities"** means stock or marketable securities and includes loan capital as defined in section 78(7) of the Finance Act 1986.

50(4-5)   [Repealed by FA 1999, s. 139 and Sch. 20, Pt. V(2).]

Prospective repeals – S. 50 repealed by FA 1990, s. 132 and Sch. 19, Pt. VI, from a date to be appointed in accordance with s. 107–111 of that Act. (See note below.)

History – In s. 50(1) the words "Part I, or paragraph 16, of Schedule 13 to the Finance Act 1999 (conveyance or transfer on sale or otherwise)" substituted for the words:
"**50**   either of the following headings in Schedule 1 to the Stamp Act 1891–
    (a)   "Conveyance or Transfer on Sale";
    (b)   "Conveyance or Transfer of any kind not hereinbefore described"."
by FA 1999, s. 112(4) and Sch. 14, para. 21, the substitution having effect in relation to instruments executed on or after 1 October 1999.
In s. 50(1) reference to option to dispose of exempt securities inserted by F(No. 2)A 1987, s. 99(1). S. 50(3) amended by F(No. 2)A 1987, s. 99(2), by inserting reference to exemption by virtue of FA 1986, s. 79(2) (loan capital).
In –
    s. 50(2) the words "Schedule 15 to the Finance Act 1999 (bearer instruments)" substituted for the words "the heading "Bearer Instrument" in Schedule 1 to the Stamp Act 1891";
    s. 50(3)(b) the words "exempt from stamp duty under paragraph 1 of Schedule 15 to the Finance Act 1999 (issue of bearer instrument) by virtue of paragraph 17 of that Schedule (certain non-sterling instruments)" substituted for the words "by virtue of section 30 of the Finance Act 1967 or section 7 of the Finance Act (Northern Ireland) 1967 or section 79(2) of the Finance Act 1986 exempt from stamp duty under the heading "Bearer Instrument" in Schedule 1 to the Stamp Act 1891"; and
    s. 50(3)(c) the words "exempt from stamp duty under that Schedule by virtue of paragraph 17 of that Schedule or section 79(2) of the Finance Act 1986" substituted for the words "by virtue of section 30 of the Finance Act 1967 or section 7 of the Finance Act (Northern Ireland) 1967 or section 79(2) of the Finance Act 1986 from stamp duty under that heading",
by FA 1999, s. 113(3) and Sch. 16, para. 10(2), (3), (4) respectively, the substitutions applying in relation to bearer instruments issued on or after 1 October 1999. (The text of s. 50 reproduced above ignores the fact that the substitution in the third bullet point would lead to the word "exempt" appearing twice in succession in the same sentence.)
S. 50(4), (5) repealed by FA 1999, s. 139 and Sch. 20, Pt. V(2), the repeal having effect in relation to instruments executed, or bearer instruments issued, on or after 1 October 1999, but as regards unit trust schemes subject to FA 1999, Sch. 20, Pt. V(2), para. 2.

Notes – S. 50 includes reference to equivalent Northern Ireland exemptions etc.

The Treasury order appointing the "abolition day" for the purposes of FA 1990, s. 107–110 was to have broadly coincided with the start of paperless trading under the Stock Exchange's planned TAURUS system (IR press release, 20 March 1990). However, on 11 March 1993 it was announced that TAURUS had been abandoned (London Stock Exchange News Release 6/93).

51   Bearer instruments relating to stock in foreign currencies

51   [Repealed by FA 1999, s. 139 and Sch. 20, Pt. V(2) in relation to instruments executed, or bearer instruments issued, on or after 1 October 1999, but as regards unit trust schemes subject to FA 1999, Sch. 20, Pt. V(2), para. 2.]

52   Clearance services

52   [Amends FA 1986, s. 70(6).]

Prospective repeals – S. 52 repealed by FA 1990, s. 132 and Sch. 19, Pt. VI, for instruments executed on or after a day to be appointed.

53   Borrowing of stock by market makers

53   [Repealed by FA 1997, s. 113 and Sch. 18, Pt. VII]

54   Shared ownership transactions

54(1)   [Amends FA 1980, s. 97(3)(b).]

54(2)   Section 97 of the Finance Act 1980 and section 108(5) and (6) of the Finance Act 1981 shall apply to a lease within subsection (3) below as they apply to a lease granted by a body mentioned in section 97(3) of the Finance Act 1980.

54(3)   A lease is within this subsection if it is granted–

(a)   by a person against whom the right to buy under Part V of the Housing Act 1985 is exercisable by virtue of section 171A of that Act (preservation of right to buy on disposal to private sector landlord), and

(b)   to a person who is the qualifying person for the purposes of the preserved right to buy and in relation to whom that dwelling-house is the qualifying dwelling-house.

54(4)   This section applies to leases granted on or after 1st August 1987.

55   Crown exemption

55(1)   Where any conveyance, transfer or lease is made or agreed to be made

(a)   to a Minister of the Crown or

(b)   to the Solicitor for the affairs of Her Majesty's Treasury, or

(c)   to the National Assembly for Wales, or

(d)   to the Northern Ireland Assembly Commission,

no stamp duty shall be chargeable "under Part I or II, or paragraph 16, of Schedule 13 to the Finance Act 1999" on the instrument by which the conveyance, transfer or lease, or the agreement for it, is effected.

55(2)   In this section **"Minister of the Crown"** has the same meaning as in the Ministers of the Crown Act 1975.

55(3)   Article 3(6) of the Secretary of State for the Environment Order 1970 and Article 4(5) of the Secretary of State for Transport Order 1976 (which exempt transfers by, to or with those Ministers) shall cease to have effect.

55(4)   This section applies to instruments executed on or after 1st August 1987.

History – In s. 55(1), the division of existing text into paragraphs and the insertion of para. (d) made by FA 2000, s. 132(2)) and 132(3) respectively, the insertion having effect in relation to instruments executed on or after 28 March 2000.

In s. 55(1), the words "under Part I or II, or paragraph 16, of Schedule 13 to the Finance Act 1999" substituted for the words:

"55   by virtue of any of the following headings in Schedule 1 to the Stamp Act 1891–

(a)   "Conveyance or Transfer on Sale"

(b)   "Conveyance or Transfer of any kind not hereinbefore described",

(c)   "Lease or Tack","

by FA 1999, s. 112(4) and Sch. 14, para. 22, the substitution having effect in relation to instruments executed on or after 1 October 1999.

In s. 55(1), the words "or to the National Assembly for Wales," inserted after the words "Her Majesty's Treasury," by the Government of Wales Act 1998, s. 125 and Sch. 12, para. 25, with effect from 1 April 1999 (SI 1999/782).

Cross references – Scotland Act 1998, s. 123: references in s. 55 to a Minister of the Crown are to be read as including the Scottish Ministers, the Lord Advocate and the Parliamentary corporation.

STAMP DUTY RESERVE TAX

56 Stamp duty reserve tax

56   Schedule 7 to this Act (which contains miscellaneous amendments of Part IV of the Finance Act 1986) shall have effect.

Prospective repeals – S. 56 repealed by FA 1990, s. 132 and Sch. 19, Pt. VII in accordance with s. 110 of that Act.

Notes – The Treasury order appointing the "abolition day" for the purposes of FA 1990, s. 107–110 was to have broadly coincided with the start of paperless trading under the Stock Exchange's planned TAURUS system (IR press release, 20 March 1990). However, on 11 March 1993 it was announced that TAURUS had been abandoned (London Stock Exchange News Release 6/93).

PART VI – MISCELLANEOUS AND SUPPLEMENTARY

72 Short title, interpretation, construction and repeals

72(1)   This Act may be cited as the Finance Act 1987.

72(2), (3)   [Not reproduced.]

72(4)   Part III of this Act, except section 56 and Schedule 7, shall be construed as one with the Stamp Act 1891.

72(5)–(7)   [Not reproduced.]

SCHEDULES

SCHEDULE 7 – STAMP DUTY RESERVE TAX

Section 56

Prospective repeal – Sch. 7 repealed by FA 1990, s. 132 and Sch. 19, Pt. VII, from a date to be appointed in accordance with s. 110 of that Act.

Notes – The Treasury order appointing the "abolition day" for the purposes of FA 1990, s. 107–110 was to have broadly coincided with the start of paperless trading under the Stock Exchange's planned TAURUS system (IR press release, 20 March 1990). However, on 11 March 1993 it was announced that TAURUS had been abandoned (London Stock Exchange News Release 6/93).

1   Part IV of the Finance Act 1986 shall be amended in accordance with the following provisions of this Schedule.

Prospective repeals – Para. 1 repealed by FA 1990, s. 132 and Sch. 19, Pt. VII, from a date to be appointed in accordance with s. 110 of that Act.

Notes – The Treasury order appointing the "abolition day" for the purposes of FA 1990, s. 107–110 was to have broadly coincided with the start of paperless trading under the Stock Exchange's planned TAURUS system (IR press release, 20 March 1990). However, on 11 March 1993 it was announced that TAURUS had been abandoned (London Stock Exchange News Release 6/93).

PRINCIPAL CHARGE

2   [Inserts FA 1986, s. 87(7A), (7B).]

Prospective repeals – Para. 2 repealed by FA 1990, s. 132 and Sch. 19, Pt. VII, from a date to be appointed in accordance with s. 110 of that Act.

Notes – The Treasury order appointing the "abolition day" for the purposes of FA 1990, s. 107–110 was to have broadly coincided with the start of paperless trading under the Stock Exchange's planned TAURUS system (IR press release, 20 March 1990). However, on 11 March 1993 it was announced that TAURUS had been abandoned (London Stock Exchange News Release 6/93).

RENOUNCEABLE LETTERS OF ALLOTMENT, ETC.

3   [Amends FA 1986, s. 88(3)(a).]

Prospective repeals – Para. 3 repealed by FA 1990, s. 132 and Sch. 19, Pt. VII, from a date to be appointed in accordance with s. 110 of that Act.

Notes – The Treasury order appointing the "abolition day" for the purposes of FA 1990, s. 107–110 was to have broadly coincided with the start of paperless trading under the Stock Exchange's planned TAURUS system (IR press release, 20 March 1990). However, on 11 March 1993 it was announced that TAURUS had been abandoned (London Stock Exchange News Release 6/93).

MARKET MAKERS IN OPTIONS

4   [Repealed by FA 1997, s. 113 and Sch. 18, Pt. VII.]

CLEARANCE SERVICES

5   [Substitutes FA 1986, s. 90(5), (6).]

Prospective repeals – Para 5 repealed by FA 1990, s. 132 and Sch. 19, Pt. VII, from a date to be appointed in accordance with s. 110 of that Act.

Notes – The Treasury order appointing the "abolition day" for the purposes of FA 1990, s. 107–110 was to have broadly coincided with the start of paperless trading under the Stock Exchange's planned TAURUS system (IR press release, 20 March 1990). However, on 11 March 1993 it was announced that TAURUS had been abandoned (London Stock Exchange News Release 6/93).

CHARITIES ETC.

6   [Inserts FA 1986, s. 90(7).]

Prospective repeals – Para. 6 repealed by FA 1990, s. 132 and Sch. 19, Pt. VII, from a date to be appointed in accordance with s. 110 of that Act.

Notes – The Treasury order appointing the "abolition day" for the purposes of FA 1990, s. 107–110 was to have broadly coincided with the start of paperless trading under the Stock Exchange's planned TAURUS system (IR press release, 20 March 1990). However, on 11 March 1993 it was announced that TAURUS had been abandoned (London Stock Exchange News Release 6/93).

INTEREST ON TAX REPAYMENTS

7   [Inserts FA 1986, s. 92(4A).]

Prospective repeals – Para. 7 repealed by FA 1990, s. 132 and Sch. 19, Pt. VII, from a date to be appointed in accordance with s. 110 of that Act.

Notes – The Treasury order appointing the "abolition day" for the purposes of FA 1990, s. 107–110 was to have broadly coincided with the start of paperless trading under the Stock Exchange's planned TAURUS system (IR press release, 20 March 1990). However, on 11 March 1993 it was announced that TAURUS had been abandoned (London Stock Exchange News Release 6/93).

FINANCE (NO. 2) ACT 1987

(1987 Chapter 51)

[23rd July 1987]

PART III – MISCELLANEOUS AND SUPPLEMENTARY

99   Stamp duty: options etc.

99   [Amends FA 1987, s. 50(1), (3).]

Prospective repeals – S. 99 repealed by FA 1990, s. 132 and Sch. 19, Pt. VI, from a date to be appointed in accordance with s. 107–111 of that Act.

Notes – The Treasury order appointing the "abolition day" for the purposes of FA 1990, s. 107–110 was to have broadly coincided with the start of paperless trading under the Stock Exchange's planned TAURUS system (IR press release, 20 March 1990). However, on 11 March 1993 it was announced that TAURUS had been abandoned (London Stock Exchange News Release 6/93).

100   Stamp duty reserve tax

100   [Inserts FA 1986, s. 89A; repeals FA 1986, s. 91(2).]

Prospective repeals – S. 100 repealed by FA 1990, s. 132 and Sch. 19, Pt. VII, from a date to be appointed in accordance with s. 110 of that Act.

Notes – The Treasury order appointing the "abolition day" for the purposes of FA 1990, s. 107–110 was to have broadly coincided with the start of paperless trading under the Stock Exchange's planned TAURUS system (IR press release, 20 March 1990). However, on 11 March 1993 it was announced that TAURUS had been abandoned (London Stock Exchange News Release 6/93).

FINANCE ACT 1988

(1988 Chapter 39)

[*29th July 1988*]

ARRANGEMENT OF SECTIONS

PART IV – MISCELLANEOUS AND GENERAL

STAMP DUTY AND STAMP DUTY RESERVE TAX

PART IV – MISCELLANEOUS AND GENERAL

STAMP DUTY AND STAMP DUTY RESERVE TAX

140   Abolition of stamp duty under the heading "Unit Trust Instrument"

140   [Repealed by FA 1999, s. 139 and Sch. 20, Pt. V(2) in relation to instruments executed, or bearer instruments issued, on or after 1 October 1999, but as regards unit trust schemes subject to FA 1999, Sch. 20, Pt. V(2), para. 2. The repeal took effect from 6 February 2000 as regards unit trust schemes, by virtue of FA 1999, s. 122(4) and FA 1999, Sch. 19.]

141   Abolition of stamp duty on documents relating to transactions of capital companies

141   [Repealed by FA 1999, s. 139 and Sch. 20, Pt. V(2) in relation to instruments executed, or bearer instruments issued, on or after 1 October 1999, but as regards unit trust schemes subject to FA 1999, Sch. 20, Pt. V(2), para. 2. The repeal took effect from 6 February 2000 as regards unit trust schemes, by virtue of FA 1999, s. 122(4) and FA 1999, Sch. 19.]

142   Stamp duty: housing action trusts

142(1)   [Inserts FA 1980, s. 97(3)(cc).]

142(2)   [Inserts FA 1981, s. 107(3)(ff).]

143   Stamp duty: paired shares

143(1)   This section applies where–

(a)   the articles of association of a company incorporated in the United Kingdom (**"the UK company"**) and the equivalent instruments governing a company which is not so incorporated (**"the foreign company"**) each provide that no share in the company to which they relate may be transferred otherwise than as part of a unit comprising one share in that company and one share in the other; and

(b)   such units are to be or have been offered for sale to the public in the United Kingdom and, at the same time, other such units are to be or, as the case may be, have been offered for sale to the public at a broadly equivalent price in the country in which the foreign company is incorporated (**"the foreign country"**).

143(2) In relation to an instrument to which this subsection applies, no duty is chargeable under paragraph 1 of Schedule 15 to the Finance Act 1999 (bearer instruments: charge on issue); but this does not affect the other requirements of that Schedule.

143(3) Subsection (2) above applies to any bearer instrument issued on or after 1st November 1987 which represents shares in the UK company, or a right to an allotment of or to subscribe for such shares, if the purpose of the issue is–

(a) to make such shares available for sale (as part of such units as are referred to in subsection (1) above) in pursuance of either of the offers referred to in subsection (1)(b) above or of any other offer for sale of such units to the public made at the same time and at a broadly equivalent price in a country other than the United Kingdom or the foreign country; or

(b) to give effect to an allotment of such shares (as part of such units) as fully or partly paid bonus shares.

143(4) In relation to an instrument to which this subsection applies–

(a) the foreign company shall be treated for the purposes of Schedule 15 to the Finance Act 1999 (stamp duty on bearer instruments) as a UK company, and

(b) paragraph 17 of that Schedule (exemption for non-sterling instruments) shall not apply.

143(5) Subsection (4) above applies to any bearer instrument issued on or after 9th December 1987 which represents shares in the foreign company, or a right to an allotment of or to subscribe for such shares; and is not issued for the purpose–

(a) of making shares in the foreign company available for sale (as part of such units as are referred to in subsection (1) above) in pursuance of either of the offers referred to in subsection (1)(b) above or of any other offer such as is mentioned in subsection (3)(a) above; or

(b) of giving effect to an allotment of such shares (as part of such units) as fully or partly paid bonus shares.

143(6) In relation to any instrument which transfers such units as are referred to in subsection (1) above and is executed on or after the date of the passing of this Act, the foreign company shall be treated for the purposes of sections 67 and 68 (depositary receipts) and 70 and 71 (clearance services) of the Finance Act 1986 as a company incorporated in the United Kingdom.

143(7) Section 3 of the Stamp Act 1891 (which requires every instrument written upon the same piece of material as another instrument to be separately stamped) shall not apply in relation to any bearer instrument issued on or after 9th December 1987 which represents shares in the UK company or the foreign company, or a right to an allotment of or to subscribe for such shares.

143(8) This section shall be construed as one with the Stamp Act 1891.

143(9) Subsections (2) and (3) above, together with subsection (1) above so far as relating to them, shall be deemed to have come into force on 1st November 1987, and subsections (4), (5) and (7) above, together with subsection (1) above so far as relating to them, shall be deemed to have come into force on 9th December 1987.

Prospective repeals – S. 143 repealed by FA 1990, s. 132 and Sch. 19, Pt. VI, in accordance with s. 107–111 of that Act. (See note below).

History – In s. 143(1)(b), the word "other" was substituted by FA 1990, s. 112.
The following amendments were made by FA 1999, s. 113(3) and Sch. 16, para. 11 in relation to bearer instruments issued on or after 1 October 1999:
     s. 143(2) substituted for the previous version;
     in s. 143(3) the words "Subsection (2) above applies" substituted for the words "This subsection applies";
     s. 143(4) substituted for the previous version; and
     in s. 143(5) the words "Subsection (4) above applies" substituted for the words "This subsection applies".

Cross references – SA 1891, s. 3: how instruments are written and stamped.

Notes – The Treasury order appointing the "abolition day" for the purposes of FA 1990, s. 107–110 was to have broadly coincided with the start of paperless trading under the Stock Exchange's planned TAURUS system (IR press release, 20 March 1990). However, on 11 March 1993 it was announced that TAURUS had been abandoned (London Stock Exchange News Release 6/93).

144   Stamp duty reserve tax: paired shares etc.

144(1)–(6) [Amends FA 1986, s. 99.]

Prospective repeals – S. 144 repealed by FA 1990, s. 132 and Sch. 19, Pt. VII, from a date to be appointed in accordance with s. 110 of that Act.

History – S. 144(3) repealed by FA 1999, s. 139 and Sch. 20, Pt. V(5), the repeal having effect in relation to instruments executed on or after 6 February 2000.

Notes – The Treasury order appointing the "abolition day" for the purposes of FA 1990, s. 107–110 was to have broadly coincided with the start of paperless trading under the Stock Exchange's planned TAURUS system (IR press release, 20 March 1990). However, on 11 March 1993 it was announced that TAURUS had been abandoned (London Stock Exchange News Release 6/93).

MISCELLANEOUS

145　Building societies: change of status

145　Schedule 12 to this Act (which makes provision in connection with the transfer of a building society's business to a company in accordance with the Building Societies Act 1986) shall have effect.

146　Post-consolidation amendments

146　The enactments specified in Schedule 13 to this Act shall have effect subject to the amendments specified in that Schedule (being amendments to correct errors in the Taxes Act 1988 and in the amendments made by the Finance Act 1987 for the purposes of the consolidation effected by the Taxes Act 1988).

SCHEDULES

SCHEDULE 12 – BUILDING SOCIETIES: CHANGE OF STATUS

Section 145

STAMP DUTY

7　[Amends Building Societies Act 1986, s. 109.]

SCHEDULE 13 – POST-CONSOLIDATION AMENDMENTS

Section 146

Part II – Amendments of Other Enactments

THE FINANCE ACT 1980 (c. 48)

19　[Amends FA 1980, s. 101.]

Prospective repeals – Para. 19 repealed by FA 1990, s. 132 and Sch. 19, Pt. VI, from a date to be appointed in accordance with s. 107–109 of that Act.

Notes – The Treasury order appointing the "abolition day" for the purposes of FA 1990, s. 107–110 was to have broadly coincided with the start of paperless trading under the Stock Exchange's planned TAURUS system (IR press release, 20 March 1990). However, on 11 March 1993 it was announced that TAURUS had been abandoned (London Stock Exchange News Release 6/93).

THE FINANCE ACT 1981 (c. 35)

21　[Para. 21 repealed by FA 1999, s. 139 and Sch. 20, Pt. V(5), the repeal having effect in relation to instruments executed on or after 6 February 2000. Former para. 21 amended FA 1981, s. 110.]

THE FINANCE ACT 1986 (c. 41)

23　[Amends FA 1986, s. 94(5).]

Prospective repeals – Para. 23 repealed by FA 1990, s. 132 and Sch. 19, Pt. VII, from a date to be appointed in accordance with s. 110 of that Act.

Notes – The Treasury order appointing the "abolition day" for the purposes of FA 1990, s. 107–110 was to have broadly coincided with the start of paperless trading under the Stock Exchange's planned TAURUS system (IR press release, 20 March 1990). However, on 11 March 1993 it was announced that TAURUS had been abandoned (London Stock Exchange News Release 6/93).

FINANCE ACT 1989

(1989 Chapter 26)

[*27th July 1989*]

PART III – MISCELLANEOUS AND GENERAL

STAMP DUTY ETC.

173 Insurance: abolition of certain duties

173 [Repealed by FA 1999, s. 139 and Sch. 20, Pt. V(2) in relation to instruments executed, or bearer instruments issued, on or after 1 October 1999, but as regards unit trust schemes subject to FA 1999, Sch. 20, Pt. V(2), para. 2. The repeal took effect from 6 February 2000 as regards unit trust schemes, by virtue of FA 1999, s. 122(4) and FA 1999, Sch. 19.]

Cross references – FA 1999, Sch. 13, para. 25(b): stamp duty not chargeable under FA 1999 Sch. 13 on any description of instrument in respect of which duty was abolished by s. 173.
FA 1999, Sch. 15, para. 15(b): stamp duty not chargeable under FA 1999, Sch. 15 on any description of instrument in respect of which duty was abolished by s. 173.

Notes – S. 173 abolished stamp duty under the following headings of SA 1891, Schedule 1 (now repealed):
- "Policy of Life Insurance", and
- para (3) of the heading "Bond, Covenant, or Instrument of any kind whatsoever" (superannuation annuities).

174 Unit trusts

174 [Repealed by FA 1999, s. 139 and Sch. 20, Pt. V(5) in relation to instruments executed on or after 6 February 2000.]

175 Stamp duty: stock exchange nominees

175(1) The Treasury may by regulations provide that where–

(a) circumstances would (apart from the regulations) give rise to a charge to stamp duty under Part I of Schedule 13 to the Finance Act 1999 (conveyance or transfer on sale) and to a charge to stamp duty reserve tax,

(b) the circumstances involve a stock exchange nominee, and

(c) the circumstances are such as are prescribed,

the charge to stamp duty shall be treated as not arising.

175(2) The power to make regulations under this section shall be exercisable by statutory instrument subject to annulment in pursuance of a resolution of the House of Commons.

175(3) In this section–

(a) **"prescribed"** means prescribed by the regulations, and

(b) **"stock exchange nominee"** means a person designated for the purposes of section 127 of the Finance Act 1976 as a nominee of The Stock Exchange by an order made by the Secretary of State under subsection (5) of that section.

Prospective repeals – S. 175 repealed by FA 1990, s. 132 and Sch. 19, Pt. VI, for instruments executed on or after a day to be appointed.

History – In s. 175(1)(a), the words "Part I of Schedule 13 to the Finance Act 1999 (conveyance or transfer on sale)" substituted for the words "the heading "Conveyance or Transfer on Sale" in Schedule 1 to the Stamp Act 1891" by FA 1999, s. 112(4) and Sch. 14, para. 23, the substitution having effect in relation to instruments executed on or after 1 October 1999.

176 Stamp duty reserve tax: stock exchange nominees

176(1) The Treasury may by regulations provide that where–

(a) circumstances would (apart from the regulations) give rise to two charges to stamp duty reserve tax,

(b) the circumstances involve a stock exchange nominee, and

(c) the circumstances are such as are prescribed,

such one of the charges as may be prescribed shall be treated as not arising.

176(2) The Treasury may by regulations provide that where–

(a) circumstances would (apart from the regulations) give rise to a charge to stamp duty reserve tax and a charge to stamp duty,

(b) the circumstances involve a stock exchange nominee, and

(c)　the circumstances are such as are prescribed,

the charge to stamp duty reserve tax shall be treated as not arising.

176(3)　The Treasury may by regulations provide that a provision of an Act by virtue of which there is no charge to stamp duty reserve tax shall also apply in circumstances which involve a stock exchange nominee and are such as are prescribed.

176(4)　The Treasury may by regulations provide that a provision of an Act by virtue of which the rate at which stamp duty reserve tax is charged is less than it would be apart from the provision shall also apply in circumstances which involve a stock exchange nominee and are such as are prescribed.

176(5)　The power to make regulations under this section shall be exercisable by statutory instrument subject to annulment in pursuance of a resolution of the House of Commons.

176(6)　In this section–

　　"prescribed" means prescribed by the regulations, and

　　"stock exchange nominee" means a person designated for the purposes of section 127 of the Finance Act 1976 as a nominee of The Stock Exchange by an order made by the Secretary of State under subsection (5) of that section.

Prospective repeals – S. 176 repealed by FA 1990, s. 132 and Sch. 19, Pt. VII, from a date to be appointed in accordance with s. 110 of that Act.

Notes – The Treasury order appointing the "abolition day" for the purposes of FA 1990, s. 107–110 was to have broadly coincided with the start of paperless trading under the Stock Exchange's planned TAURUS system (IR press release, 20 March 1990). However, on 11 March 1993 it was announced that TAURUS had been abandoned (London Stock Exchange News Release 6/93).

177　Stamp duty reserve tax: information

177　Regulations under section 98(1) of the Finance Act 1986 (administration etc. of stamp duty reserve tax) may include–

(a)　provision that notice which the regulations require to be given to the Commissioners of Inland Revenue shall be given in a manner or form specified by the Commissioners;

(b)　provision that information which the regulations require to be supplied to the Commissioners shall be supplied in a manner or form specified by the Commissioners.

Prospective repeals – S. 177 repealed by FA 1990, s. 132 and Sch. 19, Pt. VII, from a date to be appointed in accordance with s. 110 of that Act. (See note below).

Notes – SI 1986/1711, reg. 2, 4, 5: notice and information.
The Treasury order appointing the "abolition day" for the purposes of FA 1990, s. 107–110 was to have broadly coincided with the start of paperless trading under the Stock Exchange's planned TAURUS system (IR press release, 20 March 1990). However, on 11 March 1993 it was announced that TAURUS had been abandoned (London Stock Exchange News Release 6/93).

178　Setting of rates of interest

178(1)　The rate of interest applicable for the purposes of an enactment to which this section applies shall be the rate which for the purposes of that enactment is provided for by regulations made by the Treasury under this section.

178(2)　This section applies to–

(aa)　section 15A of the Stamp Act 1891;

(a)　section 8(9) of the Finance Act 1894,

(b)　section 18 of the Finance Act 1896,

(c)　section 61(5) of the Finance (1909–10) Act 1910,

(d)–(k)　[not reproduced here],

(l)　section 92 of the Finance Act 1986, [and]

(m)–(o)　[not reproduced here], and

(p)　section 110 of the Finance Act 1999.

178(3)　Regulations under this section may–

(a)　make different provision for different enactments or for different purposes of the same enactment,

(b)　either themselves specify a rate of interest for the purposes of an enactment or make provision for any such rate to be determined by reference to such rate or the average of such rates as may be referred to in the regulations,

(c)　provide for rates to be reduced below, or increased above, what they otherwise would be by specified amounts or by reference to specified formulae,

(d)　provide for rates arrived at by reference to averages to be rounded up or down,

(e) provide for circumstances in which alteration of a rate of interest is or is not to take place, and

(f) provide that alterations of rates are to have effect for periods beginning on or after a day determined in accordance with the regulations in relation to interest running from before that day as well as from or from after that day.

178(4) The power to make regulations under this section shall be exercisable by statutory instrument which shall be subject to annulment in pursuance of a resolution of the House of Commons.

178(5) Where–

(a) the rate provided for by regulations under this section as the rate applicable for the purposes of any enactment is changed, and

(b) the new rate is not specified in the regulations,

the Board shall by order specify the new rate and the day from which it has effect.

178(6) [Not reproduced here.]

178(7) Subsection (1) shall have effect for periods beginning on or after such day as the Treasury may by order made by statutory instrument appoint and shall have effect in relation to interest running from before that day as well as from or from after that day; and different days may be appointed for different enactments.

History – S. 178(2)(aa) and (p) inserted respectively for stamp duty by s. 109(2), applying to instruments executed on or after 1 October 1999 and, for interest on repayment of duty overpaid, by s. 110(9) in relation to instruments executed on or after 1 October 1999.

Statutory instruments – SI 1989/1297, as amended (see *Tax Statutes and Statutory Instruments*, vol.1B): Taxes (Interest Rate) Regulations 1989.

Notes – S. 178 is reproduced in full with relevant notes in Vol. 1A.

FINANCE ACT 1990

(1990 Chapter 29)

[*26th July 1990*]

ARRANGEMENT OF SECTIONS

PART III – STAMP DUTY AND STAMP DUTY RESERVE TAX

PART IV – MISCELLANEOUS AND GENERAL

SCHEDULES

19.   REPEALS
          Part VI – Stamp Duty
          Part VII – Stamp Duty Reserve Tax

PART III – STAMP DUTY AND STAMP DUTY RESERVE TAX

REPEALS

107   Stamp duty to be abolished on bearer instruments

107(1)   Stamp duty shall not be chargeable under Schedule 15 to the Finance Act 1999 (bearer instruments).

107(2)   Subsection (1) above applies in relation to the charge under paragraph 1 of that Schedule (charge on issue) where the instrument is issued on or after the abolition day.

107(3)   Subsection (1) above applies in relation to the charge under paragraph 2 of that Schedule (charge on transfer of stock) where the stock constituted by or transferable by means of the instrument is transferred on or after the abolition day.

History – S. 107 substituted for the previous version by FA 1999, s. 113(3) and Sch. 16, para. 12, the substitution applying in relation to bearer instruments issued on or after 1 October 1999.

Notes – The Treasury order appointing the "abolition day" for the purposes of s. 107–110 was to have broadly coincided with the start of paperless trading under the Stock Exchange's planned TAURUS system (IR press release, 20 March 1990). However, on 11 March 1993 it was announced that TAURUS had been abandoned (London Stock Exchange News Release 6/93).

S. 111(2): s. 107 to be construed as one with SA 1891.

108   Transfer of securities: abolition of stamp duty

108(1)   Where defined securities are transferred to or vested in a person by an instrument, stamp duty shall not be chargeable on the instrument.

108(2)   In this section **"defined securities"** means–

(a)   stocks, shares or loan capital,

(b)   interests in, or in dividends or other rights arising out of, stocks, shares or loan capital,

(c)   rights to allotments of or to subscribe for, or options to acquire or to dispose of, stocks, shares or loan capital, and

(d)   units under a unit trust scheme.

108(3)   In this section **"loan capital"** means–

(a)   any debenture stock, corporation stock or funded debt, by whatever name known, issued by a government or a body corporate or other body of persons (which here includes a local authority and any body whether formed or established in the United Kingdom or elsewhere);

(b)   any capital raised by a government, or by such a body as is mentioned in paragraph (a) above, if the capital is borrowed or has the character of borrowed money, and whether it is in the form of stock or any other form;

(c)   stock or marketable securities issued by a government.

108(4)   In this section **"unit"** and **"unit trust scheme"** have the same meanings as they had in Part VII of the Finance Act 1946 immediately before the abolition day.

108(5)   In this section references to a **government** include references to a government department, including a Northern Ireland department.

108(6)   In this section **"government"** means the government of the United Kingdom or of Northern Ireland or of any country or territory outside the United Kingdom.

108(7)   Subject to subsection (8) below, this section applies if the instrument is executed in pursuance of a contract made on or after the abolition day.

108(8)   In the case of an instrument–

(a)   which falls within section 67(1) or (9) of the Finance Act 1986 (depositary receipts) or section 70(1) or (9) of that Act (clearance services), or

(b)   which does not fall within section 67(1) or (9) or section 70(1) or (9) of that Act and is not executed in pursuance of a contract,

this section applies if the instrument is executed on or after the abolition day.

Notes – The Treasury order appointing the "abolition day" for the purposes of s. 107–110 was to have broadly coincided with the start of paperless trading under the Stock Exchange's planned TAURUS system (IR press release, 20 March 1990). However, on 11 March 1993 it was announced that TAURUS had been abandoned (London Stock Exchange News Release 6/93).

S. 111(2): s. 108 to be construed as one with SA 1891.

109   Stamp duty: other repeals

109(1)   Section 83 of the Stamp Act 1891 (fine for certain acts relating to securities) shall not apply where an instrument of assignment or transfer is executed, or a transfer or negotiation of the stock constituted by or transferable by means of a bearer instrument takes place, on or after the abolition day.

109(2)   The following provisions (which relate to the cancellation of certain instruments) shall not apply where the stock certificate or other instrument is entered on or after the abolition day–

(a)   section 109(1) of the Stamp Act 1891,

(b)   section 5(2) of the Finance Act 1899,

(c, d) [Repealed by FA 1999, s. 139 and Sch. 20, Pt. V(5).]

109(3)   Section 67 of the Finance Act 1963(prohibition of circulation of blank transfers) shall not apply where the sale is made on or after the abolition day; and section 16 of the Finance Act (Northern Ireland) 1963 (equivalent provision for Northern Ireland) shall not apply where the sale is made on or after the abolition day.

109(4)   No person shall be required to notify the Commissioners under section 68(1) or (2) or 71(1) or (2) of the Finance Act 1986 (depositary receipts and clearance services) if he first issues the receipts, provides the services or holds the securities as there mentioned on or after the abolition day.

109(5)   No company shall be required to notify the Commissioners under section 68(3) or 71(3) of that Act if it first becomes aware as there mentioned on or after the abolition day.

109(6)   The following provisions shall cease to have effect–

(a & b) [Repealed by FA 1999, s. 139 and Sch. 20, Pt. V(5).]

(c)   section 33 of the Finance Act 1970 (composition by financial institutions in respect of stamp duty),

(d)   section 127(7) of the Finance Act 1976 (extension of composition provisions to Northern Ireland), and

(e)   section 85 of the Finance Act 1986 (provisions about stock, marketable securities, etc.).

109(7)   The provisions mentioned in subsection (6) above shall cease to have effect as provided by the Treasury by order.

109(8)   An order under subsection (7) above–

(a)   shall be made by statutory instrument;

(b)   may make different provision for different provisions or different purposes;

(c)   may include such supplementary, incidental, consequential or transitional provisions as appear to the Treasury to be necessary or expedient.

109(9)   [Repealed by FA 1999, s. 139 and Sch. 20, Pt. V(5).]

History – The following parts of s. 109 were repealed by FA 1999, s. 139 and Sch. 20, Pt. V(5), the repeals having effect in relation to instruments executed on or after 6 February 2000: subs. (2)(c) and (d), (6)(a) and (b) and (9).

Notes – The Treasury order appointing the "abolition day" for the purposes of s. 107–110 was to have broadly coincided with the start of paperless trading under the Stock Exchange's planned TAURUS system (IR press release, 20 March 1990). However, on 11 March 1993 it was announced that TAURUS had been abandoned (London Stock Exchange News Release 6/93).

S. 111(2): s. 108 to be construed as one with SA 1891.

110   Stamp duty reserve tax: abolition

110(1)   Stamp duty reserve tax shall cease to be chargeable.

110(2)   In relation to the charge to tax under section 87 of the Finance Act 1986 subsection (1) above applies where–

(a)   the agreement to transfer is conditional and the condition is satisfied on or after the abolition day, or

(b)   the agreement is not conditional and is made on or after the abolition day.

110(3)   In relation to the charge to tax under section 93(1) of that Act subsection (1) above applies where securities are transferred, issued or appropriated on or after the abolition day (whenever the arrangement was made).

110(4)   In relation to the charge to tax under section 96(1) of that Act subsection (1) above applies where securities are transferred or issued on or after the abolition day (whenever the arrangement was made).

110(5)   In relation to the charge to tax under section 93(10) of that Act subsection (1) above applies where securities are issued or transferred on sale, under terms there mentioned, on or after the abolition day.

110(6)   In relation to the charge to tax under section 96(8) of that Act subsection (1) above applies where securities are issued or transferred on sale, under terms there mentioned, on or after the abolition day.

110(7)   Where before the abolition day securities are issued or transferred on sale under terms mentioned in section 93(10) of that Act, in construing section 93(10) the effect of subsections (1) and (3) above shall be ignored.

110(8)   Where before the abolition day securities are issued or transferred on sale under terms mentioned in section 96(8) of that Act, in construing section 96(8) the effect of subsections (1) and (4) above shall be ignored.

Notes – The Treasury order appointing the "abolition day" for the purposes of s. 107–110 was to have broadly coincided with the start of paperless trading under the Stock Exchange's planned TAURUS system (IR press release, 20 March 1990). However, on 11 March 1993 it was announced that TAURUS had been abandoned (London Stock Exchange News Release 6/93).

111   General

111(1)   In sections 107 to 110 above **"the abolition day"** means such day as may be appointed by the Treasury by order made by statutory instrument.

111(2)   Sections 107 to 109 above shall be construed as one with the Stamp Act 1891.

Cross references – FA 1991, s. 110–114: abolition of most duties other than those on land or an interest in, or right to occupy, land with effect from abolition day.
FA 1999, s. 123(3): list of provisions of FA 1999 which cease to have effect on abolition day under FA 1991, s. 111.

Notes – The Treasury order was to have broadly coincided with the start of paperless trading under the Stock Exchange's planned TAURUS system (IR press release, 20 March 1990). However, on 11 March 1993 it was announced that TAURUS had been abandoned (London Stock Exchange News Release 6/93).

PAIRED SHARES

112   Stamp duty

112(1)   [Amends FA 1988, s. 143(1)(b).]

112(2)   Subsection (1) above applies where–

(a)   the offers referred to in section 143(1) are made, or are to be made, on or after the day on which this Act is passed, and

(b)   before the offers are made, or are to be made, units comprising shares in the two companies concerned were offered (whether before or on or after the day on which this Act is passed) in circumstances where section 143 applied without the amendment made bysubsection (1) above.

113   Stamp duty reserve tax

113(1)   Section 99 of the Finance Act 1986 (stamp duty reserve tax: interpretation) shall be amended as follows.

113(2)   [Amends FA 1986, s. 99(6A)(b).]

113(3)   [Inserts FA 1986, s. 99(6B)]

113(4)   [Repealed by FA 1999, s. 139 and Sch. 20, Pt. V(5).]

113(5)   Subsection (2) above applies where–

(a)   the offers referred to in section 99(6A) are made on or after the day on which this Act is passed, and

(b)   before the offers are made, units comprising shares in the two companies concerned were offered (whether before or on or after the day on which this Act is passed) in circumstances where section 99(6A) applied without the amendment made by subsection (2) above.

113(6)   Subsections (3) and (4) above apply where–

(a)   the shares referred to in section 99(6B) are issued on or after the day on which this Act is passed, and

(b)   before they are issued, units comprising shares in the two companies concerned were offered (whether before or on or after the day on which this Act is passed) in circumstances where section 99(6A) applied without the amendment made by subsection (2) above.

History – S. 113(4), which amended FA 1986, s. 99(9), repealed by FA 1999, s. 139 and Sch. 20, Pt. V(5), the repeal having effect in relation to instruments executed on or after 6 February 2000.

INTERNATIONAL ORGANISATIONS

114   International organisations

114(1)   [Inserts FA 1984, s. 126(3)(d).]

114(2)   Where an organisation or body is designated under section 126(1) or (4) before the day on which this Act is passed, subsection (1) above applies in relation to the issue of securities by the organisation or body on or after that day.

114(3)   Where an organisation or body is designated under section 126(1) or (4) on or after the day on which this Act is passed, subsection (1) above applies in relation to the issue of securities by the organisation or body after the designation.

PART IV – MISCELLANEOUS AND GENERAL

GENERAL

132   Repeals

132(1)   The enactments specified in Schedule 19 to this Act (which include spent or unnecessary enactments) are hereby repealed to the extent specified in the third column of that Schedule, but subject to any provision at the end of any Part of that Schedule.

133   Short title

133   This Act may be cited as the Finance Act 1990.

SCHEDULES

SCHEDULE 19 – REPEALS

Section 132

Part VI – Stamp Duty

Chapter	Short title	Extent of repeal
1891 c. 39.	The Stamp Act 1891.	In section 59(1), the words "or stock, or marketable securities,". Section 83. Section 109(1). Schedule 1, the whole of the heading beginning "Bearer Instrument", and paragraph (1) of the general exemptions at the end of the Schedule.
1899 c.9.	The Finance Act 1899.	Section 5(2).
1946 c. 64	The Finance Act 1946.	Section 54(3) and (4). Section 56. Section 57(2A) to (4).
1946 c.17 (N.I.).	The Finance (No. 2) Act (Northern Ireland) 1946.	Section 25(3) and (4). Section 27. Section 28(2) to (4).
1947 c. 35.	The Finance Act 1947.	Section 57.
1948 c. 49.	The Finance Act 1948.	Section 74.

Chapter	Short title	Extent of repeal
1950 c. 32 (N.I.).	The Finance (No. 2) Act (Northern Ireland) 1950.	Section 3(1).
1951 c. 43.	The Finance Act 1951.	Section 42.
1963 c. 18.	The Stock Transfer Act 1963.	In section 2(3), in paragraph (a) the words ''and section 56(4) of the Finance Act 1946'', and paragraph (c) and the word ''and'' immediately preceeding it.
1963 c. 25.	The Finance Act 1963.	Section 55(1A).
		In section 59, subsections (1) to (4).
		Section 60.
		Section 61.
		In section 62, in subsection (1) the words from ''and any''.
		Section 65(1).
		Section 67.
1963 c. 22. (N.I.).	The Finance Act (Northern Ireland) 1963.	Section 4(1A).
		In section 8, subsections (1) to (4).
		Section 9.
		Section 10.
		In section 11, in subsection (1) the words from ''and any'' to the end, and subsection (3).
		Section 14(1).
		Section 16.
1963 c. 24 (N.I.).	The Stock Transfer Act (Northern Ireland) 1963.	In section 2(3), in paragraph (a) the words ''and section 27(4) of the Finance (No. 2) Act (Northern Ireland) 1946'', and paragraph (c) and the word ''and'' immediately preceeding.
1967 c. 54.	The Finance Act 1967.	Section 30.
1967 c. 20 (N.I.).	The Finance Act (Northern Ireland) 1967.	Section 7.
1970 c. 24.	The Finance Act 1970.	Section 33.
		In Schedule 7, paragraph 6.
1970 c. 21 (N.I.).	The Finance Act (Northern Ireland) 1970.	In Schedule 2, paragraph 6.
1974 c. 30	The Finance Act 1974.	In Schedule 11, paragraphs 2 and 12.
1975 c. 80.	The OECD Support Fund Act 1975.	Section 4(2).
1976 c. 40.	The Finance Act 1976.	In section 127, subsections (1) and (4) to (7).
		Section 131(3.
1980 c. 48.	The Finance Act 1980.	Section 101.
1984 c. 43.	The Finance Act 1984.	Section 126(3)(c) and (5).
1985 c. 6.	The Companies Act 1985.	In Schedule 14, in paragraph 8 the words from ''and, unless''.
1985 c. 54.	The Finance Act 1985.	Section 81.
1986 c. 41.	The Finance Act 1986.	Section 64(1).
		Section 65 to 72.
		Section 77.
		In section 79, subsections (2) to (8), and in subsection (12) the words ''(7), (9),''.
SI 1986/1032 (N.I.).	The Companies (Northern Ireland) Order 1986.	Schedule 14, in paragraph 7 the words from ''unless''.
1987 c. 16.	The Finance Act 1987.	Sections 50 to 53.

Chapter	Short title	Extent of repeal
1987 c. 51.	The Finance (No. 2) Act 1987.	Section 99.
1988 c. 39.	The Finance Act 1988.	Section 143.
		In Schedule 13, paragraph 19.
1989 c. 26.	The Finance Act 1989.	Sections 174 and 175.

1 So far as these repeals relate to bearer instruments, they have effect in accordance with section 107 of this Act.

2 So far as these repeals relate to instruments other than bearer instruments, they have effect in accordance with section 108 of this Act.

3 So far as these repeals relate to–

(a)   any provision mentioned in subsection (1), (2), (3), (4) or (5) of section 109 of this Act, or

(b)   any other provision to the extent that it is ancillary to or dependent on any provision so mentioned,

the repeals have effect in accordance with the subsection concerned.

4 So far as these repeals relate to–

(a)   any provision mentioned in section 109(6) of this Act, or

(b)   any other provision to the extent that it is ancillary to or dependent on any provision so mentioned,

the repeals have effect in accordance with any order under section 109(7) of this Act.

5 Paragraphs 1 and 2 above have effect subject to paragraphs 3 and 4 above.

Notes – The Treasury order appointing the "abolition day" for the purposes of s. 107–110 was to have broadly coincided with the start of paperless trading under the Stock Exchange's planned TAURUS system (IR press release, 20 March 1990). However, on 11 March 1993 it was announced that TAURUS had been abandoned (London Stock Exchange News Release 6/93).

Part VII – Stamp Duty Reserve Tax

Chapter	Short title	Extent of repeal
1986 c. 41.	The Finance Act 1986.	Part IV
1986 c. 16.	The Finance Act 1987.	Section 56
		Schedule 7.
1987 c. 51	The Finance Act (No. 2) Act 1987.	Section 100.
1988 c. 39.	The Finance Act 1988.	Section 144
		In Schedule 13, paragraph 23
1989 c. 26.	The Finance Act 1989.	Sections 176 and 177

These repeals have effect in accordance with section 110 of this Act.

Notes – The Treasury order appointing the "abolition day" for the purposes of s. 107–110 was to have broadly coincided with the start of paperless trading under the Stock Exchange's planned TAURUS system (IR press release, 20 March 1990). However, on 11 March 1993 it was announced that TAURUS had been abandoned (London Stock Exchange News Release 6/93).

FINANCE ACT 1991

(1991 Chapter 31)

[*25th July 1991*]

ARRANGEMENT OF SECTIONS

PART IV – STAMP DUTY AND STAMP DUTY RESERVE TAX

PART V – MISCELLANEOUS AND GENERAL

GENERAL

PART IV – STAMP DUTY AND STAMP DUTY RESERVE TAX

110　Stamp duty abolished in certain cases

110(1)　Where apart from this section stamp duty under any of the provisions of Schedule 13 to the Finance Act 1999 would be chargeable on an instrument, stamp duty shall not be so chargeable if the property consists entirely of exempt property.

110(2)–(4)　[Substituted by FA 1999, s. 112(4) and Sch. 14, para. 25: see history note below.]

110(5)　For the purposes of this section **exempt property** is property other than–

(a)　land,

(b)　[repealed by Trusts of Land and Appointment of Trustees Act 1996, s. 25(2) and Sch. 4],

(c)　a licence to occupy land.

110(6)　This section applies to–

(a)　an instrument executed in pursuance of a contract made on or after the abolition day;

(b)　an instrument which is not executed in pursuance of a contract and is executed on or after the abolition day.

110(7)　For the purposes of this section the **abolition day** is such day as may be appointed under section 111(1) of the Finance Act 1990 (abolition of stamp duty for securities etc).

History – S. 110(1) substituted for s. 110(1)–(4) by FA 1999, s. 112(4) and Sch. 14, para. 25, the substitution having effect in relation to instruments executed on or after 1 October 1999 but FA 1999, s. 112 and Sch. 14 do not apply to certain transfers or other instruments relating to units under a unit trust scheme (FA 1999, s. 122(1) and (2)). The repeal took effect with regards to certain transfers or other instruments relating to units under a unit trust scheme on their execution on or after 6 February 2000 (FA 1999, s. 122(4) and FA 1999, Sch. 19).

Former s. 110(3)(e) repealed and former subs. (4), amended by FA 1994, s. 258 and Sch. 26, Pt. VII(1), in relation to instruments executed after 7 December 1993, not being instruments executed in pursuance of a contract made before 30 November 1993.

S. 110(5)(b) repealed by Trusts of Land and Appointment of Trustees Act 1996, s. 25(2) and Sch. 4, with effect from 1 January 1997 (SI 1996/2974).

Note – The abolition day was to have broadly coincided with the implementation of the TAURUS system (London Stock Exchange News Release 40/91, 17 October 1991). However, on 11 March 1993 it was announced that TAURUS had been abandoned (London Stock Exchange News Release 6/93).

111　Stamp duty reduced in certain cases

111(1)　This section applies where–

(a)　stamp duty under Part I of Schedule 13 to the Finance Act 1999 (conveyance or transfer on sale) is chargeable on an instrument to which this section applies, and

(b)   part of the property concerned consists of exempt property.

111(2)   In such a case–

(a)   the consideration in respect of which duty would be charged (apart from this section) shall be apportioned, on such basis as is just and reasonable, as between the part of the property which consists of exempt property and the part which does not, and

(b)   the instrument shall be charged only in respect of the consideration attributed to such of the property as is not exempt property.

111(3)   In this section **"exempt property"** has the same meaning as in section 110 above.

111(4)   This section applies to–

(a)   an instrument executed in pursuance of a contract made on or after the abolition day;

(b)   an instrument which is not executed in pursuance of a contract and is executed on or after the abolition day.

111(5)   In this section **"the abolition day"** has the same meaning as in section 110 above.

History – In s. 111(1), the words "Part I of Schedule 13 to the Finance Act 1999 (conveyance or transfer on sale)" substituted for the words "the heading "conveyance or transfer on sale" in Schedule 1 to the Stamp Act 1891" by FA 1999, s. 112(4) and Sch. 14, para. 26, the substitution having effect in relation to instruments executed on or after 1 October 1999 but FA 1999, s. 112 and Sch. 14 do not apply to certain transfers or other instruments relating to units under a unit trust scheme (FA 1999, s. 122(1) and (2)).

Note – The abolition day was to have broadly coincided with the implementation of the TAURUS system (London Stock Exchange News Release 40/91, 17 October 1991). However, on 11 March 1993 it was announced that TAURUS had been abandoned (London Stock Exchange News Release 6/93).

112   Apportionment of consideration for stamp duty purposes

112(1)   Subsection (2) below applies where part of the property referred to in section 58(1) of the Stamp Act 1891 (consideration to be apportioned between different instruments as parties think fit) consists of exempt property.

112(2)   Section 58(1) shall have effect as if "the parties think fit" read "is just and reasonable".

112(3)   Subsection (4) below applies where–

(a)   part of the property referred to in section 58(2) of the Stamp Act 1891 (property contracted to be purchased by two or more persons etc.) consists of exempt property, and

(b)   both or (as the case may be) all the relevant persons are connected with one another.

112(4)   Section 58(2) shall have effect as if the words from "for distinct parts of the consideration" to the end of the subsection read ", the consideration is to be apportioned in such manner as is just and reasonable, so that a distinct consideration for each separate part or parcel is set forth in the conveyance relating thereto, and such conveyance is to be charged with *ad valorem* duty in respect of such distinct consideration."

112(5)   In a case where subsection (2) or (4) above applies and the consideration is apportioned in a manner that is not just and reasonable, the enactments relating to stamp duty shall have effect as if–

(a)   the consideration had been apportioned in a manner that is just and reasonable, and

(b)   the amount of any distinct consideration set forth in any conveyance relating to a separate part or parcel of property were such amount as is found by a just and reasonable apportionment (and not the amount actually set forth).

112(6)   In this section **"exempt property"** has the same meaning as in section 110 above.

112(7)   For the purposes of subsection (3) above–

(a)   a person is a **relevant person** if he is a person by or for whom the property is contracted to be purchased;

(b)   the question whether persons are **connected** with one another shall be determined in accordance with section 839 of the Taxes Act 1988.

112(8)   This section applies where the contract concerned is made on or after the abolition day.

112(9)   In this section **"the abolition day"** has the same meaning as in section 110 above.

Notes – The abolition day was to have broadly coincided with the implementation of the TAURUS system (London Stock Exchange News Release 40/91, 17 October 1991). However, on 11 March 1993 it was announced that TAURUS had been abandoned (London Stock Exchange News Release 6/93).

113   Certification of instruments for stamp duty purposes

113(1)   For the purposes of paragraph 6(1) of Schedule 13 to the Finance Act 1999 (meaning of instrument being certified at an amount)–

(a)   a sale or contract or agreement for the sale of exempt property within the meaning of section 110 above shall be disregarded; and

(b)   any statement as mentioned in that provision shall be construed as leaving out of account any matter which is to be so disregarded.

113(2)   [Substituted by FA 1999, s. 112(4)) and Sch. 14, para. 27: see history note below.]

113(3)   [Substituted by FA 1999, s. 112(4)) and Sch. 14, para. 27: see history note below.]

113(4)   This section applies to–

(a)   an instrument executed in pursuance of a contract made on or after the abolition day;

(b)   an instrument which is not executed in pursuance of a contract and is executed on or after the abolition day.

113(5)   In this section **"the abolition day"** has the same meaning as in section 110 above.

History – S. 113(1) substituted for s. 113(1)–(3) by FA 1999, s. 112(4) and Sch. 14, para. 27, the substitution having effect in relation to instruments executed on or after 1 October 1999 but FA 1999, s. 112 and Sch. 14 do not apply to certain transfers or other instruments relating to units under a unit trust scheme (FA 1999, s. 122(1) and (2)). The repeal took effect with regards to certain transfers or other instruments relating to units under a unit trust scheme on their execution on or after 6 February 2000 (FA 1999, s. 122(4) and FA 1999, Sch. 19).

Notes – The abolition day was to have broadly coincided with the implementation of the TAURUS system (London Stock Exchange News Release 40/91, 17 October 1991). However, on 11 March 1993 it was announced that TAURUS had been abandoned (London Stock Exchange News Release 6/93).

114   Acquisition under statute: exempt property

114(1)   Section 36 of the Finance Act 1949 and section 9 of the Finance Act (Northern Ireland) 1949 shall be amended as mentioned in subsections (2) and (3) below.

114(2)   In subsection (4) of each of those sections (goods not affected by section 12 of the Finance Act 1895, which relates to duty on property acquired under statute) for the words "goods, wares or merchandise" (in each place where they occur) there shall be substituted the words "exempt property".

114(3)   In each of those sections the following subsection shall be inserted after subsection (4)–

    "(5) In subsection (4) above **"exempt property"** has the same meaning as in section 110 of the Finance Act 1991."

114(4)   This section applies where the Act mentioned in section 12 of the Finance Act 1895, and by virtue of which property is vested or a person is authorised to purchase property, is passed on or after the abolition day.

114(5)   In this section **"the abolition day"** has the same meaning as in section 110 above.

Note – The abolition day was to have broadly coincided with the implementation of the TAURUS system (London Stock Exchange News Release 40/91, 17 October 1991). However, on 11 March 1993 it was announced that TAURUS had been abandoned (London Stock Exchange News Release 6/93).

115   Northern Ireland bank notes: duty abolished

115   [Repealed by FA 1999, s. 139 and Sch. 20, Pt. V(2) in relation to instruments executed, or bearer instruments issued, on or after 1 October 1999 but, as regards unit trust schemes, subject to FA 1999, Sch. 20, Pt. V(2), para. (2). The repeal took effect from 6 February 2000 as regards unit trust schemes, by virtue of FA 1999, s. 122(4) and FA 1999, Sch. 19.]

116   Investment exchanges and clearing houses: stamp duty

116(1)   The Treasury may make regulations providing as mentioned in this section with regard to any circumstances which–

(a)   would (apart from the regulations) give rise to a charge to stamp duty,

(b)   involve a prescribed recognised investment exchange or a prescribed recognised clearing house, or a member or nominee (or member or nominee of a prescribed description) of such an exchange, or a nominee (or nominee of a prescribed description) of such a clearing house, or a nominee (or nominee of a prescribed description) of a member of such an exchange, and

(c)   are such as are prescribed.

116(2)   The regulations may provide that the charge to stamp duty shall be treated as not arising or (depending on the terms of the regulations) as reduced.

116(3)   Regulations under this section–

(a)   shall be made by statutory instrument subject to annulment in pursuance of a resolution of the House of Commons;

(b)   may include such supplementary, incidental, consequential or transitional provisions as appear to the Treasury to be necessary or expedient;

(c)   may make different provision for different circumstances;

(d)   may make any provision in such way as the Treasury think fit (whether by amending enactments or otherwise).

116(4)   In this section–

(a)   **"prescribed"** means prescribed by the regulations,

(b)   **"recognised investment exchange"** means a recognised investment exchange within the meaning of the Financial Services Act 1986, and

(c)   **"recognised clearing house"** means a recognised clearing house within the meaning of that Act.

Statutory instruments – SI 1992/570 (instruments executed before 20 October 1997): introduced following the merger of two London exchanges to form LIFFE (the London International Financial Futures and Options Exchange). SI 1997/2429 (instruments executed on or after 20 October 1997): prescribed stamp duty reliefs in relation to transactions involving members of LIFFE and The London Clearing House Limited or its nominees. SI 1999/3262 (instruments executed on or after 29 December 1999): prescribed stamp duty reliefs when securities are transferred (as a result of options being exercised or under futures contracts) to OM London Exchange Limited or its nominees acting in a clearing capacity.

Notes – FA 1997, s. 98: repurchases and lending of stock.

117   Investment exchanges and clearing houses: SDRT

117(1)   The Treasury may make regulations providing as mentioned in this section with regard to any circumstances which–

(a)   would (apart from the regulations) give rise to a charge to stamp duty reserve tax,

(b)   involve a prescribed recognised investment exchange or a prescribed recognised clearing house, or a member or nominee (or member or nominee of a prescribed description) of such an exchange, or a nominee (or nominee of a prescribed description) of such a clearing house, or a nominee (or nominee of a prescribed description) of a member of such an exchange, and

(c)   are such as are prescribed.

117(2)   The regulations may provide that the charge to stamp duty reserve tax shall be treated as not arising or (depending on the terms of the regulations) as reduced.

117(3)   Subsections (3) or (4) of section 116 above shall apply for the purposes of this section as they apply for the purposes of that.

Statutory instruments – SI 1992/570 (instruments executed before 20 October 1997): introduced following the merger of two London exchanges to form LIFFE (the London International Financial Futures and Options Exchange). SI 1995/2051: prescribed exemptions from stamp duty reserve tax for the London Clearing House as clearing house for Tradepoint. SI 1997/2429 (agreements made, etc., on or after 20 October 1997): prescribed stamp duty reserve tax reliefs in relation to transactions involving members of LIFFE and The London Clearing House Limited or its nominees. SI 1999/3262 (instruments executed on or after 29 December 1999): prescribed stamp duty reserve tax reliefs for agreements to transfer securities (as a result of options being exercised or under futures contracts) to OM London Exchange Limited or its nominees acting in a clearing capacity.

Notes – FA 1986, s. 87 principal charge to SDRT.

PART V – MISCELLANEOUS AND GENERAL

GENERAL

124   Short title

124   This Act may be cited as the Finance Act 1991.

FINANCE (NO. 2) ACT 1992

(1992 Chapter 48)

[*16th July 1992*]

PART III – MISCELLANEOUS AND GENERAL

MISCELLANEOUS

77 Northern Ireland Electricity

77   Schedule 17 to this Act (which makes provision in relation to the transfer of the undertaking of Northern Ireland Electricity) shall have effect.

SCHEDULES

SCHEDULE 17 – NORTHERN IRELAND ELECTRICITY

STAMP DUTY RESERVE TAX

10(1)   No agreement made for the purposes of or for purposes connected with the transfer scheme shall give rise to a charge to stamp duty reserve tax.

10(2)   No agreement which is made in pursuance of Schedule 10 to the Order shall give rise to a charge to stamp duty reserve tax.

10(3)   This paragraph shall be deemed to have come into force on 1st April 1992.

Notes – The Order referred to in para. 10(2) is the Electricity (Northern Ireland) Order 1992 (SI 1992/231 (NI 1)).

FINANCE ACT 1993

(1993 Chapter 34)

[*27th July 1993*]

ARRANGEMENT OF SECTIONS

PART V – STAMP DUTY

PART VI – MISCELLANEOUS AND GENERAL

STATUTORY EFFECT OF RESOLUTIONS ETC.

PART V – STAMP DUTY

201   Increase in stamp duty threshold

201   [Repealed by FA 1999, s. 139 and Sch. 20, Pt. V(2) in relation to instruments executed, or bearer instruments issued, on or after 1 October 1999 but, as regards unit trust schemes, subject to FA 1999, Sch. 20, Pt. V(2), para. 2. The repeal took effect from 6 February 2000 as regards unit trust schemes, by virtue of FA 1999, s. 122(4) and FA 1999, Sch. 19.]

202   Rent to mortgage: England and Wales

202(1)   Subsection (2) below applies where–

(a)   a person exercises the right to acquire on rent to mortgage terms under Part V of the Housing Act 1985, and

(b)   in pursuance of the exercise of that right a conveyance of the freehold is executed in his favour as regards the dwelling-house concerned.

202(2)   For the purposes of the enactments relating to stamp duty chargeable under Part I of Schedule 13 to the Finance Act 1999 (conveyance or transfer on sale), the consideration for the sale shall be taken to be equal to the price which, by virtue of section 126 of the Housing Act 1985, would be payable for the dwelling-house on a conveyance if the person were exercising the right to buy under Part V of that Act.

202(3)   Subsection (4) below applies where–

(a)   a person exercises the right to acquire on rent to mortgage terms under Part V of the Housing Act 1985, and

(b)   in pursuance of the exercise of that right a lease is executed in his favour as regards the dwelling-house concerned.

202(4)   In such a case–

(a)   the lease shall not be chargeable with stamp duty under Part II of Schedule 13 to the Finance Act 1999 (lease) but shall be chargeable with stamp duty under Part I of that Schedule (conveyance or transfer on sale) as if it were a conveyance on sale;

(b)   for the purposes of the enactments relating to stamp duty chargeable under Part I of that Schedule the consideration for the sale mentioned in paragraph (a) above shall be taken to be equal to the price which, by virtue of section 126 of the Housing Act 1985, would be payable for the dwelling-house on a grant if the person were exercising the right to buy under Part V of that Act.

202(5)   This section shall apply where the conveyance or lease is executed after the day on which this Act is passed.

History – In s. 202 the following amendments were made by FA 1999, s. 112(4) and Sch. 14, para. 28 in relation to instruments executed on or after 1 October 1999:

- in subs. (2), the words "Part I of Schedule 13 to the Finance Act 1999 (conveyance or transfer on sale)" substituted for the words "the heading "Conveyance or Transfer on Sale" in Schedule 1 to the Stamp Act 1891";
- in subs. (4)(a), the words
  - (a)   "Part II of Schedule 13 to the Finance Act 1999 (lease)" substituted for the words "the heading "Lease or Tack" in Schedule 1 to the Stamp Act 1891", and
  - (b)   the words "Part I of that Schedule (conveyance or transfer on sale)" substituted for the words "the heading "Conveyance or Transfer on Sale" in that Schedule"; and
- in subs. (4)(b), the words "Part I of that Schedule" substituted for the words "the heading "Conveyance or Transfer on Sale"".

203   Rent to loan: Scotland

203(1)   Subsection (2) below applies where–

(a)   a person exercises the right to purchase a house by way of the rent to loan scheme under Part III of the Housing (Scotland) Act 1987, and

(b)   in pursuance of the exercise of that right a heritable disposition of the house is executed in favour of him.

203(2)   For the purposes of the enactments relating to stamp duty chargeable under Part I of Schedule 13 to the Finance Act 1999 (conveyance or transfer on sale), the consideration for the sale shall be taken to be equal to the price which, by virtue of section 62 of the Housing (Scotland) Act 1987, would be payable for the house if the person were exercising the right to purchase under section 61 of that Act.

203(3)   This section shall apply where the disposition is executed after the day on which this Act is passed.

History – In s. 203(2), the words "Part I of Schedule 13 to the Finance Act 1999 (conveyance or transfer on sale)" substituted for the words "the heading "Conveyance or Transfer on Sale" in Schedule 1 to the Stamp Act 1891" by FA 1999, s. 112(4) and Sch. 14, para. 29, the substitution having effect in relation to instruments executed on or after 1 October 1999.

204   Method of denoting stamp duty

204(1)   The Treasury may make regulations as to the method by which stamp duty is to be denoted.

204(2)   In particular, regulations under this section may–

(a)   provide for duty to be denoted by impressed stamps or adhesive stamps or by a record printed or made by a machine or implement or by such other method as may be prescribed;

(b)   provide for one method only to be used, whether generally or in prescribed cases;

(c)   provide for alternative methods to be available, whether generally or in prescribed cases;

(d)   make different provision for different cases;

and cases may be designated by reference to the type of instrument concerned, the geographical area involved, or such other factors as the Treasury think fit.

204(3)   Regulations under this section may provide that where stamp duty is denoted by a method which (in the case of the instrument concerned) is required or permitted by the law in force at the time it is stamped, for the purposes of section 14(4) of the Stamp Act 1891 (instruments not to be given in evidence etc. unless stamped in accordance with the law in force at the time of execution) the method shall be treated as being in accordance with the law in force at the time when the instrument was executed.

204(4)   Regulations under this section may include such supplementary, incidental, consequential or transitional provisions as appear to the Treasury to be necessary or expedient.

204(5)   Regulations under this section may make provision in such way as the Treasury think fit, and in particular may amend or repeal or modify the effect of any provision of any Act.

204(6)   In this section **"prescribed"** means prescribed by regulations under this section.

204(7)   The power to make regulations under this section shall be exercisable by statutory instrument subject to annulment in pursuance of a resolution of the House of Commons.

History – In s. 204(3) the word "first" (which appeared before the words "execution" and "executed" respectively) repealed by FA 2000, s. 156 and Sch. 40, Pt. III, the repeal having effect from 28 July 2000.

PART VI – MISCELLANEOUS AND GENERAL

STATUTORY EFFECT OF RESOLUTIONS ETC.

207   Stamp duty

207(1)   [Amends FA 1973, s. 50(2)(a) and (d).]

207(2)   This section shall apply in relation to resolutions passed after the day on which this Act is passed.

FINANCE ACT 1994

(1994 Chapter 9)

[3rd May 1994]

ARRANGEMENT OF SECTIONS

PART VI – STAMP DUTY

PART VI – STAMP DUTY

239   Execution of deeds

239(1)   In section 122 of the Stamp Act 1891 (definitions)–

(a)   [Inserts Stamp Act 1891, s. 122 (1A).]

(b)   [Amends Stamp Act 1891, s. 122(1).]

239(2)   [Amends Stamp Duties Management Act 1891, s. 27.]

239(3)   This section shall apply to any instrument except one which, on or before 7th December 1993, has been executed for the purposes of the Stamp Act 1891 as that Act has effect before amendment by this section.

240   Time for presenting agreement for lease

240(1)   This section applies if there are presented for stamping at the same time in pursuance of Schedule 13 to the Finance Act 1999–

(a)   an agreement for a lease, and

(b)   the lease which gives effect to the agreement, and the duty (if any) chargeable on the agreement is paid.

240(2)   Section 15A of that Act (interest payable on late stamping) applies in relation to the agreement as if the reference to the day on which the instrument was executed were to the day on which the lease was executed.

240(3)   For the purposes of section 15B of that Act (penalty on late stamping) the agreement is treated–

(a)   as if it had been executed at the same time and place as the lease, and

(b)   where the lease was executed outside the United Kingdom, as if it had been first received in the United Kingdom at the same time as the lease.

240(4)   For the purposes of this section a lease gives effect to an agreement if the lease is granted subsequent to the agreement and either is in conformity with the agreement or relates to substantially the same property and term as the agreement.

240(5)   References in this section to an agreement for a lease include missives of let in Scotland.

History – S. 240 and 240A substituted for the previous version of s. 240 by FA 1999, s. 109(3) and Sch. 12, para. 4, the substitution applying to instruments executed on or after 1 October 1999.

Cross reference – FA 1999, Sch. 18, para. 4: where referring to the duration of a lease, the expression "term" in relation to Scotland means "period".

Other material – Law Society's Gazette, 6 July 1994 (see Misc. 303): Revenue guidance on procedure for stamping leases and agreements for leases. Inland Revenue Tax Bulletin, Issue 18, August 1995, p. 234: presentation of the agreement with the lease, within 30 days after the execution of the lease, will be accepted as satisfying the requirement under FA 1931, s. 28 to produce the agreement.

Note – S. 240(2) and 240(3) refer to s. 15A and 15B "of that Act" respectively, i.e. of FA 1999. Apparently, they should refer to s. 15A and 15B of the Stamp Act 1891, as substituted by FA 1999, s. 109(1).

240A   Requirements before lease treated as duly stamped

240A(1)   A lease shall not be treated as duly stamped unless–

(a)   it contains a certificate that there is no agreement to which it gives effect, or

(b)   it is stamped with a stamp denoting–

       (i) that there is an agreement to which it gives effect which is not chargeable with duty, or

       (ii) the duty paid on the agreement to which it gives effect.

240A(2)   For the purposes of this section a lease gives effect to an agreement if the lease is granted subsequent to the agreement and either is in conformity with the agreement or relates to substantially the same property and term as the agreement.

240A(3)   References in this section to a lease do not include, and references in this section to an agreement do include, missives of let in Scotland.

History – S. 240A and 240 above substituted for the previous version of s. 240 by FA 1999, s. 109(3) and Sch. 12, para. 4, the substitution applying to instruments executed on or after 1 October 1999.

241   Exchange, partition, etc.

241(1)   Where–

(a)   the consideration for the transfer or vesting of any estate or interest in land or the grant of any lease consists of or includes any property, and

(b)   for the purposes of stamp duty chargeable under or by reference to Part I of Schedule 13 to the Finance Act 1999 (conveyance or transfer on sale) no amount or value is, apart from this section, attributed to that property on that transfer, vesting or grant,

then, for those purposes, the consideration or, as the case may be, the consideration so far as relating to that property shall be taken to be the market value of the property immediately before the instrument in question is executed and accordingly the instrument shall be charged with ad valorem duty under that heading.

241(2)   For the purposes of this section the market value of property at any time is the price which that property might reasonably be expected to fetch on a sale at that time in the open market.

241(3)–(5)   [Repealed by FA 1999, s. 139 and Sch. 20, Pt. V(2).]

241(6)   This section shall apply to instruments executed after 7th December 1993, not being instruments executed in pursuance of a contract made before 30th November 1993.

History – In s. 241(1)(a), the word "lease" substituted for the words "lease or tack" and, in (1)(b), the words "Part I of Schedule 13 to the Finance Act 1999 (conveyance or transfer on sale)" substituted for the words "the heading "Conveyance or Transfer on Sale" in Schedule 1 to the Stamp Act 1891" by FA 1999, s. 112(4) and Sch. 14, para. 30, the substitution having effect in relation to instruments executed on or after 1 October 1999.
S. 241(3)-(5) repealed by FA 1999, s. 139 and Sch. 20, Pt. V(2), the repeal having effect in relation to instruments executed, or bearer instruments issued, on or after 1 October 1999 but, as regards unit trust schemes, subject to FA 1999, Sch. 20, Pt. V(2), para. 2. The repeal took effect from 6 February 2000 as regards unit trust schemes, by virtue of FA 1999, s. 122(4) and FA 1999, Sch. 19.

Other material – IR press release, 18 April 1994: guidance on aspects of stamp duty charge on exchange of properties.

242   Where consideration not ascertainable from conveyance or lease

242(1)   Where, for the purposes of stamp duty chargeable under or by reference to Part I of Schedule 13 to the Finance Act 1999 (conveyance or transfer on sale), the consideration, or any part of the consideration, for–

(a)   the transfer or vesting of any estate or interest in land, or

(b)   the grant of any lease,

cannot, apart from this subsection, be ascertained at the time the instrument in question is executed, the consideration for the transfer, vesting or grant shall for those purposes be taken to be the market value immediately before the instrument is executed of the estate or interest transferred or vested or, as the case may be, the lease granted.

242(2)   Where, for the purposes of stamp duty chargeable under paragraph 12 of Schedule 13 to the Finance Act 1999, the rent, or any part of the rent, payable under any lease cannot, apart from this subsection, be ascertained at the time it is executed, the rent shall for those purposes be taken to be the market rent at that time.

242(3)   For the purposes of this section–

(a)   the cases where consideration or rent cannot be ascertained at any time do not include cases where the consideration or rent could be ascertained on the assumption that any future event mentioned in the instrument in question were or were not to occur, and

(b)   the market rent of a lease at any time is the rent which the lease might reasonably be expected to fetch at that time in the open market,

and in this section **"market value"** has the same meaning as in section 241 above.

242(4)   This section shall apply to instruments executed after 7th December 1993.

History – In s. 242, the following amendments were made by FA 1999, s. 112(4) and Sch. 14, para. 31, the amendments having effect in relation to instruments executed on or after 1 October 1999:
- in subs. (1) (twice), (2) and (3) (twice) the word "lease" substituted for the words "lease or tack";
- in the opening words of subs. (1), the words "Part I of Schedule 13 to the Finance Act 1999 (conveyance or transfer on sale)" substituted for the words "the heading "Conveyance or Transfer on Sale" in Schedule 1 to the Stamp Act 1891"; and
- in subs. (2), the words "paragraph 12 of Schedule 13 to the Finance Act 1999" substituted for the words "paragraph (3) of the heading "Lease or Tack" in Schedule 1 to that Act".

Other material – IR Tax Bulletin, Issue 18, August 1995, p. 235 (not reproduced): Revenue approach to applying contingency principle (s. 242(3)(a)).

243   Agreements to surrender leases

243(1)   Where, in pursuance of any agreement, any lease is surrendered (or, in Scotland, renounced) at any time otherwise than by deed, the agreement shall be treated for the purposes of stamp duty as if it were a deed executed at that time effecting the surrender (or, as the case may be, renunciation).

243(2)   This section shall apply to any agreement made after 7th December 1993.

History – In s. 243(1), the words "stamp duty" substituted for the words "any duty chargeable under the Stamp Act 1891" by FA 1999, s. 112(4) and Sch. 14, para. 32 in relation to instruments executed on or after 1 October 1999.

244   Production of documents on transfer of land in Northern Ireland

244(1)   Subject to section 245 below, on the occasion of–

(a)   any transfer on sale of any freehold interest in land in Northern Ireland, or

(b)   the grant, or any transfer on sale, of any lease of such land,

the transferee, lessee or proposed lessee shall produce to the Commissioners the instrument by means of which the transfer is effected or the lease granted or agreed to be granted, as the case may be.

244(2)   Any transferee, lessee or proposed lessee required to produce any instrument under subsection (1) above shall produce with it a document (signed by him or by some person on his behalf and showing his address) giving such particulars as may be prescribed.

244(3)   Any person who, within thirty days–

(a)   after the execution of an instrument which he is required under subsection (1) above to produce, or

(b)   in the case of such an instrument executed at a place outside Northern Ireland, after it is first received in Northern Ireland,

fails to comply with that subsection or subsection (2) above shall be liable on summary conviction to a fine not exceeding level 1 on the standard scale.

244(4)   Where any agreement for any lease of land in Northern Ireland is produced to the Commissioners together with a document (signed as mentioned in subsection (2) above) giving such particulars as may be prescribed–

(a)   it shall not be necessary to produce to them the instrument granting the lease, or any further such document as is referred to in that subsection, unless that instrument is inconsistent with the agreement, but

(b)   the Commissioners shall, if any such instrument is produced to them and application is made for that purpose, denote on the instrument that it has been produced to them.

244(5)   Notwithstanding anything in section 12 of the Stamp Act 1891, no instrument required by this section to be produced to the Commissioners shall be deemed, for the purposes of section 14 of that Act, to be duly stamped unless it is stamped with a stamp denoting that the instrument has been so produced.

History – S. 244 brought into force on 4 November 1996 by SI 1996/2316 (C.59).

Statutory instruments – SI 1996/2348: "relevant instrument" defined for the purposes of s. 244(1). Prescribed particulars to be given in a document produced pursuant to s. 244(2) defined.

Notes – Level 1 on the standard scale is £200 from 1 October 1992.

245   Production of documents: supplementary

245(1)   Section 244 above shall not apply to any instrument (an **"exempt instrument"**) falling within any prescribed class; but regulations may, in respect of exempt instruments or such descriptions of exempt instruments as may be prescribed, require such a document as is mentioned in subsection (2) of that section to be furnished in accordance with the regulations to the Commissioner of Valuation for Northern Ireland.

245(2)   The information contained in any document produced to the Commissioners under section 244(2) above shall be available for use by the Commissioner of Valuation for Northern Ireland.

245(3)   Any person who fails to comply with any requirement imposed by virtue of subsection (1) above shall be liable on summary conviction to a fine not exceeding level 3 on the standard scale.

245(4)   Section 244 above shall also not apply to any instrument which relates solely to–

(a)   incorporeal hereditaments or to a grave or right of burial, or

(b)   land subject to land purchase annuities which are registered in the Land Registry in Northern Ireland.

245(5)   In this section and section 244 above–

   "lease"–

   (a)   includes an underlease or other tenancy and an agreement for a lease, underlease or tenancy, but

   (b)   does not include a mortgage, charge or lien on any property for securing money or money's worth,

   and **"lessee"** and **"grant"** shall be construed accordingly,

   "prescribed" means prescribed by regulations, and

   "regulations" means regulations made by the Commissioners under this section.

245(6)   The power to make regulations under this section shall be exercisable by statutory instrument which shall be subject to annulment in pursuance of a resolution of the House of Commons.

245(7)   Regulations under this section may make different provision for different cases.

245(8)   This section and section 244 above shall come into force on such day as the Treasury may by order made by statutory instrument appoint.

History – S. 245 brought into force on 4 November 1996 by SI 1996/2316 (C.59).

Statutory instruments – SI 1996/2348: exempt instruments for the purposes of s. 245(1).

Notes – Level 3 on the standard scale is £1,000 from 1 October 1992.

FINANCE ACT 1995

(1995 Chapter 4)

[1st May 1995]

ARRANGEMENT OF SECTIONS

PART V – STAMP DUTY

PART VI – MISCELLANEOUS AND GENERAL

MISCELLANEOUS

SCHEDULES

PART V – STAMP DUTY

149   Transfer: associated bodies

149(1)   Section 42 of the Finance Act 1930 (relief from transfer stamp duty in case of transfer of property as between associated bodies corporate) shall be amended as mentioned in subsections (2) to (5) below.

149(2)   [Amends FA 1930, s. 42(2).]

149(3)   [Inserts FA 1930, s. 42(2A) and (2B).]

149(4)   [Amends FA 1930, s. 42(3).]

149(5)   [Inserts FA 1930, s. 42(4).]

149(6)   [Amends FA 1967, s. 27(3)(c).]

149(7)   This section shall apply in relation to instruments executed on or after the day on which this Act is passed.

150   Northern Ireland transfer: associated bodies

150   [Amends FA (NI) 1954, s. 11 in relation to instruments executed on or after 1 May 1995.]

151   Lease: associated bodies

151(1)   Stamp duty under Part II of Schedule 13 to the Finance Act 1999 (lease) shall not be chargeable on an instrument which is–

(a)   a lease,

(b)   an agreement for a lease, or

(c)   an agreement with respect to a letting,

as respects which the condition in subsection (2) below is satisfied.

This subsection is subject to subsection (4A) below.

151(2)   The condition is that it is shown to the satisfaction of the Commissioners of Inland Revenue that–

(a)   the lessor is a body corporate and the lessee is another body corporate,

(b)   those bodies are associated at the time the instrument is executed,

(c)   in the case of an agreement, the agreement is for the lease or letting to be granted to the lessee or to a body corporate which is associated with the lessee at the time the instrument is executed, and

(d)   the instrument is not executed in pursuance of or in connection with an arrangement falling within subsection (3) below.

151(3)   An arrangement falls within this subsection if it is one under which–

(a)   the consideration, or any part of the consideration, for the lease or agreement was to be provided or received (directly or indirectly) by a person other than a body corporate which at the relevant time was associated with either the lessor or the lessee, or

(b)   the lessor and the lessee were to cease to be associated by reason of the lessor or a third body corporate ceasing to be the lessee's parent;

and the relevant time is the time of the execution of the instrument.

151(4)   Without prejudice to the generality of paragraph (a) of subsection (3)above, an arrangement shall be treated as within that paragraph if it is one under which the lessor or the lessee or a body corporate associated with either at the relevant time was to be enabled to provide any of the consideration, or was to part with any of it, by or in consequence of the carrying out of a transaction which involved (or transactions any of which involved) a payment or other disposition by a person other than a body corporate associated with the lessor or the lessee at the relevant time.

151(4A)   An instrument shall not be exempt from stamp duty by virtue of subsection (1) above if at the time the instrument is executed arrangements are in existence by virtue of which at that or some later time any person has or could obtain, or any persons together have or could obtain, control of the lessee but not of the lessor.

151(5)   An instrument mentioned in subsection (1) above shall not be treated as duly stamped unless–

(a)   it is duly stamped in accordance with the law that would apply but for that subsection, or

(b)   it has, in accordance with section 12 of the Stamp Act 1891, been stamped with a particular stamp denoting either that it is not chargeable with any duty or that it is duly stamped.

151(6)   In this section–

(a)   references to the **lessor** are to the person granting the lease or (in the case of an agreement) agreeing to grant the lease or letting;

(b)   references to the **lessee** are to the person being granted the lease or (in the case of an agreement) agreeing for the lease or letting to be granted to him or another.

151(7)   For the purposes of this section bodies corporate are **associated** at a particular time if at that time one is the parent of the other or another body corporate is the parent of each.

151(8)   For the purposes of this section one body corporate is the **parent** of another at a particular time if at that time the first body

(a)   is beneficial owner of not less than 75 per cent of the ordinary share capital of the second body;

(b)   is beneficially entitled to not less than 75 per cent of any profits available for distribution to equity holders of the second body; and

(c)   would be beneficially entitled to not less than 75 per cent of any assets of the second body available for distribution to its equity holders on a winding-up.

151(9)   In subsection (8) above **"ordinary share capital"**, in relation to a body corporate, means all the issued share capital (by whatever name called) of the body corporate, other than capital the holders of which have a right to a dividend at a fixed rate but have no other right to share in the profits of the body corporate.

151(10)   The **ownership** referred to in paragraph (a) of subsection (8)above is ownership either directly or through another body corporate or other bodies corporate, or partly directly and partly through another body corporate or other bodies corporate; and Part I of Schedule 4 to the Finance Act 1938 (determination of amount of capital held through other bodies corporate) shall apply for the purposes of that paragraph.

151(10A)   Schedule 18 to the Income and Corporation Taxes Act 1988 shall apply for the purposes of paragraphs (b) and (c) of subsection (8) as it applies for the purposes of paragraphs (a) and (b) of section 413(7) of that Act; but this is subject to subsection (10B).

151(10B)   In determining for the purposes of this section whether a body corporate is the parent of the lessor, paragraphs 5(3) and 5B to 5E of Schedule 18 to the Income and Corporation Taxes Act 1988 shall not apply for the purposes of paragraph (b) or (c) of subsection (8) above.

151(10C)   In this section, **"control"** shall be construed in accordance with section 840 of the Income and Corporation Taxes Act 1988.

151(11)   This section shall apply in relation to instruments executed after the day on which this Act is passed.

History – In the heading to s. 151, the word "Lease" substituted for the words "Lease or tack" by FA 1999, s. 112(4) and Sch. 14, para. 33 with effect in relation to instruments executed on or after 1 October 1999.
In s. 151(1), at the end the paragraph "This subsection is subject to subsection (4A) below." was inserted by FA 2000, s. 125 (2) which has effect in relation to instruments executed after xx July 2000.
In s. 151(1), the words "Part II of Schedule 13 to the Finance Act 1999 (lease)" substituted for the words "the heading "Lease or Tack" in Schedule 1 to the Stamp Act 1891" and, in subs. (1) (twice), (2), (3) and (6) (four times) the word "lease" substituted for the words "lease or tack" by FA 1999, s. 112(4) and Sch. 14, para. 33, the substitutions having effect in relation to instruments executed on or after 1 October 1999.
S. 151 (4A) inserted by FA 2000, s. 125(3) which has effect in relation to instruments executed after xx July 2000.
In s. 151 (8) "(a)" was inserted immediately after the words "if at that time the first body" by FA 2000, s. 125 (4) which has effect in relation to instruments executed after xx July 2000.
In s. 151 (8), paragraphs (b) and (c) inserted by FA 2000, s. 125 (4) which has effect in relation to instruments executed after xx July 2000.
In s. 151(10) the words "paragraph (a) of" were inserted and the words "that paragraph" substituted in place of the words "this section" by FA 2000, s. 125 (5) which has effect in relation to instruments executed after xx July 2000.
S. 151 (10A) - (10C) inserted by FA 2000, s. 125 (6) which has effect in relation to instruments executed after xx July 2000.
Statements of practice – SP 3/98: Stamp Office approach to application of anti-avoidance rules preventing exploitation of group relief.
Notes – ICTA 1988, s. 840 and Sch. 18 appear in *Tax Statutes and Statutory Instruments*, Vol. 1A.

PART VI – MISCELLANEOUS AND GENERAL

MISCELLANEOUS

152   Open-ended investment companies

152(1)   The Treasury may, by regulations, make such provision as they consider appropriate for securing that the enactments specified in subsection (2) below have effect in relation to–

(a)   open-ended investment companies of any such description as may be specified in the regulations,

(b)   holdings in, and the assets of, such companies, and

(c)   transactions involving such companies,

in a manner corresponding, subject to such modifications as the Treasury consider appropriate, to the manner in which they have effect in relation to unit trusts, to rights under, and the assets subject to, such trusts and to transactions for purposes connected with such trusts.

152(2)   The enactments referred to in subsection (1) above are–

(a)   the Tax Acts and the Taxation of Chargeable Gains Act 1992; and

(b)   the enactments relating to stamp duty and stamp duty reserve tax.

152(3) The power of the Treasury to make regulations under this section in relation to any such enactments shall include power to make provision which does any one or more of the following, that is to say–

(a) identifies the payments which are or are not to be treated, for the purposes of any prescribed enactment, as the distributions of open-ended investment companies;

(b) modifies the operation of Chapters II, III and VA of Part VI of the Taxes Act 1988 in relation to open-ended investment companies or in relation to payments falling to be treated as the distributions of such companies;

(c) applies and adapts any of the provisions of the enactments relating to stamp duty or stamp duty reserve tax for the purpose of making in relation to transactions involving open-ended investment companies any provision corresponding (with or without modifications) to that which applies under those enactments in the case of equivalent transactions involving unit trusts;

(d) provides for any or all of the provisions of sections 75 to 77 of the Finance Act 1986 to have effect or not to have effect in relation to open-ended investment companies or the undertakings of, or any shares in, such companies;

(e) so modifies the operation of any prescribed enactment in relation to any such companies as to secure that arrangements for treating the assets of an open-ended investment company as assets comprised in separate pools are given an effect corresponding, in prescribed respects, to that of equivalent arrangements constituting the separate parts of an umbrella scheme;

(f) requires prescribed enactments to have effect in relation to an open-ended investment company as if it were, or were not, a member of the same group of companies as one or more other companies;

(g) identifies the holdings in open-ended investment companies which are, or are not, to be treated for the purposes of any prescribed enactment as comprised in the same class of holdings;

(h) preserves a continuity of tax treatment where, in connection with any scheme of re-organisation, assets of one or more unit trusts become assets of one or more open-ended investment companies, or vice versa;

(i) treats the separate parts of the undertaking of an open-ended investment company in relation to which provision is made by virtue of paragraph (e) above as distinct companies for the purposes of any regulations under this section;

(j) amends, adapts or applies the provisions of any subordinate legislation made under or by reference to any enactment modified by the regulations.

152(4) The power to make regulations under this section shall be exercisable by statutory instrument and shall include power–

(a) to make different provision for different cases; and

(b) to make such incidental, supplemental, consequential and transitional provision as the Treasury may think fit.

152(5) A statutory instrument containing regulations under this section shall be subject to annulment in pursuance of a resolution of the House of Commons.

152(6) In this section–

"**the enactments relating to stamp duty**" means the Stamp Act 1891, and any enactment (including any Northern Ireland legislation) which amends or is required to be construed together with that Act;

"**the enactments relating to stamp duty reserve tax**" means Part IV of the Finance Act 1986 and any enactment which amends or is required to be construed as one with that Part;

"**Northern Ireland legislation**" shall have the meaning given by section 24(5) of the Interpretation Act 1978;

"**open-ended investment company**" has the same meaning as in the Financial Services Act 1986;

"**prescribed**" means prescribed by regulations under this section;

"**subordinate legislation**" means any subordinate legislation within the meaning of the Interpretation Act 1978 or any order or regulations made by statutory instrument under Northern Ireland legislation; and

"**umbrella scheme**" shall have the meaning given by section 468 of the Taxes Act 1988;

and references in this section to the enactments relating to stamp duty, or to any of them, or to Part IV of the Finance Act 1986 shall have effect as including references to enactments repealed by sections 107 to 110 of the Finance Act 1990.

152(7)   Any reference in this section to unit trusts has effect–

(a)   for the purposes of so much of this section as confers power in relation to the enactments specified in paragraph (a) of subsection (2) above, as a reference to authorised unit trusts (within the meaning of section 468 of the Taxes Act 1988), and

(b)   for the purposes of so much of this section as confers power in relation to the enactments specified in paragraph (b) of that subsection, as a reference to any unit trust scheme (within the meaning given by section 57 of the Finance Act 1946).

152(8)   For the purposes of this section the enactments which shall be taken to make provision in relation to companies that are members of the same group of companies shall include any enactments which make provision in relation to a case–

(a)   where one company has, or in relation to another company is, a subsidiary, or a subsidiary of a particular description, or

(b)   where one company controls another or two or more companies are under the same control.

History – In s. 152:
   in subs. (2)(b), the words "stamp duty reserve tax" substituted for the words " Part IV of the Finance Act 1986 (stamp duty reserve tax)";
   in subs. (3)(c), the words "the enactments relating to stamp duty or stamp duty reserve tax" substituted for the words "Part IV of the Finance Act 1986" and the words "those enactments" substituted for the words "the enactments relating to stamp duty"; and
   in subs. (6), the definition of "the enactments relating to stamp duty reserve tax" inserted,
all by FA 1999, s. 122(4) and Sch. 19, para. 13, the substitutions and insertion coming into force on 6 February 2000.

Statutory instruments – Stamp Duty and Stamp Duty Reserve Tax (Open-ended Investment Companies) Regulations 1997, SI 1997/1156.
Stamp Duty and Stamp Duty Reserve Tax (Open-ended Investment Companies) (Amendment) Regulations SI 1999/1467, reg. 3: amendment of SI 1997/1156, reg. 9, 10 to remove time limit of 1 July 1999 for exemption from charge to stamp duty or stamp duty reserve tax for amalgamation of authorised unit trust with an open-ended investment company.
Stamp Duty and Stamp Duty Reserve Tax (Open-ended Investment Companies) (Amendment No.2) Regulations SI 1999/3261 (operative from 6 February 2000): amendment of SI 1997/1156 to introduce a stamp duty reserve tax regime for dealings of shares in open-ended investment companies which is equivalent to the provisions of FA 1999, Sch. 19 for unit trusts.

162   Repeals

162   The provisions specified in Schedule 29 to this Act (which include provisions which are already spent) are hereby repealed to the extent specified in the third column of that Schedule, but subject to any provision of that Schedule.

SCHEDULES

SCHEDULE 29 – REPEALS

Section 162

Part X – Stamp Duty

Chapter	Short title	Extent of repeal
1930 c. 28.	The Finance Act 1930.	In section 42(3) the words from "with the substitution" to the end.
1954 c. 23 (N.I.).	The Finance Act (Northern Ireland) 1954.	In section 11(3A) the words from "with the substitution" to the end.

These repeals have effect in accordance with sections 149 and 150 of this Act.

FINANCE ACT 1996

(1996 Chapter 8)

[29th April 1996]

ARRANGEMENT OF SECTIONS

PART VI – STAMP DUTY AND STAMP DUTY RESERVE TAX

PART VI – STAMP DUTY AND STAMP DUTY RESERVE TAX

STAMP DUTY

186   Transfers of securities to members of electronic transfer systems etc.

186(1)   Stamp duty shall not be chargeable on an instrument effecting a transfer of securities if the transferee is a member of an electronic transfer system and the instrument is in a form which will, in accordance with the rules of the system, ensure that the securities are changed from being held in certificated form to being held in uncertificated form so that title to them may become transferable by means of the system.

186(2)   In this section–

"certificated form" has the same meaning as in the relevant regulations;

"electronic transfer system" means a system and procedures which, in accordance with the relevant regulations, enable title to securities to be evidenced and transferred without a written instrument;

"member", in relation to an electronic transfer system, means a person who is permitted by the operator of the system to transfer by means of the system title to securities held by him in uncertificated form;

"operator" means a person approved by the Treasury under the relevant regulations as operator of an electronic transfer system;

"the relevant regulations" means regulations under section 207 of the Companies Act 1989 (transfer without written instrument);

"securities" means stock or marketable securities;

"uncertificated form" has the same meaning as it has in the relevant regulations.

186(3)   This section applies in relation to instruments executed on or after 1st July 1996.

186(4)   This section shall be construed as one with the Stamp Act 1891.

Prospective repeals – S. 186 repealed by FA 1996, s. 205 and Sch. 41, Pt. VII, in accordance with FA 1990, s. 108.

Cross references – FA 1999, s. 119(3): regulations may make provision for exempting UK depositary interests in foreign securities from stamp duty reserve tax where the terms of issue of the interest are such that it can only be transferred by one of two methods, one of which is by means of a transfer within s. 186.

Notes – The Treasury order appointing the "abolition day" for the purposes of FA 1990, s. 107–110 was to have broadly coincided with the start of paperless trading under the Stock Exchange's planned TAURUS system (IR press release, 20 March 1990). However, on 11 March 1993 it was announced that TAURUS had been abandoned (London Stock Exchange News Release 6/93).

STAMP DUTY RESERVE TAX

187   Territorial scope of the tax

187(1)   [Inserts FA 1986, s. 86(4).]

187(2)   The amendment made by subsection (1) above shall have effect–

(a)   in relation to an agreement, if–

(i) the agreement is conditional and the condition is satisfied on or after 1st July 1996; or

(ii) the agreement is not conditional and is made on or after that date; and

(b)   in relation to a transfer, issue or appropriation made or effected on or after that date.

Prospective repeals – S. 187 repealed by FA 1996, s. 205 and Sch. 41, Pt. VII, in accordance with FA 1990, s. 110.

Notes – The Treasury order appointing the "abolition day" for the purposes of FA 1990, s. 107–110 was to have broadly coincided with the start of paperless trading under the Stock Exchange's planned TAURUS system (IR press release, 20 March 1990). However, on 11 March 1993 it was announced that TAURUS had been abandoned (London Stock Exchange News Release 6/93).

188   Removal of the two month period

188(1)   [Amends FA 1986, s. 87(2).]

188(2)   [Repealed by FA 1999, s. 139 and Sch. 20, Pt. V(2).]

188(3)   [Repeals FA 1986, s. 88(2) and (3).]

188(4)   [Amends FA 1986, s. 92(1).]

188(5)   The amendments made by this section shall have effect in relation to an agreement to transfer securities if–

(a)   the agreement is conditional and the condition is satisfied on or after 1st July 1996; or

(b)   the agreement is not conditional and is made on or after that date.

Prospective repeals – S. 188 repealed by FA 1996, s. 205 and Sch. 41, Pt. VII, in accordance with FA 1990, s. 110.

History – S. 188(2) (which inserted FA 1986, s. 88(1)(aa) and (ab)) repealed by FA 1999, s. 139 and Sch. 20, Pt. V(2), the repeal having effect in relation to instruments executed, or bearer instruments issued, on or after 1 October 1999 but, as regards unit trust schemes, subject to FA 1999, Sch. 20, Pt. V(2), para. 2.

Notes – The Treasury order appointing the "abolition day" for the purposes of FA 1990, s. 107–110 was to have broadly coincided with the start of paperless trading under the Stock Exchange's planned TAURUS system (IR press release, 20 March 1990). However, on 11 March 1993 it was announced that TAURUS had been abandoned (London Stock Exchange News Release 6/93).

189   Transfers to members of electronic transfer systems etc.

189(1)   [Inserts FA 1986, s. 88(1A).]

189(2)   This section has effect in relation to an agreement to transfer securities if an instrument is executed on or after 1st July 1996 in pursuance of the agreement.

Prospective repeal – S. 189 repealed by FA 1996, s. 205 and Sch. 41, Pt. VII, in accordance with FA 1990, s. 110.

Notes – The Treasury order appointing the "abolition day" for the purposes of FA 1990, s. 107–110 was to have broadly coincided with the start of paperless trading under the Stock Exchange's planned TAURUS system (IR press release, 20 March 1990). However, on 11 March 1993 it was announced that TAURUS had been abandoned (London Stock Exchange News Release 6/93).

190   Transfers between associated bodies

190(1)   [Inserts FA 1986, s. 88(1B).]

190(2)   [Inserts FA 1986, s. 88(4), (5) and (6).]

190(3)   This section has effect where the instrument on which stamp duty is not chargeable by virtue of section 42 of the Finance Act 1930 or section 11 of the Finance Act (Northern Ireland) 1954 is executed on or after 4th January 1996 in pursuance of an agreement to transfer securities made on or after that date.

Prospective repeals – S. 190 repealed by FA 1996, s. 205 and Sch. 41, Pt. VII, in accordance with FA 1990, s. 110.

Notes – The Treasury order appointing the "abolition day" for the purposes of FA 1990, s. 107–110 was to have broadly coincided with the start of paperless trading under the Stock Exchange's planned TAURUS system (IR press release, 20 March 1990). However, on 11 March 1993 it was announced that TAURUS had been abandoned (London Stock Exchange News Release 6/93).

191   Stock lending and collateral security arrangements

191   [Repealed by FA 1997, s. 113 and Sch. 18, Pt. VII.]

192   Repayment or cancellation of tax

192(1)   [Repeals FA 1986, s. 87(4), (5) and (8).]

192(2)   [Amends FA 1986, s. 88(1), (1A) and (1B).]

192(3)   [Amends FA 1986, s. 92(1).]

192(4)   [Inserts FA 1986, s. 92(1A) and (1B).]

192(5)   [Inserts FA 1986, s. 92(6).]

192(6)   The amendments made by this section shall have effect in relation to an agreement to transfer securities if–

(a)   the agreement is conditional and the condition is satisfied on or after 1st July 1996; or

(b)   the agreement is not conditional and is made on or after that date.

Prospective repeals – S. 192 repealed by FA 1996, s. 205 and Sch. 41, Pt. VII, in accordance with FA 1990, s. 110.

Notes – The Treasury order appointing the "abolition day" for the purposes of FA 1990, s. 107–110 was to have broadly coincided with the start of paperless trading under the Stock Exchange's planned TAURUS system (IR press release, 20 March 1990). However, on 11 March 1993 it was announced that TAURUS had been abandoned (London Stock Exchange News Release 6/93).

193   Depositary receipts

193(1)   Section 93 of the Finance Act 1986 (depositary receipts) shall be amended in accordance with the following provisions of this section.

193(2)   [Amends FA 1986, s. 93(1).]

193(3)   [Amends FA 1986, s. 93(6)(d).]

193(4)   This section has effect–

(a)   so far as relating to the charge to tax under section 93(1) of the Finance Act 1986, where securities are transferred, issued or appropriated on or after 1st July 1996 (whenever the arrangement was made);

(b)   so far as relating to the charge to tax under section 93(10) of that Act, in relation to instalments payable on or after 1st July 1996.

Prospective repeals – S. 193 repealed by FA 1996, s. 205 and Sch. 41, Pt. VII, in accordance with FA 1990, s. 110.

Notes – The Treasury order appointing the "abolition day" for the purposes of FA 1990, s. 107–110 was to have broadly coincided with the start of paperless trading under the Stock Exchange's planned TAURUS system (IR press release, 20 March 1990). However, on 11 March 1993 it was announced that TAURUS had been abandoned (London Stock Exchange News Release 6/93).

194   Rates of charge expressed as percentages

194(1)   [Amends FA 1986, s. 87(6).]

194(2)   In section 93 of that Act (depositary receipts)–

(a)   [amends s. 93(4)];

(b) [repealed by FA 1997, s. 113 and Sch. 18, Pt. VII]

(c) [amends s. 93(10)].

194(3) [Repeals FA 1986, s. 94(8).]

194(4) In section 96 of that Act (clearance services)–

(a) [amends s. 96(2)];

(b) [repealed by FA 1997, s. 113 and Sch. 18, Pt. VII]

(c) [amends s. 96(8)].

194(5) [Repeals FA 1986, s 96(12).]

194(6) [Inserts FA 1986, s. 99(13).]

194(7) Subsections (1) to (5) above have effect in accordance with the following provisions of this subsection, that is to say–

(a) in relation to the charge to tax under section 87 of the Finance Act 1986, subsection (1) above applies where–

(i) the agreement to transfer is conditional and the condition is satisfied on or after 1st July 1996; or

(ii) the agreement is not conditional and is made on or after 1st July 1996;

(b) in relation to the charge to tax under section 93(1) of that Act, paragraphs (a) and (b) of subsection (2) above apply where securities are transferred, issued or appropriated on or after 1st July 1996 (whenever the arrangement was made) and subsection (3) above has effect accordingly;

(c) in relation to the charge to tax under section 93(10) of that Act, paragraph (c) of subsection (2) above applies in relation to instalments payable on or after 1st July 1996;

(d) in relation to the charge to tax under section 96(1) of that Act, paragraphs (a) and (b) of subsection (4) above apply where securities are transferred or issued on or after 1st July 1996 (whenever the arrangement was made) and subsection (5) above has effect accordingly;

(e) in relation to the charge to tax under section 96(8) of that Act, paragraph (c) of subsection (4) above applies in relation to instalments payable on or after 1st July 1996.

Prospective repeal – S. 194 repealed by FA 1996, s. 205 and Sch. 41, Pt. VII, in accordance with FA 1990, s. 110.

History – S. 194(2)(b) and (4)(b) repealed by FA 1997, s. 113 and Sch. 18, Pt. VII, with effect where securities are transferred on or after the day which is the commencement day for the purposes of FA 1997, s. 102, unless the securities were acquired by the transferor before that day (s. 104(5)). The appointed day for the purposes of FA 1997, s. 102(5) and (6) was 20 October 1997, the commencement day by virtue of SI 1997/2428 (C. 95). For instruments where s. 194(2)(b) and (4)(b) still applied after that date, their effect was to amend s. 93(5) (depositary receipts) and s. 96(3) (clearance services) respectively. See the history notes to those sections for further details.

The Treasury order appointing the "abolition day" for the purposes of FA 1990, s. 107–110 was to have broadly coincided with the start of paperless trading under the Stock Exchange's planned TAURUS system (IR press release, 20 March 1990). However, on 11 March 1993 it was announced that TAURUS had been abandoned (London Stock Exchange News Release 6/93).

195 Regulations concerning administration: sub-delegation to the Board

195 [Inserts FA 1986, s. 98(1A).]

Prospective repeals – S. 195 repealed by FA 1996, s. 205 and Sch. 41, Pt. VII, in accordance with FA 1990, s. 110.

Notes – The Treasury order appointing the "abolition day" for the purposes of FA 1990, s. 107–110 was to have broadly coincided with the start of paperless trading under the Stock Exchange's planned TAURUS system (IR press release, 20 March 1990). However, on 11 March 1993 it was announced that TAURUS had been abandoned (London Stock Exchange News Release 6/93).

CLEARANCE SERVICES

196 Election by operator for alternative system of charge

196(1) [Amends FA 1986, s. 70(1).]

196(2) [Amends FA 1986, s. 96(1).]

196(3) [Inserts FA 1986, s. 97A.]

196(4) [Repeals FA 1986, s. 97(2) in relation to any transfer effected on or after 1st July 1996.]

196(5) [Amends FA 1986, s. 99(10).]

196(6) Subsections (1), (2), (3) and (5) above shall come into force on 1st July 1996.

Prospective repeals – S. 196 repealed by FA 1996, s. 205 and Sch. 41, Pt. VII, in accordance with FA 1990, s. 110.

Notes – The Treasury order appointing the "abolition day" for the purposes of FA 1990, s. 107–110 was to have broadly coincided with the start of paperless trading under the Stock Exchange's planned TAURUS system (IR press release, 20 March 1990). However, on 11 March 1993 it was announced that TAURUS had been abandoned (London Stock Exchange News Release 6/93).

PART VII – MISCELLANEOUS AND SUPPLEMENTAL

MISCELLANEOUS: DIRECT TAXATION

201   Enactment of Inland Revenue concessions

201   Schedule 39 to this Act has effect for the purpose of enacting certain extra-statutory concessions relating to income tax, corporation tax, capital gains tax, and stamp duty.

MISCELLANEOUS: OTHER MATTERS

202   Gilt stripping

202(1)–(4)   [Not relevant to stamp duties.]

202(5)   The Treasury may by regulations make provision for securing that enactments and subordinate legislation which–

(a)   apply in relation to government securities or to any description of such securities, or

(b)   for any other purpose refer (in whatever terms) to such securities or to any description of them,

have effect with such modifications as the Treasury may think appropriate in consequence of the making of any provision or arrangements for, or in connection with, the issue or transfer of strips of government securities or the consolidation of such strips into other securities.

202(6)   Regulations under subsection (5) above may–

(a)   impose a charge to income tax, corporation tax, capital gains tax, inheritance tax, stamp duty or stamp duty reserve tax;

(b)   include provision applying generally to, or to any description of, enactments or subordinate legislation;

(c)   make different provision for different cases; and

(d)   contain such incidental, supplemental, consequential and transitional provision as the Treasury think appropriate.

202(7)   The power to make regulations under subsection (5) above shall be exercisable by statutory instrument subject to annulment in pursuance of a resolution of the House of Commons.

202(8)   Schedule 40 to this Act (which makes provision in relation to strips for taxation purposes) shall have effect.

202(9)   The enactments that may be modified by regulations under this section shall include section 95 above and the enactments contained in Schedule 40 to this Act.

202(10)   In this section–

"**government securities**" means any securities included in Part I of Schedule 11 to the Finance Act 1942;

"**modifications**" includes amendments, additions and omissions; and

"**subordinate legislation**" has the same meaning as in the Interpretation Act 1978;

and expressions used in this section and in section 47 of the Finance Act 1942 have the same meanings in this section as in that section.

SUPPLEMENTAL

205   Repeals

205(1)   The enactments mentioned in Schedule 41 to this Act (which include spent provisions) are hereby repealed to the extent specified in the third column of that Schedule.

205(2)   The repeals specified in that Schedule have effect subject to the commencement provisions and savings contained in, or referred to, in the notes set out in that Schedule.

206   Short title

206   This Act may be cited as the Finance Act 1996.

SCHEDULES

SCHEDULE 39 – ENACTMENT OF CERTAIN INLAND REVENUE EXTRA-STATUTORY CONCESSIONS

Section 201

Part III – Stamp Duty

LOST OR SPOILED INSTRUMENTS

10(1) The Stamp Duties Management Act 1891 (**"the Management Act"**) shall be amended as follows.

10(2) [Amends SDMA 1891, s. 9(7)(e).]

10(3) [Inserts SDMA 1891, s. 12A.]

10(4) Subject to subparagraph (5) below, the amendments made by this paragraph shall have effect from the day on which this Act is passed.

10(5) The amendments made by this paragraph shall not apply in relation to an instrument which has been accidentally spoiled if an application for allowance under section 9 of the Management Act was made before the day on which this Act is passed.

SCHEDULE 40 – GILT STRIPPING: TAXATION PROVISIONS

Section 202

THE STAMP ACT 1891 (c. 39)

1 [Amends the definition of "stock" in SA 1891, s. 122(1).]

2 [Repealed by FA 1999, s. 139 and Sch. 20, Pt. V(2) in relation to instruments executed, or bearer instruments issued, on or after 1 October 1999 but, as regards unit trust schemes, subject to FA 1999, Sch. 20, Pt. V(2), para. 2. The repeal took effect from 6 February 2000 as regards unit trust schemes, by virtue of FA 1999, s. 122(4) and FA 1999, Sch. 19.]

SCHEDULE 41 – REPEALS

Section 205

Part VII – Stamp Duty and Stamp Duty Reserve Tax

Chapter	Short title	Extent of repeal
1986 c. 41.	The Finance Act 1986.	In section 87, in subsection (2), the words "the expiry of the period of two months beginning with" and the words from "unless" to the end and subsections (4), (5) and (8). Section 88(2) and (3). Section 94(8). Section 96(12). Section 97(2).
1996 c. 8.	The Finance Act 1996.	Sections 186 to 196.

1   The repeals in sections 87 and 88 of the Finance Act 1986 have effect in accordance with sections 174 and 178 of this Act.

2   The repeals in section 94 and 96 of the Finance Act 1986 have effect in accordance with section 180 of this Act.

3   The repeal in section 97 of the Finance Act 1986 has effect in accordance with section 182(4) of this Act.

4   The repeals in the Finance Act 1996 have effect–

(a)   so far as relating to stamp duty, in accordance with section 108 of the Finance Act 1990; and

(b)   so far as relating to stamp duty reserve tax, in accordance with section 110 of the Finance Act 1990.

FINANCE ACT 1997

1997 Chapter 16

[19th March 1997]

ARRANGEMENT OF SECTIONS

PART VII – STAMP DUTY AND STAMP DUTY RESERVE TAX

STAMP DUTY

STAMP DUTY RESERVE TAX

PART VIII –
SUPPLEMENTAL

SCHEDULES

PART VII – STAMP DUTY AND STAMP DUTY RESERVE TAX

STAMP DUTY

95   Mergers of authorised unit trusts

95(1)   Stamp duty shall not be chargeable on an instrument transferring any property which is subject to the trusts of an authorised unit trust (**"the target trust"**) to the trustees of another authorised unit trust (**"the acquiring trust"**) if the conditions set out in subsection (2) below are fulfilled.

95(2)   Those conditions are that–

(a)   the transfer forms part of an arrangement under which the whole of the available property of the target trust is transferred to the trustees of the acquiring trust;

(b)   under the arrangement all the units in the target trust are extinguished;

(c)   the consideration under the arrangement consists of or includes the issue of units (**"the consideration units"**) in the acquiring trust to the persons who held the extinguished units;

(d)   the consideration units are issued to those persons in proportion to their holdings of the extinguished units; and

(e)   the consideration under the arrangement does not include anything else, other than the assumption or discharge by the trustees of the acquiring trust of liabilities of the trustees of the target trust.

95(3)   An instrument on which stamp duty is not chargeable by virtue only of this section shall not be taken to be duly stamped unless it is stamped with the duty to which it would be liable but for this section or it has, in accordance with section 12 of the Stamp Act 1891, been stamped with a particular stamp denoting that it is not chargeable with any duty.

95(4)   In this section–

"authorised unit trust" means a unit trust scheme in the case of which an order under section 78 of the Financial Services Act 1986 is in force;

"the whole of the available property of the target trust" means the whole of the property subject to the trusts of the target trust, other than any property which is retained for the purpose of discharging liabilities of the trustees of the target trust;

"unit" and **"unit trust scheme"** have the same meanings as in Part VII of the Finance Act 1946.

95(5)   Each of the parts of an umbrella scheme (and not the scheme as a whole) shall be regarded for the purposes of this section as an authorised unit trust; and in this section **"umbrella scheme"** has the same meaning as in section 468 of the Taxes Act 1988 and references to parts of an umbrella scheme shall be construed in accordance with that section.

95(6)   This section applies to any instrument which is executed–

(a)   on or after the day on which this Act is passed; but

(b)   before 1st July 1999.

96   Demutualisation of insurance companies

96(1)   This section applies where there is a relevant transfer, under a scheme, of the whole or any part of the business carried on by a mutual insurance company (**"the mutual"**) to a company which has share capital (**"the acquiring company"**).

96(2)   Stamp duty shall not be chargeable on an instrument executed for the purposes of or in connection with the transfer if the requirements of subsections (3) and (4) below are satisfied in relation to the shares of a company (**"the issuing company"**) which is either–

(a)   the acquiring company; or

(b)   a company of which the acquiring company is a wholly-owned subsidiary.

96(3)   Shares in the issuing company must be offered, under the scheme, to at least 90 per cent of the persons who immediately before the transfer are members of the mutual.

96(4)   Under the scheme, all the shares in the issuing company which will be in issue immediately after the transfer has been made, other than shares which are to be or have been issued pursuant to an offer to the public, must be offered to the persons who (at the time of the offer) are–

(a)   members of the mutual;

(b)   persons who are entitled to become members of the mutual; or

(c)   employees, former employees or pensioners of the mutual or of a company which is a wholly-owned subsidiary of the mutual.

96(5)   An instrument on which stamp duty is not chargeable by virtue only of subsection (2) above shall not be taken to be duly stamped unless it is stamped with the duty to which it would be liable but for that subsection or it has, in accordance with section 12 of the Stamp Act 1891, been stamped with a particular stamp denoting that it is not chargeable with any duty.

96(6)   For the purposes of this section, a company is a wholly-owned subsidiary of another person (**"the parent"**) if it has no members except the parent and the parent's wholly-owned subsidiaries or persons acting on behalf of the parent or its wholly-owned subsidiaries.

96(7) In this section **"relevant transfer"** means–

(a) a transfer to which Schedule 2C to the Insurance Companies Act 1982 (transfers of insurance business) applies; or

(b) a transfer to which that Schedule would apply but for section 15(1A) of that Act (provisions of Part II of that Act which do not apply to EC companies in certain circumstances).

96(8) In this section–

"employee", in relation to a mutual insurance company or its wholly-owned subsidiary, includes any officer or director of the company or subsidiary and any other person taking part in the management of the affairs of the company or subsidiary;

"insurance company" has the meaning given in section 96 of the Insurance Companies Act 1982;

"mutual insurance company" means an insurance company carrying on business without having any share capital;

"pensioner", in relation to a mutual insurance company or its wholly-owned subsidiary, means a person entitled (whether presently or prospectively) to a pension, lump sum, gratuity or other like benefit referable to the service of any person as an employee of the company or subsidiary.

96(9) The Treasury may by regulations amend subsection (3) above by substituting a lower percentage for the percentage there mentioned.

96(10) The Treasury may by regulations provide that any or all of the references in subsections (3) and (4) above to members shall be construed as references to members of a class specified in the regulations; and different provision may be made for different cases.

96(11) The power to make regulations under this section shall be exercisable by statutory instrument subject to annulment in pursuance of a resolution of the House of Commons.

96(12) This section applies in relation to instruments executed on or after the day on which this Act is passed.

97   Relief for intermediaries

97(1) [Inserts FA 1986, s. 80A, 80B.]

97(2) [Omits FA 1986, s. 81 (sales to market makers).]

97(3) [Amends FA 1986, s. 88(1B)(b)(i) .]

97(4) Subsections (1) and (2) above apply to instruments executed on or after the commencement day.

97(5) Subsection (3) above applies in relation to an agreement to transfer chargeable securities if the securities were acquired in a transaction which was given effect to by an instrument of transfer executed on or after the commencement day.

97(6) For the purposes of this section the commencement day is such day as the Treasury may by order made by statutory instrument appoint.

Prospective repeal – S. 97 repealed by FA 1997, s. 113 and Sch. 18, Pt. VII, in accordance with FA 1990, s. 108.

Statutory instruments – SI 1997/2428 (C. 95): appoints 20 October 1997 for the purposes of this section, pursuant to s. 97(6).

Notes – The Treasury order appointing the "abolition day" for the purposes of FA 1990, s. 107–110 was to have broadly coincided with the start of paperless trading under the Stock Exchange's planned TAURUS system (IR press release, 20 March 1990). However, on 11 March 1993 it was announced that TAURUS had been abandoned (London Stock Exchange News Release 6/93).

98   Repurchases and stock lending

98(1) [Inserts FA 1986, s. 80C.]

98(2) [Omits FA 1986, s. 82.]

98(3) This section applies to instruments executed on or after the commencement day.

98(4) For the purposes of this section the commencement day is such day as the Treasury may by order made by statutory instrument appoint.

Prospective repeal – S. 98 repealed by FA 1997, s. 113 and Sch. 18, Pt. VII, in accordance with FA 1990, s. 108.

Statutory instruments – SI 1997/2428 (C. 95): appoints 20 October 1997 for the purposes of this section, pursuant to s. 98(4).

Notes – The Treasury order appointing the "abolition day" for the purposes of FA 1990, s. 107–110 was to have broadly coincided with the start of paperless trading under the Stock Exchange's planned TAURUS system (IR press release, 20 March 1990). However, on 11 March 1993 it was announced that TAURUS had been abandoned (London Stock Exchange News Release 6/93).

99   Depositary receipts and clearance services

99(1)   [Repeals FA 1986, s. 67(4).]

99(2)   [Amends FA 1986, s. 67(3) and repeals s. 69(6)–(8).]

99(3)   [Repeals FA 1986, s. 70(4).]

99(4)   [Amends FA 1986, s. 70(3) and repeals s. 72(4).]

99(5)   This section applies to any instrument executed on or after the day which is the commencement day for the purposes of section 97 above, except an instrument which transfers relevant securities which were acquired by the transferor before that date.

Prospective repeal – S. 99 repealed by FA 1997, s. 113 and Sch. 18, Pt. VII, in accordance with FA 1990, s. 108.

Notes – The Treasury order appointing the "abolition day" for the purposes of FA 1990, s. 107–110 was to have broadly coincided with the start of paperless trading under the Stock Exchange's planned TAURUS system (IR press release, 20 March 1990). However, on 11 March 1993 it was announced that TAURUS had been abandoned (London Stock Exchange News Release 6/93).

STAMP DUTY RESERVE TAX

100   Mergers of authorised unit trusts

100(1)   Section 87 of the Finance Act 1986 shall not apply as regards an agreement to transfer securities which constitute property which is subject to the trusts of an authorised unit trust (**"the target trust"**) to the trustees of another authorised unit trust (**"the acquiring trust"**) if the conditions set out in subsection (2) below are fulfilled.

100(2)   Those conditions are that–

(a)   the agreement forms part of an arrangement under which the whole of the available property of the target trust is transferred to the trustees of the acquiring trust;

(b)   under the arrangement all the units in the target trust are extinguished;

(c)   the consideration under the arrangement consists of or includes the issue of units (**"the consideration units"**) in the acquiring trust to the persons who held the extinguished units;

(d)   the consideration units are issued to those persons in proportion to their holdings of the extinguished units; and

(e)   the consideration under the arrangement does not include anything else, other than the assumption or discharge by the trustees of the acquiring trust of liabilities of the trustees of the target trust.

100(3)   Where–

(a)   stamp duty is not chargeable on an instrument by virtue of section 95(1) above, or

(b)   section 87 of the Finance Act 1986 does not apply as regards an agreement by virtue of subsection (1) above,

section 87 of the Finance Act 1986 shall not apply as regards an agreement, or a deemed agreement, to transfer a unit to the managers of the target trust which is made in order that the unit may be extinguished under the arrangement mentioned in section 93(2)(a) or, as the case may be, subsection (2)(a) above.

100(4)   In this section–

"**authorised unit trust**" means a unit trust scheme in the case of which an order under section 78 of the Financial Services Act 1986 is in force;

"**the whole of the available property of the target trust**" means the whole of the property subject to the trusts of the target trust, other than any property which is retained for the purpose of discharging liabilities of the trustees of the target trust;

"**unit**" and "**unit trust scheme**" have the same meanings as in Part VII of the Finance Act 1946.

100(5)   Each of the parts of an umbrella scheme (and not the scheme as a whole) shall be regarded for the purposes of this section as an authorised unit trust; and in this section "**umbrella scheme**" has the same meaning as in section 468 of the Taxes Act 1988 and references to parts of an umbrella scheme shall be construed in accordance with that section.

100(6)   This section applies–

(a)   to an agreement which is not conditional, if the agreement is made on or after the day on which this Act is passed but before 1st July 1999; and

(b)   to a conditional agreement, if the condition is satisfied on or after the day on which this Act is passed but before 1st July 1999.

Prospective repeal – S. 100 repealed by FA 1997, s. 113 and Sch. 18, Pt. VII, in accordance with FA 1990, s. 110.

101   Direction to hold trust property on other trusts

101(1)   Where an agreement to transfer securities constituting property subject to the trusts of an authorised unit trust (**"the absorbed trust"**) is made by means of a direction by the holders of units in the absorbed trust (**"the sellers"**) to the trustees of another trust (**"the continuing trust"**) to hold the whole of the available property of the absorbed trust on the trusts of the continuing trust, section 87 of the Finance Act 1986 shall not apply as regards the agreement if the conditions set out in subsection (2) below are fulfilled.

101(2)   Those conditions are that–

(a)   the trustees of the absorbed trust are the same persons as the trustees of the continuing trust;

(b)   the agreement forms part of an arrangement under which all the units in the absorbed trust are extinguished;

(c)   the consideration for the direction by the sellers consists of or includes the issue of units (**"the consideration units"**) in the continuing trust to the sellers;

(d)   the consideration units are issued to the sellers in proportion to their holdings of the extinguished units; and

(e)   the consideration for the direction by the sellers does not include anything else, other than the assumption or discharge by the trustees of the continuing trust of liabilities of the trustees of the absorbed trust.

101(3)   Where section 87 of the Finance Act 1986 does not apply as regards an agreement by virtue of subsection (1) above, that section shall not apply as regards an agreement, or a deemed agreement, to transfer a unit to the managers of the absorbed trust which is made in order that the unit may be extinguished under the arrangement mentioned in subsection (2)(b) above.

101(4)   In this section–

"authorised unit trust" and **"unit"** have the same meanings as in section 100 above (and section 100(5) applies for the purposes of this section as it applies for the purposes of section 100);

"the whole of the available property of the absorbed trust" means the whole of the property subject to the trusts of the absorbed trust, other than any property which is retained for the purpose of discharging liabilities of the trustees of the absorbed trust.

101(5)   This section applies–

(a)   to an agreement which is not conditional, if the agreement is made on or after the day on which this Act is passed but before 1st July 1999; and

(b)   to a conditional agreement, if the condition is satisfied on or after the day on which this Act is passed but before 1st July 1999.

Prospective repeal – S. 101 repealed by FA 1997, s. 113 and Sch. 18, Pt. VII, in accordance with FA 1990, s. 110.

102   Relief for intermediaries

102(1)   [Inserts FA 1986, s. 88A, 88B.]

102(2)   [Omits FA 1986, s. 89.]

102(3)   [Amends FA 1986, s. 88(1B)(b)(ii).]

102(4)   Subsections (1) and (2) above apply to an agreement to transfer securities–

(a)   in the case of an agreement which is not conditional, if the agreement is made on or after the commencement day; and

(b)   in the case of a conditional agreement, if the condition is satisfied on or after the commencement day.

102(5)   Subsection (3) above applies in relation to property consisting of chargeable securities if the securities were acquired in pursuance of an agreement to which subsections (1) and (2) above apply (by virtue of subsection (4) above).

102(6)   For the purposes of this section the commencement day is such day as the Treasury may by order made by statutory instrument appoint.

Prospective repeal – S. 102 repealed by FA 1997, s. 113 and Sch. 18, Pt. VII, in accordance with FA 1990, s. 110.

Statutory instruments – SI 1997/2428 (C. 95): appoints 20 October 1997 for the purposes of this section, pursuant to s. 102(6).

Notes – The Treasury order appointing the "abolition day" for the purposes of FA 1990, s. 107–110 was to have broadly coincided with the start of paperless trading under the Stock Exchange's planned TAURUS system (IR press release, 20 March 1990). However, on 11 March 1993 it was announced that TAURUS had been abandoned (London Stock Exchange News Release 6/93).

103   Repurchases and stock lending

103(1)   [Inserts FA 1986, s. 89AA.]

103(2)   [Omits FA 1986, s. 89B.]

103(3)   [Substitutes FA 1986, s. 88(1B)(b)(iia) in consequence of amendments made by s. 101(1), (2).]

103(4)   [Inserts FA 1986, s. 88(1C), (1D).]

103(5)   Subsections (l) and (2) above apply to an agreement to transfer securities–

(a)   in the case of an agreement which is not conditional, if the agreement is made on or after the commencement day; and

(b)   in the case of a conditional agreement, if the condition is satisfied on or after the commencement day.

103(6)   Subsection (3) above applies in relation to property consisting of chargeable securities if the securities were acquired in pursuance of an agreement to which subsections (l) and (2) above apply (by virtue of subsection (5) above).

103(7)   Subsection (4) above applies to instruments executed on or after the commencement day.

103(8)   For the purposes of this section the commencement day is such day as the Treasury may by order made by statutory instrument appoint.

Prospective repeal – S. 103 repealed by FA 1997, s. 113 and Sch. 18, Pt. VII, in accordance with FA 1990, s. 110.

Statutory instruments – SI 1997/2428 (C. 95): appoints 20 October 1997 for the purposes of this section, pursuant to s. 102(6).

Notes – The Treasury order appointing the "abolition day" for the purposes of FA 1990, s. 107–110 was to have broadly coincided with the start of paperless trading under the Stock Exchange's planned TAURUS system (IR press release, 20 March 1990). However, on 11 March 1993 it was announced that TAURUS had been abandoned (London Stock Exchange News Release 6/93).

104   Depositary receipts and clearance services

104(1)   [Repeals FA 1986, s. 93(5).]

104(2)   [Amends FA 1986, s. 93(4) and (7)(a) and repeals s. 94(5)–(7).]

104(3)   [Repeals FA 1986, s. 96(3).]

104(4)   [Amends FA 1986, s. 96(2) and (5)(a) and repeals s. 96(11).]

104(5)   This section applies where securities are transferred on or after the day which is the commencement day for the purposes of section 102 above, unless the securities were acquired by the transferor before that day.

Prospective repeal – S. 104 repealed by FA 1997, s. 113 and Sch. 18, Pt. VII, in accordance with FA 1990, s. 110.

Notes – The Treasury order appointing the "abolition day" for the purposes of FA 1990, s. 107–110 was to have broadly coincided with the start of paperless trading under the Stock Exchange's planned TAURUS system (IR press release, 20 March 1990). However, on 11 March 1993 it was announced that TAURUS had been abandoned (London Stock Exchange News Release 6/93).

105   Inland Bearer Instruments

105(1)   [Repeals FA 1986, s. 90(3)(b).]

105(2)   [Inserts FA 1986, s. 90(3A)–(3F).]

105(3)   [Adds FA 1986, s. 90(8) and (9).]

105(4)   This section applies to an agreement if the inland bearer instrument in question was issued on or after 26th November 1996 and–

(a)   in the case of an agreement which is not conditional, the agreement is made on or after 26th November 1996; or

(b)   in the case of a conditional agreement, the condition is satisfied on or after 26th November 1996.

Prospective repeal – S. 105 repealed by FA 1997, s. 113 and Sch. 18, Pt. VII, in accordance with FA 1990, s. 110.

Notes – The Treasury order appointing the "abolition day" for the purposes of FA 1990, s. 107–110 was to have broadly coincided with the start of paperless trading under the Stock Exchange's planned TAURUS system (IR press release, 20 March 1990). However, on 11 March 1993 it was announced that TAURUS had been abandoned (London Stock Exchange News Release 6/93).

106   Repayment or cancellation of tax

106(1)   Section 87 of the Finance Act 1986 (the principal charge) shall be amended in accordance with subsections (2) and (3) below.

106(2)   [Substitutes FA 1986, s. 87(7A).]

106(3)   [Repeals FA 1986, s. 87(7B).]

106(4)   Section 88 of the Finance Act 1986 (special cases) shall be amended in accordance with subsections (5) to (7) below.

106(5)   [Amends FA 1986, s. 88(1B).]

106(6)   [Substitutes FA 1986, s. 88(4), (5) and (5A).]

106(7)   [Substitutes heading to FA 1986, s. 88.]

106(8)   [Inserts FA 1986, s. 92(7).]

106(9)   The amendments made by subsections (2), (3) and (8) above have effect in relation to an agreement to transfer securities if—

(a)   the agreement is conditional and the condition is satisfied on or after 4th January 1997; or

(b)   the agreement is not conditional and is made on or after that date.

106(10)   The amendments made by subsections (5) and (6) above have effect where the instrument on which stamp duty is not chargeable by virtue of section 42 of the Finance Act 1930 or section 11 of the Finance Act (Northern Ireland) 1954 is executed on or after 4th January 1997 in pursuance of an agreement to transfer securities made on or after that date.

Prospective repeal – S. 106 repealed by FA 1997, s. 113 and Sch. 18, Pt. VII, in accordance with FA 1990, s. 110.

Notes – The Treasury order appointing the "abolition day" for the purposes of FA 1990, s. 107–110 was to have broadly coincided with the start of paperless trading under the Stock Exchange's planned TAURUS system (IR press release, 20 March 1990). However, on 11 March 1993 it was announced that TAURUS had been abandoned (London Stock Exchange News Release 6/93).

PART VIII – MISCELLANEOUS AND SUPPLEMENTAL

SUPPLEMENTAL

113   Repeals

113(1)   The enactments mentioned in Schedule 18 to this Act (which include spent provisions) are hereby repealed to the extent specified in the third column of that Schedule.

113(2)   The repeals specified in that Schedule have effect subject to the commencement provisions and savings contained or referred to in the notes set out in that Schedule.

SCHEDULES

SCHEDULE 18 – REPEALS

Section 113

Part VII – STAMP DUTY AND STAMP DUTY RESERVE TAX

Chapter	Short title	Extent of repeal
1986 c. 41.	The Finance Act 1986.	Section 67(4).
		Section 69(6) to (8).
		Section 70(4).
		Section 72(4).
		Sections 80A to 80C.
		Sections 81 and 82.
		Section 87(7B).

Chapter	Short title	Extent of repeal
		In section 88(1B)(b), the word "or" at the end of sub-paragraph (ii).
		Sections 88A and 88B.
		Section 89.
		Section 89AA.
		Section 89B.
		Section 90(3)(b).
		Section 93(5).
		Section 94(5) to (7).
		Section 96(3) and (11).
1987 c. 16.	The Finance Act 1987.	Section 53.
		In Schedule 7, paragraph 4.
1988 c. 39.	The Finance Act 1988.	In Schedule 13, paragraph 23.
1996 c. 8.	The Finance Act 1996.	Section 191.
		Section 194(2)(b) and (4)(b).
1997 c. 16.	The Finance Act 1997.	Sections 97 to 106.

1 The repeals of sections 80A to 80C of the Finance Act 1986 and sections 97 to 99 of this Act have effect in accordance with section 108 of the Finance Act 1990.

2 The repeals in sections 67, 69, 70 and 72 of the Finance Act 1986 have effect in accordance with section 99 of this Act.

3 The repeal of section 81 of the Finance Act 1986 has effect in accordance with section 97 of this Act.

4 The repeals of section 82 of the Finance Act 1986 and section 53 of the Finance Act 1987 have effect in accordance with section 98 of this Act.

5 The repeals in sections 87 and 88 of the Finance Act 1986 have effect in accordance with section 106 of this Act.

6 The repeals of sections 88A, 88B and 89AA of the Finance Act 1986 and sections 100 to 106 of this Act have effect in accordance with section 110 of the Finance Act 1990.

7 The repeal of section 89 of the Finance Act 1986 and the repeal in Schedule 7 to the Finance Act 1987 have effect in accordance with section 102 of this Act.

8 The repeals of section 89B of the Finance Act 1986 and section 191 of the Finance Act 1996 have effect in accordance with section 103 of this Act.

9 The repeal of section 90(3)(b) of the Finance Act 1986 has effect in accordance with section 105 of this Act.

10 The repeals in sections 93, 94 and 96 of the Finance Act 1986, in Schedule 13 to the Finance Act 1988 and in section 194 of the Finance Act 1996 have effect in accordance with section 104 of this Act.

FINANCE (NO. 2) ACT 1997

(1997 Chapter 58)

[31st July 1997]

PART IV – MISCELLANEOUS AND SUPPLEMENTAL

STAMP DUTY

49   Stamp duty on conveyance or transfer on sale

49 [Repealed by FA 1999, s. 139 and Sch. 20, Pt. V(2) in relation to instruments executed, or bearer instruments issued, on or after 1 October 1999 but, as regards unit trust schemes, subject to

FA 1999, Sch. 20, Pt. V(2), para. 2. The repeal took effect from 6 February 2000 as regards unit trust schemes, by virtue of FA 1999, s. 122(4) and FA 1999, Sch. 19.]

FINANCE ACT 1998

1998 Chapter 36

[*31st July 1998*]

ARRANGEMENT OF SECTIONS

PART V – OTHER TAXES

STAMP DUTY

PART VI – MISCELLANEOUS AND SUPPLEMENTAL

SUPPLEMENTAL

SCHEDULES

PART V – OTHER TAXES

STAMP DUTY

149 Stamp duty on conveyance or transfer on sale

149 [Repealed by FA 1999, s. 139 and Sch. 20, Pt. V(2) in relation to instruments executed, or bearer instruments issued, on or after 1 October 1999 but, as regards unit trust schemes, subject to FA 1999, Sch. 20, Pt. V(2), para. 2. The repeal took effect from 6 February 2000 as regards unit trust schemes, by virtue of FA 1999, s. 122(4) and FA 1999, Sch. 19.]

150 Relief from double stamp duties etc.

150(1) Where an instrument which is chargeable with stamp duty in Great Britain and in Northern Ireland has been stamped in either of those parts of the United Kingdom–

(a)   the instrument shall, to the extent of the duty it bears be deemed to be stamped in the other part of the United Kingdom, but

(b)   if the stamp duty chargeable on the instrument in that part of the United Kingdom exceeds the stamp duty chargeable on the instrument in the part of the United Kingdom in which it has been stamped the instrument shall not be deemed to have been duly stamped in that other part of the United Kingdom unless and until stamped in accordance with the law which has effect in that part of the United Kingdom with a stamp denoting an amount equal to the excess.

150(2) An instrument which, by *virtue of paragraph (b) of subsection* (1) above, is not deemed to have been duly stamped in a part of the United Kingdom unless and until stamped with a stamp denoting an amount equal to the excess mentioned in that paragraph may, notwithstanding anything in section 15 of the Stamp Act 1891, be stamped with such a stamp without payment of any penalty at any time within 30 days after it has first been received in that part of the United Kingdom.

150(3) [Amends SDMA 1891, s. 22.]

150(4) [Repeals s. 29 of the Government of Ireland Act 1920.]

150(5) [Repeals the saving in Sch. 6, Pt. I to the Northern Ireland Constitution Act 1973 (repeals) for orders made under s. 69 of the Government of Ireland Act 1920 in relation to Part IV of the Government of Ireland (Adaptation of the Taxing Acts) Order 1922 (the provisions of which are either spent or re-enacted with modifications in (2) and (3) above).]

151   Depositary receipts and clearance services: exchanges of shares

151(1) [Amends FA 1986, s. 95(3).]

151(2) [Adds FA 1986, s. 95(5)–(7).]

151(3) [Amends FA 1986, s. 97(4).]

151(4) [Adds FA 1986, s. 97(6) and (7).]

151(5) [Amends FA 1986, s. 99(10).]

151(6) This section applies where the issue by company X referred to in section 95(3) or (6) or 97(4) or (7) of the Finance Act 1986 is an issue on or after 1st May 1998.

PART VI – MISCELLANEOUS AND SUPPLEMENTAL

SUPPLEMENTAL

165   Repeals

165(1) The enactments mentioned in Schedule 27 to this Act (which include spent provisions) are hereby repealed to the extent specified in the third column of that Schedule.

165(2) The repeals specified in that Schedule have effect subject to the commencement provisions and savings contained or referred to in the notes set out in that Schedule.

166   Short title

166 This Act may be cited as the Finance Act 1998.

SCHEDULES

SCHEDULE 27 – REPEALS

Part V – OTHER TAXES

(2) STAMP DUTY

Chapter	Short title	Extent of repeal
1920 c. 67.	The Government of Ireland Act 1920.	Section 29.

FINANCE ACT 1999

PART VI – STAMP DUTY AND STAMP DUTY RESERVE TAX

STAMP DUTY

109   Interest and penalties on late stamping

109(1)   [Substitutes SA 1891, s. 15.]

109(2)   [Inserts FA 1989, s. 178(2)(aa).]

109(3)   The consequential amendments in Schedule 12 to this Act have effect.

109(4)   This section applies to instruments executed on or after 1st October 1999.

Cross reference – FA 1999, s. 122(1): the provisions of s. 109 do not apply to transfers or other instruments relating to units under a unit trust scheme except in relation to stamp duty (s. 122(2)):
- (a)   on a conveyance or transfer on sale of property other than units under a unit trust scheme in relation to which such units form the whole or part of the consideration, or
- (b)   under FA 1999, Sch. 15 (bearer instruments).

110   Interest on repayment of duty overpaid etc.

110(1)   A payment by the Commissioners to which this section applies shall be paid with interest at the rate applicable under section 178 of the Finance Act 1989 for the period between the relevant time (as defined below) and the date on which the order for the payment is issued.

110(2)   This section applies to any repayment by the Commissioners of duty, or any penalty on late stamping, under the enactments relating to stamp duty.

In that case the relevant time is 30 days after the day on which the instrument in question was executed or, if later, the date on which the payment of duty or penalty was made.

110(3)   This section applies to a repayment by the Commissioners of an amount lodged with them in respect of the duty payable on stamping an instrument if–

(a)   the instrument is presented for stamping,

(b)   the instrument is duly stamped, and

(c)   the repayment is of an amount then repayable.

In that case the relevant time is 30 days after the day on which the instrument was executed or, if later, the date on which the amount was lodged with the Commissioners.

110(4)   This section also applies to a money payment made by the Commissioners under section 11 of the Stamp Duties Management Act 1891 (allowances for spoiled or misused stamps).

In that case the relevant time is the date on which the duty was paid for the stamp in respect of which the allowance is made.

110(5)   A payment by the Commissioners under section 12A(2)(b) of that Act (allowances for lost or spoiled instruments) is treated for the purposes of this section as a repayment of the duty or penalty by reference to which it is made.

In that case the relevant time is the date on which the payment of duty or penalty was made.

110(6)   No interest is payable under this section if the amount of the payment to which this section applies is less than £25.

110(7)   No interest is payable under this section in respect of a payment made in consequence of an order or judgment of a court having power to allow interest on the payment.

110(8)   Interest paid to any person under this section is not income of that person for any tax purposes.

110(9)   [Inserts FA 1989, s. 178(2)(p).]

110(10)   This section applies in relation to instruments executed on or after 1st October 1999.

Cross references – FA 1999, s. 122(1): the provisions of s. 110 do not apply to transfers or other instruments relating to units under a unit trust scheme; however those provisions do apply in relation to stamp duty (s. 122(2)):
- (a)   on a conveyance or transfer on sale of property other than units under a unit trust scheme in relation to which such units form the whole or part of the consideration, or
- (b)   under FA 1999, Sch. 15 (bearer instruments).

FA 2000, Sch. 33, para. 5: the provisions of s. 110 apply to a repayment of stamp duty or a penalty on late stamping where regulations under FA 2000, Sch. 33 are not approved by House of Commons and the duty or penalty would not have been payable but for those regulations.
SI 1989/1297, reg. 3AB(1)(e): applicable rate of interest under s. 110.

111   Stamp duty on conveyance or transfer on sale

111   [Repealed by FA 1999, s. 139 and Sch. 20, Pt. V(2), the repeal having effect in relation to instruments executed, or bearer instruments issued, on or after 1 October 1999 but, as regards unit trust schemes, subject to Sch. 20, Pt. V(2), para. 2. The repeal took effect from 6 February 2000 as regards unit trust schemes, by virtue of FA 1999, s. 122(4) and Sch. 19.]

112   General amendment of charging provisions

112(1)   The amount of any stamp duty chargeable ad valorem–

(a)   shall be a percentage of the amount specified in the relevant charging provision, and
(b)   shall be rounded up (if necessary) to the nearest multiple of £5.

112(2)   The amount of every fixed stamp duty shall be £5.

112(3)   The provisions of Schedule 13 to this Act have effect in place of Schedule 1 to the Stamp Act 1891, and certain related enactments, so far as they relate to the instruments (other than bearer instruments) chargeable to duty and the method of calculation and rates of duty.

112(4)   The consequential amendments in Schedule 14 to this Act have effect.

112(5)   The percentage rates specified in Schedule 13 and the enactments amended by Schedule 14 correspond to the rates of duty generally in force at the passing of this Act.

In the case of an instrument in relation to which there was then in force transitional provision in connection with an earlier change in the rate of duty having the effect that a different rate applied, the new or amended provisions have effect as if a reference to a percentage corresponding to that different rate were substituted.

112(6)   This section has effect in relation to instruments executed on or after 1st October 1999.

Cross reference – FA 1999, s. 122(1): the provisions of s. 112 do not apply to transfers or other instruments relating to units under a unit trust scheme except in relation to stamp duty (s. 122(2)):
(a)   on a conveyance or transfer on sale of property other than units under a unit trust scheme in relation to which such units form the whole or part of the consideration, or
(b)   under FA 1999, Sch. 15 (bearer instruments).

113   Bearer instruments

113(1)   The provisions of Schedule 15 to this Act have effect in place of the heading "Bearer Instruments" in Schedule 1 to the Stamp Act 1891, and certain related enactments, and incorporate amendments in relation to bearer instruments corresponding to those made by–

section 109 (interest and penalties on late stamping),
section 112 (general amendment of charging provisions), and
Part I of Schedule 17 to this Act (amendments of penalties other than on late stamping).

113(2)   The percentage rates specified in Schedule 15 correspond to the rates of duty generally in force at the passing of this Act.

In the case of an instrument in relation to which there was then in force transitional provision in connection with an earlier change in the rate of duty having the effect that a different rate applied, the new provisions have effect as if a reference to a percentage corresponding to that different rate were substituted.

113(3)   The consequential amendments specified in Schedule 16 to this Act have effect.

113(4)   This section applies in relation to bearer instruments issued on or after 1st October 1999.

Prospective repeal – S. 113 repealed by FA 1999, s. 123(3) and s. 139 and Sch. 20, Pt. V(6) with effect, so far as it relates to stamp duty on bearer instruments, in accordance with FA 1990, s. 107.

Note – The "abolition day" for the purposes of FA 1990, s. 107–110 was such day as may be appointed by Treasury order in accordance with s. 111(1) of that act. Originally, the Treasury order appointing the "abolition day" was to have coincided broadly with the start of paperless trading under the Stock Exchange's planned TAURUS system (IR press release, 20 March 1990). However, on 11 March 1993 it was announced that TAURUS had been abandoned (London Stock Exchange News Release 6/93).

114   Penalties other than on late stamping

114(1)   The provisions of Schedule 17 to this Act (stamp duty: penalties other than on late stamping) have effect.

114(2)   The provisions of that Schedule have effect in relation to penalties in respect of things done or omitted on or after 1st October 1999.

115   Minor amendments and repeal of obsolete provisions

115   Schedule 18 to this Act (stamp duty: minor amendments and repeal of obsolete provisions) has effect.

STAMP DUTY RESERVE TAX

116   Non-sterling bearer instruments issued in connection with merger or takeover

116(1)   [Substitutes FA 1986, s. 95(2).]

116(2)   [Substitutes FA 1986, s. 97(3).]

116(3)   This section applies to any instrument issued on or after 30th January 1999, except one giving effect to an agreement for a company merger or takeover entered into in writing by the companies involved before that date.

Prospective repeal – S. 116 repealed by FA 1999, s. 123(3) and s. 139 and Sch. 20, Pt. V(6) with effect, so far as it relates to stamp duty on bearer instruments, in accordance with FA 1990, s. 107.

Note – The "abolition day" for the purposes of FA 1990, s. 107–110 was such day as may be appointed by Treasury order in accordance with s. 111(1) of that act. Originally, the Treasury order appointing the "abolition day" was to have coincided broadly with the start of paperless trading under the Stock Exchange's planned TAURUS system (IR press release, 20 March 1990). However, on 11 March 1993 it was announced that TAURUS had been abandoned (London Stock Exchange News Release 6/93).

117   Scope of exceptions for certain bearer instruments

117(1)   [Substitutes FA 1986, s. 95(2)(b).]

117(2)   [Inserts FA 1986, s. 95(2A)-(2D).]

117(3)   [Substitutes FA 1986, s. 95(6).]

117(4)   [Substitutes FA 1986, s. 97(3)(b).]

117(5)   [Inserts FA 1986, s. 97(3A)-(3D).]

117(6)   [Substitutes FA 1986, s. 97(7).]

117(7)   Subsections (1) to (6) above apply in relation to any instrument issued on or after 9th March 1999, except one giving effect to an agreement for a company merger or takeover entered into in writing by the companies involved before 30th January 1999.

Prospective repeal – S. 117 repealed by FA 1999, s. 123(3) and s. 139 and Sch. 20, Pt. V(6) with effect, so far as it relates to stamp duty on bearer instruments, in accordance with FA 1990, s. 107.

Note – The "abolition day" for the purposes of FA 1990, s. 107–110 was such day as may be appointed by Treasury order in accordance with s. 111(1) of that act. Originally, the Treasury order appointing the "abolition day" was to have coincided broadly with the start of paperless trading under the Stock Exchange's planned TAURUS system (IR press release, 20 March 1990). However, on 11 March 1993 it was announced that TAURUS had been abandoned (London Stock Exchange News Release 6/93).

118   Relief in case of certain replacement securities

118(1)   [Inserts FA 1986, s. 95A.]

118(2)   [Amends FA 1986, s. 99(10).]

118(3)   [Inserts FA 1986, s. 97AA.]

118(4)   [Amends FA 1986, s. 99(10).]

118(5)   This section applies in relation to securities issued on or after 1st May 1998.

Prospective repeal – S. 118 repealed by FA 1999, s. 123(3) and s. 139 and Sch. 20, Pt. V(6) with effect, so far as it relates to stamp duty reserve tax, in accordance with FA 1990, s. 110.

Note – The "abolition day" for the purposes of FA 1990, s. 107–110 was such day as may be appointed by Treasury order in accordance with s. 111(1) of that act. Originally, the Treasury order appointing the "abolition day" was to have coincided broadly with the start of paperless trading under the Stock Exchange's planned TAURUS system (IR press release, 20 March 1990). However, on 11 March 1993 it was announced that TAURUS had been abandoned (London Stock Exchange News Release 6/93).

119   Power to exempt UK depositary interests in foreign securities

119(1)   The Treasury may by regulations make provision excluding from the definition of "chargeable securities" in Part IV of the Finance Act 1986 such rights in or in relation to securities as, in accordance with the regulations, are to be treated as exempt UK depositary interests in foreign securities.

119(2)   Subject to subsection (3), the regulations may–

(a)   define "depositary interest", "UK depositary interest" and "foreign securities" for this purpose; and

(b)   exempt such descriptions of UK depositary interests in foreign securities (as so defined) as may from time to time be specified in the regulations.

119(3)   The regulations shall not make provision for the exemption of a depositary interest unless the terms of issue of the interest are such that it can only be transferred in accordance with regulations under section 207 of the Companies Act 1989 (transfer of securities without written instrument) or by means of a transfer within section 186(1) of the Finance Act 1996 (transfer of securities to member of electronic transfer system).

119(4)   The regulations may contain such incidental, supplementary, consequential and transitional provision as appears to the Treasury to be appropriate.

This may include provision modifying the enactments relating to stamp duty reserve tax for the purpose of giving effect to the exemption conferred by regulations under this section (or, where earlier regulations are varied or revoked, withdrawing an exemption formerly conferred).

119(5)   Regulations under this section may make different provision for different cases.

119(6)   Regulations under this section shall be made by statutory instrument which shall be subject to annulment in pursuance of a resolution of the House of Commons.

Prospective repeal – S. 119 repealed by FA 1999, s. 123(3) and s. 139 and Sch. 20, Pt. V(6) with effect, so far as it relates to stamp duty reserve tax, in accordance with FA 1990, s. 110.

Statutory instruments – SI 1988/2383: regulations made under s. 98, s. 119 and s. 121.

Note – The "abolition day" for the purposes of FA 1990, s. 107–110 was such day as may be appointed by Treasury order in accordance with s. 111(1) of that act. Originally, the Treasury order appointing the "abolition day" was to have coincided broadly with the start of paperless trading under the Stock Exchange's planned TAURUS system (IR press release, 20 March 1990). However, on 11 March 1993 it was announced that TAURUS had been abandoned (London Stock Exchange News Release 6/93).

120   Minor amendments of exceptions to general charge

120(1)   Section 90 of the Finance Act 1986 (exceptions from the general charge to stamp duty reserve tax) is amended as follows.

120(2)   [Amends FA 1986, s. 90(3F)(c).]

120(3)   [Amends FA 1986, s. 90(5).]

120(4)   Subsection (2) above applies to instruments issued on or after 9th March 1999.

120(5)   Subsection (3) above applies to agreements to transfer securities made on or after 9th March 1999.

Prospective repeal – S. 120 repealed by FA 1999, s. 123(3) and s. 139 and Sch. 20, Pt. V(6) with effect, so far as it relates to stamp duty reserve tax, in accordance with FA 1990, s. 110.

Note – The "abolition day" for the purposes of FA 1990, s. 107–110 was such day as may be appointed by Treasury order in accordance with s. 111(1) of that act. Originally, the Treasury order appointing the "abolition day" was to have coincided broadly with the start of paperless trading under the Stock Exchange's planned TAURUS system (IR press release, 20 March 1990). However, on 11 March 1993 it was announced that TAURUS had been abandoned (London Stock Exchange News Release 6/93).

121   Power to make regulations with respect to administration, etc.

121(1)   The following provisions have effect with respect to the power conferred on the Treasury by section 98(1) of the Finance Act 1986 (stamp duty reserve tax: regulations with respect to administration, etc.).

121(2)   That power includes power to make provision–

(a)   applying the provisions of the Taxes Management Act 1970 relating to penalties and the payment of interest on overdue tax, and

(b)   requiring information to be provided, or books, documents or other records to be made available for inspection, and imposing a penalty for failure to do so.

121(3)   That power includes, and shall be deemed always to have included, power to make provision requiring specified descriptions of persons to account for and pay tax, and any interest on it, on behalf of the person liable to pay it.

Prospective repeal – S. 121 repealed by FA 1999, s. 123(3) and s. 139 and Sch. 20, Pt. V(6) with effect, so far as it relates to stamp duty reserve tax, in accordance with FA 1990, s. 110.

Statutory instruments – SI 1999/2383 (amending SI 1986/1711): regulations made under s. 121.
SI 1999/2536 (amending SI 1986/1711): regulations made under s. 121.
SI 1999/3264 (amending SI 1986/1711): regulations made under s. 121.

Note – The "abolition day" for the purposes of FA 1990, s. 107–110 was such day as may be appointed by Treasury order in accordance with s. 111(1) of that act. Originally, the Treasury order appointing the "abolition day" was to have coincided broadly with the start of paperless trading under the Stock Exchange's planned TAURUS system (IR press release, 20 March 1990). However, on 11 March 1993 it was announced that TAURUS had been abandoned (London Stock Exchange News Release 6/93).

UNITS IN UNIT TRUSTS

122   Stamp duty and stamp duty reserve tax: unit trusts

122(1)   The following provisions of this Act (which apply generally to instruments executed on or after 1st October 1999)–

(a)   section 109 and Schedule 12 (interest and penalties on late stamping),

(b)   section 110 (interest on duty overpaid, etc.), and

(c)   section 112 and Schedules 13 and 14 (general amendment of charging provisions),

do not apply to transfers or other instruments relating to units under a unit trust scheme.

122(2)   Subsection (1) does not affect the operation of those provisions in relation to stamp duty–

(a)   on a conveyance or transfer on sale of property other than units under a unit trust scheme in relation to which such units form the whole or part of the consideration, or

(b)   under Schedule 15 to this Act (bearer instruments).

122(3)   In subsections (1) and (2) "unit" and "unit trust scheme" have the same meaning as in Part VII of the Finance Act 1946 or Part III of the Finance (No.2) Act (Northern Ireland) 1946.

122(4)   Schedule 19 to this Act (stamp duty and stamp duty reserve tax: unit trusts) has effect.

This subsection and that Schedule come into force on 6th February 2000.

SUPPLEMENTARY PROVISIONS

123   Construction of this Part and other supplementary provisions

123(1)   This Part–

(a)   so far as it relates to stamp duty shall be construed as one with the Stamp Act 1891, and

(b)   so far as it relates to stamp duty reserve tax shall be construed as one with Part IV of the Finance Act 1986.

123(2)   In this Part–

(a)   **"the enactments relating to stamp duty"** means the Stamp Act 1891 and any enactment amending or which is to be construed as one with that Act; and

(b)   **"the enactments relating to stamp duty reserve tax"** means Part IV of the Finance Act 1986 and any enactment amending or which is to be construed as one with that Part.

123(3)   The following provisions of this Part shall cease to have effect on the day appointed under section 111(1) of the Finance Act 1990 (abolition of stamp duty for securities etc.):

section 113;

sections 116 to 121;

subsections (1)(b) and (2)(b) of this section;

in Schedule 13–

> paragraph 3,
>
> in paragraph 4 the words "in the case of any other conveyance or transfer on sale",
>
> paragraph 7(1)(b)(ii) to (iv);
>
> paragraph 24(a), (b) and (d);

in Schedule 14, paragraphs 5, 8, 12, 13, 16 to 21 and 23;

Schedule 15;

in Schedule 16, paragraphs 2 to 11;

in Schedule 17, paragraphs 6 to 8;

Parts I to III of Schedule 19;

in Part IV of that Schedule, the words "and the enactments relating to stamp duty reserve tax" in paragraphs 14(1), 15, 16, 17(1) and 18(1).

123(4)   The amendment by this Part, or the repeal in consequence of this Part, of any enactment relating to stamp duty does not affect that enactment as applied for any purpose other than stamp duty.

Prospective repeal – S. 123(1)(b) and (2)(b) repealed by FA 1999, s. 123(3) and s. 139 and Sch. 20, Pt. V(6) with effect, so far as they relate to stamp duty reserve tax, in accordance with FA 1990, s. 110.

Note – The "abolition day" for the purposes of FA 1990, s. 107–110 was such day as may be appointed by Treasury order in accordance with s. 111(1) of that act. Originally, the Treasury order appointing the "abolition day" was to have coincided broadly with the start of paperless trading under the Stock Exchange's planned TAURUS system (IR press release, 20 March 1990). However, on 11 March 1993 it was announced that TAURUS had been abandoned (London Stock Exchange News Release 6/93).

PART VIII – MISCELLANEOUS AND SUPPLEMENTAL

SUPPLEMENTAL

139   Repeals

139(1)   The enactments mentioned in Schedule 20 to this Act (which include provisions that are spent or of no practical utility) are hereby repealed to the extent specified in the third column of that Schedule.

139(2)   The repeals specified in that Schedule have effect subject to the commencement provisions and savings contained or referred to in the notes set out in that Schedule.

140   Short title

140   This Act may be cited as the Finance Act 1999.

SCHEDULES

SCHEDULE 12 – STAMP DUTY: INTEREST AND PENALTIES ON LATE STAMPING

Section 109(3)

Cross reference – FA 1999, s. 122(1): the provisions of Sch. 12 do not apply to transfers or other instruments relating to units under a unit trust scheme except in relation to stamp duty (s. 122(2)):
  (a)   on a conveyance or transfer on sale of property other than units under a unit trust scheme in relation to which such units form the whole or part of the consideration, or
  (b)   under FA 1999, Sch. 15 (bearer instruments).

STAMP ACT 1891 (c.39)

1   [Substitutes SA 1891, s. 12.]
Cross reference – FA 1999, s. 122(1): the provisions of Sch. 12 do not apply to transfers or other instruments relating to units under a unit trust scheme (see note at beginning of Sch. 12 for more details).

2   [Substitutes SA 1891, s. 13.]
Cross reference – FA 1999, s. 122(1): the provisions of Sch. 12 do not apply to transfers or other instruments relating to units under a unit trust scheme (see note at beginning of Sch. 12 for more details).

3(1)   Section 14 of the Stamp Act 1891 (terms upon which instruments not duly stamped may be received in evidence) is amended as follows.

3(2)   [Amends SA 1891, s. 14(1).]

3(3)   [Amends SA 1891, s. 14(2).]

3(4)   [Amends SA 1891, s. 14(3).]

3(5)   [Amends SA 1891, s. 14(4).]
Cross reference – FA 1999, s. 122(1): the provisions of Sch. 12 do not apply to transfers or other instruments relating to units under a unit trust scheme (see note at beginning of Sch. 12 for more details).

FINANCE ACT 1994 (c.9)

4   [Substitutes FA 1994, s. 240.]
Cross references – FA 1999, s. 122(1): the provisions of Sch. 12 do not apply to transfers or other instruments relating to units under a unit trust scheme (see note at beginning of Sch. 12 for more details).
FA 1999, Sch. 18, para. 4: where referring to the duration of a lease, the expression "term" in relation to Scotland means "period".

SCHEDULE 13 – STAMP DUTY: INSTRUMENTS CHARGEABLE AND RATES OF DUTY

Section 112(3)

History – The provisions of Sch. 13 have effect in place of those contained in SA 1891, Sch. 1 and certain related enactments, so far as they relate to the instruments (other than bearer instruments) chargeable to duty and the method and calculation of rates of duty, in relation to instruments executed on or after 1 October 1999 (s. 112).

Cross reference – FA 1999, s. 122(1): the provisions of Sch. 13 do not apply to transfers or other instruments relating to units under a unit trust scheme except in relation to stamp duty (s. 122(2)):

   (a)   on a conveyance or transfer on sale of property other than units under a unit trust scheme in relation to which such units form the whole or part of the consideration, or

   (b)   under FA 1999, Sch. 15 (bearer instruments).

Part I – Conveyance or Transfer on Sale

CHARGE

1(1) Stamp duty is chargeable on a conveyance or transfer on sale.

1(2) For this purpose **"conveyance on sale"** includes every instrument, and every decree or order of a court or commissioners, by which any property, or any estate or interest in property, is, on being sold, transferred to or vested in the purchaser or another person on behalf of or at the direction of the purchaser.

Cross references – SA 1891 s. 122(1): **"instrument"** includes every written document.

FA 1898, s. 6: conveyance on sale includes foreclosure decree.

FA 1900, s. 10: no duty in respect of further consideration by way of covenant, relating to subject matter of conveyance.

FA 1930, s. 42(1): no duty on instruments transferring beneficial interest in property between associated companies.

FA 1958, s. 35(5) (no duty on any agreement made under New Towns Act 1946, s. 14).

FA 1970, s. 33 (composition of stamp duty payable by agreement with recognised stock exchange (or, from such day to be appointed, recognised clearing house or investment exchange: FA 1986, s. 83)).

FA 1980, s. 97: shared housing ownership transactions – residential leases granted by specified bodies partly in consideration of a premium come under FA 1999, Sch. 13, Pt. I rather than Pt. II.

FA 1982, s. 129: no duty chargeable on conveyance or transfer or agreement for same to charitable body or to trustees of National Heritage Memorial Fund or the National Endowment for Science, Technology and the Arts (The Lottery Fund).

FA 1985, s. 83: exemption from duty for instruments executed in pursuance of Court Order made on grant of decree of divorce etc., though £5 duty payable.

FA 1985, s. 84: exemption from duty for instruments effecting variation by beneficiaries of dispositions by deceased within two years of latter's death or appropriation by personal representative in or towards satisfaction of a general legacy; or effecting an appropriation by a personal representative towards satisfaction of surviving spouse's interest in intestate's estate. £5 duty still payable.

FA 1986, s. 75(2): exemption from duty under FA 1999, Sch. 13, Pt. I for instruments executed in connection with acquisition of the undertaking of one company by another in pursuance of scheme of reconstruction of the former. A reduced rate applies under FA 1986, s. 76(4) in relation to such acquisitions.

FA 1986, s. 79(4): exemption from duty for certain instruments relating to loan capital.

FA 1986, s. 79(7A): exemption from duty for certain instruments relating to loan capital carrying a right to interest which reduces if the business results (or value of any property) improves (or increases), or which increases if the business results (or value of any property) deteriorates (or diminishes) (so called "ratchet loans").

FA 1986, s. 77: exemption from duty under FA 1999, Sch. 13, Pt. I for instruments which transfer shares in a target company to an acquiring company, if conditions in s. 77(3) are fulfilled.

FA 1987, s. 50(1): exemption from duty under FA 1999, Sch. 13, Pt. I of instruments transferring or vesting certain interests, rights or options (warrants) to purchase exempt securities (government and loan stocks).

FA 1987, s. 55(1): exemption from duty under FA 1999, Sch. 13, Pt. I of any conveyance or transfer (or agreement to these) to a Minister of the Crown or the Solicitor for the affairs of Her Majesty's Treasury.

FA 1989, s. 175: Treasury may, by regulations, exempt transaction involving a stock exchange nominee from charge under FA 1999, Sch. 13, Pt. I if also charged to stamp duty reserve tax.

FA 1990, s. 108: exemption for transfer of "defined securities" (abolition intended to coincide with introduction of paperless trading).

FA 1993, s. 202(4): lease chargeable to stamp duty under FA 1999, Sch. 13, Pt. I as a conveyance and not under Pt. II where a person exercises a right to acquire on rent to mortgage terms under the Housing Act 1985, Pt. V, and a lease is executed in pursuance of that right.

FA 1999, s. 122(1): the provisions of Sch. 13 do not apply to transfers or other instruments relating to units under a unit trust scheme (see note at beginning of Sch. 13 for more details).

FA 2000, s. 118: transfers etc. of land where consideration is or includes any other property.

FA 2000, s. 119: transfers of land to a company where either the transferor company is connected with the transferee or the transfer is for a consideration (some or all of) which consists of shares in a company connected with the transferor.

FA 2000, s. 122: a transfer etc. of marketable securities which would not otherwise be treated as a transfer on sale is treated as a sale for the purposes of Sch. 13, Pt. I where the consideration for the transfer is or includes any debt, stock or securities which are not "chargeable securities" for the purposes of stamp duty reserve tax within the meaning of FA 1986, Pt. IV.

FA 2000, s. 129: no stamp duty chargeable on an instrument for the sale, transfer or other disposition of intellectual property.

FA 2000, s. 130: no stamp duty chargeable on certain conveyances or transfers of land to registered social landlords (or equivalent in Scotland or Northern Ireland).

Extra-statutory concessions – G5: transfer of stock from persons to themselves operating as an executor's assent.

G6: transfer of assets between non-profit making bodies with similar objects.

Statements of practice – SP 8/93: stamp duty: new buildings.

Notes – SI 1987/516: certification of certain transactions.

RATES OF DUTY

2 Duty under this Part is chargeable by reference to the amount or value of the consideration for the sale.

Cross references – FA 1986, s. 67(2) (depository receipts) and s. 70(2) (clearance services): rate of duty chargeable under FA 1999, Sch. 13, Pt. I on instruments transferring securities of UK incorporated company to persons specified in said s. 67, 70.

FA 1993, s. 202(2): for the purposes of stamp duty under FA 1999, Sch. 13, Pt. I, consideration for sale taken to be equal to a price which, by virtue of the Housing Act 1985, s. 126 would be payable for the dwelling-house on conveyance if the person exercised the right to buy.

FA 1993, s. 203(2): for the purposes of stamp duty under FA 1999, Sch. 13, Pt. I, consideration for sale taken to be equal to the price which, by virtue of the Housing (Scotland) Act 1987, s. 62 would be payable for the house if the person were exercising the right to buy.
FA 1994, s. 242(1): duty payable under FA 1999, Sch. 13, Pt. I on open market value of property if price payable cannot be ascertained when the transfer document is executed.
FA 1999, s. 122(1): the provisions of Sch. 13 do not apply to transfers or other instruments relating to units under a unit trust scheme (see note at beginning of Sch. 13 for more details).
FA 2000, s. 118: transfers etc. of land where consideration is or includes any other property.
FA 2000, s. 119: transfers of land to a company where either the transferor company is connected with the transferee or the transfer is for a consideration (some or all of) which consists of shares in a company connected with the transferor.
Statements of practice – SP 11/91: stamp duty and value added tax (VAT) – interaction.
SP 11/91: stamp duty chargeable on VAT-inclusive consideration in respect of certain commercial property transactions.

3   In the case of a conveyance or transfer of stock or marketable securities the rate is 0.5%.

Prospective repeal – Sch. 13, para. 3 repealed by FA 1999, s. 123(3) and s. 139 and Sch. 20, Pt. V(6) with effect, so far as it relates to stamp duty on instruments other than bearer instruments, in accordance with FA 1990, s. 108. (This effectively repeats the prospective repeal of the equivalent previous provisions of FA 1963, s. 55(1A) in relation to instruments executed on or after 1 October 1999. See history note at the beginning of this Schedule.)

Cross reference – FA 1999, s. 122(1): the provisions of Sch. 13 do not apply to transfers or other instruments relating to units under a unit trust scheme (see note at beginning of Sch. 13 for more details).

Note – The "abolition day" for the purposes of FA 1990, s. 107–110 was such day as may be appointed by Treasury order in accordance with s. 111(1) of that act. Originally, the Treasury order appointing the "abolition day" was to have coincided broadly with the start of paperless trading under the Stock Exchange's planned TAURUS system (IR press release, 20 March 1990). However, on 11 March 1993 it was announced that TAURUS had been abandoned (London Stock Exchange News Release 6/93).

4   In the case of any other conveyance or transfer on sale the rates of duty are as follows–

1. Where the amount or value of the consideration is £60,000 or under and the instrument is certified at £60,000	Nil
2. Where the amount or value of the consideration is £250,000 or under and the instrument is certified at £250,000	1%
3. Where the amount or value of the consideration is £500,000 or under and the instrument is certified at £500,000	3%
4. Any other case	4%

Prospective repeal – In Sch. 13, para. 4, the words "In the case of any other conveyance or transfer on sale" repealed by FA 1999, s. 123(3) and s. 139 and Sch. 20, Pt. V(6) with effect, so far as it relates to stamp duty on instruments other than bearer instruments, in accordance with FA 1990, s. 108.

History – In Sch. 13, para. 4, 3% substituted for 2.5% in paragraph 3, and 4% substituted for 3.5% in paragraph 4 of the table by FA 2000, s. 114(1)) the substitution applying to instruments executed on or after 28 March 2000, unless the instrument gives effect to a contract made on or before 21 March 2000 except in circumstances specified in FA 2000, s. 114(3)).

Cross references – LLPA 2000, s. 12 will come into force on a date to be appointed by Statutory Instrument and it provides:
"**12(1)**   Stamp duty shall not be chargeable on an instrument by which property is conveyed or transferred by a person to a limited liability partnership in connection with its incorporation within the period of one year beginning with the date of incorporation if the following two conditions are satisfied.
12(2)   The first condition is that at the relevant time the person–
(a)   is a partner in a partnership comprised of all the persons who are or are to be members of the limited liability partnership (and no-one else), or
(b)   holds the property conveyed or transferred as nominee or bare trustee for one or more of the partners in such a partnership.
12(3)   The second condition is that–
(a)   the proportions of the property conveyed or transferred to which the persons mentioned in subsection (2)(a) are entitled immediately after the conveyance or transfer are the same as those to which they were entitled at the relevant time, or
(b)   none of the differences in those proportions has arisen as part of a scheme or arrangement of which the main purpose, or one of the main purposes, is avoidance of liability to any duty or tax.
12(4)   For the purposes of subsection (2) a person holds property as bare trustee for a partner if the partner has the exclusive right (subject only to satisfying any outstanding charge, lien or other right of the trustee to resort to the property for payment of duty, taxes, costs or other outgoings) to direct how the property shall be dealt with.
12(5)   In this section "the relevant time" means–
(a)   if the person who conveyed or transferred the property to the limited liability partnership acquired the property after its incorporation, immediately after he acquired the property, and
(b)   in any other case, immediately before its incorporation.
12(6)   An instrument in respect of which stamp duty is not chargeable by virtue of subsection (1) shall not be taken to be duly stamped unless–
(a)   it has, in accordance with section 12 of the Stamp Act 1891, been stamped with a particular stamp denoting that it is not chargeable with any duty or that it is duly stamped, or
(b)   it is stamped with the duty to which it would be liable apart from that subsection."
FA 1999, s. 122(1): the provisions of Sch. 13 do not apply to transfers or other instruments relating to units under a unit trust scheme (see note at beginning of Sch. 13 for more details).

Other material – The Stamp Office Customer Newsletter, March 1999 (not reproduced): details of changes to rates of duty introduced by FA 1999.

Note – The "abolition day" for the purposes of FA 1990, s. 107–110 was such day as may be appointed by Treasury order in accordance with s. 111(1) of that act. Originally, the Treasury order appointing the "abolition day" was to have coincided broadly with the start of paperless trading under the Stock Exchange's planned TAURUS system (IR press release, 20 March 1990). However, on 11 March 1993 it was announced that TAURUS had been abandoned (London Stock Exchange News Release 6/93).

5 The above provisions are subject to any enactment setting a different rate or setting an upper limit on the amount of duty chargeable.

Cross reference – FA 1999, s. 122(1): the provisions of Sch. 13 do not apply to transfers or other instruments relating to units under a unit trust scheme (see note at beginning of Sch. 13 for more details).

MEANING OF INSTRUMENT BEING CERTIFIED AT AN AMOUNT

6(1) The references in paragraph 4 above to an instrument being certified at a particular amount mean that it contains a statement that the transaction effected by the instrument does not form part of a larger transaction or series of transactions in respect of which the amount or value, or aggregate amount or value, of the consideration exceeds that amount.

6(2) For this purpose a sale or contract or agreement for the sale of goods, wares or merchandise shall be disregarded–

(a) in the case of an instrument which is not an actual conveyance or transfer of the goods, wares or merchandise (with or without other property);

(b) in the case of an instrument treated as such a conveyance or transfer only by virtue of paragraph 7 (contracts or agreements chargeable as conveyances on sale);

and any statement as mentioned in sub-paragraph (1) shall be construed as leaving out of account any matter which is to be so disregarded.

Cross references – FA 1991, s. 113(1): for the purposes of Sch. 13, para. 6(1) a sale or contract or agreement for the sale of exempt property within the meaning of section 110 shall be disregarded and any statement as mentioned in that provision shall be construed as leaving out of account any matter which is to be so disregarded.
FA 1999, s. 122(1): the provisions of Sch. 13 do not apply to transfers or other instruments relating to units under a unit trust scheme (see note at beginning of Sch. 13 for more details).
FA 2000, Sch. 34, para. 4: intellectual property shall be disregarded for the purposes of Sch. 13, para. 6.

Statements of practice – SP 6/90: certificate may be included in conveyance or transfer of property subject to a debt where covenant by transferee relates to part of the debt, provided the relevant amount of the debt does not exceed the amount certified; transfer may then be sent direct to Land Registry. (Statement refers to certificate under FA 1958, s. 34(4), repealed by FA 1999, s. 139 and Sch. 20, Pt. V(2). The wording of para. 6 effectively replaces the repealed legislation.)

CONTRACTS OR AGREEMENTS CHARGEABLE AS CONVEYANCES ON SALE

7(1) A contract or agreement for the sale of–

(a) any equitable estate or interest in property, or

(b) any estate or interest in property except–

   (i) land,

   (ii) goods, wares or merchandise,

   (iii) stock or marketable securities,

   (iv) any ship or vessel, or a part interest, share or property of or in any ship or vessel, or

   (v) property of any description situated outside the United Kingdom,

is chargeable with the same ad valorem duty, to be paid by the purchaser, as if it were an actual conveyance on sale of the estate, interest or property contracted or agreed to be sold.

7(2) Where the purchaser has paid ad valorem duty and before having obtained a conveyance or transfer of the property enters into a contract or agreement for the sale of the same, the contract or agreement is chargeable, if the consideration for that sale is in excess of the consideration for the original sale, with the ad valorem duty payable in respect of the excess consideration but is not otherwise chargeable.

7(3) Where duty has been paid in conformity with sub-paragraphs (1) and (2), the conveyance or transfer to the purchaser or sub-purchaser, or any other person on his behalf or by his direction, is not chargeable with any duty.

7(4) In that case, upon application and upon production of the contract or agreement (or contracts or agreements) duly stamped, the Commissioners shall either–

(a) denote the payment of the ad valorem duty upon the conveyance or transfer, or

(b) transfer the ad valorem duty to the conveyance or transfer.

Prospective repeal – Sch. 13, para. 7(1)(b)(ii)–(iv) repealed by FA 1999, s. 123(3) and s. 139 and Sch. 20, Pt. V(6) with effect, so far as it relates to stamp duty on instruments other than bearer instruments, in accordance with FA 1990, s. 108.(This effectively repeats the prospective repeal of the equivalent previous provisions of SA 1891, s. 59 in relation to instruments executed on or after 1 October 1999. See history note at the beginning of this Schedule.)

Cross references – FA 1963, s. 65: exemption in respect of applications for legal aid.
FA 1982, s. 129: no duty chargeable on conveyance, transfer or lease or agreement for same where to charitable body or to trustees of National Heritage Memorial Fund or the National Endowment for Science, Technology and the Arts (The Lottery Fund).
FA 1985, s. 83: exemption from duty for instruments executed in pursuance of Court Order made on grant of decree of divorce etc., though £5 duty payable.
FA 1985, s. 84: exemption from duty for instruments effecting variation by beneficiaries of dispositions by deceased within two years of latter's death or appropriation by personal representative in or towards satisfaction of a general legacy; or effecting an

appropriation by a personal representative towards satisfaction of surviving spouse's interest in intestate's estate. £5 duty still payable.
FA 1999, s. 122(1): the provisions of Sch. 13 do not apply to transfers or other instruments relating to units under a unit trust scheme (see note at beginning of Sch. 13 for more details).
FA 2000, s. 118: transfers etc. of land where consideration is or includes any other property.
FA 2000, s. 119: transfers of land to a company where either the transferor company is connected with the transferee or the transfer is for a consideration which consists (in full or in part) of shares in a company connected with the transferee.

Note – The "abolition day" for the purposes of FA 1990, s. 107–110 was such day as may be appointed by Treasury order in accordance with s. 111(1) of that act. Originally, the Treasury order appointing the "abolition day" was to have coincided broadly with the start of paperless trading under the Stock Exchange's planned TAURUS system (IR press release, 20 March 1990). However, on 11 March 1993 it was announced that TAURUS had been abandoned (London Stock Exchange News Release 6/93).

8(1)   Where a contract or agreement would apart from paragraph 7 not be chargeable with any duty and a conveyance or transfer made in conformity with the contract or agreement is presented to the Commissioners for stamping with the ad valorem duty chargeable on it–

(a)   within the period of six months after the execution of the contract or agreement, or

(b)   within such longer period as the Commissioners may think reasonable in the circumstances of the case,

the conveyance or transfer shall be stamped accordingly, and both it and the contract or agreement shall be deemed to be duly stamped.

8(2)   Nothing in this paragraph affects the provisions as to the stamping of a conveyance or transfer after execution.

Cross reference – FA 1999, s. 122(1): the provisions of Sch. 13 do not apply to transfers or other instruments relating to units under a unit trust scheme (see note at beginning of Sch. 13 for more details).

9   The ad valorem duty paid upon a contract or agreement by virtue of paragraph 7 shall be repaid by the Commissioners if the contract or agreement is afterwards rescinded or annulled or is for any other reason not substantially performed or carried into effect so as to operate as or be followed by a conveyance or transfer.

Cross reference – FA 1999, s. 122(1): the provisions of Sch. 13 do not apply to transfers or other instruments relating to units under a unit trust scheme (see note at beginning of Sch. 13 for more details).

Part II – Lease

Cross reference – FA 1999, Sch. 18, para. 4: where referring to the duration of a lease, the expression "term" in relation to Scotland means "period".

Other material – The Stamp Office Customer Newsletter, March 1999 (not reproduced): changes to rates of duty introduced by FA 1999.
The Stamp Office Customer Newsletter, May 1999 (not reproduced): a revised approach to "RPI" leases.

CHARGE

10   Stamp duty is chargeable on a lease.

Cross references – FA 1980, s. 97: shared housing ownership transactions – residential leases granted by specified bodies partly in consideration of a premium come under FA 1999, Sch. 13, Pt. I rather than Pt. II.
FA 1982, s. 129: no duty chargeable on a lease or agreement for a lease to charitable body or to trustees of National Heritage Memorial Fund or the National Endowment for Science, Technology and the Arts (The Lottery Fund).
FA 1987, s. 55(1): exemption from duty under FA 1999, Sch. 13, Pt. II of any or lease (or agreement to a lease) to a Minister of the Crown or the Solicitor for the affairs of Her Majesty's Treasury.
FA 1993, s. 202(4): lease chargeable to stamp duty under FA 1999, Sch. 13, Pt. I as a conveyance and not under Pt. II where a person exercises a right to acquire on rent to mortgage terms under the Housing Act 1985, Pt. V, and a lease is executed in pursuance of that right.
FA 1995, s. 151: duty not chargeable under FA 1999, Sch. 13, Pt. II on a lease, an agreement for a lease, or an agreement with respect to a letting, where the transaction is between certain associated bodies.
FA 1999, s. 122(1): the provisions of Sch. 13 do not apply to transfers or other instruments relating to units under a unit trust scheme (see note at beginning of Sch. 13 for more details).
FA 1999, Sch. 13, para. 20: an instrument which is not itself a lease:
(a)   by which it is agreed that the rent reserved by a lease should be increased, or
(b)   which confirms or records any such agreement made otherwise than in writing,
(other than an instrument giving effect to a provision in the lease for periodic review of the rent reserved by it) is chargeable with the same duty as if it were a lease in consideration of the additional rent made payable by it.
FA 2000, s. 121: lease granted to a company where either the grantor is connected with the company or the lease is granted for consideration (some or all of) which consists of shares in a company with which the grantor is connected.
FA 2000, s. 128: surrender of leases.
FA 2000, s. 130: no stamp duty chargeable on a lease of land to a registered social landlord (or equivalent in Scotland or Northern Ireland).

RATES OF DUTY

11   In the case of a lease for a definite term less than a year the duty is as follows–

1. Lease of furnished dwelling-house or apartments where the rent for the term exceeds £5,000	£5
2. Any other lease of land	The same duty as for a lease for a year at the rent reserved for the definite term

History – In para. 11 the sum of "£5,000" substituted for the sum of "£500" in paragraph 1 of the table by FA 2000, s. 115(1)(a) in relation to instruments executed on or after 28 March 2000.

Cross references – FA 1994, s. 243(1): duty chargeable on price paid in return for any agreement for the surrender (otherwise than by deed) of a lease if the agreement was made after 7 December 1993. In Scotland this applies if a lease is renounced. FA 1999, s. 122(1): the provisions of Sch. 13 do not apply to transfers or other instruments relating to units under a unit trust scheme (see note at beginning of Sch. 13 for more details).
FA 1999, Sch. 18, para. 4: where referring to the duration of a lease, the expression "term" in relation to Scotland means "period".

Other material – The Stamp Office Customer Newsletter, March 1999 (not reproduced): details of changes to rates of duty introduced by FA 1999 (including premiums paid for a lease).
The Stamp Office Customer Newsletter, May 1999 (not reproduced): revised approach to "RPI" leases – backdated claims.

12(1) In the case of a lease of land for any other definite term, or for an indefinite term, the duty is determined as follows.

12(2) If the consideration or part of the consideration moving to the lessor or to any other person consists of any money, stock, security or other property, the duty in respect of that consideration is the same as that on a conveyance on a sale for the same consideration.

But if–

(a) part of the consideration is rent, and

(b) that rent exceeds £600 a year,

the duty is calculated as if paragraph 1 of the Table in paragraph 4 of this Schedule were omitted.

12(3) If the consideration or part of the consideration is rent, the duty in respect of that consideration is determined by reference to the rate or average rate of the rent (whether reserved as a yearly rent or not), as follows.

1. Term not more than 7 years or indefinite–	
(a) if the rent is £5,000 or less	Nil
(b) if the rent is more than £5,000	1%
2. Term more than 7 years but not more than 35 years	2%
3. Term more than 35 years but not more than 100 years	12%
4. Term more than 100 years	24%

History – In Sch. 13, para. 12(3) the sum of "£5,000" substituted for the sum of "£500" in paragraph 1.(a) and (b) of the table by FA 2000, s. 115(1)(b) in relation to instruments executed on or after 28 March 2000.
In Sch. 13, para. 12(3) the words "not more than 7 years" substituted for the words "less than 7 years" in paragraph 1. of the table by FA 2000, 116(1), the substitution applying to instruments executed on or after 1 October 1999, subject to the transitional provisions of FA 2000, Sch. 32 for instruments executed on or after that date but before 28 March 2000.

Cross references – FA 1994, s. 242(2): duty payable under FA 1999, Sch. 13, para 12 on market rent if rent payable cannot be ascertained when the transfer document is executed.
FA 1999, s. 122(1): the provisions of Sch. 13 do not apply to transfers or other instruments relating to units under a unit trust scheme (see note at beginning of Sch. 13 for more details).
FA 1999, Sch. 18, para. 4: where referring to the duration of a lease, the expression "term" in relation to Scotland means "period".

Statements of practice – SP 11/91: stamp duty chargeable on VAT-inclusive consideration in respect of commercial lease agreements, except where formal notice of election not to waive exemption.
SP 11/91: where lease attracts VAT, stamp duty chargeable on VAT-inclusive consideration.

Other material – The Stamp Office Customer Newsletter, March 1999 (not reproduced): details of changes to rates of duty introduced by FA 1999 (including premiums paid for a lease).
The Stamp Office Customer Newsletter, May 1999 (not reproduced): revised approach to "RPI" leases – backdated claims.

13 Stamp duty of £5 is chargeable on a lease not within paragraph 11 or 12 above.

Cross reference – FA 1999, s. 122(1): the provisions of Sch. 13 do not apply to transfers or other instruments relating to units under a unit trust scheme (see note at beginning of Sch. 13 for more details).

AGREEMENT FOR A LEASE CHARGED AS A LEASE

14(1) An agreement for a lease is chargeable with the same duty as if it were an actual lease made for the term and consideration mentioned in the agreement.

14(2) Where duty has been duly paid on an agreement for a lease and subsequent to that agreement a lease is granted which either–

(a) is in conformity with the agreement, or

(b) relates to substantially the same property and term as the agreement, the duty which would otherwise be charged on the lease is reduced by the amount of the duty paid on the agreement.

14(3) Sub-paragraph (1) does not apply to missives of let in Scotland that constitute an actual lease.

Subject to that, references in this paragraph to an agreement for a lease include missives of let in Scotland.

Cross references – FA 1982, s. 129: no duty chargeable on an agreement for a lease to charitable body or to trustees of National Heritage Memorial Fund or the National Endowment for Science, Technology and the Arts (The Lottery Fund).
FA 1999, s. 122(1): the provisions of Sch. 13 do not apply to transfers or other instruments relating to units under a unit trust scheme (see note at beginning of Sch. 13 for more details).
FA 1999, Sch. 18, para. 4: where referring to the duration of a lease, the expression "term" in relation to Scotland means "period".

LEASE FOR FIXED TERM AND THEN UNTIL DETERMINED

15(1) For the purposes of this Part a lease granted for a fixed term and thereafter until determined is treated as a lease for a definite term equal to the fixed term together with such further period as must elapse before the earliest date at which the lease can be determined.

15(2) Paragraph 14 (agreement for a lease charged as a lease) shall be construed accordingly.

Cross references – FA 1982, s. 129: no duty chargeable on a lease or an agreement for a lease to charitable body or to trustees of National Heritage Memorial Fund or the National Endowment for Science, Technology and the Arts (The Lottery Fund).
FA 1999, s. 122(1): the provisions of Sch. 13 do not apply to transfers or other instruments relating to units under a unit trust scheme (see note at beginning of Sch. 13 for more details).
FA 1999, Sch. 18, para. 4: where referring to the duration of a lease, the expression "term" in relation to Scotland means "period".

Part III – Other Instruments

CONVEYANCE OR TRANSFER OTHERWISE THAN ON SALE

16(1) Stamp duty of £5 is chargeable on a conveyance or transfer of property otherwise than on sale.

16(2) In sub-paragraph (1) **"conveyance or transfer"** includes every instrument, and every decree or order of a court or commissioners, by which any property is transferred to or vested in any person.

Cross references – FA 1985, s. 87(2): certain fixed duties may be excluded by regulations in relation to certain instruments (see **Note** below and notes to that section for such regulations).
FA 1986, s. 67(3) (depository receipts) and s. 70(3) (clearance services): rate of duty chargeable under FA 1999, Sch. 13, para. 16 on instruments transferring securities of UK incorporated company to persons specified in said s. 67, 70.
FA 1987, s. 50(1): exemption from duty under FA 1999, Sch. 13, para. 16 of instruments transferring or vesting certain interests, rights or options (warrants) to purchase exempt securities (government and loan stocks).
FA 1987, s. 55(1): exemption from duty under FA 1999, Sch. 13, para. 16 of any conveyance or transfer (or agreement to these) to a Minister of the Crown or the Solicitor for the affairs of Her Majesty's Treasury.
FA 1999, s. 122(1): the provisions of Sch. 13 do not apply to transfers or other instruments relating to units under a unit trust scheme (see note at beginning of Sch. 13 for more details).
FA 2000, s. 130: no stamp duty chargeable under Sch. 13, para. 16 on a conveyance or transfer of land to a registered social landlord (or equivalent in Scotland or Northern Ireland).

Notes – SI 1987/516: certification of certain transactions.

DECLARATION OF USE OR TRUST

17(1) Stamp duty of £5 is chargeable on a declaration of any use or trust of or concerning property unless the instrument constitutes a conveyance or transfer on sale.

17(2) This does not apply to a will.

Cross references – FA 1985, s. 87(2): certain fixed duties may be excluded by regulations in relation to certain instruments (see notes to that section for such regulations).
FA 1999, s. 122(1): the provisions of Sch. 13 do not apply to transfers or other instruments relating to units under a unit trust scheme (see note at beginning of Sch. 13 for more details).

Other material – High Court Practice Direction (Chancery 3/89) (not reproduced): duplicate orders under Variation of Trusts Act 1958 which are not confined to the lifting of protective trusts (exempt) or do not affect voluntary dispositions inter vivos (capable of certification under SI 1987/516) fall under (what is now) FA 1999, Sch. 13, para 17.

DISPOSITIONS IN SCOTLAND

18(1) The following are chargeable with duty as a conveyance on sale–

(a) a disposition of heritable property in Scotland to singular successors or purchasers;

(b) a disposition of heritable property in Scotland to a purchaser containing a clause declaring all or any part of the purchase money a real burden upon, or affecting, the heritable property thereby disponed, or any part of it;

(c)   a disposition in Scotland containing constitution of feu or ground annual right.

18(2)   A disposition in Scotland of any property, or any right or interest in property, that is not so chargeable is chargeable with stamp duty of £5.

Cross references – FA 1985, s. 87(2): certain fixed duties may be excluded by regulations in relation to certain instruments (see notes to that section for such regulations).
FA 1999, s. 122(1): the provisions of Sch. 13 do not apply to transfers or other instruments relating to units under a unit trust scheme (see note at beginning of Sch. 13 for more details).

DUPLICATE OR COUNTERPART

19(1)   A duplicate or counterpart of an instrument chargeable with duty is chargeable with duty of £5.

19(2)   The duplicate or counterpart of an instrument chargeable with duty is not duly stamped unless–

(a)   it is stamped as an original instrument, or

(b)   it appears by some stamp impressed on it that the full and proper duty has been paid on the original instrument of which it is the duplicate or counterpart.

19(3)   Sub-paragraph (2) does not apply to the counterpart of an instrument chargeable as a lease, if that counterpart is not executed by or on behalf of any lessor or grantor.

Cross references – FA 1985, s. 87(2): certain fixed duties may be excluded by regulations in relation to certain instruments (see notes to that section for such regulations).
FA 1999, s. 122(1): the provisions of Sch. 13 do not apply to transfers or other instruments relating to units under a unit trust scheme (see note at beginning of Sch. 13 for more details).
Other material – High Court Practice Direction (Chancery 3/89) (not reproduced): duplicate orders under Variation of Trusts Act 1958 which are not confined to the lifting of protective trusts (exempt) or do not affect voluntary dispositions inter vivos (capable of certification under SI 1987/516) fall under (what is now) FA 1999, Sch. 13, para 17.

INSTRUMENT INCREASING RENT

20(1)   An instrument (not itself a lease)–

(a)   by which it is agreed that the rent reserved by a lease should be increased, or

(b)   which confirms or records any such agreement made otherwise than in writing,

is chargeable with the same duty as if it were a lease in consideration of the additional rent made payable by it.

20(2)   Sub-paragraph (1) does not apply to an instrument giving effect to provision in the lease for periodic review of the rent reserved by it.

Cross references – FA 1985, s. 87(2): certain fixed duties may be excluded by regulations in relation to certain instruments (see notes to that section for such regulations).
FA 1999, s. 122(1): the provisions of Sch. 13 do not apply to transfers or other instruments relating to units under a unit trust scheme (see note at beginning of Sch. 13 for more details).

PARTITION OR DIVISION

21(1)   Where on the partition or division of an estate or interest in land consideration exceeding £100 in amount or value is paid or given, or agreed to be paid or given, for equality, the principal or only instrument by which the partition or division is effected is chargeable with the same ad valorem duty as a conveyance on sale for the consideration, and with that duty only.

21(2)   Where there are several instruments for completing the title of either party, the principal instrument is to be ascertained, and the other instruments shall be charged with duty, as provided by sections 58(3) and 61 of the Stamp Act 1891 in the case of several instruments of conveyance.

21(3)   Stamp duty of £5 is chargeable on an instrument effecting a partition or division to which the above provisions do not apply.

Cross references – FA 1985, s. 87(2): certain fixed duties may be excluded by regulations in relation to certain instruments (see notes to that section for such regulations).
FA 1994, s. 241: exchanges of land interests treated as sales for stamp duty at market value and charged under FA 1999, Sch. 13, Pt. I accordingly.
FA 1999, s. 122(1): the provisions of Sch. 13 do not apply to transfers or other instruments relating to units under a unit trust scheme (see note at beginning of Sch. 13 for more details).

RELEASE OR RENUNCIATION

22   Stamp duty of £5 is chargeable on a release or renunciation of property unless the instrument constitutes a conveyance or transfer on sale.

Cross references – FA 1985, s. 87(2): certain fixed duties may be excluded by regulations in relation to certain instruments (see notes to that section for such regulations).
FA 1999, s. 122(1): the provisions of Sch. 13 do not apply to transfers or other instruments relating to units under a unit trust scheme (see note at beginning of Sch. 13 for more details).

SURRENDER

23　　Stamp duty of £5 is chargeable on a surrender of property unless the instrument constitutes a conveyance or transfer on sale.

Cross references – FA 1985, s. 87(2): certain fixed duties may be excluded by regulations in relation to certain instruments (see notes to that section for such regulations).
FA 1999, s. 122(1): the provisions of Sch. 13 do not apply to transfers or other instruments relating to units under a unit trust scheme (see note at beginning of Sch. 13 for more details).
FA 2000, s. 128: surrender of leases.

Part IV – General Exemptions

24　　The following are exempt from stamp duty under this Schedule–

(a)　　transfers of shares in the government or parliamentary stocks or funds or strips (within the meaning of section 47 of the Finance Act 1942) of such stocks or funds;

(b)　　instruments for the sale, transfer, or other disposition (absolutely or otherwise) of any ship or vessel, or any part, interest, share or property of or in a ship or vessel;

(c)　　testaments, testamentary instruments and dispositions mortis causa in Scotland;

(d)　　renounceable letters of allotment, letters of rights or other similar instruments where the rights under the letter or other instrument are renounceable not later than six months after its issue.

Prospective repeal – Sch. 13, para. 24(a), (b) and (d) repealed by FA 1999, s. 123(3) and s. 139 and Sch. 20, Pt. V(6) with effect, so far as it relates to stamp duty on instruments other than bearer instruments, in accordance with FA 1990, s. 108.

Cross references – FA 1942, s. 47: Treasury regulations with respect to the transfer and registration of Government stock.
FA 1985, s. 81(2): disapplication of exemption for renounceable letters of allotment etc. under FA 1999, Sch. 13, para. 24(d) for certain renunciations of rights to shares in a company under an arrangement between persons who control the company (or who will as a consequence of the arrangement).
FA 1999, s. 122(1): the provisions of Sch. 13 do not apply to transfers or other instruments relating to units under a unit trust scheme (see note at beginning of Sch. 13 for more details).

Note – The "abolition day" for the purposes of FA 1990, s. 107–110 was such day as may be appointed by Treasury order in accordance with s. 111(1) of that act. Originally, the Treasury order appointing the "abolition day" was to have coincided broadly with the start of paperless trading under the Stock Exchange's planned TAURUS system (IR press release, 20 March 1990). However, on 11 March 1993 it was announced that TAURUS had been abandoned (London Stock Exchange News Release 6/93).

25　　Stamp duty is not chargeable under this Schedule on any description of instrument in respect of which duty was abolished by–

(a)　　section 64 of the Finance Act 1971 or section 5 of the Finance Act (Northern Ireland) 1971 (abolition of duty on mortgages, bonds, debentures etc.), or

(b)　　section 173 of the Finance Act 1989 (life insurance policies and superannuation annuities).

Cross reference – FA 1999, s. 122(1): the provisions of Sch. 13 do not apply to transfers or other instruments relating to units under a unit trust scheme (see note at beginning of Sch. 13 for more details).

26　　Nothing in this Schedule affects any other enactment conferring exemption or relief from stamp duty.

Cross reference – FA 1999, s. 122(1): the provisions of Sch. 13 do not apply to transfers or other instruments relating to units under a unit trust scheme (see note at beginning of Sch. 13 for more details).

SCHEDULE 14 – STAMP DUTY: AMENDMENTS CONSEQUENTIAL ON SECTION 112

Section 112(4)

Cross reference – FA 1999, s. 122(1): the provisions of Sch. 14 do not apply to transfers or other instruments relating to units under a unit trust scheme except in relation to stamp duty (s. 122(2)):
(a)　　on a conveyance or transfer on sale of property other than units under a unit trust scheme in relation to which such units form the whole or part of the consideration, or
(b)　　under FA 1999, Sch. 15 (bearer instruments).

GENERAL AMENDMENTS

1(1)　　Any reference (express or implied) in any enactment, instrument or other document to any of the headings in Schedule 1 to the Stamp Act 1891 (other than the heading "bearer instrument") shall be construed, so far as is required for continuing its effect, as being or, as the case may require, including a reference to the corresponding provision of Schedule 13 to this Act.

1(2)　　Sub-paragraph (1)–

(a)　　has effect subject to any express amendment made by this Act, and

(b)   is without prejudice to the general application of section 17(2) of the Interpretation Act 1978 (general effect of repeal and re-enactment).

Cross reference – FA 1999, s. 122(1): the provisions of Sch. 14 do not apply to transfers or other instruments relating to units under a unit trust scheme (see note at beginning of Sch. 14 for more details).

2   In the enactments relating to stamp duty for "lease or tack", wherever occurring, substitute "lease".

Cross reference – FA 1999, s. 122(1): the provisions of Sch. 14 do not apply to transfers or other instruments relating to units under a unit trust scheme (see note at beginning of Sch. 14 for more details).

FINANCE ACT 1930 (c.28)

3   [Amends FA 1930, s. 42(1).]

Cross reference – FA 1999, s. 122(1): the provisions of Sch. 14 do not apply to transfers or other instruments relating to units under a unit trust scheme (see note at beginning of Sch. 14 for more details).

FINANCE ACT (NORTHERN IRELAND) 1954 (c.23 (N.I.))

4   [Amends FA (Northern Ireland) 1954, s. 11(1).]

Cross reference – FA 1999, s. 122(1): the provisions of Sch. 14 do not apply to transfers or other instruments relating to units under a unit trust scheme (see note at beginning of Sch. 14 for more details).

FINANCE ACT 1970 (c.24)

5   [Amends FA 1970, s. 33(1).]

Prospective repeal – Sch. 14, para. 5 repealed by FA 1999, s. 123(3) and s. 139 and Sch. 20, Pt. V(6) (see note at foot of Sch. 20, Pt. V(6) regarding errors in the table) with effect, so far as it relates to stamp duty on instruments other than bearer instruments, in accordance with FA 1990, s. 108.

Cross reference – FA 1999, s. 122(1): the provisions of Sch. 14 do not apply to transfers or other instruments relating to units under a unit trust scheme (see note at beginning of Sch. 14 for more details).

Note – The "abolition day" for the purposes of FA 1990, s. 107–110 was such day as may be appointed by Treasury order in accordance with s. 111(1) of that act. Originally, the Treasury order appointing the "abolition day" was to have coincided broadly with the start of paperless trading under the Stock Exchange's planned TAURUS system (IR press release, 20 March 1990). However, on 11 March 1993 it was announced that TAURUS had been abandoned (London Stock Exchange News Release 6/93).

FINANCE ACT 1980 (c.48)

6   [Amends FA 1980, s. 97(1).]

Cross reference – FA 1999, s. 122(1): the provisions of Sch. 14 do not apply to transfers or other instruments relating to units under a unit trust scheme (see note at beginning of Sch. 14 for more details).

FINANCE ACT 1982 (c.39)

7   [Amends FA 1982, s. 129(1).]

Cross reference – FA 1999, s. 122(1): the provisions of Sch. 14 do not apply to transfers or other instruments relating to units under a unit trust scheme (see note at beginning of Sch. 14 for more details).

FINANCE ACT 1985 (c.54)

8   [Amends FA 1985, s. 81.]

8(2)   [Substitutes FA 1985, s. 81(2).]

8(3)   [Amends FA 1985, s.81(3).]

Prospective repeal – Sch. 14, para. 8 repealed by FA 1999, s. 123(3) and s. 139 and Sch. 20, Pt. V(6) (see note at foot of Sch. 20, Pt. V(6) regarding errors in the table) with effect, so far as it relates to stamp duty on instruments other than bearer instruments, in accordance with FA 1990, s. 108.

Cross reference – FA 1999, s. 122(1): the provisions of Sch. 14 do not apply to transfers or other instruments relating to units under a unit trust scheme (see note at beginning of Sch. 14 for more details).

9   [Amends FA 1985, s. 82(5).]

Cross reference – FA 1999, s. 122(1): the provisions of Sch. 14 do not apply to transfers or other instruments relating to units under a unit trust scheme (see note at beginning of Sch. 14 for more details).

10   [Amends FA 1985, s. 83.]

(a)   [Amends FA 1985, s. 83(1).]

(b)   [Amends FA 1985, s. 83(2).]

Cross reference – FA 1999, s. 122(1): the provisions of Sch. 14 do not apply to transfers or other instruments relating to units under a unit trust scheme (see note at beginning of Sch. 14 for more details).

11   [Amends FA 1985, s. 84.]

(a)   [Amends FA 1985, s. 84(1).]

(b)   [Amends FA 1985, s. 84(8).]

Cross reference – FA 1999, s. 122(1): the provisions of Sch. 14 do not apply to transfers or other instruments relating to units under a unit trust scheme (see note at beginning of Sch. 14 for more details).

FINANCE ACT 1986 (c.41)

12   [Amends FA 1986, s. 67.]

12(2)   [Substitutes FA 1986, s. 67(2)(3).]

12(3)   [Amends FA 1986, s. 67(9).]

Prospective repeal – Sch. 14, para. 12 repealed by FA 1999, s. 123(3) and s. 139 and Sch. 20, Pt. V(6) (see note at foot of Sch. 20, Pt. V(6) regarding errors in the table) with effect, so far as it relates to stamp duty on instruments other than bearer instruments, in accordance with FA 1990, s. 108.

Cross reference – FA 1999, s. 122(1): the provisions of Sch. 14 do not apply to transfers or other instruments relating to units under a unit trust scheme (see note at beginning of Sch. 14 for more details).

Note – The "abolition day" for the purposes of FA 1990, s. 107–110 was such day as may be appointed by Treasury order in accordance with s. 111(1) of that act. Originally, the Treasury order appointing the "abolition day" was to have coincided broadly with the start of paperless trading under the Stock Exchange's planned TAURUS system (IR press release, 20 March 1990). However, on 11 March 1993 it was announced that TAURUS had been abandoned (London Stock Exchange News Release 6/93).

13   [Amends FA 1986, s. 70.]

13(2)   [Substitutes FA 1986, s. 70(2) (3).]

13(3)   [Amends FA 1986, s. 70(9).]

Prospective repeal – Sch. 14, para. 13 repealed by FA 1999, s. 123(3) and s. 139 and Sch. 20, Pt. V(6) (see note at foot of Sch. 20, Pt. V(6) regarding errors in the table) with effect, so far as it relates to stamp duty on instruments other than bearer instruments, in accordance with FA 1990, s. 108.

Cross reference – FA 1999, s. 122(1): the provisions of Sch. 14 do not apply to transfers or other instruments relating to units under a unit trust scheme (see note at beginning of Sch. 14 for more details).

Note – The "abolition day" for the purposes of FA 1990, s. 107–110 was such day as may be appointed by Treasury order in accordance with s. 111(1) of that act. Originally, the Treasury order appointing the "abolition day" was to have coincided broadly with the start of paperless trading under the Stock Exchange's planned TAURUS system (IR press release, 20 March 1990). However, on 11 March 1993 it was announced that TAURUS had been abandoned (London Stock Exchange News Release 6/93).

14   [Amends FA 1986 s. 75(2).]

Cross reference – FA 1999, s. 122(1): the provisions of Sch. 14 do not apply to transfers or other instruments relating to units under a unit trust scheme (see note at beginning of Sch. 14 for more details).

15   [Amends FA 1986, s. 76.]

15(2)   [Amends FA 1986, s. 76(2).]

15(3)   [Amends FA 1986, s. 76(4).]

Cross reference – FA 1999, s. 122(1): the provisions of Sch. 14 do not apply to transfers or other instruments relating to units under a unit trust scheme (see note at beginning of Sch. 14 for more details).

16   [Amends FA 1986, s. 77(1).]

Prospective repeal – Sch. 14, para. 16 repealed by FA 1999, s. 123(3) and s. 139 and Sch. 20, Pt. V(6) (see note at foot of Sch. 20, Pt. V(6) regarding errors in the table) with effect, so far as it relates to stamp duty on instruments other than bearer instruments, in accordance with FA 1990, s. 108.

Cross reference – FA 1999, s. 122(1): the provisions of Sch. 14 do not apply to transfers or other instruments relating to units under a unit trust scheme (see note at beginning of Sch. 14 for more details).

Note – The "abolition day" for the purposes of FA 1990, s. 107–110 was such day as may be appointed by Treasury order in accordance with s. 111(1) of that act. Originally, the Treasury order appointing the "abolition day" was to have coincided broadly with the start of paperless trading under the Stock Exchange's planned TAURUS system (IR press release, 20 March 1990). However, on 11 March 1993 it was announced that TAURUS had been abandoned (London Stock Exchange News Release 6/93).

17   [Substitutes FA 1986, s. 79(8).]

Prospective repeal – Sch. 14, para. 17 repealed by FA 1999, s. 123(3) and s. 139 and Sch. 20, Pt. V(6) (see note at foot of Sch. 20, Pt. V(6) regarding errors in the table) with effect, so far as it relates to stamp duty on instruments other than bearer instruments, in accordance with FA 1990, s. 108.

Cross reference – FA 1999, s. 122(1): the provisions of Sch. 14 do not apply to transfers or other instruments relating to units under a unit trust scheme (see note at beginning of Sch. 14 for more details).

Note – The "abolition day" for the purposes of FA 1990, s. 107–110 was such day as may be appointed by Treasury order in accordance with s. 111(1) of that act. Originally, the Treasury order appointing the "abolition day" was to have coincided broadly with the start of paperless trading under the Stock Exchange's planned TAURUS system (IR press release, 20 March 1990). However, on 11 March 1993 it was announced that TAURUS had been abandoned (London Stock Exchange News Release 6/93).

18   [Amends FA 1986, s. 80B(7).]

Prospective repeal – Sch. 14, para. 18 repealed by FA 1999, s. 123(3) and s. 139 and Sch. 20, Pt. V(6) (see note at foot of Sch. 20, Pt. V(6) regarding errors in the table) with effect, so far as it relates to stamp duty on instruments other than bearer instruments, in accordance with FA 1990, s. 108.

Cross reference – FA 1999, s. 122(1): the provisions of Sch. 14 do not apply to transfers or other instruments relating to units under a unit trust scheme (see note at beginning of Sch. 14 for more details).

Note – The "abolition day" for the purposes of FA 1990, s. 107–110 was such day as may be appointed by Treasury order in accordance with s. 111(1) of that act. Originally, the Treasury order appointing the "abolition day" was to have coincided broadly with the start of paperless trading under the Stock Exchange's planned TAURUS system (IR press release, 20 March 1990). However, on 11 March 1993 it was announced that TAURUS had been abandoned (London Stock Exchange News Release 6/93).

19   [Amends FA 1986, s. 80C(8).]

Prospective repeal – Sch. 14, para. 19 repealed by FA 1999, s. 123(3) and s. 139 and Sch. 20, Pt. V(6) (see note at foot of Sch. 20, Pt. V(6) regarding errors in the table) with effect, so far as it relates to stamp duty on instruments other than bearer instruments, in accordance with FA 1990, s. 108.

Cross reference – FA 1999, s. 122(1): the provisions of Sch. 14 do not apply to transfers or other instruments relating to units under a unit trust scheme (see note at beginning of Sch. 14 for more details).

Note – The "abolition day" for the purposes of FA 1990, s. 107–110 was such day as may be appointed by Treasury order in accordance with s. 111(1) of that act. Originally, the Treasury order appointing the "abolition day" was to have coincided broadly with the start of paperless trading under the Stock Exchange's planned TAURUS system (IR press release, 20 March 1990). However, on 11 March 1993 it was announced that TAURUS had been abandoned (London Stock Exchange News Release 6/93).

20 [Amends FA 1986, s. 88.]

20(2) [Substitutes FA 1986, s. 88 (aa),(ab).]

20(3) [Amends FA 1986, s. 88 (1A)(b).]

Prospective repeal – Sch. 14, para. 20 repealed by FA 1999, s. 123(3) and s. 139 and Sch. 20, Pt. V(6) (see note at foot of Sch. 20, Pt. V(6) regarding errors in the table) with effect, so far as it relates to stamp duty reserve tax, in accordance with FA 1990, s. 110.

Cross reference – FA 1999, s. 122(1): the provisions of Sch. 14 do not apply to transfers or other instruments relating to units under a unit trust scheme (see note at beginning of Sch. 14 for more details).

Note – The "abolition day" for the purposes of FA 1990, s. 107–110 was such day as may be appointed by Treasury order in accordance with s. 111(1) of that act. Originally, the Treasury order appointing the "abolition day" was to have coincided broadly with the start of paperless trading under the Stock Exchange's planned TAURUS system (IR press release, 20 March 1990). However, on 11 March 1993 it was announced that TAURUS had been abandoned (London Stock Exchange News Release 6/93).

FINANCE ACT 1987 (c.16)

21 [Amends FA 1987, s. 50(1).]

Prospective repeal – Sch. 14, para. 21 repealed by FA 1999, s. 123(3) and s. 139 and Sch. 20, Pt. V(6) (see note at foot of Sch. 20, Pt. V(6) regarding errors in the table) with effect, so far as it relates to stamp duty on instruments other than bearer instruments, in accordance with FA 1990, s. 108.

Cross reference – FA 1999, s. 122(1): the provisions of Sch. 14 do not apply to transfers or other instruments relating to units under a unit trust scheme (see note at beginning of Sch. 14 for more details).

Note – The "abolition day" for the purposes of FA 1990, s. 107–110 was such day as may be appointed by Treasury order in accordance with s. 111(1) of that act. Originally, the Treasury order appointing the "abolition day" was to have coincided broadly with the start of paperless trading under the Stock Exchange's planned TAURUS system (IR press release, 20 March 1990). However, on 11 March 1993 it was announced that TAURUS had been abandoned (London Stock Exchange News Release 6/93).

22 [Amends FA 1987, s. 55(1).]

Cross reference – FA 1999, s. 122(1): the provisions of Sch. 14 do not apply to transfers or other instruments relating to units under a unit trust scheme (see note at beginning of Sch. 14 for more details).

FINANCE ACT 1989 (c.26)

23 [Amends FA 1989, s. 175(1).]

Prospective repeal – Sch. 14, para. 23 repealed by FA 1999, s. 123(3) and s. 139 and Sch. 20, Pt. V(6) (see note at foot of Sch. 20, Pt. V(6) regarding errors in the table) with effect, so far as it relates to stamp duty on instruments other than bearer instruments, in accordance with FA 1990, s. 108.

Cross reference – FA 1999, s. 122(1): the provisions of Sch. 14 do not apply to transfers or other instruments relating to units under a unit trust scheme (see note at beginning of Sch. 14 for more details).

Note – The "abolition day" for the purposes of FA 1990, s. 107–110 was such day as may be appointed by Treasury order in accordance with s. 111(1) of that act. Originally, the Treasury order appointing the "abolition day" was to have coincided broadly with the start of paperless trading under the Stock Exchange's planned TAURUS system (IR press release, 20 March 1990). However, on 11 March 1993 it was announced that TAURUS had been abandoned (London Stock Exchange News Release 6/93).

NATIONAL HEALTH SERVICE AND COMMUNITY CARE ACT 1990 (c.19)

24 [Amends National Health Service and Community Care Act 1990, s. 61(3).]

Cross reference – FA 1999, s. 122(1): the provisions of Sch. 14 do not apply to transfers or other instruments relating to units under a unit trust scheme (see note at beginning of Sch. 14 for more details).

FINANCE ACT 1991 (c.31)

25 [Substitutes FA 1991, s. 110 (1) to (4).]

Cross reference – FA 1999, s. 122(1): the provisions of Sch. 14 do not apply to transfers or other instruments relating to units under a unit trust scheme (see note at beginning of Sch. 14 for more details).

26 *[Amends FA 1991, s. 111(1).]*

Cross reference – FA 1999, s. 122(1): the provisions of Sch. 14 do not apply to transfers or other instruments relating to units under a unit trust scheme (see note at beginning of Sch. 14 for more details).

27 [Substitutes FA 1991, s. 113(1) to (3).]

Cross reference – FA 1999, s. 122(1): the provisions of Sch. 14 do not apply to transfers or other instruments relating to units under a unit trust scheme (see note at beginning of Sch. 14 for more details).

FINANCE ACT 1993 (c.34)

28(1)　[Amends FA 1993, s. 202.]

28(2)　[Amends FA 1993, s. 202(2).]

28(3)　[Amends FA 1993, s. 202 (4)(a).]

28(4)　[Amends FA 1993, s. 202 (4)(b).]

Cross reference – FA 1999, s. 122(1): the provisions of Sch. 14 do not apply to transfers or other instruments relating to units under a unit trust scheme (see note at beginning of Sch. 14 for more details).

29　[Amends FA 1993, s. 203(2).]

Cross reference – FA 1999, s. 122(1): the provisions of Sch. 14 do not apply to transfers or other instruments relating to units under a unit trust scheme (see note at beginning of Sch. 14 for more details).

FINANCE ACT 1994 (c.9)

30　[Amends FA 1994, s. 241(1).]

(a)　[Amends FA 1994, s. 241(1)(a)]

(b)　[Amends FA 1994, s. 241(1)(b).]

Cross reference – FA 1999, s. 122(1): the provisions of Sch. 14 do not apply to transfers or other instruments relating to units under a unit trust scheme (see note at beginning of Sch. 14 for more details).

31(1)　[Amends FA 1994, s. 242.]

31(2)　[Amends FA 1994, s. 242(1),(2), (3).]

31(3)　[Amends FA 1994, s. 242(1).]

31(4)　[Amends FA 1994, s. 242(2).]

Cross reference – FA 1999, s. 122(1): the provisions of Sch. 14 do not apply to transfers or other instruments relating to units under a unit trust scheme (see note at beginning of Sch. 14 for more details).

32　[Amends FA 1994, s. 243.]

Cross reference – FA 1999, s. 122(1): the provisions of Sch. 14 do not apply to transfers or other instruments relating to units under a unit trust scheme (see note at beginning of Sch. 14 for more details).

FINANCE ACT 1995 (c.4)

33　[Amends FA 1995, s. 151.]

(a)　[Amends FA 1995, s. 151(1).]

(b)　[Amends FA 1995, s. 151(1),(2),(3),(6).]

Cross reference – FA 1999, s. 122(1): the provisions of Sch. 14 do not apply to transfers or other instruments relating to units under a unit trust scheme (see note at beginning of Sch. 14 for more details).

SCHEDULE 15 – STAMP DUTY: BEARER INSTRUMENTS

Section 113(1)

Prospective repeal – Sch. 15 repealed by FA 1999, s. 123(3) and s. 139 and Sch. 20, Pt. V(6) with effect, so far as it relates to stamp duty on bearer instruments, in accordance with FA 1990, s. 107.

History – The provisions of Sch. 15 (incorporating amendments in relation to bearer instruments corresponding to those elsewhere in FA 1999 for interest and penalties on late stamping (s. 109), general amendment of charging provisions (s. 112) and amendments of penalties other than on late stamping (Sch. 17, Pt I)) have effect in place of those under the heading "Bearer Instruments" in SA 1891, Sch. 1 and certain related enactments in relation to bearer instruments issued on or after 1 October 1999 (s. 113).

Cross references – FA 1988, s. 143(2): exemption from duty under Sch. 15, para. 1 of certain instruments representing shares (or rights to allotment of or to subscribe to shares) in a UK company "paired" with shares etc. in a foreign company.
FA 1988, s. 143(4): in applying FA 1988, s. 143 (paired shares), foreign company treated for the purposes of Sch. 15 as a UK company but exemption for non-sterling instruments under Sch. 15, para. 17 does not apply.
FA 1990, s. 107: abolition of stamp duty on issue or transfer of bearer instruments on or after the abolition day (see also prospective repeal note above and note below regarding the "abolition day").
FA 1999, Sch. 19, para. 1: the fact that no stamp duty is chargeable on a transfer or other instrument relating to a unit under a unit trust scheme does not affect any charge under Sch. 15.

Note – The "abolition day" for the purposes of FA 1990, s. 107–110 was such day as may be appointed by Treasury order in accordance with s. 111(1) of that act. Originally, the Treasury order appointing the "abolition day" was to have coincided broadly with the start of paperless trading under the Stock Exchange's planned TAURUS system (IR press release, 20 March 1990). However, on 11 March 1993 it was announced that TAURUS had been abandoned (London Stock Exchange News Release 6/93).

Part I – Charging Provisions

CHARGE ON ISSUE OF INSTRUMENT

1(1)   Stamp duty is chargeable–

(a)   on the issue of a bearer instrument in the United Kingdom, and

(b)   on the issue of a bearer instrument outside the United Kingdom by or on behalf of a UK company.

1(2)   This is subject to the exemptions in Part II of this Schedule.

Prospective repeal – Sch. 15 repealed by FA 1999, s. 123(3) and s. 139 and Sch. 20, Pt. V(6) with effect, so far as it relates to stamp duty on bearer instruments, in accordance with FA 1990, s. 107. (For information on the "abolition day" for the purposes of FA 1990, s. 107, see note at the start of this Schedule.)

Cross references – FA 1984, s. 126(3)(c): exclusion of certain instruments issued by designated organisations.
FA 1986, s. 79(2): exemption for bearer instruments relating to loan capital.
FA 1986, s. 90(3)–(3F), 95(2), 97(3): exemption from charges to stamp duty reserve tax on transfer, issue or appropriation or on an agreement to transfer securities constituted by or transferable by certain bearer instruments.
FA 1987, s. 50(2): exemption from duty under Sch. 15 for instruments and transfers relating to certain interests, rights and options (warrants) to purchase exempt securities (government and loan stocks).
FA 1988, s. 143(2): exemption from duty under Sch. 15, para. 1 of certain instruments representing shares (or rights to allotment of or to subscribe to shares) in a UK company "paired" with shares etc. in a foreign company, but this does not affect the other requirements of Sch. 15 (see separate note below).
FA 1988, s. 143(4)(a): treatment of foreign company as a UK company in the application of Sch. 15 (other than para. 1, see separate note above) to instruments representing shares etc. in foreign companies "paired" with UK companies.
FA 1990, s. 107(2): abolition of stamp duty on issue of bearer instruments on or after the abolition day (see prospective repeal note above).

Note – Issue of instruments by the OECD Support Fund excluded by OECD Support Fund Act 1975, s. 4(2).

CHARGE ON TRANSFER OF STOCK BY MEANS OF INSTRUMENT

2   Stamp duty is chargeable on the transfer in the United Kingdom of the stock constituted by or transferable by means of a bearer instrument if duty was not chargeable under paragraph 1 on the issue of the instrument and–

(a)   duty would be chargeable under Part I of Schedule 13 (conveyance or transfer on sale) if the transfer were effected by an instrument other than a bearer instrument, or

(b)   the stock constituted by or transferable by means of a bearer instrument consists of units under a unit trust scheme.

Prospective repeal – Sch. 15 repealed by FA 1999, s. 123(3) and s. 139 and Sch. 20, Pt. V(6) with effect, so far as it relates to stamp duty on bearer instruments, in accordance with FA 1990, s. 107. (For information on the "abolition day" for the purposes of FA 1990, s. 107, see note at the start of this Schedule.)

Cross references – FA 1984, s. 126(3)(c): exclusion of certain instruments issued by designated organisations.
FA 1986, s. 79(2): exemption for bearer instruments relating to loan capital.
FA 1986, s. 90(3)–(3F), 95(2), 97(3): exemption from charges to stamp duty reserve tax on transfer, issue or appropriation or on an agreement to transfer securities constituted by or transferable by certain bearer instruments.
FA 1987, s. 50(2): exemption from duty under Sch. 15 for instruments and transfers relating to certain interests, rights and options (warrants) to purchase exempt securities (government and loan stocks).
FA 1988, s. 143(4)(a): treatment of foreign company as a UK company in the application of Sch. 15 (other than para. 1, see notes under that paragraph) to instruments representing shares etc. in foreign companies "paired" with UK companies.
FA 1990, s. 107(3): abolition of stamp duty on transfer of bearer instruments on or after the abolition day (see prospective repeal note above).

MEANING OF "BEARER INSTRUMENT"

3   In this Schedule **"bearer instrument"** means–

(a)   a marketable security transferable by delivery;

(b)   a share warrant or stock certificate to bearer or instrument to bearer (by whatever name called) having the like effect as such a warrant or certificate;

(c)   a deposit certificate to bearer;

(d)   any other instrument to bearer by means of which stock can be transferred; or

(e)   an instrument issued by a non-UK company that is a bearer instrument by usage.

Prospective repeal – Sch. 15 repealed by FA 1999, s. 123(3) and s. 139 and Sch. 20, Pt. V(6) with effect, so far as it relates to stamp duty on bearer instruments, in accordance with FA 1990, s. 107. (For information on the "abolition day" for the purposes of FA 1990, s. 107, see note at the start of this Schedule.)

RATES OF DUTY

4   *The duty chargeable under this* Schedule is 1.5% of the market value of the stock constituted by or transferable by means of the instrument, unless paragraph 5 or 6 applies.

Prospective repeal – Sch. 15 repealed by FA 1999, s. 123(3) and s. 139 and Sch. 20, Pt. V(6) with effect, so far as it relates to stamp duty on bearer instruments, in accordance with FA 1990, s. 107. (For information on the "abolition day" for the purposes of FA 1990, s. 107, see note at the start of this Schedule.)

5   In the case of–

(a)   a deposit certificate in respect of stock of a single non-UK company, or

(b)   an instrument issued by a non-UK company that is a bearer instrument by usage (and is not otherwise within the definition of **"bearer instrument"** in paragraph 3),

the duty is 0.2% of the market value of the stock constituted by or transferable by means of the instrument.

Prospective repeal – Sch. 15 repealed by FA 1999, s. 123(3) and s. 139 and Sch. 20, Pt. V(6) with effect, so far as it relates to stamp duty on bearer instruments, in accordance with FA 1990, s. 107. (For information on the "abolition day" for the purposes of FA 1990, s. 107, see note at the start of this Schedule.)

Cross reference – FA 1963, s. 67(4A): nothing in FA 1963, s. 67 (prohibition of circulation of blank transfers) applies to an instrument which is chargeable with the rate specified in Sch. 15, para. 5 and is duly stamped.

6   In the case of an instrument given in substitution for a like instrument stamped ad valorem (whether under this Schedule or not) the duty is £5.

Prospective repeal – Sch. 15 repealed by FA 1999, s. 123(3) and s. 139 and Sch. 20, Pt. V(6) with effect, so far as it relates to stamp duty on bearer instruments, in accordance with FA 1990, s. 107. (For information on the "abolition day" for the purposes of FA 1990, s. 107, see note at the start of this Schedule.)

ASCERTAINMENT OF MARKET VALUE

7(1)   For the purposes of duty under paragraph 1 (charge on issue of instrument) the market value of the stock constituted by or transferable by means of the instrument is ascertained as follows.

7(2)   If the stock was offered for public subscription (whether in registered or in bearer form) within twelve months before the issue of the instrument, the market value shall be taken to be the amount subscribed for the stock.

7(3)   In any other case the market value shall be taken to be–

(a)   the value of the stock on the first day within one month after the issue of the instrument on which stock of that description is dealt in on a stock exchange in the United Kingdom, or

(b)   if stock of that description is not so dealt in, the value of the stock immediately after the issue of the instrument.

Prospective repeal – Sch. 15 repealed by FA 1999, s. 123(3) and s. 139 and Sch. 20, Pt. V(6) with effect, so far as it relates to stamp duty on bearer instruments, in accordance with FA 1990, s. 107. (For information on the "abolition day" for the purposes of FA 1990, s. 107, see note at the start of this Schedule.)

8(1)   For the purposes of duty under paragraph 2 (charge on transfer of stock by means of instrument) the market value of the stock constituted by or transferable by means of the instrument is ascertained as follows.

8(2)   In the case of a transfer pursuant to a contract of sale, the market value shall be taken to be the value of the stock on the date when the contract is made.

8(3)   In any other case, the market value shall be taken to be the value of the stock on the day preceding that on which the instrument is presented to the Commissioners for stamping, or, if it is not so presented, on the date of the transfer.

Prospective repeal – Sch. 15 repealed by FA 1999, s. 123(3) and s. 139 and Sch. 20, Pt. V(6) with effect, so far as it relates to stamp duty on bearer instruments, in accordance with FA 1990, s. 107. (For information on the "abolition day" for the purposes of FA 1990, s. 107, see note at the start of this Schedule.)

MEANING OF "DEPOSIT CERTIFICATE"

9   In this Schedule a **"deposit certificate"** means an instrument acknowledging the deposit of stock and entitling the bearer to rights (whether expressed as units or otherwise) in or in relation to the stock deposited or equivalent stock.

Prospective repeal – Sch. 15 repealed by FA 1999, s. 123(3) and s. 139 and Sch. 20, Pt. V(6) with effect, so far as it relates to stamp duty on bearer instruments, in accordance with FA 1990, s. 107. (For information on the "abolition day" for the purposes of FA 1990, s. 107, see note at the start of this Schedule.)

BEARER INSTRUMENTS BY USAGE

10(1)   In this Schedule a **"bearer instrument by usage"** means an instrument–

(a)   which is used for the purpose of transferring the right to stock, and

(b)   delivery of which is treated by usage as sufficient for the purposes of a sale on the market, whether that delivery constitutes a legal transfer or not.

10(2)   A bearer instrument by usage is treated–

(a)   as transferring the stock on delivery of the instrument, and

(b)   as issued by the person by whom or on whose behalf it was first issued, whether or not it was then capable of being used for transferring the right to the stock without execution by the holder.

Prospective repeal – Sch. 15 repealed by FA 1999, s. 123(3) and s. 139 and Sch. 20, Pt. V(6) with effect, so far as it relates to stamp duty on bearer instruments, in accordance with FA 1990, s. 107. (For information on the "abolition day" for the purposes of FA 1990, s. 107, see note at the start of this Schedule.)

MEANING OF "COMPANY", "UK COMPANY" AND "NON-UK COMPANY"

11   In this Schedule–

> **"company"** includes any body of persons, corporate or unincorporate;
>
> **"UK company"** means a company that is formed or established in the United Kingdom; and
>
> **"non-UK company"** means a company that is not a UK company.

Prospective repeal – Sch. 15 repealed by FA 1999, s. 123(3) and s. 139 and Sch. 20, Pt. V(6) with effect, so far as it relates to stamp duty on bearer instruments, in accordance with FA 1990, s. 107. (For information on the "abolition day" for the purposes of FA 1990, s. 107, see note at the start of this Schedule.)

MEANING OF "STOCK" AND "TRANSFER"

12(1)   In this Schedule "stock" includes securities.

12(2)   References in this Schedule to stock include any interest in, or in any fraction of, stock or in any dividends or other rights arising out of stock and any right to an allotment of or to subscribe for stock.

12(3)   In this Schedule "transfer" includes negotiation, and "transferable", "transferred" and "transferring" shall be construed accordingly.

Prospective repeal – Sch. 15 repealed by FA 1999, s. 123(3) and s. 139 and Sch. 20, Pt. V(6) with effect, so far as it relates to stamp duty on bearer instruments, in accordance with FA 1990, s. 107. (For information on the "abolition day" for the purposes of FA 1990, s. 107, see note at the start of this Schedule.)

Part II – EXEMPTIONS

FOREIGN LOAN SECURITIES

13   Stamp duty is not chargeable on a bearer instrument issued outside the United Kingdom in respect of a loan which is expressed in a currency other than sterling and which is not–

(a)   offered for subscription in the United Kingdom, or

(b)   offered for subscription with a view to an offer for sale in the United Kingdom of securities in respect of the loan.

Prospective repeal – Sch. 15 repealed by FA 1999, s. 123(3) and s. 139 and Sch. 20, Pt. V(6) with effect, so far as it relates to stamp duty on bearer instruments, in accordance with FA 1990, s. 107. (For information on the "abolition day" for the purposes of FA 1990, s. 107, see note at the start of this Schedule.)

STOCK EXEMPT FROM DUTY ON TRANSFER

14   Stamp duty is not chargeable under this Schedule on an instrument constituting, or used for transferring, stock (other than units in a unit trust) that is exempt from all stamp duties on transfer.

Prospective repeal – Sch. 15 repealed by FA 1999, s. 123(3) and s. 139 and Sch. 20, Pt. V(6) with effect, so far as it relates to stamp duty on bearer instruments, in accordance with FA 1990, s. 107. (For information on the "abolition day" for the purposes of FA 1990, s. 107, see note at the start of this Schedule.)

INSTRUMENTS IN RESPECT OF WHICH DUTY PREVIOUSLY ABOLISHED

15   Stamp duty is not chargeable under this Schedule on any description of instrument in respect of which duty was abolished by–

(a)   section 64 of the Finance Act 1971 or section 5 of the Finance Act (Northern Ireland) 1971 (abolition of duty on mortgages, bonds, debentures etc.), or

(b)   section 173 of the Finance Act 1989 (life insurance policies and superannuation annuities).

Prospective repeal – Sch. 15 repealed by FA 1999, s. 123(3) and s. 139 and Sch. 20, Pt. V(6) with effect, so far as it relates to stamp duty on bearer instruments, in accordance with FA 1990, s. 107. (For information on the "abolition day" for the purposes of FA 1990, s. 107, see note at the start of this Schedule.)

RENOUNCEABLE LETTERS OF ALLOTMENT

16   Stamp duty is not chargeable under this Schedule on renounceable letters of allotment, letters of rights or other similar instruments where the rights under the letter or other instrument are renounceable not later than six months after its issue.

Prospective repeal – Sch. 15 repealed by FA 1999, s. 123(3) and s. 139 and Sch. 20, Pt. V(6) with effect, so far as it relates to stamp duty on bearer instruments, in accordance with FA 1990, s. 107. (For information on the "abolition day" for the purposes of FA 1990, s. 107, see note at the start of this Schedule.)

Cross references – FA 1986, s. 95(2): exception from charge to stamp duty reserve tax under FA 1986, s. 93 (on entry into depositary receipt system) not applicable to an instrument within the exemption conferred by Sch. 15, para. 16.

FA 1986, s. 97(3): exception from charge to stamp duty reserve tax under FA 1986, s. 96 (on entry into clearance system) not applicable to an instrument within the exemption conferred by Sch. 15, para. 16.

INSTRUMENTS RELATING TO NON-STERLING STOCK

17(1)   Stamp duty is not chargeable under this Schedule on the issue of an instrument which relates to stock expressed–

(a)   in a currency other than sterling, or

(b)   in units of account defined by reference to more than one currency (whether or not including sterling),

or on the transfer of the stock constituted by or transferable by means of any such instrument.

17(2)   Where the stock to which the instrument relates consists of a loan for the repayment of which there is an option between sterling and one or more other currencies, sub-paragraph (1) applies if the option is exercisable only by the holder of the stock and does not apply in any other case.

Prospective repeal – Sch. 15 repealed by FA 1999, s. 123(3) and s. 139 and Sch. 20, Pt. V(6) with effect, so far as it relates to stamp duty on bearer instruments, in accordance with FA 1990, s. 107. (For information on the "abolition day" for the purposes of FA 1990, s. 107, see note at the start of this Schedule.)

Cross references – FA 1986, s. 95(2): exception from charge to stamp duty reserve tax under FA 1986, s. 93 (on entry into depositary receipt system) not applicable to an instrument within the exemption conferred by Sch. 15, para. 17 which does not raise new capital and is not issued in exchange for an instrument raising new capital.
FA 1986, s. 97(3): exception from charge to stamp duty reserve tax under FA 1986, s. 96 (on entry into clearance system) not applicable to an instrument within the exemption conferred by Sch. 15, para. 17 which does not raise new capital and is not issued in exchange for an instrument raising new capital.
FA 1988, s. 143(4)(b): for the purposes of treating a foreign company as a UK company in accordance with FA 1988, s. 143 (paired shares)(see cross-reference at beginning of Sch. 15), para. 17 does not apply.

18   Where the capital stock of a company is not expressed in terms of any currency, it shall be treated for the purposes of paragraph 17 as expressed in the currency of the territory under the law of which the company is formed or established.

Prospective repeal – Sch. 15 repealed by FA 1999, s. 123(3) and s. 139 and Sch. 20, Pt. V(6) with effect, so far as it relates to stamp duty on bearer instruments, in accordance with FA 1990, s. 107. (For information on the "abolition day" for the purposes of FA 1990, s. 107, see note at the start of this Schedule.)

19(1)   A unit under a unit trust scheme or a share in a foreign mutual fund shall be treated for the purposes of paragraph 17 as capital stock of a company formed or established in the territory by the law of which the scheme or fund is governed.

19(2)   A **"foreign mutual fund"** means a fund administered under arrangements governed by the law of a territory outside the United Kingdom under which subscribers to the fund are entitled to participate in, or receive payments by reference to, profits or income arising to the fund from the acquisition, holding, management or disposal of investments.

19(3)   In relation to a foreign mutual fund **"share"** means the right of a subscriber, or of another in his right, to participate in or receive payments by reference to profits or income so arising.

Prospective repeal – Sch. 15 repealed by FA 1999, s. 123(3) and s. 139 and Sch. 20, Pt. V(6) with effect, so far as it relates to stamp duty on bearer instruments, in accordance with FA 1990, s. 107. (For information on the "abolition day" for the purposes of FA 1990, s. 107, see note at the start of this Schedule.)

VARIATION OF ORIGINAL TERMS OR CONDITIONS

20   Where a bearer instrument issued by or on behalf of a non-UK company in respect of a loan expressed in sterling–

(a)   has been stamped ad valorem, or

(b)   has been stamped with duty under paragraph 6 above (fixed duty on instrument given in substitution for another instrument stamped ad valorem), or

(c)   has been stamped with the denoting stamp referred to in paragraph 21(2)(b)below,

duty is not chargeable under this Schedule by reason only that the instrument is amended on its face pursuant to an agreement for the variation of any of its original terms or conditions.

Prospective repeal – Sch. 15 repealed by FA 1999, s. 123(3) and s. 139 and Sch. 20, Pt. V(6) with effect, so far as it relates to stamp duty on bearer instruments, in accordance with FA 1990, s. 107. (For information on the "abolition day" for the purposes of FA 1990, s. 107, see note at the start of this Schedule.)

Part III – Supplementary Provisions

DUTY CHARGEABLE ON ISSUE OF INSTRUMENT

21(1) This paragraph applies where duty is chargeable under paragraph 1 of this Schedule.

21(2) The instrument–

(a) shall before being issued be produced to the Commissioners, together with such particulars in writing of the instrument as the Commissioners may require, and

(b) shall be deemed to be duly stamped if and only if it is stamped with a particular stamp denoting that it has been produced to the Commissioners.

21(3) Within six weeks of the date on which the instrument is issued, or such longer time as the Commissioners may allow, a statement in writing containing the date of the issue and such further particulars as the Commissioners may require in respect of the instrument shall be delivered to the Commissioners.

21(4) The duty chargeable in respect of the instrument shall be paid to the Commissioners on delivery of that statement or within such longer time as the Commissioners may allow.

Prospective repeal – Sch. 15 repealed by FA 1999, s. 123(3) and s. 139 and Sch. 20, Pt. V(6) with effect, so far as it relates to stamp duty on bearer instruments, in accordance with FA 1990, s. 107. (For information on the "abolition day" for the purposes of FA 1990, s. 107, see note at the start of this Schedule.)

22(1) If default is made in complying with paragraph 21–

(a) the person by whom or on whose behalf the instrument is issued, and

(b) any person who acts as the agent of that person for the purposes of the issue,

are each liable to a penalty not exceeding the aggregate of £300 and the duty chargeable.

22(2) Those persons are also jointly and severally liable to pay to Her Majesty–

(a) the duty chargeable, and

(b) interest on the unpaid duty from the date of the default until the duty is paid.

Prospective repeal – Sch. 15 repealed by FA 1999, s. 123(3) and s. 139 and Sch. 20, Pt. V(6) with effect, so far as it relates to stamp duty on bearer instruments, in accordance with FA 1990, s. 107. (For information on the "abolition day" for the purposes of FA 1990, s. 107, see note at the start of this Schedule.)

DUTY CHARGEABLE ON TRANSFER OF STOCK BY MEANS OF INSTRUMENT

23(1) This paragraph applies where duty is chargeable under paragraph 2 of this Schedule.

23(2) Where the instrument is presented to the Commissioners for stamping–

(a) the person presenting it, and

(b) the owner of the instrument,

shall furnish to the Commissioners such particulars in writing as the Commissioners may require for determining the amount of duty chargeable.

23(3) If the instrument is not duly stamped each person who in the United Kingdom–

(a) transfers any stock by or by means of the instrument, or

(b) is concerned as broker or agent in any such transfer,

is liable to a penalty not exceeding the aggregate of £300 and the amount of duty chargeable.

23(4) Those persons are also jointly and severally liable to pay to Her Majesty–

(a) the duty chargeable, and

(b) interest on the unpaid duty from the date of the transfer in question until the duty is paid.

Prospective repeal – Sch. 15 repealed by FA 1999, s. 123(3) and s. 139 and Sch. 20, Pt. V(6) with effect, so far as it relates to stamp duty on bearer instruments, in accordance with FA 1990, s. 107. (For information on the "abolition day" for the purposes of FA 1990, s. 107, see note at the start of this Schedule.)

SUPPLEMENTARY PROVISIONS AS TO INTEREST

24(1) The following provisions apply to interest under paragraph 22(2) or 23(4).

24(2) If an amount is lodged with the Commissioners in respect of the duty, the amount on which *interest is payable is reduced* by that amount.

24(3) Interest is payable at the rate prescribed under section 178 of the Finance Act 1989 for the purposes of section 15A of the Stamp Act 1891 (interest on late stamping).

24(4) The amount of interest shall be rounded down (if necessary) to the nearest multiple of £5. No interest is payable if the amount is less than £25.

24(5)   The interest shall be paid without any deduction of income tax and shall not be taken into account in computing income or profits for any tax purposes.

Prospective repeal – Sch. 15 repealed by FA 1999, s. 123(3) and s. 139 and Sch. 20, Pt. V(6) with effect, so far as it relates to stamp duty on bearer instruments, in accordance with FA 1990, s. 107. (For information on the "abolition day" for the purposes of FA 1990, s. 107, see note at the start of this Schedule.)

PENALTY FOR FALSE STATEMENT

25   A person who in furnishing particulars under this Part of this Schedule wilfully or negligently furnishes particulars that are false in any material respect is liable to a penalty not exceeding the aggregate of £300 and twice the amount by which the stamp duty chargeable exceeds that paid.

Prospective repeal – Sch. 15 repealed by FA 1999, s. 123(3) and s. 139 and Sch. 20, Pt. V(6) with effect, so far as it relates to stamp duty on bearer instruments, in accordance with FA 1990, s. 107. (For information on the "abolition day" for the purposes of FA 1990, s. 107, see note at the start of this Schedule.)

26   An instrument in respect of which duty is chargeable under paragraph 2 of this Schedule which–

(a)   has been stamped ad valorem, or

(b)   has been stamped with a stamp indicating that it is chargeable with a fixed duty under paragraph 6 (instrument in substitution for one stamped ad valorem) and has been stamped under that paragraph,

shall be treated as duly stamped for all purposes other than paragraph 25.

Prospective repeal – Sch. 15 repealed by FA 1999, s. 123(3) and s. 139 and Sch. 20, Pt. V(6) with effect, so far as it relates to stamp duty on bearer instruments, in accordance with FA 1990, s. 107. (For information on the "abolition day" for the purposes of FA 1990, s. 107, see note at the start of this Schedule.)

SCHEDULE 16 – STAMP DUTY: AMENDMENTS CONSEQUENTIAL ON SECTION 113

Section 113(3)

GENERAL AMENDMENT

1(1)   Any reference (express or implied) in any enactment, instrument or other document to the heading "Bearer Instrument" in Schedule 1 to the Stamp Act 1891 shall be construed, so far as is required for continuing its effect, as being or, as the case may require, including a reference to Schedule 15 to this Act.

1(2)   Sub-paragraph (1)–

(a)   has effect subject to any express amendment made by this Act, and

(b)   is without prejudice to the general application of section 17(2) of the Interpretation Act 1978 (general effect of repeal and re-enactment).

FINANCE ACT 1963 (c.25)

2   [Substitutes FA 1963, s. 67(4).]

Prospective repeal – Sch. 16, para. 2 repealed by FA 1999, s. 123(3) and s. 139 and Sch. 20, Pt. V(6) with effect, so far as it relates to stamp duty on bearer instruments, in accordance with FA 1990, s. 107.

Note – The "abolition day" for the purposes of FA 1990, s. 107–110 was such day as may be appointed by Treasury order in accordance with s. 111(1) of that act. Originally, the Treasury order appointing the "abolition day" was to have coincided broadly with the start of paperless trading under the Stock Exchange's planned TAURUS system (IR press release, 20 March 1990). However, on 11 March 1993 it was announced that TAURUS had been abandoned (London Stock Exchange News Release 6/93).

FINANCE ACT 1976 (c.40)

3   [Amends FA 1976, s. 131(3).]

Prospective repeal – Sch. 16, para. 3 repealed by FA 1999, s. 123(3) and s. 139 and Sch. 20, Pt. V(6) with effect, so far as it relates to stamp duty on bearer instruments, in accordance with FA 1990, s. 107.

Notes – FA 1976 s. 131(3) is not reproduced.
The "abolition day" for the purposes of FA 1990, s. 107–110 was such day as may be appointed by Treasury order in accordance with s. 111(1) of that act. Originally, the Treasury order appointing the "abolition day" was to have coincided broadly with the start of paperless trading under the Stock Exchange's planned TAURUS system (IR press release, 20 March 1990). However, on 11 March 1993 it was announced that TAURUS had been abandoned (London Stock Exchange News Release 6/93).

FINANCE ACT 1984 (c.43)

4   [Amends FA 1984, s. 126(3)(c) and (5).]

Prospective repeal – Sch. 16, para. 4 repealed by FA 1999, s. 123(3) and s. 139 and Sch. 20, Pt. V(6) with effect, so far as it relates to stamp duty on bearer instruments, in accordance with FA 1990, s. 107.

Note – The "abolition day" for the purposes of FA 1990, s. 107–110 was such day as may be appointed by Treasury order in accordance with s. 111(1) of that act. Originally, the Treasury order appointing the "abolition day" was to have coincided broadly with the start of paperless trading under the Stock Exchange's planned TAURUS system (IR press release, 20 March 1990). However, on 11 March 1993 it was announced that TAURUS had been abandoned (London Stock Exchange News Release 6/93).

FINANCE ACT 1986 (c.41)

5   [Amends FA 1986, s. 79(2).]

Prospective repeal – Sch. 16, para. 5 repealed by FA 1999, s. 123(3) and s. 139 and Sch. 20, Pt. V(6) with effect, so far as it relates to stamp duty on bearer instruments, in accordance with FA 1990, s. 107.

Note – The "abolition day" for the purposes of FA 1990, s. 107–110 was such day as may be appointed by Treasury order in accordance with s. 111(1) of that act. Originally, the Treasury order appointing the "abolition day" was to have coincided broadly with the start of paperless trading under the Stock Exchange's planned TAURUS system (IR press release, 20 March 1990). However, on 11 March 1993 it was announced that TAURUS had been abandoned (London Stock Exchange News Release 6/93).

6(1)   [Amends FA 1986, s. 90.]

6(2)   [Substitutes FA 1986, s. 90(3)(a).]

6(3)   [Amends FA 1986, s. 90(3A).]

6(4)   [Amends FA 1986, s. 90(3B).]

6(5)   [Substitutes FA 1986, s. 90(3C)(b).]

6(6)   [Substitutes FA 1986, s. 90(3E)(b).]

Prospective repeal – Sch. 16, para. 6 repealed by FA 1999, s. 123(3) and s. 139 and Sch. 20, Pt. V(6) with effect, so far as it relates to stamp duty reserve tax, in accordance with FA 1990, s. 110.

Note – The "abolition day" for the purposes of FA 1990, s. 107–110 was such day as may be appointed by Treasury order in accordance with s. 111(1) of that act. Originally, the Treasury order appointing the "abolition day" was to have coincided broadly with the start of paperless trading under the Stock Exchange's planned TAURUS system (IR press release, 20 March 1990). However, on 11 March 1993 it was announced that TAURUS had been abandoned (London Stock Exchange News Release 6/93).

7   [Substitutes FA 1986, s. 95(2).]

7(2)   There shall be no charge to tax under section 93 of that Act by virtue of paragraph (b) of subsection (2) of section 95 as substituted by sub-paragraph (1) above in the case of an instrument which gives effect to an agreement for a company merger or takeover entered into in writing by the companies involved before 30th January 1999.

Prospective repeal – Sch. 16, para. 7 repealed by FA 1999, s. 123(3) and s. 139 and Sch. 20, Pt. V(6) with effect, so far as it relates to stamp duty reserve tax, in accordance with FA 1990, s. 110.

Note – The "abolition day" for the purposes of FA 1990, s. 107–110 was such day as may be appointed by Treasury order in accordance with s. 111(1) of that act. Originally, the Treasury order appointing the "abolition day" was to have coincided broadly with the start of paperless trading under the Stock Exchange's planned TAURUS system (IR press release, 20 March 1990). However, on 11 March 1993 it was announced that TAURUS had been abandoned (London Stock Exchange News Release 6/93).

8(1)   [Substitutes FA 1986, s. 97(3).]

8(2)   There shall be no charge to tax under section 96 of that Act by virtue of paragraph (b) of subsection (3) of section 97 as substituted by sub-paragraph (1) above in the case of an instrument which gives effect to an agreement for a company merger or takeover entered into in writing by the companies involved before 30th January 1999.

Prospective repeal – Sch. 16, para. 8 repealed by FA 1999, s. 123(3) and s. 139 and Sch. 20, Pt. V(6) with effect, so far as it relates to stamp duty reserve tax, in accordance with FA 1990, s. 110.

Note – The "abolition day" for the purposes of FA 1990, s. 107–110 was such day as may be appointed by Treasury order in accordance with s. 111(1) of that act. Originally, the Treasury order appointing the "abolition day" was to have coincided broadly with the start of paperless trading under the Stock Exchange's planned TAURUS system (IR press release, 20 March 1990). However, on 11 March 1993 it was announced that TAURUS had been abandoned (London Stock Exchange News Release 6/93).

9   [Inserts FA 1986, s. 99(1A).]

Prospective repeal – Sch. 16, para. 9 repealed by FA 1999, s. 123(3) and s. 139 and Sch. 20, Pt. V(6) with effect, so far as it relates to stamp duty reserve tax, in accordance with FA 1990, s. 110.

Note – The "abolition day" for the purposes of FA 1990, s. 107–110 was such day as may be appointed by Treasury order in accordance with s. 111(1) of that act. Originally, the Treasury order appointing the "abolition day" was to have coincided broadly with the start of paperless trading under the Stock Exchange's planned TAURUS system (IR press release, 20 March 1990). However, on 11 March 1993 it was announced that TAURUS had been abandoned (London Stock Exchange News Release 6/93).

FINANCE ACT 1987 (c.16)

10(1)   Section 50 of the Finance Act 1987 (warrants to purchase government stock etc.: exempt securities) is amended as follows.

10(2)   [Amends FA 1987, s. 50(2).]

10(3)   [Amends FA 1987, s. 50(3)(b).]

10(4)   [Amends FA 1987, s. 50(3)(c).]

Prospective repeal – Sch. 16, para. 10 repealed by FA 1999, s. 123(3) and s. 139 and Sch. 20, Pt. V(6) with effect, so far as it relates to stamp duty on bearer instruments, in accordance with FA 1990, s. 107.

Note – The "abolition day" for the purposes of FA 1990, s. 107–110 was such day as may be appointed by Treasury order in accordance with s. 111(1) of that act. Originally, the Treasury order appointing the "abolition day" was to have coincided broadly with the start of paperless trading under the Stock Exchange's planned TAURUS system (IR press release, 20 March 1990). However, on 11 March 1993 it was announced that TAURUS had been abandoned (London Stock Exchange News Release 6/93).

FINANCE ACT 1988 (c.39)

11(1)   Section 143 of the Finance Act 1988 (paired shares) is amended as follows.

11(2)   [Substitutes FA 1988, s. 143(2).]

11(3)   [Amends FA 1988, s. 143(3).]

11(4)   [Substitutes FA 1988, s. 143(4).]

11(5)   [Amends FA 1988, s. 143(5).]

Prospective repeal – Sch. 16, para. 11 repealed by FA 1999, s. 123(3) and s. 139 and Sch. 20, Pt. V(6) with effect, so far as it relates to stamp duty on bearer instruments, in accordance with FA 1990, s. 107.

Note – The "abolition day" for the purposes of FA 1990, s. 107–110 was such day as may be appointed by Treasury order in accordance with s. 111(1) of that act. Originally, the Treasury order appointing the "abolition day" was to have coincided broadly with the start of paperless trading under the Stock Exchange's planned TAURUS system (IR press release, 20 March 1990). However, on 11 March 1993 it was announced that TAURUS had been abandoned (London Stock Exchange News Release 6/93).

FINANCE ACT 1990 (c.29)

12   [Substitutes FA 1990, s. 107(1)(2) and (3).]

SCHEDULE 17 – STAMP DUTY: PENALTIES OTHER THAN ON LATE STAMPING

Section 114

Part I – Amendments of Penalties

INTRODUCTION

1   The amendments in this Part of this Schedule–

(a)   replace administrative fines by penalties;

(b)   amend provisions imposing a fine or penalty of a specified amount so as to impose a penalty not exceeding a specified amount;

(c)   increase or modernise in certain cases the maximum penalty.

STAMP DUTIES MANAGEMENT ACT 1891 (c.38)

2(1)   The Stamp Duties Management Act 1891 is amended as follows.

2(2)   [Amends SDMA 1891, s. 12A(2)(b).]

2(3)   [Amends SDMA 1891, s. 21.]

STAMP ACT 1891 (c.39)

3(1)   The Stamp Act 1891 is amended as follows.

3(2)   [Amends SDMA 1891, s. 5.]

3(3)   [Amends SDMA 1891, s. 9(1).]

3(4)   [Amends SDMA 1891, s. 16.]

3(5)   [Amends SDMA 1891, s. 17.]

3(6)   [Amends SDMA 1891, s. 83.]

FINANCE ACT 1946 (c.64)

4 [Repealed by FA 1999, s. 139 and Sch. 20, Pt. V(5) in relation to instruments executed on or after 6 February 2000.]

FINANCE (No. 2) ACT (NORTHERN IRELAND) 1946 (c.17 (N.I.))

5 [Repealed by FA 1999, s. 139 and Sch. 20, Pt. V(5) in relation to instruments executed on or after 6 February 2000.]

FINANCE ACT 1963 (c.25)

6 [Amends FA 1963, s. 67(1).]

Prospective repeal – Sch. 17, para. 6 repealed by FA 1999, s. 123(3) and s. 139 and Sch. 20, Pt. V(6) with effect, so far as it relates to stamp duty on instruments other than bearer instruments, in accordance with FA 1990, s. 108.

Note – The "abolition day" for the purposes of FA 1990, s. 107–110 was such day as may be appointed by Treasury order in accordance with s. 111(1) of that act. Originally, the Treasury order appointing the "abolition day" was to have coincided broadly with the start of paperless trading under the Stock Exchange's planned TAURUS system (IR press release, 20 March 1990). However, on 11 March 1993 it was announced that TAURUS had been abandoned (London Stock Exchange News Release 6/93).

FINANCE ACT (NORTHERN IRELAND) 1963 (c.22 (N.I.))

7 [Amends FA (Northern Ireland) 1963, s. 16(1).]

Prospective repeal – Sch. 17, para. 7 repealed by FA 1999, s. 123(3) and s. 139 and Sch. 20, Pt. V(6) with effect, so far as it relates to stamp duty on instruments other than bearer instruments, in accordance with FA 1990, s. 108.

Note – The "abolition day" for the purposes of FA 1990, s. 107–110 was such day as may be appointed by Treasury order in accordance with s. 111(1) of that act. Originally, the Treasury order appointing the "abolition day" was to have coincided broadly with the start of paperless trading under the Stock Exchange's planned TAURUS system (IR press release, 20 March 1990). However, on 11 March 1993 it was announced that TAURUS had been abandoned (London Stock Exchange News Release 6/93).

FINANCE ACT 1986 (c.41)

8 [Amends FA 1986, s. 68(4), and (5) and s. 71(4) and (5).]

Prospective repeal – Sch. 17, para. 8 repealed by FA 1999, s. 123(3) and s. 139 and Sch. 20, Pt. V(6) with effect, so far as it relates to stamp duty on instruments other than bearer instruments, in accordance with FA 1990, s. 108.

Note – The "abolition day" for the purposes of FA 1990, s. 107–110 was such day as may be appointed by Treasury order in accordance with s. 111(1) of that act. Originally, the Treasury order appointing the "abolition day" was to have coincided broadly with the start of paperless trading under the Stock Exchange's planned TAURUS system (IR press release, 20 March 1990). However, on 11 March 1993 it was announced that TAURUS had been abandoned (London Stock Exchange News Release 6/93).

Part II – Determination of Penalty and Appeals

INTRODUCTION

9(1) This Part of this Schedule applies to penalties under the enactments relating to stamp duty, other than penalties under section 15B of the Stamp Act 1891 (penalty on late stamping).

9(2) Nothing in this Part of this Schedule affects criminal proceedings for an offence.

DETERMINATION OF PENALTY BY OFFICER OF COMMISSIONERS

10(1) An officer of the Commissioners authorised by the Commissioners for the purposes of this paragraph may make a determination–

(a) imposing the penalty, and

(b) setting it at such amount as in the officer's opinion is correct or appropriate.

10(2) Notice of the determination must be served on the person liable to the penalty.

The notice must also state–

(a) the date on which the notice is issued, and

(b) the time within which an appeal against the determination may be made.

10(3) After notice of the determination has been served, the determination cannot be altered except–

(a) in accordance with sub-paragraph (4),

(b) by agreement in writing, or

(c) on appeal.

10(4) If it is discovered by an officer of the Commissioners authorised by the Commissioners for the purposes of this paragraph that the amount of a penalty determined under this paragraph is or has become insufficient, the officer may make a determination in a further amount so that the penalty is set at the amount which in the officer's opinion is correct or appropriate.

10(5)   If a person liable to a penalty has died–

(a)   any determination which could have been made in relation to that person may be made in relation to his personal representatives, and

(b)   any penalty imposed on them is a debt due from and payable out of the person's estate.

10(6)   A penalty determined under this paragraph is due and payable at the end of the period of 30 days beginning with the date of the issue of the notice of determination.

11(1)   An appeal lies to the Special Commissioners against a determination under paragraph 10.

11(2)   Notice of appeal must be given in writing to the officer of the Commissioners by whom the determination was made within 30 days of the date of the notice of the determination.

11(3)   An appeal may be brought out of time with the consent of the Commissioners or the Special Commissioners.

The Comissioners–

(a)   shall give that consent if satisfied, on an application for that purpose, that there was a reasonable excuse for not bringing the appeal within the time limit, and

(b)   if not so satisfied, shall refer the matter for determination by the Special Commissioners.

11(4)   The notice of appeal must specify the grounds of appeal, but on the hearing of the appeal the Special Commissioners may allow the appellant to put forward a ground not specified in the notice of appeal, and take it into consideration, if satisfied that the omission was not wilful or unreasonable.

11(5)   The powers conferred by section 46A(1)(c) and (2) to (4) and sections 56B to 56D of the Taxes Management Act 1970 (power of Lord Chancellor to make regulations as to jurisdiction, practice and procedure in relation to appeals to Special Commissioners) apply in relation to appeals under this paragraph.

11(6)   On an appeal under this paragraph the Special Commissioners may–

(a)   if it appears to them that no penalty has been incurred, set the determination aside;

(b)   if the amount determined appears to them to be appropriate, confirm the determination;

(c)   if the amount determined appears to them to be excessive, reduce it to such other amount (including nil) as they consider appropriate;

(d)   if the amount determined appears to them to be insufficient, increase it to such amount not exceeding the permitted maximum as they consider appropriate.

Cross reference – SI 1994/1811 (as amended by SI 2000/288): procedures for appeals under Sch. 17, para. 11 relating to penalties (regulations came into force on 1 March 2000).

12(1)   Section 56A of the Taxes Management Act 1970 (general right of appeal on point of law) applies in relation to a decision of the Special Commissioners under paragraph 11.

12(2)   Without prejudice to that right of appeal, an appeal lies against the amount of a penalty determined by the Special Commissioners under paragraph 11, at the instance of the person liable to the penalty–

(a)   to the High Court, or

(b)   in Scotland, to the Court of Session sitting as the Court of Exchequer.

12(3)   On an appeal under sub-paragraph (2) the court has the same powers as are conferred on the Special Commissioners by paragraph 11(6) above.

PENALTY PROCEEDINGS BEFORE THE COURT

13(1)   Where in the opinion of the Commissioners the liability of a person for a penalty arises by reason of his fraud or the fraud of another person, proceedings for the penalty may be brought–

(a)   in the High Court, or

(b)   in Scotland, in the Court of Session sitting as the Court of Exchequer.

13(2)   Proceedings under this paragraph in England and Wales shall be brought–

(a)   by and in the name of the Commissioners as an authorised department for the purposes of the Crown Proceedings Act 1947, or

(b)   in the name of the Attorney General.

Any such proceedings shall be deemed to be civil proceedings by the Crown within the meaning of Part II of the Crown Proceedings Act 1947.

13(3) Proceedings under this paragraph in Scotland shall be brought in the name of the Advocate General for Scotland.

13(4) Proceedings under this paragraph in Northern Ireland shall be brought–

(a) by and in the name of the Commissioners as an authorised department for the purposes of the Crown Proceedings Act 1947 as for the time being in force in Northern Ireland, or

(b) in the name of the Attorney General for Northern Ireland.

Any such proceedings shall be deemed to be civil proceedings within the meaning of Part II of the Crown Proceedings Act 1947 as for the time being in force in Northern Ireland.

13(5) If in proceedings under this paragraph the court does not find that fraud is proved but considers that the person concerned is nevertheless liable to a penalty, the court may determine a penalty notwithstanding that, but for the opinion of the Commissioners as to fraud, the penalty would not have been a matter for the court.

13(6) Paragraph 10 above (determination of penalty by officer of Commissioners) does not apply where proceedings are brought under this paragraph.

SUPPLEMENTARY PROVISIONS

14(1) The Commissioners may in their discretion mitigate any penalty, or stay or compound any proceedings for the recovery of a penalty.

14(2) They may also, after judgment, further mitigate or entirely remit the penalty.

15 A penalty may be determined under paragraph 10, or proceedings for a penalty brought under paragraph 13, at any time within six years after the date on which the penalty was incurred.

Part III – Power to Apply Provisions as to Collection and Recovery etc

16(1) The Treasury may make regulations applying in relation to penalties to which Part II of this Schedule applies such provisions of the Taxes Management Act 1970 as they think fit.

16(2) The regulations may apply the provisions of that Act with such modifications as the Treasury think fit.

16(3) Regulations under this paragraph shall be made by statutory instrument which shall be subject to annulment in pursuance of a resolution of the House of Commons.

Statutory instruments – SI 1999/2537: regulations made under Sch. 17, para. 16.

17 Without prejudice to the generality of the power conferred by paragraph 16, regulations under that paragraph may apply–

(a) any of the provisions of Part VI of the Taxes Management Act 1970 (collection and recovery), and

(b) such of the provisions of Part XI of that Act (miscellaneous and supplemental provisions) as appear to the Treasury to be appropriate.

Statutory instruments – SI 1999/2537: regulations made under Sch. 17, para. 17.

18 Sections 21, 22 and 35 of the Inland Revenue Regulation Act 1890 (proceedings for fines, etc.) do not apply in relation to penalties to which Part II of this Schedule applies.

SCHEDULE 18 – STAMP DUTY: MINOR AMENDMENTS AND REPEAL OF OBSOLETE PROVISIONS

Section 115

Part I – Minor Amendments

INTRODUCTION

1 The provisions of this Part of this Schedule have effect for the purposes of the enactments relating to stamp duty.

PAYMENT BY CHEQUE

2(1) Where–

(a)   any payment to the Commissioners is made by cheque, and

(b)   the cheque is paid on its first presentation to the banker on whom it is drawn,

the payment is treated as made on the day on which the cheque was first received by the Commissioners.

2(2) Sub-paragraph (1) applies where the cheque was first received by the Commissioners on or after 1st October 1999.

EVIDENCE IN CASES OF FRAUDULENT CONDUCT, ETC.

3(1) Statements made or documents produced by or on behalf of a person are not inadmissible in any such proceedings as are mentioned in sub-paragraph (2) by reason only that it has been drawn to that person's attention–

(a)   that pecuniary settlements may be accepted instead of a penalty being determined, or proceedings being instituted, or

(b)   that, though no undertaking can be given as to whether or not the Commissioners will accept such a settlement in the case of any particular person, it is the practice of the Commissioners to be influenced by the fact that a person has made a full confession of any fraudulent conduct to which he had been a party and has given full facilities for investigation,

and that he was or may have been induced thereby to make the statements or produce the documents.

3(2) The proceedings mentioned in sub-paragraph (1) are–

(a)   any criminal proceedings against the person in question for any form of fraudulent conduct in connection with or in relation to stamp duty, and

(b)   any proceedings against that person for the recovery of any stamp duty or interest on unpaid stamp duty due from him, and

(c)   any proceedings for a penalty, or on appeal against the determination of a penalty, in connection with or in relation to stamp duty.

REFERENCES TO DURATION OF LEASE

4   In relation to Scotland, the expression **"term"**, where referring to the duration of a lease, means **"period"**.

Part II – Obsolete Provisions

5(1)   Section 13 of the Stamp Duties Management Act 1891 (certain offences in relation to dies and stamps provided by the Commissioners to be felonies) is amended as follows.

5(2)   For the sidenote substitute "Offences in relation to dies and stamps.".

5(3)   Make the existing provision subsection (1) and at the beginning, for "Every person who" substitute "A person commits an offence who".

5(4)   Omit the words from "shall be guilty of felony" to the end.

5(5)   [Inserts SDMA 1891, s. 13(2)]

5(6)   This paragraph has effect in relation to things done or omitted on or after 1st October 1999.

6(1)   The following provisions of the Stamp Duties Management Act 1891 shall cease to have effect–

    in section 2 (recovery of money received for duty), subsections (2) and (3);

    section 3 (power to grant licences to deal in stamps);

    section 4 (penalty for unauthorised dealing in stamps etc.);

    section 5 (provisions as to determination of a licence);

    section 6 (penalty for hawking stamps);

    section 8 (discount on sale of stamps);

    section 9(2) and (3) (cases in which allowance may be made for spoiled adhesive stamps);

    in section 11 (how allowance to be made), the words from "deducting therefrom" to the end;

    section 12 (repurchase of stamps by Commissioners);

    section 17 (proceedings for detection of stamps stolen or fraudulently obtained);

    section 18 (licensed person in possession of forged stamps to be presumed guilty);

         section 19 (mode of proceeding when stamps are seized);

         section 20 (defacement of adhesive stamps);

         section 25 (mode of granting licences).

6(2)   This paragraph comes into force on 1st October 1999.

SCHEDULE 19 – STAMP DUTY AND STAMP DUTY RESERVE TAX: UNIT TRUSTS

Section 122(4)

History – The provisions of Sch. 19 come into force on 6 February 2000 (FA 1999, s. 122(4)) and effectively replace those contained in:

- SA 1891 and certain related enactments (which remained in effect so far as they relate to transfers or other instruments relating to units under a unit trust scheme notwithstanding their general repeal on or after 1 October 1999 – FA 1999, Sch. 20 Pt. V(2), para. 2); and
- those in FA 1946, s. 54–57 and related acts (which were repealed with effect in relation to instruments executed on or after 6 February 2000 – FA 1999, Sch. 20 Pt. V(5)).

Cross reference – Stamp Duty and Stamp Duty Reserve Tax (Open-ended Investment Companies) Regulations 1997, SI 1997/1156.

Notes – SI 1992/197: common investment fund established under the Administration of Justice Act 1982, s. 42(1) is excepted from the definition of "unit trust scheme" for the purposes of stamp duty and stamp duty reserve tax from 1 March 1992.

Part I – Abolition of Stamp Duty on Transfers etc. of Units in Unit Trusts

Prospective repeal – Sch. 19, Pt I repealed by FA 1999, s. 123(3) and s. 139 and Sch. 20, Pt. V(6) with effect:
(a)   so far as it relates to stamp duty on bearer instruments, in accordance with FA 1990, s. 107; and
(b)   so far as it relates to stamp duty on instruments other than bearer instruments, in accordance with FA 1990, s. 108.

Cross reference – FA 1986, s. 88(1): instrument not charged to stamp duty by virtue of Sch. 19, Pt I disregarded for the purposes of the conditions for repayment of stamp duty reserve tax in FA 1986, s. 92(1A) and (1B).

Note – The "abolition day" for the purposes of FA 1990, s. 107–110 was such day as may be appointed by Treasury order in accordance with s. 111(1) of that act. Originally, the Treasury order appointing the "abolition day" was to have coincided broadly with the start of paperless trading under the Stock Exchange's planned TAURUS system (IR press release, 20 March 1990). However, on 11 March 1993 it was announced that TAURUS had been abandoned (London Stock Exchange News Release 6/93).

1(1)   No stamp duty is chargeable on a transfer or other instrument relating to a unit under a unit trust scheme.

1(2)   Sub-paragraph (1) does not affect any charge to stamp duty–

(a)   on a conveyance or transfer on sale of property other than units under a unit trust scheme in relation to which such units form the whole or part of the consideration, or

(b)   under Schedule 15 to this Act (bearer instruments).

1(3)   This paragraph has effect in relation to instruments executed on or after 6th February 2000.

Prospective repeal – Sch. 19, Pt I repealed by FA 1999, s. 123(3) and s. 139 and Sch. 20, Pt. V(6) with effect:
(a)   so far as it relates to stamp duty on bearer instruments, in accordance with FA 1990, s. 107; and
(b)   so far as it relates to stamp duty on instruments other than bearer instruments, in accordance with FA 1990, s. 108.
(For information on the "abolition day" for the purposes of FA 1990, s. 107–110, see note at the start of Pt I.)

Part II – Stamp Duty Reserve Tax on Dealings with Units in Unit Trusts

Prospective repeal – Sch. 19, Pt II repealed by FA 1999, s. 123(3) and s. 139 and Sch. 20, Pt. V(6) with effect, so far as it relates to stamp duty reserve tax, in accordance with FA 1990, s. 110.

Note – The "abolition day" for the purposes of FA 1990, s. 107–110 was such day as may be appointed by Treasury order in accordance with s. 111(1) of that act. Originally, the Treasury order appointing the "abolition day" was to have coincided broadly with the start of paperless trading under the Stock Exchange's planned TAURUS system (IR press release, 20 March 1990). However, on 11 March 1993 it was announced that TAURUS had been abandoned (London Stock Exchange News Release 6/93).

CHARGE TO TAX

2(1)   There is a charge to stamp duty reserve tax where–

(a)   a person authorises or requires the trustees or managers under a unit trust scheme to treat him as no longer interested in a unit under the scheme, or

(b)   a unit under a unit trust scheme is transferred to the managers of the scheme,

and the unit is a chargeable security.

Those events are referred to in this Part of this Schedule as a "surrender" of the unit to the managers.

2(2)   The tax is chargeable–

(a)   whether the surrender is made or effected in the United Kingdom or elsewhere, and

(b)   whether or not any party is resident or situate in any part of the United Kingdom.

2(3)   The persons liable for the tax are the trustees of the unit trust.

2(4)   This paragraph is subject to the exclusions provided for in paragraphs 6 and 7.

Prospective repeal – Sch. 19, Pt II repealed by FA 1999, s. 123(3) and s. 139 and Sch. 20, Pt. V(6) with effect, so far as it relates to stamp duty reserve tax, in accordance with FA 1990, s. 110.(For information on the "abolition day" for the purposes of FA 1990, s. 110, see note at the start of Pt II.)

RATE OF TAX

3(1)   Tax under this Part of this Schedule is chargeable at the rate of 0.5% of the market value of the unit.

This is subject to any reduction under paragraph 4 or 5.

3(2)   The market value of a unit means whichever is higher of–

(a)   the price the unit might reasonably be expected to fetch on a sale in the open market at the time of surrender, and

(b)   its cancellation price, or if it is redeemed its redemption price, at that time, calculated in accordance with the trust instrument.

Prospective repeal – Sch. 19, Pt II repealed by FA 1999, s. 123(3) and s. 139 and Sch. 20, Pt. V(6) with effect, so far as it relates to stamp duty reserve tax, in accordance with FA 1990, s. 110.(For information on the "abolition day" for the purposes of FA 1990, s. 110, see note at the start of Pt II.)

PROPORTIONATE REDUCTION OF TAX BY REFERENCE TO UNITS ISSUED

4(1)   The amount of tax chargeable shall be proportionately reduced if the number of units of the same class as the unit in question that are surrendered to the managers in the relevant two-week period exceeds the number of units of that class issued by the managers in that period.

4(2)   The "relevant two-week period" in relation to a surrender is the period from the beginning of the week in which the surrender occurs to the end of the following week.

For this purpose a week means a period of seven days beginning with a Sunday.

4(3)   The reduction is made by applying the following fraction to the amount otherwise chargeable–

$$\frac{I}{S}$$

Where:

I   is the number of units of the class issued by the managers in the relevant two-week period, and

S   is the number of units of the class surrendered to the managers in that period.

4(4)   If a consolidation or sub-division of units affects the comparison of the number of units surrendered and the number of units issued, the numbers shall be determined as if the consolidation or sub-division had not taken place.

"Consolidation or sub-division" includes any alteration of the number of units of the class in question otherwise than in consequence of an increase or reduction in the trust property.

4(5)   This paragraph does not apply if on the surrender of the unit the unit holder receives anything other than money; and for the purposes of this paragraph no account shall be taken of a surrender or issue that is not entirely of money.

Prospective repeal – Sch. 19, Pt II repealed by FA 1999, s. 123(3) and s. 139 and Sch. 20, Pt. V(6) with effect, so far as it relates to stamp duty reserve tax, in accordance with FA 1990, s. 110. (For information on the "abolition day" for the purposes of FA 1990, s. 110, see note at the start of Pt II.)

Cross reference – Stamp Duty and Stamp Duty Reserve Tax (Open-ended Investment Companies) Regulations 1997, SI 1997/1156, reg. 4A: modifications of Sch. 19, para. 4 in relation to open-ended investment companies.

PROPORTIONATE REDUCTION OF TAX BY REFERENCE TO ASSETS HELD

5(1)   The amount of tax chargeable after any reduction under paragraph 4 shall be further reduced if in the relevant two-week period the trust property is invested in both exempt and non-exempt investments.

5(2)   The reduction is made by applying the following fraction to that amount–

5(3)   In this paragraph **"exempt investment"** has the same meaning as in section 99(5A)(b) of the Finance Act 1986; and **"non-exempt investment"** means any investment that is not an exempt investment.

EXCLUSION OF CHARGE IN CERTAIN CASES OF CHANGE OF OWNERSHIP

6(1)   This paragraph applies where in pursuance of arrangements between the person entitled to a unit and another person ("the new owner")–

(a)   the unit is surrendered to the managers, and

(b)   the person surrendering the unit authorises or requires the managers or trustees to treat the new owner as entitled to it.

6(2)   There is no charge to tax under this Part of this Schedule if no consideration in money or money's worth is given in connection with the surrender of the unit or the new owner's becoming entitled to it.

6(3)   There is no charge to tax under this Part of this Schedule if the new owner is–

(a)   a body of persons established for charitable purposes only, or

(b)   the trustees of a trust established for those purposes only, or

(c)   the Trustees of the National Heritage Memorial Fund, or

(d)   the Historic Buildings and Monuments Commission for England.

6(4)   There is no charge to tax under this Part of this Schedule if an instrument executed at the time of the surrender–

(a)   in pursuance of arrangements between the persons entitled to the unit and the new owner, and

(b)   transferring the unit from the one to the other,

would be exempt from stamp duty (if stamp duty were otherwise chargeable) by virtue of any of the provisions mentioned in sub-paragraph (5).

6(5)   The provisions referred to in sub-paragraph (4) are–

(a)   section 42 of the Finance Act 1930 or section 11 of the Finance Act (Northern Ireland) 1954 (transfers between associated companies); and

(b)   regulations under section 87(2) of the Finance Act 1985 (power to exempt instruments from stamp duty of fixed amount).

6(6)   Where by virtue of sub-paragraph (2), (3) or (4) there is no charge to tax, both the surrender and the related issue shall be left out of account for the purposes of paragraph 4.

EXCLUSION OF CHARGE IN CASE OF IN SPECIE REDEMPTION

7   There is no charge to tax under this Part of this Schedule if on the surrender of the unit the unit holder receives only such part of each description of asset in the trust property as is proportionate to, or as nearly as practicable proportionate to, the unit holder's share.

INTERPRETATION

8(1)   For the purposes of this Part of this Schedule **"issue"** in the context of the issue of a unit by the managers under a unit trust scheme includes their transferring an existing unit or authorising or requiring the trustees to treat a person as entitled to a unit under the scheme.

8(2)   References in this Part of this Schedule to the surrender or issue of a unit under a unit trust scheme do not include a surrender or issue effected by means of, or consisting of the issue of, a certificate to bearer.

TRANSITIONAL PROVISION

9   This Part of this Schedule applies where the surrender of the unit to the managers occurs on or after 6th February 2000.

Prospective repeal – Sch. 19, Pt II repealed by FA 1999, s. 123(3) and s. 139 and Sch. 20, Pt. V(6) with effect, so far as it relates to stamp duty reserve tax, in accordance with FA 1990, s. 110.(For information on the "abolition day" for the purposes of FA 1990, s. 110, see note at the start of Pt II.)

Part III – Minor and Consequential Amendments

Prospective repeal – Sch. 19, Pt III repealed by FA 1999, s. 123(3) and s. 139 and Sch. 20, Pt. V(6) with effect:
(a)   so far as it relates to stamp duty on bearer instruments, in accordance with FA 1990, s. 107;
(b)   so far as it relates to stamp duty on instruments other than bearer instruments, in accordance with FA 1990, s. 108; and
(c)   so far as it relates to stamp duty reserve tax, in accordance with FA 1990, s. 110.

Note – The "abolition day" for the purposes of FA 1990, s. 107–110 was such day as may be appointed by Treasury order in accordance with s. 111(1) of that act. Originally, the Treasury order appointing the "abolition day" was to have coincided broadly with the start of paperless trading under the Stock Exchange's planned TAURUS system (IR press release, 20 March 1990). However, on 11 March 1993 it was announced that TAURUS had been abandoned (London Stock Exchange News Release 6/93).

FINANCE ACT 1986 (c.41)

10   [Inserts FA 1986, s. 88(1)(c).]

Prospective repeal – Sch. 19, Pt. III repealed by FA 1999, s. 123(3) and s. 139 and Sch. 20, Pt. V(6) with effect, so far as it relates to stamp duty reserve tax, in accordance with FA 1990, s. 110. (For information on the "abolition day" for the purposes of FA 1990, s. 110, see note at the start of Pt. III.)

11(1)   Section 90 of the Finance Act 1986 (exceptions from general charge to stamp duty reserve tax) is amended as follows.

11(2)   [Amends FA 1986, s. 90 (1).]

11(3)   [Inserts FA 1986, , s. 90(1A).]

11(4)   [Inserts FA 1986, s. 90(1B).]

11(5)   The amendments in sub-paragraphs (2) and (3) apply where the relevant day for purposes of section 87 of the Finance Act 1986 falls on or after 6th February 2000.

11(6)   The amendment in sub-paragraph (4) applies where the surrender (within the meaning of Part II of Schedule 19 to the Finance Act 1999) occurs on or after 6th February 2000.

Prospective repeal – Sch. 19, Pt. III repealed by FA 1999, s. 123(3) and s. 139 and Sch. 20, Pt. V(6) with effect, so far as it relates to stamp duty reserve tax, in accordance with FA 1990, s. 110. (For information on the "abolition day" for the purposes of FA 1990, s. 110, see note at the start of Pt. III.)

12(1)   Section 99 of the Finance Act 1986 (general interpretation provisions) is amended as follows.

12(2)   [Amends FA 1986, s. 99(5).]

12(3)   [Inserts FA 1986, s. 99(5A) and (5B).]

12(4)   [Substitutes FA 1986, s. 99(9).]

Prospective repeal – Sch. 19, Pt. III repealed by FA 1999, s. 123(3) and s. 139 and Sch. 20, Pt. V(6) with effect, so far as it relates to stamp duty reserve tax, in accordance with FA 1990, s. 110. (For information on the "abolition day" for the purposes of FA 1990, s. 110, see note at the start of Pt. III.)

FINANCE ACT 1995 (c.4)

13(1)   Section 152 of the Finance Act 1995 (power to apply tax legislation to open-ended investment companies) is amended as follows.

13(2)   [Amends FA 1995, s. 152 (2)(b).]

13(3)   [Amends FA 1995, s. 152(3)(c).]

13(4)   [Amends FA 1995, s. 152(6).]

Prospective repeal – Sch. 19, Pt. III repealed by FA 1999, s. 123(3) and s. 139 and Sch. 20, Pt. V(6) with effect:
(a)   so far as it relates to stamp duty on bearer instruments, in accordance with FA 1990, s. 107;
(b)   so far as it relates to stamp duty on instruments other than bearer instruments, in accordance with FA 1990, s. 108; and
(c)   so far as it relates to stamp duty reserve tax, in accordance with FA 1990, s. 110.
(For information on the "abolition day" for the purposes of FA 1990, s. 107–110, see note at the start of Pt. III.)
Stamp Duty and Stamp Duty Reserve Tax (Open-ended Investment Companies) (Amendment No. 2) Regulations SI 1999/3261 (operative from 6 February 2000): amendment of SI 1997/1156 to introduce a stamp duty reserve tax regime for dealings of shares in open-ended investment companies which is equivalent to the provisions of Sch. 19.

Part IV – General Definitions

MEANING OF "UNIT TRUST SCHEME" AND RELATED EXPRESSIONS

14(1)   The following definitions apply for the purposes of the enactments relating to stamp duty and the enactments relating to stamp duty reserve tax.

14(2) **"Unit trust scheme"** has the same meaning as in the Financial Services Act 1986, subject to paragraphs 15 to 18.

14(3) In relation to a unit trust scheme–

"trust instrument" means the trust deed or other instrument (whether under seal or not) creating or recording the trusts on which the property in question is held;

"trust property" means the property subject to the trusts of the trust instrument;

"unit" means a right or interest (whether described as a unit, as a sub-unit or otherwise) of a beneficiary under the trust instrument;

"unit holder" means a person entitled to a share of the trust property; and

"certificate to bearer", in relation to a unit, means a document by the delivery of which the unit can be transferred.

Prospective repeal – In Sch. 19, para. 14(1), the words "and the enactments relating to stamp duty reserve tax" repealed by FA 1999, s. 123(3) and s. 139 and Sch. 20, Pt. V(6) with effect in accordance with FA 1990, s. 110.

Cross references – SI 1992/197: common investment fund established under the Administration of Justice Act 1982, s. 42(1) is excepted from the definition of "unit trust scheme" for the purposes of stamp duty and stamp duty reserve tax from 1 March 1992.

Stamp Duty and Stamp Duty Reserve Tax (Open-ended Investment Companies) Regulations 1997, SI 1997/1156, reg. 4A: modifications of Sch. 19, para. 14 in relation to open-ended investment companies.

Note – The "abolition day" for the purposes of FA 1990, s. 110 was such day as may be appointed by Treasury order in accordance with s. 111(1) of that act. Originally, the Treasury order appointing the "abolition day" was to have coincided broadly with the start of paperless trading under the Stock Exchange's planned TAURUS system (IR press release, 20 March 1990). However, on 11 March 1993 it was announced that TAURUS had been abandoned (London Stock Exchange News Release 6/93).

SCHEMES NOT TREATED AS UNIT TRUST SCHEMES

15 References in the enactments relating to stamp duty and the enactments relating to stamp duty reserve tax to a unit trust scheme do not include–

15(a) a common investment scheme under section 22 of the Charities Act 1960, section 25 of the Charities Act (Northern Ireland) 1964, or section 24 of the Charities Act 1993,

15(b) a common deposit scheme under section 22A of the Charities Act 1960 or section 25 of the Charities Act 1993, or

15(c) a unit trust scheme the units in which are under the terms of the trust instrument required to be held only by bodies or persons established for charitable purposes only or trustees of trusts so established.

Prospective repeal – In Sch. 19, para. 15, the words "and the enactments relating to stamp duty reserve tax" repealed by FA 1999, s. 123(3) and s. 139 and Sch. 20, Pt. V(6) with effect in accordance with FA 1990, s. 110.

Note – The "abolition day" for the purposes of FA 1990, s. 110 was such day as may be appointed by Treasury order in accordance with s. 111(1) of that act. Originally, the Treasury order appointing the "abolition day" was to have coincided broadly with the start of paperless trading under the Stock Exchange's planned TAURUS system (IR press release, 20 March 1990). However, on 11 March 1993 it was announced that TAURUS had been abandoned (London Stock Exchange News Release 6/93).

16 References in the enactments relating to stamp duty and the enactments relating to stamp duty reserve tax to a unit trust scheme do not include common investment arrangements made by trustees of exempt approved schemes (within the meaning of section 592(1) of the Taxes Act 1988) solely for the purposes of the schemes.

Prospective repeal – In Sch. 19, para. 16, the words "and the enactments relating to stamp duty reserve tax" repealed by FA 1999, s. 123(3) and s. 139 and Sch. 20, Pt. V(6) with effect in accordance with FA 1990, s. 110.

Note – The "abolition day" for the purposes of FA 1990, s. 110 was such day as may be appointed by Treasury order in accordance with s. 111(1) of that act. Originally, the Treasury order appointing the "abolition day" was to have coincided broadly with the start of paperless trading under the Stock Exchange's planned TAURUS system (IR press release, 20 March 1990). However, on 11 March 1993 it was announced that TAURUS had been abandoned (London Stock Exchange News Release 6/93).

17(1) The Treasury may by regulations provide that any scheme of a description specified in the regulations shall be treated as not being a unit trust scheme for the purposes of the enactments relating to stamp duty and the enactments relating to stamp duty reserve tax.

17(2) Regulations under this paragraph–

(a) may contain such supplementary and transitional provisions as appear to the Treasury to be necessary or expedient, and

(b) shall be made by statutory instrument which shall be subject to annulment in pursuance of a resolution of the House of Commons.

17(3) This paragraph replaces section 57(1A) and (1B) of the Finance Act 1946 and section 28(1A) and (1B) of the Finance (No.2) Act (Northern Ireland) 1946.

17(4) Any regulations having effect under those provisions for the purposes of Part VII of the Finance Act 1946 or Part III of the Finance (No.2) Act (Northern Ireland) 1946 which are in force immediately before the commencement of this Schedule shall have effect as if made under this paragraph.

Prospective repeal – In Sch. 19, para. 17(1), the words "and the enactments relating to stamp duty reserve tax" repealed by FA 1999, s. 123(3) and s. 139 and Sch. 20, Pt. V(6) with effect in accordance with FA 1990, s. 110.

Cross reference – Stamp Duty and Stamp Duty Reserve Tax (Open-ended Investment Companies) Regulations 1997, SI 1997/1156, reg. 4A: modifications of Sch. 19, para. 17 in relation to open-ended investment companies.

Note – The "abolition day" for the purposes of FA 1990, s. 110 was such day as may be appointed by Treasury order in accordance with s. 111(1) of that act. Originally, the Treasury order appointing the "abolition day" was to have coincided broadly with the start of paperless trading under the Stock Exchange's planned TAURUS system (IR press release, 20 March 1990). However, on 11 March 1993 it was announced that TAURUS had been abandoned (London Stock Exchange News Release 6/93).

TREATMENT OF UMBRELLA SCHEMES

18(1)   For the purposes of the enactments relating to stamp duty and the enactments relating to stamp duty reserve tax each of the parts of an umbrella scheme is regarded as a unit trust scheme and the scheme as a whole is not so regarded.

18(2)   An **"umbrella scheme"** means a unit trust scheme–

(a)   which provides arrangements for separate pooling of the contributions of participants and of the profits or income out of which payments are to be made to them, and

(b)   under which the participants are entitled to exchange rights in one pool for rights in another;

and a **"part of an umbrella scheme"** means such of the arrangements as relate to a separate pool.

18(3)   In relation to part of an umbrella scheme–

(a)   any reference to the trust property has effect as a reference to such of the trust property as under the arrangements forms part of the separate pool to which the part of the umbrella scheme relates, and

(b)   any reference to a unit holder has effect as a reference to a person for the time being having rights in that separate pool.

Prospective repeal – In Sch. 19, para. 18(1), the words "and the enactments relating to stamp duty reserve tax" repealed by FA 1999, s. 123(3) and s. 139 and Sch. 20, Pt. V(6) with effect in accordance with FA 1990, s. 110.

Note – The "abolition day" for the purposes of FA 1990, s. 110 was such day as may be appointed by Treasury order in accordance with s. 111(1) of that act. Originally, the Treasury order appointing the "abolition day" was to have coincided broadly with the start of paperless trading under the Stock Exchange's planned TAURUS system (IR press release, 20 March 1990). However, on 11 March 1993 it was announced that TAURUS had been abandoned (London Stock Exchange News Release 6/93).

REFERENCES TO STOCK IN STAMP DUTY ENACTMENTS INCLUDE UNITS UNDER UNIT TRUST SCHEME

19   In the enactments relating to stamp duty–

19(a)   any reference to stock includes a unit under a unit trust scheme, and

19(b)   any reference to a stock certificate to bearer includes a certificate to bearer in relation to a unit under a unit trust scheme.

SCHEDULE 20 – REPEALS

Section 139

Part V – Stamp Duty and Stamp Duty Reserve Tax

(1) STAMP DUTY: INTEREST AND PENALTIES ON LATE STAMPING

Chapter	Short title	Extent of repeal
1933 c. 19.	The Finance Act 1933.	In section 42, the words "and subsection (1) of section 15".
1933 c. 28 (N.I.).	The Finance Act (Northern Ireland) 1933.	In section 2, the words "and subsection (1) of section fifteen".
1965 c. 25.	The Finance Act 1965.	Section 91.
1965 c. 16 (N.I.).	The Finance Act (Northern Ireland) 1965.	Section 5.

Chapter	Short title	Extent of repeal
1984 c. 43.	The Finance Act 1984.	Section 111(4).
1986 c. 41.	The Finance Act 1986.	Section 69(5). Section 72(3).

1.   These repeals have effect in relation to instruments executed on or after 1st October 1999, subject to paragraph 2.

2.   The repeals do not have effect in relation to transfers or other instruments relating to units under a unit trust scheme.

This does not affect their operation in relation to–

(a)   conveyances or transfers on sale of property other than units under a unit trust scheme in relation to which such units form the whole or part of the consideration; and

(b)   bearer instruments constituting, or used for transferring, units under a unit trust scheme.

(2) STAMP DUTY: CHARGING PROVISIONS AND RATES OF DUTY

Chapter	Short title	Extent of repeal
1891 c. 39.	The Stamp Act 1891.	Section 1. Section 54. Section 59. Section 62. Sections 72 and 73. Section 75. Section 77(5). Schedule 1.
1902 c. 7.	The Finance Act 1902.	Section 9.
1903 c. 46.	The Revenue Act 1903.	Section 7.
1949 c. 47.	The Finance Act 1949.	Section 35. Schedule 8.
1949 c. 15 (N.I.).	The Finance Act (Northern Ireland) 1949.	Section 35. Schedule 2.
1958 c. 56.	The Finance Act 1958.	Section 34(4).
1958 c. 14 (N.I.).	The Finance Act (Northern Ireland) 1958.	Section 7(4).
1963 c. 25.	The Finance Act 1963.	Sections 55 to 63. Section 65(1).
1963 c. 22 (N.I.).	The Finance Act (Northern Ireland) 1963.	Sections 4 to 12. Section 14(1).
1967 c. 54.	The Finance Act 1967.	Section 30.
1967 c. 20 (N.I.).	The Finance Act (Northern Ireland) 1967.	Section 7.
1970 c. 24.	The Finance Act 1970.	Section 32. Schedule 7.
1970 c. 21 (N.I.).	The Finance Act (Northern Ireland) 1970.	Section 6. Schedule 2.
1971 c. 68.	The Finance Act 1971.	Section 64.
1971 c. 27 (N.I.).	The Finance Act (Northern Ireland) 1971.	Section 5(1) and (3).
1972 c. 41.	The Finance Act 1972.	Section 126.
1974 c. 30.	The Finance Act 1974.	Section 49. Section 57(3)(d). Schedule 11.
1976 c. 40.	The Finance Act 1976.	In Part VI of Schedule 15, the provision amending section 33(1) of the Finance Act 1970.
1980 c. 48.	The Finance Act 1980.	Section 95.

Chapter	Short title	Extent of repeal
1982 c. 39.	The Finance Act 1982.	Section 128.
1984 c. 43.	The Finance Act 1984.	Section 109.
		Section 111(1).
1986 c. 41.	The Finance Act 1986.	Sections 64 and 65.
		Section 78(1) to (6), (8) and (10) to (14).
		In section 79–
		(a) subsection (1);
		(b) subsections (9) to (1 1); and
		(c) in subsection (12), the words ''(10) and (14)''.
		Section 80.
1987 c. 16.	The Finance Act 1987.	Section 49.
		Section 50(4) and (5).
		Section 51.
1988 c. 39.	The Finance Act 1988.	Sections 140 and 141.
1989 c. 26.	The Finance Act 1989.	Section 173.
1991 c. 31.	The Finance Act 1991.	Section 115.
1992 c. 2.	The Stamp Duty (Temporary Provisions) Act 1992.	The whole Act.
1993 c. 34.	The Finance Act 1993.	Section 201.
1994 c. 9.	The Finance Act 1994.	Section 241(3) to (5).
1996 c. 8.	The Finance Act 1996.	Section 188(2).
		In Schedule 40, paragraph 2.
1997 c. 58.	The Finance (No. 2) Act 1997.	Section 49.
1998 c. 36.	The Finance Act 1998.	Section 149.
1999 c. 00.	The Finance Act 1999.	Section 111.

1.   These repeals have effect in relation to instruments executed, or bearer instruments issued, on or after 1st October 1999, subject to paragraph 2.

2.   The repeals do not have effect in relation to transfers or other instruments relating to units under a unit trust scheme.

This does not affect their operation in relation to–

(a)   conveyances or transfers on sale of property other than units under a unit trust scheme in relation to which such units form the whole or part of the consideration; and

(b)   bearer instruments constituting, or used for transferring, units under a unit trust scheme.

(3) STAMP DUTY: PENALTIES OTHER THAN ON LATE STAMPING

Chapter	Short title	Extent of repeal
1891 c. 38.	The Stamp Duties Management Act 1891.	In section 13, the words from ''shall be guilty of felony'' to the end.
		Section 26.
1891 c. 39.	The Stamp Act 1891.	Section 121.
1898 c. 46.	The Revenue Act 1898.	Section 7(5).
1986 c. 41.	The Finance Act 1986.	Section 68(6).
		Section 71(6).

These repeals have effect in relation to things done or omitted on or after 1st October 1999.

(4) STAMP DUTY: OBSOLETE ENACTMENTS

Chapter	Short title	Extent of repeal
1891 c. 38.	The Stamp Duties Management Act 1891.	Section 2(2) and (3). Sections 3 to 6. Section 8. Section 9(2) and (3). In section 11, the words from "deducting therefrom" to the end. Section 12. Sections 17 to 20. Section 25.

These repeals come into force on 1st October 1999.

(5) STAMP DUTY: UNIT TRUSTS

Chapter	Short title	Extent of repeal
1946 c. 64.	The Finance Act 1946.	Section 54 to 57.
1946 c. 17 (N.I.).	The Finance (No. 2) Act (Northern Ireland) 1946.	Section 25 to 28.
1963 c. 18.	The Stock Transfer Act 1963.	In section 2(3)(a), the words "and section 56(4) of the Finance Act 1946".
1963 c. 24 (N.I.).	The Stock Transfer Act (Northern Ireland) 1963.	In section 2(3)(a), the words "and section 27(4) of the Finance (No. 2) Act (Northern Ireland) 1946".
1963 c. 25.	The Finance Act 1963.	Section 65(2).
1963 c. 22 (N.I.).	The Finance Act (Northern Ireland) 1963.	Section 14(2).
1980 c. 48.	The Finance Act 1980.	Section 101.
1981 c. 35.	The Finance Act 1981.	Section 110.
1986 c. 41.	The Finance Act 1986.	Section 90(2).
1988 c. 39.	The Finance Act 1988.	Section 144(3). In Schedule 13, paragraph 21.
1989 c. 26.	The Finance Act 1989.	Section 174.
1990 c. 29.	The Finance Act 1990.	In section 109– (a) subsection (2)(c) and (d); (b) subsection (6)(a) and (b); and (c) subsection (9). Section 113(4).
1992 c. 41.	The Charities Act 1992.	In Schedule 6, paragraph 2.
1993 c. 10.	The Charities Act 1993.	In Schedule 6, paragraph 5.
1999 c. 00.	The Finance Act 1999.	In Schedule 17, paragraphs 4 and 5.

1. These repeals have effect in relation to instruments executed on or after 6th February 2000.

2. The repeals of section 57(1A) and (1B) of the Finance Act 1946 and section 28(1A) and (1B) of the Finance (No.2) Act (Northern Ireland) 1946 have effect subject to paragraph 17(4) of Schedule 19 (saving for existing regulations).

(6) REPEALS HAVING EFFECT ON ABOLITION DATE

Chapter	Short title	Extent of repeal
1999 c. 00.	The Finance Act 1999.	Section 113. Section 116 to 121. In section 123(1) and (2), paragraph (b) and the word "and" immediately preceding it. In Schedule 13– (a) paragraph 3; (b) in paragraph 4, the words "in the case of any other conveyance or transfer on sale"; (c) paragraph 7(1)(b)(ii) to (iv). (d) paragraph 24(a), (b) and (d). In Schedule 14, paragraphs 4, 7, 11, 12, 15 to 20 and 22. Schedule 15. In Schedule 16, paragraphs 2 to 11. In Schedule 17, paragraphs 6 and 8. In Schedule 19– (a) Parts I to III; (b) in Part IV, the words "and the enactments relating to stamp duty reserve tax" in paragraphs 14(1), 15, 16, 17(1) and 18(1).

These repeals have effect–

(a) so far as they relate to stamp duty on bearer instruments, in accordance with section 107 of the Finance Act 1990;

(b) so far as they relate to stamp duty on instruments other than bearer instruments, in accordance with section 108 of that Act;

(c) so far as they relate to stamp duty reserve tax, in accordance with section 110 of that Act.

Note – The table in Sch. 20, Pt. V(6) above contains errors in the "Extent of repeal" column in listing the paragraphs of Sch. 14 which are to be repealed. This table is intended to reproduce those elements of Pt. VI (including associated schedules) of this act which (prospectively) cease to have effect under s. 123(3). In so doing, the paragraphs of Sch. 14 which cease to have effect under that section have not been listed correctly. The Stamp Office have confirmed informally that the correct paragraphs are, 5, 8, 12, 13, 16–21 and 23 in accordance with s. 123(3). Those paragraphs of Sch. 14 which are affected have been treated as if the table errors had been corrected in advance of Royal Assent to the Finance Bill.

FINANCE ACT 2000

(2000 Chapter 17)

[28 July 2000]

ARRANGEMENT OF SECTIONS

PART IV – STAMP DUTY AND STAMP DUTY RESERVE TAX

STAMP DUTY

PART IV – STAMP DUTY AND STAMP DUTY RESERVE TAX

STAMP DUTY

114   Rates: conveyance or transfer on sale

114(1)   In Schedule 13 to the Finance Act 1999 (instruments chargeable and rates of duty), in Part I (conveyance or transfer on sale), in the third column of the table in paragraph 4–

(a)   in the third entry, for "2.5%" substitute "3%"; and

(b)   in the fourth entry, for "3.5%" substitute "4%".

114(2)   This section applies to instruments executed on or after 28th March 2000.

114(3)   But this section does not apply to an instrument giving effect to a contract made on or before 21st March 2000, unless–

(a)   the instrument is made in consequence of the exercise after that date of any option, right of pre-emption or similar right; or

(b)   the instrument transfers the property in question to, or vests it in, a person other than the purchaser under the contract, because of an assignment (or, in Scotland, assignation) or further contract made after that date.

114(4)   This section shall be deemed to have come into force on 28th March 2000.

115   Rates: duty on lease chargeable by reference to rent

115(1)   In Schedule 13 to the Finance Act 1999 (instruments chargeable and rates of duty), in Part II (lease)–

(a)   in paragraph 11, in paragraph 1 of the table, and

(b)   in paragraph 12(3), in paragraph 1(a) and (b) of the table,

for "£500" substitute "£5,000".

115(2)   This section has effect in relation to instruments executed on or after 28th March 2000.

115(3)   This section shall be deemed to have come into force on 28th March 2000.

116   Rate of duty on seven year leases

116(1)   In paragraph 12(3) of Schedule 13 to the Finance Act 1999 (rates of stamp duty on leases where part of consideration is rent), in paragraph 1 of the table, for "less than 7 years" substitute "not more than 7 years".

116(2)   This section applies to instruments executed on or after 1st October 1999, subject to Schedule 32 to this Act (which makes transitional provision for instruments executed on or after 1st October 1999 but before 28th March 2000).

116(3)   This section shall be deemed to have come into force on 28th March 2000.

117   Power to vary stamp duties

117   Schedule 33 to this Act (power to vary stamp duties) has effect.

118   Land transferred etc. for other property

118(1)   Subsection (2) applies where–

(a)   an instrument transferring or vesting an estate or interest in land would not, apart from this section, be or fall to be treated as a conveyance or transfer on sale for the purposes of stamp duty; but

(b)   the transfer or vesting of the estate or interest is for consideration; and

(c)   the consideration is or includes any property ("the other property").

118(2)   For the purposes of Part I of Schedule 13 to the Finance Act 1999 (stamp duty on conveyance or transfer on sale) the instrument transferring or vesting the estate or interest shall be taken to be a transfer on sale of the estate or interest.

118(3)   If–

(a)   the other property is or includes one or more estates or interests in land, and

(b)   *ad valorem* duty is chargeable on the conveyance or transfer of all or any of those estates or interests,

the amount of duty that would (apart from this subsection) be chargeable in consequence of subsection (2) on the transfer on sale there mentioned shall be reduced (but not below nil) by the total of the *ad valorem* duty chargeable as mentioned in paragraph (b).

118(4)   If, for the purposes of Part I of Schedule 13 to the Finance Act 1999, the amount or value of the consideration for the transfer on sale mentioned in subsection (2) would (apart from this subsection) exceed the market value of the estate or interest immediately before the execution of the instrument transferring or vesting it, the amount or value of the consideration shall be taken for those purposes to be equal to that market value.

118(5)   For the purposes of this section, the market value of property at any time is the price which that property might reasonably be expected to fetch on a sale at that time in the open market.

118(6)   Subsection (2) has effect even though–

(a)   the transfer or vesting of the estate or interest is the whole or part of the consideration for a sale of the other property; or

(b)   the transaction is by way of exchange.

118(7)   Subsection (2) does not affect any charge to stamp duty in respect of the same or any other instrument so far as it relates to the transfer of the other property.

118(8)   This section is subject to subsection (5) of section 119.

118(9)   This section shall be construed as one with the Stamp Act 1891.

118(10)   This section applies to instruments executed on or after 28th March 2000.

118(11)   But this section does not apply to an instrument giving effect to a contract made on or before 21st March 2000, unless–

(a)   the instrument is made in consequence of the exercise after that date of any option, right of pre-emption or similar right; or

(b)   the instrument transfers the property in question to, or vests it in, a person other than the purchaser under the contract, because of an assignment (or, in Scotland, assignation) or further contract made after that date.

118(12)   This section shall be deemed to have come into force on 28th March 2000.

119   Transfer of land to connected company

119(1)   This section applies where an estate or interest in land is transferred to or vested in a company ("A") and–

(a)   the person transferring or vesting the estate or interest ("B") is connected with A; or

(b)   some or all of the consideration for the transfer or vesting consists of the issue or transfer of shares in a company with which B is connected.

119(2)   For the purposes of Part I of Schedule 13 to the Finance Act 1999 (stamp duty on conveyance or transfer on sale) an instrument transferring or vesting the estate or interest shall be taken to be a transfer on sale of the estate or interest.

119(3)   If for those purposes the amount or value of the consideration for the transfer on sale of the estate or interest would, apart from this subsection, be less than the value determined under subsection (4), the consideration shall be taken for those purposes to be the value determined under subsection (4).

119(4)   That value is–

(a)   the market value of the estate or interest immediately before the execution of the instrument transferring or vesting it; but

(b)   reduced by the value of so much of any actual consideration as does not consist of property.

119(5)   Where–

(a)   apart from this section, an instrument would be chargeable to stamp duty in accordance with section 118, and

(b)   apart from that section, the instrument would be chargeable to stamp duty in accordance with this section,

the stamp duty chargeable on the instrument shall be determined in accordance with this section (instead of that section).

119(6)   This section applies only if, in consequence of its application, the instrument transferring or vesting the estate or interest is chargeable with a greater amount of stamp duty than it would be apart from this section and section 118.

119(7)   For the purposes of this section, the market value of property at any time is the price which that property might reasonably be expected to fetch on a sale at that time in the open market.

119(8)   In this section–

    "company" means any body corporate;

    "shares" includes stock and the reference to shares in a company includes a reference to securities issued by a company.

119(9)   For the purposes of this section, the question whether any person is connected with another shall be determined in accordance with the provisions of section 839 of the Taxes Act 1988.

119(10)   This section shall be construed as one with the Stamp Act 1891.

119(11)   This section applies to instruments executed on or after 28th March 2000.

119(12)   But this section does not apply to an instrument giving effect to a contract made on or before 21st March 2000, unless–

(a)   the instrument is made in consequence of the exercise after that date of any option, right of pre-emption or similar right; or

(b)   the instrument transfers the property in question to, or vests it in, a person other than the purchaser under the contract, because of an assignment (or, in Scotland, assignation) or further contract made after that date.

119(13)   This section shall be deemed to have come into force on 28th March 2000.

120   Exceptions from section 119

120(1)   Section 119 does not apply by virtue of paragraph (a) of subsection (1) of that section in any of the following cases (any reference in this section to A or B being taken as a reference to the person referred to as A or B, as the case may be, in that subsection).

120(2)   Case 1 is where B holds the estate or interest as nominee or bare trustee for A.

120(3)   Case 2 is where A is to hold the estate or interest as nominee or bare trustee for B.

120(4)   Case 3 is where B holds the estate or interest as nominee or bare trustee for some other person and A is to hold it as nominee or bare trustee for that other person.

120(5) Case 4 is where (in a case not falling within subsection (2) or (4) above)–

(a)   the transfer or vesting is a conveyance or transfer out of a settlement in or towards satisfaction of a beneficiary's interest;

(b)   the beneficiary's interest is not an interest acquired for money or money's worth; and

(c)   the conveyance or transfer is a distribution of property in accordance with the provisions of the settlement.

120(6) Case 5 is where (in a case not falling within subsection (3) above) A–

(a)   is a person carrying on a business which consists of or includes the management of trusts; and

(b)   is to hold the estate or interest as trustee acting in the course of that business.

120(7) Case 6 is where (in a case not falling within subsection (3) above) A is to hold the estate or interest as trustee and, apart from section 839(3) of the Taxes Act 1988 (trustees as connected persons), would not be connected with B.

120(8) Case 7 is where–

(a)   B is a company;

(b)   the transfer or vesting is, or is part of, a distribution of assets (whether or not in connection with the winding up of the company); and

(c)   the estate or interest was acquired by B by virtue of an instrument which is duly stamped.

120(9) This section shall be construed as one with the Stamp Act 1891.

120(10) This section applies to instruments executed after the day on which this Act is passed.

121   Grant of lease to connected company

121(1) This section applies where a lease is granted to a company ("A") and–

(a)   the person granting the lease ("B") is connected with A; or

(b)   some or all of the consideration for the grant of the lease consists of the issue or transfer of shares in a company with which B is connected.

121(2) Subsection (3) has effect for the purposes of stamp duty chargeable under Part II of Schedule 13 to the Finance Act 1999 (stamp duty on a lease) by reference to Part I of that Schedule (conveyance or transfer on sale).

121(3) If, apart from this subsection, the amount or value of the consideration for the grant would be less than the value determined under subsection (4), the consideration shall be taken to be the value determined under subsection (4).

121(4) That value is–

(a)   the market value, immediately before the instrument granting the lease is executed, of the lease granted; but

(b)   reduced by the value of so much of any actual consideration as does not consist of property.

121(5) This section applies only if, in consequence of its application, the lease is chargeable with a greater amount of stamp duty than it would be apart from this section.

121(6) For the purposes of this section, the market value of property at any time is the price which that property might reasonably be expected to fetch on a sale at that time in the open market.

121(7) In this section–

"**company**" means any body corporate;

"**shares**" includes stock and the reference to shares in a company includes a reference to securities issued by a company.

121(8) For the purposes of this section, the question whether any person is connected with another shall be determined in accordance with the provisions of section 839 of the Taxes Act 1988.

121(9) This section shall be construed as one with the Stamp Act 1891.

121(10) This section applies to instruments executed on or after 28th March 2000.

121(11) But this section does not apply to an instrument giving effect to a contract made on or before 21st March 2000, unless–

(a)   the instrument is made in consequence of the exercise after that date of any option, right of pre-emption or similar right; or

(b)   the instrument transfers the property in question to, or vests it in, a person other than the purchaser under the contract, because of an assignment (or, in Scotland, assignation) or further contract made after that date.

121(12)   This section shall be deemed to have come into force on 28th March 2000.

122   Marketable securities transferred etc. for exempt property

122(1)   Subsection (2) applies where—

(a)   an instrument transferring marketable securities would not, apart from this section, be or fall to be treated as a transfer on sale for the purposes of stamp duty; but

(b)   the transfer of the marketable securities is for consideration; and

(c)   the consideration is or includes any qualifying property ("the other property").

122(2)   For the purposes of Part I of Schedule 13 to the Finance Act 1999 (stamp duty on conveyance or transfer on sale) the instrument transferring the marketable securities shall be taken to be a transfer on sale of those securities.

122(3)   If the amount or value of the consideration for that transfer on sale would (apart from this subsection) exceed the market value of the marketable securities immediately before the execution of the instrument transferring them, the amount or value of the consideration shall be taken to be equal to that market value.

For this purpose the market value of property at any time is the price which that property might reasonably be expected to fetch on a sale at that time in the open market.

122(4)   Subsection (2) has effect even though—

(a)   the transfer of the marketable securities is the whole or part of the consideration for a sale of the other property; or

(b)   the transaction is by way of exchange.

122(5)   Subsection (2) does not affect any charge to stamp duty in respect of the same or any other instrument so far as it relates to the transfer of the other property.

122(6)   In this section **"qualifying property"** means any debt due, stock or securities, to the extent that the debt, stock or securities are not chargeable securities, within the meaning of Part IV of the Finance Act 1986 (stamp duty reserve tax).

122(7)   This section shall be construed as one with the Stamp Act 1891.

122(8)   This section applies to instruments executed on or after 28th March 2000.

122(9)   But this section does not apply to an instrument giving effect to a contract made on or before 21st March 2000, unless—

(a)   the instrument is made in consequence of the exercise after that date of any option, right of pre-emption or similar right; or

(b)   the instrument transfers the property in question to, or vests it in, a person other than the purchaser under the contract, because of an assignment (or, in Scotland, assignation) or further contract made after that date.

122(10)   This section shall be deemed to have come into force on 28th March 2000.

123   Transfer of property between associated companies: Great Britain

123(1)   Amend section 42 of the Finance Act 1930 as follows.

123(2)   In subsection (2) (instruments on which stamp duty not chargeable) in paragraph (a) for "to another" substitute "("the transferor") to another ("the transferee")".

123(3)   In that subsection, after paragraph (b) insert—

"unless at the time the instrument is executed arrangements are in existence by virtue of which at that or some later time any person has or could obtain, or any persons together have or could obtain, control of the transferee but not of the transferor.".

123(4)   In subsection (2B) (body to be parent of another if beneficial owner of 75% of ordinary share capital) after "if at that time the first body" insert "(a)" and at the end of the subsection add—

"(b)   is beneficially entitled to not less than 75 per cent of any profits available for distribution to equity holders of the second body; and

(c)   would be beneficially entitled to not less than 75 per cent of any assets of the second body available for distribution to its equity holders on a winding-up.".

123(5) In subsection (3)–

(a) after "The ownership referred to in" insert "paragraph (a) of"; and

(b) for "this section" substitute "that paragraph".

123(6) At the end of the section add–

> "**42(5)** Schedule 18 to the Income and Corporation Taxes Act 1988 shall apply for the purposes of paragraphs (b) and (c) of subsection (2B) as it applies for the purposes of paragraphs (a) and (b) of section 413(7) of that Act; but this is subject to subsection (6).
>
> **42(6)** In determining for the purposes of this section whether a body corporate is the parent of the transferor, paragraphs 5(3) and 5B to 5E of Schedule 18 to the Income and Corporation Taxes Act 1988 shall not apply for the purposes of paragraph (b) or (c) of subsection (2B).
>
> **42(7)** In this section, **"control"** shall be construed in accordance with section 840 of the Income and Corporation Taxes Act 1988.".

123(7) This section has effect in relation to instruments executed after the day on which this Act is passed.

124 Transfer of property between associated companies: Northern Ireland

124(1) Amend section 11 of the Finance Act (Northern Ireland) 1954 as follows.

124(2) After subsection (2) (instruments on which stamp duty not chargeable) insert–

> "**11(2A)** But this section does not apply to an instrument by virtue of subsection (2)(a) if, at the time the instrument is executed, arrangements are in existence by virtue of which at that or some later time any person has or could obtain, or any persons together have or could obtain, control of the transferee but not of the transferor.".

124(3) In subsection (3AA) (body to be parent of another if beneficial owner of 75% of ordinary share capital) after "if at that time the first body" insert "(a)" and at the end of the subsection add–

> "(b) is beneficially entitled to not less than 75 per cent of any profits available for distribution to equity holders of the second body; and
>
> (c) would be beneficially entitled to not less than 75 per cent of any assets of the second body available for distribution to its equity holders on a winding-up;"

124(4) In subsection (3A)–

(a) after "The ownership referred to in" insert "paragraph (a) of"; and

(b) for "this section" substitute "that paragraph".

124(5) At the end of the section add–

> "**11(6)** Schedule 18 to the Income and Corporation Taxes Act 1988 shall apply for the purposes of paragraphs (b) and (c) of subsection (3AA) as it applies for the purposes of paragraphs (a) and (b) of section 413(7) of that Act but this is subject to subsection (7).
>
> **11(7)** In determining for the purposes of this section whether a body corporate is the parent of the transferor, paragraphs 5(3) and 5B to 5E of Schedule 18 to the Income and Corporation Taxes Act 1988 shall not apply for the purposes of paragraph (b) or (c) of subsection (3AA).
>
> **11(8)** In this section, **"control"** shall be construed in accordance with section 840 of the Income and Corporation Taxes Act 1988.".

124(6) This section has effect in relation to instruments executed after the day on which this Act is passed.

125 Grant of leases etc. between associated companies

125(1) Amend section 151 of the Finance Act 1995 as follows.

125(2) In subsection (1) (stamp duty not chargeable on leases etc) at the end insert the following paragraph–

> "This subsection is subject to subsection (4A) below."

125(3) After subsection (4) insert–

> "**151(4A)** An instrument shall not be exempt from stamp duty by virtue of subsection (1) above if at the time the instrument is executed arrangements are in existence by virtue of

which at that or some later time any person has or could obtain, or any persons together have or could obtain, control of the lessee but not of the lessor.".

125(4)   In subsection (8) (body to be parent of another if beneficial owner of 75% of ordinary share capital) after "if at that time the first body" insert "(a)" and at the end of the subsection add–

"(b)   is beneficially entitled to not less than 75 per cent of any profits available for distribution to equity holders of the second body; and

(c)   would be beneficially entitled to not less than 75 per cent of any assets of the second body available for distribution to its equity holders on a winding-up;"

125(5)   In subsection (10)–

(a)   after "The ownership referred to in" insert "paragraph (a) of"; and

(b)   for "this section" substitute "that paragraph".

125(6)   After subsection (10) insert–

"**151(10A)**   Schedule 18 to the Income and Corporation Taxes Act 1988 shall apply for the purposes of paragraphs (b) and (c) of subsection (8) as it applies for the purposes of paragraphs (a) and (b) of section 413(7) of that Act; but this is subject to subsection (10B).

151(10B)   In determining for the purposes of this section whether a body corporate is the parent of the lessor, paragraphs 5(3) and 5B to 5E of Schedule 18 to the Income and Corporation Taxes Act 1988 shall not apply for the purposes of paragraph (b) or (c) of subsection (8) above.

151(10C)   In this section, **"control"** shall be construed in accordance with section 840 of the Income and Corporation Taxes Act 1988."

125(7)   This section has effect in relation to instruments executed after the day on which this Act is passed.

126   Future issues of stock

126(1)   Amend section 55 of the Stamp Act 1891 (calculation of ad valorem duty in respect of stock and securities) as follows.

126(2)   After subsection (1) insert–

"**55(1A)**   For the purposes of subsection (1), it is immaterial–

(a)   whether, at the time of the execution of the conveyance on sale, the stock or marketable security is or has been issued or is to be issued; and

(b)   in a case where the stock or marketable security is to be issued, when it is to be, or is, issued and whether the issue is certain or contingent."

126(3)   This section has effect in relation to instruments executed after the day on which this Act is passed.

127   Company acquisition reliefs: redeemable shares

127(1)   Amend section 75 of the Finance Act 1986 (acquisitions: reliefs) in accordance with subsections (2) and (3).

127(2)   In subsection (4), in paragraph (a) (which requires that the consideration for the acquisition consists of or includes the issue of shares) after "the issue of" insert "non-redeemable".

127(3)   In subsection (4), after paragraph (b) add–

"In paragraph (a) above, **"non-redeemable shares"** means shares which are not redeemable shares."

127(4)   In section 76 of the Finance Act 1986 (acquisitions: further provisions about reliefs) in subsection (3)(a) (which requires that the consideration for the acquisition consists of or includes the issue of shares) for "shares" substitute "non-redeemable shares (within the meaning of section 75(4)(a) above)".

127(5)   This section has effect in relation to instruments executed after the day on which this Act is passed.

128   Surrender of leases

128(1)   Where a lease is or has been surrendered or, in Scotland, renounced at any time, a document evidencing the surrender or renunciation shall be treated for the purposes of stamp duty as if it were a deed executed at that time effecting the surrender or renunciation.

128(2) Stamp duty shall be chargeable by virtue of subsection (1) on a document containing a statutory declaration, notwithstanding anything in rule 316(1) of the Land Registration Rules 1925 or any other provision of those Rules or of any other rules (whenever made) under section 144 of the Land Registration Act 1925.

128(3) Stamp duty shall not be chargeable by virtue of subsection (1) on any lease or agreement for a lease or with respect to any letting if the lease or agreement—

(a)   is made in consideration of the surrender or renunciation; and

(b)   relates to the same subject matter as the lease surrendered or renounced.

128(4) Stamp duty shall not be chargeable by virtue of subsection (1) on any document if a document falling within subsection (5) has been duly stamped.

128(5) The documents that fall within this subsection are—

(a)   a deed effecting the surrender or renunciation;

(b)   an agreement which falls to be treated for the purposes of stamp duty as if it were such a deed;

(c)   any document which falls to be so treated by virtue of subsection (1); and

(d)   any lease or agreement falling within subsection (3).

128(6) A land registrar shall regard a document which by virtue of subsection (4) is not chargeable to stamp duty by virtue of subsection (1) as not duly stamped unless—

(a)   it is stamped as if it were a deed effecting the surrender or renunciation; or

(b)   it appears by some stamp impressed on it that the full and proper duty chargeable on such a deed has been paid on another document; or

(c)   it appears by some stamp impressed on it that a lease or agreement falling within subsection (3) has been duly stamped; or

(d)   the land registrar is aware of a document falling within subsection (5) which has been duly stamped.

128(7) The documents which evidence the surrender or renunciation of a lease shall be taken to include an application, in consequence of the surrender or renunciation of the lease, for—

(a)   the making in a land register, or

(b)   the removal from a land register,

of an entry relating to the lease.

128(8) In this section—

     "land register"–

        (a)   in relation to England and Wales, means the register kept under section 1 of the Land Registration Act 1925;

        (b)   in relation to Scotland, means the Land Register of Scotland or the General Register of Sasines;

        (c)   in relation to Northern Ireland, means the register maintained under section 10 of the Land Registration Act (Northern Ireland) 1970;

     "land registrar"–

        (a)   in relation to England and Wales, means the Chief Land Registrar or any other officer of Her Majesty's Land Registry exercising functions of the Chief Land Registrar;

        (b)   in relation to Scotland, means the Keeper of the Registers of Scotland;

        (c)   in relation to Northern Ireland, means the Registrar of Titles or any other official of the Land Registry exercising functions of the Registrar of Titles.

128(9) This section shall be construed as one with the Stamp Act 1891.

128(10) This section applies to documents relating to the surrender or renunciation of a lease after the day on which this Act is passed.

129   Abolition of duty on instruments relating to intellectual property

129(1) No stamp duty is chargeable on an instrument for the sale, transfer or other disposition of intellectual property.

129(2) In subsection (1) **"intellectual property"** means–

(a)   any patent, trade mark, registered design, copyright or design right,

(b)   any plant breeders' rights and rights under section 7 of the Plant Varieties Act 1997,

(c)   any licence or other right in respect of anything within paragraph (a) or (b), and

(d)   any rights under the law of a country or territory outside the United Kingdom that correspond or are similar to those within paragraph (a), (b) or (c).

129(3)   Schedule 34 to this Act (which contains provisions supplementing this section) has effect.

129(4)   This section and Schedule 34 shall be construed as one with the Stamp Act 1891.

129(5)   This section applies to instruments executed on or after 28th March 2000.

129(6)   This section shall be deemed to have come into force on that date.

130   Transfers to registered social landlords etc.

130(1)   No stamp duty shall be chargeable under Part I or II, or paragraph 16 of Part III, of Schedule 13 to the Finance Act 1999 on a conveyance or transfer of an estate or interest in land, or on a lease of land,–

(a)   to a qualifying landlord controlled by its tenants;
(b)   to a qualifying landlord by a qualifying transferor; or
(c)   to a qualifying landlord purchasing the estate or interest, or the grant of the lease, with the assistance of a public subsidy.

130(2)   For the purposes of this section the cases where a qualifying landlord is controlled by its tenants are those cases where the majority of the board members of the qualifying landlord are tenants occupying properties owned or managed by the qualifying landlord.

130(3)   For the purposes of subsection (2) a **"board member"** means–

(a)   in relation to a qualifying landlord which is a company, a director of the company;
(b)   in relation to a qualifying landlord which is a body corporate whose affairs are managed by its members, a member;
(c)   in relation to a qualifying landlord which is a body of trustees, a member of that body of trustees;
(d)   in relation to a qualifying landlord not falling within any of paragraphs (a) to (c), a member of the committee of management or other body to which is entrusted the direction of the affairs of the qualifying landlord.

130(4)   In subsection (3), **"company"** has the same meaning as in the Companies Act 1985 (see section 735(1) of that Act).

130(5)   In this section **"qualifying landlord"** means–

(a)   in relation to England and Wales, any body registered as a social landlord in a register maintained under section 1(1) of the Housing Act 1996;
(b)   in relation to Scotland–
      (i)   any housing association registered in the register maintained under section 3(1) of the Housing Associations Act 1985 by Scottish Homes; or
      (ii)   any body corporate whose objects correspond to those of a housing association and which, pursuant to a contract with Scottish Homes, is registered in a register kept for the purpose by Scottish Homes;
(c)   in relation to Northern Ireland, any housing association registered in the register maintained under Article 14 of the Housing (Northern Ireland) Order 1992.

130(6)   In this section **"qualifying transferor"** means any of the following–

(a)   a qualifying landlord;
(b)   a housing action trust established under Part III of the Housing Act 1988;
(c)   a principal council, within the meaning of the Local Government Act 1972;
(d)   the Common Council of the City of London;
(e)   a council constituted under section 2 of the Local Government etc. (Scotland) Act 1994;
(f)   Scottish Homes;
(g)   the Department for Social Development in Northern Ireland;
(h)   the Northern Ireland Housing Executive.

130(7)   In this section **"public subsidy"** means any grant or other financial assistance–

(a)   made or given by way of a distribution pursuant to section 25 of the National Lottery etc. Act 1993 (application of money by distributing bodies);
(b)   under section 18 of the Housing Act 1996 (social housing grants);
(c)   under section 126 of the Housing Grants, Construction and Regeneration Act 1996 (financial assistance for regeneration and development);

(d) under section 2 of the Housing (Scotland) Act 1988 (general functions of Scottish Homes); or

(e) under Article 33 of the Housing (Northern Ireland) Order 1992 (housing association grants).

130(8) Where stamp duty would be chargeable on an instrument but for paragraph (c) of subsection (1), that subsection shall only have effect in relation to the instrument if the instrument is certified to the Board by the qualifying landlord concerned as being an instrument on which stamp duty is by virtue of that paragraph not chargeable.

130(9) An instrument on which stamp duty is not chargeable by virtue only of this section shall not be taken to be duly stamped unless—

(a) it is stamped with the duty to which it would be liable but for this section; or

(b) it has, in accordance with section 12 of the Stamp Act 1891, been stamped with a particular stamp denoting that it is not chargeable with any duty.

130(10) This section applies to instruments executed after the day on which this Act is passed.

131 Relief for certain instruments executed before this Act has effect

131(1) This section applies to an instrument of any of the following descriptions executed in the period beginning with 22nd March 2000 and ending with the day on which this Act is passed—

(a) an instrument transferring or vesting an estate or interest in land in such circumstances as are mentioned in section 119 (transfer of land to connected company), in a case specified in section 120) (excepted cases);

(b) a conveyance or transfer of an estate or interest in land, or a lease of land, to a qualifying landlord within the meaning of section 130 (transfers to registered social landlords, etc.) from a qualifying transferor within subsection (6)(c), (d), (e), (f) or (h) of that section.

131(2) If the instrument is not stamped until after the day on which this Act is passed, the law in force at the time of its execution shall be deemed for stamp duty purposes to be that which would have applied if it had been executed after that day.

131(3) If the Commissioners are satisfied that—

(a) the instrument was stamped on or before the day on which this Act is passed,

(b) stamp duty was chargeable in respect of it, and

(c) had it been stamped after that day no stamp duty, or less stamp duty, would have been chargeable,

they shall pay to such person as they consider appropriate an amount equal to the duty (and any interest or penalty) that would not have been payable if the law in force at the time of execution of the instrument had been that which would have applied had it been executed after that day.

131(4) Any such payment must be claimed before 1st April 2001.

131(5) Entitlement to a payment is subject to compliance with such conditions as the Commissioners may determine with respect to the production of the instrument, to its being stamped so as to indicate that it has been produced under this section or to other matters.

131(6) For the purposes of section 10 of the Exchequer and Audit Departments Act 1866 (Commissioners to deduct repayments from gross revenues) any amount paid under this section shall be treated as a repayment.

131(7) This section shall be construed as one with the Stamp Act 1891.

132 The Northern Ireland Assembly Commission

132(1) Amend section 55 of the Finance Act 1987 (Crown exemption from stamp duty) as follows.

132(2) In subsection (1) (which specifies the bodies relieved from stamp duty)—

(a) after "agreed to be made" insert "(a)";

(b) after "Minister of the Crown or" insert "(b)"; and

(c) after "Treasury, or" insert "(c)".

132(3) In subsection (1), after "National Assembly for Wales," insert "or
(d) to the Northern Ireland Assembly Commission,".

132(4) Subsection (3) has effect in relation to instruments executed on or after 28th March 2000.

132(5) This section shall be deemed to have come into force on 28th March 2000.

STAMP DUTY AND STAMP DUTY RESERVE TAX

133   Loan capital where return bears inverse relationship to results

133(1)   In section 79 of the Finance Act 1986 (loan capital), after subsection (7) insert–

"**79(7A)**   Subsection (4) above shall not be prevented from applying to an instrument by virtue of subsection (6)(b) above by reason only that the loan capital concerned carries a right to interest which–

(a)   reduces in the event of the results of a business or part of a business improving, or the value of any property increasing, or

(b)   increases in the event of the results of a business or part of a business deteriorating, or the value of any property diminishing.".

133(2)   For the purposes of stamp duty, subsection (1) above has effect where the instrument is executed on or after 21st March 2000.

133(3)   For the purposes of stamp duty reserve tax, subsection (1) above has effect–

(a)   in relation to the charge to tax under section 87 of the Finance Act 1986, where–

    (i)   the agreement to transfer is conditional and the condition is satisfied on or after 21st March 2000, or

    (ii)   the agreement is not conditional and is made on or after that date;

(b)   in relation to the charge to tax under section 93(1) of that Act, where securities are transferred, issued or appropriated on or after 21st March 2000 (whenever the arrangement was made);

(c)   in relation to the charge to tax under section 96(1) of that Act, where securities are transferred or issued on or after 21st March 2000 (whenever the arrangement was made);

(d)   in relation to the charge to tax under section 93(10) of that Act, where securities are issued or transferred on sale, under terms there mentioned, on or after 21st March 2000;

(e)   in relation to the charge to tax under section 96(8) of that Act, where securities are issued or transferred on sale, under terms there mentioned, on or after 21st March 2000.

134   Transfers between depositary receipt systems and clearance systems

134(1)   In Part III of the Finance Act 1986 (stamp duty), after section 72 insert–

"TRANSFERS BETWEEN DEPOSITARY RECEIPT SYSTEM AND CLEARANCE SYSTEM

Transfers between depositary receipt system and clearance system

72A(1)   Where an instrument transfers relevant securities of a company incorporated in the United Kingdom between a depositary receipt system and a clearance system–

(a)   the provisions of section 67(2) to (5) or, as the case may be, section 70(2) to (5) above shall not apply, and

(b)   the stamp duty chargeable on the instrument is £5.

72A(2)   A transfer between a depositary receipt system and a clearance system means a transfer–

(a)   from (or to) a company that at the time of the transfer falls within section 67(6) above, and

(b)   to (or from) a company that at that time falls within section 70(6) above.

72A(3)   This section does not apply to a transfer from a clearance system (that is, from such a company as is mentioned in subsection (2)(b) above) if at the time of the transfer an election is in force under section 97A below in relation to the clearance services for the purposes of which the securities are held immediately before the transfer.".

134(2)   In Part IV of the Finance Act 1986 (stamp duty reserve tax), after section 97A insert–

"Transfer between depositary receipt system and clearance system

97B(1)   There shall be no charge to tax under section 93 or 96 above where securities are transferred between a depositary receipt system and a clearance system.

97B(2)   A transfer between a depositary receipt system and a clearance system means a transfer–

(a)   from (or to) a company which at the time of the transfer falls within section 67(6) above, and

(b)   to (or from) a company which at that time falls within section 70(6) above.

97B(3)   This section does not apply to a transfer from a clearance system (that is, from such a company as is mentioned in subsection (2)(b) above) if at the time of the transfer an election is in force under section 97A above in relation to the clearance services for the purposes of which the securities are held immediately before the transfer.".

134(3)   In sections 67(9), 70(9), 95(1) and 97(1) of the Finance Act 1986 (transfers between depositary receipt systems or between clearance systems), the words "and is resident in the United Kingdom" and "and is so resident" shall cease to have effect.

134(4)   In section 97A of that Act (clearance services: election for alternative system of charge), after subsection (12) add–

"97A(13)   Nothing in section 70(9) or 97(1) above has effect to prevent a charge to stamp duty or stamp duty reserve tax arising–

(a)   on a transfer to which subsection (5) above applies, or

(b)   on a deemed transfer under subsection (11) above.".

134(5)   The amendments in this section have effect as follows–

(a)   subsection (1), and subsections (3) and (4) as they apply for stamp duty purposes, apply in relation to instruments executed after the day on which this Act is passed;

(b)   subsection (2), and subsections (3) and (4) as they apply for the purposes of stamp duty reserve tax, apply where the securities are transferred after that day.

SCHEDULES

SCHEDULE 32 – STAMP DUTY ON SEVEN YEAR LEASES: TRANSITIONAL PROVISIONS

Section 116(2)

INTRODUCTORY

1   In this Schedule–

"additional duty", in relation to an instrument, means additional stamp duty chargeable on the instrument as a result of section 116;

"the appropriate amount of duty", in relation to an instrument, means the stamp duty that would have been chargeable on the instrument if section 116 had been in force when it was executed; and

"the commencement date" means 28th March 2000.

INSTRUMENTS TO WHICH THIS SCHEDULE APPLIES

2   The instruments to which this Schedule applies are–

(a)   leases of land for a term of seven years, and

(b)   agreements for leases of land for a term of seven years,

executed on or after 1st October 1999 and before the commencement date.

INSTRUMENTS WHICH REMAIN DULY STAMPED

3   An instrument to which this Schedule applies which is stamped with the appropriate amount of duty is duly stamped, whenever it was executed.

INSTRUMENTS WHICH CEASE TO BE DULY STAMPED

4(1)   An instrument to which this Schedule applies which–

(a)   immediately before the commencement date was duly stamped, but

(b)   was stamped with less than the appropriate amount of duty,

ceases to be duly stamped on the commencement date.

4(2) Sub-paragraph (1) applies even if the instrument has been stamped in accordance with section 12(5) of the Stamp Act 1891 with a stamp denoting that it is duly stamped.

4(3) If an instrument ceases to be duly stamped on the commencement date as a result of sub-paragraph (1)–

(a)   section 12(6) of the Stamp Act 1891 (adjudicated instruments admissible in evidence) does not apply to it at any time when it is not duly stamped, and

(b)   section 14(1) of that Act (receipt in evidence of insufficiently stamped instruments if unpaid duty paid to court) does not apply to it at any time when it is not duly stamped, unless the unpaid duty and any interest or penalty is paid in accordance with that subsection.

STAMPING FOLLOWING EARLIER ADJUDICATION

5 Section 12A(1) of the Stamp Act 1891 (adjudicated instruments not to be stamped other than in accordance with adjudication decision) does not prevent an instrument to which this Schedule applies which is stamped with less than the appropriate amount of duty from being stamped with additional duty.

USE OF INSTRUMENTS IN EVIDENCE, ETC.

6 Section 14(4) of the Stamp Act 1891 (instruments not to be used unless duly stamped in accordance with law in force when executed) applies in relation to an instrument to which this Schedule applies as if, as respects any time on or after the commencement date, the reference to the law in force at the time when it was executed were to the law in force on the commencement date.

ADJUDICATION, INTEREST AND PENALTIES

7(1) This paragraph applies for the purpose of applying sections 12 to 13B and 15 to 15B of the Stamp Act 1891 (adjudication by Commissioners and interest and penalties on late stamping) in relation to any additional duty chargeable on an instrument to which this Schedule applies.

7(2) Those sections continue to apply without modification as respects any other stamp duty chargeable on the instrument.

7(3) Those sections have effect as respects the additional duty as if–

(a)   the additional duty were the only stamp duty chargeable on the instrument;

(b)   the instrument had been executed on the commencement date; and

(c)   in the case of an instrument executed outside the United Kingdom and first received in the United Kingdom before the commencement date, the instrument had been first received in the United Kingdom on the commencement date.

7(4) Accordingly, those sections apply as respects additional duty as if–

(a)   references to duty were to additional duty;

(b)   references to stamping were to stamping with additional duty;

(c)   references to an instrument's being stamped were to its being stamped with additional duty;

(d)   references to an instrument's being duly stamped were to its being stamped with all the additional duty chargeable on it;

(e)   references to an instrument's being unstamped were to its not being stamped with any additional duty;

(f)   references to an instrument's being insufficiently stamped were to its being stamped with insufficient additional duty;

(g)   references to adjudication, or an appeal, under any of those sections were to adjudication or an appeal under the section in question as it has effect as respects additional duty; and

(h)   references to the maximum penalty were to the maximum penalty as respects additional duty.

SCHEDULE 33 – POWER TO VARY STAMP DUTIES

Section 117

POWER OF TREASURY TO MAKE PROVISION BY REGULATIONS

1(1) The Treasury may if they consider it expedient in the public interest make provision by regulations for the variation of an existing stamp duty.

1(2) The power conferred by this paragraph includes, in particular, power to alter the descriptions of document in respect of which an existing stamp duty, or an existing rate or amount of duty, is chargeable.

1(3) The power to make regulations under this paragraph is exercisable by statutory instrument.

POWER ONLY TO BE USED FOR CASES INVOLVING LAND OR SHARES ETC.

2(1) The power conferred by paragraph 1 does not include power–

(a) to vary the amount chargeable by way of stamp duty on an excepted instrument, or

(b) to cause stamp duty to become chargeable on an excepted instrument.

2(2) For the purposes of this paragraph–

(a) an **"excepted instrument"** is any document that is not a relevant property instrument, and

(b) a **"relevant property instrument"** is a document that (whether or not it also relates to any other transaction) relates to a transaction that to any extent involves–

(i) land, stock or marketable securities, or

(ii) any estate or interest in land, stock or marketable securities.

POWER NOT TO BE USED TO VARY RATES OR THRESHOLDS

3 The power conferred by paragraph 1 does not, except as mentioned in paragraph 1(2), include power to vary–

(a) the rate, or rates, of an existing *ad valorem* stamp duty,

(b) the amount of an existing fixed stamp duty,

(c) any threshold specified in paragraph 4 of Schedule 13 to the Finance Act 1999 (rate bands for conveyance or transfer on sale), or

(d) any threshold specified in paragraph 11 or 12 of that Schedule (duty on leases) in respect of rent or the term of a lease.

APPROVAL OF REGULATIONS BY HOUSE OF COMMONS

4(1) An instrument containing regulations under paragraph 1 shall be laid before the House of Commons after being made.

4(2) If the regulations are not approved by the House of Commons before the end of the period of 28 days beginning with the day on which they are made, they shall cease to have effect at the end of that period if they have not already ceased to have effect under sub-paragraph (3).

4(3) If on any day during that period of 28 days the House of Commons, in proceedings on a motion that (or to the effect that) the regulations be approved, comes to a decision rejecting the regulations, they shall cease to have effect at the end of that day.

4(4) Where regulations cease to have effect under sub-paragraph (2) or (3), their ceasing to have effect is without prejudice to anything done in reliance on them.

4(5) In reckoning any such period of 28 days take no account of any time during which–

(a) Parliament is prorogued or dissolved, or

(b) the House of Commons is adjourned for more than four days.

CLAIM FOR REPAYMENT IF REGULATIONS NOT APPROVED

5(1) Where regulations cease to have effect under paragraph 4(2) or (3), any amount paid by way of stamp duty, or interest or penalty on late stamping, that would not have been payable but for the regulations shall, on a claim, be repaid by the Commissioners.

5(2) Section 110 of the Finance Act 1999 (interest on repayment of duty overpaid etc.) applies to a repayment under this paragraph of any amount paid by way of stamp duty or penalty on late stamping.

In the case of a repayment under this paragraph, the relevant time for the purposes of that section is 30 days after the day on which the instrument in question was executed or, if later, the *date on which the payment* of duty or penalty was made.

5(3) A claim for repayment must be made within two years after the date of the instrument in question or, if it is not dated, within two years after its execution.

5(4) No repayment shall be made on a claim until the instrument in question has been produced to the Commissioners for such cancelling of stamps, and such stamping to denote the making of the repayment or the producing of the instrument under this paragraph, as the Commissioners consider appropriate.

5(5) Any repayment shall, subject to any regulations under sub-paragraph (6)(d), be made to such person as the Commissioners consider appropriate.

5(6) The Commissioners may make provision by regulations–

(a)   for varying the time limit having effect under sub-paragraph (3);

(b)   for varying or repealing the condition having effect under sub-paragraph (4);

(c)   as to any other conditions that must be met before repayment is made;

(d)   as to the person to whom repayment is to be made.

5(7) Regulations under this paragraph shall be made by statutory instrument which shall be subject to annulment in pursuance of a resolution of the House of Commons.

USE IN EVIDENCE, ETC. OF INSTRUMENTS AFFECTED BY REGULATIONS CEASING TO HAVE EFFECT

6(1) Where regulations cease to have effect under paragraph 4(2) or (3), the following provisions apply to an instrument that–

(a)   was executed at a time when the regulations were in force, and

(b)   was at that time chargeable with any amount of stamp duty with which it would not have been chargeable apart from the regulations.

6(2) If the instrument was stamped while the regulations were in force, nothing done in pursuance of paragraph 5 (repayment of duty etc.) prevents it being treated for any purpose as duly stamped in accordance with the law in force at the time when it was executed.

6(3) If the instrument was not stamped while the regulations were in force, the law in force at the time when it was executed shall be deemed to have been what the law would have been apart from the regulations.

TEMPORARY EFFECT OF REGULATIONS

7(1) Regulations under paragraph 1 shall not apply in relation to instruments executed after the end of–

(a)   the period of 18 months beginning with the day on which the regulations were made, or

(b)   such shorter period as may be specified in the regulations.

7(2) This does not affect the power to make further provision by regulations under paragraph 1 to the same or similar effect.

POWER TO MAKE TRANSITIONAL ETC. PROVISION

8 Any power to make regulations under this Schedule includes power to make such transitional, supplementary and incidental provision as appears to the authority making the regulations to be necessary or expedient.

INTERPRETATION

9(1) In relation to a bearer instrument (as defined in paragraph 3 of Schedule 15 to the Finance Act 1999), references in this Schedule to the execution of the instrument shall be read as references to its issue.

9(2) This Schedule shall be construed as one with the Stamp Act 1891.

SCHEDULE 34 – ABOLITION OF STAMP DUTY ON INSTRUMENTS RELATING TO INTELLECTUAL PROPERTY: SUPPLEMENTARY PROVISIONS

Section 129

INTRODUCTION

1   In this Schedule **"intellectual property"** has the same meaning as in section 129(1).

STAMP DUTY REDUCED IN CERTAIN OTHER CASES

2(1)   This paragraph applies where–

(a)   stamp duty under Part I of Schedule 13 to the Finance Act 1999 (conveyance or transfer on sale) is chargeable on an instrument, and

(b)   part of the property concerned consists of intellectual property.

2(2)   In such a case–

(a)   the consideration in respect of which duty would otherwise be charged shall be apportioned, on such basis as is just and reasonable, as between the part of the property which consists of intellectual property and the part which does not, and

(b)   the instrument shall be charged only in respect of the consideration attributed to such of the property as is not intellectual property.

2(3)   This paragraph applies to instruments executed on or after 28th March 2000.

APPORTIONMENT OF CONSIDERATION FOR STAMP DUTY PURPOSES

3(1)   Where part of the property referred to in section 58(1) of the Stamp Act 1891 (consideration to be apportioned between different instruments as parties think fit) consists of intellectual property, that provision shall have effect as if "the parties think fit" read "is just and reasonable".

3(2)   Where–

(a)   part of the property referred to in section 58(2) of the Stamp Act 1891 (property contracted to be purchased by two or more persons etc.) consists of intellectual property, and

(b)   both or (as the case may be) all the relevant persons are connected with one another,

that provision shall have effect as if the words from "for distinct parts of the consideration" to the end of the subsection read ", the consideration is to be apportioned in such manner as is just and reasonable, so that a distinct consideration for each separate part or parcel is set forth in the conveyance relating thereto, and such conveyance is to be charged with *ad valorem* duty in respect of such distinct consideration.".

3(3)   In a case where sub-paragraph (1) or (2) applies and the consideration is apportioned in a manner that is not just and reasonable, the enactments relating to stamp duty shall have effect as if–

(a)   the consideration had been apportioned in a manner that is just and reasonable, and

(b)   the amount of any distinct consideration set forth in any conveyance relating to a separate part or parcel of property were such amount as is found by a just and reasonable apportionment (and not the amount actually set forth).

3(4)   For the purposes of sub-paragraph (2)–

(a)   a person is a relevant person if he is a person by or for whom the property is contracted to be purchased;

(b)   the question whether persons are connected with one another shall be determined in accordance with section 839 of the Taxes Act 1988.

3(5)   In sub-paragraph (3) **"the enactments relating to stamp duty"** means the Stamp Act 1891 and any enactment amending or which is to be construed as one with that Act.

3(6)   This paragraph applies to instruments executed on or after 28th March 2000.

CERTIFICATION OF INSTRUMENTS FOR STAMP DUTY PURPOSES

4(1)   Intellectual property shall be disregarded for the purposes of paragraph 6 of Schedule 13 to the Finance Act 1999 (certification of instrument as not forming part of transaction or series of transactions exceeding specified amount).

4(2)   Any statement as mentioned in paragraph 6(1) of that Schedule shall be construed as leaving out of account any matter which is to be so disregarded.

4(3)   This paragraph applies to instruments executed on or after 28th March 2000.

ACQUISITION UNDER STATUTE

5(1)   Section 12 of the Finance Act 1895 (property vested by Act or purchased under statutory powers) does not require any person who is authorised to purchase any property as mentioned in that section on or after 28th March 2000 to include any intellectual property in the instrument of conveyance required by that section to be produced to the Commissioners.

5(2)　If the property consists wholly of intellectual property no instrument of conveyance need be produced to the Commissioners under that section.

5(3)　This paragraph applies where the Act mentioned in that section, and by virtue of which property is vested or a person is authorised to purchase property, is passed on or after 28th March 2000.

SCHEDULE 40 – REPEALS
Part III – Stamp Duty

Chapter	Short title	Extent of repeal
1949 c. 15 (N.I.).	The Finance Act (Northern Ireland) 1949.	Section 8.
1977 c. 37.	The Patents Act 1977.	Section 126.
1993 c. 34.	The Finance Act 1993.	In section 204(3), the word "first" (in each place where it occurs).
1994 c. 26.	The Trade Marks Act 1994.	Section 61.
2000 c. .	The Finance Act 2000.	Section 130. In Schedule 33, paragraph 9(1).

1.　The repeals in the Patents Act 1977 and the Trade Marks Act 1994 have effect in accordance with section 129(5) of this Act.

1A.　The repeals in the Finance Act 1986 have effect in accordance with section 134(5) of this Act.

2.　The repeals of sections 133 and 134 of this Act have effect–

(a)　so far as relating to stamp duty on bearer instruments, in accordance with section 107 of the Finance Act 1990;

(b)　so far as relating to stamp duty on instruments other than bearer instruments, in accordance with section 108 of that Act; and

(c)　so far as relating to stamp duty reserve tax, in accordance with section 110 of that Act.

3.　The repeal in Schedule 33 to this Act has effect in accordance with section 107 of the Finance Act 1990.

MISCELLANEOUS EXEMPTIONS – LIST

Note – The following list is not exhaustive. Selection has been made on the basis either of general interest or of recency.

Settled Land Act 1925, s. 12, 14, Sch. 2, para. 1(8), 2(2) (no stamp duty on vesting orders or vesting assents).

Land Registration Act 1925, s. 130 (acknowledgments by persons to registrar that latter is entitled to return of or copies of documents, not subject to stamp duty).

Administration of Estates Act 1925, s. 36 (assent by personal representative not subject to stamp duty).

Diplomatic Privileges Act 1964, Sch. 1 (general exemption under art. 23 and 34 of Vienna Convention in relation to premises of diplomatic missions and diplomatic agents respectively).

Gas Act 1972, s. 33 (Treasury guaranteed redeemable stock in British Gas Corporation exempt from duty on transfer).

Friendly Societies Act 1974, s. 105 (no duty on documents required or authorised under the Act or the rules of the society).

Industrial Injuries and Diseases (Old Cases) Act 1975, s. 12 (no duty on documents issued in connection with schemes for supplementing workmen's compensation or for industrial diseases benefit).

Industry Act 1975, Sch. 1, para. 18 (no duty on certain transfers to National Enterprise Board).

Scottish Development Agency Act 1975, Sch. 1, para. 18 (no duty on certain transfers to the Agency).

Welsh Development Agency Act 1975, Sch. 1, para. 20 (no duty on certain transfers to the Agency).

Petroleum and Submarine Pipe-lines Act 1975, s. 9 (no duty on certain transfers to British National Oil Corporation).

Development of Rural Wales Act 1976, s. 32 (no duty on transfers of property from Welsh Development Agency to Development Board for Rural Wales).

Patents Act 1977, s. 126 (exemptions for instruments relating to or applications for European patent under provisions of Community Patent Convention).

National Heritage Act 1980, s. 11 (no duty on conveyances or transfers under which property accepted in satisfaction of tax passes to specified institutions or bodies).

Industry Act 1980, s. 2 (no duty on transfers of securities or other property from National Enterprise Board, Scottish Development Agency, or Welsh Development Agency to Secretary of State).

Highways Act 1980, s. 281 (no duty on instruments which Minister certifies as expense incurred by him under that Act in relation to highway which is to become a trunk road).

Oil and Gas (Enterprise) Act 1982, s. 33 (no duty on instruments certified as executed for the purpose of disposal of any part of the undertaking, property or rights of British National Oil Corporation or British Gas Corporation).

County Courts Act 1984, s. 79 (agreement not to appeal not stampable).

Ordnance Factories and Military Services Act 1984, s. 13 (no duty on instruments certified to be schemes or in pursuance of schemes for transfer to companies).

Transport Act 1985, s. 131 (no duty on schemes or on instruments transferring property, rights or liabilities of National Bus Company to subsidiaries).

Building Societies Act 1986, s. 109 (as amended by FA 1988, Sch. 12, para. 8) (certain documents issued by or in relation to societies; transfer of property, rights and liabilities of society to successor company).

Electricity Act 1989, Sch. 11, para. 11, 12 (stamp duty and stamp duty reserve tax exemptions applying on electricity privatisation).

National Health Service and Community Care Act 1990, s. 61(3) (as amended by FA 1999, s. 103(4) and Sch. 14, para. 24) (exemption for conveyance, transfer or lease made to a National Health Service trust).

Ports Act 1991, s. 36 (no stamp duty on any transfer effected by that Act, or on transfer of property, rights and liabilities of a port authority to its successor company, etc.).

Further and Higher Education (Scotland) Act 1992, s. 58 (no stamp duty in respect of any agreement made or any transfer effected under or by virtue of any of the provisions of this Act).

Social Security Administration Act 1992, s. 188 (no duty on documents in connection with any description of business under the Act).

Friendly Societies Act 1992, s. 105 (no stamp duty chargeable upon any document required or authorised by that Act, the *Friendly Societies Act* 1974 or the constitution of a society).

Education Act 1993, s. 299 (no stamp duty chargeable in respect of certain transfers effected under certain provisions of that Act).

Agriculture Act 1993, Sch. 2, para. 28 (no stamp duty on transfers under s. 11 of that Act or on an approved scheme or on certified instruments).

Railways Act 1993, Sch. 9, para. 2 and 3 (no stamp duty or stamp duty reserve tax on certain restructuring schemes under that Act, or instruments or agreements certified as pursuant to an obligation imposed under that Act).

Broadcasting Act 1996, Sch. 7, para. 25, 26 (no stamp duty on any agreement or instrument certified as being a restructuring scheme or a restructuring scheme modification agreement, etc., and no stamp duty reserve tax on agreement to transfer chargeable securities from BBC to a wholly-owned subsidiary of the BBC where agreement is part of restructuring scheme).

Regional Development Agencies Act 1998, s. 39 (no stamp duty on a transfer scheme pursuant to an order under s. 25 of that Act or a scheme under s. 34–37 or Sch. 3, para. 1 of that Act which provide for the transfer of property, rights or liabilities, or on an instrument or agreement which is certified as made in pursuance of such a scheme).

The Visiting Forces and Allied Headquarters (Stamp Duties) (Designation) Order 1998 (SI 1999/1517) and *The Visiting Forces (Stamp Duties) (Designation) Order 1998* (SI 1999/1518) (exemption from stamp duties in relation to visiting forces of designated countries and designated allied headquarters – lists of such designated countries and headquarters. Orders made under FA 1960, s. 74 (not reproduced).).

School Standards and Framework Act 1998, s. 79 (no stamp duty on any transfer to a local authority under the various provisions of this act).

Access to Justice Act 1999, Sch. 14, para. 34(1) (no stamp duty on any scheme under paragraph 33 of Sch. 14 of that act, or on any instrument or agreement which is certified to the Commissioners of Inland Revenue by the Lord Chancellor as made in pursuance of such a scheme).

Greater London Authority Act 1999, s. 417 (no stamp duty on a transfer instrument under an order under s. 408 or 411, or a scheme under s. 409, of the act involving London Regional Transport, or an instrument or agreement which is certified to the Commissioners of Inland Revenue by a Minister of the Crown as made in pursuance of such a transfer instrument, or which is so certified as giving effect to a preparatory reorganisation).

STAMP DUTIES
STATUTORY INSTRUMENTS

Table of Contents

> **Note:** Only those statutory instruments listed below which contain substantive provisions are reproduced in this division. The other statutory instruments listed are amending instruments; the amendments made by them have been consolidated in the relevant amended regulations.

STAMP DUTY (EXEMPT INSTRUMENTS) REGULATIONS 1985

(SI 1985/1688)

Made on 4 November 1985 by the Commissioners of Inland Revenue in exercise of the powers conferred upon them by s. 89 of the Finance Act 1985.

1 These Regulations may be cited as the Stamp Duty (Exempt Instruments) Regulations 1985 and shall come into operation on 1st January 1986.

2 In these Regulations unless the context otherwise requires:–

"Her Majesty's Land Registry" and **"Chief Land Registrar"** have the same meaning as in section 126(1) of the Land Registration Act 1925 and **"Registered land"** has the same meaning as in section 3 of that Act.

3 For the purposes of section 89 of the Finance Act 1985, the following class of instrument is prescribed:–

Instruments by means of which any transfer on sale within the meaning of paragraphs (a) or (c) of section 28(1) of the Finance Act 1931 is effected and in respect of which the following conditions are fulfilled:–

(a) the instrument is executed on or after the 1st January 1986;

(b) the consideration for the sale in question is of an amount or value such that no stamp duty is chargeable and the instrument is certified in accordance with section 34(4) of the Finance Act 1958; and

(c)

(i) the land in question is registered land; or

(ii) in the case of land which is not registered land it is an instrument–

(a) to which section 123 of the Land Registration Act 1925 applies, or

(b) which effects a transfer in the case of which under rule 72 of the Land Registration Rules 1925 the transferee is deemed to be the applicant for first registration.

4 Where the instrument is of the class of instrument to which Regulation 3 above applies it shall be the duty of the applicant to deliver to the proper office of Her Majesty's Land Registry with his application for registration the instrument of transfer and a document signed by the transferee or by some person on his behalf and showing his address giving all the particulars set out in Schedule 2 to the Finance Act 1931.

5 The Chief Land Registrar shall furnish to the Commissioners of Inland Revenue the said particulars given to him under Regulation 4 above.

STAMP DUTY RESERVE TAX REGULATIONS 1986

(SI 1986/1711, as amended by SI 1988/835, SI 1989/1301, SI 1991/724, SI 1992/3287, SI 1993/1711, SI 1994/1813, SI 1997/2430 and SI 1999/2536)

Made by the Treasury on 2 October 1986 under s. 98 of the Finance Act 1986. Operative from 27 October 1986.

CITATION AND COMMENCEMENT

1 These Regulations may be cited as the Stamp Duty Reserve Tax Regulations 1986 and shall come into operation on 27th October 1986.

INTERPRETATION

2 In these Regulations unless the context otherwise requires–

"Act" means Part IV of the Finance Act 1986;

"accountable date" means–

(a) in relation to a relevant transaction–

    (i) in connection with which securities are transferred by means of a relevant system operated by the operator of that system, or

    (ii) which is reported by means of a relevant system to a recognised self-regulating organisation, a recognised professional body or an exchange by the operator of that system in a case where the securities to which the transaction relates are not transferred by means of a relevant system, or

    (iii) which is reported, otherwise than by means of a relevant system, to an exchange, in a case where the securities to which the transaction relates are not transferred by means of a relevant system,

(b) the date agreed between the Board and the operator or, if no such date is agreed, the date which is the fourteenth day following the date of the relevant transaction,

(c) in relation to interest on overdue tax arising in connection with a relevant transaction which, by virtue of a party to that transaction being a participant in a relevant system, or a member of an exchange, could have been, but was not, reported to a recognised self-regulating organisation, a recognised professional body or an exchange by means of that system, or to an exchange otherwise than by means of a relevant system, the date which is the fourteenth day following the date of the relevant transaction,

(d) in relation to a relevant transaction to which neither paragraph (a) nor paragraph (b) applies, the date which is the seventh day of the month following the month in which the charge to tax occasioned by the relevant transaction is incurred, and

(e) in relation to a surrender, the date which is the fourteenth day of the month following the month in which the relevant two week period ends;

"accountable person" means–

(a) in relation to a charge under section 87 of the Act (**"section 87"**)–

    (i) if the person mentioned as B in section 87(1) is a member of an exchange, or if a member of an exchange is acting as an agent for B who is not such a member, that member, and failing that

    (ii) if the person mentioned as A in section 87(1) is a member of an exchange, or if a member of an exchange is acting as an agent for A who is not such a member, that member, and failing that

    (iii) if the person mentioned as B in section 87(1) is a qualified dealer, or if a qualified dealer is acting as an agent for B who is not a qualified dealer, the qualified dealer, and failing that

    (iv) if the person mentioned as A in section 87(1) is a qualified dealer, or if a qualified dealer is acting as an agent for A who is not a qualified dealer, the qualified dealer, and failing that

    (v) the person mentioned as B in section 87(1),

(b) in relation to a charge under section 93(1) to (7) of the Act, the person mentioned in section 93(8) thereof: Provided that if section 93(9) is applicable, then the accountable person means the person to whom the securities are transferred,

(c) in relation to a charge under section 93(10) of the Act, the person liable to pay the instalment,

(d) in relation to a charge under section 96(1) to (5) of the Act, the person mentioned in subsection (6) thereof: Provided that if section 96(7) is applicable, then the accountable person means the person to whom the securities are transferred,

(e) in relation to a charge under section 96(8) of the Act, the person liable to pay the instalment, and

(f) in relation to a charge on the surrender of a unit under paragraph 2(1) of Schedule 19 to the Finance Act 1999–

    (i) the managers of the unit trust scheme and, failing that,

    (ii) the trustees of the unit trust scheme;

(g) in relation to a charge on the surrender of a share in an open-ended investment company under paragraph 2(1) of Schedule 19 to the Finance Act 1999–

    (i) the authorised corporate director of the company and, failing that,

    (ii) the company;

"authorised corporate director" and **"open-ended investment company"**, have the meanings given by regulation 2 of the Stamp Duty and Stamp Duty Reserve Tax (Open-ended Investment Companies) Regulations 1997;

"barrister" includes a member of the Faculty of Advocates;

"the Board" means the Commissioners of Inland Revenue;

"EEA regulated market" means a market of a kind described in paragraphs (a) and (b) of article 2 of the Financial Services Act 1986 (EEA Regulated Markets) (Exemption) Order 1995;

"exchange" means–

(a)   a recognised investment exchange within the meaning given by section 207(1) of the Financial Services Act 1986, or

(b)   an EEA regulated market.

"European institution" has the meaning given by regulation 3 of the Banking Coordination (Second Council Directive) Regulations 1992;

"General Commissioners" has the same meaning as in the Taxes Management Act 1970;

"investment business" has the meaning given by section 1(2) of the Financial Services Act 1986;

"notice" means notice in writing;

"operator" means–

(a)   a person approved by the Treasury under the Treasury Regulations as Operator of a relevant system;

(b)   subject to paragraph (c), where a relevant transaction is reported to an exchange otherwise than by means of a relevant system, the operator of that exchange or, if there is no such operator, that exchange;

(c)   where a relevant transaction is reported to more than one exchange otherwise than by means of a relevant system, the operator of the exchange of which the party who is the accountable person in relation to that transaction is a member or, if there is no such operator, that exchange;

"qualified dealer" means a person who, not being a member of an exchange–

(a)   is an authorised person under Chapter III of Part I of the Financial Services Act 1986, or

(b)   by virtue of paragraph 1 of Schedule 15 to that Act is to be treated as such a person, or

(c)   is authorised under a legislative provision of the government of a territory outside the United Kingdom to carry on investment business, or

(d)   while not required to be authorised to do so, carries on investment business;

"recognised professional body" and

"recognised self-regulating organisation" have the meanings given by section 207(1) of the Financial Services Act 1986;

"relevant system" has the meaning given by regulation 2(1) of the Treasury Regulations;

"relevant transaction" means–

(a)   an agreement falling within section 87(1) of the Act,

(b)   a transfer, issue or appropriation falling within section 93(1)(b) of the Act, or

(c)   a transfer or issue falling within section 96(1)(b) of the Act,

and in respect of which there is a charge to tax;

"relevant two-week period" has the meaning given by paragraph 4(2) of Schedule 19 to the Finance Act 1999;

"Special Commissioners" has the same meaning as in the Taxes Management Act 1970;

"surrender" shall be construed in accordance with paragraph 2(1) of Schedule 19 to the Finance Act 1999 (surrender of units to managers);

"tax" means stamp duty reserve tax.

"unit" and **"unit trust scheme"** have the meanings given by paragraph 14 of Schedule 19 to the Finance Act 1999.

"the Treasury Regulations" means the Uncertificated Securities Regulations 1995.

History – Definition of "accountable date" in Reg. 2 amended by SI 1999/3264, reg. 3(2), by inserting para. (d), with effect from 6 February 2000.
Definition of "accountable person" in reg. 2 amended by SI 1999/3264, reg. 3(3), by inserting para. (f) and para. (g), with effect from 6 February 2000; amended by SI 1988/835, reg. 1, 3, by substituting new para. (a), with effect from 27 May 1988; amended by SI 1997/2430, reg. 3(a), by substituting new para. (a), with effect from 20 October 1997.
Definition of "authorised corporate director" and "open-ended investment company" inserted by SI 1999/3264, reg. 3(4), with effect from 6 February 2000.
Definition of "the Board" inserted by SI 1997/2430, reg. 3(c), with effect from 20 October 1997.
Definition of "EEA regulated market" inserted by SI 1997/2430, reg. 3(c), with effect from 20 October 1997.
Definition of "exchange" inserted by SI 1997/2430, reg. 3(c), with effect from 20 October 1997.
Definition of "broker and dealer" inserted by SI 1988/835, reg. 1, 4, with effect from 27 May 1988; definition deleted by SI 1997/2430, reg. 3(d), with effect from 20 October 1997.
Definition of "market maker" inserted by SI 1988/835, reg. 1, 5, with effect from 27 May 1988; definition deleted by SI 1997/2430, reg. 3(d), with effect from 20 October 1997.
Definition of "operator" inserted by SI 1997/2430, reg. 3(e), with effect from 20 October 1997.
Definition of "qualified dealer" substituted by SI 1988/835, reg. 1, 6, with effect from 27 May 1988; amended by SI 1997/2430, reg. 3(f) by substituting the words "member of an exchange" for "market maker or broker and dealer" and added to the definition with effect from 20 October 1997.
Definition of "recognised professional body" inserted by SI 1997/2430, reg. 3(g), with effect from 20 October 1997.
Definition of "relevant system" inserted by SI 1997/2430, reg. 3(g), with effect from 20 October 1997.
Definition of "relevant two-week period" inserted by SI 1999/3264, reg. 3(5), with effect from 6 February 2000.
Definition of "surrender" inserted by SI 1999/3264, reg. 3(6), with effect from 6 February 2000.
Definition of "the Treasury Regulations" inserted by SI 1997/2430, reg. 3(h), with effect from 20 October 1997.
Definitions of "European institution", "investment business", and para. (c) added to definition of "qualified dealer" by SI 1992/3287, reg. 2, with effect from 1 January 1993.
Definition of "unit" and "unit trust scheme" inserted by SI 1999/3264, reg. 3(7), with effect from 6 February 2000.

2A References in these Regulations to any of the provisions of Schedule 19 to the Finance Act 1999 shall be construed as including references to those provisions as modified in relation to open-ended investment companies by the Stamp Duty and Stamp Duty Reserve Tax (Open-ended Investment Companies) Regulations 1997.

History – Reg. 2A inserted by SI 1999/3264, reg. 4, with effect from 6 February 2000.

DUE DATE FOR PAYMENT

3 Tax charged under the Act, or under paragraph 2(1) of Schedule 19 to the Finance Act 1999, shall be due and payable on the accountable date.

History – In reg. 3 words "or under paragraph 2(1) of Schedule 19 to the Finance Act 1999" inserted by SI 1999/3264, reg. 5, with effect from 6 February 2000.

NOTICE OF CHARGE AND PAYMENT

4(1) Subject to paragraph (3), an accountable person, except where different arrangements are authorised in writing by the Board, shall on or before the accountable date–

(a)   give notice of each charge to tax to the Board, and

(b)   pay the tax due.

4(2) A notice under this regulation shall be in such form as the Board may prescribe or authorise and shall contain such information as they may reasonably require for the purposes of the Act.

4(3) This regulation shall not apply where–

(a)   the tax in question has been accounted for by the operator under regulation 4A, or

(b)   regulation 4B applies to the accountable person.

History – In reg. 4(1) words "Subject to paragraph (3), an accountable person, except where" substituted for the words "An accountable person, except where the tax in question has been accounted for by the operator under regulation 4A or where" by SI 1999/3264, reg. 6, with effect from 6 February 2000.
In reg. 4(1), the words "the tax in question has been accounted for by the operator under regulation 4A or where" inserted by SI 1997/2430, reg. 4, with effect from 20 October 1997.
Reg. 4(3) inserted by SI 1999/3264, reg. 6(3), with effect from 6 February 2000.

4A(1) An operator, except where different arrangements are authorised in writing by the Board, shall on or before the accountable date–

(a)   give notice to the Board of each charge to tax arising–

    (i)   in respect of a relevant transaction in connection with which securities are transferred by means of a relevant system operated by him, or

    (ii)   in respect of a relevant transaction that is reported to a recognised self-regulating organisation, a recognised professional body or an exchange by means of a relevant system operated by him, or

    (iii)   in respect of a relevant transaction that is reported otherwise than by means of a relevant system to an exchange in relation to which he is the operator, or (as the case may be) which itself is the operator, in a case where the securities to which the transaction relates are not transferred by means of a relevant system, and

(b)   pay the tax due.

4A(2)   A notice under this regulation shall be in such form as the Board may prescribe or authorise and shall contain such information as they may reasonably require for the purposes of the Act.

4A(3)   The Board may, by notification in writing to an operator, impose such requirements, conditions or procedures as they consider necessary for the purposes of these Regulations.

History – Regulation 4A inserted by SI 1997/2430, reg. 5, with effect from 20 October 1997.

4B(1)   An accountable person in relation to a charge to tax on a surrender shall on or before the accountable date–

(a)   give notice to the Board–

    (i)   detailing all surrenders for which the relevant two-week period ends in the month preceding that in which the accountable date falls, and

    (ii)   setting out the total of any reductions under paragraphs 4 and 5 of Schedule 19 to the Finance Act 1999 of the amounts of tax chargeable on those surrenders;

    (iii)   identifying those surrenders to which paragraph 6 or 7 of Schedule 19 to the Finance Act 1999 applies, and

    (iv)   stating the total amount of tax due and payable, and

(b)   pay the tax due.

4B(2)   A notice under this regulation shall be given–

(a)   in relation to each unit trust scheme of which the accountable person is the manager or trustee; and

(b)   in relation to each open-ended investment company of which the accountable person is the authorised corporate director, or in relation to an open-ended investment company which is the accountable person.

4B(3)   A notice under this regulation shall be in such form as the Board may prescribe or authorise and shall contain such information as they may reasonably require for the purposes of the Act and Part II of Schedule 19 to the Finance Act 1999.

History – Reg. 4B inserted by SI 1999/3264, reg. 7, with effect from 6 February 2000.

POWER TO REQUIRE INFORMATION

5(1)   The Board may by notice require any person to furnish them within such time, not being less than 30 days, as may be specified in the notice with such information (including documents or records) as the Board may reasonably require for the purposes of the Act.

5(2)   A barrister or solicitor shall not be obliged in pursuance of a notice under this regulation to disclose, without his client's consent, any information with respect to which a claim to professional privilege could be maintained.

NOTICE OF DETERMINATION

6(1)   Where it appears to the Board that a relevant transaction or surrender has taken place or where a claim is made to the Board in connection with a relevant transaction or surrender, the Board may give notice to any person who appears to them in relation to that transaction or surrender to be the accountable person or, having regard to regulation 4A(1), the operator, or the person liable for any of the tax charged or to the claimant, stating that they have determined the matters specified in the notice.

6(2)   If it appears to the Board that any such matter specified in a notice of determination is, or may be, material as respects any liability under the Act of two or more persons, they may give notice of the determination to each of those persons.

6(3)   Any matter that appears to the Board to be relevant for the purposes of the Act may be determined and specified in a notice under this regulation.

6(4)   A determination for the purposes of a notice under this regulation of any fact relating to a relevant transaction or surrender –

(a)   shall, if that fact has been stated in a notice under regulation 4, 4A, or 4B and the Board are satisfied that the notice is correct, be made by the Board in accordance with that notice, but

(b)   may, in any other case, be made by the Board to the best of their judgment.

6(5)   A notice under this regulation shall state the time within which and the manner in which an appeal against any determination in it may be made.

6(6)   Subject to any variation by agreement in writing or on appeal, a determination in a notice under this regulation shall be conclusive for the purposes of the Act, and, where appropriate, Part II of Schedule 19 to the Finance Act 1999 against a person on whom the notice is served.

History – In reg. 6(1) the words "or surrender" inserted by SI 1999/3264, reg. 8(2), in three places with effect from 6 February 2000.
In reg. 6(1), the words "or, having regard to regulation 4A(1), the operator" inserted by SI 1997/2430, reg. 6(a), with effect from 20 October 1997.
In reg. 6(4) the words "or surrender" inserted by SI 1999/3264, reg. 8(3), with effect from 6 February 2000.
In reg. 6(4)(a) words "4, 4A, or 4B" substituted for the words "4 or 4A" by SI 1999/3264, reg. 8(4), with effect from 6 February 2000.
In reg. 6(4)(a), the words "or 4A" inserted by SI 1997/2430, reg. 6(b), with effect from 20 October 1997.
In reg. 6(6) words "and, where appropriate, Part II of Schedule 19 to the Finance Act 1999" inserted by SI 1999/3264, reg. 8(4), with effect from 6 February 2000.

RELIEF FROM ACCOUNTABILITY

7   If on a claim–

(a)   in relation to a charge under section 87 of the Act, an accountable person or an operator, other than a person liable under section 91 of the Act, or

(b)   in relation to a charge under paragraph 2(1) of Schedule 19 to the Finance Act 1999, an accountable person, other than a person liable under paragraph 2(3) of that Schedule,

proves to the Board's satisfaction that he has taken without success all reasonable steps, both before and after the date of the agreement, to recover from the person liable tax for which he is accountable under regulation 4, 4A, or 4B he shall be relieved of his liability to account for and pay that tax and any interest on that tax.

History – In reg. 7 words
"If on a claim–
    (a)   in relation to a charge under section 87 of the Act, an accountable person or an operator, other than a person liable under section 91 of the Act, or
    (b)   in relation to a charge under paragraph 2(1) of Schedule 19 to the Finance Act 1999, an accountable person, other than a person liable under paragraph 2(3) of that Schedule," substituted for the words "If on a claim in relation to a charge under section 87 of the Act an accountable person or an operator, other than a person liable under section 91 of the Act", by SI 1999/3264, reg. 9, with effect from 6 February 2000.
In reg. 7 words "4, 4A, or 4B" substituted for the words "4 or 4A" by SI 1999/3264, reg. 9, with effect from 6 February 2000.
In reg. 7, the words "or an operator" inserted by SI 1997/2430, reg. 7(a), with effect from 20 October 1997.
In reg. 7, the words "or 4A" inserted by SI 1997/2430, reg. 7(b), with effect from 20 October 1997.

APPEALS AGAINST DETERMINATION

8(1)   A person on whom a notice under regulation 6 has been served may, within 30 days of the date of the notice, appeal against any determination specified in it by notice given to the Board and specifying the grounds of appeal.

8(2)   Subject to the following provisions of this regulation the appeal shall be to the Special Commissioners.

8(3)   Where–

(a)   it is so agreed between the appellant and the Board, or

(b)   the High Court, on an application made by the appellant, is satisfied that the matters to be decided on the appeal are likely to be substantially confined to questions of law and gives leave for that purpose,

the appeal may be to the High Court.

8(4)   An appeal on any question as to the value of land in the United Kingdom may be to the appropriate tribunal.

8(4A)   If and so far as the question in dispute on any appeal under this regulation to the Special Commissioners or the High Court is a question as to the value of land in the United Kingdom, the question shall be determined on a reference to the appropriate tribunal.

8(4B)   In this regulation **"the appropriate tribunal"** means–

(a)   where the land is in England or Wales, the Lands Tribunal;

(b)   where the land is in Scotland, the Lands Tribunal for Scotland;

(c)   where the land is in Northern Ireland, the Lands Tribunal for Northern Ireland.

8(4C)   On the hearing of an appeal before them, the Special Commissioners may allow the appellant to put forward any ground of appeao not specified in the notice of appeal and take it into account if satisfied that the omission was not wilful or unreasonable.

8(4D)   The Special Commissioners shall on an appeal to them confirm the determination appealed against unless they are satisfied that the determination ought to be varied or quashed.

8(5)   In the application of this regulation to Scotland, for references to the High Court there shall be substituted references to the Court of Session.

History – Reg. 8(4), (4A) and (4B) where first occurring substituted by SI 1993/3110, reg. 3, operative from 1 January 1994. Reg. 8(4A), (4B), where next occurring, inserted by SI 1994/1813, reg. 2(1) and Sch. 1, para. 28, operative from 1 September 1994; subsequently renamed 4C and 4D by SI 1997/2430 reg. 8, with effect from 20 October 1997.

Cross references – SI 1994/1811, reg. 24(4): penalties under reg. 24 for failure to comply with special commissioners' direction etc. in proceedings relating to an appeal under reg. 8 above treated for all purposes as tax determined by the Board and due and payable.

APPEALS OUT OF TIME

9   An appeal under regulation 8 may be brought out of time with the consent of the Board or the Special Commissioners; and the Board–

(a)   shall give that consent if satisfied, on an application for the purpose, that there was a reasonable excuse for not bringing the appeal within the time limited and that the application was made thereafter without unreasonable delay, and

(b)   shall, if not so satisfied, refer the application for determination by the Special Commissioners.

APPEALS FROM THE SPECIAL COMMISSIONERS

10(1)   Any party to an appeal, if dissatisfied in point of law with the determination of that appeal by the Special Commissioners, may appeal against that determination to the High Court.

10(2)   The High Court shall hear and determine any question of law arising on an appeal under paragraph 1 above and may reverse, affirm or vary the determination of the Special Commissioners, or remit the matter to the Special Commissioners with the court's opinion on it, or make such other order in relation to the matter as the court thinks fit.

10(3)   This regulation shall have effect–

(a)   in its application to Scotland, with the substitution of references to the Court of Session for references to the High Court; and

(b)   in its application to Northern Ireland, with the substitution of references to the Court of Appeal in Northern Ireland for references to the High Court.

History – Reg. 10 substituted by SI 1994/1813, reg. 2(1) and Sch. 1, para. 29, operative from 1 September 1994.

INTEREST ON OVERPAID TAX

11(1)   Where tax repaid under regulation 14 is not less than £25 it shall be repaid with interest on it at the rate which is the rate applicable under section 178 of the Finance Act 1989 for the purposes of section 92(2) of the Act from the time it was paid.

11(2)   Interest paid under this regulation shall not constitute income for the purposes of income tax or corporation tax.

History – Reg. 11(1) amended by SI 1989/1301, operative from 18 August 1989.

Notes – For the rate of interest, see FA 1986, s. 92(2) and note thereto.

RECOVERY OF TAX

12(1)   The Board shall not exercise any remedy or take any proceedings for the recovery of any amount of tax which is due from any person unless the amount has been agreed in writing between that person and the Board or has been determined and specified in a notice under regulation 6.

12(2)   Where an amount has been so determined and specified, but an appeal to which this paragraph applies is pending against the determination, the Board shall not exercise any remedy or take any legal proceedings to recover the amount determined except such part of it as may be agreed in writing or determined and specified in a further notice under regulation 6 to be a part not in dispute.

12(3)   Paragraph (2) applies to any appeal under regulation 8 but not to any further appeal; and regulation 8 shall have effect, in relation to a determination made in pursuance of paragraph (2) of this regulation, as if paragraphs (4) to (4B) of that regulation were omitted.

History – In reg. 12(3), the words "paragraphs (4) to (4B)" substituted by SI 1993/3110, reg. 4, with effect from 1 January 1994.

UNDERPAYMENTS

13(1)   Subject to paragraphs (2) and (3), where too little tax has been paid in respect of a relevant transaction or surrender the tax underpaid shall be payable with interest, whether or not the amount that has been paid was that stated as payable in a notice under regulation 4, 4A or 4B.

13(2)   Where tax charged under the Act or under paragraph 2(1) of Schedule 19 to the Finance Act 1999,is paid in accordance with a notice given to the Board under regulation 4,4A or 4B and the payment is made and accepted in full satisfaction of the tax so charged, no additional amount of tax shall be determined and specified in a notice under regulation 6 after the end of the period of 6 years beginning with the later of–

(a)   the date on which the payment was made and accepted, and

(b)   the relevant accountable date;

and, subject to paragraph (3), at the end of that period any liability for the additional tax shall be extinguished.

13(3)   In any case of fraudulent or negligent conduct by or on behalf of any person in connection with or in relation to tax the period mentioned in paragraph (2) shall be the period of 6 years beginning when the fraudulent or negligent conduct comes to the knowledge of the Board.

History – In reg. 13(1) words "or surrender" inserted by SI 1999/3264, reg. 10(2), with effect from 6 February 2000.
In reg. 13(1) words "4, 4A, or 4B" substituted for the words "4 or 4A" by SI 1999/3264, reg. 10(2), with effect from 6 February 2000.
In reg. 13(1), the words "or 4A" added by SI 1997/2430, reg. 9(a), with effect from 20 October 1997.
In reg. 13(2), the words "or 4A" added by SI 1997/2430, reg. 9(b), with effect from 20 October 1997.
In reg. 13(2) words "or under paragraph 2(1) of Schedule 19 to the Finance Act 1999," inserted by SI 1999/3264, reg. 10(3), with effect from 6 February 2000.
In reg. 13(2) words "4, 4A, or 4B" substituted for the words "4 or 4A" by SI 1999/3264, reg. 10(3), with effect from 6 February 2000.
In reg. 13(3), the words "fraudulent or negligent conduct" substituted in each place by SI 1993/3110, reg. 5, with effect from 1 January 1994.

OVERPAYMENTS

14(1)   If on a claim it is proved to the Board's satisfaction that too much tax has been paid in respect of any relevant transaction or surrender the excess (and any interest paid thereon) shall be repaid by the Board.

14(2)   A claim under this regulation shall be made within a period of 6 years beginning with the later of–

(a)   the date on which the payment was made, and

(b)   the relevant accountable date.

History – In reg. 14(1) words "or surrender" inserted by SI 1999/3264, reg. 11, with effect from 6 February 2000.

INSPECTION OF RECORDS

15(1)   Every accountable person or operator shall, whenever and wherever required to do so, make available for inspection by an officer of the Board authorised for that purpose all books, documents and other records in his possession or under his control containing information relating to any relevant transaction to which he was a party or in connection with which he acted.

15(2)   Where records are maintained by computer the person required to make them available for inspection shall provide the officer making the inspection with all facilities necessary for obtaining information from them.

History – In reg. 15(1), the words "or operator" inserted after the words "accountable person" and the words "and whenever" inserted after the word "whenever" by SI 1997/2430, reg. 10, with effect from 20 October 1997.

EVIDENCE

16(1)   For the purposes of the preceding provisions of these Regulations, a notice under regulation 6 specifying any determination which can no longer be varied or quashed on appeal shall be sufficient evidence of the matters specified.

16(2)   In any proceedings for the recovery of tax or interest on tax, a certificate by an officer of the Board–

(a)   that the tax or interest is due, or

(b)   that, to the best of his knowledge and belief, it has not been paid,

shall be sufficient evidence that the sum mentioned in the certificate is due or, as the case may be, unpaid; and a document purporting to be such a certificate shall be deemed to be such a certificate unless the contrary is proved.

DETERMINATION OF QUESTIONS ON PREVIOUS VIEW OF THE LAW

17   Where any payment has been made and accepted in satisfaction of any liability for tax and on a view of the law then generally received or adopted in practice, any question whether too little or too much has been paid or what was the right amount of tax payable shall be determined on the same view, notwithstanding that it appears from a subsequent legal decision or otherwise that the view was or may have been wrong.

RECOVERY OF OVER-REPAYMENT OF TAX, ETC.

18(1)   Where an amount of tax has been repaid, or interest has been paid, to any person which ought not to have been repaid or paid to him, that amount may be determined and recovered as if it were tax due from him.

18(2)   Subject to paragraph (3) a determination under this regulation may be made before the expiration of 6 years from the date on which the amount was repaid or paid.

18(3)   In any case of fraudulent or negligent conduct the period mentioned in paragraph (2) shall be 6 years from the date on which the fraudulent or negligent conduct comes to the knowledge of the Board.

18(4)   In this regulation an amount repaid or paid includes an amount allowed by way of set off.

History – In reg. 18(3), the words "fraudulent or negligent conduct" substituted in each place by SI 1993/3110, reg. 6, with effect from 1 January 1994.

SERVICE OF DOCUMENTS

19   A notice or other document which is to be served on or given to a person under these Regulations may be delivered to him or left at his usual or last known place of residence or served by post, addressed to him at his usual or last known place of residence or place of business or employment.

TAXES MANAGEMENT ACT 1970: PROVISIONS TO APPLY

20(1)   The provisions of the Taxes Management Act 1970 specified in the first column of the Table in Part I of the Schedule to these Regulations shall apply in relation to the tax as they apply in relation to a tax within the meaning of that Act subject to any modification specified in the second column of that Table.

20(2)   Any expression to which a meaning is given by the Act or in these Regulations and which is used in a provision of the Taxes Management Act 1970 as applied by this regulation shall in that provision, as so applied, have the same meaning as in the Act or these Regulations.

20(3)   The provisions of the Taxes Management Act 1970 specified in Part I of the Schedule (as modified where appropriate) are restated as so modified and applied in Part II of the Schedule.

History – Reg. 20(3) amended by SI 1988/835, reg. 1, 7 (by omitting "the" which appeared before "Part I"), with effect from 27 May 1988.

INLAND REVENUE REGULATION ACT 1890: PROVISIONS NOT TO APPLY

21   Sections 21, 22, and 35 of the Inland Revenue Regulation Act 1890 (proceedings for fines, etc.) shall not apply in relation to stamp duty reserve tax.

SCHEDULES

Regulation 20

Part I – Table

Provision applied	Modifications
Section 23(1)	
(2)	For the words "five shillings" substitute "25 pence".
(3)	For the word ""'security'"" substitute ""'securities'""; and for the words "includes shares, stock, debentures and debenture stock" substitute "means chargeable securities".

Provision applied	Modifications
25(1)	For the words "chargeable gains an inspector" substitute "relevant transactions the Board"; and omit the words "in writing".
(2)	–
(3)	–
(4)	For the words "stock exchange in the United Kingdom, other than a market maker," substitute "recognised investment exchange or a market of the kind described in paragraphs (a) and (b) of article 2 of the Financial Services Act 1986 (EEA Regulated Markets) (Exemption) Order 1995 ("EEA regulated market")".
(5)	For the words "a stock exchange in the United Kingdom" substitute "a recognised investment exchange or an EEA regulated market"; and omit the words "after 5th April 1968 and".
(8)	–
(9)	For the words ""company"" to the end substitute ""shares or securities" means chargeable securities and "company" shall be construed accordingly".
26(2)	For the words "include" to the end substitute "are references to chargeable securities".
46A(1)	Omit paragraphs (a) and (b) and the words "General Commissioners or" in paragraph (c); and for the words "appeals or other proceedings under the Taxes Acts" substitute "an appeal against a determination".
46A(2)	–
46A(3)	–
46A(4)	–
50(3)–(6)	[Omitted by SI 1994/1813, reg. 2(1) and Sch. 1, para. 30(1), (2), and reg. 2(2) and Sch. 2, Pt. II.]
51(1), (2)	[Omitted by SI 1994/1813, reg. 2(1) and Sch. 1, para. 30(1), (2) and reg. 2(2) and Sch. 2, Pt. II.]
52(1)–(3)	[Omitted by SI 1994/1813, reg. 2(1) and Sch. 1, para. 30(1), (2), and reg. 2(2) and Sch. 2, Pt. II.]
53(1)	Before the word "Commissioners" insert "Special".
(2)	–
56B(1)	–
56B(2)	Before the word "Commissioners" wherever it occurs insert "Special".
56B(3)	Before the word "Commissioners" in both places where it occurs insert "Special".
56B(4)	–
56B(5)	–
56B(6)	–
56C	–
56D	–
60	–
61	–
63(1)	–
63(2)	–
63A(1)	–
63A(2)	–
65(1)	For paragraphs (a) and (b) there shall be substituted "the amount of any tax *for the time being due* and payable is less than £1,000.".
(4)	–
66(1)	For the words "any assessment" substitute "the Act".
(2)	–
(2A)	–

Provision applied	*Modifications*
(3)	–
(4)	–
67(1)	Omit the words "under any assessment".
(2)	–
68	–
69	For the words "Part IX of this" substitute "the"; omit the words "charged and"; and omit the words "under the assessment" to the end.
71(2)	For the words "chargeable to" substitute "accountable or liable for"; omit the word "income"; for the words "Income Tax Acts" substitute "Act"; and omit the words "for the purpose of the assessment of the body".
(3)	Omit the word "income"; for the words "charged on the body" substitute "for which the body is accountable or liable"; and for the words "Income Tax Acts" substitute "Act".
72(1)	For the words "assessable and chargeable to income" substitute "accountable or liable for"; and for the words "assessed and charged" substitute "accountable or liable".
(2)	For the word "chargeable" substitute "accountable or liable"; for the words "Income Tax Acts" substitute "Act"; and for the words "of assessment and payment of income tax" substitute "thereof".
(3)	For the words "has been charged" substitute "is accountable or liable"; for the words "Income Tax Acts" in both places in which they occur substitute "Act"; and for the word "charged" substitute "for which he is accountable or liable".
73	For the words "chargeable to income" substitute "accountable or liable for".
74(1)	For the words "chargeable to income" substitute "accountable or liable for"; and for the words "chargeable on such deceased person" substitute "for which such deceased person is accountable or liable".
(2)	–
78(1)	Omit the words from the beginning to "(Schedule A etc.)"; omit the words "whether a British subject or not"; for the words "assessable and chargeable to income" substitute "accountable or liable for"; omit the words from "whether the branch" to "or gains or not"; for the words "assessed and charged" substitute "accountable or liable"; and omit the words from "and in the actual receipt" to the end.
83(1)	For the words "in whose name" substitute "who is accountable or liable in respect of"; omit the words "is chargeable"; for the words "Income Tax Acts" substitute "Act"; and for the words "of assessment and payment of income tax" substitute "thereof".
(2)	For the words "has been charged" substitute "is accountable or liable"; for the words "Income Tax Acts" in both places in which they occur substitute "Act"; and for the word "charged" substitute "for which he is accountable or liable".
86(1)	For the words "The following" to "section 55 or 59B of this Act;" substitute "Tax which becomes due and payable"; and for the words "the relevant date" substitute "1st October 1999 or the accountable date, whichever is the later,".
(3)	For the word "relevant" substitute "accountable".
89(1)	[Omitted by SI 1989/1301.]

Provision applied	*Modifications*
(3)	[Omitted by SI 1989/1301.]
90	–
93(1)	For the words "where" to "with the notice" substitute "where any person (the taxpayer) fails to give a notice which he is required to give under regulation 4 or 4A of the Stamp Duty Reserve Tax Regulations 1986".
93(2)–(3)	Omit the words "General or".
93(5)	For the words "to (4)" substitute "and (3)"; and for the words from "if" to the end substitute "if the failure by the taxpayer to give the notice continues after the end of a period of one year beginning on the last day on which the notice should have been given, he shall be liable to a penalty of an amount not exceeding the amount of the tax which he should have paid by the date by which he should have given the notice".
93(6)	–
95(1)	In paragraph (a) for the word "delivers" substitute "gives"; and for the words from "return" to "Act)" substitute "notice under regulation 4 or 4A of the Stamp Duty Reserve Tax Regulations 1986"; in paragraph (b) omit the word "return,"; for the words "in connection with" substitute "in, or in connection with,"; omit the words "for any allowance, deduction or relief"; and for the words "income tax or capital gains" substitute "stamp duty reserve"; omit paragraph (c) and the word "or" immediately preceding it.
(2)	In paragraph (a) for the words "income tax and capital gains" substitute "stamp duty reserve"; omit the words "for" to "assessment"; and omit the words "including" to "repayable"; in paragraph (b) for the word "return" substitute "notice"; after the word "statement" insert "or"; omit the words "or accounts"; after the word "as" insert "given or"; and omit the words "or submitted".
97(1)	For the word "return" in both places in which it occurs substitute "notice"; after the word "statement" in both places in which it occurs insert "or"; omit the words "or amounts" in both places in which they occur; for the words "sections 95 and 96" substitute "section 95"; for the words "made or submitted" in both places in which they occur substitute "given or made"; and for the words "those sections" substitute "that section".
98(1)	Omit the words "Subject to the provisions of this section and section 98A below,".
98(2)	Omit the words "Subject to section 98A below".
98(3)	–
98(4)	–
Table	Omit the provisions specified in the first and second columns of the Table and the words at the end of the Table and insert the following provisions–
	Section 23 of this Act; Section 25(1), (2), (3), (4), (5), (8) and (9) of this Act; Section 26 of this Act; The Stamp Duty Reserve Tax Regulations 1986 (other than regulations 4, 4A and 4B);
	The Stamp Duty Reserve Tax Regulations 1986. Interests in Foreign Securities) Regulations 1999.
99	For the words "preparation or delivery" substitute "giving"; for the words "information, return, accounts or other document" substitute "notice under regulation 4, 4A or 4B, or any information under regulation 5, of the Stamp Duty Reserve Tax Regulations 1986"; and omit paragraph (a).
100(1)	Before the word "Commissioners" insert "Special"; and for the words "the Taxes Acts" substitute "this Act".
100(2)	In paragraph (a) for the words "section 93(1) above" onwards substitute "section 93(1)(a) above, or"; omit paragraph (b); in paragraph (c) for the words "section 98(1) above" onwards substitute "section 98(1)(i) above"; omit paragraphs (d) and (e).

Provision applied	*Modifications*
100(3)	–
100(4)	–
100(5)	–
100A(1)	–
100A(2)	–
100A(3)	Omit the words "in an assessment".
100B(1)	For the words from "this Act" onwards substitute "the Stamp Duty Reserve Tax regulations 1986 relating to appeals against determinations specified in notices under regulation 6 of those Regulations ("regulation 6 determinations") shall have effect in relation to an appeal against such a determination as they have effect in relation to appeals against regulation 6 determinations.
100B(2)	Omit the words "section 50(6) to (8) of this Act shall not apply but"; and before the word "Commissioners" in both places where it occurs insert "Special".
100B(3)	For the words "section 56 of this Act" substitute "regulation 10 of the Stamp Duty Reserve Tax Regulations 1986"; and before the word "Commissioners" in both places where it occurs insert "Special".
100C(1)	Omit the words "General or".
100C(2)	Before the word "Commissioners" insert "Special".
100C(3)	Before the word "Commissioners" insert "Special"; and omit the words "in an assessment".
100C(4)	–
100C(5)	–
100D	–
101	For the word "assessment" substitute "notice under regulation 6 of The Stamp Duty Reserve Tax Regulations 1986"; after the word "varied" insert "or quashed"; for the word "any" in the second place in which it occurs substitute "the Special"; and for the word "that" to the end substitute "of the matters specified".
102	–
103(1)	Omit the words "Subject to subsection (2) below" and the words "for any period"; and before the word "Commissioners" insert "Special".
103(3)	–
103(4)	Before the word "Commissioners" insert "Special".
104	For the words "the Taxes Acts" substitute "this Act"; and for the word "misdemeanour" substitute "offence".
105	–
108(1)	For the words "Taxes Acts" in both places in which they occur substitute "Act"; and omit the words "This subsection" to the end.
(2)	For the words from the beginning to "on" substitute "Tax for which"; and after the word "Charter" insert "is accountable or liable".
(3)	–

Provision applied	*Modifications*
111(1)	Omit the words "Capital Gains Tax"; the words "1979"; and omit the words "inspector or other" in both places in which they occur.
(2)	Omit the words "inspector or other"; and for the words "£5" substitute "level 1 on the standard scale as defined in section 75 of the Criminal Justice Act 1982".
114(1)	For the words "An assessment or determination" substitute "A notice of determination"; for the words "Taxes Acts" in both places in which they occur substitute "Act"; omit the words "or property charged or"; and the words "charged or".
(2)	For the words "An assessment or determination" substitute "A notice of determination"; in paragraph (a)(i) omit the word "liable"; in paragraph (a)(ii) for the words "the description of any profits or property" substitute "any matter specified therein"; and omit the word "or"; omit paragraph (a)(iii); omit paragraph (b).
118(1)	Omit the following expressions and the words which occur after them:
	"the Board"
	"chargeable gain"
	"chargeable period"
	"inspector"
	"return"
	"tax"
	"the Taxes Acts"
	"trade"; and
	in the words which occur after the expression "neglect" for the words "Taxes Act" substitute "Act".
(2)	Before the word "Commissioners" insert "Special"; and after the word "deemed" in the second place in which it occurs insert "not to have failed to do it unless the excuse ceased and, after the excuse ceased, he shall be deemed".

History – Entry for 25(4) substituted by SI 1997/2430, reg. 11(2), with effect from 20 October 1997.

Entry for 25(5) substituted by SI 1997/2430, reg. 11(3), with effect from 20 October 1997.

Entries for 46A(1)–(4) inserted by SI 1993/3110, reg. 7(2), with effect from 1 January 1994.

Entries for s. 50(3)–(6) omitted with effect from 1 September 1994.

Entries for s. 51(1), (2) omitted with effect from 1 September 1994.

Entries for s. 52(1)–(3) omitted with effect from 1 September 1994.

Entries for s. 53 substituted by SI 1994/1813, reg. 2(1) and Sch. 1, para. 30(1), (3), with effect from 1 September 1994.

Entries for 56B inserted by SI 1993/3110, reg. 7(3), with effect from 1 January 1994.

Entry for 56C inserted by SI 1993/3110, reg. 7(3), with effect from 1 January 1994.

Entry for 56D inserted by SI 1993/3110, reg. 7(3), with effect from 1 January 1994.

Entry for 60 inserted by SI 1993/3110, reg. 7(3), with effect from 1 January 1994.

Entry for 63 substituted by SI 1993/3110, reg. 7(4), with effect from 1 January 1994.

Entry for 63A substituted by SI 1993/3110, reg. 7(3), with effect from 1 January 1994.

Entry for 65(1) substituted by SI 1993/3110, reg. 7(5), with effect from 1 January 1994.

Entry for 66(1) substituted by SI 1993/3110, reg. 7(6), with effect from 1 January 1994

Entries for 86 substituted by SI 1999/2536, reg. 3(2), with effect from 1 October 1999.

Entries for 89(1), (3) omitted by SI 1989/1301, operative from 18 August 1989.

Entry for 93(1) amended by SI 1999/3264, reg.12(2), by substituting the words "4, 4A or 4B" for the words "4 or 4A" with effect from 6 February 2000.

Entry for 93 previously substituted by SI 1997/2430, reg. 11(4), with effect from 20 October 1997.

Entries for 93(2) and (5) substituted by SI 1993/3110, reg. 7(8), with effect from 1 January 1994.

Words "Section 51 of this Act;" omitted from entry relating to the table by SI 1994/1813, reg. 2(1) and Sch. 1, para. 30(1), (4), and reg. 2(2) and Sch. 2, Pt. II, with effect from 1 September 1994.

Entry for 95(1) amended by SI 1999/3264, reg.12(2), by substituting the words "4, 4A or 4B" for the words "4 or 4A" with effect from 6 February 2000.

Entry for 95(1) previously substituted by SI 1997/2430, reg. 11(5), with effect from 20 October 1997.

Entry for 98 amended by SI 1999/3264, reg.12(3), by substituting the words "4, 4A and 4B" for the words "4 and 4A" with effect from 6 February 2000.

Entry for 98 amended by SI 1999/2383, reg.5(2), by adding the words "The Stamp Duty Reserve Tax (UK Depositary Interests in Foreign Securities) Regulations 1999" with effect from 25 August 1999.

Entry for 98 substituted by SI 1997/2430, reg. 11(6), with effect from 20 October 1997.

Entries for 98 previously substituted by SI 1993/3110, reg. 7(9), with effect from 1 January 1994.

Entry for 99 amended by SI 1999/3264, reg.12(2), by substituting the words "4, 4A or 4B" for the words "4 or 4A" with effect from 6 February 2000.

Entry for 99 previously substituted by SI 1997/2430, reg. 11(7), with effect from 20 October 1997.

Entry for 99 previously substituted by SI 1993/3110, reg. 7(10), with effect from 1 January 1994.

Entries for 100 substituted by SI 1993/3110, reg. 7(11), with effect from 1 January 1994.

Entries for 100A substituted by SI 1993/3110, reg. 7(11), with effect from 1 January 1994.

Entries for 100B substituted by SI 1993/3110, reg. 7(11), with effect from 1 January 1994.

Entries for 100C substituted by SI 1993/3110, reg. 7(11), with effect from 1 January 1994.
Entry for 100D substituted by SI 1993/3110, reg. 7(11), with effect from 1 January 1994.
Entries for 103 substituted by SI 1993/3110, reg. 7(12), with effect from 1 January 1994.
In entry for 114(1) and (2), the words "An assessment or determination" substituted by SI 1993/3110, reg. 7(13), with effect from 1 January 1994.

Part II – Taxes Management Act 1970

Notes – This heading is to Pt. II of these regulations (i.e. the Stamp Duty Reserve Tax Regulations 1986 (SI 1986/1711)). The following headings refer to Points of the Taxes Management Act 1970, provisions of which are modified by these regulations.

Part III – Other Returns and Information

Notes – This heading is to Pt. III/V/VI/VII/VIII/IX/X/XI of the Taxes Management Act 1970. The text below is the modified version of the provision in that Part which is introduced by these regulations.

23 Power to obtain copies of registers of securities

23(1) The Board may cause to be served upon any body corporate a notice requiring them to deliver to the Board within a specified time, being not less than twenty-one days, a copy, certified by a duly authorised officer of such body, of the whole of, or any specified class of entries in, any register containing the names of the holders of any securities issued by them.

23(2) On delivery of the copy in accordance with the notice payment shall be made therefore at the rate of 25 pence in respect of each one hundred entries.

23(3) In this section **"securities"** means chargeable securities, and **"entry"** means, in relation to any register, so much thereof as relates to the securities held by any one person.

25 Issuing houses, stockbrokers, auctioneers, etc.

25(1) For the purpose of obtaining particulars of relevant transactions the Board may by notice require a return under any of the provisions of this section.

25(2) An issuing house or other person carrying on a business of effecting public issues of shares or securities in any company, or placings of shares or securities in any company, either on behalf of the company, or on behalf of holders of blocks of shares or securities which have not previously been the subject of a public issue or placing, may be required to make a return of all such public issues or placings effected by that person in the course of the business in the period specified in the notice requiring the return, giving particulars of the persons to or with whom the shares or securities are issued, allotted or placed, and the number or amount of the shares or securities so obtained by them respectively.

25(3) A person not carrying on such a business may be required to make a return as regards any such public issue or placing effected by that person and specified in the notice, giving particulars of the persons to or with whom the shares or securities are issued, allotted, or placed and the number or amount of the shares or securities so obtained by them respectively.

25(4) A member of a recognised investment exchange or a market of the kind described in paragraphs (a) and (b) of article 2 of the Financial Services Act 1986 (EEA Regulated Markets) (Exemption) Order 1995 (**"EEA regulated market"**) may be required to make a return giving particulars of any transactions effected by him in the course of his business in the period specified in the notice requiring the return and giving particulars of–

(a) the parties to the transactions,

(b) the number or amount of the shares or securities dealt with in the respective transactions, and

(c) the amount or value of the consideration.

25(5) A person (other than a member of a recognised investment exchange or an EEA regulated market) who acts as an agent or broker in the United Kingdom in transactions in shares or securities may be required to make a return giving particulars of any such transactions effected by him in the period specified in the notice, and giving particulars of–

(a) the parties to the transactions,

(b) the number or amount of the shares or securities dealt with in the respective transactions, and

(c) the amount or value of the consideration.

25(8) No person shall be required under this section to include in a return particulars of any transaction effected more than three years before the service of the notice requiring him to make the return.

25(9)   In this section **"shares or securities"** means chargeable securities and **"company"** shall be construed accordingly.

History – S. 25(4) and 25(5) substituted by SI 1997/2430, reg. 12(2), with effect from 20 October 1997.

26   Nominee shareholders

26(1)   If, for the purpose of obtaining particulars of relevant transactions, any person in whose name any shares of a company are registered is so required by notice by the Board, he shall state whether or not he is the beneficial owner of those shares and, if not the beneficial owner of those shares or any of them, shall furnish the name and address of the person or persons on whose behalf the shares are registered in his name.

26(2)   In this section references to **shares** are references to chargeable securities.

Part V – Appeal and Other Proceedings

Notes – This heading is to Pt. III/V/VI/VII/VIII/IX/X/XI of the Taxes Management Act 1970. The text below is the modified version of the provision in that Part which is introduced by these regulations.

PROCEDURE BEFORE SPECIAL COMMISSIONERS

46A   Regulations about Jurisdiction

46A(1)   The Lord Chancellor may, with the consent of the Lord Advocate, make regulations–

(c)   as to the number of Special Commissioners required or permitted to hear, or perform other functions in relation to, an appeal against a determination.

46A(2)   The Regulations may–

(a)   make different provision for different cases or different circumstances, and

(b)   contain such supplementary, incidental, consequential and transitional provision as the Lord Chancellor thinks appropriate.

46A(3)   Provision made by virtue of subsection (1) or (2) above may include provision amending this or any other Act or any instrument made under an Act.

46A(4)   Regulations under this section shall be made by statutory instrument subject to annulment in pursuance of a resolution of either House of Parliament.

History – Entries for s. 46A inserted by SI 1993/3110, reg. 8(2), with effect from 1 January 1994.

50   Procedure

50(3)–(6)   [Omitted by SI 1994/1813, reg. 2(1) and Sch. 1, para. 31(1), (2), and reg. 2(2) and Sch. 2, Pt. II.]

History – S. 50(3)–(6) omitted with effect from 1 September 1994.

51   Power of Special Commissioners to obtain information from appellant

51   [Omitted by SI 1994/1813, reg. 2(1) and Sch. 1, para. 31(1), (2), and reg. 2(2) and Sch. 2, Pt. II.]

History – S. 51 omitted with effect from 1 September 1994.

52   Evidence

52(1)   [Omitted by SI 1994/1813, reg. 2(1) and Sch. 1, para. 31(1), (2), and reg. 2(2) and Sch. 2, Pt. II.]

History – S. 52 omitted with effect from 1 September 1994.

53   Appeals against summary determination of penalties

53(1)   An appeal shall lie to the High Court or, in Scotland, the Court of Session as the Court of Exchequer in Scotland, against the summary determination by the Commissioners of any penalty pursuant to regulations under section 56B of this Act.

53(2)   On any such appeal the court may either confirm or reverse the determination of the Commissioners or reduce or increase the sum determined.

History – S. 53 (as modified) substituted by SI 1994/1813, reg. 2(1) and Sch. 1, para. 31(1), (3), with effect from 1 September 1994.

56B   Regulations about practice and procedure

56B(1)   The Lord Chancellor may, with the consent of the Lord Advocate, make regulations about the practice and procedure to be followed in connection with appeals.

56B(2)   The regulations may in particular include provision–

(a)   enabling the Special Commissioners to join as a party to an appeal a person who would not otherwise be a party;

(b)   for requiring any party to an appeal to provide information and make documents available for inspection by the Special Commissioners or by officers of the Board;

(c)   for requiring persons to attend the hearing of an appeal to give evidence and produce documents;

(d)   as to evidence generally in relation to appeals;

(e)   enabling the Special Commissioners to review their decisions;

(f)   for the imposition of penalties not exceeding an amount specified in the regulations;

(g)   for the determination and recovery of penalties (imposed by virtue of paragraph (f) above or any other enactment) and for appeals against penalties.

56B(3)   The regulations may also include provision–

(a)   authorising or requiring the Special Commissioners, in circumstances prescribed in the regulations, to state a case for the opinion of a court;

(b)   for an appeal to lie to a court on a question of law arising from a decision of the Special Commissioners;

(c)   as to the practice and procedure to be followed in connection with cases so stated or such appeals.

56B(4)   The regulations may–

(a)   make different provision for different cases or different circumstances, and

(b)   contain such supplementary, incidental, consequential and transitional provision as the Lord Chancellor thinks appropriate.

56B(5)   Provision made by virtue of any of subsections (1) to (4) above may include provision amending this or any other Act or any instrument made under an Act.

56B(6)   Regulations under this section shall be made by statutory instrument subject to annulment in pursuance of a resolution of either House of Parliament.

History – Entries for s. 56B inserted by SI 1993/3110, reg. 8(3), with effect from 1 January 1994.

56C   Power of Special Commissioners to order costs

56C(1)   Regulations made under section 56B above may include provision for–

(a)   the award by the Special Commissioners of the costs of, or incidental to, appeal hearings before them,

(b)   the recovery of costs so awarded, and

(c)   appeals against such awards.

56C(2)   Any provision made by virtue of subsection 1(a) above shall provide that the Special Commissioners shall not award costs against a party to an appeal unless they consider that he has acted wholly unreasonably in connection with the hearing in question.

History – Entries for s. 56C inserted by SI 1993/3110, reg. 8(3), with effect from 1 January 1994.

56D   Power of Special Commissioners to publish reports of decisions

56D(1)   Regulations made under section 56B above may include provision for the Special Commissioners to publish reports of such of their decisions as they consider appropriate.

56D(2)   Any provision made by virtue of subsection (1) above shall provide that any report *published*, other than a report of an appeal that was heard in public, shall be in a form that so far as possible prevents the identification of any person whose affairs are dealt with in the report.

56D(3)   No obligation of secrecy to which the Special Commissioners are subject (by virtue of this Act or otherwise) shall prevent their publishing reports of their decisions in accordance with any provision made by virtue of subsection (1) above.

History – Entries for s. 56D inserted by SI 1993/3110, reg. 8(3), with effect from 1 January 1994.

Part VI – Collection and Recovery

Notes – This heading is to Pt. III/V/VI/VII/VIII/IX/X/XI of the Taxes Management Act 1970. The text below is the modified version of the provision in that Part which is introduced by these regulations.

60   Issue of demand notes and receipts

60(1)   Every collector shall, when the tax becomes due and payable, make demand of the respective sums given to him in charge to collect, from the persons charged therewith, or at the places of their last abode, or on the premises in respect of which the tax is charged, as the case may require.

60(2)   On payment of the tax, the collector shall if requested give a receipt.

History – Entries for s. 60 inserted by SI 1993/3110, reg. 8(4), with effect from 1 January 1994.

DISTRAINT AND POINDING

61   Distraint by collectors

61(1)   If a person neglects or refuses to pay the sum charged, upon demand made by the collector, the collector shall, for non-payment thereof, distrain upon the lands, tenements and premises in respect of which the tax is charged, or distrain the person charged by his goods and chattels, and all such other goods and chattels as the collector is hereby authorised to distrain.

61(2)   For the purpose of levying any such distress, a collector may, after obtaining a warrant for the purpose signed by the General Commissioners, break open, in the daytime, any house or premises, calling to his assistance any constable.

Every such constable shall, when so required, aid and assist the collector in the execution of the warrant and in levying the distress in the house or premises.

61(3)   A levy or warrant to break open shall be executed by, or under the direction of, and in the presence of, the collector.

61(4)   A distress levied by the collector shall be kept for five days, at the costs and charges of a person neglecting or refusing to pay.

61(5)   If the person aforesaid does not pay the sum due, together with the costs and charges within the said five days, the distress shall be appraised by two or more inhabitants of the parish in which the distress is taken, or by other sufficient persons, and shall be sold by public auction by the collector for payment of the sum due and all costs and charges.

The costs and charges of taking, keeping, and selling the distress shall be retained by the collector, and any overplus coming by the distress, after the deduction of the costs and charges and of the sum due, shall be restored to the owner of the goods distrained.

63   Recovery of tax in Scotland

63(1)   Subject to subsection (3) below, in Scotland, where any tax is due and has not been paid, the sheriff, on an application by the collector accompanied by a certificate by the collector–

(a)   stating that none of the persons specified in the application has paid the tax due by him;

(b)   stating that the collector has demanded payment under section 60 of this Act from each such person of the amount due by him;

(c)   stating that 14 days have elapsed since the date of such demand without payment of the said amount; and

(d)   specifying the amount due and unpaid by each such person,

shall grant a summary warrant in a form prescribed by Act of Sederunt authorising the recovery, by any of the diligences mentioned in subsection (2) below, of the amount remaining due and unpaid.

63(2)   The diligences referred to in subsection (1) above are–

(a)   a poinding and sale in accordance with Schedule 5 to the Debtors (Scotland) Act 1987;

(b)   an earnings arrestment;

(c)   an arrestment and action of furthcoming or sale.

History – Entries for s. 63 substituted by SI 1993/3110, reg. 8(5), with effect from 1 January 1994.

63A   Sheriff officer's fees and outlays

63A(1)   Subject to subsection (2) below and without prejudice to paragraphs 25 to 34 of Schedule 5 to the Debtors (Scotland) Act 1987 (expenses of poinding and sale), the sheriff officer's fees, together with the outlays necessarily incurred by him, in connection with the execution of a summary warrant shall be chargeable against the debtor.

63A(2)   No fee shall be chargeable by the sheriff officer against the debtor for collecting, and accounting to the collector for, sums paid to him by the debtor in respect of the amount owing.

History – Entries for s. 63A inserted by SI 1993/3110, reg. 8(6), with effect from 1 January 1994.

COURT PROCEEDINGS

65   Magistrates' courts

65(1)   Where the amount of any tax for the time being due and payable is less than £1,000, the tax shall, without prejudice to any other remedy, be recoverable summarily as a civil debt by proceedings commenced in the name of a collector.

65(4)   It is hereby declared that in subsection (1) above the expression **"recoverable summarily as a civil debt"** in respect of proceedings in Northern Ireland means recoverable in proceedings under Article 62 of the Magistrates' Courts (Northern Ireland) Order 1981.

History – Entry for s. 65(1) substituted by SI 1993/3110, reg. 8(7), with effect from 1 January 1994.

66   County courts

66(1)   Tax due and payable under the Act may, in England and Wales, and in Northern Ireland where the amount does not exceed the limit specified in Article 10(1) of the County Courts (Northern Ireland) Order 1980, without prejudice to any other remedy, be sued for and recovered from the person charged therewith as a debt due to the Crown by proceedings in a county court commenced in the name of a collector.

66(2)   An officer of the Board who is authorised by the Board to do so may address the court in any proceedings under this section in a county court in England and Wales.

66(2A)   [Omitted by SI 1991/724 (L 5).]

66(3)   In this section as it applies in Northern Ireland the expression **"county court"** shall mean a county court held for a division under the County Courts (Northern Ireland) Order 1980.

66(4)   Sections 21 and 42(2) of the Interpretation Act (Northern Ireland) 1954 shall apply as if any reference in those provisions to any enactment included a reference to this section, and Part III of the County Courts (Northern Ireland) Order 1980 (general civil jurisdiction) shall apply for the purposes of this section in Northern Ireland.

History – Entry for s. 66(1) substituted by SI 1993/3110, reg. 8(8), with effect from 1 January 1994. S. 66(2A) omitted, by SI 1991/724 (L 5), reg. 2(8) and Schedule, operative from 1 July 1991.

67   Inferior courts in Scotland

67(1)   In Scotland, where the amount of tax for the time being due and payable does not exceed the sum for the time being specified in section 35(1)(a) of the Sheriff Courts (Scotland) Act 1971 the tax may, without prejudice to any other remedy, be sued for and recovered from the person charged therewith as a debt due to the Crown by proceedings commenced in the name of a collector in the sheriff court.

67(2)   Sections 65 and 66 above shall not apply in Scotland.

68   High Court etc.

68(1)   Any tax may be sued for and recovered from the person charged therewith in the High Court as a debt due to the Crown, or by any other means whereby any debt of record or otherwise due to the Crown can, or may at any time, be sued for and recovered, as well as by the other means specially provided by this Act for levying the tax.

68(2)   All matters within the jurisdiction of the High Court under this section shall be assigned in Scotland to the Court of Session sitting as the Court of Exchequer.

SUPPLEMENTAL

69   Interest on tax

69   Interest charged under the Act shall be treated for the purposes–

    (a)   of sections 61, 63 and 65 to 68 above, and

    (b)   of section 35(2)(g)(i) of the Crown Proceedings Act 1947 (rules of court to impose restrictions on set-off and counterclaim where the proceedings or set-off or counterclaim relate to taxes) and of any rules of court (including county court rules) for England and Wales or Northern Ireland, which impose such a restriction, and

    (c)   of section 35(2)(b) of the said Act of 1947 as set out in section 50 of that Act (which imposes corresponding restrictions in Scotland),

as if it were tax due and payable.

Part VII – Persons Chargeable in a Representative Capacity, etc.

Notes – This heading is to Pt. III/V/VI/VII/VIII/IX/X/XI of the Taxes Management Act 1970. The text below is the modified version of the provision in that Part which is introduced by these regulations.

71   Bodies of persons

71(1)   Subject to section 108 of this Act, the chamberlain or other officer acting as treasurer, auditor or receiver for the time being of any body of persons accountable or liable for tax shall be answerable for doing all such acts as are required to be done under the Act and for payment of the tax.

71(2)   Every such officer as aforesaid may from time to time retain, out of any money coming into his hands on behalf of the body, so much thereof as is sufficient to pay the tax for which the body is accountable or liable, and shall be indemnified for all such payments made in pursuance of the Act.

72   Trustees, guardians, etc., of incapacitated persons

72(1)   The trustee, guardian, tutor, curator or committee of any incapacitated person having the direction, control or management of the property or concern of any such person, whether such person resides in the United Kingdom or not, shall be accountable or liable for tax in like manner and to the like amount as that person would be accountable or liable if he were not an incapacitated person.

72(2)   The person who is accountable or liable in respect of an incapacitated person shall be answerable for all matters required to be done under the Act for the purpose thereof.

72(3)   Any person who is accountable or liable under the Act in respect of any incapacitated person as aforesaid may retain, out of money coming into his hands on behalf of any such person, so much thereof from time to time as is sufficient to pay the tax for which he is accountable or liable, and shall be indemnified for all such payments made in pursuance of the Act.

73   Further provision as to infants

73   If a person accountable or liable for tax is an infant, then his parent, guardian or tutor–

  (a)   shall be liable for the tax in default of payment by the infant, and

  (b)   on neglect or refusal of payment, may be proceeded against in like manner as any other defaulter, and

  (c)   if he makes such payment, shall be allowed all sums so paid in his accounts.

74   Personal representatives

74(1)   If a person accountable or liable for tax dies, the executor or administrator of the person deceased shall be liable for the tax for which such deceased person is accountable or liable, and may deduct any payments made under this section out of the assets and effects of the person deceased.

74(2)   On neglect or refusal of payment, any person liable under this section may be proceeded against in like manner as any other defaulter.

Part VIII – Charges on Non-Residents

Notes – This heading is to Pt. III/V/VI/VII/VIII/IX/X/XI of the Taxes Management Act 1970. The text below is the modified version of the provision in that Part which is introduced by these regulations.

78   Method of charging non-residents

78(1)   A person not resident in the United Kingdom shall be accountable for tax in the name of any such trustee, guardian, tutor, curator or committee as is mentioned in section 72 of this Act, or of any branch or agent, in like manner and to the like amount as such non-resident person would be accountable or liable if he were resident in the United Kingdom.

83   *Responsibilities and indemnification of persons in whose name a non-resident person is chargeable*

83(1)   A person who is accountable or liable in respect of a non-resident person shall be answerable for all matters required to be done under the Act for the purpose thereof.

83(2)   A person who is accountable or liable under the Act in respect of any non-resident person as aforesaid may retain, out of money coming into his hands on behalf of any such person, so much thereof from time to time as is sufficient to pay the tax for which he is accountable or liable, and shall be indemnified for all such payments made in pursuance of the Act.

Part IX – Interest on Overdue Tax

Notes – This heading is to Pt. III/V/VI/VII/VIII/IX/X/XI of the Taxes Management Act 1970. The text below is the modified version of the provision in that Part which is introduced by these regulations.

86   Interest on overdue tax

86(1)   Tax which becomes due and payable shall carry interest at the rate applicable under section 178 of the Finance Act 1989 from 1 October 1999 or the accountable date, whichever is the later, until payment.

86(3)   Subsection (1) above applies even if the accountable date is a non-business day within the meaning of section 92 of the Bills of Exchange Act 1882.

History – Entries for S. 86 substituted by SI 1999/2536, reg. 4(2), operative from 1 October 1999.

89   The prescribed rate of interest

89   [Omitted by SI 1989/1301, reg. 1, 5(b), operative from 18 August 1989.]

90   Disallowance of relief for interest on tax

90   Interest payable under this Part of this Act shall be paid without any deduction of income tax and shall not be allowed as a deduction in computing any income, profits or losses for any tax purposes.

Part X – Penalties, etc.

Notes – This heading is to Pt. III/V/VI/VII/VIII/IX/X/XI of the Taxes Management Act 1970. The text below is the modified version of the provision in that Part which is introduced by these regulations.

93   Failure to give notice for stamp duty reserve tax

93(1)   This section applies where any person (the taxpayer) fails to give a notice which he is required to give under regulation 4, 4A or 4B of The Stamp Duty Reserve Tax Regulations 1986

93(2)   The taxpayer shall be liable to a penalty which shall be £100.

93(3)   If, on an application made to them by an officer of the Board, the Special Commissioners so direct, the taxpayer shall be liable to a further penalty or penalties not exceeding £60 for each day on which the failure continues after the day on which he is notified of the direction (but excluding any day for which a penalty under this subsection has already been imposed).

93(5)   Without prejudice to any penalties under subsections (2) and (3) above, if the failure by the taxpayer to give the notice continues after the end of a period of one year beginning on the last day on which the notice should have been given, he shall be liable to a penalty of an amount not exceeding the amount of the tax which he should have paid by the date by which he should have given the notice.

93(6)   No penalty shall be imposed under subsection (3) above in respect of a failure at any time after the failure has been remedied.

History – Entry for 93(1) amended by SI 1999/3264, reg. 13(2), by substituting the words "4, 4A or 4B" for the words "4 or 4A" with effect from 6 February 2000.
Entries for s. 93(2) and (5) substituted by SI 1993/3110, reg. 8(10), with effect from 1 January 1994.
S. 93 subsititued by SI 1997/2430, reg. 12(3), with effect from 20 October 1997.

95   Incorrect notice etc. for stamp duty reserve tax

95(1)   Where a person fraudulently or negligently–

(a)   gives any incorrect notice under regulation 4, 4A or 4B of The Stamp Duty Reserve Tax Regulations 1986, or

(b)   makes any incorrect statement or declaration in, or in connection with, any claim in respect of stamp duty reserve tax,

he shall be liable to a penalty not exceeding the amount of the difference specified in subsection (2) below.

95(2)   The difference is that between–

(a)   the amount of stamp duty reserve tax payable by the said person, and

(b)   the amount which would have been the amount so payable if the notice, statement or declaration as given or made by him had been correct.

History – Entry for 95(1)(a) amended by SI 1999/3264, reg. 13(2), by substituting the words "4, 4A or 4B" for the words "4 or 4A" with effect from 6 February 2000.
S. 95(1) subsitituted by SI 1997/2430, reg. 12(4), with effect from 20 October 1997.

97   Incorrect notice: supplemental

97(1)   Where any such notice, statement or declaration as are mentioned in section 95 above were given or made by any person neither fraudulently nor negligently and it comes to his notice (or, if he has died, to the notice of his personal representatives) that they were incorrect, then, unless the error is remedied without unreasonable delay, the notice, statement or declaration shall be treated for the purposes of that section as having been negligently given or made by him.

98   Special returns, etc.

98(1)   Where any person–
(a)   has been required, by a notice served under or for the purposes of any of the provisions specified in the first column of the Table below, to deliver any return or other document, to furnish any particulars, to produce any document, or to make anything available for inspection, and he fails to comply with the notice, or
(b)   fails to furnish any information, give any certificate or produce any document or record in accordance with any of the provisions specified in the second column of the Table below,
he shall be liable, subject to subsections (3) and (4) below–
(i)   to a penalty not exceeding £300, and
(ii)   if the failure continues after a penalty is imposed under paragraph (i) above, to a further penalty or penalties not exceeding £60 for each day on which the failure continues after the day on which the penalty under paragraph (i) above was imposed (but excluding any day for which a penalty under this paragraph has already been imposed).

98(2)   Where a person fraudulently or negligently furnishes, gives, produces or makes any incorrect information, certificate, document, record or declaration of a kind mentioned in any of the provisions specified in either column of the Table below, he shall be liable to a penalty not exceeding £3,000.

98(3)   No penalty shall be imposed under subsection (1) above in respect of a failure within paragraph (a) of that subsection at any time after the failure has been remedied.

98(4)   No penalty shall be imposed under paragraph (ii) of subsection (1) above in respect of a failure within paragraph (b) of that subsection at any time after the failure has been remedied.

TABLE

1	2
Section 23 of this Act;	The Stamp Duty Reserve Tax Regulations 1986 (other than regulations 4, 4A and 4B);
Section 25(1), (2), (3), (4), (5), (8) and (9) of this Act;	The Stamp Duty Reserve Tax (UK Depositary Interests in Foreign Securities) Regulations 1999.
Section 26 of this Act; The Stamp Duty Reserve Tax Regulations 1986.	

History – Table in s. 98 (as modified) amended by SI 1999/3264, reg. 13(3), by substituting the words "4, 4A and 4B" for the words "4 and 4A" with effect from 6 February 2000.
Table in s. 98 (as modified) amended by SI 1999/2383, reg. 6(2), by adding the words "The Stamp Duty Reserve Tax (UK Depositary Interests in Foreign Securities) Regulations 1999" with effect from 25 August 1999.
Table in s. 98 (as modified) substituted by SI 1994/1813, reg. 2(1) and Sch. 1, para. 31(1), (4) and reg. 2(2) and Sch. 2, Pt. II, with effect from 1 September 1994.
Entries previously for 98 substituted by SI 1993/3110, reg. 8(11), with effect from 1 January 1994.
The words "regulation 4" substituted for "reg. 4 and 4A" with effect from 20 October 1997 by SI 1997/2430.

99   Assisting in giving incorrect notice etc.

99   Any person who assists in or induces the giving of any notice under regulation 4, 4A or 4B, or any information under regulation 5, of the Stamp Duty Reserve Tax Regulations 1986 which he knows to be incorrect shall be liable to a penalty not exceeding £3,000.

History – Entry for 99 amended by SI 1999/3264, reg. 13(2), by substituting the words "4, 4A or 4B" for the words "4 or 4A" with effect from 6 February 2000.
Entry for s. 99 substituted by SI 1993/3110, reg. 8(12), with effect from 1 January 1994.
The words "or 4A" inserted with effect from 20 October 1997 by SI 1997/2430.

100 Determination of penalties by officer of board

100(1) Subject to subsection (2) below and except where proceedings for a penalty have been instituted under section 100D below or a penalty has been imposed by the Special Commissioners under section 53 of this Act, an officer of the Board authorised by the Board for the purposes of this section may make a determination imposing a penalty under any provision of this Act and setting it at such amount as, in his opinion, is correct or appropriate.

100(2) Subsection (1) above does not apply where the penalty is a penalty under–

(a)   section 93(1)(a) above, or

(c)   section 98(1)(i) above.

100(3) Notice of a determination of a penalty under this section shall be served on the person liable to the penalty and shall state the date on which it is issued and the time within which an appeal against the determination may be made.

100(4) After the notice of a determination under this section has been served the determination shall not be altered except in accordance with this section or on appeal.

100(5) If it is discovered by an officer of the Board authorised by the Board for the purposes of this section that the amount of a penalty determined under this section is or has become insufficient the officer may make a determination in a further amount so that the penalty is set at the amount which, in his opinion, is correct or appropriate.

History – Entries for s. 100 substituted by SI 1993/3110, reg. 8(13), with effect from 1 January 1994.

100A Provisions supplementary to section 100

100A(1) Where a person who has incurred a penalty has died, a determination under section 100 above which could have been made in relation to him may be made in relation to his personal representatives, and any penalty imposed on personal representatives by virtue of this subsection shall be a debt due from and payable out of his estate.

100A(2) A penalty determined under section 100 above shall be due and payable at the end of the period of thirty days beginning with the date of the issue of the notice of determination.

100A(3) A penalty determined under section 100 above shall for all purposes be treated as if it were tax charged and due and payable.

History – Entries for s. 100A substituted by SI 1993/3110, reg. 8(13), with effect from 1 January 1994.

100B Appeals against penalty determinations

100B(1) An appeal may be brought against the determination of a penalty under section 100 above and, subject to the following provisions of this section, the provisions of the Stamp Duty Reserve Tax Regulations 1986 relating to appeals against determinations specified in notices under regulation 6 of those Regulations ("regulation 6 determinations") shall have effect in relation to an appeal against such a determination as they have effect in relation to appeals against regulation 6 determinations.

100B(2) On an appeal against the determination of a penalty under section 100 above–

(a)   in the case of a penalty which is required to be of a particular amount, the Special Commissioners may–

  (i)   if it appears to them that no penalty has been incurred, set the determination aside,

  (ii)   if the amount determined appears to them to be correct, confirm the determination, or

  (iii)   if the amount determined appears to them to be incorrect, increase or reduce it to the correct amount,

(b)   in the case of any other penalty, the Special Commissioners may–

  (i)   if it appears to them that no penalty has been incurred, set the determination aside,

  (ii)   if the amount determined appears to them to be appropriate, confirm the determination,

  (iii)   if the amount determined appears to them to be excessive, reduce it to such other amount (including nil) as they consider appropriate, or

  (iv)   if the amount determined appears to them to be insufficient, increase it to such amount not exceeding the permitted maximum as they consider appropriate.

100B(3) Without prejudice to regulation 10 of the Stamp Duty Reserve Tax Regulations 1986, an appeal from a decision of the Special Commissioners against the amount of a penalty which has been determined under section 100 above or this section shall lie, at the instance of the person liable to the penalty, to the High Court or, in Scotland, to the Court of Session as the Court of Exchequer in Scotland; and on that appeal the court shall have the like jurisdiction as is conferred on the Special Commissioners by virtue of this section.

History – Entries for s. 100B substituted by SI 1993/3110, reg. 8(13), with effect from 1 January 1994.

100C   Penalty proceedings before Commissioners

100C(1)   An officer of the Board authorised by the Board for the purposes of this section may commence proceedings before the Special Commissioners for any penalty to which subsection (1) of section 100 above does not apply by virtue of subsection (2) of that section.

100C(2)   Proceedings under this section shall be by way of information in writing, made to the Special Commissioners, and upon summons issued by them to the defendant (or defender) to appear before them at a time and place stated in the summons; and they shall hear and decide each case in a summary way.

100C(3)   Any penalty determined by the Special Commissioners in proceedings under this section shall for all purposes be treated as if it were tax charged and due and payable.

100C(4)   An appeal against the determination of a penalty in proceedings under this section shall lie to the High Court or, in Scotland, the Court of Session as the Court of Exchequer in Scotland–

(a)   by any party on a question of law, and

(b)   by the defendant (or, in Scotland, the defender) against the amount of the penalty.

100C(5)   On any such appeal the court may–

(a)   if it appears that no penalty has been incurred, set the determination aside,

(b)   if the amount determined appears to be appropriate, confirm the determination,

(c)   if the amount determined appears to be excessive, reduce it to such other amount (including nil) as the court considers appropriate, or

(d)   if the amount determined appears to be insufficient, increase it to such amount not exceeding the permitted maximum as the court considers appropriate.

History – Entries for s. 100C substituted by SI 1993/3110, reg. 8(13), with effect from 1 January 1994.

100D   Penalty proceedings before court

100D(1)   Where in the opinion of the Board the liability of any person for a penalty arises by reason of the fraud of that or any other person, proceedings for the penalty may be instituted before the High Court or, in Scotland, the Court of Session as the Court of Exchequer in Scotland.

100D(2)   Proceedings under this section which are not instituted (in England, Wales or Northern Ireland) under the Crown Proceedings Act 1947 by and in the name of the Board as an authorised department for the purposes of that Act shall be instituted–

(a)   in England and Wales, in the name of the Attorney General,

(b)   in Scotland, in the name of the Lord Advocate, and

(c)   in Northern Ireland, in the name of the Attorney General for Northern Ireland.

100D(3)   Any proceedings under this section instituted in England and Wales shall be deemed to be civil proceedings by the Crown within the meaning of Part II of the Crown Proceedings Act 1947 and any such proceedings instituted in Northern Ireland shall be deemed to be civil proceedings within the meaning of that Part of that Act as for the time being in force in Northern Ireland.

100D(4)   If in proceedings under this section the court does not find that fraud is proved but consider that the person concerned is nevertheless liable to a penalty, the court may determine a penalty notwithstanding that, but for the opinion of the Board as to fraud, the penalty would not have been a matter for the court.

History – Entries for s. 100D substituted by SI 1993/3110, reg. 8(13), with effect from 1 January 1994.

101   Evidence for purposes of preceding provisions of Part X

101   For the purposes of the preceding provisions of this Part of this Act, any notice under regulation 6 of The Stamp Duty Reserve Tax Regulations 1986 which can no longer be varied or quashed by the Special Commissioners on appeal or by order of any court shall be sufficient evidence of the matters specified.

102   Mitigation of penalties

102   The Board may in their discretion mitigate any penalty, or stay or compound any proceedings for recovery thereof, and may also, after judgment, further mitigate or entirely remit the penalty.

103   Time limits for penalties

103(1)   Where the amount of a penalty is to be ascertained by reference to tax payable by a person, the penalty may be determined by an officer of the Board, or proceedings for the penalty may be commenced before the Special Commissioners or a court–

(a)   at any time within six years after the date on which the penalty was incurred, or

(b)   at any later time within three years after the final determination of the amount of tax by reference to which the amount of the penalty is to be ascertained.

103(3)   A penalty under section 99 of this Act may be determined by an officer of the Board, or proceedings for such a penalty may be commenced before a court, at any time within twenty years after the date on which the penalty was incurred.

103(4)   A penalty to which neither subsection (1) nor subsection (3) above applies may be so determined, or proceedings for such a penalty may be commenced before the Special Commissioners or a court, at any time within six years after the date on which the penalty was incurred or began to be incurred.

History – Entries for s. 103 substituted by SI 1993/3110, reg. 8(14), with effect from 1 January 1994.

104   Saving for criminal proceedings

104   The provisions of this Act shall not, save so far as is otherwise provided, affect any criminal proceedings for any offence.

105   Evidence in cases of fraud and wilful default

105(1)   Statements made or documents produced by or on behalf of a person shall not be inadmissable in any such proceedings as are mentioned in subsection (2) below by reason only that it has been drawn to his attention that–

(a)   in relation to tax, the Board may accept pecuniary settlements instead of instituting proceedings, and

(b)   though no undertaking can be given as to whether or not the Board will accept such a settlement in the case of any particular person, it is the practice of the Board to be influenced by the fact that a person has made a full confession of any fraud or default to which he had been a party and has given full facilities for investigation,

and that he was or may have been induced thereby to make the statements or produce the documents.

105(2)   The proceedings mentioned in subsection (1) above are–

(a)   any criminal proceedings against the person in question for any form of fraud or wilful default in connection with or in relation to tax, and

(b)   any proceedings against him for the recovery of any sum due from him, whether by way of tax or penalty, in connection with or in relation to tax.

Part XI – Miscellaneous and Supplemental

Notes – This heading is to Pt. III/V/VI/VII/VIII/IX/X/XI of the Taxes Management Act 1970. The text below is the modified version of the provision in that Part which is introduced by these regulations.

COMPANIES

108   Responsibility of company officers

108(1)   Everything to be done by a company under the Act shall be done by the company acting through the proper officer of the company, and service on a company of any document under or in pursuance of the Act may be effected by serving it on the proper officer.

108(2)   Tax for which a company which is not a body corporate, or which is a body corporate not incorporated under the Companies Act 1985 or any other enactment forming part of the law of the United Kingdom, or by Charter, is accountable or liable, may, at any time after the tax becomes due, and without prejudice to any other method of recovery, be recovered from the proper officer of the company, and that officer may retain out of any money coming into his hands on behalf of the company sufficient sums to pay that tax, and, so far as he is not so reimbursed, shall be entitled to be indemnified by the company in respect of the liability so imposed on him.

108(3)   For the purposes of this section–

(a)   the **proper officer** of a company which is a body corporate shall be the secretary or person acting as secretary of the company, except that if a liquidator has been appointed for the company the liquidator shall be the proper officer,

(b)   the **proper officer** of a company which is not a body corporate or for which there is no proper officer within paragraph (a) above, shall be the treasurer or the person acting as treasurer, of the company.

VALUATION

111   Valuation of assets: power to inspect

111(1)   If for the purposes of the Act the Board authorise an officer of the Board to inspect any property for the purpose of ascertaining its market value the person having the custody or possession of that property shall permit the officer so authorised to inspect it at such reasonable times as the Board may consider necessary.

111(2)   If any person wilfully delays or obstructs an officer of the Board acting in pursuance of this section he shall be liable on summary conviction to a fine not exceeding level 1 on the standard scale as defined in section 75 of the Criminal Justice Act 1982.

Notes – Level of fine since 1 October 1992 is £200 (Criminal Justice Act 1982, s. 37(2); Criminal Justice Act 1991, s. 17(1), 101(1), Sch. 12, para. 6; SI 1992/333).

DOCUMENTS

114   Want of form or errors not to invalidate notice of determination, etc.

114(1)   A notice of determination, warrant or other proceeding which purports to be made in pursuance of any provision of the Act shall not be quashed, or deemed to be void or voidable, for want of form, or be affected by reason of a mistake, defect or omission therein, if the same is in substance and effect in conformity with or according to the intent and meaning of the Act, and if the person intended to be affected thereby is designated therein according to common intent and understanding.

114(2)   A notice of determination shall not be impeached or affected–

(a)   by reason of a mistake therein as to–

    (i) the name or surname of a person, or

    (ii) any matter specified therein.

INTERPRETATION

118   Interpretation

118(1)   In this Act, unless the context otherwise requires–

"**Act**" includes an Act of the Parliament of Northern Ireland and "**enactment**" shall be construed accordingly,

"**body of persons**" means any body politic, corporate or collegiate, and any company, fraternity, fellowship and society of persons, whether corporate or not corporate,

"**branch or agency**" means any factorship, agency, receivership, branch or management, and "**branch or agent**" shall be construed accordingly,

"**collector**" means any collector of taxes,

"**company**" has the meaning given by section 526(5) of the principal Act (with section 354 of that Act),

"**incapacitated person**" means any infant, person of unsound mind, lunatic, idiot or insane person,

"**neglect**" means negligence or a failure to give any notice, make any return or to produce or furnish any document or other information required by or under the Act,

"**the principal Act**" means the Income and Corporation Taxes Act 1970.

118(2)   *For the purposes of this Act, a person shall be deemed not to have failed to do anything required to be done within a limited time if he did it within such further time, if any, as the Board or the Special Commissioners or officer concerned may have allowed; and where a person had a reasonable excuse for not doing anything required to be done he shall be deemed not to have failed to do it unless the excuse ceased and, after the excuse ceased, he shall be deemed not to have failed to do it if he did it without unreasonable delay after the excuse had ceased.*

STAMP DUTY (EXEMPT INSTRUMENTS) REGULATIONS 1987

(SI 1987/516, as amended by SI 1999/2539.)

Made by the Treasury on 24 March 1987 under s. 87(2) of the Finance Act 1985. Operative from 1 May 1987.

1   These Regulations may be cited as the Stamp Duty (Exempt Instruments) Regulations 1987 and shall come into force on 1st May 1987.

1A   In these regulations **"life policy"** means–

(a)   any policy of insurance on a human life, or on the happening of a contingency dependent upon a human life, except a policy of insurance for a payment only upon the death of a person otherwise than from a natural cause, or

(b)   a grant or contract for the payment of an annuity upon a human life.

History – Reg. 1A inserted by SI 1999/2539, reg. 3, with effect in relation to instruments executed on or after 1st October 1999.

2(1)   An instrument which–

(a)   is executed on or after 1st May 1987,

(b)   is of a kind specified in the Schedule hereto for the purposes of this regulation, and

(c)   is certified by a certificate which fulfils the conditions of regulation 3 to be an instrument of that kind,

shall be exempt from duty under the provisions specified in paragraph (2) of this regulation.

2(2)   The provisions specified are–

(a)   the following paragraphs of Part III of Schedule 13 to the Finance Act 1999–

 (i) paragraph 16 (conveyance or transfer otherwise than on sale),

 (ii) paragraph 17 (declaration of use or trust),

 (iii) paragraph 18 (dispositions in Scotland);

(b)   sections 83(2) and 84(8) of the Finance Act 1985.

History – In reg. 2(2)(a), the words
"the following –" to the end of sub-para. (a) substituted by SI 1999/2539, reg. 4, with effect in relation to instruments executed on or after 1 October 1999. In relation to instruments executed before that date, reg. 2(2)(a) provides as follows:
"(a)   the headings in Schedule 1 to the Stamp Act 1891
 "Conveyance or transfer of any kind not hereinbefore described"; or
 "Disposition in Scotland of any property or of any right or interest therein not described in this Schedule";"

3   The certificate–

(a)   shall be in writing and–

 (i) be included as part of the instrument, or

 (ii) be endorsed upon or, where separate, be physically attached to the instrument concerned;

(b)   shall contain a sufficient description of–

 (i) the instrument concerned where the certificate is separate but physically attached to the instrument, and

 (ii) the category in the Schedule hereto into which the instrument falls;

(c)

 (i) shall be signed by the transferor or grantor or by his solicitor or duly authorised agent, and

 (ii) where it is not signed by the transferor or grantor or by his solicitor, it shall contain a statement by the signatory of the capacity in which he signs, that he is authorised so to sign and that he gives the certificate from his own knowledge of the facts stated in it.

4   The Schedule to these Regulations shall have effect for the specification of instruments for the purposes of regulation 2.

5   An instrument which is certified in accordance with these Regulations shall not be required under section 82(5) or section 84(9) of the Finance Act 1985 to be stamped in accordance with section 12 of the Stamp Act 1891 with a particular stamp denoting that it is duly stamped or that it is not chargeable with any duty.

SCHEDULES

Regulation 4

An instrument which effects any one or more of the following transactions only is an instrument specified for the purposes of regulation 2–

A   The vesting of property subject to a trust in the trustees of the trust on the appointment of a new trustee, or in the continuing trustees on the retirement of a trustee.

B   The conveyance or transfer of property the subject of a specific devise or legacy to the beneficiary named in the will (or his nominee).

C   The conveyance or transfer of property which forms part of an intestate's estate to the person entitled on intestacy (or his nominee).

D   The appropriation of property within section 84(4) of the Finance Act 1985 (death: appropriation in satisfaction of a general legacy of money) or section 84(5) or (7) of that Act (death: appropriation in satisfaction of any interest of surviving spouse and in Scotland also of any interest of issue).

E   The conveyance or transfer of property which forms part of the residuary estate of a testator to a beneficiary (or his nominee) entitled solely by virtue of his entitlement under the will.

F   The conveyance or transfer of property out of a settlement in or towards satisfaction of a beneficiary's interest, not being an interest acquired for money or money's worth, being a conveyance or transfer constituting a distribution of property in accordance with the provisions of the settlement.

G   The conveyance or transfer of property on and in consideration only of marriage to a party to the marriage (or his nominee) or to trustees to be held on the terms of a settlement made in consideration only of the marriage.

H   The conveyance or transfer of property within section 83(1) of the Finance Act 1985 (transfers in connection with divorce etc.)

I   The conveyance or transfer by the liquidator of property which formed part of the assets of the company in liquidation to a shareholder of that company (or his nominee) in or towards satisfaction of the shareholder's rights on a winding-up.

J   The grant in fee simple of an easement in or over land for no consideration in money or money's worth.

K   The grant of a servitude for no consideration in money or money's worth.

L   The conveyance or transfer of property operating as a voluntary disposition inter vivos for no consideration in money or money's worth nor any consideration referred to in section 57 of the Stamp Act 1891 (conveyance in consideration of a debt etc.).

M   The conveyance or transfer of property by an instrument within section 84(1) of the Finance Act 1985 (death: varying disposition).

N   The declaration of any use or trust of or concerning a life policy, or property representing, or benefits arising under, a life policy.

History – Schedule amended by SI 1999/2539, reg. 5, by inserting category N, with effect in relation to instruments executed on or after 1st October 1999.

Statements of practice – SP 6/90: transaction where transferor covenants to pay the debt to which the property is subject is within category L if the transferee does not assume any liability for it; where so certified, transfer etc. may be sent direct to the Land Registry.

Other material – High Court Practice Direction (Chancery 3/89): duplicate orders under the Variation of Trusts Act 1958 affecting voluntary dispositions inter vivos fall within category L.

STAMP DUTY AND STAMP DUTY RESERVE TAX (DEFINITIONS OF UNIT TRUST SCHEME) REGULATIONS 1988

(SI 1988/268)

Made by the Treasury on 18 February 1988 under s. 57 of the Finance Act 1946 and s. 28 of the Finance (No. 2) Act (Northern Ireland) 1946. Operative from 11 March 1988.

1   These Regulations may be cited as the Stamp Duty and Stamp Duty Reserve Tax (Definitions of Unit Trust Scheme) Regulations 1988 and shall come into force on 11th March 1988.

2   In these Regulations unless the context otherwise requires–

"**limited partnership**" means a limited partnership registered under the Limited Partnerships Act 1907 and "**general partner**" and "**limited partner**" have the same meanings as in that Act;

"**limited partnership scheme**" means a unit trust scheme of the description specified in regulation 4;

"**Part III**" means Part III of the Finance (No. 2) Act (Northern Ireland) 1946;

"**Part VII**" means Part VII of the Finance Act 1946;

"**participant**" in relation to a unit trust scheme, has the meaning given by section 75(2) of the Financial Services Act 1986;

"**scheme property**" means, in relation to a unit trust scheme, property of any description, including money, which is held on trust for the participants in the scheme;

"**unit trust scheme**" means a scheme which, apart from these Regulations, is a unit trust scheme for the purposes of Part VII or Part III as the case may be.

3   A unit trust scheme which is–

(a)   a limited partnership scheme, or

(b)   a profit sharing scheme which has been approved in accordance with Part I of Schedule 9 to the Finance Act 1978.

shall be treated as not being a unit trust scheme for the purposes of Part VII or Part III as the case may be.

Notes – For approval of profit sharing schemes, see now ICTA 1988, Sch. 9 (reproduced in *Tax Statutes and Statutory Instruments*, vol. 1A).

4   A unit trust scheme is a limited partnership scheme when the scheme property is held on trust for the general partners and the limited partners in a limited partnership.

STAMP DUTY AND STAMP DUTY RESERVE TAX (DEFINITION OF UNIT TRUST SCHEME) REGULATIONS 1992

(SI 1992/197)

Made on 6 February 1992 by the Treasury, in exercise of the powers conferred on them by s. 57(1A) and (1B) of the Finance Act 1946.

1   These Regulations may be cited as the Stamp Duty and Stamp Duty Reserve Tax (Definition of Unit Trust Scheme) Regulations 1992 and shall come into force on 1st March 1992.

2   A scheme made by the Lord Chancellor in exercise of the powers conferred on him by section 42(1) of the Administration of Justice Act 1982 shall be treated as not being a unit trust scheme for the purposes of Part VII of the Finance Act 1946.

Notes – Administration of Justice Act 1982, s. 42(1) establishes common investment fund.
FA 1946, s. 57 defines "unit trust scheme" for stamp duty purposes.
FA 1986, s. 99(9) defines "unit trust scheme" for stamp duty reserve tax purposes. Schemes to which SI 1992/197 apply will be excepted from these definitions.

ELECTRICITY (NORTHERN IRELAND CONSEQUENTIAL AMENDMENTS) ORDER 1992

(SI 1992/232)

Made on 11 February 1992 by Her Majesty the Queen in exercise of the powers conferred by s. 38(2) of the Northern Ireland Constitution Act 1973 as extended by Sch. 1 to the Northern Ireland Act 1974.

TITLE, COMMENCEMENT AND EXTENT

1(1)   This Order may be cited as the Electricity (Northern Ireland Consequential Amendments) Order 1992.

1(2)   This Order comes into force on such day or days as may be appointed by order made under Article 1(2) of the Electricity (Northern Ireland) Order 1992.

1(3)   Article 2 extends to Northern Ireland only, Article 4 extends to England and Wales and to Scotland and the remaining provisions extend to the whole of the United Kingdom.

STAMP DUTY EXEMPTION FOR CERTAIN CONTRACTS

2   Electricity shall be treated as goods for the purposes of section 59 of the Stamp Act 1891 (certain contracts chargeable as conveyances on sale).

Statutory instruments – SI 1992/231 (NI 1): Head of Department to appoint by order future day on which Order will come into force.

SPECIAL COMMISSIONERS (JURISDICTION AND PROCEDURE) REGULATIONS 1994

(SI 1994/1811, as amended by SI 1999/3292 and SI 2000/288.)

Made on 6 July 1994 by the Lord Chancellor, in exercise of the powers conferred on him by s. 46A and 56B of the Taxes Management Act 1970. Operative from 1 September 1994.

ARRANGEMENT OF REGULATIONS

REGULATION

PART I – INTRODUCTORY

CITATION, COMMENCEMENT AND APPLICATION

1(1)   These Regulations may be cited as the Special Commissioners (Jurisdiction and Procedure) Regulations 1994 and shall come into force on 1st September 1994.

1(2)   These Regulations do not apply in relation to any proceedings in respect of which notice of the place, date and time of the hearing was given, or a summons was issued, prior to 1st September 1994.

INTERPRETATION

2   In these Regulations unless the context otherwise requires–

"**the Board**" means the Commissioners of Inland Revenue;

"**the Clerk**", in relation to any proceedings, means the Clerk to the Special Commissioners;

"**costs**" includes fees, charges, disbursements, expenses and remuneration;

"**the enactments relating to stamp duty**" means section 13(4) of the Stamp Act 1891 and Part II of Schedule 17 to the Finance Act 1999;

"**final determination**" means the decision finally determining any proceedings before a Tribunal;

"**General Commissioners**" shall be construed in accordance with section 2(1) of the Management Act;

"**inspector**" means an inspector of taxes;

"**the Management Act**" means the Taxes Management Act 1970;

"**party**" means a party to any proceedings, and for the purposes of these Regulations–

(a)   where the proceedings relate to an assessment, decision or determination made by the Board, the Board and any inspector or other officer of the Board for the time being concerned with the proceedings shall together constitute a party to those proceedings;

(b)   where the proceedings relate to an assessment, decision or determination made by an inspector or other officer of the Board, that person and any other inspector or other officer of the Board for the time being concerned with the proceedings shall together constitute a party to those proceedings;

and references to "the Revenue" are references to a party within paragraph (a) or, as the case may be, paragraph (b) above;

"**proceedings**" means–

(a)   any appeal to the Special Commissioners under the Taxes Acts;

(b)   any proceedings before the Special Commissioners which under the Taxes Acts are to be heard and determined in the same way as such an appeal;

(c)   any proceedings before the Special Commissioners which relate to a penalty and are not within paragraph (a) or paragraph (b) above;

(d)   any appeal to the Special Commissioners relating to inheritance tax;

(e)   any appeal to the Special Commissioners relating to stamp duty reserve tax;

(f)   any appeal to the Special Commissioners relating to petroleum revenue tax;

(g)   any question in dispute falling to be determined by the Special Commissioners under section 46B or 46C of the Taxes Management Act 1970;

(h)   any appeal which under regulation 19(3) of the General Commissioners (Jurisdiction and Procedure) Regulations 1994 falls to be determined by the Special Commissioners;

(i)   any appeal to the Special Commissioners under the enactments relating to stamp duty;

"proceedings in Northern Ireland" means any proceedings (as defined in this regulation)–

(a)   which fall within the meaning of that expression as defined in section 58(3) of the Management Act, or

(b)   as respects which an appeal from the determination of the Special Commissioners under any enactment lies to a court in Northern Ireland;

"proceedings in Scotland" means any proceedings (as defined in this regulation) which fall to be determined by reference to the law of Scotland;

"Special Commissioners" and **"the Presiding Special Commissioner"** shall be construed in accordance with section 4(1) of the Management Act;

"the Taxes Acts" has the meaning given by section 118(1) of the Management Act;

"Tribunal", in relation to any proceedings, means the Special Commissioner or Special Commissioners by whom the proceedings are heard.

History – Definition of "the enactments relating to stamp duty" inserted by SI 2000/288, reg. 3(a), operative from 1 March 2000.
Definition of "proceedings" amended by SI 1999/3292, reg. 3, by adding paras. (g) and (h), operative from 1 January 2000.
Definition of "proceedings" amended by SI 2000/288, reg. 3(b), by adding para. (i), operative from 1 March 2000.

PART II – PREPARATION FOR A HEARING

LISTING AND NOTICE OF HEARING

3(1)   Except in relation to proceedings under section 100C of the Management Act, or section 249 of the Inheritance Tax Act 1984, any party to proceedings which are to be heard by the Special Commissioners may serve notice on the Clerk that he wishes a date for the hearing to be fixed.

3(2)   On receipt of a notice under paragraph (1) above and on being satisfied that the Special Commissioners have jurisdiction over the proceedings and that he has sufficient particulars of the proceedings and of the issues for determination, the Clerk shall, unless the Presiding Special Commissioner otherwise directs, send notice to each party of the place, date and time of the hearing.

3(3)   Unless the parties otherwise agree or the Tribunal otherwise directs, the date of the hearing specified in a notice under paragraph (2) above shall be not earlier than twenty eight days after the date on which the notice is sent to the parties.

GENERAL POWER TO GIVE DIRECTIONS

4(1)   A Special Commissioner prior to the hearing of any proceedings, for the purpose of enabling the parties to prepare for the hearing or of assisting a Tribunal to determine any of the issues in those proceedings, may on the application of a party or of his own motion, give such directions as he thinks fit.

4(2)   A Tribunal hearing any proceedings may, for the purpose of assisting the determination of any of the issues in those proceedings, on the application of a party or of its own motion, give such directions as it thinks fit.

4(3)   An application by a party for any directions under this Part of these Regulations (otherwise than during a hearing) shall be made in writing to the Clerk and, unless it is accompanied by the written consent of all the parties, shall be served by the Clerk on any other party who might be affected by such directions.

4(4)   If any such other party, by notice to the Special Commissioners and the other party or parties, objects to the directions sought in the application, the Special Commissioner concerned shall consider the objection and, if the application is not one in respect of which the parties are entitled to be heard under these Regulations, shall if he considers it necessary for the determination of the application, give the parties an opportunity to be heard.

SUMMONING OF WITNESSES

5(1)   Where a party to any proceedings requires the attendance of a person at the hearing of those proceedings to give evidence or to produce any document in his possession, custody or power relevant to the subject matter of the proceedings, a Special Commissioner may, on the application of that party, issue a summons (in this regulation referred to as a "witness summons") requiring the attendance of that person at the hearing, or the production of the document, wherever that person may be in the United Kingdom.

5(2)   A witness summons issued under paragraph (1) above shall state the name and address of, or otherwise describe, the person to be served and shall be signed by the Special Commissioner issuing it, and it shall be the responsibility of the party on whose application the summons was issued to serve it on that person.

5(3)   Service of a witness summons under this regulation shall be effected–

(a)   in the case of an individual, by leaving a copy of the summons with him;

(b)   in the case of a body corporate registered in the United Kingdom, by leaving a copy of the summons with the secretary or clerk of the body corporate;

(c)   in the case of a foreign body corporate with a place of business in the United Kingdom, by leaving a copy of the summons with a person authorised to accept service of process on the body corporate.

5(4)   A person who in obedience to a witness summons attends the hearing of any proceedings and gives evidence–

(a)   is a witness of the party on whose application the summons was issued, and

(b)   may not be cross-examined by that party without the leave of the Tribunal hearing the proceedings.

5(5)   Leave shall not be given by a Tribunal under paragraph (4)(b) above unless the Tribunal decides that the witness may be treated as a hostile witness.

5(6)   No person shall be required to attend in obedience to a witness summons unless it has been served on him at least seven days before the hearing or, if it has been served on him within that period, he has informed the Clerk that he accepts such service.

5(7)   No person shall be required to attend and give evidence or to produce any document in obedience to a witness summons unless the party serving the summons either–

(a)   pays or tenders to that person, at the time when the summons is served on him, a sum sufficient to cover his reasonable expenses of travelling to and from, and his attendance at, the hearing, or

(b)   has agreed with that person, prior to service of the summons, to pay such a sum to him at a different time.

5(8)   No person shall be compelled in obedience to a witness summons to give any evidence or produce any document that he could not be compelled to give or produce in an action in a court of law in that part of the United Kingdom by reference to the law of which the proceedings are to be determined.

5(9)   No person who has been appointed as an auditor for the purposes of any enactment or who is a tax adviser within the meaning of section 20B(10) of the Management Act shall be compelled in obedience to a witness summons to produce any document if, having regard to section 20B(9) to (13) of that Act, he would not be obliged to deliver or make available that document in response to a notice under section 20(3) or (8A)(a) of that Act.

5(10)   Where, in the case of any document, a person could under section 20B(14) of that Act comply with such a notice by delivering a copy of parts of the document and making those parts available for inspection, he shall not be compelled in obedience to a witness summons to do more at the hearing than–

(a)   produce a photographic or other facsimile copy of those parts of the document, and

(b)   make those parts of the document available for inspection by the Tribunal.

5(11)   On the application, by notice served on the Clerk, of a person on whom a witness summons has been served, a Special Commissioner may set aside the summons in whole or in part; and the party on whose application the summons was issued shall be entitled to be heard on such an application.

5(12)   This regulation shall apply to proceedings in Scotland–

(a)   with the omission of paragraphs (4) and (5) above;

(b)   with the substitution for references to issuing a summons and to a witness summons of references to issuing a citation and to a witness citation.

AGREEMENT OF DOCUMENTS

6   If a party agrees a document for the purposes of any proceedings he shall be deemed, subject to the terms of the agreement, to admit for the purposes of those proceedings–

(a)   that the document was written and signed or executed by the person by whom, and on the date on which, it purports to have been, and

(b)   if it purports to be a copy of another document, that it is a true copy of that document,

but, subject to any enactment or rule of law, in the absence of an express admission or agreement, he shall not be deemed to admit the truth of the contents of that document.

PROCEEDINGS TO BE HEARD TOGETHER OR IN SUCCESSION

7(1)   Where two or more proceedings have been brought before, but have not yet been heard by, the Special Commissioners or have been brought before, but have not yet been heard by, the Special Commissioners and any General Commissioners and it appears to the Presiding Special Commissioner–

(a)   that some common issue arises in both or all of them, or

(b)   that both or all of them are relevant to some common issue,

the Presiding Special Commissioner may, of his own motion or on application by a party to any of those proceedings, direct that those proceedings be heard at the same time or consecutively and by the same Tribunal.

7(2)   A direction shall not be given under paragraph (1) above except on notice sent to all the parties to the proceedings in question who shall be entitled to be heard before any direction is given.

7(3)   On the giving of a direction under paragraph (1) above, the Clerk shall send notice of the date and terms of the direction to all the parties to the proceedings and, where one or more of the proceedings in question was pending before the General Commissioners, to the Clerk to the division or, as the case may be, each division of General Commissioners concerned.

7(4)   References in this regulation to proceedings pending before the General Commissioners are references to proceedings in relation to which the General Commissioners (Jurisdiction and Procedure) Regulations 1994 apply.

JOINING OF ADDITIONAL PARTIES

8(1)   If it appears to a Special Commissioner, whether on the application of a party or otherwise, that it is desirable that any person other than the Revenue be made a party to any proceedings, he may direct that such person be joined as a party in the proceedings and may give such further directions for giving effect to, or in connection with, the direction as he thinks fit.

8(2)   Where–

(a)   pursuant to a direction under paragraph (1) above a person is joined as a party in any proceedings by reason of a question arising in those proceedings which may affect his liability to tax or in which he otherwise has an interest, and

(b)   pursuant to an application under regulation 15(2) by another party the hearing or, as the case may be, part of the hearing of the proceedings is to take place in private,

he shall not be entitled, unless all the other parties consent, to be present at the hearing of the proceedings or, as the case may be, the part of the hearing which is to take place in private except during such part as relates to that question, and a Tribunal shall, if necessary, hear any such question separately from the rest of the proceedings.

8(3)   Subject to paragraph (4) below, on the application of a person who has been joined as a party in the circumstances specified in paragraph (2) above, a Special Commissioner may, if he is satisfied that it would be to the convenience of the parties to do so, direct that the proceedings be transferred to the General Commissioners for the division in which the applicant ordinarily resided at the date of the application.

8(4)   No application may be made under paragraph (3) above in any case where the proceedings in question under any enactment lie only to the Special Commissioners and not to the General Commissioners.

PRELIMINARY HEARING

9(1) Where it appears to a Special Commissioner that any proceedings would be facilitated by holding a preliminary hearing, he may, on the application of a party or of his own motion, give directions for such a hearing to be held.

9(2) The Clerk shall give to the parties not less than fourteen days notice, or such shorter notice as the parties agree or the Special Commissioner sees fit to impose, of the time and place of the preliminary hearing.

9(3) On a preliminary hearing the Special Commissioner–

(a) shall give all such directions as appear necessary or desirable so as to enable the proceedings to be disposed of expeditiously, effectively and fairly;

(b) may, if the parties so agree, determine the proceedings without any further hearing.

POWER OF SPECIAL COMMISSIONERS TO OBTAIN INFORMATION

10(1) A Special Commissioner on a preliminary hearing of any proceedings, or a Tribunal in the course of the hearing of any proceedings, may serve notice on any party, other than the Revenue, directing that party within the time specified in the notice–

(a) to deliver to him or, as the case may be, the Tribunal such particulars as he or the Tribunal may consider are required for the purposes of determining any of the issues in the proceedings, and

(b) to make available for inspection by him or the Tribunal, or by an officer of the Board, all such books, accounts or other documents in the party's possession or power as may be specified or described in the notice, being books, accounts or other documents which, in the opinion of the Special Commissioner or Tribunal issuing the notice, contain or may contain information relating to the subject matter of the proceedings.

10(2) Any officer of the Board may at all reasonable times inspect and take copies of, or extracts from, any particulars delivered under paragraph (1)(a) above, and the Special Commissioner or Tribunal who issued the notice, or any officer of the Board, may take copies of, or extracts from, any books, accounts or other documents made available for inspection under paragraph (1)(b) above.

POSTPONEMENTS AND ADJOURNMENTS

11(1) A Special Commissioner may postpone the hearing of any proceedings, and the Clerk shall send notice to the parties of the place, date and time of the postponed hearing.

11(2) A Tribunal may from time to time adjourn the hearing of any proceedings and, subject to paragraph (3) below, the Clerk shall send notice to the parties of the place, date and time of the adjourned hearing.

11(3) If the place, date and time of the adjourned hearing are announced before the adjournment in the presence of the parties, no notice need be sent by the Clerk under paragraph (2) above.

11(4) When any hearing is adjourned in order that further information or evidence may be obtained, a Tribunal may give directions regarding the disclosure of such information or evidence to the parties prior to the resumption of the hearing.

EXPERT EVIDENCE

12(1) Unless a Special Commissioner otherwise directs, no expert evidence may be adduced by a party at the hearing of any proceedings unless–

(a) he has agreed with the other party or parties that the substance of the evidence shall be disclosed in the form of a written report or opinion in advance of the hearing and not later than such date as is specified in the agreement, and the substance of the evidence has been so disclosed, or

(b) where no such agreement has been reached or where the substance of the evidence has not been so disclosed, an application is made to a Special Commissioner under paragraph (2) below by the party seeking to adduce the evidence to determine whether a direction should be given under paragraph (3) below, and the party seeking to adduce the evidence complies with a direction given under that paragraph.

12(2) An application under this paragraph–

(a)   shall be made not later than twenty one days after the date on which notice is sent by the Clerk under regulation 3(2) or, if the Special Commissioner so permits, at any later time prior to or in the course of the hearing, and

(b)   shall state whether the party is willing to disclose the substance of the evidence prior to its being given at the hearing and, if not, the reasons for his objection.

12(3)   On an application under paragraph (2) above, unless he considers that there are special reasons for not doing so, the Special Commissioner shall direct that the substance of the evidence shall be disclosed in the form of a written report or opinion to such other parties and within such period as he may specify.

12(4)   This regulation shall not apply to proceedings in Scotland.

PART III – HEARING AND DETERMINATION OF PROCEEDINGS

CONSTITUTION AND SITTINGS OF TRIBUNAL

13(1)   Any one, two or three of the Special Commissioners shall constitute a Tribunal.

13(2)   Where any proceedings are before a Tribunal which comprises two or three Special Commissioners–

(a)   if the Presiding Special Commissioner is one of them, he shall preside at the hearing unless he otherwise directs and, if he is not, one of them shall be nominated by him to preside;

(b)   the proceedings may be continued by any one or more of them if all the parties give their consent and unless the Presiding Special Commissioner otherwise directs.

REPRESENTATION AT HEARING

14   At the hearing of any proceedings before a Tribunal–

(a)   a party other than the Revenue may be represented by any person whether or not legally qualified, except that if in a particular case the Tribunal is satisfied that there are good and sufficient reasons for doing so, it may refuse to permit a particular person, other than one who is legally qualified or who has been admitted a member of an incorporated society of accountants, to represent a party at the hearing;

(b)   the Revenue may be represented by a barrister, advocate, solicitor or any officer of the Board.

HEARINGS IN PUBLIC OR IN PRIVATE

15(1)   Subject to paragraph (2) below, hearings before a Tribunal shall be in public.

15(2)   Any party to proceedings may, by notice to the Clerk, apply for the hearing, or any part of the hearing, to take place in private; and where such application is made, the hearing or, as the case may be, the part of the hearing which is the subject of the application, shall take place in private–

(a)   if the application is made by a party other than the Revenue, or

(b)   if the application is made by the Revenue and a Special Commissioner so directs.

15(3)   The following persons shall be entitled to the [sic] present at the hearing of any proceedings before a Tribunal notwithstanding that the hearing or part of the hearing takes place in private, and may remain present during the deliberations of the Tribunal but shall take no part in those deliberations–

(a)   the Presiding Special Commissioner or any of the Special Commissioners notwithstanding that they do not constitute the Tribunal or part of the Tribunal for the purpose of the hearing;

(b)   the clerk and any of the staff of the Special Commissioners;

(c)   a member of the Council on Tribunals or of the Scottish Committee of that Council in the capacity of member;

(d)   a member of the Judicial Studies Board or one of its committees in the capacity of member.

15(4)   A Tribunal, with the consent of the parties, may permit any other person to be present at the hearing of proceedings before it which is to take place, or part of which is to take place, in private.

FAILURE OF PARTIES TO ATTEND HEARING

16(1)   If a party fails to attend or to be represented at a hearing of which he has been duly notified, the Tribunal may–

(a)   unless it is satisfied that there is good and sufficient reason for such absence, hear and determine the proceedings in the absence of the party or his representative, or

(b)   postpone or adjourn the hearing.

16(2)   Before deciding to hear and determine any proceedings in the absence of a party or his representative, the Tribunal shall consider any representations in writing or otherwise submitted by or on behalf of that party in response to the notice of hearing and shall give any party present at the hearing an opportunity to be heard in regard to those representations.

PROCEDURE AND EVIDENCE AT HEARING

17(1)   At the beginning of the hearing of any proceedings the Tribunal shall, except where it considers it unnecessary to do so, explain the order of proceeding which it proposes to adopt.

17(2)   The Tribunal shall conduct the hearing in such manner as it considers most suitable to the clarification and determination of the issues before it and generally to the just handling of the proceedings, and, so far as appears to it appropriate, shall seek to avoid formality in its procedure.

17(3)   The parties shall be heard in such order as the Tribunal shall determine and shall be entitled–

(a)   to give evidence,

(b)   to call witnesses,

(c)   to question any witnesses including other parties who give evidence, and

(d)   to address the Tribunal both on the evidence and generally on the subject matter of the proceedings.

17(4)   In assessing the truth and weight of any evidence, the Tribunal may take account of its nature and source, and the manner in which it is given.

17(5)   Evidence before the Tribunal may be given orally or, if the Tribunal so directs, by any affidavit or any statement made or recorded in a document, but at any stage of the hearing the Tribunal may, on the application of any party or of its own motion, require the personal attendance as a witness of–

(a)   the maker of an affidavit, or

(b)   the maker of such a statement, or

(c)   in the case of an oral statement recorded in a document, the person by whom the statement was so recorded.

17(6)   The Tribunal may receive evidence of any fact which appears to the Tribunal to be relevant to the subject matter of the proceedings notwithstanding that such evidence would be inadmissible in proceedings before a court of law in that part of the United Kingdom by reference to the law of which the proceedings before the Tribunal are to be determined, but, save in cases where claims for privilege are allowed (including, in proceedings in Scotland, claims for protection from disclosure by virtue of any rule of law relating to the confidentiality of communications), it shall not refuse to admit any evidence which would be admissible in such proceedings.

17(7)   The Tribunal may require any witness to give evidence on oath or affirmation and for that purpose there may be administered an oath or affirmation in due form.

DECISIONS OF TRIBUNAL

18(1)   Where proceedings are before a Tribunal which comprises two or three Special Commissioners, any decision of the Tribunal shall be made by the votes of the Special Commissioners comprising that Tribunal.

18(2)   Where proceedings are before a Tribunal which comprises two Special Commissioners, in the event of an equality of votes, the Special Commissioner presiding at the hearing shall be entitled to a second or casting vote.

18(3)   Where proceedings are before a Tribunal which comprises three Special Commissioners, any decision or direction of the tribunal shall be made by the votes of the majority of the Special Commissioners comprising that Tribunal.

18(4)   The final determination may be given orally by a Tribunal at the end of the hearing or may be reserved and in either event shall be recorded forthwith in a document which, subject to paragraph (7) below, shall contain a statement of the facts found by the Tribunal and the reasons for the determination and shall be signed and dated by the Tribunal.

18(5)   A Tribunal may, after reserving the final determination–

(a)   give a written decision in principle on one or more issues arising in the proceedings, and

(b)   adjourn the making of the final determination until after its decision in principle has been issued and such further questions arising from that decision have been agreed by the parties or, failing agreement, decided by the Tribunal after having heard the parties.

18(6)   A decision in principle given under paragraph (5)(a) above shall contain, in relation to the matters covered by the decision–

(a)   a statement of the facts found by the Tribunal, and

(b)   the reasons for the decision.

18(7)   In any case where a decision in principle has been given under paragraph (5)(a) above, the document recording the final determination need not contain a statement of the facts and reasons referred to in paragraph (4) above except in so far as is necessary in order to explain the final determination of the Tribunal on matters not covered in the decision in principle.

18(8)   The Clerk shall send a copy of the document recording a decision in principle, and a copy of the document recording the final determination, to each party.

18(9)   Except where the final determination is given at the end of the hearing, it shall be treated as having been made on the date on which a copy of the document recording it is sent to the parties under paragraph (8) above.

18(10)   Every copy of the document recording the final determination sent to the parties under this regulation, other than a document recording a final determination made in accordance with regulation 23(2)(b), shall be accompanied by a notification of the provisions of–

(a)   the Management Act,

(b)   these Regulations, and

(c)   rules of court, relating to appeals from the Special Commissioners, and of the time within which, and the manner in which, such appeals shall be made.

History – In reg. 18(10), words ", other than...regulation 23(2)(b)," inserted by SI 1999/3292 reg. 4 operative from 1 January 2000.

REVIEW OF TRIBUNAL'S DECISION IN PRINCIPLE OR FINAL DETERMINATION

19(1)   If, on the application of a party or of its own motion, a Tribunal is satisfied that–

(a)   a decision in principle or the final determination was wrongly made as a result of an administrative error on the part of the Clerk or any of the staff of the Special Commissioners or a party, or

(b)   a party, who was entitled to be heard at a hearing but failed to appear or to be represented, had good and sufficient reason for failing to appear or to be represented, or

(c)   accounts or other information relevant to a party's case had been sent to the Clerk or to the appropriate inspector or other officer of the Board prior to the hearing of the proceedings but had not been received by the Tribunal until after the hearing,

the Tribunal may review and set aside or vary the decision in principle or final determination (or both the decision in principle and the final determination).

19(2)   An application for the purposes of paragraph (1) above shall be made to the Tribunal not later than fourteen days after the date on which a copy of the document recording the decision in principle or, as the case may be, the final determination was sent to the parties under regulation 18(8), or by such later time as the Tribunal may allow, and shall be in writing stating the grounds in full.

19(3)   Where the Tribunal proposes to review of its own motion the decision in principle or final determination, it shall serve notice of that proposal on the parties not later than fourteen days after the date on which a copy of the document recording the decision in principle or, as the case may be, the final determination was sent to the parties under regulation 18(8).

19(4)   The parties shall have an opportunity to be heard on a review, or in relation to any application or proposal for review, under this regulation and the review shall be determined by the Tribunal which decided the case or, where it is not practicable for it to be heard by that Tribunal, by a Tribunal appointed by the Presiding Special Commissioner; and if, having reviewed the decision in principle or final determination, the Tribunal sets aside that decision or determination, it shall substitute such decision or determination as it thinks fit or order a rehearing before either the same or a differently constituted Tribunal.

19(5)   Regulation 18 shall apply to a decision by a Tribunal varying a decision in principle or final determination, or substituting a new decision in principle or final determination, as it applies to a decision in principle or final determination.

PUBLICATION OF DECISIONS IN PRINCIPLE OR FINAL DETERMINATIONS

20(1)   The Presiding Special Commissioner may make arrangements for the publication of reports of such of the decisions in principle and final determinations given by Tribunals as he considers appropriate.

20(2)   Where the Presiding Special Commissioner considers it appropriate to publish a report of a decision in principle or final determination pursuant to paragraph (1) above, and that decision or determination relates to proceedings the whole or part of which were heard in private in accordance with regulation 15(2), he shall ensure that the report is in a form which so far as possible prevents the identification of any person whose affairs are dealt with in the decision or determination.

ORDERS FOR COSTS

21(1)   Subject to paragraph (2) below, a Tribunal may make an order awarding the costs of, or incidental to, the hearing of any proceedings by it against any party to those proceedings (including a party who has withdrawn his appeal or application) if it is of the opinion that the party has acted wholly unreasonably in connection with the hearing in question.

21(2)   No order shall be made under paragraph (1) above against a party without first giving that party an opportunity of making representations against the making of the order.

21(3)   An order under paragraph (1) above may require the party against whom it is made to pay to the other party or parties the whole or part of the costs incurred by the other party or parties of, or incidental to, the hearing of the proceedings, such costs to be taxed if not otherwise agreed.

21(4)   Any costs required to be taxed pursuant to an order under this regulation shall be taxed in the county court according to such of the scales prescribed by rules of court for proceedings in the county court as may be directed by the order or, in the absence of any such direction, by the county court.

21(5)   In the application of this regulation to proceedings in Scotland–

(a)   any reference to costs shall be construed as a reference to expenses;

(b)   in paragraph (4) above, for the references to the county court there shall be substituted references to the sheriff court and for the reference to proceedings there shall be substituted a reference to civil proceedings.

21(6)   In the application of this regulation to proceedings in Northern Ireland, for paragraphs (3) and (4) above there shall be substituted–

"**21(3)**   An order under paragraph (1) above may require the party against whom it is made to pay to the other party or parties the whole or part of the costs incurred by that other party or parties of, or incidental to, the hearing of the proceedings, such costs to be taxed in the county court if not determined by the Tribunal or otherwise agreed.

21(4)   Any costs which may be determined by the Tribunal under paragraph (3) above shall be determined by reference to the scales prescribed by rules of court for proceedings in the county court and any costs required to be taxed pursuant to an order under this regulation shall be taxed in the same manner as costs in equity suits or proceedings in the county court.".

PART IV – SPECIAL PROCEDURE

PROCEEDINGS RELATING TO TAX ON CHARGEABLE GAINS

22(1)   Where the market value of an asset on a particular date or the apportionment of an amount or value is a material question in any proceedings relating to tax on chargeable gains, the Tribunal hearing the proceedings shall, if so required by any party, record in its decision in principle or final determination that market value or apportionment.

22(2) The final determination on an appeal of the market value of an asset on a particular date or of the apportionment of any amount or value may be proved in any proceedings relating to tax on chargeable gains by a certificate stating the material particulars signed by–

(a) an inspector where the appeal was settled by agreement, or

(b) the Clerk where the Special Commissioners determined the appeal, or

(c) the clerk or registrar of another tribunal where the material question was determined by that other tribunal in accordance with section 46D or 47B of the Management Act or section 222(4A) of the Inheritance Tax Act 1984,

and a document purporting to be such a certificate may be received in evidence in any such proceedings without further proof.

22(3) In this regulation the expression **"final determination on an appeal"** shall be construed in accordance with regulation 11(2) of the Capital Gains Tax Regulations 1967, and the expression **"material question in any proceedings"** shall be construed in accordance with regulation 15(a) of those Regulations.

History – In reg. 22(2)(c), "46D" was substituted by SI 1999/3292 reg. 5, operative from 1 January 2000.

REFERENCES OF QUESTIONS TO OTHER TRIBUNALS

23(1) A question in an appeal which is required to be determined in accordance with section 46D or 47B of the Taxes Management Act 1970 or section 222(4A) of the Inheritance Tax Act 1984 shall be referred to the appropriate tribunal by the Tribunal before whom the appeal is brought or, if the hearing of the appeal has not yet begun, by an inspector or other officer of the Board.

23(2) Where any question in an appeal has been referred to another tribunal in accordance with paragraph (1) above, the Tribunal before whom the appeal is brought–

(a) shall finally determine the remaining question or questions in the appeal without awaiting the determination of the question referred to the other tribunal, and

(b) shall make a final determination of the appeal (in accordance with regulation 18) once all the questions in the appeal have been finally determined.

23(3) The reference in paragraph (2)(b) above to all the questions in the appeal having being finally determined is a reference to a time when no further appeals in relation to those questions under any enactment are pending.

History – Reg. 23 substituted by SI 1999/3292 reg. 6, operative from 1 January 2000.

PENALTY FOR FAILURE TO COMPLY WITH TRIBUNAL DIRECTION

24(1) If any party or other person fails to comply with any direction of a Tribunal under these Regulations including a direction in a notice under regulation 10, the Tribunal may summarily determine a penalty against that party or other person not exceeding £10,000.

24(2) Subject to paragraphs (6) to (11) of regulation 5, if a person on whom a summons is served under that regulation–

(a) fails to attend in obedience to the summons, or

(b) attends, but refuses to be sworn or to affirm, or

(c) refuses to answer any lawful question, or

(d) refuses to produce any document which he has been required to produce,

the Tribunal may summarily determine a penalty against him not exceeding £10,000.

24(3) Subject to paragraph (4) and (5) below, any penalty determined by the Tribunal under paragraph (1) or (2) above shall for all purposes be treated as if it were tax charged in an assessment and due and payable.

24(4) Any penalty determined by the Tribunal under paragraph (1) or (2) above in proceedings relating to–

(a) an appeal under section 222 of the Inheritance Tax Act 1984, or

(b) an appeal under regulation 8 of the Stamp Duty Reserve Tax Regulations 1986,

shall for all purposes be treated as if it were tax determined by the Board and due and payable.

24(5) Any penalty determined by the Tribunal under paragraph (1) or (2) above in proceedings relating to an appeal under the enactments relating to stamp duty shall for all purposes be treated as if it were a penalty, other than a penalty under section 15B of the Stamp Act 1891 (penalty on late stamping), determined by an officer of the Board, and due and payable, under those enactments.

History – Reg. 24(5) was inserted by SI 2000/288 reg. 4, operative from 1 March 2000.

PART V – MISCELLANEOUS

IRREGULARITIES

25(1) Any irregularity resulting from any failure to comply with any provision of these Regulations or with any direction given by a Tribunal before the Tribunal has reached its decision shall not of itself render the proceedings void.

25(2) Where any such irregularity comes to the attention of a Tribunal, the Tribunal, before reaching its decision, may, and if it considers that any person may have been prejudiced by that irregularity shall, give such directions as it thinks just to cure or waive the irregularity.

25(3) Clerical mistakes in any document recording a direction or decision of a Tribunal, or errors arising in such a document from an accidental slip or omission, may be corrected by the Special Commissioner presiding at the hearing or any other of the Special Commissioners comprising the Tribunal, or by the Presiding Special Commissioner if all the Special Commissioners comprising the Tribunal have died or ceased to be Special Commissioners, by certificate under his hand.

NOTICES

26 Every notice required by these Regulations shall be in writing unless a Tribunal authorises it to be given orally.

SERVICE

27(1) Any notice or other document (other than a summons under regulation 5) required or authorised by these Regulations to be sent or delivered to, or served on, any person shall be duly sent or delivered to, or served on, that person–

(a)   if it is sent to him at his proper address by post; or

(b)   if it is sent to him at that address by facsimile transmission or other similar means which produce a document containing a text of the communication, in which event the document shall be regarded as sent when it is received in a legible form; or

(c)   if it is delivered to him or left at his proper address.

27(2) Any such document may–

(a)   in the case of a body corporate, be sent or delivered to, or left with, the secretary or clerk of that body;

(b)   in the case of a foreign body corporate, be sent or delivered to, or left with, the person authorised to accept service of process on it;

(c)   in the case of a partnership, be sent or delivered to, or left with, any partner;

(d)   in the case of an unincorporated association other than a partnership, be sent or delivered to, or left with, any member of the governing body of the association.

27(3) For the purposes of this regulation, a person's proper address is–

(a)   in the case of the secretary or clerk of a body corporate registered in the United Kingdom, the address of the registered or principal office of that body corporate;

(b)   in the case of the person authorised to accept service of process on a foreign body corporate, the address of the principal office or place of business of that body corporate in the United Kingdom;

(c)   in the case of the Special Commissioners or their Clerk, the address of the Clerk;

(d)   in the case of any other person, the usual or last known address of that person.

SUBSTITUTED SERVICE

28 If any person to or on whom any notice or other document (other than a summons under regulation 5) is required to be sent, delivered or served for the purposes of these Regulations cannot be found or has died and has no known representative, or is out of the United Kingdom, or if for any other reason service on him cannot be readily effected, a Tribunal may dispense with the requirement that the notice or other document be sent or delivered to, or served on him or may make an order for substituted service on such other person or in such other form (whether by advertisement in a newspaper or otherwise) as the Tribunal may think fit.

STAMP DUTY RESERVE TAX (TRADEPOINT) REGULATIONS 1995

(SI 1995/2051)

Made on 1 August 1995 by the Treasury, in exercise of the powers conferred on them by s. 116(3) and (4) and 117 of the Finance Act 1991. Operative from 25 August 1995.

CITATION AND COMMENCEMENT

1   These Regulations may be cited as the Stamp Duty Reserve Tax (Tradepoint) Regulations 1995 and shall come into force on 25th August 1995.

INTERPRETATION

2   In these Regulations unless the context otherwise requires–

"**Board of directors**" means the Board of directors of Tradepoint;

"**clearing participant**" means a member (as defined by this regulation) who is also a member of The London Clearing House Limited and who as such is permitted by the Board of directors and that clearing house to clear transactions made on the Exchange for a traded security;

"**client**" means a person who gives instructions to a participant for equity securities to be purchased or, as the case may be, sold on the Exchange;

"**equity securities**" means stocks and shares which are issued or raised by a company but does not include stocks and shares issued or raised by a company not incorporated in the United Kingdom unless–

(a)   they are registered in a register kept in the United Kingdom by or on behalf of the company, or

(b)   in the case of shares, they are paired, within the meaning of section 99(6A) of the Finance Act 1986, with shares issued by a company incorporated in the United Kingdom;

"**the Exchange**" means Tradepoint Investment Exchange;

"**member**" in relation to Tradepoint means a person approved by the Board of directors as a participant;

"**nominee**" means a person whose business is or includes holding equity securities as a nominee for The London Clearing House Limited acting in its capacity as a person providing clearing services in connection with a transaction made on the Exchange, or as a nominee for a clearing participant (as the case may be);

"**non-clearing participant**" means a participant other than a clearing participant;

"**participant**" means a participant in the Exchange;

"**section 117**" means section 117 of the Finance Act 1991;

"**Tradepoint**" means Tradepoint Financial Networks plc.

PRESCRIBED PERSONS FOR THE PURPOSES OF SECTION 117

3   For the purposes of section 117–

(a)   The London Clearing House Limited is a recognised clearing house which is prescribed;

(b)   Tradepoint is a recognised investment exchange which is prescribed and, in relation to that exchange, a member who is a clearing participant is prescribed as a description of member of that exchange.

PRESCRIBED CIRCUMSTANCES FOR THE PURPOSES OF SECTION 117

4(1)   In the circumstances prescribed by paragraph (2) below, a charge to stamp duty reserve tax shall be treated as not arising.

4(2)   The circumstances prescribed are where, in connection with a transaction made on the Exchange–

(a)   equity securities of a particular kind are agreed to be transferred–

(i)   from a clearing participant or a nominee of a clearing participant to another clearing participant or nominee, or

    (ii) from a non-clearing participant or a client to a clearing participant or a nominee of a clearing participant, or

    (iii) from a clearing participant or a nominee of a clearing participant to The London Clearing House Limited or to a nominee of that clearing house, or

    (iv) from a person other than a clearing participant to The London Clearing House Limited or to a nominee of that clearing house, as a result of a failure by a clearing participant to fulfil his obligations in respect of the transaction concerned to transfer equity securities to The London Clearing House Limited or to a nominee of that clearing house, or

    (v) from The London Clearing House Limited or a nominee of that clearing house to a clearing participant or a nominee of a clearing participant; and

(b)   the person to whom those securities are agreed to be transferred under any of the agreements specified in sub-paragraph (a) above (**"the relevant agreement"**) is required on receipt of those shares to transfer equity securities under a matching agreement to another person or, in the case of an agreement falling within paragraph (iv) of that sub-paragraph, would have been so required if the failure referred to in that paragraph had not occurred.

4(3)   In paragraph (2) above–

(a)   **"matching agreement"** means an agreement under which–

    (i) the equity securities agreed to be transferred are of the same kind as the equity securities agreed to be transferred under the relevant agreement, and

    (ii) the number and transfer price of the equity securities agreed to be transferred are identical to the number and transfer price of the equity securities agreed to be transferred under the relevant agreement;

(b)   references to The London Clearing House Limited are references to that clearing house in its capacity as a person providing clearing services in connection with a transaction made on the Exchange;

(c)   references to a clearing participant are references to a clearing participant in his capacity as such.

CONSEQUENTIAL PROVISION

5(1)   Equity securities which are the subject of an agreement specified in regulation 4(2)(a) shall be dealt with by a clearing participant who is a party to the agreement in a separate designated account, and not otherwise.

5(2)   In paragraph (1) above **"designated account"** means an account designated by The London Clearing House Limited for a clearing participant in connection with the equity securities concerned.

STAMP DUTY AND STAMP DUTY RESERVE TAX (PENSION FUNDS POOLING SCHEMES) REGULATIONS 1996

(SI 1996/1584)

Made on 19 June 1996 by the Treasury, in exercise of the powers conferred on them by s. 57(1A) of the Finance Act 1946, and s. 28 of the Finance (No. 2) Act (Northern Ireland) 1946. Operative from 11 July 1996.

1   These regulations may be cited as the Stamp Duty and Stamp Duty Reserve Tax (Pension Funds Pooling Schemes) Regulations 1996 and shall come into force on 11th July 1996.

2   In these regulations–

    "pension funds pooling scheme" means a unit trust scheme of the description specified in regulation 4 of the Income Tax (Pension Funds Pooling Schemes) Regulations 1996;

    "unit trust scheme" has the meaning given by section 75(8) of the Financial Services Act 1986.

3   A unit trust scheme which is a pension funds pooling scheme shall be treated as not being a unit trust scheme for the purposes of Part VII of the Finance Act 1946 or Part III of the Finance (No. 2) Act (Northern Ireland) 1946 as the case may be.

STAMP DUTY (PRODUCTION OF DOCUMENTS) (NORTHERN IRELAND) REGULATIONS 1996

(SI 1996/2348)

Made on 9 September 1996 by the Commissioners of Inland Revenue, in exercise of the powers conferred on them by s. 244(2) and s. 245(1), (5) and (7) of the Finance Act 1994. Operative from 4 November 1996.

CITATION AND COMMENCEMENT

1   These Regulations may be cited as the Stamp Duty (Production of Documents)(Northern Ireland) Regulations 1996 and shall come into force on 4th November 1996.

INTERPRETATION

2   In these Regulations unless the context otherwise requires–

"**exempt instrument**" shall be construed in accordance with regulation 4(l);

"**grant**", "**lease**" and "**lessee**" shall be construed in accordance with section 245(5) of the Finance Act 1994;

"**long leasehold interest**", in relation to a transaction, means a leasehold interest which, at the time of that transaction, was for a term of 25 years or more before expiry;

"**registered land**" has the meaning given by section 45(1) of the Interpretation Act (Northern Ireland), 1954;

"**relevant instrument**" means an instrument which a transferee, lessee or proposed lessee is required to produce to the commissioners of Inland Revenue under subsection (1) of section 244;

"**section 244**" means section 244 of the Finance Act 1994;

"**short leasehold interest**", in relation to a transaction, means a leasehold interest which, at the time of that transaction, was for a term of less than 25 years before expiry.

PRESCRIBED PARTICULARS

3   The particulars to be given in a document produced pursuant to subsection (2) of section 244 are those prescribed by the Schedule to these Regulations.

CLASSES OF EXEMPT INSTRUMENT

4(1)   Paragraphs (2) and (3) prescribe classes of instrument which are exempt instruments for the purposes of section 245(1) of the Finance Act 1994.

4(2)   The class of instrument prescribed by this paragraph is any instrument effecting any transfer on sale of any freehold interest in land in Northern Ireland where the instrument has the characteristics specified in paragraph (4).

4(3)   The class of instrument prescribed by this paragraph is any instrument effecting any transfer on sale of any lease of land in Northern Ireland where the instrument has the characteristics specified in paragraph (4).

4(4)   The characteristics specified are that–

(a)   the instrument is executed on or after 4th November 1996;

(b)   by reason of the amount or value of the consideration for the transfer effected by the instrument, no stamp duty is chargeable on the instrument; and

(c)   the instrument is certified in accordance with section 7(4) of the Finance Act (Northern Ireland), 1958.

FURNISHING OF DOCUMENTS RELATING TO REGISTERED LAND

5(1)   This regulation applies in the case of an exempt instrument which effects a transfer–

(a)   of land which is registered land, or

(b)   of land which is not registered land, and the case is one in which, as a result of the transfer, the first registration of the ownership of the land becomes compulsory by virtue of section 24 of the Land Registration Act (Northern Ireland) 1970.

5(2)   The transferee shall produce to the Registrar of Titles with the exempt instrument such a document as is mentioned in subsection (2) of section 244 and contains the particulars prescribed by the Schedule to these Regulations; and the Registrar of Titles shall furnish that document to the Commissioner of Valuation for Northern Ireland.

5(3)   In paragraph (2) **"the Registrar of Titles"** shall be construed in accordance with section 1(4) of the Land Registration Act (Northern Ireland) 1970.

FURNISHING OF DOCUMENTS RELATING TO UNREGISTERED LAND

6(1)   This regulation applies in the case of an exempt instrument which effects a transfer of land which is not registered land, and the case is one in which, as a result of the transfer, the first registration of the ownership of that land does not become compulsory by virtue of section 24 of the Land Registration Act (Northern Ireland) 1970.

6(2)   The transferee shall produce to the Registrar of Deeds with the exempt instrument such a document as is mentioned in subsection (2) of section 244 and contains the particulars prescribed by the Schedule to these Regulations; and the Registrar of Deeds shall furnish that document to the Commissioner of Valuation for Northern Ireland.

6(3)   In paragraph (2) **"the Registrar of Deeds"** means the officer having the control and management of the registry of deeds; and **"the registry of deeds"** has the meaning given by section 46(2) of the Interpretation Act (Northern Ireland), 1954.

SCHEDULE

Regulations 3, 5(2), 6(2)

PRESCRIBED PARTICULARS TO BE GIVEN IN A DOCUMENT PRODUCED PURSUANT TO SUBSECTION (2) OF SECTION 244 OR REGULATION 5(2) OR 6(2)

The particulars prescribed are particulars–

(1)   of the description of the relevant instrument;

(2)   of the date of the relevant instrument;

(3)   of the names and addresses of the transferor and the transferee or the lessor and the lessee;

(4)   of the situation and postal address of the land to which the transaction relates, including–

    (a)   in any case relating to registered land, the Folio Number, County, Townland and Area,

    (b)   in any case relating to unregistered land or land which is part of a Folio, the Folio Number and Townland, and

    (c)   if necessary for the identification of the land, a photocopy of a plan indicating boundaries and areas, and stating the size of the areas and whether those areas are measured in acres or hectares;

(5)   showing whether the interest transferred or granted by the transaction is a freehold interest, a long leasehold interest or a short leasehold interest;

(6)   showing whether the transfer or grant relates to–

    (a)   a dwelling house,

    (b)   commercial property,

    (c)   development land,

    (d)   farmland, or

    (e)   other land,
    and, in the case of a transfer or grant which relates to other land, specifying the nature of that other land;

(7)   in any case where the transfer or grant relates to commercial property, showing whether that transfer or grant relates to a single plot of land for the construction of a dwelling;

(8) in any case where the interest transferred or granted is a freehold interest or a long leasehold interest, specifying the amount of the consideration, and in any case where that amount relates to a number of separate items, the allocation of that amount among those items;

(9) showing whether the consideration for the transaction includes value added tax, and if so the amount of that value added tax;

(10) in any case where the interest transferred or granted is a short leasehold interest, specifying–

    (a) the term of the lease,

    (b) the date of commencement of the term,

    (c) the rent reserved,

    (d) the dates on which the rent is payable,

    (e) any capital payment made in connection with the transfer or grant of the lease,

    (f) whether the lease makes provision for rent reviews, and if so the dates of those rent reviews,

    (g) whether the lessee is responsible for repairs and insurance,

    (h) whether the lessee is responsible for any other matters and, if so, specifying those other matters, and

    (i) any other covenants affecting the value of the lease;

(11) of any debt released by the transaction, the amount of that debt and the person to whom that debt was owed;

(12) of the name and address of any selling or letting agent;

(13) of the name of the solicitor for the transferor or lessor;

(14) in a case where the document is signed by an individual who is not the transferee, lessee or proposed lessee, of the name, address and telephone number of that individual.

STAMP DUTY AND STAMP DUTY RESERVE TAX (OPEN-ENDED INVESTMENT COMPANIES) REGULATIONS 1997

(SI 1997/1156, as amended by SI 1999/1467 and SI 1999/3261)

Made on 3 April 1997 by the Treasury, in exercise of the powers conferred on them by s. 152 of the Finance Act 1995. Operative from 28 April 1997.

ARRANGEMENT OF REGULATIONS

REGULATION

9. AMALGAMATION OF AN AUTHORISED UNIT TRUST WITH AN OPEN-ENDED INVESTMENT COMPANY – EXEMPTION FROM STAMP DUTY CHARGE

10. AMALGAMATION OF AN AUTHORISED UNIT TRUST WITH AN OPEN-ENDED INVESTMENT COMPANY – EXEMPTION FROM STAMP DUTY RESERVE TAX CHARGE

11. DISAPPLICATION OF SECTION 42 OF THE FINANCE ACT 1930

12. DISAPPLICATION OF SECTIONS 75 TO 77 OF THE FINANCE ACT 1986

CITATION AND COMMENCEMENT

1 These Regulations may be cited as the Stamp Duty and Stamp Duty Reserve Tax (Open-ended Investment Companies) Regulations 1997 and shall come into force on 28th April 1997.

INTERPRETATION

2 In these Regulations–

"authorised corporate director", **"open-ended investment company"**, **"owner of shares"** and **"scheme property"** have the meanings given by subsection (10) of section 468 of the Income and Corporation Taxes Act 1988, read with subsections (11) to (18) of that section, as those subsections are added in relation to open-ended investment companies by regulation 10(4) of the Open-ended Investment Companies (Tax) Regulations 1997; and accordingly references in subsections (11) to (16) of that section to the **"Tax Acts"** shall be construed as if they included references both to the enactments relating to stamp duty and to the enactments relating to stamp duty reserve tax;

"authorised unit trust" means a unit trust scheme in the case of which an order under section 78 of the Financial Services Act 1986 is in force;

"the enactments relating to stamp duty" and **"the enactments relating to stamp duty reserve tax"** have the meanings given by section 152(6) of the Finance Act 1995;

"the relevant enactments relating to stamp duty or stamp duty reserve tax" means–

(a)   sections 88(1), 90(1) to (1B), 99(5A) and (5B) of the Finance Act 1986, and

(b)   section 122(1) and (2) of, and paragraphs 1 to 9, 14 and 17 of Schedule 19 to, the Finance Act 1999;

"trust instrument", **"trust property"**, **"unit"**, **"unit holder"** and **"unit trust scheme"** have the meanings given by paragraph 14 of Schedule 19 to the Finance Act 1999.

History – Definitions of "the Board", "open-ended investment company" and "authorised corporate director", and "the Taxes Act" omitted by SI 1999/3261, reg. 3(2), with effect from 6 February 2000.
Definitions of "authorised corporate director", "open-ended investment company", "owner of shares" and "scheme property", "the enactments relating to stamp duty" and "the enactments relating to stamp duty reserve tax", "the relevant enactments relating to stamp duty or stamp duty reserve tax" inserted by SI 1999/3261, reg. 3, with effect from 6 February 2000.
Definitions of "trust instrument", "trust property", "unit", "unit holder" and "unit trust scheme" substituted for the definitions of "unit" and "unit trust scheme" by SI 1999/3261, reg. 3(5), with effect from 6 February 2000.

STAMP DUTY AND STAMP DUTY RESERVE TAX TREATMENT OF OPEN-ENDED INVESTMENT COMPANIES

3 Subject to the modifications set out in regulations 4 to 4B, the relevant enactments relating to stamp duty or stamp duty reserve tax shall have effect in relation to open-ended investment companies in a manner corresponding to that in which they have effect in relation to unit trust schemes.

History – Reg. 3 substituted by SI 1999/3261, reg. 4, with effect from 6 February 2000. Former wording of reg. 3 is as follows:

"APPLICATION OF SECTION 57(1A) AND (1B) OF THE FINANCE ACT 1946 TO OPEN-ENDED INVESTMENT COMPANIES
"**3** Section 57(1A) and (1B) of the Finance Act 1946 (regulatory powers) shall have effect in relation to open-ended investment companies as they have effect in relation to unit trust schemes."

GENERAL MODIFICATIONS OF THE RELEVANT ENACTMENTS RELATING TO STAMP DUTY OR STAMP DUTY RESERVE TAX

4(1) Subject to the modifications specified in regulations 4A and 4B, the relevant enactments relating to stamp duty or stamp duty reserve tax shall be modified as follows in relation to open-ended investment companies.

4(2) References, however expressed, to–

(a)   a unit trust scheme, or

(b)   the trustees of a unit trust scheme,

shall have effect as if they were references to an open-ended investment company.

4(3)   References, however expressed, to the managers of a unit trust scheme shall have effect as if they were references to the authorised corporate director of an open-ended investment company.

4(4)   References, however expressed, to–

(a)   a unit under a unit trust scheme, or

(b)   an entitlement to a share of the trust property,

shall have effect as if they were references to a share in an open-ended investment company.

4(5)   References, however expressed, to–

(a)   a unit holder, or

(b)   a person entitled to a unit,

shall have effect as if they were references to the owner of a share in an open-ended investment company.

4(6)   References, however expressed, to trust property shall have effect as if they were references to scheme property.

4(7)   References, however expressed, to a trust instrument shall have effect as if they were references to an instrument incorporating an open-ended investment company.

History – Reg. 4 substituted by SI 1999/3261, reg. 5, with effect from 6 February 2000. Former wording of reg. 4 is as follows:

"REPURCHASE OF SHARES BY AUTHORISED CORPORATE DIRECTOR"

4(1)   Where a person authorises or requires the authorised corporate director of an open-ended investment company to treat him as no longer the owner of a share in that company and does not authorise or require the authorised corporate director to treat another person as the owner of that share, he shall be deemed, for the purposes of section 87 of the Finance Act 1986, to agree with the authorised corporate director to transfer that share to him; and any instrument whereby he gives the authority or makes the requirement shall be deemed for the purposes of the enactments relating to stamp duty to be a conveyance or transfer of the share on sale.

4(2)   Where the authorised corporate director of an open-ended investment company transfers a share in that open-ended investment company which was transferred to him within the immediately preceding two months–

(a)   any stamp duty payable in respect of the instrument of transfer relating to the transfer of the share shall not exceed 50p;

(b)   where there is no instrument of transfer, section 87 of the Finance Act 1986 shall not apply as regards the agreement to transfer.

4(3)   Where a share in an open-ended investment company is transferred to the authorised corporate director of that open-ended investment company and, before the expiration of two months from the date of the transfer, the authorised corporate director certifies that the events specified in paragraph (4) have occurred, the Board shall–

(a)   on the application of the person by or on behalf of whom stamp duty was paid in respect of the instrument of transfer or, where there was no instrument of transfer, stamp duty reserve tax was paid in relation to the agreement to transfer, and

(b)   on the production to them of the instrument of transfer (if any) and of the authorised corporate director's certificate, refund the duty or, as the case may be, the tax.

4(4)   The events specified in this paragraph are that–

(a)   the certificate (if any) in respect of the share has been cancelled,

(b)   as a consequence of the transfer, a proportionate part of the investments of the open-ended investment company concerned has been realised and the property of the company diminished accordingly, and

(c)   the share is extinguished and the authorised corporate director has no power to transfer any other share in lieu thereof.

4(5)   Paragraphs (1) to (4) shall have effect in relation to an authorised corporate director irrespective of whether he is acting on behalf of the open-ended investment company concerned or on his own account."

MODIFICATIONS OF SCHEDULE 19 TO THE FINANCE ACT 1999

4A(1)   Schedule 19 to the Finance Act 1999 shall be modified as follows in relation to open-ended investment companies.

4A(2)   In paragraph 4–

(a)   in sub-paragraph (1)–

     (i) for the words "units of the same class as the unit in question" there shall be substituted the word "shares", and

     (ii) for the words "units of that class" there shall be substituted the word "shares";

(b)   in sub-paragraph (3) for the words "units of the class" in both places where they occur there shall be substituted the word "shares";

(c)   in sub-paragraph (4) for the words "units of the class in question" there shall be substituted the word "shares";

(d)   after sub-paragraph (5) there shall be added the following sub-paragraph–

     "(6) Where there is more than one class of shares in an open-ended investment company, the proportionate reduction of tax under this paragraph shall be calculated as if all the shares in the company had been converted into shares of a single class."

4A(3) In paragraph 14–

(a)   for sub-paragraph (2) there shall be substituted the following sub-paragraph–

"(2) "**Open-ended investment company**" has, subject to paragraph 17, the meaning given by subsection (10) of section 468 of the Income and Corporation Taxes Act 1988, read with subsections (11) to (18) of that section, as those subsections are added in relation to open-ended investment companies by regulation 10(4) of the Open-ended Investment Companies (Tax) Regulations 1997; and accordingly references in subsection (11) to (16) of that section to the "Tax Acts" shall be construed as if they included references both to the enactments relating to stamp duty and to the enactments relating to stamp duty reserve tax; and those enactments shall have effect accordingly."

(b)   in sub-paragraph (3) the definitions of "trust instrument", "trust property", "unit" and "unit holder" shall be omitted.

4A(4)   In paragraph 17 sub-paragraph (4) shall be omitted.

History – Reg. 4A inserted by SI 1999/3261, reg. 5, with effect from 6 February 2000.

MODIFICATIONS OF THE FINANCE ACT 1986

4B(1)   Section 99 of the Finance Act 1986 (general interpretation provisions) shall be modified as follows in relation to open-ended investment companies.

4B(2)   In subsection (5A) paragraph (a) and the word "or" following it shall be omitted.

History – Reg. 4B inserted by SI 1999/3261, reg. 5, with effect from 6 February 2000.

BEARER SECURITIES ISSUED BY AN OPEN-ENDED INVESTMENT COMPANY IN A FOREIGN CURRENCY

5   Bearer securities issued by an open-ended investment company in a currency other than sterling shall be treated, for the purposes of the enactments relating to stamp duty and the enactments relating to stamp duty reserve tax, as if the securities had been issued in sterling.

History – In reg. 5 the words "the enactments relating to stamp duty reserve tax" substituted for the words "of Part IV of the Finance Act 1986" by SI 1999/3261, reg. 6, with effect from 6 February 2000.

SHARES IN OPEN-ENDED INVESTMENT COMPANIES DEALING IN INTEREST-BEARING INVESTMENTS

6   [Omitted by SI 1999/3261, reg. 7.]

History – Reg. 6 omitted by SI 1999/3261, reg. 7, with effect from 6 February 2000. Reg. 6 formerly read as follows:
"**6(1)**   Stamp duty shall not be chargeable on any transfer of shares of an open-ended investment company to which this regulation applies.
6(2)   This regulation applies to any open-ended investment company under whose prospectus or instrument of incorporation funds of the company–
(a)   cannot be invested in such a way that income can arise to the company which will be chargeable to tax otherwise than under Case III of Schedule D, and
(b)   cannot be invested in any investment on the transfer of which ad valorem stamp duty would be chargeable."

CONVERSION OF AN AUTHORISED UNIT TRUST TO AN OPEN-ENDED INVESTMENT COMPANY – EXEMPTION FROM STAMP DUTY CHARGE

7(1)   Stamp duty shall not be chargeable on an instrument transferring any property which is subject to the trusts of an authorised unit trust ("**the target trust**") to an open-ended investment company ("**the acquiring company**") if the conditions set out in paragraph (2) are fulfilled.

7(2)   Those conditions are that–

(a)   the transfer forms part of an arrangement for the conversion of an authorised unit trust to an open-ended investment company, whereby the whole of the available property of the target trust becomes the whole of the property of the acquiring company;

(b)   under the arrangement all the units in the target trust are extinguished;

(c)   the consideration under the arrangement consists of or includes the issue of shares ("the consideration shares") in the acquiring company to the persons who held the extinguished units;

(d)   the consideration shares are issued to those persons in proportion to their holdings of the extinguished units; and

(e)   the consideration under the arrangement does not include anything else other than the assumption or discharge by the acquiring company of liabilities of the trustees of the target trust.

7(3) An instrument on which stamp duty is not chargeable by virtue only of this regulation shall not be taken to be duly stamped unless it is stamped with the duty to which it would be liable but for this regulation or it has, in accordance with section 12 of the Stamp Act 1891, been stamped with a particular stamp denoting that it is not chargeable with any duty.

7(4) In this regulation and in regulations 8 to 10 **"the whole of the available property of the target trust"** means the whole of the property subject to the trusts of the target trust, other than any property which is retained for the purpose of discharging liabilities of the trustees of the target trust.

7(5) For the purposes of this regulation and regulations 8 to 10 each of the parts of an umbrella scheme (and not the scheme as a whole) shall be regarded as an authorised unit trust; and **"umbrella scheme"** has the same meaning as in section 468 of the Income and Corporation Taxes Act 1988.

CONVERSION OF AN AUTHORISED UNIT TRUST TO AN OPEN-ENDED INVESTMENT COMPANY – EXEMPTION FROM STAMP DUTY RESERVE TAX CHARGE

8(1) Section 87 of the Finance Act 1986 shall not apply as regards an agreement to transfer securities which constitute property which is subject to the trusts of an authorised unit trust (**"the target trust"**) to an open-ended investment company (**"the acquiring company"**) if the conditions set out in paragraph (2) are fulfilled.

8(2) Those conditions are that–

(a)   the agreement forms part of an arrangement for the conversion of an authorised unit trust to an open-ended investment company, whereby the whole of the available property of the target trust becomes the whole of the property of the acquiring company;

(b)   under the arrangement all the units in the target trust are extinguished;

(c)   the consideration under the arrangement consists of or includes the issue of shares (**"the consideration shares"**) in the acquiring company to the persons who held the extinguished units;

(d)   the consideration shares are issued to those persons in proportion to their holdings of the extinguished units; and

(e)   the consideration under the arrangement does not include anything else other than the assumption or discharge by the acquiring company of liabilities of the trustees of the target trust.

8(3) Where–

(a)   stamp duty is not chargeable on an instrument by virtue of regulation 7(1), or

(b)   section 87 of the Finance Act 1986 does not apply as regards an agreement by virtue of paragraph (1) of this regulation,

section 87 of the Finance Act 1986 shall not apply as regards an agreement, or a deemed agreement, to transfer a unit to the managers of the target trust which is made in order that the unit may be extinguished under the arrangement mentioned in regulation 7(2)(b) or, as the case may be, paragraph (2)(b) of this regulation.

AMALGAMATION OF AN AUTHORISED UNIT TRUST WITH AN OPEN-ENDED INVESTMENT COMPANY – EXEMPTION FROM STAMP DUTY CHARGE

9(1) Stamp duty shall not be chargeable on an instrument transferring any property which is subject to the trusts of an authorised unit trust (**"the target trust"**) to an open-ended investment company (**"the acquiring company"**) if the conditions set out in paragraph (2) are fulfilled.

9(2) Those conditions are that–

(a)   the transfer forms part of an arrangement for the amalgamation of an authorised unit trust with an open-ended investment company, whereby the whole of the available property of the target trust becomes part (but not the whole) of the property of the acquiring company;

(b)   under the arrangement all the units in the target trust are extinguished;

(c)   the consideration under the arrangement consists of or includes the issue of shares (**"the consideration shares"**) in the acquiring company to the persons who held the extinguished units;

(d)   the consideration shares are issued to those persons in proportion to their holdings of the extinguished units; and

(e)   the consideration under the arrangement does not include anything else other than the assumption or discharge by the acquiring company of liabilities of the trustees of the target trust.

9(3)   An instrument on which stamp duty is not chargeable by virtue only of this section shall not be taken to be duly stamped unless it is stamped with the duty to which it would be liable but for this regulation or it has, in accordance with section 12 of the Stamp Act 1891, been stamped with a particular stamp denoting that it is not chargeable with any duty.

9(4)   This regulation applies to any instrument which is executed–

(a)   on or after the date of coming into force of these Regulations.

History – In reg. 9(4) the words:
"; but (b) before 1st July 1999."which appeared after para. (a) omitted by the Stamp Duty and Stamp Duty Reserve Tax (Open-ended Investment Companies)(Amendment) Regulations 1999 (SI 1999/1467), reg. 3 which came into force on 16 June 1999.

AMALGAMATION OF AN AUTHORISED UNIT TRUST WITH AN OPEN-ENDED INVESTMENT COMPANY – EXEMPTION FROM STAMP DUTY RESERVE TAX CHARGE

10(1)   Section 87 of the Finance Act 1986 shall not apply as regards an agreement to transfer securities which constitute property which is subject to the trusts of an authorised unit trust (**"the target trust"**) to an open-ended investment company (**"the acquiring company"**) if the conditions set out in paragraph (2) are fulfilled.

10(2)   Those conditions are that–

(a)   the agreement forms part of an arrangement for the amalgamation of an authorised unit trust with an open-ended investment company, whereby the whole of the available property of the target trust becomes part (but not the whole) of the property of the acquiring company;

(b)   under the arrangement all the units in the target trust are extinguished;

(c)   the consideration under the arrangement consists of or includes the issue of shares (**"the consideration shares"**) in the acquiring company to the persons who held the extinguished units;

(d)   the consideration shares are issued to those persons in proportion to their holdings of the extinguished units; and

(e)   the consideration under the arrangement does not include anything else other than the assumption or discharge by the acquiring company of liabilities of the trustees of the target trust.

10(3)   Where–

(a)   stamp duty is not chargeable on an instrument by virtue of regulation 9(1), or

(b)   section 87 of the Finance Act 1986 does not apply as regards an agreement by virtue of paragraph (1) of this regulation,

section 87 of the Finance Act 1986 shall not apply as regards an agreement, or a deemed agreement, to transfer a unit to the managers of the target trust which is made in order that the unit may be extinguished under the arrangement mentioned in regulation 9(2)(b) or, as the case may be, paragraph (2)(b) of this regulation.

10(4)   This regulation applies–

(a)   to an agreement which is not conditional, if the agreement is made on or after the date of coming into force of these Regulations; and

(b)   to a conditional agreement, if the condition is satisfied on or after the date of coming into force of these Regulations.

History – In reg. 10(4) the words " but before 1st July 1999" which appeared (twice) after the word "Regulations" in para. (a) and (b) omitted by the Stamp Duty and Stamp Duty Reserve Tax (Open-ended Investment Companies) (Amendment) Regulations 1999 (SI 1999/1467), reg. 4 which came into force on 16 June 1999.

DISAPPLICATION OF SECTION 42 OF THE FINANCE ACT 1930

11   Section 42 of the Finance Act 1930 (relief from transfer stamp duty in case of transfer of property as between associated companies) shall not apply as regards any beneficial interest in property that is conveyed or transferred to or from an open-ended investment company.

DISAPPLICATION OF SECTIONS 75 TO 77 OF THE FINANCE ACT 1986

12   Sections 75 to 77 of the Finance Act 1986 (acquisition by a company of another company's undertaking) shall not apply as regards open-ended investment companies.

STAMP DUTY AND STAMP DUTY RESERVE TAX (INVESTMENT EXCHANGES AND CLEARING HOUSES) REGULATIONS 1997

(SI 1997/2429)

Made on 8 October 1997 by the Treasury, in exercise of the powers conferred on them by s. 116 and 117 of the Finance Act 1991. Operative from 20 October 1997.

CITATION, COMMENCEMENT AND EFFECT

1(1)   These Regulations may be cited as the Stamp Duty and Stamp Duty Reserve Tax (Investment Exchanges and Clearing Houses) Regulations 1997 and shall come into force on 20th October 1997.

1(2)   These Regulations shall have effect–

(a)   as respects the charge to stamp duty, in relation to instruments executed on or after 20th October 1997;

(b)   as respects the charge to stamp duty reserve tax–

(i)   in the case of an agreement to transfer equity securities which is not conditional, where the agreement is made on or after 20th October 1997;

(ii)   in the case of an agreement to transfer equity securities which is conditional, where the condition is satisfied on or after that date.

INTERPRETATION

2   In these Regulations unless the context otherwise requires–

"**the Board of directors**" means the Board of directors of LIFFE (A & M);

"**clearing member**" means a member (as defined by this regulation) who is also a member of The London Clearing House Limited and who as such is permitted by the Board of directors and that clearing house to clear transactions made on LIFFE for an equity security;

"**equity securities**" means stocks and shares which are issued or raised by a company but does not include stocks and shares issued or raised by a company not incorporated in the United Kingdom unless–

(a)   they are registered in a register kept in the United Kingdom by or on behalf of the company, or

(b)   in the case of shares, they are paired, within the meaning of section 99(6A) of the Finance Act 1986, with shares issued by a company incorporated in the United Kingdom;

"**LIFFE**" means The London International Financial Futures and Options Exchange;

"**LIFFE (A & M)**" means LIFFE Administration and Management;

"**member**" means a member of LIFFE (A & M) who is recognised as such by the Board of directors;

"**non-clearing**" member means a member other than a clearing member;

"**option**" means an option to buy or sell securities which is listed by and traded on LIFFE.

PRESCRIPTION OF RECOGNISED INVESTMENT EXCHANGE AND RECOGNISED CLEARING HOUSE

3   For the purposes of sections 116 and 117 of the Finance Act 1991–

(a)   LIFFE (A & M) is a recognised investment exchange which is prescribed;

(b)   The London Clearing House Limited is a recognised clearing house which is prescribed.

TRANSFERS OF SECURITIES TO THE LONDON CLEARING HOUSE LIMITED – PRESCRIBED CIRCUMSTANCES

4(1) In the circumstances prescribed by paragraph (2), a charge to stamp duty or to stamp duty reserve tax shall be treated as not arising.

4(2) The circumstances prescribed are where, as a result of the exercise of options, equity securities of a particular kind are transferred or issued or agreed to be transferred or issued–

(a) to The London Clearing House Limited; or

(b) to a person whose business is or includes holding such securities as a nominee for The London Clearing House Limited.

4(3) References in this regulation and in regulation 5 to The London Clearing House Limited are references to that clearing house in its capacity as a person providing clearing services in connection with a transaction made on LIFFE.

TRANSFERS OF SECURITIES TO OR FROM MEMBERS OF LIFFE – PRESCRIBED CIRCUMSTANCES

5(1) In the circumstances prescribed by paragraph (2), a charge to stamp duty or to stamp duty reserve tax shall be treated as not arising.

5(2) The circumstances prescribed are where, in order to meet an obligation to receive securities resulting from the exercise of options, equity securities of a particular kind are transferred or agreed to be transferred–

(a) from a non-clearing member or a nominee of a non-clearing member to a clearing member or a nominee of a clearing member; or

(b) from The London Clearing House Limited or a nominee of that clearing house to a clearing member or a nominee of a clearing member.

5(3) References in paragraph (2) to a clearing member are references to a clearing member in his capacity as such.

REVOCATION OF THE STAMP DUTY AND STAMP DUTY RESERVE TAX (INVESTMENT EXCHANGES AND CLEARING HOUSES) REGULATIONS 1992

6 The Stamp Duty and Stamp Duty Reserve Tax (Investment Exchanges and Clearing Houses) Regulations 1992 are hereby revoked as respects instruments and agreements referred to in regulation 1(2).

THE EUROPEAN SINGLE CURRENCY (TAXES) REGULATIONS 1998

(SI 1998/3177)

Made on the 17 February 1998 and laid before the House of Commons on 17 February 1998 Operative from 1 January 1999

PART I – INTRODUCTORY

CITATION AND COMMENCEMENT

1 These Regulations may be cited as the European Single Currency (Taxes) Regulations 1998 and shall come into force on 1st January 1999.

[Only those definitions which are relevant to stamp duty and stamp duty reserve tax are reproduced],

INTERPRETATION

2(1) In these Regulations unless the context otherwise requires–

"euro" means the single currency adopted or proposed to be adopted as its currency by a member State in accordance with the Treaty establishing the European Community;

"euroconversion" has the meaning given by regulation 3;

"member State" means a member State other than the United Kingdom;

"**participating member State**" means a member State that adopts the euro as its currency;

"**reconventioning**" in relation to a relevant asset means a change, consequent on simple redenomination, in the terms of the asset as a result of which the new terms become aligned to the prevailing terms of equivalent marketable relevant assets denominated in euro;

"**relevant asset**" means a debt (whether or not a debt on a security), a long-term capital asset, a long-term capital liability, an option, a qualifying contract, or any commodity or financial futures;

"**renominalisation**" in relation to a relevant asset means a change, consequent on simple redenomination, in the minimum nominal amount in which the asset can be held or traded to a new round amount;

"**security**" has the meaning given by section 132(3)(b) of the 1992 Act;

"**simple redenomination**" means the conversion of the currency in which an asset, liability, contract or instrument is expressed from the currency of a participating member State into euro, and any rounding of the resulting amount to the nearest euro cent;

2(2) [neither relevant nor reproduced],

DEFINITION OF EUROCONVERSION

3(1) "**Euroconversion**" means–

(a) in relation to any currency, or an amount expressed in any currency, of a participating member State, the conversion or restating of that currency or that amount into euro and any rounding of the resulting amount within a euro;

(b) in relation to any asset, liability, contract or instrument–

(i) the simple redenomination of that asset, liability, contract or instrument, or

(ii) in the case of a relevant asset, the simple redenomination of that asset accompanied by either or both of renominalisation and reconventioning, or

(iii) the substitution (whether by way of exchange, conversion, replacement or otherwise) for the asset, liability, contract or instrument of an equivalent replacement asset, liability, contract or instrument.

3(2) An equivalent replacement asset, liability, contract or instrument means an asset, liability, contract or instrument whose amount, terms and conditions are identical to what it is reasonable to assume would be the amount, terms and conditions of the original asset, liability, contract or instrument were it to undergo a simple redenomination, or (in the case of a relevant asset) a simple redenomination accompanied by either or both of renominalisation and reconventioning.

3(3) For the purposes of paragraphs (1) and (2) a simple redenomination is accompanied (in the case of a relevant asset) by renominalisation or reconventioning if either–

(a) the renominalisation or reconventioning is effected simultaneously, or

(b) it is effected within a period of time following the simple redenomination which is such as to enable it reasonably to be inferred that the renominalisation or reconventioning is associated with the simple redenomination.

PART II – DEDUCTIBILITY OF COSTS OF EUROCONVERSION OF SHARES AND OTHER SECURITIES

INTERPRETATION

4 [Neither relevant nor reproduced.]

TRADING COMPANIES

5 [Neither relevant nor reproduced.]

INVESTMENT COMPANIES AND INSURANCE COMPANIES - DEEMED EXPENSES OF MANAGEMENT

6 [Neither relevant nor reproduced.]

PART III – EXCHANGE GAINS AND LOSSES, INTEREST RATE AND CURRENCY CONTRACTS AND OPTIONS, DEBT CONTRACTS AND OPTIONS, AND RELEVANT DISCOUNTED SECURITIES

DEFERRAL OF UNREALISED GAINS

7 [Neither relevant nor reproduced.]

INTEREST RATE CONTRACTS (INCLUDING OPTIONS) - CHANGE IN RATE OF INTEREST

8 [Neither relevant nor reproduced.]

CURRENCY CONTRACTS (INCLUDING OPTIONS) - CHANGE IN RATE OF INTEREST

9 [Neither relevant nor reproduced.]

CURRENCY CONTRACTS (INCLUDING OPTIONS) - CONVERSION INTO EURO

10 [Neither relevant nor reproduced.]

DEBT CONTRACTS (INCLUDING OPTIONS) - CONVERSION INTO EURO

11 [Neither relevant nor reproduced.]

EXCHANGE OR CONVERSION OF RELEVANT DISCOUNTED SECURITES

12 [Neither relevant nor reproduced.]

PART IV – AGREEMENTS FOR SALE AND REPURCHASE OF SECURITIES

INTERPRETATION

13 [Neither relevant nor reproduced.]

REPLACEMENT OF SECURITIES IN A EUROCONVERSION

14 [Neither relevant nor reproduced.]

PAYMENT OR BENEFIT RECEIVED BY INTERIM HOLDER ON EUROCONVERSION

15 [Neither relevant nor reproduced.]

PAYMENT DEEMED TO BE MADE BY INTERIM HOLDER ON EUROCONVERSION

16 [Neither relevant nor reproduced.]

RENOMINALISATION RESULTING IN NEW MINIMUM DENOMINATION IN WHICH SECURITIES CAN BE HELD OR TRADED

17 [Neither relevant nor reproduced.]

PAYMENT MADE OR DEEMED TO BE MADE BY INTERIM HOLDER IN RESPECT OF EUROCONVERSION – CHARGEABLE GAINS CONSEQUENCES

18 [Neither relevant nor reproduced.]

EUROCONVERSION – LOAN RELATIONSHIPS CONSEQUENCES

19 [neither relevant nor reproduced]

PART V – STOCK LENDING ARRANGEMENTS

INTERPRETATION

20   [Neither relevant nor reproduced.]

DEEMED CAPITAL PAYMENT

21   [Neither relevant nor reproduced.]

RENOMINALISATION RESULTING IN NEW MINIMUM AMOUNT IN WHICH SECURITIES CAN BE HELD OR TRADED

22   [Neither relevant nor reproduced.]

PAYMENT MADE BY BORROWER TO LENDER IN RESPECT OF EUROCONVERSION – CHARGEABLE GAINS CONSEQUENCES

23   [Neither relevant nor reproduced.]

PART VI – REPURCHASES AND STOCK LENDING – STAMP DUTY AND STAMP DUTY RESERVE TAX

INTERPRETATION

24   In this Part of these Regulations **"capital payment"** means any payment on the euroconversion of securities other than any interest, dividend or other annual payment payable in respect of the securities.

REPLACEMENT OF STOCK IN A EUROCONVERSION

25(1)   This regulation applies in a case where–

(a)   there is an arrangement involving the transfer of stock to which subsection (1)(a) of section 80C of the Finance Act 1986 (repurchases and stock lending – exemption from stamp duty) applies, and

(b)   there is a euroconversion of that stock (**the old stock**), effected wholly or in part by the issue of new stock to replace the old stock.

25(2)   The new stock shall be regarded, for the purposes of section 80C of the Finance Act 1986, as stock of the same kind and amount as the old stock.

REPLACEMENT OF CHARGEABLE SECURITIES IN A EUROCONVERSION

26(1)   This regulation applies in a case where–

(a)   there is an arrangement involving the transfer of chargeable securities to which subsection (1)(a) of section 89AA of the Finance Act 1986 (repurchases and stock lending – exemption from stamp duty reserve tax) applies, and

(b)   there is a euroconversion of those chargeable securities (**the old chargeable securities**), effected wholly or partly by the issue of new chargeable securities to replace the old chargeable securities.

26(2)   The new chargeable securities shall be regarded, for the purposes of section 89AA of the Finance Act 1986, as chargeable securities of the same kind and amount as the old chargeable securities.

PAYMENT OR BENEFIT RECEIVED BY TRANSFEREE OF STOCK ON EUROCONVERSION

27(1)   This regulation applies in a case where–

(a)   there is an arrangement involving the transfer of stock to which subsection (1) of section 80C of the Finance Act 1986 applies,

(b)   a capital payment would, but for the arrangement, be received by the person referred to as B in that section or by his nominee on the euroconversion of that stock,

(c)   neither the person referred to as A in that section nor his nominee is required under the arrangement to pay to B or to B's nominee an amount equivalent to the amount of that capital payment, and an amount equivalent to the amount of that capital payment is not required under the arrangement to be taken into account in computing the price of stock to be transferred to B or his nominee under the arrangement, and

(d)   the amount of the capital payment would not exceed 500 euros.

27(2)   A shall not be regarded, for the purposes of section 80C of the Finance Act 1986, as a person to whom a benefit consisting of an amount equal to the capital payment referred to in paragraph (1) accrues as mentioned in subsection (4)(b) of that section.

PAYMENT OR BENEFIT RECEIVED BY TRANSFEREE OF CHARGEABLE SECURITIES ON EUROCONVERSION

28(1)   This regulation applies in a case where–

(a)   there is an arrangement involving the transfer of chargeable securities to which subsection (1) of section 89AA of the Finance Act 1986 applies,

(b)   a capital payment would, but for the arrangement, be received by the person referred to as Q in that section or by his nominee on the euroconversion of those chargeable securities,

(c)   neither the person referred to as P in that section nor his nominee is required under the arrangement to pay to Q or to Q's nominee an amount equivalent to the amount of that capital payment, and an amount equivalent to the amount of that capital payment is not required under the arrangement to be taken into account in computing the price of the chargeable securities to be transferred to Q or his nominee under the arrangement, and

(d)   the amount of the capital payment would not exceed 500 euros.

28(2)   P shall not be regarded, for the purposes of section 89AA of the Finance Act 1986, as a person to whom a benefit consisting of an amount equal to the capital payment referred to in paragraph (1) accrues as mentioned in subsection (4)(b) of that section.

RENOMINALISATION RESULTING IN NEW MINIMUM DENOMINATION IN WHICH STOCK CAN BE HELD OR TRADED

29(1)   This regulation applies in a case where–

(a)   there is an arrangement involving the transfer of stock to which subsection (1) of section 80C of the Finance Act 1986 applies,

(b)   there is a euroconversion of that stock prior to the transfer of stock under the arrangement by A or his nominee to B or his nominee as mentioned in subsection (1)(b) of that section,

(c)   the aggregate nominal value (expressed in euros) of the stock transferred by B to A or his nominee as mentioned in subsection (1)(a) of that section, or of stock issued to replace that stock in a euroconversion is, as a result of renominalisation, not a whole multiple of the new minimum denomination in which that stock can be traded at the time of the transfer of stock referred to in sub-paragraph (b),

(d)   stock the aggregate nominal value of which is equal to the largest whole multiple of the new minimum denomination which does not exceed the aggregate nominal value referred to in sub-paragraph (c) is required under the arrangement to be transferred by A or his nominee to B or his nominee, and

(e)   A or his nominee is required under the arrangement to pay to B or his nominee an amount which either–

(i)   is equal to the amount of what would, but for the arrangement, have been the proceeds of disposal of the remainder of the stock on the renominalisation received by B, or

(ii)   is equal to the value, at the time of the transfer of stock referred to in sub-paragraph (b), of the remainder of the stock if the remainder could still be held at that time though *not* traded.

29(2)   Where this regulation applies, the requirement for payment of the amount specified in paragraph (1)(e) is to be regarded, for the purposes of section 80C of the Finance Act 1986, as equivalent to a requirement for the remainder of the stock to be transferred by A or his nominee to B or his nominee.

29(3)   The value referred to in paragraph (1)(e)(i) is the appropriate proportion (based on nominal value) of the market value of the minimum amount of the original stock that, at the time of the transfer of stock referred to in sub-paragraph (b), could be traded.

29(4)   Where the amount calculated in accordance with sub-paragraph (e) of paragraph (1) does not exceed 500 euros, and the arrangement does not require payment of a sum equal to this amount, this regulation shall have effect as if the amount calculated in accordance with that sub-paragraph were nil and the requirement specified in that sub-paragraph were satisfied.

RENOMINALISATION RESULTING IN NEW MINIMUM DENOMINATION IN WHICH CHARGEABLE SECURITIES CAN BE HELD OR TRADED

30(1) This regulation applies in a case where–

(a)   there is an arrangement involving the transfer of chargeable securities to which subsection (1) of section 89AA of the Finance Act 1986 applies,

(b)   there is a euroconversion of those chargeable securities prior to the transfer of chargeable securities under the arrangement by P or his nominee to Q or his nominee as mentioned in subsection (1)(b) of that section,

(c)   the aggregate nominal value (expressed in euros) of the chargeable securities transferred by Q to P or his nominee as mentioned in subsection (1)(a) of that section, or of chargeable securities issued to replace those chargeable securities in a euroconversion is, as a result of renominalisation, not a whole multiple of the new minimum denomination in which those chargeable securities can be traded at the time of the transfer of chargeable securities referred to sub-paragraph (b),

(d)   chargeable securities the aggregate nominal value of which is equal to the largest whole multiple of the new minimum denomination which does not exceed the aggregate nominal value referred to in sub-paragraph (c) are required under the arrangement to be transferred by P or his nominee to Q or his nominee, and

(e)   P or his nominee is required under the arrangement to pay to Q or his nominee an amount which either–

(i)   is equal to the amount of what would, but for the arrangement, have been the proceeds of disposal of the remainder of the chargeable securities on the renominalisation received by Q, or

(ii)   is equal to the value, at the time of the transfer of chargeable securities referred to in sub-paragraph (b), of the remainder of the chargeable securities if the remainder could still be held at that time though not traded.

30(2) Where this regulation applies, the requirement for payment of the amount specified in paragraph (1)(e) is to be regarded, for the purposes of section 89AA of the Finance Act 1986, as equivalent to a requirement for the remainder of the chargeable securities to be transferred by P or his nominee to Q or his nominee.

30(3) The value referred to in paragraph (1)(e) is the appropriate proportion (based on nominal value) of the market value of the minimum amount of the original chargeable securities that, at the time of the transfer of chargeable securities referred to in paragraph (1)(b), could be traded.

30(4) Where the amount calculated in accordance with sub-paragraph (e) of paragraph (1) does not exceed 500 euros, and the arrangement does not require payment of a sum equal to this amount, this regulation shall have effect as if the amount calculated in accordance with that sub-paragraph were nil and the requirement specified in that sub-paragraph were satisfied.

PART VII – ACCRUED INCOME SCHEME
INTERPRETATION

31 [Neither relevant nor reproduced.]

DISAPPLICATION OF ACCRUED INCOME PROVISIONS IN RESPECT OF AN EXCHANGE OR CONVERSION OF SECURITIES RESULTING FROM A EUROCONVERSION

32 [Neither relevant nor reproduced.]

DISAPPLICATION OF VARIABLE INTEREST RATE PROVISION IN CERTAIN CIRCUMSTANCES

33 [Neither relevant nor reproduced.]

CALCULATION OF ACCRUED AMOUNT OR REBATE AMOUNT IN THE
EVENT OF A EUROCONVERSION OF SECURITIES

34 [Neither relevant nor reproduced.]

TREATMENT OF CAPITAL SUM RECEIVABLE ON EUROCONVERSION OF
SECURITIES

35 [Neither relevant nor reproduced.]

PART VIII – CHARGEABLE GAINS

EQUATION OF HOLDING OF NON-STERLING CURRENCY WITH NEW EURO
HOLDING ON EUROCONVERSION

36 [Neither relevant nor reproduced.]

EQUATION OF DEBT (OTHER THAN A DEBT ON A SECURITY) ON
EUROCONVERSION

37 [Neither relevant nor reproduced.]

DERIVATIVES OVER ASSETS THE SUBJECT OF EUROCONVERSION

38 [Neither relevant nor reproduced.]

CASH PAYMENTS RECEIVED ON EUROCONVERSION OF SECURITIES

39 [Neither relevant nor reproduced.]

PART IX – CONTROLLED FOREIGN COMPANIES

REPLACEMENT OF CURRENCY USED IN ACCOUNTS OF CONTROLLED
FOREIGN COMPANY BY EURO

40 [Neither relevant nor reproduced.]

PART X – AMENDMENTS TO THE LOCAL CURRENCY ELECTIONS REGULATIONS

INTRODUCTORY

41 [Neither relevant nor reproduced.]

PERIOD FOR DETERMINING VALIDITY OF ELECTIONS

42 [Neither relevant nor reproduced.]

EXISTING ELECTION FOR ECU OR PARTICIPATING CURRENCIES

43 [Neither relevant nor reproduced.]

TREATMENT OF EXISTING PART TRADE ELECTIONS IN PARTICIPATING
CURRENCIES

44 [Neither relevant nor reproduced.]

ELECTION FOR WHOLE TRADE EHERE PART TRADE ELECTION ALREADY
EXISTS

45 [Neither relevant nor reproduced.]

DETERMINATION OF RATE OF EXCHANGE WHERE PART TRADE
ELECTION REPLACED BY WHOLE TRADE ELECTION OR COMBINED PART
TRADE ELECTION

46 [Neither relevant nor reproduced.]

PART TRADE ELECTIONS FOR NEW PART TRADES

47 [Neither relevant nor reproduced.]

THE STAMP DUTY RESERVE TAX (UK DEPOSITARY INTERESTS IN FOREIGN SECURITIES) REGULATIONS 1999

(SI 1999/2383)

Made on 24 August 1999 by the Treasury, in exercise of the powers conferred on them by section 98 of the Finance Act 1986 and sections 119 and 121 of the Finance Act 1999. Operative from 25 August 1999.

ARRANGEMENT OF REGULATIONS

CITATION, COMMENCEMENT AND EFFECT

1   These Regulations may be cited as the Stamp Duty Reserve Tax (UK Depositary Interests in Foreign Securities) Regulations 1999 and shall come into force on 25th August 1999.

INTERPRETATION

2   In these Regulations–

"**the Board**" means the Commissioners of Inland Revenue;

"**collective investment scheme**" has the meaning given by section 75 of the Financial Services Act 1986;

"**depositary interest**" means a security which–

(a)   consists of the rights of a person in or relating to securities of a particular kind which, or entitlements to which, are held on trust for the benefit of that person by another person, and

(b)   under the terms of its issue, can only be transferred in accordance with regulations under section 207 of the Companies Act 1989 (transfer of securities without written instrument) or by means of a transfer within section 186(1) of the Finance Act 1996 (transfer of securities to member of electronic transfer system);

"**foreign securities**" means securities falling within the definition of "securities" in regulation 3(1) of the Uncertificated Securities Regulations 1995 which–

(a)   are issued or raised by a body corporate that is not incorporated, and whose central management and control is not exercised, in the United Kingdom;

(b)   are not registered in a register kept in the United Kingdom by or on behalf of the body corporate by which they are issued or raised;

(c)   are not units or shares in, or do not otherwise represent rights relating to, a collective investment scheme; and

(d)   are of the same class in the body corporate as securities which are listed on a recognised stock exchange overseas;

"**the Management Act**" means the Taxes Management Act 1970;

"**operator**" has the meaning given by regulation 2 of the principal Regulations;

"**recognised stock exchange overseas**" means any stock exchange which is–

(a)   outside the United Kingdom, and

(b)   for the time being designated for the purposes of section 841 of the Income and Corporation Taxes Act 1988 as a recognised stock exchange by order made by the Board under that section;

"**the principal Regulations**" means the Stamp Duty Reserve Tax Regulations 1986;

"**relevant day**" has the meaning given by section 87(3) of the Finance Act 1986;

"**the Schedule**" means the Schedule to the principal Regulations;

"**UK depositary interest**" means a depositary interest which is issued in the United Kingdom or registered on a register kept in the United Kingdom.

EXCLUSION OF A UK DEPOSITARY INTEREST IN FOREIGN SECURITIES FROM THE DEFINITION OF "CHARGEABLE SECURITIES" IN PART IV OF THE FINANCE ACT 1986

3(1) Subject to paragraph (2), a UK depositary interest in foreign securities is not a chargeable security for the purposes of Part IV of the Finance Act 1986.

3(2) Paragraph (1) does not apply to an agreement to transfer a security where the security ceases to be a UK depositary interest in foreign securities on or before the relevant day.

NOTICE RELATING TO UK DEPOSITARY INTERESTS IN FOREIGN SECURITIES

4(1) This regulation applies to an operator in circumstances where, for the first time, a depositary interest in a particular foreign security is issued and the operator intends to treat the depositary interest as one to which regulation 3(1) applies.

4(2) An operator shall, on or before the date which is the fourteenth day following the date of issue, give notice to the Board of–

(a) the date of issue, and

(b) the depositary interest issued.

4(3) A notice under this regulation shall be in such form as the Board may prescribe or authorise and shall contain such information as they may reasonably require for the purposes of the Finance Act 1986.

AMENDMENTS TO PART I OF THE SCHEDULE

5(1) The Table in Part I of the Schedule (which applies the provisions of the Management Act specified in the first column of that Table subject to any modification specified in the second column of that Table) shall be amended as follows.

5(2) In the entry relating to section 98 in the second column after the words "The Stamp Duty Reserve Tax Regulations 1986 (other than regulations 4 and 4A)" there shall be added the words "The Stamp Duty Reserve Tax (UK Depositary Interests in Foreign Securities) Regulations 1999".

AMENDMENTS TO PART II OF THE SCHEDULE

6(1) Part II of the Schedule (which restates the provisions of the Management Act specified in Part I of the Schedule as modified where appropriate) shall be amended as follows.

6(2) In the second column of the Table in section 98 (as modified) after the words "The Stamp Duty Reserve Tax Regulations 1986 (other than regulations 4 and 4A)" there shall be added the words "The Stamp Duty Reserve Tax (UK Depositary Interests in Foreign Securities) Regulations 1999".

THE STAMP DUTY (COLLECTION AND RECOVERY OF PENALTIES) REGULATIONS 1999

(SI 1999/2537)

Made on 9 September 1999 by the Treasury, in exercise of the powers conferred on them by paragraphs 16 and 17 of Schedule 17 to the Finance Act 1999. Operative from 1 October 1999.

ARRANGEMENT OF REGULATIONS

REGULATION

REGULATION

SCHEDULES

SCHEDULE
SCHEDULE

CITATION, COMMENCEMENT AND EFFECT

1(1)   These Regulations may be cited as the Stamp Duty (Collection and Recovery of Penalties) Regulations 1999 and shall come into force on 1st October 1999.

1(2)   These Regulations have effect in relation to penalties in respect of things done or omitted on or after 1st October 1999.

INTERPRETATION

2   In these Regulations–

"the enactments relating to stamp duty" means the Stamp Act 1981 and any enactment amending, or which is to be construed as one with, that Act;

"the Management Act" means the Taxes Management Act 1970;

"stamp duty penalty" means a penalty under the enactments relating to stamp duty, other than a penalty under section 15B of the Stamp Act 1891.

THE MANAGEMENT ACT: PROVISIONS TO APPLY

3(1)   The provisions of the Management Act specified in the first column of the Table in Part I of the Schedule to these Regulations shall apply in relation to stamp duty penalties as they apply in relation to taxes within the meaning of that Act subject to any modification specified in the second column of that Table.

3(2)   Any expression which is used in a provision of the Management Act as applied by this regulation, and to which a meaning is not given by that Act as so applied, shall in that provision have the same meaning as in the enactments relating to stamp duty or these Regulations.

3(3)   The provisions of the Management Act which are applied subject to modifications by this regulation are restated (as modified where appropriate) in Part II of the Schedule to these Regulations.

SCHEDULE

Regulation 3

Part I

Provisions applied	*Modifications*
Section 60(1)	For the words "the tax" in the first place where they occur substitute "a stamp duty penalty"; and omit the words "or on the premises in respect of which the tax is charged,".
(2)	For the word "tax" substitute "penalty".
61	
63	For the side-note to the section substitute "Recovery of stamp duty penalties in Scotland".
(1)	Omit the words "Subject to subsection (3) below,"; for the word "tax" in the first place where it occurs substitute "stamp duty penalty"; and in paragraph (a) for the word "tax" substitute "penalty".
(2)	–
63A	
65(1)	For the words "income tax, capital gains tax or corporation tax" substitute *"a stamp duty penalty"*.
(2)	For the word "tax" substitute "stamp duty penalties"; and for the words "under one assessment" substitute "in respect of the same act or omission".
(3)	–
(4)	–

Provisions applied	*Modifications*
(5)	–
66(1)	For the word "Tax" substitute "A stamp duty penalty"; and omit the words "under any assessment".
(2)	–
(3)	–
(4)	–
67(1)	For the word "tax" substitute "a stamp duty penalty"; and omit the words "under any asssessment".
(1A)	–
(2)	–
68(1)	For the word "tax" in the first place where it occurs substitute "stamp duty penalty"; and for the word "tax" in the second place where it occurs substitute "penalty".
(2)	–
69	For the side-note to the section substitute "Interest on stamp duty penalties".
	For the words from "A penalty" to "as if it were interest so charged" substitute "Interest charged under section 103A of this Act on a stamp duty penalty"; and for the words from "as if it were tax" in the first place where they occur to the end substitute "as if it were a stamp duty penalty due and payable in respect of the same act or omission as that to which the stamp duty penalty on which the interest is charged relates".
70(2)	In paragraph (a) before the word "penalty" insert "stamp duty"; and omit the words from "under Part II, VA or X" to "under Part IX of this Act"; in paragraph (b) omit the words ", surcharge or interest".
103A	For the side-note to the section substitute "Interest on stamp duty penalties".
	For the words from "penalty" to "Finance Act 1998," substitute "stamp duty penalty"; and after the words "Finance Act 1989" insert "for the purpose of section 15A of the Stamp Act 1891".
107A	For the side-note to the section substitute "Trustees".
(2)	Omit the word "relevant"; for the words from "liable" to "section 86 of this Act" substitute "liable to a stamp duty penalty, or to interest under section 103A of this Act on such a penalty,"; and for the words ", interest, payment or surcharge" substitute "or interest".
(3)	Omit "(a) or (c)"; for the words "a relevant trustee" substitute "a trustee"; and for the words from "the relevant time" to the end substitute "the time when the act or omission which caused the penalty to become payable occurred".
108(1)	For the words "Taxes Acts" in both places where they occur substitute "relevant enactments relating to stamp duty"; and omit the words from "This subsection" to the end.
(2)	For the words from the beginning to "Corporation Tax Acts on" substitute "A stamp duty penalty for which"; after the word "Charter," insert "is liable,"; for the words "the tax becomes due" substitute "the penalty becomes due"; and for the words "that tax" substitute "that penalty".

Provisions applied	*Modifications*
(3)	–
112	For the side-note to the section substitute "Loss, destruction or damage to notices of determination, etc.".
(1)	For the words from "assessment to tax" to "or any return" substitute "notice of determination,"; for the words "relating to tax" substitute "relating to a stamp duty penalty"; omit the word "inspectors,"; for the words "in relation to tax" substitute "in relation to the penalty"; for the words "assessment or duplicate of assessment" substitute "notice of determination"; for the words "the return or" substitute "the"; omit the words "made or" in both places where they occur; for the words "charged with tax" substitute "charged with a stamp duty penalty"; and for the words from "any tax for the same chargeable period" to "so charged" substitute "an amount in respect of that same penalty".
(2)	Omit the words "General or"; and omit the word "concerned".
113	For the side-note to the section substitute "Form of determinations and other documents".
(1D)	For the words "a penalty under section 100 of this Act" substitute "a stamp duty penalty".
(3)	For the words from "Every assessment" to "of determination" substitute "Every determination, warrant, notice of determination"; omit the word "assessing,"; and for the words "and levying tax or determining a penalty" substitute ", levying or determining a stamp duty penalty".
114	For the side-note to the section substitute "Want of form or errors not to invalidate determinations, etc.".
(1)	For the words "An assessment or determination" substitute "A determination"; after the word "proceeding" insert "in relation to a stamp duty penalty"; for the words "the Taxes Acts" in both places where they occur substitute "the relevant enactments relating to stamp duty"; and omit the words "or property".
(2)	For the words "An assessment or determination" substitute "A determination"; in paragraph (a)(ii) for the words "the description of any profits or property" substitute "the amount of the penalty"; in paragraph (a)(iii) for the words "the amount of the tax charged" substitute "any other matter specified therein"; and in paragraph (b) omit the words "assessment or".
115(1)	For the word "form" substitute "other document"; and for the words "the Taxes Acts" substitute "the relevant enactments relating to stamp duty".
(2)	For the words "the Taxes Acts" substitute "the relevant enactments relating to stamp duty"; before the words "by any officer of the Board" insert "or"; omit the words "or by or on behalf of any body of Commissioners"; in paragraph (b) omit the words "in the case of a company, at any other prescribed place, and"; omit the words "or any other prescribed place".
(5)	Omit the words "the General Commissioners Regulations or".
118(1)	Omit the following definitions –
	"Act"
	"branch or agency"
	"chargeable gain"
	"chargeable period"
	"the General Commissioners Regulations"
	"incapacitated person"
	"infant"
	"inspector"
	"the relevant trustees"
	"return"

Provisions applied   Modifications

"successor"

"tax"

"the Taxes Acts"

"the 1992 Act"

"trade";

and after the definition of "the principal Act" insert the following definition –

" "the relevant enactments relating to stamp duty" means this Act and –

(a) Part II of Schedule 17 to the Finance Act 1999, and

(b) the Stamp Duty (Collection and Recovery of Penalties) Regulations 1999,."

Part II – Taxes Management Act 1970

Notes – This heading is to Pt. II of these regulations (i.e. the Stamp Duty (Collection and Recovery of Penalties) Regulations 1999 (SI 1999/2537)). The following headings refer to Points of the Taxes Management Act 1970, provisions of which are modified by these regulations.

Part VI – Collection and Recovery

Notes – This heading is to Pt. VI/X/XI of the Taxes Management Act 1970. The text below is the modified version of the provision in that Part which is introduced by these regulations.

60   Issue of demand notes and receipts

60(1)   Every collector shall, when a stamp duty penalty becomes due and payable, make demand of the respective sums given to him in charge to collect, from the persons charged therewith, or at the places of their last abode, as the case may require.

60(2)   On payment of the penalty, the collector shall if so requested give a receipt.

DISTRAINT AND POINDING

61   Distraint by collectors

61(1)   If a person neglects or refuses to pay the sum charged, upon demand made by the collector, the collector may distrain upon the goods and chattels of the person charged (in this section referred to as "the person in default").

61(2)   For the purpose of levying any such distress, a justice of the peace, on being satisfied by information on oath that there is reasonable ground for believing that a person is neglecting or refusing to pay a sum charged, may issue a warrant in writing authorising a collector to break open, in the daytime, any house or premises, calling to his assistance any constable.

Every such constable shall, when so required, aid and assist the collector in the execution of the warrant and in levying the distress in the house or premises.

61(3)   A levy or warrant to break open shall be executed by, or under the direction of, and in the presence of, the collector.

61(4)   A distress levied by the collector shall be kept for five days, at the costs and charges of the person in default.

61(5)   If the person in default does not pay the sum due, together with the costs and charges, the distress shall be appraised by one or more independent persons appointed by the collector, and shall be sold by public auction by the collector for payment of the sum due and all costs and charges.

Any overplus coming by the distress, after the deduction of the costs and charges and of the sum due, shall be restored to the owner of the goods distrained.

61(6)   The Treasury may by regulations make provision with respect to –

(a)   the fees chargeable on or in connection with the levying of distress, and

(b)   the costs and charges recoverable where distress has been levied; and any such regulations shall be made by statutory instrument which shall be subject to annulment in pursuance of a resolution of the House of Commons.

63   Recovery of stamp duty penalties in Scotland

63(1)   In Scotland, where any stamp duty penalty is due and has not been paid, the sheriff, on an application by the collector accompanied by a certificate by the collector–

(a)   stating that none of the persons specified in the application has paid the penalty due by him;

(b)   stating that the collector has demanded payment under section 60 of this Act from each such person of the amount due by him;

(c)   stating that 14 days have elapsed since the date of such demand without payment of the said amount; and

(d)   specifying the amount due and unpaid by each such person, shall grant a summary warrant in a form prescribed by Act of Sederunt authorising the recovery, by any of the diligences mentioned in subsection (2) below, of the amount remaining due and unpaid.

63(2)   The diligences referred to in subsection (1) above are–

(a)   a poinding and sale in accordance with Schedule 5 to the Debtors (Scotland) Act 1987;

(b)   an earnings arrestment;

(c)   an arrestment and action of furthcoming or sale.

63A   Sheriff officer's fees and outlays

63A(1)   Subject to subsection (2) below and without prejudice to paragraphs 25 to 34 of Schedule 5 to the Debtors (Scotland) Act 1987 (expenses of poinding and sale), the sheriff officer's fees, together with the outlays necessarily incurred by him, in connection with the execution of a summary warrant shall be chargeable against the debtor.

63A(2)   No fee shall be chargeable by the sheriff officer against the debtor for collecting, and accounting to the collector for, sums paid to him by the debtor in respect of the amount owing.

COURT PROCEEDINGS

65   Magistrates' courts

65(1)   Any amount due and payable by way of a stamp duty penalty which does not exceed £2,000 shall, without prejudice to any other remedy, be recoverable summarily as a civil debt by proceedings commenced in the name of the collector.

65(2)   All or any of the sums in respect of stamp duty penalties from any one person and payable to any one collector (being sums which are by law recoverable summarily) may, whether or not they are due in respect of the same act or omission, be included in the same complaint, summons, order, warrant or other document required by law to be laid before justices or to be issued by justices, and every such document as aforesaid shall, as respects each such sum, be construed as a separate document and its invalidity as respects any one such sum shall not affect its validity as respects any other such sum.

65(3)   Proceedings under this section may be brought in England and Wales at any time within one year from the time when the matter complained of arose.

65(4)   It is hereby declared that in subsection (1) above the expression **"recoverable summarily as a civil debt"** in respect of proceedings in Northern Ireland means recoverable in proceedings under Article 62 of the Magistrates' Courts (Northern Ireland) Order 1981.

65(5)   The Treasury may by order made by statutory instrument increase the sum specified in subsection (1) above; and any such statutory instrument shall be subject to annulment in pursuance of a resolution of the Commons House of Parliament.

66   County courts

66(1)   A stamp duty penalty due and payable may, in England and Wales, and in Northern Ireland where the amount does not exceed the limit specified in Article 10(1) of the County Courts (Northern Ireland) Order 1980, without prejudice to any other remedy, be sued for and recovered from the person charged therewith as a debt due to the Crown by proceedings in a county court commenced in the name of a collector.

66(2)   An officer of the Board who is authorised by the Board to do so may address the court in proceedings under this section in a county court in England and Wales.

66(3)   In this section as it applies in Northern Ireland the expression **"county court"** shall mean a county court held for a division under the County Courts (Northern Ireland) Order 1980.

66(4)   Sections 21 and 42(2) of the Interpretation Act (Northern Ireland) 1954 shall apply as if any reference in those provisions to any enactment included a reference to this section, and Part III of the County Courts (Northern Ireland) Order 1980 (general civil jurisdiction) shall apply for the purposes of this section in Northern Ireland.

67   Inferior courts in Scotland

67(1)   In Scotland, a stamp duty penalty due and payable may, without prejudice to any other remedy, be sued for and recovered from the person charged therewith as a debt due to the Crown by proceedings commenced in the name of a collector in the sheriff court.

67(1A)   An officer of the Board who is authorised by the Board to do so may address the court in any proceedings under this section.

67(2)   Sections 65 and 66 above shall not apply in Scotland.

68   High Court, etc.

68(1)   Any stamp duty penalty may be sued for and recovered from the person charged therewith in the High Court as a debt due to the Crown, or by any other means whereby any debt of record or otherwise due to the Crown can, or may at any time, be sued for and recovered, as well as by the other means specially provided by this Act for levying the penalty.

68(2)   All matters within the jurisdiction of the High Court under this section shall be assigned in Scotland to the Court of Session sitting as the Court of Exchequer.

SUPPLEMENTAL

69   Interest on stamp duty penalties

69   Interest charged under section 103A of this Act on a stamp duty penalty shall be treated for the purposes–

    (a) of sections 61, 63 and 65 to 68 above, and

    (b) of section 35(2)(g)(i) of the Crown Proceedings Act 1947 (rules of court to impose restrictions on set-off and counterclaim where the proceedings or set-off or counterclaim relate to taxes) and of any rules of court (including county court rules) for England and Wales or Northern Ireland, which impose such a restriction, and

    (c) of section 35(2)(b) of the said Act of 1947 as set out in section 50 of that Act (which imposes corresponding restrictions in Scotland), as if it were a stamp duty penalty due and payable in respect of the same act or omission as that to which the stamp duty penalty on which the interest is charged relates.

70   Evidence

70(2)   A certificate of a collector–

(a)   that a stamp duty penalty is payable, and

(b)   that payment of the penalty has not been made to him or, to the best of his knowledge and belief, to any other collector or to any person acting on his behalf or on behalf of another collector, shall be sufficient evidence that the sum mentioned in the certificate is unpaid and is due to the Crown, and any document purporting to be such a certificate as is mentioned in this subsection shall be deemed to be such a certificate unless the contrary is proved.

Part X – Penalties Etc.

Notes – This heading is to Pt. VI/X/XI of the Taxes Management Act 1970. The text below is the modified version of the provision in that Part which is introduced by these regulations.

103A   Interest on stamp duty penalties

103A   A stamp duty penalty shall carry interest at the rate applicable under section 178 of the Finance Act 1989 for the purpose of section 15A of the Stamp Act 1891 from the date on which it becomes due and payable until payment.

Part XI – Miscellaneous and Supplemental

Notes – This heading is to Pt. VI/X/XI of the Taxes Management Act 1970. The text below is the modified version of the provision in that Part which is introduced by these regulations.

SETTLEMENTS

107A   Trustees

107A(2)   Subject to subsection (3) below, where the trustees of a settlement are liable to a stamp duty penalty, or to interest under subsection 103A of this Act on such a penalty, the penalty or interest may be recovered (but only once) from any one or more of those trustees.

107A(3)   No amount may be recovered by virtue of subsection (2) above from a person who did not become a trustee until after the time when the act or omission which caused the penalty to become payable occurred.

COMPANIES

108   Responsibility of company officers

108(1)   Everything to be done by a company under the relevant enactments relating to stamp duty shall be done by the company acting through the proper officer of the company, or, except where a liquidator has been appointed for the company, through such other person as may for the time being have the express, implied or apparent authority of the company to act on its behalf for the purpose, and service on a company of any document under or in pursuance of the relevant enactments relating to stamp duty may be effected by serving it on the proper officer.

108(2)   A stamp duty penalty for which a company which is not a body corporate, or which is a body corporate not incorporated under the Companies Act 1985 or any other enactment forming part of the law of the United Kingdom, or by Charter, is liable, may, at any time after the penalty becomes due, and without prejudice to any other method of recovery, be recovered from the proper officer of the company, and that officer may retain out of any money coming into his hands on behalf of the company sufficient sums to pay that penalty, and, so far as he is not so reimbursed, shall be entitled to be indemnified by the company in respect of the liability so imposed on him.

108(3)   For the purposes of this section–

(a)   the proper officer of a company which is a body corporate shall be the secretary or person acting as secretary of the company, except that if a liquidator has been appointed for the company the liquidator shall be the proper officer,

(b)   the proper officer of a company which is not a body corporate or for which there is no proper officer within paragraph (a) above, shall be the treasurer or the person acting as treasurer, of the company.

112   Loss, destruction or damage to notices of determination, etc.

112(1)   Where any notice of determination, or other document relating to a stamp duty penalty, has been lost or destroyed, or been so defaced or damaged as to be illegible or otherwise useless, the Commissioners, collectors and other officers having powers in relation to the penalty may, notwithstanding anything in any enactment to the contrary, do all such acts and things as they might have done, and all acts and things done under or in pursuance of this section shall be as valid and effectual for all purposes as they would have been, if the notice of determination had not been made, or the other document had not been furnished or required to be furnished:

Provided that, where any person who is charged with a stamp duty penalty in consequence or by virtue of any act or thing done under or in pursuance to this section proves to the satisfaction of the Commissioners having jurisdiction in the case that he has already paid an amount in respect of that same penalty, relief shall be given to the extent to which the liability of that person has been discharged by the payment so made either by abatement from the charge or by repayment, as the case may require.

112(2)   In this section **"the Commissioners"** *means, as the case may require,* either the Board or *the Special* Commissioners.

113   Form of determinations and other documents

113(1D)   Where an officer of the Board has decided to impose a stamp duty penalty and has taken all other decisions needed for arriving at the amount of the penalty, he may entrust to any other officer of the Board responsibility for completing the determination procedure, whether by means involving the use of a computer or otherwise, including responsibility for serving notice of the determination on the person liable to the penalty.

113(3) Every determination, warrant, notice of determination or of demand, or other document required to be used in charging, collecting, levying or determining a stamp duty penalty shall be in accordance with the forms prescribed from time to time in that behalf by the Board, and a document in the form prescribed and supplied or approved by them shall be valid and effectual.

114 Want of form or errors not to invalidate determinations, etc.

114(1) A determination, warrant or other proceeding in relation to a stamp duty penalty which purports to be made in pursuance of any provision of the relevant enactments relating to stamp duty shall not be quashed, or deemed to be void or voidable, for want of form, or be affected by reason of a mistake, defect or omission therein, if the same is in substance and effect in conformity with or according to the intent and meaning of the relevant enactments relating to stamp duty, and if the person charged or intended to be charged or affected thereby is designated therein according to common intent and understanding.

114(2) A determination shall not be impeached or affected–

(a) by reason of a mistake therein as to–

(i) the name or surname of a person liable, or

(ii) the amount of the penalty, or

(iii) any other matter specified therein, or

(b) by reason of any variance between the notice and the determination.

115 Delivery and service of documents

115(1) A notice or other document which is to be served under the relevant enactments relating to stamp duty on a person may be either delivered to him or left at his usual or last known place of residence.

115(2) Any notice or other document to be given, sent, served, or delivered under the relevant enactments relating to stamp duty may be served by post, and, if to be given, sent, served or delivered to or on any person by the Board, or by any officer of the Board, may be so served addressed to that person–

() at his usual or last known place of residence, or his place of business or employment, or

(b) in the case of a liquidator of a company, at his address for the purposes of the liquidation.

115(5) Nothing in this section applies to any notice or other document required or authorised by the Special Commissioners Regulations to be sent or delivered to, or served on, any person.

118 Interpretation

118(1) In this Act, unless the context otherwise requires–

"**the Board**" means the Commissioners of Inland Revenue,

"**body of persons**" means any body politic, corporate or collegiate, and any company, fraternity, fellowship and society of persons, whether corporate or not corporate,

"**collector**" means any collector of taxes,

"**company**" has the meaning given by section 832(1) of the principal Act (with section 468 of that Act),

"**the principal Act**" means the Income and Corporation Taxes Act 1988,

"**the relevant enactments relating to stamp duty**" means this Act and,

(a) Part II of Schedule 17 to the Finance Act 1999, and

(b) the Stamp Duty (Collection and Recovery of Penalties) Regulations 1999,

"**the Special Commissioners Regulations**"means the Special Commissioners (Jurisdiction and Procedure) Regulations 1994.

Stamp Duty and Stamp Duty Reserve Tax (Investment Exchanges and Clearing Houses) (OM London Exchange Limited) Regulations 1999

(SI 1999/3262)

Made on 7 December 1999 by the Treasury, in exercise of the powers conferred on them by s. 116 and 117 of the Finance Act 1991. Operative from 29 December 1999

ARRANGEMENT OF REGULATIONS

REGULATION
1.   CITATION, COMMENCEMENT AND EFFECT
2.   INTERPRETATION
3.   PRESCRIPTION OF RECOGNISED INVESTMENT EXCHANGE
4.   TRANSFERS AND ISSUES OF SECURITIES TO OM LONDON EXCHANGE LIMITED – PRESCRIBED CIRCUMSTANCES
5.   TRANSFERS OF SECURITIES TO OR FROM MEMBERS OF OM LONDON EXCHANGE LIMITED – PRESCRIBED CIRCUMSTANCES

CITATION, COMMENCEMENT AND EFFECT

1(1) These Regulations may be cited as the Stamp Duty and Stamp Duty Reserve Tax (Investment Exchanges and Clearing Houses) (OM London Exchange Limited) Regulations 1999 and shall come into force on 29th December 1999.

1(2) These Regulations shall have effect–

(a)   as respects the charge to stamp duty, in relation to instruments executed on or after 29th December 1999;

(b)   as respects the charge to stamp duty reserve tax–

    (i)   in the case of an agreement to transfer equity securities which is not conditional, where the agreement is made on or after 29th December 1999;

    (ii)   in the case of an agreement to transfer equity securities which is conditional, where the condition is satisfied on or after that date.

INTERPRETATION

2   In these Regulations–

"**clearing member**" means a member who is permitted by the rules of OM London Exchange Limited to clear transactions made on that exchange for an equity security;

"**equity securities**" means stocks and shares which are issued or raised by a company but does not include stocks and shares issued by a company not incorporated in the United Kingdom unless–

(a)   they are registered in a register kept in the United Kingdom by or on behalf of the company, or

(b)   in the case of shares, they are paired, within the meaning of section 99(6A) of the Finance Act 1986, with shares issued by a company incorporated in the United Kingdom;

(c)   "**member**" means a member of OM London Exchange Limited who is recognised as such by the rules of that exchange;

(d)   "**non-clearing member**" means a member other than a clearing member;

(e)   "**option**" means an option to buy or sell securities which is listed by and traded on OM London Exchange Limited;

(f)   "**futures contract**" means a futures, or a forward, contract conferring rights and obligations to buy or sell securities which is listed by and traded on OM London Exchange Limited.

PRESCRIPTION OF RECOGNISED INVESTMENT EXCHANGE

3   For the purposes of sections 116 and 117 of the Finance Act 1991 OM London Exchange Limited is a recognised investment exchange which is prescribed.

TRANSFERS AND ISSUES OF SECURITIES TO OM LONDON EXCHANGE LIMITED – PRESCRIBED CIRCUMSTANCES

4(1) In the circumstances prescribed by paragraph (2), a charge to stamp duty or to stamp duty reserve tax shall be treated as not arising.

4(2) The circumstances prescribed are where, as a result of the exercise of options, or under futures contracts, equity securities of a particular kind are transferred or issued or agreed to be transferred or issued–

(a) to OM London Exchange Limited; or

(b) to a person whose business is or includes holding such securities as a nominee for OM London Exchange Limited.

4(3) References in this regulation and in regulation 5 to OM London Exchange Limited are references to that exchange in its capacity as a person providing clearing services in connection with a transaction made on that exchange.

TRANSFERS OF SECURITIES TO OR FROM MEMBERS OF OM LONDON EXCHANGE LIMITED – PRESCRIBED CIRCUMSTANCES

5(1) In the circumstances prescribed by paragraph (2), a charge to stamp duty or to stamp duty reserve tax shall be treated as not arising.

5(2) The circumstances prescribed are where, in order to meet an obligation to receive securities resulting from the exercise of options, or under futures contracts, equity securities of a particular kind are transferred or agreed to be transferred–

(a) from a non-clearing member or a nominee of a non-clearing member to a clearing member or the nominee of a clearing member; or

(b) from OM London Exchange Limited or a nominee of OM London Exchange Limited to a clearing member or a nominee of a clearing member.

5(3) In paragraph (2) references to a clearing member are references to a clearing member in his capacity as such.

DISTRAINT BY COLLECTORS (FEES, COSTS AND CHARGES) (STAMP DUTY PENALTIES) REGULATIONS 1999

(SI 1999/3263)

Made on 7 December 1999 by the Treasury, in exercise of the powers conferred on them by s. 61(6) of the Taxes Management Act 1970. Operative from 29 December 1999

ARRANGEMENT OF REGULATIONS

REGULATION

SCHEDULES

SCHEDULE

SCHEDULE

CITATION, COMMENCEMENT AND EFFECT

1(1) These Regulations may be cited as the Distraint by Collectors (Fees, Costs and Charges) (Stamp Duty Penalties) Regulations 1999 and shall come into force on 29th December 1999.

1(2)   These Regulations have effect in relation to the levying of distress under section 61 of the Taxes Management Act 1970 where, upon demand made by a collector, a person has neglected or refused to pay a sum in respect of a stamp duty penalty.

INTERPRETATION

2   In these Regulations–

"close possession" means physical possession by the distrainor or a person acting on his behalf of the goods and chattels distrained;

"the enactments relating to stamp duty" means the Stamp Act 1891 and any enactment amending, or which is to be construed as one with, that Act;

"stamp duty penalty" means a penalty under the enactments relating to stamp duty, other than a penalty under section 15B of the Stamp Act 1891;

"walking possession" means possession in accordance with an agreement between the distrainor and the distrainee whereby, in consideration of the distrainor not remaining in close possession, the distrainor undertakes not to dispose of the goods distrained or any part thereof, or permit their removal by any person not authorised by the distrainor to remove them.

ASCERTAINMENT OF FEES, COSTS AND CHARGES

3   The fees chargeable on or in connection with the levying of distress and the costs recoverable where the distress has been levied shall be those specified in the Schedule to these Regulations, but subject to any provision of that Schedule.

DEDUCTION OF FEES, COSTS AND CHARGES BY THE COLLECTOR

4   The fees, costs and charges specified in the Schedule to these Regulations shall be deducted by the collector from the sums received on or in connection with the levying of distress or where distress has been levied.

DISPUTES AS TO FEES, COSTS AND CHARGES

5(1)   In the case of dispute as to any fees chargeable, or costs and charges recoverable under the Schedule to these Regulations, the amount of those fees, costs and charges shall be taxed.

5(2)   Such a taxation shall be carried out by the district judge of the county court for the district in which the distress is or is intended to be levied, and he may give such directions as to the costs of taxation as he thinks fit.

5(3)   In the application of paragraph (2) to Northern Ireland, there shall be substituted for the words "by the district judge of the county court for the district in which the distress is or is intended to be levied" the words "by the Master (Taxing Office)".

SCHEDULES

SCHEDULE

Action Taken	Fees, Costs and Charges
On or in connection with the levying of distress	*Fees*
For making a visit to premises with a view to levying distress (whether the levy is made or not).	A sum not exceeding £12.50.
Levying distress where the total sum charged is £100 or less.	£12.50
Levying distress where the total sum charged is more than £100.	12$\frac{1}{2}$ per cent on the first £100 of the amount to be recovered; 4 per cent on the next £400; 2$\frac{1}{2}$ per cent on the next £1,500; 1 per cent on the next £8,000; $\frac{1}{4}$ per cent on any additional sum.
Where distress has been levied	*Costs and Charges*
1. Taking possession	
Where close possession is taken.	£4.50 for the day of levy only.
Where walking possession is taken.	45p per day, payable for the day the distress is levied and up to 14 days thereafter.
2. Removal and storage of goods	The reasonable costs and charges of removal and storage.
3. Appraisement	The reasonable fees, charges and expenses of the person appraising.
4. Sale	
Where the sale is held on the auctioneer's premises, for the auctioneer's commission (to include all out-of-pocket expenses other than charges for advertising, removal and storage).	15 per cent on the sum realised plus the reasonable cost of advertising, removal and storage.
Where the sale is held on the debtor's premises, for the auctioneer's commission (not to include out-of-pocket expenses or charges for advertising).	7$\frac{1}{2}$ per cent on the sum realised plus out-of-pocket expenses actually and reasonably incurred and the reasonable costs of advertising.

1 In any case where close possession is taken, an individual left in possession must provide his own board.

2 *For the purpose of calculating any percentage fees, costs and charges, a fraction of £1 is to be reckoned as £1, but any fraction of a penny in the total amount so calculated is to be disregarded.*

3 In addition to any amount authorised by this Schedule in respect of the supply of goods or services on which value added tax is chargeable there may be added a sum equivalent to value added tax at the appropriate rate on that amount.

STAMP DUTIES EXTRA-STATUTORY MATERIAL

Table of Contents

continued over

B. CCAB/ICAEW Material

C. Miscellaneous

D. Inland Revenue Pamphlets

EXTRA-STATUTORY CONCESSIONS

Inland Revenue booklet IR 1 (Inland Revenue Extra-Statutory Concessions) (valid at 31 August 1999) contains the following caveat:

"The concessions described within are of general application, but it must be borne in mind that in a particular case there may be special circumstances which will require to be taken into account in considering the application of the concession. A concession will not be given in any case where an attempt is made to use it for tax avoidance."

G.   CONCESSIONS RELATING TO STAMP DUTIES

G1   STAMP ALLOWANCE ON LOST DOCUMENTS

[Classified obsolete by IR 131 (1996). Replaced by FA 1996, Sch. 39, para. 10 (Stamp Duties Management Act 1891, s.12A).]

Notes – Concession G1 has been put on a statutory footing: see note to SDMA 1891, s. 12A.

G2   STAMPING OF REPLICAS OF DOCUMENTS WHICH HAVE BEEN SPOILT OR LOST

[Classified obsolete by IR 131 (1996). Replaced by FA 1996, Sch. 39, para. 10 (Stamp Duties Management Act 1891, s. 12A).]

Notes – Concession G2 has been put on a statutory footing: see note to SDMA 1891, s. 12A.

G3   GROUP LIFE AND PENSION POLICIES

[Classified obsolete by IR 1 (1994). Withdrawn with effect from 1 January 1990 as a result of the abolition of stamp duty on policies of insurance.]

G4   REPAYMENT OF DUTY ON CANCELLED POLICIES OF INSURANCE

[Classified obsolete by IR 1 (1994). Withdrawn with effect from 1 January 1990 as a result of the abolition of stamp duty on policies of insurance.]

G5   TRANSFER OF STOCK FROM PERSONS TO THEMSELVES OPERATING AS AN EXECUTORS' ASSENT

Stamp duty is not claimed on transfer of stock in a company registered in England, Wales or Northern Ireland from a person to himself (or from two or more persons to themselves) which operates as an executors' assent. The point does not arise in relation to companies registered in Scotland.

G6   TRANSFER OF ASSETS BETWEEN NON-PROFIT MAKING BODIES WITH SIMILAR OBJECTS

When the reconstruction of a non-profit making body with objects in a field of public interest such as education, community work or scientific research, or the amalgamation of two or more such bodies involves a transfer to the successor body of assets for which there passes no consideration in money or money's worth, the instruments of transfer are treated as exempt from ad valorem stamp duty and charged to 50p fixed duty only. There must be sufficient identity between the members of the transferor and transferee bodies and the rules of both must prohibit the distribution of assets to members and provide that on a winding-up the assets can only be transferred to a similar body subject to like restrictions.

G7   TRANSFERS OF STOCK INTO SEPON

[Classified as obsolete by IR 131 (1996). Replaced by FA 1996, s. 191 (FA 1986, s. 89A).]

History – ESC G7 was published on 2 October 1995.

G8   STOCK LOAN RETURNS

[Classified as obsolete by IR 131 (1996). Replaced by FA 1996, s. 191 (FA 1986, s. 89A).]

History – ESC G8 was published on 2 October 1995.

G9   TRANSFERS OF COLLATERAL

[Classified as obsolete by IR 131 (1996). Replaced by FA 1996, s. 191 (FA 1986, s. 89A).]

History – ESC G9 was published on 2 October 1995.

INLAND REVENUE STATEMENTS OF PRACTICE

The statements of practice are classified according to the Inland Revenue publication "Statements of Practice" (IR 131) valid at 31 August 1999.

SP 5/78 STAMP DUTY: CONVEYANCE IN CONSIDERATION OF A DEBT
[8 November 1978]

[Deleted 10 November 1980.]

SP 3/84 STAMP DUTY: CONVERTIBLE LOAN STOCK [13 March 1984]

Transfers of certain loan capital are exempted from stamp duty by Section 79, FA 1986. Subsection (2) provides that the exemption is not available where the loan capital carries an unexpired right of conversion into shares or other securities or to the acquisition of shares or other securities, including loan capital of the same description. The Board of Inland Revenue are advised that subsection (2) does not exclude from the exemption loan capital which carries an unexpired right of conversion into or acquisition of loan capital which itself comes within the terms of the exemption.

SP 9/84 STAMP DUTY: TREATMENT OF SECURITIES DEALT IN ON THE STOCK EXCHANGE UNLISTED SECURITIES MARKET [7 December 1984]

[Classified obsolete by IR 131 (1994).]

SP 10/87 STAMP DUTY: CONVEYANCES AND LEASES OF BUILDING PLOTS
[22 December 1987]

[Superseded by SP 8/93.]

SP 6/90 STAMP DUTY: CONVEYANCES AND TRANSFERS OF PROPERTY SUBJECT TO A DEBT – SECTION 57 STAMP ACT 1891 [27 April 1990]

Introduction

1. Since the abolition of the duty on voluntary dispositions in 1985, many enquiries have been received about the stamp duty chargeable on conveyances etc. subject to a debt where no chargeable consideration (e.g. money or stock) unrelated to the debt is given by the transferee. This Statement of Practice sets out the Board's view of the correct stamp duty treatment of such conveyances.

2. For the sake of completeness it should be noted that where chargeable consideration unrelated to debt is given by the transferee, Section 57 renders the conveyance liable to ad valorem duty on the aggregate of that consideration and the debt whether the transferee assumes liability for the debt or not (*IR Commrs v City of Glasgow Bank* [1881] 8 R 389, 18 SLR 242).

Section 57, Stamp Act 1891

3. The most commonly misunderstood applications of Section 57 arise where

–   a mortgaged property held in the name of one spouse is transferred into the joint names of both spouses;

–   a mortgaged property held in the name of one spouse or in their joint names is transferred into the sole name of the other;

–   a mortgaged business property, frequently farmland, is conveyed from a sole proprietor to a family partnership or from a family partnership to a fresh partnership bringing in other members of the family.

4. The critical question is whether the transaction to which the conveyance gives effect is or is not a sale. If it is, Section 57 will apply and the conveyance will be chargeable to ad valorem duty on the amount of the debt assumed. If it is not, then Section 57 will not apply and ad valorem duty will not be payable.

Express covenants

5. Where property is transferred subject to a debt, the transferee may covenant, either in the instrument or by means of a separate written undertaking, to pay the debt or indemnify the transferor against his personal liability to the lender. Such a covenant or undertaking constitutes

valuable consideration and, in view of Section 57, establishes the transaction as a sale for stamp duty purposes.

6.   Where the transferor covenants to pay the debt and the transferee does not assume any liability for it, no chargeable consideration has been given and there is no sale. The transfer would then be a voluntary disposition – i.e. an unencumbered gift capable of being certified as Category L under the Stamp Duty (Exempt Instruments) Regulations 1987 (SI 1987/516) – and so exempt from the 50p charge that would otherwise arise.

Implied covenants

7.   Where no express covenant or undertaking is given by the transferee, the Board are advised that, except in Scotland, a covenant by the transferee may be implied. That makes the transaction a sale, as in paragraph 4 above.

8.   Such an implied covenant may be negated if there is evidence that it was the intention of the parties at the time of the transfer that the transferor should continue to be liable for the whole of the mortgage debt. Where evidence of such a contrary intention exists, the transfer would again be treated for stamp duty purposes as a voluntary disposition.

9.   Where property in joint names subject to a debt is transferred to one of the joint holders (though with no cash passing), a covenant by the transferee to indemnify the transferor may be implied even where both parties were jointly liable on the mortgage.

Amount chargeable

10.   Where a conveyance of property subject to a debt is chargeable to ad valorem duty and the express or implied covenant by the transferee relates only to part of the debt, only the amount of that part is treated as chargeable consideration within Section 57. A certificate of value under Section 34(4) FA 1958 may, where appropriate, be included in the conveyance where the relevant amount of the debt does not exceed the amount certified.

Other provisions

11.   The foregoing does not affect any statutory exemption from duty that may apply, e.g. that for transfers to a charity (Section 129, FA 1982) and that available for certain transfers of property from one party to a marriage to the other in connection with their divorce or separation (Section 83(1) FA 1985 and Category H of the Stamp Duty (Exempt Instruments) Regulations 1987).

Procedure

12.   Where the applicant is satisfied that the conveyance or transfer is made on sale, it may be sent or taken for stamping with a remittance of the duty payable. If the transfer contains an appropriate certificate of value – see paragraph 10 above – it may be sent direct to the Land Registry in the usual way if appropriate. In either case, if the amount of the debt outstanding is not given in the conveyance or transfer the amount should be stated in a covering letter.

13.   Where the conveyance or transfer contains a covenant by the transferor to pay the debt (see paragraph 6) and is certified as within Category L of the Stamp Duty (Exempt Instruments) Regulations 1987, it should also be sent direct to the Land Registry if appropriate.

14.   In any other case where the applicant believes that the conveyance or transfer effects a voluntary disposition – see paragraph 8 above – it should be presented for adjudication accompanied by a statement of the facts and any supporting evidence.

SP 6/91   STAMP DUTY AND VALUE ADDED TAX (VAT): INTERACTION
[Superseded by SP 11/91.]

SP 11/91   STAMP DUTY AND VALUE ADDED TAX (VAT): INTERACTION
[12 September 1991]

1.   This Statement is a revised version of the Statement about stamp duty and VAT issued on 22 July 1991, *SP 6/91, and replaces it.*

Introduction

2.   To comply with a judgment of the European Court of Justice in June 1988, standard rate UK VAT has been applied to non-residential construction with effect from 1 April 1989 (Section 18 Finance Act 1989). VAT is compulsory on sales of buildings treated as new for this purpose, which

Procedure for submitting documents

Where a person accepts that a conveyance or lease of a building plot is chargeable on the total price paid or payable for the land and the completed building, it should be submitted for stamping in the usual way together with a covering letter giving the aggregate price and a payment for the duty appropriate to that price.

Where the total price does not exceed the amount up to which the instrument is liable to nil duty (currently £60,000) and a certificate of value is included in the instrument, a conveyance may be sent direct to the Land Registry in England and Wales or, in Scotland, to the Keeper of the Registers of Scotland. A lease will need to be stamped in respect of the rent.

Where the total price exceeds the threshold at which duty becomes payable but the taxpayer takes the view that duty is payable on some smaller sum, the instrument should be submitted to the Stamp Office. This applies even where the taxpayer believes that the amount potentially chargeable to ad valorem duty is below the threshold and a certificate of value is included in the instrument. The instrument should be accompanied by a copy of the agreement(s) for sale etc. and a letter stating the amount which the taxpayer regards as chargeable consideration, identifying separately any amount attributable to building work. Details of any contractual arrangements not covered by the agreement(s) should also be given in the covering letter.

SP 3/98 STAMP DUTY: GROUP RELIEF [13 October 1998]

1. Section 42 Finance Act 1930 gives relief from stamp duty for transfers of property between members of the same group of companies. Section 151 Finance Act 1995 similarly gives relief from duty on the grant of a lease between members of the same group.

2. Section 27(3) Finance Act 1967 and Section 151(3) Finance Act 1995 are designed to prevent the use of group relief to avoid stamp duty when property, or an economic interest in it, passes out of the group.

3. This statement sets out the Stamp Office's current general practice in order to assist practitioners in determining whether claims to relief might qualify. The treatment of a particular case will of course depend on the precise facts. This statement is for general guidance only; and the facts of a particular transaction may, exceptionally, place it outside the guidelines. It applies also to the equivalent Northern Ireland legislation.

General

4. Broadly, Section 27(3) and the corresponding provisions in Section 151, provide that relief is not to be given if the transfer was made in pursuance of, or in connection with, an arrangement under which—

a.   all or part of the consideration for the transfer was to be provided or received, directly or indirectly, by a person outside the group; or

b.   the interest being transferred was previously transferred by a person outside the group; or

c.   the transferor and transferee were no longer to be part of the same group.

5. The person claiming the relief when the relevant instrument is adjudicated has the onus of satisfying the Stamp Office that the intra-group transaction is not carried out in pursuance of, or in connection with, an arrangement of a kind which disqualifies the transaction from relief: *Escoigne Properties Ltd v IRC* [1958] AC 549, 564.

"Arrangement"

6. *In this context*, arrangement means the plan or scheme in pursuance of which the things identified in the subparagraphs of Ss27(3) and 151(3) have been or are to be done: *Shop and Store Developments Ltd v IRC* [1967] 1 AC 472, 493–494. The arrangement need not be based in contract. It is sufficient if the intra-group transaction is made in connection with that plan or scheme. The intra-group transaction may be the first bi-lateral step by which legal rights and obligations are created in pursuance of the arrangement. If there is an expectation that a disqualifying event will happen in accordance with the arrangement and no likelihood in practice that it will not, relief will be refused.

7. The words *in connection with* are very broad. In *Escoigne*, there was a gap of four years between the two steps in issue.

Provision or receipt of consideration by a person outside the group: section 27(3)(a); section 151(3)(a) and (4)

8.   Section 27(3)(a) denies relief where the instrument was executed in pursuance of or in connection with an arrangement under which any of the consideration is to be provided or received, directly or indirectly, by a person outside the group. It also denies relief if the arrangement is one under which the transferor or transferee (or member of the same group as either of them) is to be enabled to provide any of the consideration, or is to part with it, in consequence of a transaction involving a payment or other disposition by a person outside the group. Section 151 lays down similar rules for leases.

9.   In some cases, the question arises whether loan finance for the purchase or lease will disqualify an intra-group transaction from relief. It is necessary to look at all the facts of the individual case, but the Stamp Office will interpret the provisions in the light of their general purpose of denying relief where the intra-group transaction is a means of saving stamp duty when the property, or a interest in it, moves out of the group. Accordingly, the Stamp Office are likely to be satisfied that relief is due if the intra-group transaction is not to be followed by a sale of the property transferred, or an underlease, to a person outside the group. If the intra-group transaction is to be followed by a sale underlease to a person outside the group, but the claimant can demonstrate that stamp duty will be paid in respect of that transaction in approximately the same amount as would have been payable if the intra-group transferor or lessor had itself sold the property or granted the underlease, the Stamp Office are likely to satisfied that the intra-group transaction and the transfer or lease-out are independent for stamp duty purposes and grant the relief sought.

10.   A transaction is not disqualified merely because the transferee within the group obtains a specific loan for the purchase of the asset; or the loan is secured on the asset; or arrangements are made to replace or novate an existing charge on the property transferred It will be necessary to consider the facts as a whole, especially in the loan finance is not straightforward finance on ordinary commercial terms.

11.   Intra-group transactions will be very carefully scrutinised, a relief may be refused, where, for example, the intra-group transaction involves or is to be followed by:

- the creation or transfer of loan stock or equity capital;
- a capital reorganisation of the transferee;
- a guarantee by a third party not associated with the group;
- the creation of a new charge or financial arrangement whereby title to the property is, or may be, vested in the lender otherwise than in satisfaction of all or part of the debt; or
- the assignment of the freehold reversion or the intra-group lease to a person outside the group.

12.   Similarly transactions will be very carefully scrutinised where:

- all or part of the consideration for the transaction is to remain outstanding or is represented by intra-group debt, (as the aim and effect may be to reduce the value of the transferee company on a possible future sale outside the group); or
- the existing shareholders of the transferee include shareholders outside the group and the transaction is to be followed by the declaration of a dividend in specie, or by the liquidation of the transferee.

13.   Further assurances by way of statutory declaration – the document in which the claim is made to the Stamp Office – will be required in any case in which the property transferred or vested intra-group is the only, or only substantial, asset of the transferee. Information to that effect should be provided in the statutory declaration submitted with the documents.

14.   Where group member A has granted a lease to a person outside the group, and subsequently grants an underlease to its fellow group member B, so that the rent already payable by the lessee becomes payable to B rather than A, relief is likely to be given for the intra-group underlease, provided there are no other factors which suggest that relief should be denied.

Property previously conveyed by a person outside the group: section 27(3)(b)

15.   Section 27(3)(b) was intended to prevent the avoidance of duty on the transfer of property into a group by means of a sub-sale, so as to take advantage of section 58(4) of the Stamp Act 1891. For example, suppose the property is sold to a group member by a vendor outside the group, but the sale rests in contract without a transfer of the legal title. The group member then sells the property to another member of its own group, and directs the vendor to transfer the legal title to that other member. In accordance with section 58(4) the transfer completing the sale and the sub-sale is

chargeable to duty only in relation to the sub-sale (thus relieving the effect of section 4 of the Stamp Act). However, section 27(3)(b) would deny group relief for that transfer.

16.   The Stamp Office will continue to apply section 27(3)(b) to schemes of this type and to any other scheme where an attempt has been made to avoid the duty payable on the acquisition by the group. However, where an outside vendor sells a property to a member of the group, the sale is completed by a transfer and stamp duty is paid on that transfer, the Stamp Office will normally regard any subsequent intra-group transfer as independent, and grant relief for the transfer within the purchaser's group.

Dissociation or demerger of transferee: section 27(3)(c): section 151(3)(b)

17.   Before the introduction of section 27(3), almost all the avoidance devices encountered in this area involved the transfer of property to a subsidiary, often created solely as a vehicle for that property, followed by the transfer of the shares in the subsidiary out of the group. Compared with a transfer of the property out of the group, a substantial amount of duty could be avoided even where the subsidiary paid for the property from its own resources. If the consideration for the intra-group transaction remained outstanding or was represented by debt, duty could be reduced further by reducing the value of the shares – hence section 27(3)(a).

18.   Section 27(3)(c) was introduced to counter this avoidance in relation to conveyances and transfers on sale. Section 151(3)(b) deals with leases on similar lines.

19.   In cases of this kind, the Stamp Office will need to be satisfied that the intra-group transfer or lease is not a step in pursuance of an arrangement to demerge the transferee. The existence of such an arrangement may be apparent from company documents, correspondence and other dealings between members of the group and professional advisers, or from discussions or negotiations with the potential purchasers, underwriters or minority shareholders.

20.   In practice, the Stamp Office will apply these provisions so as to preclude group relief if there is evidence of a plan or scheme to dispose of the subsidiary and there is no practical likelihood that the scheme will not be carried through. It will not be regarded as sufficient for the claimant to contend that such an arrangement which is less than contractual may possibly be frustrated by unforeseen events or unlikely occurrences. Even a contract may be frustrated.

21.   As the liability of the relevant instrument must, as a matter general principle, be determined as at the date of the instrument, the question whether an arrangement of the relevant kind exists must also be determined at that time, although the Stamp Office may have regard to what is said and done thereafter to establish the true position (*Wm Cory and Son Ltd v. IRC* [1965] AC1088). For the purposes of stamp duty, it is therefore the existence of the scheme or plan to which these provisions direct attention, not the ultimate outcome of steps which may be taken to implement that scheme. Accordingly, statements of practice in relation to other taxes have no application in this context.

REVENUE INTERPRETATIONS

IRInt. 4001   STAMP DUTY LITIGATION: (1) UNSTAMPED DOCUMENTS, OVERSEAS OR ONSHORE; (2) CONTINGENCY PRINCIPLE [August 1997, p. 459–461]

Parinv (Hatfield) Ltd v IRC [1996] STC 933 – Off-Shore Declaration Of Trust Ineffective To Avoid Ad Valorem Duty On Subsequent Transfers

This case concerned the effectiveness of an off-shore declaration of trust in avoiding ad valorem stamp duty on subsequent transfers. The High Court held that the device was ineffective. The taxpayer has lodged an appeal. In the meantme, the Stamp Office will continue to apply the law on the basis of the High Court's decision.

In the Parinv case, the taxpayer sought to rely on a copy of an unstamped overseas document to argue that the Stamp Office should stamp a transfer of property to a purchaser at 50p rather than 1%, on the basis that the transfer transferred only bare legal title and that the equitable interest in the property was transferred by the unstamped document. This argument was rejected by the Court on the grounds that the unstamped document was not admissible as evidence, inview of Section 14(4) of the Stamp Act 1891.

Unstamped Documents – Inland Revenue Practice

Following enquiries from customers, the Inland Revenue has decided to publicise its current practice with regard to unstamped documents. Under the terms of Section 14(4) Stamp Act 1891 . . .

> "an instrument executed in any part of the United Kingdom, or relating wheresoever executed, to any property situate, or to any matter or thing done or to be done, in any part of the United Kingdom, shall not, except in criminal proceedings, be given in evidence, or be available for any purpose whatever, unless it is duly stamped in accordance with the law in force at the time when it was first executed".

It has been the Inland Revenue's view that an unstamped document cannot be offered in evidence in any legal proceedings other than criminal proceedings, and that this includes hearings before the Special or General Commissioners. Following the case of Parinv (Hatfield) Ltd v CIR, the Inland Revenue's current practice will be as follows.

In the Parinv case, the Inland Revenue argued that an unstamped instrument was itself excluded from being used in civil proceedings, a view accepted by Lindsay J. Furthermore he took the view that a true copy, sometimes called a conformed copy, of an original unstamped document cannot be used to provide information or material or evidence of the original to the court.

The court then went on to consider the Inland Revenue's position in connection with copy documents. In his analysis of Section 14 (4) Stamp Act 1891 Lindsay J. considered the words "shall not ... be available for any purpose whatever". He indicated that these words were not an absolute prohibition because this would prevent an unstamped document being examined even in order to determine what should be the appropriate stamp. The Court referred to a judgement in an earlier case and endorsed the view that the words mean that one person cannot compel another person to rely on and accept an unstamped document.

The Inland Revenue in addition, argued that it was able to look at the copy document with the purpose of establishing the liability to duty of another document. The Court held that because the taxpayer is obliged by Section 5 of the Act to provide all facts and circumstances affecting the liability to duty of a document including all such evidence deemed necessary by the Board to form a view if adjudication or assessment is required, the Inland Revenue was not obliged by the Act to exclude from its consideration the contents of a copy of an unstamped document which had been supplied to it in order to meet that obligation. It was unlikely that Parliament would have imposed a fine for non-disclosure (i.e. a fraudulent act) and yet required the Revenue to ignore the disclosure. So the Inland Revenue can have regard to a document for the purpose of an assessment of duty. But that does not compel the Inland Revenue to go any further.

The Inland Revenue is aware that documents executed overseas are frequently retained there with a view to deferral or avoidance of payment of stamp duty. It will not be the Inland Revenue's practice to request sight of original documents in these or other circumstances, merely to check whether they have been duly stamped or not. However, if the documents are to be relied on by a person in support of any claim to relief, or otherwise used in evidence in relation to any liability to tax, or the amount thereof, that person should be aware that the Revenue cannot be compelled to accept in support of such claim or as evidence unstamped original or conformed unstamped copies of documents.

Penalty for fraud

Section 5 of the Stamp Act 1891 requires that all the facts and circumstances affecting the liability of an instrument to duty, or the amount of the duty chargeable, shall be fully and truly set forth in the instrument, and that any failure to do so by the parties or their advisers with intent to defraud the Crown shall attract a fine. The Stamp Office takes the view that a failure to disclose the fact that the parties are attempting to rely on an unstamped instrument, contrary to Section 14(4) of the Stamp Act, in executing a transfer which purports to convey the bare legal estate, will constitute a breach of Section 5, and appropriate action will be taken.

The Stamp Office also takes the view that any attempt by the parties to an instrument containing a certificate under the exempt instruments legislation which relied on another instrument executed overseas which was not duly stamped, would constitute a breach of Section 5.

LM Tenancies 1 Plc V CIR [1996] STC 880 – Consideration Calculated in Accordance With A Formula Ascertained By Application Of Contingency Principle

This case concerned the application of the contingency principle. The High Court held that where the calculation of duty relied on a future value, (the price of a gilt some time after execution of the document) the Stamp Office could rely on the last published figure.

The taxpayer has lodged an appeal against this decision. In the meantime the Stamp Office will apply the law on the basis of the Court's decision, subject to the normal right of appeal in any individual case. On that basis, duty is payable on an ascertainable amount where the contingency principle can be applied in the way outlined above.

The Stamp Office is of the view that the contingency principle, as it was held to apply in this case, will apply to other reference values which are unknown at the date of execution. An example is the practice of making future rent increases subject to an increase in an index, typically the RPI. The Stamp Office will apply the published increase in RPI over the 12 months prior to execution of the lease or agreement for lease to calculate the average annual rent.

Where the contingency principle does not apply, Section 242 Finance Act 1994 now provides that where the consideration for an interest in land is unascertainable, ad valorem stamp duty is chargeable on the basis of the value of the property conveyed.

The Inland Revenue *Tax Bulletin* contains the following caveat:

"... You can expect the interpretations of law contained in the Bulletin will normally be applied in relevant cases, but this is subject to a number of qualifications.

- Particular cases may turn on their facts, or context, and because every possible situation cannot be covered there may be circumstances when the interpretation given here will not apply.
- There may also be circumstances in which the Board would find it necessary to argue for a different interpretation in appeal proceedings ...".

OTHER MATERIAL

A. PRESS RELEASES

STAMP DUTY: DEPOSITARY RECEIPTS AND CLEARANCE SERVICES [Inland Revenue press release, 24 October 1986]

The Board of Inland Revenue have announced the names of nominee companies to which, on the transfer of shares to them, the one and one-half ($1\frac{1}{2}$) per cent rate of stamp duty will apply with effect from 27 October 1986.

The *Finance Act* 1986, s. 67 and 70 provide for stamp duty at the rate of £1.50 per £100 to be charged in the case of transfers (on sale or otherwise) of UK shares to certain nominee companies.

The following companies have notified the Board of Inland Revenue that they come within the terms of these provisions:

Section 67 (depositary receipt) cases

> Beech Street Nominees Ltd.
> BNY (Nominees) Ltd.
> Chembank Depositary Nominees Ltd.
> Guaranty Nominees Ltd.
> Irving Trust Company (Nominees) Ltd.
> Midland Bank (St. Magnus) Nominees Ltd.
> National City Nominees Ltd.
> Specease Ltd.

Section 70 (clearance services) cases

> EC Nominees Ltd.
> Stock Exchange (Nominees) Ltd. [now ceased, see press release, 16 April 1987]

Stamp duty at the $1\frac{1}{2}$ per cent rate will accordingly be payable on transfers to these companies executed on or after 27 October 1986.

STAMP DUTY: CLEARANCE SYSTEMS [Inland Revenue press release, 16 April 1987]

The Inland Revenue have been notified that Stock Exchange (Nominees) Ltd. will cease to act as a nominee for a clearance service operator.

A new company, SE (Global Custody) Ltd., will in future act for the clearance system previously dealt with by Stock Exchange (Nominees) Ltd.

The change takes effect from 5 May 1987.

STAMP DUTY: CLEARANCE SYSTEMS [Inland Revenue press release, 16 February 1989]

In accordance with stamp duty law, the Inland Revenue have been notified that a new company, MGT(B) Nominees Ltd., is acting as a nominee for a clearance service operator.

STAMP DUTY: DEPOSITARY RECEIPTS [Inland Revenue press release, 14 June 1989]

In accordance with stamp duty law, the Board of Inland Revenue have been notified that the following two companies are acting as nominees for persons issuing depositary receipts:

–   BT Ctag Nominees Ltd. – with effect from 15 May 1989.
–   SP Nominees Ltd. – with effect from 18 May 1989.

TAURUS [London Stock Exchange News Release 6/93, 11 March 1993]

The Board of the London Stock Exchange today (11 March) announced that it is stopping all work on the development and testing of the Taurus service with immediate effect. Following an approach by Sir Andrew Hugh Smith, Chairman of the Exchange, the Governor of the Bank of England has appointed a small task force to consider the best way forward for securities settlement in the UK. The Bank of England is issuing further details in a separate announcement today.

In the light of the Board's decision, Peter Rawlins, Chief Executive of the Exchange, has decided to stand down forthwith. Sir Andrew Hugh Smith will assume the additional role of Chief Executive and Jane Barker, currently Finance Director of the Exchange, will become Chief Operating Officer, until such time as a new Chief Executive is appointed.

The decision to stop work on Taurus was reached following a thorough review by the senior management of the Exchange and by Coopers & Lybrand, the Exchange's consultants, of the status and objectives of the project in the light of the first industry-wide testing stage. It revealed serious concerns which would have taken a minimum of fifteen months to correct before any further industry-wide testing could be resumed. This implies that it would be two to three years before Taurus could be operable.

In the view of the Board, the significantly lengthened timescales and the costs necessary to achieve a reliable service make continuation of the project unjustifiable.

The Board emphasises the continued operational effectiveness for all investors of the existing Talisman settlement service. Talisman is in no way affected by this decision.

There will obviously be painful staffing implications, but it is too early to know what decisions industry participants will take. There are some 220 Stock Exchange employees currently working on the project who have today been told their positions are now redundant. There are a further 130 individual contractors whose contracts are being terminated. The Board thanks them for all their efforts and deeply regrets this necessary consequence of its decision.

Sir Andrew Hugh Smith said

"It is with deep regret that my Board has reached the decision to stop work on Taurus. We have all been committed to the Taurus development, and the delivery of its projected benefits to the users of our markets.

I very much welcome the Governor's agreement to set up a task force. From the start, the design of Taurus reflected a compromise between many commercial interests. We very much hope that what will emerge from this task force will be the best answer to the needs of the markets.

I would like to record our gratitude to Peter Rawlins for the very significant contribution he has made."

STAMP DUTY: DEPOSITARY RECEIPTS [Inland Revenue press release, 25 February 1994]

The Inland Revenue have been notified, in accordance with Section 68(2) Finance Act 1986, that the following companies are acting as nominees for persons whose business is or includes issuing depositary receipts:

Bank America Nominees Ltd
Barclays Nominees (White Horse) Ltd.

STAMP DUTY: CLEARANCE SERVICES [Inland Revenue press release, 25 February 1994]

The Inland Revenue have been notified, in accordance with Section 71(2) Finance Act 1986, that the following company is acting as nominee for Japanese Securities Clearing Corporation (JSCC), a clearance service:

Barclays Nominees (JSCC) Limited

STAMP DUTY: PROPERTY TRANSACTIONS [Inland Revenue press release, 18 April 1994]

This Press Release gives guidance, in response to enquiries and representations, about some aspects of the stamp duty changes introduced by the Finance Bill. They are:

a.　the calculation of duty on an exchange of properties, particularly where the properties are of unequal value and a payment of money (known as equality money) is also made;

b.　the application of the £60,000 threshold to exchanges;

c.　the treatment of sales where one property is sold and another property is given in part payment of the sale price. The guidance makes clear that in these circumstances duty at one per cent is charged (subject to the threshold) on the consideration for the property being sold; the transfer of the other property which is given in part payment is liable only to the fixed duty of 50 pence.

Details

Exchanges

1.　[*Finance Act* 1994 s. 241] introduces new rules for stamp duty on exchanges of interests in land or buildings. Under the new rules duty is charged on each transfer. The duty in each case is calculated by reference to the "consideration" (ie the value) given for the transfer; where the consideration consists of property, its open market value will be taken. For example, if one house worth £100,000 is exchanged for another house worth £100,000, duty of £1,000 (one per cent of £100,000) is charged on each transfer. The £60,000 threshold is applied separately to each side of the exchange. For example, if there is a straightforward exchange of one house worth £50,000 for another worth £50,000, both transfers are within the threshold and so no duty would be payable on either (see paragraph 10 below).

2.   Where the market values of the two properties being exchanged are not equal, a payment of money (or some other consideration) may often be given with the lower value property, so as to equalise the bargain. The treatment of such cases for stamp duty purposes will depend on the facts and the effect of the relevant documents.

Examples

3.   For example, where one house worth £100,000 is exchanged for another worth £80,000 plus £20,000 money, the conveyance for the transfer of the £100,000 house will normally say that the consideration for the transfer consists of the £80,000 house and the £20,000 money; and the conveyance will be stamped accordingly with duty on £100,000.

4.   On the conveyance of the £80,000 house, the Stamp Office have charged duty under the new rules by reference to the consideration expressed in the conveyance:

a.   where the conveyance provides that the consideration for the transfer of the cheaper property is the appropriate proportion of the value of the more expensive property, stamp duty is applied accordingly. Thus if the conveyance provides that the consideration for the £80,000 house is the appropriate proportion of the £100,000 house, the amount charged to duty on the transfer of the £80,000 house is limited to £80,000;

b.   more commonly the conveyance may say simply that the consideration for the transfer of the £80,000 house consists of the £100,000 house. In these circumstances, the Stamp Office will have charged duty by reference to the value of the £100,000 house.

Representations

5.   Representations have been made that in many cases the wording of the conveyance of the cheaper property may not fully reflect the consideration expressed in the initial contract or agreement. It has been suggested that where the contract provides for an exchange and also provides for money to be paid as equality money by one party to the other, the equality money should be taken into account in deciding how much of the more expensive property is regarded as consideration for the cheaper property (even though the equality money has not been mentioned in the conveyance of the cheaper property).

Revised practice

6.   The Inland Revenue have taken legal advice on this. The conclusion is that where it is clear from the contract that the intention of the parties to the transaction is that the cheaper property should be transferred for the more expensive property *less* the equality money, the Stamp Office will limit the charge to duty accordingly. For example, if the initial contract provided for an £80,000 house to be exchanged for a £100,000 house, and for £20,000 to be paid as equality money, the amount charged to duty on the transfer of the £80,000 property would be limited to £80,000. The result in an individual case will depend on the facts of the case and the relevant documents. The Stamp Office will need to see the relevant contract with the conveyance which is to be stamped.

7.   Where there is a multiple exchange of properties, an apportionment on similar lines may be made to determine how much of the consideration is attributable to each of the transfers. For example, two or more properties may be exchanged for one larger property, with or without a payment of equality money. Here again, the precise result will depend on the facts of the case.

Past cases

8.   Where the transfer of a cheaper property has already been stamped by reference to the full value of a more expensive property, but the person who has paid the duty thinks that the duty would be reduced on the basis explained in paragraph 6 or 7 above, the Stamp Office will be prepared to review the case. Applicants should resubmit the relevant conveyance, and the contract (or a certified copy of the contract). (If it is not possible to obtain the original stamped document from the relevant Registrar, the Stamp Office should be consulted about alternative arrangements.) Where appropriate, excess duty will be repaid provided the claim is made within the 2-year time limit laid down by section 10 of the Stamp Duties Management Act 1891.

9. Claims for repayment should be made to the Stamp Office at Worthing (for England, Wales and Northern Ireland), or Edinburgh (for Scotland).

Application of £60,000 threshold

10. Sales of property (other than shares) for a price not exceeding the £60,000 threshold are exempted from duty, provided that a "certificate of value" is given stating that the transfer is not part of a larger transaction, or a series of transactions, for a total price of more than £60,000. The threshold is applied separately to each side of an exchange of properties. If in a particular case the threshold has not been applied separately to each side of an exchange, (or to two sales where the purchase prices have been set off against each other), and the person who paid the duty believes that too much duty was paid, the documents (with the certificate of value) may be returned for reconsideration to the Stamp Office on the same basis as in paragraphs 8 and 9 above.

11. Where there is a multiple exchange – for example, properties A and B are exchanged for property C – the transfers of properties A and B would be regarded as parts of a larger transaction, and the threshold would not apply to either of them if the total consideration for both was more than £60,000. The threshold would be applied separately to the transfer of property C.

Sales

12. In many cases, transactions which in the past have been structured and documented as exchanges could equally well be carried out as sales for a price which may be partly satisfied in kind. For example, when a builder offers a property for sale, he may receive the price from the buyer in the form either of money, or partly of money and partly of the buyer's old house. Such a transaction can be carried out and documented (commencing with the initial contract) as a sale. Stamp duty is charged on the consideration for the sale. So if, for example, the buyer is buying a new house for £100,000, and pays for it with £30,000 in cash plus his old house worth £70,000, duty of £1,000 (one per cent of £100,000) would be charged on the transfer of the £100,000 house. The house which the builder accepts as part payment for the sale would not be regarded as a separate sale for stamp duty purposes. It would be charged only to the fixed duty of 50 pence. The threshold would not be of relevance to this transfer as it is not a conveyance on sale.

General

13. In cases of doubt about how a particular document of the types mentioned above would be treated by the Stamp Office for stamp duty purposes, the Technical Section, The Stamp Office, Ridgeworth House, Liverpool Gardens, Worthing BN11 1XP, will be willing to help.

STAMP DUTY: NEW LEASES WITH INDEXED RENT LEVELS [Inland Revenue press release, 14 May 1999]

The Economic Secretary to the Treasury, Patricia Hewitt, today [14 May 1999] announced that the Inland Revenue have reviewed their practice in relation to the Stamp Duty treatment of new leases under which future rent levels are expressed to be dependent on future movements in an index such as the Retail Prices Index (RPI).

The change in practice, based on recent legal advice, means that in general less Stamp Duty will be payable in these cases. Many people who have paid Stamp Duty on such leases under the current basis will be entitled to a repayment. The new basis takes effect from today [14 May 1999].

In a reply to a Parliamentary Question, Mrs. Hewitt said:

> "In the light of recent legal advice given to the Inland Revenue the treatment of these leases for Stamp Duty is to be changed.

> When a new lease is taken out, Stamp Duty is charged by reference to both the premium and the rent under the lease. The premium attracts duty at the same rates as the selling price on the sale of a freehold interest. The premium gets the benefit of the £60,000 nil rate band provided that the rent does not exceed a ceiling, currently £600 per annum. The average annual rent is charged at rates of between one per cent and twenty-four per cent, depending on the length of the lease.

> Many leases provide that the rent is to increase by a fixed percentage at annual or other intervals – or they lay down the actual amounts of the increases. The average annual rent, and therefore the Stamp Duty, is straightforward to calculate in these cases. But if future rent levels are expressed in terms of future movements in a index like the RPI, it is less clear how a figure for the average annual rent can be calculated at the time the lease is taken out. In the

light of representations, on 6 November 1996 the then Economic Secretary made a statement to this House by way of Written Answer, setting out how the Stamp Office would apply Stamp Duty in such cases for the future, on the basis of legal advice (Hansard Cols 541–543).

Broadly, where the rent under a lease was to be adjusted by reference to future changes in an index, Stamp Duty would be calculated by reference to changes in that index during the year ending with the date of execution of the lease.

However, the legal validity of this approach has been challenged. Further legal advice given to the Inland Revenue is that the current system of applying a formula to allow for increases in an index number after the date of execution of a lease is not appropriate. So this practice will cease.

In future, where there is a formula expressed in the lease for rent reviews based on the RPI, only any change in the RPI up to the date of its execution will be taken into account for Stamp Duty purposes. This is expected to result, in most cases, in the average rent being little more than the initial rent.

This change means that people who have paid Stamp Duty on this type of lease may have paid more duty than they should have done. The Inland Revenue will invite those who paid duty on a lease of this kind to contact the Stamp Office and claim any repayment due to them. Details of the arrangements for repayments are set out in an Inland Revenue Press Release and on the Inland Revenue web-site."

Details

The Inland Revenue will make repayments of excess Stamp Duty paid under the practice announced in 1996 as follows:

- Repayments will be made to those who made appeals against the assessment of Stamp Duty pending the outcome of litigation challenging the Stamp Office's practice;
- repayments will also be made to those affected who present a claim to the Stamp Office within the 2 years of execution of the relevant lease provided for under the *Stamp Duties Management Act* 1891; and
- in the exceptional circumstances of this change of practice, the Stamp Office will also consider claims in respect of similar leases executed on or after 25 February 1995, provided that such claims are made within one year of the date of this Press Release.

[Note 7 to the press release gives the following further advice regarding claims:

7. Applicants for repayments should contact the Stamp Office at the following address;

Stamp Allowance Claims Section
Manchester Stamp Office
Alexandra House
Parsonage
Manchester M60 9BT
DX 14430 Manchester 2

1. Applications should where possible be accompanied by the original stamped document. If that is not in the applicant's possession, for example because it is held by a solicitor, building society or land registry, the Stamp Office should be consulted as to alternative arrangements. Duplicate and copy documents are not acceptable.

2. Information and advice are also available by telephoning the Stamp Office Helpline: 0845 6030135. (All calls to this number are charged at local rates.)]

STAMP DUTY: 7 YEAR LEASES [Inland Revenue press release, 17 September 1999]

The rate of Stamp Duty applying to the rental element of new leases for exactly 7 years is to be confirmed in the Finance Bill 2000.

This will reaffirm the Government's intention of ensuring that new leases of exactly 7 years are subject to Stamp Duty on the rent paid under the lease, and will correct a technical omission in the *Finance Act* 1999, putting an end to any uncertainty.

Annual revenue from Stamp Duty on the rental element of leases of 7 years and below is about £1 million.

Details

1.   Section 112 and Schedule 13 of *Finance Act* 1999 re-state the schedule of rates of Stamp Duty in percentage terms to correspond to the rates of duty generally in force. This is done to introduce a standardised provision for rounding up amounts of duty to multiples of £5 to streamline administration, with effect from 1 October 1999. The Stamp Duty rates on leases for periods of less than 7 years and those for more than 7 years are set at percentages of the rental which correspond to the current rates of duty. But there is no explicit reference to the rate of duty for new leases for a period of exactly 7 years, although the current legislation sets the Stamp Duty for the rental element of such leases at 50p for each £50 or part thereof (or zero in the case of annual rents of no more than £500).

2.   The effect of this would be that from 1 October 1999 leases for exactly 7 years would not be subject to Stamp Duty on the rent paid under the lease instead of being liable to the current 1% of the average annual rent – though the duty on any premium paid for the lease would not be reduced.

3.   A measure will be brought forward in next year's Finance Bill, effective from 1 October 1999, to ensure that the Government's intention (which was set out in the published *Explanatory Notes* to the 1999 *Finance Act*) is met. This will again put leases for exactly 7 years onto the same footing as those for under 7 years.

4.   There will be two possibilities for relevant documents for 7-year leases executed on or after 1 October 1999 arising in the interim:

A.   They may be presented for stamping in accordance with the lower amounts of duty specified in *Finance Act* 1999. In such cases:

- the document will be considered to be "duly stamped" for legal purposes until the new measures take effect (after the vote on Resolutions is taken at the end of next year's Budget debates);
- at this point the document will cease to be duly stamped until it is again presented for stamping so that the duty is topped up to the intended 1%;
- interest and penalties for late stamping will apply to the second stamping only if, and to the extent that, the extra duty is paid or a document is presented (again) more than 30 days after the new measures take effect.

B.   Taxpayers may, if they wish, have their documents stamped in the first place at the full 1% to ensure that the documents concerned will remain duly stamped after the new measures take effect. This entirely voluntary procedure will avoid the need for a second presentation for stamping.

B.   CCAB/ICAEW MATERIAL

RECONSTRUCTION OF A CLOSE COMPANY (FA 1986, s. 75) [ICAEW Technical Release 631, August 1986]

The Revenue stated that relief would not be available where reconstruction of a close company took place and one group of shareholders took over one part of its undertaking while another group took the remaining business.

C.   MISCELLANEOUS

MISC. 301   STAMP DUTY: ADJUDICATION [Law Society's Gazette, 18 July 1990]

The stamp office has announced an administrative modification to its adjudication procedures. Following examination of an instrument for adjudication, the stamp office's practice is to notify the applicant of the amount of duty estimated to be payable. Normally, this leads to one of two courses of action; the applicant either agrees and remits the duty, or notifies the stamp office of his disagreement. If the applicant agrees, the instrument is stamped and returned; if he disagrees, discussions by way of correspondence between the applicant and the office may follow with the aim of reaching agreement or, where necessary, a formal assessment is issued.

Sometimes, however, there is no response at all from the applicant to the stamp office's estimate – no payment of duty or indication of disagreement. Nevertheless, duty is normally eventually paid, but it may be necessary for the stamp office to issue a number of reminders. This is administratively inconvenient and wasteful of the office's resources.

The office has therefore introduced a change in procedure. It will continue to allow 28 days for applicants to respond to estimates of duty payable. If no response has been received after the 28 days, a reminder will be issued, but this will be the only reminder. The office will consider the request for adjudication as having been withdrawn once a further 14 days have elapsed after the issue of the reminder, and will then return the instrument unstamped to the applicant.

This will not prevent the applicant from representing the instrument for adjudication. However, s. 14(4) (instrument not duly stamped not to be given in evidence) and s. 15 (penalty upon stamping instruments after execution) of the Stamp Act 1891 might apply in the event of delay.

MISC. 302   STAMP DUTY: AGREEMENTS FOR LEASES [Law Society's Gazette, 6 July 1994]

The stamp office has now published guidance on the procedures to be followed when leases are presented for stamping. Readers should note that the new arrangements apply to leases executed on or after 6 May 1994, and that it will now be necessary for a lease either to contain a certificate (in the form suggested by the stamp office) to the effect that there was no prior agreement or to be denoted with the duty paid (if any) on the agreement to which the lease gives effect. The text of the stamp office's guidance is reproduced below, with its permission.

Further to the stamp office budget notes, additional guidance is now given on the new arrangements to be introduced from 6 May. The past practices [*sic*] of stamping a lease without necessarily calling for the agreement for lease has ceased.

Charges introduced

An agreement for lease is liable to stamp duty and any duty paid must be denoted on the ensuing lease. Leases executed on 6 May 1994 onwards will not be duly stamped for the purpose of the Stamp Act unless either:

(a)   they are certified to the effect that there was no prior agreement; or
(b)   they are denoted with the duty paid (if any) on the agreement to which they give effect.

The new arrangements will now enable agreements executed on or after 6 May 1994 to be submitted with the lease to which they relate without a penalty for late stamping, provided they are submitted within 30 days of the date of execution of the lease.

Where both lease and agreement are submitted more than 30 days after execution of the lease, the penalty provisions will be applied to both documents. However, the penalty on the agreement will be calculated from the date of execution of the lease, not from the date the agreement was executed.

For those agreements which were executed prior to 6 May, the stamp office will mitigate the penalty for late stamping on any agreement for lease which is submitted together with a lease in conformity with that agreement, as long as both are submitted within 30 days of the date of execution of the lease.

If, pursuant to one duly stamped agreement for lease, several leases are granted of separate parts of the property at apportioned rents, each lease will be denoted for the whole of the duty impressed on the agreement.

Form of certificate

The certificate included in a lease to which there was no agreement should be along the following lines:

> "I/We certify that there is no agreement for lease (or tack) to which this (lease or tack) gives effect."

In the absence of a certificate, the stamp office will be unable to process the lease and documents will be returned for resubmission (unless accompanied by the agreement for lease). Where certificates are not inserted in the instrument as originally drawn, they should be added to the instrument and signed by the parties who have executed the instrument. Separate certificates will not be accepted.

Documents to be submitted

Where a counterpart of a lease (no certificate) is submitted, it will be assessed under the provisions of s. 72 of the SA 1891 to 50p duty unless the duty chargeable on the lease, e.g. the total of impressed and denoting stamps, is a lesser amount.

Procedures

The existing arrangements for denoting will continue but may be changed in the light of experience. You can ask your stamp office for leases to be denoted but if urgent, send the agreement and lease (or counterpart) to London Stamp Office, South West Wing, Bush House, Strand, London WC2B 4QN; DX 1099 London/Chancery Lane. Leases which contain a certificate will continue to be dealt with by your usual stamp office.

MISC. 303   STAMP DUTY RESERVE TAX (SDRT) Penalties for failure to notify liability [Inland Revenue *Tax Bulletin*, issue 37, October 1998, p. 589]

This article explains the Stamp Office's practice in relation to the penalties to which an accountable person may be liable in the event of a failure to notify SDRT liability before the accountable date.

Background

Broadly speaking, SDRT is charged on agreements to transfer shares where no stock transfer form is used (and accordingly no Stamp Duty is paid). Most SDRT arises on transfers of dematerialised shares held in CREST, where the SDRT concerned is accounted for centrally through CREST. However not all securities are able to be held in CREST and so SDRT also arises in a variety of other situations. One common example is where such "residual" securities that have been purchased but not yet delivered are soon sold again and accordingly registered directly into the name of the second purchaser.

Where SDRT arises that is not accounted for in CREST, Regulation 4 of the SDRT Regulations SI 1986 No 1711 (as amended by SI 1997/2430) requires the accountable person to give written notice of each charge to SDRT, and to pay the SDRT due direct to the Inland Revenue, on or before the accountable date.

The written notice (which should set out the date of the agreement, and the parties, securities and consideration involved) should be sent together with the SDRT itself to the Shares Unit of the Stamp Office at the address below.

Where the shares are purchased on an exchange the accountable person, as defined by Regulation 2 of the SDRT Regulations 1986, will be one of the brokers (or qualified dealers) involved in the transaction. Otherwise the purchaser is accountable.

The accountable date is the seventh day of the month following the month in which the trade date of the transaction occurred. Interest is charged from that date on any SDRT paid late.

Penalties apply to late notices under Section 93 Taxes Management Act (TMA) 1970, as applied to SDRT by SI 1986/1711 (as amended by SI 1997/2430). The level of penalties depends on how late the notice is provided as set out below.

Notice given late but within one year of the accountable date

Section 93(2) TMA 1970 states that each Regulation 4 failure will incur a liability to a penalty of £100; that is to say that each transaction which is accounted for to the Stamp Office after the accountable date will attract a potential penalty of £100. Composite monthly notifications are very welcome, but it should be noted that a late composite notice covering say 10 transactions would potentially be liable to 10 penalties of £100.

However, to prevent the size of the potential penalty being disproportionate to the amount of SDRT involved, the amount of the statutory penalty in relation to each individual transaction will normally be limited to the lesser of:

- the total SDRT due on the transaction reported, and
- £100.

So, for example, if a late composite notice for a particular month relates to just two transactions attracting SDRT of £10 and £1000 respectively, the mitigated penalty would normally be £110 rather than £200.

Whenever an agreement to transfer chargeable securities is not reported before the accountable date the accountable person can now expect to have to account for a maximum penalty of £100 along with interest on the SDRT from the accountable date to the date of payment.

Notice given more than one year after the accountable date

In addition to the penalty described above, if the failure continues for twelve months or more the accountable person becomes liable, under Section 93(5) TMA 1970, to a tax geared penalty not exceeding the amount of SDRT which should have been paid. In the event of such a penalty becoming due, consideration will be given to mitigating the amount charged in line with the Board's established policy. Full details are given in Stamp Office leaflet SO14 (available from the address below) but, briefly, the three factors taken into consideration are; the readiness with which the disclosure is made, the amount of co-operation given and the overall gravity of the offence committed.

Cases where transfer document stamped after accountable date

SDRT arises whenever a stock transfer form relating to a transaction in securities is not stamped before the accountable date. However, in practice accountable persons handling residual securities sometimes find they cannot get stock transfer forms stamped by that time, but are nevertheless confident that such a form will be stamped shortly thereafter (which will then cancel the SDRT charge).

Where a stock transfer form relating to residual securities is stamped within 60 days of the date of the transaction the Stamp Office will not seek interest on the SDRT in the meantime and no notice need be given. This extends the practice set out at the end of paragraph 1.11 of the SDRT Notes for Guidance published in February 1998.

However, should a stock transfer form not in fact be duly stamped within this time then interest on the unpaid SDRT will still run from the accountable date. In addition, if a notice was not delivered by that date the penalties described above will apply.

It should also be noted that if the stock transfer form is presented for stamping more than 30 days after it is executed there may be a penalty for late stamping.

Contact point

SDRT Notices and payments, and requests for further information, should be sent to:

> Shares Unit
> Ground Floor
> East Block
> Barrington Road
> Worthing
> BN12 4SE
> Telephone: 01903 509467/471

MISC. 304   STAMP DUTY AND VAT UPON THE TRANSFER OF A BUSINESS [Law Society's Gazette, 15 January 1999]

Last year the Stamp Office published a customer newsletter concerning the stamp duty position on the sale of business as a going concern and this was reproduced in the Gazette (see [1998] Gazette, 16 September, 42).

The Law Society has received a number of representations concerning the Stamp Office's requirement that solicitors submitting a business sale agreement document allowing for VAT to be charged later on should provide a written undertaking to return the document to the Stamp Office for payment of the additional duty if VAT is charged later. A number of the Stamp Office's customers have suggested that it is not practical for them to give this undertaking because they would be required to ensure that the additional duty was held in their client account before giving that undertaking on behalf of the client. We accept that in the vast majority of cases no additional stamp duty will be payable and it would not be appropriate to require firms to hold this extra duty where it is unlikely to fall due. Several firms have suggested an alternative undertaking which, in the circumstances, the Stamp Office now decided to adopt. The paragraph in the previous newsletter headed 'What if VAT can be charged?' is withdrawn and is replace by the following:

> "If the document allows for VAT to be charged later on, for instance, if Customs & Excise refuse clearance, then we will stamp the document on the initial consideration stated and ask you to confirm that:
>
> - the transaction is believed to involve the transfer of a going concern and consequently no VAT has been added to the consideration stated in the document;
> - you have advised your client that they are obliged to tell the Stamp Office if that position changes, in line with their obligations under s.5 of the *Stamp Act* 1891; and
> - that the client undertakes to arrange for the document to be returned to the Stamp Office and to pay the extra duty due if VAT does become payable.
>
> A written undertaking from the client to that effect should be enclosed with your letter. The Stamp Office has special arrangements with the Land Registry for the release of documents direct to the Stamp Office where they are held by the Registry but are required for adjustment of the stamp duty they bear."

This amendment and the revised arrangements are to take immediate effect.

Questions or comments about these new arrangements should be directed to the local Stamp Office or, alternatively: Archie Brown, assistant director, The Stamp Office, 15 Floor, Cale Cross House, 156 Pilgrim Street, Newcastle-upon-Tyne, NE1 6TF; DX 61201 Newcastle-upon-Tyne; telephone: 0191 245 0232 Fax 0191 245 0229.

MISC. 305   STAMP DUTY – CHANCERY DIVISION PRACTICE DIRECTIONS
[CHANCERY GUIDE 28 August 1999, SECTION C – Extract from CDPD 12 TRUSTS – F Variation of Trusts]

(iii) Stamp Duty

(a)   An undertaking by solicitors with regard to stamping is not required to be included in an order under the Variation of Trusts Act 1958 whether made by a Judge or Master.

(b)   The Commissioners of Inland Revenue consider that the stamp duty position of duplicate orders is as follows:

    (i) Orders confined to the lifting of protective trusts. These orders are not liable for duty at all and should not be presented to a stamp office.

    (ii) Orders affecting voluntary dispositions inter vivos. These orders may be certified under the Stamp Duty (Exempt Instruments) Regulations 1987 (S.I. 1987 No. 516), as within category L in the schedule to those regulations, in which case they should not be presented to a stamp office. Without such a certificate they attract 50p duty under the head "Conveyance or transfer of any kind not hereinbefore described."

    (iii) Orders outside categories (i) and (ii) above that contain declarations of the trust, i.e. that effect no disposition of trust property. These orders attract 50p fixed duty under the head "Declaration of trust". They may be presented for stamping at any stamp office in the usual way, or sent for adjudication if preferred.

MISC. 306   STAMP DUTY RESERVE TAX: CHANGES TO INTEREST RATES; PENALTIES FOR FAILURE TO NOTIFY LIABILITY; INTERACTION WITH STAMP DUTY [Inland Revenue Tax Bulletin, October 1999.]

This article notes the changes to the arrangements for interest on late paid and overpaid SDRT from 1 October (announced in a Press Release of 10 September 1999), describes a modification to the practice about penalties for late notifications of SDRT (set out in an article in the October 1998 edition of Tax Bulletin, page 589) and highlights some points on the interaction of SDRT with Stamp Duty from 1 October.

Background

Broadly speaking, SDRT is charged on agreements to transfer shares where no stock transfer form is used (and accordingly no Stamp Duty is paid). Most SDRT arises on transfers of dematerialised shares held in CREST, where the SDRT concerned is accounted for centrally through CREST. But not all securities are able to be held in CREST and so SDRT also arises in a variety of other situations.

In such cases, the accountable person has to give written notice of each charge to SDRT, and to pay the SDRT due, on or before the accountable date. Where the shares are purchased on an exchange the accountable person will generally be one of the brokers involved in the transaction. Otherwise the purchaser is accountable.

The accountable date is the seventh day of the month following the month in which the trade date of the transaction occurred. Interest is charged from the accountable date on any SDRT paid late. Late notices may also attract penalties. The level of penalties depends on how late the notice is provided.

More detailed background information was contained in the earlier article.

Changes to SDRT interest rates from 1 October 1999

Before 1 October the rates of interest charged on late paid SDRT and paid on SDRT repayments were the same. But from 1 October, as with other taxes, the interest rates will differ. The rates for SDRT (and for Stamp Duty) will be the same as those for income tax. Details of these changes can be obtained from leaflets issued by the Stamp Office, obtainable from the Stamp Office helpline – 0845 6030135 or on the Inland Revenue website.

Penalties for failure to notify SDRT liability on time

As set out in the previous article, the rules depend on whether a late notice is provided within a year of the accountable date, or after a longer period. No changes are being made to the practice regarding notices given more than one year after the accountable date, which remains as set out in the previous article.

In the light of the changes to interest rates, and a review of the first year of operation of the practice on penalties in the previous article, the practice in the case of notices provided within a year of the accountable date is being modified in the case of multiple late notices made by an accountable person. This article sets out the revised position, which will apply in relation to notifications relating to transactions for which the accountable date was on or after 1 October 1999.

Section 93(2) TMA 1970 (as applied to SDRT by SI 1986/1711) states that each failure to give timely notification will incur a penalty of £100; that is to say that each transaction which is accounted for to the Stamp Office after the accountable date may attract a potential penalty of £100. While composite monthly notifications by an accountable person are administratively convenient, a late notice covering, say, 10 transactions is potentially liable to 10 penalties of £100. The amount of the penalty in relation to each individual transaction is in practice limited so that it does not exceed the SDRT due on the transaction concerned.

From 1 October, to coincide with the introduction of a fully up to date interest rate regime, where there is a composite notice relating to a number of transactions in a single month, the Stamp Office will normally only seek a single £100 penalty charge, provided that the accountable person takes steps to eliminate sources of recurrent error. So, if a composite notice relating to 3 transactions in one month and 4 transactions in the next month is sent in after the accountable date for the second month, the penalty would normally be £200 rather than £700.

If the total SDRT relating to the transactions in a single month is less than £100, then the lesser figure would be used, in keeping with the existing practice. So if in the example above the 3 transactions in the first month involved an aggregate amount of £50 SDRT, and the 4 transactions in the second month involved over £100 then the penalty would be £150 rather than £200.

Interaction with Stamp Duty

Where a stock transfer form relating to residual securities (securities that cannot be settled in CREST) is stamped within 60 days of the date of the transaction, it remains the case that the Stamp Office will not seek interest on the SDRT in the meantime and no notice need be given. However, should a stock transfer form not in fact be duly stamped within this time then interest on the unpaid SDRT will still run from the accountable date. In addition, if a notice was not delivered by that date the penalties described above will apply.

It should be noted here, and more generally, that if a stock transfer form is presented for stamping more than 30 days after it is executed, and the duty is paid late, then interest will run on the Stamp Duty and there may be a penalty for late stamping.

The introduction of interest on Stamp Duty from 1 October, in parallel to the changes to SDRT also means that the procedures described in paragraphs 1.13 of the (February 1998) SDRT Guidance Notes no longer apply either in "wait and see" cases or where a document has been presented for an adjudicated relief. In future the question of SDRT will only be raised where difficulty is experienced in securing the stamping of the document.

MISC. 307   PRIVATE FINANCE INITIATIVE PROJECTS: STAMP DUTY

Introduction

This article considers the correct Stamp Duty treatment of the documents likely to be encountered in a typical PFI scheme.

This article has been written following detailed consultation between Inland Revenue Head Office technical specialists and representatives from various parties advising public and private sector bodies. Background information about this working group is in the article on page 642 of the April 1999 edition of Tax Bulletin.

As indicated in that earlier article, PFI transactions are by their very nature complex. So it is important to emphasise that the Stamp Duty position in any particular case will depend on an analysis of the form of the particular documents to ascertain their true legal effect, and that what follows is based on straightforward situations and is necessarily only intended to give general advice. At the end of the day, the treatment of a particular transaction will always depend on its own particular facts.

Background – A Typical Transaction

In a typical PFI transaction, a public sector entity – e.g. an NHS trust – agrees to acquire services. Typically a specially formed private sector company agrees to carry out the project and supply the services. The public sector body is referred to as "Purchaser". The private sector supplier is referred to as "Operator".

The main documents will normally be:

(a)　an outright transfer ("Project Land Transfer"), or head lease at a peppercorn rent ("Project Land Head Lease"), of the project site and buildings from the Purchaser to the Operator;

(b)　a leaseback ("Project Land Lease") of the project site and buildings from the Operator to the Purchaser. Again, this lease is normally at a peppercorn rent;

(c)　if the Purchaser has identified surplus land which it owns and can contribute to assist the economics of the project, a transfer of such surplus land by the Purchaser to the Operator ("Surplus Land Transfer");

(d)　a master agreement ("Project Agreement"):

●　　providing for the making of the above transfers or leases;

●　　regulating the provision of all of the services which the Operator is to supply; and

●　　providing for the Purchaser to make periodic payments, called the "Unitary Charge", to the Operator in return for the facilities and services under the project.

Transfer or Lease of The Project Land

In these transactions, the consideration for the transfer of the project site under the Project Land Transfer, or for the grant of the Project Land Head Lease may well be, or include, the undertaking by the Operator to carry out building or refurbishment works on the Project Land.

If such an undertaking were the only consideration, no ad valorem duty would be chargeable, as (in particular) a contract to carry out works is not "consideration [which] consists of property" for the purpose of Section 241 FA 1994. So the Project Land Transfer or Head Lease would only attract fixed duty.

Section 241 FA 1994 charges ad valorem duty on a transfer of land or the grant of a lease in exchange for any property (alone or with other consideration). So a charge under that section would arise if the Operator's grant of the leaseback to the Purchaser – the Project Land Lease – represented part or all of the consideration for the Project Land Transfer or Head Lease.

The article in the August 1995 edition of Tax Bulletin (paragraph 16, page 234) described the situation where, in the case of a sale and leaseback, there is a contract of sale for a price and a separate agreement for lease (rather than the leaseback forming part of the consideration given for the sale, in effect by way of exchange). In such situations the sale is liable to duty by reference to the price, and the leaseback is charged by reference to any premium and rent.

It is quite possible that transactions which this article considers may fall to be treated in this way. For example, if the various documents–

●　　clearly identify the only consideration as the Operator's undertaking to carry out the building works; and

●　　do not describe the grant of the Project Land Lease as the consideration for the Project Land Transfer or Head Lease

the Stamp Office would normally expect to charge the Project Land Transfer or Head Lease only to fixed duty.

The Project Land Lease

Exemptions from ad valorem stamp duty exist for leases in favour of ministers of the Crown, the Treasury Solicitor, NHS Trusts and charities. However, where a PFI transaction involves other types of body – notably local authorities – the liability arising on such documents falls to be considered.

The Project Land Lease is likely to be expressed to be at a peppercorn rent. And so in normal circumstances, in accordance with long standing practice, only fixed duty would apply. But, as with leases generally, it is possible that in some cases another amount (here, potentially a part of the unitary charge) should also be properly regarded as forming part of the rent for Stamp Duty purposes, if that is the true legal effect of the transaction.

If, in a case where the position is doubtful, a Project Land Lease is presented for stamping on the basis of a rational apportionment of the expected unitary charge between the part to be regarded as rent and the part to be regarded as relating to services, the Stamp Office would normally expect to accept the taxpayer's approach.

It should be noted that the position for Schedule A purposes (set out in the next article) is not the same as that for Stamp Duty.

Surplus Land Transfers

A Surplus Land Transfer, by the Purchaser to the private sector Operator, will normally be made without immediate monetary consideration. The following points of interest arise:

(a) however, should there be some immediate monetary consideration, it would attract ad valorem duty. This may, for example, arise where the Purchaser has waived exemption from VAT in relation to the surplus land in question, and the Operator makes a payment of VAT on the transfer.

(b) a charge to ad valorem duty under Section 241 FA 1994 will not normally arise on the basis that there is an exchange, unless the documentation describes the grant of the Project Land Lease as consideration for the Surplus Land Transfer, or describes the Surplus Land Transfer as consideration for the grant of the Project Land Lease.

(c) in general, the transfer of the surplus land will be described as made in one of three ways:
- by way of a contribution to the Operator's cost of carrying out the project works, or
- in satisfaction of a specific monetary amount of the future unitary charge, or
- in consideration of the Operator agreeing to accept a lower level of unitary charge than it would otherwise have done.

Various matters arise from the situations described in (c) above.

(1) Where the surplus land is transferred as a contribution towards expenses of the Operator on the building works, and there is no other consideration, the Surplus Land Transfer will only attract a fixed duty. This is because the Operator's agreement to execute the building works is not "property" for the purposes of Section 241 FA 1994. Where there is other consideration, of course, it may, depending on the facts, attract duty.

(2) If the Surplus Land Transfer is made in satisfaction of an amount of the future unitary charge, or in consideration of the Operator agreeing to accept a lower level of unitary charge than it would otherwise have done, it will not normally attract ad valorem duty. Section 57, SA 1891 does charge duty on conveyances made in satisfaction of a debt, but it only applies where the debt is due or accruing due at the date of execution. Normally that will not be the case in the type of transaction which the article considers.

(3) Where surplus land is transferred under the type of arrangements described above, the project documentation will normally contain rules about what is to happen if the Operator later re-sells the land at a profit. Sometimes, the Operator will be required to pass back a proportion of the profit to the public sector Purchaser by way of a contingent price for the surplus land. In that case, for stamp duty purposes, the contingency principle applies. If the documents provide that a minimum or maximum additional amount may become payable, that amount will attract ad valorem duty. If an amount cannot be determined under the contingency principle, then ad valorem stamp duty will be payable on the market value of the surplus land, applying Section 242 FA 1994.

(4) Sometimes, any profit on a resale is to be retained by the Operator but part or all of it is to be brought into the economics of the project. The amount in question may be treated:
- (i) as itself a contribution to the Operator's cost of carrying out the project, or
- (ii) as satisfying a specific future amount on account of the unitary charge.

In either case the principles set out earlier in this article should normally mean that there will be no charge to ad valorem duty.

Project Agreement

The Project Agreement normally provides for all of the intended land transfers or leases. As an agreement for one or more leases, it will be liable to the same ad valorem stamp duty in respect of each such lease as if it were that lease itself, and it will be entitled to the same exemptions as the actual leases would have qualified for.

In the same way as for other documents, the stamp duty on a Project Agreement, as an agreement for lease, will attract interest, and may attract a penalty, if it is presented for stamping out of time.

The time allowed for stamping the Project Agreement is 30 days from the date of execution unless it is presented with the granted lease when the 30 days start to run on the execution of the lease.

If the parties intended to stamp the Project Agreement and the related leases together, but the leases were not granted because a dispute had arisen, this would be a factor we would take into account in considering the mitigation of any penalty arising on stamping the agreement late.

Credit for stamp duty paid on a Project Agreement is allowed against the duty payable on a lease granted pursuant to that agreement – provided that the lease is in conformity with the project agreement or relates to substantially the same property and term. Exceptionally, there may be a major change of plan during the course of a PFI scheme. Where difficulties occur, especially where as a result of matters beyond the parties control, we would expect to apply this rule in a common sense way.

D. INLAND REVENUE PAMPHLETS

The Inland Revenue issues, free of charge, a number of explanatory leaflets which may be obtained from local Stamp Offices or from the Inland Revenue Public Enquiry Room, West Wing, Somerset House, London WC2 1LB, or on the internet at www.inlandrevenue.gov.uk/leaflets/stof.htm. In addition, Stamp Office Customer Newsletters are issued from time to time and can be obtained from the same sources.

SO1	Stamp duty on buying a freehold house in England, Wales and Northern Ireland.
SO1Scot	Stamp duty on buying land or buildings in Scotland.
SO2	The Stamp Office customer promise and service information
SO3	If things go wrong: complaints and lost documents
SO5	Common stamp duty forms and how to complete them
SO5(Scotland)1	Common Scottish stamp duty forms and how to complete them
SO6	A short history of stamp duties
SO7	Stamp duty on buying a leasehold domestic property
SO7Scot	Stamp duty and leases in Scotland
SO8	Stamp duty on agreements securing short tenancies
SO99	Changes to stamp duty from 1 October 1999
SO10	Stamp duty interest and penalties
SO11	Stamp duty and charities
SO13	Stamp Office Audit and Compliance Unit code of practice – SDRT inspections

The Stamp Office Customer Newsletters

New Rates of Stamp Duty	March 1999
A Revised Approach to "RPI" Leases	May 1999
New Interest & Penalty Arrangements	September 1999
New Ways of Calculating Stamp Duty	September 1999
Stamp Duty Reserve Tax Regime For Unit Trusts And Open-Ended Investment Companies.	November 1999
Unit Trusts: Pro Rata in Special [sic] Redemption of Units	December 1999
New Rates of Stamp Duty	March 2000

INDEX TO STAMP DUTIES

For a list of abbreviations used in this Index see p. xii.

STAMP DUTIES LIST OF DEFINITIONS AND MEANINGS

For a list of abbreviations used in this list see p. xii.

Provision

A

Abolition day ..FA90 111(1); FA91 110(7), 111(5),
112(9), 113(5), 114(5)
Absorbed trust .... FA97 101(1)
Accountable date .... SI 1986/1711 reg. 2
Accountable person .... SI 1986/1711 reg. 2
Act .... SI 1986/1711 reg. 2
Acquiring company .... FA97 96(1)
Acquiring trust .... FA97 95(1), 100(1)
Appropriate tribunal ...... SI 1986/1711 reg. 8(4B)
Assurance IA86 190
Authorised unit trust ...FA97 95(4), 100(4), 101(4)
Authorised unit trust scheme ..FA80 101(3); FA86
99(5B)

B

Barrister .... SI 1986/1711 reg. 2
Bearer instrument .... FA99 Sch. 15, para. 3
Bearer instrument by usage ..... FA63 59(2); FA99
Sch. 15, para. 10
Board .... FA86 99(2);
SI 1986/1711 reg. 3
Board of directors .... SI 1997/2429 reg. 2
Body of persons .... SI 1986/1711 reg. 118(1)
Branch or agent .... SI 1986/1711 reg. 118(1)
Branch or agency .... SI 1986/1711 reg. 118(1)
Broker .... FA86 89(4)
Broker and dealer .... FA86 89(4);
SI 1986/1711 reg. 2

C

Capital payment .... SI 1998/3177 reg. 24
Certificate to bearer .... FA99 Sch. 19, para. 14
Certified .... FA66 45(6)
Chargeable securities ....FA86 99(3), (4), (5), (5A),
(6), (10), (11)
Charter-party SA1891 49
Chief Land Registrar .... SI 1985/1688 reg. 2
Chief office SDMA1891 27
Clearing member .... SI 1997/2429 reg. 2;
SI 1999/3262 reg. 2
Close possession .... SI 1999/3263 reg. 2
Collective investment scheme .... FA86 99(5B);
FA97 97(1), 102(1)
Collector .... SI 1986/1711 reg. 118(1)
Commissioners SA1891 122; SDMA1891 27
Company ....SI 1986/1711 reg. 118(1); FA99
Sch. 15, para. 11
Connected .... FA91 112(7)
Consideration units   FA97 95(2)(c), 100(2), 101(2)
Continuing trust .... FA97 101(1)
Control ..... FA86 95(4), 97(5), 90(9); ICTA88 840

Provision

Conveyance IA86 190
Conveyance on sale   SA1891 54; FA1898 6; FA99
Sch. 13, para. 1
Conveyance or transfer ....FA99 Sch. 13, para. 16
County court .... SI 1986/1711 reg. 66(3)

D

Day of The Stock Exchange
reforms .... FA86 66(5), 85(5), 94(8), 96(12)
Dealer in relation to securities ....FA86 89(4)
Defined securities .... FA90 108(2)
Depositary certificate for overseas
stock ....FA63 59(2)
Depositary receipt for chargeable
securities .... FA86 90(8)(a), 94(1)
Depositary receipt for stocks or
shares ....FA86 99(7)
Depositary receipt for relevant
securities ....FA86 69(1)
Depositary receipt for stocks or
shares ....FA86 99(7)
Deposit certificate ..... FA63 59(2); FA99 Sch. 15,
para. 9
Die SDMA1891 27
Duty SDMA1891 27

E

EEA exchange ...FA97 97(1), 98(1), 102(1), 103(1)
EEA regulated market .... SI 1986/1711 reg. 3
EEA State .... FA97 97(1), 102(1)
Employee ....FA97 96(8)
Enactment .... SI 1986/1711 reg. 118(1)
Enactments relating to stamp duty ...FA86 87(8);
FA95 152(6); FA99 123(2)(a);
SI 1999/3263 reg. 2
Enactments relating to stamp duty
reserve tax ......FA95 152(6); FA99 123(2)(b)
Equity securities .... SI 1997/2429 reg. 2;
SI 1999/3262 reg. 2
Euro .... SI 1998/3177 reg. 2(1)
European institution .... SI 1986/1711 reg. 2
Euroconversion .... SI 1998/3177 reg. 3(1)
Exchange .... SI 1986/1711 reg. 3
Executed SA1891 122; SDMA1891 27
Execution SA1891 122; SDMA1891 27
Exempt instrument .... SI 1996/2348 reg. 2
Exempt investment ...... FA99 Sch. 19, para. 5
Exempt property ..... FA91 110(5), 111(3), 112(6)
Exempt securities ....FA87 50(3)
Exercise of a relevant option .. FA97 97(1), 102(1)
Existing association .... F(No. 2)A83 7(2)

F

Foreign loan security FA63 60

bt62 98 sd def Mp 13548—addef

Stamp Duties List of Definitions and Meanings   **13,548**
For a list of abbreviations used in this list see p. xii.

INSURANCE PREMIUM TAX

Table of Contents

INSURANCE PREMIUM TAX

Table of Contents

INSURANCE PREMIUM TAX STATUTES

Table of Contents

Note: Only those extant parts of these Acts which relate to insurance premium tax are reproduced here. The relevant provisions of the last Finance Act have been reproduced in full text, while the previous Finance Act has been abridged by the omission of repealed provisions and of provisions which do no more than amend provisions of earlier enactments.

PROVISIONAL COLLECTION OF TAXES ACT 1968

(1968 Chapter 2)

[1st February 1968]

ARRANGEMENT OF SECTIONS

1   Temporary statutory effect of House of Commons resolutions affecting income tax, purchase tax or customs or excise duties

1(1)   This section applies only to [not relevant to insurance premium tax] insurance premium tax, and [not relevant to insurance premium tax].

1(1A)   [Repealed by FA 1993, s. 205(3), s. 213 and Sch. 23, Pt. VI.]

1(2)   Subject to that, and to the provisions of subsections (4) to (8) below, where the House of Commons passes a resolution which–

(a)   provides for the renewal for a further period of any tax in force or imposed during the previous financial year (whether at the same or a different rate, and whether with or without modifications) or for the variation or abolition of any existing tax, and

(b)   contains a declaration that it is expedient in the public interest that the resolution should have statutory effect under the provisions of this Act,

the resolution shall, for the period specified in the next following subsection, have statutory effect as if contained in an Act of Parliament and, where the resolution provides for the renewal of a tax, all enactments which were in force with reference to that tax as last imposed by Act of Parliament shall during that period have full force and effect with respect to the tax as renewed by the resolution.

In this section references to the **renewal of a tax** include references to its reimposition, and references to the abolition of a tax include references to its repeal.

1(3)   The said period is–

(a)   in the case of a resolution passed in November or December in any year, one expiring with 5th May in the next calendar year;

(aa)   in the case of a resolution passed in February or March in any year, one expiring with 5th August in the same calendar year; and

(b)   in the case of any other resolution, one expiring at the end of four months after the date on which it is expressed to take effect or, if no such date is expressed, after the date on which it is passed.

1(4)   A resolution shall cease to have statutory effect under this section unless within the next thirty days on which the House of Commons sits after the day on which the resolution is passed–

(a)   a Bill renewing, varying or, as the case may be, abolishing the tax is read a second time by the House, or

(b)   a Bill is amended by the House in Committee or on Report, or by any Standing Committee of the House so as to include provision for the renewal, variation or, as the case may be, abolition of the tax.

1(5)   A resolution shall also cease to have statutory effect under this section if–

(a)   the provisions giving effect to it are rejected during the passage of the Bill containing them through the House, or

(b)   an Act comes into operation renewing, varying or, as the case may be, abolishing the tax, or

(c)   Parliament is dissolved or prorogued.

1(6)   Where, in the case of a resolution providing for the renewal or variation of a tax, the resolution ceases to have statutory effect by virtue of subsection (4) or (5) above, or the period specified in subsection (3) above terminates, before an Act comes into operation renewing or varying the tax, any money paid in pursuance of the resolution shall be repaid or made good, and any deduction made in pursuance of the resolution shall be deemed to be an unauthorised deduction.

1(7)   Where any tax as renewed or varied by a resolution is modified by the Act renewing or varying the tax, any money paid in pursuance of the resolution which would not have been payable under the new conditions affecting the tax shall be repaid or made good, and any deduction made in pursuance of the resolution shall, so far as it would not have been authorised under the new conditions affecting the tax, be deemed to be an unauthorised deduction.

1(8)   When during any session a resolution has had statutory effect under this section, statutory effect shall not be again given under this section in the same session to the same resolution or to a resolution having the same effect.

History – In s. 1(1), the words "insurance premium tax," were inserted by FA 1994, s. 6 and Sch. 7, para. 33, in relation to resolutions passed after 3 May 1994.
S. 1(1A) repealed by FA 1993, s. 205(3) and s. 213 and Sch. 23 Pt. VI, in relation to resolutions passed after 27 July 1993. Former s. 1(1A) was inserted by FA 1985, s. 97.
In s. 1(3)(a), references to "November or December" and "5th May in the next calendar year" substituted and in s. 1(4), the word "thirty" substituted by FA 1993, s. 205(5), in relation to resolutions passed after 27 July 1993.
S. 1(3)(aa) was inserted by F(No. 2)A 1997, s. 50(1), with effect in relation to resolutions passed after 31 July 1997.
In s. 1(4)(b), the words "in Committee ... of the House" inserted by FA 1968, s. 60.
Application extended to petroleum revenue tax, stamp duty reserve tax, value added tax and car tax by OTA 1975, s. 11; FA 1986, s. 86(3); FA 1972, s. 1(5) and FA 1972, s. 52(11) and Sch. 7, para. 2(4) respectively.
References to provisions of ICTA 1988 substituted by Sch. 29, para. 32 of that Act.

Cross references – FA 1997, s. 49(9): transitional provisions for set-offs etc.

5   House of Commons resolution giving provisional effect to motions affecting taxation

5(1)   This section shall apply if the House of Commons resolves that provisional statutory effect shall be given to one or more motions to be moved by the Chancellor of the Exchequer, or some other Minister, and which, if agreed to by the House, would be resolutions–

(a)   to which statutory effect could be given under section 1 of this Act, or
(b)   to which section 3 of this Act could be applied,
(c)   [Repealed by FA 1993, s. 205(6)(a), s. 213 and Sch. 23, Pt. VI.]

5(2)   Subject to subsection (3) below, on the passing of the resolution under subsection (1) above, sections 1 to 3 of this Act and section 822 of the Income and Corporation Taxes Act 1988 (over-deductions from preference dividends before passing of annual Act) shall apply as if each motion to which the resolution applies had then been agreed to by a resolution of the House.

5(3)   Subsection (2) above shall cease to apply to a motion if that motion, or a motion containing the same proposals with modifications, is not agreed to by a resolution of the House (in this section referred to as **"a confirmatory resolution"**) within the next ten days on which the House sits after the resolution under subsection (1) above is passed, and, if it ceases to apply, all such adjustments, whether by way of discharge or repayment of tax, or discharge of security, or otherwise, shall be made as may be necessary to restore the position to what it would have been if subsection (2) above had never applied to that motion, and to make good any deductions which have become unauthorised deductions.

5(4)   The enactments specified in subsection (2) above shall have effect as if–

(a)   any confirmatory resolution passed within the said period of ten sitting days had been passed when the resolution under subsection (1) above was passed, and
(b)   everything done in pursuance of the said subsection (2) by reference to the motion to which the confirmatory resolution relates had been done by reference to the confirmatory resolution,

but any necessary adjustments shall be made, whether by way of discharge or repayment of tax, or modification of the terms of any security, or further assessment, or otherwise, where the proposals in the confirmatory resolution are not the same as those in the original motion to which that resolution relates.

History – S. 5(1)(c) and word "or" immediately preceding it and in s. 5(2), reference to ICTA 1988, s. 822 substituted by FA 1993, s. 205(6), s. 213 and Sch. 23, Pt. VI, in relation to resolutions passed after 27 July 1993.
References to provisions of ICTA 1988 substituted by Sch. 29, para. 32 of that Act.

6   Short title, repeals and saving as respects Northern Ireland

6(1)   This Act may be cited as the Provisional Collection of Taxes Act 1968.

6(2)　[Amending provision, not reproduced here.]

6(3)　[Repealed by Northern Ireland Constitution Act 1973, s. 41(1)(a) and Sch. 6, Pt. I, with effect from 18 July 1973.]

INSOLVENCY ACT 1986

(1986 Chapter 45)

[25th July 1986]

175　Preferential debts (general provisions)

175(1)　In a winding up the company's preferential debts (within the meaning given by section 386 in Part XII) shall be paid in priority to all other debts.

175(2)　Preferential debts–

(a)　rank equally among themselves after the expenses of the winding up and shall be paid in full, unless the assets are insufficient to meet them, in which case they abate in equal proportions; and

(b)　so far as the assets of the company available for payment of general creditors are insufficient to meet them, have priority over the claims of holders of debentures secured by, or holders of, any floating charge created by the company, and shall be paid accordingly out of any property comprised in or subject to that charge.

386　Categories of preferential debts

386(1)　A reference in this Act to the preferential debts of a company or an individual is to the debts listed in Schedule 6 to this Act [not relevant to insurance premium tax]; insurance premium tax [not relevant to insurance premium tax] and references to preferential creditors are to be read accordingly.

386(2)　In that Schedule **"the debtor"** means the company or the individual concerned.

386(3)　[Not relevant to insurance premium tax.]

History – In s. 386(2), the words "insurance premium tax" were inserted by FA 1994, s. 64 and Sch. 7, para. 7(2), with effect from 1 October 1994.

SCHEDULES

SCHEDULE 6 – THE CATEGORIES OF PREFERENTIAL DEBTS

Section 386

3A　Any insurance premium tax which is referable to the period of 6 months next before the relevant date (which period is referred to below as **"the 6-month period"**).

　　For the purposes of this paragraph–

(a)　where the whole of the accounting period to which any insurance premium tax is attributable falls within the 6-month period, the whole amount of that tax is referable to that period; and

(b)　in any other case the amount of any insurance premium tax which is referable to the 6-month period is the proportion of the tax which is equal to such proportion (if any) of the accounting period in question as falls within the 6-month period;

　　and references here to **accounting periods** shall be construed in accordance with Part III of the Finance Act 1994.

History – Para. 3A was inserted by FA 1994, s. 64 and Sch. 7, para. 7(2), with effect from 1 October 1994.

INCOME AND CORPORATION TAXES ACT 1988

(1988 Chapter 1)

[9th February 1988]

827   VAT penalties etc.

827(1)   [Not relevant to insurance premium tax.]

827(1A)   [Not relevant to insurance premium tax.]

827(1B)   Where a person is liable to make a payment by way of–

(a)   penalty under any of paragraphs 12 to 19 of Schedule 7 to the Finance Act 1994 (insurance premium tax), or

(b)   interest under paragraph 21 of that Schedule,

the payment shall not be allowed as a deduction in computing any income, profits or losses for any tax purposes.

827(IC)   [Not relevant to insurance premium tax.]

827(2)   [Not relevant to insurance premium tax.]

History – S. 827(1B) was inserted by FA 1994, s. 64 and Sch. 7, para. 31, consequential upon the introduction of insurance premium tax by FA 1994, Pt. III, with effect from 1 October 1994.

FINANCE ACT 1994

(1994 Chapter 9)

[3rd May 1994]

ARRANGEMENT OF SECTIONS

PART III – INSURANCE PREMIUM TAX

PART III – INSURANCE PREMIUM TAX

THE BASIC PROVISIONS

48   Insurance premium tax

48(1)   A tax, to be known as insurance premium tax, shall be charged in accordance with this Part.

48(2)   The tax shall be under the care and management of the Commissioners of Customs and Excise.

49   Charge to tax

49   Tax shall be charged on the receipt of a premium by an insurer if the premium is received–

(a)   under a taxable insurance contract, and

(b)   on or after 1st October 1994.

Official publications – Notice IPT 2, Pt. 1 (1999): a general guide to IPT, basic principles.

50   Chargeable amount

50(1)   Tax shall be charged by reference to the chargeable amount.

50(2)   For the purposes of this Part, the **chargeable amount** is such amount as, with the addition of the tax chargeable, is equal to the amount of the premium.

50(3)   Subsections (1) and (2) above shall have effect subject to section 69 below.

History – In s. 50(3), the words "Subsections (1) and (2)" were substituted by FA 1997, s. 23(2), generally with effect in relation to a premium which falls to be regarded for the purposes of FA 1994, Pt. III as received under a taxable insurance contract on or after 1 April 1997. However, the amendment does not have effect in relation to a premium if the premium–
- (1)   is in respect of a contract made before 1 April 1997; and
- (2)   falls, by virtue of regulations under s. 68, to be regarded for the purposes of Pt. III as received under the contract by the insurer on a date before 1 August 1997.

However, these two exclusions to the effective date of the amendment do not apply in relation to a premium if the premium–
- (1)   is an additional premium under the contract;
- (2)   falls as mentioned in s. 24(2)(b) to be regarded as received under the contract by the insurer on or after 1 April 1997; and
- (3)   is in respect of a risk which was not covered by the contract before 1 April 1997.

Extra-statutory concessions – 3.30 (Notice 48 (1999 edn)): de minimis provisions.

51   Rate of tax

51(1)   Tax shall be charged–

- (a)   at the higher rate, in the case of a premium which is liable to tax at that rate; and
- (b)   at the standard rate, in any other case.

51(2)   For the purposes of this Part–

- (a)   the higher rate is 17.5 per cent; and
- (b)   the standard rate is 5 per cent.

History – In s. 51(2)(b), the words "5 per cent" were substituted for the words "4 per cent" by FA 1999, s. 125(1)), generally with effect in relation to a premium which falls to be regarded for the purposes of Pt. III of FA 1994 as received under a taxable insurance contract by an insurer on or after 1 July 1999. However, the amendment does not have effect in relation to a premium if the premium–
- (1)   is in respect of a contract made before 1 July 1999, and
- (2)   falls to be regarded for the purposes of Pt. III of that Act as received under the contract by the insurer on a date before 1 January 2000, by virtue of regulations under s. 68 of that Act (special accounting schemes).

However, these two exclusions to the effective date of the amendment do not apply in relation to a premium if the premium–
- (1)   is an additional premium under a contract,
- (2)   falls to be regarded for the purposes of Pt. III of that Act as received under the contract by the insurer on or after 1 July 1999, by virtue of regulations under s. 68 of that Act, and
- (3)   is in respect of a risk which was not covered by the contract before 1 July 1999.

S. 51 was substituted by FA 1997, s. 21(1), generally with effect in relation to a premium which falls to be regarded for the purposes of FA 1994, Pt. III as received under a taxable insurance contract on or after 1 April 1997. However, the amendment does not have effect in relation to a premium if the premium–
- (1)   is in respect of a contract made before 1 April 1997; and
- (2)   falls, by virtue of regulations under s. 68, to be regarded for the purposes of Pt. III as received under the contract by the insurer on a date before 1 August 1997.

However, these two exclusions to the effective date of the amendment do not apply in relation to a premium if the premium–
- (1)   is an additional premium under the contract;
- (2)   falls as mentioned in s. 24(2)(b) to be regarded as received under the contract by the insurer on or after 1 April 1997; and
- (3)   is in respect of a risk which was not covered by the contract before 1 April 1997.

Previously there was only one rate of insurance premium tax which was 2.5 per cent.

51A   Premiums liable to tax at the higher rate

51A(1)   A premium received under a taxable insurance contract by an insurer is liable to tax at the higher rate if it falls within one or more of the paragraphs of Part II of Schedule 6A to this Act.

51A(2)   Part I of Schedule 6A to this Act shall have effect with respect to the interpretation of that Schedule.

51A(3)   Provision may be made by order amending Schedule 6A as it has effect for the time being.

51A(4)   This section is subject to section 69 below.

History – S. 51A was inserted by FA 1997, s. 22(1), generally with effect in relation to a premium which falls to be regarded for the purposes of FA 1994, Pt. III as received under a taxable insurance contract on or after 1 April 1997. However, the amendment does not have effect in relation to a premium if the premium–
- (1)   is in respect of a contract made before 1 April 1997; and
- (2)   falls, by virtue of regulations under s. 68, to be regarded for the purposes of Pt. III as received under the contract by the insurer on a date before 1 August 1997.

However, these two exclusions to the effective date of the amendment do not apply in relation to a premium if the premium–
- (1)   is an additional premium under the contract;
- (2)   falls as mentioned in s. 24(2)(b) to be regarded as received under the contract by the insurer on or after 1 April 1997; and
- (3)   is in respect of a risk which was not covered by the contract before 1 April 1997.

Extra-statutory concessions – 48 (Notice 48 (1999 edn)): 3.33: certain premiums not liable to the higher rate of tax if received before 1 October 1997 in respect of a pre-1 April 1997 contract.

Official publications – Notice IPT 2, Pt. 3 (1999 edn): a general guide to IPT, the higher rate of IPT.

Other material – Business Brief 8/99: differential rates of IPT applied to travel insurance amounted to state aid for premiums up to 1 August 1998.

52   Liability to pay tax

52(1)   Tax shall be payable by the person who is the insurer in relation to the contract under which the premium is received.

52(2) Subsection (1) above shall have effect subject to any regulations made under section 65 below.

52A   Certain fees to be treated as premiums under higher rate contracts

52A(1) This section applies where–

(a)   at or about the time when a higher rate contract is effected, and

(b)   in connection with that contract,

a fee in respect of an insurance-related service is charged by a taxable intermediary to a person who is or becomes the insured (or one of the insured) under the contract or to a person who acts for or on behalf of such a person.

52A(2) Where this section applies–

(a)   a payment in respect of the fee shall be treated for the purposes of this Part as a **premium received under a taxable insurance contract** by an insurer, and

(b)   that premium–

     (i) shall be treated for the purposes of this Part as so received at the time when the payment is made, and

     (ii) shall be chargeable to tax at the higher rate.

52A(3) Tax charged by virtue of subsection (2) above shall be payable by the taxable intermediary as if he were the insurer under the contract mentioned in paragraph (a) of that subsection.

52A(4) For the purposes of this section, a contract of insurance is a **"higher rate contract"** if–

(a)   it is a taxable insurance contract; and

(b)   the whole or any part of a premium received under the contract by the insurer is (apart from this section) liable to tax at the higher rate.

52A(5) For the purposes of this Part a **"taxable intermediary"** is a person falling within subsection (6) or (6A) below who–

(a)   at or about the time when a higher rate contract is effected, and

(b)   in connection with that contract,

charges a fee in respect of an insurance-related service to a person who is or becomes the insured (or one of the insured) under the contract or to a person who acts for or on behalf of such a person.

52A(6) A person falls within this subsection if the higher rate contract mentioned in subsection (1) above falls within paragraph 2 or 3 of Schedule 6A to this Act (motor cars or motor cycles, or relevant goods) and the person is–

(a)   within the meaning of the paragraph in question, a supplier of motor cars or motor cycles or, as the case may be, of relevant goods; or

(b)   a person connected with a person falling within paragraph (a) above; or

(c)   a person who in the course of his business pays–

     (i) the whole or any part of the premium received under that contract, or

     (ii) a fee connected with the arranging of that contract,

to a person falling within paragraph (a) or (b) above.

52A(6A) A person falls within this subsection if the higher rate contract mentioned in subsection (1) above falls within paragraph 4 of Schedule 6A to this Act (travel insurance) and the person is–

(a)   the insurer under that contract; or

(b)   a person through whom that contract is arranged in the course of his business; or

(c)   a person connected with the insurer under that contract; or

(d)   a person connected with a person falling within paragraph (b) above; or

(e)   a person who in the course of his business pays–

     (i) the whole or any part of the premium received under that contract, or

     (ii) a fee connected with the arranging of that contract, to a person falling within any of paragraphs (a) to (d) above.

52A(7) [Substituted by FA 1998, s. 147(3).]

52A(8) For the purposes of this section, any question whether a person is **connected** with another shall be determined in accordance with section 839 of the Taxes Act 1988.

52A(9) In this section–

"insurance-related service" means any service which is related to, or connected with, insurance.

History – S. 52A was inserted by FA 1997, s. 25(1), with effect in relation to payments in respect of fees charged on or after 19 March 1997.
In s. 52A(5), the words "or (6A)" were inserted by FA 1998, s. 147(2), operative in relation to payments in respect of fees charged on or after 1 August 1998.
S. 52A(6) and (6A) were substituted for former s. 52A(6) and (7) by FA 1998, s. 147(3), operative in relation to payments in respect of fees charged on or after 1 August 1998. Former s.52A(6) and (7) read as follows:
"**(6)**   A person falls within this subsection if–
  (a)   he is a supplier of goods or services falling within subsection (7) below; or
  (b)   he is connected with a supplier of goods or services falling within that subsection; or
  (c)   he is a person who pays–
      (i)   the whole or any part of the premium received under that contract, or
      (ii) a fee connected with the arranging of that contract,
    to a supplier of goods or services falling within subsection (7) below or to a person who is connected with a supplier of goods or services falling within that subsection.
(7)   A person is a supplier of goods or services falling within this subsection if–
  (a)   he is a supplier of motor cars or motor cycles, within the meaning of paragraph 2 of Schedule 6A to this Act;
  (b)   he is a supplier of relevant goods, within the meaning of paragraph 3 of that Schedule; or
  (c)   he is a tour operator or travel agent."
In s. 52A(9), the definitions of tour operator and travel agent were omitted and repealed by FA 1998, s. 147(3) and (4) and Sch. 27, Pt. V, operative in relation to payments in respect of fees charged on or after 1 August 1998. Former definitions of tour operator and travel agent are as follows: **"tour operator"** and **"travel agent"** have the same meaning as in paragraph 4 of Schedule 6A to this Act."

Cross references – SI 1994/1774, reg. 2(1): "taxable intermediary's fees".

ADMINISTRATION

53   Registration of insurers

53(1) A person who–
(a)   receives, as insurer, premiums in the course of a taxable business, and
(b)   is not registered,
is liable to be registered.

53(1A) The register kept under this section may contain such information as the Commissioners think is required for the purposes of the care and management of the tax.

53(2) A person who–
(a)   at any time forms the intention of receiving, as insurer, premiums in the course of a taxable business, and
(b)   is not already receiving, as insurer, premiums in the course of another taxable business,
shall notify the Commissioners of those facts.

53(3) A person who at any time–
(a)   ceases to have the intention of receiving, as insurer, premiums in the course of a taxable business, and
(b)   has no intention of receiving, as insurer, premiums in the course of another taxable business,
shall notify the Commissioners of those facts.

53(4) Where a person is liable to be registered by virtue of subsection (1) above the Commissioners shall register him with effect from the time when he begins to receive premiums in the course of the business concerned; and it is immaterial whether or not he notifies the Commissioners under subsection (2) above.

53(5) Where a person–
(a)   notifies the Commissioners under subsection (3) above, and
(b)   satisfies them of the facts there mentioned,
(c)   [Omitted by FA 1995, s. 34 and Sch. 5, para. 2(2) and repealed by FA 1995, s. 162 and Sch. 29, Pt. VII.]
the Commissioners shall cancel his registration with effect from the earliest practicable time after he ceases to receive, as insurer, premiums in the course of any taxable business.

53(5A) In a case where–
(a)   the Commissioners are satisfied that a person has ceased to receive, as insurer, premiums in the course of any taxable business, but
(b)   he has not notified them under subsection (3) above,
they may cancel his registration with effect from the earliest practicable time after he so ceased.

53(6) For the purposes of this section regulations may make provision–

(a)   as to the time within which a notification is to be made;

(b)   as to the circumstances in which premiums are to be taken to be received in the course of a taxable business;

(c)   as to the form and manner in which any notification is to be made and as to the information to be contained in or provided with it;

(d)   requiring a person who has made a notification to notify the Commissioners if any information contained in or provided in connection with it is or becomes inaccurate;

(e)   as to the correction of entries in the register.

53(7)   References in this section to **receiving premiums** are to receiving premiums on or after 1st October 1994.

History – S. 53(1A) was inserted by FA 1995, s. 34 and Sch. 5, para. 3.
In s. 53(5), the word "and" was inserted after para. (a) by FA 1995, s. 34 and Sch. 5, para. 2(2)(a), in relation to notifications made under s. 53(3) on or after 1 May 1995.
In s. 53(5), para. (c) and the word "and" immediately preceding it were omitted and repealed by FA 1995, s. 34 and 162 and Sch. 5, para. 2(2)(b) and Sch. 29, Pt. VII, in relation to notifications made under s. 53(3) on or after 1 May 1995.
S. 53(5A) was inserted by FA 1995, s. 34 and Sch. 5, para. 2(3).

Cross references – SI 1994/1774, reg. 2(1): interpretation of registered person and registration.
SI 1994/1774, reg. 4(1) and (2): forms to notify liability to register.
SI 1994/1774, reg. 6: notification of liability to be de-registered.
SI 1994/1774, reg. 7: transfer of a going concern.
SI 1994/1774, reg. 11: death, bankruptcy or incapacity of registrable persons.

Statutory instruments – SI 1994/1774; 1995/1587 (made under s. 53(6)).

Official publications – Notice IPT 1 "Registering for IPT".

Other material – Form IPT 1: "Insurance premium tax: Application for registration".
Form IPT 2: names, addresses and telephone number of partners who complete Form IPT 1.
Form IPT 68: joint application to transfer taxable business as a going concern so transferee becomes liable to be registered.

Notes – SI 1994/1774, reg. 5: notification to commissioners of changes in registration particulars.

53A   Information required to keep register up to date

53A(1)   Regulations may make provision requiring a **registrable person** to notify the Commissioners of particulars which–

(a)   are of changes in circumstances relating to the **registrable person** or any business carried on by him,

(b)   appear to the Commissioners to be required for the purpose of keeping the register kept under section 53 or 53AA above up to date, and

(c)   are of a prescribed description.

53A(2)   Regulations may make provision–

(a)   as to the time within which a notification is to be made;

(b)   as to the form and manner in which a notification is to be made;

(c)   requiring a person who has made a notification to notify the Commissioners if any information contained in it is inaccurate.

History – In s. 53A(1)(b), the words "or 53AA" were inserted by FA 1997, s. 27(2), with effect from 19 March 1997.
S. 53A was inserted by FA 1995, s. 34 and Sch. 5, para. 4.

Cross references – S. 73(3A): "registrable person".

Statutory instruments – SI 1995/1587 (made under s. 53A(1), (2), amending SI 1994/1774).
SI 1997/1157 (amending SI 1994/1774).

53AA   Registration of taxable intermediaries

53AA(1)   A person who–

(a)   is a taxable intermediary, and

(b)   is not registered,

is liable to be registered.

53AA(2)   The register kept under this section may contain such information as the Commissioners think is required for the purposes of the care and management of the tax.

53AA(3)   A person who–

(a)   at any time forms the intention of charging taxable intermediary's fees, and

(b)   is not already charging such fees in the course of another business,

shall notify the Commissioners of those facts.

53AA(4)   A person who at any time–

(a)   ceases to have the intention of charging taxable intermediary's fees in the course of his business, and

(b)   has no intention of charging such fees in the course of another business of his, shall notify the Commissioners of those facts.

53AA(5) Where a person is liable to be registered by virtue of subsection (1) above, the Commissioners shall register him with effect from the time when he begins to charge taxable intermediary's fees in the course of the business concerned; and it is immaterial whether or not he notifies the Commissioners under subsection (3) above.

53AA(6) Where a person–

(a)   notifies the Commissioners under subsection (4) above, and

(b)   satisfies them of the facts there mentioned,

the Commissioners shall cancel his registration with effect from the earliest practicable time after he ceases to charge taxable intermediary's fees in the course of any business of his.

53AA(7) In a case where–

(a)   the Commissioners are satisfied that a person has ceased to charge taxable intermediary's fees in the course of any business of his, but

(b)   he has not notified them under subsection (4) above,

they may cancel his registration with effect from the earliest practicable time after he so ceased.

53AA(8) For the purposes of this section regulations may make provision–

(a)   as to the time within which a notification is to be made;

(b)   as to the form and manner in which any notification is to be made and as to the information to be contained in or provided with it;

(c)   requiring a person who has made a notification to notify the Commissioners if any information contained in or provided in connection with it is or becomes inaccurate;

(d)   as to the correction of entries in the register.

53AA(9) In this Part **"taxable intermediary's fees"** means fees which, to the extent of any payment in respect of them, are chargeable to tax by virtue of section 52A above.

History – S. 53AA was inserted by FA 1997, s.26, with effect from 19 March 1997.

Cross references – S. 73(3A): "registrable person".
SI 1994/1774, reg. 2(1): "accounting period" and "registered person".
SI 1994/1774, reg. 4A(1): notification of liability to register and taxable intermediaries.
SI 1994/1774, reg. 5(5): changes in particulars.
SI 1994/1774, reg. 6A: notification of liability to be de-registered and taxable intermediaries.
SI 1994/1774, reg. 19: payments in respect of credit.

Statutory instruments – SI 1997/1157 (amending SI 1994/1774).

Official publications – Notice IPT 2, Pt. 10 (1999 edn): a general guide to IPT, taxable intermediaries.

54   Accounting for tax and time for payment

54 Regulations may provide that a **registrable person** shall–

(a)   account for tax by reference to such periods (accounting periods) as may be determined by or under the regulations;

(b)   make, in relation to accounting periods, returns in such form as may be prescribed and at such times as may be so determined;

(c)   pay tax at such times and in such manner as may be so determined.

Cross references – S. 73(3A): "registrable person".

Statutory instrument – SI 1994/1774.

Other material – Form IPT 100: "Insurance premium tax return".
Form IPT 100L: "Lloyd's composite IPT return for syndicates".
Form IPT 100L(S): "Lloyd's composite return – schedule of participating syndicates".

55   Credit

55(1) Regulations may provide that where an insurer or taxable intermediary has paid tax and all or part of the premium or taxable intermediary's fee (as the case may be) is repaid, the insurer or taxable intermediary shall be entitled to credit of such an amount as is found in accordance with prescribed rules.

55(2) Regulations may provide that where–

(a)   by virtue of regulations made under section 68 below tax is charged in relation to a premium which is shown in the accounts of an insurer as due to him,

(b)   that tax is paid, and

(c)   it is shown to the satisfaction of the Commissioners that the premium, or part of it, will never actually be received by or on behalf of the insurer, the insurer shall be entitled to credit of such an amount as is found in accordance with prescribed rules.

55(3) Regulations may make provision as to the manner in which an insurer or taxable intermediary is to benefit from credit, and in particular may make provision–

(a) that an insurer or taxable intermediary shall be entitled to credit by reference to accounting periods;

(b) that an insurer or taxable intermediary shall be entitled to deduct an amount equal to his total credit for an accounting period from the total amount of tax due from him for the period;

(c) that if no tax is due from an insurer or taxable intermediary for an accounting period but he is entitled to credit for the period, the amount of the credit shall be paid to him by the Commissioners;

(d) that if the amount of credit to which an insurer or taxable intermediary is entitled for an accounting period exceeds the amount of tax due from him for the period, an amount equal to the excess shall be paid to him by the Commissioners;

(e) for the whole or part of any credit to be held over to be credited for a subsequent accounting period;

(f) as to the manner in which a person who has ceased to be registrable (whether under section 53 or section 53AA) is to benefit from credit.

55(4) Regulations under subsection (3)(c) or (d) above may provide that where at the end of an accounting period an amount is due to an insurer or taxable intermediary who has failed to submit returns for an earlier period as required by this Part, the Commissioners may withhold payment of the amount until he has complied with that requirement.

55(5) Regulations under subsection (3)(e) above may provide for credit to be held over either on the insurer's or taxable intermediary's application or in accordance with general or special directions given by the Commissioners from time to time.

55(6) Regulations may provide that–

(a) no deduction or payment shall be made in respect of credit except on a claim made in such manner and at such time as may be determined by or under regulations;

(b) payment in respect of credit shall be made subject to such conditions (if any) as the Commissioners think fit to impose, including conditions as to repayment in specified circumstances;

(c) deduction in respect of credit shall be made subject to such conditions (if any) as the Commissioners think fit to impose, including conditions as to the payment to the Commissioners, in specified circumstances, of an amount representing the whole or part of the amount deducted.

55(7) Regulations may require a claim by an insurer or taxable intermediary to be made in a return required by provision made under section 54 above.

55(8) Regulations may provide that where–

(a) all or any of the tax payable in respect of a premium or taxable intermediary's fee has not been paid, and

(b) the circumstances are such that a person would be entitled to credit if the tax had been paid,

prescribed adjustments shall be made as regards any amount of tax due from any person.

History – In s. 55(1), (3)–(5), (7) and (8), in each place where they occur, the words "or taxable intermediary" were inserted by FA 1997, s. 27(3)(a), with effect from 19 March 1997.
In s. 55(1), the words "or taxable intermediary's fee (as the case may be)" were inserted by FA 1997, s. 27(3)(b), with effect from 19 March 1997.
In s. 55(3)(f), the words "(whether under section 53 or section 53AA)" were inserted by FA 1997, s. 27(3)(c), with effect from 19 March 1997.
In s. 55(5), the words "or taxable intermediary's" were *inserted* by FA 1997, s. 27(3)(d), with effect from 19 March 1997.
In s. 55(8)(a), the words "or taxable intermediary's fee" were inserted by FA 1997, s. 27(3)(e), with effect from 19 March 1997.
Statutory instruments – SI 1994/1774, reg. 18(3) (as amended by SI 1997/1157).

56 Power to assess

56(1) In a case where–

(a) a person has failed to make any returns required to be made under this Part,

(b) a person has failed to keep any documents necessary to verify returns required to be made under this Part,

(c) a person has failed to afford the facilities necessary to verify returns required to be made under this Part, or

(d)   it appears to the Commissioners that returns required to be made by a person under this Part are incomplete or incorrect,

the Commissioners may assess the amount of tax due from the person concerned to the best of their judgment and notify it to him.

56(2)   Where a person has for an accounting period been paid an amount to which he purports to be entitled under regulations made under section 55 above, then, to the extent that the amount ought not to have been paid or would not have been paid had the facts been known or been as they later turn out to be, the Commissioners may assess the amount as being tax due from him for that period and notify it to him accordingly.

56(3)   Where a person is assessed under subsections (1) and (2) above in respect of the same accounting period the assessments may be combined and notified to him as one assessment.

56(4)   Where the person failing to make a return, or making a return which appears to the Commissioners to be incomplete or incorrect, was required to make the return as a personal representative, trustee in bankruptcy, trustee in sequestration, receiver, liquidator or person otherwise acting in a representative capacity in relation to another person, subsection (1) above shall apply as if the reference to tax due from him included a reference to tax due from that other person.

56(5)   An assessment under subsection (1) or (2) above of an amount of tax due for an accounting period shall not be made after the later of the following–

(a)   two years after the end of the accounting period;

(b)   one year after evidence of facts, sufficient in the Commissioners' opinion to justify the making of the assessment, comes to their knowledge;

but where further such evidence comes to their knowledge after the making of an assessment under subsection (1) or (2) above another assessment may be made under the subsection concerned in addition to any earlier assessment.

56(6)   In a case where–

(a)   as a result of a person's failure to make a return for an accounting period the Commissioners have made an assessment under subsection (1) above for that period,

(b)   the tax assessed has been paid but no proper return has been made for the period to which the assessment related, and

(c)   as a result of a failure to make a return for a later accounting period, being a failure by the person referred to in paragraph (a) above or a person acting in a representative capacity in relation to him, as mentioned in subsection (4) above, the Commissioners find it necessary to make another assessment under subsection (1) above,

then, if the Commissioners think fit, having regard to the failure referred to in paragraph (a) above, they may specify in the assessment referred to in paragraph (c) above an amount of tax greater than that which they would otherwise have considered to be appropriate.

56(7)   Where an amount has been assessed and notified to any person under subsection (1) or (2) above it shall be deemed to be an amount of tax due from him and may be recovered accordingly unless, or except to the extent that, the assessment has subsequently been withdrawn or reduced.

56(8)   For the purposes of this section notification to–

(a)   a personal representative, trustee in bankruptcy, trustee in sequestration, receiver or liquidator, or

(b)   a person otherwise acting in a representative capacity in relation to another person,

shall be treated as notification to the person in relation to whom the person mentioned in paragraph (a) above, or the first person mentioned in paragraph (b) above, acts.

Cross reference – SI 1994/1774, reg. 37(1), 42(2) and 43(3).

TAX REPRESENTATIVES

57   Tax representatives

57(1)   Where at any time (**a relevant time**) a person who is an insurer or taxable intermediary–

(a)   is registered, or liable to be registered, under section 53 or, as the case may be, section 53AA above, and

(b)   does not have any business establishment or other fixed establishment in the United Kingdom, this section shall have effect with a view to securing that another person is the insurer's or taxable intermediary's tax representative at that time.

57(2) If, at the time the insurer or taxable intermediary first falls within subsection (1) above, the insurer or taxable intermediary has a representative fulfilling the requirements of section 10 of the Insurance Companies Act 1982–

(a)   the Commissioners shall be taken to approve that person at that time as the insurer's or taxable intermediary's tax representative, and

(b)   that person shall be the insurer's or taxable intermediary's tax representative at any relevant time falling after the time mentioned in paragraph (a) above and before the Commissioners' approval is withdrawn.

57(3) If, at the time the insurer or taxable intermediary first falls within subsection (1) above, the insurer or taxable intermediary does not have a representative fulfilling the requirements of section 10 of the Insurance Companies Act 1982, the insurer or taxable intermediary shall take action as mentioned in subsection (4) below.

57(4) The insurer or taxable intermediary takes action as mentioned in this subsection if–

(a)   he requests the Commissioners to approve a particular person as his tax representative, and

(b)   the request is made with a view to securing that a person approved by the Commissioners becomes the insurer's or taxable intermediary's tax representative within the relevant period.

57(5) If the Commissioners approve a person as the insurer's or taxable intermediary's tax representative in a case where action has been taken as mentioned in subsection (4) above, that person shall be the insurer's or taxable intermediary's tax representative at any relevant time falling after the Commissioners' approval is given and before their approval is withdrawn.

57(6) Subsection (7) below applies where the Commissioners believe that the revenue would not be sufficiently protected if–

(a)   a person were to become the insurer's or taxable intermediary's tax representative by virtue of subsection (2) above, or

(b)   a person who by virtue of any of the provisions of this section is the insurer's or taxable intermediary's tax representative were to continue to be so.

57(7) If the Commissioners require the insurer or taxable intermediary to take action as mentioned in subsection (4) above the insurer or taxable intermediary shall comply with that requirement.

57(8) In a case where–

(a)   a person is the insurer's or taxable intermediary's tax representative,

(b)   the insurer or taxable intermediary withdraws his agreement that that person should act as his tax representative, or that person withdraws his agreement to act as the insurer's or taxable intermediary's tax representative, or the insurer or taxable intermediary and that person agree that that person should no longer be the insurer's or taxable intermediary's tax representative, and

(c)   that person notifies the Commissioners accordingly,

the Commissioners shall be taken to have withdrawn their approval of that person at the time they inform the insurer or taxable intermediary that they have received the notification, and that person shall cease at that time to be the insurer's or taxable intermediary's tax representative.

57(9) Where subsection (8) above applies the insurer or taxable intermediary shall take action as mentioned in subsection (4) above.

57(10) If at any time after the insurer or taxable intermediary first falls within subsection (1) above–

(a)   the insurer or taxable intermediary (otherwise than in pursuance of a duty under subsection (3), (7) or (9) above) requests the Commissioners to approve a particular person as his tax representative, and

(b)   the Commissioners approve that person,

that person shall be the insurer's or taxable intermediary's tax representative at any relevant time falling after the Commissioners' approval is given and before their approval is withdrawn.

57(11) The Commissioners may at any time direct that a person who is an agent of the insurer or taxable intermediary and is specified in the direction shall be the insurer's or taxable intermediary's tax representative; and–

(a)   the direction shall be taken to signify the Commissioners' approval of that person as the insurer's or taxable intermediary's tax representative;

(b)   that person shall be the insurer's or taxable intermediary's tax representative at any relevant time falling after the Commissioners' direction is made and before their approval is withdrawn;

(c)   the direction shall not prejudice any duty of the insurer or taxable intermediary under subsection (3), (7) or (9) above;

(d)   subsection (8) above shall not apply in the case of the person specified in the direction.

57(12)   Where the Commissioners approve a person under this section as the insurer's or taxable intermediary's tax representative–

(a)   at the time the approval is given they shall be taken to withdraw their approval of any person who was the insurer's or taxable intermediary's tax representative immediately before the approval was given, and

(b)   that person shall cease at that time to be the insurer's or taxable intermediary's tax representative.

57(13)   The fact that a person ceases to be an insurer's or taxable intermediary's representative shall not prevent his subsequent approval under this section.

57(14)   The Commissioners may not withdraw their approval of a person as a tax representative except by virtue of subsection (8) or (12) above.

57(15)   Regulations may make provision as to the time at which–

(a)   the Commissioners' approval is to be treated as given in a case where action has been taken as mentioned in subsection (4) above or a request has been made as mentioned in subsection (10) above;

(b)   the Commissioners are to be taken to inform the insurer or taxable intermediary under subsection (8) above;

(c)   a direction of the Commissioners is to be treated as made under subsection (11) above.

57(16)   The **relevant period** for the purposes of subsection (4) above is–

(a)   where subsection (4) above applies by virtue of subsection (3) above, the period of 30 days beginning with the day on which the insurer or taxable intermediary first falls within subsection (1) above;

(b)   where subsection (4) above applies by virtue of subsection (7) above, the period of 30 days beginning with the day on which the requirement mentioned in subsection (7) above is made;

(c)   where subsection (4) above applies by virtue of subsection (9) above, the period of 30 days beginning with the day on which the person mentioned in subsection (8) above ceases to be the insurer's or taxable intermediary's tax representative;

but if in any case the Commissioners allow a longer period than that found under paragraphs (a) to (c) above, the **relevant period** is that longer period.

History – In s. 57 wherever occurring, the words "or taxable intermediary" were inserted by FA 1997, s. 27(4)(a), with effect from 19 March 1997.

In s. 57 wherever occurring, the words "or taxable intermediary's" were inserted by FA 1997, s. 27(4)(b), with effect from 19 March 1997.

In s. 57(1)(a), the words "or, as the case may be, section 53AA" were inserted by FA 1997, s. 27(4)(c), with effect from 19 March 1997.

Cross reference – Insurance Companies Act 1982, s. 10: requirements which representative must fulfil are as follows:
- the representative must be UK-resident and designated as applicant's representative for purposes of s. 10 of the 1982 Act;
- the representative must be authorised to act generally, and accept service of any document, on behalf of the applicant;
- the representative must not be an auditor, or a partner or employee of an auditor of any business carried on by the applicant; and
- if representative is not an individual, it must be a company (as defined in companies legislation) with its head office in the UK. The company must have a representative in the UK.

Statutory instruments – SI 1994/1774, reg. 29 and 33 (as amended by SI 1997/1157).

58   Rights and duties of tax representatives

58(1)   Where a person is an insurer's or taxable intermediary's tax representative at any time, the *tax representative*–

(a)   shall be entitled to act on the insurer's or taxable intermediary's behalf for the purposes of legislation relating to insurance premium tax,

(b)   shall secure (where appropriate by acting on the insurer's or taxable intermediary's behalf) the insurer's or taxable intermediary's compliance with and discharge of the obligations and liabilities to which the insurer or taxable intermediary is subject by virtue of legislation relating to insurance premium tax (including obligations and liabilities arising before the person became the insurer's or taxable intermediary's tax representative), and

(c)   shall be personally liable in respect of any failure to secure the insurer's or taxable intermediary's compliance with or discharge of any such obligation or liability, and in respect of anything done for purposes connected with acting on the insurer's or taxable intermediary's behalf,

as if the obligations and liabilities imposed on the insurer or taxable intermediary were imposed jointly and severally on the tax representative and the insurer or taxable intermediary.

58(2)   A tax representative shall not be liable by virtue of subsection (1) above himself to be registered under this Part, but regulations may–

(a)   require the registration of the names of tax representatives against the names of the insurers in any register kept under this Part;

(b)   make provision for the deletion of the names of persons who cease to be tax representatives.

58(3)   A tax representative shall not by virtue of subsection (1) above be guilty of any offence except in so far as–

(a)   the tax representative has consented to, or connived in, the commission of the offence by the insurer or taxable intermediary,

(b)   the commission of the offence by the insurer or taxable intermediary is attributable to any neglect on the part of the tax representative, or

(c)   the offence consists in a contravention by the tax representative of an obligation which, by virtue of that subsection, is imposed both on the tax representative and on the insurer or taxable intermediary.

58(4)   Subsection (1)(b) above shall have effect subject to such provisions as may be made by regulations.

History – In s. 58 wherever they appear, the words "or taxable intermediary" were inserted by FA 1997, s. 27(5)(a), with effect from 19 March 1997.
In s. 58 wherever they appear, the words "or taxable intermediary's" were inserted by FA 1997, s. 27(5)(b), with effect from 19 March 1997.

Statutory instruments – SI 1994/1774 (as amended by SI 1997/1157).

REVIEW AND APPEAL

Official publications – Notice IPT 2, Pt. 12 (1999 edn): a general guide to IPT, reviews and appeals.

59   Review of Commissioners' decisions

59(1)   This section applies to any decision of the Commissioners with respect to any of the following matters–

(a)   the registration or cancellation of registration of any person under this Part;

(b)   whether tax is chargeable in respect of a premium or how much tax is chargeable;

(bb)   whether a payment falls to be treated under section 52A(2) above as a premium received under a taxable insurance contract by an insurer and chargeable to tax at the higher rate;

(c)   whether a person is entitled to credit by virtue of regulations under section 55 above or how much credit a person is entitled to or the manner in which he is to benefit from credit;

(d)   an assessment falling within subsection (1A) below or the amount of such an assessment;

(e)   any refusal of an application under section 63 below;

(f)   whether a notice may be served on a person by virtue of regulations made under section 65 below;

(g)   an assessment under regulations made under section 65 below or the amount of such an assessment;

(h)   whether a scheme established by regulations under section 68 below applies to an insurer as regards an accounting period;

(i)   the requirement of any security under paragraph 24 of Schedule 7 to this Act or its amount;

(j)   any liability to a penalty under paragraphs 12 to 19 of Schedule 7 to this Act;

(k)   the amount of any penalty or interest specified in an assessment under paragraph 25 of Schedule 7 to this Act;

(l)   a claim for the repayment of an amount under paragraph 8 of Schedule 7 to this Act;

(m)   any liability of the Commissioners to pay interest under paragraph 22 of Schedule 7 to this Act or the amount of the interest payable.

59(1A) An assessment falls within this subsection if it is an assessment under section 56 above in respect of an accounting period in relation to which a return required to be made by virtue of regulations under section 54 above has been made.

59(2) Any person who is or will be affected by any decision to which this section applies may by notice in writing to the Commissioners require them to review the decision.

59(3) The Commissioners shall not be required under this section to review any decision unless the notice requiring the review is given before the end of the period of 45 days beginning with the day on which written notification of the decision, or of the assessment containing the decision, was first given to the person requiring the review.

59(4) For the purposes of subsection (3) above it shall be the duty of the Commissioners to give written notification of any decision to which this section applies to any person who–

(a)   requests such a notification,

(b)   has not previously been given written notification of that decision, and

(c)   if given such a notification, will be entitled to require a review of the decision under this section.

59(5) A person shall be entitled to give a notice under this section requiring a decision to be reviewed for a second or subsequent time only if–

(a)   the grounds on which he requires the further review are that the Commissioners did not, on any previous review, have the opportunity to consider certain facts or other matters, and

(b)   he does not, on the further review, require the Commissioners to consider any facts or matters which were considered on a previous review except in so far as they are relevant to any issue not previously considered.

59(6) Where the Commissioners are required in accordance with this section to review any decision, it shall be their duty to do so; and on the review they may withdraw, vary or confirm the decision.

59(7) In a case where–

(a)   it is the duty under this section of the Commissioners to review any decision, and

(b)   they do not, within the period of 45 days beginning with the day on which the review was required, give notice to the person requiring it of their determination on the review,

they shall be assumed for the purposes of this Part to have confirmed the decision.

59(8) The Commissioners shall not by virtue of any requirement under this section to review a decision have any power, apart from their power in pursuance of paragraph 13 of Schedule 7 to this Act, to mitigate the amount of any penalty imposed under this Part.

History – S. 59(1)(bb) was inserted by FA 1997, s. 27(6), with effect from 19 March 1997.
In s. 59(1)(d), the words "falling within subsection (1A) below" were substituted by FA 1995, s. 34 and Sch. 5, para. 5(2), in relation to assessments made on or after 1 May 1995.
S. 59(1A) was inserted by FA 1995, s. 34 and Sch. 5, para. 5(3), in relation to assessments made on or after 1 May 1995.

Cross references – FA 1997, Sch. 5, para. 19(2): assessments to recover excess payments by Commissioners.
SI 1994/1774, reg. 43(3): diligence.
SI 1997/1431, reg. 5(1)(b): restrictions on levying distress.

Statutory instruments – S. 59 came into force with effect from 1 October 1994 (SI 1994/1733 (C 32)).

60   Appeals

60(1) Subject to the following provisions of this section, an appeal shall lie to an appeal tribunal with respect to any of the following decisions–

(a)   any decision by the Commissioners on a review under section 59 above (including a deemed confirmation under subsection (7) of that section);

(b)   any decision by the Commissioners on such review of a decision referred to in section 59(1) above as the Commissioners have agreed to undertake in consequence of a request made after the end of the period mentioned in section 59(3) above.

60(2) Without prejudice to paragraph 13 of Schedule 7 to this Act, nothing in subsection (1) above shall be taken to confer on a tribunal any power to vary an amount assessed by way of penalty or interest except in so far as it is necessary to reduce it to the amount which is appropriate under paragraphs 12 to 21 of that Schedule.

60(3) Where an appeal is made under this section by a person who is required to make returns by virtue of regulations under section 54 above, the appeal shall not be entertained unless the appellant–

(a)   has made all the returns which he is required to make by virtue of those regulations, and

(b)   has paid the amounts shown in those returns as payable by him;

but the restriction in paragraph (b) above shall not apply in the case of an appeal against a decision with respect to the matter mentioned in section 59(1)(i) above.

60(4)   Where the appeal is against a decision with respect to any of the matters mentioned in paragraphs (b) and (d) of section 59(1) above it shall not be entertained unless–

(a)   the amount which the Commissioners have determined to be payable as tax has been paid or deposited with them, or

(b)   on being satisfied that the appellant would otherwise suffer hardship the Commissioners agree or the tribunal decides that it should be entertained notwithstanding that that amount has not been so paid or deposited.

60(5)   Where on an appeal against a decision with respect to any of the matters mentioned in section 59(1)(d) above–

(a)   it is found that the amount specified in the assessment is less than it ought to have been, and
(b)   the tribunal gives a direction specifying the correct amount,

the assessment shall have effect as an assessment of the amount specified in the direction and that amount shall be deemed to have been notified to the appellant.

60(6)   Where on an appeal under this section it is found that the whole or part of any amount paid or deposited in pursuance of subsection (4) above is not due, so much of that amount as is found not to be due shall be repaid with interest at such rate as the tribunal may determine.

60(7)   Where on an appeal under this section it is found that the whole or part of any amount due to the appellant by virtue of regulations under section 55(3)(c) or (d) or (f) above has not been paid, so much of that amount as is found not to have been paid shall be paid with interest at such rate as the tribunal may determine.

60(8)   Where an appeal under this section has been entertained notwithstanding that an amount determined by the Commissioners to be payable as tax has not been paid or deposited and it is found on the appeal that that amount is due the tribunal may, if it thinks fit, direct that that amount shall be paid with interest at such rate as may be specified in the direction.

60(9)   On an appeal against an assessment to a penalty under paragraph 12 of Schedule 7 to this Act, the burden of proof as to the matters specified in paragraphs (a) and (b) of sub-paragraph (1) of paragraph 12 shall lie upon the Commissioners.

60(10)   Sections 25 and 29 of the Finance Act 1985 (settling of appeals by agreement and enforcement of certain decisions of tribunal) shall have effect as if–

(a)   the references to section 40 of the Value Added Tax Act 1983 included references to this section, and

(b)   the references to **value added tax** included references to insurance premium tax.

Cross references – VATA 1994, s. 83: appeals to a VAT tribunal against the decision of the commissioners with respect to the matters specified in s. 83.
VATA 1994, s. 85: settling appeals by agreement.
VATA 1994, s. 87: enforcement of certain decisions of tribunal.
FA 1997, Sch. 5, para. 19(2): assessments to recover excess payments by Commissioners.

Statutory instruments – SI 1986/590 (as amended by SI 1986/2290, SI 1994/2617): VAT Tribunals Rules.

Notes – S. 60 came into force with effect from 1 October 1994 (SI 1994/1733 (C 32)).
VATA 1983, s. 40 is now VATA 1994, s. 83.
FA 1985, s. 25, 29 is now VATA 1994, s. 85, 87.

61   Review and appeal: commencement

61   Sections 59 and 60 above shall come into force on such day as may be appointed by order.
Statutory instrument – The appointed day is 1 October 1994 (SI 1994/1733 (C 32)).

MISCELLANEOUS

62   Partnership, bankruptcy, transfer of business, etc.

62(1)   Regulations may make provision for determining by what persons anything required by this Part to be done by an insurer or taxable intermediary is to be done where the business concerned is carried on in partnership or by another unincorporated body.

62(2)   The registration under this Part of an unincorporated body other than a partnership may be in the name of the body concerned; and in determining whether premiums are received by such a body no account shall be taken of any change in its members.

62(3) Regulations may make provision for determining by what person anything required by this Part to be done by an insurer is to be done in a case where insurance business is carried on by persons who are underwriting members of Lloyd's and are members of a syndicate of such underwriting members.

62(4) Regulations may–

(a) make provision for the registration for the purposes of this Part of a syndicate of underwriting members of Lloyd's;

(b) provide that for purposes prescribed by the regulations no account shall be taken of any change in the members of such a syndicate;

and regulations under paragraph (a) above may modify section 53 above.

62(5) As regards any case where a person carries on a business of an insurer or taxable intermediary who has died or become bankrupt or incapacitated or been sequestrated, or of an insurer or taxable intermediary which is in liquidation or receivership or in relation to which an administration order is in force, regulations may–

(a) require the person to inform the Commissioners of the fact that he is carrying on the business and of the event that has led to his carrying it on;

(b) make provision allowing the person to be treated for a limited time as if he were the insurer or taxable intermediary;

(c) make provision for securing continuity in the application of this Part where a person is so treated.

62(6) Regulations may make provision for securing continuity in the application of this Part in cases where a business carried on by a person is transferred to another person as a going concern.

62(7) Regulations under subsection (6) above may in particular provide–

(a) for liabilities and duties under this Part of the transferor to become, to such extent as may be provided by the regulations, liabilities and duties of the transferee;

(b) for any right of either of them to repayment or credit in respect of tax to be satisfied by making a repayment or allowing a credit to the other;

but the regulations may provide that no such provision as is mentioned in paragraph (a) or (b) of this subsection shall have effect in relation to any transferor and transferee unless an application in that behalf has been made by them under the regulations.

History – In s. 62(1) and (5) wherever occurring, the words "or taxable intermediary" were inserted by FA 1997, s. 27(7), with effect from 19 March 1997.

Statutory instruments – SI 1994/1774 (as amended by SI 1997/1157).

63   Groups of companies

63(1) Where under the following provisions of this section any bodies corporate are treated as members of a group, for the purposes of this Part–

(a) any taxable business carried on by a member of the group shall be treated as carried on by the representative member,

(aa) any business carried on by a member of the group who is a taxable intermediary shall be treated as carried on by the representative member,

(b) the representative member shall be taken to be the insurer in relation to any taxable insurance contract as regards which a member of the group is the actual insurer,

(bb) the representative member shall be taken to be the taxable intermediary in relation to any taxable intermediary's fees as regards which a member of the group is the actual taxable intermediary,

(c) any receipt by a member of the group of a premium under a taxable insurance contract shall be taken to be a receipt by the representative member, and

(d) all members of the group shall be jointly and severally liable for any tax due from the representative member.

63(2) Two or more bodies corporate are eligible to be treated as members of a group if each of them falls within subsection (3) below and–

(a) one of them controls each of the others,

(b) one person (whether a body corporate or an individual) controls all of them, or

(c) two or more individuals carrying on a business in partnership control all of them.

63(3) A body falls within this subsection if it is resident in the United Kingdom or it has an established place of business in the United Kingdom.

63(4) Where an application to that effect is made to the Commissioners with respect to two or more bodies corporate eligible to be treated as members of a group, then–

(a) from the beginning of an accounting period they shall be so treated, and

(b) one of them shall be the representative member,

unless the Commissioners refuse the application; and the Commissioners shall not refuse the application unless it appears to them necessary to do so for the protection of the revenue.

63(5) Where any bodies corporate are treated as members of a group and an application to that effect is made to the Commissioners, then, from the beginning of an accounting period–

(a) a further body eligible to be so treated shall be included among the bodies so treated,

(b) a body corporate shall be excluded from the bodies so treated,

(c) another member of the group shall be substituted as the representative member, or

(d) the bodies corporate shall no longer be treated as members of a group,

unless the application is to the effect mentioned in paragraph (a) or (c) above and the Commissioners refuse the application.

63(6) The Commissioners may refuse an application under subsection (5)(a) or (c) above only if it appears to them necessary to do so for the protection of the revenue.

63(7) Where a body corporate is treated as a member of a group as being controlled by any person and it appears to the Commissioners that it has ceased to be so controlled, they shall, by notice given to that person, terminate that treatment from such date as may be specified in the notice.

63(8) An application under this section with respect to any bodies corporate must be made by one of those bodies or by the person controlling them and must be made not less than 90 days before the date from which it is to take effect, or at such later time as the Commissioners may allow.

63(9) For the purposes of this section a body corporate shall be taken to **control** another body corporate if it is empowered by statute to control that body's activities or if it is that body's holding company within the meaning of section 736 of the Companies Act 1985; and an individual or individuals shall be taken to control a body corporate if he or they, were he or they a company, would be that body's holding company within the meaning of that section.

History – S. 63(1)(aa) was inserted by FA 1997, s. 27(8)(a), with effect from 19 March 1997.
S. 63(1)(bb) was inserted by FA 1997, s. 27(8)(b), with effect from 19 March 1997.

64 Information, powers, penalties, etc.

64 Schedule 7 to this Act (which contains provisions relating to information, powers, penalties and other matters) shall have effect.

65 Liability of insured in certain cases

65(1) Regulations may make provision under this section with regard to any case where at any time–

(a) an insurer does not have any business establishment or other fixed establishment in the United Kingdom, and

(b) no person is the insurer's tax representative by virtue of section 57 above.

65(2) Regulations may make provision allowing notice to be served in accordance with the regulations on–

(a) the person who is insured under a taxable insurance contract, if there is one insured person, or

(b) one or more of the persons who are insured under a taxable insurance contract, if there are two or more insured persons;

and a notice so served is referred to in this section as a **liability notice**.

65(3) Regulations may provide that if a liability notice has been served in accordance with the regulations–

(a) the Commissioners may assess to the best of their judgment the amount of any tax due in respect of premiums received by the insurer under the contract concerned after the material date and before the date of the assessment, and

(b) that amount shall be deemed to be the amount of tax so due.

65(4) The **material date** is–

(a)   where there is one person on whom a liability notice has been served in respect of the contract, the date when the notice was served or such later date as may be specified in the notice;

(b)   where there are two or more persons on whom liability notices have been served in respect of the contract, the date when the last of the notices was served or such later date as may be specified in the notices.

65(5)   Regulations may provide that where–

(a)   an assessment is made in respect of a contract under provision included in the regulations by virtue of subsection (3) above, and

(b)   the assessment is notified to the person, or each of the persons, on whom a liability notice in respect of the contract has been served,

the persons mentioned in subsection (6) below shall be jointly and severally liable to pay the tax assessed, and that tax shall be recoverable accordingly.

65(6)   The persons are–

(a)   the person or persons mentioned in subsection (5)(b) above, and

(b)   the insurer.

65(7)   Where regulations make provision under subsection (5) above they must also provide that any provision made under that subsection shall not apply if, or to the extent that, the assessment has subsequently been withdrawn or reduced.

65(8)   Regulations may make provision as to the time within which, and the manner in which, tax which has been assessed is to be paid.

65(9)   Where any amount is recovered from an insured person by virtue of regulations made under this section, the insurer shall be liable to pay to the insured person an amount equal to the amount recovered; and regulations may make provision requiring an insurer to pay interest where this subsection applies.

65(10)   Regulations may make provision for adjustments to be made of a person's liability in any case where–

(a)   an assessment is made under section 56 above in relation to the insurer, and

(b)   an assessment made by virtue of regulations under this section relates to premiums received (or assumed for the purposes of the assessment to be received) within a period which corresponds to any extent with the accounting period to which the assessment under section 56 relates.

65(11)   Regulations may make provision as regards a case where–

(a)   an assessment made in respect of a contract by virtue of regulations under this section relates to premiums received (or assumed for the purposes of the assessment to be received) within a given period, and

(b)   an amount of tax is paid by the insurer in respect of an accounting period which corresponds to any extent with that period;

and the regulations may include provision for determining whether, or how much of, any of the tax paid as mentioned in paragraph (b) above is attributable to premiums received under the contract in the period mentioned in paragraph (a) above.

65(12)   Regulations may–

(a)   make provision requiring the Commissioners, in prescribed circumstances, to furnish prescribed information to an insured person;

(b)   make provision requiring any person on whom a liability notice has been served to keep records, to furnish information, or to produce documents for inspection or cause documents to be produced for inspection;

(c)   make such provision as the Commissioners think is reasonable for the purpose of facilitating the recovery of tax from the persons having joint and several liability (rather than from the insurer alone);

(d)   modify the effect of any provision of this Part.

65(13)   Regulations may provide for an insured person to be liable to pay tax assessed by virtue of the regulations notwithstanding that he has already paid an amount representing tax as part of a premium.

Statutory instrument – SI 1994/1774, reg. 32 and 39.

66   Directions as to amounts of premiums

66(1)   This section applies where–

(a)   anything is received by way of premium under a taxable insurance contract, and

(b)   the amount of the premium is less than it would be if it were received under the contract in open market conditions.

66(2)   The Commissioners may direct that the amount of the premium shall be taken for the purposes of this Part to be such amount as it would be if it were received under the contract in open market conditions.

66(3)   A direction under subsection (2) above shall be given by notice in writing to the insurer, and no direction may be given more than three years after the time of the receipt.

66(4)   Where the Commissioners make a direction under subsection (2) above in the case of a contract they may also direct that if–

(a)   anything is received by way of premium under the contract after the giving of the notice or after such later date as may be specified in the notice, and

(b)   the amount of the premium is less than it would be if it were received under the contract in open market conditions,

the amount of the premium shall be taken for the purposes of this Part to be such amount as it would be if it were received under the contract in open market conditions.

66(5)   For the purposes of this section a **premium is received in open market conditions** if it is received–

(a)   by an insurer standing in no such relationship with the insured person as would affect the premium, and

(b)   in circumstances where there is no other contract or arrangement affecting the parties.

66(6)   For the purpose of this section it is immaterial whether what is received by way of premium is money or something other than money or both.

Cross reference – SI 1994/1774, reg. 24(1).

67   Deemed date of receipt of certain premiums

67(1)   In a case where–

(a)   a premium under a contract of insurance is received by the insurer after 30th November 1993 and before 1st October 1994, and

(b)   the period of cover for the risk begins on or after 1st October 1994,

for the purposes of this Part the premium shall be taken to be received on 1st October 1994.

67(2)   Subsection (3) below applies where–

(a)   a premium under a contract of insurance is received by the insurer after 30th November 1993 and before 1st October 1994,

(b)   the period of cover for the risk begins before 1st October 1994 and ends after 30th September 1995, and

(c)   the premium, or any part of it, is attributable to such of the period of cover as falls after 30th September 1995.

67(3)   For the purposes of this Part–

(a)   so much of the premium as is attributable to such of the period of cover as falls after 30th September 1995 shall be taken to be received on 1st October 1994;

(b)   so much as is so attributable shall be taken to be a separate premium.

67(4)   If a contract relates to more than one risk subsection (1) above shall have effect as if the reference in paragraph (b) to the risk were to any given risk.

67(5)   If a contract relates to more than one risk, subsections (2) and (3) above shall apply as follows–

(a)   so much of the premium as is attributable to any given risk shall be deemed for the purposes of those subsections to be a separate premium relating to that risk;

(b)   those subsections shall then apply separately in the case of each given risk and the separate premium relating to it;

and any further attribution required by those subsections shall be made accordingly.

67(6) Subsections (1) and (4) above do not apply in relation to a contract if the contract belongs to a class of contract as regards which the normal practice is for a premium to be received by or on behalf of the insurer before the date when cover begins.

67(7) Subsections (2), (3) and (5) above do not apply in relation to a contract if the contract belongs to a class of contract as regards which the normal practice is for cover to be provided for a period exceeding twelve months.

67(8) Any attribution under this section shall be made on such basis as is just and reasonable.

Cross reference – SI 1994/1774, reg. 23(6) and (8).

67A Announced increase in rate of tax: certain premiums treated as received on date of increase

67A(1) This section applies in any case where a proposed increase is announced by a Minister of the Crown in the rate at which tax is to be charged on a premium if it is received by the insurer on or after a date specified in the announcement (**"the date of the change"**).

67A(2) In a case where–

(a) a premium under a contract of insurance is received by the insurer on or after the date of the announcement but before the date of the change, and

(b) the period of cover for the risk begins on or after the date of the change,

for the purposes of this Part the premium shall be taken to be **received** on the date of the change.

67A(3) Subsection (4) below applies where–

(a) a premium under a contract of insurance is received by the insurer on or after the date of the announcement but before the date of the change;

(b) the period of cover for the risk begins before the date of the change and ends on or after the first anniversary of the date of the change; and

(c) the premium, or any part of it, is attributable to such of the period of cover as falls on or after the first anniversary of the date of the change.

67A(4) For the purposes of this Part–

(a) so much of the premium as is attributable to such of the period of cover as falls on or after the first anniversary of the date of the change shall be taken to be **received** on the date of the change; and

(b) so much as is so attributable shall be taken to be a separate premium.

67A(5) In determining whether the condition in subsection (2)(a) or (3)(a) above is satisfied, the provisions of regulations made by virtue of subsection (3) or (7) of section 68 below apply as they would apart from this section; but, subject to that, where subsection (2) or (4) above applies–

(a) that subsection shall have effect notwithstanding anything in section 68 below or regulations made under that section; and

(b) any regulations made under that section shall have effect as if the entry made in the accounts of the insurer showing the premium as due to him had been made as at the date of the change.

67A(6) Any attribution under this section shall be made on such basis as is just and reasonable.

67A(7) In this section–

 "increase", in relation to the rate of tax, includes the imposition of a charge to tax by adding to the descriptions of contract which are taxable insurance contracts;

 "Minister of the Crown" has the same meaning as in the Ministers of the Crown Act 1975.

History – S. 67A was inserted by FA 1997, s. 29(1), with effect on and after 26 November 1996.

Cross references – FA 1999, s. 125(5): bringing into force amended provision in FA 1994, Sch. 6A, para. 4 on travel insurance in relation to the increases in insurance premium tax–
 (1) the announcement relating to the increases, as described in s. 67A(1), and to those exceptions, as described in s. 67B(1), is taken to have been made on 9 March 1999;
 (2) the date of the change is 1 July 1999; and
 (3) the concessionary date is 1 January 2000.

FA 1998, s. 146(5): bringing into force amended provision in FA 1994, Sch. 6A, para. 4 on travel insurance in relation to the increases in insurance premium tax–
 (1) the announcement relating to the increases, as described in s. 67A(1), and to those exceptions, as described in s. 67B(1), is taken to have been made on 17 March 1998;
 (2) the date of the change is 1 August 1998; and
 (3) the concessionary date is 1 February 1999.

FA 1997, s. 29(2): in the application of s. 67A in relation to the increases in insurance premium tax–
 (1) the announcement relating to the increases, as described in s. 67A(1), and to those exceptions, as described in s. 67B(1), is taken to have been made on 26 November 1996;
 (2) the date of the change is 1 April 1997; and

(3)   the concessionary date is 1 August 1997.

Official publications – Notice IPT 2, Pt. 7 (1999 edn): a general guide to IPT, transitional arrangements for rate change.

67B   Announced increase in rate of tax: certain contracts treated as made on date of increase.

67B(1)   This section applies in any case where–

(a)   an announcement falling within section 67A(1) above is made; but

(b)   a proposed exception from the increase in question is also announced by a Minister of the Crown; and

(c)   the proposed exception is to apply in relation to a premium only if the conditions described in subsection (2) below are satisfied in respect of the premium.

67B(2)   Those conditions are–

(a)   that the premium is in respect of a contract made before the date of the change;

(b)   that the premium falls, by virtue of regulations under section 68 below, to be regarded for the purposes of this Part as received under the contract by the insurer before such date (**"the concessionary date"**) as is specified for the purpose in the announcement.

67B(3)   In a case where–

(a)   a premium under a contract of insurance is received by the insurer on or after the date of the announcement but before the concessionary date, and

(b)   the period of cover for the risk begins on or after the date of the change,

the rate of tax applicable in relation to the premium shall be determined as if the contract had been made on the date of the change.

67B(4)   Subsection (5) below applies where–

(a)   a premium under a contract of insurance is received by the insurer on or after the date of the announcement but before the concessionary date;

(b)   the period of cover for the risk begins before the date of the change and ends on or after the first anniversary of the date of the change; and

(c)   the premium, or any part of it, is attributable to such of the period of cover as falls on or after the first anniversary of the date of the change.

67B(5)   Where this subsection applies–

(a)   the rate of tax applicable in relation to so much of the premium as is attributable to such of the period of cover as falls on or after the first anniversary of the date of the change shall be determined as if the contract had been made on the date of the change; and

(b)   so much of the premium as is so attributable shall be taken to be a separate premium.

67B(6)   Any attribution under this section shall be made on such basis as is just and reasonable.

67B(7)   In this section–

     "the date of the change" has the same meaning as in section 67A above;

     "Minister of the Crown" has the same meaning as in section 67A above.

History – S. 67B was inserted by FA 1997, s. 29(1), with effect on and after 26 November 1996.

Cross references – FA 1999, s. 125(5): bringing into force amended provision in FA 1994, Sch. 6A, para. 4 on travel insurance in relation to the increases in insurance premium tax–

   (1)   the announcement relating to the increases, as described in s. 67A(1), and to those exceptions, as described in s. 67B(1), is taken to have been made on 9 March 1999;

   (2)   the date of the change is 1 July 1999; and

   (3)   the concessionary date is 1 January 2000.

FA 1998, s. 146(5): bringing into force amended provision in FA 1994, Sch. 6A, para. 4 on travel insurance in relation to the increases in insurance premium tax–

   (1)   the announcement relating to the increases, as described in s. 67A(1), and to those exceptions, as described in s. 67B(1), is taken to have been made on 17 March 1998;

   (2)   the date of the change is 1 August 1998; and

   (3)   the concessionary date is 1 February 1999.

FA 1997, s. 29(2): in the application of s. 67A in relation to the increases in insurance premium tax–

   (1)   the announcement relating to the increases, as described in s. 67A(1), and to those exceptions, as described in s. 67B(1), is taken to have been made on 26 November 1996;

   (2)   the date of the change is 1 April 1997; and

   (3)   the concessionary date is 1 August 1997.

Official publications – Notice IPT 2, Pt. 7 (1999 edn): a general guide to IPT, transitional arrangements for rate change.

67C   Announced increase in rate of tax: exceptions and apportionments

67C(1)   Sections 67A(2) and 67B(3) above do not apply in relation to a premium if the risk to which that premium relates belongs to a class of risk as regards which the normal practice is for a premium to be received by or on behalf of the insurer before the date when cover begins.

67C(2)   Sections 67A(3) and (4) and 67B(4) and (5) above do not apply in relation to a premium if the risk to which that premium relates belongs to a class of risk as regards which the normal practice is for cover to be provided for a period exceeding twelve months.

67C(3)   If a contract relates to more than one risk, then, in the application of section 67A(2), 67A(3) and (4), 67B(3) or 67B(4) and (5) above–

(a)   the reference in section 67A(2)(b) or (3)(b) or 67B(3)(b) or (4)(b), as the case may be, to the **risk** shall be taken as a reference to any given risk,

(b)   so much of the premium as is attributable to any given risk shall be taken for the purposes of section 67A(2), 67A(3) and (4), 67B(3) or 67B(4) and (5) above, as the case may be, to be a separate premium relating to that risk,

(c)   those provisions shall then apply separately in the case of each given risk and the separate premium relating to it, and

(d)   any further attribution required by section 67A(3) and (4) or 67B(4) and (5) above shall be made accordingly,

and subsections (1) and (2) above shall apply accordingly.

67C(4)   Any attribution under this section shall be made on such basis as is just and reasonable.

History – S. 67C was inserted by FA 1997, s. 29(1), with effect on and after 26 November 1996.

Cross references – FA 1999, s. 125(5): bringing into force amended provision in FA 1994, Sch. 6A, para. 4 on travel insurance in relation to the increases in insurance premium tax–
(1)   the announcement relating to the increases, as described in s. 67A(1), and to those exceptions, as described in s. 67B(1), is taken to have been made on 9 March 1999;
(2)   the date of the change is 1 July 1999; and
(3)   the concessionary date is 1 January 2000.
FA 1998, s. 146(5): bringing into force amended provision in FA 1994, Sch. 6A, para. 4 on travel insurance in relation to the increases in insurance premium tax–
(1)   the announcement relating to the increases, as described in s. 67A(1), and to those exceptions, as described in s. 67B(1), is taken to have been made on 17 March 1998;
(2)   the date of the change is 1 August 1998; and
(3)   the concessionary date is 1 February 1999.
FA 1997, s. 29(2): in the application of s. 67A in relation to the increases in insurance premium tax–
(1)   the announcement relating to the increases, as described in s. 67A(1), and to those exceptions, as described in s. 67B(1), is taken to have been made on 26 November 1996;
(2)   the date of the change is 1 April 1997; and
(3)   the concessionary date is 1 August 1997.

Official publications – Notice IPT 2, Pt. 7 (1999 edn): a general guide to IPT, transitional arrangements for rate change.

68   Special accounting schemes

68(1)   Regulations may make provision establishing a scheme in accordance with the following provisions of this section; and in this section **"a relevant accounting period"**, in relation to an insurer, means an accounting period as regards which the scheme applies to the insurer.

68(2)   Regulations may provide that if an insurer notifies the Commissioners that the scheme should apply to him as regards accounting periods beginning on or after a date specified in the notification and prescribed conditions are fulfilled, then, subject to any provision made under subsection (9) below, the scheme shall apply to the insurer as regards accounting periods beginning on or after that date.

68(3)   Regulations may provide that where–

(a)   an entry is made in the accounts of an insurer showing a premium under a taxable insurance contract as due to him, and

(b)   the entry is made as at a particular date which falls within a relevant accounting period,

then (whether or not that date is one on which the premium is actually received by the insurer or on which the premium would otherwise be treated for the purposes of this Part as received by him) the premium shall for the purposes of this Part be taken to be received by the insurer on that date or, in prescribed circumstances, to be received by him on a different date determined in accordance with the regulations.

68(4)   Where regulations make provision under subsection (3) above they may also provide that, for the purposes of this Part, the amount of the premium shall be taken to be the amount which the entry in the accounts treats as its amount.

68(5) Regulations may provide that provision made under subsections (3) and (4) above shall apply even if the premium, or part of it, is never actually received by the insurer or on his behalf; and the regulations may include provision that, where the premium is never actually received because the contract under which it would have been received is never entered into or is terminated, the premium is nonetheless to be taken for the purposes of this Part to be received under a taxable insurance contract.

68(6) Regulations may provide that any provision made under subsection (4) above shall be subject to any directions made under section 66 above.

68(7) Regulations may provide that where a premium is treated as received on a particular date by virtue of provision made under subsection (3) above and there is another date on which the premium–

(a)   is actually received by the insurer, or

(b)   would, apart from the regulations, be treated for the purposes of this Part as received by him,

the premium shall be taken for the purposes of this Part not to be received by him on that other date.

68(8) Regulations may provide that provision made under subsection (7) above shall apply only to the extent that there is no excess of the actual amount of the premium over the amount which, by virtue of regulations under this section or of a direction under section 66 above, is to be taken for the purposes of this Part to be its amount; and the regulations may include provision that where there is such an excess, the excess amount shall be taken for the purposes of this Part to be a separate premium and to be received by the insurer on a date determined in accordance with the regulations.

68(9) Regulations may provide that if a notification has been given in accordance with provision made under subsection (2) above and subsequently–

(a)   the insurer gives notice to the Commissioners that the scheme should not apply to him as regards accounting periods beginning on or after a date specified in the notice, or

(b)   the Commissioners give notice to the insurer that the scheme is not to apply to him as regards accounting periods beginning on or after a date specified in the notice,

then, if prescribed conditions are fulfilled, the scheme shall not apply to the insurer as regards an accounting period beginning on or after the date specified in the notice mentioned in paragraph (a) or (b) above unless the circumstances are such as may be prescribed.

68(10) Regulations may include provision–

(a)   enabling an insurer to whom the scheme applies as regards an accounting period to account for tax due in respect of that period on the assumption that the scheme will apply to him as regards subsequent accounting periods;

(b)   designed to secure that, where the scheme ceases to apply to an insurer, any tax which by virtue of provision made under paragraph (a) above has not been accounted for is accounted for and paid.

68(11) Regulations may provide that where–

(a)   an entry in the accounts of an insurer shows a premium as due to him,

(b)   the entry is made as at a date falling before 1st October 1994,

(c)   tax in respect of the receipt of the premium would, apart from the regulations, be charged by reference to a date (whether or not the date on which the premium is actually received by the insurer) falling on or after 1st October 1994,

(d)   the date by reference to which tax would be charged falls within a relevant accounting period, and

(e)   *prescribed conditions are fulfilled,*

the premium, or such part of it as may be found in accordance with prescribed rules, shall be taken for the purposes of this Part to have been received by the insurer before 1st October 1994.

68(12) Without prejudice to subsection (13) below, regulations may include provision modifying any provision made under this section so as to secure the effective operation of the provision in a case where a premium consists wholly or partly of anything other than money.

68(13) Regulations may modify the effect of any provision of this Part.

68(14) The reference in subsection (3)(a) above to a **premium under a taxable insurance contract** includes a reference to anything that, although not actually received by or on behalf of the insurer, would be such a premium if it were so received.

Cross references – FA 1997, s. 24(2)(b): premiums received before 1 August 1997 and commencement of new tax rate. FA 1998, s. 146(4): bringing into force amended provision in FA 1994, Sch. 6A, para. 4 on travel insurance.
Statutory instruments – SI 1994/1774.
Extra-statutory concessions – 3.29 (Notice 48 (1999 edn)): special accounting scheme – introductory provisions.

69   Charge to tax where different rates of tax apply

69(1)   This section applies for the purpose of determining the chargeable amount in a case where a contract provides cover falling within any one of the following paragraphs, that is to say–

(a)   cover for one or more exempt matters,

(b)   cover for one or more standard rate matters, or

(c)   cover for one or more higher rate matters,

and also provides cover falling within another of those paragraphs.

69(2)   In the following provisions of this section **"the non-exempt premium"** means the difference between–

(a)   the amount of the premium; and

(b)   such part of the premium as is attributable to any exempt matter or matters or, if no part is so attributable, nil.

69(3)   If the contract provides cover for one or more exempt matters and also provides cover for either–

(a)   one or more standard rate matters, or

(b)   one or more higher rate matters,

the chargeable amount is such amount as, with the addition of the tax chargeable at the standard rate or (as the case may be) the higher rate, is equal to the non-exempt premium.

69(4)   If the contract provides cover for both–

(a)   one or more standard rate matters, and

(b)   one or more higher rate matters,

the higher rate element and the standard rate element shall be found in accordance with the following provisions of this section.

69(5)   For the purposes of this section–

(a)   **"the higher rate element"** is such portion of the non-exempt premium as is attributable to the higher rate matters (including tax at the higher rate); and

(b)   **"the standard rate element"** is the difference between–

    (i) the non-exempt premium; and

    (ii) the higher rate element.

69(6)   In a case falling within subsection (4) above, tax shall be charged separately–

(a)   at the standard rate, by reference to the standard rate chargeable amount, and

(b)   at the higher rate, by reference to the higher rate chargeable amount,

and the tax chargeable in respect of the premium is the aggregate of those amounts of tax.

69(7)   For the purposes of this section–

    "the higher rate chargeable amount" is such amount as, with the addition of the tax chargeable at the higher rate, is equal to the higher rate element;

    "standard rate chargeable amount" is such amount as, with the addition of the tax chargeable at the standard rate, is equal to the standard rate element.

69(8)   References in this Part to the **chargeable amount** shall, in a case falling within subsection (4) above, be taken as referring separately to the standard rate chargeable amount and the higher rate chargeable amount.

69(9)   In applying subsection (2)(b) above, any amount that is included in the premium as being referable to tax (whether or not the amount corresponds to the actual amount of tax payable in respect of the premium) shall be taken to be wholly attributable to the non-exempt matter or matters.

69(10)   In applying subsection (5)(a) above, any amount that is included in the premium as being referable to tax at the higher rate (whether or not the amount corresponds to the actual amount of tax payable at that rate in respect of the premium) shall be taken to be wholly attributable to the higher rate element.

69(11)   Subject to subsections (9) and (10) above, any attribution under subsection (2)(b) or (5)(a) above shall be made on such basis as is just and reasonable.

69(12) For the purposes of this section–

(a) an **"exempt matter"** is any matter such that, if it were the only matter for which the contract provided cover, the contract would not be a taxable insurance contract;

(b) a **"non-exempt matter"** is a matter which is not an exempt matter;

(c) a **"standard rate matter"** is any matter such that, if it were the only matter for which the contract provided cover, tax at the standard rate would be chargeable on the chargeable amount;

(d) a **"higher rate matter"** is any matter such that, if it were the only matter for which the contract provided cover, tax at the higher rate would be chargeable on the chargeable amount.

69(13) If the contract relates to a lifeboat and lifeboat equipment, the lifeboat and the equipment shall be taken together in applying this section.

69(14) For the purposes of this section **"lifeboat"** and **"lifeboat equipment"** have the same meaning as in paragraph 6 of Schedule 7A to this Act.

History – S. 69 was substituted by FA 1997, s.23(1), generally with effect in relation to a premium which falls to be regarded for the purposes of FA 1994, Pt. III as received under a taxable insurance contract on or after 1 April 1997. However, the amendment does not have effect in relation to a premium if the premium–
(1) is in respect of a contract made before 1 April 1997; and
(2) falls, by virtue of regulations under s. 68, to be regarded for the purposes of Pt. III as received under the contract by the insurer on a date before 1 August 1997.
However, these two exclusions to the effective date of the amendment do not apply in relation to a premium if the premium–
(1) is an additional premium under the contract;
(2) falls as mentioned in s. 24(2)(b) to be regarded as received under the contract by the insurer on or after 1 April 1997; and
(3) is in respect of a risk which was not covered by the contract before 1 April 1997.
Former s. 69 reads as follows:

"69 Reduced chargeable amount
"**69(1)** Where a contract provides cover for one or more exempt matters and also provides cover for one or more non-exempt matters, for the purposes of this Part the **chargeable amount** is such amount as, with the addition of the tax chargeable, is equal to the difference between–
(a) the amount of the premium, and
(b) such part of the premium as is attributable to the exempt matter or matters.
69(2) In applying subsection (1) above, any amount that is included in the premium as being referable to tax (whether or not the amount corresponds to the actual amount of tax payable in respect of the premium) shall be taken to be wholly attributable to the non-exempt matter or matters; and, subject to that, any attribution under subsection (1) above shall be made on such basis as is just and reasonable.
69(3) For the purposes of this section an **exempt matter** is any matter such that, if it were the only matter for which the contract provided cover, the contract would not be a taxable insurance contract.
69(4) For the purposes of this section a **non-exempt matter** is a matter which is not an exempt matter.
69(5) If the contract relates to a lifeboat and lifeboat equipment, the lifeboat and the equipment shall be taken together in applying this section.
69(5A) For the purposes of this section **"lifeboat"** and **"lifeboat equipment"** have the same meaning as in paragraph 6 of Schedule 7A to this Act.
69(6) [Deleted by SI 1994/1698, art. 3(b).]"
Former s. 69(5A) was inserted by SI 1994/1698, art. 3(a), operative from 1 October 1994.
Former s. 69(6) was deleted by SI 1994/1698, art. 3(b), operative from 1 October 1994.
Extra-statutory concessions – 3.29 (Notice 48 (1999 edn)): special accounting scheme – introductory provisions.
3.30 (Notice 48 (1999 edn)): de minimis provisions.

SUPPLEMENTARY

70 Interpretation: taxable insurance contracts

70(1) Subject to subsection (1A) below, any contract of insurance is a taxable insurance contract.

70(1A) A contract is not a taxable insurance contract if it falls within one or more of the paragraphs of Part I of Schedule 7A to this Act.

70(1B) Part II of Schedule 7A to this Act (interpretation of certain provisions of Part I) shall have effect.

70(2)–(10) [Deleted by SI 1994/1698, art. 4(c).]

70(11) This section has effect subject to section 71 below.

70(12) This section and section 71 below have effect for the purposes of this Part.

History – In s. 70(1), the words "subsection (1A) below" were substituted by SI 1994/1698, art. 4(a), operative from 1 October 1994.
S. 70(1A) and (1B) were inserted by SI 1994/1698, art. 4(b), operative from 1 October 1994.
S. 70(2)–(10) were deleted by SI 1994/1698, art. 4(c), operative from 1 October 1994.

Cross references – Insurance Companies Act 1982, Sch. 1: classes of long-term business are life and annuity; marriage and birth; linked long term; permanent health, tontines; capital redemption and pension fund management.
Insurance Companies Act 1982, Sch. 2, Pt. I: Class 1: accident; Class 5: aircraft; Class 6: ships; Class 11: aircraft liability; and Class 12: liability of ships.
Export and Investment Guarantees Act 1991, s. 1(1): supplies (directly or indirectly) by persons carrying on business in the UK to persons carrying on business outside the UK.
FA 1997, s. 24: commencement of new tax rate.

Official publications – Notice IPT 2, Pt. 2 (1999 edn): a general guide to IPT, exemptions from the tax.
Notice IPT 2, Pt. 4 (1999 edn): a general guide to IPT, apportionment.

71 Taxable insurance contracts: power to change definition

71(1) Provision may be made by order that–

(a) a contract of insurance that would otherwise not be a taxable insurance contract shall be a taxable insurance contract if it falls within a particular description;

(b) a contract of insurance that would otherwise be a taxable insurance contract shall not be a taxable insurance contract if it falls within a particular description.

71(2) A description referred to in subsection (1) above may be by reference to the nature of the insured or by reference to such other factors as the Treasury think fit.

71(3) Provision under this section may be made in such way as the Treasury think fit, and in particular may be made by amending this Part.

71(4) An order under this section may amend or modify the effect of section 69 above in such way as the Treasury think fit.

Statutory instruments – SI 1994/1698.
SI 1996/2955.
SI 1997/1627.

72 Interpretation: premium

72(1) In relation to a taxable insurance contract, a **premium** is any payment received under the contract by the insurer, and in particular includes any payment wholly or partly referable to–

(a) any risk,

(b) costs of administration,

(c) commission,

(d) any facility for paying in instalments or making deferred payment (whether or not payment for the facility is called interest), or

(e) tax.

72(1A) Where an amount is charged to the insured by any person in connection with a taxable insurance contract, any payment in respect of that amount is to be regarded as a payment received under that contract by the insurer unless–

(a) the payment is chargeable to tax at the higher rate by virtue of section 52A above; or

(b) the amount is charged under a separate contract and is identified in writing to the insured as a separate amount so charged.

72(2) A premium may consist wholly or partly of anything other than money, and references to **payment** in subsection (1) above shall be construed accordingly.

72(3) Where a premium is to any extent received in a form other than money, its amount shall be taken to be–

(a) an amount equal to the value of whatever is received in a form other than money, or

(b) if money is also received, the aggregate of the amount found under paragraph (a) above and the amount received in the form of money.

72(4) The value to be taken for the purposes of subsection (3) above is open market value at the time of the receipt by the insurer.

72(5) The **open market value** of anything at any time shall be taken to be an amount equal to such consideration in money as would be payable on a sale of it at that time to a person standing in no such relationship with any person as would affect that consideration.

72(6) Where (apart from this subsection) anything received under a contract by the insurer would be taken to be an instalment of a premium, it shall be taken to be a separate premium.

72(7) Where anything is **received** by any person on behalf of the insurer–

(a) it shall be treated as received by the insurer when it is received by the other person, and

(b) *the later receipt of the whole or any part of it by the insurer shall be disregarded.*

72(7A) Where any person is authorised by or on behalf of an employee to deduct from anything due to the employee under his contract of employment an amount in respect of a payment due under a taxable insurance contract, subsection (7) above shall not apply to the receipt on behalf of the insurer by the person so authorised of the amount deducted.

72(8) In a case where–

(a)   a payment under a taxable insurance contract is made to a person (the **intermediary**) by or on behalf of the insured, and

(b)   the whole or part of the payment is referable to commission to which the intermediary is entitled,

in determining for the purposes of subsection (7) above whether, or how much of, the payment is received by the intermediary on behalf of the insurer any of the payment that is referable to that commission shall be regarded as received by the intermediary on behalf of the insurer notwithstanding the intermediary's entitlement.

72(8A)   Where, by virtue of subsection (7A) above, subsection (7) above does not apply to the receipt of an amount by a person and the whole or part of the amount is referable to commission to which he is entitled–

(a)   if the whole of the amount is so referable, the amount shall be treated as **received** by the insurer when it is deducted by that person; and

(b)   otherwise, the part of the amount that is so referable shall be treated as **received** by the insurer when the remainder of the payment concerned is or is treated as received by him.

72(9)   References in subsection (8) above to a **payment** include references to a payment in a form other than money.

72(10)   This section has effect for the purposes of this Part.

History – S. 72(1A) was inserted by FA 1997, s. 28(1), with effect in relation to payments received in respect of amounts charged on or after 1 April 1997.
S. 72(7A) was inserted by FA 1997, s. 30(1), with effect in relation to amounts deducted on or after 19 March 1997.
S. 72(8A) was inserted by FA 1997, s. 30(2), with effect in relation to amounts deducted on or after 19 March 1997.

73   Interpretation: other provisions

73(1)   Unless the context otherwise requires–

     "accounting period" shall be construed in accordance with section 54 above;

     "appeal tribunal" means a VAT and duties tribunal;

     "authorised person" means any person acting under the authority of the Commissioners;

     "the Commissioners" means the Commissioners of Customs and Excise;

     "conduct" includes any act, omission or statement;

     "the standard rate" shall be construed in accordance with section 51 above.

     "insurance business" means a business which consists of or includes the provision of insurance;

     "insurer" means a person or body of persons (whether incorporated or not) carrying on insurance business;

     "legislation relating to insurance premium tax" means this Part (as defined by subsection (9) below), any other enactment (whenever passed) relating to insurance premium tax, and any subordinate legislation made under any such enactment;

     "prescribed" means prescribed by an order or regulations under this Part;

     "the higher rate" shall be construed in accordance with section 51 above;

     "tax" means insurance premium tax;

     "tax representative" shall be construed in accordance with section 57 above;

     "taxable business" means a business which consists of or includes the provision of insurance under taxable insurance contracts;

     "taxable insurance contract" shall be construed in accordance with section 70 above;

     "taxable intermediary" shall be construed in accordance with section 52A above;

     "taxable intermediary's fees" has the meaning given by section 53AA(9) above;

73(2)   [Deleted by SI 1994/1698, art. 6.]

73(3)   Subject to subsection (3A) below, a **registrable person** is a person who–

(a)   is registered under section 53 above, or

(b)   is liable to be registered under that section.

73(3A)   References in sections 53A and 54 above and paragraphs 1, 9 and 12 of Schedule 7 to this Act to a **registrable person** include a reference to a person who–

(a)   is registered under section 53AA above; or

(b)   is liable to be registered under that section.

73(4)–(8)   [Deleted by SI 1994/1698, art. 6.]

73(9) A reference to this Part includes a reference to any order or regulations made under it and a reference to a provision of this Part includes a reference to any order or regulations made under the provision, unless otherwise required by the context or any order or regulations.

73(10) This section has effect for the purposes of this Part.

History – In s. 73(1), the definition of "taxable intermediary" was inserted by FA 1997, s. 27(9)(a), with effect from 19 March 1997.
In s. 73(1), the definition of "taxable intermediary's fees" was inserted by FA 1997, s. 27(9)(b), with effect from 19 March 1997.
In s. 73(1), the definition of "the higher rate" was inserted by FA 1997, s. 21(2)(a), generally with effect in relation to a premium which falls to be regarded for the purposes of FA 1994, Pt. III as received under a taxable insurance contract on or after 1 April 1997. However, the amendment does not have effect in relation to a premium if the premium–
  (1)   is in respect of a contract made before 1 April 1997; and
  (2)   falls, by virtue of regulations under s. 68, to be regarded for the purposes of Pt. III as received under the contract by the insurer on a date before 1 August 1997.
However, these two exclusions to the effective date of the amendment do not apply in relation to a premium if the premium–
  (1)   is an additional premium under the contract;
  (2)   falls as mentioned in s. 24(2)(b) to be regarded as received under the contract by the insurer on or after 1 April 1997; and
  (3)   is in respect of a risk which was not covered by the contract before 1 April 1997.
In s. 73(1), the definition of "the standard rate" was inserted by FA 1997, s. 21(2)(b), generally with effect in relation to a premium which falls to be regarded for the purposes of FA 1994, Pt. III as received under a taxable insurance contract on or after 1 April 1997. However, the amendment does not have effect in relation to a premium if the premium–
  (1)   is in respect of a contract made before 1 April 1997; and
  (2)   falls, by virtue of regulations under s. 68, to be regarded for the purposes of Pt. III as received under the contract by the insurer on a date before 1 August 1997.
However, these two exclusions to the effective date of the amendment do not apply in relation to a premium if the premium–
  (1)   is an additional premium under the contract;
  (2)   falls as mentioned in s. 24(2)(b) to be regarded as received under the contract by the insurer on or after 1 April 1997; and
  (3)   is in respect of a risk which was not covered by the contract before 1 April 1997.
In s. 73(3), the words "Subject to subsection (3A) below," were inserted by FA 1997, s. 27(10), with effect from 19 March 1997.
S. 73(3A) was inserted by FA 1997, s. 27(10), with effect from 19 March 1997.
In s. 73(1), the definition of "insurance business" was inserted by FA 1995, s. 34 and Sch. 5, para. 6, with effect from 1 May 1995.
S. 73(2) was deleted by SI 1994/1698, art. 6, operative from 1 October 1994.
S. 73(4)–(8) were deleted by SI 1994/1698, art. 6, operative from 1 October 1994.

Cross reference – Insurance Companies Act 1982, s. 93A(3): in determining where the risk is located, the following rules apply:
  •   insurance relating to buildings or buildings and their contents, the member state in which the property is situated;
  •   vehicle insurance, the member state of registration;
  •   policies of four months' duration or less relating to travel or holiday risks, the member state where the policyholder took out the policy;
  •   all other cases, where the policyholder is an individual, the member state in which he has his habitual residence and otherwise, the member state where the policyholder's establishment is situated.

74   Orders and regulations

74(1) The power to make an order under section 61 above shall be exercisable by the Commissioners, and the power to make an order under any other provision of this Part shall be exercisable by the Treasury.

74(2) Any power to make regulations under this Part shall be exercisable by the Commissioners.

74(3) Any power to make an order or regulations under this Part shall be exercisable by statutory instrument.

74(4) An order under section 51A or 71 above shall be laid before the House of Commons; and unless it is approved by that House before the expiration of a period of 28 days beginning with the date on which it was made it shall cease to have effect on the expiration of that period, but without prejudice to anything previously done under the order or to the making of a new order.

74(5) In reckoning any such period as is mentioned in subsection (4) above no account shall be taken of any time during which Parliament is dissolved or prorogued or during which the House of Commons is adjourned for more than four days.

74(6) A statutory instrument containing an order or regulations under this Part (other than an order under section 51A or 71 above) shall be subject to annulment in pursuance of a resolution of the House of Commons.

74(7) Any power to make an order or regulations under this Part–

(a)   may be exercised as regards prescribed cases or descriptions of case;

(b)   may be exercised differently in relation to different cases or descriptions of case.

74(8) An order or regulations under this Part may include such supplementary, incidental, consequential or transitional provisions as appear to the Treasury or the Commissioners (as the case may be) to be necessary or expedient.

74(9) No specific provision of this Part about an order or regulations shall prejudice the generality of subsections (7) and (8) above.

History – In s. 74(4) and (6), the words "51A or" were inserted by FA 1997, s. 22(2)(a), (b), generally with effect in relation to a premium which falls to be regarded for the purposes of FA 1994, Pt. III as received under a taxable insurance contract on or after 1 April 1997. However, the amendment does not have effect in relation to a premium if the premium–
  (1)   is in respect of a contract made before 1 April 1997; and
  (2)   falls, by virtue of regulations under s. 68, to be regarded for the purposes of Pt. III as received under the contract by the insurer on a date before 1 August 1997.
However, these two exclusions to the effective date of the amendment do not apply in relation to a premium if the premium–
  (1)   is an additional premium under the contract;
  (2)   falls as mentioned in s. 24(2)(b) to be regarded as received under the contract by the insurer on or after 1 April 1997; and
  (3)   is in respect of a risk which was not covered by the contract before 1 April 1997.

Statutory instruments – SI 1994/1698.
SI 1994/1733 (C 32).
SI 1994/1774.
SI 1994/1819.
SI 1996/223.

SCHEDULES

SCHEDULE 6A – PREMIUMS LIABLE TO TAX AT THE HIGHER RATE

Section 51A

History – Sch. 6A was inserted by FA 1997, s. 22(3) and Sch. 4, generally with effect in relation to a premium which falls to be regarded for the purposes of FA 1994, Pt. III as received under a taxable insurance contract on or after 1 April 1997. However, the amendment does not have effect in relation to a premium if the premium–
  (1)   is in respect of a contract made before 1 April 1997; and
  (2)   falls, by virtue of regulations under s. 68, to be regarded for the purposes of Pt. III as received under the contract by the insurer on a date before 1 August 1997.
However, these two exclusions to the effective date of the amendment do not apply in relation to a premium if the premium–
  (1)   is an additional premium under the contract;
  (2)   falls as mentioned in s. 24(2)(b) to be regarded as received under the contract by the insurer on or after 1 April 1997; and
  (3)   is in respect of a risk which was not covered by the contract before 1 April 1997.

Part I – Interpretation

1(1) In this Schedule–

"insurance-related service" means any service which is related to, or connected with, insurance;

"supply" includes all forms of supply; and **"supplier"** shall be construed accordingly.

1(2) For the purposes of this Schedule, any question whether a person is **connected** with another shall be determined in accordance with section 839 of the Taxes Act 1988.

Official publications – Notice IPT 2, Appendix C5 (1999 edn): Statement of Practice re connected persons.

Part II – Descriptions of premium

INSURANCE RELATING TO MOTOR CARS OR MOTOR CYCLES

2(1) A premium under a taxable insurance contract relating to a motor car or motor cycle falls within this paragraph if–

(a)   the contract is arranged through a person falling within sub-paragraph (2) below, or

(b)   the insurer under the contract is a person falling within that sub-paragraph,

unless the insurance is provided to the insured free of charge.

2(2) A person falls within this sub-paragraph if–

(a)   he is a supplier of motor cars or motor cycles;

(b)   he is connected with a supplier of motor cars or motor cycles; or

(c)   he pays–

    (i)   the whole or any part of the premium received under the taxable insurance contract, or

    (ii)   a fee connected with the arranging of that contract,

to a supplier of motor cars or motor cycles or to a person who is connected with a supplier of motor cars or motor cycles.

2(3) Where a taxable insurance contract relating to a motor car or motor cycle is arranged through a person who is connected with a supplier of motor cars or motor cycles, the premium does not fall within this paragraph by virtue only of sub-paragraph (2)(b) above except to the extent that the premium is attributable to cover for a risk which relates to a motor car or motor cycle supplied by a supplier of motor cars or motor cycles with whom that person is connected.

2(4) Where the insurer under a taxable insurance contract relating to a motor car or motor cycle is connected with a supplier of motor cars or motor cycles, the premium does not fall within this paragraph by virtue only of sub-paragraph (2)(b) above except to the extent that the premium is attributable to cover for a risk which relates to a motor car or motor cycle supplied by a supplier of motor cars or motor cycles with whom the insurer is connected.

2(5) For the purposes of this paragraph, the cases where insurance is provided to the insured **free of charge** are those cases where no charge (whether by way of premium or otherwise) is made–

(a)   in respect of the taxable insurance contract, or

(b)   at or about the time when the taxable insurance contract is made and in connection with that contract, in respect of any insurance-related service,

by any person falling within sub-paragraph (2) above to any person who is or becomes the insured (or one of the insured) under the contract or to any person who acts, otherwise than in the course of a business, for or on behalf of such a person.

2(6)   In this paragraph–

"motor car" and **"motor cycle"** have the meaning given–

(a)   by section 185(1) of the Road Traffic Act 1988; or

(b)   in Northern Ireland, by Article 3(1) of the Road Traffic (Northern Ireland) Order 1995;

"supplier" does not include an insurer who supplies a car or motor cycle as a means of discharging liabilities arising by reason of a claim under an insurance contract.

Extra-statutory concessions – 3.31 (Notice 48 (1999 edn)): insurance relating to motor cars or motor cycles. 3.34 (Notice 48 (1999 edn)): discounted insurance.

INSURANCE RELATING TO DOMESTIC APPLIANCES ETC.

3(1) A premium under a taxable insurance contract relating to relevant goods falls within this paragraph if–

(a)   the contract is arranged through a person falling within sub-paragraph (2) below, or

(b)   the insurer under the contract is a person falling within that sub-paragraph, unless the insurance is provided to the insured free of charge.

3(2)   A person falls within this sub-paragraph if–

(a)   he is a supplier of relevant goods;

(b)   he is connected with a supplier of relevant goods; or

(c)   he pays–

(i) the whole or any part of the premium received under the taxable insurance contract, or

(ii) a fee connected with the arranging of that contract,

to a supplier of relevant goods or to a person who is connected with a supplier of relevant goods.

3(3) Where a taxable insurance contract relating to relevant goods is arranged through a person who is connected with a supplier of relevant goods, the premium does not fall within this paragraph by virtue only of sub-paragraph (2)(b) above except to the extent that the premium is attributable to cover for a risk which relates to relevant goods supplied by a supplier of relevant goods with whom that person is connected.

3(4) Where the insurer under a taxable insurance contract relating to relevant goods is connected with a supplier of relevant goods, the premium does not fall within this paragraph by virtue only of sub-paragraph (2)(b) above except to the extent that the premium is attributable to cover for a risk which relates to relevant goods supplied by a supplier of relevant goods with whom the insurer is connected.

3(5) For the purposes of this paragraph, the cases where insurance is provided to the insured **free of charge** are those cases where no charge (whether by way of premium or otherwise) is made–

(a)   in respect of the taxable insurance contract, or

(b)   at or about the time when the taxable insurance contract is made and in connection with that contract, in respect of any insurance-related service,

by any person falling within sub-paragraph (2) above to any person who is or becomes the insured (or one of the insured) under the contract or to any person who acts, otherwise than in the course of a business, for or on behalf of such a person.

3(6)   In this paragraph–

"relevant goods" means any electrical or mechanical appliance of a kind–

(a)   which is ordinarily used in or about the home; or

(b)   which is ordinarily owned by private individuals and used by them for the purposes of leisure, amusement or entertainment;

"supplier" does not include an insurer who supplies relevant goods as a means of discharging liabilities arising by reason of a claim under an insurance contract.

3(7)   In sub-paragraph (6) above–

"appliance" includes any device, equipment or apparatus;

"the home" includes any private garden and any private garage or private workshop appurtenant to a dwelling.

Extra-statutory concessions – 3.32 (Notice 48 (1999 edn)): home contents insurance.
3.34 (Notice 48 (1999 edn)): discounted insurance.

TRAVEL INSURANCE

4(1)   A premium under a taxable insurance contract falls within this paragraph if it is in respect of the provision of cover against travel risks for a person travelling.

4(2)   Where–

(a)   a contract of insurance provides cover against both travel risks and risks other than travel risks,

(b)   the premium attributable to the cover against travel risks does not exceed 10 per cent of the total premium payable under the contract, and

(c)   the contract does not provide cover for a person travelling against travel risks falling within two or more of the paragraphs of sub-paragraph (3) below,

the premium, so far as attributable to the cover against travel risks, does not fall within this paragraph by virtue of sub-paragraph (1) above.

4(3)   The travel risks mentioned in sub-paragraph (2)(c) above are–

(a)   liability in respect of cancellation of travel or of accommodation arranged in connection with travel;

(b)   delayed or missed departure;

(c)   curtailment of travel or of the use of accommodation arranged in connection with travel;

(d)   loss or delayed arrival of baggage;

(e)   personal injury or illness or expenses of repatriation.

4(4)   A premium does not fall within this paragraph by virtue of sub-paragraph (1) above if it is payable under a taxable insurance contract relating to a motor vehicle and is attributable to cover of the kind generally known as–

(a)   fully comprehensive,

(b)   third party, fire and theft,

(c)   third party, or

(d)   roadside assistance,

or if it is payable under a taxable insurance contract relating to a caravan, boat or aircraft and is attributable to cover of a description broadly corresponding to any of those set out in paragraphs (a) to (d) above (so far as applicable) provided in respect of the caravan, boat or aircraft for a period of at least one month for the person travelling.

4(5)   In this paragraph–

"person travelling" includes a person intending to travel;

"travel risks" means risks associated with, or related to, travel or intended travel–

(a)   outside the United Kingdom,

(b)   by air within the United Kingdom,

(c)   within the United Kingdom in connection with travel falling within paragraph (a) or (b) above, or

(d)   which involves absence from home for at least one night, or risks to which a person travelling may be exposed during, or at any place at which he may be in the course of, any such travel.

History – Para. 4 was substituted by FA 1998, s. 146(2), generally with effect in relation to a premium which is received under a taxable insurance contract by an insurer on or after 1 August 1998, subject to the provisions of FA 1998, s. 146(2). Former para. 4 reads as follows:

4(1) A premium under a taxable insurance contract relating to travel risks falls within this paragraph if–
(a) the contract is arranged through a person falling within sub-paragraph (2) below, or
(b) the insurer under the contract is a person falling within that sub-paragraph,
unless the insurance is provided to the insured free of charge.

4(2) A person falls within this sub-paragraph if–
(a) he is a tour operator or travel agent;
(b) he is connected with a tour operator or travel agent; or
(c) he pays–
  (i) the whole or any part of the premium received under the contract, or
  (ii) a fee connected with the arranging of the contract,
to a tour operator or travel agent or to a person who is connected with a tour operator or travel agent.

4(3) Where a taxable insurance contract relating to travel risks is arranged through a person who is connected with a tour operator or travel agent, the premium does not fall within this paragraph by virtue only of sub-paragraph (2)(b) above except to the extent that the premium is attributable to cover for a risk which relates to services supplied by a tour operator or travel agent with whom that person is connected.

4(4) Where the insurer under a taxable insurance contract relating to travel risks is connected with a tour operator or travel agent, the premium does not fall within this paragraph by virtue only of sub-paragraph (2)(b) above except to the extent that the premium is attributable to cover for a risk which relates to services supplied by a tour operator or travel agent with whom the insurer is connected.

4(5) For the purposes of sub-paragraphs (3) and (4) above, a travel agent shall be treated as **supplying any services** whose provision he secures or arranges.

4(6) For the purposes of this paragraph, the cases where insurance is provided to the insured **free of charge** are those cases where no charge (whether by way of premium or otherwise) is made–
(a) in respect of the taxable insurance contract, or
(b) at or about the time when the taxable insurance contract is made and in connection with that contract, in respect of any insurance-related service,
by any person falling within sub-paragraph (2) above to any person who is or becomes the insured (or one of the insured) under the contract or to any person who acts, otherwise than in the course of a business, for or on behalf of such a person.

4(7) In this paragraph–
  "**tour operator**" includes any person who carries on a business which consists of or includes the provision, or the securing of the provision, of–
    (a) services for the transport of travellers; or
    (b) accommodation for travellers;
  "**travel agent**" includes any person who carries on a business which consists of or includes the making of arrangements, whether directly or indirectly, with a tour operator for the transport or accommodation of travellers;
  "**travel risks**" means–
    (a) risks associated with, or related to, travel or intended travel; or
    (b) risks to which a person travelling may be exposed at any place at which he may be in the course of his travel."

Extra-statutory concessions – 3.34 (Notice 48 (1999 edn)): discounted insurance.

Other material – Business Brief 8/99: differential rates of IPT for travel insurance held to be state aid for premiums paid up to 1 August 1998.

SCHEDULE 7 – INSURANCE PREMIUM TAX

Section 64

Part I – Information

RECORDS

1(1) Regulations may require registrable persons to keep records.

1(2) Regulations under sub-paragraph (1) above may be framed by reference to such records as may be specified in any notice published by the Commissioners in pursuance of the regulations and not withdrawn by a further notice.

1(3) Regulations may require any records kept in pursuance of the regulations to be preserved for such period not exceeding six years as may be specified in the regulations.

1(4) Any duty under regulations to preserve records may be discharged by the preservation of the information contained in them by such means as the Commissioners may approve; and where that information is so preserved a copy of any document forming part of the records shall (subject to the following provisions of this paragraph) be admissible in evidence in any proceedings, whether civil or criminal, to the same extent as the records themselves.

1(5) The Commissioners may, as a condition of approving under sub-paragraph (4) above any means of preserving information contained in any records, impose such reasonable requirements as appear to them necessary for securing that the information will be as readily available to them as if the records themselves had been preserved.

1(6) A statement contained in a document produced by a computer shall not by virtue of sub-paragraph (4) above be admissible in evidence–

(a) in civil proceedings in England and Wales, except in accordance with sections 5 and 6 of the Civil Evidence Act 1968;

(b) in criminal proceedings in England and Wales, except in accordance with sections 69 and 70 of the Police and Criminal Evidence Act 1984 and Part II of the Criminal Justice Act 1988;

(c) in civil proceedings in Scotland, except in accordance with sections 5 and 6 of the Civil Evidence (Scotland) Act 1988;

(d) in criminal proceedings in Scotland, except in accordance with Schedule 8 to the Criminal Procedure (Scotland) Act 1995;

(e) in civil proceedings in Northern Ireland, except in accordance with sections 2 and 3 of the Civil Evidence Act (Northern Ireland) 1971;

(f) in criminal proceedings in Northern Ireland, except in accordance with Article 68 of the Police and Criminal Evidence (Northern Ireland) Order 1989 and Part II of the Criminal Justice (Evidence, Etc.) (Northern Ireland) Order 1988.

History – Reference in para. 1(6)(d) to Criminal Procedure (Scotland) Act 1995, Sch. 8 substituted by Criminal Procedure (Consequential Provisions) (Scotland) Act 1995. Sch. 4, para. 89(4)(a).

Cross references – S. 73(3A): "registrable person".
Civil Evidence Act 1968, s. 5: admissibility of statements produced by computers.
Civil Evidence Act 1968, s. 6: provisions supplementary to s. 2–5.
Police and Criminal Evidence Act 1984, s. 69: evidence from computer records.
Police and Criminal Evidence Act 1984, s. 70: supplementary provisions to s. 68, 69.
Criminal Justice Act 1988, Pt. II: documentary evidence in criminal proceedings.

Statutory instruments – SI 1994/1774 (as amended by SI 1997/1157).

OTHER PROVISIONS

2(1) Every person who is concerned (in whatever capacity) in an insurance business shall furnish to the Commissioners such information relating to contracts of insurance entered into in the course of the business as the Commissioners may reasonably require.

2(2) Every person who makes arrangements for other persons to enter into any contract of insurance shall furnish to the Commissioners such information relating to that contract as the Commissioners may reasonably require.

2(3) Every person who–

(a) is concerned in a business that is not an insurance business, and

(b) has been involved in the entry into any contract of insurance providing cover for any matter associated with the business,

shall furnish to the Commissioners such information relating to that contract as the Commissioners may reasonably require.

2(4) The information mentioned in sub-paragraph (1), (2) or (3) above shall be furnished within such time and in such form as the Commissioners may reasonably require.

History – In para. 2(1)–(3), the words "an insurance business" were substituted in each place where they occur by FA 1995, s. 34 and Sch. 5, para. 7(1)(a), in relation to contracts whether entered into before or after the passing of that Act (1 May 1995). In para. 2(1)–(3), the words "contracts of insurance" and the words "contract of insurance" were substituted in each place where they occur by FA 1995, s. 34 and Sch. 5, para. 7(1)(b) and (c), in relation to contracts whether entered into before or after the passing of that Act (1 May 1995).

3(1) Every person who is concerned (in whatever capacity) in an insurance business shall upon demand made by an authorised person produce or cause to be produced for inspection by that person any documents relating to contracts of insurance entered into in the course of the business.

3(2) Every person who makes arrangements for other persons to enter into any contract of insurance shall upon demand made by an authorised person produce or cause to be produced for inspection by that person any documents relating to that contract.

3(3) Every person who–

(a) is concerned in a business that is not an insurance business, and

(b) has been involved in the entry into any contract of insurance providing cover for any matter associated with the business,

shall upon demand made by an authorised person produce or cause to be produced for inspection by that person any documents relating to that contract.

3(4) Where, by virtue of any of sub-paragraphs (1) to (3) above, an authorised person has power to require the production of any documents from any person, he shall have the like power to require production of the documents concerned from any other person who appears to the authorised person to be in possession of them; but where any such other person claims a lien on any document produced by him, the production shall be without prejudice to the lien.

3(5) The documents mentioned in sub-paragraphs (1) to (4) above shall be produced–

(a) at the principal place of business of the person on whom the demand is made or at such other place as the authorised person may reasonably require, and

(b) at such time as the authorised person may reasonably require.

3(6) An authorised person may take copies of, or make extracts from, any document produced under any of sub-paragraphs (1) to (4) above.

3(7) If it appears to him to be necessary to do so, an authorised person may, at a reasonable time and for a reasonable period, remove any document produced under any of sub-paragraphs (1) to (4) above and shall, on request, provide a receipt for any document so removed; and where a lien is claimed on a document produced under sub-paragraph (4) above the removal of the document under this sub-paragraph shall not be regarded as breaking the lien.

3(8) Where a document removed by an authorised person under sub-paragraph (7) above is reasonably required for the proper conduct of a business he shall, as soon as practicable, provide a copy of the document, free of charge, to the person by whom it was produced or caused to be produced.

3(9) Where any documents removed under the powers conferred by this paragraph are lost or damaged the Commissioners shall be liable to compensate their owner for any expenses reasonably incurred by him in replacing or repairing the document.

History – In para. 3(1)–(3), the words "an insurance business" were substituted in each place where they occurred by FA 1995, s. 34 and Sch. 5, para. 7(1)(a), in relation to contracts whether entered into before or after the passing of that Act (1 May 1995). In para. 3(1)–(3), the words "contracts of insurance" and the words "contract of insurance" were substituted in each place where they occur by FA 1995, s. 34 and Sch. 5, para. 7(1)(b) and (c), in relation to contracts whether entered into before or after the passing of that Act (1 May 1995).

Part II – Powers

ENTRY, ARREST, ETC.

History – Reference in para. 4(2) to Criminal Procedure (Scotland) Act 1995, s. 308, substituted by Criminal Procedure (Consequential Provisions) (Scotland) Act 1995, Sch. 4, para. 89(4)(b).

4(1) For the purpose of exercising any powers under this Part of this Act an authorised person may at any reasonable time enter premises used in connection with the carrying on of a business.

4(2) In a case where–

(a) a justice of the peace is satisfied on information on oath that there is reasonable ground for suspecting that a fraud offence which appears to be of a serious nature is being, has been or is about to be committed on any premises or that evidence of the commission of such an offence is to be found there, or

(b) in Scotland a justice, within the meaning of section 308 of the Criminal Procedure (Scotland) Act 1995, is satisfied by evidence on oath as mentioned in paragraph (a) above,

he may issue a warrant in writing authorising any authorised person to enter those premises, if necessary by force, at any time within one month from the time of the issue of the warrant and search them.

4(3) A person who enters the premises under the authority of the warrant may–

(a) take with him such other persons as appear to him to be necessary;

(b) seize and remove any documents or other things whatsoever found on the premises which he has reasonable cause to believe may be required as evidence for the purposes of proceedings in respect of a fraud offence which appears to him to be of a serious nature;

(c) search or cause to be searched any person found on the premises whom he has reasonable cause to believe to be in possession of any such documents or other things;

but no woman or girl shall be searched except by a woman.

4(4) The powers conferred by a warrant under this paragraph shall not be exercisable–

(a) by more than such number of authorised persons as may be specified in the warrant,

(b) outside such times of day as may be so specified, or

(c) if the warrant so provides, otherwise than in the presence of a constable in uniform.

4(5) An authorised person seeking to exercise the powers conferred by a warrant under this paragraph or, if there is more than one such authorised person, that one of them who is in charge of the search shall provide a copy of the warrant endorsed with his name as follows–

(a)   if the occupier of the premises concerned is present at the time the search is to begin, the copy shall be supplied to the occupier;

(b)   if at that time the occupier is not present but a person who appears to the authorised person to be in charge of the premises is present, the copy shall be supplied to that person;

(c)   if neither paragraph (a) nor paragraph (b) above applies, the copy shall be left in a prominent place on the premises.

4(6) Where an authorised person has reasonable grounds for suspecting that a fraud offence has been committed he may arrest anyone whom he has reasonable grounds for suspecting to be guilty of the offence.

4(7) In this paragraph **"a fraud offence"** means an offence under any provision of paragraph 9(1) to (5) below.

ORDER FOR ACCESS TO RECORDED INFORMATION ETC.

4A(1) Where, on an application by an authorised person, a justice of the peace or, in Scotland, a justice (within the meaning of section 462 of the Criminal Procedure (Scotland) Act 1975) is satisfied that there are reasonable grounds for believing–

(a)   that an offence in connection with tax is being, has been or is about to be committed, and

(b)   that any recorded information (including any document of any nature whatsoever) which may be required as evidence for the purpose of any proceedings in respect of such an offence is in the possession of any person,

he may make an order under this paragraph.

4A(2) An order under this paragraph is an order that the person who appears to the justice to be in possession of the recorded information to which the application relates shall–

(a)   give an authorised person access to it, and

(b)   permit an authorised person to remove and take away any of it which he reasonably considers necessary,

not later than the end of the period of 7 days beginning on the date of the order or the end of such longer period as the order may specify.

4A(3) The reference in sub-paragraph (2)(a) above to **giving an authorised person access to the recorded information** to which the application relates includes a reference to permitting the authorised person to take copies of it or to make extracts from it.

4A(4) Where the recorded information consists of information contained in a computer, an order under this paragraph shall have effect as an order to produce the information in a form in which it is visible and legible and, if the authorised person wishes to remove it, in a form in which it can be removed.

4A(5) This paragraph is without prejudice to paragraphs 3 and 4 above.

History – Para. 4A was inserted by FA 1995, s. 34 and Sch. 5, para. 8(1).

REMOVAL OF DOCUMENTS ETC.

5(1) An authorised person who removes anything in the exercise of a power conferred by or under paragraph 4 or 4A above shall, if so requested by a person showing himself–

(a)   to be the occupier of premises from which it was removed, or

(b)   to have had custody or control of it immediately before the removal,

provide that person with a record of what he removed.

5(2) The authorised person shall provide the record within a reasonable time from the making of the request for it.

5(3) Subject to sub-paragraph (7) below, if a request for permission to be allowed access to anything which–

(a)   has been removed by an authorised person, and

(b)   is retained by the Commissioners for the purposes of investigating an offence,

is made to the officer in overall charge of the investigation by a person who had custody or control of the thing immediately before it was so removed or by someone acting on behalf of such a person, the officer shall allow the person who made the request access to it under the supervision of an authorised person.

5(4)   Subject to sub-paragraph (7) below, if a request for a photograph or copy of any such thing is made to the officer in overall charge of the investigation by a person who had custody or control of the thing immediately before it was so removed, or by someone acting on behalf of such a person, the officer shall–

(a)   allow the person who made the request access to it under the supervision of an authorised person for the purpose of photographing it or copying it, or

(b)   photograph or copy it, or cause it to be photographed or copied.

5(5)   Subject to sub-paragraph (7) below, where anything is photographed or copied under sub-paragraph (4)(b) above the officer shall supply the photograph or copy, or cause it to be supplied, to the person who made the request.

5(6)   The photograph or copy shall be supplied within a reasonable time from the making of the request.

5(7)   There is no duty under this paragraph to allow access to, or to supply a photograph or copy of, anything if the officer in overall charge of the investigation for the purposes of which it was removed has reasonable grounds for believing that to do so would prejudice–

(a)   that investigation,

(b)   the investigation of an offence other than the offence for the purposes of the investigation of which the thing was removed, or

(c)   any criminal proceedings which may be brought as a result of the investigation of which he is in charge or any such investigation as is mentioned in paragraph (b) above.

5(8)   Any reference in this paragraph to the **officer in overall charge** of the investigation is a reference to the person whose name and address are endorsed on the warrant concerned as being the officer so in charge.

History – In para. 5(1), the words "or 4A" were inserted by FA 1995, s. 34 and Sch. 5, para. 8(2).

6(1)   Where, on an application made as mentioned in sub-paragraph (2) below, the appropriate judicial authority is satisfied that a person has failed to comply with a requirement imposed by paragraph 5 above, the authority may order that person to comply with the requirement within such time and in such manner as may be specified in the order.

6(2)   An application under sub-paragraph (1) above shall be made–

(a)   in the case of a failure to comply with any of the requirements imposed by sub-paragraphs (1) and (2) of paragraph 5 above, by the occupier of the premises from which the thing in question was removed or by the person who had custody or control of it immediately before it was so removed, and

(b)   in any other case, by the person who had such custody or control.

6(3)   In this paragraph **"the appropriate judicial authority"** means–

(a)   in England and Wales, a magistrates' court;

(b)   in Scotland, the sheriff;

(c)   in Northern Ireland, a court of summary jurisdiction, as defined in Article 2(2)(a) of the Magistrates' Court (Northern Ireland) Order 1981.

6(4)   In England and Wales and Northern Ireland, an application for an order under this paragraph shall be made by way of complaint; and sections 21 and 42(2) of the Interpretation Act (Northern Ireland) 1954 shall apply as if any reference in those provisions to any enactment included a reference to this paragraph.

Part III – Recovery

RECOVERY OF TAX ETC.

7(1)   Tax due from any person shall be recoverable as a debt due to the Crown.

7(2)   [Amends Insolvency Act 1986, s. 386(1) and inserts Insolvency Act 1986, Sch. 6, para. 3A.]

7(3)   In the Bankruptcy (Scotland) Act 1985, Schedule 3 (preferred debts) shall be amended as mentioned in sub-paragraphs (4) and (5) below.

7(4)   [Inserts Bankruptcy (Scotland) Act 1985, Sch. 3, para. 2(1A).]

7(5)   [Inserts Bankruptcy (Scotland) Act 1985, Sch. 3, para. 8A.]

7(6) [Amends Insolvency (Northern Ireland) Order 1989, art. 346(1) and inserts to that order Sch. 4, para. 3A.]

7(7–12) [Repealed by FA 1997, s. 113 and Sch. 18, Pt. V(2).]

History – Para. 7(7)–(12) repealed by FA 1997, s. 113 and Sch. 18, Pt. V(2), operative from 1 July 1997 (SI 1997/1433 (C. 55)).

Former para. 7(8)–(12) were substituted for former para. 7(8) by FA 1995, s. 34 and Sch. 5, para. 9, with effect from 1 May 1995.

Statutory instruments – SI 1994/1774, as amended by SI 1995/1587, SI 1996/2099.

RECOVERY OF OVERPAID TAX

8(1) Where a person has paid an amount to the Commissioners by way of tax which was not tax due to them, they shall be liable to repay the amount to him.

8(2) The Commissioners shall only be liable to repay an amount under this paragraph on a claim being made for the purpose.

8(3) It shall be a defence, in relation to a claim under this paragraph, that repayment of an amount would unjustly enrich the claimant.

8(4) The Commissioners shall not be liable, on a claim made under this paragraph, to repay any amount paid to them more than three years before the making of the claim.

8(5) [Substituted by FA 1997, s. 50 and Sch. 5, para. 5(2) as explained in the history note.]

8(6) A claim under this paragraph shall be made in such form and manner and shall be supported by such documentary evidence as may be prescribed by regulations.

8(7) Except as provided by this paragraph, the Commissioners shall not be liable to repay an amount paid to them by way of tax by virtue of the fact that it was not tax due to them.

History – Para. 8(4) was substituted for former para. 8(4) and (5) by FA 1997, s. 50 and Sch. 5, para. 5(2), with effect from 19 March 1997.

Cross references – FA 1997, Sch. 5, para. 1(1)(b) and (3)(b): unjust enrichment and "relevant repayment provision".
FA 1997, Sch. 5, para. 4(2): unjust enrichment and contravention of requirement to repay Commissioners.
FA 1997, Sch. 5, para. 14(3)(b): recovery of excess payments by the Commissioners.
FA 1997, Sch. 5, para. 19(2)(c): review of decisions and appeals.
SI 1994/1774, reg. 19A: claim and reimbursement arrangements.
SI 1994/1774, reg. 19B: disregarded reimbursement arrangements.
SI 1994/1774, reg. 19H: reimbursement arrangements made before 11 February 1998.

Statutory instruments – SI 1994/1774, reg. 14.

Part IV – Penalties

Official publications – Notice IPT 2, Pt. 11 (1999 edn): a general guide to IPT, penalties and interest.

CRIMINAL OFFENCES

9(1) A person is guilty of an offence if–

(a) being a registrable person, he is knowingly concerned in, or in the taking of steps with a view to, the fraudulent evasion of tax by him or another registrable person, or

(b) not being a registrable person, he is knowingly concerned in, or in the taking of steps with a view to, the fraudulent evasion of tax by a registrable person.

9(2) Any reference in sub-paragraph (1) above to the **evasion of tax** includes a reference to the obtaining of a payment under regulations under section 55(3)(c) or (d) or (f) of this Act.

9(3) A person is guilty of an offence if with the requisite intent–

(a) he produces, furnishes or sends, or causes to be produced, furnished or sent, for the purposes of this Part of this Act any document which is false in a material particular, or

(b) he otherwise makes use for those purposes of such a document;

and the requisite intent is intent to deceive or to secure that a machine will respond to the document as if it were a true document.

9(4) A person is guilty of an offence if in furnishing any information for the purposes of this Part of this Act he makes a statement which he knows to be false in a material particular or recklessly makes a statement which is false in a material particular.

9(5) A person is guilty of an offence by virtue of this sub-paragraph if his conduct during any specified period must have involved the commission by him of one or more offences under the preceding provisions of this paragraph; and the preceding provisions of this sub-paragraph apply whether or not the particulars of that offence or those offences are known.

9(6) A person is guilty of an offence if–

(a)   he enters into a taxable insurance contract, or

(b)   he makes arrangements for other persons to enter into a taxable insurance contract,

with reason to believe that tax in respect of the contract will be evaded.

9(7) A person is guilty of an offence if he enters into taxable insurance contracts without giving security (or further security) he has been required to give under paragraph 24 below.

Cross references – S. 73(3A): "registrable person".

CRIMINAL PENALTIES

10(1) A person guilty of an offence under paragraph 9(1) above shall be liable–

(a)   on summary conviction, to a penalty of the statutory maximum or of three times the amount of the tax, whichever is the greater, or to imprisonment for a term not exceeding six months or to both;

(b)   on conviction on indictment, to a penalty of any amount or to imprisonment for a term not exceeding seven years or to both.

10(2) The reference in sub-paragraph (1) above to the **amount of the tax** shall be construed, in relation to tax itself or a payment falling within paragraph 9(2) above, as a reference to the aggregate of–

(a)   the amount (if any) falsely claimed by way of credit, and

(b)   the amount (if any) by which the gross amount of tax was falsely understated.

10(3) A person guilty of an offence under paragraph 9(3) or (4) above shall be liable–

(a)   on summary conviction, to a penalty of the statutory maximum or, where sub-paragraph (4) below applies, to the alternative penalty there specified if it is greater, or to imprisonment for a term not exceeding six months or to both;

(b)   on conviction on indictment, to a penalty of any amount or to imprisonment for a term not exceeding seven years or to both.

10(4) In a case where–

(a)   the document referred to in paragraph 9(3) above is a return required under this Part of this Act, or

(b)   the information referred to in paragraph 9(4) above is contained in or otherwise relevant to such a return,

the **alternative penalty** is a penalty equal to three times the aggregate of the amount (if any) falsely claimed by way of credit and the amount (if any) by which the gross amount of tax was understated.

10(5) A person guilty of an offence under paragraph 9(5) above shall be liable–

(a)   on summary conviction, to a penalty of the statutory maximum or (if greater) three times the amount of any tax that was or was intended to be evaded by his conduct, or to imprisonment for a term not exceeding six months or to both;

(b)   on conviction on indictment, to a penalty of any amount or to imprisonment for a term not exceeding seven years or to both;

and paragraph 9(2) and sub-paragraph (2) above shall apply for the purposes of this sub-paragraph as they apply respectively for the purposes of paragraph 9(1) and sub-paragraph (1) above.

10(6) A person guilty of an offence under paragraph 9(6) above shall be liable on summary conviction to a penalty of level 5 on the standard scale or three times the amount of the tax, whichever is the greater.

10(7) A person guilty of an offence under paragraph 9(7) above shall be liable on summary conviction to a penalty of level 5 on the standard scale.

10(8) In this paragraph–

(a)   "**credit**" means credit for which provision is made by regulations under section 55 of this Act;

(b)   "**the gross amount of tax**" means the total amount of tax due before taking into account any deduction for which provision is made by regulations under section 55(3) of this Act.

Note – Level 5 on the standard scale and the statutory maximum is £5,000, with effect from 1 October 1992.

CRIMINAL PROCEEDINGS ETC.

11 Sections 145 to 155 of the Customs and Excise Management Act 1979 (proceedings for offences, mitigation of penalties and certain other matters) shall apply in relation to offences under paragraph 9 above and penalties imposed under paragraph 10 above as they apply in relation to offences and penalties under the customs and excise Acts as defined in that Act.

Cross references – CEMA 1979, s. 145–155: general provisions as to legal proceedings.

CIVIL PENALTIES

12(1) In a case where–

(a) for the purpose of evading tax, a **registrable person** does any act or omits to take any action, and

(b) his conduct involves dishonesty (whether or not it is such as to give rise to criminal liability),

he shall be liable to a penalty equal to the amount of tax evaded, or (as the case may be) sought to be evaded, by his conduct; but this is subject to sub-paragraph (7) below.

12(2) The reference in sub-paragraph (1)(a) above to **evading tax** includes a reference to obtaining a payment under regulations under section 55(3)(c) or (d) or (f) of this Act in circumstances where the person concerned is not entitled to the sum.

12(3) The reference in sub-paragraph (1) above to the **amount of tax evaded** or sought to be evaded is a reference to the aggregate of–

(a) the amount (if any) falsely claimed by way of credit, and

(b) the amount (if any) by which the gross amount of tax was falsely understated.

12(4) In this paragraph–

(a) **"credit"** means credit for which provision is made by regulations under section 55 of this Act;

(b) **"the gross amount of tax"** means the total amount of tax due before taking into account any deduction for which provision is made by regulations under section 55(3) of this Act.

12(5) Statements made or documents produced by or on behalf of a person shall not be inadmissible in any such proceedings as are mentioned in sub-paragraph (6) below by reason only that it has been drawn to his attention–

(a) that, in relation to tax, the Commissioners may assess an amount due by way of a civil penalty instead of instituting criminal proceedings and, though no undertaking can be given as to whether the Commissioners will make such an assessment in the case of any person, it is their practice to be influenced by the fact that a person has made a full confession of any dishonest conduct to which he has been a party and has given full facilities for investigation, and

(b) that the Commissioners or, on appeal, an appeal tribunal have power under paragraph 13 below to reduce a penalty under this paragraph,

and that he was or may have been induced thereby to make the statements or produce the documents.

12(6) The proceedings referred to in sub-paragraph (5) above are–

(a) any criminal proceedings against the person concerned in respect of any offence in connection with or in relation to tax, and

(b) any proceedings against him for the recovery of any sum due from him in connection with or in relation to tax.

12(7) Where, by reason of conduct falling within sub-paragraph (1) above, a person is convicted of an offence (whether under this Part of this Act or otherwise) that conduct shall not also give rise to liability to a penalty under this paragraph.

13(1) Where a person is liable to a penalty under paragraph 12 above the Commissioners or, on appeal, an appeal tribunal may reduce the penalty to such amount (including nil) as they think proper.

13(2) In the case of a penalty reduced by the Commissioners under sub-paragraph (1) above an appeal tribunal, on an appeal relating to the penalty, may cancel the whole or any part of the reduction made by the Commissioners.

13(3) None of the matters specified in sub-paragraph (4) below shall be matters which the Commissioners or any appeal tribunal shall be entitled to take into account in exercising their powers under this paragraph.

13(4)   Those matters are–

(a)   the insufficiency of the funds available to any person for paying any tax due or for paying the amount of the penalty;

(b)   the fact that there has, in the case in question or in that case taken with any other cases, been no or no significant loss of tax.

Cross references – Value Added Tax Tribunals Rules 1986 (SI 1986/590), r. 2: definition of "mitigation appeal".

14(1)   A person who fails to comply with section 53(2) or 53AA(3) of this Act shall be liable to a penalty equal to 5 per cent of the relevant tax or, if it is greater or the circumstances are such that there is no relevant tax, to a penalty of £250; but this is subject to sub-paragraphs (3) and (4) below.

14(2)   In sub-paragraph (1) above **"relevant tax"** means the tax (if any) for which the person concerned is liable for the period which–

(a)   begins on the date with effect from which he is, in accordance with section 53 or, as the case may be, section 53AA of this Act, required to be registered, and

(b)   ends on the date on which the Commissioners received notification of his liability to be registered.

14(3)   Conduct falling within sub-paragraph (1) above shall not give rise to liability to a penalty under this paragraph if the person concerned satisfies the Commissioners or, on appeal, an appeal tribunal that there is a reasonable excuse for his conduct.

14(4)   Where, by reason of conduct falling within sub-paragraph (1) above–

(a)   a person is convicted of an offence (whether under this Part of this Act or otherwise), or

(b)   a person is assessed to a penalty under paragraph 12 above,

that conduct shall not also give rise to liability to a penalty under this paragraph.

14(5)   If it appears to the Treasury that there has been a change in the value of money since the passing of this Act or, as the case may be, the last occasion when the power conferred by this sub-paragraph was exercised, they may by order substitute for the sum for the time being specified in sub-paragraph (1) above such other sum as appears to them to be justified by the change.

14(6)   An order under sub-paragraph (5) above shall not apply in relation to a failure which ended on or before the date on which the order comes into force.

History – In para. 14(1), the words "or 53AA(3)" were inserted by FA 1997, s. 27(11)(a), with effect from 19 March 1997. In para. 14(2)(a), the words "or, as the case may be, section 53AA" were inserted by FA 1997, s. 27(11)(b), with effect from 19 March 1997.

Cross references – Value Added Tax Tribunals Rules 1986 (SI 1986/590), r. 2: definition of "reasonable excuse appeal".

15(1)   This paragraph applies if a person fails to comply with–

(a)   a requirement imposed by regulations made under section 54 of this Act to pay the tax due in respect of any period within the time required by the regulations, or

(b)   a requirement imposed by regulations made under that section to furnish a return in respect of any period within the time required by the regulations;

and sub-paragraphs (2) and (3) below shall have effect subject to sub-paragraphs (5) and (6) below and paragraph 25(7) below.

15(2)   The person shall be liable to a penalty equal to 5 per cent of the tax due or, if it is greater, to a penalty of £250.

15(3)   The person–

(a)   shall be liable, in addition to an initial penalty under sub-paragraph (2) above, to a penalty of £20 for every relevant day when he fails to pay the tax or furnish the return, but

(b)   shall not in respect of the continuation of the failure be liable to further penalties under sub-paragraph (2) above;

and a **relevant day** is any day falling after the time within which the tax is required to be paid or the return is required to be furnished.

15(4)   For the purposes of sub-paragraph (2) above the **tax due** –

(a)   shall, if the person concerned has furnished a return, be taken to be the tax shown in the return as that for which he is accountable in respect of the period in question, and

(b)   shall, in any other case, be taken to be such tax as has been assessed for that period and notified to him under section 56(1) of this Act.

15(5)   A failure falling within sub-paragraph (1) or (3) above shall not give rise to liability to a penalty under this paragraph if the person concerned satisfies the Commissioners or, on appeal, an appeal tribunal that there is a reasonable excuse for the failure.

15(6) Where, by reason of a failure falling within sub-paragraph (1) or (3) above–

(a)   a person is convicted of an offence (whether under this Part of this Act or otherwise), or

(b)   a person is assessed to a penalty under paragraph 12 above,

that failure shall not also give rise to liability to a penalty under this paragraph.

15(7) If it appears to the Treasury that there has been a change in the value of money since the passing of this Act or, as the case may be, the last occasion when the power conferred by this sub-paragraph was exercised, they may by order substitute for the sums for the time being specified in sub-paragraphs (2) and (3) above such other sums as appear to them to be justified by the change.

15(8) An order under sub-paragraph (7) above shall not apply in relation to a failure which began before the date on which the order comes into force.

Cross references – Value Added Tax Tribunals Rules 1986 (SI 1986/590), r. 2: definition of "reasonable excuse appeal".

16(1) This paragraph applies where–

(a)   by virtue of regulations made under section 65 of this Act a liability notice (within the meaning of that section) is served on an insured person,

(b)   by virtue of such regulations that person is liable to pay an amount of tax which has been assessed in accordance with the regulations, and

(c)   that tax is not paid within the time required by the regulations;

and sub-paragraphs (2) and (3) below shall have effect subject to sub-paragraphs (4) and (5) below and paragraph 25(7) below.

16(2) The person shall be liable to a penalty equal to 5 per cent of the tax assessed as mentioned in sub-paragraph (1) above or, if it is greater, to a penalty of £250.

16(3) The person–

(a)   shall be liable, in addition to an initial penalty under sub-paragraph (2) above, to a penalty of £20 for every relevant day when the tax is unpaid, but

(b)   shall not in respect of the continuation of the non-payment of the tax be liable to further penalties under sub-paragraph (2) above;

and a **relevant day** is any day falling after the time within which the tax is required to be paid.

16(4) A person shall not be liable to a penalty by virtue of this paragraph if he satisfies the Commissioners or, on appeal, an appeal tribunal that he took all reasonable steps to ensure that the tax mentioned in sub-paragraph (1)(b) above was paid within the time required by the regulations.

16(5) Where, by reason of a failure to pay tax, a person is convicted of an offence (whether under this Part of this Act or otherwise), that failure shall not also give rise to liability to a penalty under this paragraph.

16(6) If it appears to the Treasury that there has been a change in the value of money since the passing of this Act or, as the case may be, the last occasion when the power conferred by this sub-paragraph was exercised, they may by order substitute for the sums for the time being specified in sub-paragraphs (2) and (3) above such other sums as appear to them to be justified by the change.

16(7) An order under sub-paragraph (6) above shall not apply in relation to any failure to pay tax that was required to be paid before the date on which the order comes into force.

Cross references – Value Added Tax Tribunals Rules 1986 (SI 1986/590), r. 2: definition of "reasonable excuse appeal".

17(1) If a person fails to comply with–

(a)   section 53(3) of this Act,

(b)   any provision of paragraph 2 or 3 above, or

(c)   a requirement imposed by any regulations made under this Part of this Act, other than a requirement falling within sub-paragraph (2) below,

he shall be liable to a penalty of £250; but this is subject to sub-paragraphs (3) and (4) below.

17(2) A requirement falls within this sub-paragraph if it is–

(a)   a requirement imposed by regulations made under section 54 of this Act to pay the tax due in respect of any period within the time required by the regulations,

(b)   a requirement imposed by regulations made under that section to furnish a return in respect of any period within the time required by the regulations,

(c)   a requirement imposed by regulations made under section 65 of this Act to pay tax within the time required by the regulations, or

(d)   a requirement specified for the purposes of this sub-paragraph by regulations.

17(3) A failure falling within sub-paragraph (1) above shall not give rise to liability to a penalty under this paragraph if the person concerned satisfies the Commissioners or, on appeal, an appeal tribunal that there is a reasonable excuse for the failure.

17(4) Where by reason of a failure falling within sub-paragraph (1) above–

(a) a person is convicted of an offence (whether under this Part of this Act or otherwise), or

(b) a person is assessed to a penalty under paragraph 12 above,

that failure shall not also give rise to liability to a penalty under this paragraph.

17(5) If it appears to the Treasury that there has been a change in the value of money since the passing of this Act or, as the case may be, the last occasion when the power conferred by this sub-paragraph was exercised, they may by order substitute for the sum for the time being specified in sub-paragraph (1) above such other sum as appears to them to be justified by the change.

17(6) An order under sub-paragraph (5) above shall not apply in relation to a failure which began before the date on which the order comes into force.

Cross references – FA 1997, Sch. 5, para. 4(2): unjust enrichment and contravention of requirement to repay Commissioners. Value Added Tax Tribunals Rules 1986 (SI 1986/590), r. 2: definition of "reasonable excuse appeal".

18(1) A person who–

(a) by virtue of subsection (3), (7) or (9) of section 57 of this Act becomes subject to a duty to take action as mentioned in subsection (4) of that section, and

(b) fails to take action as so mentioned,

shall be liable to a penalty of £10,000; but this is subject to sub-paragraph (2) below.

18(2) A failure falling within sub-paragraph (1) above shall not give rise to liability to a penalty under this paragraph if the person concerned satisfies the Commissioners or, on appeal, an appeal tribunal that there is a reasonable excuse for the failure.

18(3) If it appears to the Treasury that there has been a change in the value of money since the passing of this Act or, as the case may be, the last occasion when the power conferred by this sub-paragraph was exercised, they may by order substitute for the sum for the time being specified in sub-paragraph (1) above such other sum as appears to them to be justified by the change.

18(4) An order under sub-paragraph (3) above shall not apply in relation to a case where the duty mentioned in sub-paragraph (1) above was imposed before the date on which the order comes into force.

Cross references – Value Added Tax Tribunals Rules 1986 (SI 1986/590), r. 2: definition of "reasonable excuse appeal".

19(1) This paragraph applies where–

(a) in accordance with regulations under section 51 of the Finance Act 1997 (enforcement by distress) a distress is authorised to be levied on the goods and chattels of a person (a person in default) who has refused or neglected to pay any tax due from him or any amount recoverable as if it were tax due from him, and

(b) the person levying the distress and the person in default have entered into a walking possession agreement.

19(2) For the purposes of this paragraph a **walking possession agreement** is an agreement under which, in consideration of the property distrained upon being allowed to remain in the custody of the person in default and of the delaying of its sale, the person in default–

(a) acknowledges that the property specified in the agreement is under distraint and held in walking possession, and

(b) undertakes that, except with the consent of the Commissioners and subject to such conditions as they may impose, he will not remove or allow the removal of any of the specified property from the premises named in the agreement.

19(3) Subject to sub-paragraph (4) below, if the person in default is in breach of the undertaking contained in a walking possession agreement, he shall be liable to a penalty equal to half of the tax or other amount referred to in sub-paragraph (1)(a) above.

19(4) The person in default shall not be liable to a penalty under sub-paragraph (3) above if he satisfies the Commissioners or, on appeal, an appeal tribunal that there is a reasonable excuse for the breach in question.

19(5) This paragraph does not extend to Scotland.

History – In para. 19(1)(a), the words "section 51 of the Finance Act 1997 (enforcement by distress)" were substituted for the words "paragraph 7(7) above" by FA 1997, s. 53(5), with effect from 1 July 1997 (SI 1997/1432 (C 54)).

Cross references – Value Added Tax Tribunals Rules 1986 (SI 1986/590), r. 2: definition of "reasonable excuse appeal".

20 For the purposes of paragraphs 14(3), 15(5), 17(3), 18(2) and 19(4) above–

(a) an insufficiency of funds available for paying any amount is not a **reasonable excuse**, and
(b) where reliance is placed on any other person to perform any task, neither the fact of that reliance nor any conduct of the person relied upon is a **reasonable excuse**.

Part V – Interest

Official publications – Notice IPT 2, Pt. 11 (1999): a general guide to IPT, penalties and interest.

INTEREST ON TAX ETC.

21(1) Where an assessment is made under any provision of section 56 of this Act, the whole of the amount assessed shall carry interest at the rate applicable under section 197 of the Finance Act 1996 from the reckonable date until payment; but this is subject to sub-paragraph (2) and paragraph 25(7) below.

21(2) Sub-paragraph (1) above shall not apply in relation to an assessment under section 56(1) of this Act unless at least one of the following conditions is fulfilled, namely–

(a) that the assessment relates to an accounting period in respect of which either a return has previously been made, or an earlier assessment has already been notified to the person concerned;
(b) that the assessment relates to an accounting period which exceeds three months and begins on the date with effect from which the person was, or was required to be, registered under this Part of this Act.

21(3) In a case where–

(a) the circumstances are such that a relevant assessment could have been made, but
(b) before such an assessment was made the tax due or other amount concerned was paid (so that no such assessment was necessary),

the whole of the amount paid shall carry interest at the rate applicable under section 197 of the Finance Act 1996 from the reckonable date until the date on which it was paid; and for the purposes of this sub-paragraph a **relevant assessment** is an assessment in relation to which sub-paragraph (1) above would have applied if the assessment had been made.

21(4) The references in sub-paragraphs (1) and (3) above to the **reckonable date** shall be construed as follows–

(a) where the amount assessed or paid is such an amount as is referred to in subsection (2) of section 56 of this Act, the **reckonable date** is the seventh day after the day on which a written instruction was issued by the Commissioners directing the making of the payment of the amount which ought not to have been paid to the person concerned;
(b) in all other cases the **reckonable date** is the latest date on which (in accordance with regulations under this Part of this Act) a return is required to be made for the accounting period to which the amount assessed or paid relates;

and interest under this paragraph shall run from the reckonable date even if that date is a non-business day, within the meaning of section 92 of the Bills of Exchange Act 1882.

21(5) [Repealed by FA 1996, s. 205 and Sch. 41, Pt. VIII.]

21(6) Interest under this paragraph shall be paid without any deduction of income tax.

History – In Para. 21(1) and para. 21(3) the words "the rate applicable under section 197 of the Finance Act 1996" substitute for the words "the prescribed rate" by FA 1996, s. 197(6)(b) as respects periods beginning on or after 1 April 1997.
Para. 21(5) repealed by FA 1996, s. 205 and Sch. 41, Pt. VIII, as respects periods beginning on or after 1 April 1997. Former para. 21(5) read as follows:
"(5) In this paragraph **"the prescribed rate"** means such rate as may be prescribed by order; and such an order–
(a) may prescribe different rates for different purposes;
(b) shall apply to interest for periods beginning on or after the date when the order is expressed to come into force, whether or not interest runs from before that date."

Cross references – FA 1996, s. 197; setting of rates of interest by Treasury regulations for periods beginning on or after a day to be appointed.
Bills of Exchange Act 1882, s. 92: the following are non-business days for the purpose of the 1882 Act:
● Saturday, Sunday, Good Friday, Christmas Day;
● Bank holidays;
● a day appointed by Royal proclamation as a public fast or thanksgiving day; and
● a day declared under the Banking and Financial Dealings Act 1971 to be a non-business day.

Statutory instruments – The rate of interest has been set by statutory instrument as follows:

Period of application	%	Order
From 6 July 1998	9.50	SI 1998/1461
1 April 1997–5 July 1998	6.25	SI 1997/1016
6 February 1996–31 March 1997	6.25	SI 1996/166
1 October 1994–5 February 1996	5.50	SI 1994/1819

The basis for setting the rate of interest was amended by SI 1998/1461 with effect from 6 July 1998. Interest will be set using formulae linked to a reference rate. The reference rate will be based on an average of the base rates of six main banks rounded to the nearest whole number. For default interest, the formula used will be the reference rate plus 2.5 per cent. Application of the formulae for interest accruing on or after 6 July 1998 is as follows:

Period of application	Rate of interest
From 6 March 1999	7.5
6 January 1999–5 March 1999	8.5
6 July 1998–5 January 1999	9.5

INTEREST PAYABLE BY COMMISSIONERS

22(1) Where, due to an error on the part of the Commissioners, a person–

(a)   has paid to them by way of tax an amount which was not tax due and which they are in consequence liable to repay to him,

(b)   has failed to claim payment of an amount to the payment of which he was entitled in pursuance of provision made under section 55(3)(c), (d) or (f) of this Act, or

(c)   has suffered delay in receiving payment of an amount due to him from them in connection with tax,

then, if and to the extent that they would not be liable to do so apart from this paragraph, they shall (subject to the following provisions of this paragraph) pay interest to him on that amount for the applicable period.

22(1A) In sub-paragraph (1) above–

(a)   the reference in paragraph (a) to an amount which the Commissioners are **liable to repay** in consequence of the making of a payment that was not due is a reference to only so much of that amount as is the subject of a claim that the Commissioners are required to satisfy or have satisfied; and

(b)   the amounts referred to in paragraph (c) do not include any amount payable under this paragraph.

22(2) Interest under this paragraph shall be payable at the rate applicable under section 197 of the Finance Act 1997.

22(3) The **applicable period**, in a case falling within sub-paragraph (1)(a) above, is the period–

(a)   beginning with the date on which the payment is received by the Commissioners, and

(b)   ending with the date on which they authorise payment of the amount on which the interest is payable.

22(4) The **applicable period**, in a case falling within sub-paragraph (1)(b) or (c) above, is the period–

(a)   beginning with the date on which, apart from the error, the Commissioners might reasonably have been expected to authorise payment of the amount on which the interest is payable, and

(b)   ending with the date on which they in fact authorise payment of that amount.

22(5) In determining the **applicable period** for the purposes of this paragraph there shall be left out of account any period by which the Commissioners' authorisation of the payment of interest is delayed by the conduct of the person who claims the interest.

22(5A) The reference in sub-paragraph (5) above to a **period by which the Commissioners' authorisation of the payment of interest is delayed** by the conduct of the person who claims it includes, in particular, any period which is referable to–

(a)   any unreasonable delay in the making of the claim for interest or in the making of any claim for the payment or repayment of the amount on which interest is claimed;

(b)   any failure by that person or a person acting on his behalf or under his influence to provide the Commissioners–

  (i)   at or before the time of the making of a claim, or

  (ii) subsequently in response to a request for information by the Commissioners,

with all the information required by them to enable the existence and amount of the claimant's entitlement to a payment or repayment, and to interest on that payment or repayment, to be determined; and

(c)   the making, as part of or in association with either–

(i)   the claim for interest, or

(ii) any claim for the payment or repayment of the amount on which interest is claimed,

of a claim to anything to which the claimant was not entitled.

22(6)   In determining for the purposes of sub-paragraph (5A) above whether any period of delay is referable to a failure by any person to provide information in response to a request by the Commissioners, there shall be taken to be so referable, except so far as may be provided for by regulations, any period which–

(a)   begins with the date on which the Commissioners require that person to provide information which they reasonably consider relevant to the matter to be determined; and

(b)   ends with the earliest date on which it would be reasonable for the Commissioners to conclude–

(i)   that they have received a complete answer to their request for information;

(ii) that they have received all that they need in answer to that request; or

(iii) that it is unnecessary for them to be provided with any information in answer to that request.

22(7)   [Substituted by FA 1997, s. 50 and Sch. 5, para. 10(1), as explained in history note.]

22(8)   The Commissioners shall only be liable to pay interest under this paragraph on a claim made in writing for that purpose.

22(9)   A claim under this paragraph shall not be made more than three years after the end of the applicable period to which it relates.

22(10)   References in this paragraph to the **authorisation by the Commissioners of the payment** of any amount include references to the discharge by way of set-off of the Commissioners' liability to pay that amount.

History – Para. 22(1A) was inserted by FA 1997, s. 50 and Sch. 5, para. 9(2) and is deemed to always have had effect. In para. 22(2), the words "the rate applicable under section 197 of the Finance Act 1996" were substituted for the words: "such rate as may from time to time be prescribed by order, and–
(a)   any such order may prescribe different rates for different purposes;
(b)   any such order shall apply to interest for periods beginning on or after the date on which the order is expressed to come into force, whether or not interest runs from before that date."
by FA 1996, s. 197(6)(c), as respects periods beginning on or after 1 April 1997.
Para. 22(5), (5A) and (6) were substituted for para. 22(5)–(7) by FA 1997, s. 50 and Sch. 5, para. 10(1), with effect for the purposes of determining whether any period beginning on or after 19 March 1997 is left out of account. Former para. 22(5)–(7) read as follows:
"(5)   In determining the **applicable period** for the purposes of this paragraph, there shall be left out of account any period referable to the raising and answering of any reasonable enquiry relating to any matter giving rise to, or otherwise connected with, the person's entitlement to interest under this paragraph.
(6)   In determining for the purposes of sub-paragraph (5) above whether any period is referable to the **raising and answering of such an enquiry** as is there mentioned, there shall be taken to be so referable any period which begins with the date on which the Commissioners first consider it necessary to make such an enquiry and ends with the date on which the Commissioners–
(a)   satisfy themselves that they have received a complete answer to the enquiry, or
(b)   determine not to make the enquiry or (if they have made it) not to pursue it further;
but excluding so much of that period as may be prescribed by regulations.
(7)   For the purposes of sub-paragraph (6) above it is immaterial–
(a)   whether any enquiry is in fact made;
(b)   whether any enquiry is or might have been made of the person referred to in sub-paragraph (1) above or of an authorised person or of some other person."
Para. 22(9) was substituted by FA 1997, s. 50 and Sch. 5, para. 9(3) and is deemed to always have had effect.
Para. 22(10) was substituted by FA 1997, s. 50 and Sch. 5, para. 9(4) and is deemed to always have had effect.

Cross references – FA 1996, s. 197; setting of rates of interest by Treasury regulations for periods beginning on or after a day to be appointed.
FA 1997, Sch. 5, para. 15(2): assessment for overpaid interest.
FA 1997, Sch. 5, para. 19(2)(c): review of decisions and appeals.
FA 1997, Sch. 5, para. 20(2)(c): "relevant tax" and recovery of excess payments by the Commissioners.

Statutory instruments – The rate of interest has been set by statutory instrument as follows:

Period of application	%	Order
From 6 July 1998	6	SI 1998/1461
From 1 April 1997–5 July 1998	6	SI 1997/1016
From 1 October 1994–31 March 1997	8	SI 1994/1819

The basis of setting interest rates was amended by SI 1998/1461. For interest accruing on or after 6 July 1998 statutory interest paid in cases of official error; will be set using formulae linked to a reference rate. The reference rate will be based on an average of the base rates of six main banks rounded to the nearest whole number. For statutory interest, the formula used will be the reference rate minus 1 per cent. Application of the formulae for interest accruing on or after 6 July 1998 is as follows:

Period of application	Rate of interest
From 6 February 2000	5
6 March 1999–5 February 2000	4
6 January 1999–5 March 1999	5
6 July 1998–5 January 1999	6

23(1)   In a case where–

(a)   any interest is payable by the Commissioners to a person on a sum due to him under this Part of this Act, and

(b)   he is a person to whom regulations under section 55 of this Act apply,

the interest shall be treated as an amount to which he is entitled by way of credit in pursuance of the regulations.

23(2)   Sub-paragraph (1) above shall be disregarded for the purpose of determining a person's entitlement to interest or the amount of interest to which he is entitled.

Part VI – Miscellaneous

SECURITY FOR TAX

24   Where it appears to the Commissioners requisite to do so for the protection of the revenue they may require a registrable person, as a condition of his entering into taxable insurance contracts, to give security (or further security) of such amount and in such manner as they may determine for the payment of any tax which is or may become due from him.

ASSESSMENTS TO PENALTIES ETC.

25(1)   Where a person is liable–

(a)   to a penalty under any of paragraphs 12 to 19 above, or

(b)   for interest under paragraph 21 above,

the Commissioners may, subject to sub-paragraph (2) below, assess the amount due by way of penalty or interest (as the case may be) and notify it to him accordingly; and the fact that any conduct giving rise to a penalty under any of paragraphs 12 to 19 above may have ceased before an assessment is made under this paragraph shall not affect the power of the Commissioners to make such an assessment.

25(2)   In the case of the penalties and interest referred to in the following.paragraphs of this sub-paragraph, the assessment under this paragraph shall be of an amount due in respect of the accounting period which in the paragraph concerned is referred to as the relevant period–

(a)   in the case of a penalty under paragraph 12 above relating to the evasion of tax, the **relevant period** is the accounting period for which the tax evaded was due;

(b)   in the case of a penalty under paragraph 12 above relating to the obtaining of a payment under regulations under section 55(3)(c) or (d) or (f) of this Act, the **relevant period** is the accounting period in respect of which the payment was obtained;

(c)   in the case of interest under paragraph 21 above, the **relevant period** is the accounting period in respect of which the tax (or amount assessed as tax) was due.

25(3)   In a case where the amount of any penalty or interest falls to be calculated by reference to tax which was not paid at the time it should have been and that tax cannot be readily attributed to any one or more accounting periods, it shall be treated for the purposes of this Part of this Act as tax due for such period or periods as the Commissioners may determine to the best of their judgment and notify to the person liable for the tax and penalty or interest.

25(4)   Where a person is assessed under this paragraph to an amount due by way of any penalty or interest falling within sub-paragraph (2) above and is also assessed under subsection (1) or (2) of section 56 of this Act for the accounting period which is the relevant period under sub-paragraph (2) above, the assessments may be combined and notified to him as one assessment, but the amount of the penalty or interest shall be separately identified in the notice.

25(5)   Sub-paragraph (6) below applies in the case of–

(a)   an amount due by way of penalty under paragraph 15 or 16 above;

(b)   an amount due by way of interest under paragraph 21 above.

25(6)   Where this sub-paragraph applies in the case of an amount–

(a)   a notice of assessment under this paragraph shall specify a date, being not later than the date of the notice, to which the aggregate amount of the penalty or, as the case may be, the amount of interest which is assessed is calculated, and

(b)   if the penalty or interest continues to accrue after that date, a further assessment or further assessments may be made under this paragraph in respect of amounts which so accrue.

25(7) If, within such period as may be notified by the Commissioners to the person liable to the penalty under paragraph 15 or 16 above or for the interest under paragraph 21 above–

(a) a failure falling within paragraph 15(3) above is remedied,

(b) the tax referred to in paragraph 16(1) above is paid, or

(c) the amount referred to in paragraph 21(1) above is paid,

it shall be treated for the purposes of paragraph 15, 16 or 21 above (as the case may be) as remedied or paid on the date specified as mentioned in sub-paragraph (6)(a) above.

25(8) Where an amount has been assessed and notified to any person under this paragraph it shall be recoverable as if it were tax due from him unless, or except to the extent that, the assessment has subsequently been withdrawn or reduced.

25(9) Subsection (8) of section 56 of this Act shall apply for the purposes of this paragraph as it applies for the purposes of that section.

ASSESSMENTS: TIME LIMITS

26(1) Subject to the following provisions of this paragraph, an assessment under–

(a) any provision of section 56 of this Act, or

(b) paragraph 25 above,

shall not be made more than three years after the end of the accounting period concerned or, in the case of an assessment under paragraph 25 above of an amount due by way of a penalty which is not a penalty referred to in sub-paragraph (2) of that paragraph, three years after the event giving rise to the penalty.

26(2) An assessment under paragraph 25 above of–

(a) an amount due by way of any penalty referred to in sub-paragraph (2) of that paragraph, or

(b) an amount due by way of interest,

may be made at any time before the expiry of the period of two years beginning with the time when the amount of tax due for the accounting period concerned has been finally determined.

26(3) In relation to an assessment under paragraph 25 above, any reference in sub-paragraph (1) or (2) above to the **accounting period concerned** is a reference to that period which, in the case of the penalty or interest concerned, is the relevant period referred to in sub-paragraph (2) of that paragraph.

26(4) If tax has been lost–

(a) as a result of conduct falling within paragraph 12(1) above or for which a person has been convicted of fraud, or

(b) in circumstances giving rise to liability to a penalty under paragraph 14 above,

an assessment may be made as if, in sub-paragraph (1) above, each reference to three years were a reference to twenty years.

History – In para. 26(1) the words "three years" in both places were substituted by FA 1997, s. 50 and Sch. 5, para. 6(1) and (2)(b), with effect from 19 March 1997.

In para. 26(4) the words "three years" were substituted by FA 1997, s. 50 and Sch. 5, para. 6(1) and (2)(b), with effect from 19 March 1997.

SUPPLEMENTARY ASSESSMENTS

27 If, otherwise than in circumstances falling within subsection (5)(b) of section 56 of this Act, it appears to the Commissioners that the amount which ought to have been assessed in an assessment under any provision of that section or under paragraph 25 above exceeds the amount which was so assessed, then–

(a) under the like provision as that assessment was made, and

(b) on or before the last day on which that assessment could have been made,

the Commissioners may make a supplementary assessment of the amount of the excess and shall notify the person concerned accordingly.

DISCLOSURE OF INFORMATION

28(1) Notwithstanding any obligation not to disclose information that would otherwise apply, the Commissioners may disclose information–

(a) to the Secretary of State, or

(b) to an authorised officer of the Secretary of State,

for the purpose of assisting the Secretary of State in the performance of his duties.

28(2)   Notwithstanding any such obligation as is mentioned in sub-paragraph (1) above–

(a)   the Secretary of State, or
(b)   an authorised officer of the Secretary of State,

may disclose information to the Commissioners or to an authorised officer of the Commissioners for the purpose of assisting the Commissioners in the performance of duties in relation to tax.

28(3)   Information that has been disclosed to a person by virtue of this paragraph shall not be disclosed by him except–

(a)   to another person to whom (instead of him) disclosure could by virtue of this paragraph have been made, or
(b)   for the purpose of any proceedings connected with the operation of any provision of, or made under, any enactment in relation to insurance or to tax.

28(4)   References in the preceding provisions of this paragraph to an **authorised officer** of the Secretary of State are to any person who has been designated by the Secretary of State as a person to and by whom information may be disclosed under this paragraph.

28(5)   The Secretary of State shall notify the Commissioners in writing of the name of any person designated under sub-paragraph (4) above.

Cross reference – Transfer of Functions (Insurance) Order 1997 (SI 1997/2781), art. 4(3): the functions of the Secretary of State under para. 28 are exercisable concurrently with the Treasury.

28A(1)   Notwithstanding any obligation not to disclose information that would otherwise apply, the Commissioners may disclose information–

(a)   to the Treasury, or
(b)   to an authorised officer of the Treasury,

for the purpose of assisting the Treasury in the performance of their duties.

28A(2)   Notwithstanding any such obligation as is mentioned in sub-paragraph (1) above–

(a)   the Treasury, or
(b)   an authorised officer of the Treasury,

may disclose information to the Commissioners or to an authorised officer of the Commissioners for the purpose of assisting the Commissioners in the performance of duties in relation to tax.

28A(3)   Information that has been disclosed to a person by virtue of this paragraph shall not be disclosed by him except–

(a)   to another person to whom (instead of him) disclosure could by virtue of this paragraph have been made, or
(b)   for the purpose of any proceedings connected with the operation of any provision of, or made under, any enactment in relation to insurance or to tax.

28A(4)   References in the preceding provisions of this paragraph to an **authorised officer of the Treasury** are to any person who has been designated by the Treasury as a person to and by whom information may be disclosed under this paragraph.

28A(5)   The Treasury shall notify the Commissioners in writing of the name of any person designated under sub-paragraph (4) above.

History – Para. 28A was inserted by SI 1997/2781, art. 8 and para. 124 of the accompanying Schedule, operative from 5 January 1998.

EVIDENCE BY CERTIFICATE

29(1)   A certificate of the Commissioners–

(a)   that a person was or was not at any time registered under section 53 of this Act,
(b)   that any return required by regulations under section 54 of this Act has not been made or had not been made at any time, or
(c)   that any tax shown as due in a return made in pursuance of regulations made under *section 54 of this* Act, or in an assessment made under section 56 of this Act, has not been paid,

shall be sufficient evidence of that fact until the contrary is proved.

29(2)   Any document purporting to be a certificate under sub-paragraph (1) above shall be taken to be such a certificate until the contrary is proved.

SERVICE OF NOTICES ETC.

30   Any notice, notification or requirement to be served on, given to or made of any person for the purposes of this Part of this Act may be served, given or made by sending it by post in a letter addressed to that person or his tax representative at the last or usual residence or place of business of that person or representative.

NO DEDUCTION OF PENALTIES OR INTEREST

31   [Inserts ICTA 1988, s. 827(1B).]

DESTINATION OF RECEIPTS

32   All money and securities for money collected or received for or on account of the tax shall–

(a)   if collected or received in Great Britain, be placed to the general account of the Commissioners kept at the Bank of England under section 17 of the Customs and Excise Management Act 1979;

(b)   if collected or received in Northern Ireland, be paid into the Consolidated Fund of the United Kingdom in such manner as the Treasury may direct.

Cross reference – CEMA 1979, s. 17: commissioners' receipts and expenses – disposal of duties etc.

PROVISIONAL COLLECTION OF TAX

33   [Amends PCTA 1968, s. 1(1).]

34(1)   In a case where–

(a)   by virtue of a resolution having effect under the Provisional Collection of Taxes Act 1968 tax has been paid at a rate specified in the resolution, and

(b)   by virtue of section 1(6) or (7) or 5(3) of that Act any of that tax is repayable in consequence of the restoration in relation to the premium concerned of a lower rate,

the amount repayable shall be the difference between the tax paid by reference to the actual chargeable amount at the rate specified in the resolution and the tax that would have been payable by reference to the actual chargeable amount at the lower rate.

34(2)   In sub-paragraph (1) above the **"actual chargeable amount"** means the chargeable amount by reference to which tax was paid.

34(3)   In a case where–

(a)   by virtue of a resolution having effect under the Provisional Collection of Taxes Act 1968 tax is chargeable at a rate specified in the resolution, but

(b)   before the tax is paid it ceases to be chargeable at that rate in consequence of the restoration in relation to the premium concerned of a lower rate,

the tax chargeable at the lower rate shall be charged by reference to the same chargeable amount as that by reference to which tax would have been chargeable at the rate specified in the resolution.

Cross references – PCTA 1968, s. 1: temporary statutory effect of House of Commons resolutions affecting income tax or customs or excise duties.
PCTA 1968, s. 5: House of Commons resolution giving provisional effect to motions affecting taxation.

ADJUSTMENT OF CONTRACTS

35(1)   Where, after the making of a contract of insurance and before a given premium is received by the insurer under the contract, there is a change in the tax chargeable on the receipt of the premium, then, unless the contract otherwise provided, there shall be added to or deducted from the amount payable as the premium an amount equal to the difference between–

(a)   the tax chargeable had the change not been made, and
(b)   the tax in fact chargeable.

35(2)   References in sub-paragraph (1) above to a **change in the tax chargeable** include references to a change to or from no tax being chargeable.

35(3)   Where this paragraph applies, the amount of the premium shall not be treated as altered for the purposes of calculating tax.

SCHEDULE 7A – INSURANCE PREMIUM TAX: CONTRACTS THAT ARE NOT TAXABLE

Section 70

History – Sch. 7A was inserted by SI 1994/1698, art. 5, operative from 1 October 1994.

Official publications – Notice IPT 2, Pt. 2 (1999 edn): a general guide to IPT, exemptions from the tax.

Part I – Descriptions of Contract

CONTRACTS OF REINSURANCE

1   A contract falls within this paragraph if it is a contract of reinsurance.

CONTRACTS CONSTITUTING LONG TERM BUSINESS

2(1)   Subject to sub-paragraph (3) below, a contract falls within this paragraph if it is one whose effecting and carrying out constitutes business of one or more of the classes specified in Schedule 1 to the Insurance Companies Act 1982 (long term business) and constitutes only such business.

2(2)   In deciding whether the effecting and carrying out of a contract constitutes only such business as is mentioned in sub-paragraph (1) above where–

(a)   the contract includes cover for risks not falling within the descriptions in any of the classes specified in Schedule 1 to the Insurance Companies Act 1982;

(b)   the effecting and carrying out of the contract is treated for the purposes of that Act as constituting business of one or more of those classes and only such business by virtue of the application to it of section 1(3) of that Act; and

(c)   the contract was not entered into after 30th November 1993,

the inclusion of such cover shall be ignored.

2(3)   A contract which would otherwise fall within this paragraph does not do so if it is for medical insurance.

2(4)   Subject to sub-paragraph (5) below, for the purposes of this paragraph a contract is a contract for medical insurance if it provides one or more of the following benefits,

whether or not their provision is subject to conditions or limitations–

(a)   medical, dental or optical, consultation, diagnosis or treatment;

(b)   alternative or complementary medical treatment or therapy;

(c)   convalescent care;

(d)   goods or services related to any of the above;

(e)   payment or reimbursement of, or a grant towards, the whole or part of the cost of any of the above;

(f)   payment of a specified sum for optical, dental or medical appointments;

(g)   payment of a specified sum for each specified period of treatment as a hospital in patient;

(h)   payment of a specified sum for each specified period of convalescent care; or

(i)   payment of a specified sum, except one to which sub-paragraph (6) below applies, when a person is diagnosed as requiring or has undergone a specified medical procedure.

2(5)   A benefit which would apart from this sub-paragraph fall within sub-paragraph (4) above shall not do so if, before he can become entitled to the benefit, the insured is required–

(a)   to be suffering from a disability which so impairs his ability to carry out normal activities of daily living that he requires long term care, supervision or assistance; and

(b)   to have been suffering from the disability for a continuous period of not less than 4 weeks.

2(6)   This sub-paragraph applies to a payment of a specified sum if the contract under which it is payable provides that only one such payment in relation to each specified medical procedure will be made in respect of each person in relation to whom benefit is payable under the contract.

History – In para. 2(1), the words "Subject to sub-paragraph (3) below, a contract falls" were substituted for the words "A contract falls" by SI 1997/1627, art. 2(a), operative from 1 October 1997.
Para. 2(3) was inserted by SI 1997/1627, art. 2(b), operative from 1 October 1997.
Para. 2(4) was inserted by SI 1997/1627, art. 2(b), operative from 1 October 1997.
Para. 2(5) was inserted by SI 1997/1627, art. 2(b), operative from 1 October 1997.
Para. 2(6) was inserted by SI 1997/1627, art. 2(b), operative from 1 October 1997.

CONTRACTS RELATING TO MOTOR VEHICLES FOR USE BY HANDICAPPED PERSONS

3(1) A contract falls within this paragraph if it relates only to a motor vehicle and the conditions mentioned in sub-paragraph (2) below are satisfied.

3(2) The conditions referred to in sub-paragraph (1) above are that—

(a) the vehicle is used, or intended for use, by a handicapped person in receipt of a disability living allowance by virtue of entitlement to the mobility component or of a mobility supplement;

(b) the insured lets such vehicles on hire to such persons in the course of a business consisting predominantly of the provision of motor vehicles to such persons; and

(c) the insured does not in the course of the business let such vehicles on hire to such persons on terms other than qualifying terms.

3(3) For the purposes of sub-paragraph (2)(c) above a vehicle is let on **qualifying terms** to a person (the lessee) if the consideration for the letting consists wholly or partly of sums paid to the insured by—

(a) the Department of Social Security;

(b) the Department of Health and Social Services for Northern Ireland; or

(c) the Ministry of Defence,

on behalf of the lessee in respect of the disability living allowance or mobility supplement to which the lessee is entitled.

3(4) For the purposes of this paragraph—

(a) **"handicapped"** means chronically sick or disabled;

(b) **"disability living allowance"** means a disability living allowance within the meaning of section 71 of the Social Security Contributions and Benefits Act 1992 or section 71 of the Social Security Contributions and Benefits (Northern Ireland) Act 1992;

(c) **"mobility supplement"** means a mobility supplement within the meaning of article 26A of the Naval, Military and Air Forces etc. (Disablement and Death) Service Pensions Order 1983, article 25A of the Personal Injuries (Civilians) Scheme 1983, article 3 of the Motor Vehicles (Exemption from Vehicles Excise Duty) Order 1985 or article 3 of the Motor Vehicles (Exemption from Vehicles Excise Duty) (Northern Ireland) Order 1985.

CONTRACTS RELATING TO COMMERCIAL SHIPS

4(1) A contract falls within this paragraph if it relates only to a commercial ship and is a contract whose effecting and carrying out constitutes business of one or more of the relevant classes and constitutes only such business.

4(2) For the purposes of this paragraph the relevant classes are classes 1, 6 and 12 of the classes specified in Part I of Schedule 2 to the Insurance Companies Act 1982 (ships, accident, third-party etc.).

4(3) For the purposes of this paragraph a **commercial ship** is a ship which is—

(a) of a gross tonnage of 15 tons or more; and

(b) not designed or adapted for use for recreation or pleasure.

CONTRACTS RELATING TO LIFEBOATS AND LIFEBOAT EQUIPMENT

5(1) A contract falls within this paragraph if it relates only to a lifeboat and is a contract whose effecting and carrying out constitutes business of one or more of the relevant classes and constitutes only such business.

5(2) For the purposes of this paragraph the relevant classes are classes 1, 6 and 12 of the classes specified in Part I of Schedule 2 to the Insurance Companies Act 1982 (ships, accident, third-party etc.).

5(3) For the purposes of this paragraph a **lifeboat** is a vessel used or to be used solely for rescue or assistance at sea.

6(1) A contract falls within this paragraph if it relates only to a lifeboat and lifeboat equipment and is such that, if it related only to a lifeboat, it would fall within paragraph 5 above.

6(2) In deciding whether a contract relates to lifeboat equipment the nature of the risks concerned is immaterial, and they may (for example) be risks of dying or sustaining injury or of loss or damage.

6(3)   For the purposes of this paragraph–

(a)   **"lifeboat"** has the meaning given by paragraph 5(3) above; and

(b)   **"lifeboat equipment"** means anything used or to be used solely in connection with a lifeboat.

CONTRACTS RELATING TO COMMERCIAL AIRCRAFT

7(1)   A contract falls within this paragraph if it relates only to a commercial aircraft and is a contract whose effecting and carrying out constitutes business of one or more of the relevant classes and constitutes only such business.

7(2)   For the purposes of this paragraph the relevant classes are classes 1, 5 and 11 of the classes specified in Part I of Schedule 2 to the Insurance Companies Act 1982 (aircraft, accident, third-party etc.).

7(3)   For the purposes of this paragraph a commercial aircraft is an aircraft which is–

(a)   of a weight of 8,000 kilogrammes or more; and

(b)   not designed or adapted for use for recreation or pleasure.

CONTRACTS RELATING TO RISKS OUTSIDE THE UNITED KINGDOM

8(1)   A contract falls within this paragraph if it relates only to a risk which is situated outside the United Kingdom.

8(2)   Section 96A(3) of the Insurance Companies Act 1982 shall apply to determine whether a risk is situated in the United Kingdom for the purposes of this paragraph as it applies to determine that question for the purposes of that Act, but as if for paragraph (a) of that section there were substituted the following–

"(a)   where the insurance relates to a building, its contents or both (whether or not the contents are covered by the same policy), to the member State in which the building is situated;".

CONTRACTS RELATING TO FOREIGN OR INTERNATIONAL RAILWAY ROLLING STOCK

9(1)   A contract falls within this paragraph if it relates only to foreign or international railway rolling stock and is a contract whose effecting and carrying out constitutes business of one or more of the relevant classes and constitutes only such business.

9(2)   For the purposes of this paragraph the relevant classes are classes 4 and 13 of the classes specified in Part I of Schedule 2 to the Insurance Companies Act 1982 (railway rolling stock, third party etc.).

9(3)   For the purposes of this paragraph foreign or international railway rolling stock is railway rolling stock used principally for journeys taking place wholly or partly outside the United Kingdom.

CONTRACTS RELATING TO THE CHANNEL TUNNEL

10(1)   A contract falls within this paragraph if it relates only to the Channel tunnel system and is a contract whose effecting and carrying out constitutes business of one or more of the relevant classes and constitutes only such business.

10(2)   For the purposes of this paragraph the relevant classes are classes 8, 9 and 13 of the classes specified in Part I of Schedule 2 to the Insurance Companies Act 1982 (fire, damage to property, third party etc.).

10(3)   For the purposes of this paragraph **"the Channel tunnel system"** means–

(a)   the tunnels described in section 1(7)(a) of the Channel Tunnel Act 1987;

(b)   the control towers situated in the terminal areas described in section 1(7)(b) of that Act; and

(c)   the shuttle crossovers, wherever situated.

11(1)   A contract falls within this paragraph if it relates only to relevant Channel tunnel equipment and is a contract whose effecting and carrying out constitutes business of one or more of the relevant classes and constitutes only such business.

11(2)   For the purposes of this paragraph the relevant classes are classes 8, 9 and 13 of the classes specified in Part I of Schedule 2 to the Insurance Companies Act 1982 (fire, damage to property, third party etc.).

11(3) For the purposes of this paragraph **"the Channel tunnel system"** has the meaning given by paragraph 10(3) above.

11(4) For the purposes of this paragraph **"relevant Channel tunnel equipment"** means, subject to sub-paragraph (5) below, the fixed or movable equipment needed for the operation of the Channel tunnel system or for the operation of trains through any tunnel forming part of it and in particular includes–

(a)   any ventilation cooling or electrical plant used or to be used in connection with any such operation; and

(b)   any safety, signalling and control equipment which is or is to be so used.

11(5) Equipment which consists of or forms part of–

(a)   roads, bridges, platforms, ticket offices and other facilities for the use of passengers or motor vehicles;

(b)   administrative buildings and maintenance facilities; and

(c)   railway track or signalling equipment which is not situated in any part of the Channel tunnel system,

is not relevant Channel tunnel equipment for the purposes of this paragraph.

CONTRACTS RELATING TO GOODS IN FOREIGN OR INTERNATIONAL TRANSIT

12(1) A contract falls within this paragraph if it relates only to loss of or damage to goods in foreign or international transit and the insured enters into the contract in the course of a business carried on by him.

12(2) For the purposes of this paragraph **goods in foreign or international transit** are goods in transit, and any container in which they are carried, where their carriage–

(a)   begins and ends outside the United Kingdom;

(b)   begins outside but ends in the United Kingdom; or

(c)   ends outside but begins in the United Kingdom.

12(3) For the purposes of sub-paragraph (2) above **"container"** has the same meaning as in regulation 38(3) of the Value Added Tax (General) Regulations 1985.

Note – Value Added Tax (General) Regulations 1985, reg. 38 is now Value Added Tax Regulations 1995 (SI 1995/2518), reg. 117(2).

CONTRACTS RELATING TO CREDIT

13(1) A contract falls within this paragraph if it relates only to credit granted in relation to goods or services supplied under a relevant contract by a person carrying on business in the United Kingdom.

13(2) For the purposes of this paragraph a **relevant contract** is–

(a)   a contract to make a relevant supply of goods, or a supply of services, or both, to an overseas customer;

(b)   a contract to supply goods to a person who is to–

    (i) export those goods; or

    (ii) incorporate those goods in other goods which he is to export,

where the condition mentioned in sub-paragraph (3) below is satisfied;

(c)   a contract to supply to a person who is to export goods services consisting of the valuation or testing of, or other work carried out on, those goods where the condition mentioned in sub-paragraph (3) below is satisfied;

(d)   a contract to supply services to a person in order that he may comply with a legally binding obligation to make a supply of services to an overseas customer.

13(3) The condition referred to in sub-paragraph (2)(b) and (c) above is that the goods to be exported are to be exported in order that the person exporting them may comply with a legally binding obligation to make a relevant supply of goods to an overseas customer.

13(4) For the purposes of this paragraph–

(a)   **"export"** means export from the United Kingdom and cognate expressions shall be construed accordingly; and

(b)   any reference to a **person who is to export goods** shall be taken as including a reference to a person at whose direction the insured is to export them and the reference in sub-paragraph (3) above to the person exporting goods shall be construed accordingly.

13(5) Where a contract relates to–

(a)   credit of the description in sub-paragraph (1) above; and

(b)   loss resulting from the insured or any third party being required to pay the amount of any bond or guarantee against non-performance by the insured of the contract which involves him making the supply,

the contract shall be treated for the purposes of sub-paragraph (1) above as if it did not relate to loss of the description in paragraph (b) above.

CONTRACTS RELATING TO EXCHANGE LOSSES

14(1) A contract falls within this paragraph if–

(a)   it relates only to loss resulting from a change in the rate at which the price for a supply which is or may be made by the insured may be exchanged for another currency; and

(b)   the conditions mentioned in sub-paragraph (2) below are satisfied.

14(2) The conditions referred to in sub-paragraph (1) above are that–

(a)   the insured is a person carrying on business in the United Kingdom;

(b)   the contract of insurance concerns a contract to make a relevant supply of goods, or a supply of services, or both, to an overseas customer (whether or not the contract to make the supply is one into which the insured has entered, or one for which he has tendered or intends to tender); and

(c)   the period of cover for the risk expires no later than the date by which the whole of the price for the supply is to be paid or, where the contract has not been entered into, would be required to be paid.

14(3) Where the contract relates to–

(a)   loss of the description in sub-paragraph (1)(a) above; and

(b)   loss relating from a change in the rate at which the price of goods which the insured imports into the United Kingdom for the purpose of enabling him to make the supply concerned may be exchanged for another currency,

the contract shall be treated for the purposes of sub-paragraphs (1) and (2) above as if it did not relate to loss of the description in paragraph (b) above.

CONTRACTS RELATING TO THE PROVISION OF FINANCIAL FACILITIES

15(1) A contract falls within this paragraph if it relates only to the provision of a relevant financial facility and the conditions mentioned in sub-paragraph (2) below are satisfied.

15(2) The conditions referred to in sub-paragraph (1) above are that–

(a)   the person to whom the relevant financial facility is provided is an overseas customer;

(b)   it is provided in order that he may comply with a legally binding obligation to receive a relevant supply of goods, or a supply of services, or both, from a person carrying on business; and

(c)   the contract of insurance is a contract whose effecting and carrying out constitutes business of one or both of classes 14 and 15 of the classes specified in Part I of Schedule 2 to the Insurance Companies Act 1982 (credit, suretyship etc.).

15(3) For the purposes of this paragraph **a relevant financial facility** is–

(a)   the making of an advance;

(b)   the issue of a letter of credit or acceptance of a bill of exchange;

(c)   the giving of a guarantee or bond; or

(d)   any other similar transaction entered into in order to provide a customer with the means to pay, or a supplier with the right to call upon a third party for, the consideration for goods or services.

History – In para. 15(2)(b), words which appeared after the words "carrying on business" were omitted by SI 1996/2955, art. 2, operative from 1 January 1997.

Part II – Interpretation

16(1) This Part of this Schedule applies for the purposes of Part I of this Schedule.

16(2) A relevant supply of goods is any supply of goods where the supply is to be made outside the United Kingdom or where the goods are to be exported from the United Kingdom.

16(3) An overseas customer, in relation to a supply of goods or services, is a person who—

(a) does not have any business establishment in the United Kingdom but has such an establishment elsewhere;

(b) has such establishments both in the United Kingdom and elsewhere, provided that the establishment at which, or for the purposes of which, the goods or services which are to be supplied to him are most directly to be used is not in the United Kingdom; or

(c) has no such establishment in any place and does not have his usual place of residence in the United Kingdom.

FINANCE ACT 1995

(1995 Chapter 4)

[*1st May 1995*]

PART II – VALUE ADDED TAX AND INSURANCE PREMIUM TAX

INSURANCE PREMIUM TAX

32 Insurance premium tax

32 Schedule 5 to this Act (which relates to insurance premium tax) shall have effect.

SCHEDULES

SCHEDULE 5 – INSURANCE PREMIUM TAX

Section 34

1 Part III of the Finance Act 1994 (insurance premium tax) shall be amended as provided by this Schedule.

2(1) Section 53 (registration of insurers) shall be amended as follows.

2(2) [Amends FA 1994, s. 53(5).]

2(3) [Inserts FA 1994, s. 53(5A).]

2(4) Sub-paragraph (2) above shall apply in relation to notifications made under section 53(3) on or after the day on which this Act is passed.

3 [Inserts FA 1994, s. 53(1A).]

4 [Inserts FA 1994, s. 53A.]

5(1) Section 59 (review of Commissioners' decisions) shall be amended as follows.

5(2) [Amends FA 1994, s. 59(1)(d).]

5(3) [Inserts FA 1994, s. 59(1A).]

5(4) This paragraph shall apply in relation to assessments made on or after the day on which this Act is passed.

6 [Amends FA 1994, s. 73(1).]

7(1) [Amends FA 1994, Sch. 7, para. 2(1)–(3) and 3(1)–(3).]

7(2) This paragraph shall apply in relation to contracts whether entered into before or after the passing of this Act.

8(1) [Inserts FA 1994, Sch. 7, para. 4A.]

8(2) [Amends FA 1994, Sch. 7, para. 5(1).]

9　[Substituted FA 1994, former Sch. 7, para. 7(8). Para. 9 was repealed by FA 1997, s. 113 and Sch. 18, Pt. V(2), with effect from 1 July 1997 (SI 1997/1433 (C. 55)).]

FINANCE ACT 1996

(1996 Chapter 8)

[29th April 1996]

PART VII – MISCELLANEOUS AND SUPPLEMENTAL

MISCELLANEOUS: INDIRECT TAXATION

197　Setting of rates of interest

197(1)　The rate of interest applicable for the purposes of an enactment to which this section applies shall be the rate which for the purposes of that enactment is provided for by regulations made by the Treasury under this section.

197(2)　This section applies to–

(a)　[Not relevant to insurance premium tax.]

(b)　paragraphs 21 and 22 of Schedule 7 to [the Finance] Act [1994] (interest on amounts of insurance premium tax and on amounts payable by the Commissioners in respect of that tax);

(c)　[Not relevant to insurance premium tax.]

(d)　[Not relevant to insurance premium tax.]; and

(e)　paragraph 17 of Schedule 5 to the Finance Act 1997 (interest on amounts repayable in respect of overpayments by the Commissioners in connection with excise duties, insurance premium tax and landfill tax).

197(3)　Regulations under this section may–

(a)　make different provision for different enactments or for different purposes of the same enactment,

(b)　either themselves specify a rate of interest for the purposes of an enactment or make provision for any such rate to be determined, and to change from time to time, by reference to such rate or the average of such rates as may be referred to in the regulations,

(c)　provide for rates to be reduced below, or increased above, what they otherwise would be by specified amounts or by reference to specified formulae,

(d)　provide for rates arrived at by reference to averages or formulae to be rounded up or down,

(e)　provide for circumstances in which changes of rates of interest are or are not to take place, and

(f)　provide that changes of rates are to have effect for periods beginning on or after a day determined in accordance with the regulations in relation to interest running from before that day, as well as in relation to interest running from, or from after, that day.

197(4)　The power to make regulations under this section shall be exercisable by statutory instrument subject to annulment in pursuance of a resolution of the House of Commons.

197(5)　Where–

(a)　regulations under this section provide, without specifying the rate determined in accordance with the regulations, for a new method of determining the rate applicable for the purposes of any enactment, or

(b)　the rate which, in accordance with regulations under this section, is the rate applicable for the purposes of any enactment changes otherwise than by virtue of the making of regulations specifying a new rate,

the Commissioners of Customs and *Excise* shall make an order specifying the new rate and the day from which, in accordance with the regulations, it has effect.

197(6)

(a)　[Not relevant to insurance premium tax.]

(b)　[amends FA 1996, Sch. 7, para. 21;]

(c)   [amends FA 1996, Sch. 7, para. 22; and]

(d)   [Not relevant to insurance premium tax.]

197(7)   Subsections (1) and (6) above shall have effect for periods beginning on or after such day as the Treasury may by order made by statutory instrument appoint and shall have effect in relation to interest running from before that day, as well as in relation to interest running from, or from after, that day; and different days may be appointed under this subsection for different purposes.

History – S. 197(2)(e) was inserted by FA 1997, s. 50 and Sch. 5, para. 21, with effect from 19 March 1997.

Cross references – FA 1997, Sch. 5, para. 17(1): interest on assessment under FA 1997, Sch. 5, para. 14 or 15.

Statutory instruments – SI 1997/1015: sets 1 April 1997 as the appointed day for the purposes of s. 197(7).
SI 1997/1016: sets the rate of interest from 1 April 1997 at 6.25 per cent and 6 per cent per annum for the purposes of FA 1994, Sch. 7, para. 21 and 22 respectively.
SI 1998/1461: sets the rate of interest from 6 July 1998 at 9.5 per cent and 6 per cent per annum for the purposes of FA 1994, Sch. 7, para. 21 and 22 respectively.

Notes – References to "that Act" in s. 197(6) is to Finance Act 1994.
The basis for setting the rate of interest was amended by SI 1998/1461 with effect from 6 July 1998. Interest will be set using formulae linked to a reference rate. The reference rate will be based on an average of the base rates of six main banks rounded to the nearest whole number. For default interest, the formula used will be the reference rate plus 2.5 per cent. Application of the formulae for interest accruing on or after 6th July 1998 is as follows:

Period of application	Statutory interest FA 1994, Sch. 7, para. 22	Default interest FA 1994, Sch. 7, para. 21
From 6 February 2000	5	8.5
6 March 1999–5 February 2000	4	7.5
6 January 1999–5 March 1999	5	8.5
6 July 1998–5 January 1999	6	9.5

SI 2000/631: amended Air Passenger Duty and Other Indirect Taxes (Interest Rate) Regulations 1998 (SI 1998/1461).

SCHEDULES

SCHEDULE 41 – REPEALS

Part VIII – Miscellaneous

(1)   RATES OF INTEREST

Chapter	Short title	Extent of repeal
1994 c. 9	The Finance Act 1994.	In Schedule 7, paragraph 21(5).

Subsection (7) of section 197 of this Act applies in relation to these repeals as it applies in relation to subsection (6) of that section.

FINANCE ACT 1997

(1997 Chapter 16)

[*19th March 1997*]

ARRANGEMENT OF SECTIONS

PART II – INSURANCE PREMIUM TAX

NEW RATES OF TAX

21 Rate of Tax

21(1) [Substitutes FA 1994, s. 51.]

21(2) [Amends FA 1994, s. 73(1).]

22 Premiums liable to tax at the higher rate

22(1) [Inserts FA 1994, s. 51A.]

22(2) [Amends FA 1994, s. 74(4) and (6).]

22(3) [Inserts FA 1994, Sch. 6A.]

23 Charge to tax where different rates apply

23(1) [Substitutes FA 1994, s. 69.]

23(2) [Amends FA 1994, s. 50(3).]

24 Commencement of sections 21 to 23

24(1) Except as provided by subsection (2) below, sections 21 to 23 above have effect in relation to a premium which falls to be regarded for the purposes of Part III of the Finance Act 1994 as received under a taxable insurance contract by an insurer on or after 1st April 1997.

24(2) Sections 21 to 23 above do not have effect in relation to a premium if the premium–

(a) is in respect of a contract made before 1st April 1997; and

(b) falls, by virtue of regulations under section 68 of the Finance Act 1994 (special accounting scheme), to be regarded for the purposes of Part III of that Act as received under the contract by the insurer on a date before 1st August 1997.

24(3) Subsection (2) above does not apply in relation to a premium if the premium–

(a) is an additional premium under the contract;

(b) falls as mentioned in subsection (2)(b) above to be regarded as received under the contract by the insurer on or after 1st April 1997; and

(c) is in respect of a risk which was not covered by the contract before 1st April 1997.

24(4) Without prejudice to the generality of subsections (1) to (3) above, those subsections shall be construed in accordance with sections 67A to 67C of the Finance Act 1994 (which are inserted by section 29 below).

Official publications – Notice IPT 2, Pt. 7 (1999): a general guide to IPT, transitional arrangements for rate change.

TAXABLE INTERMEDIARIES AND THEIR FEES

25 Certain fees to be treated as premiums under higher rate contracts

25(1) [Inserts FA 1994, s. 52A.]

25(2) The amendment made by subsection (1) above has effect in relation to payments in respect of fees charged on or after the day on which this Act is passed.

26 Registration of taxable intermediaries

26 [Inserts FA 1994, s. 53AA.]

27 Supplementary provisions

27(1) The Finance Act 1994 shall be amended in accordance with the following provisions of this section.

27(2) [Amends FA 1994, s. 53A(1)(b).]

27(3) [Amends FA 1994, s. 55.]

27(4) [Amends FA 1994, s. 57.]

27(5) [Amends FA 1994, s. 58.]

27(6) [Inserts FA 1994, s. 59(1)(bb).]

27(7) [Amends FA 1994, s. 62.]

27(8)   [Inserts FA 1994, s. 63(1)(aa) and (bb).]

27(9)   [Amends FA 1994, s. 73(1).]

27(10)   [Amends FA 1994, s. 73(3) and inserts FA 1994, s. 73(3A).]

27(11)   [Amends FA 1994, Sch. 7, para. 14(1) and (2)(a).]

MISCELLANEOUS

28   Amounts charged by other intermediaries

28(1)   [Inserts FA 1994, s. 72(1A).]

28(2)   The amendment made by subsection (1) above has effect in relation to payments received in respect of amounts charged on or after 1st April 1997.

29   Prevention of pre-emption

29(1)   [Inserts FA 1994, s. 67A, 67B and 67C.]

29(2)   In the application of sections 67A to 67C of the Finance Act 1994 in relation to the increases in insurance premium tax effected by this Part and the exceptions from those increases–

(a)   the announcement relating to those increases, as described in section 67A(1), and to those exceptions, as described in section 67B(1), shall be taken to have been made on 26th November 1996;

(b)   "the date of the change" is 1st April 1997; and

(c)   "the concessionary date" is 1st August 1997.

29(3)   The amendment made by subsection (1) above has effect on and after 26th November 1996.

30   Tax point for payroll deductions

30(1)   [Inserts FA 1994, s. 72(7A).]

30(2)   [Inserts FA 1994, s. 72(8A).]

30(3)   This section applies in relation to amounts deducted on or after the day on which this Act is passed.

PART IV – PAYMENTS AND OVERPAYMENTS IN RESPECT OF INDIRECT TAXES

EXCISE DUTIES AND OTHER INDIRECT TAXES

50   Overpayments, interest, assessments, etc.

50(1)   Schedule 5 to this Act (which makes provision in relation to excise duties, insurance premium tax and landfill tax which corresponds to that made for VAT by sections 44 to 48 above) shall have effect.

50(2)   [Not relevant to insurance premium tax.]

ENFORCEMENT OF PAYMENT

51   Enforcement by distress

51(1)   The Commissioners may by regulations make provision–

(a)   for authorising distress to be levied on the goods and chattels of any person refusing or neglecting to pay–

(i)   any amount of relevant tax due from him, or

(ii)   any amount recoverable as if it were relevant tax due from him;

(b)   for the disposal of any goods or chattels on which distress is levied in pursuance of the regulations; and

(c)   for the imposition and recovery of costs, charges, expenses and fees in connection with *anything done under* the regulations.

51(2)   The provision that may be contained in regulations under this section shall include, in particular–

(a)   provision for the levying of distress, by any person authorised to do so under the regulations, on goods or chattels located at any place whatever (including on a public highway); and

(b)   provision authorising distress to be levied at any such time of the day or night, and on any such day of the week, as may be specified or described in the regulations.

51(3)   Regulations under this section may–

(a)   make different provision for different cases, and

(b)   contain any such incidental, supplemental, consequential or transitional provision as the Commissioners think fit;

and the transitional provision that may be contained in regulations under this section shall include transitional provision in connection with the coming into force of the repeal by this Act of any other power by regulations to make provision for or in connection with the levying of distress.

51(4)   The power to make regulations under this section shall be exercisable by statutory instrument subject to annulment in pursuance of a resolution of the House of Commons.

51(5)   The following are **relevant taxes** for the purposes of this section, that is to say–

(a)   any duty of customs or excise, other than vehicle excise duty;

(b)   value added tax;

(c)   insurance premium tax;

(d)   landfill tax;

(e)   any agricultural levy of the European Community.

51(6)   In this section **"the Commissioners"** means the Commissioners of Customs and Excise.

51(7)   Regulations made under this section shall not have effect in Scotland.

52   Enforcement by diligence

52(1)   Where any amount of relevant tax or any amount recoverable as if it were relevant tax is due and has not been paid, the sheriff, on an application by the Commissioners accompanied by a certificate by them–

(a)   stating that none of the persons specified in the application has paid the amount due from him;

(b)   stating that payment of the amount due from each such person has been demanded from him; and

(c)   specifying the amount due from and unpaid by each such person,

shall grant a summary warrant in a form prescribed by Act of Sederunt authorising the recovery, by any of the diligences mentioned in subsection (2) below, of the amount remaining due and unpaid.

52(2)   The diligences referred to in subsection (1) above are–

(a)   a poinding and sale in accordance with Schedule 5 to the Debtors (Scotland) Act 1987;

(b)   an earnings arrestment;

(c)   an arrestment and action of furthcoming or sale.

52(3)   Subject to subsection (4) below and without prejudice to paragraphs 25 to 34 of Schedule 5 to the Debtors (Scotland) Act 1987 (expenses of poinding and sale) the sheriff officer's fees, together with the outlays necessarily incurred by him, in connection with the execution of a summary warrant shall be chargeable against the debtor.

52(4)   No fees shall be chargeable by the sheriff officer against the debtor for collecting, and accounting to the Commissioners for, sums paid to him by the debtor in respect of the amount owing.

52(5)   The following are **relevant taxes** for the purposes of this section, that is to say–

(a)   [Not relevant to insurance premium tax.]

(b)   [Not relevant to insurance premium tax.]

(c)   insurance premium tax;

(d)   [Not relevant to insurance premium tax.]

(e)   [Not relevant to insurance premium tax.]

52(6)   In this section **"the Commissioners"** means the Commissioners of Customs and Excise.

52(7)   This section shall come into force on such day as the Commissioners of Customs and Excise may by order made by statutory instrument appoint, and different days may be appointed under this subsection for different purposes.

52(8)   This section extends only to Scotland.

Statutory instruments – Finance Act 1997, sections 52 and 53, (Appointed Day) Order 1997 (SI 1997/1432) (C 54): the appointed day is 1 July 1997.

53   Amendments consequential on sections 51 and 52

53(1)   [Not relevant to insurance premium tax.]

53(2)   [Not relevant to insurance premium tax.]

53(3)   [Not relevant to insurance premium tax.]

53(4)   [Not relevant to insurance premium tax.]

53(5)   [Amends FA 1994, Sch. 7, para. 19(1)(a).]

53(6)   [Not relevant to insurance premium tax.]

53(7)   [Not relevant to insurance premium tax.]

53(8)   [Not relevant to insurance premium tax.]

53(9)   This section shall come into force on such day as the Commissioners of Customs and Excise may by order made by statutory instrument appoint, and different days may be appointed under this subsection for different purposes.

Statutory instruments – Finance Act 1997, sections 52 and 53, (Appointed Day) Order 1997 (SI 1997/1432) (C 54): the appointed day is 1 July 1997.

PART VIII – MISCELLANEOUS AND SUPPLEMENTAL

Supplemental

113   Repeals

113(1)   The enactments mentioned in Schedule 18 to this Act (which include spent provisions) are hereby repealed to the extent specified in the third column of that Schedule.

113(2)   The repeals specified in that Schedule have effect subject to the commencement provisions and savings contained or referred to in the notes set out in that Schedule.

SCHEDULES

SCHEDULE 4 – INSURANCE PREMIUM TAX: THE HIGHER RATE

Section 22

[Inserts FA 1994, Sch. 6A.]

SCHEDULE 5 – INDIRECT TAXES: OVERPAYMENTS ETC.

Section 50

Part I – Unjust Enrichment

APPLICATION OF PART I

1(1)   This Part of this Schedule has effect for the purposes of the following provisions (which make it a defence to a claim for repayment that the repayment would unjustly enrich the claimant), namely–

(a)   [Not relevant to insurance premium tax.]

(b)   paragraph 8(3) of Schedule 7 to the Finance Act 1994 (insurance premium tax); and

(c)   [Not relevant to insurance premium tax.].

1(2)   Those provisions are referred to in this Part of this Schedule as unjust enrichment provisions.

1(3)   In this Part of this Schedule–

"the Commissioners" means the Commissioners of Customs and Excise;
"relevant repayment provision" means–
(a)   [Not relevant to insurance premium tax.]
(b)   paragraph 8 of Schedule 7 to the Finance Act 1994 (recovery of overpaid insurance premium tax); or
(c)   [Not relevant to insurance premium tax.];
"relevant tax" means any duty of excise, insurance premium tax or landfill tax; and
"subordinate legislation" has the same meaning as in the Interpretation Act 1978.

DISREGARD OF BUSINESS LOSSES

2(1)   This paragraph applies where–

(a)   there is an amount paid by way of relevant tax which (apart from an unjust enrichment provision) would fall to be repaid under a relevant repayment provision to any person (**"the taxpayer"**), and

(b)   the whole or a part of the cost of the payment of that amount to the Commissioners has, for practical purposes, been borne by a person other than the taxpayer.

2(2)   Where, in a case to which this paragraph applies, loss or damage has been or may be incurred by the taxpayer as a result of mistaken assumptions made in his case about the operation of any provisions relating to a relevant tax, that loss or damage shall be disregarded, except to the extent of the quantified amount, in the making of any determination–

(a)   of whether or to what extent the repayment of an amount to the taxpayer would enrich him; or

(b)   of whether or to what extent any enrichment of the taxpayer would be unjust.

2(3)   In sub-paragraph (2) above **"the quantified amount"** means the amount (if any) which is shown by the taxpayer to constitute the amount that would appropriately compensate him for loss or damage shown by him to have resulted, for any business carried on by him, from the making of the mistaken assumptions.

2(4)   The reference in sub-paragraph (2) above to **provisions relating to a relevant tax** is a reference to any provisions of–

(a)   any enactment, subordinate legislation or Community legislation (whether or not still in force) which relates to that tax or to any matter connected with it; or

(b)   any notice published by the Commissioners under or for the purposes of any such enactment or subordinate legislation.

2(5)   This paragraph has effect for the purposes of making any repayment on or after the day on which this Act is passed, even if the claim for that repayment was made before that day.

REIMBURSEMENT ARRANGEMENTS

3(1)   The Commissioners may by regulations make provision for reimbursement arrangements made by any person to be disregarded for the purposes of any or all of the unjust enrichment provisions except where the arrangements–

(a)   contain such provision as may be required by the regulations; and

(b)   are supported by such undertakings to comply with the provisions of the arrangements as may be required by the regulations to be given to the Commissioners.

3(2)   In this paragraph **"reimbursement arrangements"** means any arrangements for the purposes of a claim under a relevant repayment provision which–

(a)   are made by any person for the purpose of securing that he is not unjustly enriched by the repayment of any amount in pursuance of the claim; and

(b)   provide for the reimbursement of persons who have for practical purposes borne the whole or any part of the cost of the original payment of that amount to the Commissioners.

3(3)   Without prejudice to the generality of sub-paragraph (1) above, the provision that may be required by regulations under this paragraph to be contained in reimbursement arrangements includes–

(a)   provision requiring a reimbursement for which the arrangements provide to be made within such period after the repayment to which it relates as may be specified in the regulations;

(b)   provision for the repayment of amounts to the Commissioners where those amounts are not reimbursed in accordance with the arrangements;

(c)   provision requiring interest paid by the Commissioners on any amount repaid by them to be treated in the same way as that amount for the purposes of any requirement under the arrangements to make reimbursement or to repay the Commissioners;

(d)   provision requiring such records relating to the carrying out of the arrangements as may be described in the regulations to be kept and produced to the Commissioners, or to an officer of theirs.

3(4)   Regulations under this paragraph may impose obligations on such persons as may be specified in the regulations–

(a)   to make the repayments to the Commissioners that they are required to make in pursuance of any provisions contained in any reimbursement arrangements by virtue of sub-paragraph (3)(b) or (c) above;

(b)   to comply with any requirements contained in any such arrangements by virtue of sub-paragraph (3)(d) above.

3(5)   Regulations under this paragraph may make provision for the form and manner in which, and the times at which, undertakings are to be given to the Commissioners in accordance with the regulations; and any such provision may allow for those matters to be determined by the Commissioners in accordance with the regulations.

3(6)   Regulations under this paragraph may–

(a)   contain any such incidental, supplementary, consequential or transitional provision as appears to the Commissioners to be necessary or expedient; and

(b)   make different provision for different circumstances.

3(7)   Regulations under this paragraph may have effect (irrespective of when the claim for repayment was made) for the purposes of the making of any repayment by the Commissioners after the time when the regulations are made; and, accordingly, such regulations may apply to arrangements made before that time.

3(8)   Regulations under this paragraph shall be made by statutory instrument subject to annulment in pursuance of a resolution of the House of Commons.

Statutory instruments – Insurance Premium Tax (Amendment) Regulations 1998 (SI 1998/60) are the regulations referred to in para. 3(1), (3), (4), (5), (6) and (7) and describe the provisions that must be included in reimbursement arrangements made by a person making a claim under FA 1997, Sch. 7, para. 8.

CONTRAVENTION OF REQUIREMENT TO REPAY COMMISSIONERS

4(1)   [Not relevant to insurance premium tax.]

4(2)   For the purposes of Schedule 7 to the Finance Act 1994 (insurance premium tax), a contravention or failure to comply with an obligation imposed by regulations made by virtue of paragraph 3(4) above shall be deemed, to the extent that it relates to amounts repaid under paragraph 8 of that Schedule (recovery of overpaid insurance premium tax), to be a failure to comply with a requirement falling within paragraph 17(1)(c) of that Schedule (breach of regulations).

4(3)   [Not relevant to insurance premium tax.]

Part II – Time Limits

REPAYMENTS

5(1)   [Not relevant to insurance premium tax.]

5(2)   [Substitutes FA 1994, Sch. 7, para. 8(4) for former para. 8(4) and (5).]

5(3)   *[Substitutes FA 1996, Sch. 5, para. 14(4).]*

ASSESSMENTS

6   [Amends FA 1994, Sch. 7, para. 26(1) and (4) and certain provisions relating to excise duties and landfill tax.]

Part III – Interest

INTEREST ON OVERPAID AIR PASSENGER DUTY

7   [Not relevant to insurance premium tax.]

8   [Not relevant to insurance premium tax]

INTEREST ON OVERPAID INSURANCE PREMIUM TAX

9(1)   Paragraph 22 of Schedule 7 to the Finance Act 1994 (interest payable by the Commissioners in connection with insurance premium tax) shall have effect, and be deemed always to have had effect, with the amendments for which this paragraph provides.

9(2)   [Inserts FA 1994, Sch. 7, para. 22(1A).]

9(3)   [Substitutes FA 1994, Sch. 7, para. 22(9).]

9(4)   [Substitutes FA 1994, Sch. 7, para. 22(10).]

10(1)   [Substitutes FA 1994, Sch. 7, para. 22(5), (5A) and (6) for former para. 22(5)–(7).]

10(2)   Sub-paragraph (1) above shall have effect for the purposes of determining whether any period beginning on or after the day on which this Act is passed is left out of account.

INTEREST ON OVERPAID LANDFILL TAX

11   [Not relevant to insurance premium tax.]

12   [Not relevant to insurance premium tax.]

Part IV – Set-off Involving Landfill Tax

13   [Not relevant to insurance premium tax.]

Part V – Recovery of Excess Payments by the Commissioners

ASSESSMENT FOR EXCESSIVE REPAYMENT

14(1)   Where–

(a)   any amount has been paid at any time to any person by way of a repayment under a relevant repayment provision, and

(b)   the amount paid exceeded the amount which the Commissioners were liable at that time to repay to that person,

the Commissioners may, to the best of their judgment, assess the excess paid to that person and notify it to him.

14(2)   Where any person is liable to pay any amount to the Commissioners in pursuance of an obligation imposed by virtue of paragraph 3(4)(a) above, the Commissioners may, to the best of their judgment, assess the amount due from that person and notify it to him.

14(3)   In this paragraph **"relevant repayment provision"** means–

(a)   [Not relevant to insurance premium tax.]

(b)   paragraph 8 of Schedule 7 to the Finance Act 1994 (recovery of overpaid insurance premium tax); or

(c)   [Not relevant to insurance premium tax.].

ASSESSMENT FOR OVERPAYMENTS OF INTEREST

15(1)   Where–

(a)   any amount has been paid to any person by way of interest under a relevant interest provision, but

(b)   that person was not entitled to that amount under that provision,

the Commissioners may, to the best of their judgment, assess the amount so paid to which that person was not entitled and notify it to him.

15(2)   In this paragraph **"relevant interest provision"** means–

(a)   paragraph 9 of Schedule 6 to the Finance Act 1994 (interest payable by the Commissioners on overpayments of air passenger duty);

(b)   paragraph 22 of Schedule 7 to that Act (interest payable by the Commissioners on overpayments etc. of insurance premium tax); or

(c)   paragraph 29 of Schedule 5 to the Finance Act 1996 (interest payable by the Commissioners on overpayments etc. of landfill tax).

ASSESSMENTS UNDER PARAGRAPHS 14 AND 15

16(1)   An assessment under paragraph 14 or 15 above shall not be made more than two years after the time when evidence of facts sufficient in the opinion of the Commissioners to justify the making of the assessment comes to the knowledge of the Commissioners.

16(2)   Where an amount has been assessed and notified to any person under paragraph 14 or 15 above, it shall be recoverable (subject to any provision having effect in accordance with paragraph 19 below) as if it were relevant tax due from him.

16(3)   Sub-paragraph (2) above does not have effect if, or to the extent that, the assessment in question has been withdrawn or reduced.

INTEREST ON AMOUNTS ASSESSED

17(1)   Where an assessment is made under paragraph 14 or 15 above, the whole of the amount assessed shall carry interest at the rate applicable under section 197 of the Finance Act 1996 from the date on which the assessment is notified until payment.

17(2)   Where any person is liable to interest under sub-paragraph (1) above the Commissioners may assess the amount due by way of interest and notify it to him.

17(3)   Without prejudice to the power to make assessments under this paragraph for later periods, the interest to which an assessment under this paragraph may relate shall be confined to interest for a period of no more than two years ending with the time when the assessment under this paragraph is made.

17(4)   Interest under this paragraph shall be paid without any deduction of income tax.

17(5)   A notice of assessment under this paragraph shall specify a date, being not later than the date of the notice, to which the amount of interest is calculated; and, if the interest continues to accrue after that date, a further assessment or assessments may be made under this paragraph in respect of amounts which so accrue.

17(6)   If, within such period as may be notified by the Commissioners to the person liable for interest under sub-paragraph (1) above, the amount referred to in that sub-paragraph is paid, it shall be treated for the purposes of that sub-paragraph as paid on the date specified as mentioned in sub-paragraph (5) above.

17(7)   Where an amount has been assessed and notified to any person under this paragraph it shall be recoverable as if it were relevant tax due from him.

17(8)   Sub-paragraph (7) above does not have effect if, or to the extent that, the assessment in question has been withdrawn or reduced.

Cross references – FA 1994, s. 197(2)(e): setting of interest rates.

SUPPLEMENTARY ASSESSMENTS

18   If it appears to the Commissioners that the amount which ought to have been assessed in an assessment under paragraph 14, 15 or 17 above exceeds the amount which was so assessed, then–

(a)   under the same paragraph as that assessment was made, and

(b)   on or before the last day on which that assessment could have been made,

the Commissioners may make a supplementary assessment of the amount of the excess and shall notify the person concerned accordingly.

REVIEW OF DECISIONS AND APPEALS

19(1)   [Not relevant to insurance premium tax.]

19(2)   Sections 59 and 60 of that Act of 1994 (review and appeal in the case of insurance premium tax) shall have effect in relation to any decision which–

(a)   is contained in an assessment under paragraph 14, 15 or 17 above,

(b)   is a decision about whether any amount is due to the Commissioners or about how much is due, and

(c)   is made in a case in which the relevant repayment provision is paragraph 8 of Schedule 7 to that Act or the relevant interest provision is paragraph 22 of that Schedule,

as if that decision were a decision to which section 59 of that Act applies.

19(3)   [Not relevant to insurance premium tax.]

INTERPRETATION OF PART V

20(1)   In this Part of this Schedule **"the Commissioners"** means the Commissioners of Customs and Excise.

20(2)   In this Part of this Schedule **"relevant tax"**, in relation to any assessment, means–

(a)   [Not relevant to insurance premium tax.]

(b)   insurance premium tax if the assessment relates to–
  (i)   a repayment of an amount paid by way of such tax,
  (ii) an overpayment of interest under paragraph 22 of Schedule 7 to the Finance Act 1994, or
  (iii) interest on an amount specified in an assessment in relation to which the relevant tax is insurance premium tax;
  and

(c)   [Not relevant to insurance premium tax.]

20(3)   For the purposes of this Part of this Schedule notification to a personal representative, trustee in bankruptcy, interim or permanent trustee, receiver, liquidator or person otherwise acting in a representative capacity in relation to another shall be treated as notification to the person in relation to whom he so acts.

CONSEQUENTIAL AMENDMENT

21   [Inserts FA 1996, s. 197(2)(e).]

SCHEDULE 18 – REPEALS

Section 113

Part V – INDIRECT TAXES

(2) DISTRESS AND DILIGENCE

Chapter	Short title	Extent of repeal
1994 c. 9.	The Finance Act 1994.	In Schedule 7, paragraph 7(7) to (12).

These repeals come into force on such day as the Commissioners of Customs and Excise may by order made by statutory instrument appoint, and different days may be appointed for different purposes.

Statutory instruments – Finance Act 1997 (Repeal of Distress and Diligence enactments) (Appointed Day) Order 1997 (SI 1997/1433) (C 55): the appointed day for Pt. V(2) is 1 July 1997.

FINANCE ACT 1998

(1998 Chapter 36)

[*31st July 1998*]

PART V – OTHER TAXES

INSURANCE PREMIUM TAX

146   Travel insurance: higher rate tax

146(1) [Substitutes FA 1994, Sch. 6A, para. 4.]

146(3) Except as provided by subsection (4) below, Sch. 6A, para. 4(1) and (2) above have effect in relation to a premium which falls to be regarded for the purposes of Part III of the Finance Act 1994 as received under a taxable insurance contract by an insurer on or after 1st August 1998.

146(4) Subsections (1) and (2) above do not have effect in relation to a premium if the premium–

(a)   is in respect of a contract made before 1st August 1998; and
(b)   falls, by virtue of regulations under section 68 of the Finance Act 1994 (special accounting scheme), to be regarded for the purposes of Part III of that Act as received under the contract by the insurer on a date before 1st February 1999.

146(5) In the application of sections 67A to 67C of the Finance Act 1994 in relation to the increase in insurance premium tax effected by this section and the exception from that increase–

(a)   the announcement relating to that increase, as described in section 67A(1), and to that exception, as described in section 67B(1), shall be taken to have been made on 17th March 1998;
(b)   "the date of the change" is 1st August 1998; and
(c)   "the concessionary date" is 1st February 1999.

147   Taxable intermediaries

147(1) Section 52A of the Finance Act 1994 (certain fees to be treated as premiums under higher rate contracts) shall be amended as follows.

147(2) [Amends FA 1994, s. 52A(5).]

147(3) [Substitutes FA 1994, s. 52A(6) and s. 52A(6A) for former s. 52A(6) and s. 52A(7).]

147(4) [Amends FA 1994, s.52A(9).]

147(5) The amendments made by this section have effect in relation to payments in respect of fees charged on or after 1st August 1998.

PART VI – MISCELLANEOUS AND SUPPLEMENTAL

Supplemental

165   Repeals

165(1) The enactments mentioned in Schedule 27 to this Act (which include spent provisions) are hereby repealed to the extent specified in the third column of that Schedule.

165(2) *The repeals specified* in that Schedule have effect subject to the commencement provisions and savings contained or referred to in the notes set out in that Schedule.

166   Short title

166 This Act may be cited as the Finance Act 1998.

SCHEDULES

SCHEDULE 27 – REPEALS
Part V – OTHER TAXES

(1) INSURANCE PREMIUM TAX

Chapter	Short title	Extent of repeal
1994 c. 9.	The Finance Act 1994.	In section 52A(9), the definition of "tour operator" and "travel agent".

This repeal has effect in accordance with section 147 of this Act.

FINANCE ACT 1999

(1999 Chapter 16)

[*27 July 1999*]

ARRANGEMENT OF SECTIONS

PART VII –
INSURANCE PREMIUM TAX

PART VII – PART VII - OTHER TAXES

INSURANCE PREMIUM TAX

125   Rate of insurance premium tax

125(1)   [Amends FA 1994, s. 51(2)(b).]

125(2)   Subsection (1) above has effect in relation to a premium which falls to be regarded for the purposes of Part III of the Finance Act 1994 (insurance premium tax) as received under a taxable insurance contract by an insurer on or after 1st July 1999.

125(3)   Subsection (1) above does not have effect in relation to a premium which–

(a)   is in respect of a contract made before 1st July 1999, and

(b)   falls to be regarded for the purposes of Part III of that Act as received under the contract by the insurer on a date before 1st January 2000, by virtue of regulations under section 68 of that Act (special accounting schemes).

125(4)   Subsection (3) above does not apply in relation to a premium which–

(a)   is an additional premium under a contract,

(b)   falls to be regarded for the purposes of Part III of that Act as received under the contract by the insurer on or after 1st July 1999, by virtue of regulations under section 68 of that Act, and

(c)   is in respect of a risk which was not covered by the contract before 1st July 1999.

125(5)   In the application of sections 67A to 67C of that Act (announced increase in rate of insurance premium tax) in relation to the increase under subsection (1) above and the exception under subsection (3) above–

(a)   the announcement for the purpose of sections 67A(1) and 67B(1) shall be taken to have been made on 9th March 1999,

(b)   the date of the change is 1st July 1999, and
(c)   the concessionary date is 1st January 2000.

INSURANCE PREMIUM TAX STATUTORY INSTRUMENTS

Table of Contents

> **Note:** Not all current statutory instruments are reproduced in full text in this division. If a current statutory instrument merely amends an existing Act or statutory instrument, then the existing Act or statutory instrument itself is amended and a history note is added thereto. The amending statutory instrument is not reproduced in this division, but it is listed below together with a note indicating its effect. Similarly, if a statutory instrument merely brings a current provision into operation, i.e. it is a commencement order or an appointed day order, then it is also listed below together with an appropriate note. If a statutory instrument only partly relates to insurance premium tax, only that part is reproduced.

INSURANCE PREMIUM TAX REGULATIONS 1994

(SI 1994/1774, as amended by SI 1995/1587, SI 1996/2099, SI 1997/1157, SI 1997/1431, SI 1998/60)

Made on 6 July 1994 by the Commissioners of Customs and Excise, in exercise of the powers conferred on them by s. 53(6), 54, 55(1)–(8), 57(15), 58(2) and (4), 62(1) and (3)–(7), 65(1)–(3), (5) and (7)–(13), 68(1)–(11) and 74(2), (7) and (8) of, and para. 1(1)–(3), 7(7) and (8) and 8(6) of Sch. 7 to, the Finance Act 1994. Operative from 1 August 1994.

ARRANGEMENT OF REGULATIONS

PART I – PRELIMINARY

CITATION AND COMMENCEMENT

1   These Regulations may be cited as the Insurance Premium Tax Regulations 1994 and shall come into force on 1st August 1994.

INTERPRETATION

2(1)   In these Regulations–

    "accounting period" means–

    (a)   in the case of a registered person, each period of three months ending on the dates notified to him by the Commissioners, whether by means of a certificate of registration issued by them or otherwise;

    (b)   in the case of a registrable person who is not registered, each quarter; or

    (c)   in the case of any registrable person, such other period in relation to which he is required by or under regulation 12 to make a return;

    and, in every case, the first accounting period of a registrable person shall commence on the effective date determined in accordance with section 53 or 53AA of the Act upon which the person was or should have been registered;

    "the Act" means Part III of the Finance Act 1994;

    "Collector" means a Collector, Deputy Collector or Assistant Collector of Customs and Excise;

    "Lloyd's" means the society incorporated by section 3 of Lloyd's Act 1871;

    "managing agent" has the same meaning as in section 12(1) of Lloyd's Act 1982;

    "registered person" means a person who is registered under section 53 or 53AA of the Act and, except in regulation 30, **"register"** and **"registration"** shall be construed accordingly;

    "registration number" means the unique identifying number allocated to a registered person and notified to him by the Commissioners;

    "return" means a return which is required to be made in accordance with regulation 12;

"**taxable intermediary's fees**" means fees which, to the extent of any payment in respect of them, are chargeable to tax by virtue of section 52A of the Finance Act 1994 and references in these regulations to "fee" or "fees" shall be construed accordingly;

"**underwriting member**" has the same meaning as in section 2(1) of Lloyd's Act 1982.

2(2)   Any reference in these Regulations to "**this Part**" is a reference to the Part of these Regulations in which that reference is made.

2(3)   Any reference in these Regulations to a form prescribed in the Schedule to these Regulations shall include a reference to a form which the Commissioners are satisfied is a form to the like effect.

History – In reg. 2(1), in the definition of "accounting period", the words "or 53AA" were inserted by SI 1997/1157, reg. 3(a), operative from 1 May 1997.
In reg. 2(1), in the definition of "registered person", the words "or 53AA" were inserted by SI 1997/1157, reg. 3(b), operative from 1 May 1997.
In reg. 2(1), the definition of "taxable intermediary's fees" was inserted by SI 1997/1157, reg. 3(c), operative from 1 May 1997.

REQUIREMENT, DIRECTION, DEMAND OR APPROVAL

3   Any requirement, direction, demand or approval by the Commissioners under or for the purposes of these Regulations shall be made or given by a notice in writing.

PART II – REGISTRATION AND PROVISIONS FOR SPECIAL CASES

Official publications – Notice IPT 1 (1998 edn): registering for IPT.

NOTIFICATION OF LIABILITY TO REGISTER

4(1)   A person who is required by section 53(2) of the Act to notify the Commissioners of the facts there mentioned shall do so on the form numbered 1 in the Schedule to these Regulations.

4(2)   Where the notification referred to in this regulation is made by a partnership, it shall include the particulars set out on the form numbered 2 in the Schedule to these Regulations.

4(3)   The notification referred to in this regulation shall be made within thirty days of the earliest date after 31st July 1994 on which the person either forms or continues to have the intention to receive premiums in the course of a taxable business.

NOTIFICATION OF LIABILITY TO REGISTER – TAXABLE INTERMEDIARIES

4A(1)   A person who is required by section 53AA(3) of the Act to notify the Commissioners of the facts there mentioned shall do so on the form numbered 1 in the Schedule to these Regulations.

4A(2)   Where the notification referred to in this regulation is made by a partnership, it shall include the particulars set out on the form numbered 2 in the Schedule to these Regulations.

4A(3)   The notification referred to in this regulation shall be made within thirty days of the earliest date after 30th April 1997 on which the person either forms or continues to have the intention to charge taxable intermediary's fees in the course of any business of his.

History – Reg. 4A was inserted by SI 1997/1157, reg. 4, operative from 1 May 1997.

CHANGES IN PARTICULARS

5(1)   A person who has made a notification under regulation 4 or 4A, whether or not it was made in accordance with paragraph (3) of regulation 4 or 4A above, shall, within thirty days of–

(a)   discovering any inaccuracy in; or

(b)   any change occurring which causes to become inaccurate,

any information contained in or provided with the notification, notify the Commissioners in writing and furnish them with full particulars thereof.

5(2)   Without prejudice to paragraph (1) above, a registrable person shall, within thirty days of any change occurring in any of the circumstances referred to in paragraph (4) below, notify the Commissioners in writing and furnish them with particulars of–

(a)   the change; and

(b)   the date on which the change occurred.

5(3)   A registrable person who discovers that any information contained in or provided with a notification under paragraph (2) above is inaccurate shall, within thirty days of his discovering the inaccuracy, notify the Commissioners and furnish them with particulars of–

(a)   the inaccuracy;

(b)   the date on which the inaccuracy was discovered;

(c)   why the information was inaccurate; and

(d)   the correct information.

5(4)   The circumstances mentioned in paragraph (2) above are the following circumstances relating to the registrable person, any insurance business carried on by him or any business in the course of which he charges taxable intermediary's fees–

(a)   his name, his trading name (if different) and address;

(b)   the name, the trading name (if different) and address of his tax representative;

(c)   his status, namely whether he carries on business as a sole proprietor, body corporate, partnership or other unincorporated body;

(d)   in the case of a partnership, the name and address of the partners;

(e)   in the case of a syndicate of underwriting members of Lloyd's which has been registered as such, the number or other identifying feature by reference to which it was registered.

5(5)   Where in relation to a registrable person the Commissioners are satisfied that any of the information recorded in the register kept under section 53 or 53AA of the Act is or has become inaccurate they may correct the register accordingly.

5(6)   For the purposes of paragraph (5) above it is immaterial whether or not the registrable person has made any notification he was required to make under this regulation.

History – In reg. 5(1), the words "or 4A" were inserted by SI 1997/1157, reg. 5(a), operative from 1 May 1997.
In reg. 5(1), the words "of regulation 4 or 4A above" were substituted for the words "of that regulation" by SI 1997/1157, reg. 5(a), operative from 1 May 1997.
In reg. 5(4), the words ", any insurance business carried ... intermediary's fees" were substituted for the words "or any insurance business carried on by him" by SI 1997/1157, reg. 5(b), operative from 1 May 1997.
In reg. 5(5), the words "or 53AA" were inserted by SI 1997/1157, reg. 5(c4), operative from 1 May 1997.
Reg. 5 was substituted by SI 1995/1587, reg. 3, operative from 17 July 1995.

NOTIFICATION OF LIABILITY TO BE DE-REGISTERED

6   A person who is required by section 53(3) of the Act to notify the Commissioners of the facts there mentioned shall, within thirty days of his having ceased to have the intention to receive premiums in the course of any taxable business, notify the Commissioners in writing and shall therein inform them of–

(a)   the date on which he ceased to have the intention of receiving premiums in the course of any taxable business; and

(b)   if different, the date on which the last such premium was received.

NOTIFICATION OF LIABILITY TO BE DE-REGISTERED – TAXABLE INTERMEDIARIES

6A   A person who is required by section 53AA(4) of the Act to notify the Commissioners of the facts there mentioned shall, within thirty days of his having ceased to have the intention of charging taxable intermediary's fees, give notice to the Commissioners in writing –

(a)   of the date on which he ceased to charge taxable intermediary's fees in the course of any business of his; and

(b)   if different, the date on which the last such fee was received.

History – Reg. 6A was inserted by SI 1997/1157, reg. 6, operative from 1 May 1997.

TRANSFER OF A GOING CONCERN

7(1)   Where–

(a)   a taxable business is transferred as a going concern;

(b)   the registration of the transferor has not already been cancelled;

(c)   as a result of the transfer of the business the registration of the transferor is to be cancelled and the transferee becomes liable to be registered; and

(d)   an application is made on the form numbered 3 in the Schedule to these Regulations by both the transferor and the transferee,

the Commissioners may with effect from the date of the transfer cancel the registration of the transferor and register the transferee with the registration number previously allocated to the transferor.

7(2)   An application under paragraph (1) above shall be treated as the notification referred to in regulation 6.

7(3)   Where the transferee of a business has been registered under paragraph (1) above with the registration number previously allocated to the transferor–

(a)   any liability of the transferor existing at the date of the transfer to make a return or account for or pay any tax under Part III of these Regulations shall become the liability of the transferee;

(b)   any entitlement of the transferor, whether or not existing at the date of the transfer, to credit or payment under Part IV of these Regulations shall become the entitlement of the transferee.

7(4)   In addition to the provisions set out in paragraph (3) above, where the transferee of a business has been registered under paragraph (1) above with the registration number previously allocated to the transferor during an accounting period subsequent to that in which the transfer took place (but with effect from the date of the transfer) and any–

(a)   return has been made;

(b)   tax has been accounted for; or

(c)   entitlement to credit has been claimed,

by either the transferor or the transferee, it shall be treated as having been done by the transferee.

7(5)   Where–

(a)   a taxable business is transferred as a going concern;

(b)   the transferee makes a payment to a person which represents the repayment of any premium or part of a premium received in the course of that business; and

(c)   the transferor has paid tax on that premium or part,

then, whether or not the transferee has been registered under paragraph (1) above with the registration number previously allocated to the transferor, any entitlement to credit under Part IV of these Regulations shall become the entitlement of the transferee.

REGISTRATION OF LLOYD'S SYNDICATES

8(1)   Where a taxable business is carried on by persons who are underwriting members of Lloyd's who are members of a syndicate of such underwriting members the registration of those persons for the purposes of the Act may be by reference to the syndicate; and, where such a syndicate is not known by any name, the registration may be by reference to any number or other identifying feature of the syndicate.

8(2)   In determining whether premiums are received by any syndicate which has been registered in the manner described in paragraph (1) above no account shall be taken of any change in the members of the syndicate.

Official publications – Notice IPT 2, Pt. 8 (1999): a general guide to IPT, arrangements for Lloyd's.

REPRESENTATION OF LLOYD'S SYNDICATES

9(1)   Anything required to be done by or under the Act (whether by these Regulations or otherwise) by or on behalf of a syndicate of underwriting members of Lloyd's shall be the joint and several responsibility of the persons mentioned in paragraph (2) below; but if it is done by any of those persons it shall be sufficient compliance with any such requirement.

9(2)   The persons are–

(a)   the underwriting members of the syndicate;

(b)   the managing agent of the syndicate; and

(c)   as regards any accounting period for which it is required by paragraph (3) below to act as the syndicate's representative, Lloyd's.

9(3)   Where a syndicate of underwriting members of Lloyd's has made an election that Lloyd's shall act as its representative Lloyd's shall so act in relation to any accounting period as regards which–

(a)   that election has effect;

(b)   the syndicate is registered as described in regulation 8; and

(c)   the scheme established by Part V of these Regulations applies to the syndicate.

9(4)   An election under paragraph (3) above shall be made in writing and shall specify the first accounting period of the syndicate in respect of which the election is to have effect, being an accounting period beginning on or after the date the election is made.

9(5)   Subject to paragraphs (6) and (7) below, an election under paragraph (3) above shall have effect for the accounting period specified in the election and all subsequent accounting periods.

9(6)   An election under paragraph (3) above shall not have effect unless written notification of the election is given to the Commissioners before the beginning of the accounting period specified in the election.

9(7)   An election under paragraph (3) above shall cease to have effect with effect from the accounting period specified in any notice in writing given by the syndicate to the Commissioners for this purpose, being an accounting period beginning after the date the notice is given.

REPRESENTATION OF UNINCORPORATED BODY

10(1)   Where anything is required to be done by or under the Act (whether by these Regulations or otherwise) by or on behalf of an unincorporated body other than a partnership, it shall be the joint and several responsibility of–

(a)   every member holding office as president, chairman, treasurer, secretary or any similar office; or

(b)   if there is no such office, every member holding office as a member of a committee by which the affairs of the body are managed; or

(c)   if there is no such office or committee, every member;

but, subject to paragraph (2) below, if it is done by any of the persons referred to above that shall be sufficient compliance with any such requirement.

10(2)   Where an unincorporated body other than a partnership is required to make any notification such as is referred to in regulations 4 to 6, it shall not be sufficient compliance unless the notification is made by a person upon whom a responsibility for making it is imposed by paragraph (1) above.

10(3)   Where anything is required to be done by or under the Act (whether by these Regulations or otherwise) by or on behalf of a partnership, it shall be the joint and several responsibility of every partner; but if it is done by one partner or, in the case of a partnership whose principal place of business is in Scotland, by any other person authorised by the partnership with respect thereto that shall be sufficient compliance with any such requirement.

DEATH, BANKRUPTCY OR INCAPACITY OF REGISTRABLE PERSONS

11(1)   If a registrable person dies or becomes bankrupt or incapacitated, the Commissioners may, from the date on which he died or became bankrupt or incapacitated, as the case may be, treat as a registrable person any person carrying on any taxable business of his or any business in the course of which he charged taxable intermediary's fees; and any legislation relating to insurance premium tax shall apply to any person so treated as though he were a registered person.

11(2)   Any person carrying on such business as aforesaid shall, within thirty days of commencing to do so, inform the Commissioners in writing of that fact and of the date of the death or bankruptcy or of the nature of the incapacity and the date on which it began.

11(3)   Where the Commissioners have treated a person carrying on a business as a registrable person under paragraph (1) above, they shall cease so to treat him if–

(a)   the registration of the registrable person is cancelled, whether or not any other person is registered with the registration number previously allocated to him;

(b)   the bankruptcy is discharged or the incapacity ceases; or

(c)   he ceases carrying on the business of the registrable person.

11(4)   *In relation to a registrable person which is a* company, the references in this regulation to the **registrable person becoming incapacitated** shall be construed as references to its going into liquidation or receivership or to an administration order being made in relation to it; and references to the incapacity ceasing shall be construed accordingly.

History – In reg. 11(1), the words "or any business ... intermediary's fees" were inserted by SI 1997/1157, reg. 7, operative from 1 May 1997.

PART III – ACCOUNTING, PAYMENT AND RECORDS

MAKING OF RETURNS

Official publications – Notice IPT 2, Pt. 6 (1999 edn): a general guide to IPT, accounting for IPT.

12(1) Subject to paragraphs (2) and (4) below and save as the Commissioners may otherwise allow, a registrable person shall, in respect of each accounting period, make a return to the Controller, Central Collection Unit (IPT) on the form numbered 4 in the Schedule to these Regulations.

12(2) Lloyd's may, in respect of any two or more syndicates of underwriting members of Lloyd's for which it is required by regulation 9(3) to act as representative as regards an accounting period which, as regards each syndicate, begins on the same date and ends on the same date, make a return on the form numbered 5 in the Schedule to these Regulations; and, provided it is accompanied by a summary schedule on the form numbered 6 in the Schedule to these Regulations, the making of a return under this paragraph shall be treated as sufficient compliance with paragraph (1) above in relation to the accounting period of each of the syndicates concerned.

12(3) Subject to paragraph (4) below, a registrable person shall make each return not later than the last day of the month next following the end of the period to which it relates.

12(4) Where the Commissioners consider it necessary in the circumstances of any particular case, they may–

(a) vary the length of any accounting period or the date on which it begins or ends or by which any return must be made;

(b) allow or direct the registrable person to make a return in accordance with sub-paragraph (a) above;

(c) allow or direct a registrable person to make returns to a specified address;

and any person to whom the Commissioners give any direction such as is referred to in this regulation shall comply therewith.

CORRECTION OF ERRORS

13(1) In this regulation–

"credit" means credit to which a person is entitled under Part IV of these Regulations;

"overdeclaration" means, in relation to any return, the amount (if any) which was wrongly treated as tax due for the accounting period concerned and which caused either the amount of tax which was payable to be overstated or the entitlement to a payment under regulation 19(1) to be understated or both or would have caused such an overstatement or understatement were it not for the existence of an underdeclaration in relation to that return;

"underdeclaration" means, in relation to any return, the aggregate of–

(a) the amount (if any) of tax due for the accounting period concerned which was not taken into account; and

(b) the amount (if any) which was wrongly deducted as credit,

and which caused either the amount of tax which was payable to be understated or the entitlement to a payment under regulation 19(1) to be overstated or both or would have caused such an understatement or overstatement were it not for the existence of an overdeclaration in relation to that return.

13(2) This regulation applies where a registrable person has made a return which was inaccurate as the result of an overdeclaration or underdeclaration.

13(3) Where, in relation to any overdeclarations or underdeclarations that are discovered by the registrable person in an accounting period–

(a) the total of the overdeclarations discovered does not exceed £2,000, he may enter that total in the box opposite the legend "Overdeclarations from previous periods" in the return for that accounting period;

(b) the total of the underdeclarations discovered does not exceed £2,000, he may enter that total in the box opposite the legend "Underdeclarations from previous periods" in the return for that accounting period;

and, where he does so, he shall calculate the tax payable by him or the payment to which he is entitled accordingly.

13(4) Where the return for the accounting period in which the overdeclaration or underdeclaration was discovered is made by Lloyd's in accordance with regulation 12(2), paragraph (3) above shall apply as if the references to the totals of the overdeclarations or underdeclarations not exceeding £2,000 were references to each such total for each syndicate in respect of which the return is made not exceeding £2,000.

13(5) No amount shall be entered in any return in respect of any overdeclaration or underdeclaration except in accordance with this regulation.

13(6) Where any amount has been entered in a return in accordance with this regulation, that return shall be regarded as correcting any earlier return to which that amount relates.

CLAIMS FOR OVERPAID TAX

14 Except where the amount to which the claim relates has been entered in a return in accordance with regulation 13 or is included in an amount so entered, any claim under paragraph 8 of Schedule 7 to the Act shall be made in writing to the Commissioners and shall, by reference to such documentary evidence as is in the possession of the claimant, state the amount of the claim and the method by which that amount was calculated.

PAYMENT OF TAX

15 Save as the Commissioners may otherwise allow or direct, any person required to make a return shall pay to the Controller, Central Collection Unit (IPT) such amount of tax as is payable by him in respect of the accounting period to which the return relates no later than the last day on which he was required to make the return.

RECORDS

16(1) Every registrable person shall, for the purpose of accounting for tax, keep and preserve the following–

(a)　his business and accounting records;

(b)　policy documents, cover notes, endorsements and similar documents, and copies of such documents that are issued by him;

(c)　copies of all invoices, renewal notices and similar documents issued by him;

(d)　all credit or debit notes or other documents received by him which evidence an increase or decrease in the amount of any premium or fee, and copies of such documents that are issued by him;

(e)　such other records as the Commissioners may specify in a notice published by them and not withdrawn by them.

16(2) Every registrable person shall keep and preserve the records specified in paragraph (1) above for a period of six years.

16(3) The reference in paragraph (1)(d) above to **any premium** shall be construed for the purposes of that paragraph as it would be construed for the purposes of Part V of these Regulations.

History – In reg. 16(1)(d), the words "or fee" were inserted by SI 1997/1157, reg. 8, operative from 1 May 1997.

PART IV – CLAIMS IN RESPECT OF CREDIT

SCOPE

17(1) This Part applies where–

(a)　an insurer has paid tax and all or part of the premium on which the tax was charged is repaid; or

(b)　a taxable intermediary has paid tax and all or part of the fee on which the tax was charged is repaid.

17(2) *Where–*

(a)　an insurer receives a premium in an accounting period and repays that premium or part of it in that accounting period; or

(b)　a taxable intermediary receives a fee in an accounting period and repays that fee or part of it in that accounting period, this Part shall apply as if the tax on the premium or fee (as the case may be) had already been paid by him.

17(3)   This Part applies subject to regulation 7.

History – Reg. 17(1) and (2) were substituted by SI 1997/1157, reg. 9, operative from 1 May 1997. Former reg. 17(1) and (2) read as follows:
"**17(1)**   This Part applies where an insurer has paid tax and all or part of the premium on which the tax was charged is repaid.
17(2)   Where an insurer receives a premium in an accounting period and repays that premium or part of it in that accounting period, this Part shall apply as if the tax on the premium had already been paid by him."

CLAIMS IN RETURNS

18(1)   Where this Part applies, the insurer or, as the case may be, taxable intermediary shall be entitled to credit of an amount which represents the difference between the amount of tax paid by him and the amount of tax he would have been liable to pay had the premium or fee received by him been reduced or extinguished, as the case may be, by the amount of the repayment.

18(2)   Subject to paragraph (3) below, an insurer or taxable intermediary who is entitled to credit under this Part may claim it by deducting its amount from any tax due from him for the accounting period in which the premium or fee was repaid or any subsequent accounting period and, where he does so, he shall make his return for that accounting period accordingly.

18(3)   Where the Commissioners have given a special or general direction under section 55(5) of the Act prescribing rules according to which any credit may or shall be held over to an accounting period subsequent to that in which the premium or fee, or part of such premium or fee was repaid, that credit, subject to any subsequent such direction varying or withdrawing the rules, may only be claimed in accordance with those rules.

History – In reg. 18(1), the words "or, as the case may be, taxable intermediary" were inserted by SI 1997/1157, reg. 10(a)(i), operative from 1 May 1997.
In reg. 18(1), the words "or fee" were inserted by SI 1997/1157, reg. 10(a)(ii), operative from 1 May 1997.
In reg. 18(2), the words "or taxable intermediary" were inserted by SI 1997/1157, reg. 10(b)(i), operative from 1 May 1997.
In reg. 18(2), the words "or fee" were inserted by SI 1997/1157, reg. 10(b)(ii), operative from 1 May 1997.
In reg. 18(3), the words "premium or fee, or part of such premium or fee" were substituted for the words "premium or part" by SI 1997/1157, reg. 10(c), operative from 1 May 1997.

PAYMENTS IN RESPECT OF CREDIT

19(1)   Subject to paragraph (5) below, where the total credit claimed by the insurer or taxable intermediary in accordance with this Part exceeds the total of the tax due from him for the accounting period, the Commissioners shall pay to him an amount equal to the excess.

19(2)   Where the Commissioners have cancelled the registration of an insurer or taxable intermediary in accordance with section 53(5) or 53AA(6) of the Act, and he is not a registrable person, he shall make any claim in respect of credit to which this Part applies by making an application in writing.

19(3)   An insurer or taxable intermediary making an application under paragraph (2) above shall furnish to the Commissioners full particulars in relation to the credit claimed, including (but not restricted to)–

(a)   the return in which the relevant tax was accounted for;

(b)   the date and manner of payment of that tax;

(c)   the date of the repayment of the premium or fee, or part of such premium or fee; and

(d)   the amounts of both the tax which was paid and the repayment.

19(4)   Subject to paragraph (5) below, where the Commissioners are satisfied that the insurer or taxable intermediary as the case may be, is entitled to credit as claimed by him, and that he has not previously had the benefit of that credit, they shall pay to him an amount equal to the credit.

19(5)   *The Commissioners shall* not be liable to make any payment under this regulation unless and until the insurer or taxable intermediary has made all the returns which he was required to make.

History – In reg. 19(1), the words "or taxable intermediary" were inserted by SI 1997/1157, reg. 11(a), operative from 1 May 1997.
In reg. 19(2), the words "or taxable intermediary" and "or 53AA(6)" were inserted by SI 1997/1157, reg. 11(b), operative from 1 May 1997.
In reg. 19(3), the words "or taxable intermediary" were inserted by SI 1997/1157, reg. 11(c)(i), operative from 1 May 1997.
In reg. 19(3)(c), the words "premium or fee, or part of such premium or fee" were substituted for the words "premium or part" by SI 1997/1157, reg. 11(c)(ii), operative from 1 May 1997.
In reg. 19(4), the words "or taxable intermediary as the case may be," were inserted by SI 1997/1157, reg. 11(d), operative from 1 May 1997.
In reg. 19(5), the words "or taxable intermediary" were inserted by SI 1997/1157, reg. 11(e), operative from 1 May 1997.

PART IVA – REIMBURSEMENT ARRANGEMENTS

INTERPRETATION OF PART IVA

19A   In this Part–

"**claim**" means a claim made (irrespective of when it was made) under paragraph 8 of Schedule 7 to the Act for repayment of an amount paid to the Commissioners by way of tax which was not tax due to them; and "**claimed**" and "**claimant**" shall be construed accordingly;

"**reimbursement arrangements**" means any arrangements (whether made before, on or after 30th January 1998) for the purposes of a claim which–

(a)   are made by a claimant for the purpose of securing that he is not unjustly enriched by the repayment of any amount in pursuance of the claim; and

(b)   provide for the reimbursement of persons (consumers) who have, for practical purposes, borne the whole or any part of the cost of the original payment of that amount to the Commissioners;

"**relevant amount**" means that part (which may be the whole) of the amount of a claim which the claimant has reimbursed or intends to reimburse to consumers.

History – Reg. 19A was inserted by SI 1998/60, reg. 2, operative from 11 February 1998.

REIMBURSEMENT ARRANGEMENTS – GENERAL

19B   Without prejudice to regulation 19H below, for the purposes of paragraph 8(3) of Schedule 7 to the Act (defence by the Commissioners that repayment by them of an amount claimed would unjustly enrich the claimant) reimbursement arrangements made by a claimant shall be disregarded except where they–

(a)   include the provisions described in regulation 19C below; and

(b)   are supported by the undertakings described in regulation 19G below.

History – Reg. 19B was inserted by SI 1998/60, reg. 2, operative from 11 February 1998.

REIMBURSEMENT ARRANGEMENTS – PROVISIONS TO BE INCLUDED

19C   The provisions referred to in regulation 19B(a) above are that–

(a)   reimbursement for which the arrangements provide will be completed by no later than 90 days after the repayment to which it relates;

(b)   no deduction will be made from the relevant amount by way of fee or charge (howsoever expressed or effected);

(c)   reimbursement will be made only in cash or by cheque;

(d)   any part of the relevant amount that is not reimbursed by the time mentioned in paragraph (a) above will be repaid by the claimant to the Commissioners;

(e)   any interest paid by the Commissioners on any relevant amount repaid by them will also be treated by the claimant in the same way as the relevant amount falls to be treated under paragraphs (a) and (b) above; and

(f)   the records described in regulation 19E below will be kept by the claimant and produced by him to the Commissioners, or to an officer of theirs in accordance with regulation 19F below.

History – Reg. 19C was inserted by SI 1998/60, reg. 2, operative from 11 February 1998.

REPAYMENTS TO THE COMMISSIONERS

19D   The claimant shall, without prior demand, make any repayment to the Commissioners that he is required to make by virtue of regulation 19C(d) and (e) above within 14 days of the expiration of the period of 90 days referred to in regulation 19C(a) above.

History – Reg. 19D was inserted by SI 1998/60, reg. 2, operative from 11 February 1998.

RECORDS

19E   The claimant shall keep records of the following matters–

(a)   the names and addresses of those consumers whom he has reimbursed or whom he intends to reimburse;

(b)   the total amount reimbursed to each such consumer;

(c)   the amount of interest included in each total amount reimbursed to each consumer;

(d)   the date that each reimbursement is made.

History – Reg. 19E was inserted by SI 1998/60, reg. 2, operative from 11 February 1998.

PRODUCTION OF RECORDS

19F(1)   Where a claimant is given notice in accordance with paragraph (2) below, he shall, in accordance with such notice produce to the Commissioners, or to an officer of theirs, the records that he is required to keep pursuant to regulation 19E above.

19F(2)   A notice given for the purposes of paragraph (1) above shall–

(a)   be in writing;

(b)   state the place and time at which, and the date on which the records are to be produced; and

(c)   be signed and dated by the Commissioners, or by an officer of theirs,
          and may be given before or after, or both before and after the Commissioners have paid the relevant amount to the claimant.

History – Reg. 19F was inserted by SI 1998/60, reg. 2, operative from 11 February 1998.

UNDERTAKINGS

19G(1)   Without prejudice to regulation 19H(b) below, the undertakings referred to in regulation 19B(b) above shall be given to the Commissioners by the claimant no later than the time at which he makes the claim for which the reimbursement arrangements have been made.

19G(2)   The undertakings shall be in writing, shall be signed and dated by the claimant, and shall be to the effect that–

(a)   at the date of the undertakings he is able to identify the names and addresses of those consumers whom he has reimbursed or whom he intends to reimburse;

(b)   he will apply the whole of the relevant amount repaid to him, without any deduction by way of fee or charge or otherwise, to the reimbursement in cash or by cheque, of such consumers by no later than 90 days after his receipt of that amount (except insofar as he has already so reimbursed them);

(c)   he will apply any interest paid to him on the relevant amount repaid to him wholly to the reimbursement of such consumers by no later than 90 days after his receipt of that interest;

(d)   he will repay to the Commissioners without demand the whole or such part of the relevant amount repaid to him or of any interest paid to him as he fails to apply in accordance with the undertakings mentioned in sub- paragraphs (b) and (c) above;

(e)   he will keep the records described in regulation 19E above; and

(f)   he will comply with any notice given to him in accordance with regulation 19F above concerning the production of such records.

History – Reg. 19G was inserted by SI 1998/60, reg. 2, operative from 11 February 1998.

REIMBURSEMENT ARRANGEMENTS MADE BEFORE 11TH FEBRUARY 1998

19H   Reimbursement arrangements made by a claimant before 11th February 1998 shall not be disregarded for the purposes of paragraph 8(3) of Schedule 7 to the Act if; not later than 11th March 1998–

(a)   he includes in those arrangements (if they are not already included) the provisions described in regulation 19C above; and

(b)   gives the undertakings described in regulation 19G above.

History – Reg. 19H was inserted by SI 1998/60, reg. 2, operative from 11 February 1998.

PART V – SPECIAL ACCOUNTING SCHEME

INTERPRETATION

20(1)   In this Part–

"**date of receipt**", in relation to any premium, means the date on which apart from the operation of the scheme the premium is received or taken to be received by the provisions of the Act;

"**initial period**" means the first of the accounting periods which begin on or after the date specified in a notification made under regulation 21(1);

"**premium written date**", in relation to any premium, means the date as at which the insurer makes an entry in his accounts showing the premium as due to him.

20(2) Any reference in this Part to the **accounts of any person** shall be construed as a reference to—

(a) the books, accounts or other similar records which he maintains in whatever form for the purpose of enabling him to show the premiums receivable by him in the revenue account he is required to prepare by section 17(1) of the Insurance Companies Act 1982; and **"premiums receivable"** has the same meaning as in regulation 3 of the Insurance Companies (Accounts and Statements) Regulations 1983; or

(b) where he is not required to prepare the revenue account referred to in sub-paragraph (a) above, any books, accounts or other records which would enable him to prepare one.

20(3) Any reference in this Part to **a premium** shall be construed as including a reference to anything that, although not actually received by or on behalf of an insurer, would be a premium if it were so received.

20(4) In deciding whether and (if it does) how the scheme applies to an accounting period of an insurer to whom the scheme has previously applied as regards one or more accounting periods ending before the beginning of the initial period specified in a notification he has made under regulation 21(1), the fact of such previous application of the scheme shall be ignored.

NOTIFICATION BY INSURER THAT SCHEME TO APPLY

21(1) An insurer who is a registrable person and—

(a) is required to prepare the revenue account referred to in regulation 20(2)(a); or

(b) not being required to prepare such a revenue account, keeps accounts as described in regulation 20(2)(b),

may notify the Commissioners in writing that the scheme should apply to him as regards accounting periods beginning on or after a date specified in the notification, being a date falling after the date the notification is made.

21(2) An insurer who has made a notification under paragraph (1) above may notify the Commissioners in writing that he wishes to withdraw the notification and, provided he makes the notification referred to in this paragraph no later than the last day by which he is required to make the return for the initial period and before he has made that return, the scheme shall not apply to him as regards any accounting period.

21(3) The fact that an insurer has on a previous occasion withdrawn or been expelled from the scheme under regulation 26 or 27 or withdrawn a notification under paragraph (2) above shall not prevent him making a notification under paragraph (1) above.

RELEVANT ACCOUNTING PERIODS

22 Subject to regulations 21(2), 26 and 27, the scheme shall apply as regards all the accounting periods of an insurer who has made a notification under regulation 21(1) with effect from the initial period.

PREMIUMS TREATED AS RECEIVED ON PREMIUM WRITTEN DATE

23(1) Subject to paragraph (8) below, any premium in relation to which—

(a) an insurer has made an entry in his accounts showing the premium as due to him;

(b) the premium written date falls within a relevant accounting period; and

(c) the date of receipt does not fall within an accounting period which is earlier than the initial period and which is not a relevant accounting period,

shall be treated for the purposes of the Act as received by the insurer on the premium written date; and the insurer shall account for tax due in respect of the relevant accounting period concerned accordingly.

23(2) Paragraph (1) above shall apply even if the premium or any part of it is never actually received by the insurer; and, where it is never actually received because the contract under which it is or would have been received is terminated or is not entered into, the premium shall nonetheless be taken for the purposes of the Act to have been received under the contract (including, where appropriate, a taxable insurance contract) under which the insurer treated it as due.

23(3) Where in relation to any premium to which paragraph (1) above applies the premium written date is a date other than the date of receipt, the premium shall be treated for the purposes of the Act as not having been received by the insurer on the date of receipt; but this is subject to paragraph (4) below.

23(4) Paragraph (3) above shall not apply to any excess which falls to be treated as a separate premium in accordance with regulation 24(2).

23(5) An insurer to whom the scheme applies as regards an accounting period may assume that the scheme will apply as regards all subsequent accounting periods and account for tax due in respect of that period accordingly.

23(6) Subject to paragraph (7) below, where in relation to a premium–

(a)   the premium written date falls before 1st October 1994;

(b)   the premium was actually received by the insurer on or after 1st October 1994; and

(c)   the contract under which the premium was received is not a contract to which, if the premium had actually been received on the premium written date, section 67(3) of the Act would have applied,

the premium shall be treated for the purposes of the Act as received before 1st October 1994 and the insurer shall accordingly not account for any tax on that premium.

23(7) Paragraph (6) above shall not apply to any premium where–

(a)   the contract under which the premium was received relates to a risk the period of cover for which begins on or after 1st October 1994; and

(b)   it is not the normal practice as regards the class of contract to which that contract belongs for an insurer to make an entry in his accounts showing the premium as due as at a date before the period of cover begins.

23(8) Where the initial period begins on 1st October 1994, nothing in this regulation shall be taken as requiring a premium–

(a)   which was actually received by the insurer before 1st October 1994;

(b)   in respect of which the premium written date falls within a relevant accounting period;

(c)   which is not taken by virtue of section 67 of the Act to be received on 1st October 1994; and

(d)   which was received under a contract which relates to a risk the period of cover for which begins before 1st October 1994,

to be treated as received on a date other than the date of receipt.

23(9) Where in relation to any premium–

(a)   an insurer has made an entry in his accounts showing the premium as due to him;

(b)   the entry was made on a date falling within a relevant accounting period; and

(c)   the premium written date would, apart from this paragraph, fall in a relevant accounting period which is earlier than the accounting period referred to in paragraph (b) above,

the insurer shall be treated for the purposes of this regulation as if he had made the entry showing the premium as due to him as at the date on which the entry was made and that date (and no other date) shall be the premium written date accordingly.

AMOUNT OF PREMIUM

24(1) Subject to any direction made under section 66 of the Act, where in relation to any premium to which regulation 23(1) applies the amount which is entered in the accounts as due (the initial amount) is not the amount which is or would be found apart from the operation of the scheme to be the amount of the premium in accordance with the provisions of the Act the amount of the premium shall be taken to be the initial amount.

24(2) Where paragraph (1) above applies and the amount of the premium which is received exceeds the initial amount, the excess shall be treated as a separate premium and shall be treated as received on a date determined in accordance with paragraphs (3) and (4) below.

24(3) Where an amount of premium is treated as a separate premium in accordance with paragraph (2) above and–

(a)   the initial amount is not less than the amount which has been agreed with the insured by the insurer or his agent as the amount which, as at the date the entry is made, is due under the contract; and

(b)   the insurer makes an entry in his accounts showing the excess as due,

it shall be treated as received on the date he makes that entry in his accounts.

24(4)   In any case where an amount of premium is treated as a separate premium in accordance with paragraph (2) above and paragraph (3) above does not apply, the excess shall be treated as received on the date as at which the initial amount is entered in the accounts as due.

24(5)   An insurer who intends to enter in his accounts as due any excess over the initial amount of any premium which, if he were to make such an entry, would be treated as received on a date determined in accordance with paragraph (3) above may assume that it will be so treated until such time as he ceases to have that intention.

24(6)   Where in relation to an amount of premium which is treated as a separate premium in accordance with paragraph (2) above the date of receipt is a date other than the date determined in accordance with paragraphs (3) and (4) above, it shall be treated as not having been received by the insurer on the date of receipt.

CREDIT

25(1)   Subject to paragraph (2) below, where tax has been paid–

(a)   in respect of a premium to which regulation 24(1) applies and the initial amount exceeds the amount which is or would be found apart from the operation of the scheme to be the amount of the premium in accordance with the provisions of the Act; or

(b)   in respect of a premium or part of a premium which has not been received,

then, if it is shown to the satisfaction of the Commissioners that that excess, premium or part, as the case may be, will never actually be received, the amount of that excess, premium or part shall be treated as an amount of premium which the insurer has repaid on the date upon which the Commissioners are so satisfied and he shall be entitled to credit for the amount concerned in accordance with Part IV of these Regulations.

25(2)   It shall be a condition of any claim being made by an insurer in reliance upon paragraph (1) above that, if the excess, premium or part (as the case may be) or any part thereof is in fact received by the insurer, he shall pay to the Commissioners an amount equal to the tax chargeable on the amount received; and any amount which the insurer is liable to pay under this paragraph shall be treated as tax due for the accounting period in which the amount of excess or premium was received.

Extra-statutory concessions – 3.29 (Notice 48 (1999 edn)): special accounting scheme – introductory provisions.

WITHDRAWAL FROM THE SCHEME

26(1)   An insurer may notify the Commissioners in writing that the scheme should not apply to him as regards accounting periods beginning on or after a date specified in the notification (being a date falling after the date the notification is made) and the scheme shall cease to apply to him accordingly.

26(2)   The scheme shall nonetheless continue to apply to an insurer who has made a notification under paragraph (1) above unless and until–

(a)   he has made all the returns which he was required to make;

(b)   he has paid all the tax which was payable in respect of the accounting periods for which he was required to make those returns; and

(c)   the scheme has applied as regards such number of relevant accounting periods as is required in order for the scheme to have applied to him for a period of not less than twelve consecutive months beginning with the first day of the initial period;

and, when he has complied with sub-paragraphs (a) to (c) above and with any requirement to make returns or pay tax arising since the date the notification was made, the scheme shall cease to apply with effect from the first of his accounting periods which begin on or after the date of such compliance.

EXPULSION FROM THE SCHEME

27(1)   In any case where the Commissioners consider it necessary for the protection of the revenue, including (but not restricted to) a case where the revenue is prejudiced by reason of the premium written date in relation to premiums falling in accounting periods later than those in which falls the date of receipt, they may give notice to an insurer who has made the notification under regulation 21(1) that the scheme is not to apply to him; and the scheme shall accordingly not apply or cease to apply, as the case may be.

27(2)   Where a notice is given under paragraph (1) above before the last day of the initial period, the scheme shall not apply to any of the accounting periods of the insurer.

27(3) Where a notice is given under paragraph (1) above on or after the last day of the initial period, the notice shall specify the accounting period of the insurer with effect from which the scheme is not to apply to him, being an accounting period the last day of which falls after the date the notice is given.

TAX TO BE ACCOUNTED FOR ON CESSATION

28(1) Where the scheme has ceased to apply to an insurer by virtue of regulation 26 or 27, he shall account for and pay any tax chargeable on premiums in relation to which the date of receipt falls within a relevant accounting period and for which he has not accounted and which he has not paid in reliance upon the assumption referred to in regulation 23(5) as if the premiums were received in the accounting period with effect from which the scheme has ceased to apply to him.

28(2) Where the Commissioners have cancelled the registration of an insurer and the last of his accounting periods is a relevant accounting period, paragraph (1) above shall apply as if–

(a) the scheme had ceased to apply to him by virtue of regulation 26 or 27; and

(b) the reference to the accounting period with effect from which the scheme has ceased to apply to him were a reference to the last of his accounting periods.

PART VI – TAX REPRESENTATIVES

Official publications – Notice IPT 2, Pt. 9 (1999 edn): a general guide to IPT, tax representatives.

NOTIFICATION IN CERTAIN CASES

29(1) Where the Commissioners approve a person as an insurer's taxable intermediary's tax representative in a case where action has been taken as mentioned in section 57(4) of the Act or a request has been made as mentioned in section 57(10) of the Act, as the case may be, they shall be taken to have given such approval on the date they serve on the insurer taxable intermediary a notice in writing confirming their approval or on such later date as may be specified in the notice.

29(2) Where the Commissioners inform an insurer taxable intermediary that they have received a notification such as is referred to in section 57(8) of the Act, they shall be taken to have so informed him on the date they serve on him a notice in writing to that effect.

29(3) Where the Commissioners make a direction such as is described in section 57(11) of the Act, they shall be taken to have made the direction–

(a) on the date they serve on both the insurer or, as the case may be taxable intermediary, and the person who is to be his tax representative a notice in writing confirming that that person shall be his tax representative;

(b) where such notices are served on different dates, the later of them; or

(c) where such notices specify a date falling after the date on which the later of them is served, the date specified in the notices.

History – In reg. 29(1), the words "taxable intermediary's" and the words "taxable intermediary" were inserted by SI 1997/1157, reg. 12(a), operative from 1 May 1997.
In reg. 29(2), the words "taxable intermediary" were inserted by SI 1997/1157, reg. 12(b), operative from 1 May 1997.
In reg. 29(3), the words "or, as the case may be taxable intermediary," were inserted by SI 1997/1157, reg. 12(c), operative from 1 May 1997.

REGISTRATION

30(1) The Commissioners shall register alongside the name of an insurer or taxable intermediary the name of any tax representative of his for the time being.

30(2) Where the Commissioners withdraw their approval of a tax representative who has been registered by them under paragraph (1) above, they shall cancel that registration.

History – In reg. 30(1), the words "or taxable intermediary" were inserted by SI 1997/1157, reg. 13, operative from 1 May 1997.

LIABILITY TO NOTIFY

31 A tax representative shall not–

(a) be jointly and severally liable with the insurer or taxable intermediary; or

(b) be required to secure the insurer's or taxable intermediary's compliance with or the discharge of his obligation, in relation to any requirement that the insurer or taxable intermediary make a notification such as is referred to in regulation 4 or 6.

History – In reg. 31, the words "or taxable intermediary" were inserted in two places and the words "or taxable intermediary's" were inserted in one place by SI 1997/1157, reg. 14, operative from 1 May 1997.

PART VII – LIABILITY OF INSURED PERSONS

INTERPRETATION

32 In this Part–

"**contract**" means a taxable insurance contract;

"**liability notice**" means a notice served under regulation 34;

"**material date**" has the same meaning as in section 65(4) of the Act;

"**tax debt**" means a liability to pay an amount which is tax or is deemed to be or recoverable as if it were tax which, at the time of any payment, has not been discharged.

SCOPE

33 This Part applies where–

(a) an insurer who is a registrable person does not have any business establishment or other fixed establishment in the United Kingdom, and

(b) no person is that insurer's tax representative by virtue of section 57 of the Act.

LIABILITY NOTICES

34 Where this Part applies, the Commissioners may serve a notice on the person who is insured under a contract or, where there are two or more such persons, one or more of them.

POWER TO ASSESS TAX DUE

35(1) This regulation applies where–

(a) the Commissioners have served a liability notice or notices; and

(b) the insurer–

(i) has failed to make any return he was required to make or any such return appears to the Commissioners to be incomplete or incorrect; or

(ii) has failed to pay any tax or amount deemed to be tax, including an amount which he was liable to pay by virtue of this Part.

35(2) Where this regulation applies–

(a) the Commissioners may assess to the best of their judgment the amount of any tax due in respect of premiums received by the insurer under the contract after the material date and before the date of the assessment; and

(b) the amount so assessed shall be deemed to be the amount of tax due in respect of that contract for the period by reference to which the assessment is made.

PERSONS LIABLE FOR TAX ASSESSED

36(1) Where the Commissioners make an assessment under regulation 35 and notify it to the insured person, or each of the insured persons, on whom a liability notice in respect of the contract has been served–

(a) the insurer; and

(b) the insured persons mentioned in this regulation,

shall be jointly and severally liable to pay the amount of tax assessed, to the extent that the assessment has not subsequently been reduced or withdrawn, and that tax shall be recoverable accordingly.

36(2) An insured person who has been notified of an assessment made under regulation 35 shall be liable in accordance with this regulation to pay the tax so assessed notwithstanding that he has already paid an amount representing that tax or any part of it as part of a premium.

ADJUSTMENT OF ASSESSMENTS

37(1) Where–

(a) an amount of tax has been assessed under regulation 35; and

(b) the amount of that tax, or any part of it, has also been assessed under section 56 of the Act and notified to the insurer,

the assessment which has been made under regulation 35 shall be treated as reduced to the extent that the amount referred to in sub-paragraph (b) above has been included in the amount thereof.

37(2) Where an assessment such as is referred to in paragraph (1)(a) or (b) above is subsequently withdrawn, that paragraph shall not apply; and where the assessment is reduced, it shall apply as if any reference to the amount of tax which has been assessed were a reference to the reduced amount.

TIME FOR PAYMENT

38 Any insured person who is liable to pay an amount of tax which has been assessed under regulation 35 shall do so no later than thirty days after the date on which it was notified to him.

INTEREST ON REIMBURSEMENTS

39(1) Where an insurer is liable by virtue of section 65(9) of the Act to pay to an insured person an amount equal to the amount which has been recovered from him, then, if and to the extent that the insurer would not be liable to do so apart from this regulation, he shall pay interest to him.

39(2) The interest payable under paragraph (1) above shall be paid at the rate of 8 per cent per annum for the period beginning with the date on which the amount was recovered from the insured person and ending with the date the insurer paid to him an amount equal to that amount.

ALLOCATION OF PAYMENTS

40(1) This regulation applies where an insurer pays an amount of tax to the Commissioners and–

(a) at the time of the payment there exists a tax debt of his by virtue of his being liable to pay tax which has been assessed under regulation 35;

(b) at the time of the payment there exists a tax debt of his which–

    (i) is not within sub-paragraph (a) above; and

    (ii) relates to an accounting period which corresponds to any extent with the period by reference to which the assessment referred to in sub-paragraph (a) above was made; and

(c) the amount of the payment is not sufficient to satisfy all his tax debts in full.

40(2) Where this regulation applies and the payment would not otherwise be applied as described in this paragraph, the payment shall be applied to reduce or extinguish the tax debt within paragraph (1)(a) above before it is applied to any other tax debt.

40(3) Where–

(a) this regulation applies;

(b) there are two or more tax debts within paragraph (1)(a) above; and

(c) the payment is not sufficient to satisfy those tax debts in full,

there shall be applied to each such tax debt such proportion of the payment as bears the same relationship to the whole of the payment as does the tax debt to the total of those tax debts.

RECORDS

41(1) Where–

(a) an insured person has been served with a liability notice;

(b) he is carrying on a business; and

(c) *the contract provides cover for any matter associated with that business,*

the insured person shall keep and preserve the records specified in paragraph (2) below.

41(2) The records which an insured person shall keep and preserve are such of the following as relate to the contract–

(a) his business and accounting records;

(b) policy documents, cover notes, endorsements and similar documents;

(c) all invoices, renewal notices and similar documents issued to him;

(d) all credit or debit notes or other documents received by him which evidence an increase or decrease in the premium, and copies of such documents that are issued by him.

41(3) Every insured person who is required to keep and preserve records by paragraph (1) above shall do so for a period of six years.

41(4) The reference in paragraph (2)(d) above to **any premium** shall be construed for the purposes of that paragraph as it would be construed for the purposes of Part V of these Regulations.

PART VIII – DISTRESS AND DILIGENCE

A42 In this Part–

"**Job Band**" followed by a number between "1" and "12" means the band for the purposes of pay and grading in which the job an officer performs is ranked in the system applicable to Customs and Excise.

History – Reg. A42 inserted by SI 1996/2099, reg. 3, operative from 2 September 1996.

DISTRESS

42 [Repealed by SI 1997/1431, reg. 3(1) and Sch. 3, operative from 1 July 1997.]

History – Former reg. 42 reads as follows:
"**42(1)** Subject to paragraph (2) below, if upon written demand a person neglects or refuses to pay any tax due from him or any amount recoverable as if it were tax due from him, a Collector or an officer of rank not below that of Job Band 7 may distrain on the goods and chattels of that person and by warrant signed by him direct any authorised person to levy such distress.
42(2) Where–
(a)   the amount in relation to which a warrant has been issued under paragraph (1) above is not an amount assessed under section 56(1) of the Act upon failure to make a return; and
(b)   the Commissioners may be required under section 59 of the Act to review a decision which, if that decision were varied or withdrawn, would cause the amount in relation to which the warrant has been issued to be reduced or extinguished,
no distress shall be levied before the last day on which the person who is liable to pay the amount concerned is required, by rules made under paragraph 9 of Schedule 8 to the Value Added Tax Act 1983 [VATA 1994, Sch. 12, para. 9], to serve a notice of appeal with respect to that decision.
42(3) A levy shall be executed by or under the direction of, and in the presence of, the authorised person.
42(4) A person in respect of whose goods and chattels a warrant has been signed shall be liable for all costs and charges in connection with anything done under this regulation.
42(5) If the person aforesaid does not pay the amount due together with the costs and charges within five days of a levy, the distress shall be sold by the authorised person for payment of the amount due and all costs and charges; and costs and charges of taking, keeping and selling the distress shall be retained by the authorised person and any surplus remaining after the deduction of the costs and charges and of the amount due shall be restored to the owner of the goods distrained."
In former reg. 42(1), the words "Job Band 7" were substituted by SI 1996/2099, reg. 4, operative from 2 September 1996.

DILIGENCE

43 In Scotland, the following provisions shall have effect:

(a)   where the Commissioners are empowered to apply to the sheriff for a warrant to authorise a sheriff officer to recover any amount of tax or sum recoverable as if it were tax remaining due and unpaid, any application, and any certificate required to accompany that application, may be made on their behalf by a Collector or an officer of rank not below that of Job Band 7;

(b)   where, during the course of a poinding and sale in accordance with Schedule 5 to the Debtors (Scotland) Act 1987 the Commissioners are entitled as a creditor to do any act, then any such act, with the exception of the exercise of the power contained in paragraph 18(3) of that Schedule, may be done on their behalf by a Collector or an officer of rank not below that of Job Band 7.

History – In reg. 43(a) and (b), the words "Job Band 7" were substituted by SI 1996/2099, reg. 4, operative from 2 September 1996. Reg. 43 substituted by SI 1995/587, reg. 4, operative from 17 July 1995.

SCHEDULES

[Forms: not reproduced.]

History – Forms 1, 4, 5 and 6 were substituted by SI 1997/1157, reg. 15, operative from 1 May 1997.

DISTRESS FOR CUSTOMS AND EXCISE DUTIES AND OTHER INDIRECT TAXES REGULATIONS 1997

(SI 1997/1431)

Made on 9 June 1997 by the Commissioners of Customs and Excise, in exercise of the powers conferred on them by s. 51(1), (2) and (3) of the Finance Act 1997 and of all other powers enabling them in that behalf. Operative from 1 July 1997.

CITATION AND COMMENCEMENT

1   These Regulations may be cited as The Distress for Customs and Excise Duties and Other Indirect Taxes Regulations 1997 and shall come into force on 1st July 1997.

INTERPRETATION

2(1)   In these Regulations–

"**authorised person**" means a person acting under the authority of the Commissioners;

"**costs**" means any costs, charges, expenses and fees;

"**officer**" means, subject to section 8(2) of the Customs and Excise Management Act 1979, a person commissioned by the Commissioners pursuant to section 6(3) of that Act;

"**person in default**" means a person who has refused or neglected to pay any relevant tax due from him;

"**relevant tax**" means any of the following–

(a)   any duty of customs or excise, other than vehicle excise duty;

(b)   value added tax;

(c)   insurance premium tax;

(d)   landfill tax;

(e)   any agricultural levy of the European Community;

"**VAT Act**" means the Value Added Tax Act 1994;

"**walking possession agreement**" means an agreement under which, in consideration of any goods and chattels distrained upon being allowed to remain in the custody of the person in default and of the delaying of their sale, that person–

(a)   acknowledges that the goods and chattels specified in the agreement are under distraint and held in walking possession; and

(b)   undertakes that, except with the consent of the Commissioners and subject to such conditions as they may impose, he will not remove or allow the removal of any of the specified goods and chattels from the place named in the agreement;

"**1994 Act**" means Part III of the Finance Act 1994;

"**1996 Act**" means Part III of the Finance Act 1996.

2(2)   Any reference in these Regulations to an amount of **relevant tax** includes a reference to any amount recoverable as if it were an amount of that relevant tax.

REVOCATIONS AND TRANSITIONAL PROVISIONS

3(1)   The Regulations specified in Schedule 3 are hereby revoked to the extent set out there.

3(2)   Where a warrant is signed before the coming into force of these Regulations, these Regulations shall apply to anything done, after these Regulations come into force, in relation to that warrant or as a consequence of distress being levied.

LEVYING DISTRESS

4(1)   Subject to regulation 5 below, if upon written demand a person neglects or refuses to pay any relevant tax due from him an officer may levy distress on the goods and chattels of that person and by warrant signed by him direct any authorised person to levy such distress.

4(2)   Where a warrant has been signed, distress shall be levied by or under the direction of, and in the presence of, the authorised person.

4(3)   Subject to regulation 6 below, distress may be levied on any goods and chattels located at any place whatever including on a public highway.

RESTRICTIONS ON LEVYING DISTRESS

5(1) Where–

(a) [not relevant to insurance premium tax]

(b) an amount of insurance premium tax is due and the Commissioners may be required under section 59 of the 1994 Act to review a decision which, if that decision were varied or withdrawn, would cause the amount to be reduced or extinguished; or

(c) [not relevant to insurance premium tax],

no distress shall be levied before expiry of the last day on which the person who is liable to pay the amount concerned is required, by rules made under paragraph 9 of Schedule 12 to the VAT Act, to serve a notice of appeal with respect to that decision.

5(2) [Not relevant to insurance premium tax.]

GOODS AND CHATTELS NOT SUBJECT TO LEVY

6 No distress shall be levied on any goods and chattels mentioned in Schedule 1 which at the time of levy are located in a place and used for a purpose mentioned in that Schedule.

TIMES FOR LEVYING DISTRESS

7(1) Subject to paragraph (2) below, a levy of distress shall commence only during the period between eight o'clock in the morning and eight o'clock at night on any day of the week but it may be continued thereafter outside that period until the levy is completed.

7(2) Where a person holds himself out as conducting any profession, trade or business during hours which are partly within and partly outside, or wholly outside the period mentioned in paragraph (1) above, a levy of distress may be commenced at any time during that period or during the hours of any day in which he holds himself out as conducting that profession, trade or business and it may be continued thereafter outside that period or those hours until the levy is completed.

COSTS

8(1) A person in respect of whose goods and chattels a warrant has been signed shall be liable to pay to an officer or authorised person all costs, in connection with anything done under these Regulations described in column 1 of Schedule 2, as determined in accordance with column 2 of that Schedule.

8(2) An authorised person may, after deducting and accounting for the amount of relevant tax to the Commissioners, retain costs from any amount received.

SALE

9 If any person upon whose goods and chattels distress has been levied does not pay the amount of relevant tax due together with costs within 5 days of a levy, an officer or authorised person may sell the distress for payment of the amount of relevant tax and costs; and the officer or authorised person, after deducting and retaining the amount of relevant tax and costs shall restore any surplus to the owner of the goods upon which distress was levied.

DISPUTES AS TO COSTS

10(1) In the case of any dispute as to costs, the amount of those costs shall be taxed by a district judge of the county court of the district where the distress was levied, and he may make such order as he thinks fit as to the costs of the taxation.

10(2) In the application of this regulation to Northern Ireland, in the case of any dispute as to costs, the amount of those costs shall be taxed in the same manner as costs in equity suits or proceedings in the county court in Northern Ireland.

SCHEDULES

SCHEDULE 1 – GOODS AND CHATTELS NOT SUBJECT TO LEVY

Regulation 6

1(1) Any of the following goods and chattels which are located in a dwelling house at which distress is being levied and are reasonably required for the domestic needs of any person residing in that dwelling house–

(a)   beds and bedding;

(b)   household linen;

(c)   chairs and settees;

(d)   tables;

(e)   food;

(f)   lights and light fittings;

(g)   heating appliances;

(h)   curtains;

(i)   floor coverings;

(j)   furniture, equipment and utensils used for cooking, storing or eating food;

(k)   refrigerators;

(l)   articles used for cleaning, mending, or pressing clothes;

(m)   articles used for cleaning the home;

(n)   furniture used for storing–

    (i)   clothing, bedding or household linen;

    (ii) articles used for cleaning the home;

    (iii) utensils used for cooking or eating food;

(o)   articles used for safety in the home;

(p)   toys for the use of any child within the household;

(q)   medical aids and medical equipment.

1(2) Any of the following items which are located in premises used for the purposes of any profession, trade or business–

(a)   fire fighting equipment for use on the premises;

(b)   medical aids and medical equipment for use on the premises.

SCHEDULE 2 – SCALE OF COSTS

Regulation 8(1)

Matter (1)	Costs (2)
1 For attending to levy distress where payment is made of an amount of relevant tax due and distress is not levied:	£12.50
2 For levying distress–	
(a) where an amount of relevant tax demanded and due does not exceed £100:	£12.50
(b) where an amount of relevant tax demanded and due exceeds £100:	12½% on the first £100, 4% on the next £400, 2½% on the next £1,500, 1% on the next £8,000, ¼% on any additional sum.

Matter (1)	Costs (2)
3 For taking possession of distrained goods–	
(a) where a person remains in physical possession of goods at the place where distress was levied (the person to provide his own food and lodgings):	£4.50 per day.
(b) where possession is taken under a walking possession agreement:	£7.00
4 For appraising goods upon which distress has been levied:	Reasonable costs of appraisement.
5 For arranging removal and storage of goods upon which distress has been levied:	Reasonable costs of arrangement.
6 For removing and storing goods upon which distress has been levied:	Reasonable costs of removal and storage.
7 For advertising the sale of goods upon which distress has been levied:	Reasonable costs of advertising.
8 For selling the distress–	
(a) where a sale by auction is held at the auctioneer's premises:	15% of the sum realised.
(b) where a sale by auction is held elsewhere:	7½% of the sum realised and the auctioneer's reasonable costs.
(c) where a sale by other means is undertaken:	7½% of the sum realised and reasonable costs.

9 In addition to any amount specified in this scale in respect of the supply of goods or services on which value added tax is chargeable there may be added a sum equivalent to value added tax at the appropriate rate on that amount.

SCHEDULE 3 – REVOCATIONS

Regulation 3(1)

Statutory Instrument Number	Title of Regulation	Extent
SI 1994/1774	The Insurance Premium Tax Regulations 1994	regulation 42
SI 1995/2518	The Value Added Tax Regulations 1995	regulation 212
SI 1996/1527	The Landfill Tax Regulations 1996	regulation 48

AIR PASSENGER DUTY AND OTHER INDIRECT TAXES (INTEREST RATE) REGULATIONS 1998

(1998/1461, as amended by SI 2000/631)

Made on 15 June 1998 by the Treasury, in exercise of the powers conferred on them by s. 197 of the Finance Act 1996 and of all other powers enabling them in that behalf. Operative from 6 July 1998.

CITATION AND COMMENCEMENT

1 These Regulations may be cited as the Air Passenger Duty and Other Indirect Taxes (Interest Rate) Regulations 1998 and shall come into force on 6th July 1998 in relation to interest accruing on or after that date.

INTERPRETATION

2(1)   In these Regulations unless the context otherwise requires:

"**established rate**" means–

(a)   on the coming into force of these Regulations, 6 per cent per annum; and

(b)   in relation to any day after the first reference day after the coming into force of these Regulations, the reference rate found on the immediately preceding reference day;

"**operative day**" means the sixth day of each month;

"**reference day**" means the twelfth working day before the next operative day;

"**section 197**" means section 197 of the Finance Act 1996;

"**the relevant enactments**" are those referred to in regulations 4(1) and 5(1) below;

"**working day**" means any day other than a non-business day within the meaning of section 92 of the Bills of Exchange Act 1882.

2(2)   In these Regulations **the reference rate** found on a reference day is the percentage per annum found by averaging the base lending rates at close of business on that day of–

(a)   Bank of Scotland,

(b)   Barclays Bank plc.,

(c)   Lloyds Bank plc.,

(d)   HSBC Bank plc.,

(e)   National Westminster Bank plc., and

(f)   The Royal Bank of Scotland plc.

and, if the result is not a whole number, rounding the result to the nearest such number, with any result midway between two whole numbers rounded down.

History – In reg. 2(1)(a), the words "6 per cent" were substituted for the words "7 per cent" by SI 2000/631, reg. 3(a), operative from 1 April 2000.
In reg. 2(2)(d), the words "HSBC Bank plc." were substituted for the words "Midland Bank plc." by SI 2000/631, reg. 3(b), operative from 1 April 2000.

3   [Revokes SI 1997/1016.]

APPLICABLE RATE OF INTEREST PAYABLE TO THE COMMISSIONERS OF CUSTOMS AND EXCISE IN CONNECTION WITH EXCISE DUTIES, INSURANCE PREMIUM TAX, VAT, LANDFILL TAX, AND CUSTOMS DUTY

4(1)   For the purposes of–

(a)   [neither relevant nor reproduced],

(b)   paragraph 21 of Schedule 7 to [the Finance] Act [1994],

(c)   [neither relevant nor reproduced], and

(d)   [neither relevant nor reproduced],

(e)   paragraph 26 of Schedule 5 to the Finance Act 1997, and

(f)   [neither relevant nor reproduced],

the rate applicable under section 197 shall, subject to paragraph (2) below, be 8.5 per cent per annum.

4(2)   Where on any reference day after the coming into force of these Regulations, the reference rate found on that day differs from the established rate, the rate applicable under section 197 of the Finance Act 1996 for the purposes of the enactments referred to in paragraph (1) above shall, from the next operative day, be the percentage per annum determined in accordance with the formula specified in paragraph (3) below.

4(3)   The formula specified in this paragraph is–

$$RR + 2.5,$$

where–

RR is the reference rate referred to in paragraph (2) above.

History – Reg. 4 was substituted by SI 2000/631, reg. 4, operative from 1 April 2000. Former reg. 4 and its heading read as follows:

"APPLICABLE RATE OF INTEREST PAYABLE TO THE COMMISSIONERS OF CUSTOMS AND EXCISE IN CONNECTION WITH AIR PASSENGER DUTY, INSURANCE PREMIUM TAX, VAT RECOVERED OR RECOVERABLE BY ASSESSMENT AND LANDFILL TAX

4(1)   For the purposes of–

(a) [neither relevant nor reproduced],
(b) paragraph 21 of Schedule 7 to [the Finance] Act [1994],
(c) [neither relevant nor reproduced], and
(d) [neither relevant nor reproduced],
the rate applicable under section 197 shall, subject to paragraph (2) below, be 9.5 per cent per annum.

4(2) Where on any reference day after the coming into force of these Regulations, the reference rate found on that day differs from the established rate, the rate applicable under section 197 of the Finance Act 1996 for the purposes of the enactments referred to in paragraph (1) above shall, from the next operative day, be the percentage per annum determined in accordance with the formula specified in paragraph (3) below.

4(3) The formula specified in this paragraph is—

$$RR + 2.5,$$

where—
RR is the reference rate referred to in paragraph (2) above."

APPLICABLE RATE OF INTEREST PAYABLE BY THE COMMISSIONERS OF CUSTOMS AND EXCISE IN CONNECTION WITH AIR PASSENGER DUTY, INSURANCE PREMIUM TAX, VAT, LANDFILL TAX AND CUSTOMS DUTY

5(1) For the purposes of—

(a) [neither relevant nor reproduced],

(b) [neither relevant nor reproduced],

(c) section 78 of the Value Added Tax Act 1994,

(d) [neither relevant nor reproduced],

(e) [neither relevant nor reproduced],

(f) [neither relevant nor reproduced],

the rate applicable under section 197 of the Finance Act 1996 shall be 5 per cent per annum.

5(2) Where, on a reference day after the coming into force of these Regulations, the reference rate found on that date differs from the established rate, the rate applicable under section 197 for the purposes of the enactments referred to in paragraph (1) above shall, from the next operative day, be the percentage per annum determined in accordance with the formula specified in paragraph (3) below.

5(3) The formula specified in this paragraph is—

$$RR - 1,$$

where—
RR is the reference rate referred to in paragraph (2) above.

History – Reg. 5 was substituted by SI 2000/631, reg. 5, operative from 1 April 2000. Former reg. 5 and its heading read as follows:

"APPLICABLE RATE OF INTEREST PAYABLE BY THE COMMISSIONERS OF CUSTOMS AND EXCISE IN CONNECTION WITH AIR PASSENGER DUTY, INSURANCE PREMIUM TAX, CASES OF OFFICIAL ERROR IN RELATION TO VAT AND LANDFILL TAX

5(1) For the purposes of—
(a) [neither relevant nor reproduced],
(b) paragraph 22 of Schedule 7 to that Act,
(c) [neither relevant nor reproduced], and
(d) [neither relevant nor reproduced],
the rate applicable under section 197 of the Finance Act 1996 shall be 6 per cent per annum.

5(2) Where, on a reference day after the coming into force of these Regulations, the reference rate found on that date differs from the established rate, the rate applicable under section 197 for the purposes of the enactments referred to in paragraph (1) above shall, from the next operative day, be the percentage per annum determined in accordance with the formula specified in paragraph (3) below.

5(3) The formula specified in this paragraph is—

$$RR - 1,$$

where—
RR is the reference rate referred to in paragraph (2) above."

EFFECT OF CHANGE IN APPLICABLE RATE

6 Where the rate applicable under section 197 for the *purposes* of any of the relevant enactments changes on an operative *day by virtue* of these Regulations, that change shall have effect for *periods beginning* on or after the operative day in relation to interest running from before that day as well as in relation to interest running from, or from after that day.

7 Where the rate applicable under section 197 for the purposes of any of the relevant enactments changes on an operative day by virtue of these Regulations, the rate in force immediately prior to

any change shall continue to have effect for periods immediately prior to the change and so on in the case of any number of successive changes.

APPLICABLE RATE OF INTEREST PRIOR TO THE COMING INTO FORCE OF THESE REGULATIONS

8 The rate applicable under section 197 for interest running from before the date these regulations come into force in relation to periods prior to that date shall be that specified for the relevant enactments in the following Tables–

TABLE 1

[Neither relevant nor reproduced.]

TABLE 2

Paragraph 21 of Schedule 7 to the Finance Act 1994

Interest for any period	Rate %
from 1st October 1994 and before 6th February 1996	5.5
after 5th February 1996 and before 6th July 1998	6.25

TABLE 3

[Neither relevant nor reproduced.]

TABLE 4

[Neither relevant nor reproduced.]

TABLE 5

[Neither relevant nor reproduced.]

TABLE 6

Paragraph 22 of Schedule 7 to the Finance Act 1994

Interest for any period	Rate %
after 1st October 1994 and before 1st April 1997	8
after 31st March 1997 and before 6th July 1998	6

TABLE 7

[Neither relevant nor reproduced.]

TABLE 8

[Neither relevant nor reproduced.]

MINIMUM AMOUNT OF INTEREST PAYABLE IN CONNECTION WITH CUSTOMS DUTY

9 [Neither relevant nor reproduced.]

History – Reg. 9 was inserted by SI 2000/631, reg. 7, operative from 1 April 2000.

any change which is necessary to ensure rates for refunds immediately preceding the change and to obtain the rate of any monthly or subsequent change.

APPROPRIATE RATE OF INTEREST PRIOR TO THE COMING INTO FORCE OF THESE REGULATIONS

8. The rate applicable under section 197 to instalments arising from interest on the date due to enhance note into force in relation to periods prior to that date shall be that specified for the relevant enactment in the following Tables:

TABLE 1

[Neither relevant nor reproduced.]

TABLE 2

Paragraph 21 of Schedule 7 to the Finance Act 1994

Rate	Period for any period
5.5	from 1st October 1994 and before 6th February 1996
6.25	after 5th February 1996 and before 6th May 1996

TABLE 3

[Neither relevant nor reproduced.]

TABLE 4

[Neither relevant nor reproduced.]

TABLE 5

[Neither relevant nor reproduced.]

TABLE 6

Paragraph 22 of Schedule 2 to the Finance Act 1994

Rate	Period for any period
8	after 1st October 1994 and before 1st April 1997
9	since 31st March 1995 and before 6th July 1995

TABLE 7

[Neither relevant nor reproduced.]

TABLE 8

[Neither relevant nor reproduced.]

MINIMUM AMOUNT OF INTEREST PAYABLE IN CONNECTION WITH CUSTOMS DUTY

9. [Neither relevant nor reproduced.]

History—Regs...

INSURANCE PREMIUM TAX EXTRA-STATUTORY MATERIAL

Table of Contents

OFFICIAL PUBLICATIONS

Publication

AO2   The Adjudicator's Office: How to complain about Customs and Excise
IPT1   Registering for IPT
IPT2   A general guide to IPT
–   VAT and duties tribunals – Appeals and applications to the tribunals – Explanatory leaflet
48   Extra-statutory concessions
989   Visits by Customs and Excise officers
999   Catalogue of notices
1000   Complaints and putting things right: our code of practice
–   Taxpayers' charter

Note – The above publications are not reproduced.

EXTRA-STATUTORY CONCESSIONS

This section contains the text of Notice 48, "Extra-statutory concessions" (1999). Only the material relating to IPT is reproduced here.

Notice 48 – Extra-statutory concessions (1999) [IPT material only]

CONTENTS

3.   CONCESSIONS DESIGNED TO REMOVE INEQUITIES OR ANOMALIES IN ADMINISTRATION

3.29.   Insurance premium tax: Special accounting scheme introductory provisions

(Part I)

Inception written option

1 (1) Where the special accounting scheme applies to an insurer for the accounting period beginning on 1 October 1994, he need not account for any tax due on a premium:

(a)   actually received on or after 1 October 1994 and in a relevant accounting period

(b)   received under a contract that relates to a risk the period of cover for which begins before 1 October 1994, and

(c)   for which the tax point applicable under the special accounting scheme falls before 1 October 1995.

(2) Where (1) (a) and (b) above apply, but the tax point adopted by the insurer under the special accounting scheme falls on or after 1 October 1995, the insurer need not account for tax where the total premium received or written relates entirely to a risk the period of cover for which began before 1 October 1994.

(Part II)

Strict written premium option

2 (1) Where the special accounting scheme applies to an insurer for the accounting period beginning on 1 October 1994 and the insurer:

(a)   treats as tax due one forty-first of all premiums written on or after 1 October 1994 that are received (or due) under a taxable insurance contract but on which tax is not chargeable, and

(b)   does not include such amounts treated as tax in claims for overdeclarations or make a claim for refund of overpaid tax in respect of them, then he may claim as a credit against tax due one forty-first of any refund written on or after 1 October 1994 of all or part of a premium that was originally received under a taxable insurance contract but on which tax was not due.

(2) For the purposes of this paragraph, regulation 25 of the Insurance Premium Tax Regulations 1994 shall apply to premiums written on or after 1 October 1994 that are due under taxable insurance contracts but on which tax was not chargeable.

(3) For the purposes of this paragraph, a premium is written on or after 1 October 1994 if the tax point applicable under the special accounting scheme falls on or after that date; and a refund is written on or after 1 October 1994 if it is entered in the insurer's accounts as at a date falling on or after that date.

3 Nothing in this part shall require an insurer to account for tax on the portion of a premium that is attributable to exempt matters in accordance with section 69 of the Finance Act 1994, or prevent him from taking advantage of any de minimis rules.

(Part III)

4 An insurer may elect to use one or both options described in Parts I and II above but, where he chooses to use both options each option must be applied to the entirety of a clearly defined sector of business.

3.30.   Insurance premium tax: De minimis provisions

1 Where an insurer is able to demonstrate that the total premium for a taxable insurance contract which provides cover for both exempt and non-exempt matters is below the de minimis limits set out in paragraph 3 below, then:

(a)   that contract may be treated as though it were exempt, and

(b)   credit may be claimed in respect of any tax that has already been accounted for on premiums received or written under that contract (subject to the normal provisions as to the manner in which an insurer is able to claim and benefit from such credit).

2 Where an insurer applies this concession to a taxable insurance contract he must monitor payments received or due in relation to that contract. If a premium written or received by an insurer takes the total premium relating to a contract over the limits set out in paragraph 3 below, the insurer must account for tax on that total premium at the tax point applicable to the additional premium which takes the total premium over the limits set out in paragraph 3.

3 A total premium for a taxable insurance contract is below the de minimis limits if it is £500,000 or less, and 10 per cent or less of it is attributable to non-exempt matters.

4 Where the only taxable contracts under which an insurer intends to provide insurance are those in respect of which, to the best of the insurer's knowledge, the total premiums will each be below the de minimis limits, then provided:

(a)   application has been made in writing to the Commissioners for exemption from the requirement to make returns

(b)   any information as may reasonably be requested by the Commissioners about the number and value of taxable insurance contracts entered into by the insurer has been supplied to them, and

(c)   the Commissioners approve that insurer's application

the insurer will be exempted from the requirements of registrable persons to make returns.

5 For the purposes of this concession the "total premium" for a taxable insurance contract is the total of all premiums which have been received under that contract once there can be no more premium payments (either by or to the insurer) made under it.

3.31.   Insurance Premium tax: Insurance relating to motor cars or motor cycles

For the purposes of Schedule 6A to the Finance Act 1994, a premium under a taxable insurance policy relating to a motor car or motor cycle (other than a motor car or motor cycle on hire) will not be regarded as falling within paragraph 2(1) to the extent that it relates to a policy of motor vehicle insurance which provides cover of the kind generally known as:

(i)   fully comprehensive

(ii)   third party, fire and theft, or

(iii)   third party.

3.32.   Insurance premium tax: Home contents insurance

For the purposes of Schedule 6A to the Finance Act 1994 a premium under a taxable insurance contract relating to relevant goods will not fall within paragraph 3(1) to the extent that it relates to insurance of the kind generally known as household contents insurance and which principally relates to risks arising in connection with items in the private dwellings of individuals.

"Relevant goods" are as defined in paragraph 3(6) of Schedule 6A to the Finance Act 1994.

3.33.   Insurance premium tax: Special accounting scheme transitional arrangements

By concession, sections 21 to 23 of the Finance Act 1997 do not have effect in relation to a *premium if the premium*:

(a)   is in respect of a pre 1 April 1997 contract, and

(b)   falls, by virtue of regulations made under section 68 of the Finance Act 1994 (special accounting scheme) to be regarded for the purposes of Part III of that Act as received under the contract by the insurer on a date before 1 October 1997.

This concession does not apply where a contract of insurance is liable to the higher rate of insurance premium tax and provides for premiums to be paid on a monthly basis.

3.34. Insurance premium tax: Arrangements for discounted insurance

(1) By concession, where:

(a)   a premium under a taxable insurance contract is liable to insurance premium tax at the higher rate, and

(b)   the insurance is arranged or provided by one of the persons in paragraphs 2(2) or 3(2) of Schedule 6A to the Finance Act 1994 for less than the actual cost of providing that insurance to the insured,

the higher rate element of any premium received by the insurer will be the amount paid by the insured (or any person on his behalf).

(2) For the purposes of paragraph 1. above:

(a)   "higher rate element" is as defined in section 69(5) of the Finance Act 1994 (as amended), and

(b)   references to payments being made on behalf of the insured shall not be taken to include any sum paid to the insurer or any person acting on behalf of the insurer by a person mentioned in paragraphs 2(2) or 3(2) of Schedule 6A to the Finance Act 1994.

The previous concession relating to arrangements for discounting insurance was withdrawn and replaced by this concession from 1 August 1998.

OTHER MATERIAL

NEWS RELEASES

INTEREST PAID BY AND TO CUSTOMS & EXCISE [HM Customs and Excise News Release 16/98, 3 July 1998]

The way that interest rates paid by and to Customs are calculated will change from 6 July 1998.

This will bring the Customs default interest rate in line with the rate charged by the Inland Revenue for unpaid tax. As part of closer working between the two Departments, it will be future policy to continue to align the Customs rate with that of the Revenue for unpaid tax.

Default interest charged on underdeclared VAT, Air Passenger Duty (APD) Insurance Premium Tax (IPT) and Landfill Tax; and statutory interest paid in cases of official error; will be set using formulae linked to a reference rate. The reference rate will be based on an average of the base rates of six main banks rounded to the nearest whole number.

For default interest, the formula used will be the reference rate plus 2.5 per cent. For statutory interest, the formula used will be the reference rate minus 1 per cent.

Application of the formulae for the first time will result in the rate of default interest on underdeclared VAT, APD, IPT and Landfill Tax being increased to 9.5 per cent per annum on 6th July 1998 from 6.25 per cent.. The increase is necessary due to increases in bank base lending rates since the default interest rate was last changed in February 1996.

The base rate will be monitored every month and, where changes are necessary, new Departmental interest rates will be set by an order of the Commissioners of Customs & Excise. Like the Inland Revenue, these new procedures will enable Customs to react quickly to future changes in base rates and maintain a system of interest rates which reflects market rates.

NOTES TO EDITORS

The reference rate will be the percentage per annum found by averaging the base lending rates at close of business on the 12th working day before the sixth day of each month (the "reference day") of :- Bank of Scotland, Barclays Bank, Lloyds Bank, Midland Bank, National Westminster Bank and The Royal Bank of Scotland.

Section 197 of the Finance Act 1996 provides that the prescribed rate, and day from which it takes effect, for the purpose of charging interest on indirect taxes shall be set by an order of the Commissioners of Customs and Excise. SI 1998 No. 1461 was made and laid before the House of Commons on 15th June 1998 and will come into force on 6th July 1998. This Statutory Instrument sets out the procedure for setting, and formulae for calculating, Departmental interest rates.

Interest for VAT underdeclared on returns was introduced on April 1990, and is covered by Section 74 of the VAT Act 1994. Interest for IPT undeclared on returns is covered by Schedule 7 paragraph 21 of the Finance Act 1994. Interest for APD undeclared on returns is covered by Schedule 6 paragraph 7 of the Finance Act 1994. Interest for Landfill Tax undeclared on returns is covered by Schedule 5 paragraph 26 of the Finance Act 1996.

Statutory interest payments in respect of VAT is covered by Section 78 of the VAT Act 1994. Statutory interest payments in respect of IPT is covered by Schedule 7 paragraph 22 of the Finance Act 1994. Statutory interest payments in respect of APD is covered by Schedule 6 paragraph 9 of the Finance Act 1994. Statutory interest payments in respect of Landfill Tax is covered by Schedule 5 paragraph 29 of the Finance Act 1996.

NEW RATES OF INTEREST PAID BY AND TO CUSTOMS & EXCISE [HM Customs and Excise News Release 31/98, 23 December 1998]

As a result of recent reductions in base lending rates, the rates of interest paid by and to Customs will decrease from 6th January 1999.

An Order of the Commissioners of Customs and Excise was issued on 18th December 1998 stating that:

–   the rate of default interest charged on underdeclared VAT, APD (air passenger duty) IPT (insurance premium tax) and Landfill Tax will decrease by 1 per cent to 8.5 per cent per annum;

–   the rate of statutory interest paid by Customs in cases of official error will decrease by 1 per cent to 5 per cent per annum.

Notes

Section 197 of the Finance Act 1996 provides that the prescribed rate, and day from which it takes effect, for the purpose of charging interest on indirect taxes shall be set by an order of the Commissioners of Customs and Excise. SI 1998 No. 1461 was made and laid before the House of Commons on 15th June 1998 and came into force on 6th July 1998. This Statutory Instrument sets out the procedure for setting, and formulae for calculating, Departmental interest rates based on a monthly reference rate.

The reference rate will be the percentage per annum found by averaging the base lending rates at close of business on the 12th working day before the sixth day of each month (the "reference day") of - Bank of Scotland, Barclays Bank, Lloyds Bank, Midland Bank, National Westminster Bank and The Royal Bank of Scotland.

Interest for VAT underdeclared on returns is covered by Section 74 of the VAT Act 1994. Interest for IPT undeclared on returns is covered by Schedule 7 paragraph 21 of the Finance Act 1994. Interest for APD undeclared on returns is covered by Schedule 6 paragraph 7 of the Finance Act 1994. Interest for Landfill Tax undeclared on returns is covered by Schedule 5 paragraph 26 of the Finance Act 1996.

Statutory interest payments in respect of VAT is covered by Section 78 of the VAT Act 1994. Statutory interest payments in respect of IPT is covered by Schedule 7 paragraph 22 of the Finance Act 1994. Statutory interest payments in respect of APD is covered by Schedule 6 paragraph 9 of the Finance Act 1994. Statutory interest payments in respect of Landfill Tax is covered by Schedule 5 paragraph 29 of the Finance Act 1996.

NEW RATES OF INTEREST PAID BY AND TO CUSTOMS & EXCISE [HM Customs and Excise News Release 7/99, 3 March 1999]

As a result of recent reductions in base lending rates, the rates of interest paid by and to Customs will decrease from 6th March 1999.

An Order of the Commissioners of Customs and Excise was issued on 22nd February 1999 stating that:

–   the rate of default interest charged on underdeclared VAT, APD (air passenger duty) IPT (insurance premium tax) and Landfill Tax will decrease from 8.5 per cent to 7.5 per cent per annum;

–   the rate of statutory interest paid by Customs in cases of official error will decrease from 5 per cent to 4 per cent per annum.

Notes

Section 197 of the Finance Act 1996 provides that the prescribed rate, and day from which it takes effect, for the purpose of charging interest on indirect taxes shall be set by an order of the Commissioners of Customs and Excise. SI 1998 No. 1461 was made and laid before the House of Commons on 15th June 1998 and came into force on 6th July 1998. This Statutory Instrument sets out the procedure for setting, and formulae for calculating, Departmental interest rates based on a monthly reference rate.

The reference rate will be the percentage per annum found by averaging the base lending rates at close of business on the 12th working day before the sixth day of each month (the "reference day") of - Bank of Scotland, Barclays Bank, Lloyds Bank, Midland Bank, National Westminster Bank and The Royal Bank of Scotland.

Interest for VAT underdeclared on returns is covered by Section 74 of the VAT Act 1994. Interest for IPT undeclared on returns is covered by Schedule 7 paragraph 21 of the Finance Act 1994. Interest for APD undeclared on returns is covered by Schedule 6 paragraph 7 of the Finance Act 1994. Interest for Landfill Tax undeclared on returns is covered by Schedule 5 paragraph 26 of the Finance Act 1996.

Statutory interest payments in respect of VAT is covered by Section 78 of the VAT Act 1994. Statutory interest payments in respect of IPT is covered by Schedule 7 paragraph 22 of the Finance Act 1994. Statutory interest payments in respect of APD is covered by Schedule 6 paragraph 9 of the Finance Act 1994. Statutory interest payments in respect of Landfill Tax is covered by Schedule 5 paragraph 29 of the Finance Act 1996.

BUSINESS BRIEFS

LUNN-POLY LIMITED/BISHOPSGATE INSURANCE LTD – JUDICIAL REVIEW [HM Customs and Excise Business Brief 10/98, 24 April 1998]

The travel agents Lunn-Poly and their travel insurance provider, Bishopsgate Insurance, sought judicial review of the higher rate of insurance premium tax applied to travel insurance sold by travel agents and tour operators. They argued before the High Court that on four different grounds the tax was incompatible with European Law. The High Court on 2 April found for Customs on three of these grounds, but found for Lunn-Poly on one; that the application of the tax in this sector was a state aid to other travel insurers taxed at the lower rate and should have been notified to the European Commission.

The Court granted them a declaration to this effect.

Our view remains that this tax is not a state aid. We were given immediate leave to appeal against this aspect of the judgement and have now done so.

The Chancellor had already announced before the judgement that the higher rate of IPT will be extended to all sales of travel insurance in recognition of likely changes in the market in travel insurance. This change is being introduced on 1 August in line with the period of notice previously agreed with the insurance industry for introducing IPT rate changes. By removing the differential rates of IPT chargeable on travel insurance this measure also removes the features of the IPT legislation which were the subject of the concern raised by the Court in relation to state aids.

A remedy when something is found to be an illegal state aid is for the aid to be recovered. In this case the nearest equivalent would be to apply the higher rate of IPT retrospectively to those supplies of travel insurance that remained liable only to the standard rate of IPT. No such action is planned and given the above mentioned Budget change and pending appeal no further action is to be taken. In our view the judgement has no impact on higher rate tax already paid or due on travel insurance. It is also limited to travel insurance and has no effect on the higher rate of IPT paid by other sectors.

Since an appeal has now been served the matter is now sub judice and we cannot comment on the arguments relating to the case.

INSURANCE PREMIUM TAX (IPT): DETERMINING THE LOCATION OF RISK [HM Customs and Excise Business Brief 5/99, 24 February 1999]

The policy for determining location of risk for IPT liability has been revised. This may affect insurers and insurance intermediaries.

IPT is only payable on insurance premiums relating to risks located in the UK as determined by reference to the Insurance Companies Act (ICA) 1982 (see paragraph 8 of Schedule 7A to the Finance Act 1994). For certain insurance contracts the location of risk is determined by where the individual policyholder habitually resides. Shortly after IPT was introduced the relevant section of the ICA was changed to the effect that habitual residence had to be determined at the date when the contract is entered into. This change to the ICA has never been reflected in the application of IPT which has continued to determine habitual residence largely by reference to where the policyholder intends to spend the time covered by the insurance policy. Following discussions with the insurance industry and to avoid any confusion or scope for manipulation between the two pieces of legislation, Customs are now modifying their policy to fully reflect the ICA wording. From today insurers will be required to apply this revised approach when determining the IPT liability of such insurance contracts. In the great majority of cases this revised approach will not change the IPT liability.

Guidance on the revised approach has been issued to insurers via the Association of British Insurers and Lloyd's. A revised version of Public Notice IPT2 - A General Guide to IPT - will be available from VAT advice centres in March. If you require further information or have difficulties in implementing the change you should contact your local VAT advice centre listed under Customs and Excise in the telephone directory.

IPT: LUNN POLY LIMITED / BISHOPSGATE INSURANCE LTD [HM Customs and Excise Business Brief 6/99, 23 March 1999]

The travel agents Lunn-Poly and their travel insurance provider, Bishopsgate Insurance, sought judicial review of the higher rate of insurance premium tax applied to travel insurance sold by travel agents and tour operators. They argued that this measure offended a number of points of EC law.

The Court of Appeal in its judgement of 26 February dismissed Custom's appeal against the Divisional Court's decision that the differential rates of IPT applied to travel insurance amounted to a state aid to those insurers liable to account for the standard rate of 4 per cent.

Customs are still considering the implications of the judgement and whether to petition the House of Lords for leave to appeal. However, three points appear clear: - the judgement - that retention of the 4 per cent rate for certain suppliers of travel insurance amounted to an illegal State aid - has no impact on higher rate tax already paid or due on travel insurance; - the judgement is limited to travel insurance and has no effect on the higher rate of IPT paid by other sectors; and - the issue is historic in that the extension of higher rate IPT to all supplies of travel insurance on 1 August 1998 removed the features of the IPT legislation which were the subject of the concern raised by the Court in relation to State aids.

The Court of Appeal did not consider it necessary to hear arguments on the cross-appeal from Lunn Poly. The Divisional Court's judgement therefore stands that the higher rate does not infringe other EC legislation and does not amount to an illegal turnover tax.

IPT: LUNN POLY LIMITED / BISHOPSGATE INSURANCE LTD [HM Customs and Excise Business Brief 8/99, 31 March 1999]

Customs will not be petitioning the House of Lords for leave to appeal against the Court of Appeal's judgement in this case. The judgement stated that the differential rates of IPT applied to travel insurance amounted to a state aid to those insurers liable to account for the standard rate of 4 per cent. Customs are meeting with the industry to discuss implementation of the judgement.

STATEMENT OF PRACTICE

Insurance Premium Tax: connected persons [HM Customs and Excise Statement of Practice]

Schedule 6A to the Finance Act 1994 provides that the higher rate of IPT will apply to taxable insurance contracts relating to motor vehicles and domestic appliances where the insurance is arranged through or provided by a person connected (1) to (for example) a motor dealer or a retailer of domestic electrical appliances ("connected suppliers of relevant goods or services"). However, the higher rate will only apply where the insurance relates to relevant goods or services provided by the connected supplier.

> (1) Any question of whether a person is connected with another shall be determined in accordance with section 839 of the Taxes Act 1988

In many cases these "connected" transactions will be regular occurrences or easily identified, and the higher rate should be applied accordingly.

However, there will be some instances where the "connected" transactions are indistinguishable from other transactions. In such cases, Customs will accept that where the connection is co-incidental and the insurance is not provided as part of a systematic scheme to sell insurance to customers of a connected supplier of relevant goods or services, the premium will not be subject to the higher rate.

So, where there are genuine difficulties in identifying connected sales, the higher rate of IPT will only apply where there is a deliberate or systematic attempt:

(a)   by a supplier of relevant goods or services to sell insurance to purchasers of those goods or services using a connected insurer or insurance agent; or

(b)   by an insurer or insurance agent to sell insurance to customers of a connected supplier of relevant goods or services to cover relevant goods and services provided by that supplier.

Where there are genuine difficulties in identifying connected sales, Customs and Excise will not expect insurers or insurance agents who are connected to a supplier of relevant goods or services to ask each and every customer where they made their purchase of relevant goods or services, or if, and if so where, they intend to make such a purchase.

The connected persons provisions will not generally require the apportionment of premiums between that part of a premium which is deemed to relate to goods or services supplied by a "connected" supplier of relevant goods or services and that part which is deemed not to. This is because a premium will usually either be treated in its entirety as "connected" (if it is sold as part of a systematic scheme to sell insurance to customers of the "connected" supplier of relevant goods or services or if its connection is easily identifiable) or it will be treated in its entirety as completely unconnected.

This Statement of Practice will be implemented at local level by local IPT officers, with decisions taken by them. Any disputes may be referred to the Independent Adjudicator.

This Statement of Practice may be changed or disapplied if used for the purposes of avoidance of tax.

INDEX TO INSURANCE PREMIUM TAX

For a list of abbreviations used in this Index see p. xii.

Provision

Intermediaries
. amounts charged by .... FA94 s. 72(1A)
. credit, entitlement to .... FA94 s. 55
. death or bankruptcy etc. .... FA94 s. 62(5)
. de-registration, notification of
    liability .... SI 1994/1774 reg. 6A
. fees treated as premiums under
    higher rate contracts ...... FA94 s. 52A, 73(1)
. groups of companies .... FA94 s. 63
. payments to .... FA94 s. 73
. registration .... FA94 s. 53AA
. . notification of liability .... SI 1994/1774 reg. 4A
. taxable intermediary, meaning .... FA94 s. 73(1)
. taxable intermediary's fees,
    meaning .... SI 1994/1774 reg. 2(1)
. tax representatives for .... FA94 s. 57, 58

International railway rolling stock –
    see Rolling stock

L

Letters of credit
. non-taxable insurance contracts .. FA94 Sch. 7A,
    para. 15

Liability for tax
. insured persons – see Insured
    persons
. insurers .... FA94 s. 52
. tax representatives .... FA94 s. 58

Lifeboats and equipment
. contract, chargeable amount .... FA94 s. 69
. lifeboat equipment, meaning ..... FA94 Sch. 7A,
    para, 6(3)(b)
. lifeboat, meaning ...... FA94 Sch. 7A, para. 5(3)
. non-taxable insurance contracts .. FA94 Sch. 7A,
    para. 5, 6

Liquidation or receivership – see
    also Incapacity
. compliance .... FA94 s. 62(5)

Lloyd's underwriters
. compliance .... FA94 s. 62(3)
. registration of syndicates .... SI 1994/1774 reg. 8
. . representation .... SI 1994/1774 reg. 9
. returns for syndicates ....SI 1994/1774 reg. 12(2)
. . correction of errors .....SI 1994/1774 reg. 13(4)

Loans
. non-taxable insurance contracts .. FA94 Sch. 7A,
    para. 15

Location of risk
. determining ....BB 5/99

Long-term insurance
. non-taxable insurance contracts .. FA94 Sch. 7A,
    para. 2

Loss of or damage to goods
. goods in foreign or international
    transit, non-taxable insurance
    contracts .... *FA94* Sch. 7A, para. 12

M

Meanings – see Insurance Premium
    Tax List of Definitions and
    Meanings at p. 14,357

Provision

Medical insurance
. exclusion from exemption .... FA94 Sch. 7A,
    para. 2(3)

Motor vehicles
. handicapped persons,
    non-taxable insurance
    contracts .... FA94 Sch. 7A, para. 3
. higher rate premiums ....FA94 s. 52A(7),
    Sch. 6A, para. 2;
    ESC 3.31; SP

N

Non-taxable insurance contracts –
    see Contract of insurance

Northern Ireland
. recovery of tax .... FA94 Sch. 7, para. 7

O

Offences
. criminal .... FA94 Sch. 7, para. 9
. order for access to recorded
    information etc. ...... FA94 Sch. 7, para. 4A
. penalties – see Penalties
. tax representatives .... FA94 s. 58(3)

Officers
. pay and grading, Job Band .... SI 1994/1774
    reg. A42

Overdeclarations
. returns, correction of errors .... SI 1994/1774
    reg. 13

Overpaid tax
. recovery .... FA94 Sch. 7, para. 8
. . claims ....SI 1994/1774 reg. 14
. . reimbursement arrangements ..... SI 1994/1774
    reg. 19A–19H

P

Partnerships
. compliance .... FA94 s. 62
. registration
. . notification to commissioners ..... SI 1994/1774
    reg. 4–6
. . representation ....SI 1994/1774 reg. 10(3)

Payment of tax
. enforcement
. . diligence – see Diligence
. . distress – see Distress
. . walking possession agreement .... FA94 Sch. 7,
    para. 19(1)
. time for ....FA94 s. 54;
    SI 1994/1774 reg. 15

Payroll deductions
. tax point ....FA94 s. 72(7A), (8A)

Penalties
. assessments to .... FA94 Sch. 7, para. 25
. civil penalties
. . breach of a walking possession
    agreement .... FA94 Sch. 7, para. 19
. . fraudulent evasion of tax .... FA94 Sch. 7,
    para. 12

INSURANCE PREMIUM TAX
LIST OF DEFINITIONS
AND MEANINGS

For a list of abbreviations used in this Index see p. xii.

For a list of abbreviations used in this list see p. xii.

LANDFILL TAX

Table of Contents

LANDFILL TAX STATUTES

Table of Contents

Note: Only those extant parts of these Acts which relate to landfill tax are reproduced here.

PROVISIONAL COLLECTION OF TAXES ACT 1968

(1968 Chapter 2)

[*1st February 1968*]

ARRANGEMENT OF SECTIONS

1   Temporary statutory effect of House of Commons resolutions affecting income tax, purchase tax or customs or excise duties

1(1)   This section applies only to [not relevant to landfill tax] landfill tax [not relevant to landfill tax].

1(1A)   [Repealed by FA 1993, s. 205(3), s. 213 and Sch. 23, Pt. VI.]

1(2)   Subject to that, and to the provisions of subsections (4) to (8) below, where the House of Commons passes a resolution which–

(a)   provides for the renewal for a further period of any tax in force or imposed during the previous financial year (whether at the same or a different rate, and whether with or without modifications) or for the variation or abolition of any existing tax, and

(b)   contains a declaration that it is expedient in the public interest that the resolution should have statutory effect under the provisions of this Act,

the resolution shall, for the period specified in the next following subsection, have statutory effect as if contained in an Act of Parliament and, where the resolution provides for the renewal of a tax, all enactments which were in force with reference to that tax as last imposed by Act of Parliament shall during that period have full force and effect with respect to the tax as renewed by the resolution.

In this section references to the **renewal of a tax** include references to its reimposition, and references to the abolition of a tax include references to its repeal.

1(3)   The said period is–

(a)   in the case of a resolution passed in November or December in any year, one expiring with 5th May in the next calendar year;

(aa)   in the case of a resolution passed in February or March in any year, one expiring with 5th August in the same calendar year; and

(b)   in the case of any other resolution, one expiring at the end of four months after the date on which it is expressed to take effect or, if no such date is expressed, after the date on which it is passed.

1(4)   A resolution shall cease to have statutory effect under this section unless within the next thirty days on which the House of Commons sits after the day on which the resolution is passed–

(a)   a Bill renewing, varying or, as the case may be, abolishing the tax is read a second time by the House, or

(b)   a Bill is amended by the House in Committee or on Report, or by any Standing Committee of the House so as to include provision for the renewal, variation or, as the case may be, abolition of the tax.

1(5)   A resolution shall also cease to have statutory effect under this section if–

(a)   the provisions giving effect to it are rejected during the passage of the Bill containing them through the House, or

(b)   an Act comes into operation renewing, varying or, as the case may be, abolishing the tax, or

(c)   Parliament is dissolved or prorogued.

1(6)   Where, in the case of a resolution providing for the renewal or variation of a tax, the resolution ceases to have statutory effect by virtue of subsection (4) or (5) above, or the period specified in subsection (3) above terminates, before an Act comes into operation renewing or varying the tax, any money paid in pursuance of the resolution shall be repaid or made good, and any deduction made in pursuance of the resolution shall be deemed to be an unauthorised deduction.

1(7) Where any tax as renewed or varied by a resolution is modified by the Act renewing or varying the tax, any money paid in pursuance of the resolution which would not have been payable under the new conditions affecting the tax shall be repaid or made good, and any deduction made in pursuance of the resolution shall, so far as it would not have been authorised under the new conditions affecting the tax, be deemed to be an unauthorised deduction.

1(8) When during any session a resolution has had statutory effect under this section, statutory effect shall not be again given under this section in the same session to the same resolution or to a resolution having the same effect.

History – In s. 1(1), the words "landfill tax," were inserted by FA 1998, s. 148(1), in relation to resolutions passed after 2 July 1998.
S. 1(1A) repealed by FA 1993, s. 205(3) and s. 213 and Sch. 23 Pt. VI, in relation to resolutions passed after 27 July 1993. Former s. 1(1A) was inserted by FA 1985, s. 97.
In s. 1(3)(a), references to "November or December" and "5th May in the next calendar year" were substituted and in s. 1(4), the word "thirty" was substituted by FA 1993, s. 205(5), in relation to resolutions passed after 27 July 1993.
S. 1(3)(aa) was inserted by F(No. 2)A 1997, s. 50(1), with effect in relation to resolutions passed after 31 July 1997.
In s. 1(4)(b), the words "in Committee ... of the House" were inserted by FA 1968, s. 60.

Cross references – FA 1998, s. 148(2)(b): repayable landfill tax in consequence of the restoration in relation to the taxable disposal of a lower rate.

5 House of Commons resolution giving provisional effect to motions affecting taxation

5(1) This section shall apply if the House of Commons resolves that provisional statutory effect shall be given to one or more motions to be moved by the Chancellor of the Exchequer, or some other Minister, and which, if agreed to by the House, would be resolutions–

(a)   to which statutory effect could be given under section 1 of this Act, or

(b)   to which section 3 of this Act could be applied,

(c)   [Repealed by FA 1993, s. 205(6)(a), s. 213 and Sch. 23, Pt. VI.]

5(2) Subject to subsection (3) below, on the passing of the resolution under subsection (1) above, sections 1 to 3 of this Act and section 822 of the Income and Corporation Taxes Act 1988 (over-deductions from preference dividends before passing of annual Act) shall apply as if each motion to which the resolution applies had then been agreed to by a resolution of the House.

5(3) Subsection (2) above shall cease to apply to a motion if that motion, or a motion containing the same proposals with modifications, is not agreed to by a resolution of the House (in this section referred to as **"a confirmatory resolution"**) within the next ten days on which the House sits after the resolution under subsection (1) above is passed, and, if it ceases to apply, all such adjustments, whether by way of discharge or repayment of tax, or discharge of security, or otherwise, shall be made as may be necessary to restore the position to what it would have been if subsection (2) above had never applied to that motion, and to make good any deductions which have become unauthorised deductions.

5(4) The enactments specified in subsection (2) above shall have effect as if–

(a)   any confirmatory resolution passed within the said period of ten sitting days had been passed when the resolution under subsection (1) above was passed, and

(b)   everything done in pursuance of the said subsection (2) by reference to the motion to which the confirmatory resolution relates had been done by reference to the confirmatory resolution,

but any necessary adjustments shall be made, whether by way of discharge or repayment of tax, or modification of the terms of any security, or further assessment, or otherwise, where the proposals in the confirmatory resolution are not the same as those in the original motion to which that resolution relates.

History – S. 5(1)(c) and word "or" immediately preceding it and in s. 5(2), reference to ICTA 1988, s. 822 substituted by FA 1993, s. 205(6), s. 213 and Sch. 23, Pt. VI, in relation to resolutions passed after 27 July 1993.
References to provisions of ICTA 1988 substituted by Sch. 29, para. 32 of that Act.

Cross references – FA 1998, s. 148(2)(b): repayable landfill tax in consequence of the restoration in relation to the taxable disposal of a lower rate.

6 Short title, repeals and saving as respects Northern Ireland

6(1) This Act may be cited as the Provisional Collection of Taxes Act 1968.

6(2)   [Amending provision, not reproduced here.]

6(3)   [Repealed by Northern Ireland Constitution Act 1973, s. 41(1)(a) and Sch. 6, Pt. I.]

History – S. 6(3) was repealed by Northern Ireland Constitution Act 1973, s. 41(1)(a) and Sch. 6, Pt. I, with effect from 18 July 1973.

INSOLVENCY ACT 1986

(1986 Chapter 45)

[*25th July 1986*]

Notes – The Insolvency Act 1986 came into force on 29 December 1986. See also relevant parts of Bankruptcy (Scotland) Act 1985, reproduced above.

PART IV – WINDING UP OF COMPANIES REGISTERED UNDER THE COMPANIES ACTS

Chapter VIII – Provisions of General Application in Winding Up

PREFERENTIAL DEBTS

175   Preferential debts (general provision)

175(1)   In a winding up the company's preferential debts (within the meaning given by section 386 in Part XII) shall be paid in priority to all other debts.

175(2)   Preferential debts–

(a)   rank equally among themselves after the expenses of the winding up and shall be paid in full, unless the assets are insufficient to meet them, in which case they abate in equal proportions; and

(b)   so far as the assets of the company available for payment of general creditors are insufficient to meet them, have priority over the claims of holders of debentures secured by, or holders of, any floating charge created by the company, and shall be paid accordingly out of any property comprised in or subject to that charge.

PART XII – PREFERENTIAL DEBTS IN COMPANY AND INDIVIDUAL INSOLVENCY

386   Categories of preferential debts

386(1)   A reference in this Act to the **preferential debts** of a company or an individual is to the debts listed in Schedule 6 to this Act (money owed to the Inland Revenue for income tax deducted at source; VAT, insurance premium tax, landfill tax, car tax, betting and gaming duties, beer duty, lottery duty, air passenger duty; social security and pension scheme contributions; remuneration etc. of employees; levies on coal and steel production); and references to preferential creditors are *to be read accordingly.*

386(2)   In that Schedule **"the debtor"** means the company or the individual concerned.

386(3)   Schedule 6 is to be read with Schedule 4 to the Pensions Schemes Act 1993 (occupational pension scheme contributions).

History – In s. 386(1), the words "landfill tax," inserted by FA 1996, s. 60 and Sch. 5, para. 12(1) with effect from 29 April 1996.

In s. 386(1), the words "air passenger duty" inserted by FA 1995, s. 17 with effect from 1 May 1995.

In s. 386(1), the words "lottery duty" inserted by FA 1993, s. 36 with effect from 1 December 1993.

In s. 386(1), the words "insurance premium tax," inserted by FA 1994, s. 64 and Sch. 7, para. 7(2), with effect from 3 May 1994.

In s. 386(1), the words "beer duty" inserted by FA 1991, s. 7 and Sch. 2, para. 21A as inserted by F(No. 2)A 1992, s. 9(1) with effect from 16 July 1992.

In s. 386(1), the words "; levies on coal and steel production" inserted by SI 1987/2093, with effect from 1 January 1988.

In s. 386(3), the words "Schedule 4 to the Social Security Pensions Act 1975" substituted by the Pension Schemes Act 1993, Sch. 8, para. 18, with effect from 7 February 1994.

Cross reference – SI 1986/1999, reg. 3, Sch. 1, Pt. II, para. 34: application to estates of deceased person dying before presentation of bankruptcy petition.

SCHEDULES

SCHEDULE 6 – THE CATEGORIES OF PREFERENTIAL DEBTS

Section 386

CATEGORY 1: DEBTS DUE TO INLAND REVENUE

1, 2   [Not relevant to landfill tax.]

CATEGORY 2: DEBTS DUE TO CUSTOMS AND EXCISE

3   [Not relevant to landfill tax.]

3A   [Not relevant to landfill tax.]

3B   Any landfill tax which is referable to the period of 6 months next before the relevant date (which period is referred to below as **"the 6-month period"**).

For the purposes of this paragraph–

(a)   where the whole of the accounting period to which any landfill tax is attributable falls within the 6-month period, the whole amount of that tax is referable to that period; and

(b)   in any other case the amount of any landfill tax which is referable to the 6-month period is the proportion of the tax which is equal to such proportion (if any) of the accounting period in question as falls within the 6-month period;

and references here to accounting periods shall be construed in accordance with Part III of the Finance Act 1996.

History – para.3B inserted by FA 1996, s.60 and Sch.5, para.12(1) with effect from 29 April 1996.

4-16   [Not relevant to landfill tax.]

INCOME AND CORPORATION TAXES ACT 1988

(1988 Chapter 1)

[*19th February 1988*]

827   VAT penalties etc.

827(1)–(1C)   [Not relevant to landfill tax.]

827(1C)   Where a person is liable to make a payment by way of–

(a)   penalty under Part V of Schedule 5 to the Finance Act 1996 (landfill tax), or

(b)   interest under paragraph 26 or 27 of that Schedule,

the payment shall not be allowed as a deduction in computing any income, profits or losses for any *tax purposes*.

827(2)   [Not relevant to landfill tax.]

History – S. 827(1C) was inserted by FA 1994, s. 60 and Sch. 5, para. 40.

Cross references – FA 1996, Sch. 5, Pt. V: civil penalties.
FA 1996, Sch. 5, para. 26: interest on under–declared tax.
FA 1996, interest on unpaid tax. etc.

FINANCE ACT 1996

(1996 Chapter 8)

[*29th April 1996*]

ARRANGEMENT OF SECTIONS

PART III – LANDFILL TAX

THE BASIC PROVISIONS

EXEMPTIONS

ADMINISTRATION

CREDIT

REVIEW AND APPEAL

MISCELLANEOUS

INTERPRETATION

PART III – LANDFILL TAX
THE BASIC PROVISIONS

39   Landfill tax

39(1)   A tax, to be known as landfill tax, shall be charged in accordance with this Part.

39(2)   The tax shall be under the care and management of the Commissioners of Customs and Excise.

Official publications – Taxpayer's charter.
LFT1, para. 1ff. (2000 edn).

40   Charge to tax

40(1)   Tax shall be charged on a taxable disposal.

40(2)   A disposal is a **taxable disposal** if–

(a)   it is a disposal of material as waste,
(b)   it is made by way of landfill,
(c)   it is made at a landfill site, and
(d)   it is made on or after 1st October 1996.

40(3)   For this purpose a disposal is **made at a landfill site** if the land on or under which it is made constitutes or falls within land which is a landfill site at the time of the disposal.

Official publications – LFT1, para. 1.2 (2000 edn).

41   Liability to pay tax

41(1)   The person liable to pay tax charged on a taxable disposal is the landfill site operator.

41(2)   The reference here to the **landfill site operator** is to the person who is at the time of the disposal the operator of the landfill site which constitutes or contains the land on or under which the disposal is made.

Cross references – FA 1996, Sch. 5, para. 57(4): joint and several liability for a secondary liability.
Official publications – LFT1, para. 1.7 (2000 edn).

42   Amount of tax

42(1)   The amount of tax charged on a taxable disposal shall be found by taking–

(a)   £11 for each whole tonne disposed of and a proportionately reduced sum for any additional part of a tonne, or
(b)   a proportionately reduced sum if less than a tonne is disposed of.

42(2)   Where the material disposed of consists entirely of qualifying material this section applies as if the reference to £11 were to £2.

42(3)   Qualifying material is material for the time being listed for the purposes of this section in an order.

42(4)   The Treasury must have regard to the object of securing that material is listed if it is of a kind commonly described as inactive or inert.

History – In s. 42(1)(a), the figure "£11" was substituted for the figure of "£11" by FA 2000, s. 140(1), in relation to taxable disposals made, or treated as made, on or after 1 April 2000.
In s. 42(1)(a), the former figure "£10" was substituted for the figure of "£7" by FA 1999, s. 124(1), in relation to taxable disposals made, or treated as made, on or after 1 April 1999.
In s. 42(2), the figure "£11" was substituted for the figure of "£10" by FA 2000, s. 140(1), in relation to taxable disposals made, or treated as made, on or after 1 April 2000.
In s. 42(2), the former figure "£10" was substituted for the figure of "£7" by FA 1999, s. 124(1), in relation to taxable disposals made, or treated as made, on or after 1 April 1999.

Statutory instruments – Landfill Tax (Qualifying Material) Order 1996 (SI 1996/1528).
Landfill Tax (Qualifying Material) Order 1996 (SI 1996/1528): qualifying material.

Official publications – LFT1, para. 2 (2000 edn): rates of tax.

EXEMPTIONS

43   Material removed from water

43(1)   A disposal is not a **taxable disposal** for the purposes of this Part if it is shown to the satisfaction of the Commissioners that the disposal is of material all of which–

(a)   has been removed (by dredging or otherwise) from water falling within subsection (2) below, and

(b)   formed part of or projected from the bed of the water concerned before its removal.

43(2)   Water falls within this subsection if it is–

(a)   a river, canal or watercourse (whether natural or artificial), or

(b)   a dock or harbour (whether natural or artificial).

43(3)   A disposal is not a **taxable disposal** for the purposes of this Part if it is shown to the satisfaction of the Commissioners that the disposal is of material all of which–

(a)   has been removed (by dredging or otherwise) from water falling within the approaches to a harbour (whether natural or artificial),

(b)   has been removed in the interests of navigation, and

(c)   formed part of or projected from the bed of the water concerned before its removal.

43(4)   A disposal is not a **taxable disposal** for the purposes of this Part if it is shown to the satisfaction of the Commissioners that the disposal is of material all of which–

(a)   consists of naturally occurring mineral material, and

(b)   has been removed (by dredging or otherwise) from the sea in the course of commercial operations carried out to obtain substances such as sand or gravel from the seabed.

Official publications – LFT1, para. 3 (2000 edn).

43A   Contaminated land

43A(1)   A disposal is not a **taxable disposal** for the purposes of this Part if it is a disposal within subsection (2) below.

43A(2)   A disposal is within this subsection if–

(a)   it is of material all of which has been removed from land in relation to which a certificate issued under section 43B below was in force at the time of the removal;

(b)   none of that material has been removed from a part of the land in relation to which, as at the time of the removal, the qualifying period has expired;

(c)   it is a disposal in relation to which any conditions to which the certificate was made subject are satisfied; and

(d)   it is not a disposal within subsection (4) below.

43A(3)   For the purpose of subsection (2)(b) above the **qualifying period expires**, in relation to the part of the land in question–

(a)   in the case of a reclamation which qualified under section 43B(7)(a) below, where the object involves the construction of–

     (i) a building; or

     (ii) a civil engineering work,

   when the construction commences;

(b)   in any other case of a reclamation which qualified under section 43B(7)(a) below, when pollutants have been cleared to the extent that they no longer prevent the object from being fulfilled; or

(c)   in the case of a reclamation which qualified under section 43B(7)(b) below, when pollutants have been cleared to the extent that the potential for harm has been removed.

43A(4)   Subject to subsection (5) below, a disposal is within this subsection if it is of material the removal of any of which is required in order to comply with–

(a)   a works notice served under section 46A of the Control of Pollution Act 1974;

(b)   an enforcement notice served under section 13 of the Environmental Protection Act 1990;

(c)   a prohibition notice served under section 14 of the Environmental Protection Act 1990;

(d)   an order under section 26 of the Environmental Protection Act 1990;

(e)   a remediation notice served under section 78E of the Environmental Protection Act 1990,

(f)   an enforcement notice served under section 90B of the Water Resources Act 1991; or

(g)   a works notice served under section 161A of the Water Resources Act 1991.

43A(5)   A disposal shall not be regarded as falling within subsection (4) above where the removal of the material has been carried out by or on behalf of any of the following bodies:

(a)   a local authority;

(b)   a development corporation;

(c)   the Environment Agency;

(d)   the Scottish Environment Protection Agency;

(e)   English Partnerships;

(f)   Scottish Enterprise;

(g)   Highlands and Islands Enterprise;

(h)   the Welsh Development Agency.

43A(6)   In this section–

    "development corporation" means–

    (a)   in England and Wales, a corporation established under section 135 of the Local Government, Planning and Land Act 1980;

    (b)   in Scotland, a corporation established under section 2 of the New Towns (Scotland) Act 1968;

    "English Partnerships" means the Urban Regeneration Agency established by section 158 of the Leasehold Reform, Housing and Urban Development Act 1993;

    "Highlands and Islands Enterprise" means the body established by section 1(b) of the Enterprise and New Towns (Scotland) Act 1990;

    "land" includes land covered by water;

    "Scottish Enterprise" means the corporation established by section 1(a) of the Enterprise and New Towns (Scotland) Act 1990;

    "the Welsh Development Agency" means the body established by section 1 of the Welsh Development Agency Act 1975.

43A(7)   For the purposes of this section–

(a)   the **removal of material** includes its removal from one part of the land for disposal on another part of the same land;

(b)   the **clearing of pollutants** includes their being cleared from one part of the land for disposal on another part of the same land.

History – S. 43A was inserted by SI 1996/1529, art. 3, operative from 1 August 1996.

Forms – LT 1C: contaminated land - application for a certificate of exemption.

Official publications – Information Note 1/97 (1 May 1997): reclamation of contaminated land, which is due to be replaced by Notice LFT2.
LFT1, para. 3.4 (2000 edn).

43B   Contaminated land: certificates

43B(1)   Subject to subsection (2) below, the Commissioners shall issue a certificate in relation to any land where–

(a)   *an application in writing is made by a person carrying out, or intending to carry out, a reclamation of that land (the applicant);*

(b)   the applicant provides to them such information as they may direct, whether generally or as regards that particular case;

(c)   the application is made not less than 30 days before the date from which the certificate is to take effect; and

(d) the reclamation qualifies under subsection (7) below.

43B(2) The Commissioners shall not refuse an application for a certificate in a case where the conditions specified in subsection (1)(a) to (d) above are satisfied unless it appears to them–

(a) necessary to do so for the protection of the revenue; or

(b) except where the applicant is one of the bodies mentioned in subsection (5) of section 43A above, that all or part of the reclamation of land to which the application relates is required in order to comply with a notice or order mentioned in subsection (4) of that section.

43B(3) The Commissioners may make a certificate subject to such conditions set out in the certificate as they think fit, including (but not restricted to) conditions–

(a) that the certificate is to be in force only in relation to a particular quantity of material;

(b) that the certificate is to be in force only in relation to disposals made at a particular landfill site or sites;

(c) that the certificate is to be in force in relation to part only of the land to which the application relates.

43B(4) A certificate issued under this section–

(a) shall have effect from the date it is issued to the applicant or such later date as the Commissioners may specify in the certificate; and

(b) shall cease to have effect on such date as the Commissioners may set out in the certificate, but in any event no later than the day on which the person to whom the certificate was issued ceases to have the intention to carry out any activity involving reclamation of the land in relation to which the certificate was issued.

43B(5) Where a certificate has been issued to a person, the Commissioners–

(a) may vary it by issuing a further certificate to that person; or

(b) may withdraw it by giving notice in writing to that person; but this is subject to subsection (6) below.

43B(6) The Commissioners shall not withdraw a certificate unless it appears to them–

(a) necessary to do so for the protection of the revenue;

(b) that the reclamation did not in fact qualify under subsection (7) below or no longer so qualifies;

(c) that there will not be any or any more disposals within section 43A(2) above of material from the land to which the certificate relates; or

(d) except where the person to whom the certificate was issued is one of the bodies mentioned in subsection (5) of section 43A above, that the removal of material from the land to which the certificate relates is required in order to comply with a notice or order mentioned in subsection (4) of that section.

43B(7) A reclamation qualifies under this subsection if–

(a) it is, or is to be, carried out with the object of facilitating development, conservation, the provision of a public park or other amenity, or the use of the land for agriculture or forestry; or

(b) in a case other than one within paragraph (a) above, it is, or is to be, carried out with the object of reducing or removing the potential of pollutants to cause harm,

and, in either case, the conditions specified in subsection (8) below are satisfied.

43B(8) The conditions mentioned in subsection (7) above are–

(a) that the reclamation constitutes or includes clearing the land of pollutants which are causing harm or have the potential for causing harm;

(b) that, in a case within subsection (7)(a) above, those pollutants would (unless cleared) prevent the object concerned being fulfilled; and

(c) that all relevant activities have ceased or have ceased to give rise to any pollutants in relation to that land.

43B(9) For the purposes of subsection (8) above the clearing of pollutants–

(a) need not be such that all pollutants are removed;

(b) need not be such that pollutants are removed from every part of the land in which they are present;

(c) may involve their being cleared from one part of the land and disposed of on another part of the same land.

43B(10) For the purposes of subsection (8)(c) above an activity is **relevant** if–

(a)   it has at any time resulted in the presence of pollutants in, on or under the land in question otherwise than–

      (i) without the consent of the person who was the occupier of the land at the time, or

      (ii) by allowing pollutants to be carried onto the land by air or water, and

(b)   at that time it was carried out–

      (i) by the applicant or a person connected with him, or

      (ii) by any person on the land in question.

43B(11)   For the purposes of subsection (10) above–

(a)   any question whether a person is **connected** with another shall be determined in accordance with section 839 of the Taxes Act 1988;

(b)   the **occupier of land** that is not in fact occupied is the person entitled to occupy it.

43B(12)   In this section **"land"** has the meaning given by section 43A(6) above.

History – S. 43B was inserted by SI 1996/1529, art. 3, operative from 1 August 1996.

Official publications – LFT2 is due to be published in due course.

43C   Site restoration

43C(1)   A disposal is not a **taxable disposal** for the purposes of this Part if–

(a)   the disposal is of material all of which is treated for the purposes of section 42 above as qualifying material,

(b)   before the disposal the operator of the landfill site notifies the Commissioners in writing that he is commencing the restoration of all or a part of the site and provides such other written information as the Commissioners may require generally or in the particular case, and

(c)   the material is deposited on and used in the restoration of the site or part specified in the notification under paragraph (b) above.

43C(2)   In this section **"restoration"** means work, other than capping waste, which is required by a relevant instrument to be carried out to restore a landfill site to use on completion of waste disposal operations.

43C(3)   The following are **relevant instruments**–

(a)   a planning consent;

(b)   a waste management licence;

(c)   a resolution authorising the disposal of waste on or in land.

History – S. 43C was inserted by SI 2000/2075, art. 2(a), operative in respect of disposals of material taking place, or treated as taking place, on or after 1 October 1999.

Official publications – Information Note 1/99: restoring landfill sites and filling quarries.

44   Mining and quarrying

44(1)   A disposal is not a **taxable disposal** for the purposes of this Part if it is shown to the satisfaction of the Commissioners that the disposal is of material all of which fulfils each of the conditions set out in subsections (2) to (4) below.

44(2)   The material must result from commercial mining operations (whether the mining is deep or open-cast) or from commercial quarrying operations.

44(3)   The material must be naturally occurring material extracted from the earth in the course of the operations.

44(4)   The material must not have been subjected to, or result from, a non-qualifying process carried out at any stage between the extraction and the disposal.

44(5)   A **non-qualifying process** is–

(a)   a process separate from the mining or quarrying operations, or

(b)   a process forming part of those operations and permanently altering the material's chemical composition.

Official publications – LFT1, para. 3.2 (2000 edn).

44A   Quarries

44A(1)   A disposal is not a **taxable disposal** for the purposes of this Part if it is–

(a)   of material all of which is treated for the purposes of section 42 above as qualifying material,

(b)   made at a qualifying landfill site, and

(c)   made, or treated as made, on or after 1st October 1999.

44A(2)   A landfill site is a **qualifying landfill site** for the purposes of this section if at the time of the disposal–

(a)   the landfill site is or was a quarry,

(b)   subject to subsection (3) below, it is a requirement of planning consent in respect of the land in which the quarry or former quarry is situated that it be wholly or partially refilled, and

(c)   subject to subsection (4) below, the licence or, as the case may require, resolution authorising disposals on or in the land comprising the site permits only the disposal of material which comprises qualifying material.

44A(3)   Where a quarry–

(a)   was in existence before 1st October 1999, and

(b)   quarrying operations ceased before that date,

the requirement referred to in subsection (2)(b) must have been imposed on or before that date.

44A(4)   Where a licence authorising disposals on or in the land does not (apart from the application of this subsection) meet the requirements of subsection (2)(c) above and an application has been made to vary the licence in order to meet them, it shall be deemed to meet them for the period before-

(a)   the application is disposed of, or

(b)   the second anniversary of the making of the application if it occurs before the application is disposed of.

44A(5)   For the purposes of subsection (4) an **application is disposed of** if–

(a)   it is granted,

(b)   it is withdrawn,

(c)   it is refused and there is no right of appeal against the refusal,

(d)   a time limit for appeal against refusal expires without an appeal having been commenced, or

(e)   an appeal against refusal is dismissed or withdrawn and there is no further right of appeal.

History – S. 44A was inserted by SI 2000/2075, art. 2(b), operative in respect of disposals of material taking place, or treated as taking place, on or after 1 October 1999.

45   Pet cemeteries

45(1)   A disposal is not a **taxable disposal** for the purposes of this Part if–

(a)   the disposal is of material consisting entirely of the remains of dead domestic pets, and

(b)   the landfill site at which the disposal is made fulfils the test set out in subsection (2) below.

45(2)   The test is that during the relevant period–

(a)   no landfill disposal was made at the site, or

(b)   the only landfill disposals made at the site were of material consisting entirely of the remains of dead domestic pets.

45(3)   For the purposes of subsection (2) above the **relevant period**–

(a)   begins with 1st October 1996 or (if later) with the coming into force in relation to the site of the licence or resolution mentioned in section 66 below, and

(b)   ends immediately before the disposal mentioned in subsection (1) above.

Official publications – LFT1, para. 3.3 (2000 edn).

46   Power to vary

46(1)   Provision may be made by order to produce the result that–

(a)   a disposal which would otherwise be a taxable disposal (by virtue of this Part as it applies for the time being) is not a taxable disposal;

(b)   a disposal which would otherwise not be a taxable disposal (by virtue of this Part as it applies for the time being) is a taxable disposal.

46(2)   Without prejudice to the generality of subsection (1) above, an order under this section may–

(a)   confer exemption by reference to certificates issued by the Commissioners and to conditions set out in certificates;

(b)   allow the Commissioners to direct requirements to be met before certificates can be issued;

(c)   provide for the review of decisions about certificates and for appeals relating to decisions on review.

46(3) Provision may be made under this section in such way as the Treasury think fit (whether by amending this Part or otherwise).

Statutory instruments – Landfill Tax (Contaminated Land) Order 1996 (SI 1996/1529).
Landfill Tax (Site Restoration and Quarries) Order 1999 (SI 1999/2075).

ADMINISTRATION

47 Registration

47(1) The register kept under this section may contain such information as the Commissioners think is required for the purposes of the care and management of the tax.

47(2) A person who–

(a) carries out taxable activities, and

(b) is not registered,

is liable to be registered.

47(3) Where–

(a) a person at any time forms the intention of carrying out taxable activities, and

(b) he is not registered,

he shall notify the Commissioners of his intention.

47(4) A person who at any time ceases to have the intention of carrying out taxable activities shall notify the Commissioners of that fact.

47(5) Where a person is liable to be registered by virtue of subsection (2) above the Commissioners shall register him with effect from the time when he begins to carry out taxable activities; and this subsection applies whether or not he notifies the Commissioners under subsection (3) above.

47(6) Where the Commissioners are satisfied that a person has ceased to carry out taxable activities they may cancel his registration with effect from the earliest practicable time after he so ceased; and this subsection applies whether or not he notifies the Commissioners under subsection (4) above.

47(7) Where–

(a) a person notifies the Commissioners under subsection (4) above,

(b) they are satisfied that he will not carry out taxable activities,

(c) they are satisfied that no tax which he is liable to pay is unpaid,

(d) they are satisfied that no credit to which he is entitled under regulations made under section 51 below is outstanding, and

(e) subsection (8) below does not apply,

the Commissioners shall cancel his registration with effect from the earliest practicable time after he ceases to carry out taxable activities.

47(8) Where–

(a) a person notifies the Commissioners under subsection (4) above, and

(b) they are satisfied that he has not carried out, and will not carry out, taxable activities,

the Commissioners shall cancel his registration with effect from the time when he ceased to have the intention to carry out taxable activities.

47(9) For the purposes of this section regulations may make provision–

(a) as to the time within which a notification is to be made;

(b) as to the form and manner in which any notification is to be made and as to the information to be contained in or provided with it;

(c) requiring a person who has made a notification to notify the Commissioners if any information contained in or provided in connection with it is or becomes inaccurate;

(d) as to the correction of entries in the register.

47(10) References in this Part to a **registrable person** are to a person who–

(a) is registered under this section, or

(b) is liable to be registered under this section.

Cross references – Landfill Tax Regulations 1996 (SI 1996/1527), reg. 2(1): meaning of effective date of registration, registered person and registrable person.
Landfill Tax Regulations 1996 (SI 1996/1527), reg. 4(1): notification of liability to register on statutory form.
Landfill Tax Regulations 1996 (SI 1996/1527), reg. 6: notification of cessation of taxable activities.
Landfill Tax Regulations 1996 (SI 1996/1527), reg. 20(2): payments in respect of credit.

Statutory instruments – Landfill Tax Regulations 1996 (SI 1996/1527).

Official publications – LFT1, para. 11 (2000 edn).

48   Information required to keep register up to date

48(1)   Regulations may make provision requiring a registrable person to notify the Commissioners of particulars which–

(a)   are of changes in circumstances relating to the registrable person or any business carried on by him,

(b)   appear to the Commissioners to be required for the purpose of keeping the register kept under section 47 above up to date, and

(c)   are of a prescribed description.

48(2)   Regulations may make provision–

(a)   as to the time within which a notification is to be made;

(b)   as to the form and manner in which a notification is to be made;

(c)   requiring a person who has made a notification to notify the Commissioners if any information contained in it is inaccurate.

Statutory instruments – Landfill Tax Regulations 1996 (SI 1996/1527).

49   Accounting for tax and time for payment

49   Regulations may provide that a registrable person shall–

(a)   account for tax by reference to such periods (accounting periods) as may be determined by or under the regulations;

(b)   make, in relation to accounting periods, returns in such form as may be prescribed and at such times as may be so determined;

(c)   pay tax at such times and in such manner as may be so determined.

Statutory instruments – Landfill Tax Regulations 1996 (SI 1996/1527).

Official publications – LFT1, para. 5 (2000 edn): tax points.
LFT1, para. 12 (2000 edn) : accounting for tax.
LFT1, para. 13 (2000 edn): records.

50   Power to assess

50(1)   Where–

(a)   a person has failed to make any returns required to be made under this Part,

(b)   a person has failed to keep any documents necessary to verify returns required to be made under this Part,

(c)   a person has failed to afford the facilities necessary to verify returns required to be made under this Part, or

(d)   it appears to the Commissioners that returns required to be made by a person under this Part are incomplete or incorrect,

the Commissioners may assess the amount of tax due from the person concerned to the best of their judgment and notify it to him.

50(2)   Where a person has for an accounting period been paid an amount to which he purports to be entitled under regulations made under section 51 below, then, to the extent that the amount ought not to have been paid or would not have been paid had the facts been known or been as they later turn out to be, the Commissioners may assess the amount as being tax due from him for that period and notify it to him accordingly.

50(3)   Where a person is assessed under subsections (1) and (2) above in respect of the same accounting period the assessments may be combined and notified to him as one assessment.

50(4)   Where the person failing to make a return, or making a return which appears to the Commissioners to be incomplete or incorrect, was required to make the return as a personal representative, trustee in bankruptcy, receiver, liquidator or person otherwise acting in a representative capacity in relation to another person, subsection (1) above shall apply as if the reference to tax due from him included a reference to tax due from that other person.

50(5)   An assessment under subsection (1) or (2) above of an amount of tax due for an accounting period shall not be made after the later of the following

(a)   two years after the end of the accounting period;

(b)   one year after evidence of facts, sufficient in the Commissioners' opinion to justify the making of the assessment, comes to their knowledge;

but where further such evidence comes to their knowledge after the baking of an assessment under subsection (1) or (2) above another assessment may be made under the subsection concerned in addition to any earlier assessment.

50(6)   Where–

(a)   as a result of a person's failure to make a return in relation to an accounting period the Commissioners have made an assessment under subsection (1) above for that period,

(b)   the tax assessed has been paid but no proper return has been made in relation to the period to which the assessment related, and

(c)   as a result of a failure to make a return in relation to a later accounting period, being a failure by the person referred to in paragraph (a) above or a person acting in a representative capacity in relation to him, as mentioned in subsection (4) above, the Commissioners find it necessary to make another assessment under subsection (1) above,

then, if the Commissioners think fit, having regard to the failure referred to in paragraph (a) above, they may specify in the assessment referred to in paragraph (c) above an amount of tax greater than that which they would otherwise have considered to be appropriate.

50(7)   Where an amount has been assessed and notified to any person under subsection (1) or (2) above it shall be deemed to be an amount of tax due from him and may be recovered accordingly unless, or except to the extent that, the assessment has subsequently been withdrawn or reduced.

50(8)   For the purposes of this section notification to–

(a)   a personal representative, trustee in bankruptcy, receiver or liquidator, or

(b)   a person otherwise acting in a representative capacity in relation to another person,

shall be treated as notification to the person in relation to whom the person mentioned in paragraph (a) above, or the first person mentioned in paragraph (b) above, acts.

50(9)   Subsection (5) above has effect subject to paragraph 33 of Schedule 5 to this Act.

50(10)   In this section **"trustee in bankruptcy"** means, as respects Scotland, an interim or permanent trustee (within the meaning of the Bankruptcy (Scotland) Act 1985) or a trustee acting under a trust deed (within the meaning of that Act).

Cross references – FA 1996, Sch. 5, para. 52(1): assessments of secondary liability.
FA 1996, Sch. 5, para. 54(1): adjustments of secondary liability.
FA 1996, Sch. 5, para. 57(5): joint and several liability for a secondary liability.
Landfill Tax Regulations 1996 (SI 1996/1527), reg. 48(2): distress.

CREDIT

51   Credit: general

51(1)   Regulations may provide that where–

(a)   a person has paid or is liable to pay tax, and

(b)   prescribed conditions are fulfilled,

the person shall be entitled to credit of such an amount as is found in accordance with prescribed rules.

51(2)   Regulations may make provision as to the manner in which a person is to benefit from credit, and in particular may make provision–

(a)   that a person shall be entitled to credit by reference to accounting periods;

(b)   that a person shall be entitled to deduct an amount equal to his total credit for an accounting period from the total amount of tax due from him for the period;

(c)   that if no tax is due from a person for an accounting period but he is entitled to credit for the period, the amount of the credit shall be paid to him by the Commissioners;

(d)   that if the amount of credit to which a person is entitled for an accounting period exceeds the amount of tax due from him for the period, an amount equal to the excess shall be paid to him by the Commissioners;

(e)   for the whole or part of any credit to be held over to be credited for a subsequent accounting *period;*

(f)   as to the manner in which a person who has ceased to be registrable is to benefit from credit.

51(3)   Regulations under subsection (2)(c) or (d) above may provide that where at the end of an accounting period an amount is due to a person who has failed to submit returns for an earlier period as required by this Part, the Commissioners may withhold payment of the amount until he has complied with that requirement.

51(4) Regulations under subsection (2)(e) above may provide for credit to be held over either on the person's application or in accordance with directions given by the Commissioners from time to time; and the regulations may allow directions to be given generally or with regard to particular cases.

51(5) Regulations may provide that–

(a) no benefit shall be conferred in respect of credit except on a claim made in such manner and at such time as may be determined by or under regulations;

(b) payment in respect of credit shall be made subject to such conditions (if any) as the Commissioners think fit to impose, including conditions as to repayment in specified circumstances;

(c) deduction in respect of credit shall be made subject to such conditions (if any) as the Commissioners think fit to impose, including conditions as to the payment to the Commissioners, in specified circumstances, of an amount representing the whole or part of the amount deducted.

51(6) Regulations may require a claim by a person to be made in a return required by provision made under section 49 above.

51(7) Nothing in section 52 or 53 below shall be taken to derogate from the power to make regulations under this section (whether with regard to bad debts, the environment or any other matter).

Cross references – FA 1996, Sch. 5, para. 50(1): operator entitled to credit.
FA 1996, Sch. 5, para. 54(1): adjustments of secondary liability.

Statutory instruments – Landfill Tax Regulations 1996 (SI 1996/1527, as amended by SI 1999/3270).

Official publications – LFT1, para. 8 and 9 (2000 edn).

Notes – FA 1997 s. 50 and Sch. 5: indirect taxes and overpayments.

52   Bad debts

52(1) Regulations may be made under section 51 above with a view to securing that a person is entitled to credit if–

(a) he carries out a taxable activity as a result of which he becomes entitled to a debt which turns out to be bad (in whole or in part), and

(b) such other conditions as may be prescribed are fulfilled.

52(2) The regulations may include provision under section 51(5)(b) or (c) above requiring repayment or payment if it turns out that it was not justified to regard a debt as bad (or to regard it as bad to the extent that it was so regarded).

52(3) The regulations may include provision for determining whether, and to what extent, a debt is to be taken to be bad.

Statutory instruments – Landfill Tax Regulations 1996 (SI 1996/1527).

Official publications – LFT1, para. 7 (2000 edn).

53   Bodies concerned with the environment

53(1) Regulations may be made under section 51 above with a view to securing that a person is entitled to credit if–

(a) he pays a sum to a body whose objects are or include the protection of the environment, and

(b) such other conditions as may be prescribed are fulfilled.

53(2) The regulations may in particular prescribe conditions–

(a) requiring bodies to which sums are paid (environmental bodies) to be approved by another body (the regulatory body);

(b) requiring the regulatory body to be approved by the Commissioners;

(c) requiring sums to be paid with the intention that they be expended on such matters connected with the protection of the environment as may be prescribed.

53(3) The regulations may include provision under section 51(5)(b) or (c) above requiring repayment or payment if–

(a) a sum is not in fact expended on matters prescribed under subsection (2)(c) above, or

(b) a prescribed condition turns out not to have been fulfilled.

53(4) The regulations may include–

(a) provision for determining the amount of credit (including provision for limiting it);

(b) provision that matters connected with the protection of the environment include such matters as overheads (including administration) of environmental bodies and the regulatory body;

(c)   provision as to the matters by reference to which an environmental body or the regulatory body can be, and remain, approved (including matters relating to the functions and activities of any such body);

(d)   provision allowing approval of an environmental body or the regulatory body to be withdrawn (whether prospectively or retrospectively);

(e)   provision that, if approval of the regulatory body is withdrawn, another body may be approved in its place or its functions may be performed by the Commissioners;

(f)   provision allowing the Commissioners to disclose to the regulatory body information which relates to the tax affairs of persons carrying out taxable activities and which is relevant to the credit scheme established by the regulations.

Statutory instruments – Landfill Tax Regulations 1996 (SI 1996/1527, as amended by SI 1999/3270).
Official publications – LFT1, para. 10 (2000 edn): environmental bodies.

REVIEW AND APPEAL

54   Review of Commissioners' decisions

54(1)   This section applies to the following decisions of the Commissioners–

(a)   a decision as to the registration or cancellation of registration of any person under this Part;

(b)   a decision as to whether tax is chargeable in respect of a disposal or as to how much tax is chargeable;

(ba)   a decision to refuse an application for a certificate under section 43B above, or to withdraw such a certificate;

(bb)   a decision to make a certificate issued under section 43B above subject to a condition that it is to be in force in relation to part only of the land to which the application for the certificate related;

(c)   a decision as to whether a person is entitled to credit by virtue of regulations under section 51 above or as to how much credit a person is entitled to or as to the manner in which he is to benefit from credit;

(d)   a decision as to an assessment falling within subsection (2) below or as to the amount of such an assessment;

(e)   a decision to refuse a request under section 58(3) below;

(f)   a decision to refuse an application under section 59 below;

(g)   a decision as to whether conditions set out in a specification under the authority of provision made under section 68(4)(b) below are met in relation to a disposal;

(h)   a decision to give a direction under any provision contained in regulations by virtue of section 68(5) below;

(i)   a decision as to a claim for the repayment of an amount under paragraph 14 of Schedule 5 to this Act;

(j)   a decision as to liability to a penalty under Part V of that Schedule or as to the amount of such a penalty;

(k)   a decision under paragraph 19 of that Schedule (as mentioned in paragraph 19(5));

(l)   a decision as to any liability to pay interest under paragraph 26 or of that Schedule or as to the amount of the interest payable;

(m)   a decision as to any liability to pay interest under paragraph 29 of that Schedule or as to the amount of the interest payable;

(n)   a decision to require any security under paragraph 31 of that Schedule or as to its amount;

(o)   a decision as to the amount of any penalty or interest specified in an assessment under paragraph 32 of that Schedule.

54(2)   An assessment falls within this subsection if it is an assessment under section 50 above in respect of an accounting period in relation to which a return required to be made by virtue of regulations under section 49 above has been made.

54(3)   Any person who is or will be affected by any decision to which this section applies may by notice in writing to the Commissioners require them to review the decision.

54(4)   *The Commissioners shall not be required under this section to review any decision unless the notice requiring the review is given before the end of the period of 45 days beginning with the day on which written notification of the decision, or of the assessment containing the decision, was first given to the person requiring the review.*

54(5)   For the purposes of subsection (4) above it shall be the duty of the Commissioners to give written notification of any decision t6 which this section applies to any person who–

(a)   requests such a notification,

(b)   has not previously been given written notification of that decision, and

(c)   if given such a notification, will be entitled to require a review of the decision under this section.

54(6)   A person shall be entitled to give a notice under this section requiring a decision to be reviewed for a second or subsequent time only if–

(a)   the grounds on which he requires the further review are that the Commissioners did not, on any previous review, have the opportunity to consider certain facts or other matters, and

(b)   he does not, on the further review, require the Commissioners to consider any facts or matters which were considered on a previous review except in so far as they are relevant to any issue not previously considered.

54(7)   Where the Commissioners are required in accordance with this section to review any decision it shall be their duty to do so; and on the review they may withdraw, vary or confirm the decision.

54(8)   Where–

(a)   it is the duty under this section of the Commissioners to review any decision, and

(b)   they do not, within the period of 45 days beginning with the day on which the review was required, give notice to the person requiring it of their determination on the review,

they shall be deemed for the purposes of this Part to have confirmed the decision.

History – S. 54(1)(ba) and (bb) were inserted by SI 1996/1529, art. 4, operative from enactment of s. 54 on 29 April 1996.

Cross references – FA 1996, Sch. 5, para. 59: reviews and secondary liability.
FA 1997, Sch. 5, para. 19(3): review of decisions and appeals.
Value Added Tax Tribunals Rules 1986 (SI 1986/590), r. 20(1A): disclosure, inspection and production of documents.
Landfill Tax Regulations 1996 (SI 1996/1527), reg. 48(2): distress.
Distress for Customs and Excise Duties and Other Indirect Taxes Regulations (SI 1997/1431), reg. 5(1)(b): restrictions on levying distress.

55   Appeals: general

55(1)   Subject to the following provisions of this section, an appeal shall lie to an appeal tribunal with respect to any of the following decisions–

(a)   any decision by the Commissioners on a review under section 54 above (including a deemed confirmation under subsection (8) of that section);

(b)   any decision by the Commissioners on such review of a decision referred to in section 54(1) above as the Commissioners have agreed to undertake in consequence of a request made after the end of the period mentioned in section 54(4) above.

55(2)   Where an appeal is made under this section by a person who is required to make returns by virtue of regulations under section 49 above, the appeal shall not be entertained unless the appellant–

(a)   has made all the returns which he is required to make by virtue of those regulations, and

(b)   has paid the amounts shown in those returns as payable by him.

55(3)   Where an appeal is made under this section with respect to a decision falling within section 54(1)(b) or (d) above the appeal shall not be entertained unless–

(a)   the amount which the Commissioners have determined to be payable as tax has been paid or deposited with them, or

(b)   on being satisfied that the appellant would otherwise suffer hardship the Commissioners agree or the tribunal decides that it should be entertained notwithstanding that that amount has not been so paid or deposited.

55(4)   On an appeal under this section against an assessment to a penalty under paragraph 18 of Schedule 5 to this Act, the burden of proof as to the matters specified in paragraphs (a) and (b) of sub-paragraph (1) of paragraph 18 shall lie upon the Commissioners.

Cross references – FA 1997, Sch. 5, para. 19(3): review of decisions and appeals.
Value Added Tax Tribunals Rules 1986 (SI 1986/590), r. 2: definition of "appellant".

Official publications – VAT and duties tribunals – Appeals and applications to the tribunals – Explanatory leaflet.
990: Customs and excise appeals.
1000: Complaints and putting things right: our code of practice.
AO2: The Adjudicator's Office: How to complain about Customs and Excise.
LFT1, para. 15 (1997 edn): reviews and appeals.

56   Appeals: other provisions

56(1)   Subsection (2) below applies where the Commissioners make a decision falling within section 54(1)(d) above and on a review of it there is a further decision with respect to which an appeal is made under section 55 above; and the reference here to a further decision includes a reference to a deemed confirmation under section 54(8) above.

56(2)   Where on the appeal–

(a)   it is found that the amount specified in the assessment is less than it ought to have been, and

(b)   the tribunal gives a direction specifying the correct amount,

the assessment shall have effect as an assessment of the amount specified in the direction and that amount shall be deemed to have been notified to the appellant.

56(3)   Where on an appeal under section 55 above it is found that the whole or part of any amount paid or deposited in pursuance of section 55(3) above is not due, so much of that amount as is found not to be-due shall be repaid with interest at such rate as the tribunal may determine.

56(4)   Where on an appeal under section 55 above it is found that the whole or part of any amount due to the appellant by virtue of regulations under section 51(2)(c) or (d) or (f) above has not been paid, so much of that amount as is found not to have been paid shall be paid with interest at such rate as the tribunal may determine.

56(5)   Where an appeal under section 55 above has been entertained notwithstanding that an amount determined by the Commissioners to be payable as tax has not been paid or deposited and it is found on the appeal that that amount is due the tribunal may, if it thinks fit, direct that that amount shall be paid with interest at such rate as may be specified in the direction.

56(6)   Without prejudice to paragraph 25 of Schedule 5 to this Act, nothing in section 55 above shall be taken to confer on a tribunal any power to vary an amount assessed by way of penalty except in so far as it is necessary to reduce it to the amount which is appropriate under paragraphs 18 to 24 of that Schedule.

56(7)   Without prejudice to paragraph 28 of Schedule 5 to this Act, nothing in section 55 above shall be taken to confer on a tribunal any power to vary an amount assessed by way of interest except in so far as it is necessary to reduce it to the amount which is appropriate under paragraph 26 or 27 of that Schedule.

56(8)   Sections 85 and 87 of the Value Added Tax Act 1994 (settling of appeals by agreement and enforcement of certain decisions of tribunal) shall have effect as if–

(a)   the references to section 83 of that Act included references to section 55 above, and

(b)   the references to value added tax included references to landfill tax.

Cross references – FA 1997, Sch. 5, para. 19(3): review of decisions and appeals.
Value Added Tax Tribunals Rules 1986 (SI 1986/590), r. 16(2): withdrawal of an appeal or application.

57   Review and appeal: commencement

57   Sections 54 to 56 above shall come into force on–

(a)   1st October 1996, or

(b)   such earlier day as may be appointed by order.

MISCELLANEOUS

58   Partnership, bankruptcy, transfer of business, etc.

58(1)   As regards any case where a business is carried on in partnership or by another unincorporated body, regulations may make provision for determining by what persons anything required by this Part to be done by a person is to be done.

58(2)   The registration under this Part of an unincorporated body other than a partnership may be in the name of the body concerned; and in determining whether taxable activities are carried out by such a body no account shall be taken of any change in its members.

58(3)   The registration under this Part of a body corporate carrying on a business in several divisions may, if the body corporate so requests and the Commissioners see fit, be in the names of those divisions.

58(4)   As regards any case where a person carries on a business of a person who has died or become bankrupt or incapacitated or whose estate has been sequestrated, or of a person which is in liquidation or receivership or in relation to which an administration order is in force, regulations may–

(a)   require the first-mentioned person to inform the Commissioners of the fact that he is carrying on the business and of the event that has led to his carrying it on;

(b)   make provision allowing the person to be treated for a limited time as if he were the other person;

(c)   make provision for securing continuity in the application of this Part where a person is so treated.

58(5)   Regulations may make provision for securing continuity in the application of this Part in cases where a business carried on by a person is transferred to another person as a going concern.

58(6)   Regulations under subsection (5) above may in particular–

(a)   require the transferor to inform the Commissioners of the transfer;

(b)   provide for liabilities and duties under this Part of the transferor to become, to such extent as may be provided by the regulations, liabilities and duties of the transferee;

(c)   provide for any right of either of them to repayment or credit in respect of tax to be satisfied by making a repayment or allowing a credit to the other;

but the regulations may provide that no such provision as is mentioned in paragraph (b) or (c) of this subsection shall have effect in relation to any transferor and transferee unless an application in that behalf has been made by them under the regulations.

Statutory instruments – Landfill Tax Regulations 1996 (SI 1996/1527).

Official publications – LFT1, para. 11.6 (2000 edn): transfer of a business as a going concern.
LFT1, para. 11.8 (2000 edn): company registered in divisions.

59   Groups of companies

59(1)   Where under the following provisions of this section any bodies corporate are treated as members of a group, for the purposes of this Part–

(a)   any liability of a member of the group to pay tax shall be taken to be a liability of the representative member;

(b)   the representative member shall be taken to carry out any taxable activities which a member of the group would carry out (apart from this section) by virtue of section 69 below;

(c)   all members of the group shall be jointly and severally liable for any tax due from the representative member.

59(2)   Two or more bodies corporate are eligible to be treated as members of a group if the condition mentioned in subsection (3) below is fulfilled and–

(a)   one of them controls each of the others,

(b)   one person (whether a body corporate or an individual) controls all of them, or

(c)   two or more individuals carrying on a business in partnership control all of them.

59(3)   The condition is that the prospective representative member has an established place of business in the United Kingdom.

59(4)   Where an application to that effect is made to the Commissioners with respect to two or more bodies corporate eligible to be treated as members of a group, then–

(a)   from the beginning of an accounting period they shall be so treated, and

(b)   one of them shall be the representative member,

unless the Commissioners refuse the application; and the Commissioners shall not refuse the application unless it appears to them necessary to do so for the protection of the revenue.

59(5)   Where any bodies corporate are treated as members of a group and an application to that effect is made to the Commissioners, then, from the beginning of an accounting period–

(a)   a further body eligible to be so treated shall be included among the bodies so treated,

(b)   a body corporate shall be excluded from the bodies so treated,

(c)   another member of the group shall be substituted as the representative member, or

(d)   the bodies corporate shall no longer be treated as members of a group,

unless the application is to the effect mentioned in paragraph (a) or (c) above and the Commissioners refuse the application.

59(6)   The Commissioners may refuse an application under subsection (5)(a) or (c) above only if it appears to them necessary to do so for the protection of the revenue.

59(7)   Where a body corporate is treated as a member of a group as being controlled by any person and it appears to the Commissioners that it has ceased to be so controlled, they shall, by notice given to that person, terminate that treatment from such date as may be specified in the notice.

59(8) An application under this section with respect to any bodies corporate must be made by one of those bodies or by the person controlling them and must be made not less than 90 days before the date from which it is to take effect, or at such later time as the Commissioners may allow.

59(9) For the purposes of this section a body corporate shall be taken to **control** another body corporate if it is empowered by statute to control that body's activities or if it is that body's holding company within the meaning of section 736 of the Companies Act 1985; and an individual or individuals shall be taken to **control** a body corporate if he or they, were he or they a company, would be that body's holding company within the meaning of that section.

Official publications – LFT1, para. 11.7 (2000 edn).

60 Information, powers, penalties, secondary liability, etc.

60 Schedule 5 to this Act (which contains provisions relating to information, powers, penalties, secondary liability and other matters) shall have effect.

History – In s. 60, the words ", secondary liability" were inserted by FA 2000, s. 142(1), with effect from 28 July 2000. Accordingly the sidenote to s. 60 was amended with the insertion of the words ", secondary liability" by FA 2000, s. 142(2)

Official publications – 989: Visits by Customs and Excise officers.
LFT1, para. 13.4 (2000 edn): production of records.

61 Taxable disposals: special provisions

61(1) Where–

(a)   a taxable disposal is in fact made on a particular day,

(b)   within the period of 14 days beginning with that day the person liable to pay tax in respect of the disposal issues a landfill invoice in respect of the disposal, and

(c)   he has not notified the Commissioners in writing that he elects not to avail himself of this subsection,

for the purposes of this Part the disposal shall be treated as made at the time the invoice is issued.

61(2) The reference in subsection (1) above to a **landfill invoice** is to a document containing such particulars as regulations may prescribe for the purposes of that subsection.

61(3) The Commissioners may at the request of a person direct that subsection (1) above shall apply–

(a)   in relation to disposals in respect of which he is liable to pay tax, or

(b)   in relation to such of them as may be specified in the direction,

as if for the period of 14 days there were substituted such longer period as may be specified in the direction.

Cross references – FA 1996, Sch. 5, para. 49(8): secondary liability.
Landfill Tax Regulations 1996 (SI 1996/1527), reg. 23: scope of entitlement to credit.
Landfill Tax Regulations 1996 (SI 1996/1527), reg. 42(2): basic method and determination of weight of material.

Statutory instruments – Landfill Tax Regulations 1996 (SI 1996/1527).

62 Taxable disposals: regulations

62(1) For the purposes of this Part, regulations may make provision under this section in relation to a disposal which is a taxable disposal (or would be apart from the regulations).

62(2) The regulations may provide that if particular conditions are fulfilled–

(a)   the disposal shall be treated as not being a taxable disposal, or

(b)   the disposal shall, to the extent found in accordance with prescribed rules, be treated as not being a taxable disposal.

62(3) The regulations may provide that if particular conditions are fulfilled–

(a)   the disposal shall be treated as made at a time which is found in accordance with prescribed rules and which falls after the time when it would be regarded as made apart from the regulations, or

(b)   the disposal shall, to the extent found in accordance with prescribed rules, be treated as made at a time which is found in accordance with prescribed rules and which falls after the time when it would be regarded as made apart from the regulations.

62(4) In finding the time when the disposal would be regarded as made apart from the regulations, section 61(1) above and any direction under section 61(3) above shall be taken into account.

62(5) The regulations may be framed by reference to–

(a)   conditions specified in the regulations or by the Commissioners or by an authorised person, or

(b)   any combination of such conditions;

and the regulations may specify conditions, or allow conditions to be specified, generally or with regard to particular cases.

62(6)   The regulations may make provision under subsections (2)(b) and (3)(b) above in relation to the same disposal.

62(7)   The regulations may only provide that a disposal is to be treated as not being a taxable disposal if or to the extent that–

(a)   the material comprised in the disposal is held temporarily pending one or more of the following–

    (i)   the incineration or recycling of the material, or

    (ii)   the removal of the material for use elsewhere, or

    (iii)   the use of the material, if it is qualifying material within the meaning of section 42(3) above, for the restoration to use of the site at which the disposal takes place, or any part of that site, upon completion of waste disposal operations at the site, or as the case may be, that part of the site, or

    (iv)   the sorting of the material with a view to its removal elsewhere or its eventual disposal, and

(b)   the material in question is held temporarily in an area designated for the purpose by an authorised person.

History – S. 62(7)(a) was substituted by FA 2000, s. 141(2), with effect from 28 July 2000. Former s. 62(7)(a) reads as follows: "**(7)(a)**   The disposal is a temporary one pending the incineration or recycling of the material concerned, or pending the removal of the material for use elsewhere, or pending the sorting of the material with a view to its removal elsewhere or its eventual disposal"

In s. 62(7)(b), the words "the material in question is held temporarily" were substituted for the words "the temporary disposal is made" by FA 2000, s. 141(3), with effect from 28 July 2000.

Cross references – FA 1996, Sch. 5, para. 49(8): secondary liability.

Statutory instruments – Landfill Tax Regulations 1996 (SI 1996/1527).

63   Qualifying material: special provisions

63(1)   This section applies for the purposes of section 42 above.

63(2)   The Commissioners may direct that where material is disposed of it must be treated as qualifying material if it would in fact be such material but for a small quantity of non-qualifying material; and whether a quantity of non-qualifying material is small must be determined in accordance with the terms of the direction.

63(3)   The Commissioners may at the request of a person direct that where there is a disposal in respect of which he is liable to pay tax the material disposed of must be treated as qualifying material if it would in fact be such material but for a small quantity of non-qualifying material, and–

(a)   a direction may apply to all disposals in respect of which a person is liable to pay tax or to such of them as are identified in the direction;

(b)   whether a quantity of non-qualifying material is small must be determined in accordance with the terms of the direction.

63(4)   If a direction under subsection (3) above applies to a disposal any direction under subsection (2) above shall not apply to it.

63(5)   An order may provide that material must not be treated as qualifying material unless prescribed conditions are met.

63(6)   A condition may relate to any matter the Treasury think fit (such as the production of a document which includes a statement of the nature of the material).

Statutory instruments – Landfill Tax (Qualifying Material) Order 1996 (SI 1996/1528).

INTERPRETATION

64   Disposal of material as waste

64(1)   A disposal of material is a disposal of it as waste if the person making the disposal does so with the intention of discarding the material.

64(2)   The fact that the person making the disposal or any other person could benefit from or make use of the material is irrelevant.

64(3) Where a person makes a disposal on behalf of another person, for the purposes of subsections (1) and (2) above the person on whose behalf the disposal is made shall be treated as making the disposal.

64(4) The reference in subsection (3) above to a **disposal on behalf of another person** includes references to a disposal–

(a)   at the request of another person;

(b)   in pursuance of a contract with another person.

65   Disposal by way of landfill

65(1) There is a disposal of material by way of landfill if–

(a)   it is deposited on the surface of land or on a structure set into the surface, or

(b)   it is deposited under the surface of land.

65(2) Subsection (1) above applies whether or not the material is placed in a container before it is deposited.

65(3) Subsection (1)(b) above applies whether the material–

(a)   is covered with earth after it is deposited, or

(b)   is deposited in a cavity (such as a cavern or mine).

65(4) If material is deposited on the surface of land (or on a structure set into the surface) with a view to it being covered with earth the disposal must be treated as made when the material is deposited and not when it is covered.

65(5) An order may provide that the meaning of the disposal of material by way of landfill (as it applies for the time being) shall be varied.

65(6) An order under subsection (5) above may make provision in such way as the Treasury think fit, whether by amending any of subsections (1) to (4) above or otherwise.

65(7) In this section **"land"** includes land covered by water where the land is above the low water mark of ordinary spring tides.

65(8) In this section **"earth"** includes similar matter (such as sand or rocks).

66   Landfill sites

66 Land is a **landfill site** at a given time if at that time–

(a)   a licence which is a site licence for the purposes of Part II of the Environmental Protection Act 1990 (waste on land) is in force in relation to the land and authorises disposals in or on the land,

(b)   a resolution under section 54 of that Act (land occupied by waste disposal authorities in Scotland) is in force in relation to the land and authorises deposits or disposals in or on the land,

(ba)   a permit under regulations under section 2 of the Pollution Prevention and Control Act 1999 is in force in relation to the land and authorises deposits or disposals in or on the land

(c)   a disposal licence issued under Part II of the Pollution Control and Local Government (Northern Ireland) Order 1978 (waste on land) is in force in relation to the land and authorises deposits on the land,

(d)   a resolution passed under Article 13 of that Order (land occupied by district councils in Northern Ireland) is in force in relation to the land and relates to deposits on the land, or

(e)   a licence under any provision for the time being having effect in Northern Ireland and corresponding to section 35 of the Environmental Protection Act 1990 (waste management licences) is in force in relation to the land and authorises disposals in or on the land.

Prospective insertion – S. 66(ba) was to be inserted by Pollution Prevention and Control Act 1999, s. 6(1) and sch. 2, para. 19, operative with effect from 21 March 2000 in so far as it extends to England and Wales (SI 2000/800 (C. 18)). S. 66(ba) reads as follows:
"(ba) a permit under regulations under section 2 of the Pollution Prevention and Control Act 1999 is in force in relation to the land and authorises deposits or disposals in or on the land"

Cross references – Landfill Tax Regulations 1996 (SI 1996/1527), reg. 2(1): meaning of landfill site.

67   Operators of landfill sites

67 The **operator of a landfill site** at a given time is–

(a)   the person who is at the time concerned the holder of the licence, where section 66(a) above applies;

(b)   the waste disposal authority which at the time concerned occupies the landfill site, where section 66(b) above applies;

(c)   the person who is at the time concerned the holder of the licence, where section 66(c) above applies;

(d)   the district council which passed the resolution, where section 66(d) above applies;

(e)   the person who is at the time concerned the holder of the licence, where section 66(e) above applies.

Cross references – FA 1996, Sch. 5, para. 49(1): secondary liability.
FA 1996, Sch. 5, para. 52(6): assessments and secondary liability.
FA 1996, Sch. 5, para. 54(8): adjustments of secondary liability.

68   Weight of material disposed of

68(1)   The weight of the material disposed of on a taxable disposal shall be determined in accordance with regulations.

68(2)   The regulations may–

(a)   prescribe rules for determining the weight;

(b)   authorise rules for determining the weight to be specified by the Commissioners in a prescribed manner;

(c)   authorise rules for determining the weight to be agreed by the person liable to pay the tax and an authorised person.

68(3)   The regulations may in particular prescribe, or authorise the specification or agreement of, rules about–

(a)   the method by which the weight is to be determined;

(b)   the time by reference to which the weight is to be determined;

(c)   the discounting of constituents (such as water).

68(4)   The regulations may include provision that a specification authorised under subsection (2)(b) above may provide–

(a)   that it is to have effect only in relation to disposals of such descriptions as may be set out in the specification;

(b)   that it is not to have effect in relation to particular disposals; unless the Commissioners are satisfied that such conditions as may be set out in the specification are met in relation to the disposals;

and the conditions may be framed by reference to such factors as the Commissioners think fit (such as the consent of an authorised person to the specification having effect in relation to disposals).

68(5)   The regulations may include provision that–

(a)   where rules are agreed as mentioned in subsection (2)(c) above, and

(b)   the Commissioners believe that they should no longer be applied because they do not give an accurate indication of the weight or they are not being fully observed or for some other reason,

the Commissioners may direct that the agreed rules shall no longer have effect.

68(6)   The regulations shall be so framed that where in relation to a given disposal–

(a)   no specification of the Commissioners has effect, and

(b)   no agreed rules have effect,

the weight shall be determined in accordance with rules prescribed in the regulations.

Statutory instruments – Landfill Tax Regulations 1996 (SI 1996/1527).

69   Taxable activities

69(1)   A person carries out a **taxable activity** if–

(a)   he makes a taxable disposal in respect of which he is liable to pay tax, or

(b)   he permits another person to make a taxable disposal in respect of which he (the first-mentioned person) is liable to pay tax.

69(2)   Where–

(a)   a taxable disposal is made, and

(b)   it is made without the knowledge of the person who is liable to pay tax in respect of it,

that person shall for the purposes of this section be taken to permit the disposal.

70   Interpretation: other provisions

70(1)   Unless the context otherwise requires–

"**accounting period**" shall be construed in accordance with section 49 above;

"**appeal tribunal**" means a VAT and duties tribunal;

"**authorised person**" means any person acting under the authority of the Commissioners;

"**the Commissioners**" means the Commissioners of Customs and Excise;

"**conduct**" includes any act, omission or statement;

"**the Environment Agency**" means the body established by section 1 of the Environment Act 1995;

"**material**" means material of all kinds, including objects, substances and products of all kinds;

"**prescribed**" means prescribed by an order or regulations under this Part;

"**registrable person**" has the meaning given by section 47(10) above;

"**tax**" means landfill tax;

"**the Scottish Environment Protection Agency**" means the body established by section 20 of the Environment Act 1995;

"**taxable disposal**" has the meaning given by section 40 above.

70(2)   A **landfill disposal** is a disposal–

(a)   of material as waste, and

(b)   made by way of landfill.

70(2A)   A **local authority** is–

(a)   the council of a county, county borough, district, London borough, parish or group of parishes (or, in Wales, community or group of communities);

(b)   the Common Council of the City of London;

(c)   as respects the Temples, the Sub-Treasurer of the Inner Temple and the Under-Treasurer of the Middle Temple respectively;

(d)   the council of the Isles of Scilly;

(e)   any joint committee or joint board established by two or more of the foregoing;

(f)   in relation to Scotland, a council constituted under section 2 of the Local Government etc. (Scotland) Act 1994, any two or more such councils and any joint committee or joint board within the meaning of section 235(1) of the Local Government (Scotland) Act 1973.

70(3)   A reference to this Part includes a reference to any order or regulations made under it and a reference to a provision of this Part includes a reference to any order or regulations made under the provision, unless otherwise required by the context or any order or regulations.

70(4)   This section and sections 64 to 69 above apply for the purposes of this Part.

History – In s. 70(1), the definitions of "the Environment Agency" and "the Scottish Environment Protection Agency" were inserted by SI 1996/1529, art. 5, operative from 1 August 1996.
S. 70(2A) was inserted by SI 1996/1529, art. 6, operative from 1 August 1996.

Cross references – Landfill Tax Regulations 1996 (SI 1996/1527), reg. 2(1): meaning of disposal.

SUPPLEMENTARY

71   Orders and regulations

71(1)   The power to make an order under section 57 above shall be exercisable by the Commissioners, and the power to make an order under any other provision of this Part shall be exercisable by the Treasury.

71(2)   Any power to make regulations under this Part shall be exercisable by the Commissioners.

71(3)   Any power to make an order or regulations under this Part shall be exercisable by statutory instrument.

71(4)   An order to which this subsection applies shall be laid before the House of Commons; and unless it is approved by that House before the expiration of a period of 28 days beginning with the date on which it was made it shall cease to have effect on the expiration of that period, but without prejudice to anything previously done under the order or to the making of a new order.

71(5)   In reckoning any such period as is mentioned in subsection (4) above no account shall be taken of any time during which Parliament is dissolved or prorogued or during which the House of Commons is adjourned for more than four days.

71(6) A statutory instrument containing an order or regulations under this Part (other than an order under section 57 above or an order to which subsection (4) above applies) shall be subject to annulment in pursuance of a resolution of the House of Commons.

71(7) Subsection (4) above applies to–

(a) an order under section 42(3) above providing for material which would otherwise be qualifying material not to be qualifying material;

(b) an order under section 46 above which produces the result that a disposal which would otherwise not be a taxable disposal is a taxable disposal;

(c) an order under section 63(5) above other than one which provides only that an earlier order under section 63(5) is not to apply to material;

(d) an order under section 65(5) above providing for anything which would otherwise not be a disposal of material by way of landfill to be such a disposal.

71(8) Any power to make an order or regulations under this Part–

(a) may be exercised as regards prescribed cases or descriptions of case;

(b) may be exercised differently in relation to different cases or descriptions of case.

71(9) An order or regulations under this Part may include such supplementary, incidental, consequential or transitional provisions as appear to the Treasury or the Commissioners (as the case may be) to be necessary or expedient.

71(10) No specific provision of this Part about an order or regulations shall prejudice the generality of subsections (8) and (9) above.

PART VII – MISCELLANEOUS AND SUPPLEMENTAL

MISCELLANEOUS: INDIRECT TAXATION

197   Setting of rates of interest

197(1) The rate of interest applicable for the purposes of an enactment to which this section applies shall be the rate which for the purposes of that enactment is provided for by regulations made by the Treasury under this section.

197(2) This section applies to

(a) [Not relevant to landfill tax.]

(b) [Not relevant to landfill tax.]

(c) [Not relevant to landfill tax.]

(d) paragraphs 26 and 29 of Schedule 5 to this Act (interest payable to or by the Commissioners in connection with landfill tax) and

(e) paragraph 17 of Schedule 5 to the Finance Act 1997 (interest on amounts repayable in respect of overpayments by the Commissioners in connection with excise duties, insurance premium tax and landfill tax).

197(3) Regulations under this section may–

(a) make different provision for different enactments or for different purposes of the same enactment,

(b) either themselves specify a rate of interest for the purposes of an enactment or make provision for any such rate to be determined, and to change from time to time, by reference to such rate or the average of such rates as may be referred to in the regulations,

(c) provide for rates to be reduced below, or increased above, what they otherwise would be by specified amounts or by reference to specified formulae,

(d) provide for rates arrived at by reference to averages or formulae to be rounded up or down,

(e) provide for circumstances in which changes of rates of interest are or are not to take place, and

(f) provide that changes of rates are to have effect for periods beginning on or after a day determined in accordance with the regulations in relation to interest running from before that day, as well as in relation to interest running from, or from after, that day.

197(4) The power to make regulations under this section shall be exercisable by statutory instrument subject to annulment in pursuance of a resolution of the House of Commons.

197(5) Where–

(a)   regulations under this section provide, without specifying the rate determined in accordance with the regulations, for a new method of determining the rate applicable for the purposes of any enactment, or

(b)   the rate which, in accordance with regulations under this section, is the rate applicable for the purposes of any enactment changes otherwise than by virtue of the making of regulations specifying a new rate,

the Commissioners of Customs and Excise shall make an order specifying the new rate and the day from which, in accordance with the regulations, it has effect.

197(6)   [Not relevant to landfill tax.]

197(7)   Subsections (1) and (6) above shall have effect for periods beginning on or after such day as the Treasury may by order made by statutory instrument appoint and shall have effect in relation to interest running from before that day, as well as in relation to interest running from, or from after, that day; and different days may be appointed under this subsection for different purposes.

History – In s. 197(1), para. (e) was inserted by FA 1997, s. 50 and Sch. 5, para. 21, with effect from 19 March 1997.

Statutory instruments – SI 1997/1015: sets 1 April 1997 as the appointed day for the purposes of s. 197(7).
SI 1997/1016: sets rate of interest from 1 April 1997 at 6.25 per cent and 6 per cent per annum for the purposes of FA 1996, Sch. 5, para. 26 and Sch. 5, para. 29 respectively.
SI 1998/1461: sets rate of interest from 6 July 1998 at 9.5 per cent and 6 per cent per annum for the purposes of FA 1996, Sch. 5, para. 26 and Sch. 5, para. 29 respectively.
The basis for setting the rate of interest was amended by SI 1998/1461 with effect from 6 July 1998. Interest is set using formulae linked to a reference rate. The reference rate is based on an average of the base rates of six main banks rounded to the nearest whole number. For default interest, the formula used will be the reference rate plus 2.5 per cent. Application of the formulae for interest accruing on or after 6 July 1998 is as follows:

Period of application	Statutory interest FA 1996, Sch. 5, para. 29	Default interest FA 1996, Sch. 5, para. 26
From 6 February 2000	5	8.5
6 March 1999–5 February 2000	4	7.5
6 January 1999–5 March 1999	5	8.5
6 July 1998–5 January 1999	6	9.5

SI 2000/631: amended Air Passenger Duty and Other Indirect Taxes (Interest Rate) Regulations 1998 (SI 1998/1461).

SCHEDULES

SCHEDULE 5 – LANDFILL TAX

Section 60

Part I – INFORMATION

GENERAL

1(1)   Every person who is concerned (in whatever capacity) with any landfill disposal shall furnish to the Commissioners such information relating to the disposal as the Commissioners may reasonably require.

1(2)   The information mentioned in sub-paragraph (1) above shall be furnished within such time and in such form as the Commissioners may reasonably require.

RECORDS

2(1)   Regulations may require registrable persons to make records.

2(2)   Regulations under sub-paragraph (1) above may be framed by reference to such records as may be stipulated in any notice published by the Commissioners in pursuance of the regulations and not withdrawn by a further notice.

2(3)   Regulations may–

(a)   require registrable persons to preserve records of a prescribed description (whether or not the records are required to be made in pursuance of regulations) for such period not exceeding six years as may be specified in the regulations;

(b)   authorise the Commissioners to direct that any such records need only be preserved for a shorter period than that specified in the regulations;

(c)   authorise a direction to be made so as to apply generally or in such cases as the Commissioners may stipulate.

2(4) Any duty under regulations to preserve records may be discharged by the preservation of the information contained in them by such means as the Commissioners may approve; and where that information is so preserved a copy of any document forming part of the records shall (subject to the following provisions of this paragraph) be admissible in evidence in any proceedings, whether civil or criminal, to the same extent as the records themselves.

2(5) The Commissioners may, as a condition of approving under sub-paragraph (4) above any means of preserving information contained in any records, impose such reasonable requirements as appear to them necessary for securing that the information will be as readily available to them as if the records themselves had been preserved.

2(6) A statement contained in a document produced by a computer shall not by virtue of sub-paragraph (4) above be admissible in evidence–

(a)   in criminal proceedings in England and Wales, except in accordance with sections 69 and 70 of the Police and Criminal Evidence Act 1984 and Part II of the Criminal Justice Act 1988;

(b)   in civil proceedings in Scotland, except in accordance with sections 5 and 6 of the Civil Evidence (Scotland) Act 1988;

(c)   in criminal proceedings in Scotland, except in accordance with Schedule 8 to the Criminal Procedure (Scotland) Act 1995;

(d)   in civil proceedings in Northern Ireland, except in accordance with sections 2 and 3 of the Civil Evidence Act (Northern Ireland) 1971;

(e)   in criminal proceedings in Northern Ireland, except in accordance with Article 68 of the Police and Criminal Evidence (Northern Ireland) Order 1989 and Part II of the Criminal Justice (Evidence, Etc.) (Northern Ireland) Order 1988.

2(7) In the case of civil proceedings in England and Wales to which sections 5 and 6 of the Civil Evidence Act 1968 apply, a statement contained in a document produced by a computer shall not be admissible in evidence by virtue of sub-paragraph (4) above except in accordance with those sections.

Statutory instruments – Landfill Tax Regulations 1996 (SI 1996/1527).

DOCUMENTS

3(1) Every person who is concerned (in whatever capacity) with any landfill disposal shall upon demand made by an authorised person produce or cause to be produced for inspection by that person any documents relating to the disposal.

3(2) Where, by virtue of sub-paragraph (1) above, an authorised person has power to require the production of any documents from any person, he shall have the like power to require production of the documents concerned from any other person who appears to the authorised person to be in possession of them; but where any such other person claims a lien on any document produced by him, the production shall be without prejudice to the lien.

3(3) The documents mentioned in sub-paragraphs (1) and (2) above shall be produced–

(a)   at such place as the authorised person may reasonably require, and
(b)   at such time as the authorised person may reasonably require.

3(4) An authorised person may take copies of, or make extracts from, any document produced under sub-paragraph (1) or (2) above.

3(5) If it appears to him to be necessary to do so, an authorised person may, at a reasonable time and for a reasonable period, remove any document produced under sub-paragraph (1) or (2) above and shall, on request, provide a receipt for any document so removed; and where a lien is claimed on a document produced under sub-paragraph (2) above the removal of the document under this sub- paragraph shall not be regarded as breaking the lien.

3(6) Where a document removed by an authorised person under sub-paragraph (5) above is reasonably required for any purpose he shall, as soon as practicable, provide a copy of the document, free of charge, to the person by whom it was produced or caused to be produced.

3(7) Where any documents removed under the powers conferred by this paragraph are lost or damaged the Commissioners shall be liable to compensate their owner for any expenses reasonably incurred by him in replacing or repairing the documents.

Part II – POWERS

ENTRY AND INSPECTION

4   For the purpose of exercising any powers under this Part of this Act an authorised person may at any reasonable time enter and inspect premises used in connection with the carrying on of a business.

Official publications – 989: Visits by Customs and Excise officers.

ENTRY AND SEARCH

5(1)   Where–

(a)   a justice of the peace is satisfied on information on oath that there is reasonable ground for suspecting that a fraud offence which appears to be of a serious nature is being, has been or is about to be committed on any premises or that evidence of the commission of such an offence is to be found there, or

(b)   in Scotland a justice, within the meaning of section 307 of the Criminal Procedure (Scotland) Act 1995, is satisfied by evidence on oath as mentioned in paragraph (a) above,

he may issue a warrant in writing authorising any authorised person to enter those premises, if necessary by force, at any time within one month from the time of the issue of the warrant and search them.

5(2)   A person who enters the premises under the authority of the warrant may–

(a)   take with him such other persons as appear to him to be necessary;

(b)   seize and remove any documents or other things whatsoever found on the premises which he has reasonable cause to believe may be required as evidence for the purposes of proceedings in respect of a fraud offence which appears to him to be of a serious nature;

(c)   search or cause to be searched any person found on the premises whom he has reasonable cause to believe to be in possession of any such documents or other things;

but no woman or girl shall be searched except by a woman.

5(3)   The powers conferred by a warrant under this paragraph shall not be exercisable–

(a)   by more than such number of authorised persons as may be specified in the warrant,

(b)   outside such times of day as may be so specified, or

(c)   if the warrant so provides, otherwise than in the presence of a constable in uniform.

5(4)   An authorised person seeking to exercise the powers conferred by a warrant under this paragraph or, if there is more than one such authorised person, that one of them who is in charge of the search shall provide a copy of the warrant endorsed with his name as follows–

(a)   if the occupier of the premises concerned is present at the time the search is to begin, the copy shall be supplied to the occupier;

(b)   if at that time the occupier is not present but a person who appears to the authorised person to be in charge of the premises is present, the copy shall be supplied to that person;

(c)   if neither paragraph (a) nor paragraph (b) above applies, the copy shall be left in a prominent place on the premises.

5(5)   In this paragraph **"a fraud offence"** means an offence under any provision of paragraph 15(1) to (5) below.

ARREST

6(1)   Where an authorised person has reasonable grounds for suspecting that a fraud offence has been committed he may arrest anyone whom he has reasonable grounds for suspecting to be guilty of the offence.

6(2)   In this paragraph **"a fraud offence"** means an offence under any provision of paragraph 15(1) to (5) below.

ORDER FOR ACCESS TO RECORDED INFORMATION ETC.

7(1)   Where, on an application by an authorised person, a justice of the peace or, in Scotland, a justice (within the meaning of section 307 of the Criminal Procedure (Scotland) Act 1995) is satisfied that there are reasonable grounds for believing–

(a)   that an offence in connection with tax is being, has been or is about to be committed, and

(b) that any recorded information (including any document of any nature whatsoever) which may be required as evidence for the purpose of any proceedings in respect of such an offence is in the possession of any person, he may make an order under this paragraph.

7(2) An order under this paragraph is an order that the person who appears to the justice to be in possession of the recorded information to which the application relates shall–

(a) give an authorised person access to it, and

(b) permit an authorised person to remove and take away any of it which he reasonably considers necessary,

not later than the end of the period of 7 days beginning with the date of the order or the end of such longer period as the order may specify.

7(3) The reference in sub-paragraph (2)(a) above to giving an authorised person **access to the recorded information** to which the application relates includes a reference to permitting the authorised person to take copies of it or to make extracts from it.

7(4) Where the recorded information consists of information contained in a computer, an order under this paragraph shall have effect as an order to produce the information in a form in which it is visible and legible and, if the authorised person wishes to remove it, in a form in which it can be removed.

7(5) This paragraph is without prejudice to paragraphs 3 to 5 above.

REMOVAL OF DOCUMENTS ETC.

8(1) An authorised person who removes anything in the exercise of a power conferred by or under paragraph 5 or 7 above shall, if so requested by a person showing himself–

(a) to be the occupier of premises from which it was removed, or

(b) to have had custody or control of it immediately before the removal, provide that person with a record of what he removed.

8(2) The authorised person shall provide the record within a reasonable time from the making of the request for it.

8(3) Subject to sub-paragraph (7) below, if a request for permission to be allowed access to anything which–

(a) has been removed by an authorised person, and

(b) is retained by the Commissioners for the purposes of investigating an offence,

is made to the officer in overall charge of the investigation by a person who had custody or control of the thing immediately before it was so removed or by someone acting on behalf of such a person, the officer shall allow the person who made the request access to it under the supervision of an authorised person.

8(4) Subject to sub-paragraph (7) below, if a request for a photograph or copy of any such thing is made to the officer in overall charge of the investigation by a person who had custody or control of the thing immediately before it was so removed, or by someone acting on behalf of such a person, the officer shall–

(a) allow the person who made the request access to it under the supervision of an authorised person for the purpose of photographing it or copying it, or

(b) photograph or copy it, or cause it to be photographed or copied.

8(5) Subject to sub-paragraph (7) below, where anything is photographed or copied under sub-paragraph (4)(b) above the officer shall supply the photograph or copy, or cause it to be supplied, to the person who made the request.

8(6) The photograph or copy shall be supplied within a reasonable time from the making of the request.

8(7) There is no duty under this paragraph to allow access to, or to supply a photograph or copy of, anything if the officer in overall charge of the investigation for the purposes of which it was removed has reasonable grounds for believing that to do so would prejudice–

(a) that investigation,

(b) the investigation of an offence other than the offence for the purposes of the investigation of which the thing was removed, or

(c) any criminal proceedings which may be brought as a result of the investigation of which he is in charge or any such investigation as is mentioned in paragraph (b) above.

8(8) Any reference in this paragraph to the **officer in overall charge** of the investigation is a reference to the person whose name and address are endorsed on the warrant concerned as being the officer so in charge.

9(1) Where, on an application made as mentioned in sub-paragraph (2) below, the appropriate judicial authority is satisfied that a person has failed to comply with a requirement imposed by paragraph 8 above, the authority may order that person to comply with the requirement within such time and in such manner as may be specified in the order.

9(2) An application under sub-paragraph (1) above shall be made–

(a)   in the case of a failure to comply with any of the requirements imposed by sub-paragraphs (1) and (2) of paragraph 8 above, by the occupier of the premises from which the thing in question was removed or by the person who had custody or control of it immediately before it was so removed, and

(b)   in any other case, by the person who had such custody or control.

9(3) In this paragraph

"the appropriate judicial authority" means–
   (a)   in England and Wales, a magistrates' court;
   (b)   in Scotland, the sheriff;
   (c)   in Northern Ireland, a court of summary jurisdiction, as defined in Article 2(2)(a) of the Magistrates Court (Northern Ireland) Order 1981.

9(4) In England and Wales and Northern Ireland, an application for an order under this paragraph shall be made by way of complaint; and sections 21 and 42(2) of the Interpretation Act (Northern Ireland) 1954 shall apply as if any reference in those provisions to any enactment included a reference to this paragraph.

POWER TO TAKE SAMPLES

10(1) An authorised person, if it appears to him necessary for the protection of the revenue against mistake or fraud, may at any time take, from material which he has reasonable cause to believe is intended to be, is being, or has been disposed of as waste by way of landfill, such samples as he may require with a view to determining how the material ought to be or to have been treated for the purposes of tax.

10(2) Any sample taken under this paragraph shall be disposed of in such manner as the Commissioners may direct.

Part III – RECOVERY

GENERAL

11 Tax due from any person shall be recoverable as a debt due to the Crown.

PREFERENTIAL AND PREFERRED DEBTS

12(1) [Amends IA 1986, s. 386(1) and inserts IA 1986, Sch. 6, para. 3B.]

12(2) [Introduces amendments to Bankruptcy (Scotland) Act 1985, Sch. 3.]

12(3) [Inserts Bankruptcy (Scotland) Act 1985, Sch. 3, para. 2(1B).]

12(4) [Inserts Bankruptcy (Scotland) Act 1985, Sch. 3, para. 8B.]

12(5) [Amends Insolvency (Northern Ireland) Order 1989, art. 346(1) and inserts Sch. 4, para. 3B.]

DISTRESS AND DILIGENCE

13 [Omitted by FA 1997, s. 113 and Sch. 18, Pt. V(2).]

History – Para. 13 was repealed by FA 1997, s. 113 and Sch. 18, Pt. V(2), with effect from 1 July 1997 (SI 1997/1433) (C 55).

RECOVERY OF OVERPAID TAX

Statutory instruments – Landfill Tax Regulations 1996 (SI 1996/1527, as amended by SI 1996/2100).

14(1) Where a person has paid an amount to the Commissioners by way of tax which was not tax due to them, they shall be liable to repay the amount to him.

14(2) The Commissioners shall only be liable to repay an amount under this paragraph on a claim being made for the purpose.

14(3) It shall be a defence, in relation to a claim under this paragraph, that repayment of an amount would unjustly enrich the claimant.

14(4) The Commissioners shall not be liable, on a claim made under this paragraph, to repay any amount paid to them more than three years before the making of the claim.

14(5) A claim under this paragraph shall be made in such form and manner and shall be supported by such documentary evidence as may be prescribed by regulations.

14(6) Except as provided by this paragraph, the Commissioners shall not be liable to repay an amount paid to them by way of tax by virtue of the fact that it was not tax due to them.

History – Para. 14(4) was substituted by FA 1997, s. 50 and Sch. 5, para. 5(3), with effect from19 March 1997.

Cross references – FA 1997, Sch. 5, para. 1: unjust enrichment.
FA 1997, Sch. 5, para. 4(3): contravention of requirement to repay Commissioners.
FA 1997, Sch. 5, para. 14(3)(c): assessment for excessive repayment.
FA 1997, Sch. 5, para. 19(3): review of decisions and appeals.

Statutory instruments – Landfill Tax Regulations 1996 (SI 1996/1527).

Part IV – CRIMINAL PENALTIES

CRIMINAL OFFENCES

15(1) A person is guilty of an offence if–

(a) being a registrable person, he is knowingly concerned in, or in the taking of steps with a view to, the fraudulent evasion of tax by him or another registrable person, or

(b) not being a registrable person, he is knowingly concerned in, or in the taking of steps with a view to, the fraudulent evasion of tax by a registrable person.

15(2) Any reference in sub-paragraph (1) above to the **evasion of tax** includes a reference to the obtaining of a payment under regulations under section 51(2)(c) or (d) or (f) of this Act.

15(3) A person is guilty of an offence if with the requisite intent–

(a) he produces, furnishes or sends, or causes to be produced, furnished or sent, for the purposes of this Part of this Act any document which is false in a material particular, or

(b) he otherwise makes use for those purposes of such a document;

and the requisite intent is intent to deceive or to secure that a machine will respond to the document as if it were a true document.

15(4) A person is guilty of an offence if in furnishing any information for the purposes of this Part of this Act he makes a statement which he knows to be false in a material particular or recklessly makes a statement which is false in a material particular.

15(5) A person is guilty of an offence by virtue of this sub-paragraph if his conduct during any specified period must have involved the commission by him of one or more offences under the preceding provisions of this paragraph; and the preceding provisions of this sub-paragraph apply whether or not the particulars of that offence or those offences are known.

15(6) A person is guilty of an offence if–

(a) he enters into a taxable landfill contract, or

(b) he makes arrangements for other persons to enter into such a contract,

with reason to believe that tax in respect of the disposal concerned will be evaded.

15(7) A person is guilty of an offence if he carries out taxable activities without giving security (or further security) he has been required to give under paragraph 31 below.

15(8) For the purposes of this paragraph a taxable **landfill contract** is a contract under which there is to be a taxable disposal.

CRIMINAL PENALTIES

16(1) A person guilty of an offence under paragraph 15(1) above is liable–

(a) on summary conviction, to a penalty of the statutory maximum or of three times the amount of the tax, whichever is the greater, or to imprisonment for a term not exceeding six months or to both;

(b) on conviction on indictment, to a penalty of any amount or to imprisonment for a term not exceeding seven years or to both.

16(2) The reference in sub-paragraph (1) above to the **amount of the tax** shall be construed, in relation to tax itself or a payment falling within paragraph 15(2) above, as a reference to the aggregate of–

(a)   the amount (if any) falsely claimed by way of credit, and

(b)   the amount (if any) by which the gross amount of tax was falsely understated.

16(3) A person guilty of an offence under paragraph 15(3) or (4) above is liable–

(a)   on summary conviction, to a penalty of the statutory maximum (or, where sub-paragraph (4) below applies, to the alternative penalty there specified if it is greater) or to imprisonment for a term not exceeding six months or to both;

(b)   on conviction on indictment, to a penalty of any amount or to imprisonment for a term not exceeding seven years or to both.

16(4) Where–

(a)   the document referred to in paragraph 15(3) above is a return required under this Part of this Act, or

(b)   the information referred to in paragraph 15(4) above is contained in or otherwise relevant to such a return,

the alternative penalty is a penalty equal to three times the aggregate of the amount (if any) falsely claimed by way of credit and the amount (if any) by which the gross amount of tax was understated.

16(5) A person guilty of an offence under paragraph 15(5) above is liable–

(a)   on summary conviction, to a penalty of the statutory maximum (or, if greater, three times the amount of any tax that was or was intended to be evaded by his conduct) or to imprisonment for a term not exceeding six months or to both;

(b)   on conviction on indictment, to a penalty of any amount or to imprisonment for a term not exceeding seven years or to both;

and paragraph 15(2) and sub-paragraph (2) above shall apply for the purposes of this sub-paragraph as they apply respectively for the purposes of paragraph 15(1) and sub-paragraph (1) above.

16(6) A person guilty of an offence under paragraph 15(6) above is liable on summary conviction to a penalty of level 15 on the standard scale or three times the amount of the tax, whichever is the greater.

16(7) A person guilty of an offence under paragraph 15(7) above is liable on summary conviction to a penalty of level 15 on the standard scale.

16(8) In this paragraph–

(a)   **"credit"** means credit for which provision is made by regulations under section 51 of this Act;

(b)   **"the gross amount of tax"** means the total amount of tax due before taking into account any deduction for which provision is made by regulations under section 51(2) of this Act.

CRIMINAL PROCEEDINGS ETC.

17 Sections 145 to 155 of the Customs and Excise Management Act 1979 (proceedings for offences, mitigation of penalties and certain other matters) shall apply in relation to offences under paragraph 15 above and penalties imposed under paragraph 16 above as they apply in relation to offences and penalties under the customs and excise Acts as defined in that Act.

Official publications – LFT1, para. 14 (2000 edn): penalties and interest.

Part V – CIVIL PENALTIES

EVASION

18(1) Where–

(a)   for the purpose of evading tax, a registrable person does any act or omits to take any action, and

(b)   his conduct involves dishonesty (whether or not it is such as to give rise to criminal liability),

he is liable to a penalty equal to the amount of tax evaded, or (as the case may be) sought to be evaded, by his conduct; but this is subject to sub-paragraph (7) below.

18(2) The reference in sub-paragraph (1)(a) above to **evading tax** includes a reference to obtaining a payment under regulations under section 51(2)(c) or (d) or (f) of this Act in circumstances where the person concerned is not entitled to the sum.

18(3) The reference in sub-paragraph (1) above to the **amount of tax evaded** or sought to be evaded is a reference to the aggregate of–

(a)   the amount (if any) falsely claimed by way of credit, and

(b)   the amount (if any) by which the gross amount of tax was falsely understated.

18(4) In this paragraph–

(a)   **"credit"** means credit for which provision is made by regulations under section 51 of this Act;

(b)   **"the gross amount of tax"** means the total amount of tax due before taking into account any deduction for which provision is made by regulations under section 51(2) of this Act.

18(5) Statements made or documents produced by or on behalf of a person shall not be inadmissible in any such proceedings as are mentioned in sub-paragraph (6) below by reason only that it has been drawn to his attention–

(a)   that, in relation to tax, the Commissioners may assess an amount due by way of a civil penalty instead of instituting criminal proceedings and, though no undertaking can be given as to whether the Commissioners will make such an assessment in the case of any person, it is their practice to be influenced by the fact that a person has made a full confession of any dishonest conduct to which he has been a party and has given full facilities for investigation, and

(b)   that the Commissioners or, on appeal, an appeal tribunal have power under paragraph 25 below to reduce a penalty under this paragraph,

and that he was or may have been induced thereby to make the statements or produce the documents.

18(6) The proceedings referred to in sub-paragraph (5) above are–

(a)   any criminal proceedings against the person concerned in respect of any offence in connection with or in relation to tax, and

(b)   any proceedings against him for the recovery of any sum due from him in connection with or in relation to tax.

18(7) Where, by reason of conduct falling within sub-paragraph (1) above, a person is convicted of an offence (whether under this Part of this Act or otherwise) that conduct shall not also give rise to liability to a penalty under this paragraph.

Cross reference – Value Added Tax Tribunals Rules 1986 (SI 1986/590), r. 2: definition of "evasion penalty appeal".

19(1) Where it appears to the Commissioners–

(a)   that a body corporate is liable to a penalty under paragraph 18 above, and

(b)   that the conduct giving rise to that penalty is, in whole or in part, attributable to the dishonesty of a person who is, or at the material time was, a director or managing officer of the body corporate (a named officer),

the Commissioners may serve a notice under this paragraph on the body corporate and on the named officer.

19(2) A notice under this paragraph shall state–

(a)   the amount of the penalty referred to in sub-paragraph (1)(a) above (the basic penalty), and

(b)   that the Commissioners propose, in accordance with this paragraph, to recover from the named officer such portion (which may be the whole) of the basic penalty as is specified in the notice.

19(3) Where a notice is served under this paragraph, the portion of the basic penalty specified in the notice shall be recoverable from the named officer as if he were personally liable under paragraph 18 above to a penalty which corresponds to that portion; and the amount of that penalty may be assessed and notified to him accordingly under paragraph 32 below.

19(4) Where a notice is served under this paragraph–

(a)   the amount which, under paragraph 32 below, may be assessed as the amount due by way of penalty from the body corporate shall be only so much (if any) of the basic penalty as is not assessed on and notified to a named officer by virtue of sub-paragraph (3) above, and

(b)   the body corporate shall be treated as discharged from liability for so much of the basic penalty as is so assessed and notified.

19(5)   No appeal shall lie against a notice under this paragraph as such but–

(a)   where a body corporate is assessed as mentioned in sub-paragraph (4)(a) above, the body corporate may require a review of the Commissioners' decision as to its liability to a penalty and as to the amount of the basic penalty as if it were specified in the assessment;

(b)   where an assessment is made on a named officer by virtue of sub-paragraph (3) above, the named officer may require a review of the Commissioners' decision that the conduct of the body corporate referred to in sub-paragraph (1)(b) above is, in whole or in part, attributable to his dishonesty and of their decision as to the portion of the penalty which the Commissioners propose to recover from him;

(c)   sections 55 and 56 of this Act shall apply accordingly.

19(6)   In this paragraph a **"managing officer"**, in relation to a body corporate, means any manager, secretary or other similar officer of the body corporate or any person purporting to act in any such capacity or as a director; and where the affairs of a body corporate are managed by its members, this paragraph shall apply in relation to the conduct of a member in connection with his functions of management as if he were a director of the body corporate.

Cross references – Value Added Tax Tribunals Rules 1986 (SI 1986/590), r. 2: definition of "evasion penalty appeal".
Value Added Tax Tribunals Rules 1986 (SI 1986/590), r. 19(3A): power of a tribunal to strike out or dismiss an appeal.

MISDECLARATION OR NEGLECT

20(1)   Where, for an accounting period–

(a)   a return is made which understates a person's liability to tax or overstates his entitlement to credit, or

(b)   an assessment is made which understates a person's liability to tax and, at the end of the period of 30 days beginning on the date of the assessment, he has not taken all such steps as are reasonable to draw the understatement to the attention of the Commissioners,

the person concerned is liable, subject to sub-paragraphs (3) and (4) below, to a penalty equal to 5 per cent of the amount of the understatement of liability or (as the case may be) overstatement of entitlement.

20(2)   Where–

(a)   a return for an accounting period overstates or understates to any extent a person's liability to tax or his entitlement to credit, and

(b)   that return is corrected, in such circumstances and in accordance with such conditions as may be prescribed by regulations, by a return for a later accounting period which understates or overstates, to the corresponding extent, that liability or entitlement,

it shall be assumed for the purposes of this paragraph that the statement made by each such return is a correct statement for the accounting period to which the return relates.

20(3)   Conduct falling within sub-paragraph (1) above shall not give rise to liability to a penalty under this paragraph if the person concerned furnishes full information with respect to the inaccuracy concerned to the Commissioners–

(a)   at a time when he has no reason to believe that enquiries are being made by the Commissioners into his affairs, so far as they relate to tax, and

(b)   in such form and manner as may be prescribed by regulations or specified by the Commissioners in accordance with provision made by regulations.

20(4)   Where, by reason of conduct falling within sub-paragraph (1) above–

(a)   a person is convicted of an offence (whether under this Part of this Act or otherwise), or

(b)   a person is assessed to a penalty under paragraph 18 above,

that conduct shall not also give rise to liability to a penalty under this paragraph.

20(5)   In this paragraph **"credit"** means credit for which provision is made by regulations under section 51 of this Act.

Statutory instruments – Landfill Tax Regulations 1996 (SI 1996/1527).

REGISTRATION

21(1)   A person who fails to comply with section 47(3) of this Act is liable to a penalty equal to 5 per cent. of the relevant tax or, if it is greater or the circumstances are such that there is no relevant tax, to a penalty of £250; but this is subject to sub-paragraph (4) below.

21(2)   In sub-paragraph (1) above

"**relevant tax**" means the tax (if any) for which the person concerned is liable for the period which–

(a)   begins on the date with effect from which he is, in accordance with section 47 of this Act, required to be registered, and

(b)   ends on the date on which the Commissioners received notification of, or otherwise became aware of, his liability to be registered.

21(3)   A person who fails to comply with section 47(4) of this Act is liable to a penalty of £250.

21(4)   Where, by reason of conduct falling within sub-paragraph (1) above–

(a)   a person is convicted of an offence (whether under this Part of this Act or otherwise), or

(b)   a person is assessed to a penalty under paragraph 18 above,

that conduct shall not also give rise to liability to a penalty under this paragraph.

INFORMATION

22(1)   If a person–

(a)   fails to comply with any provision of paragraph 1 or 3 above, or

(b)   fails to make records as required by any provision of regulations made under paragraph 2 above,

he is liable to a penalty of £250; but this is subject to sub-paragraph (4) below.

22(2)   Where–

(a)   a penalty (an initial penalty) is imposed on a person under sub-paragraph (1) above, and

(b)   the failure which led to the initial penalty continues after its imposition,

he is (subject to sub-paragraph (4) below) liable to a further penalty of £20 for each day during which (or any part of which) the failure continues after the day on which the initial penalty was imposed.

22(3)   A person who fails to preserve records in compliance with any provision of regulations made under paragraph 2 above (read with that paragraph and any direction given under the regulations) is liable to a penalty of £250; but this is subject to sub-paragraph (4) below.

22(4)   Where by reason of a failure falling within sub-paragraph (1) or (3) above–

(a)   a person is convicted of an offence (whether under this Part of this Act or otherwise), or

a person is assessed to a penalty under paragraph 18 above,

that failure shall not also give rise to liability to a penalty under this paragraph.

BREACH OF REGULATIONS

23(1)   Where regulations made under this Part of this Act impose a requirement on any person, they may provide that if the person fails to comply with the requirement he shall be liable to a penalty of £250; but this is subject to sub-paragraphs (2) and (3) below.

23(2)   Where by reason of any conduct–

(a)   a person is convicted of an offence (whether under this Part of this Act or otherwise), or

(b)   a person is assessed to a penalty under paragraph 18 above,

that conduct shall not also give rise to liability to a penalty under the regulations.

23(3)   Sub-paragraph (1) above does not apply to any failure mentioned in paragraph 22 above.

Cross references – FA 1997, Sch. 5, para. 4(3): contravention of requirement to repay Commissioners.

Statutory instruments – Landfill Tax Regulations 1996 (SI 1996/1527).

WALKING POSSESSION AGREEMENTS

24(1)   This paragraph applies where–

(a)   in accordance with regulations under section 51 of the Finance Act 1997 (enforcement by distress)a distress is authorised to be levied on the goods and chattels of a person (a person in default) who has refused or neglected to pay any tax due from him or any amount recoverable as if it were tax due from him, and

(b)   the person levying the distress and the person in default have entered into a walking possession agreement.

24(2)   For the purposes of this paragraph a walking possession agreement is an agreement under which, in consideration of the property distrained upon being allowed to remain in the custody of the person in default and of the delaying of its sale, the person in default–

(a) acknowledges that the property specified in the agreement is under distraint and held in walking possession, and

(b) undertakes that, except with the consent of the Commissioners and subject to such conditions as they may impose, he will not remove or allow the removal of any of the specified property from the premises named in the agreement.

24(3) If the person in default is in breach of the undertaking contained in a walking possession agreement, he is liable to a penalty equal to half of the tax or other amount referred to in sub-paragraph (1)(a) above.

24(4) This paragraph does not extend to Scotland.

History – In para. 24(1)(a), the words "section 51 of the Finance Act 1997 (enforcement by distress)" were substituted by FA 1997, s. 53(8), with effect from 1 July 1997 (SI 1997/1432) (C 35).

MITIGATION OF PENALTIES

25(1) Where a person is liable to a penalty under this Part of this Schedule the Commissioners or, on appeal, an appeal tribunal may reduce the penalty to such amount (including nil) as they think proper.

25(2) Where the person concerned satisfies the Commissioners or, on appeal, an appeal tribunal that there is a reasonable excuse for any breach, failure or other conduct, that is a factor which (among other things) may be taken into account under sub-paragraph (1) above.

25(3) In the case of a penalty reduced by the Commissioners under sub-paragraph (1) above an appeal tribunal, on an appeal relating to the penalty, may cancel the whole or any part of the reduction made by the Commissioners.

Cross references – Value Added Tax Tribunals Rules 1986 (SI 1986/590), r. 2: definition of "mitigation appeal".

Official publications – LFT1, para. 14 (2000 edn): penalties and interest.

Part VI – INTEREST

INTEREST ON UNDER-DECLARED TAX

26(1) Sub-paragraph (2) below applies where–

(a) under section 50(1) of this Act the Commissioners assess an amount of tax due from a registrable person for an accounting period and notify it to him, and

(b) the assessment is made on the basis that the amount (the **additional amount**) is due from him in addition to any amount shown in a return made in relation to the accounting period.

26(2) The additional amount shall carry interest for the period which–

(a) begins with the day after that on which the person is required by provision made under section 49 of this Act to pay tax due from him for the accounting period, and

(b) ends with the day before the relevant day.

26(3) For the purposes of sub-paragraph (2) above the **relevant day** is the earlier of–

(a) the day on which the assessment is notified to the person;

(b) the day on which the additional amount is paid.

26(4) Sub-paragraph (5) below applies where under section 50(2) of this Act the Commissioners assess an amount as being tax due from a registrable person for an accounting period and notify it to him.

26(5) The amount shall carry interest for the period which–

(a) begins with the day after that on which the person is required by provision made under section 49 of this Act to pay tax due from him for the accounting period, and

(b) ends with the day before the relevant day.

26(6) For the purposes of sub-paragraph (5) above the **relevant day** is the earlier of–

(a) the day on which the assessment is notified to the person;

(b) the day on which the amount is paid.

26(7) Interest under this paragraph shall be payable at the rate applicable under section 197 of this Act.

26(8) Interest under this paragraph shall be paid without any deduction of income tax.

26(9) Sub-paragraph (10) below applies where–

(a) an amount carries interest under this paragraph (or would do so apart from that sub-paragraph), and

(b) all or part of the amount turns out not to be due.

26(10) In such a case–

(a) the amount or part (as the case may be) shall not carry interest under this paragraph and shall be treated as never having done so, and

(b) all such adjustments as are reasonable shall be made, including adjustments by way of repayment by the Commissioners where appropriate.

Statutory instruments – From 6 July 1998 the rate of interest is set using formulae linked to a reference rate. The reference rate is based on an average of the base rates of six main banks rounded to the nearest whole number. The rate of interest is the reference rate plus 2.5%, i.e. from 6 July 1998 the reference rate is set at 7% and therefore the rate of interest is 9.5% (SI 1998/1461). The base rate is monitored every month and, where changes are necessary, new interest rates are set by an order of the Commissioners of Customs & Excise (SI 1998/1461). Interest accruing on or after 6 July 1998 is as follows:

Period of application	Default interest FA 1996, Sch. 5, para. 26
From 6 February 2000	8.5
6 March 1999–5 February 2000	7.5
6 January 1999–5 March 1999	8.5
6 July 1998–5 January 1999	9.5

The rate of interest for the period 1 April 1997–5 July 1998 was 6.25% (SI 1997/1016).

INTEREST ON UNPAID TAX ETC.

27(1) Sub-paragraph (2) below applies where–

(a) a registrable person makes a return under provision made under section 49 of this Act (whether or not he makes it at the time required by such provision), and

(b) the return shows that an amount of tax is due from him for the accounting period in relation to which the return is made.

27(2) The amount shall carry interest for the period which–

(a) begins with the day after that on which the person is required by provision made under section 49 of this Act to pay tax due from him for the accounting period, and

(b) ends with the day before that on which the amount is paid.

27(3) Sub-paragraph (4) below applies where–

(a) under section 50(1) of this Act the Commissioners assess an amount of tax due from a registrable person for an accounting period and notify it to him, and

(b) the assessment is made on the basis that no return required by provision made under section 49 of this Act has been made by the person in relation to the accounting period.

27(4) The amount shall carry interest for the period which–

(a) begins with the day after that on which the person is required by provision made under section 49 of this Act to pay tax due from him for the accounting period, and

(b) ends with the day before that on which the amount is paid.

27(5) Sub-paragraph (6) below applies where–

(a) under section 50(1) of this Act the Commissioners assess an amount of tax due from a registrable person for an accounting period and notify it to him, and

(b) the assessment (the **supplementary assessment**) is made on the basis that the amount (the **additional amount**) is due from him in addition to any amount shown in a return, or in any previous assessment, made in relation to the accounting period.

27(6) The additional amount shall carry interest for the period which–

(a) begins with the day on which the supplementary assessment is notified to the person, and

(b) ends with the day before that on which the additional amount is paid.

27(7) Sub-paragraph (8) below applies where under section 50(2) of this Act the Commissioners assess an amount as being tax due from a registrable person for an accounting period and notify it to him.

27(8) The amount shall carry interest for the period which–

(a) begins with the day on which the assessment is notified to the person, and

(b) ends with the day before that on which the amount is paid.

27(9) Sub-paragraph (10) below applies where under paragraph 32 below the Commissioners–

(a) assess an amount due from a person by way of penalty under Part V of this Schedule and notify it to him, or

(b)   assess an amount due from a person by way of interest under paragraph 26 above and notify it to him.

27(10)   The amount shall carry interest for the period which–

(a)   begins with the day on which the assessment is notified to the person, and

(b)   ends with the day before that on which the amount is paid.

27(11)   Interest under this paragraph shall be compound interest calculated–

(a)   at the penalty rate, and

(b)   with monthly rests;

and the penalty rate is the rate found by taking the rate at which interest is payable under paragraph 26 above and adding 10 percentage points to that rate.

27(12)   Interest under this paragraph shall be paid without any deduction of income tax.

27(13)   Where–

(a)   the Commissioners assess and notify an amount as mentioned in sub-paragraph (5)(a) or (7) or (9)(a) or (b) above,

(b)   they also specify a date for the purposes of this sub-paragraph, and

(c)   the amount concerned is paid on or before that date,

the amount shall not carry interest by virtue of sub-paragraph (6) or (8) or (10) above (as the case may be).

27(14)   Sub-paragraph (15) below applies where–

(a)   an amount carries interest under this paragraph (or would do so apart from that sub-paragraph), and

(b)   all or part of the amount turns out not to be due.

27(15)   In such a case–

(a)   the amount or part (as the case may be) shall not carry interest under this paragraph and shall be treated as never having done so, and

(b)   all such adjustments as are reasonable shall be made, including adjustments by way of repayment by the Commissioners where appropriate.

28(1)   Where a person is liable to pay interest under paragraph 27 above the Commissioners or, on appeal, an appeal tribunal may reduce the amount payable to such amount (including nil) as they think proper.

28(2)   Where the person concerned satisfies the Commissioners or, on appeal, an appeal tribunal that there is a reasonable excuse for the conduct giving rise to the liability to pay interest, that is a fact or which (among other things) may be taken into account under sub-paragraph (1) above.

28(3)   In the case of interest reduced by the Commissioners under sub-paragraph (1) above an appeal tribunal, on an appeal relating to the interest, may cancel the whole or any part of the reduction made by the Commissioners.

Cross references – Value Added Tax Tribunals Rules 1986 (SI 1986/590), r. 2: definition of "mitigation appeal".

INTEREST PAYABLE BY COMMISSIONERS

29(1)   Where, due to an error on the part of the Commissioners, a person–

(a)   has paid to them by way of tax an amount which was not tax due and which they are in consequence liable to repay to him,

(b)   has failed to claim payment of an amount to the payment of which he was entitled in pursuance of provision made under section 51(2)(c) or (d) or (f) of this Act, or

(c)   has suffered delay in receiving payment of an amount due to him from them in connection with tax,

then, if and to the extent that they would not be liable to do so apart from this paragraph, they shall (subject to the following provisions of this paragraph) pay interest to him on that amount for the applicable period.

29(1A)   In sub-paragraph (1) above–

(a)   the reference in paragraph (a) to an amount which the **Commissioners are liable to repay** in consequence of the making of a payment that was not due is a reference to only so much of that amount as is the subject of a claim that the Commissioners are required to satisfy or have satisfied; and

(b)   the amounts referred to in paragraph (c) do not include any amount payable under this
       paragraph.

29(2)   The **applicable period**, in a case falling within sub-paragraph (1)(a) above, is the period–

(a)   beginning with the date on which the payment is received by the Commissioners, and
(b)   ending with the date on which they authorise payment of the amount on which the interest is
       payable.

29(3)   The applicable period, in a case falling within sub-paragraph (1)(b) or (c) above, is the
period–

(a)   beginning with the date on which, apart from the error, the Commissioners might reasonably
       have been expected to authorise payment of the amount on which the interest is payable, and
(b)   ending with the date on which they in fact authorise payment of that amount.

29(4)   In determining the applicable period for the purposes of this paragraph there shall be left
out of account any period by which the Commissioners' authorisation of the payment of interest is
delayed by the conduct of the person who claims the interest.

29(4A)   The reference in sub-paragraph (4) above to a period by which the Commissioners'
authorisation of the payment of interest is **delayed** by the conduct of the person who claims it
includes, in particular, any period which is referable to–

(a)   any unreasonable delay in the making of the claim for interest or in the making of any claim
       for the payment or repayment of the amount on which interest is claimed;
(b)   any failure by that person or a person acting on his behalf or under his influence to provide
       the Commissioners–
       (i)   at or before the time of the making of a claim, or
       (ii) subsequently in response to a request for information by the Commissioners,

with all the information required by them to enable the existence and amount of the claimant's
entitlement to a payment or repayment, and to interest on that payment or repayment, to be
determined; and

(c)   the making, as part of or in association with either–
       (i)   the claim for interest, or
       (ii) any claim for the payment or repayment of the amount on which interest is claimed,

of a claim to anything to which the claimant was not entitled.

29(5)   In determining for the purposes of sub-paragraph (4A) above whether any period of delay is
referable to a failure by any person to provide information in response to a request by the
Commissioners, there shall be taken to be so referable, except so far as may be provided for by
regulations, any period which–

(a)   begins with the date on which the Commissioners require that person to provide information
       which they reasonably consider relevant to the matter to be determined; and
(b)   ends with the earliest date on which it would be reasonable for the Commissioners to
       conclude–
       (i)   that they have received a complete answer to their request for information;
       (ii) that they have received all that they need in answer to that request; or
       (iii) that it is unnecessary for them to be provided with any information in answer to that
             request.

29(7)   The Commissioners shall only be liable to pay interest under this paragraph on a claim
made in writing for that purpose.

29(8)   A claim under this paragraph shall not be made more than three years after the end of the
applicable period to which it relates.

29(9)   References in this paragraph–

(a)   to **receiving payment** of any amount from the Commissioners, or
(b)   to the **authorisation** by the Commissioners of the payment of any amount,

include references to the discharge by way of set-off (whether in accordance with regulations under
paragraph 42 or 43 below or otherwise) of the Commissioners' liability to pay that amount.

29(10)   Interest under this paragraph shall be payable at the rate applicable under section 197 of
this Act.

History – Para. 29(1A) was inserted by FA 1997, s. 50 and Sch. 5, para. 11(2) and is deemed always to have had effect.
Para. 29(4), (4A) and (5) were substituted for former para. 1(4)-(6) by FA 1997, s. 50 and Sch. 5, para. 12(1), with effect for the
purposes of determining whether any period beginning on or after 19 March 1997 is left out of account.
Para. 29(8) was substituted by FA 1997, s. 50 and Sch. 5, para. 11(3) and is deemed always to have had effect.

Para. 29(9) was substituted by FA 1997, s. 50 and Sch. 5, para. 11(4) and is deemed always to have had effect.

Cross references – FA 1997, Sch. 5, para. 15(2) and 20(2)(c): assessment for overpayments of interest.
FA 1997, Sch. 5, para. 19(3): review of decisions and appeals.

Statutory instruments – From 6 July 1998 the rate of interest is set using formulae linked to a reference rate. The reference rate is based on an average of the base rates of six main banks rounded to the nearest whole number. The rate of interest is the reference rate minus 1%, i.e. from 6 July 1998 the reference rate is set at 7% and therefore the rate of interest is 6% (SI 1998/1461). The base rate is monitored every month and, where changes are necessary, new interest rates are set by an order of the Commissioners of Customs & Excise (SI 1998/1461). Interest accruing on or after 6 July 1998 is as follows:

	Statutory interest
Period of application	*FA 1996, Sch. 5, para. 29*
From 6 February 2000	5
6 March 1999–5 February 2000	4
6 January 1999–5 March 1999	5
6 July 1998–5 January 1999	6

The rate of interest for the period 1/4/97–5/7/98 was 6% (SI 1997/1016).

30(1) Where–

(a) any interest is payable by the Commissioners to a person on a sum due to him under this Part of this Act, and

(b) he is a person to whom regulations under section 51 of this Act apply,

the interest shall be treated as an amount to which he is entitled by way of credit in pursuance of the regulations.

30(2) Sub-paragraph (1) above shall be disregarded for the purpose of determining a person's entitlement to interest or the amount of interest to which he is entitled.

Official publications – LFT1, para. 14 (2000 edn): penalties and interest.

Part VII – MISCELLANEOUS

SECURITY FOR TAX

31 Where it appears to the Commissioners requisite to do so for the protection of the revenue they may require a registrable person, as a condition of his carrying out taxable activities, to give security (or further security) of such amount and in such manner as they may determine for the payment of any tax which is or may become due from him.

ASSESSMENTS TO PENALTIES ETC.

32(1) Where a person is liable–

(a) to a penalty under Part V of this Schedule, or

(b) for interest under paragraph 26 or 27 above,

the Commissioners may, subject to sub-paragraph (2) below, assess the amount due by way of penalty or interest (as the case may be) and notify it to him accordingly; and the fact that any conduct giving rise to a penalty under Part V of this Schedule may have ceased before an assessment is made under this paragraph shall not affect the power of the Commissioners to make such an assessment.

32(2) In the case of the penalties and interest referred to in the following paragraphs of this sub-paragraph, the assessment under this paragraph shall be of an amount due in respect of the accounting period which in the paragraph concerned is referred to as the relevant period–

(a) in the case of a penalty under paragraph 18 above relating to the evasion of tax, and in the case of interest under paragraph 27 above on an amount due by way of such a penalty, the relevant period is the accounting period for which the tax evaded was due;

(b) in the case of a penalty under paragraph 18 above relating to the obtaining of a payment under regulations under section 51(2)(c) or (d) or (f) of this Act, and in the case of interest under paragraph 27 above on an amount due by way of such a penalty, the relevant period is the accounting period in respect of which the payment was obtained;

(c) in the case of interest under paragraph 26 above, and in the case of interest under paragraph 27 above on an amount due by way of interest under paragraph 26 above, the relevant period is the accounting period in respect of which the tax was due;

(d) in the case of interest under paragraph 27 above on an amount of tax, the relevant period is the accounting period in respect of which the tax was due.

32(3) In a case where the amount of any penalty or interest falls to be calculated by reference to tax which was not paid at the time it should have been and that tax cannot be readily attributed to any one or more accounting periods, it shall be treated for the purposes of this Part of this Act as tax due for such period or periods as the Commissioners may determine to the best of their judgment and notify to the person liable for the tax and penalty or interest.

32(4) Where a person is assessed under this paragraph to an amount due by way of any penalty or interest falling within sub-paragraph (2) above and is also assessed under subsection (1) or (2) of section 50 of this Act for the accounting period which is the relevant period under sub-paragraph (2) above, the assessments may be combined and notified to him as one assessment, but the amount of the penalty or interest shall be separately identified in the notice.

32(5) Sub-paragraph (6) below applies in the case of an amount due by way of interest under paragraph 27 above.

32(6) Where this sub-paragraph applies in the case of an amount–

(a) a notice of assessment under this paragraph shall specify a date, being not later than the date of the notice, to which the amount of interest which is assessed is calculated, and

(b) if the interest continues to accrue after that date, a further assessment or further assessments may be made under this paragraph in respect of amounts which so accrue.

32(7) If, within such period as may be notified by the Commissioners to the person liable for the interest under paragraph 27 above, the amount referred to in paragraph 27(2), (4), (6), (8) or (10) above (as the case may be) is paid, it shall be treated for the purposes of paragraph 27 above as paid on the date specified as mentioned in sub-paragraph (6)(a) above.

32(8) Where an amount has been assessed and notified to any person under this paragraph it shall be recoverable as if it were tax due from him unless, or except to the extent that, the assessment has subsequently been withdrawn or reduced.

32(9) Subsection (8) of section 50 of this Act shall apply for the purposes of this paragraph as it applies for the purposes of that section.

ASSESSMENTS: TIME LIMITS

33(1) Subject to the following provisions of this paragraph, an assessment under–

(a) any provision of section 50 of this Act, or
(b) paragraph 32 above,

shall not be made more than three years after the end of the accounting period concerned or, in the case of an assessment under paragraph 32 above of an amount due by way of a penalty which is not a penalty referred to in sub-paragraph (2) of that paragraph, three years after the event giving rise to the penalty.

33(2) Subject to sub-paragraph (5) below, an assessment under paragraph 32 above of–

(a) an amount due by way of any penalty referred to in sub-paragraph (2) of that paragraph, or
(b) an amount due by way of interest,

may be made at any time before the expiry of the period of two years beginning with the time when the amount of tax due for the accounting period concerned has been finally determined.

33(3) In relation to an assessment under paragraph 32 above, any reference in sub-paragraph (1) or (2) above to the **accounting period concerned** is a reference to that period which, in the case of the penalty or interest concerned, is the relevant period referred to in sub-paragraph (2) of that paragraph.

33(4) Subject to sub-paragraph (5) below, if tax has been lost–

(a) as a result of conduct falling within paragraph 18(1) above or for which a person has been convicted of fraud, or
(b) in circumstances giving rise to liability to a penalty under paragraph 21 above,

an assessment may be made as if, in sub-paragraph (1) above, each reference to three years were a reference to twenty years.

33(5) Where after a person's death the Commissioners propose to assess an amount as due by reason of some conduct of the deceased–

(a) the assessment shall not be made more than three years after the death, and
(b) if the circumstances are as set out in sub-paragraph (4) above, the modification of sub-paragraph (1) above contained in that sub-paragraph shall not apply but any assessment which (from the point of view of time limits) could have been made immediately after the death may be made at any time within three years after it.

History – In para. 33(1), the words "three years" were substituted in two places for the words "six years" by FA 1997, s. 50 and Sch. 5, para. 6(2)(b), with effect from 19 March 1997.
In para. 33(4), the words "three years" were substituted for the words "six years" by FA 1997, s. 50 and Sch. 5, para. 6(2)(b), with effect from 19 March 1997.
Cross references – FA 1997, Sch. 5, para. 6(2): overpayments.

SUPPLEMENTARY ASSESSMENTS

34 If, otherwise than in circumstances falling within subsection (5)(b) of section 50 of this Act, it appears to the Commissioners that the amount which ought to have been assessed in an assessment under any provision of that section or under paragraph 32 above exceeds the amount which was so assessed, then–

(a)   under the like provision as that assessment was made, and

(b)   on or before the last day on which that assessment could have been made,

the Commissioners may make a supplementary assessment of the amount of the excess and shall notify the person concerned accordingly.

DISCLOSURE OF INFORMATION

35(1) Notwithstanding any obligation not to disclose information that would otherwise apply, the Commissioners may disclose information to–

(a)   the Secretary of State,

(b)   the Environment Agency,

(c)   the Scottish Environment Protection Agency,

(d)   the Department of the Environment for Northern Ireland,

(e)   a district council in Northern Ireland, or

(f)   an authorised officer of any person (a principal) mentioned in paragraphs (a) to (e) above,

for the purpose of assisting the principal concerned in the performance of the principal's duties.

35(2) Notwithstanding any such obligation as is mentioned in sub-paragraph (1) above, any person mentioned in sub-paragraph (1)(a) to (f) above may disclose information to the Commissioners or to an authorised officer of the Commissioners for the purpose of assisting the Commissioners in the performance of duties in relation to tax.

35(3) Information that has been disclosed to a person by virtue of this paragraph shall not be disclosed by him except–

(a)   to another person to whom (instead of him) disclosure could by virtue of this paragraph have been made, or

(b)   for the purpose of any proceedings connected with the operation of any provision of, or made under, any enactment in relation to the environment or to tax.

35(4) References in the preceding provisions of this paragraph to an authorised officer of any person (the **principal**) are to any person who has been designated by the principal as a person to and by whom information may be disclosed by virtue of this paragraph.

35(5) The Secretary of State shall notify the Commissioners in writing of the name of any person designated by the Secretary of State under sub-paragraph (4) above.

35(6) No charge may be made for a disclosure made by virtue of this paragraph.

THE REGISTER: PUBLICATION

36(1) The Commissioners may publish, by such means as they think fit, information which–

(a)   is derived from the register kept under section 47 of this Act, and

(b)   falls within any of the descriptions set out below.

36(2) The descriptions are–

(a)   the names of registered persons;

(b)   the addresses of any sites or other premises at which they carry on business;

(c)   the registration numbers assigned to them in the register;

(d)   the fact (where it is the case) that the registered person is a body corporate which under section 59 of this Act is treated as a member of a group;

(e)   the names of the other bodies corporate treated under that section as members of the group;

(f)   the addresses of any sites or other premises at which those other bodies carry on business.

36(3) Information may be published in accordance with this paragraph notwithstanding any obligation not to disclose the information that would otherwise apply.

EVIDENCE BY CERTIFICATE ETC.

37(1) A certificate of the Commissioners–

(a)   that a person was or was not at any time registered under section 47 of this Act,

(b)   that any return required by regulations made under section 49 of this Act has not been made or had not been made at any time, or

(c)   that any tax shown as due in a return made in pursuance of regulations made under section 49 of this Act, or in an assessment made under section 50 of this Act, has not been paid,

shall be sufficient evidence of that fact until the contrary is proved.

37(2) A photograph of any document furnished to the Commissioners for the purposes of this Part of this Act and certified by them to be such a photograph shall be admissible in any proceedings, whether civil or criminal, to the same extent as the document itself.

37(3) Any document purporting to be a certificate under sub-paragraph (1) or above shall be taken to be such a certificate until the contrary is proved.

SERVICE OF NOTICES ETC.

38 Any notice, notification or requirement to be served on, given to or made of any person for the purposes of this Part of this Act may be served, given or made by sending it by post in a letter addressed to that person at his last or usual residence or place of business.

39(1) This paragraph applies to directions, specifications and conditions which the Commissioners or an authorised person may give or impose under any provision of this Part.

39(2) A direction, specification or condition given or imposed by the Commissioners may be withdrawn or varied by them.

39(3) A direction, specification or condition given or imposed by an authorised person may be withdrawn or varied by him or by another authorised person.

39(4) No direction, specification or condition shall have effect as regards any person it is intended to affect unless–

(a)   a notice containing it is served on him, or

(b)   other reasonable steps are taken with a view to bringing it to his attention.

39(5) No withdrawal or variation of a direction, specification or condition shall have effect as regards any person the withdrawal or variation is intended to affect unless–

(a)   a notice containing the withdrawal or variation is served on him, or

(b)   other reasonable steps are taken with a view to bringing the withdrawal or variation to his attention.

NO DEDUCTION OF PENALTIES OR INTEREST

40 [Inserts ICTA 1988, s. 827(1C).]

DESTINATION OF RECEIPTS

41 All money and securities for money collected or received for or on account of the tax shall–

(a)   if collected or received in Great Britain, be placed to the general account of the Commissioners kept at the Bank of England under section 17 of the Customs and Excise Management Act 1979;

(b)   if collected or received in Northern Ireland, be paid into the consolidated fund of the United Kingdom in such manner as the treasury may direct.

SET-OFF OF AMOUNTS

42(1) Regulations may make provision in relation to any case where–

(a)   a person is under a duty to pay to the Commissioners at any time an amount or amounts in respect of landfill tax, and

(b)   the Commissioners are under a duty to pay to that person at the same time an amount or amounts in respect of any tax (or taxes) under their care and management.

42(2) The regulations may provide that if the total of the amount or amounts mentioned in sub-paragraph (1)(a) above exceeds the total of the amount or amounts mentioned in sub-paragraph (1)(b) above, the latter shall be set off against the former.

42(3) The regulations may provide that if the total of the amount or amounts mentioned in sub-paragraph (1)(b) above exceeds the total of the amount or amounts mentioned in sub-paragraph (1)(a) above, the Commissioners may set off the latter in paying the former.

42(4) The regulations may provide that if the total of the amount or amounts mentioned in sub-paragraph (1)(a) above is the same as the total of the amount or amounts mentioned in sub-paragraph (1)(b) above no payment need be made in respect of the former or the latter.

42(4A) The regulations may provide for any limitation on the time within which the Commissioners are entitled to take steps for recovering any amount due to them in respect of landfill tax to be disregarded, in such cases as may be described in the regulations, in determining whether any person is under such a duty to pay as is mentioned in sub-paragraph (1)(a) above.

42(5) The regulations may include provision treating any duty to pay mentioned in sub-paragraph (1) above as discharged accordingly.

42(6) References in sub-paragraph (1) above to an amount in respect of a particular tax include references not only to an amount of tax itself but also to other amounts such as interest and penalty.

42(7) In this paragraph **"tax"** includes "duty".

History – Para. 42(4A) was inserted by FA 1997, s. 50 and Sch. 5, para. 13(1), with effect from 19 March 1997.
Statutory instruments – Landfill Tax Regulations 1996 (SI 1996/1527).

43 Regulations may make provision in relation to any case where–

(a)   a person is under a duty to pay to the Commissioners at any time an amount or amounts in respect of any tax (or taxes) under their care and management, and

(b)   the Commissioners are under a duty to pay to that person at the same time an amount or amounts in respect of landfill tax.

43(2) The regulations may provide that if the total of the amount or amounts mentioned in sub-paragraph (1)(a) above exceeds the total of the amount or amounts mentioned in sub-paragraph (1)(b) above, the latter shall be set off against the former.

43(3) The regulations may provide that if the total of the amount or amounts mentioned in sub-paragraph (1)(b) above exceeds the total of the amount or amounts mentioned in sub-paragraph (1)(a) above, the Commissioners may set off the latter in paying the former.

43(4) The regulations may provide that if the total of the amount or amounts mentioned in sub-paragraph (1)(a) above is the same as the total of the amount or amounts mentioned in sub-paragraph (1)(b) above no payment need be made in respect of the former or the latter.

43(4A) The regulations may provide for any limitation on the time within which the Commissioners are entitled to take steps for recovering any amount due to them in respect of any of the taxes under their care and management to be disregarded, in such cases as may be described in the regulations, in determining whether any person is under such a duty to pay as is mentioned in sub-paragraph (1)(a) above.

43(5) The regulations may include provision treating any duty to pay mentioned in sub-paragraph (1) above as discharged accordingly.

43(6) References in sub-paragraph (1) above to an **amount in respect of a particular tax** include references not only to an amount of tax itself but also to other amounts such as interest and penalty.

43(7) In this paragraph **"tax"** includes "duty".

History – Para. 43(4A) was inserted by FA 1997, s. 50 and Sch. 5, para. 13(2), with effect from 19 March 1997.
Statutory instruments – Landfill Tax Regulations 1996 (SI 1996/1527).

AMOUNTS SHOWN AS TAX ON INVOICES

44(1) Where–

(a)   a registrable person issues an invoice showing an amount as tax chargeable on an event, and no tax is in fact chargeable on the event, an amount equal to the amount shown as tax shall be recoverable from the person as a debt due to the Crown.

44(2) Where–

(a)   a registrable person issues an invoice showing an amount as tax chargeable on a taxable disposal, and

(b)   the amount shown as tax exceeds the amount of tax in fact chargeable on the disposal,

an amount equal to the excess shall be recoverable from the person as a debt due to the Crown.

44(3) References in this paragraph to an **invoice** are to any invoice, whether or not it is a landfill invoice within the meaning of section 61 of this Act.

ADJUSTMENT OF CONTRACTS

45(1) This paragraph applies where–

(a) material undergoes a landfill disposal,

(b) a payment falls to be made under a disposal contract relating to the material, and

(c) after the making of the contract there is a change in the tax chargeable on the landfill disposal.

45(2) In such a case the amount of any payment mentioned in sub-paragraph (1)(b) above shall be adjusted, unless the disposal contract otherwise provides, so as to reflect the tax chargeable on the landfill disposal.

45(3) For the purposes of this paragraph a disposal contract relating to material is a contract providing for the disposal of the material, and it is immaterial–

(a) when the contract was made;

(b) whether the contract also provides for other matters;

(c) whether the contract provides for a method of disposal and (if it does) what method it provides for.

45(4) The reference in sub-paragraph (1) above to a **change in the tax chargeable** is a reference to a change–

(a) to or from no tax being chargeable, or

(b) in the amount of tax chargeable.

46(1) This paragraph applies where–

(a) work is carried out under a construction contract,

(b) as a result of the work, material undergoes a landfill disposal,

(c) the contract makes no provision as to the disposal of such material, and

(d) the contract was made on or before 29th November 1994 (when the proposal to create tax was announced).

46(2) In such a case the amount of any payment which falls to be made–

(a) under the construction contract, and

(b) in respect of the work, shall be adjusted, unless the contract otherwise provides, so as to reflect the tax (if any) chargeable on the disposal.

46(3) For the purposes of this paragraph a **construction contract** is a contract under which all or any of the following work is to be carried out–

(a) the preparation of a site;

(b) demolition;

(c) building;

(d) civil engineering.

ADJUSTMENT OF RENT ETC.

47(1) This paragraph applies where–

(a) an agreement with regard to any sum payable in respect of the use of land (whether the sum is called rent or royalty or otherwise) provides that the amount of the sum is to be calculated by reference to the turnover of a business,

(b) the agreement was made on or before 29th November 1994 (when the proposal to create tax was announced), and

(c) the circumstances are such that (had the agreement been made after that date) it can reasonably be expected that it would have provided that tax be ignored in calculating the turnover.

47(2) In such a case the agreement shall be taken to provide that tax be ignored in calculating the turnover.

Part VIII – Secondary Liability: Controllers of Landfill Sites

History – Pt. VIII was added by FA 2000, s. 142(3) and Sch. 37, with effect in relation to taxable disposals made on or after 28 July 2000.

MEANING OF CONTROLLER

48(1) For the purposes of this Part of this Schedule a person is the **controller** of the whole, or a part, of a landfill site at a given time if he determines, or is entitled to determine, what disposals of material, if any, may be made–

(a)   at every part of the site at that time, or

(b)   at that part of the site at that time,

as the case may be.

48(2) But a person who, because he is an employee or agent of another, determines or is entitled to determine what disposals may be made at a landfill site or any part of a landfill site is not the controller of that site or, as the case may be, that part of that site.

48(3) Where a person is the controller of the whole or a part of a landfill site, that site or, as the case may be, that part of the site is referred to in this Part of this Schedule as being under his **control**.

48(4) Any reference in this Part of this Schedule to a **controller** (without more) is a reference to a controller of the whole or a part of a landfill site.

SECONDARY LIABILITY

49(1) Where–

(a)   a taxable disposal is made at a landfill site,

(b)   at the time when that disposal is made a person is the operator of the landfill site by virtue of section 67(a), (c) or (e) of this Act, and

(c)   at that time a person other than the operator mentioned in paragraph (b) above is the controller of the whole or a part of the landfill site,

the controller shall be liable to pay to the Commissioners an amount of the landfill tax chargeable on the disposal.

49(2) The amount which the controller is liable to pay shall be determined in accordance with the following provisions of this paragraph.

49(3) In a case where the whole of the landfill site is under the control of the controller, he shall be liable to pay the whole of the landfill tax chargeable.

49(4) In a case where a part of the landfill site is under the control of the controller, he shall be liable to pay an amount of the landfill tax calculated in accordance with sub-paragraphs (5) and (6) below.

49(5) The amount of landfill tax which the controller is liable to pay is the amount which would have been chargeable had a separate taxable disposal consisting of the amount of material referred to in sub-paragraph (6) below been made at the time of the disposal mentioned in sub-paragraph (1)(a) above.

49(6) That amount of material is the amount by weight of the material comprised in the disposal mentioned in sub-paragraph (1)(a) above which was disposed of on the part of the landfill site under the control of the controller.

49(7) If the amount mentioned in sub-paragraph (6) above is nil, the controller shall have no liability under sub-paragraph (1) above in relation to landfill tax chargeable on the disposal.

49(8) For the purposes of sub-paragraph (1)(b) and (c) above–

(a)   section 61 of this Act, and

(b)   any regulations made under section 62 of this Act,

shall not apply for determining the time when the disposal in question is made.

OPERATOR ENTITLED TO CREDIT

50(1) This paragraph applies where–

(a)   the operator of a landfill site is liable to pay landfill tax on a taxable disposal by reference to a particular accounting period,

(b)   a controller of the whole or a part of that site is (apart from this paragraph) liable under paragraph 49 above to pay an amount of that tax, and

(c)   for the accounting period in question the operator is entitled to credit under regulations made under section 51 of this Act.

50(2) The amount of the tax which the controller is (apart from this sub-paragraph) liable to pay shall be reduced by the amount calculated in accordance with the following formula-

$$\frac{A \times C}{G}$$

where–

A is the amount of tax mentioned in sub-paragraph (1)(b) above;

C is the amount of credit mentioned in sub-paragraph (1)(c) above; and

G is the operator's gross tax liability for the accounting period in question.

50(3) For the purposes of sub-paragraph (2) above, the operator's **gross tax liability** for the accounting period in question is the gross amount of landfill tax–

(a) which is chargeable on disposals made at all landfill sites of which he is the operator, and

(b) for which he is required to account by reference to that accounting period.

50(4) In sub-paragraph (3) above, **the gross amount of landfill tax** means the amount of tax before any credit or any other adjustment is taken into account in the period in question.

50(5) If the amount calculated in accordance with the formula in sub-paragraph (2) above is greater than the amount of tax mentioned in sub-paragraph (1)(b) above, the amount of the tax which the controller is liable to pay shall be reduced to nil.

PAYMENT OF SECONDARY LIABILITY

51(1) This paragraph applies where a controller is liable under paragraph 49 above (after taking account of any reduction under paragraph 50 above) to pay an amount of landfill tax (**"the relevant amount"**).

51(2) The controller is required to pay the relevant amount to the Commissioners only if–

(a) a notice containing the required information is served on him, or

(b) other reasonable steps are taken with a view to bringing the required information to his attention,

before the end of the period of two years beginning with the day immediately following the relevant accounting day.

51(3) The **relevant accounting day** is the last day of the accounting period by reference to which the landfill site operator liable to pay the landfill tax in question is required to account for that tax.

51(4) If the controller is required to pay the relevant amount by virtue of this paragraph, the amount shall be paid before the end of the period of thirty days beginning with the day immediately following the notification day.

51(5) The **notification day** is–

(a) in a case where notice is served on a controller as mentioned in sub-paragraph (2)(a) above, the day on which the notice is served, or

(b) in a case where other reasonable steps are taken as mentioned in sub-paragraph (2)(b) above, the day on which the last of those steps is taken.

51(6) For the purposes of sub-paragraph (2) above the **required information** is the relevant amount and, if that amount is one reduced in accordance with paragraph 50 above, also–

(a) the amount of the controller's liability under paragraph 49 above apart from the reduction,

(b) the amount of credit to which the operator is entitled, and

(c) the operator's gross tax liability.

ASSESSMENTS

52(1) Where an amount of landfill tax is–

(a) assessed under section 50 of this Act, and

(b) notified to a licensed operator,

the Commissioners may also determine that a controller of the whole or a part of any landfill site operated by the licensed operator shall be liable to pay so much of the amount assessed as they consider just and equitable.

52(2) A controller is required to pay an amount determined under sub-paragraph (1) above only if–

(a) a notice stating the amount is served on him, or

(b)   other reasonable steps are taken with a view to bringing the amount of the liability to his attention,

before the expiry of the period of two years beginning with the day immediately following the assessment day.

52(3)   The **assessment day** is the day on which the assessment in question is notified to the licensed operator.

52(4)   If a controller is required to pay an amount by virtue of this paragraph, it shall be paid before the end of the period of thirty days beginning with the day immediately following the notification day.

52(5)   The **notification day** is–

(a)   in a case where notice is served on a controller as mentioned in sub-paragraph (2)(a) above, the day on which the notice is served, or

(b)   in a case where other reasonable steps are taken as mentioned in sub-paragraph (2)(b) above, the day on which the last of those steps is taken.

52(6)   For the purposes of this paragraph a **licensed operator** is a person who is the operator of a landfill site by virtue of section 67(a), (c) or (e) of this Act.

ASSESSMENT WITHDRAWN OR REDUCED

53(1)   Where–

(a)   a controller is liable to pay an amount determined under paragraph 52 above, and

(b)   the assessment notified to the licensed operator is withdrawn or reduced,

the Commissioners may determine that the controller's liability is to be cancelled or to be reduced to such an amount as they consider just and equitable.

53(2)   Sub-paragraphs (3) to (5) below apply where the Commissioners make a determination under sub-paragraph (1) above that the controller's liability is to be reduced (but not cancelled).

53(3)   In such a case they shall–

(a)   serve the controller with notice stating the amount of the reduced liability, or

(b)   take other reasonable steps with a view to bringing the reduced amount to the controller's attention.

53(4)   If the controller has already been served with notice of the amount determined under paragraph 52 above, or if other steps have already been taken to bring that amount to his attention–

(a)   the Commissioners shall serve the notice mentioned in sub-paragraph (3)(a) above, or take the steps mentioned in sub-paragraph (3)(b) above, before the end of the period of thirty days beginning with the day immediately following that on which they make the determination under sub-paragraph (1) above, and

(b)   the reduced amount shall be payable, or treated as having been payable, on or before the day on which the amount referred to in sub-paragraph (1)(a) above would have been payable apart from this paragraph.

53(5)   In a case where the controller has not been served with notice of the amount determined under paragraph 52 above, or no other steps have been taken to bring that amount to his attention, he shall be liable to pay the reduced amount only if–

(a)   the notice mentioned in sub-paragraph (3)(a) above is served, or

(b)   the other steps mentioned in sub-paragraph (3)(b) above are taken,

before the expiry of the period of two years beginning with the day immediately following that on which the Commissioners make the determination under sub-paragraph (1) above.

53(6)   Sub-paragraph (7) below applies where–

(a)   the Commissioners make a determination under sub-paragraph (1) above that the controller's liability is to be cancelled, and

(b)   the controller has already been served with notice of the amount determined under paragraph 52 above, or other steps have already been taken to bring that amount to his attention.

53(7)   In such a case the Commissioners shall–

(a)   serve the controller with notice stating that the liability has been cancelled, or

(b)   take other reasonable steps with a view to bringing the cancellation to the controller's attention, before the end of the period of thirty days beginning with the day immediately following that on which they make the determination that the liability is to be cancelled.

ADJUSTMENTS

54(1)   This paragraph applies in any case where the liability of a licensed operator to pay landfill tax is adjusted otherwise than by–

(a)   his being entitled to credit under regulations made under section 51 of this Act,

(b)   his being notified of an amount assessed under section 50 of this Act, or

(c)   the withdrawal or reduction of an assessment under section 50 of this Act which was notified to him.

54(2)   In such a case the Commissioners may determine that a controller of the whole or any part of a landfill site operated by the licensed operator–

(a)   shall be liable to pay to the Commissioners such an amount as they consider just and equitable, or

(b)   shall be entitled to an allowance of such an amount as they consider just and equitable.

54(3)   A controller is required to pay an amount determined under sub-paragraph (2)(a) above only if–

(a)   a notice stating the amount is served on him, or

(b)   other reasonable steps are taken with a view to bringing the amount of the liability to his attention,

before the end of the period of two years beginning with the day immediately following the relevant accounting day.

54(4)   The **relevant accounting day** is the last day of the accounting period of the operator within which the adjustment in question was taken into account.

54(5)   If a controller is required to pay an amount by virtue of sub-paragraph (3) above, it shall be paid before the end of the period of thirty days beginning with the day immediately following the notification day.

54(6)   The **notification day** is–

(a)   in a case where notice is served on a controller as mentioned in sub-paragraph (3)(a) above, the day on which the notice is served, or

(b)   in a case where other reasonable steps are taken as mentioned in sub-paragraph (3)(b) above, the day on which the last of those steps is taken.

54(7)   The Commissioners may determine in what manner a controller is to benefit from an allowance determined under sub-paragraph (2)(b) above.

54(8)   For the purposes of this paragraph a **licensed operator** is a person who is the operator of a landfill site by virtue of section 67(a), (c) or (e) of this Act.

AMOUNTS PAYABLE TO BE TREATED AS TAX

55   An amount which a controller is required to pay under paragraph 52, 53 or 54(2)(a) above or under paragraph 58 below shall be deemed to be an amount of tax due from him and shall be recoverable accordingly.

CONTROLLER NOT CARRYING OUT TAXABLE ACTIVITY

56   A controller is not to be treated for the purposes of this Act as **carrying out a taxable activity** by reason only of any liability under this Part of this Schedule.

JOINT AND SEVERAL LIABILITY

57(1)   In any case where the condition in sub-paragraph (4), (5) or (6) below is satisfied, the controller and the operator shall be jointly and severally liable for the principal liability.

57(2)   But the amount which may be recovered from the controller in consequence of such liability shall not exceed the amount of the secondary liability.

57(3)   For the purposes of this paragraph–

(a)   the **principal liability** is the amount referred to in sub-paragraph (4)(a), (5)(a) or (6)(a) below, as the case may be, and

(b)   the **secondary liability** is the amount referred to in sub-paragraph (4)(b), (5)(b) or (6)(b) below, as the case may be.

57(4)   The condition in this sub-paragraph is satisfied if–

(a)   the operator of a landfill site is liable under section 41 of this Act for landfill tax, and

(b)   a controller is liable under paragraph 49 above, after taking account of any reduction under paragraph 50 above, to pay an amount of that tax.

57(5)   The condition in this sub-paragraph is satisfied if–

(a)   the operator of a landfill site is notified of the amount of an assessment made under section 50 of this Act, and

(b)   in consequence of a determination made under paragraph 52 above by the Commissioners in connection with the assessment, a controller is liable to pay an amount (after taking account of any reduction under paragraph 53 above).

57(6)   The condition in this sub-paragraph is satisfied if–

(a)   the liability of the operator of a landfill site to pay landfill tax is adjusted in such a way that paragraph 54 above applies, and

(b)   in consequence of a determination made under paragraph 54(2)(a) above by the Commissioners in connection with the adjustment, a controller is liable to pay an amount.

INTEREST PAYABLE BY A CONTROLLER

58(1)   This paragraph applies where–

(a)   the operator of a landfill site and the controller of the whole or a part of that site are by virtue of paragraph 57 above jointly and severally liable for an amount, and

(b)   that amount carries interest by virtue of any provision of this Schedule.

58(2)   The controller and the operator shall be jointly and severally liable to pay the interest.

58(3)   But the amount which may be recovered from the controller in consequence of such liability shall not exceed the amount calculated in accordance with the following formula–

$$\frac{(I - [A + B]) \times S}{P}$$

where–

  I is the total amount of interest in question;

  A is the amount of interest carried for the period which–

  (a)   begins with the first day of the period for which interest is carried, and

  (b)   ends with the day on which the controller becomes liable to pay the secondary liability;

  B is the amount of interest carried for any day falling after that on which the secondary liability is met in full;

  S is the amount of the secondary liability;

  P is the amount of the principal liability.

   In this paragraph **secondary liability** and **principal liability** have the same meaning as in paragraph 57 above.

58(4)   The controller is liable for an amount of interest only if–

(a)   a notice stating the amount is served on him, or

(b)   other reasonable steps are taken with a view to bringing the amount of the liability to his attention,

before the end of the period of two years beginning with the day immediately following the final day.

58(5)   The **final day** is the last day of the period for which the interest in question is carried.

58(6)   If the controller is required to pay an amount in accordance with this paragraph, it shall be paid before the end of the period of thirty days beginning with the day immediately following the notification day.

58(7)   The **notification day** is–

(a)   in a case where notice is served on a controller as mentioned in sub-paragraph (4)(a) above, the day on which the notice is served, or

(b)   in a case where other reasonable steps are taken as mentioned in sub-paragraph (4)(b) above, the day on which the last of those steps is taken.

58(8) Where by virtue of sub-paragraph (2) above a controller is liable to pay interest which arises under paragraph 27 above, paragraph 28 above shall apply in relation to that interest as it applies to interest which a person is liable under paragraph 27 above to pay.

REVIEWS

59 Section 54 of this Act shall apply to a decision of the Commissioners under this Part of this Schedule–

(a)   that a person is a controller,

(b)   that a person is liable under this Part of this Schedule to pay any amount (including a penalty under paragraph 60 below),

(c)   that a person is not entitled under this Part of this Schedule to an allowance, or

(d)   as to the amount of any liability or any allowance under this Part of this Schedule,

as it applies to the other decisions of the Commissioners specified in subsection (1) of that section.

NOTICE THAT PERSON IS, OR IS NO LONGER, A CONTROLLER

60(1) This paragraph applies where–

(a)   on the date when this paragraph comes into force, a person is a controller of the whole or a part of a landfill site, or

(b)   after that date, a person becomes or ceases to be a controller of the whole or a part of a landfill site.

60(2) The controller, and the operator of the landfill site in question, shall be under a duty to secure that notice which complies with the requirements of sub-paragraph (3) below appropriate to the case in question is given to the Commissioners.

60(3) The requirements of this sub-paragraph are that the notice–

(a)   states that a person is, has become or has ceased to be a controller,

(b)   identifies that person and the site under his control or formerly under his control,

(c)   states the date when he became or ceased to be the controller, and

(d)   is given within the period of thirty days beginning with the day immediately following–

(i)   the day when this paragraph comes into force, in a case falling within sub-paragraph (1)(a) above, or

(ii)   the day when the person in question becomes or ceases to be the controller, in a case falling within sub-paragraph (1)(b) above.

60(4) If a person fails to comply with sub-paragraph (2) above, he is liable to a penalty of £250.

60(5) Paragraph 25 above applies to a penalty under sub-paragraph (4) above as it applies to a penalty under Part V of this Schedule.

EXTENSION OF TIME LIMITS WHERE NOTICE NOT SERVED

61(1) This paragraph applies where–

(a)   a person is liable under paragraph 49 above to pay an amount of landfill tax or liable under paragraph 58 above to pay interest, or

(b)   the Commissioners are entitled under paragraph 52, 53 or 54 above to determine an amount which a person is liable to pay.

61(2) The reference to two years in paragraph 51(2), 52(2), 53(5), 54(3) or 58(4) above (as the case may be) shall be treated as a reference to twenty years if the requirement of paragraph 60(2) above to give notice to the Commissioners in relation to the person mentioned in sub-paragraph (1) above being or becoming a controller has not been complied with.

FINANCE ACT 1997

(1997 Chapter 16)

[*19th March 1997*]

ARRANGEMENT OF SECTIONS

PART IV – PAYMENTS AND OVERPAYMENTS IN RESPECT OF INDIRECT TAXES

PART IV – PAYMENTS AND OVERPAYMENTS IN RESPECT OF INDIRECT TAXES

EXCISE DUTIES AND OTHER INDIRECT TAXES

50   Overpayments, interest, assessments, etc.

50(1)   Schedule 5 to this Act (which makes provision in relation to excise duties, insurance premium tax and landfill tax which corresponds to that made for VAT by sections 44 to 48 above) shall have effect.

50(2)   [Not relevant to landfill tax.]

ENFORCEMENT OF PAYMENT

51   Enforcement by distress

51(1)   The Commissioners may by regulations make provision–

(a)   for authorising distress to be levied on the goods and chattels of any person refusing or neglecting to pay–

     (i) *any amount of relevant tax due from him*, or

     (ii) any amount recoverable as if it were relevant tax due from him;

(b)   for the disposal of any goods or chattels on which distress is levied in pursuance of the regulations; and

(c)   for the imposition and recovery of costs, charges, expenses and fees in connection with anything done under the regulations.

51(2) The provision that may be contained in regulations under this section shall include, in particular–

(a) provision for the levying of distress, by any person authorised to do so under the regulations, on goods or chattels located at any place whatever (including on a public highway); and

(b) provision authorising distress to be levied at any such time of the day or night, and on any such day of the week, as may be specified or described in the regulations.

51(3) Regulations under this section may–

(a) make different provision for different cases, and

(b) contain any such incidental, supplemental, consequential or transitional provision as the Commissioners think fit;

and the transitional provision that may be contained in regulations under this section shall include transitional provision in connection with the coming into force of the repeal by this Act of any other power by regulations to make provision for or in connection with the levying of distress.

51(4) The power to make regulations under this section shall be exercisable by statutory instrument subject to annulment in pursuance of a resolution of the House of Commons.

51(5) The following are **relevant taxes** for the purposes of this section, that is to say–

(a) [Not relevant to landfill tax.]

(b) [Not relevant to landfill tax.]

(c) [Not relevant to landfill tax.]

(d) landfill tax;

(e) [Not relevant to landfill tax.]

51(6) In this section **"the Commissioners"** means the Commissioners of Customs and Excise.

51(7) Regulations made under this section shall not have effect in Scotland.

Statutory instruments – Distress for Customs and Excise Duties and Other Indirect Taxes Regulations 1997 (SI 1997/1431).

52   Enforcement by diligence

52(1) Where any amount of relevant tax or any amount recoverable as if it were relevant tax is due and has not been paid, the sheriff, on an application by the Commissioners accompanied by a certificate by them–

(a) stating that none of the persons specified in the application has paid the amount due from him;

(b) stating that payment of the amount due from each such person has been demanded from him; and

(c) specifying the amount due from and unpaid by each such person,

shall grant a summary warrant in a form prescribed by Act of Sederunt authorising the recovery, by any of the diligences mentioned in subsection (2) below, of the amount remaining due and unpaid.

52(2) The **diligences** referred to in subsection (1) above are–

(a) a poinding and sale in accordance with Schedule 5 to the Debtors (Scotland) Act 1987;

(b) an earnings arrestment;

(c) an arrestment and action of forthcoming or sale.

52(3) Subject to subsection (4) below and without prejudice to paragraphs 25 to 34 of Schedule 5 to the Debtors (Scotland) Act 1987 (expenses of poinding and sale) the sheriff officer's fees, together with the outlays necessarily incurred by him, in connection with the execution of a summary warrant shall be chargeable against the debtor.

52(4) No fees shall be chargeable by the sheriff officer against the debtor for collecting, and accounting to the Commissioners for, sums paid to him by the debtor in respect of the amount owing.

52(5) The following are **relevant taxes** for the purposes of this section, that is to say–

(a) [Not relevant to landfill tax.]

(b) [Not relevant to landfill tax.]

(c) [Not relevant to landfill tax.]

(d) landfill tax;

(e) [Not relevant to landfill tax.]

52(6) In this section **"the Commissioners"** means the Commissioners of Customs and Excise.

52(7) This section shall come into force on such day as the Commissioners of Customs and Excise may by order made by statutory instrument appoint, and different days may be appointed under this subsection for different purposes.

52(8) This section extends only to Scotland.

Statutory instruments – Finance Act 1997, sections 52 and 53, (Appointed Day) Order 1997 (SI 1997/1432) (C 54): the appointed day is 1 July 1997.

53   Amendments consequential on sections 51 and 52

53(1) [Not relevant to landfill tax.]

53(2) [Not relevant to landfill tax.]

53(3) [Not relevant to landfill tax.]

53(4) [Not relevant to landfill tax.]

53(5) [Not relevant to landfill tax.]

53(6) [Not relevant to landfill tax.]

53(7) [Not relevant to landfill tax.]

53(8) [Amends FA 1996, Sch. 5, para. 24(1)(a).]

53(9) This section shall come into force on such day as the Commissioners of Customs and Excise may by order made by statutory instrument appoint, and different days may be appointed under this subsection for different purposes.

Statutory instruments – Finance Act 1997, sections 52 and 53, (Appointed Day) Order 1997 (SI 1997/1432) (C 54): the appointed day is 1 July 1997.

PART VIII – MISCELLANEOUS AND SUPPLEMENTAL

SUPPLEMENTAL

113   Repeals

113(1) The enactments mentioned in Schedule 18 to this Act (which include spent provisions) are hereby repealed to the extent specified in the third column of that Schedule.

113(2) The repeals specified in that Schedule have effect subject to the commencement provisions and savings contained or referred to in the notes set out in that Schedule.

SCHEDULES

SCHEDULE 5 – INDIRECT TAXES: OVERPAYMENTS ETC.

Section 50

Part I – Unjust Enrichment

APPLICATION OF PART I

1(1) This Part of this Schedule has effect for the purposes of the following provisions (which make it a defence to a claim for repayment that the repayment would unjustly enrich the claimant), namely–

(a)   section 137A(3) of the Customs and Excise Management Act 1979 (excise duties);

(b)   paragraph 8(3) of Schedule 7 to the Finance Act 1994 (insurance premium tax); and

(c)   *paragraph 14(3) of Schedule 5 to the Finance Act 1996 (landfill tax).*

1(2) Those provisions are referred to in this Part of this Schedule as unjust enrichment provisions.

1(3) In this Part of this Schedule–

"**the Commissioners**" means the Commissioners of Customs and Excise;

"**relevant repayment provision**" means–

(a)   section 137A of the Customs and Excise Management Act 1979 (recovery of overpaid excise duty);

(b)   paragraph 8 of Schedule 7 to the Finance Act 1994 (recovery of overpaid insurance premium tax); or

(c)   paragraph 14 of Schedule 5 to the Finance Act 1996 (recovery of overpaid landfill tax);

"relevant tax" means any duty of excise, insurance premium tax or landfill tax; and

"subordinate legislation" has the same meaning as in the Interpretation Act 1978.

DISREGARD OF BUSINESS LOSSES

2(1)   This paragraph applies where–

(a)   there is an amount paid by way of relevant tax which (apart from an unjust enrichment provision) would fall to be repaid under a relevant repayment provision to any person (**"the taxpayer"**), and

(b)   the whole or a part of the cost of the payment of that amount to the Commissioners has, for practical purposes, been borne by a person other than the taxpayer.

2(2)   Where, in a case to which this paragraph applies, loss or damage has been or may be incurred by the taxpayer as a result of mistaken assumptions made in his case about the operation of any provisions relating to a relevant tax, that loss or damage shall be disregarded, except to the extent of the quantified amount, in the making of any determination–

(a)   of whether or to what extent the repayment of an amount to the taxpayer would enrich him; or

(b)   of whether or to what extent any enrichment of the taxpayer would be unjust.

2(3)   In sub-paragraph (2) above **"the quantified amount"** means the amount (if any) which is shown by the taxpayer to constitute the amount that would appropriately compensate him for loss or damage shown by him to have resulted, for any business carried on by him, from the making of the mistaken assumptions.

2(4)   The reference in sub-paragraph (2) above to provisions relating to a relevant tax is a reference to any provisions of–

(a)   any enactment, subordinate legislation or Community legislation (whether or not still in force) which relates to that tax or to any matter connected with it; or

(b)   any notice published by the Commissioners under or for the purposes of any such enactment or subordinate legislation.

2(5)   This paragraph has effect for the purposes of making any repayment on or after the day on which this Act is passed, even if the claim for that repayment was made before that day.

REIMBURSEMENT ARRANGEMENTS

3(1)   The Commissioners may by regulations make provision for reimbursement arrangements made by any person to be disregarded for the purposes of any or all of the unjust enrichment provisions except where the arrangements–

(a)   contain such provision as may be required by the regulations; and

(b)   are supported by such undertakings to comply with the provisions of the arrangements as may be required by the regulations to be given to the Commissioners.

3(2)   In this paragraph **"reimbursement arrangements"** means any arrangements for the purposes of a claim under a relevant repayment provision which–

(a)   are made by any person for the purpose of securing that he is not unjustly enriched by the repayment of any amount in pursuance of the claim; and

(b)   provide for the reimbursement of persons who have for practical purposes borne the whole or any part of the cost of the original payment of that amount to the Commissioners.

3(3)   Without prejudice to the generality of sub-paragraph (1) above, the provision that may be required by regulations under this paragraph to be contained in reimbursement arrangements includes–

(a)   provision requiring a reimbursement for which the arrangements provide to be made within such period after the repayment to which it relates as may be specified in the regulations;

(b)   provision for the repayment of amounts to the Commissioners where those amounts are not reimbursed in accordance with the arrangements;

(c)   provision requiring interest paid by the Commissioners on any amount repaid by them to be treated in the same way as that amount for the purposes of any requirement under the arrangements to make reimbursement or to repay the Commissioners;

(d)   provision requiring such records relating to the carrying out of the arrangements as may be described in the regulations to be kept and produced to the Commissioners, or to an officer of theirs.

3(4) Regulations under this paragraph may impose obligations on such persons as may be specified in the regulations–

(a)   to make the repayments to the Commissioners that they are required to make in pursuance of any provisions contained in any reimbursement arrangements by virtue of sub-paragraph (3)(b) or (c) above;

(b)   to comply with any requirements contained in any such arrangements by virtue of sub-paragraph (3)(d) above.

3(5) Regulations under this paragraph may make provision for the form and manner in which, and the times at which, undertakings are to be given to the Commissioners in accordance with the regulations; and any such provision may allow for those matters to be determined by the Commissioners in accordance with the regulations.

3(6) Regulations under this paragraph may–

(a)   contain any such incidental, supplementary, consequential or transitional provision as appears to the Commissioners to be necessary or expedient; and

(b)   make different provision for different circumstances.

3(7) Regulations under this paragraph may have effect (irrespective of when the claim for repayment was made) for the purposes of the making of any repayment by the Commissioners after the time when the regulations are made; and, accordingly, such regulations may apply to arrangements made before that time.

3(8) Regulations under this paragraph shall be made by statutory instrument subject to annulment in pursuance of a resolution of the House of Commons.

Statutory instruments – Landfill Tax (Amendment) Regulations 1998 (SI 1998/61).

CONTRAVENTION OF REQUIREMENT TO REPAY COMMISSIONERS

4(1) [Not relevant to landfill tax.]

4(2) [Not relevant to landfill tax.]

4(3) Paragraph 23 of Schedule 5 to the Finance Act 1996 (power to provide for penalty) shall have effect as if an obligation imposed by regulations made by virtue of paragraph 3(4) above were, to the extent that it relates to amounts repaid under paragraph 14 of that Schedule (recovery of overpaid landfill tax), a requirement imposed by regulations under Part III of that Act; and the provisions of that Schedule in relation to penalties under Part V of that Schedule shall have effect accordingly.

Part II – Time Limits

REPAYMENTS

5(1) [Not relevant to landfill tax.]

5(2) [Not relevant to landfill tax.]

5(3) *[Substitutes FA 1996, Sch. 5, para. 14(4).]*

ASSESSMENTS

6 [Amends FA 1996, Sch. 5, para. 33(1) and (4) and certain other provisions which are not relevant to landfill tax.]

Part III – Interest

7-10   [Not relevant to landfill tax.]

INTEREST ON OVERPAID LANDFILL TAX

11(1)   Paragraph 29 of Schedule 5 to the Finance Act 1996 (interest payable by the Commissioners in connection with landfill tax) shall have effect, and be deemed always to have had effect, with the amendments for which this paragraph provides.

11(2)   [Inserts FA 1996, Sch. 5, para. 29(1A).]

11(3)   [Substitutes FA 1996, Sch. 5, para. 29(8).]

11(4)   [Substitutes FA 1996, Sch. 5, para. 29(9).]

12   [Substitutes FA 1996, Sch. 5, para. 29(4), (4A) and (5) for former para. 29(4) – (6).]

12(2)   Sub-paragraph (1) above shall have effect for the purposes of determining whether any period beginning on or after the day on which this Act is passed is left out of account.

Part IV – Set-off Involving Landfill Tax

13   [Inserts FA 1996, Sch. 5, para. 42(4A).]

13(2)   [Inserts FA 1996, Sch. 5, para. 43(4A).]

Part V – Recovery of Excess Payments by the Commissioners

ASSESSMENT FOR EXCESSIVE REPAYMENT

14(1)   Where–

(a)   any amount has been paid at any time to any person by way of a repayment under a relevant repayment provision, and

(b)   the amount paid exceeded the amount which the Commissioners were liable at that time to repay to that person,

the Commissioners may, to the best of their judgment, assess the excess paid to that person and notify it to him.

14(2)   Where any person is liable to pay any amount to the Commissioners in pursuance of an obligation imposed by virtue of paragraph 3(4)(a) above, the Commissioners may, to the best of their judgment, assess the amount due from that person and notify it to him.

14(3)   In this paragraph **"relevant repayment provision"** means–

(a)   [Not relevant to landfill tax.]

(b)   [Not relevant to landfill tax.]

(c)   paragraph 14 of Schedule 5 to the Finance Act 1996 (recovery of overpaid landfill tax).

Cross references – Landfill Tax (Amendment) Regulations 1998 (SI 1998/61), reg. 14A: reimbursement arrangements.
Landfill Tax (Amendment) Regulations 1998 (SI 1998/61), reg. 14B: disregarded reimbursement arrangements.
Landfill Tax (Amendment) Regulations 1998 (SI 1998/61), reg. 14H: reimbursement arrangements made before 11 February 1998.

ASSESSMENT FOR OVERPAYMENTS OF INTEREST

15(1)   Where–

(a)   any amount has been paid to any person by way of interest under a relevant interest provision, but

(b)   that person was not entitled to that amount under that provision,

the Commissioners may, to the best of their judgment, assess the amount so paid to which that person was not entitled and notify it to him.

15(2)   In this paragraph **"relevant interest provision"** means–

(a)   [Not relevant to landfill tax.]

(b)   [Not relevant to landfill tax.]

(c)   paragraph 29 of Schedule 5 to the Finance Act 1996 (interest payable by the Commissioners on overpayments etc. of landfill tax).

ASSESSMENTS UNDER PARAGRAPHS 14 AND 15

16(1)   An assessment under paragraph 14 or 15 above shall not be made more than two years after the time when evidence of facts sufficient in the opinion of the Commissioners to justify the making of the assessment comes to the knowledge of the Commissioners.

16(2)   Where an amount has been assessed and notified to any person under paragraph 14 or 15 above, it shall be recoverable (subject to any provision having effect in accordance with paragraph 19 below) as if it were relevant tax due from him.

16(3)   Sub-paragraph (2) above does not have effect if, or to the extent that, the assessment in question has been withdrawn or reduced.

INTEREST ON AMOUNTS ASSESSED

17(1)   Where an assessment is made under paragraph 14 or 15 above, the whole of the amount assessed shall carry interest at the rate applicable under section 197 of the Finance Act 1996 from the date on which the assessment is notified until payment.

17(2)   Where any person is liable to interest under sub-paragraph (1) above the Commissioners may assess the amount due by way of interest and notify it to him.

17(3)   Without prejudice to the power to make assessments under this paragraph for later periods, the interest to which an assessment under this paragraph may relate shall be confined to interest for a period of no more than two years ending with the time when the assessment under this paragraph is made.

17(4)   Interest under this paragraph shall be paid without any deduction of income tax.

17(5)   A notice of assessment under this paragraph shall specify a date, being not later than the date of the notice, to which the amount of interest is calculated; and, if the interest continues to accrue after that date, a further assessment or assessments may be made under this paragraph in respect of amounts which so accrue.

17(6)   If, within such period as may be notified by the Commissioners to the person liable for interest under sub-paragraph (1) above, the amount referred to in that sub-paragraph is paid, it shall be treated for the purposes of that sub-paragraph as paid on the date specified as mentioned in sub-paragraph (5) above.

17(7)   Where an amount has been assessed and notified to any person under this paragraph it shall be recoverable as if it were relevant tax due from him.

17(8)   Sub-paragraph (7) above does not have effect if, or to the extent that, the assessment in question has been withdrawn or reduced.

SUPPLEMENTARY ASSESSMENTS

18   If it appears to the Commissioners that the amount which ought to have been assessed in an assessment under paragraph 14, 15 or 17 above exceeds the amount which was so assessed, then–

(a)   under the same paragraph as that assessment was made, and

(b)   on or before the last day on which that assessment could have been made,

the Commissioners may make a supplementary assessment of the amount of the excess and shall notify the person concerned accordingly.

REVIEW OF DECISIONS AND APPEALS

19(1)   [Not relevant to landfill tax.]

19(2)   [Not relevant to landfill tax.]

19(3)   Sections 54 to 56 of the Finance Act 1996 (review and appeal in the case of landfill tax) shall have effect in relation to any decision which–

(a)   is contained in an assessment under paragraph 14, 15 or 17 above,

(b)   is a decision about whether any amount is due to the Commissioners or about how much is due, and

(c)   is made in a case in which the relevant repayment provision is paragraph 14 of Schedule 5 to that Act or the relevant interest provision is paragraph 29 of that Schedule,

as if that decision were a decision to which section 54 of that Act applies.

INTERPRETATION OF PART V

20(1) In this Part of this Schedule **"the Commissioners"** means the Commissioners of Customs and Excise.

20(2) In this Part of this Schedule **"relevant tax"**, in relation to any assessment, means–

(a) [Not relevant to landfill tax.]

(b) [Not relevant to landfill tax.]

(c) landfill tax if the assessment relates to–

    (i) a repayment of an amount paid by way of such tax,

    (ii) an overpayment of interest under paragraph 29 of Schedule 5 to the Finance Act 1996, or

    (iii) interest on an amount specified in an assessment in relation to which the relevant tax is landfill tax.

20(3) For the purposes of this Part of this Schedule notification to a personal representative, trustee in bankruptcy, interim or permanent trustee, receiver, liquidator or person otherwise acting in a representative capacity in relation to another shall be treated as notification to the person in relation to whom he so acts.

CONSEQUENTIAL AMENDMENT

21 [Inserts FA 1996, s. 197(2)(e) and the word "and" after FA 1997, s. 197(2)(d).]

Part VI – Indirect Taxes

(2) DISTRESS AND DILIGENCE

Chapter	Short title	Extent of repeal
1996 c. 8.	The Finance Act 1996.	In Schedule 5, paragraph 13.

These repeals come into force on such day as the Commissioners of Customs and Excise may by order made by statutory instrument appoint, and different days may be appointed for different purposes.

Statutory instruments – Finance Act 1997 (Repeal of Distress and Diligence enactments) (Appointed Day) Order 1997 (SI 1997/1433) (C 55): the appointed day for Pt. V(2) is 1 July 1997.

FINANCE ACT 1998

1998 Chapter 36

[*31st July 1998*]

PART V – OTHER TAXES

LANDFILL TAX

148   Provisional collection of landfill tax

148(1) [Amends PCTA 1968, s. 1(1).]

148(2) Where–

(a) by virtue of a resolution having effect under the Provisional Collection of Taxes Act 1968 landfill tax has been paid at a rate specified in the resolution on a taxable disposal of material by reference to the weight of material disposed of, and

(b) by virtue of section 1(6) or (7) or 5(3) of that Act any of that tax is repayable in consequence of the restoration in relation to the taxable disposal of a lower rate, the amount repayable shall be the difference between the landfill tax paid on the taxable disposal at the rate specified in the resolution and the landfill tax that would have been payable on a taxable disposal of the same weight of material at the lower rate.

148(3) Where–

(a) by virtue of a resolution having effect under the Provisional Collection of Taxes Act 1968 landfill tax is chargeable at a rate specified in the resolution on a taxable disposal by reference to the weight of material disposed of, but

(b) before the tax is paid it ceases to be chargeable at that rate in consequence of the restoration in relation to the taxable disposal of a lower rate,

the landfill tax chargeable at the lower rate shall be charged by reference to the same weight of material as that by reference to which landfill tax would have been chargeable at the rate specified in the resolution.

148(4) Expressions used in this section and Part III of the Finance Act 1996 have the same meanings in this section as in that Part.

PART VI – MISCELLANEOUS AND SUPPLEMENTAL

SUPPLEMENTAL

166   Short title

166 This Act may be cited as the Finance Act 1998.

FINANCE ACT 1999

(1999 Chapter 16)

[(27 July 1999)]

PART VII – PART VII – OTHER TAXES

LANDFILL TAX

124   Amends FA 1996, s. 42(1)(a)and(2).

124(2) This section has effect in relation to taxable disposals made, or treated as made, on or after 1st April 1999.

FINANCE ACT 2000

(2000 Chapter 17)

ARRANGEMENT OF SECTIONS

PART V – OTHER TAXES
LANDFILL TAX

SCHEDULES

PART V – OTHER TAXES

LANDFILL TAX

140   Rate

140(1)   In section 42 of the Finance Act 1996 (amount of landfill tax), in subsections (1)(a) and (2) for "£10" substitute "£11".

140(2)   This section has effect in relation to taxable disposals made, or treated as made, on or after 1st April 2000.

141   Disposals which are not taxable

141(1)   In section 62 of the Finance Act 1996 (regulations about taxable disposals) amend subsection (7) (limit on power to make regulations providing that a disposal is not taxable) as follows.

141(2)   For paragraph (a) substitute–

"(a)   the material comprised in the disposal is held temporarily pending one or more of the following–
  (i)   the incineration or recycling of the material, or
  (ii)   the removal of the material for use elsewhere, or
  (iii) the use of the material, if it is qualifying material within the meaning of section 42(3) above, for the restoration to use of the site at which the disposal takes place, or any part of that site, upon completion of waste disposal operations at the site, or as the case may be, that part of the site, or
  (iv)   the sorting of the material with a view to its removal elsewhere or its eventual disposal, and".

141(3)   In paragraph (b) for "the temporary disposal is made" substitute "the material in question is held temporarily".

142   Secondary liability

142(1)   In section 60 of the Finance Act 1996 (which gives effect to Schedule 5 to the Act), after "penalties" insert ", secondary liability".

142(2)   Accordingly the sidenote to that section becomes "Information, powers, penalties, secondary liability, etc".

142(3)   At the end of Schedule 5 to that Act (supplementary provisions relating to landfill tax) add the Part VIII set out in Schedule 37 to this Act.

142(4)   Subsection (3) has effect in relation to taxable disposals made on or after the day on which this Act is passed.

SCHEDULES

SCHEDULE 37 – LANDFILL TAX: NEW PART VIII OF SCHEDULE 5 TO THE FINANCE ACT 1996

Section 138

"Part VIII – Secondary Liability: Controllers of Landfill Sites

MEANING OF CONTROLLER

48(1)   For the purposes of this Part of this Schedule a person is the controller of the whole, or a part, of a landfill site at a given time if he determines, or is entitled to determine, what disposals of material, if any, may be made–
(a)   at every part of the site at that time, or
(b)   at that part of the site at that time,
as the case may be.

48(2)   But a person who, because he is an employee or agent of another, determines or is entitled to determine what disposals may be made at a landfill site or any part of a landfill site is not the controller of that site or, as the case may be, that part of that site.

48(3)   Where a person is the controller of the whole or a part of a landfill site, that site or, as the case may be, that part of the site is referred to in this Part of this Schedule as being under his control.

48(4)   Any reference in this Part of this Schedule to a controller (without more) is a reference to a controller of the whole or a part of a landfill site.

SECONDARY LIABILITY

49(1)   Where–
(a)   a taxable disposal is made at a landfill site,
(b)   at the time when that disposal is made a person is the operator of the landfill site by virtue of section 67(a), (c) or (e) of this Act, and
(c)   at that time a person other than the operator mentioned in paragraph (b) above is the controller of the whole or a part of the landfill site,
the controller shall be liable to pay to the Commissioners an amount of the landfill tax chargeable on the disposal.

49(2)   The amount which the controller is liable to pay shall be determined in accordance with the following provisions of this paragraph.

49(3)   In a case where the whole of the landfill site is under the control of the controller, he shall be liable to pay the whole of the landfill tax chargeable.

49(4)   In a case where a part of the landfill site is under the control of the controller, he shall be liable to pay an amount of the landfill tax calculated in accordance with sub-paragraphs (5) and (6) below.

49(5)   The amount of landfill tax which the controller is liable to pay is the amount which would have been chargeable had a separate taxable disposal consisting of the amount of material referred to in sub-paragraph (6) below been made at the time of the disposal mentioned in sub-paragraph (1)(a) above.

49(6)   That amount of material is the amount by weight of the material comprised in the disposal mentioned in sub-paragraph (1)(a) above which was disposed of on the part of the landfill site under the control of the controller.

49(7)   If the amount mentioned in sub-paragraph (6) above is nil, the controller shall have no liability under sub-paragraph (1) above in relation to landfill tax chargeable on the disposal.

49(8)   For the purposes of sub-paragraph (1)(b) and (c) above–
(a)   section 61 of this Act, and

(b)   any regulations made under section 62 of this Act,

shall not apply for determining the time when the disposal in question is made.

OPERATOR ENTITLED TO CREDIT

50(1)   This paragraph applies where–

(a)   the operator of a landfill site is liable to pay landfill tax on a taxable disposal by reference to a particular accounting period,

(b)   a controller of the whole or a part of that site is (apart from this paragraph) liable under paragraph 49 above to pay an amount of that tax, and

(c)   for the accounting period in question the operator is entitled to credit under regulations made under section 51 of this Act.

50(2)   The amount of the tax which the controller is (apart from this sub-paragraph) liable to pay shall be reduced by the amount calculated in accordance with the following formula–

$$\frac{A \times C}{G}$$

where–

A is the amount of tax mentioned in sub-paragraph (1)(b) above;

C is the amount of credit mentioned in sub-paragraph (1)(c) above; and

G is the operator's gross tax liability for the accounting period in question.

50(3)   For the purposes of sub-paragraph (2) above, the operator's **gross tax liability** for the accounting period in question is the gross amount of landfill tax–

(a)   which is chargeable on disposals made at all landfill sites of which he is the operator, and

(b)   for which he is required to account by reference to that accounting period.

50(4)   In sub-paragraph (3) above, **the gross amount of landfill tax** means the amount of tax before any credit or any other adjustment is taken into account in the period in question.

50(5)   If the amount calculated in accordance with the formula in sub-paragraph (2) above is greater than the amount of tax mentioned in sub-paragraph (1)(b) above, the amount of the tax which the controller is liable to pay shall be reduced to nil.

PAYMENT OF SECONDARY LIABILITY

51(1)   This paragraph applies where a controller is liable under paragraph 49 above (after taking account of any reduction under paragraph 50 above) to pay an amount of landfill tax (**"the relevant amount"**).

51(2)   The controller is required to pay the relevant amount to the Commissioners only if–

(a)   a notice containing the required information is served on him, or

(b)   other reasonable steps are taken with a view to bringing the required information to his attention,

before the end of the period of two years beginning with the day immediately following the relevant accounting day.

51(3)   The **relevant accounting** day is the last day of the accounting period by reference to which the landfill site operator liable to pay the landfill tax in question is required to account for that tax.

51(4)   If the controller is required to pay the relevant amount by virtue of this paragraph, the amount shall be paid before the end of the period of thirty days beginning with the day immediately following the notification day.

51(5)   The **notification day** is–

(a)   in a case where notice is served on a controller as mentioned in sub-paragraph (2)(a) above, the day on which the notice is served, or

(b)   in a case where other reasonable steps are taken as mentioned in sub-paragraph (2)(b) above, the day on which the last of those steps is taken.

51(6)   For the purposes of sub-paragraph (2) above the **required information** is the relevant amount and, if that amount is one reduced in accordance with paragraph 50 above, also–

(a)   the amount of the controller's liability under paragraph 49 above apart from the reduction,

(b)   the amount of credit to which the operator is entitled, and

(c)   the operator's gross tax liability.

ASSESSMENTS

52(1)   Where an amount of landfill tax is–

(a)   assessed under section 50 of this Act, and

(b)   notified to a licensed operator,

the Commissioners may also determine that a controller of the whole or a part of any landfill site operated by the licensed operator shall be liable to pay so much of the amount assessed as they consider just and equitable.

52(2)   A controller is required to pay an amount determined under sub-paragraph (1) above only if–

(a)   a notice stating the amount is served on him, or

(b)   other reasonable steps are taken with a view to bringing the amount of the liability to his attention,

before the expiry of the period of two years beginning with the day immediately following the assessment day.

52(3)   The **assessment day** is the day on which the assessment in question is notified to the licensed operator.

52(4)   If a controller is required to pay an amount by virtue of this paragraph, it shall be paid before the end of the period of thirty days beginning with the day immediately following the notification day.

52(5)   The **notification day** is–

(a)   in a case where notice is served on a controller as mentioned in sub-paragraph (2)(a) above, the day on which the notice is served, or

(b)   in a case where other reasonable steps are taken as mentioned in sub-paragraph (2)(b) above, the day on which the last of those steps is taken.

52(6)   For the purposes of this paragraph a **licensed operator** is a person who is the operator of a landfill site by virtue of section 67(a), (c) or (e) of this Act.

ASSESSMENT WITHDRAWN OR REDUCED

53(1)   Where–

(a)   a controller is liable to pay an amount determined under paragraph 52 above, and

(b)   the assessment notified to the licensed operator is withdrawn or reduced,

the Commissioners may determine that the controller's liability is to be cancelled or to be reduced to such an amount as they consider just and equitable.

53(2)   Sub-paragraphs (3) to (5) below apply where the Commissioners make a determination under sub-paragraph (1) above that the controller's liability is to be reduced (but not cancelled).

53(3)   In such a case they shall–

(a)   serve the controller with notice stating the amount of the reduced liability, or

(b)   take other reasonable steps with a view to bringing the reduced amount to the controller's attention.

53(4)   If the controller has already been served with notice of the amount determined under paragraph 52 above, or if other steps have already been taken to bring that amount to his attention–

(a)   the Commissioners shall serve the notice mentioned in sub-paragraph (3)(a) above, or take the steps mentioned in sub-paragraph (3)(b) above, before the end of the period of thirty days beginning with the day immediately following that on which they make the determination under sub-paragraph (1) above, and

(b)   the reduced amount shall be payable, or treated as having been payable, on or before the day on which the amount referred to in sub-paragraph (1)(a) above would have been payable apart from this paragraph.

53(5)   In a case where the controller has not been served with notice of the amount determined under paragraph 52 above, or no other steps have been taken to bring that amount to his attention, he shall be liable to pay the reduced amount only if–

(a)   the notice mentioned in sub-paragraph (3)(a) above is served, or

(b)   the other steps mentioned in sub-paragraph (3)(b) above are taken,
before the expiry of the period of two years beginning with the day immediately following
that on which the Commissioners make the determination under sub-paragraph (1) above.

53(6)   Sub-paragraph (7) below applies where–
(a)   the Commissioners make a determination under sub-paragraph (1) above that the
controller's liability is to be cancelled, and
(b)   the controller has already been served with notice of the amount determined under
paragraph 52 above, or other steps have already been taken to bring that amount to his
attention.

53(7)   In such a case the Commissioners shall–
(a)   serve the controller with notice stating that the liability has been cancelled, or
(b)   take other reasonable steps with a view to bringing the cancellation to the controller's
attention,
before the end of the period of thirty days beginning with the day immediately following that
on which they make the determination that the liability is to be cancelled.

ADJUSTMENTS

54(1)   This paragraph applies in any case where the liability of a licensed operator to pay
landfill tax is adjusted otherwise than by–
(a)   his being entitled to credit under regulations made under section 51 of this Act,
(b)   his being notified of an amount assessed under section 50 of this Act, or
(c)   the withdrawal or reduction of an assessment under section 50 of this Act which was
notified to him.

54(2)   In such a case the Commissioners may determine that a controller of the whole or
any part of a landfill site operated by the licensed operator–
(a)   shall be liable to pay to the Commissioners such an amount as they consider just and
equitable, or
(b)   shall be entitled to an allowance of such an amount as they consider just and
equitable.

54(3)   A controller is required to pay an amount determined under sub-paragraph (2)(a)
above only if–
(a)   a notice stating the amount is served on him, or
(b)   other reasonable steps are taken with a view to bringing the amount of the liability to
his attention,
before the end of the period of two years beginning with the day immediately following the
relevant accounting day.

54(4)   The **relevant accounting day** is the last day of the accounting period of the operator
within which the adjustment in question was taken into account.

54(5)   If a controller is required to pay an amount by virtue of sub-paragraph (3) above, it
shall be paid before the end of the period of thirty days beginning with the day immediately
following the notification day.

54(6)   The **notification day is**–
(a)   in a case where notice is served on a controller as mentioned in sub-paragraph (3)(a)
above, the day on which the notice is served, or
(b)   in a case where other reasonable steps are taken as mentioned in sub-paragraph (3)(b)
above, the day on which the last of those steps is taken.

54(7)   The Commissioners may determine in what manner a controller is to benefit from an
allowance determined under sub-paragraph (2)(b) above.

54(8)   For the purposes of this paragraph a **licensed operator** is a person who is the
operator of a landfill site by virtue of section 67(a), (c) or (e) of this Act.

AMOUNTS PAYABLE TO BE TREATED AS TAX

55   An amount which a controller is required to pay under paragraph 52, 53 or 54(2)(a)
above or under paragraph 58 below shall be deemed to be an amount of tax due from him
and shall be recoverable accordingly.

CONTROLLER NOT CARRYING OUT TAXABLE ACTIVITY

56 A controller is not to be treated for the purposes of this Act as **carrying out a taxable activity** by reason only of any liability under this Part of this Schedule.

JOINT AND SEVERAL LIABILITY

57(1) In any case where the condition in sub-paragraph (4), (5) or (6) below is satisfied, the controller and the operator shall be jointly and severally liable for the principal liability.

57(2) But the amount which may be recovered from the controller in consequence of such liability shall not exceed the amount of the secondary liability.

57(3) For the purposes of this paragraph–
(a) the **principal liability** is the amount referred to in sub-paragraph (4)(a), (5)(a) or (6)(a) below, as the case may be, and
(b) the **secondary liability** is the amount referred to in sub-paragraph (4)(b), (5)(b) or (6)(b) below, as the case may be.

57(4) The condition in this sub-paragraph is satisfied if–
(a) the operator of a landfill site is liable under section 41 of this Act for landfill tax, and
(b) a controller is liable under paragraph 49 above, after taking account of any reduction under paragraph 50 above, to pay an amount of that tax.

57(5) The condition in this sub-paragraph is satisfied if–
(a) the operator of a landfill site is notified of the amount of an assessment made under section 50 of this Act, and
(b) in consequence of a determination made under paragraph 52 above by the Commissioners in connection with the assessment, a controller is liable to pay an amount (after taking account of any reduction under paragraph 53 above).

57(6) The condition in this sub-paragraph is satisfied if–
(a) the liability of the operator of a landfill site to pay landfill tax is adjusted in such a way that paragraph 54 above applies, and
(b) in consequence of a determination made under paragraph 54(2)(a) above by the Commissioners in connection with the adjustment, a controller is liable to pay an amount.

INTEREST PAYABLE BY A CONTROLLER

58(1) This paragraph applies where–
(a) the operator of a landfill site and the controller of the whole or a part of that site are by virtue of paragraph 57 above jointly and severally liable for an amount, and
(b) that amount carries interest by virtue of any provision of this Schedule.

58(2) The controller and the operator shall be jointly and severally liable to pay the interest.

58(3) But the amount which may be recovered from the controller in consequence of such liability shall not exceed the amount calculated in accordance with the following formula–

$$\frac{(I - [A + B]) \times S}{P}$$

where–
> I is the total amount of interest in question;
> A is the amount of interest carried for the period which–
> (a) begins with the first day of the period for which interest is carried, and
> (b) ends with the day on which the controller becomes liable to pay the secondary liability;
> B is the amount of interest carried for any day falling after that on which the secondary liability is met in full;
> S is the amount of the secondary liability;
> P is the amount of the principal liability.

In this paragraph **secondary liability** and **principal liability** have the same meaning as in paragraph 57 above.

58(4) The controller is liable for an amount of interest only if–
(a) a notice stating the amount is served on him, or

(b)   other reasonable steps are taken with a view to bringing the amount of the liability to his attention,

before the end of the period of two years beginning with the day immediately following the final day.

58(5)   The **final day** is the last day of the period for which the interest in question is carried.

58(6)   If the controller is required to pay an amount in accordance with this paragraph, it shall be paid before the end of the period of thirty days beginning with the day immediately following the notification day.

58(7)   The **notification day** is–

(a)   in a case where notice is served on a controller as mentioned in sub-paragraph (4)(a) above, the day on which the notice is served, or

(b)   in a case where other reasonable steps are taken as mentioned in sub-paragraph (4)(b) above, the day on which the last of those steps is taken.

58(8)   Where by virtue of sub-paragraph (2) above a controller is liable to pay interest which arises under paragraph 27 above, paragraph 28 above shall apply in relation to that interest as it applies to interest which a person is liable under paragraph 27 above to pay.

REVIEWS

59   Section 54 of this Act shall apply to a decision of the Commissioners under this Part of this Schedule–

(a)   that a person is a controller,

(b)   that a person is liable under this Part of this Schedule to pay any amount (including a penalty under paragraph 60 below),

(c)   that a person is not entitled under this Part of this Schedule to an allowance, or

(d)   as to the amount of any liability or any allowance under this Part of this Schedule,

as it applies to the other decisions of the Commissioners specified in subsection (1) of that section.

NOTICE THAT PERSON IS, OR IS NO LONGER, A CONTROLLER

60(1)   This paragraph applies where–

(a)   on the date when this paragraph comes into force, a person is a controller of the whole or a part of a landfill site, or

(b)   after that date, a person becomes or ceases to be a controller of the whole or a part of a landfill site.

60(2)   The controller, and the operator of the landfill site in question, shall be under a duty to secure that notice which complies with the requirements of sub-paragraph (3) below appropriate to the case in question is given to the Commissioners.

60(3)   The requirements of this sub-paragraph are that the notice–

(a)   states that a person is, has become or has ceased to be a controller,

(b)   identifies that person and the site under his control or formerly under his control,

(c)   states the date when he became or ceased to be the controller, and

(d)   is given within the period of thirty days beginning with the day immediately following–

     (i)   the day when this paragraph comes into force, in a case falling within sub-paragraph (1)(a) above, or

     (ii)   the day when the person in question becomes or ceases to be the controller, in a case falling within sub-paragraph (1)(b) above.

60(4)   If a person fails to comply with sub-paragraph (2) above, he is liable to a penalty of £250.

60(5)   Paragraph 25 above applies to a penalty under sub-paragraph (4) above as it applies to a penalty under Part V of this Schedule.

EXTENSION OF TIME LIMITS WHERE NOTICE NOT SERVED

61(1)   This paragraph applies where–

(a)   a person is liable under paragraph 49 above to pay an amount of landfill tax or liable under paragraph 58 above to pay interest, or

(b) the Commissioners are entitled under paragraph 52, 53 or 54 above to determine an amount which a person is liable to pay.

61(2) The reference to two years in paragraph 51(2), 52(2), 53(5), 54(3) or 58(4) above (as the case may be) shall be treated as a reference to twenty years if the requirement of paragraph 60(2) above to give notice to the Commissioners in relation to the person mentioned in sub-paragraph (1) above being or becoming a controller has not been complied with."

LANDFILL TAX
STATUTORY INSTRUMENTS

Table of Contents

Note: Not all current statutory instruments are reproduced in full text in this division. If a current statutory instrument merely amends an existing Act or statutory instrument, then the existing Act or statutory instrument itself is amended and a history note is added thereto. The amending statutory instrument is not reproduced in this division, but it is listed below together with a note indicating its effect. Similarly, if a statutory instrument merely brings a current provision into operation, i.e. it is a commencement order or an appointed day order, then it is also listed below together with an appropriate note. If a statutory instrument only partly relates to landfill tax, only that part is reproduced.

THE LANDFILL TAX REGULATIONS 1996

(1996/1527, as amended by SI 1996/2100; SI 1997/1431; SI 1998/61; SI 1999/3270)

Made on 12 June 1996 by the Commissioners of Customs and Excise, in exercise of the powers conferred on them by s. 47(9), 48(1) and (2), 49, 51(1) to (6), 52(1) to (3), 53(1) to (4), 58(1) and (4) to (6), 61(2), 62(1) to (3) and (5) and (6) and 68(1) to (6) of, and para. 2(1) to (3), 13(1) and (6), 14(5), 20(3), 23(1), 42(1) to (5) and 43(1) to (5) of Sch. 5 to, the Finance Act 1996, hereby make the following Regulations coming into force on 1 August 1996.

ARRANGEMENT OF REGULATIONS

PART I – PRELIMINARY

CITATION AND COMMENCEMENT

1   These Regulations may be cited as the Landfill Tax Regulations 1996 and shall come into force on 1st August 1996.

INTERPRETATION

2(1)   In these Regulations–

"**accounting period**" means–

(a)   in the case of a registered person, each period of three months ending on the dates notified to him by the Commissioners, whether by means of a registration certificate issued by them or otherwise;

(b)   in the case of a registrable person who is not registered, each quarter; or

(c)   in the case of any registrable person, such other period in relation to which he is required by or under regulation 11 to make a return;

and, in every case, the first accounting period of a registrable person shall begin on the effective date of registration;

"**the Act**" means the Finance Act 1996;

"**Collector**" means a Collector, Deputy Collector or Assistant Collector of Customs and Excise;

"credit", except where the context otherwise requires, means credit which a person is entitled to claim under Part IV of these Regulations;

"disposal" means a landfill disposal (which expression has the meaning given in section 70(2) of the Act) made on or after 1st October 1996 and **"disposed of"** shall be construed accordingly;

"effective date of registration" means the date determined in accordance with section 47 of the Act upon which the person was or should have been registered;

"landfill invoice" means an invoice of the description in regulation 37;

"landfill site" has the meaning given in section 66 of the Act;

"landfill tax account" has the meaning given in regulation 12;

"landfill tax bad debt account" has the meaning given in regulation 26;

"quarter" means a period of three months ending at the end of March, June, September or December;

"registered person" means a person who is registered under section 47 of the Act and "register" and "registration" shall be construed accordingly;

"registrable person" has the meaning given in section 47(10) of the Act;

"registration number" means the identifying number allocated to a registered person and notified to him by the Commissioners;

"return" means a return which is required to be made in accordance with regulation 11;

"taxable business" means a business or part of a business in the course of which taxable activities are carried out;

"transfer note" has the same meaning as in the Environmental Protection (Duty of Care) Regulations 1991;

"working day" means any day of the week except Saturday and Sunday and a bank holiday or public holiday, in either case, for England.

2(2) In these Regulations any question whether a person is **connected** with another shall be determined in accordance with section 839 of the Taxes Act 1988.

2(3) Any reference in these Regulations to **"this Part"** is a reference to the Part of these Regulations in which that reference is made.

2(4) Any reference in these Regulations to a form prescribed in the Schedule to these Regulations shall include a reference to a form which the Commissioners are satisfied is a form to the like effect.

DESIGNATION, DIRECTION OR APPROVAL

3 Any designation, direction or approval by the Commissioners under or for the purposes of these Regulations shall be made or given by a notice in writing.

PART II – REGISTRATION AND PROVISION FOR SPECIAL CASES

NOTIFICATION OF LIABILITY TO BE REGISTERED

4(1) A person who is required by section 47(3) of the Act to notify the Commissioners of his intention to carry out taxable activities shall do so on the form numbered 1 in the Schedule to these Regulations.

4(2) Where the notification referred to in this regulation is made by a person who operates or intends to operate more than one landfill site, it shall include the particulars set out on the form numbered 2 in the Schedule to these Regulations.

4(3) Where the notification referred to in this regulation is made by a partnership, it shall include the particulars set out on the form numbered 3 in the Schedule to these Regulations.

4(4) The notification referred to in this regulation shall be made within 30 days of the earliest date after 1st August 1996 on which the person either forms or continues to have the intention to carry out taxable activities.

CHANGES IN PARTICULARS

5(1) A person who has made a notification under regulation 4, whether or not it was made in accordance with paragraph (4) of that regulation, shall, within 30 days of–

(a)   discovering any inaccuracy in; or

(b)   any change occurring which causes to become inaccurate,

any of the information which was contained in or provided with the notification, notify the Commissioners in writing and furnish them with full particulars.

5(2) Without prejudice to paragraph (1) above, a registrable person shall, within 30 days of any change occurring in any of the circumstances referred to in paragraph (4) below, notify the Commissioners in writing and furnish them with particulars of–

(a)   the change; and

(b)   the date on which the change occurred.

5(3) A registrable person who discovers that any information contained in or provided with a notification under paragraph (1) or (2) above was inaccurate shall, within 30 days of his discovering the inaccuracy, notify the Commissioners in writing and furnish them with particulars of–

(a)   the inaccuracy;

(b)   the date on which the inaccuracy was discovered;

(c)   how the information was inaccurate; and

(d)   the correct information.

5(4) The circumstances mentioned in paragraph (2) above are the following circumstances relating to the registrable person or any taxable business carried on by him:

(a)   his name, his trading name (if different), his address and the landfill sites he operates;

(b)   his status, namely whether he carries on business as a sole proprietor, body corporate, partnership or other unincorporated body;

(c)   in the case of a partnership, the name and address of any partner.

5(5) Any person failing to comply with a requirement imposed in any of paragraph (1) to (3) above shall be liable to a penalty of £250.

5(6) Where in relation to a registered person the Commissioners are satisfied that any of the information recorded in the register is or has become inaccurate they may correct the register accordingly.

5(7) For the purposes of paragraph (6) above, it is immaterial whether or not the registered person has notified the Commissioners of any change which has occurred in accordance with paragraph (1) to (3) above.

NOTIFICATION OF CESSATION OF TAXABLE ACTIVITIES

6 A person who is required by section 47(4) of the Act to notify the Commissioners of his having ceased to have the intention to carry out taxable activities shall, within 30 days of his so having ceased, notify the Commissioners in writing and shall therein inform them of–

(a)   the date on which he ceased to have the intention of carrying out taxable activities; and

(b)   if different, the date on which he ceased to carry out taxable activities.

TRANSFER OF A GOING CONCERN

7(1) Where–

(a)   a taxable business is transferred as a going concern;

(b)   the registration of the transferor has not already been cancelled;

(c)   as a result of the transfer of the business the registration of the transferor is to be cancelled and the transferee has become liable to be registered; and

(d)   an application is made on the form numbered 4 in the Schedule to these Regulations by both the transferor and the transferee,

the Commissioners may with effect from the date of the transfer cancel the registration of the transferor and register the transferee with the registration number previously allocated to the transferor.

7(2) An application under paragraph (1) above shall be treated as the notification referred to in regulation 6.

7(3) Where the transferee of a business has been registered under paragraph (1) above with the registration number previously allocated to the transferor–

(a) any liability of the transferor existing at the date of the transfer to make a return or account for or pay any tax under Part III of these Regulations shall become the liability of the transferee;

(b) any entitlement of the transferor, whether or not existing at the date of the transfer, to credit or payment under Part IV of these Regulations shall become the entitlement of the transferee.

7(4) In addition to the provisions set out in paragraph (3) above, where the transferee of a business has been registered under paragraph (1) above with the registration number previously allocated to the transferor during an accounting period subsequent to that in which the transfer took place (but with effect from the date of the transfer) and any–

(a) return has been made;

(b) tax has been accounted for; or

(c) entitlement to credit has been claimed,

by either the transferor or the transferee, it shall be treated as having been done by the transferee.

7(5) Where–

(a) a taxable business is transferred as a going concern;

(b) the transferee removes material as described in regulation 21(2) or (4); and

(c) the transferor has paid tax on the disposal concerned,

then, whether or not the transferee has been registered under paragraph (1) above with the registration number previously allocated to the transferor, any entitlement to credit arising under Part V of these Regulations shall become the entitlement of the transferee.

Official publications – LFT1, para. 11.5 (1997 edn).

REPRESENTATION OF UNINCORPORATED BODY

8(1) Where anything is required to be done by or under the Act (whether by these Regulations or otherwise) by or on behalf of an unincorporated body other than a partnership, it shall be the joint and several responsibility of–

(a) every member holding office as president, chairman, treasurer, secretary or any similar office; or

(b) if there is no such office, every member holding office as a member of a committee by which the affairs of the body are managed; or

(c) if there is no such office or committee, every member;

but, subject to paragraph (2) below, if it is done by any of the persons referred to above that shall be sufficient compliance with any such requirement.

8(2) Where an unincorporated body other than a partnership is required to make any notification such as is referred to in regulation 4 to 6, it shall not be sufficient compliance unless the notification is made by a person upon whom a responsibility for making it is imposed by paragraph (1) above.

8(3) Where anything is required to be done by or under the Act (whether by these Regulations or otherwise) by or on behalf of a partnership, it shall be the joint and several responsibility of every partner; but if it is done by one partner or, in the case of a partnership whose principal place of business is in Scotland, by any other person authorised by the partnership with respect thereto that shall be sufficient compliance with any such requirement.

BANKRUPTCY OR INCAPACITY OF REGISTRABLE PERSONS

9(1) If a registrable person becomes bankrupt or incapacitated, the Commissioners may, from the date on which he became bankrupt or incapacitated, as the case may be, treat as a registrable person any person carrying on any taxable business of his; and any legislation relating to landfill tax shall apply to any person so treated as though he were a registered person.

9(2) Any person carrying on such business as aforesaid shall, within 30 days of commencing to do so, inform the Commissioners in writing of that fact and the date of the bankruptcy order or of the nature of the incapacity and the date on which it began.

9(3) Where the Commissioners have treated a person carrying on a business as a registrable person under paragraph (1) above, they shall cease so to treat him if–

(a) the registration of the registrable person is cancelled, whether or not any other person is registered with the registration number previously allocated to him;

(b) the bankruptcy is discharged or the incapacity ceases; or

(c) he ceases carrying on the business of the registrable person.

9(4) In relation to a registrable person which is a company, the references in this regulation to the registrable person becoming **incapacitated** shall be construed as references to its going into liquidation or receivership or to an administration order being made in relation to it; and references to the **incapacity ceasing** shall be construed accordingly.

PART III – ACCOUNTING, PAYMENT AND RECORDS

INTERPRETATION

10 In this Part, **"accounting period"** has the meaning given in regulation 2(1).

MAKING OF RETURNS

11(1) Subject to paragraph (3) below and save as the Commissioners may otherwise allow, a registrable person shall, in respect of each accounting period, make a return to the Controller, Central Collection Unit (LT), on the form numbered 5 in the Schedule to these Regulations.

11(2) Subject to paragraph (3) below, a registrable person shall make each return not later than the last working day of the month next following the end of the period to which it relates.

11(3) Where the Commissioners consider it necessary in the circumstances of any particular case, they may–

(a) vary the length of any accounting period or the date on which it begins or ends or by which any return must be made;

(b) allow or direct the registrable person to make a return in accordance with sub-paragraph (a) above;

(c) allow or direct a registrable person to make returns to a specified address,

and any person to whom the Commissioners give any direction such as is referred to in this regulation shall comply therewith.

Official publications – LFT1, para. 12.1 (1997 edn).

LANDFILL TAX ACCOUNT

12(1) Every registrable person shall make and maintain an account to be known as **"the landfill tax account"**.

12(2) The landfill tax account shall be in such form and contain such particulars as may be stipulated in a notice published by the Commissioners and not withdrawn by a further notice.

CORRECTION OF ERRORS

13(1) In this regulation–

"**overdeclaration**" means, in relation to any return, the amount (if any) which was wrongly treated as tax due for the accounting period concerned and which caused the amount of tax which was payable to be overstated, or the entitlement to a payment under regulation 20 to be understated (or both) or would have caused such an overstatement or understatement were it not for the existence of an underdeclaration in relation to that return;

"**underdeclaration**" means, in relation to any return, the aggregate of–

(a) the amount (if any) of tax due for the accounting period concerned which was not taken into account; and

(b) the amount (if any) which was wrongly deducted as credit,

and which caused the amount of tax which was payable to be understated, or the entitlement to a payment under regulation 20 to be overstated (or both) or would have caused such an understatement or overstatement were it not for the existence of an overdeclaration in relation to that return.

13(2) This regulation applies where a registrable person has made a return which was inaccurate as the result of an overdeclaration or underdeclaration.

13(3) Where in any accounting period a registrable person has discovered one or more overdeclarations, he may enter the overdeclarations in the return for the accounting period in which they were discovered by including their amount in the box opposite the legend "Overdeclarations from previous periods (no limit)."

13(4) Where in any accounting period–

(a) a registrable person discovers one or more underdeclarations; and

(b) having treated the amount of those underdeclarations as reduced by the amount of any overdeclarations for the same accounting periods, the total of those underdeclarations does not exceed £2,000,

he may enter the underdeclarations in his return for the accounting period in which they were discovered by including their amount in the box opposite the legend "Underdeclarations from previous periods (must not exceed £2,000, see general notes)."

13(5) Where a registrable person enters an amount in a return in accordance with paragraph (3) or (4) above he shall calculate the tax payable by him or the payment to which he is entitled accordingly.

13(6) Where an amount has been entered in accordance with this regulation in a return which has been made–

(a) the return shall be regarded as correcting any earlier return to which that amount relates; and

(b) the registrable person shall be taken to have furnished information with respect to the inaccuracy in the prescribed form and manner for the purposes of paragraph 20 of Schedule 5 to the Act.

13(7) No amount shall be entered in a return in respect of any overdeclaration or underdeclaration except in accordance with this regulation; and as regards any underdeclaration that cannot be corrected under paragraph (4) above a person shall not be taken to have furnished information with respect to an inaccuracy in the prescribed form and manner for the purposes of paragraph 20 of Schedule 5 to the Act unless he provides such information to the Commissioners in writing.

CLAIMS FOR OVERPAID TAX

14 Except where the amount to which the claim relates has been entered in a return in accordance with regulation 13 or is included in an amount so entered, any claim under paragraph 14 of Schedule 5 to the Act shall be made in writing to the Commissioners and shall, by reference to such documentary evidence as is in the possession of the claimant, state the amount of the claim and the method by which that amount was calculated.

INTERPRETATION OF REGULATIONS 14A TO 14H

14A In this regulation and in regulations 14B to 14H below–

"**claim**" means a claim made (irrespective of when it was made) under paragraph 14 of Schedule 5 to the Act for repayment of an amount paid to the Commissioners by way of tax which was not tax due to them; and "**claimed**" and "**claimant**" shall be construed accordingly;

"**reimbursement arrangements**" means any arrangements (whether made before, on or after 30th January 1998) for the purposes of a claim which–

(a) are made by a claimant for the purpose of securing that he is not unjustly enriched by the repayment of any amount in pursuance of the claim; and

(b) provide for the reimbursement of persons (consumers) who have, for practical purposes, borne the whole or any part of the cost of the original payment of that amount to the Commissioners;

"**relevant amount**" means that part (which may be the whole) of the amount of a claim which the claimant has reimbursed or intends to reimburse to consumers.

History – Reg. 14A was inserted by SI 1998/61, reg. 2, operative from 11 February 1998.

REIMBURSEMENT ARRANGEMENTS – GENERAL

14B Without prejudice to regulation 14H below, for the purposes of paragraph 14(3) of Schedule 5 to the Act (defence by the Commissioners that repayment by them of an amount claimed would unjustly enrich the claimant) reimbursement arrangements made by a claimant shall be disregarded except where they–

(a) include the provisions described in regulation 14C below; and

(b) are supported by the undertakings described in regulation 14G below.

History – Reg. 14B was inserted by SI 1998/61, reg. 2, operative from 11 February 1998.

REIMBURSEMENT ARRANGEMENTS – PROVISIONS TO BE INCLUDED

14C The provisions referred to in regulation 14B above are that–

(a) reimbursement for which the arrangements provide will be completed by no later than 90 days after the repayment to which it relates;

(b) no deduction will be made from the relevant amount by way of fee or charge (howsoever expressed or effected);

(c) reimbursement will be made only in cash or by cheque;

(d) any part of the relevant amount that is not reimbursed by the time mentioned in paragraph (a) above will be repaid by the claimant to the Commissioners;

(e) any interest paid by the Commissioners on any relevant amount repaid by them will also be treated by the claimant in the same way as the relevant amount falls to be treated under paragraphs (a) and (b) above; and

(f) the records described in regulation 14E below will be kept by the claimant and produced by him to the Commissioners, or to an officer of theirs in accordance with regulation 14F below.

History – Reg. 14C was inserted by SI 1998/61, reg. 2, operative from 11 February 1998.

REPAYMENTS TO THE COMMISSIONERS

14D The claimant shall, without prior demand, make any repayment to the Commissioners that he is required to make by virtue of regulation 14C(d) and (e) above within 14 days of the expiration of the period of 90 days referred to in regulation 14C(a) above.

History – Reg. 14D was inserted by SI 1998/61, reg. 2, operative from 11 February 1998.

RECORDS

14E The claimant shall keep records of the following matters–

(a) the names and addresses of those consumers whom he has reimbursed or whom he intends to reimburse;

(b) the total amount reimbursed to each such consumer;

(c) the amount of interest included in each total amount reimbursed to each consumer;

(d) the date that each reimbursement is made.

History – Reg. 14E was inserted by SI 1998/61, reg. 2, operative from 11 February 1998.

PRODUCTION OF RECORDS

14F(1) Where a claimant is given notice in accordance with paragraph (2) below, he shall, in accordance with such notice produce to the Commissioners, or to an officer of theirs, the records that he is required to keep pursuant to regulation 14E above.

14F(2) A notice given for the purposes of paragraph (1) above shall–

(a) be in writing;

(b) state the place and time at which, and the date on which the records are to be produced; and

(c) be signed and dated by the Commissioners, or by an officer of theirs,

and may be given before or after, or both before and after the Commissioners have paid the relevant amount to the claimant.

History – Reg. 14F was inserted by SI 1998/61, reg. 2, operative from 11 February 1998.

UNDERTAKINGS

14G(1) Without prejudice to regulation 14H(b) below, the undertakings referred to in regulation 14B(b) above shall be given to the Commissioners by the claimant no later than the time at which he makes the claim for which the reimbursement arrangements have been made.

14G(2) The undertakings shall be in writing, shall be signed and dated by the claimant, and shall be to the effect that–

(a) at the date of the undertakings he is able to identify the names and addresses of those consumers whom he has reimbursed or whom he intends to reimburse;

(b) he will apply the whole of the relevant amount repaid to him, without any deduction by way of fee or charge or otherwise, to the reimbursement in cash or by cheque, of such consumers by no later than 90 days after his receipt of that amount (except insofar as he has already so reimbursed them);

(c) he will apply any interest paid to him on the relevant amount repaid to him wholly to the reimbursement of such consumers by no later than 90 days after his receipt of that interest;

(d) he will repay to the Commissioners without demand the whole or such part of the relevant amount repaid to him or of any interest paid to him as he fails to apply in accordance with the undertakings mentioned in sub-paragraphs (b) and (c) above;

(e) he will keep the records described in regulation 14E above; and

(f) he will comply with any notice given to him in accordance with regulation 14F above concerning the production of such records.

History – Reg. 14G was inserted by SI 1998/61, reg. 2, operative from 11 February 1998.

REIMBURSEMENT ARRANGEMENTS MADE BEFORE 11TH FEBRUARY 1998

14H Reimbursement arrangements made by a claimant before 11th February 1998 shall not be disregarded for the purposes of paragraph 14(3) of Schedule 5 to the Act if, not later than 11th March 1998–

(a) he includes in those arrangements (if they are not already included) the provisions described in regulation 14C above; and

(b) gives the undertakings described in regulation 14G above.

History – Reg. 14H was inserted by SI 1998/61, reg. 2, operative from 11 February 1998.

PAYMENT OF TAX

15 Save as the Commissioners may otherwise allow or direct, any person required to make a return shall pay to the Controller, Central Collection Unit (LT), such amount of tax as is payable by him in respect of the accounting period to which the return relates no later than the last day on which he was required to make the return.

Official publications – LFT1, para. 12.2 (1997 edn).

RECORDS

16(1) Every registrable person shall, for the purpose of accounting for tax, preserve the following–

(a) his business and accounting records;

(b) his landfill tax account;

(c) transfer notes and any other original or copy records in relation to material brought onto or removed from the landfill site (including any record made for the purpose of Part IX of these Regulations);

(d) all invoices (including landfill invoices) and similar documents issued to him and copies of such invoices and similar documents issued by him;

(e) all credit or debit notes or other documents received by him which evidence an increase or decrease in the amount of any consideration for a relevant transaction, and copies of such documents that are issued by him;

(f) such other records as the Commissioners may specify in a notice published by them and not withdrawn by a further notice.

16(2) Subject to paragraphs (3) and (4) below, every registrable person shall preserve the records specified in paragraph (1) above for a period of six years.

16(3) Subject to paragraph (4) below, a registrable person who has made a landfill tax bad debt account shall preserve that account for a period of five years from the date of the claim made under Part VI of these Regulations.

16(4) The Commissioners may direct that registrable persons shall preserve the records specified in paragraph (1) above for a shorter period than that specified in this regulation; and such direction may be made so as to apply generally or in such cases as the Commissioners may stipulate.

16(5) In paragraph (1) above–

(a)   the reference to **material being brought onto a landfill site** is a reference to material that is brought onto the site for the purpose of a relevant transaction;

(b)   the reference to **material being removed from a landfill site** is a reference to material being removed that has at some previous time fallen wholly or partly within paragraph (a) above.

16(6)   In this regulation **"relevant transaction"** means a disposal or anything that would be a disposal but for the fact that the material is not disposed of as waste.
Official publications – LFT1, para. 13 (1997 edn).

PART IV – CREDIT: GENERAL
Official publications – LFT1, para. 8 and 9 (1997 edn).

INTERPRETATION

17   In this Part–

"relevant accounting period" means–

(a)   in the case of an entitlement to credit arising under Part V of these Regulations, the accounting period in which the reuse condition or, as the case may be, the enforced removal condition was satisfied;

(b)   in the case of an entitlement to credit arising under Part VI of these Regulations, the accounting period in which the period of one year from the date of the issue of the landfill invoice expired;

(c)   in the case of an entitlement arising under Part VII of these Regulations, the accounting period in which the qualifying contribution was made;

"relevant amount" means the amount of the credit as determined in accordance with Part V, VI or VII of these Regulations, as the case may be;

"relevant tax" means the tax, if any, that was required to have been paid as a condition of the entitlement to credit.

SCOPE

18(1)   This Part applies to entitlements to credit arising under Part V, VI or VII of these Regulations.

18(2)   No credit arising under any provision of these Regulations may be claimed except in accordance with this Part.

CLAIMS IN RETURNS

19(1)   Subject to paragraphs (2) and (3) below, a person entitled to credit may claim it by deducting its amount from any tax due from him for the relevant accounting period or any subsequent accounting period and, where he does so, he shall make his return for that accounting period accordingly.

19(2)   Where the entitlement to credit arises under Part VII of these Regulations paragraph (1) above shall apply as if there were substituted for "or any subsequent accounting period" the words "or any subsequent accounting period in the same contribution year as determined in relation to that person under regulation 31."

19(3)   The Commissioners may make directions generally or with regard to particular cases prescribing rules in accordance with which credit may or shall be held over to be credited in an accounting period subsequent to the relevant accounting period; and where such a direction has been made that credit, subject to any subsequent such direction varying or withdrawing the rules, may only be claimed in accordance with those rules.

PAYMENTS IN RESPECT OF CREDIT

20(1)   Subject to paragraph (5) below, where the total credit claimed by a registrable person in accordance with this Part exceeds the total of the tax due from him for the accounting period, the Commissioners shall pay to him an amount equal to the excess.

20(2)   Where the Commissioners have cancelled the registration of a person in accordance with section 47(6) of the Act, and he is not a registrable person, he shall make any claim in respect of credit to which this Part applies by making an application in writing.

20(3) A person making an application under paragraph (2) above shall furnish to the Commissioners full particulars in relation to the credit claimed, including (but not restricted to)–

(a) except in the case of an entitlement to credit arising under Part VII of these Regulations, the return in which the relevant tax was accounted for;

(b) except in the case of an entitlement to credit arising under Part VII of these Regulations, the amount of the tax and the date and manner of its payment;

(c) the events by virtue of which the entitlement to credit arose.

20(4) Subject to paragraph (5) below, where the Commissioners are satisfied that a person who has made a claim in accordance with paragraphs (2) and (3) above is entitled to credit, and that he has not previously had the benefit of that credit, they shall pay to him an amount equal to the credit.

20(5) The Commissioners shall not be liable to make any payment under this regulation unless and until the person has made all the returns which he was required to make.

PART V – CREDIT: PERMANENT REMOVALS ETC.

ENTITLEMENT TO CREDIT

Official publications – LFT1, para. 8 and 9 (1997 edn).

21(1) An entitlement to credit arises under this Part where–

(a) a registered person has accounted for an amount of tax and, except where the removal by virtue of which sub-paragraph (b) below is satisfied takes place in the accounting period in which credit arising under this Part is claimed in accordance with Part IV of these Regulations, he has paid that tax; and

(b) in relation to the disposal on which that tax was charged, either–

    (i) the reuse condition has been satisfied; or

    (ii) the enforced removal condition has been satisfied.

21(2) The **reuse condition** is satisfied where–

(a) the disposal has been made with the intention that the material comprised in it–

    (i) would be recycled or incinerated, or

    (ii) removed for use (other than by way of a further disposal) at a place other than a relevant site;

(b) that material, or some of it, has been recycled, incinerated or permanently removed from the landfill site, as the case may be, in accordance with that intention;

(c) that recycling, incineration or removal–

    (i) has taken place no later than one year after the date of the disposal; or

    (ii) where water had been added to the material in order to facilitate its disposal, has taken place no later than five years after the date of the disposal; and

(d) the registered person has, before the disposal, notified the Commissioners in writing that he intends to make one or more removals of material in relation to which sub-paragraphs (a) to (c) above will be satisfied.

21(3) For the purpose of paragraph (2)(a)(ii) above a **relevant site** is the landfill site at which the disposal was made or any other landfill site.

21(4) The **enforced removal condition** is satisfied where–

(a) the disposal is in breach of the terms of the licence or resolution, as the case may be, by virtue of which the land constitutes a landfill site;

(b) the registered person has been directed to remove the material comprised in the disposal, or some of it, by a relevant authority and he has removed it, or some of it; and

(c) a further taxable disposal of the material has been made and, except where the registered person is the person liable for the tax chargeable on that further disposal, he has paid to the site operator an amount representing that tax.

21(5) For the purpose of paragraph (4)(b) above the following are **relevant authorities**–

(a) the Environment Agency;

(b) the Scottish Environment Protection Agency;

(c) the Department of the Environment for Northern Ireland;

(d)   a district council in Northern Ireland.

21(6)   The amount of the credit arising under this Part shall be equal to the tax that was charged on the disposal; except that where only some of the material comprised in that disposal is removed, the amount of the credit shall be such proportion of that tax as the material removed forms of the total of the material.

PART VI – CREDIT: BAD DEBTS

Official publications – LFT1, para. 7 (1997 edn).

INTERPRETATION

22   In this Part–

"claim" means a claim in accordance with Part IV of these Regulations for an amount of credit arising under this Part and **"claimant"** shall be construed accordingly;

"customer" means a person for whom a taxable activity is carried out by the claimant;

"outstanding amount" means, in relation to any claim–

(a)   if at the time of the claim the claimant has received no payment in respect of the amount written off in his accounts, the amount so written off; or

(b)   if at that time he has received a payment, the amount by which the amount written off exceeds the payment (or the aggregate of the payments);

"relevant disposal" means any taxable disposal upon which a claim is based;

"security" means–

(a)   in relation to England, Wales and Northern Ireland, any mortgage, charge, lien or other security; and

(b)   in relation to Scotland, any security (whether heritable or moveable), any floating charge and any right of lien or preference and right of retention (other than a right of compensation or set-off).

SCOPE

23   An entitlement to credit arises under this Part where–

(a)   a registered person has carried out a taxable activity for a consideration in money for a customer with whom he is not connected;

(b)   he has accounted for and paid tax on the disposal concerned;

(c)   the whole or any part of the consideration for the disposal has been written off in his accounts as a bad debt;

(d)   he has issued a landfill invoice in respect of the disposal which shows the amount of tax chargeable;

(e)   that invoice was issued–

(i) within 14 days of the date of the disposal, or

(ii) within such other period as may have been specified in a direction of the Commissioners made under section 61(3) of the Act;

(f)   a period of one year (beginning with the date of the issue of that invoice) has elapsed; and

(g)   the following provisions of this Part have been complied with.

AMOUNT OF CREDIT

24   The credit arising under this Part shall be of an amount equal to such proportion of the tax charged on the relevant disposal as the outstanding amount forms of the total consideration.

EVIDENCE REQUIRED IN SUPPORT OF CLAIM

25   The claimant, before he makes a claim, shall hold in respect of each relevant disposal–

(a)   a copy of the landfill invoice issued by him;

(b)   records or any other documents showing that he has accounted for and paid tax on the disposal; and

(c)   records or any other documents showing that the consideration has been written off in his accounts as a bad debt.

RECORDS REQUIRED TO BE KEPT

26(1) Any person who makes a claim shall make a record of that claim.

26(2) The record referred to in paragraph (1) above shall contain the following information in respect of each claim made:

(a) in respect of each relevant disposal–

  (i) the amount of tax charged;

  (ii) the return in which that tax was accounted for and when it was paid;

  (iii) the date and identifying number of the landfill invoice that was issued;

  (iv) any consideration that has been received (whether before the claim was made or subsequently);

  (v) the details of any transfer note;

(b) the outstanding amount;

(c) the amount of the claim;

(d) the return in which the claim was made.

26(3) Any records made in pursuance of this regulation shall be kept in a single account known as **"the landfill tax bad debt account"**.

ATTRIBUTION OF PAYMENTS

27(1) Where–

(a) the claimant has carried out a taxable activity for a customer;

(b) there exist one or more other matters in respect of which the claimant is entitled to a debt owed by the customer (whether they involve a taxable disposal or not and whether they are connected with waste or not); and

(c) a payment has been received by the claimant from the customer,

the payment shall be attributed to the taxable activity and the other matters in accordance with the rule set out in paragraphs (2) and (3) below (and the debts arising in respect of the taxable activity and the other matters are collectively referred to in those paragraphs as debts).

27(2) The payment shall be attributed to the debt which arose earliest and, if not wholly attributed to that debt, thereafter to debts in the order of the dates on which they arose, except that attribution under this paragraph shall not be made if the payment was allocated to a debt by the customer at the time of payment and the debt was paid in full.

27(3) Where–

(a) the earliest debt and the other debts to which the whole of the payment could be attributed arose on the same day; or

(b) the debts to which the balance of the payment could be attributed in accordance with paragraph (2) above arose on the same day,

the payment shall be attributed to those debts by multiplying, for each such debt, the payment made by a fraction of which the numerator is the amount remaining unpaid in respect of that debt and the denominator is the amount remaining unpaid in respect of all those debts.

REPAYMENT OF CREDIT

28(1) Where a claimant–

(a) has benefited from an amount of credit to which he was entitled under this Part; and

(b) either–

  (i) a payment for the relevant disposal is subsequently received; or

  (ii) a payment is, by virtue of regulation 27, treated as attributed to the relevant disposal,

he shall repay to the Commissioners such amount as equals the amount of the credit, or the balance thereof, multiplied by a fraction of which the numerator is the amount so received or attributed, and the denominator is the amount of the outstanding consideration.

28(2) Where the claimant–

(a) fails to comply with the requirements of regulation 26; or

(b) in relation to the documents mentioned in that regulation, fails to comply with either–

  (i) regulation 16; or

  (ii) any obligation arising under paragraph 3 of Schedule 5 to the Act, he shall repay to the Commissioners the amount of the claim to which the failure to comply relates.

WRITING OFF DEBTS

29(1) This regulation shall apply for the purpose of determining whether, and to what extent, the consideration is to be taken to have been written off as a bad debt.

29(2) The whole or any part of the consideration for a taxable activity shall be taken to have been written off as a bad debt where–

(a)   the claimant has written it off in his accounts as a bad debt; and

(b)   he has made an entry in relation to that activity in the landfill tax bad debt account in accordance with regulation 26 (and this shall apply regardless of whether a claim can be made in relation to that activity at that time).

29(3) Where the claimant owes an amount of money to the customer which can be set off, the consideration written off in the landfill tax bad debt account shall be reduced by the amount so owed.

29(4) Where the claimant holds in relation to the customer an enforceable security, the consideration written off in the landfill tax bad debt account shall be reduced by the value of the security.

PART VII – CREDIT: BODIES CONCERNED WITH THE ENVIRONMENT

Official publications – LFT1, para. 10 (1997 edn).

INTERPRETATION AND GENERAL PROVISIONS

30(1) In this Part–

"**approved body**" means a body approved for the time being under regulation 34;

"**approved object**" has the meaning given in regulation 33;

"**contributing third party**" means a person who has made or agreed to make (whether or not under a legally binding agreement) a payment to a registered person to secure the making by him of a qualifying contribution or to reimburse him, in whole or in part, for any such contribution he has made;

"**income**" includes interest;

"**qualifying contribution**" has the meaning given in regulation 32;

"**the regulatory body**" means such body, if any, as in relation to which an approval of the Commissioners under regulation 35 has effect for the time being;

"**running costs**" includes any cost incurred in connection with the management and administration of a body or its assets.

30(2) A body shall only be taken to **spend a qualifying contribution** in the course or furtherance of its approved objects–

(a)   in a case where the contribution is made subject to a condition that it may only be invested for the purpose of generating income, where the body so spends all of that income;

(b)   in a case not falling within sub-paragraph (a) above, where the body becomes entitled to income, where it so spends both the whole of the qualifying contribution and all of that income;

(c)   in a case not falling within either of sub-paragraphs (a) and (b) above, where the body so spends the whole of the qualifying contribution; or

(d)   where–

       (i)   it transfers any qualifying contribution or income derived therefrom to another approved body, and

       (ii)   that transfer is subject to a condition that the sum transferred shall be spent only in the course or furtherance of that other body's approved objects.

30(3) Any approval, or revocation of such approval, by the Commissioners or the regulatory body shall be given by notice in writing to the body affected and shall take effect from the date the notice is given or such later date as the Commissioners or, as the case may be, the regulatory body may specify in it.

History – In reg. 30(1), the definition of "contributing third party" was inserted by SI 2000/3270, reg. 3, operative from 1 January 2000.

ENTITLEMENT TO CREDIT

31(1) Subject to the following provisions of this regulation, an entitlement to credit arises under this Part in respect of qualifying contributions made by registered persons.

31(2) Subject to paragraph (3) below, a person shall be entitled to credit in respect of 90 per cent of the amount of each qualifying contribution made by him in any accounting period; and for this purpose a qualifying contribution made–

(a)   in one accounting period;

(b)   before the return for the previous accounting period has been made; and

(c)   before the period within which that return is required to be made has expired,

shall be treated as having been made in the accounting period mentioned in sub-paragraph (b) above (and not in the accounting period in which it was in fact made).

31(3) In respect of the qualifying contributions made in each contribution year, a person shall not be entitled to credit of an amount greater than 20 per cent of his relevant tax liability.

31(4) For the purpose of paragraphs (2) and (3) above the **contribution year** of a person is his first contribution year and each period of 12 months ending on the anniversary of the end of his first contribution year; but this is subject to paragraphs (6) to (6E) below.

31(5) The reference in paragraph (4) above to the first **contribution year** of a person is a reference to–

(a)   the period of 12 months beginning with his effective date of registration; or

(b)   where that period of 12 months does not end on the last day of an accounting period, the period beginning with his effective date of registration and ending on the last day of the accounting period in which the 12 month period ends

but this is subject to paragraphs (6) to (6E) below.

31(6) Where–

(a)   the Commissioners vary the length of a person's accounting period under regulation 11(3);

(b)   as a consequence of the variation the end of any contribution year of his other than the first contribution year would not coincide with the end of an accounting period,

the contribution year thus affected shall end on the same day as the end of the accounting period in which that contribution year would apart from this regulation end; and each of the person's subsequent contribution years shall end on the anniversary of the end of that contribution year (subject to any subsequent application of this paragraph).

31(6A) Subject to paragraphs (6C) to (6E) below, a registered person may make an election that his first contribution year or any subsequent contribution year of his should be varied by ending instead on the last day of an accounting period of his which he specifies in the notice mentioned in paragraph (6C) below (and that contribution year shall so end).

31(6B) Where a contribution year has been varied by virtue of an election made under paragraph (6A) above all of the person's subsequent contribution years shall instead consist of successive periods of 12 months ending on the anniversary of the contribution year as so varied.

31(6C) An election shall not be treated as having been made under paragraph (6A) above unless and until notice of it has been given in writing to the Commissioners (and shall accordingly be treated as having been made on the day such notice is given).

31(6D) A notice under paragraph (6C) above shall specify an accounting period which does not end either before the date on which the election is made or more than 12 months after that date.

31(6E) Where a registered person has made an election under paragraph (6A) above he shall not make another election unless at least 24 months have elapsed since his previous election was made.

31(7) Subject to paragraph (8) below, the reference in paragraph (3) above to the **relevant tax liability** of a person is a reference to the aggregate of–

(a)   the tax payable by him, if any, in respect of the accounting period in relation to which that liability falls to be determined; and

(b)   the tax payable by him, if any, in respect of any earlier accounting period or periods which fall within the same contribution year as that accounting period;

and where in respect of any accounting period he is entitled to a payment under regulation 20 the aggregate of the tax payable by him in respect of the accounting periods mentioned in sub-paragraphs (a) and (b) above shall be reduced by the amount of that payment.

31(8)   Omitted by SI 1999/3270, reg. 4(f).

31(9)   Omitted by SI 1999/3270, reg. 4(f).

31(10)   For the purposes of paragraph (7) above any entitlement to credit arising under this Part shall be disregarded in determining the tax payable by a person in respect of any period.

History – Reg. 31(2)(a) was substituted by SI 2000/3270, reg. 4(a), operative from 1 January 2000. Former reg. 31(2)(a) reads as follows:
"(a)   in the first accounting period following the end of a contribution year;".
In reg. 31(4), the words "paragraphs (6) to (6E)" were substituted for the words "paragraph (6)" by SI 2000/3270, reg. 4(b), operative from 1 January 2000.
In reg. 31(5), the words "but this is subject to paragraphs (6) to (6E) below" were inserted by SI 2000/3270, reg. 4(c), operative from 1 January 2000.
Reg. 31(6A)–(6E) were inserted by SI 2000/3270, reg. 4(d), operative from 1 January 2000.
In reg. 31(7), the words "paragraph (10)" were substituted for the words "paragraphs (8) and (10)" by SI 2000/3270, reg. 4(e), operative from 1 January 2000.
Reg. 31(8) and (9) were omitted by SI 2000/3270, reg. 4(f), operative from 1 January 2000. Former reg. 31(8) and (9) read as follows:
"**(8)**   Where paragraph (5)(b) above applies so that the first contribution year of a person exceeds 12 months his **relevant tax liability** for that contribution year shall be taken to be such amount as is found by multiplying the tax payable by him in respect of that accounting period by a fraction the numerator of which is 12 and the denominator of which is the number of months comprised in the period.
(9)   For the purpose of determining the number of months comprised in an accounting period as described in paragraph (8) above–
(a)   if the period does not begin on the first day of a month, it shall be taken to begin on the nearest first day of a month;
(b)   if the period does not end on the last day of a month, it shall be taken to end on the nearest last day of a month;
(c)   if the period begins or ends on the sixteenth day of a month comprising thirty-one days, it shall be taken to begin on the first day of the following month or, as the case may be, end on the last day of the preceding month;
(d)   if the period begins or ends on the fifteenth day of February when it contains twenty- nine days, it shall be taken to begin on the first day of March or, as the case may be, end on the last day of January.".
In reg. 31(10), the words "paragraph (7)" were substituted for the words "paragraphs (7) and (8)" by SI 2000/3270, reg. 4(g), operative from 1 January 2000.

QUALIFYING CONTRIBUTIONS

32(1)   A payment is a **qualifying contribution** if–

(a)   it is made by a registered person to an approved body;

(b)   it is made subject to a condition that the body shall spend the sum paid or any income derived from it or both only in the course or furtherance of its approved objects;

(c)   the requirements of paragraphs (2) to (2B) below have been complied with in relation to that payment; and

(d)   it is not repaid to him, or a contributing third party, in the same accounting period as that in which it was made.

32(2)   A person claiming credit arising under this Part shall make a record containing the following information–

(a)   the amount and date of each payment he has made to an approved body;

(b)   the name and enrolment number of that body;

(c)   the name and address of any contributing third party; and

(d)   the amount of the payment made or to be made by the contributing third party and the date, or as the case may require, dates on which payment of the whole or any part of that amount–

    (i)   was received, or

    (ii) is expected to be received.

32(2A)   A person claiming credit under this Part for a contribution in relation to which there is a contributing third party shall have provided to the regulatory body or, if they are performing the functions specified in regulation 34(1) below, to the Commissioners the following information–

(a)   the name and address of the contributing third party;

(b)   the amount of the payment made or to be made by the contributing third party and the date, or as the case may require, dates on which payment of the whole or any part of that amount–

    (i)   was received, or

    (ii) is expected to be received;

(c)   the enrolment number of the approved body to whom the contribution was made.

32(2B) A person claiming credit under this Part for a contribution in relation to which there is a contributing third party shall have informed the approved body to which the contribution is made of the name and address of the contributing third party.

32(3) For the purposes of this Part where any qualifying contribution or income derived therefrom is transferred to a body as described in regulation 30(2)(d)–

(a) the body to whom the sum is transferred shall be treated as having received qualifying contributions of the amount concerned; and

(b) that body shall be treated as having received those qualifying contributions from the registered person or persons who originally paid them (but this shall not give rise to any further entitlement to credit in respect of those contributions).

History – In reg. 32(1)(c), the words "paragraphs (2) to (2B)" were substituted for the words "paragraph (2)" by SI 2000/3270, reg. 5(a), operative from 1 January 2000.
In reg. 32(1)(d), the words ", or a contributing third party," were inserted by SI 2000/3270, reg. 5(b), operative from 1 January 2000.
Reg. 32(2)(c) and (d) were inserted by SI 2000/3270, reg. 5(c), operative from 1 January 2000.
Reg. 32(2A) and (2B) were inserted by SI 2000/3270, reg. 5(d), operative from 1 January 2000.
Reg. 32(3) was substituted by SI 2000/3270, reg. 5(e), operative from 1 January 2000. Former reg. 32(3) reads as follows:
"**32(3)** Where any qualifying contribution or income derived therefrom is transferred to a body as described in regulation 30(2)(d)–
(a) the body to whom the sum is transferred shall be treated for the purposes of this Part as having received qualifying contributions of that amount; and
(b) that body shall be treated accordingly as having received qualifying contributions from the person or persons from whom the body making the transfer in fact received them (but this shall not give rise to any further entitlement to credit in respect of those contributions)."

BODIES ELIGIBLE FOR APPROVAL

33(1) A body is eligible to be approved if–

(a) it is–

    (i) a body corporate, or

    (ii) a trust, partnership or other unincorporated body;

(b) its objects are or include any of the objects within paragraph (2) below (approved objects);

(c) it is precluded from distributing and does not distribute any profit it makes or other income it receives;

(d) it applies any profit or other income to the furtherance of its objects (whether or not approved objects);

(e) it is precluded from applying any of its funds for the benefit of any of the persons–

    (i) who have made qualifying contributions to it, or

    (ii) who were a contributing third party in relation to such contributions,

except that such persons may benefit where they belong to a class of persons that benefits generally;

(f) it is not controlled by one or more of the persons and bodies listed in paragraphs (1A) and (1B) below;

(g) none of the persons or bodies listed in paragraph (1B) below is concerned in its management; and

(h) it pays to the regulatory body an application fee of £100 or such lesser sum as the regulatory body may require.

33(1A) The persons and bodies mentioned in paragraph (1)(f) above are:

(a) a local authority;

(b) a body corporate controlled by one or more local authorities;

(c) a registered person;

(d) a person connected with any of the persons or bodies mentioned in sub-paragraphs (a) to (c) above.

33(1B) The persons and bodies mentioned in paragraph 1(f) and (g) above are:

(a) a person who controlled or was concerned in the management of a body the approval of which was revoked otherwise than under regulation 34(1)(ee);

(b) a person who has been convicted of an indictable offence;

(c) a person who is disqualified for being a charity trustee or a trustee for a charity by virtue of section 72 of the Charities Act 1993;

(d)   a person connected with any of the persons or bodies mentioned in sub-paragraphs (a) to (c) above;

(e)   a person who is incapable by reason of mental disorder.

33(1C)   For the purpose of paragraph (1B)(e) above, a person shall be treated as **incapable by reason of mental disorder** where–

(a)   in England and Wales, the judge has exercised any of his functions under Part VII of the Mental Health Act 1983;

(b)   in Scotland, the court has appointed a curator bonis, tutor or judicial factor; or

(c)   in Northern Ireland, the court has exercised any of its powers under Part VIII of the Mental Health (Northern Ireland) Order 1986 (whether or not by virtue of Article 97(2) of that Order),

but shall cease to be so treated where the judge or court concerned has made a finding that he is not or is no longer incapable of managing and administering his property and affairs.

33(2)   The objects of a body are approved objects in so far as they are any of the following objects–

(a)   in relation to any land the use of which for any economic, social or environmental purpose has been prevented or restricted because of the carrying on of an activity on the land which has ceased–

      (i)   reclamation, remediation or restoration; or

      (ii)   any other operation intended to facilitate economic, social or environmental use;

but this is subject to paragraph (3) below;

(b)   in relation to any land the condition of which, by reason of the carrying on of an activity on the land which has ceased, is such that pollution (whether of that land or not) is being or may be caused–

      (i)   any operation intended to prevent or reduce any potential for pollution; or

      (ii)   any operation intended to remedy or mitigate the effects of any pollution that has been caused,

but this is subject to paragraph (3) below;

(c)   for the purpose of encouraging the use of more sustainable waste management practices–

      (i)   research and development;

      (ii)   education; or

      (iii)   collection and dissemination of information about waste management practices generally;

(cc)   for the purpose of encouraging the development of products from waste or the development of markets for recycled waste–

      (i)   research and development,

      (ii)   education, or

      (iii)   collection and dissemination of information about the development of products from waste or the development of markets for recycled waste;

(d)   where it is for the protection of the environment, the provision, maintenance or improvement of–

      (i)   a public park; or

      (ii)   another public amenity,

in the vicinity of a landfill site, provided the conditions in paragraph (6) below are satisfied;

(e)   where it is for the protection of the environment, the maintenance, repair or restoration of a building or other structure which–

      (i)   is a place of religious worship or of historic or architectural interest,

      (ii)   is open to the public, and

      (iii)   is situated in the vicinity of a landfill site,

provided the conditions in paragraph (6) below are satisfied;

(f)   the provision of financial, administration and other similar services to bodies which are within this regulation and only such bodies.

33(3)   An object shall not be, or shall no longer be, regarded as falling within paragraph (2)(a) or (b) above if the reclamation, remediation, restoration or other operation–

(a)   is such that any benefit from it will accrue to any person who has carried out or knowingly permitted the activity which has ceased;

(b)   involves works which are required to be carried out by a notice or order within paragraph (4) below; or

(c)   is wholly or partly required to be carried out by a relevant condition.

33(4)   The notices and order mentioned in paragraph (3) above are–

(a)   a works notice served under section 46A of the Control of Pollution Act 1974;

(b)   an enforcement notice served under section 13 of the Environmental Protection Act 1990;

(c)   a prohibition notice served under section 14 of the Environmental Protection Act 1990;

(d)   an order under section 26 of the Environmental Protection Act 1990;

(e)   a remediation notice served under section 78E of the Environmental Protection Act 1990;

(f)   an enforcement notice served under section 90B of the Water Resources Act 1991;

(g)   a works notice served under section 161A of the Water Resources Act 1991;

33(5)   In paragraph (2)(c) above **"waste management practices"** includes waste minimisation, minimisation of pollution and harm from waste, reuse of waste, recycling of waste, waste recovery activities and the clearing of pollutants from contaminated land.

33(6)   The conditions mentioned in sub-paragraphs (d) and (e) of paragraph (2) above are–

(a)   in a case falling within sub-paragraph (d), that the provision of the park or amenity is not required by a relevant condition; and

(b)   in a case falling within either of those sub-paragraphs, that the park, amenity, building or structure (as the case may be) is not to be operated with a view to profit.

33(7)   Where the objects of a body are or include any of the objects set out in paragraph (2) above, the following shall also be regarded as objects within that paragraph–

(a)   the use of qualifying contributions in paying the running costs of the body, but this is subject to paragraph (8) below;

(b)   the use of qualifying contributions in paying a contribution to the running costs of the regulatory body.

33(8)   The use of qualifying contributions in paying the running costs of the body shall only be regarded as an approved object if the body determines so to use no more than such proportion of the total of qualifying contributions, together with any income derived from them, (or, in the case of a contribution within regulation 30(2)(a), only that income) as the proportion of that total forms of the total funds at its disposal and does not in fact use a greater amount.

33(9)   For the purposes of paragraph (1) above a body or person (in either case, for the purposes of this paragraph, **"the person"**) shall be taken to **control** a body where–

(a)   in the case of a body which is a body corporate, the person is empowered by statute to control that body's activities or if he is that body's holding company within the meaning of section 736 of the Companies Act 1985, and an individual shall be taken to control a body corporate if he, were he a company, would be that body's holding company within the meaning of that Act;

(b)   in the case of a body which is a trust or a partnership, where–

      (i)   the person, taken together with any nominee of his, or

      (ii) any nominee of the person, taken together with any nominee of that nominee or any other nominee of the person,

   forms a majority of the total number of trustees or partners, as the case may be;

(c)   in the case of any other body, where the person, whether directly or through any nominee, has the power–

      (i)   to appoint or remove any officer of the body;

      (ii) to determine the objects of the body;

      (iii) to determine how any of the body's funds may be applied.

33(10)   For the purposes of paragraphs (3) and (6) above a condition is **relevant** if it is–

(a)   a condition of any planning permission or other statutory consent or approval granted on the application of any person making a qualifying contribution to the body, or

(b)   a term of an agreement made under–

> (i)   section 106 of the Town and Country Planning Act 1990,

> (ii) section 75 of the Town and Country Planning (Scotland) Act 1997, or

> (iii) article 40 of the Planning (Northern Ireland) Order 1991, to which such a person is a party.

History – In reg. 33(1), at the beginning, the words "A body is eligible to be approved if–" were substituted for the words "A body is within this regulation if–" by SI 2000/3270, reg. 6(a), operative from 1 January 2000.
Reg. 33(1)(e) was substituted by SI 2000/3270, reg. 6(b), operative from 1 January 2000. Former reg. 33(1)(e) reads as follows:
"(e)   it is precluded from applying any of its funds for the benefit of any of the persons who have made qualifying contributions to it, except that such persons may benefit where they belong to a class of persons that benefits generally;".
The word "and" after reg. 33(1)(e) was omitted by SI 2000/3270, reg. 6(c), operative from 1 January 2000.
Reg. 33(1)(f)–(h) were substituted for former reg. 33(1)(f) by SI 2000/3270, reg. 6(d), operative from 1 January 2000. Former reg. 33(1)(f) reads as follows:
"(f)   it is not controlled by one or more–
              (i)   local authorities,
bodies corporate controlled by one or more local authorities, or
registered persons."
Reg. 33(1A) was inserted by SI 2000/3270, reg. 6(e), operative from 1 January 2000.
Reg. 33(1B) was inserted by SI 2000/3270, reg. 6(e), operative from 1 January 2000.
Reg. 33(1C) was inserted by SI 2000/3270, reg. 6(e), operative from 1 January 2000.
Reg. 33(2)(cc) was inserted by SI 2000/3270, reg. 6(f), operative from 1 January 2000.
In reg. 33(5), the words "recycling of waste," were inserted by SI 2000/3270, reg. 6(g), operative from 1 January 2000.
In reg. 33(7)(b), at the beginning, the words "where the regulatory body has made the approval of the body subject to a condition to that effect," were omitted by SI 2000/3270, reg. 6(h), operative from 1 January 2000.
In reg. 33(9), the words "a body or person (in either case, for the purposes of this paragraph, **"the person"**)" were substituted for the words "a local authority, body corporate or registered person (in each case, **"the person"**)" by SI 2000/3270, reg. 6(i), operative from 1 January 2000.
Reg. 33(10)(b) was substituted by SI 2000/3270, reg. 6(j), operative from 1 January 2000. Former reg. 33(10)(b) reads as follows:
"(b)   a term of an agreement made under section 106 of the Town and Country Planning Act 1990 to which such a person is a party."

OBLIGATIONS OF APPROVED BODIES

33A(1)   An approved body shall–

(a)   continue to meet all the requirements of regulation 33 above;

(b)   apply qualifying contributions and any income derived therefrom only to approved objects;

(c)   not apply any of its funds for the benefit of any of the persons who have made qualifying contributions to it or who were contributing third parties in relation to such contributions (except to the extent that they benefit by virtue of belonging to a class of persons that benefits generally);

(d)   make and retain records of the following-

> (i)   the name, address and registration number of each registered person making a qualifying contribution to the body;

> (ii) the name and address of any contributing third party in relation to a qualifying contribution received by the body;

> (iii) the amount and date of receipt of each qualifying contribution and the amount and date of receipt of any income derived therefrom;

> (iv) in the case of a transfer of the whole or part of any qualifying contribution or income derived therefrom to or from the body, the date of the transfer, the amount transferred, the name and enrolment number of the body from or, as the case may require, to which it was transferred, the name, address and registration number of the person who made the qualifying contribution and the name and address of any contributing third party in relation to the qualifying contribution;

> (v)   in respect of each qualifying contribution and any income derived therefrom, including any such amount transferred to the body by another approved body, the date of and all other details relating to its expenditure;

(e)   provide the following information to the regulatory body or, if they are performing the functions specified in regulation 34(1) below, to the Commissioners within 7 days of the receipt by it of any qualifying contribution–

> (i)   the amount of the contribution;

> (ii) the date it was received;

     (iii) the name and registration number of the person making the contribution;

     (iv) the name and address of any contributing third party in relation to the contribution notified to it by virtue of regulation 32(2B) above;

(f)   notify the regulatory body within seven days of any transfer to or by it of qualifying contributions or of income derived therefrom of–

     (i) the date of the transfer;

     (ii) the enrolment number of the approved body by or, as the case may require, to which the transfer was made;

     (iii) the amount transferred;

     (iv) the name and registration number of the person who made the qualifying contribution;

     (v) the name and address of any contributing third party in relation to the contribution; and

     (vi) the approved objects to which the transferred funds are to be applied;

(g)   provide the regulatory body or, if they are performing the functions specified in regulation 34(1) below, the Commissioners with information from or access to the records referred to in sub-paragraph (f) above within 14 days (or such longer period as the regulatory body or, as the case may require, the Commissioners may allow) of a request being made for such information or access;

(h)   submit to the regulatory body or, if they are performing the functions specified in regulation 34(1) below, to the Commissioners within 14 days of the end of the relevant period determined in accordance with paragraph (2) below details of–

     (i) qualifying contributions and any other income or profit whatsoever received by it,

     (ii) any expenditure made by it during the period, and

     (iii) any balances held by it at the end of the period;

(i)   submit to the regulatory body within 9 months of the end of its financial year independently audited financial accounts for that year; and

(j)   pay to the regulatory body an amount equal to 5 per cent of each qualifying contribution it receives, or such lesser amount as the regulatory body may require, towards its running costs within 14 days of receipt of a demand for payment.

33A(2) For the purposes of paragraph (1)(h) above, the **relevant period** in respect of an approved body is–

(a)   in the case of the first such period–

     (i) the period of 6 months, or

     (ii) where the aggregate of the qualifying contributions and income therefrom received by the body in the period referred to in sub-paragraph (i) above is no greater than £100,000, the period of 12 months,

commencing with the date on which the body was approved; and

(b)   in the case of subsequent periods–

     (i) the period of 6 months, or

     (ii) where the aggregate of the qualifying contributions and income therefrom received by the body during the period referred to in sub-paragraph (i) above and the period of 6 months preceding that does not exceed £100,000, the period of 12 months,

commencing with the day after the end of the first or, as the case may require, a subsequent period.

History – Reg. 33A was inserted by SI 2000/3270, reg. 7, operative from 1 January 2000.

FUNCTIONS OF THE REGULATORY BODY

34(1) The regulatory body–

(a)   shall, on application being made to it by a body which is eligible to be approved under regulation 33 above, approve that body;

(b)   Omitted by SI 1999/3270, reg. 8(b).

(c)   Omitted by SI 1999/3270, reg. 8(b).

(d)   Omitted by SI 1999/3270, reg. 8(b).

(e)   may revoke the approval of any body which fails to comply with any requirement of regulation 33A(1);

(ee)   shall revoke the approval of any body which applies for its approval to be revoked;

(f)   shall maintain a roll of bodies which it has approved;

(g)   shall allocate an identifying number (the enrolment number) to each such body;

(h)   shall remove from the roll any body whose approval it has revoked;

(i)   shall satisfy itself, by reference to such records or other documents or information it thinks fit, that the qualifying contributions received by the body have been spent by it only in the course or furtherance of its approved objects;

(j)   shall publish information regarding which bodies it has approved and which approvals it has revoked; and

(k)   shall, when notified by an approved body of the transfer to or by it of the whole or part of a qualifying contribution or of income derived therefrom, notify the registered person who made the qualifying contribution, and any contributing third party in relation to it, of–

    (i)   the date of the transfer,

    (ii)   the name and enrolment number of the body by or, as the case may require, to whom the transfer was made;

    (iii)   the amount transferred; and

    (iv)   the approved objects to which the transferred funds are to be applied.

34(2)   Where–

(a)   the Commissioners revoke their approval of the regulatory body without approving another body with effect from the day after the revocation takes effect; and

(b)   they have not given notice in writing to each body which has been enrolled (and which has not been removed from the roll), no later than the date such revocation takes effect, that they will be performing any of the functions specified in paragraph (1) above,

the approval of all such bodies shall be deemed to have been revoked on the day the Commissioners revoked their approval.

History – Reg. 34(1)(a) was substituted by SI 2000/3270, reg. 8(a), operative from 1 January 2000. Former reg. 33(10)(b) reads as follows:
"(a)   may approve a body which is within regulation 33;"
Reg. 34(1)(b), (c) and (d) were omitted by SI 2000/3270, reg. 8(b), operative from 1 January 2000. Former reg. 34(1)(b), (c) and (d) read as follows:
"(b)   may require any person applying for approval to pay an application fee;
(c)   without prejudice to the generality of sub-paragraph (d) below, may require approved bodies to pay a contribution to the running costs of the regulatory body and such contribution may be required to be paid periodically;
(d)   may, either at the time of granting the approval or subsequently, make the approval subject to such conditions as it thinks fit, including conditions relating to the records and accounts the body shall keep;"
Reg. 34(1)(e) and (ee) were substituted for former reg. 34(1)(e) by SI 2000/3270, reg. 8(c), operative from 1 January 2000. Former reg. 34(1)(e) reads as follows:
"(e)   may revoke the approval;".
In reg. 34(1)(i), the word "and" at the end was omitted by SI 2000/3270, reg. 8(d), operative from 1 January 2000.
Reg. 34(1)(k) was inserted by SI 2000/3270, reg. 8(e), operative from 1 January 2000.
In reg. 34(2)(b), the words "will be" were substituted for the words "will not be" by SI 2000/3270, reg. 8(f), operative from 1 January 2000.

FUNCTIONS OF THE COMMISSIONERS

35(1)   The Commissioners–

(a)   may approve a body to carry out the functions prescribed by regulation 34(1) above;

(b)   Omitted by SI 1999/3270, reg. 9(b).

(c)   may revoke the approval;

(d)   shall not approve a body without first revoking the approval for any other body with effect from a time earlier than that for which the new approval is to take effect;

(e)   for any time as regards which no approval has effect, may perform any of the functions specified in regulation 34(1);

(f)   may disclose to the regulatory body information which relates to the tax affairs of registered persons and which is relevant to the credit scheme established by this Part; and

(g)   having regard to any information received from the regulatory body, may serve notices under regulation 36.

35(2)   Without prejudice to the generality of paragraph (1)(c) above, the Commissioners may revoke their approval of the regulatory body where it appears to them necessary to do so for the proper operation of the credit scheme established by this Part.

History – Reg. 35(1)(a) was substituted by SI 2000/3270, reg. 9(a), operative from 1 January 2000. Former reg. 35(1)(a) reads as follows:

"(a) may approve a body for the purposes of this Part;".

Reg. 35(1)(b) was omitted by SI 2000/3270, reg. 9(b), operative from 1 January 2000. Former reg. 35(1)(b) reads as follows:

"(b) may, either at the time of granting the approval or subsequently, make the approval subject to such conditions as they think fit;".

In reg. 35(1)(f) the word "regulatory" was inserted by SI 2000/3270, reg. 9(c), operative from 1 January 2000.

In reg. 35(1)(g) the word "regulatory" was inserted by SI 2000/3270, reg. 9(c), operative from 1 January 2000.

Reg. 35(2) was substituted by SI 2000/3270, reg. 9(d), operative from 1 January 2000. Former reg. 35(2) reads as follows:

"(2) Without prejudice to the generality of paragraph (1)(c) above, the Commissioners may revoke their approval of a body where it appears to them–

(a) that the body is in breach of any condition imposed under paragraph (1)(b) above; or

(b) that it is necessary to do so for the proper operation of the credit scheme established by this Part."

REPAYMENT OF CREDIT

36(1) Where a person has benefited from an amount of credit to which he was entitled under this Part and the Commissioners serve upon him a notice in relation to a qualifying contribution paid to an approved body–

(a) specifying that–

  (i) they are not satisfied that the contribution has been spent by the body only in the course or furtherance of its approved objects; or

  (ii) they are not satisfied that any income derived from the contribution has been so spent by the body;

(b) specifying a breach of a condition to which the approval of the body was made subject and which occurred before the contribution was spent by the body; or

(c) specifying that–

  (i) the approval of the body has been revoked; and

  (ii) the contribution had not been spent by the body before that revocation took effect,

he shall repay to the Commissioners the credit claimed in respect of the qualifying contribution.

36(2) For the purpose of paragraph (1) above where–

(a) repayment is required in relation to credit that has been claimed in respect of more than one qualifying contribution in an accounting period; and

(b) regulation 31(3) applied so that the amount of credit was restricted,

the person shall be deemed to have claimed credit in respect of such proportion of each contribution made in that accounting period as the total credit claimed in accordance with that regulation forms of the total of the contributions made.

36(3) Where–

(a) a person has benefited from an amount of credit to which he was entitled under this Part; and

(b) the whole or a part of the qualifying contribution in respect of which the entitlement to credit arose has been repaid to him or a person who was a contributing third party in relation to the qualifying contribution,

he shall pay to the Commissioners an amount equal to 90 per cent of the amount repaid to him or, as the case may require, to the contributing third party.

36(4) Paragraph (5) below applies where–

(a) a person has benefited from an amount of credit to which he was entitled under this Part; and

(b) he is entitled to a payment under regulation 20 in respect of a later accounting period in the same contribution year as the accounting period in respect of which that credit was claimed.

36(5) Where this paragraph applies the person shall pay to the Commissioners an amount equal to the difference between–

(a) the aggregate of–

  (i) the amount of the credit from which he has benefited, and

  (ii) any other amounts of credit arising under this Part which he is or was entitled to claim, in respect of that contribution year; and

(b) the amount of credit which he would have been entitled to claim if he had in fact claimed the aggregate amount mentioned in sub-paragraph (a) above in the return for the accounting period in respect of which he was entitled to the payment under regulation 20.

36(6) Where–

(a) a person has benefited from an amount of credit to which he was entitled under this Part;

(b) he acquires an asset from a body to which he has made a qualifying contribution for–

       (i) no consideration, or

       (ii) a consideration which is less than the open market value of the asset,

he shall pay to the Commissioners an amount equal to 90 per cent of the amount by which the open market value exceeds the consideration; but this is subject to paragraph (7) below.

36(7)   A person required to pay an amount to the Commissioners by paragraph (6) above–

(a)   shall not be required to pay more than the total amount of relevant credit;

(b)   shall not be entitled to claim any further amounts of credit in respect of qualifying contributions made by him to the body in question on or after the date on which he acquired the asset.

36(8)   For the purposes of paragraphs (6) and (7) above–

(a)   **"asset"** includes land, goods or services and any interest in any of these;

(b)   the **open market value** of an asset is the amount of the consideration in money that would be payable for the asset by a person standing in no such relationship with any person as would affect that consideration;

(c)   **"relevant credit"** means credit arising under this Part–

       (i) from which a person has benefited, and

       (ii) which has arisen in respect of qualifying contributions made by him to the body in question or treated by virtue of regulation 32(3) as having been received by that body from him.

History – Reg. 36(3) was substituted by SI 2000/3270, reg. 10, operative from 1 January 2000. Former reg. 36(3) reads as follows:
"**36(3)** Where–
(a)   a person has benefited from an amount of credit to which he was entitled under this Part; and
(b)   the whole or a part of the qualifying contribution in respect of which the entitlement to credit arose has been repaid to him,
he shall pay to the Commissioners an amount equal to 90 per cent of the amount repaid to him."

PART VIII – LANDFILL INVOICES
CONTENTS OF A LANDFILL INVOICE

37(1)   An invoice is a **landfill invoice** if it contains the following information:

(a)   an identifying number;

(b)   the date of its issue;

(c)   the date of the disposal or disposals in respect of which it is issued or, where a series of disposals is made for the same person, the dates between which the disposals were made;

(d)   the name, address and registration number of the person issuing it;

(e)   the name and address of the person to whom it is issued;

(f)   the weight of the material disposed of;

(g)   a description of the material disposed of;

(h)   the rate of tax chargeable in relation to the disposal or, if the invoice relates to more than one disposal and the rate of tax for each of them is not the same, the rate of tax chargeable for each disposal;

(i)   the total amount payable for which the invoice is issued; and

(j)   where the amount of tax is shown separately, a statement confirming that that tax may not be treated as the input tax of any person.

37(2)   In paragraph (1)(j) above **"input tax"** has the same meaning as in section 24(1) of the Value Added Tax Act 1994.

Official publications – LFT1, para. 5.4 (1997 edn).

PART IX – TEMPORARY DISPOSALS
SCOPE AND EFFECT

38(1)   A disposal to which this Part applies–

(a)   shall not be treated as made at the time when apart from this Part it would be regarded as made; and (b)　　shall be treated as having been made–

　　　　(i)　when it is treated as being an exempt disposal by virtue of regulation 39, or

　　　　(ii)　to the extent that it is not so treated, at the time when it is treated as having been made by virtue of regulation 40.

38(2)　This Part applies to a disposal where–

(a)　　an authorised person has designated an area (the **designated area**) for the purpose of this Part;

(b)　　material is disposed of in the designated area at a time when the designation has effect;

(c)　　the disposal is a temporary one pending all of the material being put to a qualifying use within the relevant period; and

(d)　　such other conditions as the Commissioners or an authorised person may specify for the purpose of this Part, whether generally or with regard to particular cases, are satisfied.

38(3)　A designation ceases to have effect if–

(a)　　notice to that effect is given in writing by the Commissioners or by an authorised person;

(b)　　any period for which the designation was to have effect by virtue of a condition specified in relation thereto expires;

(c)　　any disposal to which this Part does not apply (whether because it is not temporary or for some other reason) is made in the designated area; or

(d)　　a disposal is treated by virtue of regulation 40 as having been made at a certain time and all of the material comprised in that disposal is not removed from the designated area within seven days of that time.

38(4)　A use is a qualifying use if thereby the material is–

(a)　　recycled or incinerated;

(b)　　used (other than by way of a further disposal) at a place other than a relevant site; or

(c)　　sorted pending–

　　　　(i)　its use at a place other than a relevant site, or

　　　　(ii)　its disposal,

being a use or disposal, as the case may be, within the relevant period.

38(5)　For the purposes of paragraph (4) above–

(a)　　a use is not a **qualifying use** if it would constitute a breach of any condition relating to the use of the material to be disposed of which has been specified in relation to that designated area or generally;

(b)　　a **relevant site** is the landfill site at which the disposal was made or any other landfill site;

(c)　　the **relevant period** is the period of one year commencing with the date of the disposal or such other period as the Commissioners or an authorised person may approve or direct.

DISPOSALS TO BE TREATED AS EXEMPT

39(1)　Where there is a disposal to which this Part applies and–

(a)　　the material comprised in the disposal has been put to a qualifying use within the relevant period, if it would otherwise be a taxable disposal that disposal shall be treated as not being a taxable disposal (shall be treated as being an exempt disposal); but this is subject to paragraph (2) below;

(b)　　some of the material comprised in a disposal has been put to a qualifying use within the relevant period (and some has not), the disposal shall be treated as being an exempt disposal to the extent of the part so dealt with and the remaining part shall be treated in accordance with regulation 40.

39(2)　A disposal shall not be treated as being an **exempt disposal** unless the landfill site operator concerned has made and, in relation to that disposal, maintained the record specified in paragraph (3) below (the temporary disposal record).

39(3)　The **temporary disposal record** mentioned in paragraph (2) above is a record, in relation to the designated area, of–

(a)　　the weight and description of all material disposed of;

(b)　　the intended destination of all such material and, where any material has been removed, the actual destination of that material; and

(c)   the weight and description of any material removed.

DISPOSALS TO BE TREATED AS MADE AT CERTAIN TIMES

40(1)   Where in the case of a disposal to which this Part applies the disposal is not wholly treated as being an exempt disposal it shall, to the extent that it is not so treated, be treated as having been made at the earliest of the following times–

(a)   when the relevant period has expired;

(b)   when the designation ceases to have effect;

(c)   when there has been a breach of any condition specified by the Commissioners or an authorised person;

(d)   when there has been a failure to make the temporary disposal record;

(e)   when there has been a failure to maintain the temporary disposal record;

(f)   when any of the material concerned is used (other than by way of a further disposal) at the same or another landfill site (but not in the same designated area).

40(2)   The reference in paragraph (1)(e) above to a **"failure to maintain the temporary disposal record"** is a reference to an omission to enter in a record that has been made the information specified in regulation 39(3) in relation to any disposal made after the record was made.

PART X – DETERMINATION OF WEIGHT OF MATERIAL DISPOSED OF

SCOPE

41   This Part applies for the purpose of determining the weight of material comprised in a disposal; and references in this Part to weight shall be construed as references to the weight of such material.

BASIC METHOD

42(1)   Except where regulation 43 or 44 applies and subject to paragraph (2) below, a registrable person shall determine weight by weighing the material concerned.

42(2)   The weighing of the material shall be carried out at the time of the disposal; and for this purpose any time at which section 61 of the Act or Part IX of these Regulations require the disposal to be treated as made shall be disregarded.

SPECIFIED METHODS

43(1)   Except where regulation 44 applies, this regulation applies where the Commissioners have specified rules for determining weight in a notice published by them and not withdrawn by a further notice.

43(2)   A specification made by the Commissioners as described in paragraph (1) above may make provision for–

(a)   the method by which weight is to be determined;

(b)   the time by reference to which weight is to be determined.

43(3)   A specification made by the Commissioners as described in paragraph (1) above may provide–

(a)   that it is to have effect only in relation to disposals of such descriptions as may be set out in the specification;

(b)   that it is not to have effect in relation to particular disposals unless the Commissioners are satisfied that such conditions as may be set out in the specification are met in relation to the disposals.

43(4)   Where this regulation applies the registrable person shall determine weight in accordance with the rules in the specification (and not in accordance with the rule in regulation 42).

AGREED METHODS

44(1)   This regulation applies where–

(a)   the registrable person and an authorised person have agreed in writing that weight shall be determined in accordance with rules other than those described in regulation 42 or specified under regulation 43; and

(b)   a direction under paragraph (3) below has not been made.

44(2)   rules may be agreed under this regulation as regards–

(a)   the method by which weight is to be determined;

(b)   the time by reference to which weight is to be determined;

(c)   the discounting of water forming a constituent of material disposed of, but this is subject to paragraph (5) below.

44(3)   Where rules have been agreed under this regulation and the Commissioners believe that they should no longer be applied because they do not give an accurate indication of the weight or they are not being fully observed or for some other reason they may direct that the agreed rules shall no longer have effect.

44(4)   Where this regulation applies the registrable person shall determine weight in accordance with the rules agreed (and not in accordance with the rule in regulation 42 or 43).

44(5)   Subject to paragraphs (6) to (8) below, rules may be agreed regarding the discounting of water if, and only if–

(a)   no water is present in the material naturally and the water is present because–

> (i)   it has been added for the purpose of enabling the material to be transported for disposal;

> (ii)   it has been used for the purpose of extracting any mineral; or

> (iii)   it has arisen, or has been added, in the course of an industrial process; or

(b)   the material is the residue from the treatment of effluent or sewage by a water treatment works.

44(6)   Rules may not be agreed under paragraph (5) above where any of the material is capable of escaping from the landfill site concerned by leaching unless–

(a)   it is likely to do so in the form of water only; or

(b)   the leachate is to be collected on the site concerned and treated in order to eliminate any potential it has to cause harm.

44(7)   Where the material falls within paragraph (5)(a) above rules may not be agreed under paragraph (5) above unless the total water which has been added, or (in a case falling within paragraph (5)(a)(iii) above) has arisen or has been added or both, constitutes 25 per cent or more of the weight at the time of the disposal.

44(8)   Where the material falls within paragraph (5)(b) above rules may not be agreed under paragraph (5) above except for the discounting of water which has been added prior to disposal (and not of water which is present in the material naturally).

44(9)   For the purposes of paragraph (8) above any water which has been extracted prior to disposal shall be deemed to be water that has been added, except that where the water extracted exceeds the quantity of water added that excess shall be deemed to have been present naturally.

PART XI – SET-OFF OF AMOUNTS

LANDFILL TAX AMOUNT OWED TO COMMISSIONERS

45(1)   Subject to regulation 47, this regulation applies where–

(a)   a person is under a duty to pay to the Commissioners at any time an amount or amounts in respect of landfill tax; and

(b)   the Commissioners are under a duty to pay to that person at the same time an amount or amounts in respect of any tax or taxes under their care and management.

45(2)   Where the total of the amount or amounts mentioned in paragraph (1)(a) above exceeds the total of the amount or amounts mentioned in paragraph (1)(b) above, the latter shall be set off against the former.

45(3)   Where the total of the amount or amounts mentioned in paragraph (1)(b) above exceeds the total of the amount or amounts mentioned in paragraph (1)(a) above, the Commissioners may set off the latter in paying the former.

45(4)   Where the total of the amount or amounts mentioned in paragraph (1)(a) above is the same as the total of the amount or amounts mentioned in paragraph (1)(b) above, no payment need be made in respect of either.

45(5) Where this regulation applies and an amount has been set off in accordance with any of paragraphs (2) to (4) above, the duty of both the person and the Commissioners to pay the amount or amounts concerned shall be treated as having been discharged accordingly.

45(6) References in paragraph (1) above to an amount in respect of a particular tax include references not only to an amount of tax itself but also to amounts of penalty, surcharge or interest.

45(7) In this regulation **"tax"** includes **"duty"**.

LANDFILL TAX AMOUNT OWED BY COMMISSIONERS

46(1) Subject to regulation 47, this regulation applies where–

(a) a person is under a duty to pay to the Commissioners at any time an amount or amounts in respect of any tax or taxes under their care and management; and

(b) the Commissioners are under a duty to pay to that person at the same time an amount or amounts in respect of landfill tax.

46(2) Where the total of the amount or amounts mentioned in paragraph (1)(a) above exceeds the total of the amount or amounts mentioned in paragraph (1)(b) above, the latter shall be set off against the former.

46(3) Where the total of the amount or amounts mentioned in paragraph (1)(b) above exceeds the total of the amount or amounts mentioned in paragraph (1)(a) above, the Commissioners may set off the latter in paying the former.

46(4) Where the total of the amount or amounts mentioned in paragraph (1)(a) above is the same as the total of the amount or amounts mentioned in paragraph (1)(b) above, no payment need be made in respect of either.

46(5) Where this regulation applies and an amount has been set off in accordance with any of paragraphs (2) to (4) above, the duty of both the person and the Commissioners to pay the amount or amounts concerned shall be treated as having been discharged accordingly.

46(6) Paragraphs (6) and (7) of regulation 45 shall apply in relation to this regulation as they apply in relation to that regulation.

NO SET-OFF WHERE INSOLVENCY PROCEDURE APPLIED

47(1) Neither regulation 45 nor 46 shall require any such amount as is mentioned in paragraph (1)(b) of those regulations (in either case, **"the credit"**) to be set against any such sum as is mentioned in paragraph (1)(a) of those regulations (in either case, **"the debit"**) in any case where–

(a) an insolvency procedure has been applied to the person entitled to the credit;

(b) the credit became due after that procedure was so applied;

(c) the liability to pay the debit either arose before that procedure was so applied or (having risen afterwards) relates to, or to matters occurring in the course of–

    (i) the carrying on of any business; or

    (ii) in the case of any sum such as is mentioned in regulation 46(1)(b), the carrying out of taxable activities,

at times before the procedure was so applied.

47(2) Subject to paragraph (3) below, the following are the times when an **insolvency procedure** is to be taken, for the purposes of this regulation, to have been applied to any person, that is to say–

(a) when a bankruptcy order, winding-up order, administration order or award of sequestration is made in relation to that person;

(b) when that person is put into administrative receivership;

(c) when that person, being a corporation, passes a resolution for voluntary winding-up;

(d) when any voluntary arrangement approved in accordance with Part I or Part VIII of the Insolvency Act 1986, or Part II or Chapter II of Part VIII of the Insolvency (Northern Ireland) Order 1989, comes into force in relation to that person;

(e) when a deed of arrangement registered in accordance with the Deeds of Arrangement Act 1914 or Chapter I of Part VIII of that Order of 1989 takes effect in relation to that person;

(f) when that person's estate becomes vested in any other person as that person's trustee under a trust deed.

47(3) References in this regulation, in relation to any person, to the **application of an insolvency procedure** to that person shall not include–

(a) the making of a bankruptcy order, winding-up order, administration order or award of sequestration at a time when any such arrangements or deed as is mentioned in paragraph (2)(d) to (f) above is in force in relation to that person;

(b) the making of a winding-up order at any of the following times–

    (i) immediately upon the discharge of an administration order made in relation to that person;

    (ii) when that person is being wound-up voluntarily;

    (iii) when that person is in administrative receivership; or

(c) the making of an administration order in relation to that person at any time when that person is in administrative receivership.

47(4) For the purposes of this regulation a person shall be regarded as being in **administrative receivership** throughout any continuous period for which (disregarding any temporary vacancy in the office of receiver) there is an administrative receiver of that person, and the reference in paragraph (2) above to a person being **put into administrative receivership** shall be construed accordingly.

PART XII – DISTRESS AND DILIGENCE

DISTRESS

A48 In this Part–

"**Job Band**" followed by a number between "1" and "12" means the band for the purposes of pay and grading in which the job an officer performs is ranked in the system applicable to Customs and Excise.

History – Reg. A48 was inserted by SI 1996/2100, reg. 3, operative from 2 September 1996.

48 Repealed by SI 1997/1431, reg. 3(1) and Sch. 3, operative from 1 July 1997.

History – Former reg. 48 reads as follows:
"**48(1)** Subject to paragraph (2) below, if upon written demand a person neglects or refuses to pay any tax due from him or any amount recoverable as if it were tax due from him, a Collector or an officer of rank not below that of Job Band 7 may distrain on the goods and chattels of that person and by warrant signed by him direct any authorised person to levy such distress.
48(2) Where–
(a) the amount in relation to which a warrant has been issued under paragraph (1) above is not an amount assessed under section 50(1) of the Act upon failure to make a return; and
(b) the Commissioners may be required under section 54 of the Act to review a decision which, if that decision were varied or withdrawn, would cause the amount in relation to which the warrant has been issued to be reduced or extinguished,
no distress shall be levied before the last day on which the person who is liable to pay the amount concerned is required, by rules made under paragraph 9 of Schedule 12 to the Value Added Tax Act 1994, to serve a notice of appeal with respect to that decision.
48(3) A levy shall be executed by or under the direction of, and in the presence of, the authorised person.
48(4) A person in respect of whose goods and chattels a warrant has been signed shall be liable for all costs and charges in connection with anything done under this regulation.
48(5) If the person aforesaid does not pay the amount due together with the costs and charges within five days of a levy, the distress shall be sold by the authorised person for payment of the amount due and all costs and charges; and costs and charges of taking, keeping and selling the distress shall be retained by the authorised person and any surplus remaining after the deduction of the costs and charges and of the amount due shall be restored to the owner of the goods distrained."
In former reg. 48(1), the words "Job Band 7" were substituted by SI 1996/2100, reg. 4, operative from 2 September 1996.

DILIGENCE

49 In Scotland the following provisions shall have effect:

(a) where the Commissioners are empowered to apply to the sheriff for a warrant to authorise a sheriff officer to recover any amount of tax or sum recoverable as if it were tax remaining due and unpaid, any application, and any certificate required to accompany that application, may be made on their behalf by a Collector or an officer of rank not below that of Job Band 7;

(b) where during the course of a poinding and sale in accordance with Schedule 5 to the Debtors (Scotland) Act 1987 the Commissioners are entitled as a creditor to do any act, then any such act, with the exception of the exercise of the power contained in paragraph 18(3) of that Schedule, may be done on their behalf by a Collector or an officer of rank not below that of Job Band 7.

History – In reg. 49(a) and (b), the words "Job Band 7" were substituted by SI 1996/2100, reg. 4, operative from 2 September 1996.

SCHEDULES

Form 1: LT1
Form 2: LT1A
Form 3: LT2
Form 4: LT68
Form 5: LT100
[Forms not reproduced.]
Official publications – LFT1, Appendix D (1997 edn): landfill tax return and completion notes.

THE LANDFILL TAX (QUALIFYING MATERIAL) ORDER 1996

(SI 1996/1528)

Made on 12 June 1996 by the Treasury under s. 42 and 63 of the Finance Act 1996. Operative from 1 October 1996.

Whereas section 42(2) of the Finance Act 1996 provides for a lower rate of landfill tax to be charged where the material disposed of consists entirely of qualifying material:

Whereas section 42(3) of that Act provides that qualifying material is material for the time being listed in an Order made by the Treasury:

Whereas section 42(4) of that Act requires the Treasury to have regard to the object of securing that material is listed in that Order if it is of a kind commonly described as inactive or inert:

Whereas the Treasury have had regard to that object:

Now the Treasury, in exercise of the powers conferred on them by sections 42(3) and 63(5) and (6) of the Finance Act 1996 and of all other powers enabling them in that behalf, hereby make the following Order:

1 This Order may be cited as the Landfill Tax (Qualifying Material) Order 1996 and shall come into force on 1st October 1996.

2 Subject to articles 3 to 5 below, the material listed in column 2 of the Schedule to this Order is **qualifying material** for the purpose of section 42 of the Act.
Official publications – LFT1, para. 2.2 and Appendix A (1997 edn).

3 The Schedule to this Order shall be construed in accordance with the notes contained in it.

4 The material listed in column 2 of the Schedule to this Order must not be treated as qualifying material unless any condition set out alongside the description of the material in column 3 of that Schedule is satisfied.

5 Where the owner of the material immediately prior to the disposal and the operator of the landfill site at which the disposal is made are not the same person, material must not be treated as qualifying material unless it satisfies the relevant condition.

6 In the case of a disposal at a landfill site in Great Britain, the **relevant condition** is that a transfer note includes in relation to each type of material of which the disposal consists–

(a)   a description of the material–

    (i)   which accords with its description in column 2 of the Schedule to this Order, or

    (ii) where a note contained in that Schedule lists the material (other than by way of exclusion), which accords with that description, or

    (iii) which is some other accurate description; or

(b)   where the material is water within Group 9 of the Schedule to this Order–

    (i)   the description "water", and

    (ii) a description of the material held in suspension which, if that material had been disposed of separately, would comply with the requirements of paragraph (a) above.

7 In the case of a disposal at a landfill site in Northern Ireland, the **relevant condition** is that any document produced to evidence the transfer of the material includes, in relation to each type of material of which the disposal consists, a description of that material as specified in paragraph (a) or, as the case may be, paragraph (b) of article 6 above.

8 In article 6 above **"transfer note"** has the same meaning as in the Environmental Protection (Duty of Care) Regulations 1991.

Column 1	Column 2	Column 3
Group	*Description of material*	*Conditions*
Group 1	Rocks and soils	Naturally occurring
Group 2	Ceramic or concrete materials	
Group 3	Minerals	Processed or prepared, not used
Group 4	Furnace slags	
Group 5	Ash	
Group 6	Low activity inorganic compounds	
Group 7	Calcium sulphate	Disposed of either at site not licensed to take putrescible waste or in containment cell which takes only calcium sulphate
Group 8	Calcium hydroxide and brine	Deposited in brine cavity
Group 9	Water	Containing other qualifying material in suspension

Notes:

(1)   Group 1 includes clay, sand, gravel, sandstone, limestone, crushed stone, china clay, construction stone, stone from the demolition of buildings or structures, slate, topsoil, peat, silt and dredgings.

(2)   Group 2 comprises only the following–

   (a) glass;

   (b) ceramics;

   (c) concrete.

(3)   For the purposes of Note (2) above–

   (a) **glass** includes fritted enamel, but excludes glass fibre and glass-reinforced plastic;

   (b) **ceramics** includes bricks, bricks and mortar, tiles, clay ware, pottery, china and refractories;

   (c) **concrete** includes reinforced concrete, concrete blocks, breeze blocks and aircrete blocks, but excludes concrete plant washings.

(4)   Group 3 comprises only the following–

   (a) moulding sands;

   (b) clays;

   (c) mineral absorbents;

   (d) man-made mineral fibres;

   (e) silica;

   (f) mica;

   (g) mineral abrasives.

(5)   For the purposes of Note (4) above–

   (a) **moulding sands** excludes sands containing organic binders;

   (b) **clays** includes moulding clays and clay absorbents, including Fuller's earth and bentonite;

   (c) **man-made mineral fibres** includes glass fibres, but excludes glass-reinforced plastic and asbestos.

(6)   Group 4 includes–

   (a) vitrified wastes and residues from thermal processing of minerals where, in either case, the residue is both fused and insoluble;

   (b) slag from waste incineration.

(7)   Group 5–

      (a)   comprises only bottom ash and fly ash from wood, coal or waste combustion; and

      (b)   excludes fly ash from municipal, clinical and hazardous waste incinerators and sewage sludge incinerators.

(8)   Group 6 comprises only titanium dioxide, calcium carbonate, magnesium carbonate, magnesium oxide, magnesium hydroxide, iron oxide, ferric hydroxide, aluminium oxide, aluminium hydroxide and zirconium dioxide.

(9)   Group 7 includes gypsum and calcium sulphate based plasters, but excludes plasterboard.

DISTRESS FOR CUSTOMS AND EXCISE DUTIES AND OTHER INDIRECT TAXES REGULATIONS 1997

(SI 1997/1431)

Made on 9 June 1997 by the Commissioners of Customs and Excise, in exercise of the powers conferred on them by s. 51(1), (2) and (3) of the Finance Act 1997 and of all other powers enabling them in that behalf. Operative from 1 July 1997.

CITATION AND COMMENCEMENT

1   These Regulations may be cited as The Distress for Customs and Excise Duties and Other Indirect Taxes Regulations 1997 and shall come into force on 1st July 1997.

INTERPRETATION

2(1) In these Regulations–

    "authorised person" means a person acting under the authority of the Commissioners;

    "costs" means any costs, charges, expenses and fees;

    "officer" means, subject to section 8(2) of the Customs and Excise Management Act 1979, a person commissioned by the Commissioners pursuant to section 6(3) of that Act;

    "person in default" means a person who has refused or neglected to pay any relevant tax due from him;

    "relevant tax" means any of the following–

      (a)   [not relevant to landfill tax]

      (b)   [not relevant to landfill tax]

      (c)   [not relevant to landfill tax]

      (d)   landfill tax;

      (e)   [not relevant to landfill tax]

    "VAT Act" means the Value Added Tax Act 1994;

    "walking possession agreement" means an agreement under which, in consideration of any goods and chattels distrained upon being allowed to remain in the custody of the person in default and of the delaying of their sale, that person–

      (a)   acknowledges that the goods and chattels specified in the agreement are under distraint and held in walking possession; and

      (b)   undertakes that, except with the consent of the Commissioners and subject to such conditions as they may impose, he will not remove or allow the removal of any of the specified goods and chattels from the place named in the agreement;

    "1994 Act" means Part III of the Finance Act 1994;

    "1996 Act" means Part III of the Finance Act 1996.

2(2) Any reference in these Regulations to an amount of **relevant tax** includes a reference to any amount recoverable as if it were an amount of that relevant tax.

REVOCATIONS AND TRANSITIONAL PROVISIONS

3(1) The Regulations specified in Schedule 3 are hereby revoked to the extent set out there.

3(2) Where a warrant is signed before the coming into force of these Regulations, these Regulations shall apply to anything done, after these Regulations come into force, in relation to that warrant or as a consequence of distress being levied.

LEVYING DISTRESS

4(1) Subject to regulation 5 below, if upon written demand a person neglects or refuses to pay any relevant tax due from him an officer may levy distress on the goods and chattels of that person and by warrant signed by him direct any authorised person to levy such distress.

4(2) Where a warrant has been signed, distress shall be levied by or under the direction of, and in the presence of, the authorised person.

4(3) Subject to regulation 6 below, distress may be levied on any goods and chattels located at any place whatever including on a public highway.

RESTRICTIONS ON LEVYING DISTRESS

5(1) Where–

(a-b) [not relevant to landfill tax.]

(c) an amount of landfill tax is due and the Commissioners may be required under section 54 of the 1996 Act to review a decision which, if that decision were varied or withdrawn, would cause the amount to be reduced or extinguished,

no distress shall be levied before expiry of the last day on which the person who is liable to pay the amount concerned is required, by rules made under paragraph 9 of Schedule 12 to the VAT Act, to serve a notice of appeal with respect to that decision.

5(2) [Not relevant to landfill tax.]

GOODS AND CHATTELS NOT SUBJECT TO LEVY

6 No distress shall be levied on any goods and chattels mentioned in Schedule 1 which at the time of levy are located in a place and used for a purpose mentioned in that Schedule.

TIMES FOR LEVYING DISTRESS

7(1) Subject to paragraph (2) below, a levy of distress shall commence only during the period between eight o'clock in the morning and eight o'clock at night on any day of the week but it may be continued thereafter outside that period until the levy is completed.

7(2) Where a person holds himself out as conducting any profession, trade or business during hours which are partly within and partly outside, or wholly outside the period mentioned in paragraph (1) above, a levy of distress may be commenced at any time during that period or during the hours of any day in which he holds himself out as conducting that profession, trade or business and it may be continued thereafter outside that period or those hours until the levy is completed.

COSTS

8(1) A person in respect of whose goods and chattels a warrant has been signed shall be liable to pay to an officer or authorised person all costs, in connection with anything done under these Regulations described in column 1 of Schedule 2, as determined in accordance with column 2 of that Schedule.

8(2) An authorised person may, after deducting and accounting for the amount of relevant tax to the Commissioners, retain costs from any amount received.

SALE

9 If any person upon whose goods and chattels distress has been levied does not pay the amount of relevant tax due together with costs within 5 days of a levy, an officer or authorised person may sell the distress for payment of the amount of relevant tax and costs; and the officer or authorised person, after deducting and retaining the amount of relevant tax and costs shall restore any surplus to the owner of the goods upon which distress was levied.

DISPUTES AS TO COSTS

10(1) In the case of any dispute as to costs, the amount of those costs shall be taxed by a district judge of the county court of the district where the distress was levied, and he may make such order as he thinks fit as to the costs of the taxation.

10(2) In the application of this regulation to Northern Ireland, in the case of any dispute as to costs, the amount of those costs shall be taxed in the same manner as costs in equity suits or proceedings in the county court in Northern Ireland.

SCHEDULES

SCHEDULE 1 – GOODS AND CHATTELS NOT SUBJECT TO LEVY

Regulation 6

1 Any of the following goods and chattels which are located in a dwelling house at which distress is being levied and are reasonably required for the domestic needs of any person residing in that dwelling house–

    (a) beds and bedding;

    (b) household linen;

    (c) chairs and settees;

    (d) tables;

    (e) food;

    (f) lights and light fittings;

    (g) heating appliances;

    (h) curtains;

    (i) floor coverings;

    (j) furniture, equipment and utensils used for cooking, storing or eating food;

    (k) refrigerators;

    (l) articles used for cleaning, mending, or pressing clothes;

    (m) articles used for cleaning the home;

    (n) furniture used for storing–

      (i) clothing, bedding or household linen;

      (ii) articles used for cleaning the home;

      (iii) utensils used for cooking or eating food;

    (o) articles used for safety in the home;

    (p) toys for the use of any child within the household;

    (q) medical aids and medical equipment.

2 Any of the following items which are located in premises used for the purposes of any profession, trade or business–

    (a) fire fighting equipment for use on the premises;

    (b) medical aids and medical equipment for use on the premises.

SCHEDULE 2 – SCALE OF COSTS

Regulation 8(1)

Matter (1)	Costs (2)
1 For attending to levy distress where payment is made of an amount of relevant tax due and distress is not levied:	£12.50
2 For levying distress–	
(a) where an amount of relevant tax demanded and due *does not exceed £100:*	£12.50
(b) where an amount of relevant tax demanded and due exceeds £100:	12½% on the first £100, 4% on the next £400, 2½% on the next £1,500, 1% on the next £8,000, ¼% on any additional sum.

Matter (1)	Costs (2)
3 For taking possession of distrained goods–	
(a) where a person remains in physical possession of goods at the place where distress was levied (the person to provide his own food and lodgings):	£4.50 per day.
(b) where possession is taken under a walking possession agreement:	£7.00
4 For appraising goods upon which distress has been levied:	Reasonable costs of appraisement.
5 For arranging removal and storage of goods upon which distress has been levied:	Reasonable costs of arrangement.
6 For removing and storing goods upon which distress has been levied:	Reasonable costs of removal and storage.
7 For advertising the sale of goods upon which distress has been levied:	Reasonable costs of advertising.
8 For selling the distress–	
(a) where a sale by auction is held at the auctioneer's premises:	15% of the sum realised.
(b) where a sale by auction is held elsewhere:	7½% of the sum realised and the auctioneer's reasonable costs.
(c) where a sale by other means is undertaken:	7½% of the sum realised and reasonable costs.

9   In addition to any amount specified in this scale in respect of the supply of goods or services on which value added tax is chargeable there may be added a sum equivalent to value added tax at the appropriate rate on that amount.

SCHEDULE 3 – REVOCATIONS

Regulation 3(1)

Statutory Instrument Number	Title of Regulation	Extent
SI 1994/1774	The Insurance Premium Tax Regulations 1994	regulation 42
SI 1995/2518	The Value Added Tax Regulations 1995	regulation 212
SI 1996/1527	The Landfill Tax Regulations 1996	regulation 48

AIR PASSENGER DUTY AND OTHER INDIRECT TAXES (INTEREST RATE) REGULATIONS 1998

(1998/1461, as amended by SI 2000/631)

Made on 15 June 1998 by the Treasury, in exercise of the powers conferred on them by s. 197 of the Finance Act 1996 and of all other powers enabling them in that behalf. Operative from 6 July 1998.

CITATION AND COMMENCEMENT

1   These Regulations may be cited as the Air Passenger Duty and Other Indirect Taxes (Interest Rate) Regulations 1998 and shall come into force on 6th July 1998 in relation to interest accruing on or after that date.

INTERPRETATION

2(1) In these Regulations unless the context otherwise requires:

"**established rate**" means–

(a)   on the coming into force of these Regulations, 6 per cent per annum; and

(b)   in relation to any day after the first reference day after the coming into force of these Regulations, the reference rate found on the immediately preceding reference day;

"**operative day**" means the sixth day of each month;

"**reference day**" means the twelfth working day before the next operative day;

"**section 197**" means section 197 of the Finance Act 1996;

"**the relevant enactments**" are those referred to in regulations 4(1) and 5(1) below;

"**working day**" means any day other than a non-business day within the meaning of section 92 of the Bills of Exchange Act 1882.

2(2) In these Regulations **the reference rate** found on a reference day is the percentage per annum found by averaging the base lending rates at close of business on that day of–

(a)   Bank of Scotland,

(b)   Barclays Bank plc.,

(c)   Lloyds Bank plc.,

(d)   HSBC Bank plc.,

(e)   National Westminster Bank plc., and

(f)   The Royal Bank of Scotland plc.

and, if the result is not a whole number, rounding the result to the nearest such number, with any result midway between two whole numbers rounded down.

History – In reg. 2(1)(a), the words "6 per cent" were substituted for the words "7 per cent" by SI 2000/631, reg. 3(a), operative from 1 April 2000.
In reg. 2(2)(d), the words "HSBC Bank plc." were substituted for the words "Midland Bank plc." by SI 2000/631, reg. 3(b), operative from 1 April 2000.

3 [Revokes SI 1997/1016.]

APPLICABLE RATE OF INTEREST PAYABLE TO THE COMMISSIONERS OF CUSTOMS AND EXCISE IN CONNECTION WITH EXCISE DUTIES, INSURANCE PREMIUM TAX, VAT, LANDFILL TAX, AND CUSTOMS DUTY

4(1) For the purposes of–

(a)   [neither relevant nor reproduced],

(b)   [neither relevant nor reproduced],

(c)   section 74 of the Value Added Tax Act 1994, and

(d)   [neither relevant nor reproduced],

(e)   [neither relevant nor reproduced], and

(f)   [neither relevant nor reproduced],

the rate applicable under section 197 shall, subject to paragraph (2) below, be 8.5 per cent per annum.

4(2) Where on any reference day after the coming into force of these Regulations, the reference rate found on that day differs from the established rate, the rate applicable under section 197 of the Finance Act 1996 for the purposes of the enactments referred to in paragraph (1) above shall, from the next operative day, be the percentage per annum determined in accordance with the formula specified in paragraph (3) below.

4(3) The formula specified in this paragraph is–

$$RR + 2.5,$$

where–

    RR is the reference rate referred to in paragraph (2) above.

History – Reg. 4 was substituted by SI 2000/631, reg. 4, operative from 1 April 2000. Former reg. 4 and its heading read as follows:

"APPLICABLE RATE OF INTEREST PAYABLE TO THE COMMISSIONERS OF CUSTOMS AND EXCISE IN CONNECTION WITH AIR PASSENGER DUTY, INSURANCE PREMIUM TAX, VAT RECOVERED OR RECOVERABLE BY ASSESSMENT AND LANDFILL TAX

"**4(1)** For the purposes of–

(a)   [neither relevant nor reproduced],
(b)   [neither relevant nor reproduced],
(c)   [neither relevant nor reproduced], and
(d)   paragraph 26 of Schedule 5 to the Finance Act 1996,
the rate applicable under section 197 shall, subject to paragraph (2) below, be 9.5 per cent per annum.

4(2)   Where on any reference day after the coming into force of these Regulations, the reference rate found on that day differs from the established rate, the rate applicable under section 197 of the Finance Act 1996 for the purposes of the enactments referred to in paragraph (1) above shall, from the next operative day, be the percentage per annum determined in accordance with the formula specified in paragraph (3) below.

4(3)   The formula specified in this paragraph is—

$$RR + 2.5,$$

where—

RR is the reference rate referred to in paragraph (2) above."

APPLICABLE RATE OF INTEREST PAYABLE BY THE COMMISSIONERS OF CUSTOMS AND EXCISE IN CONNECTION WITH AIR PASSENGER DUTY, INSURANCE PREMIUM TAX, VAT, LANDFILL TAX AND CUSTOMS DUTY

5(1)   For the purposes of—

(a)   [neither relevant nor reproduced],

(b)   [neither relevant nor reproduced],

(c)   section 78 of the Value Added Tax Act 1994,

(d)   [neither relevant nor reproduced],

(e)   [neither relevant nor reproduced],

(f)   [neither relevant nor reproduced],

the rate applicable under section 197 of the Finance Act 1996 shall be 5 per cent per annum.

5(2)   Where, on a reference day after the coming into force of these Regulations, the reference rate found on that date differs from the established rate, the rate applicable under section 197 for the purposes of the enactments referred to in paragraph (1) above shall, from the next operative day, be the percentage per annum determined in accordance with the formula specified in paragraph (3) below.

5(3)   The formula specified in this paragraph is—

$$RR - 1,$$

where—

RR is the reference rate referred to in paragraph (2) above.

History – Reg. 5 was substituted by SI 2000/631, reg. 5, operative from 1 April 2000. Former reg. 5 and its heading read as follows:

"APPLICABLE RATE OF INTEREST PAYABLE BY THE COMMISSIONERS OF CUSTOMS AND EXCISE IN CONNECTION WITH AIR PASSENGER DUTY, INSURANCE PREMIUM TAX, CASES OF OFFICIAL ERROR IN RELATION TO VAT AND LANDFILL TAX

"**5(1)**   For the purposes of—
(a)   [neither relevant nor reproduced],
(b)   [neither relevant nor reproduced],
(c)   [neither relevant nor reproduced], and
(d)   paragraph 29 of Schedule 5 to the Finance Act 1996,
the rate applicable under section 197 of the Finance Act 1996 shall be 6 per cent per annum.

5(2)   Where, on a reference day after the coming into force of these Regulations, the reference rate found on that date differs from the established rate, the rate applicable under section 197 for the purposes of the enactments referred to in paragraph (1) above shall, from the next operative day, be the percentage per annum determined in accordance with the formula specified in paragraph (3) below.

5(3)   The formula specified in this paragraph is—

$$RR - 1,$$

where—

RR is the reference rate referred to in paragraph (2) above."

EFFECT OF CHANGE IN APPLICABLE RATE

6   Where the rate applicable under section 197 for the purposes of any of the relevant enactments changes on an operative day by virtue of these Regulations, that change shall have effect for periods beginning on or after the operative day in relation to interest running from before that day as well as in relation to interest running from, or from after that day.

7   Where the rate applicable under section 197 for the purposes of any of the relevant enactments changes on an operative day by virtue of these Regulations, the rate in force immediately prior to any change shall continue to have effect for periods immediately prior to the change and so on in the case of any number of successive changes.

APPLICABLE RATE OF INTEREST PRIOR TO THE COMING INTO FORCE OF THESE REGULATIONS

8 The rate applicable under section 197 for interest running from before the date these regulations come into force in relation to periods prior to that date shall be that specified for the relevant enactments in the following Tables–

TABLE 1

[Neither relevant nor reproduced.]

TABLE 2

[Neither relevant nor reproduced.]

TABLE 3

[Neither relevant nor reproduced.]

TABLE 4

Paragraph 26 of Schedule 5 to the Finance Act 1996

Interest for any period	Rate %
from 1st April 1997 and before 6th July 1998	6.25

TABLE 5

[Neither relevant nor reproduced.]

TABLE 6

[Neither relevant nor reproduced.]

TABLE 7

[Neither relevant nor reproduced.]

TABLE 8

Paragraph 29 of Schedule 5 to the Finance Act 1996

Interest for any period	Rate %
from 1st April 1997 and before 6th July 1998	6

MINIMUM AMOUNT OF INTEREST PAYABLE IN CONNECTION WITH CUSTOMS DUTY

9 [neither relevant nor reproduced].

History – Reg. 9 was inserted by SI 2000/631, reg. 7, operative from 1 April 2000.

LANDFILL TAX EXTRA-STATUTORY MATERIAL

Table of Contents

LANDFILL TAX
EXTRA-STATUTORY
MATERIAL

Table of Contents

OFFICIAL PUBLICATIONS

Publication

AO2	The Adjudicator's Office: How to complain about Customs and Excise
LFT1	A general guide to landfill tax
LFT2	Contaminated land (due to be published shortly)
X-55	Landfill Tax (Customs & Excise book of guidance)
–	VAT and duties tribunals – Appeals and applications to the tribunals – Explanatory leaflet
48	Extra-statutory concessions
989	Visits by Customs and Excise officers
999	Catalogue of publications
1000	Complaints and putting things right: our code of practice
–	Taxpayers' charter
–	Information Note 1/97: Reclamation of contaminated land
–	Information Note 1/99: Restoring landfill sites and filling quarries

Note – The above publications are not reproduced.

Notice 48 – Extra-statutory concessions (1999)
[Landfill tax material only]

3. CONCESSIONS DESIGNED TO REMOVE INEQUITIES OR ANOMALIES IN ADMINISTRATION

3.35. Landfill tax: Used foundry sand

By way of concession, used foundry sand shall be treated as falling within Group 3 (Minerals) of the Landfill Tax (Qualifying Material) Order 1996. This means that used foundry sand, when disposed to landfill, shall attract the lower rate of landfill tax.

3.36. Landfill tax: Environmental Bodies Credit Scheme: contribution year for site operators on non-standard tax periods

By way of concession, site operators who have non-standard tax period dates that result in an accounting year of 364 days or less, will be allowed to adopt a second contribution year consisting of 4 tax periods.

3.37. Landfill tax: Temporary disposal of material in designated areas for storage or sorting pending use in site restoration

1 For the purposes of Part IX of the Landfill Tax Regulations 1996:

(a) the following may be treated as a qualifying use:
(i) storage of qualifying material for later use in restoration of the landfill site, and
(ii) sorting of material into qualifying material for storage for use, or for immediate use, in restoration of the landfill site and other material for disposal, and

(b) the relevant period as defined in regulation 38(5)(c) for the purposes of the application of regulation 38(2)(c) in respect of such use may be treated as being 3 years.

2 The concession applies only to disposals of material made on or after 1 October 1999.

3 Before applying this concession to any disposal, a site operator must apply to the Commissioners for an area to be designated under regulation 38 for, or in the case of an existing designated area for its designation to be amended to permit, the temporary disposal of material in the area pending all the material being put to the qualifying use set out in the concession.

4 Application of this concession is subject to compliance with all conditions imposed by or under Part IX of the above regulations applicable to, and to the operation of, the area designated for temporary disposals of material pending its being put to the qualifying use specified in the concession, including the record keeping requirement imposed by regulation 39.

3.38. Landfill tax: Allowing landfill tax credits arising from certain qualifying contributions to environmental bodies to be claimed early

From 6 September 1999, for the purposes of Parts IV and VII of the Landfill Tax Regulations 1996, a claim to credit in respect of a qualifying contribution made before the earlier of the date on which a return is made, or a return is due to be made, may be made on that return.

3.39. Excise — hydrocarbon oil duty: Duty-paid deliveries for bonded users/distributors

When the Commissioners are satisfied that duty-paid oil has been delivered to a person approved to receive duty-free oil of the same description under the provisions of the Hydrocarbon Oil Duties Act 1979, they may repay to the supplier the duty which they are satisfied has been paid, and not repaid, on the quantity of oil so delivered subject to the conditions which would apply if the oil had been delivered without payment of duty.

3.40. Excise — hydrocarbon oil duty: Duty-paid deliveries for refinery boilers

When the Commissioners are satisfied that unused, duty-paid, hydrocarbon oil has been delivered to any premises approved as a refiners for use as fuel for the production of energy they may repay to the supplier the duty which they are satisfied has been paid, and not repaid, on the quantity of oil delivered.

3.41. Excise - hydrocarbon oil duty: Relief of duty on recovered motor spirit vapour

From 15 April 1993 duty relief may be allowed on motor spirit vapour recovered, during duty-paid deliveries of motor spirit from bonded mineral oil installations to service stations, and returned to bonded installations for conversion to liquid motor spirit.

3.42.   Excise — tobacco products duty: Imported tobacco products

Imported tobacco products may be delivered on importation without payment of tobacco products duty for deposit in premises registered under the Tobacco Products Regulations 1979 provided that the products are treated thereafter in all respects as if they had been manufactured in the United Kingdom.

3.43.   Excise — spirits duty: The Alcoholic Liquor Duties Act 1979: application of sections 18 and 21 to the recovery of spirits by authorised duty-free spirits users

Persons authorised to receive duty-free spirits under section 8 or 10 of the Alcoholic Liquor Duties Act 1979 may recover spirits by distillation provided a licence to rectify is taken out under section 18(1) of that Act. The requirements of section 21 of the Act and Part II of the Spirits (Rectifying, Compounding and Drawback) Regulations 1988 will be waived.

3.44.   Excise — spirits duty: The Methylated Spirits Regulations 1987: application of regulations 14 and 15 to the production and distribution of trade specific denatured alcohol

The denatured ethanol grade of spirits described in the Methylated Spirits Regulations 1987 regulation 14(1)(c) will be interpreted as including grades of denatured ethanol other than the statutory formulation of regulation 15(1)(c) provided

- it is demonstrated than an alternative formulation for denatured ethanol is required, and
- that such a formulation is approved by the Commissioners following evaluation of the denaturant properties of the product.

3.45.   Excise — beer duty: The Beer Regulations 1993: Amendment to Part IX, Regulations 26-33, to make provision for repayment of duty on beer that is not of satisfactory quality in the case of beer that is not currently eligible for repayment of duty.

This concession provides for the brewing industry to assume the practical control of beer of unsatisfactory quality, subject to the following conditions being observed:

- there is a complete audit trail which confirms the beer has been destroyed and that it was duty paid
- the destruction of the beer is supervised by a responsible representative of the brewery, and
- the requirements of other regulatory authorities are observed.

3.46.   Excise — amusement machine licence duty (AMLD): Extension of AMLD Summer Season Licence to 7 November 1999

The AMLD summer season licence allows operators of amusement arcades (mainly seaside arcades and theme parks) to provide licensable amusement machines for play during the months of March to October (8 months) for the cost of a 6 month licence.

This concession, which came into effect in May 1999, extends the summer season licence by 7 days in 1999, allowing traders with seasonal licences to operate until Sunday 7 November. Similar extensions have been granted in previous years.

3.47.   Excise — warehoused goods: Requirement for revenue traders to register

The Warehousekeepers and Owners of Warehoused Goods Regulations 1999 (SI 1999/1278) require revenue traders who wish to deposit dutiable goods other than hydrocarbon oil ("relevant goods") in an excise warehouse, or purchase warehoused relevant goods, to be approved as registered owners.

As a concession, from 1 October 1999 the Commissioners will treat the definition of "relevant goods" in regulation 2 as if it were amended so as to exclude wine and made-wine so that wine and made-wine will be treated in the same way as hydrocarbon oil is treated for the purposes of the Regulations. (Wine and made-wine are defined in sections 1(4) and 1(5) respectively of the Alcohol Liquor Duties Act 1979, which Act, by section 4(2), is to be construed as one Act with the Customs and Excise Management Act 1979).

INDEX TO LANDFILL TAX

For a list of abbreviations used in this Index see p. xii.

For a list of abbreviations used in this Index see p. xii.

For a list of abbreviations used in this Index see p. xii.

For a list of abbreviations used in this Index see p. xii.

LANDFILL TAX
LIST OF DEFINITIONS
AND MEANINGS

For a list of abbreviations used in this list see p. xii.

CLIMATE CHANGE LEVY

Table of Contents

CLIMATE CHANGE LEVY

Table of Contents

CLIMATE CHANGE LEVY STATUTES

Table of Contents

Note: Only those extant parts of these Acts which relate to landfill tax are reproduced here.

CLIMATE CHANGE LEVY STATUTES

Table of Contents

PROVISIONAL COLLECTION OF TAXES ACT 1968

(1968 Chapter 2)

[*1st February 1968*]

ARRANGEMENT OF SECTIONS

1   Temporary statutory effect of House of Commons resolutions affecting income tax, purchase tax or customs or excise duties

1(1)   This section applies only to income tax, corporation tax, petroleum revenue tax, stamp duty reserve tax, value added tax, climate change levy, insurance premium tax, landfill tax, and duties of customs and excise.

1(1A)   [Repealed by FA 1993, s. 205(3), s. 213 and Sch. 23, Pt. VI.]

1(2)   Subject to that, and to the provisions of subsections (4) to (8) below, where the House of Commons passes a resolution which–

(a)   provides for the renewal for a further period of any tax in force or imposed during the previous financial year (whether at the same or a different rate, and whether with or without modifications) or for the variation or abolition of any existing tax, and

(b)   contains a declaration that it is expedient in the public interest that the resolution should have statutory effect under the provisions of this Act,

the resolution shall, for the period specified in the next following subsection, have statutory effect as if contained in an Act of Parliament and, where the resolution provides for the renewal of a tax, all enactments which were in force with reference to that tax as last imposed by Act of Parliament shall during that period have full force and effect with respect to the tax as renewed by the resolution.

In this section references to the renewal of a tax include references to its reimposition, and references to the abolition of a tax include references to its repeal.

1(3)   The said period is–

(a)   in the case of a resolution passed in November or December in any year, one expiring with 5th May in the next calendar year;

(aa)   in the case of a resolution passed in February or March in any year, one expiring with 5th August in the same calendar year; and

(b)   in the case of any other resolution, one expiring at the end of four months after the date on which it is expressed to take effect or, if no such date is expressed, after the date on which it is passed.

1(4)   A resolution shall cease to have statutory effect under this section unless within the next thirty days on which the House of Commons sits after the day on which the resolution is passed–

(a)   a Bill renewing, varying or, as the case may be, abolishing the tax is read a second time by the House, or

(b)   a Bill is amended by the House in Committee or on Report, or by any Standing Committee of the House so as to include provision for the renewal, variation or, as the case may be, abolition of the tax.

1(5)   A resolution shall also cease to have statutory effect under this section if–

(a)   the provisions giving effect to it are rejected during the passage of the Bill containing them through the House, or

(b)   an Act comes into operation renewing, varying or, as the case may be, abolishing the tax, or

(c)   Parliament is dissolved or prorogued.

1(6) Where, in the case of a resolution providing for the renewal or variation of a tax, the resolution ceases to have statutory effect by virtue of subsection (4) or (5) above, or the period specified in subsection (3) above terminates, before an Act comes into operation renewing or varying the tax, any money paid in pursuance of the resolution shall be repaid or made good, and any deduction made in pursuance of the resolution shall be deemed to be an unauthorised deduction.

1(7) Where any tax as renewed or varied by a resolution is modified by the Act renewing or varying the tax, any money paid in pursuance of the resolution which would not have been payable under the new conditions affecting the tax shall be repaid or made good, and any deduction made in pursuance of the resolution shall, so far as it would not have been authorised under the new conditions affecting the tax, be deemed to be an unauthorised deduction.

1(8) When during any session a resolution has had statutory effect under this section, statutory effect shall not be again given under this section in the same session to the same resolution or to a resolution having the same effect.

History – In s. 1(1), the words, "climate change levy" inserted by FA 2000, Sch. 7, para. 1.
In s. 1(1), the words "(including advance corporation tax)" which followed "corporation tax" omitted by FA 1998, s. 31 and Sch. 3, para. 1(2), s. 165 and Sch. 27, Pt. III(2), in relation to distributions made after 5 April 1999.
In s. 1(1), the words "insurance premium tax," inserted by FA 1994, s. 64 and Sch. 7, para. 33, in relation to resolutions passed after 3 May 1994.
In s. 1(1), the words "corporation tax (including advance corporation tax)" inserted by FA 1993, s. 205 in relation to resolutions passed after 27 July 1993.
In s. 1(1), the words "car tax" repealed by FA 1993, s. 205(2) and s. 213 and Sch. 23, Pt. VI in relation to resolutions passed after 27 July 1993.
S. 1(1) amended by FA 1968, s. 51(2) but provisions including reference to purchase tax repealed by FA 1972, Sch. 28.
In s. 1(1), the words "landfill tax," inserted by FA 1998, s. 148(1).
S. 1(1A) repealed by FA 1993, s. 205(3) and s. 213 and Sch. 23, Pt. VI in relation to resolutions passed after 27 July 1993. S. 1(1A) was inserted by FA 1985, s. 97.
In s. 1(3)(a), references to "November or December" and "5th May in the next calendar year" substituted and in s. 1(4), the word "thirty" substituted by FA 1993, s. 205(5) in relation to resolutions passed after 27 July 1993.
S. 1(3)(aa) inserted by F(No. 2)A 1997, s. 50(1) in relation to resolutions passed after 31 July 1997.
In s. 1(4)(b), the words "in Committee . . . of the House" inserted by FA 1968, s. 60.
Application extended to petroleum revenue tax, stamp duty reserve tax, value added tax and car tax by OTA 1975, s. 11; FA 1986, s. 86(3); FA 1972, s. 1(5) and FA 1972, s. 52(11) and Sch. 7, para. 2(4) respectively.
References to provisions of ICTA 1988 substituted by Sch. 29, para. 32 of that Act.
Cross references – FA 1994, s. 64 and Sch. 7, para. 34(1): amount of insurance premium tax repayable by virtue of s. 1(6), (7) is the difference between the amount chargeable at the rate specified in the resolution and the amount that would have been chargeable at the lower rate.
FA 1998, s. 148(2): amount of landfill tax repayable by virtue of s. 1(6), (7) is the difference between the amount paid on the taxable disposal at the rate specified in the resolution and the amount that would have been payable on a taxable disposal of the same weight of material at the lower rate.
FA 2000, Sch. 6 para. 141(1)(b): amount of climate change levy repayable by virtue of s. 1(6), (7).

2   Payments and deductions made on account, and before renewal, of any temporary tax within s. 1

2(1) Any payment or deduction made on account of a temporary tax to which section 1 above applies and within one month after the date of its expiry shall, if the payment or deduction would have been a legal payment or deduction if the tax had not expired, be deemed to be a legal payment or deduction, subject to the condition that–

(a)   if a resolution for the renewal or reimposition of the tax is not passed by the House of Commons within that month, or such a resolution is passed within that month but ceases to have statutory effect under the said section 1, any money so paid or deducted shall be repaid or made good, and

(b)   if the tax is ultimately renewed or reimposed at a different rate, or with modifications, any amount paid or deducted which could not properly have been paid or deducted under the new conditions affecting the tax shall be repaid or made good.

2(2) In this section **"temporary tax"** means a tax which has been imposed, or renewed or reimposed, for a limited period not exceeding eighteen months, and was in force or imposed during the previous financial year.

5   House of Commons resolution giving provisional effect to motions affecting taxation

5(1) This section shall apply if the House of Commons resolves that provisional statutory effect shall be given to one or more motions to be moved by the Chancellor of the Exchequer, or some other Minister, and which, if agreed to by the House, would be resolutions–

(a)   to which statutory effect could be given under section 1 of this Act, or

(b)   to which section 3 of this Act could be applied,

(c)   [Repealed by FA 1993, s. 205(6)(a), s. 213 and Sch. 23, Pt. VI.]

5(2)   Subject to subsection (3) below, on the passing of the resolution under subsection (1) above, sections 1 to 3 of this Act and section 822 of the Income and Corporation Taxes Act 1988 (over-deductions from preference dividends before passing of annual Act) shall apply as if each motion to which the resolution applies had then been agreed to by a resolution of the House.

5(3)   Subsection (2) above shall cease to apply to a motion if that motion, or a motion containing the same proposals with modifications, is not agreed to by a resolution of the House (in this section referred to as "a confirmatory resolution") within the next ten days on which the House sits after the resolution under subsection (1) above is passed, and, if it ceases to apply, all such adjustments, whether by way of discharge or repayment of tax, or discharge of security, or otherwise, shall be made as may be necessary to restore the position to what it would have been if subsection (2) above had never applied to that motion, and to make good any deductions which have become unauthorised deductions.

5(4)   The enactments specified in subsection (2) above shall have effect as if–

(a)   any confirmatory resolution passed within the said period of ten sitting days had been passed when the resolution under subsection (1) above was passed, and

(b)   everything done in pursuance of the said subsection (2) by reference to the motion to which the confirmatory resolution relates had been done by reference to the confirmatory resolution,

but any necessary adjustments shall be made, whether by way of discharge or repayment of tax, or modification of the terms of any security, or further assessment, or otherwise, where the proposals in the confirmatory resolution are not the same as those in the original motion to which that resolution relates.

History – S. 5(1)(c) and word "or" immediately preceding it and in s. 5(2), reference to ICTA 1988, s. 822 substituted by FA 1993, s. 205(6), s. 213 and Sch. 23, Pt. VI, in relation to resolutions passed after 27 July 1993.
References to provisions of ICTA 1988 substituted by Sch. 29, para. 32 of that Act.

Cross references – S.3: provisional collection of duties of customs and excise under resolutions not having statutory effect under s.1.
FA 1973, s. 50: corresponding provisions for stamp duty.
FA 1994, s. 64 and Sch. 7, para. 34(1): amount of insurance premium tax repayable by virtue of s. 5(3) is the difference between the amount specified in the resolution and the amount that would have been chargeable at the lower rate.
FA 1998, s. 148(2): amount of landfill tax repayable by virtue of s. 5(3) is the difference between the amount paid on the taxable disposal at the rate specified in the resolution and the amount that would have been payable on a taxable disposal of the same weight of material at the lower rate.
FA 2000, Sch. 6 para. 141(1)(b): amount of climate change levy repayable by virtue of s. 5(3) is the difference between the levy paid on the supply at the rate specified in the resolution and the levy that would have been payable on a supply of the same quantity of the commodity at the lower rate.

6   Short title, repeals and saving as respects Northern Ireland

6(1)   This Act may be cited as the Provisional Collection of Taxes Act 1968.

6(2)   [Amending provision, not reproduced here.]

6(3)   [Repealed by Northern Ireland Constitution Act 1973, s. 41(1)(a) and Sch. 6, Pt. I, with effect from 18 July 1973.]

FINANCE ACT 2000

(2000 Chapter 17)

[28th July 2000]

ARRANGEMENT OF SECTIONS

PART II – CLIMATE CHANGE LEVY

PART II – CLIMATE CHANGE LEVY

30 Climate change levy

30(1)   Schedule 6 to this Act (which makes provision for a new tax that is to be known as climate change levy) shall have effect.

30(2)   Schedule 7 to this Act (climate change levy: consequential amendments) shall have effect.

30(3)   Part V of Schedule 6 to this Act (registration for the purposes of climate change levy) shall not come into force until such date as the Treasury may appoint by order made by statutory instrument; and different days may be appointed under this subsection for different purposes.

SCHEDULES

SCHEDULE 6 – CLIMATE CHANGE LEVY

Section 30

Part I – The Levy

CLIMATE CHANGE LEVY

1(1)   A tax to be known as climate change levy ("the levy") shall be charged in accordance with this Schedule.

1(2)   The levy is under the care and management of the Commissioners of Customs and Excise.

LEVY CHARGED ON TAXABLE SUPPLIES

2(1) The levy is charged on taxable supplies.

2(2) Any supply of a taxable commodity is a taxable supply, subject to the provisions of Part II of this Schedule.

MEANING OF "TAXABLE COMMODITY"

3(1) The following are taxable commodities for the purposes of this Schedule, subject to sub-paragraph (2) and to any regulations under sub-paragraph (3)–

(a) electricity;

(b) any gas in a gaseous state that is of a kind supplied by a gas utility;

(c) any petroleum gas, or other gaseous hydrocarbon, in a liquid state;

(d) coal and lignite;

(e) coke, and semi-coke, of coal or lignite;

(f) petroleum coke.

3(2) The following are not taxable commodities–

(a) hydrocarbon oil or road fuel gas within the meaning of the Hydrocarbon Oil Duties Act 1979;

(b) waste within the meaning of Part II of the Environmental Protection Act 1990 or the meaning given by Article 2(2) of the Waste and Contaminated Land (Northern Ireland) Order 1997.

3(3) The Treasury may by regulations provide that a commodity of a description specified in the regulations is, or is not, a taxable commodity for the purposes of this Schedule.

Part II – Taxable Supplies

INTRODUCTION

4(1) A supply of a taxable commodity (or part of such a supply) is a taxable supply for the purposes of the levy if levy is chargeable on the supply under–

paragraph 5 (supplies of electricity),

paragraph 6 (supplies of gas), or

paragraph 7 (other supplies in course or furtherance of business),

and the supply (or part) is not excluded under paragraphs 8 to 10 or exempt under paragraphs 11 to 21.

4(2) In this Schedule–

(a) references to a supply of a taxable commodity include a supply that is deemed to be made under paragraph 23, and

(b) references to a taxable supply include a supply that is deemed to be made under paragraph 24

but paragraphs 23 and 24 have effect subject to any exceptions provided for under paragraph 21.

SUPPLIES OF ELECTRICITY

5(1) Levy is chargeable on a supply of electricity if–

(a) the supply is made by an electricity utility, and

(b) the person to whom the supply is made–
  (i) is not an electricity utility, or
  (ii) is the utility itself.

5(2) Levy is chargeable on a supply made from a combined heat and power station of electricity produced in the station if–

(a) the station is a partly exempt combined heat and power station,

(b) the supply is not one that is deemed to be made under paragraph 23(3) (self-supply by producer), and

(c) the person to whom the supply is made is not an electricity utility.

5(3) Levy is chargeable on a supply of electricity that is deemed to be made under paragraph 23(3).

5(4) Except as provided by sub-paragraphs (1) to (3), levy is not chargeable on a supply of electricity.

SUPPLIES OF GAS

6(1) Levy is chargeable on a supply of any gas if—

(a)   the supply is made by a gas utility, and

(b)   the person to whom the supply is made–
  (i) is not a gas utility, or
  (ii) is the utility itself.

6(2) Levy is chargeable on a supply of gas that is deemed to be made under paragraph 23(3) (self-supply by producer) if the gas—

(a)   is held in a gaseous state immediately prior to being released for burning, and

(b)   is of a kind supplied by a gas utility.

6(3) Except as provided by sub-paragraphs (1) to (3), levy is not chargeable on a supply of any gas that is supplied in a gaseous state.

OTHER SUPPLIES MADE IN COURSE OR FURTHERANCE OF BUSINESS

7(1) This paragraph applies to a supply of a taxable commodity other than–

(a)   electricity, or

(b)   gas in a gaseous state.

7(2) Levy is chargeable on any such supply if the supply is made in the course or furtherance of a business.

EXCLUDED SUPPLIES: SUPPLY FOR DOMESTIC OR CHARITY USE

8(1) A supply is excluded from the levy if it is–

(a)   for domestic use (see paragraph 9), or

(b)   for charity use.

8(2) For the purposes of this paragraph, a supply is for charity use if the commodity supplied is for use by a charity otherwise than in the course or furtherance of a business.

8(3) If a supply is partly for domestic or charity use and partly not, the part of the supply that is for domestic or charity use is excluded from the levy.

8(4) Where a supply of a commodity is partly for domestic or charity use and partly not–

(a)   if at least 60 per cent. of the commodity is supplied for domestic or charity use, the whole supply is treated as a supply for domestic or charity use, and

(b)   in any other case, an apportionment shall be made to determine the extent to which the supply is for domestic or charity use.

EXCLUDED SUPPLIES: MEANING OF "FOR DOMESTIC USE"

9(1) For the purposes of paragraph 8 the following supplies are always for domestic use–

(a)   a supply of not more than one tonne of coal or coke held out for sale as domestic fuel;

(b)   a supply to a person at any premises of–
  (i) any gas in a gaseous state that is provided through pipes and is of a kind supplied by a gas utility, or
  (ii) petroleum gas in a gaseous state provided through pipes,
where the gas or petroleum gas (together with any other gas or petroleum gas provided through pipes to him at the premises by the same supplier) was not provided at a rate exceeding 4397 kilowatt hours a month;

(c)   a supply of petroleum gas in a liquid state where the petroleum gas is supplied in cylinders the net weight of each of which is less than 50 kilogrammes and either the number of cylinders supplied is 20 or fewer or the petroleum gas is not intended for sale by the *recipient;*

(d)   a supply of petroleum gas in a liquid state, otherwise than in cylinders, to a person at any premises at which he is not able to store more than two tonnes of such petroleum gas;

(e)   a metered supply of electricity to a person at any premises where the electricity (together with any other electricity provided to him at the premises by the same supplier) was not provided at a rate exceeding 1000 kilowatt hours a month;

(f)   an unmetered supply of electricity to a person where the electricity (together with any other unmetered electricity provided to him by the same supplier) was not provided at a rate exceeding 1000 kilowatt hours a month.

9(2) For the purposes of paragraph 8, supplies not within sub-paragraph (1) are for domestic use if and only if the commodity supplied is for use in–

(a)   a building, or part of a building, which consists of a dwelling or number of dwellings,

(b)   a building, or part of a building, used for a relevant residential purpose,

(c)   self-catering holiday accommodation (including any accommodation advertised or held out as such),

(d)   a caravan,

(e)   a houseboat (that is to say, a boat or other floating decked structure designed or adapted for use solely as a place of permanent habitation and not having means of, or capable of being readily adapted for, self-propulsion), or

(f)   an appliance that–

    (i)   is not part of a combined heat and power station,

    (ii)   is located otherwise than in premises of a description mentioned in any of paragraphs (a) to (e), and

    (iii) is used to heat air or water that, when heated, is supplied to premises of, or each of, such a description.

9(3) For the purposes of this paragraph use for a relevant residential purpose means use as–

(a)   a home or other institution providing residential accommodation for children,

(b)   a home or other institution providing residential accommodation with personal care for persons in need of personal care by reason of old age, disablement, past or present dependence on alcohol or drugs or past or present mental disorder,

(c)   a hospice,

(d)   residential accommodation for students or school pupils,

(e)   residential accommodation for members of any of the armed forces,

(f)   a monastery, nunnery or similar establishment, or

(g)   an institution which is the sole or main residence of at least 90 per cent. of its residents,

except use as a hospital, a prison or similar institution or an hotel or inn or similar establishment.

9(4) The power to make provision by order under section 2(1C) of the Value Added Tax Act 1994 varying, or varying any provision contained in, Schedule A1 to that Act (supplies for domestic use and non-business use by a charity that attract reduced VAT rate) includes power to make provision for any appropriate corresponding variation of, or of any provision contained in, this paragraph.

EXCLUDED SUPPLIES: SUPPLY BEFORE 1ST APRIL 2001

10 Any supply made before 1st April 2001 is excluded from the levy.

EXEMPTION: SUPPLY NOT FOR BURNING IN THE UK

11(1) A supply of a taxable commodity to which this sub-paragraph applies is exempt from the levy if the person to whom the supply is made has, before the supply is made, notified the supplier–

(a)   that he intends to use the commodity in making supplies of it to any other person, or

(b)   that he intends to cause the commodity to be exported from the United Kingdom and has no intention to cause it to be thereafter brought back into the United Kingdom.

11(2) Sub-paragraph (1) applies to supplies of a taxable commodity other than–

(a)   electricity, or

(b)   any gas in a gaseous state.

11(3) A supply of electricity, or of gas in a gaseous state, is exempt from the levy if the person to whom the supply is made has, before the supply is made, notified the supplier that–

(a)   he intends to cause the commodity to be exported from the United Kingdom, and

(b)   has no intention to cause it to be thereafter brought back into the United Kingdom.

11(4) Regulations under paragraph 22 may, in particular, include provision as to the application of sub-paragraph (3) in cases where a person who is both an exporter and an importer of a commodity intends to be a net exporter of the commodity.

EXEMPTION: SUPPLY USED IN TRANSPORT

12(1) A supply of a taxable commodity is exempt from levy if the commodity is to be burned (or, in the case of electricity, consumed)–

(a)   in order to propel a train,

(b)   in order to propel a non-railway vehicle while it is being used for, or for purposes connected with, transporting passengers,

(c)   in a railway vehicle, or a non-railway vehicle, while it is being used for, or for purposes connected with, transporting passengers,

(d)   in a railway vehicle while it is being used for, or for purposes connected with, transporting goods, or

(e)   in a ship while it is engaged on a journey any part of which is beyond the seaward limit of the territorial sea.

Paragraphs (a) to (c) are subject to the exception in sub-paragraph (3).

12(2) In this paragraph–

"railway vehicle" and **"train"** have the meaning given by section 83 of the Railways Act 1993;

"non-railway vehicle" means–

(a)   any vehicle other than a railway vehicle, or

(b)   any ship, that is designed or adapted to carry not less than 12 passengers.

12(3) Sub-paragraph (1)(a) to (c) does not apply in relation to the transporting of passengers to, from or within–

(a)   a place of entertainment, recreation or amusement, or

(b)   a place of cultural, scientific, historical or similar interest,

that is a place to which rights of admission, or where rights to use facilities at it, are supplied by the person to whom the commodity is supplied or by a person connected with him within the meaning of section 839 of the Taxes Act 1988.

EXEMPTION: SUPPLIES TO PRODUCERS OF COMMODITIES OTHER THAN ELECTRICITY

13   A supply of a taxable commodity to a person is exempt from the levy if–

(a)   the supply is not a supply of electricity that is deemed to be made under paragraph 23(3), and

(b)   the commodity is to be used by that person–

(i)   in producing taxable commodities other than electricity,

(ii)   in producing hydrocarbon oil or road fuel gas,

(iii)   in producing, for chargeable use within the meaning of section 6A of the Hydrocarbon Oil Duties Act 1979 (fuel substitutes), liquids that are not hydrocarbon oil, or

(iv)   in producing uranium for use in an electricity generating station.

For this purpose **"hydrocarbon oil"** and **"road fuel gas"** have the same meaning as in the Hydrocarbon Oil Duties Act 1979 and **"liquid"** has the same meaning as in section 6A of that Act.

EXEMPTION: SUPPLIES (OTHER THAN SELF-SUPPLIES) TO ELECTRICITY PRODUCERS

14(1) A supply of a taxable commodity to a person is exempt from the levy if–

(a)   the commodity is to be used by that person in producing electricity in a generating station that is neither–

(i)   a fully exempt combined heat and power station, nor

(ii)   a partly exempt combined heat and power station,

and

(b)   the supply is not a supply of electricity that is deemed to be made under paragraph 23(3).

14(2) Sub-paragraph (1) does not exempt a supply where the person to whom the supply is made–

(a)   is an exempt unlicensed electricity supplier of a description prescribed by regulations made by the Treasury, and

(b)   uses the commodity supplied in producing electricity.

14(3) Sub-paragraph (1) does not exempt a supply where the person to whom the supply is made–

(a)   is an auto-generator,

(b)   uses the commodity supplied in producing electricity, and

(c) uses the electricity produced otherwise than in making supplies that are excluded under paragraphs 8 to 10 or exempt under any of paragraphs 11, 12 and 18.

14(4) In this paragraph **"exempt unlicensed electricity supplier"** means a person–

(a) to whom an exemption from section 4(1)(c) of the Electricity Act 1989 (persons supplying electricity to premises) has been granted by an order under section 5 of that Act, or

(b) to whom an exemption from Article 8(1)(c) of the Electricity Supply (Northern Ireland) Order 1992 has been granted by an order under Article 9 of that Orderexcept where he is acting otherwise than for purposes connected with the carrying on of activities authorised by the exemption.

14(5) Sub-paragraph (4) applies subject to–

(a) any direction under paragraph 151(1), and

(b) any regulations under paragraph 151(2).

EXEMPTION: SUPPLIES (OTHER THAN SELF-SUPPLIES) TO COMBINED HEAT AND POWER STATIONS

15(1) A supply of a taxable commodity to a person is exempt from the levy if–

(a) the commodity is to be used by that person in–
   (i) a fully exempt combined heat and power station, or
   (ii) a partly exempt combined heat and power station,
   in producing any outputs of the station, and

(b) the supply is not a supply of electricity that is deemed to be made under paragraph 23(3).

For this purpose **"outputs"** has the meaning given by paragraph 148(9).

15(2) Where–

(a) a supply of a taxable commodity to a person would (apart from this sub-paragraph) be exempted in full by sub-paragraph (1), and

(b) at the time the supply is made, the efficiency percentage for the combined heat and power station in which the commodity is to be used by that person is less than the threshold efficiency percentage for the station,

sub-paragraph (1) only exempts the relevant fraction of the supply.

15(3) For the purposes of sub-paragraph (2), the "relevant fraction" of a supply of a taxable commodity that is to be used in a combined heat and power station is the fraction–

(a) whose numerator is the efficiency percentage for the station at the time the supply is made, and

(b) whose denominator is the threshold efficiency percentage for the station at that time.

15(4) For the purposes of this paragraph–

(a) the "threshold efficiency percentage" for a combined heat and power station is the percentage set as the threshold efficiency percentage for the station by regulations made by the Treasury;

(b) the "efficiency percentage" for a combined heat and power station is the percentage stated as the efficiency percentage for the station in a certificate in force in respect of the station under paragraph 148 (certificate given by Secretary of State that station is fully or partly exempt).

15(5) Paragraph 149 confers power to make provision by regulations for determining the efficiency percentage to be stated in a certificate under paragraph 148.

EXEMPTION: SUPPLIES (OTHER THAN SELF-SUPPLIES) OF ELECTRICITY *FROM PARTLY EXEMPT COMBINED HEAT AND POWER STATIONS*

16(1) This paragraph applies to a supply that–

(a) is a supply made from a partly exempt combined heat and power station of electricity produced in the station, and

(b) is not a supply that is deemed to be made under paragraph 23(3).

16(2) The supply is exempt from the levy if the quantity of electricity supplied by the supply is not such as causes the exceeding of any specified limit that, by virtue of regulations made by the Treasury, applies in relation to the station for any specified period.

16(3) In this paragraph **"specified"** means prescribed by, or determined in accordance with, regulations made by the Treasury.

EXEMPTION: SELF-SUPPLIES BY ELECTRICITY PRODUCERS

17(1) This paragraph applies to a supply of electricity that is deemed to be made under paragraph 23(3) by a person ("the producer") to himself.

17(2) If the producer is an auto-generator, the supply is exempt from the levy unless–

(a) it is a supply from a partly-exempt combined heat and power station of electricity produced in the station, and

(b) the quantity of electricity supplied by the supply is such as causes the exceeding of any such limit as is mentioned in paragraph 16(2) that applies in relation to the station.

17(3) If the producer is not an auto-generator, the supply is exempt from the levy if it is a supply made from a fully exempt combined heat and power station of electricity produced in the station.

17(4) If the producer is not an auto-generator, the supply is exempt from the levy if–

(a) it is a supply from a partly-exempt combined heat and power station of electricity produced in the station, and

(b) the quantity of electricity supplied by the supply is not such as causes the exceeding of any such limit as is mentioned in paragraph 16(2) that applies in relation to the station.

EXEMPTION: SUPPLY NOT USED AS FUEL

18(1) A supply of a taxable commodity is exempt from the levy if the person to whom the supply is made intends to cause the commodity to be used otherwise than as fuel.

18(2) The Treasury may by regulations specify, in relation to any commodity, uses of that commodity that, for the purposes of sub-paragraph (1), are to be taken as being, or as not being, uses of that commodity as fuel.

18(3) The uses of a commodity that may be specified under sub-paragraph (2) as being uses of that commodity as, or otherwise than as, fuel include uses ("mixed uses") of the commodity that involve it being used partly as fuel and partly not; but the Treasury must have regard to the object of securing that a mixed use is not specified as being a use of the commodity otherwise than as fuel if it involves the use of the commodity otherwise than as fuel in a way that is merely incidental to its use as fuel.

EXEMPTION: ELECTRICITY FROM RENEWABLE SOURCES

19(1) A supply of electricity is exempt from the levy if–

(a) the supply is not one that is deemed to be made under paragraph 23(3),

(b) the supply is made under a contract that contains a renewable source declaration given by the supplier,

(c) prescribed conditions are fulfilled, and

(d) the supplier, and each other person (if any) who is a generator of any renewable source electricity allocated by the supplier to supplies under the contract, has in a written notice given to the Commissioners agreed that he will fulfil those conditions so far as they may apply to him.

19(2) In this paragraph **"renewable source declaration"** means a declaration that, in each averaging period, the amount of electricity supplied by exempt renewable supplies made by the supplier in the period will not exceed the difference between–

(a) the total amount of renewable source electricity that during that period is either acquired or generated by the supplier, and

(b) so much of that total amount as is allocated by the supplier otherwise than to exempt renewable supplies made by him in the period.

In this sub-paragraph **"averaging period"** has the same meaning as in paragraph 20 and **"exempt renewable supplies"** means supplies made on the basis that they are exempt under this paragraph.

19(3) For the purposes of this paragraph and paragraph 20, electricity is "renewable source electricity" if–

(a) it is generated in a prescribed manner, and

(b) prescribed conditions are fulfilled.

A manner of generating electricity may be prescribed by reference to the means by which the electricity is generated or the materials from which it is generated (or both).

19(4) In prescribing a manner of generating electricity under sub-paragraph (3), the Commissioners must have regard to the object of securing that exemption under this paragraph is only available for supplies of electricity that has a renewable source.

19(5) The conditions that may be prescribed under sub-paragraph (1)(c) include, in particular, conditions in connection with–

(a)   the giving of effect to renewable source declarations;
(b)   the supply of information;
(c)   the inspection of records and, for that purpose, the production of records in legible form and entry into premises;
(d)   monitoring by the Gas and Electricity Markets Authority, or the Director General of Electricity Supply for Northern Ireland, of the application of provisions of, or made under, this paragraph;
(e)   the doing of things to or by a person authorised by the Authority or the Director General (as well as to or by the Authority or the Director General);
(f)   things being done at times or in ways specified by the Authority, the Director General or such an authorised person.

19(6) A condition prescribed under sub-paragraph (1)(c) may be one that is required to be fulfilled throughout a period, including a period ending after the time when a supply whose exemption turns on the fulfilment of the condition is treated as being made.

19(7) The conditions that may be prescribed under sub-paragraph (3)(b) include, in particular, conditions in connection with–

(a)   the generation of the electricity;
(b)   the materials from which the electricity is generated;
(c)   any of the matters mentioned in paragraphs (b) to (f) of sub-paragraph (5).

19(8) Each of–

(a)   the Gas and Electricity Markets Authority, and
(b)   the Director General of Electricity Supply for Northern Ireland,

shall supply the Commissioners with such information (whether or not obtained under this paragraph), and otherwise give the Commissioners such co-operation, as the Commissioners may require in connection with the application (whether generally or in relation to any particular case) of any relevant provisions.

19(9) In sub-paragraph (8) **"relevant provisions"** means provisions of or made under–

(a)   this paragraph or paragraph 20, or
(b)   paragraph 23(3) so far as relating to electricity, or paragraph 23(4).

19(10) None of–

(a)   section 57(1) of the Electricity Act 1989,
(b)   section 42(1) of the Gas Act 1986, and
(c)   Article 61(1) of the Electricity (Northern Ireland) Order 1992,

(provisions restricting disclosure of information) applies to any disclosure of information made in pursuance of sub-paragraph (8).

EXEMPTION UNDER PARAGRAPH 19: AVERAGING PERIODS

20(1) This paragraph applies where a person ("the supplier") makes supplies of electricity on the basis that they are exempt under paragraph 19 ("exempt renewable supplies").

20(2) The rules about balancing and averaging periods are–

(a)   a balancing period is a period of 3 months;
(b)   when a balancing period ends, a new one begins;
(c)   the first balancing period and the first averaging period begin at the same time;
(d)   unless the supplier specifies an earlier time, that time is the time when he is treated as making the first of the exempt renewable supplies;
(e)   when an averaging period ends, a new one begins;
(f)   an averaging period ends once it has run for 2 years (but may end sooner under paragraph (g) or sub-paragraph (4)(a) or (5)(a));
(g)   if the supplier stops making exempt renewable supplies, the end of the balancing period in which he makes the last exempt renewable supply is also the end of the averaging period in which that balancing period falls.

20(3)   At the end of each balancing period calculate–

(a)   the total of–
   (i)   the quantity of renewable source electricity that the supplier acquired or generated in that period, and
   (ii)   any balancing credit carried forward to that balancing period; and

(b)   the total of–
   (i)   the quantity of electricity supplied by exempt renewable supplies made by him in that period, and
   (ii)   any balancing debit carried forward to that balancing period.

20(4)   If the total mentioned in sub-paragraph (3)(a) exceeds that mentioned in sub-paragraph (3)(b)–

(a)   the averaging period within which the balancing period fell ends at the end of the balancing period, and

(b)   a balancing credit equal to the difference between the two totals is carried forward to the next balancing period.

20(5)   If the totals mentioned in paragraphs (a) and (b) of sub-paragraph (3) are the same–

(a)   the averaging period within which the balancing period fell ends at the end of the balancing period, and

(b)   no balancing credit or debit is carried forward to the next balancing period.

20(6)   Sub-paragraphs (7) and (8) apply if the total mentioned in sub-paragraph (3)(b) exceeds that mentioned in sub-paragraph (3)(a).

20(7)   Where the end of the balancing period is by virtue of sub-paragraph (2)(c) (averaging period ends after 2 years) the end of an averaging period, the supplier is liable to account to the Commissioners for an amount equal to the amount that would be payable by way of levy on a taxable supply that–

(a)   is made at the end of the balancing period,

(b)   is a supply of a quantity of electricity equal to the difference between the two totals, and

(c)   is treated as a reduced-rate supply to the extent (if any) that the exempt renewable supplies made by the supplier in the averaging period would have been reduced-rate supplies if they had not been made on the basis that they were exempt.

   For the purposes of this Schedule, the amount for which the supplier is liable to account shall be treated as an amount of levy for which he is liable to account for an accounting period ending at the end of the balancing period.

20(8)   Where sub-paragraph (7) does not apply, a balancing debit equal to the difference between the two totals is carried forward to the next balancing period.

REGULATIONS TO AVOID DOUBLE CHARGES TO LEVY

21(1)   The Commissioners may by regulations make provision for avoiding, counteracting or mitigating double charges to levy.

21(2)   For the purposes of this paragraph there is a double charge to levy where–

(a)   a supply of a taxable commodity ("the produced commodity")is a taxable supply, and

(b)   a taxable commodity used directly or indirectly in producing the produced commodity has been the subject of a taxable supply.

21(3)   Regulations under this paragraph may, in particular, make provision for a supply of a taxable commodity to be wholly or to any extent–

(a)   exempt from the the levy, or

(b)   deemed not a supply of the commodity.

21(4)   The provision mentioned in sub-paragraph (3) includes provision for exceptions to any of sub-paragraph (1) to (3) of paragraph 23 or paragraph 24(3).

21(5)   The powers conferred by this paragraph are in addition to the powers to make provision by tax credit regulations in relation to any such case as is mentioned in paragraph 62(1)(g).

REGULATIONS GIVING EFFECT TO EXEMPTIONS

22(1)   The Commissioners may by regulations make provision for giving effect to the exclusions and exemptions provided for by paragraphs 8 to 21.

22(2)   Regulations under this paragraph may, in particular, include provision for–

(a)   determining the extent to which a supply of a taxable commodity is, or is to be treated as being, a taxable supply;

(b)   authorising a person making supplies of a taxable commodity to another person to treat the supplies to that other person as being taxable supplies only to an extent certified by the Commissioners.

DEEMED SUPPLY: USE OF COMMODITIES BY UTILITIES AND PRODUCERS

23(1)   Where an electricity utility–

(a)   has electricity available to it, and

(b)   as regards a quantity of the electricity, makes no supply of that quantity to another person but causes it to be consumed in the United Kingdom,

the utility is for the purposes of this Schedule deemed to make a supply to itself of that quantity of the electricity.

23(2)   Where a gas utility–

(a)   holds gas in a gaseous state, and

(b)   as regards a quantity of the gas, makes no supply of that quantity to another person but causes it to be burned in the United Kingdom,

the utility is for the purposes of this Schedule deemed to make a supply to itself of that quantity of the gas.

23(3)   Where–

(a)   a person has produced a taxable commodity,

(b)   the commodity is either–

        (i)   a taxable commodity other than electricity, or

        (ii) electricity that has been produced from taxable commodities, and

(c)   as regards a quantity of the commodity, the person makes no supply of that quantity to another person but causes it to be burned (or, in the case of electricity, consumed) in the United Kingdom,

the person is for the purposes of this Schedule deemed to make a supply to himself of that quantity of the commodity.

23(4)   The Commissioners may by regulations make provision for electricity to be treated for the purposes of sub-paragraph (3)(b)(ii)–

(a)   as produced from taxable commodities unless prescribed conditions are fulfilled, or

(b)   as produced otherwise than from taxable commodities only where prescribed conditions are fulfilled.

23(5)   The conditions that may be prescribed under sub-paragraph (4) include, in particular, conditions in connection with the materials from which the electricity is produced.

DEEMED SUPPLY: CHANGE OF CIRCUMSTANCES OR INTENTIONS

24(1)   This paragraph applies where–

(a)   a supply of a taxable commodity has been made to a person on or after 1st April 2001,

(b)   the supply was not a taxable supply, and

(c)   there is such a change in circumstances or any person's intentions that, if the changed circumstances or intentions had existed at the time the supply was made, the supply would have been a taxable supply.

24(2)   This paragraph does not apply where the supply was not a taxable supply by reason of *being exempt from the levy under paragraph* 19 (exemption for supply of electricity from renewable sources, but see paragraph 20).

24(3)   The person to whom the supply was made is for the purposes of this Schedule deemed to make a taxable supply of the commodity to himself.

24(4)   Where–

(a)   a supply of a taxable commodity was not a taxable supply by virtue of being supplied for use in premises of a description mentioned in any of paragraphs (a) to (f) of paragraph 9(2), and

(b)   those premises cease to be premises of any of those descriptions,

sub-paragraph (3) only applies to so much (if any) of the commodity supplied as was not used in the premises before they ceased to be premises of any of those descriptions.

24(5) The Commissioners may by regulations make provision specifying descriptions of occurrences and non-occurrences that are to be taken as being, or as not being, changes of circumstances or intentions for the purposes of sub-paragraph (1)(c).

Part III – Time of Supply

INTRODUCTION

25 This Part of this Schedule applies to determine when a supply of a taxable commodity is treated as taking place.

ELECTRICITY OR GAS: SUPPLY WHEN CLIMATE CHANGE LEVY ACCOUNTING DOCUMENT ISSUED

26(1) This paragraph applies–

(a) to supplies of electricity, and

(b) to supplies of gas where the gas is supplied in a gaseous state and is of a kind supplied by a gas utility.

26(2) Where this paragraph applies, a supply is treated as taking place each time a climate change levy accounting document in respect of a supply is issued by the person making the supply.

26(3) A supply that is treated as taking place under this paragraph is a supply of the electricity or gas covered by the accounting document.

26(4) Nothing in this paragraph applies to any electricity or gas that is covered by a special utility scheme (see paragraph 29).

ELECTRICITY OR GAS: DUTY TO ISSUE CLIMATE CHANGE LEVY ACCOUNTING DOCUMENT

27(1) This paragraph applies where on any day–

(a) electricity, or gas that is in a gaseous state and is of a kind supplied by a gas utility, is actually supplied to a person ("the consumer"),

(b) the supply by which the electricity or gas is supplied is a taxable supply, and

(c) the person liable to account for the levy on that supply is the person making the supply ("the supplier").

27(2) A climate change levy accounting document covering the electricity or gas actually supplied on that day must be issued by the supplier no later than–

(a) the end of the period of 15 weeks beginning with that day, if on that day the consumer is a small-scale user of the commodity supplied;

(b) the end of the period of 6 weeks beginning with that day, if on that day the consumer is not a small-scale user of the commodity supplied.

27(3) A climate change levy accounting document issued under this paragraph that covers the electricity, or the gas of any kind, actually supplied on any day must also cover any electricity or (as the case may be) any gas of that kind that–

(a) has been actually supplied by the supplier to the consumer on any earlier day, and

(b) has not been covered by a previous climate change levy accounting document.

27(4) For the purposes of this paragraph–

(a) an accounting document shall be taken to cover the electricity or gas actually supplied on a day if it covers the electricity or gas actually supplied during a period that includes that day; and

(b) an accounting document shall be taken to cover the electricity or gas actually supplied on a day or during a period if it is an accounting document for a quantity of electricity or gas that is a reasonable estimate of the quantity actually supplied.

27(5) A climate change levy accounting document issued under this paragraph must contain a statement of–

(a) the quantity of electricity or gas that it covers,

(b) the period during which, or during which it is estimated that, that quantity was actually supplied,

(c) the supplier's name and address,

(d)   the customer's name and address, and

(e)   the reference number used by the supplier for the customer.

27(6)   For the purposes of this paragraph a person is, on any day, a small-scale user of a commodity if the rate at which he is taken to be supplied with that commodity on that day does not exceed the prescribed rate.

27(7)   The Commissioners may make provision by regulations as to the rate at which a person is, for the purposes of sub-paragraph (6), taken to be supplied with a commodity on any day.

27(8)   Regulations under sub-paragraph (7) may, in particular, include provision for–

(a)   rates to be determined or estimated in accordance with the regulations;

(b)   rates to be so determined or estimated by reference to the quantity of a commodity actually supplied, or estimated to have been actually supplied, during a period ending with, or at any time before or after, the day in question;

(c)   cases where a person is supplied with a commodity of any kind by two or more suppliers.

27(9)   Nothing in this paragraph applies to any electricity or gas–

(a)   that is covered by a special utility scheme (see paragraph 29), or

(b)   that is actually supplied before 1st April 2001.

27(10)   This paragraph applies subject to paragraph 36(5).

ELECTRICITY OR GAS: ACTUAL SUPPLY NOT FOLLOWED BY CLIMATE CHANGE LEVY ACCOUNTING DOCUMENT

28(1)   This paragraph applies where on any day–

(a)   electricity, or gas that is in a gaseous state and is of a kind supplied by a gas utility, is actually supplied to a person ("the consumer"),

(b)   the supply by which the electricity or gas is supplied is a taxable supply,

(c)   the person liable to account for the levy on that supply is the person making the supply ("the supplier"), and

(d)   the supplier does not within the period applicable under sub-paragraph (2) of paragraph 27 issue a climate change levy accounting document under that paragraph covering the electricity or gas.

28(2)   Where this paragraph applies, a supply is treated as taking place at the end of that period.

28(3)   A supply that is treated as taking place under this paragraph is a supply of all the electricity or (as the case may be) gas of the same kind that–

(a)   has been actually supplied by the supplier to the consumer before the end of that period, and

(b)   has not been covered by a climate change levy accounting document.

28(4)   Sub-paragraph (4) of paragraph 27 (interpretation of "covered by an accounting document") applies for the purposes of this paragraph as for those of that paragraph.

28(5)   Nothing in this paragraph applies to any electricity or gas–

(a)   that is covered by a special utility scheme (see paragraph 29),

(b)   that is actually supplied before 1st April 2001, or

(c)   that is treated under paragraph 36(3) as supplied on that day.

ELECTRICITY OR GAS: SPECIAL UTILITY SCHEMES

29(1)   For the purposes of this Schedule a "special utility scheme" is a scheme for determining when–

(a)   a supply of electricity, or

(b)   a supply of gas that is in a gaseous state and is of a kind supplied by a gas utility,

is treated as taking place in cases where the electricity or gas is covered by the scheme.

29(2)   If in the opinion of the Commissioners it is reasonable to do so, they may in accordance with the provisions of this paragraph prepare a special utility scheme for a utility or for two or more utilities.

In this paragraph **"utility"** includes a person who makes supplies on which levy is chargeable by virtue of paragraph 5(2) (partly exempt combined heat and power stations).

29(3)   A special utility scheme shall specify the period for which it is to have effect.

29(4)   No special utility scheme shall be of any effect in relation to any electricity or gas supplied by a utility unless the utility elects in writing to be bound by it for the specified period.

29(5) If a utility makes such an election–

(a) the scheme shall have effect for the specified period in relation to such electricity or gas supplied by the utility as is covered by the scheme, and

(b) during the specified period the scheme applies to determine when a supply of a taxable commodity is treated as taking place if the commodity is electricity or gas covered by the scheme.

29(6) A special utility scheme may–

(a) cover all or any of the electricity or gas supplied by a utility for which the scheme is prepared;

(b) provide for paragraph 36 or 37 not to apply, or to apply with modifications, to electricity or gas covered by the scheme.

29(7) The Commissioners may by regulations make further provision with respect to special utility schemes, including (in particular) provision amending this paragraph.

OTHER COMMODITIES: GENERAL RULES FOR SUPPLY BY UK RESIDENTS

30(1) This paragraph applies to supplies that are not of either of the descriptions mentioned in paragraphs (a) and (b) of paragraph 26(1) (electricity and gas in a gaseous state).

30(2) The general rules as to when such supplies are taken to be made are, in cases where the supply is made by a person resident in the United Kingdom, as follows–

(a) if the commodity is to be removed, the supply takes place at the time of the removal;

(b) if the commodity is not to be removed, the supply takes place when the commodity is made available to the person to whom it is supplied;

(c) if the commodity (being sent or taken on approval or sale or return or similar terms) is removed before it is known whether a supply will take place, the supply takes place when it becomes certain that the supply has taken place or, if sooner, 12 months after the removal.

30(3) These general rules are subject to–

paragraph 31 (earlier invoice),
paragraph 32 (later invoice),
paragraph 34 (deemed supplies), and
paragraph 36 (directions by Commissioners).

OTHER COMMODITIES: EARLIER INVOICE

31(1) If before the time applicable under paragraph 30(2) the person making the supply–

(a) issues an invoice in respect of the supply, or

(b) receives a payment in respect of it,

the supply is treated, to the extent that it is covered by the invoice or payment, as taking place when the invoice is issued or the payment is received.

31(2) Sub-paragraph (1) does not apply where the commodity (being sent or taken on approval or sale or return or similar terms) is removed before it is known whether a supply will take place.

31(3) Sub-paragraph (1) applies subject to any direction under paragraph 35(3).

OTHER COMMODITIES: LATER INVOICE

32(1) If within 14 days after the time applicable under paragraph 30(2) the person making the supply issues an invoice in respect of it, the supply is treated as taking place at the time the invoice is issued.

32(2) This does not apply–

(a) to the extent that the supply is treated as taking place at the time mentioned in paragraph 31(1) (earlier invoice), or

(b) if the person liable to account for any levy charged on the supply has notified the Commissioners in writing that he elects not to avail himself of sub-paragraph (1).

32(3) The Commissioners may, at the request of a person liable to account for any levy charged on any supplies, direct that sub-paragraph (1) shall apply–

(a) in relation to those supplies, or

(b) in relation to such of those supplies as may be specified in the direction,

with the substitution for the period of 14 days of such longer period as may be specified in the direction.

32(4)　Sub-paragraphs (1) to (3) apply subject to any direction under paragraph 35.

OTHER COMMODITIES: SUPPLY BY NON-UK RESIDENTS

33(1)　This paragraph applies to supplies that–

(a)　are not of either of the descriptions mentioned in paragraphs (a) and (b) of paragraph 26(1) (electricity and gas in a gaseous state), and

(b)　are made by a person who is not resident in the United Kingdom.

33(2)　The supply is treated as taking place–

(a)　when the commodity is delivered to the person to whom it is supplied, or

(b)　if earlier, when it is made available in the United Kingdom to that person.

33(3)　Sub-paragraph (2) applies subject to–

(a)　sub-paragraph (4),

(b)　paragraph 34 (deemed supplies), and

(c)　any direction under paragraph 35.

33(4)　If within 14 days after the time applicable under sub-paragraph (2) the person to whom the supply is made elects in writing for the supply to be treated as taking place at the time the election is made, the supply is treated as taking place at the time the election is made.

OTHER COMMODITIES: DEEMED SUPPLIES

34(1)　This paragraph applies to supplies that–

(a)　are not of either of the descriptions mentioned in paragraphs (a) and (b) of paragraph 26(1) (electricity and gas in a gaseous state), and

(b)　are deemed to be made under paragraph 23 or 24.

34(2)　A supply that is deemed to be made under paragraph 23 is treated as taking place when the commodity is burned (or, in the case of electricity, consumed).

34(3)　A supply that is deemed to be made under paragraph 24 is treated as taking place upon the occurrence of the change in circumstances or intentions.

OTHER COMMODITIES: DIRECTIONS BY COMMISSIONERS

35(1)　This paragraph applies to supplies that are not of either of the descriptions mentioned in paragraphs (a) and (b) of paragraph 26(1) (electricity and gas in a gaseous state).

35(2)　The Commissioners may, at the request of the person liable to account for any levy charged on any supplies to which this paragraph applies, make a direction under sub-paragraph (3) or (4) altering the time at which those supplies (or such of those supplies as may be specified in the direction) are to be treated as taking place.

35(3)　The Commissioners may direct that the supplies shall be treated as taking place–

(a)　at times or on dates determined by or by reference to the occurrence of some event described in the direction, or

(b)　at times or on dates determined by or by reference to the time when some event so described would in the ordinary course of events occur,

provided the resulting times or dates are in every case earlier than would otherwise apply.

35(4)　The Commissioners may direct that the supplies shall be treated as taking place–

(a)　at the beginning of the relevant working period (as defined in the case of the person making the request in and for the purposes of the direction), or

(b)　at the end of the relevant working period (as so defined).

35(5)　A direction under sub-paragraph (4) shall not apply to the extent that the time when the supplies in question are made is determined by paragraph 31(1).

SUPPLIES INVOICED OR PAID FOR BEFORE 1ST APRIL 2001

36(1)　This paragraph applies where–

(a)　the taxable commodities covered by an invoice issued, or payment received, before 1st April 2001 are to any extent commodities that have not been burned (or, in the case of electricity, consumed) before the invoice is issued or payment is received, and

(b)　the advance invoicing or payment is not acceptable normal practice.

It does not matter whether the invoice mentioned in paragraph (a) is, or is not, a climate change levy accounting document.

36(2)   A fair apportionment shall be made to determine the quantity of the taxable commodities covered by the invoice or payment that will not be, or was not, burned (or consumed) before 1st April 2001.

36(3)   Where this paragraph applies, a supply is treated as taking place on 1st April 2001.

That supply is a supply of the quantity of the taxable commodities that is mentioned in, and determined under, sub-paragraph (2).

36(4)   For the purposes of this paragraph advance invoicing or payment is **"acceptable normal practice"** if–

(a)   the supply is of a kind in the case of which it is normal practice for invoices to be issued, or payments made, in respect of taxable commodities not already burned (or consumed),

(b)   that practice does not involve issuing invoices, or making payments, more than 15 weeks in advance of the burning (or consumption) of any of the taxable commodities in respect of which the invoice is issued or payment is made, and

(c)   the advance invoicing or payment is in accordance with the practice.

36(5)   Nothing in paragraph 27 requires a climate change levy accounting document to be issued to cover any commodities that are supplied by a supply that, under sub-paragraph (3), is treated as made on 1st April 2001.

36(6)   This paragraph applies to invoices issued, and payments received, before the passing of this Act (as well as to those issued or received after its passing).

SUPPLIES OF ELECTRICITY OR GAS SPANNING CHANGE OF RATE ETC.

37(1)   This paragraph applies in the case of a supply of electricity, or of gas that is in a gaseous state and is of a kind supplied by a gas utility, affected by–

(a)   a change in the descriptions of supplies that are taxable supplies,

(b)   a change in any rate of levy in force,

(c)   a change consisting in the rate of levy applicable to the supply ceasing to be, or becoming, the rate that is applicable to half-rate supplies or reduced-rate supplies, or

(d)   the change consisting in the transition from 31st March 2001 to 1st April 2001.

37(2)   For the purposes of this paragraph a supply is affected by a change if the electricity or gas of which it is a supply ("the supplied commodity") is actually supplied partly before the change and partly after.

However, this paragraph does not apply in the case of a supply that, under paragraph 36(3), is treated as made on 1st April 2001.

37(3)   If the person liable to account for any levy on the supply so elects–

(a)   the rate at which levy is chargeable on any part of the supply, or

(b)   any question whether, or to what extent, the supply is a taxable supply,

shall be determined in accordance with sub-paragraph (5) or (6).

37(4)   An election for determination in accordance with sub-paragraph (6) may be made only where–

(a)   there is such a change as is mentioned in sub-paragraph (1)(c), and

(b)   all the supplied commodity is actually supplied before the supply is treated as taking place.

37(5)   Where the election is for determination in accordance with this sub-paragraph, the rules are–

A.   Treat the fraction of the supplied commodity actually supplied before the change ("the pre-change fraction") as supplied by a supply made before the change and treat the fraction of the supplied commodity actually supplied after the change ("the post-change fraction") as supplied by a supply made after the change.

B.   Where the pre-change and post-change fractions are not known (because, for example, there *are no relevant meter* readings available)–

"the pre-change fraction" is calculated by dividing–

(a)   the number of days in the period over which the supply is actually made that fall before the change, by

(b)   the number of days in that period; and

"the post-change fraction" is the difference between 1 and the pre-change fraction.

C.   If use of the fractions given by rule B would produce an inequitable result, the pre-change and post-change fractions may be derived from a reasonable estimate of the fractions of the supplied commodity actually supplied before and after the change.

37(6)   Where the election is for determination in accordance with this sub-paragraph, treat the change as taking place immediately after the time at which the last of the supplied commodity was actually supplied.

OTHER SUPPLIES SPANNING CHANGE OF RATE ETC.

38(1)   This paragraph applies where there is–

(a)   a change in the descriptions of supplies that are taxable supplies,

(b)   a change in the rate of levy in force,

(c)   a change consisting in the rate of levy applicable to any supply ceasing to be, or becoming, the rate that is applicable to half-rate supplies or reduced-rate supplies, or

(d)   the change consisting in the transition from 31st March 2001 to 1st April 2001.

38(2)   Where–

(a)   a supply affected by the change would apart from special provisions be treated under paragraph 30(2) or 33(2) as made wholly or partly at a time when it would not have been affected by the change, or

(b)   a supply not so affected would apart from special provisions be treated under paragraph 30(2) or 33(2) as made wholly or partly at a time when it would have been so affected,

the rate at which levy is chargeable on the supply, or any question whether it is a taxable supply, shall, if the person liable to account for any levy on the supply so elects, be determined without regard to the special provisions.

38(3)   In this paragraph **"special provisions"** means the provisions of paragraphs 31, 32, 33(4) and 35.

REGULATIONS AS TO TIME OF SUPPLY

39(1)   The Commissioners may make provision by regulations as to the time at which a supply is to be treated as taking place–

(a)   in cases where the supply is for a consideration and the whole or part of the consideration–

  (i)   is determined or payable periodically, or from time to time, or at the end of any period, or

  (ii) is determined at the time when the commodity is appropriated for any purpose;

(b)   in the case of a supply otherwise than for consideration;

(c)   in the case of any supply that is deemed to be made under paragraph 23 or 24.

39(2)   In any such case as is mentioned in sub-paragraph (1) the regulations may provide that a taxable commodity shall be treated as separately and successively supplied at prescribed times or intervals.

39(3)   Paragraphs 26 to 36 (main rules as to time of supply) have effect subject to any regulations under this paragraph.

39(4)   The power to make regulations under this paragraph includes power to provide for specified provisions of the regulations to be treated as special provisions for the purposes of paragraph 38 (supplies spanning change of rate etc.).

Part IV – Payment and Rate of Levy

PERSONS LIABLE TO ACCOUNT FOR LEVY

40(1)   The person liable to account for the levy charged on a taxable supply is, except in a case where sub-paragraph (2) applies, the person making the supply.

40(2)   In the case of a taxable supply made by a person who–

(a)   is not resident in the United Kingdom, and

(b)   is not a utility,

the person liable to account for the levy charged on the supply is the person to whom the supply is made.

RETURNS AND PAYMENT OF LEVY

41(1)   The Commissioners may by regulations make provision–

(a)   for persons liable to account for levy to do so by reference to such periods ("accounting periods") as may be determined by or under the regulations;

(b)   for persons who are or are required to be registered for the purposes of the levy to be subject to such obligations to make returns for those purposes for such periods, at such times and in such form as may be so determined; and

(c)   for persons who are required to account for levy for any period to become liable to pay the amounts due from them at such times and in such manner as may be so determined.

41(2)   Without prejudice to the generality of the powers conferred by sub-paragraph (1), regulations under this paragraph may contain provision–

(a)   for levy falling in accordance with the regulations to be accounted for by reference to one accounting period to be treated in prescribed circumstances, and for prescribed purposes, as levy due for a different period;

(b)   for the correction of errors made when accounting for levy by reference to any period;

(c)   for the entries to be made in any accounts in connection with the correction of any such errors and for the financial adjustments to be made in that connection;

(d)   for a person, for purposes connected with the making of any such entry or financial adjustment, to be required to provide to any prescribed person, or to retain, a document in the prescribed form containing prescribed particulars of the matters to which the entry or adjustment relates;

(e)   for enabling the Commissioners, in such cases as they may think fit, to dispense with or relax a requirement imposed by regulations made by virtue of paragraph (d);

(f)   for the amount of levy which, in accordance with the regulations, is treated as due for a later period than that by reference to which it should have been accounted for to be treated as increased by an amount representing interest at the rate applicable under section 197 of the Finance Act 1996 for such period as may be determined in accordance with the regulations.

41(3)   Subject to the following provisions of this paragraph, if any person ("the taxpayer") fails–

(a)   to comply with so much of any regulations under this paragraph as requires him, at or before a particular time, to make a return for any accounting period, or

(b)   to comply with so much of any regulations under this paragraph as requires him, at or before a particular time, to pay an amount of levy due from him,

he shall be liable to a penalty of £250.

41(4)   Liability to a penalty under sub-paragraph (3) shall not arise if the taxpayer satisfies the Commissioners or, on appeal, an appeal tribunal–

(a)   that there is a reasonable excuse for the failure to make the return or to pay the levy in accordance with the regulations; and

(b)   that there is not an occasion after the last day on which the return or payment was required by the regulations to be made when there was a failure without a reasonable excuse to make it.

41(5)   Where, by reason of any failure falling within paragraph (a) or (b) of sub-paragraph (3)–

(a)   a person is convicted of an offence (whether under this Schedule or otherwise), or

(b)   a person is assessed to a penalty under paragraph 98 (penalty for evasion),

that person shall not, by reason of that failure, be liable also to a penalty under that sub-paragraph (3).

AMOUNT PAYABLE BY WAY OF LEVY

42(1)   The amount payable by way of levy on a taxable supply is–

(a)   if the supply is neither a half-rate supply nor a reduced-rate supply, the amount ascertained from the Table in accordance with sub-paragraph (2);

(b)   if the supply is a half-rate supply, 50 per cent. of the amount that would be payable if the supply were neither a half-rate supply nor a reduced-rate supply;

(c)   if the supply is a reduced-rate supply, 20 per cent. of the amount that would be payable if the supply were neither a half-rate supply nor a reduced-rate supply.

Taxable commodity supplied	Rate at which levy payable if supply is neither a half-rate supply nor a reduced-rate supply
Electricity	£0.0043 per kilowatt hour
Gas supplied by a gas utility or any gas supplied in a gaseous state that is of a kind supplied by a gas utility	£0.0015 per kilowatt hour
Any petroleum gas, or other gaseous hydrocarbon, supplied in a liquid state	£0.0096 per kilogram
Any other taxable commodity	£0.0117 per kilogram

42(2) The levy payable on a fraction of a quantity of a commodity is that fraction of the levy payable on that quantity of the commodity.

HALF-RATE FOR SUPPLIES TO HORTICULTURAL PRODUCERS

43(1) For the purposes of this Schedule a **half-rate supply** is a taxable supply in respect of which the following conditions are satisfied–

(a)   the first condition is that the person to whom the supply is made is a horticultural producer;

(b)   the second condition is that the horticultural producer intends to use the taxable commodity supplied–

(i)   in the heating, for the growth of horticultural produce primarily with a view to the production of horticultural produce for sale, of any building or structure, or of the earth or other growing medium in it,

(ii)   in the lighting, for the growth of horticultural produce primarily with a view to the production of horticultural produce for sale, of any building or structure, or

(iii)   in the sterilisation of the earth or other growing medium to be used for the growth of horticultural produce as mentioned in sub-paragraph (i) in any building or structure.

43(2) In this paragraph **"horticultural producer"** means a person growing horticultural produce primarily for sale.

43(3) In this paragraph **"horticultural produce"** means–

(a)   fruit;

(b)   vegetables of a kind grown for human consumption, including fungi, but not including maincrop potatoes or peas grown for seed, for harvesting dry or for vining;

(c)   flowers, pot plants and decorative foliage;

(d)   herbs;

(e)   seeds other than pea seeds, and bulbs and other material, being seeds, bulbs or material for sowing or planting for the production of–

(i)   fruit,

(ii)   vegetables falling within paragraph (b),

(iii)   flowers, plants or foliage falling within paragraph (c), or

(iv)   herbs,or for reproduction of the seeds, bulbs or other material planted; or

(f)   trees and shrubs, other than trees grown for the purpose of afforestation;

but does not include hops.

43(4) The Commissioners may by regulations make provision for facilitating the enjoyment of the reduced rate of levy payable on half-rate supplies.

43(5) Regulations under sub-paragraph (4) may, in particular, include provision–

(a)   for determining the extent to which a taxable supply is, or is to be treated as being, a half-rate supply;

(b)   for authorising a person making taxable supplies to another person to treat the supplies to that other person as being half-rate supplies only to an extent certified by the Commissioners;

(c)   for a person making half-rate supplies ("the supplier") to account for levy on those supplies as if the supplies were neither half-rate supplies nor reduced-rate supplies.

43(6) Provision such as is mentioned in sub-paragraph (5)(c) may be made only where tax credit regulations provide for a horticultural producer to be entitled to a tax credit in respect of 50 per cent. of the levy accounted for by the supplier on any half-rate supplies–

(a)   that are made by the supplier to the horticultural producer, and

(b)   on which the supplier has accounted for levy on the basis mentioned in sub-paragraph (5)(c).

REDUCED-RATE FOR SUPPLIES COVERED BY CLIMATE CHANGE AGREEMENT

44(1) Where the Secretary of State gives a certificate to the Commissioners stating that, for a period specified in the certificate, a facility is to be taken as being covered by a climate change agreement, the Commissioners shall publish a notice in respect of the facility.

44(2) Such a notice shall–

(a)   state the day on which it is published,

(b)   identify the facility or facilities in respect of which it is published,

(c)   for each facility–

   (i) set out the first and last days of the period specified for the facility in the Secretary of State's certificate, and

   (ii) indicate the effect of sub-paragraph (3),

and

(d)   indicate that the notice may be varied by later notices.

44(3) For the purposes of this Schedule, a reduced-rate supply is a taxable supply in respect of which the following conditions are satisfied–

(a)   the first condition is that the taxable commodity supplied by the supply is supplied to a facility identified in a notice published under sub-paragraph (1);

(b)   the second condition is that the supply is made at a time falling in the period that begins with the later of–

   (i) the first day set out for the facility under sub-paragraph (2)(c), and

   (ii) the day on which the notice is published,

   and ends with the last day set out for the facility under sub-paragraph (2)(c).

44(4) Sub-paragraph (3) has effect subject to paragraph 45.

44(5) The Commissioners may, for the purposes of sub-paragraph (3), by regulations make provision for determining whether any taxable commodity is supplied to a facility.

44(6) The provision that may be made by regulations under sub-paragraph (5) includes, in particular, provision for a taxable commodity of any description specified in the regulations to be taken as supplied to a facility only if the commodity is delivered to the facility.

REDUCED-RATE SUPPLIES: VARIATION OF NOTICES UNDER PARAGRAPH 44

45(1) This paragraph applies where the Secretary of State, after having given in respect of a facility such a certificate as is mentioned in paragraph 44(1) ("the original certificate"), gives a certificate (a "variation certificate") to the Commissioners stating–

(a)   that, throughout the period ("the original period") specified for the facility in the original certificate, the facility is to be taken as not being covered by a climate change agreement; or

(b)   that, for so much of the original period as falls on or after a day specified in the variation certificate (being a day falling within the original period), the facility is to be taken as no longer being covered by a climate change agreement.

45(2) Where the Commissioners receive a variation certificate in respect of a facility before they have published a notice under paragraph 44(1) in response to the original certificate so far as relating to the facility, their obligation to publish a notice under paragraph 44(1) in respect of the facility shall have effect as an obligation to publish such a notice in response to the original *certificate as varied by the* variation certificate.

45(3) Where the Commissioners receive a variation certificate but sub-paragraph (2) does not apply, they shall publish a notice (a "variation notice") that–

(a)   states the day on which it is published,

(b)   identifies the facility or facilities in respect of which it is published,

(c) sets out, for each facility in respect of which the statement in the variation certificate is of the type described in sub-paragraph (1)(b), the date specified for the facility in the variation certificate, and

(d) for each facility, indicates the effect of sub-paragraphs (4) to (7) as they apply in the case of the facility.

45(4) Sub-paragraphs (5) to (7) set out the effect of a variation notice being published in respect of a facility.

45(5) If–

(a) the statement in the variation certificate in respect of the facility is of the type described in sub-paragraph (1)(a), and

(b) the day on which the variation notice is published falls before the beginning of the original period,

the notice ("the original notice") published under paragraph 44(1) in response to the original certificate has effect as if the facility had never been identified in it.

45(6) If–

(a) the statement in the variation certificate in respect of the facility is of the type described in sub-paragraph (1)(a), and

(b) the day on which the variation notice is published falls during the original period,

the original notice has effect as if the last day set out for the facility under paragraph 44(2)(c) were the day on which the variation notice is published.

45(7) If the statement in the variation certificate in respect of the facility is of the type described in sub-paragraph (1)(b), the original notice has effect as if the last day set out for the facility under paragraph 44(2)(c) were the later of–

(a) the day on which the variation notice is published, and

(b) the day set out in the variation notice for the facility under sub-paragraph (3)(c).

CLIMATE CHANGE AGREEMENTS

46 In this Schedule **"climate change agreement"** means–

(a) an agreement that falls within paragraph 47, or

(b) a combination of agreements that falls within paragraph 48.

CLIMATE CHANGE AGREEMENTS: DIRECT AGREEMENT WITH SECRETARY OF STATE

47(1) An agreement (including one entered into before the passing of this Act) falls within this paragraph if it is an agreement–

(a) entered into with the Secretary of State,

(b) expressed to be entered into for the purposes of the reduced rate of climate change levy,

(c) identifying the facilities to which it applies,

(d) to which a representative of each facility to which it applies is a party,

(e) setting, or providing for the setting of, targets for the facilities to which it applies,

(f) specifying certification periods (as to which see paragraph 49(1)) for the facilities to which it applies, and

(g) providing for five-yearly (or more frequent) reviews by the Secretary of State of targets set by or under the agreement for those facilities and for giving effect to outcomes of such reviews.

47(2) In this paragraph and paragraph 48 **"representative"**, in relation to a facility to which an agreement applies, means–

(a) the person who is the operator of the facility at–

　(i) the time the agreement is entered into, or

　(ii) if later, the time the facility last became a facility to which the agreement applies,

or

(b) a person authorised by that operator to agree to the facility being a facility to which the agreement applies.

CLIMATE CHANGE AGREEMENT: COMBINATION OF UMBRELLA AND UNDERLYING AGREEMENTS

48(1)   A combination of agreements falls within this paragraph if the following conditions are satisfied.

48(2)   The first condition is that the combination is a combination of–

(a)   an umbrella agreement (including one entered into before the passing of this Act), and

(b)   an agreement (including one entered into before the passing of this Act) that, in relation to the umbrella agreement, is an underlying agreement.

48(3)   The second condition is that between them the two agreements–

(a)   set, or provide for the setting of, targets for the facilities to which the underlying agreement applies,

(b)   specify certification periods (as to which see paragraph 49(1)) for the facilities to which the underlying agreement applies, and

(c)   provide for five-yearly (or more frequent) reviews by the Secretary of State of targets set by or under the agreements for those facilities and for giving effect to outcomes of such reviews.

48(4)   For the purposes of this paragraph an **"umbrella agreement"** is an agreement–

(a)   entered into with the Secretary of State,

(b)   expressed to be entered into for the purposes of the reduced rate of climate change levy,

(c)   identifying the facilities to which it applies, and

(d)   to which a representative of each facility to which it applies is a party.

48(5)   For the purposes of this paragraph an agreement is an **"underlying agreement"** agreement in relation to an umbrella agreement if it is an agreement–

(a)   expressed to be entered into for the purposes of the umbrella agreement,

(b)   entered into–

    (i) with the Secretary of State, or

    (ii) with a party to the umbrella agreement other than the Secretary of State,

(c)   approved by the Secretary of State if he is not a party to it,

(d)   identifying which of the facilities to which the umbrella agreement applies are the facilities to which it applies, and

(e)   to which a representative of each facility to which it applies is a party.

48(6)   In the case of a climate change agreement that is a combination of agreements that falls within this paragraph, references to the facilities to which the climate change agreement applies are references to the facilities to which the underlying agreement applies.

CLIMATE CHANGE AGREEMENT: SUPPLEMENTAL PROVISIONS

49(1)   The first certification period specified by a climate change agreement for a facility to which it applies shall begin with the later of–

(a)   the date on which the agreement, so far as relating to the facility, is expressed to take effect, and

(b)   1st April 2001;

and each subsequent certification period so specified shall begin immediately after the end of a previous certification period.

49(2)   Where a climate change agreement (the "new agreement") applies to a facility to which another climate change agreement previously applied, the first certification period specified by the new agreement for the facility shall be–

(a)   a period beginning as provided by sub-paragraph (1), or

(b)   a period that–

    (i) begins earlier than that, and

    (ii) is a period that was a certification period specified for the facility by any climate change agreement that previously applied to the facility.

A period such as is mentioned in paragraph (b) includes a period beginning, or beginning and ending, before the date on which the new agreement, so far as relating to the facility, is expressed to take effect.

49(3) For the purposes of giving certificates such as are mentioned in paragraphs 44(1) and 45(1), the Secretary of State may take a facility as being covered by a climate change agreement for a period if the facility is one to which the agreement applies and either–

(a) that period is the first certification period specified by the agreement for the facility, or

(b) that period is a subsequent certification period for the facility and it appears to the Secretary of State that progress made in the immediately preceding certification period towards meeting targets set for the facility by the agreement or by a climate change agreement that previously applied to the facility is, or is likely to be, such as under the provisions of the agreement in question is to be taken as being satisfactory.

49(4) For the purposes of sub-paragraph (3)(b) a climate change agreement may (in particular) provide that progress towards meeting any targets for a facility is to be taken as being satisfactory if, in the absence (or partial absence) of any such progress required under the agreement, alternative requirements provided for by the agreement are satisfied.

49(5) For the purposes of sub-paragraphs (2) and (3), the circumstances in which a facility to which a climate change agreement applies is one to which another such agreement previously applied include those where the facility is–

(a) a part, or a combination of parts, of a facility to which another such agreement previously applied,

(b) a combination of two or more such facilities,

(c) any combination of parts of such facilities, or

(d) any combination of such facilities and parts of such facilities.

49(6) Paragraphs 47 and 48 and sub-paragraph (4) above are not to be taken as meaning that an agreement, or combination of agreements, containing provision in addition to any mentioned in those paragraphs and that sub-paragraph is not a climate change agreement.

49(7) For the purposes of paragraphs 47 and 48 and this paragraph **"target"**, in relation to a facility to which a climate change agreement applies, means a target relating to–

(a) energy, or energy derived from a source of any description, used in the facility or an identifiable group of facilities within which the facility falls, or

(b) emissions, or emissions of any description, from the facility or such a group of facilities;

and for this purpose **"identifiable group"** means a group that is identified in the agreement or that at any relevant time can be identified under the agreement.

49(8) Nothing in this Schedule is to be taken as requiring the Secretary of State to–

(a) enter into any climate change agreement,

(b) enter into a climate change agreement with any particular person or persons, in respect of any particular facility or facilities or on any particular terms, or

(c) approve any, or any particular, proposed climate change agreement.

FACILITIES TO WHICH CLIMATE CHANGE AGREEMENTS CAN APPLY

50(1) This paragraph applies where, in connection with concluding or varying a climate change agreement, it falls to be determined whether a facility is to be, or is to continue to be, identified in the agreement as a facility to which the agreement applies.

50(2) For the purposes of such a determination **"facility"** is (subject to any regulations under sub-paragraph (3) or (4)) to be taken as meaning–

(a) an installation covered by paragraph 51; or

(b) a site on which there is or are–

   (i) such an installation or two or more such installations,

   (ii) a part, or parts, of such an installation,

   (iii) a part, or parts, of each of two or more such installations, or

   (iv) any combination of such installations and parts of such installations.

50(3) The Secretary of State may by regulations make provision for an installation covered by paragraph 51 to be taken to be a facility for those purposes only if–

(a) the taxable commodities supplied to the installation by taxable supplies are intended to be burned (or, in the case of electricity, consumed)–

   (i) in the installation, or

   (ii) on the site where the installation is situated but not in the installation,

   and

(b)   the amounts of taxable commodities, and of any other commodities specified in the regulations, subject to each of those intentions are such that any conditions specified in the regulations are satisfied.

50(4)   The Secretary of State may by regulations make provision for a site to be taken to be a facility for those purposes only if–

(a)   the taxable commodities supplied to the site by taxable supplies are intended to be burned (or, in the case of electricity, consumed)–

    (i)   in installations on the site that are covered by paragraph 51 (or in parts of such installations), or

    (ii)   on the site but not in any such installation (or part of such an installation), and

(b)   the amounts of taxable commodities, and of any other commodities specified in the regulations, subject to each of those intentions are such that any conditions specified in the regulations are satisfied.

50(5)   Regulations under sub-paragraph (3) or (4) may make provision for deeming, for the purposes of the regulations, commodities to be intended to be burned (or, in the case of electricity, consumed) in circumstances specified in the regulations.

50(6)   In this paragraph and paragraph 51 **"installation"** means a stationary technical unit.

ENERGY-INTENSIVE INSTALLATIONS

51(1)   An installation is covered by this paragraph if it falls within any one or more of the descriptions of installation set out in the Table.

51(2)   An installation is also covered by this paragraph if it is on the same site as, and ancillary to, an installation falling within any one or more of those descriptions.

51(3)   Sub-paragraphs (1) and (2) are subject to any regulations under paragraph 52.

51(4)   For the purposes of sub-paragraph (2), one installation ("the ancillary installation") is ancillary to another ("the primary installation") if–

(a)   the ancillary installation does not fall within any of those descriptions,

(b)   activities ("the ancillary activities") are carried out at the ancillary installation that are directly associated with any of the primary activities carried out at the primary installation, and

(c)   the ancillary activities–

    (i)   have a technical connection with those primary activities, and

    (ii)   could have an effect on environmental pollution or emissions capable of causing such pollution.

51(5)   However, an installation (or part of an installation) used for research, development and testing of new products and processes does not fall within any of those descriptions.

51(6)   In sub-paragraph (4)–

    "environmental pollution" has the same meaning as in the Pollution Prevention and Control Act 1999;

    "primary activity", in relation to an installation falling within any one or more of the descriptions of installation set out in the Table, means an activity the carrying out of which at the installation results in the installation falling within one or more of those descriptions.

TABLE

DESCRIPTIONS OF ENERGY-INTENSIVE INSTALLATIONS

ENERGY INDUSTRIES

1(1)   Combustion installations with a rated thermal input exceeding 50 MW.

1(2)   Combustion installations operated by the same operator on the same site with a combined rated thermal input exceeding 50 MW.

2   Mineral oil and gas refineries.

3   Coke ovens.

4   Coal gasification and liquefaction plants.

PRODUCTION AND PROCESSING OF METALS

5 Metal ore (including sulphide ore) roasting or sintering installations.

6 Installations for the production of pig iron or steel (primary or secondary fusion) including continuous casting.

7(1) The following installations for the processing of ferrous metals–
(a) hot-rolling mills;
(b) smitheries with hammers.

7(2) Installations for the processing of ferrous metals by the application of protective fused metal coats.

8 Ferrous metal foundries.

9 Installations–

(a) for the production of non-ferrous crude metals from ore, concentrates or secondary raw materials by metallurgical, chemical or electrolytic processes;

(b) for the smelting, including the alloyage, of non-ferrous metals, including recovered products (refining, foundry casting, etc.).

10 Installations for surface treatment of metals and plastic materials using an electrolytic or chemical process.

MINERAL INDUSTRY

11 Installations for the production of–

(a) cement clinker in rotary kilns, or
(b) lime in rotary kilns or other furnaces.

12 Installations for the production of asbestos and the manufacture of asbestos-based products.

13 Installations for the manufacture of glass including glass fibre.

14 Installations for melting mineral substances including the production of mineral fibres.

15 Installations for the manufacture of ceramic products by firing, in particular roofing tiles, bricks, refractory bricks, tiles, stoneware, stoneware or porcelain.

CHEMICAL INDUSTRY

16 Installations for the production, on an industrial scale by chemical processing, of basic organic chemicals such as–

(a) simple hydrocarbons (linear or cyclic, saturated or unsaturated, aliphatic or aromatic);
(b) oxygen-containing hydrocarbons such as alcohols, aldehydes, ketones, carboxylic acids, esters, acetates, ethers, peroxides, epoxy resins;
(c) sulphurous hydrocarbons;
(d) nitrogenous hydrocarbons such as amines, amides, nitrous compounds, nitro compounds or nitrate compounds, nitriles, cyanates, isocyanates;
(e) phosphorus-containing hydrocarbons;
(f) halogenic hydrocarbons;
(g) organometallic compounds;
(h) basic plastic materials (polymers, synthetic fibres and cellulose-based fibres);
(i) synthetic rubbers;
(j) dyes and pigments;
(k) surface-active agents and surfactants.

17 Installations for the production, on an industrial scale by chemical processing, of basic inorganic chemicals such as–

(a) gases, such as ammonia, chlorine or hydrogen chloride, fluorine or hydrogen fluoride, carbon oxides, sulphur compounds, nitrogen oxides, hydrogen, sulphur dioxide, carbonyl chloride;
(b) acids, such as chromic acid, hydrofluoric acid, phosphoric acid, nitric acid, hydrochloric acid, sulphuric acid, oleum, sulphurous acids;
(c) bases, such as ammonium hydroxide, potassium hydroxide, sodium hydroxide;
(d) salts, such as ammonium chloride, potassium chlorate, potassium carbonate, sodium carbonate, perborate, silver nitrate;

(e)   non-metals, metal oxides or other inorganic compounds such as calcium carbide, silicon, silicon carbide.

18   Installations for the production, on an industrial scale by chemical processing, of phosphorous-based, nitrogen-based or potassium-based fertilizers (whether simple or compound).

19   Installations for the production, on an industrial scale by chemical processing, of basic plant health products and of biocides.

20   Installations using a chemical or biological process for the production, on an industrial scale, of basic pharmaceutical products.

21   Installations for the production, on an industrial scale by chemical processing, of explosives.

WASTE MANAGEMENT

22   Installations for the disposal or recovery of hazardous waste as defined in–

(a)   the list referred to in Article 1(4) of Council Directive 91/689/EEC,

(b)   Annex IIA, and headings R1, R5, R6, R8 and R9 of Annex IIB, to Council Directive 75/442/EEC, and

(c)   Council Directive 75/439/EEC.

23   Installations for the incineration of municipal waste as defined in–

(a)   Council Directive 89/369/EEC, and

(b)   Council Directive 89/429/EEC.

24   Installations for the disposal of non-hazardous waste as defined in headings D8 and D9 of Annex IIA to Council Directive 75/442/EEC.

25   Landfills other than landfills of inert waste.

OTHER ACTIVITIES

26   Industrial plants for the production of–

(a)   pulp from timber or other fibrous materials;

(b)   paper and board.

27   Plants for the pre-treatment (operations such as washing, bleaching, mercerisation) or dyeing of fibres or textiles.

28   Plants for the tanning of hides and skins.

29(1)   Slaughterhouses.

29(2)   Installations for–

(a)   the production of food products by the treatment and processing of–

        (i) animal raw materials (other than milk), or

        (ii) vegetable raw materials;

(b)   the treatment and processing of milk.

30   Installations for the disposal or recycling of animal carcases and animal waste.

31   Installations for the intensive rearing of poultry or pigs.

32   Installations for the surface treatment of substances, objects or products using organic solvents, in particular for dressing, printing, coating, degreasing, waterproofing, sizing, painting, cleaning or impregnating.

33   Installations for the production of carbon (hard-burnt coal) or electrographite by means of incineration or graphitization.

POWER TO VARY THE INSTALLATIONS COVERED BY PARAGRAPH 51

52(1)   The Treasury may make provision by regulations for varying the installations covered by paragraph 51.

52(2)   The provision that may be made by regulations under this paragraph includes, in particular, provision–

(a)   for the installations covered by paragraph 51 to include, or not to include, any installation of a description specified in the regulations;

(b) amending the Table in paragraph 51 by adding a description of installation to the Table, removing a description of installation from the Table or altering a description of installation set out in the Table;

(c) amending paragraph 51.

Part V – Registration

REQUIREMENT TO BE REGISTERED

53(1) A person is required to be registered with the Commissioners for the purposes of the levy if a taxable supply is made in respect of which he is the person liable to account for the levy charged.

53(2) The Commissioners shall, for the purposes of sub-paragraph (1) and in accordance with the provisions of this Part of this Schedule, establish and maintain a register of persons liable to account for levy.

53(3) The Commissioners shall keep such information in the register as they consider appropriate for the care and management of the levy.

INTERPRETATION OF PART V

54 In this Part of this Schedule–

(a) references to the register are references to the register maintained under paragraph 51(2);

(b) references to registering a person are references to registering him in that register; and

(c) references to a person's registration are references to his registration in that register.

NOTIFICATION OF REGISTRABILITY ETC.

55(1) A person who–

(a) intends to make, or have made to him, any taxable supply in respect of which (if made) he will be the person liable to account for the levy charged, or

(b) is required to be registered for the purposes of the levy,

shall (if he is not so registered) notify the Commissioners of that fact.

55(2) Subject to sub-paragraphs (5) and (6), a person who fails to comply with sub-paragraph (1) shall be liable to a penalty.

55(3) The amount of the penalty shall be–

(a) the amount equal to 5 per cent. of the relevant levy; or

(b) if it is greater or the circumstances are such that there is no relevant levy, £250.

55(4) In sub-paragraph (3) **"relevant levy"** means the levy (if any) for which the person in question is liable to account in respect of taxable supplies made in the period which–

(a) begins with the date with effect from which he is required to be registered for the purposes of the levy; and

(b) ends with the date on which the Commissioners received notification of, or otherwise first became aware of, the fact that he was required to be registered.

55(5) A failure to comply with sub-paragraph (1) shall not give rise to any liability to a penalty under this paragraph if the person concerned satisfies the Commissioners or, on appeal, an appeal tribunal that there is a reasonable excuse for the failure.

55(6) Where, by reason of any conduct falling within sub-paragraph (2)–

(a) a person is convicted of an offence (whether under this Act or otherwise), or

(b) a person is assessed to a penalty under paragraph 98 (penalty for evasion),

that person shall not by reason of that conduct be liable also to a penalty under this paragraph.

FORM OF REGISTRATION

56(1) The Commissioners shall register a person if–

(a) they receive from him a notification given in pursuance of paragraph 55, or

(b) although they have not received from him such a notification, it appears to them that he is required to be registered.

Where the Commissioners register a person who is required to be registered, they shall register him with effect from the time when the requirement arose.

56(2) Where any two or more bodies corporate are members of the same group they shall be registered together as one person in the name of the representative member.

56(3) The registration of a body corporate carrying on a business in several divisions may, if the body corporate so requests and the Commissioners see fit, be in the names of those divisions.

56(4) The registration of–

(a)   any two or more persons carrying on a business in partnership, or

(b)   an unincorporated body,

may be in the name of the firm or body concerned.

NOTIFICATION OF LOSS OR PROSPECTIVE LOSS OF REGISTRABILITY

57(1) Where a person who has become liable to give a notification by virtue of paragraph 55 ceases (whether before or after being registered for the purposes of the levy) to intend to make, or to intend to have made to him, taxable supplies in respect of which (if made) he would be the person liable to account for the levy charged, he shall notify the Commissioners of that fact.

57(2) A person who fails to comply with sub-paragraph (1) shall be liable to a penalty of £250.

CANCELLATION OF REGISTRATION

58(1) If the Commissioners are satisfied that a registered person–

(a)   has ceased to make, or have made to him, taxable supplies on which he is liable to account for the levy charged, and

(b)   does not intend to make, or have made to him, any such supplies,

they may cancel his registration with effect from such time after he last made, or had made to him, taxable supplies as appears to them to be appropriate.

58(2) Sub-paragraph (1) applies whether or not the registered person has notified the Commissioners under paragraph 57.

58(3) The Commissioners shall be under a duty to exercise the power conferred by sub-paragraph (1) with effect from any time if, where the power is exercisable, they are satisfied that the conditions specified in sub-paragraph (4) are satisfied and were or will be satisfied at that time.

58(4) Those conditions are–

(a)   that the person in question has given a notification under paragraph 57;

(b)   that no levy due from that person, and no amount recoverable as if it were levy, remains unpaid;

(c)   that no tax credit to which that person is entitled by virtue of any tax credit regulations is outstanding; and

(d)   that that person is not subject to any outstanding liability to make a return for the purposes of the levy.

58(5) Where–

(a)   a registered person notifies the Commissioners under paragraph 57, and

(b)   they are satisfied that (if he had not been registered) he would not have been required to be registered at any time since the time when he was registered,

they shall cancel his registration with effect from the date of his registration.

CORRECTION OF THE REGISTER ETC.

59(1) The Commissioners may by regulations make provision for and with respect to the correction of entries in the register.

59(2) Regulations under this paragraph may, to such extent as appears to the Commissioners appropriate for keeping the register up to date, make provision requiring–

(a)   registered persons, and

(b)   persons who are required to be registered,

to notify the Commissioners of changes in circumstances relating to themselves, their businesses or any other matter with respect to which particulars are contained in the register (or would be, were the person registered).

SUPPLEMENTAL REGULATIONS ABOUT NOTIFICATIONS

60(1) For the purposes of any provision made by or under this Part of this Schedule for any matter to be notified to the Commissioners, regulations made by the Commissioners may make provision–

(a)   as to the time within which the notification is to be given;

(b)   as to the form and manner in which the notification is to be given; and

(c)   as to the information and other particulars to be contained in or provided with any notification.

60(2) For those purposes the Commissioners may also by regulations impose obligations requiring a person who has given a notification to notify the Commissioners if any information contained in or provided in connection with that notification is or becomes inaccurate.

60(3) The power under this paragraph to make regulations as to the time within which any notification is to be given shall include power to authorise the Commissioners to extend the time for the giving of a notification.

PUBLICATION OF INFORMATION ON THE REGISTER

61(1) The Commissioners may publish, by such means as they think fit, any information which–

(a)   is derived from the register; and

(b)   falls within any of the descriptions set out below.

61(2) The descriptions are–

(a)   the names of registered persons;

(b)   the fact (where it is the case) that the registered person is a body corporate which is a member of a group;

(c)   the names of the other bodies corporate which are members of the group.

61(3) Information may be published in accordance with this paragraph notwithstanding any obligation not to disclose the information that would otherwise apply.

Part VI – Credits and Repayments

TAX CREDITS

62(1) The Commissioners may, in accordance with the following provisions of this paragraph, by regulations make provision in relation to cases where–

(a)   after a taxable supply has been made, there is such a change in circumstances or any person's intentions that, if the changed circumstances or intentions had existed at the time the supply was made, the supply would not have been a taxable supply;

(b)   after a supply of a taxable commodity is made on the basis that it is a taxable supply, it is determined that the supply was not (to any extent) a taxable supply;

(c)   after a taxable supply has been made on the basis that it was neither a half-rate supply nor a reduced-rate supply, it is determined that the supply was (to any extent) a half-rate or reduced-rate supply;

(d)   levy is accounted for on a half-rate supply as if the supply were neither a half-rate supply nor a reduced-rate supply;

(e)   after a charge to levy has arisen on a supply of a taxable commodity ("the original commodity") to a person who uses the commodity supplied in producing taxable commodities primarily for his own consumption, that person makes supplies of any of the commodities in whose production he has used the original commodity;

(f)   after a person has become entitled to a debt as a result of making a taxable supply, the debt turns out to be bad (in whole or in part);

(g)   the making of a taxable supply gives rise to a double charge to levy within the meaning of paragraph 21.

62(2) The provision that may be made in relation to any such case as is mentioned in sub-paragraph (1) is provision–

(a)   for such person as may be specified in the regulations to be entitled to a tax credit in respect of any levy charged on the supply (or, in such a case as is mentioned in sub-paragraph (1)(g), one of the supplies) in question;

(b)   for a tax credit to which any person is entitled under the regulations to be brought into account when he is accounting for levy due from him for such accounting period or periods as may be determined in accordance with the regulations; and

(c)   for a person entitled to a tax credit to be entitled, in any prescribed case where he cannot bring the tax credit into account so as to set it against a liability to levy, to a repayment of levy of an amount so determined.

62(3) Regulations under this paragraph may contain any or all of the following provisions–

(a) provision making any entitlement to a tax credit conditional on the making of a claim by such person, within such period and in such manner as may be prescribed;

(b) provision making entitlement to bring a tax credit into account, or to receive a repayment in respect of such a credit, conditional on compliance with such requirements (including the making of a claim) as may be determined in accordance with the regulations;

(c) provision requiring a claim for a tax credit to be evidenced and quantified by reference to such records and other documents as may be so determined;

(d) provision requiring a person claiming any entitlement to a tax credit to keep, for such period and in such form and manner as may be so determined, those records and documents and a record of such information relating to the claim as may be so determined;

(e) provision for the withdrawal of a tax credit where any requirement of the regulations is not complied with;

(f) provision for interest at the rate applicable under section 197 of the Finance Act 1996 to be treated as added, for such period and for such purposes as may be prescribed, to the amount of any tax credit;

(g) provision for determining whether, and to what extent, a debt is to be taken as bad;

(h) provision for the withdrawal of a tax credit to which a person has become entitled in a case within sub-paragraph (1)(f) where any part of the debt that has been taken to be bad falls to be regarded as not having been bad;

(i) provision for determining whether, and to what extent, any part of a debt that has been taken to be bad should be regarded as not having been bad;

(j) provision for anything falling to be determined in accordance with the regulations to be determined by reference to a general or specific direction given in accordance with the regulations by the Commissioners.

62(4) Regulations made under this paragraph shall have effect subject to the provisions of paragraph 64.

REPAYMENTS OF OVERPAID LEVY

63(1) Where a person has paid an amount to the Commissioners by way of levy which was not levy due to them, they shall be liable to repay the amount to him.

63(2) The Commissioners shall not be liable to repay an amount under this paragraph if, or to the extent that, any person has become entitled to a tax credit in respect of that amount by virtue of tax credit regulations.

63(3) The Commissioners shall not be liable to repay an amount under this paragraph except on the making of a claim for that purpose.

63(4) A claim under this paragraph must be made in such form and manner, and must be supported by such documentary evidence, as may be required by regulations made by the Commissioners.

63(5) The preceding provisions of this paragraph are subject to the provisions of paragraph 64.

63(6) Except as provided by this paragraph or tax credit regulations, the Commissioners shall not, by virtue of the fact that it was not levy due to them, be liable to repay any amount paid to them by way of levy.

SUPPLEMENTAL PROVISIONS ABOUT REPAYMENTS ETC.

64(1) The Commissioners shall not be liable, on any claim for a repayment of levy, to repay any amount paid to them more than three years before the making of the claim.

64(2) It shall be a defence to any claim for a repayment of an amount of levy that the repayment of that amount would unjustly enrich the claimant.

64(3) Sub-paragraph (4) applies for the purposes of sub-paragraph (2) where–

(a) there is an amount paid by way of levy which (apart from sub-paragraph (2)) would fall to be the subject of a repayment of levy to any person ("person A"); and

(b) the whole or a part of the cost of the payment of that amount to the Commissioners has, for practical purposes, been borne by a person other than person A.

64(4) Where, in a case to which this sub-paragraph applies, loss or damage has been or may be incurred by person A as a result of mistaken assumptions made in his case about the operation of any provisions relating to levy, that loss or damage shall be disregarded, except to the extent of the quantified amount, in the making of any determination as to–

(a)   whether or to what extent the repayment of an amount to person A would enrich him; or

(b)   whether or to what extent any enrichment of person A would be unjust.

64(5)   In sub-paragraph (4) **"the quantified amount"** means the amount (if any) which is shown by person A to constitute the amount that would appropriately compensate him for loss or damage shown by him to have resulted, for any business carried on by him, from the making of the mistaken assumptions.

64(6)   The reference in sub-paragraph (4) to provisions relating to levy is a reference to any provisions of–

(a)   any enactment or subordinate legislation (whether or not still in force) which relates to the levy or to any matter connected with it; or

(b)   any notice published by the Commissioners under or for the purposes of any enactment or subordinate legislation relating to the levy.

REIMBURSEMENT ARRANGEMENTS

65(1)   The Commissioners may by regulations make provision for reimbursement arrangements made by any person to be disregarded for the purposes of paragraph 64(2) except where the arrangements–

(a)   contain such provision as may be required by the regulations; and

(b)   are supported by such undertakings to comply with the provisions of the arrangements as may be required by the regulations to be given to the Commissioners.

65(2)   In this paragraph **"reimbursement arrangements"** means any arrangements for the purposes of a claim to a repayment of levy which–

(a)   are made by any person for the purpose of securing that he is not unjustly enriched by the repayment of any amount in pursuance of the claim; and

(b)   provide for the reimbursement of persons who have for practical purposes borne the whole or any part of the cost of the original payment of that amount to the Commissioners.

65(3)   Without prejudice to the generality of sub-paragraph (1), the provision that may be required by regulations under this paragraph to be contained in reimbursement arrangements includes–

(a)   provision requiring a reimbursement for which the arrangements provide to be made within such period after the repayment to which it relates as may be specified in the regulations;

(b)   provision for the repayment of amounts to the Commissioners where those amounts are not reimbursed in accordance with the arrangements;

(c)   provision requiring interest paid by the Commissioners on any amount repaid by them to be treated in the same way as that amount for the purposes of any requirement under the arrangements to make reimbursement or to repay the Commissioners;

(d)   provision requiring such records relating to the carrying out of the arrangements as may be described in the regulations to be kept and produced to the Commissioners, or to an officer of theirs.

65(4)   Regulations under this paragraph may impose obligations on such persons as may be specified in the regulations–

(a)   to make the repayments to the Commissioners that they are required to make in pursuance of any provisions contained in any reimbursement arrangements by virtue of sub-paragraph (3)(b) or (c);

(b)   to comply with any requirements contained in any such arrangements by virtue of sub-paragraph (3)(d).

65(5)   Regulations under this paragraph may make provision for the form and manner in which, and the times at which, undertakings are to be given to the Commissioners in accordance with the regulations; and any such provision may allow for those matters to be determined by the Commissioners in accordance with the regulations.

INTEREST PAYABLE BY THE COMMISSIONERS

66(1)   Where, due to an error on the part of the Commissioners, a person–

(a)   has paid to them by way of levy an amount which was not levy due and which they are in consequence liable to repay to him,

(b)   has failed to claim a repayment of levy to which he was entitled, under any tax credit regulations, in respect of any tax credits, or

(c)   has suffered delay in receiving payment of an amount due to him from them in connection with levy,

then, if and to the extent that they would not be liable to do so apart from this paragraph, they shall (subject to the following provisions of this paragraph) pay interest to him on that amount for the applicable period.

66(2)   In sub-paragraph (1), the reference in paragraph (a) to an amount which the Commissioners are liable to repay in consequence of the making of a payment that was not due is a reference to only so much of that amount as is the subject of a claim that the Commissioners are required to satisfy or have satisfied.

66(3)   In that sub-paragraph the amounts referred to in paragraph (c)–

(a)   do not include any amount payable under this paragraph;

(b)   do not include the amount of any interest for which provision is made by virtue of paragraph 62(3)(f); but

(c)   do include any amount due (in respect of an adjustment of overpaid interest) by way of a repayment under paragraph 87(3) or 110(3).

66(4)   The applicable period, in a case falling within sub-paragraph (1)(a), is the period–

(a)   beginning with the date on which the payment is received by the Commissioners; and

(b)   ending with the date on which they authorise payment of the amount on which the interest is payable.

66(5)   The applicable period, in a case falling within sub-paragraph (1)(b) or (c), is the period–

(a)   beginning with the date on which, apart from the error, the Commissioners might reasonably have been expected to authorise payment of the amount on which the interest is payable; and

(b)   ending with the date on which they in fact authorise payment of that amount.

66(6)   In determining the applicable period for the purposes of this paragraph there shall be left out of account any period by which the Commissioners' authorisation of the payment of interest is delayed by circumstances beyond their control.

66(7)   The reference in sub-paragraph (6) to a period by which the Commissioners' authorisation of the payment of interest is delayed by circumstances beyond their control includes, in particular, any period which is referable to–

(a)   any unreasonable delay in the making of any claim for the payment or repayment of the amount on which interest is claimed;

(b)   any failure by any person to provide the Commissioners–

(i) at or before the time of the making of a claim, or

(ii) subsequently in response to a request for information by the Commissioners,

with all the information required by them to enable the existence and amount of the claimant's entitlement to a payment or repayment, and to interest on that payment or repayment, to be determined; and

(c)   the making, as part of or in association with any claim for the payment or repayment of the amount on which interest is claimed, of a claim to anything to which the claimant was not entitled.

66(8)   In determining for the purposes of sub-paragraph (7) whether any period of delay is referable to a failure by any person to provide information in response to a request by the Commissioners, there shall be taken to be so referable, except so far as may be provided for by regulations, any period which–

(a)   begins with the date on which the Commissioners require that person to provide information which they reasonably consider relevant to the matter to be determined; and

(b)   ends with the earliest date on which it would be reasonable for the Commissioners to conclude–

(i) *that they have received a complete answer to their request for information;*

(ii) that they have received all that they need in answer to that request; or

(iii) that it is unnecessary for them to be provided with any information in answer to that request.

66(9)   The Commissioners shall not be liable to pay interest under this paragraph except on the making of a claim for that purpose.

66(10)   A claim under this paragraph must be in writing and must be made not more than three years after the end of the applicable period to which it relates.

66(11)   References in this paragraph–

(a)   to receiving payment of any amount from the Commissioners, or

(b)   to the authorisation by the Commissioners of the payment of any amount,

include references to the discharge by way of set-off (whether in accordance with regulations under paragraph 73 or 74 or otherwise) of the Commissioners' liability to pay that amount.

66(12)   Interest under this paragraph shall be payable at the rate applicable under section 197 of the Finance Act 1996.

ASSESSMENT FOR EXCESSIVE REPAYMENT

67(1)   Where–

(a)   any amount has been paid at any time to any person by way of a repayment of levy, and

(b)   the amount paid exceeded the amount which the Commissioners were liable at that time to repay to that person,

the Commissioners may, to the best of their judgement, assess the excess paid to that person and notify it to him.

67(2)   Where–

(a)   any amount has been paid to any person by way of repayment of levy,

(b)   the repayment is in respect of a tax credit the entitlement to which arose in a case falling within paragraph 62(1)(f) (tax credit where all or part of a debt is bad),

(c)   the whole or any part of the credit is withdrawn on account of any part of the debt taken as bad falling to be regarded as not having been bad, and

(d)   the amount paid exceeded the amount which the Commissioners would have been liable to repay to that person had that withdrawal been taken into account,

the Commissioners may, to the best of their judgement, assess the excess paid to that person and notify it to him.

67(3)   Where any person is liable to pay any amount to the Commissioners in pursuance of an obligation imposed by virtue of paragraph 65(4)(a), the Commissioners may, to the best of their judgement, assess the amount due from that person and notify it to him.

67(4)   Subject to sub-paragraph (5), where–

(a)   an assessment is made on any person under this paragraph in respect of a repayment of levy made in relation to any accounting period, and

(b)   the Commissioners have power under Part VII of this Schedule to make an assessment on that person to an amount of levy due from that person for that period,

the assessments may be combined and notified to him as one assessment.

67(5)   A notice of a combined assessment under sub-paragraph (4) must separately identify the amount being assessed in respect of repayments of levy.

ASSESSMENT FOR OVERPAYMENTS OF INTEREST

68   Where–

(a)   any amount has been paid to any person by way of interest under paragraph 66, but

(b)   that person was not entitled to that amount under that paragraph,

the Commissioners may, to the best of their judgement, assess the amount so paid to which that person was not entitled and notify it to him.

ASSESSMENTS UNDER PARAGRAPHS 67 AND 68

69(1)   An assessment under paragraph 67 or 68 shall not be made more than two years after the time when evidence of facts sufficient in the opinion of the Commissioners to justify the making of the assessment comes to the knowledge of the Commissioners.

69(2)   Where an amount has been assessed and notified to any person under paragraph 67 or 68, it shall be recoverable as if it were levy due from him.

69(3)   Sub-paragraph (2) does not have effect if, or to the extent that, the assessment in question has been withdrawn or reduced.

INTEREST ON AMOUNTS ASSESSED

70(1) Where an assessment is made under paragraph 67 or 68, the whole of the amount assessed shall carry interest, for the period specified in sub-paragraph (2), as follows–

(a)   so much of that amount as represents the amount of a tax credit claimed by a person who was not entitled to it (but not any amount assessed under paragraph 67(2)) shall carry penalty interest;

(b)   so much of that amount as does not carry penalty interest under paragraph (a) shall carry interest at the rate applicable under section 197 of the Finance Act 1996.

70(2) That period is the period which–

(a)   begins with the day after that on which the person is notified of the assessment; and

(b)   ends with the day before that on which payment is made of the amount assessed.

70(3) Interest under this paragraph shall be paid without any deduction of income tax.

70(4) Penalty interest under this paragraph shall be compound interest calculated–

(a)   at the penalty rate, and

(b)   with monthly rests.

70(5) For this purpose the penalty rate is the rate found by–

(a)   taking the rate applicable under section 197 of the Finance Act 1996 for the purposes of sub-paragraph (1)(b); and

(b)   adding 10 percentage points to that rate.

70(6) Where a person is liable under this paragraph to pay any penalty interest, the Commissioners or, on appeal, an appeal tribunal may reduce the amount payable to such amount (including nil) as they think proper.

70(7) Subject to sub-paragraph (8), where the person concerned satisfies the Commissioners or, on appeal, an appeal tribunal that there is a reasonable excuse for the conduct giving rise to the liability to pay penalty interest, that is a matter which (among other things) may be taken into account under sub-paragraph (6).

70(8) In determining whether there is a reasonable excuse for the purposes of sub-paragraph (7), no account shall be taken of any of the following matters, that is to say–

(a)   the insufficiency of the funds available to any person for paying any levy due or for paying the amount of the interest;

(b)   the fact that there has, in the case in question or in that case taken with any other cases, been no or no significant loss of levy;

(c)   the fact that the person liable to pay the interest or a person acting on his behalf has acted in good faith.

70(9) In the case of interest reduced by the Commissioners under sub-paragraph (6) an appeal tribunal, on an appeal relating to the interest, may cancel the whole or any part of the reduction made by the Commissioners.

ASSESSMENTS TO INTEREST UNDER PARAGRAPH 70

71(1) Where any person is liable to interest under paragraph 70 the Commissioners may assess the amount due by way of interest and notify it to him accordingly.

71(2) Without prejudice to the power to make assessments under this paragraph for later periods, the interest to which an assessment under this paragraph may relate shall be confined to interest for a period of no more than two years ending with the time when the assessment under this paragraph is made.

71(3) Where an amount has been assessed and notified to any person under this paragraph it shall be recoverable as if it were levy due from him.

71(4) Sub-paragraph (3) does not have effect if, or to the extent that, the assessment in question has been withdrawn or reduced.

71(5) Where an assessment is made under this paragraph to an amount of interest under paragraph 70–

(a)   the notice of assessment shall specify a date, not later than the date of the notice of assessment, to which the amount of interest which is assessed is calculated; and

(b)   if the interest continues to accrue after that date, a further assessment or further assessments may be made under this paragraph in respect of the amounts so accruing.

71(6) Where–

(a)   an assessment to interest is made specifying a date for the purposes of sub-paragraph (5)(a), and

(b)   within such period as may for the purposes of this sub-paragraph have been notified by the Commissioners to the person liable for the interest, the amount on which the interest is payable is paid,

that amount shall be deemed for the purposes of any further liability to interest to have been paid on the specified date.

SUPPLEMENTARY ASSESSMENTS

72   If it appears to the Commissioners that the amount which ought to have been assessed in an assessment under paragraph 67, 68 or 71 exceeds the amount which was so assessed, then–

(a)   under the same paragraph as that assessment was made, and

(b)   on or before the last day on which that assessment could have been made,

the Commissioners may make a supplementary assessment of the amount of the excess and notify the person concerned accordingly.

SET-OFF OF OR AGAINST AMOUNTS DUE UNDER THIS SCHEDULE

73(1)   The Commissioners may by regulations make provision in relation to any case where–

(a)   a person is under a duty to pay to the Commissioners at any time an amount or amounts in respect of levy; and

(b)   the Commissioners are under a duty to pay to that person at the same time an amount or amounts in respect of levy or any of the other taxes under their care and management.

73(2)   Regulations under this paragraph may provide that if the total of the amount or amounts mentioned in sub-paragraph (1)(a) exceeds the total of the amount or amounts mentioned in sub-paragraph (1)(b), the latter shall be set off against the former.

73(3)   Regulations under this paragraph may provide that if the total of the amount or amounts mentioned in sub-paragraph (1)(b) exceeds the total of the amount or amounts mentioned in sub-paragraph (1)(a), the Commissioners may set off the latter in paying the former.

73(4)   Regulations under this paragraph may provide that if the total of the amount or amounts mentioned in sub-paragraph (1)(a) is the same as the total of the amount or amounts mentioned in sub-paragraph (1)(b) no payment need be made in respect of the former or the latter.

73(5)   Regulations under this paragraph may provide for any limitation on the time within which the Commissioners are entitled to take steps for recovering any amount due to them in respect of levy to be disregarded, in such cases as may be described in the regulations, in determining whether any person is under such a duty to pay as is mentioned in sub-paragraph (1)(a).

73(6)   Regulations under paragraph may include provision treating any duty to pay mentioned in sub-paragraph (1) as discharged accordingly.

73(7)   References in sub-paragraph (1) to an amount in respect of a particular tax include references not only to an amount of tax itself but also to other amounts such as interest and penalties that are or may be recovered as if they were amounts of tax.

73(8)   In this paragraph **"tax"** includes duty.

SET-OFF OF OR AGAINST OTHER TAXES AND DUTIES

74(1)   The Commissioners may by regulations make provision in relation to any case where–

(a)   a person is under a duty to pay to the Commissioners at any time an amount or amounts in respect of any tax (or taxes) under their care and management other than levy; and

(b)   the Commissioners are under a duty, at the same time, to make any repayment of levy to that person or to make any other payment to him of any amount or amounts in respect of levy.

74(2)   Regulations under this paragraph may provide that if the total of the amount or amounts mentioned in sub-paragraph (1)(a) exceeds the total of the amount or amounts mentioned in sub-paragraph (1)(b), the latter shall be set off against the former.

74(3)   Regulations under this paragraph may provide that if the total of the amount or amounts mentioned in sub-paragraph (1)(b) exceeds the total of the amount or amounts mentioned in sub-paragraph (1)(a), the Commissioners may set off the latter in paying the former.

74(4) Regulations under this paragraph may provide that if the total of the amount or amounts mentioned in sub-paragraph (1)(a) is the same as the total of the amount or amounts mentioned in sub-paragraph (1)(b) no payment need be made in respect of the former or the latter.

74(5) Regulations under this paragraph may provide for any limitation on the time within which the Commissioners are entitled to take steps for recovering any amount due to them in respect of any of the taxes under their care and management to be disregarded, in such cases as may be described in the regulations, in determining whether any person is under such a duty to pay as is mentioned in sub-paragraph (1)(a).

74(6) Regulations under this paragraph may include provision treating any duty to pay mentioned in sub-paragraph (1) as discharged accordingly.

74(7) References in sub-paragraph (1) to an amount in respect of a particular tax include references not only to an amount of tax itself but also to other amounts such as interest and penalties that are or may be recovered as if they were amounts of tax.

74(8) In this paragraph **"tax"** includes duty.

RESTRICTION ON POWERS TO PROVIDE FOR SET-OFF

75(1) Regulations made under paragraph 73 or 74 shall not require any such amount or amounts as are mentioned in sub-paragraph (1)(b) of that paragraph ("the credit") to be set against any such amount or amounts as are mentioned in sub-paragraph (1)(a) of that paragraph ("the debit") in any case where–

(a) an insolvency procedure has been applied to the person entitled to the credit;

(b) the credit became due after that procedure was so applied; and

(c) the liability to pay the debit either arose before that procedure was so applied or (having arisen afterwards) relates to, or to matters occurring in the course of, the carrying on of any business at times before the procedure was so applied.

75(2) For the purposes of this paragraph, an insolvency procedure is applied to a person if–

(a) a bankruptcy order, winding-up order or administration order is made in relation to that person or an award of sequestration is made on that person's estate;

(b) that person is put into administrative receivership;

(c) that person passes a resolution for voluntary winding up;

(d) any voluntary arrangement approved in accordance with–
(i) Part I or VIII of the Insolvency Act 1986, or
(ii) Part II or Chapter II of Part VIII of the Insolvency (Northern Ireland) Order 1989,
comes into force in relation to that person;

(e) a deed of arrangement registered in accordance with–
(i) the Deeds of Arrangement Act 1914, or
(ii) Chapter I of Part VIII of that Order,
takes effect in relation to that person;

(f) a person is appointed as the interim receiver of some or all of that person's property under section 286 of the Insolvency Act 1986 or Article 259 of the Insolvency (Northern Ireland) Order 1989;

(g) a person is appointed as the provisional liquidator in relation to that person under section 135 of that Act or Article 115 of that Order;

(h) an interim order is made under Part VIII of that Act, or Chapter II of Part VIII of that Order, in relation to that person; or

(i) that person's estate becomes vested in any other person as that person's trustee under a trust deed (within the meaning of the Bankruptcy (Scotland) Act 1985).

75(3) In this paragraph references, in relation to any person, to the application of an insolvency procedure to that person shall not include–

(a) the making of a bankruptcy order, winding-up order, administration order or award of sequestration at a time when any such arrangement or deed as is mentioned in paragraph (d), (e) or (i) of sub-paragraph (2) is in force in relation to that person;

(b) the making of a winding-up order at any of the following times, that is to say–
(i) immediately upon the discharge of an administration order made in relation to that person;
(ii) when that person is being wound up voluntarily;
(iii) when that person is in administrative receivership;
or

(c)   the making of an administration order in relation to that person at any time when that person is in administrative receivership.

75(4)   For the purposes of this paragraph a person shall be regarded as being in administrative receivership throughout any continuous period for which (disregarding any temporary vacancy in the office of receiver) there is an administrative receiver of that person.

75(5)   In this paragraph–

> **"administration order"** means an administration order under section 8 of the Insolvency Act 1986 or Article 21 of the Insolvency (Northern Ireland) Order 1989;
> **"administrative receiver"** means an administrative receiver within the meaning of section 251 of that Act or Article 5(1) of that Order.

PART VI: SUPPLEMENTAL PROVISIONS

76(1)   Any notification of an assessment under any provision of this Part of this Schedule to a person's representative shall be treated for the purposes of this Schedule as notification to the person in relation to whom the representative acts.

76(2)   In this paragraph **"representative"**, in relation to any person, means–

(a)   any of that person's personal representatives;
(b)   that person's trustee in bankruptcy or liquidator;
(c)   any person holding office as a receiver in relation to that person or any of his property;
(d)   that person's tax representative or any other person for the time being acting in a representative capacity in relation to that person.

76(3)   In this paragraph **"trustee in bankruptcy"** includes, as respects Scotland–

(a)   an interim or permanent trustee (within the meaning of the Bankruptcy (Scotland) Act 1985); and
(b)   a trustee acting under a trust deed (within the meaning of that Act).

76(4)   The powers conferred by paragraphs 73 and 74 are without prejudice to any power of the Commissioners to provide by tax credit regulations for any amount to be set against another.

Part VII – Recovery and Interest

RECOVERY OF LEVY AS DEBT DUE

77   Levy shall be recoverable as a debt due to the Crown.

ASSESSMENTS OF AMOUNTS OF LEVY DUE

78(1)   Where it appears to the Commissioners–

(a)   that any period is an accounting period by reference to which a person is liable to account for levy,
(b)   that any levy for which that person is liable to account by reference to that period has become due, and
(c)   that there has been a default by that person that falls within sub-paragraph (2),

they may assess the amount of levy due from that person for that period to the best of their judgement and notify that amount to that person.

78(2)   The defaults falling within this sub-paragraph are–

(a)   any failure to make a return required to be made by any provision made by or under this Schedule;
(b)   any failure to keep any documents necessary to verify returns required to be made under any such provision;
(c)   any failure to afford the facilities necessary to verify returns required to be made under any such provision;
(d)   the making, in purported compliance with any requirement of any such provision to make a return, of an incomplete or incorrect return;
(e)   any failure to comply with a requirement imposed by or under Part V of this Schedule (registration).

78(3)   Where it appears to the Commissioners that a default falling within sub-paragraph (2) is a default by a person on whom the requirement to make a return is imposed in his capacity as the representative of another person, sub-paragraph (1) shall apply as if the reference to the amount of levy due included a reference to any levy due from that other person.

78(4) In a case where–

(a) the Commissioners have made an assessment for any accounting period as a result of any person's failure to make a return for that period,

(b) the levy assessed has been paid but no proper return has been made for that period,

(c) as a result of a failure (whether by that person or a representative of his) to make a return for a later accounting period, the Commissioners find it necessary to make another assessment under this paragraph in relation to the later period, and

(d) the Commissioners think it appropriate to do so in the light of the absence of a proper return for the earlier period,

they may, in the assessment in relation to the later period, specify an amount of levy due that is greater than the amount that they would have considered to be appropriate had they had regard only to the later period.

78(5) Where an amount has been assessed and notified to any person under this paragraph, it shall be recoverable on the basis that it is an amount of levy due from him.

78(6) Sub-paragraph (5) does not have effect if, or to the extent that, the assessment in question has been withdrawn or reduced.

SUPPLEMENTARY ASSESSMENTS

79(1) If, where an assessment has been notified to any person under paragraph 78 or this paragraph, it appears to the Commissioners that the amount which ought to have been assessed as due for any accounting period exceeds the amount that has already been assessed, the Commissioners may make a supplementary assessment of the amount of the excess and notify that person accordingly.

79(2) Where an amount has been assessed and notified to any person under this paragraph it shall be recoverable on the basis that it is an amount of levy due from him.

79(3) Sub-paragraph (2) does not have effect if, or to the extent that, the assessment in question has been withdrawn or reduced.

TIME LIMITS FOR ASSESSMENTS

80(1) An assessment under paragraph 78 or 79 of an amount of levy due for any accounting period–

(a) shall not be made more than two years after the end of the accounting period unless it is made within the period mentioned in sub-paragraph (2); and

(b) subject to sub-paragraph (3), shall not in any event be made more than three years after the end of that accounting period.

80(2) The period referred to in sub-paragraph (1)(a) is the period of one year after evidence of facts sufficient in the Commissioners' opinion to justify the making of the assessment first came to their knowledge.

80(3) Subject to sub-paragraph (4), where levy has been lost–

(a) as a result of any conduct for which a person has been convicted of an offence involving fraud,

(b) in circumstances giving rise to liability to a penalty under paragraph 55 (failure to notify of registrability etc.), or

(c) as a result of conduct falling within paragraph 98(1) (evasion),

that levy may be assessed under paragraph 78 or 79 as if, in sub-paragraph (1)(b) above, for "three years" there were substituted "twenty years".

80(4) Where, after a person's death, the Commissioners propose to assess an amount of levy as due by reason of some conduct of the deceased–

(a) the assessment shall not be made more than three years after the death; and

(b) if the circumstances are as set out in sub-paragraph (3)–

(i) the modification of sub-paragraph (1) contained in that sub-paragraph shall not apply; but

(ii) any assessment which (applying that modification) could have been made immediately after the death may be made at any time within three years after it.

80(5)   Nothing in this paragraph shall prejudice the powers of the Commissioners under paragraph 78(4).

ORDINARY INTEREST ON OVERDUE LEVY PAID BEFORE ASSESSMENT

81(1)   Where–

(a)   the circumstances are such that an assessment could have been made under paragraph 78 or 79 of an amount of levy due from any person, but

(b)   before such an assessment was made and notified to that person that amount was paid (so that no such assessment was necessary),

the whole of the amount paid shall carry interest for the period specified in sub-paragraph (2).

81(2)   That period is the period which–

(a)   begins with the day after that on which the person is required in accordance with regulations under paragraph 41 to pay levy due from him for the accounting period to which the amount paid relates; and

(b)   ends with the day before that on which the amount is paid.

81(3)   Interest under this paragraph shall be payable at the rate applicable under section 197 of the Finance Act 1996.

PENALTY INTEREST ON UNPAID LEVY

82(1)   Where–

(a)   a person makes a return for the purposes of any regulations made under paragraph 41 (whether or not at the time required by the regulations), and

(b)   the return shows that an amount of levy is due from him for the accounting period for which the return is made,

that amount shall carry penalty interest for the period specified in sub-paragraph (2).

82(2)   That period is the period which–

(a)   begins with the day after that on which the person is required in accordance with regulations under paragraph 41 to pay levy due from him for the accounting period in question; and

(b)   ends with the day before that on which the amount shown in the return is paid.

PENALTY INTEREST ON LEVY WHERE NO RETURN MADE

83(1)   Where–

(a)   the Commissioners make an assessment under paragraph 78 or 79 of an amount of levy due from any person for any accounting period and notify it to him, and

(b)   the assessment is made at a time after the time by which a return is required by regulations under paragraph 41 to be made by that person for that accounting period and before any such return has been made,

that amount shall carry penalty interest for the period specified in sub-paragraph (2).

83(2)   That period is the period which–

(a)   begins with the day after that on which the person is required in accordance with regulations under paragraph 41 to pay levy due from him for the accounting period in question; and

(b)   ends with the day before that on which the assessed amount is paid.

83(3)   Where the person, after the assessment is made, makes for the purposes of any regulations under paragraph 41 a return for the accounting period in question, the assessed amount shall not carry penalty interest under this paragraph to the extent that that amount is shown in the return as an amount of levy due from him for that accounting period (and, accordingly, carries penalty interest under paragraph 82).

ORDINARY AND PENALTY INTEREST ON UNDER-DECLARED LEVY

84(1)   Subject to sub-paragraph (4), where–

(a)   the Commissioners make an assessment under paragraph 78 or 79 of an amount of levy due from any person for any accounting period and notify it to him,

(b)   the assessment is made after a return for the purposes of any regulations under paragraph 41 has been made by that person for that accounting period, and

(c)   the assessment is made on the basis that the amount ("the additional amount") is due from him in addition to any amount shown in the return, or in a previous assessment made in relation to the accounting period,

the additional amount shall carry interest for the period specified in sub-paragraph (2).

84(2)   That period is the period which–

(a)   begins with the day after that on which the person is required in accordance with regulations under paragraph 41 to pay levy due from him for the accounting period in question; and

(b)   ends with the day before the day on which the additional amount is paid.

84(3)   Interest under this paragraph–

(a)   in respect of so much of the period specified in sub-paragraph (2) as falls before the day on which the assessment is notified to the person in question, shall be payable at the rate applicable under section 197 of the Finance Act 1996 for the purposes of paragraph 81(3); and

(b)   in respect of the remainder (if any) of that period, shall be penalty interest.

84(4)   Where–

(a)   the Commissioners make an assessment under paragraph 78 or 79 of an amount of levy due from any person for any accounting period and notify it to him,

(b)   they also specify a date for the purposes of this sub-paragraph, and

(c)   the amount assessed is paid on or before that date,

the only interest carried by that amount under this paragraph shall be interest, at the rate given by sub-paragraph (3)(a), for the period before the day on which the assessment is notified.

PENALTY INTEREST ON UNPAID ORDINARY INTEREST

85(1)   Subject to sub-paragraph (2), where the Commissioners make an assessment under paragraph 88 of an amount of interest payable at the rate given by paragraph 81(3), that amount shall carry penalty interest for the period which–

(a)   begins with the day on which the assessment is notified to the person on whom the assessment is made; and

(b)   ends with the day before the day on which the assessed interest is paid.

85(2)   Where–

(a)   the Commissioners make an assessment under paragraph 88 of an amount of interest due from any person,

(b)   they also specify a date for the purposes of this sub-paragraph, and

(c)   the amount of interest assessed is paid on or before that date,

the amount paid before that date shall not carry penalty interest under this paragraph.

PENALTY INTEREST

86(1)   Penalty interest under any of paragraphs 82 to 85 shall be compound interest calculated–

(a)   at the penalty rate, and

(b)   with monthly rests.

86(2)   For this purpose the penalty rate is the rate found by–

(a)   taking the rate applicable under section 197 of the Finance Act 1996 for the purposes of paragraph 81(3); and

(b)   adding 10 percentage points to that rate.

86(3)   Where a person is liable under any of paragraphs 82 to 85 to pay any penalty interest, the Commissioners or, on appeal, an appeal tribunal may reduce the amount payable to such amount (including nil) as they think proper.

86(4)   Subject to sub-paragraph (5), where the person concerned satisfies the Commissioners or, on appeal, an appeal tribunal that there is a reasonable excuse for the conduct giving rise to the liability to pay penalty interest, that is a matter which (among other things) may be taken into account under sub-paragraph (3).

86(5)   In determining whether there is a reasonable excuse for the purposes of sub-paragraph (4), no account shall be taken of any of the following matters, that is to say–

(a)   the insufficiency of the funds available to any person for paying any levy due or for paying the amount of the interest;

(b)   the fact that there has, in the case in question or in that case taken with any other cases, been no or no significant loss of levy;

(c)   the fact that the person liable to pay the interest or a person acting on his behalf has acted in good faith.

86(6)   In the case of interest reduced by the Commissioners under sub-paragraph (3) an appeal tribunal, on an appeal relating to the interest, may cancel the whole or any part of the reduction made by the Commissioners.

SUPPLEMENTAL PROVISIONS ABOUT INTEREST

87(1)   Interest under any of paragraphs 81 to 85 shall be paid without any deduction of income tax.

87(2)   Sub-paragraph (3) applies where–

(a)   an amount carries interest under any of paragraphs 81 to 85 (or would do so apart from that sub-paragraph); and

(b)   all or part of the amount turns out not to be due.

87(3)   In such a case–

(a)   the amount or part that turns out not to be due shall not carry interest under the applicable paragraph and shall be treated as never having done so; and

(b)   all such adjustments as are reasonable shall be made, including (subject to paragraphs 64 to 76) adjustments by way of repayment.

ASSESSMENTS TO INTEREST

88(1)   Where a person is liable for interest under any of paragraphs 81 to 85, the Commissioners may assess the amount due by way of interest and notify it to him accordingly.

88(2)   If, where an assessment has been notified to any person under sub-paragraph (1) or this sub-paragraph, it appears to the Commissioners that the amount which ought to have been assessed exceeds the amount that has already been assessed, the Commissioners may make a supplementary assessment of the amount of the excess and shall notify that person accordingly.

88(3)   Where an amount has been assessed and notified to any person under this paragraph, it shall be recoverable as if it were levy due from him.

88(4)   Sub-paragraph (3)–

(a)   shall not apply so as to require any interest to be payable on interest except–

      (i) in accordance with paragraph 85, or

      (ii) in so far as it falls to be compounded in accordance with paragraph 86; and

(b)   shall not have effect if, or to the extent that, the assessment in question has been withdrawn or reduced.

88(5)   Paragraph 80 shall apply in relation to assessments under this paragraph as if any assessment to interest were an assessment under paragraph 78 to levy due for the period which is the relevant accounting period in relation to that interest.

88(6)   Subject to sub-paragraph (7), where a person–

(a)   is assessed under this paragraph to an amount due by way of any interest, and

(b)   is also assessed under paragraph 78 or 79 for the accounting period which is the relevant accounting period in relation to that interest,

the assessments may be combined and notified to him as one assessment.

88(7)   A notice of a combined assessment under sub-paragraph (6) must separately identify the interest being assessed.

88(8)   The relevant accounting period for the purposes of this paragraph is–

(a)   in the case of interest on levy due for any accounting period, that accounting period; and

(b)   in the case of interest on interest (whether under paragraph 85 or by virtue of any compounding under paragraph 86), the period which is the relevant accounting period for the interest on which the interest is payable.

88(9)   In a case where–

(a)   the amount of any interest falls to be calculated by reference to levy which was not paid at the time when it should have been, and

(b)   that levy cannot be readily attributed to any one or more accounting periods, that levy shall be treated for the purposes of interest on any of that levy as levy due for such period or periods as the Commissioners may determine to the best of their judgement and notify to the person liable.

FURTHER ASSESSMENTS TO PENALTY INTEREST

89(1) Where an assessment is made under paragraph 88 to an amount of penalty interest under any of paragraphs 82 to 85–

(a)   the notice of assessment shall specify a date, not later than the date of the notice of assessment, to which the amount of interest which is assessed is calculated; and

(b)   if the interest continues to accrue after that date, a further assessment or further assessments may be made under paragraph 88 in respect of the amounts so accruing.

89(2) Where–

(a)   an assessment to penalty interest is made specifying a date for the purposes of sub-paragraph (1)(a), and

(b)   within such period as may for the purposes of this sub-paragraph have been notified by the Commissioners to the person liable for the interest, the amount on which the interest is payable is paid,

that amount shall be deemed for the purposes of any further liability to interest to have been paid on the specified date.

WALKING POSSESSION AGREEMENTS

90(1) This paragraph applies where–

(a)   in accordance with regulations under section 51 of the Finance Act 1997 (enforcement by distress), a distress is authorised to be levied on the goods and chattels of a person ("the person in default") who has refused or neglected to pay an amount of levy due from him or an amount recoverable from him as if it were levy; and

(b)   the person levying the distress and the person in default have entered into a walking possession agreement.

90(2) For the purposes of this paragraph a walking possession agreement is an agreement under which, in consideration of the property distrained upon being allowed to remain in the custody of the person in default and of the delaying of its sale, the person in default–

(a)   acknowledges that the property specified in the agreement is under distraint and held in walking possession; and

(b)   undertakes that, except with the consent of the Commissioners and subject to such conditions as they may impose, he will not remove or allow the removal of any of the specified property from the premises named in the agreement.

90(3) Subject to sub-paragraph (4), if the person in default is in breach of the undertaking contained in a walking possession agreement, he shall be liable to a penalty equal to one half of the levy or other amount referred to in sub-paragraph (1)(a).

90(4) The person in default shall not be liable to a penalty under sub-paragraph (3) if he satisfies the Commissioners or, on appeal, an appeal tribunal that there is a reasonable excuse for the breach in question.

90(5) This paragraph does not extend to Scotland.

INTERPRETATION ETC. OF PART VII

91(1) In this Part of this Schedule **"penalty interest"** shall be construed in accordance with paragraph 86.

91(2) Any notification of an assessment under any provision of this Part of this Schedule to a person's representative shall be treated for the purposes of this Schedule as notification to the person in relation to whom the representative acts.

91(3) In this Part of this Schedule **"representative"**, in relation to any person, means–

(a)   any of that person's personal representatives;

(b)   that person's trustee in bankruptcy or liquidator;

(c)   any person holding office as a receiver in relation to that person or any of his property;

(d)   that person's tax representative or any other person for the time being acting in a representative capacity in relation to that person.

91(4) In this paragraph **"trustee in bankruptcy"** includes, as respects Scotland–

(a)   an interim or permanent trustee (within the meaning of the Bankruptcy (Scotland) Act 1985); and

(b)   a trustee acting under a trust deed (within the meaning of that Act).

Part VIII – Evasion, Misdeclaration and Neglect

CRIMINAL OFFENCES: EVASION

92(1) A person is guilty of an offence if he is knowingly concerned in, or in the taking of steps with a view to–

(a)   the fraudulent evasion by that person of any levy with which he is charged; or

(b)   the fraudulent evasion by any other person of any levy with which that other person is charged.

92(2) The references in sub-paragraph (1) to the evasion of levy include references to obtaining, in circumstances where there is no entitlement to it, either a tax credit or a repayment of levy.

92(3) A person guilty of an offence under this paragraph shall be liable (subject to sub-paragraph (4))–

(a)   on summary conviction, to a penalty of the statutory maximum or to imprisonment for a term not exceeding six months, or to both;

(b)   on conviction on indictment, to a penalty of any amount or to imprisonment for a term not exceeding seven years, or to both.

92(4) In the case of any offence under this paragraph, where the statutory maximum is less than three times the sum of the amounts of levy which are shown to be amounts that were or were intended to be evaded, the penalty on summary conviction shall be the amount equal to three times that sum (instead of the statutory maximum).

92(5) For the purposes of sub-paragraph (4) the amounts of levy that were or were intended to be evaded shall be taken to include–

(a)   the amount of any tax credit, and

(b)   the amount of any repayment of levy,

which was, or was intended to be, obtained in circumstances where there was no entitlement to it.

92(6) In determining for the purposes of sub-paragraph (4) how much levy (in addition to any amount falling within sub-paragraph (5)) was or was intended to be evaded, no account shall be taken of the extent (if any) to which any liability to levy of any person fell, or would have fallen, to be reduced by the amount of any tax credit or repayment of levy to which he was, or would have been, entitled.

CRIMINAL OFFENCES: MISSTATEMENTS

93(1) A person is guilty of an offence if, with the requisite intent and for purposes connected with the levy–

(a)   he produces or provides, or causes to be produced or provided, any document which is false in a material particular, or

(b)   he otherwise makes use of such a document;

and in this sub-paragraph **"the requisite intent"** means the intent to deceive any person or to secure that a machine will respond to the document as if it were a true document.

93(2) A person is guilty of an offence if, in providing any information under any provision made by or under this Schedule–

(a)   he makes a statement which he knows to be false in a material particular; or

(b)   he recklessly makes a statement which is false in a material particular.

93(3) A person guilty of an offence under this paragraph shall be liable (subject to sub-paragraph (4))–

(a)   on summary conviction, to a penalty of the statutory maximum or to imprisonment for a term not exceeding six months, or to both;

(b)   on conviction on indictment, to a penalty of any amount or to imprisonment for a term not exceeding seven years, or to both.

93(4)   In the case of any offence under this paragraph, where–

(a)   the document referred to in sub-paragraph (1) is a return required under any provision made by or under this Schedule, or

(b)   the information referred to in sub-paragraph (2) is contained in or otherwise relevant to such a return,

the amount of the penalty on summary conviction shall be whichever is the greater of the statutory maximum and the amount equal to three times the sum of the amounts (if any) by which the return understates any person's liability to levy.

93(5)   In sub-paragraph (4) the reference to the amount by which any person's liability to levy is understated shall be taken to be equal to the sum of–

(a)   the amount (if any) by which his gross liability was understated; and

(b)   the amount (if any) by which any entitlements of his to tax credits and repayments of levy were overstated.

93(6)   In sub-paragraph (5) **"gross liability"** means liability to levy before any deduction is made in respect of any entitlement to any tax credit or repayments of levy.

CRIMINAL OFFENCES: CONDUCT INVOLVING EVASIONS OR MISSTATEMENTS

94(1)   A person is guilty of an offence under this paragraph if his conduct during any particular period must have involved the commission by him of one or more offences under the preceding provisions of this Part of this Schedule.

94(2)   For the purposes of any proceedings for an offence under this paragraph it shall be immaterial whether the particulars of the offence or offences that must have been committed are known.

94(3)   A person guilty of an offence under this paragraph shall be liable (subject to sub-paragraph (4))–

(a)   on summary conviction, to a penalty of the statutory maximum or to imprisonment for a term not exceeding six months, or to both;

(b)   on conviction on indictment, to a penalty of any amount or to imprisonment for a term not exceeding seven years, or to both.

94(4)   In the case of any offence under this paragraph, where the statutory maximum is less than three times the sum of the amounts of levy which are shown to be amounts that were or were intended to be evaded by the conduct in question, the penalty on summary conviction shall be the amount equal to three times that sum (instead of the statutory maximum).

94(5)   For the purposes of sub-paragraph (4) the amounts of levy that were or were intended to be evaded by any conduct shall be taken to include–

(a)   the amount of any tax credit, and

(b)   the amount of any repayment of levy,

which was, or was intended to be, obtained in circumstances where there was no entitlement to it.

94(6)   In determining for the purposes of sub-paragraph (4) how much levy (in addition to any amount falling within sub-paragraph (5)) was or was intended to be evaded, no account shall be taken of the extent (if any) to which any liability to levy of any person fell, or would have fallen, to be reduced by the amount of any tax credit or repayments of levy to which he was, or would have been, entitled.

CRIMINAL OFFENCES: PREPARATIONS FOR EVASION

95(1)   Where a person–

(a)   becomes a party to any agreement under or by means of which a supply of a taxable commodity is or is to be made, or

(b)   makes arrangements for any other person to become a party to such an agreement,

he is guilty of an offence if he does so in the belief that levy chargeable on the supply will be evaded.

95(2)   Subject to sub-paragraph (3), a person guilty of an offence under this paragraph shall be liable, on summary conviction, to a penalty of level 5 on the standard scale.

95(3)   In the case of any offence under this paragraph, where level 5 on the standard scale is less than three times the sum of the amounts of levy which are shown to be amounts that were or were intended to be evaded in respect of the supply in question, the penalty shall be the amount equal to three times that sum (instead of level 5 on the standard scale).

95(4) For the purposes of sub-paragraph (3) the amounts of levy that were or were intended to be evaded shall be taken to include–

(a)   the amount of any tax credit, and

(b)   the amount of any repayment of levy,

which was, or was intended to be, obtained in circumstances where there was no entitlement to it.

95(5) In determining for the purposes of sub-paragraph (3) how much levy (in addition to any amount falling within sub-paragraph (4)) was or was intended to be evaded, no account shall be taken of the extent (if any) to which any liability to levy of any person fell, or would have fallen, to be reduced by the amount of any tax credit or repayments of levy to which he was, or would have been, entitled.

OFFENCES UNDER PARAGRAPHS 92 TO 95: PROCEDURAL MATTERS

96 Sections 145 to 155 of the Customs and Excise Management Act 1979 (proceedings for offences, mitigation of penalties and certain other matters) shall apply in relation to offences and penalties under paragraphs 92 to 95 as they apply in relation to offences and penalties under the customs and excise Acts.

ARREST FOR OFFENCES UNDER PARAGRAPHS 92 TO 94

97(1) Where an authorised person has reasonable grounds for suspecting that a fraud offence has been committed he may arrest anyone whom he has reasonable grounds for suspecting to be guilty of the offence.

97(2) In this paragraph–

    "authorised person" means any person acting under the authority of the Commissioners; and

    "a fraud offence" means an offence under any of paragraphs 92 to 94.

CIVIL PENALTIES: EVASION

98(1) Subject to sub-paragraph (5), where–

(a)   any person engages in any conduct for the purpose of evading levy, and

(b)   that conduct involves dishonesty (whether or not it is such as to give rise to criminal liability),

that person shall be liable to a penalty.

98(2) The amount of the penalty shall be–

(a)   equal to the amount of levy evaded, or (as the case may be) intended to be evaded, by the person's conduct if at the time of engaging in that conduct he was or was required to be registered for the purposes of the levy;

(b)   equal to twice that amount if at that time the person neither was nor was required to be registered for those purposes.

98(3) The references in sub-paragraph (1) to evading levy include references to obtaining, in circumstances where there is no entitlement to it, either–

(a)   a tax credit; or

(b)   a repayment of levy.

98(4) For the purposes of sub-paragraph (2) the amount of levy that was or was intended to be evaded by any conduct shall be taken to include–

(a)   the amount of any tax credit, and

(b)   the amount of any repayment of levy,

which was, or was intended to be, obtained in circumstances where there was no entitlement to it.

98(5) In determining for the purposes of sub-paragraph (2) how much levy (in addition to any amount falling within sub-paragraph (4)) was or was intended to be evaded, no account shall be taken of the extent (if any) to which any liability to levy of any person fell, or would have fallen, to be reduced by the amount of any tax credit or repayments of levy to which he was, or would have been, entitled.

98(6) Where, by reason of conduct falling within sub-paragraph (1), a person is convicted of an offence (whether under this Act or otherwise) that person shall not by reason of that conduct be liable also to a penalty under this paragraph.

LIABILITY OF DIRECTORS ETC. FOR PENALTIES UNDER PARAGRAPH 98

99(1) Where it appears to the Commissioners–

(a) that a body corporate is liable to a penalty under paragraph 98, and

(b) that the conduct giving rise to that penalty is, in whole or in part, attributable to the dishonesty of a person who is, or at the material time was, a director or managing officer of the body corporate (a "named officer"),

the Commissioners may serve a notice under this paragraph on the body corporate and on the named officer.

99(2) A notice under this paragraph shall state–

(a) the amount of the penalty referred to in sub-paragraph (1)(a) ("the basic penalty"), and

(b) that the Commissioners propose, in accordance with this paragraph, to recover from the named officer such portion of the basic penalty (which may be the whole of it) as is specified in the notice.

99(3) Where a notice is served under this paragraph, the portion of the basic penalty specified in the notice shall be recoverable from the named officer as if he were personally liable under paragraph 98 to a penalty which corresponds to that portion.

99(4) Where a notice is served under this paragraph–

(a) the amount which may be assessed under Part IX of this Schedule as the amount due by way of penalty from the body corporate shall be only so much (if any) of the basic penalty as is not assessed on and notified to a named officer; and

(b) the body corporate shall be treated as discharged from liability for so much of the basic penalty as is so assessed and notified.

99(5) Subject to the following provisions of this paragraph, the giving of a notice under this paragraph as such shall not be a decision which may be reviewed under paragraph 121.

99(6) Where a body corporate is assessed as mentioned in sub-paragraph (4)(a), the decisions of the Commissioners that may be reviewed in accordance with paragraph 121 shall include their decision–

(a) as to the liability of the body corporate to a penalty, and

(b) as to the amount of the basic penalty that is specified in the assessment;

and paragraphs 122 and 123 shall apply accordingly.

99(7) Where an assessment is made on a named officer by virtue of this paragraph, the decisions which may be reviewed under paragraph 121 at the request of the named officer shall include–

(a) the Commissioners' decisions in the case of the body corporate as to the matters mentioned in sub-paragraph (6)(a) and (b);

(b) their decision that the conduct of the body corporate referred to in sub-paragraph (1)(b) is, in whole or in part, attributable to the dishonesty of the named officer; and

(c) their decision as to the portion of the penalty which the Commissioners propose to recover from him;

and paragraphs 122 and 123 shall apply accordingly.

99(8) In this paragraph a **"managing officer"**, in relation to a body corporate, means–

(a) any manager, secretary or other similar officer of the body corporate; or

(b) any person purporting to act in any such capacity or as a director.

99(9) Where the affairs of a body corporate are managed by its members, this paragraph shall apply in relation to the conduct of a member in connection with his functions of management as if he were a director of the body corporate.

CIVIL PENALTIES: MISDECLARATION OR NEGLECT

100(1) Subject to sub-paragraphs (3) to (5), where for an accounting period–

(a) a return is made which understates a person's liability to levy or overstates his entitlement to any tax credit or repayment of levy, or

(b) at the end of the period of 30 days beginning on the date of the making of any assessment which understates a person's liability to levy, that person has not taken all such steps as are reasonable to draw the understatement to the attention of the Commissioners,

the person concerned shall be liable to a penalty equal to 5 per cent. of the amount of the understatement of liability or (as the case may be) overstatement of entitlement.

100(2) Where–

(a) a return for an accounting period–
   (i) overstates or understates to any extent a person's liability to levy, or
   (ii) understates or overstates to any extent his entitlement to any tax credits or repayments of levy,
   and
(b) that return is corrected–
   (i) in such circumstances as may be prescribed, and
   (ii) in accordance with such conditions as may be prescribed,
   by a return for a later accounting period which understates or overstates, to the corresponding extent, any liability or entitlement for the later period,

it shall be assumed for the purposes of this paragraph that the statement made by each such return is a correct statement for the accounting period to which the return relates.

100(3) Conduct falling within sub-paragraph (1) shall not give rise to liability to a penalty under this paragraph if the person concerned provides the Commissioners with full information with respect to the inaccuracy concerned–

(a) at a time when he has no reason to believe that enquiries are being made by the Commissioners into his affairs, so far as they relate to the levy; and
(b) in such form and manner as may be prescribed by regulations made by the Commissioners or specified by them in accordance with any such regulations.

100(4) Conduct falling within sub-paragraph (1) shall not give rise to liability to a penalty under this paragraph if the person concerned satisfies the Commissioners or, on appeal, an appeal tribunal that there is a reasonable excuse for his conduct.

100(5) Where, by reason of conduct falling within sub-paragraph (1)–

(a) a person is convicted of an offence (whether under this Act or otherwise), or
(b) a person is assessed to a penalty under paragraph 98,

that person shall not by reason of that conduct be liable also to a penalty under this paragraph.

CIVIL PENALTIES: INCORRECT NOTIFICATIONS ETC.

101(1) Where–

(a) a person gives a notification for the purposes of paragraph 11 in relation to any supply (or supplies) of a taxable commodity (or taxable commodities), and
(b) the notification is incorrect,

the person shall be liable to a penalty.

101(2) Where–

(a) a person gives, in relation to any supply (or supplies) of a taxable commodity (or taxable commodities) being made to him, to the supplier a certificate that the supply (or supplies) is (or are) to any extent–
   (i) for domestic or charity use,
   (ii) exempt under any of paragraphs 12, 13, 14, 18 and 21, or
   (iii) a half-rate supply (or half-rate supplies), and
(b) the certificate is incorrect,

the person shall be liable to a penalty.

101(3) The amount of the penalty to which a person is liable under sub-paragraph (1) or (2) shall be equal to 105 per cent. of the difference between–

(a) the amount of levy (which may be nil) that would have been chargeable on the supply (or supplies) if the notification or certificate had been correct, and
(b) the amount of levy actually chargeable.

101(4) The giving of a notification or certificate shall not give rise to a penalty under this paragraph if the person who gave it satisfies the Commissioners or, on appeal, an appeal tribunal that there is a reasonable excuse for his having given it.

101(5) Where by reason of giving a notification or certificate–

(a)   a person is convicted of an offence (whether under this Act or otherwise), or

(b)   a person is assessed to a penalty under paragraph 98,

that person shall not by reason of the giving of the notification or certificate be liable also to a penalty under this paragraph.

INTERPRETATION OF PART VIII

102(1)   References in this Part of this Schedule to obtaining a tax credit are references to bringing an amount into account as a tax credit for the purposes of levy on the basis that that amount is an amount which may be so brought into account in accordance with tax credit regulations.

102(2)   References in this Part of this Schedule to obtaining a repayment of levy are references to obtaining either–

(a)   the payment or repayment of any amount, or

(b)   the acknowledgement of a right to receive any amount,

on the basis that that amount is the amount of a repayment of levy to which there is an entitlement.

Part IX – Civil Penalties

PRELIMINARY

103(1)   In this Part of this Schedule **"civil penalty"** means any penalty liability to which–

(a)   is imposed by or under this Schedule, and

(b)   arises otherwise than in consequence of a person's conviction for a criminal offence.

103(2)   In this Part of this Schedule–

(a)   references to a person's being liable to a civil penalty include references to his being a person from whom the whole or any part of a civil penalty is recoverable by virtue of paragraph 99; and

(b)   references, in relation to a person from whom the whole or any part of a civil penalty is so recoverable, to the penalty to which he is liable are references to so much of the penalty as is recoverable from him.

103(3)   Any notification of an assessment under any provision of this Part of this Schedule to a person's representative shall be treated for the purposes of this Schedule as notification to the person in relation to whom the representative acts.

103(4)   In this paragraph **"representative"**, in relation to any person, means–

(a)   any of that person's personal representatives;

(b)   that person's trustee in bankruptcy or liquidator;

(c)   any person holding office as a receiver in relation to that person or any of his property;

(d)   that person's tax representative or any other person for the time being acting in a representative capacity in relation to that person.

103(5)   In this paragraph **"trustee in bankruptcy"** includes, as respects Scotland–

(a)   an interim or permanent trustee (within the meaning of the Bankruptcy (Scotland) Act 1985); and

(b)   a trustee acting under a trust deed (within the meaning of that Act).

REDUCTION OF PENALTIES

104(1)   Where a person is liable to a civil penalty–

(a)   the Commissioners or, on appeal, an appeal tribunal may reduce the penalty to such amount (including nil) as they think proper; but

(b)   on an appeal relating to any penalty reduced by the Commissioners, an appeal tribunal may cancel the whole or any part of the Commissioners' reduction.

104(2)   In determining whether a civil penalty should be, or should have been, reduced under sub-paragraph (1), no account shall be taken of any of the following matters, that is to say–

(a)   the insufficiency of the funds available to any person for paying any levy due or for paying the amount of the penalty;

(b)   the fact that there has, in the case in question or in that case taken with any other cases, been no or no significant loss of levy;

(c)   the fact that the person liable to the penalty or a person acting on his behalf has acted in good faith.

MATTERS NOT AMOUNTING TO REASONABLE EXCUSE

105 For the purposes of any provision made by or under this Schedule under which liability to a civil penalty does not arise in respect of conduct for which there is shown to be a reasonable excuse–

(a)   an insufficiency of funds available for paying any amount is not a reasonable excuse; and
(b)   where reliance has been placed on any other person to perform any task, neither the fact of that reliance nor any conduct of the person relied upon is a reasonable excuse.

ASSESSMENTS TO PENALTIES ETC.

106(1) Where a person is liable to a civil penalty, the Commissioners may assess the amount due by way of penalty and notify it to him accordingly.

106(2) If, where an assessment has been notified to any person under sub-paragraph (1) or this sub-paragraph, it appears to the Commissioners that the amount which ought to have been assessed exceeds the amount that has already been assessed, the Commissioners may make a supplementary assessment of the amount of the excess and shall notify that person accordingly.

106(3) The fact that any conduct giving rise to a civil penalty may have ceased before an assessment is made under this paragraph shall not affect the power of the Commissioners to make such an assessment.

106(4) Where an amount has been assessed and notified to any person under this paragraph, it shall be recoverable as if it were levy due from him.

106(5) Sub-paragraph (4)–

(a)   shall not apply so as to require any interest to be payable on a penalty otherwise than in accordance with this Part of this Schedule; and
(b)   shall not have effect if, or to the extent that, the assessment in question has been withdrawn or reduced.

106(6) Subject to sub-paragraph (7), where a person–

(a)   is assessed under this paragraph to an amount due by way of a penalty, and
(b)   is also assessed under any one or more provisions of Part VII of this Schedule for an accounting period to which the conduct attracting the penalty is referable,

the assessments may be combined and notified to him as one assessment.

106(7) A notice of a combined assessment under sub-paragraph (6) must separately identify the penalty being assessed.

106(8) The power to make an assessment under this paragraph is subject to paragraph 99(4).

FURTHER ASSESSMENTS TO DAILY PENALTIES

107(1) This paragraph applies where an assessment is made under paragraph 106 to an amount of a civil penalty to which any person is liable–

(a)   under paragraph 124(3) (failure to provide information); or
(b)   under paragraph 127(4) (failure to produce a document).

107(2) The notice of assessment shall specify a time, not later than the end of the day of the giving of the notice of assessment, to which the amount of any daily penalty is calculated.

107(3) For the purposes of sub-paragraph (2) **"daily penalty"** means–

(a)   in a case within sub-paragraph (1)(a), a penalty imposed by virtue of paragraph 124(3)(b); and
(b)   in a case within sub-paragraph (1)(b), a penalty imposed by virtue of paragraph 127(4)(b).

107(4) If further penalties accrue in respect of a continuing failure after that date to provide the information or, as the case may be, produce the document, a further assessment or further assessments may be made under paragraph 106 in respect of the amounts so accruing.

107(5) Where–

(a)   an assessment to a civil penalty is made specifying a date for the purposes of sub-paragraph (2), and
(b)   the failure in question is remedied within such period as may for the purposes of this sub-paragraph have been notified by the Commissioners to the person liable for the penalty,

the failure shall be deemed for the purposes of any further liability to civil penalties to have been remedied on the specified date.

TIME LIMITS ON PENALTY ASSESSMENTS

108(1)   Subject to sub-paragraphs (2) and (3), an assessment under paragraph 106 to a penalty shall not be made more than three years after the conduct to which the penalty relates.

108(2)   Subject to sub-paragraph (3), if levy has been lost–

(a)   as a result of any conduct for which a person has been convicted of an offence involving fraud,

(b)   in circumstances giving rise to liability to a penalty under paragraph 55 (failure to notify of registrability etc.), or

(c)   as a result of conduct falling within paragraph 98(1) (evasion),

an assessment may be made for any civil penalty relating to that conduct as if, in sub-paragraph (1), for "three years" there were substituted "twenty years".

108(3)   Where, after a person's death, the Commissioners propose to assess an amount of a civil penalty due by reason of some conduct of the deceased–

(a)   the assessment shall not be made more than three years after the death; and

(b)   if the circumstances are as set out in sub-paragraph (2)–

   (i)   the modification of sub-paragraph (1) contained in that sub-paragraph shall not apply; but

   (ii)   any assessment which (applying that modification) could have been made immediately after the death may be made at any time within three years after it.

PENALTY INTEREST ON UNPAID PENALTIES

109(1)   Subject to sub-paragraph (2), where the Commissioners make an assessment under paragraph 106 of any civil penalty to which a person is liable the amount of that penalty shall carry penalty interest for the period which–

(a)   begins with the day on which the assessment is notified to the person on whom the assessment is made; and

(b)   ends with the day before the day on which the assessed penalty is paid.

109(2)   Where–

(a)   the Commissioners make an assessment under paragraph 106 of an amount of any civil penalty to which any person is liable,

(b)   they also specify a date for the purposes of this sub-paragraph, and

(c)   the amount of the penalty assessed is paid on or before that date,

the amount paid before that date shall not carry penalty interest under this paragraph.

109(3)   Penalty interest under this paragraph shall be compound interest calculated–

(a)   at the penalty rate, and

(b)   with monthly rests.

109(4)   For this purpose the penalty rate is the rate found by–

(a)   taking the rate applicable under section 197 of the Finance Act 1996 for the purposes of paragraph 81(3); and

(b)   adding 10 percentage points to that rate.

109(5)   Where a person is liable under this paragraph to pay any penalty interest, the Commissioners or, on appeal, an appeal tribunal may reduce the amount payable to such amount (including nil) as they think proper.

109(6)   Subject to sub-paragraph (7), where the person concerned satisfies the Commissioners or, on appeal, an appeal tribunal that there is a reasonable excuse for the conduct giving rise to the liability to pay penalty interest, that is a matter which (among other things) may be taken into account under sub-paragraph (5).

109(7)   In determining whether there is a reasonable excuse for the purposes of sub-paragraph (6), no account shall be taken of any of the following matters, that is to say–

(a)   the insufficiency of the funds available to any person for paying any levy or penalty due or for paying the amount of the interest;

(b)   the fact that there has, in the case in question or in that case taken with any other cases, been no or no significant loss of levy;

(c)   the fact that the person liable to pay the interest or a person acting on his behalf has acted in good faith.

109(8)   In the case of interest reduced by the Commissioners under sub-paragraph (5), an appeal tribunal, on an appeal relating to the interest, may cancel the whole or any part of the reduction made by the Commissioners.

SUPPLEMENTAL PROVISIONS ABOUT INTEREST

110(1)   Interest under paragraph 109 shall be paid without any deduction of income tax.

110(2)   Sub-paragraph (3) applies where–

(a)   an amount carries interest under paragraph 109 (or would do so apart from that sub-paragraph); and

(b)   all or part of the amount turns out not to be due.

110(3)   In such a case–

(a)   the amount or part that turns out not to be due shall not carry interest under paragraph 109 and shall be treated as never having done so; and

(b)   all such adjustments as are reasonable shall be made, including (subject to paragraphs 64 to 76) adjustments by way of repayment.

ASSESSMENTS TO PENALTY INTEREST ON UNPAID PENALTIES

111(1)   Where a person is liable for interest under paragraph 109, the Commissioners may assess the amount due by way of interest and notify it to him accordingly.

111(2)   If, where an assessment has been notified to any person under sub-paragraph (1) or this sub-paragraph, it appears to the Commissioners that the amount which ought to have been assessed exceeds the amount that has already been assessed, the Commissioners may make a supplementary assessment of the amount of the excess and notify that person accordingly.

111(3)   Where an amount has been assessed and notified to any person under this paragraph, it shall be recoverable as if it were levy due from him.

111(4)   Sub-paragraph (3)–

(a)   shall not apply so as to require any interest to be payable on interest (except in so far as it falls to be compounded in accordance with paragraph 109(3)); and

(b)   shall not have effect if, or to the extent that, the assessment in question has been withdrawn or reduced.

111(5)   Paragraph 108 shall apply in relation to assessments under paragraph as if any assessment to interest on a penalty were an assessment under paragraph 106 to the penalty in question.

111(6)   Subject to sub-paragraph (7), where a person–

(a)   is assessed under this paragraph to an amount due by way of any interest on a penalty, and

(b)   is also assessed under any one or more provisions of Part VII of this Schedule for the accounting period to which the conduct attracting the penalty is referable,

the assessments may be combined and notified to him as one assessment.

111(7)   A notice of a combined assessment under sub-paragraph (6) must separately identify the interest being assessed.

FURTHER ASSESSMENTS TO INTEREST ON PENALTIES

112(1)   Where an assessment is made under paragraph 111 to an amount of penalty interest under paragraph 111–

(a)   the notice of assessment shall specify a date, not later than the date of the notice of assessment, to which the amount of interest which is assessed is calculated; and

(b)   if the interest continues to accrue after that date, a further assessment or further assessments may be made under paragraph 111 in respect of the amounts so accruing.

112(2)   Where–

(a)   an assessment to penalty interest is made specifying a date for the purposes of sub-paragraph (1)(a), and

(b)   within such period as may for the purposes of this sub-paragraph have been notified by the Commissioners to the person liable for the interest, the amount on which the interest is payable is paid, that amount shall be deemed for the purposes of any further liability to interest to have been paid on the specified date.

UP-RATING OF AMOUNTS OF PENALTIES

113(1) If it appears to the Treasury that there has been a change in the value of money since the time when the amount of a civil penalty provided for by this Schedule was fixed, they may by regulations substitute, for the amount for the time being specified as the amount of that penalty, such other sum as appears to them to be justified by the change.

113(2) In sub-paragraph (1) the reference to the time when the amount of a civil penalty was fixed is a reference–

(a)   in the case of a penalty which has not previously been modified under that sub-paragraph, to the time of the passing of this Act; and

(b)   in any other case, to the time of the making of the regulations under that sub-paragraph that made the most recent modification of the amount of that penalty.

113(3) Regulations under sub-paragraph (1) shall not apply to the penalty for any conduct before the coming into force of the regulations.

Part X – Non-Residents, Groups and Other Special Cases

NON-RESIDENT TAXPAYERS: APPOINTMENT OF TAX REPRESENTATIVES

114(1) The Commissioners may by regulations make provision for securing that every non-resident taxpayer has a person resident in the United Kingdom to act as his tax representative for the purposes of the levy.

114(2) Regulations under this paragraph may, in particular, contain any or all of the following–

(a)   provision requiring notification to be given to the Commissioners where a person becomes a non-resident taxpayer;

(b)   provision requiring the appointment of tax representatives by non-resident taxpayers;

(c)   provision for the appointment of a person as a tax representative to take effect only where the person appointed is approved by the Commissioners;

(d)   provision authorising the Commissioners to give a direction requiring the replacement of a tax representative;

(e)   provision authorising the Commissioners to give a direction requiring a person specified in the direction to be treated as the appointed tax representative of a non-resident taxpayer so specified;

(f)   provision about the circumstances in which a person ceases to be a tax representative and about the withdrawal by the Commissioners of their approval of a tax representative;

(g)   provision enabling a tax representative to act on behalf of the person for whom he is the tax representative through an agent of the representative;

(h)   provision for the purposes of any provision made by virtue of paragraphs (a) to (g) regulating the procedure to be followed in any case and imposing requirements as to the information and other particulars to be provided to the Commissioners;

(i)   provision as to the time at which things done under or for the purposes of the regulations are to take effect.

114(3) Subject to sub-paragraph (4), a person who–

(a)   becomes subject, in accordance with any regulations under this paragraph, to an obligation to request the Commissioners' approval for any person's appointment as his tax representative, but

(b)   fails (with or without making the appointment) to make the request as required by the *regulations*,

shall be liable to a penalty of £10,000.

114(4) A failure such as is mentioned in sub-paragraph (3) shall not give rise to liability to a penalty under this paragraph if the person concerned satisfies the Commissioners or, on appeal, an appeal tribunal that there is a reasonable excuse for the failure.

EFFECT OF APPOINTMENT OF TAX REPRESENTATIVES

115(1)   The tax representative of a non-resident taxpayer shall be entitled to act on the non-resident taxpayer's behalf for the purposes of any provision made by or under this Schedule.

115(2)   The tax representative of a non-resident taxpayer shall be under a duty, except to such extent as the Commissioners by regulations otherwise provide, to secure the non-resident taxpayer's compliance with, and discharge of, the obligations and liabilities to which the non-resident taxpayer is subject by virtue of any provision made by or under this Schedule (including obligations and liabilities arising or incurred before he became the non-resident taxpayer's tax representative).

115(3)   A person who is or has been the tax representative of a non-resident taxpayer shall be personally liable–

(a)   in respect of any failure while he is or was the non-resident taxpayer's tax representative to secure compliance with, or the discharge of, any obligation or liability to which sub-paragraph (2) applies, and

(b)   in respect of anything done in the course of, or for purposes connected with, acting on the non-resident taxpayer's behalf,

as if the obligations and liabilities to which sub-paragraph (2) applies were imposed jointly and severally on the tax representative and the non-resident taxpayer.

115(4)   A tax representative shall not be liable by virtue of this paragraph to be registered for the purposes of the levy; but the Commissioners may by regulations–

(a)   require the names of tax representatives to be registered against the names of the non-resident taxpayers of whom they are the representatives;

(b)   make provision for the deletion of the names so registered of persons who cease to be tax representatives.

115(5)   A tax representative shall not by virtue of this paragraph be guilty of any offence except in so far as–

(a)   he has consented to, or connived in, the commission of the offence by the non-resident taxpayer;

(b)   the commission of the offence by the non-resident taxpayer is attributable to any neglect on the part of the tax representative; or

(c)   the offence consists in a contravention by the tax representative of an obligation which, by virtue of this paragraph, is imposed both on the tax representative and on the non-resident taxpayer.

GROUPS OF COMPANIES ETC.

116(1)   The Commissioners may make provision by regulations for two or more bodies corporate to be treated as members of a group for the purposes of the Schedule.

116(2)   Regulations under sub-paragraph (1) may, in particular, make provision for or about–

(a)   eligibility for group treatment;

(b)   representative members of groups;

(c)   applications for, or the variation or ending of, group treatment;

(d)   the decisions to be made on applications;

(e)   the variation or ending of group treatment by notice given by the Commissioners otherwise than on an application;

(f)   treating a member of a group as charged with levy that would otherwise be levy with which another member of the group would be charged;

(g)   the members of a group liable for levy, or amounts recoverable as levy, due from a member of a group.

116(3)   The provision mentioned in sub-paragraph (2)(c) includes provision–

(a)   about the time within which applications are to be made,

(b)   for authorising the Commissioners to extend such time, and

(c)   for applications that seek group treatment, or its variation or ending, with effect from a time before they are made.

116(4)   The provision mentioned in sub-paragraph (2)(e) includes provision for a notice to have effect from a time before it is given.

116(5)   Regulations under sub-paragraph (1) may make provision for imposing requirements on a body corporate to notify the Commissioners of prescribed matters relating to group treatment.

116(6)   A body corporate which fails to comply with any such requirement imposed by such regulations shall be liable to a penalty of £250.

PARTNERSHIPS AND OTHER UNINCORPORATED BODIES

117(1)   The Commissioners may by regulations make provision for determining by what persons anything required to be done under this Schedule is to be done where, apart from those regulations, that requirement would fall on–

(a)   persons carrying on business in partnership; or

(b)   persons carrying on business together as an unincorporated body;

but any regulations under this sub-paragraph must be construed subject to the following provisions of this paragraph.

117(2)   In determining for the purposes of this Schedule who at any time is the person accountable for any levy in a case where, apart from this sub-paragraph, the persons accountable are persons carrying on any business–

(a)   in partnership, or

(b)   as an unincorporated body,

the firm or body shall be treated, for the purposes of that determination (and notwithstanding any changes from time to time in the members of the firm or body), as the same person and as separate from its members.

117(3)   Without prejudice to section 36 of the Partnership Act 1890 (rights of persons dealing with firm against apparent members of firm), where–

(a)   persons have been carrying on in partnership any business in the course or furtherance of which there has been done any thing that resulted in the firm becoming liable to account for any levy, and

(b)   a person ceases to be a member of the firm,

that person shall be regarded for the purposes of this Schedule (including sub-paragraph (7) below) as continuing to be a partner until the date on which the change in the partnership is notified to the Commissioners.

117(4)   Where a person ceases to be a member of a firm during an accounting period (or is treated as so ceasing by virtue of sub-paragraph (3)) any notice, whether of assessment or otherwise, which–

(a)   is served on the firm under or for the purposes of any provision made by or under this Schedule, and

(b)   relates to, or to any matter arising in, that period or any earlier period during the whole or part of which he was a member of the firm,

shall be treated as served also on him.

117(5)   Without prejudice to section 16 of the Partnership Act 1890 (notice to acting partner to be notice to the firm), any notice, whether of assessment or otherwise, which–

(a)   is addressed to a firm by the name in which it is registered, and

(b)   is served in accordance with this Schedule,

shall be treated for the purposes of this Schedule as served on the firm and, accordingly, where sub-paragraph (4) applies, as served also on the former partner.

117(6)   Subject to sub-paragraph (7), nothing in this paragraph shall affect the extent to which, under section 9 of the Partnership Act 1890 (liability of partners for debts of the firm), a partner is liable for levy owed by the firm.

117(7)   Where a person is a partner in a firm during part only of an accounting period, his personal liability for levy incurred by the firm in respect of taxable supplies made in that period shall include, but shall not exceed, such proportion of the firm's liability as may be just and reasonable in the circumstances.

DEATH AND INCAPACITY

118(1)   The Commissioners may, in accordance with sub-paragraph (2), by regulations make provision for the purposes of the levy in relation to cases where a person carries on a business of an individual who has died or become incapacitated.

118(2) The provisions that may be contained in regulations under this paragraph are–

(a) provision requiring the person who is carrying on the business to inform the Commissioners of the fact that he is carrying on the business and of the event that has led to his carrying it on;

(b) provision allowing that person to be treated for a limited time as if he and the person who has died or become incapacitated were the same person; and

(c) such other provision as the Commissioners think fit for securing continuity in the application of this Schedule where a person is so treated.

TRANSFER OF A BUSINESS AS A GOING CONCERN

119(1) The Commissioners may by regulations make provision for securing continuity in the application of this Schedule in cases where any business carried on by a person is transferred to another person as a going concern.

119(2) Regulations under this paragraph may, in particular, include any or all of the following–

(a) provision requiring the transferor to inform the Commissioners of the transfer;

(b) provision for liabilities and duties under this Schedule of the transferor to become, to such extent as may be provided by the regulations, liabilities and duties of the transferee;

(c) provision for any right of either of them to a tax credit or repayment of levy to be satisfied by allowing the credit or making the repayment to the other;

(d) provision as to the preservation of any records or accounts relating to the business which, by virtue of any regulations under paragraph 125, are required to be preserved for any period after the transfer.

119(3) Regulations under this paragraph may provide that no such provision as is mentioned in paragraph (b) or (c) of sub-paragraph (2) shall have effect in relation to any transferor and transferee unless an application for the purpose has been made by them under the regulations.

INSOLVENCY ETC.

120(1) The Commissioners may by regulations make provision in accordance with the following provisions of this paragraph for the application of this Schedule in cases in which an insolvency procedure is applied to a person or to a deceased individual's estate.

In this paragraph **"the relevant person"** means the person to whom, or the deceased individual to whose estate, the insolvency procedure is applied.

120(2) The provision that may be contained in regulations under this paragraph may include any or all of the following–

(a) provision requiring any such person as may be prescribed to give notification to the Commissioners, in the prescribed manner, of the prescribed particulars of any relevant matter;

(b) provision requiring a person to be treated, to the prescribed extent, as if he were the same person as the relevant person for the purposes of this Schedule or such of its provisions as may be prescribed; and

(c) provision for securing continuity in the application of any of the provisions of this Schedule where, by virtue of any regulations under this paragraph, any person is treated as if he were the same person as the relevant person.

120(3) In sub-paragraph (2) **"relevant matter"**, in relation to a case in which an insolvency procedure is applied to any person or to any deceased individual's estate, means–

(a) the application of that procedure to that person or estate;

(b) the appointment of any person for the purposes of the application of that procedure;

(c) any other matter relating to–

(i) the application of that procedure to the person to whom, or the estate to which, it is applied;

(ii) the holding of an appointment made for the purposes of that procedure; or

(iii) the exercise or discharge of any powers or duties conferred or imposed on any person by virtue of such an appointment.

120(4) Regulations made by virtue of sub-paragraph (2)(b) may include provision for a person to cease to be treated as if he were the same person as the relevant person on the occurrence of such an event as may be prescribed.

120(5) Regulations under this paragraph prescribing the manner in which any notification is to be given to the Commissioners may require it to be given in such manner and to contain such particulars as may be specified in a general notice published by the Commissioners in accordance with the regulations.

120(6) Regulations under this paragraph may provide that the extent to which, and the purposes for which, a person is to be treated under the regulations as if he were the same person as the relevant person may be determined by reference to a notice given in accordance with the regulations to the person so treated.

120(7) For the purposes of this paragraph, an insolvency procedure is applied to a person if–

(a)   a bankruptcy order, winding-up order or administration order is made in relation to that person or a partnership of which he is a member;

(b)   an award of sequestration is made on that person's estate or on the estate of a partnership of which he is a member;

(c)   that person is put into administrative receivership;

(d)   that person passes a resolution for voluntary winding up;

(e)   any voluntary arrangement approved in accordance with–
        (i) Part I or VIII of the Insolvency Act 1986, or
        (ii) Part II or Chapter II of Part VIII of the Insolvency (Northern Ireland) Order 1989,
        comes into force in relation to that person or a partnership of which that person is a member;

(f)   a deed of arrangement registered in accordance with–
        (i) the Deeds of Arrangement Act 1914, or
        (ii) Chapter I of Part VIII of that Order,
        takes effect in relation to that person;

(g)   a person is appointed as the receiver or manager of some or all of that person's property, or of income arising from some or all of his property;

(h)   a person is appointed as the interim receiver of some or all of that person's property under section 286 of the Insolvency Act 1986 or Article 259 of the Insolvency (Northern Ireland) Order 1989;

(i)   a person is appointed as the provisional liquidator in relation to that person under section 135 of that Act or Article 115 of that Order;

(j)   an interim order is made under Part VIII of that Act, or Chapter II of Part VIII of that Order, in relation to that person; or

(k)   that person's estate, or the estate of a partnership of which that person is a member, becomes vested in any other person as that person's, or the partnership's, trustee under a trust deed (within the meaning of the Bankruptcy (Scotland) Act 1985).

120(8) For the purposes of this paragraph, an insolvency procedure is applied to a deceased individual's estate if–

(a)   a bankruptcy order, or an order by some other name but corresponding to a bankruptcy order, is made after the individual's death in relation to his estate under provisions of–
        (i) the Insolvency Act 1986, or
        (ii) the Insolvency (Northern Ireland) Order 1989,
        as applied to the administration of the insolvent estates of deceased individuals; or

(b)   an award of sequestration is made on the individual's estate after the individual's death.

120(9) In sub-paragraph (7)–

(a)   **"administration order"** means an administration order under section 8 of the Insolvency Act 1986 or Article 21 of the Insolvency (Northern Ireland) Order 1989;

(b)   references to a member of a partnership include references to any person who is liable as a partner under section 14 of the Partnership Act 1890 (persons liable by "holding out").

Part XI – Review And Appeal

REVIEW OF COMMISSIONERS' DECISIONS

121(1) This paragraph applies to a decision of the Commissioners with respect to any of the following matters–

(a)   whether or not a person is charged in any case with an amount of levy;

(b)   the amount of levy charged in any case and the time when the charge is to be taken as having arisen;

(c)   the registration of any person for the purposes of the levy or the cancellation of any registration;

(d)   the person liable to pay the levy charged in any case, the amount of a person's liability to levy and the time by which he is required to pay an amount of levy;

(e)   whether to prepare a special utility scheme for a utility;

(f)   the imposition of a requirement on any person to give security, or further security, under paragraph 139 and the amount and manner of providing any security required under that paragraph;

(g)   whether or not liability to a penalty or to interest on any amount arises in any person's case under any provision made by or under this Schedule, and the amount of any such liability;

(h)   any matter the decision as to which is reviewable under this paragraph of this Part of this Schedule in accordance with paragraph 99(6) or (7);

(i)   the extent of any person's entitlement to any tax credit or to a repayment in respect of a tax credit and the extent of any liability of the Commissioners under this Schedule to pay interest on any amount;

(j)   whether or not any person is required to have a tax representative by virtue of any regulations under paragraph 114;

(k)   the giving, withdrawal or variation, for the purposes of any such regulations, of any approval or direction with respect to the person who is to act as another's tax representative;

(l)   the giving, withdrawal or variation of a utility direction under paragraph 151(1);

(m)   whether a body corporate is to be treated, or is to cease to be treated, as a member of a group, the times at which a body corporate is to be so treated and the body corporate which is, in relation to any time, to be the representative member for a group;

(n)   any matter not falling within the preceding paragraphs the decision with respect to which is contained in–

    (i)   an assessment under paragraph 78 or 79 in respect of an accounting period in relation to which any return required to be made by virtue of regulations under paragraph 41 has been made, or

    (ii) an assessment under any provision of this Schedule other than paragraph 78 or 79.

121(2)   Any person who is or will be affected by any decision to which this paragraph applies may by notice in writing to the Commissioners require them to review the decision.

121(3)   The Commissioners shall not be required under this paragraph to review any decision unless the notice requiring the review is given before the end of the period of forty-five days beginning with the day on which written notification of the decision, or of an assessment containing or giving effect to the decision, was first given to the person requiring the review.

121(4)   For the purposes of sub-paragraph (3) it shall be the duty of the Commissioners to give written notification of any decision to which this paragraph applies to any person who–

(a)   requests such a notification;

(b)   has not previously been given written notification of that decision; and

(c)   if given such a notification, will be entitled to require a review of the decision under this paragraph.

121(5)   A person shall be entitled to give a notice under this paragraph requiring a decision to be reviewed for a second or subsequent time only if–

(a)   the grounds on which he requires the further review are that the Commissioners did not, on any previous review, have the opportunity to consider certain facts or other matters; and

(b)   he does not, on the further review, require the Commissioners to consider any facts or matters which were considered on a previous review except in so far as they are relevant to any issue to which the facts or matters not previously considered relate.

121(6)   Where the Commissioners are required by a notice under this paragraph to review any decision, it shall be their duty to do so.

121(7)   On a review under this paragraph the Commissioners may (subject to sub-paragraph (9)) withdraw, vary or confirm the decision reviewed.

121(8)   Where–

(a)   it is the duty under this paragraph of the Commissioners to review any decision, and

(b)   they do not, within the period of forty-five days beginning with the day on which the review was required, give notice to the person requiring it of their determination on the review,

they shall be deemed to have confirmed the decision.

121(9)   Where the Commissioners decide, on a review under this paragraph, that a liability to a penalty or to an amount of interest arises, they shall not be entitled to modify the amount payable in respect of that liability except–

(a)   in exercise of a power conferred by paragraph 104(1) (penalties) or paragraph 70(6), 86(3) or 109(5) (penalty interest); or

(b)   for the purpose of making the amount payable conform to the amount of the liability imposed by this Schedule.

121(10)   This paragraph has effect subject to paragraph 99(5).

APPEALS AGAINST REVIEWED DECISIONS

122(1)   Subject to the following provisions of this paragraph, an appeal shall lie to an appeal tribunal with respect to any of the following decisions–

(a)   any decision by the Commissioners on a review under paragraph 121 (including a deemed confirmation under paragraph 121(8));

(b)   any decision by the Commissioners on any such review of a decision referred to in paragraph 121(1) as the Commissioners have agreed to undertake in consequence of a request made after the end of the period mentioned in paragraph 121(3).

122(2)   Where an appeal under this paragraph relates to a decision (whether or not contained in an assessment) that an amount of levy is due from any person, that appeal shall not be entertained unless–

(a)   the amount which the Commissioners have determined to be due has been paid or deposited with them; or

(b)   on being satisfied that the appellant would otherwise suffer hardship–
      (i) the Commissioners agree, or
      (ii) the appeal tribunal decide,
    that it should be entertained notwithstanding that that amount has not been so paid or deposited.

122(3)   On an appeal under this paragraph relating to a penalty under paragraph 98 (evasion), the burden of proof as to the matters specified in paragraphs (a) and (b) of sub-paragraph (1) of that paragraph shall lie upon the Commissioners.

DETERMINATIONS ON APPEAL

123(1)   Where, on an appeal under paragraph 122–

(a)   it is found that an assessment of the appellant made, confirmed or treated as confirmed by the Commissioners on a review under paragraph 121 ("the original assessment") is an assessment for an amount that is less than it ought to have been, and

(b)   the appeal tribunal give a direction specifying the correct amount,

the assessment shall have effect as an assessment of the amount specified in the direction and (without prejudice to any power under this Schedule to reduce the amount of interest payable on the amount of an assessment) as if it were an assessment notified to the appellant in that amount at the same time as the original assessment.

123(2)   On an appeal under paragraph 122, the powers of the appeal tribunal in relation to any decision of the Commissioners shall include a power, where the tribunal allow an appeal on the ground that the Commissioners could not reasonably have arrived at the decision, either–

(a)   to direct that the decision, so far as it remains in force, is to cease to have effect from such time as the tribunal may direct; or

(b)   to require the Commissioners to conduct, in accordance with the directions of the tribunal, a further review of the original decision.

123(3)   Where, on an appeal under paragraph 122, the appeal tribunal find that a liability to a penalty or to an amount of interest arises, the tribunal shall not give any direction for the modification of the amount payable in respect of that liability except–

(a)   in exercise of a power conferred on the tribunal by paragraph 104(1) (penalties) or paragraph 70(6) or (9), 86(3) or (6) or 109(5) or (8) (penalty interest); or

(b)   for the purpose of making the amount payable conform to the amount of the liability imposed by this Schedule.

123(4)   Where, on an appeal under paragraph 122, it is found that the whole or part of any amount paid or deposited in pursuance of paragraph 122(2) is not due, so much of that amount as is found not to be due shall be repaid with interest at such rate as the appeal tribunal may determine.

123(5)   Where, on an appeal under paragraph 122, it is found that the whole or part of any amount due to the appellant by way of any repayment in respect of a tax credit has not been paid, so much of that amount as is found not to have been paid shall be paid with interest at such rate as the appeal tribunal may determine.

123(6)   Where–

(a)   an appeal under paragraph 122 has been entertained notwithstanding that an amount determined by the Commissioners to be payable as levy has not been paid or deposited, and

(b)   it is found on the appeal that that amount is due,

the appeal tribunal may, if they think fit, direct that that amount shall be paid with interest at such rate as may be specified in the direction.

123(7)   Sections 85 and 87 of the Value Added Tax Act 1994 (settling of appeals by agreement and enforcement of certain decisions of tribunal) shall have effect as if–

(a)   the references to section 83 of that Act included references to paragraph 122; and

(b)   the references to value added tax included references to levy.

Part XII – Information and Evidence

PROVISION OF INFORMATION

124(1)   Every person involved (in whatever capacity) in making or receiving supplies of taxable commodities, or in any connected activities, shall provide the Commissioners with such information relating to the matters in which he is or has been involved as the Commissioners may reasonably require.

124(2)   Information required under sub-paragraph (1) shall be provided to the Commissioners within such period after being required, and in such form, as the Commissioners may reasonably require.

124(3)   Subject to sub-paragraphs (4) and (5) and to paragraph 107(5) (which relates to supplementary assessments of daily penalties), if a person fails to provide information which he is required to provide under this paragraph, he shall be liable–

(a)   to a penalty of £250; and

(b)   to a further penalty of £20 for every day after the last relevant date and before the day after that on which the required information is provided.

124(4)   Liability to a penalty specified in sub-paragraph (3) shall not arise if the person required to provide the information satisfies the Commissioners or, on appeal, an appeal tribunal–

(a)   in the case of the penalty under paragraph (a) of that sub-paragraph that there is a reasonable excuse–

    (i)   for the initial failure to provide the required information on or before the last relevant date; and

    (ii)   for every subsequent failure to provide it;

    and

(b)   in the case of any penalty under paragraph (b) of that sub-paragraph for any day, that there is a reasonable excuse for the failure to provide the information on or before that day.

124(5)   Where, by reason of any failure by any person to provide information required under this paragraph–

(a)   that person is convicted of an offence (whether under this Act or otherwise), or

(b)   that person is assessed to a penalty under paragraph 98 (penalty for evasion),

that person shall not by reason of that failure be liable also to a penalty under this paragraph.

124(6)   In this paragraph **"the last relevant date"** means the last day of the period within which the person in question was required to provide the information.

RECORDS

125(1)   The Commissioners may by regulations impose obligations to keep records on persons who are, or are required to be, registered.

125(2)   Regulations under this paragraph may be framed by reference to such records as may be stipulated in any notice published by the Commissioners in pursuance of the regulations and not withdrawn by a further notice.

125(3)   Regulations under this paragraph may–

(a)   require any records kept in pursuance of the regulations to be preserved for such period, not exceeding six years, as may be specified in the regulations;

(b)   authorise the Commissioners to direct that any such records need only be preserved for a shorter period than that specified in the regulations;

(c)   authorise a direction to be made so as to apply generally or in such cases as the Commissioners may stipulate.

125(4)   Any duty under regulations under this paragraph to preserve records may be discharged by the preservation of the information contained in them by such means as the Commissioners may approve.

125(5)   The Commissioners may, as a condition of approving under sub-paragraph (4) any means of preserving information contained in any records, impose such reasonable requirements as appear to them necessary for securing that the information will be as readily available to them as if the records themselves had been preserved.

125(6)   Subject to sub-paragraphs (7) and (8), a person who fails to preserve any record in compliance with–

(a)   any regulations under this paragraph, or

(b)   any notice, direction or requirement given or imposed under such regulations,

shall be liable to a penalty of £250.

125(7)   A failure such as is mentioned in sub-paragraph (6) shall not give rise to any penalty under that sub-paragraph if the person required to preserve the record satisfies the Commissioners or, on appeal, an appeal tribunal that there is a reasonable excuse for the failure.

125(8)   Where, by reason of any such failure by any person as is mentioned in sub-paragraph (6)–

(a)   that person is convicted of an offence (whether under this Act or otherwise), or

(b)   that person is assessed to a penalty under paragraph 98 (penalty for evasion),

that person shall not by reason of that failure be liable also to a penalty under this paragraph.

125(9)   The Commissioners may if they think fit at any time modify or withdraw any approval or requirement given or imposed for the purposes of this paragraph.

EVIDENCE OF RECORDS THAT ARE REQUIRED TO BE PRESERVED

126(1)   Subject to the following provisions of this paragraph, where any obligation to preserve records is discharged in accordance with paragraph 125(4), a copy of any document forming part of the records shall be admissible in evidence in any proceedings, whether civil or criminal, to the same extent as the records themselves.

126(2)   A statement contained in a document produced by a computer shall not by virtue of this paragraph be admissible in evidence–

(a)   in criminal proceedings in England and Wales, except in accordance with Part II of the Criminal Justice Act 1988;

(b)   in civil proceedings in Scotland, except in accordance with sections 5 and 6 of the Civil Evidence (Scotland) Act 1988;

(c)   in criminal proceedings in Scotland, except in accordance with Schedule 8 to the Criminal Procedure (Scotland) Act 1995;

(d)   in criminal proceedings in Northern Ireland, except in accordance with Part II of the Criminal Justice (Evidence, Etc.) (Northern Ireland) Order 1988.

PRODUCTION OF DOCUMENTS

127(1)   Every person involved (in whatever capacity) in making or receiving supplies of taxable commodities, or in any connected activities, shall upon demand made by an authorised person produce or cause to be produced for inspection by that person any documents relating to the matters in which he is or has been involved.

127(2)   Where, by virtue of sub-paragraph (1), an authorised person has power to require the production of any documents from any person—

(a)   he shall have the like power to require production of the documents concerned from any other person who appears to the authorised person to be in possession of them; and

(b)   the production of any document by that other person in pursuance of a requirement under this sub-paragraph shall be without prejudice to any lien claimed by that other person on that document.

127(3)   The documents mentioned in sub-paragraphs (1) and (2) shall be produced at such time and place as the authorised person may reasonably require.

127(4)   Subject to sub-paragraphs (5) and (6) and to paragraph 107(5) (which relates to supplementary assessments of daily penalties), if a person fails to produce any document which he is required to produce under this paragraph, he shall be liable—

(a)   to a penalty of £250; and

(b)   to a further penalty of £20 for every day after the last relevant date and before the day after that on which the document is produced.

127(5)   Liability to a penalty specified in sub-paragraph (4) shall not arise if the person required to produce the document in question satisfies the Commissioners or, on appeal, an appeal tribunal—

(a)   in the case of the penalty under paragraph (a) of that sub-paragraph, that there is a reasonable excuse—

    (i) for the initial failure to produce the document at the required time; and

    (ii) for every subsequent failure to produce it;

    and

(b)   in the case of any penalty under paragraph (b) of that sub-paragraph for any day, that there is a reasonable excuse for the failure to produce the document on or before that day.

127(6)   Where, by reason of any failure by any person to provide information required under this paragraph—

(a)   that person is convicted of an offence (whether under this Act or otherwise), or

(b)   that person is assessed to a penalty under paragraph 98 (penalty for evasion),

that person shall not by reason of that failure be liable also to a penalty under this paragraph.

127(7)   In this paragraph **"the last relevant date"** means the last day of the period within which the person in question was required to produce the document.

POWERS IN RELATION TO DOCUMENTS PRODUCED

128(1)   An authorised person may take copies of, or make extracts from, any document produced under paragraph 127.

128(2)   If it appears to him to be necessary to do so, an authorised person may, at a reasonable time and for a reasonable period, remove any document produced under paragraph 127.

128(3)   An authorised person who removes any document under sub-paragraph (2) shall, if requested to do so, provide a receipt for the document so removed.

128(4)   Where a lien is claimed on a document produced under paragraph 127(2), the removal of the document under sub-paragraph (2) shall not be regarded as breaking the lien.

128(5)   Where a document removed by an authorised person under sub-paragraph (2) is reasonably required for any purpose he shall, as soon as practicable, provide a copy of the document, free of charge, to the person by whom it was produced or caused to be produced.

128(6)   Where any documents removed under the powers conferred by this paragraph are lost or damaged, the Commissioners shall be liable to compensate their owner for any expenses reasonably incurred by him in replacing or repairing the documents.

ENTRY AND INSPECTION

129   For the purpose of exercising any powers under this Schedule, an authorised person may at any reasonable time enter and inspect premises used in connection with the carrying on of a business.

ENTRY AND SEARCH

130(1) Where–

(a)   a justice of the peace is satisfied on information on oath that there is reasonable ground for suspecting that a fraud offence which appears to be of a serious nature is being, has been or is about to be committed on any premises or that evidence of the commission of such an offence is to be found there, or

(b)   in Scotland a justice (within the meaning of section 307 of the Criminal Procedure (Scotland) Act 1995) is satisfied by evidence on oath as mentioned in paragraph (a),

he may issue a warrant in writing authorising any authorised person to enter those premises, if necessary by force, at any time within one month from the time of the issue of the warrant and to search them.

130(2) A person who enters the premises under the authority of the warrant may–

(a)   take with him such other persons as appear to him to be necessary;

(b)   seize and remove any such documents or other things at all found on the premises as he has reasonable cause to believe may be required as evidence for the purposes of proceedings in respect of a fraud offence which appears to him to be of a serious nature;

(c)   search, or cause to be searched, any person found on the premises whom he has reasonable cause to believe to be in possession of any documents or other things which may be so required.

130(3) Sub-paragraph (2) shall not authorise any person to be searched by a member of the opposite sex.

130(4) The powers conferred by a warrant under this paragraph shall not be exercisable–

(a)   by more than such number of authorised persons as may be specified in the warrant;

(b)   outside such periods of the day as may be so specified; or

(c)   if the warrant so provides, otherwise than in the presence of a constable in uniform.

130(5) An authorised person seeking to exercise the powers conferred by a warrant under this paragraph or, if there is more than one such authorised person, such one of them as is in charge of the search shall provide a copy of the warrant endorsed with his name as follows–

(a)   if the occupier of the premises concerned is present at the time the search is to begin, the copy shall be supplied to the occupier;

(b)   if at that time the occupier is not present but a person who appears to the authorised person to be in charge of the premises is present, the copy shall be supplied to that person;

(c)   if neither paragraph (a) nor paragraph (b) applies, the copy shall be left in a prominent place on the premises.

130(6) In this paragraph **"a fraud offence"** means an offence under any of paragraphs 92 to 94.

ORDER FOR ACCESS TO RECORDED INFORMATION ETC.

131(1) Where, on an application by an authorised person, a justice of the peace or, in Scotland, a justice (within the meaning of section 307 of the Criminal Procedure (Scotland) Act 1995) is satisfied that there are reasonable grounds for believing–

(a)   that an offence in connection with levy is being, has been or is about to be committed, and

(b)   that any recorded information (including any document of any nature at all) which may be required as evidence for the purpose of any proceedings in respect of such an offence is in the possession of any person,

he may make an order under this paragraph.

131(2) An order under this paragraph is an order that the person who appears to the justice to be in possession of the recorded information to which the application relates shall–

(a)   give an authorised person access to it, and

(b)   permit an authorised person to remove and take away any of it which he reasonably considers necessary,

not later than the end of the period of seven days beginning with the date of the order or the end of such longer period as the order may specify.

131(3) The reference in sub-paragraph (2)(a) to giving an authorised person access to the recorded information to which the application relates includes a reference to permitting the authorised person to take copies of it or to make extracts from it.

131(4)   Where the recorded information consists of information contained in a computer, an order under this paragraph shall have effect as an order to produce the information–

(a)   in a form in which it is visible and legible; and

(b)   if the authorised person wishes to remove it, in a form in which it can be removed.

131(5)   This paragraph is without prejudice to the preceding paragraphs of this Part of this Schedule.

REMOVAL OF DOCUMENTS ETC.

132(1)   An authorised person who removes anything in the exercise of a power conferred by or under paragraph 130 or 131 shall, if so requested by a person showing himself–

(a)   to be the occupier of premises from which it was removed, or

(b)   to have had custody or control of it immediately before the removal,

provide that person with a record of what he removed.

132(2)   The authorised person shall provide the record within a reasonable time from the making of the request for it.

132(3)   Subject to sub-paragraph (7), if a request for permission to be allowed access to anything which–

(a)   has been removed by an authorised person, and

(b)   is retained by the Commissioners for the purposes of investigating an offence,

is made to the officer in overall charge of the investigation by a person who had custody or control of the thing immediately before it was so removed, or by someone acting on behalf of such a person, the officer shall allow the person who made the request access to it under the supervision of an authorised person.

132(4)   Subject to sub-paragraph (7), if a request for a photograph or copy of any such thing is made to the officer in overall charge of the investigation by a person who had custody or control of the thing immediately before it was so removed, or by someone acting on behalf of such a person, the officer shall–

(a)   allow the person who made the request access to it under the supervision of an authorised person for the purpose of photographing it or copying it; or

(b)   photograph or copy it, or cause it to be photographed or copied.

132(5)   Subject to sub-paragraph (7), where anything is photographed or copied under sub-paragraph (4)(b), the officer shall supply the photograph or copy, or cause it to be supplied, to the person who made the request.

132(6)   The photograph or copy shall be supplied within a reasonable time from the making of the request.

132(7)   There is no duty under this paragraph to allow access to anything, or to supply a photograph or copy of anything, if the officer in overall charge of the investigation for the purposes of which it was removed has reasonable grounds for believing that to do so would prejudice–

(a)   that investigation;

(b)   the investigation of an offence other than the offence for the purposes of the investigation of which the thing was removed; or

(c)   any criminal proceedings which may be brought as a result of the investigation of which he is in charge or any such investigation as is mentioned in paragraph (b).

132(8)   Any reference in this paragraph to the officer in overall charge of the investigation is a reference to the person whose name and address are endorsed on the warrant concerned as being the officer so in charge.

ENFORCEMENT OF PARAGRAPH 132

133(1)   Where, on an application made as mentioned in sub-paragraph (2), the appropriate judicial authority is satisfied that a person has failed to comply with a requirement imposed by paragraph 132, the authority may order that person to comply with the requirement within such time and in such manner as may be specified in the order.

133(2)   An application under sub-paragraph (1) shall not be made except–

(a)   in the case of a failure to comply with any of the requirements imposed by paragraph 132(1) and (2)–

   (i) by the occupier of the premises from which the thing in question was removed, or

(ii) by the person who had custody or control of it immediately before it was so removed;

(b) in any other case, by the person who had such custody or control.

133(3) In this paragraph **"the appropriate judicial authority"** means–

(a) in England and Wales, a magistrates' court;

(b) in Scotland, the sheriff;

(c) in Northern Ireland, a court of summary jurisdiction, as defined in Article 2(2)(a) of the Magistrates' Courts (Northern Ireland) Order 1981.

133(4) In England and Wales and Northern Ireland, an application for an order under this paragraph shall be made by way of complaint; and sections 21 and 42(2) of the Interpretation Act (Northern Ireland) 1954 shall apply as if any reference in those provisions to any enactment included a reference to this paragraph.

POWER TO TAKE SAMPLES AND EXAMINE METERS

134(1) An authorised person, if it appears to him necessary for the protection of the revenue against mistake or fraud, may at any time take, from material which he has reasonable cause to believe is–

(a) a taxable commodity which is intended to be, is being or has been the subject of a taxable supply, or

(b) a product of the burning of a taxable commodity (other than electricity) which is being or has been the subject of a taxable supply,

such samples as he may require with a view to determining how the material ought to be treated, or to have been treated, for the purposes of the levy.

134(2) An authorised person, if it appears to him necessary for the protection of the revenue against mistake or fraud, may at any time examine any meter which he has reasonable cause to believe is intended to be, is being or has been used for ascertaining the quantity of any taxable commodity supplied by a taxable supply.

134(3) Any sample taken under sub-paragraph (1) shall be disposed of in such manner as the Commissioners may direct.

EVIDENCE BY CERTIFICATE

135(1) In any proceedings a certificate of the Commissioners–

(a) that a person was or was not at any time registered for the purposes of the levy,

(b) that any return required by regulations made under paragraph 41 has not been made or had not been made at any time,

(c) that any levy shown as due in a return made in pursuance of regulations made under paragraph 41 has not been paid, or

(d) that any amount shown as due in any assessment made under this Schedule has not been paid,

shall be evidence or, in Scotland, sufficient evidence of that fact.

135(2) A photograph of any document provided to the Commissioners for the purposes of this Schedule and certified by them to be such a photograph shall be admissible in any proceedings, whether civil or criminal, to the same extent as the document itself.

135(3) In any proceedings any document purporting to be a certificate under sub-paragraph (1) or (2) shall be taken to be such a certificate unless the contrary is shown.

INDUCEMENTS TO PROVIDE INFORMATION

136(1) This paragraph applies–

(a) to any criminal proceedings against a person in respect of an offence in connection with or in relation to levy; and

(b) to any proceedings against a person for the recovery of any sum due from him in connection with or in relation to levy.

136(2) Statements made or documents produced or provided by or on behalf of a person shall not be inadmissible in any proceedings to which this paragraph applies by reason only that–

(a) a matter falling within sub-paragraph (3) or (4) has been drawn to that person's attention; and

(b)   he was or may have been induced, as a result, to make the statements or to produce or provide the documents.

136(3)   The matters falling within this sub-paragraph are–

(a)   that, in relation to levy, the Commissioners may assess an amount due by way of a civil penalty instead of instituting criminal proceedings;

(b)   that it is the practice of the Commissioners (without giving any undertaking as to whether they will make such an assessment in any case) to be influenced by whether a person–

(i)   has made a full confession of any dishonest conduct to which he has been a party; and

(ii)   has otherwise co-operated to the full with any investigation.

136(4)   The matter falling within this sub-paragraph is the fact that the Commissioners or, on appeal, an appeal tribunal have power under any provision of this Schedule to reduce a penalty.

DISCLOSURE OF INFORMATION

137(1)   Notwithstanding any obligation not to disclose information that would otherwise apply, but subject to sub-paragraph (2), the Commissioners may disclose any information obtained or held by them in or in connection with the carrying out of their functions in relation to the levy to any of the following–

(a)   any Minister of the Crown;

(b)   the Scottish Ministers;

(c)   any Minister, within the meaning of the Northern Ireland Act 1998, or any Northern Ireland department;

(d)   the National Assembly for Wales;

(e)   the Environment Agency;

(f)   the Scottish Environment Protection Agency;

(g)   the Gas and Electricity Markets Authority;

(h)   the Director General of Electricity Supply for Northern Ireland;

(i)   the Director General of Gas for Northern Ireland;

(j)   an authorised officer of any person mentioned in paragraphs (a) to (i).

137(2)   Information shall not be disclosed under sub-paragraph (1) except for the purpose of assisting a person falling within paragraphs (a) to (j) of that sub-paragraph in the performance of his duties.

137(3)   Notwithstanding any such obligation as is mentioned in sub-paragraph (1), any person mentioned in sub-paragraph (1)(a) to (j) may disclose information–

(a)   to the Commissioners, or

(b)   to an authorised officer of the Commissioners,

for the purpose of assisting the Commissioners in the performance of duties in relation to the levy.

137(4)   Information that has been disclosed to a person by virtue of this paragraph shall not be disclosed by him except–

(a)   to another person to whom (instead of him) disclosure could by virtue of this paragraph have been made; or

(b)   for the purpose of any proceedings connected with the operation of any provision made by or under any enactment relating to the environment or to levy.

137(5)   References in the preceding provisions of this paragraph to an authorised officer of any person ("the principal") are to any person who has been designated by the principal as a person to and by whom information may be disclosed by virtue of this paragraph.

137(6)   Where the principal is a person falling within any of paragraphs (a) to (c) of sub-paragraph (1), the principal shall notify the Commissioners in writing of the name of any person designated by the principal for the purposes of this paragraph.

137(7)   No charge may be made for any disclosure made by virtue of this paragraph.

137(8)   In this paragraph **"enactment"** includes an enactment contained in an Act of the Scottish Parliament or in any Northern Ireland legislation.

MEANING OF "AUTHORISED PERSON"

138   In this Part of this Schedule **"authorised person"** means any person acting under the authority of the Commissioners.

Part XIII – Miscellaneous and Supplementary

SECURITY FOR LEVY

139(1)   Where it appears to the Commissioners necessary to do so for the protection of the revenue they may require any person who is or is required to be registered for the purposes of the levy to give security, or further security, for the payment of any levy which is or may become due from him.

139(2)   The power of the Commissioners to require any security, or further security, under this paragraph shall be a power to require security, or further security, of such amount and in such manner as they may determine.

139(3)   A person who is liable to account for the levy on a taxable supply that he makes is guilty of an offence if, at the time the supply is made–

(a)   he has been required to give security under this paragraph, and

(b)   he has not complied with that requirement.

139(4)   A person who is liable to account for the levy on a taxable supply that another person makes to him is guilty of an offence if he makes any arrangements for the making of the supply at a time when–

(a)   he has been required to give security under this paragraph, and

(b)   he has not complied with that requirement.

139(5)   A person guilty of an offence under this paragraph shall be liable, on summary conviction, to a penalty of level 5 on the standard scale.

139(6)   Sections 145 to 155 of the Customs and Excise Management Act 1979 (proceedings for offences, mitigation of penalties and certain other matters) shall apply in relation to an offence under this paragraph as they apply in relation to offences and penalties under the customs and excise Acts.

DESTINATION OF RECEIPTS

140   All money and securities for money collected or received for or on account of levy shall–

(a)   if collected or received in Great Britain, be placed to the general account of the Commissioners kept at the Bank of England under section 17 of the Customs and Excise Management Act 1979; and

(b)   if collected or received in Northern Ireland, be paid into the Consolidated Fund of the United Kingdom in such manner as the Treasury may direct.

PROVISIONAL COLLECTION OF LEVY

141(1)   Where–

(a)   by virtue of a resolution having effect under the Provisional Collection of Taxes Act 1968 (which is amended by Schedule 7 to this Act so as to apply in relation to levy), levy has been paid at a rate specified in the resolution on a supply of a taxable commodity, and

(b)   by virtue of section 1(6) or (7) or 5(3) of that Act, any of the levy paid is repayable in consequence of the restoration in relation to the supply of a lower rate,

the amount repayable shall be the difference between the levy paid on the supply at the rate specified in the resolution and the levy that would have been payable on a supply of the same quantity of the commodity at the lower rate.

141(2)   Where–

(a)   by virtue of a resolution having effect under that Act, levy is chargeable at a rate specified in the resolution on a supply of a taxable commodity, but

(b)   before the levy is paid it ceases to be chargeable at that rate in consequence of the restoration in relation to the supply of a lower rate,

the levy chargeable at the lower rate shall be charged by reference to the same quantity of the commodity as that by reference to which levy would have been chargeable at the rate specified in the resolution.

ADJUSTMENT OF CONTRACTS

142(1)   Sub-paragraph (2) applies in the case of a contract for the supply of a taxable commodity if–

(a)   the contract is entered into before 1st April 2001 (whether before or after the passing of this Act) or at a time when supplies such as are provided for by the contract are not taxable supplies, but

(b)   supplies falling to be made under the contract will be, or become or will become, taxable supplies.

142(2)   The supplier of the commodity may unilaterally vary the contract by adjusting the price chargeable for any supply made under the contract if he does so for the purpose of passing on, to the person liable to pay for the supply, the burden (or any part of the burden) of the levy for which the supplier is liable to account on the supply.

142(3)   Sub-paragraph (4) applies in the case of a contract for the supply of a taxable commodity if it provides (whether as a result of a variation under sub-paragraph (2) or otherwise) for the passing on, to the person liable to pay for the supply, of the burden (or any part of the burden) of any levy for which the supplier is liable to account on the supply.

142(4)   The supplier of the commodity may unilaterally vary the contract by adjusting the price chargeable for any supply made under the contract if he does so for the purpose of giving effect (to any extent) to–

(a)   any change in the rate at which levy is charged on the supply;

(b)   levy ceasing to be chargeable on the supply.

142(5)   The powers conferred by this paragraph are in addition to any contractual powers.

CLIMATE CHANGE LEVY ACCOUNTING DOCUMENTS

143(1)   Provision may be made by regulations requiring registered persons who make taxable supplies–

(a)   in prescribed cases, or

(b)   to persons of prescribed descriptions,

to provide the persons supplied with climate change levy accounting documents.

143(2)   For the purposes of this Schedule a **"climate change levy accounting document"** for a taxable supply is an invoice–

(a)   stating that it is a climate change levy accounting document (for which purpose the inclusion of the phrase "climate change levy accounting document" or the phrase "CCL accounting document", whether as shown here or with any of the letters shown here as small letters appearing as capitals, shall be sufficient),

(b)   stating the date on which it is issued, and

(c)   containing the required statements.

143(3)   For the purposes of sub-paragraph (2)(c) **"the required statements"** means–

(a)   in the case of a climate change levy accounting document issued under paragraph 27, the statements required by paragraph 27(5);

(b)   in the case of a climate change levy accounting document whose provision is required by regulations, statements of prescribed particulars of or relating to–

       (i)   the supply,

      (ii)   the persons by and to whom the supply is made, and

     (iii)   the levy chargeable.

143(4)   Where regulations make provision requiring a climate change levy accounting document to be provided in connection with any description of supply, regulations may make provision for–

(a)   requiring the accounting document to be provided within a prescribed time after, or at a prescribed time before, the supply is treated as taking place;

(b)   allowing an accounting document to be provided later than required by the regulations where it is provided in accordance with general or special directions given by the Commissioners.

143(5)   Regulations may make provision conferring power on the Commissioners to allow the requirements of any regulations as to the statements to be contained in a climate change levy accounting document to be relaxed or dispensed with.

143(6)   Regulations may make provision for allowing a climate change levy accounting document required to be issued under paragraph 27 to be issued later than the time applicable under paragraph 27(2) where it is issued in accordance with general or special directions given by the Commissioners.

143(7)   In this paragraph **"regulations"** means regulations made by the Commissioners.

SERVICE OF NOTICES ETC.

144(1) Any notice, notification or requirement that is to be or may be served on, given to or imposed on any person for the purposes of any provision made by or under this Schedule may be served, given or imposed by sending it to that person or his tax representative by post in a letter addressed to that person or his representative at the latest or usual residence or place of business of that person or representative.

144(2) Any direction required or authorised by or under this Schedule to be given by the Commissioners may be given by sending it by post in a letter addressed to each person affected by it at his latest or usual residence or place of business.

VARIATION AND WITHDRAWAL OF DIRECTIONS ETC.

145 Any direction, notice or notification required or authorised by or under this Schedule to be given by the Commissioners may be withdrawn or varied by them by a direction, notice or notification given in the same manner as the one withdrawn or varied.

REGULATIONS AND ORDERS

146(1) Any power under this Schedule to make regulations shall be exercisable by statutory instrument.

146(2) A statutory instrument that—

(a)   contains regulations made under this Schedule, and

(b)   is not subject to a requirement that a draft of the instrument be laid before Parliament and approved by a resolution of the House of Commons,

shall be subject to annulment in pursuance of a resolution of the House of Commons.

146(3) A statutory instrument that contains (whether alone or with other provisions) regulations under paragraph 3(3), 14(3), 15(4)(a), 16, 18(2), 52, 113(1), 148(4) or 149 or 151(2) (regulations made by the Treasury) shall not be made unless a draft of the statutory instrument containing the regulations has been laid before Parliament and approved by a resolution of the House of Commons.

146(4) Where regulations under this Schedule made by the Commissioners impose a relevant requirement on any person, they may provide that if the person fails to comply with the requirement he shall be liable, subject to sub-paragraph (5), to a penalty of £250.

146(5) Where by reason of any conduct—

(a)   a person is convicted of an offence (whether under this Act or otherwise), or

(b)   a person is assessed to a penalty under paragraph 98,

that person shall not by reason of that conduct be liable also to a penalty under any regulations under this Schedule.

146(6) In sub-paragraph (4) **"relevant requirement"** means any requirement other than one the penalty for a contravention of which is specified in paragraph 41(3), 114(3) or 125(6).

146(7) A power under this Schedule to make any provision by regulations—

(a)   may be exercised so as to apply the provision only in such cases as may be described in the regulations;

(b)   may be exercised so as to make different provision for different cases or descriptions of case; and

(c)   shall include power by the regulations to make such supplementary, incidental, consequential or transitional provision as the authority making the regulations may think fit.

Part XIV – Interpretation

GENERAL

147 *In this Schedule—*

"**accounting period**" means a period which, in pursuance of any regulations under paragraph 41, is an accounting period for the purposes of the levy;

"**agreement**" includes any arrangement or understanding (whether or not legally enforceable), and cognate expressions shall be construed accordingly;

"**appeal tribunal**" means a VAT and duties tribunal;

"**auto-generator**" has the meaning given by paragraph 152;

"**climate change agreement**" has the meaning given by paragraph 46;

"**climate change levy accounting document**" has the meaning given by paragraph 143(2);

"**combined heat and power station**" has the meaning given by paragraph 148(1);

"**the Commissioners**" means the Commissioners of Customs and Excise;

"**conduct**" includes acts and omissions;

"**electricity utility**" has the meaning given by paragraph 150(2) (but see paragraph 148(4));

"**fully exempt combined heat and power station**" has the meaning given by paragraph 150(2);

"**gas utility**" has the meaning given by paragraph 150(3) (but see paragraph 150(4));

"**half-rate supply**" has the meaning given by paragraph 43(1);

"**member**", in relation to a group, shall be construed in accordance with regulations under paragraph 116;

"**non-resident taxpayer**" means a person who–

(a)   is or is required to be registered for the purposes of the levy, and

(b)   is not resident in the United Kingdom;

"**partly exempt combined heat and power station**" has the meaning given by paragraph 148(3);

"**prescribed**" (except in paragraphs 14(3), 16(3) and 148(4)) means prescribed by regulations made by the Commissioners under this Schedule;

"**produced**"–

(a)   in relation to electricity, means generated, and

(b)   in relation to any other commodity, includes extracted;

"**reduced-rate supply**" has the meaning given by paragraph 44(3) (which, by virtue of paragraph 44(4), has effect subject to paragraph 45);

"**registered**" means registered in the register maintained under paragraph 53(2);

"**representative member**", in relation to a group, shall be construed in accordance with regulations under paragraph 116;

"**resident in the United Kingdom**" has the meaning given by paragraph 156;

"**ship**" includes hovercraft;

"**special utility scheme**" has the meaning given by paragraph 29(1);

"**subordinate legislation**" has the same meaning as in the Interpretation Act 1978;

"**supply for charity use**" shall be construed in accordance with paragraph 8;

"**supply for domestic use**" shall be construed in accordance with paragraphs 8 and 9;

"**tax credit**" means a tax credit for which provision is made by tax credit regulations;

"**tax credit regulations**" means regulations under paragraph 62;

"**tax representative**", in relation to any person, means the person who, in accordance with any regulations under paragraph 114, is for the time being that person's tax representative for the purposes of the levy;

"**taxable commodity**" shall be construed in accordance with paragraph 3;

"**taxable supply**" shall be construed in accordance with paragraphs 2(2) and 4;

"**the United Kingdom**" includes the territorial waters adjacent to any part of the United Kingdom;

"**utility**" has the meaning given by paragraph 150(1).

MEANING OF "COMBINED HEAT AND POWER STATION" ETC.

148(1)   In this Schedule "**combined heat and power station**" means a station producing electricity or motive power that is (or may be) operated for purposes including the supply to any premises of–

(a)   heat produced in association with electricity or motive power, or

(b)   steam produced from, or air or water heated by, such heat.

148(2)   In this Schedule "**fully exempt combined heat and power station**" means a combined heat and power station in respect of which there is in force a certificate (a "full-exemption certificate")–

(a)   given by the Secretary of State,

(b)   stating that the station is a fully exempt combined heat and power station for the purposes of the levy, and

(c)   complying with sub-paragraph (6) and (so far as applicable) any provision made by regulations under sub-paragraph (10).

148(3) In this Schedule **"partly exempt combined heat and power station"** means a combined heat and power station in respect of which there is in force a certificate (a "part-exemption certificate")–

(a)   given by the Secretary of State,

(b)   stating that the station is a partly exempt combined heat and power station for the purposes of the levy, and

(c)   complying with sub-paragraph (6) and (so far as applicable) any provision made by regulations under sub-paragraph (10).

148(4) The Secretary of State shall give a full-exemption certificate in respect of a combined heat and power station where–

(a)   an application is made for a certificate under this paragraph in respect of the station, and

(b)   it appears to him that such conditions as may be prescribed are satisfied in relation to the station.

For this purpose **"prescribed"** means prescribed by regulations made by the Treasury.

148(5) The Secretary of State shall give a part-exemption certificate in respect of a combined heat and power station where–

(a)   an application is made for a certificate under this paragraph in respect of the station, and

(b)   his decision on the application is to refuse to give a full-exemption certificate.

148(6) A full-exemption or part-exemption certificate given in respect of a combined heat and power station shall state the percentage that, for the purposes of paragraph 15, is the efficiency percentage for the station determined in accordance with any regulations under paragraph 149.

148(7) In prescribing conditions under sub-paragraph (4), the Treasury must have regard to the object of securing that a combined heat and power station will only be a fully exempt combined heat and power station for the purposes of this Schedule if it is one in which electricity or motive power is produced concurrently with heat in a manner that makes efficient use of the commodities used in their production.

148(8) A condition prescribed under sub-paragraph (4) may, in particular, relate to any of the following–

(a)   a station's outputs;

(b)   the commodities used in the production of such outputs;

(c)   the methods of producing such outputs;

(d)   the efficiency with which such outputs are produced.

148(9) For the purposes of sub-paragraph (8), a station's **"outputs"** are any electricity or motive power produced in the station and any of the following supplied from the station, namely–

(a)   heat or steam, or

(b)   air, or water, that has been heated or cooled.

148(10) The Secretary of State may by regulations make provision for or about–

(a)   certificates under this paragraph;

(b)   applications for such certificates;

(c)   the information that is to accompany such applications.

148(11) The provision that may be made by virtue of sub-paragraph (10)(a) includes in particular–

(a)   provision in respect of the periods for which certificates under this paragraph are to be in force;

(b)   provision for the (non-retrospective) variation or revocation of such certificates.

DETERMINATION OF EFFICIENCY PERCENTAGES FOR COMBINED HEAT AND POWER STATIONS

149(1) The Treasury may by regulations make provision for determining the percentage that is to be stated in a certificate under paragraph 148 as the efficiency percentage for a combined heat and power station.

149(2) (2) Regulations under this paragraph may, in particular, include–

(a)   provision in respect of methods of calculating efficiency percentages;

(b)   provision in respect of the measurements and data to be used in calculating such percentages;

(c)   provision in respect of the procedures for determining such percentages;

(d)   provision in respect of verifying–

(i)   calculations by which such percentages are produced, and

(ii) measurements and data used in such calculations;

(e)   provision that, so far as framed by reference to any document, is framed by reference to that document as from time to time in force.

149(3)   In making provision under this paragraph, the Treasury must have regard to the object of securing that the efficiency percentage for a combined heat and power station is (save for any appropriate adjustments) a percentage that reflects a fair assessment of the efficiency with which commodities are transformed in the station into electricity or motive power.

MEANING OF "UTILITY"

150(1)   In this Schedule **"utility"** means an electricity utility or a gas utility.

150(2)   In this Schedule **"electricity utility"** means the holder of–

(a)   a licence under section 6(1)(d) of the Electricity Act 1989 (supply licences), or

(b)   a licence under Article 10(1)(c) or (2) of the Electricity Supply (Northern Ireland) Order 1992,

except where the holder is acting otherwise than for purposes connected with the carrying on of activities authorised by the licence.

Until the coming into force of the substitution for section 6 of the Electricity Act 1989 provided for by the Utilities Act 2000, paragraph (a) above shall have effect as if the reference to section 6(1)(d) were to section 6(1)(c) or (2).

150(3)   In this Schedule **"gas utility"** means the holder of–

(a)   a licence under section 7A(1) of the Gas Act 1986 (supply licences), or

(b)   a licence under Article 8(1)(c) of the Gas (Northern Ireland) Order 1996,

except where the holder is acting otherwise than for purposes connected with the carrying on of activities authorised by the licence.

150(4)   Sub-paragraphs (1) to (3) have effect subject to–

(a)   any direction under paragraph 151(1), and

(b)   any regulations under paragraph 151(2).

PERSON TREATED AS, OR AS NOT BEING, A UTILITY

151(1)   The Commissioners may by direction (a "utility direction") make, in respect of a person (or persons) specified in the direction, provision authorised by sub-paragraph (3).

151(2)   The Treasury may by regulations ("utility regulations") make, in respect of any person of a description specified in the regulations, provision authorised by sub-paragraph (3).

151(3)   The provision authorised by this sub-paragraph is provision for–

(a)   a person who is an unregulated electricity supplier to be treated for levy purposes as being an electricity utility;

(b)   a person who is an unregulated gas supplier to be treated for levy purposes as being a gas utility;

(c)   a person who is an electricity utility to be treated for levy purposes as not being an electricity utility;

(d)   a person who is a gas utility to be treated for levy purposes as not being a gas utility.

151(4)   References in sub-paragraph (3) to provision for a person to be treated in a particular way for "levy purposes" are to provision for him to be treated in that way for–

(a)   the purposes of this Schedule, or

(b)   *such of those purposes as are specified in the direction or regulations by which the provision is made.*

151(5)   The power to make any provision by a utility direction or utility regulations may be exercised so that the provision applies in relation to a person only to an extent specified in, or determined under, the direction or regulations.

151(6)   A utility direction cannot take effect until it has been–

(a)   given by the Commissioners to each person in respect of whom it makes provision, and

(b)   published by the Commissioners.

151(7)   Paragraph 146(7)(b) and (c) applies to the power to make provision by a utility direction as to a power to make provision by regulations.

151(8) In this paragraph–

"unregulated electricity supplier" means a person who–

(a)   makes supplies of electricity, and

(b)   is not an electricity utility;

"unregulated gas supplier" means a person who–

(a)   makes supplies of gas that is in a gaseous state and is of a kind supplied by a gas utility, and

(b)   is not a gas utility.

MEANING OF "AUTO-GENERATOR"

152(1) In this Schedule "auto-generator" means a person who produces electricity if the electricity that he produces is primarily for his own consumption.

152(2) The Commissioners may by regulations specify requirements to be fulfilled before the electricity that a person produces is, for the purposes of sub-paragraph (1), to be taken as produced primarily for his own consumption.

152(3) For the purposes of this paragraph, electricity is for a person's own consumption if it is for consumption by him or a person connected with him within the meaning of section 839 of the Taxes Act 1988.

MEANING OF "LEVY DUE FOR AN ACCOUNTING PERIOD"

153 References in this Schedule, in relation to any accounting period, to levy due from any person for that period are references (subject to any regulations made by virtue of paragraph 41(2)(a)) to the levy for which that person is required, in accordance with regulations under paragraph 41, to account by reference to that period.

MEANING OF "REPAYMENT OF LEVY"

154 References in this Schedule to a repayment of levy or of an amount of levy are references to any repayment of an amount to any person by virtue of–

(a)   any tax credit regulations; or

(b)   paragraph 63, 87(3) or 110(3).

INTERPRETATION OF "IN THE COURSE OR FURTHERANCE OF A BUSINESS"

155(1) Anything done in connection with the termination or intended termination of a business shall, for the purposes of this Schedule, be treated as being done in the course or furtherance of the business.

155(2) Where in a disposition of a business as a going concern, or of its assets (whether or not in connection with its reorganisation or winding up), there is a supply of a taxable commodity, that supply shall for the purposes of this Schedule be taken to be made in the course or furtherance of the business.

MEANING OF "RESIDENT IN THE UNITED KINGDOM"

156 For the purposes of this Schedule a person is resident in the United Kingdom at any time if, at that time–

(a)   that person has an established place of business in the United Kingdom;

(b)   that person has a usual place of residence in the United Kingdom; or

(c)   that person is a firm or unincorporated body which (without having a relevant connection with the United Kingdom by virtue of paragraph (a)) has amongst its partners or members at least one individual with a usual place of residence in the United Kingdom.

REFERENCES TO THE GAS AND ELECTRICITY MARKETS AUTHORITY: TRANSITIONAL PROVISION

157(1) Until such time as a transfer of functions from the Director General of Electricity Supply to the Gas and Electricity Markets Authority ("the Authority") has taken effect, references in paragraph 19 to the Authority shall be taken to be references to the Director General.

157(2)   Until such time as all the functions of the Director General of Electricity Supply have been transferred in accordance with the Utilities Act 2000 (transfer to the Authority) or abolished, references to the Authority in paragraph 137 shall be taken to include the Director General.

157(3)   Until such time as all the functions of the Director General of Gas Supply have been transferred in accordance with the Utilities Act 2000 (transfer to the Authority) or abolished, references to the Authority in paragraph 137 shall be taken to include the Director General.

157(4)   The power conferred by paragraph 146(7) includes, in particular, power for regulations under paragraph 19 to make transitional provision in connection with the transfer of functions from the Director General of Electricity Supply to the Authority.

SCHEDULE 7 – CLIMATE CHANGE LEVY: CONSEQUENTIAL AMENDMENTS

Section 30

PROVISIONAL COLLECTION OF TAXES ACT 1968 (C.2)

1   In section 1(1) of the Provisional Collection of Taxes Act 1968 (taxes in relation to which resolutions may have temporary statutory effect), after "value added tax" there shall be inserted ", climate change levy,".

BANKRUPTCY (SCOTLAND) ACT 1985 (C.66)

2(1)   In paragraph 2 of Schedule 3 to the Bankruptcy (Scotland) Act 1985 (tax liabilities that are preferred debts), after sub-paragraph (1B) insert–

"**2(1C)**   Any climate change levy which is referable to the period of six months next before the relevant date."

2(2)   In that Schedule, after paragraph 8B insert–

"PERIODS TO WHICH CLIMATE CHANGE LEVY REFERABLE

8C(1)   For the purpose of paragraph 2(1C) of Part I of this Schedule–
(a)   where the whole of the accounting period to which any climate change levy is attributable falls within the period of six months next before the relevant date ("the relevant period"), the whole amount of that levy shall be referable to the relevant period; and
(b)   in any other case the amount of any climate change levy which shall be referable to the relevant period shall be the proportion of the levy which is equal to such proportion (if any) of the accounting period in question as falls within the relevant period.

8C(2)   In sub-paragraph (1) **"accounting period"** shall be construed in accordance with Schedule 6 to the Finance Act 2000."

INSOLVENCY ACT 1986 (C.45)

3(1)   In the Insolvency Act 1986–
(a)   in section 386(1) (preferential debts), after "landfill tax," insert "climate change levy,"; and
(b)   in Schedule 6 (categories of preferential debts), after paragraph 3B insert the paragraph set out in sub-paragraph (2).

3(2)   That paragraph is as follows–

"**3C**   Any climate change levy which is referable to the period of 6 months next before the relevant date (which period is referred to below as "the 6-month period").

For the purposes of this paragraph–
(a)   where the whole of the accounting period to which any climate change levy is attributable falls within the 6-month period, the whole amount of that levy is referable to that period; and
(b)   in any other case the amount of any climate change levy which is referable to the 6-month period is the proportion of the levy which is equal to such proportion (if any) of the accounting period in question as falls within the 6-month period;

and references here to accounting periods shall be construed in accordance with Schedule 6 to the Finance Act 2000."

INCOME AND CORPORATION TAXES ACT 1988 (C.1)

4   In section 827 of the Taxes Act 1988 (no deduction for penalties etc.), the following subsection shall be inserted after subsection (1C)–

"**827(1D)**   Where a person is liable to make a payment by way of–

(a)   any penalty under any provision of Schedule 6 to the Finance Act 2000 (climate change levy),

(b)   interest under paragraph 70 of that Schedule (interest on recoverable overpayments etc.),

(c)   interest under any of paragraphs 81 to 85 of that Schedule (interest on climate change levy due and on interest), or

(d)   interest under paragraph 109 of that Schedule (interest on penalties),

the payment shall not be allowed as a deduction in computing any income, profits or losses for any tax purposes."

INSOLVENCY (NORTHERN IRELAND) ORDER 1989 (N.I. 19)

5(1)   In the Insolvency (Northern Ireland) Order 1989–

(a)   in Article 346(1) (preferential debts), after "landfill tax," insert "climate change levy,"; and

(b)   in Schedule 4 (categories of preferential debts), after paragraph 3B insert the paragraph set out in sub-paragraph (2).

5(2)   That paragraph is as follows–

"**3C**   Any climate change levy which is referable to the period of 6 months next before the relevant date (which period is referred to below as "the 6-month period").

For the purposes of this paragraph–

(a)   where the whole of the accounting period to which any climate change levy is attributable falls within the 6-month period, the whole amount of that levy is referable to that period; and

(b)   in any other case the amount of any climate change levy which is referable to the 6-month period is the proportion of the levy which is equal to such proportion (if any) of the accounting period in question as falls within the 6-month period;

and references here to accounting periods shall be construed in accordance with Schedule 6 to the Finance Act 2000."

FINANCE ACT 1996 (C.8)

6   In section 197(2) of the Finance Act 1996 (enactments for which interest rates are set under section 197), after paragraph (f) there shall be inserted–

"(g)   the following provisions of Schedule 6 to the Finance Act 2000 (interest payable to or by the Commissioners in connection with climate change levy), that is to say, paragraphs 41(2)(f), 62(3)(f), 66, 70(1)(b) and 81(3)."

FINANCE ACT 1997 (C.16)

7(1)   The Finance Act 1997 is amended as follows.

7(2)   In section 51(5) (indirect taxes in respect of which the Commissioners may make regulations about enforcement by distress), after paragraph (e) insert–

"(f)   climate change levy."

7(3)   In section 52(5) (enforcement in Scotland of indirect taxes by diligence), after paragraph (e) insert–

"(f)   climate change levy."

7(4)   sub-paragraph (3) extends only to Scotland.

INDEX TO
CLIMATE CHANGE LEVY

For a list of abbreviations used in this Index see p. xii.

For a list of abbreviations used in this Index see p. xii.

For a list of abbreviations used in this Index see p. xii.

For a list of abbreviations used in this Index see p. xii.

CLIMATE CHANGE LEVY
LIST OF DEFINITIONS
AND MEANINGS

For a list of abbreviations used in this list see p. xii.